W9-BUR-983

EDITORIAL BOARD

ROBERT C. CLARK
DIRECTING EDITOR
Distinguished Service Professor and Austin Wakeman Scott
Professor of Law and Former Dean of the Law School
Harvard University

DANIEL A. FARBER
Sho Sato Professor of Law
University of California at Berkeley

HEATHER K. GERKEN
Dean and the Sol & Lillian Goldman Professor of Law
Yale University

SAMUEL ISSACHAROFF
Bonnie and Richard Reiss Professor of Constitutional Law
New York University

HAROLD HONGJU KOH
Sterling Professor of International Law and
Former Dean of the Law School
Yale University

SAUL LEVMORE
William B. Graham Distinguished Service Professor of Law and
Former Dean of the Law School
University of Chicago

THOMAS W. MERRILL
Charles Evans Hughes Professor of Law
Columbia University

ROBERT L. RABIN
A. Calder Mackay Professor of Law
Stanford University

EDITORIAL BOARD

ROBERT C. CLARK

DANIEL A. BAYNES

ELIZABETH KLEINFELD

SAMUEL ISSACHAROFF

HAROLD HONGJU KOH

SAUL LEVMORE

THOMAS W. MERRILL

ROBERT L. RABIN

UNIVERSITY CASEBOOK SERIES®

GELLHORN AND BYSE'S

ADMINISTRATIVE LAW

CASES AND COMMENTS

TWELFTH EDITION

PETER L. STRAUSS
Betts Professor of Law Emeritus,
Columbia University

TODD D. RAKOFF
Byrne Professor of Administrative Law,
Harvard University

GILLIAN E. METZGER
Stanley H. Fuld Professor of Law,
Columbia University

DAVID J. BARRON
Circuit Judge, U.S. Court of Appeals, First Circuit
Hon. S. William Green Visiting Professor of Public Law,
Harvard Law School

ANNE JOSEPH O'CONNELL
George Johnson Professor of Law,
University of California, Berkeley

FOUNDATION PRESS

The publisher is not engaged in rendering legal or other professional advice, and this publication is not a substitute for the advice of an attorney. If you require legal or other expert advice, you should seek the services of a competent attorney or other professional.

University Casebook Series is a trademark registered in the U.S. Patent and Trademark Office.

COPYRIGHT © 1940, 1947, 1954, 1960, 1970, 1974, 1979, 1987, 1995, 2003 FOUNDATION PRESS
© 2011 By THOMSON REUTERS/FOUNDATION PRESS
© 2018 LEG, Inc. d/b/a West Academic
    444 Cedar Street, Suite 700
    St. Paul, MN 55101
    1-877-888-1330

Printed in the United States of America

ISBN: 978-1-63460-819-0

PREFACE

This is primarily a book about Administrative Law—the body of general rules and principles governing federal administrative agencies and their connections to the President, the Congress, and the Courts. For some users, it may also serve as an introduction to Congress, the legislative process, and statutory interpretation. These are vital subjects for any lawyer to consider; yet public law today largely emerges from the work of the administrative state, and it is that fact that dominantly informs this book's pages.

Perhaps at no time since the New Deal has Administrative Law been as vibrant a subject as it has been in the last few years. Conservative critics of President Obama and his administration loudly claimed that he was using the agencies to override Congress's laws and create executive authoritarianism. Liberal critics of President Trump are now forcefully making much the same claim about his administration. For some time now it has been impossible even to follow the daily news intelligently without running into Executive Orders, administrative hearings, rulemaking proceedings, judicial review of agency actions, and indeed almost everything put before you in this volume.

In the midst of this clamor, are there rules governing the use of power by government that can be broadly accepted no matter who is in or out of power? Rules that provide for regularity in government and equality in its actions? Rules that provide for widespread participation in governance but also shield the rights of individuals and private entities? Rules that enable power to be used but also protect those who are out of power? We hope so.

Indeed, administrative law in the United States continues to grow and develop; as is immediately evident, this is a thick book. This development represents the continuing quest of our society to rein in naked power: to use power for the common good but to control it as well. Rules like these are a large part of what we mean when we say our society believes in the rule of law.

But what the content of these rules of proceeding should be, is without a doubt a contested issue. In this book, we have tried to develop what the law is, as it stands, without claiming that it is the best possible set of rules. Indeed, we have gone out of our way to highlight controversies and present alternative points of view. The possibility of change pervades our subject—change coming perhaps from new appointees to the Supreme Court, perhaps from new statutes passed by Congress, or perhaps from new patterns of action undertaken by the Executive branch itself. We think this possibility, and with it our subject as a whole, is exciting, even if it is at times also a little scary.

We hope that when you delve into this book you, too, will find Administrative Law to be both of great importance and of great interest.

And a note about usage: As in earlier editions, we have omitted without indication many citations and footnotes when we have reproduced opinions and other writings. The original call numbers have been used for the footnotes that we have retained. In quoted text, footnotes are quotations unless preceded by "[Ed.]." And while we have indicated omissions of text by ellipses (. . .), we have ordinarily given only one such signal; the omitted material may comprise words, phrases, sentences, or paragraphs.

PETER L. STRAUSS
TODD D. RAKOFF
GILLIAN E. METZGER
DAVID J. BARRON
ANNE JOSEPH O'CONNELL

October 15, 2017

ACKNOWLEDGMENTS

Excerpts from the following are reprinted with permission:

Frank Ackerman & Lisa Heinzerling, Pricing the Priceless: Cost-Benefit Analysis Of Environmental Protection, 150 U. Pa. L. Rev. 1553 (2002).

Kate Andrias, The President's Enforcement Power, 88 N.Y.U. L. Rev. 1031 (2013).

Michael Asimow, Five Models of Administrative Adjudication, 2015 Am. J. Comp. Law 3 (2015).

Nicholas Bagley, Remedial Restraint in Administrative Law, 117 Colum. L. Rev. 253 (2017).

Nicholas Bagley, The Puzzling Presumption of Reviewability, 127 Harv. L. Rev. 1285 (2014).

Kenneth A. Bamberger, Normative Canons in the Review of Administrative Policymaking, 118 Yale L.J. 64 (2008).

Eugene Bardach & Robert A. Kagan, Going By the Book: The Problem of Regulatory Unreasonableness (New York: The Twentieth Century Fund, 1982).

David J. Barron & Elena Kagan, Chevron's Nondelegation Doctrine, The Supreme Court Review 201 (2001).

Sam Batkins, It is Premature to Label a Regulatory Budget Unconstitutional, Regulatory Review Blog (June 26, 2017).

Lisa Schultz Bressman, Disciplining Delegation After Whitman v. American Trucking Ass'ns, 87 Cornell L. Rev. 452 (2002).

Lisa Schultz Bressman & Michael P. Vandenbergh, Inside the Administrative State: A Critical Look at the Practice of Presidential Control, 105 Mich. L. Rev. 47 (2006).

Stephen Breyer, Making Our Democracy Work: A Judge's View (Alfred A. Knopf 2010).

Rebecca L. Brown, Separated Powers and Ordered Liberty, 139 U. Pa. L. Rev. 1513 (1991).

Jessica Bulman-Pozen, Executive Federalism Comes to America, 102 Va. L. Rev. 953 (2016).

William W. Buzbee, Preemption, Hard Look Review, Regulatory Interaction, and the Quest for Stewardship and Intergenerational Equity, 77 Geo. Wash. L. Rev. 1521 (2009).

Cary Coglianese, Heather Kilmartin & Evan Mendelson, Transparency and Public Participation in the Federal Rulemaking Process: Recommendations for the New Administration, 77 Geo. Wash. L. Rev 924 (2009).

Steven R. Croley, White House Review of Agency Rulemaking: An Empirical Investigation, 70 U. Chi. L. Rev. 821 (2003).

Christopher DeMuth, Sr. & Michael S. Greve, Agency Finance in the Age of Executive Government, 24 Geo. Mason L. Rev. 555 (2017).

John D. Donahue, The Transformation of Government Work, in Government by Contract (ed. Freeman & Minow, Harvard University Press, 2009).

Christopher F. Edley, Jr., Administrative Law: Rethinking Judicial Control of Bureaucracy (Yale University Press 1990).

Harry T. Edwards & Michael A. Livermore, Pitfalls of Empirical Studies that Attempt to Understand the Factors Affecting Appellate Decisionmaking, 58 Duke L.J. 1895 (2009).

Harry T. Edwards, The Judicial Function and the Elusive Goal of Principled Decisionmaking, 1991 Wisconsin L. Rev. 837.

E. Donald Elliott, Chevron Matters: How the Chevron Doctrine Redefined the Roles of Congress, Courts, and Agencies in Environmental Law, 16 Vill. Envtl. L.J. 1 (2005).

Daniel R. Ernst, Tocqueville's Nightmare: The Administrative State Emerges in America, 1900–1940 (Oxford University Press 2014).

William N. Eskridge Jr., The New Textualism, 37 U.C.L.A. L. Rev. 621 (1990).

William N. Eskridge Jr. & Lauren E. Baer, The Continuum of Deference: Supreme Court Treatment of Agency Statutory Interpretations from Chevron to Hamdan, 96 Georgetown L.J. 1083 (2008).

Dan Farber, Courts Should Kill Trump's Pricey "2-for-1" Dergulation Order, The Hill Blog (Feb. 9, 2017).

Daniel A. Farber & Anne Joseph O'Connell, Agencies as Adversaries, 105 Cal L. Rev. 1375 (2017).

Daniel A. Farber & Anne Joseph O'Connell, The Lost World of Administrative Law, 92 Tex. L. Rev. 1137 (2014).

Cynthia R. Farina, Reporter, ABA Committee on the Status and Future of Federal e-Rulemaking, Achieving the Potential: The Future of Federal e-Rulemaking (2008).

Cynthia R. Farina, Conceiving Due Process, 3 Yale J.L. & Feminism 189 (1991).

Cynthia R. Farina, Statutory Interpretation and the Balance of Power in the Administrative State, 89 Colum. L. Rev. 452 (1989).

Cynthia R. Farina, The Consent of the Governed: Against Simple Rules for a Complex World, 72 U. Chi.-Kent L. Rev. 987 (1997).

Jody Freeman, Extending Public Law Norms through Privatization, 116 Harv. L. Rev. 1285 (2003).

Jody Freeman & Adrian Vermeule, Massachusetts v. EPA: From Politics to Expertise, 2007 Sup. Ct. Rev. 51 (2007).

Jody Freeman & Martha Minow, Reframing the Outsourcing Debates, in Government by Contract (ed. Freeman & Minow, Harvard University Press, 2009).

Ernest Gellhorn & Glen O. Robinson, Rulemaking "Due Process": An Inconclusive Dialogue, 48 U. Chi. L. Rev. 201 (1981).

Daniel J. Gifford, The Morgan Cases: A Retrospective View, 30 Ad. L. Rev. 237 (1978).

Abbe R. Gluck, Imperfect Statutes, Imperfect Courts: Understanding Congress' Plan in the Era of Unorthodox Lawmaking, 129 Harv. L. Rev. 62 (2015).

Abbe R. Gluck & Lisa Schultz Bressman, Statutory Interpretation from the Inside—An Empirical Study of Congressional Drafting, Delegation, and the Canons: Part 1, 65 Stan. L. Rev. 901 (2013).

Philip Hamburger, Is Administrative Law Unlawful? (University of Chicago Press 2014).

Lisa Heinzerling, Cost-Benefit Jumps the Shark, Georgetown Law Faculty Blog (June 13, 2012).

Kristin E. Hickman, The Three Phases of Mead, 83 Fordham L. Rev. 527 (2014).

Elena Kagan, Presidential Administration, 114 Harv. L. Rev. 2245 (2001).

Orin S. Kerr, Shedding Light on Chevron: An Empirical Study of the Chevron Doctrine in the U.S. Courts of Appeals, 15 Yale J. on Reg. 1 (1998).

Cornelius M. Kerwin & Scott R. Furlong, Rulemaking: How Government Agencies Write Law and Make Policy (4th. ed. CQ Press 2010).

James M. Landis, The Administrative Process (Yale University Press 1938).

Gary Lawson, Katherine Ferguson & Guillermo Montero, "Oh Lord, Please Don't Let Me Be Misunderstood!": Rediscovering the Mathews v. Eldridge and Penn Central Frameworks, 81 Notre Dame L. Rev. 1 (2005).

Gary Lawson, The Rise and Rise of the Administrative State, 107 Harv. L. Rev. 1231 (1994).

Lawrence Lessig & Cass R. Sunstein, The President and the Administration, 94 Colum. L. Rev. 6 (1994).

Jason A. MacDonald, Limitation Riders and Congressional Influence over Bureaucratic Policy Decisions, 104 Am. Pol. Sci. Rev. 766 (2010).

M. Elizabeth Magill, Agency Choice of Policymaking Form, 71 U. Chi. L. Rev. 1383 (2004).

John F. Manning, Separation of Powers as Ordinary Interpretation, 124 Harv. L. Rev. 1939 (2011).

John F. Manning, Textualism as a Nondelegation Doctrine, 97 Colum. L. Rev. 673 (1997).

Jerry L. Mashaw, Bureaucratic Justice: Managing Social Security Disability Claims (Yale University Press 1983).

Jerry L. Mashaw, Creating the Administrative Constitution: The Lost One Hundred Years of American Administrative Law (Yale University Press 2012).

Jerry L. Mashaw, Greed, Chaos and Governance: Using Public Choice to Improve Public Law (Yale University Press 1997).

Thomas O. McGarity, Deregulatory Riders Redux, 1 Mich. J. Envtl. & Admin. L. 33 (2012).

Thomas O. McGarity, The Internal Structure of EPA Rulemaking, 54 Law & Contemp. Probs. 57 (Autumn 1991).

McNollgast, The Political Origins of the Administrative Procedure Act, 15 J.L. Econ. & Org. 180 (1999).

Thomas W. Merrill, Rethinking Article I, Section 1: From Nondelegation to Exclusive Delegation, 104 Colum. L. Rev. 2097 (2004).

Thomas W. Merrill, Textualism and the Future of the Chevron Doctrine, 72 Wash. U. L. Q. 351 (1994).

Gillian E. Metzger, Administrative Law as the New Federalism, 57 Duke L.J. 2023 (2008).

Gillian E. Metzger, Ordinary Administrative Law as Constitutional Common Law, 110 Colum. L. Rev. 479 (2010).

Gillian E. Metzger, Privatization as Delegation, 103 Colum. L. Rev. 1367 (2003).

Gillian E. Metzger, The Constitutional Duty to Supervise, 124 Yale L.J. 1836 (2015).

Gillian E. Metzger, The Supreme Court 2016 Term—Foreword: 1930s Redux: The Administrative State Under Siege, 131 Harv. L. Rev. 1 (2017).

Jonathan T. Molot, The Judicial Perspective in the Administrative State: Reconciling Modern Doctrines of Deference with the Judiciary's Structural Role, 53 Stanford L. Rev. 1 (2000).

Alan B. Morrison, The Administrative Procedure Act: A Living and Responsive Law, 72 Va. L. Rev. 258 (1986).

Anne Joseph O'Connell, Auditing Politics or Political Auditing? (SSRN abstract no. 964656).

Anne Joseph O'Connell, Bureaucracy at the Boundary, 162 U. Pa. L. Rev. 841 (2014).

Nicholas R. Parrillo, Against the Profit Motive: The Salary Revolution in American Government, 1780–1940 (Yale University Press 2013).

Eloise Pasachoff, Budget as a Source of Agency Policy Control, 125 Yale L.J. 2182 (2016).

Richard J. Pierce, Jr., How Agencies Should Give Meaning to the Statutes They Administer: A Response to Mashaw and Strauss, 59 Admin. L. Rev. 197 (2007).

Richard J. Pierce, Jr., Making Sense of Procedural Injury, 62 Admin. L. Rev. 1 (2010).

David E. Pozen, Freedom of Information Beyond the Freedom of Information Act, 165 U. Pa. L. Rev. 1097 (2017).

David E. Pozen, The Leaky Leviathan: Why the Government Condemns and Condones Unlawful Disclosures of Information, 127 Harv. L. Rev. 512 (2013).

Todd D. Rakoff, Brock v. Roadway Express, Inc. and the New Law of Regulatory Due Process, 1987 Sup. Ct. Rev. 157.

Richard L. Revesz & Michael A. Livermore, Retaking Rationality: How Cost-Benefit Analysis Can Better Protect the Environment and Our Health (Oxford University Press 2008).

Edward L. Rubin, It's Time to Make the Administrative Procedure Act Administrative, 89 Cornell L. Rev. 95 (2003).

Antonin Scalia, The Doctrine of Standing as an Essential Element of the Separation of Powers, 17 Suffolk U.L. Rev. 881 (1983)

Antonin Scalia, Vermont Yankee: The APA, the D.C. Circuit, and the Supreme Court, 1978 Sup. Ct. Rev. 345.

Peter H. Schuck, Delegation and Democracy: Comments on David Schoenbrod, 20 Cardozo L. Rev. 775 (1999).

Mark Seidenfeld, Demystifying Deossification: Rethinking Recent Proposals to Modify Judicial Review of Notice and Comment Rulemaking, 75 Tex. L. Rev. 483 (1997).

Peter M. Shane, The Bureaucratic Due Process of Government Watch Lists, 75 Geo. Wash. L. Rev. 804 (2007).

Peter M. Shane, Empowering the Collaborative Citizen in the Administrative State: A Case Study of the Federal Communications Commission, 65 U. Miami L. Rev. 483 (2011).

Martin Shapiro, APA: Past, Present, Future, 72 Va. L. Rev. 447 (1986).

Sidney A. Shapiro & Richard Murphy, Eight Things Americans Can't Figure Out About Controlling Administrative Power, 61 Admin. L. Rev. 5 (2009).

Sidney A. Shapiro & Randy S. Rabinowitz, Punishment versus Cooperation in Regulatory Enforcement: A Case Study of OSHA, 49 Admin. L. Rev. 713 (1997).

Mathew Stephenson, A Costly Signaling Theory of "Hard Look" Judicial Review, 58 Admin. L. Rev. 753 (2006).

Richard B. Stewart, The Reformation of American Administrative Law, 88 Harv. L. Rev. 1669 (1975).

Peter L. Strauss, Changing Times: The APA at Fifty, 63 U. Chi. L. Rev. 1389 (1996).

Peter L. Strauss, Revisiting Overton Park: Political and Judicial Controls Over Administrative Actions Affecting the Community, 39 U.C.L.A. L. Rev. 1251 (1992).

Peter L. Strauss, The Place of Agencies in Government: Separation of Powers and the Fourth Branch, 84 Colum. L. Rev. 573 (1984).

Cass R. Sunstein & Thomas J. Miles, Depoliticizing Administrative Law, 58 Duke L.J. 2193 (2009).

Cass R. Sunstein, Law and Administration After Chevron, 90 Colum. L. Rev. 2071 (1990).

Cass R. Sunstein, The Cost-Benefit State: The Future of Regulatory Protection (American Bar Association 2002).

Karen M. Tani, States of Dependency: Welfare, Rights, and American Governance, 1935–1972 (Cambridge University Press 2016).

Kathryn A. Watts, Controlling Presidential Control, 114 Mich. L. Rev. 683 (2016).

Kathryn A. Watts, Proposing a Place for Politics in Arbitrary and Capricious Review, 119 Yale L.J. 2 (2009).

Stephen F. Williams, The Era of "Risk-Risk" and the Problem of Keeping the APA Up to Date, 63 U. Chi. L. Rev. 1375 (1996).

SUMMARY OF CONTENTS

PART 1. OVERVIEW

PART 2. UNDERSTANDING STATUTES

PART 4. THE AGENCY AND THE CONSTITUTION

PART 5. JUDGING THE WORK OF AGENCIES

TABLE OF CONTENTS

PART 1. OVERVIEW

PART 2. UNDERSTANDING STATUTES

PART 3. THE AGENCY AT WORK

Chapter III. Procedural Frameworks for Administrative Action

PART 4. THE AGENCY AND THE CONSTITUTION

Chapter VII. Agency Relationships with Congress, the President, and the Courts: The Structural Constitution 775

PART 5. JUDGING THE WORK OF AGENCIES

TABLE OF CASES

The principal cases are in bold type.

TABLE OF STATUTES

TABLE OF REGULATIONS AND RULES

TABLE OF URLs

TABLE OF AUTHORITIES

UNIVERSITY CASEBOOK SERIES®

GELLHORN AND BYSE'S

ADMINISTRATIVE LAW

CASES AND COMMENTS

TWELFTH EDITION

PART 1

OVERVIEW

I.   AN INTRODUCTION TO ADMINISTRATIVE LAW

CHAPTER I

AN INTRODUCTION TO ADMINISTRATIVE LAW

Sec. 1.	*An Introductory Example*
Sec. 2.	*The Basics*
Sec. 3.	*The Tasks of Administrative Law*
Sec. 4.	*Teaching and Studying Administrative Law from This Casebook*

SECTION 1.   AN INTRODUCTORY EXAMPLE

The Problem of Airplane Tarmac Delays

What follows is a real problem: the legal materials are genuine, and the facts are true. It is a real problem in another sense, too; its pieces are complex and open to multiple solutions. Of course, if you are reading this at the beginning of your study of administrative law, you do not know much of what you would need to know to answer the questions posed in the way an experienced lawyer or policymaker would. (Some of the questions are not so easy even if you do know what there is to know!) So, the purpose of the problem is twofold: first, to show you the kinds of questions administrative law tries to answer, and second, to invite you to use your imagination, along with the information given, to think about some of the complexities of the issues.

The Problem of Airplane Tarmac Delays

Most of you have taken an airplane to travel to a destination. What has been the longest delay of a flight that you have experienced? Were you stuck in the airplane at the gate or on the tarmac or even the runway for some of that time? What has been the longest amount of time that you have remained on the airplane after boarding but before taking off? These are descriptive questions. How long do you think passengers should be forced to stay on a grounded airplane before having access to food or water? Before having the opportunity to get off? These are normative queries.

In the eight months between December 2006 and July 2007, hundreds of thousands of passengers boarded airplanes that then remained grounded on airport tarmacs for more than three hours, typically because of weather and its interactions with airline operations. In December 2006, passengers sat on an American Airlines plane diverted in flight to the airport in Austin, Texas, for almost ten hours. During a February 2007 snowstorm, ten Jet Blue flights kept their wheels down, full of passengers, at New York City's John F. Kennedy International Airport. One plane scheduled to travel to Aruba remained on the ground for almost eleven hours. Another to Cancun stayed for almost nine hours before the flight was canceled. Because these airplanes were not at the gates, passengers could not get off—to walk around the airport, to use bigger bathrooms, to eat or drink in airport restaurants— in these situations.

Airline passengers were hopping mad. Airlines, though apologetic, argued that returning to the gate was not always possible and, even if possible, might have resulted in even longer delays.

Assuming it were a completely open question, where in the legal universe should we put the law of airline passenger service? Should it be a matter of tort, requiring an airline to take "reasonable care"? Should it be a matter of contract, so that passengers get what they, individually or collectively, bargain for? Should we pass statutes, state or federal, specifying things like the length of time airplanes can sit on the tarmac and when food and drink have to be provided, and stipulating civil and possibly criminal penalties? Or should we give the matter over to a state or federal administrative agency to consider and regulate? Or should we simply have no law on the subject and leave the issue to the forces of reputation and social norms?

Let's consider the solution of just relying on courts first. *Should passengers stuck on a grounded flight for hours be able to sue the airline under tort or contract law?* If such suits were permitted and plausible, plaintiffs themselves could be compensated (unlike regulatory fines, which typically go, at least in major part, to the government).

One passenger on that December 2006 American Airlines (AA) flight, Catherine Ray, tried the courts. She filed a five-count class action suit in Arkansas state court (which was later removed to federal court by the carrier) that alleged false imprisonment, intentional infliction of emotional distress, negligence, breach of contract, and deceit/fraud. These allegations come from the fact section of her complaint:

9. While confined on the ground in Austin, the toilets became full and would not flush and the stench of human excrement and body odor filled the plane.

10. While confined, in the aircraft, plaintiff and other passengers were unable to wash their hands due to the aircraft running out of water and not being re-supplied by AA.

11. Plaintiff and other passengers were provided only two soft drinks and only a few granola bars for food.

12. Plaintiff and other passengers were also deprived of access to medications, nutritional supplements and needs, and hydration especially needed by [the] infirm, elderly and children. . . .

18. Defendant had ample advanced warning of weather conditions at Dallas and knew or should have known that it was not able to land aircraft at Dallas (DFW) airport at the capacity it had scheduled on December 29, 2006, due to transient thunderstorms and could have cancelled or delayed from departing many of the flights that it diverted and stranded, thereby preventing the diversions and confinements.

19. With the exception of a few passengers whose destination was the Austin[,] Texas area, AA refused to permit passengers to exit the aircraft even though buses and available gates at the terminal were available to AA.

Complaint, Ray v. American Airlines, Civil Case No. 08–5025 (W.D. Ark. 2008) (removed from state court).

Some of Ray's claims were preempted by the Airline Deregulation Act, 47 U.S.C. § 41413(b)(1), and others were dismissed for failing to state a claim. But her false imprisonment, intentional infliction of emotional distress, and negligence claims made it to the summary judgment stage. The district court granted summary judgment to the airline, however, holding that Ray did not revoke her consent to be on the plane (and therefore was not falsely imprisoned) and that the airline "had no duty to provide Plaintiff with a stress-free flight environment" (and thus she lacked a key element for the other tort claims). Ray v. American Airlines, 2009 WL 921124 (W.D. Ark. 2009), affirmed, 609 F.3d 917 (8th Cir. 2010). In other cases, instead of assessing the elements of any tort claims, courts have held that such claims were preempted. See, e.g., Biscone v. JetBlue Corp., 103 A.D.3d 158 (N.Y. App. Div. 2012). Litigation thus seems an unlikely avenue for changing airline practices, unless Congress enacts federal statutes that permit such suits (barring preemption defenses) or force airlines to put more guarantees in their contracts of carriage with passengers (making contract claims plausible). *Would you favor such changes?*

As noted above, an alternative to litigation is new legislation. Senators Barbara Boxer (D-CA) and Olympia Snowe (R-ME) introduced S.678, the Airline Passenger Bill of Rights Act of 2007, in the Senate. In main part, the proposed bill would have amended Chapter 417 of Title 49 of the United States Code to add:

SEC. 41781. AIRLINE CUSTOMER SERVICE REQUIREMENTS.

(a) IN GENERAL.—Not later than 60 days after the date of the enactment of the Airline Passenger Bill of Rights Act of 2007, each air carrier shall institute the following practices:

(1) PROVISION OF FOOD AND WATER.—In any case in which departure of a flight of an air carrier is delayed, such air carrier shall provide—

(A) adequate food and potable water to passengers on such flight during such delay; and

(B) adequate restroom facilities to passengers on such flight during such delay.

(2) RIGHT TO DEPLANE.—

(A) IN GENERAL.—Except as provided in subparagraph (B), if more than 3 hours after passengers have boarded an air carrier and the air carrier doors are closed, the air carrier has not departed, the air carrier shall provide passengers with the option to deplane safely before the departure of such air carrier. Such option shall be provided to passengers not less often than once during each 3-hour period that the plane remains on the ground.

(B) EXCEPTIONS.—Subparagraph (A) shall not apply—

(i) if the pilot of such flight reasonably determines that such flight will depart not later than 30 minutes after the 3 hour delay; or

(ii) if the pilot of such flight reasonably determines that permitting a passenger to deplane would jeopardize passenger safety or security.

(b) AIR CARRIER.—In this section the term "air carrier" means an air carrier holding a certificate issued under section 41102 that conducts scheduled passenger air transportation.

———————————

The legislation also instructed the Secretary of Transportation to "promulgate such regulations as the Secretary determines necessary to carry out the amendments made by this Act" and imposed a tight deadline of 60 days after the Act's enactment for these rules. Similar legislation was introduced in the House.

A passenger on one of the grounded flights formed a new group, the Coalition for Airline Passengers Bill of Rights, to lobby for this legislation.[1] The Consumer Federation of America, Consumers Union, and Public Citizen, among other groups, also supported the bill. The Business Travel Coalition, which represents "the managed travel community," announced its opposition. And the airlines, as expected, voiced their alarm. The CEO of Virgin America was quoted by *USA Today* worrying about unintended consequences: "We had a situation about a month ago at (New York's JFK), where we had a plane sit out on the

———————————

[1] This specific group no longer seems to be in existence, having been replaced by FlyersRights.org.

taxiway for four hours and 10 minutes. We normally bring our planes back after four hours, unless we're certain takeoff is imminent. Well, if we had had a four-hour law in place, that plane would have gone back to the terminal and then would have been 35th or 40th in line to take off. As it was, they got in the air 10 minutes later."

The Constitution requires that a bill pass both the House of Representatives and the Senate and be signed by the President to become law—or be repassed by two-thirds majorities in each chamber to overcome a presidential veto. But traditional legislation faces other obstacles in Congress too—including having to be voted out of committees in the House and Senate (sometimes more than one in each chamber) and possibly needing 60 votes in the Senate to overcome a filibuster. In this case, the relevant committee in the Senate was the Committee on Commerce, Science, and Transportation, which held a hearing on April 11, 2007, on the proposed law.

Would you vote for this legislation? What were the legislation's chances of success in 2007? How much does party affiliation matter for this issue? Democrats held the majority of seats in both chambers of Congress at the time, the November 2006 election having shifted control from the Republicans. President George W. Bush was in the White House. After the Senate hearing, nothing else happened in either the House or Senate to advance the legislation in that congressional session. *What advantages does Congress have over the courts in addressing policy issues? Disadvantages?*

An alternative to both the courts and new legislation (almost always with tasks for the bureaucracy) is agency regulation based on existing laws. *Which federal agencies govern airlines?* The Federal Aviation Administration (FAA) and the Department of Transportation are two of the primary entities. The FAA is an agency that sits within the Transportation Department, which is one of fifteen cabinet departments. The FAA has some independent authority but often must get approval from its parent agency for action. Both are led by individuals nominated by the President and confirmed by the Senate. By statute, the Administrator of the FAA must "(1) be a citizen of the United States; (2) be a civilian; and (3) have experience in a field directly related to aviation," and serves (since 1994) a five-year term. 49 U.S.C. § 106(b)–(c). The Secretary of Transportation, a member of the President's cabinet, has no statutory term or qualifications. *Can you figure out, if you do not know already, who served as FAA Administrator and Secretary of Transportation in 2007 (and who serves in those positions now)? Why do you think they were chosen for those jobs? Should there be expertise requirements for either position? Why shouldn't a military officer be allowed to run the FAA?*

We include below the organizational charts for both these agencies so you can get a sense of the institutional complexity. The one for the

Department of Transportation comes from the U.S. Government Manual. The one for the FAA was on its web site.[2]

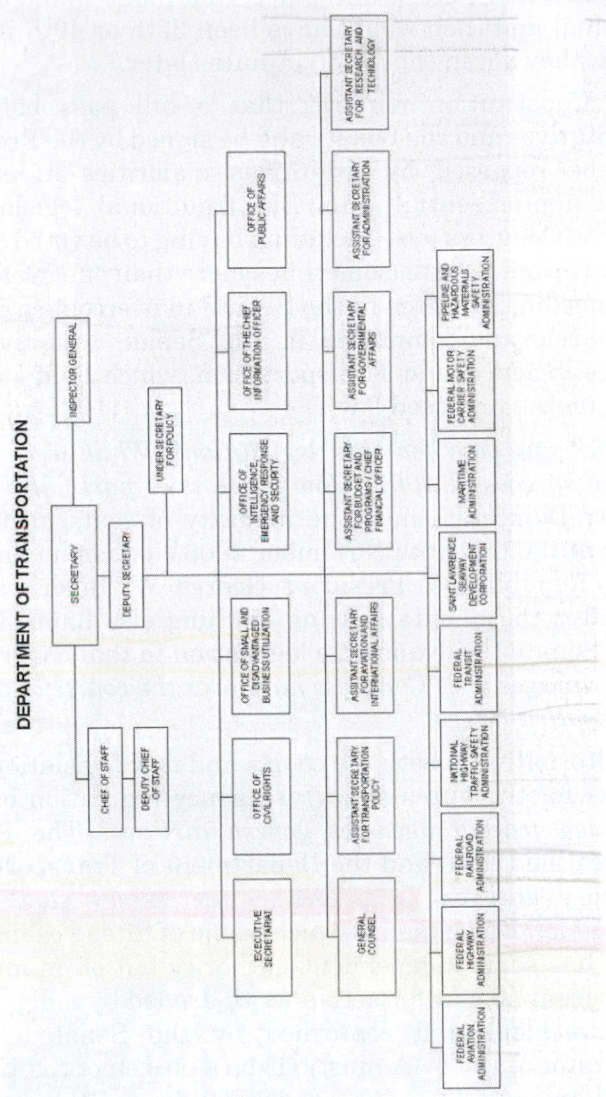

---

[2] In addition to the FAA and Department of Transportation, the National Transportation Safety Board (NTSB), an independent establishment, also oversees airlines. It investigates airlines, when they crash or get into other accidents, and issues safety recommendations. The NTSB is not located within the Transportation Department. Unlike the other two agencies, it is run by five members, all of whom are appointed by the President and confirmed by the Senate to five-year terms and can be removed only for "inefficiency, neglect of duty, or malfeasance in office." Like many independent regulatory commissions and boards, the NTSB has both party-balancing (no more than three of the five members can be from the same political party) and expertise mandates ("[a]t least 3 members shall be appointed on the basis of technical qualification, professional standing, and demonstrated knowledge in accident reconstruction, safety engineering, human factors, transportation safety, or transportation regulation"). 49 U.S.C. § 1111(b)–(c). *Should the leaders of an agency investigating airplane crashes have protection from being fired? When should an agency be headed by one person (as opposed to a group, where a majority is needed to act)?*

FEDERAL AVIATION ADMINISTRATION

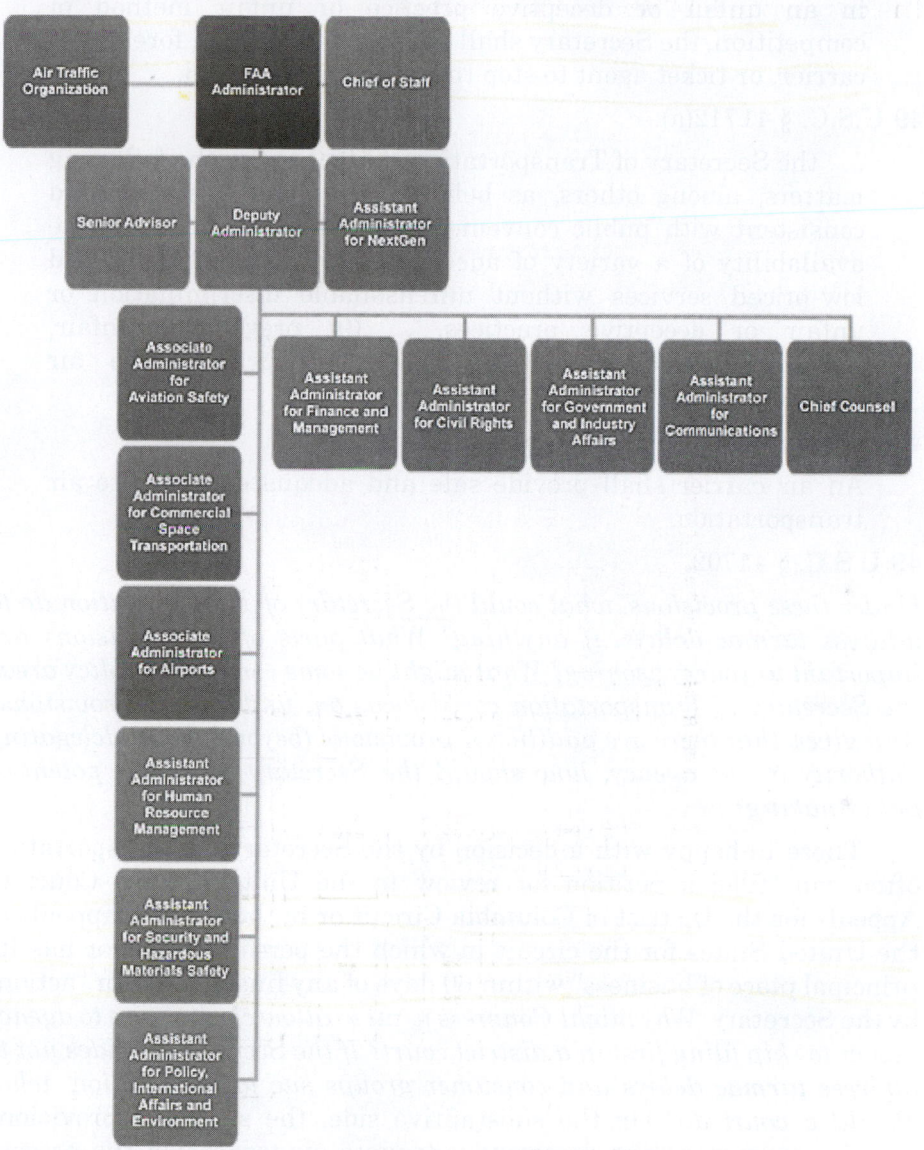

An agency needs legal authority to act. In 2007, the following statutory provisions were already on the books:

On the initiative of the Secretary of Transportation or the complaint of an air carrier, foreign air carrier, or ticket agent, and if the Secretary considers it is in the public interest, the Secretary may investigate and decide whether an air carrier, foreign air carrier, or ticket agent has been or is engaged in an unfair or deceptive practice or an unfair method of competition in air transportation or the sale of air transportation. If the Secretary, after notice and an opportunity for a hearing, finds that an air carrier, foreign air carrier, or ticket agent is engaged in an unfair or deceptive practice or unfair method of competition, the Secretary shall order the air carrier, foreign air carrier, or ticket agent to stop the practice or method.

49 U.S.C. § 41712(a).

. . . the Secretary of Transportation shall consider the following matters, among others, as being in the public interest and consistent with public convenience and necessity: . . . (4) the availability of a variety of adequate, economic, efficient, and low-priced services without unreasonable discrimination or unfair or deceptive practices. . . . (9) preventing unfair, deceptive, predatory, or anticompetitive practices in air transportation.

49 U.S.C. § 40101(a)(4), (9).

An air carrier shall provide safe and adequate interstate air transportation.

49 U.S.C. § 41702.

Under these provisions, what could the Secretary of Transportation do to address tarmac delays, if anything? What parts of the provisions are important to your reasoning? What might be some competing policy areas the Secretary of Transportation could focus on, under these provisions? And given that there are additional provisions (beyond these) delegating authority to the agency, how should the Secretary prioritize potential policymaking?

Those unhappy with a decision by the Secretary of Transportation often can "fil[e] a petition for review in the United States Court of Appeals for the District of Columbia Circuit or in the court of appeals of the United States for the circuit in which the person resides or has its principal place of business" within 60 days of any final "order" or "action" by the Secretary. *Why might Congress want to allow challengers to agency action to skip filing first in a district court? If the Secretary decides not to address tarmac delays and consumer groups sue to force action, what should a court do?* On the substantive side, the statutory provisions promise consumers non-deceptive, adequate air travel. On the process side, they provide considerable discretion to the agency. *What is the role of the judiciary in a situation like this?*

The Secretary of Transportation is, of course, a member of the President's cabinet. Insofar as high political judgment is involved in framing proper regulations, the President may well be involved. *Is this such an issue?* But the Secretary hardly has time to determine how many airplanes sat on tarmacs for how long during specific periods. Most of the work, then, is done by offices or administrations within the Department, such as the FAA and the Office of Aviation Enforcement in the General Counsel's Office. In FY 2008, the Department was allotted 55,150 full-time equivalent positions, of which only 23 were slots for Senate-confirmed presidential appointees, 41 were excepted Schedule C (political) positions, and 31 were non-career Senior Executive Service (also political) jobs. Its FY 2008 budget exceeded $63.4 billion.[3] *How much should the Secretary of Transportation rely on political appointees? On career employees?*

How would the Secretary (and subordinates) go about enacting a new policy? The Administrative Procedure Act (APA), which you will learn about in this course, briefly details procedures for notice-and-comment rulemaking: "After notice . . ., the agency shall give interested persons an opportunity to participate in the rule making through submission of written data, views, or arguments with or without opportunity for oral presentation. After consideration of the relevant matter presented, the agency shall incorporate in the rules adopted a concise general statement of their basis and purpose." 5 U.S.C. § 553. In bare bones, this translates into a notice of proposed rulemaking (often called an NPRM), a comment period, and a final rule.

Rulemaking in practice often looks far more complicated. In November 2007, the Department of Transportation issued an *Advance* NPRM (think of it as a prior notice to the notice), not discussed in the APA, asking for comment on the following seven possible measures:

1. Require Contingency Plans for Lengthy Tarmac Delays and Incorporate Them in Their Contracts of Carriage[4] [which would be tied, according to the ANPRM, to a four-hour delay]

2. Require Carriers To Respond to Consumer Problems

3. Declare the Operation of Flights That Remain Chronically Delayed To Be an Unfair and Deceptive Practice and an Unfair Method of Competition

4. Require Carriers To Publish Delay Data on Their Web Sites

5. Require Carriers To Publish Complaint Data on Their Web Sites

6. Require Carriers To Report On-Time Performance of International Flights

7. Require Carriers To Audit Their Adherence to Their Customer Service Plans

Department of Transportation, Enhancing Airline Passenger Protections, 72 Fed. Reg. 65,233, 65,234–65,236 (Nov. 20, 2007). *How would you classify each of the seven items? How many rely on disclosure*

---

[3]   For FY 2016, the Department had 51,876 full-time equivalent positions (with 22 Senate-confirmed slots, 2 positions requiring presidential appointment (with no Senate role), 39 excepted Schedule C positions, and 28 non-career Senior Executive Service jobs), and its budget exceeded $75.5 billion.

[4]   "With the contingency plan incorporated in the contract of carriage, passengers would be able to sue in court for damages if a carrier failed to adhere to its plan." Department of Transportation, Enhancing Airline Passenger Protections, 72 Fed. Reg. 65,233, 65,234 (Nov. 20, 2007).

of information to regulate? How many impose duties other than information disclosure? What are the advantages and disadvantages of specifying a particular time period for tarmac delays?

The ANPRM also listed a series of questions for commenters to answer, including on the first measure:

> What costs would it impose on the carriers? Would it have any negative consequences? Is it likely to succeed in protecting passengers from the conditions described above? If not, why not? What additional or different measures should we consider adopting? Would incorporation of the contingency plan in the contract of carriage give consumers adequate notice of what might happen in the event of a long delay on the tarmac? When prolonged delays occur, would these measures succeed in reducing the resultant uncertainty and discomfort for passengers? Should the types of carriers covered by the regulation be expanded or limited? What would be the cost or benefit of narrowing or expanding coverage? Should the requirement of coordinating the plan with airport authorities apply to all primary airports (i.e., commercial service airports that enplane more than 10,000 passengers annually) rather than only to medium hub airports (primary airports that enplane between 0.25 and 1 percent of total U.S. passengers) and large hub airports (primary airports that enplane at least 1 percent of total U.S. passengers)?

Id. at 65,235.

How many comments do you think the Department received, and from whom, on its ANPRM? Surprisingly, fewer than 10 percent (of the approximately 200 comments) came from industry. Only four airlines—Delta Air Lines, Virgin Atlantic Airways, Jet Airways (India), and China Eastern Airlines—submitted comments, though five carrier associations also provided their views. On the consumer side, 131 members of the Coalition for an Airline Passengers Bill of Rights "filed identical or nearly identical comments." Five consumer associations—the Aviation Consumer Action Project, National Business Travel Association, Federation of State Public Interest Grounds, Public Citizen, and National Consumers League—and 34 other individuals also sent in reactions. The Department summarized the views as follows:

> In general, the consumers and consumer associations maintained that the Department's proposals do not go far enough, while the carriers and carrier associations attributed the current problems mostly to factors beyond their control such as weather and the air traffic control system and tended to characterize the proposals as unnecessary and unduly burdensome. The travel agency associations expressed support for consumer protections but not at their members' expense.

Department of Transportation, Enhancing Airline Passenger Protections, 73 Fed. Reg. 74,586, 74,587 (Dec. 8, 2008).

After the November 2008 election, which changed party control of the White House from Republican President George W. Bush to Democrat President-Elect Barack Obama, but before Obama's inauguration, the Department of Transportation published an NPRM, seeking comments before February 6, 2009 (a 60-day comment period). *Should then-Secretary of Transportation Mary Peters, who knew she would no longer be in her job in January 2009, continued to have engaged in policymaking?* (President Obama chose Republican Ray LaHood, a former member of Congress, to head the Department of Transportation initially). The NPRM continued with a subset of the ANPRM's issues. The proposed regulation would:

> (1) Require air carriers to adopt contingency plans for lengthy tarmac delays and to incorporate these plans in their contracts of carriage, (2) require air carriers to respond to consumer problems, (3) declare the operation of flights that remain chronically delayed to be an unfair and deceptive practice and an unfair method of competition, (4) require air carriers to publish delay data on their Web sites, and (5) require air carriers to adopt customer service plans, incorporate these in their contracts of carriage, and audit their adherence to their plans.

Id.

Before the NPRM was published, it had to be approved by the Office of Information and Regulatory Affairs (OIRA), within the Office of Management and Budget in the Executive Office of the President, as a significant regulation under Executive Order 12,866. The Order, issued by President Bill Clinton and continued by each of his successors, Republican and Democrat, requires OIRA to sign off on significant proposed and final rules by executive agencies and departments like the two agencies we are discussing.[5] One of OIRA's duties is to ensure that a rule's benefits are greater than its costs and indeed that the agency's action maximizes net benefits, so long as a specific statute does not prevent such cost-benefit analysis. The APA makes no mention of these mandates. Because of the Executive Order, the Transportation Department performed a detailed regulatory evaluation of the proposed rule's benefits and costs. In the NPRM, the agency stated:

> On the cost side, many of the measures suggested in this NPRM would impose costs for both implementation and operation on the entities that its proposed requirements would cover. The benefits we seek to achieve entail relieving consumers of the burdens they now face due to lengthy ground delays, chronically delayed flights, and other problems discussed in the NPRM. The

---

[5] Independent agencies such as the NTSB do not need OIRA approval.

benefits would be achieved by affording consumers significantly more information than they have now about delayed and cancelled flights and about how carriers will respond to their needs in the event of lengthy ground delays. Making this information accessible should not only alleviate consumers' difficulties during long delays but also enable them to make better-informed choices when booking flights. The Regulatory Evaluation has concluded that the benefits of the proposal appear to exceed its costs. A copy of the Regulatory Evaluation has been placed in the docket.

Id. at 74,600.

Interestingly, in May 2008, then-White House Chief of Staff Joshua Bolten had told executive agencies and departments that "regulations to be finalized in this Administration should be proposed no later than June 1, 2008, and final regulations should be issued no later than November 1, 2008." The NPRM here made clear that the Transportation Department was not trying to finish the rulemaking by the time President George W. Bush left office. *Why did the agency not try to finish it before the change of Administration?*

Despite dealing with an issue that hundreds of thousands of passengers had recently experienced, only 21 comments—split essentially equally between industry on one side and consumers and consumer associations on the other—came in during the 90-day comment period for the NPRM (the agency ended up providing a 30-day extension to the original 60-day period). To be fair, one of those comments summarized the views of those who participated in a discussion on the NPRM on regulationroom.org (see p. 763). *Does the low number surprise you?* You can find information online about many rulemakings at www.regulations.gov. You can even file comments on many agencies' open rulemakings there. *How easy is it to navigate that website, compared to other online resources and services you use?*

Industry commenters supported some of the proposals, but noted concerns with the regulatory evaluations (i.e., the cost-benefit analyses) and pushed for alternatives that "address[ed] weather-related and air traffic control related issues." As with the ANPRM, consumer comments indicated that "the Department's proposals do not go far enough and contend that additional regulatory measures are needed to better protect consumers." Department of Transportation, Enhancing Airline Passenger Protections, 74 Fed. Reg. 68,983, 68,983–68,984 (Dec. 30, 2009). US Airways was one of two carriers to comment on the NPRM (it had not commented on the ANPRM). Its comment, submitted on March 9, 2009, read, in part:

Although the Department is well-intentioned, this NPRM is overreaching and attempts to regulate air carriers for situations beyond their control. US Airways already has in place many of the elements that the Department is proposing to require in this NPRM. Nevertheless, US Airways opposes other provisions of the NPRM that would impose substantial new burdens on air carriers. In these comments, US Airways will highlight two particular areas of concern—the overall rationale for the NPRM and two needed revisions to any contingency plan requirement: (a) exclusion of international operations; and (b) enhanced regulatory accountability for airports. The Company also fully supports the comments of the Air Transport Association ("ATA") filed today in this docket. . . .

As an initial proposition, the notion that air carriers want to delay or inconvenience passengers should be forever stricken as a credible argument. There is no air carrier that would ever knowingly want to put passengers on an airplane for extended periods of time. Unfortunately, there are times where gridlock occurs that causes schedule delay and passenger inconvenience. These excessive delays extending well beyond scheduled departure/arrival times usually result from extreme weather conditions beyond the control of the air carrier. Nevertheless, air carrier management makes every attempt to avert or reduce the overall number of delays by making costly and inconvenient decisions to cancel flights, reroute passengers, permit cost-free itinerary changes, and in extreme examples, suspend all operations at a hub.

When facing extended delays, air carrier management makes decisions based on the based available data at the time, but weather forecasts do not always cooperate, and passengers, unfortunately, can experience long delays. . . .

US Airways understands that it is tempting to want to regulate to give passengers some relief from the rare case of lengthy on-board delays. Even with continued improvements by all air carriers in on-time performance, passengers are still occasionally delayed. For delays that are within the control of the air carrier, the Department's effort to identify chronically delayed flights and remind air carriers of their disclosure obligations is a good example of government and industry working constructively to address a problem for the benefit of consumers. As the Department knows, US Airways worked aggressively in reviewing all of the flights that were identified as chronically delayed and has reduced the number of US Airways flights appearing on DOT Tables 5 and 6 to a very small number, if any. . . .

US Airways understands the Department's interest in imposing an inflexible return-to-gate standard to attempt to avoid lengthy tarmac delays. As described above, however, US Airways already has a contingency plan in place to deal with lengthy onboard delays. It has long been necessary to have such a "voluntary" plan because it is inevitable that when certain weather conditions occur, passengers will experience longer-than-normal delays.

US Airways' existing contingency plan is substantially similar to the contingency plan that the Department proposes, except that it leaves to the carrier's expertise the decision about when the aircraft should return to the gate. We oppose any enforceable provision that the air carrier return to the gate at a fixed time. Not only will returning to the gate at a specific time result in the possibility of additional cancellations, but it could also trigger a spillover effect to the next day. Air carriers do not have unlimited resources to recover from these types of situations. . . .

Comments of US Airways, Inc. in Docket OST–2007–0022, https://www.regulations.gov/document?D=DOT-OST-2007-0022-0246 (footnotes omitted).

What do you find persuasive in US Airways's comment? Less persuasive? The carrier filed its comment on the last possible day but knew what another industry commenter, ATA, was going to say even though it was filing at the same time. Consumer groups would not have had time to respond to either US Airways's or ATA's comment. *Is this sharing of information between US Airways and ATA, or the lack of time to respond, a problem?* As noted below, the rule was adopted. An academic study published five years after the rule took effect found the regulation "has been highly effective in reducing the frequency of occurrence of long tarmac times." On the other hand, the study also found that "another significant effect of the rule has been the rise in flight cancellation rates [and subsequent rebooking and delays to destination]." Using some data modeling, the study found "a significant increase in passenger delays, especially for passengers scheduled to travel on the flights which are at risk of long tarmac delays." Chiwei Yana et al., Tarmac delay policies: A passenger-centric analysis, 83 Transportation Research Part A: Policy and Practice 42, 42 (2016). *Does this change your mind about your reactions to US Airways's comment?*

Some proposed rules that are not finalized before a change in administration are withdrawn under new leadership. But the Department of Transportation here issued a final rule in December 2009, to take effect in April 2010, after clearing it with OIRA (then headed by administrative law scholar extraordinaire, Cass Sunstein) [hereinafter 2010 rule]. In short, according to the agency:

We have decided to adopt a final rule along the lines set forth in the NPRM, with one important exception: We are strengthening the protections for consumers from those initially proposed by setting time limits (1) for carriers to provide food and water to passengers; and (2) to deplane passengers when lengthy tarmac delays occur on domestic flights. In adopting this approach, we have carefully considered all the comments in this proceeding and believe that our action strikes the proper balance between permitting carriers the freedom to make marketplace-based decisions while ensuring consumers can count on receiving the protections they deserve in the unlikely event of an extended tarmac delay.

The final rule requires that each plan include, at a minimum, the following: (1) An assurance that, for domestic flights, the air carrier will not permit an aircraft to remain on the tarmac for more than three hours unless the pilot-in-command determines there is a safety-related or security-related impediment to deplaning passengers (e.g., . . . weather, air traffic control, a directive from an appropriate government agency, etc.), or Air Traffic Control advises the pilot-in-command that returning to the gate or permitting passengers to disembark elsewhere would significantly disrupt airport operations . . . .

Department of Transportation, Enhancing Airline Passenger Protections, 74 Fed. Reg. 68,983, 68,987 (Dec. 30, 2009). The final rule was weaker than the NPRM in some respects. Notably, the Department did not mandate that carriers incorporate their contingency plans in their contracts of carriage—which would have permitted breach of contract suits—after receiving comments that it lacked the legal authority to force such a change. Instead, the final rule "strongly encourages carriers to incorporate the terms of their contingency plans in their contracts of carriage, as most major carriers have done voluntarily with respect to their customer service plans." Id. at 68,989.

Had the final rule required a change to contracts of carriage, airlines could have sued the Transportation Department on substantive grounds, though they may not have succeeded. Theoretically, airlines could have argued that the enacted 3-hour time limit exceeded the agency's statutory authority. *Look back to the statutory provisions. Would you agree with such an argument? Are those provisions ambiguous? If so, should courts defer to the Department's interpretation of those provisions?* In other rulemakings, substantive objections may derive not only from relevant statutes but also from the U.S. Constitution.

Here, the Department of Transportation engaged in considerable process before issuing its final rule: an ANPRM with a comment period and an NPRM with a comment period. Those unhappy with the rule would not have a plausible argument that the agency should have provided more opportunity to comment (though perhaps there would have been a plausible claim if the agency had denied the request for a 30-day extension of the NPRM's comment period and there were other extenuating circumstances making the original 60-day period insufficient). But there are other potential process objections to a rulemaking. For instance, a challenger might allege that the agency did not provide sufficient information with the NPRM to permit meaningful comment. In addition, if the final rule is not identical to the proposed rule, a challenger could claim that the final rule not a "logical outgrowth" of the proposed rule, as is required. The final rule was largely stronger than the proposed rule. *Should that be permissible?* As with the substantive challenges, statutes (particularly the APA) and the Constitution can come into play for procedural objections.

The Department's final rule was followed by legislation. In 2012, Congress enacted, with support from both parties, a modified version of the proposed legislation discussed above—notably without the time limits on how long a plane can remain on the tarmac before giving passengers the opportunity to deplane. The FAA Modernization and Safety Improvement Act of 2012, a major reauthorization bill covering many issues, codified some of the earlier adopted regulatory structure. Section 415 mandates that carriers and airport operators of a certain size submit (for the Secretary of Transportation's approval) emergency contingency plans for how they will:

> (A) provide adequate food, potable water, restroom facilities, comfortable cabin temperatures, and access to medical treatment for passengers onboard an aircraft at the airport when the departure of a flight is delayed or the disembarkation of passengers is delayed; (B) share facilities and make gates available at the airport in an emergency; and (C) allow passengers to deplane following an excessive tarmac delay in accordance with [another section].

Although the legislation did not adopt the three-hour cut-off mandate that appears in the Department's final rule, it also did not repeal the regulation. Section 415 also requires the Secretary to "establish a consumer complaints toll-free hotline telephone number for the use of passengers in air transportation and shall take actions to notify the public of—(1) that telephone number; and (2) the Internet Web site of the Aviation Consumer Protection Division of the Department of Transportation." It also mandates covered carriers to provide information on the telephone hotline and the Aviation Consumer Protection Division, among other items. Public Law No. 112–95, 126 Stat. 11, § 415.

In fact, as with much significant agency regulation, no legal challenges were filed against this major rulemaking. It is a myth—largely held by commentators, even in administrative law—that most rules result in legal challenges in federal courts.

Having a regulation in place, of course, is not the end of the story. It may not be followed. *Should the agency that has authority to regulate also have authority to enforce? Or should another agency be in charge of enforcement? What kind of enforcement regime would you desire? For instance, should the agency be able to issue penalties itself or should the agency have to take the matter to a federal court? Should an enforcement agency go after every violation? Could it as a practical matter do so?*

By statute, the "Secretary of Transportation may impose a civil penalty for . . . [certain] violations [including of the 2010 rule] only after notice and an opportunity for a hearing." 49 U.S.C. § 46301. The Department learns of violations from carriers themselves (as the rule has reporting mandates) and from consumer complaints (see: https://www. transportation.gov/airconsumer/file-consumer-complaint).

The Department's Office of Aviation Enforcement and Proceedings came after American Airlines for violating the 2010 rule, among other provisions. The parties settled in 2016. The agreement began:

> This consent order concerns violations by American Airlines, Inc. (American Airlines) of 14 CFR 259.4 (the Department's tarmac delay rule), 49 U.S.C. § 41712 (prohibition against unfair and deceptive practices), and 49 U.S.C. § 42301 (requirement to adhere to a carrier's tarmac delay contingency plan). American Airlines failed to adhere to the assurances in its contingency plan for lengthy tarmac delays for twenty domestic flights at Charlotte International Airport (CLT) on February 16, 2013, six domestic flights at Dallas/Fort Worth International Airport (DFW) on February 27, 2015, and one domestic flight at Shreveport Regional Airport (SHV) on October 22, 2015. Specifically, the carrier permitted the flights to remain on the tarmac for more than three hours without providing passengers an opportunity to deplane. This order directs American Airlines to cease and desist from future similar violations of Part 259 and sections 41712 and 42301 and assesses American Airlines $1.6 million in civil penalties.

Department of Transportation, Consent Order with American Airlines (Dec. 14, 2016), at 1, https://www.transportation.gov/sites/dot.gov/files/docs/eo-2016-12-10.pdf (footnotes omitted).

The fine is steep. But unlike successful contract or tort litigation where any damages would go entirely to the plaintiff (and her attorneys), only $602,000 of the fine gets "credited to American Airlines for compensation provided to passengers on the affected flights"; another $303,000 goes back to the carrier for part of "the carrier's expended costs of acquiring, operating and maintaining a surface management and surveillance system at CLT and DFW to monitor the location of each aircraft on the airfield." Id. at 15. *Does the fine, as structured, strike you as appropriate?*

The 2010 rule and 2012 legislation, of course, did not make air travel trouble free. In April 2016, President Obama issued an Executive Order, Steps to Increase Competition and Better Inform Consumers and Workers to Support Continued Growth of the American Economy. In part, it directed executive departments and agencies "with authorities that could be used to enhance competition (agencies)" to, "where consistent with other laws, use those authorities to promote competition, arm consumers and workers with the information they need to make informed choices, and eliminate regulations that restrict competition without corresponding benefits to the American public." Exec. Order No. 13,725, 81 Fed. Reg. 23,417 (April 20, 2016). *Should the President be able to order agencies to undertake particular rulemakings in this manner?*

Following the White House's directive, the Department of Transportation finalized rules requiring more information disclosure by airlines and barring "cherry picking" of data for certain performance metrics. It also issued an ANPRM mandating that airlines refund baggage fees when the baggage is "substantially delayed." The White House touted both actions in a released fact sheet titled "Obama Administration Announces New Actions to Spur Competition in the Airline Industry, Give Consumers the Information They Need to Make Informed Choices." *What are the benefits and costs of having such coordination between the White House and a cabinet department on agency regulation?*

In the first few months of President Trump's Administration, overbooking of airplane flights and poor customer service has generated considerable media attention (and You Tube hits). For instance, David Dao was physically dragged off a United Airlines flight (operated by a regional carrier) in April 2017. He eventually settled with the airline before filing an actual suit, but after obtaining an attorney. Some are calling for additional legislation, and others for more regulation. The House Transportation and Infrastructure Committee and the Senate Subcommittee on Aviation (of the Transportation Committee) held hearings in May 2017. And so, the circle of potential policymaking continues. *If you were advising President Trump and you know that one of the President's programs is to eliminate two regulations for every new regulation, would you advise him to pressure the Transportation Department to get rid of the 2010 tarmac rule?*

SECTION 2.   THE BASICS

> *Frequently Asked Questions*

If you were to log on to a hypothetical website—www.admin law.gov—to find some fundamental background for understanding administrative law in general (or the preceding problem in particular) you might find something like the following. As with most sets of Frequently Asked Questions, the responses to these FAQs are only initial entry points for more sophisticated questions and answers that will arise throughout this book.

Frequently Asked Questions

- What is administrative law?

- What entities are administrative agencies?

- Is everything the government does considered agency action?

- Is administrative law important?

- Is administrative law just politics by another name?

- How are administrative agencies organized?

- How do administrative agencies do their work?

- How do administrative agencies make regulations?

- How do administrative agencies decide cases?

- How do courts review the work of administrative agencies?

- How do the White House and Congress oversee the actions of administrative agencies?

- How does administrative law contribute to social welfare?

- How does administrative law contribute to freedom?

- How does administrative law contribute to social justice?

What is administrative law?

Administrative law comprises the body of general rules and principles governing administrative agencies—governing both how they do their own work and how the results of that work will be viewed, or reviewed, by the President, Congress, and the federal courts. It exists in every country and at all levels of government—federal, state, and local—in our system and there are some emerging principles of international (or global as it is sometimes called) administrative law, too. Federal administrative law, the subject of this book (and website), can be found in many sources: the Constitution, federal statutes, executive orders, and decisions of the federal courts—as well as in the legal materials, decisions and rules of all sorts, developed by the agencies themselves.

Administrative law, as a body of general principles, needs to be distinguished from the particular substantive law implemented by each individual agency—distinguished, that is, from the tax law practiced by the Internal Revenue Service, the labor law of the National Labor Relations Board, or the occupational safety and health law of the Occupational Safety and Health Administration. Administrative law takes place on a more general, and more process-oriented, plane. The distinction is somewhat analogous to that between civil procedure and torts or contracts. Every torts or contracts case, because it came from a judicial proceeding, has a civil procedure matrix, even if the principal topic of dispute concerns a substantive torts or contracts doctrine. Similarly, administrative law treats general questions like the process by which agency regulations must be made, or the authority agency regulations will have if reviewed in court, rather than of the more particular questions regarding labor or tax policy.

What entities are administrative agencies?

Administrative agencies are all of the authorities and operating units of the government except for the constitutionally established entities in the first three Articles: that is, except for Congress, the President and Vice President, and the Supreme Court. They are sometimes called "agencies," but sometimes "departments," sometimes "boards," sometimes "commissions"—they are all still agencies. Just as agents, in the ordinary sense of the term, carry out tasks for their principals, so, too, do agencies carry out the instructions of, and are responsible to, the three great constitutionally established, institutional "principals." Because administrative agencies largely are not established or even mentioned by the Constitution, they have to be created by statute or, in some cases, by presidential order.

There are five major categories of agencies. First, White House agencies, such as the Office of Management and Budget (which houses OIRA, described in the example above), sit within the Executive Office of the President. Second, there are fifteen cabinet departments. The most recent addition was the Department of Homeland Security, which started operations in 2003. Their leaders, along with the Vice President, make up the President's Cabinet. Third, executive agencies are sometimes housed within cabinet departments, like the FAA discussed above. Others are freestanding, like the Environmental Protection Agency. A few of their leaders (along with some leaders of the White House agencies) are often considered "cabinet-level," at the discretion of the President. Fourth, independent regulatory commissions and boards, like the National Transportation Safety Board (another transportation agency described briefly in a footnote above), are run by multi-member leadership and excluded from some administrative procedures imposed by the White House. As with cabinet departments and executive agencies, they cover a wide range of policy areas. Finally, there are agencies that are only partly federal in nature, including public-private entities like government corporations, federal-state organizations like those established under the Compact Clause, and federal-foreign institutions like those created by treaties.

Sometimes, agencies change type. The Postal Service, one of the country's oldest agencies (even pre-dating the country's founding), started as a freestanding executive agency, with its leader considered cabinet-level for decades. Since 1971, it has functioned as a government corporation. It is the largest employer of nonmilitary government employees and the second largest employer of civilians in either the public or private sector, after Walmart.

Is everything the government does considered agency action?

Almost. When Congress passes a statute, that is not agency action, nor is a court making a decision or the President giving a speech or issuing a pardon. But when the Internal Revenue Service collects taxes, the Bureau of Land Management leases public lands, the National Labor Relations Board supervises a workplace election, the Centers for Disease Control collect epidemiological data, Immigration and Customs Enforcement deports an undocumented immigrant, the Environmental Protection Agency sets a new air quality standard, or the Social Security Administration pays disability benefits—these all are agency action.

However, some agency action is so given over to the discretion of the officials involved that it almost disappears from the ken of administrative law. The decisions of the Air Force as to what jets to order, a federal prosecutor as to whether to press charges, or the State Department trying to set foreign policy in the Middle East are all in some sense agency action, but they are unlikely to raise issues subject to traditional forms of administrative law control covered in this book. Some raise unique issues of law, such as government contracting, with bid disputes in front of the Government Accountability Office or the Court of Federal Claims, for example. And sometimes the length or breadth of agency discretion, in this large sense of the term "discretion," is uncertain, as, for example, in the degree to which Congress intended to give individual agencies the complete freedom to decide what priorities they should establish in carrying out their general mandates.

Is administrative law important?

Indeed! Given what has already been said, it is clear that it is almost impossible to be a lawyer for the government (except perhaps for those who prosecute ordinary crimes) without some knowledge of administrative law. But the same is really true for most practitioners with private clients. Most transactions these days have a regulatory aspect to them, and understanding any regulatory framework requires knowledge not merely of the substantive policies but also of the types of processes and materials involved—the knowledge, in short, of administrative law. A recent survey by the National Council of Bar Examiners found that over 20 percent of new law school graduates listed administrative law as a primary practice area (and over 70 percent did some work in the field).

One might even go a bit further and say that it is hard even to follow the news knowledgeably without some understanding of administrative law. To speak of matters growing out the events of September 11, 2001: the implications of making airport security into a matter handled by a federal agency, the proper distribution of emergency funds to airlines in need of bailout and to the families of those killed, the powers and limits of a new Department of Homeland Security—these were all deeply affected by the doctrines of administrative law. The same could be said of the responses to the recent "Great Recession" (the financial crisis of 2007–2009): the handling of the Troubled Asset Relief Program and other bailout funds, the augmentation of the powers of the Federal Reserve Board and the Securities and Exchange Commission, and the establishment of a new agency, the Consumer Financial Protection Bureau. Given the growth of federal regulation over the last century or so, administrative law is one of the best places to see how law works in the modern world. (Two members of the current Supreme Court— Justices Breyer and Kagan—used to be professors of administrative law. And the late Justice Scalia also taught administrative law.)

Is administrative law just politics by another name?

Some say so. Because administrative agencies wield the government's power, they are of course intimately connected with many issues that are the subject of political debate. They are subject to frequent oversight by the President and Congress at the federal level and by states and localities beneath. But because administrative law deals with the proper legal structure for that use of power and that process of oversight, it brings to bear the values of the law: values such as regularity, consistency, evenhandedness, and participation. This tension—or if you like, this persistent problem of how to encapsulate political will in legal norms—bedevils administrative law. But this very closeness to, but separation from, politics also helps make the subject both interesting and important.

How are administrative agencies organized?

The Constitution says very little about the details of the structure of the federal government, so each agency is basically organized by the statute (or sometimes, by presidential directive) that puts it in business and tells it what its basic tasks are—this is often called the agency's "organic" statute (or founding memorandum). (Many times, but not always, the statute and the agency are eponyms: for example, the National Labor Relations Act establishing the National Labor Relations Board.) Nevertheless, and not surprisingly, there are many commonalities among most administrative agencies. There is a head of the agency, with a small cadre of advisers immediately responsible to that office, but the great bulk of agency personnel serve in "administrations," "services," "offices," or the like—subordinate units each with its own particular responsibilities and hierarchical organization. Thus, for example, the problem of controlling the gypsy moth is the immediate responsibility of a group of specialists in the Animal and Plant Health Inspection Service, headed by an Administrator and itself one of several bureaus under the authority of the Under Secretary for Marketing and Regulatory Programs, who is one of several undersecretaries under the authority of the Secretary of Agriculture. Legal staffs within agencies are typically segregated into special law offices. In any agency with substantial adjudicatory responsibilities, the administrative law judges (or other first-level adjudicators) and any appellate agency tribunal are separated from both the staff and the legal counsel of the agency. (Descriptions of the various federal departments and agencies, and organizational charts of their various units, can be found in the U.S. Government Manual, online at www.usgovernmentmanual.gov.)

At the top of the agencies are Senate-confirmed presidential appointees. There are, however, two different general patterns for these leadership structures. As described above, some agencies are regulatory commissions or boards, almost always headed by multi-member bodies, whose members can be removed from office by the President only for "cause," and accordingly are sometimes called "independent" agencies. The NTSB is such an example. Other entities—White House agencies, cabinet departments, and executive agencies—are typically headed by a single administrator who serves at the President's pleasure without any term specified at the start. There are agencies with unusual leadership arrangements. The new CFPB, for example, is headed by an administrator appointed to a five-year term, who can be fired only for cause (at the time when this casebook went to press, the constitutionality of this structure was under en banc review at the U.S. Court of Appeals for the D.C. Circuit, with oral arguments having taken place in May 2017). The Postal Service's entire Board of Governors is appointed by the President and confirmed by the Senate; that Board (and not the President) then chooses the Postmaster General (and then the Board and Postmaster General select the Deputy Postmaster General).

To determine who has what specific substantive responsibilities within an agency, one has to work with statutes that delegate authority and with presidential directives and agency rules that redelegate it. Some of the procedural requirements of administrative law also vary by the form of organization of an agency—for example, the Government in the Sunshine Act applies to agencies headed by multi-member boards but not to those headed by single administrators, and the Federal Vacancies Reform Act largely permits acting officials only in agencies that are not run by multi-member boards. But the overwhelming majority of administrative law requirements do not turn on the particularities of each agency's organization. Rather, they are responsibilities placed on all agencies simply because they are agencies.

How do administrative agencies do their work?

Agencies act in many ways. The Chairman of the Federal Reserve Board may well influence the course of the economy—or at least the financial markets—simply by giving a speech. The Department of Defense takes a more direct route to the same end—it spends a lot of money. According to a new government website (www.usaspending.gov) that brings spending across the government together for the first time in one place, the federal government spent $3.85 trillion in 2016 (about half of that went to Social Security, Medicare, and national defense)—of the total, individuals received 30 percent; for profit entities obtained 19 percent, and states and localities took in 17 percent. Even spending actions have a legal structure, depending as they do on delegated authority, not to mention appropriations.

But agencies also do things that look more "law" like, and it is those things that mostly come to mind when one speaks of administrative law. Agencies make regulations. A quick look at the Code of Federal Regulations (CFR) (available in hard copy or online at www.ecfr.gov) will show that agencies make a great many regulations. According to the Congressional Review Service, between 1976 and 2015, agencies published between 3,410 (in 2015) and 7,745 (in 1980) final rules in the Federal Register. In addition, in the period of 1997 to 2015, "major rules," which are rules expected to have an annual economic impact of at least $100 million or other significant economic effects, ranged between an annual low of 51 (in 1999 and 2002) and a high of 100 (in 2010). To compare, looking at two-year Congresses between 1977 and 2014, enacted laws ranged from 284 (for 2011 and 2012 together) to 804 (for 1977 and 1978).

Agencies also adjudicate. In Fiscal Year 2014, the Social Security Administration decided over 2.8 million initial claims for disability benefits (and presided over 680,000 hearings). In the same year, the Veterans Administration processed over 1.3 million initial disability and pension claims for benefits, and immigration courts, under the Department of Justice, completed over 184,000 cases. All of these agencies have considerable backlogs of claims. To compare, in that year, including both civil and criminal matters, the federal appellate courts saw nearly 55,000 filings and district courts received over 376,000 filings. Many of these matters, particularly at the district court level, are settled out of court.

Agencies license activities or individuals too. One cannot just decide to be a pilot and start carrying passengers for hire! And agencies enforce their statutes and regulations—by sending out inspectors, revoking licenses, levying penalties, or bringing criminal actions in court. Any particular agency can do only the things that its governing statutes authorize it to do, but the typical agency will have many of these powers. Or, in other words, individual agencies—say, the Securities and Exchange Commission—can set priorities, administer budgets, make rules, decide cases, and pursue enforcement actions, and in doing so exercise legislative, executive, and judicial powers that at the constitutional level would be split up among Congress, the President, and the federal courts.

Finally, although administrative law often assumes only one agency is acting in a particular issue area, there are considerable overlaps in regulatory authority across agencies. Sometimes, agencies work together to produce joint action; other times, they fight with each other over turf and policy outcomes.

How do administrative agencies make regulations?

Needless to say, this is in some respects a technical question that can only be answered after considerable study. In general, administrative rulemaking begins as you might expect—with a decision on the part of an agency to do something to carry out one of its statutory responsibilities. Because agencies usually have more they could do than they have time or money for, this is not necessarily an easy decision to make. Thus setting priorities, although usually thought of as a purely executive task, has important legal consequences. And along with the decision to do something is, of course, the issue of what to do. Here, most commonly, a team within the agency—some with technical expertise, some with legal expertise, and so forth—will develop a more-or-less worked out proposal. The archetypal procedure is then to conduct a "notice-and-comment" rulemaking—that is, to give notice that a rule is in the offing and to allow for those outside the agency to comment on the proposal. Staff then review that rulemaking record before making any rule final. The White House is often involved in big rulemakings by cabinet departments and executive agencies from the very start (in terms of prompting action) through to the very end (reviewing proposed and final rules). Assuming that the proper procedures have been followed, and that the rule is substantively within the agency's statutory authority, final administrative rules have full legislative force, binding courts, agencies, and citizens alike to their terms.

How do administrative agencies decide cases?

If by "cases" you mean the application of statutes or rules to individual circumstances, administrative agencies decide cases informally, and by the millions, all the time. (If, for example, you have been away from the United States and, on returning, turned in a customs form (now often electronic) and passed through customs without paying duty, you have successfully "won" an administrative adjudication.) If by "cases" you instead mean the relatively formal proceedings that lead to final determinations of contested matters and may form precedents for future agency action, then you will not be mistaken if you think of them as trial-type proceedings—with some differences. The most formal agency cases are heard in the first instance before administrative law judges, officials who are not judges as understood in Article III of the Constitution but have substantial civil service protections to help them maintain their independence. Often there is an intermediate level of review before a reasonably sheltered appeals panel. But if the case is important, or has significant contested issues, the ultimate decision may be made by the head of the agency (the head may be a single person or a multi-member board or commission). These officials also have political and policy responsibilities; they are not the same as appellate judges. But they are empowered to decide the issues in the adjudication. In short, there is often a closer connection between overt policy authority and case decision in administrative adjudication than in courtroom adjudication.

This might be viewed as the genius of administrative adjudication, or as its fatal flaw. (Sometimes, Congress has shied away from this standard arrangement and separated adjudicatory matters from the rest of the agency's responsibilities. The Occupational Health and Safety Act, for example, created both a regulatory and an enforcement agency in one, the well-known OSHA, and a separate case-hearing agency, the lesser-known OSHRC (Occupational Safety and Health Review Commission).)

How do courts review the work of administrative agencies?

Almost every statute that creates an administrative agency and delegates authority to it also provides for the major final decisions of the agency—the rules it makes and the cases it decides—to be reviewed by a federal court. Occasionally this review is de novo, for example, when a court reviews an agency's decision to withhold information that has been requested by someone under the Freedom of Information Act. And sometimes the matter on review can raise an issue, such as a constitutional issue, on which a court will displace completely the agency's judgment. But on most matters, the fact that the agency has decided one way or another has some weight before the court; to put the point another way, the court will to some extent defer to the agency's initial judgment. In part, this is a straightforward reflection of the reality that, in both rulemaking and adjudication, most often review takes place on the record the agency has built, which necessarily reflects how the agency framed the issue. (Indeed, Congress often provides for agency decisions to be reviewed for the first time in a federal Court of Appeals, that is, in a court that hears argument but doesn't take new evidence.) But deference to the agency is also grounded on the belief that on many matters the agency may have made a better decision than the judges would if they substituted their own judgment. This might be because the agency understands the factual matrix better because of its daily involvement with the problem at hand, because the agency gets more political input on a matter that turns on a value-laden choice among possible policies, because the agency has a set of experts who understand the science or economics of the problem better than generalist judges, or perhaps some other reason. What the grounds of deference are, and how far they go, are a matter of considerable debate among scholars, judges, and politicians. Chevron, U.S.A., Inc. v. Natural Resources Defense Council, Inc., 467 U.S. 837—the Chevron case, decided in 1984, which you will hear much about—held that judges should even defer to an agency's interpretation of Congress's statutory language if the language is ambiguous and the view of the agency delegated to act under the statute is reasonable. It is both the most cited case in modern administrative law and one of the most controversial.

How do the White House and Congress oversee the actions of administrative agencies?

Most agency actions are not reviewed by a court, though agencies, like private parties, act in the "shadow of the law." In addition, agencies face considerable non-judicial oversight, within and outside the federal government, and a fair number of pages in these materials deal with this. At the front end, top agency leaders are selected by the President and confirmed by the Senate. On the one hand, Congress orders agencies to perform tasks, and at times even imposes deadlines on them; on the other, its appropriations of operating funds may not suffice for agencies to perform these tasks. The White House also "directs" certain agencies to undertake particular programs. In the middle, OIRA reviews significant regulations by cabinet departments and executive agencies before they are issued. The President (and another agency leader for that matter) can also ask an agency—of any type—to consider her views in a particular policy area. Congress can withhold funding for particular agency programs through appropriations riders and can hold hearings to question agency officials on their plans.

At the back end, the President can fire almost all political officials not located in independent regulatory commissions and boards for any reason. In addition, the President can express her displeasure, short of firing, in public or private forums. Congress too can attack agency decisions at the back end. Congress can repeal certain important agency regulations under the Congressional Review Act, which then prevents an agency from issuing a rule in the future in "substantially the same form". Until 2017, only one regulation had been overturned through the CRA. In 2017, with unified Republican government, Congress repealed 14 rules issued by agencies during President Obama's Administration (and one rule issued by the Consumer Financial Protection Bureau, which was still led by a President Obama appointee after President Trump took office) under the CRA's fast track procedures. Congress can also launch formal investigations, hold hearings, and engage in less formal mechanisms.

How much force the White House's views should carry is a matter of considerable dispute, depending on agency type and other factors. (There is also conflict, although less, about congressional pressure). These tensions generally do not play themselves out in court.

How does administrative law contribute to social welfare?

The programs run by administrative agencies have considerable effects on our economy and on other aspects of our welfare as a society. The Federal Reserve Board sets interest rates; the Securities and Exchange Commission tries to keep securities markets free of fraud; the Environmental Protection Agency establishes and enforces pollution standards; the National Park Service maintains many of our greatest natural treasures. Administrative law, as the law of the process by which these things happen, contributes to social welfare insofar as it improves the performance of these functions—insofar as it contributes to agency decisions being better thought through, taking account of more varied interests, being better communicated to those affected, paying greater attention to human dignity, being more rationally enforced, *and* by not creating enormous burdens such as making things costlier, more cumbersome, or too slow. The cost-benefit analysis required by OIRA for significant rulemakings by many agencies appears, at first blush, to guarantee an improvement in social welfare. But the regulatory analysis is overseen by a White House agency, with close ties to presidential priorities, and it is only one component of what the agency considers in signing off on major rulemakings. Whether administrative law improves social welfare—or, perhaps better put, what the doctrines of administrative law should be so it will have this beneficial effect—is one of the persistent problems of the subject.

How does administrative law contribute to freedom?

Many administrative agencies regulate private activity. Regulation inherently reduces the freedom of some people compared to what they would have had if only common law rules applied. At the same time, regulation can increase freedom—of regulatory beneficiaries and even of regulated entities that receive permission to undertake particular actions. Whether any particular regulatory regime increases or decreases individual freedom overall is thus a program-by-program question. But freedom is not just an individual matter; it also is a matter of the working of our governmental institutions. Administrative law serves to increase this social or political freedom when it makes the workings of the government more transparent to citizens and when it provides increased opportunities for them to participate in governmental affairs. Whether American administrative law adequately does this or whether it overdoes this are persistent questions. But it is at least worth noting that many foreign legal scholars and law reformers consider some of the doctrines of American administrative law—for instance, the wide comment possibilities available during much rulemaking and the Freedom of Information Act—to be considerably better in this regard than their own existing arrangements.

How does administrative law contribute to social justice?

The programs run by administrative agencies also have tremendous consequences for how benefits and burdens are distributed throughout the society—benefits as disparate as disability pensions, minimum wages, cleanups of toxic wastes, and admission to the United States itself, and burdens as disparate as filing forms, reengineering production processes, and, of course, paying taxes. The very disciplining of these activities to the regularity of the law—the reduction in arbitrariness of the distribution of either benefits or burdens—might be considered a considerable contribution to social justice. That administrative law doctrines make some real contribution of this sort is hard to deny. More difficult is the question whether administrative law conduces toward or away from social equality, or if not equality, then toward or away from the fair distribution of society's benefits. Seemingly technical doctrines can have distributive effects. Indeed, those effects have fueled some of the major disputes in the history of administrative law. As to what the overall balance is, perhaps all that can be said with safety is that the issue is contentious.

SECTION 3.   THE TASKS OF ADMINISTRATIVE LAW

> *a. Historical Perspectives on the Administrative State*
> *b. Legal Perspectives on the Administrative State*
> *c. Contemporary Perspectives on the Administrative State*

Administrative law begins with the statutes that establish and empower administrative agencies—decisions taken by the political branches of government that define the scope of each agency's authority and mandate the modes through which that authority is to be exercised. Have Congress and the President acted wisely? Given the ubiquity of agencies in the modern world, these decisions are probably best evaluated not in absolute terms (administrative agencies are "good" or "bad") but in comparative terms (they are "better" or "worse").

Better or worse than what? When a new agency is being considered—such as the recently established and controversial Consumer Financial Protection Bureau—political rhetoric usually frames the choice in terms of action, inaction, or reverse action: administrative agencies are equated with "regulation" and contrasted with the choices of "doing nothing" or "deregulation." From the standpoint of legal analysis, however, this is insufficient. The difficulty can be seen most clearly if we ask: what in the legal universe does Congress's "doing nothing" equate with? It doesn't equate with "no law," if only because there are very few things on which there is ever "no law." There may be state statutes, state regulations, or common law requirements that govern, for example. Indeed, "doing nothing" from the political point of view might well leave in place a highly articulated and demanding set of legal norms.

In the American legal system, there are three likely alternatives to the establishment of administrative agencies. First, there are common law regimes, created and implemented through the courts. Products liability law is, by and large, an example of a common-law legal regime. Second, there are statutory law regimes, in which legislatures establish rules that are directly enforceable in court. The law of sales under the

Uniform Commercial Code is an example of this type of legal regime. Third, there are privatization regimes, where legislatures or agencies contract with private entities to provide goods or services that the government could have dispensed. The use of private prisons and detention facilities to confine inmates and immigrants without proper documentation, respectively, is an example of the third regime. It is also important to keep in mind that agencies exist at the federal, state, and local levels, and that one alternative to federal regulation is state or local regulation. This book focuses on federal agencies, but many of the lessons also apply, at least in part, to nonfederal agencies.

To decide the value of establishing an administrative law regime to handle a particular topic, it is thus necessary to compare the advantages or disadvantages of it to each of these other possibilities. These pluses and minuses are of two general varieties. One is institutional: what are the advantages or disadvantages of creating special-purpose agencies staffed by appointed and career personnel rather than relying on general-purpose legislatures and courts or, alternatively, on a specialized private organization. The other is in terms of conferred powers: legislatures generally make rules, while courts usually decide cases; agencies can be given both these powers within their jurisdictions *and* the powers to conduct inspections, grant licenses, broadcast information, undertake research, and do other things as well. One might then ask overall whether the probable use of a panoply of powers by a specialized organ of government resting on delegated powers is likely to be better or worse, in addressing the matter at hand, than having the legislature itself establish a set of directly legally effective rules or than leaving the whole matter to the courts to work out as cases arise. In addition, one might query what decisions should be governmental decisions as opposed to private decisions with some or no governmental oversight.

These are complex questions. In addition, administrative agencies are not static. Their design, authority, and oversight can change through time. Below is a scholarly introduction to some of the issues. We begin with some brief histories of the federal administrative state, presented in chronological order of the periods they describe, from the founding of our country to the 1960s. And then we turn to some fundamental legal perspectives on the tasks and legitimacy of the administrative state, listed in chronological order of publication. Finally, we conclude with more recent views of the modern federal bureaucracy, also provided in publication order.

a. Historical Perspectives on the Administrative State

(1) NICHOLAS R. PARRILLO, AGAINST THE PROFIT MOTIVE: THE SALARY REVOLUTION IN AMERICAN GOVERNMENT, 1780–1940, at 1–4 (2013): "In America today, the lawful income of a public official consists of a salary. However, in the eighteenth century and often far into the nineteenth and

early twentieth centuries, American law authorized a wider variety of ways for officials to make money. Judges charged fees for transactions in the cases they heard. District attorneys won a fee for each criminal they convicted. Tax investigators received a percentage of the evasions they discovered. Naval officers were awarded a percentage of the value of the ships they captured, plus bounties for the enemy sailors on board ships they sank. Militiamen enjoyed rewards for capturing Indians or taking their scalps. Policemen were allowed rewards for recovering stolen property or arresting suspects. Jailors collected fees from inmates for permitting them various privileges, and the managers of penitentiaries had a share of the product of inmates' labor. Clerks deciding immigrants' applications for citizenship took a fee for every application. Government doctors deciding veterans' applications for benefits did the same, as did federal land officers deciding settlers' applications for homesteads. Even diplomats could lawfully accept a 'gift' from a foreign government upon finalizing a treaty.

"What these arrangements had in common was that the officers' incomes depended, immediately and objectively, on the delivery of services and the achievement of outputs. By a gradual yet profound transformation extending from the late eighteenth century through the early twentieth century, American lawmakers abolished all these forms of income and replaced them with the fixed salaries that we now take for granted in government service, thus attenuating the relationship of officials' income to their conduct. In so doing, they made the absence of the profit motive a defining feature of government.

"The key to comprehending this transformation is to understand the nonsalary forms of pay that initially predominated. There were two basic types, which I term *facilitative payments* and *bounties*. A facilitative payment was a sum that an officer received for performing a service that the affected person wanted or needed, such as processing an application or issuing a permit. A bounty was a sum that an officer received for performing a task that the affected person did not want and might resist, such as arresting a suspect, discovering tax delinquencies, or forcing an inmate to do hard labor.

"The two forms of payment tended to give rise to two very different social relationships between officials and the people with whom they dealt. The facilitative payment tended to promote reciprocal exchange between the officer and the recipient of the service, working to the benefit of both. It fostered mutual accommodation. . . . In contrast, the bounty tended to promote adversarialism. The officer gained by the affected person's loss-by taking state-mandated action that the affected person wanted left undone. . . .

"The two different social dynamics generated by facilitative payments and bounties inspired, respectively, two different arguments for why officials' profitseeking was incompatible with the needs and values of a liberal-democratic republic and therefore had to be abolished.

The critique of facilitative payments was essentially that customer-seller accommodation no longer had a rightful place in government. . . . The critique of bounties was quite different. . . . The officer's monetary incentive to impose sanctions on laypersons placed him in such an adversarial posture toward them as to vitiate their trust in government and elicit from them a mirror-image adversarial response. In addition, officers' profit motive discouraged them from making the kind of subjective and discretionary decisions not to enforce the law that were (and are) necessary to sand off the hard edges of modern slate power so it can win acceptance by the population. As lawmakers vested officials with more power and charged them with more ambitious missions, selflessness and forbearance became necessary to vest the officialdom with legitimacy and to foster the essential minimum of lay cooperation that makes the modem state workable."

(2)   DANIEL R. ERNST, TOCQUEVILLE'S NIGHTMARE: THE ADMINISTRATIVE STATE EMERGES IN AMERICA, 1900–1940, at 1–3, 7–8 (2014): "When the French aristocrat Alexis de Tocqueville visited America in the 1830s, he discovered that although the United States had 'centralized government,' it had little in the way of 'centralized administration,' bureaucracies through which federal officials could impose their will on a dispersed and factious people. This seeming shortcoming, Tocqueville decided, was a very good thing. . . .

"By 1940, America was still not Europe, but it had acquired a great deal of centralized administration. Teams of administrators resolved disputes; regulated agriculture and industry; collected taxes; and distributed grants, loans, and other benefits. . . . Something about the 'machinery of government' that Americans had built for themselves had confounded Tocqueville's expectations.

"That something was the rule of law. . . .

"Americans' belief that courts might deliver them from Tocqueville's nightmare gave a distinctly legalistic cast to the administrative state they created after 1900. Although courts accorded administrators great freedom when acting within their legislative and constitutional limits, they insisted on retaining the power to call wayward administrators to account, much as they would farmers who let their cattle forage on the land of others. Further, the agencies themselves usually acted by deciding individual cases rather than making rules and regulations, their most controversial activity today. Even when engaged in the 'legislative' act of prospectively setting rates for public utilities, administrators proceeded case by case. Judges readily assumed that norms of due process that had been worked out in the courts ought also to govern the 'quasi-adjudication' of administrative agencies, and they condemned administrators who violated these norms. In particular, they expected administrators to maintain a judicial aloofness from subordinates presenting the government's case against a respondent. To do otherwise would violate the ancient maxim that no man should be the judge in his own cause. It would also mix powers that, as Montesquieu and John Adams had insisted, must be kept separate if a government were to be one 'of laws and not of men.'

"The courts' influence went beyond the structure of an agency; it reached deep into the thought processes of administrators and taught them to justify their actions in a peculiarly legalistic way. . . .

"The story of how Americans faced down Tocqueville's nightmare still matters, but not because the solution they settled on by the end of the 1930s can or should be ours today. New forms of governance have emerged since 1940, in response, in part, to problems, such as expense, delay, and the 'capture' of regulators, that resulted after the rule of law became a rule of lawyers. Even so, the story told here answers a complaint that has gained in popularity since the eruption of the Tea Party movement in 2009: the statebuilders of the early twentieth century abandoned an American tradition of individualism in what amounted to 'the decisive wrong turn in the nation's history.' This claim overlooks a crucial fact: the reformers who supposedly sent the Constitution into exile, actually designed the principles of individual rights, limited government, and due process into the administrative state."

(3) KAREN M. TANI, STATES OF DEPENDENCY: WELFARE, RIGHTS, AND AMERICAN GOVERNANCE, 1935–1972, at 9–10 (2016): "Most scholars associate the concept of welfare rights with the second half of the 1960s: with the broadening of the modern civil rights movement, the establishment of the War on Poverty's Legal Services Program, the flourishing of grassroots welfare rights organizations, and a series of bold pronouncements from the Supreme Court about the constitutional rights of poor citizens. . . . In fact, however, the idea of welfare as a right—and the related but distinct idea of welfare recipients as rights holders—has a longer history, one that both helps us understand why rights language appealed to poor Americans and their allies in the 1960s and why rights claims met such fierce resistance from other parts of the polity.

"This longer history has been obscured from view by a construct that continues to dominate our understanding of U.S. social welfare provision: the 'two-track welfare state.' Historically, national-level insurance-based programs—constituting what scholars call the upper track—have been more generous, better administered, and more secure. Old Age Insurance ('Social Security') is the classic example. Payments from these programs have generally been framed as earned rights or entitlements, and white men and their dependents have benefited disproportionately. 'Means-tested' programs, in contrast, such as Aid to Dependent Children (ADC) (now Temporary Aid to Needy Families), have historically been less generous and secure, more vulnerable to maladministration, and more stigmatizing. This lower track has disproportionately served women and racial minorities, and its benefits, according to the two-track account, are decidedly not rights. . . .

"Peering underneath the hood of this two-track welfare state, [this book] reveals that well before the War on Poverty or the modern welfare rights movement some government officials eagerly introduced rights concepts into the world of welfare. The Social Security Act, we tend to forget, was not just about Social Security; it also authorized matching grants to states for programs of need-based income support. These 'welfare' programs encompassed large categories of the poor: dependent (i.e., fatherless) children, the aged, and the blind. Desperate for funds and overwhelmed by their citizens' needs, nearly all states applied for grants—and thereby enabled the federal government to claim an ongoing role in the administration of a jealously guarded local function. . . . The task facing New Deal administrators was to reform and supplant what they self-servingly referred to as the 'old poor law,' a localized, nonuniform system of poor relief with very deep roots. Rights language appeared to be a useful tool for reaching uncomprehending and at times uncooperative state and local officials. The old poor law, federal administrators explained in speeches, guidance documents, and training sessions, understood relief as charity or a gratuity; that is why poor relief could at one time be administered by nonexperts, in a highly discretionary fashion, with little regard for the individual in need. The benefits of the new public assistance programs, in contrast, came to recipients as a matter of right, and therefore had to be administered in a more systematic and professional way, with due regard for the recipient's other rights—to fair and equal treatment, to autonomy in his or her spending choices, and to some degree of privacy."

b.   Legal Perspectives on the Administrative State

(1)   FELIX FRANKFURTER, THE TASK OF ADMINISTRATIVE LAW, 75 U. Pa. L. Rev. 614, 614–15 (1927): "The widening area of what in effect is law-making authority, exercised by officials whose actions are not subject to ordinary court review, constitutes perhaps the most striking contemporary tendency of the Anglo-American legal order. The massive volumes of Statutory Rules and Orders, published annually since 1890, testify to the pervasive domain of delegated legislation in Great Britain. The formulation and publication of executive orders and rules and regulations are in this country still in a primitive stage, which only serves to render more portentous the operation of these forms of law. But the range of control conferred by Congress and the State legislatures upon subsidiary law-making bodies, variously denominated as heads of departments, commissions and boards, penetrates in the United States, as in Great Britain and the Dominions, the whole gamut of human affairs. Hardly a measure passes Congress the effective execution of which is not conditioned upon rules and regulations emanating from the enforcing authorities. These administrative complements are euphemistically called 'filling in the details' of a policy set forth in statutes. But the 'details' are of the essence; they give meaning and

content to vague contours. The control of banking, insurance, public utilities, finance, industry, the professions, health and morals, in sum, the manifold response of government to the forces and needs of modern society, is building up a body of laws not written by legislatures, and of adjudications not made by courts and not subject to their revision. These powers are lodged in a vast congeries of agencies. We are in the midst of a process, largely unconscious and certainly unscientific, of adjusting the exercise of these powers to the traditional system of Anglo-American law and courts. A systematic scrutiny of these issues and a conscious effort towards their wise solution are the concerns of administrative law. The broad boundaries and far-reaching implications of these problems may be indicated by saying that administrative law deals with the field of legal control exercised by law-administering agencies other than courts, and the field of control exercised by courts over such agencies."

(2) JAMES M. LANDIS, THE ADMINISTRATIVE PROCESS 7, 30–38, 46, 154–55 (1938): "Two tendencies in the expanding civilization of the late nineteenth century seem to me to foreshadow the need for methods of government different in kind from those that had prevailed in the past. These are the rise of industrialism and the rise of democracy. Naturally, these two tendencies combined and interacted each upon the other, so that it becomes difficult to isolate cause and effect. . . . The rise of industrialism and the rise of democracy, however, brought new and difficult problems to government. A world that scarcely a hundred years ago could listen to Wordsworth's denunciation of railroads because their building despoiled the beauty of his northern landscapes is different, very different, from one that in 1938 has to determine lanes and flight levels for air traffic. While it was true that advances in transportation, communication, and mass production were in themselves disturbing elements, the profound problems were the social and economic questions that flowed from the era of mechanical invention. To their solution some contribution derived from the rise of humanitarianism. But the driving force was the recognition by the governing classes of our civilization of their growing dependence upon the promotion of the welfare of the governed. Concessions to rectify social mal-adjustments thus had to be made, however grudgingly. And as the demands for positive solutions increased and, in the form of legislative measures, were precipitated upon the cathodes of governmental activity, *laissez faire*—the simple belief that only good could come by giving economic forces free play—came to an end.

". . . [T]he reasons which prompted a resort to the administrative process . . . would seem to be reasonably clear. In large measure these reasons sprang from a distrust of the ability of the judicial process to make the necessary adjustments in the development of both law and regulatory methods as they related to particular industrial problems.

"Admittedly, the judicial process suffers from several basic and more or less unchangeable characteristics. One of these is its inability to maintain a longtime, uninterrupted interest in a relatively narrow and carefully defined area of economic and social activity. . . . A general jurisdiction leaves the resolution of an infinite variety of matters within the hands of courts. In the disposition of these claims judges are uninhibited in their discretion except for legislative rules of guidance or such other rules as they themselves may distill out of that vast reserve of materials that we call the common law. This breadth of jurisdiction and freedom of disposition tends somewhat to make judges jacks-of-all-trades and masters of none. . . .

"To these considerations must be added two others. The first is the recognition that there are certain fields where the making of law springs less from generalizations and principles drawn from the majestic authority of textbooks and cases, than from a 'practical' judgment which is based upon all the available considerations and which has in mind the most desirable and pragmatic method of solving that particular problem. . . . The second consideration is, perhaps, even more important. It is the fact that the common-law system left too much in the way of the enforcement of claims and interests to private initiative. . . .

"The administrative process is, in essence, our generation's answer to the inadequacy of the judicial and the legislative processes. It represents our effort to find an answer to those inadequacies by some other method than merely increasing executive power. If the doctrine of the separation of power implies division, it also implies balance, and balance calls for equality. The creation of administrative power may be the means for the preservation of that balance, so that paradoxically enough, though it may seem in theoretic violation of the doctrine of the separation of power, it may in matter of fact be the means for the preservation of the content of that doctrine. . . .

"The grandeur that is law loses nothing from such a prospect. . . . 'Courts,' as Mr. Justice Stone has reminded us, 'are not the only agency of government that must be assumed to have capacity to govern'; nor are they, one can add, the only agency moved by the desire for justice. The power of judicial review under our traditions of government lies with the courts because of a deep belief that the heritage they hold makes them experts in the synthesis of design. Such difficulties as have arisen have come because courts cast aside that role to assume to themselves expertness in matters of industrial health, utility engineering, railroad management, even bread baking. The rise of the administrative process represented the hope that policies to shape such fields could most adequately be developed by men bred to the facts. That hope is still dominant, but its possession bears no threat to our ideal of the 'supremacy of law.' Instead, it lifts it to new heights where the great judge, like a conductor of a many-tongued symphony, from what would otherwise be discord, makes known through the voice of many instruments the vision that has been given him of man's destiny upon this earth."

(3) RICHARD B. STEWART, THE REFORMATION OF AMERICAN ADMINISTRATIVE LAW, 88 Harv. L. Rev. 1669, 1683–85, 1760–62 (1975): "Today, the exercise of agency discretion is inevitably seen as the essentially legislative process of adjusting the competing claims of various private interests affected by agency policy. The unravelling of the notion of an objective goal for administration is reflected in statements by judges and legal commentators that the 'public interest is a texture of multiple strands,' that it 'is not a monolith,' and 'involves a balance of many interests.' Courts have asserted that agencies must consider all of the various interests affected by their decisions as an essential predicate to 'balancing all elements essential to a just determination of the public interest.' . . .

"The sense of uneasiness aroused by this resurgence of discretion is heightened by perceived biases in the results of the agency balancing process as it is currently carried on. Critics have repeatedly asserted, with a dogmatic tone that reflects settled opinion, that in carrying out broad legislative directives, agencies unduly favor organized interests, especially the interests of regulated or client business firms and other organized groups at the expense of diffuse, comparatively unorganized interests such as consumers, environmentalists, and the poor. In the midst of a 'growing sense of disillusion with the role which regulatory agencies play,' many legislators, judges, and legal and economic commentators have accepted the thesis of persistent bias in agency policies. At its crudest, this thesis is based on the 'capture' scenario, in which administrations are systematically controlled, sometimes corruptly, by the business firms within their orbit of responsibility. . . .

"The expansion of the traditional model to afford participation rights in the process of agency decision and judicial review to a wide variety of affected interests must ultimately rest on the premise that such procedural changes will be an effective and workable means of assuring improved agency decisions. Advocates of extended access believe that an enlarged system of formal proceedings can, by securing adequate consideration of the interests of all affected persons, yield outcomes that better serve society as a whole. The credibility of this belief must now be considered.

"Although the courts have displayed caution in expanding and reworking administrative law doctrine to ensure the representation of all affected interests, the thrust of decisions over the past decade supports the assessment of the Court of Appeals for the District of Columbia Circuit that: 'In recent years, the concept that public participation in decisions which involve the public interest is not only valuable but indispensable has gained increasing support.' . . . Such participation, it is claimed, will not only improve the quality of agency decisions and make them more responsive to the needs of the various participating interests, but is valuable in itself because it gives citizens a sense of involvement in the process of government, and increases confidence in the fairness of government decisions. Indeed, litigation on behalf of widely-shared 'public' interests is explicitly defended as a substitute political process that enables the 'citizen to cast a different kind of vote, [which] informs the court that . . . a particular point of view is being ignored or underestimated' by the agency. Its ultimate aim is seen as 'a basic reordering of governmental institutions so that access and influence may be had by all.' . . .

"The time has come for a critical assessment of this prescription for asserted biases and inadequacies in agency decisions. The judges' incipient transformation of administrative law into a scheme of interest representation is responding to powerful needs that have been neglected by other branches of government. There are serious perceived inadequacies in agency performance, and this perception must be addressed if attitudes towards government are not to degenerate into cynicism or despair. Moreover, the realities of agency performance may often indeed be far short of what is desirable or even tolerable. But whether a judicially implemented system of interest representation is an adequate or workable response to these needs is a question deserving the most careful consideration."

(4) CHRISTOPHER F. EDLEY, JR., ADMINISTRATIVE LAW: RETHINKING JUDICIAL CONTROL OF BUREAUCRACY 4–7 (1990): "Historically, the separation of powers bulwarks were intended to minimize the risk of arbitrary government. Beginning in the late nineteenth century, however, and culminating with the Supreme Court's acquiescence in the New Deal's suggestion of administrative hegemony, courts and commentators increasingly recognized that a less rigid design was necessary to accommodate modern exigencies. In response, a variety of modern judicial doctrines and attitudes developed. The elements of this new approach to constraining bureaucratic discretion were the regularization of administrative processes, the presumptive availability of judicial review, and judicial deference to administrative expertise— expertise being itself a rational and professional constraint against arbitrariness. These elements were eventually reflected in the Administrative Procedure Act of 1946 (APA). . . . The 'administrative' state is now inevitable because of the ever-lengthening agenda of complex public policy problems and the institutional limitations of legislatures. The broad delegations of power to those agencies—make the workplace 'reasonably' safe, assist the disabled who cannot engage in 'substantial gainful activity,' award licenses and allocate scarce resources in accordance with the 'public interest, convenience and necessity,' and similar formulas—create administrative discretion far more sweeping in scope and pervasiveness than the familiar and inherent ministerial discretion of the executive.

"As if to codify sweeping discretion, many statutes include a catchall delegation of substantive rule making authority to the agency, instructing the administrator to make any rules 'necessary' or 'appropriate' to accomplish the purposes of the statute. The sense that this discretion must be controlled continues to animate administrative law. As the bureaucracy's role has grown, so have the risks and benefits associated with official action. The stakes involved in judicial intervention to check malfeasance and misfeasance have also grown, so that familiar postures of judicial review now assume unfamiliar dimensions. In a way, discontent with judicial activism and the powerful social role of unelected judges is only a derivative problem, the principal one being awesome agency power.

"The Rule of Law approach to constraining discretion, which achieved maturity with the enactment of the APA, entails a strong role for subconstitutional judicial review. Such oversight by the unelected branch, however, is itself problematic in terms of those same values that cause us to fear official abuses in the first place. Thus, the continuing dilemma for administrative law has been that the effort to impose Rule of Law constraints on agencies must contend with the critique that judicial review simply replaces the *objectionable discretion of the administrator* with the *objectionable discretion of the judge*.

"There is a hopeful response to that critique. We have a continuing project of constructing and reforming a matrix of legal doctrines and attitudes intended to discipline the judges. That project reflects our powerful commitment to legal formality. If it is successful, the discipline judges themselves impose on administrators will not be simply another form of arbitrariness. But that is a rather large 'if.' "

(5) CYNTHIA R. FARINA, THE CONSENT OF THE GOVERNED: AGAINST SIMPLE RULES FOR A COMPLEX WORLD, 72 U. Chi.-Kent L. Rev. 987, 987–89 (1997): "The 1980s saw the emergence of a rich separation of powers jurisprudence that has been channeled, in this decade, into more focused attention on strengthening the hand of the President. . . . The ideological sources drawn upon are diverse—original intent, civic republicanism, public choice theory—but the central argument is consistent: The President, and the President alone, represents the entire citizenry. The President, uniquely, is situated to infuse into regulatory policymaking the will of the whole people.

"I argue here that this latest effort at making peace between regulatory government and representative democracy is fatally flawed. Despite the ingenuity and intensity with which strong presidentialism is advanced, it is premised upon a fundamentally untenable conception of the consent of the governed. The 'will of the people,' as invoked in that effort, is artificially bounded in time, homogenized, shorn of ambiguities—in short, fabricated. It obscures complex problems (recognized elsewhere in administrative law scholarship) of information, prediction, and risk perception. It slides over vexed questions (recognized elsewhere in scholarly literature about democracy) of when leaders should lead rather than follow and of how the act of governing becomes a process in which the collective will is formed, rather than merely implemented.

"My counter-proposition is a broad, and perhaps uncomfortably indeterminate one: No single mode of democratic legitimation can serve to mediate between the conflicted, protean, often inchoate will of the people and the modern regulatory enterprise. No single institution or practice is capable of performing the multiple tasks of registering, interpreting, educating, adapting, affording participation, facilitating deliberation, brokering accommodation, and umpiring conflict that are (or at least ought to be) entailed in shaping the public policy of a post-industrialized democracy with an activist regulatory government. There are no simple rules for this complex world. Rather, we must necessarily look to a plurality of institutions and practices as contributors to an ongoing process of legitimizing the regulatory state. Each of those institutions and practices will be partial and, of itself, insufficient. Each imposes its own kind of costs on the regulatory process. Each is capable, if overemphasized, of introducing its own kind of distortion.

"In sum, I am suggesting that the reconciliatory effort must abandon its yearning for a neat solution to the legitimacy problem and, instead, come to terms with 'the ugliness of democracy.'"

(6) PHILIP HAMBURGER, IS ADMINISTRATIVE LAW UNLAWFUL? 3–5 (2014): "Traditionally, under the U.S. Constitution, the government could bind its subjects only through its legislative and judicial powers. And because the Constitution granted these powers, respectively, to Congress and the courts, only the acts of these institutions could impose legally obligatory constraints on persons who were subject to the laws. In contrast, the executive's acts could not create this binding effect. Although the executive could implement the confining obligation of acts of Congress or the courts, it itself could not bind, but at most could impose force, whether by bringing matters to the courts or, ultimately, by physically carrying out their binding acts. Lawful executive power thus was very different from the two types of binding power authorized by the Constitution, and when the executive makes binding edicts and thereby strays into legislative and judicial power, it is exercising what, from a historical perspective, this book understands as administrative law.

"What exactly were the binding acts that the executive traditionally could not adopt? The secretary of the treasury, for example, could authorize the distribution of government largess, and could make regulations that instructed treasury officers, but he could not promulgate regulations altering tax rates. Although the Post Office could refuse a request to mail a letter, it could not issue regulations requiring subjects to avoid private carriers; and although the Interior Department could deny access to confidential government information, it could not issue an order compelling a business to supply information.

"Of course, the executive decisions granting or denying government money, services, information, and other benefits were very important.

Yet they could be executive decisions precisely because they did not bind Americans.

"Nowadays, however, the executive enjoys binding legislative and judicial power. First, its agencies make legislative rules dictating what Americans can grow, manufacture, transport, smoke, eat, and drink. Second, the agencies make binding adjudications—initially demanding information about violations of the rules, and then reaching conclusions about guilt and imposing fines. Only then, third, does the executive exercise its own power—that of coercion—to enforce its legislation and adjudication. . . .

"And this points to the danger. The power to bind is a power to constrain liberty. Although only Congress and the courts have the power to bind and thereby confine liberty, this is exactly what executive and other administrative bodies claim to do through administrative law."

c.   Contemporary Perspectives on the Administrative State

(1) ELENA KAGAN, PRESIDENTIAL ADMINISTRATION, 114 Harv. L. Rev. 2245, 2246–2249 (2001): "The history of the American administrative state is the history of competition among different entities for control of its policies. All three branches of government—the President, Congress, and Judiciary—have participated in this competition; so too have the external constituencies and internal staff of the agencies. Because of the stakes of the contest and the strength of the claims and weapons possessed by the contestants, no single entity has emerged finally triumphant, or is ever likely to do so. But at different times, one or another has come to the fore and asserted at least a comparative primacy in setting the direction and influencing the outcome of administrative process. In this time, that institution is the Presidency. We live today in an era of presidential administration. . . .

"For administrative law scholars, the claim of presidential administration may seem puzzling. . . . These scholars—concerned as they are with the actual practices of administrative control, as carried out in executive branch as well as independent agencies—may well have viewed the claim as arguable, though perhaps premature, if made ten or fifteen years ago, when President Reagan or Bush was in office. In the first month of his tenure, Reagan issued an executive order creating a mechanism by which the Office of Management and Budget (OMB), an entity within the Executive Office of the President (EOP), would review all major regulations of executive branch agencies. As Reagan's and then Bush's terms proceeded, and the antiregulatory effects of this system of review became increasingly evident, administrative law scholars took part in a sharp debate about its propriety. With the advent of the Clinton Administration, however, this debate receded. Although President Clinton issued his own executive order providing for OMB review of regulations, the terms of this order struck most observers as moderating the aggressive approach to oversight of administration taken in the Reagan and Bush Presidencies. Perhaps as important, the Clinton OMB chose to implement the order in a way generally sympathetic to regulatory efforts. Because objections to OMB review in the Reagan and Bush era arose in large part from its deregulatory tendencies, this reversal of substantive direction contributed to the waning of interest in, and even recognition of, the involvement of the President and his EOP staff in administration.

"In fact, as this Article will show, presidential control of administration, in critical respects, expanded dramatically during the Clinton years, making the regulatory activity of the executive branch agencies more and more an extension of the President's own policy and political agenda. Faced for most of his time in office with a hostile Congress but eager to show progress on domestic issues, Clinton and his White House staff turned to the bureaucracy to achieve, to the extent it could, the full panoply of his domestic policy goals. Whether the subject was health care, welfare reform, tobacco, or guns, a self-conscious and central object of the White House was to devise, direct, and/or finally announce administrative actions—regulations, guidance, enforcement strategies, and reports—to showcase and advance presidential policies. In executing this strategy, the White House in large measure set the administrative agenda for key agencies, heavily influencing what they would (or would not) spend time on and what they would (or would not) generate as regulatory product.

"The resulting policy orientation diverged substantially from that of the Reagan and Bush years, disproving the assumption some scholars have made, primarily on the basis of that earlier experience, that presidential supervision of administration inherently cuts in a deregulatory direction. Where once presidential supervision had worked to dilute or delay regulatory initiatives, it served in the Clinton years as part of a distinctly activist and pro-regulatory governing agenda. Where once presidential supervision had tended to favor politically conservative positions, it generally operated during the Clinton Presidency as a mechanism to achieve progressive goals. Or expressed in the terms most sympathetic to all these Presidents (and therefore most contestable), if Reagan and Bush showed that presidential supervision could thwart regulators intent on regulating no matter what the cost, Clinton showed that presidential supervision could jolt into action bureaucrats suffering from bureaucratic inertia in the face of unmet needs and challenges."

(2) JODY FREEMAN & MARTHA MINOW, REFRAMING THE OUTSOURCING DEBATES IN GOVERNMENT BY CONTRACT (Freeman & Minow, eds.) 7–9, 15, 20 (2009): "Government in the nineteenth and twentieth centuries did purchase goods—including armaments—from private companies. In areas like human services, local governments also regularly arranged contracts to provide counseling, foster care, and sanitation. But toward

the end of the twentieth century and the start of the twenty-first, federal and state governments have relied heavily on ongoing contracts with private providers for a much broader range of government functions, making contract the primary mechanism of government action, and arguably government's most important means of control over the provision of public services. This development makes the contracting process—from negotiation to oversight to remedies for breach—a key accountability mechanism in modern government. It also exposes the critical need for capacity *within* the government to develop and monitor such contracts. In this sense, outsourcing does not lessen government's burden; it changes it and may even increase it.

"Present-day outsourcing cannot be understood, however, without locating it as a reaction to an intervening period—beginning with the Progressive Era and lasting through the New Deal. After the Great Depression, widespread disillusionment with the private sector led to popular support for entrusting public institutions with greater responsibilities, and the government grew dramatically. By the late 1970s, however, the pendulum had swung in the other direction: there was newfound enthusiasm for private markets and competitive practices. . . . In the 1980 presidential campaign, Ronald Reagan ran on an explicit agenda of downsizing a wasteful and bloated public sector. Since then, outsourcing has been embraced with greater or lesser enthusiasm by both Democratic and Republican administrations. In the 1990s, the Clinton administration sought to 'reinvent government' largely by shrinking the federal workforce and infusing it with private-sector methods and metrics. . . . The administration of President George W. Bush has pursued outsourcing even more aggressively. . . .

"This account suggests how far contemporary expectations of government have evolved since the Progressive Era and the New Deal. In the United States today, government is just one among alternative forms of organization. Private for-profit, private not-for-profit, and hybrid state-sponsored enterprises each deliver services to the public. The government is not indispensable—even for functions we might think of as 'inherently governmental.' There is also a perceptible and relatively new understanding of the citizen as customer: someone who pays taxes and expects value in return, and who cares less about the identity of the provider than about the timely and affordable provision of the good or service. It is hard to know whether this shift in public attitudes helped fuel the demand for smaller government and more outsourcing, or vice versa. Likely it is both. . . .

"It may seem easiest to advance public values by keeping all government work within government. But a significant amount of outsourcing will persist in the United States for the simple reason that government cannot do everything its citizens want done without growing into a behemoth they refuse to support. Of course, the contracting regime we now have is not necessarily inevitable. What the public 'wants' is not exogenous to government; public preferences reflect choices the government has already made and which it has the power to reverse. Still, we think it unlikely that the American public is prepared to abandon outsourcing in favor of a larger and more powerful state. . . .

"With contractual governance here to stay, the real question is not whether to outsource at all, but to what ends, using which strategies, and under what constraints. New energy must be devoted to determining which essential functions must remain not only formally directed by the government in theory, but actually performed by the government in fact. The 'inherently governmental' designation used for this purpose for over half a century has proven woefully inadequate, both conceptually and in practice. . . .

"Our current government contracting system does not work. It is largely invisible and unresponsive to the public in whose name it is undertaken. The existing rules and procedures fail to guard adequately against inefficiency, conflict of interest, and abuse. And much of the power being exercised through contracting is largely unaccountable to *any* regime of oversight—market, legal, or political. Yet government by contract has arrived, and it is here to stay. This fact should prompt serious and sustained public dialogue about the short- and long-term implications of outsourcing for American democracy."

(3)   DANIEL A. FARBER & ANNE JOSEPH O'CONNELL, THE LOST WORLD OF ADMINISTRATIVE LAW, 92 Tex. L. Rev. 1137, 1137, 1188–89 (2014): "The reality of the modern administrative state diverges considerably from the series of assumptions underlying the Administrative Procedure Act (APA) and classic judicial decisions that followed the APA reviewing agency actions. Those assumptions call for statutory directives to be implemented by one agency led by Senate-confirmed presidential appointees with decision-making authority. The implementation (in the form of a discrete action) is presumed to be through statutorily mandated procedures and criteria, with judicial review to determine whether the reasons given by the agency at the time of its action match the delegated directions. This is the lost world of administrative law, though it is what students largely still learn. Today, there are often statutory and executive directives to be implemented by multiple agencies often missing confirmed leaders, where ultimate decision-making authority may rest outside of those agencies. The process of implementation is also through mandates in both statutes and executive orders, where the final result faces limited, if any, oversight by the courts. . . .

"The lost world of the APA and administrative law and the real world of modern administrative practice do share the same overall focus: the exercise of discretion. The cleavages, some rather deep, turn on the sources, the wielders, and the reviewers of that discretion. Almost forty years ago, Richard Stewart posited that interest groups might become the basis of a 'fully-articulated model' of administrative discretion. In his view, if a wide range of interests could be captured in the administrative state, 'policy choices would presumably reflect an appropriate consideration of all affected interests and the pluralist solution to the problem of agency discretion might prove both workable and convincing.'

"Today, pluralism or some wider form of democratic legitimacy is just one goal of not only administrative law but administrative practice as well. These goals include agency efficiency and effectiveness, democratic legitimacy, and the rule of law. With such complex ends, it should not be surprising that the sources, exercise, and review of discretion are not simple, either as a descriptive or as a normative matter. We not only need to acknowledge the increasingly fictional yet deeply engrained account of administrative law, but also need to think seriously about how that account can better reflect current practices while still retaining its tractability and original objectives."

(4) JESSICA BULMAN-POZEN, EXECUTIVE FEDERALISM COMES TO AMERICA, 102 Va. L. Rev. 953, 954–56 (2016): "Executive federalism— 'processes of intergovernmental negotiation that are dominated by the executives of the different governments within the federal system'—is pervasive in parliamentary federations, such as Canada, Australia, and the European Union. Given the American separation of powers arrangement, executive federalism has been thought absent, even 'impossible,' in the United States. But the partisan dynamics that have gridlocked Congress and empowered both federal and state executives have generated a distinctive American variant.

"Viewing American law and politics through the lens of executive federalism brings four key features into focus. First, executives have become dominant actors at both the state and federal levels. They formulate policy and manage intergovernmental relations. Although executive negotiations have shaped American federalism at least since the New Deal, Congress once superintended them. Today, from healthcare to marijuana to climate change, federal and state executives negotiate without Congress. Second, there is a substantial degree of mutuality among these executives, much more than is suggested by the federal government's legal supremacy. Federal and state actors turn to state law as well as federal law to further their agendas; sometimes this amplifies conflict, but it also enables officials to find paths to compromise. Third, national policy frequently comes to look different across the states as a result of executive negotiations. Some states more strongly press a position shared by the federal executive, while others offer competing views. Finally, horizontal relationships among the states are critical in setting national policy, as the federal executive builds on interstate agreements and reshapes them in turn. . . .

"The practice enhances the federal executive's capacity to act amid congressional dysfunction, but so too does it entail the multiplicity and pushback endemic to state-federal relations. Perhaps most notably, it facilitates a form of governance suited to polarization: state-differentiated national policy. . . . Executive federalism also offers a needed forum for bipartisan compromise. Rather than require a grand deal that satisfies an aggregate national body, executive federalism unfolds through many negotiations among disaggregated political actors. These discrete conversations facilitate intraparty difference at the same time as the process of implementation further complicates, and may attenuate, partisan commitments. . . .

"Any approach to national policymaking that leaves Congress on the sidelines has a clear strike against it as a matter of democratic representation, and the deficiencies of executive federalism in this respect are apparent. Yet, as recent work in political theory shows, representation is a more complicated process than the law's standard delegate models suggest. . . . If executive federalism is a potentially valuable practice, so too is it vulnerable. Challenges raising a host of doctrinal objections are already flooding the courts, and more can be expected."

SECTION 4. TEACHING AND STUDYING ADMINISTRATIVE LAW FROM THIS CASEBOOK

Administrative law is a big subject, and this is a big book. It would take a very big course of many semester hours to cover everything contained in the following chapters. None of your editors has ever given so large a course. We expect our users to be selective among the topics addressed, as we are. We have edited the book to facilitate this selectivity. Some instructors will use it for a first-year introductory course to legislation and regulation. Others will use it for a more traditional, basic administrative law course in law schools that do not offer an introductory "leg-reg" class. And some will turn to it for an advanced administrative law class.

We have also edited this book to allow different users to take up its topics in varying sequences. Many administrative law topics are interrelated, to a degree you may not have encountered in other courses. "What are the standards to be applied on judicial review?" interacts with "When is judicial review available?" and with "What agency procedures are required in developing agency rules?" Cases presenting one of these issues explicitly or implicitly deal with the others. It is not reasonable to attempt to present the issues all at once, and different instructors will find one or another path through them to be appropriate. We have tried to edit the materials of this casebook to focus on the particular questions at hand, but also, in various ways, to signal or briefly anticipate the related issues you may not yet have dealt with in detail. By the end of the course, we trust, the interrelationships will emerge, and your review of the course will bring fresh understanding of your course's earliest topics.

In sum, we have tried to treat most topics in this book thoroughly and with intellectual rigor. We have done so in the belief that what is not directly covered in your course might still prove helpful to you in gaining fuller understanding of what *is* covered and in the hope that after you have finished your course, our book will remain useful to you as a reference.

PART 2

UNDERSTANDING STATUTES

II.   STATUTORY INTERPRETATION

CHAPTER II
STATUTORY INTERPRETATION

Federal agencies are, first and foremost, creatures of congressional statutes. Their powers and procedures are defined both by the statutes that create them, and pertain especially to them, and by other statutes that generally regulate their behavior, such as the Administrative Procedures Act. Statutory interpretation, then, is the bread and butter task of lawyers who work within the agencies, or who represent clients that interact with and are affected by agencies, and of courts that resolve disputes over what agencies have done or may do. Indeed, because, as the scholar William Eskridge has put it, we live in a republic of statutes, statutory interpretation is central to all law practice today. And, as you may know, it is the subject of considerable dispute among lawyers and judges. For this reason, it is critical to understand not just the details of these particular statutes but also how one goes about interpreting them. And to understand how to do that, it is important to understand how one goes about interpreting statutes generally—an endeavor known as statutory interpretation. The materials of this chapter address statutory interpretation generally, leaving to Chapter VIII the special considerations that may arise when agencies themselves interpret statutes and when courts encounter statutory interpretations that agencies advance.

SECTION 1.   HOW STATUTES ARE MADE[1]

> a. *The Legislative Process*
> b. *Other Participants in the Legislative Process*

To understand how to interpret the federal statutes that govern federal administrative agencies, it is important first to understand the process for enacting federal statutes generally. That process is complex—

---

[1] Much of the information in this section is drawn from Chs. 15 and 16 of CQ PRESS, GUIDE TO CONGRESS (2008). Another brief summary appears in the opening pages of Robert Katzmann, Interpreting Statutes (2015)—a short, thorough, and balanced exploration of the contemporaneous issues about statutory interpretation written by the present Chief Judge of the United States Court of Appeals for the Second Circuit.

at times, byzantine. It is the product of many detailed rules. The Constitution mandates some of them. The House and Senate establish the rest.

These rules govern every step of the legislative process, from the introduction of a bill to its enactment into law. Along the way, at least if the usual rules are followed (which by no means always happens), hearings are held, reports are produced, bills are proposed, floor debates take place, amendments are proposed, and, after bills are passed by each chamber, differing versions are reconciled until a final bill is sent to the President to be either signed into law or vetoed. And, if the latter occurs, the chambers may vote again to override the veto and thereby enact the bill into law.

While you read the following material, think about why the American legislative process is so complicated. What do we gain from making it difficult to turn a bill into law? What are the downsides of this complicated process? Consider also how the process might affect statutory interpretation. What should we make of the dozens of reports and other congressional and executive statements that may be generated by a bill? What do we make of the fact that actors other than Senators and Representatives play key roles in the process of creating the legislative text? Does the fact that some legislation is not actually drafted by elected officials or their aides change how you view the text of a statute? Does knowledge of the process change how we should read the text or understand the purpose of a statute? In particular, does the fact that this process is so complex bear on whether judges should view themselves as partners in trying to ensure the legislation at issue results in sensible outcomes or does it instead indicate that judges should interpret statutes in a manner most likely to require drafters to be precise going forward?

a. The Legislative Process

Article I, Section 7 of the Constitution sets out the basic legislative process:

> Every bill which shall have passed the House of Representatives and the Senate, shall, before it become a law, be presented to the President of the United States; if he approve he shall sign it, but if not he shall return it, with his objections to that House in which it shall have originated . . . .
>
> Every order, resolution, or vote to which the concurrence of the Senate and House of Representatives may be necessary (except on a question of adjournment) shall be presented to the President of the United States; and before the same shall take effect, shall be approved by him, or being disapproved by him, shall be repassed by two thirds of the Senate and House of

Representatives, according to the rules and limitations prescribed in the case of a bill.

U.S. Const. Art. I, § 7, cls. 2–3. A bill, then, must reach the end of a daunting path in order to be enacted. It must first be passed by each chamber of the United States' bicameral legislature: the House and the Senate. Next, the bill is presented to the President. The President may either sign the bill, turning it into law, or veto the bill. If vetoed, Congress can override the President by a two-thirds supermajority in each chamber.

Although Section 7 articulates a broad outline of the legislative process, notice how little it says about congressional structure and process; the congressional committees, for example, are nowhere mentioned. Just as the Constitution leaves it to Congress to create the American government by statute, Article I, § 5, cl. 2 leaves it to each chamber to "determine the rules of its proceedings." The total body of Congressional procedures and rules is vast, and governs the legislative process's nuts-and-bolts: introduction of a bill and referral to committee, amendment and debate during committee consideration, debate on the floor of the chambers, or reconciliation between competing versions of a bill passed by the two chambers. Even a glance at some of the more important rules highlights just how involved the legislative process really is.

For a bill to go anywhere, it must first be introduced. A bill may be introduced by any member of either chamber and may have one or more "sponsors." Many bills are not actually drafted by elected legislators; much actual drafting occurs in professional offices maintained by each chamber, and members of Congress also can introduce bills written by lobbyists, special interest groups, or the White House. Once introduced, a bill is referred to a Congressional committee for further consideration. Each chamber has its own committees, and each committee—such as Armed Services, Commerce, or Foreign Relations (among many, many others)—has jurisdiction over a discrete subject matter. Sometimes it is obvious which committee has jurisdiction. More often, a bill could justifiably be considered by a number of committees. The final referral decision rests with the leadership of each chamber—the Senate Majority Leader or the Speaker of the House.

Once a bill has been referred to a committee, that committee takes control and begins to consider the bill. Most often, the bill will be referred to a specialized subcommittee for initial consideration. While in subcommittee or, later, the full committee, a bill may be rewritten, amended, rejected, or reported to the full chamber for consideration. Typically, one of the first steps taken is to conduct hearings. These hearings, which may or may not be printed, are used to take testimony from experts and interested parties (and sometimes even other legislators) and gather evidence about the bill. Hearings are followed by "mark up" sessions, where the bill is revised, amended, and prepared to be sent from subcommittee to committee, or from the full committee to the chamber. The last step in committee is the final committee vote. If approved, the committee reports the bill to the chamber, and a detailed "House or Senate Report" describing the bill and some of the committee's deliberations accompanies the bill. Minority views are often attached.

Next, a bill must be scheduled for floor consideration. The majority party in each chamber handles the scheduling for such consideration in that chamber. It may be days or weeks before a bill is actually sent to the floor. (Notably, the House and Senate have very different procedures for scheduling, as well as for floor discussion, bill amendments, and voting.) In the House, these matters are tightly controlled by a unique committee, the Rules Committee, that sets their terms. In the less numerous Senate, debate is not controlled in this way, and that opens the possibility that opponents will "filibuster"—that is, engage in continuous debate that can be ended only by a supermajority vote.

After a bill makes it to the floor and passes in the chamber in which it was introduced, the bill is sent to the other chamber, where—again—the process begins with referral to committee. Even if it then emerges from committee for floor consideration, it will often have modified the bill, or modification may happen in debate. And to become law, both chambers must agree on identical language.

Once adopted by the second chamber, if it does vary from the bill that passed the first, it will be returned to that chamber, where the simplest outcome is for the first chamber to accept the bill in the form the second has adopted. But if this does not happen, in order to reconcile the two versions of the bill and to send a unified bill to the President, each chamber designates members for a "conference committee" with the responsibility of creating a unified bill. The conference committee is made up of members of both the House and the Senate, and the conferees debate the two competing versions of the bill and make revisions until a majority of the conference committee reach an agreement on a revised bill. This revised version is then sent to each chamber for final approval with a conference report describing the bill and any compromises that have been made. If both chambers agree to the revised bill, the bill—at last—is sent to the President. If signed, the bill becomes law. If vetoed, the bill becomes law only if Congress can override the President's veto with a two-thirds majority.

The legislative process has been complicated further by an increase in the use of "omnibus" bills since the 1970s. Omnibus bills are massive pieces of legislation combining many smaller bills. Often, these smaller bills are drafted by different committees (sometimes without any contact among the various committees) then joined together before moving to the floor. These large omnibus bills may contain provisions that—on their own—would attract far greater attention. For example, a recent omnibus appropriations bill contained a provision that quietly rolled back a provision of the Dodd-Frank financial reform legislation. *See* Abbe Gluck,

Anne Joseph O'Connell and Rosa Po, Unorthodox Lawmaking, Unorthodox Rulemaking, 115 Colum. L. Rev. 1789, 1805 (2015).

One particularly common type of omnibus legislation, the budget reconciliation bill, involves a unique and complex process. Each year, when adopting its annual budget resolution, Congress has the option of including "reconciliation instructions." These instructions trigger reconciliation procedures that allow Congress to more quickly craft and approve budget legislation. For instance, reconciliation limits the number and type of amendments that may be added to the budget legislation, restricts floor debate in the Senate to twenty hours, and prohibits filibustering the legislation. *See* Megan S. Lynch & James V. Saturno, Cong. Research Serv., R44058, The Budget Reconciliation Process: Stages of Consideration 6–9 (2017). The use of the reconciliation process often courts controversy. In a high-profile recent example, in 2010, some key portions of the Affordable Care Act (ACA) were enacted through budget reconciliation. *See* Abbe R. Gluck, Imperfect Statutes, Imperfect Courts: Understanding Congress's Plan in the Era of Unorthodox Lawmaking, 129 Harv. L. Rev. 62, 69–70, 78–79 (2015).

But even aside from omnibus bills, there are all kinds of exceptions to the standard process for passing a bill out of the House and the Senate. A recent study found, for example, that "in the first year of the 112th Congress, fewer than 10% of enacted laws proceeded through the 'textbook' legislative process (first passing through committees on each side, then moving to debate and vote in each chamber, followed by conference between the chambers, and concluding with a final vote by both chambers before passage). More than 40% of enacted statutes did not go through the committee process in either chamber, but proceeded directly from the floor or were shepherded through by party leadership or the White House." Gluck, O'Connell, and Po, Unorthodox Lawmaking, Unorthodox Lawmaking, at 1800. And, it appears, this trend is on an upward trajectory. Id.

Once a bill passes out of the House and Senate (whether in textbook fashion or not), it goes to the President. Sometimes, upon signing a bill, the President issues a signing statement. Such statements may do nothing more than sing the praises of the legislation. They may also offer the President's view of the purpose of the legislation. In some instances, the statement may offer an interpretive gloss on key provisions of the law. And, in still others, the statement may even announce the President's view that a particular provision is unconstitutional. See Symposium: The Last Word? The Constitutional Implications of Presidential Signing Statements, 16 Wm. & Mary Bill Rts. J. 1 (2007), Curtis A. Bradley & Eric A. Posner, Presidential Signing Statements and Executive Power, 23 Const. Comment. 307, 312 (2006).

b. Other Participants in the Legislative Process

Although not often considered when discussing statutory interpretation, many institutional actors besides Congress and the President routinely interact with fledgling laws and play a significant role in the legislative process. One of the most important of these actors is the nonpartisan Congressional Budget Office (CBO). The CBO produces "formal cost estimate[s] for nearly every bill that is approved by a full committee of either the House or the Senate." Cong. Budget Office, Processes, https://www.cbo.gov/about/processes. These cost estimates, or "CBO scores," have a powerful influence on legislators—as well as on the ability of a bill to make it out of committee and survive in a full-chamber vote—and legislators often draft bills with the CBO score firmly in mind. Indeed, given the importance of CBO calculations, some scholars have gone so far as to propose that courts adopt a new principle of interpretation: construe statutes consistently with their CBO scores. *See* Lisa Schultz Bressman & Abbe R. Gluck, Statutory Interpretation from the Inside—An Empirical Study of Congressional Drafting, Delegation, and the Canons: Part II, 66 Stan. L. Rev. 725, 782 (2014). In their view, this principle "could help courts reflect congressional expectations in resolving disputes that implicate the score." *Id.*

Other budgetary and oversight entities are also heavily involved in the legislative process. For example, the Government Accountability Office (GAO) prepares reports on the desirability of enacting a bill into law, usually at the request of a committee. And the Office of Management and Budget (OMB), an executive agency, reviews legislation that agencies wish to propose to Congress to ensure that the legislation is consistent with the President's priorities. In addition, OMB makes sure that agencies have a chance to comment on a bill before the President signs it.

Perhaps most crucial to the day-to-day work of the House and Senate are the Offices of Legislative Counsel. These offices provide nonpartisan, confidential legislative drafting services to the two chambers. They assist legislators in drafting new bills, amending bills during committee or conference, and preparing motions to use on the floor of the House or Senate. *See, e.g.,* Office of the Legislative Counsel, U.S. House of Representatives, Our Services, http://legcounsel.house.gov/HOLC/About _Our_Office/Our_Services.html. A recent survey of legislative staffers revealed that much—maybe even a majority—of legislative drafting is done by these two offices. According to the survey, staffers give Legislative Counsel "rough outlines of statutory text, which Legislative Counsel then turns into legislative language." Bressman & Gluck, *supra,* at 740. The results of the survey suggest that there may often be a real disconnect, then, between legislators (and their staffers) and the statutory text. *Id.*

SECTION 2.   THEORIES OF STATUTORY INTERPRETATION

> *a. Textualism*
> *b. Purposivism*
> *c. Pragmatic and Dynamic Statutory Interpretation*

Once a bill becomes law, questions inevitably arise about how the resulting statute should be interpreted. Here is a problem to spark your appreciation of the kinds of issues that can arise:

The Case of the Negligently Placed Mail

Here's the statutory pattern:

(a)   Under the Postal Reorganization Act, the Federal Tort Claims Act "shall apply to tort claims arising out of the activities of the Postal Service."

(b)   The Federal Tort Claims Act provides that the United States waives sovereign immunity (that is, immunity from being sued), and confers jurisdiction on the federal courts, for

> claims against the United States, for money damages, accruing on and after January 1, 1945, for injury or loss of property, or personal injury or death caused by the negligent or wrongful act or omission of any employee of the Government while acting within the scope of his office or employment, under circumstances where the United States, if a private person, would be liable to the claimant in accordance with the law of the place where the act or omission occurred.

As to these claims:

> The United States shall be liable . . . in the same manner and to the same extent as a private individual under like circumstances, but shall not be liable for interest prior to judgment or for punitive damages.

However,

> The provisions of this [waiver] shall not apply to—[thirteen items including] . . .
>
> Any claim arising out of the loss, miscarriage, or negligent transmission of letters or postal matter.

Here are the facts:

The plaintiff was injured when she tripped on a package that had been sent to her but was negligently placed by a postman on her steps where she would not see it. The parties stipulate that under state law she would have a cause of action for damages. The Postal Service pleads sovereign immunity and moves to dismiss the suit.

Does the Postal Service prevail in its motion? Why? How sure are you of the result?

And here are some additional points:

Are the following points, individually or cumulatively, relevant to deciding the case? Do they, individually or cumulatively, change your mind one way or the other as to the outcome, or as to the certainty with which you espouse it?

(a)   In an earlier case, the Supreme Court had ruled that the postal service was not immune—that is, had waived immunity—in regard to the negligent handling of postal motor vehicles.

(b)   A dictionary defines "transmission" as "an act, process, or instance of transmitting"; and "transmit" as "to cause to go or be conveyed to another person or place."

(c)   The other items on the list of thirteen "shall not apply" situations include "any claim arising from the activities of the Tennessee Valley Authority," "any claim arising out of the combatant activities of the military forces during time of war" and "any claim arising in a foreign country."

(d)   Each day the Postal Service delivers 660 million pieces of mail to 142 million delivery points.

(e)   At a hearing held before a Senate subcommittee considering the Federal Tort Claims Act, a Special Assistant to the Attorney General had testified: "Every person who sends a piece of postal matter can protect himself by registering it, as provided by the postal laws and regulations. It would be intolerable, of course, if in any case of loss or delay the Government could be sued for damages. Consequently, this provision was inserted."

Problem over. If you want to see what the judges said, you can look at Raila v. United States, 355 F.3d 118 (2d Cir. 2004) (cause of action survives); Dolan v. United States Postal Service, 377 F.3d 285 (3d Cir. 2004) (cause of action dismissed); Dolan v. United States Postal Service, 546 U.S. 481 (2006) (cause of action revived). For commentary, see Robert Katzmann, Judging Statutes 58 ff. (2014).

Various theories of statutory interpretation have developed over time to structure thinking about how to resolve problems like this. Should the focus be on resolving the issue in the way that is most faithful to the text of the provision? To Congress's purpose when it passed the measure? That best addresses pragmatic concerns about what would make the most sense from a policy perspective? That reflects what Congress would have done if it had known how society would look at the time the interpretive dispute actually arises?

Theories of statutory interpretation aim to explain why one might give one answer rather than another to such questions. And these theories can matter in practice. Two judges interpreting the same statute could decide a case regarding a dispute over the meaning of a statutory provision differently, for example, simply based on whether they place more emphasis on the plain text of the statute or on the legislature's purpose in enacting the statute. Thus, a theoretical argument for opting for one approach rather than another can have very real practical consequences.

In reading the following materials on the leading theories of statutory interpretation—textualism, purposivism, pragmatism, and dynamic statutory interpretation—think about how each of the theories relates to what you have learned about the legislative process. Consider also the role that judges are assuming when applying each of the theories. Should judges be faithful to the text of the statute alone? Does the legislative purpose matter? The practical consequences? And how should we consider older statutes when they are applied in new contexts?

Here is one caution before you begin. The modes of statutory interpretation that are described below are approaches rather than doctrines; to put the point in another way, these modes of statutory interpretation are not mandated or forbidden by binding precedents. The Supreme Court—and lower courts, too—can decide a case on one day using approach A, and on the next day using approach B, and that is accepted by the institution. Usually that happens because different Justices have different approaches, and they write as they see fit (subject of course to being able to gain the assent of the rest of the majority). So one cannot expect to learn a mode of interpretation that as a matter of precedent must be followed. One can instead expect to learn a variety of modes of interpretation that will be met, again and again, in the practice of the law.

a. Textualism

> *WEST VIRGINIA UNIVERSITY*
> *   HOSPITALS, INC. v. CASEY*
> *TENNESSEE VALLEY AUTHORITY v.*
> *   HILL*
> *BAKER BOTTS L.L.P. v. ASARCO LLC*
> *Notes on Textualism*

Quite obviously, a statute's text matters. Less obvious is why the text matters and whether it is all that matters. In recent decades, a school of statutory interpretation known as "textualism" has emerged and had great influence. Defining "textualism" is not so easy. But while "textualism does not admit of a simple definition, . . . in practice [it] is associated with the basic proposition that judges must seek and abide by the public meaning of the enacted text, understood in context (as all texts must be)." John F. Manning, Textualism and Legislative Intent, 91 Va. L. Rev. 419 (2005).

Textualism's leading modern champion was the late Justice Scalia. But, as the materials below reveal, judges of all stripes have at times sung the praises of faithful adherence to the legislative text, consequences be damned. A key question such praise raises, however, is why the text should matter? Is it because only a theory of interpretation that privileges the text in some very strong manner is likely to constrain judges and thus preserve the role of the political branches in actually enacting statutes? Is it because the legislators that enact laws actually intend for the text—and the text alone—to express their intentions? Is it because laws have no intentions, only words that comprise them, and so any search for the legislature's intention in drafting the measure is a hopeless one?

As you read the three cases that follow, consider why strict adherence to the statutory language might make sense and why it might not. How does textualism relate to the legislative process and the statute produced? Should a judge confine her decision to the statutory language when a legislative purpose may be discerned that conflicts with the text? Is that last question one that even makes sense?

The first case considers the import of language added to a provision in the United States Code—42 U.S.C. § 1988—by the Civil Rights Attorney's Fees Award Act of 1976. The Act provided that "[i]n any action or proceeding to enforce" various identified civil rights statutes, "the court, in its discretion, may allow the prevailing party, other than the United States, a reasonable attorney's fee as part of the costs." The question presented is cleanly stated in the very first sentence of the opinion.

WEST VIRGINIA UNIVERSITY HOSPITALS, INC. v. CASEY

Supreme Court of the United States (1991).
499 U.S. 83.

■ JUSTICE SCALIA delivered the opinion of the Court.

This case presents the question whether fees for services rendered by experts in civil rights litigation may be shifted to the losing party pursuant to 42 U.S.C. § 1988, which permits the award of "a reasonable attorney's fee."

I

Petitioner West Virginia University Hospitals, Inc. (WVUH), operates a hospital in Morgantown, W. Va., near the Pennsylvania border. The hospital is often used by Medicaid recipients living in southwestern Pennsylvania. In January 1986, Pennsylvania's

Department of Public Welfare notified WVUH of new Medicaid reimbursement schedules for services provided to Pennsylvania residents by the Morgantown hospital. In administrative proceedings, WVUH unsuccessfully objected to the new reimbursement rates on both federal statutory and federal constitutional grounds. After exhausting administrative remedies, WVUH filed suit in Federal District Court. . .

. . . Counsel for WVUH employed Coopers & Lybrand, a national accounting firm, and three doctors specializing in hospital finance to assist in the preparation of the lawsuit and to testify at trial. WVUH prevailed at trial in May 1988. The District Court subsequently awarded fees pursuant to 42 U.S.C. § 1988, including over $ 100,000 in fees attributable to expert services. The District Court found these services to have been "essential" to presentation of the case—a finding not disputed by respondents.

Respondents appealed both the judgment on the merits and the fee award. The Court of Appeals for the Third Circuit affirmed as to the former, but reversed as to the expert fees, disallowing them except to the extent that they fell within the $ 30-per-day fees for witnesses prescribed by 28 U.S.C. § 1821. . . .

II

. . . In Crawford Fitting Co. v. J. T. Gibbons, Inc., 482 U.S. 437 (1987), we held that [the general "costs" and "witness fees" statutes, not covering the claimed expert fees] define the full extent of a federal court's power to shift litigation costs absent express statutory authority to go further. The question before us, then, is—with regard to both testimonial and nontestimonial expert fees—whether the term "attorney's fee" in § 1988 provides the "explicit statutory authority" required by Crawford Fitting.

III

The record of statutory usage demonstrates convincingly that attorney's fees and expert fees are regarded as separate elements of litigation cost. While some fee-shifting provisions, like § 1988, refer only to "attorney's fees," see, e. g., Civil Rights Act of 1964, 42 U.S.C. § 2000e–5(k), many others explicitly shift expert witness fees as well as attorney's fees. In 1976, just over a week prior to the enactment of § 1988, Congress passed those provisions of the Toxic Substances Control Act, 15 U.S.C. §§ 2618(d), 2619(c)(2), which provide that a prevailing party may recover "the costs of suit and reasonable fees for attorneys and expert witnesses." (Emphasis added.) Also in 1976, Congress amended the Consumer Product Safety Act, 15 U.S.C. §§ 2060(c), 2072(a), 2073, which as originally enacted in 1972 shifted to the losing party "costs of suit, including a reasonable attorney's fee," see 86 Stat. 1226. In the 1976 amendment, Congress altered the fee-shifting provisions to their present form by adding a phrase shifting expert witness fees in addition to attorney's fees. See Pub. L. 94–284, § 10, 90 Stat. 506, 507. Two other significant Acts passed in 1976 contain similar phrasing: the Resource Conservation and Recovery Act of 1976, 42 U.S.C. § 6972(e) ("costs of litigation (including reasonable attorney and expert witness fees)"), and the Natural Gas Pipeline Safety Act Amendments of 1976, 49 U.S.C. App. § 1686(e) ("costs of suit, including reasonable attorney's fees and reasonable expert witnesses fees").

Congress enacted similarly phrased fee-shifting provisions in numerous statutes both before 1976, see, *e. g.*, Endangered Species Act of 1973, 16 U.S.C. § 1540(g)(4) ("costs of litigation (including reasonable attorney and expert witness fees)"), and afterwards, see, *e.g.*, Public Utility Regulatory Policies Act of 1978, 16 U.S.C. § 2632 (a)(1) ("reasonable attorneys' fees, expert witness fees, and other reasonable costs incurred in preparation and advocacy of [the litigant's] position"). These statutes encompass diverse categories of legislation . . . . At least 34 statutes in 10 different titles of the U.S. Code explicitly shift attorney's fees *and* expert witness fees.

The laws that refer to fees for nontestimonial expert services are less common, but they establish a similar usage both before and after 1976: Such fees are referred to *in addition to* attorney's fees when a shift is intended: Such fees are referred to *in addition to* attorney's fees when a shift is intended. . . .

. . . We think this statutory usage shows beyond question that attorney's fees and expert fees are distinct items of expense. If, as WVUH argues, the one includes the other, dozens of statutes referring to the two separately become an inexplicable exercise in redundancy. . . .

IV

[Extended discussion of pre-1976 cases omitted.] In sum, we conclude that at the time this provision was enacted neither statutory nor judicial usage regarded the phrase "attorney's fees" as embracing fees for experts' services.

V

. . . . WVUH further argues that the congressional purpose in enacting § 1988 must prevail over the ordinary meaning of the statutory terms. It quotes, for example, the House Committee Report to the effect that "the judicial remedy [must be] full and complete," H. R. Rep. No. 94–1558, p. 1 (1976), and the Senate Committee Report to the effect that "citizens must have the opportunity to recover what it costs them to vindicate [civil] rights in court," S. Rep. No. 94–1011, *supra*, at 2. As we have observed before, however, the purpose of a statute includes not only what it sets out to change, but also what it resolves to leave alone. See Rodriguez v. United States, 480 U.S. 522, 525–526 (1987). The best evidence of that purpose is the statutory text adopted by both Houses of Congress and submitted to the President. Where that contains a phrase that is unambiguous—that has a clearly accepted meaning in both legislative and judicial practice—we do not permit it to be expanded or contracted by the statements of individual legislators or committees during the course of the enactment process. See United States v. Ron Pair Enterprises, Inc., 489 U.S. 235, 241 (1989) ("Where, as here, the statute's language is plain, 'the sole function of the court is to enforce it according to its terms' "), quoting Caminetti v. United States, 242 U.S. 470, 485 (1917). Congress could easily have shifted "attorney's fees and expert witness fees," or "reasonable litigation expenses," as it did in contemporaneous statutes; it chose instead to enact more restrictive language, and we are bound by that restriction.

. . . [WVUH also contends] that, even if Congress plainly did not include expert fees in the fee-shifting provisions of § 1988, it would have done so had it thought about it. Most of the pre-§ 1988 statutes that explicitly shifted expert fees dealt with environmental litigation, where the necessity of expert advice was readily apparent; and when Congress later enacted the EAJA, the federal counterpart of § 1988, it explicitly included expert fees. Thus, the argument runs, the 94th Congress simply forgot; it is our duty to ask how they would have decided had they actually considered the question. See Friedrich v. Chicago, 888 F. 2d 511, 514 (CA7 1989) (awarding expert fees under § 1988 because a court should "complete . . . the statute by reading it to bring about the end that the legislators would have specified had they thought about it more clearly").

This argument profoundly mistakes our role. Where a statutory term presented to us for the first time is ambiguous, we construe it to contain that permissible meaning which fits most logically and comfortably into the body of both previously and subsequently enacted law. See 2 J. Sutherland, Statutory Construction § 5201 (3d F. Horack ed. 1943). We do so not because that precise accommodative meaning is what the lawmakers must have had in mind (how could an earlier Congress know what a later Congress would enact?), but because it is our role to make sense rather than nonsense out of the *corpus juris*. But where, as here, the meaning of the term prevents such accommodation, it is not our function to eliminate clearly expressed inconsistency of policy and to treat alike subjects that different Congresses have chosen to treat differently. The facile attribution of congressional "forgetfulness" cannot justify such a usurpation. Where what is at issue is not a contradictory disposition within the same enactment, but merely a difference between the more parsimonious policy of an earlier enactment and the more generous policy of a later one, there is no more basis for saying that the earlier Congress forgot than for saying that the earlier Congress felt differently. In such circumstances, the attribution of forgetfulness rests in reality upon the judge's assessment that the later statute contains the *better* disposition. But that is not for judges to prescribe. We thus reject this last argument for the same reason that Justice Brandeis, writing for the Court, once rejected a similar (though less explicit) argument by the United States:

"[The statute's] language is plain and unambiguous. What the Government asks is not a construction of a statute, but, in effect, an enlargement of it by the court, so that what was omitted, presumably by inadvertence, may be included within its scope. To supply omissions transcends the judicial function." Iselin v. United States, 270 U.S. 245, 250–251 (1926). . . .

The judgment of the Court of Appeals is affirmed.

■ JUSTICE MARSHALL, dissenting.

As Justice Stevens demonstrates, the Court uses the implements of literalism to wound, rather than to minister to, congressional intent in this case. That is a dangerous usurpation of congressional power when any statute is involved. It is troubling for special reasons, however, when the statute at issue is clearly designed to give access to the federal courts to persons and groups attempting to vindicate vital civil rights. . . .

■ JUSTICE STEVENS, with whom JUSTICE MARSHALL and JUSTICE BLACKMUN join, dissenting.

. . . In the early 1970's, Congress began to focus on the importance of public interest litigation, and since that time, it has enacted numerous fee-shifting statutes. In many of these statutes, which the majority cites at length, Congress has expressly authorized the recovery of expert witness fees as part of the costs of litigation. The question in this case is whether, notwithstanding the omission of such an express authorization in 42 U.S.C. § 1988, Congress intended to authorize such recovery when it provided for "a reasonable attorney's fee as part of the costs." In my view, just as the omission of express authorization in a will does not preclude compensation to an estate's attorney, the omission of express authorization for expert witness fees in a fee-shifting provision should not preclude the award of expert witness fees. We should look at the way in which the Court has interpreted the text of this statute in the past, as well as this statute's legislative history, to resolve the question before us, rather than looking at the text of the many other statutes that the majority cites in which Congress expressly recognized the need for compensating expert witnesses. . . .

. . . On those occasions . . . when the Court has put on its thick grammarian's spectacles and ignored the available evidence of congressional purpose and the teaching of prior cases construing a statute, the congressional response has been [dramatic, citing six prominent examples]. . . . In the domain of statutory interpretation, Congress is the master. It obviously has the power to correct our mistakes, but we do the country a disservice when we needlessly ignore persuasive evidence of Congress' actual purpose and require it "to take the time to revisit the matter" and to restate its purpose in more precise English whenever its work product suffers from an omission or inadvertent error. As JUDGE LEARNED HAND explained, statutes are likely to be imprecise.

"All [legislators] have done is to write down certain words which they mean to apply generally to situations of that kind. To apply these literally may either pervert what was plainly their general meaning, or leave undisposed of what there is every reason to suppose they meant to provide for. Thus it is not enough for the judge just to use a dictionary. If he should do no more, he might come out with a result which every sensible man would recognize to be quite the opposite of what was really intended; which would contradict or leave unfulfilled its plain purpose." L. Hand, How Far Is a Judge Free in Rendering a Decision?, in The Spirit of Liberty 103, 106 (I. Dilliard ed. 1952).

The Court concludes its opinion with the suggestion that disagreement with its textual analysis could only be based on the dissenters' preference for a "better" statute, ante. It overlooks the possibility that a different view may be more faithful to Congress' command. The fact that Congress has consistently provided for the inclusion of expert witness fees in fee-shifting statutes when it considered the matter is a weak reed on which to rest the conclusion that the omission of such a provision represents a deliberate decision to forbid such awards. Only time will tell whether the Court, with its literal reading of § 1988, has correctly interpreted the will of Congress with respect to the issue it has resolved today. . . .

NOTES

(1) ***What Is the Background of This Case?*** The fact that, as Justice Scalia recites, Congress had passed a slew of statutes concerning attorney's fees in 1976 was not just an accident of history. Congress was reacting to a Supreme Court decision of the prior year. That case concerned whether there might be an exception to what is known as the American Rule. Under that rule, each party to litigation pays their own fees and costs. The rule—which deviates from the British Rule, under which the loser pays for the winning party's attorney as well as his own—was thought to ensure that poorer litigants were not deterred by the prospects of losing and assuming the fees and costs of the winner. But the question then arose as to whether there should be an equitable exception to the American Rule in order to account for public interest litigation that seeks equitable rather than monetary relief. And that issue came before the Supreme Court in ALYESKA PIPELINE SERVICE CO. V. WILDERNESS SOCIETY, 421 U.S. 240 (1975). There, several environmental organizations had successfully sought an injunction directing the Department of the Interior to perform legally required environmental analyses, and properly to apply federal land use laws, in connection with oil companies' application for permission to construct the Alaska Pipeline connecting the newly discovered oil fields of Alaska's North Slope to the port of Valdez. Because the plaintiffs had acted to vindicate "important rights of all citizens" by bringing an action to ensure that the government system functioned properly, the D.C. Circuit found them entitled to reimbursement for "the reasonable value of their services." Alaska Wilderness Soc. v.

Morton, 495 F.2d 1026, 1032 (D.C. Cir.1974) (en banc). Otherwise, the court reasoned, the cost of such litigation—especially against well-financed parties such as Alyeska—might deter private parties from seeking to have environmental statutes properly enforced. Statutorily precluded from entering such an award against the United States, the court held that the pipeline company Alyeska, an intervenor supporting the government's (wrongful) approval of its pipeline, was responsible for half of those costs. But, JUSTICE WHITE, writing for a majority, reversed the D.C. Circuit, emphasizing the need for legislative action given Congress's longstanding general endorsement of the American rule.

> In the United States, the prevailing litigant is ordinarily not entitled to collect a reasonable attorneys' fee from the loser. We are asked to fashion a far-reaching exception to this "American Rule"; but having considered its origin and development, we are convinced that it would be inappropriate for the Judiciary, without legislative guidance, to reallocate the burdens of litigation in the manner and to the extent urged by respondents and approved by the Court of Appeals. . . .

> We do not purport to assess the merits or demerits of the "American Rule" with respect to the allowance of attorneys' fees. It has been criticized in recent years, and courts have been urged to find exceptions to it. It is also apparent from our national experience that the encouragement of private action to implement public policy has been viewed as desirable in a variety of circumstances. But the rule followed in our courts with respect to attorneys' fees has survived. It is deeply rooted in our history and in congressional policy; and it is not for us to invade the legislature's province by redistributing litigation costs in the manner suggested by respondents and followed by the Court of Appeals.

421 U.S. at 247, 263–4, 270–1. Justices Marshall and Brennan dissented.

The Civil Rights Attorney's Fees Award Act, at stake in the West Virginia University Hospitals, like the other attorney's fees acts of 1976, was a response to this decision.

(2) *And What Happened After This Case?* Congress responded strongly to West Virginia University Hospitals. The Civil Rights Act Amendments of 1990 broadly authorized reimbursement of expert witness fees in a civil rights context. And when President George H.W. Bush vetoed that legislation, Congress then enacted the Civil Rights Act Amendments of 1991, which he signed into law. Its new subsection, 1988(c), explicitly provided reimbursement for expert witness expenses "as part of the attorney's fee" for successful litigation under *some, but not all*, of the statutes mentioned in the amended provision, a pattern that has continued. What does this history of congressional responses to Supreme Court decisions suggest about the merits of textualism? Does it show the virtues of textualism, in the sense that Congress is perfectly capable of making itself clear and that when in these instances it did make itself clear, it did not take an absolutist view one way or the other? Or does this history show the gap between text and

legislative intent and thus the ways in which textualism may result in outcomes Congress never had in mind?

TENNESSEE VALLEY AUTHORITY v. HILL

Supreme Court of the United States (1978).
437 U.S. 153.

■ CHIEF JUSTICE BURGER delivered the opinion of the Court.

I

. . . In this area of the Little Tennessee River the Tennessee Valley Authority [TVA], a wholly owned public corporation of the United States, began constructing the Tellico Dam and Reservoir Project in 1967, shortly after Congress appropriated initial funds for its development. Tellico is a multipurpose regional development project designed principally to stimulate shoreline development, generate sufficient electric current to heat 20,000 homes, and provide flatwater recreation and flood control, as well as improve economic conditions in "an area characterized by underutilization of human resources and outmigration of young people." Of particular relevance to this case is one aspect of the project, a dam. . .

The Tellico Dam has never opened, however, despite the fact that construction has been virtually completed and the dam is essentially ready for operation. Although Congress has appropriated monies for Tellico every year since 1967, progress was delayed, and ultimately stopped, by a tangle of lawsuits and administrative proceedings. After unsuccessfully urging TVA to consider alternatives to damming the Little Tennessee, local citizens and national conservation groups brought suit in the District Court, claiming that the project did not conform to the requirements of the National Environmental Policy Act of 1969 (NEPA). . .

A few months prior to the District Court's decision dissolving the NEPA injunction, a discovery was made in the waters of the Little Tennessee which would profoundly affect the Tellico Project. Exploring the area around Coytee Springs, which is about seven miles from the mouth of the river, a University of Tennessee ichthyologist, Dr. David A. Etnier, found a previously unknown species of perch, the snail darter, or *Percina (Imostoma) tanasi*. This three-inch, tannish-colored fish, whose numbers are estimated to be in the range of 10,000 to 15,000, would soon engage the attention of environmentalists, the TVA, the Department of the Interior, the Congress of the United States, and ultimately the federal courts, as a new and additional basis to halt construction of the dam.

Until recently the finding of a new species of animal life would hardly generate a cause celebre. This is particularly so in the case of darters, of which there are approximately 130 known species, 8 to 10 of these having been identified only in the last five years. The moving force behind the snail darter's sudden fame came some four months after its discovery, when the Congress passed the Endangered Species Act of 1973 (Act), 87 Stat. 884, 16 U.S.C. § 1531 *et seq.* (1976 ed.). This legislation, among other things, authorizes the Secretary of the Interior to declare species of animal life "endangered" and to identify the "critical habitat" of these creatures. When a species or its habitat is so listed, the following portion of the Act—relevant here—becomes effective:

"The Secretary [of the Interior] shall review other programs administered by him and utilize such programs in furtherance of the purposes of this chapter. All other Federal departments and agencies shall, in consultation with and with the assistance of the Secretary, utilize their authorities in furtherance of the purposes of this chapter by carrying out programs for the conservation of endangered species and threatened species listed pursuant to section 1533 of this title and by taking such action necessary to insure that actions authorized, funded, or carried out by them do not jeopardize the continued existence of such endangered species and threatened species or result in the destruction or modification of habitat of such species which is determined by the Secretary, after consultation as appropriate with the affected States, to be critical."

In January 1975, the respondents in this case and others petitioned the Secretary of the Interior to list the snail darter as an endangered species. After receiving comments from various interested parties, including TVA and the State of Tennessee, the Secretary formally listed the snail darter as an endangered species on October 8, 1975. . . . [T]he Secretary determined that the snail darter apparently lives only in that portion of the Little Tennessee River which would be completely inundated by the reservoir created as a consequence of the Tellico Dam's completion. The Secretary went on to explain the significance of the dam to the habitat of the snail darter: . . . "The proposed impoundment of water behind the proposed Tellico Dam would result in total destruction of the snail darter's habitat."

Subsequent to this determination, the Secretary declared the area of the Little Tennessee which would be affected by the Tellico Dam to be the "critical habitat" of the snail darter. Using these determinations as a predicate, and notwithstanding the near completion of the dam, the Secretary declared that pursuant to § 7 of the Act, "all Federal agencies must take such action as is necessary to insure that actions authorized, funded, or carried out by them do not result in the destruction or modification of this critical habitat area." This notice, of course, was pointedly directed at TVA and clearly aimed at halting completion or operation of the dam. . . .

. . . Meanwhile, Congress had also become involved in the fate of the snail darter. Appearing before a Subcommittee of the House Committee on Appropriations in April 1975—some seven months before the snail darter was listed as endangered—TVA representatives described the discovery of the fish and the relevance of the Endangered Species Act to the Tellico Project. . . . At that time TVA presented a position which it would advance in successive forums thereafter, namely, that the Act did not prohibit the completion of a project authorized, funded, and substantially constructed before the Act was passed. TVA also described its efforts to transplant the snail darter, but contended that the dam should be finished regardless of the experiment's success. Thereafter, the House Committee on Appropriations, in its June 20, 1975, Report, stated the following in the course of recommending that an additional $ 29 million be appropriated for Tellico:

"The *Committee* directs that the project, for which an environmental impact statement has been completed and provided the Committee, should be completed as promptly as possible . . . ." H. R. Rep. No. 94–319, p. 76 (1975). (Emphasis added.)

Congress then approved the TVA general budget, which contained funds for continued construction of the Tellico Project. In December 1975, one month after the snail darter was declared an endangered species, the President signed the bill into law. . . .

In February 1976, pursuant to § 11 (g) of the Endangered Species Act, 87 Stat. 900, 16 U.S.C. § 1540 (g) (1976 ed.), respondents filed the case now under review, seeking to enjoin completion of the dam and impoundment of the reservoir on the ground that those actions would violate the Act by directly causing the extinction of the species. . . .

II

. . . It may seem curious to some that the survival of a relatively small number of three-inch fish among all the countless millions of species extant would require the permanent halting of a virtually completed dam for which Congress has expended more than $ 100 million. The paradox is not minimized by the fact that Congress continued to appropriate large sums of public money for the project, even after congressional Appropriations Committees were apprised of its apparent impact upon the survival of the snail darter. We conclude, however, that the explicit provisions of the Endangered Species Act require precisely that result.

One would be hard pressed to find a statutory provision whose terms were any plainer than those in § 7 of the Endangered Species Act. Its very words affirmatively command all federal agencies "to *insure* that actions *authorized, funded,* or *carried out* by them do not *jeopardize* the continued existence" of an endangered species or "*result* in the destruction or modification of habitat of such species . . . ." 16 U.S.C. § 1536 (1976 ed.). (Emphasis added.) This language admits of no exception. Nonetheless, petitioner urges, as do the dissenters, that the Act cannot reasonably be interpreted as applying to a federal project which was well under way when Congress passed the Endangered Species Act of 1973. To sustain that position, however, we would be forced to ignore the ordinary meaning of plain language. It has not been shown, for example, how TVA can close the gates of the Tellico Dam without "carrying out" an action that has been "authorized" and "funded" by a federal agency. Nor can we understand how such action will "*insure*" that the snail darter's habitat is not disrupted. Accepting the Secretary's determinations, as we must, it is clear that TVA's proposed operation of the dam will have precisely the opposite effect, namely the *eradication* of an endangered species.

Concededly, this view of the Act will produce results requiring the sacrifice of the anticipated benefits of the project and of many millions of dollars in public funds. But examination of the language, history, and structure of the legislation under review here indicates beyond doubt that Congress intended endangered species to be afforded the highest of priorities. . . .

By 1973, when Congress held hearings on what would later become the Endangered Species Act of 1973, it was informed that species were still being lost at the rate of about one per year. . .

As it was finally passed, the Endangered Species Act of 1973 represented the most comprehensive legislation for the preservation of endangered species ever enacted by any nation. Its stated purposes were "to provide a means whereby the ecosystems upon which endangered species and threatened species depend may be conserved," and "to provide a program for the conservation of such . . . species . . . ." In furtherance of these goals, Congress expressly stated in § 2 (c) that "all Federal departments and agencies shall seek to conserve endangered species and threatened species . . . ." Lest there be any ambiguity as to the meaning of this statutory directive, the Act specifically defined "conserve" as meaning "to use and the use of all methods and procedures which are necessary to bring any endangered species or threatened species to the point at which the measures provided pursuant to this chapter are no longer necessary." . . .

Section 7 of the Act, which of course is relied upon by respondents in this case, provides a particularly good gauge of congressional intent. . . . Explaining the idea behind this language, an administration spokesman told Congress that it "would further signal to all . . . agencies of the Government that this is the first priority, consistent with their primary objectives." 1973 House Hearings 213 (statement of Deputy Assistant Secretary of the Interior). . . .

It is against this legislative background that we must measure TVA's claim that the Act was not intended to stop operation of a project which, like Tellico Dam, was near completion when an endangered species was discovered in its path. While there is no discussion in the legislative history of precisely this problem, the totality of congressional action makes it abundantly clear that the result we reach today is wholly in accord with both the words of the statute and the intent of Congress. The plain intent of Congress in enacting this statute was to halt and reverse the trend toward species extinction, whatever the cost. This is reflected not only in the stated policies of the Act, but in literally every section of the statute. All persons, including federal agencies, are specifically instructed not to "take" endangered species, meaning that no one is "to harass, harm, pursue, hunt, shoot, wound, kill, trap, capture, or collect" such life forms. Agencies in particular are directed by §§ 2 (c) and 3 (2) of the Act to "use . . . *all methods and* procedures which are necessary" to preserve endangered species. In addition, the legislative history undergirding § 7 reveals an explicit congressional decision to require agencies to afford first priority to the declared national policy of saving endangered species. The pointed omission of the type of qualifying language previously included in endangered species legislation reveals a conscious decision by Congress to give endangered species priority over the "primary missions" of federal agencies.

It is not for us to speculate, much less act, on whether Congress would have altered its stance had the specific events of this case been anticipated. In any event, we discern no hint in the deliberations of Congress relating to the 1973 Act that would compel a different result than we reach here. Indeed, the repeated expressions of congressional concern over what it saw as the potentially enormous danger presented by the eradication of *any* endangered species suggest how the balance would have been struck had the issue been presented to Congress in 1973. . . .

[N]either the Endangered Species Act nor Art. III of the Constitution provides federal courts with authority to make such fine utilitarian calculations. On the contrary, the plain language of the Act, buttressed by its legislative history, shows clearly that Congress viewed the value of endangered species as "incalculable." Quite obviously, it would be difficult for a court to balance the loss of a sum certain—even $ 100 million—against a congressionally declared "incalculable" value, even assuming we had the power to engage in such a weighing process, which we emphatically do not. . . .

Notwithstanding Congress' expression of intent in 1973, we are urged to find that the continuing appropriations for Tellico Dam constitute an implied repeal of the 1973 Act, at least insofar as it applies to the Tellico Project. In support of this view, TVA points to the statements found in various House and Senate Appropriations Committees' Reports; those Reports generally reflected the attitude of the *Committees* either that the Act did not apply to Tellico or that the dam should be completed regardless of the provisions of the Act. Since we are unwilling to assume that these latter Committee statements constituted advice to ignore the provisions of a duly enacted law, we assume that these Committees believed that the Act simply was not applicable in this situation. But even under this interpretation of the Committees' actions, we are unable to conclude that the Act has been in any respect amended or repealed.

Perhaps mindful of the fact that it is "swimming upstream" against a strong current of well-established precedent, TVA argues for an exception to the rule against implied repealers in a circumstance where, as here, Appropriations Committees have expressly stated their "understanding" that the earlier legislation would not prohibit the proposed expenditure. We cannot accept such a proposition. Expressions of committees dealing with requests for appropriations cannot be equated with statutes enacted by Congress, particularly not in the circumstances presented by this case. . . .

Second, there is no indication that Congress as a whole was aware of TVA's position, although the Appropriations Committees apparently agreed with petitioner's views.

(B)

. . . . Here we are urged to view the Endangered Species Act "reasonably," and hence shape a remedy "that accords with some modicum of common sense and the public weal." *Post*, at 196. But is that our function? . . .

Our individual appraisal of the wisdom or unwisdom of a particular course consciously selected by the Congress is to be put aside in the process of interpreting a statute. Once the meaning of an enactment is discerned and its constitutionality determined, the judicial process comes to an end. We do not sit as a committee of review, nor are we vested with the power of veto. The lines ascribed to Sir Thomas More by Robert Bolt are not without relevance here:

"The law, Roper, the law. I know what's legal, not what's right. And I'll stick to what's legal. . . . I'm *not* God. The currents and eddies right and wrong, which you find such plain-sailing, I can't navigate, I'm no voyager. But in the thickets of the law, oh there I'm a forester. . . . What would you do? Cut a great road through the law to get after the Devil? . . . And when the last law was down, and the Devil turned round on you—where would you hide, Roper, the laws all being flat? . . . This country's planted thick with laws from coast to coast—Man's laws, not God's—and if you cut them down . . . d'you really think you could stand upright in the winds that would below then? . . . Yes, I'd give the Devil benefit of law, for my own safety's sake." R. Bolt, A Man for All Seasons, Act I, p. 147 (Three Plays, Heinemann ed. 1967). . . .

[The Court of Appeals' injunction against building the dam is affirmed.]

■ JUSTICE POWELL, with whom JUSTICE BLACKMUN joins, dissenting.

. . . . This decision casts a long shadow over the operation of even the most important projects, serving vital needs of society and national defense, whenever it is determined that continued operation would threaten extinction of an endangered species or its habitat. This result is said to be required by the "plain intent of Congress" as well as by the language of the statute.

In my view § 7 cannot reasonably be interpreted as applying to a project that is completed or substantially completed when its threat to an endangered species is discovered. Nor can I believe that Congress could have intended this Act to produce the "absurd result"—in the words of the District Court—of this case. If it were clear from the language of the Act and its legislative history that Congress intended to authorize this result, this Court would be compelled to enforce it. It is not our province to rectify policy or political judgments by the Legislative Branch, however egregiously they may disserve the public interest. But where the statutory language and legislative history, as in this case, need not be construed to reach such a result, I view it as the duty of this Court to adopt a permissible construction that accords with some modicum of common sense and the public weal.

[Dissent of Justice Rehnquist omitted.]

NOTE

Partly as a response to the Court's opinion, Congress in 1978 created the Endangered Species Committee, a high level group authorized under certain circumstances to grant exemptions from the operation of the Endangered Species Act. However, when this Committee reviewed the Tellico Dam project, it did not grant an exemption because it determined that the project was uneconomic in any case. Not to be deterred, Congress in 1979 passed a rider to an appropriations bill directing TVA to complete construction, which was done. Meanwhile, some other populations of the snail darter were found elsewhere in the river, so completion did not in fact annihilate the species.

BAKER BOTTS L.L.P. v. ASARCO LLC

Supreme Court of the United States (2015).
135 S.Ct. 2158.

■ JUSTICE THOMAS delivered the opinion of the Court.

Section 327(a) of the Bankruptcy Code allows bankruptcy trustees to hire attorneys, accountants, and other professionals to assist them in carrying out their statutory duties. 11 U.S.C. § 327(a). Another provision, § 330(a)(1), states that a bankruptcy court "may award . . . reasonable compensation for actual, necessary services rendered by" those professionals. The question before us is whether § 330(a)(1) permits a bankruptcy court to award attorney's fees for work performed in defending a fee application in court. We hold that it does not and therefore [affirm the judgment of the Court of Appeals.

I

In 2005, respondent ASARCO LLC, a copper mining, smelting, and refining company, found itself in financial trouble. Faced with falling copper prices, debt, cash flow deficiencies, environmental liabilities, and a striking work force, ASARCO filed for Chapter 11 bankruptcy. . . .

Relying on § 327(a) of the Bankruptcy Code, . . ., ASARCO obtained the Bankruptcy Court's permission to hire two law firms, petitioners Baker Botts L.L.P. and Jordan, Hyden, Womble, Culbreth & Holzer, P.C., to provide legal representation during the bankruptcy.

Among other services, the firms prosecuted fraudulent-transfer claims against ASARCO's parent company and ultimately obtained a judgment against it worth between $7 and $10 billion. This judgment contributed to a successful reorganization in which all of ASARCO's creditors were paid in full. After over four years in bankruptcy, ASARCO emerged in 2009 with $1.4 billion in cash, little debt, and resolution of its environmental liabilities.

The law firms sought compensation under § 330(a)(1) . . . ASARCO, controlled once again by its parent company, challenged the compensation requested in the applications. After extensive discovery and a 6-day trial on fees, the Bankruptcy Court rejected ASARCO's objections and awarded the firms approximately $120 million for their work in the bankruptcy proceeding plus a $4.1 million enhancement for exceptional performance. The court also awarded the firms over $5 million for time spent litigating in defense of their fee applications.

ASARCO appealed various aspects of the award to the District Court. As relevant here, the court held that the firms could recover fees for defending their fee application. . . .

II

A

"Our basic point of reference when considering the award of attorney's fees is the bedrock principle known as the American Rule: Each litigant pays his own attorney's fees, win or lose, unless a statute or contract provides otherwise." Hardt v. Reliance Standard Life Ins. Co., 560 U.S. 242, 252–253 (2010). The American Rule has roots in our common law reaching back to at least the 18th century, and "[s]tatutes which invade the common law are to be read with a presumption favoring the retention of long-established and familiar [legal] principles," Fogerty v. Fantasy, Inc., 510 U.S. 517, 534 (1994). We consequently will not deviate from the American Rule " 'absent explicit statutory authority.' " . . .

The attorney's fees provision of the Equal Access to Justice Act offers a good example of the clarity we have required to deviate from the American Rule. See 28 U.S.C. § 2412(d)(1)(A). That section provides that "a court shall award to a prevailing party other than the United States fees and other expenses . . . incurred by that party in any civil action (other than cases sounding in tort) . . . brought by or against the United States" under certain conditions. *Ibid*. . . .[T]here could be little dispute that this provision—which mentions "fees," a "prevailing party," and a "civil action"—is a "fee-shifting statut[e]" that trumps the American Rule.

B

Congress did not expressly depart from the American Rule to permit compensation for fee-defense litigation by professionals hired to assist trustees in bankruptcy proceedings. Section 327(a) . . . professionals are hired to serve the administrator of the estate for the benefit of the estate.

Section 330(a)(1) . . . cannot displace the American Rule with respect to fee-defense litigation. To be sure, the phrase "reasonable compensation for actual, necessary services rendered" permits courts to award fees to attorneys for work done to assist the administrator of the estate, as the Bankruptcy Court did here when it ordered ASARCO to pay roughly $120 million for the firms' work in the bankruptcy proceeding. No one disputes that § 330(a)(1) authorizes an award of attorney's fees for that kind of work. But the phrase "reasonable compensation for actual, necessary services rendered" neither specifically nor explicitly authorizes courts to shift the costs of adversarial litigation from one side to the other—in this case, from the attorneys seeking fees to the administrator of the estate—as most statutes that displace the American Rule do.

Instead, § 330(a)(1) provides compensation for all § 327(a) professionals—whether accountant, attorney, or auctioneer—for all manner of work done *in service of* the estate administrator. More specifically, § 330(a)(1) allows "reasonable compensation" only for *"actual, necessary services rendered."* (Emphasis added.) That qualification is significant. The word "services" ordinarily refers to "labor performed for another." [citing dictionary definitions][2] . . . Time spent litigating a fee application against the administrator of a bankruptcy estate cannot be fairly described as "labor performed for"—let alone "disinterested service to"—that administrator.

This legislative decision to limit "compensation" to "services rendered" is particularly telling given that other provisions of the Bankruptcy Code expressly transfer the costs of litigation from one adversarial party to the other. Section 110(i), for instance, provides that "[i]f a bankruptcy petition preparer . . . commits any act that the court finds to be fraudulent, unfair, or deceptive, on the motion of the debtor, trustee, United States trustee (or the bankruptcy administrator, if any)," the bankruptcy court must "order the bankruptcy petition preparer to pay the debtor . . . reasonable attorneys' fees and costs in moving for damages under this subsection." § 110(i)(1)(C). Had Congress wished to shift the burdens of fee-defense litigation under § 330(a)(1) in a similar manner, it easily could have done so. We accordingly refuse "to invade the legislature's province by redistributing litigation costs" here.

---

[2]   Congress added the phrase "reasonable compensation for the services rendered" to federal bankruptcy law in 1934. Act of June 7, 1934, § 77B(c)(9), 48 Stat. 917. We look to the ordinary meaning of those words at that time.

III

The law firms, the United States as *amicus curiae*, and the dissent resist this straightforward interpretation of the statute. The law firms and the Government each offer a theory for why § 330(a)(1) expressly overrides the American Rule in the context of litigation in defense of a fee application, and the dissent embraces the latter. Neither theory is persuasive. [Discussion of law firm argument omitted.] . . .

B

The Government's theory, embraced by the dissent, fares no better. Although the United States agrees that "the defense of a fee application does not *itself* qualify as an independently compensable service," it nonetheless contends that "compensation for such work is properly viewed as part of the compensation *for the underlying services* in the bankruptcy proceeding." Brief for United States as *Amicus Curiae* 25. According to the Government, if an attorney is not repaid for his time spent successfully litigating fees, his compensation for his actual "services rendered" to the estate administrator in the underlying proceeding will be diluted. The United States thus urges us to treat fees for fee-defense work "as a component of 'reasonable compensation.' " *Id.*, at 33. We refuse to do so for several reasons.

1

First and foremost, the Government's theory cannot be reconciled with the relevant text. Section 330(a)(1) does not authorize courts to award "reasonable compensation" *simpliciter*, but "reasonable compensation *for actual, necessary services rendered by*" the § 327(a) professional. § 330(a)(1)(A) (emphasis added). Here, the contested award was tied to the firms' work on the fee-defense litigation and is correctly understood only as compensation for that work. The Government and the dissent properly concede that litigation in defense of a fee application is not a "service" within the meaning of § 330(a)(1); it follows that the contested award was not "compensation" for a "service." Thus, the only way to reach their reading of the statute would be to excise the phrase "for actual, necessary services rendered" from the statute.[3] . . . In any event, the Government's textual foothold for its argument is too insubstantial to support a deviation from the American Rule. The open-ended phrase "reasonable compensation," standing alone, is not the sort of "specific and explicit provisio[n]" that Congress must provide in order to alter this default rule.

2

Ultimately, the Government's theory rests on a flawed and irrelevant policy argument. The United States contends that awarding fees for fee-defense litigation is a "judicial exception" necessary to the

---

[3]   The dissent's focus on reasonable compensation is therefore a red herring. See *post.* The question is not whether an award for fee-defense work would be "reasonable," but whether such work is compensable in the first place.

proper functioning of the Bankruptcy Code. Absent this exception, it warns, fee-defense litigation will dilute attorney's fees . . . undermining the congressional aim of ensuring that talented attorneys will take on bankruptcy work. . . . [But] *no* attorneys, regardless of whether they practice in bankruptcy, are entitled to receive fees for fee-defense litigation absent express statutory authorization. Requiring bankruptcy attorneys to pay for the defense of their fees thus will not result in any disparity between bankruptcy and nonbankruptcy lawyers. . . .

More importantly, we would lack the authority to rewrite the statute even if we believed that uncompensated fee litigation would fall particularly hard on the bankruptcy bar. "Our unwillingness to soften the import of Congress' chosen words even if we believe the words lead to a harsh outcome is longstanding," and that is no less true in bankruptcy than it is elsewhere. . . . Congress has not granted us "roving authority . . . to allow counsel fees . . . whenever [we] might deem them warranted. Our job is to follow the text even if doing so will supposedly "undercut a basic objective of the statute." Section 330(a)(1) itself does not authorize the award of fees for defending a fee application, and that is the end of the matter. . . .

Affirmed

■ JUSTICE SOTOMAYOR, concurring in part and concurring in the judgment.

As the Court's opinion explains, there is no textual, contextual, or other support for reading 11 U.S.C. § 330(a)(1) in the way advocated by petitioners and the United States. Given the clarity of the statutory language, it would be improper to allow policy considerations to undermine the American Rule in this case. On that understanding, I join all but Part III-B-2 of the Court's opinion.

■ JUSTICE BREYER, with whom JUSTICE GINSBURG and JUSTICE KAGAN join, dissenting.

The Bankruptcy Code authorizes a court to award "*reasonable compensation* for actual, necessary services rendered by" various "professional person[s]," including "attorneys," whom a bankruptcy "trustee [has] employ[ed] . . . to represent or assist the trustee in carrying out the trustee's duties." 11 U.S.C. §§ 327(a), 330(a) (emphasis added). I agree with the Court that a professional's defense of a fee application is not a "service" within the meaning of the Code. But I agree with the Government that compensation for fee-defense work "is properly viewed as part of the compensation *for the underlying services* in [a] bankruptcy proceeding.". In my view, when a bankruptcy court determines "reasonable compensation," it may take into account the expenses that a professional has incurred in defending his or her application for fees. . . . Consider a bankruptcy attorney who earns $50,000—a fee that reflects her hours, rates, and expertise—but is forced to spend $20,000 defending her fee application against meritless objections. It is within a bankruptcy court's discretion to decide that, taking into account the extensive fee litigation, $50,000 is an insufficient award. The attorney has effectively been paid $30,000, and the bankruptcy court might understandably conclude that such a fee is not "reasonable." . . .

A contrary interpretation of "reasonable compensation" would undercut a basic objective of the statute. Congress intended to ensure that high-quality attorneys and other professionals would be available to assist trustees in representing and administering bankruptcy estates. . . .In some cases, the extensive process through which a bankruptcy professional defends his or her fees may be so burdensome that additional fees are necessary in order to maintain comparability of compensation. In order to be paid, a professional assisting a trustee must file with the court a detailed application seeking compensation. Fed. Rule Bkrtcy. Proc. 2016(a). . . [I]n order to maintain comparable compensation, a court may find it necessary to account for the relatively burdensome fee-defense process required by the Bankruptcy Code. Accounting for this process ensures that a professional is paid "reasonable compensation."

II

The majority rests its conclusion upon an interpretation of the statutory language that I find neither legally necessary nor convincing. The majority says that Congress, in writing the reasonable-compensation statute, did not "displace the American Rule with respect to fee-defense litigation." . . . But the American Rule is a default rule that applies only where "a statute or contract" does not "provid[e] otherwise." And here, the statute "provides otherwise." *Ibid.* Section 330(a)(1)(A) permits a "court [to] award . . . reasonable compensation for actual, necessary services rendered by the trustee, examiner, ombudsman, professional person, or attorney and by any paraprofessional person employed by any such person." This Court has recognized that through § 330(a), Congress "ma[d]e specific and explicit [its] provisio[n] for the allowance of attorneys' fees," and thus displaced the American Rule. Alyeska Pipeline Service Co. v. Wilderness Society, 421 U.S. 240, 260 and n. 33 (1975). . . .

Indeed, to the extent that the majority bases its decision on the specific words of § 330(a), its argument seems weak. The majority disregards direct statutory evidence that Congress intended to give courts the authority to account for reasonable fee-litigation costs. Section 330(a)(6) states that "any compensation awarded for the preparation of a fee application shall be based on the level and skill reasonably required to prepare the application." This provision does not authorize compensation, but rather *assumes* (through the words "any compensation awarded") pre-existing authorization under § 330(a). And the majority cannot convincingly explain why, under its reading of the statute, fee-application is a compensable "actual, necessary servic[e] rendered" to the estate. . . . In my view, the majority is wrong to distinguish between the costs of fee preparation and the costs of fee litigation. . . . Its decision to do so creates anomalies and undermines the basic purpose of the Bankruptcy Code's fee award provision.

For these reasons, I respectfully dissent.

NOTES ON TEXTUALISM

(1) *Consider the Cases.* We have just read three cases: West Virginia University Hospital, TVA v. Hill, and Baker Botts. All three are textualist in the sense that the majority opinion in each relies on the particular wording of the statute involved to reach a decision opposed by other Justices who in dissent claim to follow a broader understanding of what Congress meant to do. But that does not mean that the method used in each of the cases is exactly alike. Textualism should perhaps be seen as a family of approaches, perhaps closely related, rather than as a single methodology. Before going on, consider these questions: How do each of the opinions treat the relationship between statutory text and common language? Between statutory text and the text of other statutes? Between statutory text and the intent of Congress? Between statutory text and the rest of the legal system?

(2) *What Distinguishes Textualism?* JOHN F. MANNING, TEXTUALISM AND LEGISLATIVE INTENT, 91 Va. L. Rev. 419 (2005): ". . . classical intentionalists emphasize that meaning depends on what the speaker actually intends to convey. In that sense, classical intentionalists treat Congress much as they would treat an individual speaker: If an individual uses a term that has multiple potential meanings, the true meaning of that term as used on a particular occasion depends on the meaning intended by the speaker. So when the words of a statute leave a residue of ambiguity, intentionalists find it appropriate to examine the bill's internal legislative history for further evidence of what members of Congress "intended." More important, because people often speak loosely, listeners must adjust their understanding when circumstances suggest that an individual has poorly expressed his or her intentions. By the same token, intentionalists insist that judges enforce the spirit rather than the letter of the law when the enacted words fail to capture the legislature's apparent purposes, as revealed by the tenor of the legislation as a whole, the mischiefs giving rise to its enactment, the policy expressed in similar statutes, and whatever other circumstances may shed light on the policy of the enactment. Classical intentionalism thus presupposes that interpreters should try to ascertain how the legislative majority would have handled a problem that the fair import of the enacted text either does not resolve or resolves in a manner that does not adequately reflect the legislature's apparent aims.

"Like classical intentionalists, textualists work within the faithful agent framework; they believe that in our system of government, federal judges have a duty to ascertain and implement as accurately as possible the instructions set down by Congress (within constitutional bounds). . . But textualists deny that a legislature has any shared intention that lies behind but differs from the reasonable import of the words adopted; that is, they think it impossible to tell how the body as a whole actually intended (or, more accurately, would have intended) to resolve a policy question not clearly or satisfactorily settled by the text. Building upon the realist tradition, textualists do not believe that the premises governing an individual's intended meaning translate well to a complex, multi-member legislative process. As one author has put it, Congress is a "they," not an "it," and legislative policies are reduced to law only through a cumbersome and highly intricate lawmaking process. . . .

"So . . . textualists reject perhaps the most important premise of classical intentionalism: the idea that behind most legislation lies some sort of policy judgment that is meaningfully identifiable, shared by a legislative majority, and yet imprecisely expressed in the public meaning of the text that has made its way through Congress's many filters. Textualists focus on the end product of the legislative process, as reflected in the way a reasonable person conversant with applicable conventions would read the enacted words in context. Because of the fractured, tortuous, and often concealed nature of legislative bargaining, textualists believe that such a construct is the best that interpreters can do—that objectified intent provides the most, if not the only, plausible way for a faithful agent to show fidelity to his principal."

(3) ANTONIN SCALIA, A MATTER OF INTERPRETATION (1997): "[T]hough I have no quarrel with the common law and its process, I do question whether the *attitude* of the common-law judge—the mind-set that asks, 'What is the most desirable resolution of this case, and how can any impediments to the achievement of that resolution be evaded?'—is appropriate for most of the work that I do, and much of the work that state judges do. We live in an age of legislation, and most new law is statutory law. As [Lawrence M. Friedman] has put it, in modern time 'the main business of government, and therefore of law, [is] legislative and executive. . . . Even private law, so-called, [has been] turning statutory. The lion's share of the norms and rules that actually govern[ ] the country [come] out of Congress and the legislatures. . . . The rules of the countless administrative agencies [are] themselves an important, even crucial, source of law.' This is particularly true in the federal courts, where, with a qualification so small it does not bear mentioning, there is no such thing as common law. Every issue of law resolved by a federal judge involves interpretation of text—the text of a regulation, or of a statute, or of the Constitution. . . .

". . . To be a textualist in good standing, one need not be too dull to perceive the broader social purposes that a statute is designed, or could be designed to serve; or to hidebound to realize that new times require new laws. One need only hold the belief that judges have no authority to pursue those broader purposes or write those new laws. . . .

"Of all the criticisms leveled against textualism, the most mindless is that it is 'formalistic.' The answer to that is, *of course it's formalistic*! The rule of law is *about* form. If, for example, a citizen performs an act—let us say the sale of certain technology to a foreign country—which is prohibited by a widely publicized bill proposed by the administration and passed by both houses of Congress, *but not yet signed by the President*, that sale is lawful. It is of no consequence that everyone knows both houses of Congress and the President wish to prevent that sale. Before the wish becomes binding law, it must be embodied in a bill that passes both houses and is signed by the

President. Is that not formalism? A murderer has been caught with blood on his hands, bending over the body of his victim; a neighbor with a video camera has filmed the crime; and the murderer has confessed in writing and on videotape. We nonetheless insist that before the state can punish this miscreant, it must conduct a full-dress criminal trial that results in a verdict of guilty. Is that not formalism? Long live formalism. It is what makes a government a government of laws and not of men."

(4) *Another View?* STEPHEN D. SMITH, LAW WITHOUT MIND, 88 Mich L. Rev. 104, 112, 117–18 (1989): ". . . If the statute is understood not as the expression of a collective decision by the established political authority but rather as a kind of thing-in-itself, a free-floating text, then why is its right to command any greater than that of, say, the political treatise or the science fiction novel? . . .

". . . The result comes close to achieving, at least in aspiration, a law that is in the most literal sense "mindless." Of course, the law would still be the product of mental processes, just as decisions based on interpreting astrological configurations or on reading palms or tea leaves are the result of (perhaps very intricate) mental processes. But such decisions are not, at least not in the most important sense, based on "mind." Similarly, when statutes are understood as "texts" but not as the expression of actual, conscious, temporally situated decisions, the connection to "mind" is cut; the statute becomes a kind of Rorschach blot; it constrains—there are thousands of things that an observer just can't see in a Rorshach blot [sic]—but its constraints are fortuitous, not the product of conscious deliberation. And the critical question, more vexing now than in its earlier appearances, is not whether such a statute *can* guide judges, but whether there is any conceivable reason why it *should*. A person might search for answers to vital personal questions in a Rorschach blot; he might even *find* answers there. But who wants to turn his life over to a Rorschach blot?"

b.　Purposivism

> *CHURCH OF THE HOLY TRINITY v.*
> *　UNITED STATES*
> *UNITED STEELWORKERS v. WEBER*
> *KING v. BURWELL*
> *Notes on Purposivism*

The leading counter-theory to textualism is purposivism. The purposivist approach need not ignore the legislative text. But this theory does necessarily encourage judges to ask about the legislature's purpose or reason for enacting the statute. A key question concerns just how strongly they should be encouraged to do so. Only when the text is unclear? Always?

As with textualism, there are defenders and critics of purposivism. And, as with textualism, there are deep questions about why legislative purpose should matter. After all, if that purpose has not been made manifest in the text, how is that purpose entitled to be given legal effect? On the other hand, statutory texts are rarely if ever perfectly clear in all respects. When an ambiguity arises, what is a judge to do if not search for the purpose underlying the statute? Moreover, why should the judge start with the text rather than the purpose? If the purpose of the statute is clear, but the text does not appear to reflect it, why should one assume that the text means what it seems to say?

As you read the materials on purposivism that follow, consider how a judge should determine the legislature's purpose. What if the statute has more than one purpose? Should the court be more concerned with the specific or general intent of those who drafted a statute? And, most fundamentally, is the purpose relevant only when the text is unclear or is the text relevant only insofar as it tracks the clear legislative purpose?

To sharpen your mind, consider (before reading the Court's opinion) the statute, quite old, involved in the next case, 23 Stat. 332, ch. 164 (Feb. 26, 1885):

> *Be it enacted by the Senate and House of Representatives of the United States of America in Congress assembled*, That from and after the passage of this act it shall be unlawful for any person, company, partnership, or corporation, in any manner whatsoever, to prepay the transportation, or in any way assist or encourage the importation or migration of any alien or aliens, any foreigner or foreigners, into the United States, its Territories, or the District of Columbia, under contract or agreement, parol or special, express or implied, made previous to the importation or migration of such alien or aliens, foreigner or foreigners, to perform labor or service of any kind in the United States, its Territories, or the District of Columbia.
>
> SEC. 2. That all contracts or agreements, express or implied, parol, or special, which may hereafter be made by and between any person, company, partnership, or corporation, and any foreigner or foreigners, alien or aliens, to perform labor or service or having reference to the performance of labor or service by any person in the United states, its Territories, or the District of Columbia previous to the migration or importation of the person or persons whose labor or service is contracted for into the United States, shall be utterly void and of no effect,
>
> SEC. 3. That for every violation of any of the provisions of section one of this act the person, partnership, company, or corporation violating the same, by knowingly assisting, encouraging or soliciting the migration or importation of any alien or aliens, foreigner or foreigners, into the United States, its Territories, or the District of Columbia, to perform labor or service of any kind under contract or agreement, express or implied, parol or special, with such alien or aliens, foreigner or foreigners, previous to becoming residents or citizens of the

United States, shall forfeit and pay for every such offence the sum of one thousand dollars. . .

SEC. 4. That the master of any vessel who shall knowingly bring within the United States on any such vessel, and land, or permit to be landed, from any foreign port or place, any alien laborer, mechanic, or artisan who, previous to embarkation on such vessel, had entered into contract or agreement, parol or special, express or implied, to perform labor or service in the United States, shall be deemed guilty of a misdemeanor. . .

SEC. 5. That nothing in this act shall be so construed. . .to prevent any person, or persons, partnership, or corporation from engaging, under contract or agreement, skilled workmen in foreign countries to perform labor in the United States in or upon any new industry not at present established in the United States: *Provided,* That skilled labor for that purpose cannot be otherwise obtained; nor shall the provisions of this act apply to professional actors, artists, lecturers, or singers, nor to persons employed strictly as personal or domestic servants. . .

The question of the case is whether a church that contracts with a pastor from abroad to come to the United States and serve violates the statute.

CHURCH OF THE HOLY TRINITY v. UNITED STATES

Supreme Court of the United States (1892).
143 U.S. 457.

■ JUSTICE BREWER delivered the opinion of the court.

Plaintiff in error is a corporation, duly organized and incorporated as a religious society under the laws of the State of New York. E. Walpole Warren was, prior to September, 1887, an alien residing in England. In that month the plaintiff in error made a contract with him, by which he was to remove to the city of New York and enter into its service as rector and pastor; and in pursuance of such contract, Warren did so remove and enter upon such service. It is claimed by the United States that this contract on the part of the plaintiff in error was forbidden by the act of February 26, 1885, 23 Stat. 332, c. 164, and an action was commenced to recover the penalty prescribed by that act. The Circuit Court held that the contract was within the prohibition of the statute, and rendered judgment accordingly, (36 Fed. Rep. 303;) and the single question presented for our determination is whether it erred in that conclusion.

The first section describes the act forbidden, and is in these words:

"Be it enacted by the Senate and House of Representatives of the United States of America in Congress assembled, That from and after the passage of this act it shall be unlawful for any person, company, partnership, or corporation, in any manner whatsoever, to prepay the transportation, or in any way assist or encourage the importation or migration of any alien or aliens, any foreigner or foreigners, into the United States, its Territories, or the District of Columbia, under contract or agreement, parol or special, express or implied, made previous to the importation or migration of such alien or aliens, foreigner or foreigners, to perform labor or service of any kind in the United States, its Territories, or the District of Columbia."

It must be conceded that the act of the corporation is within the letter of this section, for the relation of rector to his church is one of service, and implies labor on the one side with compensation on the other. Not only are the general words labor and service both used, but also, as it were to guard against any narrow interpretation and emphasize a breadth of meaning, to them is added "of any kind;" and, further, as noticed by the Circuit Judge in his opinion, the fifth section, which makes specific exceptions, among them professional actors, artists, lecturers, singers and domestic servants, strengthens the idea that every other kind of labor and service was intended to be reached by the first section. While there is great force to this reasoning, we cannot think Congress intended to denounce with penalties a transaction like that in the present case. It is a familiar rule, that a thing may be within the letter of the statute and yet not within the statute, because not within its spirit, nor within the intention of its makers. This has been often asserted, and the reports are full of cases illustrating its application. This is not the substitution of the will of the judge for that of the legislator, for frequently words of general meaning are used in a statute, words broad enough to include an act in question, and yet a consideration of the whole legislation, or of the circumstances surrounding its enactment, or of the absurd results which follow from giving such broad meaning to the words, makes it unreasonable to believe that the legislator intended to include the particular act. . .

In [United States v. Kirby, 7 Wall. 482] the court says: "All laws should receive a sensible construction. General terms should be so limited in their application as not to lead to injustice, oppression or an absurd consequence. It will always, therefore, be presumed that the legislature intended exceptions to its language which would avoid results of this character. The reason of the law in such cases should prevail over its letter. The common sense of man approves the judgment mentioned by Puffendorf, that the Bolognian law which enacted 'that whoever drew blood in the streets should be punished with the utmost severity,' did not extend to the surgeon who opened the vein of a person that fell down in the street in a fit. The same common sense accepts the ruling, cited by Plowden, that the statute of 1st Edward II., which enacts that a prisoner who breaks prison shall be guilty of felony, does not extend to a prisoner who breaks out when the prison is on fire, 'for he is not to be hanged because he would not stay to be burnt.' And we think that a like common sense will sanction the ruling we make . . . ."

Among other things which may be considered in determining the intent of the legislature is the title of the act . . . .

It will be seen that words as general as those used in the first section of this act were by that decision limited, and the intent of Congress with respect to the act was gathered partially, at least, from its title. Now, the title of this act is, "An act to prohibit the importation and migration of foreigners and aliens under contract or agreement to perform labor in the United States, its Territories and the District of Columbia." Obviously the thought expressed in this reaches only to the work of the manual laborer, as distinguished from that of the professional man. No one reading such a title would suppose that Congress had in its mind any purpose of staying the coming into this country of ministers of the gospel, or, indeed, of any class whose toil is that of the brain. The common understanding of the terms labor and laborers does not include preaching and preachers; and it is to be assumed that words and phrases are used in their ordinary meaning. So whatever of light is thrown upon the statute by the language of the title indicates an exclusion from its penal provisions of all contracts for the employment of ministers, rectors and pastors.

Again, another guide to the meaning of a statute is found in the evil which it is designed to remedy; and for this the court properly looks at contemporaneous events, the situation as it existed, and as it was pressed upon the attention of the legislative body. United States v. Union Pacific Railroad, 91 U.S. 72, 79. The situation which called for this statute was briefly but fully stated by Justice Brown when, as District Judge, he decided the case of United States v. Craig, 28 Fed. Rep. 795, 798: "The motives and history of the act are matters of common knowledge. It had become the practice for large capitalists in this country to contract with their agents abroad for the shipment of great numbers of an ignorant and servile class of foreign laborers, under contracts, by which the employer agreed, upon the one hand, to prepay their passage, while, upon the other hand, the laborers agreed to work after their arrival for a certain time at a low rate of wages. The effect of this was to break down the labor market, and to reduce other laborers engaged in like occupations to the level of the assisted immigrant. The evil finally became so flagrant that an appeal was made to Congress for relief by the passage of the act in question, the design of which was to raise the standard of foreign immigrants, and to discountenance the migration of those who had not sufficient means in their own hands, or those of their friends, to pay their passage."

It appears, also, from the petitions, and in the testimony presented before the committees of Congress, that it was this cheap unskilled labor which was making the trouble, and the influx of which Congress sought to prevent. It was never suggested that we had in this country a surplus of brain toilers, and, least of all, that the market for the services of Christian ministers was depressed by foreign competition. Those were matters to which the attention of Congress, or of the people, was not directed. So far, then, as the evil which was sought to be remedied interprets the statute, it also guides to an exclusion of this contract from the penalties of the act.

A singular circumstance, throwing light upon the intent of Congress, is found in this extract from the report of the Senate Committee on Education and Labor, recommending the passage of the bill: "The general facts and considerations which induce the committee to recommend the passage of this bill are set forth in the Report of the Committee of the House. The committee report the bill back without amendment, although there are certain features thereof which might well be changed or modified, in the hope that the bill may not fail of passage during the present session. Especially would the committee have otherwise recommended amendments, substituting for the expression 'labor and service,' whenever it occurs in the body of the bill, the words 'manual labor' or 'manual service,' as sufficiently broad to accomplish the purposes of the bill, and that such amendments would remove objections which a sharp and perhaps unfriendly criticism may urge to the proposed legislation. The committee, however, believing that the bill in its present form will be construed as including only those whose labor or service is manual in character, and being very desirous that the bill become a law before the adjournment, have reported the bill without change." 6059, Congressional Record, 48th Congress. And, referring back to the report of the Committee of the House, there appears this language: "It seeks to restrain and prohibit the immigration or importation of laborers who would have never seen our shores but for the inducements and allurements of men whose only object is to obtain labor at the lowest possible rate, regardless of the social and material well-being of our own citizens and regardless of the evil consequences which result to American laborers from such immigration. This class of immigrants care nothing about our institutions, and in many instances never even heard of them; they are men whose passage is paid by the importers; they come here under contract to labor for a certain number of years; they are ignorant of our social condition, and that they may remain so they are isolated and prevented from coming into contact with Americans. They are generally from the lowest social stratum, and live upon the coarsest food and in hovels of a character before unknown to American workmen. They, as a rule, do not become citizens, and are certainly not a desirable acquisition to the body politic. The inevitable tendency of their presence among us is to degrade American labor, and to reduce it to the level of the imported pauper labor." Page 5359, Congressional Record, 48th Congress. . . .

Suppose in the Congress that passed this act some member had offered a bill which in terms declared that, if any Roman Catholic church in this country should contract with Cardinal Manning to come to this country and enter into its service as pastor and priest; or any Episcopal church should enter into a like contract with Canon Farrar; or any Baptist church should make similar arrangements with Rev. Mr. Spurgeon; or any Jewish synagogue with some eminent Rabbi, such contract should be adjudged unlawful and void, and the church making it be subject to prosecution and punishment, can it be believed that it would have received a minute of approving thought or a single vote? Yet it is contended that such was in effect the meaning of this statute. The construction invoked cannot be accepted as correct. It is a case where there was presented a definite evil, in view of which the legislature used general terms with the purpose of reaching all phases of that evil, and thereafter, unexpectedly, it is developed that the general language thus employed is broad enough to reach cases and acts which the whole history and life of the country affirm could not have been intentionally legislated against. It is the duty of the counts, under those circumstances, to say that, however broad the language of the statute may be, the act, although within the letter, is not within the intention of the legislature, and therefore cannot be within the statute.

The judgment will be reversed, and the case remanded for further proceedings in accordance with this opinion.

UNITED STEELWORKERS v. WEBER

Supreme Court of the United States (1979).
443 U.S. 193.

■ JUSTICE BRENNAN delivered the opinion of the Court.

Challenged here is the legality of an affirmative action plan— collectively bargained by an employer and a union—that reserves for black employees 50% of the openings in an in-plant craft-training program until the percentage of black craftworkers in the plant is commensurate with the percentage of blacks in the local labor force. The question for decision is whether Congress, in Title VII of the Civil Rights Act of 1964, 78 Stat. 253, as amended, 42 U.S.C. § 2000e *et seq.*, left employers and unions in the private sector free to take such race-conscious steps to eliminate manifest racial imbalances in traditionally segregated job categories. We hold that Title VII does not prohibit such race-conscious affirmative action plans.

I

In 1974, petitioner United Steelworkers of America (USWA) and petitioner Kaiser Aluminum & Chemical Corp. (Kaiser) entered into a master collective-bargaining agreement covering terms and conditions of employment at 15 Kaiser plants. The agreement contained, *inter alia*, an affirmative action plan designed to eliminate conspicuous racial imbalances in Kaiser's then almost exclusively white craftwork forces. Black craft-hiring goals were set for each Kaiser plant equal to the percentage of blacks in the respective local labor forces. To enable plants to meet these goals, on-the-job training programs were established to teach unskilled production workers—black and white—the skills necessary to become craftworkers. The plan reserved for black employees 50% of the openings in these newly created in-plant training programs.

This case arose from the operation of the plan at Kaiser's plant in Gramercy, La. Until 1974, Kaiser hired as craftworkers for that plant only persons who had had prior craft experience. Because blacks had long been excluded from craft unions, few were able to present such credentials. As a consequence, prior to 1974 only 1.83% (5 out of 273) of the skilled craftworkers at the Gramercy plant were black, even though the work force in the Gramercy area was approximately 39% black.

Pursuant to the national agreement Kaiser altered its craft-hiring practice in the Gramercy plant. Rather than hiring already trained outsiders, Kaiser established a training program to train its production workers to fill craft openings. Selection of craft trainees was made on the basis of seniority, with the proviso that at least 50% of the new trainees were to be black until the percentage of black skilled craftworkers in the Gramercy plant approximated the percentage of blacks in the local labor force.

During 1974, the first year of the operation of the Kaiser-USWA affirmative action plan, 13 craft trainees were selected from Gramercy's production work force. Of these, seven were black and six white. The most senior black selected into the program had less seniority than several white production workers whose bids for admission were rejected. Thereafter one of those white production workers, respondent Brian Weber (hereafter respondent), instituted this class action in the United States District Court for the Eastern District of Louisiana.

The complaint alleged that the filling of craft trainee positions at the Gramercy plant pursuant to the affirmative action program had resulted in junior black employees' receiving training in preference to senior white employees, thus discriminating against respondent and other similarly situated white employees in violation of §§ 703(a) and (d) of Title VII. . . .

II

. . . The only question before us is the narrow statutory issue of whether Title VII *forbids* private employers and unions from voluntarily agreeing upon bona fide affirmative action plans that accord racial preferences in the manner and for the purpose provided in the Kaiser-USWA plan. That question was expressly left open in McDonald v. Santa Fe Trail Transp. Co., 427 U.S. 273 (1976), which held, in a case not involving affirmative action, that Title VII protects whites as well as blacks from certain forms of racial discrimination.

Respondent argues that Congress intended in Title VII to prohibit all race-conscious affirmative action plans. Respondent's argument rests upon a literal interpretation of §§ 703(a) and (d) of the Act. Those sections make it unlawful to "discriminate . . . because of . . . race" in hiring and in the selection of apprentices for training programs. Since, the argument runs, McDonald v. Santa Fe Trail Transp. Co., settled that Title VII forbids discrimination against whites as well as blacks, and since the Kaiser-USWA affirmative action plan operates to discriminate against white employees solely because they are white, it follows that the Kaiser-USWA plan violates Title VII.

Respondent's argument is not without force. But it overlooks the significance of the fact that the Kaiser-USWA plan is an affirmative action plan voluntarily adopted by private parties to eliminate traditional patterns of racial segregation. In this context respondent's reliance upon a literal construction of §§ 703(a) and (d) and upon McDonald is misplaced. . . .It is a "familiar rule, that a thing may be within the letter of the statute and yet not within the statute, because not within its spirit, nor within the intention of its makers." Holy Trinity Church v. United States, 143 U.S. 457, 459 (1892). The prohibition against racial discrimination in §§ 703(a) and (d) of Title VII must therefore be read against the background of the legislative history of Title VII and the historical context from which the Act arose. Examination of those sources makes clear that an interpretation of the sections that forbade all race-conscious affirmative action would "bring about an end completely at variance with the purpose of the statute" and must be rejected.

Congress' primary concern in enacting the prohibition against racial discrimination in Title VII of the Civil Rights Act of 1964 was with "the plight of the Negro in our economy." 110 Cong. Rec. 6548 (1964) (remarks of Sen. Humphrey). Before 1964, blacks were largely relegated to "unskilled and semi-skilled jobs." Ibid. (remarks of Sen. Humphrey); id., at 7204 (remarks of Sen. Clark); id., at 7379–7380 (remarks of Sen. Kennedy). Because of automation the number of such jobs was rapidly decreasing. See id., at 6548 (remarks of Sen. Humphrey); id., at 7204 (remarks of Sen. Clark). As a consequence, "the relative position of the Negro worker [was] steadily worsening. In 1947 the nonwhite unemployment rate was only 64 percent higher than the white rate; in 1962 it was 124 percent higher." Id., at 6547 (remarks of Sen. Humphrey). See also id., at 7204 (remarks of Sen. Clark). Congress considered this a serious social problem. . . .

Congress feared that the goals of the Civil Rights Act—the integration of blacks into the mainstream of American society—could not be achieved unless this trend were reversed. And Congress recognized that that would not be possible unless blacks were able to secure jobs "which have a future." Id., at 7204 (remarks of Sen. Clark). See also id., at 7379–7380 (remarks of Sen. Kennedy). . . .

It plainly appears from the House Report accompanying the Civil Rights Act that Congress did not intend wholly to prohibit private and voluntary affirmative action efforts as one method of solving this problem. The Report provides:

"No bill can or should lay claim to eliminating all of the causes and consequences of racial and other types of discrimination against minorities. There is reason to believe, however, that national leadership provided by the enactment of Federal legislation dealing with the most troublesome problems *will create an atmosphere conducive to voluntary or local resolution of other forms of discrimination.*" H. R. Rep. No. 914, 88th Cong., 1st Sess., pt. 1, p. 18 (1963).

Given this legislative history, we cannot agree with respondent that Congress intended to prohibit the private sector from taking effective steps to accomplish the goal that Congress designed Title VII to achieve. The very statutory words intended as a spur or catalyst to cause "employers and unions to self-examine and to self-evaluate their employment practices and to endeavor to eliminate, so far as possible, the last vestiges of an unfortunate and ignominious page in this country's history," Albemarle Paper Co. v. Moody, 422 U.S. 405, 418 (1975), cannot be interpreted as an absolute prohibition against all private, voluntary, race-conscious affirmative action efforts to hasten the elimination of such vestiges. It would be ironic indeed if a law triggered by a Nation's concern over centuries of racial injustice and intended to improve the lot of those who had "been excluded from the American dream for so long," 110 Cong. Rec. 6552 (1964) (remarks of Sen. Humphrey), constituted the first legislative prohibition of all voluntary, private, race-conscious efforts to abolish traditional patterns of racial segregation and hierarchy.

Our conclusion is further reinforced by examination of the language and legislative history of § 703(j) of Title VII. Opponents of Title VII raised two related arguments against the bill. First, they argued that the Act would be interpreted to *require* employers with racially imbalanced work forces to grant preferential treatment to racial minorities in order to integrate. Second, they argued that employers with racially imbalanced work forces would grant preferential treatment to racial minorities, even if not required to do so by the Act. Had Congress meant to prohibit all race-conscious affirmative action, as respondent urges, it easily could have answered both objections by providing that Title VII would not require or *permit* racially preferential integration efforts. But Congress did not choose such a course. Rather, Congress added § 703(j) which addresses only the first objection. The section provides that nothing contained in Title VII "shall be interpreted to *require* any employer . . . to grant preferential treatment . . . to any group because of the race . . . of such . . . group on account of" a *de facto* racial imbalance in the employer's work force. The section does *not* state that "nothing in Title VII shall be interpreted to *permit*" voluntary affirmative efforts to correct racial imbalances. The natural inference is that Congress chose not to forbid all voluntary race-conscious affirmative action.

The reasons for this choice are evident from the legislative record. Title VII could not have been enacted into law without substantial support from legislators in both Houses who traditionally resisted federal regulation of private business. Those legislators demanded as a price for their support that "management prerogatives, and union freedoms . . . be left undisturbed to the greatest extent possible." H. R. Rep. No. 914, 88th Cong., 1st Sess., pt. 2, p. 29 (1963). Section 703(j) was proposed by Senator Dirksen to allay any fears that the Act might be interpreted in such a way as to upset this compromise. The section was designed to prevent § 703 of Title VII from being interpreted in such a way as to lead to undue "Federal Government interference with private businesses because of some Federal employee's ideas about racial balance or racial imbalance." 110 Cong. Rec. 14314 (1964) (remarks of Sen. Miller). See also *id.*, at 9881 (remarks of Sen. Allott); *id.*, at 10520 (remarks of Sen. Carlson); *id.*, at 11471 (remarks of Sen. Javits); *id.*, at 12817 (remarks of Sen. Dirksen). Clearly, a prohibition against all voluntary, race-conscious, affirmative action efforts would disserve these ends. Such a prohibition would augment the powers of the Federal Government and diminish traditional management prerogatives while at the same time impeding attainment of the ultimate statutory goals. In view of this legislative history and in view of Congress' desire to avoid undue federal regulation of private businesses, use of the word "require" rather than the phrase "require or permit" in § 703(j) fortifies the conclusion that Congress did not intend to limit traditional business freedom to such a degree as to prohibit all voluntary, race-conscious affirmative action. . . .

We conclude, therefore, that the adoption of the Kaiser-USWA plan for the Gramercy plant falls within the area of discretion left by Title VII to the private sector voluntarily to adopt affirmative action plans designed to eliminate conspicuous racial imbalance in traditionally segregated job categories. Accordingly, the judgment of the Court of Appeals for the Fifth Circuit is

Reversed.

■ JUSTICE POWELL and JUSTICE STEVENS took no part in the consideration or decision of these cases.

■ CHIEF JUSTICE BURGER, dissenting.

. . . .Often we have difficulty interpreting statutes either because of imprecise drafting or because legislative compromises have produced genuine ambiguities. But here there is no lack of clarity, no ambiguity. The quota embodied in the collective-bargaining agreement between Kaiser and the Steelworkers unquestionably discriminates on the basis of race against individual employees seeking admission to on-the-job training programs. And, under the plain language of § 703(d), that is "an *unlawful* employment practice." . . .

Arguably, Congress may not have gone far enough in correcting the effects of past discrimination when it enacted Title VII. The gross discrimination against minorities to which the Court adverts— particularly against Negroes in the building trades and craft unions—is one of the dark chapters in the otherwise great history of the American labor movement. And, I do not question the importance of encouraging voluntary compliance with the purposes and policies of Title VII. But that statute was conceived and enacted to make discrimination against *any* individual illegal, and I fail to see how "voluntary compliance" with the no-discrimination principle that is the heart and soul of Title VII as currently written will be achieved by permitting employers to discriminate against some individuals to give preferential treatment to others. . . .

It is often observed that hard cases make bad law. I suspect there is some truth to that adage, for the "hard" cases always tempt judges to exceed the limits of their authority, as the Court does today by totally rewriting a crucial part of Title VII to reach a "desirable" result. . . .

■ JUSTICE REHNQUIST, with whom THE CHIEF JUSTICE joins, dissenting.

. . .

Today's decision represents an equally dramatic and equally unremarked switch in this Court's interpretation of Title VII.

The operative sections of Title VII prohibit racial discrimination in employment *simpliciter*. Taken in its normal meaning, and as understood by all Members of Congress who spoke to the issue during the legislative debates, this language prohibits a covered employer from considering race when making an employment decision, whether the race be black or white. Several years ago, however, a United States District Court held that "the dismissal of white employees charged with misappropriating company property while not dismissing a similarly charged Negro employee does not raise a claim upon which Title VII relief may be granted." McDonald v. Santa Fe Trail Transp. Co., 427 U.S. 273, 278 (1976). This Court unanimously reversed, concluding from the "uncontradicted legislative history" that "Title VII prohibits racial discrimination against the white petitioners in this case upon the same standards as would be applicable were they Negroes . . . ."

We have never wavered in our understanding that Title VII "prohibits *all* racial discrimination in employment, without exception for any group of particular employees." In Griggs v. Duke Power Co., 401 U.S. 424, 431 (1971), our first occasion to interpret Title VII, a unanimous Court observed that "[discriminatory] preference, for any group, minority or majority, is precisely and only what Congress has proscribed." And in our most recent discussion of the issue, we uttered words seemingly dispositive of this case: "It is clear beyond cavil that the obligation imposed by Title VII is to provide an equal opportunity for *each* applicant regardless of race, without regard to whether members of the applicant's race are already proportionately represented in the work force." Furnco Construction Corp. v. Waters, 438 U.S. 567, 579 (1978).

. . . [Here,] without even a break in syntax, the Court rejects "a literal construction of § 703 (a)" in favor of newly discovered "legislative history," which leads it to a conclusion directly contrary to that compelled by the "uncontradicted legislative history" unearthed in *McDonald* and our other prior decisions. Now we are told that the legislative history of Title VII shows that employers are free to discriminate on the basis of race: an employer may, in the Court's words, "trammel the interests of the white employees" in favor of black employees in order to eliminate "racial imbalance." Our earlier interpretations of Title VII, . . . were all wrong.

As if this were not enough to make a reasonable observer question this Court's adherence to the oft-stated principle that our duty is to construe rather than rewrite legislation, the Court also seizes upon § 703(j) of Title VII as an independent, or at least partially independent, basis for its holding. Totally ignoring the wording of that section, which is obviously addressed to those charged with the responsibility of interpreting the law rather than those who are subject to its proscriptions, and totally ignoring the months of legislative debates preceding the section's introduction and passage, which demonstrate clearly that it was enacted to prevent precisely what occurred in this case, the Court infers from § 703(j) that "Congress chose not to forbid all voluntary race-conscious affirmative action."

Thus, by a *tour de force* reminiscent not of jurists such as Hale, Holmes, and Hughes, but of escape artists such as Houdini, the Court eludes clear statutory language, "uncontradicted" legislative history, and uniform precedent in concluding that employers are, after all, permitted to consider race in making employment decisions. It may be that one or more of the principal sponsors of Title VII would have preferred to see a provision allowing preferential treatment of minorities written into the bill. Such a provision, however, would have to have been expressly or impliedly excepted from Title VII's explicit prohibition on all racial discrimination in employment. There is no such exception in the Act. And a reading of the legislative debates concerning Title VII, in which proponents and opponents alike uniformly denounced discrimination in favor of, as well as discrimination against, Negroes, demonstrates clearly that any legislator harboring an unspoken desire for such a provision could not possibly have succeeded in enacting it into law. . . .

[In the intervening sections of his opinion, Justice Rehnquist reviews the facts of this case and, at length, the legislative history of the statute.]

IV

Reading the language of Title VII, as the Court purports to do, "against the background of [its] legislative history . . . and the historical context from which the Act arose," one is led inescapably to the conclusion that Congress fully understood what it was saying and meant precisely what it said. Opponents of the civil rights bill did not argue that employers would be permitted under Title VII voluntarily to grant preferential treatment to minorities to correct racial imbalance. The plain language of the statute too clearly prohibited such racial discrimination to admit of any doubt. They argued, tirelessly, that Title

VII would be interpreted by federal agencies and their agents to require unwilling employers to racially balance their work forces by granting preferential treatment to minorities. Supporters of H. R. 7152 responded, equally tirelessly, that the Act would not be so interpreted because not only does it not require preferential treatment of minorities, it also does not *permit* preferential treatment of any race for any reason. It cannot be doubted that the proponents of Title VII understood the meaning of their words, for "[seldom] has similar legislation been debated with greater consciousness of the need for 'legislative history,' or with greater care in the making thereof, to guide the courts in interpreting and applying the law."

To put an end to the dispute, supporters of the civil rights bill drafted and introduced § 703(j). Specifically addressed to the opposition's charge, § 703(j) simply enjoins federal agencies and courts from interpreting Title VII to require an employer to prefer certain racial groups to correct imbalances in his work force. The section says nothing about voluntary preferential treatment of minorities because such racial discrimination is plainly proscribed by §§ 703(a) and (d). Indeed, had Congress intended to except voluntary, race-conscious preferential treatment from the blanket prohibition of racial discrimination in §§ 703(a) and (d), it surely could have drafted language better suited to the task than § 703(j). It knew how. Section 703(i) provides:

"Nothing contained in [Title VII] shall apply to any business or enterprise on or near an Indian reservation with respect to any publicly announced employment practice of such business or enterprise under which a preferential treatment is given to any individual because he is an Indian living on or near a reservation."

V

Our task in this case, like any other case involving the construction of a statute, is to give effect to the intent of Congress. To divine that intent, we traditionally look first to the words of the statute and, if they are unclear, then to the statute's legislative history. Finding the desired result hopelessly foreclosed by these conventional sources, the Court turns to a third source—the "spirit" of the Act. But close examination of what the Court proffers as the spirit of the Act reveals it as the spirit animating the present majority, not the 88th Congress. For if the spirit of the Act eludes the cold words of the statute itself, it rings out with unmistakable clarity in the words of the elected representatives who made the Act law. It is *equality*. . . .

There is perhaps no device more destructive to the notion of equality than the *numerus clausus*—the quota. Whether described as "benign discrimination" or "affirmative action," the racial quota is nonetheless a creator of castes, a two-edged sword that must demean one in order to prefer another. In passing Title VII, Congress outlawed *all* racial discrimination, recognizing that no discrimination based on race is benign, that no action disadvantaging a person because of his color is affirmative. With today's holding, the Court introduces into Title VII a tolerance for the very evil that the law was intended to eradicate, without offering even a clue as to what the limits on that tolerance may be. We are told simply that Kaiser's racially discriminatory admission quota "falls on the permissible side of the line." By going not merely *beyond*, but directly *against* Title VII's language and legislative history, the Court has sown the wind. Later courts will face the impossible task of reaping the whirlwind.

KING v. BURWELL

Supreme Court of the United States (2015).
135 S.Ct. 2480.

■ CHIEF JUSTICE ROBERTS delivered the opinion of the Court.

The Patient Protection and Affordable Care Act adopts a series of interlocking reforms designed to expand coverage in the individual health insurance market. First, the Act bars insurers from taking a person's health into account when deciding whether to sell health insurance or how much to charge. Second, the Act generally requires each person to maintain insurance coverage or make a payment to the Internal Revenue Service. And third, the Act gives tax credits to certain people to make insurance more affordable.

In addition to those reforms, the Act requires the creation of an "Exchange" in each State—basically, a marketplace that allows people to compare and purchase insurance plans. The Act gives each State the opportunity to establish its own Exchange, but provides that the Federal Government will establish the Exchange if the State does not.

This case is about whether the Act's interlocking reforms apply equally in each State no matter who establishes the State's Exchange. Specifically, the question presented is whether the Act's tax credits are available in States that have a Federal Exchange.

I

A

The Patient Protection and Affordable Care Act, 124 Stat. 119, grew out of a long history of failed health insurance reform. In the 1990s, several States began experimenting with ways to expand people's access to coverage. One common approach was to impose a pair of insurance market regulations—a "guaranteed issue" requirement, which barred insurers from denying coverage to any person because of his health, and a "community rating" requirement, which barred insurers from charging a person higher premiums for the same reason. Together, those requirements were designed to ensure that anyone who wanted to buy health insurance could do so.

The guaranteed issue and community rating requirements achieved that goal, but they had an unintended consequence: They encouraged people to wait until they got sick to buy insurance. Why buy insurance coverage when you are healthy, if you can buy the same coverage for the same price when you become ill? This consequence—known as "adverse selection"—led to a second: Insurers were forced to increase premiums to account for the fact that, more and more, it was the sick rather than the healthy who were buying insurance. And that consequence fed back into the first: As the cost of insurance rose, even more people waited until they became ill to buy it.

This led to an economic "death spiral." As premiums rose higher and higher, and the number of people buying insurance sank lower and lower, insurers began to leave the market entirely. As a result, the number of people without insurance increased dramatically. . . .

B

The Affordable Care Act adopts . . . guaranteed issue and community rating requirements. The Act provides that "each health insurance issuer that offers health insurance coverage in the individual . . . market in a State must accept every . . . individual in the State that applies for such coverage." The Act also bars insurers from charging higher premiums on the basis of a person's health.

Second, the Act generally requires individuals to maintain health insurance coverage or make a payment to the IRS. Congress recognized that, without an incentive, "many individuals would wait to purchase health insurance until they needed care." So Congress adopted a coverage requirement to "minimize this adverse selection and broaden the health insurance risk pool to include healthy individuals, which will lower health insurance premiums." In Congress's view, that coverage requirement was "essential to creating effective health insurance markets." Congress also provided an exemption from the coverage requirement for anyone who has to spend more than eight percent of his income on health insurance.

Third, the Act seeks to make insurance more affordable by giving refundable tax credits to individuals with household incomes between 100 percent and 400 percent of the federal poverty line. Individuals who meet the Act's requirements may purchase insurance with the tax credits, which are provided in advance directly to the individual's insurer.

These three reforms are closely intertwined. As noted, Congress found that the guaranteed issue and community rating requirements would not work without the coverage requirement. And the coverage requirement would not work without the tax credits. The reason is that, without the tax credits, the cost of buying insurance would exceed eight percent of income for a large number of individuals, which would exempt them from the coverage requirement. Given the relationship between these three reforms, the Act provided that they should take effect on the same day—January 1, 2014.

C

In addition to those three reforms, the Act requires the creation of an "Exchange" in each State where people can shop for insurance, usually online. An Exchange may be created in one of two ways. First, the Act provides that "[e]ach State shall . . . establish an American Health Benefit Exchange . . . for the State." Second, if a State nonetheless chooses not to establish its own Exchange, the Act provides that the Secretary of Health and Human Services "shall . . . establish and operate such Exchange within the State."

The issue in this case is whether the Act's tax credits are available in States that have a Federal Exchange rather than a State Exchange. The Act initially provides that tax credits "shall be allowed" for any "applicable taxpayer." The Act then provides that the amount of the tax credit depends in part on whether the taxpayer has enrolled in an insurance plan through "an Exchange *established by the State* under section 1311 of the Patient Protection and Affordable Care Act."

The IRS addressed the availability of tax credits by promulgating a rule that made them available on both State and Federal Exchanges. As relevant here, the IRS Rule provides that a taxpayer is eligible for a tax credit if he enrolled in an insurance plan through "an Exchange," which is defined as "an Exchange serving the individual market . . . regardless of whether the Exchange is established and operated by a State . . . or by HHS," At this point, 16 States and the District of Columbia have established their own Exchanges; the other 34 States have elected to have HHS do so. . . .

II

The Affordable Care Act addresses tax credits in what is now Section 36B of the Internal Revenue Code. . . . The parties dispute whether Section 36B authorizes tax credits for individuals who enroll in an insurance plan through a Federal Exchange. Petitioners argue that a Federal Exchange is not "an Exchange established by the State under [42 U.S.C. § 18031]," and that the IRS Rule therefore contradicts Section 36B. The Government responds that the IRS Rule is lawful because the phrase "an Exchange established by the State under [42 U.S.C. § 18031]" should be read to include Federal Exchanges. . . .

A

We begin with the text of Section 36B. As relevant here, Section 36B allows an individual to receive tax credits only if the individual enrolls in an insurance plan through "an Exchange established by the State under [42 U.S.C. § 18031]." In other words, three things must be true: First, the individual must enroll in an insurance plan through "an Exchange." Second, that Exchange must be "established by the State." And third, that Exchange must be established "under [42 U.S.C. § 18031]." We address each requirement in turn.

First, all parties agree that a Federal Exchange qualifies as "an Exchange" for purposes of Section 36B. . . .

Second, we must determine whether a Federal Exchange is "established by the State" for purposes of Section 36B. At the outset, it might seem that a Federal Exchange cannot fulfill this requirement. After all, the Act defines "State" to mean "each of the 50 States and the District of Columbia"—a definition that does not include the Federal Government. 42 U.S.C. § 18024(d). But when read in context, "with a view to [its] place in the overall statutory scheme," the meaning of the phrase "established by the State" is not so clear.

After telling each State to establish an Exchange, Section 18031 provides that all Exchanges "shall make available qualified health plans to qualified individuals." 42 U.S.C. § 18031(d)(2)(A). Section 18032 then defines the term "qualified individual" in part as an individual who "resides in the State that established the Exchange." § 18032(f)(1)(A). And that's a problem: If we give the phrase "the State that established the Exchange" its most natural meaning, there would be *no* "qualified individuals" on Federal Exchanges. But the Act clearly contemplates that there will be qualified individuals on *every* Exchange. As we just mentioned, the Act requires all Exchanges to "make available qualified health plans to qualified individuals"—something an Exchange could not do if there were no such individuals. § 18031(d)(2)(A). And the Act tells the Exchange, in deciding which health plans to offer, to consider "the interests of qualified individuals . . . in the State or States in which such Exchange operates"—again, something the Exchange could not do if qualified individuals did not exist. § 18031(e)(1)(B). This problem arises repeatedly throughout the Act. . . .

These provisions suggest that the Act may not always use the phrase "established by the State" in its most natural sense. Thus, the meaning of that phrase may not be as clear as it appears when read out of context.

Third, we must determine whether a Federal Exchange is established "under [42 U.S.C. § 18031]." This too might seem a requirement that a Federal Exchange cannot fulfill, because it is Section 18041 that tells the Secretary when to "establish and operate such Exchange." But here again, the way different provisions in the statute interact suggests otherwise.

The Act defines the term "Exchange" to mean "an American Health Benefit Exchange established under section 18031." § 300gg–91(d)(21). If we import that definition into Section 18041, the Act tells the Secretary to "establish and operate such 'American Health Benefit Exchange established under section 18031.'" That suggests that Section 18041 authorizes the Secretary to establish an Exchange under Section 18031, not (or not only) under Section 18041. Otherwise, the Federal Exchange, by definition, would not be an "Exchange" at all.

This interpretation of "under [42 U.S.C. § 18031]" fits best with the statutory context. All of the requirements that an Exchange must meet are in Section 18031, so it is sensible to regard all Exchanges as established under that provision. In addition, every time the Act uses the word "Exchange," the definitional provision requires that we substitute the phrase "Exchange established under section 18031." If Federal Exchanges were not established under Section 18031, therefore, literally none of the Act's requirements would apply to them. Finally, the Act repeatedly uses the phrase "established under [42 U.S.C. § 18031]" in situations where it would make no sense to distinguish between State and Federal Exchanges. . . .

The upshot of all this is that the phrase "an Exchange established by the State under [42 U.S.C. § 18031]" is properly viewed as ambiguous. The phrase may be limited in its reach to State Exchanges. But it is also possible that the phrase refers to *all* Exchanges—both State and Federal—at least for purposes of the tax credits. If a State chooses not to follow the directive in Section 18031 that it establish an Exchange, the Act tells the Secretary to establish "such Exchange." § 18041. And by using the words "such Exchange," the Act indicates that State and Federal Exchanges should be the same. But State and Federal Exchanges would differ in a fundamental way if tax credits were available only on State Exchanges—one type of Exchange would help make insurance more affordable by providing billions of dollars to the States' citizens; the other type of Exchange would not.

The conclusion that Section 36B is ambiguous is further supported by several provisions that assume tax credits will be available on both State and Federal Exchanges. . . .

Petitioners and the dissent respond that the words "established by the State" would be unnecessary if Congress meant to extend tax credits to both State and Federal Exchanges. But "our preference for avoiding surplusage constructions is not absolute." *Lamie v. United States Trustee,* 540 U.S. 526, 536 (2004). And specifically with respect to this Act, rigorous application of the canon does not seem a particularly useful guide to a fair construction of the statute.

The Affordable Care Act contains more than a few examples of inartful drafting. (To cite just one, the Act creates three separate Section 1563s. See 124 Stat. 270, 911, 912.) Several features of the Act's passage contributed to that unfortunate reality. Congress wrote key parts of the Act behind closed doors, rather than through "the traditional legislative process." And Congress passed much of the Act using a complicated budgetary procedure known as "reconciliation," which limited opportunities for debate and amendment, and bypassed the Senate's normal 60-vote filibuster requirement. As a result, the Act does not reflect the type of care and deliberation that one might expect of such significant legislation.

Anyway, we "must do our best, bearing in mind the fundamental canon of statutory construction that the words of a statute must be read in their context and with a view to their place in the overall statutory scheme." Utility Air Regulatory Group, 573 U.S., at ___. After reading Section 36B along with other related provisions in the Act, we cannot conclude that the phrase "an Exchange established by the State under [Section 18031]" is unambiguous.

B

Given that the text is ambiguous, we must turn to the broader structure of the Act to determine the meaning of Section 36B. "A provision that may seem ambiguous in isolation is often clarified by the remainder of the statutory scheme . . . because only one of the permissible meanings produces a substantive effect that is compatible with the rest of the law." Here, the statutory scheme compels us to reject petitioners' interpretation because it would destabilize the individual insurance market in any State with a Federal Exchange, and likely create the very "death spirals" that Congress designed the Act to avoid. See New York State Dept. of Social Servs. v. Dublino, 413 U.S. 405, 419–420 (1973) ("We cannot interpret federal statutes to negate their own stated purposes.").

As discussed above, Congress based the Affordable Care Act on three major reforms: first, the guaranteed issue and community rating requirements; second, a requirement that individuals maintain health insurance coverage or make a payment to the IRS; and third, the tax credits for individuals with household incomes between 100 percent and 400 percent of the federal poverty line. In a State that establishes its own Exchange, these three reforms work together to expand insurance coverage. The guaranteed issue and community rating requirements ensure that anyone can buy insurance; the coverage requirement creates an incentive for people to do so before they get sick; and the tax credits—it is hoped—make insurance more affordable. Together, those reforms "minimize . . . adverse selection and broaden the health insurance risk pool to include healthy individuals, which will lower health insurance premiums."

Under petitioners' reading, however, the Act would operate quite differently in a State with a Federal Exchange. As they see it, one of the Act's three major reforms—the tax credits—would not apply. And a second major reform—the coverage requirement—would not apply in a meaningful way. As explained earlier, the coverage requirement applies only when the cost of buying health insurance (minus the amount of the tax credits) is less than eight percent of an individual's income. So without the tax credits, the coverage requirement would apply to fewer individuals. And it would be a *lot* fewer. In 2014, approximately 87 percent of people who bought insurance on a Federal Exchange did so with tax credits, and virtually all of those people would become exempt.

If petitioners are right, therefore, only one of the Act's three major reforms would apply in States with a Federal Exchange.

The combination of no tax credits and an ineffective coverage requirement could well push a State's individual insurance market into a death spiral. One study predicts that premiums would increase by 47 percent and enrollment would decrease by 70 percent. E. Saltzman & C. Eibner, The Effect of Eliminating the Affordable Care Act's Tax Credits in Federally Facilitated Marketplaces (2015). Another study predicts that premiums would increase by 35 percent and enrollment would decrease by 69 percent. L. Blumberg, M. Buettgens, & J. Holahan, The Implications of a Supreme Court Finding for the Plaintiff in King vs. Burwell: 8.2 Million More Uninsured and 35% Higher Premiums (2015). . . .

It is implausible that Congress meant the Act to operate in this manner. Congress made the guaranteed issue and community rating requirements applicable in every State in the Nation. But those requirements only work when combined with the coverage requirement and the tax credits. So it stands to reason that Congress meant for those provisions to apply in every State as well. . . .

C

Finally, the structure of Section 36B itself suggests that tax credits are not limited to State Exchanges . . .

D

Petitioners' arguments about the plain meaning of Section 36B are strong. But while the meaning of the phrase "an Exchange established by the State under [42 U.S.C. § 18031]" may seem plain "when viewed in isolation," such a reading turns out to be "untenable in light of [the statute] as a whole." In this instance, the context and structure of the Act compel us to depart from what would otherwise be the most natural reading of the pertinent statutory phrase.

Reliance on context and structure in statutory interpretation is a "subtle business, calling for great wariness lest what professes to be mere rendering becomes creation and attempted interpretation of legislation becomes legislation itself." Palmer v. Massachusetts, 308 U.S. 79, 83 (1939). For the reasons we have given, however, such reliance is appropriate in this case, and leads us to conclude that Section 36B allows tax credits for insurance purchased on any Exchange created under the Act. Those credits are necessary for the Federal Exchanges to function like their State Exchange counterparts, and to avoid the type of calamitous result that Congress plainly meant to avoid.

* * *

In a democracy, the power to make the law rests with those chosen by the people. Our role is more confined—"to say what the law is." Marbury v. Madison, 1 Cranch 137, 177 (1803). That is easier in some cases than in others. But in every case we must respect the role of the Legislature, and take care not to undo what it has done. A fair reading of legislation demands a fair understanding of the legislative plan.

Congress passed the Affordable Care Act to improve health insurance markets, not to destroy them. If at all possible, we must interpret the Act in a way that is consistent with the former, and avoids the latter. Section 36B can fairly be read consistent with what we see as Congress's plan, and that is the reading we adopt. . . .

[The judgment of the Fourth circuit, upholding the Act, is affirmed.]

■ JUSTICE SCALIA, with whom JUSTICE THOMAS and JUSTICE ALITO join, dissenting.

The Court holds that when the Patient Protection and Affordable Care Act says "Exchange established by the State" it means "Exchange established by the State or the Federal Government." That is of course quite absurd, and the Court's 21 pages of explanation make it no less so.

I

. . . This case requires us to decide whether someone who buys insurance on an Exchange established by the Secretary gets tax credits. You would think the answer would be obvious—so obvious there would hardly be a need for the Supreme Court to hear a case about it. In order to receive any money under § 36B, an individual must enroll in an insurance plan through an "Exchange established by the State." The Secretary of Health and Human Services is not a State. So an Exchange established by the Secretary is not an Exchange established by the State—which means people who buy health insurance through such an Exchange get no money under § 36B.

Words no longer have meaning if an Exchange that is *not* established by a State is "established by the State." It is hard to come up with a clearer way to limit tax credits to state Exchanges than to use the words "established by the State." And it is hard to come up with a reason to include the words "by the State" other than the purpose of limiting credits to state Exchanges. . . . Under all the usual rules of interpretation, in short, the Government should lose this case. But normal rules of interpretation seem always to yield to the overriding principle of the present Court: The Affordable Care Act must be saved. . . .

III

For its next defense of the indefensible, the Court turns to the Affordable Care Act's design and purposes. . . .

To begin with, "even the most formidable argument concerning the statute's purposes could not overcome the clarity [of] the statute's text." Statutory design and purpose matter only to the extent they help clarify an otherwise ambiguous provision. Could anyone maintain with a straight face that § 36B is unclear? To mention just the highlights, the Court's interpretation clashes with a statutory definition, renders words inoperative in at least seven separate provisions of the Act, overlooks the contrast between provisions that say "Exchange" and those that say "Exchange established by the State," gives the same phrase one meaning for purposes of tax credits but an entirely different meaning for other purposes, and (let us not forget) contradicts the ordinary meaning of the words Congress used. On the other side of the ledger, the Court has come up with nothing more than a general provision that turns out to be controlled by a specific one, a handful of clauses that are consistent with either understanding of establishment by the State, and a resemblance between the tax-credit provision and the rest of the Tax Code. If that is all it takes to make something ambiguous, everything is ambiguous.

Having gone wrong in consulting statutory purpose at all, the Court goes wrong again in analyzing it. The purposes of a law must be "collected chiefly from its words," not "from extrinsic circumstances." Only by concentrating on the law's terms can a judge hope to uncover the scheme *of the statute,* rather than some other scheme that the judge thinks desirable. Like it or not, the express terms of the Affordable Care Act make only two of the three reforms mentioned by the Court applicable in States that do not establish Exchanges. It is perfectly possible for them to operate independently of tax credits. The guaranteed-issue and community-rating requirements continue to ensure that insurance companies treat all customers the same no matter their health, and the individual mandate continues to encourage people to maintain coverage, lest they be "taxed."

The Court protests that without the tax credits, the number of people covered by the individual mandate shrinks, and without a broadly applicable individual mandate the guaranteed-issue and community-rating requirements "would destabilize the individual insurance market." *Ante,* at 2493. If true, these projections would show only that the statutory scheme contains a flaw; they would not show that the statute means the opposite of what it says. . . .

Compounding its errors, the Court forgets that it is no more appropriate to consider one of a statute's purposes in isolation than it is to consider one of its words that way. No law pursues just one purpose at all costs, and no statutory scheme encompasses just one element. Most relevant here, the Affordable Care Act displays a congressional preference for state participation in the establishment of Exchanges: Each State gets the first opportunity to set up its Exchange, 42 U.S.C. § 18031(b); States that take up the opportunity receive federal funding for "activities . . . related to establishing" an Exchange; and the Secretary may establish an Exchange in a State only as a fallback, § 18041(c). But setting up and running an Exchange involve significant burdens— meeting strict deadlines, § 18041(b), implementing requirements related to the offering of insurance plans, § 18031(d)(4), setting up outreach programs, § 18031(i), and ensuring that the Exchange is self-sustaining by 2015, § 18031(d)(5)(A). A State would have much less reason to take on these burdens if its citizens could receive tax credits no matter who establishes its Exchange. (Now that the Internal Revenue Service has interpreted § 36B to authorize tax credits everywhere, by the way, 34 States have failed to set up their own Exchanges. *Ante,* at 2487.) So even if making credits available on all Exchanges advances the goal of improving healthcare markets, it frustrates the goal of encouraging state involvement in the implementation of the Act. *This* is what justifies going out of our way to read "established by the State" to mean "established by the State or not established by the State"? . . . All in all, the Court's arguments about the law's purpose and design are no more convincing than its arguments about context. . . .

NOTES ON PURPOSIVISM

(1)   ***Consider the Cases.*** There is an understandable tendency to think of "purposivism" as a unitary theory, defined by its opposition to "textualism." But a more careful analysis might show that there are many varieties of "purposivism." The three preceding cases—Holy Trinity Church, Weber, and King v. Burwell—might be arranged along several different dimensions. How do they differ in the level of generality or specificity of the "purpose" they are trying to locate? How do they differ as to the evidence they use to establish the "purpose" they find? How do they use that "purpose" in relation to the text they also construe? Is there a form of "purposivism" that is attractive, and a form that is not? It is perhaps worth noting that each of these cases has, among serious scholars, both its defenders and its detractors.

(2)   ***A Classic Statement.*** HENRY M. HART and ALBERT M. SACKS, THE LEGAL PROCESS: BASIC PROBLEMS IN THE MAKING AND APPLICATION OF LAW 1374 ff: (1958; ed. Eskridge and Frickey, 1994):

> "In interpreting a statute a court should:
>
> > 1.   Decide what purpose ought to be attributed to the statute and to any subordinate provision of it which may be involved; and then
> >
> > 2.   Interpret the words of the statute immediately in question so as to carry out the purpose as best it can, making sure, however, that it does not give the words either—
> >
> > > a.   a meaning they will not bear, or
> > >
> > > b.   a meaning which would violate any established policy of clear statement. . . .
>
> ". . . The words of a statute, taken in their context, serve both as guides in the attribution of general purpose, and as factors limiting the particular meanings that can be properly attributed. . . . A formally enacted statement of purpose in a statute should be accepted by the court if it appears to have been designed to serve as a guide to interpretation, is consistent with the words and context of the statute, and is relevant to the question of meaning at issue. . . .

"... In drawing such inferences [about purpose] the court needs to be aware that the concept of purpose is not simple.

a.   Purposes may be shaped with differing degrees of definiteness.

The definiteness may be such that resolution of a doubtful about purpose resolves, without more, a question of specific application. . . . Or purpose may be deliberately formulated with great generality, openly contemplating the exercise of further judgment by the interpreter even after he has fully grasped the legislature's thought.

b.   Purposes, moreover, may exist in hierarchies or constellations. E.g. (to give a very simple illustration), to do <u>this</u> only so far as possible without doing <u>that</u>.

c.   One form of such a constellation or relationship is invariable in the law and of immense importance. The purpose of statute must always be treated as including not only an immediate purpose or group of related purposes but a larger and subtler purpose as to how the particular statute is to be fitted into the legal system as a whole. . . .

"... In determining the more immediate purpose which ought to be attributed to a statute, and to any subordinate provision of it which may be involved, a court should try to put itself in imagination in the position of the legislature which enacted the measure. The court, however, should not do this in the mood of a cynical political observer, taking account of all short-run currents of political expedience that swirl around any legislative session. It should assume, unless the contrary unmistakably appears, that the legislature was made up of reasonable persons pursuing reasonable purposes reasonably. It should presume conclusively that these persons, whether or not entertaining concepts of reasonableness shared by the court, were trying responsibly and in good faith to discharge their constitutional powers and duties. . . .

"... The degree of definiteness to be attributed to the legislative purpose in the enactment of the statute is decisive of the nature of the task of interpretation which remains after the purpose has been grasped. . . . [The court] should give sympathetic attention to indications in the legislative history of the lines of contemplated growth, if the history is available. It should give weight to popular construction of self-operating elements of the statute, if that is uniform. Primarily, it should strive to develop a coherent and reasoned pattern of applications intelligibly related to the general purpose."

(3)   ***A Modern Statement.*** STEPHEN BREYER, MAKING OUR DEMOCRACY WORK 94–98 (2010): "I believe a purpose-oriented approach is better than a purely text-oriented approach. Three sets of considerations, taken together, explain why I believe the Court is obliged to follow a purpose-oriented approach.

"First, judicial consideration of a statute's purposes helps to further the Constitution's democratic goals. In a representative democracy, legislators must ultimately act in ways that voters find acceptable. But voters are unaware of the detailed language that legislators write. They can do no more than consider whether a legislator's work corresponds roughly to their own views, typically expressed in terms of general objectives, say peace, prosperity, healthy environment, and economizing.

"A legislator whose statute furthers a popular objective will seek credit at election time—at least if the statute works reasonably well. But suppose the statute does not work well. Then whom should the voters blame? If courts have interpreted the statute in accordance with the legislator's purposes, there is no one to blame but the legislator. But if courts disregard the statute's purposes, it is much harder for the voter to know who is responsible when results go awry. . . .

"No single court decision will make a difference. But over time, where vast numbers of statutory provisions are at issue, the following generalizations seem fair. The more the Court relies on text-based methods alone to interpret statutes, the easier it will be for legislators to avoid responsibility for a badly written statute simply by saying that the Court reached results they did not favor. The more the Court seeks realistically to ascertain the purposes of a statute and interprets its provisions in ways that further those purposes, the harder it will be for the legislator to escape responsibility for the statute's objectives, and the easier it will be for voters to hold their legislators responsible for their legislative decisions, including the consequences of the statutes for which they vote.

"Second, a purpose-oriented approach helps individual statutes work better for those whom Congress intended to help. . . .

"Third, and most important, by emphasizing purpose the Court will help Congress better accomplish its own legislative work. Congress does not, cannot, and need not write statutes that precisely and exhaustively explain where and how each of the statute's provisions will apply. For one thing, doing so would require too many words. Who wants statutory encyclopedias that spell out in excruciating detail all potential applications in all potential circumstances? Who could read them?

"For another thing, linguistic imprecision, vagueness, and ambiguity are often useful, even necessary, statutory instruments. Congress may not know just how its statute should apply in future circumstances where it can see that future only dimly, and new situations will always emerge. Congress may want to consider only one aspect of a complex, detailed subject, an aspect that warrants a few general words that simply point a court in the right direction. Congress may want to use a general standard, such as "restraint of trade," while intending courts to develop more specific content on a case-by-case common-law basis. Or, the English language may lack words that succinctly express, say, the necessary quantitative measurement, as, for example, when Congress seeks to punish more severely those who commit "serious" or "violent" crimes.

"In these circumstances, congressional drafting staffs may well use general or imprecise words while relying on committee reports, statements of members delivered on the floor of Congress, legislative hearings, and similar materials to convey intended purposes, hence meaning, scope, and reference. Congress can use that drafting system if, and only if, it can count on the courts to consider legislative purposes when interpreting statutes and look at the associated legislative materials to help determine legislative purpose. When courts do so, drafters, legislators, and judges can work together. They act in tandem with Congress, carrying out the legislators' objectives in even the most complex statutes, such as those dealing with bankruptcy, transit system mergers, or pension benefit guarantees.

"Without such teamwork, legislators and their staffs would face a drafting task that is daunting and even impractical. . . .

"In saying all this, I recognize that the political complexion of Congress can change. By looking at the purposes of those who once enacted a statute as I would do, the Court might produce an interpretation that a more recent Congress would disapprove. But in doing so, the Court emphasizes the need for *legislation*, to depart from an earlier statute, and it thereby also assures the present Congress that their own intentions will be honored later when the Court considers the meaning of a statute that they have passed."

(4) ***Another View.*** ANTONIN SCALIA, A MATTER OF INTERPRETATION 17–18 (1997): "[I]t is simply incompatible with democratic government, or indeed, even with fair government, to have the meaning of a law determined by what the lawgiver meant, rather than by what the lawgiver promulgated. That seems to me one step worse than the trick the emperor Nero was said to engage in: posting edicts high up on the pillars, so that they could not easily be read. Government by unexpressed intent is similarly tyrannical. It is the *law* that governs, not the intent of the lawgiver. That seems to me the essence of the famous American ideal set forth in the Massachusetts constitution: A government of laws, not of men. Men may intend what they will; but it is only the laws that they enact which bind us.

"In reality, however, if one accepts the principle that the object of judicial interpretation is to determine the intent of the legislature, being bound by genuine but unexpressed legislative intent rather than the law is only the *theoretical* threat. The *practical* threat is that, under the guise or even the self-delusion of pursuing unexpressed legislative intents, common-law judges will in fact pursue their own objectives and desires, extending their lawmaking proclivities from the common law to the statutory field. When you are told to decide, not on the basis of what the legislature said, but on the basis of what it *meant*, and are assured that there is no necessary connection between the two, your best shot at figuring out what the legislature meant is to ask yourself what a wise and intelligent person *should* have meant; and that will surely bring you to the conclusion that the law means what you think it *ought* to mean—which is precisely how judges decide things under the common law."

c. Pragmatic and Dynamic Statutory Interpretation

> **HIVELY v. IVY TECH COMMUNITY COLLEGE**
> **Notes on Dynamic Statutory Interpretation**

As we have seen, textualism focuses on the words of the statute and purposivism focuses on the purpose underlying those words. A different theory of statutory interpretation focuses on the practical consequences that would follow from a given interpretation—whether that interpretation is based on the statute's text or its seeming purpose (perhaps as divined from the applicable legislative history). Such an approach is often described as pragmatic statutory interpretation. Judge Richard A. Posner describes legal pragmatism as "a heightened concern with consequences" and "a disposition to ground policy judgments on facts and consequences rather than on conceptualisms, generalities, pieties, and slogans." This approach has achieved special recognition as applied to the problem of statutes passed many years ago. Statutory interpretation, says Prof. William Eskridge, should respond to changes in "societal, political, and legal context"; we should embrace (to use the term he coined) "dynamic statutory interpretation."

The excerpted case that follows, Hively v. Ivy Tech Community College, directly engages with the questions Posner and Eskridge raise. The statute at stake is a core provision of the 1964 Civil Rights Act, 42 U.S.C. § 2000e–2(a):

It shall be an unlawful employment practice for an employer—

(1) to fail or refuse to hire or to discharge any individual, or otherwise to discriminate against any individual with respect to his compensation, terms, conditions, or privileges of employment, because of such individual's race, color, religion, sex, or national origin. . . .

And here's the question: As of 2017, does this statute outlaw discrimination by an employer on the basis of sexual orientation? And here's enough, could the answer possiblty be "yes" if it were clear that in 1964 no one would have thought so?

As you read *Hively* and the excerpts that follow, think about how the methods of statutory interpretation used by the majority and by Judge Posner differ from the textualism employed in West Virginia University Hosp., Inc. v. Casey and the purposivism in Weber. Should judges consider the consequences of their holdings? Should changing social, political, and legal contexts impact statutory interpretation? In light of the country's deliberate legislative process, are pragmatism and dynamic statutory interpretation legitimate methods of statutory interpretation?

HIVELY v. IVY TECH COMMUNITY COLLEGE

United States Court of Appeals for the Seventh Circuit, en banc (2017).
853 F.3d 339.

■ JUDGE WOOD.

Title VII of the Civil Rights Act of 1964 makes it unlawful for employers subject to the Act to discriminate on the basis of a person's "race, color, religion, sex, or national origin . . . ." 42 U.S.C. § 2000e–2(a). For many years, the courts of appeals of this country understood the prohibition against sex discrimination to exclude discrimination on the basis of a person's sexual orientation. The Supreme Court, however, has never spoken to that question. In this case, we have been asked to take a fresh look at our position in light of developments at the Supreme Court extending over two decades. We have done so, and we conclude today that discrimination on the basis of sexual orientation is a form of sex discrimination. We therefore reverse the district court's judgment dismissing Kimberly Hively's suit against Ivy Tech Community College and remand for further proceedings.

I

Hively is openly lesbian. She began teaching as a part-time, adjunct professor at Ivy Tech Community College's South Bend campus in 2000. Hoping to improve her lot, she applied for at least six full-time positions between 2009 and 2014. These efforts were unsuccessful; worse yet, in July 2014 her part-time contract was not renewed. . . .

. . . .

II
A

The question before us is not whether this court can, or should, "amend" Title VII to add a new protected category to the familiar list of "race, color, religion, sex, or national origin." 42 U.S.C. § 2000e–2(a). Obviously that lies beyond our power. We must decide instead what it means to discriminate on the basis of sex, and in particular, whether actions taken on the basis of sexual orientation are a subset of actions taken on the basis of sex. This is a pure question of statutory interpretation and thus well within the judiciary's competence.

Much ink has been spilled about the proper way to go about the task of statutory interpretation. One can stick, to the greatest extent possible, to the language enacted by the legislature; one could consult the legislative history that led up to the bill that became law; one could examine later actions of the legislature (*i.e.* efforts to amend the law and later enactments) for whatever light they may shed; and one could use a combination of these methods.

Few people would insist that there is a need to delve into secondary sources if the statute is plain on its face. Even if it is not pellucid, the best source for disambiguation is the broader context of the statute that the legislature—in this case, Congress—passed. This is uncontroversial when the reading seems consistent with the conventional wisdom about the reach of the law. It becomes somewhat harder to swallow if the language reveals suspected or actual unintended consequences. It is then that some have thought that legislative history should be used to block a particular reading of a statute. Legislative history, however, is notoriously malleable. Even worse is the temptation to try to divine the significance of unsuccessful legislative efforts to change the law. Those failures can mean almost anything, ranging from the lack of necessity for a proposed change because the law already accomplishes the desired goal, to the undesirability of the change because a majority of the legislature is happy with the way the courts are currently interpreting the law, to the irrelevance of the non-enactment, when it is attributable to nothing more than legislative logrolling or gridlock that had nothing to do with its merits.

Ivy Tech sets great store on the fact that Congress has frequently considered amending Title VII to add the words "sexual orientation" to the list of prohibited characteristics, yet it has never done so. Many of our sister circuits have also noted this fact. In our view, however, it is simply too difficult to draw a reliable inference from these truncated legislative initiatives to rest our opinion on them. The goalposts have been moving over the years, as the Supreme Court has shed more light on the scope of the language that already is in the statute: no *sex* discrimination.

The dissent makes much of the fact that Congresses acting more than thirty years after the passage of Title VII made use of the term "sexual orientation" to prohibit discrimination or violence on that basis in statutes such as the Violence Against Women Act and the federal Hate Crimes Act. But this gets us no closer to answering the question at hand, for Congress may certainly choose to use both a belt and suspenders to achieve its objectives, and the fact that "sex" and "sexual orientation" discrimination may overlap in later statutes is of no help in determining whether sexual orientation discrimination *is* discrimination on the basis of sex for the purposes of Title VII.

Moreover, the agency most closely associated with this law, the Equal Employment Opportunity Commission, in 2015 announced that it now takes the position that Title VII's prohibition against sex discrimination encompasses discrimination on the basis of sexual orientation. Our point here is not that we have a duty to defer to the EEOC's position. We assume for present purposes that no such duty exists. But the Commission's position may have caused some in Congress to think that legislation is needed to carve sexual orientation *out* of the statute, not to put it *in*. In the end, we have no idea what inference to draw from congressional inaction or later enactments, because there is no way of knowing what explains each individual member's votes, much less what explains the failure of the body as a whole to change this 1964 statute.

Our interpretive task is guided instead by the Supreme Court's approach in the closely related case of Oncale v. Sundowner Offshore Services, Inc., 523 U.S. 75 (1998) where it had this to say as it addressed the question whether Title VII covers sexual harassment inflicted by a man on a male victim:

> We see no justification in the statutory language or our precedents for a categorical rule excluding same-sex harassment claims from the coverage of Title VII. As some courts have observed, male-on-male sexual harassment in the workplace was assuredly not the principal evil Congress was concerned with when it enacted Title VII. But statutory prohibitions often go beyond the principal evil to cover reasonably comparable evils, and it is ultimately the provisions of our laws rather than the principal concerns of our legislators by which we are governed. Title VII prohibits "discriminat[ion] ... because of ... sex" in the "terms" or "conditions" of employment. Our holding that this includes sexual harassment must extend to sexual harassment of any kind that meets the statutory requirements. 523 U.S. at 79–80.

The Court could not have been clearer: the fact that the enacting Congress may not have anticipated a particular application of the law cannot stand in the way of the provisions of the law that are on the books.

It is therefore neither here nor there that the Congress that enacted the Civil Rights Act in 1964 and chose to include sex as a prohibited basis for employment discrimination (no matter why it did so) may not have realized or understood the full scope of the words it chose. Indeed, in the years since 1964, Title VII has been understood to cover far more than the simple decision of an employer not to hire a woman for Job A, or a man for Job B. . . . It is quite possible that these interpretations may also have surprised some who served in the 88th Congress. Nevertheless, experience with the law has led the Supreme Court to recognize that each of these examples is a covered form of sex discrimination.

B

. . . . Hively alleges that if she had been a man married to a woman (or living with a woman, or dating a woman) and everything else had stayed the same, Ivy Tech would not have refused to promote her and would not have fired her. . . . This describes paradigmatic sex discrimination. . . . Ivy Tech is disadvantaging her *because she is a woman*. Nothing in the complaint hints that Ivy Tech has an anti-marriage policy that extends to heterosexual relationships, or for that matter even an anti-partnership policy that is gender-neutral.

Viewed through the lens of the gender nonconformity line of cases, Hively represents the ultimate case of failure to conform to the female stereotype (at least as understood in a place such as modern America, which views heterosexuality as the norm and other forms of sexuality as exceptional): she is not heterosexual. Our panel described the line between a gender nonconformity claim and one based on sexual orientation as gossamer-thin; we conclude that it does not exist at all. Hively's claim is no different from the claims brought by women who were rejected for jobs in traditionally male workplaces, such as fire departments, construction, and policing. The employers in those cases were policing the boundaries of what jobs or behaviors they found acceptable for a woman (or in some cases, for a man).

The virtue of looking at comparators and paying heed to gender non-conformity is that this process sheds light on the interpretive question raised by Hively's case: is sexual-orientation discrimination a form of sex discrimination, given the way in which the Supreme Court has interpreted the word "sex" in the statute? The dissent criticizes us for not trying to *rule out* sexual-orientation discrimination by controlling for it in our comparator example and for not placing any weight on the fact that if someone had asked Ivy Tech what its reasons were at the time of the discriminatory conduct, it probably would have said "sexual orientation," not "sex." We assume that this is true, but this thought experiment does not answer the question before us—instead, it begs that question. It commits the logical fallacy of assuming the conclusion it sets out to prove. . . .

Hively also has argued that action based on sexual orientation is sex discrimination under the associational theory. It is now accepted that a person who is discriminated against because of the protected characteristic of one with whom she associates is actually being disadvantaged because of her own traits. This line of cases began with *Loving*, in which the Supreme Court held that "restricting the freedom to marry solely because of racial classifications violates the central meaning of the Equal Protection Clause." The Court rejected the argument that miscegenation statutes do not violate equal protection because they "punish equally both the white and the Negro participants in an interracial marriage." When dealing with a statute containing racial classifications, it wrote, "the fact of equal application does not immunize the statute from the very heavy burden of justification" required by the Fourteenth Amendment for lines drawn by race. . . .

The fact that we now accept this analysis tells us nothing, however, about the world in 1967, when *Loving* reached the Supreme Court. The dissent implies that we are adopting an anachronistic view of Title VII, enacted just three years before *Loving*, but it is the dissent's understanding of *Loving* and the miscegenation laws that is an anachronism. Thanks to *Loving* and [additional cases discussed] society understands now that such laws are (and always were) inherently racist. But as of 1967 (and thus as of 1964), Virginia and 15 other states had anti-miscegenation laws on the books. *Loving*, 388 U.S. at 6. These laws were long defended and understood as non-discriminatory because the legal obstacle affected *both* partners. The Court in *Loving* recognized that equal application of a law that prohibited conduct only between members of different races did not save it. Changing the race of one partner made a difference in determining the legality of the conduct, and so the law rested on "distinctions drawn according to race," which were unjustifiable and racially discriminatory. *Loving*, 388 U.S. at 11. So too, here. If we were to change the sex of one partner in a lesbian relationship, the outcome would be different. This reveals that the discrimination rests on distinctions drawn according to sex.

III

Today's decision must be understood against the backdrop of the Supreme Court's decisions, not only in the field of employment discrimination, but also in the area of broader discrimination on the basis of sexual orientation. . . .

The logic of the Supreme Court's decisions, as well as the common-sense reality that it is actually impossible to discriminate on the basis of sexual orientation without discriminating on the basis of sex, persuade us that the time has come to overrule our previous cases that have endeavored to find and observe that line. . . .

We hold only that a person who alleges that she experienced employment discrimination on the basis of her sexual orientation has put forth a case of sex discrimination for Title VII purposes. It was therefore wrong to dismiss Hively's complaint for failure to state a claim. The judgment of the district court is reversed and the case is remanded for further proceedings.

■ JUDGE POSNER, concurring.

It is helpful to note at the outset that the interpretation of statutes comes in three flavors. The first and most conventional is the extraction of the original meaning of the statute—the meaning intended by the legislators—and corresponds to interpretation in ordinary discourse. Knowing English I can usually determine swiftly and straightforwardly the meaning of a statement, oral or written, made to me in English (not always, because the statement may be garbled, grammatically intricate or inaccurate, obtuse, or complex beyond my ability to understand).

The second form of interpretation, illustrated by the commonplace local ordinance which commands "no vehicles in the park," is interpretation by unexpressed intent, whereby we understand that although an ambulance is a vehicle, the ordinance was not intended to include ambulances among the "vehicles" forbidden to enter the park. This mode of interpretation received its definitive statement in Blackstone's analysis of the medieval law of Bologna which stated that "whoever drew blood in the streets should be punished with the utmost severity." William Blackstone, Commentaries on the Laws of England *60 (1765). Blackstone asked whether the law should have been interpreted to make punishable a surgeon "who opened the vein of a person that fell down in the street with a fit." (Bleeding a sick or injured person was a common form of medical treatment in those days.) Blackstone thought not, remarking that as to "the effects and consequence, or the spirit and reason of the law . . . the rule is, where words bear either none, or a very absurd signification, if literally understood, we must a little deviate from the received sense of them." The law didn't mention surgeons, but Blackstone thought it obvious that the legislators, who must have known something about the medical activities of surgeons, had not intended the law to apply to them. And so it is with ambulances in parks that prohibit vehicles.

Finally and most controversially, interpretation can mean giving a fresh meaning to a statement (which can be a statement found in a constitutional or statutory text)—a meaning that infuses the statement with vitality and significance today. An example of this last form of interpretation—the form that in my mind is most clearly applicable to the present case—is the Sherman Antitrust Act, enacted in 1890, long before there was a sophisticated understanding of the economics of monopoly and competition. Times have changed; and for more than thirty years the Act has been interpreted in conformity to the modern, not the nineteenth-century, understanding of the relevant economics. The Act has thus been updated by, or in the name of, judicial interpretation—the form of interpretation that consists of making old law satisfy modern needs and understandings. And a common form of interpretation it is, despite its flouting "original meaning." Statutes and constitutional provisions frequently are interpreted on the basis of present need and present understanding rather than original meaning—constitutional provisions even more frequently, because most of them are older than most statutes.

Title VII of the Civil Rights Act of 1964, now more than half a century old, invites an interpretation that will update it to the present, a present that differs markedly from the era in which the Act was enacted. But I need to emphasize that this third form of interpretation—call it judicial interpretive updating—presupposes a lengthy interval between enactment and (re)interpretation. A statute when passed has an understood meaning; it takes years, often many years, for a shift in the political and cultural environment to change the understanding of the statute.

Hively, the plaintiff, claims that because she's a lesbian her employer declined to either promote her to fulltime employment or renew her part-time employment contract. She seeks redress on the basis of the provision of Title VII that forbids an employer "to fail or refuse to hire[,] or to discharge[,] any individual, or otherwise to discriminate against any individual with respect to his compensation, terms, conditions, or privileges of employment, because of such individual's . . . sex . . . ." 42 U.S.C. § 2000e–2(a)(1).

The argument that firing a woman on account of her being a lesbian does *not* violate Title VII is that the term "sex" in the statute, when enacted in 1964, undoubtedly meant "man or woman," and so at the time people would have thought that a woman who was fired for being a lesbian was not being fired for being a woman unless her employer would not have fired on grounds of homosexuality a man he knew to be homosexual; for in that event the only difference between the two would be the gender of the one he fired. Title VII does not mention discrimination on the basis of sexual orientation, and so an explanation is needed for how 53 years later the meaning of the statute has changed and the word "sex" in it now connotes both gender *and* sexual orientation.

It is well-nigh certain that homosexuality, male or female, did not figure in the minds of the legislators who enacted Title VII. I had graduated from law school two years before the law was enacted. Had I been asked then whether I had ever met a male homosexual, I would have answered: probably not; had I been asked whether I had ever met a lesbian I would have answered "only in the pages of *À la recherche du temps perdu.*" Homosexuality was almost invisible in the 1960s. It became visible in the 1980s as a consequence of the AIDS epidemic; today it is regarded by a large swathe of the American population as normal. But what is certain is that the word "sex" in Title VII had no immediate reference to homosexuality; many years would elapse before it could be understood to include homosexuality.

A diehard "originalist" would argue that what was believed in 1964 defines the scope of the statute for as long as the statutory text remains unchanged, and therefore until changed by Congress's amending or replacing the statute. But . . . statutory and constitutional provisions frequently are interpreted on the basis of present need and understanding rather than original meaning.

The majority opinion states that Congress in 1964 "may not have realized or understood the full scope of the words it chose." This could be understood to imply that the statute forbade discrimination against homosexuals but the framers and ratifiers of the statute were not smart enough to realize that. I would prefer to say that theirs was the then-current understanding of the key word—sex. "Sex" in 1964 meant gender, not sexual orientation. What the framers and ratifiers understandably didn't understand was how attitudes toward homosexuals would change in the following half century. They shouldn't be blamed for that failure of foresight. *We* understand the words of Title VII differently not because we're smarter than the statute's framers and ratifiers but because we live in a different era, a different culture. Congress in the 1960s did not foresee the sexual revolution of the 2000s. . . .

I would prefer to see us acknowledge openly that today we, who are judges rather than members of Congress, are imposing on a half-century-old statute a meaning of "sex discrimination" that the Congress that enacted it would not have accepted. This is something courts do fairly frequently to avoid statutory obsolescence and concomitantly to avoid placing the entire burden of updating old statutes on the legislative branch. We should not leave the impression that we are merely the obedient servants of the 88th Congress (1963–1965), carrying out their wishes. We are not. We are taking advantage of what the last half century has taught.

■ JUDGE FLAUM, with whom JUDGE RIPPLE, joins, concurring.

. . . . I find the issue before us is simply whether discriminating against an employee for being homosexual violates Title VII's prohibition against discriminating against that employee because of their sex. In my view, the answer is yes, and the statute's text commands as much. . . . Ivy Tech allegedly refused to promote Professor Hively because she was homosexual—or (A) a woman who is (B) sexually attracted to women. Thus, the College allegedly discriminated against Professor Hively, at least in part, because of her sex. I conclude that Title VII, as its text provides, does not allow this.

■ JUDGE SYKES, with whom JUDGE BAUER and JUDGE KANNE, join, dissenting.

. . . . The majority deploys a judge-empowering, common-law decision method that leaves a great deal of room for judicial discretion. So does Judge Posner in his concurrence. Neither is faithful to the statutory text, read fairly, as a reasonable person would have understood it when it was adopted. The result is a statutory amendment courtesy of unelected judges. Judge Posner admits this; he embraces and argues for this conception of judicial power. The majority does not, preferring instead to smuggle in the statutory amendment under cover of an aggressive reading of loosely related Supreme Court precedents. Either way, the result is the same: the circumvention of the legislative process by which the people govern themselves.

Respect for the constraints imposed on the judiciary by a system of written law must begin with fidelity to the traditional first principle of statutory interpretation: When a statute supplies the rule of decision, our role is to give effect to the enacted text, interpreting the statutory language as a reasonable person would have understood it at the time of enactment. We are not authorized to infuse the text with a new or unconventional meaning or to update it to respond to changed social, economic, or political conditions.

In a handful of statutory contexts, Congress has vested the federal courts with authority to consider and make new rules of law in the common-law way. The Sherman Act is the archetype of the so-called "common-law statutes," but there are very few of these and Title VII is not one of them. So our role is interpretive only; we lack the discretion to ascribe to Title VII a meaning it did not bear at its inception. . . .

Judicial statutory updating, whether overt or covert, cannot be reconciled with the constitutional design. The Constitution establishes a procedure for enacting and amending statutes: bicameralism and presentment. *See* U.S. CONST. art. I, § 7. Needless to say, statutory amendments brought to you by the judiciary do not pass through this process. That is why a textualist decision method matters: When we assume the power to alter the original public meaning of a statute through the process of interpretation, we assume a power that is not ours. The Constitution assigns the power to make and amend statutory law to the elected representatives of the people. However welcome today's decision might be as a policy matter, it comes at a great cost to representative self-government.

I

... Sexual orientation is not on the list of forbidden categories of employment discrimination, and we have long and consistently held that employment decisions based on a person's sexual orientation do not classify people on the basis of sex and thus are not covered by Title VII's prohibition of discrimination "because of sex.". . . .

Today the court jettisons the prevailing interpretation and installs the polar opposite. Suddenly sexual-orientation discrimination *is* sex discrimination and thus is actionable under Title VII. What justification is offered for this radical change in a well-established, uniform interpretation of an important—indeed, transformational—statute? My colleagues take note of the Supreme Court's "absence from the debate." What debate? There is no debate, at least not in the relevant sense. . . .

Of course there *is* a robust debate on this subject in our culture, media, and politics. Attitudes about gay rights have dramatically shifted in the 53 years since the Civil Rights Act was adopted. Lambda Legal's proposed new reading of Title VII—offered on behalf of plaintiff Kimberly Hively at the appellate stage of this litigation—has a strong foothold in current popular opinion.

This striking cultural change informs a case for legislative change and might eventually persuade the people's representatives to amend the statute to implement a new public policy. But it does not bear on the sole inquiry properly before the en banc court: Is the prevailing interpretation of Title VII—that discrimination on the basis of sexual orientation is different in kind and not a form of sex discrimination—*wrong as an original matter*?

A

... To be clear, I agree with my colleagues that the proposed new interpretation is not necessarily incorrect simply because no one in the 1964 Congress that adopted Title VII intended or anticipated its application to sexual-orientation discrimination. The subjective intentions of the legislators do not matter. Statutory interpretation is an objective inquiry that looks for the meaning the statutory language conveyed to a reasonable person at the time of enactment. The objective meaning of the text is not delimited by what individual lawmakers specifically had in mind when they voted for the statute. . . .

B

That is where our agreement ends. . . .

Is it even remotely plausible that in 1964, when Title VII was adopted, a reasonable person competent in the English language would have understood that a law banning employment discrimination "because of sex" also banned discrimination because of sexual orientation? The answer is no, of course not. . . .

Title VII does not define discrimination "because of sex." In common, ordinary usage in 1964—and now, for that matter—the word "sex" means biologically *male* or *female*; it does not also refer to sexual orientation. *See, e.g., Sex*, THE AMERICAN HERITAGE DICTIONARY OF THE ENGLISH LANGUAGE (1st ed. 1969) (defining "sex" as "[t]he property or quality by which organisms are classified according to their reproductive functions[;] [e]ither of two divisions, designated *male* and *female*, of this classification"); *Sex*, NEW OXFORD AMERICAN DICTIONARY (3d ed. 2010) (defining "sex" as "either of the two main categories (male and female) into which humans and many other living things are divided on the basis of their reproductive functions"); *Sex*, THE AMERICAN HERITAGE DESK DICTIONARY (5th ed. 2013) (defining "sex" as "[e]ither of the two divisions, female and male, by which most organisms are classified on the basis of their reproductive organs and functions[;] [t]he condition or character of being female or male").

To a fluent speaker of the English language—then and now—the ordinary meaning of the word "sex" does not fairly include the concept of "sexual orientation." The two terms are never used interchangeably, and the latter is not subsumed within the former; there is no overlap in meaning. Contrary to the majority's vivid rhetorical claim, it does not take "considerable calisthenics" to separate the two. The words plainly describe different traits, and the separate and distinct meaning of each term is easily grasped. More specifically to the point here, discrimination "because of sex" is not reasonably understood to include discrimination based on sexual orientation, a different immutable characteristic. Classifying people by sexual orientation is different than classifying them by sex. The two traits are categorically distinct and widely recognized as such. There is no ambiguity or vagueness here. . . .

C

This commonsense understanding is confirmed by the language Congress uses when it *does* legislate against sexual-orientation discrimination. For example, the Violence Against Women Act prohibits funded programs and activities from discriminating "on the basis of actual or perceived race, color, religion, national origin, *sex*, gender identity, . . . *sexual orientation*, or disability." 42 U.S.C. § 13925(b)(13)(A) (emphases added). If sex discrimination is commonly understood to encompass sexual-orientation discrimination, then listing the two categories separately, as this statute does, is needless surplusage. The federal Hate Crimes Act is another example. It imposes a heightened punishment for causing or attempting to cause bodily injury "to any person, because of the actual or perceived religion, national origin, *gender, sexual orientation*, gender identity, or disability of any person." 18 U.S.C. § 249(a)(2)(A) (emphases added). . . .

II

. . . An employer who refuses to hire homosexuals is not drawing a line based on the job applicant's sex. He is not excluding gay men because they are men and lesbians because they are women. His discriminatory motivation is independent of and unrelated to the applicant's sex. Sexism (misandry and misogyny) and homophobia are separate kinds of prejudice that classify people in distinct ways based on different immutable characteristics. Simply put, sexual-orientation discrimination doesn't classify people by sex; it doesn't draw male/female distinctions but instead targets homosexual men and women for harsher treatment than heterosexual men and women. . . .

Here the majority is not using the comparative method to isolate whether Ivy Tech was *actually* motivated by Hively's sex when it refused to promote her to full-time professor and canceled her part-time teaching contract. To repeat, Hively does not make that allegation. Her factual claim is that Ivy Tech refused to promote her and canceled her contract because she is a lesbian. The only question for us is whether *that* claim—her *real* claim—is actionable under Title VII *as a matter of law*. That's a pure question of statutory interpretation.

But the comparative method of proof is an evidentiary test; it is not an interpretive tool. It tells us *nothing* about the meaning or scope of Title VII. In ordinary English usage, sexual-orientation discrimination is a distinct form of discrimination and is not synonymous with sex discrimination. That's the plain meaning of Title VII's text as originally understood. An *evidentiary test* like the comparative method of proof has no work to do here and is utterly out of place.

III

. . . Finally, drawing especially on *Obergefell*, my colleagues worry that adhering to the long-settled interpretation of Title VII "creates 'a paradoxical legal landscape in which a person can be married on Saturday and then fired on Monday for just that act.'" The concern is understandable, but my colleagues conflate the distinction between state action, which is subject to constitutional limits, and private action, which is regulated by statute. The Due Process and Equal Protection Clauses are constitutional restraints on government. Title VII is a statutory restraint on employers. The legal regimes differ accordingly. Any discrepancy is a matter for legislative, not judicial, correction.

* * *

If Kimberly Hively was denied a job because of her sexual orientation, she was treated unjustly. But Title VII does not provide a remedy for this kind of discrimination. The argument that it *should* must be addressed to Congress. . . .

NOTES ON DYNAMIC STATUTORY INTERPRETATION

(1) *In This Corner.* WILLIAM N. ESKRIDGE JR., DYNAMIC STATUTORY INTERPRETATION, 135 U. Pa. L. Rev. 1479 (1987): "Federal judges interpreting the Constitution typically consider not only the constitutional text and its historical background, but also its subsequent interpretational history, related constitutional developments, and current societal facts. Similarly, judges interpreting common law precedents normally consider not only the text of the precedents and their historical context, but also their subsequent history, related legal developments, and current societal context. In light of this, it is odd that many judges and commentators believe judges should consider only the text and historical context when interpreting statutes, the third main source of law. Statutes, however, should—like the Constitution and the common law—be interpreted "dynamically," that is, in light of their present societal, political, and legal context. . . .

". . . The dialectic of statutory interpretation is the process of understanding a text created in the past and applying it to a present problem. This process cannot be described simply as the recreation of past events and past expectations, for the "best" interpretation of a statute is typically the one that is most consonant with our current "web of beliefs" and policies surrounding the statute. That is, statutory interpretation involves the present-day interpreter's understanding and reconciliation of three different perspectives, no one of which will always control. These three perspectives relate to (1) the statutory text, which is the formal focus of interpretation and a constraint on the range of interpretive options available (textual perspective); (2) the original legislative expectations surrounding the statute's creation, including compromises reached (historical perspective); and (3) the subsequent evolution of the statute and its present context, especially the ways in which the societal and legal environment of the statute has materially changed over time (evolutive perspective). . . .

". . . The three perspectives implicated in dynamic interpretation . . . suggest a continuum. In many cases, the text of the statute will provide determinate answers, though we should trust our reading of the text primarily when the statute is recent and the context of enactment represents considered legislative deliberation and decision on the interpretive issue. This is one end of the continuum: the text controls. At the opposite end of the continuum are those cases where neither the text nor the historical context of the statute clearly resolves the interpretive question, and the societal and legal context of the statute has changed materially. In those cases, the evolutive context controls. In general, the more detailed the text is, the greater weight the interpreter will give to textual considerations; the more recent the statute and the clearer the legislative expectations, the greater weight the interpreter will give to historical considerations; the more striking the changes in circumstances (changes in public values count more than factual changes in society), the greater weight the interpreter will give to evolutive considerations."

(2) *And in the Other Corner.* MARTIN H. REDISH and THEODORE CHUNG, DEMOCRATIC THEORY AND THE LEGISLATIVE PROCESS: MOURNING THE DEATH OF ORIGINALISM IN STATUTORY INTERPRETATION, 68 Tul. L. Rev. 803, 807–08 (1994): "Despite its claim that it carves out only a minor exception to the general rule of judicial deference to the legislature in the realm of statutory interpretation, dynamic statutory interpretation effectively represents a dramatic and pernicious reordering of our democratic form of government. In short, dynamic statutory interpretation would establish the judiciary as a largely unaccountable ruling elite, the virtual equivalent of philosopher kings. Robert Dahl has labeled judges operating under such a model "guardians," empowered to pass judgment not merely on the constitutionality of legislative enactments but on their wisdom and morality as well.

"The judiciary that dynamic scholars envision for purposes of statutory interpretation bears little resemblance to the judiciary posited by either new textualist or originalist commentators. Instead of deciphering and implementing the decisions of a coordinate branch, the judiciary, from the dynamist perspective, acts as an adjunct in the legislative process or, more precisely, a super legislature.

"Underlying dynamic statutory interpretation, then, is an ominously antidemocratic conception of our system of government. Notions of separation of powers that typify traditional interpretive models are, in the eyes of dynamic scholars, impediments to good government. Indeed, dynamic scholars insist, the citizenry cannot afford to entrust its well-being to a Congress beholden to special interests. Because the federal judiciary remains insulated from special-interest and constituent pressures, dynamists further contend that it is the branch best suited to ascertain and protect the common good. However, by conferring on judges wide-ranging discretion to ignore what would otherwise be discernible legislative directives in favor of interpretations more consistent with their own notions of the common good, dynamic interpretation runs afoul of the normative political premise of self-determination that undergirds our representative democracy."

(3) *The Administrative Law Stakes.* Should you study the Notes on Interpreting the APA in Chapter III, or the development of the "paper hearing" in Chapter IV, you'll quickly come to understand the stakes of this debate for interpretation of the federal Administrative Procedure Act, enacted in 1946 and not much amended by Congress since. See Peter L. Strauss, Statutes That Are Not Static—The Case of the APA, 14 J. Contemp. Leg. Issues 767 (2005).

SECTION 3.   TOOLS OF STATUTORY INTERPRETATION

> a. *Dictionaries*
> b. *Custom and Usage*
> c. *Canons of Construction*
> d. *Statutory Structure*
> e. *Legislative History*

Theories of statutory interpretation are helpful in structuring thinking about how to approach an interpretive issue raised by a statute. But one still needs to know how to actually go about resolving the interpretive issue at hand. And that requires one to be aware of the relevant tools that may be deployed in the course of applying an interpretive theory, including, in particular, dictionaries, custom and usage, canons of construction, both linguistic and substantive, statutory structure, and legislative history.

As you read the following excerpts, consider the affinity between the major theories of statutory interpretation and the characteristic tools that may be associated with each of those theories—for instance, the relationship between textualism and the plain meaning rule, linguistic canons, and dictionaries; between purposivism and legislative history; between pragmatic and dynamic approaches and some of the substantive canons. Consider, too, the hazards presented by the deployment of some of these tools. Does it make sense to assume the drafters of the legislation understood that the tool being deployed would be deployed? If so, is that because the assumption accurately reflects the understandings of the drafters? Or is it because the assumption is legitimate even if it is not based on the realty of the drafting process? Why would such an assumption then be legitimate?

a.   Dictionaries

> *TANIGUCHI v. KAN PACIFIC SAIPAN, LTD.*

An intuitive and obvious means of discerning a word's ordinary meaning is to look it up in a dictionary. This trend has increased in recent years. But are dictionaries useful? Judge Learned Hand famously cautioned that "it is one of the surest indexes of a mature and developed jurisprudence not to make a fortress out of the dictionary." Cabell v. Markham, 148 F.2d 737, 739 (2d Cir. 1945). As you think about the following problem and case, consider Hand's caution and consider whether a general definition of a word in a dictionary can (or should) really lend much insight into how to construe the federal criminal statute at issue, given the unique penalties it imposes and the particular purposes it was designed to serve.

WHAT DOES IT MEAN TO BE AN "INTERPRETER"?

The plaintiff in a tort action was visiting from Japan when he allegedly was injured by the negligence of the defendant. During pretrial discovery proceedings, and in response to the defendant's proper demand, the plaintiff supplied the defendant with a number of documents written in Japanese, which the defendant then had translated. The defendant prevailed at trial and so sought to recover its "costs" as defined by 28 U.S.C. 1920, including the substantial costs of these documentary translations.

Until 1978, Section 1920 contained no provision that would have supported recovery of translation costs. In that year, the Court Interpreters Act added subsection (6) to Section 1920:

A judge or clerk of any court of the United States may tax as costs the following: . . .

(6) Compensation of court appointed experts, compensation of interpreters, and salaries, fees, expenses, and costs of special interpretation services under section 1828 of this title [concerning criminal actions and in civil actions initiated by the United States (including petitions for writs of habeas corpus initiated in the name of the United States by relators) in a United States district court].

A bill of costs shall be filed in the case and, upon allowance, included in the judgment or decree.

Are the defendants entitled to recover their translation costs?

TANIGUCHI v. KAN PACIFIC SAIPAN, LTD.

Supreme Court of the United States (2012).
566 U.S. 560.

■ JUSTICE ALITO delivered the opinion of the Court.

The costs that may be awarded to prevailing parties in lawsuits brought in federal court are set forth in 28 U.S.C. § 1920. The Court Interpreters Act amended that statute to include "compensation of interpreters." § 1920(6). The question presented in this case is whether "compensation of interpreters" covers the cost of translating documents. Because the ordinary meaning of the word "interpreter" is a person who translates orally from one language to another, we hold that "compensation of interpreters" is limited to the cost of oral translation and does not include the cost of document translation.

I

. . . Petitioner was injured when his leg broke through a wooden deck during a tour of respondent's resort property. Initially, petitioner said that he needed no medical attention, but two weeks later, he informed respondent that he had suffered cuts, bruises, and torn ligaments from the accident. Due to these alleged injuries, he claimed damages for medical expenses and for lost income from contracts he was unable to honor. [Defendants successfully moved for summary judgment] on the ground that petitioner offered no evidence that respondent knew of the defective deck or otherwise failed to exercise reasonable care.

In preparing its defense, respondent paid to have various documents translated from Japanese to English . . . [and] submitted a bill for those costs. Over petitioner's objection, the District Court awarded the costs to respondent as "compensation of interpreters" under § 1920(6). . . . The United States Court of Appeals for the Ninth Circuit affirmed both the District Court's grant of summary judgment and its award of costs. . . .

II

A

. . . Not until 1853 did Congress enact legislation specifying the costs allowable in federal court . . . which we have described as a "far-reaching Act specifying in detail the nature and amount of the taxable items of cost in the federal courts." *Alyeska Pipeline Service Co. v. Wilderness Society*, 421 U.S. 240 (1975), at 251–252. . . .

Federal Rule of Civil Procedure 54(d) gives courts the discretion to award costs to prevailing parties. . . . We have held that "§ 1920 defines the term 'costs' as used in Rule 54(d)." *Crawford Fitting*, 482 U.S.437 (1987), at 441. In so doing, we rejected the view that "the discretion granted by Rule 54(d) is a separate source of power to tax as costs expenses not enumerated in § 1920." *Ibid.*

As originally configured, § 1920 contained five categories of taxable costs . . . In 1978, Congress enacted the Court Interpreters Act, which amended § 1920 to add a sixth category: "Compensation of court appointed experts, compensation of interpreters, and salaries, fees, expenses, and costs of special interpretation services under section 1828 of this title." 28 U.S.C. § 1920(6); see also § 7, 92 Stat. 2044. We are concerned here with this sixth category, specifically the item of taxable costs identified as "compensation of interpreters."

B

. . . "[I]nterpreter" . . . is not defined in the Court Interpreters Act or in any other relevant statutory provision. When a term goes undefined in a statute, we give the term its ordinary meaning.

Many dictionaries in use when Congress enacted the Court Interpreters Act in 1978 defined "interpreter" as one who translates spoken, as opposed to written, language. The American Heritage Dictionary, for instance, defined the term as "[o]ne who translates orally from one language into another." American Heritage Dictionary 685 (1978). The Scribner-Bantam English Dictionary defined the related word "interpret" as "to translate orally." Scribner-Bantam English Dictionary 476 (1977). Similarly, the Random House Dictionary defined the intransitive form of "interpret" as "to translate what is *said* in a foreign language." Random House Dictionary of the English Language 744 (1973) (emphasis added). And, notably, the Oxford English Dictionary defined "interpreter" as "[o]ne who translates languages," but then divided that definition into two senses: "a. [a] translator of books or writings," which it designated as obsolete, and "b. [o]ne who translates the communications of persons speaking different languages; *spec.* one whose office it is to do so orally in the presence of the persons; a dragoman." 5 Oxford English Dictionary 416 (1933); see also Concise Oxford Dictionary of Current English 566 (6th ed. 1976) ("One who interprets; one whose office it is to translate the words of persons speaking different languages, esp. orally in their presence"); Chambers Twentieth Century Dictionary 686 (1973) ("one who translates orally for the benefit of two or more parties speaking different languages: . . . a translator (*obs.*).").

Pre-1978 legal dictionaries also generally defined the words "interpreter" and "interpret" in terms of oral translation. The then-current edition of Black's Law Dictionary, for example, defined "interpreter" as "[a] person sworn at a trial to interpret the evidence of a foreigner . . .to the court," and it defined "interpret" in relevant part as "to translate orally from one tongue to another." Black's Law Dictionary 954, 953 (rev. 4th ed. 1968); see also W. Anderson, A Dictionary of Law 565 (1888) ("One who translates the testimony of witnesses speaking a foreign tongue, for the benefit of the court and jury"); 1 B. Abbott, Dictionary of Terms and Phrases Used in American or English Jurisprudence 639 (1878) ("one who restates the testimony of a witness testifying in a foreign tongue, to the court and jury, in their language"). But see Ballentine's Law Dictionary 655, 654 (3d ed. 1969) (defining "interpreter" as "[o]ne who interprets, particularly one who interprets words written or spoken in a foreign language," and "interpret" as "to translate from a foreign language").

Against these authorities, respondent relies almost exclusively on Webster's Third New International Dictionary (hereinafter Webster's Third). The version of that dictionary in print when Congress enacted the Court Interpreters Act defined "interpreter" as "one that translates; *esp*: a person who translates orally for parties conversing in different tongues." Webster's Third 1182 (1976). The sense divider *esp* (for especially) indicates that the most common meaning of the term is one "who translates orally," but that meaning is subsumed within the more general definition "one that translates." . . . For respondent, the general definition suffices to establish that the term "interpreter" ordinarily includes persons who translate the written word. . . . We disagree.

That a definition is broad enough to encompass one sense of a word does not establish that the word is *ordinarily* understood in that sense. . . . It is telling that all the dictionaries cited above defined "interpreter" at the time of the statute's enactment as including persons who translate orally, but only a handful defined the word broadly enough to encompass translators of written material. Although the Oxford English Dictionary, one of the most authoritative on the English language, recognized that "interpreter" *can* mean one who translates writings, it expressly designated that meaning as obsolete. . . .

To be sure, the word "interpreter" can encompass persons who translate documents, but because that is not the ordinary meaning of the word, it does not control unless the context in which the word appears indicates that it does. . . . If anything, the statutory context suggests the opposite: that the word "interpreter" applies only to those who translate orally. As previously mentioned, Congress enacted § 1920(6) as part of the Court Interpreters Act. The main provision of that Act is § 2(a), codified in 28 U.S.C. §§ 1827 and 1828. See 92 Stat. 2040–2042. Particularly relevant here is § 1827. As it now reads, that statute provides for the establishment of "a program to facilitate the use of certified and otherwise qualified interpreters in judicial proceedings instituted by the United States." § 1827(a). Subsection (d) directs courts to use an interpreter in any criminal or civil action instituted by the United States if a party or witness "speaks only or primarily a language other than the English language" or "suffers from a hearing impairment" "so as to inhibit such party's comprehension of the proceedings or communication with counsel or the presiding judicial officer, or so as to inhibit such witness' comprehension of questions and the presentation of such testimony." § 1827(d)(1). As originally enacted, subsection (k) mandated that the "interpretation provided by certified interpreters . . . shall be in the consecutive mode except that the presiding judicial officer . . . may authorize a simultaneous or summary interpretation." § 1827(k) (1976 ed., Supp. II); see also 92 Stat. 2042. In its current form, subsection (k) provides that interpretation "shall be in the simultaneous mode for any party . . . and in the consecutive mode for witnesses," unless the court directs otherwise. The simultaneous, consecutive, and summary modes are all methods of oral interpretation and have nothing to do with the translation of writings. Taken together, these provisions are a strong contextual clue that Congress was dealing only with oral translation in the Court Interpreters Act and that it intended to use the term "interpreter" throughout the Act in its ordinary sense as someone who translates the spoken word. . . .

The references to technical terminology in the Court Interpreters Act further suggest that Congress used "interpreter" in a technical sense, and it is therefore significant that relevant professional literature draws a line between "interpreters," who "are used for oral conversations," and "translators," who "are used for written communications." [citations omitted] That Congress specified "interpreters" but not "translators" is yet another signal that it intended to limit § 1920(6) to the costs of oral, instead of written, translation.[6] . . .

C

No other rule of construction compels us to depart from the ordinary meaning of "interpreter.". . . Our decision is in keeping with the narrow scope of taxable costs. "Although 'costs' has an everyday meaning synonymous with 'expenses,' the concept of taxable costs under Rule 54(d) is more limited and represents those expenses, including, for example, court fees, that a court will assess against a litigant." 10 C. Wright, A. Miller, & M. Kane, Federal Practice and Procedure § 2666, pp. 202–203 (3d ed. 1998). . . . Because taxable costs are limited by statute and are modest in scope, we see no compelling reason to stretch the ordinary meaning of the cost items Congress authorized in § 1920.

As for respondent's extratextual arguments, they are more properly directed at Congress. . . .

* * *

Because the ordinary meaning of "interpreter" is someone who translates orally from one language to another, we hold that the category "compensation of interpreters" in § 1920(6) does not include costs for document translation. We therefore vacate the judgment of the United States Court of Appeals for the Ninth Circuit and remand the case for further proceedings consistent with this opinion.

It is so ordered.

■ JUSTICE GINSBURG, with whom JUSTICE BREYER and JUSTICE SOTOMAYOR join, dissenting.

To be comprehended by the parties, the witnesses, and the court, expression in foreign languages must be translated into English. Congress therefore provided, in 28 U.S.C. § 1920(6), that the prevailing party may recoup compensation paid to "interpreters." The word "interpreters," the Court emphasizes, commonly refers to translators of oral speech. But as the Court acknowledges, "interpreters" is more than occasionally used to encompass those who translate written speech as well. . . . In short, employing the word "interpreters" to include translators of written as well as oral speech, if not "the most common usage," is at least an "acceptable" usage. Moreover, the word "interpret" is generally understood to mean "to explain or tell the meaning of: translate into intelligible or familiar language or terms," while

---

[6] Some provisions within the United States Code use both "interpreter" and "translator" together, thus implying that Congress understands the terms to have the distinct meanings described above. See, *e.g.,* 8 U.S.C. § 1555(b) (providing that appropriations for the Immigration and Naturalization Service "shall be available for payment of . . . interpreters and translators who are not citizens of the United States"); 28 U.S.C. § 530C(b)(1)(I) (providing that Department of Justice funds may be used for "[p]ayment of interpreters and translators who are not citizens of the United States").

"translate" commonly means "to turn into one's own or another language." Webster's 1182, 2429. . . .

Most federal courts of appeals confronted with the question have held that costs may be awarded under § 1920(6) for the translation of documents necessary to, or in preparation for, litigation. [citing cases].

In practice, federal trial courts have awarded document translation costs in cases spanning several decades. Before the Court Interpreters Act added § 1920(6) to the taxation of costs statute in 1978, district courts awarded costs for document translation under § 1920(4), which allowed taxation of "[f]ees for exemplification and copies of papers," 28 U.S.C. § 1920(4) (1976 ed.), or under § 1920's predecessor, 28 U.S.C. § 830 (1925 ed.). Pre-1978, district courts also awarded costs for oral translation of witness testimony. Nothing in the Court Interpreters Act, a measure intended to expand access to interpretation services, indicates a design to eliminate the availability of costs awards for document translation. Post-1978, rulings awarding document translation costs under § 1920(6) indicate the courts' understanding both that the term "interpreter" can readily encompass oral and written translation, and that Congress did not otherwise instruct.[2] I agree that context should guide the determination whether § 1920(6) is most sensibly read to encompass persons who translate documents. But the context key for me is the practice of federal courts both before and after § 1920(6)'s enactment.

The purpose of translation, after all, is to make relevant foreign-language communication accessible to the litigants and the court. See S. Rep., at 1 (The Court Interpreters Act is intended "to insure that all participants in our Federal courts can meaningfully take part."). Documentary evidence in a foreign language, no less than oral statements, must be translated to equip the parties to present their case clearly and the court to decide the merits intelligently.[3] And it is not extraordinary that what documents say, more than what witnesses testify, may make or break a case.

Distinguishing written from oral translation for cost-award purposes, moreover, is an endeavor all the more dubious, for, as the Court acknowledges, some translation tasks do not fall neatly into one category or the other. An interpreter, for example, may be called upon to "sight translate" a written document, i.e., to convey a written foreign-language document's content orally in English. . . . Similarly hard to categorize is the common court-interpreter task of listening to a recording in a foreign language, transcribing it, then translating it into English. . . . [And

---

[2] Currently, some federal district courts make the practice of allowing fees for translation of documents explicit in their local rules. [providing numerous examples].

[3] Noteworthy, other paragraphs Congress placed in § 1920 cover written documents. See 28 U.S.C. § 1920(2) (2006 ed., Supp. IV) ("Fees for printed or electronically recorded transcripts"); § 1920(3) (2006 ed.) ("Fees and disbursements for printing and witnesses"); § 1920(4) ("Fees for exemplification and the costs of making copies of any [necessary] materials"). Nothing indicates that Congress intended paragraph (6), unlike paragraphs (2)–(4), to apply exclusively to oral communications.

c]urrent practice in awarding translation costs ... has shown that district judges are up to the task of confining awards to translation services necessary to present or defeat a claim. [citing cases]

In short, § 1920(6)'s prescription on "interpreters" is not so clear as to leave no room for interpretation. Given the purpose served by translation and the practice prevailing in district courts, there is no good reason to exclude from taxable costs payments for placing written words within the grasp of parties, jurors, and judges. . . .

NOTE

LOOKING IT UP: DICTIONARIES AND STATUTORY INTERPRETATION, NOTE, 107 Harv. L. Rev. 1437 (1994): "Over the past decade, the Supreme Court's use of dictionaries in its published opinions has increased dramatically. Although the Court has consulted dictionaries almost since its inception, it rarely did so more than a handful of times per Term before the 1980s. In the quarter-century between 1958 and 1983, the Court cited dictionaries only 125 times—an average of five times per Term. Prior to 1980, in fact, the word "dictionary" never appeared more than fifteen times in a single volume of the Supreme Court Reporter.

"By contrast, in the six Terms between 1987 and 1992, the Court never cited dictionaries fewer than fifteen times, with a high point of thirty-two references during the 1992 Term. Dictionary definitions appeared in twenty-eight percent of the 107 Supreme Court cases decided by published opinion in the 1992 Term—a fourteen-fold increase over the 1981 Term. . . .

"The Court's growing faith in dictionaries is tied to a broader methodological shift toward textualism in statutory interpretation. . . .

"Adherents to the plain meaning approach have long assumed that dictionaries are the best source of the common understanding of words. . . .

"The Court has rarely paused to consider the wisdom or the implications of relying on dictionaries in statutory interpretation. Of the opinions that do make explicit arguments about the practice, most are dissents that criticize the majority for its excessive reliance on dictionaries. Even when ... the Justices acknowledge the limitations of their interpretive method, the assumption that dictionaries reveal ordinary meaning is usually left unquestioned. For some members of the Court, the dictionary has become a sort of default source, presumptively decisive unless there is specific evidence to the contrary. Yet dictionaries are neither as neutral nor as reductive as the Court supposes them to be, and they do not provide the sort of meaning the Court seeks to determine. . . .

"Individual judges must make subjective decisions about which dictionary and which definition to use. The same arguments about manipulability and arbitrariness that textualists use to attack the examination of legislative history can therefore be applied to dictionaries. The fiction that the particular definitions cited by the Court accurately capture statutory meaning is as tenuous as the assumption that scraps of legislative history reveal the intent of legislatures. Subjectivity may be an ineradicable component of the interpretive process; the point is that the use of dictionaries cannot eliminate this element, and may even exacerbate it. An opinion based on a dictionary must justify not only its chosen meaning for statutory terms, but also the choice of a particular dictionary definition to reach that conclusion."

b.   Custom and Usage

NIX v. HEDDEN

NIX v. HEDDEN

Supreme Court of the United States (1893).
149 U.S. 304.

This was an action brought February 4, 1887, against the collector of the port of New York to recover back duties paid under protest on tomatoes imported by the plaintiff from the West Indies in the spring of 1886, which the collector assessed under 'Schedule G.-Provisions,' of the tariff act of March 3, 1883, (chapter 121,) imposing a duty on 'vegetables in their natural state, or in salt or brine, not specially enumerated or provided for in this act, ten per centum ad valorem;' and which the plaintiffs contended came within the clause in the free list of the same act, 'Fruits, green, ripe, or dried, not specially enumerated or provided for in this act.' 22 Stat. 504, 519.

At the trial the plaintiff's counsel, after reading in evidence definitions of the words 'fruit' and 'vegetables' from Webster's Dictionary, Worcester's Dictionary, and the Imperial Dictionary, called two witnesses, who had been for 30 years in the business of selling fruit and vegetables, and asked them, after hearing these definitions, to say whether these words had 'any special meaning in trade or commerce, different from those read.'

One of the witnesses answered as follows: 'Well, it does not classify all things there, but they are correct as far as they go. It does not take all kinds of fruit or vegetables; it takes a portion of them. I think the words 'fruit' and 'vegetable' have the same meaning in trade to-day that they had on March 1, 1883. I understand that the term 'fruit' is applied in trade only to such plants or parts of plants as contain the seeds. There are more vegetables than those in the enumeration given in Webster's Dictionary under the term 'vegetable,' as 'cabbage, cauliflower, turnips, potatoes, peas, beans, and the like,' probably covered by the words 'and the like."

The other witness testified: 'I don't think the term 'fruit' or the term 'vegetables' had, in March, 1883, and prior thereto, any special meaning in trade and commerce in this country different from that which I have read here from the dictionaries.'

The plaintiff's counsel then read in evidence from the same dictionaries the definitions of the word 'tomato.'

The defendant's counsel then read in evidence from Webster's Dictionary the definitions of the words 'pea,' 'egg plant,' 'cucumber,' 'squash,' and 'pepper.'

The plaintiff then read in evidence from Webster's and Worcester's dictionaries the definitions of 'potato,' 'turnip,' 'parsnip,' 'cauliflower,' 'cabbage,' 'carrot,' and 'bean.'

No other evidence was offered by either party. The court, upon the defendant's motion, directed a verdict for him, which was returned, and judgment rendered thereon. The plaintiffs duly excepted to the instruction, and sued out this writ of error.

■ JUSTICE GRAY, after stating the facts in the foregoing language, delivered the opinion of the court.

The single question in this case is whether tomatoes, considered as provisions, are to be classed as 'vegetables' or as 'fruit,' within the meaning of the tariff act of 1883.

The only witnesses called at the trial testified that neither 'vegetables' nor 'fruit' had any special meaning in trade or commerce different from that given in the dictionaries, and that they had the same meaning in trade to-day that they had in March, 1883.

The passages cited from the dictionaries define the word 'fruit' as the seed of plants, or that part of plants which contains the seed, and especially the juicy, pulpy products of certain plants, covering and containing the seed. These definitions have no tendency to show that tomatoes are 'fruit,' as distinguished from 'vegetables,' in common speech, or within the meaning of the tariff act.

There being no evidence that the words 'fruit' and 'vegetables' have acquired any special meaning in trade or commerce, they must receive their ordinary meaning. Of that meaning the court is bound to take judicial notice, as it does in regard to all words in our own tongue; and upon such a question dictionaries are admitted, not as evidence, but only as aids to the memory and understanding of the court.

Botanically speaking, tomatoes are the fruit of a vine, just as are cucumbers, squashes, beans, and peas. But in the common language of the people, whether sellers or consumers of provisions, all these are vegetables which are grown in kitchen gardens, and which, whether eaten cooked or raw, are, like potatoes, carrots, parsnips, turnips, beets, cauliflower, cabbage, celery, and lettuce, usually served at dinner in, with, or after the soup, fish, or meats which constitute the principal part of the repast, and not, like fruits generally, as dessert.

The attempt to class tomatoes as fruit is not unlike a recent attempt to class beans as seeds, of which Justice Bradley, speaking for this court, said: 'We do not see why they should be classified as seeds, any more than walnuts should be so classified. Both are seeds, in the language of botany or natural history, but not in commerce nor in common parlance. On the other hand in speaking generally of provisions, beans may well be included under the term 'vegetables.' As an article of food on our tables, whether baked or boiled, or forming the basis of soup, they are used as a vegetable, as well when ripe as when green. This is the principal use to which they are put. Beyond the common knowledge which we have on this subject, very little evidence is necessary, or can be produced.' Robertson v. Salomon, 130 U.S. 412, 414.

Judgment affirmed.

NOTES

(1)   Interpretation of statutory terms by reference to usages is not limited to general customs. If a statute, for instance, regulates a particular trade or trade practice, its terms can be understood by reference to the meaning of those terms within the trade. See, e.g., Corning Glass Works v. Brennan, 417 U.S. 188 (1974) ("working conditions" interpreted "in the language of industrial relations.")

(2)   TODD D. RAKOFF, STATUTORY INTERPRETATION AS A MULTIFARIOUS ENTERPRISE, 104 Nw. U. L. Rev. 1559, 1572–75 (2010): "[M]ost statutory interpretation is not done by judges. Judges necessarily act after the fact—after the interpretive work done by ordinary citizens trying to comply with the law, by private lawyers advising clients, by public prosecutors deciding what charges (if any) to bring, by administrative agencies enforcing statutes or making rules, and so on. In most instances, these nonjudicial determinations will have a determinative effect, either as a matter of law under a principle of deference or nonreviewability, or as a matter of practice because the determination will never be tested in court. . . .

"Because issues of statutory interpretation do not arise unless a statute has been passed, we are tempted to look at any statute from the point of view of the enactors of the legislation. Because of our predisposition to favor fully enacted statutes, we tend to try to see how the enactors might have resolved the particular ambiguity or uncertainty that has arisen. This approach has always been subject to the criticism that the point of view of those subject to the legislation—its readers—ought to count for something. To put the matter in language more commonly applied to private documents, there has long been a dispute between the "subjective" and the "objective" readings of statutory language. But we need now to recognize that in addition to enactors and readers, there is another legitimate category: the active users of statutes who have both the need and the authority, delegated or recognized, to interpret statutes within some significant leeway. These users are highly variegated, ranging from administrative agencies to organized trade groups, to more loosely constructed foci of expertise, on to ordinary people creating ordinary customs.

"Indeed, one could go further to argue that among the desirable design criteria for the legal system as a whole we should include keeping statutory law close to social practices, rather than distantly formal (recognizing that, at times, closeness implies changing common practice, too). Much can be said for the proposition that legal systems in which customs, social norms, and legislatively specified rules flow together are the most successful. Certainly the judge-made common law has traditionally taken a similar point of view."

c.   Canons of Construction

> *(1) Linguistic Canons*
> *(2) Substantive Canons*
> *(3) The Absurdity Doctrine*

Courts have identified various rules of thumb for decoding statutory language—the so-called "canons of construction." These canons come in two types—linguistic canons and substantive canons. We separately then consider what might be thought of as a substantive canon, sometimes treated as a separate doctrine, which counsels interpreters to avoid attributing to Congress a meaning that would yield an absurd result.

(1) Linguistic Canons

> *YATES v. UNITED STATES*
> *LOCKHART v. UNITED STATES*
> *Notes on Linguistic Canons of Construction*

Linguistic canons are said to merely reflect linguistic conventions about how the English language is generally used and understood. For that reason, one might think that these canons must be deployed to determine a statute's plain meaning, for without them the words in a given statute cannot be understood at all. Such words have meaning only because they are read in light of the ordinary way we understand any collection of words to be used in relation to one another. Alternatively, one might question whether that is right. Linguistic canons might in fact be too rigid. Perhaps people sometimes use words in ways that do not track the way the canons assume they will be used. If so, does it make sense for judges to insist that the words in a statute always were intended to be used in the manner that the canons anticipate they were intended to be used?

There are literally dozens of rules that have been asserted as "canons." Here are some of the most common ones:

Expressio unius est exclusio alterius. Expression of one thing implies the exclusion of others.

Noscitur a sociis. A term is known by its associates.

Ejusdem generis. A general term is interpreted to include things of the same type as the more specific listed examples.

refer[red] to documents of wide dissemination." And we did so even though the list began with the word "any."

The *noscitur a sociis* canon operates in a similar manner here. "Tangible object" is the last in a list of terms that begins "any record [or] document." The term is therefore appropriately read to refer, not to any tangible object, but specifically to the subset of tangible objects involving records and documents, *i.e.*, objects used to record or preserve information.

This moderate interpretation of "tangible object" accords with the list of actions § 1519 proscribes. The section applies to anyone who "alters, destroys, mutilates, conceals, covers up, *falsifies*, or *makes a false entry in* any record, document, or tangible object" with the requisite obstructive intent. (Emphasis added.) The last two verbs, "falsif[y]" and "mak[e] a false entry in," typically take as grammatical objects records, documents, or things used to record or preserve information, such as logbooks or hard drives. See, *e.g.*, Black's Law Dictionary 720 (10th ed. 2014) (defining "falsify" as "[t]o make deceptive; to counterfeit, forge, or misrepresent; esp., to tamper with (a document, record, etc.)"). It would be unnatural, for example, to describe a killer's act of wiping his fingerprints from a gun as "falsifying" the murder weapon. But it would not be strange to refer to "falsifying" data stored on a hard drive as simply "falsifying" a hard drive. . . .

A canon related to *noscitur a sociis, ejusdem generis,* counsels: "Where general words follow specific words in a statutory enumeration, the general words are [usually] construed to embrace only objects similar in nature to those objects enumerated by the preceding specific words." In Begay v. United States, 553 U.S. 137, 142–143 (2008), for example, we relied on this principle to determine what crimes were covered by the statutory phrase "any crime . . . that . . . is burglary, arson, or extortion, involves use of explosives, or otherwise involves conduct that presents a serious potential risk of physical injury to another," 18 U.S.C. § 924(e)(2)(B)(ii). The enumeration of specific crimes, we explained, indicates that the "otherwise involves" provision covers "only *similar* crimes, rather than *every* crime that 'presents a serious potential risk of physical injury to another.'" 553 U.S., at 142, 128 S.Ct. 1581. Had Congress intended the latter "all encompassing" meaning, we observed, "it is hard to see why it would have needed to include the examples at all." Just so here. Had Congress intended "tangible object" in § 1519 to be interpreted so generically as to capture physical objects as dissimilar as documents and fish, Congress would have had no reason to refer specifically to "record" or "document." The Government's unbounded reading of "tangible object" would render those words misleading surplusage.

Having used traditional tools of statutory interpretation to examine markers of congressional intent within the Sarbanes-Oxley Act and § 1519 itself, we are persuaded that an aggressive interpretation of "tangible object" must be rejected. It is highly improbable that Congress would have buried a general spoliation statute covering objects of any and every kind in a provision targeting fraud in financial record-keeping. . . .

[The Court reversed the judgment of the Eleventh Circuit, which had upheld the trial court's conviction.]

■ JUSTICE ALITO, concurring in the judgment.

This case can and should be resolved on narrow grounds. And though the question is close, traditional tools of statutory construction confirm that John Yates has the better of the argument. . . .

Section 1519 refers to "any record, document, or tangible object." The *noscitur a sociis* canon instructs that when a statute contains a list, each word in that list presumptively has a "similar" meaning. A related canon, *ejusdem generis* teaches that general words following a list of specific words should usually be read in light of those specific words to mean something "similar." Applying these canons to § 1519's list of nouns, the term "tangible object" should refer to something similar to records or documents. A fish does not spring to mind—nor does an antelope, a colonial farmhouse, a hydrofoil, or an oil derrick. All are "objects" that are "tangible." But who wouldn't raise an eyebrow if a neighbor, when asked to identify something similar to a "record" or "document," said "crocodile"?

■ JUSTICE KAGAN, with whom JUSTICE SCALIA, JUSTICE KENNEDY, and JUSTICE THOMAS join, dissenting.

. . . I would begin with § 1519's text. When Congress has not supplied a definition, we generally give a statutory term its ordinary meaning. As the plurality must acknowledge, the ordinary meaning of "tangible object" is "a discrete thing that possesses physical form." A fish is, of course, a discrete thing that possesses physical form. See generally Dr. Seuss, One Fish Two Fish Red Fish Blue Fish (1960). So the ordinary meaning of the term "tangible object" in § 1519, as no one here disputes, covers fish (including too-small red grouper). . . .

That is not necessarily the end of the matter; I agree with the plurality (really, who does not?) that context matters in interpreting statutes. [But] here the text and its context point the same way. Stepping back from the words "tangible object" provides only further evidence that Congress said what it meant and meant what it said.

Begin with the way the surrounding words in § 1519 reinforce the breadth of the term at issue. Section 1519 refers to "any" tangible object, thus indicating (in line with *that* word's plain meaning) a tangible object "of whatever kind." This Court has time and again recognized that "any" has "an expansive meaning," bringing within a statute's reach *all* types of the item (here, "tangible object") to which the law refers. And the adjacent laundry list of verbs in § 1519 ("alters, destroys, mutilates, conceals, covers up, falsifies, or makes a false entry") further shows that

Congress wrote a statute with a wide scope. Those words are supposed to ensure—just as "tangible object" is meant to—that § 1519 covers the whole world of evidence-tampering, in all its prodigious variety. . . .

II

A

The plurality searches far and wide for anything—*anything*—to support its interpretation of § 1519. But its fishing expedition comes up empty.

. . . [T]he plurality [hopes] that *noscitur a sociis* and *ejusdem generis* will save it. The first of those related canons advises that words grouped in a list be given similar meanings. The second counsels that a general term following specific words embraces only things of a similar kind. According to the plurality, those Latin maxims change the English meaning of "tangible object" to only things, like records and documents, "used to record or preserve information." But understood as this Court always has, the canons have no such transformative effect on the workaday language Congress chose.

[A]ssigning "tangible object" its ordinary meaning comports with *noscitur a sociis* and *ejusdem generis* when applied, as they should be, with attention to § 1519's subject and purpose. Those canons require identifying a common trait that links all the words in a statutory phrase. In responding to that demand, the plurality characterizes records and documents as things that preserve information—and so they are. But just as much, they are things that provide information, and thus potentially serve as evidence relevant to matters under review. And in a statute pertaining to obstruction of federal investigations, that evidentiary function comes to the fore. The destruction of records and documents prevents law enforcement agents from gathering facts relevant to official inquiries. And so too does the destruction of tangible objects—of whatever kind. Whether the item is a fisherman's ledger or an undersized fish, throwing it overboard has the identical effect on the administration of justice. For purposes of § 1519, records, documents, and (all) tangible objects are therefore alike. . . .

And the plurality's invocation of § 1519's verbs does nothing to buttress its canon-based argument. The plurality observes that § 1519 prohibits "falsif[ying]" or "mak[ing] a false entry in" a tangible object, and no one can do those things to, say, a murder weapon (or a fish). But of course someone can alter, destroy, mutilate, conceal, or cover up such a tangible object, and § 1519 prohibits those actions too. The Court has never before suggested that all the verbs in a statute need to match up with all the nouns. And for good reason. It is exactly when Congress sets out to draft a statute broadly—to include every imaginable variation on a theme—that such mismatches will arise. To respond by narrowing the law, as the plurality does, is thus to flout both what Congress wrote and what Congress wanted. . . .

LOCKHART v. UNITED STATES

Supreme Court of the United States (2016).
136 S.Ct. 958.

■ JUSTICE SOTOMAYOR delivered the opinion of the Court.

Defendants convicted of possessing child pornography in violation of 18 U.S.C. § 2252(a)(4) are subject to a 10-year mandatory minimum sentence and an increased maximum sentence if they have "a prior conviction . . . under the laws of any State relating to aggravated sexual abuse, sexual abuse, or abusive sexual conduct involving a minor or ward." § 2252(b)(2). [Defendants had prior convictions for sexual abuse involving an adult.]

The question before us is whether the phrase "involving a minor or ward" modifies all items in the list of predicate crimes ("aggravated sexual abuse," "sexual abuse," and "abusive sexual conduct") or only the one item that immediately precedes it ("abusive sexual conduct"). . . . We affirm the Second Circuit's holding that the phrase "involving a minor or ward" in § 2252(b)(2) modifies only "abusive sexual conduct." . . .

I

[The Court reviewed the proceeding below that resulted in Lockhart's being sentenced to the enhanced mandatory minimum.]

II

Section 2252(b)(2) reads in full:

"Whoever violates, or attempts or conspires to violate [18 U.S.C. § 2252(a)(4)] shall be fined under this title or imprisoned not more than 10 years, or both, but . . . if such person has a prior conviction . . . under the laws of any State relating to aggravated sexual abuse, sexual abuse, or abusive sexual conduct involving a minor or ward, . . . such person shall be fined under this title and imprisoned for not less than 10 years nor more than 20 years."

. . . The issue before us is whether the limiting phrase that appears at the end of that list—"involving a minor or ward"—applies to all three predicate crimes preceding it in the list or only the final predicate crime. We hold that "involving a minor or ward" modifies only "abusive sexual conduct," the antecedent immediately preceding it. . . .

A

Consider the text. When this Court has interpreted statutes that include a list of terms or phrases followed by a limiting clause, we have typically applied an interpretive strategy called the "rule of the last antecedent." The rule provides that "a limiting clause or phrase . . . should ordinarily be read as modifying only the noun or phrase that it immediately follows."

. . . The rule reflects the basic intuition that when a modifier appears at the end of a list, it is easier to apply that modifier only to the item directly before it. That is particularly true where it takes more than a little mental energy to process the individual entries in the list, making it a heavy lift to carry the modifier across them all. For example, imagine you are the general manager of the Yankees and you are rounding out your 2016 roster. You tell your scouts to find a defensive catcher, a quick-footed shortstop, or a pitcher from last year's World Champion Kansas City Royals. It would be natural for your scouts to confine their search for a pitcher to last year's championship team, but to look more broadly for catchers and shortstops.

Applied here, the last antecedent principle suggests that the phrase "involving a minor or ward" modifies only the phrase that it immediately follows: "abusive sexual conduct." As a corollary, it also suggests that the phrases "aggravated sexual abuse" and "sexual abuse" are not so constrained.

Of course, as with any canon of statutory interpretation, the rule of the last antecedent "is not an absolute and can assuredly be overcome by other indicia of meaning." Barnhart, 540 U.S., at 26. For instance, take " 'the laws, the treaties, and the constitution of the United States.' " *Post* (Kagan, J., dissenting). A reader intuitively applies "of the United States" to "the laws," "the treaties" and "the constitution" because (among other things) laws, treaties, and the constitution are often cited together, because readers are used to seeing "of the United States" modify each of them, and because the listed items are simple and parallel without unexpected internal modifiers or structure. Section 2252(b)(2), by contrast, does not contain items that readers are used to seeing listed together or a concluding modifier that readers are accustomed to applying to each of them. And the varied syntax of each item in the list makes it hard for the reader to carry the final modifying clause across all three.

More importantly, here the interpretation urged by the rule of the last antecedent is not overcome by other indicia of meaning. To the contrary, § 2252(b)(2)'s context fortifies the meaning that principle commands.

B

[The pattern of § 2252(b)(2) parallels the pattern of Chapter 109A of the Federal Criminal Code, where "aggravated sexual abuse," "sexual abuse," and "sexual abuse of a minor or ward" are set out as three distinct, separate offenses.]

This similarity appears to be more than a coincidence. We cannot state with certainty that Congress used Chapter 109A as a template for the list of state predicates set out in § 2252(b)(2), but we cannot ignore the parallel, particularly because the headings in Chapter 109A were in place when Congress amended the statute to add § 2252(b)(2)'s state sexual-abuse predicates.

If Congress had intended to limit each of the state predicates to conduct "involving a minor or ward," we doubt it would have followed, or thought it needed to follow, so closely the structure and language of Chapter 109A. . . .

III

A

Lockhart argues, to the contrary, that the phrase "involving a minor or ward" should be interpreted to modify all three state sexual-abuse predicates. He first contends, as does our dissenting colleague, that the so-called series-qualifier principle supports his reading. This principle, Lockhart says, requires a modifier to apply to all items in a series when such an application would represent a natural construction.

This Court has long acknowledged that structural or contextual evidence may "rebut the last antecedent inference." . . . But in none of those cases did the Court describe, much less apply, a countervailing grammatical mandate that could bear the weight that either Lockhart or the dissent places on the series qualifier principle. Instead, the Court simply observed that sometimes context weighs against the application of the rule of the last antecedent. Whether a modifier is "applicable as much to the first . . . as to the last" words in a list, whether a set of items form a "single, integrated list," and whether the application of the rule would require acceptance of an "unlikely premise" are fundamentally contextual questions.

Lockhart attempts to identify contextual indicia that he says rebut the rule of the last antecedent, but those indicia hurt rather than help his prospects. He points out that the final two state predicates, "sexual abuse" and "abusive sexual conduct," are "nearly synonymous as a matter of everyday speech." And, of course, anyone who commits "aggravated sexual abuse" has also necessarily committed "sexual abuse." So, he posits, the items in the list are sufficiently similar that a limiting phrase could apply equally to all three of them.

But Lockhart's effort to demonstrate some similarity among the items in the list of state predicates reveals far too much similarity. The three state predicate crimes are not just related on Lockhart's reading; they are hopelessly redundant. Any conduct that would qualify as "aggravated sexual abuse . . . involving a minor or ward" or "sexual abuse . . . involving a minor or ward" would also qualify as "abusive sexual conduct involving a minor or ward." We take no position today on the meaning of the terms "aggravated sexual abuse," "sexual abuse," and "abusive sexual conduct," including their similarities and differences. But it is clear that applying the limiting phrase to all three items would risk running headlong into the rule against superfluity by transforming

the whole list boasts a fancy name—the "series-qualifier canon"—but, as my opening examples show, it reflects the completely ordinary way that people speak and listen, write and read.

Even the exception to the series-qualifier principle is intuitive, emphasizing both its common-sensical basis and its customary usage. When the nouns in a list are so disparate that the modifying clause does not make sense when applied to them all, then the last-antecedent rule takes over. Suppose your friend told you not that she wants to meet "an actor, director, or producer involved with Star Wars," but instead that she hopes someday to meet "a President, Supreme Court Justice, or actor involved with Star Wars." Presumably, you would know that she wants to meet a President or Justice even if that person has no connection to the famed film franchise. But so long as the modifying clause "is applicable as much to the first and other words as to the last," this Court has stated, "the natural construction of the language demands that the clause be read as applicable to all." In other words, the modifier then qualifies not just the last antecedent but the whole series.

. . . The relevant language—"aggravated sexual abuse, sexual abuse, or abusive sexual conduct involving a minor or ward"—contains a "single, integrated list" of parallel terms (*i.e.,* sex crimes) followed by a modifying clause. Given the close relation among the terms in the series, the modifier makes sense "as much to the first and other words as to the last." In other words, the reference to a minor or ward applies as well to sexual abuse and aggravated sexual abuse as to abusive sexual conduct. (The case would be different if, for example, the statute established a mandatory minimum for any person previously convicted of "arson, receipt of stolen property, or abusive sexual conduct involving a minor or ward.") So interpreting the modifier "as applicable to all" the preceding terms is what "the natural construction of the language" requires.

The majority responds to all this by claiming that the "inelegant phrasing" of § 2252(b)(2) renders it somehow exempt from a grammatical rule reflecting "how people ordinarily" use the English language. But to begin with, the majority is wrong to suggest that the series-qualifier canon is only about "colloquial" or "conversational" English. In fact, it applies to both speech and writing, in both their informal and their formal varieties. Here is a way to test my point: Pick up a journal, or a book, or for that matter a Supreme Court opinion—most of which keep "everyday" colloquialisms at a far distance. You'll come across many sentences having the structure of the statutory provision at issue here: a few nouns followed by a modifying clause. And you'll discover, again and yet again, that the clause modifies every noun in the series, not just the last—in other words, that even (especially?) in formal writing, the series-qualifier principle works.[2] And the majority is wrong too in suggesting

---

[2] Too busy to carry out this homework assignment? Consider some examples (there are many more) from just the last few months of this Court's work. In *OBB Personenverkehr AG v. Sachs,* this Court described a lawsuit as alleging "wrongful arrest, imprisonment, and torture

that the "odd repetition" in § 2252(b)(2)'s list of state predicates causes the series-qualifier principle to lose its force. *Ibid*. The majority's own made-up sentence proves that much. If a friend asked you "to get her tart lemons, sour lemons, or sour fruit from Mexico," you might well think her list of terms perplexing: You might puzzle over the difference between tart and sour lemons, and wonder why she had specifically mentioned lemons when she apparently would be happy with sour fruit of any kind. But of one thing, you would have no doubt: Your friend wants some produce *from Mexico*; it would not do to get her, say, sour lemons from Vietnam. However weird the way she listed fruits—or the way § 2252(b)(2) lists offenses—the modifying clause still refers to them all.

The majority as well seeks refuge in the idea that applying the series-qualifier canon to § 2252(b)(2) would violate the rule against superfluity. Says the majority: "Any conduct that would qualify as 'aggravated sexual abuse . . . involving a minor or ward' or 'sexual abuse . . . involving a minor or ward' would also qualify as 'abusive sexual conduct involving a minor or ward.'" But that rejoinder doesn't work. "[T]he canon against superfluity," this Court has often stated, "assists only where a competing interpretation gives effect to every clause and word of a statute." And the majority's approach (as it admits) produces superfluity too—and in equal measure. Now (to rearrange the majority's sentence) any conduct that would qualify as "abusive sexual conduct involving a minor or ward" or "aggravated sexual abuse" would also qualify as "sexual abuse." In other words, on the majority's reading as well, two listed crimes become subsets of a third, so that the three could have been written as one. And indeed, the majority's superfluity has an especially odd quality, because it relates to the modifying clause itself: The majority, that is, makes the term "involving a minor or ward" wholly unnecessary. Remember the old adage about the pot and the kettle? That is why the rule against superfluity cannot excuse the majority from reading § 2252(b)(2)'s modifier, as ordinary usage demands, to pertain to all the terms in the preceding series. . . .

IV

Suppose, for a moment, that this case is not as clear as I've suggested. Assume there is no way to know whether to apply the last-antecedent or the series-qualifier rule. Imagine, too, that the legislative

---

by *Saudi police*." In *James v. Boise*, this Court affirmed that state courts must follow its interpretations of "the laws, the treaties, and the constitution *of the United States*." In *Musacchio v. United States*, this Court noted that in interpreting statutes it looks to the "text, context, and relevant historical treatment *of the provision at issue*." In *FERC v. Electric Power Supply Assn.*, this Court applied a statute addressing "any rule, regulation, practice, or contract *affecting [a wholesale] rate [or] charge*." And in *Montanile v. Board of Trustees of Nat. Elevator Industry Health Benefit Plan*, this Court interpreted an employee benefits plan requiring reimbursement "for attorneys' fees, costs, expenses or damages *claimed by the covered person*." In each case, of course, the italicized modifying clause refers to every item in the preceding list. That is because the series-qualifier rule reflects how all of us use language, in writing and in speech, in formal and informal contexts, all the time.

history is not quite so compelling and the majority's "template" argument not quite so strained. Who, then, should prevail?

This Court has a rule for how to resolve genuine ambiguity in criminal statutes: in favor of the criminal defendant. As the majority puts the point, the rule of lenity insists that courts side with the defendant "when the ordinary canons of statutory construction have revealed no satisfactory construction." At the very least, that principle should tip the scales in Lockhart's favor, because nothing the majority has said shows that the modifying clause in § 2252(b)(2) *unambiguously* applies to only the last term in the preceding series.

But in fact, Lockhart's case is stronger. Consider the following sentence, summarizing various points made above: "The series-qualifier principle, the legislative history, and the rule of lenity discussed in this opinion all point in the same direction." Now answer the following question: Has only the rule of lenity been discussed in this opinion, or have the series-qualifier principle and the legislative history been discussed as well? Even had you not read the preceding 16-plus pages, you would know the right answer—because of the ordinary way all of us use language. That, in the end, is why Lockhart should win.

NOTES ON LINGUISTIC CANONS OF CONSTRUCTION

(1) KARL N. LLEWELLYN, REMARKS ON THE THEORY OF APPELLATE DECISION AND THE RULES OR CANONS ABOUT HOW STATUTES ARE TO BE CONSTRUED, 3 Vand. L. Rev. 395 (1950): "When it comes to presenting a proposed construction in court, there is an accepted conventional vocabulary. As in argument over points of case-law, the accepted convention still, unhappily requires discussion as if only one single correct meaning could exist. Hence there are two opposing canons on almost every point. . . .Every lawyer must be familiar with them all: they are still needed tools of argument. . . . Plainly, to make any canon take hold in a particular instance, the construction contended for must be sold, essentially, by means other than the use of the canon: The good sense of the situation and a simple construction of the available language to achieve that sense, by tenable means, out of the statutory language.

(2)   What is the actual relationship between canons of construction and the way statutes are drafted? In STATUTORY INTERPRETATION FROM THE INSIDE—AN EMPIRICAL STUDY OF CONGRESSIONAL DRAFTING, DELEGATION, AND THE CANONS: PART I, 65 Stan. L. Rev. 901 (2013), ABBE GLUCK & LISA SCHULTZ BRESSMAN interviewed 137 congressional counsels—staff members with responsibility for drafting—to try to answer this question. Here's a part of what they found, 65 Stan. L. Rev. at 930–936:

"We asked first by concept and then by name about the six textual canons most commonly deployed by courts and scholars:

> *Noscitura sociis* (construe ambiguous terms in a list in reference to other terms on the list)

Ejusdem generis (construe general, often catch-all, terms in a list in reference to other, more specific, terms in a list)

Expressio/Inclusiounius est exclusio alterius (the inclusion of specific terms or exceptions indicates an intent to exclude terms or exceptions not included)?

The rule against superfluities (construe statutes to avoid redundancy; when there are two overlapping terms, construe to give an independent meaning to each)?

The whole act rule (statutory terms are presumed to have a consistent meaning throughout a statute)?

The whole code rule (statutory terms are presumed to have a consistent meaning throughout the U.S. Code)?

"We also inquired directly into the use of dictionaries (dictionaries should be consulted to determine the ordinary or plain meaning of statutory terms) and the *in pari material* rule (similar statutory provisions should be interpreted similarly).

"[O]ur respondents displayed a high degree of familiarity with the concepts underlying the textual canons, but much less familiarity with their formal names. Our respondents also appeared to regularly use several of these canons in the drafting process. But, of particular note, the concepts that our respondents indicated they used most often—for example, the concept underlying the *expressio unius* canon—are among the least consistently utilized textual canons by the courts, and they have come under criticism (even from textualist judges) about the extent to which they reflect drafting reality. In contrast, the canons most commonly employed by courts, including the rule against superfluities, the whole act rule, and the use of dictionaries, appear to be used the least often by our drafters-despite our respondents' awareness that the courts use them—due to a host of political or institutional factors that courts rarely take into account."

As to those canons drafters did use:

"*Concepts in use:* expressio, noscitur, *and* ejusdem

"Approximately 33% of our respondents told us that the assumption underlying the *expressio unius* canon-that the inclusion of specific terms signifies the exclusion of terms not mentioned-always or often applies. Five percent more agreed that the default rule is always exclusivity unless language indicates otherwise, and most of the remaining respondents likewise validated the assumption by explaining that they 'signaled' whether they wished a list to be something other than exclusive, usually through the use of the word 'including' or a catch-all term. Only 10% of respondents indicated that the presumption typically goes in the other direction, toward inclusivity.

"*Expressio* was also one of the most recognized textual canons by name (along with the rule against superfluities). But when asked about the rule by name, most of our respondents told us that they did not employ it (several respondents made statements such as 'we don't know any Latin'), even though, when asked about the concept, they already had substantiated their use of the assumptions underlying it. A number of respondents (18%) got at this disconnect by describing the ideas embraced by the textual canons as 'intuitive.' As one stated: 'We consider them not expressly but intuitively: how does this legislation interact with existing code? Is it inclusive, exclusive, are like things treated alike—those values are thought about here.'

"With respect to the general concept underlying both the *noscitur* and *ejusdem* rules, 71% of respondents (ninety-seven) said that terms in a statutory list always or often relate to one another, and only two respondents said they rarely or never did. The vast majority of respondents, however, did not know those rules when asked by name (85% did not know *noscitur* and 65% did not know *ejusdem*)."

And why were some canons that were known still not used? Here's one example:

"*Superfluities: redundancy to satisfy political stakeholders*

"For instance, even though 62% of our respondents knew the rule against superfluities by name, 18% of respondents told us it rarely applies, and 45% more told us it only sometimes does. Eighteen percent also explained the relative weakness of this rule's application by reference to two recurring reasons, one practical and one political. From a practical perspective, our respondents focused on the need to ensure that the statute covers the intended terrain. They told us that drafters intentionally err on the side of redundancy to 'capture the universe' or 'because you just want to be sure you hit it.'

"These respondents also pointed out that the *political interests* of the audience often demand redundancy. They told us, for example, that 'sometimes politically for compromise they must include certain words in the statute—that senator, that constituent, that lobbyist wants to see that word'; similarly, they said that 'sometimes the lists are in there to satisfy groups, certain phrases are needed to satisfy political interests and they might overlap' or that 'sometimes you have it in there because someone had to see their phrase in the bill to get it passed.' One example provided was a statute drafted to cover 'medical service providers' that had to be amended to include a specific (and redundant) reference to 'hospitals' to satisfy stakeholders.

"We were not surprised to see pragmatic considerations trumping application of the rule against superfluities. Common sense tells us that, despite the popularity of this rule with judges, there is likely to be redundancy, especially in exceedingly long statutes. (We have seen no evidence, however, that judges take the length of statutes into account when applying the rule.) But what respondents told us was different from that common-sense assumption: namely, terms are often *purposefully redundant to satisfy audiences other than courts.*

"This is an argument that has been made in other contexts. Scholars have argued that the audience for legislative language or legislative history is much broader than judges, or even agencies, and that these statutory materials are sometimes expressly directed at noninterpreters, such as lobbyists and other stakeholders. Whether this 'audience' issue should have an effect on how courts interpret statutes is a different matter—after all, how will courts be able to discern when drafters are talking to them as opposed to other audiences? A fictitious interpretive rule may be required precisely *because* investigating the intended audience would be too difficult. But that has not been the main judicial justification for the rule against superfluities.

"Our findings certainly call into question what *has* been the rule's primary justification: namely that, because it reflects how Congress drafts and also because Congress is aware of it, the rule helps faithful-agent judges effectuate congressional intent. We note also that, in several recent cases, the Court has divided over application of the rule—with the majority relying on the rule to decide the case over the objection of dissenters who have argued, like some of our respondents, that Congress is often intentionally redundant to be certain that it has made its point. We have seen no case, however, in which the Court acknowledged the political considerations, like satisfying stakeholders, that some of our respondents also mentioned. Our findings suggest that those considerations likewise may mean that judicial application of the rule does precisely the opposite of effectuating drafter intent."

(2) Substantive Canons

> ### BOND v. UNITED STATES

Unlike the semantic canons, which purport to reflect neutral principles about everyday language use, the substantive canons of construction are different. These canons take the form of clear statement rules, requiring the legislature to clearly indicate its intent before courts interpret a statute to conflict with a favored policy outcome. Are such canons best understood as means of ensuring that statutes are construed in a manner faithful to the intentions of their drafters on the theory that the drafters would not want the statute to be construed in a manner that would infringe the substantive policy reflected in the canon? Or are such canons best understood as constraints on legislative drafters that, for reasons of policy, ensure that drafters enact statutes that trench on certain policies only when they do so clearly? Is one understanding of the role that such canons play more defensible as a matter of constitutional structure than another?

One well-known substantive canon is the canon of constitutional avoidance. This canon instructs that statutes should be construed, when unclear, to avoid giving rise to serious constitutional questions. But there are many others—from canons favoring the rights of Native Americans to the rule of lenity, which aims to protect the notice rights of criminal defendants. Consider the following case:

BOND v. UNITED STATES

Supreme Court of the United States (2014).
134 S.Ct. 2077.

■ CHIEF JUSTICE ROBERTS delivered the opinion of the Court.

. . .

I

A

. . . . In 1997, the President of the United States, upon the advice and consent of the Senate, ratified the Convention on the Prohibition of the Development, Production, Stockpiling, and Use of Chemical Weapons and on Their Destruction. . . . The Convention was conceived as an effort to update the Geneva Protocol's protections and to expand the prohibition on chemical weapons beyond state actors in wartime. The Convention aimed to achieve that objective by prohibiting the development, stockpiling, or use of chemical weapons by any State Party or person within a State Party's jurisdiction. . . .

Congress gave the Convention domestic effect in 1998 when it passed the Chemical Weapons Convention Implementation Act. The Act . . . forbids any person knowingly "to develop, produce, otherwise acquire, transfer directly or indirectly, receive, stockpile, retain, own, possess, or use, or threaten to use, any chemical weapon." 18 U.S.C. § 229(a)(1). It defines "chemical weapon" in relevant part as "[a] toxic chemical and its precursors, except where intended for a purpose not prohibited under this chapter as long as the type and quantity is consistent with such a purpose." § 229F(1)(A). "Toxic chemical," in turn, is defined in general as "any chemical which through its chemical action on life processes can cause death, temporary incapacitation or permanent harm to humans or animals. . . .

B

Petitioner Carol Anne Bond is a microbiologist from Lansdale, Pennsylvania. In 2006, Bond's closest friend, Myrlinda Haynes, announced that she was pregnant. When Bond discovered that her husband was the child's father, she sought revenge against Haynes. Bond stole a quantity of 10–chloro–10H–phenoxarsine (an arsenic-based compound) from her employer, a chemical manufacturer. She also ordered a vial of potassium dichromate (a chemical commonly used in printing photographs or cleaning laboratory equipment) on Amazon.com. Both chemicals are toxic to humans and, in high enough doses, potentially lethal. It is undisputed, however, that Bond did not intend to kill Haynes. She instead hoped that Haynes would touch the chemicals and develop an uncomfortable rash.

Between November 2006 and June 2007, Bond went to Haynes's home on at least 24 occasions and spread the chemicals on her car door, mailbox, and door knob. These attempted assaults were almost entirely unsuccessful. . . . Haynes repeatedly called the local police to report the suspicious substances . . . . [P]ostal inspectors placed surveillance cameras around her home. The cameras caught Bond opening Haynes's mailbox, stealing an envelope, and stuffing potassium dichromate inside the muffler of Haynes's car.

Federal prosecutors naturally charged Bond with two counts of mail theft, in violation of 18 U.S.C. § 1708. More surprising, they also charged her with two counts of possessing and using a chemical weapon, in violation of section 229(a). Bond moved to dismiss the chemical weapon counts on the ground that section 229 exceeded Congress's enumerated powers and invaded powers reserved to the States by the Tenth Amendment. . . .

II

. . . [I]t is "a well-established principle governing the prudent exercise of this Court's jurisdiction that normally the Court will not decide a constitutional question if there is some other ground upon which to dispose of the case." Bond argues that section 229 does not cover her conduct. So we consider that argument first.

III

. . .

A

. . . In the Government's view, the conclusion that Bond "knowingly" "use[d]" a "chemical weapon" in violation of section 229(a) is simple: The chemicals that Bond placed on Haynes's home and car are "toxic chemical[s]" as defined by the statute, and Bond's attempt to assault Haynes was not a "peaceful purpose." §§ 229F(1), (8), (7) . The problem with this interpretation is that it would "dramatically intrude[ ] upon traditional state criminal jurisdiction," and we avoid reading statutes to have such reach in the absence of a clear indication that they do.

Part of a fair reading of statutory text is recognizing that "Congress legislates against the backdrop" of certain unexpressed presumptions. As Justice Frankfurter put it in his famous essay on statutory interpretation, correctly reading a statute "demands awareness of certain presuppositions." . . .

Among the background principles of construction that our cases have recognized are those grounded in the relationship between the Federal Government and the States under our Constitution. . . . [One of] these is the well-established principle that " 'it is incumbent upon the federal courts to be certain of Congress' intent before finding that federal law overrides' " the "usual constitutional balance of federal and state powers." Gregory v. Ashcroft, 501 U.S. 452, 460 (1991). . . .

We have applied this background principle when construing federal statutes that touched on several areas of traditional state responsibility. Perhaps the clearest example of traditional state authority is the punishment of local criminal activity. Thus, "we will not be quick to assume that Congress has meant to effect a significant change in the sensitive relation between federal and state criminal jurisdiction." . . .

These precedents make clear that it is appropriate to refer to basic principles of federalism embodied in the Constitution to resolve ambiguity in a federal statute. In this case, the ambiguity derives from the improbably broad reach of the key statutory definition given the term—"chemical weapon"—being defined; the deeply serious consequences of adopting such a boundless reading; and the lack of any apparent need to do so in light of the context from which the statute arose—a treaty about chemical warfare and terrorism. We conclude that, in this curious case, we can insist on a clear indication that Congress meant to reach purely local crimes, before interpreting the statute's expansive language in a way that intrudes on the police power of the States.

B

We do not find any such clear indication in section 229. "Chemical weapon" is the key term that defines the statute's reach, and it is defined extremely broadly. But that general definition does not constitute a clear statement that Congress meant the statute to reach local criminal conduct. . . .

The Government would have us . . . adopt a reading of section 229 that would sweep in everything from the detergent under the kitchen sink to the stain remover in the laundry room. Yet no one would ordinarily describe those substances as "chemical weapons." The Government responds that because Bond used "specialized, highly toxic" (though legal) chemicals, "this case presents no occasion to address whether Congress intended [section 229] to apply to common household substances." That the statute *would* apply so broadly, however, is the inescapable conclusion of the Government's position: Any parent would be guilty of a serious federal offense—possession of a chemical weapon—when, exasperated by the children's repeated failure to clean the goldfish tank, he considers poisoning the fish with a few drops of vinegar. We are reluctant to ignore the ordinary meaning of "chemical weapon" when doing so would transform a statute passed to implement the international Convention on Chemical Weapons into one that also makes it a federal offense to poison goldfish. That would not be a "realistic assessment[ ] of congressional intent."

In light of all of this, it is fully appropriate to apply the background assumption that Congress normally preserves "the constitutional balance between the National Government and the States." That assumption is grounded in the very structure of the Constitution. And as we explained when this case was first before us, maintaining that constitutional balance is not merely an end unto itself. Rather, "[b]y denying any one government complete jurisdiction over all the concerns of public life, federalism protects the liberty of the individual from arbitrary power."

The Government's reading of section 229 would " 'alter sensitive federal-state relationships,' " convert an astonishing amount of "traditionally local criminal conduct" into "a matter for federal enforcement," and "involve a substantial extension of federal police resources." It would transform the statute from one whose core concerns are acts of war, assassination, and terrorism into a massive federal anti-poisoning regime that reaches the simplest of assaults. As the Government reads section 229, "hardly" a poisoning "in the land would fall outside the federal statute's domain." Of course Bond's conduct is serious and unacceptable—and against the laws of Pennsylvania. But the background principle that Congress does not normally intrude upon the police power of the States is critically important. In light of that principle, we are reluctant to conclude that Congress meant to punish Bond's crime with a federal prosecution for a chemical weapons attack. . . .

The judgment of the Court of Appeals [sustaining her conviction] is reversed, and the case is remanded for further proceedings consistent with this opinion.

■ JUSTICE SCALIA, with whom JUSTICE THOMAS joins, and with whom JUSTICE ALITO joins as to Part I, concurring in the judgment.

Somewhere in Norristown, Pennsylvania, a husband's paramour suffered a minor thumb burn at the hands of a betrayed wife. The United States Congress—"every where extending the sphere of its activity, and drawing all power into its impetuous vortex"—has made a federal case out of it. What are we to do?

It is the responsibility of "the legislature, not the Court, . . . to define a crime, and ordain its punishment." Today, the Court shirks its job and performs Congress's. As sweeping and unsettling as the Chemical Weapons Convention Implementation Act of 1998 may be, it is clear beyond doubt that it covers what Bond did; and we have no authority to amend it. . . .

The meaning of the Act is plain. No person may knowingly "develop, produce, otherwise acquire, transfer directly or indirectly, receive, stockpile, retain, own, possess, or use, or threaten to use, any chemical weapon." 18 U.S.C. § 229(a)(1). A "chemical weapon" is "[a] toxic chemical and its precursors, except where intended for a purpose not prohibited under this chapter as long as the type and quantity is consistent with such a purpose." § 229F(1)(A). A "toxic chemical" is "any chemical which through its chemical action on life processes can cause death, temporary incapacitation or permanent harm to humans or animals. The term includes all such chemicals, regardless of their origin or of their method of production, and regardless of whether they are produced in facilities, in munitions or elsewhere." § 229F(8)(A). A "purpose not prohibited" is "[a]ny peaceful purpose related to an industrial, agricultural, research, medical, or pharmaceutical activity or other activity." § 229F(7)(A).

Applying those provisions to this case is hardly complicated. Bond possessed and used "chemical[s] which through [their] chemical action on life processes can cause death, temporary incapacitation or permanent harm." Thus, she possessed "toxic chemicals." And, because they were not possessed or used only for a "purpose not prohibited," § 229F(1)(A), they were "chemical weapons." Ergo, Bond violated the Act. End of statutory analysis, I would have thought.

The Court does not think the interpretive exercise so simple. But that is only because its result-driven antitextualism befogs what is evident.

[The Court] *starts* with the federalism-related consequences of the statute's meaning and reasons backwards, holding that, if the statute has what the Court considers a disruptive effect on the "federal-state balance" of criminal jurisdiction, *ante,* that effect causes the text, even if clear on its face, to be ambiguous. Just ponder what the Court says: "[The Act's] ambiguity *derives* from the improbably broad reach of the key statutory definition . . . the deeply serious consequences of adopting such a boundless reading; and the lack of any apparent need to do so. . . ." *Ibid.* (emphasis added). Imagine what future courts can do with that judge-empowering principle: Whatever has improbably broad, deeply serious, and apparently unnecessary consequences . . . *is ambiguous*! . . .

In this case, . . . the ordinary meaning of the term being defined is irrelevant, because the statute's own definition—however expansive—is utterly clear: any "chemical which through its chemical action on life processes can cause death, temporary incapacitation or permanent harm to humans or animals," § 229F(8)(A), unless the chemical is possessed or used for a "peaceful purpose," § 229F(1)(A), (7)(A). The statute parses itself. There is no opinion of ours, and none written by any court or put forward by any commentator since Aristotle, which says, or even suggests, that "dissonance" between ordinary meaning and the unambiguous words of a definition is to be resolved in favor of ordinary meaning. If that were the case, there would hardly be any use in providing a definition. No, the true rule is entirely clear: "When a statute includes an explicit definition, we must follow that definition, *even if it varies from that term's ordinary meaning.*" Stenberg v. Carhart, 530 U.S. 914, 942 (2000) (emphasis added). Once again, contemplate the judge-empowering consequences of the new interpretive rule the Court today announces: When there is "dissonance" between the statutory definition and the ordinary meaning of the defined word, the latter may prevail.

But even text clear on its face, the Court suggests, must be read against the backdrop of established interpretive presumptions. Thus, we presume "that a criminal statute derived from the common law carries with it the requirement of a culpable mental state—even if no such limitation appears in the text." And we presume that "federal statutes do not apply outside the United States." Both of those are, indeed, established interpretive presumptions that are (1) based upon realistic assessments of congressional intent, and (2) well known to Congress— thus furthering rather than subverting genuine legislative intent. To apply these presumptions, then, is not to rewrite clear text; it is to interpret words fairly, in light of their statutory context. But there is nothing either (1) realistic or (2) well known about the presumption the Court shoves down the throat of a resisting statute today. Who in the world would have thought that a definition is inoperative if it contradicts ordinary meaning? When this statute was enacted, there was not yet a "*Bond* presumption" to that effect—though presumably Congress will have to take account of the *Bond* presumption in the future, perhaps by adding at the end of all its definitions that depart from ordinary connotation "and we really mean it.". . .

[Justice Scalia went on to say that even though the statute applied to the defendant's behavior, it was unconstitutional for entirely other reasons; thus he concurred in the judgment.]

[Justice Thomas's concurrence is omitted.]

[Justice Alito's concurrence is omitted.]

NOTES

(1)   WILLIAM N. ESKRIDGE, JR. & PHILIP P. FRICKEY, QUASI-CONSTITUTIONAL LAW: CLEAR STATEMENT RULES AS CONSTITUTIONAL LAWMAKING, 45 Vand. L. Rev. 593 (1992): ". . . . [T]he current Court emphasizes a different array of clear statement rules than did the Court in the 1970s. The current Court is less inclined to protect individual rights through cautious statutory interpretation than the Court was a decade ago, and more inclined to protect constitutional structures through cautious interpretation. Moreover, consistent with its interest in textualism as its dominant interpretive methodology, the current Court emphasizes clear statement rules much more than presumptions. Indeed, the most striking innovation of the recent Court has been its creation of a series of new "super-strong clear statement rules" protecting constitutional structures, especially structures associated with federalism.

"These super-strong clear statement rules are remarkable. On the one hand, they require a clearer, more explicit statement from Congress in the text of the statute, without reference to legislative history, than prior clear statement rules have required. This would suggest that such rules are protecting particularly important constitutional values. But, on the other hand, the super-strong clear statement rules the Court has actually adopted protect constitutional values that are virtually never enforced through constitutional interpretation. That is, the Court in the 1980s has tended to create the strongest clear statement rules to confine Congress's power in areas in which Congress has the constitutional power to do virtually anything. What the Court is doing is creating a domain of "quasi-constitutional law" in certain areas: Judicial review does not prevent

Congress from legislating, but judicial interpretation of the resulting legislation requires an extraordinarily specific statement on the face of the statute for Congress to limit the states or the executive department.

"That the Court's super-strong clear statement rules are new does not mean they are undesirable, of course. In fact, a good case can be made for such quasi-constitutional law: structural constitutional protections, especially those of federalism, are underenforced constitutional norms. They are essentially unenforceable by the Court as a direct limitation upon Congress's power, and are best left to the political process. But the Court may have a legitimate role in forcing the political process to pay attention to the constitutional values at stake, and super-strong clear statement rules are a practical way for the Court to focus legislative attention on these values. . . ."

(2)   CASS R. SUNSTEIN, INTERPRETING STATUTES IN THE REGULATORY STATE, 103 Harv. L. Rev. 405,452–54 (1989): "The canons of construction continue to be a prominent feature in the federal and state courts. The use of general guides to construction—in the form of "clear-statement" principles and background understandings—can be found in every area of modern law.

"An analogy may be helpful here. The law of contracts is pervaded by— indeed, it consists largely of—a set of principles filling contractual gaps when the parties have been silent, or when the meaning of their words is unclear. Imagine, for example, that the parties have been silent on the time of performance, damages in the event of breach, or the consequences of dramatically changed circumstances and partial default. The use of implied terms, or "off-the-rack" provisions, is a familiar part of the law of contract; and it would be most peculiar to say that they are an illegitimate incursion into the usual process of "interpreting" the parties' intent. Without implied terms of some sort, contracts simply would not be susceptible to construction. Implied terms also provide the background against which people enter into agreements.

"To a large degree, interpretive principles—including the traditional "canons"—serve the same function in public law. They too help judges to construe both statements and silences; they too should not be seen as the intrusion of controversial judgments into "ordinary" interpretation. There are, however, differences as well as similarities. In the law of contracts, it is often said that implied terms should attempt to "mimic the market" by doing what the parties would do if they had made provision on the subject. In this respect, contract law is pervaded by a background norm in favor of party autonomy and the market. In statutory construction, by contrast, the notion of "mimicking the market" is unavailable, and the idea that one should do what Congress would have done is far from a complete guide. As we have seen, how Congress would have resolved the question is sometimes unclear; sometimes the resolution of the enacting Congress would produce difficulties as a result of changed circumstances; sometimes courts properly call into play principles—many of them constitutionally inspired—that push statutes in directions that diverge from the conclusion that Congress would have reached if it had resolved the matter. Despite these differences, the critical point is that, as in contract law, the interpretation of a text requires courts to refer to background norms in interpreting terms."

---

(3) The Absurdity Doctrine

> *PUBLIC CITIZEN v. U.S. DEP'T OF*
> *JUSTICE*

We close our consideration of canons by considering an unusually powerful and controversial rule of thumb: the absurdity doctrine, which directs courts not to read statutes so as to produce absurd results. From one vantage point, this would seem to be uncontroversial. Why would one construe a statute to create an absurdity? From another vantage point, though, this doctrine is itself absurd because it invites interpreters to ignore what the text actually says. The same can be said of an analogous doctrine telling judges to ignore typos: the scrivener's error doctrine. These doctrines test textualism. Must a textualist reject the scrivener's error and the absurdity doctrines? Or, rather, are these the doctrines that save textualism from itself being deemed absurd? Relatedly, are the scrivener's error and absurdity doctrines just the natural consequence of a commitment to purposivism? Or are they instead an indication of the illegitimacy of purposivism? After all, isn't there a risk that an error or an absurdity is in the eye of the beholder?

PUBLIC CITIZEN v. U.S. DEP'T OF JUSTICE

Supreme Court of the United States (1989).
491 U.S. 440.

■ JUSTICE BRENNAN delivered the opinion of the Court.

. . . Since 1952 the President, through the Department of Justice, has requested advice from the American Bar Association's Standing Committee on Federal Judiciary (ABA Committee) in making [judicial] nominations.

The American Bar Association is a private voluntary professional association of approximately 343,000 attorneys. It has several working committees, among them the advisory body whose work is at issue here. The ABA Committee consists of 14 persons belonging to, and chosen by, the American Bar Association. Each of the 12 federal judicial Circuits (not including the Federal Circuit) has one representative on the ABA Committee, except for the Ninth Circuit, which has two; in addition, one member is chosen at large. The ABA Committee receives no federal funds. It does not recommend persons for appointment to the federal bench of its own initiative.

Prior to announcing the names of nominees for judgeships on the courts of appeals, the district courts, or the Court of International Trade, the President, acting through the Department of Justice, routinely requests a potential nominee to complete a questionnaire drawn up by the ABA Committee and to submit it to the Assistant Attorney General for the Office of Legal Policy, to the chair of the ABA Committee, and to the committee member (usually the representative of the relevant judicial Circuit) charged with investigating the nominee. . . .

B

[The Federal Advisory Committee Act (FACA)] was born of a desire to assess the need for the "numerous committees, boards, commissions, councils, and similar groups which have been established to advise officers and agencies in the executive branch of the Federal Government." Its purpose was to ensure that new advisory committees be established only when essential and that their number be minimized; that they be terminated when they have outlived their usefulness; that their creation, operation, and duration be subject to uniform standards and procedures; that Congress and the public remain apprised of their existence, activities, and cost; and that their work be exclusively advisory in nature.

. . . FACA requires that each advisory committee file a charter, § 9(c), and keep detailed minutes of its meetings. Those meetings must be chaired or attended by an officer or employee of the Federal Government who is authorized to adjourn any meeting when he or she deems its adjournment in the public interest. FACA also requires advisory committees to provide advance notice of their meetings and to open them to the public, unless the President or the agency head to which an advisory committee reports determines that it may be closed to the public in accordance with the Government in the Sunshine Act. In addition, FACA stipulates that advisory committee minutes, records, and reports be made available to the public, provided they do not fall within one of the Freedom of Information Act's exemptions, and the Government does not choose to withhold them. Advisory committees established by legislation or created by the President or other federal officials must also be "fairly balanced in terms of the points of view represented and the functions" they perform. Their existence is limited to two years, unless specifically exempted by the entity establishing them.

C

In October 1986, appellant Washington Legal Foundation (WLF) brought suit against the Department of Justice after the ABA Committee refused WLF's request for the names of potential judicial nominees it was considering and for the ABA Committee's reports and minutes of its meetings. WLF asked the District Court for the District of Columbia to declare the ABA Committee an "advisory committee" as FACA defines that term. WLF further sought an injunction ordering the Justice Department to cease utilizing the ABA Committee as an advisory committee until it complied with FACA. . . .

III

Section 3(2) of FACA, defines "advisory committee" as follows: . . .

> "(2) The term 'advisory committee' means any committee, board, commission, council, conference, panel, task force, or other similar group, or any subcommittee or other subgroup thereof (hereafter in this paragraph referred to as 'committee'), which is—. . .

> (B) established or utilized by the President, . . ."

. . . Whether the ABA Committee constitutes an "advisory committee" for purposes of FACA therefore depends upon whether it is "utilized" by the President or the Justice Department as Congress intended that term to be understood.

A

There is no doubt that the Executive makes use of the ABA Committee, and thus "utilizes" it in one common sense of the term. As the District Court recognized, however, "reliance on the plain language of FACA alone is not entirely satisfactory." "Utilize" is a woolly verb, its contours left undefined by the statute itself. Read unqualifiedly, it would extend FACA's requirements to any group of two or more persons, or at least any formal organization, from which the President or an Executive agency seeks advice. We are convinced that Congress did not intend that result. A nodding acquaintance with FACA's purposes, as manifested by its legislative history and as recited in § 2 of the Act, reveals that it cannot have been Congress' intention, for example, to require the filing of a charter, the presence of a controlling federal official, and detailed minutes any time the President seeks the views of the National Association for the Advancement of Colored People (NAACP) before nominating Commissioners to the Equal Employment Opportunity Commission, or asks the leaders of an American Legion Post he is visiting for the organization's opinion on some aspect of military policy.

Nor can Congress have meant—as a straightforward reading of "utilize" would appear to require—that all of FACA's restrictions apply if a President consults with his own political party before picking his Cabinet. It was unmistakably *not* Congress' intention to intrude on a political party's freedom to conduct its affairs as it chooses, or its ability to advise elected officials who belong to that party, by placing a federal employee in charge of each advisory group meeting and making its minutes public property. FACA was enacted to cure specific ills, above all the wasteful expenditure of public funds for worthless committee meetings and biased proposals; although its reach is extensive, we cannot believe that it was intended to cover every formal and informal consultation between the President or an Executive agency and a group rendering advice. As we said in Church of the Holy Trinity v. United States: "[F]requently words of general meaning are used in a statute, words broad enough to include an act in question, and yet a consideration of the whole legislation, or of the circumstances surrounding its enactment, or of the absurd results which follow from giving such broad meaning to the words, makes it unreasonable to believe that the legislator intended to include the particular act."

Where the literal reading of a statutory term would "compel an odd result," we must search for other evidence of congressional intent to lend the term its proper scope. "The circumstances of the enactment of particular legislation," for example, "may persuade a court that Congress did not intend words of common meaning to have their literal effect." Even though, as Judge Learned Hand said, "the words used, even in their literal sense, are the primary, and ordinarily the most reliable, source of interpreting the meaning of any writing," nevertheless "it is one of the surest indexes of a mature and developed jurisprudence not to make a fortress out of the dictionary; but to remember that statutes always have some purpose or object to accomplish, whose sympathetic and imaginative discovery is the surest guide to their meaning." Cabell v. Markham, 148 F.2d 737, 739 (CA2), aff'd, 326 U.S. 404 (1945). Looking beyond the naked text for guidance is perfectly proper when the result it apparently decrees is difficult to fathom or where it seems inconsistent with Congress' intention . . . .

B

[A] literalistic reading of § 3(2) would bring the Justice Department's advisory relationship with the ABA Committee within FACA's terms, particularly given FACA's objective of opening many advisory relationships to public scrutiny except in certain narrowly defined situations. A literalistic reading, however, would catch far more groups and consulting arrangements than Congress could conceivably have intended. And the careful review which this interpretive difficulty warrants of earlier efforts to regulate federal advisory committees and the circumstances surrounding FACA's adoption strongly suggests that FACA's definition of "advisory committee" was not meant to encompass the ABA Committee's relationship with the Justice Department. That relationship seems not to have been within the contemplation of Executive Order No. 11007. And FACA's legislative history does not display an intent to widen the Order's application to encircle it. Weighing the deliberately inclusive statutory language against other evidence of congressional intent, it seems to us a close question whether FACA should be construed to apply to the ABA Committee, although on the whole we are fairly confident it should not. . . .

■ JUSTICE SCALIA took no part in the consideration or decision of these cases.

■ JUSTICE KENNEDY, with whom THE CHIEF JUSTICE and JUSTICE O'CONNOR join, concurring in the judgment.

[T]his suit presents [a] distinct issue[ ] of the separation of powers. [It] concerns the rules this Court must follow in interpreting a statute passed by Congress and signed by the President. On this subject, I cannot join the Court's conclusion that the Federal Advisory Committee Act (FACA), does not cover the activities of the American Bar Association's Standing Committee on Federal Judiciary in advising the Department of Justice regarding potential nominees for federal judgeships. The result seems sensible in the abstract; but I cannot accept the method by which the Court arrives at its interpretation of FACA, which does not accord proper respect to the finality and binding effect of legislative enactments. . . .

I

. . . Although I believe the Court's result is quite sensible, I cannot go along with the unhealthy process of amending the statute by judicial interpretation. Where the language of a statute is clear in its application, the normal rule is that we are bound by it. There is, of course, a legitimate exception to this rule, which the Court invokes, and with which I have no quarrel. Where the plain language of the statute would lead to "patently absurd consequences," *United States v. Brown,* 333 U.S. 18, 27 (1948), that "Congress could not *possibly* have intended," *FBI v. Abramson,* 456 U.S. 615, 640 (1982) (O'Connor, J., dissenting) (emphasis added), we need not apply the language in such a fashion. When used in a proper manner, this narrow exception to our normal rule of statutory construction does not intrude upon the lawmaking powers of Congress, but rather demonstrates a respect for the coequal Legislative Branch, which we assume would not act in an absurd way.

This exception remains a legitimate tool of the Judiciary, however, only as long as the Court acts with self-discipline by limiting the exception to situations where the result of applying the plain language would be, in a genuine sense, absurd, *i.e.,* where it is quite impossible that Congress could have intended the result, and where the alleged absurdity is so clear as to be obvious to most anyone. . . . In today's opinion, however, the Court disregards the plain language of the statute not because its application would be patently absurd, but rather because, on the basis of its view of the legislative history, the Court is "fairly confident" that "FACA should [not] be construed to apply to the ABA Committee." I believe the Court's loose invocation of the "absurd result" canon of statutory construction creates too great a risk that the Court is exercising its own "WILL instead of JUDGMENT," with the consequence of "substituti[ng] [its own] pleasure to that of the legislative body." The Federalist No. 78 (A. Hamilton).

The Court makes only a passing effort to show that it would be absurd to apply the term "utilize" to the ABA Committee according to its commonsense meaning. It offers three examples that we can assume are meant to demonstrate this point: the application of FACA to an American Legion Post should the President visit that organization and happen to ask its opinion on some aspect of military policy; the application of FACA to the meetings of the National Association for the Advancement of

Colored People (NAACP) should the President seek its views in nominating Commissioners to the Equal Employment Opportunity Commission; and the application of FACA to the national committee of the President's political party should he consult it for advice and recommendations before picking his Cabinet.

None of these examples demonstrate the kind of absurd consequences that would justify departure from the plain language of the statute. A commonsense interpretation of the term "utilize" would not necessarily reach the kind of ad hoc contact with a private group that is contemplated by the Court's American Legion hypothetical. . . . As for the more regular use contemplated by the Court's examples concerning the NAACP and the national committee of the President's political party, it would not be at all absurd to say that, under the Court's hypothetical, these groups would be "utilized" by the President to obtain "advice or recommendations" on appointments, and therefore would fall within the coverage of the statute. Rather, what is troublesome about these examples is that they raise the very same serious constitutional questions that confront us here (and perhaps others as well). The Court confuses the two points. The fact that a particular application of the clear terms of a statute might be unconstitutional does not, in and of itself, render a straightforward application of the language absurd, so as to allow us to conclude that the statute does not apply. . . .

NOTES

(1)   JOHN F. MANNING, THE ABSURDITY DOCTRINE, 116 Harv. L. Rev. 2387 (2003): ". . . . The standard justification for the absurdity doctrine is straightforward. In a system marked by legislative supremacy (within constitutional boundaries), federal courts act as faithful agents of Congress. For that reason, legislative intent is widely assumed to be the touchstone of statutory interpretation. While the enacted text is generally considered the best evidence of such intent, Congress does not always accurately reduce its intentions to words because legislators necessarily draft statutes within the constraints of bounded foresight, limited resources, and imperfect language. The absurdity doctrine builds on that idea: If a given statutory application sharply contradicts commonly held social values, then the Supreme Court presumes that this absurd result reflects imprecise drafting that Congress could and would have corrected had the issue come up during the enactment process. Accordingly, standard interpretive doctrine (perhaps tautologically) defines an "absurd result" as an outcome so contrary to perceived social values that Congress could not have "intended" it. So understood, the absurdity doctrine is merely a version of strong intentionalism, which permits a court to adjust a clear statute in the rare case in which the court finds that the statutory text diverges from the legislature's true intent, as derived from sources such as the legislative history or the purpose of the statute as a whole.

"Despite the absurdity doctrine's deep roots, recent intellectual and judicial developments have undermined the doctrine's strong intentionalist foundations. Modern textualism, which emerged in the late twentieth century, maintains that, contrary to the tenets of strong intentionalism, respect for the legislative process requires judges to adhere to the precise terms of statutory texts. In particular, textualists argue that the (often unseen) complexities of the legislative process make it meaningless to speak of "legislative intent" as distinct from the meaning conveyed by a clearly expressed statutory command. . . .

"Notwithstanding these considerations, even the staunchest modern textualists still embrace and apply, even if rarely, at least some version of the absurdity doctrine. The Supreme Court, at least until recently, has followed suit. One can readily understand why. No one, of course, is for absurd results. And the examples most frequently cited to justify the absurdity doctrine seem to reflect a compelling, if imprecise, intuition. The currently dominant version of textualism seems relatively attractive precisely because the absurdity doctrine provides an all-purpose backstop to the principle that judges must follow a clear text wherever it takes them. But this version of textualism is, I believe, wrong. If textualists object to strong intentionalism in general, the absurdity doctrine is particularly problematic because it permits judges to alter clear statutory language based on vaguely defined social values, rather than sources (such as legislative history) that are more immediately linked to the legislative process. And if one accepts the previously discussed inferences from the constitutional structure, then one cannot simply re-rationalize the absurdity doctrine as an inherent attribute of judicial power. . . ."

(2) *A Problem to Consider.*

The Case of the Very Last Day

For a very long time, mining has been permitted on federal public lands. In order to keep track of the various mining claims, in 1976 Congress enacted the Federal Land Policy and Management Act. This Act established a recording system that required each year the claimant to file a notice of his intention to continue to hold the claim. The notice had to be filed, said Congress, "prior to December 31 of each year." Nothing in the Act or its legislative history explains why this language was chosen. The Act also provided that failure to file on time "shall be deemed conclusively to constitute an abandonment of the mining claim . . . by the owner." In the event, a miner filed his notice on December 31. Did he forfeit his claim?

(To find the authoritative answer, see United States v. Locke, 471 U.S. 84 (1985)).

d. Statutory Structure

The meaning of a statute may also be discerned from its structure. A frequent justification courts provide for a particular interpretation of a statutory provision is that an alternative would be in tension with other provisions located elsewhere in the statute. Some have read King v. Burwell, excerpted above, to be an exemplar of the use of structure as a tool of construction. If so, does King reveal the virtues—or the perils—of using such a tool?

ABBE R. GLUCK, IMPERFECT STATUTES, IMPERFECT COURTS: UNDERSTANDING CONGRESS'S PLAN IN THE ERA OF UNORTHODOX LAWMAKING, 129 Harv. L. Rev. 62 (2015): ". . . . Whereas the Court's recent statutory interpretation jurisprudence has been marked by a targeted focus on a few contested words, *King* responds by looking at the full picture, at Congress's "plan"—a term that itself sends a strong message about Congress's rationality and the inherent purposiveness and functionality of legislation. . . .

"Justice Scalia's dissent decries these moves as an activist departure from "the normal rules of interpretation." But imposing perfection on an imperfect statute, as the canons would have, would itself have been a kind of aggressive judicial legislation. Nor does *King's* emphasis on the "plan" mean a resort to legislative history or other subjective factors maligned by textualists. The opinion derives its understanding of the ACA's scheme from its text, structure, and the statute's own, codified "stated purposes" (not legislative history). . . . One way to understand *King* is that the Chief Justice chooses the holistic side of textualism, one that has always shared with purposivism the assumption that Congress legislates rationally, with means to an end. . . .

"The *King* challenge was . . . grounded in a particular view of the Court's inability, or unwillingness, to deal with legislative complexity. The challengers' vision of how the Court should see Congress, adopted by Justice Scalia in dissent, embraces a profound tension at the heart of modern statutory interpretation doctrine: Congress is assumed to be both irrational and perfect at once. Congress can never be understood, but when courts interpret statutes, they should hold Congress to standards of omniscience, precision, perfection, and simplicity. Textualism has deeply influenced this vision, but it is important to recognize that it has now come to be adopted by most judges, because it is embodied in the canons of interpretation that most judges (and all of the Justices) now deploy in virtually every statutory case. . . .

"Instead, the *King* majority responds with a different vision of both Congress's and the Court's capacities. Congress is imperfect, but it has a "plan"—the most important word in the opinion, because it signals that Congress is nevertheless rational, that its work product is comprehensible, and that a laser focus on a few words is not the right perspective. Plans, as Professor Scott Shapiro has noted, are meant to be read by someone; they form the basis of relationships between those who write the plans and those who implement them. Plans also provide the whole story, all the pieces of the big picture. The *King* majority elevates the Court by putting the Court (and not the agency) on the receiving end of the plan; tells us that Congress can trust the Court to understand it; takes a macro, functionalist, view of how all the pieces of the ACA work together; and concludes that the Court has a duty not to "undo what [Congress] has done."

"Many courtwatchers saw these moves and cried "purposivism!" Labels matter because the term "purposivism" today means something different, as a term of art, from the mere use of purpose in interpretation. The term is a loaded one—a textualist foil—and tends to be coupled with charges of legislative-history use, atextual interpretation, and judicial activism. Indeed, critics have accused the majority of "legislative gap-filling" for ignoring the "usual rules of interpretation." But what has escaped attention is that the kind of objectified, text-derived purpose the Court utilizes has textualist foundations, along with Legal Process ones. So does the concept of a comprehensive legislative plan. That concept has appeared in more than 100 cases in the U.S. Reports—it is a particular kind of purpose that derives from statutory text and structure, and so is different from the concept of "purposivism" as we have come to know it. . . .

"*King* seems to be invoking a third way. It does not seem a coincidence that the *King* majority reaches back to 1973 for a citation on the value of a statute's "stated purposes." It also cites many other pretextualist era decisions—decisions not commonly cited by the Court in statutory cases—to support its interpretive choices. The Court seems to be looking to entrenched, earlier ways of using text and purposiveness together—and choosing a different term (the "plan") to signal that it is doing something different—rather than aligning its view with one side or the other in the modern textualism-purposivism debates."

e. Legislative History

> **BABBITT v. SWEET HOME CHAPTER OF COMMUNITIES FOR A GREAT OREGON**
> *Notes on Legislative History*
> *The Case of the Educational Expert*

One of the biggest bones of contention between textualists and those who subscribe to other interpretive philosophies is the use of legislative history. Legislative history is a broad category that includes records of congressional debates, committee reports, and any other documents generated during the legislative process. (It should not be confused with the history of a piece of legislation in the broader sense of the social problem Congress meant to address or the events in the public arena that made the problem salient—matters to which judges of all stripes often refer.) Textualists (or at least the most diehard ones) shun the use of legislative history, while adherents to some other philosophies find it a useful tool for understanding the words of a statute. Consider the following materials.

BABBITT v. SWEET HOME CHAPTER OF COMMUNITIES FOR A GREAT OREGON

Supreme Court of the United States, 1995.
515 U.S. 687.

■ JUSTICE STEVENS delivered the opinion of the Court.

The Endangered Species Act of 1973 (ESA or Act) contains a variety of protections designed to save from extinction species that the Secretary of the Interior designates as endangered or threatened. Section 9 of the Act makes it unlawful for any person to "take" any endangered or threatened species. The Secretary has promulgated a regulation that defines the statute's prohibition on takings to include "significant habitat modification or degradation where it actually kills or injures wildlife." This case presents the question whether the Secretary exceeded his authority under the Act by promulgating that regulation.

I

Section 9(a)(1) of the Act provides the following protection for endangered species:

Except as provided in sections 1535(g)(2) and 1539 of this title, with respect to any endangered species of fish or wildlife listed pursuant to section 1533 of this title it is unlawful for any person subject to the jurisdiction of the United States to—. . .

(B) take any such species within the United States or the territorial sea of the United States. 16 U.S.C. § 1538(a)(1).

Section 3(19) of the Act defines the statutory term "take":

The term 'take' means to harass, harm, pursue, hunt, shoot, wound, kill, trap, capture, or collect, or to attempt to engage in any such conduct. 16 U.S.C. § 1532(19).

The Act does not further define the terms it uses to define "take." The Interior Department regulations that implement the statute, however, define the statutory term "harm":

Harm in the definition of 'take' in the Act means an act which actually kills or injures wildlife. Such act may include significant habitat modification or degradation where it actually kills or injures wildlife by significantly impairing essential behavioral patterns, including breeding, feeding, or sheltering. 50 CFR § 17.3 (1994).

This regulation has been in place since 1975.

A limitation on the § 9 "take" prohibition appears in § 10(a)(1)(B) of the Act, which Congress added by amendment in 1982. That section authorizes the Secretary to grant a permit for any taking otherwise prohibited by § 9(a)(1)(B) "if such taking is incidental to, and not the purpose of, the carrying out of an otherwise lawful activity."

In addition to the prohibition on takings, the Act provides several other protections for endangered species. Section 4 commands the Secretary to identify species of fish or wildlife that are in danger of extinction and to publish from time to time lists of all species he determines to be endangered or threatened. Section 5 authorizes the Secretary, in cooperation with the States, to acquire land to aid in preserving such species. Section 7 requires federal agencies to ensure that none of their activities, including the granting of licenses and permits, will jeopardize the continued existence of endangered species "or result in the destruction or adverse modification of habitat of such species which is determined by the Secretary . . . to be critical."

Respondents in this action are small landowners, logging companies, and families dependent on the forest products industries in the Pacific Northwest and in the Southeast, and organizations that represent their interests. They brought this declaratory judgment action against petitioners, the Secretary of the Interior and the Director of the Fish and Wildlife Service, in the United States District Court for the District of Columbia to challenge the statutory validity of the Secretary's regulation defining "harm," particularly the inclusion of habitat modification and degradation in the definition. Respondents challenged the regulation on its face. Their complaint alleged that application of the "harm" regulation to the red-cockaded woodpecker, an endangered species, and the northern spotted owl, a threatened species, had injured them economically. . . .

II

. . . The text of the Act provides three reasons for concluding that the Secretary's interpretation is reasonable. First, an ordinary understanding of the word "harm" supports it. The dictionary definition of the verb form of "harm" is "to cause hurt or damage to: injure." Webster's Third New International Dictionary 1034 (1966). In the context of the ESA, that definition naturally encompasses habitat modification that results in actual injury or death to members of an endangered or threatened species. . . .

Second, the broad purpose of the ESA supports the Secretary's decision to extend protection against activities that cause the precise harms Congress enacted the statute to avoid. . . .

Third, the fact that Congress in 1982 authorized the Secretary to issue permits for takings that § 9(a)(1)(B) would otherwise prohibit, "if such taking is incidental to, and not the purpose of, the carrying out of an otherwise lawful activity," strongly suggests that Congress understood § 9(a)(1)(B) to prohibit indirect as well as deliberate takings . . .

III

Our conclusion that the Secretary's definition of "harm" rests on a permissible construction of the ESA gains further support from the legislative history of the statute. The Committee Reports accompanying the bills that became the ESA do not specifically discuss the meaning of "harm," but they make clear that Congress intended "take" to apply broadly to cover indirect as well as purposeful actions. The Senate Report stressed that " '[t]ake' is defined . . . in the broadest possible manner to include every conceivable way in which a person can 'take' or attempt to 'take' any fish or wildlife." S. Rep. No. 93–307, p. 7 (1973). U.S. Code Cong. & Admin. News 1973, pp. 2989, 2995. The House Report stated that "the broadest possible terms" were used to define restrictions on takings. H.R. Rep. No. 93–412, p. 15 (1973). The House Report underscored the breadth of the "take" definition by noting that it included "harassment, whether intentional or not." *Id.* at 11 (emphasis added). The Report explained that the definition "would allow, for example, the Secretary to regulate or prohibit the activities of birdwatchers where the effect of those activities might disturb the birds and make it difficult for them to hatch or raise their young." *Ibid.* These comments, ignored in the dissent's welcome but selective foray into legislative history, support the Secretary's interpretation that the term "take" in § 9 reached far more than the deliberate actions of hunters and trappers.

Two endangered species bills, S. 1592 and S. 1983, were introduced in the Senate and referred to the Commerce Committee. Neither bill included the word "harm" in its definition of "take," although the definitions otherwise closely resembled the one that appeared in the bill as ultimately enacted. *See* Hearings on S. 1592 and S. 1983 before the Subcommittee on Environment of the Senate Committee on Commerce, 93d Cong., 1st Sess., pp. 7, 27 (1973) (hereinafter Hearings). Senator Tunney, the floor manager of the bill in the Senate, subsequently introduced a floor amendment that added "harm" to the definition, noting that this and accompanying amendments would "help to achieve the purposes of the bill." 119 Cong. Rec. 25683 (1973). Respondents argue that the lack of debate about the amendment that added "harm" counsels in favor of a narrow interpretation. We disagree. An obviously broad word that the Senate went out of its way to add to an important statutory definition is precisely the sort of provision that deserves a respectful reading.

The definition of "take" that originally appeared in S. 1983 differed from the definition as ultimately enacted in one other significant respect: It included "the destruction, modification, or curtailment of [the] habitat or range" of fish and wildlife. Hearings, at 27. Respondents make much of the fact that the Commerce Committee removed this phrase from the "take" definition before S. 1983 went to the floor. *See* 119 Cong. Rec. 25663 (1973). We do not find that fact especially significant. The legislative materials contain no indication why the habitat protection provision was deleted. That provision differed greatly from the regulation at issue today. Most notably, the habitat protection provision in S. 1983 would have applied far more broadly than the regulation does because it made adverse habitat modification a categorical violation of the "take" prohibition, unbounded by the regulation's limitation to habitat modifications that actually kill or injure wildlife. The S. 1983 language also failed to qualify "modification" with the regulation's limiting adjective "significant." We do not believe the Senate's unelaborated disavowal of the provision in S. 1983 undermines the reasonableness of the more moderate habitat protection in the Secretary's "harm" regulation.

The history of the 1982 amendment that gave the Secretary authority to grant permits for "incidental" takings provides further support for his reading of the Act. The House Report expressly states that "[b]y use of the word 'incidental' the Committee intends to cover situations in which it is known that a taking will occur if the other activity is engaged in but such taking is incidental to, and not the purpose of, the activity." H.R. Rep. No. 97–567, p. 31 (1982). U.S. Code Cong. & Admin. News 1982, pp. 2807, 2831. This reference to the foreseeability of incidental takings undermines respondents' argument that the 1982 amendment covered only accidental killings of endangered and threatened animals that might occur in the course of hunting or trapping other animals. Indeed, Congress had habitat modification directly in mind: Both the Senate Report and the House Conference Report identified as the model for the permit process a cooperative state-federal response to a case in California where a development project threatened incidental harm to a species of endangered butterfly by modification of its habitat. *See* S. Rep. No. 97–418, p. 10 (1982); H.R. Conf. Rep. No. 97–835, pp. 30–32 (1982). Thus, Congress in 1982 focused squarely on the aspect of the "harm" regulation at issue in this litigation. Congress' implementation of a permit program is consistent with the Secretary's interpretation of the term "harm." . . . .

[The judgment of the Court of Appeals, favoring the landowners, is reversed.]

■ JUSTICE SCALIA, with whom THE CHIEF JUSTICE and JUSTICE THOMAS join, dissenting.

. . . [T]he Court maintains that the legislative history of the 1973 Act supports the Secretary's definition. Even if legislative history were a legitimate and reliable tool of interpretation (which I shall assume in order to rebut the Court's claim); and even if it could appropriately be resorted to when the enacted text is as clear as this, here it shows quite the opposite of what the Court says. I shall not pause to discuss the Court's reliance on such statements in the Committee Reports as "[t]ake' is defined . . . in the broadest possible manner to include every conceivable way in which a person can 'take' or attempt to 'take' any fish or wildlife." S. Rep. No. 93–307, p. 7 (1973) U.S. Code Cong. & Admin. News 1973, pg. 2995. This sort of empty flourish—to the effect that "this statute means what it means all the way"—counts for little even when enacted into the law itself.

Much of the Court's discussion of legislative history is devoted to two items: first, the Senate floor manager's introduction of an amendment that added the word "harm" to the definition of "take," with the observation that (along with other amendments) it would "help to achieve the purposes of the bill"; second, the relevant Committee's removal from the definition of a provision stating that "take" includes "the destruction, modification or curtailment of [the] habitat or range" of fish and wildlife. The Court inflates the first and belittles the second, even though the second is on its face far more pertinent. But this elaborate inference from various pre-enactment actions and inactions is quite unnecessary, since we have direct evidence of what those who brought the legislation to the floor thought it meant—evidence as solid as any ever to be found in legislative history, but which the Court banishes to a footnote.

Both the Senate and House floor managers of the bill explained it in terms which leave no doubt that the problem of habitat destruction on private lands was to be solved principally by the land acquisition program of § 1534, while § 1538 solved a different problem altogether— the problem of takings. Senator Tunney stated:

> *Through [the] land acquisition provisions, we will be able to conserve habitats necessary to protect fish and wildlife from further destruction.*
>
> Although most endangered species are threatened primarily by the destruction of their natural habitats, a significant portion of these animals are subject to *predation by man for commercial, sport, consumption, or other purposes.* The provisions of [the bill] would prohibit the commerce in or the importation, exportation, or taking of endangered species . . . .
> 119 Cong. Rec. 25669 (1973) (emphasis added).

The House floor manager, Representative Sullivan, put the same thought in this way:

> [T]he principal threat to animals stems from destruction of their habitat. . . . *[The bill] will meet this problem by providing funds for acquisition of critical habitat.* . . . It will also enable the Department of Agriculture to cooperate with willing landowners who desire to assist in the protection of endangered species, *but who are understandably unwilling to do so at excessive cost to themselves.*
>
> Another hazard to endangered species arises from those who would *capture or kill them for pleasure or profit.* There is no way that the Congress can make it less pleasurable for a person to take an animal, but we can certainly make it less profitable for them to do so. *Id.* at 30162 (emphasis added).

Habitat modification and takings, in other words, were viewed as different problems, addressed by different provisions of the Act. The Court really has no explanation for these statements. All it can say is that "[n]either statement even suggested that [the habitat acquisition funding provision in § 1534] would be the Act's exclusive remedy for habitat modification by private landowners or that habitat modification by private landowners stood outside the ambit of [§ 1538]." That is to say, the statements are not as bad as they might have been. Little in life is. They are, however, quite bad enough to destroy the Court's legislative-history case, since they display the clear understanding (1) that habitat modification is separate from "taking," and (2) that habitat destruction on private lands is to be remedied by public acquisition, and not by making particular unlucky landowners incur "excessive cost to themselves." The Court points out triumphantly that they do not display the understanding (3) that the land acquisition program is "the [Act's] only response to habitat modification." Of course not, since that is not so (all public lands are subject to habitat-modification restrictions); but (1) and (2) are quite enough to exclude the Court's interpretation. They identify the land acquisition program as the Act's only response to habitat modification by private landowners, and thus do not in the least "contradic[t]," the fact that § 1536 prohibits habitat modification by federal agencies.

. . . [T]he Court seeks support from a provision that was added to the Act in 1982, the year after the Secretary promulgated the current regulation. The provision states:

> [T]he Secretary may permit, under such terms and conditions as he shall prescribe—. . .

> any taking otherwise prohibited by section 1538(a)(1)(B) . . . if such taking is incidental to, and not the purpose of, the carrying out of an otherwise lawful activity." 16 U.S.C. § 1539(a)(1)(B).

This provision does not, of course, implicate our doctrine that reenactment of a statutory provision ratifies an extant judicial or administrative interpretation, for neither the taking prohibition in § 1538(a)(1)(B) nor the definition in § 1532(19) was reenacted. The Court claims, however, that the provision "strongly suggests that Congress understood [§ 1538(a)(1)(B)] to prohibit indirect as well as deliberate takings." That would be a valid inference if habitat modification were the only substantial "otherwise lawful activity" that might incidentally and nonpurposefully cause a prohibited "taking." Of course it is not. This provision applies to the many otherwise lawful takings that incidentally take a protected species—as when fishing for unprotected salmon also takes an endangered species of salmon. . . .

This is enough to show, in my view, that the 1982 permit provision does not support the regulation. I must acknowledge that the Senate Committee Report on this provision, and the House Conference Committee Report, clearly contemplate that it will enable the Secretary to permit environmental modification. *See* S. Rep. No. 97–418, p. 10 (1982); H.R. Conf. Rep. No. 97–835, pp. 30–32 (1982). But the text of the amendment cannot possibly bear that asserted meaning, when placed within the context of an Act that must be interpreted (as we have seen) not to prohibit private environmental modification. The neutral language of the amendment cannot possibly alter that interpretation, nor can its legislative history be summoned forth to contradict, rather than clarify, what is in its totality an unambiguous statutory text. There is little fear, of course, that giving no effect to the relevant portions of the Committee Reports will frustrate the real-life expectations of a majority of the Members of Congress. If they read and relied on such tedious detail on such an obscure point (it was not, after all, presented as a revision of the statute's prohibitory scope, but as a discretionary-waiver provision) the Republic would be in grave peril. . . .

NOTES ON LEGISLATIVE HISTORY

(1) *What Counts?* WILLIAM N. ESKRIDGE, JR., THE NEW TEXTUALISM, 37 UCLA L. Rev. 621 (1990): ". . . [T]he Court has worked out a rough hierarchy of evidence to resolve conflicts [between portions of the legislative history of a statute]. The hierarchy is based upon the comparative reliability of each source: How likely does this source reflect the views or assumptions of the enacting Congress? Is there a danger of strategic manipulation by individual Members or biased groups seeking to 'pack' the legislative history? How well-informed is the source? The figure below, which Professor Frickey and I have developed in teaching Legislation at the University of Minnesota School of Law and at the Georgetown University Law Center (respectively), reflects this hierarchy.

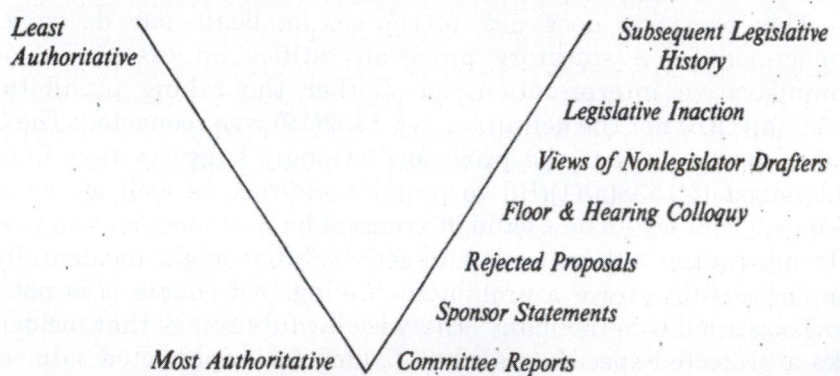

HIERARCHY OF LEGISLATIVE HISTORY SOURCES
(THE FRICKEY & ESKRIDGE MINI-FUNNEL)

Least Authoritative

Subsequent Legislative History

Legislative Inaction

Views of Nonlegislator Drafters

Floor & Hearing Colloquy

Rejected Proposals

Sponsor Statements

Most Authoritative   Committee Reports

1. Committee Reports

". . . Committee reports are the most frequently cited and relied-upon sources of legislative history, and in the Court's traditional view the most authoritative source. 'A committee report represents the considered and collective understanding of those Congressmen involved in drafting and studying proposed legislation. Floor debates reflect at best the understanding of individual Congressmen. It would take extensive and thoughtful debate to detract from the plain thrust of a committee report . . . .' [Citations in article to quotes from Court cases are omitted.] Committee reports are often the best evidence of bicameral agreement, either because the House and Senate reports are identical, or because a conference report explicates the chambers' resolution of differences.

2. Sponsor Statements

". . . Next only to committee reports in reliability are statements by sponsors and/or floor managers, and the Court relies on their statements routinely. '[R]emarks . . . of the sponsor of the language ultimately enacted, are an authoritative guide to the statute's construction,' because the sponsors are the Members of Congress most likely to know what the proposed legislation is all about, and other Members can be expected to pay special heed to their characterizations of the legislation. 'While the views of a sponsor of legislation are by no means conclusive, they are entitled to considerable weight, particularly in the absence of a committee report.'

3. Rejected Proposals

". . . 'Few principles of statutory construction are more compelling than the proposition that Congress does not intend sub silentio to enact statutory language that it has earlier discarded in favor of other language.' . . . This is a slight overstatement of the Court's practice. Oftentimes, the rejection of proposed language by the committee, on the floor of the House or Senate, or in conference is quite probative, since it is direct evidence that Congress considered an issue and agreed not to adopt a specified policy. But other times it is unclear that the rejection was truly a referendum on the issue later before the Court. The Court usually does not rely on evidence concerning rejected proposals as its primary legislative history.

4. Floor and Hearing Colloquy

" 'In construing laws [the Court has] been extremely wary of testimony before committee hearings and of debates on the floor of Congress save for precise analyses of statutory phrases by the sponsors of the proposed laws.' Thus, statements by legislators at hearings or on the floor are not as authoritative as those of sponsors and floor managers, unless the speakers can be identified as 'players' on that particular bill. According to the conventional wisdom, nonplayers are less likely to know what the consensus view is on the bill, and are more likely to behave strategically (engaging in the famed 'planned colloquy'). Further, the views of those unsupportive of the proposed legislation 'are no authoritative guide to the construction of legislation. It is the sponsors that we look to when the meaning of the statutory words is in doubt.' This conventional wisdom has been relaxed somewhat in the last twenty years, for the Court frequently looks to legislative colloquy, especially to discern the general assumptions made at the time a law was enacted. Moreover, where the sponsor's statements are either too general or suspicious, the Court will rely on more specific colloquy instead. Even the views of opponents have sometimes been considered.

5. Nonlegislative Drafters and Sponsors

"In [two Supreme Court cases], the testimony of nonlegislative supporters of the legislation (executive officials, law professors, environmental groups) was counted as relevant but not critical. Such use is typical of this evidence. The Court will usually invoke these statements as further evidence in support of conclusions gleaned from the statutory text, committee reports, and sponsors' statements. Nonlegislator evidence will be most important in cases where it is clear that the statute was a careful compromise reached outside the legislative process and merely ratified by the legislature, and sometimes in cases where there is virtually no other evidence.

6.   Legislative Silence and Subsequent History

"For the reasons developed above, evidence of legislative silence and subsequent history is usually too ambiguous to count as legislative history, but in some contexts the sources are considered by the Court. '[W]hile the views of subsequent Congresses cannot override the unmistakable intent of the enacting one, such views are entitled to significant weight, and particularly so when the precise intent of the enacting Congress is obscure.' Much the same can be said of the dog that doesn't bark argument: Legislative silence will usually be supporting evidence of legislative intent and will be the main evidence only when there is virtually no other evidence of legislative intent."

(2) *A Bad Idea.* J~ohn~ F. M~anning~, T~extualism~ A~s~ A N~ondelegation~ D~octrine~, 97 Colum. L. Rev. 673 (1997): ". . . . In contrast with an old Supreme Court case that contains the common law meaning of a term of legal art, legislative history is endogenous to the legislative process; as an exercise of delegated law elaboration authority, it violates an important prophylactic safeguard of bicameralism and presentment—the constitutional choice to deny Congress authority to construe its own laws, except through the enactment of further law. When Congress enacts a statute containing an externally defined term of art, it takes the details of the art as it finds them. When, however, the Court gives authoritative weight to a committee's subjective understanding of statutory meaning (announced outside the statutory text), it empowers Congress to specify statutory details—without the structurally-mandated cost of getting two Houses of Congress and the President to approve them. Although neither a pre-enactment Supreme Court case nor a committee report formally goes through bicameralism and presentment, crediting a legislatively created source of meaning offers Congress a more substantial temptation to shift the specification of detail outside the cumbersome legislative process.

"To appreciate the importance of adopting interpretive rules designed to preserve the integrity of the constitutionally prescribed legislative process, it is helpful to recall the context that gave rise to the inclusion of bicameralism and presentment in the Constitution. Adopted in an era when many had lost confidence in the capacity of (unchecked) legislatures to safeguard liberty and respect law, the constitutional checks of bicameralism and presentment, codified in Article I, Section 7, comprised a key element of the Constitution's scheme to preserve individual liberty. Those requirements serve evident and well-understood purposes, which require only brief mention here. First, by dividing the legislative power between two chambers, bicameralism and presentment make it more difficult for factions to usurp legislative authority, ensuring a diffusion of governmental power and preserving the liberty and security of the governed. In this regard, the division of legislative power into distinct parts effectively operates 'to balance interest against interest, ambition against ambition, the combinations and spirit of dominion of one body against the like combinations and spirit of another.' Second, the requirements of Article I, Section 7 promote caution and deliberation; by mandating that each piece of legislation clear an intricate process involving distinct constitutional actors, bicameralism and presentment reduce the incidence of hasty and ill-considered legislation. Third, by relying on multiple, potentially antagonistic constitutional decisionmakers, the legislative process prescribed by Article I often produces conflict and friction, enhancing the prospects for a full and open discussion of matters of public import.

"These protections come at considerable expense. By design, they raise the decision costs associated with lawmaking, safeguarding liberty through a deliberate sacrifice of governmental efficiency. The Federalists recognized as much. They acknowledged that 'this complicated check on legislation may in some instances be injurious as well as beneficial,' and that 'the power of preventing bad laws includes that of preventing good ones.' However, they saw the risks of ill-advised governmental action as far greater than the risks of inaction. Madison thus contended that 'the facility and excess of law-making,' and not the converse, 'seem to be the diseases to which our governments are most liable.' Hamilton similarly contended that '[t]he injury which may possibly be done by defeating a few good laws will be amply compensated by the advantage of preventing a number of bad ones.' This trade-off, manifest in the constitutional structure, did not go unnoticed in the debate over the Constitution and was in fact expressly conceded by its strongest defenders. . . .

"Textualism's simple ambition is to require legislators to accept responsibility for their legislative acts. The authoritative use of legislative history undermines this objective; as things now stand, no legislator ever has to vote for any piece of legislative history. No legislator (other than a member of the relevant committee) is responsible for the understandings expressed in a committee report. No legislator, other than the sponsor, is responsible for the contents of a sponsor's explanation of a bill. Yet these documents may prove decisive in interpretation . . ."

(3) ***A Good Idea.*** STEPHEN BREYER, ON THE USES OF LEGISLATIVE HISTORY IN INTERPRETING STATUTES, 65 S. Cal. L. Rev. 845 (1992): "[One constitutional argument against the use of legislative history] concerns the Constitution's requirements for enacting a law. A bill must pass both houses of Congress and obtain the President's signature or a veto override. The result, says the Constitution, is a statute; and that statute, not a floor speech or committee report or testimony or presidential message or congressional 'intent,' is the law. The use of legislative history, according to this argument, tends to make these other matters—report language and floor speeches—the 'law' even though they had received neither a majority vote nor a presidential signature. . . .

"The 'statute-is-the-only-law' argument misses the point. No one claims that legislative history is a statute, or even that, in any strong sense, it is 'law.' Rather, legislative history is helpful in trying to understand the meaning of the words that do make up the statute or the 'law.' A judge cannot interpret the words of an ambiguous statute without looking beyond its words for the words have simply ceased to provide univocal guidance to decide the case at hand. Can the judge, for example, ignore a dictionary or the historical interpretive practice of the agency that customarily applies some words? Is a dictionary or an historic agency interpretive practice 'law?' It is 'law' only in a weak sense that does not claim the status of a statute, and in a sense that violates neither the letter nor the spirit of the Constitution. . . .

(4) ROBERT A. KATZMANN, JUDGING STATUTES 48 (2014): "As to constraining judicial preferences, it seems to me that excluding legislative history when interpreting ambiguous statutes is just as likely to expand a judge's discretion as reduce it. When a statute is unambiguous, resorting to legislative history is generally not necessary; in that circumstance, the inquiry ordinarily ends. But when a statute is ambiguous, barring legislative history leaves a judge only with words that could be interpreted in a variety of ways without contextual guidance as to what legislators may have thought. Lacking such guidance increases the probability that a judge will construe a law in a manner that the legislators did not intend. It is seemingly inconsistent that textualists, who look to such extratextual materials as the records of the Constitutional Convention and *The Federalist* in interpreting the Constitution, would look askance at the use of legislative history sources when interpreting legislation."

(5) *A Problem.* To decide between the various pro or con claims regarding the use of legislative history, and about how legislative history intersects with other modes of statutory interpretation, it is helpful to have some experience in using it. What follows is a statutory problem and the legislative history that might be relevant. The history has been somewhat shortened for comprehensibility within the usual dimensions of a law school class, but the editors have removed nothing of consequence for the problem and hopefully have left enough of the whole to give you an appreciation for the lawyerly tasks involved.

The Case of the Educational Expert[2]

The statute involved in this case is the Handicapped Children's Protection Act of 1986, an amendment to the Education for All Handicapped Children Act of 1975 (EAHCA), which was also then known as the Education of the Handicapped Act (EHA). Sympathetic to contemporary reactions to the word "Handicapped," Congress renamed the whole act the Individuals with Disabilities Education Act (IDEA) when reenacting it in 1990 for reasons unimportant to the issues

---

[2]   These materials are adapted from Peter L. Strauss, Congress at Work (Foundation 2016).

addressed here. Because it predates that welcome change, the legislative history that follows does use the term "handicapped," and the authors hope readers sensitive to this issue will accept that they, like the Congress, would today have chosen a different descriptor.

The EAHCA offered to the states federal funds in exchange for their establishing programs that would assure mentally and physically disabled children appropriate educational opportunities. It also required the states to establish administrative procedures for resolving any disputes about the services parents claimed for their children. And it authorized federal judicial review of the outcomes of these procedures and permitted the reviewing court to "grant such relief as the court determines is appropriate."

When parents who had successfully challenged a school board's rejection of their child's need for special education sought reimbursement of their attorney's fees, the Supreme Court held that this remedy was not available. Smith v. Robinson, 468 U.S. 992 (1984). There the Court reaffirmed the Alyeska decision—see Note 1 p. 67 above—despite both the general congressional reaction to that decision and the intervention of statutory changes that might have supported an award in this particular domain. The majority emphasized the need for Congress to be explicit in effecting any departures from "the American Rule." The opinions in the case discussed only "attorneys' fees." Justice Brennan bitterly dissented for himself and Justices Marshall and Stevens, 468 U.S. at 1030–31:

> . . . [W]ith today's decision coming as it does after Congress has spoken on the subject of attorney's fees, Congress will now have to take the time to revisit the matter. And until it does, the handicapped children of this country whose difficulties are compounded by discrimination and by other deprivations of constitutional rights will have to pay the costs. It is at best ironic that the Court has managed to impose this burden on handicapped children in the course of interpreting a statute wholly intended to promote the educational rights of those children.

Two years later, Congress *did* revisit the matter, enacting the Handicapped Children's Protection Act of 1986. It definitely authorized courts to award attorney's fees in these situations.

But that is not the problem you are facing. You are representing the parents of a high school student with special needs. The local school district contended that his needs could be met in the local high school; his parents contended that the appropriate individualized education program for their son, under the now-renamed Individuals with Disabilities Education Act, was in a specialized private school. On review, you have succeeded in convincing the district court that under the IDEA the school district should pay for him to attend that private school. In other words, you won—except that it cost nearly $30,000 in fees for the services of an expert educational consultant who assisted you throughout the proceedings. Her testing and testimony was, if anything, more important than your own help in successfully contesting the adequacy of what the school board proposed to do for the child's special education needs. Can that $30,000, in addition to your own fees, be recovered?

Here's the relevant statute, as finally enacted, in full:

THE HANDICAPPED CHILDREN'S PROTECTION ACT OF 1986

Sec. 1.   This Act may be cited as the "Handicapped Children's Protection Act of 1986".

Sec. 2.   Section 615(e)(4) of the Education of the Handicapped Act is amended by inserting "(A)" after the paragraph designation and by adding at the end thereof the following new subparagraphs:

"(B) In any action or proceeding brought under this subsection, the court, in its discretion, may award reasonable attorneys' fees as part of the costs to the parents or guardian of a handicapped child or youth who is the prevailing party.

"(C) For the purpose of this subsection, fees awarded under this subsection shall be based on rates prevailing in the community in which the action or proceeding arose for the kind and quality of services furnished. No bonus or multiplier may be used in calculating the fees awarded under this subsection.

"(D) No award of attorneys' fees and related costs may be made in any action or proceeding under this subsection for services performed subsequent to the time of a written offer of settlement to a parent or guardian, if—

"i)   the offer is made within the time prescribed by Rule 68 of the Federal Rules of Civil Procedure or, in the case of an administrative proceeding, at any time more than ten days before the proceeding begins;

"ii) the offer is not accepted within ten days; and

"iii) the court or administrative officer finds that the relief finally obtained by the parents or guardian is not more favorable to the parents or guardian than the offer of settlement.

"(E) Notwithstanding the provisions of subparagraph (D), an award of attorneys' fees and related costs may be made to a parent or guardian who is the prevailing party and who was substantially justified in rejecting the settlement offer.

"(F) Whenever the court finds that—

"i)   the parent or guardian, during the course of the action or proceeding, unreasonably protracted the final resolution of the controversy;

"ii) the amount of the attorneys' fees otherwise authorized to be awarded unreasonably exceeds the hourly rate prevailing in the community for similar services by attorneys of reasonably comparable skill, experience, and reputation; or

"(iii) the time spent and legal services furnished were excessive considering the nature of the action or proceeding the court shall reduce, accordingly, the amount of the attorneys' fees awarded under this subsection.

"(G) The provisions of subparagraph (F) shall not apply in any action or proceeding if the court finds that the State or local educational agency unreasonably protracted the final resolution of the action or proceeding or there was a violation of section 615 of this Act."

Sec. 3.   Section 615 of the Education of the Handicapped Act is amended by adding at the end thereof the following new subsection.

"(f) Nothing in this title shall be construed to restrict or limit the rights, procedures, and remedies available under the Constitution, title V of the Rehabilitation Act of 1973, or other Federal statutes protecting the rights of handicapped children and youth, except that before the filing of a civil action under such laws seeking relief that is also available under this part, the procedures under subsections (b)(2) and (c) shall be exhausted to the same extent as would be required had the action been brought under this part."

Sec. 4. (a)   The Comptroller General of the United States, through the General Accounting Office, shall conduct a study of the impact of the amendments to the Education of the Handicapped Act made under section 2 of this Act. Not later than June 30, 1989, the Comptroller General shall submit a report containing the findings of such study to the Committee on Education and Labor of the House of Representatives and the Committee on Labor and Human Resources of the Senate. The Comptroller General shall conduct a formal briefing for such Committees on the status of the study not later than March 1, 1988. Such report shall include the information described in subsection (b).

(b) The report authorized under subsection (a) shall include the following information:

(1) The number, in the aggregate and by State, of written decisions under section 615 (b)(2) and (c) transmitted to State advisory panels under section 615(d)(4) for fiscal years 1984 through 1988, the prevailing party in each such decision, and the type of complaint. For fiscal year 1986, the report shall designate which decisions concern complaints filed after the date of the enactment of this Act.

(2) the number, in the aggregate and by State, of civil actions brought under section 615(e)(2), the prevailing party in each action, and the type of complaint for fiscal years 1984 through 1988. For fiscal year 1986 the report shall designate which decisions concern complaints filed after the date of enactment.

(3) Data, for a geographically representative selective sample of states, indicating (A) the specific amount of attorneys' fees, costs, and expenses awarded to the prevailing party, in each action and proceeding under section 615(e)(4)(B) from the date of the enactment of this Act through fiscal year 1988, and the range of such fees, costs, and expenses awarded in the actions and proceedings under such section, categorized by type of complaint and (B) for the same sample as in (A) the number of hours spent by personnel, including attorneys and consultants, involved in the action or proceeding, and expenses incurred by the parents and the State educational agency and local educational agency.

(4) Data, for a geographically representative sample of States, on the experience of educational agencies in resolving complaints informally under section 615(b)(2), from the date of the enactment of this Act through fiscal year 1988.

Sec. 5.   The amendment made by section 2 shall apply with respect to actions or proceedings brought under section 615(e) of the Education of the Handicapped Act after July 3, 1984, and actions or proceedings brought prior to July 4, 1984, under such section which was pending on July 4, 1984."

––––––––––––

Having thought about the possible uses of the statute you and your opponent might make, you then looked to see what the legislative history looked like. You found potentially relevant history in the following places:

- Hearings in both Houses regarding potential legislation to overrule the result in Smith v. Robinson.

- Report of the Senate Committee on Labor and Human Resources to accompany proposed Senate bill S. 415.

- Senate debate regarding S. 415.

- Report of the House Committee on Education and Labor to accompany proposed House bill H.R. 1523.

- House debate regarding H.R. 1523.

- Conference Committee Report on the Handicapped Children's Protection Act of 1986.

a.   Hearings in both Houses regarding potential legislation to overrule the result in Smith v. Robinson.

Committees in both House and Senate held hearings on bills intended to overrule *Smith v. Robinson* within a year of the decision. The House hearings are not conveniently available. In the Senate, subcommittee chair Weicker (R. Conn.) and three other Senators appeared in support of the bill, and Senator Thurmond (R. S.C.) made a brief appearance counseling caution (but not opposition) in light of possible financial consequences. Two panels testified on behalf of proponents of the measure; the committee called no opponents as witnesses. The National Association of School Boards, however, was in the audience and submitted a statement suggesting concerns with possible financial consequences for local boards required to fund parents' attorneys and the impact of funding on the nature of the underlying process—that it might become more adversarial.

In the hearings overall you would find emphatic repudiation of *Smith,* attention to the importance and expense of attorneys, and no particular concern about the components of litigating cost. As close as one gets to detailed attention to the components of costs are statements like this one from the letter of The [Florida] Governor's Commission on Advocacy for Persons with Disabilities supporting the proposed draft:

> Unfortunately, legal process is also highly technical, costly, time consuming, and largely inaccessible to the average family. The extent of discovery and expert testimony that can be utilized in a typical educational due process hearing can rival a medical malpractice case.

Handicapped Children's Protection Act of 1985, Sen. Comm. on Labor and Human Resources, Subcomm. on the Handicapped 92, 93 (Thurs. May 16, 1985).

b. Report of the Senate Committee on Labor and Human Resources to accompany proposed Senate bill S. 415.

99TH CONGRESS   SENATE   REPORT 99–112
    1st Session

Handicapped Children's Protection Act of 1985

———

July 25 (legislative day, July 16), 1985.—Ordered to be printed

———

Mr. Hatch, from the Committee on Labor and Human Resources, submitted the following

REPORT

(To accompany S. 415) together with ADDITIONAL VIEWS

The Committee on Labor and Human Resources, to which was referred the bill (S. 415) to amend the Education of the Handicapped Act to authorize the award of reasonable attorneys' fees to certain prevailing parties; and to clarify the effect of the Education of the Handicapped Act on rights, procedures, and remedies under other laws relating to the prohibition of discrimination, having considered the same, reports favorably thereon with an amendment and recommends that the bill as amended do pass.

I.   Background of S. 415

In passing the Education of All Handicapped Children Act of 1975 (Public Law 94–142) Congress indicated that "it is in the national interest that the Federal Government assist State and local efforts to provide programs to meet the educational needs of handicapped children in order to assure equal protection of the law." In those States which accept funds under Part B of the Education of the Handicapped Act [EHA], as amended by Public Law 94–142, the Act established an enforceable right to a free appropriate public education for all handicapped children and established due process procedures, including the right to judicial review, to protect those rights.

Congress' original intent was that due process procedures, including the right to litigation if that became necessary, be available to all parents. On July 5, 1984, the Supreme Court, in Smith v. Robinson, 468 U.S. 992, 104 S.Ct. 3457 (1984), determined that Congress intended that the EHA provide the exclusive source of rights and remedies in special education cases covered by that act. The effect of this decision was to preclude parents from bringing special education cases under section 504 of the Rehabilitation Act of 1973, and recovering attorney's fees available under section 505 of that act, where relief was available under the EHA. . . .

The situation which has resulted from the Smith v. Robinson decision was summarized by Justices Brennan, Marshall, and Stevens in their dissenting opinion: "Congress will now have to take the time to revisit the matter." Seeking to clarify the intent of Congress with respect to the educational rights of handicapped children guaranteed by the EHA, the Handicapped Children's Protection Act of 1985 was introduced on February 6, 1985. The Subcommittee on the Handicapped held a hearing on March 16, 1985, to receive testimony from parents of handicapped children, attorneys who have represented parents of handicapped children in EHA litigation (including the Smith v. Robinson case), and Edwin Martin, former Assistant Secretary of Education for Special Education and Rehabilitative Services. Written testimony was also received from the National School Boards Association and various parent, advocacy, and professional education groups. On June 11, 1985, the Subcommittee unanimously reported S. 415 with amendment to the full Committee. On July 10, 1985, the full Committee unanimously moved to order the bill, as amended, reported to the Senate.

II.   Section-by Section Analysis

S. 415 as reported by the full Committee consists of six sections. Throughout the remainder of this report the word "school" should be interpreted to include State or local educational agencies or intermediate educational units, as appropriate; the phrase "parent or legal representative" includes a person acting as a parent of a child or a surrogate parent who has been appointed in accordance with section 615(b)(1) of the EHA; and the words "reasonable attorney's fees" simply mean fees appropriate in the circumstances of each case as determined by court.

Section 1 provides that this Act be cited as the Handicapped Children's Protection Act of 1985.

Section 2 provides for the award of reasonable attorney's fees to prevailing parents in EHA civil actions and in administrative proceedings to parents in certain specified circumstances.

Section 3 provides that the court cases will be heard de novo if attorneys are not used at the due process hearing level.

Section 4 provides that the EHA does not limit the applicability of other laws which protect handicapped children and youth except that when a parent brings suit under another law when that suit could have been brought under the EHA, the parent will be required to exhaust EHA administrative remedies to the same degree as would have been required had the suit been under the EHA.

Section 5 authorizes parent training centers under section 631 of the EHA to train parents better to understand and participate in due process proceedings and requires the establishment of at least one parent training center in each State.

Section 6 established a general effective date as the date of enactment and also authorizes courts retroactively to award attorney's fees for civil court actions to parents who prevailed in EHA cases pending on or brought after the date of the Smith v. Robinson decision.

IV. Tabulation of Votes Cast in Committee

The motion to report the bill favorably to the Senate was passed unanimously by voice of the Committee. An earlier motion to strike the provision placing conditions upon fee awards for publicly funded attorneys who represent prevailing parents in EHA cases was defeated by a vote of 9 to 7.

V.   Regulatory Impact Statement

The Committee has determined that there will be minimal increase in regulatory burden imposed by this bill. While new regulations will need to be promulgated to reflect the new provisions in the bill, those regulations build on existing regulations.

VI. Changes in Existing Law

In compliance with rule XXVI paragraph 12 of the Standard Rules of the Senate, the following provides a print of the statute or the part or section thereof to be amended or replaced (existing law proposed to be omitted is enclosed in black brackets, new matter is printed in italic, existing law in which no change is proposed is shown in roman):

Education of the Handicapped Act

* * *

[The Report then sets out the language of the bill as approved by the full committee. Quite complex and for our problem's purpose largely irrelevant, the Report included the following language from the bill as the full committee had approved it:

Sec. 615(f)   The provisions of section 615A shall govern the award of a reasonable attorney's fee, reasonable witness fees, and other reasonable expenses in connection with any impartial due process hearing [conducted by the state or local educational agency] under subsection (b) of this section, any impartial review [conducted by the state educational agency] under subsection (c), and the bringing of the civil action [in federal district court] under subsection (e).

Fees and Expenses

Sec. 615A. (a)(1)(A)   Except as provided in subparagraphs (B) and (C), in any civil action brought under section 615(e), the court may, in its discretion, award a reasonable attorney's fee, reasonable witness fees, and other reasonable expenses of the civil action, in addition to the costs to a parent or legal representative of a handicapped child or youth who is the prevailing party.

(B)   Whenever

(i)   the decision of the impartial due process hearing under section 615(b) or the impartial review of such hearing under section 615(c) is in favor of the parent or legal representative of a handicapped child or youth, and

(ii)   the State or local educational agency or intermediate educational unit appeals the decision pursuant to section 615(e), the parent or legal representative of the handicapped child or youth shall be awarded a reasonable attorney's fee, reasonable witness fees, and other reasonable expenses of the civil action.

(C)   Whenever—

(i)   the decision of the impartial due process hearing under section 615(b) or the impartial review of such hearing under section 615(c), and the decision of the courts, is in favor of the parent or legal representative of a handicapped child or youth, and

(ii)   the State of local educational agency or intermediate educational unit appeals the decision of the courts pursuant to section 615(e)

the parent or legal representative of the handicapped child or youth shall be awarded a reasonable attorney's fees, reasonable witness fees, and other reasonable expenses of such appeal.

(2)   Whenever the parent or legal representative—

(A)   is awarded fees under subparagraph (A), (B), or (C), and

(B)   is represented by a publicly funded organization which provides legal services,

the reasonable attorney's fee which is awarded pursuant to this subsection shall be computed based upon the actual cost related to the bringing of the civil action under section 615(e) to the publicly funded organization, including the proportion of the compensation of the attorney so related, other reasonable expenses which can be documented, and the proportion of the annual overhead costs of the publicly funded organization attributable to the number of hours reasonably spent on such civil action.

     * * *

     . . . .

VII. Additional Views of Senators Hatch, Weicker, Stafford, Dole, Pell, Matsunaga, Simon, Kerry, Kennedy, Metzenbaum, Dodd, and Grassley

While the full committee (at the markup of July 10, 1985) voted unanimously to report S. 415 as amended, there were numerous expressions of concerns that further work would need to be done prior to Senate consideration of the bill.

As a result, Senator Hatch, as chairman of the full committee and Senator Weicker, as chairman of the Subcommittee on the Handicapped, met with representatives of the administration and other interested parties, and, with the agreement of the Department of Education decided to offer an amendment in the form of a substitute when S. 415 is considered on the Senate floor. This amended version of S. 415 is considered by Senators Stafford, Dole, Pell, Matsunaga, Simon, Kerry, Kennedy, Metzenbaum, Dodd, and Grassley.

Throughout remainder of this section of the report the word "school" should be interpreted to include State or local educational agencies or intermediate educational units, as appropriate; the phrase "parent or legal representative" includes a person acting as a parent of a child or a surrogate parent who has been appointed in accordance with section 615(b)(1)(B) of the EHA; and the words "reasonable attorney's fees" simply mean fees appropriate in the circumstances of each case as determined by the Court.

Section-by-Section Analysis of Proposed Amendment

The bill described below, which will be offered as an amendment in the nature of a substitute to S. 415 on the Senate floor, is similar to the original version of S. 415, introduced on February 6, 1985, with two substantive additions. A section-by-section analysis of the substitute amendment to be offered on the Senate floor follows.

Section 1 provides that this Act may be known as the Handicapped Children's Protection Act of 1985.

Section 2 provides the award of reasonable attorney fees to prevailing parents in an EHA action or proceeding. In those cases where the prevailing parent is represented by an attorney who is employed by an organization which receives its operating expenses from Federal, State, or local governmental sources for the purpose of providing legal services, the organization shall be compensated based on the organization's costs.

Section 3 provides that the EHA does not limit the applicability of other laws which protect handicapped children and youth, except that when a parent brings suit under another law when that suit could have been brought under the EHA, the parent will be required to exhaust EHA administrative remedies to the same degree as would have been required had the suit been brought under the EHA.

Section 4 authorizes courts to award attorney's fees in conjunction with any EHA action or proceeding brought after July 3, 1984, or brought before July 4, 1984, but still pending on July 4, 1984. This provision would thus apply to cases brought on or pending on the date of the Smith v. Robinson decision.

Discussion of Substitute Bill

General

The Committee believes that the substitute bill provides fee awards to handicapped children on a basis similar to other fee shifting statutes when securing the right guaranteed to them by the EHA.

Award of Fees and Expenses

Section 2 of the bill amends section 615(e)(4) of the EHA to permit a court, in its discretion, to award reasonable attorney's fees to parents or legal representatives of a handicapped child or youth who is the prevailing party in any action or proceeding brought under this subsection.

It is the committee's intention that a parent or legal representative should be free to select and be represented by the attorney of his/her choice.

The committee understands and intends that State and local agencies may not use funds made available to them under part B of the EHA to pay attorney's fees or other costs incurred by parents that a court assesses against those agencies under the bill. Using these funds for those costs would divert scarce resources from direct services to handicapped children.

It is the committee's intent that the terms "prevailing party" and "reasonable" be construed consistent with the U.S. Supreme Court's decision in Hensley v. Eckerhart, 461 U.S. 424, 440 (1983). In this case, the Court held that:

> the extent of a plaintiff's success is a crucial factor in determining the proper amount of an award of attorney's fees. Where the plaintiff has failed to prevail on a claim that is distinct in all respects from his successful claims, the hours spent on the unsuccessful claim should be excluded in

considering the amount of a reasonable fee. Where a lawsuit consists of related claims, a plaintiff who has won substantial relief should not have his attorney's fee reduced simply because the district court did not adopt each contention raised. But where the plaintiff achieved only limited success, the district court should award only that amount of fees that is reasonable in relation to the results obtained.

It is also the committee's intent that, consistent with section 300.10 of Title 34 (EHA regulations) the term "parent or legal representative" includes a person acting as a parent of a child or a surrogate parent who has been appointed in accordance with section 615(b)(1)(B) of the EHA. The term does not include the State if the child is a ward of the State. Under appropriate circumstances, a child or youth may also bring an action under the EHA and receive an award of attorney's fees to the extent that he/she prevails.

The committee also intends that section 2 should be interpreted consistent with fee provisions of statutes such as title VII of Civil Rights Act of 1964 which authorizes courts to award fees for time spent by counsel in mandatory administrative proceedings under those statutes. See New York Gaslight Club, Inc. v. Carey, 447 U.S. 54 (1980) (compare Webb v. Board of Education for Dyer County, 471 U.S. 234 (1985) in which the court declined to award fees for work done at the administrative level because the statute under which the suit was brought did not require the exhaustion of administrative remedies prior to going to court).

The committee intends that S. 415 will allow the Court, but not the hearing officer, to award fees for time spent by counsel in mandatory EHA administrative proceedings. This is consistent with the committee's position that handicapped children should be provided fee awards on a basis similar to other fee shifting statutes when securing the rights guaranteed to them by the EHA.

It is the intention of the committee to adopt the policy of Christiansburg Garment Co. v. EEOC, 434 U.S. 412 (1978), which is that a party which brings an action that is "frivolous, unreasonable, or without foundation" may be held liable for the prevailing defendant's attorney fees. Nothing in S. 415 should override this established principle concerning frivolous lawsuits. While the committee has no evidence that parents bring EHA suits which are frivolous, unreasonable, or without foundation, in the rare instance where this occurs, this provision would apply.

The committee included subsection (c) to ensure that in those cases where the prevailing party is represented by an attorney who is employed by an organization which receives funds, other than attorney fees awards, from Federal, State, or local governmental sources, the party should be awarded fees on the basis of the actual costs of the litigation to the organization. This limits "double-dipping" or providing attorney fee awards out of governmental funds to organizations already receiving some funding from governmental sources.

Effective Date of Enactment

The bill would be effective on enactment. However, the bill also provides that parents who filed after Smith v. Robinson or whose action or proceeding was pending at the time of Smith v. Robinson may be awarded fees on the same grounds as parents whose action or proceeding is brought after the enactment of S. 415.

Text of Amendment Proposed to be Substituted for Committee Reported Version of S. 415

S. 415

To amend the Education of the Handicapped Act to authorize the award of reasonable attorneys' fees to certain prevailing parties, and to clarify the effect of the Education of the Handicapped Act on rights, procedures, and remedies under other laws relating to the prohibition of discrimination.

In lieu of the matter proposed to be inserted by the committee amendment insert the following:

That this Act may be cited as the "Handicapped Children's Protection Act of 1985".

Sec. 2.   Section 615(e)(4) of the Education of the Handicapped Act amended by inserting "(A)" after the paragraph designation and by adding at the end thereof the following new subparagraphs:

"(B) In any action or proceeding brought under this subsection, the court, in its discretion, may award a reasonable attorney's fee in addition to the costs to a parent or legal representative of a handicapped child or youth who is the prevailing party.

"(C) Whenever the parent or legal representative of a handicapped child or youth—

(i)   is awarded fees under subparagraph (B), and

(ii)   is represented by a publicly funded organization which provides legal services,

the reasonable attorney's fee which is awarded pursuant to this subsection shall be computed based upon the actual cost related to the bringing of the civil action under this subsection to the publicly funded organization, including the proportion of the compensation of the attorney so related, other reasonable expenses which can be documented, and the proportion of the annual overhead costs of the publicly funded organization attributable to the number of hours reasonably spent on such civil action.

"(D) For the purpose of this paragraph, the term 'publicly funded organization' means any organization which receives funds, other than attorney fee awards, from Federal, State, or local governmental sources which are available for use during any fiscal year in which the action or proceeding is pending to enable the organization to provide legal counsel or representation."

Sec. 3. Section 615 of the Education of the Handicapped Act is amended by adding at the end thereof the following new subsection:

"(f) Nothing in this title shall be construed to restrict or limit the rights, procedures, and remedies available under the Constitution, title V of the Rehabilitation Act of 1973, or other Federal statutes protecting the rights of handicapped children and youth, except that before the filing of a civil action under such laws seeking relief that is also available under this part, the procedures under subsections (b)(2) and (c) shall be exhausted to the same extent as would be required had the action been brought under this part."

Sec. 4. The amendment made by section 2 shall apply with respect to actions or proceedings brought under section 615(e) of the Education of the Handicapped Act after July 3, 1984, and actions or proceedings brought prior to July 4, 1984, under such section which were pending on July 4, 1984.

VIII. Additional Views of Kerry, Kennedy, Pell, Dodd, Simon, Metzenbaum, and Matsunaga

Although strongly endorsing the principle that parents or legal representatives of handicapped children must be able to access the full range of available remedies in order to protect their handicapped children's educational rights, seven members of the committee (Kerry, Kennedy, Pell, Dodd, Simon, Metzenbaum, and Matsunaga) believe that one provision should be deleted from the legislation. Language exists in the bill which limits attorney's fees available to nonprofit, publicly funded organizations who provide legal assistance, yet will not limit fees to privately funded attorneys. Undoubtedly, this creates a blatant double standard which will have a particularly negative impact on lower income handicapped children most dependent on legal representation by publicly funded attorneys. Furthermore, by requiring that attorneys' fees awarded to publicly funded attorneys be computed according the cost based standard rather than the prevailing market based standard used by private attorneys, a dangerous precedent for all future cases litigated in this area will be set.

c. Senate debate regarding S. 415.

131 Congressional Record (Senate)

Tuesday, July 30, 1985; (Legislative day of Tuesday, July 16, 1985)

99th Cong. 1st Sess. 131 Cong. Rec. S. 10396, 10465

EDUCATION OF THE HANDICAPPED ACT AMENDMENTS; WEICKER (AND OTHERS) AMENDMENT NO. 561

Mr. Dole (for Mr. Weicker, for himself, Mr. Hatch, Mr. Kennedy, Mr. Dole, Mr. Stafford, Mr. Grassley, Mr. Pell, Mr. Simon, Mr. Metzenbaum, and Mr. Dodd) proposed an amendment to the bill (S. 415) to amend the Education of the Handicapped Act to authorize the award of reasonable attorneys' fees to certain prevailing parties, and to clarify the effect of the Education of the Handicapped Act on rights, procedures, and remedies under other laws relating to prohibition of discrimination; as follows:

[The text of the substitute set out in section VII of the Committee Report was printed here, with a slight change unimportant to our consideration.]

. . .

Mr. Weicker. Mr. President, I rise today to offer an amendment in the form of a substitute bill to S. 415 as it was reported out of the Labor and Human Resources Committee on July 10, 1985. This amendment is cosponsored by Senators Hatch, Stafford, Grassley, Dole, Kennedy, Kerry, Pell, Metzenbaum, Dodd, Matsunaga, and Simon, and has been developed in conjunction with and agreed to by the Department of Education and the Department of Justice. The passage of this substitute bill will bring to fruition months of intensive work and negotiation among Senators and Representatives of the administration. . . .

The purpose of S. 415 is simple—to overturn the Smith versus Robinson decision and thereby to clarify congressional intent regarding these matters. The fact that Congress did not intend to leave unprotected the rights of handicapped children and their parents to secure the free appropriate public education promised to them by EHA was made clear in the 1978 passage of section 505(b) of the Rehabilitation Act which makes attorney's fees available under section 504. Section 505(b) clearly does not make an exception for handicapped children seeking an appropriate education. Indeed, the 1978 Senate and House reports accompanying section 505(b) explain that disabled individuals were one of the very few minority groups in this country who had not been specifically authorized by Congress to seek attorney's fees. The purpose of section 505(b) was "to correct this omission and thereby assist handicapped individuals in securing the legal protection guaranteed them." . . . .

Allowing courts to award attorney's fees to prevailing plaintiffs is not an unusual congressional remedy. In fact, according to the Congressional Research Service (Rept. No. 85–126A), Congress has already enacted more than 130 fee shifting statutes which provide for the award of attorneys' fees to parties who prevail in court to obtain what is guaranteed to them by law. Many of these statutes are civil rights statutes—that is, Age Discrimination Employment Act through 29 U.S.C. sec. 626(b); the Equal Pay Act through 29 U.S.C. sec. 216(b); the Fair Housing Act through 42 U.S.C. sec. 3612(c); title II and title VII of the Civil Rights Act of 1964 through 42 U.S.C. sec. 2000a–3(b) and 2000e–5(k); and the Civil Rights Attorney's Fees Awards Act of 1976 through 42 U.S.C. sec. 1988; but similar attorney's fees statutes exist for a wide variety of laws ranging from the Safe Drinking Water Act through

42 U.S.C. sec. 300j–8(d), to the Deepwater Ports Act through 33 U.S.C. sec. 1515(d), to the National Historic Preservation Act through 16 U.S.C. sec. 470w–4.

. . .

With this amendment, S. 415 will enable courts to compensate parents for whatever reasonable cost they had to incur to fully secure what was guaranteed to them by the EHA. As in other fee shifting statutes, it is our intent that such awards will include, at the discretion of the court, reasonable attorney's fees, necessary expert witness fees, and other reasonable expenses which were necessary for parent to vindicate their claim to a free appropriate public education for their handicapped child. . . .

Mr. Stafford. Mr. President, I rise in support of S. 415, the Handicapped Children's Protection Act of 1985.

. . .

Critics of S. 415 are fearful that the availability of attorney's fees awards to prevailing parents will increase litigation. It is my belief that the opposite situation will occur. State and local education agencies will be more inclined to work out effective compromises with parents before court action becomes necessary.

Parents must have every opportunity to participate with local school personnel to develop programs for their handicapped children if 94–142 [the EHA] is to provide the free and appropriate education that it promised. That includes making reasonable legal fees available if the services of an attorney are necessary.

A law that mandates a free and appropriate public education to handicapped children, that at the same time denies the awarding of legal fees incurred to uphold that mandate, is a hollow promise at best. It hurts the families most that can least afford it.

I urge my colleagues to vote in favor of S. 415. Senator Weicker is to be commended for his leadership on this important legislation.

Mr. Hatch. Mr. President, S. 415, the Handicapped Children's Protection Act, was drafted in response to the Supreme Court's 1984 opinion in Smith versus Robinson.

. . .

The Hatch-Weicker substitute we are considering today is a modification of the committee bill reported by my Labor and Human Resources Committee on July 10. It is similar to S. 415 as originally introduced with two substantive changes. The first requires exhaustion of administration remedies before pursuing litigation. The second places conditions upon fee awards for publicly funded attorneys representing parents who prevailed in EHA cases.

. . .

Mr. Kerry. Mr. President, I would like to rise in strong support of S. 415 the Handicapped Children's Protection Act and urge that my colleagues join me in passing this vital legislation. . . . However, there is one provision in the legislation which greatly undermines the strength of this bill and should be deleted. Language exists in the bill which limits attorneys' fees available to nonprofit, publicly funded organizations who provide legal services, yet will not place these same limitations on privately funded attorneys. To some this is considered double dipping; quite frankly Mr. President I view this as a double standard. This blatant double standard will have a particularly negative impact on lower income handicapped children most dependent on legal representation by publicly funded attorneys. . . . As a lawyer who has worked in a public attorney's office, I have witnessed firsthand that under our present system, offices which provide legal assistance to indigent handicapped children encounter an overwhelming demand for their services and unfortunately have very limited resources to meet this demand. I emphatically believe that any additional funds made available to expand legal services to our Nation's disabled poor citizens is money well spent.

. . .

Mr. President, I offered an amendment in the Labor and Human Resources Committee that would have deleted the provision to cap publicly funded attorneys' fees. The amendment was narrowly defeated by a 7 to 9 vote. . . . This double standard weakens the legislation and while I urge my colleagues to vote for the Handicapped Children's Protection Act, I strongly urge that when this bill goes to conference committee, that we do all we can to uphold the educational rights of all handicapped children, rich and poor, and delete this provision.

Mr. Simon. . . . The Supreme Court's decision on July 5, 1984, in Smith versus Robinson, jeopardizes the educational rights provided under Public Law 94–142 and negates the intent of Congress to assure equal protection for all handicapped children. In eliminating a parent's ability to be reimbursed for attorney fees under Public Law 94–142, the Court has made the due process guarantees of that act, including the right to go to court when necessary, meaningless for all but the wealthy and well informed. . . .

The provisions of S. 415 reaffirm and clarify the original intent of Congress in providing a variety of effective avenues for parents to use in resolving questions concerning the appropriate educational services their handicapped children should receive. . . . Mr. President, I wish that I could endorse S. 415 without qualification. There is one provision, however, that does not deserve our support and which I am hopeful will be removed in conference with the House. Under this provision, any organization which receives public funds for the purpose of providing legal assistance would be eligible for attorney fee awards only in the amount that could be documented to be the actual cost of the case. Attorneys awarded fees under the many other fee-shifting statutes—

including such wide-ranging statutes as the Deepwater Ports Act, the National Historic Preservation Act, the Equal Pay Act and the Fair Housing Act—may be compensated on the basis of the prevailing market-based standard used by private attorneys. A serious question must be raised as to why this limit is being imposed on handicapped cases and on the seriously inadequate legal services available to the poor. This provision will hurt most those whom this bill as a whole is most intended to help. . . .

I support prompt passage of this much needed legislation.

The Presiding Officer. The bill is open to further amendment. If there be no further amendment to be proposed, the question is on agreeing to the committee amendment in the nature of a substitute, as amended.

The committee amendment, as amended, was agreed to.

The bill was ordered to be engrossed for a third reading and was read the third time.

The Presiding Officer. The bill having been read the third time, the question is, Shall it pass?

So the bill (S. 415) was passed.

d. Report of the House Committee on Education and Labor to accompany proposed House bill H.R. 1523.

99TH CONGRESS	HOUSE OF	REPORT 99–296
1st Session	REPRESENTATIVES	

HANDICAPPED CHILDREN'S PROTECTION ACT OF 1985

October 2, 1985.—Committed to the Committee of the Whole House on the State of the Union and ordered to be printed

Mr. Hawkins, from the Committee on Education and Labor, submitted the following together with Supplemental Views [To accompany H.R. 1523]

[Including cost estimate of the Congressional Budget Office]

The Committee on Education and Labor, to whom was referred the bill (H.R. 1523) to amend the Education of the Handicapped Act to authorize the award of reasonable attorneys' fees to certain prevailing parties, to clarify the effect of the Education of the Handicapped Act on rights, procedures, and remedies under other laws relating to the prohibition of discrimination, and for other purposes, having considered the same, report favorably thereon with amendment and recommend that the bill as amended do pass.

The amendment is as follows:

Strike out all after the enacting clause and insert in lieu thereof the following:

SECTION 1. SHORT TITLE

This Act may be cited as the "Handicapped Children's Protection Act of 1985".

SEC. 2. AWARD OF ATTORNEYS' FEES.

Section 615(e)(4) of the Education of the Handicapped Act (hereinafter in this Act referred to as the "Act") as amended by inserting "(A)" after the paragraph designation and by adding at the end thereof the following:

"(B) In any action or proceeding brought under this subsection, the court, in its discretion, may award reasonable attorneys' fees, expenses, and costs to the parents or guardian of a handicapped child or youth who is the prevailing party.

(5)   For purposes of this subsection—

"(A) fees awarded under this subsection shall be based on rates prevailing in the community in which the action or proceeding arose for the kind and quality of services furnished; and

"(B) fees, expenses, and costs awarded under this subsection to a prevailing part may not be paid with funds provided to the State under this Act.". . .

SEC. 5. EFFECTIVE DATE.

(a)   General Provision.—Except as provided in subsection (b), the provisions of this Act shall take effect on the date of enactment of this Act.

(b)   Limited Retroactive Application.—The amendments made by sections 2 and 3 shall apply with respect to actions or proceedings brought under section 615(e) of the Education of the Handicapped Act after July 3, 1984, and actions or proceedings brought prior to July 4, 1984, under such section which were pending on July 4, 1984.

Committee Action

On March 7, 1985 Congressman Williams introduced H.R. 1523, the Handicapped Children's Protection Act of 1985. On March 12 1985, the Subcommittee on Select Education held a hearing at which members of the Subcommittee heard testimony from the American Association of School Administrators, the National School Boards Association, the Council for Exceptional Children, the Consortium for Citizens with Developmental Disabilities, and a parent. On April 3, 1985, the Subcommittee marked-up the bill. On September 11th and 19th, 1985, the Committee on Education and Labor considered the bill and on the latter date ordered reported by voice vote an Amendment in the Nature of a Substitute.

Background and Need for Legislation

In 1971 and 1972 two landmark cases established the constitutional rights of handicapped children to a free appropriate public education. The courts found, among other things, that handicapped children's rights under 42 U.S.C. 1983 had been abridged. Section 1983 prohibits, among other things, an agency acting under color of state law from abridging a handicapped person's rights under the Constitution. The cases were Pennsylvania Ass'n for Retarded Children v. Commonwealth, 343 F.Supp. 279 (E.D. Pa. 1972) and Mills v. Bd. Of Education, 349 F.Supp. 866 (D.D.C. 1972).

In 1973 Congress enacted section 504 of the Rehabilitation Act of 1973. Section 504 prohibits recipients of federal financial assistance from discriminating against persons on the basis of their handicaps. The original legislation defined a handicapped person in terms of employment and ability to benefit from rehabilitation services. In 1974 Congress clarified its intent that section 504 was not limited to employment but rather covered all handicapped persons, including children and youth in relation to education.

In 1975 Congress passed the Education for All Handicapped Children Act (P.L. 94–142), amending the Education of the Handicapped Act (EHA). EHA, as amended, guarantees a free appropriate public education to every handicapped child in a state that accepts EHA funds. EHA includes a process approach for determining what constitutes an "appropriate" education. . . .

In 1976, Congress adopted 42 U.S.C. 1988, which authorizes a court, at its discretion, to award reasonable attorneys' fees under, among other statutes, 42 U.S.C. 1983 to a party prevailing in any action or proceeding claiming abridgement of his/her constitutional rights.

In 1977 the Department of Health, Education, and Welfare issued regulations implementing section 504 and EHA. The Section 504 regulations were published in the *Federal Register* on May 4, 1977 and the regulations implementing Part B of EHA were published on August 23, 1977. Each regulation recognized the existence of the other and in explaining the relationship between the two each recognized that Congress intended that the other law constituted a separate but equally viable statement of the rights of handicapped children and youth to a free appropriate public education. . . .

In 1978, Congress amended title V of the Rehabilitation Act of 1973 to include a new section (section 505) that provides reasonable attorneys' fees to the prevailing party in any action or proceeding brought under section 504.

In sum, since 1978, it has been Congress' intent to permit parents or guardians to pursue the rights of handicapped children through EHA, section 504, and section 1983. . . .

Congressional intent was ignored by the U.S. Supreme Court when, on July 5, 1984, it handed down its decision in Smith v. Robinson, 468 U.S. 992 (1984). . . .

H.R. 1523 is designed to: (1) authorize courts to award reasonable attorneys' fees to parents of handicapped children who prevail in actions or proceedings under EHA; (2) re-establish statutory rights repealed by the U.S. Supreme Court in Smith v. Robinson; (3) reaffirm, in light of this decision, the viability of section 504, 42 U.S.C. 1983, and other statutes as separate vehicles for ensuring the rights of handicapped children, and the role of OCR in investigating complaints of handicapped discrimination under section 504; and (4) improve the due process procedures available to handicapped children under EHA.

Award of Attorneys' Fees

Section 2 of the bill amends section 615(e)(4) of EHA to permit a court, in its discretion, to award reasonable attorneys' fees, costs, and expenses to the parents or guardian of a handicapped child or youth who is the prevailing party in an action or proceeding (a due process hearing or a state level review) brought under Part B of EHA.

The "action or proceeding" language in section 2 of the bill is identical to the language in title VII of the Civil Rights Act of 1964, interpreted by the Supreme Court in New York Gaslight Club v. Carey, 447 U.S. 54 (1980). In Gaslight, the Court held that the use of the phrase "action or proceeding" indicates an intent to subject the losing party to an award of attorneys' fees, expenses and costs incurred in court. The Court's decision also established a similar right under title VII to obtain an award of fees, costs, and expenses incurred in mandatory state and local administrative proceedings, even where no lawsuit is filed.

Consistent with the Supreme Court's reasoning in Gaslight, since EHA, like title VII, requires parents to exhaust administrative remedies before seeking judicial relief, if a parent loses at the local or state administrative proceeding but wins on appeal in federal court, the court may award reasonable fees for services performed in connection with both the administrative proceedings and the civil action.

Further, if a parent prevails on the merits at an administrative proceeding (and the agency does not appeal the decision), the parent may be awarded reasonable attorneys' fees, costs, and expenses incurred in such administrative proceeding.

. . .

The phrase "expenses and costs" includes expenses of expert witnesses; the reasonable costs of any study, report, test, or project which is found to be necessary for the preparation of the parents' or guardian's due process hearing, state administrative review or civil action; as well as traditional costs and expenses incurred in the course of litigating a case (e.g., depositions and interrogatories). . . .

It is also the Committee's intent that, consistent with section 300.10 of title 34 (EHA regulations), the term "parent" includes a person acting as a parent of a child or a surrogate parent who has been appointed in accordance with section 615(b)(1)(B) of EHA. The term does not include the State if the child is the ward of the State. Of course, under appropriate circumstances a child or youth may also bring an action or proceeding under EHA and receive an award of attorney's fees to the extent he/she prevails.

. . .

Section-by-Section Analysis

Short Title

Section 1 of the bill cites the title as the "Handicapped Children's Protection Act of 1985".

Award of Attorneys' Fees

Section 2 of the bill amends section 615(e)(4) of the Education of Handicapped Act (EHA) to authorize the court, at its discretion to award reasonable attorneys' fees, costs, and expenses to a parent who prevails in an action or proceeding brought under such section. Section 2 also specifies that fee awards should be based on the prevailing community rates for the kind and quality of services furnished and prohibits the use of EHA funds to pay the fees, costs and expenses awarded. . . .

Effective Date

Section 5 of the bill specifies the effective date of the bill as the date of enactment, except that sections 2 and 3 apply with respect to actions or proceedings brought under section 615(e) of the EHA after July 3, 1984 and actions or proceedings brought prior to July 4 1984, under such sections which were pending on July 4, 1984.

. . .

SUPPLEMENTAL VIEWS (H.R. 1523), THE HANDICAPPED CHILDREN'S PROTECTION ACT OF 1985

. . . We support the major objective of H.R. 1523 which appropriately responds to *Smith* by amending P.L. 94–142 to allow Courts to authorize an award of reasonable attorneys' fees to parents who prevail in P.L. 94–142 court actions.

. . .

Unwisely, H.R. 1523 extends, without limitation, the right to recover attorneys' fees to the administrative procedures available under P.L. 94–142 for the first time. This provision could radically alter the delicate balance that currently exists in P.L. 94–142's due process system, resulting in a severe financial burden for state educational agencies and local school systems. . . . H.R. 1523, by allowing for the recovery by a prevailing parent of attorneys' fees at the administrative level without limitation, invites the use of attorneys into a proceeding which does not require either party to be represented by counsel. The increased participation of attorneys in these procedures will lead to a more adversarial relationship between parents and educators and force school systems to use their precious educational dollars to pay lawyers whose participation is not only not required by law, but also may prove counterproductive. In effect, the Federal government, which presently contributes approximately 8 percent of the cost of educating a handicapped child, would, under H.R. 1523, require state education agencies and local school systems to spend their educational funds . . . to pay attorneys' fees in a Federally mandated administrative hearing system in those instances when the state and local educational agencies were carrying out their public responsibility of providing what they considered to be an appropriate education.

As voted unanimously out of the Subcommittee on Select Education, H.R. 1523 contained provisions which set certain limitations on fees at the administrative level and represented a bipartisan compromise. To the chagrin of Members who had forged this agreement, a substitute version of H.R. 1523 was introduced at the Full Committee, containing the current controversial provision on fees at the administrative level. Members of the Subcommittee who had marked-up and unanimously passed out of Subcommittee a bill in April of 1985 were confronted in September, 1985, with a radically different substitute bill at the Full Committee, without explanation or benefit to consider the new provision as a Subcommittee.

. . .

The failure of the Committee on Education and Labor to demonstrate reasonable restraint on this legislation should not be repeated by the House. We encourage Members to support efforts that will address these issues.

Jim Jeffords.
Bill Goodling.
Thomas E. Petril.
Marge Roukema.
Steve Gunderson.
Steve Bartlett.
Rod Chandler.
Tom Tauke.
Dick Armey.

e.   House debate regarding H.R. 1523.

131 Congressional Record (House of Representatives)

Tuesday, November 12, 1985

99th Cong. 1st Sess. 26 131 Cong. Rec. H9964

HANDICAPPED CHILDREN'S PROTECTION ACT OF 1985

Mr. Williams. . . .

Madam Speaker, on March 7, 1985, H.R. 1523, the Handicapped Children's Protection Act was introduced. The original bill was designed to accomplish four basic objectives.

First, to authorize courts to award reasonable attorneys' fees to parents of handicapped children who prevail in specified circumstances under Part B of the Education of the Handicapped Act.

Second, to reestablish statutory rights repealed by the U.S. Supreme Court in the decision in Smith versus Robinson.

Third, to reaffirm, in light of this decision, the viability of section 504 of the Rehabilitation Act of 1973, 42 U.S.C. 1983 and other statutes as separate vehicles for ensuring the rights of handicapped children.

. . .

Fourth, to improve the due process procedures available under part B of the Education of the Handicapped Act.

Today, we are considering an amendment in the nature of a substitute which satisfies all of these objectives. The road traveled to reach this bipartisan compromise has not been smooth. The issues involved in the legislation are extremely complex and affect all participants in our educational system: Handicapped children and their families, teachers, and school officials. However, Members on both sides of the aisle have worked long and hard to reach this bipartisan compromise. Special recognition must go to Mr. Hawkins, Mr. Biaggi, Mr. Jeffords, and Mr. Bartlett. My personal thanks for all your efforts.

In the course of drafting this legislation, organizations representing handicapped children, parents, educators, administrators, boards of education have often expressed strong and often divergent positions on the provisions in the bill. The consequences of including or excluding particular provisions were expressed and then debated at length.

The bill we present today for passage represents a consensus which achieves the needed balance between the rights of handicapped children and local and State educational agencies. I urge my colleagues to support this bipartisan substitute.

Let me briefly describe the key components of the legislation.

First, it amends part B of EHA to provide that a parent or guardian of a handicapped child who prevails against a school district or State educational agency in a civil action in Federal or State court, or an administrative proceeding such as a due process hearing or State appeal, may be awarded reasonable attorney's fees, costs and expenses by the court.

Second, it provides for the submission to Congress of a GAO study on the impact of this provision no later than 3 ½ years after the date of enactment of the legislation.

Third, the legislation contains a sunset provision under which a court's authority to award fees to parents who prevail in administrative proceedings terminates 4 years after the date of enactment of this legislation if the GAO report is submitted on schedule: Thus, after 4 years, unless Congress passes additional legislation, a court's authority to award fees will be limited to civil actions in State or Federal courts in which parents prevail.

Fourth, it overturns the U.S. Supreme Court's decision in Smith versus Robinson by reestablishing the viability of Section 504 of the Rehabilitation Act of 1973 and other statutes as separate vehicles for ensuring the rights of handicapped children and youth.

. . .

Finally, the bill specifies that the provisions concerning the awarding of attorneys fees and the effect of the Education of the Handicapped Act on other laws apply retroactively with respect to actions or proceedings after July 3, 1984, and actions or proceedings brought prior to July 4, 1984, which were pending on July 4, 1984.

The Congressional Budget Office states that there will be no increase in Federal cost as a result of this bill.

Public Law 94–142 was hailed upon passage as a significant step forward in ensuring the educational rights of persons with handicaps and it is living up to its promises. This legislation before you today only strengthens that capability. I urge my colleagues to support the compromise.

Madam Speaker, I reserve the balance of my time.

The Speaker pro tempore. (Mr. Garcia). The Chair recognizes the gentleman from Texas [Mr. Bartlett].

Mr. Bartlett. Mr. Speaker, I yield myself 14 ½ minutes.

(Mr. Bartlett asked and was given permission to revise and extend his remarks.)

Mr. Bartlett. . . .

Mr. Speaker, H.R. 1523 constructively addresses the issue of the recovery of attorneys' fees for civil action under Public Law 94–142 in response to the Smith decision. It properly authorizes courts to award reasonable attorneys' fees to parents of handicapped children who prevail in civil actions. I support without reservation, this portion of H.R. 1523, believing that not only the families of handicapped children will be served by this amendment but also the public interest of ensuring the provision of a free and appropriate education for all handicapped children.

Saying this, Mr. Speaker, I must raise what I consider to be a serious flaw in H.R. 1523 which taints its contributions to Public Law 94–142. H.R. 1523 mistakenly extends the authority for the recovery of attorneys' fees into Public Law 94–142's administrative hearing process. Public Law 94–142 is essentially a grant-in-aid statute that provides an informal process by which parents and educators can mutually determine what is an appropriate education for a handicapped student. The system for identifying, evaluating, developing, and administering the individualized educational program rests upon the ability of parents and educators to meet, share information, and agree upon a program. . . .

There are a number of very good reasons why this provision is both unnecessary and could be destructive. Foremost is an indisputable fact that the number of administrative hearings held each year to resolve disputes between parents and educators is decreasing. According to a survey by the National Association of State Directors of Special Education the number of first-level hearings decreased by 39 percent between 1979–80 and 1983–84. For the school year 1983–84 only 1 out of every 3,000 of the approximately 4 million students was involved in a first-level hearing and only 1 in every 64,800 was the subject of litigation.

. . .

H.R. 1523, by allowing for the recovery of fees at the administrative level, removes the incentive to resolve disputes informally because schools will be as liable for attorneys' fees under the administrative system as they are in court. The complications resulting from this part of H.R. 1523 become even clearer when one considers the impact of fees at the administrative level on the mediation or informal complaint procedure that is also part of H. R. 1523.

The principle that I advocate on this issue is a simple one: Congress should not do anything to encourage the participation of lawyers in a conflict resolution situation which does not require their participation. By allowing for the recovery of attorneys' fees under Public Law 94–142 at the administrative level, H.R. 1523 will increase the participation of attorneys and decrease the likelihood that parents and educators will resolve their disputes informally and inexpensively.

. . .

I support H.R. 1523 at this time for two reasons: First, I do believe Congress should act to restore attorneys' fees to court level, and second, the bill includes sunset on the provision authorizing fees at the administrative level. This sunset will mean that after a sufficient period of time, Congress will be able to examine the impact of the bill as presently constituted and act accordingly. If this provision were not in H.R. 1523, I could not support the bill.

Mr. Speaker, H.R. 1523 serves a vital purpose of allowing courts to authorize attorneys' fees to parents who prevail in Public Law 94–142 litigation. H.R. 1523 also jeopardizes Public Law 94–142's administrative hearing system and the process by which parents and educators informally determine what is appropriate for a handicapped student.

. . .

Mr. Speaker, at this time, I would ask the gentleman from Montana [Mr. Williams] if he would engage in a colloquy.

. . .

Mr. Williams. Mr. Speaker, I will be pleased to join with my colleague in a colloquy.

Mr. Bartlett. Mr. Speaker, section 2 of H.R. 1523 amends section 615(e)(4) of the Education of the Handicapped Act by adding the following new provision:

In any action or proceeding brought under this subsection, the court, in its discretion, may award reasonable attorneys' fees, expenses, and costs to the parents or guardian of a handicapped child or youth who is the prevailing party.

Could you clarify the meaning of the terms "action" and "proceeding?"

Mr. Williams. The term "action" is intended to include a civil action filed in a State or Federal court. The term "proceeding" is limited to the due process hearing that parents are required to exhaust under 615(b)(2) and the State appeal under section 615(c). The term "proceeding" is not intended to include meetings held to develop individualized education programs or meetings to make decisions concerning such matters as the identification, evaluation, or placement of handicapped children.

Mr. Bartlett. It is my understanding that parents are not entitled to any fees, costs, or expenses when they are declared the prevailing party in any action or proceeding but at the final appeal of such action or proceeding the school district is declared the prevailing party. Do you agree with this statement?

Mr. Williams. Yes, I do agree with that.

Mr. Bartlett. Similarly, where the parents lose in any action or proceeding but at the final appeal of such action or proceeding the parents are declared the prevailing party, do you agree that they are entitled to reasonable fees, costs, and expenses related to all prior actions and proceedings as well as the final appeal?

Mr. Williams. Yes, I do. . . . The part of the bill that the gentleman from Texas says is flawed I regard as its strength. What we are talking about is providing attorneys' fees for those individuals who are being denied access to the educational system; access as provided by Public Law 94–142.

It is argued that the hearings are informal and that the school boards are generally cooperative. The reality of the matter is this: We are talking about Mr. or Mrs. John Doe who have a problem with a child gaining access, who then come before a school board. While most of us have experience, testifying in one forum or another; so hence we are not impressed nor more intimidated by a school board. Do we fully understand the psychological impact and burden it places on the parents appearing before a quasi-judicial body? There is an inhibition placed; they do not have the ability nor experience to argue and to make their case.

At the same time, the school board has present, on staff, their own attorneys; but absent that, members of the school board are not burdened with the same lack of experience. They have been subjected to election; they have been through the process time and time again; they come in an adversarial position, and that is the critical nature of this legislation and of this situation.

They are there to say that the child should not be in the school. The parents want the child in the program. So clearly, confrontation exists. It is important to establish a record, whether the parents prevail at this point or not, the record must be established. Most parents, by themselves, cannot effectively establish the record on which a step forward into the courts can be based. They do not have that knowledge or skills.

For the most part, they will not prevail, and oftentimes when they are rejected at that point, they leave and give up the fight, to the detriment of the child.

. . .

Mr. Bartlett. Mr. Speaker, I yield 4 minutes to the gentleman from Vermont [Mr. Jeffords], the ranking member of the Education and Labor Committee.

(Mr. Jeffords asked and was given permission to revise and extend his remarks.)

Mr. Jeffords. Mr. Speaker, the bill before us today, H.R. 1523, the Handicapped Children's Protection Act, is necessary because of a Supreme Court decision in the case of Smith versus Robinson. There is no doubt that there is agreement among all of us that the decision rendered by the court in July 1984 must be overturned. . . . I must congratulate the chairman of the subcommittee, Mr. Williams, and the ranking Republican, Mr. Bartlett, for their efforts on this bill. The results of their labors is a bill that continues to support a handicapped child's rights, and the enforcement of those rights, to an appropriate education.

. . .

Currently there is no prohibition against the use of an attorney by either party at the administrative proceedings level. . . . Our action in this bill may draw in the use of an attorney at an earlier stage in the proceedings than has been the norm to date. In this way, we may be disrupting a system of proven effectiveness. . . . The seriousness of this issue deserves discussion by this body. Our debate on the issue though, has been precluded somewhat by the action taken by the other body. Instead, concerns regarding the wisdom of providing for attorneys' fees at the administrative proceedings level have been partially addressed in H.R. 523 by the inclusion of a sunset provision. I appreciate the willingness of the majority to work with the minority on this point. By including a 4-year sunset provision directed toward the payment of attorney's fees at the hearing level, and requiring a GAO study to assess the effects of the provision, we can review the outcome and make the appropriate changes if they are necessary. I hope that my fears are proven wrong. It would be nice to be able to come to this body 4 years from now and heartily endorse the payment of attorneys' fees at the administrative level. I am not sure that such an action will be supported by our findings.

. . .

The Speaker pro tempore. The question is on the motion offered by the gentleman from Montana [Mr. Williams] that the House suspend the rules and pass the bill, H.R. 1523, as amended.

The question was taken; and (two-thirds having voted in favor thereof) the rules were suspended, and the bill, as amended, was passed.

A motion to reconsider was laid on the table.

[At this point, following an established House procedure, the text of H.R. 1523 was substituted for that of S. 415, and S. 415, as thus amended, was approved. S. 415, as passed by the House, thus contained the language of H.R. 1523.]

APPOINTMENT OF CONFEREES ON S. 415

Mr. Williams. Mr. Speaker, I ask unanimous consent that the House insist on its amendment to the Senate bill, S. 415, and request a conference with the Senate thereon.

The Speaker pro tempore. Is there objection to the request of the gentleman from Montana? The Chair hears none and, without objection, appoints the following conferees: Messrs. Hawkins, Biaggi, Williams, Hayes, Martinez, Eckart of Ohio, Jeffords, Goodling, Coleman of Missouri, and Bartlett.

There was no objection.

f.   Conference Committee Report on the Handicapped Children's Protection Act of 1986

[House and Senate representatives met and resolved their differences, as reported below.]

99TH CONGRESS	HOUSE OF	REPORT 99–687
2nd Session	REPRESENTATIVES	

Handicapped Children's Protection Act of 1986

———

JULY 16, 1986.—Ordered to be printed

———

Mr. Hawkins, from the committee of conference, submitted the following

CONFERENCE REPORT [To accompany S. 415]

The committee of conference on the disagreeing votes of the two Houses on the amendments of the House to the bill (S. 415), to amend the Education of the Handicapped Act to authorize the award of reasonable attorneys' fees to certain prevailing parties, and to clarify the effect of the Education of the Handicapped Act on rights, procedures, and remedies under other laws relating to the prohibition of discrimination, having met, after full and free conference, have agreed to recommend and do recommend to their respective Houses as follows:

That the Senate recede from its disagreement to the amendment of the House to the text of the bill and agree to the same with an amendment as follows:

In lieu of the matter proposed to be inserted by the House amendment, insert the following:

[Here appears the text of the statute as finally enacted, set out above at ___.]

And the House agree to the same.

That the Senate recede from its disagreement to the amendment of the House to the title of the bill, and agree to the same.

Augustus F. Hawkins,
Mario Biaggi,
Pat Williams,
Charles A. Hayes,
Matthew H. Martinez,
Dennis E. Eckart,
Managers on the Part of the House.

Orrin Hatch,
Lowell. P. Weicker, Jr.,
Don Nickles,
Ted Kennedy,
John F. Kerry,
Managers on the Part of the Senate.

JOINT EXPLANATORY STATEMENT OF
THE COMMITTEE OF CONFERENCE

The managers on the part of the House and the Senate at the conference on the disagreeing votes of the two Houses on the amendment of the House to the bill (S. 415) to authorize the award of attorneys' fees to certain prevailing parties, and to clarify the effect of the Education of the Handicapped Act on rights, procedures and remedies under other laws relating to the prohibition of discrimination and for other purposes, submit the following joint statement to the House and the Senate in explanation of the effect of the action agreed upon by the managers and recommended in the accompanying conference report. The differences between the Senate bill and the House amendment and the substitute agreed to at the conference, are noted below, except for clerical corrections, conforming changes made necessary by agreements reached by the conferees, and minor drafting and clarifying changes.

The Senate bill provides for "a reasonable attorney's fee."

The House amendment provides for "reasonable attorneys' fees." The Senate recedes.

With slightly different wording, both the Senate bill and the House amendment provide for the awarding of attorneys' fees in addition to costs.

The Senate recedes to the House and the House recedes to the Senate with an amendment clarifying that "the court, in its discretion, may award reasonable attorneys' fees as part of the costs. . . ." This change in wording incorporates the Supreme Court Marek v. Chesny decision (473 U.S. 1, 87 L.Ed.2d 1).

The conferees intend that the term "attorneys' fees as part of the costs" include reasonable expenses and fees of expert witnesses and reasonable costs of any test or evaluation which is found to be necessary for the preparation of the parent or guardian's case in the action or proceeding, as well as traditional costs incurred in the course of litigating a case.

The Senate bill provides for the award of attorney's fees "to a parent or legal representative."

The House amendment provides for the award of attorneys' fees "to the parents or guardian."

The Senate recedes.

The Senate bill limits the amount of the fee awarded whenever a parent or legal representative is represented by a publicly funded organization which provides legal services.

The House amendment provides that fee awards shall be based on prevailing rates in the community.

The House recedes to the Senate and the Senate recedes to the House with an amendment clarifying that "fees awarded under this subsection shall be based on rates prevailing in the community in which the action or proceeding arose for the kind and quality of the services furnished." See, Hensley v. Eckerhart, 461 U.S. 424 (1983); Marek v. Chesny, 473 U.S. 1, 87 L.Ed.2d 1 (1985); and Blum v. Stenson, 465 U.S. 886, 104 S.Ct. 1541 (1984). However, no such awards of attorneys' fees shall be calculated by using bonuses or multipliers. The conferees want to make it clear that the inclusion of the prohibition against calculation of fees using bonuses and multipliers is limited to cases brought only under part B of the Education of the Handicapped Act. The conferees do not intend in any way to diminish the applicability of interpretation by the U.S. Supreme Court regarding bonuses and multipliers to other statutes such as 42 U.S.C. 1988. See, Hensley v. Eckerhart, Blum v. Stenson, Evans v. Jeff D., 475 U.S. 717, 106 S.Ct. 1531 (1986). In addition, several new sections would be added to clarify that under part B of the Education of the Handicapped Act, no award of attorneys' fees and related costs subject to the provision of the act may be made for services performed subsequent to the time a written offer of settlement is made to a party (if the offer is made at least 10 days prior to the date of the action or proceeding) if the offer is not accepted within ten days and a court or administrative officer finds that the relief finally obtained by the party is not more favorable to the parent or guardian than the offer of settlement. However, attorneys' fees may be awarded to a prevailing parent or guardian who was substantially justified in rejecting the settlement offer. Furthermore, the court shall reduce accordingly the amount of attorneys' fees and related expenses otherwise allowable if they determine that:

(1) the parent or guardian, during the course of the action or proceeding unreasonably protracted the final resolution of the controversy;

(2) the amount of attorneys' fees otherwise authorized to be awarded unreasonably exceeds the hourly rate prevailing in the community for similar services by attorneys of reasonably comparable skills experience and reputation; or

(3) the time spent and legal services furnished were excessive considering the nature of the action or proceeding.

Finally, the preceding situations in which the court reduces the amount of fees and related expenses otherwise allowable shall not apply if the local or state educational agency is determined to have unreasonably protracted the final resolution of the action or proceeding or if a violation of section 615 of the Education of the Handicapped Act is found.

The conferees intend that this provision clarify the application of the Marek v. Chesny decision to the Handicapped Children's Protection Act. One exception is made to the applicability of the Marek v. Chesny decision. When the parent or guardian is substantially justified in rejecting the settlement offer, the Marek v. Chesny decision would not apply. Substantial justification for rejection would include relevant pending court decisions which could have an impact on the case in question.

In enumerating three conditions under which the amount of attorneys' fees would be reduced, the committee intends to protect against excessive reimbursement. The second condition is a codification of the policy for awarding fees in footnote 11 of Blum v. Stenson.

5.   The House amendment, but not the Senate bill, specifies that fees, expenses, and costs awarded to the prevailing party may not be paid with the funds provided under part B of EHA. The report accompanying the Senate's bill restates existing policy that bars the payment of such fees and the costs under part B.

The House recedes. The conferees wish to emphasize that existing law bars payment of attorneys' fees with funds appropriated under B of EHA.

6.   The House amendment, but not the Senate bill, provides for a GAO study of the impact of the bill authorizing the awarding of fees and costs.

The Senate recedes to the House with an amendment expanding the data collection requirements of the GAO study to include information regarding the amount of funds expended by local educational agencies and state educational agencies on civil actions and administrative proceedings.

7.   The House amendment, but not the Senate bill, sunsets the court's authority to award fees at the administrative level after a period of time specified in the legislation.

The House recedes.

8.   With slightly different wording, both the Senate bill and the House amendment authorize the filing of civil actions under legal authorities other than part B of EHA so long as parents first exhaust administrative remedies available under part B of EHA to the same extent as would be required under that part.

The House recedes. It is the conferees' intent that actions brought under 42 U.S.C. 1983 are governed by this provision.

9.   The House amendment, but not the Senate bill requires public access to hearing decisions.

The House recedes. The conferees wish to emphasize that public access to hearing decisions is existing law.

10. The House amendment, but not the Senate bill, requires that the public educational agency provide parents with an opportunity to meet informally in an attempt to resolve a complaint.

The House recedes.

11. The House amendment, but not the Senate bill, includes an anti-retaliation provision.

The House recedes. It is the conferees' intent that no person may discharge, intimidate, retaliate, threaten, coerce, or otherwise take an adverse action against any person because such person has filed a complaint, testified, furnished information, assisted or participated in any manner in a meeting, hearing, review, investigation, or other activity related to the administration of, exercise of authority under, or right secured by part B of EHA. The term "person" the first time it is used means a state educational agency, local educational agency, intermediate educational unit or any official or employee thereof.

12. The House amendment, but not the Senate bill, makes retroactive its provision regarding the effect of EHA on other laws (section 3).

The House recedes.

Augustus F. Hawkins,
Mario Biaggi,
Pat Williams,
Charles A. Hayes,
Matthew H. Martinez,
Dennis E. Eckart,
Managers on the Part of the House.

Orrin Hatch,
Lowell. P. Weicker, Jr.,
Don Nickles,
Ted Kennedy,
John F. Kerry,
Managers on the Part of the Senate.

[The House and Senate promptly voted approval of the report, and with it the bill, that was then sent to the President for signature, promptly provided There were largely self-congratulatory debates in each chamber, and no amendments were offered or voted upon.]

* * *

What parts of this legislative history will you use to buttress your claim that the Handicapped Children's Protection Act of 1986 covers the cost of the expert who helped you prepare and present your case? What parts of this legislative history will your opponent use to try to defeat that claim? What is your prediction as to how it turned out?

(If you want to read what the various Justices of the Supreme Court had to say, read Arlington Central School Dist. Bd. Of Education v. Murphy, 548 U.S. 291 (2006).

PART 3

THE AGENCY AT WORK

CHAPTER III
PROCEDURAL FRAMEWORKS
FOR ADMINISTRATIVE ACTION

> **Sec. 1.** *The Fundamental Procedural Categories of Administrative Action: Rulemaking and Adjudication*
>
> **Sec. 2.** *Constraints on an Agency's Option to Use Either Adjudication or Rulemaking*
>
> **Sec. 3.** *Procedures Outside the Fundamental Procedural Categories: Information Gathering and Inspection*

At the core of administrative law is the agency. A creature of statute and executive branch action, it stands in a complex relationship to the named constitutional branches of the federal government—Congress, the President, and the Supreme Court. Parts 3 and 4 of these materials explore these relationships. This Part, by contrast, is devoted to exploring the agency itself, how it operates and the legal constraints that govern its procedures.

As Chapter I notes, the U.S. Constitution says very little about the structure of the federal government beyond occasional references to "Departments," "Heads of Departments," and principal and inferior Officers. Instead, the agencies that dominate modern federal government—the Departments of State, Treasury, and Health and Human Services, for instance, or the Federal Communications Commission and the Securities and Exchange Commission—owe their creation and powers to Congress. Congress has broad authority to structure agencies as it sees fit, subject to constitutional limitations discussed in Chapter VII. And Congress has developed a number of different agency structures and forms. The most common form for executive agencies and departments, like the Department of Health and Human Services, the Environmental Protection Agency, and the Federal Aviation Administration, is to have a single agency head who is nominated by the President with Senate consent and is removable by the President at will. Another common form is an agency like the Federal Communications Commission, often termed an "independent regulatory commission," that is headed by a collegial body, whose members are presidentially nominated with Senate confirmation for staggered, fixed terms and who are removable only for cause.

These two categories hardly exhaust the different agency structures you will find in the federal government. Sometimes, as in the case of the Social Security Administration, an independent agency will be headed by a single individual who enjoys term tenure and for-cause removal protection. Sometimes independent commissions are located within executive agencies. An example of this is the Federal Energy Regulatory Commission, a body charged with regulating the interstate transmission of electricity, gas, and oil that is located in the Department of Energy (and thus ostensibly subject to oversight by the Secretary of Energy), but whose five members have the term appointments and removal protection that denote "independence." Congress has also at times created "private" corporations to serve its policy goals, such as the Federal Deposit Insurance Corporation, the Tennessee Valley Authority, Amtrak, and the U.S. Postal Service. Further, many federal programs are implemented by state agencies subject to federal administrative oversight—Social Security Disability Insurance and Medicaid are two prime examples— with the result that much of these programs' front-line administration is not undertaken by federal agencies at all.

Congress generally assigns agencies a wide array of roles and responsibilities. Agencies provide benefits, generate information, issue licenses, promulgate rules that govern private conduct, enforce federal law, adjudicate disputes, develop and operate infrastructure, award grants and contracts, manage their internal administration, and much more. You can readily see this by exploring any busy agency's website— for example, http://www.osha.gov, the website of the Occupational Safety and Health Administration. There you will find links for filing complaints or required reports, voluntary programs, statistical data, enforcement guidance and more—a wide range of matters beyond the regulations whose generation is a principal emphasis of these materials. Any lawyer working with workplace health and safety matters would, of necessity, become intimately familiar with much of this—which represents, if you like, the internal law of administration.[1] That internal law will generally be unique to the agency involved, however, and this casebook, like other law school teaching materials, stresses common problems and general legal principles, the issues that are most likely to wind up in court, on the President's desk, or before a congressional committee.

In the organization of this casebook, the law-making functions of agency rulemaking and agency adjudication dominate its attention to agency action, and these are the two basic categories of agency action the federal Administrative Procedure Act deals with—for executive and independent agencies alike. Since rulemaking results in a statute-like governing text, one's intuitive understanding readily equates it with a legislature's enactment of general policy; since it involves an arbiter

---

[1]   The subject of agency internal law is well considered in Nicholas Parillo, ed., American Administrative Law from the Inside Out (Cambridge U.P. 2017), a festschrift volume celebrating Prof. Jerry Mashaw's extraordinary contributions to understanding.

resolving disputed questions after a hearing between parties, one easily analogizes agency adjudication to the processes of judicial trial. Yet as the materials that follow suggest, the reality is much more complicated and the line between these two procedural forms is not always clear. Adopting a rule specifying some parameters necessary to assure the safety of a nuclear reactor will turn on questions of scientific fact, dispute about which might also arise in litigation; agencies sometimes use adjudication as courts sometimes use common-law decisionmaking to set general policy that will affect a large number of individuals. Note that the APA procedures for rulemaking and adjudication are inapplicable to a substantial amount of government activity affecting citizens' interests, such as information gathering and dispersal, setting general policy, contracting, and grant-making;[2] only some of these topics will be addressed in the following pages.

In the particular case of OSHA, Congress has chosen to place the responsibility for administrative adjudication of possible federal occupational safety and health statute and rule violations in a separate agency, the Occupational Safety and Health Review Commission.[3] (Consider why Congress might structure an agency this way.) OSHA itself only promulgates regulations and brings enforcement actions before OSHRC. For most prominent federal agencies, the combination of rulemaking, executing, *and* adjudicating functions is a key feature of their responsibilities. Operating under what are frequently broad authorizations, agencies like the EPA simultaneously develop and promulgate binding regulatory standards, investigate and prosecute violations of those standards, and adjudicate the resultant disputes. It is a basic precept of administrative law that agencies can only exercise the powers they have been delegated, but Congress frequently entrusts agencies with extensive policy-setting powers, subject only to broad limitations such as that they must regulate "in the public interest" or set emission standards "requisite to protect the public health."

These combinations of functions and broad delegations may be necessary to meet the needs of contemporary governance, yet they create enduring tensions between the constitutional framework and modern administrative government. Those tensions are explored in detail in Part 3 but surface as well, if less overtly, in the following materials on agency procedure. For example, judicial assessment, whether agencies have violated governing procedural requirements, occurs against a background of anxiety about the tremendous power that agencies wield and the profound impact their regulations can have on our nation's society and economy. In reading the materials of this Part, try not to lose sight of these larger constitutional tensions and how they may be

---

[2]   Some of these, as a formal matter, would fit within the APA's definitions of rulemaking and adjudication, but the procedures the APA requires are generally limited to acts with a capacity to make general law, which these do not.

[3]   http://www.oshrc.gov.

influencing the development of what appears on the surface to be non-constitutional or ordinary administrative law.[4]

Section 1 of this Chapter begins by identifying the *constitutional distinction between rulemaking and adjudication.* It then turns to describing how the rulemaking-adjudication divide factors into the APA and providing a more general overview on the APA's adoption and interpretation over the years. Section 2 addresses the principles that may constrain agency ability to use one or the other of these two modes of action. Section 3 offers the briefest of glances at information collection and inspection, two essential agency activities that largely fall outside of standard understandings of rulemaking and adjudication.

SECTION 1.   THE FUNDAMENTAL PROCEDURAL CATEGORIES OF ADMINISTRATIVE ACTION: RULEMAKING AND ADJUDICATION

> *a. The Constitution*
> *b. The Fundamental Statute*
> *c. Additional Sources of Procedural Constraint*

a.   The Constitution

> ***LONDONER v. DENVER***
> ***BI-METALLIC INVESTMENT CO. v. STATE BD. OF EQUALIZATION OF COLORADO***
> *Notes on the Londoner/Bi-Metallic Distinction*

LONDONER v. DENVER

Supreme Court of the United States (1908).
210 U.S. 373.

■ JUSTICE MOODY delivered the opinion of the Court.

The plaintiffs in error began this proceeding in a state court of Colorado to relieve lands owned by them from an assessment of a tax for the cost of paving a street upon which the lands abutted. The relief sought was granted by the trial court, but its action was reversed by the Supreme Court of the State. . . . The [Colorado] Supreme Court held that the tax was assessed in conformity with the constitution and laws of the State, and its decision on that question is conclusive. . . .

---

[4]   For a more sustained discussion of this point, see Gillian E. Metzger, Ordinary Administrative Law as Constitutional Common Law, 110 Colum. L. Rev. 479 (2010).

The tax complained of was assessed under the provisions of the charter of the city of Denver, which confers upon the city the power to make local improvements and to assess the cost upon property specially benefited. . . . It appears from the charter that, in the execution of the power to make local improvements and assess the cost upon the property specially benefited, the main steps to be taken by the city authorities are plainly marked and separated:

1. The board of public works must transmit to the city council a resolution ordering the work to be done and the form of an ordinance authorizing it and creating an assessment district. This it can do only upon certain conditions, one of which is that there shall first be filed a petition asking the improvement, signed by the owners of the majority of the frontage to be assessed.

2. The passage of that ordinance by the city council, which is given authority to determine conclusively whether the action of the board was duly taken.

3. The assessment of the cost upon the landowners after due notice and opportunity for hearing.

In the case before us the board took the first step by transmitting to the council the resolution to do the work and the form of an ordinance authorizing it. It is contended, however, that there was wanting an essential condition of the jurisdiction of the board, namely, such a petition from the owners as the law requires. The trial court found this contention to be true. But, as has been seen, the charter gave the city council the authority to determine conclusively that the improvements were duly ordered by the board after due notice and a proper petition. In the exercise of this authority the city council, in the ordinance directing the improvement to be made, adjudged, in effect, that a proper petition had been filed. . . . The state Supreme Court held that the determination of the city council was conclusive that a proper petition was filed, and that decision must be accepted by us as the law of the State. The only question for this court is whether the charter provision authorizing such a finding, without notice to the landowners, denies to them due process of law. We think it does not. The proceedings, from the beginning up to and including the passage of the ordinance authorizing the work did not include any assessment or necessitate any assessment, although they laid the foundation for an assessment, which might or might not subsequently be made. Clearly all this might validly be done without hearing to the landowners, provided a hearing upon the assessment itself is afforded. The legislature might have authorized the making of improvements by the city council without any petition. If it chose to exact a petition as a security for wise and just action it could, so far as the Federal Constitution is concerned, accompany that condition with a provision that the council, with or without notice, should determine finally whether it had been performed. This disposes of the first assignment of error, which is overruled. . . .

The fifth assignment, though general, vague and obscure, fairly raises, we think, the question whether the assessment was made without notice and opportunity for hearing to those affected by it, thereby denying to them due process of law. The trial court found as a fact that no opportunity for hearing was afforded, and the Supreme Court did not disturb this finding. The record discloses what was actually done, and there seems to be no dispute about it. After the improvement was completed the board of public works, in compliance with § 29 of the charter, certified to the city clerk a statement of the cost, and an apportionment of it to the lots of land to be assessed. Thereupon the city clerk, in compliance with § 30, published a notice stating, inter alia, that the written complaints or objections of the owners, if filed within thirty days, would be "heard and determined by the city council before the passage of any ordinance assessing the cost." Those interested, therefore, were informed that if they reduced their complaints and objections to writing, and filed them within thirty days, those complaints and objections would be heard, and would be heard before any assessment was made. . . . Resting upon the assurance that they would be heard, the plaintiffs in error filed within the thirty days the following paper:

"Denver, Colorado, January 13, 1900.

"To the Honorable Board of Public Works and the Honorable Mayor and City Council of the City of Denver:

"The undersigned, by Joshua Grozier, their attorney, do hereby most earnestly and strenuously protest and object to the passage of the contemplated or any assessing ordinance against the property in Eighth Avenue Paving District No. 1, so called, for each of the following reasons, to wit:

"1st.   That said assessment and all and each of the proceedings leading up to the same were and are illegal, voidable and void, and the attempted assessment if made will be void and uncollectible.

"2nd.   That said assessment and the cost of said pretended improvement should be collected, if at all, as a general tax against the city at large and not as a special assessment.

"3rd.   That property in said city not assessed is benefited by the said pretended improvement and certain property assessed is not benefited by said pretended improvement and other property assessed is not benefited by said pretended improvement to the extent of the assessment; that the individual pieces of property in said district are not benefited to the extent assessed against them and each of them respectively; that the assessment is arbitrary and property assessed in an equal amount is not benefited equally; that the boundaries of said pretended district were arbitrarily created without regard to the benefits or any other method of assessment known to law; that said assessment is outrageously large. . . .

"8th.   Because the city had no jurisdiction in the premises. No petition subscribed by the owners of a majority of the frontage in the district to be assessed for said improvements was ever obtained or presented. . . .

"Wherefore, because of the foregoing and numerous other good and sufficient reasons, the undersigned object and protest against the passage of the said proposed assessing ordinance."

This certainly was a complaint against and objection to the proposed assessment. Instead of affording the plaintiffs in error an opportunity to be heard upon its allegations, the city council, without notice to them, met as a board of equalization, not in a stated but in a specially called session, and, without any hearing, adopted the following resolution:

"Whereas, complaints have been filed by the various persons and firms as the owners of real estate included within the Eighth Avenue Paving District No. 1, of the city of Denver against the proposed assessments on said property for the cost of said paving, . . . and Whereas, no complaint or objection has been filed or made against the apportionment of said assessment made by the board of public works of the city of Denver, but the complaints and objections filed deny wholly the right of the city to assess any district or portion of the assessable property of the city of Denver; therefore, be it

"Resolved, by the city council of the city of Denver, sitting as a board of equalization, that the apportionments of said assessment made by said board of public works be, and the same are hereby, confirmed and approved."

Subsequently, without further notice or hearing, the city council enacted the ordinance of assessment whose validity is to be determined in this case. The facts out of which the question on this assignment arises may be compressed into small compass. The first step in the assessment proceedings was by the certificate of the board of public works of the cost of the improvement and a preliminary apportionment of it. The last step was the enactment of the assessment ordinance. From beginning to end of the proceedings the landowners, although allowed to formulate and file complaints and objections, were not afforded an opportunity to be heard upon them. Upon these facts was there a denial by the State of the due process of law guaranteed by the Fourteenth Amendment to the Constitution of the United States?

In the assessment, apportionment and collection of taxes upon property within their jurisdiction the Constitution of the United States imposes few restrictions upon the States. In the enforcement of such restrictions as the Constitution does impose this court has regarded substance and not form. But where the legislature of a State, instead of fixing the tax itself, commits to some subordinate body the duty of determining whether, in what amount, and upon whom it shall be levied, and of making its assessment and apportionment, due process of law requires that at some stage of the proceedings before the tax becomes irrevocably fixed, the taxpayer shall have an opportunity to be heard, of which he must have notice, either personal, by publication, or by a law fixing the time and place of the hearing. It must be remembered that the law of Colorado denies the landowner the right to object in the courts to the assessment, upon the ground that the objections are cognizable only by the board of equalization.

If it is enough that, under such circumstances, an opportunity is given to submit in writing all objections to and complaints of the tax to the board, then there was a hearing afforded in the case at bar. But we think that something more than that, even in proceedings for taxation, is required by due process of law. Many requirements essential in strictly judicial proceedings may be dispensed with in proceedings of this nature. But even here a hearing in its very essence demands that he who is entitled to it shall have the right to support his allegations by argument however brief, and, if need be, by proof, however informal. Pittsburgh, C. C. & St. L. R. Co. v. Backus, 154 U.S. 421, 426; Fallbrook Irrigation District v. Bradley, 164 U.S. 112, 171, et seq. It is apparent that such a hearing was denied to the plaintiffs in error. The denial was by the city council, which, while acting as a board of equalization, represents the State. The assessment was therefore void, and the plaintiffs in error were entitled to a decree discharging their lands from a lien on account of it. . . . Judgment reversed.

■ THE CHIEF JUSTICE and JUSTICE HOLMES dissent.

BI-METALLIC INVESTMENT CO. v. STATE BD. OF EQUALIZATION OF COLORADO

Supreme Court of the United States (1915).
239 U.S. 441.

■ JUSTICE HOLMES delivered the opinion of the Court.

This is a suit to enjoin the State Board of Equalization and the Colorado Tax Commission from putting in force, and the defendant Pitcher as assessor of Denver from obeying, an order of the boards increasing the valuation of all taxable property in Denver forty per cent. The order was sustained and the suit directed to be dismissed by the Supreme Court of the State. 56 Colo. 512, 138 P. 1010. See 56 Colo. 343, 138 P. 509. The plaintiff is the owner of real estate in Denver and brings the case here on the ground that it was given no opportunity to be heard and that therefore its property will be taken without due process of law, contrary to the Fourteenth Amendment of the Constitution of the United States. That is the only question with which we have to deal. . . .

For the purposes of decision we assume that the constitutional question is presented in the baldest way—that neither the plaintiff nor the assessor of Denver, who presents a brief on the plaintiff's side, nor any representative of the city and county, was given an opportunity to be heard, other than such as they may have had by reason of the fact that the time of meeting of the boards is fixed by law. On this assumption it is obvious that injustice may be suffered if some property in the county already has been valued at its full worth. But if certain property has been valued at a rate different from that generally prevailing in the county the owner has had his opportunity to protest and appeal as usual in our system of taxation, Hagar v. Reclamation District, 111 U.S. 701, 709, 710, so that it must be assumed that the property owners in the county all stand alike. The question then is whether all individuals have a constitutional right to be heard before a matter can be decided in which all are equally concerned—here, for instance, before a superior board decides that the local taxing officers have adopted a system of undervaluation throughout a county, as notoriously often has been the case. The answer of this court in the State Railroad Tax Cases, 92 U.S. 575, at least as to any further notice, was that it was hard to believe that the proposition was seriously made.

Where a rule of conduct applies to more than a few people it is impracticable that every one should have a direct voice in its adoption. The Constitution does not require all public acts to be done in town meeting or an assembly of the whole. General statutes within the state power are passed that affect the person or property of individuals, sometimes to the point of ruin, without giving them a chance to be heard. Their rights are protected in the only way that they can be in a complex society, by their power, immediate or remote, over those who make the rule. If the result in this case had been reached as it might have been by the State's doubling the rate of taxation, no one would suggest that the Fourteenth Amendment was violated unless every person affected had been allowed an opportunity to raise his voice against it before the body entrusted by the state constitution with the power. In considering this case in this court we must assume that the proper state machinery has been used, and the question is whether, if the state constitution had declared that Denver had been undervalued as compared with the rest of the State and had decreed that for the current year the valuation should be forty per cent higher, the objection now urged could prevail. It appears to us that to put the question is to answer it. There must be a limit to individual argument in such matters if government is to go on. In Londoner v. Denver, 210 U.S. 373, 385, a local board had to determine "whether, in what amount, and upon whom" a tax for paving a street should be levied for special benefits. A relatively small number of persons was concerned, who were exceptionally affected, in each case upon individual grounds, and it was held that they had a right to a hearing. But that decision is far from reaching a general determination dealing only with the principle upon which all the assessments in a county had been laid.

Judgment affirmed.

NOTES ON THE LONDONER/BI-METALLIC DISTINCTION

(1) *Just What Is the Nature of the Londoner/Bi-Metallic Distinction?* Suppose that, to address a growing problem of alcoholism and public drinking in certain neighborhoods, a city passed a statute authorizing its Liquor Commission to impose limits on alcohol sales in areas with high rates of public drinking and public disturbance.[5] The Commission can impose a variety of limits, ranging from restrictions on the quantity and timing of alcoholic sales to flat bans on sales of certain beverages or by particular liquor establishments.

At what point in the following series of actions, if any, do you think due process would obligate the Commission to provide notice and some opportunity to be heard to liquor stores affected by its actions:

- The Commission designates an area as having a high rate of public drinking and public disturbance.

- The Commission determines that sales of single beer bottles and flask or single-serving bottles of other alcoholic beverages are particularly likely to lead to public drinking.

- The Commission enacts a ban on sales of single-serving bottles of alcoholic beverages (single-serving beer bottles or flasks) by those stores in a designated area whose sales of this nature produce more than 10% of their gross income.

- The Commission concludes that sales by a particular store in the area bring it under this ban.

In determining if or when the Londoner hearing right applies in each of the preceding scenarios, would it matter if there were only a few stores affected by the Commission's actions or instead the number was in the hundreds? Would it matter if single alcohol sales represented such a significant part of one liquor store's business that the ban force it to close?

The answer to these questions depends on how we read Justice Holmes' description of Londoner as a case where "[a] relatively small number of persons was concerned, who were exceptionally affected, in each case upon individual grounds." If we conclude that "a relatively small number" is key, then the Londoner right would seem not to apply if a large number of liquor stores are affected. But is it plausible to think Londoner would have been decided differently if the street to be paved had been many miles in length and the affected plots had numbered in the thousands? How could a court determine when the number affected is large enough to extinguish the due process hearing right?

---

5   This problem is based on Decatur Liquors v. District of Columbia, noted at p. 228 below.

An alternative reading would put more emphasis on Holmes' observation that, however many persons were concerned, they were persons "who were exceptionally affected, in each case upon individual grounds." Recall that Londoner confined the right to a hearing to those facts bearing on the appropriate assessment for each particular lot. This reading would suggest that the hearing right is independent of the numbers involved but would obtain only when the Commission makes factual determinations with respect to a particular liquor store's sales volume.

Note that characterization of a matter as requiring "facts" to be decided is not, in itself, sufficient. Agencies are often called upon to decide scientific or general facts that are independent of particular parties—for example, in the hypothetical above, the Commission's determination that single alcohol sales are likely to lead to public drinking. An agency may need to determine whether a certain chemical is a human carcinogen; if so, how much cancer is likely to be caused at what concentrations, and what would be the feasibility and/or cost of controlling exposure to a given level in different types of industrial settings. Facts like these are neither party-specific (the sort of fact frequently styled "adjudicative") nor so general as the kind of proposition often styled as "legislative fact"—whether, for example, smoking is hazardous to human health. Particularly as applied to these expert matters, the adjudicative-legislative fact distinction is imperfect. While one might conclude that not all factfinding requires a Londoner "hearing," calling a given kind of fact "legislative" hardly suggests that its determination by a legislature's political vote rather than trial techniques would be ideal. For these issues of general fact, Cass Sunstein, The Most Knowledgeable Branch, 164 U. Pa. L. Rev. 1607 (2016), strongly defends executive branch factfinding techniques as superior to those of either legislature or court, though perhaps glossing over the potentials for political influence that also exist in this context.[6]

Yet a third reading might understand "in each case upon individual grounds" as signaling the inadequacy of political avenues for relief. "When . . . government singles out an individual for adverse action, the political process provides little protection. Individuals singled out for adverse action can be protected only by forcing the government to use a decisionmaking process that ensures fairness to the individual. That is the purpose of the Due Process Clause." 2 Richard J. Pierce, Jr., Administrative Law Treatise § 9.2 at 743 (5th ed. 2010); see also John Hart Ely, Democracy and Distrust 87 (1980). Indeed, political intervention and influence on individual decisions seems inappropriate in many contexts. See INS v. Chadha, 462 U.S. 919, 959 (1983) (Powell, J., concurring in the judgment), p. 837. On this view, the political process provides adequate protection against abuse of governmental power when broader policy is at stake and large numbers of people are concerned. But will political processes prove adequate when the policy being set will particularly affect a relatively small or politically disadvantaged group of people? Should additional procedural protections then be required?

---

6   Peter L. Strauss, Things Left Unsaid, Questions Not Asked, 164 U. Pa. L. Rev. 1607 (2016).

Shortly after his inauguration, President Trump issued an executive order categorically revoking visas and closing the country's borders to persons from seven nations that had been identified by statute or a pre-existing executive order as harboring potential terrorist threats. Amongst the arguments made in reaction to what had proved an extremely disruptive event in the lives of many already in the air, or believing that they had a legal right of return to the United States (as, for example, green card holders), was the claim that this action deprived affected individuals of their rights without due process of law. How would the Londoner/Bi-Metallic distinction apply to this action? If you conclude that it was a quasi-legislative action, might the absence of any public procedures attending its adoption (even, reportedly, significant internal government consultation) persuade you that "due process of lawmaking" had been violated? See Peter Shane, Back to the Future of the American State, p. 232 below.

PETER L. STRAUSS, REVISITING *OVERTON PARK*: POLITICAL AND JUDICIAL CONTROLS OVER ADMINISTRATIVE ACTIONS AFFECTING THE COMMUNITY, 39 UCLA L. Rev. 1251, 1256–57 (1992): "A . . . prominent distinction between the worlds of politics and law appears in Justice Holmes' opinion for the Court in the still influential Bi-Metallic Investment Co. v. State Board of Equalization. . . . Although Holmes' conclusion was procedural—at issue was the application of the Due Process Clause of the Constitution to require quasi-adjudicatory process—the contrast he drew was grounded in conventional notions regarding the relative strengths and weaknesses of legal and political process. Politicians, not judges, should be responsible for setting the dimensions of social policy that may involve trades among the interests of broad groupings of citizens; judges' strengths lie in resolving discrete controversies between individuals, in which one wins, another loses, and broad social adjustments are secondary to the outcome of their concrete dispute. That contrast was given later, influential expression by Professor Lon Fuller, who noted the difference between the 'bi-polar' disputes characterizing typical judicial action and the 'polycentric' controversies that characterize legislatures and the policy-making side of administrative action. The give-and-take resolutions typical of the latter are more readily achieved by meliorative than winner-take-all procedures and are less easily justified in terms of a system structured as rational analysis than one grounded in accommodation."

(2) *How Has the Distinction Fared in the Courts?*

(a) O'CONNOR, J., speaking for the Court in MINNESOTA STATE BOARD FOR COMMUNITY COLLEGES v. KNIGHT, 465 U.S. 271, 283–287 (1984):

"The Constitution does not grant to members of the public generally a right to be heard by public bodies making decisions of policy. . . . Policymaking organs in our system of government have never operated under a constitutional constraint requiring them to afford every interested member of the public an opportunity to present testimony before any policy is adopted. Legislatures throughout the nation, including Congress, frequently enact bills on which no hearings have been held or on which testimony has been received from only a select group. Executive agencies likewise make policy decisions of widespread application without permitting unrestricted public testimony. Public officials at all levels of government daily make policy decisions based only on the advice they decide they need and choose to hear. To recognize a constitutional right to participate directly in government policymaking would work a revolution in existing government practices.

"Not least among the reasons for refusing to recognize such a right is the impossibility of its judicial definition and enforcement. Both federalism and separation-of-powers concerns would be implicated in the massive intrusion into state and federal policymaking that recognition of the claimed right would entail. Moreover, the pragmatic considerations identified by Justice Holmes in Bi-Metallic Investment Co. v. State Board of Equalization are as weighty today as they were in 1915. Government makes so many policy decisions affecting so many people that it would likely grind to a halt were policymaking constrained by constitutional requirements on whose voices must be heard. 'There must be a limit to individual argument in such matters if government is to go on.' Absent statutory restrictions, the state must be free to consult or not to consult whomever it pleases.

"However wise or practicable various levels of public participation in various kinds of policy decisions may be, this Court has never held, and nothing in the Constitution suggests it should hold, that government must provide for such participation. In Bi-Metallic the Court rejected due process as a source of an obligation to listen. Nothing in the First Amendment or in this Court's case law interpreting it suggests that the rights to speak, associate, and petition require government policymakers to listen or respond to individuals' communications on public issues. . . . No other constitutional provision has been advanced as a source of such a requirement. Nor, finally, can the structure of government established and approved by the Constitution provide the source. It is inherent in a republican form of government that direct public participation in government policymaking is limited. See The Federalist No. 10 (Madison). Disagreement with public policy and disapproval of officials' responsiveness, as Justice Holmes suggested in Bi-Metallic, is to be registered principally at the polls."

(b) In ONYX PROPS. LLC v. BD. OF CNTY. COMM'RS, 838 F.3d 1039 (10th Cir. 2016), the Board of County Commissioners of Elbert County, Colorado, discovered that the County zoning map had been lost and created a new one without following the procedures required by state law for doing so. That violation of state procedural requirements was not, however, a violation of the federal due process rights of property owners who had been required to comply with the new map in seeking a rezoning that would permit them to subdivide their properties. "Early in the last century the Supreme Court held that constitutional procedural due process does not govern the enactment of legislation. In *Bi-Metallic* the . . . Court held that a hearing was not constitutionally required for each affected landowner before the adoption of a generally applicable tax increase. It explained that such a requirement would be too burdensome, and the public had other means of influencing legislative decisions . . . As the Supreme Court wrote decades after *Bi-Metallic*:

In altering substantive rights through enactment of rules of general applicability, a legislature generally provides constitutionally adequate process simply by enacting the statute, publishing it, and, to the extent the statute regulates private conduct, affording those within the statute's reach a reasonable opportunity both to familiarize themselves with the general requirements imposed and to comply with those requirements.

United States v. Locke, 471 U.S. 84, 108 (1985). We recognize that not all actions by municipal boards are legislative. When the action has a limited focus (only a few people or properties are affected) and is based on grounds that are individually assessed, it may be more adjudicative than legislative and therefore subject to traditional procedural requirements of notice and hearing. . . . In such circumstances the need for additional procedural protections is greater because political remedies are often unattainable by individuals or small groups and the grant of procedural safeguards to a few does not impose as great a burden on government.

Bi-Metallic controls here because . . . the adoption of a comprehensive zoning ordinance is a legislative act. A zoning plan is based on community-wide development goals, not on the particular facts of individual situations. It involves the discretionary implementation of prospective policies rather than the application of an existing policy to a specific landowner."

(c)   In DECATUR LIQUORS, INC. v. DISTRICT OF COLUMBIA, 478 F.3d 360 (D.C. Cir. 2007), holders of liquor licenses sued the District of Columbia, claiming inter alia that an amendment to the liquor code declaring a moratorium on off-premises single unit sales of beer, malt liquor, and ale in a specified geographic area violated the U.S. Constitution. The court held that the District of Columbia did not violate holders' due process rights by denying the affected licensees individualized notice and an opportunity to be heard. "Here, the moratorium zone covered all 73 liquor stores in Ward 4. This is the classic Bi-Metallic scenario—the statute prohibits the same conduct by all 73 licensees. Not only would individualized hearings be impractical, they would be unnecessary, as the only disputable issue would be the link between the forbidden sales and the District's legislative goal. Although there might be situations where the Due Process Clause entitled a party to a hearing on whether the relevant legislative purposes called for inclusion of the party's property within a special geographic zone, this is not such a case; the purpose of the moratorium zone was clear, and there is no dispute that encompassing all Ward 4 licensees matched the legislative goal."

(3)   **The Elements of the Distinction.** The distinction between making a rule and adjudicating a case is one of the most basic in all of jurisprudence. As you may see, p. 233, the APA's definitions of rule and adjudication, 5 U.S.C. § 551(4, 5, 6 and 7) quite fudge the issue. They include in "rule" a statement of "particular applicability" and give "adjudication" a catchall meaning for any final disposition "other than rulemaking but including licensing." It might occur to you that to grant a license is to make a statement of "particular applicability and future effect." Here are some materials that

bear on the question of how the distinction is, as a general matter, to be drawn, and on the difficulties in doing so:

(a)   The element of prospectivity:

(*i*)   5 U.S.C. § 551(4):

> "rule" means the whole or a part of an agency statement of general or particular applicability *and future effect* designed to implement, interpret, or prescribe law or policy or describing the organization, procedure, or practice requirements of an agency and includes the approval or prescription for the future of rates, wages, corporate or financial structures or reorganizations thereof, prices, facilities, appliances, services or allowances therefor or of valuations, costs, or accounting, or practices bearing on any of the foregoing (Emphasis added).

(*ii*)   HOLMES, J., in PRENTIS V. ATLANTIC COAST LINE CO., 211 U.S. 210, 226 (1908):

"A judicial inquiry investigates, declares and enforces liabilities as they stand on present or past facts and under laws supposed already to exist. That is its purpose and end. Legislation on the other hand looks to the future and changes existing conditions by making a new rule to be applied thereafter to all or some part of those subject to its power. The establishment of a rate is the making of a rule for the future, and therefore is an act legislative not judicial in kind."

(*iii*)   THOMAS M. COOLEY, A TREATISE ON THE CONSTITUTIONAL LIMITATIONS WHICH REST UPON THE LEGISLATIVE POWER OF THE STATES OF THE AMERICAN UNION 132 (7th ed. 1903 (Victor H. Lane, ed.)):

"[I]t is said that that which distinguishes a judicial from a legislative act is, that the one is a determination of what the existing law is in relation to some existing thing already done or happened, while the other is a predetermination of what the law shall be for the regulation of all future cases falling under its provisions."

(*iv*)   FREDERICK SCHAUER, A BRIEF NOTE ON THE LOGIC OF RULES, WITH SPECIAL REFERENCE TO *BOWEN V. GEORGETOWN UNIVERSITY HOSPITAL*, 42 Admin.L.Rev. 447, 454 (1990):

"[N]othing . . . [in the distinction between whether a decision speaks forward or not] suggests one answer or another to the question of when 'the future' starts. Some decisions will pertain to a certain narrow temporal time frame, and these will be the 'orders,' and others will pertain to an open-ended time frame, and these are the 'rules,' but *that* distinction has nothing to do with when that time frame is or starts and nothing to do with the relationship between the time frame and the time of the making of the decision. To put the same point differently (and perhaps slightly more clearly), we are now able to appreciate that the creation of an open-ended rule and the designation of the starting time for the open-ended period encompassed by that rule are two distinct issues."

(b)   The element of generality:

(i)   RALPH F. FUCHS, PROCEDURE IN ADMINISTRATIVE RULE-MAKING, 52 Harv. L. Rev. 259, 263–64 (1938):

"The most obvious definition of rule-making and the one most often employed in the literature of administrative law asserts simply that it is the function of laying down general regulations as distinguished from orders that apply to named persons or to specific situations. Most acts of legislatures, although by no means all, establish rights and duties with respect either to people generally or to classes of people or situations that are defined but not enumerated. Conversely, the judgments of courts usually are addressed to particular individuals or to situations that are definitely specified. Similarly, administrative action can be classified into general regulations, including determinations whose effect is to bring general regulations into operation, and orders or acts of specific application.

". . . [I]t is feasible to distinguish a general regulation from an order of specific application on the basis of the manner in which the parties subject to it are designated. If they are named, or if they are in effect identified by their relation to a piece of property or transaction or institution which is specified, the order is one of specific application. If they are not named, but the order applies to a designated class of persons or situations, the order is a general regulation or a rule."

(ii)   JOHN DICKINSON, ADMINISTRATIVE JUSTICE AND THE SUPREMACY OF LAW 17–20 (1927):

"Our constitutional distinction between 'legislative,' 'executive' and 'judicial' powers draws the courts frequently into discussions in which the 'legislative' or 'executive' aspect of an administrative act is generally emphasized at the expense of the 'judicial.' Thus, for example, the act of a public-utilities commission in fixing a rate has been held to be 'legislative' for constitutional purposes.

"From one aspect of juristic analysis, legislative it no doubt is—that is, from the aspect of its future operation and its applicability to a whole class of cases. But the writ of mandamus is future in its operation, and yet is not for that reason regarded as legislative; and if we examine rate-fixing from the standpoint of the general applicability of the resulting rate to an indefinite number of future cases as a class, we observe the significant peculiarity that, while the rate applies indifferently, indeed, as against all future shippers, it applies only to the particular carrier or carriers who were parties to the hearing and other proceedings before the commission, and for whom, as the outcome of those proceedings, the rate is prescribed. From the standpoint of shippers, therefore, the rate may no doubt be regarded as legislation, but from the standpoint of the carriers it seems quite as truly adjudication. Even with respect to the shippers, however, it may be likened to the procedure whereby an injunction is obtained against a group of persons designated by a class-description and not named personally in the bill. If the latter procedure is judicial, there is certainly an element of adjudication in administrative rate-fixing; and that is all I wish to insist on here. There is no intention to deny that rate-fixing involves as one of its elements the exercise of a function which may as well as not be called 'legislative.' The whole discussion should go to demonstrate the futility of trying to classify a particular exercise of administrative power as either wholly legislative or wholly judicial. The tendency of the administrative procedure is to foreshorten both functions into a continuous governmental act."

(iii) RONALD M. LEVIN, THE CASE FOR (FINALLY) FIXING THE APA's DEFINITION OF "RULE," 56 Admin. L. Rev. 1077 (2004):

"[T]he ordinary understanding of a 'rule' is a governmental pronouncement that takes the form of a statute—a 'quasi-legislative' act that has 'general applicability.' Indeed, the due process foundations of the distinction between rules and adjudicative orders, reflected in a tradition that dates back to the venerable case of Bi-Metallic Investment Co. v. State Board of Equalization are rooted in the distinction between generalized and particularized action. The classic doctrine holds that a regulated person has little if any constitutional right to a hearing in rulemaking, as opposed to adjudication, because of the impracticability of giving a hearing to numerous affected persons, and because 'legislative' rather than 'adjudicative' facts are likely to be involved. These rationales relate to generality, not prospectivity."

(c) The element of "the rule of law":

(i) FRIEDRICH A. HAYEK, THE CONSTITUTION OF LIBERTY 153–54 (1960):

"The conception of freedom under the law . . . rests on the contention that when we obey laws, in the sense of general abstract rules laid down irrespective of their application to us, we are not subject to another man's will and are therefore free. It is because the lawgiver does not know the particular cases to which his rules will apply, and it is because the judge who applies them has no choice in drawing the conclusions that follow from the existing body of rules and the particular facts of the case, that it can be said that laws and not men rule. Because the rule is laid down in ignorance of the particular case and no man's will decides the coercion used to enforce it, the law is not arbitrary. This, however, is true only if by 'law' we mean the general rules that apply equally to everybody. This generality is probably the most important aspect of that attribute of law which we have called its 'abstractness.' As a true law should not name any particulars, so it should especially not single out any specific persons or group of persons."

(ii) KATIE R. EYER, ADMINISTRATIVE ADJUDICATION AND THE RULE OF LAW, 60 Admin. L. Rev. 647, 651 (2008):

". . .[A]djudicative lawmaking theoretically has the potential to further a number of important rule-of-law goals. . . . [A]djudicative lawmaking by administrative agencies theoretically has the capacity to increase consistency in the legal standards applied to individual cases, promote predictability through rule creation, and restrain otherwise arbitrary discretion. . . . [T]he historically tepid academic view of adjudicative lawmaking by administrative agencies. . . . is unwarranted—and is, in fact, dangerous—in cases where a decline in adjudicative lawmaking is unlikely to be accompanied by the creation of a legislative lawmaking program of comparable scope and vigor. Where such comparable substitutes are unlikely to be forthcoming, a reduction in an agency's use of adjudicative lawmaking is likely to have substantial negative effects, which should be cause for concern. . . .

". . .[C]ritiques of adjudicative lawmaking from a prospectivity perspective . . . may be of less importance than many authors have previously suggested. . . .[A]djudicative lawmaking—while it does create some prospectivity concerns in the short term and, in particular, as applied to the individual parties involved in the dispute—does not create a major deviation from the prospectivity norm over the long term. Most individuals will be subject to preexisting rules, and even those parties subject to ostensibly "new" rules created through adjudication will rarely be without forewarning that the new rule was forthcoming."

(iii) ROBERTO M. UNGER, KNOWLEDGE AND POLITICS 89–90 (1975):

"To understand the nature of adjudication one must distinguish two different ways of ordering human relations. One way is to establish rules to govern general categories of acts and persons, and then to decide particular disputes among persons on the basis of the established rules. This is legal justice. The other way is to determine goals and then, quite independently of rules, to decide particular cases by a judgment of what decision is most likely to contribute to the predetermined goals, a judgment of instrumental rationality. This is substantive justice.

"In the situation of legal justice, the laws are made against the background of the ends they are designed to promote, even if the sole permissible end is liberty itself. Only after the rules have been formulated do decisions 'under the rules' become possible. Hence, the possibility of some sort of distinction between legislation and adjudication is precisely what defines legal justice. The main task of the theory of adjudication is to say when a decision can truly be said to stand 'under a rule,' if the rule we have in mind is the law of the state, applied by a judge. Only decisions 'under a rule' are consistent with freedom; others constitute arbitrary exercises of judicial power. . . .

"The distinctive feature of substantive justice is the nonexistence of any line between legislation and adjudication. In the pure case of substantive justice, there is neither rulemaking nor rule applying, because rather than prescriptive rules there are only choices as to what should be accomplished and judgments of instrumental rationality about how to get it done."

(4) ***Should Legislative Action Be Subject to Procedural Due Process Constraints?*** PETER M. SHANE, BACK TO THE FUTURE OF THE AMERICAN STATE: OVERRULING BUCKLEY V. VALEO AND OTHER MADISONIAN STEPS, 57 U. Pitt. L. Rev. 443, 455 (1996): "Under the current state of due process law, the Due Process Clauses exercise no procedural leverage over legislative deliberations. Under the relevant precedents, it is black-letter judicial interpretation that procedural due process attaches only to the government's adjudicatory processes and not to legislative-style decision making, even when conducted by an administrative agency. . . . But such a reading of the Due Process Clauses seems facially wrong. A proper analysis should begin

with the proposition that limiting the reach of procedural due process to adjudication does not accord with the Constitution's text. The point seems self-evident because the Due Process Clauses are routinely applied to the legislature in substantive due process cases. The question then ought to be posed whether legislative decisions that affect the rights and responsibilities of persons outside Congress deny liberty arbitrarily if such decisions are made under conditions in which no attention is given to the rudiments of sound decision-making procedure."

Prof. Shane's argument echoes one earlier made in Hans A. Linde, Due Process of Lawmaking, 55 Neb. L. Rev. 197 (1976). Many believe the rulemaking procedures imposed by the APA, that you may study in Ch. IV, have denatured this question for rulemaking (which lacks legislation's direct political connection). Keep this issue in mind as you study the materials of that chapter.

b. The Fundamental Statute

> *ADMINISTRATIVE PROCEDURE ACT*
> *OF 1946*
> *Notes on the APA Definitions*
> *Notes on the History of the APA*
> *Notes on Interpreting the APA*

ADMINISTRATIVE PROCEDURE ACT OF 1946

The full text of the APA appears in the Appendix, at p. 1464.

§ 551   Definitions . . .

(4) "rule" means the whole or a part of an agency statement of general or particular applicability and future effect designed to implement, interpret, or prescribe law or policy or describing the organization, procedure, or practice requirements of an agency and includes the approval or prescription for the future of rates, wages, corporate or financial structures or reorganization thereof, prices, facilities, appliances, services or allowances therefor or of valuations, costs, or accounting, or practices bearing on any of the foregoing;

(5) "rule making" means agency process for formulating, amending, or repealing a rule;

(6) "order" means the whole or a part of a final disposition, whether affirmative, negative, injunctive, or declaratory in form, of an agency in a matter other than rule making but including licensing;

(7) "adjudication" means agency process for the formulation of an order.

NOTES ON THE APA DEFINITIONS

(1) *Either a Rule or an Order.* Note that the APA's definitions render *every* agency "final disposition, whether affirmative, negative, injunctive, or declaratory in form" *either* a rule *or* an order. The latter—i.e., the products of "adjudication"—is the residual category. Chapter IV explores the difficulties presented by the definition of "rule." Here, observe that the definition sections give two concrete examples of their application: The definition of an "order" includes "licensing," and the definition of a "rule" includes "the approval or prescription for the future of rates, wages, corporate or financial structures or reorganization thereof, prices, facilities, appliances, services or allowances therefor or of valuations, costs, or accounting, or practices." Both of these activities are somewhat ambiguous in Londoner/Bi-Metallic terms; each typically involves particular applicants for rate approvals or licenses whose individual facts will be central to decision, on one side, and broadly diverse community interests and more social (polycentric) issues of fact on the other. Moreover, APA licensing procedures are more lenient in important ways than the ordinary APA procedures for on-the-record adjudication, and APA ratemaking procedures are more formal than the notice-and-comment procedures typically used to specify, for example, requirements of safety equipment for automobiles. Even though licensing is explicitly mentioned in the general definition of adjudication, various portions of §§ 554(d), 556(d) and 557(b) make special provisions for initial licensing, the application process. So does § 558 of the Act. Similarly, ratemaking gets special treatment as a type of formal rulemaking—and is even mentioned in § 554(d), a provision about "adjudication." These procedural variations are roughly equivalent and create a formal procedure of somewhat lesser intensity than ordinary on-the-record adjudication for both that kind of "adjudication" that is action on an initial license application and that kind of "rulemaking" that is ratemaking. In this concrete way, the Act's provisions accommodate the ambiguities of both the definitional sections and the constitutional test.

(2) *Formal and Informal Agency Proceedings.* The APA distinguishes between formal and informal versions of both rulemaking and adjudication. This is done not by means of additional definitions, but rather by making those sections of the Act which define formal hearings (§§ 556 and 557) applicable only to certain proceedings: proceedings required to be "on the record." Thus, we find within § 553, "Rule making," that an informal procedure is defined in § 553(c) but that the subsection ends by saying: "When rules are required by statute to be made on the record after opportunity for an agency hearing, sections 556 and 557 of this title apply instead of this subsection." Ratemaking proceedings, defined as rulemaking, are the most common form for which such requirements appear. As to adjudication, § 554, "Adjudications," starts right off by saying that it only applies "in every case of adjudication required by statute to be determined on the record after opportunity for an agency hearing"; later on, in § 554(c)(2), we find adjudications referred over for "hearing and decision on notice and in accordance with sections 556 and 557 of this title." For adjudications that are *not* "required by statute to be determined on the

record after opportunity for an agency hearing," the only arguably applicable provision of the APA is § 555(e), requiring prompt notice of denials of requests, "accompanied by a brief statement of the grounds for denial" unless the denial is self-explanatory or in affirmation of a previous denial.

NOTES ON THE HISTORY OF THE APA

(1) **The Background of the APA.** The Court's early views of the APA were showcased in WONG YANG SUNG V. MCGRATH, 339 U.S. 33 (1950). Wong Yang Sung, a citizen of China, was arrested and charged with being unlawfully in the United States through overstaying his shore leave as a member of a shipping crew. After an administrative hearing, an immigration inspector recommended deportation; the Acting Commissioner approved and the Board of Immigration Appeals affirmed. Wong Yang Sung then filed a habeas corpus proceeding in District Court for the District of Columbia, claiming that the administrative hearing was not conducted in conformity with §§ 5 and 11 of the APA, codified at 5 U.S.C. § 554 and scattered other sections addressing ALJs. Those sections provide, inter alia, that officers presiding at formal hearings under the APA shall be independent of officers engaged in prosecution or investigation and shall have protection against dismissal. Although the government admitted that the hearing did not comply with the APA, it asserted that the Act did not apply to deportation hearings. In holding that the APA did apply, the Supreme Court in an opinion by JUSTICE JACKSON discussed in detail the history and purposes of the Act:

"Multiplication of federal administrative agencies and expansion of their functions to include adjudications which have serious impact on private rights has been one of the dramatic legal developments of the past half-century. Partly from restriction by statute, partly from judicial self-restraint, and partly by necessity—from the nature of their multitudinous and semi-legislative or executive tasks—the decisions of administrative tribunals were accorded considerable finality, and especially with respect to fact finding. The conviction developed, particularly within the legal profession, that this power was not sufficiently safeguarded and sometimes was put to arbitrary and biased use.

"Concern over administrative impartiality and response to growing discontent was reflected in Congress as early as 1929, when Senator Norris introduced a bill to create a separate administrative court. . . . The Executive Branch of the Federal Government also became concerned as to whether the structure and procedure of these bodies was conducive to fairness in the administrative process. . . . The President early in 1939 . . . directed the Attorney General to name 'a committee of eminent lawyers, jurists, scholars, and administrators to review the entire administrative process in the various departments of the executive Government and to recommend improvements, including the suggestion of any needed legislation.' . . . So strong was the demand for reform, however, that Congress did not await the Committee's report but passed what was known as the Walter-Logan bill, a comprehensive and rigid prescription of standardized procedures for administrative agencies. This bill was vetoed by President Roosevelt December 18, 1940 . . .

"The McCarran-Sumners bill, which evolved into the present Act, was introduced in 1945. Its consideration and hearing, especially of agency interests, was painstaking. . . . It passed both Houses without opposition and was signed by President Truman June 11, 1946. . . . The Act thus represents a long period of study and strife; it settles long-continued and hard-fought contentions, and enacts a formula upon which opposing social and political forces have come to rest. It contains many compromises and generalities and, no doubt, some ambiguities. Experience may reveal defects. But it would be a disservice to our form of government and to the administrative process itself if the courts should fail, so far as the terms of the Act warrant, to give effect to its remedial purposes where the evils it was aimed at appear. . . .

"Of the several administrative evils sought to be cured or minimized, only two are particularly relevant to issues before us today. One purpose was to introduce greater uniformity of procedure and standardization of administrative practice among the diverse agencies whose customs had departed widely from each other. We pursue this no further than to note that any exception we may find to its applicability would tend to defeat this purpose.

"More fundamental, however, was the purpose to curtail and change the practice of embodying in one person or agency the duties of prosecutor and judge. . . . [T]he Attorney General's Committee on Administrative Procedure, which divided as to the appropriate remedy, was unanimous that this evil existed. Its Final Report said: 'These types of commingling of functions of investigation or advocacy with the function of deciding are thus plainly undesirable. But they are also avoidable and should be avoided by appropriate internal division of labor. For the disqualifications produced by investigation or advocacy are personal psychological ones which result from engaging in those types of activity; and the problem is simply one of isolating those who engage in the activity.' Rep. Atty. Gen. Comm. Ad. Proc. 56 (1941), S. Doc. No. 8, 77th Cong., 1st Sess. 56 (1941). . . .

"Turning now to the case before us, we find the administrative hearing a perfect exemplification of the practices so unanimously condemned. . . . This hearing, which followed the uniform practice of the Immigration Service, was before an immigrant inspector, who, for purposes of the hearing, is called the 'presiding inspector.' Except with consent of the alien, the presiding inspector may not be the one who investigated the case. 8 C.F.R. 150.6(b). But the inspector's duties include investigation of like cases; and while he is today hearing cases investigated by a colleague, tomorrow his investigation of a case may be heard before the [examining] inspector whose case he passes on today. . . . The presiding inspector, when no examining inspector is present, is required to 'conduct the interrogation of the alien and the witnesses in behalf of the Government and shall cross-examine the alien's witnesses and present such evidence as is necessary to support the charges in the warrant of arrest.' 8 C.F.R. 150.6(b). . . .

"The Administrative Procedure Act did not go so far as to require a complete separation of investigating and prosecuting functions from adjudicating functions. But that the safeguards it did set up were intended to ameliorate the evils from the commingling of functions as exemplified here is beyond doubt. And this commingling, if objectionable anywhere, would seem to be particularly so in the deportation proceeding, where we frequently meet with a voteless class of litigants who not only lack the influence of citizens, but who are strangers to the laws and customs in which they find themselves involved and who often do not even understand the tongue in which they are accused. Nothing in the nature of the parties or proceedings suggests that we should strain to exempt deportation proceedings from reforms in administrative procedure applicable generally to federal agencies.

"Nor can we accord any weight to the argument that to apply the Act to such hearings will cause inconvenience and added expense to the Immigration Service. Of course it will, as it will to nearly every agency to which it is applied. But the power of the purse belongs to Congress, and Congress has determined that the price for greater fairness is not too high. The agencies, unlike the aliens, have ready and persuasive access to the legislative ear and if error is made by including them, relief from Congress is a simple matter. . . .

"[T]he difficulty with . . . [the government's] argument . . . that the deportation statute does not require a hearing is that, without such hearing, there would be no constitutional authority for deportation. . . . When the Constitution requires a hearing, it requires a fair one, one before a tribunal which meets at least currently prevailing standards of impartiality. A deportation hearing involves issues basic to human liberty and happiness and, in the present upheavals in lands to which aliens may be returned, perhaps to life itself. It might be difficult to justify as measuring up to constitutional standards of impartiality a hearing tribunal for deportation proceedings the like of which has been condemned by Congress as unfair even where less vital matters of property rights are at stake."

The Court's confidence about Congress's purposes was apparently misplaced, for the specific holding of Wong Yang Sung that § 554 of the APA applies to deportation proceedings was promptly reversed by legislation, and that reversal was subsequently upheld against constitutional challenge. See Marcello v. Bonds, 349 U.S. 302 (1955). Courts continue to cite Wong Yang Sung for the general proposition that aliens have due process rights in deportation hearings, but they no longer reason that the APA embodies Congress's assessment of the procedures the Constitution requires. Chapter V of these materials explores the reasoning courts now use in giving concrete content to the procedures fairness requires for the hearings it necessitates.

(2) *On the APA's Adoption.* Unanimously passed in both House and Senate in 1946, the APA emerged after a lengthy period of debate and development.[7] Justice Jackson, President Roosevelt's Attorney General from 1940 to 1941, participated in the development of the APA at an early stage.

---

[7] A full legislative history, including hearings and debates, appears in S. Doc. 248, 79th Cong. 2d Sess., 1946.

Thus, his opinion in Wang Yang Sung reflects the knowledge possessed by the generation of its framers. As the excerpts from that opinion note, it emerged from a long political back and forth in reaction to the New Deal that, in 1939, led President Roosevelt to direct the Attorney General to form a committee to study administrative reform and propose legislation. The director of the Attorney General's Committee on Administrative Procedure was Walter Gellhorn, the first editor of this casebook; the Committee's final report, Sen. Doc. 8, 77th Cong. 1st Sess. (1941), has long been regarded as an exemplar of empirical study of government functioning.[8] World War II then intervened, and the Act was passed after "a most rigorous and lengthy sieve of consideration"[9] that began as that war drew to a close.

Subsequent scholarly accounts offered additional views on the political context of the APA's adoption. Here are three excerpts:

(a)   MARTIN SHAPIRO, APA: PAST, PRESENT, FUTURE, 72 Va. L. Rev. 447, 452–54 (1986): "Turning to the APA itself, . . . most . . . contributors to this symposium rightly characterize it as a deal struck between opposing political forces. One should consider, however, who struck the deal and what its terms were. The battle of the thirties was between Republicans and conservative Democrats on the one hand and New Deal Democrats on the other, at a time when the New Deal consensus was not yet dominant in American politics. Consequently, the New Dealers were loath to compromise and loath to allow congressional initiatives against the president. . . .

"By 1946, the New Deal consensus was absolutely and unassailably established, so the battle was by then really an internal one among New Dealers—between conservative and liberal Democrats, both of whom were firmly harnessed to the New Deal vision of the administrative state. At this point, the liberal New Dealers could afford to compromise in a statute that no longer appeared to threaten the strong presidency . . .

"The APA as originally enacted divided all administrative law into three parts. For matters requiring adjudication, in which government action was directly detrimental to the specific legal interests of particular parties, the compromise was heavily weighted in favor of the conservatives. The . . . demand for totally separate tribunals was ignored: the agencies themselves adjudicated these matters. But the agencies' processes were to be considered quasi-adjudication and were to be governed by adjudicative-style procedures, presided over by a relatively independent hearing officer, and freely subject to relatively strict judicial review.

"The second part, rulemaking, constituted an almost total victory for the liberal New Deal forces. Congress' delegation of vast lawmaking power to the agencies was acknowledged and legitimated. Rulemaking was to be quasi-legislative, not quasi-judicial. No adjudicatory-style hearings or hearing officers were required. Those not directly and immediately affected by the rule could not easily obtain judicial review. Under the APA [as understood when enacted], rulemaking generated no record to be reviewed, and the

---

[8]   Virginia Legal Studies published an abridged edition, "Administrative Procedure in Government Agencies," in 1968.

[9]   S. Doc. 248 at iii (Statement of Sen. McCarran, Chair, Sen. Judiciary Committee).

standard of review made an agency's decisions irreversible unless it had acted insanely. Although the agencies were acting in a quasi-legislative capacity, they were not required to jump through as many procedural hoops as Congress typically did in legislating. Congress normally held oral hearings on pending legislation, a full draft of which was already on the docket, and issued a rather elaborate committee report to explain a bill as it went to the floor of the House or Senate. In contrast, the APA simply required an agency to give notice only of its intention to make a rule. It did not have to submit a draft. It had to receive written comments, but no hearing was required. It merely had to provide a 'concise' and 'general' statement accompanying its rule.

"In the absence of a rulemaking record, reviewing courts were forced to presume that the agency had the facts to support its rule. Given the extremely broad and standardless delegations in most of the New Deal legislation of the thirties and forties, courts rarely found that a rule violated the terms of its parent statute. And it was rare indeed for a New Deal-appointed judge reviewing the work of a New Deal-staffed agency to find that the agency had acted like a lunatic, that is that it had been, in the words of the APA, 'arbitrary' and 'capricious.' Therefore, in the political bargain judicial review of rulemaking is about all the conservatives got, and they got very little of that.

"The third part of administrative law originally conceived by the APA included everything that government did that was neither adjudication nor rulemaking."

Prof. Shapiro goes on to explain that this large mass of diverse activities fell into the default APA category of "adjudication." In the absence of some other statute requiring a hearing on the record, it was left without significant procedural requirements.

(b) In "A 'Bill of Rights' for the American State," the second chapter of her THE UNWIELDY AMERICAN STATE: ADMINISTRATIVE POLITICS SINCE THE NEW DEAL 59–108 (2012), JOANNA L. GRISINGER gives a historical account that is less of fierce political struggles than of progressive moderation of ABA perspectives resulting in accommodations, and in a "bill of rights for the administrative process . . . more complicated than that hopeful language suggested. Comparing the rhetoric that surrounded the APA with its practical effects suggests that the act did more to change opinions about the administrative process than to change the inner workings of the agencies. . . . Triumphalist language surrounding the APA did serve to insulate subsequent administrative activity and administrative reform from attack. . . . 'The battle over fundamentals had ceased. The federal administrative process was secure.'"

(c) MCNOLLGAST, THE POLITICAL ORIGINS OF THE ADMINISTRATIVE PROCEDURE ACT, 15 J.L. Econ. & Org. 180, 182–83 (1999): ". . . [T]he passage and structure of the APA presents many puzzles . . . . For example, why did New Deal Democrats change their position on procedural due process and agree to pass procedural limitations on agencies in 1946? Furthermore, why did the parties in Congress form a 'grand coalition' in favor of the APA? Why did it take until 1946 to codify procedural due process, given that much of the APA had been proposed a decade before? Why did Congress enact some proposals regarding procedural due process but not others? . . .

"Two profound partisan changes that took place in the 1940s provide answers to many of these questions. First, New Deal Democrats realized that their prospects for retaining the presidency were growing increasingly dim after Roosevelt's death in 1945. The New Dealers could no longer count on an executive administration that was sympathetic to New Deal policies and that would continue to implement its policies more or less in the ways that New Dealers preferred. This fear provided New Deal supporters with the incentive to consolidate the gains of the New Deal thus far. Second, following 13 years of unbroken Democratic control of the presidency, the character of the judiciary had changed substantially from the high point of conflict between 1932 and 1937. As a result, the New Dealers no longer feared a combative relationship with the courts if they delegated to them the responsibility to enforce the procedural due process requirements. In sum, by 1946, the New Dealers in Congress had an interest in consolidating their policy gains against the possible antipathy of a Republican presidency, and they could finally count on the courts to favor New Deal programs in adjudicating procedural provisions.

"The importance of this argument, if true, is that it demonstrates that more was at stake in the establishment of administrative procedure than fairness, equity, concern for individual liberties, and administrative efficiency. Because the very future of the New Deal was at stake, political preferences over economic outcomes as well as prosaic political strategizing and coalition building played major roles in shaping the foundations for the present administrative state. Liberal Democrats accepted legislative formalization of procedural due process and a greater role for judicial review only when it appeared to be advantageous to their interests and when combined in a logroll that consolidated the gains of the New Deal and empowered Congress vis-à-vis the executive."

(3) *The APA's Continued Relevance?*

(a)   Save for the Freedom of Information Act that the APA incorporates, that you may study in Ch. VI, the APA as such has been little amended in the more than 70 years since its enactment—and this despite changes that have made notice-and-comment rulemaking rather than ratemaking and complex formal adjudication the dominant procedures of concern. These changes have contributed to caselaw developments you may encounter in the chapters on rulemaking (IV) and standards of review (VIII), as well as assertions of presidential control you may also meet there and in Chapter VII. Congress has provided separately for regulatory negotiation and for alternative dispute resolution methods you may study in the chapters on rulemaking (IV) and adjudication (V); occasional statutes, such as the Unfunded Mandates Reform Act of 1995, 2 U.S.C. §§ 1531–52 and Small Business Regulatory Enforcement Fairness Act, 5 U.S.C. § 601 ff., impose particular analytic requirements in defined cases, and it has occasionally required additional rulemaking procedures in particular statutory regimes, such as the Occupational Safety and Health Act. At this writing, however,

§ 553 remains as it was in 1946. Legislative proposals pending in Congress, however—proposed but not finally enacted in several preceding sessions—may significantly revise the required procedures for all rulemaking. See, e.g., pp. 286, 844 and 848.

(b) EDWARD RUBIN, IT'S TIME TO MAKE THE ADMINISTRATIVE PROCEDURE ACT ADMINISTRATIVE, 89 Cornell L. Rev. 95, 96, 101–05 (2003): ". . . [T]he APA was out of date at the time it was enacted. The cause of this premature obsolescence was the American government's epochal transformation in the half century preceding the APA's enactment. This change was the advent of the administrative state itself, the transition from a system of rules elaborated and implemented by the judiciary to a system of comprehensive regulation elaborated and implemented by administrative agencies. . . .

". . . [T]he structure of the APA itself reveals that the statute is essentially a one-trick pony. All of its basic provisions rely on a single method for controlling the actions of administrative agencies, namely, participation by private parties. . . . Any other methods of controlling administrative action, including executive, legislative, and internal supervision, are largely absent from the statute. . . . This represents a significant lacuna because an Administrative Procedure Act should address the entire range.

"One obvious difficulty with the APA's reliance on public participation is that it forces the statute to depend for its effectiveness on large organizations—business firms, labor unions and, most characteristically, organized interest groups. . . . The disadvantages of the APA's monochromatic approach to agency control goes well beyond the obvious unfairness of relying on large private organizations, however. Supervision exercised by private parties is necessarily external, and usually adversarial as well. . . . Perhaps the most serious limitation of private party participation, however, is that it is almost always incremental. . . .

"The inherently incremental nature of the control functions that the APA prescribes is hardly accidental. Rather, it emerges from the conception of government that prevailed in premodern times, and that survives in contemporary governance as the rationale for common law. The administrative state displaces this approach. Its defining feature is conscious policy intervention in the economic and social system by various means, among them the promulgation of explicitly new laws. While incremental decision making is not necessarily precluded, the hallmarks of the administrative state—the rationale behind the creation of administrative agencies—are its comprehensive programs and long-term planning in pursuit of these policy objectives. Thus, by relying on the necessarily incremental device of private party participation, the APA ignores the essential feature of the administrative state and adopts a means of control characterized by a specifically pre-administrative approach to governance."

(c) Numerous other important writings trace not only the APA's history but its changes with continuing national development and its omissions—in particular, the unaddressed world of internal administrative law. See, for example, Nicholas Parillo, ed., Administrative Law from the

Inside Out: Essays on Themes in the Work of Jerry L. Mashaw (2017); Joanna L. Grisinger, The Unwieldy American State: Administrative Politics Since the New Deal (2012); Daniel A. Farber and Anne Joseph O'Connell, The Lost World of Administrative Law, 82 Tex. L. Rev. 1137 (2014).

NOTES ON INTERPRETING THE APA

(1) *A Note on Sources.* Shortly after the APA was enacted, the Department of Justice prepared an Attorney General's Manual on the Administrative Procedure Act (1947), primarily for the benefit of other government agencies. Although those agencies and their legal adviser were in important respects parties in interest, the Supreme Court has drawn upon this manual as "a contemporaneous interpretation" of the APA that is entitled to "some deference . . . because of the role played by the Department of Justice in drafting the legislation." Vermont Yankee Nuclear Power Corp. v. Natural Resources Defense Council, 435 U.S. 519 (1978). Also often cited are the Senate and House Judiciary Committee Reports on the APA, S. Rep. No. 752, 79th Cong., 1st Sess. (1945) and H. Rep. No. 1980, 79th Cong. 2d Sess. (1946).

(2) *A Static or Evolving Statute?* WILLIAM ESKRIDGE and JOHN FEREJOHN, SUPER STATUTES, 50 Duke L.J. 1215 (2001), identifies a kind of statute that "successfully penetrate[s] public normative and institutional culture in a deep way. . . . A super-statute is a law or series of laws that (1) seeks to establish a new normative or institutional framework for state policy and (2) over time does "stick" in the public culture such that (3) the super-statute and its institutional or normative principles have a broad effect on the law—including an effect beyond the four corners of the statute. Super-statutes are typically enacted only after lengthy normative debate about a vexing social or economic problem . . . . The law must also prove robust as a solution, a standard, or a norm over time, such that its earlier critics are discredited and its policy and principles become axiomatic for the public culture." Is the APA such a statute? As a statute of general application, and considerable importance to contemporary issues, should it be interpreted today as a statute of its times, or as an evolving text whose language takes meaning from ongoing circumstances?

In Leegin Creative Leather Products v. PSKS, Inc., 551 U.S. 877 (2007), a closely divided Court, viewing the Sherman Anti-Trust Act as a framework for common-law development of antitrust principles, overruled prior decisions and reinterpreted the Act in light of modern developments and understandings. In Milner v. Department of the Navy, 562 U.S. 562 (2011), p. 683, the Court in an 8–1 decision took a very different stance towards the Freedom of Information Act (FOIA), adhering to original understandings of the Act's text and rejecting several decades of contrary judicial interpretations and government practice. Which model is most appropriate for the APA? As the materials in Section 2 of Chapter IV detail, the Court appeared to reject quite so freewheeling an approach to the APA in Vermont Yankee Nuclear Power Corp. v. Natural Resources Defense Council, 435 U.S. 519 (1978), a decision addressing the requirements for notice-and-comment rulemaking. Yet, as you may also learn there, current doctrine on these requirements has made them a far cry from what the 1946 Congress likely understood the APA to demand, and one might identify three broad approaches the Court has used in interpreting the APA.

PETER L. STRAUSS, CHANGING TIMES: THE APA AT FIFTY, 63 U.Chi. L. Rev. 1389, 1392–93 (1996): "[T]his is a story of change, albeit one mostly led, rather than followed, by the Court. It falls roughly into three phases. [The APA] was produced against a backdrop of empirical study and political contention; it used broad strokes, in the language of those who had participated in the studies and struggles, to address practical problems. In its first years, the lawyers and judges who litigated and decided issues about its meaning had been, to a greater or lesser extent, witnesses to its creation, and they evidently expected their experiences to contribute to the statute's interpretation; . . . the habits of using legislative materials to illuminate statutory text were firmly in place.

"In the middle period, represented here by the procedural ferment and paradigm shifts of the seventies, lawyers' arguments were less likely to draw upon the debates of the forties, and the Court proved willing to reinterpret the text to fit contemporary developments. The apparent exception to that trend, Vermont Yankee Nuclear Power Corp. v. NRDC, [p. 295,] might be thought to have involved a lower court's effort to give the statute meaning outside any reasonable possibility offered by the text, rather than a more general refusal to accommodate that text to contemporary understandings.

"Most recently, in the third phase, the Court has turned to formalism in matters of textual interpretation. Rejecting partnership assumptions about its relation with Congress that have characterized thinking about statutes since early in this century, it takes text as both time-bound and limiting. For the APA, that makes decisions turn on what its words would have been understood to mean as a matter of standard usage in 1946—usage independent of the political context and debates."

(3) DIRECTOR, OFFICE OF WORKERS' COMPENSATION PROGRAMS V. GREENWICH COLLIERIES, 512 U.S. 267 (1994). This issue of whether the APA should be read as a static or evolving statute could be understood to underlie this case, which Strauss connects to "the turn to formalist, originalist approaches to textual interpretation." Its issue was whether the phrase "burden of proof" in 5 U.S.C. § 556(d) (§ 7(c) of the APA) refers to the "burden of going forward" (i.e., the burden of initially establishing a prima facie claim, shifting to the other side the obligation to rebut) or to the "burden of persuasion" (i.e., the burden of ultimately establishing a simple preponderance of evidence in one's own favor). The text would permit either meaning, and the choice between them could be significant. In adjudicating benefits claims under the Black Lung Benefits Act (BLBA), 30 U.S.C. § 901 et seq., and the Longshore and Harbor Workers' Compensation Act (LHWCA), 33 U.S.C. § 901 et seq., the Department of Labor had long followed what it called a "true doubt" rule. Under this approach, a claimant had the burden of going forward; once she had carried that burden, however, the burden of persuasion shifted to the party opposing the benefits claim. As a result, the benefits claimant would win any case in which the factfinder

found the evidence to be evenly balanced. The effect, which the Department grounded in statutory policy, was somewhat to favor benefit claimants.

After concluding that neither statute in question provided for an exception to § 556(d), JUSTICE O'CONNOR'S opinion for the Court turned to the meaning of "burden of proof": "Because the term 'burden of proof' is nowhere defined in the APA, our task is to construe it in accord with its ordinary or natural meaning. It is easier to state this task than to accomplish it, for the meaning of words may change over time, and many words have several meanings even at a fixed point in time. Here we must seek to ascertain the ordinary meaning of 'burden of proof' in 1946, the year the APA was enacted."

An extensive review of the cases and literature leading up to 1946—little of which had appeared in the briefs—persuaded the majority that "the emerging [1946] consensus on a definition of burden of proof" had fixed on the burden of persuasion. "We . . . presume Congress intended the phrase to have the meaning generally accepted in the legal community at the time of enactment. These principles lead us to conclude that the drafters of the APA used the term 'burden of proof' to mean the burden of persuasion. . . .

". . . [While] the Department relies on the Senate and House Judiciary Committee Reports on the APA to support its claim that burden of proof means only burden of production[,] . . . [this] legislative history . . . is imprecise and only marginally relevant. Congress chose to use the term 'burden of proof' in the text of the statute, and given the substantial evidence that the ordinary meaning of burden of proof was burden of persuasion, this legislative history cannot carry the day."

The majority acknowledged Congress's recognition of both the merits of claims under the two statutes and the difficulty in proving them—and the consequent merit of departmental policies reflecting solicitude for benefits claimants. But the "true doubt" approach went a step too far. ". . . [I]t runs afoul of the APA, a statute designed 'to introduce greater uniformity of procedure and standardization of administrative practice among the diverse agencies whose customs had departed widely from each other.' Wong Yang Sung v. McGrath, 339 U.S. 33, 41 (1950). That concern is directly implicated here, for under the Department's reading each agency would be free to decide who shall bear the burden of persuasion. Accordingly, the Department cannot allocate the burden of persuasion in a manner that conflicts with the APA." Justice Souter, with Justices Blackmun and Stevens joining him, strongly dissented, relying both on the agency's long practice under the statutes and on his own reading of the historical understandings leading up to the APA's enactment.

(4) *On the Merits of the Greenwich Collieries Approach to the APA.*

(a) STRAUSS, CHANGING TIMES, supra p. 243, at 1420. After detailing the Court's turn to a formalist, originalist, and static account of the APA's meaning in *Greenwich Collieries*, Strauss voiced criticism of this approach: "If the Court seriously intended to return the APA to its 1946 meanings, we will have been left with a far less flexible instrument of government than we had previously thought we possessed. Recall that in Wong Yang Sung,

Justice Jackson characterized the Court's role as being 'so far as the terms of the Act warrant, to give effect to its remedial purposes where the evils it was aimed at appear.' Effecting 'remedial purposes' within a range that 'terms . . . warrant,' appropriately to the interpretive conventions of the time, reflects a far more fluid approach to meaning over the years than the effort to find 'ordinary meaning . . . in 1946.' And the intervening cases, as we have seen, unselfconsciously assumed an evolving statute—one whose evolution, to be sure, was limited by the possibilities of its text, but that nonetheless accommodated the shifting currents of administrative law development across the years. The APA's endurance for fifty years as a central reference point for the manifold activities of the federal government, like the Constitution's endurance for more than two hundred, can be understood only as a product of that flexibility. An interpretive theory that makes of statutes such static events undercuts the very project of having an APA."

(b) Judge Stephen Williams had somewhat different thoughts. STEPHEN F. WILLIAMS, THE ERA OF "RISK-RISK" AND THE PROBLEM OF KEEPING THE APA UP TO DATE, 63 U. Chi. L. Rev. 1375, 1385–87 (1996):

". . . I will step back a minute and ask more generally what the consuming public might reasonably expect from courts in their interpretation of a statute such as the APA—intended to guide the procedures of countless arms of the administrative state.

"Congress's decision to adopt the APA expressed, presumably, its belief that the courts—and perhaps the citizenry—needed some help. If Congress had fully embraced the judicial answers to the questions posed by administrative proliferation, a statute would not have been necessary. I apologize for mentioning the obvious, but anxiety over obsolescence tends to obscure the point. Absent constitutional imperatives, the congressional voice is decisive. Thus, to state the obvious, one criterion for sound interpretation of the APA must be fidelity to what Congress meant.

"A second criterion is that interpretations should lend themselves to reasonable application across the range of agencies and agency activities governed by the statute. . . . If one size must fit all, as in some sense it must under the APA, then those who define the permissible size must either build flexibility into the definition (for example, 'reasonable' availability) or find some other solution to the problem of variability. As applied to Greenwich Collieries, this principle might support reading 'burden of proof' as burden of production only. Because that reading leaves the more significant issue, burden of persuasion, untouched, it enables individual agencies to resolve it separately with a focus on context.

"Notice that each of these approaches to agency diversity has its costs. A pliable standard provides relatively little advance guidance. But a clear universal standard, deliberately set in lax terms (ones that leave agencies relatively unconstrained), may jeopardize private interests that Congress meant to protect.

"Third, there is surely an interest—the one that Strauss singles out for emphasis—in interpretations that fit current circumstances." Yet "[w]hile Strauss focuses on keeping the APA current, I wonder if the central fault of

Greenwich Collieries, by his lights, is really the Court's asserted failure to allow the meaning of the APA to flow with the times. . . . Strauss's real complaint—still a serious one—lies in regard to the second criterion that I hypothesized for APA interpretation, namely, the need to embrace disparate agencies and disparate activities. On that criterion, none of the options open to the Court was particularly appetizing . . . The Court could not adopt an elastic interpretation such as might be embodied in a concept of 'reasonableness.' It had to decide between two discrete possibilities, burden of production or burden of persuasion; Congress surely could not have meant the term to shift its meaning back and forth, from agency to agency, at the will of the courts. So long as the Court was forced to choose a one-size-fits-all meaning, the option with the advantage of being less intrusive upon agency choice (mere burden of production) came at the price of allowing agencies to deny some private parties the benefit of forcing their adversaries to carry the burden of persuasion—a benefit Congress intended them to have if the Court's reading of Congress's 1946 meaning was correct."

(c) In TEXTUALISM AND CONTEXTUALISM IN ADMINISTRATIVE LAW, 78 B. U. L. Rev. 1023 (1998), Professor JONATHAN SIEGEL argued that "a dominant force in the construction of many administrative law statutes is neither the statutes' text nor the intentions of their authors, but background principles of administrative law." The Greenwich Collieries "opinion is inordinately focused on the abstract meaning of the three words, 'burden of proof,' to the exclusion of all other considerations. We hear a great deal in the Court's opinion about what these words meant to Lemuel Shaw in 1833 and how Justice Holmes credited that meaning on behalf of the Supreme Court ninety years later. Wholly absent from the Court's opinion, however, is any discussion of the background principles of administrative law that are usually so important in interpreting administrative law statutes. . . . The Court treated the phrase 'burden of proof' as a universal, indivisible atom that would necessarily have the same meaning wherever it might appear, so that its meaning in a federal statute about administrative law could be gleaned from its usage in a state supreme court opinion dealing with ordinary civil procedure."

(5) *The Impact of Subsequent Statutory Developments.* To what extent are courts justified in attending to intervening statutory developments in interpreting the APA? PETER L. STRAUSS, STATUTES THAT ARE NOT STATIC—THE CASE OF THE APA, 14 J. Contemp. Leg. Issues 767, 789–90, 798–99 (2005), argues that FOIA's "strong and unequivocal commitment to information exposure" legitimates interpreting the APA to require disclosure of data relied on in rulemaking, notwithstanding that neither FOIA nor the APA contains any such express mandate. "The Congresses that adopted FOIA and its amendments were of course not the legislators of 1946; but they were legislators crafting a considerably more contemporary set of instructions to the judiciary, also relying on the judges' faithfulness as servants of the law as they understand it to be."

c. Additional Sources of Procedural Constraint

These materials focus on the Administrative Procedure Act and a few other general procedural enactments folded into its structure, such as the Freedom of Information Act and Government in the Sunshine Act, see Chapter VI. Yet administrative lawyers need to be aware that a number of other statutes provide general structure for certain aspects of administrative procedure or judicial review. Title 28 of the U.S. Code and implementing rules of civil and appellate procedure contain enforcement procedures for subpoenas, provisions respecting jurisdiction and venue for judicial review, and the delegation of litigating responsibility to the Department of Justice and its officers. The Paperwork Reduction Act of 1980, briefly discussed at p. 269 places generalized agency information-gathering under the supervision of the Office of Management and Budget (OMB), a White House agency we meet frequently in these pages. The Federal Advisory Committee Act (FACA), discussed at p. 747, makes the White House also responsible to regulate agency use of private-public committees for consultation and policy development, and requires any such committees to work openly. Statutes and executive orders creating additional procedural obligations for rulemaking have become a major source of added complexity.

More important, an awareness of general procedural requirements is just the beginning of solving any concrete problem of administrative procedure. It is essential to always consult the specific statutes under which the agency acts. Those "organic" or substantive statutes may establish additional or differing procedural requirements—and may also indicate which general procedural requirements are triggered. A number of the APA's requirements, such as the provisions for formal rulemaking and adjudication in §§ 556–557, are triggered by the organic statute. See § 553(c). The potential applicability of specific statutory procedural requirements is signaled by § 559's proviso that the APA's procedural requirements "do not limit or repeal additional requirements imposed by statute or otherwise recognized by law."

Within statutory and constitutional limits, agencies generally enjoy substantial freedom to shape the procedures they employ. Agencies often adopt detailed procedural regulations, which will usually be found in an early chapter of the agency's volume of the Code of Federal Regulations (CFR)—the official annual compendium of regulations adopted by federal agencies, which is organized along the lines of the United States Code and is several times as large. Once adopted through notice-and-comment rulemaking, these procedural regulations are binding on the agency. Any attorney involved with a particular agency or proceeding must pay careful attention to its procedural regulations and any internal interpretations those regulations may have received.

One useful resource for considering agency procedural issues both generally and in some specific cases is the work of the Administrative

Conference of the United States (ACUS), frequently cited in this casebook. Created in 1968, abolished by the 104th Congress in 1995, Pub. L. No. 104–52, tit. IV, 109 Stat. 468 (1995), and more recently reinstated, Pub. L. 111–8, 123 Stat. 656 (2009), this small agency is charged with responsibility for continuing analysis and development of federal administrative procedures. Like the American Law Institute, it commissions scholarly studies of discrete issues, both general and in relation to particular agency actors. Committee recommendations developed from the resulting reports and approved by its Council are debated and adopted by a numerous assembly divided between public and private members. This process has often produced significant change at the administrative level and—as important—permitted professional views on administrative procedural matters to coalesce in a relatively apolitical setting. You can find ACUS's work, searchable for the topics it has acted on and the reports on which they are based, at http://www.acus.gov.

SECTION 2.   CONSTRAINTS ON AN AGENCY'S OPTION TO USE EITHER ADJUDICATION OR RULEMAKING

> **SECURITIES & EXCHANGE COMMISSION v. CHENERY CORP.**
> **Notes on the Chenery Decisions**
> **Notes on the Problem of Retroactivity**

M. ELIZABETH MAGILL, AGENCY CHOICE OF POLICYMAKING FORM, 71 U. Chi. L. Rev. 1383 (2004): "An administrative agency delegated some task-protect the environment, assure the integrity of the securities markets, improve auto safety—might carry out that obligation by adopting a rule, bringing or deciding a case, or announcing its interpretation of a statute. In fact, it might rely on all of those quite distinct tools in the course of implementing its statutory mandate. Agencies are unique institutions in this respect. Most government actors are not free to select from a menu of policymaking tools. The legislature adopts statutes; prosecutors bring cases; courts decide cases brought to them by parties. Confining legislatures, prosecutors, and courts to particular ways of doing their jobs is no accident. Those assignments spring from the most essential aspects of the Constitution's design. But the typical administrative agency is not so constrained. Most agencies can rely on policymaking tools that look like legislating, enforcing, and adjudicating. . . . To be sure, the peculiar mix of powers—part legislative, part executive, part judicial—that Congress is constitutionally permitted to bestow on administrative agencies generates much of the heat in the debate over their constitutional status. But that is usually where interest in the issue ends. The nonconstitutional dimensions of agencies' ability to rely on a mix of policymaking tools generate little interest or investigation. This Article aims to rectify that by identifying, evaluating, and coming to terms with . . . [a] phenomenon [that] can be simply stated: the typical administrative agency is authorized to use a range of distinct policymaking forms to effectuate its statutory mandate, and its choice about which tool to rely on appears, at first glance at least, to be unregulated by courts."

The earlier materials in this chapter introduce the constitutional distinction between adjudication and rulemaking, and the Administrative Procedure Act as the fundamental federal statute governing administrative procedures. Adjudication and rulemaking are the APA's two fundamental categories of agency procedure, and later chapters explore their characteristics in some detail. You might wonder, however, whether and in what ways the "rule of law" issues instinct in the distinction affect an agency's use of these two procedural options, if its organic statute would leave it free to take either route to a desired end. We begin with SEC v. Chenery Corp., a dispute that arose in the New Deal era (thus, not under the APA) and reached the Supreme Court twice. Each of those Court decisions grounds important contemporary understandings of administrative law. We set out the second set of opinions; it clearly states, as well, the enduring lesson of the first.

SECURITIES & EXCHANGE COMMISSION v. CHENERY CORP.

Supreme Court of the United States (1947).
332 U.S. 194.

■ JUSTICE MURPHY delivered the opinion of the Court.

[The Public Utility Holding Company Act of 1935 aimed at dismantling the complex, highly leveraged pyramid structures common in the public utility industry; the collapse of many of these companies in the 1929 stock market crash had contributed to the Great Depression. Section 11(b) directed the SEC "as soon as practicable after January 1, 1938 . . . [to] require by order, after notice and opportunity for hearing, that each registered holding company . . . shall take such action as the Commission shall find necessary to limit the operations of the holding-company system of which such company is a part to a single integrated public-utility system . . . ." Section 11(e) permitted companies to forestall mandatory reorganization by proposing a "voluntary" plan. The SEC would then determine, after hearing, whether the proposal was "necessary to effectuate the provisions of [§ 11(b)] and fair and equitable to the persons affected by such plan." The Chenerys—officers, directors, and controlling shareholders of Federal Water Service Corporation (Federal)—had attempted voluntary reorganization under a plan in which they would retain a substantial role in the new enterprise. But the SEC refused to approve reorganization on these terms.]

This case is here for the second time. In SEC v. Chenery Corp., 318 U.S. 80 (1943) [Chenery I], we held that an order of the Securities and Exchange Commission could not be sustained on the grounds upon which that agency acted. We therefore directed that the case be remanded to the Commission for such further proceedings as might be appropriate. On remand, the Commission reexamined the problem, recast its rationale and reached the same result. The issue now is whether the Commission's action is proper in light of the principles established in our prior decision.

When the case was first here, we emphasized a simple but fundamental rule of administrative law. That rule is to the effect that a reviewing court, in dealing with a determination or judgment which an administrative agency alone is authorized to make, must judge the propriety of such action solely by the grounds invoked by the agency. If those grounds are inadequate or improper, the court is powerless to affirm the administrative action by substituting what it considers to be a more adequate or proper basis. To do so would propel the court into the domain which Congress has set aside exclusively for the administrative agency.

We also emphasized in our prior decision an important corollary of the foregoing rule. If the administrative action is to be tested by the basis upon which it purports to rest, that basis must be set forth with such clarity as to be understandable. It will not do for a court to be compelled to guess at the theory underlying the agency's action . . .

Applying this rule and its corollary, the Court was unable to sustain the Commission's original action. . . . During the period when successive reorganization plans proposed by the management were before the Commission, the officers, directors and controlling stockholders of Federal purchased a substantial amount of Federal's preferred stock on the over-the-counter market. Under the [proposed] plan, this preferred stock was to be converted into common stock of a new corporation; on the basis of the purchases of preferred stock, the management would have received more than 10% of this new common stock. It was frankly admitted that the management's purpose in buying the preferred stock was to protect its interest in the new company. It was also plain that there was no fraud or lack of disclosure in making these purchases.

But the Commission would not approve the [proposed] plan so long as the preferred stock purchased by the management was to be treated on a parity with the other preferred stock. It felt that the officers and directors of a holding company in process of reorganization under the Act were fiduciaries and were under a duty not to trade in the securities of that company during the reorganization period. And so the plan was amended to provide that the preferred stock acquired by the management, unlike that held by others, was not to be converted into the new common stock; instead, it was to be surrendered at cost plus dividends accumulated since the purchase dates. As amended, the plan was approved by the Commission over the management's objections.

The Court interpreted the Commission's order approving this amended plan as grounded solely upon judicial authority. The Commission appeared to have treated the preferred stock acquired by the management in accordance with what it thought were standards theretofore recognized by courts. If it intended to create new standards growing out of its experience in effectuating the legislative policy, it failed to express itself with sufficient clarity and precision to be so understood. Hence the order was judged by the only standards clearly invoked by the Commission. On that basis, the order could not stand. The opinion pointed out that courts do not impose upon officers and directors of a corporation any fiduciary duty to its stockholders which precludes them, merely because they are officers and directors, from buying and selling the corporation's stock. Nor was it felt that the cases upon which the Commission relied established any principles of law or equity which in themselves would be sufficient to justify this order. The opinion further noted that neither Congress nor the Commission had promulgated any general rule proscribing such action as the purchase of preferred stock by Federal's management. And the only judge-made rule of equity which might have justified the Commission's order related to fraud or mismanagement of the reorganization by the officers and directors, matters which were admittedly absent in this situation.

[On remand from Chenery I, Federal's management again sought approval of a plan in which they would participate in the reorganized enterprise through conversion of the preferred stock they had acquired. The SEC again refused to approve such participation. The D.C. Circuit reversed, believing this to be inconsistent with Chenery I.]

The latest order of the Commission definitely avoids the fatal error of relying on judicial precedents which do not sustain it. This time, after a thorough reexamination of the problem in light of the purposes and standards of the Holding Company Act, the Commission has concluded that the proposed transaction is inconsistent with the . . . Act. It has drawn heavily upon its accumulated experience in dealing with utility reorganizations. And it has expressed its reasons with a clarity and thoroughness that admit of no doubt as to the underlying basis of its order.

The argument is pressed upon us, however, that the Commission was foreclosed from taking such a step following our prior decision. It is said that, in the absence of findings of conscious wrongdoing on the part of Federal's management, the Commission could not determine by an order in this particular case that it was inconsistent with the statutory standards to permit Federal's management to realize a profit through the reorganization purchases. All that it could do was to enter an order allowing an amendment to the plan so that the proposed transaction could be consummated. Under this view, the Commission would be free only to promulgate a general rule outlawing such profits in future utility reorganizations; but such a rule would have to be prospective in nature and have no retroactive effect upon the instant situation.

We reject this contention, for it grows out of a misapprehension of our prior decision and of the Commission's statutory duties. We held no more and no less than that the Commission's first order was unsupportable for the reasons supplied by that agency. But when the case left this Court, the problem whether Federal's management should be treated equally with other preferred stockholders still lacked a final and complete answer. It was clear that the Commission could not give a negative answer by resort to prior judicial declarations. And it was also clear that the Commission was not bound by settled judicial precedents in a situation of this nature. Still unsettled, however, was the answer the Commission might give were it to bring to bear on the facts the proper administrative and statutory considerations, a function which belongs exclusively to the Commission in the first instance. The administrative process had taken an erroneous rather than a final turn. Hence we carefully refrained from expressing any views as to the propriety of an order rooted in the proper and relevant considerations.

. . . The fact that the Commission had committed a legal error in its first disposition of the case certainly gave Federal's management no vested right to receive the benefits of such an order. After the remand was made, therefore, the Commission was bound to deal with the problem afresh, performing the function delegated to it by Congress. . . .

The absence of a general rule or regulation governing management trading during reorganization did not affect the Commission's duties in relation to the particular proposal before it. The Commission was asked to grant or deny effectiveness to a proposed amendment to Federal's reorganization plan whereby the management would be accorded parity treatment on its holdings. It could do that only in the form of an order, entered after a due consideration of the particular facts in light of the relevant and proper standards. That was true regardless of whether those standards previously had been spelled out in a general rule or regulation. Indeed, if the Commission rightly felt that the proposed amendment was inconsistent with those standards, an order giving effect to the amendment merely because there was no general rule or regulation covering the matter would be unjustified.

It is true that our prior decision explicitly recognized the possibility that the Commission might have promulgated a general rule dealing with this problem under its statutory rule-making powers, in which case the issue for our consideration would have been entirely different from that which did confront us. But we did not mean to imply thereby that the failure of the Commission to anticipate this problem and to promulgate a general rule withdrew all power from that agency to perform its statutory duty in this case. To hold that the Commission had no alternative in this proceeding but to approve the proposed transaction, while formulating any general rules it might desire for use in future cases of this nature, would be to stultify the administrative process. That we refuse to do.

Since the Commission, unlike a court, does have the ability to make new law prospectively through the exercise of its rule-making powers, it has less reason to rely upon ad hoc adjudication to formulate new standards of conduct within the framework of the Holding Company Act. The function of filling in the interstices of the Act should be performed, as much as possible, through this quasi-legislative promulgation of rules to be applied in the future. But any rigid requirement to that effect would make the administrative process inflexible and incapable of dealing with many of the specialized problems which arise. Not every principle essential to the effective administration of a statute can or should be cast immediately into the mold of a general rule. Some principles must await their own development, while others must be adjusted to meet particular, unforeseeable situations. In performing its important functions in these respects, therefore, an administrative agency must be equipped to act either by general rule or by individual order. To insist upon one form of action to the exclusion of the other is to exalt form over necessity.

In other words, problems may arise in a case which the administrative agency could not reasonably foresee, problems which must be solved despite the absence of a relevant general rule. Or the agency may not have had sufficient experience with a particular problem to warrant rigidifying its tentative judgment into a hard and fast rule. Or the problem may be so specialized and varying in nature as to be impossible of capture within the boundaries of a general rule. In those situations, the agency must retain power to deal with the problems on a case-to-case basis if the administrative process is to be effective. There is thus a very definite place for the case-by-case evolution of statutory standards. And the choice made between proceeding by general rule or by individual, ad hoc litigation is one that lies primarily in the informed discretion of the administrative agency.

Hence we refuse to say that the Commission, which had not previously been confronted with the problem of management trading during reorganization, was forbidden from utilizing this particular proceeding for announcing and applying a new standard of conduct. That such action might have a retroactive effect was not necessarily fatal to its validity. Every case of first impression has a retroactive effect, whether the new principle is announced by a court or by an administrative agency. But such retroactivity must be balanced against the mischief of producing a result which is contrary to a statutory design or to legal and equitable principles. If that mischief is greater than the ill effect of the retroactive application of a new standard, it is not the type of retroactivity which is condemned by law.

    . . . [The Commission's] view was that the amended plan would involve the issuance of securities on terms "detrimental to the public interest or the interest of investors" . . . and would result in an "unfair or inequitable distribution of voting power" among the Federal security holders . . . It was led to this result "not by proof that the [Chenerys] committed acts of conscious wrongdoing but by the character of the conflicting interests created by the interveners' program of stock purchases carried out while plans for reorganization were under consideration." [The Commission had emphasized both the "normal powers" possessed by management and the "special powers" management obtains during voluntary reorganization; it "felt that a management program of stock purchases would give rise to the temptation and the opportunity to shape the reorganization proceeding so as to encourage public selling on the market at low prices."]

The Commission further felt that its answer should be the same even where proof of intentional wrongdoing on the management's part is lacking. Assuming a conflict of interests, the Commission thought that the absence of actual misconduct is immaterial; injury to the public investors and to the corporation may result just as readily. "Questionable transactions may be explained away, and an abuse of investors and the administrative process may be perpetrated without evil intent, yet the injury will remain." Moreover, the Commission was of the view that the delays and the difficulties involved in probing the mental processes and personal integrity of corporate officials do not warrant any distinction on the basis of evil intent, the plain fact being "that an absence of unfairness or detriment in cases of this sort would be practically impossible to establish by proof." . . .

The scope of our review of an administrative order wherein a new principle is announced and applied is no different from that which pertains to ordinary administrative action. The wisdom of the principle adopted is none of our concern. Our duty is at an end when it becomes evident that the Commission's action is based upon substantial evidence and is consistent with the authority granted by Congress. . . .

The Commission's conclusion here rests squarely in that area where administrative judgments are entitled to the greatest amount of weight by appellate courts. It is the product of administrative experience, appreciation of the complexities of the problem, realization of the statutory policies, and responsible treatment of the uncontested facts. It is the type of judgment which administrative agencies are best equipped to make and which justifies the use of the administrative process. Whether we agree or disagree with the result reached, it is an allowable judgment which we cannot disturb.

Reversed.

■ JUSTICE JACKSON, dissenting [joined by JUSTICE FRANKFURTER].

The Court by this present decision sustains the identical administrative order which only recently it held invalid. As the Court correctly notes, the Commission has only "recast its rationale and reached the same result." There being no change in the order, no additional evidence in the record and no amendment of relevant legislation, it is clear that there has been a shift in attitude between that of the controlling membership of the Court when the case was first here and that of those who have the power of decision on this second review.[10]

I feel constrained to disagree with the reasoning offered to rationalize this shift. It makes judicial review of administrative orders a hopeless formality for the litigant . . . It reduces the judicial process in such cases to a mere feint. . . .

. . . The basic assumption of the earlier opinion as therein stated was, *"But before transactions otherwise legal can be outlawed or denied their usual business consequences, they must fall under the ban of some standards of conduct prescribed by an agency of government authorized to prescribe such standards . . ."* The basic assumption of the present opinion is stated thus: *"The absence of a general rule or regulation governing management trading during reorganization did not affect the Commission's duties in relation to the particular proposal before it."* This puts in juxtaposition the two conflicting philosophies which produce opposite results in the same case and on the same facts. The difference between the first and the latest decision of the Court is thus simply the difference between holding that administrative orders must have a basis in law and a holding that absence of a legal basis is no ground on which courts may annul them.

As there admittedly is no law or regulation to support this order, we peruse the Court's opinion diligently to find on what grounds it is now held that the Court of Appeals, on pain of being reversed for error, was required to stamp this order with its approval. We find but one. That is the principle of judicial deference to administrative experience. That argument is five times stressed in as many different contexts . . .

What are we to make of this reiterated deference to "administrative experience" when in another context the Court says, "Hence, we refuse to say that the Commission, *which had not previously been confronted with the problem of management trading during reorganization,* was forbidden from utilizing this particular proceeding for announcing and applying *a new standard of conduct."*? (Emphasis supplied.)

The Court's reasoning adds up to this: The Commission must be sustained because of its accumulated experience in solving a problem with which it had never before been confronted!

---

10   [Ed.] Chenery I had been a 4–3 decision, in which Justice Frankfurter wrote for himself, Chief Justice Stone, and Justices Roberts and Jackson. Justices Black, Reed, and Murphy dissented. Justice Douglas had not participated, and there had been one vacancy. By the time of Chenery II, Vinson had replaced Stone, Burton had replaced Roberts, and Rutledge had filled the vacancy. Justice Rutledge joined the three Chenery I dissenters to form the Chenery II majority, Justice Burton concurred in the judgment without opinion, and Chief Justice Vinson joined Justice Douglas in not participating. Of the original Chenery I majority, this left only Justices Frankfurter and Jackson to dissent.

Of course, thus to uphold the Commission by professing to find that it has enunciated a "new standard of conduct" brings the Court squarely against the invalidity of retroactive law-making. But the Court does not falter. "That such action might have a retroactive effect was not necessarily fatal to its validity." "But such retroactivity must be balanced against the mischief of producing a result which is contrary to a statutory design or to legal and equitable principles." Of course, if what these parties did really was condemned by "statutory design" or "legal and equitable principles," it could be stopped without resort to a new rule and there would be no retroactivity to condone. But if it had been the Court's view that some law already prohibited the purchases, it would hardly have been necessary three sentences earlier to hold that the Commission was not prohibited "from utilizing this particular proceeding for announcing and applying a *new standard of conduct.*" (Emphasis supplied.)

I give up. Now I realize fully what Mark Twain meant when he said, "The more you explain it, the more I don't understand it."

. . . [A]dministrative experience is of weight in judicial review only to this point—it is a persuasive reason for deference to the Commission in the exercise of its discretionary powers under and within the law. It cannot be invoked to support action outside of the law. . . .

The truth is that in this decision the Court approves the Commission's assertion of power to govern the matter *without* law, power to force surrender of stock so purchased whenever it will, and power also to overlook such acquisitions if it so chooses. The reasons which will lead it to take one course as against the other remain locked in its own breast, and it has not and apparently does not intend to commit them to any rule or regulation. This administrative authoritarianism, this power to decide without law, is what the Court seems to approve in so many words: "The absence of a general rule or regulation governing management trading during reorganization did not affect the Commission's duties . . ." This seems to me to undervalue and to belittle the place of law, even in the system of administrative justice. It calls to mind Mr. Justice Cardozo's statement that "Law as a guide to conduct is reduced to the level of mere futility if it is unknown and unknowable." . . .

NOTES ON THE CHENERY DECISIONS

(1) **Chenery I.** The enduring proposition from the *first* round of the Chenery litigation has shaped much administrative law concerning the agency-court relationship:

When the case was first here, we emphasized a simple but fundamental rule of administrative law. That rule is to the effect that a reviewing court, in dealing with a determination or judgment which an administrative agency alone is authorized to make, must judge the propriety of such action solely by the grounds invoked by the agency. If those grounds are inadequate or improper, the court is powerless to affirm the administrative action by substituting what it considers to be a more adequate or proper basis. To do so would propel the court into the domain which Congress has set aside exclusively for the administrative agency.

We also emphasized in our prior decision an important corollary of the foregoing rule. If the administrative action is to be tested by the basis upon which it purports to rest, that basis must be set forth with such clarity as to be understandable. It will not do for a court to be compelled to guess at the theory underlying the agency's action. . . .

The first paragraph describes a relationship between reviewing court and agency that differs markedly from that between reviewing court and trial court. Decisions from trial or intermediate appellate courts are regularly sustained for reasons other than these lower courts give. The last sentence of the paragraph offers an explanation for this difference: responsibility for setting policy has been allocated to the agency, not the courts.

This basic principle, that courts must base their review of administrative action on the reasons the agency actually gave, underlies much contemporary administrative law doctrine. Chapter VIII, on standards of review, treats its implications for the nature of judicial review in detail, and you may find echoes elsewhere in these materials. But this principle may also create imperatives for agencies. In THE CONSTITUTIONAL FOUNDATIONS OF CHENERY, 116 YALE L.J. 952, 958–59 (2007), KEVIN M. STACK argues that "the Chenery principle . . . has a constitutional foundation. Specifically, the Chenery principle is a default rule of statutory construction that implements the nondelegation doctrine in ways that complement and reinforce that doctrine's other modes of enforcement." This casebook treats the question whether a nondelegation principle limits the permissible creation of agency authority in some detail in Chapter VI; there you will learn that, as conventionally stated, the principle requires only that an authorizing statute must contain an "intelligible principle" on the basis of which the legality of the agency's action can be determined. Professor Stack, however, suggests that, traditionally, it also involved evaluation "whether the statutory grant conditioned the exercise of authority upon an agency's stating the grounds for its invocation of the statutory authority." A legislature, of course, is under no such obligation; Congress can and does establish binding norms without having to state its justification for doing so. He argues: "While this requirement of an express statement of the agency's predicate grounds for action has slipped from constitutional doctrine, the Chenery principle's prohibition on post hoc rationales enforces this arm of the nondelegation doctrine. . . . [It also] operates both to bolster the political accountability of the agency's action and to prevent arbitrariness in the agency's exercise of its discretion. It provides assurance that accountable agency decision-makers, not merely courts and agency lawyers, have embraced the grounds for the agency's actions, and that the agency decisionmakers have exercised their judgment on the issue in the first instance."

(2) *It Can Pay to Settle.* ROY SCHOTLAND, A SPORTING PROPOSITION—SEC v. CHENERY, ADMINISTRATIVE LAW STORIES 168 (P. STRAUSS, ED. 2006)

recounts a settlement conference between the SEC and Mr. Chenery (perhaps most famous as the owner of remarkable racehorses, including Secretariat, winner of the Triple Crown). The SEC offered to permit reorganization in a way that would have protected his ownership control, if he were willing to accept a reasonable interest rate on his investment in lieu of what might have been regarded as insider profits. While he thought this fair, his lawyer advised him heatedly that it was "unconstitutional!" He then declined the settlement offer and litigated—at the eventual cost of paying for nine years of litigation and losing perhaps $25,000,000 2017 dollars in investment value.

Prof. Schotland noted, too, that Justice Jackson's fierce rule-of-law objections came shortly after his return from Nuremberg, where he had served as Lead Prosecutor in the war crimes trials there—a role some of his colleagues had strongly criticized on "retroactive lawmaking" grounds. Just as one might defend the war crimes trials by reference to understandings reflected in the "law of war," does the SEC's action gain credibility from the closeness of the issue on the first appeal, whether traditional judicial authority justified its initial rejection of the proposed reorganization? As editorial footnote 10, p. 255, remarks, Chenery I was closely divided over the question whether equity cases defining the obligations of fiduciaries supported the SEC's initial decision. If equity precedents placed the legality of Mr. Chenery's conduct so close to the line, shouldn't competent counsel have advised him at the outset that rejection of their application on equitable grounds was possible?

(3)   ***Should Adjudication or Rulemaking Be Preferred?*** Independent of any constitutional fairness question, you might think that the procedural characteristics of adjudication and rulemaking counsel the appropriateness of using one or the other process—a question you will be better placed to assess after you have had a chance to study the materials of Chapters IV and V. We provide here the briefest of introductions to scholarly views:

(a)   RICHARD J. PIERCE, JR., TWO PROBLEMS IN ADMINISTRATIVE LAW: POLITICAL POLARITY ON THE DISTRICT OF COLUMBIA CIRCUIT AND JUDICIAL DETERRENCE OF AGENCY RULEMAKING, 1988 Duke L.J. 300, 308–09: ". . . Rulemaking yields higher quality policy decisions than adjudication because it invites broad participation in the policymaking process by all affected entities and groups, and because it encourages the agency to focus on the broad effects of its policy rather than the often idiosyncratic adjudicative facts of a specific dispute. . . . It eliminates the need to relitigate policy issues . . . and it yields much clearer 'rules' than can be extracted from a decision resolving a specific dispute."

(b)   MARK H. GRUNEWALD, THE NLRB'S FIRST RULEMAKING: AN EXERCISE IN PRAGMATISM, 41 Duke L.J. 274, 281–82 (1991): "[P]olicy formulated in [adjudication] . . . is formulated exclusively from *argument* and *evidence* that the *parties* to the proceeding offer (evaluated in light of the Board's expertise). Consequently, it formally lacks as a basis the breadth of data that rulemaking submissions can provide, and even the data upon which it is based is presented by a limited number of participants. . . . Rulemaking . . . provides clarity, not in the sense of the specificity of policy (which may vary from rule to rule), but in the identification of a decision as a policy choice. It also provides stability, not in the sense of unchangeable policy, but in policy that cannot be changed without a process focused on the policy choice."

(c) E. DONALD ELLIOTT, RE-INVENTING RULEMAKING, 41 Duke L.J. 1490, 1492 (1992): "There can be no abstract answer to the question whether rulemaking or case-by-case evolution is the better way to make policy; in each case the answer depends on a variety of factors, including: how sure the agency is about what policy it wishes to adopt, how frequently the agency anticipates the question will come up, whether the issue is inherently entangled with other issues that can best be addressed comprehensively, and what other issues are currently pressing for the agency's attention."

(d) LISA SCHULTZ BRESSMAN, BEYOND ACCOUNTABILITY: ARBITRARINESS AND LEGITIMACY IN THE ADMINISTRATIVE STATE, 78 N.Y.U. L. Rev. 461, 535–36 (2003): "If notice-and-comment rulemaking typically is the best method for making general policy, then a refusal to use it might be arbitrary. It might lack any justification whatsoever. Or it might indicate improper motives, such as a desire to avoid committing broadly or visibly, or to retain room for departures that serve narrow interests. . . . [A]gencies should be required to take affirmative steps to justify a departure from rulemaking. At a minimum, they should articulate the reasons for using other procedures. This brings choice of procedure into compliance with the reasoned-decisionmaking requirement."

(e) PETER L. STRAUSS, RULES, ADJUDICATIONS, AND OTHER SOURCES OF LAW IN AN EXECUTIVE DEPARTMENT: REFLECTIONS ON THE INTERIOR DEPARTMENT'S ADMINISTRATION OF THE MINING LAW, 74 Colum. L. Rev. 1231 (1974), after studying the Department of the Interior's Bureau of Land Management for the Administrative Conference of the United States, questioned whether the ascription of "choice" to agency heads is always, or even often, appropriate. "The failure to use rulemaking," he found, "is far less a product of conscious departmental choice than a result of impediments to the making of rules created by the Department's internal procedures. The channels which lead to rulemaking . . . are so clogged with obstacles, and the flow through them so sluggish, that staff members hesitate to use them. . . . As a result, rulemaking may be consciously avoided by an individual with an idea for policy change when other means for achieving the same policy ends appear to be available." In Chenery, recall, the occasion for policymaking arose definitively only when the Chenery application was in hand and exploration of it revealed certain issues. If the SEC had then paused its consideration of the application in order to develop a rule, would "fairness" issues have been any different? Should the SEC have been obliged to permit the desired reorganization in the face of issues it had not previously anticipated?

(f) ALAN B. MORRISON, THE ADMINISTRATIVE PROCEDURE ACT: A LIVING AND RESPONSIVE LAW, 72 Va. L. Rev. 253, 255–56 (1986). Finally, as always, consider how agencies might be influenced in any degree of choice they do exercise by the fact of political as well as judicial influences on their behavior. Rulemaking is discrete, focused, and policy-centered in a way that adjudication is not. Prof. Morrison, who for many years was the lead attorney for Ralph Nader's NGO, Public Citizen, suggested in this essay that its clearer, more accessible articulation of policy "makes an agency's actions and policies more visible and hence more vulnerable to public and congressional criticism. . . .[R]ulemakings are often more controversial than adjudications, whose very processes are hidden from outsiders." Congress and the President, then, as later materials will reveal, may have considerably more notice and leverage over the one than the other. In particular, as those pages will reveal, a presidential executive order requires White House coordination when agencies undertake "significant" rulemakings; no similar structured oversight exists for coordination or clearance of adjudications, and indeed White house participation in decisions about particular adjudicatory undertakings can have a regrettable odor. And when Cary Coglianese and Daniel E. Walters recently reported the results of a recent workshop on Agenda-Setting in the Regulatory State: Theory and Evidence, 68 Admin. L. Rev. 865 (2016), their much broader consideration of this process was, again, limited to the rulemaking context.

(4) NLRB v. BELL AEROSPACE, 416 U.S. 267 (1974). For a brief while, a confused set of opinions in a 1969 decision of the Court, NLRB v. Wyman-Gordon, 394 U.S. 759 (1969), made it appear that the Court might be willing to develop "arbitrariness" standards that could result in requiring agencies to use rulemaking for the setting of agency policy.[11] That prospect receded with the decision in this case, which reversed a Second Circuit opinion that would have required the NLRB to use rulemaking to change a long-standing interpretation, developed in adjudication, that corporate buyers were necessarily "managerial employees" excluded from the protections of the National Labor Relations Act. "[T]he Board is not precluded from announcing new principles in an adjudicative proceeding and . . . the choice between rulemaking and adjudication lies in the first instance within the Board's discretion. Although there may be situations where the Board's reliance on adjudication would amount to an abuse of discretion or a violation of the Act, . . . there is ample indication that adjudication is especially appropriate in the instant context. As the Court of Appeals noted, '[t]here must be tens of thousands of manufacturing, wholesale and retail units which employ buyers, and hundreds of thousands of the latter.' Moreover, duties of buyers vary widely depending on the company or industry. It is doubtful whether any generalized standard could be framed which would have more than marginal utility. The Board thus has reason to proceed with caution, developing its standards in a case-by-case manner with attention to the specific character of the buyers' authority and duties in each company. The Board's judgment that adjudication best serves this purpose is entitled to great weight."

---

[11] In his concurrence in Bowen v. Georgetown University Hospital, briefly discussed at p. 264 below, Justice Scalia characterized the decision in Wyman-Gordon in terms that do endure: "And just as Chenery suggested that rulemaking was prospective, the opinions in NLRB v. Wyman-Gordon Co., suggested the obverse: that adjudication could *not* be purely prospective, since otherwise it would constitute rulemaking. . . . Side by side these two cases, Chenery and Wyman-Gordon, set forth quite nicely the "dichotomy between rulemaking and adjudication" upon which "the entire [APA] is based." 1947 Attorney General's Manual on the APA. . . ."

NOTES ON THE PROBLEM OF RETROACTIVITY

The judicial power typically operates on the parties to the action before it—consequently applying "new law" to parties who when acting had not been aware of it.[12] Having thus to apply a holding to the present parties operates as an important constraint on common-law courts' law-generating capacities, since its tendency is to constrain their actions to interstitial change that, as in Chenery itself, a thoughtful lawyer might have anticipated.[13] Legislation, on the other hand, is rarely retrospective in application—the usual exceptions being statutes that relieve individuals from prior burdens. Legislatures may also, on occasion, date the application of changes in laws, such as tax laws, to their introduction as legislative business, in order to protect against evasion in anticipation of their enactment. If an agency, adjudicating, applies "new law" to the parties before it (as the judicial model suggests it should), may a court nonetheless determine that the new rule can be applied only prospectively? Or if an agency has made a rule that is to operate prospectively, but a reviewing court finds it inadequately supported, may the agency on repairing the defect make its rule applicable as of the original date of its promulgation?

(1) *On Permitting Only Prospective Application of New Policies Developed in Adjudication.* In EPILEPSY FOUNDATION OF NORTHEAST OHIO v. NLRB, 268 F.3d 1095 (D.C.Cir. 2001), the NLRB decision had characterized as unfair labor practices actions that, when they had been taken, prevailing Board decisions clearly permitted. Section 7 of the National Labor Relations Act, 29 U.S.C. § 157 states that "employees shall have the right . . . to engage in other concerted activities for the purpose of collective bargaining or other mutual aid or protection." Over the years, the NLRB had vacillated over its interpretation of this right, but for a decade had clearly permitted the challenged employer conduct. In reinterpreting § 7, the Board had repudiated that view and found the conduct forbidden. Judge Edwards, formerly a professor of Labor Law, wrote for the reviewing court, acknowledging that "the Board's decision in this case is a reasonable reading of § 7 of the NLRA. An otherwise reasonable interpretation of § 7 is not made legally infirm because the Board gives *renewed*, rather than new, meaning to a disputed statutory provision. It is a fact of life in NLRB lore that certain substantive provisions of the NLRA invariably fluctuate with the changing compositions of the Board. . . . The Board's conclusion obviously is debatable (because the Board has 'changed its mind' several times in addressing this issue); but the rationale underlying the decision in this case is both clear and reasonable. That is all that is necessary to garner deference from the court.

---

[12] The Supreme Court has increasingly insisted on retroactive decisionmaking in civil cases by Article III courts, with some Justices going so far as to suggest that "prospective decisionmaking is quite incompatible with the judicial power . . . and courts have no authority to engage in the practice." Harper v. Virginia Dep't of Taxation, 509 U.S. 86, 107 (1993) (Scalia, J., concurring).

[13] Viz., Justice Holmes oft-quoted dissenting remark in Southern Pacific Co. v. Jensen, 244 U.S. 205, 221 (1917): "I recognize without hesitation that judges do and must legislate, but they can do so only interstitially; they are confined from molar to molecular motions. A common-law judge could not say I think the doctrine of consideration a bit of historical nonsense and shall not enforce it in my court."

'When a challenge to an agency construction of a statutory provision, fairly conceptualized, really centers on the wisdom of the agency's policy, rather than whether it is a reasonable choice within a gap left open by Congress, the challenge must fail.' Chevron U.S.A. Inc. v. Natural Res. Def. Council, Inc., 467 U.S. 837, 866 (1984) [p. 1129]. The Foundation's challenge here is merely an attack on the wisdom of the agency's policy, and, therefore, the challenge must fail." Nonetheless, "when there is a 'substitution of new law for old law that was reasonably clear,' the new rule may justifiably be given prospectively-only effect in order to 'protect the settled expectations of those who had relied on the preexisting rule.' Williams Natural Gas Co. v. FERC, 3 F.3d 1544, 1554 (D.C. Cir. 1993). . . . In light of this governing principle, there is little doubt here that the Board erred in giving retroactive effect to its new interpretation of § 7. At the time when this case arose, the Board's policy . . . was absolutely clear . . . Indeed, it would be a 'manifest injustice' to require the Foundation to pay damages to an employee who, without legal right, flagrantly defied his employer's *lawful* instructions."[14]

Many factors conjoined to produce a similar outcome in DE NIZ ROBLES V. LYNCH, 803 F.3d 1165 (10th Cir. 2015), an opinion written by Judge Gorsuch before his elevation to the Supreme Court. In 2006, the Tenth Circuit had resolved a statutory tension between 8 U.S.C. § 1255(i), permitting the Attorney General to adjust the status of illegal immigrants, and 8 U.S.C. § 1182(a), prohibiting certain persons from winning lawful residency, in a manner that would have authorized the Attorney General to adjust De Niz Robles's status—as he promptly sought. Before it acted on his petition, however, the Board of Immigration Appeals ruled in another proceeding that the statutory tension had to be resolved to favor the prohibition, and it thus denied De Niz Robles's petition. In Chapter VIII you will encounter the Supreme Court decisions, Chevron, U.S.A., Inc. v. NRDC, 467 U.S. 837 (1984) and National Cable & Telecommunications Ass'n v. Brand X Internet Services, 545 U.S. 967 (2005), that now caused the Tenth Circuit to accept that, at least as to BIA rulings on petitions filed *after* its decision in that other proceeding, the BIA's reconciliation of the two statutes would control, and not the Tenth Circuit's 2006 decision. But could the BIA apply its new view "retroactively" to a petition filed in reliance on the Tenth Circuit's earlier reading? No, Judge Gorsuch concluded.

"When it comes to retroactivity and the law we can say a couple things with certainty. First and foremost, we know that legislation is rarely afforded retroactive effect. . . . To overcome the presumption of prospectivity, the Supreme Court has held that Congress must declare unequivocally its intention to regulate past conduct—and even then due process and equal protection demands may sometimes bar its way. . . .

"Quite the opposite from legislation (and with equal certainty) we can say that judicial decisions 'have had retrospective operation for near a

---

[14] On the other hand, as the D.C. Circuit has reiterated, "[u]nder this Circuit's law, 'retroactive effect is appropriate' for adjudicatory rules . . . that are 'new applications of existing law, clarifications, and additions' rather than the 'substitution of new law for old law that was reasonably clear.' Verizon Tel. Cos. v. FCC, 269 F.3d 1098, 1109, 348 U.S. App. D.C. 98 (D.C. Cir. 2001)," HealthBridge Mgmt., LLC v. NLRB, 798 F.3d 1059 (2015).

thousand years.' Kuhn v. Fairmont Coal Co., 215 U.S. 349, 372 (1910) (Holmes, J., dissenting). You might wonder why the due process and equal protection concerns that counsel in favor of prospectivity in legislation don't operate similarly when it comes to judicial decisions. The answer, we think, lies in the fact that for civil society to function the people need courts to provide backward-looking resolutions for their disputes. And accepting this premise, the Constitution has sought to mitigate the due process and equal protection concerns associated with retroactive decisionmaking in other ways, by rules circumscribing the nature of the judicial function and the judicial actor. . . .

"So when it comes to Congress we know its handiwork is presumptively prospective. And when it comes to the judiciary we know its decisions are presumptively retroactive. But what does the law have to say when the decision at issue comes from an executive agency? . . . The Constitution speaks far less directly to that peculiar question. Perhaps because the framers anticipated an Executive charged with enforcing the decisions of the other branches—not with exercising delegated legislative authority, let alone exercising that authority in a quasi-judicial tribunal empowered to overrule judicial decisions. . . . Coming at it from another angle, if the separation of powers doesn't forbid this form of decision-making outright, might second-order constitutional protections sounding in due process and equal protection, as embodied in our longstanding traditions and precedents addressing retroactivity in the law, sometimes constrain the retroactive application of its results?

"We think the answer yes. In light of the principles and precedents we've outlined, it seems to us that the more an agency acts like a judge—applying preexisting rules of general applicability to discrete cases and controversies—the closer it comes to the norm of adjudication and the stronger the case may be for retroactive application of the agency's decision. But the more an agency acts like a legislator—announcing new rules of general applicability—the closer it comes to the norm of legislation and the stronger the case becomes for limiting application of the agency's decision to future conduct. The presumption of prospectivity attaches to Congress's own work unless it plainly indicates an intention to act retroactively. That same presumption, we think, should attach when Congress's delegates seek to exercise delegated legislative policymaking authority: their rules too should be presumed prospective in operation unless Congress has clearly authorized retroactive application. And this logic, we believe, suffices to resolve our case. . . ."

(2) *On Applying New Precedent to Other Parties.* Vacillation such as preceded (and followed[15]) the NLRB's decision in Epilepsy Foundation is perhaps extreme, yet we are accustomed to thinking of the law developed by adjudication, the common law, as more malleable than statutes. Any party to a common-law proceeding has the right to argue that a precedent ostensibly applicable to its situation should be distinguished or overruled.

---

[15] The NLRB had made the challenged decision during the Clinton administration. Three years after the Epilepsy Foundation decision, during the Bush administration, it returned to its prior interpretation. IBM Corporation, 341 NLRB 1288 (2004).

When, in SHELL OIL CO. V. FERC, 707 F.2d 230 (5th Cir. 1983), the agency refused to reconsider a policy adopted in an earlier adjudication in the face of arguments that the factual circumstances now before it differed from those of the precedential decision, the court vacated the decision and remanded it for reconsideration. "Agencies may establish rules of general application in a statutory rulemaking or an individual adjudication. The choice of methods is a matter within the agency's informed discretion. But we must be mindful that these two methods of making rules differ fundamentally in the due process safeguards they provide. Rulemaking procedures require public notice and an opportunity for all interested parties to participate. . . . By contrast, no due process guarantees are extended to non-parties in an individual adjudication, although non-parties may be greatly affected by a general rule an agency adopts in such a proceeding. Shell was afforded no meaningful opportunity in [the precedential decision] to challenge [its] factual assumption . . . Due process requires that Shell be allowed to challenge that assumption here and now."

Whether or not "due process" was actually at stake, the court's observation reflects general truths about the contrast between adjudication and rulemaking as instruments for policy development. In the former, other similarly situated regulated entities are at the mercy of the skills and circumstances of the particular litigants; they rarely receive notice that an issue of importance to them about to be decided, and their ability to participate, is in any event constrained. The opportunity to argue for distinction or overruling—at least for the first few following cases—is a natural corollary. Normally, though, this is put in terms of an opportunity to argue, not a right to a hearing in the full sense, and lawyers know that adjudicators' tempers (and explanations) will grow short once the new doctrine has become firmly rooted. The final footnote of the court's opinion states: "Our decision of course does not preclude the Commission from establishing the identical rule on remand if it adduces sufficient evidence to support the underlying assumption."

(3) ***If an Agency Has Corrected a Rulemaking Previously Vacated for Error, Can It Apply the Rule as of the Rule's Initial Effectiveness Date?*** BOWEN V. GEORGETOWN UNIVERSITY HOSPITAL, 488 U.S. 204 (1988), considered a schedule the Secretary of Health and Human Services had adopted by rulemaking to govern Medicare cost reimbursements. Initially, it had acted without using the APA's notice and comment procedures,[16] and a district court rejected its use of the new schedule on the ground that that use was required. HHS then reimbursed costs that had been submitted under the old schedule, but used notice and comment rulemaking again to adopt the same new schedule, providing for "retroactive corrective adjustments" to recapture excess amounts paid after its initial adoption of the schedule. That, the Court concluded, was impermissible. "Retroactivity is not favored in the law. Greene v. United States, 376 U.S. 149, 160 (1964). Thus, congressional

---

[16] When you consider APA rulemaking in detail, you will see that the Act excepts "a matter relating to agency management or personnel or to public property, loans, grants, benefits or contracts" from the obligation to use these procedures, 5 U.S.C. § 553(a)(2), but this exception has been criticized and is often waived.

enactments and administrative rules will not be construed to have retroactive effect unless their language requires this result. By the same principle, a statutory grant of legislative rulemaking authority will not, as a general matter, be understood to encompass the power to promulgate retroactive rules unless that power is conveyed by Congress in express terms. Even where some substantial justification for retroactive rulemaking is presented, courts should be reluctant to find such authority absent an express statutory grant." And, in the legislative history of the applicable statute, "the House and Senate Committee Reports expressed a desire to forbid retroactive cost-limit rules . . . 'so that the provider would know in advance the limits to Government recognition of incurred costs and have the opportunity to act to avoid having costs that are not reimbursable.' The Secretary's past administrative practice is consistent with this interpretation of the statute. . . ."

Justice Scalia, concurring, insisted that the APA's definition of a rule as "an agency statement of general or particular applicability *and future effect*" 5 U.S.C. § 551(4) (emphasis added) "required that rules have legal consequences only for the future. It could not possibly mean that merely *some* of their legal consequences must be for the future, though they may also have legal consequences for the past, since that description would . . . destroy the entire dichotomy upon which the most significant portions of the APA are based. . . .

". . . [The House] Report [accompanying the APA] states that '[t]he phrase "future effect" does not preclude agencies from considering and, so far as legally authorized, dealing with past transactions in prescribing rules for the future.' The Treasury Department might prescribe, for example, that for purposes of assessing future income tax liability, income from certain trusts that has previously been considered nontaxable will be taxable—whether those trusts were established before or after the effective date of the regulation. That is not retroactivity in the sense at issue here, *i.e.*, in the sense of altering the *past* legal consequences of past actions. Rather, it is what has been characterized as 'secondary' retroactivity. A rule with exclusively future effect (taxation of future trust income) can unquestionably *affect* past transactions (rendering the previously established trusts less desirable in the future), but it does not for that reason cease to be a rule under the APA. Thus, with respect to the present matter, there is no question that the Secretary could have applied her new wage-index formulas to respondents in the future, even though respondents may have been operating under long-term labor and supply contracts negotiated in reliance upon the pre-existing rule. . . ."

(4) *On Sending a Rule Back to the Adopting Agency for Correction without Eliminating Its Effectiveness.* As may be evident to you, the Bowen decision, by casting doubt on agencies' legal authority to cure defective rulemakings retrospectively, created an incentive for those wishing to postpone the effectiveness of regulation to seek review of rulemakings, even for readily corrected and relatively immaterial errors. HHS's unhappy odyssey in Bowen began when a reviewing court struck down the revised cost formula because of a procedural flaw. By the time the agency had again

adopted the new formula, now through a legally unexceptionable process, three years had passed. This was the fact that generated the "need" for retroactive application of the rule. In reaction, as the material on rulemaking, p. 353, notes, courts have sometimes used practice of remand without vacatur, under which they remand a rule infected by readily corrected error without vacating it. See also p. 1437 (discussing remedies).

The courts' awareness of the Bowen incentive is illustrated by ICORE v. FCC, 985 F.2d 1075, 1081–82 (D.C. Cir. 1993). In 1986, the FCC had adopted a rule that revised the formula by which local telephone companies were compensated for the interconnections they provide their customers with interstate long-distance carriers. The following year, the D.C. Circuit found that the Commission had failed to demonstrate a rational basis for the new formula. The court remanded the case to the agency without vacating the rule. The FCC reopened comment on the revised formula and, in 1991, readopted it with an augmented explanation. This time, the court found the explanation adequate. It then turned to petitioners' argument that use of the revised formula to govern compensation for the period 1986–91 constituted impermissible retroactive rulemaking:

"Here, of course, in contrast to [Bowen], the court considering the rule initially found it inappropriate to set the rule aside. The court's decision on that point represented a careful consideration of the risk of disruption and of the likelihood that the rule was altogether sound at the core. . . . Petitioners offer no reason why a rule so treated, and in fact applied during the entire interim period, should be treated the same as the rule initially 'struck down' in [Bowen]. Petitioners cite no case employing [Bowen] to cancel the effect of rules deliberately left standing by a court pending a remand. . . ."

(5) *On Primary and Secondary Retroactivity.* Justice Scalia's distinction between primary and secondary retroactivity is well-established but its application can be problematic. Consider WILLIAM V. LUNEBURG, RETROACTIVITY AND ADMINISTRATIVE RULEMAKING, 1991 Duke L.J. 106, 109–10: "At the outset it should be noted that the formulation of a definition of retroactivity is no easy task, as the literature demonstrates. Take these relatively simple cases:

1.   The Environmental Protection Agency (EPA) for the first time adopts a standard for the release of sulfur dioxide from existing power plants. The regulation imposes civil penalties for pre-adoption releases of that pollutant in violation of the new standard.

2.   The EPA promulgates a new sulfur dioxide standard with a compliance date two years in the future. Most or all plants within the scope of the regulation will need to dismantle pollution-control technology installed in response to a prior, less stringent EPA regulation and invest in new stack gas cleaning equipment.

3.   A newly constructed power plant applies to the EPA for a permit to operate. The permit would have been granted under EPA regulations in effect during the construction phase of the facility,

but it is denied based on new EPA regulations adopted between the time of application and final agency action on the permit.

"Under one common definition, a retroactive regulation gives pre-adoption conduct a different legal effect from the one it would have had without the adoption of the regulation. Under this view, only the first case posed above is clearly a case of formal retroactivity. The third case is somewhat problematic in that regard, and the second case would fall outside this account of retroactivity. Yet all of these cases and variations provoke concern for the same reasons: They create 'surprise' and a potential for undermining 'reasonable' reliance by affected parties. When a certain activity occurred, apparently applicable legal principles either signaled approval or at least did not suggest disapproval. Retroactivity may threaten these expectations with 'disappointment' and unforeseen costs. The destabilizing effects of retroactive regulation suggest the need to come to terms with the permissible parameters of retroactivity. The impact of Bowen . . . depends, to a great degree, on the Court's concept of retroactivity, the contours of which are still obscure."

SECTION 3. PROCEDURES OUTSIDE THE FUNDAMENTAL PROCEDURAL CATEGORIES: INFORMATION GATHERING AND INSPECTION

> *a.* **Required Forms and Reports**
> *b.* **Information Collection by Inspection**
> *c.* **Resisting Inspection and Information Demands**

Rulemaking and adjudication are the fundamental categories of agency action under the APA. But the great bulk of government activity affecting citizen interests occurs outside of and prior to the relatively structured interchanges that are the principal focus of this casebook—that is, before a notice of proposed rulemaking is published, a license application filed, or a complaint seeking a sanction issued. Agencies gather information, make general policy, and enter contracts or make government grants outside these frameworks. The great diversity of these types of agency actions and the different settings involved makes it difficult to discuss them helpfully in a few paragraphs. In addition, such earlier agency activities are not often litigated. As a result, courses in administrative law, like the APA, tend to grant them only passing mention. Yet information gathering, in particular, may be the context in which most citizens most often come into contact with administrative agencies, and that makes it worthy of some exploration here.

Administrative agencies gather information in many ways—through inspections, through requiring reports such as tax returns or factory emissions filings, through more formal subpoenas, and so on. Moreover, the mere flow of information to government is only part of the significance of requiring information, and in many settings it is the lesser part. Business and individuals often change their primary conduct in response to being subject to inspection or having to report data. As Chapter VI discusses at p. 748, the government's making that information available to the public, without further official action, may itself be a spur to change; disclosure itself can be a form of regulation.

Information is the raw material for the implementation and shaping of policy. Information may be required in the course of adjudication or rulemaking, in advance of either of these activities, or in the service of other important but less formal agency functions, such as staff action on requests for governmental action, i.e. licensing or public grants; identifying industry problems or policy issues that may require agency response; monitoring circumstances in which enforcement activity may be required; and preparing for dealings with the legislature or the executive on issues of policy or oversight. As you proceed through the following pages, consider what goals are being enforced and where information demands fit in furthering those goals.

Collection of information raises a number of important policy questions, such as how to make the most effective use of an agency's limited resources or the potential advantages and pitfalls of a more cooperative approach to inspection and enforcement. The materials that follow, focusing on the activities of the Occupational Safety and Health Administration, begin by considering these policy questions and briefly review statutory constraints on the government's activities. But information gathering, particularly through inspection, can also trigger constitutional constraints. Thus, the materials also briefly discuss the limits imposed on the government's activities in this area by the Fourth Amendment's protection "against unreasonable searches and seizures" and the Fifth Amendment's provision that "[n]o person . . .shall be compelled in any criminal case to be a witness against himself."

a.   Required Forms and Reports

Perhaps the most commonplace feature of regulatory regimes is an obligation to supply the government with information, either directly or by keeping it on hand for possible inspection. Experience with required forms and reports is as common as filing an annual tax return, applying for Social Security benefits, or, in a pharmacy, keeping prescription records. To be valid, the information requirement must be established by statute or an authorized regulation. Sanctions for non-compliance must be similarly defined; some, such as denial of a requested benefit, may be administered by the agency itself; others, such as criminal penalties, require judicial assistance. By contrast, the forms on which information is requested—paper or (increasingly) electronic—will likely be generated by purely internal bureaucratic routine.

For citizens and regulated entities alike, the burdens of such requirements are substantial. At the federal level, the Paperwork Reduction Act, 44 U.S.C. §§ 3501–3520, makes OMB's Office of Information and Regulatory Affairs (OIRA) responsible both for controlling and reducing the cumulating, expensive, sometimes even disturbing character of the paperwork burden, and for assuring its conversion into electronic form. OIRA maintains a "dashboard" providing information about its activities, www.reginfo.gov, and on April 7, 2017, that dashboard reported the existence of 9,482 active federal information requirements of persons or organizations outside government. These requirements, it reported, elicited over 110 billion annual responses, produced in over 11.6 billion hours of labor, at a cost of $128 billion dollars. For the Department of the Treasury alone, home of the Internal Revenue Service, 1074 forms elicited 2.7 billion responses taking 8.2 billion hours to complete, at a cost of $33.8 billion. Despite the PRA's hopeful title, these numbers have been steadily growing over the years. "[G]overnment information . . . can be the means by which the dedicated public servant uncovers problems, reaches decisions, enforces laws, delivers services, and informs the public. But it also can be the means by which the faceless bureaucrat asks time-consuming or intrusive questions, forces seemingly arbitrary changes in business practices or personal behavior, and imposes significant costs on the economy."[17]

The next few paragraphs give a brief introduction to the PRA. Paperwork reduction may seem a dull topic, but the struggles over it have large implications. Any effort at control quickly confronts the reality that much of the government's curiosity is firmly rooted in the programs it seeks to administer.[18] Information is required to assure that the rules of government programs are being respected, to permit intelligent decisions about the future course of policy, to understand the workings and needs of the part of the private sector being subject to regulation, and to inform the public about matters of common concern. Indeed, the lack of information critical to analyzing issues and controlling costs has led to "poor service quality, high costs, low productivity, unnecessary risks and burdens, and unexploited opportunities for improvement. . . ."[19]

If an agency wishes to collect information from outside government by asking identical questions of ten or more sources, the Act requires it

---

[17] S. Rep. 103–392, Paperwork Reduction Act of 1994, Committee on Governmental Affairs 18 (1994). The National Performance Review gave many examples of "industrial-era bureaucracies in an information age," such as the requirement of 14 different forms for every import transaction and as many as 40 for a single export transaction, at an estimated cost of at least $150–200 per transaction. National Performance Review, Accompanying Report on Reengineering Through Information Technology 38 (1993).

[18] "Maybe we could suppress [red tape] if it were merely the nefarious work of a small group of villains or if it were a waste product easily separated from the things we want to government, but it is neither. . . . What we need is a detached clinical approach rather than heated attacks, the delicate wielding of a scalpel rather than furious flailing about with a meat ax." Herbert Kaufman, Red Tape: Its Origins, Uses, and Abuses 97–98 (1977).

[19] S. Rep. 103–392, above n. 17 at 19, 30.

to obtain OIRA's approval before doing so. The governing standard is "whether the collection of information by the agency is necessary for the proper performance of the functions of the agency, including whether the information shall have practical utility." 44 U.S.C. § 3508. If the agency uses the public procedures of rulemaking to create its collection requirement, OIRA enjoys participatory rights and substantial oversight of that process;[20] if the agency proceeds only bureaucratically, OIRA determines its necessity and may itself conduct informal proceedings to that end. Anyone can track the requests made to OIRA (as well as find other information about the Act) at the OIRA website. OIRA can withhold permission to collect information or make it subject to a condition that the information be obtained through a central collection agency able to coordinate this request with the requests of other agencies interested in similar data. OIRA's participation in agency rulemaking is protected from judicial review, 44 U.S.C. § 3507(d)(6), and review of decisions outside that framework has rarely been sought. See Action All. of Senior Citizens v. Sullivan, 930 F.2d 77 (D.C. Cir. 1991). Even the independent regulatory commissions are subject to OIRA's constraints under the Act, although a commission may override OIRA by a publicly explained majority vote. 44 U.S.C. § 3507(f).

Approved information requests are given an OMB control number, and you find that number on any federal government form you receive. If the number is not there on an information request required to be approved in this manner, you cannot be required to comply with it. The implications of a failure to show that number can be quite dramatic.[21]

This centralization of control over information requirements in the presidency (through OIRA) is a presidential political control and coordination mechanism of surprising strength—and it is one that Congress, perhaps in frustration at the continued size of information requirements, has steadily made stronger. You might consider whether it animates the non-statutory presidential controls over rulemaking you may come to consider in Chapters IV, Section 4.d and VII, Section 3.c. While OIRA's function is focused on coordination and cost reduction, and the statute explicitly disclaims any purpose to enlarge its authority over

---

[20] If OIRA comments publicly in the rulemaking, § 3507(d)(4) permits the Director, "in the Director's discretion," to disapprove a collection (A) "not specifically required by an agency rule," (B) if the agency failed to comply with statutory requirements, (C) "if the Director finds within 60 days after the publication of the rule that the agency's response to the Director's comments . . . was unreasonable," or (D) if the Director finds the agency in its final rule has substantially modified what it initially proposed, without resubmitting the modified collection requirement at least 60 days before issuing the final rule.

[21] 44 U.S.C. § 3512 provides: "(a) Notwithstanding any other provision of law, no person shall be subject to any penalty for failing to comply with a collection of information that is subject to this chapter if—"(1) the collection of information does not display a valid control number assigned by the Director [of the OMB] in accordance with this chapter;. . . . *(b) The protection provided by this section may be raised in the form of a complete defense, bar, or otherwise at any time during the agency administrative process or judicial action applicable thereto.*" (emphasis added). In Saco River Cellular, Inc. v. FCC, 133 F.3d 25 (D. C. Cir. 1998), this provision required the unwinding of licensing proceedings ostensibly completed in 1986 but on the basis of information supplied on forms that did not bear a valid control number.

an agency's "substantive policies and programs," 44 U.S.C. § 3518(e), compliance with that limitation is itself in the hands of the White House and OMB. Is the statute a salutary recognition of the need for presidential coordination and of the benefits of sharing information across government (including the benefit of reducing duplicative information demands from agencies that may be unaware of each others' activities)? Or is it an invitation for influential regulated interests to undermine agency functioning by making covert use of White House friends? Similar questions about political controls are presented in some depth in the later discussion of the rulemaking controls created by executive order, but those controls are not created by statute; the PRA statutorily recognizes a level of presidential direction of agency affairs that, to date, is highly unusual.

b. Information Collection by Inspection

Recordkeeping requirements sometimes require maintaining records in office files that may be subject to inspection on request, rather than submitted to the government. In the digital age, as may seem obvious, requiring submission of such records in digital form has the advantage of freeing the requirement from the need to inspect and permitting creation of a comprehensive database that may facilitate government or even private analysis. The EPA's Toxic Resource Inventory, that you may consider in Chapter VI, is a striking example— permitting citizens to acquire information about toxic materials emitted by industry in any zip code and, in consequence, encouraging voluntary controls by industry interested to cultivate local goodwill. OSHA has long required employers to maintain records of industrial illnesses and injuries at their worksites, subject to inspection; in 2016 it adopted an amendment to its rules requiring annual digital submission of these records, 29 C.F.R. Part 1904, a change that had been vigorously resisted by the U.S. Chamber of Commerce. 89 FR 29623 (May 12, 2016). As of April 7, 2017, OSHA's website reported, "OSHA is not accepting electronic submissions at this time." Consider what may have been the reasons for the Chamber's resistance, and the possible actions of President Trump's administration, responsible for implementing this change, in effecting it.

The reality, of course—even before any budget cuts in 2017—is that OSHA's resources for physical inspection of workplaces have long been extremely limited. OSHA's budget for federal enforcement in 2017 was $208 million, about 38% of the whole OSHA budget. Writing in 2010, THOMAS MCGARITY, RENA STEINZOR, SIDNEY SHAPIRO, AND MATTHEW SHUDTZ, WORKERS AT RISK: REGULATORY DYSFUNCTION AT OSHA (Ctr. for Progressive Reform Feb. 2010) had observed: "Often, the most difficult and most important work for a regulatory agency is the most resource-intensive. Enforcement that has a meaningful deterrent effect is the prime example. Inspectors must be trained and deployed across the entire country. OSHA must develop fair and effective mechanisms for targeting the most dangerous worksites for inspection by trained personnel. If conducted properly, a compliance assessment at a very large worksite might take 2,000 employee-hours. The accompanying legal proceedings can drag on for months or years. In Fiscal Year 2010, OSHA will spend about $227 million on federal enforcement programs, but will only have the capacity to inspect 40,000 of the nation's more than 8 million workplaces. . . OSHA's $513 million budget for Fiscal Year 2009 is less than 0.02 percent of the year's $3.1 trillion total federal outlays . . ." Since the 2016 budget allocated fewer dollars to enforcement, this concern has hardy diminished. And from it you can readily understand the difference between record retention and record submission—a difference considerably underscored when in the spring of 2017 Congress used the Congressional Review Act to disapprove a rule adopted in the closing days of the Obama administration that might have permitted OSHA to cite recordkeeping violations occurring within the five-year period it requires injury and illness records to be kept on the work site; as a result of this disapproval, OSHA must charge violations within six months of their occurrence. For an industry unlikely to be inspected, the requirement of inspection rather than submission substantially lowers if it does not eliminate enforcement risks.

In 2015, the Bureau of Labor Statistics reported almost 5,000 workers suffered fatal workplace injuries (20% in the construction industry) and employers reported that 2.9 million workers—3% of the workforce—had suffered nonfatal workplace injuries and illnesses;[22] latent injuries, such as might be produced by workplace carcinogens, are at best underreported in these figures. ORLY LOBEL, INTERLOCKING REGULATORY AND INDUSTRIAL RELATIONS: THE GOVERNANCE OF WORKPLACE SAFETY, 57 Admin. L. Rev. 1071, 1074, 1080 (2005): "Despite an image of intrusiveness and omnipresence, OSHA is actually a low-budget, understaffed, overextended agency. In today's American labor market, OSHA is responsible for the safety of more than 115 million workers at over eight million worksites. The agency currently has a staff of over 2,000 employees,[23] which is actually fewer workers than the agency had at its inception. . . . Because of its limited resources, the agency can conduct inspections at only a small fraction of all worksites. Recent budgetary cuts have further limited the agency's capabilities and effectiveness. In effect, OSHA is able to inspect every workplace that it oversees less than once each century. OSHA manages to investigate only one-quarter of the workplaces with reported fatalities. Even the most at-risk industries, such as construction sites, are inspected, on average, once every ten years. . . ."

---

[22]   https://www.bls.gov/iif/ (visited 4/8/2017).

[23]   2,173 in FY 2016. https://www.dol.gov/sites/default/files/documents/general/budget/FY 2017BIB_0.pdf (visited September 15, 2017).

Within these constraints, choices of enforcement strategy and style can significantly impact the effectiveness of the agency in controlling workplace injury, its statutory responsibility. A visit to OSHA's website will reveal many programs aimed at education and securing voluntary compliance, and also policies for setting enforcement priorities— identifying particularly hazardous industries, particular workplaces where deaths and serious injuries have occurred at a high rate, and so forth. The choice between cooperative and police styles of enforcement is itself a fraught one. Should the agency's inspectors be envisioned as expert consultants, granted substantial discretion so that they can work collaboratively and creatively with management and labor to efficiently address health and safety problems as they arise? Or instead should they be viewed as street-level bureaucrats lacking the education necessary for trustworthy exercise of broad discretion, and possibly prone to graft (to supplement inferior wages)—persons who had better be given a detailed manual specifying their activities? Or perhaps as the equivalent of police officers, with primary responsibility to detect violations and issue citations rather than proactively assist employers to improve the safety of their workplaces? The costs and benefits of proceeding "by the book" are explored in a provocative literature, which includes Bardach and Robert A. Kagan, Going By the Book: The Problem of Regulatory Unreasonableness (1982); Sidney A. Shapiro and Randy S. Rabinowitz, Punishment versus Cooperation in Regulatory Enforcement: A Case Study of OSHA, 49 Admin. L. Rev. 713, 720–24 (1997) ; and Steven Kelman, Regulating America, Regulating Sweden: A Comparative Study of Occupational Safety and Health Policy 196 (1981).

The state of Maine at one point sought to marry the two approaches. (Occupational safety and health is one of those areas in which cooperative federalism can play a role, with states taking on federal responsibilities under OSHA's supervision; the general effectiveness of these programs, a separate issue, has been questioned. Alison D. Morantz, Has Devolution Injured American Workers? 25 J.L. Econ & Org. 183 (2009).) Finding that stepped-up inspections and enforcement were not yielding fewer worker injuries and illnesses, the Maine OSHA office developed a "partnership" approach. It invited the 200 industries with the highest reported number of workers' compensation claims—1% of Maine's employers, but 30% of its workforce and 45% of its claims—to participate in a cooperative program that would work to identify and correct safety problems. Those who accepted were promised a reduction in the incidence of "wall-to-wall inspections"; good faith efforts to stay with the program would also eliminate fines and sanctions. Of these 200 firms, all but two joined the program, and their workers' compensation claim experience fell by 47.3%; the state as a whole saw a 27% drop in claims—a drop substantially explained by this performance in a group previously responsible for almost half the claims filed. For OSHA's Maine area director, the program also brought substantial rewards in agency efficiency: a wall-to-wall inspection at a high hazard plant might involve six to nine officers on site for three months, then time to write findings, and months or years of litigation—with little sign, on later inspections, of permanent change. In three years, he thought, the new program had resulted in the identification and elimination of seven times as many safety hazards as his agency could have found in a more adversary setting. See Charles Oliver, "Executive Update F," Investor's Business Daily 4, Sept. 10, 1996; see also Lobel, supra, at 1116–18.

The success of this and other programs prompted OSHA to issue a directive establishing a cooperative compliance program in high-hazard industries nationwide; over 12,000 were invited to join, under threat of immediate priority for comprehensive inspection if they did not. Given OSHA's constrained resources, of course, the reality of this threat depended on the degree of cooperation it would be able to secure. (There is also the possibility, as Shapiro and Rabinowitz suggest, 49 Admin. L. Rev. at 741, that "OSHA appears to be rewarding those employers with the worst safety records, which sends the wrong message.") On judicial review, this initiative was struck down, because OSHA had not used what the D.C. Circuit determined were necessary notice-and-comment rulemaking procedures for adopting it, see Chamber of Commerce of the United States v. Dep't of Labor, 174 F.3d 206 (1999); the case is discussed in the materials on rulemaking in Chapter IV, p. 374.

c.   Resisting Inspection and Information Demands

(1) *Inspections.* Neither inspection nor information demands are always willingly received. In an effort to control the size of this book, the editors decided to eschew an extended treatment of Fourth Amendment issues, which had been presented in earlier editions. But a summary, underscoring the differences with the treatment of searches for evidence of crime, still seems appropriate.

The Fourth Amendment to the U.S. Constitution, applicable as well to state and local governments through the Fourteenth Amendment, provides:

> The right of the people to be secure in their persons, houses, papers, and effects, against unreasonable searches and seizures, shall not be violated, and no Warrants shall issue, but upon probable cause, supported by Oath or affirmation, and particularly describing the place to be searched, and the persons or things to be seized.

Its application in criminal matters remains a constant source of litigation, even at the Supreme Court level, particularly in response to automobiles with locked compartments, and issues (such as surveillance techniques) arising with modern technology. Administrative searches (i.e., inspections) present an additional problem, as agencies often conduct them for programmatic and preventative reasons. Section 8(a) of the Occupational Safety and Health Act of 1970 (OSHA) is typical; it provides:

> In order to carry out the purposes of this chapter, the Secretary, upon presenting appropriate credentials to the owner, operator, or agent in charge, is authorized—
>
> (1) to enter without delay and at reasonable times any factory, plant, establishment, construction site, or other area, workplace or environment where work is performed by an employee of an employer; and
>
> (2) to inspect and investigate during regular working hours and at other reasonable times, and within reasonable limits and in a reasonable manner, any such place of employment and all pertinent conditions, structures, machines, apparatus, devices, equipment, and materials therein, and to question privately any such employer, owner, operator, agent, or employee.

84 Stat. 1590, 29 U.S.C. § 657(a) (1970). It may be evident that a program for inspecting (searching) without "probable cause, supported by Oath or affirmation, and particularly describing the place to be searched, and the persons or things to be seized" is in some tension with the Constitution's words. Although in the criminal context warrantless searches are sometimes accepted as not "unreasonable," that is generally because exigent circumstances make obtaining a warrant impractical and the need for search strong. Administrative searches, in general, present no such imperatives.

Eight years after five Justices had ruled that a municipal health inspector's demand to enter a home in response to signs of rat infestation "touch[ed] at most upon the periphery" of Fourth Amendment concerns, Frank v. Maryland, 359 U.S. 360 (1959), six Justices upheld two citizens' refusals to permit administrative searches—in one case, of an apartment, in the other, of a warehouse. Camara v. Municipal Court, 387 U.S. 523 (1967), See v. Seattle, 387 U.S. 541 (1967). In 1978, Marshall v. Barlow's Inc., 436 U.S. 307 found the OSHA statute "unconstitutional insofar as it purports to authorize inspections without warrant or its equivalent." Accommodating the realities and needs of the administrative state, however, the Court indicated that it would be sufficient to show that the inspection would occur in conformity with a reasonable plan, without any need to "particularly describe[e] the place to be searched, and the persons or things to be seized." In itself a striking accommodation to the information needs for the administrative state, even this watered-down warrant requirement is not requisite for a "closely regulated industry"— a category that seemed quite narrow in its first expression but has subsequently broadened considerably. Donovan v. Dewey, 452 U.S. 494 (1981) (stone quarry); New York v. Burger, 482 U.S. 691 (1987) (automobile junk yard). In practice, moreover, those to be inspected must take the trouble (and attention-drawing risk) of demanding a warrant, and few do.

Would imposing standards for administrative searches under the APA be a better approach? EDWARD RUBIN, IT'S TIME TO MAKE THE ADMINISTRATIVE PROCEDURE ACT ADMINISTRATIVE, 89 Cornell L. Rev. 95, 130–31 (2003): ". . .[A]dministrative inspection cases are a doctrinal farrago. The recognized meaning of the warrant requirement is that a police officer must demonstrate to a judge that there is probable cause to conclude that the person has committed an offense before searching the person's residence or business. If one eliminates probable cause and substitutes a completely different standard, such as 'a general administrative plan,' there is little reason to describe the new requirement as a warrant. While this can certainly be regarded as diluting Fourth Amendment protection, the accusation is beside the point. The judges who decided these cases had no intention of undermining the use of warrants in criminal law; rather, they were using the claim that a warrant is required to fashion an essentially new procedural requirement for one form of informal adjudication. Federal judges are fully aware that administrative agencies must collect large quantities of information, and they know that the probable cause requirement, designed for criminal cases, would be unacceptably disruptive in a regulatory context. However, they are also aware that such inspections can serve as an independent sanction and can be used in an unfair or abusive manner. Unfortunately, the APA provides no standards whatsoever for assessing the propriety of on-site inspections or most other forms of informal adjudication. So the judges fashioned the new requirement of a general administrative plan and used the Fourth Amendment as a vehicle to impose it on administrative agencies. This provides some measure of supervision for on-site inspections, but it is something of a gimmick . . . ."

(2) *Subpoenas.* The need to balance concerns of individual privacy and regulatory enforcement has also played out in the context of administrative subpoenas, with the Supreme Court adopting a standard that grants agencies broad powers to subpoena documents. The leading decision is OKLAHOMA PRESS PUB. CO. V. WALLING, 327 U.S. 186, 208–09 (1946): ". . . It is not necessary, as in the case of a warrant, that a specific charge or complaint of violation of law be pending or that the order be made pursuant to one. It is enough that the investigation be for a lawfully authorized purpose, within the power of Congress to command. . . . The requirement of 'probable cause, supported by oath or affirmation' literally applicable in the case of a warrant is satisfied, in that of an order for production, by the court's determination that the investigation is authorized by Congress, is for a purpose Congress can order, and the documents sought are relevant to the inquiry. . . . Beyond this the requirement of reasonableness, including particularity in 'describing the place to be searched, and the persons or things to be seized,' also literally applicable to warrants, comes down to specification of the documents to be produced adequate, but not excessive, for the purposes of the relevant inquiry."

Subpoena enforcement, like warrant issuance, generally requires a court action, but (as with the warrant) the burden of justification for the agency is not severe. When the Equal Employment Opportunity Commission subpoenaed certain records in the course of its investigation into allegations of employment discrimination, the Supreme Court reiterated its understanding of the permissive approach that should be taken by district courts where enforcement was sought, MCLANE CO. V. EEOC, 137 S.Ct. 1159 (2017): "A district court's role in an EEOC subpoena enforcement proceeding, we have twice explained, is a straightforward one. See Univ. of Pa. v. EEOC, 493 U.S. 182, 191 (1990); EEOC v. Shell Oil Co., 466 U.S., 54, 72 n. 26 (1984). A district court is not to use an enforcement proceeding as an opportunity to test the strength of the underlying complaint. Rather, a district court should 'satisfy itself that the charge is valid and that the material requested is "relevant" to the charge.' Univ. of Pa., 493 U.S., at 191. It should do so cognizant of the 'generou[s]' construction that courts have given the term 'relevant.' If the charge is proper and the material requested is relevant, the district court should enforce the subpoena unless the employer establishes that the subpoena is 'too indefinite,' has been issued for an 'illegitimate purpose,' or is unduly burdensome."

(3) *And the Fifth Amendment Too?* One can without difficulty tell a similar story of stress and accommodation respecting the Fifth Amendment's assurance that "no person . . . shall be compelled in any criminal case to be a witness against himself." Thus, when a "person" can point to a crime and believably assert that her response to some demand for information might serve as a link in a chain of evidence tending to convict her of that crime, she will be excused from responding. As a general matter, this privilege has been a strong one in American political history; fear of police coercion in criminal interrogations initially marked understanding of its scope. The widespread use of the Fifth Amendment by witnesses at congressional and administrative hearings during the anti-Communist hysteria of the early 1950s, and the political demagoguery that usually followed invocation of the privilege, have assured a broad reading of the amendment in other investigative contexts as well. The Supreme Court has strongly resisted efforts to punish invocation of the privilege, as by, for example, making use of the privilege a ground for removal from a public job.[24]

Nevertheless, recognizing the privilege's power to frustrate much regulatory activity, the courts have rarely found it available to resist information demands made in ordinary administrative contexts. In the first place, the privilege cannot be asserted by corporations or other artificial "persons,"[25] although such entities *are* protected as "persons" by

---

[24] Gardner v. Broderick, 392 U.S. 273 (1968). A public employee could, however, be fired for refusing to answer questions directly and narrowly relating to the performance of her duties.

[25] Such as partnerships, unions, or unincorporated associations. Hale v. Henkel, 201 U.S. 43 (1906); Bellis v. United States, 417 U.S. 85 (1974).

the Fifth Amendment's guarantees of due process and of "just compensation" when property is taken for public use. The Court reasons that the privilege seeks to protect the individual from having her will overborne by the state, an interest in personal integrity that artificial persons do not share.

Even real persons face numerous obstacles to using the privilege in the regulatory context. First, they may assert it only by affirmatively claiming it. For example, if a taxpayer's sources of income were unlawful, she could not use the privilege to excuse her failure to file an income tax return but would have to file the return invoking the privilege on the line where earned income is to be reported. This is a more conspicuous gesture than most would wish to make. And any other response, if false, opens the citizen to prosecution for "false statement."[26] Second, the claim can be made only for "testimonial" communications. It is unavailable, for example, as a basis for resisting the taking of a fingerprint or other physical evidence. Third, it can be made only on the basis of potential criminal liability, not merely a tendency to bring about undesired regulatory consequences. Finally, the circumstances in which a claim can be made are highly limited: the papers must both belong to the claimant and be in her possession. Thus, if my papers are subpoenaed from my accountant or my bank, the privilege is not available, for I am not the one being required to produce them; if my accountant's papers are sought from me, the fact that they incriminate me is irrelevant. Only if I can establish that the very fact of producing the papers in response to the subpoena is a testimonial act that might incriminate me, can a claim be made.[27] In a hearing process, eliciting oral statements, the application of the privilege is more obvious. But the risk is that the claimant will be thought to have waived it by earlier answers indicating cooperation with the relevant line of the inquiry. Braswell v. United States, 487 U.S. 99 (1988) exemplifies these pressures and the arguable compromises that have resulted, holding that the sole shareholder and only active officer of a small company, and thus the custodian of its corporate records, could not resist a subpoena for them on self-incrimination grounds. He was entitled only to have kept from the jury the potentially incriminating fact that *he* was the one who produced the records.[28]

---

[26] Brogan v. United States, 522 U.S. 398 (1998).

[27] United States v. Doe, 465 U.S. 605 (1984); Baltimore City Dep't Social Services v. Bouknight, 493 U.S. 549 (1990).

[28] "Because the custodian acts as a representative, the act is deemed one of the corporation and not the individual. Therefore, the Government concedes, as it must, that it may make no evidentiary use of the "individual act" against the individual. For example, in a criminal prosecution against the custodian, the Government may not introduce into evidence before the jury the fact that the subpoena was served upon and the corporation's documents were delivered by one particular individual, the custodian."

CHAPTER IV
RULEMAKING

Imagine a visitor who seeks to catalog the variety of written texts the American federal government uses to communicate its powers and its citizens' rights and obligations. She might organize those texts into the following pyramid:

One Constitution, ratified
by "the people"

Hundreds of statutes, enacted by an
elected Congress

Thousands of regulations, adopted by politically
responsible agency heads

Tens of thousands of interpretations and other guidance
documents, issued by agency bureaus

Countless advice letters, press releases, and other statements of
understanding generated by individual bureaucrats

The pyramid shape is descriptively accurate. The relative sizes of the Constitution and the Statutes at Large are obvious. The Code of Federal Regulations (CFR), the annual compilation of the documents described by the third level above (and some other materials), is considerably larger than the United States Code (which captures only part of the Statutes at Large). At any technologically sophisticated agency (e.g., the Environmental Protection Agency) the volume of its own interpretations and guidance documents, the fourth level, may exceed that of the entire CFR.

This Chapter is principally concerned with the procedures used to create regulations (the third level). With some exceptions, § 553 of the Administrative Procedure Act (APA) provides two possible procedures: (1) "formal rulemaking," an on-the-record process verging on trial, rarely encountered these days but being pushed again in Congress, and

(2) "informal" or "notice-and-comment" rulemaking, the procedure most commonly employed today. (Indeed, informal rulemaking has become so dominant that it is the process generally meant when the term "rulemaking" is used.) Agency use of the APA's exceptions, meant to be limited, is considerable, with over one-third of major rules forgoing even notice-and-comment procedures in a recent study by the Government Accountability Office.

In the materials that follow, Section 1 provides an introduction to § 553 and the APA's approach to rulemaking. Section 2 then considers the requirements for notice-and-comment rulemaking in some detail. We begin with some basic judicial parameters, in particular the Supreme Court's insistence that judges may only rarely impose procedural requirements beyond those required by the APA, the specific substantive statute under which the agency acts, or the agency's own regulations. The flip side of this resistance to judicial imposed procedures is the demand that agencies adhere to procedural requirements that are imposed by statute and regulation, and we examine the specific demands courts have read § 553 to contain. Section 3 examines the exceptions to § 553's requirements, focusing both on the more informal agency issuances (the fourth level) that play an important role in guiding agency regulatory activities and informing the public of the agency's views, and binding rulemaking that may, in particular instances, be improperly evading the notice-and-comment rulemaking process.

Then we take a step back and situate the § 553 process in the wider course of making a rule. Section 4 examines the initiation of rulemaking, especially the process for centralized review of executive agencies' rulemaking efforts by the Office for Information and Regulatory Affairs (OIRA) in the Office of Management and Budget (OMB). Such centralized review offers Presidents an opportunity to insert their political priorities into the rulemaking process and in general assert close supervision of agency regulation. In this chapter, however, we focus on outlining the current procedures for centralized review; Chapter VII considers the constitutional and political implications of such presidential oversight. Finally, Section 5 takes up a set of issues that may arise during the finalization of a rule, including ex parte contacts and allegedly biased decisionmakers.

SECTION 1.   INTRODUCTION

If authorized by statute, consistent with the Constitution, and adopted through the required procedures, regulations have legally binding effect on the government and citizens alike, until displaced by statute or other validly adopted regulations. Thus, rulemaking is an extremely important process in modern regulatory programs.

Two sets of broader issues repeatedly surface that you may find helpful to think about in considering the materials in this chapter. First, what kinds of procedures should be required for contemporary rulemaking? Does your answer to this question vary with the type of policy or rule at stake, or by the type of agency (and its oversight by the White House or Congress)? Have the courts done a good job in interpreting § 553 and applying it to current rulemaking contexts? To what extent are the procedures now required for notice-and-comment rulemaking adequate and effective mechanisms for addressing what are referred to below as questions of "general facts"—factual matters that do not vary with particular parties but do involve specific factual issues and thus are distinct from general policy propositions. Is the current procedural framework excessively rigidified and formalistic—or, alternatively, are agencies allowed too much room for action that evades important constraints? And what about fairness concerns: are they adequately addressed through prevailing procedures?

Second, what roles should different institutions play in setting those procedural requirements and overseeing the rulemaking process? To what extent should this be a central responsibility of the courts as opposed to the political branches of the federal government (Congress and the President)? In thinking about institutional roles, remember that the range of institutional players here is potentially quite broad and also includes state and local governments, private or nongovernmental institutions, experts, regulated parties, regulatory beneficiaries, and interested members of the general public. Another critical player is of course the agency. Should agencies be entrusted with primary responsibility for developing adequate rulemaking procedures, given their substantive area expertise, or do agencies have too great an interest in minimizing the procedural constraints they face?

5 U.S.C. § 553

§ 553.   Rule making

(a) This section applies, according to the provisions thereof, except to the extent that there is involved—

    (1)   a military or foreign affairs function of the United States; or

    (2)   a matter relating to agency management or personnel or to public property, loans, grants, benefits, or contracts.

(b) General notice of proposed rulemaking shall be published in the Federal Register, unless persons subject thereto are named and either personally served or otherwise have actual notice thereof in accordance with law. The notice shall include—

    (1)   a statement of the time, place, and nature of public rule making proceedings;

    (2)   reference to the legal authority under which the rule is proposed; and

    (3)   either the terms or substance of the proposed rule or a description of the subjects and issues involved.

Except when notice or hearing is required by statute, this subsection does not apply—

(A) to interpretative rules, general statements of policy, or rules of agency organization, procedure, or practice; or

(B) when the agency for good cause finds (and incorporates the finding and a brief statement of reasons therefor in the rules issued) that notice and public procedure thereon are impracticable, unnecessary, or contrary to the public interest.

(c) After notice required by this section, the agency shall give interested persons an opportunity to participate in the rule making through submission of written data, views, or arguments with or without opportunity for oral presentation. After consideration of the relevant matter presented, the agency shall incorporate in the rules adopted a concise general statement of their basis and purpose. When rules are required by statute to be made on the record after opportunity for an agency hearing, sections 556 and 557 of this title apply instead of this subsection.

(d) The required publication or service of a substantive rule shall be made not less than 30 days before its effective date, except—

(1) a substantive rule which grants or recognizes an exemption or relieves a restriction;

(2) interpretative rules and statements of policy; or

(3) as otherwise provided by the agency for good cause found and published with the rule.

(e) Each agency shall give an interested person the right to petition for the issuance, amendment, or repeal of a rule.

NOTES

(1) **What Is a Rule?** One point worth noting at the outset is the breadth of the APA's definition of a rule. The definition comes in § 551(4), which provides:

"[R]ule" means the whole or a part of an agency statement of general or particular applicability and future effect designed to implement, interpret, or prescribe law or policy or describing the organization, procedure, or practice requirements of an agency and includes the approval or prescription for the future of rates, wages, corporate or financial structures or reorganization thereof, prices, facilities, appliances, services or allowances therefor or of valuations, costs, or accounting, or practices bearing on any of the foregoing[.]

Under this definition, which is contrasted with the term "order" in § 551(6), the term "rule" is not limited to measures promulgated under notice-and-comment or formal rulemaking. Instead, it also includes a vast array of agency documents, including many of the guidance documents, advice letters, and other statements placed in the two lowest levels of the pyramid above. Note that this definition of a rule for APA purposes as including "an agency statement of . . . particular applicability" differs from the emphasis in constitutional analysis on rules being generally applicable, which you may have seen if you read the material on Londoner and Bi-Metallic in Chapter III starting on p. 218.

Is an announcement outlining the terms of a payment-in-kind program a rule under the APA's definition? SUGAR CANE GROWERS COOPERATIVE V. VENEMAN, 289 F.3d 89 (D.C. Cir. 2002), involved a sugar payment-in-kind program run by the Department of Agriculture. Under the program, farmers bid for the right to receive sugar from the government-owned surplus to sell on the market in return for plowing under a given acreage of already planted sugar-producing crops. Important to the program's success was an assurance that participating farmers would not increase their future production over what they might have expected absent participation in the program. Thus, participants were told they could not participate in future payment-in-kind programs if they increased their future planted acreage. In August 2001, the Department announced by press release that it had decided to implement a payment-in-kind program for the 2001 sugar crop without APA rulemaking and subsequently published a "Notice of Program Implementation" in the Federal Register. Sugar cane growers disadvantaged by the program's payment-per-producer cap sued, alleging that the Department had violated the APA by promulgating a rule without notice-and-comment rulemaking.

JUDGE SILBERMAN wrote the panel's decision: "The APA defines a rule very broadly. . . . We have recognized that notwithstanding the breadth of the APA's definition an agency pronouncement that lacks the firmness of a proscribed standard . . . is not a rule. . . . [T]he government . . . argues that because the announcement of the . . . program was an 'isolated agency act' that did not propose to affect subsequent Department acts and had 'no future effect on any other party before the agency' it was not a rule. The government would have us see its announcement of the . . . program as analogous to an agency's award of a contract pursuant to an invitation of bids or an agency's decision to approve an application or a proposal—in administrative law terms an informal adjudication (which is the technical term for an executive action). We have little difficulty . . . in rejecting this argument. The August . . . press release. . . and . . . Notice of Program Implementation set forth the bid submission procedures which all applicants must follow, the payment limitations of the program, and the sanctions that will be imposed on participants if they plant more in future years than in 2001. It is simply absurd to call this anything but a rule 'by any other name.' " Do you agree?

(2) *Formal Rulemaking and* **Florida East Coast Railway.** The procedures for informal rulemaking are fully provided in § 553, whereas formal rulemaking involves compliance with §§ 556 and 557 instead of § 553(c).[1] In brief, formal rulemaking requires additional procedures for the

---

[1]   Specific agency statutes can also provide for hybrid procedures between informal and formal rulemaking. See Note 4 (Legislatively Required Hybrid Rulemaking) below on p. 305 for more discussion of these mixed procedures, which cannot be imposed by the courts (unless in the rare circumstance the Constitution requires them).

submission and adjudication of evidence, though in some contexts it can be conducted without an *oral* hearing. As the text of § 553(c) makes clear, whether an agency must use formal rulemaking procedures is determined by whether "rules are required by statute to be made on the record after opportunity for an agency hearing." The "statute" here is the law delegating authority under which the agency is operating.

In the early years of the APA, formal rulemaking was relatively common. Indeed, the first edition of Kenneth Culp Davis's casebook on administrative law in 1951 devoted only three pages to notice-and-comment rulemaking but spent an entire chapter on formal rulemaking.

Much early agency rulemaking concerned economic matters, fitting § 551(4)'s definition of "rule" as including "the approval or prescription for the future of rates, wages, corporate or financial structures or reorganization thereof, prices, facilities, appliances, services or allowances therefor or of valuations, costs, or accounting, or practices bearing on any of the foregoing." It had long been settled that while legislatures might enact rates through the normal lawmaking process, the Constitution's Due Process Clauses required individualized oral hearings if agencies were to be given the task of setting firm-specific rates. See, e.g., ICC v. Louisville & Nashville R. Co., 227 U.S. 88, 93 (1913). Under the APA, then, it was readily understood that such proceedings fit the "formal rulemaking" mode. From the perspective of the firm whose rates were set, the agency's determination turns on the firm's own particular, individual circumstances and this suggests the virtues of trial-type process. From the public's perspective, however, rate setting raises a host of competing, "polycentric" policy issues whose resolution we would ordinarily expect to entrust to politics, if interests had equal access to that space. (This same mix is present in initial licensing. The APA defines licensing as "adjudication," but because of special provisions contained in §§ 554–558, the initial licensing process is essentially the same as formal rulemaking.)

In the last four decades, formal rulemakings have become quite rare. The formal rulemaking process was criticized for being a voracious consumer of agency resources and giving excessive control over the development of the rule to the parties to the proceeding. For example, a Food and Drug Administration (FDA) formal rulemaking to determine the percentage of peanuts a substance must contain in order to be labeled "peanut butter" took nine years (including twenty weeks of hearings, generating close to 8,000 pages of hearing record) to produce a six-page opinion to justify a decision to require at least 90 percent peanuts, which the courts upheld (along with a ceiling of 55 percent fat). According to an FDA history, "A prominent attorney on the case wryly observed that the peanut butter standards 'put many lawyers' children through college.'" Many commentators believe formal rulemaking takes considerably longer than notice-and-comment rulemaking, though that view has recently been challenged. See Aaron L. Nielson, In Defense of Formal Rulemaking, 75 Ohio State L.J. 237 (2014).

ROBERT W. HAMILTON, PROCEDURES FOR THE ADOPTION OF RULES OF GENERAL APPLICABILITY: THE NEED FOR PROCEDURAL INNOVATION IN ADMINISTRATIVE RULEMAKING, 60 Cal. L. Rev. 1276, 1312–13 (1972) reported more generally: "It is surprising to discover that most agencies required to conduct formal hearings in connection with rulemaking in fact did not do so during the previous five years. . . . Thus, the primary impact of these procedural requirements is often not, as one might otherwise have expected, the testing of agency assumptions by cross-examination, or the testing of agency conclusions by courts on the basis of substantial evidence of record. Rather these procedures either cause the abandonment of the program (as in the Department of Labor), the development of techniques to reach the same regulatory goal but without a hearing (as FDA is now trying to do), or the promulgation of noncontroversial regulations by a process of negotiation and compromise (as FDA historically has done and Interior is encouraged to do). In practice, therefore, the principal effect of imposing rulemaking on a record has often been the dilution of the regulatory process rather than the protection of persons from arbitrary action."

In 1973, one year after publication of Hamilton's study, the Supreme Court cemented the marginalization of formal rulemaking with its decision in UNITED STATES v. FLORIDA EAST COAST RAILWAY CO., 410 U.S. 224. The Interstate Commerce Commission (ICC) had by regulation established "incentive" rates to encourage railroads to send empty freight cars back to their owners. Without such rates, railroads had no particular reason to return the cars, and cars that tended to go full in only one direction— refrigerator cars, for example, carrying produce to urban markets—often pooled at their destination and created artificial and unnecessary shortages. The Interstate Commerce Act directed the ICC to act "after hearing," and the ICC had initially contemplated oral trial-type procedures for its regulatory effort. However, after intense congressional pressure to move more quickly, the agency limited the railroads to written submissions in informal rulemaking.

The Supreme Court upheld this procedural choice. It held that the simple reference to "hearing" in the Act was not enough to activate § 553(c)'s reference to cases in which "rules are required by statute to be made on the record after opportunity for an agency hearing." The Court noted that, in reaching the opposite conclusion, "[t]he District Court observed that it was 'rather hard to believe that the last sentence of § 553(c) was directed only to the few legislative sports where the words "on the record" or their equivalent had found their way into the statute book.' 318 F.Supp., at 496. This is, however, the language which Congress used, and since there are statutes on the books that do use these very words, see, e.g., the Fulbright Amendment to the Walsh-Healey Act, 41 U.S.C. § 43a, and 21 U.S.C. § 371(e)(3), the regulations provision of the Food and Drug Act, adherence to that language cannot be said to render the provision nugatory or ineffectual. We recognized in United States v. Allegheny-Ludlum Steel Corp., 406 U.S. 742 (1972) that the actual words 'on the record' and 'after . . . hearing' used in § 553 were not words of art, and that other statutory language having the same meaning could trigger the provisions of §§ 556 and 557 in rulemaking proceedings. But we adhere to our conclusion, expressed in that case, that the phrase 'after hearing' in § 1(14)(a) of the Interstate Commerce Act does not have such an effect."

Earlier cases like ICC v. Louisville & Nashville R. Co., which as noted above required a hearing in ratemaking contexts, were distinguished as involving the rates of a single railroad grounded in its individual financial circumstances, and not uniform and nationwide incentive payments ordered to be made by all railroads subject to the regulation.

Subsequent cases do appear to treat the terms in § 553 ("on the record after opportunity for an agency hearing") as "words of art," requiring all of them before mandating formal procedures. When a statute refers simply to "hearing" in the context of adjudication, rather than rulemaking, should the court similarly presume that informal procedures were intended? As discussed below, in Ch. V, Sec. 3 (p. 528), this question has provoked debate in the lower courts over the years.

(3)   *A Return of Formal Rulemaking?* Despite its marginalization post-Florida East Coast Railway, formal rulemaking, at least as a proposal, has reappeared in White House and congressional initiatives. As discussed below in Subsection 4.d, for several decades the Office of Information and Regulatory Affairs (OIRA) in the Office of Management and Budget (OMB) has undertaken centralized review of much executive branch rulemaking. President George W. Bush's Executive Order 13422, issued in January 2007, amended the process for review of regulations in various ways, including by imposing a requirement that agencies consider the use of formal rulemaking procedures. Agencies may have considered this option, but if so they rejected it; no agency proposed using formal rulemaking when not statutorily required in the period when the Order was in force. 72 Fed. Reg. 2763 (Jan. 23, 2007). President Obama rescinded Executive Order 13422 soon after he assumed office in January 2009. E.O. 13497, 74 Fed. Reg. 6113 (Feb. 4, 2009).

More recently, in April 2017, Republican Senator Rob Portman (Ohio) and Democrat Senator Heidi Heitkamp (North Dakota) introduced the Regulatory Accountability Act (S. 951), which, among other items, calls for:

(e)   Public Hearing for High-Impact Rules[2] and Certain Major Rules[3].—

(1)   PETITION FOR PUBLIC HEARING.—

(A)   IN GENERAL.—Before the date on which the comment period closes with respect to a proposed high-impact rule or a proposed

---

[2]   [Ed.] The Act defines "high impact rule" as follows:

"[H]igh-impact rule" means any rule that the Administrator determines is likely to cause an annual effect on the economy of $1,000,000,000 or more, adjusted once every 5 years to reflect increases in the Consumer Price Index for All Urban Consumers, as published by the Bureau of Labor Statistics of the Department of Labor[.]

S. 951 (115th Cong.), § 2.

[3]   [Ed.] The Act defines "major rule" as follows:

"[M]ajor rule" means any rule that the Administrator determines is likely to cause—

(A) an annual effect on the economy of $100,000,000 or more, adjusted once every 5 years to reflect increases in the Consumer Price Index for All Urban Consumers, as published by the Bureau of Labor Statistics of the Department of Labor;

(B) a major increase in costs or prices for consumers, individual industries, Federal, State, local, or tribal government agencies, or geographic regions; or

(C) significant adverse effects on competition, employment, investment, productivity, innovation, public health and safety, or the ability of United States-based enterprises to compete with foreign-based enterprises in domestic and export markets[.]

major rule described in [notes 2 & 3], an interested person may petition the agency that proposed the rule to hold a public hearing in accordance with this subsection.

(B) PETITION FOR PUBLIC HEARING FOR HIGH-IMPACT RULES.—

(i) GRANTING OF PETITION.—Not later than 30 days after the date on which an agency receives a petition submitted under subparagraph (A) with respect to a high-impact rule, the agency shall grant the petition if the petition shows that—

(I) the proposed rule is based on conclusions with respect to 1 or more specific scientific, technical, economic, or other complex factual issues that are genuinely disputed;

[Ed. (II) omitted, relevant to a sub-class of rules that agencies have to reissue]

(III) the resolution of the disputed factual issues described in subclause (I) would likely have an effect on—

(aa) the costs and benefits of the proposed rule; or

(bb) whether the proposed rule achieves the statutory purpose.

(ii) DENIAL OF PETITION.—If an agency denies a petition submitted under clause (i) in whole or in part, the agency shall include in the rulemaking record an explanation for the denial sufficient for judicial review, including—

(I) findings by the agency that—

(aa) there is no genuine dispute as to the factual issues raised by the petition; or

[Ed. (bb) omitted, relevant to a sub-class of rules that agencies have to reissue]; and

(II) a reasoned determination by the agency that the factual issues raised by the petition, even if subject to genuine dispute and not subject to subclause (I)(bb), will not have an effect on—

(aa) the costs and benefits of the proposed rule; or

(bb) whether the proposed rule achieves the statutory purpose.

(iii) INCLUSION IN THE RECORD.—A petition submitted under subparagraph (A) with respect to a high-impact rule and the decision of an agency with respect to the petition shall be included in the rulemaking record.

S. 951 (115th Cong.), § 2.

(C) PETITION FOR PUBLIC HEARING FOR CERTAIN MAJOR RULES.—

(i) IN GENERAL.—In the case of a major rule described in [note 3], any interested person may petition for a hearing under this subsection on the grounds and within the time limitation described in subparagraph (B)(i).

(ii) AGENCY AUTHORITY TO DENY PETITION.—An agency may deny a petition submitted to the agency under clause (i) if the agency reasonably determines that—

(I) a hearing—

(aa) would not advance the consideration of the proposed rule by the agency; or

(bb) would, in light of the need for agency action, unreasonably delay completion of the rulemaking; or

[Ed. (II) omitted, relevant to a sub-class of rules that agencies have to reissue].

(iii) INCLUSION IN THE RECORD.—A petition submitted under clause (i) and the decision of an agency with respect to the petition shall be included in the rulemaking record.

(2) NOTICE OF HEARING.—Not later than 45 days before the date on which a hearing is held under this subsection, an agency shall publish in the Federal Register a notice specifying—

(A) the proposed rule to be considered at the hearing; and

(B) the factual issues to be considered at the hearing.

(3) HEARING REQUIREMENTS.—

(A) LIMITED NATURE OF HEARING.—A hearing held under this subsection shall be limited to—

(i) the specific factual issues raised in a petition granted in whole or in part under paragraph (1); and

(ii) any other factual issues the resolution of which an agency, in the discretion of the agency, determines will advance consideration by the agency of the proposed rule.

(B) PROCEDURES.—

(i) BURDEN OF PROOF.—Except as otherwise provided by statute, a proponent of a rule has the burden of proof in a hearing held under this subsection.

(ii) ADMISSION OF EVIDENCE.—In a hearing held under this subsection, any documentary or oral evidence may be received, except that an agency, as a matter of policy, shall provide for the exclusion of immaterial or unduly repetitious evidence.

(iii) ADOPTION OF RULES GOVERNING HEARINGS.—To govern a hearing held under this subsection, each agency shall adopt rules that provide for—

> (I) the appointment of an agency official or administrative law judge to preside at the hearing;

> (II) the presentation by interested parties of relevant documentary or oral evidence, unless the evidence is immaterial or unduly repetitious;

> (III) a reasonable and adequate opportunity for cross-examination by interested parties concerning genuinely disputed factual issues raised by the petition, provided that, in the case of multiple interested parties with the same or similar interests, the agency may require the use of common counsel where the common counsel may adequately represent the interests that will be significantly affected by the proposed rule; and

> (IV) when appropriate, and to the extent practicable, the consolidation of proceedings with respect to multiple petitions submitted under this subsection into a single hearing.

(C) RECORD OF HEARING.—A transcript of testimony and exhibits, together with all papers and requests filed in the hearing, shall constitute the exclusive record for decision of the factual issues addressed in a hearing held under this subsection.

Estimates of how many rulemakings would qualify under this proposed legislation vary. In 2017, the U.S. Chamber of Commerce, looking at only stated costs (which an older form of the legislation used), had pegged high-impact rules at no more than 4 per year and major rules at between 15 and 25 per year (with 2016 being an outlier at 34).[4] But the proposed statutory definitions are in terms of "annual effects," not stated costs, which would presumably shift the estimates upward. The definition in the RAA for "major" rules closely parallels the definition in the Congressional Review Act, 5 U.S.C. §§ 801–808 (see p. 846). According to the Congressional Research Service, major rules under the CRA have varied between 50 and 100 from 1997 to 2015.[5] CRS and other government entities do not have similar counts for high impact rules as defined in S. 951.

How does this proposal differ from formal rulemaking in the APA, §§ 556–557? What do you think motivates this proposal? Simply a desire for

---

[4] U.S. Chamber of Commerce, Taming the Administrative State: Identifying Regulations that Impact Jobs and the Economy, at 2 (March 2017), available at: http://www.uschamber.com/sites/default/files/taming_the_administrative_state_report_march_2017.pdf. In earlier congressional testimony, the Chamber of Commerce pegged the number of high-impact rules at 5 to 7 per year.

[5] Maeve P. Carey, Counting Regulations: An Overview of Rulemaking, Types of Federal Regulations, and Pages in the Federal Register, Cong. Research Service Report 43056 (Oct. 2016), at 8, available at: http://fas.org/sgp/crs/misc/R43056.pdf.

less regulation? A wish for more consideration of options? Should rulemaking procedures vary with the importance of the undertaking? As you will see later in this chapter, the executive branch's review of agency rulemaking distinguishes among types of rulemakings. Would you vote for this provision of the RAA? What if it were limited only to high-impact rules (and thus did not include major rules)? Should agencies have more discretion to deny hearings for high-impact rules (along the lines of what is provided for major rules)?

(4) *A Flowchart for § 553 Notice-and-Comment Rulemaking.* Although legislation and adjudication are likely well-known processes for most law students, notice-and-comment rulemaking may be an unfamiliar procedure for those who have not spent time studying or working in administrative agencies. The following is a flowchart describing what rulemaking entails, assuming it is finished. The steps in the right column are actions taken internally by the agency; the steps to the left are actions mostly involving other governmental actors (though as explained in Subsection 4.b below, petitions typically come from outside the federal government). In addition, the steps above the dotted line, whether internal to the agency or involving other governmental actors, all occur before the notice-and-comment process outlined in § 553 commences; the steps below the dotted line include § 553's requirements as well as requirements imposed by executive order. Additional charts and descriptions of the rulemaking process are available from RegInfo.gov, at http://www.reginfo.gov/public/reginfo/Regmap/index.jsp (detailed map of process), and Regulation Room, at http://regulationroom.org/learn/what-rulemaking.

We make two observations here. First, a rule is not final until it is published in the Federal Register. When a new President of the opposing party takes office, one of the first actions of the White House is to direct executive agencies and departments to withdraw any items sent to the Federal Register under the previous administration that have not yet been published. See Kennecott Utah Copper Corp. v. Dep't of Interior, 88 F.3d 1191, 1206 (D.C. Cir. 1996) (allowing agencies to withdraw regulations "until virtually the last minute before public release").

Second, the flowchart (and almost all materials on rulemaking) conveys an incorrect presumption—that every notice of proposed rulemaking (NPRM) results in a final rule. In a recent study of rulemakings appearing in the Unified Agenda of Federal Regulatory and Deregulatory Actions from Fall 1988 to Spring 2010, more than ten percent of final actions that had a previous NPRM ended in a withdrawal of the NPRM, as opposed to a final rule. Anne Joseph O'Connell, Agency Rulemaking and Political Transitions, 105 Nw. U. L. Rev. 471, 520 (2015). The odds of a proposed rule being withdrawn (relative to being finished) increase after a presidential transition. Id. at 523.

Rulemaking

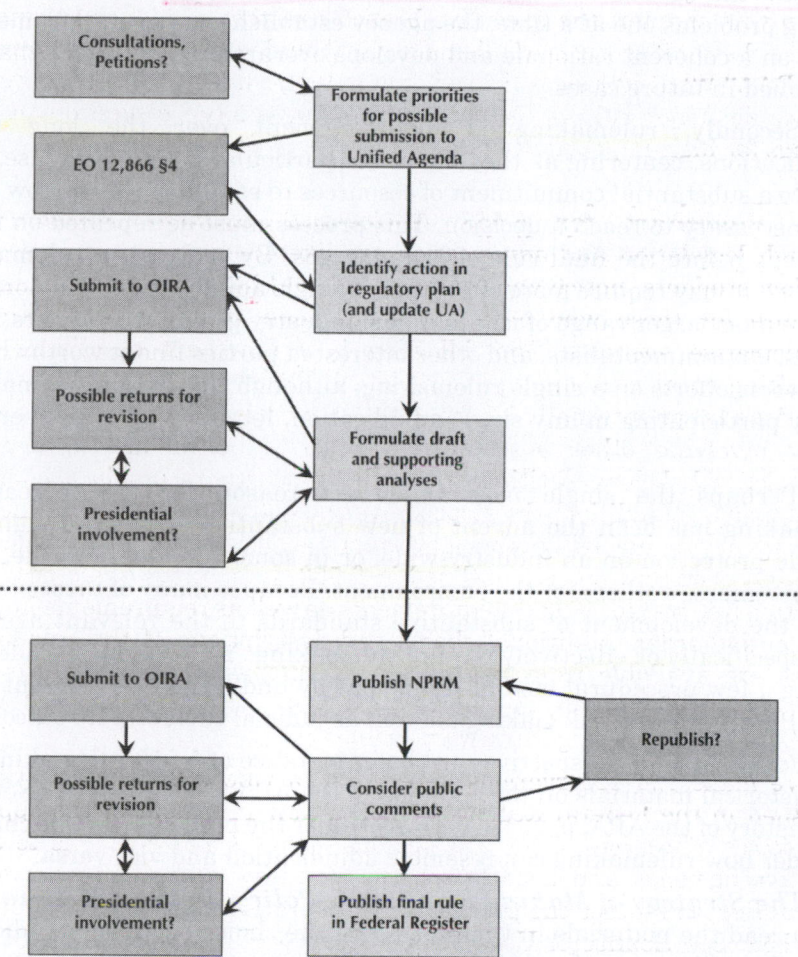

(5) *The Virtues of Making Regulatory Policy through Rulemaking.*
ALAN B. MORRISON, THE ADMINISTRATIVE PROCEDURE ACT: A LIVING AND
RESPONSIVE LAW, 72 Va. L. Rev. 253, 256–258 (1986): "... I have little doubt
that anyone would disagree with the conclusion reached by then law
professor and now ... [Justice] Antonin Scalia, who observed that 'perhaps
the most notable development in federal government administration during
the last two decades is the constant and accelerating flight away from
individualized, adjudicatory proceedings to generalized disposition through
rulemaking.'[2] This shift has occurred for a number of reasons.

"First, rulemaking is likely to produce a more rationally coherent rule
for general application. Unlike adjudications, which are often focused on a
single party, rulemaking allows an opportunity for all interested parties to
comment. While results in adjudications are often determined by the

---

[2]   Scalia, Vermont Yankee: The APA, the D.C. Circuit, and the Supreme Court, 1978 Sup.
Ct. Rev. 345, 376.

particular facts before the agency, rulemaking allows, if not actually requires, the agency to take a broader look at an issue. Thus, instead of solving problems one at a time, the agency establishes an overall framework based on a coherent rationale and develops overarching principles that can be applied in future cases.

"Secondly, rulemaking is more efficient over the long term. Adjudications, centering as they do on the particulars of a given case, may require a substantial commitment of resources to establish the narrow set of facts necessary to reach a decision. This process must be repeated on many occasions before the final rule of law emerges. By contrast, a rulemaking, although it may require more effort than a single adjudication, will normally resolve a far larger range of issues. Thus, industry groups, consumers, labor unions, environmentalists, and other interested parties find it worthwhile to focus their efforts on a single rulemaking, although they might be unable to justify participating in any single adjudication, let alone an entire series of them. . . .

"Perhaps the single most important reason for the increase in rulemaking has been the advent of new substantive statutes designed to provide protection on an industry-wide, or in some cases nationwide, basis for consumers, workers, or the environment. Because many of these statutes leave the development of substantive standards to the relevant agencies, they specifically or effectively require rulemaking. Yet Congress, aside from adding a few procedural modifications, has by and large been content to let the APA govern this rulemaking, as well as judicial review of its outcomes."

For additional perspectives on the importance of § 553 rulemaking, see the historical materials on the adoption of the APA in Chapter III (Notes on the History of the APA, p. 235). As you consider the materials in this chapter, consider how rulemaking can resemble adjudication and vice versa.

(6) **The Strategy of Making Regulatory Policy through Rulemaking.** If you read the materials in Chapter III on the choice between adjudication and rulemaking, you should recall the classic case SEC v. Chenery Corp., 332 U.S. 194 (1947) (Chenery II) (p. 249), which permits agencies to choose the form of policymaking, subject to constitutional and agency-specific statutory constraints. Also in Chapter III, you may have encountered an excerpt from Professor M. Elizabeth Magill. Here is another, well suited to the work of this chapter. M. ELIZABETH MAGILL, AGENCY CHOICE OF POLICYMAKING FORM, 71 U. Chi. L. Rev. 1383, 1384 (2004): "Consider, for an illustrative example, the Securities and Exchange Commission (SEC), which is authorized by various statutes to regulate the securities markets. Imagine that the SEC is concerned that a certain kind of financial transaction may violate the anti-fraud provisions of those laws. The SEC is authorized by statute and governing precedent to take the following actions. It might promulgate a legislative rule prohibiting the transaction. If valid, the rule would operate just like a statute; private parties would be required to refrain from engaging in the transaction or face sanctions. The SEC might also bring an administrative enforcement action against an individual who has engaged in the transaction. That proceeding would be conducted before an SEC adjudicator; if the adjudicator vindicated the agency's action, the object

of the enforcement action would face the authorized sanctions. The SEC might also choose to bring a judicial enforcement action. This route would be much like the administrative enforcement action—the agency would select the object of the action and, if the court vindicated the agency's position, sanctions would follow—but the proceeding would take place in the federal courts. Finally, the SEC might choose to provide guidance—for example, through congressional testimony, speeches, or a more formalized 'release'—advising interested parties of its concerns about the transaction. Though it would surely influence the behavior of private actors, that guidance would be advisory only; it would not on its own have binding legal effect. The SEC is thus authorized to take one of four paths to address the transaction with which it is concerned: legislative rule, administrative adjudication, judicial enforcement, or guidance. The SEC is not alone in this respect. Many agencies can rely on an assortment of policymaking forms—often something like this standard set—to effectuate their policy judgments.

"The agency's choice among these policymaking forms matters because, as suggested above, each is distinct. The differences are significant and they run along three dimensions: the process the agency follows, the legal effect of the instrument, and the availability and nature of judicial examination of the agency's action." Who in the agency makes this choice? The Commissioners by majority vote? Senior staff? For a longer discussion of the benefits and costs of trying to use the APA's exceptions to rulemaking, see Connor Raso, Agency Avoidance of Rulemaking, 67 Admin. L. Rev. 65 (2015).

This chapter focuses on the first two dimensions Professor Magill mentions, while also considering presidential examination of rulemaking; Chapters VIII and IX take up the third issue. At the end of your course, you should be able to delineate contexts in which agencies likely will choose to engage in rulemaking and those in which they will often turn to some other mechanism.

(7) ***Rulemaking Requires Statutory Authority.*** The APA sets out the procedures agencies must generally follow in issuing regulations but does not itself authorize agencies to engage in rulemaking. Instead, such a grant of rulemaking authority must be found in a substantive statute the agency is implementing. (Those statutes can also impose procedural mandates on the agency that are more extensive than the APA's requirements.) Absent such a grant of authority, often found in the agency's "organic" statute, agency rules cannot claim the force of law (i.e., be "legislative rules"); although they may function as precedent within the agency, courts will treat them as at best persuasive rather than binding on the public. (We take up this difference in Section 3, below.)

Courts tend to be permissive in finding rulemaking authority in generally worded statutory provisions. Professors Thomas Merrill and Kathryn Watts have argued that this is a relatively recent development, part of an effort by scholars and judges in the 1960s and 1970s to encourage greater use of rulemaking. An example of this phenomenon is National Petroleum Refiners Ass'n v. FTC, 482 F.2d 672 (D.C. Cir. 1973), in which the D.C. Circuit read a statutory provision granting the FTC general authority "to make rules and regulations for the purposes of carrying out" the Federal

Trade Commission Act, 15 U.S.C. § 46(g), as empowering the agency to issue substantive rules that could be enforced through the adjudications the FTC was expressly authorized to undertake. According to Merrill and Watts, the effect was to adopt a new canon: "unless the legislative history reveals a clear intent to the contrary, courts should resolve any uncertainty about the scope of an agency's rulemaking authority in favor of finding a delegation of the full measure of power to the agency." Merrill and Watts fault this approach for ignoring Congress's prior practice of signaling when it meant agencies to have power to make rules with the force of law by including a provision imposing sanctions on those who violated agency rules. THOMAS W. MERRILL & KATHRYN TONGUE WATTS, AGENCY RULES WITH THE FORCE OF LAW: THE ORIGINAL CONVENTION, 116 Harv. L. Rev. 472, 557 (2002).

In 2012, the Patent and Trademark Office issued a regulation prescribing a standard of review for a third-party claim about a previously issued patent. Patent holders challenged the rule, arguing, in part, that the agency lacked statutory authority to issue it. In Cuozzo Speed Technologies, LLC v. Lee, 136 S.Ct. 2131, 2144 (2016), the Supreme Court applied Chevron deference to the PTO's interpretation of the Leahy-Smith America Invents Act and held the agency had rulemaking authority: "The upshot is, whether we look at statutory language alone, or that language in context of the statute's purpose, we find an express delegation of rulemaking authority, a 'gap' that rules might fill, and 'ambiguity' in respect to the boundaries of that gap."

SECTION 2.   THE REQUIREMENTS OF § 553 NOTICE-AND-COMMENT RULEMAKING

> a. *No More than § 553 Requires?*
> b. *Notice*
> c. *An Opportunity to Comment and a Concise General Statement of the Rule's Basis and Purpose*

This section outlines the procedural demands that § 553 imposes on rulemaking. It begins with an iconic decision rejecting judicial efforts to impose procedural requirements not constitutionally mandated or contained in the APA, other statutes, or agency regulations. But that leaves courts free to insist on adherence to the APA's rulemaking procedures. Thus, a core question becomes determining exactly what § 553 requires. As detailed in Subsections b and c, over the years the courts have added quite a significant gloss to § 553's spare statutory terms.

a.   No More than § 553 Requires?

> **VERMONT YANKEE NUCLEAR POWER CORP. v. NRDC**
>
> **Notes on the Problems of Finding and Reviewing Contested "General" Facts**

VERMONT YANKEE NUCLEAR POWER CORP. v. NATURAL RESOURCES DEFENSE COUNCIL, INC.

Supreme Court of the United States (1978).
435 U.S. 519.

[In December 1967, the Atomic Energy Commission (replaced by the Nuclear Regulatory Commission (NRC) by the time the case reached the Supreme Court) issued Vermont Yankee Nuclear Power Company a license to build a nuclear power plant in Vernon, Vermont. At that time, the licensing of nuclear power plants occurred in two stages. The first authorized construction of the plant; the second stage licensed the plant's operation once built. These mandatory adjudicatory hearings were often quite extensive and involved community voices and nongovernmental groups like the Natural Resources Defense Council (NRDC), often in adamant opposition. A wide range of factual issues might have been contested at these hearings—from matters specific to the particular plant for which a construction or operating license was sought to questions of a more general character that did not turn on facts about either the particular plant's location or the people who would be operating it or exposed to its effects.

Over the NRDC's objection, the environmental effects of reprocessing spent fuel and disposing of reprocessing wastes were excluded from consideration at the hearing on Vermont Yankee's operating license. This exclusion was affirmed by the Appeals Board, but then the Commission, expressly referencing the Vermont Yankee proceeding, began a rulemaking to "specifically deal with the question of consideration of environmental effects associated with the uranium fuel cycle in the individual cost-benefit analyses for light water cooled nuclear power reactors." This question concerned the environmental impact the nuclear fuel cycle could be expected to have *outside* a plant's grounds. For electricity to be generated at a nuclear plant, uranium had to be mined, processed to enhance its potential as fuel, embodied in fuel elements, and then transported to the plant. After the fuel's potential to generate power had been exhausted, the resulting highly radioactive waste somehow had to be transported, processed, and stored safely. Each of these operations could be expected to have environmental and safety impacts, but they would not be impacts specific to a particular plant. For instance, workers could be injured, or the public threatened, in Utah where the mines were or in the Ohio River valley where enrichment occurred. The expectable impacts, moreover, could be expressed in relationship to units of power to be generated or, perhaps, to numbers of fuel rods made or used. Once these impacts had been determined, the impact attributable to a particular plant could be straightforwardly calculated on the basis of its generating capacity.

The NPRM suggested two alternatives: (1) no quantitative evaluation of the environmental hazards because an "Environmental Survey of the Nuclear Fuel Cycle" prepared by Commission staff had concluded that the hazards were slight, or (2) a specified set of numerical values for environmental impacts, which would then be incorporated into a table to determine the overall cost-benefit balance for each particular operating license. These proposed values were also derived from the staff Environmental Survey.

The statute granted the Commission rulemaking authority, and no one questioned its authority to deal with fuel cycle issues by informal rulemaking as opposed to adjudication. For the Commission, using rulemaking to determine such environmental impacts promised to take these factual questions out of individual licensing proceedings, where they would be repetitive and could perhaps be used simply for delay. The agency might also have believed that a one-time process for determining these matters, open to any member of the public interested to participate, could be advantageous to accurate determination of the matters in issue. In addition, the agency's line staff, using an institutional decision process, would be better able than individual judicial officers lacking focused expertise to come to appropriate judgments. Still, for parties opposing the licensing of specific nuclear reactors, this route would substitute the procedural rights of informal rulemaking for the procedural rights of formal adjudication. In their view, the procedures of rulemaking were insufficiently rigorous and open to public participation to be trustworthy in determining factual questions of large public moment. To what extent could the courts be persuaded to require processes for resolving such portentous factual issues in rulemaking that would be like those otherwise available in agency adjudication?

When the Commission issued a final rule and applied it to reaffirm the grant of Vermont Yankee's operating license, the NRDC and other environmental groups sought judicial review in the D.C. Circuit. They challenged (1) the rule as procedurally defective and substantively arbitrary, and (2) the licensing decision as unsustainable given the flawed rule. Procedurally, they wanted to engage in discovery and cross-examine agency witnesses. Chief Judge David Bazelon wrote the court's opinion in this and a companion case involving licensing of two reactors by Consumers Power Company. Both opinions remanded the cases to the Commission for further proceedings, the precise nature of which was somewhat disputed. Vermont Yankee (whose license would be lost if the D.C. Circuit's decision prevailed) took the initiative in petitioning for certiorari. The Supreme Court's practice of retitling cases according to how the parties are aligned in the petition for review accounts for the fact (not uncommon in regulatory cases) that no agency is named in the caption of what was in fact review of the Commission's work.]

■ JUSTICE REHNQUIST delivered the opinion of the Court.

In 1946, Congress enacted the Administrative Procedure Act, which as we have noted elsewhere was not only "a new, basic and comprehensive regulation of procedures in many agencies," Wong Yang Sung v. McGrath, 339 U.S. 33 (1950), but was also a legislative enactment which settled "long-continued and hard-fought contentions, and enacts a formula upon which opposing social and political forces have come to rest." Id., at 40. Section 4 of the Act, 5 U.S.C. § 553 (1976 ed.), dealing with rulemaking, requires in subsection (b) that "notice of proposed rulemaking shall be published in the Federal Register . . . ," describes the contents of that notice, and goes on to require in subsection (c) that after the notice the agency "shall give interested persons an opportunity to participate in the rule making through submission of written data, views, or arguments with or without opportunity for oral presentation. After consideration of the relevant matter presented, the agency shall incorporate in the rules adopted a concise general statement of their basis and purpose." Interpreting this provision of the Act in United States v. Allegheny-Ludlum Steel Corp., 406 U.S. 742 (1972), and United States v. Florida East Coast Ry. Co., 410 U.S. 224 (1973) [p. 285], we held that generally speaking this section of the Act established the maximum procedural requirements which Congress was willing to have the courts impose upon agencies in conducting rulemaking procedures. Agencies are free to grant additional procedural rights in the exercise of their discretion, but reviewing courts are generally not free to impose them if the agencies have not chosen to grant them. This is not to say necessarily that there are no circumstances which would ever justify a court in overturning agency action because of a failure to employ procedures beyond those required by the statute. But such circumstances, if they exist, are extremely rare.

Even apart from the Administrative Procedure Act this Court has for more than four decades emphasized that the formulation of procedures was basically to be left within the discretion of the agencies to which Congress had confided the responsibility for substantive judgments. In FCC v. Schreiber, 381 U.S. 279, 290 (1965), the Court explicated this principle, describing it as "an outgrowth of the congressional determination that administrative agencies and administrators will be familiar with the industries which they regulate and will be in a better position than federal courts or Congress itself to design procedural rules adapted to the peculiarities of the industry and the tasks of the agency involved." . . .

I

. . . Much of the controversy in this case revolves around the procedures used in the rulemaking hearing which commenced in

New Procedures

February 1973. In a supplemental notice of hearing the Commission indicated that while discovery or cross-examination would not be utilized, the Environmental Survey would be available to the public before the hearing along with the extensive background documents cited therein. All participants would be given a reasonable opportunity to present their position and could be represented by counsel if they so desired. Written and, time permitting, oral statements would be received and incorporated into the record. All persons giving oral statements would be subject to questioning by the Commission. At the conclusion of the hearing, a transcript would be made available to the public and the record would remain open for 30 days to allow the filing of supplemental written statements. More than 40 individuals and organizations representing a wide variety of interests submitted written comments. . . . The hearing was held on February 1 and 2, with participation by a number of groups, including the Commission's staff, the United States Environmental Protection Agency, a manufacturer of reactor equipment, a trade association from the nuclear industry, a group of electric utility companies, and a group called Consolidated National Intervenors which represented 79 groups and individuals including respondent NRDC.

[At the hearing Dr. Frank Pittman, director of the Commission's waste management and transportation division, submitted a twenty-page statement describing techniques for storing and disposing of nuclear wastes, a subject not addressed by the Environmental Survey. In the statement, Dr. Pittman outlined the Commission's plan to rely on reprocessing and long-term storage of high-level wastes at a permanent facility it would construct but provided few specifics on the Commission's plans. However, he characterized concerns about the environmental risks associated with management of nuclear wastes as a "bugaboo" and the possibility of a significant release of radioactivity at such a facility as "incredible." His statement was subsequently characterized by the D.C. Circuit as little more than "conclusory reassurances." The Licensing Board asked Dr. Pittman some questions, and in their subsequent testimony representatives of environmental groups noted problems the Commission had encountered with waste disposal.]

After the hearing, the Commission's staff filed a supplemental document for the purpose of clarifying and revising the Environmental Survey. Then the Licensing Board forwarded its report to the Commission without rendering any decision. The Licensing Board identified as the principal procedural question the propriety of declining to use full formal adjudicatory procedures. The major substantive issue was the technical adequacy of the Environmental Survey.

In April 1974, the Commission issued a rule which adopted the second of the two proposed alternatives described above. The

Commission also approved the procedures used at the hearing,[7] and indicated that the record, including the Environmental Survey, provided an "adequate data base for the regulation adopted." Finally, the Commission ruled that to the extent the rule differed from the Appeal Board decisions in Vermont Yankee "those decisions have no further precedential significance," but that [it was unnecessary to reconsider the decisions] since "the environmental effects of the uranium fuel cycle have been shown to be relatively insignificant . . . ."

Respondents appealed from both the Commission's adoption of the rule and its decision to grant Vermont Yankee's license to the Court of Appeals for the District of Columbia Circuit. With respect to the challenge of Vermont Yankee's license, the court first ruled that in the absence of effective rulemaking proceedings,[13] the Commission must deal with the environmental impact of fuel reprocessing and disposal in individual licensing proceedings. The court then examined the rulemaking proceedings and, despite the fact that it appeared that the agency employed all the procedures required by 5 U.S.C. § 553 and more, the court determined the proceedings to be inadequate and overturned the rule. Accordingly, the Commission's determination with respect to Vermont Yankee's license was also remanded for further proceedings.[14]

. . .

II

[The Court first addressed] whether the Commission may consider the environmental impact of the fuel processes when licensing nuclear reactors. In addition to the weight which normally attaches to the

---

[7]   The Commission stated:

"In our view, the procedures adopted provide a more than adequate basis for formulation of the rule we adopted. All parties were fully heard. Nothing offered was excluded. The record does not indicate that any evidentiary material would have been received under different procedures. Nor did the proponent of the strict 'adjudicatory' approach make an offer of proof—or even remotely suggest—what substantive matters it would develop under different procedures. In addition, we note that 11 documents including the Survey were available to the parties several weeks before the hearing, and the Regulatory staff, though not requested to do so, made available various drafts and handwritten notes. Under all of the circumstances, we conclude that adjudicatory type procedures were not warranted here."

[13]   In the Court of Appeals no one questioned the Commission's authority to deal with fuel cycle issues by informal rulemaking as opposed to adjudication. Neither does anyone seriously question before this Court the Commission's authority in this respect.

[14]   After the decision of the Court of Appeals the Commission promulgated a new interim rule pending issuance of a final rule. 42 Fed. Reg. 13803 (1977). . . . As we read the opinion of the Court of Appeals, its view that reviewing courts may in the absence of special circumstances justifying such a course of action impose additional procedural requirements on agency action raises questions of such significance in this area of the law as to warrant our granting certiorari and deciding the case. Since the vast majority of challenges to administrative agency action are brought to the Court of Appeals for the District of Columbia Circuit, the decision of that court in this case will serve as precedent for many more proceedings for judicial review of agency actions than would the decision of another Court of Appeals. Finally, this decision will continue to play a major role in the instant litigation regardless of the Commission's decision to press ahead with further rulemaking proceedings. . . .

agency's determination of such a question, other reasons support the Commission's conclusion.

Vermont Yankee will produce annually well over 100 pounds of radioactive wastes, some of which will be highly toxic. The Commission itself . . . clearly recognizes that these wastes "pose the most severe potential health hazard. . . ." Many of these substances must be isolated for anywhere from 600 to hundreds of thousands of years. It is hard to argue that these wastes do not constitute "adverse environmental effects which cannot be avoided should the proposal be implemented," or that by operating nuclear power plants we are not making "irreversible and irretrievable commitments of resources." . . . For these reasons we hold that the Commission acted well within its statutory authority when it considered the back end of the fuel cycle in individual licensing proceedings.

We next turn to the invalidation of the fuel cycle rule. But before determining whether the Court of Appeals reached a permissible result, we must determine exactly what result it did reach, and in this case that is no mean feat. . . .

After a thorough examination of the opinion itself, we conclude that while the matter is not entirely free from doubt, the majority of the Court of Appeals struck down the rule because of the perceived inadequacies of the procedures employed in the rulemaking proceedings. The court first determined the intervenors' primary argument to be "that the decision to preclude 'discovery or cross-examination' denied them a meaningful opportunity to participate in the proceedings as guaranteed by due process." The court then went on to frame the issue for decision thus:

> "Thus, we are called upon to decide whether the procedures provided by the agency were sufficient to ventilate the issues."

. . . [T]here is little doubt in our minds that the ineluctable mandate of the court's decision is that the procedures afforded during the hearings were inadequate. This conclusion is particularly buttressed by the fact that after the court examined the record, particularly the testimony of Dr. Pittman, and declared it insufficient, the court proceeded to discuss at some length the necessity for further procedural devices or a more "sensitive" application of those devices employed during the proceedings. The exploration of the record and the statement regarding its insufficiency might initially lead one to conclude that the court was only examining the sufficiency of the evidence, but the remaining portions of the opinion dispel any doubt that this was certainly not the sole or even the principal basis of the decision. Accordingly, we feel compelled to address the opinion on its own terms, and we conclude that it was wrong.

In prior opinions we have intimated that even in a rulemaking proceeding when an agency is making a " 'quasi-judicial' " determination by which a very small number of persons are " 'exceptionally affected, in each case upon individual grounds,' " in some circumstances additional procedures may be required in order to afford the aggrieved individuals due process.[16] United States v. Florida East Coast Ry. Co., 410 U.S., at 242, 245, quoting from Bi-Metallic Investment Co. v. State Board of Equalization, 239 U.S. 441, 446 (1915) [p. 222]. It might also be true, although we do not think the issue is presented in this case and accordingly do not decide it, that a totally unjustified departure from well-settled agency procedures of long standing might require judicial correction.

But this much is absolutely clear. Absent constitutional constraints or extremely compelling circumstances the "administrative agencies 'should be free to fashion their own rules of procedure and to pursue methods of inquiry capable of permitting them to discharge their multitudinous duties.'" FCC v. Schreiber, 381 U.S., at 290, quoting from FCC v. Pottsville Broadcasting Co., 309 U.S., at 143. . . .

Respondent NRDC argues that § 4 of the Administrative Procedure Act, 5 U.S.C. § 553, merely establishes lower procedural bounds and that a court may routinely require more than the minimum when an agency's proposed rule addresses complex or technical factual issues or "Issues of Great Public Import." We have, however, previously shown that our decisions reject this view. We also think the legislative history, even the part which it cites, does not bear out its contention. The Senate Report explains what eventually became § 4 thus:

> This subsection states . . . the minimum requirements of public rule making procedure short of statutory hearing. Under it agencies might in addition confer with industry advisory committees, consult organizations, hold informal "hearings," and the like. Considerations of practicality, necessity, and public interest . . . will naturally govern the agency's determination of the extent to which public proceedings should go. Matters of great import, or those where the public submission of facts will be either useful to the agency or a protection to the public, should naturally be accorded more elaborate public procedures. S. Rep. No. 752, 79th Cong., 1st Sess., 14–15 (1945).

The House Report is in complete accord. . . . And the Attorney General's Manual on the Administrative Procedure Act 31, 35 (1947), a contemporaneous interpretation previously given some deference by this Court because of the role played by the Department of Justice in drafting the legislation, further confirms that view. In short, all of this leaves little doubt that Congress intended that the discretion of the *agencies* and not that of the courts be exercised in determining when extra procedural devices should be employed.

---

16 Respondent NRDC does not now argue that additional procedural devices were required under the Constitution. Since this was clearly a rulemaking proceeding in its purest form, we see nothing to support such a view.

There are compelling reasons for construing § 4 in this manner. In the first place, if courts continually review agency proceedings to determine whether the agency employed procedures which were, in the court's opinion, perfectly tailored to reach what the court perceives to be the "best" or "correct" result, judicial review would be totally unpredictable. And the agencies, operating under this vague injunction to employ the "best" procedures and facing the threat of reversal if they did not, would undoubtedly adopt full adjudicatory procedures in every instance. Not only would this totally disrupt the statutory scheme, through which Congress enacted "a formula upon which opposing social and political forces have come to rest," Wong Yang Sung v. McGrath, 339 U.S., at 40, but all the inherent advantages of informal rulemaking would be totally lost.

Secondly, it is obvious that the court in these cases reviewed the agency's choice of procedures on the basis of the record actually produced at the hearing, and not on the basis of the information available to the agency when it made the decision to structure the proceedings in a certain way. This sort of Monday morning quarterbacking not only encourages but almost compels the agency to conduct all rulemaking proceedings with the full panoply of procedural devices normally associated only with adjudicatory hearings.

Finally, and perhaps most importantly, this sort of review fundamentally misconceives the nature of the standard for judicial review of an agency rule. The court below uncritically assumed that additional procedures will automatically result in a more adequate record because it will give interested parties more of an opportunity to participate in and contribute to the proceedings. But informal rulemaking need not be based solely on the transcript of a hearing held before an agency. Indeed, the agency need not even hold a formal hearing. See 5 U.S.C. § 553(c). Thus, the adequacy of the "record" in this type of proceeding is not correlated directly to the type of procedural devices employed, but rather turns on whether the agency has followed the statutory mandate of the Administrative Procedure Act or other relevant statutes. If the agency is compelled to support the rule which it ultimately adopts with the type of record produced only after a full adjudicatory hearing, it simply will have no choice but to conduct a full adjudicatory hearing prior to promulgating every rule. In sum, this sort of unwarranted judicial examination of perceived procedural shortcomings of a rulemaking proceeding can do nothing but seriously interfere with that process prescribed by Congress. . . .

In short, nothing in the APA, . . . the circumstances of this case, the nature of the issues being considered, past agency practice, or the statutory mandate under which the Commission operates permitted the court to review and overturn the rulemaking proceeding on the basis of the procedural devices employed (or not employed) by the Commission so long as the Commission employed at least the statutory *minima,* a matter about which there is no doubt in this case.

There remains, of course, the question of whether the challenged rule finds sufficient justification in the administrative proceedings that it should be upheld by the reviewing court. Judge Tamm, concurring in the result reached by the majority of the Court of Appeals, thought that it did not. There are also intimations in the majority opinion which suggest that the judges who joined it likewise may have thought the administrative proceedings an insufficient basis upon which to predicate the rule in question. We accordingly remand so that the Court of Appeals may review the rule as the Administrative Procedure Act provides. We have made it abundantly clear before that when there is a contemporaneous explanation of the agency decision, the validity of that action must "stand or fall on the propriety of that finding, judged, of course, by the appropriate standard of review. If that finding is not sustainable on the administrative record made, then the Comptroller's decision must be vacated and the matter remanded to him for further consideration." Camp v. Pitts, 411 U.S. 138, 143 (1973). See also SEC v. Chenery Corp., 318 U.S. 80 (1943). The court should engage in this kind of review and not stray beyond the judicial province to explore the procedural format or to impose upon the agency its own notion of which procedures are "best" or most likely to further some vague, undefined public good.

III

[The Court's analysis of the companion case Consumers Power Co. is omitted, except for the following peroration:] All this leads us to make one further observation of some relevance to this case. To say that the Court of Appeals' final reason for remanding is insubstantial at best is a gross understatement. Consumers Power first applied in 1969 for a construction permit—not even an operating license, just a construction permit. The proposed plant underwent an incredibly extensive review. The reports filed and reviewed literally fill books. The proceedings took years, and the actual hearings themselves over two weeks. To then nullify that effort seven years later because one report refers to other problems, which problems admittedly have been discussed at length in other reports available to the public, borders on the Kafkaesque. Nuclear energy may some day be a cheap, safe source of power or it may not. But Congress has made a choice to at least try nuclear energy, establishing a reasonable review process in which courts are to play only a limited role. The fundamental policy questions appropriately resolved in Congress and in the state legislatures are *not* subject to reexamination in the federal courts under the guise of judicial review of agency action. Time may prove wrong the decision to develop nuclear energy, but it is Congress or the States within their appropriate agencies which must eventually make that judgment. In the meantime courts should perform their appointed function. . . . And a single alleged oversight on a peripheral issue, urged by parties who never fully cooperated or indeed raised the issue below, must not be made the basis for overturning a decision properly made after an otherwise exhaustive proceeding.

Reversed and remanded.[6]

■ JUSTICE BLACKMUN and JUSTICE POWELL took no part in the consideration or decision of these cases.

NOTES

(1) ***The Decision That Nearly Wasn't.*** Recent examination of the Supreme Court files of Justice Thurgood Marshall reveals that Justice Brennan came one vote short of getting the Vermont Yankee case dismissed without decision because the NRC had indicated it would go forward with a new rulemaking on the fuel cycle rule regardless of the Court's decision. See GILLIAN E. METZGER, THE STORY OF VERMONT YANKEE: A CAUTIONARY TALE OF JUDICIAL REVIEW AND NUCLEAR WASTE, in Administrative Law Stories 125, 158–60 (Peter L. Strauss, ed. 2006). The saga of Vermont Yankee continued until recently. In February 2010, the Vermont Senate voted to close the reactor, citing leaks and other problems with the plant. See Matthew L. Wald, State Senate in Vermont Votes to Close Nuclear Plant, N.Y. Times, Feb. 25, 2010, at A14. According to the NRC, "[t]he reactor was permanently shut down on December 29, 2014, and the fuel was removed from the reactor on January 12, 2015."

(2) ***"A [F]ormula upon Which [O]pposing [S]ocial and [P]olitical [F]orces [H]ave [C]ome to [R]est."*** In Vermont Yankee, the Court insisted on reading the APA in a static fashion, reflecting the political compromises reached in 1946 when the statute was enacted. Yet no one in 1946 was imagining the extent of environmental, health, and safety regulation that would be called for a quarter-century later. Was the Court correct to view the APA's rulemaking provisions as unaffected by the dramatic expansion in the importance of rulemaking over time? For discussion of different approaches to reading the APA, see Ch. III (Notes on Interpreting the APA, p. 242) (reading it as enacted, as changing as historical circumstances warrant, and as text). The materials in the following pages discuss the creation of what Professor Richard Stewart called a "paper hearing," which many believe the Court to have affirmed by its decision in Motor Vehicles Manufacturers Ass'n v. State Farm, 463 U.S. 29 (1983) (p. 1069). In reading them, ask yourself whether the holding of Vermont Yankee might be described in a more limited way—rejecting the judicialization of rulemaking but not procedural requirements unimagined in 1946 (such as an obligation to share data and reports with commenters) that reflected the increasing importance of rulemaking without converting it to the judicial model.

(3) ***Within the Confines of Vermont Yankee.*** The Court allows judicially imposed constraints outside of agency statutory and regulatory mandates if required by the Constitution. Could the challengers to the NRC's rulemaking

---

[6]   [Ed.] For further events in this effort to litigate the life cycle of nuclear wastes, see Baltimore Gas & Electric Co. v. Natural Resources Defense Council, Inc., 462 U.S. 87 (1983).

have phrased their procedural arguments in constitutional terms? Would they have been successful? In addition, the Court assumes the agency will produce a record for judicial review. Does § 553 require the agency to produce a record? Does the Constitution? How is the record requirement not a violation of the holding in the case?

(4) ***Legislatively Required Hybrid Rulemaking.*** Vermont Yankee is a screed against judicial improvisation with legislatively set procedures. Of course, Congress can add to § 553's procedural requirements, and it has often done so in agency-specific legislation. In the 1970s, both before and after Florida East Coast Railway, p. 285, Congress passed several important regulatory statutes that built on the notice-and-comment process without moving fully to the trial-type process of formal rulemaking. These statutes created what are termed "hybrid" rulemaking processes.[7] The FTC Improvement Act was among the most detailed of these statutes. Harry & Bryant Co. v. FTC, 726 F.2d 993, 996 (4th Cir. 1984), describes an FTC rulemaking on funeral industry practices as follows: "In response to the FTC's notice [in 1972], more than 9000 documents, comprising in excess of 20,000 pages, were submitted by interested parties, including consumers and industry representatives. During the fifty-two days of hearings [in 1976] 315 witnesses testified. The witnesses also presented exhibits and underwent cross-examination by participating parties or the FTC's Presiding Officer. The hearings generated 14,719 pages of transcripts and approximately 4,000 additional pages of exhibits. Thereafter, another comment period was held for rebuttal of any materials previously admitted into evidence. Forty-seven rebuttal submissions were received."

Then Professor ANTONIN SCALIA, in VERMONT YANKEE: THE APA, THE D.C. CIRCUIT, AND THE SUPREME COURT, 1978 Sup. Ct. Rev. 345, 404–08, had this to say about the legislative fashioning of hybrid procedures: "[O]ne of the functions of procedure is to limit power—not just the power to be unfair, but the power to act in a political mode, or the power to act at all. Such limitation is sometimes an incidental result of pursuing other functions, such as efficiency and fairness; but it may be an end in itself. . . .

"Of course, once it is accepted that procedures are to be used as a means of expanding or restricting the power to act, the idea of any genuinely stable APA based on fairness and efficiency alone becomes visionary. It also becomes unrealistic to expect the framework of any such superstatute to contain only a few options of procedure among which later legislation must choose—such as the stark choice between formal and informal rulemaking offered under the current APA. . . . The degrees of activism and of political decision making which the Congress expects from (or, more precisely, which the legislative struggle finally induces its divergent factions to accord to) the FTC, the ICC, the INS, the FDA, and the CPSC may vary enormously—and so will the procedures which reflect those expectations. . . . While 'hybrid rulemaking' may no longer be devised by the courts under the APA, it will

---

[7]   See, e.g., the Occupational Safety and Health Act of 1970, 29 U.S.C. § 651; the Consumer Product Safety Act of 1972, 15 U.S.C. § 2051; the Federal Trade Commission Improvement Act of 1975, 15 U.S.C. § 57a; the Toxic Substances Control Act of 1976, 15 U.S.C. § 2601; and the Clear Air Act Amendments of 1977, 42 U.S.C. § 7401.

continue to flourish in a multiplicity of special statutes that modify the APA's dispositions, at least so long as the APA itself provides so few variants (and those based on considerations of fairness and efficiency alone) from which to select. And there is a theoretical reason why this ought to be so. Congress can, indeed, refrain from making use of the connection between procedure and power, but it cannot make that connection itself disappear. Thus, to the extent that the choice of procedures is left to the agencies themselves, to that same extent the agencies are left to determine a substantial aspect of their own power. . . .

"It seems to me, therefore, that if the continuing fragmentation of mandated administrative procedure is to be abated, what is called for is a more modest expectation of what the APA can and should achieve, and a design that will accord with the realities. . . . I would settle for an APA that contains not merely three but ten or fifteen basic procedural formats—an inventory large enough to provide the basis for a whole spectrum of legislative compromises without the necessity for shopping elsewhere."

(5) **Assessing Vermont Yankee.** Vermont Yankee remains a central decision interpreting the rulemaking provisions of the APA and was recognized as such at the time. Here are two contrasting assessments out of a large literature:

(a) CLARK BYSE, VERMONT YANKEE AND THE EVOLUTION OF ADMINISTRATIVE PROCEDURE: A SOMEWHAT DIFFERENT VIEW, 91 Harv. L. Rev. 1823, 1828–29 (1978): "If the court is convinced that an adequate record for review can best be achieved by utilization of an additional procedural device, why should it not save everyone's time and energy by ordering the agency to utilize that device?

"There are at least three answers to such an argument. First, although the reviewing court may have convinced itself that an additional procedural device is indispensable, its conviction may well be erroneous. A particular procedural device is a means to an end, not the end itself. If the court has explained in what ways the record is inadequate, very likely there will be various means by which it can be made adequate. By prescribing a particular procedure the court prevents the agency, which has the firstline responsibility and experience in administering the statute, from utilizing that experience to provide the needed record in the most cost-effective fashion.

"Second, even if the judicially prescribed procedural device might, in some abstract sense, be thought to be the indispensable *modus operandi,* is it necessary or appropriate for the court to *order* the agency [to adopt it]? I think not. If, as I believe and courts occasionally proclaim, courts and agencies constitute a 'partnership' in furtherance of the public interest and are 'collaborative instrumentalities of justice,' the judicial partner should be mindful of the sensitivities and responsibilities of the administrative partner; to the extent possible, the relationship should be one of collaboration, not command. This is not simply a matter of etiquette or abstract *noblesse oblige.* Rather it relates to an important aspect of our legal system that is sometimes overlooked, namely, that although the judiciary has a duty to uphold the law, it also has a duty to recognize and defer to the responsibilities of other components of government, including the administrative component. . . .

"Third, and most important, in enacting APA section 553 in 1946, Congress established a new general model of rulemaking procedure. There is no suggestion in the legislative history of the section that it was declaratory of the common law or that it was a delegation of power to the courts to develop desirable procedural models. On the contrary, the legislative history indicates that the question whether additional procedural devices are to be employed is an *agency* question, not a *judicial* question: '[c]onsiderations of practicality, necessity, and public interest . . . will naturally govern the *agency's* determination of the extent to which public proceedings should go.' "

(b) CHRISTOPHER F. EDLEY, JR., ADMINISTRATIVE LAW: RETHINKING JUDICIAL CONTROL OF BUREAUCRACY 228 (1990): "Because substance and procedure can be transmuted so readily, the effect of Vermont Yankee is simply to make a court that is inclined toward interventionism express its concerns and its remand instructions in quasi-procedural language that has a substantive resonance: explore more alternatives, give a more detailed explanation, disclose considerations and staff information, demonstrate adequate consideration of statutory factors, and so on. The risk is that the reviewing court may use modes of rhetoric and intervention that miscommunicate the course and nature of its dissatisfaction with the administrative action—all because in any particular circumstance, the court is concerned that its legitimate purview is somehow delimited by the substance-procedure categorization. This approach is misleading and self-defeating, in view of both the boundary problem in these two categories and the related and more fundamental point that proper evaluation of agency action requires an eye to both procedure and substance."

(6) ***Rulemaking's Effect on Statutory Hearing Rights.*** Although not figuring in the Supreme Court's discussion, an interesting feature of the Vermont Yankee litigation is the interaction of rulemaking and adjudication. The agency had to engage in individual adjudications over each potential reactor license. In these proceedings, it repeatedly confronted the issue of environmental effects of nuclear fuel. In the middle of Vermont Yankee's licensing proceedings, the agency conducted a rulemaking on how (if at all) certain of these environmental effects should be taken into account. Assuming a court did not strike down the rule, the agency could then use it in all subsequent licensing proceedings without challenge (except to how it was applied to particular facts in the adjudication).

How far can an agency use rules in this fashion to limit the scope of a statutorily required hearing? The Court faced this question in HECKLER v. CAMPBELL, 461 U.S. 458 (1983), involving medical-vocational guidelines promulgated using § 553 procedures by the Secretary of Health and Human Services to determine eligibility for Social Security disability benefits. Eligibility for these benefits turns not only on the personal characteristics of the applicant, but also on the absence of jobs in the national economy that a person of the applicant's age and abilities could hold—regardless of whether those jobs are conveniently located to the applicant or unfilled. The guidelines, promulgated using notice-and-comment procedures, took the form of a matrix of the factors the statute made relevant to work availability determinations (physical ability, age, education, and work experience). The ALJ in a particular dispute over eligibility for benefits would plug the claimant's factors into the matrix to determine whether jobs for someone with the claimant's profile exist in significant numbers in the national economy. In the past, vocational experts had testified at hearings on a particular applicant's eligibility for benefits on whether suitable available jobs existed in the national economy. Thus, the guidelines made much testimony unnecessary. The guidelines were challenged as violating an applicant's statutory rights to an individualized determination based on evidence adduced at a hearing.

In an opinion written by JUSTICE POWELL, the Court upheld the guidelines: "It is true that the statutory scheme contemplates that disability hearings will be individualized determinations based on evidence adduced at a hearing. But this does not bar the Secretary from relying on rulemaking to resolve certain classes of issues. The Court has recognized that even where an agency's enabling statute expressly requires it to hold a hearing, the agency may rely on its rulemaking authority to determine issues that do not require case-by-case consideration. See FPC v. Texaco, Inc., 377 U.S. 33, 41–44 (1964); United States v. Storer Broadcasting Co., 351 U.S. 192, 205 (1956). A contrary holding would require the agency continually to relitigate issues that may be established fairly and efficiently in a single rulemaking proceeding. . . . As the Secretary has argued, the use of published guidelines brings with it a uniformity that previously had been perceived as lacking. To require the Secretary to relitigate the existence of jobs in the national economy at each hearing would hinder needlessly an already overburdened agency."

In upholding the guidelines, the Court emphasized that the agency was still required to "assess each claimant's individual abilities . . . on the basis of evidence adduced at a hearing. We note that the regulations afford claimant ample opportunities to present evidence relating to their own abilities and to offer evidence that the guidelines do not apply to them." Should that make a difference? Is an agency's resort to rulemaking harder to square with statutory hearing rights if it operates to preclude the need for the agency to hold a hearing at all? Or should the same logic—that rulemaking can be used to pretermit issues—also apply when the effect of the rulemaking is to remove any need for a hearing at all? If the opportunity to seek a waiver of the rule is not constitutionally required, FCC v. WNCN Listeners Guild, 450 U.S. 582 (1981), should courts nonetheless give careful attention to refusals to waive? See BellSouth Corp v. FCC, 162 F.3d 1215 (D.C. Cir. 1999); Harold Krent, Reviewing Agency Action for Inconsistency with Prior Rules and Regulations, 72 Chi-Kent L. Rev. 1187 (1997).

(7) **_Enforceability of Agency Procedural Regulations._** One additional point worth emphasizing is Vermont Yankee's acknowledgment that agency procedural regulations can be judicially enforceable, just like other agency regulations. This is often termed the Accardi principle (discussed on p. 1042),

after its appearance in United States ex rel. Accardi v. Shaughnessy, 347 U.S. 260 (1964). The principle applies to agency rules intended to be binding but that can include procedural rules adopted under the exception in § 553(b)(A). See, e.g., Morton v. Ruiz, 415 U.S. 199, 235 (1974) (p. 592); Vietnam Veterans of Am. v. Sec'y of the Navy, 843 F.2d 528, 536–38 (D.C. Cir. 1988).

NOTES ON THE PROBLEMS OF FINDING AND REVIEWING CONTESTED "GENERAL" FACTS

(1) *Regulations, Fact-finding, and Procedures Familiar to Judges.* One way to understand the Supreme Court's opinion in Vermont Yankee might be that the Court feared the D.C. Circuit had imported adjudicatory values into rulemaking. Legislatures do not typically proceed by hearing live testimony about factual issues. When they hold hearings, the predominant discussion is often about policy issues. Committee members or staff may ask questions, even belligerently at times; yet interested members of the public who are present in the hearing room (perhaps waiting to deliver their own views) never have the chance to ask questions themselves. At best, they can send a note to a member or staffer suggesting them. Should a statute be enacted, any arguable failures of inquiry are of no concern to the courts.

Perhaps, however, the D.C. Circuit opinion came not from a bias toward judicialized procedures but rather from concern about the particular problems of finding "general" facts. The Vermont Yankee regulation stated a series of values for health and other consequences to be expected from the fuel cycle processes occurring outside nuclear power plants. These are not questions concerning individuals "who were exceptionally affected, in each case upon individual grounds," as the Vermont Yankee Court remarks in invoking the Bi-Metallic decision, p. 222. At the same time however, *neither* are they the kinds of questions that we would likely think well resolved by legislative processes. Such general facts might be thought akin to what are sometimes called legislative facts (and contrasted with what are sometimes called adjudicatory facts), facts that are used to create general policy and are not limited to the immediate parties to a proceeding. Yet, general facts can involve fairly specific questions on which substantial scientific and technological uncertainty exists, and legislative decision of such questions by political vote would be inappropriate.

(2) *The D.C. Circuit Debate.* We take up judicial review of agency fact-finding in Chapter VIII but want to flag its connections to agency rulemaking procedures here. At the time of Vermont Yankee, the D.C. Circuit was deeply enmeshed in internal debate over how courts ought to respond to challenges to regulations that turned on technical and scientific questions that judges lacked the expertise to resolve—or perhaps even understand. This debate was captured best in an en banc decision, ETHYL CORP. V. EPA, 541 F.2d 1 (D.C. Cir. 1976), reviewing an EPA regulation requiring annual reductions in the lead content of leaded gasoline. (This regulation is now often presented as a paradigm of a regulation whose costs are strongly justified by its benefits.) In adopting the regulation, EPA had been required to decide a number of highly controverted factual propositions, make projections based

on imperfect data, and in other ways reach technical or scientific judgments that the makers of lead additives strongly challenged. Ethyl Corp. contains separate opinions by the two main participants in the D.C. Circuit debate, Chief Judge David Bazelon and Judge Harold Leventhal. Chief Judge Bazelon would shortly thereafter be the author of the D.C. Circuit's decision in Vermont Yankee, and Judge Leventhal was the author of several opinions urging considerably expanded notice, comment opportunity, and explanation—a concept that came to be called a "paper hearing," p. 329.

JUDGE BAZELON: "I agree with the court's construction of the statute that the Administrator is called upon to make 'essentially legislative policy judgments' in assessing risks to public health. But I cannot agree that this automatically relieves the Administrator's decision from the 'procedural . . . rigor proper for questions of fact.' Quite the contrary, this case strengthens my view that '. . . in cases of great technological complexity, the best way for courts to guard against unreasonable or erroneous administrative decisions is not for the judges themselves to scrutinize the technical merits of each decision. Rather, it is to establish a decision-making process that assures a reasoned decision that can be held up to the scrutiny of the scientific community and the public.' This record provides vivid demonstration of the dangers implicit in the contrary view, ably espoused by Judge Leventhal, which would have judges 'steeping' themselves 'in technical matters to determine whether the agency "has exercised a reasoned discretion." ' It is one thing for judges to scrutinize FCC judgments concerning diversification of media ownership to determine if they are rational. But I doubt judges contribute much to improving the quality of the difficult decisions which must be made in highly technical areas when they take it upon themselves to decide, as did the panel in this case, that 'in assessing the scientific and medical data the Administrator made clear errors of judgment.' The process [of] making a de novo evaluation of the scientific evidence inevitably invites judges of opposing views to make plausible-sounding, but simplistic, judgments of the relative weight to be afforded various pieces of technical data. . . .

"Because substantive review of mathematical and scientific evidence by technically illiterate judges is dangerously unreliable, I continue to believe we will do more to improve administrative decision-making by concentrating our efforts on strengthening administrative procedures: 'When administrators provide a framework for principled decision-making, the result will be to diminish the importance of judicial review by enhancing the integrity of the administrative process, and to improve the quality of judicial review in those cases where judicial review is sought.' Environmental Defense Fund, Inc. v. Ruckelshaus, 439 F.2d 584, 598 (D.C. Cir. 1971) (Bazelon, C.J.). It does not follow that courts may never properly find that an administrative decision in a scientific area is irrational. But I do believe that in highly technical areas, where our understanding of the import of the evidence is attenuated, our readiness to review evidentiary support for decisions must be correspondingly restrained."

JUDGE LEVENTHAL: "Taking [Chief Judge Bazelon's] opinion in its fair implication, as a signal to judges to abstain from any substantive review, it is my view that while giving up is the easier course, it is not legitimately open to us at present. In the case of legislative enactments, the sole responsibility of the courts is constitutional due process review. In the case of agency decision-making the courts have an additional responsibility set by Congress. Congress has been willing to delegate its legislative powers broadly—and courts have upheld such delegation—because there is court review to assure that the agency exercises the delegated power within statutory limits, and that it fleshes out objectives within those limits by an administration that is not irrational or discriminatory. . . .

"Our present system of review assumes judges will acquire whatever technical knowledge is necessary as background for decision of the legal questions. . . . The aim of the judges is not to exercise expertise or decide technical questions, but simply to gain sufficient background orientation. Our obligation is not to be jettisoned because our initial technical understanding may be meager when compared to our initial grasp of FCC or freedom of speech questions. When called upon to make de novo decisions, individual judges have had to acquire the learning pertinent to complex technical questions in such fields as economics, science, technology and psychology. Our role is not as demanding when we are engaged in review of agency decisions, where we exercise restraint, and affirm even if we would have decided otherwise so long as the agency's decisionmaking is not irrational or discriminatory.

"The substantive review of administrative action is modest, but it cannot be carried out in a vacuum of understanding. Better no judicial review at all than a charade that gives the imprimatur without the substance of judicial confirmation that the agency is not acting unreasonably. Once the presumption of regularity in agency action is challenged with a factual submission, and even to determine whether such a challenge has been made, the agency's record and reasoning has to be looked at. If there is some factual support for the challenge, there must be either evidence or judicial notice available explicating the agency's result, or a remand to supply the gap. . . .

"Restraint, yes, abdication, no."

Judge Leventhal frequently remarked that he understood the Supreme Court's decision in Vermont Yankee to mean that he had won the debate. Do you agree?

(3) *Science Policy Questions and Institutional Design.* THOMAS O. MCGARITY, SUBSTANTIVE AND PROCEDURAL DISCRETION IN ADMINISTRATIVE RESOLUTION OF SCIENCE POLICY QUESTIONS: REGULATING CARCINOGENS IN EPA AND OSHA, 67 Geo. L.J. 729, 750 (1979): ". . . [S]cience policy questions are by their very nature policy-dominated. . . . Further, the inherent uncertainties surrounding science policy questions dictate that the agency will never be able to reduce its solution of these questions to 'findings of fact' within the traditional legal meaning of that term. . . . Moreover, close judicial scrutiny of the administrative record, even if it results from formal procedures, will not reveal unequivocal support for the agency's decision. Scouring the record of an agency's resolution of science policy questions will only reveal unresolved conflicts between qualified scientists on highly

technical questions, and strict judicial insistence upon formal 'findings of fact' will impose an impossible burden upon the agency. Finally, to the extent that a reviewing court is willing to defer to agency 'expertise' in choosing between the theories of equally respectable scientists, the court will simply force the agency to disguise policy decisions as factual determinations. Ultimately, this will result in less stringent judicial review of the legal and policy determinations upon which the agency in reality grounds its decisions."

A number of institutional arrangements, both public and private, are possible for resolving the issues Professor McGarity raises. Thus, in the Benzene case, p. 812, Congress had established the National Institute of Occupational Safety and Health (NIOSH) as one of the National Institutes of Health, a group of agencies directing scientific research, in the Department of Health and Human Services. NIOSH is charged with advising the Department of Labor's Occupational Safety and Health Administration about particular workplace risks that warrant regulatory attention. Similarly, in Whitman v. American Trucking Ass'ns, p. 791, Congress had established a Clean Air Special Advisory Panel to assist in the assessment of air pollution risks. Yet another institutional mechanism is peer review (see Note 8 on p. 443).

Do these legislative and executive measures adopt Judge Bazelon's side of the Bazelon-Leventhal debate? So long as such mechanisms have been implemented, is there less reason for courts to adopt Judge Leventhal's approach and engage in searching substantive scrutiny of their own? As you work through the materials in this chapter, keep the Bazelon-Leventhal debate in mind. How does its resolution affect the advice agency counsel should give agency staff and decisionmakers about the procedural course they should follow in rulemakings? How does its resolution affect the opportunities available to counsel for private parties seeking to influence the outcome of a rulemaking?

b. Notice

> **VETERANS JUSTICE GROUP v.
> SECRETARY OF VETERANS
> AFFAIRS**

The notice shall include . . . either the terms or substance of the proposed rule or a description of the subjects and issues involved.

5 U.S.C. § 553(b)

Notices of Proposed Rulemaking ("NPRMs"—or sometimes "NOPRs" or "NPRs") appear in the Federal Register, which the federal government publishes every business day online and in hard copy. They are also often accessible through the federal government's online rulemaking portal, regulations.gov, and typically appear on agency websites. Agencies may also issue press releases and even directly notify organizations and individuals of proposed rulemakings of likely interest to them.

VETERANS JUSTICE GROUP v. SECRETARY OF VETERANS AFFAIRS

United States Court of Appeals for the Federal Circuit (2016).
818 F.3d 1336.

■ WALLACH, CIRCUIT JUDGE.

BACKGROUND

To understand the issues relevant to this appeal, we discuss, in turn, the [Veterans Administration (VA)]'s prior regulation [and] the Final Rule . . . .

I.   Prior Regulation

A.   Claim Initiation

Veterans are entitled to compensation "[f]or disability resulting from personal injury suffered or disease contracted in line of duty, or for aggravation of a preexisting injury suffered or disease contracted in line of duty . . . during a period of war." 38 U.S.C. § 1110 (1998). For veterans to receive compensation under the laws administered by the VA, "[a] specific claim in the form prescribed by the Secretary . . . must be filed." Id. § 5101(a)(1). The VA's prior regulation implemented this authority by providing that "[a]ny communication or action, indicating an intent to apply for . . . benefits[,] . . . may be considered an informal claim." 38 C.F.R. § 3.155(a) (2014) (emphasis added) ("Prior Regulation"). Under the Prior Regulation, a veteran could establish a claim's effective date (i.e., when the claimant begins to receive compensation) by filing an informal claim, so long as a formal application was received by the VA "within [one] year from the date [the formal application form] was sent to the claimant." Id.

B.   Appeal

If a claimant perfected an informal claim by filing a formal application within the one-year time period, a VA Agency of Original Jurisdiction, typically a VA regional office ("RO"), considered the claim, gave notice to the claimant of its decision, and informed the claimant of his or her right to appeal. See 38 U.S.C. § 5104 (1998); 38 C.F.R. § 3.103(b)(1) (2014). An appeal could be initiated by filing a Notice of Disagreement ("NOD"), see 38 U.S.C. § 7105(a) (1998), and unless the requested benefit was granted or the NOD withdrawn, the VA would issue a "statement of the case" ("SOC") summarizing the reasons for the VA's decision on each issue, id. § 7105(d)(1). Following issuance of the SOC, the "claimant [would] be afforded a period of sixty days from the date of the [SOC] to file a formal appeal" with the Board of Veterans' Appeals ("Veterans Board"). Id. § 7105(d)(3). The statute provides that the "appeal should set out specific allegations of error of fact or law, such allegations related to specific items in the [SOC]." Id. . . .

The NOD is required to be: (1) filed within one year of the mailing of notice of the RO's decision; and (2) in writing. Id. § 7105(b)(1). . . .

II.   Final Rule

In September 2014, the VA promulgated the Final Rule, which sought to "strike a balance between standardizing, modernizing, and streamlining" the claim initiation and appellate process, while providing "claimants . . . with a process that remains veteran-friendly and informal." Final Rule, 79 Fed.Reg. at 57,664.

Although the Final Rule incorporated a majority of the amendments originally proposed by the VA in 2013, it altered the proposed rule in one important respect. See Standard Claims and Appeals Forms, 78 Fed.Reg. 65,490, 65,492 (Dep't of Veterans Affairs Oct. 31, 2013) ("Proposed Rule"). Under the Proposed Rule, submission of an informal claim—e.g., a narrative submission—would no longer serve as an effective date placeholder that could later be perfected by the filing of a formal claim. See id. at 65,495 (altering the Prior Regulation's definition of "claim" under 38 C.F.R. § 3.1(p) to exclude informal communications). Instead, an "incomplete claim" would provide the effective date placeholder function formerly provided by an informal claim, if perfected by the filing of a standard application form within one year. Id. at 65,494. However, in contrast to the flexible nature of the prior "informal claim" system, under the Proposed Rule, a submission would be considered an "incomplete claim" only if a claimant filled out, completely or incompletely, an online application via the VA's web-based electronic claims application system, but "d[id] not transmit the online application for processing." Id. Otherwise, claims would be considered received as of the date they were filed on a standard paper application form.

When it published the Proposed Rule in 2013, the VA explained it was "facing an unprecedented volume of compensation claims" resulting in "unacceptable delays at every phase of [the] process for adjudicating claims and appeals." Id. at 65,492. The VA received fifty-three comments in response to the Proposed Rule. While some commenters expressed approval of the agency's attempt to bring increased clarity and efficiency, others expressed concern with certain aspects of the Proposed Rule, including the VA's proposed interpretation of "incomplete claim," which some perceived as unnecessarily parochial.

In lieu of the Proposed Rule's "incomplete claim" concept, the Final Rule establishes an "intent to file"[3] process, which allows claimants to establish the effective date of an award in any of three ways. First, under

---

[3]   "An intent to file a claim must provide sufficient identifiable or biographical information to identify the claimant." Final Rule, 79 Fed.Reg. at 57,665. In contrast to informal claims, an intent to file a claim does not require the claimant "to identify the specific benefit sought," id., but does require an identification of the general benefit sought (such as compensation versus pension), 38 C.F.R. § 3.155(b)(2) (2015).

the Final Rule, an intent to file may be established by saving an electronic application within a VA web-based electronic claims application system before submitting it for actual processing. 38 C.F.R. § 3.155(b)(1)(i) (2015). Second, a claimant may submit a VA standard form ("VAF 21–0966") in either paper or electronic form. Id. § 3.155(b)(1)(ii); Final Rule, 79 Fed.Reg. at 57,666. Third, a claimant may establish intent to file by communicating orally with certain designated VA personnel "either in person or by telephone," who will document the claimant's intent. Final Rule, 79 Fed.Reg. at 57,666; see 38 C.F.R. § 3.155(b)(1)(iii) (2015). So long as a formal application is filed within one year of the submission, the VA will deem the effective date to be the date the "intent to file" submission was received.

Lastly, the Final Rule specifies that, where the RO "provides, in connection with its decision, a form identified as being for the purpose of initiating an appeal, an NOD would consist of a completed and timely submitted copy of that form." Final Rule, 79 Fed.Reg. at 57,679; see 38 C.F.R. § 20.201(a)(1) (2015). The Final Rule further clarifies the "VA will not accept as [an NOD] an expression of dissatisfaction . . . that is submitted in any other format, including on a different VA form." Final Rule, 79 Fed.Reg. at 57,679; see 38 C.F.R. § 20.201(a)(1) (2015). . . .

DISCUSSION. . .

II.   The Final Rule Is a "Logical Outgrowth" of the Proposed Rule

"The APA's rulemaking provisions generally require that notice of proposed rules be published in the Federal Register and that 'interested persons' be given the 'opportunity to participate in the rule making through submission of written data, views, or arguments.'" AFL-CIO v. Chao, 496 F.Supp.2d 76, 83 (D.D.C.2007) (quoting 5 U.S.C. § 553(c)). Although the APA does not explicitly address the relationship the notice of proposed rulemaking must have to the final rule, it provides some guidance when it states that agencies must publish in their notice of proposed rulemaking "either the terms or substance of the proposed rule or a description of the subjects and issues involved." 5 U.S.C. § 553(b)(3).

Under this standard, an agency's final rule need not be identical to the proposed rule. Indeed, "[t]he whole rationale of notice and comment rests on the expectation that the final rules will be somewhat different and improved from the rules originally proposed by the agency." Trans-Pac. Freight Conference of Japan/Korea v. Fed. Mar. Comm'n, 650 F.2d 1235, 1249 (D.C.Cir.1980).

Where a proposed rule is modified in light of public comment, the modified rule may be promulgated as a final rule without additional notice and opportunity for comment, so long as the final rule is a "logical outgrowth" of the proposed rule. CSX Transp., Inc. v. Surface Transp. Bd., 584 F.3d 1076, 1079 (D.C.Cir.2009); see also Long Island Care at Home, Ltd. v. Coke, 551 U.S. 158, 174 (2007) ("Courts of Appeals have generally interpreted [certain language in 5 U.S.C. § 553] to mean that

No addt'l notice after comment

the final rule . . . must be a logical outgrowth of the rule proposed." (internal quotation marks and citations omitted)) [p. 318]. "A final rule is a logical outgrowth of [a] proposed rule 'only if interested parties should have anticipated that the change was possible, (and) thus reasonably should have filed their comments on the subject during the notice-and-comment period.'" Int'l Union, United Mine Workers of Am. v. Mine Safety & Health Admin., 626 F.3d 84, 94–95 (D.C.Cir.2010) (quoting Int'l Union, United Mine Workers of Am. v. Mine Safety Health Admin., 407 F.3d 1250, 1259 (D.C.Cir.2005)).

American Legion contends "[t]he Final Rule's intent-to-file [provision] should be set aside . . . because it is not a logical outgrowth of the Proposed Rule." American Legion (15–7061) Br. 46 (citation omitted). According to American Legion, the Proposed Rule "did not propose [the] creat[ion] [of] a new '[i]ntent to [f]ile' form for initiating claims." Id. at 47. Instead, American Legion asserts the VA's Proposed Rule sought to modify "the informal claims process and replace it with a system where (i) existing application forms are designated as 'complete' or 'incomplete'; and (ii) electronic claims receive preferential treatment over paper [claims]." Id. (citing Proposed Rule, 78 Fed.Reg. at 65,490, 65,494–97; Final Rule, 79 Fed.Reg. at 57,663). Accordingly, American Legion contends that, because "[t]he Final Rule replaces [the Proposed Rule] with something very different[, namely,] a new intent-to-file 'concept' based on a 'new form' that was never mentioned in the Proposed Rule," id. (quoting Final Rule, 79 Fed.Reg. at 57,664), it could not have "'anticipated that the change was possible,'" id. at 46 (quoting United Mine Workers of Am., 626 F.3d at 94–95).

In response, the VA argues it "has not switched direction from the substance of the [P]roposed [R]ule, but has declined to go as far as originally proposed, following consideration of the public comments." VA (15–7061) Br. 37 (internal quotation marks and citation omitted). The VA asserts the potential results of the Proposed Rule that could have been anticipated include "declin[ing] to totally eliminate effective date placeholders for paper claims," and "attempt [ing] to reconcile [the effective date placeholder] policy with its need for standard inputs." Id. at 38. Accordingly, the VA asserts that, although "[t]he [F]inal [R]ule uses different terminology and structure," it "effects a policy urged to reconcile these issues." Id.

We conclude that, under the circumstances of this case, "interested parties should have anticipated that the change" reflected in the "intent to file" provision of the Final Rule was possible in light of the notice provided in the Proposed Rule. United Mine Workers of Am., 626 F.3d at 94–95. In lieu of the Proposed Rule's introduction of the "incomplete claim" concept, the VA adopted an "intent to file" process. Final Rule, 79 Fed.Reg. at 57,664–67. In addition to allowing a claimant to establish a claim's effective date through the submission of an application on a VA web-based electronic application system, as under the Proposed Rule, the

Final Rule expanded a claimant's options by also allowing an effective date to be established by the submission of a written intent to file a claim on a standard VA form, see 38 C.F.R. § 3.155(b)(1)(ii) (2015), or via a telephone call or in person, see id. § 3.155(b)(1)(iii). Final Rule, 79 Fed.Reg. at 57,664–67.

Contrary to American Legion's contention, the VA's substitution of the "intent to file" process for the proposed "incomplete claim" concept does not constitute a change in the basic approach of the Proposed Rule— the standardization of the claim initiation process. See Griffin Indus., Inc. v. United States, 27 Fed.Cl. 183, 196 (1992) ("The approach . . . adopted by the [agency], while different from the [P]roposed [R]egulation, was a logical outgrowth of the original proposal" because "[t]he [F]inal [R]ule changed neither the substance nor the approach" of the proposed regulation). What is more, not only were the "changes . . . in character with the original scheme[,] [they] were additionally foreshadowed in proposals and comments advanced during the rulemaking" and public comment period. S. Terminal Corp. v. EPA, 504 F.2d 646, 658 (1st Cir.1974); see also Final Rule, 79 Fed.Reg. at 57,663–64 (many commenters expressed dissatisfaction with the Proposed Rule's elimination of an effective date "placeholder" for paper claims). "[I]t would be antithetical to the purposes of the notice and comment provisions of the [APA] . . . to tax an agency with 'inconsistency' whenever it circulates a proposal that it has not firmly decided to put into effect and that it subsequently reconsiders in response to public comment." Commodity Futures Trading Com'n v. Schor, 478 U.S. 833, 845 (1986).

Lastly, we find American Legion's assertion puzzling because it is incongruent with the contentions it proffers regarding the substantive validity of the Final Rule. Unlike the Proposed Rule, the Final Rule introduces multiple avenues by which claimants may establish an effective date placeholder, thereby creating increased opportunities for claimants to establish a claim's effective date. The Final Rule does not go as far as the Proposed Rule because it does not limit the intent to file process to a VA web-based electronic claims application system. See Final Rule, 79 Fed.Reg. at 57,666. However, "[o]ne logical outgrowth of a proposal is surely . . . to refrain from taking the proposed step." Am. Iron & Steel Inst. v. EPA, 886 F.2d 390, 400 (D.C.Cir.1989). Accordingly, we find that the Final Rule is a logical outgrowth of the Proposed Rule.

NOTES

(1) *Procedural Argument as Strategy.* According to their petitions for review, the challengers objected to the substance of the VA's final rule, arguing that the rule did not match the "paternalistic, veteran friendly, and non-adversarial nature of veterans benefits adjudication." But the challengers presumably preferred the VA's final rule over the proposed version. Why did they bring this procedural challenge? If they had succeeded,

the remedy would have been procedural in nature, requiring the agency to take comments on the changes.

(2) *The Logical Outgrowth Test at the Supreme Court.* LONG ISLAND CARE. V. COKE, 551 U.S. 158 (2007), posed the question whether the Fair Labor Standards Act's "domestic services" exemption to wage and hour rules applied to domestic workers who provide companionship services and are employed by an agency other than the family or household for whom they work. Although the case turned largely on the degree of deference due to the agency's statutory interpretation, the Court also had an opportunity to address the question of when an agency's change in course might render initial notice inadequate. Although the case marked the first time the Court had used the term "logical outgrowth," lower courts, particularly the D.C. Circuit, had employed the term for decades.

JUSTICE BREYER wrote for a unanimous Court: "The Courts of Appeals have generally interpreted . . . [§ 553(b)(3)] to mean that the final rule the agency adopts must be 'a "logical outgrowth" of the rule proposed.' National Black Media Coalition v. FCC, 791 F.2d 1016, 1022 (C.A.2 1986). . . . The object, in short, is one of fair notice.

"Initially the Department [of Labor] proposed a rule of the kind that respondent seeks, namely a rule that would have placed outside the [domestic services] exemption (and hence left subject to FLSA wage and hour rules) individuals employed by third-party employers whom the Act had covered prior to 1974. The clear implication of the proposed rule was that companionship workers employed by third-party enterprises that were not covered by the FLSA prior to the 1974 Amendments (e.g., most smaller private agencies) would be included within the § 213(a)(15) exemption." According to the Court, "since the proposed rule was simply a proposal, its presence meant that the Department was considering the matter; after that consideration the Department might choose to adopt the proposal or to withdraw it. As it turned out, the Department did withdraw the proposal. . . . The result was a determination that exempted all third-party-employed companionship workers from the Act. We do not understand why such a possibility was not reasonably foreseeable."

Long Island Care thus underscores a feature about rulemaking notice that distinguishes it from adjudicatory notice: those who like the approach in a proposed rule cannot just sit back and not comment. They would be mistaken to assume that they will be notified and have a chance to voice their views in the future before the agency adopts a different path (including, possibly, a path opposite to its proposal).

(3) *Reasonably Foreseeable by Whom?* Should the test of what is "reasonably foreseeable" be based on what the public generally might anticipate from the terms of an agency's notice, or instead on what those involved in a regulatory area should know to be the issues in play? In ALTO DAIRY V. VENEMAN, 336 F.3d 560, 569–70 (7th Cir. 2003), Wisconsin dairy farmers sought to enjoin an amendment made to federal rules regulating the price of milk. Pursuant to the Milk Marketing Act, these rules are termed "orders," are set after a public hearing, and are issued separately for different

regions of the country. The notice that the Department issued stated that "[a] public hearing is being held to consider proposals to amend pooling and related provisions of the Mideast order" and listed a variety of specific proposals. The amendment actually adopted at the end of the proceeding was not identical to any of the proposals listed in the notice. No matter, wrote JUDGE POSNER: "The purpose of a rulemaking proceeding is not merely to vote up or down the specific proposals advanced before the proceeding begins, but to refine, modify, and supplement the proposals in the light of evidence and arguments presented in the course of the proceeding. If every modification is to require a further hearing at which that modification is set forth in the notice, agencies will be loath to modify initial proposals, and the rulemaking process will be degraded. . . .

"Though [the language of the notice] is gobbledygook to an outsider, insiders such as the plaintiffs would realize that the focus of the proceeding would be on their eligibility to be pooled with the Mideast producers [and thereby obtain the benefit of the higher price paid to the Mideast region]. [N]one of the proposals was identical to the amendment that the Department adopted at the end of the proceeding, namely the prohibition of paper pooling with distant plants. ["Paper pooling" was a practice under which a supply plant in one region was allowed to associate with dairy farmers in another region and, without the farmers being required to actually ship their milk to the supply plant, have those farmers' sales count towards percentage of sales the supply plant must make in a region for all of its sales to be included in that region's pool.] But paper pooling was one of the principal methods by which the plaintiffs got to pool with the Mideast producers, so that they had to assume that it would be one of the issues in the proceeding and a possible target for reform. They knew their aggressive inroads into the Mideast were controversial; they knew that in engaging in paper pooling with Mideast farmers they were exploiting the loophole created by [a 2000 regulatory change]; they knew therefore that a curtailment of their access to the Mideast blended price was a likely outcome of a rulemaking proceeding expressly concerned with the criteria for eligibility for pooling with the Mideast producers. They knew enough to know that if they wanted to protect their participation in the Mideast pool they would have to participate in the rulemaking proceeding."

This seems a sensible result, doesn't it? Should the result have been different if an "outsider" challenged the sufficiency of notice? To be sure, if the challenger were too far "outside," she might have difficulty establishing standing to complain in court. See Block v. Community Nutrition Institute 467 U.S. 340 (1984) (p. 1390). But many open government efforts are aimed at increasing the participation of stakeholders who do not typically participate in the conventional process. Specifically, the APA does not impose Article III standing hurdles for participating in the agency's notice-and-comment process. How meaningful could such efforts be if concepts like "fair notice" are contextually defined by what "insiders" know?

(4) *A Failure of Notice.* Given that the Supreme Court in the Long Island case, Note 2 above, upheld a final rule that took the opposite position of the proposed rule as a "logical outgrowth," you might assume that it would be

very hard now to win a procedural argument about notice. While the Supreme Court may see many outcomes as "reasonably foreseeable," the lower courts, particularly the D.C. Circuit, have been more exacting.

Because of statutory ambiguity and confusion among regulated entities, HHS considered whether patients with Medicare Advantage insurance (previously known as Medicare + Choice) should be counted in the "Medicare fraction" or "Medicaid fraction" for hospital reimbursement calculations. In a 2003 NPRM, HHS proposed the Medicaid fraction, under which hospitals stood to receive far more funds but noted that "there should not be a major [financial] impact associated with this proposed change." The next year, HHS issued a final rule that placed these patients instead in the Medicare fraction. In Allina Health Services v. Sebelius, 746 F.3d 1102, 1106 (D.C. Cir. 2014), Judge Silberman held that: "An agency may promulgate a rule that differs from a proposed rule only if the final rule is a 'logical outgrowth' of the proposed rule. . . . A final rule is a logical outgrowth if affected parties should have anticipated that the relevant modification was possible. . . .

"The Secretary points out that the 2003 notice proposed to codify one of only two possible interpretations of the statute . . . . Therefore, the Secretary argues, the hospitals should have been on notice that the Secretary might adopt either interpretation. The hospitals counter by arguing that the notice did not actually 'propose' adopting a rule; rather, the notice proposed merely to 'clarify' an existing practice. There is nothing in the text of the notice, the hospitals argue, to suggest that the Secretary was thinking of reconsidering a longstanding practice. Moreover, the notice indicated that 'there should not be a major impact associated with this change.' 68 Fed.Reg. at 27416. . . .

"This case is similar to one we decided in 2005. In Environmental Integrity Project v. E.P.A., the EPA issued a notice in which it 'proposed to codify' an interpretation of a regulation that the agency had applied in previous adjudications. 425 F.3d 992, 994 (D.C.Cir.2005). In its final rule, however, the agency adopted an interpretation precisely opposite to the one it had proposed codifying. We held that this was unlawful, explaining that there was no indication in the notice that the agency was open to reconsidering the interpretation that it has previously adopted through adjudication. Id. at 998. We said that agencies may not 'pull a surprise switcheroo on regulated entities.' Id. at 996.

"So, too, here. The hospitals should not be held to have anticipated that the Secretary's 'proposal to clarify' could have meant that the Secretary was open to reconsidering existing policy. The word 'clarify' does not suggest that a potential underlying major issue is open for discussion. . . .

"The Secretary's estimated financial impact of its proposal—that there should not be a major impact associated with this proposed change— supports our conclusion. See 68 Fed.Reg. at 27416. If, as the government contends, the 2003 notice had actually suggested a binary choice, between maintaining a preexisting policy and reversing that policy, then the potential estimated financial impact should have been stated in the hundreds of millions of dollars. That would doubtless have triggered an avalanche of comments, in contrast to the mere 26 pages that were actually submitted.

"It should be noted that since the Secretary was disposed to codify an interpretation that was favorable to the hospitals, there was no reason for the hospitals to fear that another party would offer comments opposed to such an interpretation. (There is no obvious constituency opposed to greater compensation for hospitals.) In that regard, this case differs from, for example, environmental regulation cases, where regulated industries can usually anticipate fierce opposition from environmental groups, and it might be thought prudent to submit comments in support of favorable proposed rules.

"We are sympathetic to the view expressed by the Seventh Circuit that proposed rules that might seem obscure to the average reader should alert members of the regulated class to the possible options that an examination of a policy would imply. See Alto Dairy v. Veneman, 336 F.3d 560, 570 (7th Cir.2003) [p. 318]; but see Natural Res. Def. Council v. U.S. E.P.A., 279 F.3d 1180, 1188 (9th Cir.2002). But we ask ourselves, would a reasonable member of the regulated class—even a good lawyer—anticipate that such a volte-face with enormous financial implications would follow the Secretary's proposed rule. Indeed, such a lawyer might well advise a hospital client not to comment opposing such a possible change for fear of giving the Secretary the very idea.

"In sum, we agree with the district court that the Secretary's final rule was not a logical outgrowth of the proposed rule."

Do you agree with the court's inferences about notice from what happened in the commenting process? (From the opinion: "Only a smattering of hospitals even bothered to comment [on the NPRM]; their commentary totaled just 26 pages, and a number of them did not understand the proposal.")

(5)   *The APA's Text.* Focus on the general and disjunctive character of the text of § 553(b)(3). Notice must include "*either* the terms *or* substance of the proposed rule *or* a description of the subjects and issues involved" (emphasis added). Do you believe that the 1946 Congress would have found a final rule that contradicted a proposed rule surprising? Even if so, would the Supreme Court (in Long Island Care) then be in error? Why or why not?

c.   An Opportunity to Comment and a Concise General Statement of a Rule's Basis and Purpose

> *U.S. v. NOVA SCOTIA FOOD PRODS. CORP.*
> *Notes on the Paper Hearing*
> *Notes on the Opportunity to Participate*
> *Notes on the Concise General Statement of the Rule's Basis and Purpose*

After notice required by this section, the agency shall give interested persons an opportunity to participate in the rule making through submission of written data, views, or arguments with or without opportunity for oral presentation. After consideration of the relevant matter presented, the agency shall incorporate in the rules adopted a concise general statement of their basis and purpose.

5 U.S.C. § 553(c)

UNITED STATES v. NOVA SCOTIA FOOD PRODUCTS CORP.

United States Court of Appeals for the Second Circuit (1977).
568 F.2d 240.

■ GURFEIN, CIRCUIT JUDGE.

[In October 1969, after several incidents of foodborne botulism, a serious and potentially fatal illness, the Food and Drug Administration (FDA) issued an NPRM concerning the processing of fish commonly sold as smoked and/or salted fish. The proposed rule reached all species of fish commercially handled this way—chub, eel, herring, salmon, sturgeon, trout, whitefish, etc. The FDA issued the rule in 1970, modifying its initial proposal in response to some comments it had received. However, the agency declined to make special provisions for particular species of fish until processors of a given species proposed a substitute they could prove adequate to protect the public from botulism. Whitefish processors apparently attempted no such demonstration. Six years later, the FDA successfully brought a district court action to enforce its rule against a whitefish processor, Nova Scotia Food Products Corp., which had not changed its processing methods to comply with the rule.]

This appeal involving a regulation of the [FDA] is not here upon a direct review of agency action. It is an appeal from a judgment of the District Court for the Eastern District of New York enjoining the appellants, after a hearing, from processing hot smoked whitefish except in accordance with time-temperature-salinity (T-T-S) regulations contained in 21 C.F.R. Part 122 (1977). The injunction was sought and granted on the ground that smoked whitefish which has been processed in violation of the T-T-S regulation is "adulterated." Food, Drug and Cosmetics Act ("the Act"), 21 U.S.C. §§ 332(a), 331(k).

The regulations cited above require that hot-process smoked fish be heated by a controlled heat process that provides a monitoring system positioned in as many strategic locations in the oven as necessary to assure a continuous temperature through each fish of not less than 180° F. for a minimum of 30 minutes for fish which have been brined to contain 3.5% Water phase salt or at 150° F. for a minimum of 30 minutes if the salinity was at 5% Water phase. Since each fish must meet these requirements, it is necessary to heat an entire batch of fish to even higher temperatures so that the lowest temperature for any fish will meet the minimum requirements.

Government inspection of appellants' plant established without question that the minimum T-T-S requirements were not being met.

There is no substantial claim that the plant was processing whitefish under "insanitary conditions" in any other material respect. Appellants, on their part, do not defend on the ground that they were in compliance, but rather that the requirements could not be met if a marketable whitefish was to be produced. They defend upon the grounds that the regulation is invalid (1) because it is beyond the authority delegated by the statute; (2) because the FDA improperly relied upon undisclosed evidence in promulgating the regulation and because it is not supported by the administrative record; and (3) because there was no adequate statement setting forth the basis of the regulation. We reject the contention that the regulation is beyond the authority delegated by the statute, but we find serious inadequacies in the procedure followed in the promulgation of the regulation and hold it to be invalid as applied to the appellants herein.

The hazard which the FDA sought to minimize was the outgrowth and toxin formation of Clostridium botulinum Type E spores of the bacteria which sometimes inhabit fish. There had been an occurrence of several cases of botulism traced to consumption of fish from inland waters in 1960 and 1963 which stimulated considerable bacteriological research. These bacteria can be present in the soil and water of various regions. They can invade fish in their natural habitat and can be further disseminated in the course of evisceration and preparation of the fish for cooking. A failure to destroy such spores through an adequate brining, thermal, and refrigeration process was found to be dangerous to public health.

The Commissioner of Food and Drugs ("Commissioner"), employing informal "notice-and-comment" procedures under 21 U.S.C. § 371(a), issued a proposal for the control of C. botulinum bacteria Type E in fish. 34 F.R. 17,176 (Oct. 23, 1969). For his statutory authority to promulgate the regulations, the Commissioner specifically relied only upon § 342(a)(4) of the Act which provides: "A food shall be deemed to be adulterated— . . . (4) if it has been prepared, packed, or held under insanitary conditions whereby it may have become contaminated with filth, or whereby it may have been rendered injurious to health." . . . Responding to the Commissioner's invitation in the notice of proposed rulemaking, members of the industry, including appellants and the intervenor-appellant, submitted comments on the proposed regulation.

The Commissioner thereafter issued the final regulations in which he adopted certain suggestions made in the comments, including a suggestion by the National Fisheries Institute, Inc. ("the Institute"), the intervenor herein. 35 F.R. 17,401 (Nov. 13, 1970). The original proposal provided that the fish would have to be cooked to a temperature of 180° F. for at least 30 minutes, if the fish have been brined to contain 3.5% Water phase salt, with no alternative. In the final regulation, an alternative suggested by the intervenor "that the parameter of 150° F. for 30 minutes and 5% Salt in the water phase be established as an alternate procedure to that stated in the proposed regulation for an interim period until specific parameters can be established" was accepted, but as a permanent part of the regulation rather than for an interim period.

The intervenor suggested that "specific parameters" be established. This referred to particular processing parameters for different species of fish on a "species by species" basis. Such "species by species" determination was proposed not only by the intervenor but also by the Bureau of Commercial Fisheries of the Department of the Interior. That Bureau objected to the general application of the T-T-S requirement proposed by the FDA on the ground that application of the regulation to all species of fish being smoked was not commercially feasible, and that the regulation should therefore specify time-temperature-salinity requirements, as developed by research and study, on a species-by-species basis. The Bureau suggested that "wholesomeness considerations could be more practically and adequately realized by reducing processing temperature and using suitable concentrations of nitrite and salt." The Commissioner took cognizance of the suggestion, but decided, nevertheless, to impose the T-T-S requirement on all species of fish (except chub, which were regulated by 21 C.F.R. 172.177 (1977) (dealing with food additives)).

He did acknowledge, however, in his "basis and purpose" statement required by the Administrative Procedure Act ("APA"), 5 U.S.C. § 553(c), that "adequate times, temperatures and salt concentrations have not been demonstrated for each individual species of fish presently smoked." 35 F.R. 17,401 (Nov. 13, 1970). The Commissioner concluded, nevertheless, that "the processing requirements of the proposed regulations are the safest now known to prevent the outgrowth and toxin formation of C. botulinum Type E." He determined that "the conditions of current good manufacturing practice for this industry should be established without further delay." Id.

The Commissioner did not answer the suggestion by the Bureau of Fisheries that nitrite and salt as additives could safely lower the high temperature otherwise required, a solution which the FDA had accepted in the case of chub. Nor did the Commissioner respond to the claim of Nova Scotia through its trade association, the Association of Smoked Fish Processors, Inc., Technical Center that "(t)he proposed process requirements suggested by the FDA for hot processed smoked fish are neither commercially feasible nor based on sound scientific evidence obtained with the variety of smoked fish products to be included under this regulation." (Exhibit D, Tab A).

Nova Scotia, in its own comment, wrote to the Commissioner that "the heating of certain types of fish to high temperatures will completely destroy the product." It suggested, as an alternative, that "specific processing procedures could be established for each species after adequate work and experimentation (sic) has been done—but not before."

(Id.). We have noted above that the response given by the Commissioner was in general terms. He did not specifically aver that the T-T-S requirements as applied to whitefish were, in fact, commercially feasible.

When, after several inspections and warnings, Nova Scotia failed to comply with the regulation, an action by the United States Attorney for injunctive relief was filed on April 7, 1976, six years later, and resulted in the judgment here on appeal. . . .

II

Appellants contend that there is an inadequate administrative record upon which to predicate judicial review, and that the failure to disclose to interested persons the factual material upon which the agency was relying vitiates the element of fairness which is essential to any kind of administrative action. Moreover, they argue that the "concise general statement of . . . basis and purpose" by the Commissioner was inadequate. 5 U.S.C. § 553.

The question of what is an adequate "record" in informal rulemaking has engaged the attention of commentators for several years. The extent of the administrative record required for judicial review of informal rulemaking is largely a function of the scope of judicial review. Even when the standard of review is whether the promulgation of the rule was "arbitrary, capricious, an abuse of discretion, or otherwise not in accordance with law," as specified in 5 U.S.C. § 706(2)(A), judicial review must nevertheless, be based on the "whole record" (id.). Adequate review of a determination requires an adequate record, if the review is to be meaningful. What will constitute an adequate record for meaningful review may vary with the nature of the administrative action to be reviewed. Review must be based on the whole record even when the judgment is one of policy, except that findings of fact such as would be required in an adjudicatory proceeding or in a formal "on the record" hearing for rulemaking need not be made. Citizens to Preserve Overton Park v. Volpe, 401 U.S. 402, 416–18 (1971) [p. 1085]. Though the action was informal, without an evidentiary record, the review must be "thorough, probing, [and] in depth." Id., 401 U.S. at 415. . . .

A

With respect to the content of the administrative "record," the Supreme Court has told us that in informal rulemaking, "the focal point for judicial review should be the administrative record already in existence, not some new record made initially in the reviewing court." See Camp v. Pitts, 411 U.S. 138, 142 (1973) [p. 1087].

No contemporaneous record was made or certified.[13] When, during the enforcement action, the basis for the regulation was sought through

---

[13] A practice developed in the early years of the APA of not making a formal contemporaneous record, but rather, when challenged, to put together a historical record of what had been available for agency consideration at the time the regulation was promulgated. . . . Professor Davis in a balanced review, has stated: "When the facts are of central importance and might be challenged, parties adversely affected by them should have a chance to respond to

pretrial discovery, the record was created by searching the files of the FDA and the memories of those who participated in the process of rulemaking. This resulted in what became Exhibit D at the trial of the injunction action. Exhibit D consists of (1) Tab A containing the comments received from outside parties during the administrative "notice-and-comment" proceeding and (2) Tabs B through L consisting of scientific data and the like upon which the Commissioner now says he relied but which were not made known to the interested parties. . . .

In an enforcement action, we must rely exclusively on the record made before the agency to determine the validity of the regulation. The exception to the exclusivity of that record is that "there may be independent judicial fact-finding when issues that were not before the agency are raised in a proceeding to *enforce* non-adjudicatory agency action." Overton Park, supra, 401 U.S. at 415 (1971). (Emphasis added.)

Though this is an enforcement proceeding and the question is close, we think that the "issues" were fairly before the agency and hence that de novo evidence was properly excluded by Judge Dooling. Our concern is, rather, with the manner in which the agency treated the issues tendered.

B

The key issues were (1) whether, in the light of the rather scant history of botulism in whitefish, that species should have been considered separately rather than included in a general regulation which failed to distinguish species from species; (2) whether the application of the proposed T-T-S requirements to smoked whitefish made the whitefish commercially unsaleable; and (3) whether the agency recognized that prospect, but nevertheless decided that the public health needs should prevail even if that meant commercial death for the whitefish industry. The procedural issues were whether, in the light of these key questions, the agency procedure was inadequate because (i) it failed to disclose to interested parties the scientific data and the methodology upon which it relied; and (ii) because it failed utterly to address itself to the pertinent question of commercial feasibility.

1.   The History of Botulism in Whitefish

. . . [Since] [t]he industry . . . abandoned vacuum-packing, . . . there has not been a single case of botulism associated with commercially prepared whitefish since 1963, though 2,750,000 pounds of whitefish are processed annually. . . .

2.   The Scientific Data

Interested parties were not informed of the scientific data, or at least of a selection of such data deemed important by the agency, so that

them. Clearly, whatever factual information the agency has considered should be a part of the record for judicial review." K. Davis, Administrative Law of the Seventies, § 29.01–6, pp. 672–73 (1976).

comments could be addressed to the data. Appellants argue that unless the scientific data relied upon by the agency are spread upon the public records, criticism of the methodology used or the meaning to be inferred from the data is rendered impossible.

We agree with appellants in this case, for although we recognize that an agency may resort to its own expertise outside the record in an informal rulemaking procedure, we do not believe that when the pertinent research material is readily available and the agency has no special expertise on the precise parameters involved, there is any reason to conceal the scientific data relied upon from the interested parties. As Judge Leventhal said in Portland Cement Ass'n v. Ruckelshaus, 486 F.2d 375, 393 (1973) [p. 330]: "It is not consonant with the purpose of a rulemaking proceeding to promulgate rules on the basis of inadequate data, or on data that [in] critical degree, *is known only to the agency.*" (Emphasis added.) This is not a case where the agency methodology was based on material supplied by the interested parties themselves. International Harvester Co. v. Ruckelshaus, 478 F.2d 615, 632 (1973). Here all the scientific research was collected by the agency, and none of it was disclosed to interested parties as the material upon which the proposed rule would be fashioned.[15] Nor was an articulate effort made to connect the scientific requirements to available technology that would make commercial survival possible, though the burden of proof was on the agency. This required it to "bear a burden of adducing a reasoned presentation supporting the reliability of its methodology." International Harvester, supra, 478 F.2d at 643 . . . .

If the failure to notify interested persons of the scientific research upon which the agency was relying actually prevented the presentation of relevant comment, the agency may be held not to have considered all "the relevant factors." We can think of no sound reasons for secrecy or reluctance to expose to public view (with an exception for trade secrets or national security) the ingredients of the deliberative process. Indeed, the FDA's own regulations now specifically require that every notice of proposed rulemaking contain "references to all data and information on which the Commissioner relies for the proposal (copies or a full list of which shall be a part of the administrative file on the matter . . .)." 21 C.F.R. § 10.40(b)(1) (1977). And this is, undoubtedly, the trend.

We think that the scientific data should have been disclosed to focus on the proper interpretation of "insanitary conditions." When the basis for a proposed rule is a scientific decision, the scientific material which is believed to support the rule should be exposed to the view of interested parties for their comment. One cannot ask for comment on a scientific paper without allowing the participants to read the paper. Scientific

---

[15] We recognize the problem posed by Judge Leventhal in International Harvester, supra, that a proceeding might never end if such submission required a reply ad infinitum, ibid. Here the exposure of the scientific research relied on simply would have required a single round of comment addressed thereto.

research is sometimes rejected for diverse inadequacies of methodology; and statistical results are sometimes rebutted because of a lack of adequate gathering technique or of supportable extrapolation. Such is the stuff of scientific debate. To suppress meaningful comment by failure to disclose the basic data relied upon is akin to rejecting comment altogether. For unless there is common ground, the comments are unlikely to be of a quality that might impress a careful agency. The inadequacy of comment in turn leads in the direction of arbitrary decision-making. We do not speak of findings of fact, for such are not technically required in the informal rulemaking procedures. We speak rather of what the agency should make known so as to elicit comments that probe the fundamentals. Informal rulemaking does not lend itself to a rigid pattern. Especially, in the circumstance of our broad reading of statutory authority in support of the agency, we conclude that the failure to disclose to interested persons the scientific data upon which the FDA relied was procedurally erroneous. Moreover, the burden was upon the agency to articulate rationally why the rule should apply to a large and diverse class, with the same T-T-S parameters made applicable to all species.

C

Appellants additionally attack the "concise general statement" required by APA, 5 U.S.C. § 553, as inadequate. We think that, in the circumstances, it was less than adequate. It is not in keeping with the rational process to leave vital questions, raised by comments which are of cogent materiality, completely unanswered. The agencies certainly have a good deal of discretion in expressing the basis of a rule, but the agencies do not have quite the prerogative of obscurantism reserved to legislatures. . . .

The test of adequacy of the "concise general statement" was expressed by Judge McGowan in the following terms: "We do not expect the agency to discuss every item of fact or opinion included in the submissions made to it in informal rulemaking. We do expect that, if the judicial review which Congress has thought it important to provide is to be meaningful, the 'concise general statement of . . . basis and purpose' mandated by Section 4 will enable us to see what major issues of policy were ventilated by the informal proceedings and why the agency reacted to them as it did." Automotive Parts & Accessories Ass'n v. Boyd, 407 F.2d 330, 338 (1968). . . .

The Secretary was squarely faced with the question whether it was necessary to formulate a rule with specific parameters that applied to all species of fish, and particularly whether lower temperatures with the addition of nitrite and salt would not be sufficient. Though this alternative was suggested by an agency of the federal government, its suggestion, though acknowledged, was never answered.

Moreover, the comment that to apply the proposed T-T-S requirements to whitefish would destroy the commercial product was neither discussed nor answered. We think that to sanction silence in the face of such vital questions would be to make the statutory requirement of a "concise general statement" less than an adequate safeguard against arbitrary decision-making. . . .

One may recognize that even commercial infeasibility cannot stand in the way of an overwhelming public interest. Yet the administrative process should disclose, at least, whether the proposed regulation is considered to be commercially feasible, or whether other considerations prevail even if commercial infeasibility is acknowledged. This kind of forthright disclosure and basic statement was lacking in the formulation of the T-T-S standard made applicable to whitefish. It is easy enough for an administrator to ban everything. In the regulation of food processing, the worldwide need for food also must be taken into account in formulating measures taken for the protection of health. In the light of the history of smoked whitefish to which we have referred, we find no articulate balancing here sufficient to make the procedure followed less than arbitrary.

After seven years of relative inaction, the FDA has apparently not reviewed the T-T-S regulations in the light of present scientific knowledge and experience. In the absence of a new statutory directive by Congress regarding control of micro-organisms, which we hope will be worthy of its consideration, we think that the T-T-S standards should be reviewed again by the FDA.

We cannot, on this appeal, remand to the agency to allow further comments by interested parties, addressed to the scientific data now disclosed at the trial below. We hold in this enforcement proceeding, therefore, that the regulation, as it affects non-vacuum-packed hot-smoked whitefish, was promulgated in an arbitrary manner and is invalid. . . .

In view of our conclusion . . . we must reverse the grant of the injunction and direct that the complaint be dismissed.

NOTES ON THE PAPER HEARING

(1) **The Paper Hearing.** Writing a year before the Vermont Yankee decision, Professor Richard Stewart saw in the expansion of agency records and the "requirement of reasoned elaboration" (including the requirement of responding to contrary arguments and evidence) that followed the Supreme Court's decision in Florida East Coast Railway (p. 285) the basis for a "paper hearing" that "combines many of the advantages of a trial-type adversary process (excepting oral testimony and cross-examination) while avoiding undue delay and cost." RICHARD B. STEWART, THE DEVELOPMENT OF ADMINISTRATIVE AND QUASI-CONSTITUTIONAL LAW IN JUDICIAL REVIEW OF ENVIRONMENTAL DECISION-MAKING: LESSONS FROM THE CLEAN AIR ACT, 62 Iowa L. Rev. 713, 731–33 (1977): "The development of a 'paper hearing' procedure and the related requirement that the Agency explain in detail the bases for its decision have contributed significantly to the improvement of

EPA decisionmaking because the Agency must be prepared to expose the factual and methodological bases for its decision and face judicial review on a record that encompasses the contentions and evidence of the Agency and its opponents, including responses by the Agency to criticism of its decision. Far more controversial are occasional court decisions that have gone beyond the requirements of detailed explanation and a 'paper hearing' to require, on a largely ad hoc basis, that EPA grant a limited trial-type hearing on specified issues . . .

"Recognition of a 'paper hearing' procedure as a third standard model of administrative decision is likely to represent a better solution to the inadequacies of the two traditional paradigms (notice-and-comment procedures and adjudicatory procedures) than a series of ad hoc responses. The development of 'paper hearing' procedures at other agencies, and proposals by commentators, legislators, and the Administrative Conference, indicate that the 'paper hearing' model may well be widely imitated and eventually accepted as a procedural *tertium quid*."

(2) ***Disclosure Demands and Vermont Yankee.*** "It is not consonant with the purpose of a rulemaking proceeding to promulgate rules on the basis of inadequate data, or on data that[, to a] critical degree, is known only to the agency." This phrase is quoted by Judge Gurfein from JUDGE HAROLD LEVENTHAL'S influential opinion in PORTLAND CEMENT ASS'N V. RUCKELSHAUS, 486 F.2d 375, 393 (D.C. Cir. 1973). In that case, challengers took issue with how the EPA set a stationary source standard for new and modified Portland cement plants, in part because they had not received information about the agency's methodology in time to comment on it. The D.C. Circuit found the agency process lacking: "We find a critical defect in the decision-making process in arriving at the standard under review in the initial inability of petitioners to obtain—in timely fashion—the test results and procedures used on existing plants which formed a partial basis for the emission control level adopted, and in the subsequent seeming refusal of the agency to respond to what seem to be legitimate problems with the methodology of these tests." Thus, putting Portland Cement and Nova Scotia together, disclosure requirements are not limited to data disclosure but include methodologies used in reasoning from data as well.

Both Portland Cement and Nova Scotia predate Vermont Yankee. Do they survive it? This issue arose in the D.C. Circuit decision, AMERICAN RADIO RELAY LEAGUE V. FCC, 524 F.3d 237 (D.C. Cir. 2008). The FCC adopted a rule approving the installation of devices on electric power lines that would transmit broadband Internet access. This technology also had the potential to interfere with the transmission and reception of amateur "ham" radio operators. The FCC concluded that existing safeguards and certain new protective measures would be adequate to prevent the problem, but the American Radio Relay League disagreed and challenged the rule. A Freedom of Information Act (FOIA) request had uncovered five studies consisting of technical data gathered from field tests performed by FCC staff. The FCC ultimately placed these in the rulemaking record, but in redacted form and after the rule had been promulgated.

JUDGE ROGERS'S opinion for the panel held that the FCC had violated § 553:"It would appear to be a fairly obvious proposition that studies upon which an agency relies in promulgating a rule must be made available during the rulemaking in order to afford interested persons meaningful notice and an opportunity for comment [quoting Judge Leventhal's opinion in Portland Cement] . . . Where, as here, an agency's determination 'is based upon "a complex mix of controversial and uncommented upon data and calculations,' " there is no APA precedent allowing an agency to cherry-pick a study on which it has chosen to rely in part." The opinion noted that the court had reviewed the partially redacted pages *in camera* in unredacted form, and that they included staff summaries of test data, scientific recommendations, test analyses, and conclusions regarding the methodology used in the studies. It concluded that the League might have something useful to say if given the opportunity to comment on the unredacted studies.

Judge Rogers rejected the suggestion that requiring disclosure of the studies was at odds with Vermont Yankee: ". . . [T]he procedures invalidated in Vermont Yankee were not anchored to any statutory provision. By contrast, the court does not impose any new procedures for the regulatory process, but merely applies settled law to the facts. The Commission made the choice to engage in notice-and-comment rulemaking and to rely on parts of its redacted studies as a basis for the rule. The court, consequently, is not imposing new procedures but enforcing the agency's procedural choice by ensuring that it conforms to APA requirements. It is one thing for the Commission to give notice and make available for comment the studies on which it relied in formulating the rule while explaining its non-reliance on certain parts. It is quite another thing to provide notice and an opportunity for comment on only those parts of the studies that the Commission likes best."

Concurring, JUDGE TATEL linked the disclosure requirement to § 706 of the APA: "That provision requires us to set aside arbitrary and capricious agency action after reviewing 'the whole record,' 5 U.S.C. § 706, and the 'whole record' in this case includes the complete content of the staff reports the Commission relied upon in promulgating the challenged rule. . . . [G]iven that the Commission relied on the studies at issue, there can be no doubt that they form part of the administrative record—a proposition unaffected by the Commission's claim that it chose not to rely on various parts of the studies. . . . Nor is there any doubt that, as our case law makes clear, the APA means exactly what it says: an agency must make the '*whole* record' available, especially where, as here, the undisclosed portions might very well undercut the agency's ultimate decision."

JUDGE KAVANAUGH wrote separately "to underscore that Portland Cement stands on a shaky legal foundation (even though it may make sense as a policy matter in some cases). Put bluntly, the Portland Cement doctrine cannot be squared with the text of § 553 of the APA.": "The APA requires only that an agency provide public notice and a comment period before the agency issues a rule. The notice must include 'the terms or substance of the proposed rule *or* a description of the subjects and issues involved.' § 553(b)(3) (emphasis added). After issuing a notice and allowing time for interested persons to comment, the agency must issue a 'concise general statement' of the rule's 'basis and purpose' along with the final rule. § 553(c). One searches the text of APA § 553 in vain for a requirement that an agency disclose other agency information as part of the notice or later in the rulemaking process. . . . Portland Cement's lack of roots in the statutory text creates a serious jurisprudential problem because the Supreme Court later rejected this kind of freeform interpretation of the APA [in Vermont Yankee].

". . . In appropriate cases or controversies, courts of course must be vigilant in ensuring that agencies adhere to the plain text of statutes imposing substantive and procedural obligations. But [c]ourts have incrementally expanded those APA procedural requirements well beyond what the text provides [and] simultaneously have grown . . . 'narrow' § 706 arbitrary-and-capricious review into a far more demanding test. . . . [These] twin lines of decisions have gradually transformed rulemaking—whether regulatory or deregulatory rulemaking—from the simple and speedy practice contemplated by the APA into a laborious, seemingly never-ending process. The judicially created obstacle course can hinder executive branch agencies from rapidly and effectively responding to changing or emerging issues within their authority, such as consumer access to broadband, or effectuating policy or philosophical changes in the Executive's approach to the subject matter at hand. The trend has not been good as a jurisprudential matter, and it continues to have significant practical consequences for the operation of the Federal Government and those affected by federal regulation and deregulation."

Is Judge Kavanaugh correct that the disclosure requirements imposed by Portland Cement and Nova Scotia are at odds with the text of § 553? Or are you persuaded by Judge Rogers's contention (echoing the line of argument articulated in Nova Scotia) that such requirements have a firmer home in § 553 than the procedures at issue in Vermont Yankee? Does the textual reference in § 553(b)(3)—"an opportunity to participate"—suffice to support such a disclosure requirement? Are the disclosure requirements instead best justified, as Judge Tatel claimed, on the basis of § 706's "whole record" requirement for judicial review? Finally, would it be better to justify data disclosure requirements on a theory that the APA should not be read in a static fashion, particularly given subsequent developments such as the tremendous growth in informal rulemaking (and the fading of formal rulemaking) after Florida East Coast Railway, p. 285? For more on the contrast between static and more evolving interpretations of the APA, see Chapter III (p. 242) and the discussion of dynamic statutory interpretation in Chapter II (p. 110).

The proposed Regulatory Accountability Act, discussed in Section 1 above (p. 286), would also amend § 553 to explicitly require agencies to disclose relevant information: "(A) IN GENERAL.—Except as provided in subparagraph (B), not later than the date on which an agency publishes a notice of proposed rulemaking . . ., all studies, models, scientific literature, and other information developed or relied upon by the agency, and actions taken by the agency to obtain that information, in connection with the determination of the agency to propose the rule that is the subject of the rulemaking shall be placed in the docket for the proposed rule and made accessible to the public. (B) EXCEPTION.—Subparagraph (A) shall not apply with respect to information that is exempt from disclosure under section 552(b) [FOIA exemptions, see p. 673]." S. 951 (115th Cong.), § 3.

(3) *The Contrast with Original Understandings.* Notwithstanding its advantages, the paper hearing represents a considerable elaboration of § 553's requirements, well beyond what any 1946 legislator would have thought was demanded of agencies, as evident from the following description of informal rulemaking contained in an influential commentary on the APA issued by the Department of Justice shortly after the statute's enactment.

ATTORNEY GENERAL'S MANUAL ON THE ADMINISTRATIVE PROCEDURE ACT 31–35 (1947): "*Informal rule making.* In every case of proposed informal rule making subject to the notice requirements of section 4(a) [i.e., § 553(b)], section 4(b) [§ 553(c)] provides that 'the agency shall afford interested persons an opportunity to participate in the rule making through submission of written data, views, or arguments with or without opportunity to present the same orally in any manner.' The quoted language confers discretion upon the agency, except where statutes require 'formal' rule making subject to sections 7 and 8 [§§ 556 & 557], to designate in each case the procedure for public participation in rule making. Such informal rule making procedure may take a variety of forms: informal hearings (with or without a stenographic transcript), conferences, consultation with industry committees, submission of written views, or any combination of these. These informal procedures have already been extensively employed by Federal agencies. In each case, the selection of the procedure to be followed will depend largely upon the nature of the rules involved. The objective should be to assure informed administrative action and adequate protection to private interests.

"Each agency is affirmatively required to consider 'all relevant matter presented' in the proceeding; it is recommended that all rules issued after such informal proceedings be accompanied by an express recital that such material has been considered. It is entirely clear, however, that section 4(b) does not require the formulation of rules upon the exclusive basis of any 'record' made in informal rule making proceedings. Senate Hearings (1941) p. 444. Accordingly, except in formal rule making governed by sections 7 and 8, an agency is free to formulate rules upon the basis of materials in its files and the knowledge and experience of the agency, in addition to the materials adduced in public rule making proceedings.

"Section 4(b) provides that upon the completion of public rule making proceedings 'after consideration of all relevant matter presented, the agency shall incorporate in any rules adopted a concise general statement of their basis and purpose.' The required statement will be important in that the courts and the public may be expected to use such statements in the interpretation of the agency's rules. The statement is to be 'concise' and 'general.' Except as required by statutes providing for 'formal' rule making procedure, findings of fact and conclusions of law are not necessary. Nor is there required an elaborate analysis of the rules or of the considerations upon which the rules were issued. Rather, the statement is intended to advise the public of the general basis and purpose of the rules."

Today, both a "blackletter" statement of administrative law published by the Administrative Law and Regulatory Practice Section of the ABA, A Blackletter Statement of Federal Administrative Law, 54 Admin. L. Rev. 1, 30–35 (2002), and its popular publication, A Guide to Federal Agency Rulemaking, present the paper hearing as an established, uncontroversial part of the law. For a discussion of the impact of these elaborations on § 553, including the concern that they "ossify" rulemaking by making it a time and resource intensive process, see the discussion of "hard look" review in Chapter VIII, Subsec. 2.b (p. 1069).

(4) **The Freedom of Information Act as Amendment.** Another important subsequent development was enactment in 1966 of FOIA as an amendment to the APA. (See Ch. VI, Sec. 3, p. 672). FOIA requires agencies to make public, on request, any properly identified factual data in agency records that do not fit one of nine narrowly defined exemptions. 5 U.S.C. §§ 552(a)(3), 552(b). Does this mean that a Notice of Proposed Rulemaking issued under § 553(b) must contain references to and make available any factual data (studies, etc.) known to the agency as arguably bearing upon its proposal? As you will learn if you study Chapter VI, where FOIA is considered in detail, "please disclose all factual studies and data in agency records that the agency has thus far considered in connection with the rulemaking on [subject] announced in the Federal Register on [date] at [page]" is a sufficiently definite (and otherwise proper) FOIA request. As American Radio Relay League demonstrates, persons interested in a rulemaking could (and certainly do) make such requests promptly on learning of a proposal. Although a requester couldn't count on getting the agency's response in time to inform her comments, the agency's obligation to disclose is evident, as is the likelihood that it would receive requests to do so. Can you convert this juxtaposition of statutory remedies into an argument that such data must be revealed during the notice-and-comment process?

(5) **The Three "Records" of Agency Rulemaking.** It is possible to identify at least three different collections of material that might be thought of in "record" terms: the record for participation, the record for decision, and the record for judicial review. The record for participation represents the material available to be used by the public as the basis for commenting upon a proposed rule during the proceeding, together with such comments as may be received and made publicly available before the end of the comment period. The record for decision consists of the mass of materials that informs the agency's own decisionmaking processes generally and in the particular rulemaking. The record for review is the documentary collection presented to a court as the basis for deciding whether the rule has sufficient basis to satisfy the applicable standard of judicial review. See Jeffrey S. Lubbers, A Guide to Federal Agency Rulemaking 287–302 (5th ed. 2012).

What are the relationships among the record for participation, the record for decision, and the record for review? Can the record for decision be larger than the record for participation, or must the agency disclose to the public everything that it considers? Can the record for decision be larger than the record for review, or must the agency produce in court all information it is aware of having considered, even information discarded as unreliable or outweighed? How, in this context, is the agency's acquired expertise (distributed among the many members of its staff) to be memorialized? Alternatively, can the record for decision be smaller than the record for review? That is, can the agency produce in court later-arising information that supports the rule it adopted but was not known at the time the rule was made? Questions such as these have provoked a considerable amount of litigation but no easy-to-state result. On the other hand, decisions such as Nova Scotia established that agencies need to make available for public comment studies and other data on which they rely and Vermont Yankee assumed that the agency would produce a record for judicial review. As a result, agencies today are very conscious of the need to keep a record during the rulemaking process and usually would not leave the record to be compiled later in an enforcement proceeding or on judicial review.

NOTES ON THE OPPORTUNITY TO PARTICIPATE

(1) *Participation in Rulemaking.* It is not surprising that the subject of the enforcement action in the case—Nova Scotia, a private party—submitted tough comments to the FDA. An industry trade group, the National Fisheries Institute, participated as well in the rulemaking process. (Often, public interest groups file views too but did not in this case.[8]) Commenting can also come from within the government. The Department of Interior's Bureau of Commercial Fisheries challenged the FDA's proposal; indeed, although it did not focus on the source of the challenge, the court found the FDA's response to this sister agency insufficient. The Small Business Administration's Office of Advocacy, which by statute is tasked with representing the interests of small business within the federal government, often files comments in other agencies' rulemakings.

Section 553(c) provides that the opportunity to participate in informal rulemaking shall be given to "interested persons." Section 551(2) defines "person" inclusively, excepting only the agency itself. Section 551(3) then defines "party" as a "person or agency" admitted or entitled to be admitted as a "party" "in an agency proceeding"; and § 551(12) defines "agency proceeding" to include rulemaking. Arguably, party status is relevant for *formal* rulemaking, where an oral hearing usually occurs and the procedures of §§ 556 and 557 generally apply, but the reference to "interested persons" in § 553 suggests that any person or group who files timely comments is entitled to participate. Filing a comment with an agency, of course, is different than being able to challenge the final result in court.

The APA does not discuss how long the commenting period should last. Rather, recent Executive Orders have set a 60-day floor for "most" rulemakings.[9] In practice, the length of comment periods varies widely,

---

[8] "In response [to the FDA's NPRM], comments were received from two trade associations, eight manufacturers, and the Bureau of Commercial Fisheries, Department of Interior." 35 Fed. Reg. 17,401 (Nov. 13, 1970).

[9] "In addition, each agency should afford the public a meaningful opportunity to comment on any proposed regulation, which in most cases should include a comment period of not less

including shrinking near the end of a presidential administration. Interested persons (including members of Congress) also often seek extensions in the length of the comment period (for instance, for "collection of information" or to "improve the quality of responses"), which agencies sometime grant. See, e.g., Tom Zanki, SEC Extends Comment Period of Mining Disclosure Rule, Law360, Jan. 22, 2016; Enhancing Airline Passenger Protections rule discussed in Chapter I, p. 14. For some information on how to submit an effective comment, see http://regulationroom.org/learn/what-effective-commenting.

(2) *Necessity of Raising Issues with the Agency and Strategic Considerations.* Often, the failure to comment on an issue counts as procedural "default," barring certain challenges in court. Thus, commenters often have an incentive to raise matters initially before the agency. For further discussion, see below, Ch. IX, Subsec. 2.c, on exhaustion of administrative remedies (p. 1413). Consider JUDGE STEPHEN WILLIAMS'S concurrence in KORETOFF V. VILSACK, 707 F.3d 394, 401 (D.C. Cir. 2013): "Generally speaking, then, the price for a ticket to facial review is to raise objections in the rulemaking. This system probably operates quite well for large industry associations and consumer or environmental groups (and the firms and individuals thus represented). But for some the impact is more severe. Firms filling niche markets, for example, as appellants appear to be, may be ill-represented by broad industry groups and unlikely to be adequately lawyered-up at the rulemaking stage. As the Fifth Circuit observed, we presumably do not want to 'require everyone who wishes to protect himself from arbitrary agency action not only to become a faithful reader of the notices of proposed rulemaking published each day in the Federal Register, but a psychic able to predict the possible changes that could be made in the proposal when the rule is finally promulgated.' City of Seabrook, 659 F.2d at 1360–61." When, if ever, should there be a procedural default rule for those who fail to comment? Commenting is not costless. How should entities consider the costs and benefits to participating in a rulemaking?

Agencies can generally waive an objection to failure to participate in the rulemaking. The Supreme Court, in EPA v. EME Homer City Generation L.P., 134 S.Ct. 1584 (2014), addressed whether a court can consider an argument that was not raised during rulemaking proceedings. The Court held that the Clean Air Act's requirement that "[o]nly an objection to a rule . . . raised with reasonable specificity during the period for public comment . . . may be raised during judicial review," 42 U.S.C. § 7607(d)(7)(B), was not a jurisdictional requirement and could be waived by the agency.

(3) *A Never-Ending Circle?* Are there limits on the scope of an agency's obligation to disclose and provide an opportunity to comment? RYBACHEK V. EPA, 904 F.2d 1276, 1281, 1286 (9th Cir. 1990), dealt with multiple challenges to EPA regulations issued under the Clean Water Act. The regulations addressed discharges into streams from placer mining operations; they had, in the judge's words, "particular impact on the gold-

---

than 60 days." E.O. 12866, § 6(a), 58 Fed. Reg. 51,735 (Sept. 30, 1993). This Order is discussed in more detail in Section 4.d below.

rich streambeds of Alaska." The first named challenger was "Rosalie A. Rybachek, North Pole, Alaska, pro se.": "The Rybacheks allege that the EPA's addition of over 6,000 pages to the administrative record, after the public review-and-comment period had ended, violated their right to comment on the record.

"We disagree. The EPA has not violated the Rybacheks' right to meaningful public participation. The additional material was the EPA's response to comments made during a public-comment period. Nothing prohibits the Agency from adding supporting documentation for a final rule in response to public comments. In fact, adherence to the Rybacheks' view might result in the EPA's never being able to issue a final rule capable of standing up to review: every time the Agency responded to public comments, such as those in this rulemaking, it would trigger a new comment period. Thus, either the comment period would continue in a never-ending circle, or, if the EPA chose not to respond to the last set of public comments, any final rule could be struck down for lack of support in the record. The Rybacheks' unviolated right was to comment on the proposed regulations, not to comment in a never-ending way on the EPA's responses to their comments."

Contrast Rybachek with OBER V. EPA, 84 F.3d 304, 314 (9th Cir. 1996). The EPA proposed to approve Arizona's plan for implementing the Clean Air Act, which included controls on particulate matter in Phoenix. In December, four months after the deadline for public comment passed, at the EPA's request, the state submitted an additional 300 pages of information responding to various comments that had suggested that additional control measures could be, and legally had to be, taken. The EPA accepted the state's justifications for not taking those measures and approved the proposed plan. The opinion for the court by JUDGE TROTT held that acceptance of this submission without offering others a chance to comment on it violated the APA:

"In Rybachek, the added materials were the EPA's own responses to comments received during the public comment period. Here, in contrast, the additional documentation was submitted by the State in response to the EPA's request for further information related to the rejection of control measures. Thus, the additional materials in Rybachek involved the EPA's internal assessment of comments from the public; whereas, here, the new information was solicited by the EPA from an interested party. . . . [I]n Rybachek, the EPA's responses related to the economic impact of the regulations on one group of miners. The additional information was not relied on or critical to the EPA's decision. Instead, the EPA decided not to alter the regulation based on the additional information it developed in response to the comments. Here, on the other hand, the added material related to the Implementation Plan's compliance with a critical statutory provision. . . ."

Do these distinctions make sense? Do they have a basis in § 553? If the EPA had made its request as part of its initial NPRM, and the state had submitted its documentation as part of its comment package on the final day of comments—as is typical on long comments filed by sophisticated rulemaking commenters (see US Airways's comment in the Introductory example on p. 14), to what procedural rights should Ober have had to respond? For more on proposals on interactive commenting, see Ch. VI, Sec. 6 (p. 763).

(4) ***The Impact of e-Rulemaking.*** Since 2008, virtually all agencies that engage in any appreciable amount of rulemaking do so electronically. Many—except for a few independent agencies, such as the Federal Communications Commission, who use their own websites—use the government's central portal, www.regulations.gov, to post their notices of proposed rulemaking and accept comments. We take up this topic in Ch. VI, Sec. 6 (p. 757). For now, we quickly raise several issues covered in more depth there.

First, under the E-Government Act of 2002, there are supposed to be "e-dockets" containing "public submissions [i.e., comments] and other materials that by agency rule or practice are included in the rulemaking docket . . . whether or not submitted electronically." In addition, in 2011, President Obama, by Executive Order 13563, ordered agencies to "provide, for both proposed and final rules, timely online access to the rulemaking docket on regulations.gov." If you look at www.regulations.gov, however, this still has not been fully accomplished. The completeness of the supporting materials and the speed and completeness of posting public comments vary dramatically from agency to agency.

Second, some administrative law scholars predicted that e-rulemaking would significantly expand public participation. See, e.g., Beth Simone Noveck, The Electronic Revolution in Rulemaking, 53 Emory L.J. 433 (2004). An early review of empirical data, however, found no "dramatic changes in the general level or quality of public participation in the rulemaking process. Most rules still garner relatively few overall comments and even fewer comments from individual citizens. As in the past, the occasional rulemaking does continue to attract a large number of citizen comments, but most of these comments remain quite unsophisticated, if not duplicative." Cary Coglianese, Citizen Participation in Rulemaking: Past, Present, and Future, 55 Duke L.J. 943, 958–59 (2006). More recently, in Executive Order 13563, President Obama also directed agencies "[t]o the extent feasible and permitted by law, . . . [to] afford the public a meaningful opportunity to comment through the Internet on any proposed regulation, with a comment period that should generally be at least 60 days." There have been some high-profile examples of e-rulemaking, including the FCC's net neutrality rulemaking in 2014 (see p. 765). That rulemaking crashed the FCC's website (after late-night host John Oliver encouraged his viewers to comment) and in the end produced approximately four million comments, many of which lacked any meaningful content.

NOTES ON THE CONCISE GENERAL STATEMENT OF THE RULE'S BASIS AND PURPOSE

(1) ***An Inadequate Statement?*** In Nova Scotia, the FDA issued its final rule in November 1970; it ran under two pages in the Federal Register. (The

proposed rule in 1969 ran under two pages as well). The complete prelude to the actual regulatory terms in the final rule read as follows:

> Current good manufacturing practice (sanitation) in manufacture, processing, packing, or holding of smoked and smoke-flavored fish for human food.

> In the Federal Register of October 23, 1969 (34 F.R. 17176), the Commissioner of Food and Drugs proposed regulations (Subpart A, Part 128a) covering current good manufacturing practice (sanitation) in the manufacture, processing, packing, or holding of smoked fish. In response, comments were received from two trade associations, eight manufacturers, and the Bureau of Commercial Fisheries, Department of Interior. The comments include opposition to certain requirements and suggestions for clarifying and technical changes.

> The principal objection is that the process requirements in the proposed regulations cannot be applied to all species of fish presently being smoked by the industry and that the regulations should therefore specify time-temperature requirements, as developed by research and study, on a species-by-species basis.

> The Commissioner finds: (1) That although adequate times, temperatures, and salt concentrations have not been demonstrated for each individual species of fish presently smoked, the processing requirements of the proposed regulations are the safest now known to prevent the outgrowth and toxin formation of C. botulinum Type E; and (2) that since the public health hazard of C. botulinum Type E in smoked fish is not restricted to a single species of fish, the conditions of current good manufacturing practice for this industry should be established without further delay.

> Therefore, having considered the comments received and other relevant material, the Commissioner concludes that the proposed regulations, with most of the suggested clarifying and technical changes incorporated, should be adopted as set forth below. Accordingly, pursuant to provisions of the Federal Food, Drug, and Cosmetic Act (secs. 402(a) (4), 701(a), 52 Stat. 1046, 1055: 21 U.S.C. 342(a) (4), 371(a)) and under authority delegated to the Commissioner (21 CFR 2.120), the following new Subpart A is added to Part 128a. . . .

35 Fed. Reg. 17,401 (1970).

In addition to faulting the FDA for not disclosing its underlying data, the Nova Scotia court also concluded that the agency had violated § 553's concise general statement requirement by not adequately considering (i) whether it was necessary to promulgate a rule applicable to all species of fish, and (ii) the claim that application of the T-T-S regulation rendered whitefish commercially unsaleable. Do you agree with the court's conclusion? Although the FDA did not respond to these claims in detail, it did note that safe species-by-species parameters did not exist and stressed the need to address potential health risks without delay. (It did, however, end up regulating chub separately.) Should that have sufficed? Today it is not uncommon for the "Preamble" to a final rule, where the agency makes its "concise general statement of basis and purpose," to run to dozens of pages.

(2) ***Statutes versus Regulations.*** Imagine that Congress had debated and then enacted precisely the same text as the FDA adopted as its regulation— that is, statutorily preferring the administrative convenience of a provision reaching all forms of smoked and/or salted fish to species-by-species requirements. The only procedural rights Nova Scotia would have had in that process would be those provided by congressional rules and practice; under the Londoner/Bi-Metallic distinction, see p. 218, Nova Scotia would have had no constitutional claim to individualized process. Moreover, the claim that Congress should have adopted more species-specific measures would seem destined to fail under the lenient rationality review that ordinarily applies to economic and social legislation. Should this legislative analogy be relevant in assessing the APA's requirements? To the extent differences exist between the legislative analogy and the procedural requirements courts have imposed on rulemaking, can they be justified?

(3) ***Timing and Inadequate Consideration of Alternatives.*** An unusual feature of Nova Scotia, which the court notes, is that the challenge to the rule came as a defense to an enforcement proceeding. Since Abbott Laboratories v. Gardner, 387 U.S. 136 (1967) (p. 1375), the more common form of judicial review of rulemaking has been a preenforcement action challenging the rule before it can be applied (see Ch. IX, Sec. 2, p. 1368). Interestingly, Abbott was decided in time for Nova Scotia to bring a preenforcement challenge, but it did not do so.

Does the enforcement posture heighten the potential for unfair hindsight in concluding that the agency should have considered alternatives that would have addressed the challenging party's circumstances—and help to explain the FDA's lack of response to concerns specific to whitefish? At the time of the rulemaking, the agency is focused on the general problem, but a court entertaining a challenge to the regulation years later in an enforcement proceeding is more likely to see matters through the prism of whitefish in particular.

STEPHEN BREYER, JUDICIAL REVIEW OF QUESTIONS OF LAW AND POLICY, 38 Admin. L. Rev. 363, 393 (1986): "The reason agencies do not explore all arguments or consider all alternatives is one of practical limits of time and resources. Yet, to have to explain and to prove all this to a reviewing court risks imposing much of the very burden that not considering alternatives aims to escape. Of course, the reviewing courts may respond that only *important* alternatives and arguments must be considered. But, what counts as 'important'? District courts often find that parties, having barely mentioned a legal point at the trial level, suddenly make it the heart of their case on appeal, emphasizing its (sudden but) supreme importance. Appellate courts typically consider such arguments as long as they have been at least mentioned in the district court. But district courts, unlike agencies dealing with policy change, do not face, say, 10,000 comments challenging different aspects of complex policies. And, when appellate courts 'answer' an argument they write a few words or paragraphs, perhaps citing a case or two. A satisfactory answer in the agency context may mean factfinding, empirical research, detailed investigation. Accordingly, one result of strict judicial review of agency policy decisions is a strong conservative pressure in favor of the status quo."

To the extent that an agency's obligation to consider various points, or to explain its resolution of them, is determined by the issues raised during the notice-and-comment proceeding, the nature of "reasoned decisionmaking" will be contingent on the history of the particular proceeding. Yet the agency ought to address *some* matters regardless whether anyone has commented on them—for example, its basic legal authority for promulgating the regulation. See the State Farm case, p. 1069. The dividing line between these two sorts of issues is likely to be tested only when someone seeks judicial review on an issue not pressed before the agency itself.

(4) ***Consideration of Statutory Objectives.*** Must an adequate "concise general statement" address how a regulation furthers the goals of the statute pursuant to which it is issued? INDEPENDENT U.S. TANKER OWNERS COMMITTEE V. DOLE, 809 F.2d 847 (D.C. Cir. 1987), involved a "payback rule" promulgated by the Secretary of Transportation, under which tanker vessels built with the assistance of a federal subsidy, and barred from competing in domestic trade as a result, could undertake domestic operations if they agreed to pay back the unamortized amount of the subsidy, plus interest, during a one-year period. The background to the rule was that, even with government subsidies up to half the cost of construction, American ships had great difficulty competing in foreign commerce. The opening of the Trans-Alaska Pipeline in 1976 led to a great demand for large tankers in the domestic shipping market to transport Alaskan oil to other points in the country. In 1985, the Maritime Administration responded with the payback rule, and owners of unsubsidized ships operating in the domestic trade sued. The rule was promulgated under the Merchant Marine Act, codified at 46 U.S.C. § 50101 et seq., which delegated "broad power . . . to foster the development and encourage the maintenance of an American merchant marine" that was, among other items, "sufficient to carry the waterborne domestic commerce and a substantial portion of the waterborne export and import foreign commerce of the United States . . . at all times" and "capable of serving as a naval and military auxiliary in time of war or national emergency."

In a unanimous opinion written by JUDGE BORK, the D.C. Circuit held that the payback rule was arbitrary and capricious because the Secretary had failed to comply with § 553's concise general statement requirement in issuing it: "This statement need not be an exhaustive, detailed account of every aspect of the rulemaking proceedings; it is not meant to be the more elaborate document, complete with findings of fact and conclusions of law, that is required in an on-the-record rulemaking. See id. § 557(c). On the other hand, this court has cautioned against 'an overly literal reading of the statutory terms "concise" and "general" . . . [which] must be accommodated to the realities of judicial scrutiny.' Automotive Parts & Accessories Ass'n v. Boyd, 407 F.2d 330, 338 (D.C. Cir. 1968). At the least, such a statement should indicate the major issues of policy that were raised in the proceedings and explain why the agency decided to respond to these issues as it did, particularly in light of the statutory objectives that the rule must serve. . . .

"The Secretary's statement of basis and purpose fails to give an adequate account of how the payback rule serves [the statutory] objectives and why alternative measures were rejected in light of them. The Secretary's treatment of these objectives, and of the concerns raised about them in the comment proceedings, is cursory at best. For example, concerns about whether this rule meets the statutory objective of maintaining an American merchant marine 'sufficient to carry its domestic water-borne commerce and a substantial portion of the water-borne export and import foreign commerce' are met with the statement: 'The Department believes that the [rule] will benefit the U.S. Merchant Marine.' . . . On the more dubious proposition that the fleet will remain able to carry 'a substantial portion' of foreign commerce, the Secretary candidly acknowledges that 'the final rule merely recognizes the existing condition of the U.S. tanker fleet. There currently exist few foreign trade employment opportunities for those vessels and the prospects for future employment in the foreign trade are far from bright.' . . . Though this statement strongly suggests the view that this rule will hasten an American retreat from carriage of foreign commerce, the Secretary surprisingly asserts that the fleet will remain 'more than adequate to carry an appropriate share of the U.S. foreign oil commerce if such opportunities should arise.' . . . This remark is hard to fathom. If there is currently little hope for the employment of American vessels in foreign trade, then the payback rule will permit the total size of the American fleet to follow its natural tendency to decrease toward the level required by the domestic market. Under present conditions, therefore, the rule will make it impossible to retain a fleet that can carry all domestic traffic and 'a substantial portion' of foreign traffic 'at all times,' which is explicitly set out as an objective in section (a) of the statute. . . .

"Rather than providing a more extensive discussion of the Merchant Marine Act's objectives, the Secretary chooses to rely on other policies in defending the rule. She identifies some of the 'most important' reasons for the rule as being 'economic efficiency,' 'use of underemployed resources,' 'increased competition,' and 'deregulation.' As she later elaborates: 'It is the Department's position that the competitive forces of the market, rather than government regulation, should be relied upon, whenever feasible, to allocate transportation capacity and resources in domestic trade. This rule reflects that position.' The central thrust of her approach, quite obviously, is to subject the merchant marine fleet to the discipline of the free market.

". . . This policy may well be defensible, yet it is not among the objectives specified in the Act, and if the Secretary has decided that it is implicit in or compatible with the statutory objectives, it would be useful for her to explain this decision somewhat more fully. She had failed to do so. . . ."

In Independent Tankers, the Secretary seems to have provided considerably more by way of explanation than would accompany a statute, but in the eyes of the court the explanation is insufficient. What would it have taken for the Secretary adequately to have explained herself in light of her statutory authority? The court did note that if "present conditions in the world shipping market make it impossible for the Secretary to find a way to meet all of the statutory objectives," "she should discuss it frankly and directly. . . ." The court also unanimously rejected the claim that the payback rule was outside the Secretary's authority under the Merchant Marine Act, even though the rule would appear to make achievement of some statutory objectives impossible. Do you think the court would have been satisfied had the Secretary been more candid about the results of the rule and the impossibility of achieving the statute's goals under current conditions? Or is the problem that an agency can't substitute nonstatutory goals reflecting a different regulatory philosophy for statutory ones? Interestingly, although the court vacated the rule, it delayed the issuance of its mandate for six months "to avoid further disruptions in the domestic market and to allow the Secretary to undertake further proceedings to address the problems of the merchant marine trade."

SECTION 3.　　EXCEPTIONS TO § 553 NOTICE-AND-COMMENT REQUIREMENTS

> **a.　The Good Cause Exception**
> **b.　The Exception for Interpretive Rules, Guidance, and Policy Statements**
> **c.　The Other Exceptions**

Section 553 also contains several provisions exempting certain rules from its requirements. The agency bears the burden of showing that any particular provision applies. These provisions include rules falling under § 553(b)'s "good cause" exception or § 553(a)'s exclusion for matters involving "a military or foreign affairs function" or "relating to agency management or personnel or to public property, loans, grants, benefits or contracts." The exception that has proved the most important and controversial in recent years, however, is § 553(b)'s exception for interpretive rules and policy statements.

a.　The Good Cause Exception

> **UNITED STATES v. DEAN**
> **Notes on Interim Final and Direct Final Rulemaking; Remand Without Vacatur**

[T]his subsection does not apply . . . when the agency for good cause finds (and incorporates the finding and a brief statement of reasons therefor in

the rules issued) that notice and public procedure thereon are impracticable, unnecessary, or contrary to the public interest.

5 U.S.C. § 553(b)(B)

UNITED STATES v. DEAN

United States Court of Appeals for the Eleventh Circuit (2010).
604 F.3d 1275.

■ FARRIS, SENIOR CIRCUIT JUDGE.

[Christopher Dean pleaded guilty to the federal offense of traveling in interstate commerce and knowingly failing to register as a sex offender under the Sex Offender Registration and Notification Act (SORNA), in violation of 18 U.S.C. § 2250(a) (2006). SORNA, which became effective on July 27, 2006, requires states to maintain a sex offender registry and requires individuals convicted of covered offenses to register in whatever state they are located or wherever they relocate. SORNA provides that: "The Attorney General shall have the authority to specify the applicability of the requirements [for registration] to sex offenders convicted before [the statute's effective date] . . . or its implementation in a particular jurisdiction, and to prescribe rules for the registration of any such sex offenders . . . ." 42 U.S.C. §§ 16913(b), (d). In February 2007, the Attorney General promulgated an interim rule, making SORNA fully retroactive. In promulgating the rule, the Attorney General invoked the "good cause" exception and did not provide pre-promulgation notice and a comment period. The Attorney General issued the following statement with the interim rule:

The immediate effectiveness of this rule is necessary to eliminate any possible uncertainty about the applicability of the Act's requirements—and related means of enforcement, including criminal liability under 18 U.S.C. 2250 for sex offenders who knowingly fail to register as required—to sex offenders whose predicate convictions predate the enactment of SORNA. Delay in the implementation of this rule would impede the effective registration of such sex offenders and would impair immediate efforts to protect the public from sex offenders who fail to register through prosecution and the imposition of criminal sanctions. The resulting practical dangers include the commission of additional sexual assaults and child sexual abuse or exploitation offenses by sex offenders that could have been prevented had local authorities and the community been aware of their presence, in addition to greater difficulty in apprehending perpetrators who have not been registered and tracked as provided by SORNA. This would thwart the legislative objective of "protect[ing] the public from sex offenders and offenders against children" by establishing "a comprehensive national system for the registration of those offenders," SORNA Sec. 102, because a substantial class of sex offenders could evade the Act's registration requirements and enforcement mechanisms during the pendency of a proposed rule and delay in the effectiveness of a final rule.

It would accordingly be contrary to the public interest to adopt this rule with the prior notice and comment period normally required under 5 U.S.C. 553(b) or with the delayed effective date normally required under 5 U.S.C. 553(d).

72 Fed. Reg. 8894, 8896–97 (2007). The Attorney General accepted post-promulgation comments on the rule through April 30, 2007. These comments were addressed in proposed National Guidelines issued in May 2007; the final version of the Guidelines issued a year later.

Dean, who had been convicted of the underlying offense in 1994, challenged his SORNA conviction on several grounds, including that the Attorney General erred in adopting the rule making SORNA retroactive without notice and comment under § 553(b)'s "good cause" exception. Other circuit circuits had split on the legality of the Attorney General's invocation of the exception.] . . .

We have indicated previously that the good cause exception "should be read narrowly," . . . [but the] exception is . . . "an important safety valve to be used where delay would do real harm." United States Steel Corp. v. EPA, 595 F.2d 207, 214 (5th Cir. 1979). In United States Steel Corp., we noted that "[u]se of the exception has repeatedly been approved, for example, in cases involving government price controls, because of the market distortions caused by the announcement of future controls. The exception was also held applicable to regulations concerning gas stations, where temporary shortages and discriminatory practices were found to have deprived some users of any supply and led to violence." Id. at 214 n. 15 (citations omitted). . . .

Only two other circuits have addressed this issue, and they reached different conclusions. United States v. Gould, 568 F.3d 459, 470 (4th Cir. 2009), upheld the Attorney General's invocation of good cause . . . [concluding] that "[t]here was a need for legal certainty about SORNA's 'retroactive' application to sex offenders convicted before SORNA and a concern for public safety that these offenders be registered in accordance with SORNA as quickly as possible." In particular the court found that "[d]elaying implementation of the regulation to accommodate notice and comment could reasonably be found to put the public safety at greater risk." . . .

The Sixth Circuit disagreed in United States v. Cain, 583 F.3d 408 (6th Cir. 2009). . . . [It] concluded that uncertainty was not good cause because every regulation is designed to provide some type of guidance. It also concluded that Congress had already built in some amount of uncertainty and delay into the design of the statute . . . [and] highlighted the Attorney General's own seven-month delay in issuing the regulation.

The court concluded that Congress had already balanced the costs and benefits of delay in not exempting SORNA from APA procedures . . . [and emphasized that the agency was not] facing a statutory deadline. The *Cain* court . . . indicated that the safety concern had previously been used when the "emergency situation arose *after* the statutory enactment at issue" . . . and noted that agencies have previously given specific reasons "to conclude that [their] regulations insufficiently protected public safety, and those reasons arose after the existing regulations went into effect." The court concluded that the "Attorney General gave no specific evidence of actual harm to the public in his conclusory statement of reasons, and gave no explanation for why he could act in an emergency fashion when Congress had not deemed the situation so critical seven months earlier."

We address the Attorney General's guidance argument first. . . . In United States Steel Corp., the EPA alleged that an immediate rule without notice and comment was necessary to provide guidance to the states. We found the need to provide guidance rationale faltered because States already had most of the information the EPA rule provided, the designations at issue were actually based on submissions by the States, and the EPA's role "is limited to reviewing the state designations and modifying them where necessary." In stark contrast, the agency here was **No guidance** granted sole discretion to determine whether SORNA applies retroactively, and there was no guidance at all in place in that matter. The guidance rationale is particularly important here as the persons who were affected by the rule were already convicted of their prior crimes and need to know whether to register. . . . While this reason alone may not have established the good cause exception, it does count to some extent.

We do, however, find unpersuasive the argument that post-promulgation comments were sufficient to ameliorate the lack of pre-promulgation notice and comment. We previously rejected this harmless error argument in United States Steel Corp., . . . [on the grounds] that allowing post-promulgation comments to resolve any harm caused by a lack of notice and comment would render the notice and comment provision toothless.

Holding . . . We conclude that the public safety argument advanced by the Attorney General is good cause for bypassing the notice and comment period. Retroactive application of the rule allowed the federal government to immediately start prosecuting sex offenders who failed to register in state registries. In practical terms, the retroactive rule reduced the risk of additional sexual assaults and sexual abuse by sex offenders by allowing federal authorities to apprehend and prosecute them. The retroactive application of SORNA also removes a barrier to timely apprehension of sex offenders. . . . [Cain held] that the safety prong of the good cause exception can only be invoked in emergency situations. However, the D.C. Circuit has noted that "the exception excuses notice and comment in emergency situations, *or* where delay could result in serious harm." *Jifry v. FAA*, 370 F.3d 1174, 1179 (D.C.

Cir. 2004) [p. 351]. . . . We hold that there does not need to be an emergency situation and the Attorney General only has to show that there is good cause to believe that delay would do real harm.

Holding

. . . Cain also reasoned that Congress built in a period of delay and the Attorney General delayed seven-months; therefore delay cannot constitute good cause. We disagree. All Congressional directives to an agency to implement rules are subject to delay as the agency considers the rule and then promulgates it. If Congress were required to create the substantive administrative rules by itself to avoid notice and comment, then the good cause exception would be meaningless. An agency could never demonstrate good cause since delay is inevitably built in as the agency brings its expertise to bear on the issue. The question is whether further delay will cause harm, and here it was reasonably determined that waiting thirty additional days for the notice and comment period to pass would do real harm.

The final argument advanced against bypassing notice and comment is that "the harm to the general public would result from delay assumes that it was inevitable that [the Attorney General] would declare that SORNA applied retroactively." Gould, 568 F.3d at 479 (Michael, J., dissenting). This is true of any rule that bypasses the notice and comment provision. The harm to the public from delay is premised on the promulgated rule staying as is even through the notice and comment phase. This argument is also premised on the idea that the rule creates the harm. . . . However, the harm exists already. Sex offenders are not registering with state jurisdictions. Since the good cause exception already assumes that the regulation will remain in place, this argument is not a reason to reject an invocation of the exception. . . .

Affirmed.

■ WILSON, CIRCUIT JUDGE, concurring in the result.

The Attorney General failed to show good cause to avoid the notice and comment requirements of the Administrative Procedure Act. At oral argument, the government conceded that at the time of his arrest Dean could have been charged with failing to register under either of two existing laws. The first was the Alabama law that provides for up to ten years in prison, a sentence as long as the one provided by SORNA. The second was "Megan's Law," the federal law that provides for up to one year in prison. The government's concession highlights the lack of an emergency or threat of real harm attending the promulgation of the regulation. There was little if any support for the Attorney General's public safety justification that notice and comment "would impair immediate efforts to protect the public from sex offenders who fail to register *through prosecution and the imposition of criminal sanctions*." The issue is not whether sex offenders should register, but rather whether the addition of one more layer of federal protection atop a substantial quilt of existing state and federal laws merited emergency treatment. . . .

While I take seriously Congress's mandate that sex offenders register their whereabouts, I accord equal respect to Congress's requirement that executive agencies provide notice and accept comment before binding this nation with their rules. The majority opinion quotes but does not give due weight to our circuit's law requiring us to construe narrowly the good cause exceptions to notice and comment.... "Certainly, a criminal prosecution founded on an agency rule should be held to the strict letter of the APA." United States v. Picciotto, 875 F.2d 345, 346 (D.C. Cir. 1989).[8] ...

The bottom line is that Congress factored delay into SORNA when it wrote the law. To this point the majority opinion has no good reply.... Congress unquestionably had the power to release the Attorney General from the requirements of the APA. Indeed, Congress could have decided on its own to make SORNA apply to pre-enactment convictions, instead of delegating that decision to the Attorney General. Congress however unambiguously declined to adopt either option. Congress balanced the costs and benefits of allowing the Attorney General to determine SORNA's pre-enactment reach, and in doing so it countenanced the inevitable delays of administrative rulemaking.... What's more, Congress's allocation of three years, plus extensions, to the states to comply with SORNA means Congress did not perceive an emergency....

... [H]owever, ... I concur in the result upholding [Dean's] conviction because another, equally potent requirement of the APA compels it: harmless error review. The passage of five months between promulgation of the regulation and Dean's arrest rendered harmless the lack of pre-enactment notice and comment.... [T]here was nothing in Dean's appellate briefs or his counsel's presentation at oral argument that suggested a reason he could have offered that might have persuaded the Attorney General not to extend SORNA to cover pre-enactment convictions.

NOTES

(1) **SORNA's Circuit Split.** Courts continue to face substantive and procedural challenges to the validity of the Attorney General's regulation making SORNA fully retroactive. In United States v. Lott, 750 F.3d 214, 219 & n. 6 (2d Cir. 2014), the Second Circuit held that the Attorney General complied with the APA's good cause exception, but in United States v. Reynolds, 710 F.3d 498 (3d Cir. 2013), the Third Circuit held that the Attorney General did not show good cause for issuing the rule without notice and comment. In so holding, the Third Circuit noted that the Fifth, Sixth,

---

[8] The majority opinion [gives] little credit to another justification from the Attorney General: a desire to provide guidance justified emergency treatment. The argument may not deserve even that much credit. In his powerful dissent in United States v. Gould, Judge Michael noted that an agency that wishes to eliminate uncertainty should not label its regulation an "interim rule" or issue a call for post-promulgation comments, "because the possibility of an alteration to the interim rule after its promulgation increases rather than eliminates uncertainty." 568 F.3d 459, 479 (4th Cir. 2009) (Michael, J., dissenting).

and Ninth Circuits agreed that good cause was lacking, while the Fourth and Eleventh Circuits have held that the Attorney General did have good cause. Most recently, the D.C. Circuit joined the majority of circuits that have considered the issue in United States v. Ross, 848 F.3d 1129 (D.C. Cir, 2017). Construing the exception narrowly, the D.C. Circuit relied on Reynolds, holding that the actions of Congress—providing a three-year period for implementation—and the "Attorney General's own behavior also undercuts the current claim of urgency: as Reynolds observed, he waited over half a year—217 days—after the effective date of the act to publish the Interim Rule." The Supreme Court has not granted certiorari on the issue.

(2) *A Narrow Exception?* Was Judge Wilson correct in faulting the majority for taking too expansive a view of the good cause exception? Should the exception be viewed narrowly? Or has judicial elaboration of § 553's requirements made a broad reading of the exception more appropriate? Put differently, should courts treat § 553's requirements and exceptions consistently, reading both either narrowly or expansively, or is there a reason to distinguish between these two components of § 553?

(3) *Prevalent Use of Exception and Ongoing Concerns.* The GOVERNMENT ACCOUNTABILITY OFFICE (GAO) recently investigated the process (or lack thereof) used by agencies in rulemaking. Its findings are surprising: "During calendar years 2003 through 2010, agencies published 568 major rules and about 30,000 nonmajor rules. . . . [A]gencies published about 35 percent of major rules and about 44 percent of nonmajor rules without an NPRM during those years. Examples of major rules without an NPRM include a May 2010 Department of the Treasury final rule prohibiting certain consumer credit practices, for which the agency invoked the good cause exception, and a September 2008 Department of Health and Human Services (HHS) notice that announced Medicare cost-sharing amounts, for which the agency cited an exception in the Social Security Act and good cause. . . . [M]any nonmajor rules without an NPRM appeared to involve routine, administrative, or technical issues. . . . [E]xamples of nonmajor rules without an NPRM that we identified during this review included a January 2007 Department of Homeland Security (DHS) temporary final rule changing drawbridge operation hours for certain bridges in Florida, and a July 2009 Federal Election Commission rule allowing a committee that is being audited by the Commission to have a hearing prior to the Commission's adoption of a final audit report. . . . The agencies that published rules in our sample claimed the good cause exception in 77 (plus or minus 11) percent of major rules and 61 (plus or minus 10) percent of nonmajor rules without an NPRM . . . ." GAO, FEDERAL RULEMAKING: AGENCIES COULD TAKE ADDITIONAL STEPS TO RESPOND TO PUBLIC COMMENTS, GAO–13–21 (December 2012), at 8–10, 15.[10] For more on post-promulgation commenting, see discussion of interim rules in the next set of Notes below, p. 353.

(4) *Mistake as Good Cause and Harmless Error from Lack of Process?* In UTILITY SOLID WASTE ACTIVITIES GROUP V. EPA, 236 F.3d 749 (D.C. Cir. 2000), which involved EPA cleanup and decontamination

---

[10]   www.gao.gov/assets/660/651052.pdf.

standards for PCB spills, the D.C. Circuit considered whether correcting a mistake could qualify as good cause. The EPA had long prohibited any further use of porous surfaces contaminated by PCB spills at concentrations of 50 parts per million (ppm) or more that could not be cleaned to a surface concentration of 10 micrograms PCBs per square centimeters ("10 mcg/100 cm2"). In a 1998 rulemaking, responding to comments that this prohibition was overly severe, the EPA promulgated a new rule allowing use of "porous surfaces contaminated by spills of liquid PCBs at concentrations greater than or equal to 10 mcg/100 cm2 for the remainder of the useful life of the surfaces and subsurface material," provided certain conditions for cleaning, painting, and marking the surface were met. Note that this new standard set as the *trigger* for requiring cleanup the 10 microgram *surface concentration* level the EPA previously required as a result of a cleanup, rather than the 50 ppm *spill concentration* level that had previously been the trigger. The EPA's statement of basis and purpose did not mention this change of parameter and apparently it was an error. Without using § 553's notice-and-comment procedures, the EPA soon amended § 761.30(p)(1) to return to the 50 ppm spill cleanup trigger. It characterized the change as a "minor technical amendment" to correct an obvious drafting error which, it credibly asserted, had resulted from careless use of a word processing find/replace command.

The D.C. Circuit held that the exception did not apply, emphasizing that the good cause exception "is not an escape clause" and "is to be narrowly construed and only reluctantly countenanced." In particular, the court insisted that there was "no threat to the environment or human health or . . . some sort of emergency" to allow invocation of the impracticability ground, and concluded that the public interest ground only applied in instances in which the goal of the regulation would be defeated by prior notice. Quoting the Attorney General's Manual, it further held that " 'unnecessary' refers to the issuance of a minor rule in which the public is not particularly interested,' " which was not the case here, as some surfaces that would have been unregulated under the issued rule were now subject to regulation, "something about which these members of the public were greatly interested." Interestingly, the court also refused to hold the failure to engage in notice and comment was harmless error: "This seems to us merely another way of saying that the change in the rule was unimportant, having no significant impact. We have already rejected that position." Should the D.C. Circuit have been more willing to allow the EPA's change? Does your answer to that turn at all on whether the question of the appropriateness of the 50 ppm spill trigger was raised in the original rulemaking? Do you think the court should have sustained the change on harmless error grounds, even if it found the good cause exception inapplicable? Would remand without vacatur, p. 355, be an appropriate remedy in this situation?

(5) *Deference to Agency's Determination that Good Cause Exists?* Should a court defer to an agency's determination that good cause exists? The Third Circuit's decision on the SORNA rule summarized the issue in this way: "(1) What is the appropriate standard of review of an agency's assertion of good cause in waiving the APA's notice and comment requirements? . . .

On the first question, the Fifth and Eleventh Circuits have determined that the arbitrary and capricious standard is the appropriate standard for reviewing the Attorney General's actions, the Fourth and Sixth Circuits have not stated a standard but appear to use de novo review, and the Ninth Circuit has explicitly avoided the question." 710 F.3d at 502.

Contrast two cases from the D.C. Circuit. In SORENSEN COMMUNICATIONS LTD. V. FCC, 755 F.3d 702, 706 (D.C. Cir. 2014), the D.C. Circuit held that the standard of review for an agency's invocation of the good cause exception was de novo, rejecting the FCC's call for deference: "To accord deference would be to run afoul of congressional intent. From the outset, we note an agency has no interpretive authority over the APA, see Envirocare of Utah, Inc. v. NRC, 194 F.3d 72 (D.C.Cir.1999); we cannot find that an exception applies simply because the agency says we should. Moreover, the good-cause inquiry is meticulous and demanding, [and our] caselaw indicates we are to narrowly construe and reluctantly countenance the exception. Deference to an agency's invocation of good cause—particularly when its reasoning is potentially capacious, as is the case here—would conflict with this court's deliberate and careful treatment of the exception in the past. Therefore, our review of the agency's legal conclusion of good cause is de novo." The Sorensen court proceeded to reject the FCC's invocation of good cause at issue, noting that the FCC cited "the threat of impending fiscal peril as cause for waiving notice and comment" of its rule regulating provision of captioning telephones and services for the hearing impaired, but "[c]uriously . . . there were no factual findings supporting the reality of the threat" to the federal fund that pays for captioning services. The court added: "[W]e do not exclude the possibility that a fiscal calamity could conceivably justify bypassing the notice-and-comment requirement, [but] this case does not provide evidence of such an exigency. . . . Though no particular catechism is necessary to establish good cause, something more than an unsupported assertion is required." Id. at 706–07.

By contrast, in JIFRY V. FAA, 370 F.3d 1174, 1179–80 (D.C. Cir. 2004), the D.C. Circuit upheld regulations providing for automatic suspension of a pilot's airman certificate—without which a pilot cannot fly in the United States—upon the FAA's being notified by the Transportation Security Administration (TSA) that the pilot poses a security threat. The regulations were issued without notice and comment, and the agency invoked the good cause exception in justification. In sustaining the FAA's action, the D.C. Circuit rejected the argument that the FAA's preexisting unlimited power to revoke a certificate immediately if it believed a pilot to be a security threat precluded good cause from existing here: "[A]t the time the challenged regulations were adopted, the FAA's power to suspend or revoke certificates was permissive only. Congress had not yet enacted [statutory provisions] formaliz[ing] the requirement that the FAA shall suspend, modify, or revoke a certificate if notified by the TSA that the individual posed a security risk. . . . The TSA and FAA deemed [automatic suspension or revocation] . . . necessary 'in order to minimize security threats and potential security vulnerabilities to the fullest extent possible.' Given [their] legitimate concern over the threat of further terrorist acts involving aircraft in the aftermath of

September 11, 2001, the agencies had 'good cause' for not offering advance public participation."

Are public safety contexts more deserving of deference? For the view that the courts have taken a very deferential view of agency good cause determinations based on national security post-September 11, see Adrian Vermeule, Our Schmittian Administrative Law, 122 Harv. L. Rev. 1095, 1122–25 (2009).

(6) *Repeated Assertion of Good Cause.* Can an agency's repeated assertion of the good cause exception in the same context ever be anything other than an effort to avoid notice-and-comment rulemaking? In OREGON TROLLERS ASS'N V. GUTIERREZ, 452 F.3d 1104, 1123–25 (9th Cir. 2006), the Ninth Circuit held that an agency's repeated annual invocation of the good cause exception does not render the exception unavailable, provided the agency justifies its decision to forego public notice and comment with specific reasons related to the year at issue and "not generic complaints about time pressure and data collection difficulties." It found that the National Marine Fisheries Service had done so in regard to its issuance of fishery management measures for the Klamath River in 2005. The agency emphasized the importance of setting fishing regulations based on current salmon stock projections. Those projections, however, are not finalized until early April each year and the fishing season must begin on May 1. Therefore, requiring a sixty-day comment period would require fishing regulations to be completed the previous year without access to complete data on the current stock numbers. In addition, the agency emphasized the need to substantially restrict fishing in 2005 in order to meet fishery plan requirements regarding the minimum number of salmon escaping to spawn. Thus, not granting the good cause exception would contradict the purpose of setting fishing regulations—limiting fishing to a sustainable level in order to protect the salmon population in the Klamath River.

(7) *Alternative Forms of a Good Cause Exception.* Consider this alternative to the APA's good cause exception, from the 2010 Model State Administrative Procedure Act: "SECTION 309. EMERGENCY RULE. If an agency finds that an imminent peril to the public health, safety, or welfare or the loss of federal funding for an agency program requires the immediate adoption of an emergency rule and publishes in a record its reasons for that finding, the agency, without prior notice or hearing or on any abbreviated notice and hearing that it finds practicable, may adopt an emergency rule without complying with [notice-and-comment procedures]. The emergency rule may be effective for not longer than [180] days [renewable once for no more than [180] days]. The adoption of an emergency rule does not preclude the adoption of a rule under [notice-and-comment procedures]. The agency shall file with the [publisher] a rule adopted under this section as soon as practicable given the nature of the emergency, publish the rule on its Internet website, and notify persons that have requested notice of rules related to that subject matter. This section does not prohibit the adoption of a new emergency rule if, at the end of the effective period of the original emergency rule, the agency finds that the imminent peril to the public health, safety, or welfare or the loss of federal funding for an agency program

still exists." Should the APA be amended to impose a time limit on rules promulgated under the good cause exception? California requires agencies issuing "emergency rules" to provide five calendar days for commenting, unless the "the emergency situation clearly poses such an immediate, serious harm that delaying action to allow public comment would be inconsistent with the public interest." For more information on California's process, see http://oal.ca.gov/regulations/emergency_regulations/Emergency_Regulation_Process/. The proposed Regulatory Accountability Act, discussed above, also contains time limits on "good cause" rules. See S. 951, § 3. Should the APA be amended to impose a minimal comment period for most good cause rules?

NOTES ON INTERIM FINAL AND DIRECT FINAL RULEMAKING AND REMAND WITHOUT VACATUR

(1) *Direct Final and Interim Final Rulemaking Defined.* Over the last decade, agencies have increasingly employed two innovative techniques, direct final rulemaking and interim final rulemaking, as a way of mitigating some of the burdens associated with notice-and-comment rulemaking. Neither of these forms of rulemaking is expressly mentioned in the APA, and their use is usually based on the good cause exception, on the ground that either undertaking notice-and-comment rulemaking prior to implementation is unnecessary or that foregoing normal procedures is justified because of an immediate need. Interim rules also help mitigate problems of retroactive rulemaking (see p. 264), because they go into effect immediately and thus may avert regulatory gaps.

Direct final rulemaking is meant to be used for uncontroversial rules that the agency predicts are unlikely to generate significant adverse comment. In its ideal form, an agency publishes its rule as a direct final rule in the Federal Register and includes a statement indicating that the rule will become final unless significant adverse comment is received by a certain deadline. See also § 553(d). If significant adverse comment is submitted— even if only one comment (though it has to be material)—the agency immediately withdraws the direct final rule and proceeds through notice-and-comment rulemaking. Properly used, Professor Ronald Levin argues, direct final rulemaking should be exempt from "the usual public participation requirements of the APA, because such participation would be 'unnecessary' within the meaning of the good cause exemption of § 553(b)(B)." RONALD M. LEVIN, DIRECT FINAL RULEMAKING, 64 Geo. Wash. L. Rev. 1, 11 (1995).

In contrast, in interim final rulemaking, an agency adopts a rule without public comment, typically makes it immediately effective (using "good cause" under § 553(d)), and then seeks comments post-promulgation. MICHAEL ASIMOW, INTERIM-FINAL RULES: MAKING HASTE SLOWLY, 51 Admin. L. Rev. 703, 710–11 (1999): In determining whether to use interim final rulemaking, an agency "[f]irst decides that it is legally entitled to adopt a rule without engaging in the normal process of pre-adoption public participation. Although several APA exceptions might apply, the occasion for adopting an interim-final rule is often the presence of some exigency that provides good cause for dispensing with public participation. . . . Second, the agency decides that it should solicit post-effective comments and make a commitment to consider those comments at the time it makes the interim-final rule final. Note that this part of the agency's decision is not legally obligatory. Except where statutes require utilization of interim-final methodology, an agency is never required to engage in further process after adopting a rule under the good cause exemption (or any other APA exemption). Solicitation of post-effective comments, consideration of such comments, preparation of a basis and purpose statement, and adoption of a final-final rule modifying the interim-final rule are all time consuming chores that an agency assumes voluntarily."

Professor Levin summarizes the distinction between these two forms of rulemaking in this way: ". . . [I]nterim final rulemaking . . . is generally used because of some felt urgency in instituting a regulation immediately. It frequently involves regulations that are deeply controversial; the agency solicits comment for its own edification or to identify possible bases of legal challenge, but will not alter the rule unless the comment *persuades* it to do so. . . . [In] direct final rulemaking . . . the agency undertakes to withdraw its rule if *anyone* objects. By using direct final rulemaking, the agency is gambling that no one will object. Such universal acquiescence is unlikely in the case of a regulation that is considered urgent enough to warrant interim final rulemaking." Levin, supra, at 3.

(2) *Current Usage and Issues.* Professor Anne Joseph O'Connell conducted a detailed empirical survey of agency rulemaking activities from 1983–2003: "[D]irect and interim final rulemaking have been increasing over time. . . . The 1989, 1993 and 2001 upticks in interim final rulemaking may . . . show that agencies rely on interim final rulemaking in the first year of a presidential administration to achieve regulatory objectives more quickly than they could with notice-and-comment rulemaking." She lists the EPA as reporting by far the greatest number of direct final rules, whereas a number of agencies reported significant usage of interim final rulemaking. Anne Joseph O'Connell, Political Cycles of Rulemaking: An Empirical Portrait of the Modern Administrative State, 94 Va. L. Rev. 889, 930, 933 (2008). There has been some more recent empirical research. A study of FDA rulemaking between 1997 and 2007 determined that the FDA proposed 38 direct final rules. Michael Kolber, Rulemaking without Rules: An Empirical Study of Direct Final Rulemaking, 72 Alb. L. Rev. 79, 82 (2009). The GAO found that between 2003 and 2010, "agencies issued 47 percent of all major final rules and 8 percent of all nonmajor rules without an NPRM as interim rules." GAO, Federal Rulemaking: Agencies Could Take Additional Steps to Respond to Public Comments, supra, at 13.

Debate over direct final rulemaking centers on whether it complies with § 553 and whether agencies are employing it appropriately. For contrasting views on legality, compare Levin, supra, and Ronald M. Levin, More on Direct Final Rulemaking: Streamlining, Not Corner-Cutting, 51 Admin. L. Rev. 757 (1999), with Lars Noah, Doubts About Direct Final Rulemaking, 51 Admin. L. Rev. 401 (1999). The FDA study above concluded that between 1997 and 2007 the agency had to withdraw forty percent of the rules it proposed for direct final rulemaking because it received significant adverse comments. This high rate of withdrawal may be atypical. "Other experiences with direct final rulemaking at the EPA, the Federal Aviation Administration and elsewhere have produced withdrawal rates of less than ten or twenty percent. A withdrawal rate of forty percent is shocking. It suggests either the FDA is dramatically off when predicting which of its rules are likely to be controversial or the FDA is using direct final rulemaking for purposes it was not intended." Kolber, supra, at 82.

The concern raised about interim final rulemaking is that many interim rules remain in effect for years without the issuance of a final rule subject to public comment. Because agency decisions to respond to comments and issue a final-final rule are voluntary, agencies often lack incentives to issue a final rule. "Inertia is at work; the rule is already in effect and nothing really needs to be done about it. Members of the public subject to the rule are complying with it. Busy members of the agency staff feel no pressure to deal with the comments received (if any) or to figure out how to modify the rule in light of the comments or administrative experience. . . . If rules dangle indefinitely in interim limbo, the post-adoption comment period was a waste of everyone's time. Desirable modifications in the rule will not occur." Asimow, supra, at 736–37. The GAO has additional concerns: "When it is unclear whether agencies considered comments, rulemaking is less transparent to the public, and, as courts have recognized, the opportunity to comment is meaningless unless the agency responds to significant points raised by the public." GAO, Federal Rulemaking: Agencies Could Take Additional Steps to Respond to Public Comments, supra, at 29.

One response to this problem would be to require that any interim regulation also be issued as a proposed regulation and expire within a three-year period of its adoption, the approach Congress took in regard to the Internal Revenue Service, see 26 U.S.C. § 7805(e). Should this solution be adopted for all interim-final regulations? For other alternatives, see p. 352.

(3) ***Remand Without Vacatur.*** Another major development is courts' use of remand without vacatur, which tells the agency to reconsider its rule while allowing the rule to stay in effect. We discuss its legality and desirability when we address the availability of judicial review in Chapter IX, Sec. 2 (p. 1437). Here, we address its prevalence and recommendations for when courts should employ the remedy. The Administrative Conference of the United States (ACUS) recently determined that the remedy had been used in "more than seventy decisions of the Court of Appeals for the District of Columbia Circuit involving over twenty federal agencies . . . ." Remand without Vacatur, Administrative Conference Recommendation 2013–6 (adopted Dec. 5, 2013), at 1 (also finding its use in other courts of appeals).[11] See, e.g., Heartland Regional Med. Ctr. v. Sebelius, 566 F.3d 193, 197–98 (D.C. Cir. 2009); Sugar Cane Growers Cooperative v. Veneman, 289 F.3d 89, 98 (D.C. Cir. 2002) (p. 283). In its 2013 recommendation on the remedy, ACUS held: "In determining whether the remedy of remand without vacatur is appropriate, courts should consider equitable factors, including whether: (a) correction is reasonably achievable in light of the nature of the

---

[11] http://www.acus.gov/sites/default/files/documents/Remand%20Without%20Vacatur %20_%20Final%20Recommendation.pdf.

deficiencies in the agency's rule or order; (b) the consequences of vacatur would be disruptive; and (c) the interests of the parties who prevailed against the agency in the litigation would be served by allowing the agency action to remain in place. . . . When a court has decided to remand an agency action, it should consider hearing parties' views on whether to vacate the agency action and on any related remedial issues." Id. at 5–6.

b.   The Exception for Interpretive Rules, Guidance, and Policy Statements

> *TEXAS v. UNITED STATES*
> *Gen. Elec. Co. v. EPA*
> *Center for Auto Safety v. NHTSA*
> *Notes on Doctrinal Test(s)*
> *Notes on the Exception's Scope, Desirability, Requirements, and Judicial Review*
> *Notes on Interpretive Rules and Regulatory Vagueness*

[T]his subsection does not apply . . . to interpretative rules, general statements of policy . . . .

5 U.S.C. § 553(b)(A)

The terms "interpretive rule" (or as § 553 would have it, "interpretative rule") and "general statements of policy" encompass a wide range of what is commonly called "soft law"—relatively formal agency actions that, if published, Section 552(a)(2) permit to be relied upon in taking action affecting private interests. Such materials are often referred to generally as "guidance" documents or "nonlegislative rules" in contrast to regulations that have gone through notice and comment (or that the agency had good cause to issue without such process), which are frequently called "legislative rules."

Trying to contrast categories within "nonlegislative rules," specifically between interpretive rules, on one hand, and policy statements and guidance, on the other, is often a frustrating exercise. The D.C. Circuit recently tried to distinguish the terms in NATIONAL MINING ASS'N v. McCARTHY, 758 F.3d 243, 252 (D.C. Cir. 2014): "As to interpretive rules, an agency action that merely interprets a prior statute or regulation, and does not itself purport to impose new obligations or prohibitions or requirements on regulated parties, is an interpretive rule. An agency action that merely explains how the agency will enforce a statute or regulation—in other words, how it will exercise its broad enforcement discretion or permitting discretion under some extant statute or rule—is a general statement of policy." Yet, what may be possible to state in words is often hard to apply to particular contexts.

To some extent, different lines of doctrine have developed for interpretive rules and policy statements (and guidance). Briefly (discussed more at p. 382), courts often consider whether an interpretive rule "clarifies" existing legal obligations. If it does more, in the sense of imposing duties on its own, it is a legislative rule. For policy statements and guidance (discussed more at p. 371), courts generally focus on whether the agency action is "binding" (though on whom is contested). If so, it is a legislative rule. Reviewability may also turn on the type of action. In the D.C. Circuit, policy statements (unlike interpretive rules) are typically not considered to be "final" actions that can be reviewed under the APA (see section on finality in Chapter IX, p. 1418).

[handwritten margin note: Legisl rule - R clarifies existing legal obligs]

For now, we recommend that you focus on the larger distinction—between legislative and nonlegislative rules—rather than on the smaller differences within the latter group. Consider the following questions as you make your way through the material:

Why, as a policy matter, might (or might not) an architect of administrative law determine that certain agency pronouncements need notice and comment and others do not? How, within the structure of the APA, should we read the governing text? And if the answers to preceding two questions are not the same, what should we do?

We start with one primary, recent high-profile case, along with two significant, classic cases, that involve challenges to the procedural legitimacy of agency policy statements that were issued without prior notice or the opportunity to comment.

TEXAS v. UNITED STATES

United States Court of Appeals for the Fifth Circuit (2015).
809 F.3d 134, affirmed by an equally divided court, 136 S.Ct. 2271 (2016).

■ SMITH, CIRCUIT JUDGE.

[The politics of immigration are complicated and contested. In 2010, during President Obama's first term, the Dream Act, which would have provided legal status to individuals brought here as children failed in the Senate after being passed in the House. It was not the first or last time some sort of legislative protection for this group had failed to get the requisite support. In response, at the President's urging, the Department of Homeland Security (DHS) established the Deferred Action for Childhood Arrivals program in 2012. Known as DACA, the program allowed teenagers and young adults who had been brought to United States as children without proper documentation (and who met other criteria) to be protected from deportation and to work legally. After he was reelected in November 2012, President Obama tried again to work with Congress on more comprehensive immigration legislation. Although Democrats controlled the Senate, they did not have a filibuster proof majority, and Republicans controlled the House of Representatives. Attempts at bipartisan reform failed, and the President said in August

2014 that he had to "act alone" on the issue. Several months later, DHS enacted the Deferred Action for Parents of Americans and Lawful Permanent Residents program. Known as DAPA, this program provided parents without proper documentation who had children who were citizens or lawful permanent residents similar benefits to DACA. Although no judicial challenges were brought to DACA at the time it was put in place, that was not true for DAPA.

Twenty-six states (or their representatives) filed suit, including Texas, seeking an injunction to stop DAPA. In doing so, they raised a series of statutory and constitutional claims. As summarized by the Fifth Circuit: "First, they asserted that DAPA violated the procedural requirements of the APA as a substantive rule that did not undergo the requisite notice-and-comment rulemaking. See 5 U.S.C. § 553. Second, the states claimed that DHS lacked the authority to implement the program even if it followed the correct rulemaking process, such that DAPA was substantively unlawful under the APA. See 5 U.S.C. § 706(2)(A)–(C). Third, the states urged that DAPA was an abrogation of the President's constitutional duty to 'take Care that the Laws be faithfully executed.' U.S. Const. art. II, § 3."

Judge Andrew S. Hanen in the Southern District of Texas, where the states had chosen to sue, sided with the states and issued a preliminary injunction. He determined that the states had standing to sue, the agency action was reviewable under the APA, and the states had shown a substantial likelihood of success on their claim that the DHS policy was subject to the APA's notice-and-comment requirements. Texas v. United States, 86 F.Supp.3d 591 (S.D. Tex. 2015).

Below are excerpts from the Fifth Circuit's decision on only the APA procedural issue. The Supreme Court granted the United States' petition for certiorari before Justice Scalia's death but heard oral arguments after his passing. The parties devoted considerable space in their briefs (as did the Court in its questions in oral argument) to issues of standing and reviewability, though they also discussed the APA and constitutional claims. The Court subsequently split evenly (4–4) on the case, and thus summarily affirmed the Fifth Circuit's decision. In light of the many issues, it is hard to draw any lessons on the Court's take on nonlegislative rules.]

In June 2012, the Department of Homeland Security ("DHS") implemented the Deferred Action for Childhood Arrivals program ("DACA"). In the DACA Memo to agency heads, the DHS Secretary "set[ ] forth how, in the exercise of . . . prosecutorial discretion, [DHS] should enforce the Nation's immigration laws against certain young people" and listed five "criteria [that] should be satisfied before an individual is considered for an exercise of prosecutorial discretion." . . . Although stating that "[f]or individuals who are granted deferred action . . ., [U.S. Citizenship and Immigration Services ('USCIS')] shall accept applications to determine whether these individuals qualify for work authorization," the DACA Memo purported to "confer[ ] no substantive right, immigration status or pathway to citizenship." At least 1.2 million persons qualify for DACA, and approximately 636,000 applications were approved through 2014. Dist. Ct. Op., 86 F.Supp.3d at 609.

In November 2014, by what is termed the "DAPA Memo," DHS expanded DACA by making millions more persons eligible for the program and extending "[t]he period for which DACA and the accompanying employment authorization is granted . . . to three-year increments, rather than the current two-year increments." The Secretary also "direct[ed] USCIS to establish a process, similar to DACA," known as DAPA, which applies to "individuals who . . . have, [as of November 20, 2014], a son or daughter who is a U.S. citizen or lawful permanent resident" and meet five additional criteria. The Secretary stated that, although "[d]eferred action does not confer any form of legal status in this country, much less citizenship [,] it [does] mean[ ] that, for a specified period of time, an individual is permitted to be lawfully present in the United States." Of the approximately 11.3 million illegal aliens in the United States, 4.3 million would be eligible for lawful presence pursuant to DAPA. Dist. Ct. Op., 86 F.Supp.3d at 612 n. 11, 670. . . .

The government advances the notion that DAPA is exempt from notice and comment as a policy statement. We evaluate two criteria to distinguish policy statements from substantive rules: whether the rule (1) "impose[s] any rights and obligations" and (2) "genuinely leaves the agency and its decision-makers free to exercise discretion." There is some overlap in the analysis of those prongs "because '[i]f a statement denies the decisionmaker discretion in the area of its coverage . . . then the statement is binding, and creates rights or obligations.'" "While mindful but suspicious of the agency's own characterization, we . . . focus[ ] primarily on whether the rule has binding effect on agency discretion or severely restricts it." "[A]n agency pronouncement will be considered binding as a practical matter if it either appears on its face to be binding, or is applied by the agency in a way that indicates it is binding." Gen. Elec., 290 F.3d at 383 (citation omitted) [p. 365].

Although the DAPA Memo facially purports to confer discretion, the district court determined that "[n]othing about DAPA 'genuinely leaves the agency and its [employees] free to exercise discretion,'" a factual finding that we review for clear error. That finding was partly informed by analysis of the implementation of DACA, the precursor to DAPA.

Like the DAPA Memo, the DACA Memo instructed agencies to review applications on a case-by-case basis and exercise discretion, but the district court found that those statements were "merely pretext" because only about 5% of the 723,000 applications accepted for evaluation had been denied, and "[d]espite a request by the [district] [c]ourt, the [g]overnment's counsel did not provide the number, if any, of requests that were denied [for discretionary reasons] even though the applicant met the DACA criteria. . . ." The finding of pretext was also based on a declaration by Kenneth Palinkas, the president of the union representing the USCIS employees processing the DACA applications, that "DHS management has taken multiple steps to ensure that DACA applications are simply rubberstamped if the applicants meet the necessary criteria"; DACA's Operating Procedures, which "contain[ ] nearly 150 pages of specific instructions for granting or denying deferred action"; and some mandatory language in the DAPA Memo itself. In denying the government's motion for a stay of the injunction, the district court further noted that the President had made public statements suggesting that in reviewing applications pursuant to DAPA, DHS officials who "don't follow the policy" will face "consequences," and "they've got a problem."

The DACA and DAPA Memos purport to grant discretion, but a rule can be binding if it is "applied by the agency in a way that indicates it is binding," and there was evidence from DACA's implementation that DAPA's discretionary language was pretextual. For a number of reasons, any extrapolation from DACA must be done carefully.

First, DACA involved issuing benefits to self-selecting applicants, and persons who expected to be denied relief would seem unlikely to apply. But the issue of self-selection is partially mitigated by the finding that "the [g]overnment has publicly declared that it will make no attempt to enforce the law against even those who are denied deferred action (absent extraordinary circumstances)." Dist. Ct. Op., 86 F.Supp.3d at 663 (footnote omitted).

Second, DACA and DAPA are not identical: Eligibility for DACA was restricted to a younger and less numerous population, which suggests that DACA applicants are less likely to have backgrounds that would warrant a discretionary denial. Further, the DAPA Memo contains additional discretionary criteria . . . But despite those differences, there are important similarities: The Secretary "direct[ed] USCIS to establish a process, similar to DACA, for exercising prosecutorial discretion," id. (emphasis added), and there was evidence that the DACA application process itself did not allow for discretion, regardless of the rates of approval and denial.

Instead of relying solely on the lack of evidence that any DACA application had been denied for discretionary reasons, the district court found pretext for additional reasons. It observed that "the 'Operating Procedures' for implementation of DACA contains nearly 150 pages of specific instructions for granting or denying deferred action to applicants" and that "[d]enials are recorded in a 'check the box' standardized form, for which USCIS personnel are provided templates. Certain denials of DAPA must be sent to a supervisor for approval[, and] there is no option for granting DAPA to an individual who does not meet each criterion." Dist. Ct. Op., 86 F.Supp.3d at 669 (footnotes omitted). The finding was also based on the declaration from Palinkas that, as with DACA, the DAPA application process itself would preclude discretion: "[R]outing DAPA applications through service centers instead of field offices . . . created an application process that bypasses traditional in-person investigatory interviews with trained USCIS adjudications officers" and "prevents officers from conducting case-by-case investigations, undermines officers' abilities to detect fraud and national-security risks, and ensures that applications will be rubber-stamped." See id. at 609–10 (citing that declaration).

As the government points out, there was conflicting evidence on the degree to which DACA allowed for discretion. Donald Neufeld, the Associate Director for Service Center Operations for USCIS, declared that "deferred action under DACA is a . . . case-specific process" that "necessarily involves the exercise of the agency's discretion," and he purported to identify several instances of discretionary denials. Although Neufeld stated that approximately 200,000 requests for additional evidence had been made upon receipt of DACA applications, the government does not know the number, if any, that related to discretionary factors rather than the objective criteria. Similarly, the government did not provide the number of cases that service-center officials referred to field offices for interviews.

Although the district court did not make a formal credibility determination or hold an evidentiary hearing on the conflicting statements by Neufeld and Palinkas, the record indicates that it did not view the Neufeld declaration as creating a material factual dispute. Further, the government did not seek an evidentiary hearing, nor does it argue on appeal that it was error not to conduct such a hearing. Reviewing for clear error, we conclude that the states have established a substantial likelihood that DAPA would not genuinely leave the agency and its employees free to exercise discretion. . . .

The district court did not err and most assuredly did not abuse its discretion. The order granting the preliminary injunction is AFFIRMED.

■ KING, CIRCUIT JUDGE, dissenting. . . .

IV. APA Procedural Claim

Our precedent is clear: "As long as the agency remains free to consider the individual facts in the various cases that arise, then the agency action in question has not established a binding norm," and thus need not go through the procedures of notice-and-comment. Prof'ls & Patients for Customized Care v. Shalala, 56 F.3d 592, 596–97 (5th Cir.1995) (citation omitted). Therefore, in order for Plaintiffs to establish a substantial likelihood of success on the merits . . . Plaintiffs bore the burden of demonstrating that the Memorandum was non-discretionary. As the majority admits, the Memorandum "facially purports to confer discretion." Majority Op. at 171. But the district court ignored this clear language, concluding that agency officials implementing DAPA will defy the Memorandum and simply rubberstamp applications. In so doing, the district court disregarded a mountain of highly probative evidence from DHS officials charged with implementing DAPA, relying instead on selected excerpts of the President's public statements, facts relating to a program materially distinguishable from the one at issue here, and improper burden-shifting. The majority now adopts the district court's conclusions wholesale and without question. Id. at 175. For the reasons set out below, I would hold that the Memorandum is nothing more than a general statement of policy and that the district court's findings cannot stand, even under clear error review.

A.　The Language and Substance of the DAPA Memorandum

In determining whether the DAPA Memorandum constitutes a substantive rule, we must begin with the words of the Memorandum itself. . . . The Memorandum states that it reflects "new policies," Appx. A, at 1, and "guidance for case-by-case use of deferred action," Appx. A, at 3. Accordingly, the Secretary characterizes the Memorandum as a "general statement[ ] of policy"—which is not subject to the notice-and-comment process. 5 U.S.C. § 553(b)(3)(A) . . . . The Memorandum also repeatedly references (more than ten times) the discretionary, "case-by-case" determinations to be made by agents in deciding whether to grant deferred action. It emphasizes that, despite the criteria contained therein, "the ultimate judgment as to whether an immigrant is granted deferred action will be determined on a case-by-case basis."33 Appx. A, at 5; see also Ass'n of Flight Attendants-CWA v. Huerta, 785 F.3d 710, 717 (D.C.Cir.2015) (stating that a document "riddled with caveats is not" likely to constitute a substantive rule). . . .

The discretionary nature of the DAPA Memorandum is further supported by the policy's substance. Although some of the Memorandum's criteria can be routinely applied, many will require agents to make discretionary judgments as to the application of the respective criteria to the facts of a particular case. For example, agents must determine whether an applicant "pose[s] a danger to national security," Appx. B, at 3, whether the applicant is "a threat to . . . border security" or "public safety," Appx. B, at 4, and whether the applicant has "significantly abused the visa or visa waiver programs,"35 Appx. B, at 4. Such criteria cannot be mechanically applied, but rather entail a degree of judgment; in other words, they are "imprecise and discretionary—not exact and certain." . . . .

Most strikingly, the last criterion contained in the DAPA Memorandum is entirely open-ended, stating that deferred action should be granted only if the applicant "present[s] no other factors that, in the exercise of discretion, makes the grant of deferred action inappropriate." Appx. A, at 4. The Memorandum does not elaborate on what such "other factors" should be considered—leaving this analysis entirely to the judgment of the agents processing the applications. This court has held that such a caveat "express[ing] that [a] list of . . . factors is neither dispositive nor exhaustive," "clearly leaves to the sound discretion of the agency in each case the ultimate decision whether to bring an enforcement action." Prof'ls & Patients, 56 F.3d at 600–01. . . .

As Judge Kavanaugh, writing for the D.C. Circuit, has stated, "[t]he most important factor" in distinguishing between a substantive rule and a general statement of policy "concerns the actual legal effect (or lack thereof) of the agency action in question on regulated entities." Nat'l Mining Ass'n v. McCarthy, 758 F.3d 243, 252 (D.C.Cir.2014). Here, the Memorandum makes clear that it "confers no substantive right, immigration status or pathway to citizenship." Appx. A, at 5. The majority suggests that DAPA "modifies substantive rights and interests," by "conferring lawful presence on 500,000 illegal aliens" and forcing Texas to change its laws. Majority Op. at 175–76. None of this appears on the face of the Memorandum though. In fact, nothing in the Memorandum indicates that it is legally binding—i.e., that an applicant who is not granted deferred action can challenge that decision in court, or that DHS would be barred from removing an applicant who appears to satisfy the Memorandum's criteria. . . . Nor does anyone assert that the Memorandum "impose[s] any obligation or prohibition on regulated entities," i.e., the potential DAPA applicants. . . .Moreover, even absent the DAPA Memorandum, DHS would have the authority to take the action of which Plaintiffs complain—i.e., by granting deferred action on an ad hoc basis. See McCarthy, 758 F.3d at 253 ("When the agency applies a general statement of policy in a particular situation, it must be prepared to support the policy just as if the policy statement had never been issued." (internal brackets omitted)). Accordingly, based on its language and substance, the Memorandum does not constitute a binding substantive rule subject to the requirements of notice-and-comment.

The majority recognizes that the plain language of Memorandum "facially purports to confer discretion" and does not argue that DAPA creates a substantive rule from its four corners alone. . . . Nonetheless, the district court reached the opposite conclusion. And it bears identifying the errors committed by the district court in holding that DAPA was a substantive rule on its face.

The district court focused on the Memorandum's "mandatory term[s], instruction[s], [and] command[s]"—in particular, the Secretary's "direct[ion]" to USCIS to begin implementing DAPA. Dist. Ct. Op., 86 F.Supp.3d at 671 n. 103. But it should be no surprise that the Memorandum "direct[s]" the USCIS to establish a process for implementing this guidance, Appx. A, at 4; certainly the Secretary did not intend for it to be ignored . . . . Although "the mandatory tone of the factors is undoubtedly calculated to encourage compliance," such language does not transform a statement of policy into a substantive rule so long as there is "an opportunity for individualized determinations." Id. at 597. . . .

Rather than relying on the language of the Memorandum, the majority concludes that DAPA is a substantive rule because it "would not genuinely leave [DHS] and its employees free to exercise discretion" in practice. Majority Op. at 175 . . . . But in doing so, the majority relies unquestioningly on the district court's finding that the discretionary language in DAPA was "merely pretext" and that DHS officials would not exercise case-by-case discretion of removals under DAPA. . . . The district court's finding was clearly erroneous, however, and I turn to it next.

B. Evidence of Pretext

. . . . "[c]lear error exists when this court is left with the definite and firm conviction that a mistake has been made." Ogden v. Comm'r, 244 F.3d 970, 971 (5th Cir.2001) (per curiam). I am left with such a conviction for three independent reasons: (1) the record lacks any probative evidence of DAPA's implementation; (2) the district court erroneously equated DAPA with DACA; and (3) even assuming DAPA and DACA can be equated, the evidence of DACA's implementation fails to establish pretext. . . .

How, then, did the district court reach the conclusion that the DAPA Memorandum's express inclusion of case-by-case discretion is "merely pretext"? First, the district court selectively relied on public statements the President made in describing the DAPA Memorandum to the public. Majority Op. at 173. But there is no precedent for a court relying on such general pronouncements in determining a program's effect on the agency and on those being regulated. . . . More importantly, the statements relied upon by the district court are not inconsistent with the DAPA Memorandum's grant of discretion to agency decision makers. For example, the President's statement that those who "meet the [DAPA] criteria . . . can come out of the shadows," Dist. Ct. Op., 86 F.Supp.3d at 668, does not suggest that applications will be rubberstamped, given that (as discussed above) those very criteria involve the exercise of discretion. . . .

Thus, even assuming DACA and DAPA applications are reviewed using the exact same administrative process, the district court had no basis for concluding that the results of that process—a process that would involve the application of markedly different, discretionary criteria—would be the same. For this reason alone—that is, the district court's heavy reliance upon this minimally probative evidence—I would conclude that the district court clearly erred. . . .

The district court also relied on a four-page declaration by Kenneth Palinkas, President of the National Citizenship and Immigration Services Council (the union representing USCIS employees processing DACA applications), for the proposition that "DACA applications are simply rubberstamped if the applicants meet the necessary criteria." Dist. Ct. Op., 86 F.Supp.3d at 610. Yet lay witness conclusions are only competent evidence if rationally drawn from facts personally observed. See Fed.R.Evid. 701. Here, Palinkas's conclusion was supported only by the fact that DACA applications are routed to "service centers instead of field offices," and that "USCIS officers in service centers . . . do not interview applicants"—a weak basis on which to conclude that DHS's representations (both to the public and to the courts) are "merely pretext." . . .

Indeed, Palinkas's assertions are rebutted—and the step-by-step process for reviewing DACA applications is explained—in the detailed affidavit filed by Donald Neufeld, the head of those very USCIS service centers. Neufeld declares that the service centers "are designed to adjudicate applications, petitions and requests" for various programs "that have higher-volume caseloads." Neufeld goes on to describe the "multi-step, case-specific process" for reviewing DACA applications . . . .

The majority accepts the district court's factual conclusions almost *carte blanche*. But clear error review is not a rubber stamp, and the litany of errors committed by the district court become readily apparent from a review of the record. The record before us, when read properly, shows that DAPA is merely a general statement of policy. As such, it is exempt from the notice-and-comment requirements of 5 U.S.C. § 553.

SIGNIFICANT CASES

GENERAL ELECTRIC CO. v. ENVIRONMENTAL PROTECTION AGENCY
290 F.3d 377 (D.C. Cir. 2002).

■ GINSBURG, CHIEF JUDGE.

General Electric Co. petitions for review of the "PCB Risk Assessment Review Guidance Document" issued by the Environmental Protection Agency. The parties dispute . . . whether the Agency should have followed the procedures required for rulemaking in the TSCA and in the Administrative Procedure Act when it promulgated the Document. We conclude . . . that . . . the Document should not have been issued without prior notice and an opportunity for public comment.

I.   Background

The TSCA prohibits the manufacture, processing, distribution, and use (other than in a "totally enclosed manner") of polychlorinated biphenyls (PCBs) unless the EPA determines that the activity will not result in an "unreasonable risk of injury to health or the environment." 15 U.S.C. § 2605(e)(2) & (3). The Guidance Document governs the application of two regulations promulgated by the EPA under the TSCA to provide respectively for the cleanup and disposal of PCB remediation waste and for the disposal of PCB bulk product waste. See 40 C.F.R. §§ 761.61 ("cleanup and disposal options for PCB remediation waste"), 761.62 (how "PCB bulk product waste shall be disposed").

Under subsection (c) of each regulation a party may apply for permission to use a method other than one of the generic methods set out in the regulations for sampling, cleaning up, or disposing of PCB remediation waste, or for sampling or disposing of PCB bulk product waste. The EPA will approve applications under these subsections if the alternative method proposed does "not pose an unreasonable risk of injury to health or the environment." Id. The regulations do not, however, tell applicants how to conduct the necessary risk assessment.

That is where the Guidance Document comes in. It "provides an overview of risk assessment techniques, and guidance for reviewing risk assessment documents submitted under the final PCB disposal rule." Guidance Document at 10. Of particular relevance to this case, in the Guidance Document the EPA also explains that an applicant seeking to use an alternative method under § 761.61(c) may take either of two approaches to risk assessment. First, the applicant may calculate cancer and non-cancer risks separately. Id. To calculate cancer risks the applicant would have to use a cancer potency factor recognized by the EPA. Such cancer potency factors range, depending upon the exposure pathway and upon the composition of the PCB mixture, from .04 to 2.0 (mg/kg/day)–1. Id., Table 9, at 64. To calculate the non-cancer risks a different type of toxicity value—a reference dose, for example—would have to be used, and certain specified non-cancer risks would have to be taken into account. Id. at 21, 42.

The second approach endorsed in the Guidance Document is to use a "total toxicity factor" of 4.0 (mg/kg/day)–1 to account for cancer and non-cancer risks together. Id. In its brief the EPA explains that this approach "provides the applicant an opportunity to reduce the time and expense associated with the risk assessment" because the Agency is willing "to accept this 'default' toxicity value of 4.0 (mg/kg/ day)–1[ ] without requiring further justification."

II. Analysis

GE's primary argument is that the Guidance Document is a legislative rule and therefore should have been promulgated only after public notice and an opportunity for comment. . . .

GE argues that the Guidance Document is a legislative rule rather than a statement of policy or an interpretive rule because it gives substance to the vague language of 40 C.F.R. § 761.61(c) ("unreasonable risk of injury to health or the environment"), does so in an obligatory fashion, and is treated by the EPA as "controlling in the field." See Community Nutrition Inst. v. Young, 818 F.2d 943, 946 (D.C. Cir. 1987); Appalachian Power, 208 F.3d at 1021. . . . Although it is not entirely clear what in the EPA's view the Document is, the EPA comes closest to characterizing it as a statement of policy . . . With the Agency's argument so understood, the question before us can be framed as whether the Guidance Document is a legislative rule or a statement of policy.

As GE argues, in cases where we have attempted to draw the line between legislative rules and statements of policy, we have considered whether the agency action (1) "imposes any rights and obligations" or (2) "genuinely leaves the agency and its decisionmakers free to exercise discretion." Community Nutrition Inst., 818 F.2d at 946; Chamber of Commerce v. Dep't of Labor, 174 F.3d 206, 212 (D.C. Cir. 1999). . . .

The EPA urges the court to consider three factors: "(1) the Agency's own characterization of its action; (2) whether the action was published in the Federal Register or the Code of Federal Regulations; and (3) whether the action has binding effects on private parties or on the agency." Molycorp, Inc. v. EPA, 197 F.3d 543, 545 (D.C. Cir. 1999). As the EPA concedes, however, the third factor is the most important: "The ultimate focus of the inquiry is whether the agency action partakes of the fundamental characteristic of a regulation, i.e., that it has the force of law."

The two tests overlap at step three of the Molycorp formulation—in which the court determines whether the agency action binds private parties or the agency itself with the "force of law." This common standard has been well stated as follows:

If a document expresses a change in substantive law or policy (that is not an interpretation) which the agency intends to make binding, or administers with binding effect, the agency may not rely upon the statutory exemption for policy statements, but must observe the APA's legislative rulemaking procedures.

Robert A. Anthony, Interpretive Rules, Policy Statements, Guidances, Manuals, and the Like—Should Federal Agencies Use Them to Bind the Public?, 41 Duke L.J. 1311, 1355 (1992).

Our cases likewise make clear that an agency pronouncement will be considered binding as a practical matter if it either appears on its face to be binding or is applied by the agency in a way that indicates it is binding. . . .

GE argues that the Guidance Document is binding both because it facially requires an applicant for a risk-based variance to calculate toxicity by one of two methods—either use a total toxicity factor of 4.0 (mg/kg/day)–1 or use a cancer potency factor and account for the specified non-cancer health risks—and because, considering the cost, delay, and uncertainty entailed in the latter course, "for all practical purposes, the Guidance is a rule that directs PCB toxicity to be measured by a 4.0 (mg/kg/day)–1 CPF."

The EPA counters that the Guidance Document lacks the force of law because it does not purport to be binding and because it has not been applied as though it were binding. . . . We think it clear that the Guidance Document does purport to bind applicants for approval of a risk-based cleanup plan under 40 C.F.R. § 761.61(c). Consider the principal directives: "When developing a risk-based cleanup application . . . both the cancer and non-cancer endpoints must be addressed. . . ." Guidance Document at 21. If an applicant chooses not to use the 4.0 total toxicity factor, then it "must, at a minimum account for the risk from non-cancer endpoints for neurotoxicity, reproductive and developmental toxicity, immune system suppression, liver damage, skin irritation, and endocrine disruption for each of the commercial mixtures found at the cleanup site." Id. Although the Guidance Document does, as noted, anticipate and acknowledge that "some risk assessments may have components that require the use of non-standard . . . unique . . . or unconventional methods for estimating risk," id. at 44, that does not undermine the binding force of the Guidance Document in standard cases. Furthermore, even though the Guidance Document gives applicants the option of calculating risk in either of two ways (assuming both are practical) it still requires them to conform to one or the other, that is, not to submit an application based upon a third way. And if an applicant does choose to calculate cancer and non-cancer risks separately, then it must consider the non-cancer risks specified in the Guidance Document. To the applicant reading the Guidance Document the message is clear: in reviewing applications the Agency will not be open to considering approaches other than those prescribed in the Document.

The Guidance Document also appears to bind the Agency to accept applications using a total toxicity factor of 4.0 (mg/kg/day)–1 to calculate the risk from both cancer and noncancer endpoints. Guidance Document at 21. . . .

Furthermore, the EPA does not contend that in practice it has not treated the Guidance Document as binding in the ways described above. . . .

In sum, the commands of the Guidance Document indicate that it has the force of law.

CENTER FOR AUTO SAFETY v. NATIONAL HIGHWAY TRAFFIC SAFETY ADMINISTRATION
452 F.3d 798 (D.C. Cir. 2006).

■ EDWARDS, SENIOR CIRCUIT JUDGE.

[Under the National Traffic and Motor Vehicle Safety Act, a manufacturer is required to issue a recall notifying consumers and offering a free remedy whenever its equipment contains a safety-related defect or fails to comply with a safety standard. Recalls can be mandated by the National Highway Traffic Safety Administration (NHTSA) or issued voluntarily by a manufacturer. During any recall, manufacturers must notify vehicle owners and provide detailed information about the defect involved, risk to motor vehicle safety, and measures to be taken to remedy the problem. NHTSA retains full authority under the Act to oversee and regulate any recall. The Act allows interested persons to petition NHTSA to initiate a proceeding over whether to order a recall and to petition for a hearing to determine if a manufacturer's recall met the statutory notice and remedy requirements. Beginning in the mid-1980s, manufacturers began issuing voluntary recalls on a geographically limited basis when a defect or noncompliance was caused by atypical climatic conditions. NHTSA did not object to such regional recalls for many years, but in 1997 it sent letters to several manufacturers expressing concerns about geographic limits on recalls. A year later, NHTSA sent letters outlining its new policy on regional recalls.]

The 1998 policy guidelines distinguish between "circumstances: (1) when the consequences of the defect occur as the result of a short-term or single exposure to a particular meteorological condition; and (2) when the consequences of the defect generally occur only after long-term or recurring exposure to environmental conditions." The guidelines indicate that, as to the former, a regional recall generally is "not appropriate." However, they also indicate that NHTSA may, "in some cases," be willing to modify the manufacturer's notification duties. Thus, the guidelines state that "the agency may act favorably on requests by manufacturers to include language in the letters to owners of vehicles in 'low-risk' states . . . that indicates that the defect is unlikely to cause a safety problem if the vehicle is not exposed to the meteorological condition at issue." As to defects that arise from long-term exposure, the guidelines say that "if the manufacturer is able to demonstrate that the relevant environmental factor (or factors) is significantly more likely to exist in the area proposed for inclusion than in the rest of the United States, NHTSA will approve a regional recall." There is a caveat that "the manufacturer's justification for such a proposal should be based on objective factors" . . . [and the] guidelines also indicate that . . . "manufacturers must assure that vehicles from outside the designated area that experience a problem due to the defect are taken care of appropriately." Finally, the guidelines state that the agency "[has] determined that, at a minimum, vehicles originally sold in or currently registered in [20 designated] states [and the District of Columbia] must be included in any regional recall related to corrosion caused by road salt." The guidelines conclude with the following words of caution: "[M]anufacturers must discuss all proposals to limit the geographic scope of any recall [with NHTSA]" . . .

[In 2004, the Center for Auto Safety and Public Citizen sued, arguing that NHTSA's policy of allowing regional recalls violated the Safety Act and that the 1998 regional recall policy guidelines violated the APA because they were issued without undertaking notice-and-comment rulemaking.]

As the case law reveals, it is not always easy to distinguish between those "general statements of policy" . . . and agency "rules" that establish binding norms or agency actions that occasion legal consequences. . . . Nevertheless, the distinction between "general statements of policy" and "rules" is critical. If the 1998 policy guidelines constitute a de facto rule, as appellants claim, then . . . § 553 of the APA would require the agency to afford notice of a proposed rulemaking and an opportunity for public comment prior to promulgating the rule. If the guidelines are no more than "general statements of policy," as NHTSA would have it, then they would neither determine rights or obligations nor occasion legal consequences and, thus, would be exempt from the APA's notice-and-comment requirement. . . . [A]n important caveat with respect to "general statements of policy" that bears mention here: if NHTSA applies the 1998 policy guidelines in a particular situation, it must be prepared to support the policy. . . . But the instant case does not involve a challenge to threats of enforcement by NHTSA. . . .

. . . [U]nder Bennett [v. Spear, 520 U.S. 154 (1997)], the 1998 policy guidelines cannot be viewed as "final agency action" under § 704 of the APA unless they "mark the consummation of the agency's decisionmaking process" *and* either determine "rights or obligations" or result in "legal consequences." Bennett, 520 U.S. at 178 (citations and internal quotation marks omitted). It is possible to view the guidelines as meeting the first part of the Bennett test, but not the second. The guidelines are nothing more than general policy statements with no legal force. They do not determine any rights or obligations, nor do they have any legal consequences. Therefore, the guidelines cannot be taken as "final agency action," nor can they otherwise be seen to constitute a binding legal norm. . . . There is no doubt that the guidelines reflect NHTSA's views on the legality of regional recalls. But this does not change the character of the guidelines from a policy statement to a binding rule. . . .

. . . NHTSA's position here is nothing more than a privileged viewpoint in the legal debate [over whether the Safety Act prohibits regional recalls]. The guidelines do not purport to carry the force of law. They have not been published in the Code of Federal Regulations. They do not define "rights or obligations." They are labeled "policy guidelines," not rules. And they read as *guidelines*, not binding regulations, [using conditional language and general prescriptions]. . . . NHTSA has not commanded, required, ordered, or dictated. And there is nothing in the record to indicate that officials in NHTSA's Office of Defects Investigation are bound to apply the guidelines in an enforcement action. The agency remains free to exercise discretion in assessing proposed recalls and in enforcing the Act. There is also nothing to indicate that automakers can rely on the guidelines as "a norm or safe harbor by which to shape their actions," see Gen. Elec. Co. v. EPA, 290 F.3d 377, 383 (D.C. Cir. 2002), which might suggest that the guidelines are binding as a practical matter. And it does not matter that agency officials have *encouraged* automakers to comply with the guidelines. . . . Our conclusion that the guidelines amount to a general statement of policy, rather than a binding rule, is further fortified by the limited authority of the Associate Administrator for Safety Assurance[,] . . . the apparent author of the guidelines, [who] had authority to issue policy guidance . . . [but not] to issue guidelines with binding effect. . . .

Appellants' final argument is that even if the guidelines do not determine rights and obligations, they had legal consequences.

Appellants contend that the agency has altered the legal regime with consequence both for automakers—who now allegedly conform their practices to the agency's standards—and for automobile consumers—who allegedly own "defective" vehicles that do not qualify for recall remedies under the Act. They say that, for seven years, the agency and automakers have followed the standards announced in the guidelines. Appellants thus urge that, under a flexible and pragmatic approach to finality . . . the agency's 1998 policy guidelines must be seen to have legal consequences that confirm final agency action.

The flaw in appellants' argument is that the 'consequences' to which they allude are practical, not legal. It may be that, to the extent that they actually prescribe anything, the agency's guidelines have been voluntarily followed by automakers and have become a *de facto* industry standard for how to conduct regional recalls. . . . But *de facto* compliance is not enough to establish that the guidelines have had *legal* consequences. . . . It may be that some car owners continue to be disadvantaged by automakers' regional recall practices. But automobile manufacturers adhered to these practices long before NHTSA issued the 1998 policy guidelines. The adverse effects flowing from the regional recall practices surely are not a *legal consequence* of the guidelines, not only because the effects preceded the guidelines, but, more importantly, because the agency has never codified the practices in binding regulations. . . . We therefore affirm the District Court's judgment dismissing appellants' action.

[Ed. Concurring opinion of Circuit Judge Randolph omitted.]

NOTES ON DOCTRINAL TEST(S)

(1) *Competing Views of Administrative Law Scholars in the Texas DAPA Case.* Consider excerpts from two competing amicus briefs filed in United States v. Texas at the Supreme Court:

From a group of administrative law scholars (including three editors of this book) in support of the United States: "The Fifth Circuit adopted an erroneous legal standard in reaching the conclusion that the DAPA Memo was not a general statement of policy. First, the court mistakenly held that the DAPA Memo was subject to notice and comment because it did not 'genuinely leave the agency and its employees free to exercise discretion.' . . . Regardless of whether the underlying factual premise of this assertion is accurate, the fact that an agency pronouncement binds lower-level agency officials does not mean it is a legislative rule rather than a policy statement for APA purposes. Indeed, a central purpose of general policy statements is to permit the agency head to direct the implementation of agency policy by lower-level officials. As amici and other administrative law scholars have explained, it is critical for agency heads to be able to bind lower-level agency employees to ensure that the agency's policies are reliably carried out. . . . Requiring notice and comment every time an agency head promulgates binding internal guidance would fundamentally impair agency heads' ability to direct the agencies they are statutorily charged with overseeing. Discretion at the level of the agency head, not discretion by lower-level staff, is therefore the essential factor. Second, the Fifth Circuit erred to the extent it stated that a policy statement's 'substantial impact' on third parties is a basis to require notice and comment."[12] See also GILLIAN E. METZGER, THE CONSTITUTIONAL DUTY TO SUPERVISE, 124 Yale L.J. 1836, 1929 (2015): "[B]y openly stating a generally applicable policy and then instituting an administrative scheme to implement that policy, the President and DHS Secretaries Napolitano and Johnson were actually fulfilling their constitutional duties to supervise. Given current budget and personnel constraints, full enforcement of the immigration laws is simply not a possibility. Hence, the alternative to the Obama Administration's approach is not full enforcement, but rather case-by-case discretionary decisions by low-level officials over which meaningful supervision is very hard to exercise. The public articulation of the administration's policies ensured that enforcement choices would be more transparent, thereby enhancing political accountability, as well as more consistent across the nation and among immigration personnel. Precluding prospective and categorical articulation of immigration enforcement policy and priorities is tantamount to insisting that nonenforcement decisions be made by lower-level officials, a requirement as much at odds with constitutional structure as a presidential dispensation power."

In contrast, from administrative law experts in support of Texas: "Because the Secretary's program establishes a new 'agency process respecting the grant . . . of a license,' 5 U.S.C. § 551(9), the Secretary was obligated to comply with the APA's notice-and-comment requirements. The Secretary's attempt to escape those requirements conflicts with the APA's text, structure, and purpose. . . . DAPA is a rule under the APA, and the Secretary does not contend otherwise. Through this rule, the Secretary has sought to establish a new process for granting exemptions and relieving restrictions for a broad class of millions of aliens who are unlawfully present in the United States. . . . Through that process, aliens may obtain lawful presence, work authorization, and other benefits. . . . Aliens who under DAPA are deemed eligible to receive benefits are invited to file applications with the United States Citizenship and Immigration Services ('USCIS'), which is directed to 'begin accepting' those applications. Pet. App. 418a. A rule of that description has substantive effect. It (i) establishes a new licensing process for exempting millions of individuals from applicable law; (ii) imposes numerical criteria to govern future licensing proceedings that are not derived from the statute; and (iii) binds agency officials."[13]

Both briefs advance arguments not made by the majority or dissent in Texas v. United States. Do you find any of them compelling?

---

[12] This amicus brief is available at: http://www.scotusblog.com/wp-content/uploads/2016/03/15-674tsacAdminLawScholars.pdf.

[13] This amicus brief is available at: http://www.scotusblog.com/wp-content/uploads/2016/04/ACFrOgAgBKywb7IMm1ybsFYe-YSU_zDynmvqnoPkJzkkFLbqUZnOAkyT2yWAsgcL0Xv6GNlERcOdH-51mGA1155UntKvsMOH0zYW9UQLuWqEd6kTKLXOeubfeeY-2Cc1.pdf.

(2) *Consistent Distinctions?* How do you explain the different outcomes in these three cases? Specifically, are General Electric and Center for Auto Safety as distinguishable as Judge Edwards maintained? Is it true that the NHTSA letter does not provide car manufacturers with a safe harbor, as the EPA Guidance Document did? The letter certainly appears to guarantee that NHTSA will approve a regional recall if the manufacturer proves, using objective factors, that an environmental factor is significantly more likely to exist in the geographic area of the recall than elsewhere in the country. Do its terms really suggest that manufacturers are free to issue a recall without consulting with NHTSA beforehand or to issue a regional recall connected to road salt that covered fewer than the twenty states NHTSA identified? Consider also the three decisions' treatment of practical effect—on both the agency and the "regulated." Which decision has the best approach to the reality of de facto compliance?

(3) *Binding on Whom and in What Ways?* All three cases emphasize "binding legal effect" as the distinction between legislative rules and general policy statements, reflecting the key characteristic of valid legislative rules that they have the force of law and bind both the public and agencies in the same fashion as statutes. But "binding" effect can be understood in a number of different ways.

One question concerns whether binding effects *on the agency* should be treated the same as binding effects *on the public* for purposes of identifying a legislative rule. The General Electric and Texas courts conclude yes; part of their rationale for finding the agency actions to constitute legislative rules was that the agencies had bound their own discretion. By contrast, Center for Auto Safety emphasizes that NHTSA remained free to exercise discretion in enforcing the act and that nothing in the record suggested that NHTSA's inspectors were bound to apply the recall guidelines in an enforcement action. The two potential objects of binding effect—the public and the agency—may seem impossible to separate: mandatory constraints on the agency will constrain the public, who will know how the agency is going to react and guide their actions accordingly. Yet a regulated party does retain the option of following an alternative approach and, if need be, challenging the agency's position in an enforcement proceeding. Does this argument work for persons without proper documentation in the Texas case? More importantly, if guidance cannot "bind" the agency, then one of the main potential benefits of agency guidance—curtailing the discretion of lower-level officials and staff—is lost. Should the courts be more willing to tolerate guidance that curtails agency discretion, such as EPA's creation of the "total toxicity factor" approach to measuring risk, which functions essentially as a safe harbor in that regulated entities know that EPA staff will accept this approach?

There is a connected second issue—*how should a court assess whether an agency, or the regulated entity, is sufficiently constrained to require notice-and-comment procedures?* The courts in General Electric and Center for Auto Safety take an ex ante approach, focusing on the terms in the agency action in assessing constraints on the agency and regulated parties. The court in Texas evaluates, in part, ex post, examining how the agency actually acts in practice. Do you agree with Center for Auto Safety that the focus should be on legal consequences for the regulated, and not the practical impact? For a contrasting case to Center for Auto Safety, consider CHAMBER OF COMMERCE V. DEP'T OF LABOR, 174 F.3d 206 (D.C. Cir. 1999). In a "policy statement" Directive, OSHA announced a plan to target the 12,500 most hazardous workplaces in the country for aggressive inspections, which was well beyond its capacity (due to the number of inspectors it had). Essential to the plan was the "carrot" of a promise to reduce greatly the chance a workplace would be inspected if the employer agreed to participate in a "Cooperative Compliance Program" that satisfied OSHA guidelines. In an earlier program in Maine, 99 percent of employers chose the carrot. For the D.C. Circuit, this was not an offer OSHA was entitled to make without first undertaking notice-and-comment rulemaking: "The Directive is . . . the practical equivalent of a rule that obliges an employer to comply or to suffer the consequences; the voluntary form of the rule is but a veil for the threat it obscures. . . . The Directive will affect employers' interests in the same way that a plainly substantive rule mandating a comprehensive safety program would affect their rights; that it so operates without having the force of law is therefore of little, if any, significance. In practical terms, the Directive places the burden of inspection upon those employers that fail to adopt a [comprehensive safety and health program], and will have a substantial impact upon all employers within its purview—including those that acquiesce in the agency's use of 'leverage' against them. Consequently, we conclude that the Directive is a substantive rather than a procedural rule."

As a practical matter, agency guidance seems likely to have a substantial impact on how regulated parties behave, particularly statements suggesting how the agency will undertake enforcement. Should such practical effects suffice to transform agency guidance into a legislative rule requiring use of notice-and-comment procedures? What room would then be left for § 553(b)(A)'s exception for policy statements and interpretive rules? Yet focusing only on legal effect may mean that "guidance" with major consequences in practice—impacts likely anticipated by the agencies involved—does not go through the public rulemaking procedures of § 553. For an argument that a "practically binding" test violates Vermont Yankee, see Cass Sunstein, "Practically Binding": General Policy Statements and Notice-and-Comment Rulemaking, 68 Admin. L. Rev. 491 (2016).

In addition, as Center for Auto Safety reveals, using legal effect as the sole measure of a legislative rule can heighten asymmetries between regulated entities and regulatory beneficiaries. The former can always refuse to adhere to the agency's policy statement and then challenge the agency's position on the merits if it brings an enforcement proceeding. Regulatory beneficiaries, however, may have few options for forcing review of an agency's policy views if regulated entities adhere in practice, particularly given some courts' insistence that policy statements are not "final agency action" and thus not subject to suit under the APA. See Nina A. Mendelson, Regulatory Beneficiaries and Informal Agency Policymaking, 92 Cornell L. Rev. 397, 420–24 (2007).

A third connected issue relates to *how guidance might bind an agency.* All three cases focus on whether ostensible guidance documents are having binding legal effect in the form of legislative rules. But administrative law recognizes another way in which guidance could be thought to be "binding," specifically the more limited force accorded agency adjudicative precedent. Although agencies can rely on such precedent, they must remain open to counterarguments and be prepared to justify any changes in their approach. See John F. Manning, Nonlegislative Rules, 72 Geo. Wash. L. Rev. 893, 934–36 (2003); Peter L. Strauss, Publication Rules in the Rulemaking Spectrum: Assuring Proper Respect for an Essential Element, 53 Admin. L. Rev. 803, 829–33 (2001). Moreover, as noted above, the APA expressly states that, if published or made publicly available, guidance may be "cited as precedent." 5 U.S.C. § 552(a)(2). Does the precedential model justify allowing guidance to have some binding effect after all? Does it alleviate the concern that agencies can evade their procedural obligations under the APA? In answering these questions, does it matter that, under well-established doctrine, agencies have broad discretion to choose to set policy by rulemaking or by case-by-case adjudication (see p. 248)?

(4) *Other Tests.* Courts have struggled to implement the distinction between legislative rules and nonlegislative rules, describing it as "blurred," "baffling," and even "enshrouded in considerable smog." Consider three alternative tests that are arguably easier to apply than the often-used binding effects standard.

First, looking specifically at interpretive rules, JUDGE STEPHEN WILLIAMS suggested the following test in AMERICAN MINING CONGRESS V. MINE SAFETY & HEALTH ADMIN., 995 F.2d 1106, 1112 (1993): "[I]nsofar as our cases can be reconciled at all, we think it almost exclusively on the basis of whether the purported interpretive rule has 'legal effect', which in turn is best ascertained by asking (1) whether in the absence of the rule there would not be an adequate legislative basis for enforcement action or other agency action to confer benefits or ensure the performance of duties, (2) whether the agency has published the rule in the Code of Federal Regulations, (3) whether the agency has explicitly invoked its general legislative authority, or (4) whether the rule effectively amends a prior legislative rule. If the answer to any of these questions is affirmative, we have a legislative, not an interpretive rule." The D.C. Circuit subsequently deemed publication in the CFR as no more than "a snippet of evidence of agency intent." Health Ins. Ass'n of Am. Inc. v. Shalala, 23 F.3d 412, 423 (D.C. Cir. 1994); see also Hemp Industries Ass'n v. DEA, 333 F.3d 1082, 1087–88 (9th Cir. 2003) (formulating an inquiry similar to the approach of American Mining).

Second, considering an FDA policy statement, JUDGE KENNETH STARR, in a partially dissenting opinion in COMMUNITY NUTRITION INSTITUTE V. YOUNG, 818 F.2d 943, 951–52 (D.C. Cir. 1987), proposed a more radical alternative, which has not gained much traction (except to help support the third alternative proposed in academic articles): "Inasmuch as our decisional law over the last decade avowedly reflects considerable uncertainty in discerning the line between agency pronouncements that are 'law' and those that are 'policy,' . . . it seems advisable to return to the pristine teaching of

Pacific Gas [Pacific Gas & Elec. Co. v. Fed. Power Comm'n, 506 F.2d 33 (D.C. Cir. 1974)]. In that case, this court articulated a rule which is clearly preferable to the present muddy state of the law. . . . We should reembrace our Pacific Gas test as the determinative factor in analyzing whether a particular pronouncement is legislative or interpretative in nature. If the pronouncement has the force of law in future proceedings, it is a legislative rule. Unless that critical feature is present, however, the agency statement should be considered to be a lower form of pronouncement, a 'non-law' as it were, or in APA terms an 'interpretative rule' or 'general statement of policy.' The correct measure of a pronouncement's force in subsequent proceedings is a practical one: must the agency merely show that the pronouncement has been violated or must the agency, if its hand is called, show that the pronouncement itself is justified in light of the underlying statute and the facts."

Third, lumping all nonlegislative items together, several scholars have suggested an even more radical (in the sense of distance from current doctrine) and even simpler approach: "Rather than asking whether a rule is legislative to answer whether notice and comment procedures should have been used, courts should simply ask whether notice and comment procedures were used. If they were, the rule should be deemed legislative and binding if otherwise lawful. If they were not, the rule is nonlegislative. If the rule is nonlegislative, a party may challenge the validity of the rule in any subsequent enforcement proceeding . . . ." JACOB E. GERSEN, LEGISLATIVE RULES REVISITED, 74 U. Chi. L. Rev. 1705, 1719 (2007); see also E. Donald Elliott, Re-Inventing Rulemaking, 41 Duke L.J. 1490 (1992); William Funk, When Is a "Rule" a Regulation? Marking a Clear Line Between Nonlegislative Rules and Legislative Rules, 54 Admin. L. Rev. 659 (2002).

Do you prefer any of these alternatives? Professor DAVID L. FRANKLIN criticizes the second and third suggestions in LEGISLATIVE RULES, NONLEGISLATIVE RULES, AND THE PERILS OF THE SHORT CUT, 120 Yale L.J. 276, 316 (2010). Professor Franklin maintains that subsequent scrutiny of guidance by the judiciary on review of enforcement actions often does not take place, as for example "when an agency pronouncement sets forth the conditions under which the agency will not take action" or "because many regulated entities choose . . . to comply with nonlegislative rules rather than incur [the costs of pre-enforcement challenges and] . . . the risks associated with noncompliance." He also contends that agencies lose little from a narrower interpretation of the § 553(b)(A) exception, as they have the ability to set policy on a case-by-case basis in adjudication. His "most fundamental" objection, however, is that "the public scrutiny that comes with notice and comment and the judicial scrutiny that comes with post-enforcement review are fundamentally dissimilar." According to Franklin, "notice and comment was designed to ensure an opportunity for interested members of the public to participate in the process of agency policymaking by making comments, raising objections, and suggesting alternatives. . . . While post-enforcement judicial review can mimic these features, it cannot fully recreate them because it occurs in the factual context of a particular enforcement action, before generalist judges, and at the behest of the regulated entity." Moreover, "robust public participation enhances the later process of judicial review by bringing to light technical issues that generalist judges might not otherwise spot, thereby enabling courts to engage in meaningful scrutiny of the resulting rules," and such scrutiny would not be "fully practicable without public input elicited by notice and comment procedures." Do you agree?

(5) ***Presidential Statements as Source of Evidence.*** In the Texas DAPA challenge, the Fifth Circuit (and district court) relied on statements by President Obama in evaluating the discretion of DHS. Is this wise? Compare Hawaii v. Trump, 859 F.3d 741 (9th Cir. 2017) (relying, in part, on President Trump's tweets in striking down his second executive order barring entry of nationals from six Muslim-majority countries rather than relying on the Order's text). For a larger discussion of judicial treatment of presidential speech, see Katherine Shaw, Beyond the Bully Pulpit: Presidential Speech in the Courts, 96 Tex. L. Rev. (forthcoming 2017), available at: http://papers. ssrn.com/sol3/papers.cfm?abstract_id=2981475.

NOTES ON THE EXCEPTION'S SCOPE, DESIRABILITY, REQUIREMENTS, AND JUDICIAL REVIEW

(1) ***The Exception's Significance.*** The amount of agency guidance has long greatly exceeded the number of agency regulations adopted using notice-and-comment procedures. Today, guidance plays an increasingly important role. TODD D. RAKOFF, THE CHOICE BETWEEN FORMAL AND INFORMAL MODES OF ADMINISTRATIVE REGULATION, 52 Admin. L. Rev. 159, 159–70 (2000): "Since the 1960s . . . administrative law in the United States has exhausted the possibilities for developing an easily workable system of regulation within the procedural forms articulated in the APA. Agencies interested in pursuing their programs, rather than just slowing down, must search for ways to escape from [its] models of rulemaking and adjudication. We are in the midst of another round of discovering the virtues of informality. There is renewed interest in resolving particular disputes short of formal adjudication. Of greater general import, there is a trend toward setting regulatory policy in less formal ways. Techniques that previously were used as preliminaries to rulemaking or adjudication under the APA are now being used on the assumption that they will constitute the final disposition."

Professor Rakoff provides data from FDA practice to support this point: "If we compare the mid-1990s with the late 1970s or early 1980s, we find that the number of FDA regulations adopted each year in accordance with the APA's rulemaking procedures declined by about fifty percent. By contrast, since the start of this decade there has been a striking increase in the number of FDA-issued documents intended to give guidance to the regulated industry but not adopted through public procedures. The rate per year for the 1990s is about four hundred percent greater than the rate for the 1980s." Id. at 168. A recent student note, drawing on data gathered under President George W. Bush's Executive Order 13422 imposing centralized review of "significant" guidance, p. 423, concludes that "[a]gencies do not commonly use guidance to make important policy decisions outside of the notice and comment process . . . [and] significant guidance is issued infrequently relative to legislative rulemaking." Connor Raso, Note, Strategic or Sincere? Analyzing Agency Use of Guidance Documents, 119 Yale L.J. 782, 815, 821–22 (2010). Yet the proportion of legislative rules that qualify as significant under the centralized review definition is relatively low (around 20 percent of issued rules, p. 418), and guidance could still be used for policy choices that do not reach this threshold but nonetheless are quite important. Raso acknowledges that "[s]ome agencies, such as the FDA and the IRS, clearly use guidance much more frequently than others" while in some other agencies, in particular "EPA and OSHA[,] . . . used most of their guidance for technical purposes." Id.

(2) ***Benefits and Costs of Agency Use of Interpretive Rules, Policy Statements, and Guidance.*** How courts should determine whether an agency action is indeed an interpretive rule or statement of policy or, instead, an improperly promulgated binding legislative rule has generated a great deal of case law and far more scholarly commentary than any other § 553 exception. This debate reflects not only the difficulty in distinguishing between these different types of rules but also the stakes that ride on the distinction. On one side is the concern that agencies will be able to exploit the exception to circumvent notice-and-comment requirements. Robert Anthony, whose work was quoted at length by the General Electric court, has emphasized this danger, arguing that the exception risks "overregulation [and] bureaucratic overreaching" by evading the disciplining aspects of the APA rulemaking. Anthony, supra, at 1373–74 (1992). Others have stressed that expanded use of interpretive rules and policy statements may undermine public participation in policymaking, particularly by regulatory beneficiaries who may lack opportunities to challenge agency policies adopted in the form of guidance. See Nina A. Mendelson, Regulatory Beneficiaries and Informal Agency Policymaking, 92 Cornell L. Rev. 397 (2007). Finally, some worry that the ability to interpret its regulations without notice-and-comment formality may tempt an agency to be less precise than it should be in drafting legislative rules—"to promulgate mush," as one court put it. Paralyzed Veterans of Am. v. D.C. Arena L.P., 117 F.3d 579, 585 (D.C. Cir. 1997).

On the other side of the equation are the important benefits that nonlegislative documents can bring to those affected by agency action and to agencies themselves. One such benefit is notifying the public of the agency's understanding of governing requirements and its regulatory responsibilities. Affected private persons can be expected to value advice on how the agency will approach the statutes and regulations it implements. Indeed, regulated entities sometimes petition agencies to issue such advice. In addition, the increasing formalization and burdens associated with notice-and-comment rulemaking may create a legitimate agency need for more flexible and less costly mechanisms to supplement its legislative rules as new issues and problems arise.

Equally important is the role of guidance in cabining the enforcement discretion of lower-level agency personnel. "The usual interface between a member of the public and an agency does not involve the agency head, but a relatively low-level member of staff; . . . the postal clerk, . . . the welfare worker, the District Forester, the IRS examiner, the Food and Drug Administration (FDA) inspector, or the application desk officer . . . [all share] responsibility for initial processing of the public's business. . . . [T]he choice the public faces is between having the clerk apply his own interpretation of the agency's legislative rules, or having his decisions and actions further controlled by the agency's [guidance]. . . . [T]he affected public (especially the repeat players among them) will almost certainly prefer a state of affairs in which . . . instructions [for applying legislative rules] are publicly given and may be relied upon—that is, the lower-level bureaucrats are to follow them, and higher levels are to depart from them only with an explanation." PETER L. STRAUSS, THE RULEMAKING CONTINUUM, 41 Duke L.J. 1463, 1482–83 (1992). Professor Gillian Metzger argues that this supervisory component to guidance has a constitutional dimension as well: "Put starkly, bureaucratic and managerial accountability in the form of internal executive branch supervision is an essential precondition for political and legal accountability given the phenomenon of delegation. . . . [C]ourts should give agencies more leeway to issue informal guidance without running afoul of the APA's notice-and-comment requirements, on the grounds that such guidance is a crucial part of agency efforts to fulfill their internal oversight responsibilities and curtail lower-level discretion. . . . Acknowledging the constitutional status of administration is . . . a crucial step in the development of models of constitutional interpretation and enforcement that better accord with the reality of administrative constitutionalism." GILLIAN E. METZGER, THE CONSTITUTIONAL DUTY TO SUPERVISE, 124 Yale L.J. 1836, 1895, 1919–20, 1933 (2015).

The availability of guidance also may have significance for the mode regulation takes. Contemporary writing about regulation often emphasizes the advantages of agencies setting performance standards rather than mandating specific mechanisms that regulated entities must employ. But the success of standards as a method of regulation may turn on an agency's ability to provide advice on what approaches will suffice to meet the governing standard. Such guidance is likely to prove particularly important for those who lack resources to devise their own methods for achieving compliance. If, as in General Electric, agencies are limited in their ability to indicate acceptable approaches to meeting a standard in common contexts, standards may carry too much uncertainty and too high transaction costs to be a workable mode of regulation. Although agencies could seek to address this problem by issuing their "guidance" through notice-and-comment proceedings, doing so may undermine the very flexibility in governing requirements that the agency sought in adopting a standard in the first place.

(3) ***Encouraging Greater Use of Contemporary Guidance and Advisory Preemption.*** ACUS recently offered a new angle on how agencies use guidance, with a report and recommendations urging agencies to rely more on contemporary guidance. See ACUS, Guidance in the Rulemaking Process, Recommendation 2014–3 (adopted June 6, 2014).[14] The key

---

[14] The recommendation and supporting materials are available at: http://www.acus.gov/recommendation/guidance-rulemaking-process.

characteristic of contemporary guidance, as its name implies, is that the guidance is issued contemporaneously with the regulation the guidance helps clarify. ACUS identified several forms that contemporary guidance may take: Agencies might provide guidance about the meaning and application of rules that agencies provide in explanatory "statement[s] of their basis and purpose" that constitute the bulk of the "preambles" issued with final rules. Alternatively, agencies might include guidance in the regulation's text, in the form of notes and examples, or in general appendixes to a rule contained in the CFR. A third example is the freestanding guidance documents that agencies sometimes issue when they promulgate a rule. ACUS advocated that agencies make better use of contemporaneous guidance, particularly in the form of the statement of basis and purpose in a rule's preamble, encouraging agencies to address how the rule advances statutory objectives and to be careful to avoid using the preamble as a substitute for regulatory language. In this regard, ACUS urged agencies to "avoid use of mandatory language in the preambles to final rules, unless an agency is using these words to describe a statutory, regulatory, or constitutional requirement, or the language is addressed to agency staff and will not foreclose agency consideration of positions advanced by affected parties." Id.

In addition, Professor Sarah Light has argued that federal agencies may use guidance as "advisory preemption" to states. In September 2016, NHTSA issued its Federal Automated Vehicles Policy, which "strongly encourages States to allow DOT alone to regulate." The Policy conceded that states may not follow the agency's advice and asked states to consult with NHTSA. Sarah E. Light, Advisory Nonpreemption, 95 Wash. U. L. Rev. 325, 332 (2017). Is such action desirable as a matter of federalism?

(4) *Current APA and Presidential Requirements Outside of Notice and Comment.* Although the APA exempts interpretive rules, general policy statements, and "rules of agency organization, procedure, or practice" from the notice-and-comment requirements of § 553, it has long subjected such measures to publication requirements. Under § 552(a)(1), agencies are required to publish such rules and policy statements in the Federal Register, and absent such publication or actual and timely notice, "a person may not in any manner be required to resort to, or be adversely affected by" these materials. Section 552(a)(2) further provides that "[a] final order, opinion, statement of policy, interpretation, or staff manual or instruction that affects a member of the public may be relied on, used, or cited as precedent by an agency against a party other than an agency only if—(i) . . .indexed and either made available or published . . . or (ii) the party has actual and timely notice of the terms thereof."

Professor Nina Mendelson has suggested creating a procedure, akin to § 553(e) of the APA, under which "citizens could be entitled to receive notice of a guidance document's issuance and to petition the agency to revise or repeal the document." She also has proposed requiring notice-and-comment rulemaking for important policy decisions, or at least demanding that agencies solicit comment on important guidance—even if not imposing a requirement of agency response. Mendelson, supra, at 444–45. Do you think such procedural measures would be an improvement?

Although Congress has not amended the APA to address this issue, the White House has imposed additional mandates on agency guidance (though these requirements do not create any private rights). In a BULLETIN FOR AGENCY GOOD GUIDANCE PRACTICES issued in January 2007 (and still in effect),[15] 72 Fed. Reg. 3432 (Jan. 25, 2007), OMB imposed transparency, participation, and review requirements on "significant guidance documents," defined to largely track the definition of significant regulatory actions requiring OMB review under Executive Order 12866, p. 1496. Each agency must maintain a current list of such guidance documents on its web site and develop "a means for the public to submit comments electronically . . . and to submit a request electronically for issuance, reconsideration, modification, or rescission of significant guidance documents . . . . [N]o formal response by the agency is required." § III. For economically significant guidance, however—guidance that may reasonably be anticipated to have an annual impact of $100 million or more, or materially and adversely affect the economy—agencies are required to provide notice and an opportunity for comment prior to promulgation of the final guidance, and in addition to post on their websites a response to the comments received. § IV. The Bulletin also requires agencies to develop procedures to ensure that significant guidance documents are approved by senior agency officials, and agency employees are instructed not to deviate from this guidance without "appropriate justification and supervisory concurrence." § II.1. These procedures were based in part on good guidance procedures that the FDA initially developed in 1997 and that subsequently received congressional approval in the Food and Drug Administration Modernization Act of 1997, 21 U.S.C. § 371(h)(1) (2006); see also Rakoff, supra, at 169–70 (describing the FDA's procedures).

As noted in Subsection 4.d below, OMB has long undertaken centralized review of agency rulemaking pursuant to executive orders. In the past, agency guidance documents were exempt from such review. In 2007, however, President Bush allowed OMB to demand consultation with an agency before the agency issues a significant guidance document, defined similarly to significant regulatory actions. See EO 13422, 72 Fed. Reg. 2703 (Jan. 18, 2007). Although President Obama repealed that Order, OMB continued to review significant agency guidance documents in his Administration.

(5) *Availability of Judicial Review.* The determination of whether an agency issuance is really a policy statement may affect the availability of judicial review under the APA. Sometimes, only legislative rules can be reviewed under a specific agency statute in an appellate court in the first instance. More generally, under the APA, courts can review only "final" agency actions. Some courts have made it almost impossible for policy statements to be considered final and therefore reviewable by equating the second prong of the finality test with legislative rules. See, for example,

---

[15] http://www.gpo.gov/fdsys/pkg/FR-2007-01-25/pdf/E7-1066.pdf.

NATIONAL MINING ASS'N V. MCCARTHY, 758 F.3d 243, 250–51 (D.C. Cir. 2014): "One might think that an agency memo entitled 'Final Guidance' would be final. But that would be wrong, at least under the sometimes-byzantine case law. An agency action is final only if it is both 'the consummation of the agency's decisionmaking process' and a decision by which 'rights or obligations have been determined' or from which 'legal consequences will flow.' Bennett v. Spear, 520 U.S. 154, 177–78 (1997) (internal quotation marks omitted). EPA concedes that the Final Guidance is the consummation of EPA's decisionmaking process. But EPA characterizes the Final Guidance as a general policy statement that has no 'legal consequences.' Therefore, according to EPA, we cannot review its legality at this time; EPA says that judicial review must wait until a permit applicant has had a permit denied and seeks review of that permit denial. . . . [T]he reviewability issue turns on one question: Is the Final Guidance a legislative rule or a general statement of policy?" Finally, the form of agency action may be relevant in assessments of ripeness. For an argument contrary to the D.C. Circuit's position, see Peter L. Strauss, Publication Rules in the Rulemaking Spectrum: Assuring Proper Respect for an Essential Element. 53 Admin. L. Rev. 803 (2001).

We discuss the issues of finality and ripeness in Chapter IX, Subsec. 2.c (p. 1418). But it is worth considering whether the risk that guidance may not be subject to judicial review provides a strong reason to be cautious about expanding the ability of agencies to use this exception from notice-and-comment procedures. An alternative would be to amend the APA to clarify that interpretive rules and policy statements constitute final agency action, clearing the way for judicial review. For a proposal to this effect, see William Funk, Legislating for Nonlegislative Rules, 56 Admin. L. Rev. 1023 (2004).

NOTES ON INTERPRETIVE RULES AND REGULATORY VAGUENESS

(1) *The Binding Effect of Interpretive Rules.* Section 553(b) does not differentiate between policy statements, interpretive rules, or rules of agency organization, procedure, or practice. Yet rules of agency organization, procedure, and practice (see p. 390) can bind both the agency and the public—indeed, they would serve little purpose if they could not.

More complicated questions arise over the binding effect of interpretive rules. Existing case law applies essentially the same inquiry to distinguish between legislative rules and interpretive rules as is used to distinguish between legislative rules and policy statements: a valid interpretive rule cannot carry the force and effect of law on its own. But in practice the inquiry can look different. As discussed before, policy statements and guidance are assessed to see whether they create binding effects. By contrast, an interpretive rule can be valid even if it clarifies preexisting vague statutory duties or has the effect of creating new duties. Therefore, the courts assess whether the interpretation is "fairly encompassed" within the statute or regulation being construed. Air Transport Assn. v. Federal Aviation Admin., 291 F.3d 49, 55–56 (D.C. Cir. 2002). As a result, an agency may use an interpretive rule to promulgate guidance with more binding effect than a policy statement, "but only if the agency's position can be characterized as an 'interpretation' of a statute or legislative regulation rather than as an exercise of independent policymaking authority." Manning, supra, at 916. As we noted at the start of Subsection 3.b, the terminology of categories of nonlegislative rules—notably interpretive rules and policy statements/guidance—can be confusing. For a thorough discussion of the relevant lines of doctrine (the clarifying law doctrine for interpretive rules and the binding norm doctrine for guidance and policy) and a call for more uniformity across the categories, see Ronald M. Levin, Rulemaking and the Guidance Exemption, available at: http://papers.ssrn.com/sol3/papers.cfm?abstract_id=2958267. To help see how it all fits together, we discuss a case that analyzes an agency action under several categories of exceptions to notice-and-comment rulemaking (including interpretive rules and policy statements) in Subsection 3.c (p. 392).

(2) *Incentives "to Promulgate Mush."* Section 553(b)'s exception for interpretive rules, particularly combined with deference to agency interpretations of their own regulations, "creates concerns that agencies will have incentives to promulgate mush" through the notice-and-comment process and then fill in more contestable details through subsequent less formal "interpretations." Paralyzed Veterans, 117 F.3d at 584. Or as the D.C. Circuit put the point in APPALACHIAN POWER CO. V. EPA, 208 F.3d 1015 (D.C. Cir. 2000): "The phenomenon we see in this case is familiar. Congress passes a broadly worded statute. The agency follows with regulations containing broad language, open-ended phrases, ambiguous standards and the like. Then as years pass, the agency issues circulars or guidance or memoranda, explaining, interpreting, defining and often expanding the commands in the regulations. One guidance document may yield another and then another and so on. Several words in a regulation may spawn hundreds of pages of text as the agency offers more and more detail regarding what its regulations demand of regulated entities. Law is made, without notice and comment, without public participation, and without publication in the Federal Register or the Code of Federal Regulations. With the advent of the Internet, the agency does not need these official publications to ensure widespread circulation; it can inform those affected simply by posting its new guidance or memoranda or policy statement on its web site. An agency operating in this way gains a large advantage. 'It can issue or amend its real rules, i.e., its interpretative rules and policy statements, quickly and inexpensively without following any statutorily prescribed procedures.' Richard J. Pierce, Jr., Seven Ways to Deossify Agency Rulemaking, 47 Admin. L. Rev. 59, 85 (1995)." Should courts be more willing to tell agencies than Congress (in the delegation context) that they have not worked hard enough?

(3) *Problems of Fair Notice.* A separate reason to be concerned about enactment of vague regulations is the concern that regulated entities may lack fair notice of their regulatory obligations. Such a concern appears to figure prominently in CHIEF JUDGE EDWARDS'S opinion in UNITED STATES V. CHRYSLER CORP., 158 F.3d 1350 (D.C. Cir. 1998). Chrysler had refused to recall 91,000 cars that NHTSA asserted were not in compliance with its standards respecting seat belts. The relevant standard specified a test the

belt assemblies must pass but did not specify the exact placement of the testing equipment. Chrysler's belt assemblies passed the test with the equipment in one position. NHTSA subsequently performed the test with the assemblies in another position that it interpreted its standard to require, and they failed that test. "[A] manufacturer cannot be found to be out of compliance with a standard if NHTSA has failed to give fair notice of what is required by the standard." That notice had not been given under the governing regulatory standard, and thus the court held Chrysler could not be required to recall the cars in question. Significantly, however, the court based its requirement of fair notice on due process and implied that a clear interpretive rule setting forth the agency's view of the regulation would have sufficed.

(4) *The D.C. Circuit's One-Bite Rule and Its Rejection by the Supreme Court.* For about a quarter century, the D.C. Circuit had a prohibition on using an interpretive rule to revise an earlier interpretive rule. This prohibition, often referred to as the D.C. Circuit's "one-bite rule," was based on the view that once an agency has issued guidance giving a regulation a definitive interpretation, subsequent revision of that interpretation in effect amends the regulation, requiring § 553 procedures. In ALASKA PROFESSIONAL HUNTERS ASS'N V. FAA, 177 F.3d 1030 (D.C. Cir. 1999), for example, the FAA issued a "Notice to Operators" that brought professional "hunting and fishing guides" in Alaska within certain FAA flight regulations. For almost thirty years, the FAA's Alaskan Region had interpreted the regulations as not applying to the guides and provided official advice to that effect. The D.C. Circuit held that the FAA was required to use notice-and-comment rulemaking to now apply the regulations to these Alaskan guides. An earlier case often cited as establishing the rule is PARALYZED VETERANS OF AMERICA V. D.C. ARENA L.P., 117 F.3d 579, 586 (D.C. Cir 1997): "The government argues that an agency has the same latitude to modify its interpretation of a regulation as it does its interpretation of a statute under Chevron. We think the government is wrong. . . . Under the APA, agencies are obliged to engage in notice and comment before formulating regulations, which applies as well to 'repeals' or 'amendments.' See 5 U.S.C. § 551(5). To allow an agency to make a fundamental change in its interpretation of a substantive regulation without notice and comment obviously would undermine those APA requirements."

Is a one-bite rule an appropriate response to concerns about evasion of the notice-and-comment process? UNITED STATES V. MAGNESIUM CORP. OF AMERICA, 616 F.3d 1129, 1139–41 (10th Cir. 2010): "The implicit reasoning appears to be this: if an agency amends its interpretation of a rule, it is effectively 'amending [the] rule' itself, 5 U.S.C. § 551(5), and the APA by its own terms defines this amendment as a kind of rulemaking, something the agency may not accomplish without notice and comment procedures." Noting that a substantial circuit split existed on the propriety of the one-bite rule, the Tenth Circuit concluded it did not need to choose a side in the debate, because "[b]y its terms the Alaska Hunters doctrine applies only to *definitive* regulatory interpretations; even under Alaska Hunters an agency remains free to disavow and amend a *tentative* interpretation of one of its rules without notice and comment." Accord MidWest Inc. v. Sec'y of Labor, 560 F.3d 506, 509–10 (D.C. Cir. 2009). The court concluded that only such a tentative interpretation was involved in the case before it.

In 2015, the Supreme Court rejected the D.C. Circuit's one-bite rule in PEREZ V. MORTGAGE BANKERS ASS'N, 135 S.Ct. 1199: "The Paralyzed Veterans doctrine is contrary to the clear text of the APA's rulemaking provisions, and it improperly imposes on agencies an obligation beyond the 'maximum procedural requirements' specified in the APA, Vermont Yankee Nuclear Power Corp. v. Natural Resources Defense Council, Inc., 435 U.S. 519, 524 (1978). The text of the APA answers the question presented. Section 4 of the APA provides that 'notice of proposed rule making shall be published in the Federal Register.' 5 U.S.C. § 553(b). When such notice is required by the APA, 'the agency shall give interested persons an opportunity to participate in the rule making.' § 553(c). But § 4 further states that unless 'notice or hearing is required by statute,' the Act's notice-and-comment requirement 'does not apply . . . to interpretative rules.' § 553(b)(A). This exemption of interpretive rules from the notice-and-comment process is categorical, and it is fatal to the rule announced in Paralyzed Veterans. . . .

"The Paralyzed Veterans doctrine creates just such a judge-made procedural right: the right to notice and an opportunity to comment when an agency changes its interpretation of one of the regulations it enforces. That requirement may be wise policy. Or it may not. Regardless, imposing such an obligation is the responsibility of Congress or the administrative agencies, not the courts. We trust that Congress weighed the costs and benefits of placing more rigorous procedural restrictions on the issuance of interpretive rules. In the end, Congress decided to adopt standards that permit agencies to promulgate freely such rules—whether or not they are consistent with earlier interpretations. That the D.C. Circuit would have struck the balance differently does not permit that court or this one to overturn Congress' contrary judgment."

Again mimicking the Vermont Yankee decision, the Perez Court underscored that those objecting to a new agency interpretation can still challenge the agency's change in view as arbitrary and capricious—in other words, even if the agency's action procedurally conforms to the APA, a substantive challenge to an agency's reasoning remains available. Do you think arbitrary-and-capricious review is the appropriate frame through which to address an agency's alleged excessive use of a procedural exemption? As the Court makes clear, under arbitrary-and-capricious review, an agency will have to explain and justify its decision to change a governing interpretation (see FCC v. Fox Television Stations, Inc., 556 U.S. 502 (2009), p. 1100). But given Perez's holding on the scope of § 553(b), will an agency also have to explain and justify a decision to issue its new interpretation outside of notice-and-comment procedures, at least beyond stating that such procedures are not required by the APA?

(5) ***Interpretive Rules and Judicial Deference***. The debate in Perez centered not on the validity of the one-bite rule but instead on whether an

agency's interpretation of its own regulations should trigger deference. Under currently governing doctrine—alternatively referred to as Seminole Rock or Auer deference—an agency's interpretation of its own regulation is given "controlling weight unless it is plainly erroneous or inconsistent with the regulation." In their concurrences in Perez, Justices Alito, Scalia, and Thomas all called for overturning Seminole Rock/Auer deference. Justice Scalia insisted that "[b]y deferring to interpretive rules, we have allowed agencies to make binding rules unhampered by notice-and-comment procedures." He also argued that deferring to agency regulatory interpretations is at odds with the APA's provisions on judicial review. Justice Thomas maintained that such deference is unconstitutional and violates separation of powers. For further discussion of this aspect of the concurrences and Seminole Rock and Auer deference, see Ch. VIII (p. 1247).

Note that the concurring justices' rejection of deference is not limited to interpretations issued outside of notice-and-comment procedures but would apply to all agency regulatory interpretations. Would it be better to tie the availability of deference for agency regulatory interpretations to the procedures used in their promulgation? The Court took such an approach with respect to deference for agency statutory interpretations in United States v. Mead Corp., 533 U.S. 218 (2001), p. 1221.

c. The Other Exceptions

> **USDA'S "PUBLIC PARTICIPATION IN RULEMAKING" POLICY FOR "PUBLIC PROPERTY, LOANS, GRANTS, BENEFITS, OR CONTRACTS" AND ITS REVOCATION**
> *Notes on Subject-Based and Agency Operation Exceptions*
> *Putting Items Together*

This section applies, according to the provisions thereof, except to the extent that there is involved—

> *(1) a military or foreign affairs function of the United States; or*
>
> *(2) a matter relating to agency management or personnel or to public property, loans, grants, benefits, or contracts.*

5 U.S.C. § 553(a)

Except when notice or hearing is required by statute, this subsection does not apply—(A) to . . . rules of agency organization, procedure, or practice . . .

5 U.S.C. § 553(b)

USDA POLICY ON "PUBLIC PARTICIPATION IN RULEMAKING" FOR "PUBLIC PROPERTY, LOANS, GRANTS, BENEFITS, OR CONTRACTS" AND ITS REVOCATION

36 Fed. Reg. 13804 (July 24, 1971).
78 Fed. Reg. 64194 (Oct. 28, 2013).

[Agencies can voluntarily agree to use notice-and-comment procedures when they are not required to do so. Consider the following two announcements by the Department of Agriculture, one from July 1971 and the other from October 2013:]

Public Participation in Rulemaking: Statement of Policy (1971)

Notice is hereby given of the policy of the Department of Agriculture to give notice of proposed rule making and to invite the public to participate in rule making where not required by law.

5 U.S.C. 553 provides generally that before rules are issued by Government agencies, notice of proposed rule making must be published in the Federal Register, and interested persons must be given an opportunity to participate in the rule making through submission of data, views, or arguments.

The law exempts from this requirement rules relating to public property, loans, grants, benefits, or contracts.

The Administrative Conference of the United States has recommended that Government agencies provide for public participation when formulating rules relating to public property, loans, grants, benefits, or contracts as a matter of policy.

The advantages of implementing the Conference's recommendation that the public be afforded an opportunity for greater participation in the formulation of rules relating to public property, loans, grants, benefits, or contracts will outweigh any disadvantages such as increased costs or delays.

The public participation requirements prescribed by 5 U.S.C. 553 (b) and (c) will be followed by all agencies of the Department in rule making relating to public property, loans, grants, benefits, or contracts. The exemptions permitted from such requirements where an agency finds for good cause that compliance would be impracticable, unnecessary or contrary to the public interest will be used sparingly, that is, only when there is a substantial basis therefor. Where such a finding is made, the finding and a statement of the reasons therefore will be published with the rule.

Revocation of Statement of Policy on Public Participation in Rulemaking (2013)

SUMMARY: The U.S. Department of Agriculture (USDA) is revoking the Statement of Policy titled "Public Participation in

Rulemaking," published in the Federal Register on July 24, 1971 (36 FR 13804), which required agencies in USDA to follow the Administrative Procedure Act's (APA) notice-and-comment rulemaking procedures in situations where the APA does not require it. The Statement of Policy implemented a 1969 recommendation by the Administrative Conference of the United States (ACUS), which urged Congress to amend the APA to remove the exemption from the notice-and-comment requirement for rulemakings relating to "public property, loans, grants, benefits, or contracts," adding that agencies should follow the notice-and-comment procedures pending amendment of the APA. By revoking the 1971 Statement of Policy, USDA restores the discretion to use notice-and-comment procedures when appropriate, unless otherwise required by law, with regard to this class of rulemakings. This action also improves USDA's ability to implement programs efficiently.

NOTES ON SUBJECT-BASED AND AGENCY OPERATION EXCEPTIONS

(1) **The USDA's Decision.** The USDA provided prior notice and took comments on the policy revocation. Only two comments were filed before the agency deadline: an individual who was worried about the word "appropriate" and the Humane Society of the United States, which raised a number of policy and legal points. Why did so few people comment? What are the benefits and costs—to the agency,[16] to regulated entities, and to the public—from the USDA's recent decision to forgo notice-and-comment procedures for a set of its actions?

(2) **Relief from Deportation as a Benefit?** In defending its DAPA policy providing relief from deportation for certain parents without proper documentation if they had children who were citizens or legally permanent residents, DHS also relied, in part, on the process exception for public benefits. The Fifth Circuit rejected that argument in Texas v. United States, 809 F.3d 134, 148, 177 (2015), though it noted that "persons granted lawful presence pursuant to DAPA are no longer 'bar[red] . . . from receiving social security retirement benefits, social security disability benefits, or health insurance under Part A of the Medicare program": "Section 553(a)(2) exempts rules from notice and comment 'to the extent that there is involved . . . a matter relating to . . . public property, loans, grants, benefits, or contracts.' To avoid 'carv[ing] the heart out of the notice provisions of Section 553', the courts construe the public-benefits exception very narrowly as applying only to agency action that 'clearly and directly relate[s] to "benefits" as that word is used in section 553(a)(2).' DAPA does not 'clearly and directly' relate to public benefits as that term is used in § 553(a)(2). That subsection suggests that 'rulemaking requirements for agencies managing benefit programs are . . . voluntarily imposed,' but USCIS—the agency tasked with evaluating DAPA applications—is not an agency managing benefit programs. Persons who meet the DAPA criteria do not directly receive the

---

[16] Recall the agency's experience in Sugar Cane Growers Cooperative v. Veneman, 289 F.3d 89 (D.C. Cir. 2002), p. 283, which was not cited explicitly in the revocation.

kind of public benefit that has been recognized, or was likely to have been included, under this exception." These parents, if granted "lawful presence" status under the program, could have applied for certain Social Security and Medicare programs managed by other agencies (and been able to work lawfully). Why shouldn't this be enough to meet the exception?

(3) *Statutes Can Override the APA.* Congress can always eliminate the APA's exceptions in particular contexts. For example, Congress has limited the scope of exemptions for the Education Department: "The exemption for public property, loans, grants and benefits in section 553(a)(2) of Title 5 shall apply only to regulations—(1) that govern the first grant competition under a new or substantially revised program authority as determined by the Secretary, or (2) where the Secretary determines that the requirements of this subsection will cause extreme hardship to the intended beneficiaries of the program affected by such regulations." 20 U.S.C. § 1232. There are other such statutory provisions, often in agency organic statutes, which force agencies to use notice-and-comment rulemaking for actions the APA would not mandate such process. See 1 Richard J. Pierce, Jr., Administrative Law Treatise § 7.10 at 669 (5th ed. 2010).

(4) *The Foreign Affairs Exception.* Similar deference to national security concerns as the D.C. Circuit displayed in Jifry, see p. 351, is evident in RAJAH V. MUKASEY, 544 F.3d 427 (2d Cir. 2008), a decision upholding a special registration program instituted by the Attorney General after September 11, 2001. Under the National Security Entry-Exit Registration System (NSEERS), alien males from certain countries had to appear for registration, fingerprinting, and presentation of immigration-related documents if they were over the age of 16 and had not qualified for permanent residence. Those who did not appear risked arrest. Those who did appear but whose immigration status was irregular risked deportation. Four men who appeared for registration and were placed in deportation proceedings challenged their deportations in part on the ground that the Attorney General had failed to comply with § 553 in instituting the program. Although the Attorney General had used notice-and-comment proceedings to promulgate a general enabling regulation that set forth the framework of the program, he had not done so in issuing the notices that designated which specific groups had to register.

According to the Second Circuit, however, the group specifications fell within the scope of § 553(a)(1): "There are at least three definitely undesirable international consequences that would follow from notice and comment rulemaking. First, sensitive foreign intelligence might be revealed in the course of explaining why some of a particular nation's citizens are regarded as a threat. Second, relations with other countries might be impaired if the government were to conduct and resolve a public debate over why some citizens of particular countries were a potential danger to our security. Third, the process would be slow and cumbersome, diminishing our ability to collect intelligence regarding, and enhance defenses in anticipation of, a potential attack by foreign terrorists." The court also held that the rule itself need not state the potential undesirable consequences stemming from use of § 553 procedures for the exception to apply, and that the Attorney

General need not prove that the group specifications were tied to "the President's conduct of foreign affairs where the relevance to international relations is facially plain."

NSEERS, at its height, applied to 25 countries (24 of which were Muslin-majority; the other was North Korea). Until it was stopped informally in 2011,[17] the program led to the deportation of about 13,000 people but did not produce any convictions for terrorism or related crimes. Even if the APA's procedural exception for foreign affairs applies to the program, what are some of the costs to the government's decision to forgo notice and comment?

(5) ***Agency Organization and Procedure.*** Under § 553(b), agencies do not have to provide prior notice and comment for "rules of agency organization, procedure, or practice." Determining what counts as "procedure" has bedeviled the lower courts, and the Supreme Court has not weighed in. In AIR TRANSPORT ASS'N OF AMERICA V. DEP'T OF TRANSPORTATION, 900 F.2d 369 (D.C. Cir. 1990),[18] the court reviewed FAA regulations concerning the "adjudication of administrative civil penalty actions," which had been issued without prior notice and comment, and found them procedurally deficient. JUDGE EDWARDS explained: "In sum, the FAA's contention that it did not affect the 'substantive' obligations of aviators under the Federal Aviation Act is irrelevant. 'The characterizations "substantive" and "procedural"—no more here than elsewhere in the law—do not guide inexorably to the right result, nor do they really advance the inquiry very far.' . . . In using the terms 'rules of agency organization, procedure, or practice,' Congress intended to distinguish not between rules affecting different classes of rights—'substantive' and 'procedural'—but rather to distinguish between rules affecting different subject matters—'the rights or interests of regulated' parties, . . . and agencies' 'internal operations,'. . . . Because the Penalty Rules substantially affect civil penalty defendants' 'right to avail [themselves] of an administrative adjudication,' members of the aviation community had a legitimate interest in participating in the rulemaking process." In a dissenting opinion, JUDGE SILBERMAN proposed a different test from the majority's substantial effects reasoning: "If we assume a spectrum of rules running from the most substantive to the most procedural, I would describe the former as those that regulate 'primary conduct' in the way that term is used in Toilet Goods Ass'n, Inc. v. Gardner, 387 U.S. 158, 164 (1967), and the latter are those furthest away from primary conduct. In other words, if a given regulation purports to direct, control, or condition the behavior of those institutions or individuals subject to regulation by the authorizing statute it is not procedural, it is substantive. At the other end of the spectrum are those rules, such as the ones before us in this case, which deal with enforcement or adjudication of claims of violations of the substantive norm but which do not purport to affect the substantive norm. These kinds of rules are, in my view, clearly procedural."

---

[17] DHS formally repealed the program in December 2016, amid calls by Republicans to restart it after President Trump took office.

[18] The decision was later vacated for mootness.

More recently, in PUBLIC CITIZEN V. DEP'T OF STATE, 276 F.3d 634 (D.C. Cir. 2002), the D.C. Circuit held that the Department of State's regulation (issued without prior notice and comment) for processing FOIA requests that limited searches to records created before the request was received (in other words, searches would not include records created between the time the request was filed and the time the search for relevant records was conducted) was procedurally permitted: "As we recognized in American Hospital Ass'n v. Bowen, '[o]ver time, our circuit in applying the § 553 exemption for procedural rules has gradually shifted focus from asking whether a given procedure has a "substantial impact" on parties to . . . inquiring more broadly whether the agency action . . . encodes a substantive value judgment.' 834 F.2d 1037, 1047 (D.C.Cir.1987) (citation omitted). This 'gradual move,' we noted, 'reflects a candid recognition that even unambiguously procedural measures affect parties to some degree.' Id. . . . Because the Department's cut-off policy applies to all FOIA requests, making no distinction between requests on the basis of subject matter, it clearly encodes no 'substantive value judgment'. . ." Would discussions about the substance-procedure distinction from Civil Procedure (specifically, over whether the Federal Rules of Civil Procedure should govern state-law claims) be helpful here?

The Fifth Circuit has held onto the "substantial impact" test. In Texas v. United States, this exception also arose: "A binding rule is not required to undergo notice and comment if it is one 'of agency organization, procedure, or practice.' § 553(b)(A). '[T]he substantial impact test is the primary means by which [we] look beyond the label 'procedural' to determine whether a rule is of the type Congress thought appropriate for public participation.' 'An agency rule that modifies substantive rights and interests can only be nominally procedural, and the exemption for such rules of agency procedure cannot apply.' DAPA undoubtedly meets that test—conferring lawful presence on 500,000 illegal aliens residing in Texas forces the state to choose between spending millions of dollars to subsidize driver's licenses and amending its statutes." 809 F.3d at 176.

(6) *Agency Management and Personnel and the Special Counsel Regulation.* The Department of Justice promulgated a regulation concerning the selection and service of a Special Counsel under the Independent Counsel Reorganization Act of 1994, without providing prior notice and comment, effective July 1, 1999. The rule addressed the lack of process:[19] "This rule relates to matters of agency management or personnel, and is therefore exempt from the usual requirements of prior notice and comment and a 30-day delay in the effective date. See 5 U.S.C. 553(a)(2). Moreover, to the extent that rulemaking procedures would otherwise be applicable, the Department finds that this rule would be exempted from the requirements of prior notice and comment as a rule of agency organization, procedure, or practice. See 5 U.S.C. 553(b)(A)." 64 Fed. Reg. 37,038, 37,041 (July 9, 1999). The appointment of Special Counsel Robert Mueller to investigate interference by Russia in the 2016 election was made pursuant to this regulation. If the regulation properly falls under the "agency

---

[19]   DOJ also cited good cause as a back-up position in light of the statute expiring on June 30, 1999.

management or personnel exception," it could be repealed immediately with notice in the Federal Register. If the regulation falls under the "agency organization, procedure, or practice," any such repeal would take effect 30 days after publication, absent "good cause."

(7) ***American Bar Association Resolution 106b.*** In February 2016, the American Bar Association's House of Delegates passed a resolution (106b), which included the following paragraph: "(8). Repeal the exemptions from the notice-and-comment process for 'public . . . loans, grants [and] benefits' and narrow the exemptions for 'public property [and] contracts' and for 'military or foreign affairs functions.'" Do you support this proposal?

PUTTING ITEMS TOGETHER

Under 49 U.S.C. §§ 44901(a), 44902(a)(1), the Transportation Security Administration (TSA) must screen individuals who want to board a commercial airline flight to make sure that they are not "carrying unlawfully a dangerous weapon, explosive, or other destructive substance." Congress left many details of this process to the agency to determine. But not all. In the Intelligence Reform and Terrorism Prevention Act of 2004, Congress told the TSA to "give a high priority to developing, testing, improving, and deploying" at airport screening checkpoints a new technology "that detects nonmetallic, chemical, biological, and radiological weapons, and explosives, in all forms." 49 U.S.C. § 44925(a). In response, the TSA worked with private contractors to develop advanced imaging technology (AIT), which produces (by various means) a "crude image of an unclothed person, who must stand in the scanner for several seconds while it generates the image."

In 2010, after experimenting with using AIT as a primary screening device at a subset of airports, the TSA decided to use these full-body scanners at all airports, without providing the public prior notice and opportunity to comment. The Electronic Privacy Information Center sued to stop the program, in part relying on § 553. The resulting decision, ELECTRONIC PRIVACY INFORMATION CENTER V. U.S. DEP'T OF HOMELAND SEC., 653 F.3d 1 (D.C. Cir. 2011), written by JUDGE GINSBURG, addresses several issues discussed thus far in this chapter.

(1) ***Is the Program a Rule of Agency Procedure?*** The TSA argued that under D.C. Circuit case law, the program merely "alter[ed] the manner in which the parties present themselves . . . to the agency" and therefore qualified to be adopted without notice and comment under § 553(b). The court disagreed: "We consider first the TSA's argument it has announced a rule of 'agency organization, procedure, or practice,' which our cases refer to as a 'procedural rule.' In general, a procedural rule 'does not itself "alter the rights or interests of parties, although it may alter the manner in which the parties present themselves or their viewpoints to the agency." 'Chamber of Commerce of U.S. v. DOL, 174 F.3d 206, 211 (D.C.Cir.1999) (quoting Batterton v. Marshall, 648 F.2d 694, 707 (D.C.Cir.1980)). That is, the rule does 'not impose new substantive burdens.' Aulenback, Inc. v. Fed. Highway Admin., 103 F.3d 156, 169 (D.C.Cir.1997). As we have noted before, however, a rule with a 'substantial impact' upon the persons subject to it is not

necessarily a substantive rule under § 553(b)(3)(A). See Pub. Citizen v. Dep't of State, 276 F.3d 634, 640–41 (2002) [p. 391]. Further, the distinction between substantive and procedural rules is 'one of degree' depending upon 'whether the substantive effect is sufficiently grave so that notice and comment are needed to safeguard the policies underlying the APA.' Lamoille Valley R.R. Co. v. ICC, 711 F.2d 295, 328 (D.C.Cir.1983). Those policies, as we have elsewhere observed, are to serve 'the need for public participation in agency decisionmaking,' Chamber of Commerce, 174 F.3d at 211, and to ensure the agency has all pertinent information before it when making a decision, Am. Hosp. Ass'n v. Bowen, 834 F.2d 1037, 1044 (1987). In order to further these policies, the exception for procedural rules 'must be narrowly construed.' United States v. Picciotto, 875 F.2d 345, 347 (D.C.Cir.1989).

"Of course, stated at a high enough level of generality, the new policy imposes no new substantive obligations upon airline passengers: The requirement that a passenger pass through a security checkpoint is hardly novel, the prohibition against boarding a plane with a weapon or an explosive device even less so. But this overly abstract account of the change in procedure at the checkpoint elides the privacy interests at the heart of the petitioners' concern with AIT. Despite the precautions taken by the TSA, it is clear that by producing an image of the unclothed passenger, an AIT scanner intrudes upon his or her personal privacy in a way a magnetometer does not. Therefore, regardless whether this is a 'new substantive burden,' see Aulenback, 103 F.3d at 169, the change substantively affects the public to a degree sufficient to implicate the policy interests animating notice-and-comment rulemaking. Cf. Pickus v. Bd. of Parole, 507 F.2d 1107, 1113–14 (D.C.Cir.1974) (rules governing parole hearings not procedural because they went 'beyond formality and substantially affect[ed]' prisoners' liberty). Indeed, few if any regulatory procedures impose directly and significantly upon so many members of the public. Not surprisingly, therefore, much public concern and media coverage have been focused upon issues of privacy, safety, and efficacy, each of which no doubt would have been the subject of many comments had the TSA seen fit to solicit comments upon a proposal to use AIT for primary screening. To confirm these issues were relevant to the TSA's deliberations about AIT, we need look no further than its assurances to that effect in its response to the petitioners' 2010 letter: 'AIT screening has proven effective in addressing ever-changing security threats, and numerous independent studies have addressed health concerns. TSA has carefully considered the important . . . privacy issues.' For these reasons, the TSA's use of AIT for primary screening has the hallmark of a substantive rule and, therefore, unless the rule comes within some other exception, it should have been the subject of notice and comment."

(2) **Is the Program a Valid Interpretive Rule?** The TSA also argued the adoption of the scanners qualified as an interpretive rule under § 553(b), permitting the agency to forgo notice and comment. Again, the court disagreed, though it noted the issue was not entirely clear cut: "The TSA next tries to justify having proceeded without notice and comment on the ground that it announced only an 'interpretative' rule advising the public of its current understanding of the statutory charge to develop and deploy new

technologies for the detection of terrorist weapons. For their part, the petitioners argue the rule is legislative rather than interpretive because it 'effectively amends a prior legislative rule,' Am. Mining Congress v. Mine Safety & Health Admin., 995 F.2d 1106, 1112 (D.C.Cir.1993), to wit, the secondary use of AIT only to back-up primary screening performed with magnetometers. See also Sprint Corp. v. FCC, 315 F.3d 369, 374 (D.C.Cir.2003) ('an amendment to a legislative rule must itself be legislative' (internal quotation marks omitted)).

"The practical question inherent in the distinction between legislative and interpretive regulations is whether the new rule effects 'a substantive regulatory change' to the statutory or regulatory regime. U.S. Telecom Ass'n, 400 F.3d at 34–40 (FCC effected substantive change when it required wireline telephone carriers to permit customers to transfer their telephone numbers to wireless carriers). For the reasons discussed [above on the agency procedure exception], we conclude the TSA's policy substantially changes the experience of airline passengers and is therefore not merely 'interpretative' either of the statute directing the TSA to detect weapons likely to be used by terrorists or of the general regulation requiring that passengers comply with all TSA screening procedures. Although the statute, 49 U.S.C. § 44925, does require the TSA to develop and test advanced screening technology, it does not specifically require the TSA to deploy AIT scanners let alone use them for primary screening. Concededly, there is some merit in the TSA's argument it has done no more than resolve an ambiguity inherent in its statutory and regulatory authority, but the purpose of the APA would be disserved if an agency with a broad statutory command (here, to detect weapons) could avoid notice-and-comment rulemaking simply by promulgating a comparably broad regulation (here, requiring passengers to clear a checkpoint) and then invoking its power to interpret that statute and regulation in binding the public to a strict and specific set of obligations."

(3) *Is the Program a Valid Policy Statement?* Finally, the TSA argued that the adoption of the scanners qualified as a policy statement that did not need to go through notice and comment. The court had little patience for that claim: "The question raised by the policy exception 'is whether a statement is . . . of present binding effect'; if it is, then the APA calls for notice and comment. McLouth Steel Prods. Corp. v. Thomas, 838 F.2d 1317, 1320 (D.C.Cir.1988). Our cases 'make clear that an agency pronouncement will be considered binding as a practical matter if it either appears on its face to be binding, or is applied by the agency in a way that indicates it is binding.' Gen. Elec. Co. v. EPA, 290 F.3d 377, 383 (D.C.Cir.2002) [p. 365] (internal citation omitted); see also Chamber of Commerce, 174 F.3d at 212–13. It is enough for the agency's statement to 'purport to bind' those subject to it, that is, to be cast in 'mandatory language' so 'the affected private parties are reasonably led to believe that failure to conform will bring adverse consequences.' Gen. Elec., 290 F.3d at 383–84 (internal quotation marks omitted).

"The TSA seems to think it significant that there are no AIT scanners at some airports and the agency retains the discretion to stop using the scanners where they are in place. More clearly significant is that a passenger is bound to comply with whatever screening procedure the TSA is using on the date he is to fly at the airport from which his flight departs. 49 C.F.R. § 1540.105(a)(2) (no passenger may enter the 'sterile area' of an airport 'without complying with the systems, measures, or procedures being applied to control access to' that area). To be sure, he can opt for a patdown but, as the TSA conceded at oral argument, the agency has not argued that option makes its screening procedures nonbinding and we therefore do not consider the possibility. We are left, then, with the argument that a passenger is not bound to comply with the set of choices presented by the TSA when he arrives at the security checkpoint, which is absurd."

(4) *Remand Without Vacatur Remedy and a Possible Good Cause Argument.* Despite ruling against the TSA on all of its arguments for why it skipped notice-and-comment procedures, the court did not vacate the program: "In sum, the TSA has advanced no justification for having failed to conduct a notice-and-comment rulemaking. We therefore remand this matter to the agency for further proceedings. Because vacating the present rule would severely disrupt an essential security operation, however, and the rule is, as we explain below, otherwise lawful, we shall not vacate the rule, but we do nonetheless expect the agency to act promptly on remand to cure the defect in its promulgation. See Allied-Signal, Inc. v. Nuclear Regulatory Comm'n, 988 F.2d 146, 150–51 (D.C.Cir.1993). The agency asks us to 'make clear that on remand, TSA is free to invoke the APA's "good cause" exception' to notice-and-comment rulemaking, 5 U.S.C. § 553(b)(B) (exception 'when the agency for good cause finds . . . that notice and public procedure thereon are impracticable, unnecessary, or contrary to the public interest'). We have no occasion to express a view upon this possibility other than to note we do not reach it."

(5) *Subsequent Events and TSA's and EPIC's Strategic Decisions.* Why didn't the agency use notice and comment to establish the AIT primary screening program? Alternatively, why didn't the agency rely on the "good cause" exception? The TSA made its policy decision in early 2010. The D.C. Circuit handed down its decision in July 2011. Almost two years later, while keeping the body scanner screening program in place, the agency issued an NPRM, which it finalized a year later. The final rule did not expressly allow passengers to opt out of screening by the body scanners in all contexts. Should the agency have waited that long given the D.C. Circuit's opinion that it "act promptly on remand to cure the defect in [the program's] promulgation"? EPIC submitted a detailed comment in the rulemaking and filed suit (along with others) against the final rule in 2016, raising procedural and substantive challenges. The D.C. Circuit dismissed the challenge in an unpublished opinion: "Petitioners essentially oppose the encroachment into individual privacy the body scanners present. They argue, generally, that the TSA insufficiently considered the privacy interests of passengers. Specifically, it was also contended that the agency inadequately responded to the proposition that passengers who did not wish to experience the body scanner might choose to drive—which is statistically more dangerous than airline travel—and that the TSA did not provide evidence that body scanners were the best method of screening passengers. Finally, one of the petitioners

contended that the final agency rule, which did not provide a pat-down option in all cases, was not a 'logical outgrowth' of the Notice of Proposed Rulemaking. We think the agency adequately responded to petitioners' contentions in the final rule. We defer to TSA's judgment on such an issue of national security. E.g., Olivares v. TSA, 819 F.3d 454, 462 (D.C. Cir. 2016). And the final rule was indeed a logical outgrowth of the Notice of Proposed Rulemaking; the opt-out notion was expressly at issue." COMPETITIVE ENTERPRISE INSTITUTE V. U.S. DEP'T OF HOMELAND SEC., 2017 WL 2347676 (D.C. Cir. 2017).

EPIC's fundamental interest was about passenger privacy. How did it use procedural claims to advance that substantive interest in the course of its litigation?

SECTION 4.   GETTING RULEMAKING STARTED

> a. *Rulemaking Initiation and Development Within the Agency*
> b. *Public Initiation of Rulemaking*
> c. *Negotiated Rulemaking*
> d. *Regulatory Planning and Review*

An agency that is going to engage in rulemaking commits to that effort well before the first event § 553 mentions, publication in the Federal Register of an NPRM. Here we discuss three routes to getting rulemaking started: initiation within the agency, public initiation, and negotiated rulemaking. Congress often mandates the first, sometimes imposing deadlines on the issuance of the NPRM, and on occasion requires the last. The White House too plays a role in the first, directing rulemaking efforts, particularly in recent years. A significant factor in an executive agency's initiation of rulemaking—whether in response to a public petition or on the agency's own initiative (the latter, to be certain, is frequently at the push of Congress or the White House)—is centralized review by the Office of Information and Regulatory Affairs (OIRA) in OMB under Executive Order 12866. Independent regulatory commissions and boards face far less scrutiny by OIRA. Such centralized review is discussed at the end of the section. Keep two caveats in mind. First, although this section (and indeed, the book as a whole) typically refers to a single agency, agencies engage in important joint rulemaking from time to time. Second, while this section (and again, the book as well) often assumes a rulemaking imposes new obligations, rulemakings can also repeal previous regulations.

a. Rulemaking Initiation and Development Within the Agency

Save for § 553(e)'s invitation to the public to petition for rulemaking, the APA says little about what happens up to the point when an NPRM is published in the Federal Register. (The 1990 Negotiated Rulemaking Act amendments are a significant but infrequently used exception, see Subsection c, below on p. 405). As might be expected, however, both agencies and their political overseers do a great deal of work in the pre-NPRM period. Increasingly, this work is the subject of statutory and executive order requirements, which we take up in Section d. Here we focus on legislative and executive pressures on the agency to start rulemaking and the internal structures of agency decisionmaking.

Legislative, presidential, and agency decisions can launch the rulemaking process. To start, a statute may compel an agency to undertake a particular rulemaking. Some statutes also impose deadlines, both on the start and completion of agency rulemaking. Consider two recent examples. The 2010 Dodd-Frank Wall Street Reform and Consumer Protection Act set close to 400 deadlines on financial agencies for proposing and finalizing various regulations, with many of these statutory mandates tasking agencies to jointly engage in the rulemaking process. The 2011 Food Safety Modernization Act gave the FDA, with input from the Departments of Agriculture and Homeland Security, one year to propose rules concerning safety mandates for the cultivating and picking of farm produce, among other issues. A study of rulemakings between 1987 and 2003 in the Unified Agenda of Federal Regulatory and Deregulatory Actions (Unified Agenda) found that the Department of Commerce faced the most statutory deadlines, followed by the EPA and the Departments of Transportation and Agriculture. Jacob E. Gersen & Anne Joseph O'Connell, Deadlines in Administrative Law, 156 U. Penn. L. Rev. 923, 981 (2008). If an agency misses a deadline, which often occurs, courts can impose a judicial deadline for agency action under the threat of contempt, including the publication of an NPRM. Some evidence suggests that deadlines may drive an agency to rely on exceptions to notice-and-comment procedures (such as the good cause exemption) discussed in the previous section to speed up the process. Gersen & O'Connell, supra, at 944–45.

The White House may also direct an agency to initiate rulemaking proceedings and even set deadlines (though these timelines are not judicially enforceable). The Introduction to this casebook (p. 19) provides one example in the regulation of passengers' experience on commercial airline flights, through an executive order. As discussed in Chapter VII (p. 951), President Obama in a June 2013 memorandum "direct[ed]" the EPA to issue a "new [rulemaking] proposal by no later than September 20, 2013" for "Carbon Pollution Standards for Future Power Plants," in addition to other NPRMs for other power plants, and to finalize those proposed rules soon thereafter. In a March 2017 Executive Order (p. 953), President Trump instructed that "the head of the relevant agency shall, as soon as practicable, suspend, revise, or rescind, or publish for notice and comment proposed rules suspending, revising, or rescinding, those actions [taken under the June 2013 memorandum], as appropriate and consistent with law." OIRA also issued "prompt" letters in President George W. Bush's Administration, suggesting specific rulemakings to agencies. The first such letter was sent to OSHA in 2001, to encourage the agency to mandate certain workplaces have automated external defibrillators. For copies of prompt letters, see: http://www.reg info.gov/public/jsp/EO/promptLetters.jsp.[20] (On the other hand, the White House, particularly at the start of a new administration, and Congress, often using appropriation riders, can impose regulatory moratoria on agencies to prevent rulemaking.) These legislative and presidential efforts to direct regulatory policymaking raise important constitutional, statutory, and policy issues that are explored in Ch. VII, Sections 2–4.

An agency can also initiate rulemaking without confronting a deadline or other statutory command—relying on its organic statute and other acts delegating authority. The agency must decide what issues warrant rulemaking. This decision, in turn, requires both the setting of regulatory priorities—policy judgments that may transcend the agency's own substantive mandate—and the use of those priorities to identify appropriate subjects for regulations.

Whether propelled by legislation, presidential directive or prompt, or internal agency decisions, the agency must develop concrete proposals. Most often, these proposals are developed within the agency, albeit with substantial consultation both inside and outside the government. We turn now to understanding structurally how rulemaking proposals are developed within an agency: Who participates, and in what form? How much control does an agency's political leadership exert over the rulemaking process? To what extent do agency heads pay attention to managing the regulatory process? Executive Order 12866, which we discuss in more detail in Subsection d, has had an important impact here as well. Its requirements that all agencies identify regulatory actions under development or review for the semiannual Unified Agenda and annual Regulatory Plan have led to greater emphasis on regulatory planning within agencies. Also significant is its mandate that each

---

[20] OIRA during President Obama's Administration did not issue prompt letters, relying on presidential directives instead. For a debate over the desirability of prompt letters, see John D. Graham, Saving Lives Through Administrative Law And Economics, 395 U. Pa. L. Rev. 395, 460 (2008) (arguing the letters were an important tool for forcing regulation); Nicholas Bagley & Richard L. Revesz, Centralized Oversight of the Regulatory State, 106 Colum. L. Rev. 1260, 1277–80 (2006) (arguing that "OIRA publicly touts the prompt letter as a proregulatory and proactive mechanism for regulatory reform while lavishing most of its attention on rolling back regulatory burdens on industry").

executive agency have a Regulatory Policy Officer who will be involved at each stage of the regulatory process. See EO 12866, §§ 4, 6(a).

Drawing on agency documents, interviews of agency officials and a symposium of senior agency officials, CORNELIUS M. KERWIN and SCOTT R. FURLONG describe key aspects of the early stages of rulemaking within the agency in RULEMAKING: HOW GOVERNMENT AGENCIES WRITE LAW AND MAKE POLICY 131, 134–36, 150, 155–56, 162–63 (4th. ed. 2010): "*A Process for Selling Priorities.* By setting priorities throughout its domain, an agency can control the types and sequencing of the rules that it produces. . . . Agencies vary considerably in their attention to setting priorities. At one extreme is a fully centralized system in which the priorities are set at the top of the agency; at the other is a fully decentralized system in which no overarching set of priorities is imposed on the operating units of the agency. Between these extremes one might find a system in which agency leadership designates some rules as high-priority projects, leaving the operating units to determine the rest of the rulemaking agenda. Still another is an essentially decentralized approach that allows for intervention by agency leadership when an emergency, political or otherwise, arises. . . .

"Changes in priorities divert resources for months or more, making them difficult if not impossible to reassemble. Diversions of resources are momentum killers that also threaten the often tenuous internal and external coalitions that the writers of significant rules rely on to produce the consensus their superiors usually seek to achieve. The optimal priority-setting system is one that balances the conflicting pressures that put careful planning and the ability to adapt at odds. . . .

"*A Process for Initiating Rules and Securing Early Input.* Virtually all agencies require some form of approval, even if it is nothing more than inclusion in the agency's priorities or a semiannual agenda. . . . Permission nearly always has to be requested in writing. . . . Several agencies rely on a formal structure, such as a committee or board, to approve the start of rules. . . .

"The results of the original survey yielded four categories of agencies: those that require guidance by senior officials for all rules; those that require guidance only on rules deemed important enough for all rules [sic]; those that require guidance only on rules deemed important enough for senior management's attention; and those that have no system of this sort. Today, virtually all agencies have systems that fall into the first two categories. . . .

"*Preparation of Planning Documents.* The significance of planning documents may not be immediately apparent, but they can be effective management tools. A detailed work plan forces those responsible for writing rules to make their intentions clear and known to all who read them. Combined with a system for approving the initiation of rules, a work plan can give senior management officials sufficient information to intervene at the early stages of a rulemaking if it appears that the rule writers are pursuing an unacceptable or infeasible course of action. Even when work plans do not serve as an instrument for oversight, they can still be useful. Depending on their content, they can force those writing the rule to consider the full range of policy, technical, operational, and resource issues that will arise and must be resolved during the rulemaking. . . .

"*Summary*. . . . The creation and institutionalization of 'rulemaking offices' marked an important milestone in the management of rulemaking. Exemplified by the work of the assistant general counsel for regulation at DOT, these offices may shepherd working groups, monitor schedules, and expedite concurrence and required analysis. They generally serve as visible, organizational reminders of the importance of rulemaking management. But there is little consistency across the government in structure, function, and importance. . . .

"*The Role of Work Groups*. . . . [W]ork groups are likely to be found in all agencies that have significant rulemaking responsibilities. Their composition and size, however, are functions of the programs the agency administers and its internal organizational culture. . . . In larger, more complex agencies that administer multiple, overlapping statutes, work groups tend to be larger and have a more diverse membership. In these cases many program offices may be represented. In addition to attorneys from the Office of the General Counsel, lawyers concerned with the enforcement dimension of the rule may also participate. . . . Representatives from offices concerned with research and policy analysis are likely to be members of the work group. . . . The field personnel who are responsible for implementing the rule once it is complete may wish to be involved to ensure that what is written is feasible and easy to administer. . . . The experiences of the EPA, the FAA, and other rulemaking agencies during the past thirty-five years indicate that the management of work groups hinges on three key variables: leadership, membership, and integration with senior management of the agency. . . .

"*Evolution of the Work Group Model.* Developments in recent years at the [EPA] suggest one way the work group model of individual rule management will evolve. It has moved away from its practice of appointing a work group for all rules. This move was prompted by the gradual realization that a full work group approach was not needed for many rules. Facing significant resource constraints and criticisms of long delays in issuing rules, the agency fashioned a new, more sophisticated tier system. The first tier contains a few rules that are classified as Administrator's Priority Actions because of unusually serious concerns over crossmedia effects and the general impact on the public. These rules arc developed in work groups composed of high-level EPA staff, with early involvement and close monitoring by the administrator or deputy administrator. The second tier, larger than the first, contains rules with major crossmedia or crossagency concerns and high levels of interest from external groups. These rules are developed by work groups as well, but generally with lower-level staff; the involvement of senior officials is determined on a case-by-case basis. Most rules belong in the third tier, which consists of regulations that can safely be developed by a single EPA office because of the nature of the issues and the relative lack of controversy that attends them. The lead office need not convene a work group; it can determine independently the types of guidance and consultation with other offices that are needed to produce a rule of acceptable quality. Such consultations will most often take the form of 'side agreements' with interested or affected offices reached early in the regulation development process. When nearing completion of the rulemaking, the lead office must certify that all side agreements have in fact been honored. . . .

"Given the wide variations in rulemaking across government agencies and the different political conditions under which they currently labor, it is certainly plausible that many will gravitate toward the new EPA paradigm. In effect, it tailors the management of individual rules to the degree of exposure and conflict agency leaders anticipate from them, based on the magnitude and complexity of the issues involved. In this regard the tiering approach is consistent with general approaches to regulation; small entities have been regulated less stringently than large ones because their behavior poses less significant threats to health and safety and because they are less able to absorb compliance costs. The tiering model also allows agencies facing the twin pressures of tight resources and even tighter schedules to invest their people power in rational ways."

For case studies on 16 recent rulemakings, including initial planning, see GAO, Federal Rulemaking: Improvements Needed to Monitoring and Evaluation of Rules Development as Well as to the Transparency of OMB Regulatory Review, GAO–09–205 (April 2009) (noting that "[a]gency officials reported that this initial work on a rule is of indeterminate length and sometimes constitutes a major portion of the process").[21] Scholars have also considered the benefits and costs to various internal agency arrangements for rulemaking. See, e.g., Jennifer Nou, Intra-Agency Coordination, 129 Harv. L. Rev. 421 (2015) (developing a "theory of how administrative leaders use internal hierarchies and procedures to process information in light of their individual preferences and exogenous uncertainties" and calling for "judicially enforceable disclosure of agencies' internal rule-drafting processes"); Thomas O. McGarity, The Internal Structure of EPA Rulemaking, 54 Law & Contemp. Probs. 57 (Autumn 1991) (evaluating four patterns of internal staff organization: the "Team Model," the "Hierarchical Model," the "Outside Advisor Model," and the "Adversarial Model").

---

[21] http://www.gao.gov/assets/290/288538.pdf.

This initiation process ultimately has to develop a product or lead to a decision not to continue efforts. Under the APA, the product is often an NPRM (assuming one of the exceptions to notice-and-comment rulemaking does not apply), but as we shall see in Subsection 4.d, an agency typically has to produce much more before it can reach that step.

b. Public Initiation of Rulemaking

Each agency shall give an interested person the right to petition for the issuance, amendment, or repeal of a rule.

5 U.S.C. § 553(e)

(1) *Sources of Petitions and Success Rates.* Section 553(e)'s express provision for public petitioning of rulemaking represents another mechanism by which rulemaking can be initiated. For instance, FlyersRights.org, (which was also a participant in the Introductory Example on the Department of Transportation's Enhancing Airline Passenger Protections rule (p. 3)) petitioned the FAA in August 2015 to issue a rule establishing standards for the minimum size of a seat—both the width and pitch—on a commercial airline. (The FAA denied the petition after receiving more than 140 comments.) Petitions can come from regulated entities or regulatory beneficiaries. Appendix C to the 2014 ACUS Report,[22] Petitions for Rulemaking,[23] by Jason A. Schwartz and Richard L. Revesz, provides some recent statistics (and comparisons to 1986 data compiled for ACUS) on rulemaking petitions. Over all the agencies examined, the sources of petitions broke down as follows: 52 percent business, 27 percent organized public interest groups, 13 percent loosely organized public interest groups or individuals, 5 percent labor organizations, and 3 percent state, local, and tribal governments. (Compared to the earlier 1986 data, business petitions have declined, relatively, to other sources, although they still make up the majority). As to individuals, who "submit a tenth to a quarter of the petitions at some agencies," the report noted: "[M]ost agency officials and stakeholders interviewed for this study assumed that average U.S. citizens were generally unaware of the right to petition for rulemaking and were unlikely to submit petitions. In practice, many of the individual petitioners are former agency staffers, lawyers, or academics, especially scientists and law professors. It is not surprising that such individuals are more likely to be aware of the right to petition for rulemakings." ACUS Report, supra, at 46–47. Most rulemaking petitions appear to be denied (though fewer in percentage terms than in 1986). But some agencies—for instance, the EPA, Department of Energy, Federal Motor Carrier Safety Administration (DOT), and Surface Transportation Board (DOT)—grant more petitions than they deny. Appendix C to ACUS

---

[22] http://www.acus.gov/appendix/petitions-rulemaking-final-report-appendix-c.

[23] http://www.acus.gov/report/petitions-rulemaking-final-report.

Report, supra. Some of these granted petitions involve significant regulations: for instance, the FDA's attempt in the mid-1990s to regulate tobacco, which is the subject of FDA v. Brown & Williamson Tobacco Corp., 529 U.S. 120 (2000) (p. 1191), started after an anti-smoking group filed a petition for rulemaking.

(2) ***Agency Practices for Rulemaking Petitions.*** Although the APA explicitly provides for rulemaking petitions, it does not specify any specific procedures for the petitioning process except that notice of any denial must be provided "accompanied by a brief statement of the grounds for denial." 5 U.S.C. § 555(e). Nevertheless, drawing from § 555 and other provisions, courts have held that the APA does mandate "agencies to respond to petitions for rulemaking 'within a reasonable time,' and to give petitioners 'prompt notice' when a petition is denied in whole or in part, along with 'a brief statement of the grounds for denial.'" ACUS, Petitions for Rulemaking, Recommendation 2014–06 (adopted Dec. 2014), at 1. In 1986, ACUS called for "basic procedures to help agencies meet the APA's minimum requirements and respond promptly to petitions for rulemaking." But nearly 30 years later, ACUS found much remained to be done: "[F]ew agencies have in place official procedures for accepting, processing, and responding to petitions for rulemaking. How petitions are received and treated varies across—and even within—agencies. In some cases, agency personnel do not even know what their agency's procedures are for handling petitions. Although the petitioning process can be a tool for enhancing public engagement in rulemaking, in practice most petitions for rulemaking are filed by sophisticated stakeholders and not by other interested members of the public. Some petitioners report that it can be difficult to learn the status of a previously filed petition, agency communication throughout the process can be poor, response times can be slow, and agency explanations for denials can be minimal and predominantly non-substantive." Id. at 2.

[handwritten margin note: No uniformity]

(3) ***Judicial Review of Rulemaking Petition Denials.*** How potent a tool § 553(e) is for prodding agency action depends to large extent on how rigorously courts review petition denials. As noted above, the FAA rejected the petition for rulemaking by FlyerRights.org on airline seat width and pitch. The petitioning organization sued in the U.S. Court of Appeals for the D.C. Circuit, arguing the denial was arbitrary and capricious based on safety considerations in an evacuation. The agency countered by claiming that the issues in the petition "do not raise an immediate safety or security concern" and arguing that it has considerable discretion on what rulemakings to undertake. The D.C. Circuit took the middle ground, finding that the FAA had "relied materially on information it had not disclosed" and remanding the matter to the agency "to adequately address the petition and the emergency egress concerns it raises." Flyers Rights Education Fund, Inc. v. Federal Aviation Administration, 864 F.3d 738 (D.C. Cir. 2017). In general, as is further developed in the materials on reviewability in Ch.

IX (p. 1370), agency refusals to initiate rulemaking are reviewable, but under a very lenient standard—particularly when "the agency has chosen not to regulate for reasons ill-suited to judicial resolution, e.g., because of internal management considerations as to budget and personnel or for reasons made after a weighing of competing policies." PROFESSIONAL PILOTS FED. V. FAA, 118 F.3d 758, 763 (D.C. Cir. 1997).

Circumstances sometimes lead agencies to explain their refusals on the merits, and when this happens the result can be more intense judicial attention to the decision. Thus, the petition in Professional Pilots (a different case against the FAA than the one by FlyerRights.org) sought revision of the FAA's Age 60 Rule, which, originally adopted in 1959, mandated that commercial pilots stop flying when they turn 60. Although the agency had frequently reconsidered the rule and acknowledged that 60 had no special medical significance, it had continued to retain the rule on the ground that no measure existed by which "to distinguish those pilots who, as a consequence of aging, present a threat to air safety from those who do not." The Federation filed its petition in 1993 and on its denial sought judicial review, arguing that the FAA had thereby violated the APA and the Age Discrimination in Employment Act (ADEA).

The D.C. Circuit determined that an extremely lenient review normally reserved for petition denials was not appropriate here, because "the decision not to institute a rulemaking looking toward repeal of the Age 60 Rule was purportedly based upon the merits of the existing Rule." Nonetheless, by a 2–1 vote the court rejected the pilot organization's challenge, concluding that the FAA's continued retention of the Rule and distinctions among different groups of pilots was rational:

> The FAA may seem to have created something of a Catch-22 by announcing that it will not allow older pilots to fly until it has experiential data demonstrating the continued ability of such pilots to fly safely. On the other hand, it hardly seems reasonable to require that the Administrator periodically put his hand into the fire in order to ensure that he has precisely assessed the danger that it poses. If the FAA was justified in imposing the Rule in the first place then we cannot say that, simply because it is the Rule itself that blocks the generation of data necessary to reconsider the Rule, it was unreasonable for the FAA to find that it lacks those data.

The majority also rejected the ADEA challenge. Dissenting, Judge Wald concluded that the FAA's justifications for the petition denial did not pass muster under the APA, particularly in light of the agency's refusal to try to obtain medical and performance data on older pilots, which she argued the agency was obligated to try to do given the ADEA's condemnation of across-the-board age discrimination. The Age 60 Rule stayed in place until December 2007, when Congress passed the Fair Treatment of Experienced Pilots Act, which raised the mandatory retirement age for pilots to 65. See 49 U.S.C. §§ 44729(a), (e)(2).

MASSACHUSETTS V. EPA, 549 U.S. 497, 527–28 (2007) [pp. 1253, 1349, 1355], provides another recent instance of less deferential scrutiny of a petition denial. There, the Supreme Court in a closely divided 5–4 decision reviewed the EPA's refusal to initiate a rulemaking on greenhouse gases with a level of scrutiny that resulted in a remand to the EPA to reconsider its decision. In so doing, the Court remarked:

> There are key differences between a denial of a petition for rulemaking and an agency's decision not to initiate an enforcement action. See American Horse Protection Assn., Inc. v. Lyng, 812 F.2d 1, 3–4 [D.C. Cir. 1987]. In contrast to nonenforcement decisions, agency refusals to initiate rulemaking "are less frequent, more apt to involve legal as opposed to factual analysis, and subject to special formalities, including a public explanation." Id., at 4; see also 5 U.S.C. § 555(e). They moreover arise out of denials of petitions for rulemaking which (at least in the circumstances here) the affected party had an undoubted procedural right to file in the first instance. Refusals to promulgate rules are thus susceptible to judicial review, though such review is "extremely limited" and "highly deferential." National Customs Brokers & Forwarders Assn. of Am., Inc. v. United States, 883 F.2d 93, 96 [D.C. Cir. 1989].

Massachusetts v. EPA is considered in Ch. IX, Sec. 1 for its discussion of standing, and in Ch. VIII, Sec. 3 for judicial review of agency statutory interpretations.

c. Negotiated Rulemaking

(1) *The Negotiated Rulemaking Process.* The Negotiated Rulemaking Act, adopted in 1990, added a new Subchapter III to the APA (now, 5 U.S.C. §§ 561–70a) "to establish a framework for the conduct of negotiated rulemaking, consistent with section 553 of this title, to encourage agencies to use the process when it enhances the informal rulemaking process." 5 U.S.C. § 561. Negotiated rulemaking—"reg-neg" in the frequent shorthand—is a process for generating rulemaking proposals, not final rules. As a result, the product of a successful reg-neg must be published in the Federal Register and undergo the normal § 553 process. In addition, reg-neg committees must follow the mandates of the Federal Advisory Committee Act, 5 U.S.C. App. 2. § 565. But Congress also provided that "[a]ny agency action relating to establishing, assisting, or terminating a negotiated rulemaking committee . . . shall not be subject to judicial review." § 570. Executive Order 12866, signed by President Clinton and still in effect, encourages agencies to "explore and, where appropriate, use consensual mechanisms for developing regulations, including negotiated rulemaking." § 6(a)(1).

PHILIP HARTER, ASSESSING THE ASSESSORS: THE ACTUAL PERFORMANCE OF NEGOTIATED RULEMAKING, 9 N.Y.U. Envtl. L.J. 32, 33–35 (2001): "... [N]egotiated rulemaking is a process by which representatives of the interests that would be substantially affected by a rule, including the agency responsible for issuing the rule, negotiate in good faith to reach consensus on a proposed rule.... [If an] agency decides to go forward with a negotiated rulemaking, it publishes a Notice of Intent in the Federal Register and other publications likely to be read by those interested in the subject matter, announcing its intention . . ., describing the subjects and scope of the rule to be developed, and listing the people or interests that will be on the committee. The notice also solicits comments on the decision to use reg-neg to develop the rule, and it invites those who believe they will be substantially affected by the rule, but who are not adequately represented on the committee, to apply for committee membership.... Following the Notice of Intent, the committee is established and the actual negotiations begin. The members of the negotiated rulemaking committee determine what factual information or other data is necessary for them to make a reasoned decision, develop . . . [and] analyze the information, examine the legal and policy issues involved . . ., and reach a consensus on the recommendation to make to the agency. As part of the consensus, each private interest agrees to support the recommendation and resulting rule to the extent that it reflects the agreement . . .

"Several implicit elements of this process merit emphasis: First, a senior representative of the agency is a full participant in the negotiations and deliberations of the negotiated rulemaking committee. Second, the committee makes its decision by consensus . . . [and] each participating interest has veto power over the decision. Third, the agency agrees to use the consensus as the basis of a proposed rule, which necessarily means that the agency will follow the traditional process of publishing the proposal as a Notice of Proposed Rulemaking (NPRM) and receive comments on the proposal before issuing a final rule.... [T]he agency alone retains the authority to issue the rule and may modify the proposal in response to comments or otherwise. That said, however, a negotiated rulemaking is a means by which the representatives of the affected interests actually share in making the regulatory decision, subject to the agency's constitutional responsibility to make the final decision. The resulting consensus is far more than a mere recommendation, especially since the agency itself endorses it during the deliberations."

(2) *Criticisms and Defenses of Reg-Neg.* WILLIAM FUNK, in WHEN SMOKE GETS IN YOUR EYES: REGULATORY NEGOTIATION AND THE PUBLIC INTEREST—EPA'S WOODSTOVE STANDARDS, 18 Envtl. L. 55, 57 (1987), criticizes reg-neg for "submerg[ing] public interest values, as reflected in the terms and conditions of the statute, to the special interests of the parties involved in the negotiation." According to Professor Funk, ". . .

the theory and principles of regulatory negotiation are at war with the theory and principles of American administrative law applicable to rulemaking" and "the goal of reasoned decision making to achieve the public interest. . . . Discretion delegated to the agency by Congress is effectively exercised by the group of interested parties, constrained only by the need to obtain consensus. The law no longer directs or even necessarily constrains the outcome but has become merely a factor in the give-and-take necessary to achieve consensus."

Are the concerns that Professor Funk raises overstated? Is the risk of agency capture through regulatory negotiation any greater than in conventional rulemaking contexts? Professor Susan Rose-Ackerman has suggested that loss of expertise may be more of a problem, emphasizing that some issues like environmental policy require "a knowledge base derived from scientific principles" and negotiation is not a methodology that helps the participants acquire technical expertise. Susan Rose-Ackerman, American Administrative Law Under Siege: Is Germany a Model?, 107 Harv. L. Rev. 1279, 1283 (1994). Is this concern met by agencies exercising thoughtful discretion in determining what rules they will attempt to negotiate? Does Professor Funk give adequate weight to the fact that any regulation ultimately produced through regulatory negotiation must go through the notice-and-comment process and is potentially subject to judicial reversal if a significant issue is raised to which the agency does not respond—or if the resulting rule exceeds the agency's authority? On the other hand, how often will legal challenges be brought against regulations that represent a consensus negotiated by the stakeholders involved?

A closely related issue concerns whether all affected interests are adequately represented in the negotiating group; lack of such representation may heighten fears of agency capture and undermine the legitimacy of the regulatory negotiation process. Does negotiated rulemaking's explicit focus on interest representation provide the best procedural chance for identifying the politically powerless and enhancing their voice in regulatory policymaking? Or is there something in the conventional rulemaking process that works to protect the interests of the politically powerless that is lost, or overridden, in regulatory negotiation? Professor Funk suggests that this "something" is the agency's independent judgment of where the public interest lies. Do you agree?

In addition, Professor Cary Coglianese analyzed EPA final rules started with reg-neg committees between 1983 and 1996 and found that the agency's reg-neg rules took longer to complete and produced more litigation than other agency rules in that time period. Such results—*if* reg-neg rules and non-reg-neg rules are comparable—suggest that the process neither saves time nor avoids litigation. Cary Coglianese, Assessing Consensus: The Promise and Performance of Negotiated Rulemaking, 46 Duke L.J. 1255 (1997).

Supporters of reg-neg, by contrast, have emphasized the benefits that the process can bring to rulemaking. JODY FREEMAN & LAURA I. LANGBEIN, REGULATORY NEGOTIATION AND THE LEGITIMACY BENEFIT, 9 N.Y.U. Envtl. L.J. 60, 62–63, 138 (2000): "In our view, empirical studies of negotiated rulemaking that examine cost, time, and litigation tell only part of the study and, we believe, not the most important part. . . . Along virtually every important qualitative dimension, all participants in this study—whether business, environmental, or government—reacted more favorably to their experience with negotiated rules than do participants in conventional rulemaking. . . . Regulatory negotiation clearly emerges, moreover, as a superior process for generating information, facilitating learning, and building trust. Most significantly, consensus-based negotiation increases legitimacy, defined as the acceptability of the regulation to those involved in its development. This legitimacy benefit . . . is no small accomplishment and . . . is more important than reducing transaction costs." Do you agree that such legitimacy benefits deserve more weight in assessing the merits of reg-neg?

(3) *The Waning of Reg-Neg?* Professor Jeffrey Lubbers identified a decline in the use of negotiated rulemaking from the 1990s. JEFFREY S. LUBBERS, ACHIEVING POLICYMAKING CONSENSUS: THE (UNFORTUNATE) WANING OF NEGOTIATED RULEMAKING, 49 S. Tex. L. Rev. 987, 996 (2008): "[F]rom the beginning of 1991 (the year after the NRA was enacted) through the end of 1999, sixty-three separate such committees were created, while from 2000 to the end of 2007, there were only twenty-two. . . . More tellingly, the number of statutorily mandated committees was only twenty-three of sixty-three (36.5%) in the first period but fifteen of twenty-two (68%) in the most recent period." According to Professor Lubbers, factors contributing to this decline were lack of funding for the Administrative Conference of the United States since the mid-1990s (which had provided support to agencies for some aspects of the process and wasn't refunded until 2010), the greater costs of reg-neg, a lack of enthusiasm for the procedure by OIRA, applicability of Federal Advisory Committee Act requirements (which require committee negotiations to be open to the public), and scholarly criticism. Professor Harter, often recognized as the "father" of reg-neg and a talented facilitator, offered another explanation at a panel sponsored by the Administrative Law Section of the ABA: fundamental conflict during President George W. Bush's Administration between political appointees and career staff. He described several instances in which a negotiated solution was rejected by political appointees at the agency management level. How does this observation fit with Professor Funk's concerns?

Professors Peter Schuck and Steven Kochevar found a further decline in reg-neg in the 2007–2013 period: only thirteen reg-neg committees were formed, with all but two statutorily required. Peter H. Schuck & Steven Kochevar, Reg Neg Redux: The Career of a Procedural Reform, 15 Theoretical Inquiries in Law 417, 439 (2014). In recent years, however, the use of reg-neg has increased, with twenty-three reg-neg committees formed between April 29, 2013, and May 31, 2017 (and a majority of those were done voluntarily, i.e., not required by statute). A 2017 ACUS Report, Negotiated Rulemaking,[24] observed: "In the last few years, the procedure has enjoyed something of a mini-resurgence, as the Departments of Transportation and Energy have deployed it in a handful of high-profile rulemakings, but it has not come close to recapturing the popularity it enjoyed in its heyday." Id. at 2.

In June 2017, ACUS adopted additional recommendations concerning reg-neg, including that agencies "consider using negotiated rulemaking when it determines that the procedure is in the public interest, will advance the agency's statutory objectives, and is consistent with the factors outlined in the Negotiated Rulemaking Act." Because these factors are wide ranging, ACUS noted that "the choice should generally reside within the agency's discretion." ACUS also encouraged agencies to keep their OIRA desk officers informed about the process (including their ability to observe meetings) and called for Congress to exempt reg-neg committees from FACA's chartering and reporting mandates. ACUS, Negotiated Rulemaking and Other Options for Public Engagement, Recommendation 2017–2 (adopted June 2017).[25] It will be interesting to see if President Trump's Administration encourages its use.

d. Regulatory Planning and Review

> *EXECUTIVE ORDER 12866*
>
> *EXECUTIVE ORDER 13771*
>
> *Notes on the Mechanics of Executive Orders 12866 and 13771*
>
> *Notes on Ongoing Issues with Executive Order 12866 and Initial Views on Executive Order 13771*
>
> *Notes on Cost-Benefit Analysis and Risk Assessment*

EXECUTIVE ORDER 12866

58 Fed. Reg. 51735 (Oct. 4, 1993).

EXECUTIVE ORDER 13771

82 Fed. Reg. 9339 (Feb. 3, 2017).

[The Executive Orders appear in the Appendix at pp. 1496, 1510. They are the principal texts for this subsection of materials. In reading

---

[24] http://www.acus.gov/report/negotiated-rulemaking-final-report.

[25] http://www.acus.gov/sites/default/files/documents/Recommendation%202017-2_Negotiated%20Rulemaking.pdf.

Executive Order 12866, focus on Sections 1, 4, and 6 through 10. Recall from the chart on p. 291 that there are considerable rulemaking requirements placed on agencies outside the APA's mandates.]

NOTES

(1) ***Meet the Players.*** As the text of Executive Order 12866 indicates, two White House offices (one of which is contained within the other) play a particularly important role in contemporary rulemaking:

(a) The Office of Management and Budget (OMB) is part of the professional White House bureaucracy in the Executive Office of the President, with a permanent staff of about 450 that, except for its top leadership (including seven Senate-confirmed presidential appointees, one of whom heads OIRA), continues through changing administrations. With limited exceptions for some (but not all) of the independent regulatory commissions, OMB controls agency submissions to Congress of draft legislation, testimony on proposed legislation, and budgetary requests. It also oversees the spending of congressional appropriations and develops management mechanisms for the executive branch. For a thorough examination of OMB's important budgetary and management functions as a form of agency control, see Eloise Pasachoff, The President's Budget as a Source of Agency Policy Control, 125 Yale L.J. 2182 (2016). As the Executive Order suggests, OMB also frequently serves as the tribunal before which inter-agency conflicts over regulatory policy are resolved.[26] In short, "OMB plays a pivotal role in developing and supporting the President's management, budget, and legislative agenda." OMB, Fiscal Year 2017 Budget, at 3.[27]

(b) The Office of Information and Regulatory Affairs (OIRA, pronounced "oh-eye-ruh") is the subdivision of OMB with the greatest responsibility for regulatory affairs. Operating with a professional staff of about 45, it is statutorily responsible for the coordination of government information policy, including the clearance of agency information demands under the Paperwork Reduction Act. Under Executive Order 12866 (and its predecessors), it writes an introduction to the government's regulatory agenda (which the General Services Administration compiles from agency submissions) and clears the draft and final regulatory impact statements that are prepared for particular rulemakings. Presidents have generally appointed as its head accomplished professionals with significant experience in policy analysis and/or law. President Trump picked Neomi Rao, a professor at George Mason University's Antonin Scalia Law School and a public member of ACUS, as his OIRA Administrator; she was confirmed by the Senate in July 2017.

(2) ***The History of Executive Order 12866 and Centralized Regulatory Review.*** The White House has taken increasingly formal

---

[26] The Office of Legal Counsel in the Department of Justice serves this function for legal conflicts.

[27] http://obamawhitehouse.archives.gov/sites/default/files/omb/assets/organization/fy 2017_omb_budget.pdf.

control of important ("significant") rulemakings since President Nixon's Administration. It has asserted at least a supervisory, if not a directory, role in shaping the analysis of issues put on the rulemaking table, and even in assessing the justifications for particular conclusions. RICHARD H. PILDES & CASS R. SUNSTEIN, REINVENTING THE REGULATORY STATE, 62 U. Chi. L. Rev. 1 (1995): "[P]residential oversight of the regulatory process, though relatively new, has become a permanent part of the institutional design of American government. This new institutional arrangement has occurred for reasons parallel to the development of a centralized budget in the 1920s. All Presidents are likely to seek assurance that an unwieldy federal bureaucracy conforms its actions to their basic principles. Any President is likely to be concerned about excessive public and private costs. And any President is likely to want to be able to coordinate agency activity so as to ensure consistency and coherence and to guard against the imposition of conflicting duties on people who must comply with the law. The result of these forces is that a centralizing and rationalizing body, housed within OMB and devoted to regulation, has emerged as an enduring, major, but insufficiently appreciated part of the national government."

The device predominantly used to accomplish this, the "regulatory impact analysis" (RIA), draws on the example legislatively set in the National Environmental Policy Act of 1969, 42 U.S.C. § 4321 et seq. NEPA requires agencies to create an Environmental Impact Statement (or at least an Environmental Assessment) that anticipates adverse environmental changes potentially caused by agency projects and considers means of reducing or avoiding them. During President Carter's Administration, Executive Order 12044 required justifications and analysis of anticipated economic impacts for a limited number of important rulemakings. President Reagan built upon this with Executive Orders 12291 and 12498, which placed a much wider range of rulemaking activities under the supervision of OIRA. Executive Order 12291 specified analytic principles for rulemaking and provided for their enforcement through OIRA. Executive Order 12498 created an annual regulatory agenda, also under OIRA supervision. Other impact analysis requirements followed, some from the White House and some from Congress; an example of the latter is the Regulatory Flexibility Act, enacted in 1980 and codified at 5 U.S.C. §§ 601–612, which encourages attention to the impact of regulations on small businesses. Presidents have avoided making the regulatory impact obligation judicially enforceable and have relied instead on enforcement from within the Executive Office of the President.

In an era of divided government, with a Democratic Congress considerably more enthusiastic about regulation than a conservative Republican White House, OIRA became a lightning rod for concerns that the President was obstructing the "necessary" work of government agencies. Contributing to these concerns was the secrecy that characterized OIRA review under President Reagan. Congress reacted by making future heads of OIRA subject to Senate confirmation in the FY 1987 omnibus spending bill, and understandings about transparency in the process were negotiated. Even so, responding to concerns about the direction regulation was (or wasn't) taking, as well as feelings that OIRA's processes were still insufficiently transparent and accountable, the Senate refused to confirm the President George H.W. Bush's nominee for the position of OIRA Administrator. President Bush responded by creating a controversial "Council on Competitiveness" chaired by Vice President Quayle. The Council was responsible for political oversight of OIRA and the resolution of important disputes. It made little pretense of operating in public. "As a result," reported ELENA KAGAN, PRESIDENTIAL ADMINISTRATION, 114 Harv. L. Rev. 2281–82 (2001) (also discussed on p. 958), "the Council provoked the same criticisms, except perhaps still more heated, formerly lodged against OIRA. . . .

"In light of this criticism, observers might have predicted that when a Democratic President assumed office in 1993, a radical curtailment of presidential supervision of administrative action would follow. Instead, the very opposite occurred. President Clinton, to be sure, replaced Reagan's executive orders on regulatory review [with Executive Order 12866] and eliminated Bush's Competitiveness Council. But . . . presidential control of administration . . . expanded significantly during the Clinton Presidency, moving in this eight-year period to the center of the regulatory landscape.

". . . Clinton came to view administration as perhaps the single most critical—in part because the single most available—vehicle to achieve his domestic policy goals. He accordingly developed a set of practices that enhanced his ability to influence or even dictate the content of administrative initiatives. He exercised this power with respect to a wide variety of agency action—rulemakings, more informal means of policymaking, and even certain enforcement activities. The new practices, to be sure, had significant limits, some internally and others externally imposed, and they left untouched a wide swath of regulatory activity. But to a considerable extent, Clinton built on the legacy Reagan had left him to devise a new and newly efficacious way of setting the policy direction of agencies—of converting administrative activity into an extension of his own policy and political agenda. In so doing, Clinton also showed that presidential supervision of administration could operate, contrary to much opinion, to trigger, not just react to, agency action and to drive this action in a regulatory, not deregulatory, direction."

President George W. Bush kept Executive Order 12866 in place, with OIRA under the initial direction of John Graham, who had headed Harvard's Center for Risk Analysis. Administrator Graham added considerably to the transparency of OIRA's procedures, including by putting information online. The most significant alteration to regulatory review came with adoption of Executive Order 13422 in January 2007, which made four major changes: (1) expanding Executive Order 12866's reach to include significant agency guidance documents; (2) heightening the specificity of the analysis required of agencies under § 1(b)(1) of Executive Order 12866; (3) enlarging the role of each agency's regulatory policy officer and mandating that agencies designate a presidential appointee to serve in that capacity; and (4) requiring that agencies consider the use of formal rulemaking procedures in coordination with OIRA (see p. 286). These changes proved contentious and were criticized for giving the President too much decisional control over the regulatory process.

One of President Obama's first actions upon assuming office was to issue Executive Order 13497, revoking Executive Order 13422 and restoring Executive Order 12866 to its earlier form under President Clinton. President Obama also instructed the OMB Director to undertake an assessment of the regulatory review process under Executive Order 12866. In January 2011, President Obama issued Executive Order 13563, Improving Regulation and Regulatory Review, 76 Fed. Reg. 3821 (Jan. 21, 2011). Rather than comprehensively revising the existing process, the new executive order "is supplemental to and reaffirms the principles, structures, and definitions governing contemporary regulatory review that were established in Executive Order 12866." Executive Order 13563 emphasized public participation, reiterating Executive Order 12866's requirement that public comment periods should generally be at least 60 days and requiring agencies to ensure a "meaningful opportunity to comment through the Internet on any proposed regulation" and "timely online access to the rulemaking docket." § 2(b). It also incorporated a focus on behavioral economics, encouraging agencies to adopt flexible regulatory approaches including "warnings, appropriate default rules, and disclosure requirements." § 4; see also Cass R. Sunstein, Adm'r, OIRA, Memorandum for the Heads of Exec. Dep'ts & Agencies (June 18, 2010) (encouraging use of disclosure and simplification as regulatory tools) (p. 748). The new order also reiterated agencies' obligation to engage in retrospective analysis of existing rules to determine if they are "outmoded, ineffective, insufficient, or excessively burdensome" and required agencies to develop plans for how they will conduct such retrospective review within 120 days. § 6. President Obama simultaneously issued a memorandum directing heads of "agencies with broad regulatory compliance and administrative enforcement responsibilities, . . . to the extent feasible and permitted by law, . . . [to] develop plans to make public information concerning their regulatory compliance and enforcement activities accessible, downloadable, and searchable online." Memorandum to the Heads of Exec. Dep'ts & Agencies, Jan. 18, 2011.

President Trump has not revoked any part of Executive Order 12866 or 13563 as of October 2017. He, however, issued additional requirements related to agency regulation in Executive Order 13771, which specifically refers to Executive Order 12866 in several places. The new order requires agencies to eliminate at least two existing regulations for every new one issued and establishes a regulatory "budget" for agencies. For more information on the new executive order's mechanics, see Notes 1 and 4 below on pp. 415, 421. For a detailed history of centralized regulatory review and OIRA's role in the rulemaking process through the start of President Obama's Administration, see Curtis W. Copeland, Federal Rulemaking: The Role of the Office of Information and Regulatory Affairs, Cong. Research Serv. Report RL32397 (June 9, 2009).[28]

---

[28] The report is available at: http://fas.org/sgp/crs/misc/RL32397.pdf.

(3) *Regulatory Review in Context: The Case of Greenhouse Gas Emissions.* Regulatory review under Executive Order 12866 can seem a dry topic. But such centralized review is at the center of current administrative law debates and scholarship because of its importance to ultimate regulatory outcomes. Some sense of that import comes from an episode during President George W. Bush's Administration involving EPA's efforts to respond to the Supreme Court's decision in Massachusetts v. EPA, 549 U.S. 497 (2007), pp. 1253, 1349, 1355, which held that greenhouse gases were air pollutants under the Clean Air Act and rejected the agency's reasons for refusing to regulate them.

HEIDI KITROSSER, ACCOUNTABILITY AND ADMINISTRATIVE STRUCTURE, 45 Willamette L. Rev. 607 (2008): "The EPA's initial reaction to the ruling was quite vigorous. EPA administrator Stephen L. Johnson convened at least 60 EPA officials to respond to the [C]ourt's instructions. The effort resulted in a December 2007 draft finding that greenhouse gases endanger the environment. The EPA also used Energy Department data from 2007 to conclude that it would be cost effective to require the nation's motor vehicle fleet to average 37.7 miles per gallon in 2018. These findings were reflected in a nearly 300 page document prepared by EPA staffers. The document, which was approved by [Administrator] Johnson, included a proposed rule to effectuate the emissions requirement.

"Given the statutory and judicial directives to the EPA and the EPA's subsequent efforts, one might assume that the next steps were routine and predictable. Specifically, one might assume that the EPA publicly issued its draft document as a Notice of Proposed Rulemaking (NPRM), that public comments followed, and that the comments were followed by a final, publicly explained and judicially reviewable decision to enact a rule or to refrain from so doing. Yet none of this occurred.

"Instead, the EPA's scientific analysis and regulatory proposals were literally willed away by the White House. As with the proverbial tree falling in a forest, the White House refused to see the EPA's plans and did their best to ensure that others could not see them. This was effectuated very simply. When the EPA e-mailed the document to . . . [OMB] for pre-rule-making review, the White House declined to open it and ordered its retraction. The White House since has claimed executive privilege against congressional attempts to discover the e-mail and related communications. Although much remains unknown, the facts detailed here have come to light as a result of disclosures from EPA staffers to journalists and to members of Congress. It also is now known that EPA shelved the scientific endangerment finding and proposed rule it had sent to the White House. Instead, it issued an Advance Notice of Proposed Rulemaking (ANPRM)—a step preliminary to an NPRM—in June of 2008 merely seeking public comment on potential use of the Clean Air Act to address climate change." The EPA finally issued the endangerment finding in December 2009, after the White House had changed hands.

(4) *Regulatory Review in Context: The 2012 Election.* Regulatory interference by OIRA also occurs under Democratic Presidents. JULIET EILPERIN, WHITE HOUSE DELAYED ENACTING RULES AHEAD OF 2012

ELECTION TO AVOID CONTROVERSY, Wash. Post (Dec. 14, 2013): "The White House systematically delayed enacting a series of rules on the environment, worker safety and health care to prevent them from becoming points of contention before the 2012 election, according to documents and interviews with current and former administration officials. Some agency officials were instructed to hold off submitting proposals to the White House for up to a year to ensure that they would not be issued before voters went to the polls, the current and former officials said. The delays meant that rules were postponed or never issued. The stalled regulations included crucial elements of the Affordable Care Act, what bodies of water deserved federal protection, pollution controls for industrial boilers and limits on dangerous silica exposure in the workplace. The Obama administration has repeatedly said that any delays until after the election were coincidental and that such decisions were made without regard to politics. But seven current and former administration officials told The Washington Post that the motives behind many of the delays were clearly political, as Obama's top aides focused on avoiding controversy before his reelection." For more on delay and OIRA, see Note 4 below on p. 428.

(5) *Presidential Control of Rulemaking.* As the example of EPA's aborted greenhouse gas regulatory effort under President George W. Bush's Administration and OIRA's delays surrounding the 2012 election suggest, a central issue underlying the regulatory review process concerns the appropriate role of the President in rulemaking. Perhaps the most controversial aspect of the Executive Order is its interjection of the President into the regulatory sphere, giving White House officials a potential veto over regulations that do not accord with the President's policy priorities. This important aspect of the regulatory review process is inseparable from constitutional arguments about the scope of presidential powers and the appropriate role of the President vis-a-vis the executive branch. As a result, presidential directive authority is discussed in detail in Ch. VII, Sec. 3 (p. 950).

NOTES ON THE MECHANICS OF EXECUTIVE ORDERS 12866 AND 13771

(1) *Regulatory Planning.* An important feature of Executive Order 12866 is its attention to regulatory planning. Section 4 is the critical section here, and it imposes two central obligations on both executive and independent agencies, "to the extent permitted by law." First, agencies are required to identify "all regulations under development or review" for inclusion in a semiannual Unified Regulatory Agenda. § 4(b). The requirement that agencies publish a Regulatory Agenda twice a year was subsequently codified in the Small Business Regulatory Enforcement Fairness Act of 1996, 5 U.S.C. § 602. Second, as part of the Unified Agenda, agencies must "prepare a Regulatory Plan . . . of the most important significant regulatory actions that the agency reasonably expects to issue in proposed or final form that fiscal year or thereafter." Agencies must include additional information on each significant regulation in the Plan beyond that required for the Unified Agenda, including the agency's objectives; the need for the

regulation; to the extent possible, alternatives to be considered; and a preliminary estimate of costs and benefits. § 4(c). Available and searchable in electronic form, the Unified Agenda lists agency actions in four stages.[29] The earliest, the "Pre-rule Stage," contains actions to be undertaken within the next twelve months to determine whether to initiate rulemaking; it is thus substantially in advance even of the second stage, actions for which an NPRM is in the offing.

Executive Order 13771 imposes additional reporting by agencies, starting with their regulatory plans in FY 2018: "each agency shall identify, for each regulation that increases incremental cost, the offsetting regulations [the agency plans to repeal] [see Note 4 on p. 421], and provide the agency's best approximation of the total costs or savings associated with each new regulation or repealed regulation." § 3(a). It also bars agencies from issuing a regulation "[u]nless otherwise required by law . . . if it was not included on the most recent version or update of the published Unified Regulatory Agenda as required under Executive Order 12866 . . . . unless the issuance of such regulation was approved in advance in writing by the Director." § 3(c).

Assuming the Unified Agenda is accurate,[30] one effect of these requirements is to allow greater public awareness of rulemaking activities before the NPRM stage. The requirement that agencies provide "the name and telephone number of an agency official knowledgeable concerning the items listed" invites immediate engagement in agency processes for those wishing it. (For more information on ex parte communications, see Section 5 below). As significant, these requirements allow for greater OIRA involvement in setting agency regulatory priorities and in the early stages of regulatory actions. This feature rose to the fore in President George W. Bush's Executive Order 13422, which replaced the requirement that agency heads must approve the regulatory plan with one mandating approval of the plan by the agency's regulatory policy officer and further required that such officers be presidential appointees.

The Bush Executive Order, which is no longer in effect, exploited the potential for greater presidential control at the expense of agency heads, but could regulatory planning requirements also benefit agency leadership? The single person (or multimember commission) in charge of a complex organization often may not learn of new policy initiatives under

---

[29] http://www.reginfo.gov/public/do/eAgendaMain.

[30] In 2015, ACUS evaluated the accuracy of the Unified Agenda. It found:

> The Unified Agenda functions reasonably well as a predictor of some agency actions, but is less accurate in other areas. For example, estimated action dates may prove incorrect, the significance of a regulation may be misclassified, and jointly issued rules may inappropriately be characterized differently by different agencies. Additionally, some rules are classified as long-term actions when regulatory activity is imminent, while others remain listed as long-term actions after work on them has ceased. Occasionally, entries are removed from the Unified Agenda without explanation. Finally, a number of regulatory actions have recently been placed in a "pending" category that is not included in the published Unified Agenda.

ACUS, Promoting Accuracy and Transparency in the Unified Agenda, Recommendation 2015–1 (adopted June 4, 2015), at 2. See also Jennifer Nou & Edward Stiglitz, Strategic Rulemaking Disclosure, 89 S. Cal. L. Rev. 733 (2016).

consideration in her agency until after they have taken definitive shape—a point at which it is considerably more difficult to get attention to issues, or alternatives, of interest to her or the Administration. Does the Regulatory Plan enhance the control of an agency's political head over her career bureaucrats by requiring her to confront at an early stage competing views about priorities for her agency?

(2) *Regulatory Review and the Distinction among Nonsignificant, Significant, and Yet More Significant Regulations.* OIRA reviews agencies' draft rules at both the proposed and final stages of rulemaking.[31] Executive Order 12866 creates three different categories of regulations, determinable by the agency *or* the Administrator of OIRA. Under § 3(f),

> "Significant regulatory action" means any regulatory action that is likely to result in a rule that may:
>
> (1)   Have an annual effect on the economy of $100 million or more or adversely affect in a material way the economy, a sector of the economy, productivity, competition, jobs, the environment, public health or safety, or State, local, or tribal governments or communities;
>
> (2)   Create a serious inconsistency or otherwise interfere with an action taken or planned by another agency;
>
> (3)   Materially alter the budgetary impact of entitlements, grants, user fees, or loan programs or the rights and obligations of recipients thereof; or
>
> (4)   Raise novel legal or policy issues arising out of legal mandates, the President's priorities, or the principles set forth in this Executive order.

The procedural obligations attached to each category of regulatory action vary significantly under the Executive Order. Regulations that do not meet these thresholds for significance are not subject to further review. For "significant" actions, the agency must document the need for the regulation and assess "the potential costs and benefits of the regulatory action, including an explanation of the manner in which the regulatory action is consistent with a statutory mandate and, to the extent possible, the President's priorities and avoids undue interference with State, local, and tribal governments. . . ." § 6(a)(3)(B). Actions meeting the economic impact standard of § 3(f)(1)— "economically significant" rulemakings—are treated as more significant than the rest and face additional requirements, including more extensive assessment and quantification of costs and benefits associated with the proposed regulation and also with reasonably feasible alternatives.

Note that unlike the regulatory planning process outlined in Section 4 of the Executive Order, these assessment commands are directed only to executive agencies and not to independent regulatory commissions and

---

[31]   This review is triggered by an agency taking a "regulatory action," defined in § 3(e) to mean "any substantive action by an agency (normally published in the Federal Register) that promulgates or is expected to lead to the promulgation of a final rule or regulation, including notices of inquiry, advance notices of proposed rulemaking, and notices of proposed rulemaking."

boards.[32] The extent to which Presidents should be able to subject these latter agencies to the centralized regulatory review process is considered in Chapter VII, Subsec. 3.c (p. 950). Current OIRA Administrator Rao has previously endorsed extending the more intensive OIRA review to independent agencies but President Trump has not yet ordered it (and indeed OIRA has explicitly noted that Executive Order 13771's main mandates do not apply to such agencies, see Note 4 below on p. 421). See Neomi Rao, Regulatory Review for Independent Agencies, Notice & Comment Blog (Dec. 14, 2016).[33] An alternative, also in discussion, is for Congress to require such review by statute. See S. 1448 (The Independent Regulatory Analysis Act of 2017), 115th Cong.[34]

OIRA has shifted its review over time to focus on significant rulemakings. According to a 2003 GAO report, "by focusing OIRA's reviews on significant rules, the number of draft proposed and final rules that OIRA examined fell from between 2,000 and 3,000 per year under the Executive Order 12291 to between 500 and 700 rules per year under Executive Order 12866." GAO, Rulemaking: OMB's Role in Reviews of Agencies' Draft Rules and the Transparency of Those Reviews, GAO–03–929 (Sept. 2003), at 24.[35] Just where to set the dividing lines among nonsignificant, significant, and more significant regulations is open to debate. And agencies may try to underplay the importance of a rulemaking to avoid OIRA review. See Jennifer Nou, Agency Self-Insulation Under Presidential Review, 126 Harv. L. Rev. 1755 (2013); Note, OIRA Avoidance, 124 Harv. L. Rev. 994 (2011). For a skeptical view of this argument, see Nina A. Mendelson & Jonathan B. Wiener, Responding to Agency Avoidance of OIRA, 37 Harv. J.L. & Pub. Pol'y 447 (2014) (noting that "it remains unclear whether avoidance of OIRA is actually widespread and serious" and maintaining, in light of the repeat-player nature of agencies' relationships with OIRA, that "[a]gencies may have good reasons and incentives to cooperate with OIRA review").

Information on OIRA's regulatory reviews is available at www.reg info.gov. According to data listed there and in GAO's Federal Rules Database, the following chart provides information on OIRA review of agency rulemaking during the past two completed Administrations:

	Total Rules Issued	OIRA Reviewed	Economically Significant
Obama Yrs. 1–8	23,630	4,376 (19% of total)	973 (22% of reviewed rules, 4% of total)
Bush Yrs. 1–8	27,039	5,124 (19% of total)	755 (15% of reviewed rules, 3% of total)

---

[32] See § 3(b) (defining "agency"); § 4(b) (extending this definition to "those considered to be independent regulatory agencies" in the regulatory planning context).

[33] http://yalejreg.com/nc/regulatory-review-for-independent-agencies-by-neomi-rao/.

[34] http://www.congress.gov/bill/115th-congress/senate-bill/1448.

[35] http://www.gao.gov/assets/160/157476.pdf.

(3) ***The OIRA Review Process Under Executive Order 12866.*** In 2003, the GAO provided a detailed summary of OIRA's formal and informal review processes, which then OIRA Administrator Graham characterized as "an excellent overview of the regulatory review process." GAO, RULEMAKING: OMB'S ROLE IN REVIEWS OF AGENCIES' DRAFT RULES AND THE TRANSPARENCY OF THOSE REVIEWS, supra, at 31–37: "According to OIRA representatives, the formal regulatory review process begins when the rulemaking agency sends the draft rule to the OIRA docket librarian (either electronically or hand carried), who logs the receipt of the rule and forwards it to the appropriate desk officer. The representatives said that OIRA desk officers do not use a standard 'checklist' to review agencies' rules, but indicated that most reviews are similar in certain respects. Section 6 of Executive Order 12866 states that the OIRA Administrator is to provide meaningful guidance and oversight 'so that each agency's regulatory actions are consistent with applicable law, the President's priorities, and the principles set forth in this Executive order, and do not conflict with the policies or actions of another agency.' The laws applicable to specific regulations vary, but always include the specific statutory authority under which each regulation is being developed (e.g., the Clean Air Act or the Occupational Safety and Health Act) as well as a variety of crosscutting regulatory statutes (e.g., the APA and the Regulatory Flexibility Act). . . .

"The type of review that OIRA conducts sometimes depends on the type of draft rule submitted. For example, if the draft rule contains a collection of information covered by the Paperwork Reduction Act, OIRA representatives said that the desk officer would also review it for compliance with the act. (They indicated that conducting both reviews simultaneously can be more difficult if different offices within the rulemaking agencies are responsible for the rule and the information collection.) If the draft rule is 'economically significant' (e.g., has an annual impact on the economy of at least $100 million), the executive order requires agencies to prepare an economic analysis describing, among other things, the alternatives that the agency considered and the costs and benefits of those alternatives. For those economically significant rules, the desk officers review the economic analyses using the 'best practices' document developed in January 1996 and the related guidance document issued in 2000. . . .

"OIRA representatives said that there is usually some type of communication (often via e-mail or telephone) between the desk officer and the rulemaking agency regarding specific issues in the draft rule. The representatives said briefings and meetings are sometimes held between OIRA and the agency during the review process, with branch chiefs, the Deputy Administrator, and/or the Administrator involved in some of these meetings. They also said that the desk officers always consult with the resource management officers on the budget side of OMB as part of their reviews, and reviews of draft rules are not completed until those resource management officers sign off. (In fact, they said that the resource management offices might take the lead in the review for rules involving the 'transfer' of federal funds within society.) If the draft rule is economically significant, they said the desk officer would also consult with an economist to help review the required economic analysis. For other rules the OIRA representatives said the desk officer might consult with other OIRA staff on issues involving statistics and surveys, information technology and systems, or privacy issues. In certain cases, OIRA may circulate a draft rule to other parts of the Executive Office of the President (e.g., the Office of Science and Technology Policy or the Council on Environmental Quality) or other agencies (e.g. SBA for rules having an impact on small businesses, or DOE, DOT, the Department of Agriculture, and the Department of the Interior for certain EPA rules). In those cases, OIRA may not only review the rule itself, but also manage an interagency review process. . . .

"[A] draft rule that has been reviewed and judged consistent with the executive order may be coded in the office's database as 'consistent with no change' (meaning that OIRA considered the draft rule as submitted to be consistent with all applicable requirements) or 'consistent with change' (which means that the draft rule was changed at either the issuing agency's initiation or at the suggestion of OIRA, and that OIRA then considered the changed rule to be consistent with all applicable requirements). If the rule is returned to the issuing agency for reconsideration, the executive order requires OIRA to provide a written explanation for the return. Section 7 of Executive Order 12866 originally required the President or the Vice President to resolve any disagreements or conflicts between or among agency heads or between OMB and any agency that cannot be resolved by the OIRA Administrator. However, in February 2002, Executive Order 13258 reassigned the Vice President's responsibilities in this area to the President's chief of staff. . . .

"OIRA representatives told us that a variety of factors could trigger informal discussions about a forthcoming rule. For example, they said informal reviews are sometimes used when there is a statutory or legal deadline for a rule or when the rule has a large impact on society and requires discussion with not only OMB but also other federal agencies. Therefore, they said informal review is more likely regarding rules issued by certain agencies (e.g., EPA, DOT, the Department of Agriculture, and the Department of Health and Human Services) that issue those types of rules. OIRA representatives also said there is an important distinction between informal consultations between OIRA and agency staff that may occur at any time and informal reviews that occur when OIRA is provided a substantive draft of a rule. There have been some indications that OIRA has increased its use of informal reviews in recent years."

The GAO illustrated the process as follows:

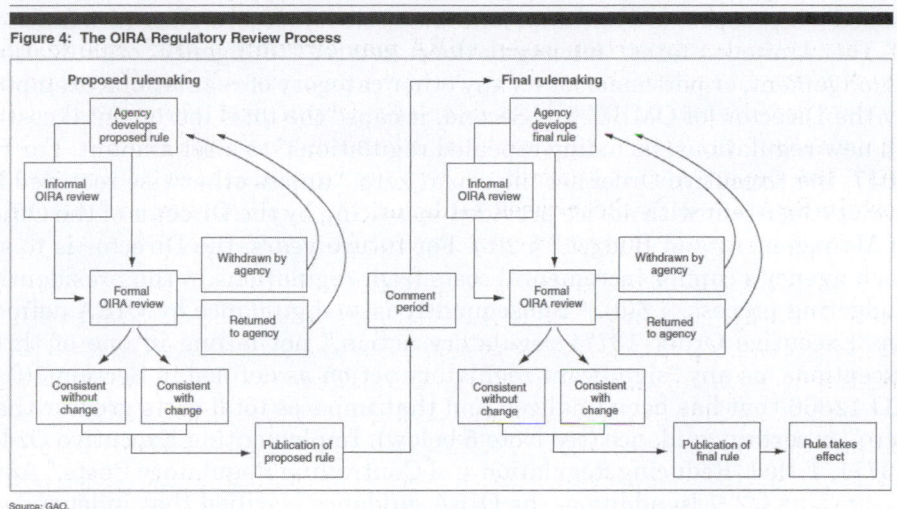

Figure 4: The OIRA Regulatory Review Process

Source: GAO.

Id. at 30.

Two notes on this process, one on outcomes and one on staff. First, you can track what OIRA does with the rules it reviews on reginfo.gov. In President Obama's Administration, OIRA marked 492 rules as consistent (with the Executive Order) without change and 3,558 as consistent with change; it formally returned only 3 rules as inconsistent with the Executive Order, and agencies withdrew 242 rules. In President George W. Bush's Administration, OIRA marked 1,402 rules as consistent without change and 3,168 as consistent with change; OIRA sent return letters for 33 rules, and 436 rules were withdrawn by the agency. Recall that OIRA typically reviews significant rules twice—at the proposal and final stages. Informal review by OIRA, however, does not appear in this tracking. Second, OIRA staff has varied expertise for the demands of their review. "Historically, OIRA staff had strong backgrounds in economics, statistics, and policy analysis. The nature of federal regulation, however, has changed since OIRA was created in 1981. Most classic economic regulation has been rescinded or is produced by independent agencies which are not subject to OIRA regulatory oversight. The fastest area of growth has been public health, safety, and environmental regulation, sometimes referred to as science-based or social regulation. To respond to this trend, [under the second Bush Administration] OIRA hired highly trained experts in fields such as environmental science, engineering, epidemiology, toxicology, public health, and health policy." JOHN D. GRAHAM ET AL., MANAGING THE REGULATORY STATE: THE EXPERIENCE OF THE BUSH ADMINISTRATION, 33 Fordham Urb. L.J. 953, 968–69 (2006). Of course, the agencies promulgating the rules often have greater subject-matter expertise.

(4) ***New Mandates from Executive Order 13771.*** President Trump issued Executive Order 13771 soon after taking office, on January 30, 2017. 82 Fed. Reg. 9339 (Feb. 3, 2017). The Executive Order imposes two sets of obligations. First, "[u]nless prohibited by law," it requires that whenever an agency "publicly proposes for notice and comment or otherwise promulgates

a new regulation, it shall identify at least two existing regulations to be repealed." § 2(a). This 2-for-1 mandate does not apply to "(a) regulations issued with respect to a military, national security, or foreign affairs function of the United States; (b) regulations related to agency organization, management, or personnel; or (c) any other category of regulations exempted by the Director [of OMB]." § 4. Second, it caps "the total incremental cost of all new regulations, including repealed regulations" to a set amount. For FY 2017, the Executive Order set the cap at zero, "unless otherwise required by law or consistent with advice provided in writing by the Director of the Office of Management and Budget." § 2(b). For future years, the Director is to set each agency's cap for incremental costs from regulations in the presidential budgeting process. § 3(d).[36] Subsequently issued guidance by OIRA defined an "Executive Order 13771 regulatory action," not falling in one of three exceptions, as any "significant regulatory action as defined in Section 3(f) of EO 12866 that has been finalized and that imposes total costs greater than zero" or certain guidance (see Note 5 below). Implementing Executive Order 13771, Titled "Reducing Regulation and Controlling Regulatory Costs," April 5, 2017, at Q2.[37] In addition, the OIRA guidance clarified that independent regulatory commissions and boards are not bound by the Executive Order's mandates. Id. at Q1. These mandates have some connection to retrospective review of rulemaking (to see if existing regulations could be repealed) that agencies were already supposed to be doing. See Executive Order 13563 § 6; Connor Raso, Assessing Regulatory Retrospective Review under the Obama Administration, Brookings Institution (June 15, 2017).[38]

In late February 2017, President Trump issued Executive Order 13777 (Enforcing the Regulatory Reform Agenda), 82 Fed. Reg. 12285 (Feb. 24, 2017). It provides some details for the implementation of Executive Order 13771. Specifically, agency heads must appoint "Regulatory Reform Officers . . . to oversee the implementation of regulatory reform initiatives and policies to ensure that agencies effectively carry out regulatory reforms, consistent with applicable law" and establish "Regulatory Reform Task Forces . . . to evaluate existing regulations (as defined in section 4 of Executive Order 13771) and make recommendations to the agency head regarding their repeal, replacement, or modification, consistent with applicable law." §§ 2–3. But many details are not provided in the two Executive Orders or the OIRA guidance. For example, what happens if the courts strike down the repeal of one of the two regulations that have to be cut under Executive Order 13771? Does the agency have to find another regulation to undo? OIRA's guidance acknowledged the issue but provided little information: "[S]uch decisions may happen years after a rule is finalized, and may affect compliance with both the cost allowances and the

---

[36] In September 2017, OIRA Administrator Rao instructed executive agencies "to submit [their] proposed total incremental cost allowance for FY 2018 to [their] OIRA Desk Officer, along with any supporting explanation, at the time [they] make [their] submissions for the Fall 2017 Regulatory Plan and Unified Agenda. . . ." http://www.whitehouse.gov/sites/whitehouse.gov/files/omb/memoranda/2017/FY%202018%20Regulatory%20Cost%20Allowances.pdf.

[37] http://www.whitehouse.gov/the-press-office/2017/04/05/memorandum-implementing-executive-order-13771-titled-reducing-regulation.

[38] http://www.brookings.edu/research/assessing-regulatory-retrospective-review-under-the-obama-administration/.

repeal provisions established pursuant to EO 13771. The agency should contact OIRA to determine how a remand or vacatur of an EO 13771 deregulatory action affects the agency's obligations under EO 13771." Id. at Q17.

(5) ***Application of Executive Orders 12866 and 13771 to Agency Guidance.*** As written, Executive Order 12866 appears not to apply to agency guidance. It defines "regulation" or "rule" as "an agency statement of general applicability and future effect, which the agency intends to have the force and effect of law" and "regulatory action" as "any substantive action by an agency (normally published in the Federal Register) that promulgates or is expected to lead to the promulgation of a final rule or regulation." § 3(d)– (e). As noted above, President Bush's Executive Order 13422 extended the regulatory review process to include "significant guidance documents," with significance defined the same as with respect to regulatory actions. A guidance document was defined as an "agency statement of general applicability and future effect, other than regulatory action, that sets forth a policy on a statutory, regulatory, or technical issue or an interpretation of a statutory or regulatory issue." EO 13422 § 3(g). In particular, agencies were required to notify OIRA in advance before issuing any significant guidance, and at OIRA's request supply "the content of the draft guidance document, together with a brief explanation of the need for the guidance document and how it will meet that need," with OIRA authorized to require further consultation before the guidance could be issued. Id. § 7. For discussion of the requirements imposed by OMB's subsequent Bulletin on Good Guidance Practices, see p. 381.

Note that both Executive Order 13422 and the Bulletin considered the practical effect of certain guidance documents sufficient to trigger OIRA review and other procedural requirements, even though such documents by definition lacked legal effect, a different approach from that taken by some of the case law on agency guidance, see Center for Auto Safety, p. 368; but see Texas v. United States, p. 357. Although President Obama revoked Executive Order 13422, and by its terms Executive Order 12866 does not appear to apply to guidance documents, OMB has asserted that significant agency guidance remains subject to OIRA review. See Peter R. Orszag, Director, OMB, M–09–13, Memorandum for the Heads & Acting Heads of Exec. Dept's & Agencies, Guidance for Regulatory Review (Mar. 4, 2009).

By its terms, Executive Order 13771 applies to any "agency statement of general or particular applicability and future effect designed to implement, interpret, or prescribe law or policy or to describe the procedure or practice requirements of an agency," with the three exceptions listed above in Note 4. § 4. It notably lacks the "force and effect of law" language included in Executive Order 12866. The subsequent OIRA guidance narrowed the covered actions to a "significant regulatory action as defined in Section 3(f) of EO 12866 that has been finalized and that imposes total costs greater than zero," as noted above, or a "significant guidance document (e.g., significant interpretive guidance) reviewed by OIRA under the procedures of EO 12866 that has been finalized and that imposes total costs greater than zero."

Implementing Executive Order 13771, Titled "Reducing Regulation and Controlling Regulatory Costs," April 5, 2017, at Q2.

(6) ***Executive Orders 12866 and 13771 and Notice-and-Comment Rulemaking.*** Look at the figure in Note 3 above. How many boxes correspond to the text of § 553? Executive Order 12866, in particular, adds much to § 553's skeletal procedures. For example, compare § 553's silence prior to the NPRM with Executive Order 12866 § 4's requirements of advance notice of potential regulatory actions and § 6(a)(1)'s demand that "*before issuing a notice of proposed rulemaking*, each agency should, where appropriate, seek the involvement of those who are intended to benefit from and those expected to be burdened by any regulation (including, specifically, State, local, and tribal officials)" (emphasis added; see also EO 13563 § 2 (same)). Also striking is the comparison of § 553(b)'s minimal notice requirement—"either the terms or substance of the proposed rule or a description of the subjects and issues involved"—with § 6(a)(3)(B)'s requirements for agency submission to OIRA, in connection with *any* "significant regulatory action," of the "text of the draft regulatory action, together with a reasonably detailed description of the need for the regulatory action, and an explanation of how the regulatory action will meet that need" as well as the assessments of the proposed action's costs and benefits quoted above. Application of some OIRA review procedures to significant agency guidance is another difference, as is the emphasis on the impact of guidance in practice.

Executive Order 13771 mandates that certain notice-and-comment rulemakings occur essentially simultaneously (as for every new significant regulation there need to be at least two previous significant rules repealed). It does not change the notice-and-comment process, expressly noting that "[a]ny agency eliminating existing costs associated with prior regulations under this [2 for 1] subsection shall do so in accordance with the Administrative Procedure Act and other applicable law." § 2(c). Most critically, a repeal of an existing regulation typically requires notice and comment, unless one of the exceptions applies (and the new Executive Order on its own would not qualify as good cause).

Equally notable is the contrast between the Executive Orders' distinctions among rulemakings (mainly, significant and nonsignificant) and the Supreme Court's decision in Vermont Yankee, p. 295, which read § 553 as establishing a one-size-fits-all set of procedures. Then-Professor Antonin Scalia had criticized the Court's decision precisely for its failure to recognize that some rulemakings are more equal than others, see p. 305. Putting aside for the moment questions about White House control, do these expanded provisions for notice and targeting of more important regulations for additional procedures structure the rulemaking process better than § 553?

(7) ***The Executive Orders and Judicial Review.*** Each Executive Order expressly notes that it is not creating judicially enforceable obligations. Executive Order 13771 § 5(c): "This order is not intended to, and does not, create any right or benefit, substantive or procedural, enforceable at law or in equity by any party against the United States, its departments, agencies, or entities, its officers, employees, or agents, or any other person." Executive

Order 12866 § 10: "Nothing in this Executive order shall affect any otherwise available judicial review of agency action. This Executive order is intended only to improve the internal management of the Federal Government and does not create any right or benefit, substantive or procedural, enforceable at law or equity by a party against the United States, its agencies or instrumentalities, its officers or employees, or any other person."

Yet won't the Executive Orders affect judicial review in practice by generating assessments of proposed regulations or by noting that particular regulations are being repealed so that another regulation can be issued— which become part of the rulemaking record? Consider first Executive Order 12866: Under § 6(b)(4)(D), after the regulatory action has been published or the agency has announced its intention not to go forward, "OIRA shall make available to the public all documents exchanged between OIRA and the agency during the review by OIRA under this section." In addition, the agency must make public the assessments and other information it provided OIRA on significant or economically significant rules, identify substantive changes between the draft submitted to OIRA and the action subsequently announced, and identify "those changes in the regulatory action made at the suggestion or recommendation of OIRA." § 6(a)(3)(E). Take next Executive Order 13371: Presuming the agency's disclosures to OIRA under § 2(a) are made public (which may not occur, see Note 6 in Section 5 below (p. 453) on issues with OIRA's transparency) and included in the record (see Note 8 below), challenges may be brought to agency actions that seem to rely on factors outside the relevant statutory framework (see p. 1271).

(8) ***Other Planning and Assessment Requirements.*** Agencies face regulatory planning and assessment requirements outside of those in these two Executive Orders. Some come from other executive orders, such as the requirements that agencies analyze regulatory impacts on federalism. Executive Order 13132, 64 Fed. Reg. 43255 (Aug. 10, 1999). Congress has also imposed potentially significant requirements. For example, the Unfunded Mandates Reform Act of 1995 put legislative muscle behind the requirement that—"unless otherwise prohibited by law"—agencies consider impacts on state, local, and tribal governments or the private sector for rules that might "result in the expenditure . . . of $100,000,000 or more (adjusted annually for inflation) in any 1 year." 2 U.S.C. §§ 1531–32. The Small Business Regulatory Enforcement Fairness Act (SBREFA) requires agencies to publish a regulatory flexibility agenda that contains "a brief description of the subject area of any rule which the agency expects to propose or promulgate which is likely to have a significant economic impact on a substantial number of small entities," along with a summary of the action, its objectives and legal basis, an approximate schedule for completing it, and an agency contact. 5 U.S.C. § 602. In addition, SBREFA amended the Regulatory Flexibility Act to allow judicial review of the RFA's requirement that an agency must prepare a regulatory flexibility analysis whenever it determines that a rule will have a "significant economic impact on a substantial number of small entities." § 611(b). Life has been made somewhat simpler than this sounds, although still complex, by permitting one "impact statement" generally to be used for all applicable impact

analysis requirements. Typically, NPRMs (and final rules) have a section near the end, "Regulatory Notices," where each mandate is briefly addressed (even if simply to say it is not applicable). See, for example, the NPRM for the Tarmac Rule discussed in the Introduction (p. 13) at 74,600–02.[39]

NOTES ON ONGOING ISSUES WITH EXECUTIVE ORDER 12866 AND INITIAL VIEWS ON EXECUTIVE ORDER 13771

(1) *Openness of the Process.* Much of the political battling in the early years of the regulatory review process concerned its lack of transparency and, correspondingly, fears that it was serving as a conduit for the views of the White House's political friends. This criticism was raised in particular about the Council on Competitiveness that Vice President Dan Quayle headed during the first Bush Administration. See Peter M. Shane, Political Accountability in a System of Checks and Balances: The Case of Presidential Review of Rulemaking, 48 Ark. L. Rev. 161 (1995). In this respect, Executive Order 12866 differed substantially from its predecessors, with agencies being required to: (1) identify substantive changes between the action they announce and the draft action they submitted to OIRA for review, and (2) indicate those changes made at OIRA's behest once the regulatory action is published or otherwise resolved. OIRA in turn is required to make publicly available all documents it exchanged with the agency during review. §§ 6(a)(3)(E), 6(b)(4)(D). Note 6 in Subsection 5.a below (p. 453) discusses the mandates concerning communications in detail. Transparency in regulatory review was enhanced during the second Bush Administration, with the disclosures required by Executive Order 12866 being made available online, and the Obama Administration expanded online access further. Using the OIRA dashboard at www.reginfo.gov, it is now possible to easily access information on any regulatory action currently under review or for which review has been completed. Will transparency increase under the Trump Administration? On one hand, as described in Chapter VI (p. 658), the new Administration is off to a more secretive start. On the other hand, it may want to tout deregulatory actions to garner political support from conservatives.

Nonetheless, concerns have continued to be voiced about insufficient openness in the OIRA process, particularly when rules are under informal review. A 2009 GAO report concluded that "there are opportunities to improve the transparency of OIRA's reviews," emphasizing that "agencies did not always clearly attribute changes made at the suggestion of OIRA" and that OIRA had not extended its transparency requirements to informal review periods. GAO, Federal Rulemaking: Improvements Needed to Monitoring and Evaluation of Rules Development as Well as to the Transparency of OMB Regulatory Reviews, GAO–09–205 (April 2009), at 6, 32. For more on substantial concerns of noncompliance with the Executive Order's communications mandates, see Note 6 in Subsection 5.a below (p. 453).

---

[39] http://www.gpo.gov/fdsys/pkg/FR-2008-12-08/pdf/E8-28527.pdf.

(2) ***Communications between OIRA and White House Officials.*** Also shielded from public disclosure are OIRA's interactions with other White House offices. LISA SCHULTZ BRESSMAN and MICHAEL P. VANDENBERGH emphasize this point in a study that focused on how top political officials at the EPA during the Bush I and Clinton Administrations perceived the regulatory review process: "White House involvement seldom was transparent to the public, either in an absolute sense or compared to the actions of the EPA. A large majority of EPA respondents scored White House involvement relatively low on all measures of transparency, including visibility to the public, opportunities for public view, media coverage, and availability of information in the administrative record." The authors argue that this undermines political accountability: "To the extent that White House offices other than OIRA are the ones handling the high-level issues, we have a particular need to know much more about how they perform this function to ensure that they perform it well." As a result, they conclude, "White House involvement should be more transparent. Such transparency may depend, more than anything, on the willingness of the President to insist that non-OIRA White House offices voluntarily document their interactions with the EPA and with interest groups regarding EPA rulemakings." INSIDE THE ADMINISTRATIVE STATE: A CRITICAL LOOK AT THE PRACTICE OF PRESIDENTIAL CONTROL, 105 Mich. L. Rev. 47, 82, 84, 92 (2006).

Do you agree that greater disclosure of general White House involvement in regulatory review is needed to reap the greater political accountability of rulemaking that is often promoted as one of the justifications for OIRA review? Or is it more important to preserve opportunities for "some candid deliberations in the secluded quarters of the Old Executive Office Building"? John D. Graham, Adm'r, OIRA, Address Before Weidenbaum Center Forum: Executive Regulatory Review: Surveying the Record, Making It Work (Dec. 17, 2001). Professor Mendelson has proposed a middle ground: "require that a significant rule include at least a summary of the substance of executive supervision." Nina A. Mendelson, Disclosing "Political" Oversight of Agency Decision Making, 108 Mich. L. Rev. 1127, 1150 (2010). See also Note 5 in Subsection 5.a (p. 453).

(3) ***Executive Order 12866's Impact on Regulatory Outcomes.*** To some extent, the question of whether greater openness is needed turns on the degree to which White House involvement (including OIRA) and outside groups through the OIRA process alter regulatory outcomes. Little hard data are available on that score with respect to White House staff and presidential aides, though their interventions could be expected to be quite influential. Professor Croley's empirical study of OIRA meetings during the Clinton Administration, however, found that "White House attendance at a[n OIRA] meeting [where the agency is invited] is . . . not associated with a greater likelihood that a rule will be changed." Steven P. Croley, White House Review of Agency Rulemaking: An Empirical Investigation, 70 U. Chi. L. Rev. 821, 861 (2003). But White House staff can meet with OIRA outside of the discussions governed by the Executive Order. OIRA itself clearly seems to influence regulatory outcomes. As described in Note 3 above (p. 419), in President Obama's Administration, the dominant outcome of OIRA review

yielded changes to the agency's regulation (indeed, there were more than seven-fold reviews yielding changes than reviews with no changes). Those figures likely understate OIRA's influence, as changes made through informal review occurring before any formal oversight are not included in the counts.

Some of OIRA's influence derives from pressure emanating from the White House; other influence comes from outside groups participating in the OIRA process. As for the latter, Professors SIMON F. HAEDER and SUSAN WEBB YACKEE recently published an extensive study of 1,500 final regulations submitted to OIRA for review, using software to analyze changes in regulatory text: "[O]urs is the first quantitative study to investigate the magnitude (and in sensitivity analyses the substantive importance) of policy change during OMB review. The main independent variables tap the volume of interest group lobbying, both overall, as well as for select types of lobbying entities. We find that more interest group lobbying is associated with more regulatory change. We also demonstrate that, when only industry groups lobby, we are more likely to see rule change; however, the same is not true for public interest groups." INFLUENCE AND THE ADMINISTRATIVE PROCESS: LOBBYING THE U.S. PRESIDENT'S OFFICE OF MANAGEMENT AND BUDGET, 109 Am. Pol. Sci. Rev. 507, 517–18 (2015).

(4) **Delay.** Another concern raised about OIRA review under Executive Order 12866 is that it adds delay to the already lengthy rulemaking process, especially for major rules. Again, this was a complaint raised against OIRA review early on, with some critics concluding that "[b]ecause OMB was unable effectively to assess the wide range of regulations submitted to it, its principal function was to slow things down." Richard H. Pildes & Cass R. Sunstein, Reinventing the Regulatory State, 62 U. Chi. L. Rev. 1, 5 (1995). Consider in this respect the early decision in ENVIRONMENTAL DEFENSE FUND V. THOMAS, 627 F.Supp. 566 (D.D.C. 1986). The EPA's adoption of rules to regulate underground storage tanks for hazardous waste had been delayed well past a statutory deadline—in part, it transpired, because of the need to obtain OMB clearance under Executive Order 12291. On the basis of internal documents released under seal, District Court Judge Thomas Flannery found this delay substantially attributable to policy disagreements between the OMB and the EPA over the approach to be taken. While accepting the timetable now proposed by the agency for completion of the rules, Judge Flannery addressed these words to OMB: "This court declares that OMB has no authority to use its regulatory review under EO 12291 to delay promulgation of EPA regulations arising from the 1984 Amendments of the RCRA beyond the date of a statutory deadline. Thus, if a deadline already has expired, OMB has no authority to delay regulations subject to the deadline in order to review them under the executive order. If the deadline is about to expire, OMB may review the regulations only until the time at which OMB review will result in the deadline being missed. . . . While this may be an intrusion into the degree of flexibility the executive agencies have in taking their time about promulgating these regulations, this is simply a judicial recognition of law as passed by Congress and of the method for dealing with deadlines laid down by the President himself."

Executive Order 12866 not only caps OIRA review at 90 days (with a possible 30-day extension), it also directs the agency to "notify OIRA as soon as possible" and comply with the review process "to the extent possible" in instances "when an agency is obligated by law to act more quickly than normal review procedures allow" or when regulatory actions "are governed by statutory or court-imposed deadlines." §§ 6(a)(3)(D), 6(b)(2). Executive Order 13771 presumably will add time to the review process but it does not include any new deadlines for OIRA review. Do the existing provisions suggest acceptance of the holding in the Environmental Defense Fund case? Do they adequately address the timing problem?

Recent research suggests delay at OIRA is still an issue. In 2013, ACUS flagged problems in the Obama Administration: "Historically, OIRA has completed most of its reviews of agency rules well within the 90-day review period. For example, from 1994–2011, the average time for OIRA review was 50 days for all rules. Since 2011, however, average OIRA review times have trended significantly upward. In 2012, the average time for OIRA review for all rules rose to 79 days, and in the first half of 2013, the average review time increased even further to 140 days. It is important to note that, as OIRA completes review for rules that have been in the backlog for some time, the average review times will likely increase, which evidences an improving situation. Approximately four dozen reviews completed in 2013 have taken more than a year." ACUS, Improving the Timeliness of OIRA Review, Administrative Conference Statement #18 (adopted Dec. 2013), at 3–4.[40] In light of these delays, ACUS issued "principles" calling for OIRA to "whenever possible, adhere to the timeliness provisions of Executive Order (EO) 12,866" and to "inform the public as to the reasons for the delay or return the rule to the submitting agency" if more than 180 days have passed since submission. Id. at 6–7. In his June 2013 confirmation hearing to be OIRA Administrator, Howard Shelanski promised to reduce the delays, noting it would be one of his highest priorities. In 2015 and 2016, reginfo.gov shows that the average review time for economically significant rules was 84 days (83 days for other rules).

OIRA delays, of course, contribute to overall delays in rulemaking. A report issued by Public Citizen in June 2016, Unsafe Delays, analyzed data from over twenty years of the federal Unified Agenda to assess changes in the length of rulemakings and other trends.[41] The report concluded that additional procedural requirements on rulemaking, including the assessment requirements of the Executive Order 12866, are causing significant delays. It found that "rules deemed to be of the highest importance (based on the priority assigned and number of requirements attached) take the longest to complete—sometimes longer than one presidential term." More specifically, economically significant rules "have taken 2.4 years, 41 percent longer than the overall average (1.7 years)," and take even longer if a regulatory flexibility analysis was required (2.5 years),

---

[40] http://www.acus.gov/sites/default/files/documents/OIRA%20Statement%20FINAL%20 POSTED%2012-9-13.pdf.

[41] http://www.citizen.org/documents/Unsafe-Delays-Report.pdf.

an advanced notice of proposed rulemaking was issued (4.4 years), or both (almost 5 years).

(5) *An Antiregulatory Bias in Executive Order 12866?* Put Executive Order 13771 to the side. Is OIRA review under Executive Order 12866 antiregulatory? Professor NICHOLAS BAGLEY and then Dean RICHARD L. REVESZ argue that it is in CENTRALIZED OVERSIGHT OF THE REGULATORY STATE, 106 Colum. L. Rev. 1260, 1267–68 (2006): "Executive Order 12,866—based as it is on an order designed explicitly to promote an antiregulatory agenda—contains within it several structural and institutional biases against regulation. First, OIRA reviews agency regulations only to determine whether their benefits outweigh their costs—in other words, to ensure that the regulation is not too stringent. But, of course, the regulation could be too lax, and cost-benefit analysis might call for a more robust regulatory response. Second, OIRA rarely reviews agency decisions to deregulate with the same rigor with which it reviews new regulations. OIRA thus stands as a structural roadblock on the path of regulation, but not deregulation—an asymmetry which cannot be justified on cost-benefit grounds. Third, perhaps most importantly, OIRA generally does not review agency inaction. Agency inertia is therefore privileged under the current system of OIRA review, and many regulations that would have positive net benefits are never enacted. Fourth, at least two procedural features of OIRA review cut against regulation: the delay associated with OIRA review (exacerbated by OIRA's small size), and OIRA's exemption from the constraints of the Administrative Procedure Act (APA). To be sure, some of OIRA's antiregulatory bent can be attributed to politics; after all, Republican Presidents have overseen OIRA for all but eight of its twenty-five-year existence. But whatever the political affiliation of the President . . . several aspects of OIRA's institutional design work together to impose a sizeable drag on the regulatory state."

Not surprisingly, former OIRA head John Graham disagrees: "Perhaps because of the stridently deregulatory stance taken by OIRA in the early years of the Reagan administration, a perception remains today that the exclusive role of OIRA is to foster deregulation or cost reduction. Indeed, benefit-cost analysis (BCA) counsels avoidance of inefficient lifesaving rules—but it also counsels acceleration of efficient investments in lifesaving. . . . [K]ey rulemakings from the 2001–2006 period . . . [illustrate] that OIRA plays a much more complex role than legal scholars appreciate. Using findings from BCA, OIRA served as a crucial advocate of several lifesaving regulations that, in the absence of OIRA's support, might not have survived White House oversight in a pro-business Republican administration. . . . What is missing from the legal literature is recognition of OIRA's proregulation role." JOHN D. GRAHAM, SAVING LIVES THROUGH ADMINISTRATIVE LAW AND ECONOMICS, 395 U. Pa. L. Rev. 395, 404, 450 (2008).

Do you agree that OIRA review under Executive Order 12866 is institutionally biased against regulation, or is any anti-regulatory tilt better viewed as a reflection of presidential policies? If such a bias does exist, would you expect prompt letters or presidential directives to be an effective counter?

(6) *Are the Advantages of OIRA Review under Executive Order 12866 Exaggerated?* Another area of extensive debate is whether OIRA review under Executive Order 12866 produces regulatory benefits that could potentially justify the practice notwithstanding allegations of an antiregulatory bias. Croley, supra, at 831: "Proponents of expanded White House control defend greater control over agency rulemaking on several grounds. First, such control promotes consistency across the executive branch. Furthermore, while OMB is not an expert in any substantive regulatory field, it has become an expert in the field of regulation itself. Accordingly, OIRA has developed a special institutional capacity for distinguishing between, on the one hand, regulation likely to advance sound regulatory policy, and on the other, regulation that—however well intentioned—may lead to unintended and undesirable consequences. In addition to mere coordination, in other words, White House review provides a 'quality check' on pending rules. . . . Defenders of greater White House control further argue that the president is uniquely situated to advance national interests, as opposed to the factional interests that are often promoted by Congress, and that consequently find expression in agency decisions. . . . Another version of the argument in favor of a strong president, the unitary executive thesis, insists that presidential control over agencies is necessary not just to promote a national orientation in agency rulemaking, but also to preserve the political and constitutional legitimacy of the regulatory state."

Cass Sunstein, OIRA's Administrator from September 2009 to August 2012, in an essay on how OIRA functions, plays up its consistency and accountability role: "[M]ost of OIRA's day-to-day work is usually spent not on costs and benefits, but on working through interagency concerns, promoting receipt of public comments (for proposed rules), ensuring discussion of alternatives, and promoting consideration of public comments (for final rules)." Cass R. Sunstein, The Office of Information and Regulatory Affairs: Myths and Realities, 126 Harv. L. Rev. 1838, 1842 (2013); see also Cass R. Sunstein, Simpler: The Future of Government (2013).

These accounts of OIRA promoting consistency and accountability have been challenged. Based on interviews with EPA officials from the Bush I and Clinton Administrations, Professors Bressman and Vandenbergh contend that these purported benefits are more theoretical than real: ". . .OIRA review appears to advance inter-agency coordination somewhat, minimizing overlaps and conflicts between or among the regulations of different federal agencies. But OIRA review does not achieve what might be called 'intra-agency coherence,' which includes reducing redundancies, avoiding inconsistencies, and eliminating unintended consequences between or among the regulations of a particular agency. . . . Perhaps even more noteworthy, we question whether presidential control facilitates political accountability. EPA respondents believed that they were more transparent and responsive than the White House. When asked to identify the aspects of the EPA process that provided greater public view and representation, respondents emphasized the notice-and-comment rule-making procedures of the [APA], various stakeholder and regional meetings, and Federal Advisory Committee Act requirements. Respondents also indicated that the general media and trade press reported far less often on White House involvement in EPA rule-making. We conclude, somewhat paradoxically, that agencies, though not comprising elected officials, may better promote political accountability than the White House." BRESSMAN & VANDERBERGH, supra, at 74–76.[42]

More recently, Professor LISA HEINZERLING, who was Associate Administrator of EPA's Office of Policy during the Obama Administration's first term—a role that meant she was the primary EPA liaison with OIRA— has expressed skepticism about Sunstein's account, discussed above, of OIRA review: "From my vantage point at EPA, it certainly often appeared that OIRA—not other White House offices, not other agencies—was calling the shots. OIRA decided what to review, offered line-by-line edits of regulatory proposals, convened meetings with outside parties, mediated disputes among the agencies, decided whether an agency's cost-benefit analysis was up to snuff, and more. It often appeared, from the agency's perspective, that other White House offices were brought in to bolster, not to question, OIRA's position on regulatory matters." INSIDE EPA: A FORMER INSIDER'S REFLECTIONS ON THE RELATIONSHIP BETWEEN THE OBAMA EPA AND THE OBAMA WHITE HOUSE, 31 Pace Envt'l. L. Rev. 325 (2014). See also discussion of transparency issues and delays in Notes 1 and 4 above (pp. 426, 428) and Note 6 in Subsection 5.a below (p. 453).

What changes would you make to the review process under Executive Order 12866, if any? Do you favor OIRA engaging in informal reviews, as described in Note 3 above on p. 419? Should those reviews be included in the Executive Order? What changes could be made to improve the timeliness and transparency of OIRA reviews, through modifying the Executive Order or other mechanisms? What about having OIRA review agency inaction, which might prompt more regulation? Do you see greater obstacles to effective OIRA review of inaction than of actual rulemaking? How should OIRA's coordination role, which emphasizes cost-benefit analysis, fit with other coordinating entities in the executive branch, like the Office of Legal Counsel, which focuses on legality, and the Domestic Policy Council, which emphasizes political implications?

(7) *Are Regulatory Caps in Executive Order 13771 Good or Bad?* Executive Order 13771 imposes on agencies, for the first time, regulatory caps and the mandate that every new regulation be matched with two

---

[42] Sally Katzen, OIRA Administrator under President Clinton, disagrees with their assessment: "I see it very differently. The agencies focus like a laser, as they should, on their statutory missions—in the case of EPA, protecting the environment. The White House and OIRA take a broader view and consider how, for example, an environmental proposal will affect energy resources, tax revenues, health policy, etc. Stated another way, EPA is pursuing a parochial interest; OIRA is tempering that with the national interest, as it should." Ms. Katzen also argues that ensuring intra-agency consistency was the agency's responsibility, and OIRA should instead focus on achieving inter-agency consistency, an area in which the former EPA officials interviewed by Professors Bressman and Vanderbergh gave OIRA better marks. Sally Katzen, A Reality Check on an Empirical Study: Comments on "Inside The Administrative State," 105 Mich. L. Rev. 1497, 1505–06 (2006).

repeals of existing rules. Consider two opposing views on these devices as a matter of public policy (as opposed to legality). SAM BATKINS, IT IS PREMATURE TO LABEL A REGULATORY BUDGET UNCONSTITUTIONAL, Regulatory Review Blog (June 26, 2017):[43] "Marcus Peacock, who led the 'landing team' at the Office of Information and Regulatory Affairs during the first few months of 2017, offered some hints about how the one-in, two-out budget might work at a recent Resources for the Future event. He cited both Canada and the United Kingdom, which have operated regulatory budgets without abandoning clean air or water standards. In those countries, reducing paperwork—through recordkeeping and reporting requirements— dominates the deregulatory actions. Peacock predicted similar actions for the United States. He stated, 'I'm guessing we're going to find something similar. And a lot of the deregulatory actions that people will focus on first are those that simply make it easier for people to fill out paperwork or just fill out less paperwork, probably.' . . . Indeed, with every administration, regulators trim paperwork and reduce regulatory costs without flouting the intent of Congress or their statutory directives. For example, during the Obama Administration, the U.S. Department of Transportation revised its rule on driver vehicle inspection reports. This rulemaking relieved truck drivers from having to file 'no defect' reports. Essentially, they no longer had to report that their trips from one city to another occurred without incident. According to the Obama Administration, this saved $1.7 billion annually by cutting 46.6 million paperwork burden hours. This is not to say that implementation of the executive order will be a walk in the park. On the contrary, it will be difficult. Fulfilling the executive order's requirements will demand a robust retrospective review and program evaluation initiative from agencies. Perhaps this effort might give rise to new agencies that will aid in the effort."

DAN FARBER, COURTS SHOULD KILL TRUMP'S PRICEY "2-FOR-1" DEREGULATION ORDER, The Hill Blog (Feb. 9, 2017):[44] "The number of regulations, apart from what they do or don't accomplish, really matters to no one except the government printing office. The cap on compliance costs ignores the fact that existing regulations have already had to pass a cost-benefit analysis. So if an existing regulation has a cost of $100 million, that means that the government already found the benefits were even higher—in other words, the existing regulation pays for itself in societal benefits. If you get rid of $100 million in costs by throwing away $120 million in benefits, just how is society better off? The regulatory process is very elaborate, and adopting a new regulation is a very expensive, time-consuming process. This executive order effectively triples the cost, because agencies not only have to enact new regulations but go through equally complex proceedings to eliminate two old ones. Basically, agencies will be able to propose about a third as many new rules as before. . . . The agency's regulatory agenda will be dominated by the need to find 'sacrificial rules' to repeal, and the agency

---

[43] http://www.theregreview.org/2017/06/26/batkins-premature-regulatory-budget-unconstitutional/.

[44] http://thehill.com/blogs/pundits-blog/the-administration/318725-courts-should-kill-trumps-pricey-2-for-1-deregulation.

may not even try to issues new rules or will abandon rule making efforts in midstream."

Could positive regulatory caps for each agency be a middle ground between these positions? How would you set the cap for the EPA? (see note 36, supra)

(8) *Agency Capacity and Independence from Emphasis on Costs and Benefits?* Another potential benefit of OIRA's emphasis on cost-benefit analysis is the effect it has on the rulemaking process within agencies. "The first two administrators of OIRA saw as perhaps the greatest benefit of OMB review improved agency ability to 'respond to the kinds of questions that OMB raises.' This was achieved when agencies either established or enhanced their in-house capabilities to analyze their regulatory decisions. Thus, the very existence of external review can improve an agency's decisionmaking process by keeping the agency on its analytical toes. There is a value in keeping agency bureaucratic decisions intellectually honest and analytically rigorous, and external, centralized presidential regulatory review can bring this about by bringing to bear a new set of perspectives and analytical tools." JAMES L. BLUMSTEIN, REGULATORY REVIEW BY THE EXECUTIVE OFFICE OF THE PRESIDENT: AN OVERVIEW AND POLICY ANALYSIS OF CURRENT ISSUES, 51 Duke L.J. 851, 879 (2001).

Some caution may be warranted, however. In COST-BENEFIT ANALYSIS AND AGENCY INDEPENDENCE, 81 U. Chi. L. Rev. 609 (2014), Professor MICHAEL LIVERMORE focuses on how agencies can use cost-benefit analysis to shield their regulatory choices. Livermore argues that "[t]here are hard methodological choices in any sophisticated analysis. How these choices are made can have extremely important effects on the results of cost-benefit analysis. . . . [A]gencies have played an important role in the evolution of cost-benefit analysis, which poses a challenge to the prevailing view of cost-benefit analysis as primarily a means for the center to exert control over the periphery." Moreover, "regularization of cost-benefit analysis into a standardized methodology actually constrains OIRA review, creating a safe harbor in which agencies are relatively protected from interference." Livermore bases his claims on a close examination of the EPA, which has "built [a] substantial in-house economics capacity . . . [that] far dwarfs that of OIRA, and has made significant methodological contributions, fostering the elaboration of concepts such as nonuse value and discounting that are fundamental to how cost-benefit analysis is carried out."

NOTES ON COST-BENEFIT ANALYSIS
AND RISK ASSESSMENT

(1) *The Practice of Cost-Benefit Analysis.* A prominent feature of the regulatory review process is its emphasis on cost-benefit analysis, particularly for economically significant rules. A good initial introduction to and justification of the practice is provided by CASS R. SUNSTEIN, past Administrator of OIRA, in THE COST-BENEFIT STATE: THE FUTURE OF REGULATORY PROTECTION 20–22 (2002): "First and foremost, a government committed to cost-benefit analysis will attempt to analyze the consequences

of regulations, on both the cost and benefit side. Such an analysis will include quantitative and qualitative accounts of expected effects, including, for example, a statement of the expected lives saved, curable cancers prevented, asthma attacks averted, and much more. . . .

". . . Many regulations do not impose substantial costs, and for routine or low-cost measures a formal analysis should not be required (and it has not been under the relevant executive orders). The central point is that the extent of the requisite analysis should depend on the magnitude of the regulation—and that a formal analysis should be required for all regulations imposing costs beyond some identified point. Quantification will be difficult or even impossible in some cases. For arsenic in drinking water, government cannot really come up with specific numbers to link exposure levels to deaths and illnesses. At this stage, science is able to produce only ranges of anticipated benefits, which are not precise but are nonetheless highly illuminating. For regulations protecting airport security in the face of terrorist threats, quantification of the benefits is at best a guess. We do not know the magnitude of the risks, and a full scale cost-benefit analysis would be silly. But even here, an effort to be as specific as possible about costs and anticipated efficacy is likely to help us to promote airport security in the most reasonable manner.

". . . [T]he cost-benefit state imposes a substantive requirement as well. In order to proceed, an agency should be required to conclude, in ordinary circumstances, that the benefits justify the costs, and to explain why. If, for example, a regulation is expected to save 80 lives, each valued at $6 million, and if it would cost $200 million, it is fully justified. But if a regulation is expected to save four lives and cost $400 million, an agency should ordinarily be barred from issuing it. If an agency seeks to proceed even though the benefits do not justify the costs, it should have to explain itself—by saying, for example, that those at risk are young children, and that because they cannot protect themselves, and because a number of years of life are involved, unusual steps should be taken.

"At this point, it might be possible to question whether a large amount of money (say, $400 million) would really be too much to spend to save a small number of lives (say, two). Who is to say that $400 million is too much? The best answer is heavily pragmatic. Each of us has limited resources, and we do not spend all of our budget on statistically low risks. We spend a certain amount, and not more, to protect against the risks associated with poor diet, motor vehicle accidents, fires, floods, and much more. In allocating our resources, we set priorities, partly to use resources to prevent the more serious safety problems and partly to use them on other things we care about, such as education, recreation, food, and entertainment. The same is true for governments, which cannot sensibly spend huge amounts on small hazards. If an agency requires a $400 million expenditure to save two lives, it will be expending resources that might well be spent on other matters, including the saving of more lives. Indeed, evidence suggests that high expenditures—of perhaps $15 million or more—will cause the loss of a statistical life, and hence that regulations with high costs and low benefits may cause more deaths than they prevent. . . .

"None of this suggests that the government should be rigidly bound to the 'bottom line.' Cost-benefit analysis ought not to place agencies in an arithmetic straightjacket. The benefits should ordinarily be required to exceed the costs, but regulators might reasonably decide that the numbers are not decisive if, for example, children are mostly at risk, or if the relevant hazard is faced mostly by poor people, or if the hazard at issue is involuntarily incurred or extremely difficult to control. . . . The basic ideas are simple: Agencies should be required to investigate both costs and benefits, to show that benefits justify costs in most circumstances, and to offer a reasonable explanation for any decision to proceed when costs exceed benefits. [T]hese requirements should help to overcome problems that we all face in thinking about risk while at the same time reducing interest-group power and promoting accountability in government."

Also look back at § 1 of Executive Order 12866. Among other items, it tells agencies that: "Costs and benefits shall be understood to include both quantifiable measures (to the fullest extent that these can be usefully estimated) and qualitative measures of costs and benefits that are difficult to quantify, but nevertheless essential to consider." Applying § 1 in actual rulemakings raises a number of analytical challenges.

(2) ***Critiques of Cost-Benefit Analysis.*** Despite its dominance, cost-benefit analysis has come in for continued critique, in no small part as a result of its role in regulatory review. Below is a sampling of the debate:

(a) FRANK ACKERMAN & LISA HEINZERLING, PRICING THE PRICELESS: COST-BENEFIT ANALYSIS OF ENVIRONMENTAL PROTECTION, 150 U. Pa. L. Rev. 1553 (2002): "[C]ost-benefit analysis involves the creation of artificial markets for things—like good health, long life, and clean air—that are not bought and sold. It also involves the devaluation of future events through discounting. So described, the mindset of the cost-benefit analyst is likely to seem quite foreign. The translation of all good things into dollars and the devaluation of the future are inconsistent with the way many people view the world. . . .

"Most people view risks imposed by others, without an individual's consent, as more worthy of government intervention than risks that an individual knowingly accepts. . . . In short, even for ultimate values such as life and death, the social context is decisive in our evaluation of risks. Cost-benefit analysis assumes the existence of generic, acontextual risk and thereby ignores the contextual information that determines the manner in which many people, in practice, think about real risks to real people. . . .

"Cost-benefit analysis is exceedingly time- and resource-intensive, and its flaws are so deep and so large that this time and these resources are wasted on it. Once a cost-benefit analysis is performed, its bottom line number offers an irresistible sound bite that inevitably drowns out more reasoned deliberation. Moreover, given the intrinsic conflict between cost-benefit analysis and the principles of fairness that animate, or should animate, our national policy toward protecting people from being hurt by other people, the results of cost-benefit analysis cannot simply be 'given some weight' along with other factors, without undermining the fundamental equality of all citizens-rich and poor, young and old, healthy and sick.

"Cost-benefit analysis cannot overcome its fatal flaw: it is completely reliant on the impossible attempt to price the priceless values of life, health, nature, and the future. Better public policy decisions can be made without cost-benefit analysis, by combining the successes of traditional regulation with the best of the innovative and flexible approaches that have gained ground in recent years."

(b) RICHARD L. REVESZ & MICHAEL A. LIVERMORE, RETAKING RATIONALITY: HOW COST-BENEFIT ANALYSIS CAN BETTER PROTECT THE ENVIRONMENT AND OUR HEALTH (2008): "Although cost-benefit analysis, as currently practiced, is indeed biased against regulation, those biases are not inherent in the methodology. If those biases were identified and eliminated, cost-benefit analysis would become a powerful tool for neutral policy analysis. . . . They stem from a shunning of cost-benefit analysis by proregulatory interests—such as consumer, environmental, and labor groups—which had the unintended effect of leaving antiregulatory interests free to shape the use of the technique to their purposes. . . .

"Proregulatory interests can no longer cling to the possibility that a boycott can shut down the game. Cost-benefit analysis has enormous currency in the federal policymaking apparatus. It is statutorily required for important environmental, health and safety programs. . . . Cost-benefit analysis, then, can be an enormously powerful tool for proregulatory groups. It can show that the interests they represent—the environment, consumers, or workers—are not opposed to the economy. Instead, regulation is necessary to preserve economic value and maximize wealth because protecting the environment and protecting health and safety are an essential part of a well-functioning economy. Without regulation, we would all be much poorer. And if cost-benefit analysis shows that regulations are justified, proregulatory groups have a strong argument that the obstacles are not competing values, but simply the failures of politicians or regulators to serve the interests of the American public. Cost-benefit analysis, then, can be a radical tool, useful to challenge the existing order."

Revesz and Livermore identify several "substantive fallacies within cost-benefit analysis that bias the technique against regulation" as well as institutional biases in how the regulatory review process is structured (see also Note 5 above, p. 430). They therefore advocate "reformed" cost-benefit analysis that, they argue, has an important role to play in centralized review, but not exclusively to check agencies. It must also spur them to action when needed. In addition, "[d]istributional analysis is a necessary corollary to cost-benefit analysis. Cost-benefit analysis, on its own terms, excludes concern for the distribution of the benefits and burdens of regulations. This omission is acceptable only if a separate effort is undertaken to account for these effects. Increasing aggregate wealth is a perfectly legitimate goal of regulation, but ignoring the distributional impacts of governmental action, and risking the perpetuation and exacerbation of socio-economic inequality is not tolerable. Critics of cost-benefit analysis are indeed correct that without efforts to distribute the burdens and benefits of regulations fairly, cost-benefit analysis loses much of its normative allure."

(3)   ***Cost-Benefit Analysis in Statutory Context.*** Can an agency be forced to engage in cost-benefit analysis in the regulatory review process when it doesn't have to perform such analysis (or indeed cannot make decisions based on such evaluation) in the context of judicial review? In some circumstances Congress appears to have forbidden costs to be taken into account in regulatory decisionmaking about health and safety issues (for example, the Clean Air Act, see Whitman v. American Trucking Ass'ns, p. 791, and the Occupational Safety and Health Act, see the Benzene case, p. 812) or to have allowed consideration of economic impact only a limited role in the regulatory equation (for instance, the Prison Rape Elimination Act, Note 4 below). In these circumstances, can agencies nevertheless be required to assess the costs and benefits of their proposed regulatory actions under Executive Order 12866? To what extent does Executive Order 12866 take such statutory limitations into account? We consider the legal implications of requiring agencies to perform such analyses in more detail in Ch. VII (p. 950). By contrast, in other regulatory settings, cost-benefit analysis may be statutorily required and, in consequence, the agency's calculations may be closely scrutinized on judicial review. See Note 5 below; Ch. VIII, p. 1093. Proposals are pending in Congress to impose cost-benefit analysis much more widely. S. 1448 (The Independent Regulatory Analysis Act of 2017), 115th Cong.[45]

(4)   ***Examples of Cost-Benefit Analysis under Executive Order 12866.*** Consider the regulatory impact analysis performed by the Department of Transportation for the Tarmac Rule discussed in the Introduction. The rule was deemed significant under the Executive Order. The agency concluded: "The total present value of benefits over a 20 year period at a 7% discount rate is $169.7 million and the total present value of costs over a 20 year period at a 7% discount rate is $100.6 million. The net present value of the rule for 20 years at a 7% discount rate is $69.1 million." Enhancing Airline Passenger Protections (Final Rule), 74 Fed. Reg. 68983, 69000 (2009). You can look at the over 100-page final Regulatory Impact Analysis, which analyzes the final rule and five alternatives (some more strict and some more lax), at http://www.regulations.gov/document?D=DOT-OST-2007-0022-0265.

Consider here the RIA's quantification of passengers' time and comfort: "Certain components of the Final Rule . . . will result in time saved (or lost) for individuals. In addition, certain components . . . will result in improved travel conditions for passengers, through greater physical comfort or increased confidence in on-time arrival. Economists measure the value of time saved using set estimates derived from average wages to reflect the cost to the individual of time spent in transit instead of on another activity. DOT has developed values to calculate air travel time savings for leisure and business passengers, with a range of high to low values . . . . This RIA uses these figures to estimate the value of passenger time saved or lost based on carriers' compliance with the Final Rule. In addition, time saved by persons

---

[45]   http://www.congress.gov/bill/115th-congress/senate-bill/1448.

coming to meet arriving passengers is also calculated and valued at $10.60 per hour, the DOT-recommended value for local personal travel. . . .

"Several aspects of the Final Rule are designed to increase traveler comfort during delays. Transportation economists have conducted studies of consumer behavior and different aspects of user experience in transit systems. These analyses have led to estimates of premiums on the value of user time based on the value people place on quicker/easier access to move from one place to another and analysis of the value of improved comfort during a travel experience. For example, studies show that transit riders value sitting more than standing without regard to any change in total travel time required. Travelers also prefer to spend time in transit rather than part of the time waiting for service if total trip length is the same.

"Several aspects of the Final Rule will shift the portion of total trip time spent in less comfortable conditions (such as the fourth hour on a plane spent sitting on the tarmac) to time spent in more comfortable conditions (the fourth hour spent in a terminal). This RIA assumes no change in overall trip time except in cases of cancellation . . . . The value of the difference in comfort is estimated using the base value of travel time saved (as noted above) and applying a 'premium' to that time. Estimates for this 'comfort premium' are developed from research literature in transportation economics. These premiums were derived from survey-based data that reflect travel time values that incorporate the quality of waiting, walking and transfer conditions.

" 'Level of service' ratings are used to determine the value of different levels. Since no specific estimate of time values for level of service ratings for airline travel are available, values were taken from other modal studies. The most applicable study estimated a time value premium based on differing levels of service that incorporated factors such as comfort, convenience and reliability . . . for various categories of public transportation and auto users. . . . Based on this study, a premium of .34 was used for the greater comfort derived from access to food, water and clean lavatory facilities; a premium of .68 was used for the greater comfort of waiting in the terminal rather than in a plane on the tarmac. These premiums are similar to those found for the value transit passengers place on being able to sit versus stand, which range from .20 to .87 in two studies that address measuring the quality of travel experience. . . .

"No data was found to quantify the value of decreased anxiety during extended wait periods. Based on the studies of auto and public transit passengers' value of levels of service summarized above, a .01 premium was selected as a proxy for the value of decreased anxiety/discomfort based on knowledge that a contingency plan exists during time greater than one hour spent on the tarmac and until allowed to deplane." Id. at 20–22.

For a much more controversial recent example, see the nearly 200-page final Regulatory Impact Analysis for the Attorney General's standards under the Prison Rape Elimination Act, which can be found at: http://www.prearesourcecenter.org/sites/default/files/library/prearia.pdf. Professor LISA HEINZERLING severely criticized the Administration's RIA in a blog post:

"Most awful is the Department's effort to put a monetary value on avoiding rape and other forms of sexual abuse in prison. To even try to understand the Department's analysis, you need first to understand how cost-benefit analysis works. . . . Thus, it came to pass that . . . the DOJ found itself in the remarkable position of asking how much money the victims of rape would be willing to pay to avoid rape and also asking how much money these victims would be willing to accept in exchange for being raped. . . . Never mind that rape is a serious crime, not a market transaction. Never mind that framing rape as a market transaction strips it of the coercion that defines it. Never mind that the law under which DOJ was acting is the Prison Rape Elimination Act, not the Prison Rape Optimization Act. In the topsy-turvy world of cost-benefit analysis, DOJ was compelled to treat rape as just another market exchange, coercion as a side note, and the elimination of prison rape as a good idea only if the economic numbers happened to come out that way.

"Compounding the outrage, DOJ went on to develop 17 different categories of rape and sexual assault and to provide monetary values of the benefit of avoiding each of these categories—thus providing, in its words, a 'hierarchy' of the different ways of sexually violating prisoners. Reading DOJ's analysis itself feels like a violation. For example, to justify giving rape committed without physical force the same economic value as rape with physical force, DOJ offered a belabored treatment of why rape can be bad even if no physical force is used, relying substantially on public comments critical of DOJ's initial suggestion that rape without physical force was only one-fifth as bad as rape with such force. One must wonder: was it really so hard for DOJ to realize that rape without physical force can be as devastating as rape with it? Did DOJ—the Department of Justice, the legal arm of the U.S. government—really not understand this until the public comment period for this rule?" LISA HEINZERLING, COST-BENEFIT JUMPS THE SHARK, Georgetown Law Faculty Blog (June 13, 2012).[46]

Interesting, the RIA for the PREA was done only because of the Executive Order. Under the Act, according to Heinzerling, "the only limit that Congress placed on DOJ's national standards was that the standards were not to impose 'substantial additional costs' beyond the present expenditures of the covered facilities. In its final rule setting the national standards called for by PREA, DOJ easily found that its standards complied with this statutory constraint. In three quick sentences, DOJ found that even full compliance with DOJ's standards would increase total expenditures by less than 1 percent and that this additional expenditure did not exceed the statutory limit of 'substantial additional costs.' " Id.

(5) **Cost-Benefit Analysis in Financial Regulation.** The use of cost-benefit analysis in financial regulation is currently receiving considerable attention, prompted in part by D.C. Circuit case law and in part by recent legislation. In a series of cases, culminating in a 2011 decision, Business Roundtable v. SEC, 647 F.3d 1144, the D.C. Circuit read the requirement that the Securities and Exchange Commission (SEC) "consider . . . whether

---

[46] http://gulcfac.typepad.com/georgetown_university_law/2012/06/cost-benefit-jumps-the-shark.html.

[regulatory] action will promote efficiency, competition, and capital formation," 15 U.S.C. § 80a–2(c), a requirement added to the Investment Company Act in 1996, to require that the SEC specifically estimate a proposed rule's costs. The Business Roundtable decision and extensive financial regulatory activity in the aftermath of the 2010 Dodd-Frank Wall Street Reform and Consumer Protection Act have sparked a vigorous scholarly debate about the propriety of requiring cost-benefit analysis (CBA) for financial regulation (FR).

In a leading article, COST-BENEFIT ANALYSIS OF FINANCIAL REGULATION: CASE STUDIES AND IMPLICATIONS, 124 Yale L.J. 882, 927–1003 (2015), Professor JOHN COATES contends that "quantitative CBA/FR is not currently feasible with any degree of precision and reliability for representative types of financial regulation." Coates emphasizes several "features of CBA/FR that make it more difficult to perform effectively than CBA in other domains," including the fact that "finance is at the heart of the economy," with financial regulation having "large and complex effects on welfare" and no agreement on how to include finance in macroeconomic models; "finance is social and political," with financial regulation operating on groups rather than objects or individuals; and "finance is non-statutory," with most relationships in finance changing through time, often rapidly. Other scholars agree that cost-benefit analysis for financial regulation is difficult but maintain that "uncertain valuations is a commonplace of regulation" and cost-benefit analysis for financial regulation is advisable, even if techniques need to be developed to make it work. See Eric A. Posner & E. Glen Weyl, Cost-Benefit Analysis of Financial Regulations: A Response to Criticisms, 124 Yale L.J. F. 246 (2015); Cass R. Sunstein, Financial Regulation and Cost-Benefit Analysis, 124 Yale L.J. F. 263, 270, 274–75 (2015); see also Symposium, The Administrative Law of Financial Regulation, 78 Law & Contemp. Probs. 1 (2015). We discuss cost-benefit analysis and judicial review in more depth in Chapter VIII (p. 1093).

(6) *Problems of Risk Assessment and Selection.* Closely intertwined with the debate over cost-benefit analysis are the difficulties agencies face in selecting which risks merit regulatory response and prioritizing their regulatory efforts. Defenders of cost-benefit analysis argue that it plays an important role in guarding against agency tendencies to overregulate, while critics deny that any such tendency exists and emphasize the uncertainties and difficulties involved in quantifying risk.

Breaking the Vicious Circle: Toward Effective Risk Regulation (1993), an important book by Stephen Breyer, written before he became a member of the Supreme Court, suggests that much of the seeming irrationality of governmental response to risk (at the legislative and agency levels) is the product of innate human difficulties in assessing and choosing among relatively small risks. Designing effective governmental institutions that will, first, assess the level of risk in the face of usually incomplete information; second, accurately assess the effect of a proposed means of dealing with the risks (the unintended consequences problem); and, finally, avoid responses driven by popular (mis)perceptions—these challenges are as difficult as any that legal institutions face and easily fall victim to the fears of the moment. Professor Jerry Mashaw and David Harfst provide a concrete example in their book The Struggle for Auto Safety 140–46 (1990). In the same legislative breath, amendments to the National Traffic and Motor Vehicle Safety Act helped stymie the development of air bags for a decade or more and required a highly questionable commitment of regulatory resources to school bus safety. Risk assessment advanced that much greater gains were to be had from safety investments in cars than in school buses. Risk management techniques suggested that at least the immediate effect of making school buses more expensive would be to keep older buses on the road. Yet members of Congress and their constituents were unmoved. They preferred personal freedom in automobiles for themselves—despite quite substantial risks of death and serious injury that were cheaply avoidable. They were horrified that anyone could propose to balance the possible saving of a child's life by making school buses safer against the relatively high regulatory costs of doing so.

RICHARD H. PILDES & CASS R. SUNSTEIN, REINVENTING THE REGULATORY STATE, 62 U. CHI. L. REV. 1, 52–53, 57 (1995): "It is hard to challenge the view that law and policy should be assessed on the basis of inquiries into the advantages and disadvantages of different courses of action. . . . Yet this process of seeking consistency can incorporate contentious assumptions about what it would mean for policy choices to be consistent and rational. In particular, this approach requires regulators to create a single metric along which diverse regulatory policies can be compared. . . . However, for laypeople, the most salient contextual features include: (1) the catastrophic nature of the risk; (2) whether the risk is uncontrollable; (3) whether the risk involves irretrievable or permanent losses; (4) the social conditions under which a particular risk is generated and managed, a point that connects to issues of consent, voluntariness, and democratic control; (5) how equitably distributed the danger is or how concentrated on identifiable, innocent, or traditionally disadvantaged victims, which ties to both notions of community and moral ideals; (6) how well understood the risk process in question is, a point that bears on the psychological disturbance produced by different risks; (7) whether the risk would be faced by future generations; and (8) how familiar the risk is. . . .

"The important point is that it can be fully rational to attend to contextual differences of this sort. . . . It is fully plausible to believe that expenditures per life saved ought to vary in accordance with (for example) the voluntariness of the risk or its catastrophic quality. Such beliefs appear widespread. Interviews with workers, for example, reveal that their valuations of workplace risks depend upon such contextual features as the overall structure of workplace relations, how much say workers have in how the risks are managed, and the nature of the particular jobs performed."

(7) *OIRA's Role in Risk Selection and OMB's Role in the Information Quality Act.* Some scholars argue that OIRA could play an important role in addressing difficulties in risk assessment. "A centralized agency armed with substantial scientific expertise might in many cases be better situated than single-mission agencies to set generic guidelines as to how science should be employed in agency risk assessments. . . . The science upon which regulatory agencies must rely in setting health-and-safety standards is inadequate to ground clear conclusions about the scope of actual risks, particularly with respect to low-dose human exposure to carcinogenic substances. . . . In undertaking carcinogenic risk assessment, different agencies currently rely on different assumptions. The result can be widely divergent risk assessments for the same carcinogen, with potentially enormous impacts on the stringency of regulation. Such assumptions, therefore, are particularly good candidates for a centralizing influence." NICHOLAS BAGLEY & RICHARD L. REVESZ, CENTRALIZED OVERSIGHT OF THE REGULATORY STATE, 106 Colum. L. Rev. 1260, 1314–17 (2006).

OIRA has begun to play such a role, issuing guidance to agencies on appropriate principles to follow in risk analysis. See Susan E. Dudley (OIRA) & Sharon L. Hays (OSTP), Memorandum for the Heads of Exec. Dep'ts & Agencies on Updated Principles for Risk Analysis (Sept. 19, 2007).[47]

OMB also plays a role. Although it withdrew a 2006 proposed Risk Assessment Bulletin, after comment, OMB has published government-wide guidelines on information disseminated by agencies, as required by the Information Quality Act. See Guidelines for Ensuring and Maximizing the Quality, Objectivity, Utility, and Integrity of Information Disseminated by Federal Agencies, 67 Fed. Reg. 8452 (Feb. 22, 2002). The Act, enacted in 2001 with little discussion, provides that all federal agencies must create administrative mechanisms by which affected persons can seek correction of information that does not comply with the guidelines. § 515(b), codified at 44 U.S.C. § 3516 note.

(8) *Is Peer Review a Solution?* In addition to its guidelines on information quality, OMB issued a bulletin providing that, "[t]o the extent permitted by law, each agency shall conduct a peer review on all influential scientific information that the agency intends to disseminate." Influential scientific information is defined as "scientific information that the agency reasonably can determine will have or does have a clear and substantial impact on important public policies or private sector decisions." The bulletin imposes additional requirements for peer review of influential scientific information that could have a $500 million annual impact or is novel, controversial, or precedent setting or has significant inter-agency interest. Final Information Quality Bulletin for Peer Review, 70 Fed. Reg. 2664, 2675–76 (Jan. 14, 2005). OMB has also recommended in the past that agencies subject regulatory impact analyses and supporting technical documents for economically significant and major rulemakings to independent, external peer review. "OMB Regulatory Review: Principles and Procedures," attached to John D. Graham, Adm'r, OIRA, Memorandum for the President's Management Council, Presidential Review of Agency Rulemaking by OIRA, Sept. 20, 2001.[48]

Does peer review offer a useful mechanism for improving the quality of regulatory decisionmaking generally? LARS NOAH, SCIENTIFIC

---

[47] http://georgewbush-whitehouse.archives.gov/omb/memoranda/fy2007/m07-24.pdf.

[48] http://obamawhitehouse.archives.gov/sites/default/files/omb/assets/omb/pubpress/2001-38-attach.pdf.

"REPUBLICANISM": EXPERT PEER REVIEW AND THE QUEST FOR REGULATORY DELIBERATION, 49 Emory L.J. 1033, 1067, 1083 (2000): "Concerns about the potential for added administrative burdens . . . deserve serious attention. If it does not help steer an agency early in the process, peer review of regulatory decisionmaking may become an ominous hurdle for agencies to surmount, both in terms of the difficulty of undergoing that scrutiny and because of the prospect of judicial invalidation triggered by the inevitable criticisms from expert peer reviewers. Moreover, if agencies sense that the blessing of outside scientists is necessary before proceeding with a rule, they may decide to settle for second-best regulatory options simply because these generate the least disagreement among the experts. . . . Involving outside scientists in the process undoubtedly will promote greater care and reflection, and these peer reviewers may help steer agencies clear of embarrassing and costly mistakes, but ultimately the independent experts cannot and should not displace the broader deliberative process about hard policy questions that science cannot answer." Professor Noah concludes that "[s]o long as independent peer review does not become a substitute for public participation or judicial review, it may provide a forum for genuine deliberation that can facilitate subsequent steps in the administrative process and help to better focus other forms of external scrutiny of agency decisionmaking."

(9) *A Cautionary Note.* It is perhaps worth noting a distortion that the political and scholarly focus on cost-benefit analysis and risk assessment can bring. Much rulemaking is not about risk in any sensible sense, even making allowances for the ways in which some analysts might see things like "deceptive practices" as matters of error risk. Much is not about maximizing welfare but rather about providing minimum standards or redistributing power or income. Watch out for any tendency of the writing in the field to take the core examples where risk assessment or cost-benefit approaches may make sense—environmental, health, and safety regulation—and rewrite all of administrative law in that model. How does Executive Order 12866 § 1 try to address this worry? Are you convinced?

SECTION 5.   AFTER THE COMMENTS ARE IN—THE DECISIONMAKING PROCESS IN RULEMAKING

> a. *Ex Parte Contacts*
> b. *An Open-Minded Decisionmaker?*

a.   Ex Parte Contacts

> *HBO, INC. v. FCC*

In distinguishing rulemaking from adjudication for due process purposes, Justice Holmes's opinion in Bi-Metallic Investment Co. v. State Bd. of Equalization of Colorado, p. 222, rejected the familiar judicial model as an inappropriate analogy when government is involved in making general policy. The APA notice-and-comment process reflects that judgment, and subsequent Supreme Court decisions such as Vermont Yankee, p. 295, have reinforced it. Ordinarily, rulemaking is thoroughly institutional from start to finish, involving whoever in the agency (and as you now know from the materials on OMB regulatory review, some outside the agency) has a relevant perspective to contribute. Decisions are taken not all at once but over sometimes substantial lengths of time. They are highly dependent on organizational decisionmaking processes. Although the cases have required agencies to share important information in the interest of effective comment, see Nova Scotia (p. 322), the institutional character of rulemaking means that the decisionmaker's "record" will vary widely from what even the most energetic participant (or reviewing judge) can know—both in content and in the conversations that have shaped it. (See Note 5, p. 334.) All this seems fairly to follow from the proposition that these are *not* proceedings required to be decided "*on the record.*" It follows as well from Justice Holmes's Bi-Metallic conclusion that citizens' protection in such proceedings is to be found, not in the procedural apparatus of trial-type hearings, but in "their [political] power, immediate or remote, over those who make the rule." And as we have seen in, for example, Executive Order 12866, an elaborate political apparatus has grown up to channel such efforts in the most important rulemakings.

Complications arise, however, if the agency uses rulemaking to make decisions that seem equally appropriate (if not more so) for adjudication, leading courts to fear that it is attempting to escape the usual constraints on "off the record" activities that apply to adjudicatory decisionmaking. SANGAMON VALLEY TELEVISION CORP. V. UNITED STATES, 269 F.2d 221 (D.C. Cir. 1959) was such a case. In that early, pre-cable television era, it was much more advantageous to have a franchise for one of the twelve "VHF" channels, 2–13, than one of the greater number of "UHF" channels. Not all televisions could receive UHF signals; those that could, often did not receive them as well as VHF, because a VHF signal could be broadcast to a larger geographic area. The "rule" the FCC proposed would have had the effect of awarding a particular VHF franchise (Channel 2) to a particular St. Louis, Missouri, television station in lieu of the UHF channel that station was currently assigned. It would also have reassigned the St. Louis station's UHF channel to Springfield, Illinois, to replace a franchise for Channel 2, currently in use. These assignments would have implemented an FCC policy to avoid intermixing VHF and UHF transmission in the same television market. Congressional testimony disclosed that the St. Louis station's president had personally called on, written, and telephoned FCC Commissioners to advocate shifting Channel 2 to St. Louis. Moreover, he had taken them to lunch and had sent them turkeys as Christmas presents while the matter was still under consideration. Apprised of this behavior, the D.C. Circuit concluded that "whatever the proceeding may be called, it involved not only allocation of TV channels among communities but also resolution of conflicting private claims to a valuable privilege, and that basic fairness requires such a proceeding to be carried on in the open. . . . Accordingly the private approaches to the members of the Commission vitiated its action and the proceeding must be reopened."

The next principal case threatened to generalize this understandable holding in Sangamon Valley to virtually all rulemaking. Decided on the eve of Vermont Yankee, it has been sharply criticized—particularly for its tendency to judicialize rulemaking and for its confusion about rulemaking procedures and records. So long as you approach it as a problematic case to be read less for its "law" than for insight into a set of enduring tensions and problems, it makes a good starting point for the materials of this section.

HOME BOX OFFICE, INC. v. FEDERAL COMMUNICATIONS COMMISSION

United States Court of Appeals for the District of Columbia Circuit (1977).
567 F.2d 9.

PER CURIAM.[49]

[In March 1975, the FCC ended a three-year notice-and-comment rulemaking proceeding by adopting four amendments to its rules governing the programs that could be shown by paid television services like HBO. If these services could show contemporary films and sports, commercial broadcasters feared, the quality of conventional television would inevitably be reduced. Viewers who could not be reached by (or afford to pay for) subscription television would be injured by this change. On the other hand, metropolitan viewers and paid service owners both denied that this harm would occur and asserted that restricting the material shown by subscription services would inhibit their commercial growth and deprive viewers of diversity. In this particular rulemaking, the FCC had held oral arguments in October 1974. Ultimately, the Commission decided to reduce somewhat the prior restrictions on paid television services. The amendments satisfied neither the commercial nor the subscription broadcast interests (including associated viewer groups) and all promptly sought review in the D.C. Circuit. Henry Geller, General Counsel of the FCC until 1973 (by which time the rulemaking was well under way) and chairperson of a public interest group concentrating on broadcast matters, was one of those seeking review. He suggested to the court that participants in the rulemaking had frequently engaged in private contacts with Commissioners and others at the FCC.]

. . . In an attempt to clarify the facts this court sua sponte ordered the Commission to provide "a list of all of the ex parte presentations, together with the details of each, made to it, or to any of its members or

---

[49] [Ed.] The court issued the opinion per curiam "because the complexity of the issues raised on appeal made it useful to share the effort required to draft this opinion among the members of the panel"; the part reproduced here was written by Judge J. Skelly Wright.

representatives, during the rulemaking proceedings." In response to this order the Commission filed a document over 60 pages long which revealed, albeit imprecisely, widespread ex parte communications involving virtually every party before this court, including amicus Geller.[107]

. . . "[I]n early 1974, then-Chairman Burch sought to complete action in this proceeding. Because the Commission was 'leaning' in its deliberations towards relaxing the existing rules . . . American Broadcasting Company's representatives contacted 'key members of Congress,' who in turn successfully pressured the Commission not to take such action. . . ." [Quoting Geller's brief.] [I]n the crucial period between the close of oral argument on October 25, 1974 and the adoption of the First Report and Order on March 20, 1975, when the rulemaking record should have been closed while the Commission was deciding what rules to promulgate, . . . broadcast interests met some 18 times with Commission personnel, cable interests some nine times, motion picture and sports interests five times each, and "public interest" intervenors not at all. . . . [W]e are particularly concerned that the final shaping of the rules we are reviewing here may have been by compromise among the contending industry forces, rather than by exercise of the independent discretion in the public interest the Communications Act vests in individual commissioners. Our concern is heightened by the submission of the Commission's Broadcast Bureau to this court which states that in December 1974 broadcast representatives "described the kind of pay cable regulation that, in their view, broadcasters 'could live with.'" If actual positions were not revealed in public comments, . . . the elaborate public discussion in these dockets has been reduced to a sham.

Even the possibility that there is here one administrative record for the public and this court and another for the Commission and those "in the know" is intolerable. . . . [I]mplicit in the decision to treat the promulgation of rules as a "final" event in an ongoing process of administration is an assumption that an act of reasoned judgment has occurred, an assumption which further contemplates the existence of a body of material—documents, comments, transcripts, and statements in various forms declaring agency expertise or policy—with reference to which such judgment was exercised. Against this material, "the full administrative record that was before [an agency official] at the time he made his decision," Citizens to Preserve Overton Park v. Volpe, [401 U.S. 402 (1971), p. 1085], . . . it is the obligation of this court to test the actions of the Commission for arbitrariness or inconsistency with delegated authority. . . . This course is obviously foreclosed if communications are made to the agency in secret and the agency itself does not disclose the information presented. . . . [A] reviewing court cannot presume that the

---

[107] . . . There can be no waiver or estoppel raised here against our consideration of an issue vital to the public as a whole. Therefore, Mr. Geller's "dirty hands," if such they be, present no bar. . . .

agency has acted properly, but must treat the agency's justifications as a fictional account of the actual decisionmaking process and must perforce find its actions arbitrary.

. . . Even if the Commission had disclosed to this court . . . what was said to it ex parte, . . . we would not have the benefit of an adversarial discussion among the parties. . . . We have insisted, for example, that [relevant] information in agency files or consultants' reports . . . be disclosed to the parties for adversarial comment. Similarly, we have required agencies to set out their thinking in notices of proposed rulemaking. This requirement not only allows adversarial critique of the agency but is perhaps one of the few ways that the public may be apprised of what the agency thinks it knows in its capacity as a repository of expert opinion. From a functional standpoint, we see no difference between assertions of fact and expert opinion tendered by the public, as here, and that generated internally in an agency: each may be biased, inaccurate, or incomplete—failings which adversary comment may illuminate. Indeed, the potential for bias in private presentations in rulemakings which resolve "conflicting private claims to a valuable privilege," seems to us greater than in cases where we have reversed agencies for failure to disclose internal studies. . . .

Equally important is the inconsistency of secrecy with fundamental notions of fairness implicit in due process and with the ideal of reasoned decisionmaking on the merits which undergirds all of our administrative law. This inconsistency was recognized in Sangamon Valley Television Corp. v. United States, 269 F.2d 221 (D.C. Cir. 1959) [p. 445], and . . . [c]ertainly any ambiguity . . . has been removed by recent congressional and presidential actions. In the Government in the Sunshine Act, for example, Congress has declared it to be "the policy of the United States that the public is entitled to the fullest practicable information regarding the decisionmaking processes of the Federal Government," and has taken steps to guard against ex parte contacts in formal agency proceedings.[125] Perhaps more closely on point is Executive Order 11920, 12 Weekly Comp. of Presidential Documents 1040 (1976), which prohibits ex parte contacts with members of the White House staff by those seeking to influence allocation of international air routes during the time route certifications are before the President for his approval. . . . Thus this is a time when all branches of government have taken steps "designed to better assure fairness and to avoid suspicions of impropriety," White House Fact Sheet on Executive Order 11920 (June 10, 1976), and consequently we have no hesitation in concluding . . . that due process requires us to set aside the Commission's rules here.

---

[125] Of course, the Sunshine Act by its terms does not apply here. Its ex parte contact provisions are couched as an amendment to 5 U.S.C. § 557, and as such the rules do not apply to rulemaking under § 4 of the Administrative Procedure Act, 5 U.S.C. § 553. Moreover, the Act was not in effect at the time of the events in question here.

. . . [W]e recognize that informal contacts between agencies and the public are the "bread and butter" of the process of administration and are completely appropriate so long as they do not frustrate judicial review or raise serious questions of fairness. Reconciliation of these considerations in a manner which will reduce procedural uncertainty leads us to conclude that communications which are received prior to issuance of a formal notice of rulemaking do not, in general, have to be put in a public file. Of course, if the information contained in such a communication forms the basis for agency action, then, under well established principles, that information must be disclosed to the public in some form. Once a notice of proposed rulemaking has been issued, however, any agency official or employee who is or may reasonably be expected to be involved in the decisional process of the rulemaking proceeding, should "refus[e] to discuss matters relating to the disposition of a [rulemaking proceeding] with any interested private party, or an attorney or agent for any such party, prior to the [agency's] decision . . .," Executive Order 11920, § 4, supra, at 1041. If ex parte contacts nonetheless occur, we think that any written document or a summary of any oral communication must be placed in the public file established for each rulemaking docket immediately after the communication is received so that interested parties may comment thereon. Compare Executive Order 11920, § 5.

. . . [W]e today remand the record to the Commission for supplementation . . . with the aid of a specially appointed hearing examiner . . .[50]

■ MACKINNON, CIRCUIT JUDGE [belatedly filed a special concurrence].

. . . [I]n this case . . . the rulemaking undeniably involved competitive interests of great monetary value and conferred preferential advantages on vast segments of the broadcast industry to the detriment of other competing business interests. The rule as issued was in effect an adjudication of the respective rights of the parties vis-a-vis each other. And since that is the nature of the case and controversy that we are deciding and to which our opinion is limited, I would make it clear that that is all we are deciding. I would not make an excessively broad statement to include dictum that could be interpreted to cover the entire universe of informal rulemaking.

NOTES

(1) *A Sound Result?* ERNEST GELLHORN & GLEN O. ROBINSON, RULEMAKING "DUE PROCESS": AN INCONCLUSIVE DIALOGUE, 48 U. Chi. L. Rev. 201 (1981):

"[*Publius*:] [E]x parte contacts . . . operate as an important check on the reliability of staff information and interpretation. Given the potential unreliability of staff-provided information, ex parte contacts with persons

---

[50] [Ed.] The concurrence by Judge Weigel, on other grounds, is omitted.

outside the agency are an important means of avoiding 'staff capture.' To be sure, one does not want an agency to rely entirely on outside informants, but neither does one want it to be the prisoner of agency staff. . . .

". . . Obtaining information is not the problem. Agencies seldom want for information or argument in a quantitative sense. If anything, they suffer from the opposite, what Alvin Toffler has described as 'information overload.' . . . What the agency rulemaker needs is both a means to get to the heart of the case, and an exchange of views with the advocates of competing positions in which he can test his, and their, understanding of the issues. It is somewhat ironic that one of the principal proponents of a ban on ex parte contacts, Judge Wright, should also interpret the APA as requiring rulemaking to provide 'a genuine dialogue between agency experts and concerned members of the public.' The formal submission of documents to an agency, in response to a formal public notice, seems unlikely to constitute a 'genuine' dialogue—but this would be the only permissible communication between the agency and the parties if the ban on ex parte contacts stands. . . . [T]o evaluate the true demand for different outcomes . . . is a vital component of rulemaking, just as it is of legislative lawmaking. . . . An agency is not simply an issuer of edicts; it is also an arbitrator of interests. Again Home Box Office is illustrative. Some of the ex parte contacts involved in that case apparently took place partly for the purpose of exploring possible compromises among the competing groups. It is difficult to envision how such compromise efforts, which are clearly desirable, could be made without some informal contacts. . . .

"[*Brutus*:] . . . [T]he rulemaker-as-arbitrator is not an appropriate model for agencies. No doubt rules often reflect compromises among competing interest groups. I do not deplore that. Even where rulemaking is a zero-sum game among different interests, agencies are properly sensitive to minimizing the losses to any particular group as a consequence of the rule being adopted. Bargaining is not objectionable except where it is done without rules, which would allow the decision to be unfairly skewed by irrelevant factors such as who was able to contact whom, when, and so forth. On the other hand, why do we have a structured rulemaking process with notice and comment and, in the Home Box Office case, even oral argument? Is this just a warmup for negotiations? I think not. It would seem to be an attempt to require rulemakers to do more than rubberstamp agreements by the affected parties. Instead, they must independently assure themselves, from the evidence produced by these procedures, that the rule is in fact in the public interest. That determination could be rendered illusory by unregulated ex parte contacts creating a predisposition in the rulemaker's mind.

"Moreover, I think it is somewhat naive to suppose that it is necessary for an agency rulemaker to have informal discussions with particular parties in order to gain an adequate understanding of their 'bottom line.' For example, I think your FCC commissioner in Home Box Office would, from the outset, have a pretty good sense of what was soft and what was firm in the positions of the parties as a result of his familiarity with the industry. If he did not, I doubt he would obtain it from ex parte discussions. The parties would be just as likely to seize such an opportunity to impress him with the fervor of their opinions and the rational basis thereof in hopes of securing a completely favorable decision, as they would be to reveal which of their claims they would be willing to concede without any quid pro quo."

(2) **The Judicial Retreat from Home Box Office.** The tensions between HBO's concern for the state of the rulemaking record on review and the institutional, legislative character of rulemaking led to a prompt retreat. In ACTION FOR CHILDREN'S TELEVISION [ACT] V. FCC, 564 F.2d 458 (D.C. Cir. 1977), a different panel of the D.C. Circuit refused to apply HBO to an FCC rulemaking involving children's television programming and advertising practices. Over 100,000 comments had been filed; six days of panel discussions and arguments had been held. Early on, the broadcast industry had undertaken "limited self-regulation"; after a private meeting with the FCC's Chairman following the Commission hearings, the industry adopted further measures to control advertising practices. When the Commission suspended its rulemaking, promising to monitor these self-regulatory measures, ACT sought review.

Holding only that HBO's "broad prescription is not to be applied retroactively," the panel's lengthy opinion left little doubt that it generally disapproved of that earlier case's prescription: "We do not propose to argue . . . that ex parte contacts always are permissible in informal rulemaking proceedings—they are of course not—but we do think . . . that ex parte contacts do not per se vitiate agency informal rulemaking action, but only do so if it appears from the administrative record under review that they may have materially influenced the action ultimately taken. . . .

"If we go as far as Home Box Office does in its ex parte ruling in ensuring a 'whole record' for our review, why not go further to require the decisionmaker to summarize and make available for public comment every status inquiry from a Congressman or any germane material—say a newspaper editorial—that he or she reads or their evening-hour ruminations? In the end, why not administer a lie-detector test to ascertain whether the required summary is an accurate and complete one? The problem is obviously a matter of degree, and the appropriate line must be drawn somewhere. In light of what must be presumed to be Congress' intent not to prohibit or require disclosure of all ex parte contacts during or after the public comment stage, we would draw that line at the point where the rulemaking proceedings involve 'competing claims to a valuable privilege.' It is at that point where the potential for unfair advantage outweighs the practical burdens, which we imagine would not be insubstantial, that such a judicially conceived rule would place upon administrators."

(3) **Home Box Office and Vermont Yankee.** The decision in Home Box Office predates Vermont Yankee by a year. If the D.C. Circuit had not already retreated from the decision, could its broad requirement of disclosure for ex parte contacts be squared with Vermont Yankee? To what extent does the text of the APA, both in its provisions for notice-and-comment rulemaking under § 553 and in its restrictions on ex parte comments in formal proceedings in § 557(d), support or undercut the Home Box Office decision?

JACK M. BEERMAN & GARY LAWSON, REPROCESSING VERMONT YANKEE, 75 Geo. Wash. L. Rev. 856, 886–88 (2007): "There is no plausible basis in the APA for prohibiting ex parte contacts during informal proceedings. To the contrary, the carefully delineated prohibitions on such contacts in formal proceedings, coupled with the absence of any remotely comparable provisions for informal proceedings, renders any such claim frivolous. Organic statutes or agency regulations could, of course, forbid or limit ex parte contacts in rulemakings in specific cases, but the D.C. Circuit's doctrine in Home Box Office purports to be general law rather than something peculiar to FCC statutes or regulations. Nor can one ground the doctrine in the requirements of substantive review, as Home Box Office seemed to suggest. This would be precisely the sort of use of substantive review to require specific agency procedures that Vermont Yankee forbids . . . [Moreover,] nothing suggests that the D.C. Circuit means to limit its doctrine only to those rule-makings that actually count as adjudications for constitutional purposes." On this last point Professor Richard Pierce disagrees, concluding that in ACT and subsequent decisions the D.C. Circuit "limited the scope of its prohibition [on ex parte comments] to cases in which an agency is resolving a dispute between two individuals who are 'competing for a specific valuable privilege,'" (i.e. the context of Sangamon Valley), where the prohibition "is rooted in an entirely plausible interpretation of the Due Process Clause." Richard J. Pierce, Jr., Reply, Waiting for Vermont Yankee III, IV, and V? A Response to Beerman and Lawson, 75 Geo. Wash. L. Rev. 902, 912 (2007).

(4) *Agency Practices and Latest ACUS Recommendations.* ACUS recently surveyed staff members at eight executive agencies and four independent regulatory commissions and found that agency practices regarding ex parte communications varied considerably—both in terms of the form of the agency policy concerning the issue (rulemaking, policy statement, or unwritten practice) and the substance (restrictive, neutral, welcoming). For instance, the Department of Labor's written policy strongly discourages such communications after an NPRM is published and requires disclosing all communications that occur, including oral ones. The Federal Election Commission's neutral regulation mandates Commissioners and their staff to quickly report any ex parte contacts and their substance, written or oral, in the period between the petition for rulemaking being circulated to the Commission (or the issuance of an NPRM) and the final action by the Commission. And the Environmental Protection Agency, by written and unwritten policy, encourages meetings in the rulemaking process (and even conducts them after the comment period is closed to get clarification of items submitted to the docket).[51] Statutes can also impose constraints on ex parte communications. For instance, the Clean Air Act requires that such communications be documented in the rulemaking docket, see Note 5 below.

---

[51] Esa L. Sferra-Bonistalli, Ex Parte Communications in Informal Rulemaking, Final Report to ACUS (May 1, 2014), available at: http://www.acus.gov/sites/default/files/documents/Final%20Ex%20Parte%20Communications%20in%20Informal%20Rulemaking%20%5B5-1-14%5D_0.pdf.

(5) *Presidential and Congressional Ex Parte Contacts.* Ex parte comments made by members of Congress, the President, or White House aides might seem to be particularly problematic, given the influence such comments could be expected to have on agency decisionmakers. On the other hand, mandating disclosure of such comments also raises concerns of undermining important political controls on agencies and more specifically of unduly infringing on the President's constitutionally protected supervision of the executive branch. The D.C. Circuit addressed ex parte congressional and presidential comments and White House meetings in SIERRA CLUB V. COSTLE, 657 F.2d 298 (D.C. Cir. 1981), considered at greater length in Ch. VII (p. 987).

The Sierra Club court refused to overturn the EPA rule on emissions from coal-fired power stations based on the agency's meetings with White House staff and the President that the agency had not disclosed in the docket: "The authority of the President to control and supervise executive policymaking is derived from the Constitution; the desirability of such control is demonstrable from the practical realities of administrative rulemaking. Regulations such as those involved here demand a careful weighing of cost, environmental, and energy considerations. They also have broad implications for national economic policy. Our form of government simply could not function effectively or rationally if key executive policymakers were isolated from each other and from the Chief Executive." Although recognizing that the docketing of such communications might be necessary in some instances to ensure due process or when a statute specifically requires, the court found no need to do so here "since EPA makes no effort to base the rule on any 'data or information' arising from that meeting."

The court further refused invalidation based on charges that agency officials had been pressured in meetings with Senator Robert Byrd, an influential coal-state senator: "We believe it entirely proper for Congressional representatives vigorously to represent the interests of their constituents before administrative agencies engaged in informal, general policy rulemaking, so long as individual Congressmen do not frustrate the intent of Congress as a whole as expressed in statute, nor undermine applicable rules of procedure. Where Congressmen keep their comments focused on the substance of the proposed rule—and we have no substantial evidence to cause us to believe Senator Byrd did not do so here—administrative agencies are expected to balance Congressional pressure with the pressures emanating from all other sources. To hold otherwise would deprive the agencies of legitimate sources of information and call into question the validity of nearly every controversial rulemaking." Noting that the only suggestions of congressional "threats" came in a Washington Post article, the opinion also stated: "We do not believe that a single newspaper account of strong 'hint[s]' represents substantial evidence of extraneous pressure significant enough to warrant a finding of unlawful congressional interference."

(6) *Ex Parte Contacts and Regulatory Review.* The Constitution may prevent courts from mandating certain communications with the White

House be disclosed. But the White House can bind itself. EO 12866 addresses "ex parte" communications in several ways. To start, it stopped a practice of communications between the White House and private interests in the OIRA review process where the rulemaking agency was purposefully excluded. Now, a "representative from the issuing agency shall be invited to any meeting between OIRA personnel and such person(s)." In addition "OIRA shall forward to the issuing agency, within 10 working days of receipt of the communication(s), all written communications, regardless of format, between OIRA personnel and any person who is not employed by the executive branch of the Federal Government, and the dates and names of individuals involved in all substantive oral communications (including meetings to which an agency representative was invited, but did not attend, and telephone conversations between OIRA personnel and any such persons)." EO 12866, § 6(b)(4)(B). With respect to disclosure to the public, the Executive Order requires OIRA to keep "a publicly available log" of "[t]he dates and names of individuals involved in all substantive oral communications, including meetings and telephone conversations, between OIRA personnel and any person not employed by the executive branch of the Federal Government, and the subject matter discussed during such communications." § 6(b)(4)(C). The subject matter is not a summary of the conversation but rather the regulation's name that was discussed. Finally, after the rule is finalized or formally withdrawn, "OIRA shall make available to the public all *documents* exchanged between OIRA and the agency during the review by OIRA under this section." § 6(b)(4)(D) (emphasis added).

The public logs appear robust, at least through President Obama's Administration—displaying many meetings, mostly with regulated entities rather than regulatory beneficiaries.[52] Rena Steinzor et al., Ctr for Progressive Reform, Behind Closed Doors at the White House: How Politics Trumps Protection of Public Health, Worker Safety, and the Environment 2–15 (2011); Steven P. Croley, White House Review of Agency Rulemaking: An Empirical Investigation, 70 U. Chi. L. Rev. 821 (2003). By contrast, few documents between OIRA and rulemaking agencies have been disclosed. Sam Abbott, Disclosure at the Office of Information and Regulatory Affairs: Written Comments and Telephone Records Suspiciously Absent, Center for Effective Gov't (Feb. 26, 2013), http://www.foreffectivegov.org/disclosure-at-oira-written-comments-and-telephone-records-suspiciously-absent.

(7) ***Conflict of Interest Constraints.*** Should former General Counsel Geller have been participating in a private capacity in a rulemaking proceeding that had been well under way while he was a high-level Commission employee? The case arose before the Ethics in Government Act defined "rulemaking" as a "particular matter" that triggers constraints on activities former officials can undertake. 18 U.S.C. § 207(i)(3). Today, it seems unlikely that he could play any role on behalf of a client—whether he actually participated in the rulemaking, which involved specific parties (lifetime ban, § 207(a)(1)), had official responsibility for it (two year cooling off period, § 207(a)(2)), or was an officer of sufficiently high status (one-year

---

[52] As of October 2017, OIRA in President Trump's Administration still did not have a working web site. But meetings were being recorded, as usual, on reginfo.gov.

general ban on contact with one's former agency, § 207(c)). But at that time, no established principle of ethical conduct forbade his appearance. The Ethics in Government Act and conflict restrictions on government officials to address the "revolving door" problem are described in more detail in Ch. V (p. 526).

b. An Open-Minded Decisionmaker?

C&W FISH CO. v. FOX

C & W FISH CO., INC. v. FOX

United States Court of Appeals for the D.C. Circuit (1991).
931 F.2d 1556.

■ HENDERSON, CIRCUIT JUDGE.

On April 13, 1990, the Department of Commerce (Department), National Oceanic and Atmospheric Administration (NOAA), issued a final rule which, in part, bans the use of drift gillnets in the Atlantic King Mackerel Fishery. See 55 Fed. Reg. 14,833 (April 19, 1990). Various individuals involved in the fishing industry challenged the final rule on several grounds, including its allegedly ultra vires promulgation. The district court rejected all of the plaintiffs' challenges, granting summary judgment to the defendants. We affirm.

[The Magnuson Fishery Conservation and Management Act (Magnuson Act or Act), 16 U.S.C. §§ 1801–82, gives the Department authority to create national programs for fish conservation and management, while also preserving state roles. Eight Regional Fishery Management Councils representing state interests are granted authority over specific geographic regions. A Council can propose a Fishery Management Plan (FMP) subject to the Secretary's final approval and must be given an opportunity to comment on any FMP the Secretary himself proposes. Within the Department, the Secretary's authority has been subdelegated in ways that may further promote state interests, as well as foster the development of departmental expertise. The Assistant Administrator for Fisheries (Assistant Administrator) of NOAA, who is also the Director of the National Marine Fisheries Service (NMFS), is an important intermediary recipient of this authority.

For years, the South Atlantic Regional Council and the Gulf Regional Council had been trying to ban gillnet fishing for various species,[53] including the Atlantic King Mackerel. In 1989, after a regional administrator had blocked several other efforts, they succeeded in getting

---

[53] [Ed.] As its name suggests, a gillnet is a net that traps fish who swim into it by catching their gills; although the size of openings in the nets offers some control, they inevitably catch unwanted fish (and other marine life); drift gillnets, a particular target of the Councils, are large nets permitted to drift through a fishing area, whose size may contribute to threats of overfishing.

a rule that imposed limited constraints but permitted continued drift gillnet fishing for the Atlantic King Mackerel. In 1990, the Councils submitted a renewed proposal to ban this practice, which the regional administrator rejected. He reasoned that "the evidence presented to support the new submission . . . had not changed since the first submission and did not warrant a change in agency policy."]

When the Regional Director's decision reached Dr. William Fox, the newly appointed NOAA Assistant Administrator, the rejected portions of the amendment gained new life. Fox—who before his appointment had been a strong advocate of the drift gillnet ban—inexplicably reported that the Regional Director had "approved" the new Amendment 3 and then, himself, approved the full plan, explaining the appropriateness of the ban. The Under Secretary and the Secretary subsequently approved the Councils' proposal, and NOAA implemented appropriate notice and comment rulemaking, 55 Fed. Reg. 5,242 (February 14, 1990) (proposed rule); 55 Fed. Reg. 14,833 (April 19, 1990) (final rule).

The issuance of the drift gillnet ban set the stage for this litigation. Immediately after the final rule was issued, two fish wholesalers and two individual fishermen filed suit against the Secretary of Commerce, Robert Mosbacher, and Assistant Administrator Fox in district court . . .

[After disposing of a number of other challenges, the court turned to appellants' contention] that Assistant Administrator Fox had an "unalterably closed mind" when he passed on the drift gillnet ban and, consequently, their due process right to an impartial decisionmaker was denied them. To support this claim, the appellants point to the fact that, immediately before his appointment, Fox was the chairman of the Florida Marine Fisheries Commission, an outspoken advocate of the drift gillnet ban. They also point to an article published after Fox was appointed, quoting Fox as stating " '[t]here's just no question that this kind of gear [i.e., drift gillnets] should be eliminated. . . . The drift nets run counter to everything we're trying to do for the fisheries.' " Wickstrom, "The Fox Goes to Washington," Florida Sportsman (Oct. 1989). Last, the appellants claim that Fox's bias is demonstrated by his failure to conduct an adequate review of the issues or to consider the positions of his staff advisors.

First we reject the suggestion that we look to the adequacy of Fox's examination of the facts and issues in order to determine whether he was biased. In Association of National Advertisers, Inc. v. FTC, 627 F.2d 1151, 1170 (D.C. Cir. 1979),[54] we held that an individual should be

---

[54] [Ed.] This rulemaking regulated the advertising of sugared cereals on children's television programs. The motions for disqualification relied on a letter the FTC's Chairman, Michael Pertschuk, had sent to the head of the Food and Drug Administration, seeking to enlist his interest: "Setting legal theory aside, the truth is that we've been drawn into this issue because of the conviction which I know you share, that one of the evils flowing from the unfairness of children's advertising is the resulting distortion of children's perception of nutritional values. I see, at this point, our logical process as follows—Children's advertising is inherently unfair . . ."

disqualified from rulemaking "only when there has been a clear and convincing showing that the Department member has an unalterably closed mind on matters critical to the disposition of the proceeding." . . . This showing should focus on the agency member's prejudgment, if any, rather than a failure to weigh the issues fairly. Whether Fox weighed the facts properly is to be examined only in determining if his decision was arbitrary or capricious. As we have often explained, this court will not second guess an agency decision or question whether the decision made was the best one.

The facts in this case do not even approach a "clear and convincing showing" that Fox had an "unalterably closed mind." As we reasoned in Association of National Advertisers, "[t]he mere discussion of policy or advocacy on a legal question . . . is not sufficient to disqualify an administrator." 627 F.2d at 1171 (footnote omitted). The harm that would result were courts to disqualify agency members whenever they express views in public, as Fox did here, is readily apparent: We would eviscerate the proper evolution of policymaking were we to disqualify every administrator who has opinions on the correct course of his agency's future actions. Administrators, and even judges, may hold policy views on questions of law prior to participating in a proceeding. The factual basis for a rulemaking is so closely intertwined with policy judgments that we would obliterate rulemaking were we to equate a statement on an issue of legislative fact with unconstitutional prejudgment.

An administrator's presence within an agency reflects the political judgment of the President and the Senate. . . . A Commission's view of what is best in the public interest may change from time to time. Commissions themselves change, underlying philosophies differ, and experience often dictates changes. We conclude that neither Fox's earlier advocacy nor his policy view as publicly expressed demonstrates an unalterably closed mind that would disqualify him as an impartial decisionmaker.

NOTES

(1) **Impartiality in Rulemaking.** In light of this decision, what does it mean to have an "impartial decisionmaker" in rulemaking? How satisfactory do you find the political explanation for weak disqualification rules in rulemaking? The rule here, like that in the cited case of Ass'n of National Advertisers, reflects the action of an unusually outspoken, pro-regulation administrator, who may have been put in office for his or her views. Do the fairness claims of those who may be subjected to the regulation in question deserve more respect than these cases afford? See ABA Committee on Government Standards, Cynthia Farina, Reporter, Keeping Faith: Government Ethics and Government Ethics Regulation, 45 Admin. L. Rev. 287 (1993). Standards for decisionmakers in adjudication are tougher. The D.C. Circuit has "held that the standard for disqualifying an administrator in an adjudicatory proceeding because of prejudgment is whether 'a

disinterested observer may conclude that (the decisionmaker) has in some measure adjudged the facts as well as the law of a particular case in advance of hearing it.' " Ass'n of Nat. Advertisers, Inc. v. FTC, 627 F.2d 1151 (D.C. Cir. 1979).

(2) ***Social Media Campaigns in Rulemaking.*** A related issue to decisionmaking "bias" in rulemaking involves the extent to which an agency can encourage support for its proposed regulations. The GAO concluded that the EPA had "violated publicity or propaganda and anti-lobbying provisions contained in appropriation acts" in its social media use campaigns surrounding the Waters of the United States rulemaking in FY 2014 and 2015.[55] The GAO found specifically that the agency's use of Thunderclap (specifically, a widely shared message linked to the proposed rule that did not identify the EPA as the sender) constituted "covert propaganda" and its links to external sites that advocated contacting members of Congress qualified as "grassroots lobbying." But the GAO determined that the agency's #DitchtheMyth and #CleanWaterRules campaigns, which extolled the benefits of clean water and the proposed rule, were permissible. For information on proposed legislation to counter agency social media campaigns, see Ch. VI, Sec. 6 (p. 767).

(3) ***Impartiality of Agency Staff.*** The reasoning of the Fox court depends in good part on an argument from the legitimacy provided by "the political judgment of the President and the Senate" in making appointments. Should different considerations govern as one descends into the "expert" levels of the civil service, where institutional decisions will be strongly shaped?

UNITED STEELWORKERS OF AM. V. MARSHALL, 647 F.2d 1189 (D.C. Cir. 1980), addressed the question of alleged bias in agency staff, in an opinion written by then-CHIEF JUDGE J. SKELLY WRIGHT, author of the portion of the Home Box Office decision addressing ex parte contacts. The case arose at an intermediate stage of a massive OSHA rulemaking to regulate worker exposure to airborne lead. Virtually every aspect of the standard was subsequently challenged. Lead Industries Association (LIA), the main industrial challenger, contended that OSHA staff attorneys had acted essentially as advocates for a stringent lead standard with the Assistant Secretary in consultations that it claimed amounted to ex parte, off-the-record contacts with one of the adverse sides in the rulemaking, thereby rendering the proceedings unfair.

"The key agency employee in question was Richard Gross, a lawyer in the Office of the Solicitor at OSHA, who served as a so-called 'standard's attorney' throughout the rulemaking. . . . The standard's attorney was at the center of activity throughout the rulemaking. He worked with the regular OSHA staff in reviewing preliminary research and drafting the proposed standard, all the while offering informal legal advice. He helped organize the public hearings and, having immersed himself in the scientific literature and in the submitted public comments, he communicated regularly with the prospective expert witnesses. In these communications he briefed the witnesses on the issues they were to address in their testimony, explained

---

[55] http://www.gao.gov/products/B-326944.

the positions of the agency, the industry, and the unions on key questions, discussed the likely criticism of the experts' testimony, and asked the experts for any new information that supported or contradicted the OSHA proposal. During the hearing itself he conducted all initial questioning of OSHA witnesses and cross-examined all other witnesses. After the hearings he assisted the Assistant Secretary by reviewing the evidence in the record, preparing summaries, analyses, and recommendations, and helping draft the Preamble to the final standard.

"In a proceeding to create a general rule it makes little sense to speak of an agency employee advocating for 'one side' over another. However contentious the proceeding, the concept of advocacy does not apply easily where the agency is not determining the specific rights of a specific party, and where the proposed rule undergoes detailed change in its journey toward a final rule. . . . Nevertheless, the adversary tone and format of the proceedings are obvious. . . . The Assistant Secretary might well have been able to assess the record more objectively—if less efficiently—had the standard's attorney not been constantly at her side. Therefore, although we have some doubt about calling the standard's attorney an 'advocate' in the context of such rulemaking, we will *assume* he played that role so we can measure his conduct against the legal constraints on the agency.

"We note at the outset that nothing in the Administrative Procedure Act bars a staff advocate from advising the decisionmaker in setting a final rule. . . . Moreover, in establishing the special hybrid procedures in the OSH Act, Congress never intended to impose the separation-of-functions requirement it imposes in adjudications. [See Ch. V, Sec. 2, p. 504.] The legislative history shows that Congress consistently turned back efforts to impose such formal procedures on OSHA standard-setting. . . . [U]nder the Supreme Court's decision in Vermont Yankee that is virtually the end of the inquiry. . . .

"Rulemaking is essentially an institutional, not an individual, process, and it is not vulnerable to communication within an agency in the same sense as it is to communication from without. In an enormously complex proceeding like an OSHA standard setting, it may simply be unrealistic to expect an official facing a massive, almost inchoate, record to isolate herself from the people with whom she worked in generating the record. In any event, we rest our decision not on our own theory of agency management, but on the state of the law."

(4) *Reliance on Subordinates and Contractors.* Separate from concerns of staff bias, agency decisionmakers simply cannot do much of the work needed in a rulemaking themselves. To what extent can decisionmakers rely on subordinates? In a series of cases, known as the Morgan cases (discussed in Chapter IV, p. 502), the Supreme Court wrestled with this question in the context of a ratemaking by the Department of Agriculture under the Packers and Stockyards Act. In MORGAN V. UNITED STATES, 298 U.S. 468 (1936) (MORGAN I), the Court held that the decisionmaking "cannot be performed by one who has not considered evidence or argument. It is not an impersonal obligation. It is a duty akin to that of a judge. The one who decides must hear. This necessary rule does not preclude practicable administrative

procedure in obtaining the aid of assistants in the department. Assistants may prosecute inquiries. Evidence may be taken by an examiner. Evidence thus taken may be sifted and analyzed by competent subordinates. . . . That duty undoubtedly may be an onerous one, but the performance of it in a substantial manner is inseparable from the exercise of the important authority conferred." Later cases in the dispute centered on the extent of judicial review of the decisionmaker's actions. Morgan v. United States, 304 U.S. 1 (1938) (Morgan II), took a more aggressive approach, which the district court used to allow the Secretary to be questioned under oath. But by the final case, UNITED STATES V. MORGAN, 313 U.S. 409 (1941) (MORGAN IV), the Court determined the questioning of the decisionmaker had gone too far: "But the short of the business is that the Secretary should never have been subjected to this examination. . . . Such an examination of a judge would be destructive of judicial responsibility. We have explicitly held in this very litigation that 'it was not the function of the court to probe the mental processes of the Secretary'. . . . Just as a judge cannot be subjected to such a scrutiny, . . . so the integrity of the administrative process must be equally respected."

For a more recent case in the rulemaking context, see NATIONAL NUTRITIONAL FOODS ASS'N V. FDA, 491 F.2d 1141 (2d Cir. 1974). After "almost two years" of hearings that "produced over 32,000 pages of testimony and thousands of pages of exhibits" the new FDA Commissioner signed off on a complex final regulation 13 days after taking office. "Conceding that it is not the function of this court 'to probe the mental processes' of the Commissioner, Morgan v. United States, 304 U.S. 1, 18 (1938) (Morgan II), petitioners insist they are entitled to probe whether he exercised his own mental processes at all. . . . The facts of this case do not constitute nearly the showing of bad faith necessary to justify further inquiry; indeed they vividly illustrate the necessity of adhering to the presumption of regularity with respect to the participation of the officer authorized to sign administrative orders, especially in the context of the promulgation of legislative rules as distinguished from adjudication. . . . It would suffice under the circumstances that [the new] Commissioner . . . considered the summaries of the objections and of the answers contained in the elaborate preambles and conferred with his staff about them. There is no reason why he could not have done this even in the limited time available, ... although we do not envy him the task. In any event, absent the most powerful preliminary showing to the contrary, effective government requires us to presume that he did."

What if those subordinates are not government employees but contractors? This issue arose in UNITED STEELWORKERS, supra. The court rejected procedural complaints against OSHA's use of consultants to summarize and evaluate data in the record, as well as to draft parts of the preamble and final standard. LIA maintained that this violated the Morgan principle that "the one who decides must hear," but the court disagreed, noting that the Assistant Secretary had "reviewed the evidence and explained the evidentiary bases for each part of the standard" in the preamble and attachments to the final standard and had "demonstrated her independence from the consultants by strongly criticizing some of their conclusions on the key issue of feasibility." More generally, the court insisted that "the unsupported allegation that hired consultants might have an incentive to act dishonestly cannot overcome the presumption that agency officials and those who assist them have acted properly. . . . [W]e generally see no reason to force agencies to hire enormous regular staffs versed in all conceivable technological issues, rather than use their appropriations to hire specific consultants for specific problems."

(5) *No Guaranteed Consideration of Staff Views.* To what extent can a regulated party challenge exclusion of staff views favorable to its cause? NAT. SMALL SHIPMENTS TRAFFIC CONF., INC. V. ICC, 725 F.2d 1442 (D.C. Cir. 1984), involved a rulemaking that reexamined how carriers allocate handling costs at freight truck terminals, among shippers of high and low bulk commodities. The final rule placed a higher proportion of the costs on smaller-size shippers, and they complained that the bureaucratic decision process within the ICC had prevented staff analyses favorable to smaller-size shippers from reaching the Commission. The court rejected this claim. It noted that the shippers may have "a legal right that their comments reach Commission members in at least summary form, and that those comments be considered before final action is taken," subject to "the longstanding rule that courts will not probe the mental processes of administrative decisionmakers absent strong evidence of bad faith or other misconduct." But staff comments were different: "Neither the APA nor the due process clause, however, accords similar treatment to staff evaluations that move beyond a mere summary of record comments to express the independent judgments of subordinate agency personnel. An agency is free to structure its internal policy debate in any manner it deems appropriate. Midlevel managers may therefore filter out the evaluations of lower-level personnel if they so choose, so long as relevant record comments are not eliminated in the process as well." But if opposing staff views become part of the decisionmaking process (and record), such "[e]vidence . . . often triggers more rigorous [judicial] review." Gillian E. Metzger, The Interdependent Relationship Between Internal and External Separation of Powers, 59 Emory L.J. 423, 445 (2009).

CHAPTER V
ADJUDICATION

> Sec. 1. *The Institutional Framework of Agency Adjudication*
>
> Sec. 2. *Formal Adjudication Under the APA*
>
> Sec. 3. *Informal Adjudication Under the APA*
>
> Sec. 4. *Due Process as a Source of Procedural Rights in Adjudication*

Adjudication is a large part of what administrative agencies do, and agency adjudication has a large impact on the ordinary lives of many of us. Sometimes this happens in incidental ways, as when someone passes through customs on returning from abroad, and the customs inspector accepts her declaration of what she has bought—thereby completing, to put it in administrative law terms, an informal adjudication. Sometimes it is much more serious and consequential, as when the Social Security Administration holds a more formal proceeding to determine whether a claimant deserves disability benefits. Yet this, too, occurs with great frequency: 652,241 times in 2016, to be precise.

Besides deciding who owes or deserves what, many agencies use adjudication as a means of establishing policy. For example, the "rules" governing who can unionize or what constitutes an unfair labor practice exist almost entirely in the cases of the National Labor Relations Board, applied as precedents. (As the Supreme Court held in the Chenery case, p. 249 above, an agency that decides cases can use them to formulate policy even if that agency also has rulemaking powers.) Indeed, regulating by deciding cases might be called the traditional way to regulate in the American legal system—following, of course, on the pattern of the courts in determining and applying the common law.

When procedures are fashioned for the conduct of agency adjudication, then, there are two, sometimes competing, general criteria in play: (1) What process will be fair to the individual parties? (2) What process will produce the best regulatory result? To which we should add, what process for adjudication will fit with the other tasks the agency must also carry out?

FEDERAL TRADE COMMISSION v.
CEMENT INSTITUTE

FEDERAL TRADE COMMISSION v. CEMENT INSTITUTE

Supreme Court of the United States (1948).
333 U.S. 683.

■ JUSTICE BLACK delivered the opinion of the Court.

We granted certiorari to review the decree of the Circuit Court of Appeals which, with one judge dissenting, vacated and set aside a cease and desist order issued by the Federal Trade Commission against the respondents. Those respondents are: The Cement Institute, an unincorporated trade association composed of 74 corporations which manufacture, sell and distribute cement; the 74 corporate members of the Institute; and 21 individuals who are associated with the Institute. It took three years for a trial examiner to hear the evidence which consists of about 49,000 pages of oral testimony and 50,000 pages of exhibits. Even the findings and conclusions of the Commission cover 176 pages. The briefs with accompanying appendixes submitted by the parties contain more than 4,000 pages. The legal questions raised by the Commission and by the different respondents are many and varied. . . .

The proceedings were begun by a Commission complaint of two counts. The first charged that certain alleged conduct set out at length constituted an unfair method of competition in violation of § 5 of the Federal Trade Commission Act. 15 U.S.C. § 45. The core of the charge was that the respondents had restrained and hindered competition in the sale and distribution of cement by means of a combination among themselves made effective through mutual understanding or agreement to employ a multiple basing point system of pricing. It was alleged that this system resulted in the quotation of identical terms of sale and identical prices for cement by the respondents at any given point in the United States. This system had worked so successfully, it was further charged, that for many years prior to the filing of the complaint, all cement buyers throughout the nation, with rare exceptions, had been unable to purchase cement for delivery in any given locality from any one of the respondents at a lower price or on more favorable terms than from any of the other respondents.

The second count of the complaint, resting chiefly on the same allegations of fact set out in Count I, charged that the multiple basing point system of sales resulted in [violations of the antitrust laws].

Resting upon its findings, the Commission ordered that respondents cease and desist from 'carrying out any planned common course of action, understanding, agreement, combination, or conspiracy' to do a number of things, all of which things, the Commission argues, had to be restrained in order effectively to restore individual freedom of action among the separate units in the cement industry. . . .

Jurisdiction.—At the very beginning we are met with a challenge to the Commission's jurisdiction to entertain the complaint and to act on it. This contention is pressed by respondent Marquette Cement Manufacturing Co. and is relied upon by other respondents. Count I of the complaint is drawn under the provision in § 5 of the Federal Trade Commission Act which declares that 'Unfair methods of competition * * * are hereby declared unlawful.' Marquette contends that the facts alleged in Count I do not constitute an 'unfair method of competition' within the meaning of § 5. Its argument runs this way: Count I in reality charges a combination to restrain trade. Such a combination constitutes an offense under § 1 of the Sherman Act which outlaws 'Every * * * combination * * * in restraint of trade.' 15 U.S.C. § 1. Section 4 of the Sherman Act provides that the attorney general shall institute suits under the Act on behalf of the United States, and that the federal district courts shall have exclusive jurisdiction of such suits. Hence, continue respondents, the Commission, whose jurisdiction is limited to 'unfair methods of competition,' is without power to institute proceedings or to issue an order with regard to the combination in restraint of trade charged in Count I. Marquette then argues that since the fact allegations of Count I are the chief reliance for the charge in Count II, this latter count also must be interpreted as charging a violation of the Sherman Act. Assuming, without deciding, that the conduct charged in each count constitutes a violation of the Sherman Act, we hold that the Commission does have jurisdiction to conclude that such conduct may also be an unfair method of competition and hence constitute a violation of § 5 of the Federal Trade Commission Act. . . .

The Multiple Basing Point Delivered Price System.—[The "multiple basing point delivered price system" of fixing prices and terms of cement sales worked as follows: The companies quoted prices of cement as delivered to the customer. They based these prices on the general market price at one of several fixed points, plus freight charges to the customer's location, regardless of whether the cement was actually shipped from that point. All sellers used the same system, and therefore quoted identical prices, regardless of their actual costs of production or of shipment.]

Alleged Bias of the Commission.—One year after the taking of testimony had been concluded and while these proceedings were still pending before the Commission, the respondent Marquette asked the Commission to disqualify itself from passing upon the issues involved. Marquette charged that the Commission had previously prejudged the issues, was 'prejudiced and biased against the Portland cement industry generally,' and that the industry and Marquette in particular could not receive a fair hearing from the Commission. After hearing oral argument the Commission refused to disqualify itself. . . .

Marquette introduced numerous exhibits intended to support its charges. In the main these exhibits were copies of the Commission's reports made to Congress or to the President, as required by § 6 of the Trade Commission Act. These reports, as well as the testimony given by members of the Commission before congressional committees, make it clear that long before the filing of this complaint the members of the Commission at that time, or at least some of them, were of the opinion that the operation of the multiple basing point system as they had studied it was the equivalent of a price fixing restraint of trade in violation of the Sherman Act. We therefore decide this contention, as did the Circuit Court of Appeals, on the assumption that such an opinion had been formed by the entire membership of the Commission as a result of its prior official investigations. But we also agree with that court's holding that this belief did not disqualify the Commission.

In the first place, the fact that the Commission had entertained such views as the result of its prior ex parte investigations did not necessarily mean that the minds of its members were irrevocably closed on the subject of the respondents' basing point practices. Here, in contrast to the Commission's investigations, members of the cement industry were legally authorized participants in the hearings. They produced evidence—volumes of it. They were free to point out to the Commission by testimony, by cross-examination of witnesses, and by arguments, conditions of the trade practices under attack which they thought kept these practices within the range of legally permissible business activities.

Moreover, Marquette's position, if sustained, would to a large extent defeat the congressional purposes which prompted passage of the Trade Commission Act. Had the entire membership of the Commission disqualified in the proceedings against these respondents, this complaint could not have been acted upon by the Commission or by any other government agency. Congress has provided for no such contingency. It has not directed that the Commission disqualify itself under any circumstances, has not provided for substitute commissioners should any of its members disqualify, and has not authorized any other government agency to hold hearings, make findings, and issue cease and desist orders in proceedings against unfair trade practices. Yet if Marquette is right, the Commission, by making studies and filing reports in obedience to congressional command, completely immunized the practices investigated, even though they are 'unfair,' from any cease and desist order by the Commission or any other governmental agency.

There is no warrant in the Act for reaching a conclusion which would thus frustrate its purposes. If the Commission's opinions expressed in congressionally required reports would bar its members from acting in unfair trade proceedings, it would appear that opinions expressed in the first basing point unfair trade proceeding would similarly disqualify them from ever passing on another. Thus experience acquired from their work as commissioners would be a handicap instead of an advantage. Such was not the intendment of Congress. For Congress acted on a committee report stating: 'It is manifestly desirable that the terms of the commissioners shall be long enough to give them an opportunity to acquire the expertness in dealing with these special questions concerning industry that comes from experience.' Report of Committee on Interstate Commerce, No. 597, June 13, 1914, 63d Cong., 2d Sess. 10–11.

Marquette also seems to argue that it was a denial of due process for the Commission to act in these proceedings after having expressed the view that industry-wide use of the basing point system was illegal. A number of cases are cited as giving support to this contention. . . .[No] decision of this Court would require us to hold that it would be a violation of procedural due process for a judge to sit in a case after he had expressed an opinion as to whether certain types of conduct were prohibited by law. In fact, judges frequently try the same case more than once and decide identical issues each time, although these issues involved questions both of law and fact. Certainly, the Federal Trade Commission cannot possibly be under stronger constitutional compulsions in this respect than a court.

The Commission properly refused to disqualify itself. . .

Findings and Evidence.—It is strongly urged that the Commission failed to find, as charged in both counts of the complaint, that the respondents had by combination, agreements, or understandings among themselves utilized the multiple basing point delivered price system as a restraint to accomplish uniform prices and terms of sale. A subsidiary contention is that assuming the Commission did so find, there is no substantial evidence to support such a finding. We think that adequate findings of combination were made and that the findings have support in the evidence. . . .

Although there is much more evidence to which reference could be made, we think that the following facts shown by evidence in the record, some of which are in dispute, are sufficient to warrant the Commission's finding of concerted action.

When the Commission rendered its decision there were about 80 cement manufacturing companies in the United States operating about 150 mills. Ten companies controlled more than half of the mills and there were substantial corporate affiliations among many of the others. This concentration of productive capacity made concerted action far less difficult than it would otherwise have been. The belief is prevalent in the industry that because of the standardized nature of cement, among other reasons, price competition is wholly unsuited to it. That belief is historic. It has resulted in concerted activities to devise means and measures to do away with competition in the industry. Out of those activities came the multiple basing point delivered price system. Evidence shows it to be a handy instrument to bring about elimination of any kind of price competition. The use of the multiple basing point delivered price system by the cement producers has been coincident with a situation whereby for many years, with rare exceptions, cement has been offered for sale in every given locality at identical prices and terms by all producers. Thousands of secret sealed bids have been received by public agencies which corresponded in prices of cement down to a fractional part of a penny.[15] . . .

The foregoing are but illustrations of the practices shown to have been utilized to maintain the basing point price system. Respondents offered testimony that cement is a standardized product, that 'cement is cement,' that no differences existed in quality or usefulness, and that purchasers demanded delivered price quotations because of the high cost of transportation from mill to dealer. . . . Respondents introduced the testimony of economists to the effect that competition alone could lead to the evolution of a multiple basing point system of uniform delivered prices and terms of sale for an industry with a standardized product and with relatively high freight costs. These economists testified that for the above reasons no inferences of collusion, agreement, or understanding could be drawn from the admitted fact that cement prices of all United States producers had for many years almost invariably been the same in every given locality in the country. There was also considerable testimony by other economic experts that the multiple basing point system of delivered prices as employed by respondents contravened accepted economic principles and could only have been maintained through collusion.

The Commission did not adopt the views of the economists produced by the respondents. It decided that even though competition might tend to drive the price of standardized products to a uniform level, such a tendency alone could not account for the almost perfect identity in prices,

---

[15] The following is one among many of the Commission's findings as to the identity of sealed bids: An abstract of the bids for 6,000 barrels of cement to the United States Engineer Office at Tucumcari, New Mexico, opened April 23, 1936, shows the following:

Name of Bidder	Price per Bbl.
Monarch	$3.286854
Ash Grove	3.286854
Lehigh	3.286854
Southwestern	3.286854
U.S. Portland Cement Co	3.286854
Oklahoma	3.286854
Consolidated	3.286854
Trinity	3.286854
Lone Star	3.286854
Universal	3.286854
Colorado	3.286854

All bids subject to 10 cents per barrel discount for payment in 15 days. (Com.Ex. 175–A.)

discounts, and cement containers which had prevailed for so long a time in the cement industry. The Commission held that the uniformity and absence of competition in the industry were the results of understandings or agreements entered into or carried out by concert of the Institute and the other respondents. It may possibly be true, as respondents' economists testified, that cement producers will, without agreement express or implied and without understanding explicit or tacit, always and at all times (for such has been substantially the case here) charge for their cement precisely, to the fractional part of a penny, the price their competitors charge. Certainly it runs counter to what many people have believed, namely, that without agreement, prices will vary—that the desire to sell will sometimes be so strong that a seller will be willing to lower his prices and take his chances. We therefore hold that the Commission was not compelled to accept the views of respondents' economist-witnesses that active competition was bound to produce uniform cement prices. The Commission was authorized to find understanding, express or implied, from evidence that the industry's Institute actively worked, in cooperation with various of its members, to maintain the multiple basing point delivered price system; that this pricing system is calculated to produce, and has produced, uniform prices and terms of sale throughout the country; and that all of the respondents have sold their cement substantially in accord with the pattern required by the multiple basing point system. . . .

We sustain the Commission's holding that concerted maintenance of the basing point delivered price system is an unfair method of competition prohibited by the Federal Trade Commission Act. . . .

The Commission's order should not have been set aside by the Circuit Court of Appeals. Its judgment is reversed and the cause is remanded to that court with directions to enforce the order.

■ JUSTICE DOUGLAS and JUSTICE JACKSON took no part in the consideration or decision of these cases.

■ JUSTICE BURTON, dissenting.

[Omitted]

NOTES

(1) *Framing the Issue.* Speaking broadly, the cement companies in the case we just read make the following argument: the matter at hand—the validity of their pricing scheme—could be tried either in a court under the antitrust statutes or before the agency under the Federal Trade Commission Act; it ought to be tried in a court, they say, because the agency is biased. The case is unusual in that there are two separate statutes that, the Court is willing to assume, would provide parallel causes of action in different venues. Let's consider the simpler case where there is one regulatory statute, for which we need to provide a process to determine when it has been violated. How do we know what process applies? In the first instance, we look

to see what process Congress has stipulated—and what we find is that different statutes come with different processes. Congress can provide, as in the Federal Election Campaign Act, for an agency to investigate and bring charges, but for the charges to be brought, and the case to be decided, in a federal district court. Congress can provide, as in the Occupational Safety and Health Act, for one agency to bring charges, but for another administrative agency to conduct the actual trial. Congress can provide, as in the Family and Medical Leave Act, for ordinary citizens to enforce a statute and its accompanying regulations in court (alongside of an agency that can also sue in court to enforce). Or, as in the Federal Trade Commission Act at stake in Cement Institute, Congress can empower an agency to investigate and bring charges in a process pursuant to which the same agency will then adjudicate and pronounce judgment. This last possibility constitutes the archetype of administrative adjudication, both in the sense that it is the one most commonly met in regulatory statutes and in the sense that it is the model that is assumed to be in play in the APA's treatment of adjudicatory procedures. (It is perhaps worth noting that this plasticity disappears when criminal sanctions are at stake; criminal cases must be brought in the ordinary courts, if only because that's where the juries are.)

(2) *Are Agencies Inherently Biased?* In other words, the problem of Cement Institute arises because of the way the process of adjudication has been set into the institutional structure of an administrative agency. The Federal Trade Commission Act established the FTC as an instrument of government, told it to investigate and pursue unfair acts in commerce, and told it, if warranted, to order the perpetrators to stop what they were doing. Historically, it dated back to the Progressive era. Politically it was part of the twentieth century's positive use of government to control the excesses of the market. Procedurally it was based on the investigation and decision of individual cases. Put differently, by means of deciding cases the agency was supposed to forward a positive agenda.

The cement companies emphasized that, before charging them, the FTC had made reports to Congress that criticized the basing point pricing system—perhaps because that was their clearest evidence of prejudgment. But considering the adjudicatory process as a whole, the FTC was even more—we might say, much more—implicated in what took place. One or another employee of the FTC:

- Investigated the situation;

- Became convinced there was wrongdoing;

- Formally voted to bring charges;

- Presented, as prosecutor, the case against the companies;

- Perhaps testified as an expert witness against the companies;

- Acted as the hearing examiner receiving the evidence;

- Made findings of fact and proposed rulings of law;

- Heard an internal appeal; and

- Rendered the final decision.

If we consider "the FTC" as a unitary actor, the agency as a whole clearly crossed over a line, rigorously policed in ordinary courtroom adjudication, separating those who charge and present (e.g., the prosecutor) from those who hear and decide (e.g., the judge and jury). Is this unfair? To make that question more doctrinally precise, does this satisfy the constitutional requirement of due process (applicable to administrative adjudication per Londoner v. Denver, p. 218 above)? Or can we rely on officials, as we rely on many people in all walks of life, to change their minds, if warranted, once they find out in detail what the facts actually are?

Another possibility is to not consider "the FTC" to be a unitary actor, but instead to notice that it, like most organizations, comprises many people, who are more or less subject to each other's control depending on how the organization is organized. We might then ask what lines of connection are permissible between those who prosecute and those who hear the case, or between those who hear the case and those who decide on any internal appeal. This, as we shall see, is one of the ways the APA (which was passed three years after the FTC reached its decision in Cement Institute in 1943) "solves" the question of fairness.

But even after the APA, the five named Commissioners at the top of the FTC are (and were in Cement Institute) themselves on both sides of the line. By the explicit terms of the FTC Act, they both formally vote to bring charges and also render the final decision. Because, one might argue, if they do not remain in control of what cases the agency brings, and what precedents the agency sets, they will not have the tools needed to be able to carry out the agenda Congress has handed them.

Justice Black's answer—taking the case as applicable, not just to the question of reports to Congress but to the situation as a whole—seems to take this point of view. The FTC's combination of functions is not per se in violation of the Constitution. A more particular bias needs to be shown. Otherwise Congress's purposes in establishing an expert, experienced Commission would be thwarted.

This point of view also prevailed in WITHROW V. LARKIN, 421 U.S. 35 (1975). There, a doctor who performed abortions (criminally prohibited at the time) was the subject of an investigatory hearing by the Wisconsin Medical Examining Board. Although the agency was presumably a much smaller and less differentiated body than the FTC, a similar result obtained. The doctor's counsel was present at a preliminary hearing and invited to explain any of the evidence that had been presented, but not otherwise allowed to participate. After the hearing, the Board formally charged the doctor with a number of violations and scheduled a contested hearing that could lead to temporary license suspension. The doctor sued in federal court, alleging that the combination of investigatory and adjudicatory roles in the Board violated due process. A three-judge district court agreed, but the Supreme Court reversed in an opinion by JUSTICE WHITE:

"The contention that the combination of investigative and adjudicative functions necessarily creates an unconstitutional risk of bias in administrative adjudication has a . . . difficult burden of persuasion to carry.

It must overcome a presumption of honesty and integrity in those serving as adjudicators; and it must convince that, under a realistic appraisal of psychological tendencies and human weakness, conferring investigative and adjudicative powers on the same individuals poses such a risk of actual bias or prejudgment that the practice must be forbidden if the guarantee of due process is to be adequately implemented. . . .

". . . [O]ur cases, although they reflect the substance of the problem, offer no support for the bald proposition applied in this case by the District Court that agency members who participate in an investigation are disqualified from adjudicating. The incredible variety of administrative mechanisms in this country will not yield to any single organizing principle. . . .

". . . [I]n this case . . . there was no more evidence of bias or the risk of bias or prejudgment than inhered in the very fact that the Board had investigated and would now adjudicate. . . . The processes utilized by the Board . . . do not in themselves contain an unacceptable risk of bias. The investigative proceeding had been closed to the public, but appellee and his counsel were permitted to be present throughout; counsel actually attended the hearings and knew the facts presented to the Board. No specific foundation has been presented for suspecting that the Board had been prejudiced by its investigation or would be disabled from hearing and deciding on the basis of the evidence to be presented at the contested hearing. . . . Without a showing to the contrary, state administrators 'are assumed to be men of conscience and intellectual discipline, capable of judging a particular controversy fairly on the basis of its own circumstances.' United States v. Morgan, 313 U.S. 409, 421 (1941). . . .

"Judges repeatedly issue arrest warrants on the basis that there is probable cause to believe that a crime has been committed and that the person named in the warrant has committed it. Judges also preside at preliminary hearings where they must decide whether the evidence is sufficient to hold a defendant for trial. Neither of these pretrial involvements has been thought to raise any constitutional barrier against the judge presiding over the criminal trial and, if the trial is without a jury, against making the necessary determination of guilt or innocence. . . . It is also very typical for the members of administrative agencies to receive the results of investigations, to approve the filing of charges or formal complaints instituting enforcement proceedings, and then to participate in the ensuing hearings. This mode of procedure does not violate the [APA], and it does not violate due process of law. We should also remember that it is not contrary to due process to allow judges and administrators . . . reversed on appeal to confront the same questions a second time around. . . .

"That the combination of investigative and adjudicatory functions does not, without more, constitute a due process violation, does not, of course, preclude a court from determining from the special facts and circumstances present in the case before it that the risk of unfairness is intolerably high."

Is this basic judicial acceptance of agencies' having a multiplicity of functions sound? Even if it meets the basics of due process, ought it to be avoided or ameliorated where possible? As we shall see, the possibility of answering yes to both of these questions forms a good part of the explanation for much of the APA's statutory treatment of administrative adjudication.

(3) *What about the "Separation of Powers"?* Even if we accept Cement Institute's answer to the question of bias, is the result consistent with the structure of our Constitution? Here are two opposing answers:

GARY LAWSON, THE RISE AND RISE OF THE ADMINISTRATIVE STATE, 107 Harv. L. Rev. 1231, 1248–49 (1994): "The constitutional separation of powers is a means to safeguard the liberty of the people. In Madison's famous words, "[t]he accumulation of all powers, legislative, executive, and judiciary, in the same hands, whether of one, a few, or many, and whether hereditary, self-appointed, or elective, may justly be pronounced the very definition of tyranny. [Federalist No.47.] The destruction of this principle of separation of powers is perhaps the crowning jewel of the modern administrative revolution. Administrative agencies routinely combine all three governmental functions in the same body, and even in the same people with that body. . . .

"This is probably the most jarring way in which the administrative state departs from the Constitution, and it typically does not even raise eyebrows. . . ."

ADRIAN VERMEULE, LAW'S ABNEGATION 42 (2016): "Lawson's view is unpersuasive . . . . The inescapable fact is that *the institutional innovations that appall Lawson were themselves generated by the very system of lawmaking-by-separation-of-powers that he wants to defend. . . .* [E]verything Lawson deems inconsistent with the Constitution of 1789 emerged *through and by means of the* operation of that very Constitution, not despite it.

"Here is another way of putting the issue. Suppose magically that the American constitutional order of 1789 were somehow restored to the baseline of 1789, . . . Would we have any reason to expect a different outcome? The same classical lawmaking, through the same classical separation-of-powers system, might well generate the same administrative state that it generated before, or some functionally equivalent substitute. . . . Legislators legislating by virtue of Article I, Presidents exercising their functions under Article II, judges judging under Article III—these, not some sinister cabal of New Deal lawyers, were the source of all the institutional innovations, like agencies exercising combined functions, that Lawson abhors."

(4) Justice Black's argument rests, in part, on the particular configuration of the Federal Trade Commission: it comprises five members, appointed for seven year terms, who can be fired only for "inefficiency, neglect of duty, or malfeasance in office." It is, in other words, an "independent agency." The case has not been so confined. Is the result fairly applicable to agencies that are "executive" agencies?

(5) *The Agency as Policymaker.* Justice Black seems to think not only that agency commingling of functions is tolerable, but that it is desirable. Here's one classic statement of that position: JAMES M. LANDIS, THE ADMINISTRATIVE PROCESS 35–39 (1938):

"The power to initiate action exists because it fulfills a long-felt need in our law. To restrict governmental intervention, in the determination of claims, to the position of an umpire deciding the merits upon the basis of the record as established by the parties, presumes the existence of an equality in the way of the respective power of the litigants to get at the facts. . . . In some spheres the absence of equal economic power generally is so prevalent that the umpire theory of administering law is almost certain to fail. Here government tends to offer its aid to a claimant, not so much because of the grave social import of the particular injury, but because the atmosphere and conditions created by an accumulation of such unredressed claims is of itself a serious social threat. . . .

"One other significant distinction between the administrative and the judicial processes is the power of 'independent' investigation possessed by the former. The test of the judicial process, traditionally, is not the fair disposition of the controversy; it is the fair disposition of the controversy *upon the record as made by the parties*. True, there are collateral sources of information which often affect judicial determinations. There is the more or less limited discretion under the doctrine of judicial notice; and there is the unarticulated but nonetheless substantial power to choose between competing premises based upon off-the-record considerations. But, in strictness, the judge must not know of the events of the controversy except as these may have been presented to him, in due form, by the parties. . . .

"On the other hand, these characteristics, conspicuously absent from the judicial process, do attend the administrative process. For that process to be successful in a particular field, it is imperative that controversies be decided as 'rightly' as possible, independently of the formal record the parties themselves produce. The ultimate test of the administrative is the policy that it formulates; not the fairness as between the parties of the disposition of a controversy on a record of their own making."

(6) *A Current Controversy.* The SEC, like the FTC in Cement Institute, has long possessed the authority to bring certain enforcement actions either in federal courts or before the agency itself in an administrative proceeding. But the Dodd-Frank Wall Street Reform and Consumer Protection Act ("Dodd-Frank"), passed during the Obama administration, significantly expanded the kinds of cases that the SEC could try internally. Here's an explanation by Professor Joseph Grundfest, a former SEC Commissioner, of some of the issues raised by this shift:

> The [SEC] often can choose between two forums when it files enforcement actions. One option is to sue in federal district court, where defendants have a right to a jury trial, can take depositions, and testimony is subject to the Federal Rules of Evidence. . . . Alternatively, the Commission can file an administrative proceeding that is heard by an administrative law judge (ALJ). There is no right to a jury trial in an administrative proceeding. Discovery is severely restricted, depositions are limited, hearings proceed on a schedule that is far more rapid than in most federal trials, and the Federal Rules of Evidence do not apply. Prosecutors and ALJs in administrative proceedings are all Commission

employees. Initial appeals from ALJ rulings are to the Commission itself, the same body that issued the order instituting the proceeding. . . . Only after the Commission rules on the appeal does a respondent gain the right to be heard by a federal judge unaffiliated with the Commission. . . .

The debate over the fairness of the Commission's administrative procedures, and over the discretion the Commission exercises when allocating litigation between federal and administrative venues, ran at a low simmer for decades with only occasional outbursts. However, this relative calm ended in 2013, when the Commission's staff announced plans to rely on expanded administrative remedies created by [Dodd-Frank] and to shift litigation that had traditionally been brought in federal court to its in-house administrative proceedings. . . . This announcement kicked over a hornet's nest of protest as critics trumpeted a long list of complaints about the fairness of the SEC's internal process and its Kafkaesque dimensions. They pointed to data suggesting that the Commission enjoyed a significant home-court advantage when litigating before its own and challenged the constitutionality of the process by which the Commission appointed its ALJs. Critics also waxed poetic about the Commission's internal procedures as an affront to the principles of due process that can be traced back to the Magna Carta. It was as though a dam holding back pent up rage about the fairness of the Commission's administrative proceedings had suddenly burst.

JOSEPH A. GRUNDFEST, FAIR OR FOUL?: SEC ADMINISTRATIVE PROCEEDINGS AND PROSPECTS FOR REFORM THROUGH REMOVAL LEGISLATION, 85 Fordham L. Rev. 1143, 1144–48 (2016).

Whether the data actually showed the SEC having a "home-court" advantage when it proceeded administratively depended on how you massaged the data. See id., 1175 ff. But the belief was widespread. One Wall Street Journal article was entitled "SEC Wins With In-House Judges" and claimed that over a five year period the SEC won 90% of the time before the ALJs compared to 69% before the courts. True or not, claims like these did not escape the notice of Congress. In a 2015 oversight hearing, then-Subcommittee Chairman Scott Garrett observed that the hurdles regulated parties face (including deferential review) "coupled with the SEC's . . . success rate . . . illustrates a very troubling pattern of the SEC's attempting to stack the rules and process in a way that the outcome of the case is, well, predetermined. This is not appropriate in a country that values appropriate due process for its citizens. Due process is a fair process, and fair process is fair play." Oversight of the SEC's Division of Enforcement Before the Subcomm. on Capital Mkts & Gov't Sponsored Enters. of the H. Comm. on Fin. Servs., 114th Cong. 3 (2015).

Andrew Ceresny, then-Director of the SEC's Enforcement Division, mounted a spirited defense, *Id.* at 8–10:

[I]n cases where we need quick relief, where we want to get a bar very quickly, or we want to get investors relief quickly, administrative proceedings can be much quicker than district court actions. District court actions will often take years to get a resolution in. . . . And another important point is where we have technical rules, where we have complicated rules, some of our rules are very complicated, we have sophisticated fact-finders who are the ALJs; whereas with a jury, it would be much more difficult for them to grasp those very, very complicated issues. . . .

Administrative proceedings have additional protections that actually defendants don't necessarily have in district court. . . . We turn over the investigative files, usually within 7 days of filing our cases, which we do not do in district court proceedings. There also are exhibit lists and witness lists provided typically in administrative proceedings. . . . [D]efendants also get subpoenas if they show good cause, and they [ ] subpoena documents. The one major difference is obviously the lack of depositions.

Nevertheless, Congress is considering legislation to restrict the SEC. The proposed Financial CHOICE Act of 2017—the bill at the center of recent efforts to repeal and replace the Dodd-Frank Act—includes a provision that curtails the SEC's autonomy to bring an enforcement action in its preferred forum. Section 823 permits the subject of an SEC administrative adjudication to compel the agency to terminate the in-house proceeding; the SEC can then bring the same case as a civil action. See Financial CHOICE Act of 2017, H.R. 10, 115th Cong. (2017). Whether this is justified by the deficiencies of administrative adjudication, or whether it has simply become part of a political program to get rid of as much as possible of the Dodd-Frank Act, is of course open to debate. The Bill passed the House on June 8, 2017.

This controversy about the SEC's use of the administrative process has also spawned litigation as to whether the way the SEC's ALJs are appointed and removed is consistent with the Constitution's Appointments Clause or the separation of powers, as well as whether the use of SEC adjudication comports with the Seventh Amendment. See pp. 886, 945, and 1027 below.

(7) *Other Possibilities.* Needless to say, the American way of conducting administrative adjudication is not the only way. In FIVE MODELS OF ADMINISTRATIVE ADJUDICATION, 2015 Am. J. Comp. Law 3, 6–7 (2015), Professor MICHAEL ASIMOW, in considering systems in common use around the world, says:

"There are *four key variables*. Each requires a choice. The first two variables relate to the initial decision and [agency] reconsideration phases. The second two relate to the judicial review phase.

(1) "Is the adjudicating body a combined-function agency or a separate tribunal? A combined-function agency combines investigation, prosecution, initial decisionmaking, and reconsideration. A separate tribunal conducts reconsideration but does not engage in investigation or prosecution.

(2) "Is the proceeding adversarial or inquisitorial? Adversarial proceedings resemble the trial-type process employed in U.S. or U.K.

criminal cases—meaning a lawyer-controlled proceeding before a relatively passive and independent adjudicator. The trial is sharply distinguished from the investigation phase of the case. Inquisitorial proceedings resemble European or Latin American criminal process, meaning that an investigator assembles a dossier and comes to a conclusion about guilt or innocence. In inquisitorial systems, the initial decision phase is controlled by the investigators rather than the lawyers. The initial decision provides the private party a written or oral opportunity to change the minds of the investigators. Similarly, an inquisitorial reconsideration proceeding is unstructured and controlled by the reconsidering officials. Of course, no system is purely adversarial or purely inquisitorial. Nevertheless, procedures can be arrayed on this axis and will tend to fall nearer either the adversarial or inquisitorial poles.

(3) "Is judicial review open or closed? In an open system, either party can introduce new evidence in court (in addition to the evidence introduced during earlier stages) or the court can request the parties to produce new evidence. Either party can offer new arguments that were not advanced at earlier stages, and the government can offer new reasons for its actions that were not adduced at an earlier stage. In other words, in an open system, the record does not crystallize until the judicial review stage. In a closed system, the parties cannot introduce new evidence, new reasons, or new arguments. The record has already crystallized either at the initial decision or reconsideration stage.

(4) "Does a reviewing court have generalized jurisdiction or is it a specialized administrative court?"

The most common, although not exclusive, U.S. combination of these variables (as exemplified by the FTC in Cement Institutes) is (1) combined function; (2) adversarial; (3) closed review; and (4) generalized court. The most common combination in the U.K. and Australia, reports Asimov, is the same except for the use of (1) separate tribunals to provide reconsideration. By contrast, in Japan, China, and Argentina, the usual combination is (1) combined function; (2) inquisitorial; (3) open review; and (4) generalized court. And in France and Germany, (1) combined function; (2) inquisitorial; (3) open review; and (4) specialized court. For another comparative view, this time of the United States, the United Kingdom, and Australia, see Peter Cane, Administrative Tribunals and Adjudication (2010). A useful website cataloging the various differences among the practices of U.S. administrative agencies is available at https://acus.law.stanford.edu/.

SECTION 2.   FORMAL ADJUDICATION UNDER THE APA

The provisions of the APA entitled "Adjudications," 5 U.S.C. § 554, apply only to cases of "adjudication required by statute to be determined on the record after opportunity for an agency hearing." This stipulation divides the universe of agency adjudications into two groups: those subject to § 554—which eventually will transfer the case to § 556 and § 557—and those not. The first group is known as formal adjudication because those parts of the APA specify a considerable set of procedures to be followed. The other group is called, not surprisingly, informal adjudication.

Since adjudications are, generally speaking, subject to the demands of due process, we might ask whether making a distinction between formal and informal adjudication, and linking that distinction to the terms of other statutes, is consistent with the constitutional demand. It was thought at the time the APA was enacted that the constitutional demand of due process sometimes required a full trial-type process, and sometimes not. What the Constitution was thought to require often turned on the various traditional processes that had developed in different corners of the law, and those processes were reflected in the statutes enacted in each area. Whether looked at as a matter of statute or as a matter of the Constitution, then, it was common to think that some administrative decisions would be made after something resembling a courtroom trial, and some would not. (For today's treatment of due process, see below, starting at p. 544.

Reliance on the requirements called for by existing statutes to determine the degree of formality meant, of course, that the APA would not have a revolutionary impact on existing practice. At the same time, there were complaints about existing practice—many of them coming out of the potentially "biased" impact of administrative structures as discussed in the preceding section. Indeed, formal adjudication was the form of administrative proceeding on which the APA's drafters lavished the greatest attention. Theirs, then, was a reformist effort—to start with the existing procedures and regularize and improve them.

Formal adjudication might be schematically represented as follows:

FLOW OF FORMAL ADJUDICATION IN AN AGENCY SETTING

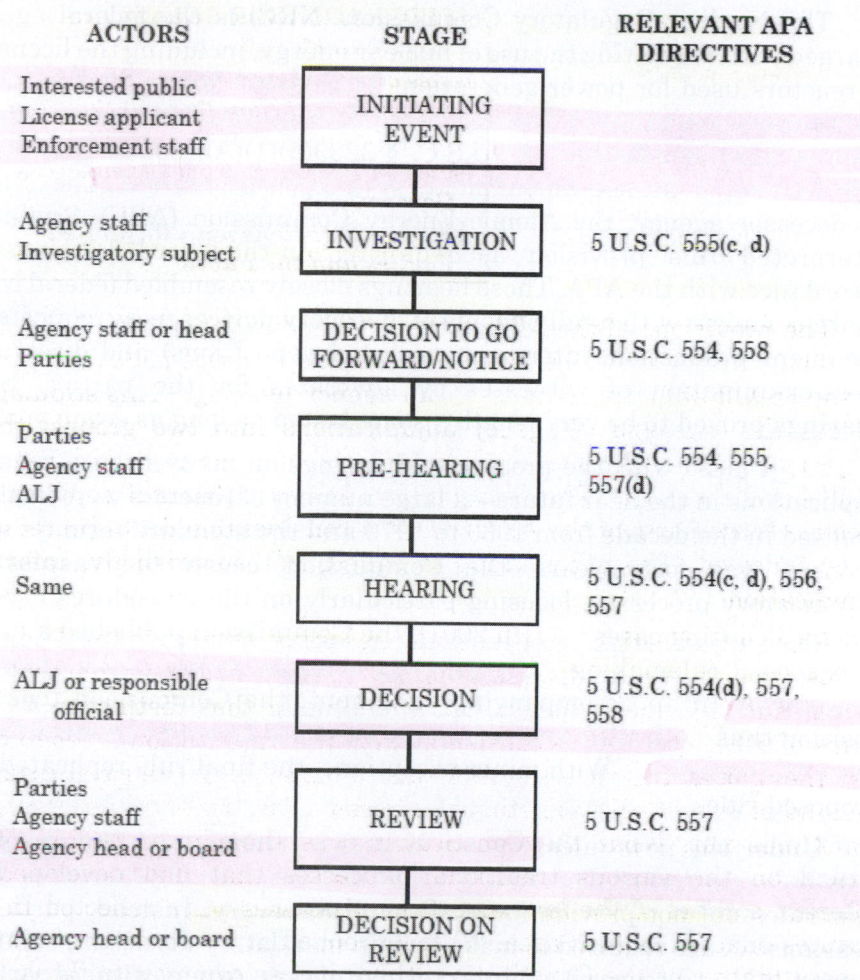

ACTORS	STAGE	RELEVANT APA DIRECTIVES
Interested public License applicant Enforcement staff	INITIATING EVENT	
Agency staff Investigatory subject	INVESTIGATION	5 U.S.C. 555(c, d)
Agency staff or head Parties	DECISION TO GO FORWARD/NOTICE	5 U.S.C. 554, 558
Parties Agency staff ALJ	PRE-HEARING	5 U.S.C. 554, 555, 557(d)
Same	HEARING	5 U.S.C. 554(c, d), 556, 557
ALJ or responsible official	DECISION	5 U.S.C. 554(d), 557, 558
Parties Agency staff Agency head or board	REVIEW	5 U.S.C. 557
Agency head or board	DECISION ON REVIEW	5 U.S.C. 557

We might, preliminarily, notice three things apparent in this diagram. First, administrative adjudication, as its name suggests, bears a family resemblance to adjudication as we know it in the courts. Second, there are specific APA provisions applicable to various stages of the process;

the generality of "family resemblance" is not going to substitute for an investigation of the statutory particulars. And third, the statute pays particular attention to who it is that carries out the various processes of adjudication. Perhaps the structural organization of adjudication specified by the APA helps answers some of the concerns left open by the due process analysis of Cement Institute.

CITIZENS AWARENESS NETWORK, INC. v. UNITED STATES

United States Court of Appeals for the First Circuit (2004).
391 F.3d 338.

■ SELYA, CIRCUIT JUDGE.

The Nuclear Regulatory Commission (NRC) is the federal agency charged with regulating the use of nuclear energy, including the licensing of reactors used for power generation. The Atomic Energy Act requires the Commission to hold a hearing "upon the request of any person whose interest may be affected," 42 U.S.C. § 2239(a)(1)(A), before granting a new license, a license amendment, or a license renewal. The NRC's predecessor agency, the Atomic Energy Commission (AEC), originally interpreted this provision as requiring on-the-record hearings in accordance with the APA. These hearings closely resembled federal court trials, complete with a full panoply of discovery devices (e.g., requests for document production, interrogatories, and depositions) and direct and cross-examination of witnesses by advocates for the parties. Such hearings proved to be very lengthy; some lasted as long as seven years.

. . . [F]aced with the prospect of hearings on many license renewal applications in the near future—a large number of reactors were initially licensed in the decade from 1960 to 1970 and the standard term for such licenses was forty years—the Commission began to reassess its adjudicatory processes, focusing particularly on the procedures used in reactor licensing cases. . . . [In 2001], the Commission published a notice of proposed rulemaking . . . suggesting a major revision of its hearing procedures. In an accompanying statement, the Commission took the position that . . . § 2239 does not require reactor licensing proceedings to be on the record. . . . With minor exceptions, the final rule replicated the proposed rule . . .

Under the new rules, reactor licensing hearings are, for the most part, to be conducted according to a less elaborate set of procedures. [The new rules do] not provide for traditional discovery. Instead, parties in hearings . . . are required to make certain mandatory disclosures (akin to "open file" . . . discovery) anent expert witnesses, expert witness reports, relevant documents, data compilations, and claims of privilege. The hearings themselves also differ. . . . Parties are allowed to submit proposed questions in advance of the hearing, but the presiding officer is under no compulsion to pose them. Parties are not allowed to submit proposed questions during the hearing unless requested to do so by the presiding officer. Cross-examination is not available as of right, although a party may request permission to conduct cross-examination that it deems "necessary to ensure the development of an adequate record for decision." 10 C.F.R. § 2.1204.

The petitioners[, several public interest groups,] . . . took umbrage at these changes and brought these petitions for judicial review. . . . The mainstay of the petitioners' challenge is the proposition that the new rules exceed the Commission's statutory authority. The petitioners start with the premise that 42 U.S.C. § 2239 requires the NRC to conduct licensing hearings on the record, that is, in strict accordance with the relevant provisions of the APA. In their view, the new rules fail to satisfy that requirement and, therefore, must be pole-axed. . . . Section 2239 requires the Commission, "upon the request of any person whose interest may be affected" by certain agency actions, to hold "a hearing." It does not explicitly require that the hearing be on the record. We have held, however, that the degree of formality that a hearing must afford does not necessarily turn on the presence or absence of an explicit statutory directive. If, even absent such a directive, the nature of the hearing that Congress intended to grant is clear, then that intention governs. Seacoast Anti-Pollution League v. Costle, 572 F.2d 872, 876 (1st Cir. 1978). We assume arguendo, favorably to the petitioners, that the Seacoast rule still obtains.[1]

The petitioners advance several arguments for holding that Congress, in enacting § 2239, purposed to require on-the-record hearings in reactor licensing cases. In addition to canvassing the legislative history and cataloging the relevant amendments to the statute, they point out that for approximately four decades the NRC and its predecessor agency, the AEC, interpreted the statute as requiring on-the-record hearings in reactor licensing proceedings. In response, the NRC highlights the ambiguity of the statute and attempts to situate the latest round of changes in a larger history of procedural experimentation. . . . For years, the courts of appeals have avoided the question of whether § 2239 requires reactor licensing hearings to be on the record. We too decline to resolve this issue. Because the new rules adopted by the Commission meet the requirements of the APA it does not matter what type of hearing the NRC is required to conduct in reactor licensing cases. . . .

We exercise plenary review over the Commission's compliance with the APA. The APA lays out only the most skeletal framework for conducting agency adjudications, leaving broad discretion to the affected agencies in formulating detailed procedural rules. In specific terms, the APA requires only that the agency provide a hearing before a neutral decisionmaker and allow each party an opportunity "to present his case

---

[1]   [Ed.] The First Circuit subsequently rejected the Seacoast rule in Dominion Energy Brayton Point LLC v. Johnson, 443 F.3d 12 (1st Cir. 2006). See p. 528 below.

or defense by oral or documentary evidence, to submit rebuttal evidence, and to conduct such cross-examination as may be required for a full and true disclosure of the facts." 5 U.S.C. § 556(d).

The petitioners urge that the magnitude of the risks involved in reactor licensing proceedings warrant the imposition of a more elaborate set of safeguards. It is beyond cavil, however, that, short of constitutional constraints, a court may not impose procedural requirements in administrative cases above and beyond those mandated by statute (here, the APA). Vermont Yankee Nuclear Power Corp. v. Natural Res. Def. Council, Inc., 435 U.S. 519, 543–44 (1978). [See p. 295.] Accordingly, we are not at liberty to impress on the Commission (or any other agency, for that matter) a procedural regime not mandated by Congress. The NRC's new rules will, therefore, succumb to the petitioners' . . . attack only if they fail to provide the minimal procedural safeguards actually demanded by the APA.

We turn now from the general to the particular. The rulemaking at issue here effected several changes in the Commission's procedures. The petitioners focus their challenge on two aspects of the newly minted process. First, they object to the Commission's decision to eliminate discovery. Second, they complain about the Commission's decision to circumscribe the availability of cross-examination. Because these are the only issues on which the petitioners have offered developed argumentation, we confine our analysis to those portions of the new rules.

We begin with the question of whether the new rules fall below the APA's minimum requirements by eliminating discovery. The Commission points out, and the petitioners do not seriously contest, that the APA does not explicitly require the provision of any discovery devices in formal adjudications. See 5 U.S.C. § 556. Thus, if the APA requires the Commission to provide any discovery to satisfy the standards for formal adjudications, that discovery must be necessary either to effectuate some other procedural right guaranteed by the APA or to ensure an adequate record for judicial review. The petitioners suggest that discovery is necessary to realize the right of citizen-intervenors to present their case and submit an informed rebuttal. If discovery is unavailable, this thesis runs, citizen-intervenors will be unable to gather the evidence needed to support their contentions and, thus, will be shut out of meaningful participation in licensing hearings.

This thesis is composed of more cry than wool. The petitioners argue as if the new rules have eliminated all access to information from opposing parties—but that is a gross distortion. The new rules provide meaningful access to information from adverse parties in the form of a system of mandatory disclosure. Although there might well be less information available to citizen-intervenors under the new rules, the difference is one of degree. There is simply no principled way that we can say that the difference occasioned by replacing traditional discovery methods with mandatory disclosure is such that citizen-intervenors are left with no means of adequately presenting their case.

Nor do we think that full-dress discovery is essential to ensure a satisfactory record for judicial review. The Commission's final decision in any hearing must survive review based on the evidence adduced in the hearing. 5 U.S.C. § 556(e). The applicant bears the burden of proof in any licensing hearing, id. § 556(d), and it will have every incentive to proffer sufficient information to allow the agency to reach a reasoned decision. That same quantum of information should be adequate for a reviewing court to determine whether the agency's action is supportable.

To say more on this point would be to paint the lily. There is simply no discovery-linked conflict between the new rules and the APA's on-the-record adjudication requirement. The petitioners' first line of argument is, therefore, a dead end.

Turning to cross-examination, the petitioners' contentions fare no better: the new rules meet the APA's requirements. . . . It is important to understand that, contrary to the petitioners' importunings, the new rules do not extirpate cross-examination. Rather, they restrict its use to situations in which it is "necessary to ensure an adequate record for decision." 10 C.F.R. § 2.1204. The legitimacy of this restriction must be weighed in light of the fact that the APA does not provide an absolute right of cross-examination in on-the-record hearings. The APA affords a right only to such cross-examination as may be necessary for a full and fair adjudication of the facts. Equally to the point, the party seeking to cross-examine bears the burden of showing that cross-examination is in fact necessary.

The Commission represents that, despite the difference in language, it interprets the standard for allowing cross-examination under the new rules to be equivalent to the APA standard. . . . Given the Commission's stated interpretation, the new rules on cross-examination cannot be termed inconsistent with the dictates of the APA. Nor do we see how cross-examination that is not "necessary to ensure an adequate record for decision" could be necessary to ensure appropriate judicial review. . . . We do, however, add a caveat. The APA does require that cross-examination be available when "required for a full and true disclosure of the facts." If the new procedures are to comply in practice with the APA, cross-examination must be allowed in appropriate instances. Should the agency's administration of the new rules contradict its present representations or otherwise flout this principle, nothing in this opinion will inoculate the rules against future challenges.

Procedural flexibility is one of the great hallmarks of the administrative process-and it is a feature that courts must be reluctant to curtail. Though the Commission's new rules may approach the outer bounds of what is permissible under the APA, we find the statute sufficiently broad to accommodate them. Similarly, the Commission's judgments as to when its procedures need fine-tuning and how they should be retooled are ones to which we accord great respect. We cannot say that the Commission's desire for more expeditious adjudications is unreasonable, nor can we say that the changes embodied in the new rules are an eccentric or a plainly inadequate means for achieving the Commission's goals.

■ LIPEZ, CIRCUIT JUDGE, concurring.

Although I concur fully in Judge Selya's thoughtful and comprehensive opinion, I write separately to describe some oddities about this case which should not go unnoticed. The basic proposition of Judge Selya's decision is indisputably correct: the new rules promulgated by the NRC to reduce the level of formality in reactor licensing proceedings comply with the "on-the-record" requirements of the [APA]. Yet that legal proposition was largely an afterthought of the NRC in the effort to justify its new rules. Instead, the NRC principally argued in the long run-up to this case that 42 U.S.C. § 2239, which simply requires the Commission to hold a hearing "upon the request of any person whose interest may be affected" before granting a new license, did not invoke the requirements for formal adjudication (commonly referred to as "on-the-record" hearings) under the APA. . . .

The terminology for hearings under the APA can be imprecise and confusing. The everyday meaning of terms like "formal" and "informal" sometimes creeps into the discussion, although those terms have specific, functional definitions under the APA. As Judge Selya notes, the terms "formal" and "on-the-record" are generally used as shorthand for hearings that must be conducted pursuant to the requirements of 5 U.S.C. §§ 554, 556, and 557 of the APA. Other terms, too, are sometimes used to refer to such procedures—"trial-type" and "quasi-judicial." These vague and indefinite terms are particularly mischievous because they evoke images of courtroom trials, and they have contributed to the false impression that the APA's requirement of on-the-record hearings involves procedures more akin to civil trials than is actually the case.

To be specific, § 554 requires that, in cases of an "adjudication required by statute to be determined on the record after opportunity for an agency hearing," the agency must follow the procedures outlined in §§ 556 and 557. Although the statutory text at issue here is itself rather pithy, these procedures can be usefully condensed into the following ten points:

1. The agency must give notice of legal authority and matters of fact and law asserted. § 554(b).

2. The oral evidentiary hearing must be presided over by an officer who can be disqualified for bias. § 556(b).

3. Presiding officers cannot have ex parte communications. §§ 554(d), 557(d)(1).

4. Parties are entitled to be represented by attorneys. § 555(b).

5.   The proponent of an order has the burden of proof. § 556(d).

6.   A party is entitled to present oral or documentary evidence. § 556(d).

7.   A party is entitled "to conduct such cross-examination as may be required for a full and true disclosure of the facts." § 556(d).

8.   Orders can be issued only on consideration of the record of the hearing. § 556(d).

9.   The transcript of testimony and exhibits is the exclusive record for decision and shall be made available to parties. § 556(e).

10.   The decision must include "findings and conclusions, and the reasons or basis therefor, on all the material issues of fact, law, or discretion presented on the record." § 557(c)(3)(A).

Strikingly, there is no reference to discovery in these statutory provisions of the APA, and cross-examination is assured only if necessary "for a full and true disclosure of the facts." 5 U.S.C. § 556(d). Most of these provisions relate to the conduct and responsibilities of the presiding officer or the basis for agency orders (on the record). Only a few relate to the conduct of the hearing itself. These APA requirements leave agencies with a great deal of flexibility in tailoring on-the-record hearing procedures to suit their perceived needs. . . .

From the beginning of its proposed rulemaking, the NRC repeatedly referred to the procedures outlined in the new regulations as "informal," as opposed to the outmoded formal procedures of the past. The clear implication was that the new informal procedures would not meet the APA's requirements for formal, on-the-record hearings. Thus, the NRC believed that it first had to establish that its authorizing statute, the Atomic Energy Act (AEA), did not require it to hold on-the-record hearings for reactor licensing. . . .

The NRC's belated recognition that the new licensing procedures might in fact comply with the on-the-record requirements of the APA is all the more surprising because sources contemporaneous with the APA's passage suggest that flexibility has always been a hallmark of the APA, and that agencies have always had considerable discretion to structure on-the-record hearings to suit their particular needs. This flexibility is nowhere more evident than in determining the role of cross-examination in on-the-record hearings. . . .

The Attorney General's Manual on the Administrative Procedure Act (1947) is a "key document" for interpreting the APA. The Manual begins by stressing the general importance of cross-examination in on-the-record hearings, cautioning that "it is clear that the 'right to present his case or defense by oral or documentary evidence' does not extend to presenting evidence in affidavit or other written form so as to deprive the agency or opposing parties of opportunity for cross-examination." . . . The Attorney General's Manual goes on, however, to acknowledge that the general opportunity to cross-examine is subject to restrictions which become more salient as the complexity of the hearing's subject matter increases. On this point, the Manual quotes from the Report of the House Committee on the Judiciary on the APA . . . The Attorney General's Manual and the House Report serve as good indicators that Congress, when it passed the APA, understood that agencies needed a considerable amount of flexibility in fashioning hearing procedures for on-the-record hearings. Despite the frequent use of terms like "trial-type" and "quasi-judicial" over the years to refer to on-the-record hearings, agencies have always been able to adapt their procedures for on-the-record hearings under the APA. . . .

NOTES ON CITIZEN AWARENESS NETWORK'S APPROACH TO THE APA

(1) *How "Skeletal" Is Formal Adjudication?* Judge Selya characterizes the APA's provisions for on-the-record adjudication as "skeletal." Does this accord with your reading of the relevant statutory provisions, §§ 554, 556, and 557? Even if the text of these provisions is minimal and flexible, does the First Circuit's account fairly capture the understanding and intent behind these provisions? In his concurrence, Judge Lipez offers a list of ten requirements that he concludes the APA requires for on-the-record adjudication. Does he provide a less flexible view of on-the-record adjudication, or do his ten requirements in practice impose only limited constraint?

(2) RICHARD PIERCE, WAITING FOR VERMONT YANKEE II, 57 Admin. L. Rev. 669, 676–77 (2005): "The First Circuit concluded that the provision in the NRC rules that confers on a presiding officer the power to grant a motion for cross-examination is legally equivalent to the APA formal adjudication right to 'such cross-examination as may be necessary for a full and fair adjudication of the facts.' That conclusion is inconsistent with the NRC's description of its rules and with the entire purpose of the rules. The NRC emphasized that it expected its presiding officers to grant motions for cross-examination only in 'rare circumstance[s].' [The NRC] expected its presiding officers to distinguish between the many disputes with respect to legislative facts that are not appropriate for cross-examination and the rare disputes with respect to adjudicative facts that are appropriate for cross-examination. It illustrated the latter class of disputes by referring to only two classes of disputes that might justify the grant of a motion to cross-examine a witness under its new rules: '(a) [i]ssues of material fact relating to the occurrence of a past activity, where the credibility of an eyewitness may reasonably be expected to be at issue, and/or (b) issues of motive or intent of the party or eyewitness material to the resolution of the contested factual matter.' The NRC noted that few licensing proceedings were likely to raise issues of that type 'such that cross-examination is an appropriate tool for issue resolution.' If the NRC had prevailed on its theory of the case, it could have made good

on its commitment to allow cross-examination rarely, if at all, in licensing cases. . . .

"The First Circuit's description of the qualified right of cross-examination that it determined to be applicable to NRC licensing proceedings differs dramatically from the rare right to cross-examination described by the NRC. The court emphasized that a court, not the NRC, will determine when cross-examination is appropriate in a licensing proceeding."

As the title of Professor Pierce's article suggests, the approach to cross-examination taken in Citizen Awareness Network can be contrasted with (and partly understood in light of) the Supreme Court's earlier decision in the Vermont Yankee case, see p. 295.

NOTES ON OTHER FEATURES OF "FORMAL ADJUDICATION"

(1) *Hearsay Evidence.* The APA says: "Any oral or documentary evidence may be received, but the agency as a matter of policy shall provide for the exclusion of irrelevant, immaterial, or unduly repetitious evidence." 5 U.S.C. § 556(d). For agencies where there is no further restriction in their statutes or regulations, this standard is understood—and rightly so, in light of its legislative history—to provide for the admission of hearsay evidence as a routine matter, although the weight of such evidence remains open to argument. Even in ordinary courts, hearsay rules have much less bite when (as in agency adjudication) there is no jury. But more can be said: Richard J. Pierce, Use of the Federal Rules of Evidence in Federal Agency Adjudications, 39 Admin. L. Rev. 1, 17–19 (1987): ". . . [I]t makes little sense to take the risk of erroneous exclusion of reliable evidence through application of highly technical exclusionary rules in the context of agency adjudications. . . . Agencies and ALJs are required to state the bases for their findings of fact. Their findings are then subject to judicial review under the substantial evidence standard. If an agency finding is based on unreliable evidence, the agency's action is reversed. Thus, there is a mechanism available in agency adjudications independent of rulings on the admissibility of evidence to insure that agency findings are based only on reliable evidence."

(2) *A Statement of Findings and Conclusions.* Another feature of APA on-the-record adjudication is § 557(c)'s requirement that agency decisions "shall include a statement of . . . findings and conclusions, and the reasons or basis therefor, on *all* the material issues of fact, law, or discretion presented on the record." (emphasis added). This might seem to demand a compulsive attention to detail, but when put to it, courts are frequently less demanding than such statutory phrases suggest, stressing simply the need to understand the administrative decision. A communication (in whatever form) that indicates precisely what has been decided will suffice, provided that even if "the findings of the Commission . . . leave much to be desired . . . the path which it followed can be discerned." Colorado Interstate Gas Co. v. Fed. Power Comm'n, 324 U.S. 581 (1945). Courts have also noted the practical difference between the agency that renders relatively few decisions in a year, each of which may have substantial precedential significance, and

the agency given the task of processing thousands upon thousands of particularistic cases. As Judge Easterbrook pointed out in Stephens v. Heckler, 766 F.2d 284 (7th Cir. 1985), regarding the enormous job of processing claims for disability benefits, when agency decisionmakers "slow down to write better opinions, that holds up the queue and prevents deserving people from receiving benefits."

At the same time, mere conclusory statements or statements that fail to identify what the agency decided will not do. Armstrong v. Commodity Futures Trading Comm'n, 12 F.3d 401 (3rd Cir. 1993), involved a decision of the CFTC concluding that Martin Armstrong controlled corporations found to have violated Commission regulations and holding him individually responsible for the violations. Rather than issue a separate statement, the CFTC had summarily affirmed the ALJ's decision finding Armstrong guilty, stating "[o]ur review of the record and the briefs submitted by the parties establishes that the ALJ reached a substantially correct result . . . [and] that the parties have not raised important questions of law or policy concerning the ALJ's findings of fact and conclusions." But it added that the decision should not be cited as precedent or considered "an expression of the Commission's views on the issues raised." The Third Circuit held this mode of proceeding to be a violation of § 557(c): "Summarily affirming the ALJ's opinion as 'substantially correct' is insufficient because it does not permit intelligent appellate review. . . . We hold that a summary affirmance of all or part of an ALJ's opinion must leave no guesswork regarding what the agency has adopted."

The appeals court found a second § 557(c) violation in the failure of both the ALJ's decision and the CFTC's opinion to address the requirements of the governing statute, § 13(b) of the Commodity Exchange Act: "The only theory under which Armstrong was charged with individual liability in the second complaint was as a controlling person as defined in § 13(b) . . . We do not understand how a statement of conclusion on a material issue of law can be adequate [under § 557(c)] without mentioning the statutory provision or its language. Section 13(b) requires at least two findings before concluding a respondent is liable as a controlling person: (1) that the respondent controlled a violator; and (2) that the controlling person did not act in good faith or knowingly induced the violation. . . . [Although] the Commission's appeal brief recites evidence in the record from which the ALJ could have found that Armstrong knowingly induced the violations[,] . . . there is still no finding by the ALJ or the Commission that Armstrong did knowingly induce the violations. Finally, and most importantly, there is no conclusion that Armstrong is liable as a controlling person under § 13(b). Without a conclusion that Armstrong is liable for violations with which he was charged, Armstrong may not be individually penalized."

In the words of Judge Henry J. Friendly, ("Some Kind of Hearing," 123 U. Pa. L. Rev. 1267, 1292 (1975)): "A written statement of reasons, almost essential if there is to be judicial review, is desirable on many other grounds. The necessity for justification is a powerful preventive of wrong decisions. The requirement also tends to effectuate intra-agency uniformity. . . . A statement of reasons may even make a decision somewhat more acceptable to a losing claimant."

(3) GUNDERSON V. DEP'T OF LABOR, 601 F.3d 1013 (10th Cir. 2010), involved a coal miner's claim for benefits under the Black Lung Benefits Act. The District Director of the Department of Labor's Office of Workers' Compensation Programs granted the claim, and the coal company that had employed the miner appealed to an ALJ. After a hearing, the ALJ rejected the miner's claim, finding that the conflicting doctors' reports were all "well-reasoned," "well-documented," and "well-supported," and entitled to equal weight. The ALJ therefore denied the claim on the ground that Mr. Gunderson had not met his burden of proving that his chronic pulmonary disease was caused by his work as a coal miner. The Department of Labor's Benefits Review Board affirmed the ALJ's decision.

The Tenth Circuit reversed: "Section 557(c)(3)(A) . . . requires an agency's adjudicative decision to be 'accompanied by a clear and satisfactory explication of the basis on which it rests.' Barren Creek Coal Co. v. Witmer, 111 F.3d 352, 356 (3d Cir. 1997). This duty of explanation has added importance for cases in which medical or scientific evidence has been presented. . . . [Agency] expertise allows agencies to relax the rules of evidence because they are deemed to 'have the skill needed to handle evidence that might mislead a jury. They have a corresponding obligation to *use* that skill when evaluating technical evidence.' Peabody Coal Co. v. McCandless, 255 F.3d 465, 469 (7th Cir. 2001) (citation omitted). [Here,] we cannot discern 'the reasons or basis,' 5 U.S.C. § 557(c)(3)(A), for the ALJ's rejection of Mr. Gunderson's claim . . . [F]rom the ALJ's statement that the conflicting opinions are 'evenly balanced, and should receive equal weight,' we cannot tell how he evaluated their opinions. The mere fact that equally qualified experts gave conflicting testimony does not authorize the ALJ to avoid the scientific controversy by declaring a tie. In reaching this conclusion, we reject . . . [the] contention that requiring a more detailed, scientifically-grounded explanation from the ALJ sets the bar too high. The ALJ's task is not to resolve general scientific controversies, but instead to determine the facts of the case at hand and apply the law accordingly. This is a task that is routinely assigned to judges and to juries . . . Moreover, with regard to disputes concerning the existence and causes of pneumoconiosis, an ALJ has the benefit of . . . Department of Labor [regulations, and] . . . may properly rely on those regulations when assessing scientific testimony."

Judge O'Brien dissented: "Even though intimately familiar with the issues and knowledgeable as to the scientific principles presented in a case, an . . . ALJ is not an expert. The ALJ is not expected, nor permitted, to meld expert opinion into his own unified theory, which he then independently applies to the facts. And it is beyond the ken of an ALJ to resolve a scientific debate. Instead, . . . [w]hen expert opinion is diametrically opposed, the ALJ must, based on all of the evidence, make a reasoned choice, if possible, as to which expert opinion is more probably correct. But a principled choice cannot always be achieved. . . . This is such a case. When he could do so, the ALJ made credibility choices among the experts; when he could not, he candidly confessed his inability. . . . [T]he ALJ [need not] do more than explain why expert opinion is in equipoise and hold the proponent of an issue to his burden of proof."

Did the majority in Gunderson ask too much of a non-expert ALJ? Or is Judge O'Brien's approach at odds with the reasoned explanation requirement embodied in § 557(c)?

(4) *Who Can Participate?* The APA draws a clear distinction between those who can participate in rulemaking proceedings and those who can participate in adjudications. In notice and comment proceedings, "the agency shall give interested persons an opportunity to participate," § 553(c). "Person" is in turn defined to include both individuals and organizations, except for the agency itself—a very large and undefined group of potential commenters. In formal adjudications, by contrast, the participants are called "parties," and "party" is defined as "a person or agency named or admitted as a party. . . in an agency proceeding, and a person or agency admitted by an agency as a party for limited purposes[.]" § 551(3). While this is, confessedly, a somewhat unhelpful definition, it does tell us two things: first, agencies can be "parties," and second, we should expect to see some formal process determining (and limiting) who will be "admitted as a party."

Taking the first point first, not only can agencies be parties—they routinely are one of the parties. In the Cement Institute case, for example, the FTC brought and prosecuted the complaint before the ALJ—becoming one party—and the complaint named a long list of entities that assertedly had violated the FTC Act—and they became the opposing parties. But not all agency proceedings have this form. In the licensing proceedings whose rules are at stake in Citizens Awareness Network, hearings are initiated, as Judge Selya states, "upon the request of any person whose interest may be affected," 42 U.S.C. § 2239(a)(1)(A).

Once a proceeding has been initiated, with whatever parties the applicable statute suggests, the question is whether other persons or entities can also participate in the hearing or on agency review of what the ALJ decides. The greatest such status would be to intervene with full procedural rights to make motions, introduce witnesses, take appeals, and so forth. (Intervenors in ordinary court proceedings, if allowed, usually have these full rights.) Another possibility, sometimes found in agency adjudications and recognized in the APA's definition of "party," is to allow intervention for a more limited purpose. Finally, at the other end of the scale, but often still valuable to potential parties, is participation as an amicus curiae—not participating in building the record, but rather arguing, usually in a brief, as to the proper policy to apply to it.

As a matter of organizing an effective proceeding, one might consider the possible advantages to be gained from letting in additional participants—in terms of additional interests to be protected, points of view to be articulated, or non-agency sources of expertise to be accessed—against the possible disadvantages of conducting a proceeding with less clearly organized voices, and of delay. As a general result, one might expect less intervention in cases for imposing a sanction against a particular party and greater intervention in cases raising large matters of policy—but, of course, there are some cases that share both characteristics. (Indeed, if the question is largely a matter of policy, and many non-parties are allowed to submit amicus briefs, an adjudication can start to resemble a rulemaking proceeding. See, for example, F.C.C. v. Fox Television Stations, p. 1100.

As a matter of the relationship between the agencies and the courts, one has the further question of who should decide who gets to participate. The APA is silent on the matter. In the famous case of Office of Communications of the United Church of Christ v. FCC, 359 F.2d 994 (D.C. Cir. 1966), the court required the FCC to allow participation in a TV license-renewal proceeding by some viewers' groups; the FCC itself had limited participation to those who might be economically harmed by the renewal. The theory of the case was that the participation of viewers was necessary if the public interest was to be achieved; more broadly speaking, that the beneficiaries of regulation, and not just those who would be harmed, were appropriate participants in a licensing proceeding.

More recently, courts have tended to leave this procedural question to the agencies themselves. The rather free approach of the Office of Communications case itself was disapproved in Envirocare of Utah, Inc. v. Nuclear Regulatory Com., 194 F3d. 72 (D.C. Cir. 1999). There, the underlying issue concerned the licensing of companies dealing with radioactive wastes. Envirocare wanted to intervene in a proceeding that threatened to grant a license to one of its competitors on terms, said Envirocare, that were less rigorous than the terms in Envirocare's own license. The Atomic Energy Act provided that "any person whose interest may be affected" was entitled to be a party in the proceeding. The Commission ruled that this language referred to parties with public health and safety interests, and not to the interests of economic competitors. The court, for its part, found the statutory language to be ambiguous, and then relied on Vermont Yankee [p. 295] and on Chevron [p. 1129] as supporting agency discretion in these matters.

Of course, one might think that the Office of Communications of the United Church of Christ is a more attractive intervenor than Envirocare of Utah, Inc. If the applicable organic statute does talk about who can participate, it is always possible that a court will find the statutory language to be unambiguous, and therefore binding on the agency. But under current doctrine, potential parties are more likely to have recourse to the procedural rules and practices of the agency involved.

(It is worth noting that the right to participate in an agency proceeding is different from the right to seek judicial review of it—that is, different from "standing" in court. As to the standards for that, see p. 1300 within).

LUDWIG v. ASTRUE

United States Court of Appeals for the Ninth Circuit (2011).
681 F.3d 1047.

■ KLEINFELD, SENIOR CIRCUIT JUDGE.

We address whether an administrative law judge's handling of an ex parte contact was error, and if so, whether it was harmless.

I.   Facts

Ludwig claimed social security disability,[1] his claim was denied, and his appeal to the district court was unsuccessful.

A.   The Medical Evidence

Ludwig told the Social Security Administration in his May 2006 application that he could not work because of epilepsy, bipolar disease, depression, insomnia, and social anxiety. He had not worked since getting fired at his last job as a cook earlier the same year. He had previously worked on a fishing tender, and as a welder and a cook. In his initial interview, Ludwig attributed his inability to work to his psychiatric problems, not his physical condition. But at his hearing, he claimed disabling arthritis in his knees, hips, and ankles, and degenerative disease in his low back. He testified that he had severe pain if he lifted as much as 15 pounds.

Ludwig had extensive medical records from correctional facilities and community health facilities. He had complained of knee problems for ten years, starting when he was in military service. A year before his social security application, he told a medical provider that he could "press 1,000 pounds," and exercised. His description of his symptoms, together with X-rays and MRIs, led to a diagnosis of chronic pain in both knees and possible tears in the meniscus of the left knee. In 2007, the Department of Veterans Affairs (VA) awarded Ludwig ten percent service-connected disability compensation on account of his knee. Two months before Ludwig's social security hearing, a VA examining physician described Ludwig's knee problems as "minimal." Around the same time, a chiropractic report said that Ludwig was walking normally.

Ludwig also complained of back pain. On June 14, 2007, Ludwig told a medical provider that he had been experiencing low back pain since trying to pick up a dishwasher the previous month. Two weeks later, he reported to a different examiner that he had endured chronic back pain since straining his back eleven years earlier, but had suffered no recent injury. He was diagnosed with lumbar strain and mild disc herniation. Ludwig said to one medical provider that Vicodin was "the only thing that helped before" with the back pain, but was instead prescribed

---

[1]   Disability under the Social Security Act is defined as the "inability to engage in any substantial gainful activity by reason of any medically determinable physical or mental impairment which can be expected to result in death or which has lasted or can be expected to last for a continuous period of not less than 12 months." 42 U.S.C. § 423(d)(1)(A)

methadone. The prescription was later changed to morphine sulphate, after Ludwig complained of side effects from the methadone. Physical therapy was prescribed, but Ludwig did not complete the sessions.

Ludwig was diagnosed with bipolar disorder in 2002. Medication successfully controlled it. Ludwig reported to his doctor in early 2006, the same year he applied for social security disability benefits, that, so long as he stayed away from alcohol, his medication kept him reasonably stable. After he got fired from his job as a cook, he enrolled in a drug and alcohol treatment program.

He also had a seizure disorder, controlled by medication. An emergency department record shows that Ludwig was admitted to the emergency room in March 2006, after having had a "witnessed seizure while working at the local Denny's restaurant." He testified at his social security hearing that this was an anxiety attack, not a seizure. But he also testified to far more frequent and recent seizures than what he had told his medical providers.

Ludwig's social security application was denied in July 2006. The Social Security Administration's medical consultant, after reviewing Ludwig's records, concluded that Ludwig's mental impairments caused mild restrictions and difficulties. He opined that Ludwig could lift or carry 25 pounds frequently, 50 pounds occasionally, stand or walk for about 6 hours in an 8-hour workday, and sit for the same amount of time. After the initial denial, Ludwig requested a hearing.

At his hearing, Ludwig testified that he could not lift more than 15 pounds without severe pain, and that it was very painful to sit for more than half an hour. But he also testified that he carried his own firewood into his cabin for heat. He testified that his bipolar disorder made it difficult for him to control his anger, and that he became anxious in crowds of more than ten people. He said he had been fired from his job at Denny's because he could not get along with his coworkers. Ludwig claimed that he suffered three or four grand mal seizures a year, the last one about a month before the hearing. He testified that his petit mal seizures occurred too frequently for him to count. But medical records from 2007 show that he claimed there were three to five year periods where he had no seizures.

B. Ex Parte Communication

Right after the hearing, and before the ALJ had issued his decision, an FBI agent told the ALJ that Ludwig was apparently faking his physical disability. The ALJ immediately sent a letter to Ludwig's lawyer, disclosing the ex parte contact. The ALJ suggested that counsel could contact the FBI agent if he wished, though he did not represent that the agent had agreed to talk to counsel:

> Shortly after your client's hearing . . . a special agent with the F.B.I. [ ] informed me that, earlier, he had observed Mr. Ludwig in the parking lot walking with normal gait and station; and

when he observed Mr. Ludwig walking inside of the Federal Courthouse (where our hearing was held) he was walking with an exaggerated limp (which I also observed as he left the hearing room).

Should you wish to inquire further, [the special agent] can be reached at the F.B.I. office at:

101 12th Ave # 329

Fairbanks, AK, 99701

Counsel responded, objecting to any weight being given to what the FBI agent had said.

Counsel asked that unless the ALJ gave assurance that no weight would be given to the ex parte communication, he receive a supplementary hearing at which counsel could cross-examine the agent. Counsel intended to address whether, among other things, the FBI agent really had observed Ludwig as he thought, since around a dozen people had been in and out of the several hearings that morning. He questioned the accuracy of the FBI agent's observations, since Ludwig's knee problem was well-documented in the medical records. Counsel also expected to ask whether his client had been under some sort of surveillance, making him recognizable to the FBI agent.

C.   The ALJ's Decision

The ALJ found that although Ludwig had a "longstanding seizure disorder," it was "controlled when he takes medication as prescribed." He noted conflicting evidence on Ludwig's physical condition, including Ludwig's claim that he could press 1,000 pounds, the chiropractor's observation that Ludwig walked normally, and evidence of damage to Ludwig's left knee.

The ALJ found that the seizure disorder and diseased tissue in the left knee were "severe" for social security purposes. As for Ludwig's back pain, the ALJ found that Ludwig's "contradictory accounts" and minimal objective findings established that Ludwig "was exaggerating symptoms." He found that Ludwig's bipolar disorder was "well controlled" so long as Ludwig took his medicine and abstained from alcohol, so it caused only "mild" restriction of activities of daily living and functioning.

The ALJ found that none of Ludwig's impairments, separately or together, met the criteria of a listed impairment, and that Ludwig had the capacity to perform "medium" work. Most importantly, the ALJ found that Ludwig was not credible, and had exaggerated how intense, persistent, and limiting his impairments were.

The decision notes that the FBI agent told the ALJ after the hearing that the agent had seen Ludwig in the parking lot "with a normal gait and station and subsequently observed the claimant walking with an exaggerated limp once inside the Federal Courthouse." The ALJ wrote that he did "not assign significant weight" to the agent's statements because the FBI agent was not familiar with Ludwig's medical history and observed Ludwig "only briefly." The ALJ did not say, as Ludwig's counsel had requested as an alternative to a supplementary hearing, that the ALJ had not assigned "any" weight to what the FBI agent told him, just that whatever weight he gave it was not "significant."

The ALJ explained that the record contained "other evidence showing [Ludwig had] exaggerated symptoms." Ludwig's testimony about his seizures was clearly exaggerated "based on what he told health providers." Ludwig had claimed for compensation purposes in March 2008 that he could walk "no more than a few yards," but had reported a month before to a medical provider that he had walked two miles in sub-zero temperatures and suffered frostbite. (Ludwig lives in Fairbanks, Alaska.) Ludwig's back and knee claims were inconsistent with his claim to health care providers that he could press 1,000 pounds. He had exaggerated various parts of his medical history to various providers. Likewise, Ludwig contradicted himself in different contexts about his claimed difficulty with social interactions. His statements that he walked for exercise, cut wood for heat, and stood for nine hours a day as a cook, contradicted his claimed physical limitations. The ALJ found that Ludwig could still work as a cook, as he had before he was fired for not getting along, and was not disabled under the Social Security Act. The district court affirmed.

II. Analysis

A. Standard of Review

. . .

B. The Ex Parte Contact

The ex parte contact in this case is troubling. Judges are supposed to get their evidence from the testimony and exhibits, not private chats. The judge should have refused to hear the ex parte communication. Ordinarily, if someone says to a judge, "Judge, you know that case you heard this morning?", a judge responds, "Don't tell me anything about it. I can't listen to evidence out of court."

The FBI agent's statements went to the heart of the case. Part of Ludwig's disability claim was his knee problem that he said made it hard to walk. He limped in the courtroom. The FBI agent told the ALJ that he saw Ludwig walking in the parking lot without limping. That is to say, the FBI agent told the ALJ privately that Ludwig was faking.

An FBI agent, by virtue of his employment, is likely to have more credibility with a trier of fact than a felon like Ludwig, with conflicting medical records and a history of substance abuse. To impeach the FBI agent, Ludwig's lawyer wanted to ask the agent in a supplementary hearing, "How do you know the person you saw in the parking lot was Ludwig?" That is a good question, and counsel doubtless had reasons for wanting to ask the FBI agent in front of the ALJ. The FBI agent was under no obligation to talk to Ludwig's attorney, and might have refused to answer his questions without a scheduled hearing. Even if the FBI agent did respond to counsel's inquiries, he would have plenty of time to improve how his answers sounded if he got a private rehearsal with claimant's counsel. Without a hearing, the ALJ would not be able to see the agent's demeanor when answering questions.

Ludwig's lawyer asked for either an assurance that the ALJ would give no weight to the ex parte communication, or else a supplementary hearing to explore what force it should have. He got neither. The ALJ said in his decision that he did not give "significant" weight to the FBI agent's information, not that he disregarded it or gave it no weight. Congress has commanded that the ALJ's decision be "on the basis of evidence adduced at the hearing," not on the basis, even in part, of private chats outside the hearing.

. . .

Allowing the FBI agent to speak to the judge outside the presence of counsel, with no opportunity for counsel to cross-examine the agent, and no assurance that the communication had no influence on the result, was error. "Notice and [a meaningful] opportunity to be heard are the hallmarks of procedural due process." Guenther v. Comm'r, 889 F.2d 882, 884 (9th Cir.1989) Though Ludwig was given notice of the evidence against him, he was not given a meaningful opportunity to be heard on it. The ALJ offered his own impeachment that the FBI agent's observation was brief and that the agent was unfamiliar with Ludwig's medical records. But Ludwig's lawyer might have done better. Where, as here, the communication is ex parte, is not disregarded by the judge, and may be subject to significant factual questions, we cannot see what justification there could be for denying a request for an evidentiary hearing. Receipt of the ex parte communication, assignment of some weight to it, and denial of a supplementary hearing to address it, was error.

C.   Harmlessness

Because the judge erred by considering the ex parte evidence without allowing a supplementary hearing, we are required to evaluate whether there was prejudice. We need not decide whether, in these circumstances, a statement that the judge disregarded the evidence would suffice to establish absence of prejudice, because the ALJ made no such statement. We do not suggest that private chats with witnesses are purged of any taint by a rote recitation that they were given "no" weight. But here we do not have even that assurance. No "significant" weight, perhaps a more candid statement than "no" weight, carries a negative pregnant, that the communication received some weight.

. . . Reversal on account of error is not automatic, but requires a determination of prejudice. . . .

[T]he factors that inform a reviewing court's "harmless-error" determination are various, potentially involving, among other case-specific factors, an estimation of the likelihood that the result would have been different, an awareness of what body (jury, lower court, administrative agency) has the authority to reach that result, a consideration of the error's likely effects on the perceived fairness, integrity, or public reputation of judicial proceedings, and a hesitancy to generalize too broadly about particular kinds of errors when the specific factual circumstances in which the error arises may well make all the difference. Shinseki v. Sanders, 556 U.S. 396, 411–12 (2009).

. . . [W]e conclude that there was no prejudice from the error. The contradictions between what Ludwig said when he testified in his disability hearing, and what he had said on other occasions, were dramatic. He had to have spoken falsely for many years to medical personnel for him to be speaking truthfully at his hearing. Considering the record as a whole, and the ALJ's explanation of his decision, we are convinced that Ludwig has not demonstrated that the decision would have been any different without the ex parte communication.

How could the ALJ give some weight to the FBI agent's communication, but not a "significant" enough amount to affect the outcome? Any judge with an adequate amount of humility makes many decisions about which he has varying degrees of confidence in his own judgment. Learning after a firm conviction has been formed that one's conviction is supported by additional evidence can affect the judge's level of confidence in his decision, without affecting the outcome of the decision. The ALJ's decision, and the record of Ludwig's contradictions, make it plain that the ALJ would have reached the same conclusion— that Ludwig was fit to resume work like his last job as a cook—had the FBI agent not spoken to him about his observations of Ludwig.

An ex parte contact can be quite egregious without being prejudicial. In the absence of actual prejudice from the error, we are required . . . to conclude that the ex parte communication does not entitle Ludwig to a reversal.

. . .

Affirmed.

NOTES ON THE INTEGRITY OF THE RECORD

(1) **The Exclusive Record.** The Ludwig case was decided using the due process clause, but it is hard to see that it would be any different if it applied APA § 554(d): "The employee who presides at the reception of evidence . . . may not (1) consult a person or party on a fact in issue, unless on notice and opportunity for all parties to participate" or APA § 556(e): "The transcript of testimony and exhibits, together with all papers and requests filed in the proceeding, constitutes the exclusive record for decision. . . ."

(2)   ALJs, being human, are going to make mistakes just like the rest of us do. A rule of harmless error seems to be a sensible recognition of the need to conserve society's resources in the face of human frailty. But in a proceeding whose hallmark is that it is "on the record," learning of relevant facts through a conversation off the record is not just "another error," and Judge Kleinfeld is clear that the ALJ should have acted differently. If that is so, should there simply be a per se rule that, in situations like this one, a new proceeding is warranted?

(3)   *What About Expertise?* In SEACOAST ANTI-POLLUTION LEAGUE V. COSTLE, 572 F.2d 872 (1st Cir. 1978), the Public Service Company of New Hampshire (PSCO) had sought a permit to discharge heated water into the Hampton-Seabrook Estuary, which runs into the Gulf of Maine. Water taken from the Gulf would be run through PSCO's proposed nuclear generating station to remove waste heat generated by the reactor; it would then be discharged back into the Gulf 39 degrees Fahrenheit warmer than at intake. Occasional discharges would be as hot as 120 degrees Fahrenheit, during a "backflushing" process intended to kill any organisms living in the intake system. Section 301 of the Federal Water Pollution Control Act (FWPCA, more commonly referred to today as the Clean Water Act or CWA) prohibits the discharge of any pollutant—and heat is a pollutant—without obtaining an EPA permit. PSCO's proposed cooling system would result in discharge of water hotter than EPA's effluent standard for heat; therefore, PSCO applied for an exemption under § 316 as well as a discharge permit under § 402. To qualify for the exemption, it had to demonstrate that the applicable effluent standard was "more stringent than necessary to assure the projection [sic] and propagation of a balanced, indigenous population of shellfish, fish, and wildlife in and on the body of water."

The EPA Regional Administrator initially approved PSCO's application, then reversed his decision after holding a public hearing. PSCO appealed to the EPA Administrator, who convened a panel of six in-house advisors and ultimately approved PSCO's application.

"Petitioners [opponents of the power plant] object to the Administrator's use of a panel of EPA scientists to assist him in reviewing the Regional Administrator's initial decision. . . . The Administrator is charged with making highly technical decisions in fields far beyond his individual expertise. . . . The decision ultimately reached is no less the Administrator's simply because agency experts helped him to reach it.

"A different question is presented, however, if the agency experts do not merely sift and analyze [the record,] but also add to the evidence properly before the Administrator. . . . To the extent the technical review panel's Report included information not in the record on which the Administrator relied, § 556(e) was violated. In effect the agency's staff would have made up for PSCO's failure to carry its burden of proof.

"Our review of the Report indicates that such violations did occur. The most serious instance is on page 19 of the Report where the technical panel rebuts the Regional Administrator's finding that PSCO had failed to supply enough data on species' thermal tolerances by saying: 'There is little information in the record on the thermal tolerances of marine organisms exposed to the specific temperature fluctuation associated with the Seabrook operation. However, the scientific literature does contain many references to the thermal sensitivity of members of the local biota.' Whether or not these references do exist and whether or not they support the conclusions the panel goes on to draw does not concern us here. What is important is that the record did not support the conclusion until supplemented by the panel. The panel's work found its way directly into the Administrator's decision. . . . [T]hey supplied the information. They are free to do that as witnesses, but not as deciders.

"The appropriate remedy under these circumstances is to remand the decision to the Administrator because he based his decision on material not part of the record. . . . The Administrator will have the options of trying to reach a new decision not dependent on the panel's supplementation of the record; of holding a hearing at which all parties will have the opportunity to cross-examine the panel members and at which the panel will have an opportunity to amplify its position; or of taking any other action within his power and consistent with this opinion."

(4) **Official Notice.** An exception to requiring evidence in the record occurs when an agency legitimately takes official notice of facts not otherwise proven. The APA provides: "When an agency decision rests on official notice of a material fact not appearing in the evidence in the record, a party is entitled, on timely request, to an opportunity to show the contrary." § 556(e). But it says nothing more specific about when official notice is appropriate.

The rules governing official notice by a federal trial court, set out in Rule 201 of the Federal Rules of Evidence, are much more explicit—but inapplicable to agency proceedings. By their terms, the Federal Rules of Evidence apply to federal courts, bankruptcy judges, and magistrates—not agencies. Rule 101. Congress can, of course, stipulate differently—e.g., 29 U.S.C. § 160(B), requiring the NLRB to rely on the rules of courtroom procedure "so far as practicable"—or agencies can similarly bind themselves through their own rules of procedure. But those rules often simply parrot or paraphrase the APA provision.

In CASTILLO-VILLAGRA V. IMMIGRATION AND NATURALIZATION SERVICE, 972 F.2d 1017 (1992), Teresa de Jesus Castillo-Villagra and her two adult daughters entered the United States, conceded deportability, and sought asylum. They claimed to have been members of a political group that opposed the Sandinista regime in Nicaragua. The Immigration Judge denied asylum in an oral decision, finding that the mother was lying and none of the three had a well-founded fear of persecution because of their political opinions. The Board of Immigration Appeals affirmed, taking administrative notice that an anti-Sandinista coalition now controlled the government and Violeta Chamorro had been elected president, so that the record did not support a finding that the petitioners would have a well-founded fear of persecution were they to return to Nicaragua.

Applying the law applicable to immigration matters, but speaking of administrative hearings in general, the Ninth Circuit vacated and remanded the BIA decision. The court said that notice in administrative proceedings should indeed be broader than the judicial "not subject to reasonable dispute" test, and instead endorsed what it called a "rule of convenience" based on what the trier of fact thinks he knows.

> While in proceedings in court notice is quite restricted for adjudicative facts, it is broader in administrative proceedings. A case before an administrative agency, unlike one before a court, "is rarely an isolated phenomenon, but is rather merely one unit in a mass of related cases . . . [which] often involve fact questions which have frequently been explored by the same tribunal." Walter Gellhorn, Official Notice in Administrative Adjudication, 20 Tex. L. Rev. 131, 136 (1941). The tribunal learns from its cases. Moreover, volume and repetition affect peoples' ability to pay attention. Because of the quantity of similar cases before an agency such as the INS, if notice is not taken more broadly in administrative hearings, litigants may have an uphill battle maintaining the attention of the administrative judges. Even if the law allows people to tell officials the exact same and obvious thing hundreds of times, the officials may find it very hard to listen attentively after the first dozen or two repetitions. Hearings may degenerate into an empty form if the adjudicators cannot focus attention upon what is noteworthy about the particular case. The broader notice available in administrative hearings may, if properly used, facilitate more genuine hearings, as opposed to "hearings" in which the finder of fact hears, but cannot, because of the repetition, listen.

On this basis, said the court, the agency was justified in taking notice that Chamorro had won the election.

But the agency was not justified in deciding that this proposition concluded the case. Whether notice can be taken, and whether rebuttal evidence must be allowed, are different questions.

> The agency should . . . have warned, prior to final decision, that it intended to take notice that the Sandinistas were out of power, and that any well-founded fear of persecution the applicants might have had before the election could no longer be well-founded, and then given the parties an opportunity to show cause why notice should not be taken of these propositions. Depending on the showing made, fairness might or might not have required that the parties be allowed to present evidence on these propositions. . . .

> In the case at bar, the applicants had a plausible claim that they might still have a well-founded fear of persecution despite the Chamorro election. The record they developed before the election allowed for the conclusion that Nicaragua had been dominated by the Sandinista party, and that Sandinista power flowed from the party, not just from the government. It may be that the party's permeation of society enables it to persecute opponents, even with the presidency and some departments of government in other hands. Perhaps the Nicaraguan government is not so strong and

hierarchical as to render impotent any political movement which does not control the presidency. . . .

. . . The point is, the propositions that the Sandinistas retain sufficient power to persecute petitioners, and that the petitioners have a well-founded fear of such persecution should they return . . . were seriously debatable, despite the election. Petitioners were never allowed to be heard on these propositions. . . .

Many other courts have reached comparable conclusions. E.g., Chhetry v. U.S. Dep't of Justice, 490 F.3d 196 (2d Cir. 2007).

OHIO BELL TELEPHONE CO. v. PUBLIC UTILITIES COMM'N OF OHIO, 301 U.S. 292 (1937), cited in Castillo-Villagra, is still, despite its age, probably the leading Supreme Court decision concerning official notice in on-the-record proceedings. The Ohio Public Utilities Commission had adjusted the value of a utility's property downward, for ratemaking purposes, to reflect the Great Depression, which had begun in the middle of a nearly decade-long ratemaking. The Commission had stated that it would fix the property value as of 1925 and received "thousands of printed pages" directed to the property's value at that time. The Commission subsequently took notice of price trends during the period 1926–1933, deriving its data from a variety of sources such as trade journals, tax lists, and findings by an Illinois district court regarding an affiliated company. The Court, in an opinion by Justice Cardozo, found no difficulty with the commission's taking notice of the depression as such, or of the general decline in market values as "one of its concomitants." But what the Commission had done denied the company the "fundamentals of a trial":

Without warning or even the hint of warning that the case would be considered or determined upon any other basis than the evidence submitted, the Commission cut down the values for the years after the date certain upon the strength of information secretly collected and never yet disclosed. The company . . . asked disclosure of the documents indicative of price trends, and an opportunity to examine them, to analyze them, to explain and to rebut them. The response was a curt refusal. Upon the strength of these unknown documents refunds have been ordered for sums mounting into millions, the Commission reporting its conclusion, but not the underlying proofs. . . . This is not the fair hearing essential to due process. It is condemnation without trial.

What was done by the Commission is subject, however, to an objection even deeper. There has been more than an expansion of the concept of notoriety beyond reasonable limits. . . . [A] deeper vice is . . . that even now we do not know the particular or evidential facts of which the Commission took judicial notice and on which it rested its conclusion. Not only are the facts unknown; there is no way to find them out. . . . The Commission, withholding from the record the evidential facts that it has gathered here and there, contents itself with saying that in gathering them it went to journals and tax lists, as if a judge were to tell us, 'I looked at the statistics in the Library of Congress, and they teach me thus and so.' This will never do if hearings and appeals are to be more than empty forms.

(5) ***Decision in a Hierarchical Organization.*** APA § 557(b) says that "On appeal from or review of the initial decision, the agency has all the powers which it would have in making the initial decision except as it may limit the issues on notice or by rule." "The agency" in this sentence must mean not the ALJ (who, after all, made the initial decision being reviewed) but those at the top of the organization: the Secretary of this or that, or the members of this Board or that Commission. This language recognizes that final decisions in formal agency proceedings often present policy choices that should be made by those politically responsible persons, appointed by the President and confirmed by the Senate, on whom Congress has conferred regulatory authority. But how does this authority at the top mesh with the idea that Congress has also provided that the decision shall be made after a hearing on the record?

This problem most famously came before the Supreme Court in a series of four cases sometimes called MORGAN V. UNITED STATES and sometimes UNITED STATES V. MORGAN, all preceding (and helping to shape) the APA: 298 U.S. 468 (1936), 304 U.S. 1 (1938), 307 U.S. 183 (1939), and 313 U.S. 409 (1941). The underlying issue was the rates to be charged for selling cattle by businesses at the Kansas City stockyards; the Packers and Stockyards Act gave the Secretary of Agriculture authority to set those rates "after full hearing," which the Supreme Court understood to mean after a formal adjudication. The evidence—the transcript contained about 10,000 pages of oral testimony and there were over 1,000 pages of statistical exhibits, too— had been taken before a hearing examiner. There was no intermediate report, oral argument was had before the Acting Secretary of Agriculture, a brief was filed on behalf of the businesses, and the Secretary of Agriculture then signed an order making findings of fact and conclusions of law and prescribing rates. The rates the Secretary ordered would have seriously hurt many of the businesses involved. Did this process give them the hearing Congress had mandated?

It would be fair to say that the Supreme Court was feeling its way in handling the issues involved—in deciding, that is, how a large agency (the Department of Agriculture, among its other duties, administered 42 regulatory statutes at the time), the tradition of a fair hearing, and the principal of political responsibility ought to coalesce. Among the major points the Court made were these:

a.   The authority to set rates was not delegated to the Department as a whole in some impersonal way. The authority to decide could be, perhaps, sub-delegated from the Secretary to someone else. But whoever signed the order had to be personally involved—to a point. In the words of Chief Justice Hughes from the first Morgan case:

> . . . [T]he weight ascribed by the law to the findings—their conclusiveness when made within the sphere of the authority conferred—rests upon the assumption that the officer who makes

the findings has addressed himself to the evidence and upon that evidence has conscientiously reached the conclusions which he deems it to justify. That duty cannot be performed by one who has not considered evidence or argument. It is not an impersonal obligation. It is a duty akin to that of a judge. The one who decides must hear.

This necessary rule does not preclude practicable administrative procedure in obtaining the aid of assistants in the department. Assistants may prosecute inquiries. Evidence may be taken by an examiner. Evidence thus taken may be sifted and analyzed by competent subordinates. Argument may be oral or written. The requirements are not technical. But there must be a hearing in a substantial sense. And to give the substance of a hearing, which is for the purpose of making determinations upon evidence, the officer who makes the determinations must consider and appraise the evidence which justifies them.

b.   The Department could not just inquire into what was going on in the Stockyards and then make its decision; it had to formulate its contentions so that the regulated parties on the other side of the statutorily required "full hearing" could meet the government's case. In the words of Justice Hughes, again, this time from the second case:

> The right to a hearing embraces not only the right to present evidence but also a reasonable opportunity to know the claims of the opposing party and to meet them. The right to submit argument implies that opportunity; otherwise the right may be but a barren one. Those who are brought into contest with the Government in a quasi-judicial proceeding aimed at the control of their activities are entitled to be fairly advised of what the Government proposes and to be heard upon its proposals before it issues its final command.

> No such reasonable opportunity was accorded appellants. The administrative proceeding was initiated by a notice of inquiry into the reasonableness of appellants' rates. No specific complaint was formulated. . . . In the absence of any report by the examiner or any findings proposed by the Government, and thus without any concrete statement of the Government's claims, the parties approached the oral argument. Nor did the oral argument reveal these claims in any appropriate manner. The discussion by counsel for the Government . . . dealt with generalities both as to principles and procedure.

> . . . The requirements of fairness are not exhausted in the taking or consideration of evidence but extend to the concluding parts of the procedure as well as to the beginning and intermediate steps.

c.   Assuming the agency did give a hearing that followed the formal requirements of a "full hearing," it was not the business of the courts (absent, we may suppose, an unusual showing of bias) to look into the mental processes of the decision maker. (On this point, see also p. 1087 within.) From the fourth Morgan case, this time in the words of Justice Frankfurter:

Over the Government's objection the district court authorized the market agencies to take the deposition of the Secretary. The Secretary thereupon appeared in person at the trial. He was questioned at length regarding the process by which he reached the conclusions of his order. . . . [T]he short of the business is that the Secretary should never have been subjected to this examination. The proceeding before the Secretary 'has a quality resembling that of a judicial proceeding'. Such an examination of a judge would be destructive of judicial responsibility. We have explicitly held in this very litigation that 'it was not the function of the court to probe the mental processes of the Secretary'. Just as a judge cannot be subjected to such a scrutiny . . . so the integrity of the administrative process must be equally respected.

The APA, written a few years later, had to handle the issues the Morgan cases raised. Since those cases were based on statutory authority, Congress did not have to mimic the Court. But much of the detail of §§ 554, 556, and 557 can be seen as responsive to the same problem—how to handle the flow of a case in a way that respects the programmatic obligations of the agency, makes institutional sense, and also responds to the evidence in a fair way.

NOTES ON THE IMPARTIALITY OF THE ALJ

(1) *The Separation of Functions.* APA § 554(d) goes further than prohibiting ex parte communications about facts in issue. It also provides that ALJs may not be supervised by agency personnel "engaged in the performance of investigative or prosecuting functions," and, the other way around, it states that "an employee . . . engaged in the performance of investigative or prosecuting functions . . . in a case may not, in that or a factually related case, participate or advise in the decision . . . except as witness or counsel in public proceedings." This "separation of functions" was one of the principal ways in which the drafters of the APA responded to the dangers of combining functions within an individual agency. As stated in Grolier, Inc. v. FTC, 615 F.2d 1215, 1219 (9th Cir. 1980), "[The provisions reflect a recommendation contained in the Report of the Attorney General's Committee on Administrative Procedure 50 (1941), S. Doc. No. 8, 77th Cong., 1st Sess. 50 (1941), which gave at least] two reasons . . . for this recommended separation: 'the investigators, if allowed to participate [in adjudication], would be likely to interpolate facts and information discovered by them ex parte and not adduced at the hearing, where the testimony is sworn and subject to cross-examination and rebuttal'; and '[a] man who has buried himself in one side of an issue is disabled from bringing to its decision that dispassionate judgment which Anglo-American tradition demands of officials who decide questions.' . . . We conclude that . . . Congress intended to preclude from decisionmaking in a particular case . . . all persons who had, in that or a factually related case, been involved with ex parte information, or who had developed, by prior involvement with the case, a 'will to win.' "

Is this separation of functions, or something like it, a mandate not only of the statute, but also of due process? In Williams v. Pennsylvania, 136 S.Ct. 1899, 1905 (2016), a district attorney who had authorized seeking the death penalty against a defendant almost thirty years earlier had become, by the time the same defendant's request for a new trial based on newly found evidence reached the state Supreme Court, Chief Justice of that court. The Supreme Court of the United States said he had to recuse himself: "under the Due Process Clause there is an impermissible risk of actual bias when a judge earlier had significant, personal involvement as a prosecutor in a critical decision regarding the defendant's case." Note that the Chief Justice's prior exposure to the case had been *as prosecutor*, a role in which he may have learned matters not part of any judicial record, and may have developed a commitment to "winning." Suppose instead the petition for a new trial had come before the same judge as heard the first trial. Same result?

(2) ***The APA's Exceptions for Ratemaking and Initial Licensing.*** Section 554(d) does not, by its own terms, apply to proceedings regarding rates or initial licenses. Why not? DANIEL J. GIFFORD, THE MORGAN CASES: A RETROSPECTIVE VIEW, 30 Admin. L. Rev. 237, 241–243 (1978): "When the [Supreme Court in Morgan v. United States, 298 U.S. 468 (1936) and successor cases] seemingly equated a 'judicial model' of decisionmaking with a 'full hearing' and perhaps with the fair procedure demanded by the due process clause, it made no distinction about the types of proceedings to which its strictures would apply. . . . [It] became apparent in the aftermath of the Morgan decisions that the pristine judicial model by which the Court seemed to be guided was inappropriate for ratemaking cases like the Morgan cases themselves, and perhaps was also inappropriate for other kinds of highly technical and complex cases. . . .

"These assessments profoundly affected the design of the [APA]. . . . These exemptions from [§ 554(d)] were justified on two grounds; first, that the hearing officer would be likely to need expert assistance in the decision of complex and technical issues and, second, that the isolation of the decision maker which a strict judicial decisionmaking model would impose would not be as necessary in non-accusatory proceedings where no stigma attached to an adverse determination."

(3) ***Bias in General.*** The most obvious reason for disqualifying a judge of any sort is that he or she has a pecuniary interest in the outcome. For the federal judiciary, disqualification rules are set in some detail by 28 U.S.C. § 455. They state the matter much more broadly: they require, inter alia, disqualification "in any proceeding in which [the judge's] impartiality might reasonably be questioned," § 455(a). Several circuit courts have stated that the appearance of impropriety standard is not applicable to ALJs. "[ALJs] are employed by the agency whose action they review. . . . If the 'appearance of impropriety' standard of 28 U.S.C. § 445(a) was applicable to [ALJs] they would be forced to recuse themselves in every case." Bunnell v. Barnhart, 336 F.3d 1112, 1114 (9th Cir. 2003); see also Greenberg v. Board of Governors of Fed. Reserve Sys., 968 F.2d 164, 166–67 (2d Cir. 1992). Yet it is not clear why this argument should lead to preclusion of *all* appearance of impropriety claims, as opposed to just those stemming from an ALJ's agency connections. Are there alternative reasons, such as the availability of judicial review, that justify limiting recusal of ALJs to instances of actual bias? As a matter of practice, § 455 and the ABA Code of Judicial Conduct are regularly looked to

for substantial guidance on what may serve to disqualify administrative judges.

(4) ***The Tension between Impartiality and Expertise.*** Although federal agencies cannot select ALJs based on their specialized expertise, "[o]nce they become ALJs, their expertise in the subject matter of the agency deepens because most of them adjudicate disputes involving only the agency for which they work, meaning they hear similar matters over and over again." Chris Guthrie et al., The "Hidden Judiciary": An Empirical Examination of Executive Branch Justice, 58 Duke L.J. 1477, 1484–85 (2009). Indeed, this reality is sometimes given as one reason why official notice should be more broadly available in administrative hearings than in judicial ones. But is there a danger that expertise can undermine impartiality? In MILES V. CHATER, 84 F.3d 1397, 1401 (11th Cir. 1996), an ALJ had rejected the plaintiff's application for disability benefits, discounting the testimony of the plaintiff's medical expert on the grounds that this particular expert "almost invariably" finds the claimant totally disabled. The Eleventh Circuit upheld the plaintiff's claim that the ALJ was biased and remanded for proceedings before another ALJ: "The ALJ plays a critical role in the disability review process. Not only is he duty-bound to develop a full and fair record, he must carefully weigh the evidence giving individualized consideration to each claim that comes before him. . . . The impartiality of the ALJ is . . . integral to the integrity of the system. . . . The ALJ's observations here [about the medical expert], without any evidence in support thereof, reflect that the process was compromised in this case."

(5) ***ALJs as Agency Employees.*** As of June 2016, federal agencies employed 1,770 ALJs. The agencies that employ ALJs are very diverse, including cabinet-level agencies such as the Department of Health and Human Services or the Department of the Interior, and independent agencies such as the Social Security Administration (SSA), the National Transportation Safety Board, the National Labor Relations Board, or the Securities and Exchange Commission. The overwhelming majority of ALJs— about 85 percent—are employed by SSA. Thus, for most ALJs today daily work consists not of complex regulatory cases but of reconciling the need for efficiency and dispatch in dealing with a sizable caseload. This marks a change from the situation when the APA was enacted. In 1947, for example, 125 (64%) of the federal government's 196 hearing officers worked in independent regulatory commissions deciding regulatory matters; the remainder worked for cabinet agencies, including only 13 who worked for the SSA (which was not, at that time, set up as an independent agency). For discussions of the historical origins of the modern ALJ, see Daniel J. Gifford, Federal Administrative Law Judges: The Relevance of Past Choices to Future Directions, 49 Admin. L. Rev. 1 (1997); Michael Asimow, The Administrative Judiciary: ALJ's in Historical Perspective, 20 J. Nat'l Ass'n Admin. L. Judges 157 (2000).

The APA includes numerous provisions to ensure ALJs' impartiality and independence. 5 U.S.C. §§ 554a, 1305, 3105, 3344, 5372, 7521. As a result, federal ALJs are an unusually well-insulated cadre of civil servants. They are paid at the level of the senior executive service, but—although formally located within the particular agencies they serve—are virtually beyond agency control. Appointments must be made on a competitive basis, from the top few names on a list supplied by civil service authorities. (This competition, it should be noted, by statute includes a "veterans preference" that increases the scores of veterans; this has led over the years to complaints that this system favors male applicants.) Once made, appointments are permanent, without a probationary period. Agencies do not control ALJ salaries or assignments, and formal proceedings before the federal Merit Systems Protection Board are required to impose serious disciplinary measures on an ALJ.

Bandimere v. S.E.C., 844 F.3d 1168 (10th Cir. 2016), ruled that ALJs working for the SEC were not just employees, but in fact "inferior officers" for the purpose of Article II, Section 2 of the Constitution; the existing hiring system did not "vest the Appointment . . . in the President alone, in the Courts of Law, or in the Heads of Departments" as the Constitution required, and therefore their appointments were invalid. Whether this decision will stand, and if so, how far it extends beyond ALJs working for the SEC, remains to be seen. Raymond J. Lucia Cos., Inc. v. S.E.C., 832 F.3d 277 (D.C. Cir. 2016), reached the contrary conclusion. It was vacated, and rehearing en banc granted; but the en banc court then let the original decision stand, by an equally-divided vote. 868 F.3f 1021. For discussion, see p. 886 below.

(6) ***Formal Adjudication without an ALJ.*** While the APA's provisions provide the archetype for formal agency adjudication, a fair number of federal agencies hold formal evidentiary hearings even though they are not subject to the APA's commands. This might happen because a class of proceedings is overtly exempted by the agency's organic statute, or, more commonly, because the terms of the statute do not meet the test of § 554. Even so, by the terms of the statute or by the terms of the agency's own regulations, or perhaps even by the terms of an executive order, the agency might hold a recognizably formal proceeding: evidence can be introduced by each side and the decision has to be based on the record so produced. The types of cases involved are eclectic: they range from a small number of hearings conducted each year by the Department of Energy to determine whether employees (or contractors' employees) get security clearance; to cases brought by benefits claimants and heard by the Board of Veterans Appeals at a yearly rate in the tens of thousands; to the hundreds of thousands of cases heard each year by the Immigration Courts run by the Department of Justice. As a general matter, it is customary to refer to the hearing officers in such cases as "AJs," Administrative Judges, to distinguish them from the "ALJs" who apply (and are given elevated status by) the APA. As the largest category of such cases, immigration hearings deserve a special mention. Not long after the APA was passed, the Supreme Court held that it applied to deportation hearings. Wong Yang Sung v. McGrath, 339 U.S. 33 (1950). Congress quickly overturned that ruling, and the Court accepted Congress's judgment. In fiscal year 2013, more than 250,000 immigration cases were heard in more than 50 Immigration Courts nationwide, presided over by more than 200 Immigration Judges (IJs). These hearings are not controlled by the APA—but they are often quite formal, involving, for

example, the cross-examination of witnesses. As to the particularities of the procedural rights accorded (or not accorded) in any such non-APA procedure, one has to have recourse to the statutes, regulations, and decisions of the particular regime. A recent comprehensive study recommended, as a general principle, that procedures in these types of cases "should resemble those in [APA formal adjudications] unless there is a good reason for the contrary conclusion." Michael Asimow, Evidentiary Hearings Outside the Administrative Procedure Act 18 (Final Report 11/10/2016, Administrative Conference of the United States).

PROFESSIONAL AIR TRAFFIC CONTROLLERS ORGANIZATION v. FEDERAL LABOR RELATIONS AUTHORITY

United States Court of Appeals for the District of Columbia Circuit (1982).
685 F.2d 547.

■ EDWARDS, CIRCUIT JUDGE.

[The Professional Air Traffic Controllers Organization called its members out on strike August 3, 1981, in violation of a statute forbidding federal employees to strike their employer. Among the several proceedings that resulted was an unfair labor practice hearing before the Federal Labor Relations Authority, threatening the revocation of PATCO's certification as the recognized union for the nation's air traffic controllers. That hearing was held before an FLRA ALJ on August 10–11, and a recommended decision was quickly announced stripping PATCO of its certification. Oral argument on review was held before the three members of the FLRA on September 16, and the ALJ's decision was affirmed October 22. Members Frazier and Applewhaite voted unconditionally to revoke PATCO's certification; Chairman Haughton would have permitted PATCO a brief period to end the strike before that revocation but joined the other two when that period elapsed without an appropriate PATCO response. The case was then brought to the D.C. Circuit for expedited judicial review.]

II.   Ex Parte Communications During the FLRA Proceedings

Unfortunately, allegations of improprieties during the FLRA's consideration of this case forced us to delay our review on the merits. Only a day before oral argument, the Department of Justice, which represents the [Federal Aviation Administration] in this review, informed the court that the Department of Justice Criminal Division and the FBI had investigated allegations of an improper contact between a "well-known labor leader" and FLRA Member Applewhaite during the pendency of the PATCO case. . . . [W]e invoked a procedure that this court has occasionally employed in like situations in the past. Without assuming that anything improper had in fact occurred or had affected the FLRA Decision in this case, we ordered the FLRA "to hold, with the aid of a specially-appointed administrative law judge, an evidentiary hearing to determine the nature, extent, source and effect of any and all ex parte communications and other approaches that may have been made to any member or members of the FLRA while the PATCO case was pending before it."

Following our remand on the ex parte communications issue, John M. Vittone, an Administrative Law Judge with the Civil Aeronautics Board, was appointed to preside over an evidentiary proceeding. . . . ALJ Vittone's inquiry led to the disclosure of a number of communications with FLRA Members that were at least arguably related to the Authority's consideration of the PATCO case. We find the vast majority of these communications unobjectionable. Three occurrences, however, are somewhat more troubling and require our careful review and discussion. We first summarize ALJ Vittone's findings regarding them.

1. The Meeting Between Member Applewhaite and FLRA General Counsel Gordon

On August 10, 1981 (one week after the unfair labor practice complaint against PATCO was filed), H. Stephan Gordon, the FLRA General Counsel, was in Member Applewhaite's office discussing administrative matters unrelated to the PATCO case. During Gordon's discussion with Member Applewhaite, Ms. Ellen Stern, an attorney with the FLRA Solicitor's office, entered Member Applewhaite's office to deliver a copy of a memorandum . . . Ms. Stern had prepared at the request of Member Frazier.[23] With General Counsel Gordon present, Ms. Stern proceeded to discuss her memorandum, which dealt with whether the Civil Service Reform Act makes revocation of a striking union's exclusive recognition status mandatory or discretionary and, assuming it is discretionary, what other disciplinary actions might be taken.

During Ms. Stern's discussion, both Member Applewhaite and General Counsel Gordon asked her general questions (e.g., regarding the availability of other remedies and whether she had researched the relevant legislative history). . . . While the conversation at least implicitly focused on the PATCO case, the facts of the case and the appropriate disposition were not discussed. The discussion ended after ten or fifteen minutes.

ALJ Vittone concluded that "[t]he conversation had no effect or impact on Member Applewhaite's ultimate decision in the PATCO case."

2. Secretary Lewis' Telephone Calls to Members Frazier and Applewhaite

During the morning of August 13, 1981, Secretary of Transportation Andrew L. Lewis, Jr. telephoned Member Frazier. Secretary Lewis stated that he was not calling about the substance of the PATCO case, but wanted Member Frazier to know that, contrary to some news reports, no

---

[23] The Solicitor is the general legal advisor of the FLRA, including the Members. The Solicitor also represents the FLRA on appeals from FLRA orders and in other legal proceedings. [Ed. The General Counsel, by contrast, represents FLRA staff in appearances before the FLRA.]

meaningful efforts to settle the strike were underway. Secretary Lewis also stated that the Department of Transportation would appreciate expeditious handling of the case. Not wanting to discuss the PATCO case with Secretary Lewis, Member Frazier replied, "I understand your position perfectly, Mr. Secretary." . . .

Member Frazier also advised Member Applewhaite of Secretary Lewis' telephone call. In anticipation of a call, Member Applewhaite located the FLRA Rules regarding the time limits for processing an appeal from an ALJ decision in an unfair labor practice case. When Secretary Lewis telephoned and stated his concern that the case not be delayed, Member Applewhaite interrupted the Secretary to inform him that if he wished to obtain expedited handling of the case, he would have to comply with the FLRA Rules and file a written motion. Secretary Lewis stated that he was unaware that papers had to be filed and that he would contact his General Counsel immediately. The conversation ended without further discussion.

During the afternoon of August 13, the FAA filed a Motion to Modify Time Limits for Filing Exceptions, requesting that the time limit be reduced from the usual twenty-five days to seven days. On August 14, the FLRA General Counsel filed a similar motion. On August 17, PATCO filed an opposition to these motions and a motion to extend the time for filing exceptions to sixty days. On August 18, 1981, the FLRA Members considered the three pending motions, denied all three, and decided instead to reduce the usual twenty-five day period for filing exceptions to nineteen days.

Upon considering this evidence, Judge Vittone concluded that: (1) the FAA's filing of a motion to expedite may have been in response to Secretary Lewis' conversation with Member Applewhaite; (2) Chairman Haughton was unaware of Secretary Lewis' telephone calls when he considered the motions on August 18; (3) "Secretary Lewis' call had an undetermined effect on Member Applewhaite's and Member Frazier's decision to reduce the time period for filing exceptions,"; and (4) the telephone calls "had no effect on Member Applewhaite's or Member Frazier's ultimate decision on the merits of the PATCO case."

3.   Member Applewhaite's Dinner With Albert Shanker

Since 1974 Albert Shanker has been President of the American Federation of Teachers, a large public-sector labor union, and a member of the Executive Council of the AFL-CIO.[26] Since 1964 Mr. Shanker has been President of the AFT's New York City Local, the United Federation of Teachers. Before joining the FLRA, Member Applewhaite had been associated with the New York Public Employment Relations Board.

---

[26] The AFL-CIO presented oral argument to the FLRA in the PATCO case as amicus curiae. Mr. Shanker, however, was unaware of the amicus status of the AFL-CIO at all times relevant to our consideration.

Through their contacts in New York, Mr. Shanker and Member Applewhaite had become professional and social friends.

During the week of September 20, 1981, Mr. Shanker was in Washington, D.C. on business. On September 21, Mr. Shanker made arrangements to have dinner with Member Applewhaite that evening. Although he did not inform Member Applewhaite of his intentions when he made the arrangements, Mr. Shanker candidly admitted that he wanted to have dinner with Member Applewhaite because he felt strongly about the PATCO case and wanted to communicate directly to Member Applewhaite his sentiments, previously expressed in public statements, that PATCO should not be severely punished for its strike. . . . After accepting the invitation, Member Applewhaite informed Member Frazier and Chairman Haughton that he was having dinner with Mr. Shanker.

Member Applewhaite and Mr. Shanker talked for about an hour and a half during their dinner on September 21. Most of the discussion concerned the preceding Saturday's Solidarity Day Rally, an upcoming tuition tax credit referendum in the District of Columbia, and mutual friends from New York. Near the end of the dinner, however, the conversation turned to labor law matters relevant to the PATCO case. The two men discussed various approaches to public employee strikes in New York, Pennsylvania and the federal government. Mr. Shanker expressed his view that the punishment of a striking union should fit the crime and that revocation of certification as a punishment for an illegal strike was tantamount to "killing a union." The record is clear that Mr. Shanker made no threats or promises to Member Applewhaite; likewise, the evidence also indicates that Member Applewhaite never revealed his position regarding the PATCO case.

Near the end of their conversation, Member Applewhaite commented that because the PATCO case was hotly contested, he would be viewed with disfavor by whichever side he voted against. Member Applewhaite also observed that he was concerned about his prospects for reappointment to the FLRA in July 1982. Mr. Shanker, in turn, responded that Member Applewhaite had no commitments from anyone and urged him to vote without regard to personal considerations. The dinner concluded and the two men departed.

The FLRA Decisional Process. On the afternoon of September 21, before the Applewhaite/Shanker dinner, the FLRA Members had had their first formal conference on the PATCO case, which had been argued to them five days earlier. Members Frazier and Applewhaite both favored revocation of PATCO's exclusive recognition status and took the position that PATCO would no longer be a labor organization within the meaning of the Civil Service Reform Act. Member Frazier favored an indefinite revocation; Member Applewhaite favored a revocation for a fixed period of one to three years. Chairman Haughton agreed that an illegal strike had occurred, but favored suspension, not revocation, of PATCO's collective bargaining status.

After September 21, Member Applewhaite considered other remedies, short of revocation, to deal with the PATCO strike. For over two weeks Member Applewhaite sought to find common ground with Chairman Haughton. Those efforts to agree on an alternative solution failed and, on October 9, Member Applewhaite finally decided to vote with Member Frazier for revocation. (Member Applewhaite apparently was concerned that the FLRA have a majority favoring one remedy, rather than render three opinions favoring three different dispositions.) . . . While these negotiations within the Authority were going on, Member Frazier became concerned that Mr. Shanker might have influenced Member Applewhaite's position in the case. On September 22, Member Frazier visited Member Applewhaite to inquire about his dinner with Mr. Shanker. Member Frazier understood Member Applewhaite to say that Shanker had said that if Member Applewhaite voted against PATCO, then Applewhaite would be unable to get work as an arbitrator when he left the FLRA. Member Frazier also understood Member Applewhaite to say that he was then leaning against voting for revocation. (ALJ Vittone found that Shanker had made no such threats during the dinner, and concluded that Member Frazier reached this conclusion based on some miscommunication or misunderstanding.)

On September 22 and again on September 28, Member Frazier advised Member Applewhaite to talk to Solicitor Freehling about his dinner with Mr. Shanker. . . . Member Frazier later asked Solicitor Freehling if Member Applewhaite had discussed his dinner with Mr. Shanker. Solicitor Freehling told Member Frazier that they had talked and that Member Applewhaite had concluded that there were no problems involved. Despite these assurances, Member Frazier contacted his personal attorney. Sometime in early October, Member Frazier's attorney contacted the FBI. The FBI interviewed Member Frazier on October 17 and then other FLRA Members and staff. FBI agents interviewed Member Applewhaite on October 22, the day the FLRA Decision issued. (Member Applewhaite was thus unaware of the FBI investigation until after he reached his final decision in the PATCO case.) . . .

C.   Applicable Legal Standards

1.   The Statutory Prohibition of Ex Parte Contacts and the FLRA Rules

The Civil Service Reform Act requires that FLRA unfair labor practice hearings, to the extent practicable, be conducted in accordance with the provisions of the Administrative Procedure Act. 5 U.S.C. § 7118(a)(6). Since FLRA unfair labor practice hearings are formal adjudications within the meaning of the APA, section 557(d) governs ex parte communications. Id. § 557(d). . . .

Three features of the prohibition on ex parte communications in agency adjudications are particularly relevant to the contacts here at issue. First, by its terms, section 557(d) applies only to ex parte communications to or from an "interested person." . . . Second, the Government in the Sunshine Act defines an "ex parte communication" as "an oral or written communication not on the public record to which reasonable prior notice to all parties is not given, but . . . not includ[ing] requests for status reports on any matter or proceeding. . . ." 5 U.S.C. § 551(14) (1976). Requests for status reports are thus allowed under the statute, even when directed to an agency decisionmaker rather than to another agency employee. . . . Third, and in direct contrast to status reports, section 557(d) explicitly prohibits communications "relevant to the merits of the proceeding." The congressional reports state that the phrase should "be construed broadly and . . . include more than the phrase 'fact in issue' currently used in [section 554(d)(1) of] the Administrative Procedure Act." . . .

The disclosure of ex parte communications serves two distinct interests. Disclosure is important in its own right to prevent the appearance of impropriety from secret communications in a proceeding that is required to be decided on the record. Disclosure is also important as an instrument of fair decisionmaking; only if a party knows the arguments presented to a decisionmaker can the party respond effectively and ensure that its position is fairly considered. When these interests of openness and opportunity for response are threatened by an ex parte communication, the communication must be disclosed. . . .

2.   Remedies for Ex Parte Communications

Section 557(d) contains two possible administrative remedies for improper ex parte communications. The first is disclosure of the communication and its content. The second requires the violating party to "show cause why his claim or interest in the proceeding should not be dismissed, denied, disregarded, or otherwise adversely affected on account of [the] violation." . . . Under the case law in this Circuit, improper ex parte communications, even when undisclosed during agency proceedings, do not necessarily void an agency decision. . . . [A] court must consider whether, as a result of improper ex parte communications, the agency's decisionmaking process was irrevocably tainted so as to make the ultimate judgment of the agency unfair, either to an innocent party or to the public interest that the agency was obliged to protect.[32] In making this determination, a number of considerations may be relevant: the gravity of the ex parte communications;[33] whether

---

[32] We have also considered the effect of ex parte communications on the availability of meaningful judicial review. . . . If the off-the-record communications regard critical facts, the court will be particularly ill-equipped to resolve in the first instance any controversy between the parties. . . .

[33] If the ex parte contacts are of such severity that an agency decision-maker should have disqualified himself, vacation of the agency decision and remand to an impartial tribunal is mandatory. Cf. Cinderella Career & Finishing Schools v. FTC, 425 F.2d 583, 591–92 (D.C. Cir.

the contacts may have influenced the agency's ultimate decision; whether the party making the improper contacts benefited from the agency's ultimate decision; whether the contents of the communications were unknown to opposing parties, who therefore had no opportunity to respond; and whether vacation of the agency's decision and remand for new proceedings would serve a useful purpose. . . . [A]ny such decision must of necessity be an exercise of equitable discretion.

D. Analysis of the Alleged Ex Parte Communications With FLRA Members

1. The Meeting Between Member Applewhaite and FLRA General Counsel Gordon

When General Counsel Gordon met with Member Applewhaite on August 10, the General Counsel's office was prosecuting the unfair labor practice complaint against PATCO before Chief ALJ Fenton. General Counsel Gordon was therefore a "person outside the agency" within the meaning of section 557(d) and the FLRA Rules. 5 C.F.R. § 2414.3(a) (1981). Still, the undisputed purpose of the meeting was to discuss budgetary and administrative matters. It was therefore entirely appropriate. The shared concerns of the Authority are not put on hold whenever the General Counsel prosecutes an unfair labor practice complaint.

The discussion relevant to the PATCO case arose only when Ms. Stern delivered a copy of her memorandum regarding decertification of striking unions to Member Applewhaite. . . . Some occasional and inadvertent contacts between the prosecuting and adjudicating arms of a small agency like the FLRA may be inevitable. . . . In hindsight, it may have been preferable if Member Applewhaite had postponed even this general conversation with Ms. Stern or if General Counsel Gordon had temporarily excused himself from Member Applewhaite's office. Nonetheless, we do not believe that this contact tainted the proceeding or unfairly advantaged the General Counsel in the prosecution of the case. Thus, we conclude that the conversation at issue here, even though possibly indiscreet and undesirable, does not void the FLRA Decision in this case.

2. Secretary Lewis' Telephone Calls to Members Frazier and Applewhaite

Transportation Secretary Lewis was undoubtedly an "interested person" within the meaning of section 557(d) and the FLRA Rules when he called Members Frazier and Applewhaite on August 13. Secretary Lewis' call clearly would have been an improper ex parte communication if he had sought to discuss the merits of the PATCO case. . . . Although Secretary Lewis did not in fact discuss the merits of the case, even a procedural inquiry may be a subtle effort to influence an agency

---

1970) (failure of single member of agency to disqualify himself for bias requires vacation of agency decision).

decision. . . . We need not decide, however, whether Secretary Lewis' contacts were in fact improper. . . . Member Applewhaite explicitly told Secretary Lewis that if he wanted the case handled more quickly than the normal course of FLRA business, then the FAA would have to file a written request. If . . . Member Applewhaite's comments led to the FAA's Motion to Modify Time Limits, *that was exactly the desired result.* . . . In these circumstances, and given ALJ Vittone's inability to find any effect of the calls on the Members' decision, we cannot find that the disposition of the motions was improperly influenced. . . .

3.   Member Applewhaite's Dinner With Albert Shanker

. . . At the outset, we are faced with the question whether Mr. Shanker was an "interested person" to the proceeding under section 557(d) and the FLRA Rules. . . . The House and Senate Reports agreed that the term covers "any individual or other person with an interest in the agency proceeding that is greater than the general interest the public as a whole may have." . . . Mr. Shanker was (and is) the President of a major public-sector labor union. As such, he has a special and well-known interest in the union movement and the developing law of labor relations in the public sector. . . . From August 3, 1981 to September 21, 1981, Mr. Shanker and his union made a series of widely publicized statements in support of PATCO. . . . Thus, Mr. Shanker's actions, as well as his union office, belie his implicit claim that he had no greater interest in the case than a member of the general public. . . .

Even if we were to adopt Mr. Shanker's position that he was not an interested person, we are astonished at his claim that he did nothing wrong.[47] Mr. Shanker frankly concedes that he "desired to have dinner with Member Applewhaite because he felt strongly about the PATCO case and he wished to communicate directly to Member Applewhaite sentiments he had previously expressed in public." . . . *It is simply unacceptable behavior for any person directly to attempt to influence the decision of a judicial officer in a pending case outside of the formal, public proceedings.* This is true for the general public, for "interested persons," and for the formal parties to the case. This rule applies to administrative adjudications as well as to cases in Article III courts. . . .

We do not hold, however, that Member Applewhaite committed an impropriety when he accepted Mr. Shanker's dinner invitation. Member Applewhaite and Mr. Shanker were professional and social friends. We recognize, of course, that a judge "must have neighbors, friends and acquaintances, business and social relations, and be a part of his day and generation." . . . Member Applewhaite was unaware of Mr. Shanker's

---

[47] Mr. Shanker suggests that "[s]ince there is no sanction available against amici, it is reasonable to assume that the ex parte rules are not intended to apply in these circumstances." This argument is simply a non sequitur. The principal purpose of the ex parte rules is not to punish violators, but to preserve the integrity of the administrative process. Even when a nonparty is the source of an ex parte communication, a proceeding may be voided if the decision is irrevocably tainted. . . .

purpose in arranging the dinner. He therefore had no reason to reject the invitation.

The majority of the dinner conversation was unrelated to the PATCO case. Only in the last fifteen minutes of the dinner did the discussion become relevant to the PATCO dispute . . . At this point, . . . Member Applewhaite should have promptly terminated the discussion. . . . We now know that Mr. Shanker did *not* in any way threaten Member Applewhaite during their dinner. Mr. Shanker did *not* tell Member Applewhaite that if he voted to decertify PATCO he would be unable to get cases as an arbitrator if and when he left the FLRA. Mr. Shanker did *not* say that he was speaking "for top AFLCIO officials" or that Member Applewhaite would need labor support to secure reappointment. Moreover, Mr. Shanker did *not* make any promises of any kind to Member Applewhaite, and Member Applewhaite did *not* reveal how he intended to vote in the PATCO case.

In these circumstances, we do not believe that it is necessary to vacate the FLRA Decision and remand the case. . . . Though plainly inappropriate, the ex parte communication was limited to a ten or fifteen minute discussion, often couched in general terms, of the appropriate discipline for a striking public employee union. This behavior falls short of the "corrupt tampering with the adjudicatory process" found by this court in WKAT, Inc. v. FCC, 296 F.2d 375, 383 (D.C.Cir.), cert. denied, 368 U.S. 841 (1961). . . . [T]he Applewhaite/Shanker dinner had no effect on the ultimate decision of Member Applewhaite or of the FLRA as a whole in the PATCO case. . . . No party benefited from the improper contact. . . . Finally, we cannot say that the parties were unfairly deprived of an opportunity to refute the arguments propounded in the ex parte communication. . . .

E.   Member Applewhaite's Alleged "Personal Interest" in the PATCO Case . . .

Based essentially on [member Applewhaite's brief conversation with Mr. Shanker about his reappointment prospects,] Member Frazier now proposes that Member Applewhaite had a personal interest in the outcome of the PATCO case . . . [and] argues that Member Applewhaite was disqualified from hearing the PATCO case.

We do not read as much into this conversation as does Member Frazier. It is not surprising that an agency member appointed by the President might be concerned about his prospects for reappointment. . . . The appropriate question here is not whether Member Applewhaite recognized that his decision might not be universally approved; rather, the correct inquiry is whether Member Applewhaite's concerns rendered him incapable of reaching a fair decision on the merits of the case before him.

The . . . conversation between Member Applewhaite and Mr. Shanker does not demonstrate an inability to fairly decide the case.

Courts have long recognized "a presumption of honesty and integrity in those serving as adjudicators." Absent a strong showing to the contrary, an agency adjudicator is presumed to act in good faith and to be capable of ignoring considerations not on the record. . . . Member Applewhaite explained that this was no different from any arbitration case in which he had ruled—one party wins and the other loses. He testified: "I have always faced that problem[,] so I just have to call it like it is and . . . take my chances." Tr. 744. We have no reason to doubt this testimony. A remand on the basis of personal interest is therefore unnecessary.

[On the merits, the court upheld the FLRA order.]

■ ROBINSON, CHIEF JUDGE, concurring in part, and concurring in the judgment. . . .

From the special hearing emerges an appalling chronicle of attorneys, high government officials, and interested outsiders apparently without compunction about intervening in the course of FLRA's decisionmaking by means of private communications with those charged with resolving the case on the merits. We have an even more distressing picture of agency decisionmakers—whose role in this formal adjudication concededly approximated that of judges—seemingly ignorant of the substance of the ex parte rules, insensitive to the compromising potentialities of certain official and social contacts, and unwilling to silence peremptorily and firmly improper discussions that did transpire. . . . [T]he court's opinion administers a mild chiding where a ringing condemnation is in order.

I. The Applewhaite-Gordon Incident

. . . [A]gencies such as FLRA fulfill, often simultaneously, the several roles of investigator, prosecutor, adjudicator, and policy formulator. Undoubtedly, this commingling of functions makes it more difficult to maintain a strict separation between those personnel who, on any given case, are cast in the role of advocate from those who occupy the position of judge in the matter. Once the agency is engaged in formal adjudication, however, such a separation is mandated by the APA, and is essential to the integrity of the administrative process. The perils of laxness on this point are well illustrated by the Applewhaite—Gordon incident. . . . The conversation was not merely indiscreet or undesirable; it was, purely and simply, a prohibited ex parte contact that should never have occurred. Gordon had no business remaining in the room once he realized that PATCO was the object of discussion. Applewhaite had no business permitting him to remain, and certainly was grossly at fault in soliciting Gordon's opinion. . . .

II. Secretary Lewis' Calls to Members Frazier and Applewhaite

. . . Secretary Lewis' calls were highly unusual. Both [Frazier and Applewhaite] stated that they had never before been contacted by a Cabinet member on a pending case. Applewhaite also explained that persons seeking status information normally contact the staff in lieu of discussing such matters directly with the members. . . .

Agencies, like courts, promulgate rules of practice to assist outsiders in communicating in proper fashion with decisionmakers. These channels are quite adequate to accommodate any information that legitimately could be sought from or provided to those who will judge the case. For a high government officer to bypass established procedures and approach, directly and privately, members of an independent decisionmaking body about a case in which he has an official interest and on which they will be called to rule suggests, at the minimum, a deplorable indifference toward safeguarding the purity of the formal adjudicatory process. Regardless of the officer's actual intent, such a call could be felt by the recipient as political pressure; regardless of its actual effect, such a call could be perceived by the public as political pressure. . . .

IV. The Applewhaite-Shanker Dinner

. . . Can the public really be expected to believe in the fairness and neutrality of the agency's formal adjudicatory processes when one of its decisionmakers permits an outspoken, highly visible official of a participating union to wine and dine him during deliberations on the case? . . . [T]hose who take on this judicial role may no longer participate in the daily intercourse of life as freely as do others. They have a duty to the judicial system in which they have accepted membership fastidiously to safeguard their integrity—at the expense, if need be, of "neighbors, friends and acquaintances, business and social relations." This *is* their "part" in their "day and generation," and one who is unwilling to make the sacrifice is unsuited to the office. . . .

■ MACKINNON, CIRCUIT JUDGE, concurring. . . .

The number of ex parte contacts that were disclosed at the remand hearing is appalling, as are the statements by counsel that such contacts were nothing more than what is normal and usual in administrative agencies and even in courts of law. . . . In this connection 18 U.S.C. § 1505 should be noted. This section of the Criminal Code provides that it is an offense if one "corruptly . . . *endeavors to influence,* obstruct or impede the due and proper administration of the law under which [a] proceeding is being had before [an] . . . agency of the United States . . ." (emphasis added). Private contacts with agency officials, with respect to pending adjudicatory matters, by interested parties or their agents, that endeavor to affect the decisional process, however subtle such contacts may be, are *corrupt* endeavors to influence the "due and proper administration of the law" and those who so attempt may be indicted. The authorized punishment is imprisonment for not more than five years, or a $5,000 fine, or both. 18 U.S.C. § 1505.

NOTES

(1)   Casebook editors sometimes suspect that opinions they encounter were written with the classroom in mind, particularly when those opinion have been authored by former academic colleagues like Judge Edwards.[2] PATCO is remarkable for capturing so many related questions in one place. Here, those questions concern the relationship of agency heads to the people around them—staff, other government officials, and private citizens who may be both personal friends and "interested persons." It catches, too, the influence of accidental interactions among agency staff, high profile events, internal politics (consider Member Frazier's decision to turn Member Applewhaite over to the FBI), and "the rotating door" through which agency leaders move in and out of government. It does so in the context of an unusual government agency: the FLRA, like the NLRB, is an almost wholly adjudicatory body and one that *always* has a government agency on one side of the issues before it, with government employees on the other.

(2)   Most government agencies will not be so wholly committed to adjudication, and in adjudication will generally be dealing only with their own staff, not other government agencies, as a party. For them, even more than for the FLRA, the PATCO issues are real ones. These issues cross the lives of agency officials daily and lurk behind every "chance" conversation. They are addressed by §§ 554(d) and 557(d) of the APA, as well as independent conflict of interest legislation and agency regulations. The pages below explore the three conversations that sparked this controversy: one within the agency, one with another government official, and the third with an interested "friend."

NOTES ON INTERESTED AGENCY STAFF & SEPARATION OF FUNCTIONS AT THE AGENCY LEVEL

(1)   *The Governing APA Requirements.* General Counsel Gordon's participation in the conversation between Ms. Stern and Member Applewhaite suggests the difficulties that can arise, perhaps especially in a small agency, from the limited pool of expertise available, the variety of tasks agency staff are asked to perform, and the frequent informality with which work within an agency is done. As seems likely often the case, the conversation among these three appears unplanned, even unconscious. In an enforcement proceeding like PATCO, agency participants would and should have little doubt that separation of functions constraints have to be observed. The FLRA's own rules, as the court remarked, treated the General Counsel's office as if it were outside the agency for purposes of these proceedings, thus bringing § 557(d) into play. Even if the agency's regulations had not extended § 557(d) in this fashion, § 554(d) would have been understood to apply. Although § 554(d)(C) appears to exclude "the agency or a member or members of the body comprising the agency" from the ex parte ban, that exclusion serves only to permit those members themselves to serve multiple functions—not to authorize prosecuting counsel to have private

---

[2]   Before his appointment to the bench, Judge Edwards was a Professor at the University of Michigan Law School, specializing in Labor Law.

conversations with them. Attorney General's Manual on the Administrative Procedure Act 58 (1947).

All § 554(d) excludes for agency prosecutors, however, are off-the-record consultations about a "fact in issue" and participation or advice about "the decision, recommended decision, or agency review." Reading this language as reaching general policy conversations in which the whole agency may be engaged, if those conversations might also bear on particular matters in litigation, would introduce layers of formality into the day-to-day functioning of the agency, an arguably unwarranted cost. Many cases are pending all the time in traditional regulatory agencies, raising issues that implicate the full range of their responsibilities.

If we think that § 554(d) precludes conversations dominated by a pending case but not those focused on a general policy question, how should we understand the Gordon/Stern/Applewhaite conversation? Does the broader preclusion of § 557(d), applying to communications "relevant to the merits of the proceeding," further complicate matters, if the agency has defined General Counsel Gordon as being "outside the agency" for these purposes?

(2) *Are Sharp Lines of Division Required for Fairness?* Even if not required by the APA or due process, is it unfair to allow staff who participate in the initial stages of a proceeding to advise agency officials who ultimately decide the case for the agency? Does the answer to that question turn at all on the resources available to the agency and the practical exigencies it may face in needing to render an informed decision? Does it depend on whether the issues involved are more matters of adjudicative or "general" fact, or on the extent of the staff's participation and advocacy for a particular position?

A strong argument against extending separation-of-functions requirements is offered by WILLIAM F. PEDERSEN, JR., THE DECLINE OF SEPARATION OF FUNCTIONS IN REGULATORY AGENCIES, 64 Va. L. Rev. 991 (1978): "Admittedly, a separation-of-functions rule has its place in an 'accusatory' proceeding, in which one group of agency employees prosecutes a private party for a violation of the law and another group must sit in judgment. Most significant decisions by government agencies, however, simply do not fit this model. Instead, they involve the formulation or the application of policy, without any connotation of wrongdoing, regarding persons who are being regulated. Agencies and their staffs exist to make policy decisions, and there is no reason to suspect that staff members who work on the early stages of a non-accusatory proceeding view the choices confronting them in a manner any less valid than do those who handle succeeding stages. . . .

"Five independent characteristics of formal adjudication may contribute to a fair disposition of a particular case: (1) a decision based on a publicly defined and publicly accessible record, (2) a mechanism for confrontation between opposing points of view, (3) a mechanism for probing and, where possible, resolving differences on factual and other matters, (4) separation-of-functions requirements, and (5) an independent, judge-like hearing officer. The framers of the APA concluded that all five of these elements must be present in accusatory cases but only the first three in policy decisions. They undermined their own work, however, by requiring the factual probing to take the form of a trial-type hearing even in policy-dominated cases.

"Whether a decision requires separation of functions depends not only upon its basic nature but also upon the procedures used to make it. Trial-type hearings cast the agency's trial staff in an adversarial role, which almost inevitably calls forth a partisan attitude, but the APA also expressly sanctions informal reliance on the advice of these same staff members in reaching a final decision. Naturally enough, private lawyers who have confronted this staff in the hearing object fiercely to its taking any part in the subsequent deliberations within the agency. Accordingly, in the years since passage of the APA, agencies gradually have adopted rules to bar those who take part in the hearing from playing any role in the preparation of the resulting decision, even when the APA would permit their involvement. . . .

"Clothing non-accusatory administrative hearings with more of the trappings of adjudicatory proceedings may make better theater, but it probably reduces their substantive importance. Agency trial staffs, because of the separation-of-functions rules, and hearing examiners, because of their misconceptions of their proper role, do not participate in the informal discussions that often generate the agency's governing policies. Unawareness of these policies or simple separation from their development may prevent the outcome of the initial hearing from reflecting what the agency as an institution would consider to be the proper result." Pedersen thus concluded that separation-of-functions requirements "can hinder efficient agency operation and lower the quality of final administrative decisions."

NOTES ON PRESSURE FROM OTHER PARTS OF GOVERNMENT

(1)   Secretary Lewis's telephone calls in PATCO point to another common characteristic of agency life: agencies frequently act in the unruly world of politics, subject to a range of official and unofficial controls courts simply do not encounter. To what extent should courts seek to control these external influences on agency decisionmaking in on-the-record proceedings?

(2)   ***Congressional Influence on Agency Adjudication.*** Suppose that an agency's decisions suggest to its congressional oversight committee— responsible under the Legislative Reorganization Act of 1970, § 118, 84 Stat. 1156 to "review and study, on a continuing basis, the application, administration, and execution of those laws, or parts of laws, the subject matter of which is within the jurisdiction of that committee"—that the agency is straying from the correct policy path. May oversight hearings be convened while aspects of the policy issues remain unresolved before the agency? Should legislators be able to express their views on highly important policy questions that might be pending in a proceeding before the agency? Or should they scrupulously abstain from indicating their positions until the

administrators have finally announced their own conclusion?[3] A major change in contemporary mores would be effected if members of Congress were to be rigorously precluded from asking questions about or making remarks concerning current administrative cases. But where should the line be drawn between legislative vigilance and legislative intermeddling?

The leading case on this question is PILLSBURY CO. V. FTC, 354 F.2d 952 (5th Cir. 1966). There, the FTC had filed a complaint against Pillsbury challenging its acquisition of competing flour millers as being anticompetitive; the case put in issue the application of § 7 of the Clayton Act. The FTC's trial examiner dismissed the complaint, but the Commission itself reinstated it. Then, while the reinstated proceedings were pending before the agency, the Senate Judiciary Committee summoned the FTC Chairman and members of his staff to appear. The Senators were volubly dissatisfied with the agency's interpretation of § 7, as shown in the theory of the reinstated complaint, which they considered too weak. The case or the Pillsbury name was referred to more than 100 times in the series of congressional hearings. When the FTC ultimately ordered Pillsbury to divest itself of the acquired companies, Pillsbury sought review, alleging a lack of due process. The alleged interference, as the reviewing court later remarked, was not an impropriety concealed from public view, but consisted, rather, of "questions and statements made by members of two Senate and House subcommittees having responsibility for legislation dealing with antitrust matters all clearly spread upon the record."

". . . We conclude that the proceedings just outlined constituted an improper intrusion into the adjudicatory processes of the Commission and were of such a damaging character as to have required at least some of the members . . . to disqualify themselves. . . .

"At times . . . statements of official position are elicited in Congressional hearings. In this context, the agencies are sometimes called to task for failing to adhere to the 'intent of Congress' in supplying meaning to the often broad statutory standards from which the agencies derive their authority, e.g., 'substantially to lessen competition' or 'to tend to create a monopoly.' . . . Although such investigatory methods raise serious policy questions as to the de facto 'independence' of the federal regulatory agencies, it seems doubtful that they raise any constitutional issues. However, when such an investigation focuses directly and substantially upon the mental decisional processes of a Commission in a case which is pending before it, Congress is no longer intervening in the agency's legislative function, but rather, in its *judicial* function. . . .

"To subject an administrator to a searching examination as to how and why he reached his decision in a case still pending before him, and to criticize him for reaching the 'wrong' decision, as the Senate subcommittee did in this case, sacrifices the appearance of impartiality-the sine qua non of American judicial justice-in favor of some short-run notions regarding the

---

[3]   Note that 18 U.S.C. § 203(a) prohibits direct or indirect compensation to a Member of Congress in any proceeding in which the United States is a party or has a "substantial interest" before any department or agency. Other statutes explicitly prohibit members of Congress from practicing before named tribunals.

Congressional intent underlying an amendment to a statute, unfettered administration of which was committed by Congress to the Federal Trade Commission (see 15 U.S.C. § 21).

"It may be argued that such officials as members of the Federal Trade Commission are sufficiently aware of the realities of governmental, not to say 'political,' life as to be able to withstand such questioning as we have outlined here. However, this court is not so 'sophisticated' that it can shrug off such a procedural due process claim merely because the officials involved should be able to discount what is said and to disregard the force of the intrusion into the adjudicatory process. We conclude that we can preserve the rights of the litigants in a case such as this without having any adverse effect upon the legitimate exercise of the investigative power of Congress. What we do is to preserve the integrity of the judicial aspect of the administrative process."

If the General Counsel of the FTC had foreseen what the hearing before the Senate committee would entail, would it have been appropriate for him to call committee counsel, to suggest that questioning be limited to the FTC's interpretation of § 7, and to suggest that the Pillsbury case not be mentioned by name? If the committee observed that constraint, but was just as forceful in conveying its sense how § 7 ought to be interpreted, would that have avoided any § 557(d) problem? Would it make any real difference to the agency's perception of the political forces bearing on it? To the public's or Pillsbury's perception of the fairness of the hearing in which it was engaged? See Ronald M. Levin, Congressional Ethics and Constituent Advocacy in an Age of Mistrust, 95 Mich. L. Rev. 1, 39 (1996).

It is a fact of life for agency officials that they must appear before congressional committees (as well as speak at lunches and other events), all of which can give rise to claims of bias. Cases like Pillsbury don't arise very often, despite these appearances, perhaps because over time agency officials have learned how to speak and have educated members of Congress and their staff about how to engage in these conversations.

(3) **Presidential Influence on Administrative Adjudication.** Are efforts by the President to influence agency adjudication to be treated the same as congressional interventions? Does it matter if the adjudication involves a determination turning on more "general" fact and carrying broad policy implications? To what extent can Congress constitutionally insulate administrative adjudication from presidential oversight or presidential control? These issues were explored in PORTLAND AUDUBON SOCIETY V. THE ENDANGERED SPECIES COMMITTEE, 984 F.3d 1534 (9th Cir. 1993), [see also p. 980]. Under the Endangered Species Act, only a committee composed of high-level officials (cabinet members, agency administrators, and the like) can grant exemptions from the ESA's requirements, based on a record compiled in an on-the-record hearing before an ALJ, a report by the Secretary of the Interior, and any other hearings or written submissions called for by the Endangered Species Committee. The Committee authorized exemptions allowing timber sales affecting the habitat of the northern spotted owl and Portland Audubon sued, noting that news stories reported White House pressure to approve the sales and seeking discovery into alleged

White House contacts that might have changed committee members' votes. The Ninth Circuit held that § 557(d)'s ban on ex parte communications applied to Committee proceedings and that the President and his aides were appropriately considered "outside the agency" for purposes of § 557(d). It also ruled that including presidential communications within the ban on ex parte contacts would not violate separation of powers by interfering with the President's ability to supervise executive branch officials, concluding that "the general principle the President may not interfere with quasi-adjudicatory agency actions is well-settled." As a result, it remanded to the Committee to hold a hearing on whether there were such contacts and their effects on the Committee's decision.

NOTES ON RELATIONS WITH REGULATED PARTIES AND THE PUBLIC

The final element in PATCO concerned member Applewhaite's dinner with Albert Shanker, an old friend and also—as head of a major union of public employees—a person with obvious and strong interests in the outcome of the PATCO matter. That they discussed the pending case and, in close proximity, Applewhaite's employment concerns, understandably troubled the reviewing judges. Here, the more political and temporary character of an agency head's work brings the contrasts with a judicial model, and concomitant concerns about fairness, into the sharpest relief.

Agency officials cannot stay as aloof from the worlds of politics and constituencies as can judges. For agencies, continuing contact with a regulated industry, the public, and the press can have central importance for effective regulation. Informal contacts, press interviews, convention addresses, and the like may help the agency win needed support, reduce future enforcement requirements (by helping industry anticipate and plan for compliance), float a trial balloon, spur the provision of needed information, signal their staff about their preferences, or otherwise achieve wholly understandable and worthy ends. Courts are not faced with the need to motivate and inform a staff, defend their policies before a concerned legislature, impress the public, or enlist reluctant support of industry.

Commissioner Applewhaite's concern for his employment future was not simply inappropriate self-interest but the natural product of our public policy choices. We have chosen to have persons who are *not* part of a permanent bureaucracy lead the government. As a result, for an agency's top personnel who are outside the Civil Service, tenure in office is anything but assured. Even at levels below that of the agency head, we encourage people to use a "revolving door" from and to the private sector. This choice risks that individuals will be tempted into acting with an eye to their future benefit while they are in government service or that they later will use information or contacts acquired in government service for private benefit. But the choice also has benefits, in improving communication between government and the private sector and maintaining citizen and political control of the bureaucracy. Having made the choice, we render concerns like Applewhaite's inevitable.

(1) *Remedies for Inappropriate Contacts.* As the PATCO decision noted, the APA outlines remedies for ex parte contacts available at the administrative level. Section 557(d) requires the agency to disclose such communications and authorizes the agency to demand that the party violating ex parte prohibitions demonstrate why his claim or interest in the proceedings should not be dismissed. Section 556(d) further authorizes the agency to consider a violation of the ex parte rules as "sufficient grounds for a decision adverse to a party who has knowingly committed such violation or knowingly caused such violation to occur." Disclosure and resultant publicity can be a remedy on their own. PATCO also underscores that in some instances inappropriate ex parte contacts may lead to criminal investigation and prosecution. See 18 U.S.C. § 1505 (prohibition on obstructing agency proceedings); see also 18 U.S.C. § 201 (prohibition on bribery of federal officials).

A harder question is whether inappropriate contacts should lead a court to set aside the agency's decision. Should PATCO be heard to complain about a contact that, presumably, would have worked in its favor? On the other hand, should actions by Shanker—not a party and not apparently acting at PATCO's behest—have been held against PATCO? The court avoided this issue by concluding that no remedy was required for the indiscretions that had occurred. In some cases, disqualification has been administered, and plainly the threat that the agency will withhold whatever the communicator is seeking to gain can serve as a significant control. Thus, in WKAT, Inc. v. FCC, 296 F.2d 375 (D.C. Cir. 1961)—not a case actually involving § 557(d) but cited by the PATCO court—the court disqualified a successful applicant for a television license worth millions because of its improper ex parte efforts to influence the role of an FCC commissioner. This sanction cannot be applied invariably, however, without risking harm to the public interest.

(2) *Prohibited Actions while in Office.* The problems of government ethics regulation are far subtler than criminal prohibitions against bribery. An ethics regime can have significant implications for government employees' morale and futures outside government. In general, such matters are the domain of the Office of Government Ethics, initially a part of the Office of Personnel Management but now a separate agency. Its regulations are binding on executive branch employees and notably detailed—for example, they not only declare a $20 maximum value for acceptable "gifts," but also indicate that retail value must be observed and state principles on which the values of several trivial gifts must be amalgamated. Were an official today to be contemplating a dinner akin to Commissioner Appelwhaite's dinner with Albert Shanker, these regulations would suggest ample basis for caution.

One of the first acts President Obama undertook upon assuming office was to issue an executive order extending ethics limits on government officials, including a prohibition on officials accepting any gifts from registered lobbyists or lobbying organizations. More significantly, the order imposed new restrictions on the ability of officials to participate in matters related to their former employment and particular limitations on former lobbyists. The latter were required to pledge that they will not "seek or accept employment with any executive agency that [the individual] ... lobbied within the 2 years before . . . appointment." E.O. 13409 § 1 (Jan. 21, 2009). Not to be outdone, President Trump shortly after taking office issued a superseding executive order covering "Ethics Commitments by Executive Branch Appointees." E.O. 13770 (Jan. 28, 2017). Many of the provisions are similar to President Obama's, but the two-year restrictions on former lobbyists were limited to participation in particular matters or specific issue areas involving former clients, rather than to employment in the agency altogether. § 1(6)(7). President Trump also issued waivers to particular appointees as to some of these obligations; these waivers were, after some pressure from the Office of Government Ethics, posted on the Whitehouse website.

(3) ***Prohibited Actions upon Leaving Office.*** Federal criminal law has long provided that a former official may not appear for a private client after leaving government in a distinct matter (adjudication, grant, contract—but *not* rule) in which she had been "personally and substantially" involved while in government, and she may not appear for a year respecting any like matter for which she had official "responsibility" during the year before she left government. See 18 U.S.C. §§ 205, 207. A moment's reflection will show that these prohibitions are limited—there is no bar to advising a client so long as one does not appear; one's partner may appear; appearance is acceptable so long as it is not in connection with a "matter" within reach of one or the other rule; and, finally, waivers could on occasion be obtained.

The Ethics in Government Act, enacted in 1978, tightened post-employment constraints in some respects. As amended, 18 U.S.C. § 207 now extends the lifetime ban on participation in particular matters in which the former employee was "personally and substantially" involved to informal as well as formal appearances. In addition, for two years she is forbidden to directly appear or communicate on all matters formally under her official responsibility. High-level former employees also face a one-year ban on making any approach to the agency, formal or informal, oral or written, seeking to influence outcomes (including in rulemaking proceedings) regardless of whether the matter was pending during their tenure or within their responsibility. The Act initially also prohibited former employees from counseling, aiding, consulting, advising, or assisting others who communicate or appear during the two years immediately following their government service, but this prohibition was repealed in 1989. Provision is made for the agency to seek its former employee's advice where the agency wants that advice, and the agency is also authorized to impose a sanction as large as five years' disqualification to appear before it on former employees who violate the Act's requirements, in addition to criminal sanctions.

President Obama's Executive Order tightened post-employment prohibitions as well. That Executive Order contained a "Revolving Door Ban" under which officials pledged "upon leaving Government service, not to lobby any covered executive branch official or non-career Senior Executive Service appointee for the remainder of the Administration." President Trump's, in addition to repeating that pledge, also requires employees to pledge to "not, within 5 years after the termination of my employment as an appointee in any executive agency in which I am appointed to serve, engage in lobbying activities with respect to that agency." E.O. 13770, § 1(1). For the counter-argument, that the "revolving door" is not something much to worry about, see David Zaring, Against Being Against the Revolving Door, 2013 U. Ill. L. Rev. 507.

(4)   The problems of government ethics regulation were the subject of study by a special ABA Committee on Government Standards, CYNTHIA R. FARINA, REPORTER, KEEPING FAITH: GOVERNMENT ETHICS AND GOVERNMENT ETHICS REGULATION, 45 Admin. L. Rev. 287, 296–97, 327 (1993): "Of all areas of substantive ethics law, the rules defining and remedying conflicts of interest are the most central, and the most vexing. Here, the longstanding American commitment to citizen governance comes up against several fundamental ideals of ethical public service. The result is considerable tension and ambivalence. On the one hand, a continual stream of people entering government from the private sector is perceived as highly desirable. The current popularity of term-limitation laws reflects this perception. Movement between government and the private sector is valued as injecting energy, experience, practicality and perspective that would be lacking in government-by-professional-bureaucracy. On the other hand, there is an equally strong conviction that neither elected nor appointed officials should have financial interests or relationships outside government that compromise their exercise of power. . . .

". . . [E]thics regulation will be both redundant and inadequate if it focuses merely on condemning the deliberate abuse of trust. It will be redundant because the criminal law (through the vehicles of bribery, illegal gratuities, embezzlement, etc.) already proscribes such behavior. It will be inadequate because the overwhelming majority of government employees, knowing themselves to be honorable persons who would never consciously misuse their position, can readily dismiss such proscriptions as irrelevant to their own professional lives—and so fail to reflect upon the insidious ways in which bias and self-interest can infect, almost unwittingly, the exercise of power. Hence, ethics regulation can make its most meaningful contribution by helping government employees to recognize, and take steps to defuse, situations that invite compromised behavior."

The Report also addressed regulation of the activities of individuals as they leave government service, noting that "it is not always clear precisely what . . . is the answer to the question 'Which use of advantage in which situation is actually unethical?' Surely we are not prepared to say that *any* use at *any* time of *any* knowledge or influence acquired during government service on behalf of a party other than the federal government, is an abuse of the public trust. Taking such a position would mean that a lawyer who had clerked for the Supreme Court could never draft a certiorari petition for a private client, or that a scientist who had worked for the FDA could never take a job in commercial new drug development, or that an MBA who had worked for the SEC could never join an investment banking house. Neither sound ethics policy nor good government supports an approach in which individuals can enter government service only at the cost of radically reconfiguring their subsequent professional lives."

The Report argued that whether using advantages of former government employment is ethical turns largely on three factors: the nature of the former official's responsibility, the nature of the matter, and the nature of the aid given the new employer or client. "Of greatest concern are situations in which the former employee had significant decisional responsibility, had access to sensitive information, or otherwise functioned in an influential role as draftsperson, strategizer or counselor[;] situations that resemble adjudicatory 'cases'[;]" and "situations in which the former employee functions directly or indirectly as advocate . . . to help advance her new employer's position in an ongoing matter with the government."

SECTION 3.   INFORMAL AGENCY ADJUDICATION UNDER THE APA

> *DOMINION ENERGY BRAYTON POINT, LLC v. JOHNSON*
> *PENSION BENEFIT GUARANTY CORP. v. LTV CORP.*
> *OLIVARES v. TRANSPORTATION SECURITY ADMINISTRATION*

On-the-record adjudication is the focus of the APA's provisions on adjudication; as you have seen, § 554 on "Adjudications" opens by stipulating that it applies whenever adjudication is "required by statute to be determined on the record after an opportunity for an agency hearing," with a few listed exceptions. Yet at the same time, the APA broadly defines adjudication as including licensing and any other agency action leading to a final disposition that is not rulemaking. §§ 551(6)–(7). This means that there is a broad array of agency actions that qualify as adjudication, yet fall outside the APA's on-the-record procedures. These are lumped into the category of "informal adjudication," but they represent a vast and extremely diverse assortment of activities.

DOMINION ENERGY BRAYTON POINT, LLC v. JOHNSON

United States Court of Appeals for the First Circuit (2006).
443 F.3d 12.

■ SELYA, CIRCUIT JUDGE.

USGen New England, Inc., now Dominion Energy Brayton Point, LLC (Dominion), filed suit against the U.S. Environmental Protection Agency, its administrator, and its regional office (collectively, the EPA), alleging that the EPA failed to perform a non-discretionary duty when it refused to grant Dominion's request for a formal evidentiary hearing after issuing a proposed final National Pollution Discharge Elimination System (NPDES) permit. . . .

I. BACKGROUND

Dominion owns an electrical generating facility in Somerset, Massachusetts (the station). The station opened in the 1960s and, like most power plants of its era, utilizes an "open-cycle" cooling system. Specifically, the station withdraws water from the Lees and Taunton Rivers, circulates that water through the plant's generating equipment as a coolant, and then discharges the water (which, by then, has attained an elevated temperature) into Mount Hope Bay.

The withdrawals and discharges of water are regulated by the Clean Water Act (CWA), 33 U.S.C. §§ 1251–1387. For the last three decades, these actions have been authorized by a series of NPDES permits issued by the EPA pursuant to section 402(a) of the CWA. The standards incorporated into those permits are determined under the thermal variance procedures laid out in section 316(a).

In 1998, the station applied for renewal of its NPDES permit and thermal variance authorization. The EPA issued a proposed final permit on October 6, 2003, in which it rejected the requested thermal variance. On November 4, Dominion sought review before the Environmental Appeals Board (the Board) and asked for an evidentiary hearing. The Board accepted the petition for review but declined to convene an evidentiary hearing. . . .

II. THE LEGAL LANDSCAPE

We set the stage for our substantive discussion by undertaking a brief review of the legal rules that frame the controversy at hand.

Before the EPA either issues an NPDES permit or authorizes a thermal variance, it must offer an "opportunity for public hearing." 33 U.S.C. §§ 1326(a), 1342(a). No definition of "public hearing" is contained within the four corners of the CWA.

The Administrative Procedure Act (APA), 5 U.S.C. § 551 *et seq.*, is also part of the relevant legal landscape. Most pertinent here are those sections that combine to describe the procedures for formal administrative adjudications. See id. §§ 554, 556, 557. These procedures apply "in every case of adjudication required by statute to be determined on the record after opportunity for an agency hearing." *Id.* § 554(a). The APA does not directly address whether these procedures apply when a statute simply calls for an "opportunity for public hearing" without any specific indication that the hearing should be "on the record."

In Seacoast Anti-Pollution League v. Costle, 572 F.2d 872 (1st Cir. 1978), this court interpreted "public hearing" (as used in sections 402(a) and 316(a) of the CWA) to mean "evidentiary hearing"—in other words, a hearing that comports with the APA's requirements for a formal adjudication. Examining the legislative history of the APA, we adopted a presumption that "unless a statute otherwise specifies, an adjudicatory hearing subject to judicial review must be [an evidentiary hearing] on the record." Id. at 877. Applying that presumption to the CWA, we concluded that "the statute certainly does not indicate that the determination need *not* be on the record." Id. at 878 (emphasis in original).

So viewed, Seacoast established a rebuttable presumption that, in the context of an adjudication, an organic statute that calls for a "public hearing" should be read to require an evidentiary hearing in compliance with the formal adjudication provisions of the APA. Two other circuit courts reached the same conclusion, albeit through different reasoning. Acquiescing in this construction, the EPA promulgated regulations that memorialized the use of formal evidentiary hearings in the NPDES permit process. *See* NPDES, Revision of Regulations, 44 Fed.Reg. 32,854, 32,938 (June 7, 1979).

In 1984, a sea change occurred in administrative law and, specifically, in the interpretation of organic statutes such as the CWA. The Supreme Court held that "[w]hen a court reviews an agency's construction of the statute which it administers," the reviewing court first must ask "whether Congress has directly spoken to the precise question at issue." Chevron U.S.A. Inc. v. NRDC, 467 U.S. 837, 842. If Congress's intent is clear, that intent governs—both the court and the agency must give it full effect. If, however, Congress has not directly addressed the question and the agency has stepped into the vacuum by promulgating an interpretive regulation, a reviewing court may "not simply impose its own construction on the statute," but, rather, ought to ask "whether the agency's answer is based on a permissible construction of the statute." Id. at 843. . . .

Armed with the Chevron decision and a presidential directive to streamline regulatory programs, the EPA advanced a proposal to eliminate formal evidentiary hearings from the NPDES permitting process. In due course, the EPA adopted that proposal as a final rule. *See* Amendments to Streamline the NPDES Program Regulations: Round Two, 65 Fed.Reg. 30,886, 30,900 (May 15, 2000).

This revision depended heavily on a Chevron analysis. The agency began by "finding no evidence that Congress intended to require formal evidentiary hearings or that the text [of section 402(a)] precludes informal adjudication of permit review petitions." Id. at 30,896. Then, it weighed the risks and benefits of employing informal hearing procedures for NPDES permit review, "determining that these procedures would not violate the Due Process Clause." Id. Finally, it "concluded that informal hearing procedures satisfy the hearing requirement of section 402(a)." Id.

It was under this new regulatory scheme that the EPA considered Dominion's request to renew its NPDES permit and to authorize a thermal variance. Thus, it was under this scheme that the EPA denied Dominion's request for an evidentiary hearing.

III. ANALYSIS

. . . For present purposes, the critical precedent is National Cable & Telecommunications Ass'n v. Brand X Internet Services, 545 U.S. 967

(2005). There, the Court examined the relationship between the stare decisis effect of an appellate court's statutory interpretation and the Chevron deference due to an administrative agency's subsequent, but contrary, interpretation. Echoing Chevron, the Court reiterated that "[f]illing [statutory] gaps . . . involves difficult policy choices that agencies are better equipped to make than courts." Id. at 2699. Then, concluding that Chevron's application should not turn on the order in which judicial and agency interpretations issue, the Justices held squarely that "[a] court's prior judicial construction of a statute trumps an agency construction otherwise entitled to Chevron deference only if the prior court decision holds that its construction follows from the unambiguous terms of the statute and thus leaves no room for agency discretion." Id. at 2700. . . .

Once this mode of analysis is understood and applied, Dominion's argument collapses. Seacoast simply does not hold that Congress clearly intended the term "public hearing" in sections 402(a) and 316(a) of the CWA to mean "evidentiary hearing." To the contrary, the Seacoast court based its interpretation of the CWA on a presumption derived from the legislative history of the APA—a presumption that would hold sway only in the absence of a showing of a contrary congressional intent. In other words, the court resorted to the presumption only because it could find no sign of a plainly discernible congressional intent. . . .

The short of it is that the Seacoast court, faced with an opaque statute, settled upon what it sensibly thought was the best construction of the CWA's "public hearing" language. . . . Consequently, under *Brand X*, Seacoast must yield to a reasonable agency interpretation of the CWA's "public hearing" requirement.

The only piece left to this puzzle is to confirm that the EPA's new regulations are, in fact, entitled to Chevron deference. This inquiry is a straightforward one. As our earlier discussion suggests (and as the Seacoast court correctly deduced), Congress has not spoken directly to the precise question at issue here. See, e.g., United States v. Fla. E. Coast Ry. Co., 410 U.S. 224, 239 (1973) ("The term 'hearing' in its legal context undoubtedly has a host of meanings.") Accordingly, we must defer to the EPA's interpretation of the CWA as long as that interpretation is reasonable.

In this instance, the administrative interpretation took into account the relevant universe of factors. *See* 65 Fed.Reg. at 30,898–30,900 (considering "(1) [t]he private interests at stake, (2) the risk of erroneous decision-making, and (3) the nature of the government interest," and concluding that its new regulation was a reasonable interpretation of the CWA). The agency's conclusion that evidentiary hearings are unnecessary and that Congress, in using the phrase "opportunity for public hearing," did not mean to mandate evidentiary hearings seems reasonable—and Dominion, to its credit, has conceded the point. . . .

Dominion exhorts us to find that *Seacoast's* holding is actually an interpretation of the APA, not the CWA (and, therefore, the EPA's regulation is also an interpretation of the APA, not entitled to Chevron deference). See, e.g., Metro. Stevedore Co. v. Rambo, 521 U.S. 121, 137 n. 9 (1997) (noting that Chevron deference is inappropriate vis-à-vis an agency interpretation of the APA's burden-of-proof provision). Such a reading of *Seacoast* is plainly incorrect. While the *Seacoast* court relied on a presumption borrowed from the APA, the court's holding is an interpretation of the CWA and, specifically, of the term "public hearing" contained in sections 402(a) and 316(a). . . . Because those changes implicate the statute that the EPA administers (i.e., the CWA), *Chevron* deference is appropriate.

IV. CONCLUSION

We summarize succinctly. Although we in no way disparage the soundness of *Seacoast's* reasoning, the *Chevron* and *Brand X* opinions and the interposition of a new and reasonable agency interpretation of the disputed statutory language have changed the picture. Because we, like the *Seacoast* court, cannot discern a clear and unambiguous congressional intent behind the words "public hearing" in the CWA and because the EPA's interpretation of that term constitutes a reasonable construction of the statute, deference is due. . . .

[W]e conclude that the district court did not err in dismissing Dominion's action.

Affirmed.

NOTES

(1) *What Is Being Interpreted?* If the Clean Water Act requires holding a "public hearing" and the APA says "required by statute to be determined on the record after opportunity for an agency hearing," is the First Circuit right when it now says that what is at issue is an interpretation of the CWA and not an interpretation of the APA? (Remember that Chevron does not cover an agency's interpretation of the APA, which is meant to bring uniformity to procedures across multiple agencies.)

The Seacoast opinion, overturned by the principal case, relied heavily on the ATTORNEY GENERAL'S MANUAL ON THE APA 42–43 (1947): "It is believed that with respect to adjudication the specific statutory requirement of a hearing, without anything more, carries with it the further requirement of decision on the basis of the evidence adduced at the hearing. With respect to rule making, it was concluded that a statutory provision that rules be issued after a hearing, without more, should not be construed as requiring agency action 'on the record,' but rather as merely requiring an opportunity for the expression of views. That conclusion was based on the legislative nature of rule making, from which it was inferred, unless a statute requires otherwise, that an agency hearing on proposed rules would be similar to a hearing before a legislative committee, with neither the legislature nor the agency being limited to the material adduced at the hearing. No such rationale applies to administrative adjudication. In fact, it is assumed that where a statute specifically provides for administrative adjudication (such as the suspension or revocation of a license) after opportunity for an agency hearing, such specific requirement for a hearing ordinarily implies the further requirement of decision in accordance with evidence adduced at the hearing. Of course, the foregoing discussion is inapplicable to any situation in which the legislative history or the context of the pertinent statute indicates a contrary congressional intent." Is this a better view?

(2) Even if what is at stake is the meaning of the Clean Water Act, should the court defer to the agency's interpretation on the theory that the agency knows best what type of hearing will best balance costs with improved results? Or should it refuse to defer, on the theory that statutorily stipulated procedures (in the CWA as well as the APA) are meant to restrain the agency and to protect outside parties? The Chevron case [p. 1129] that the court relies on involved deference to an agency determination regarding a substantive matter.

(3) Congress could, of course, change the result of this case. In 2000, the ABA passed a resolution saying:

> Resolved, that in order to preserve the uniformity of provisions and of qualifications of presiding officers contemplated by the APA, Congress should amend the APA to provide prospectively that, absent a statutory requirement to the contrary, in any future legislation that creates the opportunity for a hearing in an adjudication, such a hearing should follow the APA's formal adjudication procedures.

If you were in Congress, would you sponsor this legislation?

(4) Of course, even with the decision in this case, the EPA is still required to hold a "public hearing" by the terms of the Clean Water Act. Whether its regulations defining that "public hearing" are proper would be, in an appropriate case, subject to judicial review—presumably under the Chevron standard.

PENSION BENEFIT GUARANTY CORP. v. LTV CORP.

Supreme Court of the United States (1990).
496 U.S. 633.

■ JUSTICE BLACKMUN delivered the opinion of the Court.

[Private sector pension benefits in the United States come in two basic forms: "defined contribution" and "defined benefit." In the "defined contribution" form, employers put a specified amount of money into an account individually identified to the particular employee; the pension the employee ultimately receives depends on how much is contributed over the years and how it is invested. In the "defined benefit" form, the employee is guaranteed a specific amount per year after retirement, often related to how many years the employee worked and what his final salary was—for example, a pension of 60% of the average of his last five years' earnings. The money to pay "defined benefit" pensions is accumulated in the employer's general pension plan; because the benefit to be paid is not directly correlated to contributions to the plan, nor to how it has been invested, there is always the danger that the plan will not be large enough to cover all the promised benefits. As part of the Employee Retirement Income Security Act of 1974 (commonly known as ERISA), Congress established a mandatory government insurance program, funded by employer-paid premiums, to protect these promised defined-pension benefits. The Pension Benefit Guaranty Corporation (PBGC)—plaintiff in this case—is a wholly owned U.S. Government corporation, modeled after the Federal Deposit Insurance Corporation, that administers this program. When it acts pursuant to ERISA, it is treated as an "agency" for APA purposes.

LTV Corp.—defendant in this case—is a steel company. In 1986, it filed for bankruptcy. Its pension plan was grossly underfunded. As part of the ensuing proceedings, PBGC "terminated" the company's plan—i.e., took over its assets and its much greater existing liabilities. This had the effect both of costing the PBGC insurance fund a pretty penny and of reducing some of the benefits LTV's workers would have accrued had the old pension plan continued in effect.

As part of the bankruptcy reorganization, LTV negotiated new pension arrangements with its unions, free of the old liabilities. To PBGC's eye, these new arrangements would have the effect of putting LTV plan participants in the same financial position they would have occupied had the prior plan never been terminated. Now, however, a substantial part of their pre-existing benefits would be paid by public sources through PBGC, rather than through LTV. PBGC's fixed policy was to object to what it termed "follow-on" plans designed to wrap around the insurance benefits it provided; in its view, they resulted in the insurance fund subsidizing an employer's ongoing operations in a way not contemplated by ERISA. As a result, PBGC "restored" the plans it had previously terminated, which had the effect of making LTV again liable for the pension costs PBGC had assumed.

Before deciding to restore the plans, PBGC met with LTV to "consider any additional information [LTV] might wish to supply." When LTV refused to comply with PBGC's restoration decision, PBGC brought an action in District Court. The District Court refused enforcement and PBGC appealed to the Second Circuit, which agreed with the District Court.

In reversing, the Supreme Court first considered the Court of Appeal's substantive objections, and held (1) that the agency was not to be faulted for focusing on its responsibilities under ERISA rather than considering factors involved in bankruptcy law and labor law [see p. 1081 below]; and (2) that the agency's interpretation of ERISA should be sustained under the Chevron doctrine [see p. 1129 below]. But what concerns us here is the Court's approval of the procedure the agency had used, which the Second Circuit had also faulted. Justice Blackmun wrote:]

. . .Relying upon a passage in Bowman Transportation, Inc. v. Arkansas-Best Freight System, Inc., 419 U.S. 281, 288 n. 4 (1974), the court [below] held that the PBGC's decision was arbitrary and capricious because the 'PBGC neither apprised LTV of the material on which it was to base its decision, gave LTV an adequate opportunity to offer contrary evidence, proceeded in accordance with ascertainable standards . . ., nor provided [LTV] a statement showing its reasoning in applying those standards.' 875 F.2d, at 1021. The court suggested that on remand the agency was required to do each of these things.

The PBGC argues that this holding conflicts with Vermont Yankee Nuclear Power Corp. v. Natural Resources Defense Council, Inc. [p. 295], where, the PBGC contends, this Court made clear that when the Due Process Clause is not implicated and an agency's governing statute contains no specific procedural mandates, the [APA] establishes the maximum procedural requirements a reviewing court may impose on agencies. Although Vermont Yankee concerned additional procedures imposed . . . on the Atomic Energy Commission when the agency was engaging in informal rulemaking, the PBGC argues that the informal adjudication process by which the restoration decision was made should be governed by the same principles.

Respondents counter by arguing that courts, under some circumstances, do require agencies to undertake additional procedures. As support for this proposition, they rely on Citizens to Preserve Overton Park, Inc. v. Volpe, 401 U.S. 402 (1971). In Overton Park, the Court concluded that the Secretary of Transportation's "post hoc rationalizations" regarding a decision to authorize the construction of a highway did not provide "an [a]dequate basis for [judicial] review" for purposes of § 706 of the APA. Id., at 419. Accordingly, the Court directed the District Court on remand to consider evidence that shed light on the Secretary's reasoning at the time he made the decision. Of particular relevance for present purposes, the Court in Overton Park intimated that one recourse for the District Court might be a remand to the agency for a fuller explanation of the agency's reasoning at the time of the agency action. Subsequent cases have made clear that remanding to the agency in fact is the preferred course. Respondents contend that the instant case is controlled by Overton Park rather than Vermont Yankee, and that the Court of Appeals' ruling was thus correct.

We believe that respondents' argument is wide of the mark. We begin by noting that although one initially might feel that there is some tension between Vermont Yankee and Overton Park, the two cases are not necessarily inconsistent. Vermont Yankee stands for the general proposition that courts are not free to impose upon agencies specific procedural requirements that have no basis in the APA. At most, Overton

Park suggests that § 706(2)(A) of the APA, which directs a court to ensure that an agency action is not arbitrary and capricious or otherwise contrary to law, imposes a general "procedural" requirement of sorts by mandating that an agency take whatever steps it needs to provide an explanation that will enable the court to evaluate the agency's rationale at the time of decision.

Here, unlike in Overton Park, the Court of Appeals did not suggest that the administrative record was inadequate to enable the court to fulfill its duties under § 706. Rather, to support its ruling, the court focused on "fundamental fairness" to LTV. With the possible exception of the absence of "ascertainable standards"—by which we are not exactly sure what the Court of Appeals meant—the procedural inadequacies cited by the court all relate to LTV's role in the PBGC's decisionmaking process. But the court did not point to any provision in ERISA or the APA which gives LTV the procedural rights the court identified. Thus, the court's holding runs afoul of Vermont Yankee and finds no support in Overton Park.

Nor is Arkansas-Best, the case on which the Court of Appeals relied, to the contrary. The statement relied upon (which was dictum) said: "A party is entitled, of course, to know the issues on which decision will turn and to be apprised of the factual material on which the agency relies for decision so that he may rebut it." That statement was entirely correct in the context of Arkansas-Best, which involved a formal adjudication by the Interstate Commerce Commission pursuant to the trial-type procedures set forth in §§ 5, 7 and 8 of the APA, 5 U.S.C. §§ 554, 556–557, which include requirements that parties be given notice of "the matters of fact and law asserted," § 554(b)(3), an opportunity for "the submission and consideration of facts [and] arguments," § 554(c)(1), and an opportunity to submit "proposed findings and conclusions" or "exceptions," § 557(c)(1), (2). The determination in this case, however, was lawfully made by informal adjudication, the minimal requirements for which are set forth in § 555 of the APA, and do not include such elements. A failure to provide them where the Due Process Clause itself does not require them (which has not been asserted here) is therefore not unlawful.

We conclude that the PBGC's failure to consider all potentially relevant areas of law did not render its restoration decision arbitrary and capricious. We also conclude that the PBGC's anti-follow-on policy, an asserted basis for the restoration decision, is not contrary to clear congressional intent and is based on a permissible construction of [the statute]. Finally, we find the procedures employed by the PBGC to be consistent with the APA. Accordingly, the judgment of the Court of Appeals is reversed, and the case is remanded for further proceedings consistent with this opinion.

NOTES

(1)   *What Does the APA Say?* Here is § 555:

Ancillary matters

(a)   This section applies, according to the provisions thereof, except as otherwise provided by this subchapter.

(b)   A person compelled to appear in person before an agency or representative thereof is entitled to be accompanied, represented, and advised by counsel or, if permitted by the agency, by other qualified representative. A party is entitled to appear in person or by or with counsel or other duly qualified representative in an agency proceeding. So far as the orderly conduct of public business permits, an interested person may appear before an agency or its responsible employees for the presentation, adjustment, or determination of an issue, request, or controversy in a proceeding, whether interlocutory, summary, or otherwise, or in connection with an agency function. With due regard for the convenience and necessity of the parties or their representatives and within a reasonable time, each agency shall proceed to conclude a matter presented to it. This subsection does not grant or deny a person who is not a lawyer the right to appear for or represent others before an agency or in an agency proceeding.

(c)   [Investigative acts; copies of submitted evidence.]

(d)   [Agency subpoenas.]

(e)   Prompt notice shall be given of the denial in whole or in part of a written application, petition, or other request of an interested person made in connection with any agency proceeding. Except in affirming a prior denial or when the denial is self-explanatory, the notice shall be accompanied by a brief statement of the grounds for denial.

---

(2)   The title of the section is "Ancillary matters." The individual parts seem to assume that an "agency proceeding" already exists. Only a few particular details are specified. Is the Pension Benefit Guaranty Corp. Court right to see § 555 as the specification of "informal adjudication" in the same way that other, much more detailed provisions of the APA specify the processes for formal rulemaking, informal rulemaking, and formal adjudication?

(3)   Even if we say that the Court was right as to that, was it also right to apply Vermont Yankee's strictures to informal adjudication per § 555—to decide, that is, that § 555 is so complete that judges can add to it only if the due process clause so requires? Or should it have been treated as more open-ended?

(4)   Alternatively, should the APA be amended to provide a specific model of informal adjudication, rather than leaving most of the details to agencies to decide?

OLIVARES v. TRANSPORTATION SECURITY ADMINISTRATION

United States Court of Appeals for the District of Columbia Circuit (2016).
819 F.3d 454.

■ EDWARDS, SENIOR CIRCUIT JUDGE.

Alberto Ardila Olivares, the Petitioner before the court, is a foreign alien from Venezuela. In 2014, he applied to attend a Federal Aviation Administration ("FAA")-certified flight school in France to obtain a pilot certification to fly large, U.S.-registered aircraft. After conducting a background check, the Transportation Security Administration ("TSA") determined that Petitioner was a risk to aviation and national security and denied his application for training. Petitioner now seeks review of TSA's action, invoking the court's jurisdiction under 49 U.S.C. § 46110(a), and asserting causes of action under the Administrative Procedure Act ("APA"), 5 U.S.C. §§ 555(e), 702, 704, 706(2). . . .

I.   BACKGROUND

In the aftermath of the tragic terrorist attacks on September 11, 2001, Congress created the Transportation Security Administration to shore up our nation's civil aviation security. TSA was initially housed in the Department of Transportation and headed by the Under Secretary of Transportation for Security. In 2002, TSA was moved to the newly created Department of Homeland Security under the direction of the Secretary of Homeland Security.

This case involves TSA's role in determining whether alien pilots may be certified to operate large, U.S.-registered aircraft. "Large aircraft means aircraft of more than 12,500 pounds, maximum certificated takeoff weight." 14 C.F.R. § 1.1 (emphasis omitted). No pilot may "serve in any capacity as an airman with respect to a civil aircraft . . . in air commerce . . . without an airman certificate" from FAA. 49 U.S.C. § 44711(a)(2); see also 14 C.F.R. § 61.3(a). For large aircraft, pilots must obtain additional certification known as a Type Rating. 14 C.F.R. § 61.31(a)(1). Aliens who seek training and certification to operate large, U.S.-registered aircraft must first secure clearance by TSA. See 49 U.S.C. § 44939(a). If TSA "determine[s] that [an alien applicant] presents a risk to aviation or national security," then that applicant is ineligible to receive the training necessary to secure a large aircraft Type Rating from FAA. See id.; see also 49 C.F.R. § 1552.3(a)(4), (e).

Petitioner is an alien pilot who formerly lived and worked in the United States. On February 14, 2007, he was convicted in federal court of conspiracy to possess with intent to distribute controlled substances in violation of 21 U.S.C. § 846. He was sentenced to serve 80 months in prison, followed by 60 months of supervised release. On December 17, 2007, FAA sent Petitioner a letter revoking his pilot certification, effective January 7, 2008. Petitioner was subsequently deported on March 3, 2010.

After being deported, Petitioner worked as a pilot in Venezuela. In 2011, he was presented with an opportunity to fly a large, U.S.-registered aircraft, which required him to receive training for the appropriate Type Rating and then seek the appropriate certification from FAA. To achieve these ends, Petitioner applied for admission to an FAA-certified flight school in France. TSA then conducted a background investigation of Petitioner. Although TSA uncovered Petitioner's 2007 drug conviction, TSA granted him permission to attend flight school. Petitioner successfully completed flight school and obtained his Type Rating as well as various other FAA certifications.

In 2012, the U.S. Government Accountability Office ("GAO") published a report criticizing TSA's background investigations of alien pilots. GAO, Weaknesses Exist In TSA's Process For Ensuring Foreign Flight Students Do Not Pose A Security Threat (July 2012) ("GAO Report" or "Report"). The Report highlighted that TSA's investigation methods did not always thoroughly examine an alien's immigration status, and expressed concern that, as a result, the investigation might not identify all alien flight-school applicants presenting a security threat. In response to the Report, TSA revised its background check procedures. . . .

In 2014, Petitioner received another opportunity to pilot a large, U.S.-registered aircraft. Although his general FAA credentials remained valid, Petitioner's Type Rating had expired. As before, Petitioner applied to attend an FAA-certified flight school in France, and TSA conducted a background investigation.

Pursuant to TSA's new procedures, the agency's investigation flagged that Petitioner was inadmissible to enter the United States due to his 2007 drug conviction. As a result, Petitioner's application was referred for further investigation. The investigation uncovered that, in addition to his 2007 drug conviction, Petitioner had been suspected of firearms trafficking in 1998 in Aruba. TSA also discovered that, even though he had been deported with no right to return to the United States, Petitioner maintained a local address in Massachusetts. . . .

On November 5, 2014, TSA sent an email to Petitioner denying his application. The email stated:

> Pursuant to Title 49 of the Code of Federal Regulations [§]1552.3(e), your training request has been denied as TSA is unable to determine that you do not pose a threat to aviation or national security. This letter constitutes TSA's final determination.

TSA's email gave no further explanation for its denial of Petitioner's application.

On January 5, 2015, Petitioner filed his petition for review with this court. On March 26, 2015, Andrea Vara executed a sworn declaration explaining TSA's grounds for denying Petitioner's application for training. Ms. Vara is employed by the U.S. Department of Homeland Security, Transportation Security Administration, as the Alien Flight Student Program Manager. . . .

The Vara Declaration makes it clear that Ms. Vara was the Government official who made the determination that Petitioner's application should be denied because he presented a risk to aviation and national security. The Declaration not only explains the agency's rationale, it also cites internal materials that TSA had before it at the time when the determination was made to deny Petitioner's application. . . .

The entire Vara Declaration was included in the parties' Joint Appendix that was submitted to the court. Both parties discuss the Vara Declaration in their briefs to the court. And, as noted above, Petitioner does not question the authenticity of the Vara Declaration or the authority of the declarant; and we do not have any reason to doubt the veracity of TSA's account of the grounds justifying the agency's denial of Petitioner's application for flight training.

II. ANALYSIS

A. THE COURT'S JURISDICTION

[We have jurisdiction.]

B. STANDARD OF REVIEW

["In cases of this sort, we must defer to TSA actions that reasonably interpret and enforce the safety and security obligations of the agency."]

C. PETITIONER'S CLAIM UNDER SECTION 555(e) OF THE APA

Section 555(e) of the APA provides:

> Prompt notice shall be given of the denial in whole or in part of a written application, petition, or other request of an interested person made in connection with any agency proceeding. Except in affirming a prior denial or when the denial is self-explanatory, the notice shall be accompanied by a brief statement of the grounds for denial.

5 U.S.C. § 555(e). Petitioner claims that TSA's November 5, 2014 email to him denying his application for flight training violated the requirements of § 555(e) because the email offered no statement of the grounds for the agency's denial. As noted above, Petitioner's claim, at least at first blush, is compelling.

In Tourus Records, Inc. v. DEA, 259 F.3d 731, 737 (D.C. Cir. 2001) we explained:

> A "fundamental" requirement of administrative law is that an agency "set forth its reasons" for decision; an agency's failure to do so constitutes arbitrary and capricious agency action. That fundamental requirement is codified in section 6(d) of the APA, 5 U.S.C. § 555(e). Section 6(d) mandates that whenever an

agency denies "a written application, petition, or other request of an interested person made in connection with any agency proceeding," the agency must provide "a brief statement of the grounds for denial," unless the denial is "self-explanatory." This requirement not only ensures the agency's careful consideration of such requests, but also gives parties the opportunity to apprise the agency of any errors it may have made and, if the agency persists in its decision, facilitates judicial review. Although nothing more than a "brief statement" is necessary, the core requirement is that the agency explain "why it chose to do what it did." Henry J. Friendly, Chenery Revisited: Reflections on Reversal and Remand of Administrative Orders, 1969 Duke L.J. 199, 222.

TSA's email to Petitioner denying his application for flight training did not meet this APA standard. The email simply parroted the words of 49 U.S.C. § 44939(a), without offering anything to explain why TSA had determined that Petitioner presented a risk to aviation or national security. And TSA has not argued that the reasons behind the denial of Petitioner's application were "self-explanatory." 5 U.S.C. § 555(e). "The [email] thus provides no basis upon which we could conclude that it was the product of reasoned decisionmaking." *Tourus Records,* 259 F.3d at 737.

"When an agency provides a statement of reasons insufficient to permit a court to discern its rationale, or states no reasons at all, the usual remedy is a 'remand to the agency for additional investigation or explanation.'" *Id.* (quoting Fla. Power & Light Co. v. Lorion, 470 U.S. 729, 744 (1985)). This case presents an unusual situation, however, because, after Petitioner filed his petition for review, TSA submitted the Vara Declaration and other internal agency documents that, together, offer a clear statement of the grounds and rationale upon which TSA relied in denying Petitioner's application for flight training. The internal materials include the findings of TSA's background investigation of Petitioner as well as internal agency communications. And, as explained by the Vara Declaration, these internal materials express TSA's reasoned, contemporaneous explanation for its decision. The internal materials are not impermissible "*post hoc* rationalizations" for agency action. *Tourus Records,* 259 F.3d at 738 (quoting Burlington Truck Lines, Inc. v. United States, 371 U.S. 156 (1962)). Rather, they "represent the 'contemporaneous explanation of the agency decision,'" and, therefore, they are "appropriate subjects for our consideration." *Id.* . . .

Although we find that the internal agency materials, as illuminated by the Vara Declaration, satisfy the requirements of § 555(e), we add a word of caution. In the future, agencies will be well advised to obey the explicit command of § 555(e), rather than counting on being able to salvage their actions later, after the losing party has been forced to seek redress in court. Persistent scofflaw behavior might cause the courts to insist that the contemporaneous explanation actually be expressed to the complaining party, as the statute requires, on pain of vacatur and remand. Or the courts might insist on progressively more compelling indications that the reasons offered were in fact the reasons governing the decision when it was made. The offending agency action in this case was mitigated somewhat because the internal materials and the Vara Declaration were included in the parties' Joint Appendix, and Petitioner had an opportunity to review these materials before briefing and oral argument. This may not be sufficient in future cases involving agency defiance of § 555(e).

D.   PETITIONER'S OTHER APA CLAIMS

In addition to his claim under § 555(e), Petitioner also contends that TSA's action was "arbitrary, capricious, an abuse of discretion, or otherwise not in accordance with law," 5 U.S.C. § 706(2)(A), because TSA failed to consider all relevant factors regarding his application for flight training. We disagree. . . .

TSA was not required to show that Petitioner *would* engage in activities designed to compromise aviation or national security. Rather, the agency was merely required to give a reasonable explanation as to why it believed that Petitioner *presented a risk* to aviation or national security. The Vara Declaration satisfies this legal obligation.

III. CONCLUSION

For the reasons set forth above, the petition for review is denied.

NOTES

(1) *Other Rights in Informal Adjudication?* Most of the reported litigation under § 555 has arisen, as in the Olivares case, under the requirement of § 555(e) that the agency give "a brief statement of the grounds for denial." What other rights might lurk in § 555? FRIENDS OF THE BOW V. THOMPSON, 124 F.3d 1210, 1220–21 (10th Cir. 1997). In the course of a dispute involving the sale of timber from Medicine Bow National Forest, an environmental group, Friends of the Bow, sent a letter to the Forest Supervisor requesting that the Environmental Assessment (EA) on which the sale was based be updated because of changed circumstances. No direct response to this letter was given, but the Forest Service did prepare a 26-page "Supplemental Information Report" (SIR) explaining why no new environmental report was needed; this SIR was issued about a year after the letter in question, and a copy was given to the group. In subsequent litigation, one of the claims made by Friends was that this course of behavior violated section 555(b) of the APA, which requires an agency "within a reasonable time . . . to conclude a matter presented to it."

EBEL, J.: "The government maintains, and the district court agreed, that Friends' letter is not the sort of matter to which § 555(b) applies. There is little case law on this issue. However, we believe there is a substantial argument that § 555(b) does apply to Friends' letter, which is an explicit and colorably valid request for the Service to take action arguably required of it by law to prepare a supplemental EA. First, by its terms, § 555(b) applies to all 'matters' presented to the agency. Contrary to the government's position that the provision only applies to 'proceedings' in which a person is compelled to appear, the section specifically speaks to 'agency proceedings' in which a person is 'entitled to appear,' as well as 'agency functions' and 'matters,' terms which would appear to encompass all forms of agency action. Second, while the government points out that 'agency proceedings' only includes the rulemakings, adjudications, and licensings defined in § 551 of the APA, it fails to acknowledge that § 551 defines 'adjudication' as 'the formulation of an order,' and in turn defines 'order' expansively to include the 'whole or part of a final disposition . . . other than rule making but including licensing.' That section further defines 'agency action' broadly to include not only rule makings, licensings, and orders, but also the 'failure to act.' Id. § 551(13). Thus, we assume, for the purposes of this opinion, that § 555(b) applies to the letter.

"Nonetheless, even assuming § 555(b) applies to Friends' letter, the agency's response to the letter substantially complied with the requirements of the section, as well as with the 'brief statement' requirement of § 555(e). Friends does not dispute that the SIR is an adequate 'brief statement' of the agency's reasons for not conducting a supplemental EA. Thus, the only question is whether the SIR was issued within a 'reasonable time' as is required by § 555(b).

"Friends has not pointed to a single case in which a court has reversed an agency action under § 555(b) for failure to comply with the 'reasonable time' requirements. More typically, courts have occasionally granted mandamus to force agencies to act when there has been no response to a request for agency action. But, in this case, the agency did act, by issuing the SIR. In cases where agencies acted, courts have declined to overturn agency action on the basis of the delay in situations where the agency took much longer to respond than the approximately one year period at issue here, particularly where as here the party opposing the action benefitted from the delay. Accordingly, we conclude the agency acted within a reasonable time in producing the SIR, particularly in light of the lengthy, detailed nature of Friends' request for action, and the thoroughness of the agency's eventual response."

(2) *Yet More Informal Action?* As already mentioned, informal adjudication appears to be the APA's residual category, negatively defined: adjudication is the formulation of an "order," which occurs "in a matter *other* than rule making," and adjudication is informal when it is *not* "required by statute to be determined on the record after opportunity for an agency hearing." But much—perhaps most—of what agencies do falls outside of even this residual category: most simply, someone answers the telephone; yet more complexly, someone does the initial work of investigation that will ultimately lead to the initiation of a rulemaking or adjudication. If one wanted to defend these exclusions on the text of the APA, one could pay attention to the fact that to be within the category of adjudication at all, an agency has to be formulating an "order," which is defined to be "a final disposition . . . in a matter." But the fact that such yet-more-informal agency

action has no procedural pedigree does not mean that it is inherently unimportant. Answering a routine inquiry may not matter much—but when the Chairman of the Federal Reserve Board gives a speech detailing her views of the economy, markets can shake. Procedurally speaking, one can only hope that she has her facts right.

SECTION 4.   DUE PROCESS AS A SOURCE OF PROCEDURAL RIGHTS IN ADJUDICATION

> a. *The Doctrinal Framework*
> b. *Applications*
> c. *Post-Deprivation Process*
> d. *Due Process and "Private" Administration*

In earlier pages we have seen that due process has long been understood to stipulate procedural requirements in adjudication. See Londoner v. Denver, 210 U.S. 373 (1908), reprinted at p. 218 above, and Bi-Metallic Investment Co. v. State Bd. Of Equalization of Colorado, reprinted at p. 222 above. As stated by the Supreme Court in 1950: "Many controversies have raged about the cryptic and abstract words of the Due Process Clause but there can be no doubt that at a minimum they require that deprivation of life, liberty or property by adjudication be preceded by notice and opportunity for hearing appropriate to the nature of the case." Mullane v. Central Hanover Bank & Trust Co., 339 U.S. 306, 313 (1950). We have also noted (p. 478 above) that historically what was considered an "appropriate" hearing varied widely from subject to subject, and that the drafters of the APA attempted to capture that variety in the distinctions they drew between formal and informal adjudication, and in the subsidiary details of sections 554, 556, and 557.

The traditional law of administrative due process was reformed—some would say revolutionized—in the 1950s and 1960s, roughly at the same time that the Constitutional demands on criminal procedure were also being refashioned. Perhaps the issue most raising administrative due process concerns in the earlier part of the period was the Cold War and the excesses it spawned regarding determinations of "loyalty" and "security." One element of the ensuing debate was whether due process was to be regarded as an amalgam of particular doctrinal elements or regarded more holistically. There was Supreme Court support for both sides. In an important case decided in 1950, BAILEY V. RICHARDSON, 341 U.S. 918 (1951), the Court, by an equally divided vote, affirmed a lower court opinion upholding the discharge of a government employee for failure to pass a loyalty procedure that was very short of fair—on the basis, said the D. C. Circuit, that government employment was a "privilege" not a "right," and therefore not part of the "life, liberty, or property" protected by the due process clause. On the same day, 5–3, in

JOINT ANTI-FASCIST REFUGEE COMM. V. MCGRATH, 341 U.S. 123 (1951), the Court said that three organizations challenging the government's designation of them as "Communist" had a cause of action. Espousing the more fluid view, JUSTICE FRANKFURTER wrote:

> . . . "[D]ue process," unlike some legal rules, is not a technical conception with a fixed content unrelated to time, place and circumstances. Expressing as it does in its ultimate analysis respect enforced by law for that feeling of just treatment which has been evolved through centuries of Anglo-American constitutional history and civilization, "due process" cannot be imprisoned within the treacherous limits of any formula. Representing a profound attitude of fairness between man and man, and more particularly between the individual and government, "due process" is compounded of history, reason, the past course of decisions, and stout confidence in the strength of the democratic faith which we profess. Due process is not a mechanical instrument. It is not a yardstick. It is a process. It is a delicate process of adjustment inescapably involving the exercise of judgment by those whom the Constitution entrusted with the unfolding of the process.
>
> . . . The precise nature of the interest that has been adversely affected, the manner in which this was done, the reasons for doing it, the available alternatives to the procedure that was followed, the protection implicit in the office of the functionary whose conduct is challenged, the balance of hurt complained of and good accomplished—these are some of the considerations that must enter into the judicial judgment . . .
>
> This Court is not alone in recognizing that the right to be heard before being condemned to grievous loss of any kind . . . is a principle basic to our society . . . .

This contest between doctrinalism and a more nuanced view persisted throughout the period. But as the 1950s moved into the 1960s, the principal foci changed. Moving beyond McCarthyism, the rights of those questioning the government became a matter of how to treat the civil rights movement and anti-Vietnam war demonstrators, often students. And then, in 1970, the Supreme Court decided GOLDBERG V. KELLY, 397 U.S. 254, recognizing claims to fair process of those who were recipients of government welfare. Welfare, from the older doctrinal point of view, was the ultimate "privilege" to which the recipient had no "right." Either the law of due process had shed any aspiration to doctrinal statement or a new doctrine had to be created.

(A note: There are two clauses in the Constitution that prohibit deprivation of "life, liberty, or property, without due process of law": in the Fifth Amendment, applicable to federal government action, and in the Fourteenth Amendment, applicable to the States. As far as adjudicatory procedure is concerned, they have always been treated as having the same content, and cases under each clause are properly cited as precedents applicable to the other. Thus, important cases arising out of state, as well as federal, administrative action are included in what follows.)

a.   The Doctrinal Framework

> ***BOARD OF REGENTS OF STATE***
> ***COLLEGES v. ROTH***
> ***PERRY v. SINDERMANN***
> *Notes on the Roth and Sindermann*
> *Cases*
> *Notes on Assessments of the*
> *Roth/Sindermann Doctrine*
> ***MATHEWS v. ELDRIDGE***
> *Notes on How the Mathews v. Eldridge*
> *Doctrine Is Constructed*
> *Notes on What Should Count in the*
> *Mathews Three-Part Test*

BOARD OF REGENTS OF STATE COLLEGES v. ROTH

Supreme Court of the United States (1972).
408 U.S. 564.

■ JUSTICE STEWART delivered the opinion of the Court.

In 1968 the respondent, David Roth, was hired for his first teaching job as assistant professor of political science at Wisconsin State University-Oshkosh. He was hired for a fixed term of one academic year. The notice of his faculty appointment specified that his employment would begin on September 1, 1968, and would end on June 30, 1969.[1] The respondent completed that term. But he was informed that he would not be rehired for the next academic year.

The respondent had no tenure rights to continued employment. Under Wisconsin statutory law a state university teacher can acquire tenure as a "permanent" employee only after four years of year-to-year employment. Having acquired tenure, a teacher is entitled to continued employment "during efficiency and good behavior." A relatively new teacher without tenure, however, is under Wisconsin law entitled to nothing beyond his one-year appointment. There are no statutory or

---

[1] The respondent had no contract of employment. Rather, his formal notice of appointment was the equivalent of an employment contract.

The notice of his appointment provided that: "David F. Roth is hereby appointed to the faculty of the Wisconsin State University Position number 0262. (Location:) Oshkosh as (Rank:) Assistant Professor of (Department:) Political Science this (Date:) first day of (Month:) September (Year:) 1968." The notice went on to specify that the respondent's "appointment basis" was for the "academic year." And it provided that "[r]egulations governing tenure are in accord with Chapter 37.31, Wisconsin Statutes. The employment of any staff member for an academic year shall not be for a term beyond June 30th of the fiscal year in which the appointment is made."

administrative standards defining eligibility for re-employment. State law thus clearly leaves the decision whether to rehire a nontenured teacher for another year to the unfettered discretion of university officials.

The procedural protection afforded a Wisconsin State University teacher before he is separated from the University corresponds to his job security. As a matter of statutory law, a tenured teacher cannot be "discharged except for cause upon written charges" and pursuant to certain procedures. A nontenured teacher, similarly, is protected to some extent *during* his one-year term. Rules promulgated by the Board of Regents provide that a nontenured teacher "dismissed" before the end of the year may have some opportunity for review of the "dismissal." But the Rules provide no real protection for a nontenured teacher who simply is not re-employed for the next year. He must be informed by February 1 "concerning retention or nonretention for the ensuing year." But "no reason for non-retention need be given. No review or appeal is provided in such case."

In conformance with these Rules, the President of Wisconsin State University-Oshkosh informed the respondent before February 1, 1969, that he would not be rehired for the 1969–1970 academic year. He gave the respondent no reason for the decision and no opportunity to challenge it at any sort of hearing.

The respondent then brought this action in Federal District Court alleging that the decision not to rehire him for the next year infringed his Fourteenth Amendment rights. He attacked the decision both in substance and procedure. First, he alleged that the true reason for the decision was to punish him for certain statements critical of the University administration, and that it therefore violated his right to freedom of speech.[5] Second, he alleged that the failure of University officials to give him notice of any reason for nonretention and an opportunity for a hearing violated his right to procedural due process of law.

The District Court granted summary judgment for the respondent on the procedural issue, ordering the University officials to provide him with reasons and a hearing. The Court of Appeals, with one judge dissenting, affirmed this partial summary judgment. We granted certiorari. The only question presented to us at this stage in the case is whether the respondent had a constitutional right to a statement of reasons and a hearing on the University's decision not to rehire him for another year. We hold that he did not.

---

    [5] While the respondent alleged that he was not rehired because of his exercise of free speech, the petitioners insisted that the non-retention decision was based on other, constitutionally valid grounds. The District Court came to no conclusion whatever regarding the true reason for the University President's decision. "In the present case," it stated, "it appears that a determination as to the actual bases of [the] decision must await amplification of the facts at trial. . . . Summary judgment is inappropriate." 310 F.Supp. 972, 982.

I

The requirements of procedural due process apply only to the deprivation of interests encompassed by the Fourteenth Amendment's protection of liberty and property. When protected interests are implicated, the right to some kind of prior hearing is paramount.[7] But the range of interests protected by procedural due process is not infinite.

The District Court decided that procedural due process guarantees apply in this case by assessing and balancing the weights of the particular interests involved. It concluded that the respondent's interest in re-employment at Wisconsin State University-Oshkosh outweighed the University's interest in denying him re-employment summarily. Undeniably, the respondent's re-employment prospects were of major concern to him—concern that we surely cannot say was insignificant. And a weighing process has long been a part of any determination of the *form* of hearing required in particular situations by procedural due process.[8] But, to determine whether due process requirements apply in the first place, we must look not to the "weight" but to the *nature* of the interest at stake. We must look to see if the interest is within the Fourteenth Amendment's protection of liberty and property.

"Liberty" and "property" are broad and majestic terms. They are among the "[g]reat [constitutional] concepts . . . purposely left to gather meaning from experience. . . . [T]hey relate to the whole domain of social and economic fact, and the statesmen who founded this Nation knew too well that only a stagnant society remains unchanged." National Ins. Co. v. Tidewater Co., 337 U.S. 582, 646 (Frankfurter, J., dissenting). For that reason, the Court has fully and finally rejected the wooden distinction between "rights" and "privileges" that once seemed to govern the applicability of procedural due process rights.[9] The Court has also made

---

[7] Before a person is deprived of a protected interest, he must be afforded opportunity for some kind of a hearing, "except for extraordinary situations where some valid governmental interest is at stake that justifies postponing the hearing until after the event." Boddie v. Connecticut, 401 U.S. 371, 379. "While '[m]any controversies have raged about . . . the Due Process Clause,' . . . it is fundamental that except in emergency situations (and this is not one) due process requires that when a State seeks to terminate [a protected] interest . . ., it must afford 'notice and opportunity for hearing appropriate to the nature of the case' before the termination becomes effective." Bell v. Burson, 402 U.S. 535, 542. For the rare and extraordinary situations in which we have held that deprivation of a protected interest need not be preceded by opportunity for some kind of hearing, see, e.g., Phillips v. Commissioner of Internal Revenue, 283 U.S. 589, 597.

[8] "The formality and procedural requisites for the hearing can vary, depending upon the importance of the interests involved and the nature of the subsequent proceedings." Boddie v. Connecticut, 401 U.S. 371, 378 (1971). See, e.g., Goldberg v. Kelly, 397 U.S. 254, 263. The constitutional requirement of opportunity for some form of hearing before deprivation of a protected interest, of course, does not depend upon such a narrow balancing process.

[9] In a leading case decided many years ago, the Court of Appeals for the District of Columbia Circuit held that public employment in general was a "privilege," not a "right," and that procedural due process guarantees therefore were inapplicable. Bailey v. Richardson, 182 F.2d 46, aff'd by an equally divided Court, 341 U.S. 918. The basis of this holding has been thoroughly undermined in the ensuing years. For, as Justice Blackmun wrote for the Court only last year, "this Court now has rejected the concept that constitutional rights turn upon whether a governmental benefit is characterized as a 'right' or as a 'privilege.' " Graham v. Richardson, 403 U.S. 365, 374.

clear that the property interests protected by procedural due process extend well beyond actual ownership of real estate, chattels, or money. By the same token, the Court has required due process protection for deprivations of liberty beyond the sort of formal constraints imposed by the criminal process.

Yet, while the Court has eschewed rigid or formalistic limitations on the protection of procedural due process, it has at the same time observed certain boundaries. For the words "liberty" and "property" in the Due Process Clause of the Fourteenth Amendment must be given some meaning.

II

"While this Court has not attempted to define with exactness the liberty . . . guaranteed [by the Fourteenth Amendment], the term has received much consideration and some of the included things have been definitely stated. Without doubt, it denotes not merely freedom from bodily restraint but also the right of the individual to contract, to engage in any of the common occupations of life, to acquire useful knowledge, to marry, establish a home and bring up children, to worship God according to the dictates of his own conscience, and generally to enjoy those privileges long recognized . . . as essential to the orderly pursuit of happiness by free men." Meyer v. Nebraska, 262 U.S. 390, 399. In a Constitution for a free people, there can be no doubt that the meaning of "liberty" must be broad indeed.

There might be cases in which a State refused to re-employ a person under such circumstances that interests in liberty would be implicated. But this is not such a case.

The State, in declining to rehire the respondent, did not make any charge against him that might seriously damage his standing and associations in his community. It did not base the nonrenewal of his contract on a charge, for example, that he had been guilty of dishonesty, or immorality. Had it done so, this would be a different case. For "[w]here a person's good name, reputation, honor, or integrity is at stake because of what the government is doing to him, notice and an opportunity to be heard are essential." Wisconsin v. Constantineau, 400 U.S. 433, 437 . . . In such a case, due process would accord an opportunity to refute the charge before University officials.[12] In the present case, however, there is no suggestion whatever that the respondent's "good name, reputation, honor, or integrity" is at stake.

Similarly, there is no suggestion that the State, in declining to reemploy the respondent, imposed on him a stigma or other disability that foreclosed his freedom to take advantage of other employment opportunities. The State, for example, did not invoke any regulations to

---

[12] The purpose of such notice and hearing is to provide the person an opportunity to clear his name. Once a person has cleared his name at a hearing, his employer, of course, may remain free to deny him future employment for other reasons.

bar the respondent from all other public employment in state universities. Had it done so, this, again, would be a different case. . . .[13]

To be sure, the respondent has alleged that the nonrenewal of his contract was based on his exercise of his right to freedom of speech. But this allegation is not now before us. The District Court stayed proceedings on this issue, and the respondent has yet to prove that the decision not to rehire him was, in fact, based on his free speech activities.

Hence, on the record before us, all that clearly appears is that the respondent was not rehired for one year at one university. It stretches the concept too far to suggest that a person is deprived of "liberty" when he simply is not rehired in one job but remains as free as before to seek another.

III

The Fourteenth Amendment's procedural protection of property is a safeguard of the security of interests that a person has already acquired in specific benefits. These interests—property interests—may take many forms.

Thus, the Court has held that a person receiving welfare benefits under statutory and administrative standards defining eligibility for them has an interest in continued receipt of those benefits that is safeguarded by procedural due process. Goldberg v. Kelly. Similarly, in the area of public employment, the Court has held that a public college professor dismissed from an office held under tenure provisions, Slochower v. Board of Education, 350 U.S. 551, and college professors and staff members dismissed during the terms of their contracts, Wieman v. Updegraff, 344 U.S. 183, have interests in continued employment that are safeguarded by due process. Only last year, the Court held that this principle "proscribing summary dismissal from public employment without hearing or inquiry required by due process" also applied to a teacher recently hired without tenure or a formal contract, but nonetheless with a clearly implied promise of continued employment. Connell v. Higginbotham, 403 U.S. 207, 208.

Certain attributes of "property" interests protected by procedural due process emerge from these decisions. To have a property interest in a benefit, a person clearly must have more than an abstract need or desire for it. He must have more than a unilateral expectation of it. He

---

[13] The District Court made an assumption "that non-retention by one university or college creates concrete and practical difficulties for a professor in his subsequent academic career." 310 F.Supp., at 979. And the Court of Appeals based its affirmance of the summary judgment largely on the premise that "the substantial adverse effect non-retention is likely to have upon the career interests of an individual professor" amounts to a limitation on future employment opportunities sufficient to invoke procedural due process guarantees. 446 F.2d, at 809. But even assuming, arguendo, that such a "substantial adverse effect" under these circumstances would constitute a state-imposed restriction on liberty, the record contains no support for these assumptions. There is no suggestion of how nonretention might affect the respondent's future employment prospects. Mere proof, for example, that his record of nonretention in one job, taken alone, might make him somewhat less attractive to some other employers would hardly establish the kind of foreclosure of opportunities amounting to a deprivation of "liberty."

must, instead, have a legitimate claim of entitlement to it. It is a purpose of the ancient institution of property to protect those claims upon which people rely in their daily lives, reliance that must not be arbitrarily undermined. It is a purpose of the constitutional right to a hearing to provide an opportunity for a person to vindicate those claims.

Property interests, of course, are not created by the Constitution. Rather, they are created and their dimensions are defined by existing rules or understandings that stem from an independent source such as state law—rules or understandings that secure certain benefits and that support claims of entitlement to those benefits. Thus, the welfare recipients in Goldberg v. Kelly had a claim of entitlement to welfare payments that was grounded in the statute defining eligibility for them. The recipients had not yet shown that they were, in fact, within the statutory terms of eligibility. But we held that they had a right to a hearing at which they might attempt to do so.

Just as the welfare recipients' "property" interest in welfare payments was created and defined by statutory terms, so the respondent's "property" interest in employment at Wisconsin State University-Oshkosh was created and defined by the terms of his appointment. Those terms secured his interest in employment up to June 30, 1969. But the important fact in this case is that they specifically provided that the respondent's employment was to terminate on June 30. They did not provide for contract renewal absent "sufficient cause." Indeed, they made no provision for renewal whatsoever.

Thus, the terms of the respondent's appointment secured absolutely no interest in re-employment for the next year. They supported absolutely no possible claim of entitlement to re-employment. Nor, significantly, was there any state statute or University rule or policy that secured his interest in reemployment or that created any legitimate claim to it.[16] In these circumstances, the respondent surely had an abstract concern in being rehired, but he did not have a *property* interest sufficient to require the University authorities to give him a hearing when they declined to renew his contract of employment.

IV

Our analysis of the respondent's constitutional rights in this case in no way indicates a view that an opportunity for a hearing or a statement of reasons for nonretention would, or would not, be appropriate or wise in public colleges and universities. For it is a written Constitution that we apply. Our role is confined to interpretation of that Constitution.

We must conclude that the summary judgment for the respondent should not have been granted, since the respondent has not shown that

---

[16] To be sure, the respondent does suggest that most teachers hired on a year-to-year basis by Wisconsin State University-Oshkosh are, in fact, rehired. But the District Court has not found that there is anything approaching a "common law" of re-employment, see Perry v. Sindermann, so strong as to require University officials to give the respondent a statement of reasons and a hearing on their decision not to rehire him.

he was deprived of liberty or property protected by the Fourteenth Amendment. The judgment of the Court of Appeals, accordingly, is reversed and the case is remanded for further proceedings consistent with this opinion.[4]

■ JUSTICE MARSHALL, dissenting.

. . . While I agree with Part I of the Court's opinion, setting forth the proper framework for consideration of the issue presented, and also with those portions of Parts II and III of the Court's opinion that assert that a public employee is entitled to procedural due process whenever a State stigmatizes him by denying employment, or injures his future employment prospects severely, or whenever the State deprives him of a property interest, I would go further than the Court does in defining the terms "liberty" and "property."

. . . [W]hether or not a private employer is free to act capriciously or unreasonably with respect to employment practices, at least absent statutory or contractual controls, a government employer is different. The government may only act fairly and reasonably.

In my view, every citizen who applies for a government job is entitled to it unless the government can establish some reason for denying the employment. This is the "property" right that I believe is protected by the Fourteenth Amendment and that cannot be denied "without due process of law." And it is also liberty—liberty to work—which is the "very essence of the personal freedom and opportunity" secured by the Fourteenth Amendment. This Court has often had occasion to note that the denial of public employment is a serious blow to any citizen. Thus, when an application for public employment is denied or the contract of a government employee is not renewed, the government must say why, for it is only when the reasons underlying government action are known that citizens feel secure and protected against arbitrary government action.

Employment is one of the greatest, if not the greatest, benefits that governments offer in modern-day life. When something as valuable as the opportunity to work is at stake, the government may not reward some citizens and not others without demonstrating that its actions are fair and equitable. And it is procedural due process that is our fundamental guarantee of fairness, our protection against arbitrary, capricious, and unreasonable government action.

It may be argued that to provide procedural due process to all public employees or prospective employees would place an intolerable burden on the machinery of government. Cf. Goldberg v. Kelly. The short answer to that argument is that it is not burdensome to give reasons when

---

4   [Ed.] See the Chronicle of Higher Education, Nov. 26, 1973, p. 3, col. 1: "David F. Roth . . . has been awarded $6,746 in damages in federal district court. . . . A six-person jury found that Mr. Roth's constitutional right to free speech was violated by [Wisconsin State University at Oshkosh]. . . . Judge Doyle also has yet to rule on requests from Mr. Roth for reinstatement in his position at Oshkosh. . . . Even if Judge Doyle orders his reinstatement, Mr. Roth is not likely to return to Oshkosh, since he now teaches at Purdue University."

reasons exist. Whenever an application for employment is denied, an employee is discharged, or a decision not to rehire an employee is made, there should be some reason for the decision. It can scarcely be argued that government would be crippled by a requirement that the reason be communicated to the person most directly affected by the government's action.

Where there are numerous applicants for jobs, it is likely that few will choose to demand reasons for not being hired. But, if the demand for reasons is exceptionally great, summary procedures can be devised that would provide fair and adequate information to all persons. As long as the government has a good reason for its actions it need not fear disclosure. It is only where the government acts improperly that procedural due process is truly burdensome. And that is precisely when it is most necessary . . .

[CHIEF JUSTICE BURGER and JUSTICES WHITE, BLACKMUN, and REHNQUIST joined JUSTICE STEWART. JUSTICE POWELL took no part in the case. JUSTICES BRENNAN and DOUGLAS were, like JUSTICE MARSHALL, dissenters; their opinions have not been reproduced. Finally, CHIEF JUSTICE BURGER also filed a concurring opinion, reproduced following the next case.]

PERRY v. SINDERMANN

Supreme Court of the United States (1972).
408 U.S. 593.

■ JUSTICE STEWART delivered the opinion of the Court.

[In this case, considered with Board of Regents v. Roth, Robert Sindermann had worked for the state college system of Texas for ten years, during the last four of which he was a full professor at Odessa Junior College. He had successive one-year contracts, as Odessa had no tenure system. In the 1968–69 academic year, he was elected president of the Texas Junior College Teachers Association and, as such, publicly opposed policies of the Board of Regents. In May 1969, his contract expired and the Regents voted not to offer him a new one. They issued a press release claiming he had been insubordinate but gave him no official statement of reasons for nonrenewal and held no hearing in which he might challenge his discharge. Sindermann sued the Regents and the college's president, claiming a violation of his rights to free speech and procedural due process. The defendants denied that he had been fired in retaliation for his public criticism and argued that they had no obligation to give him a hearing.

Based on a very slim record, the district court granted summary judgment for the college officials. The court of appeals reversed. As to free speech, it remanded for trial as to the actual reason for the Regents' decision. As to due process, it remanded to allow Sindermann to show that he had an "expectancy" of reemployment. The Supreme Court first considered the First Amendment claim and held that this claim could be proved even if Sindermann lacked a contractual or tenure right to re-employment:]

For at least a quarter-century, this Court has made clear that even though a person has no "right" to a valuable governmental benefit and even though the government may deny him the benefit for any number of reasons, there are some reasons upon which the government may not rely. It may not deny a benefit to a person on a basis that infringes his constitutionally protected interests—especially, his interest in freedom of speech. . . . [On remand, Sindermann must be given the opportunity to prove his allegations of retaliatory refusal to rehire. The Court then continued:]

The respondent's lack of formal contractual or tenure security in continued employment at Odessa Junior College, though irrelevant to his free speech claim, is highly relevant to his procedural due process claim. But it may not be entirely dispositive.

We have held today in Board of Regents v. Roth that the Constitution does not require opportunity for a hearing before the nonrenewal of a nontenured teacher's contract, unless he can show that the decision not to rehire him somehow deprived him of an interest in "liberty" or that he had a "property" interest in continued employment, despite the lack of tenure or a formal contract. In Roth the teacher had not made a showing on either point to justify summary judgment in his favor.

Similarly, the respondent here has yet to show that he has been deprived of an interest that could invoke procedural due process protection. As in Roth, the mere showing that he was not rehired in one particular job, without more, did not amount to a showing of a loss of liberty. Nor did it amount to a showing of a loss of property.

But the respondent's allegations—which we must construe most favorably to the respondent at this stage of the litigation—do raise a genuine issue as to his interest in continued employment at Odessa Junior College. He alleged that this interest, though not secured by a formal contractual tenure provision, was secured by a no less binding understanding fostered by the college administration. In particular, the respondent alleged that the college had a *de facto* tenure program, and that he had tenure under that program. He claimed that he and others legitimately relied upon an unusual provision that had been in the college's official Faculty Guide for many years:

Teacher Tenure: Odessa College has no tenure system. The Administration of the College wishes the faculty member to feel that he has permanent tenure as long as his teaching services are satisfactory and as long as he displays a cooperative attitude toward his co-workers and his superiors, and as long as he is happy in his work.

Moreover, the respondent claimed legitimate reliance upon guidelines promulgated by the Coordinating Board of the Texas College and University System that provided that a person, like himself, who had been employed as a teacher in the state college and university system for seven years or more has some form of job tenure. Thus, the respondent offered to prove that a teacher with his long period of service at this particular State College had no less a "property" interest in continued employment than a formally tenured teacher at other colleges, and had no less a procedural due process right to a statement of reasons and a hearing before college officials upon their decision not to retain him.

We have made clear in Roth that "property" interests subject to procedural due process protection are not limited by a few rigid, technical forms. Rather, "property" denotes a broad range of interests that are secured by "existing rules or understandings." A person's interest in a benefit is a "property" interest for due process purposes if there are such rules or mutually explicit understandings that support his claim of entitlement to the benefit and that he may invoke at a hearing.

A written contract with an explicit tenure provision clearly is evidence of a formal understanding that supports a teacher's claim of entitlement to continued employment unless sufficient "cause" is shown. Yet absence of such an explicit contractual provision may not always foreclose the possibility that a teacher has a "property" interest in re-employment. For example, the law of contracts in most, if not all, jurisdictions long has employed a process by which agreements, though not formalized in writing, may be "implied." 3 A. Corbin on Contracts §§ 561–572A (1960). Explicit contractual provisions may be supplemented by other agreements implied from "the promisor's words and conduct in the light of the surrounding circumstances." Id., at § 562. And, "[t]he meaning of [the promisor's] words and acts is found by relating them to the usage of the past." Ibid.

A teacher, like the respondent, who has held his position for a number of years, might be able to show from the circumstances of this service—and from other relevant facts—that he has a legitimate claim of entitlement to job tenure . . . This is particularly likely in a college or university, like Odessa Junior College, that has no explicit tenure system even for senior members of its faculty, but that nonetheless may have created such a system in practice. See C. Byse & L. Joughin, Tenure in American Higher Education 17–28 (1959).[7]

In this case, the respondent has alleged the existence of rules and understandings, promulgated and fostered by state officials, that may justify his legitimate claim of entitlement to continued employment

---

[7]   We do not now hold that the respondent has any such legitimate claim of entitlement to job tenure. For "[p]roperty interests . . . are not created by the Constitution. Rather, they are created and their dimensions are defined by existing rules or understandings that stem from an independent source such as state law. . . ." Board of Regents v. Roth, at 577. If it is the law of Texas that a teacher in the respondent's position has no contractual or other claim to job tenure, the respondent's claim would be defeated.

absent "sufficient cause." We disagree with the Court of Appeals insofar as it held that a mere subjective "expectancy" is protected by procedural due process, but we agree that the respondent must be given an opportunity to prove the legitimacy of his claim of such entitlement in light of "the policies and practices of the institution." 430 F.2d, at 943. Proof of such a property interest would not, of course, entitle him to reinstatement. But such proof would obligate college officials to grant a hearing at his request, where he could be informed of the grounds for his nonretention and challenge their sufficiency.

Therefore, while we do not wholly agree with the opinion of the Court of Appeals, its judgment remanding this case to the District Court is Affirmed.[5]

■ CHIEF JUSTICE BURGER, concurring.

I concur in the Court's judgments and opinions in Sindermann and Roth, but there is one central point in both decisions that I would like to underscore. . . . [T]he relationship between a state institution and one of its teachers is essentially a matter of state concern and state law. The Court holds today only that a state-employed teacher who has a right to re-employment under state law, arising from either an express or implied contract, has, in turn, a right guaranteed by the Fourteenth Amendment to some form of prior administrative or academic hearing on the cause for nonrenewal of his contract. Thus, whether a particular teacher in a particular context has any right to such administrative hearing hinges on a question of state law. . . .

[JUSTICES BRENNAN, DOUGLAS, and MARSHALL agreed with the First Amendment portion of the Court's opinion but also voted "to direct the District Court to enter summary judgment for respondent entitling him to a statement of reasons why his contract was not renewed and a hearing on disputed issues of fact." JUSTICE POWELL took no part in the case.]

NOTES ON THE ROTH AND SINDERMANN CASES

(1) *Where Are Roth and Sindermann Coming From?* Roth and Sindermann were decided two years after—and in response to—the Supreme Court's famous decision in GOLDBERG V. KELLY, 397 U.S. 254 (1970). There, in the words of JUSTICE BRENNAN, "the question for decision [was] whether a State that terminates public assistance payments to a particular recipient without affording him the opportunity for an evidentiary hearing prior to termination denies the recipient procedural due process in violation of the Due Process Clause of the Fourteenth Amendment." 397 U.S. at 255. The Court answered in the affirmative. 397 U.S. at 263–66:

---

[5]   [Ed.] See the Odessa American, Nov. 12, 1972, p. 1, col. 1: "Robert P. Sindermann flew to Odessa Saturday and picked up the $48,000 check made out to him by Odessa College in settlement of his lawsuit stemming from the college's refusal to rehire him in 1969. . . .

"The 43-year-old former Odessa College government teacher said one of the conditions of the settlement was that the college offered to reinstate him. 'I have politely declined the invitation,' Sindermann grinned."

"It is true, of course, that some governmental benefits may be administratively terminated without affording the recipient a pre-termination evidentiary hearing. But we agree with the District Court that when welfare is discontinued, only a pre-termination evidentiary hearing provides the recipient with procedural due process. For qualified recipients, welfare provides the means to obtain essential food, clothing, housing, and medical care. Thus the crucial factor in this context—a factor not present in the case of the blacklisted government contractor, the discharged government employee, the taxpayer denied a tax exemption, or virtually anyone else whose governmental entitlements are ended—is that termination of aid pending resolution of a controversy over eligibility may deprive an eligible recipient of the very means by which to live while he waits. Since he lacks independent resources, his situation becomes immediately desperate. His need to concentrate upon finding the means for daily subsistence, in turn, adversely affects his ability to seek redress from the welfare bureaucracy.

"Moreover, important governmental interests are promoted by affording recipients a pre-termination evidentiary hearing. From its founding the Nation's basic commitment has been to foster the dignity and well-being of all persons within its borders. We have come to recognize that forces not within the control of the poor contribute to their poverty. This perception, against the background of our traditions, has significantly influenced the development of the contemporary public assistance system. Welfare, by meeting the basic demands of subsistence, can help bring within the reach of the poor the same opportunities that are available to others to participate meaningfully in the life of the community. At the same time, welfare guards against the societal malaise that may flow from a widespread sense of unjustified frustration and insecurity. Public assistance, then, is not mere charity, but a means to 'promote the general Welfare, and secure the Blessings of Liberty to ourselves and our Posterity.' The same governmental interests that counsel the provision of welfare, counsel as well its uninterrupted provision to those eligible to receive it; pre-termination evidentiary hearings are indispensable to that end.

"Appellant does not challenge the force of these considerations but argues that they are outweighed by countervailing governmental interests in conserving fiscal and administrative resources. These interests, the argument goes, justify the delay of any evidentiary hearing until after discontinuance of the grants. Summary adjudication protects the public fisc by stopping payments promptly upon discovery of reason to believe that a recipient is no longer eligible. Since most terminations are accepted without challenge, summary adjudication also conserves both the fisc and administrative time and energy by reducing the number of evidentiary hearings actually held.

"We agree with the District Court, however, that these governmental interests are not overriding in the welfare context. . . ."

The Court proceeded to specify the pre-termination procedure that would be needed. Although it stated that it was not requiring a "judicial or quasi-judicial trial," the Court's demands appeared to many readers to be quite formal; evidence had to be presented orally, cross-examination had to be permitted, and the outcome had to be based on the record so made.

Goldberg was understood, by both the dissenting judges and the commentators, to be making a sharp break with tradition by extending constitutional protection to something—the provision of welfare grants—that had previously been seen as a "privilege" rather than a "right." On this doctrinal question, JUSTICE BRENNAN answered, 397 U.S. at 261–63:

"[The State] does not contend that procedural due process is not applicable to the termination of welfare benefits. Such benefits are a matter of statutory entitlement for persons qualified to receive them.[8] Their termination involves state action that adjudicates important rights. The constitutional challenge cannot be answered by an argument that public assistance benefits are 'a privilege' and not a 'right.' " Shapiro v. Thompson, 394 U.S. 618, 627 n. 6 (1969). Relevant constitutional restraints apply as much to the withdrawal of public assistance benefits as to disqualification for unemployment compensation, Sherbert v. Verner, 374 U.S. 398 (1963); or to denial of a tax exemption, Speiser v. Randall, 357 U.S. 513 (1958); or to discharge from public employment, Slochower v. Board of Higher Education, 350 U.S. 551 (1956). The extent to which procedural due process must be afforded the recipient is influenced by the extent to which he may be "condemned to suffer grievous loss," Joint Anti-Fascist Refugee Committee v. McGrath, 341 U.S. 123, 168 (1951) (Frankfurter, J., concurring), and depends upon whether the recipient's interest in avoiding that loss outweighs the governmental interest in summary adjudication. Accordingly, as we said in Cafeteria & Restaurant Workers Union v. McElroy, 367 U.S. 886, 895 (1961), "consideration of what procedures due process may require under any given set of circumstances must begin with a determination of the precise nature of the government function involved as well as of the private interest that has been affected by governmental action."

How far did this language go? Was fair procedure constitutionally required because of the immediate needs of recipients—in effect accepting Justice Frankfurter's view that due process is triggered whenever the government imposes "grievous loss" on the individual? Or was the constitutionally crucial fact that "[s]uch benefits are a matter of statutory entitlement for persons qualified to receive them"? Or was the whole matter

---

8   [Note by the Court] It may be realistic today to regard welfare entitlements as more like "property" than a "gratuity." Much of the existing wealth in this country takes the form of rights that do not fall within traditional common-law concepts of property. It has been aptly noted that

> [s]ociety today is built around entitlement. The automobile dealer has his franchise, the doctor and lawyer their professional licenses, the worker his union membership, contract, and pension rights, the executive his contract and stock options; all are devices to aid security and independence. Many of the most important of these entitlements now flow from government: subsidies to farmers and businessmen, routes for airlines and channels for television stations; long term contracts for defense, space, and education; social security pensions for individuals. Such sources of security, whether private or public, are no longer regarded as luxuries or gratuities; to the recipients they are essentials, fully deserved, and in no sense a form of charity. It is only the poor whose entitlements, although recognized by public policy, have not been effectively enforced.

Reich, Individual Rights and Social Welfare: The Emerging Legal Issues, 74 Yale L.J. 1245, 1255 (1965). See also Reich, The New Property, 73 Yale L.J. 733 (1964).

contingent on the concession of the defendants that due process was applicable? Roth and Sindermann may be seen as an effort to answer those questions.

(2) **What Is the Constitutional Basis of the Roth/Sindermann Doctrine?** If the constitutional phrase *deprive any person of life, liberty, or property* "must be given some meaning" (Justice Stewart's phrase), is the meaning announced by Roth any stronger textually than the meaning asserted by the older cases? Isn't a distinction between "rights" (claims thought to exist prior to governmental action) and "privileges" (claims that depend on governmental grant) a perfectly good reading of the text? If the reason for rejecting this old distinction is that "only a stagnant society remains unchanged," as the Roth opinion suggests, why do we have to give an independent doctrinal significance to *each* element of the constitutional text?

(3)   Assuming we do give an independent significance to each element, why does the Court feel able to describe "liberty" interests using its own voice, yet as to "property" interests it says that "they are created and their dimensions are defined by existing rules or understandings that stem from an independent source such as state law."

(4)   **The Bitter with the Sweet?** Roth and Sindermann plainly say that statutorily created property interests "count" for due process purposes. At the same time, they assume that the procedural consequences of having a property interest are set by the due process clause. What if the very statute that creates a property interest also specifies the procedure by which it is to be tested? ARNETT V. KENNEDY, 416 U.S. 134 (1974), dealt with a federal civil-service statute that had that very character. Two members of a badly split Supreme Court majority upheld the statute because they thought its procedures were sufficiently full to meet due process standards. But the other three—with Justice Rehnquist writing, but including Justice Stewart, author of the cases we just read—said that a federal employee, in such circumstances, had no due process claim independent of the statutory procedures Congress had chosen. 416 U.S. at 152:

> Congress was obviously intent on according a measure of statutory job security to governmental employees which they had not previously enjoyed, but was likewise intent on excluding more elaborate procedural requirements which it felt would make the operation of the new scheme unnecessarily burdensome in practice. Where the focus of legislation was thus strongly on the procedural mechanism for enforcing the substantive right which was simultaneously conferred, we decline to conclude that the substantive right may be viewed wholly apart from the procedure provided for its enforcement. The employee's statutorily defined right is not a guarantee against removal without cause in the abstract, but such a guarantee as enforced by the procedures which Congress has designated for the determination of cause.

Or, as Rehnquist more pithily continued, "[W]here the grant of a substantive right is inextricably intertwined with the limitations on the procedures which are to be employed in determining that right, a litigant in the position of appellee must take the bitter with the sweet." 416 U.S. at 153–54.

This theory, however, did not last. In CLEVELAND BOARD OF EDUCATION V. LOUDERMILL, 470 U.S. 532 (1985), the Court explicitly eschewed it. 470 U.S. at 541:

> [T]he "bitter with the sweet" approach misconceives the constitutional guarantee. If a clearer holding is needed, we provide it today. The point is straight-forward: the Due Process Clause provides that certain substantive rights—life, liberty, and property—cannot be deprived except pursuant to constitutionally adequate procedures. The categories of substance and procedure are distinct. Were the rule otherwise, the Clause would be reduced to a mere tautology. "Property" cannot be defined by the procedures provided for its deprivation any more than can life or liberty. . . . In short, once it is determined that the Due Process Clause applies, "the question remains what process is due." Morrissey v. Brewer, 408 U.S. 471, 481 (1972). The answer to that question is not to be found in the . . . statute.

In short, under the Court's current doctrine, due process questions entail two levels of analysis: is "life, liberty or property" at stake? If so, is the process provided adequate (which is to say, "due") process?

(5) *How Far Does Roth/Sindermann Go?* Both of these cases dealt with the question of when government employment constitutes a property interest for the due process clause. Goldberg dealt with welfare benefits. What about other types of relationships to government? The archetypical administrative relationship—being subject to governmental regulation—is the least difficult to analyze. The very idea of "regulation" assumes that the party being regulated could have acted differently if government had not intervened. In legal terms, that is almost always equivalent to saying that the party being regulated had a common law right to do something different: because of the property it owned, or its freedom to contract, or based on other common law rights. In other words, when "regulation" is enforced through adjudication it ordinarily deprives someone of a common law "right" and is therefore subject to the demands of due process.

(6) *Government Contracts.* Do contracts with governmental entities also create "property" in the Roth-Sindermann sense? The answer cannot be "No": the Court in Sindermann explicitly references principles of contract law in explaining why Sindermann may have a provable claim to tenure. The answer cannot be "Yes": that would mean that every federal, state, and local government procurement contract—from stealth bombers to bus transportation for school children to paperclips—would support a due process claim to an administrative hearing if a dispute arose about payment. So the answer must be "Sometimes." But when? Would you distinguish Sindermann's claim from the claim for damages made by a construction contractor doing government work who has been thrown off the job halfway through the contract? Questions of this sort have been discussed by the

courts largely in terms of what process is appropriately due in the different kinds of cases and is treated more fully below at p. 619.

(7) **Prisons.** There is a long line of Supreme Court cases dealing with prisoners' claims, especially state prisoners' claims, that they were being subjected to harsh conditions—for example, solitary confinement—without proper process. Claims like these first have to address the fact that such prisoners have already had a fair full-dress trial (or had the right to one but waived it to plead guilty), and what that full process authorized was precisely a deprivation of their constitutionally grounded liberty. Were there limitations on what the state could do, after such a conviction, without holding a further hearing?

Many of the earlier cases analyzed this question on analogy to the difference between Roth and Sindermann: states could, for example, reassign prisoners to different conditions of confinement at will if no substantive standards existed that controlled prison officials, but if the states established substantive standards for reassignment, then the prisoners had a state-created liberty interest sufficient to warrant investigating whether the process by which those standards were applied was adequate. This doctrine was subject to the work-a-day criticism that it required judges to decide whether various state laws that told prison officials what to do, did or did not create "entitlements" for prisoners. It was subject to the root-and-branch criticism that it created an incentive for establishing statutorily authorized official arbitrariness in the prisons. And it was subject to the institutional criticism that it deeply enmeshed the federal courts in the conduct of state penal institutions.

In SANDIN V. CONNER, 515 U.S. 472 (1995), and WILKINSON V. AUSTIN, 545 U.S. 209 (2005), the Court crafted a new analysis. The question now is whether what the prison is doing "imposes atypical and significant hardship on the inmate in relation to the ordinary incidents of prison life." Sandin, 515 U.S. at 484. If so, further process is required because what is at issue is a deprivation of "liberty" beyond that authorized by the original trial. In Sandin, the Court held that thirty days of segregated confinement did not dramatically depart from the ordinary conditions of prison confinement; in Wilkinson, the Court said that indefinite solitary confinement, with "especially severe limitations on all human contact" and associated loss of eligibility for parole, were sufficiently atypical to constitute an infringement on liberty beyond that expected from just having been convicted of a crime. So in Wilkinson, fourteenth amendment "liberty" was at stake—but the state procedures already in place to determine whether the deprivation was justified were found to be sufficient to count as the process that was "due."

Some circuits have read the Sandin test to be in addition to, rather than a complete substitute for, the prior entitlement test. On this view, prisoners get to the question of "What process is due?" only by passing both tests. E.g., Prieto v. Clarke, 780 F.3d 245, 248-9 (4th Cir. 2015).

(8) **What about Living with a Spouse**? In KERRY V. DIN, 135 S.Ct. 2128 (2015), Kanishka Berashk, an Afghan citizen, was denied a visa to come to the United States to live with his wife, Fauzia Din, a U.S. citizen. Given his

status as a foreigner, he had no claim available to contest the proceeding. So she sued, claiming that the cursory explanation he had been given operated to deprive her, without due process, of the liberty to live in the United States with her husband. Was the "liberty" protected by the Constitution—which Justice Stewart said in Roth "must be broad indeed"—indeed this broad? The court split three ways. For Justice Scalia and two others, considering this claim to be a constitutionally protected liberty interest went too far beyond traditional understandings or decided cases. For Justice Breyer and three others, the importance of marriage, and the various ways the law acted to preserve the ability of married persons to live together, was sufficient to justify the plaintiff's claim to greater process. And the other two Justices? In an opinion by Justice Kennedy, they ruled that the issue did not need to be decided because the government had already given all the process that, in a case involving the exclusion of an alien, it was required to give.

NOTES ON ASSESSMENTS OF THE ROTH/SINDERMANN DOCTRINE

(1) *What Have the Scholars Thought of Entitlement Analysis?* Here's a sample: HENRY P. MONAGHAN, OF "LIBERTY" AND "PROPERTY", 62 Cornell L. Rev. 405, 409 (1977): "Prior to Roth, Supreme Court definitions of 'liberty' and 'property' had amounted to taking the words 'life, liberty, and property' as a unitary concept embracing all interests valued by sensible men. After Roth, however, each word of the clause must be examined separately; so examined, we find that they do not embrace the full range of state conduct having serious impact upon individual interests."

(2) WILLIAM VAN ALSTYNE, CRACKS IN "THE NEW PROPERTY": ADJUDICATIVE DUE PROCESS IN THE ADMINISTRATIVE STATE, 62 Cornell L. Rev. 445, 484 (1977): "The concept of public sector status as property both overstates and understates the problem. It overstates the problem by carrying with it additional notions of personal entitlement and of sinecurism that no constitutional court since Lochner should desire to encourage. At the same time, it understates the problem by ignoring a vast number of situations in which it is impossible to describe the relationship as one giving rise to property, but in which the government's procedural grossness is nevertheless profoundly unfair and objectionable."

(3) JERRY L. MASHAW, DIGNITARY PROCESS: A POLITICAL PSYCHOLOGY OF LIBERAL DEMOCRATIC CITIZENSHIP, 39 U. Fla. L. Rev. 433, 437 (1987): "Such an approach is functionally inadequate to address the problems of governmental or bureaucratic discretion that the due process clause was meant to address. The positive law trigger approach gives legal protection, or at least due process attention, where some legal protection already exists, while excluding due process concern where a legal regime seems to permit official arbitrariness. Although many have a taste for irony, few would choose Kafka or Ionesco as constitutional draftsmen."

(4) RICHARD B. STEWART and CASS R. SUNSTEIN, PUBLIC PROGRAMS AND PRIVATE RIGHTS, 95 Harv. L. Rev. 1195, 1257–58 (1982): "A formal definition of entitlements was not inevitable. The Court might have sought to identify

those interests that are as central to individual well-being in contemporary society as were the interests protected at common law in a different era. The judicial discretion inherent in any such task has been a major factor in the Court's refusal to follow a functional approach. Moreover, if courts were to select certain 'important' interests as those deserving due process protection, they might be driven to give those interests substantive as well as procedural protection; procedural rights alone might be of little value if administrators were free to decide cases as they pleased as long as procedural formalities were observed. A functional approach could thus invite courts to rule the welfare state through a new form of substantive due process."

(5)   PATRICIA M. WALD, GOVERNMENT BENEFITS: A NEW LOOK AT AN OLD GIFTHORSE, 65 N.Y.U. L. Rev. 247, 260 (1990): "The Court's decision was hardly a renunciation of the right-privilege distinction. It simply redefined the boundary between the two."

MATHEWS v. ELDRIDGE

Supreme Court of the United States (1976).
424 U.S. 319.

■ JUSTICE POWELL delivered the opinion of the Court.

The issue in this case is whether the Due Process Clause of the Fifth Amendment requires that prior to the termination of Social Security disability benefit payments the recipient be afforded an opportunity for an evidentiary hearing.

I

Cash benefits are provided to workers during periods in which they are completely disabled under the disability insurance benefits program created by the 1956 amendments to Title II of the Social Security Act. 42 U.S.C. § 423.[1] Respondent Eldridge was first awarded benefits in June 1968. In March 1972, he received a questionnaire from the state agency charged with monitoring his medical condition. Eldridge completed the questionnaire, indicating that his condition had not improved and identifying the medical sources, including physicians, from whom he had received treatment recently. The state agency then obtained reports from his physician and a psychiatric consultant. After considering these reports and other information in his file the agency informed Eldridge by letter that it had made a tentative determination that his disability had ceased in May 1972. The letter included a statement of reasons for the proposed termination of benefits, and advised Eldridge that he might

---

[1]   The program is financed by revenues derived from employee and employer payroll taxes. It provides monthly benefits to disabled persons who have worked sufficiently long to have an insured status, and who have had substantial work experience in a specified interval directly preceding the onset of disability. Benefits also are provided to the worker's dependents under specified circumstances. When the recipient reaches age 65 his disability benefits are automatically converted to retirement benefits. In fiscal 1974 approximately 3,700,000 persons received assistance under the program. Social Security Administration, The Year in Review 21 (1974).

Procedures offered

request reasonable time in which to obtain and submit additional information pertaining to his condition.

In his written response, Eldridge disputed one characterization of his medical condition and indicated that the agency already had enough evidence to establish his disability.[2] The state agency then made its final determination that he had ceased to be disabled in May 1972. This determination was accepted by the Social Security Administration (SSA), which notified Eldridge in July that his benefits would terminate after that month. The notification also advised him of his right to seek reconsideration by the state agency of this initial determination within six months.

Instead of requesting reconsideration Eldridge commenced this action . . . The District Court concluded that the administrative procedures pursuant to which the Secretary had terminated Eldridge's benefits abridged his right to procedural due process. [T]he Court of Appeals for the Fourth Circuit affirmed.

II

[The courts have jurisdiction.]

III

A

. . . The Secretary does not contend that procedural due process is inapplicable to terminations of Social Security disability benefits. . . . Rather, the Secretary contends that the existing administrative procedures . . . provide all the process that is constitutionally due before a recipient can be deprived of that interest. . . . Eldridge agrees that the review procedures . . . would be adequate if disability benefits were not terminated until after the evidentiary hearing stage of the administrative process. The dispute centers upon what process is due prior to the initial termination of benefits, pending review.

In recent years this Court increasingly has had occasion to consider the extent to which due process requires an evidentiary hearing prior to the deprivation of some type of property interest even if such a hearing is provided thereafter. In only one case, Goldberg v. Kelly, has the Court held that a hearing closely approximating a judicial trial is necessary.

. . . "Due process, unlike some legal rules, is not a technical conception with a fixed content unrelated to time, place and circumstances." Cafeteria Workers v. McElroy, 367 U.S. 886, 895 (1961). . . . Accordingly, resolution of the issue whether the

---

[2] Eldridge originally was disabled due to chronic anxiety and back strain. He subsequently was found to have diabetes. The tentative determination letter indicated that aid would be terminated because available medical evidence indicated that his diabetes was under control, that there existed no limitations on his back movements which would impose severe functional restrictions, and that he no longer suffered emotional problems that would preclude him from all work for which he was qualified. In his reply letter he claimed to have arthritis of the spine rather than a strained back.

administrative procedures provided here are constitutionally sufficient requires analysis of the governmental and private interests that are affected. Goldberg v. Kelly, 397 U.S. 254, 263–266; Cafeteria Workers v. McElroy, above, at 895. More precisely, our prior decisions indicate that identification of the specific dictates of due process generally requires consideration of three distinct factors: First, the private interest that will be affected by the official action; second, the risk of an erroneous deprivation of such interest through the procedures used, and the probable value, if any, of additional or substitute procedural safeguards; and finally, the Government's interest, including the function involved and the fiscal and administrative burdens that the additional or substitute procedural requirement would entail. See, e.g., Goldberg v. Kelly, above, at 263–271.

We turn first to a description of the procedures for the termination of Social Security disability benefits, and thereafter consider the factors bearing upon the constitutional adequacy of these procedures.

B

The disability insurance program is administered jointly by state and federal agencies. State agencies make the initial determination whether a disability exists, when it began, and when it ceased. The standards applied and the procedures followed are prescribed by the Secretary, who has delegated his responsibilities and powers under the Act to the SSA.

In order to establish initial and continued entitlement to disability benefits a worker must demonstrate that he is unable

> to engage in any substantial gainful activity by reason of any medically determinable physical or mental impairment which can be expected to result in death or which has lasted or can be expected to last for a continuous period of not less than 12 months . . . 42 U.S.C. § 423(d)(1)(A).

To satisfy this test the worker bears a continuing burden of showing, by means of "medically acceptable clinical and laboratory diagnostic techniques," § 423(d)(3), that he has a physical or mental impairment of such severity that

> he is not only unable to do his previous work but cannot, considering his age, education, and work experience, engage in any other kind of substantial gainful work which exists in the national economy, regardless of whether such work exists in the immediate area in which he lives, or whether a specific job vacancy exists for him, or whether he would be hired if he applied for work. § 423(d)(2)(A) . . .

The continuing-eligibility investigation is made by a state agency acting through a "team" consisting of a physician and a nonmedical person trained in disability evaluation. The agency periodically communicates with the disabled worker, usually by mail—in which case he is sent a detailed questionnaire—or by telephone, and requests information concerning his present condition, including current medical restrictions and sources of treatment, and any additional information that he considers relevant to his continued entitlement to benefits.

Information regarding the recipient's current condition is also obtained from his sources of medical treatment. If there is a conflict between the information provided by the beneficiary and that obtained from medical sources such as his physician, or between two sources of treatment, the agency may arrange for an examination by an independent consulting physician. Whenever the agency's tentative assessment of the beneficiary's condition differs from his own assessment, the beneficiary is informed that benefits may be terminated, provided a summary of the evidence upon which the proposed determination to terminate is based, and afforded an opportunity to review the medical reports and other evidence in his case file. He also may respond in writing and submit additional evidence.

The state agency then makes its final determination, which is reviewed by an examiner in the SSA Bureau of Disability Insurance. If, as is usually the case, the SSA accepts the agency determination it notifies the recipient in writing, informing him of the reasons for the decision, and of his right to seek de novo reconsideration by the state agency.[20] Upon acceptance by the SSA, benefits are terminated effective two months after the month in which medical recovery is found to have occurred.

If the recipient seeks reconsideration by the state agency and the determination is adverse, the SSA reviews the reconsideration determination and notifies the recipient of the decision. He then has a right to an evidentiary hearing before an SSA administrative law judge. The hearing is non-adversary, and the SSA is not represented by counsel. As at all prior and subsequent stages of the administrative process, however, the claimant may be represented by counsel or other spokesmen. If this hearing results in an adverse decision, the claimant is entitled to request discretionary review by the SSA Appeals Council, and finally may obtain judicial review.

Should it be determined at any point after termination of benefits, that the claimant's disability extended beyond the date of cessation initially established, the worker is entitled to retroactive payments. If, on the other hand, a beneficiary receives any payments to which he is later determined not to be entitled, the statute authorizes the Secretary to attempt to recoup these funds in specified circumstances.

---

[20] The reconsideration assessment is initially made by the state agency, but usually not by the same persons who considered the case originally. R. Dixon, Social Security Disability and Mass Justice 32 (1973). Both the recipient and the agency may adduce new evidence.

C

Despite the elaborate character of the administrative procedures provided by the Secretary, the courts below held them to be constitutionally inadequate, concluding that due process requires an evidentiary hearing prior to termination. In light of the private and governmental interests at stake here and the nature of the existing procedures, we think this was error.

Since a recipient whose benefits are terminated is awarded full retroactive relief if he ultimately prevails, his sole interest is in the uninterrupted receipt of this source of income pending final administrative decision on his claim. His potential injury is thus similar in nature to that of the welfare recipient in Goldberg . . .

Only in Goldberg has the Court held that due process requires an evidentiary hearing prior to a temporary deprivation. It was emphasized there that welfare assistance is given to persons on the very margin of subsistence. . . Eligibility for disability benefits, in contrast, is not based upon financial need.[24] Indeed, it is wholly unrelated to the worker's income or support from many other sources, such as earnings of other family members, workmen's compensation awards, tort claims awards, savings, private insurance, public or private pensions, veterans' benefits, food stamps, public assistance, or the "many other important programs, both public and private, which contain provisions for disability payments affecting a substantial portion of the work force. . . ." Richardson v. Belcher, 404 U.S. 78, 85–87 (Douglas, J., dissenting).

As Goldberg illustrates, the degree of potential deprivation that may be created by a particular decision is a factor to be considered in assessing the validity of any administrative decisionmaking process. The potential deprivation here is generally likely to be less than in Goldberg, although the degree of difference can be overstated. As the District Court emphasized, to remain eligible for benefits a recipient must be "unable to engage in substantial gainful activity." Thus, . . . there is little possibility that the terminated recipient will be able to find even temporary employment to ameliorate the interim loss.

As we recognized last Term in Fusari v. Steinberg, 419 U.S. 379, 389 (1975), "the possible length of wrongful deprivation of . . . benefits [also] is an important factor in assessing the impact of official action on the private interests." The Secretary concedes that the delay between a request for a hearing before an administrative law judge and a decision on the claim is currently between 10 and 11 months. Since a terminated recipient must first obtain a reconsideration decision as a prerequisite to invoking his right to an evidentiary hearing, the delay between the actual cutoff of benefits and final decision after a hearing exceeds one year.

---

24 The level of benefits is determined by the worker's average monthly earnings during the period prior to disability, his age, and other factors not directly related to financial need. . . .

In view of the torpidity of this administrative review process and the typically modest resources of the family unit of the physically disabled worker,[26] the hardship imposed upon the erroneously terminated disability recipient may be significant. Still, the disabled worker's need is likely to be less than that of a welfare recipient. In addition to the possibility of access to private resources, other forms of government assistance will become available where the termination of disability benefits places a worker or his family below the subsistence level. In view of these potential sources of temporary income, there is less reason here than in Goldberg to depart from the ordinary principle, established by our decisions, that something less than an evidentiary hearing is sufficient prior to adverse administrative action.

D

An additional factor to be considered here is the fairness and reliability of the existing pretermination procedures, and the probable value, if any, of additional procedural safeguards. Central to the evaluation of any administrative process is the nature of the relevant inquiry. See Friendly, "Some Kind of Hearing," 123 U. Pa. L. Rev. 1267, 1281 (1975). In order to remain eligible for benefits the disabled worker must demonstrate by means of "medically acceptable clinical and laboratory diagnostic techniques," 42 U.S.C. § 423(d)(3), that he is unable "to engage in any substantial gainful activity by reason of any *medically determinable* physical or mental impairment . . ." § 423(d)(1)(A) (emphasis supplied). In short, a medical assessment of the worker's physical or mental condition is required. This is a more sharply focused and easily documented decision than the typical determination of welfare entitlement. In the latter case, a wide variety of information may be deemed relevant and issues of witness credibility and veracity often are critical to the decisionmaking process. Goldberg noted that in such circumstances "written submissions are a wholly unsatisfactory basis for decision."

By contrast, the decision whether to discontinue disability benefits will turn, in most cases, upon "routine, standard, and unbiased medical reports by physician specialists," Richardson v. Perales, 402 U.S. 389, 404 (1971), concerning a subject whom they have personally examined.[28]

---

[26] Amici cite statistics compiled by the Secretary which indicate that in 1965 the mean income of the family unit of a disabled worker was $3,803, while the median income for the unit was $2,836. The mean liquid assets—i.e., cash, stocks, bonds—of these family units was $4,862; the median was $940. These statistics do not take into account the family unit's nonliquid assets—i.e., automobile, real estate, and the like. Brief for AFL-CIO et al. as Amici Curiae App. 4a

[28] The decision is not purely a question of the accuracy of a medical diagnosis since the ultimate issue which the state agency must resolve is whether in light of the particular worker's "age, education, and work experience" he cannot "engage in any . . . substantial gainful work which exists in the national economy. . ." 42 U.S.C. § 423(d)(2)(A). Yet information concerning each of these worker characteristics is amenable to effective written presentation. The value of an evidentiary hearing, or even a limited oral presentation, to an accurate presentation of those factors to the decisionmaker does not appear substantial. Similarly, resolution of the inquiry as to the types of employment opportunities that exist in the national economy for a physically

In Richardson the Court recognized the "reliability and probative worth of written medical reports," emphasizing that while there may be "professional disagreement with the medical conclusions" the "specter of questionable credibility and veracity is not present." To be sure, credibility and veracity may be a factor in the ultimate disability assessment in some cases. But procedural due process rules are shaped by the risk of error inherent in the truthfinding process as applied to the generality of cases, not the rare exceptions. The potential value of an evidentiary hearing, or even oral presentation to the decisionmaker, is substantially less in this context than in Goldberg.

The decision in Goldberg also was based on the Court's conclusion that written submissions were an inadequate substitute for oral presentation because they did not provide an effective means for the recipient to communicate his case to the decisionmaker. Written submissions were viewed as an unrealistic option, for most recipients lacked the "educational attainment necessary to write effectively" and could not afford professional assistance. In addition, such submissions would not provide the "flexibility of oral presentations" or "permit the recipient to mold his argument to the issues the decision maker appears to regard as important." In the context of the disability-benefits-entitlement assessment the administrative procedures under review here fully answer these objections.

The detailed questionnaire which the state agency periodically sends the recipient identifies with particularity the information relevant to the entitlement decision, and the recipient is invited to obtain assistance from the local SSA office in completing the questionnaire. More important, the information critical to the entitlement decision usually is derived from medical sources, such as the treating physician. Such sources are likely to be able to communicate more effectively through written documents than are welfare recipients or the lay witnesses supporting their cause. The conclusions of physicians often are supported by X-rays and the results of clinical or laboratory tests, information typically more amenable to written than to oral presentation.

A further safeguard against mistake is the policy of allowing the disability recipient's representative full access to all information relied upon by the state agency. In addition, prior to the cutoff of benefits the agency informs the recipient of its tentative assessment, the reasons therefor, and provides a summary of the evidence that it considers most relevant. Opportunity is then afforded the recipient to submit additional evidence or arguments, enabling him to challenge directly the accuracy of information in his file as well as the correctness of the agency's tentative conclusions. These procedures, again as contrasted with those

---

impaired worker with a particular set of skills would not necessarily be advanced by an evidentiary hearing. Cf. 1 K. Davis, Administrative Law Treatise § 7.06, p. 429 (1958). The statistical information relevant to this judgment is more amenable to written than to oral presentation.

before the Court in Goldberg, enable the recipient to "mold" his argument to respond to the precise issues which the decisionmaker regards as crucial.

Despite these carefully structured procedures, amici point to the significant reversal rate for appealed cases as clear evidence that the current process is inadequate. Depending upon the base selected and the line of analysis followed, the relevant reversal rates urged by the contending parties vary from a high of 58.6% for appealed reconsideration decisions to an overall reversal rate of only 3.3%.[29] Bare statistics rarely provide a satisfactory measure of the fairness of a decisionmaking process. Their adequacy is especially suspect here since the administrative review system is operated on an open-file basis. A recipient may always submit new evidence, and such submissions may result in additional medical examinations. Such fresh examinations were held in approximately 30% to 40% of the appealed cases in fiscal 1973, either at the reconsideration or evidentiary hearing stage of the administrative process. In this context, the value of reversal rate statistics as one means of evaluating the adequacy of the pretermination process is diminished. Thus, although we view such information as relevant, it is certainly not controlling in this case.

E

In striking the appropriate due process balance the final factor to be assessed is the public interest. This includes the administrative burden and other societal costs that would be associated with requiring, as a matter of constitutional right, an evidentiary hearing upon demand in all cases prior to the termination of disability benefits. The most visible burden would be the incremental cost resulting from the increased number of hearings and the expense of providing benefits to ineligible recipients pending decision. No one can predict the extent of the increase, but the fact that full benefits would continue until after such hearings would assure the exhaustion in most cases of this attractive option. Nor would the theoretical right of the Secretary to recover undeserved benefits result, as a practical matter, in any substantial offset to the added outlay of public funds. The parties submit widely varying estimates of the probable additional financial cost. We only need say that experience with the constitutionalizing of government procedures suggests that the ultimate additional cost in terms of money and administrative burden would not be insubstantial.

---

[29] By focusing solely on the reversal rate for appealed reconsideration determinations amici overstate the relevant reversal rate. [I]n order fully to assess the reliability and fairness of a system of procedure, one must also consider the overall rate of error for all denials of benefits. Here that overall rate is 12.2%. Moreover, about 75% of these reversals occur at the reconsideration stage of the administrative process. Since the median period between a request for reconsideration review and decision is only two months, Brief for AFL-CIO et al. as Amici Curiae App. 4a, the deprivation is significantly less than that concomitant to the lengthier delay before an evidentiary hearing. Netting out these reconsideration reversals, the overall reversal rate falls to 3.3%. See Supplemental and Reply Brief for Petitioner 14.

Financial cost alone is not a controlling weight in determining whether due process requires a particular procedural safeguard prior to some administrative decision. But the Government's interest, and hence that of the public, in conserving scarce fiscal and administrative resources is a factor that must be weighed. At some point the benefit of an additional safeguard to the individual affected by the administrative action and to society in terms of increased assurance that the action is just, may be outweighed by the cost. Significantly, the cost of protecting those whom the preliminary administrative process has identified as likely to be found undeserving may in the end come out of the pockets of the deserving since resources available for any particular program of social welfare are not unlimited.

But more is implicated in cases of this type than ad hoc weighing of fiscal and administrative burdens against the interests of a particular category of claimants. The ultimate balance involves a determination as to when, under our constitutional system, judicial-type procedures must be imposed upon administrative action to assure fairness . . . The judicial model of an evidentiary hearing is neither a required, nor even the most effective, method of decisionmaking in all circumstances. The essence of due process is the requirement that "a person in jeopardy of serious loss [be given] notice of the case against him and opportunity to meet it." Joint Anti-Fascist Comm. v. McGrath, 341 U.S., at 171–172 (Frankfurter, J., concurring). All that is necessary is that the procedures be tailored, in light of the decision to be made, to "the capacities and circumstances of those who are to be heard," Goldberg v. Kelly, 397 U.S., at 268–269, to insure that they are given a meaningful opportunity to present their case. In assessing what process is due in this case, substantial weight must be given to the good-faith judgments of the individuals charged by Congress with the administration of social welfare programs that the procedures they have provided assure fair consideration of the entitlement claims of individuals. This is especially so where, as here, the prescribed procedures not only provide the claimant with an effective process for asserting his claim prior to any administrative action, but also assure a right to an evidentiary hearing, as well as to subsequent judicial review, before the denial of his claim becomes final.

We conclude that an evidentiary hearing is not required prior to the termination of disability benefits and that the present administrative procedures fully comport with due process.

The judgment of the Court of Appeals is reversed.

■ JUSTICE STEVENS took no part in the consideration or decision of this case.

■ JUSTICE BRENNAN, with whom JUSTICE MARSHALL concurs, dissenting.

. . . [T]he Court's consideration that a discontinuance of disability benefits may cause the recipient to suffer only a limited deprivation is no argument. It is speculative. Moreover, the very legislative determination to provide disability benefits, without any prerequisite determination of need in fact, presumes a need by the recipient which is not this Court's function to denigrate. Indeed, in the present case, it is indicated that because disability benefits were terminated there was a foreclosure upon the Eldridge home and the family's furniture was repossessed, forcing Eldridge, his wife, and their children to sleep in one bed. Finally, it is also no argument that a worker, who has been placed in the untenable position of having been denied disability benefits, may still seek other forms of public assistance.

NOTES ON HOW THE MATHEWS V. ELDRIDGE DOCTRINE IS CONSTRUCTED

(1) *How Does Justice Powell Frame His Inquiry?* "[T]here is less reason here than in Goldberg to depart from *the ordinary principle*, . . . that something less than an evidentiary hearing is sufficient prior to adverse administrative action." (emphasis added). Does Mathews invert the traditional understanding of what process is due process? If a private citizen has an interest sufficiently dignified to be within the constitutional trio of "life, liberty, or property," should we not start by assuming that "the ordinary principle" is that the citizen is entitled to a trial before the state deprives him of that interest—and then see if there are reasons for saying that providing a trial is, in context, too much? Todd D. Rakoff, Brock v. Roadway Express, Inc., And The New Law Of Regulatory Due Process, 1987 Sup. Ct. Rev. 157, 162, hypothesizing the reaction of the "typical American lawyer" to the Mathews balance: "No man's liberty or property are safe when the court simply asks case by case what procedures seem worthwhile and not too costly."

(2) *What is the Right Baseline?* Should it be the courtroom trial as just suggested—or is making that the archetype of due process wrong in principle? Compare the views of JUDGE HENRY J. FRIENDLY in a famous article, published shortly before Mathews, that appears to have had significant impact on the majority's thinking in the case. In "SOME KIND OF HEARING," 123 U. Pa. L. Rev. 1267 (1975), Judge Friendly decried "the tendency to judicialize administrative procedures" that Goldberg and succeeding cases had produced. Instead, he suggested, "[T]he required degree of procedural safeguards varies directly with the importance of the private interest affected and the need for and usefulness of the particular safeguard in the given circumstances and inversely with the burden and any other adverse consequences of affording it."

A balancing test, he admitted, might seem "uncertain and subjective," but he argued that "more elaborate specification of the relevant factors may help to produce more principled and predictable decisions." He offered the following list of "factors that have been considered to be elements of a fair hearing, roughly in order of priority":

1.   An Unbiased Tribunal

2.   Notice of the Proposed Action and the Grounds Asserted for It

3. An Opportunity to Present Reasons Why the Proposed Action Should Not be Taken

4. The Right to Call Witnesses

5. The Right To Know the Evidence Against One

6. The Right To Have Decision Based Only on the Evidence Presented

7. Counsel

8. The Making of a Record

9. A Statement of Reasons

10. Public Attendance

11. Judicial Review

He concluded: "In the mass justice area the Supreme Court has yielded too readily to the notions that the adversary system is the only appropriate model and that there is only one acceptable solution to any problem, and consequently has been too prone to indulge in constitutional codification. There is need for experimentation, particularly for the use of the investigative model, for empirical studies, and for avoiding absolutes."

(3) **The Programmatic Context.** Justice Powell clearly analyzes not the case of a single claimant, but an entire system of benefits adjudication. What are its features?

One important point, surely, is that there are an enormous number of disability determinations to be made. Even counting only those cases that go to an ALJ hearing (because the claimant has been turned down in the prior steps of the process, and he appeals the termination of his benefits), in recent years the number of such cases has exceeded three quarters of a million cases per year.

Another point—pointed out at the very end of the opinion—is that in addition to the procedures provided prior to initial termination of the claimant, "the prescribed procedures . . . also assure a right to an evidentiary hearing, as well as to subsequent judicial review, before the denial of his claim becomes final." Does the determination at stake more resemble, to use a criminal law analogy, a "probable cause" proceeding?

A third point is that the record stays open throughout this process—that the ALJ considers new evidence and makes a de novo decision.

A fourth point is that this ALJ process differs a good bit from many other APA formal hearings; the ALJ is responsible for seeing the government's information into the record, for the identification and examination of government witnesses, and for cross-examination of the claimant's witnesses. As the Court says, "[T]he hearing is non-adversary and the SSA is not represented by counsel."

And a final point, as discussed in the opinion, is that many such hearings result in the granting of benefits that had been previously denied.

Does the result in the case turn on any of these facts? If so, should the Mathews test be different in a situation in which one or more of these facts is different?

(4)   *Is Mathews Balancing Capable of Principled Application?* Even as formulated, the Mathew's test abjures stating a "one size fits all" answer to the question "what process is due in administrative proceedings?" By disaggregating the very large bundle of procedures comprised in a trial-type judicial hearing, and by accepting that some procedures can follow rather than precede deprivation, or perhaps be excluded altogether, judges gain flexibility to respond to the range of administrative contexts. However, this flexibility comes at a cost. If each stick in the process bundle plus its timing is independently considered, a very large number of process combinations is possible. Can the doctrine structure judicial choice in a manner both defensible in principle and predictable in practice?

(Speaking of doctrinal regularity, does the Mathews balance apply to the many contexts not related to ordinary administrative law in which procedural due process also is relevant? The answer is sometimes yes, sometimes no. For example, it is not the test to be used in evaluating the constitutionality of procedures for determining criminal guilt, Medina v. California, 505 U.S. 437 (1992); it was the test used by the Court in deciding whether due process requires a state to provide counsel for an indigent parent in a proceeding in court to terminate her parental rights, Lassiter v. Department of Social Services, 452 U.S. 18 (1981); and it was the test used in Hamdi v. Rumsfeld, 542 U.S. 507 (2004), to judge the process to be used in determining whether the grounds existed to justify holding a U.S. citizen as a military prisoner in Guantanamo Bay. The proposition that "the Mathews test was . . . conceived to address due process claims arising in the context of administrative law," Medina, 505 U.S. at 444, is not the whole story.)

(5)   *Whose Interests Count?* That Mathews is about administering a program of government benefits does appear to show up in its identifying the government's interest as "including the function involved and the fiscal and administrative burdens that the additional or substitute procedural requirement would entail." What about administrative law cases in which the government's interest is not so much in minimizing its own "fiscal and administrative burdens" as in protecting a beneficiary class against the regulated party? Can the benefits to that group be added to the government's direct interests in figuring out how strong the third branch of the balance is, compared to the burdens put on the regulated party that comprise the first branch? There has not been much litigation raising the point, probably because this scenario—the direct imposition of regulation on a regulated party through adjudication—is the scenario most likely to have been placed by Congress within the category of formal adjudication under the APA; procedural issues then become a matter of construing the APA rather than applying the Constitution. The one Supreme Court decision raising the issue is Brock v. Roadway Express, Inc., 481 U.S. 252 (1987), which considered a statute protecting trucking industry employees from being discharged for reporting safety violations. There, a fractured Court speaking in several

opinions seemed to consider (without much argument) that the interests of the beneficiary of the regulation at issue (the truck driver) should count along with the government's interest against the interests of the regulated party (the trucking company); accordingly, it was constitutional for the statute to authorize the Secretary of Labor to order a driver's reinstatement after a summary process or, in other words, to require the company to continue to spend the money to employ someone it didn't want to employ during the longer evidentiary proceeding needed to decide the ultimate rights and wrongs. This contrasts with the normal rule for formal agency adjudications, in which (as in the usual courtroom case) the remedy—for example, the cease and desist order, or the reinstatement order—is issued only after the formal evidentiary hearing. Does this mean that the formal adjudication requirements of APA 554, 556, and 557 are more stringent than due process requires? For commentary, see TODD D. RAKOFF, BROCK V. ROADWAY EXPRESS, INC., AND THE NEW LAW OF REGULATORY DUE PROCESS, 1987 Sup. Ct. Rev. 157.

(6)   *Deference?* It is also worth noting that Mathews begins its analysis not from an idealized conception of what procedure should be used but rather from the procedure stipulated by the statutes and regulations already in use. The second branch of the test asks, really, two questions: about "the risk of an erroneous deprivation" entailed in using those existing procedures and about "the probable value ... of additional ... procedural safeguards." Justice Powell spends many words detailing and evaluating both these matters. Beyond this nod to the agency built into the announced doctrine, he also (this time without elaboration) says, at the end, that "substantial weight must be given to the good-faith judgments of the individuals charged by Congress with the administration of social welfare programs that the procedures they have provided assure fair consideration of the entitlement claims of individuals." Does Mathews defer too much on what is, after all, a constitutional question? Does it reach toward, although not fully invoking, taking "the bitter with the sweet"? Or, given the resources available to judges to determine questions such as this, and the responsibility for assuring fairness that might rest on legislative as well as judicial shoulders, does it state a sensible proposition? For an argument that deference is appropriate here, see Adrian Vermeule, Deference and Due Process, 129 Harv. L. Rev. 1890 (2016).

(7)   For a retelling of Mathews v. Eldridge and an assessment of each element of the calculus, from the perspectives of the various participants based on the record, transcript, briefs and other historical materials, see CYNTHIA R. FARINA, DUE PROCESS AT RASHOMON GATE: THE STORIES OF MATHEWS V. ELDRIGE, IN ADMINISTRATIVE LAW STORIES 229, 257 (P. Strauss ed. 2006). Professor Farina concludes: "This doctrine has not been the constitutional catalyst radically to reform the relationship between the citizen and modern regulatory government. But neither has it brought regulatory government to its knees—and so triggered a political backlash in which social welfare programs were defunded and entitlements dismantled. At a crucial moment, when the emergent new procedural due process jurisprudence was highly vulnerable, the Court chose a restrained,

pragmatic solidification. It did what it could—given what it had, and where it found itself.

"Easy for us to say that what it did, wasn't much. Hard for us to argue—almost three decades later—that what it did, wasn't enough. With the *Mathews* solution, the government often wins, as it did in the case itself. But the government doesn't *always* win. *Mathews* has given lawyers a structure for telling the story of their clients (and the people like them) in a way that judges can locate, and assess, within the constitutional framework. And so we continue to experience procedural due process as a "real" right: a claim that can be made, with meaning, by a single citizen against even the most powerful agencies. As we enter the 21st century, and all momentum is towards transnationally integrated regulatory policy, and government structures that transcend conventional national boundaries, we start out with at least this.

"Perhaps that is not, after all, such a modest accomplishment."

NOTES ON WHAT SHOULD COUNT IN THE MATHEWS THREE-PART TEST

(1) *The Cost-Benefit Constitution?* "The use of cost-benefit analysis to determine due process is not to every constitutional scholar's or judge's taste," says JUDGE POSNER, "but it is the analysis prescribed by the Supreme Court" VAN HARKEN V. CITY OF CHICAGO, 103 F.3d 1346, 1351 (7th Cir. 1997). Here's what he has in mind: In 1987, Illinois joined a number of other states in authorizing municipalities to decriminalize parking violations. Chicago exercised this authority. So long as the violation had been technically criminal, there were trial-type procedures to determine guilt consistent with conviction for other misdemeanors. Once the violation became merely civil, the city wanted to use truncated hearing procedures. Under its rules, the parking ticket was deemed prima facie evidence of a violation. The owner could either pay the fine (which could not exceed $100) or challenge the ticket in writing or in person. The police officer was not required to appear; the ticket was treated as an affidavit. Thus, the only witness was usually the vehicle owner, whom the hearing officer was instructed to cross-examine searchingly. The hearing officer could (but was not required to) subpoena witnesses, including the police officer. If the owner's challenge was denied, he could seek review in the Circuit Court of Cook County by paying the normal filing fee: $200. Consistent with due process? Yes, according to the panel opinion written by Judge Posner. The supposed judicial review was, given its price, illusory—but unnecessary because the basic procedure complied with the Mathews test:

"The costs of procedural safeguards are fairly straightforward, which is not to say easy to quantify. For example, the cost of requiring the police officer who writes the ticket to appear in person at every hearing at which the ticket is challenged—one of the procedural safeguards that the plaintiffs in this case claim is required by the due process clause—depends on the number and length of hearings, the average time the police officer requires to get to and from the hearing, the reduction in his productivity from the interruption of his normal workday that attendance at such hearings requires, and the expense to the City of hiring additional policemen. We were told at argument without contradiction that the City issues 4 million parking tickets a year, of which 5 percent are challenged (200,000), a third of those in person rather than by mail and thus requiring an oral hearing (67,000). If the ticketing officer were required to attend, the number of hearings requested would undoubtedly be higher, because respondents would think it likely that the officer wouldn't show up—a frequent occurrence at hearings on moving violations. Suppose the number of hearings would be double what it is under the challenged procedures (that is, would be 134,000), but the police would show up at only half, putting us back to 67,000; and suppose that a hearing at which a police officer showed up cost him on average 2 hours away from his other work. Then this procedural safeguard for which the plaintiffs are contending would cost the City 134,000 police hours a year, the equivalent of 67 full-time police officers at 2,000 hours a year per officer. In addition, more hearing officers would be required, at some additional cost to the City, because each hearing would be longer as a result of the presence of another live witness. And all these are simply the monetary costs. Acquittals of violators due solely to the ticketing officer's failure to appear would undermine the deterrent efficacy of the parking laws and deprive the City of revenues to which it was entitled as a matter of substantive justice.

"The benefits of a procedural safeguard are even trickier to estimate than the costs. The benefits depend on the harm that the safeguard will avert in cases in which it prevents an erroneous result and the likelihood that it will prevent an erroneous result. We know the harm here to the innocent car owner found 'guilty' and forced to pay a fine: it is the fine, and it can be anywhere from $10 to $100, for an average of $55. We must ask how likely it is that error would be averted if the ticketing officer were present at the hearing and therefore subject to cross-examination. Suppose that in his absence the probability of an erroneous determination that the respondent really did commit a parking violation is 5 percent, and the officer's presence would cut that probability in half, to 2.5 percent. Then the average saving to the innocent respondent from this additional procedural safeguard would be only $1.38 ($55 × .025)—a trivial amount.

"These calculations are inexact, to say the least; but they help to show, what is pretty obvious without them, that the benefits of requiring the police officer to appear at every hearing are unlikely to exceed the costs."

Do you agree with Judge Posner that this is what Mathews requires?

(2) *Does Mathews Make What Really Matters, Matter?* JERRY L. MASHAW, THE SUPREME COURT'S DUE PROCESS CALCULUS FOR ADMINISTRATIVE ADJUDICATION IN MATHEWS V. ELDRIDGE: THREE FACTORS IN SEARCH OF A THEORY OF VALUE, 44 U. Chi. L. Rev. 28, 48–49 (1976): "The Eldridge Court conceives of the values of procedure too narrowly: it views the sole purpose of procedural protections as enhancing accuracy, and thus limits its calculus to the benefits or costs that flow from correct or incorrect decisions. No attention is paid to 'process values' that might inhere in oral proceedings or to the demoralization costs that may result from the grant-withdrawal-grant-withdrawal sequence to which claimants like Eldridge are

subjected. Perhaps more important, as the Court seeks to make sense of a calculus in which accuracy is the sole goal of procedure, it tends erroneously to characterize disability hearings as concerned almost exclusively with medical impairment and thus concludes that such hearings involve only medical evidence, whose reliability would be little enhanced by oral procedure. As applied by the Eldridge Court the utilitarian calculus tends, as cost-benefit analyses typically do, to 'dwarf soft variables' and to ignore complexities and ambiguities.

"The problem with a utilitarian calculus is not merely that the Court may define the relevant costs and benefits too narrowly. However broadly conceived, the calculus asks unanswerable questions. For example, what is the social value, and the social cost, of continuing disability payments until after an oral hearing for persons initially determined to be ineligible? Answers to those questions require a technique for measuring the social value and social cost of government income transfers, but no such technique exists. Even if such formidable tasks of social accounting could be accomplished, the effectiveness of oral hearings in forestalling the losses that result from erroneous terminations would remain uncertain. In the face of these pervasive indeterminacies the Eldridge Court was forced to retreat to a presumption of constitutionality."

(3)   CYNTHIA R. FARINA, CONCEIVING DUE PROCESS, 3 Yale J. L. & Feminism 189, 234–35 (1991): "If due process is to mark out and defend a sphere in which the individual is reliably preserved from the demands of the collective, how can the extent of the protection the individual receives turn on some calculus explicitly designed to maximize aggregate welfare? When the claim of the individual is pitted against 'the sheer magnitude of the collective interests at stake,'[219] how often will the collective good not predominate? . . . The unnaturalness of using a social welfare balance to set the content of due process protection becomes apparent . . . if we imagine employing the Mathews approach to decide what process is due parties in traditional civil adjudication. And yet, the Court's tacit recognition that due process in the regulatory context must, somehow, be differently understood is grounded in an inescapable reality: Providing mass justice is a staggering task. . . . If the Court is to avoid dictating a massive reordering of state and federal fiscal priorities, it must, it seems, weigh individual claims to process against the systematic costs of proceduralization.

"To venture into social welfare accounting is, however, to crack the lid of Pandora's box. . . . What is the judiciary doing second-guessing the political branches' judgment on how much should be spend to implement a given regulatory program? 'If the greatest good for the greatest number is the test for constitutionality under the due process clause, then it is hard to escape the notion that the best evidence of social welfare will always be the judgment of the legislature or its delegate.'[223] To engage, at this stage of the [due process] analysis, in an inevitably ad hoc and standardless assessment of the importance of the individual interest, and to use that assessment as

---

[219] Richard Saphire, Specifying Due Process Values: Toward a More Responsive Approach to Procedural Protection, 127 U. Pa. L. Rev. 111, 155 (1978).

[223] Jerry L. Mashaw, Due Process in the Administrative State 152 (1985).

the basis for restructuring administrative behavior, seems precisely the undisciplined judicial interference in local and national governance that the Court embraced entitlement analysis to avoid."

(4) *Or Is It a Reasonable Framework?* GARY LAWSON, KATHERINE FERGUSON, & GUILLERMO MONTERO, "OH LORD, PLEASE DON'T LET ME BE MISUNDERSTOOD!": REDISCOVERING THE *MATHEWS V. ELDRIDGE* AND *PENN CENTRAL* FRAMEWORKS, 81 Notre Dame L. Rev. 1, 22–23 (2005): "Modern scholars . . . generally treat the Mathews framework as though it were an outcome-determinative test. The Court also seems to have accepted the idea that the sole justification for procedures is 'to minimize the risk of erroneous decisions' although there have been occasional dissenting voices on that score.

"Critics have, with considerable justification, roundly attacked the Mathews framework's efficacy as a decisionmaking tool. Some have pointed out that one can only weigh factors against each other if the factors are commensurable, which the Mathews factors do not appear to be. As one critic has stated, '[t]his reliance upon "weight," which is a useful approach for dealing with bananas, leaves something to be desired where factors such as those in Mathews are concerned.'[87] Others have criticized the narrow focus on decisional accuracy that the Mathews framework seems to require. Jerry Mashaw has famously argued that by identifying decisional accuracy as the holy grail of due process law, the Mathews formulation disregards the important value that individuals place on being heard: 'a lack of personal participation causes alienation and a loss of that dignity and self-respect that society properly deems independently valuable.' . . .

"All of these criticisms of Mathews have merit, but none of the developments in the evolution of Mathews that spawned these criticisms were inevitable. Mathews does not have to be viewed as anything other than a potentially useful way of structuring dialogue about fairness, in which case criticisms of Mathews for failing to direct or predict decisions are misplaced. Nor must Mathews be construed to constrict the perceived value of procedures solely to their ability to reduce the risk of erroneous substantive decisions. One could, of course, independently reach the conclusion that procedures are only valuable for their role in reaching correct substantive outcomes, but nothing in Mathews compels that result. If Mathews is best viewed solely as a means for starting (not finishing) a stylized legal conversation about fairness, it should be judged on those terms.

"Does the Mathews formulation do a serviceable job of providing a common frame of reference for legal argumentation? We think that it does. It would fail in that task if the factors that it identified were wildly inappropriate to the ultimate inquiry, which they clearly are not. It would also fail in that task if the factors themselves were so vague that they could not serve as a tool for communication. We do not see that problem either. Mathews has many critics, but we do not see the critics complaining that they do not know what the Mathews factors mean. Quite to the contrary, the

---

[87]   Edward L. Rubin, Due Process and the Administrative State, 72 Cal. L. Rev. 1044, 1138 (1984).

critics know exactly what the Mathews factors are getting at and don't like it one bit. Mathews is a perfectly respectable jurisprudential and doctrinal vehicle for promoting adversarial dialogue about fairness.

"The process by which Mathews was transformed from a device for facilitating discussion into an outcome-determinative test is to some extent understandable—formulations tend to take on lives of their own independently of their terms or justifications—but it is also regrettable. A great deal of scholarly and judicial time and energy has been spent on problems that need never have arisen."

b.   Applications

> KAPPS v. WING
> Notes on the Decision in Kapps v. Wing
> Notes on an Alternative Line of Doctrine
> LATIF v. HOLDER
> Notes on the No-Fly List Issue

KAPPS v. WING

United States Court of Appeals for the Second Circuit (2005).
404 F.3d 105.

■ CALABRESI, CIRCUIT JUDGE.

. . .

I.   BACKGROUND

A.   Statutory Framework

Congress enacted the Low Income Home Energy Assistance Act ("LIHEAA") in 1981 in response to the rising costs of oil-based energy. LIHEAA was intended to, and has since its passage, assisted the states in providing home energy assistance to low income families. Participating states are given a block grant, which may be used for two primary purposes: 1) to assist poor families in meeting their regular heating costs ("regular HEAP benefits"); and 2) to intervene in energy crises to prevent any interruption in needy households' heat ("emergency HEAP benefits"). While state LIHEAA programs must comply with certain federal statutory requirements, the states are, as a general matter, afforded substantial discretion in defining the specific contours of their LIHEAA program.

Levels of LIHEAA funding are set by Congress on an annual basis. See 42 U.S.C. § 8621. Allocated funds are distributed among participating states on the basis of a complicated statutory formula. See 42 U.S.C. § 8623. States may, but need not, choose to supplement federal funds with state monies, in order to ensure that all eligible households are provided with benefits. New York, like some other states, has opted not to supplement federal funds, and hence provides benefits only to the extent that federal funding is available in any given program year. See N.Y. Soc. Serv. L. § 97[2].

New York's Home Energy Assistance Program ("HEAP") was created by the New York State Legislature in 1983, in order to allow the state to take advantage of the LIHEAA block grant program. Like many of New York's other social services programs, HEAP is administered jointly by the state and by local social service districts. At the state level, the Office of Temporary and Disability Assistance ("OTDA") annually sets standard eligibility criteria and benefits levels for the forthcoming year. The OTDA is also responsible for establishing a "program year," within which all HEAP applications must be received. Local social service districts are responsible for the actual processing of HEAP applications, and for notifying applicants of benefits eligibility.

Under regulations passed by the OTDA, there are two categories of households which may be eligible for regular HEAP benefits: 1) "[c]ategorically income eligible households"; and 2) "[i]ncome tested households." "Categorically eligible" households are those that include at least one household member who receives at least one of several specified federal or state benefits. Households that are not categorically eligible may qualify for HEAP benefits by demonstrating income eligibility, in accordance with standards set by the state on an annual basis. Once found eligible, a household's HEAP benefits allocation is determined in accordance with a complicated payment matrix, or point system. This "payment matrix" takes into account such factors as family income, the energy burden ratio of the household, the amount of federal funds allocated for the year, and the presence of "vulnerable" household members.

The regulations in effect at the time of the district court's decision required the defendants to process all HEAP applications within 30 business days. Historically, however, actual processing times have deviated considerably from this regulatory goal. During the pendency of this litigation, average processing times for New York City HEAP applications have varied between 21 and 122 days. At the time that the parties briefed the motion for summary judgment in the district court, most, but not all, New York City applications were being processed within the 30 day period mandated by the state.

HEAP applicants are notified of the granting or the denial of HEAP benefits in a notice issued by the social service district . . . If the applicant has been found ineligible for benefits, this notice usually, but not always, includes very basic information on why benefits have been denied. Applicants who have been found eligible for HEAP benefits are sometimes informed of the amount of benefits they will receive. But, apart from that, they are given no information, other than that their benefits application has been approved. In all cases, the notice advises applicants that they can obtain further information in a number of ways, including by calling the social service district, or by setting up a meeting with a benefits specialist.

Ordinarily, applicants have 60 days from the date of the HEAP notice, during which they may request an administrative "fair hearing" to challenge the agency's eligibility and/or benefits level determination. Under state regulations, however, fair hearings may not be requested more than 105 days after the close of the HEAP program year. As such, when HEAP applicants receive notice of the grant or denial of HEAP benefits more than 105 days after the termination of the program year, they are totally foreclosed from seeking a fair hearing. And, those applicants who receive notice of HEAP eligibility more than 45 days after the close of the program year will have less than the full 60 days within which to request a fair hearing.

B.   Facts/Procedural History

Named plaintiffs Eileen Kapps, Geraldine Boyland, Alice Costello, Joan Ford, Joanne Karl and Margaret Riley filed this action in 1998. In their complaint, they alleged various violations inter alia of the LIHEAA and of the federal Due Process Clause in the defendants' administration of the New York City HEAP program. Specifically, as relevant to this appeal, plaintiffs contended below that the denial of the right to a fair hearing (by virtue of the operation of the 105 day rule, when combined with delays in providing notification of benefits) violated due process and the LIHEAA. Plaintiffs also claimed that the HEAP notices—by failing to provide information on how the applicant's benefits eligibility and allotment was calculated—did not meet the requirements of due process.

Plaintiffs named as defendants Brian J. Wing, the Commissioner of the OTDA, Jason A. Turner, the Commissioner of the New York City Department of Social Services, and Martin Oesterreich, the Commissioner of the New York City Department of Youth and Community Development. Plaintiffs sought to represent themselves, and all other applicants for regular HEAP benefits in the City of New York who had been denied certain procedural protections in the processing of their HEAP applications.

. . . The district court, in a carefully reasoned opinion . . . granted class certification, and gave summary judgment in part to the plaintiffs and in part to the defendants . . . The defendants appealed.

II.   DISCUSSION

A.   Standard of Review

We review a district court's grant of summary judgment de novo. . . .

B.   Due Process

The plaintiffs have alleged that the defendants' practices in administering New York City's HEAP program violate the procedural requirements of the Due Process Clause of the Fourteenth Amendment. In adjudicating such a claim, we consider two distinct issues: 1) whether plaintiffs possess a liberty or property interest protected by the Due Process Clause; and, if so, 2) whether existing state procedures are constitutionally adequate. The defendants argue that the plaintiffs possess no property interest in HEAP benefits, and that we therefore need not consider the second step of the due process inquiry. They also contend that—even assuming the plaintiffs have some constitutionally protected interest—the plaintiffs were afforded all the process that is required. Because an award of HEAP benefits to qualified applicants is mandatory and not discretionary (at least to the extent the program is funded in any given year), we conclude that the plaintiffs possess a sufficient property interest in the receipt of HEAP benefits to warrant due process protection in their demonstration of eligibility. We also conclude that the district court properly found existing procedures to be inadequate as a matter of federal constitutional law.

i.   Property Interest

Social welfare benefits have long been afforded constitutional protection as a species of property protected by the federal Due Process Clause. See Goldberg v. Kelly. While not all benefits programs create constitutional property interests, procedural due process protections ordinarily attach where state or federal law confers an entitlement to benefits. A mere "unilateral expectation" of receiving a benefit is not, however, enough; a property interest arises only where one has a "legitimate claim of entitlement" to the benefit. Board of Regents of State Colleges v. Roth.

In determining whether a given benefits regime creates a property interest protected by the Due Process Clause, we look to the statutes and regulations governing the distribution of benefits. Where those statutes or regulations "meaningfully channel[ ] official discretion by mandating a defined administrative outcome," a property interest will be found to exist. Sealed v. Sealed, 332 F.3d 51, 56 (2d Cir. 2003). Thus, to the extent that state or federal law "meaningfully channels" the discretion of state or local officials by mandating an award of HEAP benefits to applicants who satisfy prescribed eligibility criteria, plaintiff-applicants possess a property interest, protected by the federal Due Process Clause.

We agree with the defendants that the LIHEAA does not, by itself, create a property interest. The LIHEAA affords substantial discretion to the states, both in deciding whether to participate in the home energy program, and, if they choose to participate, in crafting their own state-level home energy laws. See 42 U.S.C. § 8624. While the Act does require participating states to certify that they agree to target certain populations, and to allocate at least some of their benefits to specified goals of the Act, it dictates no particular result as to any given benefits applicant. Accordingly, the LIHEAA itself cannot be considered to "channel" official discretion sufficiently "meaningfully" so as to confer a due process protected property right.

Property interests, however, do not arise only from federal law. To the extent that state law imposes "substantive predicates" that limit the decision-making of HEAP officials, it too may confer a constitutionally protected property right. See Roth. As a result, we must also look to New York law to determine whether plaintiffs possess a property right in the receipt of HEAP benefits. Even a cursory examination of that law reveals that it provides precisely the type of discretion-limiting "substantive predicates" that are the hallmarks of protected property rights.

Like other statutory frameworks that we have found to create property interests, New York state law sets fixed eligibility criteria for the receipt of HEAP benefits. See N.Y. Comp. Codes R. & Regs. tit. 18, § 393.4(c) (setting forth standard eligibility criteria for the receipt of HEAP benefits, and indicating that "once determined eligible a household *will* receive a regular HEAP benefit") (emphasis added). Similarly, the amount of benefits provided to eligible applicants is determined in accordance with a standard benefits matrix. See N.Y. Comp. Codes R. & Regs. tit. 18, § 393.4(c) (eligible households will receive a HEAP benefit in accordance with an annually established payment matrix); see also [trial exhibit 39] (reproduction of the defendants' "Heating Benefit Calculation Worksheet"). And, there has been no intimation in the course of this litigation that discretionary factors enter into the determination of HEAP eligibility or of benefits amount. On the contrary, it appears that all of the factors considered by the state in assessing individual HEAP eligibility are objective, and as such are ones over which HEAP administrators have no discretionary control.

Notwithstanding this mandatory statutory and regulatory framework, defendants contend that some characteristics of the HEAP program render the plaintiffs' receipt of HEAP benefits too uncertain to give plaintiffs a property interest subject to due process protection. Specifically, defendants allege that the fact that the plaintiffs are *applicants* for benefits, rather than current recipients of benefits, renders their interest in the benefits too tenuous to qualify for due process protection. Defendants also argue that the HEAP program's dependence on federal funds means that no individual plaintiff can be assured of receiving benefits, thus rendering any individual's anticipation of benefits a mere "unilateral expectation," rather than a "legitimate claim of entitlement." See Roth.

In light of these two factors, defendants suggest, it does not matter whether or not state law sets forth discretion-restricting guidelines for the operation of the HEAP program, since any individual plaintiff's interest remains too contingent to constitute a property interest . . .

a)   *Applicants for Benefits*

The Supreme Court has repeatedly reserved decision on the question of whether *applicants* for benefits (in contradistinction to *current recipients* of benefits) possess a property interest protected by the Due Process Clause. See, e.g., Lyng v. Payne, 476 U.S. 926, 942 (1986). Every circuit to address the question, however, has concluded that applicants for benefits, no less than current benefits recipients, may possess a property interest in the receipt of public welfare entitlements. And, our own circuit has indicated on at least three occasions that benefits applicants may possess a property interest, albeit in circumstances that differ somewhat from the instant case. Indeed, we have explained that "[w]hether a benefit invests the applicant with a 'claim of entitlement' or merely a 'unilateral expectation' is determined by the amount of discretion the disbursing agency retains" . . . *Colson ex rel. Colson v. Sillman*, 35 F.3d 106, 108–09 (2d Cir. 1994). . . .

The rationale for recognizing applicants' due process rights in these cases is apparent. Statutory language may so specifically mandate benefits awards upon demonstration of certain qualifications that an applicant must fairly be recognized to have a limited property interest entitling him, at least, to process sufficient to permit a demonstration of eligibility.

Defendants argue, however, that plaintiffs as applicants cannot possess a due process protected interest in the receipt of benefits, because they have not yet been shown to fulfill the eligibility criteria for HEAP benefits. This contention is without merit.

We note as an initial matter that, as to past violations of due process, all of the named plaintiffs were found eligible for benefits, and hence, even under defendants' argument, possessed a protected property interest in the receipt of benefits.[15] More fundamentally, the defendants' position misapprehends the purpose of requiring the state to afford adequate procedural due process protections in determining eligibility for benefits that state law makes a matter of entitlement. For, as the Tenth Circuit recently observed, the aim of proper procedures is precisely to allow the state to decide *properly* whether the applicant in fact has a legitimate claim of entitlement.

It is for this reason that, in cases involving the termination of benefits, federal courts do not ask whether the plaintiffs are entitled to the continuation of benefits, or whether they are, as the agency found, no longer eligible. Instead, the focus of the federal courts is on the adequacy of the procedures used to make that determination.

Comparably, our property interest analysis in the instant case extends only to the consideration of whether-were an applicant able to make out the requirements for HEAP eligibility-he or she would be entitled to benefits as a matter of law. If he or she would be so entitled, state law creates a property interest, and an applicant must be afforded procedural protections under the Due Process Clause to demonstrate his

---

[15] While the named plaintiffs were all adjudged eligible in the past, this is not necessarily true of the class as a whole, which was certified to include all households "who have applied or will apply for HEAP benefits . . ." Under the circumstances, it is particularly important that we explain why an applicant for benefits may possess a property interest regardless of whether he or she has received benefits in the past.

or her eligibility. We therefore reject the defendants' argument that plaintiffs' status as benefits applicants renders their interest in HEAP benefits insufficiently definite to constitute a "property" interest for the purposes of federal law.

b) Benefits Contingent on the Availability of Federal Funds

Under New York State law, no HEAP applicant can be certified as eligible for, and entitled to, HEAP benefits, if federal LIHEAA funds have been exhausted. It follows that not all HEAP applicants who are technically "eligible" for state benefits, will be entitled to receive those benefits. The defendants contend that this fact renders plaintiffs' interest in the receipt of benefits too tenuous to constitute a property interest. Specifically, they contend that the fact that no individual applicant can be assured of the receipt of benefits renders the interest a mere "unilateral expectation," rather than "a legitimate [claim of] entitlement." See Roth.

Relatively few courts have addressed the question of whether a social services program's contingency on the availability of funding renders it too indefinite to create a property interest. Those courts that have have generally concluded that—*to the extent that funds are available*—statutes that would create protected property interests apart from funding limits do so regardless of these limits. See, e.g., Alexander v. Polk, 750 F.2d 250, 260–61 (3d Cir. 1984); Weston v. Cassata, 37 P.3d 469, 476–77 (Colo. Ct. App. 2001). But cf. Washington Legal Clinic for the Homeless v. Barry, 107 F.3d 32, 37 (D.C. Cir. 1997) (concluding that a property interest in the receipt of shelter resources did not exist *where D.C. law did not mandate any particular priority system for the distribution of limited shelter resources*).

We agree with these other courts' approach. Under state law, eligible HEAP applicants are entitled to receive benefits, so long as funding for such benefits remains available. To the extent that LIHEAA program funds are available, the fact that the HEAP program is, as a general matter, limited to the extent of federal funding does not matter. Plaintiffs' claim of entitlement-while funds remain available-is the same as it would be were the program not contingent on the availability of sufficient funds.

We therefore conclude that plaintiffs possess a valid property interest in the receipt of regular HEAP benefits.

ii. Process Due

Having determined that plaintiffs possessed a protected property interest, we must determine "what process plaintiffs were due before they could be deprived of that interest." *Sealed*, 332 F.3d at 55. In doing so, we apply the Supreme Court's familiar Mathews v. Eldridge test. Pursuant to this test, we conclude that the process due to applicants for HEAP benefits is notice of the reasons for the agency's preliminary determination, and an opportunity to be heard in response.

Under *Mathews,* three factors guide our decision. . . .

As the district court properly found, "the importance of the private interest at stake in this case is high." *Kapps,* 283 F.Supp.2d at 875. While HEAP grants are small in dollar amounts, they are targeted to those households that "are among the poorest in America." Sen. Rep. No. 103–251, 103rd Cong., 2d Sess. at *9 (1994). By design, the HEAP program affords relief only to those who might otherwise risk a shut-off in heating services. Thus, the erroneous denial of HEAP benefits may well result in a household being left without heat.

The adverse effects of an erroneous cut off of heat services are "self-evident." Memphis Light, Gas & Water Div. v. Craft, 436 U.S. 1, 18 (1978). As noted by the Supreme Court in *Memphis Light,* "[u]tility service is a necessity of modern life . . . . [T]he discontinuance of water or heating for even short periods of time may threaten health and safety." *Id.* The gravity of the health risks posed by a discontinuation of heating services is even greater for many HEAP recipients than for the general public, as the program specifically targets households which include potentially frail individuals. In addition, many other collateral effects may result from the termination of heat, including frozen plumbing, eviction and homelessness. *See* Sen. Rep. No. 103–251, 103rd Cong., 2d Sess. at *10 (1994). Clearly, then, the plaintiffs' interest in not being erroneously denied HEAP benefits is substantial.

In contrast, the government's interest in avoiding the procedures imposed by the district court is less significant. The district court ordered the defendants to modify their HEAP procedures in two respects: 1) by making post-determination fair hearings available to *all* HEAP claimants; and 2) by providing more extensive notice information to benefits claimants. *See Kapps,* 283 F.Supp.2d at 883. . . .

a)   Requirement of a Post-Determination Hearing

[The court upheld the district court's requirement that the defendants issue their determination of HEAP eligibility no more than 45 days after the close of the program year, so that the claimants would have their full time under the statute to request a hearing.]

b)   Notice Relief

In addition to awarding fair hearing relief, the district court found the defendants' HEAP eligibility notices to be constitutionally inadequate. Specifically, the court found that the defendants violated the requirements of due process by their failure to provide budgetary information[27], or other information which was sufficiently detailed as to

---

[27] The district court ordered the provision of information about the agency's HEAP determination "in such detail as is necessary to permit a reasonable person to understand the basis for the agency's action, including: information about the household's annual income, annual energy costs, statewide energy cost standards, energy burden ratio, the presence of vulnerable household members, and income tier, as well as benefit computations in worksheet form." *Kapps,* 283 F.Supp.2d at 882. Like the parties, we refer to the totality of the additional information ordered by the district court as "budgetary information."

allow HEAP applicants to understand the reasons for the defendants' benefits determination. The defendants contend that existing HEAP notices are sufficient, or that, at a minimum, genuine issues of material fact exist as to whether more detailed notices were warranted.

In order to be constitutionally adequate, notice of benefits determinations must provide claimants with enough information to understand the reasons for the agency's action. This requirement, like the right to a fair hearing, is a basic requirement of procedural due process. Claimants cannot know *whether* a challenge to an agency's action is warranted, much less formulate an effective challenge, if they are not provided with sufficient information to understand the basis for the agency's action. Thus, in the absence of effective notice, the other due process rights afforded a benefits claimant—such as the right to a timely hearing—are rendered fundamentally hollow.

While claimants must, therefore, be afforded enough information to understand the basis for the agency's action in all instances, the specific type of notice required will vary depending on the circumstances of each given case. Under *Mathews v. Eldridge,* the cost to the government, the claimant's interest, as well as the availability of alternative means of obtaining information, must all enter into the analysis. As a result, what may be constitutionally required in one context, may not be in another.

In the instant case, the defendants suggest that two factors rendered the district court's award of notice relief improper: 1) the allegedly prohibitive cost of providing the notice mandated by the district court; and 2) the availability to claimants of additional means of seeking out information. For the reasons set forth below, we disagree.

1)   The Cost of Providing the Notice Mandated by the District Court

Much of the defendants' arguments against notice relief focus on the allegedly prohibitive cost of providing additional budgetary information. Specifically, the defendants allege that the cost of manually mating budgetary information to automatically generated notices would be exorbitant, and that the district court's conclusion that budgetary information could easily be included in the automated system (thus obviating the need for such manual pairing) was based on "pure speculation." . . .

Under *Mathews,* the cost to the defendants of providing improved notice is a relevant consideration. And we have, at times, relied on that consideration to place limits on the scope of due process notice relief. . . . Here, there is no evidence in the record from which we can conclude that the burden of affording improved notice would be unreasonable. The City Defendants' primary information technology expert, the Director of New York City's Office of Systems Development, testified in deposition that the HEAP computer system could be modified appropriately in 7–10 months, at the relatively modest cost of $75,000. And, the defendants have not identified any evidence to the contrary that was introduced below. Under the circumstances, the district court properly concluded that the expense of automatically including budgetary information in HEAP notices would not be unduly high. . . .

2)   The Availability to Claimants of Additional Means of Seeking Out Information

As the defendants point out, existing HEAP notices inform claimants that they may seek out additional information about their HEAP eligibility in a number of ways. Thus, for example, existing notices provide claimants with a number to call, and inform claimants of the availability of meetings with benefits specialists. In addition, HEAP notices indicate that plaintiffs can access their case record, and may be able to obtain copies of certain documents in that record. Defendants contend that these alternate means of securing adequate information weigh heavily, under the second *Mathews* factor, in favor of finding the defendants' HEAP notice scheme to be constitutionally adequate.

The existence of alternate state procedures, which protect against a deprivation of due process, is without doubt relevant to, and may even be dispositive of, the Mathews v. Eldridge inquiry. This is particularly so where the plaintiffs' preferred procedures would impose a significant additional cost burden on the state. Where such a cost burden is likely, and the preferred procedure seems unlikely to constitute a material improvement over existing state processes, we are unlikely to find a due process violation.

Here, however, the addition of budgetary information to HEAP notices does not entail the placing of a major financial burden on the defendants. And, the addition of such information will, in all probability, increase significantly the ability of HEAP claimants to determine accurately whether an administrative appeal is warranted. As noted by the Seventh Circuit in a comparable context, it is common sense that a scheme which relies on beneficiaries to seek out basic information on why the agency took the action it did will result in "only the aggressive receiv[ing] their due process right to be advised of the reasons for the proposed action." *See Vargas,* 508 F.2d 485, 490 (1974); "The meek and submissive," in contrast, will "remain in the dark . . . ." *Vargas,* 508 F.2d at 490. Such an outcome seems particularly likely where, as here, many HEAP claimants face obstacles, such as advanced age, or disability, which make the process of seeking further information difficult.

iii.   Conclusion

For all of the foregoing reasons, we hold that the district court appropriately granted the plaintiffs summary judgment on their due process claims . . .

NOTES ON THE DECISION IN KAPPS v. WING

(1) ***Should Applicants for Benefits Get Constitutionally Mandated Process?*** As Judge Calabresi says, the Supreme Court has refused to decide this question, although several Justices have dissented from denials of certiorari in cases presenting the issue. E.g., Gregory v. Pittsfield, 470 U.S. 1018, 1021 (1985) (O'Connor, J., joined by Brennan, J., and Marshall, J.). The Kapps decision presents the issue as being, in effect, an easy one. To the same effect, see Cushman v. Shinseki, 576 F.3d 1290 (Fed. Cir. 2009) ("a veteran alleging a service-connected disability has a due process right to fair adjudication of his claim for benefits"). What might be said on the other side? Here are three possible arguments against holding that applicants are entitled to due process:

(a) The Constitutional requirement of due process by its terms comes into play only when government acts to "deprive"; not giving something to someone is different from depriving them of it.

(b) There is a considerable body of experimental psychology that shows that most people exhibit an "endowment effect" and are averse to loss: losing something they already have hurts more than not gaining something they might have had.

(c) Many more people apply for government benefits than get them. In Kapps the cost of providing process to the extra applicants who prove unworthy comes from the limited money available to help those who really need heat in the winter. In Goldberg, by contrast, the Court was only considering the by-definition smaller class of people who had at one time been judged eligible.

(2) In Roth, Justice Marshall said: "In my view, every citizen who applies for a government job is entitled to it unless the government can establish some reason for denying the employment. This is the 'property' right that I believe is protected by the Fourteenth Amendment." But that was said in dissent and was necessarily rejected by the majority when it held that an untenured teacher who wanted to be rehired had no property right and deserved no hearing. Evidently the applicants-get-a-hearing principle goes only so far. How far?

(3) ***What About Discretion?*** Judge Calabresi spends a lot of energy investigating the precise details of the state and local rules underlying the heat assistance program. His purpose in doing this is to determine whether due process comes into play. It does if "life, liberty or property" are at stake; for this program, only "property" is potentially relevant, and to find "property," in the words of the Roth case, the claimant must have "a legitimate claim of entitlement." The judge says that if he were considering only the federal Low Income Home Energy Assistance Act he would decide that plaintiffs had no case: "the LIHEAA itself cannot be considered to 'channel' official discretion sufficiently 'meaningfully' so as to confer a due process protected property right." But it is different when he considers New York law as well: "Even a cursory examination of that law reveals that it provides precisely the type of discretion-limiting 'substantive predicates' that are the hallmarks of protected property rights." The Roth doctrine, then,

is understood to divide the world of government benefits into those that are discretionary, and consequently not to be tested through due process, and those that are sufficiently cabined that a procedure to test them is warranted. Applying the same approach, the court in Ridgely v. Federal Emergency Management Agency, 512 F.3d 727, 736 (5th Cir. 2008), decided that the distribution of federal housing assistance following hurricane Katrina was not subject to the demands of due process. "[A]lthough [the statute] and the regulations set out eligibility criteria for the receipt of continued rent assistance, they contain no 'explicitly mandatory language' that *entitles* an individual to receive benefits if he satisfies that criteria. Because no 'specific directives' limit FEMA's discretion by compelling it to provide assistance upon a showing of eligibility, these provisions do not give rise to a property interest."

This approach might be defended by saying that, if all that is at stake is a discretionary judgment, the accurate determination of the facts that the second branch of the Mathews' test seems to emphasize loses importance. Against that would be the idea that there is a difference between blind discretion and informed discretion, and requiring some process to inform the use of discretion is thus still warranted. Which view is the better view?

(4) STEPHEN F. WILLIAMS, LIBERTY AND PROPERTY: THE PROBLEM OF GOVERNMENT BENEFITS, 12 J. Legal Stud. 3, 13–14 (1983): "Besides drawing false analogies between [statutory] entitlements and property, entitlement theory has some adverse practical consequences. The first is that the entitlements theory is highly formalistic. By no intelligible criterion of value can it be said to sift out the more valuable from the less valuable interests in conditioned benefits. . . . [S]ince it expressly rejects an evaluation of the weight of the interest, entitlements theory would only by coincidence protect the more weighty ones . . .

"Second, because of its formalistic character, the entitlements analysis imposes perverse incentives upon the legislative and executive branches. So long as the government keeps a 'beneficiary' on tenterhooks by making receipt of loss of a benefit discretionary, it can keep free of the trammels of due process. . . . [T]he rule against unduly broad delegations will in some contexts prevent the use of totally discretionary criteria. Nonetheless, at the margin the entitlements approach sets up incentives against the evolution of clear substantive criteria for government allocation (or termination) of benefits—an odd way of protecting people from government."

NOTES ON AN ALTERNATIVE LINE OF DOCTRINE

(1) *Is Entitlements Analysis the Best Way to Go?* Judge Calabresi cites, and asks us to compare, Washington Legal Clinic for the Homeless v. Barry, 107 F.3d 32 (D.C. Cir.1997), which he describes as "concluding that a property interest in the receipt of shelter resources did not exist *where D.C. law did not mandate any particular priority system for the distribution of limited shelter resources*." That is a correct description of the case, and based on the language Calabresi italicized, the case is consistent with Kapps v. Wing. But does it represent an acceptable principle of law? If the legislative

and executive branches are content to have officials exercise completely discretionary power, is that the end of the matter? This question might be analyzed as a matter of what constitutes an acceptable delegation of authority from Congress to an agency, but the non-delegation doctrine can be satisfied with statutes far more general than the specificity required in Kapps. See Ch. VII, Sec. 2. There is, however, another line of authority that suggests that due process itself has something to say about standardless administrative discretion.

(2)   HOLMES V. NEW YORK CITY HOUSING AUTHORITY, 398 F.2d 262 (2d Cir. 1968): Each year the Authority received approximately 90,000 applications for public housing, out of which it could select only 10,000 families for admission. In federally aided projects, it was required to follow an objective scoring system to choose among applicants. For projects built with state and local money, however, there was no similar requirement. Plaintiffs alleged that they had applied for public housing, that they had never been advised of their eligibility or ineligibility, and that applications filed with the Authority were not processed according to any reasonable, or even ascertainable, system—not even by following a simple chronological waiting list. On interlocutory appeal, the court held that they stated a constitutional cause of action: "One charge made against the defendant, which has merit at least in connection with state-aided projects where the Authority has adopted no standards for selection among non-preference candidates, is that it thereby failed to establish the fair and orderly procedure for allocating its scarce supply of housing which due process requires. It hardly need be said that the existence of an absolute and uncontrolled discretion in an agency of government vested with the administration of a vast program, such as public housing, would be an intolerable invitation to abuse. See Hornsby v. Allen, 326 F.2d 605, 609–610 (5th Cir. 1964). For this reason alone due process requires that selections among applicants be made in accordance with 'ascertainable standards,' id. at 612, and, in cases where many candidates are equally qualified under these standards, that further selections be made in some reasonable manner such as 'by lot or on the basis of the chronological order of application.' Hornsby v. Allen, 330 F.2d 55, 56 (5th Cir. 1964) (on petition for rehearing). Due process is a flexible concept which would certainly also leave room for the employment of a scheme such as the 'objective scoring system' suggested in the resolution adopted by the Authority for federal-aided projects."

HORNSBY V. ALLEN, 326 F.2d 605 (5th Cir. 1964), on which Holmes relied, involved similar issues regarding the procedures used by a liquor licensing board to distribute liquor licenses. Both cases preceded Board of Regents v. Roth.

(3)   Fans of the Holmes-Hornsby approach, when looking for Supreme Court authority, usually cite MORTON V. RUIZ, 415 U.S. 199 (1974), decided after Roth. Ruiz and his family, Papago Indians, moved 15 miles off the Papago reservation so that he could live and work at the Phelps-Dodge copper mines at Ajo, Arizona. They maintained close ties with the reservation and, said the Court, "have not been assimilated into the dominant culture." Twenty-seven years after the Ruizes moved, the miners went on strike, the state of

Arizona refused general assistance to striking workers, and Ruiz applied for general assistance from the Bureau of Indian Affairs. The sole ground given for denying his application was that, although he lived *near* the reservation, the relevant portion of the BIA's internal Field Manual limited general assistance benefits to "Indians living *on* reservations." The statutory basis for the assistance program was phrased in very general language, and the annual appropriations acts were similarly vague. On appeal, the government argued that BIA's formal budget requests had always stated that "[g]eneral assistance will be provided to needy Indians on reservations." However, as confirmed by page after page of the agency's testimony before Congress, the BIA had always represented that "on" included "near."

In one sense, this was the end of the case. The BIA's central defense was that Congress had appropriated funds only for those living on reservations. This defense had failed. There was little doubt that if anyone "near" reservations would qualify, the Ruizes would. Instead of stopping there, however, JUSTICE BLACKMUN's opinion for a unanimous Court went on to consider whether the agency's Field Manual might have some binding legal effect:

"Having found that the congressional appropriation was intended to cover welfare services at least to those Indians residing 'on or near' the reservation, it does not necessarily follow that the Secretary is without power to create reasonable classifications and eligibility requirements in order to allocate the limited funds available to him for this purpose. Thus, if there were only enough funds appropriated to provide meaningfully for 10,000 needy Indian beneficiaries and the entire class of eligible beneficiaries numbered 20,000, it would be incumbent upon the BIA to develop an eligibility standard to deal with this problem, and the standard, if rational and proper, might leave some of the class otherwise encompassed by the appropriation without benefits. But in such a case the agency must, at a minimum, let the standard be generally known so as to assure that it is being applied consistently and so as to avoid both the reality and the appearance of arbitrary denial of benefits to potential beneficiaries.

"Assuming, arguendo, that the Secretary rationally could limit the 'on or near' appropriation to include only the smaller class of Indians who lived directly 'on' the reservation . . ., the question that remains is whether this has been validly accomplished. The power of an administrative agency to administer a congressionally created and funded program necessarily requires the formulation of policy and the making of rules to fill any gap left, implicitly or explicitly, by Congress. In the area of Indian affairs, the Executive has long been empowered to promulgate rules and policies, and the power has been given explicitly to the Secretary and his delegates at the BIA. This agency power to make rules that affect substantial individual rights and obligations carries with it the responsibility not only to remain consistent with the governing legislation, but also to employ procedures that conform to the law. No matter how rational or consistent with congressional intent a particular decision might be, the determination of eligibility cannot be made on an ad hoc basis by the dispenser of the funds."

Commentators have been perplexed ever since about exactly what this condemnation of "ad hoc" agency behavior entails. Justice Blackmun did not state the legal basis for his approach. Does the BIA have to develop a legal framework for distributing funds because this is what Congress intended? Because this is a requirement of some federal common law of administrative procedure? Because this forestalls a conclusion under the APA that the agency has acted arbitrarily and capriciously? Or because due process so requires?

Occasional lower court cases have followed Ruiz in requiring agencies to develop self-disciplining standards where the stakes for individuals are high—and also in being less than clear on the legal basis of this requirement. The Eighth Circuit in two cases compelled the Secretary of Agriculture to promulgate standards implementing discretionary farm aid programs. See Iowa ex rel. Miller v. Block, 771 F.2d 347 (8th Cir. 1985) (suit to compel implementing regulations for statute that provided that the Secretary "may make disaster payments" whenever he determines that farms within the federal crop insurance program have suffered "substantial uncompensated disaster losses"); Allison v. Block, 723 F.2d 631 (8th Cir. 1983) (suit to compel implementing policies and procedures for exercising statutory discretion to defer foreclosure of farmers in default on federal loans). More recently, the Tenth Circuit, in Hobbs ex rel. Hobbs v. Zenderman, 579 F.3d 1171, 1185–86 (10th Cir. 2009), said that cases like Ruiz "establish, at most, a due process right to be free from eligibility determinations made without reference to any publicly-available standard." On the facts at hand, however, "we need not delineate the precise boundary of the right Hobbs alleges because the standards applied by defendants here are a far cry from no standards at all."

(4) LIGHTFOOT V. DISTRICT OF COLUMBIA, 448 F.3d 392 (D.C. Cir. 2006)— the case Judge Calabresi referred to in Kapps v. Wing—squarely presented the question whether due process requires the creation of discretion-constraining standards—until the issue was mooted out by the government's adopting such standards.

The plaintiffs were a class of D.C. employees whose disability benefits had been terminated, suspended, or reduced pursuant to the statutory power of the Mayor, or his designee, to modify the benefit award if he "has reason to believe that a change of condition has occurred." The district court granted summary judgment on the plaintiff's claim that the District had "failed to adopt written and consistently applied standards, policies and procedures governing the termination, suspension and modification of benefits in violation of the Due Process Clause." It "remanded" the case to the District for rulemaking and ordered the plaintiffs' benefits reinstated until modification or termination decisions could be made under validly promulgated rules. Before the case could be considered by the D.C. Circuit on appeal, a combination of statutory amendments and emergency rules, accomplished by actions of the D.C. Council and the District's Office of Risk Management, had fulfilled the substance of the remand order. Additional claims were still pending, however, and the Court of Appeals took the opportunity to express skepticism about the lower court's analysis (448 F.3d at 398):

"It may well be the case that an agency that terminates such statutorily-entitled benefits without any reason violates due process, because that would deprive a beneficiary of the capacity to challenge the termination. More controversial . . . is the claim that the Due Process Clause may impose a requirement of substantive standards—independent of statutory standards—that may be used to restrict an administrative agency's decision to terminate or modify a protected liberty or property interest. Assuming arguendo that such a cause of action can be made out, we think it is wholly without merit here because the [disability benefit statute] and D.C. court of appeals decisions themselves provide ample standards that would satisfy any such due process claim. There is certainly no conceivable due process claim that could be predicated on the notion that an agency must proceed to establish such standards through rulemaking rather than case-by-case determinations."

JUDGE SILBERMAN, concurring, was less restrained (448 F.3d at 400–01):

"The district court thought to import the APA scope of review into this § 1983 due process suit by relying on two rather old circuit court cases: White v. Roughton, 530 F.2d 750 (7th Cir. 1976), and Holmes v. New York City Housing Authority, 398 F.2d 262 (2d Cir. 1968). See also Peter L. Strauss et al., Gellhorn and Byse's Administrative Law 833 (10th ed. 2003). . . . [T]hese cases did not apply the Mathews v. Eldridge framework because Holmes preceded Mathews by almost eight years and White issued only three days after Mathews.

"It is quite understandable that appellees and the district court would see Holmes and White as somehow outside the Mathews v. Eldridge framework because the truth is that neither case is a proper interpretation of the Due Process Clause. Their focus . . . is not on process but on substance. Yet the Supreme Court's due process jurisprudence carefully distinguishes process from substance. The issue is always, in its due process cases, whether or not the claimant has had a fair opportunity—sometimes rather informal—to present his case and not whether the agency's substantive decision was reasonable. To be sure, as we today recognize, if an agency refused to give any reason for an initial deprivation, it would be impossible for the claimant to present an argument that the agency's decision was incorrect. So procedure is implicated. But that assuredly does not mean that the Due Process Clause can be used as a looming super-arbitrary-and-capricious standard governing the substantive decisions of an administrative agency no matter how much discretion the agency enjoys. The quality of an agency's reasoning is decidedly not a process issue.

"Granted, some Supreme Court justices in dissenting opinions have sought to expand due process analysis to include challenges to government substantive decisions. See, e.g., Bd. of Regents v. Roth (Marshall, J., dissenting). But the Court has never accepted that effort to transform the

Due Process Clause. In short, Holmes and White are not only irrelevant to this case, they were also wrongly decided and simply do not survive . . .”

Compare the view of leading scholar Jerry L. Mashaw, Dignitary Process: A Political Psychology of Liberal Democratic Citizenship, 39 U. Fla. L. Rev. 433, 437 (1987): while cases like Holmes are “virtually moribund authorities,” they were in fact “correctly decided.”

LATIF v. HOLDER

United States District Court, D. Oregon (2014).
28 F.Supp.3d 1134.

■ BROWN, DISTRICT JUDGE.

This matter comes before the Court on Defendants’ Motion for Partial Summary Judgment and Plaintiffs’ Cross-Motion for Partial Summary Judgment. . . . For the reasons that follow, the Court grants Plaintiffs’ Cross-Motion and denies Defendants’ Motion.

PLAINTIFFS’ CLAIMS

Plaintiffs are citizens and lawful permanent residents of the United States (including four veterans of the United States Armed Forces) who were not allowed to board flights to or from the United States or over United States airspace. Plaintiffs believe they were denied boarding because they are on the No-Fly List, a government terrorist watch list of individuals who are prohibited from boarding commercial flights that will pass through or over United States airspace. Federal and/or local government officials told some Plaintiffs that they are on the No-Fly List.

Each Plaintiff submitted applications for redress through the Department of Homeland Security Traveler Redress Inquiry Program (DHS TRIP). Despite Plaintiffs’ requests to officials and agencies for explanations as to why they were not permitted to board flights, explanations have not been provided and Plaintiffs do not know whether they will be permitted to fly in the future.

Plaintiffs allege in their Third Amended Complaint, Claim One, that Defendants have violated Plaintiffs’ Fifth Amendment right to procedural due process because Defendants have not given Plaintiffs any post-deprivation notice nor any meaningful opportunity to contest their continued inclusion on the No-Fly List. . . .

FACTUAL BACKGROUND

The following facts are undisputed unless otherwise noted:

I.   The No-Fly List

The Federal Bureau of Investigation (FBI), which administers the Terrorist Screening Center (TSC), develops and maintains the federal government’s consolidated Terrorist Screening Database (TSDB or sometimes referred to as “the watch list”). The No-Fly List is a subset of the TSDB.

TSC provides the No-Fly List to TSA [Transportation Security Administration], a component of the Department of Homeland Security (DHS), for use in pre-screening airline passengers. TSC receives nominations for inclusion in the TSDB and generally accepts those nominations on a showing of "reasonable suspicion" that the individuals are known or suspected terrorists based on the totality of the information. TSC defines its reasonable-suspicion standard as requiring "articulable facts which, taken together with rational inferences, reasonably warrant the determination that an individual 'is known or suspected to be, or has been engaged in conduct constituting, in preparation for, in aid of or related to, terrorism or terrorist activities.' " Joint Statement of Stipulated Facts (# 84) at 4.

The government also has its own "Watchlisting Guidance" for internal law-enforcement and intelligence use, and the No-Fly List has its own minimum substantive derogatory criteria. The government does not release these documents.

II. DHS TRIP Redress Process

DHS TRIP is the mechanism available for individuals to seek redress for any travel-related screening issues experienced at airports or while crossing United States borders; *i.e.,* denial of or delayed airline boarding, denial of or delayed entry into or exit from the United States, or continuous referral for additional (secondary) screening.

A.   Administrative Review

Travelers who have faced such difficulties may submit a Traveler Inquiry Form to DHS TRIP online, by email, or by regular mail. The form prompts travelers to describe their complaint, to produce documentation relating to the issue, and to provide identification and their contact information. If the traveler is an exact or near match to an identity within the TSDB, DHS TRIP deems the complaint to be TSDB-related and forwards the traveler's complaint to TSC Redress for further review.

On receipt of the complaint, TSC Redress reviews the available information, including the information and documentation provided by the traveler, and determines (1) whether the traveler is an exact match to an identity in the TSDB and (2) whether the traveler should continue to be in the TSDB if the traveler is an exact match. When making this determination, TSC coordinates with the agency that originally nominated the individual to be included in the TSDB. If the traveler has been misidentified as someone who is an exact match to an identity in the TSDB, TSC Redress informs DHS of the misidentification. DHS, in conjunction with any other relevant agency, then addresses the misidentification by correcting information in the traveler's records or taking other appropriate action.

When DHS and/or TSC finish their review, DHS TRIP sends a determination letter advising the traveler that DHS TRIP has completed its review. A DHS TRIP determination letter neither confirms nor denies that the complainant is in the TSDB or on the No-Fly List and does not provide any further details about why the complainant may or may not be in the TSDB or on the No-Fly List. In some cases a DHS TRIP determination letter advises the recipient that he or she can pursue an administrative appeal of the determination letter with TSA or can seek judicial review in a United States court of appeals pursuant to 49 U.S.C. § 46110.

Determination letters, however, do not provide assurances about the complainant's ability to undertake future travel. In fact, DHS does not tell a complainant whether he or she is in the TSDB or a subset of the TSDB or give any explanation for inclusion on such a list at any point in the available administrative process. Thus, the complainant does not have an opportunity to contest or knowingly to offer corrections to the record on which any such determination may be based.

B.   Judicial Review

When a final determination letter indicates the complainant may seek judicial review of the decisions represented in the letter, it does not advise whether the complainant is on the No-Fly List or provide the legal or factual basis for such inclusion. If the complainant submits a petition for review to the appropriate court, the government furnishes the court (but not the petitioner) with the administrative record.

If the administrative DHS TRIP review of a petitioner's redress file resulted in a final determination that the petitioner is not on the No-Fly List, the administrative record will inform the court of that fact. If, on the other hand, the administrative DHS TRIP review of a petitioner's redress file resulted in a final determination that the petitioner is and should remain on the No-Fly List, the administrative record will include the information that the government relied on to maintain that listing. The government may have obtained this information from human sources, foreign governments, and/or "signals intelligence." The government may provide to the court *ex parte* and *in camera* information that is part of the administrative record and that the government has determined is classified, Sensitive Security Information, law-enforcement investigative information, and/or information otherwise privileged or protected from disclosure by statute or regulation.

The administrative record also includes any information that the petitioner submitted to the government as part of his or her DHS TRIP request, and the petitioner has access to that portion of the record. As noted, at no point during the judicial-review process does the government provide the petitioner with confirmation as to whether the petitioner is on the No-Fly List, set out the reasons for including petitioner's name on the List, or identify any information or evidence relied on to maintain the petitioner's name on the List.

For a petitioner who is on the No-Fly List, the court will review the administrative record submitted by the government in order to determine whether the government reasonably determined the petitioner satisfied the minimum substantive derogatory criteria for inclusion on the List. If after review the court determines the administrative record supports the petitioner's inclusion on the No-Fly List, it will deny the petition for review. If the court determines the administrative record contains insufficient evidence to satisfy the substantive derogatory criteria, however, the government takes the position that the court may remand the matter to the government for appropriate action.

III. Plaintiffs' Pertinent History

Solely for purposes of the parties' Motions presently before the Court, Defendants do not contest the following facts as asserted by Plaintiffs:[5]

Plaintiffs are thirteen United States citizens who were denied boarding on flights over United States airspace after January 1, 2009, and who believe they are on the United States government's No-Fly List. Airline representatives, FBI agents, or other government officials told some Plaintiffs that they are on the No-Fly List.

Each Plaintiff filed DHS TRIP complaints after being denied boarding and each received a determination letter that does not confirm or deny any Plaintiff's name is on any terrorist watch list nor provide a reason for any Plaintiff to be included in the TSDB or on the No-Fly List.

Many of these Plaintiffs cannot travel overseas by any mode other than air because such journeys by boat or by land would be cost-prohibitive, would be time-consuming to a degree that Plaintiffs could not take the necessary time off from work, or would put Plaintiffs at risk of interrogation and detention by foreign authorities. In addition, some Plaintiffs are not physically well enough to endure such infeasible modes of travel.

While Plaintiffs' circumstances are similar in many ways, each of their experiences and difficulties relating to and arising from their alleged inclusion on the No-Fly List is unique as set forth in their Declarations filed in support of their Motion and summarized briefly below.

Ayman Latif: Latif is a United States Marine Corps veteran and lives in Stone Mountain, Georgia, with his wife and children. Between November 2008 and April 2010 Latif and his family were living in Egypt. When Latif and his family attempted to return to the United States in April 2010, Latif was not allowed to board the first leg of their flight from Cairo to Madrid. One month later Latif was questioned by FBI agents

---

[5]   As a matter of policy, the United States government does not confirm or deny whether an individual is on the No-Fly List nor does it provide any other details as to that issue. Accordingly, Defendants have chosen not to refute Plaintiffs' allegations that they are on the No-Fly List for purposes of these Motions only. The Court, therefore, assumes for purposes of these Motions only that Plaintiffs' assertions regarding their inclusion on the No-Fly List are true.

and told he was on the No-Fly List. Because he was unable to board a flight to the United States, Latif's United States veteran disability benefits were reduced from $899.00 per month to zero as the result of being unable to attend the scheduled evaluations required to keep his benefits. In August 2010 Latif returned home after the United States government granted him a "one-time waiver" to fly to the United States. Because the waiver was for "one time," Latif cannot fly again, and therefore, he is unable to travel from the United States to Egypt to resume studies or to Saudi Arabia to perform a *hajj,* a religious pilgrimage and Islamic obligation.

Mohamed Sheikh Abdirahm Kariye: Kariye lives in Portland, Oregon, with his wife and children. In March 2010 Kariye was not allowed to board a flight from Portland to Amsterdam, was surrounded in public by government officials at the airport, and was told by an airline employee that he was on a government watch list. Because Kariye is prohibited from boarding flights out of the United States, he could not fly to visit his daughter who was studying in Dubai and cannot travel to Saudi Arabia to accompany his mother on the *hajj* pilgrimage.

Raymond Earl Knaeble IV: Knaeble is a United States Army veteran and lives in Chicago, Illinois. In 2006 Knaeble was working in Kuwait. In March 2010 Knaeble flew from Kuwait to Bogota, Colombia, to marry his wife, a Colombian citizen, and to spend time with her family. On March 14, 2010, Knaeble was not allowed to board his flight from Bogota to Miami. Knaeble was subsequently questioned numerous times by FBI agents in Colombia. Because Knaeble was unable to fly home for a required medical examination, his employer rescinded its job offer for a position in Qatar. Knaeble attempted to return to the United States through Mexico where he was detained for over 15 hours, questioned, and forced to return to Bogota. Knaeble eventually returned to the United States in August 2010 by traveling for 12 days from Santa Marta, Colombia, to Panama City and then to Mexicali, California. United States and foreign authorities detained, interrogated, and searched Knaeble on numerous occasions during that journey.

[The court gives similar descriptions for ten other plaintiffs.]

. . .

DISCUSSION

As noted, Plaintiffs allege Defendants have violated Plaintiffs' Fifth Amendment rights to procedural due process because Defendants have not provided Plaintiffs with any post-deprivation notice nor any meaningful opportunity to contest their continued inclusion on the No-Fly List. . . .

The court must weigh three factors when evaluating the sufficiency of procedural protections. . . .

A.   First Factor: Private Interest

Plaintiffs contend the first factor under Mathews weighs in their favor because Defendants' inclusion of Plaintiffs on the No-Fly List has deprived Plaintiffs of their constitutionally-protected liberty interests in travel and reputation.

1.   Right to Travel

"The right to travel is a part of the 'liberty' of which the citizen cannot be deprived without due process of law under the Fifth Amendment." Kent v. Dulles, 357 U.S. 116, 125 (1958). . . . Defendants argue there is not a constitutional right to travel by airplane or by the most convenient form of travel. Defendants, therefore, contend Plaintiffs' rights to travel are not constitutionally burdened because the No-Fly List only prohibits travel by commercial aviation. . . . Although there are viable alternatives to flying for domestic travel within the continental United States such as traveling by car or train, the Court disagrees with Defendants' contention that international air travel is a mere convenience in light of the realities of our modern world. Such an argument ignores the numerous reasons that an individual may have for wanting or needing to travel overseas quickly such as the birth of a child, the death of a loved one, a business opportunity, or a religious obligation. . . .

As Plaintiffs' difficulties with international travel demonstrate, placement on the No-Fly List is a significant impediment to international travel. It is undisputed that inclusion on the No-Fly List completely bans listed persons from boarding commercial flights to or from the United States or over United States airspace. In addition, the realistic implications of being on the No-Fly List are far-reaching. For example, TSC shares watch-list information with 22 foreign governments, and United States Customs and Border Protection makes recommendations to ship captains as to whether a passenger poses a risk to transportation security. Thus, having one's name on the watch list can also result in interference with an individual's ability to travel by means other than commercial airlines as evidenced by some Plaintiffs' experiences as they attempted to travel internationally or return to the United States by sea and by land. In addition, the ban on air travel has exposed some Plaintiffs to extensive detention and interrogation at the hands of foreign authorities. With perhaps the exception of travel to a small number of countries in North and Central America, a prohibition on flying turns routine international travel into an odyssey that imposes significant logistical, economic, and physical demands on travelers. . . .

Accordingly, the Court concludes on this record that Plaintiffs have constitutionally-protected liberty interests in traveling internationally by air, which are significantly affected by being placed on the No-Fly List.

The first step of the Mathews inquiry, however, does not end with mere recognition of a liberty interest. The Court must also weigh the liberty interest deprived against the other factors.

As noted, placement on the No-Fly List renders most international travel very difficult or impossible. One need not look beyond the hardships suffered by Plaintiffs to understand the significance of the deprivation of the right to travel internationally. Due to the major burden imposed by inclusion on the No-Fly List, Plaintiffs have suffered significantly including long-term separation from spouses and children; the inability to access desired medical and prenatal care; the inability to pursue an education of their choosing; the inability to participate in important religious rites; loss of employment opportunities; loss of government entitlements; the inability to visit family; and the inability to attend important personal and family events such as graduations, weddings, and funerals. The Court concludes international travel is not a mere convenience or luxury in this modern world. Indeed, for many international travel is a necessary aspect of liberties sacred to members of a free society.

Accordingly, on this record the Court concludes Plaintiffs' inclusion on the No-Fly List constitutes a significant deprivation of their liberty interests in international travel.

2.   Stigma-Plus-Reputation

Plaintiffs also assert the first factor under Mathews has been satisfied because Plaintiffs have been stigmatized "in conjunction with their right to travel on the same terms as other travelers." First Am. Compl. ¶ 141.

Under the "stigma-plus" doctrine, the Supreme Court has recognized a constitutionally-protected interest in "a person's good name, reputation, honor, or integrity." Wisconsin v. Constantineau, 400 U.S. 433, 437 (1971). "To prevail on a claim under the stigma-plus doctrine, Plaintiffs must show (1) public disclosure of a stigmatizing statement by the government, the accuracy of which is contested; *plus* (2) the denial of some more tangible interest such as employment, or the alteration of a right or status recognized by state law." Green v. Transp. Sec. Admin., 351 F.Supp.2d 1119, 1129 (W.D.Wash.2005) (emphasis added). Plaintiffs contend, and Defendants do not dispute, that placement on the No-Fly List satisfies the "stigma" prong because it carries with it the stigma of being a suspected terrorist that is publicly disclosed to airline employees and other travelers near the ticket counter. . . .

As noted, the Court has concluded Plaintiffs have constitutionally-protected liberty interests in the right to travel internationally by air. In addition, the Court concludes Plaintiffs have satisfied the "plus" prong because being on the No-Fly List means Plaintiffs are legally barred from traveling by air at least to and from the United States and over United States airspace, which they would be able to do but for their inclusion on the No-Fly List. . . . Plaintiffs have constitutionally-protected liberty interests in their reputations.

On the other hand, Plaintiffs' private interests at the heart of their stigma-plus claim are not as strong. Although placement on the No-Fly List carries with it the significant stigma of being a suspected terrorist and Defendants do not contest the fact that the public disclosure involved may be sufficient to satisfy the stigma-plus test, the Court notes the limited nature of the public disclosure in this case mitigates Plaintiffs' claims of injury to their reputations. Because the No-Fly List is not released publicly, the "public" disclosure is limited to a relatively small group of individuals in the same area of the airport as the traveler when the traveler is denied boarding. Notwithstanding the fact that being denied boarding an airplane and, in some instances, being arrested or surrounded by security officials in an airport is doubtlessly stigmatizing, the Court notes the breadth and specificity of the public disclosure in this case is more limited than in the ordinary "stigma-plus" case. . . . Nevertheless, the Court concludes the injury to Plaintiffs' reputations is sufficient to implicate Plaintiffs' constitutionally-protected interests in their reputations.

On this record the Court concludes Plaintiffs' claims raise constitutionally-protected liberty interests both in international air travel and in reputation, and, therefore, the first factor under the *Mathews* test weighs heavily in Plaintiffs' favor.

B.   Second Factor: Risk of Erroneous Deprivation

. . .

1.   Risk of Erroneous Deprivation

When considering the risk of erroneous deprivation, the Court considers both the substantive standard that the government uses to make its decision as well as the procedural processes in place. As noted, nominations to the TSDB are generally accepted based on a "reasonable suspicion" that requires "articulable facts which, taken together with rational inferences, reasonably warrant the determination that an individual" meets the substantive derogatory criteria. Joint Statement of Stipulated Facts (# 84) ¶ 16. This "reasonable suspicion" standard is the same as the traditional reasonable suspicion standard commonly applied by the courts. See Terry v. Ohio, 392 U.S. 1, 21 (1968) (permitting investigatory stops based on a reasonable suspicion supported by "articulable facts which, taken together with rational inferences from those facts, reasonably warrant the intrusion."). Although reasonable suspicion requires more than "a mere 'hunch,'" the evidence available "need not rise to the level required for probable cause, and . . . falls considerably short of satisfying a preponderance of the evidence standard." United States v. Arvizu, 534 U.S. 266, 274 (2002).

It is against the backdrop of this substantive standard that the Court considers the risk of erroneous deprivation of the protected interests; *i.e.,* the risk that travelers will be placed on the No-Fly List under Defendants' procedures despite not having a connection to terrorism or terrorist activities.

Defendants argue there is little risk of erroneous deprivation because the TSC has implemented extensive quality controls to ensure that the TSDB includes only individuals who are properly placed there. Defendants point out that the TSDB is updated daily and audited for accuracy and currentness on a regular basis and that each entry into the TSDB receives individualized review if the individual files a DHS TRIP inquiry. Finally, Defendants argue judicial review of the DHS TRIP determination further diminishes the risk of erroneous deprivation.

Plaintiffs, in turn, cite a 2007 report by the United States Government Accountability Office and a 2009 report by the Department of Justice Office of the Inspector General that concludes the TSDB contains many errors and that the TSC has failed to take adequate steps to remove or to modify records in a timely manner even when necessary. In addition, Plaintiffs maintain the lack of notice of inclusion on the No-Fly List or the reasons therefor forces aggrieved travelers to guess about the evidence that they should submit in their defense and, by definition, creates a one-sided and insufficient record at both the administrative and judicial level that does not provide a genuine opportunity to present exculpatory evidence for the correction of errors.

Defendants point out that the information on which Plaintiffs rely to support their contention that the TSC has failed to modify adequately or to remove records when necessary is outdated and that the 2009 report indicated significant progress in maintenance of the TSDB. Although Defendants are correct that the TSC appears to have made improvements in ensuring the TSDB is current and accurate, Plaintiffs' contention that the TSDB carries with it a risk of error, nevertheless, carries significant weight. . . .

In any event, the DHS TRIP process suffers from an even more fundamental deficiency. As noted, the reasonable suspicion standard used to accept nominations to the TSDB is a low evidentiary threshold. This low standard is particularly significant in light of Defendants' refusal to reveal whether travelers who have been denied boarding and who submit DHS TRIP inquiries are on the No-Fly List and, if they are on the List, to provide the travelers with reasons for their inclusion on the List. "Without knowledge of a charge, even simple factual errors may go uncorrected despite potentially easy, ready, and persuasive explanations." Al Haramain Islamic Found., Inc. v. United States Dep't of Treasury, 686 F.3d 965, 982 (9th Cir.2012).

The availability of judicial review does little to cure this risk of error. While judicial review provides an independent examination of the existing administrative record, that review is of the same one-sided and potentially insufficient administrative record that TSC relied on in its listing decision without any additional meaningful opportunity for the aggrieved traveler to submit evidence intelligently in order to correct anticipated errors in the record. Moreover, judicial review only extends to whether the government reasonably determined the traveler meets the minimum substantive derogatory criteria; *i.e.,* the reasonable suspicion standard. Thus, the fundamental flaw at the administrative-review stage (the combination of a one-sided record and a low evidentiary standard) carries over to the judicial-review stage.

Accordingly, on this record the Court concludes the DHS TRIP redress process, including the judicial review of DHS TRIP determinations, contains a high risk of erroneous deprivation of Plaintiffs' constitutionally-protected interests.

2.   Utility of Substitute Procedural Safeguards

In its analysis of the second Mathews factor, the Court also considers the probative value of additional procedural safeguards. Plaintiffs contend due process requires Defendants to provide post-deprivation notice of their placement on the No-Fly List; notice of the reasons they have been placed on the List; and a post-deprivation, in-person hearing to permit Plaintiffs to present exculpatory evidence. Notably, Plaintiffs argue these additional safeguards are only necessary after a traveler has been denied boarding. Defendants, in turn, assert the current procedures are sufficient in light of the compelling government interests in national security and protection of classified information.

Clearly, additional procedural safeguards would provide significant probative value. In particular, notice of inclusion on the No-Fly List through the DHS TRIP process after a traveler has been denied boarding would permit the complainant to make an intelligent decision about whether to pursue an administrative or judicial appeal. In addition, notice of the reasons for inclusion on the No-Fly List as well as an opportunity to present exculpatory evidence would help ensure the accuracy and completeness of the record to be considered at both the administrative and judicial stages and, at the very least, would provide aggrieved travelers the opportunity to correct "simple factual errors" with "potentially easy, ready, and persuasive explanations." See Al Haramain Islamic Found., 686 F.3d at 982. Thus, the Court concludes additional procedural safeguards would have significant probative value.

In summary, on this record the Court concludes the DHS TRIP process presently carries with it a high risk of erroneous deprivation in light of the low evidentiary standard required for placement on the No-Fly List together with the lack of a meaningful opportunity for individuals on the No-Fly List to provide exculpatory evidence in an effort to be taken off of the List. Moreover, the Court finds additional procedural safeguards would have significant probative value in ensuring that individuals are not erroneously deprived of their constitutionally-protected liberty interests. Accordingly, the Court concludes the second Mathews factor weighs heavily in favor of Plaintiffs.

C.   The Government's Interest

When considering the third Mathews factor, the Court weighs "the Government's interest, including the function involved and the fiscal and administrative burdens that the additional or substitute procedural requirement would entail." Mathews, 424 U.S. at 335.

"[T]he Government's interest in combating terrorism is an urgent objective of the highest order." Holder v. Humanitarian Law Project, 561 U.S. 1, 28 (2010). "It is 'obvious and unarguable' that no governmental interest is more compelling than the security of the Nation." Haig v. Agee, 453 U.S. 280, 307 (1981).

"[T]he Constitution certainly does not require that the government take actions that would endanger national security." Al Haramain, 686 F.3d at 980.... Obviously, the Court cannot and will not order Defendants to disclose classified information to Plaintiffs.

On this record the Court concludes the governmental interests in combating terrorism and protecting classified information are particularly compelling, and, viewed in isolation, the third Mathews factor weighs heavily in Defendants' favor.

D.   Balancing the Mathews Factors

" '[D]ue process, unlike some legal rules, is not a technical conception with a fixed content unrelated to time, place and circumstances.' " Gilbert v. Homar, 520 U.S. 924, 930 (1997). ... " 'The fundamental requisite of due process of law is the opportunity to be heard.' " Mullane v. Cent. Hanover Bank & Trust Co., 339 U.S. 306, 314 (1950). "This right to be heard has little reality or worth unless one is informed that the matter is pending and can choose for himself whether to appear or default, acquiesce or contest." Mullane, 339 U.S. at 314. "An elementary and fundamental requirement of due process in any proceeding which is to be accorded finality is notice reasonably calculated, under all the circumstances, to apprise interested parties of the pendency of the action and afford them an opportunity to present objections." Circu v. Gonzales, 450 F.3d 990, 993 (9th Cir.2006).

1.   Applicable Caselaw

Although balancing the Mathews factors is especially difficult in this case involving compelling interests on both sides, the Court, fortunately, does not have to paint on an empty canvass when balancing such interests. Indeed, several other courts have done so in circumstances that also required balancing a plaintiff's due-process right to contest the deprivation of important private interests with the government's interest in protecting national security and classified information. See, e.g., Al Haramain Islamic Foundation, Inc. v. U.S. Dep't of Treasury, 686 F.3d 965 (9 Cir. 2012); Jifry v. Fed. Aviation Admin., 370 F.3d 1174 (D.C.Cir.2004); NCORI v. Dep't of State, 251 F.3d 192 (D.C.Cir.2001); Ibrahim v. Dep't of Homeland Security, 2014 WL 1493561 (N.D.Cal.

2014); KindHearts for Charitable and Humanitarian Dev., Inc. v. Geithner, 647 F.Supp.2d 857 (N.D.Ohio 2009).

[The court proceeded to analyze each of the cited cases individually, reaching the following overall conclusions:]

2.   Application to the DHS TRIP Process

. . .

A comparison of the procedural protections provided in this case with those provided in Al Haramain, Jifry, KindHearts, and NCORI reveals the DHS TRIP process falls far short of satisfying the requirements of due process. In Al Haramain, Jifry, and KindHearts the defendants provided the plaintiffs with some materials relevant to the respective agencies' reasons for the deprivation at some point in the proceedings. . . .

Unlike the plaintiffs in Al Haramain, KindHearts, and Jifry, however, Plaintiffs in this case were not given any notice of the reasons for their placement on the No-Fly List nor any evidence to support their inclusion on the No-Fly List. . . .

Defendants' failure to provide any notice of the reasons for Plaintiffs' placement on the No-Fly List is especially important in light of the low evidentiary standard required to place an individual in the TSDB in the first place. When only an *ex parte* showing of reasonable suspicion supported by "articulable facts . . . taken together with rational inferences" is necessary to place an individual in the TSDB, it is certainly possible, and probably likely, that "simple factual errors" with "potentially easy, ready, and persuasive explanations" could go uncorrected. See Al Haramain, 686 F.3d at 982. Thus, without proper notice and an opportunity to be heard, an individual could be doomed to indefinite placement on the No-Fly List. Moreover, there is nothing in the DHS TRIP administrative or judicial-review procedures that remedies this fundamental deficiency. The procedures afforded to Plaintiffs through the DHS TRIP process are wholly ineffective and, therefore, fall short of the "elementary and fundamental requirement of due process" to be afforded "notice reasonably calculated, under all the circumstances, to apprise interested parties of the pendency of the action and afford them an opportunity to present objections." See Mullane, 339 U.S. at 314.

Accordingly, on this record the Court concludes the absence of any meaningful procedures to afford Plaintiffs the opportunity to contest their placement on the No-Fly List violates Plaintiffs' rights to procedural due process.

3.   Due-Process Requirements

Although the Court holds Defendants must provide a new process that satisfies the constitutional requirements for due process, the Court concludes Defendants (and not the Court) must fashion new procedures that provide Plaintiffs with the requisite due process described herein without jeopardizing national security.

Because due process requires Defendants to provide Plaintiffs (who have all been denied boarding flights and who have submitted DHS TRIP inquiries without success) with notice regarding their status on the No-Fly List and the reasons for placement on that List, it follows that such notice must be reasonably calculated to permit each Plaintiff to submit evidence relevant to the reasons for their respective inclusions on the No-Fly List. In addition, Defendants must include any responsive evidence that Plaintiffs submit in the record to be considered at both the administrative and judicial stages of review. As noted, such procedures could include, but are not limited to, the procedures identified by the Ninth Circuit in *Al Haramain;* that is, Defendants may choose to provide Plaintiffs with unclassified summaries of the reasons for their respective placement on the No-Fly List or disclose the classified reasons to properly-cleared counsel.

Although this Court cannot foreclose the possibility that in some cases such disclosures may be limited or withheld altogether because any such disclosure would create an undue risk to national security, Defendants must make such a determination on a case-by-case basis . . .

CONCLUSION

For these reasons, the Court denies Defendants' Motion for Partial Summary Judgment and grants Plaintiffs' Cross-Motion for Partial Summary Judgment . . .

The Court directs the parties to confer as to the next steps in this litigation and to file no later than July 14, 2014, a Joint Status Report with their respective proposals and schedules. The Court will schedule a Status Conference thereafter at which primary counsel for the parties should plan to attend in person.

NOTES ON THE NO-FLY LIST ISSUE

(1) **The Statutory and Regulatory Context.** The plaintiffs do not claim that they should have gotten notice when they were put on the no-fly list; their complaint, says Judge Brown, is that they were neither given "any post-deprivation notice nor any meaningful opportunity to contest their continued inclusion on the No-Fly List." As part of the statute setting up the no-fly list system, Congress directed the Assistant Secretary for Homeland Security to "establish a procedure to enable airline passengers, who are delayed or prohibited from boarding a flight because the advanced passenger prescreening system determined that they might pose a security threat, to appeal such determination and correct information contained in the system." 49 U.S.C. § 44903(j)(2)(C)(iii)(I). The implementing regulations, 49 CFR 1560.205, provide: "If an individual believes he or she has been improperly or unfairly delayed or prohibited from boarding an aircraft or entering a sterile area as a result of the Secure Flight program, the individual may seek assistance through the redress process established under this section." This

"redress process" involves the passenger's filing a form giving identifying information and specifying the complaint. Then, per the regulations, "TSA, in coordination with the TSC and other appropriate Federal law enforcement or intelligence agencies, if necessary, will review all the documentation and information requested from the individual, correct any erroneous information, and provide the individual with a timely written response." The process is not further specified. Does the regulation—unchanged since 2008—satisfy the statute? Does it satisfy § 555 of the APA, assuming it is applicable? Could a court interpreting the statute and applying the APA reach the same result Judge Brown reached—or is reliance on the due process clause, and Mathews balancing, necessary to the result?

(2)   *The Next Steps.* Following Judge Brown's opinion, the government disclosed that seven of the thirteen plaintiffs were not on the no-fly list. It then "sent to each of the remaining six Plaintiffs a notification letter that identified the applicable substantive criteria and provided an unclassified summary that included some reasons for placement of each individual on the No-Fly List. Although the unclassified summaries varied in length and detail, the letters did not disclose all of the reasons or information on which Defendants relied to maintain each Plaintiff's placement on the No-Fly List. Defendants stated they were 'unable to provide additional disclosures.' " LATIF V. LYNCH, 2016 WL 1239925 (slip op. at 5). (This is a later opinion in the same case; the name changed because the Attorney General, the first-named defendant, changed.) The remaining plaintiffs then moved for summary judgment that the government's procedures violated due process for the following reasons, id. at 1:

> 1.   The reasonable-suspicion standard that Defendants employed when placing an individual on the No-Fly List is insufficiently rigorous, and Defendants should only be permitted to place an individual on the No-Fly List if there is clear and convincing evidence to support such listing.
>
> 2.   Defendants failed to provide Plaintiffs with a full statement of the reasons for each Plaintiff's placement on the No-Fly List;
>
> 3.   Defendants failed to provide Plaintiffs with all material evidence concerning their placement on the No-Fly List;
>
> 4.   Defendants failed to provide Plaintiffs with all exculpatory evidence concerning their placement on the No-Fly List;
>
> 5.   Defendants failed to provide Plaintiffs with a live hearing before a neutral decision-maker at which Plaintiffs could confront and cross-examine witnesses; and
>
> 6.   Defendants failed to provide Plaintiffs with additional disclosures using procedures . . . which include making disclosures to counsel who have security clearances, issuing protective orders, and presenting unclassified summaries of classified information.

The court responded to these claims as follows, id. at 2:

> 1.   Due process does not require Defendants to apply the clear and convincing evidence standard to the No-Fly List determinations

that Defendants made as to these Plaintiffs nor to provide original evidence to support such determinations. The reasonable-suspicion standard does not violate procedural due process when applied to a particular Plaintiff as long as Defendants provide such Plaintiff with (1) a statement of reasons that is sufficient to permit such Plaintiff to respond meaningfully and (2) any material exculpatory or inculpatory information in Defendants' possession that is necessary for such a meaningful response.

2.   In some instances, however, Defendants may limit or withhold disclosures altogether in the event that such disclosures would create an undue risk to national security. In such instances Defendants must implement procedures to minimize the amount of material information withheld. In particular, Defendants must determine whether the information can be summarized in an unclassified summary and/or whether additional disclosures can be made to Plaintiffs' counsel who have the appropriate security clearances. When possible, Defendants must do so. When it is not possible, Defendants must so certify through a competent witness with personal knowledge of the reasons for Defendants' conclusion that they cannot make such additional disclosures.

3.   Procedural due process in this context does not require Defendants to provide Plaintiffs with a live hearing before a neutral decision-maker at which Plaintiffs could confront and cross-examine witnesses.

Judge Brown then ruled that she needed further factual development before she could decide whether the notice the government gave the plaintiffs met these standards.

(3) In addition to the letters the government sent to the particular plaintiffs, it also filed in the case a "Notice" of new procedures under the DHS TRIP program that would be "made available to similarly situated U.S. persons" (Notice Regarding Revisions to DHS TRIP Procedures at 2–3, Latif v. Holder, Case: 3:10–cv–00750–BR (D. Or. Apr. 13, 2015)):

Under the previous redress procedures, individuals who had submitted inquiries to DHS TRIP generally received a letter responding to their inquiry that neither confirmed nor denied their No Fly status. Under the newly revised procedures, a U.S. person who purchases a ticket, is denied boarding at the airport, subsequently applies for redress through DHS TRIP about the denial of boarding, and is on the No Fly List after a redress review, will now receive a letter providing his or her status on the No Fly List and the option to receive and/or submit additional information. If such an individual opts to receive and/or submit further information after receiving this initial response, DHS TRIP will provide a second, more detailed response. This second letter will identify the specific criterion under which the individual has been placed on the No Fly List and, consistent with the Court's June 24, 2014 decision, will include an unclassified summary of information supporting the individual's No Fly List status, to the extent feasible, consistent with the national security and law enforcement interests at stake. The amount and type of information provided will vary on a case-by-case basis, depending on the facts and circumstances. In some circumstances, an unclassified summary may not be able to be provided when the national security and law enforcement interests at stake are taken into account.

This second letter will also provide the requester an opportunity to be heard further concerning their status. Written responses from such individuals may be submitted and may include exhibits or other materials the individual deems relevant. Upon DHS TRIP's receipt of an individual's submission in response to the second letter, the matter will be reviewed by the Administrator of the Transportation Security Administration (TSA) or his/her designee in coordination with other relevant agencies, who will review the submission, as well as the unclassified and classified information that is being relied upon to support the No Fly listing, and will issue a final determination. TSA will provide the individual with a final written determination, providing the basis for the decision (to the extent feasible in light of the national security and law enforcement interests at stake) and will notify the individual of the ability to seek further judicial review under 49 U.S.C. § 46110.

In a more recent filing in the case (now called Latif v. Sessions) the plaintiffs make the following point: "The revised redress process is not formally codified. It has not been subject to a rule-making process and is not published in the Federal Register or the Code of Federal Regulations, nor is there a complete, publicly available description of the process. The government has publicly revealed details about the process only through court filings in lawsuits such as this one. The government may change the process at any time with no notice . . . ." Does this, too, state a cognizable due process claim?

(4) **An Earlier Look.** The refusal of the court to require the live hearing for which plaintiffs asked can perhaps be evaluated by considering what such a hearing might look like. Would informants be asked to testify—and thereby become known? Or would they be allowed to supply anonymous information—and thereby not be subject to challenge? The most famous case to raise this issue was BAILEY V. RICHARDSON, 182 F.2d 46 (D.C. Cir. 1950), aff'd by an equally divided Court, 341 U.S. 918 (1951). Having been discharged from federal government employment "due to reduction in force," Dorothy Bailey was denied reinstatement a year later, as the Cold War began, because "reasonable grounds" existed to believe her disloyal. Here is a description of her administrative hearing, as detailed by one of the D.C. Circuit judges:

"Appellant appeared and testified before a panel of the Loyalty Review Board. She submitted her own affidavit and the affidavits of some 70 persons who knew her, including bankers, corporate officials, federal and state officials, union members, and others. Again no one testified against her. She proved she had publicly and to the knowledge of a number of the affiants taken positions inconsistent with Communist sympathies. She showed not only by her own testimony but by that of other persons that she favored the Marshall Plan, which the Communist Party notoriously opposed, and that in 1940, during the Nazi-Soviet Pact, she favored Lend-Lease and was very critical of the Soviet position. In her union she urged its officers to execute noncommunist affidavits, opposed a foreign policy resolution widely publicized as pro-Russian, and favored what was then the official CIO resolution on foreign policy.

"Against all this, there were only the unsworn reports in the secret files to the effect that unsworn statements of a general sort, purporting to connect appellant with Communism, had been made by unnamed persons. Some if not all of these statements did not purport to be based on knowledge, but only on belief. Appellant sought to learn the names of the informants or, if their names were confidential, then at least whether they had been active in appellant's union, in which there were factional quarrels. The Board did not furnish or even have this information. Chairman Richardson said: 'I haven't the slightest knowledge as to who they were or how active they have been in anything.' All that the Board knew or we know about the informants is that unidentified members of the Federal Bureau of Investigation, who did not appear before the Board, believed them to be reliable. To quote again from the record: 'Chairman Richardson: I can only say to you that five or six of the reports come from informants certified to us by the Federal Bureau of Investigation as experienced and entirely reliable.' "

The D.C. Circuit ruled, two to one, that although Bailey "was not given a trial in any sense of the word," due process was not violated because government employment constituted neither life, nor liberty, nor property, so the due process clause did not apply. Hence the court did not have to do the more particular procedural analysis exemplified by the no-fly-list cases. The Bailey view of government employment has been replaced by the Roth/Sindermann analysis, and indeed a footnote in the Roth opinion (Note 9 at p. 548 above) reads: "In a leading case decided many years ago, the Court of Appeals for the District of Columbia Circuit held that public employment in general was a 'privilege,' not a 'right,' and that procedural due process guarantees therefore were inapplicable. Bailey v. Richardson, 182 F.2d 46, aff'd by an equally divided Court, 341 U.S. 918. The basis of this holding has been thoroughly undermined in the ensuing years." If that is so, what should the process in Bailey have looked like? Or what do you think of Judge Brown's effort in Latif to get the agency to build a record—that will ultimately be subject to judicial review—without requiring "a live hearing before a neutral decision-maker at which Plaintiffs could confront and cross-examine witnesses."

(5) One of the techniques Judge Brown endorses is the disclosure of sensitive information to a counsel for the no-fly designee who has the necessary security clearance. If you were that lawyer, how would you act vis-à-vis your own client?

(6) **_Bureaucratic Justice?_** Are individualized hearings the answer to the issues raised by security programs? Consider PETER M. SHANE, THE BUREAUCRATIC DUE PROCESS OF GOVERNMENT WATCH LISTS, 75 Geo. Wash. L. Rev. 804, 805–10 (2007): "Since the terrorist attacks of September 11,

2001, watch lists have become increasingly important tools for law enforcement and the protection of homeland security. The press has widely reported their existence, especially in relation to the screening of airline passengers. Each list is rooted in one or more databases that match information about persons suspected of terrorism-related activities or other criminal activity with directions for government action appropriate to that individual . . .

"The rationale for watch lists is straightforward. Both the United States as a nation and its citizens as individuals have the most profound stake in including on appropriate watch lists those persons who pose genuine threats to our national security, including the threat of terrorism. Properly managed watch lists can help ensure that persons connected with terrorist activity are denied both entry to the United States and dangerous access to vulnerable networks and other physical facilities. They can help focus legally permissible surveillance on fruitful targets and assist in the coordination of multi-agency efforts to track potential threats and prevent them from ripening into attacks.

"These interests are served, however, only to the extent that watch lists are accurate. Watch list errors are especially troubling because of the gravity of interests affected. The mistaken targeting of innocent persons subtracts from the limited resources available to pursue genuinely productive law enforcement and national security initiatives. To the extent that watch lists impede travel or immigration by noncitizens who present no actual threat to the United States, they can exact substantial cultural, political, and economic costs, in both the short and long term.

"The interests of individuals in avoiding erroneous listing are similarly compelling. For the person mistakenly targeted, costs may range from minor inconvenience to serious reputational damage or substantial limitations on privacy and freedom of action. The burdens could range from clandestine surveillance to a prohibition on entry into the United States or other travel. Perhaps the most publicized uses of watch lists have involved passenger screening on commercial airlines, which may result in intensified identity checks, personal inspection, and (for persons on the 'No-Fly' List) an effective ban on commercial air travel altogether.

"More than merely instrumental values are at stake, however, in the maintenance of watch list accuracy: the misuse of watch lists threatens our society's fundamental values. Secret programs of any kind strain the norms of openness and transparency on which democratic legitimacy is based . . . It is therefore crucial for government, in deploying secret watch lists as tools of law enforcement and national security, to address the inevitability of watch list error in a way that maintains individual dignity and our collective values of mutual trust and democratic accountability.

"To American lawyers, the problems posed by watch lists are readily perceived as problems of 'procedural due process.' The federal government has established what amounts to a system of informal adjudication—namely, the identification of persons to include on terrorist watch lists—which if performed in error threatens significant harm to individual persons. The conventional 'due process' response to this risk of adjudicative error is typically 'some kind of hearing,' either to prevent or redress the error through additional adjudicative formalities. The adjudication of individual disputes, whether administratively or in judicial forums, however, cannot be the sole component of a program to pursue watch list fairness. On the one hand, the very aim of the watch list program is likely to preclude the possibility of preinclusion hearings for many of those persons proposed for listing. Presumably, affording a suspect notice that he or she might be the subject of covert surveillance would be self-defeating. On the other hand, redress through postinclusion mechanisms would succeed only retrospectively and only for those individuals who become aware of their inclusion. Thousands of individuals might remain unjustifiably disadvantaged by the watch lists through decisionmaking procedures of which they are unaware. It ought to be viewed as intolerable in a democratic society for large numbers of innocent people to be stigmatized by the government under a largely secret program, even if such cases can be 'redressed' through postinclusion individual review.

"What is needed is a more robust form of what Professor Jerry Mashaw has labeled 'bureaucratic justice': an institutional blending of 'positive administration, bureaucratically organized' with law-like constraints on the exercise of discretion designed to secure important public values . . ."

(7) *Or How about This?* SHIRIN SINNAR, TOWARD A FAIRER TERRORIST WATCHLIST, 40 Admin. and Reg. L. News 4, 5 (2015): "[P]olicymakers and courts should question the premise of the No Fly List itself: that certain individuals who are not charged with any crime are nonetheless too dangerous to fly under any circumstances. Is it truly the case that no set of extra security procedures, especially with respect to U.S. citizens and residents, could sufficiently mitigate the threat posed? The government has sometimes granted 'one-time waivers' allowing Americans abroad to fly back to the United States, especially after they filed suit; in such cases, the government conditioned air travel on special security measures, such as advance submission of travel itineraries and extra screening (and perhaps also seated the individuals next to undisclosed federal air marshals). Even for individuals who are judged to meet the standards for inclusion on the No Fly List, measures short of total air travel bans might be available without compromising security."

c.   Post-Deprivation Process

> ***NORTH AMERICAN COLD STORAGE***
> ***CO. v. CHICAGO***
> ***Notes on the Reach of Post-Deprivation***
> ***Process***
> ***INGRAHAM v. WRIGHT***

NORTH AMERICAN COLD STORAGE CO. v. CHICAGO

Supreme Court of the United States (1908).
211 U.S. 306.

[Section 1161 of the Revised Municipal Code of the City of Chicago required owners of facilities for cold storage of any perishable food item to "put, preserve and keep such article of food supply in a clean and wholesome condition, and . . . not allow the same, nor any part thereof, to become putrid, decayed, poisoned, infected, or in any other manner rendered or made unsafe or unwholesome for human food." Further, health department inspectors were authorized "to enter any and all such premises . . . at any time of any day and to forthwith seize, condemn and destroy any such putrid, decayed, poisoned and infected food, which any such inspector may find in and upon said premises." Pursuant to this ordinance, city officials ordered North American Cold Storage to deliver to them, for purposes of destruction, forty-seven barrels of poultry that allegedly had become putrid. The Company refused. The City then threatened to destroy summarily anything in the warehouse deemed unfit for human consumption; it banned further deliveries to or from the warehouse and promised to imprison anyone attempting to avoid the ban. Business was completely halted, and the Company sought an injunction.]

■ JUSTICE PECKHAM . . . delivered the opinion of the Court.

. . . The general power of the State to legislate upon the subject embraced in the above ordinance of the city of Chicago, counsel does not deny. Nor does he deny the right to seize and destroy unwholesome or putrid food, provided that notice and opportunity to be heard be given the owner or custodian of the property before it is destroyed. We are of opinion, however, that provision for a hearing before seizure and condemnation and destruction of food which is unwholesome and unfit for use, is not necessary. . . . The right to so seize and destroy is, of course, based upon the fact that the food is not fit to be eaten. Food that is in such a condition, if kept for sale or in danger of being sold, is in itself a nuisance, and a nuisance of the most dangerous kind, involving, as it does, the health, if not the lives, of persons who may eat it. A determination on the part of the seizing officers that food is in an unfit condition to be eaten is not a decision which concludes the owner. The ex parte finding of the health officers as to the fact is not in any way binding upon those who own or claim the right to sell the food. If a party cannot get his hearing in advance of the seizure and destruction he has the right to have it afterward, which right may be claimed upon the trial in an action brought for the destruction of his property, and in that action those who destroyed it can only successfully defend if the jury shall find the fact of unwholesomeness as claimed by them. . . .

Miller v. Horton, 152 Mass. 540, 26 N.E. 100, is in principle like the case before us. It was an action brought for killing the plaintiff's horse. The defendants admitted the killing but justified the act under an order of the board of health, which declared that the horse had the glanders, and directed it to be killed. The court held that the decision of the board of health was not conclusive as to whether or not the horse was diseased, and said that: "Of course there cannot be a trial by jury before killing an animal supposed to have a contagious disease, and we assume that the legislature may authorize its destruction in such emergencies without a hearing beforehand. But it does not follow that it can throw the loss upon the owner without a hearing. If he cannot be heard beforehand he may be heard afterward. The statute may provide for paying him in case it should appear that his property was not what the legislature had declared to be a nuisance and may give him his hearing in that way. If it does not do so, the statute may leave those who act under it to proceed at their peril, and the owner gets his hearing in an action against them." . . .

Complainant, however, contends that there was no emergency requiring speedy action for the destruction of the poultry in order to protect the public health from danger resulting from consumption of such poultry. It is said that the food was in cold storage, and that it would continue in the same condition it then was for three months, if properly stored, and that therefore the defendants had ample time in which to give notice to complainant or the owner and have a hearing of the question as to the condition of the poultry, and as the ordinance provided for no hearing, it was void. But we think this is not required. The power of the legislature to enact laws in relation to the public health being conceded, as it must be, it is to a great extent within legislative discretion as to whether any hearing need be given before the destruction of unwholesome food which is unfit for human consumption. If a hearing were to be always necessary, even under the circumstances of this case, the question at once arises as to what is to be done with the food in the meantime. Is it to remain with the cold storage company, and if so under what security that it will not be removed? To be sure that it will not be removed during the time necessary for the hearing, which might frequently be indefinitely prolonged, some guard would probably have to be placed over the subject-matter of investigation, which would involve expense, and might not even then prove effectual. What is the emergency which would render a hearing unnecessary? We think when the question is one regarding the destruction of food which is not fit for human use the emergency must be one which would fairly appeal to the reasonable discretion of the legislature as to the necessity for a prior hearing, and in that case its decision would not be a subject for review by the courts. As the owner of the food or its custodian is amply protected against the party seizing the food, who must in a subsequent action against him show as a fact that it was within the statute, we think that due process of law is not denied the owner or custodian by the destruction of the food alleged to be unwholesome and unfit for human food without a preliminary hearing. . . .

Affirmed.

■ JUSTICE BREWER dissents.

NOTES ON THE REACH OF POST-DEPRIVATION PROCESS

(1) **How Far Does Cold Storage Go?** Even after a century of doctrinal evolution, the North American Cold Storage principle remains a vital aspect of procedural due process. FEDERAL DEPOSIT INS. CORP. V. MALLEN, 486 U.S. 230 (1988): As part of its charge to guard against losses from bank failures, the Federal Deposit Insurance Corporation is authorized to suspend summarily an officer of an insured bank who has been indicted for a felony involving dishonesty or breach of trust and whose continued service could pose a threat to the depositors or to public confidence in the bank. The statute provides that an administrative hearing need not be given until 30 days after the suspension and might not be concluded for an additional 60 days. Held, by a unanimous Court: no violation of due process. "An important government interest, accompanied by a substantial assurance that the deprivation is not baseless or unwarranted, may in limited cases demanding prompt action justify postponing the opportunity to be heard until after the initial deprivation. See North American Cold Storage Co. v. Chicago." As to the possible 90-day delay, the length of time was a proper item of concern, but in this case the Court was not convinced that Congress had over-stepped its limits.

GILBERT V. HOMAR, 520 U.S. 924 (1997), in turn relied on North American Cold Storage and Mallen in holding that a state university could, consistent with the Constitution, summarily suspend without pay a police officer arrested for and charged with a drug felony. JUSTICE SCALIA wrote for a unanimous Court. The purpose of a pre-suspension hearing—to assure that there are reasonable grounds to support the suspension—has already been determined by the arrest and charge. The State has a significant interest in immediately suspending employees charged with felonies who occupy positions of public trust and visibility, such as police officers. So long as the lost income is relatively insubstantial and the post-suspension hearing is prompt, due process "does not require the government to give an employee charged with a felony a paid leave at taxpayer expense."

(2) **Need There Be Exigent Circumstances?** A long line of cases affirms the power of state and federal governments to require taxpayers to pay a contested assessment and then bring an action for refund. JUSTICE BRANDEIS for a unanimous Court in PHILLIPS V. COMMISSIONER, 283 U.S. 589 (1931),

had this to say: "Where only property rights are involved, mere postponement of the judicial enquiry is not a denial of due process, if the opportunity given for the ultimate judicial determination of the liability is adequate. Delay in the judicial determination of property rights is not uncommon where it is essential that governmental needs be immediately satisfied. For the protection of public health, a State may order the summary destruction of property by administrative authorities without antecedent notice or hearing. North American Cold Storage Co. v. Chicago. . . . Because of the public necessity, the property of citizens may be summarily seized in war-time. And at any time, the United States may acquire property by eminent domain, without paying, or determining the amount of the compensation before the taking."

On the other hand, in UNITED STATES V. JAMES DANIEL GOOD REAL PROPERTY, 510 U.S. 43 (1993), the Court split 5–4 on whether a civil forfeiture of real property could be done summarily in the absence of exigent circumstances. Four and one-half years after James Good pleaded guilty to drug offenses (and three and one-half years after he had completed his jail sentence), the government convinced a magistrate, in an ex parte proceeding, that it had probable cause to seize the house and land on which the drugs had been found. The government then seized the property without prior notice to Good or the tenants then occupying it. The Court (JUSTICE KENNEDY writing) held that where property is seized, not to preserve evidence of criminal wrongdoing but to assert ownership and control, "[w]e tolerate some exceptions to the general rule requiring predeprivation notice and hearing, . . . only in extraordinary situations where some valid governmental interest is at stake that justifies postponing the hearing until after the event" (internal quotes omitted). "It is true that, in cases decided over a century ago, we permitted the ex parte seizure of real property when the Government was collecting debts or revenue. Without revisiting these cases, it suffices to say that their apparent rationale—like that for allowing summary seizures during wartime, . . . and seizures of contaminated food, see North American Cold Storage Co. v. Chicago,—was one of executive urgency. 'The prompt payment of taxes,' we noted, 'may be vital to the existence of a government.' Springer v. United States, 102 U.S. 586, 594 (1880). See also G.M. Leasing Corp. v. United States, 429 U.S. 338, 352, n. 18 (1977) ('The rationale underlying [the revenue] decisions, of course, is that the very existence of government depends upon the prompt collection of the revenues')." Here, no such executive urgency existed. Unlike such personal property as the boats and automobiles that had been involved in other cases, real property could not leave the jurisdiction. However, for dissenting Chief Justice Rehnquist and Justice Scalia, the majority opinion both disregarded the long history of ex parte seizures of real and personal property through civil forfeiture and failed convincingly to distinguish the tax cases. For Justices O'Connor and Thomas, it was also relevant that Good had been convicted at the time the forfeiture began; the majority's concern that the property rights of an "innocent owner" might be forfeited before hearing was thus, in their view, completely misplaced.

(3) *Is a Full Post-Deprivation Remedy Required?* The proposition in the Massachusetts horse-with-glanders case discussed in North American Cold Storage—that the responsible officials would be personally liable in tort to the owner if the horse were not, in fact, diseased—was overruled by Gildea v. Ellershaw, 363 Mass. 800, 298 N.E.2d 847 (1973). The Supreme Judicial Court held that under Massachusetts law a public official who acts in good faith within the scope of his official duty is not liable for "negligence or other error . . . at the suit of a private individual claiming to have been damaged thereby." Federal law similarly recognizes a variety of official immunities that wholly or partially shield state and federal actors from having to pay damages for acts that turn out to have been unjustified by law. See p. 1440. And, when the property owner attempts to recover her loss from the governmental entity itself, she may well encounter the barrier of sovereign immunity. Supreme Court cases in the tax area have stated that adequate post-payment remedies must be provided if the government denies pre-deprivation process; see, e.g., Reich v. Collins, 513 U.S. 106 (1994); McKesson Corp. v. Division of Alcoholic Beverages & Tobacco, 496 U.S. 18, 36–37 (1990).

(4) *Government Contracts.* You will recall that one of the most vexing questions raised by entitlement reasoning is whether government contracts have become "property" for due process purposes (p. 560). In LUJAN V. G & G FIRE SPRINKLERS, INC., 532 U.S. 189 (2001), plaintiff challenged a provision of the California Labor Code that permitted governmental units to withhold payments from a contractor on a public works project if the contractor or any of its subcontractors failed to comply with Code requirements. Without conducting any sort of hearing before or after its determination, the state's Division of Labor Standards Enforcement (DSLE) concluded that G & G, a subcontractor on several projects, had failed to pay its workers the "prevailing wage" as the Code requires. It therefore directed that amounts equal to the underpayment, plus penalties, be withheld from contract payments to the prime contractors who used G & G. The prime contractors in turn (as required by the Code) withheld the disputed amount from payments to G & G on the subcontracts. The Court of Appeals held that G & G had a property interest in being paid in full for the work completed and that due process required the DLSE to provide a hearing on the issue of Code violation, either before the withholding order or promptly thereafter. The Supreme Court unanimously reversed.

CHIEF JUSTICE REHNQUIST's opinion "assume[d] without deciding that the withholding of money due [G & G] under its contracts occurred under color of state law, and that . . . [G & G] has a property interest . . . in its claim for payments under its contracts." However: "In [prior cases such as FDIC v. Mallen and U.S. v. James Daniel Good Real Property], the claimant was denied a right by virtue of which he was presently entitled either to exercise ownership dominion over real or personal property, or to pursue a gainful occupation. Unlike those claimants, respondent has not been denied any present entitlement. G & G has been deprived of payment that it contends it is owed under a contract, based on the State's determination that G & G failed to comply with the contract's terms. G & G has only a claim that it did comply with those terms and therefore that it is entitled to be paid in full. Though we assume for purposes of decision here that G & G has a property interest in its claim for payment, it is an interest, unlike the interests discussed above, that can be fully protected by an ordinary breach-of-contract suit. . . . We hold that if California makes ordinary judicial process available to respondent for resolving its contractual dispute, that process is due process."

The Fire Sprinklers case thus has the effect of moving the issue from whether a particular contract right is "property" to whether a particular contract right is the kind of "property" that comprises a "present entitlement." If it is a "present entitlement," then we have to ask the kinds of questions suggested in the preceding notes; if it is not, ordinary breach-of-contract remedies are, it seems, per se sufficient. Judge Cudahy of the Seventh Circuit: "[A] fine line distinguishes factual scenarios in which a judicial remedy for breach of contract is adequate from those in which it is not. Not all injuries are equal, and not all parties can be made whole through a breach of contract action. The somewhat obscure quality that separates one from the other is important and yet eludes precise definition. The Supreme Court has referred to this mysterious element as a 'present entitlement.'" Baird v. Bd. of Educ. for Warren Community Unit School Dist. No. 205, 389 F.3d 685, 691 (7th Cir. 2004). The cases are very fact specific; among the factors lower courts have mentioned are whether the contract is purely financial or involves elements of personality, and whether the need for a remedy is time-sensitive.

(5) Sindermann (p. 553), unlike Roth, had "alleged the existence of rules and understandings, promulgated and fostered by state officials, that may justify his legitimate claim of entitlement to continued employment absent 'sufficient cause'"; proof of such would entitle him to a hearing before termination, while "[i]f it is the law of Texas that a teacher in the respondent's position has no contractual or other claim to job tenure, the respondent's claim would be defeated." If Sindermann can prove that he has a claim under Texas contract law, does that very proof also establish that he has an adequate remedy in court and has no need of an administrative hearing? Assuming that is not the law—why not?

(6) So far we have been considering property. What, if anything, do these cases mean for summary deprivation of liberty?

INGRAHAM v. WRIGHT

Supreme Court of the United States (1977).
430 U.S. 651.

■ JUSTICE POWELL delivered the opinion of the Court.

I

[Plaintiffs James Ingraham and Roosevelt Andrews, eighth and ninth graders at Drew Junior High in Dade County, Fla., sued various school officials. After plaintiffs' evidence was in, the district court dismissed the case.]

. . . Petitioners' evidence may be summarized briefly. In the 1970–1971 school year many of the 237 schools in Dade County used corporal punishment as a means of maintaining discipline pursuant to Florida legislation and a local School Board regulation. . . . The authorized punishment consisted of paddling the recalcitrant student on the buttocks with a flat wooden paddle measuring less than two feet long, three to four inches wide, and about one-half inch thick. The normal punishment was limited to one to five "licks" or blows with the paddle and resulted in no apparent physical injury to the student. School authorities viewed corporal punishment as a less drastic means of discipline than suspension or expulsion. . . .

. . . The evidence, consisting mainly of the testimony of 16 students, suggests that the regime at Drew was exceptionally harsh. The testimony of Ingraham and Andrews, in support of their individual claims for damages, is illustrative. Because he was slow to respond to his teacher's instructions, Ingraham was subjected to more than 20 licks with a paddle while being held over a table in the principal's office. The paddling was so severe that he suffered a hematoma requiring medical attention and keeping him out of school for several days. Andrews was paddled several times for minor infractions. On two occasions he was struck on his arms, once depriving him of the full use of his arm for a week.

The District Court made no findings on the credibility of the students' testimony. Rather, assuming their testimony to be credible, the court found no constitutional basis for relief. [A panel of the Fifth Circuit voted to reverse but, upon rehearing en banc, the judgment of the district court was affirmed.]

We granted certiorari, limited to the questions of cruel and unusual punishment and procedural due process.

II

[Corporal punishment dates back to colonial times, as does the common law principle (now incorporated in the Restatement (Second) of Torts) that teachers are privileged to use reasonable but not excessive force to discipline children.]

III

. . . An examination of the history of the [Eighth] Amendment and the decisions of this Court construing the proscription against cruel and unusual punishment confirms that it was designed to protect those convicted of crimes. We adhere to this longstanding limitation and hold that the Eighth Amendment does not apply to the paddling of children as a means of maintaining discipline in public schools. . . .

IV

The Fourteenth Amendment prohibits any state deprivation of life, liberty, or property without due process of law. Application of this prohibition requires the familiar two-stage analysis: We must first ask whether the asserted individual interests are encompassed within the Fourteenth Amendment's protection of "life, liberty or property"; if protected interests are implicated, we then must decide what procedures constitute "due process of law." Following that analysis here, we find that corporal punishment in public schools implicates a constitutionally protected liberty interest, but we hold that the traditional common-law remedies are fully adequate to afford due process.

A

"[T]he range of interests protected by procedural due process is not infinite." Board of Regents v. Roth, 408 U.S. at 570. We have repeatedly rejected "the notion that *any* grievous loss visited upon a person by the State is sufficient to invoke the procedural protections of the Due Process Clause." Meachum v. Fano, 427 U.S., at 224. Due process is required only when a decision of the State implicates an interest within the protection of the Fourteenth Amendment. And "to determine whether due process requirements apply in the first place, we must look not to the 'weight' but to the *nature* of the interest at stake." Roth, at 570–571.

The Due Process Clause of the Fifth Amendment, later incorporated into the Fourteenth, was intended to give Americans at least the protection against governmental power that they had enjoyed as Englishmen against the power of the Crown. The liberty preserved from deprivation without due process included the right "generally to enjoy those privileges long recognized at common law as essential to the orderly pursuit of happiness by free men." Meyer v. Nebraska, 262 U.S. 390, 399 (1923). Among the historic liberties so protected was a right to be free from, and to obtain judicial relief for, unjustified intrusions on personal security.

While the contours of this historic liberty interest in the context of our federal system of government have not been defined precisely, they always have been thought to encompass freedom from bodily restraint and punishment. It is fundamental that the state cannot hold and physically punish an individual except in accordance with due process of law.

This constitutionally protected liberty interest is at stake in this case. There is, of course, a *de minimis* level of imposition with which the Constitution is not concerned. But at least where school authorities, acting under color of state law, deliberately decide to punish a child for misconduct by restraining the child and inflicting appreciable physical pain, we hold that Fourteenth Amendment liberty interests are implicated.[43]

---

[43] Unlike Goss v. Lopez, this case does not involve the state-created property interest in public education. The purpose of corporal punishment is to correct a child's behavior without interrupting his education. That corporal punishment may, in a rare case, have the unintended effect of temporarily removing a child from school affords no basis for concluding that the practice itself deprives students of property protected by the Fourteenth Amendment. . . .

B

The question remains what process is due. Were it not for the common-law privilege permitting teachers to inflict reasonable corporal punishment on children in their care, and the availability of the traditional remedies for abuse, the case for requiring advance procedural safeguards would be strong indeed. But here we deal with a punishment—paddling—within that tradition, and the question is whether the common-law remedies are adequate to afford due process.

. . . Whether in this case the common-law remedies for excessive corporal punishment constitute due process of law must turn on an analysis of the competing interests at stake, viewed against the background of "history, reason, [and] the past course of decisions." The analysis requires consideration of three distinct factors: "First, the private interest that will be affected . . .; second, the risk of an erroneous deprivation of such interest . . . and the probable value, if any, of additional or substitute procedural safeguards; and finally, the [state] interest, including the function involved and the fiscal and administrative burdens that the additional or substitute procedural requirement would entail." Mathews v. Eldridge, 424 U.S. 319, 335 (1976).

1

Because it is rooted in history, the child's liberty interest in avoiding corporal punishment while in the care of public school authorities is subject to historical limitations. . . .

The concept that reasonable corporal punishment in school is justifiable continues to be recognized in the laws of most States. . . .

This is not to say that the child's interest in procedural safeguards is insubstantial. . . .

We turn now to a consideration of the safeguards that are available under applicable Florida law.

2

Florida has continued to recognize, and indeed has strengthened by statute, the common-law right of a child not to be subjected to excessive corporal punishment in school. Under Florida law the teacher and principal of the school decide in the first instance whether corporal punishment is reasonably necessary under the circumstances in order to discipline a child who has misbehaved. But they must exercise prudence and restraint. For Florida has preserved the traditional judicial proceedings for determining whether the punishment was justified. If the punishment inflicted is later found to have been excessive—not reasonably believed at the time to be necessary for the child's discipline or training—the school authorities inflicting it may be held liable in damages to the child and, if malice is shown, they may be subject to criminal penalties.[45]

Although students have testified in this case to specific instances of abuse, there is every reason to believe that such mistreatment is an aberration. The uncontradicted evidence suggests that corporal punishment in the Dade County schools was, "[w]ith the exception of a few cases, . . . unremarkable in physical severity." Moreover, because paddlings are usually inflicted in response to conduct directly observed by teachers in their presence, the risk that a child will be paddled without cause is typically insignificant. In the ordinary case, a disciplinary paddling neither threatens seriously to violate any substantive rights nor condemns the child "to suffer grievous loss of any kind." Anti-Fascist Comm. v. McGrath, 341 U.S., at 168 (Frankfurter, J., concurring).

In those cases where severe punishment is contemplated, the available civil and criminal sanctions for abuse-considered in light of the openness of the school environment-afford significant protection against unjustified corporal punishment. Teachers and school authorities are unlikely to inflict corporal punishment unnecessarily or excessively when a possible consequence of doing so is the institution of civil or criminal proceedings against them.[46]

It still may be argued, of course, that the child's liberty interest would be better protected if the common-law remedies were supplemented by the administrative safeguards of prior notice and a hearing. . . . But where the State has preserved what "has always been the law of the land," United States v. Barnett, 376 U.S. 681 (1964), the case for administrative safeguards is significantly less compelling.[47] . . .

---

[45] . . . Both the District Court and the Court of Appeals expressed the view that the commonlaw tort remedy was available to the petitioners in this case. And petitioners conceded in this Court that a teacher who inflicts excessive punishment on a child may be held both civilly and criminally liable under Florida law. . . .

[46] The low incidence of abuse, and the availability of established judicial remedies in the event of abuse, distinguish this case from Goss v. Lopez, 419 U.S. 565 (1975). The Ohio law struck down in Goss provided for suspensions from public school of up to 10 days without "any written procedure applicable to suspensions." Id., at 567. Although Ohio law provided generally for administrative review, the Court assumed that the short suspensions would not be stayed pending review, with the result that the review proceeding could serve neither a deterrent nor a remedial function. 419 U.S., at 581 n. 10. In these circumstances, the Court held the law authorizing suspensions unconstitutional for failure to require "that there be at least an informal give-and-take between student and disciplinarian, preferably prior to the suspension. . . ." Id., at 584. The subsequent civil and criminal proceedings available in this case may be viewed as affording substantially greater protection to the child than the informal conference mandated by Goss.

[47] "[P]rior hearings might well be dispensed with in many circumstances in which the state's conduct, if not adequately justified, would constitute a common-law tort. This would leave the injured plaintiff in precisely the same posture as a common-law plaintiff, and this procedural consequence would be quite harmonious with the substantive view that the fourteenth amendment encompasses the same liberties as those protected by the common law." Monaghan, Of "Liberty" and "Property," 62 Cornell L.Rev. 405, 431 (1977) (footnote omitted). . . .

3

But even if the need for advance procedural safeguards were clear, the question would remain whether the incremental benefit could justify the cost. Acceptance of petitioners' claims would work a transformation in the law governing corporal punishment in Florida and most other States. Given the impracticability of formulating a rule of procedural due process that varies with the severity of the particular imposition, the prior hearing petitioners seek would have to precede *any* paddling, however moderate or trivial.

Such a universal constitutional requirement would significantly burden the use of corporal punishment as a disciplinary measure. . . . Teachers, properly concerned with maintaining authority in the classroom, may well prefer to rely on other disciplinary measures-which they may view as less effective-rather than confront the possible disruption that prior notice and a hearing may entail.[50] Paradoxically, such an alteration of disciplinary policy is most likely to occur in the ordinary case where the contemplated punishment is well within the common-law privilege.[51] . . .

"At some point the benefit of an additional safeguard to the individual affected . . . and to society in terms of increased assurance that the action is just, may be outweighed by the cost." Mathews v. Eldridge, 424 U.S., at 348. We think that point has been reached in this case. In view of the low incidence of abuse, the openness of our schools, and the common-law safeguards that already exist, the risk of error that may result in violation of a schoolchild's substantive rights can only be regarded as minimal. Imposing additional administrative safeguards as a constitutional requirement might reduce that risk marginally, but would also entail a significant intrusion into an area of primary educational responsibility. We conclude that the Due Process Clause does not require notice and a hearing prior to the imposition of corporal punishment in the public schools, as that practice is authorized and limited by the common law. . . .

Affirmed.

■ JUSTICE WHITE, with whom JUSTICE BRENNAN, JUSTICE MARSHALL, and JUSTICE STEVENS join, dissenting.

Today the Court holds that corporal punishment in public schools, no matter how severe, can never be the subject of the protections afforded by the Eighth Amendment. It also holds that students in the public school

---

[50] If a prior hearing, with the inevitable attendant publicity within the school, resulted in rejection of the teacher's recommendation, the consequent impairment of the teacher's ability to maintain discipline in the classroom would not be insubstantial.

[51] The effect of interposing prior procedural safeguards may well be to make the punishment more severe by increasing the anxiety of the child. For this reason, the school authorities in Dade County found it desirable that the punishment be inflicted as soon as possible after the infraction.

systems are not constitutionally entitled to a hearing of any sort before beatings can be inflicted on them. . . .

The reason that the Constitution requires a State to provide "due process of law" when it punishes an individual for misconduct is to protect the individual from erroneous or mistaken punishment that the State would not have inflicted had it found the facts in a more reliable way. In Goss v. Lopez, 419 U.S. 565 (1975), the Court applied this principle to the school disciplinary process, holding that a student must be given an informal opportunity to be heard before he is finally suspended from public school.

> *Disciplinarians, although proceeding in utmost good faith, frequently act on the reports and advice of others;* and the controlling facts and the nature of the conduct under challenge are often disputed. *The risk of error is not at all trivial,* and it should be guarded against if that may be done without prohibitive cost or interference with the educational process. Id., at 580. (Emphasis added.)

To guard against this risk of punishing an innocent child, the Due Process Clause requires, not an "elaborate hearing" before a neutral party, but simply "an informal give-and-take between student and disciplinarian" which gives the student "an opportunity to explain his version of the facts."

The Court now holds that these "rudimentary precautions against unfair or mistaken findings of misconduct," id., at 581, are not required if the student is punished with "appreciable physical pain" rather than with a suspension, even though both punishments deprive the student of a constitutionally protected interest. . . .

[The Florida] tort action is utterly inadequate to protect against erroneous infliction of punishment for two reasons. First, under Florida law, a student . . . has no remedy at all for punishment imposed on the basis of mistaken facts . . .[11] The "traditional common-law remedies" on which the majority relies thus do nothing to protect the student from the danger that concerned the Court in Goss—the risk of reasonable, good-faith mistake in the school disciplinary process.

Second, and more important, even if the student could sue for good faith error in the infliction of punishment, the lawsuit occurs after the punishment has been finally imposed. The infliction of physical pain is final and irreparable; it cannot be undone in a subsequent proceeding. There is every reason to require, as the Court did in Goss, a few minutes of "informal give-and-take between student and disciplinarian" as a

---

[11] The majority's assurances to the contrary, it is unclear to me whether and to what extent Florida law provides a damages action against school officials for excessive corporal punishment. Giving the majority the benefit of every doubt, I think it is fair to say that the most a student punished on the basis of mistaken allegations of misconduct can hope for in Florida is a recovery for unreasonable or bad-faith error. But I strongly suspect that even this remedy is not available. . . .

"meaningful hedge" against the erroneous infliction of irreparable injury. 419 U.S., at 583–584.

The majority's conclusion that a damages remedy for excessive corporal punishment affords adequate process rests on the novel theory that the State may punish an individual without giving him any opportunity to present his side of the story, as long as he can later recover damages from a state official if he is innocent. . . . There is no authority for this theory, nor does the majority purport to find any, in the procedural due process decisions of this Court. . . .

I would reverse the judgment below.

■ JUSTICE STEVENS, dissenting.

. . . Notwithstanding my disagreement with the Court's holding . . . my respect for Justice Powell's reasoning in Part IV-B of his opinion for the Court prompts these comments.

The constitutional prohibition of state deprivations of life, liberty, or property without due process of law does not, by its express language, require that a hearing be provided *before* any deprivation may occur. To be sure, the timing of the process may be a critical element in determining its adequacy—that is, in deciding what process is due in a particular context. Generally, adequate notice and a fair opportunity to be heard in advance of any deprivation of a constitutionally protected interest are essential. The Court has recognized, however, that the wording of the command that there shall be no deprivation "without" due process of law is consistent with the conclusion that a postdeprivation remedy is sometimes constitutionally sufficient.

When only an invasion of a property interest is involved, there is a greater likelihood that a damages award will make a person completely whole than when an invasion of the individual's interest in freedom from bodily restraint and punishment has occurred. . . .

NOTES

(1) ***Rightly Decided?*** As the opinions in Ingraham indicate, the case was written against the background of GOSS V. LOPEZ, 419 U.S. 565 (1975), the Court's first brush with the procedures applicable to school discipline. Like other states, Ohio had a statutory scheme for compulsory education of children up to a certain age. One section authorized the suspension of a student for up to 10 days with no process beyond a letter from the principal to the student's parents explaining why the action had been taken. In a 5–4 opinion written by Justice White, the Court held that the lack of any pre-suspension process rendered the statute unconstitutional. Deprivation of the statutory entitlement to an education for up to 10 days is not, he said, de minimis. Moreover, suspension can tarnish a student's reputation, thus depriving him of a liberty interest. As to the process required, however, the Court departed strikingly from prior cases. All that is constitutionally required, in light of the interests implicated, the desire to avoid error, and

the functional requisites of the institutional setting, is "an informal give-and-take between student and disciplinarian." The student must be given "notice of the charges against him and, if he denies them, an explanation of the evidence the authorities have and an opportunity to present his side of the story." (If the student's conduct creates an immediate threat of institutional disruption, the school can remove him first as long as it provides an opportunity for discussion immediately afterward.) The opinion sparked speculation that "Goss process" represented the due process minimum: a four-line dialogue containing reasons ("You started the food fight in the cafeteria."); opportunity for denial ("No way!"); explanation of evidence ("Five people saw you."); opportunity to respond ("No way!!! I was at my locker when it happened.").[6] Why didn't Ingraham just adopt it?

(2)   ROBERT A. BURT, THE CONSTITUTION OF THE FAMILY, 1979 Sup. Ct. Rev. 329, 341–42: "[I]n Ingraham v. Wright, Justice Powell identified a problem of central concern to him. . . .: 'If a prior hearing, with the inevitable attendant publicity within the school, resulted in rejection of the teacher's recommendation, the consequent impairment of the teacher's ability to maintain discipline in the classroom would not be insubstantial.' . . .

"It would be unfair, however, to portray the Court in Ingraham or its conservative nucleus as intending to condone or encourage brutality by teachers, parents, or judges. This nucleus intends to encourage an unquestioning attitude toward, and a reciprocally firm and self-confident attitude by, constituted authority. An idealized image of conflict-free interpersonal relations appears to lie beneath this intention. Justice Powell reveals this in his Goss v. Lopez dissent: 'The role of the teacher in our society historically has been an honored and respected one, rooted in the experience of decades that has left for most of us warm memories of our teachers, especially those of the formative years of primary and secondary education.' It might thus appear an insult to these honored memories if the Supreme Court were now to abandon '[our reliance] for generations upon the experience, good faith and dedication of those who staff our public schools.' "

(3)   JANE RUTHERFORD, THE MYTH OF DUE PROCESS, 72 B.U. L. Rev. 1, 41 (1992): "[T]he 'law of the land' is merely a myth in both senses of the word. It is a cultural story because its content depends on which time period the law is drawn from, how elastically we read that law, and whether we define that law specifically or generally. By characterizing law as historical fact, however, the Court has managed to define the law in favor of more powerful parties. As a result, due process has been transformed from a shield for the powerless to a weapon for the powerful. Accordingly, historical due process is also a myth that carries false promises of protection. One way to balance the power more fairly is to ensure that relatively powerless parties can participate on an equal footing."

(4)   Is it legitimate, in considering the reach of constitutional due process, to take into account the degree to which an extension of procedural rights

---

[6]   An in-class experiment by one of your editors proved that Goss process can take as little as 12 seconds to accomplish.

will alter institutional power relationships? Is it responsible not to consider these possible consequences?

(5)   Most states have abolished corporal punishment in public schools. In at least some of these states, a motivating factor was the large damages that had been awarded in tort suits against schools, based on unreasonable discipline. Do you think the majority was right that the underlying power dynamics of the situation could be left to the common law rules?

(6)   More broadly, the Court relies at several places on the history of the practice whose "due process" it is assessing. It also cites and relies on Mathews. Are these two approaches compatible with each other?

d.   Due Process and "Private" Administration

> *RENDELL-BAKER v. KOHN*
> *Notes on "State Action"*
> *THOMAS M. COOLEY LAW SCHOOL v.*
>   *AMERICAN BAR ASSOCIATION*
> *Notes on "Common Law Due Process"*

RENDELL-BAKER v. KOHN

Supreme Court of the United States (1982).
457 U.S. 830.

■ CHIEF JUSTICE BURGER delivered the opinion of the Court.

We granted certiorari to decide whether a private school, whose income is derived primarily from public sources and which is regulated by public authorities, acted under color of state law when it discharged certain employees.

I

A

Respondent Kohn is the director of the New Perspectives School, a nonprofit institution located on privately owned property in Brookline, Massachusetts. The school was founded as a private institution and is operated by a board of directors, none of whom are public officials or are chosen by public officials. The school specializes in dealing with students who have experienced difficulty completing public high schools; many have drug, alcohol, or behavioral problems, or other special needs. In recent years, nearly all of the students at the school have been referred to it by the Brookline or Boston School Committees, or by the Drug Rehabilitation Division of the Massachusetts Department of Mental Health. The school issues high school diplomas certified by the Brookline School Committee.

When students are referred to the school by Brookline or Boston under Chapter 766 of the Massachusetts Acts of 1972, the School

Committees in those cities pay for the students' education.[1] The school also receives funds from a number of other state and federal agencies. In recent years, public funds have accounted for at least 90%, and in one year 99%, of respondent school's operating budget. There were approximately 50 students at the school in those years and none paid tuition.[2]

To be eligible for tuition funding under Chapter 766, the school must comply with a variety of regulations, many of which are common to all schools. The State has issued detailed regulations concerning matters ranging from recordkeeping to student-teacher ratios. Concerning personnel policies, the Chapter 766 regulations require the school to maintain written job descriptions and written statements describing personnel standards and procedures, but they impose few specific requirements.

The school is also regulated by Boston and Brookline as a result of its Chapter 766 funding. By its contract with the Boston School Committee, which refers to the school as a "contractor," the school must agree to carry out the individualized plan developed for each student referred to the school by the Committee. The contract specifies that school employees are not city employees.

The school also has a contract with the State Drug Rehabilitation Division. Like the contract with the Boston School Committee, that agreement refers to the school as a "contractor." It provides for reimbursement for services provided for students referred to the school by the Drug Rehabilitation Division, and includes requirements concerning the services to be provided. Except for general requirements, such as an equal employment opportunity requirement, the agreement does not cover personnel policies.

While five of the six petitioners were teachers at the school, petitioner Rendell-Baker was a vocational counselor hired under a grant from the federal Law Enforcement Assistance Administration, whose funds are distributed in Massachusetts through the State Committee on Criminal Justice. As a condition of the grant, the Committee on Criminal Justice must approve the school's initial hiring decisions. The purpose of this requirement is to insure that the school hires vocational counselors who meet the qualifications described in the school's grant proposal to the Committee; the Committee does not interview applicants for counselor positions.

---

[1]   Chapter 766, 1972 Mass. Acts, Mass. Gen. Laws, ch. 71B, § 3 (West Supp.1981), requires school committees to identify students with special needs and to develop suitable educational programs for such students. Massachusetts Gen. Laws, ch. 71B, § 4, provides that school committees may "enter into an agreement with any public or private school, agency, or institution to provide the necessary special education" for these students . . .

[2]   Amicus curiae Massachusetts Association of 766 Approved Private Schools, Inc., of which the New Perspectives School is a member, informs the Court that many of its members have a student population which is more or less evenly divided between students referred and paid for by the State and students referred and paid for by their parents or guardians.

B

[The Petitioners were all discharged following disputes they had with Director Kohn. Rendell-Baker's dispute concerned the proper role of a student-staff council in making hiring decisions. The other five had, in a separate matter, written a letter to the school's board of directors recommending Kohn's dismissal and had also taken their grievances to the local newspaper. All were discharged by Kohn without her, or anyone else's, having held a hearing. In separate lawsuits Rendell-Baker and the other five sought relief under 42 U.S.C. § 1983 for alleged violations of the First, Fifth, and Fourteenth Amendments.]

C

On April 16, 1980, the District Court for the District of Massachusetts, 488 F.Supp. 764, granted the defendant's motion for summary judgment in the suit brought by Rendell-Baker. A claim may be brought under § 1983 only if the defendant acted "under color" of state law.[4] . . . [T]he District Court concluded that the nexus between the school and the State was not sufficiently close so that the action of the school in discharging Rendell-Baker could be considered action of the Commonwealth of Massachusetts.

Nine days earlier, on April 7, 1980, a different judge of the District Court for the District of Massachusetts had reached a contrary conclusion on the same question in the case brought by the other five petitioners. . . . Accordingly, it held that the defendants acted under color of state law and denied the motion to dismiss. However, on June 13, 1980, noting that there was substantial ground for disagreement on that holding, the District Court certified its order as immediately appealable pursuant to 28 U.S.C. § 1292(b).

D

The Court of Appeals for the First Circuit consolidated the two actions. It noted that the school's funding, regulation, and function show that it has a close relationship with the State. However, it stressed that the school is managed by a private board and that the State has relatively little involvement in personnel matters. It concluded that the school, although regulated by the State, was not dominated by the State, especially with respect to decisions involving the discharge of personnel. The Court of Appeals then concluded that the District Court which certified the question in the action brought by the five teachers had erred in concluding that the defendants acted under color of state law. . . .

We granted certiorari, and we affirm.

---

[4]   Title 42 U.S.C. § 1983 provides:

"Every person who, under color of any statute, ordinance, regulation, custom, or usage, of any State or Territory, subjects, or causes to be subjected, any citizen of the United States or other person within the jurisdiction thereof to the deprivation of any rights, privileges, or immunities secured by the Constitution and laws, shall be liable to the party injured in an action at law, suit in equity, or other proper proceeding for redress."

II

A

Petitioners do not claim that their discharges were discriminatory in violation of Title VII of the Civil Rights Act of 1964. Nor do they claim that their discharges were unfair labor practices in violation of the National Labor Relations Act. Rather, they allege that respondents violated 42 U.S.C. § 1983 by discharging them because of their exercise of their First Amendment right of free speech and without the process due them under the Fourteenth Amendment. . . . The ultimate issue in determining whether a person is subject to suit under § 1983 is the same question posed in cases arising under the Fourteenth Amendment: is the alleged infringement of federal rights "fairly attributable to the State?" Lugar v. Edmondson Oil Co., 457 U.S. 922, 937 (1982). The core issue presented in this case is not whether petitioners were discharged because of their speech or without adequate procedural protections, but whether the school's action in discharging them can fairly be seen as state action. If the action of the respondent school is not state action, our inquiry ends.

B

In Blum v. Yaretsky, 457 U.S. 991 (1982), the Court analyzed the state action requirement of the Fourteenth Amendment. The Court considered whether certain nursing homes were state actors for the purpose of determining whether decisions regarding transfers of patients could be fairly attributed to the State, and hence be subjected to Fourteenth Amendment due process requirements. The challenged transfers primarily involved decisions, made by physicians and nursing home administrators, to move patients from "skilled nursing facilities" to less expensive "health related facilities." Like the New Perspectives School, the nursing homes were privately owned and operated. Relying on [several cases] the Court held that, "a State normally can be held responsible for a private decision only when it has exercised coercive power or has provided such significant encouragement, either overt or covert, that the choice must in law be deemed to be that of the State." In determining that the transfer decisions were not actions of the State, the Court considered each of the factors alleged by petitioners here to make the discharge decisions of the New Perspectives School fairly attributable to the State.

First, the nursing homes, like the school, depended on the State for funds; the State subsidized the operating and capital costs of the nursing homes, and paid the medical expenses of more than 90% of the patients. Here the Court of Appeals concluded that the fact that virtually all of the school's income was derived from government funding was the strongest factor to support a claim of state action. But in Blum v. Yaretsky, we held that the similar dependence of the nursing homes did not make the acts of the physicians and nursing home administrators acts of the State, and we conclude that the school's receipt of public funds does not make the discharge decisions acts of the State.

The school, like the nursing homes, is not fundamentally different from many private corporations whose business depends primarily on contracts to build roads, bridges, dams, ships, or submarines for the government. Acts of such private contractors do not become acts of the government by reason of their significant or even total engagement in performing public contracts.

The school is also analogous to the public defender found not to be a state actor in Polk County v. Dodson, 454 U.S. 312 (1981). There we concluded that, although the State paid the public defender, her relationship with her client was "identical to that existing between any other lawyer and client." Id., at 318. Here the relationship between the school and its teachers and counselors is not changed because the State pays the tuition of the students.

A second factor considered in Blum v. Yaretsky was the extensive regulation of the nursing homes by the State. There the State was indirectly involved in the transfer decisions challenged in that case because a primary goal of the State in regulating nursing homes was to keep costs down by transferring patients from intensive treatment centers to less expensive facilities when possible. Both state and federal regulations encouraged the nursing homes to transfer patients to less expensive facilities when appropriate. The nursing homes were extensively regulated in many other ways as well. The Court relied on Jackson v. Metropolitan Edison Co., 419 U.S. 345 (1974) where we held that state regulation, even if "extensive and detailed," 419 U.S., at 350, did not make a utility's actions state action.

Here the decisions to discharge the petitioners were not compelled or even influenced by any state regulation. Indeed, in contrast to the extensive regulation of the school generally, the various regulators showed relatively little interest in the school's personnel matters. The most intrusive personnel regulation promulgated by the various government agencies was the requirement that the Committee on Criminal Justice had the power to approve persons hired as vocational counselors. Such a regulation is not sufficient to make a decision to discharge, made by private management, state action.

The third factor asserted to show that the school is a state actor is that it performs a "public function." However, our holdings have made clear that the relevant question is not simply whether a private group is serving a "public function." We have held that the question is whether the function performed has been "traditionally the *exclusive* prerogative of the State." Jackson, supra, at 353; quoted in Blum v. Yaretsky, 457 U.S., at 1011 (emphasis added). There can be no doubt that the education of maladjusted high school students is a public function, but that is only the beginning of the inquiry. Chapter 766 of the Massachusetts Acts of 1972 demonstrates that the State intends to provide services for such students at public expense. That legislative policy choice in no way makes these services the exclusive province of the State. Indeed, the Court of

Appeals noted that until recently the State had not undertaken to provide education for students who could not be served by traditional public schools. That a private entity performs a function which serves the public does not make its acts state action.

Fourth, petitioners argue that there is a "symbiotic relationship" between the school and the State similar to the relationship involved in Burton v. Wilmington Parking Authority, 365 U.S. 715 (1961). Such a claim is rejected in Blum v. Yaretsky, and we reject it here. In Burton, the Court held that the refusal of a restaurant located in a public parking garage to serve Negroes constituted state action. The Court stressed that the restaurant was located on public property and that the rent from the restaurant contributed to the support of the garage. In response to the argument that the restaurant's profits, and hence the State's financial position, would suffer if it did not discriminate, the Court concluded that this showed that the State profited from the restaurant's discriminatory conduct. The Court viewed this as support for the conclusion that the State should be charged with the discriminatory actions. Here the school's fiscal relationship with the State is not different from that of many contractors performing services for the government. No symbiotic relationship such as existed in Burton exists here.

C

We hold that petitioners have not stated a claim for relief under 42 U.S.C. § 1983; accordingly, the judgment of the Court of Appeals for the First Circuit is

Affirmed.

■ JUSTICE WHITE, concurring in the judgments.

[Opinion omitted]

■ JUSTICE MARSHALL, with whom JUSTICE BRENNAN joins, dissenting.

Petitioners in these consolidated cases, former teachers and a counselor at the New Perspectives School in Brookline, Mass., were discharged by the school's administrators when they criticized certain school policies. They commenced actions under 42 U.S.C. § 1983, claiming that they had been discharged in violation of the First, Fifth, and Fourteenth Amendments. The Court today holds that their suits must be dismissed because the school did not act "under color" of state law. According to the majority, the decision of the school to discharge petitioners cannot fairly be regarded as a decision of the Commonwealth of Massachusetts.

In my view, this holding simply cannot be justified. The State has delegated to the New Perspectives School its statutory duty to educate children with special needs. The school receives almost all of its funds from the State, and is heavily regulated. This nexus between the school and the State is so substantial that the school's action must be considered state action. I therefore dissent. . . .

The decisions of this Court clearly establish that where there is a symbiotic relationship between the State and a privately owned enterprise, so that the State and a privately owned enterprise are participants in a joint venture, the actions of the private enterprise may be attributable to the State. "Conduct that is formally 'private' may become so entwined with governmental policies or so impregnated with a governmental character" that it can be regarded as governmental action. Evans v. Newton, 382 U.S. 296 (1966). The question whether such a relationship exists "can be determined only in the framework of the peculiar facts or circumstances present." Burton v. Wilmington Parking Authority, 365 U.S. 715, 726 (1961). Here, an examination of the facts and circumstances leads inexorably to the conclusion that the actions of the New Perspectives School should be attributed to the State; it is difficult to imagine a closer relationship between a government and a private enterprise.

The New Perspectives School receives virtually all of its funds from state sources. This financial dependence on the State is an important indicium of governmental involvement. The school's very survival depends on the State. If the State chooses, it may exercise complete control over the school's operations simply by threatening to withdraw financial support if the school takes action that it considers objectionable.

The school is heavily regulated and closely supervised by the State. This fact provides further support for the conclusion that its actions should be attributed to the State. The school's freedom of decisionmaking is substantially circumscribed by the Massachusetts Department of Education's guidelines and the various contracts with state agencies. For example, the school is required to develop and comply with written rules for hiring and dismissal of personnel. Almost every decision the school makes is substantially affected in some way by the State's regulations.[1]
. . .

The school's provision of a substitute for public education deserves particular emphasis because of the role of Chapter 766. Under this statute, the State is *required* to provide a free education to all children, including those with special needs. Clearly, if the State had decided to provide the service itself, its conduct would be measured against constitutional standards. The State should not be permitted to avoid constitutional requirements simply by delegating its statutory duty to a private entity.[3] In my view, such a delegation does not convert the

---

[1]   The majority argues that the fact that the school receives almost all of its funds from the state is not enough, by itself, to justify a finding of state action. It also contends that the fact that the school is closely supervised and heavily regulated is not enough, by itself, to justify such a finding. I am in general agreement with both propositions. However, when these two factors are present in the same case, and when other indicia of state action are also present, a finding of state action may very well be justified. By analyzing the various indicia of state action separately, without considering their cumulative impact, the majority commits a fundamental error.

[3]   A State may not deliberately delegate a task to a private entity in order to avoid its constitutional obligations. Terry v. Adams, 345 U.S. 461 (1953). But a State's decision to

performance of the duty from public to private action when the duty is specific and the private institution's decisionmaking authority is significantly curtailed.

When an entity is not only heavily regulated and funded by the State, but also provides a service that the State is required to provide, there is a very close nexus with the State. Under these circumstances, it is entirely appropriate to treat the entity as an arm of the State. Here, since the New Perspectives School exists solely to fulfill the State's obligations under Chapter 766, I think it fully reasonable to conclude that the school is a state actor. . . .

NOTES ON "STATE ACTION"

(1)   *Where Is the "State Action" Line?* Compare BRENTWOOD ACADEMY V. TENNESSEE SECONDARY SCHOOL ATHLETIC ASS'N, 531 U.S. 288 (2001): The Athletic Association found Brentwood Academy, a private parochial high school, to have committed recruiting violations. It placed Brentwood's athletic program on probation for four years, declared its football and boys' basketball teams ineligible to compete in playoffs for two years, and imposed a $3,000 fine. Brentwood sued under § 1983, alleging, among other things, due process violations. Held: the suit could proceed because, even though the Association was a separately incorporated membership organization, its "regulatory activity may and should be treated as state action." Id. at 291. SOUTER, J., for the Court:

"The nominally private character of the Association is overborne by the pervasive entwinement of public institutions and public officials in its composition and workings, and there is no substantial reason to claim unfairness in applying constitutional standards to it.

"The Association is not an organization of natural persons acting on their own, but of schools, and of public schools to the extent of 84% of the total. Under the Association's bylaws, each member school is represented by its principal or a faculty member, who has a vote in selecting members of the governing legislative council and board of control from eligible principals, assistant principals, and superintendents.

"Although the findings and prior opinions in this case include no express conclusion of law that public school officials act within the scope of their duties when they represent their institutions, no other view would be rational, the official nature of their involvement being shown in any number of ways. Interscholastic athletics obviously play an integral part in the public education of Tennessee, where nearly every public high school spends money on competitions among schools. Since a pickup system of interscholastic games would not do, these public teams need some mechanism to produce rules and regulate competition. The mechanism is an organization overwhelmingly   composed   of   public   school   officials   who   select

---

delegate a duty to a private entity should be carefully examined even when it has acted, not in bad faith, but for reasons of convenience. The doctrinal basis for the state action requirement is that exercises of state authority pose a special threat to constitutional values. A private entity vested with state authority poses that threat just as clearly as a state agency.

representatives (all of them public officials at the time in question here), who in turn adopt and enforce the rules that make the system work. Thus, by giving these jobs to the Association, the 290 public schools of Tennessee belonging to it can sensibly be seen as exercising their own authority to meet their own responsibilities. Unsurprisingly, then, the record indicates that half the council or board meetings documented here were held during official school hours, and that public schools have largely provided for the Association's financial support. A small portion of the Association's revenue comes from membership dues paid by the schools, and the principal part from gate receipts at tournaments among the member schools. Unlike mere public buyers of contract services, whose payments for services rendered do not convert the service providers into public actors, see Rendell-Baker, 457 U.S., at 839–843, the schools here obtain membership in the service organization and give up sources of their own income to their collective association. The Association thus exercises the authority of the predominantly public schools to charge for admission to their games; the Association does not receive this money from the schools, but enjoys the schools' moneymaking capacity as its own.

"In sum, to the extent of 84% of its membership, the Association is an organization of public schools represented by their officials acting in their official capacity to provide an integral element of secondary public schooling. There would be no recognizable Association, legal or tangible, without the public school officials, who do not merely control but overwhelmingly perform all but the purely ministerial acts by which the Association exists and functions in practical terms. Only the 16% minority of private school memberships prevents this entwinement of the Association and the public school system from being total and their identities totally indistinguishable." 531 U.S. at 298–300.

In contrast, JUSTICE THOMAS for four dissenting Justices:

". . . [C]ommon sense dictates that the TSSAA's actions cannot fairly be attributed to the State, and thus cannot constitute state action. The TSSAA was formed in 1925 as a private corporation to organize interscholastic athletics and to sponsor tournaments among its member schools. Any private or public secondary school may join the TSSAA by signing a contract agreeing to comply with its rules and decisions. Although public schools currently compose 84% of the TSSAA's membership, the TSSAA does not require that public schools constitute a set percentage of its membership, and, indeed, no public school need join the TSSAA. The TSSAA's rules are enforced not by a state agency but by its own board of control, which comprises high school principals, assistant principals, and superintendents, none of whom must work at a public school. Of course, at the time the recruiting rule was enforced in this case, all of the board members happened to be public school officials. However, each board member acts in a representative capacity on behalf of all the private and public schools in his region of Tennessee, and not simply his individual school.

"The State of Tennessee did not create the TSSAA. The State does not fund the TSSAA and does not pay its employees. In fact, only 4% of the TSSAA's revenue comes from the dues paid by member schools; the bulk of its operating budget is derived from gate receipts at tournaments it sponsors. The State does not permit the TSSAA to use state-owned facilities for a discounted fee, and it does not exempt the TSSAA from state taxation. No Tennessee law authorizes the State to coordinate interscholastic athletics or empowers another entity to organize interscholastic athletics on behalf of the State. The only state pronouncement acknowledging the TSSAA's existence is a rule providing that the State Board of Education permits public schools to maintain membership in the TSSAA if they so choose.

"Moreover, the State of Tennessee has never had any involvement in the particular action taken by the TSSAA in this case: the enforcement of the TSSAA's recruiting rule prohibiting members from using 'undue influence' on students or their parents or guardians 'to secure or to retain a student for athletic purposes.' App. 115. There is no indication that the State has ever had any interest in how schools choose to regulate recruiting. In fact, the TSSAA's authority to enforce its recruiting rule arises solely from the voluntary membership contract that each member school signs, agreeing to conduct its athletics in accordance with the rules and decisions of the TSSAA." 531 U.S. at 306–08.

(2) ***The Phenomenon of Privatization*** Governments have always relied on private parties; it is hard to imagine a government that itself would make all of its military equipment or build and furnish every one of its buildings. But alongside the growth of governmental responsibilities in the modern world there has also been a growing reliance on private parties to carry out some of these responsibilities: when the U.S. army operates in Iraq and Afghanistan, so too do many contractors brought there on government contracts, and in many states various prisoners are now housed in prisons run by corporations. To say that every private party doing something for the government is thereby made subject to the Due Process Clause would be too broad; to say that no nominally private party is subject to the strictures of the Constitution would be too narrow. Hence the Justices' problem. Moreover, the problem arises not only with respect to the due process clause but also, and historically more importantly, with respect to the equal protection clause. Hence the Justices' further headache. As both the Rendell-Baker principal case and the Brentwood Academy note case suggest, the resulting opinions are often fact-intensive and the outcomes often hotly contested. To again quote Justice Souter in Brentwood Academy, 531 U.S. at 295:

> Our cases try to plot a line between state action subject to Fourteenth Amendment scrutiny and private conduct (however exceptionable) that is not. The judicial obligation is not only to " 'preserv[e] an area of individual freedom by limiting the reach of federal law' and avoi[d] the imposition of responsibility on a State for conduct it could not control," but also to assure that constitutional standards are invoked "when it can be said that the State is *responsible* for the specific conduct of which the plaintiff complains." If the Fourteenth Amendment is not to be displaced, therefore, its ambit cannot be a simple line between States and people operating outside formally governmental organizations, and

the deed of an ostensibly private organization or individual is to be treated sometimes as if a State had caused it to be performed. Thus, we say that state action may be found if, though only if, there is such a "close nexus between the State and the challenged action" that seemingly private behavior "may be fairly treated as that of the State itself."

What is fairly attributable is a matter of normative judgment, and the criteria lack rigid simplicity.

(3) ***The Broader Context of "Privatization."*** Taken as a matter of administrative law, the issue is not merely that constitutional requirements of due process are limited to "state action"; statutory requirements are limited, too. The subject of the APA, for example, is "agency action," where "agency" is defined as "each authority of the Government of the United States." FOIA is similarly constrained. Are there ways to address the concerns of administrative law—such as participation, the control of discretion, and even-handedness—even when tasks are "privatized"?

One alternative is to privatize only in those situations whose institutional features favor retaining effective public control. JOHN D. DONAHUE, THE TRANSFORMATION OF GOVERNMENT WORK in eds. Jody Freeman and Martha Minow, Government by Contract 41, 44–45 (2009): "[There are] three characteristics whose presence makes a task appropriate for delegation and whose absence renders privatization hazardous: specificity, ease of evaluation, and competition.

"Specificity. You can only delegate what you can define. Splitting off a function requires specifying it in sufficient detail to solicit bids, select a provider, and structure a meaningful contract. . . . It is hard to write a sturdy contract for the performance of tasks that are entangled with other functions and subject to continual revision. . . . as circumstances change. . . .

"Ease of Evaluation. To outsource a function you not only need to be able to say what you want (specificity), but you also need to be in a position to know what you've gotten—clearly enough and early enough to take corrective action if what's delivered isn't what was promised. Otherwise, there can be no assurance that government is equipped to perform, as it must, as the agent of the people in ensuring that public value is produced in exchange for public resources. The easier it is to monitor performance and assess the quality of the work, the more safely can a task be delegated. . . .

"Competition. Private providers tend to outscore government on productive efficiency not because there is something magic about the private sector, but because competition eliminates, or at least narrows, the opportunities to survive without being efficient. . . . The whole point of privatization is to harness for the government the salutary effects of competition. Contracting out can transplant into public undertakings some of the intensive accountability that characterizes the private sector."

But as Professor Donahue himself argues, the actual pattern of privatization in recent years has not matched these criteria. Some very sophisticated, complex, hard to evaluate and unique tasks—such as a large part of the management of the space shuttle program—have been contracted out to private companies, as have highly judgmental decisions that control access to various government-paid-for benefits, such as nursing home care.

(4) It is sometimes said that part of the reason for governments' contracting with outside parties for services they could themselves provide is to avoid the very strictures on governmental action provided by the Constitution and laws such as the APA. In context, such a decision might seem obnoxious—or it might seem to represent a quest for efficiency and governmental savings. In a footnote included above, Justice Marshall says, "A State may not deliberately delegate a task to a private entity in order to avoid its constitutional obligations. . . . But a State's decision to delegate a duty to a private entity should be carefully examined even when it has acted, not in bad faith, but for reasons of convenience." Do you agree? Or once bad faith is put to one side, should the political branches have free rein to decide what "convenience" requires?

(5) Or should we develop a more aggressive due process doctrine to use when government privatizes? GILLIAN E. METZGER, PRIVATE DELEGATIONS, DUE PROCESS, AND THE DUTY TO SUPERVISE in eds. Jody Freeman and Martha Minow, Government by Contract 291, 307–08 (2009): "In short, significant gaps exist in the extent to which tweaking current due process rules can address the concerns with self-interested abuse of power as well as the lack of accountability and transparency in privatized governance. Instead, a more fundamental revision of current doctrine is needed. One change that appears particularly warranted is the development of a due process-based duty to supervise, under which the government must actively oversee decision making by its private delegates, at least when that decision making directly affects third parties. Imposing such a duty to supervise offers a means of checking the potential for arbitrary action and abuse of power that privatization presents, without unduly limiting private flexibility in specific cases. . . . Stated in private delegation terms, the justification for a duty to supervise is that only government supervision can ensure against self-interested decision making and ensure that due process demands of regularity and fairness are met in contexts of privatized governance. Government supervision is also essential to ensure that public officials remain ultimately responsible for exercise of government power.

"... Public administration and public contracts scholars are strikingly united on the importance of government management of its private contractors if privatization is to succeed as a tool of modern governance. . . . The focus of this scholarship is management and policy-based, but the same conclusion results: increasing privatization demands greater recognition of government's oversight and supervision responsibilities. One advantage of developing a due process-based duty to supervise is that doing so adds the force of constitutional law to those efforts at managerial reform, with the potential for constitutional invalidation giving both the government and its private contractors an incentive to ensure adequate oversight."

(6) There are a large number of federally created entities that in one way or another straddle a conceptual line between "public" and "private"—for instance, the U.S. Postal Service and Amtrak. Because of this straddle, they raise problems for a large number of legal doctrines—ranging from whether

they are "agencies" for purposes of the APA, to whether they violate the constitutional law doctrine against delegation of public power to private entities, to, as here discussed, whether they are subject to due process constraints. The applicable law is still being worked out, and there is no reason to expect the answer for one doctrine to mirror the answer for another. For discussion, see Anne Joseph O'Connell, Bureaucracy at the Boundary, 162 U. Pa. L. Rev. 841 (2014).

(7) If, as the Rendell-Baker Court says, the ultimate issue under current doctrine is whether the private entity's action is "fairly attributable to the State," and if, as the Brentwood Academy Court says, that attribution is more likely to be made when there is "entwinement" of governmental with non-governmental actors, doesn't that create an incentive for government, when it outsources one of its needs or functions, to keep its hands off of the private entity involved? If we want government to be present, through regulation, supervision, or contract, in order to represent various public values that the marketplace might otherwise submerge, is that incentive perverse?

THOMAS M. COOLEY LAW SCHOOL v. AMERICAN BAR ASSOCIATION

United States Court of Appeals for the Sixth Circuit (2006).
459 F.3d 705.

■ GIBBONS, CIRCUIT JUDGE.

This case arises from a dispute between the American Bar Association, the national accrediting body for law schools and its Consultant on Legal Education John Sebert (collectively "ABA"), and the Thomas M. Cooley Law School ("Cooley" or "the school"), an accredited law school located in Lansing, Michigan. The dispute centers on Cooley's attempts to begin two satellite programs—one at Oakland University in Rochester ("Oakland campus") and one in Grand Rapids ("Grand Rapids campus"). Cooley claims that the ABA denied Cooley due process in failing to accredit the two proposed satellites and in imposing sanctions on Cooley for operating the satellites without ABA prior acquiescence. The district court denied these claims and granted judgment to the defendants. As we find that the ABA afforded Cooley all due process in making its rulings, we affirm.

I.

The federal government does not directly accredit institutions of higher education. Rather, the Secretary of Education approves accrediting agencies for different types of educational programs, and these accrediting bodies set independent standards for accreditation. Accreditation is important to a school for a number of reasons, not the least of which is that it allows the students of the school to receive federally-backed financial aid. In addition, the majority of states use ABA accreditation to determine whether an individual applying for admission to the Bar has satisfied the state's legal education requirement.

The ABA's Council on the Section of Legal Education ("Council") is the organization charged with accrediting law schools. The Council makes its decisions following a review and recommendation by the ABA's Accreditation Committee ("Committee"). The process is governed by written Standards, Rules, and Interpretations that are adopted after both public review and comment and review by the ABA House of Delegates ("House"). The Standards describe the requirements that a law school must meet to obtain and retain ABA approval. Standard 105 states: "Before a law school makes a major change in its program of legal education or organizational structure it shall obtain the acquiescence of the Council for the change." The opening of an additional campus falls under Standard 105. Under ABA rules, a school may offer up to 20% of its legal program at a separate campus without this being a "major change" requiring prior approval. If a school offers more than 20% of its program, however, this does constitute a major change and the ABA must grant acquiescence.

[In 2002, Cooley applied to the ABA for approval of two satellite campuses. While the ABA was considering the application, it opened one of the sites but operated it below the 20% threshold. The Accreditation Committee determined that the proposal fell short in several ways; the Council adopted the Committee's recommendation and denied Cooley's application. At the same time, Cooley, relying on a doubtful reading of an ABA Rule that it claimed gave it authority to run more completely the satellite campuses so that the ABA could make an onsite evaluation of its proposal, increased its program at both campuses above the 20% level. The ABA rejected Cooley's reading of the rule and warned Cooley that it was in violation of Rule 105's requirement of prior approval for a major change. Cooley persisted, and the Accreditation Committee asked Cooley to appear at its next meeting to show cause why it should not be sanctioned.]

On March 30, 2004, Cooley filed the instant lawsuit. After Cooley filed a motion for a preliminary injunction, the parties entered into a Stipulation and Agreed Order, by which Cooley agreed to reduce its offerings at Oakland and Grand Rapids to comply with the 20% limit on non-approved programs. Cooley further agreed not to expand the programs without ABA approval. The ABA agreed to move the show-cause hearing to June. Both parties complied with the Order.

At the June 2004 show-cause hearing, Cooley argued that the ABA did not have the authority to impose sanctions under its own rules, because the school had reduced its program offerings and was now "in compliance" with all ABA rules. The Committee disagreed and recommended sanctions. The Council adopted the Committee's recommendation, censuring Cooley for its "substantial and persistent noncompliance" with ABA standards and directives and ruling that the school would be ineligible to operate branch or satellite campuses until July 31, 2006. The Council also declined to address the merits of Cooley's branch applications, noting its doubts about the school's ability to maintain a sound legal educational program and stating that any decision regarding opening a satellite campus in 2006 would have to be made with more current information. The Council informed Cooley that it could file a new application for a satellite or branch campus in the summer or fall of 2005.

Following this decision, Cooley filed an amended complaint, again challenging the ABA's refusal to acquiesce in its satellite programs and adding claims relating to the imposition of sanctions. Specifically, Cooley claimed that the ABA denied its common law right to due process and requested judicial review of the ABA's decision. Cooley also brought claims under the Higher Education Act ("HEA"), 20 U.S.C. § 1099b, and under state law. The district court dismissed the HEA claim and state law claims for failure to state a claim, Fed.R.Civ.P. 12(b)(6), and granted summary judgment on the common law due process claim. Cooley filed a timely appeal.

II.

Only the common law claims are properly before this court. . .

III.

We thus turn to the only remaining issue—Cooley's claim that the ABA's rejection of its proposals and imposition of sanctions violated the school's common law right to due process. The district court granted summary judgment to the ABA, and we review this ruling *de novo*.

A.

Many courts, including this one, recognize that "quasi-public" professional organizations and accrediting agencies such as the ABA have a common law duty to employ fair procedures when making decisions affecting their members. See Foundation for Interior Design Education Research v. Savannah Coll. of Art & Design, 244 F.3d 521, 527–28 (6th Cir. 2001); Chicago School of Automatic Transmissions, Inc. v. Accreditation Alliance of Career Schools and Colleges, 44 F.3d 447, 450 (7th Cir. 1994); Wilfred Acad. of Hair & Beauty Culture v. Southern Ass'n of Colls. & Schools, 957 F.2d 210, 214 (5th Cir. 1992); Medical Inst. of Minnesota v. National Ass'n of Trade & Technical Schools, 817 F.2d 1310, 1314 (8th Cir. 1987). Courts developed the right to common law due process as a check on organizations that exercise significant authority in areas of public concern such as accreditation and professional licensing. See Majorie Webster Junior Coll., Inc. v. Middle States Ass'n of Colls. & Secondary Sch., Inc., 432 F.2d 650, 655–56 (D.C. Cir. 1970); Falcone v. Middlesex County Medical Soc., 34 N.J. 582, 170 A.2d 791, 799 (1961). The ABA is such an organization, and we must therefore determine whether the ABA afforded Cooley adequate process in denying the applications for satellite programs and imposing sanctions.

To answer this question, we look to federal law. Although this court in Foundation applied state law to resolve a similar dispute, the agency in that case was not at that time approved by the Secretary of Education and thus was not subject to the HEA. Federal courts have exclusive jurisdiction over any action brought by a school challenging an accreditation decision made by an organization approved by the Secretary (such as the ABA). 20 U.S.C. § 1099b(f). This grant of exclusive federal jurisdiction necessarily implies that federal law should govern disputes relating to decisions made by those bodies. It would make little sense for state law to govern claims that could not be heard in any state court. "It is hard enough to be a ventriloquist's dummy in diversity suits under *Erie;* it is all but impossible to see how federal courts could apply state law to the actions of accrediting agencies when state courts have been silenced by the provision for exclusive jurisdiction." Chicago School, 44 F.3d at 449. If a grant of federal jurisdiction can justify the creation of federal common law, see, e.g., Textile Workers v. Lincoln Mills, 353 U.S. 448, 456–57 (1957), a grant of exclusive jurisdiction necessarily implies the application of federal law.

We must next determine under what principles of federal law we review a decision by an accrediting agency. Both Cooley and the ABA argue that the Administrative Procedure Act ("Act"), 5 U.S.C. § 701, provides the proper framework for reviewing the accreditation process. If the decision was made directly by the Secretary of Education, the presumption would be to review the case under the principles set forth in the Act. The Secretary, however, has delegated his authority regarding law school accreditation to the ABA, which is not a government authority and thus is not governed by the Act. Despite this delegation, however, the ABA does act on behalf of the Secretary and wields the quasi-governmental power of deciding which law schools are eligible for federal funds. Thus, while the Act does not specifically apply to the ABA, principles of administrative law are useful in determining the standard by which we review the ABA's decisionmaking process.

A number of courts have used these principles in fashioning a standard of review. Though some of the cases applied state law, see Foundation, 244 F.3d at 527, and others have left the choice-of-law question unanswered, see Wilfred Acad., 957 F.2d at 214; Medical Institute of Minnesota, 817 F.2d at 1314–15, courts have uniformly looked to administrative law in reviewing accreditation decisions. We agree and apply the standard of review that has developed in the common law. This court reviews only whether the decision of an accrediting agency such as the ABA is arbitrary and unreasonable or an abuse of discretion and whether the decision is based on substantial evidence.

This standard of review resembles the review applied under the Act. See 5 U.S.C. § 706(2)(A) ("arbitrary, capricious, an abuse of discretion, or otherwise not in accordance with the law"). We emphasize, however, that while principles of federal administrative law provide guidance in our analysis, judicial review of accreditation decisions is more limited than review under the Act. Although accrediting agencies perform a quasi-governmental function, they are still private organizations. Courts have made the policy decision to ensure that these organizations act in the public interest and do not abuse their power, but judicial review is limited to protecting the public interest. Recognizing that "the standards of accreditation are not guides for the layman but for professionals in the field of education," Wilfred Acad., 957 F.2d at 214, great deference should be afforded the substantive rules of these bodies and courts should focus on whether an accrediting agency such as the ABA followed a fair procedure in reaching its conclusions. We are not free to conduct a *de novo* review or substitute our judgment for that of the ABA or its Council. Rather, in analyzing whether the ABA abused its discretion or reached a decision that was arbitrary or unreasonable, we focus on whether the agency "conform[ed] its actions to fundamental principles of fairness." Medical Institute of Minnesota, 817 F.2d at 1314.

B.

Cooley argues that the ABA abused its discretion in refusing to consider the merits of its satellite application at the 2004 hearing and in imposing sanctions in violation of the ABA's own rules. Cooley also alleges that a number of due process violations occurred during the three rounds of hearings in 2002–2004.

1.   Imposition of Sanctions

Cooley makes two arguments regarding the ABA's decision to impose sanctions that prevented Cooley from operating a satellite or branch campus until July 31, 2006. First, Cooley argues that the ABA abused its discretion by sanctioning the school in violation of its own rules. Second, Cooley alleges that the sanction was arbitrary and unreasonable and violated due process. An abuse of discretion can only be found if no evidence supports the decision or if the agency misapplied the law. National Engineering & Contracting Co. v. OSHA, 928 F.2d 762, 768 (6th Cir. 1991).

Cooley argues that the plain language of ABA Rule 13, which outlines hearings on show-cause orders, prohibited the Council from imposing sanctions because, at the time of the hearing, Cooley was in compliance with all ABA governing standards. Rule 13 states in relevant part:

(b) Representatives of the law school, including legal counsel, may appear at the hearing and submit information to demonstrate that the school is currently in compliance with all the Standards or to present a reliable plan for bringing the school into compliance with all of the Standards within a reasonable time.

(d) After the hearing, the Committee shall determine whether the law school is in compliance with the Standards and, if not, it shall direct the law school to take remedial action or shall impose sanctions as appropriate.

(1) . . .

(2) If matters of noncompliance are substantial or have been persistent, then the Committee may recommend to the Council that the school be subjected to sanctions other than removal from the list of approved law schools regardless of whether the school has presented a reliable plan for bringing the school into compliance.

(3) . . .

(e) If the Committee determines that the law school is in compliance, it shall conclude the matter by adopting an appropriate resolution. . . .

Cooley reads these subsections as stating that the purpose of the show cause hearing is not to determine whether the school has previously violated ABA rules, but rather to determine whether the school "is currently in compliance" with the Standards. Regardless of its previous actions, Cooley argues it had reduced its course offerings below the 20% level at the time of the show-cause hearing; thus, it was "currently in compliance" and the ABA should have "conclude[d] the matter." By not doing so, Cooley contends, the ABA failed to follow the plain language of its own rules, and thus, the decision is not entitled to deference.

We agree with the ABA that Rule 13 cannot be given such a literal interpretation. . . .

Cooley's interpretation of Rule 13 would also allow schools to come in and out of compliance to avoid sanctions. . . . Cooley's actions demonstrate the danger of its reading of Rule 13, which would render the ABA powerless to sanction such blatant disregard of its rules and standards. This court must defer to an agency's interpretation of its own rules unless plainly erroneous. See A.D. Transport Express, Inc. v. United States, 290 F.3d 761, 766 (6th Cir. 2002). While Cooley's proposed interpretation of Rule 13 is perhaps plausible, the ABA's reading is not clearly erroneous and in fact is more logical. Thus, the ABA's imposition of sanctions despite Cooley's compliance with ABA standards at the time of the hearing does not constitute an abuse of discretion.

Cooley also argues that the sanction itself was arbitrary and unreasonable and violated due process. . . . Even though the sanction may have had significant impact on Cooley, it cannot be described as arbitrary and unreasonable, especially given the highly deferential standard of review and the evidence of Cooley's blatant and intentional noncompliance with ABA rules.

2.   *The Acquiescence and Sanctioning Hearings*

Cooley next contends that the district court erred in failing to address its claims that the ABA abused its discretion in denying the satellite applications in 2002 and 2003, before the school's noncompliance. The district court did, however, address these claims, and in any case, they are meritless. Cooley was afforded ample process at each of the ABA hearings—it was notified well in advance, afforded the opportunity to submit evidence to supports its case, and permitted to appear before the body with counsel present. After each group of hearings, the Committee issued a detailed written report outlining its findings and recommendations. The Council in turn wrote a letter outlining its conclusions, referencing the findings of the Committee and the applicable rules and standards.

Cooley's claim that the ABA erred in not using the new interpretations of Standard 105 in the December 2002 and January 2003 evaluations of the school's satellite applications, when those interpretations were not officially adopted until February 2003, is equally baseless . . . The other errors alleged by Cooley—a conflict of interest by one Committee member and the use of an incorrect fact sheet during one of the hearings—do not amount to a due process violation. The supposed conflict of interest arose because one Committee member was the dean of another law school. After considering the matter, the Committee denied the request that the member be replaced, finding no danger of bias and reasoning that Cooley's logic would disqualify almost any member of the Committee. As to the incorrect fact sheet, it was quickly corrected and there is no evidence that the Committee relied on it in reaching its conclusion. As both of these claims of error were duly considered by the ABA and rejected with sufficient reasoning, they do not constitute an abuse of discretion and do not in any way violate Cooley's right to a fair process. . . .

Finally, Cooley raises a number of alleged procedural problems with the sanctions hearing: the denial of its request to cross-examine witnesses, the combined prosecutorial and adjudicative functions, and the possible introduction of ex parte evidence. As the district court correctly noted, these allegations "do not even hint at the existence of prejudicial error" that would be needed to justify relief. In light of the undisputed evidence of substantial and persistent noncompliance, Cooley cannot show that it would not have been sanctioned had these alleged errors not occurred.

IV.

For the foregoing reasons, the decision of the district court is affirmed.

[Concurring opinion omitted.]

NOTES ON "COMMON LAW DUE PROCESS"

(1) **What's Going On?** The court accepts the parties' idea that the Administrative Procedure Act "provides the proper framework for reviewing the accreditation process," cites as authority cases arising out of actions of the Occupational Safety and Health Administration and the Federal Motor Carrier Safety Administration, and (as will be evident to you if you have

already studied Chapter VIII on standards of review) defers to the judgments of the ABA in much the way courts defer to the judgments of governmental agencies. Would this case be any different, in analysis or in outcome, if the ABA had been a governmental agency and its actions had met the "state action" test?

(2)   Does treating the ABA as subject to the requirements of "common law due process" depend on its being recognized by the Department of Education as having the power to accredit schools, which in turn means that the students at those schools can get federally backed financial aid? On ABA accreditation being used by many states as part of the bar admissions process? In a case involving university accreditation, the court elaborated on the connection between accreditation and financial aid:

> The federal government became involved in the accreditation process when the government required institutes of higher education to be accredited in order for the school and its students to qualify for federal financial aid. The predecessor to the Department of Education was first given statutory authority to "recognize" accrediting agencies in the G.I. Bill passed during the Korean War. Congress wanted to assure that federal money was not being spent on "fly by night" educational programs . . . Federal financial aid, however, increased in importance when Congress passed the Higher Education Act of 1965, which established federal financial aid programs beyond students who were veterans of the armed services.

Auburn Univ. v. Southern Ass'n of Coll. and Sch., Inc., 489 F.Supp.2d 1362, 1368 (N.D. Ga. 2002). Given the importance of federal financial aid and the control that accrediting agencies have over the distribution of this money, can you justify the imposition of common law due process in these contexts as a sort of half-step to constitutional due process based on a near miss of the state action requirement? If you can, how much public financial influence must exist before common law due process applies? Why is this any more compelling than the situation in Rendell-Baker, where public funds accounted for more than 90 percent of the school's budget?

(3)   *How Far Does It Go?* In one of the cases cited by the Cooley court, Falcone v. Middlesex County Medical Society, 170 A.2d 791 (N.J. 1961), there was not even a tenuous connection between the defendant and governmental action. The Falcone court nonetheless held that a private professional organization in an area of public concern needed to provide applicants common law due process when membership was an "economic necessity." In the Cooley opinion, Judge Gibbons defines her understanding of the relevant domain represented by such cases as "organizations that exercise significant authority in areas of public concern such as accreditation and professional licensing." But some cases seem to have gone even further. E.g., Curran v. Mount Diablo Council of the Boy Scouts of America, 147 Cal.App.3d 712, 195 Cal.Rptr. 325 (1983), appeal dismissed 468 U.S. 1205 (1984), holding that the alleged expulsion of an Eagle Scout from the Boy Scouts on grounds of his homosexuality, without conducting a hearing on the issue of whether there was likely to be "any significant harm to the association," stated a

claim for "wrongful denial of the common law right of fair procedure"; Brounstein v. American Cat Fanciers Ass'n, 839 F.Supp. 1100 (D.N.J. 1993) (applying New Jersey law), recognizing a cause of action for "wrongful discipline by a private organization" after a cat show judge alleged that she had had her prestigious designation as an "allbreed" judge revoked on account of her religion without procedures that accorded her "fundamental fairness." One commentator has suggested that "the actual human interests which suffer from an expulsion . . . in many cases . . . are chiefly interests of personality." Zechariah Chafee, Jr., The Internal Affairs of Associations Not for Profit, 43 Harv. L. Rev. 993, 998 (1930).

(4) At the same time, it seems that the doctrine of "common law due process" (or, as it is sometimes also called, the doctrine of "natural justice") does not apply to every situation in the non-governmental world that parallels a situation to which constitutional "due process" applies in the governmental world. For example, a private business would probably not have to accord the same procedural rights to an employee it fires that Texas would have to accord Sindermann (see p. 553) even if the employee had a contractual claim to further employment; all the private employee would have would be the right to sue for breach of contract. Indeed, it seems the just-preceding case, Rendell-Baker, was litigated and decided on such an assumption. So what is the principle that both informs and limits the doctrine? Could this principle be extended to encompass some of the concerns about "privatization" we saw in the notes after Rendell-Baker?

(5) *A Timely Controversy.* Title IX of the Education Amendments of 1972, 20 U.S.C. § 1681, provides, with some exceptions, that "No person in the United States shall, on the basis of sex, be excluded from participation in, be denied the benefits of, or be subjected to discrimination under any education program or activity receiving Federal financial assistance." Sexual harassment is considered to be a form of discrimination. On April 4, 2011, the Department of Education, Office of Civil Rights [OCR] wrote a letter—addressed "Dear Colleague"—to educational institutions outlining the Department's views of the schools' responsibilities regarding "student-on-student sexual harassment, including sexual violence." Included were stipulations as to the procedures schools had to adopt to handle complaints. "[S]chools," said the letter, "generally conduct investigations and hearings to determine whether sexual harassment or violence occurred." "In order for a school's grievance procedures to be consistent with Title IX standards," the letter continued, "the school must use a preponderance of the evidence standard . . . The 'clear and convincing' standard currently used by some schools, is a higher standard of proof [and] . . . not equitable under Title IX." The letter also said, "OCR strongly discourages schools from allowing the parties personally to question or cross-examine each other during the hearing. Allowing an alleged perpetrator to question an alleged victim directly may be traumatic or intimidating." There were other stipulations as well. The letter also said that "Public and state-supported schools must provide due process to the alleged perpetrator."

Many schools—perhaps because they did not want to jeopardize in any way their federal financial assistance—simply followed the procedures set out in OCR's letter or negotiated similar rules to settle disputes with the Department. Some schools objected, as did some individual students who were the subject of the proceedings envisioned in the letter. One ground of objection was that the letter was not put through the notice-and-comment process; for materials on when "guidance" has to be treated as a "rule," see Ch. IV, Sec. 3b. Another ground was that the requirements the letter stipulated—or the procedures that schools in fact used—did not give the accused a fair shake. Do you think the details mentioned above were consistent with due process? For one court's opinion, see John Doe v. Univ. of Cincinnati, 2017 WL 4228791 (6th Cir. 2017).

The letter was withdrawn by the Department of Education on September 22, 2017, in a new letter that promised to hold "a rulemaking process that responds to public comment."

Whatever answer you gave to the question as to merits of the letter of April 4, 2011, here's a different question: Should the rules used in public schools and colleges be different from those used in private schools and colleges? If you say no—that in practice, schools and colleges of all sorts are fundamentally alike—is it because you think that carrying out OCR's mandates to make sure of receiving federal money makes the action even of otherwise private institutions "state action"? (Jacob Gersen and Jeannie Suk, The Sex Bureaucracy, 104 Cal. L. Rev. 881, 911 (2016), say this is a "plausible argument" that has not yet been accepted in court.) Or is it because, whichever side of the state action line you are on, you think that "due process" of some ilk ought to apply to this situation?

(6) *Due Process Beyond the Law.* Consider PAUL R. VERKUIL, PRIVATIZING DUE PROCESS, 57 Admin. L. Rev. 963, 975 (2005): "The creation of a private due process regime is not limited to national associations like the NCAA. Other prominent private associations and membership groups have undertaken similar activities. Private universities provide a prime example. Unlike public institutions, private universities are outside the reach of state action-based due process requirements. Though these institutions are technically free to limit procedures by private agreement, student and faculty pressures force them into providing basic fair procedures in decisionmaking. Since these institutions serve purposes identical to public ones, it is hard to rationalize relying upon the state action distinction to deny procedures in one case and not the other. As a result, universities have established procedures for disciplinary cases irrespective of their status. The procedural codes at these institutions reveal few differences between them based on the public-private distinction.

"Thus, many private institutions have been forced, by custom, politics, or state law, to behave procedurally as if they were public. Where there is a public analogue, private institutions have less room to maneuver procedurally. They are, like private associations such as the NCAA, held to procedural expectations that reflect due process values, if not requirements. In effect, these institutions are bargaining in the shadow of the law. The shadow can be cast either by the Constitution, by state law requirements, or by social or community pressures from the entities themselves. Decisions on due process therefore depend on a host of legal and social factors of which the 'state action' designation is only one. For many institutions, both private and public, due process has become a matter of bargaining with constituents."

(7) **In The Future?** Due process is a doctrine that stretches back as far as Magna Carta, but as the Cooley Law School case shows, it is still being used to generate legal decency. The quest for due process is one of the great protean forces in the law.

CHAPTER VI

TRANSPARENCY, E-GOVERNANCE, AND THE INFORMATION AGE

> **Sec. 1.** *Introduction*
> **Sec. 2.** *Secret Law*
> **Sec. 3.** *Freedom of Information Legislation*
> **Sec. 4.** *Government in the Sunshine*
> **Sec. 5.** *Internet Disclosure as Regulation*
> **Sec. 6.** *The Promise and Problems of E-Rulemaking*

"Publicity is justly commended as a remedy for social and industrial diseases. Sunlight is said to be the best of disinfectants; electric light the most efficient policeman."[1]

SECTION 1.   INTRODUCTION

> ### *Senate Bill 721: MAR-A-LAGO Act*

Senate Bill 721:   MAR-A-LAGO Act

Introduced in the Senate on March 23, 2017, by Senators Udall, Carper, and Whitehouse

A BILL

To require the disclosure of certain visitor access records.

Section 1.   Short title

This Act may be cited as the "Making Access Records Available to Lead American Government Openness Act" or the "MAR-A-LAGO Act".

Section 2.   Findings

Congress finds the following:

(1) Beginning in 2009, the Obama administration instituted a policy to release the visitor access records for the White House complex.

---

[1]   Louis Brandeis, Other People's Money 62 (1933).

(2) This policy was responsible for making public the names of nearly 6,000,000 visitors to the White House in the 8 years of the Obama administration.

(3) This policy provided the people of the United States with insight into who influences the White House and transparency regarding efforts by lobbyists to effect policies, legislation, and Presidential actions.

(4) To date, the Trump administration has not indicated whether it will continue the policy of publicly releasing White House visitor access records. [Ed. After this bill was introduced, the White House disclosed that it would no longer provide visitor logs, citing "the grave national security risks and privacy concerns of the hundreds of thousands of visitors annually."]

(5) Since taking office on January 20, 2017, President Trump has conducted official business not only in the White House, but also at several of his privately owned clubs and resorts.

(6) President Trump's Mar-a-Lago Club in Palm Beach, Florida, has been dubbed the "Winter White House" and the "Southern White House".

(7) President Trump has spent 5 of his first 9 weekends in office at Mar-a-Lago.

(8) Mar-a-Lago is a private membership facility open to members, their guests, and others who have been invited as guests for special events.

(9) Visitors to Mar-a-Lago do not undergo the same background checks as White House visitors and visitor access records to the club have not been released to the public.

(10) The President has conducted official business and hosted international leaders at Mar-a-Lago.

(11) Media reports have shown President Trump and members of his Cabinet at Mar-a-Lago and nearby Trump International Golf Club interacting with members and guests, providing access unavailable to the general public.

(12) President Trump owns many other properties that offer similar amenities and membership-only access where he is likely to conduct official business during his term in office.

(13) On March 11, 2017, President Trump hosted several members of his Cabinet at his Trump National Golf Club in Potomac Falls, Virginia, to discuss homeland security, health care, and the economy according to media reports.

(14) Media reports have indicated that the President may use his Bedminster, New Jersey, resort as a "Summer White House".

(15) The people of the United States expect and deserve transparency in government. The policy to release visitor access records instituted by the previous administration appropriately balanced transparency with the need for confidentiality in government actions.

(16) To the extent Mar-a-Lago and any other private facilities become locations where the President conducts business and interacts with individuals who are not government officials, the same disclosures should apply.

Section 3. Improving access to influential visitor access records

(a) Definitions

In this section:

(1) Covered location

The term covered location means—

(A) the White House;

(B) the residence of the Vice President; and

(C) any other location at which the President or the Vice President regularly conducts official business.

(2) Covered records

The term covered records means information relating to a visit at a covered location, which shall include—

(A) the name of each visitor at the covered location;

(B) the name of each individual with whom each visitor described in subparagraph (A) met at the covered location; and

(C) the purpose of the visit.

(b) Requirement

Except as provided in subsection (c), not later than 30 days after the date of enactment of this Act, the President shall establish, and update every 90 days, a publicly available database that contains covered records for the preceding 90-day period.

(c) Exceptions

(1) In general

The President shall not include in the database established under subsection (b) any covered record—

(A) the posting of which would implicate personal privacy or law enforcement concerns or threaten national security; or

(B) relating to a purely personal guest at a covered location.

(2) Sensitive meetings

With respect to a particularly sensitive meeting at a covered location, the President shall—

(A) include the number of visitors at the covered location in the database established under subsection (b); and

(B) post the applicable covered records in the database established under subsection (b) when the President determines that release of the covered records is no longer sensitive.

NOTES

(1) *How Much of a Contrast? The Obama Administration and Visitor Logs.* In August 2009, Judicial Watch, Inc. submitted a Freedom of Information Act (FOIA) request to the Secret Service seeking all White House visitor logs from President Obama's inauguration to "the present." The agency refused to provide the records on the grounds that although the Secret Service is subject to FOIA, the requested items (from the Workers and Visitors Entry System) do not qualify as "agency records" under the Act. While the Obama Administration fought the request in district court and in the court of appeals (and won), see p. 679 for a brief discussion of the FOIA issues, it voluntarily provided access to many parts of the logs. The Administration made exceptions for national security, sensitive meetings (e.g., Supreme Court candidates), people visiting the President's daughters, and the President and his wife's personal guests.[2] Staff could simply mark on visitors' clearances to flag the record of their presence for non-disclosure. The last set of disclosures in December 2016 captured visits in September. Visitors from October 2016 to January 2017 were not released. In addition, POLITICO reported that White House staff often met with lobbyists outside the White House complex.[3] According to POLITICO's report, the White House claimed there was not space to hold these meetings on site, but lobbyists believed the offsite locations were chosen to avoid their meetings being disclosed. What sort of disclosures should the White House make about its employees and their meetings, onsite or offsite, if any? Do you support S. 721?

(2) *Presidential Promises and Hedges.* Typically, new Presidents issue directives on government transparency. As of October 2017, President Trump had not done so, despite campaigning to "drain the swamp" of lobbyists and other special interests. (He did issue an executive order establishing an American Technology Council, to "coordinate the vision, strategy, and direction for the Federal Government's use of information technology and the delivery of services through information technology," among other objectives.)[4] At the start of May 2017, in an opinion to the President's Counsel, the Office of Legal Counsel instructed agencies to "accommodate[e] congressional requests for information only when those requests come from a committee, subcommittee, or chairman authorized to conduct oversight."[5] This opinion angered both Democrats and Republicans in Congress.

---

[2] Julie Hirschfeld Davis, White House to Keep Its Visitor Logs Secret, N.Y. Times, April 14, 2017, http://nyti.ms/2pBPaRQ; Peter Baker, White House to Open Visitor Logs to Public, N.Y. Times, Sept. 5, 2009, http://nyti.ms/2quJ8nD.

[3] Chris Frates, W.H. Meets Lobbyists Off Campus, POLITICO, Feb. 24, 2011, http://www.politico.com/story/2011/02/wh-meets-lobbyists-off-campus-050081.

[4] Exec. Order No. 13,794, 82 Fed. Reg. 20,811 (May 3, 2017).

[5] https://www.justice.gov/olc/file/966326/download.

By contrast, President Obama's first directive to agencies, *Transparency and Open Government*,[6] promised that he was "committed to creating an unprecedented level of openness in Government." Nevertheless, the President's directive and subsequent Office of Management and Budget (OMB) memorandum[7] on the topic explicitly noted that there would be restrictions on disclosure, relevant to materials of interest to administrative law. For instance, OMB observed: "With respect to information, the presumption shall be in favor of openness (to the extent permitted by law *and subject to valid privacy, confidentiality, security, or other restrictions*). . ." It went on:

> Nothing in this Directive shall be construed to supersede existing requirements for review and clearance of pre-decisional information by the Director of the Office of Management and Budget relating to legislative, budgetary, administrative, and regulatory materials. Moreover, nothing in this Directive shall be construed to suggest that the presumption of openness precludes the legitimate protection of information whose release would threaten national security, invade personal privacy, breach confidentiality, or damage other genuinely compelling interests.

Do such exceptions significantly undermine the broad promises of openness?

(3) ***Assessing Transparency.*** You will want to assess for yourself how far ostensible commitments to open government have been observed and, indeed, whether any reservations have merit.[8] In addressing the implementation of the Freedom of Information Act, a transparency commitment made as the Information Age was barely dawning, then-Acting Attorney General Robert Bork is reported to have remarked that it presented problems akin to those "of the most difficult constitutional issues. . . . [A]djustment of [its] basic and conflicting values in individual cases, I find at least, a nerve-wracking task."[9] Decades earlier President Harry S. Truman had observed, "The President cannot function without advisers or without advice, written or oral. But just as soon as he is required to show what kind of advice he has had, who said what to him, or what kind of records he has, the advice received will be worthless."[10] The disclosures of hundreds of thousands of properly classified (so far as appears) American documents by the rogue organization WikiLeaks[11] also made clear that the subsequent exposure of this candor can be embarrassing.[12]

---

[6]   https://www.archives.gov/files/cui/documents/2009-WH-memo-on-transparency-and-open-government.pdf.

[7]   https://www.treasury.gov/open/Documents/m10-06.pdf.

[8]   Nongovernmental organizations can assist in this regard. See, e.g., www.openthegovernment.org.

[9]   Robert Saloschin, The FOIA-A Governmental Perspective, 35 Pub. Admin. Rev. 10, 13 (1975).

[10]   II Harry Truman, Memoirs: Years of Trial and Hope 454 (1956).

[11]   http://wikileaks.org.

[12]   For example, one cable confirmed that the government of Yemen was publicly taking responsibility for anti-terrorist actions actually being taken by the United States. Scott Shane and Andrew Lehren, Leaked Cables Offer Raw Look at U.S. Diplomacy, N.Y. Times, Nov. 29, 2010. In addition, ambassadors' cables characterized the heads of two major American allies as

The current Administration's start has not pleased transparency advocates. At the five-month mark, the Washington Post declared in a news article: "More and more in the Trump era, business in Washington is happening behind closed doors. The federal government's leaders are hiding from public scrutiny—and their penchant for secrecy represents a stark departure from the campaign promises of Trump and his fellow Republicans to usher in newfound transparency."[13] By contrast, President Obama's initial directive may suggest that the former Administration was exceptionally open. But the Obama Administration's commitment to transparency had the expectable limits. State secrets were defended. President Obama's White House was reported to be as concerned about "leaks" as its predecessors.[14] The Administration vigorously fought back against some FOIA requests.[15] With regard to regulatory matters, as had its predecessor, Obama's Office of Regulatory and Information Affairs exerted considerable pressure so as not to disclose its work. According to the Washington Post, OIRA "systematically delayed enacting a series of rules on the environment, worker safety and health care to prevent them from becoming points of contention before the 2012 election," by telling agencies not to submit rulemaking proposals and taking longer to do reviews once actions were submitted.[16] In addition, although OIRA posted all 183 *public* comments it received in response to its early inquiry about possible revision of Executive Order 12866, not one agency comment appears in its released materials.[17] For a longer account of how even under a mandate for open government OIRA avoided disclosing some of its actions (including those covered by EO 12866's transparency mandates), see Lisa Heinzerling, Inside EPA: A Former Insider's Reflections on the Relationship Between the Obama EPA and the Obama White House, 31 Pace Envtl. L. Rev. 325 (2014).

As suggested above, measuring transparency is difficult. Nevertheless, we do have information on FOIA compliance, discussed in Note 2 on p. 676.

It also may be helpful to distinguish between agency process (inputs) and outcomes (outputs). Professor Cass Sunstein has recently argued for increased transparency of outputs. By contrast, he is more cautious about making inputs transparent, though he notes that the costs to input transparency decline over time for a particular decision.[18]

(4) *Standardizing Agency Internet Use.* Agency use of the Internet for various governmental purposes, notably including rulemaking, has been in

---

"thin-skinned and authoritarian" (Prime Minister Sarkozy of France) and "risk averse and rarely creative" (Chancellor Merkel of Germany). BBC News, WikiLeaks Diplomatic Cables Release 'attack on world,' Nov. 29, 2010, http://www.bbc.com/news/world-us-canada-11868838.

[13] Philip Rucker & Ed O'Keefe, In Trump's Washington, Public Business Increasingly Handled Behind Closed Doors, Wash. Post, June 19, 2017, http://wapo.st/2sjz6bO?tid=ss_tw&utm_term=.befe3a702e0e.

[14] Robert Woodward, Obama's Wars 198–99 (2010).

[15] See Fox News v. Treasury, 739 F.Supp.2d 515 (S.D.N.Y. 2010).

[16] Juliet Eilperin, White House Delayed Enacting Rules Ahead of 2012 Election to Avoid Controversy, Wash. Post, Dec. 14, 2013, http://wapo.st/1hTTmFU?tid=ss_tw.

[17] http://www.reginfo.gov/public/jsp/EO/fedRegReview/fedRegReview.jsp.

[18] Cass R. Sunstein, Output Transparency vs. Input Transparency (May 2017), available at: https://papers.ssrn.com/sol3/papers.cfm?abstract_id=2826009.

evidence ever since the interactive features of Internet use became established. Initially (and still, for many purposes, for the independent regulatory commissions) each agency built its website and its utilities on its own. One result was a conspicuous lack of uniformity; another, considerable experimentation and innovation. THE E-GOVERNMENT ACT OF 2002 (Pub. L. No. 107–347, 116 Stat. 2899, codified chiefly in 44 U.S.C. § 3601 ff., also scattered sections elsewhere in U.S.C.) created a central office in OMB, the Office of Electronic Government, headed by a Chief Information Officer who would seek coordination with the information officers of departments and agencies through a Council. An E-Government strategy announced by President Bush in the same year began a process of consolidation and centralized development that continues to this day. As the statute requires, OMB has filed annual reports of its implementation, which are available online.[19] As of October 2017, the website for the Office of Electronic Government in the White House was no longer working but will presumably be fixed at some point. Section 5 of this chapter contains discussion of e-rulemaking developments.

(5) *Federal Internet Sites.* This chapter invites you to consider some of the many ways in which government transparency—particularly through transformative use of the Internet—has changed administrative law (and during your professional life it doubtless will change it further). As Vivek Kundra, the Obama Administration's Chief Information Officer, remarked at a press conference in San Francisco: "[T]echnology deployed for public service can fundamentally change how a government and its people interact."[20] At the time, in early 2010, he and the others were addressing the delivery of government services; they were celebrating a common platform for municipal service calls (311) that would permit using Twitter in any city to report a need for pothole repair. The focus in this chapter is on a different set of developments—not on the delivery of government services but on the transparency of government activity, the formation and (to a lesser extent) the implementation of policy through agency rulemaking, and the possibilities of using the provision of information as a regulatory tool.

There already exist a wide range of crosscutting governmental websites, which you may want to explore as part of your work in confronting these aspects of administrative law:

- www.regulations.gov, the central website for federal agency rulemaking, where proposals for rulemaking, supporting data, and filed comments may all be located; where one can register for notice of postings by particular agencies, or in particular dockets; and where comments may be electronically submitted.[21]

---

[19] https://www.whitehouse.gov/omb/offices/e-gov/recent_reports_and_documents.

[20] http://sanfrancisco.granicus.com/MediaPlayer.php?publish_id=557.

[21] This site is now considerably more developed than it was when critiqued by the ABA's Committee on the Status and Future of Federal e-Rulemaking, Achieving the Potential: The Future of Federal e-Rulemaking (2008), but many of the limitations and criticisms to be found there remain valid. The website www.regulationroom.org is a Cornell University site associated

- www.reginfo.gov, where the Office of Information and Regulatory Affairs' public activities are catalogued; and where current and past editions of Regulatory Plans and the Unified Agenda of Regulatory and Deregulatory actions can be found.

- www.foia.gov, the central governmental site for Freedom of Information Act issues.

- www.justice.gov/oip/doj-guide-freedom-information-act-0, an online FOIA treatise that is updated on a rolling basis.

- www.archives.gov/ogis, the site for the independent FOIA "ombudsman" created by the Openness Promotes Effectiveness in our National Government Act of 2007.

- www.data.gov, where (as of October 2017), close to 200,000 federal, state, and local government datasets are available for the use of researchers and the development of applications.[22]

- www.usaspending.gov, a "dashboard" for government spending required by the Federal Funding Accountability and Transparency Act of 2006.

These links may well be replaced by others, as the new Administration continues before the next edition of these materials are published, but it seems unlikely that their functions will be discontinued. In addition, established links that are no longer operating nine months into the new Administration—most notably, OIRA's own web site—presumably will be reactivated at some point. For a look at the discontinued Obama Administration's transparency website, go to http://open.obamawhitehouse.archives.gov/.

This chapter, as others in this book, addresses issues in a general way. Here, in particular, you can enhance your understanding by choosing an agency whose work is of interest to you and using its website (for it will surely have one) to explore the topics this chapter and the rest of the casebook consider. To name but a few, who runs the agency? What experience do they have? How is the agency organized? What initiatives is the agency pursuing? How can you participate in those initiatives? Federal agencies that are important rulemakers on health and safety issues, such as EPA, FAA, FDA, NRC, or OSHA, may offer the greatest scope for these explorations, but it is likely that any active federal agency (and some state or municipal agencies, depending on your location) will serve this purpose. Among the documents you might look for are your chosen agency's "open government plan," developed in response to President Obama's directives, and any changes under the new Trump Administration. Although these plans will undoubtedly develop considerably over the useful life of this casebook, as of this writing, EPA's Open Government Plan[23] was widely

---

with the Legal Information Institute pursuing the continued development of public participation in electronic rulemaking, in cooperation with the Department of Transportation.

[22] For example, there is an application, eRecall, showing recalls of food, drugs, medical devices, vehicles, and other products. https://www.erecall.net/Home/Index. The data sets may be better adapted to expert than general public use, however.

[23] http://www.epa.gov/open/read-plan.

praised. While the focus here, as in this book generally, is on the federal level, be aware that similar developments are occurring at the state[24] and local[25] levels as well.

SECTION 2. SECRET LAW

> ### CERVASE v. OFFICE OF THE
> ### FEDERAL REGISTER

"We hear of tyrants, and those cruel ones: but, whatever we may have felt, we have never heard of any tyrant in such sort cruel, as to punish men for disobedience to laws or orders which he had kept them from the knowledge of."[26]

As you may already have learned, p. 810, Panama Refining Co. v. Ryan, 293 U.S. 388 (1935)—the first case in which the U.S. Supreme Court held a congressional statute to be invalid as an excessive delegation of authority—dramatized the problem of secret law. A depression-era statute had given the President certain authority to control interstate commerce in petroleum and its products as a means of stabilizing prices, and he and the Secretary of the Interior (to whom he had subdelegated this power) had adopted rules in the exercise of that authority. When the validity of this statute came before the Supreme Court (all but one of whose members would find it to be a standardless and therefore unconstitutional delegation of authority), the government was embarrassed to admit that a reexamination of the relevant documents (which at the time were not publicly available) had revealed that the Secretary had inadvertently revoked the relevant regulation before the lawsuit had been filed.[27] "[I]t was shocking that the government attorneys, the private parties, and the courts had not been aware of the status of the regulation. 'The furor resulting from the hot oil case provided the final impetus for the enactment of remedial legislation [the Federal Register Act] in 1935.' "[28] Just the prior year, only weeks before the argument and decision in the case—perhaps even sensing what would likely transpire—Erwin Griswold (later to become Dean of Harvard Law School and also Solicitor General of the United States) had argued passionately and persuasively for "a reasonable means of distributing and preserving the texts of . . . executive-made law."[29] The

---

[24] E.g., http://www.openbooknewyork.com/.

[25] E.g., http://cityofmanor.org/.

[26] 5 Bentham, Works 547 (1843); Erwin N. Griswold used this as the epigram to his article, Government in Ignorance of the Law—A Plea for Better Publication of Executive Legislation, 48 Harv. L. Rev. 198 (1934), discussed in text at n. 29.

[27] Id. at 412–413.

[28] Mary Whisner, Practicing Reference . . . : A Manual "to Inform Every Citizen," 99 Law Libr. J. 159, 160 (2007), citing Morris L. Cohen, Robert C. Berring & Kent C. Olson, How to Find the Law 265 (9th ed. 1989).

[29] Erwin N. Griswold, Government in Ignorance of the Law—A Plea for Better Publication of Executive Legislation, 48 Harv. L. Rev. 198 (1934). Griswold was on the staff of the Solicitor

Federal Register, a daily gazette of executive branch documents including rules and rulemaking proposals, was the result.

The Federal Register, like such publications generally, was a useful but imperfect response to the problem of secret law. A bulky daily publication, with an ambitious yet (necessarily) limited index, its effective use required lawyers and librarians. It has never been, moreover, a *compilation* of regulations—rather it is to the publication of regulations what the Statutes at Large is to the publication of public laws. Like the Statutes at Large, it is organized chronologically. There soon appeared the analog to the United States Code, the Code of Federal Regulations (CFR). The CFR proceeds by agency and topical chapters. Nevertheless, as the following case may reveal, the task of finding relevant regulations remained difficult in an era without personal computers, easy to access databases, and the Internet.

CERVASE v. OFFICE OF THE FEDERAL REGISTER

United States Court of Appeals for the Third Circuit (1978).
580 F.2d 1166.

■ GIBBONS, CIRCUIT JUDGE.

[John Cervase, an attorney appearing pro se, brought an action seeking to force the Office of the Federal Register to create an analytical subject matter index to the Code of Federal Regulations (CFR). At the time of his suit, the 120-volume CFR had only a 164-page table of contents for the entire contents. Cervase asserted that the Office had an obligation to create an index as well, and that its breach of this duty had injured him and the public at large by making it almost impossible for them to know which federal regulations apply to them. The district court dismissed Cervase's complaint on grounds not necessary to consider here. The U.S. Court of Appeals for the Third Circuit reversed and remanded, having determined that "such a summary disposition of Cervase's complaint was improper . . . ."]

I

Cervase claims that the duty to prepare an analytical subject index arises out of two important federal statutes: the Federal Register Act of 1935 and the Freedom of Information Act of 1974. As amended, § 11 of the Federal Register Act provides in relevant part:

(b) A codification published under subsection (a) of this section shall be printed and bound in permanent form and shall be designated as the "Code of Federal Regulations." The Administrative Committee shall regulate the binding of the printed codifications into separate books with a view to practical

---

General's office until 1934, when Panama Refining was briefed. He, therefore, could easily have been aware of the coming firestorm; his article was published in the December 1934 issue of the Law Review; argument in Panama Refining was held that month; and the decision announced in January 1935.

usefulness and economical manufacture. Each book shall contain an explanation of its coverage and other aids to users that the Administration Committee may require. *A general index to the entire Code of Federal Regulations shall be separately printed and bound.*

* * * *

(d)   The Office of the Federal Register shall prepare and publish the codifications, supplements, collations, and indexes authorized by this section.

Act of Oct. 22, 1968, Pub. L. No. 90–620, ch. 15, § 11, 82 Stat. 1277 (codified at 44 U.S.C. § 1510) (emphasis added). . . .

The original Federal Register Act provided for a compilation of all existing agency regulations of general applicability and legal effect. In 1937, however, that Act was amended to provide for codification instead of compilation. . . . In the 1937 amendment Congress, for the first time, imposed the indexing obligation on those responsible for preparing the periodic codifications. The significance of this obligation within the framework of what is commonly referred to as the Federal Register System is obvious. Codification of a document is prima facie evidence both of its text and of its continuing legal effect. Publication of the document in the Federal Register makes it effective against the world. But without the retrieval mechanism provided by an adequate index, a person might never be aware of a document containing a regulation affecting him until some federal bureaucrat produced a copy of the document and attempted to apply it to him. Indeed, the affected individual might already have changed his position in complete ignorance of the existence of the regulation. Such ignorance would avail him not, however, since publication in the Federal Register gives him constructive notice of the existence of the regulation. The Federal Register Act was enacted because of widespread dissatisfaction with the unsystematic manner in which executive orders, agency regulations, and similar materials were being made available to the public. The basic object of this statutory reform was to eliminate secret law. We think that the indexing obligation is a central and essential feature of this congressional plan. Without that obligation the periodic codification of regulations cannot serve the congressional purpose of providing public access to what has been published in the Federal Register. . . .

Cervase claims that the 164-page table of contents is so totally inadequate that it cannot be considered to be in compliance with [the] mandatory duty. In his brief to the district court Cervase observed that the 1938 codification [Ed. the first codification] consisted of 14 volumes, with a general index of 513 pages. The current codification has grown to 120 volumes covering fifty titles, while what passes for an index has actually shrunk to 164 pages. By contrast, the general index to the fifty titles of the annotated United States Code comprises eight bound volumes and eight supplements, or a total of 9024 pages.

Although his complaint alleged only a violation of 44 U.S.C. §§ 1510(b) and (d), in his brief to the district court Cervase also relied on the Administrative Procedure Act, as amended by the Freedom of Information Act. This Act imposes a separate indexing obligation on federal agencies:

> *Each agency shall also maintain and make available for public inspection and copying current indexes* providing identifying information for the public as to any matter issued, adopted, or promulgated after July 4, 1967, and required by this paragraph to be made available or published. Each agency shall promptly publish, quarterly or more frequently, and distribute (by sale or otherwise) copies of each index or supplements thereto unless it determines by order published in the Federal Register that the publication would be unnecessary and impracticable, in which case the agency shall nonetheless provide copies of such index on request at a cost not to exceed the direct cost of duplication. A final order, opinion, statement of policy, interpretation, or staff manual or instruction that affects a member of the public may be relied on, used, or cited as precedent by an agency against a party other than an agency only if—
>
> (i)   it has been indexed and either made available or published as provided by this paragraph; or
>
> (ii) the party has actual and timely notice of the terms thereof.

5 U.S.C. § 552(a)(2) (emphasis supplied). . . . [Cervase argues] that § 1510(b) should be construed in pari materia with the Freedom of Information Act. That Act reaffirmed Congress' commitment to the principle of meaningful public access, by means of indexing, to records of agency action. . . .

NOTES

(1) ***Pre-Internet Access to Agency Materials.*** Although the Federal Register and the CFR were a meaningful advance, they were incomplete. Although the APA initially required the publication in the Federal Register of the most important matters and forbade their use to the prejudice of any person unless published there,[30] much "soft law" could not be found in its

---

[30] Section 3 of the original APA provided: Except to the extent that there is involved (1) any function of the United States requiring secrecy in the public interest or (2) any matter relating solely to the internal management of an agency—

(a) Rules.—Every agency shall separately state and currently publish in the Federal Register (1) descriptions of its central and field organization including delegations by the agency of final authority and the established places at which, and methods whereby, the public may secure information or make submittals or requests; (2) statements of the general course and method by which its functions are channeled and determined, including the nature and requirements of all formal or informal procedures available as well as forms and instructions as to the scope and contents of all papers, reports, or examinations; and (3) substantive rules adopted as authorized by law and statements of general policy or interpretations formulated and adopted by the agency for the guidance of the public, but not rules addressed to and served upon

pages. Access to soft law, such as agency opinions and orders, might be possible at the agency itself, but other publication was haphazard.

The 1967 codification of the 1966 Freedom of Information Act[31] brought § 552(a)(1)–(2) of the APA towards their current form, encouraging public availability and indexing by extending to materials that had *not* been published in the Federal Register the prohibition on use to the disadvantage of private parties *unless* they were publicly available and indexed.[32] Even so, before the Internet, that access might require travel to one of a limited number of agency reading rooms, or perhaps to a specific agency office. Just what might constitute a qualifying index was nowhere specified, and one can readily imagine many obstacles to it being highly detailed. If not precisely secret, then, regulatory law was often obscure and access to it expensive.

(2) *The Internet's Contributions.* Perhaps the most obvious use of the Internet is to provide further relief from the problems both of secret law and of the limitations of indexing. In 1994 the Federal Register and in 1996 the CFR were embedded and made readily searchable at the website of the Government Printing Office,[33] one of the first important federal e-government projects. They are now available as well on for-profit and non-profit sites such as Lexis/Westlaw and Cornell's Legal Information Institute,[34] respectively. Recent revisions to the Federal Register's own website[35] have begun to integrate it with the federal e-rulemaking site, regulations.gov, and improve its usability.[36] You can search the Federal Register on its website by type of document, agency, and CFR index terms, along with more advanced options.

---

named persons in accordance with law. No person shall in any manner be required to resort to organization or procedure not so published.

(b) Opinions and orders.—Every agency shall publish, or, in accordance with published rule, make available to public inspection all final opinions or orders in the adjudication of cases (except those required for good cause to be held confidential and not cited as precedents) and all rules.

(c) Public records.—Save as otherwise required by statute, matters of official record shall in accordance with published rule be made available to persons properly and directly concerned except information held confidential for good cause found.

60 Stat. 237 (1946).

[31]   Pub. L. No. 90–23, 81 Stat. 54 (1967).

[32]   Their text may be found at p. 1466 in the Appendix. The FOIA Improvement Act of 2016 limited the agency's obligation to make material available under Section 552(a)(2) to "public inspection in an electronic format," essentially eliminating any need to maintain paper libraries and indexes for the public's use.

[33]   These documents and an increasing proportion of GPO documents are available at http://www.gpo.gov/fdsys/.

[34]   http://www.law.cornell.edu/cfr/.

[35]   http://www.FederalRegister.gov.

[36]   Matt Madia, Big Upgrade for Federal Register Online, Aug. 4, 2010, available at: http://www.foreffectivegov.org/node/11200: "The site, dubbed Federal Register 2.0, now allows users to sort Federal Register documents in a variety of ways.... The redesign makes FederalRegister.gov more relevant to the government's broader e-rulemaking system. Federal e-rulemaking efforts have tended to focus on participation, allowing citizens to comment on regulations through websites, but finding basic information on regulations has often been too difficult a prerequisite to complete.... But, for Federal Register documents, the new FederalRegister.gov should provide quicker and easier access to documents."

Soft law, in particular, has become much more readily available and searchable. The Electronic Freedom of Information Act Amendments of 1996[37] required each agency to maintain an electronic reading room containing its regulations, guidance, interpretations, staff manuals—any quasi-legislative document in which the public might be interested[38]—as well as documents released in response to FOIA requests that "the agency determines have become or are likely to become the subject of subsequent requests for substantially the same records."[39] If advanced search options are enabled, the documents are not only on that agency's website but also nicely indexed, in a manner no print edition or document filing system could hope to achieve. The interventions of librarians and lawyers are no longer required (although they may still be useful); if a document is in the electronic library, it is accessible to all. It cannot any longer be "off the shelf" and unavailable.

To be certain, wider access remains a work in progress. There is no *uniform* way to access American agencies' soft law files.[40] In 2017, the Administrative Conference of the United States (ACUS), an independent federal agency dedicated to improving the administrative process and agency procedures, published its findings from a survey of 24 agency websites' treatment of federal adjudication materials. ACUS examined not only the navigability and search functions of each website but also the scope of disclosed materials (for example, formal decisions only versus submissions to the agency as well). In response to agency variation, ACUS flagged some best practices and made a series of recommendations to improve agency disclosure.[41]

If you have chosen an agency to follow, consult its electronic library to see what materials can be found there, and assess their searchability.

(3) *An Example of the Transformation.* Here is an example that may make dramatic the changes that have occurred: One of the more important regulations issued by the Department of Transportation's National Highway Traffic Safety Administration (NHTSA) has been its Standard 208, requiring the installation first of seatbelts and then of airbags in American automobiles.[42] Understandably, manufacturers and others have had questions about the requirements of the standard and interpretation of its

---

[37] Pub. L. No. 104–231, 110 Stat. 3048 (1996) (amending 5 U.S.C. § 552(a)(2)).

[38] See, for example, http://www.faa.gov/regulations_policies/, collecting a wide range of soft law documents as well as FAA regulations.

[39] 5 U.S.C. § 552(a)(2)(D). On this as on most issues regarding the Freedom of Information Act, an excellent first source to consult is the U.S. Department of Justice's Freedom of Information Act Guide, which can be found at: www.justice.gov/oip/doj-guide-freedom-information-act-0. This treatise used to be published every several years but is now updated on a rolling basis online.

[40] In the Department of Transportation, for example, enter "FAA guidance" and "NHTSA guidance" in the search box to compare accessibility of soft law of two agencies within the same cabinet department.

[41] ACUS, Adjudication Materials on Agency Websites, Recommendation 2017–1 (adopted June 2017); http://www.acus.gov/research-projects/adjudication-materials-agency-websites.

[42] 49 CFR Parts 552, 571, 585, and 595. Standard 208 came before the Supreme Court in Motor Vehicle Mfrs Ass'n v. State Farm Mut. Auto. Ins. Co., 463 U.S. 29 (1983), which you will almost certainly read if you study standards of review, p. 1069 below.

provisions, which they have addressed to NHTSA's General Counsel. The General Counsel's interpretive letters responding to their inquiries had long been public documents,[43] but access to them once depended on either visiting the Counsel's office in Washington, D.C. or finding an industry group or member that had made its own collection. One can imagine both the expense of hiring a lawyer to perform that search, and the imperfections of the filing system she would encounter. The website NHTSA has been maintaining for years now collects the opinion letters of its Chief Counsel, making them available for basic searches,[44] and perhaps promising some reliability.[45] This undertaking so impressed General Motors and an industry group that had begun electronic recordkeeping years before NHTSA supplemented its paper files, that each donated their electronic records of earlier letters for inclusion in the searchable repository. Now, using an Internet connection half a continent (or half the world) away from Washington, anyone wishing to learn about NHTSA's interpretations of Standard 208 (or any of its other regulations) reliably has that information in seconds. The visibility of government law, hard and soft, has been exponentially increased.

(4) ***Copyright and Like Restraints?*** Getting materials onto the Internet may be difficult and, even once there, they may be protected by copyright. Consider CARL MALAMUD,[46] A SHINING CITY UPON A HILL (Remarks to the 14th Law.Gov Workshop Center for American Progress, June 15, 2010, Washington, D.C.): "If you want to make juice in California, you need much more than a good supply of mangos. You need to know about these laws:

"Title 17 of the California Code of Regulations deals with Sanitation in Food Plants. The Office of Administrative Law of the State of California asserts copyright over the California Code of Regulations, and contracts with Barclays to publish the document. You can view the provisions on their web site, but I can't make a copy that looks differently, say one that is aimed specifically at juice guys.

"For your juice business, you also need to be very familiar with the California Health and Safety Code, Part 6, the California Food Sanitation Act. You also want to be familiar with Title 21 of the Code of Federal

---

[43] Compare Mark P. Schlefer v. United States, 702 F.2d 233 (D.C. Cir. 1983) (Maritime Administration required to release Chief Counsel Opinions interpreting statutes under FOIA, as operative soft law).

[44] http://isearch.nhtsa.gov/.

[45] While the agency used to assert that the Chief Counsel's interpretations "represent the definitive view of the agency on the questions addressed and may be relied upon by the regulated industry and members of the public," it now has a more cautious statement, similar to other agencies' warnings: "These letters of interpretation, signed by the Chief Counsel, represent the opinion of the agency on the questions addressed at the time of signature and may be helpful in determining how the agency might answer a question that you have if that question is similar to a previously-considered question. Please remember, however, that interpretation letters represent the opinion of the Chief Counsel based on the facts of individual cases at the time the letter was written. Do not assume that a prior interpretation will necessarily apply to your situation!" Id.

[46] Carl Malamud is the driving force behind a number of efforts to expand government-created, law-related materials available on the Internet, and to resist copyright restrictions and/or the sale of exclusive rights of electronic access to private entrepreneurs such as West. See http://public.resource.org. Public Safety Codes, for example, can be found at http://law.resource.org/pub/us/code/safety.html.

Regulations, particularly the sections on 'packaging or holding human food' and on 'sanitation standard operating procedures.'

"Of course, you also need to be fully familiar with the HACCP regulations, a series of detailed standards on Hazard Analysis and Critical Control Points from the Food and Drug Administration. The HACCP regulations, in turn, incorporate by reference a raft of technical standards, such as ANSI/ NSF Standard Number 7 for Commercial Refrigerators and Storage Freezers, which is $100 per copy, if you want to do due diligence on your freezer.

"These documents are just a start for the serious juice professional. You must, of course, consult your public safety codes, all of which are only available from a designated exclusive vendor such as the National Electrical Code from the National Fire Protection Association, likewise the building codes in your jurisdiction, the fuel and gas code, the plumbing code, the fire code, and the elevator safety code.

"You'll also need your local municipal code, particular the sections on zoning, factories, and employment practices. Most of the municipal codes of California belong to one of the three major outsourcing companies, and over 50 percent of municipal codes in California have copyright restrictions.[47]

"My point is not that the ambitious juice entrepreneur is totally without resources to learn the law, but that if I wanted to create a new product or nonprofit site aimed at the juice people of California . . . I'd have a hard time gathering the materials I'd need to set that site up. There are too many copyright restrictions, pay walls, and other impediments to access bulk legal documents needed to create a useful site. . . .

"John Adams, in his Thoughts on Government, said 'a republic is an empire of laws, and not of men.' If our republic is an empire, it is an empire that has been balkanized by a complicated set of deeds, exclusive tenancies, and contractual fences."

(5) ***Dispute over Private Standards at the Federal Level.*** The copyright issue was prominent in the 2014 revision of 1 C.F.R. Part 51, "Incorporation by Reference," 79 Fed. Reg. 66278. Incorporation by reference is a process by which standards created by private organizations are converted into legal obligations without their text being revealed. Comments in the notice and comment proceedings on possible revision of the governing OMB Guidance, Circular A–119, called attention to the European practice, which treats standards not as legal obligations in and of themselves but rather as guidance on how regulations whose essential requirements are independently stated may be fulfilled. The revisions (in both Part 51 and Circular A–119) did not take this path. While they somewhat improve the likely content of notices of proposed rulemaking and statements of basis and purpose associated with incorporations by reference, the availability of

---

47 The same problem can exist at the state as well as the municipal level. ". . . [Twenty-one] 21 states assert copyright over state regulations. . . . [I]n California, to access the official reports of the courts, you have to accept a click-through license agreement where you agree not to share any of the materials, with a specific prohibition against public and nonprofit use." Carl Malamud, The Raw Materials of Our Democracy—Remarks to the Government 2.0 Exposition, May 27, 2010, Washington, D.C.

incorporated standards, at what price and on what terms, remains in the hands of the responsible private organization. The dockets in the two proceedings can be found at regulations.gov, see OMB–2014–0001 and OFR–2013–0001; critical appraisals of the revisions to Part 51 at http://www.reg blog.org/2015/01/26/series-incorporation-by-reference/.

Malamud's organization, Public Resource, posted online many private standards from the American Society for Testing and Materials that had been incorporated into federal rules. The private organization then sued to get them removed. In early 2017, a federal district court, while noting "the need for an informed citizenry to have a full understanding of how to comply with the nation's legal requirements," sided with the copyright holder. The court held that Congress had permitted such standards groups to maintain their copyrights even when their standards are incorporated into public law. American Society for Testing and Materials v. Public.Resource.org, Inc., 2017 WL 473822 (D.D.C. 2017). Public Resource has appealed.

(6) *Secret Law and the "War on Terror."* The Internet has not eliminated secret law. Indeed, the "War on Terror" commenced at the start of the century may have generated an increase. In 2016, the Brennan Center for Justice at NYU issued a report, The New Era of Secret Law, which documents the use of secret law, motivated by national security concerns, across all three branches of government. The study finds that in the legislative branch, in addition to classified committee reports, sometimes "bills incorporate provisions [which 'include not just funding or personnel allocations, but substantive regulations'] of classified reports by reference, bestowing on them the status of law." In the executive branch, some national security directives, opinions by Office of Legal Counsel, agreements with foreign nations, and national security regulations remain secret. [Ed. Perhaps more relevant to administrative law, also in the executive branch, the "No-Fly" and other watch lists are kept secret (under classification rules), see p. 596, and government attorneys sometimes rely on classified evidence in immigration proceedings that only the immigration judge can see.] And in the judicial branch, national security litigation in the federal courts often produces sealed or redacted filings; in addition, "significant pre-Snowden FISA case law remains undisclosed." The report makes a number of proposals, including: "Decisions to withhold legal rules and authoritative legal interpretations from the public should be made by an inter-agency body of senior officials"; "The standard for keeping law secret should be more stringent than the current standard for classifying information"; "Certain categories ['disclosure of pure legal analysis', '[l]egal interpretations that purport to exempt the executive branch from compliance with statutes'] of law should never be secret"; "When the executive branch issues secret law, it should immediately share the law with the other branches and with independent oversight bodies"; "Indefinite secret law is constitutionally intolerable. There should be a four-year time limit on the secrecy of legal rules and authoritative legal interpretations. Renewals [limited to two] should require the unanimous approval of the inter-agency body charged with making secrecy

determinations"; "Americans should know how much secret law exists and the general areas where it is being applied."

Is there a constitutional right to information? How far can the government restrict access of the press under the First Amendment? See Nation Magazine v. U.S. Dep't of Defense, 762 F. Supp. 1558 (S.D.N.Y. 1991). Does the common law right to "inspect and copy public records" apply to federal agencies? The White House? Congress? Courts? See Nixon v. Warner Commc'ns, 435 U.S. 589 (1978); Schwartz v. U.S. Dep't of Justice, 435 F. Supp. 1203 (D.D.C. 1977), affirmed, 595 F.2d 888 (D.C. Cir. 1979).

(7) ***Keeping Government Records.*** Several statutes require the government to preserve official records. The Presidential Records Act mandates that the President "assure that the activities, deliberations, decisions, and policies that reflect the performance of the President's constitutional, statutory, or other official or ceremonial duties are adequately documented and that such records are preserved and maintained as Presidential records. . . ." 44 U.S.C. § 2203(a). These records are then handed over to the Archivist of the United States, who then generally releases them (subject to exemptions) according to the Act's timetable and other provisions. Soon after President Trump took office, the Archivist informed two Democratic senators who had raised concerns under the Act (after the President deleted and modified some of his tweets) that he "has advised the White House that it should capture and preserve all tweets that the president posts in the course of his official duties, including those that are subsequently deleted, as presidential records."

The Federal Records Act requires agencies to preserve, for set time periods, "all recorded information, regardless of form or characteristics, made or received by a Federal agency under Federal law or in connection with the transaction of public business . . . as evidence of the organization, functions, policies, decisions, procedures, operations, or other activities of the United States Government or because of the informational value of data in them." 44 U.S.C. § 3301. The State Department's Inspector General and the FBI determined that then-Secretary of State Hillary Clinton's use of a private email server violated "the Department's policies that were implemented in accordance with the Federal Records Act," but the FBI recommended that prosecutors not file criminal charges under the Act.

(8) ***Government Leaks—Authorized and Unauthorized.*** At times, government employees disclose information outside of FOIA. Some disclosures—typically to others within the government—are permitted by law and practice. The Whistleblower Protection Act immunizes federal employees from retaliatory personnel actions taken for communications with their agency's Inspector General or leader about serious agency misconduct. 5 U.S.C. § 2302(b). A few days after President Trump entered the White House, the office in charge of protecting government whistleblowers issued a press release noting that "agencies cannot impose nondisclosure

agreements and policies that fail to include required language" on employees' rights.[48]

Outside of formal whistleblowing, there are often other disclosures to individuals outside the government. Some are part and parcel of the administrative process and therefore authorized—informal, permitted discussions between an agency and regulated entities and regulatory beneficiaries, for example. Some are unauthorized, in that they do not expose agency misbehavior covered by whistleblower protections or fall within a particular agency's permitted practices. Amanda Leiter terms disclosures that "concer[n] not agency malfeasance but internal dissent about an agency's policy course" "soft whistleblowing" and argues that they "tend to improve agency transparency and augment congressional oversight." Amanda C. Leiter, Soft Whistleblowing, 48 Ga. L. Rev. 425 (2014).

Leaks in the national security context are of particular interest to secret law. Classified material is supposed to be kept secret. Those who disclose such information face potential criminal sanctions under the Espionage Act and other statutes. As of 2013, the government, however, has brought only eleven prosecutions, where the last eight were done under the Obama Administration. (In 2017, the Trump Administration charged a government contractor for releasing classified information of attempted Russian interference in the 2016 election.) David Pozen, in a fascinating treatment based in part on interviews with national security officials, argues that the "story behind the U.S. government's longstanding failure to enforce the laws against leaking is far more complicated, and far more interesting, than has been appreciated." He argues "that most components of the executive branch have never prioritized criminal, civil, or administrative enforcement against leakers; that a nuanced set of informal social controls has come to supplement, and nearly supplant, the formal disciplinary scheme; that much of what we call leaking occurs in a gray area between full authorization and no authorization, so that it is neither 'leaks' nor 'plants' but what [he] . . . term[s] pleaks that dominate this discursive space; that the executive's toleration of these disclosures is a rational, power-enhancing strategy and not simply a product of prosecutorial limitations, a feature, not a bug, of the system; and that to untangle these dynamics is to illuminate important facets of presidential power, bureaucratic governance, and the national security state in America today." David E. Pozen, The Leaky Leviathan: Why the Government Condemns and Condones Unlawful Disclosures of Information, 127 Harv. L. Rev. 512 (2013).

---

[48] U.S. Office of Special Counsel, Press Release, OSC's Enforcement of the Anti-Gag Order Provision in Whistleblower Law (Jan. 25. 2017).

SECTION 3.   Freedom of Information Legislation

> *a. FOIA Overview*
> *b. FOIA's General Characteristics*
> *c. FOIA in Operation*
> *d. The Reverse FOIA Action*

a. FOIA Overview

> ***THE FREEDOM OF INFORMATION ACT***
> ***Notes on Agencies, Records, and Requesters***

THE FEDERAL FREEDOM OF INFORMATION ACT, 5 U.S.C. § 552

[The Act is set out in full in the Appendix, p. 1479. The following excerpts establish the usual right of "any person" to demand the production of reasonably identified government records and the limited exemptions to that right.]

5 U.S.C. § 552. Public information; agency rules, opinions, orders, records, and proceedings

. . .

(a)(3)(A) Except with respect to the records made available under paragraphs (1) and (2) of this subsection, and except as provided in subparagraph (E), each agency, upon any request for records which

(i) reasonably describes such records and

(ii) is made in accordance with published rules stating the time, place, fees (if any), and procedures to be followed, shall make the records promptly available to any person. . . .

(a)(8)(A) An agency shall—

(i) withhold information under this section only if—

(I) the agency reasonably foresees that disclosure would harm an interest protected by an exemption described in subsection (b); or

(II) disclosure is prohibited by law; and

(ii)

(I) consider whether partial disclosure of information is possible whenever the agency determines that a full disclosure of a requested record is not possible; and

(II) take reasonable steps necessary to segregate and release nonexempt information; and

(a)(8)(B) Nothing in this paragraph requires disclosure of information that is otherwise prohibited from disclosure by law, or otherwise exempted from disclosure under subsection (b)(3). . . .

(b) This section does not apply to matters that are—

(1)(A)   specifically authorized under criteria established by an Executive order to be kept secret in the interest of national defense or foreign policy and (B) are in fact properly classified pursuant to such Executive order;

(2)   related solely to the internal personnel rules and practices of an agency;

(3)   specifically exempted from disclosure by statute (other than section 552b of this title), if that statute—

(A) (i)   requires that the matters be withheld from the public in such a manner as to leave no discretion on the issue; or

(ii)   establishes particular criteria for withholding or refers to particular types of matters to be withheld; and

(B) if enacted after the date of enactment of the OPEN FOIA Act of 2009, specifically cites to this paragraph.

(4)   trade secrets and commercial or financial information obtained from a person and privileged or confidential;

(5)   inter-agency or intra-agency memorandums or letters which would not be available by law to a party other than an agency in litigation with the agency, provided that the deliberative process privilege shall not apply to records created 25 years or more before the date on which the records were requested;

(6)   personnel and medical files and similar files the disclosure of which would constitute a clearly unwarranted invasion of personal privacy;

(7)   records or information compiled for law enforcement purposes, but only to the extent that the production of such law enforcement records or information

(A) could reasonably be expected to interfere with enforcement proceedings,

(B) would deprive a person of a right to a fair trial or an impartial adjudication,

(C) could reasonably be expected to constitute an unwarranted invasion of personal privacy,

(D) could reasonably be expected to disclose the identity of a confidential source, including a State, local, or foreign agency or authority or any private institution which furnished

United States scored 83 points (out of a possible 150), which placed it in the middle range of the ranked countries.

New disclosure laws have generated frivolous as well as deadly serious requests. On the former, in a ten-year look back at Britain's statute, the New York Times noted the "appalling regularity" of requests like: "How many residents in Sutton own an ostrich?" "What procedures are in place for a zombie invasion of Cumbria?" "How many people have been banned from Birmingham Library because they smell?" The article also reported that "[i]n Wigan, the council was asked what plans were in place to protect the town from a dragon attack, while Worthing Borough Council had to outline its preparations for an asteroid crash."[56]

By contrast, the New York Times noted the "heavy price" some requesters under India's new law have paid:[57]

> Amit Jethwa had just left his lawyer's office after discussing a lawsuit he had filed to stop an illicit limestone quarry with ties to powerful local politicians. That is when the assassins struck, speeding out of the darkness on a roaring motorbike, pistols blazing. He died on the spot, blood pouring from his mouth and nose. He was 38.
>
> Mr. Jethwa was one of millions of Indians who had embraced the country's five-year-old Right to Information Act, which allows citizens to demand almost any government information. People use the law to stop petty corruption and to solve their most basic problems, like getting access to subsidized food for the poor or a government pension without having to pay a bribe, or determining whether government doctors and teachers are actually showing up for work.
>
> But activists like Mr. Jethwa who have tried to push such disclosures further—making pointed inquiries at the dangerous intersection of high-stakes business and power politics—have paid a heavy price. Perhaps a dozen have been killed since 2005, when the law was enacted, and countless others have been beaten and harassed.

NOTES ON AGENCIES, RECORDS, AND REQUESTERS

(1) **Scope of FOIA: Agencies and Records.** FOIA is limited to "agency records". As to the first word, under the statute, "agency . . . includes any executive department, military department, Government corporation, Government controlled corporation, or other establishment in the executive branch of the Government (including the Executive Office of the President), or any independent regulatory agency." 5 U.S.C. § 552(f)(1). Compare the definition of agency for the APA. Courts have had to resolve whether certain quasi agencies (for example, the Red Cross) are subject to FOIA. The

---

[56] Bryton Clarke, From A to Z (Asteroids to Zombies), British Just Want Facts, N.Y. Times, April 12, 2015.

[57] Lydia Polgreen, High Price for India's Information Law, N.Y. Times, Jan. 22, 2011.

President is not subject to FOIA (or the APA), generating litigation over whether an entity is part of the White House (not covered) or is part of the Executive Office of the President (covered). See, e.g., Meyer v. Bush, 981 F.2d 1288 (D.C. 1993) (distinguishing between OMB and the Reagan Task Force on Regulatory Relief). As to the second word, under the statute, "record . . . includes (A) any information that would be an agency record subject to the requirements of this section when maintained by an agency in any format, including an electronic format; and (B) any information described under subparagraph (A) that is maintained for an agency by an entity under Government contract, for the purposes of records management." 5 U.S.C. § 552(f)(2).

Judicial Watch v. Secret Service, 726 F.3d 208 (D.C. Cir. 2013), rejected a FOIA request for the Secret Service's White House Access Control System records that would have revealed visitors to the President and his assistants. As they could not be obtained directly from the President or his close advisors (as they are not agencies under FOIA), they were not to be regarded as agency records; yet if they recorded visits to others in the White House Complex who were agencies—visits to OMB, for example—then the same records would be considered agency records subject to disclosure (unless some qualifying exemption applied). Ordinarily, whether records are "agency records" is governed by a four-part test explicated in Tax Analysts v. U.S. Dep't of Justice, 845 F.2d 1060, 1069 (D.C. Cir. 1988), aff'd, 492 U.S. 136 (1989):[58] "[1] the intent of the document's creator to retain or relinquish control over the records; [2] the ability of the agency to use and dispose of the record as it sees fit; [3] the extent to which agency personnel have read or relied upon the document; and [4] the degree to which the document was integrated into the agency's record system or files." In assessing Judicial Watch's request, the court found the application of this test indeterminate and noted that permitting indirect access to presidential records would raise serious separation of powers concerns. For undoubted FOIA agencies,

---

[58] In Kissinger v. Reporters Committee for Freedom of the Press, 445 U.S. 136 (1980), the Supreme Court focused on four factors to determine whether items were agency records: whether the documents were (1) in the agency's control; (2) generated within the agency; (3) placed into the agency's files; and (4) used by the agency "for any purpose." The case involved three separate FOIA requests for the transcripts and summaries of Henry Kissinger's telephone conversations that were maintained while he was Secretary of State and national security advisor to the President. Dr. Kissinger treated the notes as his own personal papers. While still in the State Department, he transferred them to a private location before two of the three FOIA requests were filed, and he entered an agreement deeding the notes to the Library of Congress. As to those two requests, the Court found that the State Department had not "withheld" anything because the documents had been removed from the State Department's possession prior to the filing of a FOIA request. "[T]he agency ha[d] neither the custody nor the control to enable it to withhold." The third FOIA request, filed before the telephone notes were removed from the State Department, sought notes of telephone conversations Dr. Kissinger had while he was in the Office of the President prior to becoming Secretary of State. Because FOIA does not include presidential assistants in the definition of "agency," the records of those phone conversations were not "agency" records, and the mere physical transfer of those documents to the State Department did not by itself render them "agency records" because the "papers were not in the control of the State Department at any time. They were not generated in the State Department. They never entered the State Department's files, and they were not used by the Department for any purpose. If mere physical location of papers and materials could confer status as an 'agency record' Kissinger's personal books, speeches, and all other memorabilia stored in his office would have been agency records subject to disclosure under the FOIA."

however, no such concerns arose; and in their absence, the indeterminacy of the Tax Analysts test favored Judicial Watch's claim, given the agency's burden to demonstrate, not the requester's to disprove, that the materials sought are not agency records.

Control is critical in assessing whether a record is an *agency* record. Courts have upheld non-disclosure of congressional documents provided to an agency where Congress has made clear that the materials remain congressional records. See American Civil Liberties Union v. CIA, 823 F.3d 655 (D.C. Cir. 2016) (Senate Select Committee on Intelligence report). The D.C. Circuit recently compelled searches of the private emails of an agency's director because he controlled the nongovernment email account when working for the agency. Competitive Enter. Inst. v. Office of Sci. & Technology Policy, 827 F.3d 145 (D.C. Cir. 2016).

While the text of the statute *authorizes* non-disclosure of agency records in certain circumstances, it does not itself *require* non-disclosure.[59] Further, it provides that if only parts of a record are exempt from disclosure, "any reasonably segregable portion" that does not share the infirmity must be produced. Both provisions seem to tell the agency that it will be easier to produce its records than not to produce them.

(2) **FOIA Requesters.** Interestingly, FOIA places almost no limits on who can request information (though the requester's identity is relevant to how much she will pay in fees for disclosures).[60] A requester of records needs only to "reasonably describe[e]" the records wanted but need not give any reason for wanting them and his description need not be in great detail. For example: "All records considered by the agency in connection with its proposed rulemaking, XY Fed. Reg. ABCD (date), on the treatment of smoked fish" would be a sufficiently detailed request. The statutory grounds for refusing to surrender records, with very limited exceptions, also do not depend on any balance between the requester's possible reason for wanting the records produced and the considerations supporting withholding.

Although commercial entities may dominate FOIA requesters, see Note 3 below, journalists have relied on FOIA to break major stories, including in recent years the abuse of detainees in Guantánamo Bay, Iraq, and Afghanistan; the failure of getting benefits to veterans; and the eavesdropping by intelligence agencies on American citizens' communications. One of two FOIA lawyers for the New York Times recently described his experience: "We know better than anyone that FOIA cases are

---

[59] This characteristic has particular importance to the supplier of commercially valuable information, who may fear its discretionary or accidental disclosure. See Notes on Exemptions Protecting Information Supplied to Government below, p. 720. Although the Act's exemptions include materials whose continued secrecy would be of interest to persons outside the agency— materials as varied as a corporation's process for making a miracle drug and an individual's tax return—the statute makes no explicit provision for these outsiders to be heard in the agency's (or the court's) consideration of what should be disclosed.

[60] After the September 11, 2001, attacks, Congress did amend FOIA to bar intelligence agencies from disclosing records to "(i) any government entity, other than a State, territory, commonwealth, or district of the United States, or any subdivision thereof; or (ii) a representative of a government entity described in clause (i)." 5 U.S.C. § 552(a)(3)(E). Compare McBurney v. Young, 569 U.S. 221 (2013) (upholding Virginia's Freedom of Information Act that restricts disclosure to Virginia citizens).

frustrating, the deck is stacked against us, and the lawsuits drag on for months and years. It can feel Sisyphean, pushing a huge legal rock up a sizable legal hill. Only unlike Sisyphus, we sometimes get to the top. We win. Between settlements and successful court decisions, we regularly make a small dent in governmental secrecy. . . . [W]e . . . forced the Pentagon to release a trove of eye-opening documents about the Bush administration's stealth campaign to sell the war in Iraq to the American people. They became central to the meticulous reporting that won David Barstow a Pulitzer Prize in 2009. . . . We have won important rulings on the Obama administration's investigation into the use of torture after 9/11 and the government's campaign to kill terrorism suspects abroad. And we don't just get documents. One of FOIA's few delightful twists is that the government pays us for our time and effort when we prevail."[61]

(3) **Commercial Requesters.** The prompt emergence of a commercial FOIA request business led to concerns that mining for competitors' trade secrets was among the Act's principal uses. This characteristic, together with FOIA's costs, discussed below at p. 727, prompted then-professor Antonin Scalia to characterize FOIA as "the Taj Mahal of the doctrine of unanticipated consequences, the Sistine Chapel of cost-benefit analysis ignored." The Freedom of Information Act Has No Clothes, Regulation, March/April 1982, at 14.

In a 2006 study,[62] the Coalition of Journalists for Open Government (which no longer exists) "analyzed 6,439 FOIA requests to 11 Cabinet-level departments and six large agencies in September 2005, the closing month of the last federal budget year." It "found that more than 60 percent of the requests came from commercial interests, with one-fourth of those filed by professional data brokers working on behalf of clients who wanted such information as the asbestos level on old Navy ships, cockpit recordings from crashed airliners and background data on prospective employees." "Other," which mostly included individuals, made up the second largest group, with one-third of the total requests. "Even accounting for a spike in journalistic activity last September, when the devastation from Hurricane Katrina prompted media requests for records on environmental and health issues," the report noted that such requests made up only 6 percent of the total received.

More recently, Professor MARGARET KWOKA examined FOIA requests received by six agencies in FY 2013: Defense Logistics Agency (4,420 requests), Environmental Protection Agency (9,737), Federal Trade Commission (1,538), Food and Drug Administration (10,167), National Institutes of Health (1,198), and Securities and Exchange Commission (12,091). Margaret B. Kwoka, FOIA, Inc., 65 Duke L.J. 1361 (2016). Here are some of her important findings, as summarized for JOTWELL:[63]

---

[61] David McCraw, Think FOIA Is a Paper Tiger? The New York Times Gives It Some Bite, N.Y. Times, June 13, 2017, http://nyti.ms/2tgPur4.

[62] CJOG, Frequent Filers: Businesses Make FOIA Their Business (2006), available at: http://perma.cc/BFD9-VZ2L.

[63] Anne Joseph O'Connell, Disclosure about Disclosure, JOTWELL (May 2016), http://adlaw.jotwell.com/disclosure-about-disclosure/.

Although a smaller FOIA operation, all but four percent of DLA's requests were categorized as commercial. Day & Day, one information reseller, charges $1800 for an annual subscription to an online database of FOIA documents from DLA (specifically, procurements and contracts).

Nearly eighty percent of EPA's requests were submitted by commercial requesters. Compared to other agencies, frequent requesters were, well, less frequent. Only six sources made more than 100 requests and none put in more than 180.

By contrast to four of the other agencies, only about one-third of FTC requests fell into the commercial category. Over half of those commercial requests (and twenty percent of all requests) came from law firms. Nearly half of the total requests were made by individuals, almost all of whom wanted information about their own consumer complaints to the agency.

Three-quarters of FDA's requests came from commercial sources. . . . [T]he "most frequent requesters are not . . . pharmaceutical companies, but information resellers." These resellers make good money. FDA News charges $997 for a one-year subscription for FDA Form 483s and $117 for a particular form. The only high-volume pharmaceutical requester, Merck & Co., overwhelmingly asked (more than 80 percent of its 373 requests) about others' FOIA requests.

Like the FTC, a little more than one-third of NIH's requests were labeled commercial. Fifteen percent came from educational institutions.

SECProbes accounted for 12 percent of all SEC requests. These 2498 requests from SECProbes were labeled as coming from news media but should have been placed in the commercial category (from impressive online sleuthing by Kwoka). If they are removed from the news media pile, only 309 requests remain in that category.

Should FOIA be amended to take account of a particular requester's identity and need for information, not only (as at present) in relation to the urgency of response to the request and the size, if any, of search fees, but also as to the very meaning of the exemptions? Alternatively, could agencies disclose more materials online in useful formats, so that information resellers would have fewer products to sell, as Kwoka proposes?

b. FOIA's General Characteristics

> **MILNER v. DEP'T OF THE NAVY**
> **Notes on Comparing FOIA and**
> **Traditional APA**

MILNER v. DEP'T OF THE NAVY

Supreme Court of the United States (2011).
562 U.S. 562.

■ JUSTICE KAGAN delivered the opinion of the Court.

The Freedom of Information Act (FOIA), 5 U.S.C. § 552, requires federal agencies to make Government records available to the public, subject to nine exemptions for specific categories of material. This case concerns the scope of Exemption 2, which protects from disclosure material that is "related solely to the internal personnel rules and practices of an agency." § 552(b)(2). Respondent Department of the Navy (Navy or Government) invoked Exemption 2 to deny a FOIA request for data and maps used to help store explosives at a naval base in Washington State. We hold that Exemption 2 does not stretch so far.

I

Congress enacted FOIA to overhaul the public-disclosure section of the Administrative Procedure Act (APA), 5 U.S.C. § 1002 (1964 ed.). That section of the APA "was plagued with vague phrases" and gradually became more "a withholding statute than a disclosure statute." EPA v. Mink, 410 U.S. 73, 79 (1973). Congress intended FOIA to "permit access to official information long shielded unnecessarily from public view." Id., at 80. FOIA thus mandates that an agency disclose records on request, unless they fall within one of nine exemptions. These exemptions are "explicitly made exclusive," id., at 79, and must be "narrowly construed," FBI v. Abramson, 456 U.S. 615, 630 (1982).

At issue here is Exemption 2, which shields from compelled disclosure documents "related solely to the internal personnel rules and practices of an agency." § 552(b)(2). Congress enacted Exemption 2 to replace the APA's exemption for "any matter relating solely to the internal management of an agency," 5 U.S.C. § 1002 (1964 ed.). Believing that the "sweep" of the phrase "internal management" had led to excessive withholding, Congress drafted Exemption 2 "to have a narrower reach." Department of Air Force v. Rose, 425 U.S. 352, 362–363 (1976).

We considered the extent of that reach in Department of Air Force v. Rose. There, we rejected the Government's invocation of Exemption 2 to withhold case summaries of honor and ethics hearings at the United States Air Force Academy. The exemption, we suggested, primarily targets material concerning employee relations or human resources: "use of parking facilities or regulations of lunch hours, statements of policy as to sick leave, and the like." Id., at 363. . . . But we stated a possible caveat to our interpretation of Exemption 2: That understanding of the provision's coverage governed, we wrote, "at least where the situation is not one where disclosure may risk circumvention of agency regulation." Id., at 369.

In Crooker v. Bureau of Alcohol, Tobacco & Firearms, 670 F.2d 1051 (1981), the D.C. Circuit . . . approved the use of Exemption 2 to shield a manual designed to train Government agents in law enforcement surveillance techniques . . . [reasoning that] Exemption 2 should . . . cover any "predominantly internal" materials[1] whose disclosure would "significantly ris[k] circumvention of agency regulations or statutes," id., at 1074. This construction of Exemption 2, the court reasoned, flowed from FOIA's "overall design," its legislative history, "and even common sense," because Congress could not have meant to "enac[t] a statute whose provisions undermined . . . the effectiveness of law enforcement agencies." Ibid.[64]

In the ensuing years, three Courts of Appeals adopted the D.C. Circuit's interpretation of Exemption 2. See 575 F.3d 959, 965 (CA9 2009) (case below); Massey v. FBI, 3 F.3d 620, 622 (CA2 1993); Kaganove v. EPA, 856 F.2d 884, 889 (CA7 1988).[2] And that interpretation spawned a new terminology: Courts applying the Crooker approach now refer to the "Low 2" exemption when discussing materials concerning human resources and employee relations, and to the "High 2" exemption when assessing records whose disclosure would risk circumvention of the law. Congress, as well, took notice of the D.C. Circuit's decision, borrowing language from Crooker to amend Exemption 7(E) when next enacting revisions to FOIA [in 1986]. The amended version of Exemption 7(E) shields certain "records or information compiled for law enforcement purposes" if their disclosure "could reasonably be expected to risk circumvention of the law."

II

The FOIA request at issue here arises from the Navy's operations at Naval Magazine Indian Island, a base in Puget Sound, Washington. The Navy keeps weapons, ammunition, and explosives on the island. To aid

---

[1] The court adopted the "predominantly internal" standard as a way of implementing the exemption's requirement that materials "relat[e] solely to" an agency's internal personnel rules and practices. The word "solely," the court reasoned, "has to be given the construction, consonant with reasonableness, of 'predominantly' " because otherwise "solely" would conflict with the expansive term "related." 670 F.2d at 1056 (some internal quotation marks omitted).

[64] [Ed.] Crooker was a 25-page majority en banc opinion, joined at the time by Judge (as she then was) Ruth Bader Ginsburg, that explored the legislative history of Exemption 2 at great length, with a depth and intensity common enough in its time but today virtually abandoned.

[2] Three other Courts of Appeals had previously taken a narrower view of Exemption 2's scope. . . . See Cox v. Department of Justice, 576 F.2d 1302, 1309–1310 (CA8 1978); Stokes v. Brennan, 476 F.2d 699, 703 (CA5 1973); Hawkes v. IRS, 467 F.2d 787, 797 (CA6 1972). These Circuits have never revised their understandings of the exemption. See [n. 7 below].

in the storage and transport of these munitions, the Navy uses data known as Explosive Safety Quantity Distance (ESQD) information. ESQD information prescribes "minimum separation distances" for explosives and helps the Navy design and construct storage facilities to prevent chain reactions in case of detonation. The ESQD calculations are often incorporated into specialized maps depicting the effects of hypothetical explosions.

In 2003 and 2004, petitioner Glen Milner, a Puget Sound resident, submitted FOIA requests for all ESQD information relating to Indian Island. The Navy refused to release the data, stating that disclosure would threaten the security of the base and surrounding community. In support of its decision to withhold the records, the Navy invoked Exemption 2.

The District Court granted summary judgment to the Navy, and the Court of Appeals affirmed, relying on the High 2 interpretation developed in Crooker. The Court of Appeals explained that the ESQD information "is predominantly used for the internal purpose of instructing agency personnel on how to do their jobs." And disclosure of the material, the court determined, "would risk circumvention of the law" by "point[ing] out the best targets for those bent on wreaking havoc"—for example, "[a] terrorist who wished to hit the most damaging target." Id., at 971. The ESQD information, the court concluded, therefore qualified for a High 2 exemption.

We granted certiorari in light of the Circuit split respecting Exemption 2's meaning, and we now reverse.

III

Our consideration of Exemption 2's scope starts with its text. Judicial decisions since FOIA's enactment have analyzed and reanalyzed the meaning of the exemption. But comparatively little attention has focused on the provision's 12 simple words: "related solely to the internal personnel rules and practices of an agency."

The key word in that dozen—the one that most clearly marks the provision's boundaries—is "personnel." When used as an adjective, as it is here to modify "rules and practices," that term refers to human resources matters. "Personnel," in this common parlance, means "the selection, placement, and training of employees and . . . the formulation of policies, procedures, and relations with [or involving] employees or their representatives." Webster's Third New International Dictionary 1687 (1966) (hereinafter Webster's). So, for example, a "personnel department" is "the department of a business firm that deals with problems affecting the employees of the firm and that usually interviews applicants for jobs." Random House Dictionary 1075 (1966) (hereinafter Random House). "Personnel management" is similarly "the phase of management concerned with the engagement and effective utilization of manpower to obtain optimum efficiency of human resources." Webster's

1687. And a "personnel agency" is "an agency for placing employable persons in jobs; employment agency." Random House 1075.

FOIA itself provides an additional example in Exemption 6. See Ratzlaf v. United States, 510 U.S. 135, 143 (1994) ("A term appearing in several places in a statutory text is generally read the same way each time it appears"). That exemption . . . protects from disclosure "personnel and medical files and similar files the disclosure of which would constitute a clearly unwarranted invasion of personal privacy." § 552(b)(6). Here too, the statute uses the term "personnel" as a modifier meaning "human resources." As we recognized in Rose, "the common and congressional meaning of . . . 'personnel file' " is the file "showing, for example, where [an employee] was born, the names of his parents, where he has lived from time to time, his . . . school records, results of examinations, [and] evaluations of his work performance." 425 U.S., at 377. It is the file typically maintained in the human resources office—otherwise known (to recall an example offered above) as the "personnel department."

Exemption 2 uses "personnel" in the exact same way. . . . [A]ll the rules and practices referenced in Exemption 2 share a critical feature: They concern the conditions of employment in federal agencies—such matters as hiring and firing, work rules and discipline, compensation and benefits. Courts in practice have had little difficulty identifying the records that qualify for withholding under this reading: They are what now commonly fall within the Low 2 exemption. Our construction of the statutory language simply makes clear that Low 2 is all of 2 (and that High 2 is not 2 at all).

The statute's purpose reinforces this understanding of the exemption. We have often noted "the Act's goal of broad disclosure" and insisted that the exemptions be "given a narrow compass." Department of Justice v. Tax Analysts, 492 U.S. 136, 151 (1989). . . .[5] This practice . . . stands on especially firm footing with respect to Exemption 2. . . . Congress worded that provision to hem in the prior APA exemption for "any matter relating solely to the internal management of an agency," which agencies had used to prevent access to masses of documents. We would ill-serve Congress's purpose by construing Exemption 2 to reauthorize the expansive withholding that Congress wanted to halt. . . .

The Government resists giving "personnel" its plain meaning on the ground that Congress, when drafting Exemption 2, considered but chose

---

[5]   The dissent would reject this longstanding rule of construction in favor of an approach asking courts "to turn Congress' public information objectives into workable agency practice." But nothing in FOIA either explicitly or implicitly grants courts discretion to expand (or contract) an exemption on this basis. In enacting FOIA, Congress struck the balance it thought right—generally favoring disclosure, subject only to a handful of specified exemptions—and did so across the length and breadth of the Federal Government. The judicial role is to enforce that congressionally determined balance rather than, as the dissent suggests, to assess case by case, department by department, and task by task whether disclosure interferes with good government.

not to enact language exempting "internal employment rules and practices." This drafting history, the Navy maintains, proves that Congress did not wish "to limit the Exemption to employment-related matters," even if the adjective "personnel" conveys that meaning in other contexts. But we think . . . [t]he scant history concerning this word change as easily supports the inference that Congress merely swapped one synonym for another. . . . Those of us who make use of legislative history believe that clear evidence of congressional intent may illuminate ambiguous text. We will not take the opposite tack of allowing ambiguous legislative history to muddy clear statutory language.

Exemption 2, as we have construed it, does not reach the ESQD information at issue here. These data and maps calculate and visually portray the magnitude of hypothetical detonations. By no stretch of imagination do they relate to "personnel rules and practices," as that term is most naturally understood. They concern the physical rules governing explosives, not the workplace rules governing sailors; they address the handling of dangerous materials, not the treatment of employees. The Navy therefore may not use Exemption 2, interpreted in accord with its plain meaning to cover human resources matters, to prevent disclosure of the requested maps and data.

IV

[The Court rejected two alternative readings of Exemption 2 offered by the government, as inconsistent with the statute's language.]

The dissent offers one last reason to embrace High 2, and indeed stakes most of its wager on this argument. Crooker, the dissent asserts, "has been consistently relied upon and followed for 30 years" by other lower courts. But this claim, too, trips at the starting gate. It would be immaterial even if true, because we have no warrant to ignore clear statutory language on the ground that other courts have done so. And in any event, it is not true. Prior to Crooker, three Circuits adopted the reading of Exemption 2 we think right, and they have not changed their minds.[7] Three other Courts of Appeals had previously taken a narrower view of Exemption 2's scope. . . . These Circuits have never revised their understandings of the exemption. See n. 2, supra.

---

[7]   The dissent's view that "two of th[ese] Circuits [have] not adher[ed] to their early positions" is incorrect. In Abraham & Rose, P.L.C. v. United States, cited by the dissent, . . . [t]he court nowhere discussed the High 2 versus Low 2 question at issue here. Its only reference to Crooker concerned the part of that decision interpreting "solely" to mean "predominantly." . . . In Sladek v. Bensinger, which the dissent also cites, the Fifth Circuit insisted that the Government disclose a Drug Enforcement Administration agent's manual because it "is not the type of trivial rule, such as allocation of parking facilities, that is covered by Exemption 2." In confirming this Low 2 interpretation of the statute, the court acknowledged that another Circuit had embraced the High 2 standard. The court, however, declined to consider this alternative interpretation because it would not have changed the case's outcome. . . . The dissent is surely right to say that Crooker "has guided nearly every FOIA case decided over the last 30 years" in Circuits applying Crooker; but that statement does not hold in the Circuits using the Low 2 approach.

Since Crooker, three other Circuits have accepted the High 2 reading. One Circuit has reserved judgment on the High 2-Low 2 debate. See Audubon Society v. Forest Serv., 104 F.3d 1201, 1203–1204 (CA10 1997). And the rest have not considered the matter. (No one should think Crooker has been extensively discussed or debated in the Courts of Appeals. In the past three decades, Crooker's analysis of Exemption 2 has been cited a sum total of five times in federal appellate decisions outside the D.C. Circuit—on average, once every six years.) The result is a 4 to 3 split among the Circuits. We will not flout all usual rules of statutory interpretation to take the side of the bare majority.

[To a further Government argument, that the exemption "encompasses records concerning an agency's internal rules and practices for its personnel to follow in the discharge of their governmental functions," the Court responded that "the purported logic in the Government's definition eludes us. We would not say, in ordinary parlance, that a 'personnel file' is any file an employee uses, or that a 'personnel department' is any department in which an employee serves. No more would we say that a 'personnel rule or practice' is any rule or practice that assists an employee in doing her job. The use of the term 'personnel' in each of these phrases connotes not that the file or department or practice/rule is for personnel, but rather that the file or department or practice/rule is about personnel—i.e., that it relates to employee relations or human resources. This case well illustrates the point. The records requested, as earlier noted, are explosives data and maps showing the distances that potential blasts travel. This information no doubt assists Navy personnel in storing munitions. But that is not to say that the data and maps relate to 'personnel rules and practices.' No one staring at these charts of explosions and using ordinary language would describe them in this manner.... [T]his odd reading would produce a sweeping exemption, posing the risk that FOIA would become less a disclosure than 'a withholding statute.'... Indeed, an agency could use Exemption 2 as an all-purpose back-up provision to withhold sensitive records that do not fall within any of FOIA's more targeted exemptions."[9]]

---

[9]   The dissent asserts that "30 years of experience" with a more expansive interpretation of the exemption suggests no "seriou[s] interfere[nce] with ... FOIA's informational objectives." But those objectives suffer any time an agency denies a FOIA request based on an improper interpretation of the statute. To give just one example, the U.S. Forest Service has wrongly invoked Exemption 2 on multiple occasions to withhold information about (of all things) bird nesting sites. See Audubon Society v. Forest Serv., 104 F.3d 1201, 1203 (CA10 1997); Maricopa Audubon Soc. v. Forest Serv., 108 F.3d 1082, 1084 (CA9 1997). And recent statistics raise a concern that federal agencies may too readily use Exemption 2 to refuse disclosure. According to amicus Public Citizen, "while reliance on exemptions overall rose 83% from 1998 to 2006, reliance on Exemption 2 rose 344% during that same time period." Brief for Public Citizen et al. as Amici Curiae 24. In 2009 alone, federal departments cited Exemption 2 more than 72,000 times to prevent access to records. See Brief for Allied Daily Newspapers of Washington et al. as Amici Curiae 3. We do not doubt that many of these FOIA denials were appropriate. But we are unable to accept the dissent's unsupported declaration that a sweeping construction of Exemption 2 has not interfered with Congress's goal of broad disclosure.

V

Although we cannot interpret Exemption 2 as the Government proposes, we recognize the strength of the Navy's interest in protecting the ESQD data and maps and other similar information. The Ninth Circuit . . . cautioned that disclosure of this information could be used to "wrea[k] havoc" and "make catastrophe more likely." Concerns of this kind—a sense that certain sensitive information should be exempt from disclosure—in part led the Crooker court to formulate the High 2 standard. And we acknowledge that our decision today upsets three decades of agency practice relying on Crooker, and therefore may force considerable adjustments.

We also note, however, that the Government has other tools at hand to shield national security information and other sensitive materials. Most notably, Exemption 1 of FOIA prevents access to classified documents. § 552(b)(1). The Government generally may classify material even after receiving a FOIA request, see Exec. Order No. 13526, § 1.7(d), 75 Fed. Reg. 711 (2009); an agency therefore may wait until that time to decide whether the dangers of disclosure outweigh the costs of classification. Exemption 3 also may mitigate the Government's security concerns. That provision applies to records that any other statute exempts from disclosure, thus offering Congress an established, streamlined method to authorize the withholding of specific records that FOIA would not otherwise protect. And Exemption 7, as already noted, protects "information compiled for law enforcement purposes" that meets one of six criteria, including if its release "could reasonably be expected to endanger the life or physical safety of any individual." § 552(b)(7)(F). The Navy argued below that the ESQD data and maps fall within Exemption 7(F), and that claim remains open for the Ninth Circuit to address on remand.

If these or other exemptions do not cover records whose release would threaten the Nation's vital interests, the Government may of course seek relief from Congress. All we hold today is that Congress has not enacted the FOIA exemption the Government desires. We leave to Congress, as is appropriate, the question whether it should do so.

Reversed and remanded.

[JUSTICE ALITO, concurring, explored at some length the possibility of treating the ESQD data and maps as information "compiled for law enforcement purposes" within the meaning of FOIA's seventh exemption—in particular as documents that, if disclosed, "could reasonably be expected to endanger the life or physical safety of any individual." § 552(b)(7)(F). He suggested that "law enforcement purposes," the evident hurdle to be surmounted, might be understood to encompass "proactive steps designed to prevent criminal activity and to maintain security. . . . Crime prevention and security measures are critical to effective law enforcement as we know it. There can be no doubt, for example, that the Secret Service acts with a law enforcement purpose when it protects federal officials from attack, even though no investigation may be ongoing." And, unlike the text of Exemption 2, "[t]he text of Exemption 7 does not require that the information be compiled *solely* for law enforcement purposes." [Ed. emphasis added] "If, indeed, the ESQD information was compiled as part of an effort to prevent crimes of terrorism and to maintain security, there is a reasonable argument that the information has been "compiled for law enforcement purposes."]

■ Justice Breyer, dissenting.

Justice Stevens has explained that, once "a statute has been construed, either by this Court *or by a consistent course of decision by other federal judges* and agencies," it can acquire a clear meaning that this Court should hesitate to change. See Shearson/American Express Inc. v. McMahon, 482 U.S. 220, 268 (1987) (opinion concurring in part and dissenting in part) (emphasis added). See also B. Cardozo, The Nature of the Judicial Process 149 (1921). I would apply that principle to this case and accept the 30-year-old decision by the D.C. Circuit in Crooker as properly stating the law.

For one thing, the Crooker decision, joined by 9 of the 10 sitting Circuit Judges, has been consistently followed, or favorably cited, by every Court of Appeals to have considered the matter during the past 30 years. Three Circuits adopted a different approach in the 1970's before Crooker was decided, but I read subsequent decisions in two of those Circuits as not adhering to their early positions. See Abraham & Rose, PLC v. United States, 138 F.3d 1075, 1080–1081 (CA6 1998) (finding Crooker's textual analysis "sound and persuasive," and noting that FBI symbols "used internally to identify confidential sources" may be withheld); Sladek v. Bensinger, 605 F.2d 899, 902 (CA5 1979) (expressly reserving judgment on the Crooker issue). As for the remaining Circuit, its district courts understand Crooker now to apply. See, e.g., Gavin v. SEC, No. 04–4522, 2007 U.S. Dist. LEXIS 62252, 2007 WL 2454156, *5–*6 (D Minn., Aug. 23, 2007). I recognize that there is reasonable ground for disagreement over the precise status of certain pre-Crooker precedents, but the Crooker interpretation of Exemption 2 has guided nearly every Freedom of Information Act (FOIA) case decided over the last 30 years. See generally Dept. of Justice, Guide to Freedom of Information Act, pp. 184–206 (2009) (FOIA Guide) (identifying over 100 district court decisions applying the Crooker approach, and one appearing to reject it).

Congress, moreover, well aware of Crooker, left Exemption 2, 5 U.S.C. § 552(b)(2), untouched when it amended the FOIA five years later. See S. Rep. No. 98–221, p. 25 (1983) (discussing Crooker); Freedom of Information Reform Act of 1986, 100 Stat. 3207–48 (amending Exemption 7, 5 U.S.C. § 552(b)(7)).

This Court has found that circumstances of this kind offer significant support for retaining an interpretation of a statute that has been settled by the lower courts. [citing numerous cases] . . . [E]ven if the majority's analysis would have persuaded me if written on a blank slate, Crooker's analysis was careful and its holding reasonable. . . . The D. C. Circuit agreed with today's Court that the Senate Report described the exemption as referring to " 'internal personnel' " matters, giving as examples " 'personnel's use of parking facilities, . . . sick leave, and the like.' " But it also noted that the House Report described the exemption as protecting from disclosure " '[o]perating rules, guidelines, and manuals of procedure for Government investigators or examiners.' " "[U]pon reflection," it thought the views of the two Houses "reconcilable" if one understood both sets of examples as referring to internal staff information (both minor personnel matters and staff instruction matters) that the public had no legitimate interest in learning about. And it accepted this view in light of its hesitation to "apply individual provisions of the statute woodenly, oblivious to Congress' intention that FOIA not frustrate law enforcement efforts." [I]t found no other exemption that would protect internal documents in which there is no legitimate public interest in disclosure—a category that includes, say, building plans, safe combinations, computer passwords, evacuation plans, and the like. . . . [Such reasoning,] based upon Congress' broader FOIA objectives and a "common sense" view of what information Congress did and did not want to make available, takes the "practical approach" that this Court has "consistently . . . taken" when interpreting the FOIA, John Doe Agency v. John Doe Corp., 493 U.S. 146, 157 (1989). . . . [T]his "practical approach" . . . reflects this Court's longstanding recognition that it cannot interpret the FOIA (and the Administrative Procedure Act (APA) of which it is a part) with the linguistic literalism fit for interpretations of the tax code. That in large part is because the FOIA (like the APA but unlike the tax code) must govern the affairs of a vast Executive Branch with numerous different agencies, bureaus, and departments, performing numerous tasks of many different kinds. Too narrow an interpretation, while working well in the case of one agency, may seriously interfere with congressional objectives when applied to another. . . .

Further, 30 years of experience with Crooker's holding suggests that it has not seriously interfered with the FOIA's informational objectives, while at the same time it has permitted agencies to withhold much information which, in my view, Congress would not have wanted to force into the public realm. To focus only on the case law, courts have held that that information protected by Exemption 2 includes blueprints for Department of Agriculture buildings that store biological agents, documents that would help hackers access National Aeronautics and Space Administration computers, agency credit card numbers, . . . guidelines for settling cases, "trigger figures" that alert the Department of Education to possible mismanagement of federal funds, security plans for the Supreme Court Building and Supreme Court Justices, vulnerability assessments of Commerce Department computer security plans, Bureau of Prisons guidelines for controlling riots and for storing hazardous chemicals, guidelines for assessing the sensitivity of military programs, and guidelines for processing Medicare reimbursement claims.[65]

In other Exemption 2 cases, where withholding may seem less reasonable, the courts have ordered disclosure. Cf. [n. 9] (citing Audubon Society v. Forest Serv., 104 F.3d 1201, 1203 (CA10 1997), and Maricopa Audubon Soc. v. Forest Serv., 108 F.3d 1082, 1084 (CA9 1997)).

The majority acknowledges that "our decision today upsets three decades of agency practice relying on Crooker, and therefore may force considerable adjustments." But how are these adjustments to be made? Should the Government rely upon other exemptions to provide the protection it believes necessary? As JUSTICE ALITO notes, Exemption 7 applies where the documents consist of "records or information compiled for law enforcement purposes" . . . But what about information that is not compiled for law enforcement purposes, such as building plans, computer passwords, credit card numbers, or safe deposit combinations? The Government, which has much experience litigating FOIA cases, warns us that Exemption 7 "targets only a subset of the important agency functions that may be circumvented." Today's decision only confirms this point, as the Court's insistence on narrow construction might persuade judges to avoid reading Exemption 7 broadly enough to provide Crooker-type protection.

The majority suggests that the Government can classify documents that should remain private. But classification is at best a partial solution. It takes time. It is subject to its own rules. As the Government points out, it would hinder the sharing of information about Government buildings with "first responders," such as local fire and police departments. And both Congress and the President believe the Nation currently faces a problem of too much, not too little, classified material. . . . [I]t is "over-classification," not Crooker, that poses the more serious threat to the FOIA's public information objectives.

That leaves congressional action. . . . But legislative action takes time; Congress has much to do; and other matters, when compared with a FOIA revision, may warrant higher legislative priority. In my view, it is for the courts, through appropriate interpretation, to turn Congress' public information objectives into workable agency practice, and to adhere to such interpretations once they are settled.

That is why: Where the courts have already interpreted Exemption 2, where that interpretation has been consistently relied upon and followed for 30 years, where Congress has taken note of that interpretation in amending other parts of the statute, where that interpretation is reasonable, where it has proved practically helpful and achieved commonsense results, where it is consistent with the FOIA's overall statutory goals, where a new and different interpretation raises

---

[65] [Ed.] Citations omitted.

serious problems of its own, and where that new interpretation would require Congress to act just to preserve a decades-long status quo, I would let sleeping legal dogs lie.

For these reasons, with respect, I dissent.

NOTES

(1) *Textualism and FOIA (and the APA).* Justice Breyer, alone, writes of a "practical" approach to interpretation that "reflects this Court's longstanding recognition that it cannot interpret the FOIA (and the Administrative Procedure Act (APA) of which it is a part) with the linguistic literalism fit for interpretations of the tax code." Milner was the second of two Supreme Court opinions issued in March 2011 to emphasize the place of ordinary linguistic meaning, and the primacy of text, in interpreting FOIA. FCC v. AT&T, 562 U.S. 397 (2011), noted briefly later at p. 725, was concerned with the meaning of "personal" in Exemption 7(C)'s reference to "personal privacy"—did that include a corporation?—rather than "personnel" in Exemption 2, and it was unanimous. Chief Justice Roberts's opinion, like Justice Kagan's, stressed ordinary meanings, linguistic usages, and the necessity of faithfulness to text.

You may take up questions about contemporary statutory interpretation techniques, generally, as an element of your studies in Chapters II or VIII. Note that Justice Breyer essentially concedes the textual issue, making virtually no attempt to make a consistent-with-the-text argument. Assuming that he is basically right on the underlying cases, how much should a settled 30-year practice count? Given the hundred-plus district court opinions cited by the Department of Justice's FOIA guide and (perhaps) Congress's arguable acceptance of Crooker when amending FOIA in 1983, is the infrequency of appellate court consideration of Exemption 2 that Justice Kagan mentions better taken as a signal of the unimportance of the question, as she suggests, or of how settled the issue had become, as he does? If the latter is the case, does it matter ("we have no warrant to ignore clear statutory language on the ground that other courts have done so")? As Justice Breyer notes, the "settled practice" banner was also carried by Justice Stevens, no longer sitting at the time of Milner; and he, too, did not prevail. In 1994, not long before Justice Breyer joined the Court, five Justices had reached out to decide, over Justice Stevens's dissent for four, that the text of the Securities Exchange Act of 1934 did not permit private plaintiffs to maintain an aiding and abetting suit; such suits had previously been upheld by all eleven circuits considering the issue and constituted 15 percent of the SEC's own enforcement docket. Central Bank of Denver v. First Interstate Bank of Denver, 511 U.S. 164, 199 (1994). "[W]e should . . . be reluctant to lop off rights of action that have been recognized for decades," Justice Stevens wrote, "even if the judicial methodology that gave them birth is now out of favor. Caution is particularly appropriate here, because the judicially recognized right in question accords with the longstanding construction of the agency Congress has assigned to enforce the securities laws."

(2) **Work for Congress?** Do you agree with Justice Breyer that "building plans, computer passwords, credit card numbers, or safe deposit combinations" will no more readily fit the language of Exemption 7 than Exemption 2 (as the majority interprets it)—particularly if Exemption 7 is to be interpreted as parsimoniously as Exemption 2? And that they are not readily (or desirably) brought within the rubric of national security classification (Exemption 1)? If you also agree that their disclosure to "any person" who might request them would be inappropriate, can you draft statutory language to guarantee their protection? Note in this regard that Congress too has recently emphasized the desirability of parsimony in interpreting FOIA. As amended in 2009, Exemption 3 is emphatic that specific statutory exemptions must be explicit; it exempts documents that are

> (3)   specifically exempted from disclosure by statute (other than section 552b of this title), if that statute—
>
>> (A) (i)   requires that the matters be withheld from the public in such a manner as to leave no discretion on the issue; or
>>
>>> (ii) establishes particular criteria for withholding or refers to particular types of matters to be withheld; *and*
>>
>> (B) if enacted after the date of enactment of the OPEN FOIA Act of 2009, specifically cites to this paragraph.

(Emphasis added).

(3) **A Quick Appraisal?** Here is an initial assessment of the case: "As to FOIA, Milner is a great illustration of both the impossibility of framing an acceptable statute in the 'disclose everything/ except' form that FOIA takes (responding to fears that the government won't disclose unless the rules are clear), and the danger of the more freewheeling response Breyer endorses." Do you agree? What do you think of Justice Breyer's test? One element requires deciding whether or not a document is of "legitimate public interest." Isn't that exactly the thing FOIA advocates don't want the government (or even judges) deciding?

(4) **The Aftermath of Milner with No High 2.** As the majority predicted, agencies now use other exemptions where they might have previously turned to the "high" Exemption 2. In National Association of Criminal Defense Lawyers v. Dep't of Justice Executive Office for United States Attorneys, the D.C. Circuit upheld DOJ's refusal to release its prosecutors' "Blue Book" (a manual on discovery in federal criminal proceedings) under Exemption 5, finding it to be protected attorney work product. 844 F.3d 246 (D.C. Cir. 2016).

NOTES ON COMPARING FOIA AND TRADITIONAL APA

(1) **Disclosure before and after FOIA.** FOIA, codified at 5 U.S.C. § 552 as a sub-part of the APA, departs further from the original APA than most of the other provisions studied in this book. As you may have read in the Notes in the preceding section on Secret Law, the APA initially provided limited "Public Information." It required agencies to publish their rules—

substantive rules, some general interpretations and statements of policy, and rules of procedure—in the Federal Register; to publish or make available for public inspection final opinions and orders in adjudicated cases, and rules of lesser generality; and to make available "matters of official record" "to persons properly and directly concerned," except where there was good cause for confidentiality (that is, to a small group of outsiders, who had a demonstrably direct connection to the information at issue). The 1967 codification of the Freedom of Information Act[66] is particularly notable for making available material in an agency's possession that does not have the quality of law—factual matter, studies, submissions by regulated parties, personal information collected by government agencies, and the like. Section 552 from subsection (a)(3) on directs agencies to make most of its non-law records available "to any person," based simply upon a request which "reasonably describes such records."

At the outset it may be useful to consider what might lie behind this emphatic departure from the original view that, beyond the legal materials generated by an agency, public access should be highly restricted. One possibility is that the APA now adopts a different view of what constitutes legally relevant materials: that it starts with the presumption that anything in an agency's files or databases might influence agency action in pursuance of its statutory responsibilities, and thus from a purely operational viewpoint have legal importance and indeed would be included in the agency's record for judicial review. Although FOIA requests are independent of (and in themselves do not operate to stay) other agency proceedings, such as rulemakings,[67] this view might be seen to have animated judicial demands for expanded agency disclosure in rulemakings that began in the 1970s, as you may have read about in the Notes on the Paper Hearing at p. 329 above.[68] Another possibility is that, as the administrative state has grown larger, it has also grown potentially more fearsome; full disclosure is on this view a starting point for a process of policing agencies through public opinion and political pressure. And a third possibility is that governmental information is a resource that ought to be available to all for their own benefit, unless there is a reason to withhold it. On this view, disclosure of records in general is just a larger case of the many overt ways in which government collects information and provides it to private businesses and organizations, from Census data on down. Congress has been consistently attentive to the second of these possibilities in its amendments to FOIA.

(2) ***Ombudsmen for FOIA but not the APA.*** Among other changes to FOIA, the OPENNESS PROMOTES EFFECTIVENESS IN OUR NATIONAL GOVERNMENT ACT OF 2007, 121 Stat. 2524, created alternative dispute resolution techniques that may avoid the necessity of litigation. Each agency is to make its FOIA Public Liaison available to requesters to "assist in the resolution of any disputes" respecting possible modification of a request to permit earlier action on it. § 552(a)(6)(B)(ii). New provisions, § 552(h)–(*l*),

---

[66]   Pub. L. No. 90–23, 81 Stat. 54 (1967).

[67]   See Note 5 (FOIA as Litigation Strategy for Non-FOIA Claims) on p. 729 below.

[68]   This theme is explored in Peter L. Strauss, Statutes that are not Static—The Case of the APA, 14 J. Contemp. Leg. Iss. 767, 786–800 (2005).

reprinted in the Appendix on p. 1490, establish a new Office of Government Information Services (OGIS) within the National Archives and Records Administration, in addition to requiring agency designation of a Chief FOIA Officer "at the Assistant Secretary or equivalent level" and one or more FOIA Public Liaisons. OGIS functions as a FOIA ombudsman—instructed both to be a general overseer of agency implementation of FOIA, reporting to the President and Congress, and to "offer mediation services to resolve disputes between persons making requests under this section and administrative agencies as a non-exclusive alternative to litigation." Its "Final Response Letters," which "document the outcome and any resolution the parties reached" are posted, if the parties permit, on its website, http://ogis. archives.gov/. Might OGIS's mediation services provide a context in which considerations of need or other considerations foreign to legal rights under FOIA, but motivating to requesters and suppliers of information, could enter into its implementation? Should there be an ombudsman for non-FOIA APA disputes?

(3) *Judicial Treatment of Agency Interpretations of FOIA and (the Rest of the) APA.* Although Chapter VIII takes up judicial review in detail, courts generally treat agency interpretations of FOIA and the APA—for instance, whether an agency's action is covered by an exemption or whether a particular statutory procedure applies—differently than interpretations of statutes that delegate specific authority to no more than a few agencies. As the D.C. Circuit has explained, "For generic statutes like the APA, FOIA, and FACA [discussed below in Section 4 on p. 746], the broadly sprawling applicability undermines any basis for deference, and courts must therefore review interpretative questions de novo." Collins v. NTSB, 351 F.3d. 1246, 1252 (D.C. Cir. 2003). There are some exceptions. Under FOIA, courts typically give some deference to agency determinations under Exemptions 1 and 3; the first applies to classified materials, and the third references specific agency statutes. But courts are divided on whether deference should be given to agency determinations of harm for Exemption 7, particularly outside the national security context. See Ctr. for Nat'l Sec. Studies v. DOJ, 331 F.3d 918, 928 (D.C. Cir. 2003); Shearson v. U.S. Dep't of Homeland Security, 2007 WL 764026 (N.D. Ohio 2007). Similarly, courts are split as to whether to defer to an agency's determination that "good cause" exists, permitting the agency to forgo notice and comment procedures under § 553 of the APA. In litigation over whether the Attorney General could issue an interim rule under the Sex Offender and Registration Act (see Note 5 (Deference to Agency's Determination that Good Cause Exists?) on p. 350), some courts reviewed the agency's good cause finding de novo, others examined it to see if it was arbitrary and capricious, and some did not decide on a standard of review (striking it down as arbitrary and capricious).

There are some key differences between the two statutory regimes. While FOIA explicitly provides that courts are to review "de novo" an agency's decision not to release records, the APA generally permits agency decisions to be reviewed under the "arbitrary, capricious, an abuse of discretion, or otherwise not in accordance with law" standard of Section 706(2)(A). How, if at all, would you change these standards of review?

(4) *Agency Regulations under FOIA.* Under FOIA, agencies may (and in some cases, must) issue regulations on a number of matters, including how requests can be aggregated, what fees will be charged, what requests will receive expedited processing, and how requests will be placed into tracks (simple, complex) for processing. For many of these items, FOIA explicitly requires agencies to use prior notice and comment. See, e.g., 5 U.S.C. § 552(a)(6)(B)(iv); Dep't of Homeland Security, Freedom of Information Act Regulations, 81 Fed. Reg. 83,625 (Nov. 22, 2016) (new rules updating its FOIA procedures, on which 15 comments were submitted). Courts have found where FOIA does not require notice and comment agencies can promulgate some regulations on how they will process FOIA requests without prior notice and comment, as "rules of agency organization, procedure, or practice" under 5 U.S.C. § 553(b). See, e.g., Public Citizen v. Dep't of State, 276 F.3d 634 (D.C. Cir. 2002) (finding that agency's "cut-off policy applies to all FOIA requests" and thus "encodes no 'substantive value judgment'" but also finding that the agency's procedurally permitted policy was unreasonable).

(5) *Exceptions for Congress in FOIA and the APA and Congressional Power over Information.* Both FOIA and the APA have carve outs for disclosure to Congress. FOIA states that the Act's bars on disclosure are "not authority to withhold information from Congress." 5 U.S.C. § 557(d)(2). Subsection 557(d)(2) of the APA, governing ex parte communications in formal proceedings, states that the framework "does not constitute authority to withhold information from Congress." Should Congress have more access than the media, in all contexts?

Even the strongest claims of "executive privilege" have often been compromised in battles between the White House and Congress, see p. 720. Moreover, legislation can force disclosure of particular information that might be FOIA defensible. The Dodd-Frank Wall Street Reform and Consumer Protection Act of 2010 explicitly required the Federal Reserve to publish on its website *all* documents "with respect to all loans and other financial assistance provided during the period beginning on December 1, 2007 and ending on the date of enactment of this Act"[69] and on December 1, 2010, it published over 21,000 unredacted documents there, revealing transactions having a value greatly exceeding the $700 billion involved in the Toxic Asset Relief Program that animates the next principal case.[70]

---

[69] Pub. L. No. 111–203, § 1109(c).

[70] Sewell Chan & Jo Craven McGinty, Fed Documents Breadth of Emergency Measures, N.Y. Times, Dec. 1, 2010, http://www.nytimes.com/2010/12/02/business/economy/02fed.html?_r=0.

c.   FOIA in Operation

> *FOX NEWS NETWORK, LLC v. DEP'T OF THE TREASURY*
>
> *Notes on Exemptions Protecting the Operational Needs of Agencies in and Outside FOIA*
>
> *Notes on Exemptions Protecting Information Supplied to the Government*
>
> *Notes on Privacy and Disclosure*
>
> *Notes on FOIA Costs, Delays, and Litigation*

FOX NEWS NETWORK, LLC v. DEP'T OF THE TREASURY

United States District Court for the Southern District of New York (2010).
739 F.Supp.2d 515.

■ MAAS, MAGISTRATE JUDGE.

In this action under the Freedom of Information Act, Plaintiff Fox News Network, LLC seeks agency records from the United States Department of the Treasury related to the intervention of the federal government two years ago to prevent the impending financial collapse of American Insurance Group ("AIG") and Citigroup, Inc. ("Citigroup" or "Citi"). Treasury provided over 10,000 pages of documents to Fox, but withheld all or portions of approximately 7,000 pages under applicable FOIA exemptions. The parties have cross-moved for summary judgment with respect to approximately 300 documents that Fox argues were improperly withheld. For the reasons detailed below and in Appendix A to this Decision and Order, both motions are granted in part and denied in part.

[Your understanding of this dispute may be helped by a brief introduction to the main actors and a short chronology of events, which we largely take directly from the opinion:

- AIG, the American Insurance Group, was a major player in American financial markets and was perhaps "too big to fail."

- BONY, the Bank of New York Mellon, was retained by Treasury to act as custodian of funds under the Troubled Asset Relief Program (TARP) and to help Treasury with custodial, accounting, auction management, and other infrastructure services needed to administer the complex portfolio of "troubled assets" that Treasury had purchased through TARP.

- Citi or Citigroup, Citigroup, Inc., a major American financial services company based in New York City, has the world's largest financial services network.

- Cleary, the law firm of Cleary Gottlieb Steen & Hamilton LLP, advised NYFRB in connection with Citigroup transactions after November 25, 2008.

- DPW, the law firm of Davis Polk & Wardwell LLP, was hired to assist both Treasury and NYFRB with respect to the AIG transaction.

- E & Y, the Ernst & Young accounting firm, assisted NYFRB in conducting due diligence on the AIG transaction.

- FDIC, the Federal Deposit Insurance Corporation, insures certain deposits in federal banks that would be threatened by bank failures.

- FRB, the Federal Reserve Board, the main governing body of the nation's central banks (the Federal Reserve System), oversees twelve regional national reserve banks, such as NYFRB, sets national monetary policy, and supervises and regulates the U.S. banking system in general.

- Morgan Stanley, Morgan Stanley & Co., Inc., served as financial advisor to NYFRB on the AIG transaction.

- NYFRB, the New York Federal Reserve Bank, like other federal reserve banks is a public-private entity, has the largest assets of any of the twelve regional reserve banks, and has been the place where national monetary policy is implemented, through the buying and selling of U.S. Treasury securities.

- PwC, the accounting firm of Pricewaterhouse Coopers, assisted Treasury with the AIG transaction.

- STB, the law firm Simpson Thacher & Bartlett (STB), was Treasury's legal counsel in connection with the Citigroup transactions.

- The Sutherland, Asbill & Brennan, LLP firm served as legal counsel for FDIC with respect to the Citigroup transactions.

Treasury worked with all the private firms mentioned above.

- September 2008—when events signaled the imminent collapse of AIG, FRB authorized NYFRB to provide an "$85 billion credit facility" to AIG. This led to a credit agreement secured by all of AIG's assets and the creation of a trust holding 79.9 percent equity interest in AIG.

- October 2008—Congress enacted the Emergency Economic Stabilization Act (EESA), which authorized TARP. After a competitive proposal process, Treasury retained BONY to act as the custodian of TARP funds. On October 28, 2008. Treasury invested $25 billion in Citigroup through the Capital Purchase Program (CPP).

- November 2008—On the Monday following the 2008 presidential election, further deterioration in AIG's financial position led to an agreement under which Treasury purchased $40 billion of senior preferred AIG stock under the Systematically Significant Failing Institution Program (SSFI). When Citigroup's "financial prospects and viability" continued to create concern, Treasury began working closely with FRB, NYFRB, and FDIC and announced additional programs of investment in Citigroup.

- December 31, 2008—Treasury invested another $20 billion in Citigroup by purchasing perpetual preferred stock and warrants through the Targeted Investment Program (TIP).

- January 2009—just prior to President Obama's inauguration, Treasury, FDIC, and NYFRB entered into loss sharing arrangements with Citigroup as part of the Asset Guarantee Program (AGP) to "provide protection against the possibility of Citigroup's suffering large losses on an asset pool of approximately $301 billion of primarily mortgage-related assets."

Fox sent Treasury two FOIA requests. The first, dated November 25, 2008 ("November Request"), sought documents concerning BONY and AIG that were generated after July 1, 2008. The first six items in that Request sought the disclosure of an unredacted copy of Treasury's custodian agreement with BONY, as well as records related to the compensation paid to BONY pursuant to that agreement, and any records relating to actions either BONY or Treasury took in connection with BONY's obligations under the agreement. The remaining ten items sought records "relating to funds paid to and assets acquired from AIG pursuant to TARP, as well as records pertaining to the terms of any TARP-related transactions with AIG, including executive compensation, oversight procedures, and pledged collateral." The second request, dated December 1, 2008 ("December Request"), sought records concerning any data collected regarding the effect of TARP funds on the availability of credit for consumers and small businesses, documents generated after September 1, 2008, concerning the Citigroup TARP transactions, and any documents submitted by Citigroup "in connection with Citigroup's request for assistance pursuant to TARP," together with any records related to agreements entered into between Treasury and Citigroup, including records concerning the terms, conditions, obligations, and restrictions of those agreements. Fox sought expedited processing of both requests[71] and in mid-December sued and sought a preliminary injunction when Treasury failed to respond. In mid-February, U.S. District Court Judge Holwell directed Treasury to comply with Fox's FOIA request within thirty days and to provide a Vaughn index of any withheld materials within forty-five days.

A Vaughn index is an affidavit submitted by government attorneys that describes in as much detail as is possible, without revealing the information being sought, the reasons for redacting or withholding documents meeting the description of a FOIA request. The statute provides for submission of the documents to the court for in camera inspection. After the Supreme Court had suggested that in camera review was not necessary in every instance,[72] the D.C. Circuit held in Vaughn v. Rosen[73] that the government could meet its FOIA obligations by submitting an index containing detailed descriptions of any documents redacted or withheld.

In response to Fox's request and Judge Holwell's order, Treasury produced 10,113 pages of material, of which approximately 4,000 were partially redacted; 3,358 pages of documents were withheld in full. In April 2009, Treasury provided an initial 334-page Vaughn index to Fox. In late May, after a conference Judge Holwell had required, Fox identified approximately 300 documents still in dispute. Cross motions for summary judgment were soon filed, and, with the parties' eventual consent, Judge Holwell referred these to Magistrate Judge Maas. In December 2009, Magistrate Judge Maas directed Treasury to supplement its Vaughn index with additional descriptions and to explain its failure to use the search term "BONY" in all of the offices it searched. Treasury responded by showing, inter alia, the results of a "BONY" search in most of its relevant offices. After oral argument, and his in camera review of fifty-two documents that he thought had been insufficiently described in the revised Vaughn index, Magistrate Judge Maas wrote the following opinion. Much shortened here, it is a virtual Baedeker to FOIA. It should convey the nature, delicacy, difficulty, tedium, and expense of FOIA litigation, for requesters, agencies, and the courts alike, in a manner appellate cases hardly can.]

II. *FOIA*

Through its passage of FOIA, Congress endorsed "a general philosophy of full agency disclosure." Dep't of Air Force v. Rose, 425 U.S. 352, 360 (1976) "[FOIA] seeks to permit access to official information long shielded unnecessarily from public view and attempts to create a

---

[71] [Ed.] 5 U.S.C. § 552(a)(6)(E) gives priority to requests for which there is a "compelling need"—an imminent threat to life or physical safety, or "urgency" on the part of a "person primarily engaged in disseminating information . . . to inform the public concerning actual or alleged Federal Government activity." The second possibility, a recognition of the statute's initial "sunshine" justification, is frequently cited in seeking expedited treatment.

[72] [Ed.] Environmental Protection Agency v. Mink, 410 U.S. 73, 93 (1973).

[73] [Ed.] 484 F.2d 820, 826–28 (D.C. Cir. 1973).

judicially enforceable public right to secure such information from possibly unwilling official hands." Environmental Protection Agency v. Mink, 410 U.S. 73, 80 (1973). . . . Summary judgment is the preferred vehicle for resolving FOIA cases. "In order to prevail on a motion for summary judgment in a FOIA case, the defending agency has the burden of showing that its search was adequate and that any withheld documents fall within an exemption to the FOIA." Carney v. U.S. Dep't of Justice, 19 F.3d 807, 812 (2d Cir. 1994). The agency can meet this burden through affidavits and declarations "giving reasonably detailed explanations why any withheld documents fall within an exemption." Id. Typically the agency will submit a Vaughn index containing descriptions of the withheld documents, along with affidavits or declarations from relevant officials. If the agency's submissions are adequate on their face, the district court may "forgo discovery and award summary judgment" to the agency, unless the plaintiff makes a showing of bad faith sufficient to impugn the agency's declarations, provides tangible evidence that an exemption claimed should not apply, or establishes that summary judgment is otherwise inappropriate. Id. . . . In keeping with FOIA's goal of full disclosure, all doubts should be resolved in favor of disclosure.

III.   *Adequacy of Search* . . .

A.   *Search Terms*

Fox contends that Treasury erred by not using the terms "TARP" or "BONY" as part of its electronic search of certain offices within Treasury, and it questions Treasury's use of different search terms in different offices. . . . [T]he question is not whether Treasury's search was perfect, but whether Fox has identified any flaws that would reveal that Treasury's search was not "reasonable." Weisberg v. U.S. Dep't of Justice, 745 F.2d 1476, 1485. . . . Treasury employs a "decentralized method" of processing FOIA requests . . . through a sub-office known as "Disclosure Services." . . . Disclosure Services referred the Fox requests to five offices; the Office of Financial Stability ("OFS"), the Executive Secretary's Office ("OES"), the Office of Legislative Affairs ("OLA"), the Office of the General Counsel ("OGC"), and the Office of Public Affairs ("OPA"). Treasury has submitted additional detailed affidavits from the FOIA coordinators for each of these five offices. . . . For example, OLA searched primarily for documents concerning EESA, as its involvement was primarily related to the passage of EESA. . . . [T]here is no reason to believe a search conducted with uniform search terms across its offices would have yielded a greater number of responsive documents. . . .

Although Treasury's search admittedly may not have been perfect, the declarations submitted by each of the five offices adequately describe a search that was reasonably calculated to find responsive documents. . . .

IV. *Preliminary Observations*

Before turning to a discussion of specific documents or groups of documents, a few words are in order regarding the approach I have taken in addressing the FOIA exemptions claimed and the nomenclature I have used.

First, throughout this Decision and Order, the document numbers used refer to the document numbers in the Revised Vaughn Index. Document numbers that begin with a "W" originally were withheld in full, although Treasury has since made "discretionary releases" of portions of some of these documents.

Additionally, unless otherwise specified, any document descriptions in quotes are taken from the corresponding entry in the Revised Vaughn Index. Citations to "Document," on the other hand, refer to the actual text of the documents. . . .

V. *Exemption 5*

Exemption 5 protects "inter-agency or intra-agency memorandums or letters which would not be available by law to a party . . . in litigation with the agency." 5 U.S.C. § 552(b)(5). "To qualify, a document must thus satisfy two conditions: its source must be a Government agency, and it must fall within the ambit of a privilege against discovery under judicial standards that would govern litigation against the agency that holds it." Dep't of Interior v. Klamath Water Users Protective Ass'n, 532 U.S. 1, 8 (2001). By incorporating the second requirement, Congress evinced its intention that Exemption 5 be coterminous with traditional discovery privileges.

Citing Exemption 5, Treasury has withheld documents pursuant to the attorney-client, deliberative process, and executive privileges. The 210 documents withheld under Exemption 5 constitute the bulk of the disputed documents in this case. Fox does not challenge the withholding of documents under the "executive privilege." . . .

A. *Intra- or Inter-Agency Requirement*

The documents withheld under Exemption 5 were exchanged between or among Treasury, the White House, FRB, the FDIC, NYFRB, Morgan Stanley, PwC, E & Y, and several law firms. Of these, Fox only challenges whether the documents exchanged between or among Treasury and NYFRB, Morgan Stanley, PwC, and E & Y can properly be considered "intra-agency.". . . Treasury claims that PwC, E & Y, Cleary, and Morgan Stanley are consultants to NYFRB, which, in turn, serves as a consultant to Treasury.

"The question at issue regarding the intra or inter-agency requirement is whether the document either originated from or was provided to an entity that is not a federal government agency, in which case the document is not protected by the exemption." Tigue v. U.S. Dep't of Justice, 312 F.3d 70, 77 (2d Cir. 2002). In 1971, the District of

Columbia Circuit recognized the "consultant corollary" to the intra-agency definition, which treats documents exchanged with agency consultants as intra-agency for purposes of Exemption 5. It subsequently expanded the application of this corollary beyond the context of paid consultants in a line of cases beginning with Ryan v. Dep't of Justice, 617 F.2d 781 (D.C. Cir. 1980). . . . [Ryan held] that questionnaire responses that United States Senators had submitted to the Department of Justice ("DOJ") to enable the Attorney General to monitor compliance with President Carter's merit selection guidelines for federal judges were agency records for FOIA purposes, even though the Senators were not "agencies" within the meaning of FOIA. As the court explained, "an agency often needs to rely on the opinions and recommendations of temporary consultants, as well as its own employees." Id. at 789. Accordingly, "[w]hen an agency record is submitted by outside consultants as part of the deliberative process, and it was solicited by the agency, . . . [it is] reasonable to deem the resulting document to be an 'intra-agency' memorandum for purposes of determining the applicability of Exemption 5." . . . In contrast, although the Second Circuit accepted the . . . "consultant corollary" . . ., it has never endorsed the broader Ryan line of cases, which would exempt the NYFRB records from disclosure even though NYFRB was not a disinterested consultant to Treasury.

In the absence of clear authority in this Circuit, both sides focus their arguments on Klamath. In that case, the Supreme Court noted that consultants whose communications have typically been held exempt have not been communicating with the Government in their own interest or on behalf of any person or group whose interests might be affected by the Government action addressed by the consultant. In that regard, consultants may be enough like the agency's own personnel to justify calling their communications "intra-agency." Klamath, 532 U.S. at 12. . . . Fox argues that NYFRB was not "brought in to carry out functions of [Treasury,] which is the essence of a consultant's services to an agency," but rather to serve its own interests as a secured lender to AIG. It is, of course, clear that NYFRB had an "interest" in the AIG transaction that differed from Treasury's interest. Specifically, Treasury used TARP funds to retire AIG's debt to NYFRB, incurred when NYFRB extended its loan in September 2008 before Congress passed EESA. Treasury contends that this type of "interest" is not what the Supreme Court had in mind, because NYFRB is a federal institution that does not actually compete in the marketplace.

Notwithstanding Fox's contentions, it is clear that NYFRB functioned "enough like" Treasury's own personnel during these transactions "to justify calling their communications 'intra-agency.'" NYFRB and Treasury worked side-by-side in developing the terms of these transactions, and I have no reason to doubt their representations that the fundamental concern of both entities was stabilizing the economy. Since they clearly were on the same team, I find that their communications were "intra-agency" communications within the meaning of Exemption 5.[5]

PwC, E & Y, and Morgan Stanley, in turn, functioned . . . as consultants to NYFRB. . . . [C]ommunications between an agency's consultant and a consultant to a consultant may be considered "intra-agency" for purposes of Exemption 5. See Tigue, 312 F.3d at 80. Thus, Treasury also is entitled to claim that these sub-consultant's communications fall within Exemption 5.

For these reasons, Treasury properly withheld as "intra-" or "interagency" all but two of the documents for which it relies on Exemption 5. The two exceptions, documents W2719 and 8972–8983, dated November 10, 2008, are email threads "discuss[ing] the proposed mechanics of how Treasury will fund the $40 billion purchase of senior preferred stock in AIG." . . . The unredacted documents show that it was NYFRB that required an answer, not AIG. In fact, in these emails NYFRB is stating a preference for how an aspect of the transaction— specifically, the transfer of funds to NYFRB—should be conducted. Thus, in this instance NYFRB was not acting as a consultant, but, rather, was functioning as a party to the transaction negotiating with Treasury. Accordingly, the email from NYFRB to Treasury at the top of W2719 (repeated at the bottom of 8979 and bottom of 8982) must be released.

B. *Deliberative Process Privilege*

Treasury has withheld all or some of 197 intra- or inter-agency documents pursuant to the deliberative process privilege. The deliberative process privilege applies to materials that are part and parcel of the process of internal agency decisionmaking. See N.L.R.B. v. Sears, Roebuck & Co., 421 U.S. 132, 150 (1975). The main purpose of this privilege is to promote better policymaking by encouraging candor in internal deliberations; thus it typically protects memoranda, drafts, recommendations, proposals, and other documents that reflect the opinions of their authors, rather than those of the agency. However, in order to be covered under the deliberative process exception, a document must not only be inter- or intra-agency, but also both "predecisional" and "deliberative."

" 'A document is predecisional when it is prepared in order to assist an agency decisionmaker in arriving at his decision.' " Tigue, 312 F.3d at 80. Although an agency need not "pinpoint" an exact decision made in reliance on the document, it must show, ex ante, that the document "related to a specific decision facing the agency." Id. This test is designed

---

[5] If NYFRB were a federal agency, its communications would be considered inter-agency even if its employees were representing separate interests or taking policy positions different than those of Treasury's employees. . . . Both Treasury and the FRB, however, have consistently maintained that NYFRB is not an agency for FOIA purposes. . . . [I]t is unnecessary to reach this question in this case because, even if it is not an agency, NYFRB is properly considered a consultant to Treasury, to which the consultant corollary to Exemption 5 applies.

to distinguish predecisional documents from those that are "merely part of a routine and ongoing process of agency self-evaluation." Id.

To be deliberative, a document must actually be "related to the process by which policies are formulated." Grand Cent. P'ship., Inc. v. Cuomo, 166 F.3d 473, 482 (2d Cir. 1999). Among the factors that courts have considered in this regard are whether the document forms an essential link in a specific consultative process, whether it reflects the personal opinion of the writer rather than the policy of the agency, and whether, if released, it would inaccurately reflect or prematurely disclose the views of the agency. Id. Thus, Treasury must actually identify and explain the role that a given document has played in the decisionmaking process. Because deliberative documents reflect the "give-and-take" of agency decisionmaking, factual material is not covered by the deliberative process privilege. Purely factual material that is severable "without compromising the private remainder of the documents" consequently must be released. . . .

1. *Transactional Documents*

Many of the withheld documents are either internal drafts of transactional documents, such as asset purchase agreements or term sheets, or emails reflecting internal discussion about the terms of the AIG or Citigroup transactional documents. Although decisions about the terms of a financial transaction may not be typical of those made by a federal agency, the decisions that Treasury made regarding the use of TARP monies and the structure of the transactions with AIG and Citigroup clearly are policy decisions. Accordingly, any such documents created before the transactions were finalized are predecisional, and, to the extent that they represent internal deliberation as to the appropriate terms of the transactions, are protected by the deliberative process privilege.[8]

Of course, transactional document drafts that eventually were shared with AIG or Citigroup are not exempt. Indeed, Treasury agrees and has represented that it did not claim deliberative process privilege for any such documents.[9] On the other hand, drafts circulated solely between or among agency personnel (and agency consultants) do potentially fall within this exemption. This includes "redlines" or comparisons of two or more drafts, if at least one of the comparison drafts

---

[8]   Fox has challenged Treasury's claim that factual content within the transactional draft documents cannot be severed and produced. The unredacted documents confirm, however, that there is no way to separate the factual material from the deliberative material. To the extent that the drafts contain language that did not exist in the final transactional documents, disclosure would reveal options that the agency did not select—which is precisely the sort of information that is protected by the deliberative process privilege.

[9]   . . . There is one exception. Documents 8548–8550 and 8567–8569 contain multiple copies of a single email from a DPW attorney to a Treasury attorney that states: "Please see below a revision that was just sent to us by Anthony Valoroso at AIG." The remainder of the email, which provides an edit suggested by AIG, was redacted. . . . Since Treasury cannot redact information received from AIG on the theory that it is protected by the deliberative process (or attorney-client) privilege, Treasury must provide an unredacted copy of this email to Fox.

was not circulated to anyone other than Treasury personnel and Treasury consultants. In addition, portions of transactional documents— such as the executive compensation provisions of the term sheet—fall within this protection, even if they were pasted into the text of an internal email. . . .

2. *Talking Points, Press Releases, and Other Public Relations Materials*

Fox argues that documents such as draft talking points and draft press releases are not exempt from disclosure under the deliberative process privilege. (Fox has identified 22 such documents.) . . . First, Fox contends that these documents were meant to explain previously-made decisions and thus are post-decisional. In its response, Treasury alleges that at the time these remarks or press releases were prepared, the details of the AIG and Citigroup transactions had not been finalized, so there were decisions remaining to be made. Second, Fox argues that even if the withheld material is predecisional, the deliberative decisions reflected in revisions to proposed remarks for a press conference are not substantive policy decisions, but, rather, decisions about how to present the agency's decisions to the press. Whether an agency's discussions about how to package its views for presentation to the public should be covered by the deliberative process privilege is a subject that has yet to be addressed by either the District of Columbia or Second Circuit Courts of Appeal.

. . . [I]t is appropriate to focus on the policy underlying the deliberative process privilege. As the Supreme Court has stated: "The point, plainly made in the Senate Report, is that the 'frank discussion of legal or policy matters' in writing might be inhibited if the discussion were made public; and that the 'decisions' and 'policies formulated' would be the poorer as a result." Sears, Roebuck & Co., 421 U.S. at 150 (quoting S. Rep. No. 813, p. 9). . . . Communications regarding how to present agency policies to Congress, the press, or the public, while deliberative, typically do not relate to the type of substantive policy decisions Congress intended to enhance through frank discussion. Nevertheless, such documents are properly withheld if their release would reveal the status of internal deliberations on substantive policy matters. Here, Treasury claims privilege with respect to four categories of documents relating to press or public relations, each of which merits separate consideration.

i. *Draft Press Release and Accompanying Comments*

Nine documents reflect discussions about, and revisions to, a single draft press release.[13] [As Treasury has described the draft, it]

was prepared in anticipation of the contemplated release of the AIG/SSFI term sheet, which was not finalized until November

---

[13] . . . The final press release, captioned "Treasury to Invest in AIG Restructuring Under the Emergency Economic Stabilization Act" (Nov. 10, 2008) is available at http://www.treas.gov /press/releases/hp1261.htm (visited Sept. 2, 2010).

10, 2008. The draft includes placeholders in anticipation of the Department's final decisions related to certain additional limitations, restrictions, and taxpayer protections to be made part of the AIG/SSFI transaction. The remaining documents are subsequent email threads (the latest of which is November 9, 2008), which attach further drafts of the draft release, suggest additional revisions in light of ensuing changes in the proposed terms, and offer opinions and recommendations regarding anticipated press inquiries about the not-yet finalized transaction.

The draft press releases were withheld in full; the email discussions were released in part. . . . [D]isclosure of the various drafts of the press release at issue here would reveal how Treasury's deliberations with respect to the underlying substantive policy progressed over the course of several days . . ., for example, alternatives that were not adopted and discussions regarding the rationale for provisions that were adopted which may not accurately reflect the ultimate rationale for their adoption. Accordingly, the draft press release and emails related thereto were properly withheld pursuant to the deliberative process privilege. . . .

iii.   *Congressional Relations Materials*

. . . Document W792–W794 is a draft letter to Congressional leaders from Secretary Paulson regarding the administration of TARP, dated December 12, 2008, intended as a 'response to inquiries received from Republican congressional leaders regarding Treasury's administration of TARP and its efforts to address the financial market crisis.' . . . [It] primarily explains and defends actions that Treasury had taken over the preceding several months. Thus, most of this document . . . does not reflect deliberation on substantive policy-oriented matters. The two paragraphs on the top of W793, however, are forward-looking statements about Treasury's actions and thus are predecisional. Similarly, because the document is a draft, these paragraphs are also predeliberative, since they do not represent the final view of the agency, but rather, only the suggestions of the author. . . Accordingly, these two paragraphs may be redacted, but the remainder of the document must be released. . . .

3.   *AIG Justification Memo and Systemic Risk Analyses*

. . . [Nine documents and email chains addressed the "systemic risk" potentially resulting from a disorderly failure of AIG and forecast the effect of Treasury's intervention. For example, as Treasury characterized it, one memo "includ[es], for example, the rationale for Treasury's proposed investment, contemplated investment considerations, an analysis of how such investment comports with EESA, and the individual analysis, opinions, and assessments of the author."] All of these documents involve analyses and assessments of the financial condition of AIG and the effect that its collapse would have on the financial system. These documents also assess the impact of Treasury's proposed intervention. Although Fox objects that Treasury "does not identify a policy decision" to which these documents relate "other than generally whether to bail out AIG," this itself sufficiently identifies a policy decision—indeed, a rather significant one.[18] Moreover, these memoranda all predate Treasury's final decision to invest in AIG, and thus played a role in the deliberative process leading to that decision. . . . Accordingly, these memoranda are both predecisional and deliberative. Finally, because the emails commenting on the memos also were part of the process by which the deliberative memoranda discussed above were refined, they, too, are covered by the deliberative process privilege. . . .

6. *AIG Workstream*

[Another email thread discussed "work streams related to [the] proposed AIG transaction." Only limited portions had been voluntarily revealed; the remainder had been redacted.] As . . . redacted portions of the email confirm, the three emails, which span less than one-half hour, reflect the attempts of senior Treasury officials—predominantly those concerned with international markets—to understand what had happened that morning regarding AIG. Nothing about the email thread is deliberative; rather, the redacted email consists of a factual recitation from a Treasury official, relaying information obtained from NYFRB. The document must be released in full. . . .

11. *Discussion Regarding An AIG Executive's Compensation*

Document W2791–W2793 is an email thread among several DPW and Treasury attorneys as well as individuals from E & Y and NYFRB. According to Treasury, "the withheld material details potential approaches to restructuring the vesting of [a] pending equity award of a senior AIG executive in light of the contemplated AIG TARP Transaction, and was prepared by Treasury's outside counsel to assist Treasury's in-house counsel in advising Treasury decisionmakers on the proposed restructuring in light of the executive compensation requirements of Section 111 of [the] EESA." Document W2799–W2803 is an email thread with an attached spreadsheet. According to Treasury, "the email summarizes share price calculations found on the attached spreadsheet prepared in response to the analysis (set forth in W2791–W2793) of potential approaches to restructuring the vesting of [a] pending equity award for a senior AIG executive in light of the contemplated AIG TARP transaction."

The email discussion and spreadsheet analysis are clearly deliberative since they are designed to help Treasury decide how to deal with the particular problem of one AIG executive's equity compensation. Although not expressly stated in Treasury's Revised Vaughn Index, it also seems apparent that this analysis occurred prior to any final decision regarding the executive's compensation. Accordingly, these two

---

[18] Fox also contends that W272 is "factual in nature." Suffice it to say, a "forecast" with respect to such unprecedented circumstances cannot fairly be described as merely factual.

documents were properly withheld pursuant to the deliberative process privilege. . . .

13. *Miscellaneous Documents . . .*

Many other documents withheld or redacted by Treasury do not fit into broad categories and therefore are considered individually. . . . [Ed. We have removed virtually all discussion of the FOIA status of these documents, approving refusals to disclose them after the Magistrate Judge's in camera reading.]

Document W5–W6/W174–175 is a "[d]raft analysis of AIG's Insurance-Retail Operations, Capital of Insurance Subsidiaries, Ratings, Constraints and other insurance companies." According to Treasury, the draft "provides an assessment of the risks to AIG policyholders and for the broader financial markets resulting from a disorderly failure of AIG." Treasury does not identify the author or the recipient of the document, but describes both as "Treasury Staff." Additionally, the only date on the document is the year 2008. Although the analysis appears to be deliberative, Treasury has not carried its burden of showing that the document predates Treasury's decision to intervene in AIG's financial collapse. Accordingly, the document must be released in full to Fox. . . .

Document W327–W328/W1583–1584 consists of multiple copies of an "interagency draft paper discussing AIG and systemic risk." The paper "provides the FRB's assessment of its grant of authority to NYFRB to establish a revolving credit facility for AIG." . . . However, even if the document is deliberative, it is not predecisional. Instead, the document, dated October 30, 2008, explains the reasoning behind FRB's decision on September 16, 2008, to authorize NYFRB to provide a credit facility to AIG. The document consequently explains a decision already made and cannot be predecisional. It therefore must be released in full. . . .

Document 8875–8881/8883–8889 is an email thread, on December 22 and 23, 2008, "regarding proposed revisions to draft 8–K filing and to draft press release related to an anticipated NYFRB sponsored transaction with AIG not involving TARP funds." . . . The redacted emails, however, are from NYFRB staff or DPW, not from Treasury. Treasury has not identified a Treasury policy decision implicated in the discussion. Moreover, because Treasury maintains that NYFRB is not an agency, it cannot withhold NYFRB's deliberations as to policy decisions. This document therefore cannot be withheld under the deliberative process privilege. . . .

C. *Attorney-Client Privilege*

. . . Treasury's attorney-client privilege claims in this FOIA case are governed by federal law. See Fed. R. Evid. 501 (privilege in federal question cases "shall be governed by the principles of the common law as they may be interpreted by the courts of the United States in the light of reason and experience"). Accordingly, to withhold a document based upon the attorney-client privilege, Treasury must show that it reflects "(1) a communication between client and counsel, which (2) was intended to be and was in fact kept confidential, and (3) made for the purpose of obtaining or providing legal advice." United States v. Constr. Prods. Research, Inc., 73 F.3d 464, 473 (2d Cir. 1996). The privilege is generally intended to "encourage clients to make full disclosure to their attorneys" to ensure the quality of subsequent legal advice. Fisher v. United States, 425 U.S. 391, 403 (1976). In the governmental context, "[a]ccess to legal advice by officials responsible for formulating, implementing and monitoring governmental policy is fundamental to 'promot[ing] broader public interests in the observance of law and administration of justice.' " In re County of Erie, 473 F.3d 413, 419 (2d Cir. 2007).

1. Policy vs. Legal Advice

It bears emphasis that the attorney-client privilege protects only legal advice, not economic, business, or policy advice. Thus, to the extent attorneys were advising Treasury about such topics as complying with EESA or how the new statute interacted with existing law, their communications plainly were privileged. On the other hand, advice about "risks or costs in terms of expense, politics, insurance, commerce, morals, and appearances" typically is not legal advice. County of Erie, 473 F.3d at 420. . . . Where [legal advice] is the predominant purpose, other "considerations and caveats" are not severable and the entire communication is privileged. Id. Moreover, when the legal advice is "incidental to the nonlegal advice that is the predominant purpose of the communication," redaction may be appropriate to preserve the privileged information. . . .

. . . [A]n email thread involving two Treasury in-house attorneys and three Treasury staff members . . . "respond[s] to questions regarding Citi's lobbying activities and offer[s] opinion[s] as to possible future course of action." Treasury indicates that the email thread discusses Citigroup's lobbying activities "in light of the TARP transactions." In fact, the redacted text contains only a Treasury attorney's factual prediction regarding Citigroup's future activities, rather than any legal advice. This document therefore must be released in full. . . . [Other email threads are similarly analyzed.]

2. The "Common Interest" Doctrine

NYFRB was a party to certain communications for which Treasury claims attorney-client privilege. Treasury contends that the presence of NYFRB, a third-party to Treasury's attorney-client relationship, should not defeat the privilege because these communications are covered by the "common interest" doctrine.

The common interest doctrine "is an exception to the general rule that voluntary disclosure of confidential, privileged material to a third party waives any applicable privilege." Sokol v. Wyeth, Inc., U.S. Dist. LEXIS 60976, 2008 WL 3166662, at *5 (S.D.N.Y. Aug. 4, 2008). For the "common interest" doctrine to apply, a party must show that "[(a)] the communications were made in the course of a joint defense effort or that the clients share a common legal interest; [(b)] the statements were designed to further the common effort; and [(c)] the privilege has not been waived." Strougo v. BEA Assocs., 199 F.R.D. 515, 525 (S.D.N.Y. 2001) (internal citation omitted). . . .

Document 8875–8881/8883–8889, consists of several email threads among DPW attorneys and NYFRB attorneys and staff regarding the disclosures AIG was required to make to the SEC in its Form 8–K. The predominant purpose of these communications unquestionably was to seek legal advice. Thus the document is an attorney-client communication. The entity to which legal advice was being provided, however, was NYFRB. Albrecht, a Treasury attorney, also is copied on the emails, although he does not take part in the discussion. Accordingly, NYFRB's privilege has been waived unless Treasury can invoke the common interest doctrine. Here, NYFRB and Treasury shared a common legal interest in having AIG make a proper disclosure to the SEC. Moreover, the communications were made in furtherance of that common legal interest. The involvement of Albrecht, a third party to the attorney-client relationship, therefore does not destroy the privilege because the communications are covered by the common interest doctrine.

VI. *Exemption 4*

Exemption 4 protects "the confidentiality of information which is obtained by the Government through questionnaires or other inquiries, but which would customarily not be released to the public by the person from whom it was obtained." Nat'l Parks and Conservation Ass'n v. Morton, 498 F.2d 765, 766 (D.C. Cir. 1974). . . For Exemption 4 to apply, the information "must be a trade secret or commercial or financial in character," must be "obtained from a person," and must be "privileged or confidential." Inner City Press/Cmty on the Move v. Bd. of Governors of the Fed. Reserve Sys., 463 F.3d 239, 244 (2d Cir. 2006).

A. *Commercial or Financial*

There is no dispute that the information that Treasury seeks to withhold under Exemption 4 is "commercial or financial in character." . . .

C. *Confidential*

To determine whether information is "confidential" within the meaning of Exemption 4, courts in this Circuit traditionally apply a two-part test. Under this test, information is confidential for purposes of Exemption 4 if disclosure "would have the effect either: '(1) of impairing the government's ability to obtain information—necessary information— in the future, or (2) of causing substantial harm to the competitive position of the person from whom the information was obtained.' " Inner City Press, 463 F.3d at 244. Treasury contends that at least one of these alternatives is applicable to each of the documents it seeks to withhold under Exemption 4.

1.   *Impairment of Information-Gathering*

In four documents, Treasury has redacted the bank account information of the entities that received TARP funds under Exemption 4, contending that these and other entities would be reluctant to provide this information in the future if it were to be released. . . . "[W]here the Government has obligated itself in good faith not to disclose documents or information which it receives, it should be able to honor such obligations." *Nat'l Parks*, 498 F.2d at 768. . . . Treasury needs to be able to maintain the confidentiality of sensitive banking records to ensure that it will continue to have an effective working relationship with banks and other similar entities. These redactions therefore were appropriate.

2.   *Competitive Harm*

The second category of confidential information protected by Exemption 4 is that which, if disclosed, would cause competitive harm to the "person" who provided the information to the agency. Although it is not necessary to show that disclosure "certainly" would cause substantial competitive harm, Treasury must show that disclosure is "likely" to do so. McDonnell Douglas v. U.S. Dep't of the Air Force, 375 F.3d 1182, 1187 (D.C. Cir. 2004). Moreover, competitive harm is "limited to harm flowing from the affirmative use of proprietary information by competitors," and does not include injury from "customer or employee disgruntlement" or "embarrassing publicity." Pub. Citizen Health Research Grp. v. FDA, 704 F.2d 1280, 1291 n. 30 (D.C. Cir. 1983).

i.   *Identification of bank that applied for CPP funds*

On two documents otherwise released in full, Treasury has redacted the name of a commercial bank that "applied for [CPP] funding but subsequently withdrew its application." . . . Treasury argues that "[d]isclosure of this information would likely give rise to speculation or rumors about the reasons why the application was withdrawn. Such speculation could reasonably be expected to harm the institution in question, by causing a loss of confidence in the institution, resulting in an outflow of deposits, a decline in the institution's stock price[,] or other adverse consequences. Any of these events is likely to result in substantial competitive harm to the institution's position in the market." In response, Fox argues that Exemption 4 cannot shield the name of a bank that applied for CPP because the record was generated by the agency, not the bank. Thus, the information was not obtained from a person.

. . . [I]n Bloomberg, L.P. v. Board of Governors of the Federal Reserve System, 601 F.3d 143 (2d Cir. 2010) . . ., the plaintiff sought "detail about loans that the twelve Federal Reserve Banks made to private banks in April and May 2008 at the Discount Window," but the agency withheld responsive records under Exemption 4. The Second Circuit held that the requested information, including the identities of the borrowing banks, "was not 'obtained from' the borrowing banks within the meaning of

FOIA Exemption 4." . . . Bloomberg is dispositive here. The name of the borrowing bank that later withdrew, which was contained in a letter generated by Treasury listing CPP fund recipients, "was generated within [Treasury] upon its decision to grant a loan. Like the loan itself, [the information requested] did not come into existence until [Treasury] made the decision to approve the loan request." Id. at 148. Accordingly, the information must be produced. . . .

iii. *AIG*

Treasury also withholds a substantial number of documents based on AIG's objection that their release would cause competitive harm to AIG. AIG propounds several different theories of competitive harm, each of which is considered below.

a. *Compensation Data*

Treasury withholds numerous documents on the theory that the release of compensation-related information would allow AIG's competitors to "poach" key AIG employees. These documents appear to contain both actual compensation data as well as information about "confidential negotiations" between the government and AIG relating to executive compensation. . . . Fox contends that . . . a competitor wishing to outbid AIG for an employee can simply contact the employee, determine how much they earn, and extend an offer of more money. . . . When actual compensation information for individual employees is set forth in a document, Treasury has redacted the information pursuant to Exemption 6, not Exemption 5. Fox further represented at oral argument that it did not challenge the Exemption 6 redactions. Accordingly, the actual individual compensation data need not be disclosed. . . . [Magistrate Judge Maas then rejected arguments that release of other materials] would likely result in the loss of key employees to AIG's competitors at this late date. Accordingly, Treasury must release these documents in full to Fox (except for the Exemption 6 redactions).

b. *Negotiation Positions*

Treasury withholds many other documents at AIG's request because they allegedly reveal sensitive information which would put potential purchasers of AIG's assets in a stronger negotiating position vis-a-vis AIG. . . . As the December 4 Order noted, a generic statement that each document contains some sort of sensitive information which would harm AIG is insufficient to sustain Treasury's burden. Accordingly, I directed Treasury to "specify the type of sensitive information allegedly contained in each document, and how that particular information could be used to the competitive disadvantage of the person from whom the information was obtained." In response, Treasury detailed the information that would be revealed by disclosure. For example, the Revised Vaughn Index for Document W2774–2783, added that "release [of the transactional draft document] would reveal changes to voting provisions and to repurchase rights provisions of agreement; email release would reveal what items remain open: compensation, board recommendation of shareholder vote, and transfer agent appointment." The revised entry for another document, W3215–W3241, added that "release would reveal factors outside advisors determined were important in valuing equity interest at AIG."

Despite these modifications, the Revised Vaughn Index does not adequately address how "particular information could be used to the competitive disadvantage of the person from whom the information was obtained," as the December 4 Order required. Rather, Treasury simply added to each entry the boilerplate phrase that release "could potentially put purchasers of AIG businesses and assets, including industry competitors, in a stronger negotiating position." As Fox correctly observes, it also does not appear that Treasury obtained any additional information from AIG since the Revised Vaughn Index is not accompanied by any additional declarations from AIG officers or employees. In the absence of such supplementation, the description of the harm remains utterly speculative. . . .

Moreover, while AIG's argument might make sense if an entity were negotiating a series of similar contracts—and disclosure of the entity's pricing strategy or other guideposts might prove damaging—that is not the situation here. Instead, AIG and Treasury engaged in a unique transaction not typically available in the marketplace. The exposure of AIG's bottom line, i.e., the favorable terms it gave Treasury, might be helpful to those seeking to purchase AIG assets, but those terms have already been made public through the release of the final transaction documents. AIG has not adequately explained how the disclosure of additional information, such as the details of the negotiations over the voting rights of the unique class of preferred stock created for this transaction, would put AIG at a disadvantage in future negotiations with non-governmental entities.[34]

Accordingly, Treasury must release these documents in full to Fox.

iv. *Citigroup*

Treasury relies on Exemption 4 on behalf of Citigroup with respect to three categories of documents: (a) fifteen "documents reflecting negotiations between Citigroup and Treasury . . . concerning restrictions on executive compensation;" (b) four "documents reflecting information regarding individual Citigroup employees' waivers of rights relating to their personal compensation;" and (c) one "draft presentation provided by Citigroup to Treasury as an example of the type of finance/risk reporting Citigroup intended to prepare for government regulators." . . .

---

[34] Documents assessing the true value of AIG's assets might be harmful to it in future transactions. Although some of the documents apparently contain information about factors important for valuing AIG's assets, Treasury and AIG have not argued that the documents contain actual confidential valuations of AIG assets.

c. *Draft Presentation*

Document W3176–W3191, prepared in November or December 2008, is a presentation that Citigroup provided to Treasury—apparently as an exemplar of the finance/risk-reporting it proposed to provide to Treasury pursuant to the loss-sharing arrangement it entered into with Treasury in January 2009 as part of the AGP transaction. Although the document was intended to serve as an illustration, it contains actual data from Citigroup's operations. In its Revised Vaughn Index, Treasury contends this document "contains sensitive and confidential commercial information relating to Citigroup's financial position and operations as of late 2008, and would likely cause substantial competitive harm to Citigroup." . . . This document does not merely concern negotiations over terms that eventually were made public. Rather, it contains confidential, proprietary information about Citigroup assets, business plans, and risk management strategies. Citigroup therefore has demonstrated a sufficiently likely competitive injury. This document therefore was properly withheld.

VII. *Conclusion*

For the foregoing reasons . . . both Treasury's motion for summary judgment (Docket No. 22) and Fox's cross-motion for summary (Docket No. 43) judgment are granted in part and denied in part. . . .

So Ordered.

NOTES ON EXEMPTIONS PROTECTING THE OPERATIONAL NEEDS OF AGENCIES IN AND OUTSIDE FOIA

(1) ***Change of Administrations and the Fox Case.*** Recall the earlier discussion of FOIA policies under different Administrations at the start of Section 3. That discussion suggests, but perhaps does not make concrete, the tensions of FOIA for government actors. The massive FOIA request at issue in this case came in under President George W. Bush's Administration, which had created the Troubled Asset Relief Program (TARP) in 2008 to respond to the threatened collapse of the American economy. By the time President Obama took office, litigation was in the very preliminary stages. Attorney General Holder's Justice Department thus inherited the dispute. One might think the Obama Administration would readily accept the invitation to expose materials that might prove embarrassing to its predecessor. Yet, DOJ vigorously defended the action, prevailing as to some but not all of the documents or partial documents it sought to withhold. Does this case change your initial assessment of the Ashcroft and Holder memoranda in Section 3?

(2) ***The Deliberative Process Privilege.*** NLRB v. SEARS, ROEBUCK & CO., 421 U.S. 132, 155–56 (1975), cited in the Fox opinion, was an early case exploring a tension that has often arisen in the cases between documents reflecting what is effectively an agency's internal "law," which *must* be revealed if the Act's purpose to avoid "secret law" is to be served, and documents concerning internal policy discussions that have not reached the

point of finality. In that case, the NLRB's General Counsel generated decision memoranda on the question whether or not to prosecute cases before the Board—memoranda that were available within the agency and instructive to its personnel how later cases might be handled. If the memorandum concluded that a proceeding should be commenced, the Court said, that fell within Exemption 5's protection of "predecisional" processes and the memorandum did not have to be revealed. But if the General Counsel decided not to go forward, that judgment of his was final and "precisely the kind of agency law in which the public is so vitally interested and which Congress sought to prevent the agency from keeping secret." See also Wolfe v. HHS, 839 F.2d 768, 775 (D.C. Cir. 1988) (en banc) (holding that the deliberative process exemption covers records indicating completed FDA actions that still needed final decisions by HHS or OMB).

According to DOJ, the deliberative process privilege, which unlike the attorney-client privilege is unique to the government, is the "most commonly invoked privilege incorporated within Exemption 5." In addition to being predecisional, records falling under the privilege must also be deliberative, in that they must be "a direct part of the deliberative process in that it makes recommendations or expresses opinions on legal or policy matters." Vaughn v. Rosen, 523 F.2d 1136, 1143–44 (D.C. Cir. 1975). Is the privilege the same as Sunstein's distinction between inputs and outputs in government decisionmaking discussed in this chapter's Introduction?

The FOIA Improvement Act of 2016 places a 25-year time limit on claims of deliberative privilege under Exemption 5, adopting the approach of the British Official Secrets Act, but makes no such adjustments in either Exemption 1 or Exemption 7. Do you think this change, permitting historians but not the media to be informed of advice given, is more likely to enhance or to inhibit the integrity of candid advice?

(3) *The Deliberative Process Privilege and Adopted Advice.* Governmental advice that is incorporated into official policy will not be protected under the deliberative process privilege. In April 2002, the Office of Legal Counsel (OLC) at DOJ wrote a memorandum evaluating whether "state and local law enforcement may lawfully enforce certain provisions of federal immigration law." The memorandum reversed the OLC's earlier position from the Clinton Administration, and the Attorney General and his staff explicitly cited it publicly on a number of occasions as defending and pushing the agency's new policy on the matter. The government tried to withhold the memorandum under FOIA, citing deliberative process (and attorney-client privilege). The Second Circuit rejected the government's position in NATIONAL COUNCIL OF LA RAZA V. DEP'T OF JUSTICE, 411 F.3d 350, 358–60 (2nd Cir. 2005): "To be sure, had the Department simply adopted only the conclusions of the OLC Memorandum, the district court could not have required that the Memorandum be disclosed. Mere reliance on a document's conclusions does not necessarily involve reliance on a document's analysis; both will ordinarily be needed before a court may properly find adoption or incorporation by reference. . . . The instant case, however, is different. The record makes clear that the Department embraced the OLC's reasoning as its own. . . . Like the deliberative process privilege, the attorney-client

privilege may not be invoked to protect a document adopted as, or incorporated by reference into, an agency's policy." See also New York Times Co. v. U.S. Dep't of Justice, 756 F.3d 100, 116–17 (2d Cir. 2014) (relying on La Raza to hold that the legal reasoning in a 2010 OLC-DoD memorandum on a contemplated drone strike against Shaykh Anwar al-Aulaqi could not be withheld under the deliberative process privilege as the government had "publicly assert[ed] that OLC advice 'establishes the legal boundaries within which we can operate' ").

(4) ***Opinion v. Facts.*** Magistrate Judge Maas at several points deals with the difficulties that may be faced in redacting documents to reveal facts but protect privileged "opinion." Then-JUDGE RUTH BADER GINSBURG dealt with this issue in PETROLEUM INFORMATION CORP. V. DEP'T OF INTERIOR, 976 F.2d 1429, 1434–35 (D.C. Cir. 1992): "Under [Exemption 5], factual information generally must be disclosed, but materials embodying officials' opinions are ordinarily exempt. . . . Quarles v. Department of Navy, 893 F.2d 390 (D.C. Cir. 1990) (observing that 'the prospect of disclosure is less likely to make an adviser omit or fudge raw facts, while it is quite likely to have just such an effect' on materials reflecting agency deliberations). The fact/opinion distinction, however, is not always dispositive; in some instances, 'the disclosure of even purely factual material may so expose the deliberative process within an agency' that the material is appropriately held privileged. [For example, Quarles] held exempt from FOIA disclosure Navy cost estimates prepared in the course of selecting a port for a battleship group. [We] explained that the estimates reflected a 'complex set of judgments' that 'partake of just that elasticity that has persuaded courts to provide shelter for opinions generally.' [D]isclosure of the estimates could 'chill' or distort eventual Navy deliberations concerning the award of a contract to construct the port . . . [T]he 'key question' in these cases [is] whether disclosure would tend to diminish candor within an agency."

(5) ***The Two Varieties of Executive Privilege Applied to FOIA.*** Courts have long recognized two general types of executive privilege.[74] The first, corresponding roughly to Exemption 1, relates to what have been often described as state secrets—that is, matters relating to national security, either military or diplomatic. The second, reflected mainly in Exemptions 5 and 7, consists of "official information." The right to disclosure differs markedly with the two classifications. Because state secrets pose patent dangers to the public interest, "disclosures that would impair national security or diplomatic relations are not required by the courts." Environmental Protection Agency v. Mink, 410 U.S. 73 (1973). Redaction of such documents to segregate the disclosable and the privileged is far less frequent. On the other hand, the disclosure of "official information" involves

---

[74] A noted legal scholar, once Attorney General of the United States, observed that "[T]he term executive privilege . . . fails to express the nature of the interests at issue; its emotive value presently exceeds and consumes what cognitive value it might have possessed. The need for confidentiality is old, common to all governments, essential to ours since its formation." Edward Levi, Confidentiality and Democratic Government, 30 The Record 323 (1975). There seems little doubt that in its details, if not its core, this aspect of executive privilege is subject to statutory modification. Nixon v. Warner Communications, 435 U.S. 589 (1978); Nixon v. Administrator of General Services, 433 U.S. 425 (1977).

a far lesser danger to the public interest. Accordingly, courts have long given lesser scope to withholding under Exemptions 5 and 7 and, as in Fox, have been quick to order redaction so at least part of records could be disclosed. See United States v. Nixon, 418 U.S. 683, 705–707, 710–711 (1974).

FOIA limits the reach of the stronger privilege to national defense or foreign policy matters that are "(A) specifically authorized under criteria established by an Executive order to be kept secret . . . and (B) are in fact properly classified pursuant to such Executive order." (Executive Order 13,526, 75 Fed. Reg. 707, issued by President Obama at the end of December 2009, is the latest order as of this writing, but each President has issued his own.) Courts are to evaluate these issues, like all others, de novo, with the burden on the agency to sustain its action. This might appear to threaten the integrity of genuine state secrets—if, for example, the executive branch is now required to provide any classified document a person requests under FOIA to a district court for its independent judgment whether the document has been properly classified—in operation. In practice, however, courts typically defer to agency expertise on national security despite FOIA's explicit de novo standard of review, as it is inherently hard for a FOIA requester to produce contrary evidence. See Susan Nevelow Mart & Tom Ginsburg, [Dis-]Informing the People's Discretion: Judicial Deference Under the National Security Exemption of the Freedom of Information Act, 66 Admin. L. Rev. 725 (2014) (empirical investigation), Laura K. Donohue, The Shadow of State Secrets, 159 U. Pa. L. Rev. 77 (2010). The D.C. Circuit, for example, will grant summary judgment to the agency under Exemption 1 "[i]f an agency's statements . . . contain reasonable specificity of detail . . . and evidence in the record does not suggest otherwise"; the court will "not conduct a more detailed inquiry to test the agency's judgment and expertise or to evaluate whether the court agrees with the agency's opinions." Larson v. Dep't of State, 565 F.3d 857, 865 (D.C. Cir. 2009). While Exemption 1 claims may be the most difficult for requesters to defeat, it is one of the least used exemptions by agencies. In FY 2016, of exemptions cited for nondisclosure, Exemption 6 appeared in nearly 30 percent of redaction explanations, Exemption 7(C) and 7(E) in over 50 percent, and Exemption 5 in almost 9 percent, but Exemption 1 made up less than 1 percent.

(6) ***Presidential Communications Privilege and Testimonial Immunity Outside of FOIA.*** The need to protect government deliberations also arises outside FOIA. IN RE SEALED CASE, 121 F.3d 729 (D.C. Cir. 1997), concerns privileges before a criminal grand jury. Nonetheless the similarities of the issues (the impact of denying confidentiality to predecisional matters on the receipt of advice within the executive branch) and procedures (district court in camera inspection of White House documents for which privilege was being asserted, and FOIA-like redaction of factual material) makes the extensive discussion of both substantive and procedural issues highly suggestive for FOIA litigation. The court found a "presidential communications privilege" for predecisional analyses intended to inform the President's judgment, whether or not these were written directly for his eyes: "Presidential advisers do not explore alternatives only in conversations with the President or pull their final advice to him out of thin air—if they do, their

advice is not likely to be worth much. Rather, the most valuable advisers will investigate the factual context of a problem in detail, obtain input from all others with significant expertise in the area, and perform detailed analyses of several different policy options before coming to closure on a recommendation for the Chief Executive." The court nonetheless restricted this presidential communications privilege, which it characterized as broader and stronger than the deliberative process privilege, to communications made or solicited by immediate presidential advisers, and intended specifically to aid them in "advising the President on official governmental matters."

The White House, under both parties, sometimes refuses to let officials testify in front of Congress; it also, on occasion, withholds documents from Congress. For instance, the White House barred Harriet Miers, former Counsel to President George W. Bush, from appearing in front of the House Judiciary Committee to address the firings of nine U.S. attorneys. The dispute ended up in court, the first time Congress sought to enforce a subpoena with only a resolution by a single chamber. In COMMITTEE ON JUDICIARY V. MIERS, 558 F.Supp.2d 53, 105–06 (D.D.C. 2008), JUDGE BATES first held the court had jurisdiction and then rejected the White House's claim of "absolute immunity for senior presidential aides": "The Court holds only that Ms. Miers (and other senior presidential advisors) do not have absolute immunity from compelled congressional process in the context of this particular subpoena dispute. There may be some instances where absolute (or qualified) immunity is appropriate for such advisors, but this is not one of them. For instance, where national security or foreign affairs form the basis for the Executive's assertion of privilege, it may be that absolute immunity is appropriate. Similarly, this decision applies only to advisors, not to the President. The Court has no occasion to address whether the President can be subject to compelled congressional process—the Supreme Court held in Harlow that the immunity inquiries for the President and senior advisors are analytically distinct. . . . Most importantly, Ms. Miers may assert executive privilege in response to any specific questions posed by the Committee. The Court does not at this time pass judgment on any specific assertion of executive privilege."

For an overview of presidential claims of executive privilege, see Todd Garvey, Presidential Claims of Executive Privilege: History, Law, Practice, and Recent Developments (CRS Report R42670, Dec. 15, 2014).[75]

NOTES ON EXEMPTIONS PROTECTING INFORMATION SUPPLIED TO GOVERNMENT

(1) *Connections to Other Sections.* Recall that a competitor seeking information about an adversary's business is no less a "person" entitled to demand information under FOIA than the most compelling public-interest claimant. Indeed, as discussed in the Note on Commercial Requesters on p. 681, competitors and information resellers make up the majority of FOIA requesters at many agencies. Obviously, submitters of information often

---

[75] http://fas.org/sgp/crs/secrecy/R42670.pdf.

have a profound interest in ensuring that agencies do not provide requested information if the agency could deny it. As discussed in more detail in Subsection 3.d below, under Executive Order 12600, agencies have to implement procedures allowing submitters to mark documents "confidential." Submitters can also bring reverse-FOIA actions to protect their interests if the agency believes it has to disclose the information, despite it being marked as confidential. We focus here on Exemptions 3 and 4 outside of the reverse-FOIA context. The next set of Notes addresses information covered by FOIA's privacy-related exemptions.

(2) *Does It Make a Difference Whether Information Is Supplied Voluntarily or under Compulsion?* The government is a demanding consumer of information from the private sector. Banks cannot be regulated, nuclear power plants licensed, new drugs authorized, taxes collected, or censuses taken without detailed information that people do not readily share with others. Where the government must solicit cooperation rather than force disclosure, confidentiality may have to be guaranteed before cooperation is forthcoming. Even if disclosure could be forced or bargained for, as in rate regulation or technology licensing, sound public policy may support preserving confidentiality of some kinds of data (e.g., to foster innovation or to avoid creating circumstances conducive to unfair competition).

Should volunteered information receive more protection under Exemption 4 than information whose submission the government has compelled? In National Parks and Conservation Ass'n v. Morton, 498 F.2d 765 (D.C. Cir. 1974), which Magistrate Judge Maas uses to frame his inquiry into Exemption 4, the applicants for concessions in the National Parks had to provide the information being sought as a condition of being considered for or retaining concessions. No such distinction was made there, and Magistrate Judge Maas's opinion does not suggest one.

The D.C. Circuit, however, made such a distinction in CRITICAL MASS ENERGY PROJECT V. NUCLEAR REGULATORY COMMISSION, 975 F.2d 871 (D.C. Cir. 1992) (en banc). In that case, the requester was seeking information about nuclear power plant "incidents" with possible safety implications that had been gathered by an industry group and then voluntarily shared with the NRC—on the condition that the agency would not release the information to other parties without the group's consent. Reaffirming the National Parks test for information supplied under government compulsion, the court, in a 7–4 decision, announced a different standard for information given to the government voluntarily:

> [I]t will be treated as confidential under Exemption 4 if it is of a kind that the provider would not customarily make available to the public. . . . [T]he presumption is that [the government's] interest will be threatened by disclosure as the persons whose confidences have been betrayed will, in all likelihood, refuse further cooperation.

Four dissenters from this en banc decision objected to this much stronger level of protection:

> Henceforth, in this circuit, it will do for an agency official to agree with the submitter's ascription of confidential status to the information. There will be no objective check on, no judicial review alert to, 'the temptation of government and business officials to follow the path of least resistance and say "confidential" whenever they seek to satisfy the government's vast information needs.' 9 to 5 Organization for Women Office Workers, 721 F.2d at 12 (Breyer, J. dissenting). . . . The FOIA request we face seeks no "information about private citizens that happens to be in the warehouse of the Government"; disclosure is sought not primarily "in the commercial interest of the requester," but to advance public understanding of the nature and quality of the NRC's oversight operations or activities.

The Critical Mass distinction has been adopted by "numerous other district court decisions," where much FOIA law is developed, according to DOJ's FOIA treatise, but not by other courts of appeals. Do you support the distinction?

(3) *The Supreme Court and Exemption 4.* In 2011, after New Hampshire decided to stop providing funds to Planned Parenthood of Northern New England, the organization sought and received money from the federal Department of Health and Human Services. In that process, Planned Parenthood submitted information on several of its practices. New Hampshire Right to Life sought that information from HHS under FOIA, which the agency refused to provide, citing Exemptions 4 and 5. The First Circuit affirmed the agency's decision not to disclose, finding that Planned Parenthood, although a nonprofit, possesses "commercial information" and that the information was "confidential" and entitled to protection. New Hampshire Right to Life v. U.S. Dept. of Health and Human Services, 778 F.3d 43 (1st Cir. 2015). The Supreme Court denied New Hampshire Right to Life's petition for certiorari. Justice Thomas, joined by Justice Scalia, dissented from that decision. Justice Thomas noted that the Supreme Court had never interpreted Exemption 4, and, citing both National Parks and Critical Mass, that "Courts of Appeals have embraced varying versions of a convoluted test that rests on judicial speculation about whether disclosure will cause competitive harm to the entity from which the information was obtained." 136 S.Ct. 383 (2015).

(4) *Mosaic Theory of Commercial Information Under FOIA.* How much proprietary information has in fact been released under FOIA is a matter of dispute. As discussed on p. 681 (Note on Commercial Requesters), the persistence of an active FOIA "industry" and the dominance of commercial sources as requesters suggest that valuable ore, deposited by other firms, is in fact being mined. As in other contexts, such as national security,[76] commercial data that are quite harmless standing alone may be

---

[76] CIA v. Sims, 471 U.S. 159, 178 (1985) ("[B]its and pieces of data may aid in piecing together bits of other information even when the individual piece is not of obvious importance in itself. Thus, what may seem trivial to the uninformed, may appear of great moment to one who has a broad view of the scene and may put the questioned item of information in its proper context.").

very revealing when combined with other information publicly available or separately sought. See Gilda Industries, Inc. v. United States Customs & Border Prot. Bureau, 457 F.Supp.2d 6, 12 (D.D.C. 2006) ("[E]ven if the information subject to a FOIA request would not itself threaten competitive injury, it is properly protected if the requester has other, public sources of information that would could complete the picture of its competitors.").

An environmental lawyer advises submitters of information to the government that the interrelated nature of information makes "[a] submission . . . like a crossword puzzle: knowing the answer to one clue helps in answering the next." For example, if a firm obtains publicly available data on a competing manufacturer's emissions, it may be able to estimate the facility's production. Submitters are advised to "draft the impossible crossword puzzle," test it for vulnerability, and then take such steps as pre-submission marking, negotiating with the agency, and following-up with other agencies to which the information is forwarded. See David R. Andrews, Confidential Business Information Provided in Reports to the EPA May Ultimately be Disclosed Under [FOIA], Nat'l L.J., Nov. 21, 1994, at B4, B7. We take up privacy issues below in the Notes on Privacy and Disclosure.

(5) ***Exemption 3: Specific Statutory Protection of Information from Release.*** Amended more often than the rest of the APA, the evolution of FOIA has often reflected the tensions between the Act's emphatic pursuit of "open government" and needs for confidentiality felt in particular settings. Thus, concerns about commercial data (and national security) issues have resulted in a number of statutes specifically exempting certain kinds of information from disclosure—the matter dealt with in FOIA's Exemption 3. Prior liberal judicial treatment of these statutes has led to Congress considerably tightening the exemption's language.[77] In 2009, Congress amended Exemption 3 to require any future statute creating an exemption to contain both an explicit, clear statement of intent to provide a qualifying statutory exemption, and an explicit reference to Exemption 3. 5 U.S.C. § 552(b)(3). The following summer, the Dodd-Frank Act contained three broad exemptions for information the SEC might acquire in investigating entities, such as hedge funds, newly subject to its regulation—all containing the required reference.[78] And, soon after that, concerns that these provisions would too extensively shield SEC operations from public view produced their emphatic repeal[79]—with worries now that the SEC's regulatory task could be significantly impeded by compromising the confidentiality of information it might seek to acquire.

NOTES ON PRIVACY AND DISCLOSURE

(1) ***"Unwarranted [I]nvasion of [P]ersonal [P]rivacy" under FOIA.*** FOIA asks agencies to consider the privacy needs of individuals. Exemption 6 applies to "personnel and medical files and similar files" when disclosure

---

[77] Gina Stevens, The Freedom of Information Act and Nondisclosure Provisions in Other Federal Laws, Congressional Research Service R41406 (Sept. 24, 2010), http://fas.org/sgp/crs/secrecy/R41406.pdf.

[78] Pub. L. No. 111–203, § 929I, 124 Stat.1377.

[79] Pub. L. No. 111–257, § 1, 124 Stat. 2646.

"would constitute a clearly unwarranted invasion of personal privacy," and Exemption 7 applies to law enforcement records when (among other things) disclosure "could reasonably be expected to constitute an unwarranted invasion of personal privacy." The structure of the Act initially forced the courts to determine what is "unwarranted" without regard to the identity or particular purpose of the party requesting information (except when someone requests information about herself). The result was the formulation of rules organized by the type of information at issue. In U.S. DEP'T OF JUSTICE V. REPORTERS COMMITTEE FOR FREEDOM OF THE PRESS, 489 U.S. 749, 774, 780 (1989), reporters requested the FBI "rap sheet" for a specific individual claimed to have organized crime connections. Stating that "the FOIA's central purpose is to ensure that the *Government's* activities be opened to the sharp eye of public scrutiny, not that information about *private citizens* that happens to be in the warehouse of the Government be so disclosed," JUSTICE STEVENS'S opinion upheld the agency in refusing to produce the requested information: "We hold as a categorical matter that a third party's request for law-enforcement records or information about a private citizen can reasonably be expected to invade that citizen's privacy, and that when the request seeks no 'official information' about a Government agency, but merely records that the Government happens to be storing, the invasion of privacy is 'unwarranted.'"

In NATIONAL ARCHIVES AND RECORDS ADMINISTRATION V. FAVISH, 541 U.S. 157, 171–72, 174–75 (2004), the Court revised its approach to determining what invasions of privacy were "unwarranted." Favish sought the release of photographs of the body of Vincent Foster, Deputy Counsel to President Clinton, whom investigators concluded had committed suicide in a public park in Northern Virginia. Did his surviving family have a protected privacy interest in their non-disclosure? JUSTICE KENNEDY, for a unanimous Court, easily found that "the personal privacy protected by Exemption 7(C) extends to family members who object to the disclosure of graphic details surrounding their relative's death . . . ." Perhaps the more difficult question was whether, unlike all other exemptions except for Exemption 6, the privacy exemption in 7(C) entailed balancing between the interests of the requester and those of the person or persons whose privacy would be violated. Upholding the agency's nondisclosure, JUSTICE KENNEDY reasoned:

> . . . [A]s a general rule, when documents are within FOIA's disclosure provisions, citizens should not be required to explain why they seek the information. A person requesting the information needs no preconceived idea of the uses the data might serve. The information belongs to citizens to do with as they choose. Furthermore, as we have noted, the disclosure does not depend on the identity of the requester. As a general rule, if the information is subject to disclosure, it belongs to all.

> When disclosure touches upon certain areas defined in the exemptions, however, the statute recognizes limitations that compete with the general interest in disclosure, and that, in appropriate cases, can overcome it. In the case of Exemption 7(C), the statute requires us to protect, in the proper degree, the personal

privacy of citizens against the uncontrolled release of information compiled through the power of the State. The statutory direction that the information not be released if the invasion of personal privacy could reasonably be expected to be unwarranted requires the courts to balance the competing interests in privacy and disclosure. To effect this balance and to give practical meaning to the exemption, the usual rule that the citizen need not offer a reason for requesting the information must be inapplicable.

Where the privacy concerns addressed by Exemption 7(C) are present, the exemption requires the person requesting the information to establish a sufficient reason for the disclosure. First, the citizen must show that the public interest sought to be advanced is a significant one, an interest more specific than having the information for its own sake. Second, the citizen must show the information is likely to advance that interest. Otherwise, the invasion of privacy is unwarranted. . . .

We hold that, where there is a privacy interest protected by Exemption 7(C) and the public interest being asserted is to show that responsible officials acted negligently or otherwise improperly in the performance of their duties, the requester must establish more than a bare suspicion in order to obtain disclosure. Rather, the requester must produce evidence that would warrant a belief by a reasonable person that the alleged Government impropriety might have occurred. . . . Only when the FOIA requester has produced evidence sufficient to satisfy this standard will there exist a counterweight on the FOIA scale for the court to balance against the cognizable privacy interests in the requested records. . . . Favish has not produced any evidence that would warrant a belief by a reasonable person that the alleged Government impropriety might have occurred to put the balance into play.

(2) ***Are FOIA's Privacy Exemptions Applicable to Corporate Information?*** You may have learned, in this course or elsewhere, that although a corporation *is* a "person" for purposes of the Due Process clauses of the Fifth and Fourteenth Amendments, it is *not* a "person" for purposes of claiming the privilege against self-incrimination under the same amendments. An artificial person lacks a will capable of being overborne. See Braswell v. United States, 487 U.S. 99 (1988). When a trade association sought FOIA access to information obtained by the FCC's Enforcement Bureau during its investigation of American Telephone & Telegraph Co. (AT&T), the FCC withheld some information under Exemption 4, and personal information identifying AT&T's staff and customers under Exemption 7(C), but denied AT&T's other claims based on its assertion of *corporate* privacy interests. The Court of Appeals for the Third Circuit reversed, AT&T v. FCC, 582 F.3d 490 (3d Cir. 2009), reasoning that because a "person" includes a corporation under FOIA, and a corporation can suffer "public embarrassment, harassment, and stigma" for investigative disclosures, a corporation may have a personal privacy interest within Exemption 7(C)'s meaning. The Supreme Court unanimously reversed, in an

opinion by Chief Justice Roberts. 562 U.S. 397 (2011). His opinion reasoned, at considerable length, that while "person" is defined by the APA to include a corporation, so that a corporation is a "person" for the purposes of Exemption 4 (and, for that matter, the making of FOIA requests, as the Fox case illustrates), "personal" is not defined and its consistent usage in common language and in the APA (Exemption 6) refers to human individuals. The Braswell problem was not mentioned. "We trust," the Court concluded, "that AT&T will not take it personally." Compare the reasoning in the majority opinion in the Milner case, p. 683.

(3) ***Privacy for Those Who Comment in Rulemakings?*** Can agencies legitimately refuse to disclose the names and addresses (whether mailing or electronic) of those who submit comments in rulemaking proceedings? Commenters certainly might face bad publicity or other forms of harassment for taking unpopular stands on controversial issues. At the same time, knowing who said what in the proceeding is one of the ways in which the public can monitor and evaluate the final outcome. In the ordinary case, the interest in full disclosure will prevail. All. for Wild Rockies v. Dep't of the Interior, 53 F.Supp.2d 32, 36–37 (D.D.C. 1999) (stating issue was one of first impression). The Alliance for Wild Rockies court did note "that in certain circumstances, an individual has a privacy interest in his or her name and address. See, e.g., Reed v. National Labor Relations Bd., 927 F.2d 1249, 1251 (D.C.Cir.1991)." But for that information not to be disclosed under FOIA, the court required "a showing that a disclosure of the commenters' names and addresses would result in a '*clearly unwarranted* invasion of personal privacy.'" The case, however, did not involve any commenters who had expressly requested anonymity. In 2006, the Solicitor of the Department of the Interior issued guidance advising that "objective evidence of either a threat to the privacy interests of the commenters or the lack of public interest in disclosure" should be sought as a prerequisite to withholding commenters' personal identifying information. Compare Doe v. Reed, 561 U.S. 186 (2010) (Washington Public Records Act validly required publication of the names of signatories to state ballot initiatives).

(4) ***Privacy for Agency Decision-Makers?*** The Department of Justice redacted the names of immigration judges from every document it released under a FOIA request from the American Immigration Lawyers Association for records concerning alleged misconduct by immigration judges, claiming the names were protected by Exemption 6. The D.C. Circuit rejected the agency's "across-the-board approach" and remanded "for a more individualized inquiry into the propriety of redacting judges' names." Am. Immigration Lawyers Ass'n v. Exec. Office for Immigration Review, 830 F.3d 667 (D.C. Cir. 2016). When should agencies be able to redact the identities of agency decisionmakers? Should it matter whether the person is a career employee or political appointee?

(5) ***The Privacy Act.*** Another avenue for getting personal information about oneself from the government is to pursue one's rights under the Privacy Act, codified at 5 U.S.C. § 552a. This detailed Act is especially addressed to government records of routine personal information—about education, medical history, financial transactions, criminal record, and so on. It specifies

a mechanism, not only for seeing what the government knows, but also for having those records corrected if they are inaccurate. See 5 U.S.C. § 552a(d). With regard to records it governs, the Privacy Act starts from the opposite point of view of FOIA: it prohibits disclosure except to, or with the permission of, the person to whom the record pertains, or except as authorized under various specified (and restricted) conditions of disclosure. But a cross-reference to FOIA contained in the Privacy Act, 5 U.S.C. § 552a(b)(2), tells agencies that they should release under FOIA that which FOIA requires to be released. Protection of privacy from the eyes of others thus depends on the scope of the FOIA exemptions. FOIA's Exemption 6 is generally met by the redaction of identifying information. For a detailed discussion of the Privacy Act, consult DOJ's treatise: http://www.justice.gov/opcl/overview-privacy-act-1974-2015-edition.

NOTES ON FOIA COSTS, DELAYS, AND LITIGATION

(1) *Costs of FOIA.* Although FOIA allows agencies to collect certain fees from requesters (depending on type),[80] 5 U.S.C. § 552(a)(4)(A), those fees do not come anywhere close to compensating agencies for their FOIA costs. For FY 2016, DOJ reported:

> ... 4,263.76 "full-time FOIA staff" were devoted to the administration of the FOIA throughout the government. The total estimated cost of all FOIA related activities across the government was $514,614,589.00. Nearly 93% ($478,455,050.17) of the total costs was attributed to the processing of requests and appeals by agencies. Roughly 7% was reported to have been spent on litigation-related activities. By the end of the fiscal year, agencies reported collecting a total of $3,870,921.51 in FOIA fees. The FOIA fees collected in FY 2016 amounts to less than 1% of the total costs related to the government's FOIA activities.[81]

To take just one agency, the FDA, of six she studied, Margaret Kwoka reports:

> In FY 2013, FDA reported spending a whopping $33,570,981.00 on FOIA processing, having dedicated eighty-two full-time personnel and additional 52.15 full-time equivalents to the task. As approximately 75 percent of their requests are from commercial interests, approximately $25 million would be attributable to commercial interests. And yet, in 2013, FDA collected a mere $327,075 from commercial requesters in fees, representing only a little more than 1 percent of the approximate cost to FDA of processing commercial FOIA requests. In fact, out of 7596 commercial requests, FDA fulfilled 3261 (or 43 percent) free of any charge.

---

[80] See, e.g., Sack v. U.S. Dept. of Defense, 823 F.3d 687 (D.C. Cir. 2016) (ruling that, contrary to OMB guidelines and Defense Department policy, students qualified as "educational institutions" under FOIA and hence were exempted from search costs).

[81] http://www.justice.gov/oip/reports/fy_2016_annual_report_summary.pdf/download.

FOIA, Inc., 65 Duke L.J. 1361, 1417 (2016). Try to track down the FOIA expenses of (and fees received by) the agency you are tracking from its annual FOIA report.

Consider that the expense of FOIA administration reduces the funds available to agencies for other purposes. The FOIA Improvement Act of 2016 considerably revised the administrative sections of FOIA (adding numerous reporting requirements that seem intended to permit more intensive congressional oversight), somewhat reduced the possibility of fee collection (by making it ordinarily contingent on compliance with the Act's ostensibly stringent time limitations for compliance), and added, "No additional funds are authorized to carry out the requirements of this Act or the amendments made by this Act. The requirements of this Act and the amendments made by this Act shall be carried out using amounts otherwise authorized or appropriated."

(2) *Agency Delays in Processing FOIA Requests and Open America Stays.* FOIA imposes tight deadlines on an agency's processing of a request: 20 days with one 10-day extension ("[i]n unusual circumstances"). After those deadlines pass, an unanswered request is labeled "backlogged." At the end of FY 2016, there were over 115,000 backlogged requests across the federal government (for a sense of scale, nearly 800,000 requests were submitted in that year, though some backlogged requests were submitted in a previous year). The Department of Homeland Security, which received over 325,000 requests in FY 2016, reported nearly 47,000 backlogged requests *at the end of the year*; it did not meet the statutory deadlines in many more cases (but did complete them before the year's end).[82] According to the agency's FY 2016 report, DHS took, on average, 33 days for simple requests (a few days longer than the 28-day average for all agencies) and 90 days for complex requests (over a month shorter than the 128-day average for all agencies) for those requests they granted, at least in part. In FY 2016, agencies granted only 1,483 requests for expedited processing (out of over 10,000 processed requests asking for such treatment). Expedited requests, which could be simple or complex, took 52 days to process, on average, in that year.[83]

FOIA reporting demonstrates that the deadlines are aspirational, at best. In addition, courts can grant agencies formal extensions from the short statutory deadlines, sometimes for years, to process FOIA requests in litigation if the agency "can show exceptional circumstances exist and that the agency is exercising due diligence in responding to the request" and there is no "exceptional need or urgency" for processing a request out of turn. 5 U.S.C. § 552(a)(6)(C)(i)–(iii); Open America v. Watergate Special Prosecution Force, 547 F.2d 605, 616 (D.C. Cir. 1976).

(3) *Scope of FOIA Litigation.* On one hand, FOIA encourages litigation. The Act allows quick filing of litigation, 5 U.S.C. § 552(a)(6)(C)(i), and wide

---

[82] Many of these requests are from persons desiring information about themselves. See Margaret B. Kwoka, First-Person FOIA, 127 Yale L.J. (forthcoming 2018).

[83] For government-wide figures, see: http://www.justice.gov/oip/reports/fy_2016_annual_report_summary.pdf/download. For DHS figures, enter the agency's name in: http://www.foia.gov/data.html.

choice of venue, § 552(a)(4)(B), and permits the court to award "reasonable attorney fees and other litigation costs" if the requester "has substantially prevailed" in her suit (through "judicial order" but also through a "voluntary or unilateral change in position by the agency"), § 552(a)(4)(E)(i). Yet, very few requesters file suit—compared to the potential pool. DOJ is required to report annually to Congress on FOIA litigation. § 552(e)(6)(A). Its searches of PACER revealed that 448 FOIA cases were filed in 2016, "a fraction of one percent of the hundreds of thousands of FOIA requests agencies have historically received every year."[84] Its 43-page summary of FOIA case dispositions in 2016 is interesting reading. It reveals that FOIA litigants are typically individuals or issue-oriented organizations, the government often prevails, and attorney's fees or costs are awarded in under one-quarter of the cases (specifically, in 2016, they were awarded in only 77 cases, many of which were brought by entities like the ACLU, Judicial Watch, and other environmental groups).[85] Although commercial entities are the most frequent requesters at many agencies, they typically are not prepared to litigate. Rather, they are happy to pick up some intelligence at not much cost. In addition, the length of litigation likely dissuades media requesters from suing; only a handful of cases resolved in 2016 involved media organizations, like the New York Times.[86]

(4) ***The Difficulties of Litigating over the Disclosure of Documents a Requester Has Not Yet Seen.*** A FOIA requester or her attorney could not see disputed withheld documents in the course of litigation without mooting the dispute. And agencies don't want to have to disclose documents in order to litigate whether they ought to be disclosed. The statute therefore provides for the judge to consider the disputed records in camera. 5 U.S.C. § 552(a)(4)(B). But this in turn means first, that opposing counsel cannot easily argue the merits, and second, that the judge may have to review hundreds or thousands of pages by herself against a general claim that they fall into one exemption or another. Whether impressed by the first problem or not, judges early on responded to the second one. Litigation under FOIA now usually proceeds on the basis of a "Vaughn index," named after the first case to require it, Vaughn v. Rosen, 484 F.2d 820 (D.C. Cir. 1973), cert. denied, 415 U.S. 977 (1974). In the Vaughn index, the agency itemizes and describes the records it does not want to produce, presents its justifications for not producing them, and cross-references the specific records with the particular justifications. These specified and indexed claims then become the basis for contest in court.

(5) ***FOIA as Litigation Strategy for Non-FOIA Claims.*** Anticipated and actual litigants in non-FOIA disputes may turn to FOIA for advancing their interests in those other matters. For example, imagine you work for "an association of non-profit consumer organizations that was established in 1968 to advance the consumer interest through research, advocacy, and

---

[84] http://www.justice.gov/oip/reports/2016_foia_litigation_compliance_report/download.

[85] http://www.justice.gov/2016_list_foia_cases_with_decision_rendered/download.

[86] For a fascinating treatment of Bloomberg's litigation to compel disclosure from the Federal Reserve Board, see Alan Feuer, Battle over the Bailout, N.Y. Times, Feb. 12, 2010, http://www.nytimes.com/2010/02/14/nyregion/14fed.html?pagewanted=all&_r=0.

education." As part of your duties, you track and try to influence agency rulemakings on food safety. One of the agencies, the Department of Agriculture, proposes a rule on listeria, a foodborne bacterium that can cause illness and death. The agency then issues a final rule, which is much weaker than what it had proposed. You think that industry representatives pressured the agency in ex parte meetings to reach the weaker result (and that the agency met only with those favoring such a result) but you do not have proof. And any challenge to the rulemaking will, if the presumption of regularity holds, be assessed on the record the agency produces. What do you do? You could file a FOIA request seeking the calendars of certain agency officials during that time. See Consumer Federation of America v. Dep't of Agriculture, 455 F.3d 283 (D.C. Cir. 2006). For a more recent example, see Eric Lipton & Lisa Friedman, E.P.A. Chief's Calendar: A Stream of Industry Meetings and Trips Home, N.Y Times, Oct. 3, 2017.

FOIA, however, generally provides no special treatment for requesters pursuing other objectives. FOIA exemptions still apply. See Abtew v. U.S. Dep't of Homeland Security, 808 F.3d 895 (D.C. Cir. 2015) (upholding the agency's refusal to disclose to an asylum applicant its Assessment to Refer, "a short document prepared by a Department official after interviewing an asylum applicant" under the deliberative process privilege).

Remedies under FOIA are also limited. The other side of the detailed procedures provided by the statute for enforcement of the claims it authorizes, and the absence of any requirement ordinarily to demonstrate a personal need for the documents requested, is a strong implication that most actual personal needs for information that might be demonstrated—in particular, that the information requested could prove useful in litigation with the government, or in connection with a pending rulemaking on which the requester wished to comment—create no claim to additional remedies. In early litigation, Renegotiation Board v. Bannercraft Clothing Co., 415 U.S. 1, 20 (1974), the Supreme Court, in a 5–4 decision, indicated a limited willingness to permit trial courts, using "the inherent powers of an equity court," to reject the argument that FOIA's remedies were exclusive. The Court reasoned that equitable considerations might on occasion permit a trial court to suspend independent administrative proceedings pending the agency's response to a FOIA request that might produce information central to those proceedings, but refused that remedy in the case before it. Congress has since, in § 552(a)(6)(E), provided for "expedited processing" for a requester "who demonstrates a compelling need." But that speedier processing generally does not apply to requesters seeking to convert FOIA into a discovery tool for use in agency proceedings. See, e.g., Kelcee Griffis, Looming Net Neutrality Decision May Overtake FOIA Actions, Law360, Sept. 22, 2017 (nothing that the FCC "may decide whether to roll back the legal underpinnings for its net neutrality rule before it releases documents that journalists and watchdogs claim are game-changers").

d. The Reverse FOIA Action

> **CHRYSLER CORP. v. BROWN**
>
> *Notes on the Ability of Suppliers to*
> *Ensure the Protection of Information*
> *They Provide the Government*

CHRYSLER CORP. v. BROWN

Supreme Court of the United States (1979).
441 U.S. 281.

■ JUSTICE REHNQUIST delivered the opinion of the Court.

[As a major defense contractor, the Chrysler Corporation was required by Executive Orders 11246 and 11375 to observe non-discriminatory hiring practices and to furnish reports and other information about its programs to the Defense Logistics Agency (DLA), an agency within the Defense Department, pursuant to regulations of the Department of Labor's Office of Federal Contract Compliance Programs (OFCCP). Some of the information provided was commercially sensitive data—for example, "manning tables," listing job titles and the number of people performing each job—which might be useful to a competitor. OFCCP regulations stated that even though such information might be exempt from mandatory disclosure under FOIA, "records obtained or generated pursuant to Executive Order 11246 (as amended) . . . shall be made available for inspection and copying . . . if it is determined that the requested inspection or copying furthers the public interest and does not impede any of the functions of the OFCC[P] or the Compliance Agencies except in the case of records disclosure of which is prohibited by law." Persons interested in monitoring Chrysler's employment practices filed FOIA requests for reports concerning two of its facilities. Pursuant to its regulations, DLA notified Chrysler of the requests and, later, of its intention to honor them. Chrysler then sought to enjoin the release of information that it asserted lay within the protection of Exemption 4. In district court it succeeded; the Third Circuit reversed, broadly sustaining the government's contentions: that FOIA created no right to withholding of information within its exemptions; that other confidentiality statutes created no private right of action; that the OFCCP regulations created any necessary authority to disclose, and were themselves within the Department of Labor's authority to adopt; and that, given authority to disclose, judicial review of the exercise of that authority would be limited to assuring procedural regularity and checking abuses of discretion. Since the administrative record was insufficient to perform such review, the Third Circuit directed the district court to remand the case to the agency for supplementation. At this point, the Supreme Court granted certiorari.]

In contending that the FOIA bars disclosure of the requested equal employment opportunity information, Chrysler relies . . . specifically on Exemption 4. . . . Chrysler contends that the nine exemptions in general, and Exemption 4 in particular, reflect a sensitivity to the privacy interests of private individuals and nongovernmental entities. That contention may be conceded without inexorably requiring the conclusion that the exemptions impose affirmative duties on an agency to withhold information sought. In fact, that conclusion is not supported by the language, logic or history of the Act. . . . By its terms, subsection (b) [Ed. the list of exemptions] demarcates the agency's obligation to disclose; it does not foreclose disclosure.

That the FOIA is exclusively a disclosure statute is, perhaps, demonstrated most convincingly by examining its provision for judicial relief. Subsection (a)(4)(B) gives federal district courts "jurisdiction to enjoin the agency from withholding agency records and to order the production of any agency records improperly withheld from the complainant." 5 U.S.C. § 552(a)(4)(B). That provision does not give the authority to bar disclosure, and thus fortifies our belief that Chrysler, and courts which have shared its view, have incorrectly interpreted the exemption provisions of the FOIA. The Act is an attempt to meet the demand for open government while preserving workable confidentiality in governmental decision-making. Congress appreciated that with the expanding sphere of governmental regulation and enterprise, much of the information within Government files has been submitted by private entities seeking Government contracts or responding to unconditional reporting obligations imposed by law. There was sentiment that Government agencies should have the latitude, in certain circumstances, to afford the confidentiality desired by these submitters. But the congressional concern was with the *agency's* need or preference for confidentiality; the FOIA by itself protects the submitters' interest in confidentiality only to the extent that this interest is endorsed by the agency collecting the information.

Enlarged access to governmental information undoubtedly cuts against the privacy concerns of nongovernmental entities, and as a matter of policy some balancing and accommodation may well be desirable. We simply hold here that Congress did not design the FOIA exemptions to be mandatory bars to disclosure.[14] . . . Chrysler contends,

---

[14] It is informative in this regard to compare the FOIA with the Privacy Act of 1974, 5 U.S.C. § 552a. In the latter Act Congress explicitly requires agencies to withhold records about an individual from most third parties unless the subject gives his permission. Even more telling is 49 U.S.C. § 1357, a section which authorizes the Administrator of the FAA to take antihijacking measures, including research and development into protection devices.

"Notwithstanding [FOIA], the Administrator shall prescribe such regulations as he may deem necessary to prohibit disclosure of any information obtained or developed in the conduct of research and development activities under this subsection if, in the opinion of the Administrator, the disclosure of such information. . .

"(B) would reveal trade secrets or privileged or confidential commercial or financial information obtained from any person . . ." Id. § 1357(d)(2)(B).

however, that even if its suit for injunctive relief cannot be based on the FOIA, such an action can be premised on the Trade Secrets Act, 18 U.S.C. § 1905. The Act provides:

> Whoever, being an officer or employee of the United States or of any department or agency thereof, publishes, divulges, discloses, or makes known in any manner or to any extent not authorized by law any information coming to him in the course of his employment or official duties or by reason of any examination or investigation made by, or return, report or record made to or filed with, such department or agency or officer or employee thereof, which information concerns or relates to the trade secrets, processes, operations, style of work, or apparatus, or to the identity, confidential statistical data, amount or source of any income, profits, losses, or expenditures of any person, firm, partnership, corporation, or association; or permits any income return or copy thereof or any book containing any abstract or particulars thereof to be seen or examined by any person except as provided by law; shall be fined not more than $1,000 or imprisoned not more than one year, or both; and shall be removed from office or employment.

There are necessarily two parts to Chrysler's argument: that § 1905 is applicable to the type of disclosure threatened in this case, and that it affords Chrysler a private right of action to obtain injunctive relief.

A

The Court of Appeals held that § 1905 was not applicable to the agency disclosure at issue here because such disclosure was "authorized by law" within the meaning of the Act. The court found the source of that authorization to be the OFCCP regulations that DLA relied on in deciding to disclose information on the . . . plants. Chrysler contends here that these agency regulations are not "law" within the meaning of § 1905.

It has been established in a variety of contexts that properly promulgated substantive regulations have the "force and effect of law." . . . It would . . . take a clear showing of contrary legislative intent before the phrase "authorized by law" in § 1905 could be held to have a narrower ambit than the traditional understanding. [After examining the relevant legislative history and finding no such clear showing, the Court rejected a Government argument that § 1905 was only an anti-leak statute applying to surreptitious, unofficial acts, and was therefore irrelevant to "official" agency actions, taken within channels. That reading, the Court thought, would "require an expansive and unprecedented holding that any agency action directed or approved by an agency head is 'authorized by law'"; such a holding would be contrary to repeated assurances to Congress that § 1905 reached formal agency action as well as employee skullduggery. The Court then resumed discussion of whether the OFCCP regulations provided the required authorization.]

In order for a regulation to have the "force and effect of law," it must have certain substantive characteristics and be the product of certain procedural requisites. . . . We [have] described a substantive rule—or a "legislative-type rule,"—as one "affecting individual rights and obligations." This characteristic is an important touchstone for distinguishing those rules that may be "binding" or have the "force of law."

Likewise the promulgation of these regulations must conform with any procedural requirements imposed by Congress. . . . The pertinent procedural limitations in this case are those found in the APA.

The regulations relied on by the Government in this case as providing "authoriz[ation] by law" within the meaning of § 1905 certainly affect individual rights and obligations; they govern the public's right to information in records obtained under Executive Order 11246 and the confidentiality rights of those who submit information to OFCCP and its compliance agencies. It is a much closer question, however, whether they are the product of a congressional grant of legislative authority.

[The Court concluded that Congress had *not* authorized the OFCCP to adopt rules having the force and effect of law on information disclosure. (That holding, Justice Marshall emphasized in a concurrence, did not call into question the validity of OFCCP regulations as a whole.) The Court found also that the Secretary of Labor had not used notice and comment rulemaking procedures in adopting the regulations—thus confirming their character as merely interpretative regulations, "not the product of procedures which Congress prescribed as necessary prerequisites to giving a regulation the binding effect of law. An interpretative regulation or general statement of agency policy cannot be the 'authoriz[ation] by law' required by § 1905."]

B

[The Court rejected Chrysler's contention that § 1905 afforded a private right of action to enjoin disclosure in violation of the statute.] [T]his Court has rarely implied a private right of action under a criminal statute and where it has done so "there was at least a statutory basis for inferring that a civil cause of action of some sort lay in favor of someone." Nothing in § 1905 prompts such an inference. . . . Most importantly, a private right of action under § 1905 is not "necessary to make effective the congressional purpose," J.I. Case Co. v. Borak, 377 U.S. 426, 433 (1964), for we find that review of DLA's decision to disclose Chrysler's employment data is available under the APA.

. . . Section 10(a) of the APA provides that "[a] person suffering legal wrong because of agency action, or adversely affected or aggrieved by agency action . . ., is entitled to judicial review thereof." 5 U.S.C. § 702. [The Court held DLA's decision to disclose reviewable because] § 1905 and any "authoriz[ation] by law" contemplated by that section place substantive limits on agency action. Therefore, we conclude that DLA's decision . . . is reviewable agency action and Chrysler is a person "adversely affected or aggrieved" within the meaning of § 10(a).

Both Chrysler and the Government agree that there is APA review of DLA's decision. They disagree on the proper scope of review. Chrysler argues that there should be de novo review, while the Government contends that such review is only available in extraordinary cases and this is not such a case.

The pertinent provisions of § 10(e) of the APA, 5 U.S.C. § 706 (1976), provide that a reviewing court shall

> (2) hold unlawful and set aside agency action, findings, and conclusions found to be—
>
>> (A) arbitrary, capricious, an abuse of discretion, or otherwise not in accordance with law; . . .
>>
>> (F) unwarranted by the facts to the extent that the facts are subject to trial de novo by the reviewing court.

For the reasons previously stated, we believe any disclosure that violates § 1905 is "not in accordance with law" within the meaning of 5 U.S.C. § 706(2)(A). De novo review by the District Court is ordinarily not necessary to decide whether a contemplated disclosure runs afoul of § 1905. The District Court in this case concluded that disclosure of some of Chrysler's documents was barred by § 1905, but the Court of Appeals did not reach the issue. We shall therefore vacate the Court of Appeals' judgment and remand for further proceedings consistent with this opinion in order that the Court of Appeals may consider whether the contemplated disclosures would violate the prohibition of § 1905.[49] Since the decision regarding this substantive issue—the scope of § 1905—will necessarily have some effect on the proper form of judicial review pursuant to § 706(2), we think it unnecessary, and therefore unwise, at the present stage of this case for us to express any additional views on that issue.

Vacated and remanded.

[Justice Marshall's concurrence is omitted.]

---

[49] Since the Court of Appeals assumed for purposes of argument that the material in question was within an exemption to the FOIA, that court found it unnecessary expressly to decide that issue and it is open on remand. We, of course, do not here attempt to determine the relative ambits of Exemption 4 and § 1905, or to determine whether § 1905 is an exempting statute within the terms of the amended Exemption 3, 5 U.S.C. § 552(b)(3) (1976). Although there is a theoretical possibility that material might be outside Exemption 4 yet within the substantive provisions of § 1905, and that therefore the FOIA might provide the necessary "authoriz[ation] by law" for purposes of § 1905, that possibility is at most of limited practical significance in view of the similarity of language between Exemption 4 and the substantive provisions of § 1905.

NOTES ON THE ABILITY OF SUPPLIERS TO ENSURE THE PROTECTION OF INFORMATION THEY PROVIDE THE GOVERNMENT

(1) *Information Suppliers as Parties.* You may now be able to understand why Magistrate Judge Maas on p. 712 permitted the suppliers of the information (for example, Citibank), as well as the government body holding it, to speak to the Exemption 4 claims, even though FOIA, as such, creates no such right. So also for AT&T in AT&T v. FCC, noted above on p. 725, on the question of the privacy of corporate information. Note that cases like these—Fox, Chrysler, AT&T—often seem to involve FOIA claimants who are at the heart of the Act's rationale—a news organization, persons interested in what Chrysler's reports to the Defense Department might show about its compliance with non-discrimination regulations applicable to major defense contractors, and an NGO seeking to assess FCC enforcement actions. The motivation for reverse-FOIA actions, as these are called, may well be the avoidance of corporate "embarrassment" rather than the protection of corporate secrets. In any event, Chrysler opened the door to such litigation.

(2) *Standards of Review.* The Chrysler case can make one's head spin with the number of sources of law it discusses and its variety of standards of judicial review. On comparison with earlier cases in this chapter, however, a fundamental contrast seems clear: On the one hand, a refusal to disclose information to a requester is to be reviewed by a court according to the procedures set out in FOIA itself—that is, *de novo* review with the agency bearing the burden of justifying non-disclosure. On the other hand, a complaint by a private supplier of information in an agency's files, that the agency is ready to disclose something it should hold secret, is to be reviewed by a court according to the standards set forth for ordinary judicial review in the APA. In the ordinary case, the court assesses whether the agency's decision to disclose information is *arbitrary or capricious*. This process, as described more fully in the materials on judicial review in Chapter VIII, normally is based on the record before the agency (rather than on material assembled through litigation) and begins with a presumption in favor of the correctness of the agency's decision (although to varying degrees of intensity).

(3) *Establishing a Framework for Reverse FOIA Actions.* President Reagan's Executive Order 12600, still in effect, facilitates reverse-FOIA actions by requiring "Executive" agencies to establish procedures permitting submitters to mark documents "confidential," and provides for notification and an opportunity to explain why the agency should deny a request for them, should their disclosure be sought. 52 Fed. Reg. 23781 (June 25, 1987). Commercially valuable information might not otherwise be identified for Exemption 4 consideration by the busy agency functionary handling a request for information. She may not recognize its implications, having little sense of the supplier's business, or of the sophisticated analyses that might be made of what seem to be harmless data. The Executive Order creates a procedure for notifying submitters of the request and an opportunity to justify the claim for confidentiality, and Chrysler then opens the courthouse

door for review. Although the order does not direct independent regulatory commissions, they often have their own policies on notifying suppliers of information.

(4) ***Applying Chrysler.*** BARTHOLDI CABLE CO. V. FCC, 114 F.3d 274 (D.C. Cir. 1997), provides an example of how APA review works in practice in a reverse-FOIA case, applying the directions of Chrysler. Bartholdi sold microwave video distribution services to apartment buildings in New York City, which had to be licensed by the FCC installation-by-installation. In the course of applying for some new licenses, the company discovered that it had already been providing some services without the needed license. The company conducted a comprehensive audit of its unauthorized operations, the report of which it transmitted to the FCC along with a request that the submission remain confidential. The agency refused to give the requested assurance, and Bartholdi went to court. The D.C. Circuit (JUDGE SENTELLE) discussed FOIA's Exemption 4 in some detail (114 F.3d at 281–82):

"Exemption 4 of FOIA provides that an agency need not disclose information that is 'trade secrets and commercial or financial information obtained from a person and privileged or confidential.' 5 U.S.C. § 552(b)(4). The test for whether information is 'confidential' depends in part on whether the information was voluntarily or involuntarily disclosed to the government. If the information was voluntarily disclosed to the government, it will be considered confidential 'if it is of a kind that would customarily not be released to the public by the person from whom it was obtained.' Critical Mass Energy Project v. NRC, 975 F.2d 871, 879 (D.C.Cir.1992) (en banc) . . . . If the information was obtained under compulsion, it will be considered confidential only 'if disclosure . . . is likely to have either of the following effects: (1) to impair the Government's ability to obtain necessary information in the future; or (2) to cause substantial harm to the competitive position of the person from whom the information was obtained.' National Parks and Conservation Ass'n v. Morton, 498 F.2d 765, 770 (D.C.Cir.1974).

"Of course, the mere fact that information falls within a FOIA exemption does not of itself bar an agency from disclosing the information. Chrysler Corp. v. Brown. But we have held that information falling within Exemption 4 of FOIA also comes within the Trade Secrets Act, 18 U.S.C. § 1905, which prohibits the disclosure of, inter alia, 'trade secrets' and 'confidential statistical data.' CNA Fin. Corp. v. Donovan, 830 F.2d 1132, 1151 (D.C. Cir. 1987) (holding that 'the scope of the [Trade Secrets] Act is at least co-extensive with that of Exemption 4 of FOIA'), cert. denied, 485 U.S. 977. Thus, generally when 'a party succeeds in demonstrating that its materials fall within Exemption 4, the government is precluded from releasing the information by virtue of the Trade Secrets Act.' McDonnell Douglas Corp. v. Widnall, 57 F.3d 1162, 1164 (D.C. Cir. 1995). However, information otherwise protected by the Trade Secrets Act may be disclosed if 'authorized by law.' See 18 U.S.C. § 1905. The Supreme Court has held that the release of otherwise protected information to the public is 'authorized by law' if permitted by a regulation that is: (1) 'rooted in a grant of power by the Congress' to limit the scope of the Trade Secrets Act; (2) 'substantive,' rather than interpretive or procedural; and (3) consistent 'with any procedural requirements imposed by Congress' such as the APA. Chrysler.'

"Section 0.457 of the Commission's regulations permits disclosure of exempt materials to the extent 'the policy considerations favoring non-disclosure' are outweighed by factors favoring disclosure. 47 C.F.R. § 0.457. The Commission has held that this regulation is 'authorized by law' as that phrase was defined by the Supreme Court in Chrysler. Pursuant to § 0.457, the [Commission's personnel] ruled that 'the public interest in disclosure of [Bartholdi's] materials would justify disclosure as a matter of our discretion even if the materials could be withheld under the FOIA.' The Commission affirmed this conclusion in its order, holding that 'public interest considerations favoring openness in our licensing proceedings outweigh any potential difficulty that the Government might experience in obtaining access to information in similar circumstances.' 11 F.C.C.R. at 2477.

"Bartholdi argues that § 0.457 of the Commission's regulations does not meet the definition of 'authorized by law' under Chrysler. But Bartholdi did not raise this challenge before the Commission. Bartholdi's application for review made no mention of Chrysler. Because Bartholdi failed to challenge the validity of § 0.457 before the Commission, we decline to consider the issue.

"Therefore, assuming the validity of § 0.457, we cannot conclude that the Commission acted arbitrarily in concluding that the public interest considerations in disclosure outweighed those in favor of confidentiality. As the Commission now explains, much of the information for which Bartholdi seeks confidential treatment is already publicly available. Moreover, the Commission concluded that the public has a compelling interest in the information at issue as it bears directly on Bartholdi's fitness as a license applicant. Bartholdi chastises the Commission for failing to articulate these rationales in its order. But a more explicit discussion in the Commission's order would have risked disclosure of the information Bartholdi was attempting to keep confidential. We cannot fault the Commission for attempting to maintain the confidentiality of Bartholdi's submissions pending judicial review."

(5) *A Reverse FOIA Complaint.* In October 2016, Students for Fair Admissions, an organization opposed to the use of race in college admissions, sued the Department of Education to compel under FOIA the disclosure of "[a]ll documents concerning the investigation of Princeton University['s]" admission practices. The agency had concluded in 2015, after years of investigation, that there was not sufficient evidence that Princeton had unlawfully treated Asian and Asian American students who had applied for admission. In March 2017, Princeton University brought a reverse-FOIA action after the Department gave notice that it planned to release the University's submissions to the agency (but would redact personally identifiable information of applicants). The agency denied that the information was protected by Exemption 4. From the University's complaint:

1.   The University brings this "reverse FOIA" action pursuant to the Administrative Procedure Act, 5 U.S.C. §§ 701–706, the

Freedom of Information Act ("FOIA"), 5 U.S.C. § 552, and the Trade Secrets Act, 18 U.S.C. § 1905, to prevent the disclosure of certain confidential and commercially sensitive documents and information relating to the University's undergraduate admissions program submitted to [Education's Office of Civil Rights (OCR)] in the course of an OCR compliance review. These materials fall generally into two categories: (1) documents and information about undergraduate applicants to the University ("Applicant Documents and Information"), and (2) documents and information about the University's proprietary admissions processes ("Admissions Documents and Information"). The University does not object to OCR producing documents that OCR itself generated in the course of its compliance review, to the extent OCR generated documents do not incorporate or quote those documents the University is seeking to protect. . . .

4. The University has at all times maintained that the Applicant Documents and Information and Admissions Documents and Information are exempt from disclosure pursuant to FOIA Exemption 4, which exempts from disclosure "trade secrets and commercial or financial information obtained from a person and privileged or confidential." 5 U.S.C. § 552(b)(4). To that end, each of the documents the University seeks to withhold from release was designated and marked, "Confidential, Private, Personal and Proprietary—Exempt from Mandatory Disclosure Under FOIA" at the time it was produced to OCR. At no time during the compliance review did OCR object to or question these designations. . . .

27. Taken separately and together, the Applicant Documents and Information and Admissions Documents and Information reveal commercially sensitive information that is kept highly confidential by the University, and would cause substantial competitive harm to the University if disclosed. Specifically, disclosure of these materials would:

a. Permit applicants and their advisers who become aware of these materials to tailor applications to what they would perceive to be the admissions priorities and preferences of the University. These applicants (as distinct from other applicants) would use the disclosed materials to create applications that they believed fit what the University was looking for in admitted students. The University's ability to see applicants' true records and promise and make fair comparisons would be substantially hampered by this tailoring of applications to the University's perceived criteria for admissions. This, in turn, would substantially impair the University's ability to identify, recruit, admit, and enroll the strongest candidates each year, to its competitive disadvantage as compared with other colleges and universities.

b. Permit other colleges and universities with which the University competes to admit and enroll students to utilize the University's confidential admissions information and processes.

The Applicant Documents and Information and the Admissions Documents and Information reveal the University's strategies and methods to identify, recruit, and enroll the strongest candidates for admission. Disclosure of this information would allow colleges and universities with whom the University competes for students to utilize these materials to place the University at a substantial competitive disadvantage. . . .

How should the court determine if the Education Department can release the materials it received from Princeton University under current doctrine? How, if at all, would you change the procedure (agency and court) for determining if private information submitted to an agency should be released to a FOIA requester?

SECTION 4.   GOVERNMENT IN THE SUNSHINE

> *Letter to Congress from Federal Communications Commission*

Letter to Congress from Federal Communications Commission

Federal Communications Commission[87]

February 2, 2005

The Honorable Ted Stevens, Chairman
Committee on Commerce, Science and Transportation
United States Senate
508 Dirksen Senate Office Building
Washington, D.C. 20510

Dear Chairman Stevens:

As Congress contemplates revision of the nation's telecommunications laws, we write regarding a proposal that enjoys bipartisan support among the Commissioners of the Federal Communications Commission: reform of the open meeting requirement of the Government in Sunshine Act ("Sunshine Act" or "Act"). We fully support the Act's goal of informing the public about the decision making processes of multi-member agencies. However, we believe amendments to the Act could enhance the efficiency and soundness of the process. At the same time, safeguards could be devised that would ensure that the goal of open government is not jeopardized.

The open-meeting provision of the Sunshine Act currently requires every portion of every meeting not falling within an exception to be open to public observation when at least a quorum of Commissioners jointly

---

[87] This document is available at http://apps.fcc.gov/edocs_public/attachmatch/DOC-2566 55A1.pdf.

conducts or disposes of official agency business.[1] Both Republican and Democratic Commissioners are on record in recent testimony before Congress that the Commission's decisional processes are impaired by this requirement, and their conclusions about the detrimental effects of the open meeting requirement are echoed by a substantial body of scholarship.[2]

We note initially that the Act is not necessary to the goal of ensuring that federal agencies explain their actions to the public. Judicial review statutes like the Administrative Procedure Act ("APA") impose "a general 'procedural' requirement of sorts by mandating that an agency take whatever steps it needs to provide an explanation . . . [of its] rationale at the time of decision." Pension Benefit Guar. Corp. v. LTV Corp., 496 U.S. 633, 654 (1990).

Nor has the open-meeting requirement generally achieved its goal of having Commissioners help shape each other's views in the course of public deliberations. In fact, this requirement is a barrier to the substantive exchange of ideas among Commissioners, hampering our abilities to obtain the benefit of each other's views, input, or comments, and hampering efforts to maximize consensus on the complex issues before us. Due to the prohibition on private collective deliberations, we rely on written communications, staff, or one-on-one meetings with each other. These indirect methods of communicating clearly do not foster frank, open discussion, and they are less efficient than in-person interchange among three or more Commissioners would be. Finally, and perhaps most significantly, Commission decisions are in some cases less well informed and well explained than they would be if we each had the benefit of the others' expertise and perspective.[3]

For these reasons, we urge amending the open meeting provision of the Sunshine Act to permit closed deliberations among Commissioners in appropriate circumstances. Scholars and other agency heads have suggested various modification models,[4] some of which include safeguards that may be desirable. For example, some models include a

---

[1]   See 5 U.S.C. § 552b; 47 C.F.R. §§ 0.601–0.607.

[2]   See, e.g., Randolph May, Reforming the Sunshine Act, 49 Admin. L. Rev. 415 (1997) ("there appears to be a fairly widespread consensus that the Sunshine Act is not achieving its principal—and obviously salutary—goal of enhancing public knowledge and understanding of agency decisionmaking"); James H. Cawley, Sunshine Law Overexposure and the Demise of Independent Agency Collegiality, 1 Widener J. Pub. L. 43 (1992). These conclusions were also echoed by the Administrative Conference of the United States ("ACUS")—a body of experts established to advise Congress on administrative law. See David M. Welborn et al., Implementation and Effects of the Federal Government in the Sunshine Act, in Administrative Conference of the United States: Recommendation and Reports (1984). The ACUS ceased operations in 1995 because Congress eliminated funding, but many of its proposals have been implemented, and scholars such as those listed here still cite its conclusions about the Sunshine Act. [Ed. ACUS was restarted in 2010.]

[3]   Scholars and other agencies agree. See, e.g., May, supra note 2; Federal Trade Commission Prepared Statement Before the Special Committee to Review the Government In the Sunshine Act, Administrative Conference of the United States, 1995 WL 540529 (1995).

[4]   See, e.g., id.; Cawley, supra note 2.

requirement that brief summaries of topics discussed at meetings between all decision makers be recorded and placed in relevant administrative records.

In closing, we want to stress that we are in complete agreement with the Sunshine Act's goal of providing the public with reliable information about the basis for Commission decisions. We support amendment of the Act because we have learned from 28 years experience that we can satisfy this goal through other means that better serve the public interest by promoting bi-partisan deliberation and more efficient decision-making.

We look forward to working with the Committee Chairman, Ranking, and Members of the Committee to resolve this issue.

> SINCERELY,
> MICHAEL K. POWELL
> *CHAIRMAN*
>
> MICHAEL J. COPPS
> *COMMISSIONER*

NOTES

(1) ***GITSA-FOIA Contrast.*** The Government in the Sunshine Act (GITSA) (reprinted at p. 1494 in the Appendix) was passed in 1976 and is codified primarily at 5 U.S.C. § 552b. It was modeled on open meetings statutes already universal in the states (where the multi-member body limitation is not always present). Its legislative history suggests that Congress thought FOIA did not provide enough information to enable the public to "understand the reasons an agency has acted in a certain way, or even what exactly it has decided to do," because "[f]ormal statements in support of agency action are frequently too brief, or too general, to fully explain [a] Commission's reasoning, of the compromises that were made. By requiring important decisions to be made openly, [the new law] will create better public understanding of agency decisions." S.Rep. No. 94–354, at 5. Would you expect members of the public to attend agency public meetings? Journalists for the New York Times or the Washington Post? Interested industry representatives? Reporters for trade press publications that, at substantial cost, provide their readers with "the inside scoop" on agency doings?

The Act requires all multi-member agencies (but not single-administrator agencies like EPA, FDA, FAA, or OSHA)[88] to give a week's public notice of their meetings and to make most portions of their meetings open to public observation. A "meeting" occurs whenever a quorum of the agency deliberates in a way that "determine[s] or result[s] in the joint conduct or disposition of official agency business," excluding decisions taken in determining issues (scheduling, closure) arising under the Act itself. 5 U.S.C. § 552b(a)(2). With multiple agency vacancies, which we see particularly at the end or beginning of an administration, or with three-

---

[88] For a list of agencies covered by the Act, see Richard Berg et al., An Interpretative Guide to the Government in the Sunshine Act app. D (2d ed. 2005).

member agencies, this can be mean that any conversation between two members may qualify as a meeting. A majority of the body has the right to close a meeting to the extent it meets one of the Act's ten exemptions, which generally mirror FOIA's exemptions. Of course, even closed meetings may be transcribed, and if the transcript cannot be had under this Act or FOIA, perhaps it can be secured by an inquiring member of Congress. See San Luis Obispo Mothers for Peace v. NRC, 751 F.2d 1287 (D.C. Cir. 1984). Moreover, while discussions of most agency adjudicatory matters may be closed, GITSA contains no exemption corresponding to FOIA's Exemption 5, the exemption for predecisional matters that figures so prominently in the Fox case on p. 703. Thus, the Act requires discussions of rulemakings and other non-adjudicatory proposed matters to be discussed on advance notice and in public view, though it does permit non-public staff-level meetings. Judicial enforcement proceedings require the agency to prove the correctness of closure decisions, but the remedies provided all go to enforcing openness; the statute does not provide for invalidation of an agency decision improperly taken at a closed meeting.

For a recent summary of the Act, its application in a world of reply-all emails, electronic chat rooms, and webcasting, and agency best practices, see Reeve T. Bull, The Government in the Sunshine Act in the 21st Century (Administrative Conference of the United States Report, March 10, 2014).[89]

(2) ***Some GITSA Problems.*** Do you find the FCC's petition to Congress surprising? What would you expect the consequences of the proposed legislation would be on the way agency business is conducted? Should only the FCC benefit? Why did it not make its arguments for change generally, rather than as a matter of special pleading?

(a) As General Counsel of the FCC, how would you advise the commissioners to treat their forthcoming trip to Europe, where they will be discussing possible coordinating measures with counterpart agencies, and thus possibly reaching preliminary conclusions about courses for the Commission to follow? FCC v. ITT World Communications, 466 U.S. 463 (1984).

The Commissioners also meet occasionally with representatives of regulated bodies or public interest advocates—a practice that, as you may have read in connection with the Home Box Office case in Chapter IV, p. 446, led to severe criticism when many such meetings occurred in the post-comment period of a rulemaking. Would you advise them that such meetings must now be conducted openly, after a week's prior public notice, or may they continue so long as they do not "determine or result in the joint conduct or disposition of official agency business"?

(b) The Nuclear Regulatory Commission must decide on the budget request it will be submitting to OMB and to Congress. Some bureaus will win and others will lose as priorities are set. Must this meeting be open? Common Cause v. NRC, 674 F.2d 921 (D.C. Cir. 1982).

---

[89] http://www.acus.gov/report/final-sunshine-act-report.

(c) The SEC's Division of Trading and Markets has been given the responsibility for drafting the final text of a recently proposed rule that generated hundreds of extensive comments from consumer groups, brokerage houses, and others. The comments raise two or three issues in which the comments are in equipoise and Commission resolution or guidance is required. Public discussion of the matter, the Division's administrator (reasonably) fears, could have significant market effects. Which course would you advise her to follow:

i) Put the matter on the Commission's calendar for its next public meeting, with a view to having these matters decided.

ii) Have a closed briefing session for the Commissioners (or their assistants), at which no decisions will be taken, and then go office to office to learn how each Commissioner would decide the matters.

iii) Submit option papers to the Commissioners, with the suggestion that they exchange written views with each other and then each report their views to her orally or in writing.

iv) Focus her attention on the Commission chairperson, whose "meetings with the staff have a powerful tendency to shape the staff's responses and recommendations, which might well be different if it were possible for the other members to be present."[90]

(3) ***The Impact of GITSA.*** Whatever may have been the cause, following passage of GITSA the number of meetings at 59 executive and independent multi-member agencies declined 31 percent between 1979 and 1986. Just under 40 percent of those meetings were open, just over 40 percent closed, and the remainder were partly closed. Rogelio Garcia, Public Access to Meetings Held under the Government in the Sunshine Act, 1979–1984, Congressional Research Service Report (1986), reprinted in Senate Comm. on Governmental Affairs, Government in the Sunshine Act: History and Recent Issues, S. Rep. No. 101–54, at 58 (1989). According to DAVID M. WELBORN ET AL., IMPLEMENTATION AND EFFECTS OF THE FEDERAL GOVERNMENT IN THE SUNSHINE ACT (1984), in the study that the FCC letter cites, (1) members tended to behave somewhat differently in open than in closed meetings. They prepared more thoroughly for the open meetings but used them more often to appeal to special interests; they refrained from asking important questions and engaged less frequently in candid exchange, sharp debate, or efforts at reconciling conflicts. (2) The authors believed there was "a shift in patterns of decision-making behavior, at least in some agencies, away from collegial processes toward segmented, individualized processes in which, in the words of one commissioner, 'members are isolated from one another.'" Of 18 agencies surveyed, only officials at the Federal Election Commission thought "that the act had strengthened the collegium." The importance of meetings declined apparently "from an aversion to public discussion of certain topics." In addition, when open meetings with collegial interactions did occur, "meetings often ha[d] no bearing on results." Over 83 percent of survey respondents from agencies with full-time membership

---

90 A Little Shade, Please—The Government-in-the-Sunshine Act Isn't Working, Washington Post, July 25, 1983 (quoting then SEC Commissioner Bevis Longstreth).

believed that "members now typically made up their minds on matters dealt with in open meetings *prior* to collective discussions." Further "the focus of decision-making activity has shifted toward the offices of individual members and to the staff level and involves three key sets of interactions. The first is between staff at the operating level who are handling a particular matter and the offices of the chairman and other members. The second is between members one-on-one, except presumably in three member agencies. The third is among staff assistants to members acting as surrogates for their principals. . . . All have distinct limitations as substitutes for collegial discussions."

More recent surveys were conducted under the direction of ACUS. Responses from 56 top members at 24 agencies and general counsels from 40 agencies supported four conclusions: "(1) agency members place comparatively little emphasis on meetings of board members as a source of information about the views and positions of fellow members, whether those meetings are conducted openly or are closed pursuant to one of the Sunshine Act exceptions; (2) agency members find somewhat greater value in interactions that occur outside of such meetings, including informal discussions amongst board or commission members and conferences between such members and staff; (3) agencies have more or less reconciled themselves to the existence of the Sunshine Act and do not generally recommend repealing or fundamentally altering it; and (4) notwithstanding the lack of any overarching objections to the Act, agencies do have a number of specific complaints and suggestions for improving the Act." Reeve T. Bull, The Government in the Sunshine Act in the 21st Century, supra, at 17. ACUS also found that the "surveys produced little evidence that commission or board members avoided discussion of certain issues in open meetings or were otherwise chilled in their interactions as a result of the Act." Id. at 20. Notably, about 40 percent of surveyed agencies disclosed that they used notational voting, which is not covered by the Act, to dispose of more than 75 percent of matters. ACUS, Government in the Sunshine Act, Recommendation 2014–2 (adopted June 2014).

(4)   *A Proposed Legislative Response.* S. 760, a legislative proposal before the 114th Congress in 2015 that was not enacted, would have provided to the FCC:

(2)   Authority to hold meetings.—

Notwithstanding section 552b of title 5, United States Code, a bipartisan majority of Commissioners may hold a meeting that is closed to the public to discuss official business if—

(A) a vote or any other agency action is not taken at the meeting;

(B) each person present at the meeting is a Commissioner, an employee of the Commission, a member of a joint board or conference established under [particular provisions], or a person on the staff of such a joint board or conference or of a member of such a joint board or conference; and

(C) an attorney from the Office of General Counsel of the Commission is present at the meeting.

Subsequent provisions would have required public disclosure of the meeting, attendees, and "a summary of the matters discussed at the meeting, except for any matters that the Commission determines may be withheld under section 552b(c) of title 5." Should such legislation be enacted? Just for the FCC?

(5) *Sunshine at the State and Local Levels.* That state governments led the federal government in adopting open-meetings laws may reflect more immediate practical impacts at the local level. Citizens are more likely to attend municipal meetings or go to the state capitol. The media, an acknowledged major beneficiary of the laws, finds at the federal level that the daily actions of the National Labor Relations Board compete with many significant "national news" items for attention. At the state or local level, reporters in Atlantic City may find meetings to revise the city charter well worth coverage. See Polillo v. Deane, 379 A.2d 211 (1977). An extensive database of information on the content, implementation, and litigation of sunshine laws in states, counties, and cities can be found at https://ballotpedia.org/ (for open records, see: https://ballotpedia.org/State_sunshine_laws; for open meetings, see: https://ballotpedia.org/State_open_meetings_laws) and a recent survey and comparison of state open meetings laws in Suzanne J. Piotrowski & Erin Borry, An Analytic Framework for Open Meetings and Transparency, 15 Pub. Admin. & Mgmt. 138 (2010).

The number of reported state cases reflects both the interest in open meetings and the potency of these laws. Violations in some states are grounds for invalidating action, including in Ohio where action is taken in an open meeting but "result[ing] from deliberations in a meeting not open to the public." See State ex rel. Delph v. Barr, 541 N.E.2d 59 (1989). Some states provide for award of attorney's fees and costs. Even criminal enforcement occurs. In 2004, a Florida county commissioner, formerly a state legislative leader, served 49 days of a 60-day jail sentence for violating the open-meetings law; the following year, officials of a community near Miami, after pleading no contest to misdemeanor charges that they had conspired to oust the city manager, were given probation, community service, and fines or court costs that ranged up to $20,000.[91] You can search some examples of fines and jail sentences handed out in Florida online.[92]

(6) *Federal Advisory Committees.* As you may recall from Chapter II (p. 159), agencies often turn to committees of experts and citizens in the development and/or application of policy. From the observation that these committees were becoming numerous and that their membership was sometimes dominated by special interests, Congress developed in 1972 the

---

[91] Robert Tanner, On Sunshine Laws, Governments Talk Loudly; Stick Rarely Used, Associated Press, March 11, 2007, http://legacy.sandiegouniontribune.com/news/nation/20070310-1053-sunshineweek.html.

[92] http://brechner.org/db_prosecutions.asp. See also Daxton R. Stewart. Let the Sunshine In, or Else: An Examination of the "Teeth" of State and Federal Open Meetings and Open Records Laws, 15 Comm. L. & Pol'y 265 (2010) (state-by-state compilation and comparative analysis of penalty and remedy provisions in open-meetings and open-records laws).

FEDERAL ADVISORY COMMITTEE ACT, 5 U.S.C. App., which seeks to control their growth and operation through OMB clearance, public process, and requirements of balance in membership. Before an advisory committee can meet or take any action, it must file a detailed charter and give advance notice in the Federal Register; it also must hold all meetings in public, keep detailed minutes, and make its records available to the public—along with any reports, records, or other documents it uses—unless they fall within GITSA or FOIA exemptions. Committees must be "fairly balanced in terms of the points of view represented," § 5(b)(2), and the Act requires precautions to ensure that their advice and recommendations "will not be inappropriately influenced by the appointing authority or by any special interest." § 5(b)(3). Steven P. Croley and William F. Funk, The Federal Advisory Committee Act and Good Government, 14 Yale J. Reg. 452 (1997), provides an excellent analysis of the Act.

"Balance" and "openness" may strike you as unmitigated public goods. Are there countervailing considerations? The first Bush, Clinton, and second Bush presidencies found themselves embroiled in FACA litigation with heavy constitutional overtones—specifically, arguable impingement on the President's actions. Public Citizen challenged presidential consultations by the first Bush's White House with the ABA over judicial appointments, Public Citizen v. U.S. Dep't of Justice, 491 U.S. 440 (1989) (p. 159); a medical society, opposing President Clinton's efforts at health care reform, claimed that Mrs. Clinton's presence on the working group charged to prepare proposed legislation rendered it an advisory committee, Ass'n of American Physicians and Surgeons v. Hillary Rodham Clinton, 997 F.2d 898 (D.C. Cir. 1993); and Public Citizen attacked closed meetings of the National Energy Policy Development Group, headed by Vice President Cheney, In re Cheney, 406 F.3d 723 (DC. Cir. 2005) (en banc). None of the decisions found that FACA applied; all noted considerable separation of powers issues if the action fell under the Act. Should these entities with ties to the President and the President's advisors (who are typically shielded from disclosure mandates) be protected from transparency obligations? How do you balance the levels of candor necessary for effective government policy-making and levels of transparency requisite for presidential accountability?

Even absent such weighty considerations, recall that as is evident throughout this book (especially in the materials on rulemaking), agency personnel must be in constant contact with those on the outside, many of whom have an interest or bias regarding the issue at hand. Could requiring advisory committees to be "fairly balanced" and operate in the open overly inhibit agency use of sources on which we should encourage agencies to rely? And do interest groups on all sides play too large a role? One study found that EPA was more likely to choose members for its National Drinking Water Advisory Council who had been endorsed by interest groups than those who were not backed.[93] An agency's selection of particular members is generally unreviewable by the courts. But a change in agency procedures governing qualifications of committee members might be reviewable. Cf. Timothy

---

[93] Steven J. Balla & John R. Wright, Interest Groups, Advisory Committees, and Congressional Control of the Bureaucracy, 45 Am. J. Pol. Sci. 799 (2001).

Cama, EPA, Pruitt May Face Lawsuits over Advisory Board Changes, The Hill, Nov. 7, 2017 (discussing potential lawsuits to EPA Administrator Scott Pruitt's decision to bar agency grant recipients, who are often academic researchers, from the agency's advisory committees).

In addition, should federally registered lobbyists be excluded from advisory committees (and other boards and commissions of private individuals serving federal functions)? Or will that produce the subterfuge of deregistration as a lobbyist to be able to serve? Asserting a purpose to reduce "the undue influence of special interests that for too long has shaped the national agenda and drowned out the voices of ordinary Americans," President Obama issued a directive excluding federally registered lobbyists from being appointed to advisory committees (but not removing already present members) on June 18, 2010.[94] OMB followed up with proposed guidance; after a commenting period, OMB finalized its stance in October 2011, with subsequent modifications in August 2014, which adopted the President's initial position for those serving in an individual capacity but allowed lobbyists serving in particular representative capacities.[95] As of October 2017, the guidance remains in effect under the Trump Administration. Just politics, or common sense?

SECTION 5.   INTERNET DISCLOSURE AS REGULATION

> *OIRA Memo: Disclosure &*
> *Simplification As Regulatory Tools*

OIRA Memo: Disclosure & Simplification As Regulatory Tools

EXECUTIVE OFFICE OF THE PRESIDENT
OFFICE OF INFORMATION AND REGULATORY AFFAIRS
OFFICE OF MANAGEMENT AND BUDGET

June 18, 2010

MEMORANDUM FOR THE HEADS OF EXECUTIVE DEPARTMENTS AND AGENCIES

FROM: Cass R. Sunstein, Administrator

SUBJECT: Disclosure and Simplification as Regulatory Tools

. . . The purpose of the following documents is to set out guidance to inform the use of disclosure and simplification in the regulatory process. To the extent permitted by law, and where appropriate in light of the

---

[94] http://obamawhitehouse.archives.gov/realitycheck/the-press-office/presidential-memorandum-lobbyists-agency-boards-and-commissions.

[95] Office of Management and Budget, "Revised Guidance on Appointment of Lobbyists to Federal Advisory Committees, Boards, and Commissions," 79 Fed. Reg. 47,482 (Aug. 13, 2014); Office of Management and Budget, "Final Guidance of Appointment of Lobbyists to Federal Boards and Commissions," 76 Fed. Reg. 61,756 (Oct. 5, 2011).

problem to which they are attempting to respond, agencies should follow the relevant principles.

Disclosure as a Regulatory Tool

<u>Purpose</u>. In many statutes, Congress requires or permits agencies to use disclosure as a regulatory tool. Executive Order 12866 provides, "Each agency shall identify and assess available alternatives to direct regulation, including . . . providing information upon which choices can be made by the public." The Open Government Directive of the Office of Management and Budget calls for disclosures that will "further the core mission of the agency." The purpose of this guidance is to set forth principles designed to assist agencies in their efforts to use information disclosure to achieve their regulatory objectives. Agencies should follow the principles outlined here in accordance with their own authorities, judgments, and goals, to the extent permitted by law.

<u>Disclosure as a Regulatory Tool</u>. Sometimes Congress requires or authorizes agencies to impose disclosure requirements instead of, or in addition to, mandates, subsidies, or bans. For example, automobile companies are required by law to disclose miles per gallon (MPG) ratings for new vehicles, and a standardized Nutrition Facts panel must be included on most food packages. The goal of disclosing such information is to provide members of the public with relevant information at the right moment in time, usually when a decision is made. Often that decision is whether to purchase a particular product. . . .

There are two general types of release that Congress may require or permit: summary disclosure and full disclosure. With summary disclosure, often required at the point of purchase, agencies highlight the most relevant information in order to increase the likelihood that people will see it, understand it, and act in accordance with what they have learned. Full disclosure is more comprehensive; it occurs when agencies release, or require others to release, all relevant information (often including underlying data).

<u>Summary Disclosure</u>. . . . Examples include nutritional labeling, energy efficiency labeling, tobacco warnings,[96] and government provision of information (e.g., fact sheets, telephone hotlines, and public interest announcements).

---

[96] [Ed.] Here are three of thirty-six alternative designs for cigarette warnings proposed by the FDA on Nov. 10, 2010, to implement § 201 of the Tobacco Control Act of 2009, P.L. 111–31, 123 Stat. 1976, 75 Fed. Reg. 69524 (2010). The mandated designs were struck down by the D.C. Circuit as violating the First Amendment. R.J. Reynolds Tobacco Co. v. FDA, 696 F.3d 1205 (D.C. Cir. 2012). As of this writing, the FDA has not renewed its effort to comply with its statutory obligation to require "color graphics depicting the negative health consequences of smoking." In 2014, the agency did run its own advertising campaign with graphic images, The Real Cost, on multiple media platforms; in addition, the agency is conducting two multi-year

Principle One: In order to select which information to highlight and how to present that information, agencies should explicitly identify their goals.

Explicit identification of goals will have important implications for the nature of disclosure. . . . If the goal is to present a warning, then graphic messages might be justified; the same is not true when the aim is simply to inform. And if the goal is to present a warning, it will often be useful to inform users of the precise steps that they might take, or the plans that they might formulate, to avoid the risk in question. . . .

Principle Two: Summary disclosure should generally be simple and specific, and should avoid undue detail or excessive complexity.

Summary disclosure should focus on the central issues and should be presented in a manner that is straightforward and easy to understand. Simple, specific disclosure is generally preferable. People have limited time and attention, and their reactions to new information are not always predictable. . . . Summary disclosure should be designed so as to be relevant to the affected population, enabling people to know why and how the information is pertinent to their own choices.

Principle Three: Summary disclosure should be accurate and in plain language. . . .

Principle Four: Disclosed information should be properly placed and timed.

. . . Agencies should attempt to offer the information that users need when they need it. To this end, they should take steps to provide people with relevant information when they are actually making the decision or taking the action in question. For example, information about fuel

---

studies, which could provide the evidence the D.C. Circuit found was lacking to justify compelling speech.

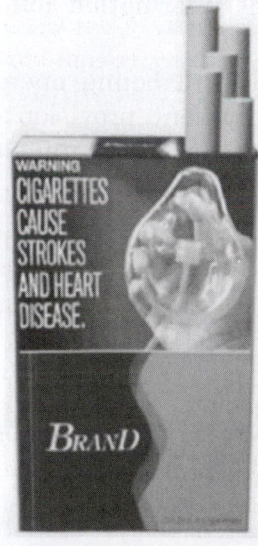  

economy is most useful if it is present and visible when people are shopping for motor vehicles. . . .

Principle Five: Summary disclosure through ratings or scales should be meaningful.

Summary disclosure may involve numerical ratings or scales, because these are convenient ways to simplify and display complicated information. For nutrition, percent daily values are a common example of this sort of summary disclosure. When users understand what such scales mean, they can be among the most effective ways to communicate information. . . . For example, the Energy Guide label provides an estimate of annual operating cost, along with a cost range for similar models. Annual savings or benefits, measured in terms of dollars, provide a metric that is both meaningful and easy to understand. . . .

Principle Six: To the extent feasible, agencies should test, in advance, the likely effects of summary disclosure, and should also monitor the effects of such disclosure over time. . . .

Principle Seven: Where feasible and appropriate, agencies should identify and consider the likely costs and benefits of disclosure requirements.

Executive Order 12866 requires agencies, to the extent permitted by law, "to assess both the costs and the benefits of the intended regulation" and "recognizing that some costs and benefits are difficult to quantify," to proceed only "upon a reasoned determination that the benefits of the intended regulation justify the costs." In accordance with this requirement, and where feasible and appropriate in the circumstances, agencies should adopt disclosure requirements only after considering both qualitative and quantitative benefits and costs. That assessment should, in turn, help agencies to decide which requirements to select.

It is important to acknowledge that in some contexts, the costs and benefits of disclosure may be difficult or even impossible to specify, and a formal analysis may not be feasible or appropriate. Quantitative assessment of benefits may involve a high degree of speculation, and a qualitative discussion, based on available evidence, may be all that is feasible. In assessing benefits, agencies should consider the fact that improvements in welfare are a central goal of disclosure requirements, but should also note that informed choice is a value in itself (even if it is difficult to quantify that value).

It is also important to recognize that people may react differently to disclosure requirements. While some consumers might use calorie information to reduce their overall calorie intake, others might not. Heterogeneity can have potentially significant effects; those who have the most to gain or to lose may or may not be benefitting from the relevant disclosure. Agencies should attempt to take divergent behavior and preferences into account when formulating disclosure policies and assessing their likely consequences.

Full Disclosure. Sometimes Congress requires or authorizes agencies to promote regulatory goals by disclosing, or by requiring others to disclose, a wide range of information about existing practices and their effects. Full disclosure will include far more detail than is available in a summary. It may well include multiple variables, supporting data, and materials that extend over long periods of time. For example, agencies use the Internet to provide detailed information about fuel economy and nutrition; such information is far more comprehensive than what is provided through summary disclosure.

Full disclosure can often promote the purposes of open government, including transparency, participation, and collaboration. The central goals of full disclosure are to allow individuals and organizations to view the data and to analyze, use, and repackage it in multiple ways, typically taking advantage of emerging technological capacities (perhaps including social media). To promote those goals, agencies should consider the following principles.

Principle One: Disclosed information should be as accessible as possible. For that reason, the Internet should ordinarily be used as a means of disclosing information, to the extent feasible and consistent with law.

Transparency is generally good practice, and agencies cannot always know which information will be most useful and in what format it will prove most valuable. Engaging in full disclosure (to the extent feasible, subject to valid restrictions, and to the extent permitted by law) is often both desirable and important.

Full disclosure will frequently involve large amounts of complicated data, and most people may not find it worth their time to seek out and analyze all or most of it. In such cases, the data may be most directly useful to groups and organizations with technical capabilities and with an interest in obtaining, analyzing, and repackaging relevant information. Such groups and organizations may reorganize and disseminate the information in ways that turn out to be highly beneficial to the general public (sometimes by improving the operation of markets). At the same time, agencies should strive to make full disclosure as useful as possible, and should therefore promote clarity and accessibility.

Principle Two: Disclosed information should be as usable as possible. For that reason, information should usually be released in an electronic format that does not require specialized software.

Consistent with the goals of open government, it is important to make information not merely available but also usable. If information is made available electronically, it will be easier for people to sift through it and to analyze or repackage it in various ways. Agencies should select an electronic format that is suitable to achieving that goal. The best method should be chosen in light of existing technology. . . .

Principle Three: Agencies should consider making periodic assessments of whether full disclosure is as accurate and useful as possible.

Where feasible and to the extent consistent with relevant laws, regulations, and policies (including protection of privacy), agencies should consider steps to investigate whether current disclosure policies are fulfilling their intended purposes. They might explore, for example, what information is being frequently used by the public and how those in the private sector are adapting and presenting information. . . . Agencies should also consider whether it might be useful to seek public comment on significant disclosures. . . .

Principle Four: Where feasible and appropriate, agencies should consider the costs and benefits of full disclosure.

As noted above, Executive Order 12866 requires agencies, to the extent permitted by law, "to assess both the costs and the benefits of the intended regulation" and to proceed only upon "a reasoned determination that the benefits of the intended regulation justify the costs." In addition, the Paperwork Reduction Act of 1995 imposes a series of requirements on efforts to collect information; these requirements are designed (among other things) to increase the practical utility of information collections and to minimize burdens on the private sector. In accordance with these requirements, and to the extent feasible and appropriate, agencies should evaluate full disclosure in terms of both qualitative and quantitative benefits and costs.

Here, as with summary disclosure, quantitative assessment of benefits may involve a degree of speculation, and a qualitative discussion, based on available evidence, may be all that is feasible. . . .

Summary Disclosure and Full Disclosure. Congress may require or authorize agencies to require summary disclosure but not full disclosure; alternatively, Congress may require or authorize agencies to require full disclosure but not summary disclosure. When Congress grants agencies discretion, and to the extent feasible, they should consider the likely effects—including the qualitative and quantitative costs and benefits—of both approaches.

Summary disclosure is the best method for informing consumers at the point of decision. Full disclosure is the best method of allowing groups and individuals access to a broad range of information, allowing them to analyze and disseminate that information in creative ways, and to use it to inform private and public decisions or otherwise to promote statutory goals. The two approaches may well be complementary. For example, it may be desirable to use summary disclosure at the point of purchase while also making full information available on the Internet.

Simplification As A Regulatory Tool [Ed. Omitted]

NOTES

(1) ***The "Regulatory" Impacts of Disclosure as Consumer Information.*** The June 2010 Sunstein memorandum addresses only the benefits of disclosure for consumer choice, suggesting that (at least within certain parameters) it may be preferable to inform consumers about their choices rather than to restrict the choices themselves. It does not discuss the possible impact of disclosure on choices that are made by sellers or other potentially regulated persons. What incentive does prominent display of miles per gallon ratings create for automobile manufacturers? The knowledge that each model will receive a crash safety rating ranging from one to five stars, based on its performance in standardized tests? Regulation by disclosure does not dictate particular design elements manufacturers must use; command and control measures that do specify necessary elements have long been criticized both for embedding yesterday's technology and for taking design decisions away from those best able to make them. Regulation by disclosure, in contrast, is said to create incentives for manufacturers to determine for themselves, in the most efficient way, the design features that will best advantage their models in the disclosures made. The memorandum also does not discuss any disadvantages to disclosure in any depth. Are there any for the examples discussed?

(2) ***Other Potential "Regulatory" Uses of Disclosure.*** The potential of disclosure to address social problems that could be dealt with by regulation is not limited to the incentives that may be created by informing consumer purchase choices. Disclosure's creation of incentives for regulated entities can be a major output without regard to consumer choice. Consider the experience under EPA's Toxics Release Inventory Program (TRI). For more than 650 toxic chemicals that are being used, manufactured, treated, transported, or released into the environment, those responsible must file annual reports with state and local governments, giving the locations and quantities of these chemicals being released. The reports are submitted to the EPA, and it compiles the data into an online, publicly accessible database. See https://www.epa.gov/toxics-release-inventory-tri-program. Any person with access to the Internet can search this database by geographic location, chemical name, or industry classification code. For establishments seeking good will from their workforce and in their communities, the resulting exposure provides an incentive for change that, again, can be met by their own thoughtful innovation. The result may be to improve their performance beyond requirements government agencies may have been able to set, while avoiding any need to comply with standardized designs or other requirements. (Indeed, rulemaking to set formal limits for each of 650 toxics may be beyond EPA's administrative capacities; as you may already have read in Chapter III, the Occupational Safety and Health Administration's failure to set workplace limits on more than a handful of toxics has been a poster child for the ossification of rulemaking, the chronic underfunding of that agency, and the impacts of aggressive judicial review.[97]) The success of the TRI program in promoting toxics controls has

---

[97] Ossification: p. 1090; underfunding: p. 271; judicial review: AFL-CIO v. OSHA, 965 F.2d 962 (11th Cir. 1992).

been well documented. See, e.g., Bradley C. Karkkainen, Information as Environmental Regulation: TRI and Performance Benchmarking, Precursor to a New Paradigm? 89 Geo. L. J. 257 (2001).

More generally, the "regulatory" advantages to disclosure include potential competition that enhances social welfare, incentives to avoid undesirable actions, and fostering of public confidence. For a defense of disclosure, see Eric W. Orts, Defending Disclosure, http://www.regblog.org/2015/06/18/orts-defending-disclosure/. On the other hand, its disadvantages include costs to regulated entities (such as reputational harm), which are magnified if disclosures are not accurate, as well as questionable or lack of efficacy in some settings. For an argument that information overload and other factors generally make disclosure ineffective as a regulatory tool, see Omri Ben-Shahar & Carl E. Schneider, More Than You Wanted to Know: The Failure of Mandated Disclosure (2015). In addition, disclosure mandates can shape market power. The Beer Institute's Voluntary Disclosure Initiative, for example, arguably benefits large brewers, which "are losing market share to the hundreds of small craft brewers that have sprung up in recent years in the United States" and which can more easily absorb the costs of calorie testing.[98] For a discussion of the benefits and costs in the database context, see Nathan Cortez, Regulation by Database, 89 Colo. L. Rev. (forthcoming). Finally, there are legal factors to consider. To what extent can the government require disclosure (whether summary or full, in Sunstein's terms) under the First Amendment?

(3) *The Data Quality Act.* The Data Quality Act, also known as the Information Quality Act, was enacted as a few hardly noticed lines of text in section 515 of the Treasury and General Government Appropriations Act for Fiscal Year 2001 (P.L. 106–554; H.R. 5658). It directs the OMB to issue government-wide guidelines that "provide policy and procedural guidance to Federal agencies for ensuring and maximizing the quality, objectivity, utility, and integrity of information (including statistical information) disseminated by Federal agencies." These guidelines, which define "information" broadly as "any communication or representation of knowledge such as facts or data, in any medium or form," require each agency not only to issue guidelines to these ends about information it disseminates but also to "establish administrative mechanisms allowing affected persons to seek and obtain correction" of non-compliant information. The Director of OMB is also to monitor agency handling of complaints. If this provides not merely a spur to useful discipline but also an opportunity for diversion and cost infliction, the result would be to make programs like TRI less timely and cost-effective. A recent account, however, finds that "industry use of the Act was put under the spotlight because of concerns about abuse. As a result, and much to the disappointment of its proponents, the Data Quality Act falls short of providing a judicially enforced mechanism for launching additional, information-based challenges to agency rulemakings."[99] GAO recently reviewed 30 agencies' performance under the Act. It found that 16 of those

---

[98] E. Frank Stephenson, Bootleggers, Baptists, and Beer Labels, Regulation (Fall 2016).

[99] Wendy Wagner, Administrative Law, Filter Failure, and Information Capture, 59 Duke L.J. 1321, 1401 (2010).

agencies reported a total of 87 correction requests in the FY 2010–2014 period (EPA, HHS, and Interior listed 61 of those 87 requests). For 59 of those 87 requests, the relevant agency made no correction to the flagged information. GAO, Information Quality Act: Actions Needed to Improve Transparency and Reporting of Correction Requests, GAO–16–110 (Dec. 2015).[100]

(4) *Other Uses of the Internet as Alternatives to Direct Regulation.* Returning to the introductory example in Chapter I, DOT's website, www.transportation.gov, contains, among others, the following links that are highly facilitative and/or supportive of regulation, if not directly the products of information disclosure by the regulated. If you are following another agency, see if you can find analogs on its website:

- Flight delay information, https://www.transtats.bts.gov/OT_Delay/OT_DelayCause1.asp, which "tracks the on-time performance of domestic flights operated by large air carriers" and discloses the provided cause for any delay.

- Airline accident and incident reports, https://www.faa.gov/data_research/accident_incident/, where you can read about emergency landings and other events as well as listen to recordings from air traffic control. There is also a database of airline accidents and some incidents, https://www.ntsb.gov/_layouts/ntsb.aviation/index.aspx.

- Instructions on filing a complaint, https://www.transportation.gov/airconsumer/file-consumer-complaint, whether safety, security, service, disability, or discrimination related. Online links for complaint filing (by type) are provided. According to the website, complaints are "entered in DOT's computerized aviation industry monitoring system, and are charged to the company in question in the monthly Air Travel Consumer Report. . . . These complaints are reviewed to determine the extent to which carriers are in compliance with federal aviation consumer protection regulations. This system also serves as a basis for rulemaking, legislation and research. Where appropriate, letters and web form submissions will be forwarded to an official at the airline for further consideration."

- Airworthiness Directives, https://www.faa.gov/regulations_policies/airworthiness_directives, which are "legally enforceable regulations issued by the FAA in accordance with 14 CFR part 39 to correct an unsafe condition in a product."

- Rating programs for vehicles, car seats, and tires, https://www.nhtsa.gov/ratings, "to help consumers make smart decisions about safety."

(5) *Uses of Information Disclosure for Regulation That Do Not Necessarily Involve the Internet.* Suppose a regulatory statute imposes

---

[100] http://www.gao.gov/assets/680/674386.pdf.

relatively harsh consequences on failures of compliance but at the same time offers an easier path in return for cooperation in providing useful information or undertaking mitigation measures. Professor BRADLEY C. KARKKAINEN offers several examples of information-forcing regulation in his chapter, INFORMATION-FORCING REGULATION AND ENVIRONMENTAL GOVERNANCE, in Grainne de Burca and Joanna Scott, eds, Law and New Governance in the EU and the US, 300–01, 304–05 (Hart Publishing, 2006). California's 1986 Proposition 65, the Safe Drinking Water and Toxic Enforcement Act,[101] for example, requires "clear and reasonable warnings" to persons exposed to any "significant risk" posed to them by carcinogens and reproductive toxins listed in the Act. Compliance with these rather indefinite requirements is enforced by jury determination, hardly a comfortable prospect for the businesses concerned. "Just when things look bleakest from the polluter's perspective," he writes, "Proposition 65 throws a lifeline, authorizing a regulatory agency, the Office of Environmental Health Hazard Assessment (OEHHA), to establish numerical thresholds that will be deemed to meet the 'no significant risk' test. By voluntarily meeting these standards, polluters can avoid the duty to warn and inoculate themselves against liability. But first, the standards must be established. This gives toxic polluters in California an unusual incentive to cooperate with regulators in setting and justifying regulatory standards, and to produce and disclose credible toxicity and exposure information to advance the regulatory process. Under Proposition 65, California has established nearly 300 regulatory standards for toxic pollutants at a far faster pace and with lower administrative costs than under conventional regulatory approaches. . . ."

The National Environmental Policy Act, Professor Karkkainen suggests, creates similar incentives for federal agencies. Environmental Impact Statements are expensive to produce and often lead to litigation; simpler Environmental Assessments can be created if the agency can find that its project will have no significant impact [FONSI], and in "all but the most extreme cases . . . federal agencies can avoid NEPA's EIS requirement by redefining projects to keep the expected environmental impacts below the statutory threshold of 'significant.'" This "mitigated FONSI" amounts to "a simplified way to achieve NEPA's core objective." Neither EIS's nor FONSI's nor EA's—all public documents—are readily available to the public on the Internet. What would you imagine to be the impact if they did appear there?

SECTION 6.   THE PROMISE AND PROBLEMS OF E-RULEMAKING

> **a. The Public's Participation**
> **b. Management Issues**

As you must already have learned if you have been assigned this Section, binding rulemaking at the federal level is the statutory responsibility of individual agencies under the APA's notice and comment

---

[101] Cal. Health and Safety Code §§ 25249.5–.13.

procedures (with occasional statutory modifications). Under Executive Orders 12866 and 13771, the Office of Management and Budget's Office of Information and Regulatory Affairs (OIRA) oversees the initiation of important rulemakings by all agencies through their participation in an annual Regulatory Plan and then reviews important rulemakings at "executive branch" agencies through their submission of draft and final cost-benefit analyses.[102] The following pages direct your attention to the implications of the Internet for rulemaking activities.

Under the mandate of § 206 of the E-Government Act of 2002, Pub. L. No. 107–347, 116 Stat. 2899, the government established an e-rulemaking program to create a unified Internet site for electronic rulemaking. This program has, to date, operated under the aegis of the EPA, joining the efforts of 40 "partners" comprising every cabinet department, EPA, SSA, several independent regulatory commissions (including the CPSC, FTC, and NRC), and a handful of quasi agencies (government corporations and banks). It has established regulations.gov as the government's centralized portal for rulemaking activity. The 40 "partners" in regulations.gov post notices of proposed rulemakings, receive comments, and maintain electronic rulemaking dockets searchable there by the Regulation Identifier Number (RIN) each projected regulation acquires on appearing in the Regulatory Agenda.[103] This is accomplished through a Federal Data Management System (FDMS), a shared electronic depository that is to include all public documents associated with a rulemaking—studies, published OIRA submissions, logs of external contacts, etc., as well as filed comments. Nearly 300 other agencies, including major independent regulatory commissions such as the CFTC, FCC, and SEC are "non-participating agencies"; these agencies post NPRMs on and may receive comments through regulations.gov, but they do not participate in the FDMS. Any electronic comments they receive, either from regulations.gov or on their own website, will be posted, if at all, to the agency's own website. As a result, their rulemaking dockets cannot be searched through the FDMS, and practice may vary from agency to agency.

Regulations.gov and the associated FDMS are among the constantly changing sites (in terms of their content) the government maintains, so you will want to make your own assessment, as you are studying these materials.[104] Because regulations.gov and FDMS involve the central

---

[102] Other statutes and executive orders require different analyses—of impacts on small business, federalism considerations, etc.—that to date have been folded into the Executive Order 12866 analyses and not often proven important. To search current and past Regulatory Plans and Unified Agendas of Regulatory and Deregulatory Actions, go to: www.reginfo.gov.

[103] See Memorandum for the President's Management Council, "Increasing Openness in the Rulemaking Process—Use of the Regulation Identifier Number" (April 7, 2010), http://obamawhitehouse.archives.gov/sites/default/files/omb/assets/inforeg/IncreasingOpenness_04072010.pdf.

[104] E-Rulemaking.Org (http://www.law.upenn.edu/institutes/ppr/erulemaking/), a website maintained at the University of Pennsylvania Law School, dedicates itself to "technological and institutional issues related to E-Rulemaking," making "research papers, policy documents,

management of facilities used by and useful to a wide range of government agencies, as well as the public, they provide a conducive setting for the use of the "best practices" approaches so prominent in the new, or collaborative, governance literature. In November 2010, the E-rulemaking Program published "Improving Electronic Dockets on Regulations.gov and the Federal Docket Management System—Best Practices for Federal Agencies" on regulations.gov, which "develops strategic goals and best practices for using the eRulemaking [FDMS] and the Regulations.gov website to allow agencies and the public to review regulatory content and to participate in the regulatory process."[105] Keynoting a Brookings Institution conference on e-rulemaking, then OIRA Administrator Cass Sunstein offered the following test for evaluating the use of the Internet in rulemaking: "If regulatory choices are based on careful analysis and subject to public scrutiny and review, we're going to be able to identify new and creative ways to maintain and to promote entrepreneurship, innovation, competitiveness, and economic growth. With that claim in mind, one of my primary points is that e-rulemaking and associated steps should be evaluated largely, it would probably be too strong to say exclusively, but largely by asking a single empirical question. Are we taking steps that are actually improving regulations?"[106]

a.   The Public's Participation

E-rulemaking has been widely heralded both for its potential to increase participation in rulemaking and to improve the quality of comments. Consider, as against the shape of regulations.gov and the FDMS as you may now find them, the following subset of tributes, criticisms, and issues:

(1) ***Regulations.gov as Democratic Mechanism.*** CASS R. SUNSTEIN, DEMOCRATIZING REGULATION, DIGITALLY, DEMOCRACY: A JOURNAL OF IDEAS (Fall 2014): "Regulations.gov may not be everyone's favorite website, and it isn't a lot of fun, but it is worth a look, because what appears there has significant consequences for the nation (and sometimes many nations) and because it is transforming notice-and-comment rule-making. When an agency proposes a rule, all the world can find it and see it, usually with great ease. If a proposal has a mistake, or veers in a bad direction, there is a genuine opportunity to comment and to get the problem fixed. When I served as administrator of the White House Office of Information and Regulatory Affairs from 2009 to 2012, I was surprised by one thing above all: A lot of regulators pay exceedingly

---

conference materials, and key websites accessible to anyone who is interested in the use of information technology in the regulatory process."

[105] http://www.regulations.gov/docs/FactSheet_eRulemaking_Best_Practices.pdf.

[106] The Future of E-rulemaking: Promoting Public Participation and Efficiency, November 30, 2010, transcript online at http://www.brookings.edu/events/the-future-of-e-rulemaking-promoting-public-participation-and-efficiency/.

close attention to public comments, and they spend a great deal of time on Regulations.gov. Such comments are carefully read, typically by people who have the authority to move regulations in better directions. Commenters often fear that what they say will go into a black hole but, in general, the fear is misplaced. People with authority end up reading what they write."

(2) *Tension between e-Rulemaking and the Expert Agency.* Peter M. Shane, Empowering the Collaborative Citizen in the Administrative State: A Case Study of the Federal Communications Commission, 65 U. Miami L. Rev. 483 (2011): ". . . The most important strategic issue for the agency is figuring out how to generate public interest in and demand for new interaction opportunities. My informal conversations with agency staff surfaced recurrent expressions of a hope for some effective public voice to serve as a counterbalance, or at least a reality check, on the voices of industry and inside-the-beltway insiders, who hardly need new media to make their views effectively known within the agency. The question is how to alert potential contributors that the FCC is prepared to listen to their input. . . .

"Persuading agency leadership and staff of the wisdom of such outreach, however, touches on perhaps the most important issue of governance philosophy underpinning these efforts: what exactly is the role of public input in an expert agency? Agencies are required to make regulatory judgments that, in APA terms, are neither 'arbitrary,' nor 'capricious.' Key agency decision makers are presumably appointed with an eye towards their expertise and qualifications regarding frequently complex subjects. Given how decision makers are chosen and that the relevant standard of judicial review requires agencies to defend the substantive rationality of their decision making, it seems obvious what public input *cannot* be. It cannot serve as some sort of plebiscite that will determine the agency's judgment.[74] If public comments, however, are not simply votes to be counted, that re-raises the question of their relevance and utility. The role of what may typically be anecdotal public comments in reaching agency decisions based on general social and economic conditions may not be obvious. The FCC staff and leadership to whom I spoke seemed uniformly willing to weigh public input according to its inherent thoughtfulness, analytic rigor, or empirical verifiability. How that is to be insured, however, and how such a commitment is to be effectively conveyed to the public are challenging issues."

---

[74] In what surely seems an overabundance of caution, OIRA recently cautioned executive agencies not to give decision-making weight to "social media tools that allow the public to rate, rank, vote on, flag, tag, label, or similarly assess the value of ideas, solutions, suggestions, questions, and comments posted by website users." According to OIRA: "[A]gency use of the information generated by these tools should be limited to organizing, ranking, and sorting comments. Because, in general, the results of online rankings, ratings, and tagging (e.g., number of votes or top rank) are not statistically generalizable, they should not be used as the basis for policy or planning."

(3) *Criticisms of Regulations.gov and FDMA.* ABA COMMITTEE ON THE STATUTE AND FUTURE OF FEDERAL E-RULEMAKING, ACHIEVING THE POTENTIAL: THE FUTURE OF FEDERAL E-RULEMAKING 4–6 (2008)[107]: "Lacking sustained and systematic involvement of non-federal users in the design of the public website, regulations.gov continues to reflect an 'insider' perspective—i.e., the viewpoint of someone familiar with rulemaking and the agencies that conduct it. The website design also . . . remains neither intuitive nor easy to use, even for those knowledgeable about rulemaking. Recent additions (e.g., e-mail notification, full-text search, RSS feed) are highly desirable improvements, but these important functionalities are not as convenient, effective, or powerful as what is needed and possible.

"A deeper problem (and one that limits the government's as well as the public's benefit from the system) is that many agencies are not using FDMS to provide the comprehensive online rulemaking docket contemplated by both the Initiative and the E-Government Act of 2002. No document—even a public comment submitted through regulations.gov—can be viewed by the public (or, for that matter, by other agencies) unless and until the responsible agency approves it for 'posting' to the public side of the system.

". . . The regulations.gov website should be completely redesigned, making creative use of web capabilities and state-of-the-art web design practices (i) to provide information in formats readily accessible to and comprehensible by the full range of potential users, and (ii) to interact efficiently and effectively with rulemaking information on agency sites. Active engagement in this process by the public users and experts of the public e-rulemaking advisory committee is essential."

(4) *ACUS Survey and Latest Recommendations.* ADMINISTRATIVE CONFERENCE OF THE UNITED STATES, AGENCY INNOVATIONS IN E-RULEMAKING, Recommendation 2011–8 (adopted Dec. 2011): ACUS examined "websites and e-rulemaking initiatives of 90 agencies, each of which had reported completing an average of two or more rulemakings" during a six-month period. It found both innovation, "often at no great cost to the government," and difficulty in locating comments, among other items. It made five types of recommendations: "Increasing the Visibility of Rulemakings," "Making Comment Policies Easy to Locate," "Improving Access to Agency Websites," "Ensuring Access to Materials from Completed Rulemakings," and "Periodically Evaluating Agency Use of the Internet in Rulemaking."

(5) *Complexity of Fostering Public Input.* CARY COGLIANESE, HEATHER KILMARTIN & EVAN MENDELSON, TRANSPARENCY AND PUBLIC PARTICIPATION IN THE FEDERAL RULEMAKING PROCESS: RECOMMENDATIONS FOR THE NEW ADMINISTRATION, 77 Geo. Wash. L.

---

[107] This excerpt was also published in 62 Admin. L. Rev. 279, 284–85, 287–88 (2010); the full text can also be found at http://www.lawschool.cornell.edu/ceri/publications-and-working-papers.cfm.

Rev. 924, 928–29, 933, 947–48 (2009): ". . . [I]improved transparency and public participation are not necessarily unmitigated goods. Even if increasing participation and transparency makes the rulemaking process and its resulting rules more legitimate, too much transparency and public participation can very well detract from making quality decisions in a timely manner. Increasing public participation requires an agency to expend more resources on filtering through and reading the comments submitted. These resources may be well spent to the extent that the additional comments contribute to better policies, but many comments are likely to be duplicative of earlier submissions. There may be, in other words, an optimal level of participation beyond which the costs and associated delays of dealing with public comments exceed the marginal benefits of processing them. For this reason, the quantitative level of participation should not be given greater priority than the quality and balance of participation. It is more important that the agency hear from all distinct viewpoints than that it hear from large numbers of individuals or groups expressing the same arguments or conveying the same information. Although agencies should never prohibit or actively discourage public comments, they need not affirmatively seek to expand participation for every rulemaking nor treat rulemaking as a mere popularity contest based on the comments received. . . .

"[A] commitment to transparency could reduce the likelihood that private firms would voluntarily provide agencies with potentially helpful information, especially if doing so were to mean that the agencies must disclose confidential business information obtained from such regulated firms. Because rulemaking demands extensive gathering of information held by regulated firms, rulemakers need to strike a balance between the critical objective of letting the public know the full basis for the agency's decisions on the one hand, and the protection of confidential business information on the other. . . .

"[S]ome observers complain that agencies fail to make information available to the public in a timely fashion and in a manner that allows for its meaningful use, especially as a prerequisite for public participation. For example, important data might not be included in a rulemaking docket until late in the comment process, or the data might be buried in voluminous records that are not available electronically. The lack of meaningful access to important information detracts from the public's ability to contribute to the formulation of better rules. And the participation that does occur will likely be less informed and therefore potentially less helpful or meaningful than it otherwise could be. The lack of information is a problem both for the average citizen and for the sophisticated 'repeat player' in the rulemaking process who is typically better able to overcome informational obstacles. A fairer process would give all parties the opportunity to file meaningful and informed comments. . . .

"To enhance the value of public comments, the new administration should encourage pilot experiments ['on a small scale'] with interactive comment processes. Interactive comment periods would appear to be most appropriate for rulemakings in which (1) the issues involved are extremely technical or complex; (2) comments filed in the initial round of commenting raise new or unanticipated issues; or (3) comments filed in the initial round of commenting contain significantly conflicting data. In these rulemakings, agencies could usefully provide two rounds of commenting to allow for interaction among commenters. Persons who submit comments during the first round would be eligible to respond to opposing comments or to agency queries in the second round. . . . Such a two-round approach also may well have a secondary effect of removing the strategic incentives to make extreme or unsupported claims or to file last-minute commentary."

(6) *Evidence from Sustained Efforts to Obtain Public Input.* CYNTHIA R. FARINA, MARY J. NEWHART, CLAIRE CARDIE & DAN COSLEY, RULEMAKING 2.0, 65 Miami L. Rev. 395 (2011), and RULEMAKING IN 140 CHARACTERS OR LESS: SOCIAL NETWORKING AND PUBLIC PARTICIPATION IN RULEMAKING, 31 Pace L. Rev. 382 (2011), provide an early account of the Cornell e-Rulemaking Initiative [CeRI],[108] an interdisciplinary effort which in collaboration with the Departments of Commerce and Transportation under a National Science Foundation grant has explored possible future lines of development in e-rulemaking that might prove successful in engaging broader segments of the public in rulemakings of interest through outreach, simplification, education, revised commenting techniques, and the like. Among CeRI's declared purposes is to "[a]ssist[ ], and actively promot[e] agency experimentation in Internet-based ways to elicit public participation beyond just the notice-and-comment process." These two articles report its initial efforts, in cooperation with the Department of Transportation, to enlist "outsiders" in two rulemakings likely to prove interesting to a broad spectrum of the public—one involving commercial drivers' texting while driving; the other, airline passenger rights, some of which is featured in the Introduction to this casebook. CeRI sought to reach individuals both directly and through groups (e.g., association of airline pilots, travel agents, automobile clubs) with which they were likely to be associated. On a site dedicated to this purpose,[109] it provided simplified accounts of the rulemaking proposals, broken down topically and presented for discussion/comment in a manner that would facilitate attention to particular issues that might be of concern to a commenter. Its moderators sought to facilitate discussion and comment while it was open and to summarize the results in a comment document, itself provided to participants for their review prior to submission, which was then

---

[108] http://www.lawschool.cornell.edu/ceri/.

[109] http://www.regulationroom.org.

submitted to the Department of Transportation as a comment in the rulemaking.

The articles suggest success in reaching members of the public who had not previously participated in rulemakings, but at substantial cost and with arguably limited benefit. As reported on the dedicated website after the airline passenger rights rule comment period ended:

- During the 110 days the rule was open on Regulation Room, a total of 19,320 unique visitors came to the site. There were 24,441 total visits, with people spending an average of 3.17 minutes on the site. Of the issue posts, the average time on the page was longest for Peanut Allergies (4.14 minutes) and shortest for Cost & Benefits (1.55 minutes). The Notice of Proposed Rulemaking was viewed 891 times; the proposed rule text was viewed 212 times.

- Anyone could read material on the site, but registration was required to participate in the discussion. A total of 1189 people registered during the time the rule was open.

- Based on answers to a survey at registration, only 6 percent of those who registered and answered the question (70 of 1094) said that they had previously submitted a comment in a federal rulemaking. A second survey question (which appeared the first time a user wanted to submit a comment) asked people to describe their interest in the rule. A total of 621 people chose to answer this optional question. Here are the responses:

    * air traveler: 566

    * other: 36

    * work for US air carrier: 7

    * researcher or expert: 7

    * work for travel agent or Global Distribution Systems (GDSs): 4

    * advocacy group: 1[110]

Note the lack of success in reaching air travel professionals for individual comments despite focused outreach to them through their constituent organizations. Those who did comment tended to prefer "voting"—the plebiscitary behavior Professor Shane, Note 2, suggests "it seems obvious . . . public input *cannot* be"—over the submission of data or reasoned views. The resource commitments needed for translating unreadable NPRMs into manageable statements the general public can

---

[110] http://archive.regulationroom.org/airline-passenger-rights/final-summary/.

understand,[111] for facilitative moderation, and—were outreach to be successful—for managing comment volume would be substantial.

(7) *A Model for Public Participation in Rulemaking?* When the FCC proposed rules for net neutrality in 2014 that would have permitted differentiations in service speed, late-night host John Oliver encouraged his viewers—particularly "trolls"—to comment against the proposal in a 13-minute comedic rant.[112] According to the Washington Post, "By Monday, the FCC's commenting system had stopped working, thanks to more than 45,000 new comments on net neutrality likely sparked by Oliver." The final rule, finalized after about four million comments were filed and upheld by the D.C. Circuit, did not adopt the proposed service differentiations, instead providing equitable access. Do you think those comments were "carefully read"? More recently, after the FCC's new chairman, Ajit Pai, proposed to roll back the final rule after the White House changed hands in 2017, Oliver appealed to his viewers again, telling them to visit the website www.gofccyourself.com, which automatically took them to the FCC's docket for filing comments on net neutrality.[113] The agency's website stopped working again (this time, apparently due to a cyberattack), but it was operating by the next day. By mid-May, the FCC had received over 1.2 million comments on its proposed repeal. What lessons can you draw from Oliver's efforts for public participation in rulemaking?

b. Management Issues

Implementing e-rulemaking presents issues both for the individual rulemaking agency and for the government as a whole.

(1) *A Government Lawyer's View.* Neil Eisner was for years the Assistant General Counsel for Regulation and Enforcement at the Department of Transportation, widely respected for his knowledge of the subject and substantially responsible for the Department's connection with CeRI (see Note 6 in the previous set). Addressing the Brookings Institution at its November 2010 Conference on E-Rulemaking, he suggested that the following were among the legal issues any agency using e-rulemaking would be obliged to consider:

". . . [A] lot of the hard copy record problems we have are still problems on the Internet, and some problems that we didn't have before are becoming problems on the Internet. Some problems, for example, censorship, should we sensor obscenity, that was always a problem when you had a hard copy record, but you didn't have too many 10 year olds or

---

[111] The reading difficulty of the typical notice of proposed rulemaking, the authors report, is at the post-graduate level; the American public reads and comprehends, on average, at the eighth-grade level.

[112] http://youtu.be/fpbOEoRrHyU.

[113] http://youtu.be/92vuuZt7wak.

12 year olds coming in and asking the docket clerk for a copy of the docket. Now they have easy access on the Internet. . . .

"What about the legal record, what has to go into the docket, . . . can [it] be the electronic record or do we still have to maintain a paper record of everything that's in there[?] . . . People believe that electronic dockets can be tampered with. Well, hard copy records could be tampered with also. . . .

"And what must the agency put in the docket? . . . For example, if an agency is not doing the blogging, a private enterprise is doing it, must the agency put in just the summary that it receives from the person who's conducting the blog, or must it put in the entire record of the blog, which could be 100 times or 1,000 times greater than the one summary that is submitted? Do we have to put in every standard form comment that we get, or if they are exactly alike, can we put in one and say we've received several thousand more like this? Do we have to put in every document to which there is a link in a document that is sent to us in case some people can't get access to the linked document?

"What about signatures, can commenters be anonymous . . .? Do I have some obligation to make sure that the signature on the docket is from a real person, or am I allowed to just go on the basis of the fact that they made a good point and I should make that change to the proposed rule regardless of who they are?

"Obscenity, should I delete everything from the docket that is obscene? Does this mean that I have to review everything that comes into the docket before I can post it online? Because this would be a tremendous burden . . ., and if I do, what are the standards I apply to what is obscene? . . . What about copyrighted material? If the federal agency relies on copyrighted material and it's not readily available to the public, should the agency post the copyrighted material on the docket considering it to be a fair use, especially if it reasonably limits it to that part on which it relied? . . . Does the agency have an obligation to determine whether it has copyrighted protection? And what conditions should be applied to the decision as to what to put in the docket? . . .

"Then there are the privacy issues that come up, especially when you have a more easily accessible and accessed docket, where you can search, for example, by people's names. Do people expect privacy when they submit a comment to the agency? . . . Must I review all comments again before I can post them online simply because they may have privacy information in them? . . . Do I have to, if I make a scan of an e-mail and place it in the docket, do I have to delete the address, the e-mail address, of the person who is the commenter? And does it matter whether I warn people in my rulemaking document that everything will be placed online as received?

"Then there's electronic participation. Can I require all participants to submit their comments electronically or do I have to accept paper copies? And may I require all comments to be submitted in an easily searched electronic or standard format? Can I ask specific questions on the form and put specific headings in and say, if you don't fill out this form, I will not review your comment?"

(2) *Agency Obligations and Social Media.* Agency use of social media raises several legal issues. To start, is an agency blog subject to the mandates of the Paperwork Reduction Act? It appears the answer is no, according to Obama Administration attorneys; blogs and web postings are like public meetings, which are not subject to the Act. See Peter Shane, Empowering the Collaborative Citizen in the Administrative State: A Case Study of the Federal Communications Commission, 65 U. Miami L. Rev. 483 (2011). In addition, are "informal comment submissions via blogs and similar applications" required to be placed in the agency record? The FCC has told commenters on blogs that their statements "*will* be considered part of the record, requiring the agency to designate staff to analyze, organize and summarize those comments for further consideration." Id.

To what extent can an agency use social media to encourage support for proposed rulemakings? The GAO found that the EPA had "violated publicity or propaganda and anti-lobbying provisions contained in appropriation acts" in its social media use campaigns surrounding the Waters of the United States rulemaking in FY 2014 and 2015. GAO, Environmental Protection Agency—Application of Publicity or Propaganda and Anti-Lobbying Provisions, B-326944 (Dec 14, 2015).[114] Specifically, according to the GAO, the EPA's use of Thunderclap (specifically, a widely shared message linked to the proposed rule that did not identify the EPA as the sender) constituted "covert propaganda" and its links to external sites that advocated contacting members of Congress qualified as "grassroots lobbying." But the GAO determined that the agency's #DitchtheMyth and #CleanWaterRules campaigns, which extolled the benefits of clean water and the proposed rule, were permissible.

In March 2017, the House of Representatives passed H.R. 1004, known as the Regulatory Integrity Act, which would require agencies to post information about all their public communications on pending regulatory actions (encompassing rules, adjudications, guidance, and policy statements), including the "intended audience," "method of communication," and a "copy of the communication"). The Act would also constrain agency public communications as follows:

(1) IN GENERAL.—Any public communication issued by an Executive agency that refers to a pending agency regulatory action—

(A) shall specify whether the Executive agency is considering alternatives;

---

[114] http://www.gao.gov/products/B-326944.

(B) shall specify whether the Executive agency is accepting or will be accepting comments; and

(C) shall expressly disclose that the Executive agency is the source of the information to the intended recipients.

(2) RESTRICTION.—Any public communication issued by an Executive agency that refers to a pending agency regulatory action, other than an impartial communication that requests comment on or provides information regarding the pending agency regulatory action, may not—

(A) directly advocate, in support of or against the pending agency regulatory action, for the submission of information to form part of the record of review for the pending agency regulatory action;

(B) appeal to the public, or solicit a third party, to undertake advocacy in support of or against the pending agency regulatory action; or

(C) be directly or indirectly for publicity or propaganda purposes within the United States unless otherwise authorized by law.

It is unlikely that the Senate will pass it (as it has not passed similar legislation in previous years). What do you like and dislike about the proposed legislation?

(3) *Identifying and Controlling Politicized Responses.* Submitting a comment by traditional mail requires the effort of putting it on paper, individually addressing the envelope in which it will be sent, and applying necessary postage; postmarks will identify the place from which it has come. Anyone who has received a computer virus or electronic advertisement ostensibly sent by a friend understands both how costless they are to send and how difficult they are to trace. Even if each electronic comment comes in fact from a different real person, an organization's membership base can now be mobilized to submit views without the organization or its members having to pay for postage. In addition, the commenter often does not need to generate the text of most if not all of the comment she will submit. How should agencies handle electronic postcard campaigns and, in general, analyze possibly enormous volumes of electronic commentary for possibly useful information or views? This has been the particular concern of Stuart Shulman, a political scientist now at the University of Massachusetts in Amherst, who has created computer programming capable of sorting large volumes of electronic submissions to reveal their similarities *and* their unique contributions. See, e.g., Stuart W. Shulman, The Case Against Mass E-mails: Perverse Incentives and Low Quality Public Participation in U.S. Federal Rulemaking, 1 Pol'y & Internet, Issue 1 (2009); Stuart W. Shulman, Whither Deliberation? Mass e-Mail Campaigns and U.S. Regulatory Rulemaking 3 J. of E-Government No. 3, p. 41 (2006).

(4) ***Managing e-Rulemaking in Second Best World.*** The ABA Committee on the Status and Future of Federal Rulemaking noted in 2008 that if an electronic rulemaking system were being designed from scratch, the result would not be regulations.gov and FDMS. Given that a brand new system was unlikely to be developed, the Committee made a number of recommendations:[115]

"Governance

"A single agency should be given responsibility for specifying and implementing the new architecture [of the system]. To minimize concerns from even the perception that one agency is being empowered to impose its particular rulemaking practices on the entire system, this new lead agency should not be one of the major rulemaking agencies.

"An interagency E-rulemaking committee should be created, funded, and charged to provide regular, ongoing advice to the new lead agency about agency needs and preferences. A parallel advisory committee of public users and various relevant outside experts should be created, funded, and charged to provide regular, ongoing advice to the lead agency about the needs and preferences of the wide range of non-federal government users.

"Data Standardization

"The new lead agency should oversee a process of facilitated discussions among participating agencies, the object of which is to establish the common data and metadata standards and to define the quality information practices essential to effective cross-government electronic rulemaking. This process must be done independently of any effort that might be undertaken to conform underlying rulemaking practices to a standard model. If agreement still cannot be achieved, the lead agency must be empowered to establish the necessary standards and practices, and OMB must unambiguously support their implementation and use.

"Funding

"A separate appropriation to the new lead agency for developing and maintaining the core e-rulemaking system should be authorized and funded. The appropriation should include an amount for further modernization and enhancement.

"Agency Practice

"The online docket should become the authoritative rulemaking record for all agencies, with clear indication and adequate identification of any portions of that record not being made publicly available. Agencies should be expected to create comprehensive, accurate electronic dockets that are well-indexed and effectively searchable. They should be expected

---

[115] This excerpt was also published in 62 Admin. L. Rev. 279, 286–87 (2010); the full text can also be found at http://scholarship.law.cornell.edu/cgi/viewcontent.cgi?article=2505&context=facpub.

to post supporting materials and comments in a prompt and timely manner, and they should receive adequate resources for this and other preparation and entry of data.

"Existing communication mechanisms should be used and new ones created to increase communication between agency personnel with technical expertise and those with regulatory program expertise, within as well as across agencies. The goals include identifying both good practices in, and legal or institutional obstacles to, e-rulemaking; creating the basis for collaboration among agencies in developing new e-tools and applications; and sharing of experience with innovative uses of technology in rulemaking."

(5) ***OIRA and Transparency.*** In his Brookings remarks, see p. 759, then-OIRA Director Sunstein emphasized the connection between transparent process and good rulemaking: "This point about information that people can readily find and use bears directly on e-rulemaking and the . . . role of analysis. If [agencies] are providing, in an accessible clear and transparent manner, both the content of rules and the analysis that support rules, they are providing something that people can find and use in part in order to improve and criticize and reform rules if the proposed form isn't ideal and in part to provide people information in advance because advance notice promotes predictability and avoids unfair surprise."

To what extent does this involve OIRA's central management role in rulemaking? You might check the docket for a recent important rulemaking on regulations.gov to see to what extent, if any, the agency's dealings with OIRA are recorded there. Should they be? Or does OIRA's participation, or any other agency's views that might be communicated to the rulemaking agency, constitute predecisional, intra-governmental deliberation properly falling with FOIA's Exemption 5?[116] Under E.O. 12866, what must OIRA disclose on its role? Commentators suggest that OIRA largely doesn't comply with these mandates.[117]

The preceding discussion, like most discussions of the changes comprehensive electronic dockets might make through their potential transformation of the commenting process, has focused (as Sunstein does) on the information they make available to the participating public. But, of course, this information is now equally accessible to OIRA, and that too is a transformation. Previously, the scientific studies on which an agency might rely, and the comments it may have received, were essentially available only to it; and OIRA's limited staff could not readily scour a physical record of substantial dimensions located at agency

---

[116] Interestingly, on some occasions, agencies submit formal comments on another agency's proposed rulemaking, which then do appear on the docket.

[117] See, e.g., Sam Abbott, Disclosure at the Office of Information and Regulatory Affairs: Written Comments and Telephone Records Suspiciously Absent (Center for Effective Government, Feb. 26, 2013), http://www.foreffectivegov.org/disclosure-at-oira-written-comments-and-telephone-records-suspiciously-absent.

headquarters. Now those materials are in the computers on their desks, and anyone else's. In the bureaucratic world, information is power. Are the implications (further centralization of decisionmaking) in the rulemaking process that this suggests a troubling, or a welcome, prospect?

THE AGENCY AND THE CONSTITUTION

CHAPTER VII

AGENCY RELATIONSHIPS WITH CONGRESS, THE PRESIDENT, AND THE COURTS: THE STRUCTURAL CONSTITUTION

Sec. 1. Introduction
Sec. 2. Congress and Administrative Agencies
Sec. 3. The President, Administrative Agencies, and the Executive Branch
Sec. 4. Constitutional Frameworks for Administrative Adjudication

Agencies are almost as old as the Constitution itself, but from the outset their relationship with the Congress, the President, and the courts has been controversial. The Constitution does not specify the structure of the national government below the level of Congress, the President, and the Supreme Court.[1] Those of you who reach these materials after studying the chapters on "the Agency at Work" will appreciate the challenge of trying to map the volume and complexity of modern administrative government onto this paucity of constitutional text. For those who are beginning your study of administrative law with this Chapter, consider how little guidance the Constitution's text gives for designing agencies as diverse as the Transportation Safety Administration, the Environmental Protection Agency, the Office of Federal Student Aid (Department of Education), the Consumer Financial Protection Bureau (created by the Dodd-Frank Wall Street Reform and Consumer Protection Act) and the Patient-Centered Outcomes Research Institute (created by the Patient Protection and Affordable Care Act).

The first Congress promptly created the Departments of Foreign Affairs, War, and Treasury. The Post Office and the Department of the Navy followed within a few years. Intense debate preceded these acts, particularly around whether the Senate could require its consent to the removal of agency heads. Although many early members of Congress had played key roles in the Philadelphia Convention and/or the ratification process, they disagreed passionately about whether removal was solely

---

[1] Early drafts of the Constitution specified a number of cabinet departments and vested them with particular responsibilities. This language was removed in the final days of drafting; one small vestige is the reference, in the Necessary and Proper Clause, to powers "vested by this Constitution in the Government of the United States, or in any Department or Officer thereof."

the President's constitutional prerogative. On another constitutional front, before the federal government was 25 years old, litigants were arguing to the Supreme Court that Congress had unconstitutionally delegated national policymaking power to another part of the government. That such fundamental questions were disputed even among those so close to the founding is, from an historical perspective, unremarkable: The Constitution was creating a new, and largely unprecedented, kind of government. In all the debate that accompanied the Convention and the ratification processes in every state, many novel and complex questions were resolved imperfectly, if at all. Gordon S. Wood, one of the preeminent historians of the period, puts it pithily: "there was not in 1787–1788 one 'correct' or 'true' meaning of the Constitution." Ideology and the Origins of Liberal America, 44 Wm. & Mary Q. 628, 632 (1987).

From a legal perspective however, the American understanding of the significance of a constitution impels us to seek determinate, authoritative meaning against which to measure the legality of government structures and practices. Controversies over congressional choices about governmental structure are, as we will see, hardly new. And a new wave of structural constitutional challenges to the administrative state originated in the presidency of Ronald Reagan. Over the last four decades, in a series of cases as potentially far-reaching as they are jurisprudentially novel, litigants have insisted that a variety of administrative arrangements violate particular provisions of Articles I, II, or III and, more generally, the principle of separation of powers. Some of the challenged arrangements are recent innovations, as Congress has tackled thorny problems like the budget deficit or misbehavior in the financial markets; others are longstanding aspects of regulatory structure or oversight that have come under new constitutional attack.

President Reagan was a vocal critic of federal regulation and the people who implemented it, but more significantly his administration fostered a renaissance of conservative constitutional theory. With very different policy preferences than the Democrats who controlled Congress through much of his presidency, Reagan sought control over agencies and regulatory programs with an aggressiveness that laid groundwork for the pro-president "unitary executive" constitutionalism of the George W. Bush administration. And, although Democrat Presidents Bill Clinton and Barack Obama disavowed the most extravagant constitutional claims of unitary executive power, their practice continued the trend of deepening and extending presidential control over the officials and the decisions of regulatory agencies. Though it is early days yet, President Trump appears to be following suit, issuing 29 executive orders in his first 100 days in office.

As Congress and the President venture into new regulatory structures and relationships, and as litigants advocate constitutional interpretations in which Article II has newfound prominence, the contemporary Court finds itself in a position uncomfortably like that of the first Supreme Court under John Marshall: building constitutional doctrine from the ground up. Perhaps this is why the cases in this Chapter seem frustratingly ad hoc—methodology swings from formalism to functionalism with little rhyme or reason, while outcomes turn on unexpected alignments of individual justices. Among democracies, the United States is remarkable for the age and minimal amendment of its national constitution and for the power of its national constitutional court. In no context are these distinctive characteristics more evident than when the Justices look to spare constitutional text to decide whether Congress or the President have overstepped some line.

SECTION 1.   INTRODUCTION

> a. *Is the Administrative State Constitutional?*
>
> b. *Separation of Powers Methodology*

The topics covered in subsequent Sections—delegation, legislative appropriations, vetoes and presidential directives, appointment and removal—are pieces of a larger puzzle: How can we reconcile the modern regulatory state with a Constitution that is more than 200 years old yet still serves as our fundamental benchmark of political legitimacy? The first set of materials in this section dips selectively into the vast body of work on separation of powers to offer several opposing views on this overarching question. The second set introduces you to general features of separation of powers analysis.

a.   Is the Administrative State Constitutional?

> *Gary Lawson, The Rise and Rise of the Administrative State*
>
> *Peter L. Strauss, The Place of Agencies in Government: Separation of Powers and the Fourth Branch*
>
> *Jerry L. Mashaw, Creating the Administrative Constitution: The Lost One Hundred Years of American Administrative Law*
>
> *Gillian E. Metzger, The Supreme Court 2016 Term—Foreword: 1930s Redux: The Administrative State Under Siege*

Gary Lawson, The Rise and Rise of the Administrative State
107 Harv. L. Rev. 1231 (1994)

The post-New Deal administrative state is unconstitutional, and its validation by the legal system amounts to nothing less than a bloodless constitutional revolution. . . .

A. The Death of Limited Government

The advocates of the Constitution of 1789 were very clear about the kind of national government they sought to create. As James Madison put it: "The powers delegated by the proposed Constitution to the federal government are few and defined." Those national powers, Madison suggested, would be "exercised principally on external objects, as war, peace, negotiation, and foreign commerce," and the states would be the principal units of government for most internal matters. . . . [I]n this day and age, discussing the doctrine of enumerated powers is like discussing the redemption of Imperial Chinese bonds. There is now virtually no significant aspect of life that is not in some way regulated by the federal government. . . .

B. The Death of the Nondelegation Doctrine

The Constitution both confines the national government to certain enumerated powers and defines the institutions of the national government that can permissibly exercise those powers. Article I of the Constitution provides that "[a]ll legislative Powers herein granted shall be vested in a Congress of the United States, which shall consist of a Senate and House of Representatives." Article II provides that "[t]he executive Power shall be vested in a President of the United States of America." Article III specifies that "the judicial Power of the United States, shall be vested in one supreme Court, and in such inferior Courts as the Congress may from time to time ordain and establish." The Constitution thus divides the powers of the national government into three categories—legislative, executive, and judicial—and vests such powers in three separate institutions. . . .

Although the Constitution does not tell us how to distinguish the legislative, executive, and judicial powers from each other, there is clearly some differentiation among the three governmental functions, which at least generates some easy cases. Consider, for example, a statute creating the Goodness and Niceness Commission and giving it power "to promulgate rules for the promotion of goodness and niceness in all areas within the power of Congress under the Constitution." If the "executive power" means simply the power to carry out legislative commands regardless of their substance, then the Goodness and Niceness Commission's rulemaking authority is executive rather than legislative power and is therefore valid. But if that is true, then there never was and never could be such a thing as a constitutional principle of nondelegation—a proposition that is belied by all available evidence about the meaning of the Constitution. . . . Certain powers simply cannot be given to executive (or judicial) officials, because those powers are *legislative* in character. . . .

. . . The United States Code is filled with statutes that create little Goodness and Niceness Commissions—each confined to a limited subject area such as securities, broadcast licenses, or (my personal favorite) imported tea.[2] These statutes are easy kills under any plausible interpretation of the Constitution's nondelegation principle. The Supreme Court, however, has rejected so many delegation challenges to so many utterly vacuous statutes that modern nondelegation decisions now simply recite these past holdings and wearily move on. Anything short of the Goodness and Niceness Commission, it seems, is permissible.

C.   The Death of the Unitary Executive

Article II states that "[t]he executive Power shall be vested in a President of the United States of America." Although the precise contours of this "executive Power" are not entirely clear, at a minimum it includes the power to execute the laws of the United States. Other clauses of the Constitution, such as the requirement that the President "take Care that the Laws be faithfully executed," assume and constrain this power to execute the laws, but the Article II Vesting Clause is the constitutional source of this power—just as the Article III Vesting Clause is the constitutional source of the federal judiciary's power to decide cases.

Significantly, that power to execute the laws is vested, not in the executive department of the national government, but in "a President of the United States of America." The Constitution thus creates a unitary executive. Any plausible theory of the federal executive power must acknowledge and account for this vesting of the executive power in the person of the President.

Of course, the President cannot be expected personally to execute all laws. Congress, pursuant to its power to make all laws "necessary and proper for carrying into Execution" the national government's powers, can create administrative machinery to assist the President in carrying out legislatively prescribed tasks. But if a statute vests discretionary authority directly in an agency official (as do most regulatory statutes) rather than in the President, the Article II Vesting Clause seems to require that such discretionary authority be subject to the President's control. . . . [D]ebate has focused almost exclusively on whether and when the President must have unlimited power to remove subordinate executive officials. That is an interesting and important question, but it does not address the central issue concerning the executive power. . . .

D.   The Death of the Independent Judiciary

Article III provides that "[t]he judicial Power of the United States, shall be vested in one supreme Court, and in such inferior Courts as the Congress may from time to time ordain and establish." The judges of all such federal courts are constitutionally guaranteed tenure during good behavior as well as assurance that their salaries will not be diminished during their time in office. One of the principal functions of

---

[2]   [Ed.] The particular example invoked by Prof. Lawson illustrates the historical point made at the outset of this Section: The Board of Tea Experts, charged with preventing the importation of substandard tea, was a 19th century creation. See Tea Importation Act, Section 41, acts Mar. 2, 1897, ch. 358, Sec. 1, 29 Stat. 604. Its existence ended with Pub. L. 104–128, the Federal Tea Tasters Repeal Act of 1996.

administrative agencies is to adjudicate disputes, yet administrative adjudicators plainly lack the essential attributes that Article III requires of any decisionmaker invested with "the judicial Power of the United States." . . .

Agency adjudication is therefore constitutionally permissible under Article III as long as the activity in question can fairly fit the definition of executive power, even if it also fairly fits the definition of judicial power. . . . Wherever the line is drawn, however, at least some modern administrative adjudication undoubtedly falls squarely on the judicial side. . . .

E. The Death of Separation of Powers

The constitutional separation of powers is a means to safeguard the liberty of the people. In Madison's famous words, "[t]he accumulation of all powers, legislative, executive, and judiciary, in the same hands, whether of one, a few, or many, and whether hereditary, self-appointed, or elective, may justly be pronounced the very definition of tyranny." [Federalist 47] The destruction of this principle of separation of powers is perhaps the crowning jewel of the modern administrative revolution. Administrative agencies routinely combine all three governmental functions in the same body, and even in the same people within that body.

Consider the typical enforcement activities of a typical federal agency—for example, of the Federal Trade Commission. The Commission promulgates substantive rules of conduct. The Commission then considers whether to authorize investigations into whether the Commission's rules have been violated. If the Commission authorizes an investigation, the investigation is conducted by the Commission, which reports its findings to the Commission. If the Commission thinks that the Commission's findings warrant an enforcement action, the Commission issues a complaint. The Commission's complaint that a Commission rule has been violated is then prosecuted by the Commission and adjudicated by the Commission. This Commission adjudication can either take place before the full Commission or before a semi-autonomous Commission administrative law judge. If the Commission chooses to adjudicate before an administrative law judge rather than before the Commission and the decision is adverse to the Commission, the Commission can appeal to the Commission. If the Commission ultimately finds a violation, then, and only then, the affected private party can appeal to an Article III court. But the agency decision, even before the bona fide Article III tribunal, possesses a very strong presumption of correctness on matters both of fact and of law. . . .

Peter L. Strauss, The Place of Agencies in Government: Separation of Powers and the Fourth Branch

84 Colum. L. Rev. 573 (1984)

For the past few years the Supreme Court has been struggling with issues of government structure so fundamental that they might have been thought textbook simple, yet with results that seem to imperil the everyday exercise of law-administration. . . .

At the root of these problems lies a difficulty in understanding the relationships between the agencies that actually do the work of law-administration, whose existence is barely hinted at in the Constitution, and the three constitutionally named repositories of all governmental power—Congress, President, and Supreme Court. When, for example, a federal agency adopts a legislative "rule" following the procedures of the Administrative Procedure Act, how is this act to be understood constitutionally? In a colloquial sense, the agency is acting legislatively— that is, creating general statements of positive law whose application to an indefinite class awaits future acts and proceedings. Validly adopted legislative rules are identical to statutes in their impact on all relevant legal actors—those subject to their constraints, those responsible for their administration, and judges or others who may have occasion to consider them in the course of their activities. Does it follow that in the constitutional sense what the agency is doing should be regarded as an exercise of the "legislative Powers . . . granted" by article I, "all" of which are vested in Congress? Or, given statutory authorization, is it to be regarded as an exercise of the executive authority vested in the President by article II, the judicial power placed in the Supreme Court (and statutorily created inferior courts) by article III, or authority merely statutory in provenance? The Constitution names and ascribes functions only to the Congress, President and Supreme Court, sitting in uneasy relation at the apex of the governmental structure; it leaves undiscussed what might be the necessary and permissible relationships of each of these three constitutional bodies to the agency making the rule. Is it significant for any of these purposes whether the rulemaking authority has been assigned to a cabinet department or to an independent regulatory commission? Indeed, does it make sense to look to the Constitution, written so many years ago, for contemporary guidance or limits on the sorts of arrangements Congress can make?

Three differing approaches have been used in the effort to understand issues such as these. The first, "separation of powers," supposes that what government does can be characterized in terms of the kind of act performed—legislating, enforcing, and determining the particular application of law—and that for the safety of the citizenry from tyrannous government these three functions must be kept in distinct places. Congress legislates, and it only legislates; the President sees to the faithful execution of those laws and, in the domestic context at least, that is all he does; the courts decide specific cases of law-application, and that is their sole function. These three powers of government are kept radically separate, because if the same body exercised all three of them, or even two, it might no longer be possible to keep it within the constraints of law.

"Separation of functions" suggests a somewhat different idea, grounded more in considerations of individual fairness in particular proceedings than in the need for structural protection against tyrannical government generally. It admits that for agencies (as distinct from the constitutionally named heads of government) the same body often does exercise all three of the characteristic governmental powers, albeit in a web of other controls—judicial review and legislative and executive oversight. As these controls are thought to give reasonable assurance against systemic lawlessness, the separation-of-functions inquiry asks to what extent constitutional due process for the particular individual(s) who may be involved with an agency in a given proceeding requires special measures to assure the objectivity or impartiality of that proceeding. The powers are not kept separate, at least in general, but certain procedural protections—for example, the requirement of an on-the-record hearing before an "impartial" trier—may be afforded.

"Checks and balances" is the third idea, one that to a degree bridges the gap between these two domains. Like separation of powers, it seeks to protect the citizens from the emergence of tyrannical government by establishing multiple heads of authority in government, which are then pitted one against another in a continuous struggle; the intent of that struggle is to deny to any one (or two) of them the capacity ever to consolidate all governmental authority in itself, while permitting the whole effectively to carry forward the work of government. Unlike separation of powers, however, the checks-and-balances idea does not suppose a radical division of government into three parts, with particular functions neatly parceled out among them. Rather, the focus is on relationships and interconnections, on maintaining the conditions in which the intended struggle at the apex may continue. From this perspective, as from the perspective of separation of functions, it is not important how powers below the apex are treated; the important question is whether the relationship of each of the three named actors of the Constitution to the exercise of those powers is such as to promise a continuation of their effective independence and interdependence.

. . . I argue that, for any consideration of the structure given law-administration below the very apex of the governmental structure, the rigid separation-of-powers compartmentalization of governmental functions should be abandoned in favor of analysis in terms of separation of functions and checks and balances. . . . A shorthand way of putting the argument is that we should stop pretending that all our government (as distinct from its highest levels) can be allocated into three neat parts.

The theory of separation-of-powers breaks down when attempting to locate administrative and regulatory agencies within one of the three branches; its vitality, rather, lies in the formulation and specification of the controls that Congress, the Supreme Court and the President may exercise over administration and regulation. . . .

[T]he important fact is that an agency is neither Congress nor President nor Court, but an inferior part of government. Each agency is subject to control relationships with some or all of the three constitutionally named branches, and those relationships give an assurance—functionally similar to that provided by the separation-of-powers notion for the constitutionally named bodies—that they will not pass out of control.[18] Powerful and potentially arbitrary as they may be, the Secretary of Agriculture and the Chairman of the SEC for this reason do not present the threat that led the framers to insist on a splitting of the authority of government at its very top. What we have, then, are three named repositories of authorizing power and control, and an infinity of institutions to which parts of the authority of each may be lent. The three must share the reins of control; means must be found of assuring that no one of them becomes dominant. But it is not terribly important to number or allocate the horses that pull the carriage of government. . . .

[G]iven the realities of contemporary government and the inescapable constraints of constitutional text and context, we can achieve the worthy ends of those who drafted our Constitution only if we give up the notion that it embodies a neat division of all government into three separate branches, each endowed with a unique portion of governmental power and employing no other. The apportionment was made, but it was made only as to those actors occupying the very apex of government—Congress, President, and Supreme Court. The remainder of government was left undefined, in the expectation that congressional judgments about appropriate structure would serve so long as they observed the two prescriptive judgments embodied in the Constitution: that the work of law-administration be under the supervision of a unitary, politically accountable chief executive; and that the structures chosen permit, even encourage, the continuation of rivalries and tensions among the three named heads of government, in order that no one body becomes irreversibly dominant and thus threatens to deprive the people themselves of their voice and control.

---

[18]   For example, one may understand the delegation doctrine in this functional way, rather than as an indication "where" in government rulemaking occurs. That doctrine requires both statutory authorization (a relationship with Congress) and a capacity on the part of the courts to assure legality (a relationship with the courts). . . .

Jerry L. Mashaw, Creating the Administrative Constitution: The Lost One Hundred Years of American Administrative Law

(Yale 2012)

The conventional conception of administrative law in the United States has long suffered from several misperceptions. Indeed I am tempted to describe them as governing myths. The first is that the national government, from 1787 until the late nineteenth century, was a government of courts and parties. In such a government, administration, and as a corollary administrative law, is a backwater—a place of little importance in the grand scheme of governance. The second is that administrative law is the law of judicial review of administrative action. . . .

A corollary of this self-executing-laws thesis is that administration in modern forms, that is, administrative officers adjudicating cases and making rules, appeared only in the late-nineteenth and early-twentieth centuries with the creation of so-called "independent" agencies like the [Interstate Commerce Commission] and the Federal Trade Commission. Administration, the execution of laws, is in this imagined world of sharply delineated powers largely limited to prosecutorial functions. And prosecution—which we now view as a quintessentially executive function—is further imagined to have been under the direct control of the President through the Attorney General.

It is but a short step from these images of our administrative constitution in the first century of the Republic to deep concerns about the legitimacy of the modern administrative state. If these images of our constitutional practices and commitments are true, then our current arrangements represent a radical departure from original understandings. . . .

These conventional characterizations capture some essential truths about national administrative organization and administrative law in nineteenth-century America. But . . . these generalizations are quite often simply wrong. Self-executing laws requiring only prosecutorial administration did not exhaust Congress's repertoire of legislative forms. From the earliest days of the Republic, Congress delegated broad authority to administrators, armed them with extrajudicial coercive powers, created systems of administrative adjudication, and specifically authorized administrative rulemaking. Nor was execution of the law lodged firmly and exclusively in the offer we now often refer to as the "Chief Executive." Lack of authority to control prosecution was a constant lament of early presidents and attorneys general. . . . While there have, indeed, been massive changes in the size and scope of the general government over the course of the twentieth century, . . . there has been no precipitous fall from a historical position of separation-of-powers grace. . . .

The Federalist or Hamiltonian wing of the founding generation was keenly aware of the need to create a government with broad authority that could command the respect and the loyalty of the populace.... Federalist principles and aspirations, however, confronted the "Antifederalist" or "Virginia Republican" tradition.... For Jeffersonians, central government involvement in internal affairs was a formula for recreating the oppression and corruption of English rule. The Constitution would have to be a compromise between or paper over these radically divergent positions. The vacuousness of Article II of the Constitution was a part of that compromise.... The American Constitution of 1787 left a hole where administration might have been.

Administration is missing? To be sure, the Constitution establishes an executive branch. But it has only two constitutionally prescribed officers.... The Constitution presumes that there will be heads of departments and other officers of the United States and provides that the President will appoint them. And the President is charged with seeing "that the Laws be faithfully executed." But the only power explicitly given to the President with respect to executing the laws is the power to require reports in writing from the heads of departments—whatever "departments" might be.

...[T]he Constitution's silence on most matters administrative provides extremely modest textual support for the notion that all administration was to be firmly and exclusively in the control of the President. Not only are the President's stated constitutional powers feeble, but Congress's powers are broad.... And, text aside, the practice of early Congresses when creating the basic machinery of government belied the notion that the founding generation imagined the President as an all-powerful administrator-in-chief.

Gillian E. Metzger, The Supreme Court 2016 Term—Foreword: 1930s Redux: The Administrative State Under Siege

131 Harv. L. Rev. 1 (2017)

Anti-administrativists paint the administrative state as fundamentally at odds with the Constitution's separation of powers system, combining together in agencies the legislative, executive, and judicial authorities that the Constitution vests in different branches and producing unaccountable and aggrandized power in the process.... But [this] ... analysis gets the constitutional diagnosis almost exactly backward.... The administrative state—with its bureaucracy, expert and professional personnel, and internal institutional complexity—performs critical constitutional functions and is the key to an accountable, constrained, and effective executive branch....

... [T]he point can be taken even further: The modern national administrative state is now constitutionally obligatory, rendered necessary by the reality of delegation. . . . [B]oth [opponents] and supporters of administrative government should agree that the phenomenon of broad delegation is not at risk of judicial invalidation. Justice Thomas aside, little support exists on the Court for invalidating delegations to the executive branch on constitutional grounds. . . . The relevant constitutional question then becomes what the separation of powers requires in a world of substantial delegation of policymaking authority. It is in this context that the administrative state is constitutionally obligatory.

. . . To see why, begin with the Constitution's requirement that the President shall "take Care that the Laws be faithfully executed." It follows that the administrative capacity the President needs in order to satisfy the take care duty is also required. So far, few would disagree. What does that administrative capacity entail in the context of broad delegations? For starters, it means sufficient bureaucratic apparatus and supervisory mechanisms to adequately oversee execution of these delegated powers. It also requires sufficient administrative resources and personnel, in particular adequate executive branch expertise and specialization, to be able to faithfully execute these delegated responsibilities in contexts of tremendous uncertainty and complexity. Arguably, this means that professional and expert government employees are now constitutionally required as well, and perhaps also the civil service, insofar as such career staff are necessary to ensure expertise and institutional stability in agencies.

Simply from the proposition that delegated power must be faithfully executed, then, the outlines of a constitutionally mandated administrative state begin to emerge. Moreover, from this proposition some proposed anti-administrative measures, such as massively underfunding the EPA without altering its statutory responsibilities or repealing environmental rules necessary to implement delegated authority without adopting an alternative enforcement regime, begin to look constitutionally suspect.

Admittedly, the claim that the Constitution necessitates some level of administrative resources, personnel, and activity seems to impute more of a positive rights aspect to our generally negative rights constitutional order. An alternative view might insist that all the Constitution requires is that the President ensure the laws are executed as faithfully as possible given the resources Congress has provided, and that the Constitution grants Congress discretion over whether and how much to fund. Yet such a view ignores the extent to which, combined with delegation, the take care duty and broader duty to supervise do carry an affirmative dimension. Delegation comes with constitutional strings attached. Having chosen to delegate broad responsibilities to the executive branch, Congress has a duty to provide the resources necessary for the executive branch to adequately fulfill its constitutional functions.

b. Separation of Powers Methodology

Courts and scholars have adopted various approaches in analyzing separation of powers questions, but two have emerged as dominant: formalism and functionalism. In reading through the cases in this chapter, you'll see a fair bit of seeming inconsistency in the Court's approach, with the Court oscillating between formalism and functionalism and many cases having strong elements of both. Think about why this might be: Is it inconsistency over time, or are the same justices taking varying stances? If the latter, are there features about the cases or the separation of powers questions at issue that could explain the variation?

(1) *Formalism and Functionalism in a Nutshell.* REBECCA BROWN, SEPARATED POWERS AND ORDERED LIBERTY, 139 U. Pa. L. Rev. 1513 (1991): "Those who espouse the formalist view of separated powers seek judicial legitimacy by insisting upon a firm textual basis in the Constitution for any governmental act. They posit that the structural provisions of the Constitution should be understood solely by their literal language and the drafters' original intent regarding their application, giving little or no weight to the influence of changed circumstances or broad objectives such as good or efficient government. The formalist approach is committed to strong substantive separations between the branches of government, finding support in the traditional expositions of the theme of 'pure' separated powers, such as the maxim that 'the legislature makes, the executive executes, and the judiciary construes the law.' Thus the formalists attempt to ensure that exercise of governmental power comports strictly with the original blueprint laid down in articles I, II, and III of the Constitution. Under formalist thinking, the creation of independent administrative agencies, for example, is considered a violation of the Constitution because such agencies require the exercise of governmental power in ways that involve an overlap of expressly assigned functions, subject to the control of none of the three branches. . . .

"In contrast, advocates of the 'functionalist' approach urge the Court to ask a different question: whether an action of one branch interferes with one of the core functions of another. The sharing of powers, in itself, is not repugnant to the functionalists, nor is the formation of alliances among the branches repugnant, as long as the basic principles of separated powers are not impaired. The functionalist view follows a different strand of separation-of-powers tradition from that of the formalists: the American variant that stresses not the independence, but the interdependence of the branches. 'While the Constitution diffuses power the better to secure liberty, it also contemplates that practice will integrate the dispersed powers into a workable government. It enjoins upon its branches separateness but interdependence, autonomy but reciprocity.' [Youngstown, Jackson, J. concurring.]" For a recent argument that the distinction between formalism and functionalism obscures as much as it illuminates and should be reconceptualized in terms of the familiar difference between rules and standards, see Aziz Z. Huq & Jon D. Michaels, The Cycles of Separation-of-Powers Jurisprudence, 126 Yale L.J. 342 (2016).

(2) *On the Relationship between Separation of Powers and Checks and Balances.* CYNTHIA R. FARINA, STATUTORY INTERPRETATION AND THE BALANCE OF POWER IN THE ADMINISTRATIVE STATE, 89 Colum. L. Rev. 452 (1989): "[O]ur tendency to describe the constitutional scheme as one of 'separation of powers and checks and balances' can be misleading. This conventional, bifurcated phrasing obscures the fact that the latter represented, for those who drafted and defended the Constitution, a vital and indispensable aspect of the former. By the time of the ratification, the prevailing understanding of separation of powers was no longer a simplistic call for absolute segregation of conceptually distinct functions. The experience between independence and the Constitutional Convention had caused American political theorists to rethink the nature of governmental authority. They came to conclude that political power was, in [historian] Gordon Wood's words, 'essentially homogenous.' [The Creation of the American Republic, 1776–87, at 604 (1969)]. Whether manifested as lawmaking, execution or adjudication, whether exercised by officials who were elected popularly, elected indirectly or appointed, all power in government shared the same fundamental quality: it was dangerous unless adequately offset and controlled. And so, notwithstanding their literal sense, the words 'separation of powers' came to connote something far more subtle and intricate than a mere abstractly logical division. The phrase expressed the expectation that, through the carefully orchestrated disposition and sharing of authority, restraint would be found in power counterbalancing power.

"This complexity of American separation of powers theory is critical . . . Those who forged the structural theory of the Constitution did not, of course, foresee the modern administrative agency—with its potent concentration of law making, law executing and adjudicating power—any more than they anticipated the federal commitment to social and economic intervention that created it. They were, however, acutely self-conscious that they were designing a plan for the future. . . . The peculiarly American conception of separation of powers that they developed sought balance, not stasis. The genius of a system in which authority was shared rather than rigidly divided was, Madison explained, that each part could respond to the movement of power over time. Change would simply prompt a readjustment, so long as each part retained 'the necessary constitutional means . . . to resist encroachments of the others.' " [Federalist No. 51.]

"We can thus understand the structural model as one of dynamic equilibrium: As power flows among the power centers in government, new patterns of counterbalance emerge to provide restraint. The movement of power can be accepted so long as equilibrium can then be reestablished. The model is inherently flexible; new configurations of power may be formed. But its pliancy is not to be mistaken for unconditional license. Innovation in one area may call for a responsive shift in other areas. An exercise of authority by one branch may become constitutionally necessary because of a realignment of power elsewhere in government."

(3) *Is there a General Separation of Powers Principle?* JOHN F. MANNING, SEPARATION OF POWERS AS ORDINARY INTERPRETATION, 124 Harv. L. Rev. 1939, 1944–45 (2011): "Contrary to [the] understandings of [both] functionalism and formalism, the Constitution adopts no freestanding principle of separation of powers. The idea of separated powers unmistakably lies behind the Constitution, but it was not adopted wholesale. The Constitution contains no Separation of Powers Clause. The historical record, moreover, reveals no one baseline for inferring what a reasonable constitutionmaker would have understood 'the separation of powers' to mean in the abstract. Rather, in the Constitution, the idea of separation of powers, properly understood, reflects many particular decisions about how to allocate and condition the exercise of federal power. Indeed, the document not only separates powers, but also blends them in many ways in order to ensure that the branches have the means and motives to check one another. Viewed in isolation from the constitutionmakers' many discrete choices, the concept of separation of powers as such can tell us little, if anything, about where, how, or to what degree the various powers were, in fact, separated (and blended) in the Philadelphia Convention's countless compromises.

"Of particular importance, like most political compromises, the ones evident in the first seven articles of the Constitution find expression at many different levels of generality. Some provisions—such as the Bicameralism and Presentment Clauses, the Appointments Clause, or the Impeachment Clauses—speak in specific terms, both about the locus of a given power and about the manner in which it is to be exercised. Other provisions are more open-ended, perhaps leaving some play in the joints. Most prominently, the Vesting Clauses speak in general terms about the legislative, executive, and judicial powers, and say nothing about how these clauses intersect with Congress's broad coordinate power to compose the government under the Necessary and Proper Clause. Like most bargained-for texts, the Constitution's structural provisions thus leave many important questions unaddressed. Because the structural provisions come in many shapes and sizes, no one-size-fits-all theory can do them justice. It is precisely this feature of the Constitution that functionalists and formalists misapprehend when they imagine that the document embraces any overarching separation of powers doctrine."

SECTION 2.   CONGRESS AND ADMINISTRATIVE AGENCIES

> a. **Delegation of Regulatory Power**
> b. **Congressional Control of Regulatory Policy**

A study of the administrative state's constitutional structure logically begins with the relationship of Congress and administrative agencies, in particular with congressional power to delegate policymaking authority to the executive branch. Such delegations are the backbone of the modern administrative state; a basic premise of our constitutional order is that an administrative agency has no inherent or independent authority to act but instead can exercise only the policymaking authority delegated to it by Congress. If you have already studied the materials in Chapter IV, you will be familiar with rulemaking, which is the most prominent way in which agencies set policy today. (Agencies also set policy through administrative adjudication, the constitutionality of which is discussed in Section 4.)

The constitutionality of congressional delegations to the executive is the subject of the nondelegation doctrine. Although almost never invoked to invalidate a statute, the nondelegation doctrine has spurred extensive case law and scholarship and is the first topic addressed in this section. Congress both delegates and then tries to exercise control over the exercise of delegated power. The ways in which Congress constitutionally can exercise such control is the subject of the second set of materials in this section.

a.   Delegation of Regulatory Power

> (1) **The Constitutionality of Regulatory Delegations**
> (2) **The Past and Future of Nondelegation Doctrine**

All legislative Powers herein granted shall be vested in a Congress of the United States, which shall consist of a Senate and House of Representatives.

U.S. Const., Art. I, § 1

The Congress shall have Power . . . To make all Laws which shall be necessary and proper for carrying into Execution the foregoing Powers, and all other Powers vested by this Constitution in the Government of the United States, or in any Department or Officer thereof.

U.S. Const., Art. I, § 8, cl. 18

(1) The Constitutionality of Regulatory Delegations

> ***WHITMAN v. AMERICAN TRUCKING ASS'NS***
>
> ***DOT v. Ass'n of American Railroads***

WHITMAN v. AMERICAN TRUCKING ASS'NS., INC.

Supreme Court of the United States (2001).
531 U.S. 457.

■ JUSTICE SCALIA delivered the opinion of the Court.

These cases present the following questions: (1) Whether § 109(b)(1) of the Clean Air Act (CAA) delegates legislative power to the Administrator of the Environmental Protection Agency (EPA). (2) Whether the Administrator may consider the costs of implementation in setting national ambient air quality standards (NAAQS) under § 109(b)(1).[3] . . . American Trucking Associations, Inc., and its co-respondents—which include, in addition to other private companies, the States of Michigan, Ohio, and West Virginia—challenged the new standards. . . .

II

[Respondents argue that the court of appeals erred in holding that] "economic considerations [may] play no part in the promulgation of ambient air quality standards under Section 109" of the CAA. . . . Section 109(b)(1) instructs the EPA to set primary ambient air quality standards

---

[3] [Ed.] The Clean Air Act §§ 108–09 (42 U.S.C. §§ 7408–09) are closely linked. Section 108 requires the EPA to: (1) publish and periodically revise a list of each air pollutant, "emissions of which, in his judgment, cause or contribute to air pollution which may reasonably be anticipated to endanger public health or welfare" and that result from numerous or mobile sources, and (2) issue air quality criteria for each pollutant, identifying in detail the information on effects of the pollutant.

Section 109 addresses the promulgation of the NAAQS. Section 109(a) requires that the EPA simultaneously publish proposed national primary and secondary ambient air quality standards for each pollutant with the criteria and information mandated by Section 108. Section 109(b), the provision at issue here, provides:

(1) National primary ambient air quality standards prescribed under subsection (a) of this section shall be ambient air quality standards the attainment and maintenance of which in the judgment of the Administrator, based on such criteria and allowing an adequate margin of safety, are requisite to protect the public health. Such primary standards may be revised in the same manner as promulgated.

(2) Any national secondary ambient air quality standard prescribed under subsection (a) of this section shall specify a level of air quality the attainment and maintenance of which in the judgment of the Administrator, based on such criteria, is requisite to protect the public welfare from any known or anticipated adverse effects associated with the presence of such air pollutant in the ambient air. Such secondary standards may be revised in the same manner as promulgated. . . .

"the attainment and maintenance of which . . . are requisite to protect the public health" with "an adequate margin of safety." Were it not for the hundreds of pages of briefing respondents have submitted on the issue, one would have thought it fairly clear that this text does not permit the EPA to consider costs in setting the standards. . . . The EPA, "based on" the information about health effects contained in the technical "criteria" documents compiled under § 108(a)(2) is to identify the maximum airborne concentration of a pollutant that the public health can tolerate, decrease the concentration to provide an "adequate" margin of safety, and set the standard at that level. Nowhere are the costs of achieving such a standard made part of that initial calculation.

Against this most natural of readings, respondents make a lengthy, spirited, but ultimately unsuccessful attack. They begin with the object of § 109(b)(1)'s focus, the "public health." . . . [R]espondents argue [that] many more factors than air pollution affect public health. In particular, the economic cost of implementing a very stringent standard might produce health losses sufficient to offset the health gains achieved in cleaning the air—for example, by closing down whole industries and thereby impoverishing the workers and consumers dependent upon those industries. That is unquestionably true, and Congress . . . not only anticipated that compliance costs could injure the public health, but provided for that precise exigency. Section 110(f)(1) of the CAA permitted the Administrator to waive the compliance deadline for stationary sources if, inter alia, sufficient control measures were simply unavailable and "the continued operation of such sources is essential . . . to the public health or welfare." [Justice Scalia cited half a dozen sections from other parts of the CAA that expressly direct the Administrator to consider cost in setting a standard.] . . . We have therefore refused to find implicit in ambiguous sections of the CAA an authorization to consider costs that has elsewhere, and so often, been expressly granted.

Accordingly, to prevail in their present challenge, respondents must show a textual commitment of authority to the EPA to consider costs in setting NAAQS under § 109(b)(1). And because § 109(b)(1) and the NAAQS for which it provides are the engine that drives nearly all of Title I of the CAA, that textual commitment must be a clear one. Congress, we have held, does not alter the fundamental details of a regulatory scheme in vague terms or ancillary provisions—it does not, one might say, hide elephants in mouseholes. See MCI Telecommunications Corp. v. American Telephone & Telegraph Co., 512 U.S. 218, 231 (1994) [p. 1171]; FDA v. Brown & Williamson Tobacco Corp., [529 U.S. 120], 159–60 [(2000) p. 1191]. . . .

It should be clear from what we have said that the canon requiring texts to be so construed as to avoid serious constitutional problems has no application here. No matter how severe the constitutional doubt, courts may choose only between reasonably available interpretations of a text. The text of § 109(b), interpreted in its statutory and historical context and with appreciation for its importance to the CAA as a whole, unambiguously bars cost considerations from the NAAQS-setting process, and thus ends the matter for us as well as the EPA.[4] We therefore affirm the judgment of the Court of Appeals on this point.

III

Section 109(b)(1) of the CAA instructs the EPA to set "ambient air quality standards the attainment and maintenance of which in the judgment of the Administrator, based on [the] criteria [documents of § 108] and allowing an adequate margin of safety, are requisite to protect the public health." The Court of Appeals held ... the EPA's interpretation (but not the statute itself) violated the nondelegation doctrine. We disagree.

In a delegation challenge, the constitutional question is whether the statute has delegated legislative power to the agency. Article I, § 1, of the Constitution vests "[a]ll legislative Powers herein granted ... in a Congress of the United States." This text permits no delegation of those powers, and so we repeatedly have said that when Congress confers decisionmaking authority upon agencies *Congress* must "lay down by legislative act an intelligible principle to which the person or body authorized to [act] is directed to conform." J.W. Hampton, Jr., & Co. v. United States, 276 U.S. 394, 409 (1928) [p. 809]. We have never suggested that an agency can cure an unlawful delegation of legislative power by adopting in its discretion a limiting construction of the statute. . . . The idea that an agency can cure an unconstitutionally standardless delegation of power by declining to exercise some of that power seems to us internally contradictory. The very choice of which portion of the power to exercise—that is to say, the prescription of the standard that Congress had omitted—would *itself* be an exercise of the forbidden legislative authority. . . .

We agree with the Solicitor General that the text of § 109(b)(1) of the CAA at a minimum requires that "[f]or a discrete set of pollutants and based on published air quality criteria that reflect the latest scientific knowledge, [the] EPA must establish uniform national standards at a level that is requisite to protect public health from the adverse effects of the pollutant in the ambient air." Requisite, in turn, "mean[s] sufficient, but not more than necessary." These limits on the EPA's discretion are strikingly similar to the ones we approved in Touby v. United States, 500 U.S. 160 (1991), which permitted the Attorney General to designate a drug as a controlled substance for purposes of criminal drug enforcement if doing so was "necessary to avoid an imminent hazard to the public safety." They also resemble the Occupational Safety and Health Act provision requiring the agency to "set the standard which most

---

[4]   Respondents' speculation that the EPA is secretly considering the costs of attainment without telling anyone is irrelevant to our interpretive inquiry. If such an allegation could be proved, it would be grounds for vacating the NAAQS, because the Administrator had not followed the law. It would not, however, be grounds for this Court's changing the law.

adequately assures, to the extent feasible, on the basis of the best available evidence, that no employee will suffer any impairment of health"—which the Court upheld in [Benzene, p. 812], and which even then-Justice Rehnquist, who alone in that case thought the statute violated the nondelegation doctrine, would have upheld if, like the statute here, it did not permit economic costs to be considered.

The scope of discretion § 109(b)(1) allows is in fact well within the outer limits of our nondelegation precedents. In the history of the Court we have found the requisite "intelligible principle" lacking in only two statutes, one of which provided literally no guidance for the exercise of discretion, and the other of which conferred authority to regulate the entire economy on the basis of no more precise a standard than stimulating the economy by assuring "fair competition." See Panama Refining Co. v. Ryan, 293 U.S. 388 (1935) [p. 810]; A.L.A. Schechter Poultry Corp. v. United States, 295 U.S. 495 (1935) [p. 810]. We have, on the other hand, upheld the validity of § 11(b)(2) of the Public Utility Holding Company Act of 1935, which gave the Securities and Exchange Commission authority to modify the structure of holding company systems so as to ensure that they are not "unduly or unnecessarily complicate[d]" and do not "unfairly or inequitably distribute voting power among security holders." American Power & Light Co. v. SEC, 329 U.S. 90, 104 (1946). We have approved the wartime conferral of agency power to fix the prices of commodities at a level that "will be generally fair and equitable and will effectuate the [in some respects conflicting] purposes of th[e] Act." Yakus v. United States, 321 U.S. 414, 420, 423–26 (1944) [p. 811]. And we have found an "intelligible principle" in various statutes authorizing regulation in the "public interest." See, e.g., National Broadcasting Co. v. United States, 319 U.S. 190 (1943) (Federal Communications Commission's power to regulate airwaves); New York Central Securities Corp. v. United States, 287 U.S. 12 (1932) (Interstate Commerce Commission's power to approve railroad consolidations). In short, we have "almost never felt qualified to second-guess Congress regarding the permissible degree of policy judgment that can be left to those executing or applying the law." Mistretta v. United States, 488 U.S. 361, 416 (1989) (Scalia, J., dissenting) [p. 802].

It is true enough that the degree of agency discretion that is acceptable varies according to the scope of the power congressionally conferred. While Congress need not provide any direction to the EPA regarding the manner in which it is to define "country elevators," which are to be exempt from newstationary-source regulations governing grain elevators, see 42 U.S.C. § 7411(i), it must provide substantial guidance on setting air standards that affect the entire national economy. But even in sweeping regulatory schemes we have never demanded, as the Court of Appeals did here, that statutes provide a "determinate criterion" for saying "how much [of the regulated harm] is too much." . . . It is therefore not conclusive for delegation purposes that, as respondents argue, ozone and particulate matter are "nonthreshold" pollutants that inflict a continuum of adverse health effects at any airborne concentration greater than zero, and hence require the EPA to make judgments of degree. "[A] certain degree of discretion, and thus of lawmaking, inheres in most executive or judicial action." Mistretta v. United States, supra, at 417 (Scalia, J., dissenting) (emphasis deleted). Section 109(b)(1) of the CAA, which to repeat we interpret as requiring the EPA to set air quality standards at the level that is "requisite"—that is, not lower or higher than is necessary—to protect the public health with an adequate margin of safety, fits comfortably within the scope of discretion permitted by our precedent. . . .

The judgment of the Court of Appeals is affirmed in part and reversed in part. [The Court remanded the case for further proceedings on different grounds.]

■ JUSTICE THOMAS, concurring.

I agree with the majority that § 109's directive to the agency is no less an "intelligible principle" than a host of other directives that we have approved. . . . Although this Court since 1928 has treated the "intelligible principle" requirement as the only constitutional limit on congressional grants of power to administrative agencies, the Constitution does not speak of "intelligible principles." Rather, it speaks in much simpler terms: "*All* legislative Powers herein granted shall be vested in a Congress." I am not convinced that the intelligible principle doctrine serves to prevent all cessions of legislative power. I believe that there are cases in which the principle is intelligible and yet the significance of the delegated decision is simply too great for the decision to be called anything other than "legislative."

As it is, none of the parties to these cases has examined the text of the Constitution or asked us to reconsider our precedents on cessions of legislative power. On a future day, however, I would be willing to address the question whether our delegation jurisprudence has strayed too far from our Founders' understanding of separation of powers.

■ JUSTICE STEVENS, with whom JUSTICE SOUTER joins, concurring in part and concurring in the judgment.

. . . I wholeheartedly endorse the Court's result and endorse its explanation of its reasons, albeit with the following caveat. The Court has two choices. We could choose to articulate our ultimate disposition of this issue by frankly acknowledging that the power delegated to the EPA is "legislative" but nevertheless conclude that the delegation is constitutional because adequately limited by the terms of the authorizing statute. Alternatively, we could pretend, as the Court does, that the authority delegated to the EPA is somehow not "legislative power." Despite the fact that there is language in our opinions that supports the Court's articulation of our holding, I am persuaded that it would be both wiser and more faithful to what we have actually done in delegation cases to admit that agency rulemaking authority is "legislative power."

The proper characterization of governmental power should generally depend on the nature of the power, not on the identity of the person exercising it. See Black's Law Dictionary 899 (6th ed.1990) (defining "legislation" as, inter alia, "[f]ormulation of rule[s] for the future"). If the NAAQS that the EPA promulgated had been prescribed by Congress, everyone would agree that those rules would be the product of an exercise of "legislative power." The same characterization is appropriate when an agency exercises rulemaking authority pursuant to a permissible delegation from Congress.

My view is not only more faithful to normal English usage, but is also fully consistent with the text of the Constitution. In Article I, the Framers vested "All legislative Powers" in the Congress, Art. I, § 1, just as in Article II they vested the "executive Power" in the President, Art. II, § 1. Those provisions do not purport to limit the authority of either recipient of power to delegate authority to others. See 1 Davis & Pierce, Administrative Law Treatise 2.6, 66 ("The Court was probably mistaken from the outset in interpreting Article I's grant of power to Congress as an implicit limit on Congress' authority to delegate legislative power"). . . .

It seems clear that an executive agency's exercise of rulemaking authority pursuant to a valid delegation from Congress is "legislative." As long as the delegation provides a sufficiently intelligible principle, there is nothing inherently unconstitutional about it. . . .

[Justice Breyer concurred in part and concurred in the judgment, stating that "other things being equal, we should read silences or ambiguities in the language of regulatory statutes as permitting, not forbidding," consideration of the "economic costs of implementation. . . . In this case, however, other things are not equal" and "legislative history, along with the statute's structure, indicates that § 109's language reflects a congressional decision not to delegate to the agency the legal authority to consider economic costs."]

SIGNIFICANT CASE

DOT v. ASS'N OF AMERICAN RAILROADS
135 S.Ct. 1225 (2015).

In 1970, Congress created Amtrak to provide passenger rail service and granted its trains primary right-of-way over freight railroad tracks. Nearly forty years later, in response to unreliability and other problems with Amtrak service, Congress enacted the Passenger Rail Investment and Improvement Act (PRIIA). Section 207(a) of the PRIIA granted Amtrak and the Federal Railroad Administration (FRA) joint authority to issue "metrics and standards" that address the performance and scheduling of passenger railroad services, after consulting with other entities such as the rail carriers over whose lines Amtrak trains operate and the Surface Transportation Board (STB). The FRA, housed in the Department of Transportation (DOT), is charged with ensuring railroad safety, reliability, and efficiency; its primary activities are issuing railroad safety regulations and investing in railroad corridors. The STB is an independent agency with adjudicatory jurisdiction over railroad rate and service issues and also oversees railroad carriers to ensure they comply with governing requirements. By contrast, Amtrak is statutorily deemed a not-for-profit corporation and headed by a ten-person board, consisting of eight members appointed by the President with Senate confirmation, the Secretary of Transportation (also appointed by the President with Senate confirmation), and Amtrak's President, who is chosen by the other members of Amtrak's board.

The PRIIA specifies that the metrics and standards created under § 207(a) are to be used for a variety of purposes, including prompting investigations by the STB and in subsequent enforcement actions. The act also instructs that the metrics and standards should be incorporated into the access and service contracts between Amtrak and host rail carriers. Section 207(d) of the PRIIA further provided that if the required metrics and standards were not completed within 180 days, any party involved in their development could petition the STB to appoint an arbitrator to resolve the disputes through binding arbitration. In 2010, Amtrak and the FRA jointly issued a final version of the metrics and standards required by § 207 and the Association of American Railroads sued. Claiming that its railroad members would have to modify their operations to satisfy the new metrics and standards, the Association claimed that § 207 violated the nondelegation doctrine, the separation of powers, and due process by placing legislative and rulemaking authority in the hands of an interested private entity (Amtrak), and it also raised Appointment Clause claims with respect to the appointment of Amtrak's President. The D.C. Circuit upheld the Association's claim that § 207 represented an unconstitutional private delegation, concluding that under the Supreme Court's decision in Carter v. Carter Coal Co., 298 U.S. 238 (1936) (p. 810), it was impermissible for Congress to delegate regulatory authority to a private entity.

The Supreme Court, in an opinion by JUSTICE KENNEDY, reversed, holding that for purposes of determining the constitutional validity of the metrics and standards, Amtrak was a governmental entity. That holding was not surprising, given that the Court had previously found Amtrak to be part of government for purposes of the First Amendment. Lebron v. National Railroad Passenger Corporation, 513 U.S. 374 (1995). More surprising were the concurring opinions of Justice Alito and Thomas which both expressed grave doubts about the constitutionality of the § 207 regime on delegation and other grounds.

JUSTICE ALITO, agreeing that Amtrak was a governmental entity, argued that the appointment mechanism for Amtrak's president and for a public arbitrator violated the Appointments Clause. He also argued that "[i]f the arbitrator can be a private person, this law is unconstitutional. . . . Congress 'cannot delegate regulatory authority to a private entity.' 721 F.3d, at 670. Indeed, Congress, vested with enumerated 'legislative Powers,' Art. I, § 1, cannot delegate its "exclusively legislative" authority at all. Wayman v. Southard, 10 Wheat. 1, 42–43 (1825) (Marshall, C.J.).

"The principle that Congress cannot delegate away its vested powers exists to protect liberty. Our Constitution, by careful design, prescribes a process for making law, and within that process there are many accountability checkpoints. See INS v. Chadha, 462 U.S. 919, 959 (1983) [p. 831]. It would dash the whole scheme if Congress could give its power away to an entity that is not constrained by those checkpoints. The Constitution's deliberative process was viewed by the Framers as a valuable feature, . . . not something to be lamented and evaded. . . .

"[T]he formal reason why the Court does not enforce the nondelegation doctrine with more vigilance is that the other branches of Government have vested powers of their own that can be used in ways that resemble lawmaking. See, e.g., Arlington v. FCC, 133 S.Ct. 1863, 1873, n. 4 (2013) [p. 1279] . . . When it comes to private entities, however, there is not even a fig leaf of constitutional justification. Private entities are not vested with 'legislative Powers.' Art. I, § 1. Nor are they vested with the 'executive Power,' Art. II, § 1, cl. 1, which belongs to the President. Indeed, it raises '[d]ifficult and fundamental questions' about 'the delegation of Executive power' when Congress authorizes citizen suits. Friends of the Earth, Inc. v. Laidlaw Environmental Services (TOC), Inc., 528 U.S. 167, 197 (2000) (Kennedy, J., concurring) [p. 1347]. A citizen suit to enforce existing law, however, is nothing compared to delegated power to create new law. By any measure, handing off regulatory power to a private entity is 'legislative delegation in its most obnoxious form.' Carter v. Carter Coal Co., 298 U.S. 238, 311 (1936). For these reasons, it is hard to imagine how delegating 'binding' tie-breaking authority to a private arbitrator to resolve a dispute between Amtrak and the FRA could be constitutional."

JUSTICE THOMAS, who concurred only in the judgment, took the occasion to offer a broader attack on current nondelegation doctrine: "The allocation of powers in the Constitution is absolute, but it does not follow that there is no overlap between the three categories of governmental power. Certain functions may be performed by two or more branches without either exceeding its enumerated powers under the Constitution. . . . The question is whether the particular function requires the exercise of a certain type of power; if it does, then only the branch in which that power is vested can perform it. . . . The function at issue here is the formulation of generally applicable rules of private conduct. Under the original understanding of the Constitution, that function requires the exercise of legislative power. By corollary, the discretion inherent in executive power does not comprehend the discretion to formulate generally applicable rules of private conduct." Justice Thomas then traced the history of the distinction between legislative and executive power, arguing that "[t]he idea that the Executive may not formulate generally applicable rules of private conduct . . . has ancient roots in the concept of the 'rule of law,' which has been understood since Greek and Roman times to mean that a ruler must be subject to the law in exercising his power and may not govern by will alone. . . . An early expression of this idea in England is seen in the constitutional law concerning crown proclamations. Even before a more formal separation of powers came about during the English Civil War, it was generally thought that the King could not use his proclamation power to alter the rights and duties of his subjects. P. Hamburger, Is Administrative Law Unlawful? 33–34 (2014). . . ."

Justice Thomas provided a lengthy analysis of the Court's delegation precedents from which the intelligible principle test was derived and argued that they do not support the current version of the test. In particular, he argued that cases like J.W. Hampton, Jr. & Co. v. United States, 276 U.S. 394(1928) (p. 809), involved "conditional legislation," which made the operation or suspension of legislation depend upon findings made by the President. According to Justice Thomas, "the practice of conditional legislation does not seem to call on the President to exercise a core function that demands an exercise of legislative power. Congress creates the rule of private conduct, and the President makes the factual determination that causes that rule to go into effect. That type of factual determination seems similar to the type of factual determination on which an enforcement action is conditioned: Neither involves an exercise of policy discretion, and both are subject to review by a court." . . . Justice Thomas similarly reinterpreted Chief Justice Marshall's 1826 opinion in Wayman v. Southard, p. 808, as resting on the difference between the setting rules of conduct for officers of the court in giving effect to judgments, which the courts constitutionally could do, and setting rules that regulated private conduct, which the legislature must do.

He concluded: "Today, the Court has abandoned all pretense of enforcing a qualitative distinction between legislative and executive power. To the extent that the 'intelligible principle' test was ever an adequate means of enforcing that distinction, it has been decoupled from the historical understanding of the legislative and executive powers and thus does not keep executive 'lawmaking' within the bounds of inherent executive discretion. . . . Under the guise of the intelligible-principle test, the Court has allowed the Executive to go beyond the safe realm of factual investigation to make political judgments about what is 'unfair' or 'unnecessary.' Our reluctance to second-guess Congress on the degree of policy judgment is understandable; our mistake lies in assuming that *any* degree of policy judgment is permissible when it comes to establishing generally applicable rules governing private conduct. To understand the 'intelligible principle' test as permitting Congress to delegate policy judgment in this context is to divorce that test from its history. It may never be possible perfectly to distinguish between legislative and executive power, but that does not mean we may look the other way when the Government asks us to apply a legally binding rule that is not enacted by Congress pursuant to Article I.

"We should return to the original meaning of the Constitution: The Government may create generally applicable rules of private conduct only through the proper exercise of legislative power. I accept that this would inhibit the Government from acting with the speed and efficiency Congress has sometimes found desirable."

NOTES

(1) ***Formalist and Functionalist Approaches.*** The opinions in Whitman and American Railroads offer very different approaches to the constitutionality of delegations of regulatory power. Writing for the majority in Whitman, Justice Scalia is adamant that the Constitution prohibits delegations of legislative power. He invokes the Vesting Clause of Article I as incontrovertible textual proof that the Constitution prohibits Congress from delegating legislative power to others. Yet Justice Scalia is also emphatic that Congress can authorize the executive branch to exercise broad policymaking and regulatory authority, maintaining that executive power can contain substantial discretion. According to Justice Thomas in American Railroads—following up on his concurrence in Whitman—these two positions are incompatible; in his view the prohibition of delegating legislative power prohibits delegation of "*any* degree of policy judgment . . . when it comes to establishing generally applicable rules governing private conduct." He therefore rejects the majority's characterization of Congress's action as authorizing the exercise of executive power. Note that Justice Stevens offers a similar definition of legislative power, identifying it as the specification of rules for the future and focusing on the nature of the power at stake, not who is wielding it. (Watch for his analogous argument in Bowsher v. Synar, p. 863). But Justice Stevens also contends that the Constitution does not prohibit delegation of legislative power, emphasizing that nothing in the Constitution expressly prohibits redelegation of legislative power provided that power is adequately limited by the terms of the governing statute.

One clear axis of differentiation among these approaches concerns methodology. Justice Thomas's approach is resolutely formalist. He insists on enforcing a clear distinction among different types of powers and on minimizing overlap, reflecting the conviction that the Constitution "divide[s] the world of governmental powers into a finite set of three, each of which is assigned to one and only one governmental actor." Steven G. Calabresi, The Vesting Clauses as Power Grants, 88 Nw. U. L. Rev. 1377, 1390 n. 45 (1994).

And he insists on adhering to formalist principle, no matter what the result. Justice Stevens, by contrast, displays a functionalist impatience with refusals to recognize rulemaking as legislative action. Finally, Justice Scalia's approach is both, combining a formalist prohibition on delegation of legislative power and insistence on characterizing rulemaking as an exercise of executive power with a functional recognition of the difficulty courts face enforcing that prohibition and acceptance of broad rulemaking authority.

Which approach, formalist or functionalist or a combination thereof, is the most appropriate to take here? Does the Constitution impose a clear textual distinction among the three types of power and grant one type exclusively to each branch? Note that scholars disagree on whether the Constitution's vesting clauses should be seen as grants of power or as simply distinguishing among the branches; you'll see this debate later on with respect to the scope of presidential power (see Sec. 3). Professors Eric A. Posner and Adrian Vermeule, Interring the Nondelegation Doctrine, 69 U. Chi. L. Rev. 1721 (2002), maintain that all the Vesting Clause of Article I means is that the "[n]either Congress nor its members may delegate to anyone else the authority to vote on federal statutes or to exercise other de jure powers of federal legislators." On this view, "a statutory grant of authority to the executive branch or other agents can never amount to a delegation of legislative power." Is their approach a plausible reading of the Clause? For criticism, see Larry Alexander & Saikrishna Prakash, Reports of Nondelegation Doctrine's Death Are Greatly Exaggerated, 70 U. Chi. L. Rev. 1297 (2003).

Even if Justice Stevens' approach can accord with the text of the vesting clauses, does an open functionalist embrace of redelegation square with the Constitution's separation-of-powers structure? After all, why have the Constitution identify certain powers with particular branches if Congress could just redistribute them. On the other hand, can't Justice Thomas be faulted for unduly restricting the legitimate scope of executive power in a misguided effort to prevent delegation of legislative power? Think about traditionally core exercises of executive power, such as law enforcement; aren't there necessarily policy choices involved? Or, as Justice Scalia put the point in Whitman, doesn't "a certain degree of discretion, and thus of lawmaking, inheres in most executive or judicial action." Does that recognition give some support to Scalia's position that what is being delegated here (and whenever a court finds an intelligible principle) can and should be viewed as executive power?

Moreover, the disruptive effect of Justice Thomas' approach in American Railroads cannot be overstated; a constitutional prohibition on policymaking by the executive branch would bring modern American government to a screeching halt. Can separation of powers justify such a dramatic overturning of decades of legislation and practice given other important constitutional goals, such as ensuring effective and politically accountable government? See Cass R. Sunstein & Adrian Vermeule, The New Coke: On the Plural Aims of Administrative Law, 2015 Sup. Ct. Rev. 41 (2016).

Arguably, Justice Scalia's approach in Whitman represents a reasonable compromise effort to combine adherence to constitutional structure with sensitivity to practical reality. But is its internal methodological inconsistency simply too great? Given Justice Scalia's sanction of delegations as broad as a statutory instruction to legislate "in the public interest," does his insistence that legislative power cannot be delegated simply ring empty? Would following Justice Stevens and being more forthright about delegation of legislative power at least have the benefit of constitutional honesty?

(2)   *Is the Prohibition on Delegation a Political Question?* One way to square the Court's insistence on a constitutional prohibition on delegating legislative power with its practice of sustaining broad policymaking and lawmaking by the executive branch would be to see the nondelegation prohibition as a political question. On this view, the prohibition on delegation would be a constitutional requirement that is for Congress and the President to enforce, not the courts. Two longstanding bases for finding a political question, emphasized recently by Court, are the presence of "a textually demonstrable constitutional commitment of the issue to a coordinate political department; or a lack of judicially discoverable and manageable standards for resolving it." Zivotofsky v. Clinton, 566 U.S. 189, 195 (2012) (quoting Baker v. Carr, 369 U.S. 186, 217 (1962)).

Are those tests met in the delegation context? Consider in this regard the following statement from Justice Scalia's dissenting opinion in MISTRETTA V. UNITED STATES, 488 U.S. 361 (1989): "[W]hile the doctrine of unconstitutional delegation is unquestionably a fundamental element of our constitutional system, it is not an element readily enforceable by the courts. Once it is conceded, as it must be, that no statute can be entirely precise, and that some judgments, even some judgments involving policy considerations, must be left to the officers executing the law and to the judges applying it, the debate over unconstitutional delegation becomes a debate not over a point of principle, but over a question of degree. As Chief Justice Taft expressed the point for the Court in the landmark case of J.W. Hampton Jr. & Co. v. United States, 276 U.S. 394 (1928) (p. 809), the limits of delegation 'must be fixed according to common sense and the inherent necessities of the governmental co-ordination.' Since Congress is no less endowed with common sense than we are, and better equipped to inform itself of the 'necessities' of government; and since the factors bearing upon those necessities are both multifarious and (in the nonpartisan sense) highly political, . . . it is small wonder that we have almost never felt qualified to second-guess Congress regarding the permissible degree of policy judgment that can be left to those executing or applying the law."

This sounds similar to concluding that judicially manageable standards are lacking for distinguishing between constitutional and excessive delegations. But the Court has not pursued this path, instead (as in Whitman) assuming jurisdiction over delegation challenges and applying the intelligible principle test. Why might that be? Cf. Zivotofsky, 566 U.S., at 196, 301 (insisting that resolving a constitutional challenge to a statute was "a familiar judicial exercise" and not a political question).

(3) *Does the Intelligible Principle Test Have Any Bite?* In American Railroads, Justice Thomas condemns the current intelligible principle test as failing to enforce "any qualitative distinction between legislative and executive power." Is he right? In light of Justice Scalia's exposition of the intelligible principle inquiry in Whitman, can you identify any delegations that would fail it?

Consider, in this regard, § 102 of the Real ID Act of 2005, Pub. L. 104–208, directing the Department of Homeland Security to construct physical barriers and roads "in the vicinity of the United States border to deter illegal crossings in areas of high illegal entry into the United States." Section 102(c)(1) provides: "Notwithstanding any other provision of law, the Secretary of Homeland Security shall have the authority to waive all legal requirements [in his/her] sole discretion, determines necessary to ensure expeditious construction of the barriers and roads . . ." Judicial review is expressly limited to constitutional claims, thereby apparently precluding challenges based on the waived statutes. In Defenders of Wildlife v. Chertoff, 526 F.Supp.2d 119 (D.D.C. 2007), the district court concluded that the quoted sections of Section 102 provide intelligible principles adequate to support the delegation. (Pursuant to a provision that sent appeals immediately to the Supreme Court, the Court denied certiorari. 554 U.S. 922 (2008).) Do you agree?

Perhaps the intelligible principle test is most effective indirectly, in ensuring that statutes will be read in a way that fosters judicial review. In SOUTH DAKOTA V. DEP'T OF THE INTERIOR, 69 F.3d 878 (8th Cir. 1995), South Dakota challenged the Interior Department's acquisition of certain lands in trust for the Lower Brule Sioux Tribe. The Department defended by claiming that the authorizing statute, Section 5 of the Indian Reorganization Act of 1934, contained no standard by which a court could assess the legality of its decision and thus its action was unreviewable. (For a discussion of when judicial review is precluded because an action is committed to agency discretion, see Ch. IX, Sec. 2.b.3.) The Eighth Circuit accepted the Department's interpretation and held that Section 5 therefore was an unconstitutional delegation, noting in particular the lack of an intelligible principle to constrain the agency: "The result is an agency fiefdom whose boundaries were never established by Congress, and whose exercise of unrestrained power is free of judicial review. It is hard to imagine a program more at odds with separation of powers principles." In the Supreme Court, the government discovered that there was indeed a judicially manageable intelligible principle in Section 5, conceded reviewability, and requested a remand for that review to occur, which the Court granted, 519 U.S. 919 (1996).

(4) *Was the D.C. Circuit So Wrong?* In its decision below, AMERICAN TRUCKING ASS'NS V. EPA, 175 F.3d 1027 (D.C. Cir. 1999), the D.C. Circuit had concluded that "that EPA has construed §§ 108 and 109 of the Clean Air Act so loosely as to render them unconstitutional delegations of legislative power. . . . Although the factors EPA uses in determining the degree of public health concern associated with different levels of ozone and PM are reasonable, EPA appears to have articulated no 'intelligible principle' to

channel its application of these factors; nor is one apparent from the statute. . . . Here it is as though Congress commanded EPA to select 'big guys,' and EPA announced that it would evaluate candidates based on height and weight, but revealed no cutoff point. The announcement, though sensible in what it does say, is fatally incomplete. The reasonable person responds, 'How tall? How heavy?' . . .

"Where (as here) statutory language and an existing agency interpretation involve an unconstitutional delegation of power, but an interpretation without the constitutional weakness is or may be available, our response is not to strike down the statute but to give the agency an opportunity to extract a determinate standard on its own. Doing so serves at least two of three basic rationales for the nondelegation doctrine. If the agency develops determinate, binding standards for itself, it is less likely to exercise the delegated authority arbitrarily. See Amalgamated Meat Cutters v. Connally, 337 F.Supp. 737, 758–59 (D.D.C. 1971) (Leventhal, J., for three-judge panel). And such standards enhance the likelihood that meaningful judicial review will prove feasible. A remand of this sort of course does not serve the third key function of non-delegation doctrine, to 'ensure[ ] to the extent consistent with orderly governmental administration that important choices of social policy are made by Congress, the branch of our Government most responsive to the popular will,' Industrial Union Dep't, AFL-CIO v. American Petroleum Inst., 448 U.S. 607, 685 (1980) ('Benzene') (Rehnquist, J., concurring) [p. 812]. The agency will make the fundamental policy choices. But the remand does ensure that the courts not hold unconstitutional a statute that an agency, with the application of its special expertise, could salvage."

Disagreeing with the majority both on whether the statutory language was unconstitutionally broad and whether EPA had adequately explained the emission levels it chose, Judge Tatel emphasized the role played by the Clean Air Scientific Advisory Committee (CASAC), created pursuant to § 109: "CASAC must consist of at least one member of the National Academy of Sciences, one physician, and one person representing state air pollution control agencies. In this case, CASAC also included medical doctors, epidemiologists, toxicologists and environmental scientists from leading research universities and institutions throughout the country. EPA must explain any departures from CASAC's recommendations. See 42 U.S.C. § 7607(d)(3). Bringing scientific methods to their evaluation of the Agency's Criteria Document and Staff Paper, CASAC provides an objective justification for the pollution standards the Agency selects."

The Supreme Court dismissed out of hand the D.C. Circuit's suggestion that EPA could remedy an overbroad delegation by adopting a narrower interpretation of the statutory language. But was the D.C. Circuit's approach so mistaken? If, as Justice Scalia acknowledged, courts are almost never able to police whether a delegation goes too far, are the constitutional concerns underlying the nondelegation doctrine best served by requiring agencies to limit their discretion instead? See Lisa Schultz Bressman, Schechter Poultry at the Millennium: A Delegation Doctrine for the Administrative State, 109 Yale L.J. 1399 (2000). What about Judge Tatel's emphasis on CASAC; in concluding that § 109(b)(1) was a constitutional delegation: No member of the Supreme Court made any reference to CASAC's role under the statute. Should the Supreme Court have given more weight to the fact that the statute requires the EPA to explain when it deviates from this expert body's recommendations for emission levels?

(5) *Narrowing Statutory Constructions and Administrative Law.* An alternative remedial strategy is to read statutes narrowly so as to avoid delegation problems where possible. This practice, sometimes described as a "nondelegation canon" of statutory construction, see Cass R. Sunstein, Nondelegation Canons, 67 U. Chi. L. Rev. 315, 322 (2000), is a species of constitutional avoidance that can be traced back at least to mid-century cases such as Kent v. Dulles, 357 U.S. 116 (1958) (interpreting the passport statute as not delegating power to the Secretary of State to refuse a passport solely on grounds of membership in or support of the Communist Party); see also Edward J. DeBartolo Corp. v. Fla. Gulf Coast Bldg. & Constr. Trades Council, 485 U.S. 568, 575 (1988) "[W]here an otherwise acceptable construction of a statute would raise serious constitutional problems, the Court will construe the statute to avoid such problems unless such construction is plainly contrary to the intent of Congress." The challengers in Whitman sought to use this strategy to their advantage, arguing that § 109 should be read to require consideration of costs, and thereby cabining EPA's authority and avoiding a nondelegation problem. Justice Scalia's majority opinion refused to follow this route, concluding the statute's text was clear in rejecting consideration of costs.[4] (For a discussion of Whitman's holding on costs, see Craig N. Oren, Run Over by American Trucking, Part I: Can EPA Revive Its Air Quality Standards, 30 Envtl. L. Rep. 10653, 10660 (Nov. 1999)).

The D.C. Circuit below had debated a separate question, namely whether any such nondelegation canon was displaced by Chevron's requirement of deference to an agency's reasonable statutory interpretation of ambiguous statutory provisions it is charged with implementing.[5] In a per

---

[4] This aspect of Whitman stands in some contrast with more recent statutory interpretation decisions by the Supreme Court emphasizing the importance of agency consideration of costs. See, e.g., Michigan v. EPA, 135 S.Ct. 2699, 2709 (2015) (p. 1149) (reading Whitman as "establish[ing] the modest principle that where the [CAA] expressly directs EPA to regulate on the basis of a factor that on its face does not include cost, the Act normally should not be read as implicitly allowing the Agency to consider cost anyway" and holding "that principle has no application" to a statutory provision directing EPA to regulate power plant emissions if it finds such regulation to be "reasonable and appropriate," as that phrase "read fairly and in context . . . plainly subsumes consideration of cost").

[5] If you haven't yet encountered Chevron v. NRDC, 467 U.S. 837 (1984), you'll see in Chapter VIII, p. 1129, that Chevron is an important doctrine governing judicial review of agency statutory interpretations. In relevant part, the case provides:

When a court reviews an agency's construction of the statute which it administers, it is confronted with two questions. First, always, is the question whether Congress has directly spoken to the precise question at issue. If the intent of Congress is clear, that is the end of the matter; for the court, as well as the agency, must give effect to the unambiguously expressed intent of Congress. If, however, the court determines Congress has not directly addressed the precise question at issue, the court does not simply impose its own construction on the statute, as would be necessary in the absence of an administrative interpretation. Rather, if the statute is silent or ambiguous with respect to the specific issue, the question for the court is whether the agency's answer is based on a permissible construction of the statute.

curiam opinion denying rehearing, the Whitman panel stated: "[J]ust as we must defer to an agency's reasonable interpretation of an ambiguous statutory term, we must defer to an agency's reasonable interpretation of a statute containing only an ambiguous principle by which to guide its exercise of delegated authority. . . . In sum, the approach of the Benzene case, in which the Supreme Court itself identified an intelligible principle in an ambiguous statute, has given way to the approach of Chevron." Subsequently dissenting from the D.C. Circuit's denial of rehearing en banc denial, Judge Silberman insisted that "the constitutional avoidance canon trumps Chevron deference." 195 F.3d 4 (D.C. Cir. 1999).

Judge Silberman's view appears to have borne the test of time. The practice of narrow construction in response to delegation challenges seems to be alive and well. In Gonzales v. Oregon, 546 U.S. 243 (2006), Justice Kennedy's opinion for the six-person majority construed the Controlled Substances Act as not authorizing the Attorney General to prohibit doctors from prescribing regulated drugs for use in physician-assisted suicide under the recently enacted Oregon Death With Dignity Act, rejecting the agency's contrary view. Otherwise, the statute would "delegate to a single Executive officer the power to effect a radical shift of authority from the States to the Federal Government to define general standards of medical practice in every locality." Hence even post-Chevron, a court nervous about regulatory authority may find a way to construe the statute against the possible delegation. E.g., MCI Telecommunications Co. v. American Telephone & Telegraph Co. (p. 1171). But see Jacob Loshin & Aaron Nielson, Hiding Nondelegation in Mouseholes, 62 Admin. L. Rev. 19 (2010) (criticizing MCI and other recent narrow interpretations of regulatory statutes as an approach no more "susceptible of consistent application" than the nondelegation doctrine itself); John F. Manning, The Nondelegation Doctrine as a Canon of Avoidance, 2000 Sup. Ct. Rev. 223, 227 (arguing that "enforcing the nondelegation doctrine through the canon of avoidance undermines, rather than furthers, the constitutional aims of that doctrine").

Scholars have also identified nondelegation concerns as the motivation behind a number of administrative law doctrines. Professor KATHRYN WATTS, in RULEMAKING AS LEGISLATING, 103 Geo. L.J. 1003, 1008 (2015), "concludes that even though the nondelegation doctrine's central premise prohibiting the delegation of legislative power has little bite in the context of the nondelegation doctrine itself, its continual appearance in the case law has confused administrative law as a whole. Some existing administrative law doctrines at least implicitly embrace the legislative role of agencies, putting them in direct tension with the nondelegation doctrine. These include Chevron deference, procedural due process, and the test used to define legislative rules [that require use of notice-and-comment procedures]. In contrast, consistent with the nondelegation doctrine's prohibition on the delegation of legislative powers, other major doctrines fail to view rulemaking as legislative in nature. These include hard look [arbitrary-and-capriciousness] review, procedural review, and Auer deference." See also

Lisa Schultz Bressman, Disciplining Delegation After Whitman v. American Trucking Ass'ns, 87 Cornell L. Rev. 452 (2002).

(6) ***American Railroads on Remand.*** As both Whitman and American Railroads indicate, the D.C. Circuit has repeatedly diverged from the Supreme Court on delegation. That pattern held true as well in the D.C. Circuit's subsequent decision in American Railroads. In overturning the D.C. Circuit, Justice Kennedy's majority opinion had returned the case for the D.C. Circuit to consider the challengers' additional constitutional challenges. On remand, the same panel of the D.C. Circuit again invalidated the statute. Ass'n of American Railroads v. DOT, 821 F.3d 19 (2016). The appellate court first held that the delegation of standard setting power to Amtrak violated due process, because it allowed an economically self-interested party, Amtrak, to set the regulatory standards that would govern itself and others. The D.C. Circuit also followed Justice Alito's opinion in holding that the provision for appointing an arbitrator was unconstitutional because it either constituted a prohibited private delegation of regulatory power or, if a public arbitrator, represented an appointment of a principal officer outside of the Article II specified mechanisms (p. 888). The government decided not to seek certiorari.

Is the D.C. Circuit's decision on remand consistent with the Supreme Court's? Although the Supreme Court remanded the due process question, does it make sense to view Amtrak as self-interested if it is part of government? In holding that it does, the D.C. Circuit emphasized the statutory requirement that Amtrak be profit-maximizing and Amtrak's obligations to its shareholders. Given the extent of Congress's control over Amtrak and ownership of Amtrak's shares, as well as the fact that Amtrak runs an annual deficit in the order of $1 billion that Congress funds, whether this statutory directive makes Amtrak more self-interested than other parts of government is open to question. Even if the D.C. Circuit's characterization of Amtrak as self-interested is correct, however, does a due process violation follow? As discussed in Chapter V (p. 505), it is well established that financial incentives can invalidate an adjudicator. But is regulation the same? The Court has upheld involvement of financially interested parties in creating a regulatory scheme, provided the parties act subject to governmental supervision. Here, any metrics and standards that Amtrak devises cannot go into effect without the FRA's assent. By holding that such governmental supervision is insufficient for due processes purposes, the D.C. Circuit's decision could have significant implications for regulatory approaches, such as reg-neg or self-regulation, that involve regulated entities in the process of designing regulation.

(2) The Past and Future of Nondelegation Doctrine

> **(i) *The Evolution of Nondelegation Doctrine***
>
> **(ii) *Competing Reactions to Current Nondelegation Doctrine***
>
> **(iii) *Delegation to Other Institutional Actors***

In this Subsection, we first consider important cases in the development of current nondelegation doctrine, some of which play a significant role in recent separation-of-powers challenges. Then, to help you formulate your own thinking in this area, we look briefly at competing positions in the scholarly debate about the state of nondelegation law. Finally, we explore some of the newer institutional arrangements in which delegation occurs: delegation to private entities and international organizations. Sprinkled throughout are state cases that reveal a path not taken by the federal courts.

(i) The Evolution of Nondelegation Doctrine

Professor Gary Lawson has described the nondelegation doctrine as "the Energizer Bunny of constitutional law: No matter how many times it gets broken, beaten, or buried, it just keeps on going and going." *Delegation and Original Meaning*, 88 Va. L. Rev. 327, 330 (2002). The materials that follow prove his point, demonstrating a long history of failed delegation challenges. As you read these materials, think about whether they make a consistent line or instead their similar results mask important differences in reasoning and the nature of the delegation at issue. These decisions can be divided into three periods.

The first period extends from the founding to the New Deal and contains many delegation decisions still referred to in current cases. These delegations often arose in the area of foreign trade. The earliest reported nondelegation challenge appears to be THE BRIG AURORA, 11 U.S. (7 Cranch) 382 (1813), which sustained a statute authorizing the President to "revive" an earlier measure giving favorable trading status to France and Britain, commerce with whom had been barred during the War of 1812 by the Non-Intercourse Act. Another early decision, WAYMAN V. SOUTHARD, 10 Wheat. 42 (1826), provided an occasion for Chief Justice Marshall to weigh in on the constitutionality of delegation. In sustaining a statute delegating to the courts authority to make rules governing their proceedings, he said: "It will not be contended that Congress can delegate to the courts, or to any other tribunals, powers which are strictly and exclusively legislative. But Congress may certainly delegate to others powers which the legislature may rightfully exercise itself." Marshall added: "The line has not been exactly drawn which separates those important subjects which must be entirely regulated by the legislature itself from those of less interest in which a general provision may be made and power given to those who are to act under such general provisions to fill up the details."

Two other late nineteenth and early twentieth century cases involved delegations more akin to today's regulatory statutes. FIELD V. CLARK, 143 U.S. 649 (1892) upheld the Tariff Act of 1890, which contained a provision authorizing certain articles to be imported duty-free but gave the President power—and duty—to suspend the provision if he was "satisfied" that any country producing and exporting these articles imposed duties on U.S. products that the President "deem[s] to be reciprocally unequal and unreasonable." Writing for the court, JUSTICE HARLAN noted the long history of Congress granting similar powers to the President in the area of trade and commerce before concluding that the Act "does not in any real sense invest the President with the power of legislation. . . . As the suspension was absolutely required when the President ascertained the existence of a particular fact, it cannot be said that in ascertaining that fact, and in issuing his proclamation in obedience to the legislative will, he exercised the function of making laws. Legislative power was exercised when Congress declared that the suspension should take effect upon a named contingency." In UNITED STATES V. GRIMAUD, 220 U.S. 506 (1911), the Court again upheld the delegation in question, a grant of authority to the Secretary of Agriculture to "make such rules and regulations" governing land set aside by the President for public forest reserves "as will insure the objects of such reservations." Strikingly, Congress had provided that violation of these rules and regulations would be a criminal (misdemeanor) offense. JUSTICE LAMAR noted that "[f]rom the beginning of the government, various acts have been passed conferring upon executive officers power to make rules and regulations. . . . None of these statutes could confer legislative power. But when Congress had legislated and indicated its will, it could give to those who were to act under such general provisions 'power to fill up the details' by the establishment of administrative rules and regulations, the violation of which could be punished by fine or imprisonment fixed by Congress, or by penalties fixed by Congress, or measured by the injury done."

Yet a third important decision from this period was J.W. HAMPTON, JR. & CO. V. UNITED STATES, 276 U.S. 394 (1928), from which the language of "intelligible principles" is derived. The case again involved a tariff measure, the Tariff Act of 1922, which directed the President to change the original statutory schedule of tariffs on various goods whenever the President, after investigating costs for articles produced domestically compared to similar articles made abroad, "shall find . . . that the duties fixed in this Act do not equalize the said differences in costs of production in the United States and the principal competing country." Moving tariff-setting more towards the bureaucratic mode of modern regulation, the Act authorized the President to act only after receiving the report of a new Tariff Commission. CHIEF JUSTICE TAFT wrote for a unanimous Court sustaining this delegation: "It is conceded by counsel that Congress may use executive officers in the application and enforcement of a policy declared in law by Congress . . . [b]ut it is said that this never has been permitted [with respect to] the power to levy taxes and fix customs duties. The authorities make no such distinction. The same principle that permits Congress to exercise its ratemaking power in interstate commerce by declaring the rule which shall prevail in the legislative fixing of rates, and enables it to remit to a ratemaking body created in accordance with its provisions the fixing of such rates, justifies a similar provision for the fixing of customs duties on imported merchandise. If Congress shall lay down by legislative act an intelligible principle to which the person or body authorized to fix such rates is directed to conform, such legislative action is not a forbidden delegation of legislative power." Taft concluded that what the statute sought to do here was "perfectly clear and intelligible": it sought to impose customs duties that would "enable domestic producers to compete on terms of equality with foreign producers in the markets of the United States." The President's role was not the making of law. He was the mere agent of the lawmaking department to ascertain and declare the event upon which its expressed will was to take effect.

The second period was much shorter, spanning a few years at the outset of the New Deal. This period was nondelegation doctrine's moment in the sun, when in three cases the Court invalidated delegations as unconstitutional delegations—the first and last times it has done so. Two cases involved the National Industrial Recovery Act (NIRA), a key measure enacted during President Roosevelt's first one hundred days in office to address the economic crisis of the Depression. (The third, Carter v. Carter Coal, 298 U.S. 238 (1936), involved a similar early New Deal measure to stabilize the coal industry.) The first case, PANAMA REFINING CO. V. RYAN, 293 U.S. 388, involved a section of the NIRA aimed at stabilizing the petroleum industry by stemming overproduction from vast, newly tapped oil fields in Texas. It authorized the President to enforce conservation orders from state boards attempting to deal with the problem. The majority found no standard for the President to follow in deciding whether to close interstate commerce to "hot oil." Only Justice Cardozo dissented.

Five months later, A.L.A. SCHECHTER POULTRY CORP. V. UNITED STATES, 295 U.S. 495 (1935), the Court considered § 3 of the NIRA, which authorized the President to approve "codes of fair competition" for a trade or industry, upon application by one or more trade or industrial associations or groups. To approve a code, the President had to find (1) that such associations or groups "impose no inequitable restrictions on admission to membership therein and are truly representative;" and (2) that such codes were not designed "to promote monopolies or to eliminate or oppress small enterprises and will not operate to discriminate against them, and will tend to effectuate the policy" of the Act. The Schechter company was indicted on multiple counts of violating the "Live Poultry Code" which had been approved by the President under § 3. CHIEF JUSTICE HUGHES wrote for a unanimous Court in invalidating § 3: "Undoubtedly, the conditions to which power is addressed are always to be considered when the exercise of power is challenged. Extraordinary conditions may call for extraordinary remedies. But . . . [e]xtraordinary conditions do not create or enlarge constitutional power . . . We think the conclusion is inescapable that the authority sought to be conferred by § 3 was not merely to deal with 'unfair competitive practices' [but] to authorize new and controlling prohibitions through codes of laws which would embrace what the formulators would propose, and what the President would approve, or prescribe, as wise and beneficent measures for the government of trades and industries in order to bring about their rehabilitation, correction and development. . . . But Congress cannot delegate legislative power to the President to exercise an unfettered discretion to make whatever laws he thinks may be needed or advisable for the rehabilitation and expansion of trade or industry. . . ."

Acknowledging that the Court had "repeatedly recognized the necessity of adapting legislation to complex conditions involving a host of details with which the national legislature cannot deal directly," Hughes concluded, "Section 3 of the Recovery Act is without precedent. It supplies no standards for any trade, industry or activity. It does not undertake to prescribe rules of conduct to be applied to particular states of fact determined by appropriate administrative procedure. Instead of prescribing rules of conduct, it authorizes the making of codes to prescribe them. For that legislative undertaking, § 3 sets up no standards, aside from the statement of the general aims of rehabilitation, correction and expansion described in section one. In view of the scope of that broad declaration, and of the nature of the few restrictions that are imposed, the discretion of the President in approving or prescribing codes, and thus enacting laws for the government of trade and industry throughout the country, is virtually unfettered. We think that the code-making authority this conferred is an unconstitutional delegation of legislative power. . . ." JUSTICE CARDOZO agreed that this delegation crossed the line: "The delegated power of legislation which has found expression in this code is not canalized within banks that keep it from overflowing. It is unconfined and vagrant . . . This is delegation running riot."

The Schechter Poultry Court was not content to invalidate § 3 on nondelegation grounds; it also held the statute exceeded Congress's regulatory authority under the Commerce Clause. Soon thereafter, the Supreme Court changed course and began to take a broader view of the commerce power. It also returned to its practice of upholding delegations. YAKUS V. UNITED STATES, 321 U.S. 414 (1944), is a prime case in point. There the Court upheld a provision of the Emergency Price Control Act of 1942, a temporary measure during World War II enacted to address inflation. The Act created an Office of Price Administration headed by a Price Administrator who, after consulting with industry to the extent practicable, was authorized to promulgate regulations fixing prices of commodities which "in his judgment will be generally fair and equitable and will effectuate the purposes of this Act," giving due weight to prices prevailing in October 1941. Writing for all but one member of the Court, CHIEF JUSTICE STONE stated: "The essentials of the legislative function are the determination of the legislative policy and its formulation and promulgation as a defined and binding rule of conduct . . . These essentials are preserved when Congress has specified the basic conditions of fact upon whose existence or occurrence, ascertained from relevant data by a designated administrative agency, it directs that its statutory command shall be effective. It is no objection that the determination of facts and the inferences to be drawn from them . . . call for the exercise of judgment . . . Only if we could say that there is an absence of standards for the guidance of the Administrator's action, so that it would be impossible in a proper proceeding to ascertain whether the will of Congress has been obeyed, would we be justified in overriding its choice of means for effecting its declared purpose of preventing inflation. The standards prescribed by the present Act, with the aid of the 'statement of considerations' required to be made by the Administrator, are sufficiently definite and precise to enable Congress, the courts and the public to ascertain whether the Administrator, in fixing the designated prices, has conformed to those standards."

Yakus marks the third period in the Court's delegation jurisprudence, which continues to this day. Its central characteristic is the Court's willingness to sustain very broad delegations. Whitman, and many of the decisions that Justice Scalia cites there, fall into this period. The delegations upheld included instructions to an agency to regulate "in the public interest." See, e.g., National Broadcasting Company v. United States, 319 U.S. 190 (1942). Other cases sustained delegation of taxing authority, Skinner v. Mid-American Pipeline Co., 490 U.S. 212 (1986), and authority to determine factors triggering imposition of statutory death penalty in military capital cases, Loving v. United States, 517 U.S. 748 (1996).

In one case, however—INDUSTRIAL UNION DEP'T, AFL-CIO V. AMERICAN PETROLEUM INST., 448 U.S. 607 (1980) (Benzene), the Court cited nondelegation concerns in invalidating agency action. At issue was a decision by the Occupational Safety and Health Administration (OSHA) to lower the maximum permissible exposure for benzene, a confirmed carcinogen, from 10 ppm to 1 ppm. The National Institute for Occupational Safety and Health (NIOSH), an independent, science-dominated agency located in the Centers for Disease Control & Prevention charged with advising OSHA about regulatory priorities, had long pushed for this regulatory change, which was extremely costly for the petroleum refining industry. A plurality written by JUSTICE STEVENS invalidated the new standard on the grounds that OSHA needed "to make a threshold finding that a place of employment is unsafe—in the sense that significant risks are present and can be eliminated or lessened by a change in practices"—before issuing any permanent health or safety standard. This "significant risk" requirement was not expressly in the statute but read into a provision defining such standards as those conditions "reasonably necessary or appropriate to provide safe or healthful employment and places of employment." Justice Stevens justified this aggressive reading on the grounds that otherwise "the statute would make such a 'sweeping delegation of legislative power' that it might be unconstitutional under the Court's reasoning in [Schechter Poultry] and [Panama Refining]."

Then-JUSTICE REHNQUIST'S opinion concurring in the judgment went further and said that § 6(b)(5) of the Act, under which OSHA regulates toxic chemicals like Benzene, was an unconstitutional delegation of legislative power: "As formulated and enforced by this Court, the nondelegation doctrine serves three important functions. First, and most abstractly, it ensures to the extent consistent with orderly governmental administration that important choices of social policy are made by Congress, the branch of our Government most responsive to the popular will. Second, the doctrine guarantees that, to the extent Congress finds it necessary to delegate authority, it provides the recipient of that authority with an intelligible principle to guide the exercise of the delegated discretion. Third, and derivative of the second, the doctrine ensures that courts charged with reviewing the exercise of delegated legislative discretion will be able to test that exercise against ascertainable standards. I believe the legislation at issue here fails on all three counts."

Section 6(b)(5) directs the Secretary to "set the standard which most adequately assures, to the extent feasible, on the basis of the best available evidence, that no employee will suffer material impairment of health or functional capacity even if such employee has regular exposure to the hazard dealt with by such standard for the period of his working life." According to Justice Rehnquist, "the language 'to the extent feasible' . . . render[s] what had been a clear, if somewhat unrealistic, standard largely, if not entirely, precatory." He added: "The decision whether the law of diminishing returns should have any place in the regulation of toxic substances is quintessentially one of legislative policy. . . . It is difficult to imagine a more obvious example of Congress simply avoiding a choice which was both fundamental for purposes of the statute and yet politically so divisive that the necessary decision or compromise was difficult, if not impossible, to hammer out in the legislative forge. . . . It is the hard choices, and not the filling in of the blanks, which must be made by the elected representatives of the people."

NOTES

(1) *Is the Nondelegation Doctrine a Myth?* Does this history of almost entirely unsuccessful delegation challenges make you question whether there really is a nondelegation doctrine? KEITH WHITTINGTON and JASON IULIANO, in THE MYTH OF THE NONDELEGATION DOCTRINE, 165 U. Pa. L. Rev. 379, 404–05, 419–20, 429 (2017), argue that the historical record demonstrates the doctrine is a myth: "A review of the Court's treatment of challenges to federal and state statutes on the grounds that they had impermissibly delegated legislative power to nonlegislative actors does not provide much basis for thinking that there was ever a seriously confining nondelegation doctrine as part of the effective constitutional order." Noting that most delegation challenges were heard in state and lower federal courts, the authors compiled a dataset of around 2500 cases involving claims of improper delegations decided in the period from the Founding to 1940. They report that delegation challenges remained "relatively rare until the antebellum period. Over the course of the second half of the nineteenth century, nondelegation cases made a regular appearance on judicial dockets . . . Nondelegation cases surged at the opening of the twentieth century, plateauing at a new level that was several times the pace at which such cases were heard in the nineteenth century. In keeping with the traditional narrative of the battles of the New Deal, the number of nondelegation cases surged again in the 1930s. . . . Despite the growth of nondelegation as an area of litigation, the number of judicial invalidations hardly budged. . . . The early 1930s do . . . stand out as an outlier, with a brief eruption of cases striking down legislation—an eruption that subsided as quickly as it arose. . . . The creation of agencies and commissions filled with experts who could effectively make the regulatory policy that shaped the economy was no doubt innovative and required significant rethinking of traditional governmental forms. But state and federal judges did not hesitate to give their stamp of approval to those institutional innovations. Traditional constitutional principles were thought to be capacious enough to accommodate the new administrative structures."

Compare the view of Professor GARY LAWSON, DELEGATION AND ORIGINAL MEANING, 88 Va. L. Rev. 327, 355, 360, 371–72 (2002): "The first serious effort to define a nondelegation principle was put forth by Chief Justice Marshall in 1825 in Wayman v. Southard . . . Chief Justice Marshall put forth his ultimate methodology for resolving delegation issues in one cryptic sentence: 'The line has not been exactly drawn which separates those important subjects, which must be entirely regulated by the legislature itself, from those of less interest, in which . . . power [may be] given to those who are to act under such general provisions to fill up the details.' . . . As far as the courts are concerned, no one has improved upon, or even elaborated upon, Chief Justice Marshall's 1825 declaration that the Constitution requires Congress to make whatever decisions are important enough that the Constitution requires Congress to make them."

(2) *How the Court Assesses Delegation.* Note that the Court used two different approaches—the contingency rationale of Field v. Clark and the "filling in the details" rationale of Grimaud—before settling on the

"intelligible principle" formulation. Why did these earlier approaches not survive as the modern standard for permissible delegation? Think about the delegation at issue in Whitman: Could it easily be sustained on these earlier grounds? Some scholars see modern cases such as Yakus as offering yet another more functionalist, approach, one that emphasized the availability of effective *checks* on delegated power. See Cynthia R. Farina, Statutory Interpretation and the Balance of Power in the Administrative State, 89 Colum. L. Rev. 452 (1989); Kevin M. Stack, The Constitutional Foundations of Chenery, 116 Yale L.J. 952 (2007).

(3) *Who Is the Delegee?* In several of these earlier cases the statutory delegation was to the President personally. The far more common modern pattern is for the statute to delegate power to the head of a Cabinet department (e.g., the Secretary of Transportation) or a freestanding agency (the Commissioners of the Federal Communications Commission); these officials then may subdelegate actual implementation of the statute to the heads of internal units (e.g., the Secretary of Transportation may subdelegate to the Administrator of the Federal Aviation Administration).

What, if any, difference does it make that the delegee is the President himself? For formalist separation-of-powers theory, none. If an intelligible principle is present, then delegated power is not "legislative" but rather "executive." For functionalist separation-of-powers theorists, however, it could matter a great deal. The identity of the delegee becomes relevant because most of the checks on administrative power that regularize agency decisionmaking and render it more transparent and participatory do not apply, or apply in the same way, to the President. Presidential decisionmaking is not subject to the Administrative Procedure Act or any of the "sunshine" statutes,[6] and courts are understandably loathe to review decisions made by the President personally.[7] A functionalist might still find the delegation constitutional but would approach it with greater wariness. See, e.g., Clinton v. New York (dissenting op. of Justice Breyer) (p. 843).

Note also that two of the three cases in which the Supreme Court has found delegations invalid—Schecter Poultry and Panama Refining—were delegations to the President personally, at a time when the strength of executive authority being manifested in Berlin and Moscow might have raised caution flags. (For another constitutional area in which international events leading up to World War II may have affected judicial perceptions about executive-centered government, see the removal cases, Myers (p. 918) and Humphrey's Executor (p. 920).)

(4) *A Road Not Taken: Delegation in the States.* The separation-of-powers and checks-and-balances principles of the U.S. Constitution apply

---

[6]   Franklin v. Massachusetts, 505 U.S. 788, 801 (1992), held that the President is not an "agency" within the meaning of the Administrative Procedure Act, 5 U.S.C. § 551; this definition also applies to the Freedom of Information Act and the Government in the Sunshine Act.

[7]   The Court has traditionally held that the federal courts may not entertain requests for an injunction against the President. Marbury v. Madison, 5 U.S. 137 (1803), one of the few cases in which the President is challenged by name rather than through the device of suing the official who implements his/her directions, is a rare example of the prerogative writs functioning for this purpose. See Ch. IX, Sec. 2.a; Jonathan R. Siegel, Suing the President: Nonstatutory Review Revisited, 97 Colum. L. Rev. 1612 (1997).

only to the national government. States are free to accept or reject these principles in whole or part and, while doubtless affected by U.S. Supreme Court views, can give them whatever interpretation seems appropriate.[8] Many state courts have discerned a nondelegation principle in their own constitutions and are more likely than the federal courts to find it violated. However, according to WHITTINGTON and IULIANO, supra, at 432, although state courts traditionally "were more active than the U.S. Supreme Court, and often more articulate and elaborate in explaining the logic of the Constitution's nondelegation principle," they "likewise refrained from imposing sharp limits on legislative discretion to shift important swaths of policymaking to other government officials, and they too erected few practical barriers to the rise of the modern administrative state and the expansive executive role in initiating and designing regulatory policy."

Two recent cases from the New York Court of Appeals, New York's highest court, demonstrate both this state impulse to limit delegation and also sanction of executive discretion. In MATTER OF NEW YORK STATEWIDE COALITION OF HISPANIC CHAMBERS OF COMMERCE V. NEW YORK CITY DEPARTMENT OF HEALTH AND MENTAL HYGIENE, 23 N.Y.3d 681, 690, 699, 16 N.E.3d 538 (2014), the New York City Board of Health, an 11-member board of mayoral appointments in the City's Department of Health and Mental Hygiene, voted to amend the City Health Code, restricting the size of containers used by food service establishments to provide sugary beverages. The rule—known as the Portion Cap Rule—prohibited certain food service establishments, including restaurants and movie theaters but not others, namely supermarkets and convenience stores, from selling sugary beverages in containers larger than 16 fluid ounces. The Court of Appeals applied a four-factor test from an earlier decision, Boreali v. Axelrod, 71 N.Y.2d 1, 517 N.E.2d 1350 (1987), and concluded that the rule went beyond the constitutional bounds of the Board's authority. These factors were: (1) whether the agency "more than simply balanc[ed] costs and benefits according to preexisting guidelines" or instead "ma[de] value judgments entail[ing] difficult and complex choices between broad policy goals"; (2) whether the agency "simply fill[ed] in details guided by independent legislation" or instead acted "without benefit of legislative guidance"; (3) "whether the challenged rule governs an area in which the Legislature has repeatedly tried to reach agreement in the face of substantial public debate"; (4) and "whether special expertise or technical competence was involved in the development of the rule." Without reaching the fourth factor, the Court in Statewide Coalition concluded, "[b]y choosing among competing policy goals, without any legislative delegation or guidance, the Board engaged in law-making and thus infringed upon the legislative jurisdiction of the City Council of New York." According to the Court, "[a]n agency that adopts a regulation, such as the Portion Cap Rule ... that interferes with

---

[8] In theory, a state's choice of government structure might be so anomalous as to offend the federal constitution's guaranty to the states of a "republican form of government." U.S. Const. Art. IV, § 4. However, since Luther v. Borden, 7 How. 1, 12 L.Ed. 581 (1849), claims under the Guaranty Clause have been regarded as nonjusticiable political questions (although the Clause was invoked to support a constitutional prohibition on the national government commandeering state legislatures, see New York v. United States, 505 U.S. 144, 183–86 (1992)).

commonplace daily activities preferred by large numbers of people must necessarily wrestle with complex value judgments concerning personal autonomy and economics. That is policymaking, not rulemaking."

When the Court of Appeals faced a similar challenge the next year in GREATER NEW YORK TAXI ASSOCIATION V. NEW YORK CITY TAXI AND LIMOUSINE COMMISSION, 25 N.Y.3d 600, 36 N.E.3d 632 (2015), it was more accepting of legislative delegation. In 2007, the NYC Taxi and Limousine Commission (TLC) commenced its "Taxi of Tomorrow" ("TOT") program, aiming to create uniformity and modernize its taxi fleet. After a four-year process involving committee and public hearings, stakeholder involvement, and bid solicitation, the TLC chose the Nissan NV200 as the TOT. Under the regulation, every new taxi, with limited exceptions, was required to be the Nissan NV200. The court analyzed the regulation under the Boreali factors but noted, "these factors are not mandatory, need not be weighed evenly, and are essentially guidelines for conducting an analysis of an agency's exercise of power." Instead, the court emphasized an "overall focus" of "whether the challenged regulation attempted to resolve difficult social problems concerning matters of personal autonomy." Concluding it did not, the court held "that the TLC engaged in proper rulemaking, rather than improper legislating." See also Nestor M. Davidson, Localist Administrative Law, 126 Yale L.J. 564 (2017).

States are also sensitive to particular issues raised private delegations, see Note 1, p. 826, perhaps because those empowered to act at the state or local level often have part-time government appointments and distinct private financial or other interests in the issues that come before them. A particularly detailed analysis is offered in Texas Boll Weevil Eradication Found., Inc. v. Lewellen, 952 S.W.2d 454 (Texas, 1997).

(ii) Competing Reactions to Current Nondelegation Doctrine

> ### Notes on Political Science Approaches to Delegation

Professor Peter Schuck poses four questions to those who engage in the continuing debate about delegation: "What is the nature of the delegation problem?; What should be our goals in seeking to control delegation?; In the absence of a nondelegation doctrine, is agency lawmaking effectively constrained?; What would be the consequences of reviving the nondelegation doctrine?" Peter H. Schuck, Delegation and Democracy: Comments on David Schoenbrod, 20 Cardozo L. Rev. 775, 776 (1999). Here is a selection of views on these questions.

(1) TODD D. RAKOFF, THE SHAPE OF THE LAW IN THE AMERICAN ADMINISTRATIVE STATE, 11 Tel Aviv U. Studies in Law 9, 20, 21–23, 24, 39 (1992): "There is . . . more than one way to divide up the power of government. The Constitution establishes three branches of government, legislative, executive and judicial; each has some power over a very large range of subject matters, but is often unable to act effectively without the participation of one or both of the other branches. This is the 'separation

of powers': branches of government that are 'omnicompetent' as regards subject-matter but 'unipowered' as regards the tools at their disposal. One could divide power the other way around. One could create organs of government that were 'omnipowered'—able to legislate, execute, adjudicate—but 'unicompetent'—entitled to exercise their many powers over only a small terrain. It is this second path that has been chosen in the fashioning of American regulatory agencies. . . .

"If the maxim that the only safe power is divided power is indeed a cultural norm, what would be taboo would be the creation of an organ of government at once omnipowered and omnicompetent. Congress would appear to operate on that maxim, as it has almost never tried to bring such an agency into being. The closest it has come was in the middle of the Great Depression, with the passage of the National Industrial Recovery Act. . . . But this example, far from disproving the force of the principle, in fact establishes it, for this Act is also the only one the Supreme Court has ever invalidated on that ground that it was, simply, an unlawful delegation of power. . . . Omnicompetence, or something near it, cannot, it seems, be delegated."

(2) DAVID SCHOENBROD, POWER WITHOUT RESPONSIBILITY 183–84 (1993): "In making laws, Congress has to allocate both rights and duties in the very course of stating what conduct it prohibits, and so must make manifest the benefits and costs of regulation. When Congress delegates, it tends to do only half its job—to distribute rights without imposing the commensurate duties. So it promises clean air without restricting polluters and higher incomes for farmers without increasing the price of groceries. In striking poses popular to each and every constituency, Congress ducks the key conflicts. Those conflicts, however, will inevitably surface when the agency tries to translate the popular abstractions of the statutory goals—such as 'clean' air or 'orderly' agricultural markets—into rules of conduct. . . . [D]elegation allows legislators to claim credit for the benefits which a regulatory statute promises yet escape the blame for the burdens it will impose . . . The public inevitably must suffer regulatory burdens to realize regulatory benefits, but the laws will come from an agency that legislators can then criticize for imposing excessive burdens on their constituents."

Compare PETER H. SCHUCK, DELEGATION AND DEMOCRACY: COMMENTS ON DAVID SCHOENBROD, 20 Cardozo L. Rev., 775, 781 (1999): "[Professor Schoenbrod] fails to see . . . that the particular attributes of the legislature's delegation—its breadth, type, and level-are themselves fundamental policy choices. . . . The optimal specificity and other delegation-related features of the legislation are among the questions on which almost all of the parties to these legislative struggles—congressional committees, legislative staffs, the White House, regulated firms, 'public interest' groups, state and local governments, and others—tend to stake out clear positions, for they know the resolution of these questions may well determine the nature and effectiveness of the regulatory scheme being established."

Neither Schoenbrod nor Schuck differentiates between delegation's effects on individual legislators and Congress as a whole. For the argument that such a distinction is critical, see now-OIRA Administrator NEOMI RAO, ADMINISTRATIVE COLLUSION: HOW DELEGATION DIMINISHES THE COLLECTIVE CONGRESS, 90 N.Y.U. L. Rev. 1463, 1465–66 (2015): "Delegation undermines separation of powers, not only by expanding the power of executive agencies, but also by unraveling the institutional interests of Congress. The Constitution creates what I term the 'collective Congress'—the people's representatives may exercise legislative power only collectively. This serves important republican principles and aligns the myriad particular interests of congressmen with the institutional interests of Congress. Members will be invested in the difficult process of lawmaking for the public good because this is the only way to exercise power. Delegation, however, provides numerous benefits to legislators by allowing them to influence and to control administration. Individual legislators thus have persistent incentives to delegate, because they can serve their personal interests by shaping how agencies exercise their delegated authority. By providing individual opportunities for legislators, delegation realigns the ambitions of congressmen away from Congress and the constitutional lawmaking process. Lawmakers may prefer to collude, rather than compete, with executive agencies over administrative power and so the Madisonian checks and balances will not prevent excessive delegations."

(3) THOMAS W. MERRILL, RETHINKING ARTICLE I, SECTION 1: FROM NONDELEGATION TO EXCLUSIVE DELEGATION, 104 Colum. L. Rev. 2097, 2098–101 (2004): "Th[e] 'Vesting Clause' . . . of Article I, Section 1 is associated with two postulates about the allocation of legislative power. The first says, 'Congress may not constitutionally delegate its legislative power to another branch of Government.' The second says, 'It is axiomatic that an administrative agency's power to promulgate legislative regulations is limited to the authority delegated by Congress.' Both postulates ascribe exclusive authority to Congress with respect to the exercise of legislative power. Otherwise, the two postulates are in significant tension with one another. The first says only Congress may exercise legislative power. The second says only Congress may delegate legislative power. In short, Article I, Section 1 has been read as imposing both a nondelegation doctrine and what may be called an 'exclusive delegation doctrine.' . . .

". . .[T]he prominence given to nondelegation, combined with the courts' unwillingness to enforce that postulate, has generated a low-level but persistent crisis of legitimacy for modern government. If we take seriously the idea that Congress may not delegate legislative power—as the nondelegation doctrine seems to invite us to do—then all three branches of government appear to be engaged in unconstitutional behavior. Congress is shirking its duty to legislate, executive agencies are exercising forbidden authority, and judges are violating their oaths by letting both of them get away with it. This massive breach of the Constitution can only encourage cynicism about government. If, however, it turns out that Article I, Section 1 is correctly understood to incorporate the exclusive delegation postulate rather than the nondelegation postulate, this legitimacy problem largely goes away. Congress has created the administrative state and has given its far-flung agencies extensive powers to adopt legislative rules. But there is nothing constitutionally problematic about this if Article I, Section 1 tells us not that only Congress can legislate, but only Congress can delegate."

(4) LISA SCHULTZ BRESSMAN, DISCIPLINING DELEGATION AFTER WHITMAN V. AMERICAN TRUCKING ASS'NS, 87 Cornell L. Rev. 452, 460, 461–62 (2002): "Administrative law is a more effective tool [than constitutional law] for addressing the delegation issue. . . . [C]ourts owe Congress a greater degree of leeway to formulate delegations under constitutional law than they owe agencies to exercise those delegations under administrative law. . . . [They] should not 'second-guess' Congress on an issue that involves consideration of factors 'both multifarious and (in the nonpartisan sense) highly political' [Mistretta, 458 U.S. at 416 (Scalia, J., dissenting]. That is not to say that Congress always has good motives for delegating. But courts must give Congress the benefit of the doubt if we are to have modern government. . . .

"At the same time, courts must insist that some governmental actor take responsibility for the hard choices of regulatory policy. Responsibility in this context means articulating the standards that direct and cabin administrative discretion. . . . If courts allow Congress implicitly to delegate such responsibility, they must require agencies expressly to assume it. . . . Using administrative law as a delegation doctrine [not only avoids declaring a congressional judgment unconstitutional but also] provides theoretical grounding and practical guidance for requiring administrative standards. As a theoretical matter, administrative law already contains principles that fit comfortably with an administrative-standards requirement. These principles . . . require agencies, in exchange for broad grants of policymaking authority, to demonstrate that they have used their authority in an open, regular, and rational fashion. They require agencies in general to articulate a basis for their policy determinations and, in particular, to articulate the standards for those determinations. In the absence of these principles, there is no protection (or recourse) against arbitrary lawmaking at any level of government."

(5) CYNTHIA R. FARINA, DECONSTRUCTING NONDELEGATION, 33 Harv. J.L. & Pub. Pol'y 1, 87, 95 (2010): "[T]he indefatigable fervor with which we cling to nondelegation arguments is difficult to justify based on either the language of the Constitution or the background understandings of agency law from which the *delegata potestas* maxim derives. Rather, it

appears to be anxiety about the consequences of two centuries of statutory delegation to agencies that keeps the delegation debate alive. This disquiet about modern regulatory government comprises several distinct concerns," including the limited government/federalism concern that broad delegation has created "a regime of unconstitutional federal regulatory overreaching [affecting] virtually every significant aspect of our social and economic lives," and the control/legitimacy concern that "agencies are making policy with little external oversight and less democratic accountability to the people."

". . . The real problem with framing concerns about regulatory government as a question of [constitutional power to delegate] is that when the inevitable confirmation of congressional authority comes, we tend to act as if there is nothing more to say. Debates about whether Congress *can* delegate have crowded out debates about whether Congress *ought* to delegate. Do we really believe that the sum and substance of congressional and presidential responsibility is to avoid doing that which they are prohibited from doing? Surely the power that we, the people, have given them through the Constitution comes impressed with an obligation to reflect carefully upon whether what *may* be done *should* be done."

(6) EVAN J. CRIDDLE, WHEN DELEGATION BEGETS DOMINATION: DUE PROCESS IN THE ADMINISTRATIVE STATE, 44 Ga. L. Rev. 117, 211 (2011): "[F]ederal courts should abandon the traditional nondelegation doctrine and embrace due process as the primary constitutional constraint on congressional delegation. According to the due process model, Congress may delegate lawmaking authority to administrative agencies if it channels that authority through a combination of substantive, procedural, and structural safeguards that prevent delegation from manifestly increasing the federal government's capacity for arbitrary lawmaking. Congressional delegations meet this standard when they include an 'intelligible principle' to guide agency discretion, together with deliberative procedural requirements and structural constraints such as political accountability and judicial review. In most contexts, the APA easily satisfies procedural due process, avoiding the need for further judicial intrusion into administrative rulemaking procedure. Where an agency's lawmaking procedures do not satisfy the constitutional minimum of due process, however, courts should set aside the agency's regulations and withhold Chevron deference to protect the public from administrative domination. The due process model thus takes seriously the nondelegation doctrine's republican ideals while reframing the Supreme Court's current delegation jurisprudence to better reconcile congressional delegation with the Constitution's enduring commitment to individual liberty."

NOTES ON POLITICAL SCIENCE
APPROACHES TO DELEGATION

Delegation has sparked extensive scholarship in political science as well as law. Where lawyers and legal academics often analyze delegation from a constitutional and normative perspective, political scientists generally take a more positive approach, examining the political dynamics underlying delegation. Political scientists have focused on understanding when Congress delegates and how it structures its delegations, as well as which of the political branches—Congress or the President—ends up controlling the exercise of delegated power.

(1) *Is Delegation Really Running Riot?* A recurrent theme in much political science scholarship on delegation is to reject "the assumption that Congress does in fact delegate, either de jure or de facto, unrestrainedly." According to DAVID EPSTEIN and SHARYN O'HALLORAN, THE NONDELEGATION DOCTRINE AND THE SEPARATION OF POWERS, 20 Cardozo L. Rev. 947, 950 (1999), "[l]egislators delegate authority in those areas—such as pork barreling in appropriations bills, military base closings, and trade policy—where the legislative process produces inefficient outcomes. Congress is also wary, though, of ceding too much authority to executive branch actors who may pursue their own policy goals rather than those of the enacting legislative coalition. Legislators therefore set the limits of executive branch discretion so that these costs and benefits of delegation balance at the margin."

Based on an empirical investigation of the scope of delegations in major legislation from 1947 to 1993, Epstein and O'Halloran conclude that "[e]xecutive discretion increases when it better suits legislators' need for reelection, and it decreases when legislative policymaking becomes politically more efficient. Combined with the finding that in major legislation the norm is for Congress not to delegate large amounts of its authority[,] . . . our findings imply a measured view of delegation. It certainly exists, but it does not overwhelm congressional policymaking, and, if anything, the trend over time shows it to be decreasing rather than increasing." They also emphasize the importance of unified government in determining the scope of delegation, concluding that Congress delegates more to executive agencies under unified government but more to independent agencies when control of the political branches is divided. They further found that Congress delegates more when legislative committees are outliers and when issue area at hand is characterized by informational intensity or uncertainty; and Congress oversees more intensely those issues on which they delegate the greatest amount of discretion. See David Epstein & Sharyn O'Halloran, Delegating Powers (1999). A more recent study by Sean Farhang and Miranda Yaver, Divided Government and the Fragmentation of American Law, 60 Am. L. Pol. Sci. 401 (2016), argues that divided government also leads Congress to fragment its delegations—by delegating to a larger number of administrative actors and providing multiple sources of distinct authority—in order to inhibit presidential subversion of congressional preferences in implementation.

(2) ***The Structure and Process of Delegated Power: Of Police Patrols and Fire Alarms.*** A substantial political science literature, often called positive political theory or PPT, exists on the means and extent to which Congress exercises control over delegated power. LISA BRESSMAN, PROCEDURES AS POLITICS IN ADMINISTRATIVE LAW, 107 Colum. L. Rev. 1749, 1767–68 (2007): Political scientists "start from the premise that delegation creates a principal-agent problem. In particular, Congress knows that agencies may implement their own policy preferences rather than legislative preferences. Political scientists identify two sorts of difficulties: 'coalitional drift' and 'bureaucratic drift.' Bureaucratic drift arises when agency officials act in ways inconsistent with the original deal or coalitional arrangement struck between interest groups and politicians. Coalitional drift occurs when agency officials, even if reflecting the preferences of the enacting Congress, depart from the preferences of future Congresses. For both sorts of problems, legislative monitoring is the antidote. . . . But . . . Congress has trouble monitoring its agents directly. Such oversight is costly, requiring both time and resources. Moreover, Congress frequently lacks the information necessary to assess whether agencies have selected policies that diverge from the ones that it would have chosen."

Yet some political scientists argue that the difficulty Congress faces in monitoring its agency delegates "ex post," or after it has delegated, doesn't mean it cedes control over delegated power. The reason is that Congress can impose indirect controls "ex ante," through the structure and process it imposes on an agency when it delegates. DAVID B. SPENCE, MANAGING DELEGATION EX ANTE: USING LAW TO STEER ADMINISTRATIVE AGENCIES, 28 J. Legal Stud. 413, 415 (1999): "Put simply, the structure and process hypothesis states that while Congress cannot foresee many of the important policy decisions it delegates to the agency, it can use enabling legislation to shape the agency policy-making process in ways that influence subsequent agency policy decisions. These means of influence include (1) providing for interest group representation in the administrative process; (2) 'stacking the deck' in favor of the interest groups supporting the original legislation (the 'enacting coalition') by specifying how the statutory mandate will be implemented; and (3) structuring the agency so that it tends to favor particular interests . . . These design decisions establish both ex ante predispositions in the agency and ex ante procedural rights for the enacting coalition, both of which can ensure that the enacting coalition's goals will be met in the agency policy-making process."

According to this view, Congress can use structure and process to alleviate its oversight difficulties and is a far more active overseer of agencies than many suppose. To make this argument, scholars distinguish between two forms of ex-post congressional oversight: Police patrols and fire alarms. Police patrols are a form of direct oversight: "at its own initiative, Congress examines a sample of executive—agency activities, with the aim of detecting and remedying any violations of legislative goals and, by its surveillance, discouraging such violations." By contrast, "fire-alarm oversight is less centralized and involves less active and direct intervention than police-patrol oversight: instead of examining a sample of administrative decisions, looking for violations of legislative goals, Congress establishes a system of rules, procedures, and informal practices that enable individual citizens and organized interest groups to examine administrative decisions[,] . . . to charge executive agencies with violating congressional goals, and to seek remedies from agencies, courts, and Congress itself." MATHEW D. MCCUBBINS & THOMAS SCHWARTZ, CONGRESSIONAL OVERSIGHT OVERLOOKED: POLICE PATROLS VERSUS FIRE ALARMS, 28 Am. J. Pol. Sci. 165, 165–66 (1984). On this view, "[w]hat has appeared to scholars to be a neglect of oversight, we argue, really is a preference for one form of oversight [fire alarms] over another, less-effective form [police patrols]."

Three scholars—MATHEW MCCUBBINS, ROGER NOLL, and BARRY WEINGAST (sometimes referred to collectively as MCNOLLGAST)—are most centrally responsible for developing PPT and the focus on structure and process. ADMINISTRATIVE PROCEDURES AS INSTRUMENTS OF POLITICAL CONTROL, 3 J. L. Econ. & Org. 243, 244, 246 (1987) "The traditional study of administrative law . . . views administrative procedures as means of assuring fairness and legitimacy in decisions by administrators. . . . The hypothesis we put forth is that much of administrative law—indeed, most administrative law that is not derived from judicial interpretation of the Constitution and common law principles of administrative fairness—is written for the purpose of helping elected politicians retain control of policymaking." Turning their attention to the APA, they argue that "[t]he legal constraints imposed in the [APA] and elsewhere enable political officials to overcome certain informational inequalities between themselves and administrative officers. By requiring agencies to collect and disseminate politically relevant information, Congress and the president make the threat of sanctions a more efficacious control device. Moreover, the administrative system is designed so that some of the costs of enforcement are borne not by politicians, but by constituents and the courts. Finally, administrative procedures affect the costs to agencies of implementing policies that are opposed by groups enfranchised by these procedures. This alters the incentive structure of the agencies and thereby shapes their decisions." See also Mathew D. McCubbins, Roger G. Noll, & Barry R. Weingast, Structure and Process, Politics and Policy: Administrative Arrangements and the Political Control of Agencies, 75 Va. L. Rev. 431 (1989).

(3) *Congressional versus Presidential Control.* Other political scientists are less persuaded by the structure and process theory and dispute the effectiveness of mechanisms for ongoing congressional control. They argue that the President enjoys several institutional advantages that those arguing for congressional dominance ignore. Keith E. Whittington & Daniel P. Carpenter, Executive Power in American Institutional Development, 1 Persp. On Politics 495, 496, 508 (2003): "[T]he narrative of congressional dominance ignores three entrenched properties of the American political system: (1) the power of the president as party leader. . . (2) the ability of the executive branch to engage in autonomous policy innovation, and (3) the ability of the executive to shape the national policy agenda. . . . The executive may be constrained by Congress, but it has not simply represented congressional interests." The scope of presidential power over administration

is discussed in detail in Section 3. See also Terry M. Moe, An Assessment of the Positive Theory of 'Congressional Dominance,' 12 Leg. Stud. Q. 475 (1987).

(iii) Delegations to Other Institutional Actors

The prior materials focused largely on delegations to public agencies. But Congress delegates to a wide array of actors, including private entities, state governments, and international actors, to name just a few, as well as many entities that straddle categories. ANNE JOSEPH O'CONNELL, BUREAUCRACY AT THE BOUNDARY, 162 U. Pa. L. Rev. 841, 846–51 (2014), analyzes "the considerable bureaucracy, including the [U.S. Postal Service], that is neither an executive agency nor an independent regulatory commission, yet is still at least partially federal. Other examples include the only major operator of passenger trains in the country, Amtrak . . .; the organization that ended the career of cyclist Lance Armstrong, the U.S. Anti-Doping Agency; the primary responder to domestic emergencies, the National Guard; the major international lender to developing countries, part of the World Bank (officially the International Bank for Reconstruction and Development (IBRD)); and the federal government's primary oversight agency, the Government Accountability Office (GAO). Most of these entities have significant ties to the federal government, but they reside at the border between the federal government and either the private sector or another government, whether state, foreign, or Native American tribal. . . . Not only are these often longstanding organizations numerous and diverse in structure, but many also play critical roles in the administrative state . . . [and] have considerable power. For example, Fannie Mae and Freddie Mac, the two largest government-sponsored enterprises (GSEs), . . . [are] among the largest financial institutions in the United States . . . [and the] GAO regularly rules on multi-million-dollar government procurement disputes."

The use of private entities as regulatory decision makers is almost as old as the modern regulatory state. Key New Deal programs relied on industry, professional, and other groups to propose, and sometimes even to set, standards of behavior backed up by the force of federal law. In the last three decades, however, reliance on private entities has expanded so radically that contemporary regimes seem qualitatively, as well as quantitatively, different from New Deal practice. Whether termed "privatization," "outsourcing" or, most recently, "collaboration," the result is a system in which private actors are deeply embedded in public governance. Sometimes these arrangements are contractual. For-profit contractors now wield government-conferred power in areas ranging from running prisons and providing military security to operating charter schools and "managing" the care given to Medicare and Medicaid recipients. In other instances, the private element is so interwoven with governmental decisionmaking that it can be difficult to discern where one ends and the other begins. Self-regulation by the stock exchanges and the private Financial Industry Regulatory Association (FINRA) are central to national securities regulation, and the government itself created what it statutorily denominated a nonprofit corporation, the Public Company Accounting Oversight Board (PCAOB) (p. 922) to play a regulatory role.

Should the fact that a state government, a private entity, or a mixed public-private entity is the recipient of delegated power affect the constitutionality of a delegation, and if so how? Private delegations have received the greatest scrutiny, and so are the focus of much of what follows. But similar issues can arise with respect to a variety of delegations. Section 3.c of this chapter looks at the issue of delegation to institutions other than federal agencies through the lens of appointment and removal.

(1) **Private Delegations.** Recall the insistence of Justice Alito in American Railroads, quoting the D.C. Circuit below, that "Congress 'cannot delegate regulatory authority to a private' entity.'" Justice Alito insisted there was no justification for "not enforce[ing] the nondelegation doctrine with more vigilance" in this context, compared to public delegations, because private entities do not enjoy any constitutional legislative or executive powers "of their own that can be used in ways that resemble lawmaking." Are you convinced? Can't private entities wield private powers in ways that resemble lawmaking? Think about private universities that adopt rules regulating student activities or shopping malls that regulate demonstrations and protests on their premises. Is it clear that these entities are just wielding private power, as opposed to being instances when the government, through its rules regulating private property, has delegated to them power to control others? See Louis L. Jaffe, Law Making by Private Groups, 51 Harv. L. Rev. 201, 220–21(1937).

Another argument for treating private delegations differently is the concern that private entities "may escape the checks and balances woven into the Constitution," Harold J. Krent, The Private Performing the Public: Delimiting Delegations to Private Parties, 65 U. Miami L. Rev. 507, 511 (2011). Justice Alito emphasized that the "Constitution, by careful design, prescribes a process for making law, and within that process there are many accountability checkpoints. . . . It would dash the whole scheme if Congress could give its power away to an entity that is not constrained by those checkpoints." But isn't the same point true of delegations to the executive branch? Alternatively, the Court has sometimes expressed concern that private entities might be biased and use delegated public powers to advance their own self-interest. See Gibson v. Berryhill, 411 U.S. 564 (1973). But again, is that concern unique to private delegations? Note that the D.C. Circuit insisted on remand that allowing Amtrak to develop metrics and standards that would affect other railroad companies violated due process because Amtrak, although a governmental entity, was self-interested. For a discussion of privatization from a due process standpoint, see Ch. V, Sec. 4.d.

One feature that does distinguish private delegates from their public counterparts is the fact that private delegates are exempt Constitution's individual rights protections, unless they are deemed to be state actors for constitutional purposes—as the Supreme Court concluded Amtrak was in American Railroads. But the Court does not make the constitutionality of a delegation turn on whether the delegee is subject to constitutional constraints in wielding its powers.

GILLIAN E. METZGER, PRIVATIZATION AS DELEGATION, 103 Colum. L. Rev. 1367, 1400–08 (2003): "Modern privatized government does not fit easily within the paradigms of U.S. constitutional law . . . [, which] strictly compartmentalizes society into public and private spheres, and does not acknowledge any substantial blurring between the two. . . . As a result, the move to greater government privatization poses a serious threat to the principle of constitutional accountability. . . . The danger is that handing over government programs to private entities will operate to place these programs outside the ambit of constitutional constraints . . . Applying constitutional norms to the government's private partners could solve this problem, but at a significant cost . . . 'Constitutionalizing' the government's private partners effectively transfers the power to decide what rules should bind these private actors from the political branches of government to the federal courts . . . [P]reserving the political branches' regulatory flexibility in privatization contexts is particularly important. . . . The government's ability to tailor regulatory structures to address identified abuses while exploiting private strengths is likely to be pivotal to successful reliance on privatization. Equally important will be allowing governments room to experiment with different approaches to privatization, so that practical experience can inform regulatory choices and governments can address new problems as they emerge."

In a similar vein, JODY FREEMAN, EXTENDING PUBLIC LAW NORMS THROUGH PRIVATIZATION, 116 Harv. L. Rev. 1285, 1285, 1290–91 (2003), argues that "instead of seeing privatization as a means of shrinking government, I imagine it as a mechanism for expanding government's reach into realms traditionally thought private. In other words, privatization can be a means of 'publicization,' through which private actors increasingly commit themselves to traditionally public goals as the price of access to lucrative opportunities to deliver goods and services that might otherwise be provided directly by the state. . . . [The debate over privatization has tended to] pit[ ] economic claims of greater productive efficiency against legal or political arguments that privatization might compromise democratic norms. Unfortunately, this opposition of economic and noneconomic values suggests that privatization represents a zero-sum game between public norms and private power. This oversimplifies the choices presented by any privatization decision. It erroneously suggests that we must sacrifice one set of goals entirely to the other because the two sets are fundamentally incompatible. I maintain that we might find ways to structure privatization that allow us to have some of each." Freeman argues that "[t]he argument for publicization is strongest in instances when services are highly contentious, value-laden, and hard to specify, and when providers enjoy significant discretion; when services affect vulnerable populations with few exit options and little political clout; and/or when the motivation for privatization is explicitly ideological or clearly corrupt. These are not the exclusive factors to consider, but they reflect the most pressing concerns of the public law perspective on privatization, and this perspective must be given voice in a way that will facilitate engagement with adherents of the economic view. . . ."

Yet another constitutional concern with privatization is that it may serve to aggrandize executive power, "provid[ing an] outsourcing agency with the means of achieving distinct public policy goals that—but for the pretext of technocratic outsourcing—would be impossible or much more difficult to attain in the ordinary course of nonprivatized public administration." Jon D. Michaels, Privatization's Pretensions, 77 U. Chi. L. Rev. 717 (2010).

(2) ***Delegation to States or State/Federal Entities.*** Delegations to states are perhaps the most common. States play critical roles in implementing a broad array of federal regulatory schemes and programs. For example, the states are responsible for incorporating the NAAQS that EPA issues under the Clean Air Act, which were at issue in Whitman, into state implementation plans that apply to emissions within their borders. Similarly, Medicaid and Social Security Disability are implemented by state agencies. Jessica Bulman-Pozen, in Federalism as a Safeguard of the Separation of Powers, 112 Colum. L. Rev. 475 (2012), notes that "when Congress gives states a role in executing federal law, it tends to delegate not exclusively but rather concurrently: States may implement federal law by conforming to standards set by the federal executive; state and federal agencies may implement the same regulatory provisions or enforce the same statutes; or state officials may execute federal law under the supervision of a federal agency." Congress also delegates power to a range of joint federal-state entities, like the National Guard. Each state has a national guard, commanded by the state's governor, but these state national guards are regulated and funded by the federal government and the President can call it into service under the President's command. See O'CONNELL, supra, at 862.

Should congressional delegations to states be treated the same as private delegations? The same as delegations to federal agencies? Some other standard? What about delegations to joint federal-state entities? In his dissent in Whitman at the D.C. Circuit, Judge Tatel argued that "[b]ecause the Clean Air Act gives politically accountable state governments primary responsibility for determining how to distribute the burdens of pollution reduction and therefore how the NAAQS will affect specific industries and individual businesses, courts have less reason to second-guess the specificity of the congressional delegation." Do you agree?

(3) ***Delegations to International Bodies.*** "Most nations today participate in a dense network of international cooperation that requires them to grant authority to international actors. At varying levels this means that the individual state surrenders some autonomy to international bodies or other states by authorizing them to participate in decisionmaking processes and to take actions that affect the state. . . . What distinguishes international delegations from mere international commitments is the existence of an entity that has been granted the authority to make decisions or take actions that bind the state or commit its resources." Curtis A. Bradley & Judith G. Kelley, The Concept of International Delegation, 71 Law & Contemp. Probs. 1, 3 (2008). In the United States, "[t]he practice of delegating to international institutions— vesting them with the authority to develop binding rules—sometimes looks like the next New Deal. Despite its continuing mistrust of international engagements, the United States continues to vest new authority in established organizations, such as the United Nations, the Organisation for Economic Co-operation and Development, and the International Labour Organization, and to create new institutions, like the World Trade Organization and the North American Free Trade Agreement, that exercise considerable power over U.S. affairs. The march seems inexorable." Edward T. Swaine, The Constitutionality of International Delegations, 104 Colum L. Rev. 1492, 1492 (2004).

International entities with delegated legal authority can include:

- Adjudicatory bodies, such as the World Trade Organization's Dispute Settlement Body, which decides the outcome of trade disputes, based on recommendation of a Dispute Panel (which is virtually guaranteed acceptance because rejection requires a consensus of members, including the losing nation), and the North American Free Trade Association's arbitral panels, which decide appeals of "dumping" cases from the Court of International Trade.

- Monitoring and enforcement bodies, such as the International Atomic Energy Association and the Organization for the Prohibition of Chemical Weapons, which can order states to allow inspections and make binding determinations about compliance with obligations under relevant treaties and international agreements.

- Policymaking bodies, such as the World Trade Organization, which can adopt binding interpretations of the often broad principles of WTO trade agreements on a supermajority vote of members.

The intense controversy over the legality and wisdom of these developments involves scholars of international law as well as constitutional law and has been bitter even by academic standards. For example, Jeb Rubenfeld's assertion that "[t]he antidemocratic qualities of the United Nations, the International Monetary Fund, and other international governance organizations—their centralization, their opacity, their remoteness from popular or representative politics, their elitism, their unaccountability-are well known," The Two World Orders, 27 Wilson Q. 22, 34 (2003), prompted Anne-Marie Slaughter to lambaste his analysis as "historically inaccurate[,] politically naïve [and] unrecognizable to an international lawyer." A Dangerous Myth, Prospect, Jan. 22, 2004, at 11, 11. The issues posed by delegations to international bodies are largely beyond the scope of this book, but the interested student can find provocative reading in The Law and Politics of International Delegation, 71 Law & Contemp. Probs. 1 (2008) (collecting articles from two Duke Law School workshops); Julian G. Ku, The Delegation of Federal Power to International Organizations: New Problems with Old Solutions, 85 Minn. L. Rev. 71 (2000); John C. Yoo, The New Sovereignty and the Old Constitution: The Chemical Weapons Convention and the Appointments Clause, 15 Const. Comment. 87 (1998).

b. Congressional Control of Regulatory Policy

> *(1) Legislation and Vetoes*
> *(2) Appropriations and Spending*
> *(3) Oversight and Investigations*
> *(4) Direct Control over Regulatory Actors*

One of the most fundamental ways in which contemporary U.S. government differs from what the Framers imagined is the relative importance of statutes and the common law. At every level of government, the common law has been displaced as the dominant system of social regulation. Initially, statutes themselves set the legal rules that supplemented or supplanted the law made by courts. Now, statutes set in motion administrative processes, and agencies make the rules that regulate economic and social activity.[9]

Nondelegation jurisprudence effectively endorsed this transformation as a constitutional matter, but the shift to administrative government also transformed the roles of Congress and the President— and here the course of constitutional reconciliation has been far more contentious. "From their originally contemplated role as initiators of policy, the House and Senate now often occupy a reactive role, responding

---

[9] See Edward L. Rubin, Law and Legislation in the Administrative State, 89 Colum. L. Rev. 369 (1989).

in formal and informal ways to policy generated by agencies. From this originally contemplated role as check upon hasty and imprudent legislation, the President as chief administrator now often forces Congress into the position of checking policy specified by the executive." Cynthia R. Farina, The Consent of the Governed: Against Simple Rules for a Complex World, 72 Chi.-Kent L. Rev. 987, 1018 (1997). Both Congress and the President recognize that the stakes are high—and the contemporary pattern of divided government (one party controlling the presidency, the other controlling one or both houses of Congress), coupled with increasing polarization of Republican and Democratic policy preferences, produce more competition than cooperation.

Here we focus on methods used by Congress to direct and influence regulatory outcomes, including legislation and vetoes, appropriations and spending, investigations, and control over executive officers. The central factual background underlying all of these topics is the reality of pervasive delegations. Having granted the executive branch broad authority and discretion, how does Congress continue to exert control and ensure agencies pay attention to governing statutory requirements and congressional preferences?

(1) Legislation and Vetoes

> *INS v. CHADHA*
> **Notes on Direction by Legislation**

Every Bill which shall have passed the House of Representatives and the Senate, shall, before it becomes a Law, be presented to the President of the United States ... Every Order, Resolution, or Vote to which the Concurrence of the Senate and House of Representatives may be necessary (except on a question of Adjournment) shall be presented to the President of the United States; and before the Same shall take Effect, shall be approved by him, or being disapproved by him, shall be repassed by two thirds of the Senate and House of Representatives, according to the Rules and Limitations prescribed in the Case of a Bill.

U.S. Const., Art. I, § 7

IMMIGRATION AND NATURALIZATION SERVICE v. CHADHA

Supreme Court of the United States (1983).
462 U.S. 919.

■ CHIEF JUSTICE BURGER delivered the opinion of the Court.

[For most of our Nation's history, an alien found deportable under relevant immigration law could remain in the United States only if some member of Congress obtained a private bill (that is, legislation that applied uniquely to the individual(s) named). The Immigration and

Nationality Act of 1952 changed this, delegating to the Attorney General (who in turn delegated to the INS)[10] the discretion to "suspend deportation" of an alien who has been physically present in the United States for at least seven years, is of good moral character, and "is a person whose deportation would, in the opinion of the Attorney General, result in extreme hardship to the alien, or to his spouse, parent, or child who is a citizen of the United States or an alien lawfully admitted for permanent residence." However, this power was conditioned upon neither house of Congress disagreeing. Subsection (c) of § 244 provides:

> (1) Upon application by any alien who is found by the Attorney General to meet [these] requirements . . . the Attorney General may in his discretion suspend deportation of such alien. If the deportation of any alien is suspended under the provisions of this subsection, a complete and detailed statement of the facts and pertinent provisions of law in the case shall be reported to the Congress with the reasons for such suspension. . . .

> (2) [I]f during the session of the Congress at which a case is reported, or prior to the close of the session of the Congress next following the session at which a case is reported, either the Senate or the House of Representatives passes a resolution stating in substance that it does not favor the suspension of such deportation, the Attorney General shall thereupon deport such alien or authorize the alien's voluntary departure at his own expense under the order of deportation in the manner provided by law. If, within the time above specified, neither the Senate nor the House of Representatives shall pass such a resolution, the Attorney General shall cancel deportation proceedings.[11]

Chadha, an East Indian born in Kenya, was deportable for overstaying his nonimmigrant student visa. He applied for and received a suspension of deportation, and his case was laid before Congress. The House Judiciary Committee reported out a resolution opposing "the granting of permanent residence in the United States to [six] aliens" including Chadha. Representative Eilberg, Chair of the Subcommittee on Immigration, Citizenship, and International Law, made a brief statement that

> [i]t was the feeling of the committee, after reviewing 340 cases, that the aliens contained in the resolution [Chadha and five others] did not meet these statutory requirements, particularly

---

[10] [Ed.] In 2003, the responsibilities of the INS were transferred to the Immigration and Customs Enforcement (ICE), Customs and Border Protection (CBP), and the Citizenship and Immigration Services (CIS). See the Homeland Security Act of 2002, Pub. L. No. 107–296, 116 Stat. 2135.

[11] [Ed.] Prior to the 1952 Act, Congress experimented briefly with a system in which deportation could be suspended on the Attorney General's recommendation if Congress affirmatively approved by concurrent resolution. This proved not significantly less burdensome than the private bill system.

as it relates to hardship; and it is the opinion of the committee that their deportation should not be suspended.

The resolution was passed without debate or recorded vote. After deportation proceedings were instituted, Chadha appealed to the Ninth Circuit, which held the legislative veto unconstitutional and enjoined Chadha's deportation. The Supreme Court granted certiorari and first disposed of several justiciability issues.]

III

We turn now to the question whether action of one House of Congress under § 244(c)(2) violates strictures of the Constitution. We begin, of course, with the presumption that the challenged statute is valid. Its wisdom is not the concern of the courts; if a challenged action does not violate the Constitution, it must be sustained. . . . By the same token, the fact that a given law or procedure is efficient, convenient, and useful in facilitating functions of government, standing alone, will not save it if it is contrary to the Constitution.

. . . The decision to provide the President with a limited and qualified power to nullify proposed legislation by veto was based on the profound conviction of the Framers that the powers conferred on Congress were the powers to be most carefully circumscribed. It is beyond doubt that lawmaking was a power to be shared by both Houses and the President. . . . The President's role in the lawmaking process also reflects the Framers' careful efforts to check whatever propensity a particular Congress might have to enact oppressive, improvident, or ill-considered measures. . . . The Court also has observed that the Presentment Clauses serve the important purpose of assuring that a "national" perspective is grafted on the legislative process: "The President is a representative of the people just as the members of the Senate and of the House are, and it may be, at some times, on some subjects, that the President elected by all the people is rather more representative of them all than are the members of either body of the Legislature whose constituencies are local and not countrywide. . . ." Myers v. United States, 272 U.S. [52,] 123 [(1926)] [p. 918].

The bicameral requirement of Art. I, §§ 1, 7 was of scarcely less concern to the Framers than was the Presidential veto and indeed the two concepts are interdependent. By providing that no law could take effect without the concurrence of the prescribed majority of the Members of both Houses, the Framers reemphasized their belief, already remarked upon in connection with the Presentment Clauses, that legislation should not be enacted unless it has been carefully and fully considered by the Nation's elected officials. . . . [I]n Federalist No. 51 Hamilton . . . point[ed] up the need to divide and disperse power in order to protect liberty: "In republican government, the legislative authority necessarily predominates. The remedy for this inconveniency is to divide the legislature into different branches; and to render them, by different modes of election and different principles of action, as little connected with each other as the nature of their common functions and their common dependence on the society will admit." . . .

We see therefore that the Framers were acutely conscious that the bicameral requirement and the Presentment Clauses would serve essential constitutional functions. The President's participation in the legislative process was to protect the Executive Branch from Congress and to protect the whole people from improvident laws. The division of the Congress into two distinctive bodies assures that the legislative power would be exercised only after opportunity for full study and debate in separate settings. The President's unilateral veto power, in turn, was limited by the power of two thirds of both Houses of Congress to overrule a veto thereby precluding final arbitrary action of one person. It emerges clearly that the prescription for legislative action in Art. I, §§ 1, 7 represents the Framers' decision that the legislative power of the Federal government be exercised in accord with a single, finely wrought and exhaustively considered, procedure.

IV

The Constitution sought to divide the delegated powers of the new federal government into three defined categories, legislative, executive and judicial, to assure, as nearly as possible, that each Branch of government would confine itself to its assigned responsibility. The hydraulic pressure inherent within each of the separate Branches to exceed the outer limits of its power, even to accomplish desirable objectives, must be resisted. Although not "hermetically" sealed from one another, Buckley v. Valeo, 424 U.S. [1,] 126 [(1976), p. 891], the powers delegated to the three Branches are functionally identifiable. When any Branch acts, it is presumptively exercising the power the Constitution has delegated to it. When the Executive acts, it presumptively acts in an executive or administrative capacity as defined in Art. II. And when, as here, one House of Congress purports to act, it is presumptively acting within its assigned sphere.

Beginning with this presumption, we must nevertheless establish that the challenged action under § 244(c)(2) is of the kind to which the procedural requirements of Art. I, § 7 apply. Not every action taken by either House is subject to the bicameralism and presentment requirements of Art. I. Whether actions taken by either House are, in law and fact, an exercise of legislative power depends not on their form but upon "whether they contain matter which is properly to be regarded as legislative in its character and effect." S.Rep. No. 1335, 54th Cong., 2d Sess., 8 (1897).[12]

---

[12] [Ed.] This Judiciary Committee Report considered whether presentment was constitutionally required in connection with a "resolution" referred to in the River and Harbors Act of 1892. The Act limited surveys and preliminary estimates for building or repairing bridges to a list designated in the Act. It further provided that once a report was submitted on a listed project, no further report or estimate could be made in the fiscal year "unless ordered by a resolution of Congress." The Report concluded that this provision "partakes of the character of

Examination of the action taken here by one House pursuant to § 244(c)(2) reveals that it was essentially legislative in purpose and effect. [T]he House took action that had the purpose and effect of altering the legal rights, duties and relations of persons, including the Attorney General, Executive Branch officials and Chadha, all outside the legislative branch. Section 244(c)(2) purports to authorize one House of Congress to require the Attorney General to deport an individual alien whose deportation otherwise would be cancelled under § 244. The one-House veto operated in this case to overrule the Attorney General and mandate Chadha's deportation; absent the House action, Chadha would remain in the United States. Congress has acted and its action has altered Chadha's status.

The legislative character of the one-House veto in this case is confirmed by the character of the Congressional action it supplants. Neither the House of Representatives nor the Senate contends that, absent the veto provision in § 244(c)(2), either of them, or both of them acting together, could effectively require the Attorney General to deport an alien once the Attorney General, in the exercise of legislatively delegated authority,[16] had determined the alien should remain in the United States. Without the challenged provision in § 244(c)(2), this could

---

an ordinary request for information from a Department which has never been deemed to require the approval of the President."

[16] Congress protests that affirming the Court of Appeals in this case will sanction "lawmaking by the Attorney General. . . . Why is the Attorney General exempt from submitting his proposed changes in the law to the full bicameral process?" Brief of the United States House of Representatives 40. To be sure, some administrative agency action—rule making, for example—may resemble "lawmaking." See 5 U.S.C. § 551(4), which defines an agency's "rule" as "the whole or part of an agency statement of general or particular applicability and future effect designed to implement, interpret, or prescribe law or policy . . ." This Court has referred to agency activity as being "quasi-legislative" in character. Humphrey's Executor v. United States, 295 U.S. 602, 628 (1935) [p. 920]. Clearly, however, "[i]n the framework of our Constitution, the President's power to see that the laws are faithfully executed refutes the idea that he is to be a lawmaker." Youngstown Sheet & Tube Co. v. Sawyer, 343 U.S. 579, 587 (1952) [p. 871]. When the Attorney General performs his duties pursuant to § 244, he does not exercise "legislative" power. The bicameral process is not necessary as a check on the Executive's administration of the laws because his administrative activity cannot reach beyond the limits of the statute that created it-a statute duly enacted pursuant to Art. I, §§ 1, 7. The constitutionality of the Attorney General's execution of the authority delegated to him by § 244 involves only a question of delegation doctrine. The courts, when a case or controversy arises, can always "ascertain whether the will of Congress has been obeyed," Yakus v. United States, 321 U.S. 414, 425 (1944) [p. 811], and can enforce adherence to statutory standards. See Ethyl Corp. v. EPA, 541 F.2d 1, 68 (CADC) (en banc) (separate statement of Leventhal, J.), cert. denied, 426 U.S. 941 (1976). It is clear, therefore, that the Attorney General acts in his presumptively Art. II capacity when he administers the Immigration and Nationality Act. Executive action under legislatively delegated authority that might resemble "legislative" action in some respects is not subject to the approval of both Houses of Congress and the President for the reason that the Constitution does not so require. That kind of Executive action is always subject to check by the terms of the legislation that authorized it; and if that authority is exceeded it is open to judicial review as well as the power of Congress to modify or revoke the authority entirely. A one-House veto is clearly legislative in both character and effect and is not so checked; the need for the check provided by Art. I, §§ 1, 7 is therefore clear. Congress' authority to delegate portions of its power to administrative agencies provides no support for the argument that Congress can constitutionally control administration of the laws by way of a Congressional veto.

have been achieved, if at all, only by legislation requiring deportation.[17] Similarly, a veto by one House of Congress under § 244(c)(2) cannot be justified as an attempt at amending the standards set out in § 244(a)(1), or as a repeal of § 244 as applied to Chadha. Amendment and repeal of statutes, no less than enactment, must conform with Art. I.

The nature of the decision implemented by the one-House veto in this case further manifests its legislative character. After long experience with the clumsy, time consuming private bill procedure, Congress made a deliberate choice to delegate to the Executive Branch, and specifically to the Attorney General, the authority to allow deportable aliens to remain in this country in certain specified circumstances. It is not disputed that this choice to delegate authority is precisely the kind of decision that can be implemented only in accordance with the procedures set out in Art. I. Disagreement with the Attorney General's decision on Chadha's deportation—that is, Congress' decision to deport Chadha—no less than Congress' original choice to delegate to the Attorney General the authority to make that decision, involves determinations of policy that Congress can implement in only one way: bicameral passage followed by presentment to the President. Congress must abide by its delegation of authority until that delegation is legislatively altered or revoked.

Finally, we see that when the Framers intended to authorize either House of Congress to act alone and outside of its prescribed bicameral legislative role, they narrowly and precisely defined the procedure for such action. There are but four provisions in the Constitution, explicit and unambiguous, by which one House may act alone with the unreviewable force of law, not subject to the President's veto: (a) The House of Representatives alone was given the power to initiate impeachments; (b) The Senate alone was given the power to conduct trials following impeachment on charges initiated by the House and to convict following trial; (c) The Senate alone was given final unreviewable power to approve or to disapprove presidential appointments; (d) The Senate alone was given unreviewable power to ratify treaties negotiated by the President. Clearly, when the Draftsmen sought to confer special powers on one House, independent of the other House, or of the President, they did so in explicit, unambiguous terms. . . .

The veto authorized by § 244(c)(2) doubtless has been in many respects a convenient shortcut; the "sharing" with the Executive by Congress of its authority over aliens in this manner is, on its face, an appealing compromise. . . . The choices we discern as having been made in the Constitutional Convention impose burdens on governmental processes that often seem clumsy, inefficient, even unworkable, but those hard choices were consciously made by men who had lived under a form of government that permitted arbitrary governmental acts to go

---

[17] We express no opinion as to whether such legislation would violate any constitutional provision.

unchecked. There is no support in the Constitution or decisions of this Court for the proposition that the cumbersomeness and delays often encountered in complying with explicit Constitutional standards may be avoided, either by the Congress or by the President. With all the obvious flaws of delay, untidiness, and potential for abuse, we have not yet found a better way to preserve freedom than by making the exercise of power subject to the carefully crafted restraints spelled out in the Constitution.

We hold that the Congressional veto provision in § 244(c)(2) is severable from the Act and that it is unconstitutional. Accordingly, the judgment of the Court of Appeals is

Affirmed.

■ JUSTICE POWELL, concurring in the judgment.

The Court's decision . . . apparently will invalidate every use of the legislative veto. The breadth of this holding gives one pause. Congress has included the veto in literally hundreds of statutes, dating back to the 1930s. Congress clearly views this procedure as essential to controlling the delegation of power to administrative agencies. One reasonably may disagree with Congress' assessment of the veto's utility, but the respect due its judgment as a coordinate branch of Government cautions that our holding should be no more extensive than necessary to decide this case. In my view, the case may be decided on a narrower ground. When Congress finds that a particular person does not satisfy the statutory criteria for permanent residence in this country it has assumed a judicial function in violation of the principle of separation of powers. . . .

. . . One abuse that was prevalent during the Confederation was the exercise of judicial power by the state legislatures. The Framers were well acquainted with the danger of subjecting the determination of the rights of one person to the "tyranny of shifting majorities." . . . Their concern that a legislature should not be able unilaterally to impose a substantial deprivation on one person was expressed [in] specific provisions, such as the Bill of Attainder Clause, Art. I, § 9, cl. 3. . . . This Clause, and the separation of powers doctrine generally, reflect the Framers' concern that trial by a legislature lacks the safeguards necessary to prevent the abuse of power. . . .

On its face, the House's action appears clearly adjudicatory.[7] The House did not enact a general rule; rather it made its own determination

---

[7] The Court concludes that Congress' action was legislative in character because each branch "presumptively act[s] within its assigned sphere." The Court's presumption provides a useful starting point, but does not conclude the inquiry. Nor does the fact that the House's action alters an individual's legal status indicate, as the Court reasons, that the action is legislative rather than adjudicative in nature. In determining whether one branch unconstitutionally has assumed a power central to another branch, the traditional characterization of the assumed power as legislative, executive, or judicial may provide some guidance. But reasonable minds may disagree over the character of an act and the more helpful inquiry, in my view, is whether the act in question raises the dangers the Framers sought to avoid.

that six specific persons did not comply with certain statutory criteria. . . .

The impropriety of the House's assumption of this function is confirmed by the fact that its action raises the very danger the Framers sought to avoid—the exercise of unchecked power. In deciding whether Chadha deserves to be deported, Congress is not subject to any internal constraints that prevent it from arbitrarily depriving him of the right to remain in this country.[9] Unlike the judiciary or an administrative agency, Congress is not bound by established substantive rules. Nor is it subject to the procedural safeguards, such as the right to counsel and a hearing before an impartial tribunal, that are present when a court or an agency[10] adjudicates individual rights. The only effective constraint on Congress' power is political, but Congress is most accountable politically when it prescribes rules of general applicability. When it decides rights of specific persons, those rights are subject to "the tyranny of a shifting majority." . . .

■ JUSTICE WHITE, dissenting.

. . . Without the legislative veto, Congress is faced with a Hobson's choice: either to refrain from delegating the necessary authority, leaving itself with a hopeless task of writing laws with the requisite specificity to cover endless special circumstances across the entire policy landscape, or in the alternative, to abdicate its law-making function to the executive branch and independent agencies. To choose the former leaves major national problems unresolved; to opt for the latter risks unaccountable policymaking by those not elected to fill that role. . . .

The legislative veto developed initially in response to the problems of reorganizing the sprawling government structure created in response to the Depression. The Reorganization Acts established the chief model for the legislative veto. When President Hoover requested authority to reorganize the government in 1929, he coupled his request that the "Congress be willing to delegate its authority over the problem (subject to defined principles) to the Executive" with a proposal for legislative review. He proposed that the Executive "should act upon approval of a joint committee of Congress or with the reservation of power of revision by Congress within some limited period adequate for its consideration." Pub. Papers 432 (1929) [Justice White then describes how the legislative veto was part of an accommodation between Congress and President

---

[9] When Congress grants particular individuals relief or benefits under its spending power, the danger of oppressive action that the separation of powers was designed to avoid is not implicated. Similarly, Congress may authorize the admission of individual aliens by special acts, but it does not follow that Congress unilaterally may make a judgment that a particular alien has no legal right to remain in this country. . . .

[10] We have recognized that independent regulatory agencies and departments of the Executive Branch often exercise authority that is "judicial in nature." Buckley v. Valeo, 424 U.S. 1, 140–141 (1976). This function, however, forms part of the agencies' execution of public law and is subject to the procedural safeguards, including judicial review, provided by the Administrative Procedure Act.

Roosevelt in which more than 30 statutes conferred "exceptional" wartime powers on the President. The legislative veto "balanced" delegations of statutory authority in new areas including the space program and international agreements on nuclear energy. During the 1970s, it was part of statutory resolutions of "major constitutional disputes between the President and Congress" in the area of war powers, emergency power, foreign arms sale, and exports of nuclear technology. It "balance[d] broad delegations in legislation emerging from the energy crisis of the 1970's," and was a condition of broad rulemaking granted the Commissioner of Education to supersede "fragmented and narrow grant programs [that] inevitably lead to Executive-Legislative confrontations."]

Even this brief review suffices to demonstrate that the legislative veto is more than "efficient, convenient, and useful." It is an important if not indispensable political invention that allows the President and Congress to resolve major constitutional and policy differences, assures the accountability of independent regulatory agencies, and preserves Congress' control over lawmaking. Perhaps there are other means of accommodation and accountability, but the increasing reliance of Congress upon the legislative veto suggests that the alternatives to which Congress must now turn are not entirely satisfactory.

. . . The power to exercise a legislative veto is not the power to write new law without bicameral approval or presidential consideration. The veto must be authorized by statute and may only negative what an Executive department or independent agency has proposed. On its face, the legislative veto no more allows one House of Congress to make law than does the presidential veto confer such power upon the President. . . .

. . . The Court's holding today that all legislative-type action must be enacted through the lawmaking process ignores that legislative authority is routinely delegated to the Executive branch, to the independent regulatory agencies, and to private individuals and groups. . . . This Court's decisions sanctioning such delegations make clear that Article I does not require all action with the effect of legislation to be passed as a law. . . . If Congress may delegate lawmaking power to independent and executive agencies, it is most difficult to understand Article I as forbidding Congress from also reserving a check on legislative power for itself. Absent the veto, the agencies receiving delegations of legislative or quasi-legislative power may issue regulations having the force of law without bicameral approval and without the President's signature. It is thus not apparent why the reservation of a veto over the exercise of that legislative power must be subject to a more exacting test. In both cases, it is enough that the initial statutory authorizations comply with the Article I requirements. . . .

. . . Today's decision strikes down in one fell swoop provisions in more laws enacted by Congress than the Court has cumulatively invalidated in its history. I fear it will now be more difficult "to insure that the fundamental policy decisions in our society will be made not by an appointed official but by the body immediately responsible to the people," Arizona v. California, 373 U.S. 546, 626.

I must dissent.

NOTES

(1) **Methodology.** Chief Justice Burger's majority opinion is a classic example of formalist separation-of-powers analysis. Yet the opinion adopts a fully functionalist mode (Part III) in exploring the functions of the bicameral and presentment requirements to check legislative power. What work does Part III do in the Chief Justice's analysis? Justice White's dissent is generally seen as an example of functionalist analysis, but most of his opinion might be better described as a pragmatic assessment of the veto's role in the development of the regulatory state. The real functionalist seems to be Justice Powell, who identifies the goals and values embedded in the constitutional structure and concludes that the veto in the context of adjudication cannot be reconciled with those goals and values. (Note particularly footnote 7 in Powell's opinion.)

Justice White's central point is that the constitutionality of the legislative veto needed to be assessed against the baseline of delegation; having sanctioned the broad legislative delegations of authority that gave birth to the modern administrative state, separation of powers concerns necessitated that the Court be similarly flexible in assessing the techniques Congress could use to still exert policymaking control. White's point could be translated into a claim about methodological consistency: Having taken a functionalist stance on delegation, the Court should not turn formalist in addressing the aftermath of delegation. Are you convinced?

Could Congress constitutionally accomplish the deportation of Chadha, by name, through the full Art. I, § 7 process? Almost certainly not: private bills benefiting only specified individuals are constitutionally different from legislation burdening only named individuals. (Such legislation in Chadha's case might not be a bill of attainder given Congress's extensive power over immigration, but surely the due process clause would come into play.) To a functionalist, this would make a difference in assessing the veto's constitutionality here. Might it also matter to a formalist, insofar as it indicates Congress is seeking to wield power it lacks constitutionally? Isn't this, at root, Justice Powell's argument?

(2) **Does Context Matter?** For Justice Powell, the most important factor in *Chadha* was the use of the legislative veto with respect to specified individuals, which in his view made the House's action adjudicatory. If you have studied the materials in Chapter III on the distinction between legislation and adjudication, you've seen that drawing the line between these two functions is hard. Does the fact that Congress historically provided relief from deportation via a private bill call Justice Powell's characterization into question?

Although Chadha involved adjudication, rulemaking was also an important setting for legislative veto provisions, particularly starting in the 1970s. Should the constitutional analysis change in that context? If agencies acting under rulemaking delegations are understood to wield legislative power, does that make the legislative veto more constitutional? For an argument that it does, see Ilan Wurman, Constitutional Administration, 69 Stan. L. Rev. 359, 385 (2017).

PETER L. STRAUSS, IN WAS THERE A BABY IN THE BATHWATER? A COMMENT ON THE SUPREME COURT'S LEGISLATIVE VETO DECISION, 1983 Duke L.J. 789, 805–807, 816, argues more broadly that substantive context should have received more attention in Chadha: "[P]olitical uses of legislative vetoes warrant special analysis. . . . [These] concern chiefly public measures primarily related to the internal organization of government and affecting the interests of private persons only indirectly; they reflect areas of direct presidential initiative and responsibility. . . . Reorganization acts, measures concerned with budgetary adjustment (impoundment), foreign relations, and war (matters of the character Chief Justice Marshall long ago referred to as 'questions in their nature political,' [Marbury v. Madison, 5 U.S. at 137], . . . may all be described fairly as a setting for horse-trading between the President and Congress: the authority subject to the veto will be that of the President himself; no alternative means of control is obvious; precise congressional standard-setting or structural arrangements are probably inadvisable; and a sharing of political authority is warranted by Congress' legitimate interests in the subject matter and the consequent desirability of committing Congress to support of the action to be taken. . . .

". . . In . . . a continuing relationship [such as the budget process], limiting one participant to episodic, formal, even clumsy acts is likely to produce rigidity and a covetousness about power that will hamper the effective conduct of government and may weaken the presidency far more than the alternative. The same is true for reorganization acts; in a government premised on the selection of a single executive as its head, it is internally sensible and externally non-threatening for the President to be the prime shaper of the internal structures of government, subject to congressional disapproval. . . ."

(3) **The Aftermath in the Courts.** Two weeks after Chadha, the Court summarily affirmed two D.C. Circuit decisions that invalidated the one-house and the two-house veto in the context of rulemaking. Process Gas Consumers Group v. Consumer Energy Council of Am., 463 U.S. 1216 (1983), affirming Consumers Energy Council of Am. v. FERC, 673 F.2d 425 (D.C. Cir. 1982) and Consumers Union of the United States v. FTC, 691 F.2d 575 (D.C. Cir. 1982). Justice Powell did not participate in the decision; only Justice Rehnquist would have set the cases for argument. Note that the lawyer who represented Chadha, Alan Morrison of Public Citizen, also represented the anti-legislative-veto petitioners in these two cases. Given how central rulemaking had become by then, were these two rulemaking cases really the "aftermath" to Chadha, or were they the main show?

Lower courts then struggled to clean up the mess created by 200+ statutes containing a veto. The issue was whether the invalid provision was severable—traditionally determined by asking whether the legislature would have wanted the balance of the statutory scheme to remain effective even without the unconstitutional portion. Justice White's account of the history emphasizes that the veto was often the condition on which Congress agreed to the Executive's request for significant delegation of power. Nonetheless, courts generally severed veto provisions. Is this surprising, given the profound disruption of invalidating established regulatory programs? Compare Free Enterprise Fund v. PCAOB (p. 922). However, in contexts closer to the historical core of the veto's development, courts sometimes recognized that the veto was the quid pro quo for delegation and struck down the entire scheme. For one such case, involving presidential power to refuse to spend (impound) appropriated funds, see p. 855.

(4) *The Aftermath in Congress.* An aspect of U.S. constitutional history that we take for granted (but which lawyers from aspiring constitutional democracies recognize as remarkable) is the routine willingness of Congress and the President to acquiesce in even quite unpalatable judicial decisions. Official defiance of Supreme Court constitutional holdings is an extraordinary event for us. In the case of Chadha, the extraordinary occurred. Between the time Chadha was decided and 2004, more than 400 new legislative vetoes appeared in legislation signed into law by Presidents Reagan, George H. W. Bush, Clinton, and George W. Bush. The vast majority of these attached committee and subcommittee veto conditions to agency use of appropriated funds. Louis Fisher, Cong. Res. Serv., RS22132, Legislative Vetoes After Chadha 2, 4 (2005).

When President Reagan signed a 1984 appropriations bill containing committee veto provisions, he issued a signing statement (see Sec. 3.c) that the Administration considered the veto provision legally nonbinding. In other words, agencies would spend appropriated funds without regard to appropriator approval. NEAL DEVINS & LOUIS FISHER, THE DEMOCRATIC CONSTITUTION 94–96 (2004): "The House Appropriations Committee knew how to respond. It threatened to repeal legislation that allowed the National Aeronautics and Space Administration (NASA) to exceed its spending caps subject to committee approval. Because of Reagan's statement, the committee told NASA that it could exceed its caps only through the enactment of supplemental legislation, requiring approval from both houses of Congress and presentment to the President. Not surprisingly, NASA head James M. Beggs much preferred the limited legislative veto check to the onerous demand that NASA obtain formal positive law approval before it exceeds its spending caps. Beggs successfully pleaded his case to Congress, seeking 'an informal agreement' and promising 'not to exceed amounts for Committee designated programs without the approval of the Committee of Appropriations.'

"In addition to informal legislative vetoes, Congress continues to put committee vetoes in public laws, and agencies comply out of self-interest. They know that any attempt on their part to defy committee control is likely to produce the kind of backlash seen in the NASA dispute. Executive agencies have to live with their review committees year after year and have a much greater incentive to make accommodations and stick by them. Presidents and their legal advisors can indulge in dramatic confrontations with Congress on these issues; agencies, however, do not want bloody dogfights with the committees that authorize their programs and provide funds. . . .

"By misreading the history of legislative vetoes and failing to comprehend the subtleties of the legislative process, the Court directed the executive and legislative branches to adhere to procedures that would be impracticable and unworkable. Neither Congress nor the executive branch wanted the static model of government offered by the Court . . . [Chadha] simply drove underground a set of legislative and committee vetoes that used to operate in plain sight."

Do you agree with this criticism of Chadha? Requiring notification is plainly lawful, and this history indicates it is often just as effective. If so, is limiting Congress to requiring notification such a big deal? See also Edward H. Stiglitz, Unitary Innovations and Political Accountability, 99 Cornell Law Review 1133 (2014) (concluding, based on a dataset of state session laws, that "legislatures respond to a judicial invalidation of the legislative veto by augmenting alternative tools of administrative control").

(5) **Clinton v. New York and The Line Item Veto Act: Article I, § 7 Strikes Again.** In 1996, with great political fanfare, Congress enacted a statute that authorized the President to sign a bill into law but then, in specified circumstances, "cancel" portions of it. Specifically, the President could "cancel in whole" (1) any dollar amount of discretionary budget authority; (2) any item of new direct spending; or (3) any limited tax benefit. The power had to be exercised within five days of signing and was conditioned on a number of substantive and procedural requirements. In identifying items for cancellation the President was required to consider the legislative history, purposes, and other relevant information about the items. The President had to find, with respect to each cancellation, that it would: "(i) reduce the Federal budget deficit; (ii) not impair any essential Government functions; and (iii) not harm the national interest." Moreover, the President had to transmit a special message to Congress notifying it of each cancellation within five calendar days (excluding Sundays) after enactment of the canceled provision. Although the cancellation authority was an amendment to the Anti-Deficiency Act, which regulates presidential impoundment of funds, see p. 855, it was named (and publicized as) The Line Item Veto Act.

CLINTON V. CITY OF NEW YORK, 524 U.S. 417 (1998), involved use of this authority by President Clinton. He followed all the statutory requirements in cancelling provisions that would have relieved New York City of an obligation to repay $2.6 billion in Medicare overpayments and that would have given advantageous tax treatment to certain farmer cooperatives. The City and the Snake River Potato Growers sued, alleging that the cancellation authority was unconstitutional.

For Justice Stevens, who wrote for six members of the Court, it was an attempt to authorize the President to amend a statute, by repealing a portion of it, through a process that did not comply with Article I, § 7's bicameral and presentment requirements. Under INS v. Chadha, which is taken up in Section 3, the attempt was clearly unconstitutional. For Justices Scalia,

Breyer, and O'Connor, however, the "line item veto" label was a red herring. They would have sustained the authorization as a delegation of power to the President not to spend money.

Isn't the Line Item Veto Act the polar opposite of the legislative veto in practical effect? Whereas the legislative veto expanded Congress's power to control executive action outside of the legislative process laid out in Article I, § 7 and could be seen as congressional aggrandizement, on its face the Line Item Veto Act looked more like congressional abdication. Perhaps it could be said to expand congressional power by allowing Congress to avoid tough trade-offs in budget choices and push them onto the President. But isn't that complaint also true of delegations? Do you think that the Line Item Veto Act went beyond the contours of a constitutional delegation under the current intelligible principle test? Were the dissenters correct to argue the Act should have been upheld as a constitutional delegation?

(6) **The Proposed REINS Act.** Congress's latest proposal to replace the legislative veto, the Regulations from the Executive in Need of Scrutiny (REINS) Act, would require legislation affirmatively approving rules with a large economic impact before the rule could go into effect. Do you think that would pass constitutional muster? No, argues Ronald M. Levin in The REINS Act: Unbridled Impediment to Regulation, 83 Geo. Wash. L. Rev. 1446, 1468 (2015): "The problem with the REINS Act is that, with regard to major rules, it would accomplish virtually the same result as the 'traditional' one-house veto—namely, it would enable a single house of Congress to nullify an agency rule, regardless of the wishes of the other house, let alone the President. The question, then, is whether the Supreme Court would accept what amounts to a 180 degree change of direction if the one-house veto were repackaged in a different format, even though the risks of unchecked action by the legislative branch would be as great in the later version as in the earlier one. My suggestion is that it would not." Yes, counters Professor Jonathan R. Siegel, in The REINS Act and the Struggle to Control Agency Rulemaking, 16 N.Y.U. J. Legis. & Pub. Pol'y 131, 134 (2013), who argues that the Act is "perfectly constitutional," albeit in his view a bad policy choice: "[T]he attacks on the Act's constitutionality are not only mistaken, but ironic, because the REINS Act would, if anything, put the federal government on a sounder constitutional footing than that on which it rests now. If anything is constitutionally surprising, it is not Congress's efforts to assert authority over rulemaking, but rather its massive, wholesale delegation of that authority, which the courts have for so long tolerated."

NOTES ON DIRECTION BY LEGISLATION

(1) **New Legislation.** After Chadha, what alternative mechanisms are available to Congress for overriding a particular regulatory policy choice? Subject to the caveat about legislation that burdens a specified individual, Congress surely remains free to redirect an agency's course by new legislation. Sometimes it does so, giving very specific directions designed to change patterns of agency action, or inaction, with which it is displeased. Still, two major barriers mean that "corrective" legislation is unlikely to occur.

The first barrier is institutional. WILLIAM N. ESKRIDGE, JR., PHILIP P. FRICKEY & ELIZABETH GARRETT, LEGISLATION AND STATUTORY INTERPRETATION 70 (2d ed. 2006): "The most salient aspect of the modern legislative process is that it is filled with a complex set of hurdles that proponents of a new policy must overcome before their bill becomes law. At each stage in the legislative process, a proposal can be changed or halted, new coalitions must be formed, and opportunities for logrolling, strategic behaviors, and deliberation are presented. Because those who control each of these choke points have the ability to kill a proposal, some political scientists have termed them *vetogates*. Vetogates emanate from a number of sources: some result from constitutional provisions, some from rules adopted formally by a legislative body, and some from norm or practices that are more informal." As commentators on the Constitution have been observing since the ratification debates, see, e.g., Federalist No. 73, "bicameralism and presentment make lawmaking difficult *by design*." John Manning, Lawmaking Made Easy, 10 Green Bag 2d 202 (2007). But the Senate filibuster, a particularly potent vetogate that often makes it necessary to reach a supermajority of sixty votes to enact legislation, comes from Senate rules. See Josh Chafetz, The Unconstitutionality of the Filibuster, 43 Conn. L. Rev. 1003 (2011); Emmet J. Bondurant, The Senate Filibuster: The Politics of Destruction, 48 Harv. J. on Legis. 467 (2011).

The second barrier is political. In times of divided government, when control of the three national branches of government are in the hands of different political parties, enacting legislation becomes extremely difficult. Political polarization is a further important contributor to legislative gridlock. As the ideological distance between the two parties grows, it becomes increasingly unlikely that legislators will vote across party lines. As a result, it becomes increasingly difficult for a party that lacks a large majority to meet the supermajority thresholds needed to end a filibuster or overturn a veto, and the instances of gridlock grow. Political scientists have documented a significant increase in political polarization in the country since the 1970s. See Gary C. Jacobson, Partisan Polarization in American Politics, 43 Pres. Stud. 688, 700–03 (2013). For an important argument that from early on competition between the two major parties displaced competition between the legislative and executive branches as the main driver of national government, see Daryl J. Levinson & Richard H. Pildes, Separation of Parties, Not Powers, 119 Harv. L. Rev. 2311 (2006).

Political polarization has had several effects on how Congress functions. One effect is a significant decline in Congress's ability to enact legislation. According to Sarah Binder in The Dysfunctional Congress, 18 Ann. Rev. Pol. Sci. 85, 95–96 (2015), "the frequency of deadlock shows a secular increase over time. . . . By this measure, the 112th Congress (2011–2012) can claim to be the 'worst Congress ever' over the postwar period, although the title is shared with the last Congress of the Clinton administration in 1999–2000." See also Thomas E. Mann & Norman J. Ornstein, The Broken Branch: How Congress Is Failing America and How to Get It Back on Track (2008). Another effect is a dramatic increase in Congress's resort to what has been called "unorthodox lawmaking," with significant use of omnibus bills and fewer than 10 percent of enacted laws proceeding through the textbook legislative process. See Abbe R. Gluck, Anne J. O'Connell, & Rosa Po, Unorthodox Lawmaking, Unorthodox Rulemaking, 115 Colum. L. Rev. 1789 (2015). For a discussion of textbook and unorthodox legislative processes, see Ch. II, Sec. 1.a.

Some dispute whether Congress is as dysfunctional as critics allege. "The stalemate/gridlock argument is misleading not only because it ignores so many [legislative] accomplishments, but also because it focuses so intently on just one small part of domestic policy, namely passage of major pieces of legislation at the national level. . . . Critics of the Constitution overlook the fact that by creating multiple 'veto points,' our political system simultaneously creates multiple points of access for policy entrepreneurs and claimants. Every 'veto point' that can be used to block action is also an 'opportunity point' that can be used to initiate or augment government activity." R. Shep Melnick, The Gridlock Illusion, Wilson Q. (Winter 2013). In a similar vein, Professor Josh Chafetz argues that claims of congressional dysfunction take too narrow a view of the numerous powers Congress has and uses outside of enacting legislation to assert itself against the other branches. Congress's Constitution: Legislative Authority and the Separation of Powers (2017).

(2) ***The Congressional Review Act (CRA).*** In 1995, Congress amended the Regulatory Flexibility Act to require that "major" rules (defined essentially in terms of large economic impact, see 5 U.S.C. § 804(2)) be laid before Congress for sixty days—specifically, sixty legislative days in the House and sixty session days in the Senate, both of which are much longer periods than sixty calendar days—before taking effect. Moreover, if a rule is submitted to Congress less than sixty days before Congress adjourns a session, then the rule is carried over to the next session of Congress and treated as if it had been submitted to Congress or published in the Federal Register on the fifteenth legislative/session day of the new session. See 5 U.S.C. § 801 et seq.; Curtis W. Copeland & Richard S. Beth, Cong. Res. Serv. RL 34633, Congressional Review Act: Disapproval of Rules (2008). Because of Chadha, any disapproval must come via a *joint resolution* (passed by both houses and presented to the President), but a special, fast-track procedure limits debate and amendments, and curtails normal committee powers. If the joint resolution is adopted, the rule may not take effect.[13] Moreover, a rule that has been disapproved "may not be reissued in substantially the same form, and a new rule that is substantially the same as such a rule may not be issued, unless the reissued or new rule is specifically authorized by a law enacted after the date of the joint resolution disapproving the original rule." 5 U.S.C. § 801(b)(2). Thus, the resolution of disapproval is intended not only to invalidate the particular rule but also to narrow the agency's original statutory authority.[14]

---

[13] If a proposed resolution of disapproval is defeated in either chamber, the sixty-day waiting period is terminated and the rule can become immediately effective. 5 U.S.C. § 801(a)(5).

[14] For an argument that this aspect of the Act has significant nondelegation problems—in that it delegates to courts the responsibility to determine the new bounds of agency authority

Use of the CRA ordinarily faces the realities of presidential veto authority as any new legislation. Prior to 2016, the Act had been used only once to invalidate a rule in its over twenty-year history—after President Bush had been elected in 2002 with control of both House and Senate; the CRA was then invoked to disapprove an OSHA rule on ergonomic (repetitive motion) injuries promulgated in the waning days of the Clinton's administration. The 2016 election revived the CRA as a potent weapon. It ushered in a Republican president and Republican control over both houses after two terms of a Democratic administration and years of Republican complaints about expanding regulation. In the new session of Congress following the election, 14 rules were overturned during the period allowed for disapprovals under the CRA, which lasted until May 18, 2017. The House sought to increase the CRA's functionality even further by adopting the Midnight Rules Review Act of 2017, H.R. 21, 115th Cong., 1st Sess., which would amend the CRA to allow for several rules to be considered at once, but the measure failed to pass the Senate.

Moreover, the CRA may prove more potent yet. The text of the CRA provides that a major rule "shall take effect on the latest of" sixty days after a report on the rule is submitted to Congress or the rule is published in the Federal Register. 5 U.S.C. § 801(a)(3). But agencies routinely fail to send new rules to Congress; a 2014 report estimates that only 71 percentof rules were being submitted for review, down from a historical rate of 88 percent. Curtis W. Copeland, Implementation of the Congressional Review Act and Possible Reforms, 40 Admin. & Reg. L. News 7, 10 (2014). This opens the possibility that any rule not submitted—even rules in effect for years—might be open to congressional disapproval under the CRA. A Brookings Institution Report, Philip A. Wallach & Nicholas W. Zeppos, How Powerful is the Congressional Review Act (Apr. 7, 2017), estimates that "348 significant rules passed during the last two decades could be vulnerable to reversal through CRA resolution," though other estimates are much higher. Thus far, most courts have dismissed claims that failure to comply with the CRA invalidates (or at least suspends the effective date of) new rules. Sean D. Croston, Congress and the Courts Close their Eyes: The Continuing Abdication of the Duty to Review Agencies' Noncompliance with the Congressional Review Act, 62 Admin. L. Rev. 907 (2010).

(3) *Additional Congressional Measures.* Over the last decade, Republicans in Congress have proposed a large number of administrative reform measures. The goal of these measures is to curb administrative action, generally by requiring imposing new approval and procedural requirements on agencies or eliminating judicial deference to agency determinations. In January 2017, the House passed H.R.5—Regulatory Accountability Act of 2017, in which many previously proposed measures were combined. The House version of the Regulatory Accountability Act would impose, for all rulemaking, expanded notice, comment, and analysis requirements, including requiring agencies to base on factual evidence and assess the costs and benefits of alternatives. For "major" rules ($100 million

without any intelligible principle—see Daniel Cohen & Peter L. Strauss, Congressional Review of Agency Regulations, 49 Admin. L. Rev. 95 (1997).

annual costs or other criteria) the Act would mandate advance notice as well, and for "high impact" rules ($1 billion in annual costs) it would demand formal hearings under 5 U.S.C. §§ 556–557. Other provisions would limit agencies' adoption of interim rules, provide interests parties and opportunity to challenge an agency's data at a hearing, and put procedural limits on the use of guidance. The Act also incorporates a measure, previously proposed as the Separation of Powers Restoration Act, that would require courts to determine all questions of law de novo. A bipartisan Regulatory Accountability Act was recently introduced in the Senate as well, which differs from the House bill in a few ways but would preserve the ability to seek a hearing for high impact rules. See p. 286.

An even more extreme pending measure is the Regulations from the Executive in Need of Scrutiny (REINS) Act, discussed at p. 844, which would prevent any major rule (as defined under the CRA) from going into effect unless Congress affirmatively approved it by a joint resolution that would need to be passed by both houses of Congress and signed by the President (or repassed by a two-thirds vote in each chamber in the event of a presidential veto). H.R. 427, 114th Cong. (2015). For the view that the Reins Act offers the "decidedly unattractive prospect" that "the dysfunction that now afflicts Congress in the enactment of laws would spread to the implementation of laws[,] . . . leave[ing] an agency unable to implement important building blocks in programs it has been directed to put in place," see Ronald M. Levin, The REINS Act: Unbridled Impediment to Regulation, 83 Geo. Wash. L. Rev. 1446, 1486 (2015). For a contrasting endorsement of the REINS Act as improving accountability, see Jonathan H. Adler, Placing "Reins" on Regulations: Assessing the Proposed REINS Act, 16 N.Y.U. J. Legis. & Pub. Pol'y 1, 24–29 (2013).

(2) Appropriations and Spending

All Bills for raising Revenue shall originate in the House of Representatives; but the Senate may propose or concur with Amendments as on other Bills.

U.S. Const., Art. I, § 7, cl. 1

No money shall be drawn from the Treasury, but in Consequence of Appropriations made by Law . . .

U.S. Const., Art. I, § 9, cl. 7

Regulatory programs require statutory authority, but authorizing a program is only the first step. Even if the authorizing statute sets a funding level, those funds must be actually appropriated in the separate, annual process of enacting the roughly dozen large statutes that fund the various units of the federal government. The appropriations process provides significant opportunity for Congress to direct regulatory action. The length and complexity of appropriations bills, coupled with special House procedures for such bills and their "must pass" nature, allow insertion of provisions that would founder in the normal institutional and political constraints of the legislative process. Lacking an item veto (see Clinton v. City of New York, p. 843), the President can reject this direction only at the usually prohibitive cost of losing the entire funding package.

For budgeting purposes, an important distinction lies between mandatory spending (also called direct spending) and discretionary spending. Whether an item of spending is mandatory or discretionary depends on the underlying substantive legislation that authorizes it, and changing mandatory spending requires a change in substantive law and can't be done by an appropriations act alone. U.S. Gov't Accountability Office, GAO–05–734sp, A Glossary of Terms Used in the Federal Budget Process 42, 55–56 (2005). Most federal spending is mandatory; in recent years only 35–39 percent of total federal spending has been discretionary. If Congress does not adopt a regular appropriations bill by the beginning of the new fiscal year, Congress adopts continuing resolutions to continue funding until the regular bill is enacted. Jessica Tollestrup, Cong. Research Serv., 97–684, The Congressional Appropriations Process: An Introduction (2012). For a useful government website on federal spending, see USASpending.gov.

For a number of years, intense partisan division and polarization has prevented the regular appropriations process from functioning. See Nolan McCarty, The Decline of Regular Order in Appropriations: Does It Matter? (draft manuscript, Dec. 12, 2014), available at: https://www.princeton.edu/~nmccarty/appropriations.pdf; see also Peter Hanson, Restoring Regular Order in Congressional Appropriations 1 (Brookings, Nov. 2015). In 2013, the collapse of the regular process—along with a deep fight over raising the debt ceiling[15]—led to a 16-day shutdown of the federal government. Such a lengthy shutdown is rare; the last prior shutdown, one that lasted 21 days, occurred from December 1995 to January 1996.[16] Article I, Section 9 of the Constitution provides that "No Money shall be drawn from the Treasury, but in Consequence of Appropriations made by Law." The cause of a shutdown is a funding gap, created by Congress and the President's failure to pass appropriations bills or a continuing resolution before the government's existing spending

---

[15] The debt ceiling is an upper limit imposed by statute "on the amount of debt that the U.S. government can owe at any time. . . . As history has unfolded in the years since the debt ceiling statute was first enacted, Congress has generally acted to increase the debt ceiling as necessary." But starting in 2011, amidst political battles over spending and the deficit, the debt ceiling became an area of legislative brinksmanship, and for "the first time that it appeared that Congress might simply refuse to increase the debt ceiling, even though its own budget required more borrowing to fund its required spending levels." Neil H. Buchanan & Michael C. Dorf, How to Choose the Least Unconstitutional Option: Lessons for the President (and Others) from the Debt Ceiling Standoff, 112 Colum. L. Rev. 1175, 1186–88 (2012).

[16] For discussions of the 2013 shutdown, see U.S. Gov't Accountability Office, GAO–15–86, 2013 Government Shutdown: Three Departments Reported Varying Degrees of Impacts on Operations, Grants, and Contracts (2014); Marc Labonte, The FY2014 Government Shutdown: Economic Effects (Cong. Research Serv., 2013). For discussion of the 1995–96 shutdown, see Roy T. Meyers, Late Appropriations and Government Shutdowns: Frequency, Causes, Consequences, and Remedies, 17 Pub. Budget & Fin. 25 (1997); Kevin R. Kosar, Shutdown of the Federal Government: Causes, Effects, and Process (Cong. Research Serv., 2004).

authority expires. Under the Anti-Deficiency Act, which dates back to 1884 and is codified at 31 U.S.C. § 1341 et seq., all federal officials and employees are prohibited from spending or obligating funds beyond the amount already appropriated. The Act also prohibits accepting voluntary services, "except for emergencies involving the safety of human life or the protection of property." 31 U.S.C. § 1342. The Act has been read strictly and its effect is to require the furlough of all non-essential personnel until new funding authority is enacted.[17] Violating the Anti-Deficiency Act is punishable through administrative and criminal penalties. Although a funding gap does not directly affect mandatory spending, it can result in delays because the government employees responsible for operating mandatory spending programs may be furloughed. See Clinton T. Brass, Cong. Research Serv., 7–5700, Shutdown of the Federal Government: Causes, Processes, and Effects (Sept. 8, 2014).

NOTES

The following notes explore the extent to which Congress can use the appropriations process to direct regulatory outcomes and the mechanisms it uses to do so.

(1) *Appropriations Riders: Limitation Riders and Legislative Riders.* One central mechanism of congressional control through appropriations is the appropriation rider. THOMAS O. MCGARITY, DEREGULATORY RIDERS REDUX, 1 Mich. J. Envtl. & Admin. L. 33, 36–38 (2012): A rider is "a provision added to an unrelated bill that 'rides' the targeted bill through the legislative process and becomes law when the President signs the bill. . . . Riders come in two broad varieties—limitation riders and legislative riders. The limitation rider is associated exclusively with appropriation bills, and it prohibits the relevant agency from expending any of the appropriated funds to engage in a proscribed activity. . . . A legislative rider modifies existing law by amending an existing statute, changing existing common law, or directing a federal agency to take a particular affirmative action (thereby rendering lawful administrative action that might otherwise have been unlawful)." Riders have been around since the early nineteenth century and "have always played a role in enacting controversial laws." But "they have become far more common since the 1990s," and "[i]n . . .[a] toxic legislative environment, [represent] one of the more effective strategies for securing legislative victories and imposing political pain."

Legislative riders are the more controversial form of rider. Legislative riders are not limited in time to the annual appropriations cycle and need not have any relationship to appropriations other than being part of an appropriations bill. "A rider can, in effect, be nothing less than authorization legislation attached to appropriations legislation . . . In other words, the legislation may in every respect be the kind of law traditionally considered

---

[17]   The leading authorities interpreting the Act are two opinions from the early 1980s from the Office of Legal Counsel in the Department of Justice. See 43 Op. Att'y Gen. 224 (April 25, 1980, 43 Op. Att'y Gen. 293 (January 16, 1981).

the province of an authorization committee. Yet, it becomes law once Congress passes the appropriations legislation to which it is attached and the President signs it into law (or Congress overrides a presidential veto)." RICHARD J. LAZARUS, CONGRESSIONAL DESCENT: THE DEMISE OF DELIBERATIVE DEMOCRACY IN ENVIRONMENTAL LAW, 94 Geo. L.J. 619, 635, 637 (2006); McGARITY, supra, at 37–39.

Limitation riders are the classic form of appropriation rider. These typically take the form of saying that "the agency may not spend any of the monies Congress is appropriating to engage in a specific activity." Lazarus, supra, at 637. A Congressional Research Service Report reviewing the Consolidated Appropriations Act for 2008 identified nearly two dozen such provisions in the act. CURTIS W. COPELAND, CONGRESSIONAL INFLUENCE ON RULEMAKING AND REGULATION THROUGH APPROPRIATIONS RESTRICTIONS 7, 11 (Cong. Research Serv., 2008). Riders continue to surface with great frequency, though they are not always enacted. For example, starting in 2011 appropriations riders prohibited the Department of Agriculture's Grain Inspection, Packers and Stockyards Administration (GIPSA) from finalizing regulations aimed at giving poultry and swine growers certain rights in their contracts with processing companies. The GIPSA Rider gained fame as the target of an episode of John Oliver's Last Week Tonight, https://www.you tube.com/watch?v=X9wHzt6gBgI, and was dropped from the FY 2016 appropriations bill. Despite passing the House the next year, the GIPSA Rider did not make it into the enacted FY 2017 appropriations bill.

Riders are most often used to stop action, but they can be used to spur action as well. "Although appropriations provisions that are designed to prevent or restrict the development, implementation, or enforcement of particular rules or types of rules are common, other types of appropriation measures are also prevalent. . . . Some appropriations provisions direct federal agencies to develop rules in particular areas, or to take particular enforcement actions. For example, a provision in the Consolidated Appropriations Act for 2008 amends the Homeland Security Act of 2002 and requires the Secretary of the Department of Homeland Security to 'regulate the sale and transfer of ammonium nitrate by an ammonium nitrate facility in accordance with the subtitle to prevent the misappropriation or use of ammonium nitrate in an act of terrorism.' The provision delineates what the regulations must contain (e.g., a registration process for owners, records that must be maintained, and an appeals process); and mandates that the Secretary '(1) shall issue a proposed rule implementing this subtitle not later than 6 months after the date of the enactment of this subtitle; and (2) shall issue a final rule implementing this subtitle not later than 1 year after such date of enactment.' " COPELAND, supra, at 2–3.

(2) *The Institutional Advantages of Control via Appropriation Riders.* JASON A. MACDONALD, LIMITATION RIDERS AND CONGRESSIONAL INFLUENCE OVER BUREAUCRATIC POLICY DECISIONS, 104 Am. Pol. Sci. Rev. 766, 767, 773 (2010), points out that appropriations riders limiting agency action have procedural and political qualities that make them "effective and frequently used tools" for Congress to influence regulatory decisionmaking. Procedurally, riders that prohibit spending for designated activities are

always "in order" because they fall within a provision of House Rule XXI (known as the "Holman rule") that allows for spending "retrenchments." Also, unlike ordinary substantive legislation, "appropriation bills do not require special orders from the House Rules Committee to reach the floor." Politically, the "must-pass" nature of appropriations bills increases their value as vehicles for congressional instructions because the President's ability to engage in veto bargaining to remove individual riders is constrained: "[N]ot passing appropriations legislation and shutting down the government, a decision accompanied by intensive media coverage that scrutinizes the motives behind the positions of both major parties and their leaders, and potentially leads the electorate to attach blame to one or both parties, is costly politically."

But are such instructions appropriately considered congressional direction—or are they no more than the idiosyncratic preferences of individual sponsors? Professor MacDonald continues: "Of course, for limitation riders to serve as a mechanism that limits the legislative majority's agency losses, the appropriations committee's ideal policy must be . . . close to [that of the median legislator.] . . . [R]esearch on the representativeness of the House Appropriations Committee [and subcommittees] indicates that the preferences of appropriators are similar to those of the floor.

"One clear implication . . . is that the availability of limitation riders improves policy outcomes for congressional majorities more under divided government than under unified government. Under divided government, the president's ideal policy, p, is farther from the chamber's median member, m, than under unified government. Assuming that the appropriations committee is a good agent of the chamber median . . . how much limitation riders improve policy for the chamber median depends on m's proximity to p." Analyzing data from 1989 to 2009, Professor MacDonald found that a greater number of limitations riders occurred in periods of divided government than unified government. He also found some support for the hypothesis that the number of riders increased as the distance between p (the President's ideal policy) and m (the preference of the median legislator) increased.

(3) *The Wisdom of Riders.* Commentators are generally skeptical (or worse) about the wisdom of directing regulatory policy via appropriations. Professor Neal Devins, although acknowledging that "Congress's use of limitation riders is sometimes necessary," finds the practice "troublesome." "The use of the appropriations process to accomplish substantive objectives that have not been considered previously or that contravene established statutory objectives may prevent the appropriate authorizing committee from applying its expertise. Exacerbating this problem, appropriations are often acted on quickly, providing little opportunity for thoughtful deliberation of the issues raised by such measures." Neal E. Devins, Regulation of Government Agencies through Limitation Riders, 1987 Duke L.J. 456, 458 (1987).

Professor LAZARUS, supra, at 622, charges that the effects have been especially devastating for environmental law regulation: "Earlier Congresses were celebrated for enacting sweeping, demanding environmental laws and for passing significant amendments in response to subsequent developments in executive branch agencies, federal courts, and the states. Now, Congress passes almost no coherent, comprehensive environmental legislation and displays no ability to deliberate openly and systematically in response to changing circumstances and new information. Instead, when Congress exercises its lawmaking authority to influence environmental protection policy, it does so primarily through the appropriations process: the sphere of its responsibility that, ironically, has proven to be the least conducive to the kind of deliberative democracy that justifies legislative supremacy in environmental lawmaking and the most susceptible to the kind of narrow, special interest factionalism that the Framers sought for the national government to be able to resist."

Professor MCGARITY, supra, at 36–37, identifies "a particular class of riders" as a source of concern: those "that are designed to stall, modify, or eliminate an ongoing regulatory program that is being implemented by a regulatory agency pursuant to duly enacted authorizing legislation. Usually pursued at the behest of affected regulated industries, these 'deregulatory riders' threaten to derail ongoing regulatory programs that are highly popular with the general public and therefore not likely to be dismantled through the normal legislative processes." Drawing on a close study of the use of riders during the 112th Congress, McGarity condemns "their extortionate use by a determined minority of legislators to advance special interests at the expense of the broader public interest."

On the other hand, "[a]s a legislative tool, the rider is not inherently good or evil. Riders can be abused in ways that defeat democracy, but they also make it possible for legislation having the support of a large majority of the national population to prevail over an obstructionist minority." McGarity, supra, at 70. Professor MacDonald, supra, at 766, argues for the potential democracy-reinforcing benefits of riders. After examining 20 years of legislative data, he concluded that riders lead to "policy outcomes that are preferable to a majority of legislators compared to outcomes that would occur if this tool did not exist" and that this effect is heightened in periods of divided government.

(4) *Agency Reliance on Non-Appropriated Funds.* Professors CHRISTOPHER DEMUTH, SR. and MICHAEL S. GREVE, AGENCY FINANCE IN THE AGE OF EXECUTIVE GOVERNMENT, 24 Geo. Mason L. Rev. 555, 555–56, 561–62 (2017), argue that recent increases in agency self-financing are fundamentally transforming basic features of how the federal government operates: "The written Constitution is unequivocal, indeed emphatic, in committing fiscal powers to Congress and in withholding them from the executive . . . Public expenditures must be appropriated by Congress. And with some exceptions, government agencies may not raise or spend funds that have not been appropriated . . . Increasingly, however, the picture is at war with reality. To an unprecedented extent, regulatory agencies rely on non-appropriated funds for their ordinary operations. Many have become self-financing; some have become profit centers for wider executive exertions—and for Congress. Correspondingly, the general assumption that

Congress will jealously guard the power of the purse as its ultimate means of checking and balancing the executive has become open to serious doubt: in many respects, those powers have fallen into disuse."

The rise in agency self-financing they document comes in many varieties. "Some of the money comes from government activities that might as well be left to private commerce, such as military PX stores ('post exchanges') and the U.S. Mint; other comes from a wide range of user fees— for using national parks and applying for licenses, permits, visas, patents, and regulatory approvals. . . . The device of the 'revolving fund' permits agencies to continuously collect user fees and spend them on specified purposes, thereby establishing 'permanent indefinite appropriations.' Revolving funds are increasingly used to permit regulatory and enforcement agencies to use fines and settlements to operate their own spending programs."

(5) ***Legality and Presidential Pushback.*** No Supreme Court decision specifically addresses whether appropriations provisions directing agencies to act (or not act) unconstitutionally infringes the President's authority. Scholarly commentary is sharply divided. Compare, e.g., Kate Stith, Congress' Power of the Purse, 97 Yale L.J. 1352 (1988) (arguing that Congress has "a constitutional duty to limit the amount and duration of each grant of spending authority" and that historical appropriations practice in the colonies included not only setting amounts but also specifying the "powers, activities, and purposes" for which appropriated funds might be used) with Jacques B. LeBoeuf, Limitations on the Use of Appropriations Riders by Congress to Effectuate Substantive Policy Changes, 19 Hastings Const. L.Q. 493 (1992) (arguing that "[a]ppropriations riders that attempt to influence executive discretion in the area of law enforcement prevent the executive branch from carrying out its constitutionally mandated activities.")

Both President Reagan and President George W. Bush asserted the unconstitutionality of such restrictions in signing statements. E.g., Statement on signing H.R. 1827 into law, 23 Weekly Comp. Pres. Doc. 800 (July 11, 1987) ("Article II of the Constitution assigns responsibility for executing the law to the President. While Congress is empowered to enact new or different laws, it may not indirectly interpret and implement existing laws, which is an essential function allocated by the Constitution to the executive branch."). See also Statement of Administration Policy, H.R. 5576—Transportation, Treasury, Housing, the Judiciary, the District of Columbia appropriations bill, FY 2007 (June 14, 2006) (limitation provision "should be deleted as inconsistent with the President's constitutional authority to supervise the unitary executive branch."). Although President Obama was more limited in his use of signing statements, see p. 962, he repeatedly challenged riders attached to defense spending that limited his ability to transfer detainees from the Guantanamo Bay facility, such as §§ 1033–35 of the FY2014 National Defense Authorization Act. Obama subsequently released five Guantanamo detainees in exchange for U.S. soldier Bowe Bergdahl, who was held by the Taliban, without providing congressional committees the advance notice required by § 1035. Soon after coming into office, President Trump issued a signing statement objecting to seventy-six spending restrictions in the Consolidated Appropriations Act of 2017, including provisions restricting transfer of Guantanamo detainees and prohibiting DOJ from interfering with states implementing medical marijuana laws.

(6) *Impoundment.* Although a tool used by the *President*, rather than Congress, to control regulatory action via spending decisions, impoundment is so intimately related to appropriations that it is sensibly considered here. Conflict over the President's power to refuse to spend appropriated funds, or to transfer them to other purposes, has been part of our history since at least the late 19th century, when President Grant set off a furor in Congress by refusing to spend appropriated river and harbor funds for what we would now term pork barrel projects. See Peter M. Shane & Harold H. Bruff, Separation of Powers Law (1996) (quoting one House Member's Shakespearian ranting, "Upon what meat hath this our Caesar fed?").

Congress cannot specifically itemize the amounts and purposes of all the monies needed to run the federal government. Even if it had time, the specification would become obsolete almost immediately, as events vary needs and costs. Therefore, while the degree of appropriations specificity has varied with the times (and the level of trust between a particular legislature and administration), executive discretion is an inevitable part of the funding process. Some exercises of this discretion are uncontroversial. If the government can accomplish a desired result for less than the projected expenditure, or if changed circumstances render the planned action unnecessary, it would be absurd to interpret the relevant appropriation as a mandate that all the money be spent, regardless. The Executive has long been permitted to make such "programmatic impoundments" with relatively little legislative involvement. (It is not hard to see these impoundments as simply effectuating congressional intent—or, at least, what Congress would have intended had it known.) This discretion was codified in the Impoundment Control Act of 1974, as amended in 1987.

The real apple of discord is a very different sort of executive refusal to spend appropriated money, "policy impoundments." Largely a post-World War II phenomenon, policy impoundments reflect a president's disagreement with the purposes for which Congress appropriates money. In order to prevent, or at least minimize, a policy result Congress favors, the President simply refuses to spend the money appropriated to accomplish it. Initially, Presidents used this strategy in the area of defense appropriations for weapons. Here, the constitutional Commander-in-Chief power arguably provides a basis for the President to assert and enforce a policy preference independent of Congress. By the presidency of Lyndon Johnson, however, policy impoundments were becoming a strategic weapon in the domestic policymaking arena. Richard Nixon impounded nearly 20 percent of non-entitlement federal expenditures; in the process, several regulatory programs were terminated. His rationale was inflation control, but the particular programs chosen for economization reflected the regulatory policy disagreements between a Republican President and a Democratic Congress. This presidential strategy did finally produce litigation about the impoundment power, and several lower court opinions rejected the argument that policy impoundments were either authorized by statute or within the President's inherent constitutional authority. See, e.g., Missouri Highway Comm. v. Volpe, 479 F.2d 1099 (8th Cir. 1973). The one case taken by the Supreme Court did not produce a definitive resolution.[18]

In the Congressional Budget and Impoundment Control Act of 1974, Congress responded to the Nixon controversy by deleting the phrase "other developments" from the Anti-Deficiency Act and setting up a procedure for policy impoundments: If the President proposed to rescind an appropriation entirely, the proposal must be submitted to Congress and would be ineffective unless approved by a bill passed within a specified period. If he or she proposed only to defer spending within the fiscal year, the proposal must be submitted to Congress and would become effective unless disapproved by a one-house veto. Of course, a decade later INS v. Chadha, p. 831, rendered this provision invalid. The D.C. Circuit then held that the veto was not severable. The legislative history, it concluded, "completely refutes the notion that Congress would have granted the President statutory authority to implement deferrals, thereby forcing itself to reenact an appropriations bill each time it disapproved of a deferral." City of New Haven v. United States, 809 F.2d 900 (D.C. Cir. 1987). There the legal status of policy impoundments remained until the next amendment to the Anti-Deficiency Act: the perhaps fatally misnamed Line Item Veto Act of 1996. See Clinton v. City of N.Y., p. 843.

(3) Oversight and Investigations

Committee Oversight. Even though Congress as a whole may find it difficult to direct agency regulatory choices, subparts of Congress can be very actively engaged in review and response. In the 1960–70s, Congress responded to growing federal regulatory ambitions by developing a complex system of committees that divided the labor of overseeing agencies.[19] One study found that between 1961 and 1983, the number of committee "oversight days" rose from about 150 per year to close to 600 per year.[20] Since then, the number of hearing days has continued to climb, reaching nearly 1,000 at its high point before 2010.[21] Political scientists identify congressional oversight as a critical tool of congressional control of the executive branch and often divide up oversight into two types: "police patrols," where Congress investigates

---

[18] In Train v. New York, 420 U.S. 35 (1975), New York City challenged President Nixon's instructions to EPA not to spend most of a sum appropriated, pursuant to the Federal Water Pollution Control Act, for federal financing of municipal sewage treatment facilities. By the time the case reached the Court, Nixon had resigned and the executive branch had abandoned its claim to inherent presidential impoundment authority. The only issues decided were statutory ones of whether the Act intended to confer discretion as to the timing of expending the funds.

[19] See, e.g., Nelson W. Polsby, The Institutionalization of the House of Representatives, 62 Am. Pol. Sci. Rev. 144 (1968).

[20] Joel Aberbach, Keeping a Watchful Eye 34–37 (1990).

[21] Jason A. MacDonald & Robert C. McGrath, Retrospective Congressional Oversight and the Dynamics of Legislative Influence over the Bureaucracy, 41 Leg. Stud. Q. 899, 903 figure 1 (2016).

based on its own initiative, and "fire alarms," where Congress investigates in response to concerns raised by interested parties. See Note 2, p. 823. For a detailed analysis of congressional investigations over time, see Douglas L. Kriner & Eric Schickler, Investigating the President: Congressional Checks on Presidential Power (2016).

JACK BEERMAN, CONGRESSIONAL ADMINISTRATION, 43 San Diego L. Rev. 61, 124, 126 (2006): "The machinery of congressional oversight is enormous. Each House of Congress has numerous committees and subcommittees, almost all of which engage in oversight activities . . . [and] [e]ach of these committees and subcommittees has professional staff to perform oversight. . . . To support its investigations, Congress has the power to subpoena witnesses and require them to bring records and other documents. These tools are quite broad, and many confrontations between Congress and the President involve actual or threatened claims of executive privilege against congressional attempts to procure information from the executive branch. [See p. 720] Congressional investigations run the gamut, from looking into the administration of regulatory programs to investigations of whether the Department of Justice is acting properly in ongoing criminal investigations and prosecutions, where disclosure of information can harm law enforcement and prejudice the rights of subjects."[22]

Scholars have vigorously debated the desirability of the proliferation of committees—and the burgeoning of congressional staff that support their work. On one view, committees (and, particularly, their chairs) are opportunistic entrepreneurs of regional and other special interests whose preferences can diverge significantly from those of the median legislator. If this view is accurate, oversight by committee might be a bad thing and certainly should not be equated with oversight by Congress as a whole. On the other hand, considerable empirical and theoretical work challenges this negative picture as overly simplistic. At least with respect to salient committees, some researchers argue that the data reveal committees acting as faithful agents of the chamber majority.[23] Studies also demonstrate that partisanship plays a significant role in the extent of congressional oversight, with a shift from unified to divided government—when each of the two parties controls one house of Congress or the executive branch—"yield[ing] a five-fold increase in the number of hearings held and quadrupl[ing] their duration." Douglas Kriner & Liam Schwartz. Divided Government and Congressional Investigations. 43 Leg. Stud. Q. 295, 295, 297 (2008); see also David C.W. Parker & Mathew Dull, Divided We Govern: The Politics of

---

[22] See also Walter Olesek, Cong. Res. Serv. Rep. R41079, Congressional Oversight: An Overview (2010).

[23] The literature on both views is collected in Jeffrey J. Rachlinski & Cynthia R. Farina, Cognitive Psychology & Optimal Government Design, 87 Cornell L. Rev. 549, 573–74 n. 101 (2002). On the representativeness of appropriations committee oversight, see Section 3.c.

Congressional Investigations, 1947–2004, 34 Leg. Stud. Q. 319, 321–22 (2009).

A separate question concerns how effective committee oversight is. One recent study found that "when it occurs, oversight often is effective, changing agency behavior for a statistically significant 19.7 percent of infractions, relative to otherwise similar infractions for which oversight does not occur," with infractions defined as "the set of issues from which Congress tends to select its subjects for oversight hearings." Brian D. Feinstein, Congress in the Administrative State, 95 Wash. U. L. Rev. (2018). Other studies suggest that having multiple committees with jurisdiction over all or part of a regulatory problem can undermine the effectiveness of oversight, because "the more congressional committees involved in the oversight of an agency, the weaker Congress is relative to the president." Professors Joshua L. Clinton, David E. Lewis, & Jennifer L. Selin, Influencing the Bureaucracy: The Irony of Congressional Oversight, 58 Am. J. Pol. Sci. 387, 387, 399 (2014). On the other hand, "granting a single committee the near-exclusive right to oversee a given agency reduces the likelihood that the agency will be subject to oversight if congressional, committee, and agency preferences [are] not properly aligned." Feinstein, supra.

Oversight by other Congressional Institutions: GAO, CRS, and CBO. Congress relies on several institutions to assist it in its oversight activities. You've probably seen reports from two of these institutions, the Governmental Accountability Office (GAO)[24] and the Congressional Research Services (CRS), cited in this casebook. Both are sizeable entities: CRS, located in the Library of Congress, has a staff of around 600 and GAO has a staff of around 3000. Both investigate at the request of congressional committees, subcommittees, or individual members of Congress and cover the gamut of topics and policy areas. One difference, however, is that CRS works solely for Congress while GAO can undertake investigations on its own initiative and also adjudicates bid protests as part of the federal contracting process. The Congressional Budget Office (CBO), with a staff of around 235, has a more specialized ambit; it produces independent analyses of budgetary and economic issues to support the congressional budget process. All three are avowedly nonpartisan.[25]

GAO is worth looking at in more detail, given its size, unique functions, and prominence in the next lead case. Anne Joseph O'Connell, Auditing Politics or Political Auditing? 1–2 (February 21, 2007), available at https://ssrn.com/abstract=964656 "Congress created the GAO in 1921 to take over the Treasury Department's role in

---

[24] GAO's name was changed from the Government Accounting Office to the Government Accountability Office in 2004.

[25] Information on staffing and responsibilities are available on their websites: https://www.cbo.gov/about/overview, https://www.cbo.gov/about/organization-and-staffing, https://www.loc.gov/crsinfo/about/structure.html, https://www.loc.gov/crsinfo/about/, https://www.gao.gov/about/index.html, https://www.gao.gov/about/gglance.html.

auditing government disbursements. Congress subsequently gave the GAO substantial additional authority after Watergate. Led by the Comptroller General, who is appointed for a 15-year term, the GAO now investigates, culls, and synthesizes stances on a multitude of policy programs and expenditures on its own initiative, by legislative mandate, and at the request of congressional committees and individual members of Congress." In its bid protest function, GAO adjudicates challenges to federal agency contract awards by disappointed bidders and others.

GAO emphasizes its independent and nonpartisan status and describes itself as the "congressional watchdog." But as O'Connell notes, "[a]lmost all would agree that the GAO is neither a simple accountant of unambiguous financial statements nor an uncontroversial provider of agency information. The auditor is often subject to scathing attacks by administrative agency officials and members of Congress who contest its conclusions. . . . When the Republicans took control of Congress in 1995, the GAO suffered a 25 percent budget cut that pared its personnel roster from approximately 5,300 in 1992 to 3,500 by October, 1996." GAO also has triggered the ire of the executive branch. A particularly prominent example came in 2002, when the Comptroller General filed a lawsuit against Vice President Cheney to obtain detailed information on the Vice President's Energy Task Force for a congressionally requested investigation.[26]

(4) Direct Control over Regulatory Actors

> **BOWSHER v. SYNAR**
>
> **Notes on Direct Congressional Participation in Regulatory Decisionmaking**
>
> **Notes on the Differences Between Parliamentary and Presidential Systems**

The House of Representatives . . . shall have the sole Power of Impeachment.

U.S. Const., Art. I, § 2, cl. 5

The Senate shall have the sole Power to try all Impeachments. . . . And no Person shall be convicted without the Concurrence of two thirds of the Members present.

U.S. Const., Art. I, § 3, cl. 6

---

[26] Walker v. Cheney, 230 F.Supp.2d 51 (D.D.C. 2002). The district court dismissed for lack of standing, id. at 65, 70, and the Comptroller General did not appeal.

*. . . [N]o person holding any Office under the United States, shall be a
member of either House during his Continuance in Office.*

U.S. Const., Art. I, § 6, cl. 2

*The President, Vice President and all civil Officers of the United States,
shall be removed from Office on Impeachment for, and Conviction of,
Treason, Bribery, or other high Crimes and Misdemeanors.*

U.S. Const., Art. II, § 4

BOWSHER v. SYNAR

Supreme Court of the United States (1986).
478 U.S. 714.

■ CHIEF JUSTICE BURGER delivered the opinion of the Court.

[The Vietnam War, politically ambitious social programs, and
politically popular tax cuts combined to quadruple the national debt
between 1970 and the 1990s. Before the economic boom of the late 20th
century produced unpredicted budget surpluses, conventional wisdom
held that the federal budget could not be balanced through any "normal"
political means. Congress had tried, for many years, to find reliable ways
to tie itself to the mast of spending reduction. The challenge was finding
some mechanism that kept all members securely in the cost-cutting boat,
when each was eager to gain credit with his or her own constituencies by
providing financial benefits to them. In 1985, with great political fanfare
(and controversy), it enacted the Balanced Budget and Emergency Deficit
Control Act—the Gramm-Rudman-Hollings Act.

The Act contained a schedule of annual "maximum deficit amounts,"
which declined over five years to $0. Each year, the White House Office
of Management and Budget and the Congressional Budget Office were
independently to estimate the federal budget deficit for the coming year
and report their findings to the Comptroller General. As you might infer
from the provision for separate estimates by agencies living at opposite
ends of Pennsylvania Avenue, this process entailed highly debatable
assumptions and predictions. The Comptroller was to review these
reports and, if he concluded that the projected deficit would exceed
statutory limits, he was to identify a set of "across the board" cuts, half
of which (the Act specified) were to come from defense programs. On
receiving the Comptroller's report, the President was to issue an order of
"sequestration" requiring these reductions. If Congress did not legislate
alternative reduction measures during a specified brief period, that order
took effect.

The Comptroller General heads the Government Accountability
Office (GAO, at that time the General Accounting Office), an agency of
now around 3,000 people that engages in audit and oversight activities
on direction from Congress, its committees and, sometimes, individual
members. The GAO was created as part of the Budget and Accounting

Act of 1921. For the first time in American history, this Act had established an executive budget function centralized in the White House; the Act simultaneously created the Comptroller and the GAO to balance this newly created executive authority.]

... The Constitution does not contemplate an active role for Congress in the supervision of officers charged with the execution of the laws it enacts. The President appoints "Officers of the United States" with the "Advice and Consent of the Senate." Once the appointment has been made and confirmed, however, the Constitution explicitly provides for removal of Officers of the United States by Congress only upon impeachment by the House of Representatives and conviction by the Senate. An impeachment by the House and trial by the Senate can rest only on "Treason, Bribery or other high Crimes and Misdemeanors." A direct congressional role in the removal of officers charged with the execution of the laws beyond this limited one is inconsistent with separation of powers. ... The structure of the Constitution does not permit Congress to execute the laws; it follows that Congress cannot grant to an officer under its control what it does not possess. ... With these principles in mind, we turn to consideration of whether the Comptroller General is controlled by Congress.

... The critical factor lies in the provisions of the statute defining the Comptroller General's office relating to removability. Although the Comptroller General is nominated by the President from a list of three individuals recommended by the Speaker of the House of Representatives and the President pro tempore of the Senate, and confirmed by the Senate, he is removable only at the initiative of Congress. He may be removed not only by impeachment but also by Joint Resolution of Congress ["at any time" for "(i) permanent disability; (ii) inefficiency; (iii) neglect of duty; (iv) malfeasance; or (v) a felony or conduct involving moral turpitude." 31 U.S.C. § 703(e)(1).][7] This provision was included, as one Congressman explained in urging passage of the Act, because Congress "felt that [the Comptroller General] should be brought under the sole control of Congress, so that Congress at the moment when it found he was inefficient and was not carrying on the duties of his office as he should and as the Congress expected, could remove him without the long, tedious process of a trial by impeachment." 61 Cong. Rec. 1081 (1921). ... The ultimate design was to "give the legislative branch of the Government control of the audit, not through the power of appointment, but through the power of removal." 58 Cong. Rec. 7211 (1919).

... [T]he dissent's assessment of the statute fails to recognize the breadth of the grounds for removal. The statute permits removal for

---

[7] Although the President could veto such a joint resolution, the veto could be overridden by a two-thirds vote of both Houses of Congress. Thus, the Comptroller General could be removed in the face of Presidential opposition. Like the District Court, we therefore read the removal provision as authorizing removal by Congress alone.

"inefficiency," "neglect of duty," or "malfeasance." These terms are very broad and, as interpreted by Congress, could sustain removal of a Comptroller General for any number of actual or perceived transgressions of the legislative will. . . . [We must also add that the dissent is simply in error to suggest that the political realities reveal that the Comptroller General is free from influence by Congress. . . . It is clear the Congress has consistently viewed the Comptroller General as an officer of the Legislative Branch.

Against this background, we see no escape from the conclusion that, because Congress had retained removal authority over the Comptroller General, he may not be entrusted with executive powers. The remaining question is whether the Comptroller General has been assigned such powers in the Balanced Budget and Emergency Deficit Control Act of 1985.

The primary responsibility of the Comptroller General under the instant Act is the preparation of a "report." This report must contain detailed estimates of projected federal revenues and expenditures. The report must also specify the reductions, if any, necessary to reduce the deficit to the target for the appropriate fiscal year. The reductions must be set forth on a program-by-program basis. . . .

Appellants suggest that the duties assigned to the Comptroller General in the Act are essentially ministerial and mechanical so that their performance does not constitute "execution of the law" in a meaningful sense. On the contrary, we view these functions as plainly entailing execution of the law in constitutional terms. Interpreting a law enacted by Congress to implement the legislative mandate is the very essence of "execution" of the law. Under § 251, the Comptroller General must exercise judgment concerning facts that affect the application of the Act. He must also interpret the provisions of the Act to determine precisely what budgetary calculations are required. Decisions of that kind are typically made by officers charged with executing a statute. . . . [And] § 252(a)(3) . . . gives the Comptroller General the ultimate authority to determine the budget cuts to be made. . . .

. . . By placing the responsibility for execution of the Balanced Budget and Emergency Deficit Control Act in the hands of an officer who is subject to removal only by itself, Congress in effect has retained control over the execution of the Act and has intruded into the executive function. The Constitution does not permit such intrusion.

We now turn to the final issue of remedy. . . . The language of the Balanced Budget and Emergency Deficit Control Act itself settles the issue. In § 274(f), Congress has explicitly provided "fallback" provisions in the Act that take effect "[i]n the event . . . *any* of the reporting procedures described in section 251 are invalidated." § 274(f)(1)(emphasis added). . . . Assuming that appellants are correct in urging that this matter must be resolved on the basis of congressional intent, the intent appears to have been for § 274(f) to be given effect in this situation. . . .

Our judgment is stayed for a period not to exceed 60 days to permit Congress to implement the fallback provisions.

■ JUSTICE STEVENS, with whom JUSTICE MARSHALL joins, concurring in the judgment.

. . . [W]hen Congress, or a component or an agent of Congress, seeks to make policy that will bind the Nation, it must follow the procedures mandated by Article I of the Constitution-through passage by both Houses and presentment to the President. . . . That principle, I believe, is applicable to the Comptroller General. . . . [O]ne of the identifying characteristics of the Comptroller General is his statutorily required relationship to the Legislative Branch. . . . In the Reorganization Act[s] of 1945 [and 1949], Congress specified that the Comptroller General and the General Accounting Office "are a part of the legislative branch of the Government." 59 Stat. 616. [I]n the Budget and Accounting Procedures Act of 1950, Congress referred to the "auditing for the Government, conducted by the Comptroller General of the United States as an agent of the Congress." 64 Stat. 835. . . .

[Justice Stevens argued that in addition to the Comptroller General's "longstanding statutory responsibilities" to Congress, "the fact that Congress had retained for itself the power to remove the Comptroller Geneeral is important evidence supporting the conclusion that he is a member of the Legislative Branch."]

The Court concludes that the Gramm-Rudman-Hollings Act impermissibly assigns the Comptroller General "executive powers." . . . This conclusion is not only far from obvious but also rests on the unstated and unsound premise that there is a definite line that distinguishes executive power from legislative power. . . .

One reason that the exercise of legislative, executive, and judicial powers cannot be categorically distributed among three mutually exclusive branches of Government is that governmental power cannot always be readily characterized with only one of those three labels. On the contrary, as our cases demonstrate, a particular function, like a chameleon, will often take on the aspect of the office to which it is assigned. For this reason, "[w]hen any Branch acts, it is presumptively exercising the power the Constitution has delegated to it." INS v. Chadha, 462 U.S. at 951.[13] . . .

---

[13] "Perhaps as a matter of political science we could say that Congress should only concern itself with broad principles of policy and leave their application in particular cases to the executive branch. But no such rule can be found in the Constitution itself or in legislative practice. It is fruitless, therefore, to try to draw any sharp and logical line between legislative and executive functions. Characteristically, the draftsmen of 1787 did not even attempt doctrinaire definitions, but placed their reliance in the mechanics of the Constitution. One of their principal devices was to vest the legislative powers in the two Houses of Congress and to make the President a part of the legislative process by requiring that all bills passed by the two Houses be submitted to him for his approval or disapproval, his disapproval or veto to be

The powers delegated to the Comptroller General by § 251 of the Act before us today have [this] chameleon-like quality. . . . [W]hen that delegation is held invalid, the "fallback provision" provides that the report that would otherwise be issued by the Comptroller General shall be issued by Congress itself. [S]urely no one would suggest that Congress had acted in any capacity other than "legislative." . . . Under the District Court's analysis, and the analysis adopted by the majority today, it would therefore appear that the function at issue is "executive" if performed by the Comptroller General but "legislative" if performed by the Congress. In my view, however, the function may appropriately be labeled "legislative" even if performed by the Comptroller General or by an executive agency. . . .

The Gramm-Rudman-Hollings Act assigns to the Comptroller General the duty to make policy decisions that have the force of law. . . . If Congress were free to delegate its policymaking authority to one of its components, or to one of its agents, it would be able to evade "the carefully crafted restraints spelled out in the Constitution." Chadha, at 959. That danger—congressional action that evades constitutional restraints—is not present when Congress delegates lawmaking power to the executive or to an independent agency. . . .

■ JUSTICE WHITE, dissenting [disagreed that the removal provision made the Comptroller General an agent of Congress]

. . . Any removal under the statute would presumably be subject to post-termination judicial review to ensure that a hearing had in fact been held and that the finding of cause for removal was not arbitrary. These procedural and substantive limitations on the removal power militate strongly against the characterization of the Comptroller as a mere agent of Congress by virtue of the removal authority. . . . More importantly, the substantial role played by the President in the process of removal through joint resolution . . . obviates the possibility that the Comptroller will perceive himself as so completely at the mercy of Congress that he will function as its tool.[9] If the Comptroller's conduct in office is not so unsatisfactory to the President as to convince the latter that removal is required under the statutory standard, Congress will have no independent power to coerce the Comptroller unless it can muster a two-thirds majority in both Houses—a feat of bipartisanship more difficult than that required to impeach and convict. The incremental in terrorem effect of the possibility of congressional removal in the face of a

---

overridden only by a two-thirds vote of each House. It is in such checks upon powers, rather than in the classifications of powers, that our governmental system finds equilibrium." Ginnane, The Control of Federal Administration by Congressional Resolutions and Committees, 66 Harv. L. Rev. 569, 571 (1953) (footnote omitted).

[9] The Court cites statements made by supporters of the Budget and Accounting Act indicating their belief that the Act's removal provisions would render the Comptroller subservient to Congress by giving Congress "absolute control of the man's destiny in office." The Court's scholarship, however, is faulty: at the time all of these statements were made-including Representative Sisson's statement of May 3, 1921—the proposed legislation provided for removal by concurrent resolution, with no Presidential role.

presidential veto is therefore exceedingly unlikely to have any discernible impact on the extent of congressional influence over the Comptroller. . . .

■ JUSTICE BLACKMUN, dissenting [argued that the only appropriate remedy in the case was to strike down the statutory removal provisions of the 1921 statute, *not* the Gramm-Rudman-Hollings Act]

. . . I cannot see the sense of invalidating legislation of this magnitude in order to preserve a cumbersome, 65-year-old removal power that has never been exercised and appears to have been all but forgotten until this litigation.

NOTES

(1) ***Joint Resolutions vs. Ordinary Legislation.*** Consider carefully the allocation of power in removal by joint resolution. If the President disagrees that removal is warranted, Congress can act only if two-thirds of both Representatives and Senators support removal. Because of the override provision, Chief Justice Burger reasons, the Court should "read the removal provision as authorizing removal by Congress alone." This same reasoning would suggest—contrary to 200 years of political reality—that laws are enacted by Congress alone. How does this allocation of power in the Comptroller removal provision differ from the following hypothetical alternative:

> Assume that the statutory removal provision vests "for cause" removal power in the President alone. Faced with an unsatisfactory (to it) Comptroller General, Congress presses the President to exercise her removal power, but she refuses to act. Congress then, by statute passed over the President's veto, abolishes the office. It promptly by statute (overriding a veto, if necessary) recreates it, and the Senate will confirm only a person named on the statutory list of three (a list, recall, prepared by the Speaker of the House and President pro tem of the Senate.)

Wouldn't this hypothetical course of events clearly be a constitutional way for Congress to control the Comptroller General? Does it differ in any constitutionally significant way from the actual removal provision?

(2) ***Why the Choice of Formalism?*** Bowsher was decided the same day as CFTC v. Schor, p. 1018, rejecting an Article III challenge to administrative adjudication of securities-fraud claims and common-law counterclaims. Bowsher is resolutely formalist; Schor explicitly rejects formalism in favor of functionalist analysis. Justice O'Connor, writing for Schor Court, tried to explain the difference: "Unlike Bowsher, this case raises no question of the aggrandizement of congressional power at the expense of a coordinate branch. Instead, the separation of powers question presented in this case is whether Congress impermissibly undermined, without appreciable expansion of its own power, the role of the Judicial Branch. In any case, we have, consistent with Bowsher, looked to a number of factors in evaluating the extent to which the congressional scheme endangers separation of

powers principles under the circumstances presented, but have found no genuine threat to those principles to be present in this case."

PETER L. STRAUSS, FORMAL AND FUNCTIONAL APPROACHES TO SEPARATION OF POWERS QUESTIONS—A FOOLISH INCONSISTENCY? 72 Cornell L. Rev. 488, 518–19 (1987): "[The CFTC] enjoys a strong relationship with each of the constitutional actors it has thus, to some extent, displaced. It acts within the framework of congressional statutes, under the constraints of congressional appropriations, and subject to the ordinary routine of congressional oversight and political chaffering. The President appoints its members, who doubtless respond to his requests for advice or suggestions as to national policy, cooperate in his councils, depend upon him for logistic support, and suffer his discipline when they depart from their duty.

"Most important, . . . the CFTC's decisions are subject to judicial controls in the usual fashion. . . . Given these arrangements, one can easily conclude that courts have been assured all the essentials of judicial power, in circumstances that do not threaten 'separation-of-powers' policy; one cannot see how either the President or Congress has been enlarged vis-a-vis the courts, or made more threatening in relation to them, or how the courts' capacity to maintain their relationship with the political heads of government has been diminished. Only formalism [could support] a negative judgment.

". . . [T]he problem underlying Bowsher cannot be understood in the same way. It is not simply that Congress chose a particular mechanism for protecting the 'independence' and 'objectivity' of the Comptroller General. . . . The Comptroller General's relationships with the President, from the proposing of his appointment onward, are strikingly weaker than those that characterize other agencies; the President and the courts both are utterly divorced from participating in the control of the particular functions under review; and the relationship between Congress and the Comptroller General is far more embracive and proprietary than the relationships that characterize the rest of government. Here one could fairly describe Congress as having appropriated to itself the President's characteristic functions (and made nugatory those of the courts). Functionalist and formalist could be equally concerned with these outcomes; that the Court chose a formalist analysis speaks to possible rhetorical advantages, but not to outcome."

NOTES ON DIRECT CONGRESSIONAL PARTICIPATION IN REGULATORY DECISIONMAKING

No Senator or Representative shall, during the Time for which he was elected, be appointed to any civil Office under the Authority of the United States, which shall have been created, or the Emoluments whereof shall have been increased during such time; and no Person holding any Office

*under the United States, shall be a Member of either House during his
Continuance in Office.*

U.S. Const., Art I, § 6, cl. 2

The Incompatibility Clause is a strong textual reminder that ours is not
a parliamentary system in which there is little separation of personnel
between the executive and the legislature. This clause, along with its textual
sibling the Emoluments Clause, seems central to the Framers' concern with
preserving the independence of the legislature. Historians of the framing
note the importance that the British Parliament continued to have in early
Americans' thinking about government structure. A key reason Parliament
failed to check the excesses of the Executive was understood to be the
Crown's "corruption" of its members by deft use of patronage appointments
to executive and judicial offices.[27] The Incompatibility and Emoluments
Clauses reflect a determination to prevent the lure of office from
undermining legislative integrity and independent judgment. What room, if
any, do these clauses leave for direct Congressional participation in
regulatory decisions?

(1) *Jawboning.* One of the most ubiquitous mechanisms through which
Congress tries to influence regulatory outcomes is direct phone calls or
letters to the agency. Challenges to allegedly overaggressive congressional
intervention in particular regulatory decisions are more typically framed as
violation of fairness or legality norms. But occasionally a litigant alleges that
advocacy by a Member crosses the line into unconstitutional direction. U.S.
v. MARDIS, 670 F.Supp.2d 696 (W.D. Tenn. 2009), aff'd on other grounds 600
F.3d 693 (6th Cir.): Mardis was federally indicted for murder under 18 U.S.C.
§ 245 for allegedly killing a local code enforcement officer on account of his
race and color. Prior to the federal charges, Mardis had entered a nolo
contendere plea to second-degree murder in state court. He moved to dismiss
the federal case, arguing among other things that the local Congressman,
Steven Cohen, violated separation of powers by causing the Department of
Justice to bring charges against him. Mardis claimed that Congressman
Cohen repeatedly contacted the FBI and the U.S. Attorney and had publicly
promised to obtain a federal prosecution of the defendant. The government
argued that even if all the allegations were true, there was no separation-of-
powers violation. Held: Motion denied. "Legislators routinely express their
opinions to executive branch officials about matters for which their
departments or agencies are responsible." Cohen's conduct is
distinguishable from Bowsher because it did not involve an official act of
Congress or the passage of legislation allowing an officer of Congress to
direct the President to take action. "The court is dubious that an individual
legislator's interaction with executive branch officials could ever interfere
with the authority of the executive in a way that would violate the
separation of powers." See also Sierra Club v. Costle, 657 F.2d 298 (D.C.
Cir. 1981) (p. 987).

---

[27] See Gordon S. Wood, The Creation of the American Republic: 1776–1787 (2d ed. 1998);
Jack N. Rakove, Original Meanings: Politics and Ideas in the Making of the Constitution 209–
10 (1996).

(2) ***Becoming an Administrative Decision Maker.*** Given the Incompatibility Clause and Bowsher, it might seem obvious that Congress cannot designate its members as agency decision makers. Nonetheless, in a regulatory area in which members were keenly interested, Congress tried to work around these obstacles. METROPOLITAN WASHINGTON AIRPORTS AUTH. V. CITIZENS FOR THE ABATEMENT OF AIRCRAFT NOISE, 501 U.S. 252 (1991): Two of the three Washington, D.C. area airports were federally owned and managed. A congressionally approved interstate compact transferred their ownership to a Commission operated by Virginia, Maryland, and the District of Columbia. The Commission, in turn, acted under the watchful eye of a Review Board, which could veto its decisions. The Board consisted of nine members of Congress from committees having jurisdiction over transportation issues. This scheme was defended on grounds that the Members were serving in their "individual capacities" as representatives of airport users and that the Board was actually a state, rather than a federal, entity. Three Justices (an unusual alignment of White, Rehnquist, and Marshall) accepted the latter argument. The balance of the Court was unpersuaded. JUSTICE STEVENS' opinion rested heavily on Bowsher and Chadha. To forestall the danger of encroachment into the executive sphere, the Constitution imposes two basic and related constraints on Congress: (1) It may not invest itself, its Members, or its agents with executive power; (2) When it exercises its legislative power, it must follow the "single, finely wrought and exhaustively considered procedures" specified in Article I. If the Board's power was considered "executive," a member or agent of Congress may not exercise it. If the power was considered "legislative," it was not being exercised in conformity with Article I, § 7. "Admittedly, Congress imposed its will on the regional authority created by the District of Columbia and the Commonwealth of Virginia by means that are unique and that might prove to be innocuous. However, the statutory scheme challenged today provides a blueprint for extensive expansion of the legislative power beyond its constitutionally-confined role."

NOTES ON THE DIFFERENCES BETWEEN PARLIAMENTARY AND PRESIDENTIAL SYSTEMS

Empowering (and constraining) the executive is an issue for all forms of government, whether democratic or not. Among democracies, parliamentary and presidential forms predominate (with semi-presidential hybrids possible, as in the case of France or continuing monarchies, like the UK, in which a monarch is the nominal or ceremonial leader and a prime minister is the actual leader of the functioning government). In global terms, generalization is problematic, but contrasts are commonly drawn with the Westminster parliamentary system originating in Great Britain and common among other jurisdictions associated with prior British rule. In these systems, unlike ours:

- All executive and legislative officials stand for election at the same time.

- There is a set or understood maximum period of time that must be observed between elections (five years is common), but an election may occur earlier than that, if the political party (or parties) in power either (1) suffer an important defeat—a "loss of confidence"—in the parliament or loses the capacity to command a majority; or (2) conclude that it would be politically advantageous to call an immediate election, rather than wait for the expiration of the maximum period to be observed between elections.

- The parliament—or more specifically, the party or coalition of parties able to command a majority of votes there—selects the chief executive, a "prime minister," to form a government of ministers to head the various elements of the executive branch. "Divided government," with the executive controlled by one political party or coalition of parties and the parliament controlled by opposing political forces, thus does not occur.

- Deciding on a prime minister and peopling important government positions may be easier or harder to accomplish, depending on the election results (whether it results in a majority or a coalition government), but once a parliamentary majority has been obtained to support it, the government is constituted immediately, without the delays that can be associated with the nomination, vetting, and confirmation processes of our presidential system. This is in part because Westminster parliamentary systems often have shadow cabinets, in which senior members of parliament from the opposition party (or parties) form an alternative cabinet, led by the leader of the opposition party, and each member "shadows" a minister of the ruling cabinet.

- Ministers are typically, although not invariably, members of the parliament, and the most important among them constitute a "cabinet" that acts collectively, under the leadership of the prime minister, to approve legislative submissions and other important government actions. (The U.S. cabinet is not a collective, mutually responsible body in this sense.) Since they will thus have previously won the approval of the government, legislative resistance to them is unlikely—and if such resistance were to be successful, that could cause a new election. Since legislation will not occur without majority (government) support, the prime minister requires no veto power.

- Ministers are directly responsible to the parliament for the work of their ministries, including such regulations (called "secondary legislation") as they may adopt. As a result of this direct political responsibility to the legislature, public rulemaking procedures are uncommon, although consultation on important regulations may often occur.

- The political layer at the top of ministries is considerably thinner than in the United States, where thousands of responsible positions exist outside the civil service—around 1,200 requiring nomination and consent, and the rest by direct presidential or secretarial appointment.

- "Independent" bodies in a parliamentary system, outside the ambit of control by prime minister, cabinet, minister, or parliament, are both less frequent and more troublesome in democratic perspective than U.S, "independent" agencies, with their distinctive political relationships to President and Congress.

You may have come to appreciate how little the U.S. Constitution has to say about the authority of the President and, especially, the executive branch of the government. Constitutions providing for parliamentary government also give their greatest attention to the authority of the legislature. Just as Article I of the U.S. Constitution states congressional powers in much greater detail then Article II defines presidential authority, Article 51 of the Australian constitution, a century younger, lists forty areas of national legislative authority. Then, Article 61 on executive authority, says only: "The executive power of the Commonwealth is vested in the Queen and is exercisable by the Governor-General as the Queen's representative, and extends to the execution and maintenance of this Constitution, and of the laws of the Commonwealth."

The prime minister and the cabinet appear not at all, being creatures only of statute. The situation under the Canadian constitution is similar. The United Kingdom's unwritten constitution, too, scarcely deals with executive authority. The unconstrained power of its Parliament to enact any law it chooses is, ostensibly, the most significant occasion for constitutional concern. But if legislatures were once the most feared sources of government authority, today's reality is that the executive holds that position—given both the circumstances of modern warfare and the complexity and breadth of issues with which today's governments must deal.

SECTION 3.   THE PRESIDENT, ADMINISTRATIVE AGENCIES, AND THE EXECUTIVE BRANCH

> a. *Introduction*
> b. *Appointment and Removal*
> c. *Presidential Direction of Regulatory Outcomes*
> d. *The Internal Separation of Powers*

The executive Power shall be vested in a President of the United States of America.

U.S. Const., Art. II, § 1

The President shall be Commander in Chief of the Army and Navy of the United States, and of the Militia of the several States, when called into the actual Service of the United States; he may require the Opinion, in writing, of the principal Officer in each of the executive Departments, upon any Subject relating to the Duties of their respective Offices . . .

U.S. Const., Art. II, § 2

[H]e shall take Care that the Laws be faithfully executed . . .

U.S. Const., Art. II, § 3

a. Introduction

YOUNGSTOWN SHEET & TUBE v. SAWYER

YOUNGSTOWN SHEET & TUBE CO. v. SAWYER

Supreme Court of the United States (1952).
343 U.S. 579.

■ JUSTICE BLACK delivered the opinion of the Court.

[In late 1951, during the Korean War, a labor dispute developed between steel companies and the United Steelworkers Union over the terms of a new collective bargaining agreement. Several months of mediation and a federal investigation failed to resolve the dispute, and the union called a strike for April 9, 1952. A few hours before the strike was to start, President Truman issued Executive Order 10340, stating that "steel is an indispensable component of substantially all . . . weapons and materials" needed by U.S. armed forces in Korea and "a work stoppage would immediately jeopardize and imperil our national defense . . . and would add to the continuing danger of our soldiers, sailors, and airmen engaged in combat in the field." The order directed the Secretary of Commerce to take possession of the steel companies "as he may deem necessary in the interests of national defense" and set terms and conditions of employment. The Secretary immediately issued his own orders taking possession of most of the steel mills and directing the presidents of the companies to maintain their operations. The next morning the President sent a message to Congress reporting his action and sent a second message twelve days later. Congress took no action.

Obeying the Secretary's orders under protest, the companies brought proceedings against him in the District Court. The District Court ruled in their favor and issued a preliminary injunction restraining the Secretary from "continuing the seizure and possession of the plants . . . and from acting under the purported authority of Executive Order No. 10340." On the same day, the Court of Appeals stayed the District Court's injunction. The Supreme Court granted certiorari on May 3 and set the cause for argument on May 12 and issued its decision on June 2.]

We are asked to decide whether the President was acting within his constitutional power when he issued an order directing the Secretary of Commerce to take possession of and operate most of the Nation's steel mills. The mill owners argue that the President's order amounts to lawmaking, a legislative function which the Constitution has expressly confided to the Congress, and not to the President. The Government's position is that the order was made on findings of the President that his action was necessary to avert a national catastrophe which would inevitably result from a stoppage of steel production, and that, in meeting this grave emergency, the President was acting within the aggregate of his constitutional powers as the Nation's Chief Executive and the Commander in Chief of the Armed Forces of the United States. [In the district court, the Government had made a similar argument, contending that the danger to "the wellbeing and safety of the Nation that the President had 'inherent power' to do what he had done—power "supported by the Constitution, by historical precedent, and by court decisions."] . . .

II

The President's power, if any, to issue the order must stem either from an act of Congress or from the Constitution itself. There is no statute that expressly authorizes the President to take possession of property as he did here. Nor is there any act of Congress to which our attention has been directed from which such a power can fairly be implied. Indeed, we do not understand the Government to rely on statutory authorization for this seizure. There are two statutes which do authorize the President to take both personal and real property under certain conditions. However, the Government admits that these conditions were not met, and that the President's order was not rooted in either of the statutes. The Government refers to the seizure provisions of one of these statutes (§ 201(b) of the Defense Production Act) as "much too cumbersome, involved, and time-consuming for the crisis which was at hand."

Moreover, the use of the seizure technique to solve labor disputes in order to prevent work stoppages was not only unauthorized by any congressional enactment; prior to this controversy, Congress had refused to adopt that method of settling labor disputes. When the Taft-Hartley Act was under consideration in 1947, Congress rejected an amendment which would have authorized such governmental seizures in cases of emergency. Apparently it was thought that the technique of seizure, like that of compulsory arbitration, would interfere with the process of collective bargaining. Consequently, the plan Congress adopted in that Act did not provide for seizure under any circumstances. Instead, the plan sought to bring about settlements by use of the customary devices of mediation, conciliation, investigation by boards of inquiry, and public reports. In some instances, temporary injunctions were authorized to provide cooling-off periods. All this failing, unions were left free to strike after a secret vote by employees as to whether they wished to accept their employers' final settlement offer.

It is clear that, if the President had authority to issue the order he did, it must be found in some provision of the Constitution. And it is not claimed that express constitutional language grants this power to the President. The contention is that presidential power should be implied from the aggregate of his powers under the Constitution. Particular reliance is placed on provisions in Article II which say that "The executive Power shall be vested in a President . . ."; that "he shall take Care that the Laws be faithfully executed," and that he "shall be Commander in Chief of the Army and Navy of the United States."

① The order cannot properly be sustained as an exercise of the President's military power as Commander in Chief of the Armed Forces. The Government attempts to do so by citing a number of cases upholding broad powers in military commanders engaged in day-to-day fighting in a theater of war. Such cases need not concern us here. Even though "theater of war" be an expanding concept, we cannot with faithfulness to our constitutional system hold that the Commander in Chief of the Armed Forces has the ultimate power as such to take possession of private property in order to keep labor disputes from stopping production. This is a job for the Nation's lawmakers, not for its military authorities.

② Nor can the seizure order be sustained because of the several constitutional provisions that grant executive power to the President. In the framework of our Constitution, the President's power to see that the laws are faithfully executed refutes the idea that he is to be a lawmaker. The Constitution limits his functions in the lawmaking process to the recommending of laws he thinks wise and the vetoing of laws he thinks bad. And the Constitution is neither silent nor equivocal about who shall make laws which the President is to execute. The first section of the first article says that "All legislative Powers herein granted shall be vested in a Congress of the United States." After granting many powers to the Congress, Article I goes on to provide that Congress may "make all Laws which shall be necessary and proper for carrying into Execution the foregoing Powers, and all other Powers vested by this Constitution in the Government of the United States, or in any Department or Officer thereof."

The President's order does not direct that a congressional policy be executed in a manner prescribed by Congress—it directs that a presidential policy be executed in a manner prescribed by the President. The preamble of the order itself, like that of many statutes, sets out reasons why the President believes certain policies should be adopted, proclaims these policies as rules of conduct to be followed, and again, like a statute, authorizes a government official to promulgate additional rules and regulations consistent with the policy proclaimed and needed to carry that policy into execution. The power of Congress to adopt such public policies as those proclaimed by the order is beyond question. It can authorize the taking of private property for public use. It can make laws regulating the relationships between employers and employees, prescribing rules designed to settle labor disputes, and fixing wages and working conditions in certain fields of our economy. The Constitution does not subject this lawmaking power of Congress to presidential or military supervision or control.

It is said that other Presidents, without congressional authority, have taken possession of private business enterprises in order to settle labor disputes. But even if this be true, Congress has not thereby lost its exclusive constitutional authority to make laws necessary and proper to carry out the powers vested by the Constitution "in the Government of the United States, or any Department or Officer thereof."

The Founders of this Nation entrusted the lawmaking power to the Congress alone in both good and bad times. It would do no good to recall the historical events, the fears of power, and the hopes for freedom that lay behind their choice. Such a review would but confirm our holding that this seizure order cannot stand.

The judgment of the District Court is affirmed.

■ JUSTICE JACKSON, concurring in the judgment and opinion of the Court.

That comprehensive and undefined presidential powers hold both practical advantages and grave dangers for the country will impress anyone who has served as legal adviser to a President in time of transition and public anxiety. While an interval of detached reflection may temper teachings of that experience, they probably are a more realistic influence on my views than the conventional materials of judicial decision which seem unduly to accentuate doctrine and legal fiction. . . .

A judge, like an executive adviser, may be surprised at the poverty of really useful and unambiguous authority applicable to concrete problems of executive power as they actually present themselves. Just what our forefathers did envision, or would have envisioned had they foreseen modern conditions, must be divined from materials almost as enigmatic as the dreams Joseph was called upon to interpret for Pharaoh. A century and a half of partisan debate and scholarly speculation yields no net result, but only supplies more or less apt quotations from respected sources on each side of any question.[1] They largely cancel each other. And court decisions are indecisive because of the judicial practice of dealing with the largest questions in the most narrow way.

---

[1] A Hamilton may be matched against a Madison. 7 The Works of Alexander Hamilton, 76–117; 1 Madison, Letters and Other Writings, 611–654. Professor Taft is counterbalanced by Theodore Roosevelt. Taft, Our Chief Magistrate and His Powers, 139–140; Theodore Roosevelt, Autobiography, 388–389. It even seems that President Taft cancels out Professor Taft. Compare his "Temporary Petroleum Withdrawal No. 5" of September 27, 1909, United States v. Midwest Oil Co., 236 U.S. 459, 467, 468, with his appraisal of executive power in "Our Chief Magistrate and His Powers" 139–140.

The actual art of governing under our Constitution does not, and cannot, conform to judicial definitions of the power of any of its branches based on isolated clauses, or even single Articles torn from context. While the Constitution diffuses power the better to secure liberty, it also contemplates that practice will integrate the dispersed powers into a workable government. It enjoins upon its branches separateness but interdependence, autonomy but reciprocity. Presidential powers are not fixed but fluctuate depending upon their disjunction or conjunction with those of Congress. We may well begin by a somewhat over-simplified grouping of practical situations in which a President may doubt, or others may challenge, his powers, and by distinguishing roughly the legal consequences of this factor of relativity.

1. When the President acts pursuant to an express or implied authorization of Congress, his authority is at its maximum, for it includes all that he possesses in his own right plus all that Congress can delegate. In these circumstances, and in these only, may he be said (for what it may be worth) to personify the federal sovereignty. If his act is held unconstitutional under these circumstances, it usually means that the Federal Government, as an undivided whole, lacks power. A seizure executed by the President pursuant to an Act of Congress would be supported by the strongest of presumptions and the widest latitude of judicial interpretation, and the burden of persuasion would rest heavily upon any who might attack it.

2. When the President acts in absence of either a congressional grant or denial of authority, he can only rely upon his own independent powers, but there is a zone of twilight in which he and Congress may have concurrent authority, or in which its distribution is uncertain. Therefore, congressional inertia, indifference or quiescence may sometimes, at least, as a practical matter, enable, if not invite, measures on independent presidential responsibility. In this area, any actual test of power is likely to depend on the imperatives of events and contemporary imponderables, rather than on abstract theories of law.

3. When the President takes measures incompatible with the expressed or implied will of Congress, his power is at its lowest ebb, for then he can rely only upon his own constitutional powers minus any constitutional powers of Congress over the matter. Courts can sustain exclusive presidential control in such a case only by disabling the Congress from acting upon the subject. Presidential claim to a power at once so conclusive and preclusive must be scrutinized with caution, for what is at stake is the equilibrium established by our constitutional system.

Into which of these classifications does this executive seizure of the steel industry fit? It is eliminated from the first by admission, for it is conceded that no congressional authorization exists for this seizure. That takes away also the support of the many precedents and declarations which were made in relation, and must be confined, to this category.

Can it then be defended under flexible tests available to the second category? It seems clearly eliminated from that class, because Congress has not left seizure of private property an open field, but has covered it by three statutory policies inconsistent with this seizure. In cases where the purpose is to supply needs of the Government itself, two courses are provided: one, seizure of a plant which fails to comply with obligatory orders placed by the Government; another, condemnation of facilities, including temporary use under the power of eminent domain. The third is applicable where it is the general economy of the country that is to be protected, rather than exclusive governmental interests. None of these were invoked. In choosing a different and inconsistent way of his own, the President cannot claim that it is necessitated or invited by failure of Congress to legislate upon the occasions, grounds and methods for seizure of industrial properties.

This leaves the current seizure to be justified only by the severe tests under the third grouping, where it can be supported only by any remainder of executive power after subtraction of such powers as Congress may have over the subject. In short, we can sustain the President only by holding that seizure of such strike-bound industries is within his domain and beyond control by Congress. Thus, this Court's first review of such seizures occurs under circumstances which leave presidential power most vulnerable to attack and in the least favorable of possible constitutional postures. . . .

The Solicitor General seeks the power of seizure in three clauses of the Executive Article, the first reading, "The executive Power shall be vested in a President of the United States of America." Lest I be thought to exaggerate, I quote the interpretation which his brief puts upon it: "In our view, this clause constitutes a grant of all the executive powers of which the Government is capable." If that be true, it is difficult to see why the forefathers bothered to add several specific items, including some trifling ones.[9]

The example of such unlimited executive power that must have most impressed the forefathers was the prerogative exercised by George III, and the description of its evils in the Declaration of Independence leads me to doubt that they were creating their new Executive in his image. Continental European examples were no more appealing. And, if we seek instruction from our own times, we can match it only from the executive powers in those governments we disparagingly describe as totalitarian. I

---

[9] ". . .he may require the Opinion, in writing, of the principal Officer in each of the executive Departments, upon any Subject relating to the Duties of their respective Offices . . ." U.S. Const. Art. II, § 2. He ". . . shall Commission all the Officers of the United States." U.S. Const. Art. II, § 3. Matters such as those would seem to be inherent in the Executive if anything is.

cannot accept the view that this clause is a grant in bulk of all conceivable executive power, but regard it as an allocation to the presidential office of the generic powers thereafter stated.

The clause on which the Government next relies is that "The President shall be Commander in Chief of the Army and Navy of the United States . . ." These cryptic words have given rise to some of the most persistent controversies in our constitutional history. . . . It undoubtedly puts the Nation's armed forces under presidential command. Hence, this loose appellation is sometimes advanced as support for any presidential action, internal or external, involving use of force, the idea being that it vests power to do anything, anywhere, that can be done with an army or navy. That seems to be the logic of an argument tendered at our bar—that the President having, on his own responsibility, sent American troops abroad derives from that act "affirmative power" to seize the means of producing a supply of steel for them. . . . Thus, it is said, he has invested himself with "war powers."

I cannot foresee all that it might entail if the Court should indorse this argument. . . . [N]o doctrine that the Court could promulgate would seem to me more sinister and alarming than that a President whose conduct of foreign affairs is so largely uncontrolled, and often even is unknown, can vastly enlarge his mastery over the internal affairs of the country by his own commitment of the Nation's armed forces to some foreign venture. . . .

The third clause in which the Solicitor General finds seizure powers is that "he shall take Care that the Laws be faithfully executed." That authority must be matched against words of the Fifth Amendment that "No person shall be . . . deprived of life, liberty or property, without due process of law . . ." One gives a governmental authority that reaches so far as there is law, the other gives a private right that authority shall go no farther. These signify about all there is of the principle that ours is a government of laws, not of men, and that we submit ourselves to rulers only if under rules.

The Solicitor General lastly grounds support of the seizure upon nebulous, inherent powers never expressly granted, but said to have accrued to the office from the customs and claims of preceding administrations. The plea is for a resulting power to deal with a crisis or an emergency according to the necessities of the case, the unarticulated assumption being that necessity knows no law. . . .

The appeal, however, that we declare the existence of inherent powers *ex necessitate* to meet an emergency asks us to do what many think would be wise, although it is something the forefathers omitted. They knew what emergencies were, knew the pressures they engender for authoritative action, knew, too, how they afford a ready pretext for usurpation. . . . [M]any modern nations have forthrightly recognized that war and economic crises may upset the normal balance between liberty and authority. Their experience with emergency powers may not be irrelevant to the argument here that we should say that the Executive, of his own volition, can invest himself with undefined emergency powers. . . .

[I]t is relevant to note the gap that exists between the President's paper powers and his real powers. The Constitution does not disclose the measure of the actual controls wielded by the modern presidential office. That instrument must be understood as an Eighteenth-Century sketch of a government hoped for, not as a blueprint of the Government that is. Vast accretions of federal power, eroded from that reserved by the States, have magnified the scope of presidential activity. Subtle shifts take place in the centers of real power that do not show on the face of the Constitution.

Executive power has the advantage of concentration in a single head in whose choice the whole Nation has a part, making him the focus of public hopes and expectations. In drama, magnitude and finality, his decisions so far overshadow any others that, almost alone, he fills the public eye and ear. No other personality in public life can begin to compete with him in access to the public mind through modern methods of communications. By his prestige as head of state and his influence upon public opinion, he exerts a leverage upon those who are supposed to check and balance his power which often cancels their effectiveness. . . .

I cannot be brought to believe that this country will suffer if the Court refuses further to aggrandize the presidential office, already so potent and so relatively immune from judicial review, at the expense of Congress. But I have no illusion that any decision by this Court can keep power in the hands of Congress if it is not wise and timely in meeting its problems. A crisis that challenges the President equally, or perhaps primarily, challenges Congress. If not good law, there was worldly wisdom in the maxim attributed to Napoleon that "The tools belong to the man who can use them." We may say that power to legislate for emergencies belongs in the hands of Congress, but only Congress itself can prevent power from slipping through its fingers. . . .

■ JUSTICE FRANKFURTER, concurring.

Although the considerations relevant to the legal enforcement of the principle of separation of powers seem to me more complicated and flexible than any appear from what Mr. Justice Black has written, I join his opinion because I thoroughly agree with the application of the principle to the circumstances of this case. . . .

The issue before us can be met, and therefore should be, without attempting to define the President's powers comprehensively. I shall not attempt to delineate what belongs to him by virtue of his office beyond the power even of Congress to contract; what authority belongs to him until Congress acts; what kind of problems may be dealt with either by the Congress or by the President or by both, what power must be exercised by the Congress and cannot be delegated to the President. . . . The judiciary may, as this case proves, have to intervene in determining where authority lies as between the democratic forces in our scheme of government. But in doing so we should be wary and humble. Such is the teaching of this Court's role in the history of the country. . . .

It cannot be contended that the President would have had power to issue this order had Congress explicitly negated such authority in formal legislation. Congress has expressed its will to withhold this power from the President as though it had said so in so many words. . . . By the Labor Management Relations Act of 1947, Congress said to the President, "You may not seize. Please report to us and ask for seizure power if you think it is needed in a specific situation." . . .

To be sure, the content of the three authorities of government is not to be derived from an abstract analysis. The areas are partly interacting, not wholly disjointed. The Constitution is a framework for government. Therefore the way the framework has consistently operated fairly establishes that it has operated according to its true nature. Deeply embedded traditional ways of conducting government cannot supplant the Constitution or legislation, but they give meaning to the words of a text or supply them. It is an inadmissibly narrow conception of American constitutional law to confine it to the words of the Constitution and to disregard the gloss which life has written upon them. In short, a systematic, unbroken, executive practice, long pursued to the knowledge of the Congress and never before questioned, engaged in by Presidents who have also sworn to uphold the Constitution, making as it were such exercise of power part of the structure of our government, may be treated as a gloss on "executive Power" vested in the President by § 1 of Art. II. [But no such] practice can be vouched for executive seizure of property at a time when this country was not at war . . .

■ CHIEF JUSTICE VINSON, with whom JUSTICE REED and JUSTICE MINTON join, dissenting.

[Chief Justice Vinson began by outlining statutes Congress had enacted to ensure support for the Korean War, arguing that] [t]heir successful execution depends upon continued production of steel and stabilized prices for steel. . . . One is not here called upon even to consider the possibility of executive seizure of a farm, a corner grocery store or even a single industrial plant. Such considerations arise only when one ignores the central fact of this case—that the Nation's entire basic steel production would have shut down completely if there had been no Government seizure. . . .

[M]uch of the argument in this case has been directed at straw men. We do not now have before us the case of a President acting solely on the basis of his own notions of the public welfare. Nor is there any question of unlimited executive power in this case. The President himself closed the door to any such claim when he sent his Message to Congress stating his purpose to abide by any action of Congress, whether approving or disapproving his seizure action. . . . The absence of a specific statute authorizing seizure of the steel mills as a mode of executing the laws—both the military procurement program and the anti-inflation program—has not until today been thought to prevent the President from executing the laws. Unlike an administrative commission confined to the enforcement of the statute under which it was created, or the head to a department when administering a particular statute, the President is a constitutional officer charged with taking care that a "mass of legislation" be executed. . . .

The broad executive power granted by Article II to an officer on duty 365 days a year cannot, it is said, be invoked to avert disaster. Instead, the President must confine himself to sending a message to Congress recommending action. Under this messenger-boy concept of the Office, the President cannot even act to preserve legislative programs from destruction so that Congress will have something left to act upon. . . . Presidents have been in the past, and any man worthy of the Office should be in the future, free to take at least interim action necessary to execute legislative programs essential to survival of the Nation. . . . The President immediately informed Congress of his action and clearly stated his intention to abide by the legislative will. No basis for claims of arbitrary action, unlimited powers or dictatorial usurpation of congressional power appears from the facts of this case. On the contrary, judicial, legislative and executive precedents throughout our history demonstrate that in this case the President acted in full conformity with his duties under the Constitution. . . .

NOTES

(1) *Early Separation of Powers Formalism and Functionalism.* Notice how the contrasting opinions in Youngstown map onto current formalist and functionalist approaches to the separation of powers, although those terms were not in use when Youngstown was decided. Justice Black, who wrote the opinion for the Court, took a "formalist" approach, carefully delineating possible bases for presidential authority and rejecting arguments from necessity as a basis for expanding presidential power. Can you reconcile agency rulemaking with Justice Black's assertion that "[i]n the framework of our Constitution, the President's power to see that the laws are faithfully executed refutes the idea that he is to be a lawmaker"?

By comparison, Justice Jackson described his view of the separation of powers in terms that are invoked by functionalists to this day, insisting that actual governance does not conform to formal separation of clearly defined powers and that interdependence of the branches is at the core of the constitutional scheme. Justice Frankfurter also insisted on viewing separation of powers in context and not abstractly, emphasizing the importance of historical practice as helping to elucidate the meaning of executive power.

(2) *Justice Jackson's Tripartite Framework.* Over time, the three-part framework that Justice Jackson laid out in his concurrence has come to dominate judicial assessment of presidential power. As the Supreme Court recently stated in Zivotofsky v. Kerry, 135 S.Ct. 2076, 2083 (2015): "In considering claims of Presidential power this Court refers to Justice Jackson's familiar tripartite framework from Youngstown Sheet & Tube Co. v. Sawyer, 343 U.S. 579, 635–638 (1952) (concurring opinion)." Jackson's framework surfaces particularly frequently in foreign affairs contexts, see Zivotofsky and Medellin v. Texas, 552 U.S. 491 (2008), and the President's detention authority, see Hamdan v. Rumsfeld, 548 U.S. 557 (2006). Jackson's concurrence is not the only part of Youngstown having a lasting impact; the Supreme Court recently endorsed Justice Frankfurter's emphasis on historical practice as a central focus in separation of powers disputes. See NLRB v. Noel Canning, [p. 892], 134 S.Ct. 2550, 2559 (2014).

Yet when the decision was issued in 1952, the initial response to Youngstown was quite negative. Several leading constitutional scholars castigated it as "a judicial brick without straw," "destined to be ignored," and "so much out of step with the way in which the American system of government functions that it cannot long stand as a guidepost in the development of United States constitutional law." Patricia L. Bellia, Executive Power in Youngstown's Shadow, 19 Const. Comment. 87, 88 & n. 3 (2002) (internal quotations omitted) (collecting criticisms).

(3) *The Dispute over Inherent Presidential Power.* The central dispute in Youngstown was over the question of whether the President enjoys implicit or inherent authority under the Constitution, as the Government claimed. Justice Black firmly denied the Government's claim, ruling President Truman's action unconstitutional because not authorized by statute or by any of the express constitutional grants of presidential authority. Chief Justice Vinson, in dissent, rejected what he called a "messenger-boy concept of the office," insisting that the "broad executive power granted by Article II" authorized the President "to take at least interim action necessary to execute legislative programs essential to survival of the Nation."

Where do Justices Jackson and Frankfurter come out on this question? Both are clearly uneasy over the breadth of the Government's claim and the suggestion that necessity is a sufficient basis for any presidential action. But both also reject Black's effort to restrict the President to express powers, suggesting both that the divide among powers is not as clear-cut in the Constitution as Black suggests and often will be affected by actual practice. Note though the difference even between Jackson and Frankfurter: while Jackson maintains that a "gap . . . exists between the President's paper powers and his real powers," Frankfurter argues that "historical gloss" over time may change the scope of the President's constitutional powers.

(4) *Youngstown's Relevance for Administrative Law.* The scope of presidential power to make law is not the focus of presidential authority disputes in administrative law. Instead, questions here turn on the scope of presidential power to exercise control over the executive branch. In terms of Jackson's tripartite framework, administrative law cases generally concern

whether Congress has authorized the President to exercise such control, whether the President has such control even though Congress has been silent, or whether the President may exercise such control even though Congress has tried to bar the president from doing so. In this third zone, the question is whether a statute violates the President's Article II authority and thus falls outside Congress's power to structure the executive branch under Article I's Necessary and Proper Clause. But the President's Article II power may also be relevant to construing what Congress has done as Congress is often less than express in addressing the extent to which the President may direct or supervise officials in the executive branch.

In this context, debates over inherent presidential authority surface as disputes over both what congress has actually done and how to read Article II's Vesting Clause, which states that "[t]he executive Power shall be vested in a President of the United States." Advocates of strong executive power read this Clause as an express grant of all executive authority in the President—often called the "unitary executive" theory. The opposing view, following Jackson in Youngstown, rejects the claim that the Vesting Clause can be read so broadly. This debate has arisen in particular in the context of limits on the President's ability to remove executive officers and is discussed below in Sec. 3.b. But a variant of the debate arises outside the context of the power to remove in connection with the President's ability to countermand or direct an executive branch official's exercise of his or her duties, discussed below in Sec. 3.c.

b. Appointment and Removal

> **(1) Appointment and Confirmation**
> **(2) The Removal Power**

Our discussion of presidential and congressional efforts to control regulatory power by controlling agency personnel begins with appointment. The question of who appoints the officers of government provoked intense disagreement both during the Constitution's drafting and in the ratification debates. The Appointments Clause represents a rare textual reference to administration in the Constitution and over the centuries has spawned a steady if thin stream of litigation. The discussion next turns to the President's removal power, which appears nowhere in the Constitution's text; the only reference to removal of civil officers is in connection to impeachment, which solely involves the House and the Senate. The President's removal power was barely mentioned in the drafting and ratification debates, but it quickly became an issue once the hard work of building a government began. The first Congress struggled with the issue and the debate begun there continues to the present day.

(1) Appboxintment and Confirmation

> *Notes on the Structure and Reach of the*
> *Appointments Clause*
> **NATIONAL LABOR RELATIONS**
> **BOARD v. NOEL CANNING**

. . . [The President] shall nominate, and by and with the Advice and Consent of the Senate, shall appoint Ambassadors, other public Ministers and Consuls, Judges of the supreme Court, and all other Officers of the United States, whose Appointments are not herein otherwise provided for, and which shall be established by Law; but the Congress may by Law vest the Appointment of such inferior Officers, as they think proper, in the President alone, in the Courts of Law, or in the Heads of Departments.

U.S. Const., Art. II, § 2, cl. 2

The President shall have Power to fill up all Vacancies that may happen during the Recess of the Senate, by granting Commissions which shall expire at the End of their next Session.

U.S. Const., Art. II, § 2, cl. 3

[H]e shall take Care that the Laws be faithfully executed . . .

U.S. Const., Art. II, § 3

The Framers were baffled by how to allocate the power to appoint the officers of government. The history of oppression by officials appointed by the Crown and the colonial governors was still fresh in their memory—but so was the unhappy experience in the states with government dominated by the legislature. In early drafts of the Constitution the power was assigned to the Senate, which was seen as something of a middle ground between the popular legislature (the House) and the Executive. Some delegates became concerned, however, that the Senate would become "a real & dangerous Aristocracy." Jack Rakove, Original Meanings: Politics and Ideas in the Making of the Constitution 265 (1996). The final draft adopted an intricate power-sharing approach: "Officers of the United States" (now generally referred to as "principal" officers) would be appointed by the President with Senate advice and consent. As to "inferior Officers," Congress could by ordinary legislation determine whether appointment would be made by the President without Senate involvement, or by "Courts of Law" or "Heads of Departments." In addition, the President was given power to make temporary appointments "to fill up all vacancies that may happen during the recess of the Senate."

This solution was accepted by almost all the delegates as combining the "responsibility" of presidential nomination with the "security" of Senatorial advice and consent. Id. at 266. During the ratification debates, however, the anti-Federalists vehemently objected to what they foresaw as a monarchical President colluding with an aristocratic Senate to overwhelm the people's representatives in the House. Instead of elites against the masses, the factor that soon became the basis for Presidential-Senate "collusion"—and indeed came to dominate the constitutional separation of powers system more broadly—was political party. See Daryl J. Levinson & Richard H. Pildes, Separation of Parties, Not Powers, 119 Harv. L. Rev. 2311 (2006). As this section details, partisan polarization has a tremendous impact on the appointments system today.

NOTES ON THE STRUCTURE AND REACH OF THE APPOINTMENTS CLAUSE

(1) **The Constitutional Norm for Appointments.** As the text of the Appointments Clause makes clear, the primary method for appointment of principal officers is presidential nomination and Senate confirmation. For inferior officers, the Constitution is more flexible, allowing appointment by the President (without requiring Senate confirmation), department heads, or courts. However, presidential nomination and Senate confirmation remains the default method of appointment; Congress must affirmatively exercise, "by law," its Appointments Clause power to exempt officers from confirmation by assigning their appointment to one of the other allowed methods. Congress has chosen to retain confirmation for a large number of executive offices, often expressly stating this in the relevant statutes. According to the 2016 "Plum Book," issued by the Senate Committee on Homeland Security and Governmental Affairs, there are over 1,200 agency positions requiring both presidential nomination and Senate confirmation.

(2) **"Principal" vs. "Inferior" Officers.** The distinction between principal officers and inferior officers is obviously crucial to the Appointments Clause's careful calibration of congressional and presidential power. EDMOND V. UNITED STATES, 520 U.S. 651 (1997), raised the question of whether a member of the Coast Guard Court of Criminal Appeals (a military court) was an inferior or principal officer. Writing for all the justices but Justice Souter, JUSTICE SCALIA acknowledged that "[o]ur cases have not set forth an exclusive criterion for distinguishing between principal and inferior officers for Appointments Clause purposes." He continued: "Generally speaking, the term 'inferior officer' connotes a relationship with some higher ranking officer or officers below the President: whether one is an 'inferior' officer depends on whether he has a superior. It is not enough that other officers may be identified who formally maintain a higher rank, or possess responsibilities of a greater magnitude. If that were the intention, the Constitution might have used the phrase 'lesser officer.' Rather, in the context of a clause designed to preserve political accountability relative to important government assignments, we think it evident that 'inferior officers' are officers whose work is directed and supervised at some level by others who were appointed by presidential nomination with the advice and consent of the Senate." Emphasizing that "the judges of the Court of Criminal Appeals have no power to render a final decision on behalf of the

United States unless permitted to do so by other Executive officers," Justice Scalia concluded that members of the Court of Criminal Appeals were inferior officers and sustained their appointment by the Secretary of Transportation. Justice Souter was unwilling to decide the question based solely on whether the officer has a "relationship of [supervision and direction] with some higher ranking officer or officers below the President."

In emphasizing the factor of supervision, the Edmond Court distinguished MORRISON V. OLSON, 487 U.S. 654 (1988) (p. 934), in which the Court, in a 7–1 opinion written by CHIEF JUSTICE REHNQUIST, had concluded that independent counsels under the Ethics in Government Act of 1978 were inferior officers. In Morrison, the Court had stated that "[t]he line between 'inferior' and 'principal' officers is one that is far from clear, and the Framers provided little guidance into where it should be drawn." Eschewing the need to specify such a line to determine the status of independent counsels, the Court held that "[s]everal factors lead to th[e] conclusion" that independent counsels were inferior officers: "First, [the independent counsel] is subject to removal by a higher Executive Branch official. Although she possesses a degree of independent discretion to exercise the powers delegated to her under the Act, the fact that she can be removed by the Attorney General indicates that she is to some degree "inferior" in rank and authority. Second, appellant is empowered by the Act to perform only certain, limited duties. An independent counsel's role is restricted primarily to investigation and, if appropriate, prosecution for certain federal crimes. . . . The Act specifically provides that in policy matters appellant is to comply to the extent possible with the policies of the Department. Third, appellant's office is limited in jurisdiction. Not only is the Act itself restricted in applicability to certain federal officials suspected of certain serious federal crimes, but an independent counsel can only act within the scope of the jurisdiction that has been granted by the Special Division pursuant to a request by the Attorney General. Finally, appellant's office is limited in tenure."

Edmond acknowledged that the Coast Guard judges were not limited in tenure or jurisdiction but distinguished Morrison on the grounds that "Morrison did not purport to set forth a definitive test for whether an office is 'inferior' under the Appointments Clause." Are you persuaded that the two cases are compatible? Doesn't Edmond give us the type of definitive test that Morrison eschewed in favor of a multifactor analysis? Which approach do you think is more appropriate? Is it particularly important to give Congress a clear line against which to legislate here? Or does a multifactor test better accommodate the Appointments Clause's goals of ensuring sufficient Senate role in appointments without unduly impeding the government's ability to function? In a more recent decision, Free Enterprise Foundation v. Public Company Accounting Oversight Board, 561 U.S. 477 (2010), the Court invoked Edmond, concluding that because members of the Board were removable at will by the Securities and Exchange Commission and subject to other oversight by the Commission, "we have no hesitation in concluding that under Edmond the Board members are inferior officers."

(3) *"Officers" vs. "Employees."* The Court has long acknowledged that the categories of principal officer and inferior officer do not encompass the entire

federal workforce. The vast majority of federal workers fall into a third category, "employees." BUCKLEY V. VALEO, 424 U.S. 1 (1976), addressed the line between officers, who must be appointed in accordance with the Appointments Clause, and employees, whose appointment process is left for Congress to specify under its Necessary and Proper Clause power: Officers are "any appointee exercising *significant* authority pursuant to the laws of the United States;" employees are "lesser functionaries subordinate to officers of the United States." (Note the reappearance of subordinateness. Does this portend further problems for Justice Scalia's criterion for distinguishing inferior from principal officers?) A line the Court might have drawn was whether the position carries the authority to enter final decisions or otherwise bind the government. But in Freytag v. Commissioner, 501 U.S. 868 (1991) (p. 889), a unanimous Court held that special trial judges of the Tax Court—who hear cases and prepare proposed opinions for the regular judges on the Court but have no final decisional authority—are officers because of the "significant discretion" they exercise.

(4)   *The Uncertain Status of ALJs.* Uncertainty over how to differentiate officers and employees is central to ongoing debates over the status of administrative law judges (ALJs), particularly at the Securities and Exchange Commission (SEC). The Dodd-Frank Wall Street Reform and Consumer Protection Act of 2010 authorized the SEC to impose civil penalties on any person in proceedings before an ALJ; prior to this point, the SEC's authority to impose civil penalties in administrative adjudication was limited to SEC-registered entities and associated individuals, primarily broker-dealers and investment advisors. For other defendants, the SEC had to file a civil enforcement action in federal court. The Dodd-Frank change led to a sharp increase in the SEC's use of administrative proceedings and a surge in constitutional challenges to administrative adjudication. Among the many constitutional claims raised in these suits that you'll see referenced in this chapter (pp. 945, 1027) and in Chapter V (p. 507), perhaps the claim getting the most traction asserts that ALJs are unconstitutionally appointed inferior officers. For background on SEC adjudication and the recent changes, see Gideon Mark, SEC and CFTC Administrative Proceedings 19 U. Pa. J. Const. L. 45 (2016).

The Supreme Court noted the debate over ALJs' status in Free Enterprise Foundation v. Public Company Accounting Board, 561 U.S. 477, 507 n. 10 (2010) (p. 922), but has yet to resolve it, so lower courts have taken the lead. In BANDIMERE V. SEC, 844 F.3d 1168 (10th Cir. 2016), the Tenth Circuit concluded, "SEC ALJs are inferior officers under the Appointments Clause. . . . First, the office of the SEC ALJ was established by law. The APA established the ALJ position. 5 U.S.C. § 556(b)(3). In addition, the Securities and Exchange Act of 1934 authorizes the SEC to delegate any of its functions with the exception of rulemaking to ALJs . . . Second, statutes set forth SEC ALJs' duties, salaries, and means of appointment. SEC ALJs are not hired on a temporary, episodic basis. They receive career appointments and can be removed only for good cause. . . . Third, SEC ALJs exercise significant discretion in performing important functions . . . SEC ALJs have authority to do all things necessary and appropriate to discharge his or her duties, which includes authority to shape the administrative record[,] . . . rul[e] on dispositive and procedural motions, issu[e] subpoenas, and presid[e] over trial-like hearings. . . .They also have authority to issue initial decisions that declare respondents liable and impose sanctions. When a respondent does not timely seek agency review, the action of [the ALJ] shall, for all purposes, including appeal or review thereof, be deemed the action of the Commission. . . . Further, SEC ALJs have power to enter default judgments and . . .authority to set aside, make permanent, limit, or suspend temporary sanctions that the SEC itself has imposed." (internal quotations and alterations omitted).

The D.C. Circuit reached the opposite conclusion about the status of SEC ALJs in RAYMOND J. LUCIA COS., INC. V. SEC, 832 F.3d 277 (D.C. Cir. 2016). Relying on an earlier D.C. Circuit decision that had held FDIC ALJs were employees rather than inferior officers, Landry v. FDIC, 204 F.3d 1125 (D.C. Cir. 2000), the panel held the same was true of SEC ALJs: "[T]he main criteria for drawing the line between inferior Officers and employees not covered by the Clause are (1) the significance of the matters resolved by the officials, (2) the discretion they exercise in reaching their decisions, and (3) the finality of those decisions. In Landry, the court held that the [FDIC] ALJs . . . were not Officers because they did not satisfy the third criterion; . . . the FDIC ALJs could not issue final decisions." The panel held that finality for ALJ decisions was also lacking at the SEC, noting that SEC rules preserve time for the Commission to decide whether to order review when no petition for review is filed and require that if the agency decides not to review, it issues an order to that effect. According to these rules, "the initial [ALJ] decision becomes final when, and only when, the Commission issues the finality order, and not before then. . . . Thus, the Commission must affirmatively act—by issuing the order—in every case. The Commission's final action is either in the form of a new decision after de novo review or, by declining to grant or order review, its embrace of the ALJ's initial decision as its own. . . . Put otherwise, the Commission's ALJs neither have been delegated sovereign authority to act independently of the Commission nor, by other means established by Congress, do they have the power to bind third parties, or the government itself, for the public benefit." Although the D.C. Circuit took the decision en banc, ultimately the panel was affirmed by an equally divided en banc court, 868 F.3d 1021 (D.C.Cir. 2017), and a petition for certiorari was pending when this casebook went to print. For recent scholarship on this issue, see Kent Barnett, Resolving the ALJ Quandary, 66 Vand. L. Rev. 797 804–05 (2013); Jennifer L. Mascott, Who are 'Officers of the United States'?, 70 Stanford L Rev. (forthcoming 2017–2018).

(5) *"Employees" vs. "Contractors."* Just as in private law, it is sometimes unclear whether an individual performing services is a government employee or an independent contractor. UNITED STATES V. HARTWELL, 73 U.S. (6 Wall.) 385 (1868), identified "ideas of tenure, duration, emolument, and duties" as central to the distinction. "A government office is different from a government contract. The latter from its nature is necessarily limited in its duration and specific in its objects. The terms agreed upon define the rights and obligations of both parties, and neither may depart from them without

the assent of the other." Id. at 393. The difference was further elaborated in United States v. Germaine, 99 U.S. 508 (1879). The Court held that a surgeon appointment by the Commissioner of Pensions to examine pension applicants was not a federal employee. His duties were "occasional and intermittent," and "*not* continuing and permanent;" he "only . . . act[ed] when called on by the Commissioner . . . in some special case," was paid only a fee per examination, took no oath, posted no bond, and was not required to keep a "place of business for public use."

An influential separation-of-powers opinion from the Clinton Administration Office of Legal Counsel concluded, "The Appointments Clause is simply not implicated when significant authority is devolved upon non-federal actors." The Constitutional Separation of Powers Between the President and Congress, 20 Op. O.L.C. 124 (1996) (Walter Dellinger). Is it troubling that individuals exercising "significant authority" on behalf of the United States are not within the constitutional appointments structure? Note that the Supreme Court cases establishing this principle long predate the expanding federal practice of privatizing functions that are conventionally considered governmental. A growing literature calls for reexamination of the law in this area. However, Free Enterprise fits comfortably with the Appointments Clause precedent. The New York Stock Exchange, on which the PCAOB was modeled, is statutorily entrusted with rulemaking, investigative, and disciplinary responsibilities, but no government official can directly appoint its officers, who also enjoy for-cause removal protection. Chief Justice Roberts, responding to the argument that members of the PCAOB were less insulated from presidential control than officers of the NYSE: "While we need not decide the question here, a removal standard appropriate for limiting Government control over private bodies may be inappropriate for officers wielding the executive power of the United States." Should the contracting out of federal regulatory authority to private actors call for less political accountability than the Appointments Clause provides for government actors?

Recently, concurring in DOT V. ASS'N OF AMERICAN RAILROADS, 135 S.Ct. 1225 (2015), Justice Alito raised questions about the status of arbitrators in disputes involving the government. The governing regulatory scheme called for the Surface Transportation Board (a federal agency) to appoint an arbitrator to resolve disputes between the Federal Railroad Administration (another federal agency) and Amtrak (a government passenger rail corporation deemed part of government for constitutional purposes) over the "metrics and standards" that would govern Amtrak's performance. According to Justice Alito, if the arbitrator were private, his or her ability to exercise binding regulatory authority would represent an unconstitutional private delegation of governmental power. On the other hand, if the arbitrator were public, Justice Alito contended that the ability to exercise binding authority would make the arbitrator a principal officer under Edmond, and thus the arbitrator's appointment by the Surface Transportation Board, rather than by the President with Senate advice and consent, would be unconstitutional. The Supreme Court remanded to the D.C. Circuit to consider this among other issues, and that court agreed with

Justice Alito that an arbitrator appointed under the statute was a principal officer and the statute violated the Appointments Clause, 821 F.3d 19, 38–39 (2016). The government decided not to seek certiorari. For a contrary view, see Office of Legal Counsel, Constitutional Limitations on Federal Government Participation in Binding Arbitration, 19 Op. O.L.C. 208 (1995) (Walter Dellinger) (arbitrators not appointed via the Appointments Clause can be used for binding arbitration involving the federal government because while they do exercise "significant authority" but "are retained for a single matter, their service expires at the resolution of that matter, and they fix their own compensation").

(6) *International Tribunals and Non-Federal Entities Implementing Federal Law.* Similar to private officials or contractors are members of international tribunals and non-federal entities. These individuals can exercise significant authority by virtue of their roles in federal regulation and programs or in applying U.S. law. But is the authority they wield federal authority? And are their positions federal offices? Following OLC's view and that of the Clinton administration, "the Ninth Circuit ruled that state officials on the Pacific Northwest Electric Power Conservation Planning Council (an organization formed by an interstate compact) are not officers, regardless of whether they exercise federal power." Anne Joseph O'Connell, Bureaucracy at the Boundary, 162 U. Pa. L. Rev. 841, 903 (2014). But others disagree, arguing that appointed individuals exercising significant federal authority should count as officers under Buckley. See, e.g., John C. Yoo, The New Sovereignty and the Old Constitution: The Chemical Weapons Convention and the Appointments Clause, 15 Const. Comment. 87 (1998).

A source of recent Appointments Clause controversy on this front involves international tribunals such as the International Court of Justice or the North American Free Trade Agreement (NAFTA) dispute settlement process overseen by the NAFTA Secretariat. These tribunals are attacked on the grounds, inter alia, that "international delegations with direct domestic effect permit international agents to change the rights of U.S. citizens under domestic law. But only individuals appointed under the Appointments Clause can exercise such authority under U.S. law," and members of the tribunals were not appointed in accordance with the Clause. John O. McGinnis, Medellin and the Future of International Delegation, 118 Yale L.J. 1712 (2009). See also David Zaring, Sovereignty Mismatch and the New Administrative Law, 91 Wash. U. L. Rev. 59, 87–89 (2013).

(7) *Who Can Appoint? "Heads" of "Departments" and "Courts of Law."* In FREYTAG V. COMMISSIONER OF INTERNAL REVENUE, 501 U.S. 868 (1991), the question was whether the Tax Court (a legislative, Article I court[28]) qualifies as a "department" or a "court of law," so that special trial judges (who function much like ALJs) could be appointed by the chief judge of the court. As mentioned in Note 2, all the Justices agreed that special trial judges are inferior officers; all also agreed that the chief judge could be given

---

[28] As discussed below in Section 4, a legislative court is one whose judges do not have the requisite life tenure and protection against salary diminution required in those who exercise the Article III judicial power. Tax Court judges, for example, are appointed for a 15-year term.

the power of appointment, but they sharply divided over the reason. Writing for the 5–4 majority, JUSTICE BLACKMUN reviewed the history of the Appointments Clause to conclude that "[t]he term 'Department' refers only to a part or division of the executive government, as the Department of State, or of the Treasury, expressly created and given the name of a department by Congress." This interpretation was necessary to avoid "excessively diffusing" the power of appointment, with a corresponding loss of accountability "to political force and the will of the people." "Confining the term 'Heads of Departments' in the Appointments Clause to executive divisions like the Cabinet-level departments constrains the distribution of the appointment power." He went on to conclude, however, that the Tax Court *is* a "Court[ ] of law" for appointments purposes. The remaining four Justices would have taken the opposite approach: In what seems to be the better of the argument, JUSTICE SCALIA insisted that "Courts of law" refers to only Article III courts. On the other hand, "Department" should be understood as comprising any "freestanding, self-contained entity in the Executive Branch, whose [head] is removable by the President (and, save impeachment, no one else)."

Freytag's narrow definition of "Department" created considerable problems for common administrative structures: neither the independent agencies nor a number of freestanding executive agencies (including the CIA, the Federal Reserve Board, and the EPA, which Congress deliberately refused to give Cabinet department status) appeared to meet the definition. FREE ENTERPRISE FOUNDATION V. PUBLIC COMPANY ACCOUNTING BOARD, 561 U.S. 477, 511 (2010) (p. 928), finally put the issue largely to rest, holding that the SEC, an independent agency, "constitutes a "Departmen[t]" for the purposes of the Appointments Clause" because it "is a freestanding component of the Executive Branch, not subordinate to or contained within any other such component," adding:

> In Freytag, we specifically reserved the question whether a "principal agenc[y], such as . . . the Securities and Exchange Commission," is a "Departmen[t]" under the Appointments Clause. Four Justices, however, would have concluded that the Commission is indeed such a "Departmen[t]," . . . because it is a "free-standing, self-contained entity in the Executive Branch." . . . Respondents urge us to adopt this reasoning . . . and we do. Respondents' reading of the Appointments Clause is consistent with the common, near-contemporary definition of a "department" as a "separate allotment or part of business; a distinct province, in which a class of duties are allotted to a particular person." 1 N. Webster, American Dictionary of the English Language *3163 (1828) (def.2) (1995 facsimile ed.). It is also consistent with the early practice of Congress.

As a sign of Free Enterprise's impact, the D.C. Circuit relied on it to conclude that "the Library of Congress is a freestanding entity that clearly meets the definition of 'Department.' To be sure, it performs a range of different functions, including some, such as the Congressional Research Service, that are exercised primarily for legislative purposes. But as we have mentioned, the Librarian is appointed by the President with advice and consent of the Senate, . . . and is subject to unrestricted removal by the President . . . Further, the powers in the Library and the Board to promulgate copyright regulations, to apply the statute to affected parties, and to set rates and terms case by case are ones generally associated in modern times with executive agencies rather than legislators. In this role the Library is undoubtedly a 'component of the Executive Branch.'" Intercollegiate Broad. Sys., Inc. v. Copyright Royalty Bd., 684 F.3d 1332, 1341–42 (D.C. Cir. 2012). Can an agency be an executive department under the Appointments Clause for some functions and not others?

Note that Free Enterprise also quickly dispensed with the further claim that even if the SEC were a "Department," the SEC Chair alone had to be its "Head" for Appointments Clause purposes: "As a constitutional matter, we see no reason why a multimember body may not be the Head of a Department that it governs. The Appointments Clause necessarily contemplates collective appointments by the Courts of Law, and each House of Congress, too, appoints its officers collectively. Petitioners argue that the Framers vested the nomination of principal officers in the President to avoid the perceived evils of collective appointments, but they reveal no similar concern with respect to inferior officers, whose appointments may be vested elsewhere, including in multimember bodies. Practice has also sanctioned the appointment of inferior officers by multimember agencies."

(8) **Who Can Appoint? No Direct Congressional Involvement.** BUCKLEY V. VALEO, 424 U.S. 1 (1976) (see also p. 886): The Federal Election Act of 1971 attempted campaign finance reform by imposing various limitations on contributions and spending, to be overseen by a new eight-member agency, the Federal Election Commission. The extraordinary political sensitivity of this regulatory program was reflected in the equally extraordinary provisions for the FEC's selection: two members appointed by the President pro tempore of the Senate, two by the Speaker of the House, and two by the President (all subject to confirmation by *both* Houses of Congress), with the Secretary of the Senate and the Clerk of the House to be ex officio nonvoting members. All three appointing authorities were forbidden to choose both of their appointees from the same political party.

The case produced multiple conflicting opinions on the First Amendment implications of the contribution and spending limits, but no Justice thought that the Act's appointment scheme could be sustained. Even Justice White, predictably the most sympathetic to innovative institutional solutions in regulatory programs, found it an easy case: "I . . . find singularly unpersuasive the proposition that because the FEC is implementing statutory policies with respect to the conduct of elections . . . its members may be appointed by Congress. . . . Congress clearly has the power to create federal offices and to define the powers and duties of those offices, Myers v. United States, 272 U.S. 52, 128–129 (1926) [p. 918], but no case in this Court even remotely supports the power of Congress to appoint an officer of the United States aside from those officers each House is authorized by Art. I to appoint to assist in the legislative processes." To similar effect is Hechinger v. Metropolitan Washington Airports Auth., 36 F.3d 97 (D.C. Cir. 1994), the second round of controversy over congressional involvement in the newly created Metropolitan Washington Airports Authority. Forbidden to place its own Members on the statutorily-created Board of Review for the Authority (p. 868), Congress tried requiring that the Board consist of nine individuals who travel frequently, have experience in aviation, are registered as voters outside D.C., Maryland, or Virginia, and are included in lists of candidates supplied to the Commission by House and Senate leaders. The D.C. Circuit struck down the new arrangement, and the Supreme Court refused to consider the matter again.

NATIONAL LABOR RELATIONS BOARD v. NOEL CANNING

Supreme Court of the United States (2014).
134 S.Ct. 2550.

■ JUSTICE BREYER delivered the opinion of the Court.

Ordinarily the President must obtain "the Advice and Consent of the Senate" before appointing an "Office[r] of the United States." U.S. Const., Art. II, § 2, cl. 2. But the Recess Appointments Clause creates an exception. It gives the President alone the power "to fill up all Vacancies that may happen during the Recess of the Senate, by granting Commissions which shall expire at the End of their next Session." Art. II, § 2, cl. 3. We here consider three questions about the application of this Clause.

The first concerns the scope of the words "recess of the Senate." Does that phrase refer only to an inter-session recess (i.e., a break between formal sessions of Congress), or does it also include an intra-session recess, such as a summer recess in the midst of a session? We conclude that the Clause applies to both kinds of recess.

The second question concerns the scope of the words "vacancies that may happen." Does that phrase refer only to vacancies that first come into existence during a recess, or does it also include vacancies that arise prior to a recess but continue to exist during the recess? We conclude that the Clause applies to both kinds of vacancy.

The third question concerns calculation of the length of a "recess." The President made the appointments here at issue on January 4, 2012. At that time the Senate was in recess pursuant to a December 17, 2011, resolution providing for a series of brief recesses punctuated by "pro forma session[s]," with "no business . . . transacted," every Tuesday and Friday through January 20, 2012. S. J., 112th Cong., 1st Sess., 923 (2011) (hereinafter 2011 S. J.). In calculating the length of a recess are we to ignore the pro forma sessions, thereby treating the series of brief recesses as a single, month-long recess? We conclude that we cannot ignore these pro forma sessions.

Our answer to the third question means that, when the appointments before us took place, the Senate was in the midst of a 3-day recess. Three days is too short a time to bring a recess within the scope of the Clause. Thus we conclude that the President lacked the power to make the recess appointments here at issue.

I

The case before us arises out of a labor dispute. The National Labor Relations Board (NLRB) found that a Pepsi-Cola distributor, Noel Canning, had unlawfully refused to reduce to writing and execute a collective-bargaining agreement with a labor union. The Board ordered the distributor to execute the agreement and to make employees whole for any losses[, and the] . . . distributor . . . asked the . . . Court of Appeals . . . to set the Board's order aside. It claimed that three of the five Board members had been invalidly appointed, leaving the Board without the three lawfully appointed members necessary for it to act. See . . . New Process Steel, L. P. v. NLRB, 560 U.S. 674–688 (2010) (in the absence of a lawfully appointed quorum, the Board cannot exercise its powers).

The three members in question were Sharon Block, Richard Griffin, and Terence Flynn. In 2011 the President had nominated each of them to the Board . . . [and on] January 4, 2012, the President, invoking the Recess Appointments Clause, appointed all three to the Board. The distributor argued that the Recess Appointments Clause did not authorize those appointments . . . [because] on December 17, 2011, the Senate, by unanimous consent, had adopted a resolution providing that it would take a series of brief recesses beginning the following day. Pursuant to that resolution, the Senate held pro forma sessions every Tuesday and Friday until it returned for ordinary business on January 23, 2012. The President's January 4 appointments were made between the January 3 and January 6 pro forma sessions. In the distributor's view, each pro forma session terminated the immediately preceding recess. Accordingly, the appointments were made during a 3-day adjournment, which is not long enough to trigger the Recess Appointments Clause.

The Court of Appeals agreed that the appointments fell outside the scope of the Clause. But the court set forth different reasons. It held that the Clause's words "the recess of the Senate" do not include recesses that occur within a formal session of Congress, i.e., intra-session recesses. Rather those words apply only to recesses between those formal sessions, i.e., inter-session recesses. Since the second session of the 112th Congress began on January 3, 2012, the day before the President's appointments, those appointments occurred during an intra-session recess, and the appointments consequently fell outside the scope of the Clause. The Court of Appeals added that, in any event, the phrase "vacancies that may happen during the recess" applies only to vacancies that come into existence during a recess. The vacancies that Members Block, Griffin, and Flynn were appointed to fill had arisen before the beginning of the recess during which they were appointed. . . . We granted the Solicitor General's petition for certiorari. . . .

II

Before turning to the specific questions presented, we shall mention two background considerations that we find relevant to all three. First, *the Recess Appointments Clause sets forth a subsidiary, not a primary, method for appointing officers of the United States*. The immediately preceding Clause—Article II, Section 2, Clause 2—provides the primary method of appointment. It says that the President "shall nominate, *and by and with the Advice and Consent of the Senate,* shall appoint Ambassadors, other public Ministers and Consuls, Judges of the supreme Court, and all other Officers of the United States" (emphasis added).

The Federalist Papers make clear that the Founders intended this method of appointment, requiring Senate approval, to be the norm (at least for principal officers). Alexander Hamilton wrote that the Constitution vests the power of *nomination* in the President alone because "one man of discernment is better fitted to analise and estimate the peculiar qualities adapted to particular offices, than a body of men of equal, or perhaps even of superior discernment." The Federalist No. 76, p. 510 (J. Cooke ed. 1961). At the same time, the need to secure Senate approval provides "an excellent check upon a spirit of favoritism in the President, and would tend greatly to preventing the appointment of unfit characters from State prejudice, from family connection, from personal attachment, or from a view to popularity." Id., at 513. Hamilton further explained that the

> ordinary power of appointment is confided to the President and Senate *jointly*, and can therefore only be exercised during the session of the Senate; but as it would have been improper to oblige this body to be continually in session for the appointment of officers; and as vacancies might happen *in their recess*, which it might be necessary for the public service to fill without delay, the succeeding clause is evidently intended to authorise the President *singly* to make temporary appointments.

Id., No. 67, at 455. Thus the Recess Appointments Clause reflects the tension between, on the one hand, the President's continuous need for "the assistance of subordinates," Myers v. United States, 272 U.S. 52, 117 (1926), and, on the other, the Senate's practice, particularly during the Republic's early years, of meeting for a single brief session each year . . .

Second, *in interpreting the Clause, we put significant weight upon historical practice.* For one thing, the interpretive questions before us concern the allocation of power between two elected branches of Government. Long ago Chief Justice Marshall wrote that

> a doubtful question, one on which human reason may pause, and the human judgment be suspended, in the decision of which the great principles of liberty are not concerned, but the respective powers of those who are equally the representatives of the people, are to be adjusted; if not put at rest by the practice

of the government, ought to receive a considerable impression from that practice.

McCulloch v. Maryland, 4 Wheat. 316, 401 (1819). . . . We recognize, of course, that the separation of powers can serve to safeguard individual liberty, Clinton v. City of New York, 524 U.S. 417–450 (1998) (Kennedy, J., concurring), and that it is the "duty of the judicial department"—in a separation-of-powers case as in any other—"to say what the law is," Marbury v. Madison, 1 Cranch 137, 177 (1803). But it is equally true that the longstanding "practice of the government," McCulloch, supra, at 401, can inform our determination of "what the law is," Marbury, supra, at 177. That principle is neither new nor controversial. . . . [T]his Court has treated practice as an important interpretive factor even when the nature or longevity of that practice is subject to dispute, and even when that practice began after the founding era. . . .

There is a great deal of history to consider here. Presidents have made recess appointments since the beginning of the Republic. Their frequency suggests that the Senate and President have recognized that recess appointments can be both necessary and appropriate in certain circumstances. We have not previously interpreted the Clause, and, when doing so for the first time in more than 200 years, we must hesitate to upset the compromises and working arrangements that the elected branches of Government themselves have reached.

III

The first question concerns the scope of the phrase "*the recess* of the Senate." Art. II, § 2, cl. 3 (emphasis added). The Constitution provides for congressional elections every two years. And the 2-year life of each elected Congress typically consists of two formal 1-year sessions, each separated from the next by an "inter-session recess." The Senate or the House of Representatives announces an inter-session recess by approving a resolution stating that it will "adjourn sine die," i.e., without specifying a date to return (in which case Congress will reconvene when the next formal session is scheduled to begin). The Senate and the House also take breaks in the midst of a session. The Senate or the House announces any such "intra-session recess" by adopting a resolution stating that it will "adjourn" to a fixed date, a few days or weeks or even months later. All agree that the phrase "the recess of the Senate" covers inter-session recesses. The question is whether it includes intra-session recesses as well.

In our view, the phrase "the recess" includes an intra-session recess of substantial length. Its words taken literally can refer to both types of recess. Founding-era dictionaries define the word "recess," much as we do today, simply as "a period of cessation from usual work." 13 The Oxford English Dictionary 322–323 (2d ed. 1989) (hereinafter OED) (citing 18th- and 19th-century sources for that definition of "recess").[29] . . . The Founders themselves used the word to refer to intra-session, as well as to inter-session, breaks. See, e.g., 3 Records of the Federal Convention of 1787, p. 76 (M. Farrand rev. 1966) (hereinafter Farrand) . . .

We recognize that the word "the" in "*the* recess" might suggest that the phrase refers to the single break separating formal sessions of Congress. That is because the word "the" frequently (but not always) indicates "a particular thing." 2 Johnson 2003. But the word can also refer "to a term used generically or universally." 17 OED 879. The Constitution, for example, directs the Senate to choose a President pro tempore "in *the* Absence of the Vice-President." Art. I, § 3, cl. 5 (emphasis added). . . . Reading "the" generically in this way, there is no linguistic problem applying the Clause's phrase to both kinds of recess. And, in fact, the phrase "the recess" was used to refer to intra-session recesses at the time of the founding. . . .

The constitutional text is thus ambiguous. And we believe the Clause's purpose demands the broader interpretation. The Clause gives the President authority to make appointments during "the recess of the Senate" so that the President can ensure the continued functioning of the Federal Government when the Senate is away. The Senate is equally away during both an inter-session and an intra-session recess, and its capacity to participate in the appointments process has nothing to do with the words it uses to signal its departure.

History also offers strong support for the broad interpretation. We concede that pre-Civil War history is not helpful. But it shows only that Congress generally took long breaks between sessions, while taking no significant intra-session breaks at all . . . Obviously, if there are no significant intra-session recesses, there will be no intra-session recess appointments. In 1867 and 1868, Congress for the first time took substantial, nonholiday intra-session breaks, and President Andrew Johnson made dozens of recess appointments. The Federal Court of Claims upheld one of those specific appointments . . . Attorney General Evarts also issued three opinions concerning the constitutionality of President Johnson's appointments, and it apparently did not occur to him that the distinction between intra-session and inter-session recesses was significant. See 12 Op. Atty. Gen. 449 (1868); 12 Op. Atty. Gen. 455 (1868); 12 Op. Atty. Gen. 469 (1868). Similarly, though the 40th Congress impeached President Johnson on charges relating to his appointment power, he was not accused of violating the Constitution by making intra-session recess appointments.

---

[29]   [Ed] The majority cited a number of early dictionaries, including 2 N. Webster, An American Dictionary of the English Language (1828) ("[r]emission or suspension of business or procedure") and 2 S. Johnson, A Dictionary of the English Language 1602–1603 (4th ed. 1773) (hereinafter Johnson) (same).

In all, between the founding and the Great Depression, Congress took substantial intra-session breaks (other than holiday breaks) in four years: 1867, 1868, 1921, and 1929. And in each of those years the President made intra-session recess appointments. Since 1929, and particularly since the end of World War II, Congress has shortened its inter-session breaks as it has taken longer and more frequent intra-session breaks; Presidents have correspondingly made more intra-session recess appointments. Indeed, if we include military appointments, Presidents have made thousands of intra-session recess appointments. . . . Not surprisingly, the publicly available opinions of Presidential legal advisers that we have found are nearly unanimous in determining that the Clause authorizes these appointments. . . .

What about the Senate? Since Presidents began making intra-session recess appointments, individual Senators have taken differing views about the proper definition of "the recess." See, e.g., 130 Cong. Rec. 23234 (1984) (resolution introduced by Senator Byrd urging limits on the length of applicable intra-session recesses) . . . But neither the Senate considered as a body nor its committees, despite opportunities to express opposition to the practice of intra-session recess appointments, has done so. Rather, to the extent that the Senate or a Senate committee has expressed a view, that view has favored a functional definition of "recess," and a functional definition encompasses intra-session recesses. . . . We recognize that the Senate cannot easily register opposition as a body to every governmental action that many, perhaps most, Senators oppose. . . . And yet we are not aware of any formal action it has taken to call into question the broad and functional definition of "recess" . . . followed by the Executive Branch since at least 1921. Nor has Justice Scalia identified any. All the while, the President has made countless recess appointments during intra-session recesses.

The upshot is that restricting the Clause to inter-session recesses would frustrate its purpose. It would make the President's recess-appointment power dependent on a formalistic distinction of Senate procedure. Moreover, the President has consistently and frequently interpreted the word "recess" to apply to intra-session recesses, and has acted on that interpretation. The Senate as a body has done nothing to deny the validity of this practice for at least three-quarters of a century. And three-quarters of a century of settled practice is long enough to entitle a practice to "great weight in a proper interpretation" of the constitutional provision. The Pocket Veto Case, 279 U.S., at 689.

We are aware of, but we are not persuaded by, three important arguments to the contrary. First, some argue that the Founders would likely have intended the Clause to apply only to inter-session recesses, for they hardly knew any other. . . . The problem with this argument, however, is that it does not fully describe the relevant founding intent. . . . We . . . think the Framers likely did intend the Clause to apply to a new circumstance that so clearly falls within its essential purposes where doing so is consistent with the Clause's language. Second, some argue that the intra-session interpretation permits the President to make "illogic[ally]" long recess appointments. . . . We agree that the intra-session interpretation permits somewhat longer recess appointments, but we do not agree that this consequence is "illogical." . . . Third, the Court of Appeals believed that application of the Clause to intra-session recesses would introduce "vagueness" into a Clause that was otherwise clear. One can find problems of uncertainty, however, either way. . . .

The greater interpretive problem is determining how long a recess must be in order to fall within the Clause. Is a break of a week, or a day, or an hour too short to count as a "recess"? The Clause itself does not say. And Justice Scalia claims that this silence itself shows that the Framers intended the Clause to apply only to an inter-session recess.

We disagree. For one thing, the most likely reason the Framers did not place a textual floor underneath the word "recess" is that they did not foresee the need for one. . . . The Framers' lack of clairvoyance on that point is not dispositive. Unlike Justice Scalia, we think it most consistent with our constitutional structure to presume that the Framers would have allowed intra-session recess appointments where there was a long history of such practice. Moreover, the lack of a textual floor raises a problem that plagues both interpretations—Justice Scalia's and ours. Today a brief inter-session recess is just as possible as a brief intra-session recess. . . . Even the Solicitor General . . . acknowledges that there is a lower limit applicable to both kinds of recess. He argues that the lower limit should be three days by analogy to the Adjournments Clause of the Constitution. That Clause says: "Neither House, during the Session of Congress, shall, without the Consent of the other, adjourn for more than three days." Art. I, § 5, cl. 4.

We agree with the Solicitor General that a 3-day recess would be too short. . . . The Adjournments Clause reflects the fact that a 3-day break is not a significant interruption of legislative business. . . . A Senate recess that is so short that it does not require the consent of the House is not long enough to trigger the President's recess-appointment power. That is not to say that the President may make recess appointments during any recess that is "more than three days." Art. I, § 5, cl. 4. The Recess Appointments Clause seeks to permit the Executive Branch to function smoothly when Congress is unavailable. And though Congress has taken short breaks for almost 200 years, and there have been many thousands of recess appointments in that time, we have not found a single example of a recess appointment made during an intra-session recess that was shorter than 10 days. . . . The lack of examples suggests that the recess-appointment power is not needed in that context. . . .

In sum, we conclude that the phrase "the recess" applies to both intra-session and inter-session recesses. If a Senate recess is so short that it does not require the consent of the House, it is too short to trigger the

Recess Appointments Clause. See Art. I, § 5, cl. 4. And a recess lasting less than 10 days is presumptively too short as well.

IV

The second question concerns the scope of the phrase "vacancies *that may happen* during the recess of the Senate." Art. II, § 2, cl. 3 (emphasis added). All agree that the phrase applies to vacancies that initially occur during a recess. But does it also apply to vacancies that initially occur before a recess and continue to exist during the recess? In our view the phrase applies to both kinds of vacancy. We believe that the Clause's language, read literally, permits, though it does not naturally favor, our broader interpretation. We concede that the most natural meaning of "happens" as applied to a "vacancy" (at least to a modern ear) is that the vacancy "happens" when it initially occurs. See 1 Johnson 913 (defining "happen" in relevant part as meaning "[t]o fall out; to chance; to come to pass"). But that is not the only possible way to use the word. . . . [W]hen Attorney General William Wirt advised President Monroe to follow the broader interpretation, he wrote that the "expression seems not perfectly clear. It may mean 'happen to take place:' that is, '*to originate*,'" or it "may mean, also, without violence to the sense, 'happen to exist.'" 1 Op. Atty. Gen. 631, 631–632 (1823). . . . In any event, the linguistic question here is not whether the phrase can be, but whether it must be, read more narrowly. The question is whether the Clause is ambiguous. The Pocket Veto Case, 279 U.S., at 690. And the broader reading, we believe, is at least a permissible reading of a "doubtful" phrase. Ibid. We consequently go on to consider the Clause's purpose and historical practice.

The Clause's purpose strongly supports the broader interpretation. That purpose is to permit the President to obtain the assistance of subordinate officers when the Senate, due to its recess, cannot confirm them. Attorney General Wirt clearly described how the narrower interpretation would undermine this purpose:

> Put the case of a vacancy occurring in an office, held in a distant part of the country, on the last day of the Senate's session. Before the vacancy is made known to the President, the Senate rises. The office may be an important one; the vacancy may paralyze a whole line of action in some essential branch of our internal police; the public interests may imperiously demand that it shall be immediately filled. But the vacancy happened to occur during the session of the Senate; and if the President's power is to be limited to such vacancies only as happen to occur during the recess of the Senate, the vacancy in the case put must continue, however ruinous the consequences may be to the public.

1 Op. Atty. Gen., at 632. . . . We do not agree with Justice Scalia's suggestion that the Framers would have accepted the catastrophe envisioned by Wirt because Congress can always provide for acting officers, see 5 U.S.C. § 3345, and the President can always convene a

special session of Congress, see U.S. Const., Art. II, § 3. Acting officers may have less authority than Presidential appointments . . . [and] to rely on acting officers would lessen the President's ability to staff the Executive Branch with people of his own choosing, . . . thereby limit[ing] the President's control and political accountability. Cf. Free Enterprise Fund v. Public Company Accounting Oversight Bd., 561 U.S. 477–498 (2010) [p. 922]. Special sessions are burdensome (and would have been especially so at the time of the founding). The point of the Recess Appointments Clause was to avoid reliance on these inadequate expedients.

At the same time, we recognize one important purpose-related consideration that argues in the opposite direction. A broad interpretation might permit a President to avoid Senate confirmations as a matter of course. If the Clause gives the President the power to "fill up all vacancies" that occur before, and continue to exist during, the Senate's recess, a President might not submit any nominations to the Senate. . . . Wirt thought considerations of character and politics would prevent Presidents from abusing the Clause in this way. 1 Op. Atty. Gen., at 634. He might have added that such temptations should not often arise. It is often less desirable for a President to make a recess appointment. A recess appointee only serves a limited term. . . . In any event, the Executive Branch has adhered to the broader interpretation for two centuries, and Senate confirmation has always remained the norm for officers that require it. . . .

Historical practice over the past 200 years strongly favors the broader interpretation. The tradition of applying the Clause to pre-recess vacancies dates at least to President James Madison. . . . [T]he evidence suggests that James Madison—as familiar as anyone with the workings of the Constitutional Convention—appointed Theodore Gaillard to replace a district judge who had left office before a recess began. It also appears that in 1815 Madison signed a bill that created two new offices prior to a recess which he then filled later during the recess. He also made recess appointments to "territorial" United States attorney and marshal positions, both of which had been created when the Senate was in session more than two years before. Justice Scalia refers to "written evidence of Madison's own beliefs," post, at 36, but in fact we have no direct evidence of what President Madison believed. . . . The next President, James Monroe, received and presumably acted upon Attorney General Wirt's advice, namely that "all vacancies which, from any casualty, happen to exist at a time when the Senate cannot be consulted as to filling them, may be temporarily filled by the President." 1 Op. Atty. Gen., at 633. Nearly every subsequent Attorney General to consider the question throughout the Nation's history has thought the same. . . .

This power is important. The Congressional Research Service is "unaware of any official source of information tracking the dates of vacancies in federal offices." The Noel Canning Decision 3, n. 6.

Nonetheless, we have enough information to believe that the Presidents since Madison have made many recess appointments filling vacancies that initially occurred prior to a recess. . . . Moreover, the Solicitor General has compiled a list of 102 (mostly uncontested) recess appointments made by Presidents going back to the founding. . . .

Did the Senate object? Early on, there was some sporadic disagreement with the broad interpretation. . . . Then in 1863 the Senate Judiciary Committee disagreed with the broad interpretation. It issued a report concluding that a vacancy "must have its inceptive point after one session has closed and before another session has begun." S. Rep. No. 80, 37th Cong., 3d Sess., p. 3. And the Senate then passed the Pay Act, which provided that "no money shall be paid . . . as a salary, to any person appointed during the recess of the Senate, to fill a vacancy . . . which . . . existed while the Senate was in session." Act of Feb. 9, 1863, § 2, 12 Stat. 646. Relying upon the floor statement of a single Senator, Justice Scalia suggests that the passage of the Pay Act indicates that the Senate as a whole endorsed the position in the 1863 Report. But the circumstances are more equivocal. . . .

In any event, the Senate subsequently abandoned its hostility. In the debate preceding the 1905 Senate Report regarding President Roosevelt's "constructive" recess appointments, Senator Tillman—who chaired the Committee that authored the 1905 Report—brought up the 1863 Report, and another Senator responded: "Whatever that report may have said in 1863, I do not think that has been the view the Senate has taken" of the issue. 38 Cong. Rec. 1606 (1904). Senator Tillman then agreed that "the Senate has acquiesced" in the President's "power to fill" pre-recess vacancies. Ibid. . . . In 1916 the Senate debated whether to pay a recess appointee who had filled a pre-recess vacancy and had not subsequently been confirmed. Both Senators to address the question—one on each side of the payment debate—agreed that the President had the constitutional power to make the appointment, and the Senate voted to pay the appointee for his service. . . . Then in 1940 Congress amended the Pay Act to authorize salary payments (with some exceptions) where (1) the "vacancy arose within thirty days prior to the termination of the session," (2) "at the termination of the session" a nomination was "pending," or (3) a nominee was "rejected by the Senate within thirty days prior to the termination of the session." Act of July 11, 54 Stat. 751 (codified, as amended, at 5 U.S.C. § 5503). All three circumstances concern a vacancy that did not initially occur during a recess but happened to exist during that recess. By paying salaries to this kind of recess appointee, the 1940 Senate (and later Senates) in effect supported the President's interpretation of the Clause.

The upshot is that the President has consistently and frequently interpreted the Recess Appointments Clause to apply to vacancies that initially occur before, but continue to exist during, a recess of the Senate. The Senate as a body has not countered this practice for nearly three-quarters of a century, perhaps longer. . . . The tradition is long enough to entitle the practice "to great regard in determining the true construction" of the constitutional provision. The Pocket Veto Case, 279 U.S., at 690. And we are reluctant to upset this traditional practice where doing so would seriously shrink the authority that Presidents have believed existed and have exercised for so long. . . .

V

The third question concerns the calculation of the length of the Senate's "recess." On December 17, 2011, the Senate by unanimous consent adopted a resolution to convene "pro forma session[s]" only, with "no business . . . transacted," on every Tuesday and Friday from December 20, 2011, through January 20, 2012. 2011 S. J. 923. . . . The Solicitor General argues that we must treat the pro forma sessions as periods of recess. He says that these "sessions" were sessions in name only because the Senate was in recess as a functional matter. . . .

In our view, however, the pro forma sessions count as sessions, not as periods of recess. We hold that, for purposes of the Recess Appointments Clause, the Senate is in session when it says it is, provided that, under its own rules, it retains the capacity to transact Senate business. . . . [W]e must give great weight to the Senate's own determination of when it is and when it is not in session. But our deference to the Senate cannot be absolute. When the Senate is without the capacity to act, under its own rules, it is not in session even if it so declares. Accordingly, we conclude that when the Senate declares that it is in session and possesses the capacity, under its own rules, to conduct business, it is in session for purposes of the Clause.

Applying this standard, we find that the pro forma sessions were sessions for purposes of the Clause. First, the Senate said it was in session. The Journal of the Senate and the Congressional Record indicate that the Senate convened for a series of twice-weekly "sessions" from December 20 through January 20. 2011 . . . Second, the Senate's rules make clear that during its pro forma sessions, despite its resolution that it would conduct no business, the Senate retained the power to conduct business. During any pro forma session, the Senate could have conducted business simply by passing a unanimous consent agreement. . . . Indeed, the Senate passed a bill by unanimous consent during the second pro forma session after its December 17 adjournment. 2011 S. J. 924. And that bill quickly became law. Pub. L. 112–78, 125 Stat. 1280. . . .

The Solicitor General . . . contends that what counts is not the Senate's capacity to conduct business but what the Senate actually does (or here, did) during its pro forma sessions. . . . Even were we, for argument's sake, to accept all of these criteria as authoritative, they would here be met. . . . [D]uring its pro forma sessions, [the Senate could] "participate as a body in making appointments" . . . It could ["receive communications from the President"]. . . .

The Solicitor General asks us to engage in a more realistic appraisal[, . . .] argu[ing] that, during the relevant pro forma sessions, business was not in fact conducted. . . . We do not believe, however, that engaging in the kind of factual appraisal that the Solicitor General suggests is either legally or practically appropriate. . . .

As the Solicitor General concedes, the Senate could preclude the President from making recess appointments by holding a series of twice-a-week ordinary (not pro forma) sessions. And the nature of the business conducted at those ordinary sessions . . . is a matter for the Senate to decide. The Constitution also gives the President (if he has enough allies in Congress) a way to force a recess. Art. II, § 3 ("[I]n Case of Disagreement between [the Houses], with Respect to the Time of Adjournment, [the President] may adjourn them to such Time as he shall think proper. . . . That structure foresees resolution not only through judicial interpretation and compromise among the branches but also by the ballot box.

VI

The Recess Appointments Clause responds to a structural difference between the Executive and Legislative Branches: The Executive Branch is perpetually in operation, while the Legislature only acts in intervals separated by recesses. The purpose of the Clause is to allow the Executive to continue operating while the Senate is unavailable. We believe that the Clause's text, standing alone, is ambiguous. It does not resolve whether the President may make appointments during intra-session recesses, or whether he may fill pre-recess vacancies. But the broader reading better serves the Clause's structural function. Moreover, that broader reading is reinforced by centuries of history, which we are hesitant to disturb. We thus hold that the Constitution empowers the President to fill any existing vacancy during any recess—intra-session or inter-session—of sufficient length.

Justice Scalia would render illegitimate thousands of recess appointments reaching all the way back to the founding era. More than that: Calling the Clause an "anachronism," he would basically read it out of the Constitution. He performs this act of judicial excision in the name of liberty. We fail to see how excising the Recess Appointments Clause preserves freedom. In fact, Alexander Hamilton observed in the very first Federalist Paper that "the vigour of government is essential to the security of liberty." The Federalist No. 1, at 5. And the Framers included the Recess Appointments Clause to preserve the "vigour of government" at times when an important organ of Government, the United States Senate, is in recess. Justice Scalia's interpretation of the Clause would defeat the power of the Clause to achieve that objective. . . .

■ JUSTICE SCALIA, with whom The CHIEF JUSTICE, JUSTICE THOMAS, and JUSTICE ALITO join, concurring in the judgment.

. . . To prevent the President's recess-appointment power from nullifying the Senate's role in the appointment process, the Constitution cabins that power in two significant ways. First, it may be exercised only in "the Recess of the Senate," that is, the intermission between two formal legislative sessions. Second, it may be used to fill only those vacancies that "happen during the Recess," that is, offices that become vacant during that intermission. Both conditions are clear from the Constitution's text and structure, and both were well understood at the founding. . . .

. . . The majority justifies [its contrary] atextual results on an adverse-possession theory of executive authority: Presidents have long claimed the powers in question, and the Senate has not disputed those claims with sufficient vigor, so the Court should not "upset the compromises and working arrangements that the elected branches of Government themselves have reached." The Court's decision transforms the recess-appointment power from a tool carefully designed to fill a narrow and specific need into a weapon to be wielded by future Presidents against future Senates. To reach that result, the majority casts aside the plain, original meaning of the constitutional text in deference to late-arising historical practices that are ambiguous at best. The majority's insistence on deferring to the Executive's untenably broad interpretation of the power is in clear conflict with our precedent and forebodes a diminution of this Court's role in controversies involving the separation of powers and the structure of government. I concur in the judgment only.

I. Our Responsibility

Today's majority disregards two overarching principles that ought to guide our consideration of the questions presented here. First, the Constitution's core, government-structuring provisions are no less critical to preserving liberty than are the later adopted provisions of the Bill of Rights. Indeed, "[s]o convinced were the Framers that liberty of the person inheres in structure that at first they did not consider a Bill of Rights necessary." Clinton v. City of New York, 524 U.S. 417, 450 (1998) (Kennedy, J., concurring). Those structural provisions reflect the founding generation's deep conviction that "checks and balances were the foundation of a structure of government that would protect liberty." Bowsher v. Synar, 478 U.S. 714, 722 (1986). . . . Second and relatedly, when questions involving the Constitution's government-structuring provisions are presented in a justiciable case, it is the solemn responsibility of the Judicial Branch " 'to say what the law is.' " Zivotofsky v. Clinton, 566 U.S. [189, 196] (2012) . . . (quoting Marbury v. Madison, 1 Cranch 137, 177 (1803)). . . . [P]olicing the "enduring structure" of constitutional government when the political branches fail to do so is "one of the most vital functions of this Court." Public Citizen

v. Department of Justice, 491 U.S. 440, 468 (1989) (Kennedy, J., concurring in judgment). . . .

Of course, where a governmental practice has been open, widespread, and unchallenged since the early days of the Republic, the practice should guide our interpretation of an ambiguous constitutional provision. . . . But "'[p]ast practice does not, by itself, create power.'" Medellín v. Texas, 552 U.S. 491, 532 (2008) (quoting Dames & Moore v. Regan, 453 U.S. 654, 686 (1981)). That is a necessary corollary of the principle that the political branches cannot by agreement alter the constitutional structure. Plainly, then, a self-aggrandizing practice adopted by one branch well after the founding, often challenged, and never before blessed by this Court—in other words, the sort of practice on which the majority relies in this case—does not relieve us of our duty to interpret the Constitution in light of its text, structure, and original understanding. . . .

II.   Intra-Session Breaks

The first question presented is whether "the Recess of the Senate," during which the President's recess-appointment power is active, is (a) the period between two of the Senate's formal sessions, or (b) any break in the Senate's proceedings. I would hold that "the Recess" is the gap between sessions and that the appointments at issue here are invalid because they undisputedly were made during the Senate's session. The Court's contrary conclusion—that "the Recess" includes "breaks in the midst of a session,"—is inconsistent with the Constitution's text and structure, and it requires judicial fabrication of vague, unadministrable limits on the recess-appointment power (thus defined) that overstep the judicial role. And although the majority relies heavily on "historical practice," no practice worthy of our deference supports the majority's conclusion on this issue. . . .

A sensible interpretation of the Recess Appointments Clause should start by recognizing that the Clause uses the term "Recess" in contradistinction to the term "Session." . . . In the founding era, the terms "recess" and "session" had well-understood meanings in the marking-out of legislative time. The life of each elected Congress typically consisted (as it still does) of two or more formal sessions separated by adjournments "sine die," that is, without a specified return date. The period between two sessions was known as "the recess." As one scholar has thoroughly demonstrated, "in government practice the phrase 'the Recess' always referred to the gap between sessions." Natelson, The Origins and Meaning of "Vacancies that May Happen During the Recess" in the Constitution's Recess Appointments Clause, 37 Harv. J. L. & Pub. Pol'y 199, 213 (2014). By contrast, other provisions of the Constitution use the verb "adjourn" rather than "recess" to refer to the commencement of breaks during a formal legislative session. See, e.g., Art. I, § 5, cl. 1; id., § 5, cl. 4. . . .

Besides being linguistically unsound, the majority's reading yields the strange result that an appointment made during a short break near the beginning of one official session will not terminate until the end of the following official session, enabling the appointment to last for up to two years. . . . [Not giving the term "recess" its formal meaning] leaves the recess-appointment power without a textually grounded principle limiting the time of its exercise. The dictionary definitions of "recess" on which the majority relies provide no such principle. On the contrary, they make clear that in colloquial usage, a recess could include any suspension of legislative business, no matter how short. . . . The notion that the Constitution empowers the President to make unilateral appointments every time the Senate takes a half-hour lunch break is so absurd as to be self-refuting. But that, in the majority's view, is what the text authorizes. . . . To avoid the absurd results that follow from its colloquial reading of "the Recess," the majority is forced to declare that some intra-session breaks—though undisputedly within the phrase's colloquial meaning—are simply "too short to trigger the Recess Appointments Clause." But it identifies no textual basis whatsoever for limiting the length of "the Recess," nor does it point to any clear standard for determining how short is too short. It is inconceivable that the Framers would have left the circumstances in which the President could exercise such a significant and potentially dangerous power so utterly indeterminate. . . .

And what about breaks longer than three days? The majority says that a break of four to nine days is "presumptively too short" but that the presumption may be rebutted in an "unusual circumstance," such as a "national catastrophe . . . that renders the Senate unavailable but calls for an urgent response." The majority must hope that the in terrorem effect of its "presumptively too short" pronouncement will deter future Presidents from making any recess appointments during 4-to-9-day breaks and thus save us from the absurd spectacle of unelected judges evaluating (after an evidentiary hearing?) whether an alleged "catastrophe" was sufficiently "urgent" to trigger the recess-appointment power. . . . An interpretation that calls for this kind of judicial adventurism cannot be correct. . . .

. . . The historical practice of the political branches is, of course, irrelevant when the Constitution is clear. But even if the Constitution were thought ambiguous on this point, history does not support the majority's interpretation. [Justice Scalia disputes all aspects of the majority's reading of the history, concluding:] What does all this amount to? In short: Intra-session recess appointments were virtually unheard of for the first 130 years of the Republic, were deemed unconstitutional by the first Attorney General to address them, were not openly defended by the Executive until 1921, were not made in significant numbers until after World War II, and have been repeatedly criticized as unconstitutional by Senators of both parties.

. . . In any controversy between the political branches over a separation-of-powers question, staking out a position and defending it over time is far easier for the Executive Branch than for the Legislative Branch. All Presidents have a high interest in expanding the powers of their office, since the more power the President can wield, the more effectively he can implement his political agenda; whereas individual Senators may have little interest in opposing Presidential encroachment on legislative prerogatives, especially when the encroacher is a President who is the leader of their own party. . . . And when the President wants to assert a power and establish a precedent, he faces neither the collective-action problems nor the procedural inertia inherent in the legislative process. The majority's methodology thus all but guarantees the continuing aggrandizement of the Executive Branch.

III. Pre-Recess Vacancies

. . . I would hold that the recess-appointment power is limited to vacancies that arise during the recess in which they are filled. . . . As the majority concedes, "the most natural meaning of 'happens' as applied to a 'vacancy' . . . is that the vacancy 'happens' when it initially occurs." . . . Thus, a vacancy that happened during the Recess was most reasonably understood as one that arose during the recess. . . . In any event, no reasonable reader would have understood the Recess Appointments Clause to use the word "happen" in the majority's "happen to be" sense, and thus to empower the President to fill all vacancies that might exist during a recess, regardless of when they arose. For one thing, the Clause's language would have been a surpassingly odd way of giving the President that power. The Clause easily could have been written to convey that meaning clearly . . . For another thing, the majority's reading not only strains the Clause's language but distorts its constitutional role, which was meant to be subordinate. . . .

If, however, the Clause had allowed the President to fill all pre-existing vacancies during the recess by granting commissions that would last throughout the following session, it would have been impossible to regard it—as the Framers plainly did—as a mere codicil to the Constitution's principal, power-sharing scheme for filling federal offices. On the majority's reading, the President would have had no need ever to seek the Senate's advice and consent for his appointments: Whenever there was a fair prospect of the Senate's rejecting his preferred nominee, the President could have appointed that individual unilaterally during the recess, allowed the appointment to expire at the end of the next session, renewed the appointment the following day, and so on ad infinitum. . . . It is unthinkable that such an obvious means for the Executive to expand its power would have been overlooked during the ratification debates.

[Justice Scalia reviews early history to conclude that early Presidents and Congresses followed the plain meaning.] The majority, however, relies heavily on a contrary account of the Clause given by

Attorney General William Wirt in 1823. . . . Wirt's argument is doubly flawed. To begin, the Constitution provides ample means, short of rewriting its text, for dealing with the hypothetical dilemma Wirt posed [of the " 'embarrassing inconvenience' if a distant office were to become vacant during the Senate's session, but news of the vacancy were not to reach the President until the recess."] Congress can authorize "acting" officers to perform the duties associated with a temporarily vacant office—and has done that, in one form or another, since 1792. And on "extraordinary Occasions" the President can call the Senate back into session to consider a nomination. Art. II, § 3. If the Framers had thought those options insufficient and preferred to authorize the President to make recess appointments to fill vacancies arising late in the session, they would have known how to do so. . . .

. . . More fundamentally, Wirt and the majority are mistaken to say that the Constitution's "substantial purpose" is to "keep . . . offices filled." The Constitution is not a road map for maximally efficient government, but a system of "carefully crafted restraints" designed to "protect the people from the improvident exercise of power." Chadha, 462 U.S., at 957, 959. . . . As we have recognized, while the Constitution's government-structuring provisions can seem "clumsy" and "inefficient," they reflect "hard choices . . . consciously made by men who had lived under a form of government that permitted arbitrary governmental acts to go unchecked." Chadha, supra, at 959. . . .

For the reasons just given, it is clear that the Constitution authorizes the President to fill unilaterally only those vacancies that arise during a recess, not every vacancy that happens to exist during a recess. Again, however, the majority says "[h]istorical practice" requires the broader interpretation. Ante, at 26. And again the majority is mistaken. Even if the Constitution were wrongly thought to be ambiguous on this point, a fair recounting of the relevant history does not support the majority's interpretation. . . . In sum: Washington's and Adams' Attorneys General read the Constitution to restrict recess appointments to vacancies arising during the recess, and there is no evidence that any of the first four Presidents consciously departed from that reading. The contrary reading was first defended by an executive official in 1823, was vehemently rejected by the Senate in 1863, was vigorously resisted by legislation in place from 1863 until 1940, and is arguably inconsistent with legislation in place from 1940 to the present. The Solicitor General has identified only about 100 appointments that have ever been made under the broader reading, and while it seems likely that a good deal more have been made in the last few decades, there is good reason to doubt that many were made before 1940 (since the appointees could not have been compensated). I can conceive of no sane constitutional theory under which this evidence of "historical practice"— which is actually evidence of a long-simmering inter-branch conflict— would require us to defer to the views of the Executive Branch. . . .

IV. Conclusion

. . . The majority replaces the Constitution's text with a new set of judge-made rules to govern recess appointments. Henceforth, the Senate can avoid triggering the President's now-vast recess-appointment power by the odd contrivance of never adjourning for more than three days without holding a pro forma session at which it is understood that no business will be conducted. How this new regime will work in practice remains to be seen. Perhaps it will reduce the prevalence of recess appointments. But perhaps not: Members of the President's party in Congress may be able to prevent the Senate from holding pro forma sessions with the necessary frequency, and if the House and Senate disagree, the President may be able to adjourn both "to such Time as he shall think proper." U.S. Const., Art. II, § 3. In any event, the limitation upon the President's appointment power is there not for the benefit of the Senate, but for the protection of the people; it should not be dependent on Senate action for its existence.

The real tragedy of today's decision is not simply the abolition of the Constitution's limits on the recess-appointment power and the substitution of a novel framework invented by this Court. It is the damage done to our separation-of-powers jurisprudence more generally. It is not every day that we encounter a proper case or controversy requiring interpretation of the Constitution's structural provisions. Most of the time, the interpretation of those provisions is left to the political branches—which, in deciding how much respect to afford the constitutional text, often take their cues from this Court. We should therefore take every opportunity to affirm the primacy of the Constitution's enduring principles over the politics of the moment. Our failure to do so today will resonate well beyond the particular dispute at hand. . . .

NOTES

(1) ***Dueling Accounts of the Recess Appointments Clause.*** Justice Breyer's majority opinion and Justice Scalia's dissent consider the same sources to determine the meaning of the Recess Appointments Clause. Why then do they reach such opposite results? One evident difference is that the majority insists the constitutional text is ambiguous, whereas Justice Scalia views it as clearly precluding appointments during intrasession recesses or applying when a vacancy predates the start of a recess. Which opinion do you think has the better account of the constitutional text? Is the text clearer on one of these issues—the meaning of "recess" or of "happens to exist"?

Another way to see the difference between the two opinions is in terms of the formalism-functionalism methodological divide discussed earlier (p. 787). Justice Scalia's emphasis on the Clause's plain meaning and his refusal to accord weight to contrary practices, even if well established, or pragmatic considerations such as the potential for disruption his interpretation might cause, is on a par with the formalism of Chief Justice

Burger in *Chadha*. By contrast, Justice Breyer's insistence on textual ambiguity, heavy reliance on historical practice, and concern that the Clause fit current conditions—where intrasession recesses dominate—belies a strongly functionalist stance. Which approach, formalism or functionalism, do you think is more appropriate here?

(2) ***The Use of Historical Practice in Separation of Powers Analysis.*** The two opinions also disagree about whether well-established practice exists on the meaning of the Recess Appointments Clause. Which opinion has the better of the argument: Do you think a longstanding practice exists on whether the Clause can be used during intrasession recesses? On whether the Clause can be used to fill vacancies that already existed when a recess occurred?

The opinions also disagree on the broader question of how much weight to accord such practice if it does exist. (For discussion of this issue in a statutory context, see *Milner v. Dep't of Navy* (p. 683).) The opinions' different approaches to historical practice reflects, in large part, the two opinions' contrasting functionalist and formalist stances. But can a functionalist argument be made for skepticism about the weight to be given historical practice? Justice Scalia also argued that "staking out a position [on a separation of powers issue] and defending it over time is far easier for the Executive Branch than for the Legislative Branch" because Presidents are not hamstrung by the collective action problems that bedevil Congress and have a consistent interest in expanding the powers of their office. Do you agree? Even if Presidents do have an advantage in creating practice, should this preclude reliance on political branch practice or should courts instead require substantial evidence before concluding that Congress has acquiesced in a practice that expands presidential power? Does it suggest that political branch practice should be given particular weight when it represents a curtailment of presidential power, as for example in the case of presidential acceptance of limitations on their removal authority with respect to independent agencies? For a discussion of these issues, see Curtis A. Bradley & Trevor W. Morrison, Historical Gloss and the Separation of Powers, 126 Harv. L. Rev. 411 (2012).

(3) ***Pro Forma Sessions.*** Both opinions agree that President Obama's use of the Recess Appointments Clause during the Senate's pro forma sessions was unconstitutional. Are you persuaded? Is there a meaningful difference between an 11-day intrasession recess that occurs when the Senate has declared itself in recess and an 11-day break in legislative business that is punctuated by one-minute sessions every three days in which one member of the Senate gavels the Senate into session and then immediately gavels it out? If the critical difference is that the Senate has not acknowledged that it is in recess, why should the Senate's view be allowed to control here, particularly if the purpose of a pro forma session is to stymie the President's exercise of the recess appointments' power? Is that tantamount to sanctioning Senate and congressional aggrandizement, as President Obama argued, or does deference to the Senate follow from the fact that the Recess Appointments Clause is a constitutional back-up plan, with the primary mode of appointment being presidential nomination and Senate approval?

To be sure, deferring to the Senate's view avoids the difficulty of determining when the Senate could undertake legislative business during a pro forma session and when it is really unavailable, but the majority does not shirk in undertaking that inquiry in determining that break of between three and ten days is presumptively too short to count as an intrasession recess. Is the inquiry here that much harder—or did you think the difficulty in determining what counts as an intrasession recess weighed in favor of limiting the Clause to intersession recesses, as Justice Scalia argued? More basically, if the focus is on the Senate's unavailability, should the broader conclusion be that in our contemporary world of instantaneous communication and quick travel, the Recess Appointments Clause has become a constitutional anachronism?

Note that the recess appointments that President Obama made were all nominations that he had proposed for several months when the Senate was in actual session but had been blocked by Senate rules. Given that both the Senate and the presidency were in Democratic hands at the time, an obvious alternative was for the Senate to get rid of the filibuster, which indeed it subsequently did. (The Senate could also have told the President that it could not reach agreement with the House on when to adjourn, thereby triggering the President's express constitutional power to adjourn Congress when the two houses cannot agree on when to adjourn, U.S. Const. Art. I, § 3, though that constitutional power has never been invoked.) Perhaps, therefore, part of what animated the unanimous rejection of these recess appointments was the shared perception that a solution to the dangers of pro forma sessions was available, if the Senate had the political will to use it. If so, Noel Canning may bear close similarities to Steel Seizure, where the Justices' sense that President Truman was trying to avoid antagonizing his supporters in organized labor may have animated their rejection of his actions.

(4) **Career Officials and Acting Heads.** How is it that agencies can keep functioning even without an appointed agency head? Part of the answer is career officials, in particular the Senior Executive Service, which includes often very senior agency officials with civil service status. (See Note 1, p. 992.) In addition, governing statutes and agency rules delegate responsibility for various agency functions to divisions and subunits within the agency, so that approval of the agency head is often not required for agency actions. But another important reason is that Congress has long given the President power to appoint acting officers who serve on a temporary basis, with statutes to this effect going back to 1792, including the longstanding Vacancies Act of 1868, which was replaced by the Federal Vacancies Reform Act (FVRA) in 1998. The FVRA establishes a default rule that the first assistant to the vacant office takes over in an acting capacity but provides that the President can appoint certain other officials as the acting head.

The Supreme Court considered the FVRA in NLRB v. SW GENERAL, INC., 137 S.Ct. 929 (2017), and in a 7–2 opinion by CHIEF JUSTICE ROBERTS held that the statute prohibits anyone from occupying an office in an acting capacity once nominated by the President as a permanent appointment for the office, unless the nominee held the position of first assistant to the office for ninety days in the year before the office became vacant. The majority's decision was at odds with established executive branch interpretations of the FVRA. More dramatic was JUSTICE THOMAS's concurrence, solely for himself, which argued that the appointment of acting principal officers without presidential nomination and Senate confirmation violated the Appointments Clause: "The Appointments Clause prescribes the exclusive process by which the President may appoint 'officers of the United States.' . . . When the President directs someone to serve as an officer pursuant to the FVRA, he is 'appoint[ing]' that person as an 'officer of the United States' within the meaning of the Appointments Clause. . . . The FVRA authorizes the President to appoint both inferior and principal officers without first obtaining the advice and consent of the Senate. Appointing inferior officers in this manner raises no constitutional problems. . . . Appointing principal officers under the FVRA, however, raises grave constitutional concerns because the Appointments Clause forbids the President to appoint principal officers without the advice and consent of the Senate." Justice Thomas concluded that the General Counsel to the NLRB, the position at issue, "plainly is an officer of the United States. I also think he is likely a principal officer."

Do you agree that the Appointments Clause prohibits Congress from authorizing temporary presidential appointments of acting officials to vacant principal officer positions? What are the likely practical implications of Justice Thomas' position?

(5) ***Political Polarization and the Appointments Process.*** President Obama's decision to make recess appointments during pro forma Senate sessions was a novel use of the appointments power, but so was the use pro forma sessions as a way to stymie recess appointments. Both are reflections of the increasing partisan divide that in recent years have led to congressional gridlock and dysfunction.

Professor ANNE JOSEPH O'CONNELL has carefully documented changes to the appointments process for Senate-confirmed positions over time. BROOKINGS REPORT: STAFFING FEDERAL AGENCIES: LESSONS FROM 1981–2016, www.brookings.edu/research/staffing-federal-agencies-lessons-from-1981-2016: "[F]rom the start of President Reagan's administration to the end of President Obama's[,] . . . over one-fifth of submitted agency nominations failed to get confirmed . . ., with President Obama's nominations failing close to one-third of the time. It took the Senate almost three months, on average, to confirm nominations, with President Reagan's nominations requiring about a month less and President Obama's requiring about a month more. . . . Although there were variations over time, some corresponding to party control and some to timing within an administration, the appointments process was more difficult for the most recent administrations. While both President Reagan's and President George H.W. Bush's agency nominations had 16 percent failure rates, that figure jumped to 21 percent for President Clinton. President George W. Bush saw 25 percent of his nominations fail to get confirmed, and President Obama's failure rate climbed to 30 percent."

In a similar vein, for successful submitted nominations, "[t]he average period between the Senate's receipt of the nomination and confirmation varied, from a low of 31 days in 1981 to a high of 166 days in 2011. And, as with nomination failures, confirmation delays were worse for the most recent administrations. Both Presidents Reagan and George H.W. Bush faced about two-month delays, on average (60 and 62 days, respectively). Successful nominations by Presidents Clinton and George W. Bush took almost an additional month (86 and 90 total days, respectively). President Obama's confirmed nominations required slightly more than an additional month beyond that (122 days)."

Does this data on the increasing difficulties of the appointments process change your views on President Obama's use of the recess appointments power during a pro forma recess? Is this use better viewed as an effort to aggrandize presidential power by shortcutting the constitutional appointments process or as an act of self-help to use a constitutional work-around in the face of Senate intransigence and abuse of power? Cf. David E. Pozen, Self-Help and the Separation of Powers, 124 Yale L.J. 2 (2014).

(6) *Causes of Delay.* The general public explanation for delays in filling executive positions is Senate confirmation (mis)behavior. And the data above indicates that Senate confirmation plays an important role. But experts identify several additional contributing factors:

- The sheer number of positions that now must be filled: Currently, there are over 1,200 positions requiring presidential nomination and Senate confirmation. "We are just forcing too many people through a system in the White House and on Capitol Hill that cannot process that many people." William A. Galston & E.J. Dionne, Jr., A Half-Empty Government Can't Govern: Why Everyone Wants to Fix The Appointments Process, Why It Never Happens, and How We Can Get It Done at 7 (Brookings Inst. Dec. 2010) (quoting Paul C. Light).

- The vetting process: "The time required to fill each of these positions has expanded exponentially in recent decades . . . In part this results from the more thorough and professional recruitment procedures employed by recent administrations. But most of the elongation . . . is the consequence of a steady accumulation of inquiries, investigations, and reviews aimed at avoiding political embarrassment. These include extensive vetting, lengthy interviews, background checks, examinations of government computer records, completion of questionnaires and forms composed of hundreds of questions, FBI full-field investigations, public financial disclosure and conflicts of interest analysis. Much of the process is duplicated when a nomination goes to the Senate and is subjected to the confirmation process." 2003 Report of the National Commission on the Public Service (the Volcker Commission) at 18.

- The unwillingness of potential nominees to risk (or actual nominees to endure) a media and political gauntlet that political scientist G. Calvin Mackenzie summarized as "nasty & brutish without being short": numerous experts have warned that the rigors of the process dissuade many excellent candidates.

- The "nomination lag": After one year, President Obama had only submitted 326 nominations for cabinet and agency positions, and Obama took an "average of 130.5 days to nominate individuals for Senate-confirmed executive agency positions in his first year." Anne J. O'Connell, Center for Am. Progress, Waiting for Leadership: President Obama's Record in Staffing Key Agency Positions and How to Improve the Appointments Process (Apr. 2010).

- A desire to "deconstruct" administrative government: The Trump administration's promise to "deconstruct the administrative state" suggests that a desire to slow down administrative government might be another factor contributing to appointments delay. As of Trump's one-hundredth day in office, his administration was off to a slow start on appointments, having submitted only 72 non-judicial nominations and received 27 confirmations. But White House officials claimed to have many nominations in the pipeline. Anne J. O'Connell, Brookings Report: Trump's staffing record in the first 100 days was slow, but not catastrophic (May 2017).

Efforts to reform the appointments process to address Senate confirmation delays can have unexpected consequences. In November 2013, the Democratic-controlled Senate voted to end the filibuster for all confirmations other than to the Supreme Court; in April 2017, the now Republican-controlled Senate ended the filibuster for Supreme Court confirmations as well in order to confirm Justice Neil Gorsuch. Anne Joseph O'Connell, in Shortening Agency and Judicial Vacancies through Filibuster Reform? An Examination of Confirmation Rates and Delays from 1981 to 2014, 64 Duke L.J. 1645, 1680–81 (2015), reports that the November 2013 "filibuster reform has had more complicated effects on the confirmation process than may have been predicted. The change does seem to have uniformly aided judicial nominations: fewer were returned to (or withdrawn by) the President, and successful nominations came more quickly. . . . But the change had conflicting effects for many agencies and agency positions: fewer nominations failed but successful nominations took longer to be confirmed."

(7) *Impact and Causes of Vacancies.* Vacancies in agency leadership positions can be substantial. In one study, top jobs in executive and independent agencies were "not filled with appointees between 15 and 25 percent of the time, on average. In other words, in one four-year term, positions are empty or staffed with acting officials between 219 days and an entire year." ANNE JOSEPH O'CONNELL, VACANT OFFICES: DELAYS IN STAFFING TOP AGENCY POSITIONS, 82 S. Cal. L. Rev. 913, 965 (2009). Although delays associated with the appointments process are a major reason for vacancies, another important factor is the short period that many

agency leaders stay in their positions, with the result that "a year or two after the start of an administration, presidents are often looking to fill critical agency jobs a second time. And near the end of an administration, these political positions empty out yet again." Id. at 919.

Professor O'Connell argues that "[v]acancies in key executive agency positions have several deleterious consequences for policymaking. . . . The absence of appointed agency leaders fosters agency inaction. If agencies are missing important managers, they will make fewer policy decisions. For instance, agencies will undertake fewer rulemaking proceedings; they will also launch fewer controversial enforcement actions. Even if there are acting officials in place, such officials often lack sufficient stature to implement significant new programs or regulations. . . . Vacancies in high-level agency positions also create confusion within the agency, particularly for careerists. . . . Confusion still exists with acting officials, though it may be less pronounced. Acting officials will generally lack sufficient authority to direct careerists beyond the most basic agency functions. . . . Gaps in agency leadership also ultimately undermine agency accountability and public trust in the administrative state. The legitimacy of modern agencies derives, in significant part, from their accountability to the president and to Congress . . . Agency claims of public representation that derive from the nomination and confirmation process are far less convincing if there are large periods of time when there are few officials who have gone through that process." Yet "[a]gency vacancies are not always costly. They may actually be desirable for policymaking in at least four circumstances[,] . . . includ[ing] the ability to select better appointees, potentially better performance from frequent turnover, the need or preference for agency inaction in particular policy areas, and the advantages of temporary officials over proper appointees in certain contexts. . . . On net, [however,] . . . the risks of agency inaction, confusion or lack of motivation among careerists, and decreased legitimacy likely outweigh the potential benefits of keeping critical agency jobs empty or staffed with acting officials." Id. at 937–52.

A somewhat more optimistic assessment is offered by Professor NINA MENDELSON, in THE UNCERTAIN EFFECTS OF SENATE CONFIRMATION DELAYS IN THE AGENCIES, 64 Duke L.J. 1571, 1574 (2015): "First, confirmation delays are not evenly spread across appointees, but affect heads of agencies far less than those lower down in the hierarchy. Second, the impact of confirmation delays can vary by agency function. Commentators focus most on the costs to presidential influence over broad policies, as compared to simple management of program implementation. But even for such significant regulatory activity, given the gestation period required for a new policy and other factors, reliance on acting career officials to fill a position or an outright vacancy may be less costly than expected. That said, confirmation delay certainly entails significant costs to agency function, including reductions in agency personnel resources and increased personnel turnover. Potential positive effects are not wholly lacking, but the list is short. Confirmation delay's most positive consequence may be to prompt closer examination of agency decision making patterns and career and political officials' qualifications, and to consider more seriously reforms to our current bureaucratic structure."

(2) The Removal Power

> Notes on the Removal Power Through Time
> FREE ENTERPRISE FUND v. PCAOB
> Morrison v. Olson
> Notes on the Implications of Free Enterprise for Independent Agencies

The House . . . shall have the sole Power of Impeachment. . . . The Senate shall have the sole Power to try all Impeachments.

U.S. Const., Art. I, § 2, cl. 5; § 3, cl. 6

The Congress shall have Power . . . To make all Laws which shall be necessary and proper for carrying into Execution the foregoing Powers, and all other Powers vested by this Constitution in the Government of the United States, or in any Department or Officer thereof.

U.S. Const., Art. I, § 8, cl. 18

The executive Power shall be vested in a President of the United States of America.

U.S. Const., Art. II, § 1

. . . [The President] shall nominate, and by and with the Advice and Consent of the Senate, shall appoint Ambassadors, other public Ministers and Consuls, Judges of the supreme Court, and all other Officers of the United States, whose Appointments are not herein otherwise provided for, and which shall be established by Law; but the Congress may by Law vest the appointment of such inferior Officers, as they think proper, in the President alone, in the Courts of Law, or in the Heads of Departments.

U.S. Const., Art. II, § 2, cl. 2

[H]e shall take Care that the Laws be faithfully executed. . . .

U.S. Const., Art. II, § 3

The President, Vice President and all civil Officers of the United States, shall be removed from Office on Impeachment for, and Conviction of, Treason, Bribery, or other high Crimes and Misdemeanors.

U.S. Const., Art. II, § 4

NOTES ON THE REMOVAL POWER THROUGH TIME

The Constitution is silent on removal, save for impeachment. Debates over the scope of the President's removal power go back to the First Congress. Congress created the first Cabinet department (Foreign Affairs) in 1789. Everyone knew how the Secretary of State must be appointed, but the House could not agree on what the Constitution meant for how the Secretary could be removed. In particular, could the Senate demand its consent to removal, given that its consent was required for appointment? The uncertainty created by constitutional silence is evident in Representative James Madison's change in view. During the initial debate he asserted, "Congress may establish the office by law; therefore, most certainly, it is in the discretion of the Legislature to say upon what terms the office should be held, either during good behavior or during pleasure"—although he urged that presidential removal at will was the best *policy*, for it concentrated responsibility for the Secretary's conduct solely in the President.[30] Within a month, Madison had switched to the position that removal is an exclusively presidential prerogative. He explained: "I have, since the subject was last before the House, examined the Constitution with attention, and I acknowledge that it does not perfectly correspond with the ideas I entertained of it from the first glance."[31] Ultimately, the House settled on presidential removal at will—through the combined votes of those who believed it was the President's constitutional right and those who believed it was the soundest policy.[32] No reliable record exists of debate in the Senate, but comparable lack of consensus can be inferred from the fact that the removal provision passed only on the Vice-President's tie-breaking vote.

The second department (War) was structured in the same way as Foreign Affairs, but the first Congress proceeded differently when it created the Department of the Treasury. Unlike the other two, Treasury was not denominated "an executive department." Moreover, one of its key officials— the Comptroller of the Treasury—was shielded from presidential direction and removal.[33] The next department, the Post Office, followed the Treasury model. Thus, early practice in structuring the entities that would administer government established a diversity of organizational forms: One pattern was quite closely allied to the President through officers serving at his pleasure.

---

[30] Annals of Congress 389, 393–95 (1789).

[31] Id. at 480. Madison was not the only prominent Framer to equivocate on removal. In Federalist 77, Alexander Hamilton argued that "stability of administration" (a key Federalist theme in advocating ratification) will be enhanced by the fact that "[t]he consent of [the Senate] would be necessary to displace as well as to appoint." However by 1793, when Hamilton as Secretary of Treasury was writing as Pacificus in defense of a broad construction of Article II, he cited removal as an illustration of the scope of the executive power. The 1810 edition of the Federalist Papers included a note to No. 77, apparently supplied by Hamilton, challenging the original version.

[32] Legal historians report that the House was divided into four major positions on the removal power: (1) a very small group who believed impeachment to be the only constitutionally authorized removal device, and three groups of virtually equal size who concluded that (2) removal was the constitutional prerogative of the President alone; (3) removal paralleled appointment, and therefore was vested jointly in President and Senate; and (4) removal was not constitutionally determined, and hence could be settled by Congress under its Necessary and Proper power. The classic account is Edward S. Corwin, Tenure of Office & The Removal Power Under the Constitution, 27 Colum. L. Rev. 353 (1927). For more recent scholarship, see David P. Currie, The Constitution in Congress: The Federalist Period, 1789–1801, at 36–40 (1997); Saikrishna Prakash, New Light on the Decision of 1789, 91 Cornell L. Rev. 1021 (2006).

[33] Ironically, Representative James Madison was the strongest initial proponent of shielding the Comptroller from Presidential control. He argued, "[T]here may be strong reasons why an officer of this kind should not hold his office at the pleasure of the executive branch." 1 Annals of Congress at 635–36. When his allies in the Foreign Affairs debate bemoaned his switching sides yet again, he retreated. Id. at 638.

The other had more independence and a greater orientation towards Congress.[34]

In the wake of the Civil War, removal became part of the feud between an overwhelmingly Republican Congress and Andrew Johnson, a Democrat President bent on thwarting any significant restructuring of race-relations through post-Civil War Reconstruction. The Tenure in Office Act of 1867 specified that members of the Cabinet would hold their office until the end of the presidential term (which in Johnson's case was the term he was completing as Lincoln's successor after Lincoln was assassinated) unless the Senate consented to their earlier removal. The provision aimed at securing the continued tenure of Secretary of War Edwin Stanton, who had been appointed by Lincoln and who supported Congress's position on Reconstruction. When President Andrew Johnson nonetheless removed Stanton, the House impeached him on this, and other, grounds. His defense included the argument that the Act was unconstitutional. Ultimately the Senate failed by one vote to convict. Congress continued to enact protections against removal, including the Pendleton Act in 1883 that established federal civil service protections. In 1886, the Court upheld the constitutionality of removal protection for a naval engineer who was deemed to be an inferior officer. See United States v. Perkins, 116 U.S. 483 (1886).

The removal issue reappeared in the waning days of President Woodrow Wilson's administration. MYERS V. UNITED STATES, 272 U.S. 52 (1926), arose out of the Postmaster General's firing of Frank Myers, Postmaster of Portland, Oregon, before the end of his statutory 4-year term. According to one version of the story, Myers was suspected of having committed fraud; other versions paint the Postmaster General as something of a tin pot dictator with a personal grudge against Myers.[35] The pertinent statute[36] provided: "Postmasters . . . shall be appointed and may be removed by the President *by and with the advice and consent of the Senate,* and shall hold their offices for four years unless sooner removed or suspended according to law." (emphasis added). President Wilson refused to seek Senate consent, and Myers sued for lost salary.

Former president and now CHIEF JUSTICE WILLIAM TAFT'S opinion for the Court rejected Myers' claim in a seventy-page opinion: "Made responsible under the Constitution for the effective enforcement of the law, the President needs as an indispensable aid to meet it the disciplinary influence upon those who act under him of a reserve power of removal. But it is contended that executive officers appointed by the President with the consent of the Senate are bound by the statutory law, and are not his servants to do his will, and that his obligation to care for the faithful execution of the laws does not authorize him to treat them as such. The degree of guidance in the discharge

---

[34] See Lawrence Lessig & Cass R. Sunstein, The President and the Administration, 94 Colum. L. Rev. 1, 71 (1994).

[35] For recent discussions of the case, see Jonathan L. Entin, The Pompous Postmaster and Presidential Power: The Story of Myers v. United States, 65 Case W. L. Rev. 1059 (2015); Saikrishna Prakash, The Story of *Myers* and Its Wayward Successors: Going Postal on the Removal Power in Presidential Power Stories (Christopher H. Schroeder & Curtis A. Bradley, eds. 2009).

[36] Section 6 of the Act of July 1, 1876.

of their duties that the President may exercise over executive officers varies with the character of their service as prescribed in the law under which they act. The highest and most important duties which his subordinates perform are those in which they act for him. In such cases they are exercising not their own but his discretion. This field is a very large one. It is sometimes described as political. Each head of a department is and must be the President's alter ego in the matters of that department where the President is required by law to exercise authority. . . .

"In all such cases, the discretion to be exercised is that of the President in determining the national public interest and in directing the action to be taken by his executive subordinates to protect it. In this field his cabinet officers must do his will. . . . The moment that he loses confidence in the intelligence, ability, judgment, or loyalty of any one of them, he must have the power to remove him without delay. To require him to file charges and submit them to the consideration of the Senate might make impossible that unity and co-ordination in executive administration essential to effective action.

". . . There is nothing in the Constitution which permits a distinction between the removal of the head of a department or a bureau, when he discharges a political duty of the President or exercises his discretion, and the removal of executive officers engaged in the . . . ordinary duties . . . prescribed by statute[. These latter duties] come under the general administrative control of the President . . . in order to secure that unitary and uniform execution of the laws which article II of the Constitution evidently contemplated in vesting general executive power in the President alone. Laws are often passed with specific provision for adoption of regulations by a department or bureau head to make the law workable and effective. The ability and judgment manifested by the official thus empowered, as well as his energy and stimulation of his subordinates, are subjects which the President must consider and supervise in his administrative control. Finding such officers to be negligent and inefficient, the President should have the power to remove them. Of course there may be duties so peculiarly and specifically committed to the discretion of a particular officer as to raise a question whether the President may overrule or revise the officer's interpretation of his statutory duty in a particular instance. Then there may be duties of a quasi judicial character imposed on executive officers and members of executive tribunals whose decisions after hearing affect interests of individuals, the discharge of which the President cannot in a particular case properly influence or control. But even in such a case he may consider the decision after its rendition as a reason for removing the officer, on the ground that the discretion regularly entrusted to that officer by statute has not been on the whole intelligently or wisely exercised. Otherwise he does not discharge his own constitutional duty of seeing that the laws be faithfully executed. . . ."

The Court then considered the argument that the removal provision could be sustained because postmasters were "inferior officers" within the meaning of the Appointments Clause: "The power to remove inferior executive officers, like that to remove superior executive officers, is an incident of the power to appoint them, and is in its nature an executive power. . . . The court . . . has recognized in the Perkins Case, 116 U.S. 483 (1886), that Congress, in committing the appointment of such inferior officers to the heads of departments, may prescribe incidental regulations controlling and restricting the latter in the exercise of the power of removal. But the court never has held, nor reasonably could hold, . . . that the excepting clause enables Congress to draw to itself, or to either branch of it, the power to remove or the right to participate in the exercise of that power. To do this would be to go beyond the words and implications of that clause, and to infringe the constitutional principle of the separation of governmental powers."[37]

The waters were muddied when, only nine years later, in HUMPHREY'S EXECUTOR V. UNITED STATES, 295 U.S. 602 (1935), a unanimous Court upheld a for cause removal protection for members of an independent commission. In 1933, President Franklin Delano Roosevelt removed William Humphrey from his position as Commissioner of the Federal Trade Commission. Humphrey had been appointed by President Hoover, Roosevelt's predecessor, and his notorious right-wing views were out of step with those of the new Administration.[38] Humphrey's estate sued for backpay. Under the FTC Act, Commissioners served for a seven-year term and could "be removed by the President for inefficiency, neglect of duty, or malfeasance in office." Based on this language and the legislative history, JUSTICE SUTHERLAND concluded that "congressional intent [was] to create a body of experts who shall gain experience by length of service; a body which shall be independent of executive authority, except in its selection, and free to exercise its judgment without the leave or hindrance of any other official or any department of the government. . . . [T]o hold that, nevertheless, the members of the commission continue in office at the mere will of the President, might be to thwart, in large measure, the very ends which Congress sought to realize by definitely fixing the term of office."

Distinguishing Myers, Justice Sutherland stated that "the narrow point actually decided was only that the President had power to remove a postmaster of the first class, without the advice and consent of the Senate as required by act of Congress. . . . A postmaster is an executive officer restricted to the performance of executive functions. He is charged with no duty at all related to either the legislative or judicial power. The actual decision in the Myers Case finds support in the theory that such an officer is merely one of the units in the executive department and, hence, inherently subject to the exclusive and illimitable power of removal by the Chief Executive, whose subordinate and aid he is. . . . [T]he necessary reach of the

---

[37] Dissenting, Justice McReynolds took issue with the argument that removal was inherently executive, while Justice Brandeis insisted that Myers was an inferior officer, and Justice Holmes argued (Brandeis agreeing) that "[t]he duty of the President to see that the laws be executed is a duty that does not go beyond the laws or require him to achieve more than Congress sees fit to leave within his power."

[38] Before firing Humphrey, FDR wrote to him expressing the hope that his resignation would be forthcoming: "You will, I know, realize that I do not feel that your mind and my mind go along together on either the policies or the administering of the Federal Trade Commission, and, frankly, I think it is best for the people of this country that I should have a full confidence." Humphrey did not concur, and the President removed him from office.

decision goes far enough to include all purely executive officers. It goes no farther; much less does it include an officer who occupies no place in the executive department and who exercises no part of the executive power vested by the Constitution in the President.

"The Federal Trade Commission is an administrative body created by Congress to carry into effect legislative policies embodied in the statute in accordance with the legislative standard therein prescribed, and to perform other specified duties as a legislative or as a judicial aid. . . . In administering the provisions of the statute in respect of 'unfair methods of competition,' that is to say, in filling in and administering the details embodied by that general standard, the commission acts in part quasi-legislatively and in part quasi-judicially. . . . To the extent that it exercises any executive function, as distinguished from executive power in the constitutional sense, it does so in the discharge and effectuation of its quasi-legislative or quasi-judicial powers, or as an agency of the legislative or judicial departments of the government. . . . [T]he Myers decision, affirming the power of the President alone to make the removal, is confined to purely executive officers; and as to officers of the kind here under consideration, we hold that no removal can be made during the prescribed term for which the officer is appointed, except for one or more of the causes named in the applicable statute."[39]

Note the curious willingness of the majority to place the FTC in both the legislative and judicial branches, and the blind eye it turns to what even then had to be conceded an executive branch function. Might it be a sufficient distinction of Myers that the precise issue there, not present here, was "only that the President had power to remove a postmaster of the first class, without the advice and consent of the Senate as required by act of Congress"? So argued Professor Strauss in The Place of Agencies in Government: Separation of Powers and the Fourth Branch, 84 Colum. L. Rev. 573 (1984), and, as you may have read in Whitman v. American Trucking Ass'ns, p. 791, the contemporary understanding is that the administrative functions the Humphrey's Executor opinion linked to Congress and the judiciary are properly characterized as executive functions.

---

[39] What changed in the nine years between Myers and Humphrey's Executor? For one thing, the Court's composition: Two members of Taft's majority—including Taft himself—had been replaced. But while the new Chief Justice, Charles Hughes, lacked Taft's presidential experience, he came from a career in the executive branch and appeared generally sympathetic to Roosevelt, or at least the needs of a Chief Executive. Another new appointee, Benjamin Cardozo, was a supporter of the New Deal. Moreover, four Justices (Van Deventer, Sutherland, Butler, and Stone) joined the opinion of the Court in both cases. Another possibility is that Humphrey's Executor was part of the Court's early resistance to President Roosevelt's assertions of regulatory authority in the New Deal. This defeat for the President's efforts to exert more control over the independent agencies (which by then included the ICC, SEC, FCC, and FTC among others) came on the same day as Schechter Poultry Corp. v. United States, p. 810 above, invalidated significant portions of the National Industrial Recovery Act on nondelegation grounds. Yet another possibility looks to international developments. Myers was decided during the early years of movements in Germany and Italy towards strong executive government. Indeed, the New York Times, reporting the decision, quoted a reference to some people's belief "that what this country needs is another Mussolini." The New York Times, Nov. 7, 1926, p. 5, § 1. By the time of Humphrey's Executor, Hitler had ended democratic government in Germany, Mussolini had embarked on the conquest of Ethiopia, and the potential dangers of strong centralized executive government were more at the fore.

Over the next 50 years, the line drawn by the combination of Myers and Humphrey's Executor held, despite occasional sniping between the President and Congress. When Ronald Reagan took office, his administration asserted a broad view of presidential power (now known as the "unitary executive theory") and insisted that many conventionally accepted limits on presidential authority were unconstitutional.[40] Meanwhile, Congress became more venturesome in devising agency structures that did not fit neatly into the Myers/Humphrey's Executive framework. The result was two modern decisions, two decades apart, that attempt again to define the constitutional contours of removal. Consider, after you read Free Enterprise Fund v. PCAOB (2010) and Morrison v. Olson (1988), whether we are any closer than was the first Congress to definitive resolution of the question.

FREE ENTERPRISE FUND v. PUBLIC COMPANY ACCOUNTING OVERSIGHT BOARD

Supreme Court of the United States (2010).
561 U.S. 477.

■ CHIEF JUSTICE ROBERTS delivered the opinion of the Court.

Our Constitution divided the "powers of the new Federal Government into three defined categories, Legislative, Executive, and Judicial." INS v. Chadha, 462 U.S. 919, 951 (1983) [p. 831]. Article II vests "[t]he executive Power . . . in a President of the United States of America," who must "take Care that the Laws be faithfully executed." In light of "[t]he impossibility that one man should be able to perform all the great business of the State," the Constitution provides for executive officers to "assist the supreme Magistrate in discharging the duties of his trust." 30 Writings of George Washington 334 (J. Fitzpatrick ed. 1939). Since 1789, the Constitution has been understood to empower the President to keep these officers accountable-by removing them from office, if necessary. This Court has determined, however, that this authority is not without limit. In Humphrey's Executor v. United States, 295 U.S. 602 (1935) [p. 920], we held that Congress can, under certain circumstances, create independent agencies run by principal officers appointed by the President, whom the President may not remove at will but only for good cause. Likewise, in United States v. Perkins, 116 U.S. 483 (1886), and Morrison v. Olson, 487 U.S. 654 (1988) [p. 934], the Court sustained similar restrictions on the power of principal executive officers—themselves responsible to the President—to remove their own inferiors. The parties do not ask us to reexamine any of these precedents, and we do not do so.

We are asked, however, to consider a new situation not yet encountered by the Court. The question is whether these separate layers of protection may be combined. May the President be restricted in his

---

[40] See Harold J. Krent, From a Unitary to a Unilateral Presidency, 88 B.U.L. Rev. 523 (2008). See also Symposium: Presidential Power in Historical Perspective: Reflections on Calabresi & Yoo's The Unitary Executive, 12 U. Pa. J. Const. L. 241 (2010).

ability to remove a principal officer, who is in turn restricted in his ability to remove an inferior officer, even though that inferior officer determines the policy and enforces the laws of the United States? We hold that such multilevel protection from removal is contrary to Article II's vesting of the executive power in the President. The President cannot "take Care that the Laws be faithfully executed" if he cannot oversee the faithfulness of the officers who execute them. . . .

I

After a series of celebrated accounting debacles, Congress enacted the Sarbanes-Oxley Act of 2002 (or Act). Among other measures, the Act introduced tighter regulation of the accounting industry under a new Public Company Accounting Oversight Board. The Board is composed of five members, appointed to staggered 5-year terms by the Securities and Exchange Commission. It was modeled on private self-regulatory organizations in the securities industry—such as the New York Stock Exchange—that investigate and discipline their own members subject to Commission oversight. Congress created the Board as a private "nonprofit corporation." . . . Unlike the self-regulatory organizations, however, the Board is a Government-created, Government-appointed entity, with expansive powers to govern an entire industry. . . . Despite the provisions specifying that Board members are not Government officials for statutory purposes, the parties agree that the Board is "part of the Government" for constitutional purposes and that its members are "'Officers of the United States'" who "exercis[e] significant authority pursuant to the laws of the United States," Buckley v. Valeo, 424 U.S. 1, 125–126 (1976) (per curiam).

The Act places the Board under the SEC's oversight, particularly with respect to the issuance of rules or the imposition of sanctions (both of which are subject to Commission approval and alteration). But the individual members of the Board—like the officers and directors of the self-regulatory organizations—are substantially insulated from the Commission's control. The Commission cannot remove Board members at will, but only "for good cause shown," "in accordance with" certain procedures. § 7211(e)(6). . . . The parties agree that the Commissioners cannot themselves be removed by the President except under the Humphrey's Executor standard of "inefficiency, neglect of duty, or malfeasance in office," 295 U.S. at 620, and we decide the case with that understanding.

Beckstead and Watts, LLP, is a Nevada accounting firm registered with the Board. The Board inspected the firm, released a report critical of its auditing procedures, and began a formal investigation. Beckstead and Watts and the Free Enterprise Fund, a nonprofit organization of which the firm is a member, then sued the Board and its members, seeking (among other things) a declaratory judgment that the Board is unconstitutional and an injunction preventing the Board from exercising its powers. . . . [T]he District Court determined that it had jurisdiction and granted summary judgment to respondents[, and a] divided Court of Appeals affirmed. . . .

III

. . . The landmark case of Myers v. United States reaffirmed the principle that Article II confers on the President "the general administrative control of those executing the laws." 272 U.S. at 164. It is *his* responsibility to take care that the laws be faithfully executed. The buck stops with the President, in Harry Truman's famous phrase. . . . [W]e have previously upheld [in Humphrey's Executor, Perkins, and Morrison] limited restrictions on the President's removal power. In those cases, however, only one level of protected tenure separated the President from an officer exercising executive power. It was the President—or a subordinate he could remove at will—who decided whether the officer's conduct merited removal under the good-cause standard. The Act before us does something quite different. It not only protects Board members from removal except for good cause, but withdraws from the President any decision on whether that good cause exists. That decision is vested instead in other tenured officers—the Commissioners—none of whom is subject to the President's direct control. The result is a Board that is not accountable to the President, and a President who is not responsible for the Board.

The added layer of tenure protection makes a difference. Without a layer of insulation between the Commission and the Board, the Commission could remove a Board member at any time, and therefore would be fully responsible for what the Board does. The President could then hold the Commission to account for its supervision of the Board, to the same extent that he may hold the Commission to account for everything else it does. A second level of tenure protection changes the nature of the President's review. Now the Commission cannot remove a Board member at will. The President therefore cannot hold the Commission fully accountable for the Board's conduct, to the same extent that he may hold the Commission accountable for everything else that it does. . . . This novel structure does not merely add to the Board's independence, but transforms it. Neither the President, nor anyone directly responsible to him, nor even an officer whose conduct he may review only for good cause, has full control over the Board. . . .

That arrangement is contrary to Article II's vesting of the executive power in the President. Without the ability to oversee the Board, or to attribute the Board's failings to those whom he *can* oversee, the President . . . can neither ensure that the laws are faithfully executed, nor be held responsible for a Board member's breach of faith. This violates the basic principle that the President "cannot delegate ultimate responsibility or the active obligation to supervise that goes with it," because Article II "makes a single President responsible for the actions of the Executive Branch." Clinton v. Jones, 520 U.S. 681, 712–713 (1997) (Breyer, J., concurring in judgment). . . . The diffusion of power carries with it a diffusion of accountability. The people do not vote for the "Officers of the United States." They instead look to the President to guide the "assistants or deputies . . . subject to his superintendence." The Federalist No. 72 (A. Hamilton). Without a clear and effective chain of command, the public cannot "determine on whom the blame or the punishment of a pernicious measure, or series of pernicious measures ought really to fall." Id., No. 70 (same). By granting the Board executive power without the Executive's oversight, this Act subverts the President's ability to ensure that the laws are faithfully executed—as well as the public's ability to pass judgment on his efforts. The Act's restrictions are incompatible with the Constitution's separation of powers.

Respondents and the dissent resist this conclusion, portraying the Board as "the kind of practical accommodation between the Legislature and the Executive that should be permitted in a 'workable government.'" Metropolitan Washington Airports Authority v. Citizens for Abatement of Aircraft Noise, Inc., 501 U.S. 252, 276 (1991) (quoting Youngstown Sheet & Tube Co. v. Sawyer, 343 U.S. 579, 635 (1952) (Jackson, J., concurring) [p. 871]). . . .

No one doubts Congress's power to create a vast and varied federal bureaucracy. But where, in all this, is the role for oversight by an elected President? . . . One can have a government that functions without being ruled by functionaries, and a government that benefits from expertise without being ruled by experts. Our Constitution was adopted to enable the people to govern themselves, through their elected leaders. The growth of the Executive Branch, which now wields vast power and touches almost every aspect of daily life, heightens the concern that it may slip from the Executive's control, and thus from that of the people. This concern is largely absent from the dissent's paean to the administrative state. . . .

In fact, the multilevel protection that the dissent endorses "provides a blueprint for extensive expansion of the legislative power." [Metropolitan Washington Airports Auth., 501 U.S. at] 277. In a system of checks and balances, "[p]ower abhors a vacuum," and one branch's handicap is another's strength. 537 F.3d, at 695, n. 4 (Kavanaugh, J., dissenting). . . . Congress has plenary control over the salary, duties, and even existence of executive offices. Only Presidential oversight can counter its influence. . . .

The Framers created a structure in which "[a] dependence on the people" would be the "primary control on the government." The Federalist No. 51 (J. Madison). That dependence is maintained, not just by "parchment barriers," id., No. 48 (same), but by letting "[a]mbition . . . counteract ambition," giving each branch "the necessary constitutional means, and personal motives, to resist encroachments of the others," id., No. 51. A key "constitutional means" vested in the President—perhaps *the* key means—was "the power of appointing, overseeing, and

controlling those who execute the laws." 1 Annals of Cong., at 463. . . .
The President has been given the power to oversee executive officers; he
is not limited, as in Harry Truman's lament, to "persuad[ing]" his
unelected subordinates "to do what they ought to do without persuasion."
In its pursuit of a "workable government," Congress cannot reduce the
Chief Magistrate to a cajoler-in-chief.

. . . [T]he Government argues that the Commission's removal power
over the Board is "broad," and could be construed as broader still, if
necessary to avoid invalidation. But the Government does not contend
that simple disagreement with the Board's policies or priorities could
constitute "good cause" for its removal. Nor do our precedents suggest as
much. Humphrey's Executor, for example, rejected a removal premised
on a lack of agreement " 'on either the policies or the administering of the
Federal Trade Commission,' " because the FTC was designed to be
" 'independent in character,' " "free from 'political domination or
control,' " and not " 'subject to anybody in the government' " or " 'to the
orders of the President.' " 295 U.S., at 619. . . . And here there is judicial
review of any effort to remove Board members, so the Commission will
not have the final word on the propriety of its own removal orders. . . .
Indeed, this case presents an even more serious threat to executive
control than an "ordinary" dual for-cause standard. Congress enacted an
unusually high standard that must be met before Board members may
be removed. A Board member cannot be removed except for willful
violations of the Act, Board rules, or the securities laws; willful abuse of
authority; or unreasonable failure to enforce compliance—as determined
in a formal Commission order, rendered on the record and after notice
and an opportunity for a hearing. . . . The rigorous standard that must
be met before a Board member may be removed was drawn from statutes
concerning private organizations like the New York Stock Exchange.
While we need not decide the question here, a removal standard
appropriate for limiting Government control over private bodies may be
inappropriate for officers wielding the executive power of the United
States.

Alternatively, respondents portray the Act's limitations on removal
as irrelevant, because—as the Court of Appeals held—the Commission
wields "at-will removal power over Board functions if not Board
members." 537 F.3d, at 683 (emphasis added). . . . Broad power over
Board functions is not equivalent to the power to remove Board
members. . . . Even if Commission power over Board activities could
substitute for authority over its members, we would still reject
respondents' premise that the Commission's power in this regard is
plenary. . . . [T]he Board is empowered to take significant enforcement
actions, and does so largely independently of the Commission. Its powers
are, of course, subject to some latent Commission control. But the Act
nowhere gives the Commission effective power to start, stop, or alter
individual Board investigations . . .

Finally, respondents suggest that our conclusion is contradicted by the past practice of Congress. But the Sarbanes-Oxley Act is highly unusual in committing substantial executive authority to officers protected by two layers of for-cause removal. . . . The parties have identified only a handful of isolated positions in which inferior officers might be protected by two levels of good-cause tenure. . . . The dissent here suggests that other such positions might exist, and complains that we do not resolve their status in this opinion. The dissent itself, however, stresses the very size and variety of the Federal Government, and those features discourage general pronouncements on matters neither briefed nor argued here. In any event, the dissent fails to support its premonitions of doom; none of the positions it identifies are similarly situated to the Board. For example, many civil servants within independent agencies would not qualify as "Officers of the United States," who "exercis[e] significant authority pursuant to the laws of the United States," Buckley, 424 U.S., at 126 . . . We do not decide the status of other Government employees, nor do we decide whether "lesser functionaries subordinate to officers of the United States" must be subject to the same sort of control as those who exercise "significant authority pursuant to the laws." . . . Nothing in our opinion, therefore, should be read to cast doubt on the use of what is colloquially known as the civil service system within independent agencies.[10] . . . [T]he dissent wanders far afield when it suggests that today's opinion might increase the President's authority to remove military officers. Without expressing any view whatever on the scope of that authority, it is enough to note that we see little analogy between our Nation's armed services and the Public Company Accounting Oversight Board. . . .

IV

Petitioners' complaint argued that the Board's "freedom from Presidential oversight and control" rendered it "and all power and authority exercised by it" in violation of the Constitution. App. 46. We reject such a broad holding. Instead, we agree with the Government that the unconstitutional tenure provisions are severable from the remainder of the statute. . . . Putting to one side petitioners' Appointments Clause challenges (addressed below), the existence of the Board does not violate the separation of powers, but the substantive removal restrictions imposed by §§ 7211(e)(6) and 7217(d)(3) do. Under the traditional default rule, removal is incident to the power of appointment. Concluding that the removal restrictions are invalid leaves the Board removable by the Commission at will, and leaves the President separated from Board members by only a single level of good-cause tenure. The Commission is

---

[10] For similar reasons, our holding also does not address that subset of independent agency employees who serve as administrative law judges. Whether administrative law judges are necessarily "Officers of the United States" is disputed. See, e.g., Landry v. FDIC, 204 F.3d 1125 (C.A.D.C. 2000). And unlike members of the Board, many administrative law judges of course perform adjudicative rather than enforcement or policymaking functions, or possess purely recommendatory powers. . . .

then fully responsible for the Board's actions, which are no less subject than the Commission's own functions to Presidential oversight. The Sarbanes-Oxley Act remains "'fully operative as a law'" with these tenure restrictions excised. . . .

It is true that the language providing for good-cause removal is only one of a number of statutory provisions that, working together, produce a constitutional violation. In theory, perhaps, the Court might blue-pencil a sufficient number of the Board's responsibilities so that its members would no longer be "Officers of the United States." Or we could restrict the Board's enforcement powers, so that it would be a purely recommendatory panel. Or the Board members could in future be made removable by the President, for good cause or at will. But such editorial freedom—far more extensive than our holding today—belongs to the Legislature, not the Judiciary. Congress of course remains free to pursue any of these options going forward.

V

Petitioners raise three more challenges to the Board under the Appointments Clause. None has merit. First, petitioners argue that Board members are principal officers requiring Presidential appointment with the Senate's advice and consent. . . . Given that the Commission is properly viewed, under the Constitution, as possessing the power to remove Board members at will, and given the Commission's other oversight authority, we have no hesitation in concluding that under Edmond [v. United States, 520 U.S. 651 (1997), p. 884] the Board members are inferior officers whose appointment Congress may permissibly vest in a "Hea[d] of Departmen[t]." . . . [Moreover, because] the Commission is a freestanding component of the Executive Branch, not subordinate to or contained within any other such component, it constitutes a "Departmen[t]" for the purposes of the Appointments Clause.[11] [Petitioners also] argue that the full Commission cannot constitutionally appoint Board members, because only the Chairman of the Commission is the Commission's "Hea[d]." The Commission's powers, however, are generally vested in the Commissioners jointly, not the Chairman alone. . . . As a constitutional matter, we see no reason why a multimember body may not be the "Hea[d]" of a "Departmen[t]" that it governs.

* * *

The Constitution that makes the President accountable to the people for executing the laws also gives him the power to do so. That power includes, as a general matter, the authority to remove those who assist him in carrying out his duties. Without such power, the President could not be held fully accountable for discharging his own responsibilities; the

---

[11] We express no view on whether the Commission is thus an "executive Departmen[t]" under the Opinions Clause, or under Section 4 of the Twenty-Fifth Amendment. See Freytag v. Commissioner, 501 U.S. 868, 886–887 (1991) [p. 889].

buck would stop somewhere else. Such diffusion of authority "would greatly diminish the intended and necessary responsibility of the chief magistrate himself." The Federalist No. 70. While we have sustained in certain cases limits on the President's removal power, the Act before us imposes a new type of restriction-two levels of protection from removal for those who nonetheless exercise significant executive power. Congress cannot limit the President's authority in this way.

■ JUSTICE BREYER, with whom JUSTICE STEVENS, JUSTICE GINSBURG, and JUSTICE SOTOMAYOR join, dissenting.

The legal question before us arises at the intersection of two general constitutional principles. On the one hand, Congress has broad power to enact statutes "necessary and proper" to the exercise of its specifically enumerated constitutional authority. . . . [T]he Necessary and Proper Clause affords Congress broad authority to "create" governmental "offices" and to structure those offices "as it chooses." Buckley v. Valeo, 424 U.S. 1, 138 (1976) (per curiam). On the other hand, the opening sections of Articles I, II, and III of the Constitution separately and respectively vest "all legislative Powers" in Congress, the "executive Power" in the President, and the "judicial Power" in the Supreme Court (and such "inferior Courts as Congress may from time to time ordain and establish"). In doing so, these provisions imply a structural separation-of-powers principle. And that principle, along with the instruction in Article II, § 3 that the President "shall take Care that the Laws be faithfully executed," limits Congress' power to structure the Federal Government. . . .

But neither of these two principles is absolute in its application to removal cases. The Necessary and Proper Clause does not grant Congress power to free *all* Executive Branch officials from dismissal at the will of the President. Nor does the separation-of-powers principle grant the President an absolute authority to remove *any and all* Executive Branch officials at will. Rather, depending on, say, the nature of the office, its function, or its subject matter, Congress sometimes may, consistent with the Constitution, limit the President's authority to remove an officer from his post. And we must here decide whether the circumstances surrounding the statute at issue justify such a limitation. In answering the question presented, we cannot look to more specific constitutional text, such as the text of the Appointments Clause or the Presentment Clause, upon which the Court has relied in other separation-of-powers cases. That is because, with the exception of the general "vesting" and "take care" language, the Constitution is completely "silent with respect to the power of removal from office." Ex parte Hennen, 13 Pet. 230, 258 (1839). Nor does history . . . [or] this Court's precedent fully answer the question presented.

When previously deciding this kind of nontextual question, the Court has emphasized the importance of examining how a particular provision, taken in context, is likely to function. . . . The Court has thereby written into law Justice Jackson's wise perception that "the Constitution . . . contemplates that practice will integrate the dispersed powers into *a workable government*." Youngstown Sheet & Tube Co. v. Sawyer, 343 U.S. 579, 635 (1952) (opinion concurring in the judgment) (emphasis added). It is not surprising that the Court in these circumstances has looked to function and context, and not to bright-line rules. For one thing, that approach embodies the intent of the Framers. . . . For another, a functional approach permits Congress and the President the flexibility needed to adapt statutory law to changing circumstances. . . . [T]he Federal Government at the time of the founding consisted of about 2,000 employees and served a population of about 4 million. Today, however, the Federal Government employs about *4.4 million workers* who serve a Nation of more than 310 million people living in a society characterized by rapid technological, economic, and social change. . . . [V]ast numbers of statutes governing vast numbers of subjects, concerned with vast numbers of different problems, provide for, or foresee, their execution or administration through the work of administrators organized within many different kinds of administrative structures, exercising different kinds of administrative authority, to achieve their legislatively mandated objectives. . . .

The functional approach required by our precedents recognizes this administrative complexity and, more importantly, recognizes the various ways presidential power operates within this context—and the various ways in which a removal provision might affect that power. . . . These practical reasons not only support our precedents' determination that cases such as this should examine the specific functions and context at issue; they also indicate that judges should hesitate before second-guessing a "for cause" decision made by the other branches. Compared to Congress and the President, the Judiciary possesses an inferior understanding of the realities of administration, and the manner in which power, including and most especially political power, operates in context.

II

To what extent then is the Act's "for cause" provision likely, as a practical matter, to limit the President's exercise of executive authority? In practical terms no "for cause" provision can, in isolation, define the full measure of executive power. This is because a legislative decision to place ultimate administrative authority in, say, the Secretary of Agriculture rather than the President, the way in which the statute defines the scope of the power the relevant administrator can exercise, the decision as to who controls the agency's budget requests and funding, the relationships between one agency or department and another, as well as more purely political factors (including Congress' ability to assert influence) are more likely to affect the President's power to get something done. . . . Indeed, notwithstanding the majority's assertion that the removal authority is "*the* key" mechanism by which the President oversees inferior officers in the independent agencies, it appears that no President has ever actually sought to exercise that power by testing the scope of a "for cause" provision.

But even if we put all these other matters to the side, we should still conclude that the "for cause" restriction before us will not restrict presidential power significantly. For one thing, the restriction directly limits, not the President's power, but the power of an already independent agency. The Court seems to have forgotten that fact when it identifies its central constitutional problem: According to the Court, the President "is powerless to intervene" if he has determined that the Board members' "conduct merit[s] removal" because "[t]hat decision is vested instead in other tenured officers—the Commissioners—none of whom is subject to the President's direct control." But so long as the President is *legitimately* foreclosed from removing the *Commissioners* except for cause (as the majority assumes), nullifying the Commission's power to remove Board members only for cause will not resolve the problem the Court has identified. . . .

. . . [O]nce we leave the realm of hypothetical logic and view the removal provision at issue in the context of the entire Act, its lack of practical effect becomes readily apparent. That is because the statute provides the Commission with full authority and virtually comprehensive control over all of the Board's functions. . . . [T]he Court is simply wrong when it says that "the Act nowhere gives the Commission effective power to start, stop, or alter" Board investigations. On the contrary, the Commission's control over the Board's investigatory and legal functions is virtually absolute. Moreover, the Commission has general supervisory powers over the Accounting Board itself: It controls the Board's budget, §§ 7219(b), (d)(1); it can assign to the Board any "duties or functions" that it "determines are necessary or appropriate," § 7211(c)(5); it has full "oversight and enforcement authority over the Board," § 7217(a), *including the authority to inspect the Board's activities whenever it believes it "appropriate" to do so*, § 7217(d)(2) (emphasis added). And it can censure the Board or its members, as well as remove the members from office, if the members, for example, fail to enforce the Act, violate any provisions of the Act, or abuse the authority granted to them under the Act, § 7217(d)(3).

What is left? The Commission's inability to remove a Board member whose perfectly *reasonable* actions cause the Commission to overrule him with great frequency? What is the practical likelihood of that occurring, or, if it does, of the President's serious concern about such a matter? Everyone concedes that the President's control over the Commission is constitutionally sufficient. And if the President's control over the Commission is sufficient, and the Commission's control over the Board is virtually absolute, then, as a practical matter, the President's control over the Board should prove sufficient as well. . . .

Where a "for cause" provision is so unlikely to restrict presidential power and so likely to further a legitimate institutional need, precedent strongly supports its constitutionality. . . . [I]n considering a related issue in Nixon v. Administrator of General Services, 433 U.S. 425 (1977), the Court made clear that when "determining whether the Act disrupts the proper balance between the coordinate branches, the proper inquiry focuses on the extent to which it prevents the Executive Branch from accomplishing its constitutionally assigned functions." Id., at 443. . . . Here, the removal restriction may somewhat diminish the *Commission's* ability to control the Board, but it will have little, if any, negative effect in respect to the President's ability to control the Board, let alone to coordinate the Executive Branch. Indeed, given Morrison, where the Court upheld a restriction that significantly interfered with the President's important historic power to control criminal prosecutions, a "purely executive" function, 487 U.S., at 687–689, the constitutionality of the present restriction would seem to follow a fortiori. . . .

[T]his Court has repeatedly upheld "for cause" provisions where they restrict the President's power to remove an officer with adjudicatory responsibilities. . . . [and Perkins, Myers, Morrison, Humphrey's Executor and Freytag] fit together in a way that logically compels a holding of constitutionality here. . . . [T]he Court has said that "[o]ur separation-of-powers jurisprudence generally focuses on the danger of one branch's *aggrandizing its power* at the expense of another branch." Freytag supra, at 878 (emphasis added). . . . Congress here has "drawn" no power to itself to remove the Board members. It has instead sought to *limit* its own power, by, for example, providing the Accounting Board with a revenue stream independent of the congressional appropriations process. And this case thereby falls outside the ambit of the Court's most serious constitutional concern. . . .

. . . Even if the "for cause" provision before us does not itself significantly interfere with the President's authority or aggrandize Congress' power, is it nonetheless necessary to adopt a bright-line rule forbidding the provision lest, through a series of such provisions, each itself upheld as reasonable, Congress might undercut the President's central constitutional role? The answer to this question is that no such need has been shown. Moreover, insofar as the Court seeks to create such a rule, it fails. . . . because of considerable uncertainty about the scope of its holding—an uncertainty that the Court's opinion both reflects and generates. . . . The Court begins to reveal the practical problems inherent in its double for-cause rule when it suggests that its rule may not apply to "the civil service." The "civil service" is defined by statute to include "all appointive positions in . . . the Government of the United States," excluding the military, but including *all* civil "officer[s]" up to and including those who are subject to Senate confirmation. 5 U.S.C. §§ 2101, 2102(a)(1)(B), 2104. The civil service thus includes many officers indistinguishable from the members of both the Commission and the

Accounting Board. . . . [E]ven if I assume that the majority categorically excludes the competitive service from the scope of its new rule, the exclusion would be insufficient. This is because the Court's "double for-cause" rule applies to appointees who are "inferior officer[s]." . . . And who are they? Courts and scholars have struggled for more than a century to define the constitutional term "inferior officers," without much success. The Court does not clarify the concept. . . .

The problem is not simply that the term "inferior officer" is indefinite but also that efforts to define it inevitably conclude that the term's sweep is unusually broad. . . . I . . . see no way to avoid sweeping hundreds, perhaps thousands of high level government officials within the scope of the Court's holding, putting their job security and their administrative actions and decisions constitutionally at risk. To make even a conservative estimate, one would have to begin by listing federal departments, offices, bureaus and other agencies whose heads are by statute removable only "for cause." I have found 48 such agencies. . . . Then it would be necessary to identify the senior officials in those agencies (just below the top) who themselves are removable only "for cause." I have identified 573 such high-ranking officials. This list is a conservative estimate because it consists only of career appointees in the Senior Executive Service (SES), see 5 U.S.C. §§ 2101a, 3132(a)(2), a group of high-ranking officials distinct from the "competitive service," see § 2101(a)(1)(C), who "serve in the key positions just below the top Presidential appointees," Office of Personnel Management, About the Senior Executive Service, online at http://www.opm.gov/ses/about_ses/index.asp; § 2102(a)(1)(C), and who are, without exception, subject to "removal" only for cause. §§ 7542–7543. And by virtually any definition, essentially all SES officials qualify as "inferior officers," for their duties, as defined by statute, require them to "direc[t] the work of an organizational unit," carry out highlevel managerial functions, or "*otherwise exercis[e] important policy-making, policy-determining, or other executive functions.*" § 3132(a)(2) (emphasis added). The potential list of those whom today's decision affects . . . [also includes] administrative law judges (ALJs). . . . And what about the military? Commissioned military officers "are 'inferior officers.' " Weiss [v. United States, 510 U.S. 163, 182 (1994), who by statute] may not be removed from office except for cause (at least in peacetime), . . . [and] can generally be so removed only by *other* commissioned officers who themselves enjoy the same career protections. The majority sees "no reason . . . to address whether" any of "these positions," "or any others," might be deemed unconstitutional under its new rule, preferring instead to leave these matters for a future case. But what is to happen in the meantime? . . .

III

One last question: How can the Court simply *assume* without deciding that the SEC Commissioners themselves are removable only "for cause?" Unless the Commissioners themselves are *in fact* protected by a "for cause" requirement, the Accounting Board statute, on the Court's own reasoning, is not constitutionally defective. . . . It is certainly not obvious that the SEC Commissioners enjoy "for cause" protection. . . . [T]he statue that established the Commission says nothing about removal. . . . Nor is the absence of a "for cause" provision in the statute that created the Commission likely to have been inadvertent. . . . Congress created the SEC at a time when, under this Court's precedents, it would have been *unconstitutional* to make the Commissioners removable only for cause. . . . The Court then, by assumption, reads *into* the statute books a "for cause removal" phrase that does not appear in the relevant statute and which Congress probably did not intend to write. And it does so in order to strike down, not to uphold, another statute. This is not a statutory construction that seeks to avoid a constitutional question, but its opposite. . . .

SIGNIFICANT CASE

MORRISON v. OLSON
487 U.S. 654 (1988).

In response to the Watergate scandal that eventually forced President Nixon's resignation, the Ethics in Government Act created an "independent counsel" to investigate and prosecute high executive officials for violations of federal criminal laws. Under the Act—this portion of which has since expired without renewal—the Attorney General would preliminarily investigate accusations of criminal wrongdoing; if he concluded that further investigation was required, he was to inform a "Special Division" of three D.C. Circuit judges, who were in turn to appoint an independent counsel (IC). The IC was given "full power and independent authority to exercise all investigative and prosecutorial functions and powers of the Department of Justice, the Attorney General, and any other officer or employee of the Department of Justice." The Special Division could determine if an investigation had reached a point justifying termination; beyond this, the power to remove was specified as "the personal action of the Attorney General and only for good cause, physical disability, mental incapacity, or any other condition that substantially impairs the performance of such independent counsel's duties." The Attorney General was required to report any such removal in detail to both the Special Division and the Judiciary Committees of the Senate and the House, and the independent counsel could obtain judicial review.

In 1986, Alexia Morrison was appointed independent counsel to investigate whether Assistant Attorney General Theodore Olson had lied while testifying under oath before a House Judiciary Committee investigating an earlier dispute between Congress and the Administrator of EPA. Olson challenged the constitutionality of the independent counsel. CHIEF JUSTICE REHNQUIST wrote for all members of the Court except Justice Scalia, who dissented, and Justice Kennedy, who did not participate. The Court first determined that the independent counsel was an "inferior officer," see p. 884, and then that appointment by the Special Division was not an unconstitutional "inter-branch" appointment:

"We now turn to consider whether the Act is invalid under the constitutional principle of separation of powers. . . . Unlike both Bowsher [p. 860], and Myers [p. 918], this case does not involve an attempt by Congress itself to gain a role in the removal of executive officials other than its established powers of impeachment and conviction. The Act instead puts the removal power squarely in the hands of the Executive Branch; an independent counsel may be removed from office, 'only by the personal action of the Attorney General, and only for good cause.' There is no requirement of congressional approval of the Attorney General's removal decision, though the decision is subject to judicial review. In our view, the removal provisions of the Act make this case more analogous to Humphrey's Executor v. United States, 295 U.S. 602 (1935) [p. 920], and Wiener v. United States, 357 U.S. 349 (1958)[41], than to Myers or Bowsher.

". . . We undoubtedly did rely on the terms 'quasi-legislative' and 'quasijudicial' to distinguish the officials involved in Humphrey's Executor and Wiener from those in Myers, but our present considered view is that the determination of whether the Constitution allows Congress to impose a 'good cause'-type restriction on the President's power to remove an official cannot be made to turn on whether or not that official is classified as 'purely executive.' The analysis contained in our removal cases is designed not to define rigid categories of those officials who may or may not be removed at will by the President,[28] but to ensure that Congress does not interfere with the President's exercise of the 'executive power' and his constitutionally appointed duty to 'take care that the laws be faithfully executed' under Article II. Myers was undoubtedly correct in its holding, and in its broader suggestion that there are some 'purely executive' officials who must be removable by the President at will if he is to be able to accomplish his constitutional role.[29] . . . We do not mean to suggest that an analysis of the functions served

---

[41] [Ed.] Wiener held that neither the Constitution nor the underlying statute gave the President at-will removal power over a member of the War Claims Commission, which was an adjudicatory body.

[28] The difficulty of defining such categories of 'executive' or 'quasi-legislative' officials is illustrated by a comparison of our decisions in cases such as Humphrey's Executor, Buckley v. Valeo, 424 U.S. 1, 140–141 (1976), and Bowsher, supra, 478 U.S. at 732–34. . . As Justice White noted in his dissent in Bowsher, it is hard to dispute that the powers of the FTC at the time of Humphrey's Executor would at the present time be considered "executive," at least to some degree. See 478 U.S. at 761, n. 3.

[29] The dissent says that the language of Article II vesting the executive power of the United States in the President requires that every officer of the United States exercising any part of that power must serve at the pleasure of the President and be removable by him at will. This rigid demarcation—a demarcation incapable of being altered by law in the slightest degree, and applicable to tens of thousands of holders of offices neither known nor foreseen by the Framers—depends upon an extrapolation from general constitutional language which we think is more than the text will bear.

by the officials at issue is irrelevant. But the real question is whether the removal restrictions are of such a nature that they impede the President's ability to perform his constitutional duty, and the functions of the officials in question must be analyzed in that light.

"[W]e cannot say that the imposition of a 'good cause' standard for removal by itself unduly trammels on executive authority. . . . [Although the independent counsel performs] law enforcement functions that typically have been undertaken by officials within the Executive Branch . . . [and] the counsel exercises no small amount of discretion and judgment in deciding how to carry out her duties under the Act, we simply do not see how the President's need to control the exercise of that discretion is so central to the functioning of the Executive Branch as to require as a matter of constitutional law that the counsel be terminable at will by the President.

"Nor do we think that the 'good cause' removal provision at issue here impermissibly burdens the President's power to control or supervise the independent counsel, as an executive official, in the execution of her duties under the Act. . . . [B]ecause the independent counsel may be terminated for 'good cause,' the Executive, through the Attorney General, retains ample authority to assure that the counsel is competently performing her statutory responsibilities in a manner that comports with the provisions of the Act. . . . [T]he legislative history of the removal provision also makes clear that the Attorney General may remove an independent counsel for 'misconduct.' We do not think that this limitation as it presently stands sufficiently deprives the President of control over the independent counsel to interfere impermissibly with his constitutional obligation to ensure the faithful execution of the laws. . . .

"Finally, we do not think that the Act 'impermissibly undermine[s]' the powers of the Executive Branch, or 'disrupts the proper balance between the coordinate branches [by] prevent[ing] the Executive Branch from accomplishing its constitutionally assigned functions,' Nixon v. Administrator of General Services, 433 U.S. [425,] 443 [(1977)]. It is undeniable that the Act reduces the amount of control or supervision that the Attorney General and, through him, the President exercises over the investigation and prosecution of a certain class of alleged criminal activity. . . . Nonetheless, the Act does give the Attorney General several means of supervising or controlling the prosecutorial powers that may be wielded by an independent counsel. Most importantly, the Attorney General retains the power to remove the counsel for 'good cause'. . . . No independent counsel may be appointed without a specific request by the Attorney General, and the Attorney General's decision not to request appointment if he finds 'no reasonable grounds to believe that further investigation is warranted' is committed to his unreviewable discretion. . . . In addition, the jurisdiction of the independent counsel is defined with reference to the facts submitted by the Attorney General, and once a counsel is appointed, the Act requires that the counsel abide by Justice Department policy unless it is not 'possible' to do so. . . ."

JUSTICE SCALIA wrote a stinging and—given the subsequent concerns about Independent Counsel excesses that led Congress to let the Act expire when it came up for renewal—prescient dissent: "[T]his suit is about. . . . [t]he allocation of power among Congress, the President, and the courts in such fashion as to preserve the equilibrium the Constitution sought to establish—so that 'a gradual concentration of the several powers in the same department,' Federalist No. 51, p. 321 (J. Madison), can effectively be resisted. Frequently an issue of this sort will come before the Court clad, so to speak, in sheep's clothing: the potential of the asserted principle to effect important change in the equilibrium of power is not immediately evident, and must be discerned by a careful and perceptive analysis. But this wolf comes as a wolf.

". . . Art. II, § 1, cl. 1 of the Constitution provides: 'The executive Power shall be vested in a President of the United States.' . . . [T]his does not mean *some* of the executive power, but *all of* the executive power. [Thus, decision here turns on two questions:] (1) Is the conduct of a criminal prosecution . . . the exercise of purely executive power? (2) Does the statute deprive the President of the United States of exclusive control over the exercise of that power? . . .

"The Court concedes that '[t]here is no real dispute that the functions performed by the independent counsel are "executive"'" . . . As for . . . whether the statute before us deprives the President of exclusive control, . . . [t]hat is indeed the whole object of the statute. Instead, the Court points out that the President, through his Attorney General, has at least *some* control. . . . [T]he Court greatly exaggerates the extent of that 'some' presidential control. . . . As we recognized in Humphrey's Executor v. United States—indeed, what Humphrey's Executor was all about—limiting removal power to 'good cause' is an impediment to, not an effective grant of, presidential control. . . .

". . . [It] effects a revolution in our constitutional jurisprudence for the Court . . . to sit in judgment of whether 'the President's need to control the exercise of [the independent counsel's] discretion is *so central* to the functioning of the Executive Branch' as to require complete control.' (emphasis added) . . . It is not for us to determine, and we have never presumed to determine, how much of the purely executive powers of government must be within the full control of the President. The Constitution prescribes that they *all* are. . . .

"The Court could have resolved the removal power issue in this case by simply relying upon its erroneous conclusion that the independent counsel was an inferior officer, and then extending our holding that the removal of inferior officers appointed by the Executive can be restricted, to a new holding that even the removal of inferior officers appointed by the courts can be restricted. That would in my view be a considerable and unjustified extension, giving the Executive full discretion in neither the selection nor the removal of a purely executive officer. The course the Court has chosen, however, is even worse. . . .

"Since our 1935 decision in Humphrey's Executor v. United States—which was considered by many at the time the product of an activist, anti-New Deal Court bent on reducing the power of President Franklin Roosevelt—it has been established that the line of permissible restriction upon removal of principal officers lies at the point at which the powers exercised by those officers are no longer purely executive. . . . It has often been observed, correctly in my view, that the line between 'purely executive' functions and 'quasi-legislative' or 'quasi-judicial' functions is not a clear one or even a rational one. . . . But at least it permitted the identification of certain officers, and certain agencies, whose functions were entirely within the control of the President. Congress had to be aware of that restriction in its legislation. Today, however, Humphrey's Executor is swept into the dustbin of repudiated constitutional principles. . . . What Humphrey's Executor (and presumably Myers) really means, we are now told, is not that there are any 'rigid categories of those officials who may or may not be removed at will by the President,' but simply that Congress cannot 'interfere with the President's exercise of the executive power and his constitutionally appointed duty to take care that the laws be faithfully executed.' This is an open invitation for Congress to experiment. . . .

"Under our system of government, the primary check against prosecutorial abuse is a political one. The prosecutors who exercise this awesome discretion are selected and can be removed by a President, whom the people have trusted enough to elect. Moreover, when crimes are not investigated and prosecuted fairly, nonselectively, with a reasonable sense of proportion, . . . the unfairness will come home to roost in the Oval Office. . . . The people know whom to blame, whereas 'one of the weightiest objections to a plurality in the executive . . . is that it tends to conceal faults and destroy responsibility.' The Federalist No. 70.

". . . A government of laws means a government of rules. Today's decision on the basic issue of fragmentation of executive power is ungoverned by rule, and hence ungoverned by law. . . . Taking all things into account, we conclude that the power taken away from the President here is not really *too* much. . . . This is not analysis; it is ad hoc judgment. . . . I prefer to rely upon the judgment of the wise men who constructed our system, and of the people who approved it, and of two centuries of history that have shown it to be sound. Like it or not, that judgment says, quite plainly, that '[t]he executive Power shall be vested in a President of the United States.'"

NOTES

(1) **Mining the Text.** Myers, Humphrey's Executor, and Morrison all contain assertions about the type of power wielded by the officer whose removal is at issue. (Humphrey's Executor also makes a distinction between

executive "power" and executive "functions.") Compare Justice Scalia's distinction between "legislative power" and "lawmaking" in Whitman v. American Trucking Assn (p. 791). The Morrison Court explicitly minimizes the importance of categorizing the power involved. Does Free Enterprise follow the Morrison majority or Justice Scalia's dissent—or does it take yet a third approach?

Justice Scalia's formalist dissent in Morrison rests on the textualist argument that Article II, § 1 vests *the* executive power in *a* President. The Morrison majority responds that this claim "depends upon an extrapolation from general constitutional language which we think is more than the text will bear." Who has the better of the argument from the Constitution's text? Does the "strong" reading of the Article II Vesting Clause play a significant role in Free Enterprise? Note that the only constitutional provision expressly addressing removal is the Impeachment Clause, Art. II, § 4, a congressional mechanism. Should the absence of an expressly conferred presidential removal power matter? Is unlimited removal power a necessary prerequisite for "tak[ing] Care that the laws be faithfully executed"—or are the dissenting Myers justices right that the duty conferred by this clause is defined *by*, not *in spite of*, the statute as written? What are the implications for a broad reading of the Vesting Clause that Article II also contains a specific list of presidential powers, including the power to "require the Opinion, in writing, of the principal Officers in each of the executive Departments, upon any subject relating to the Duties of their respective Offices," and to appoint principal officers with the Senate's consent? What follows from the powers granted to Congress, including the Necessary and Proper Clause (originally referred to as the "Sweeping Clause") and its power to vest the appointment of "inferior Officers" in the courts or department heads, as an alternative to the President? After considering all these provisions, do you think that constitutional text and structure offer a clear answer to questions about the removal power?

(2) ***Functionalism v. Formalism.*** The Morrison Court rejected Justice Scalia's formalist focus on type of power in favor of a functionalist inquiry: "the real question is whether the removal restrictions are of such a nature that they impede the President's ability to perform his constitutional duty." Does the Free Enterprise Court adopt a more formalist stance in holding that the Vesting and Take Care clauses absolutely bar multiple layers of removal protection *without regard* to their practical impact? Note that the Court rejects the accuracy, rather than the relevance, of the claim that the SEC's oversight powers are functionally the same as removal power. And it insists that double for-cause protections make a practical difference in the President's ability to oversee the Board. Does this leave open the possibility of sustaining what appear to be double for-cause removal structures in other regulatory contexts?

Justice Breyer's avowedly functionalist Free Enterprise dissent rejects reliance on "bright-line rules." He emphasizes both the extensive degree of SEC oversight of Board decisions and the lack of congressional "aggrandizement." Functionalism is often criticized, as a separation-of-powers methodology, for being too quick to sustain whatever innovative structure Congress has created. But does a functionalist approach necessarily lead to sustaining the for-cause restriction on removing Board members? Functionalist PETER L. STRAUSS emphasizes that "Congress's creation of a 'for cause'-protected *institution* (the PCAOB) within another 'for cause'-protection *institution* (the SEC) . . . [was] virtually unique." Other institutions meeting this description, such as "the Atomic Safety and Licensing Board of the Nuclear Regulatory Commission, have only adjudicatory responsibilities. . . . The PCAOB, on the other hand, is not a committed adjudicator. It has the same full range of responsibilities government agencies commonly possess—rulemaking and enforcement in addition to adjudication. For an entity operating over that full range, the argument for presidential oversight is considerably stronger. . . . Had the majority clearly held only that Congress could not constitutionally create one fully-functioned 'for cause'-protected agency within another such agency, there would have been little to write about. It is hard to imagine such a conclusion doing much mischief." ON THE DIFFICULTIES OF GENERALIZATION, *PCAOB* IN THE FOOTSTEPS OF *MYERS, HUMPHREY'S EXECUTOR, MORRISON* AND *FREYTAG*, 32 Cardozo L. Rev. No. 6 (2011).

(3) ***The Remedial Dimension.*** Central to the majority's conclusion is its assumption that SEC Commissioners enjoy for-cause removal protection. The 1934 Securities Exchange Act provides, "Each commissioner shall hold office for a term of five years," 15 U.S.C. § 78d(a). Thus, the statute is silent on removal. As Justice Breyer notes, this is probably because the SEC was created during the nine-year gap between Myers and Humphrey's Executor, when any limits on removal appeared unconstitutional. Given this history, he argues that any constitutional problem should be cured by refusing to imply a for-cause restriction into the 1934 Act. Do you agree? Note the Court's reference to the parties conceding that SEC Commissioners enjoyed removal protection. (Should this matter to the Court's interpretation of the statute? Those close to the case say that the Board wanted to argue that the 1934 Act did not confer for-cause protection but was prevented by the SEC (using its oversight powers) from doing so.)

When the Court concludes that an innovative regulatory structure or practice is unconstitutional, it often faces hard choices about how to remedy the problem. In deciding whether to sever the double for-cause removal provision from the rest of the Sarbanes Oxley Act, the Court did not explicitly consider the basic severability inquiry: What would Congress have done if it had known that the challenged provision was unconstitutional? Should the Court simply have accepted "the Government's"—i.e., the Executive's—assurance that severing the provision was preferable to invalidating the whole Act? Compare the analogous remedial problem in Bowsher, p. 860, where the Court chose to invalidate the Comptroller General's central role in a novel and complicated statutory scheme for balancing the federal budget, rather than the problematic but never used statutory method for removing him.

What about simply declaring the current structure unconstitutional and leaving it up to Congress to decide how to fix the problem? What would be the status of SEC actions in the interim? In Northern Pipeline, p. 1022, the

Court declared the bankruptcy system unconstitutional because of its use of non-Article III judges. To avoid chaos, it stayed its judgment for four months to allow Congress to act; at the Solicitor General's request, it extended the stay for two additional months. As Congress remained silent, the federal courts themselves adopted an Emergency Interim Rule taking steps responsive to the Supreme Court decision. These events occurred in 1982; Congress finally provided a statutory solution in 1984.

Finally, in terms of questions left undecided, what of the Court's statement in footnote 11 that although holding the SEC was a Department for Appointment Clause purposes, it was "express[ing] no view on whether the Commission is thus an 'executive Departmen[t]' under the Opinions Clause." How, if the SEC is part of the executive branch, could it possibly be beyond Opinions Clause, which is the one power the Constitution explicitly gives the President over elements of the executive branch.

(4) **_The Next Free Enterprise? PHH Corp. v. CFPB._** Free Enterprise set the stage for the latest high-profile removal challenge involving a constitutional challenge to the removal protections for the Director of the Consumer Financial Protection Bureau (CFPB). The CFPB was created by the Dodd-Frank Wall Street Reform Act of 2010 in the face of failures by existing bank regulators, whose main responsibility is prudential regulation of banks, to ensure their financial soundness and to adequately protect consumers of financial products. The CFPB has an unusual design: it is headed by a single director with for-cause removal protection identical to that granted FTC Commissioners and sustained in Humphrey's Executor. Although located in the Federal Reserve, the Fed has no ability to supervise the CFPB. Instead, regulations issued by the CFPB can only be set aside by a two-thirds vote (including the Treasury Secretary) of the Financial Stability Oversight Council (FSOC).[42] The CFPB is statutorily guaranteed a percentage of the Fed's budget and thus is not dependent on the annual appropriations process for funding. It is required to consult with other financial regulators before issuing rules and also works with states. (For recent scholarly takes on the CFPB's structure, see Rachel E. Barkow, Insulating Agencies: Avoiding Capture through Institutional Design, 89 Tex. L. Rev. 15 (2010); Jacob E. Gersen, Administrative Law Goes to Wall Street: The New Administrative Process, 65 Admin. L. Rev. 689 (2013).)

In PHH CORP. V. CFPB, 839 F.3d 1 (D.C. Cir. 2016), a decision that was vacated and taken en banc with an en banc decision still pending when this edition went to press, a panel of the D.C. Circuit held that the CFPB Director's removal protection was unconstitutional. JUDGE KAVANAUGH wrote a lengthy opinion for the court, including an extensive review of the background on independent agencies. But the following excerpt from the decision's opening pages suffices to convey the court's reasoning:

"The independent agencies collectively constitute, in effect, a headless fourth branch of the U.S. Government. They exercise enormous power over

---

[42] Also created by Dodd-Frank, FSOC is chaired by Treasury Secretary and consists of the chairs and heads of major national financial regulators (like the Fed, the Federal Deposit Insurance Corporation, the SEC, the CFTC, and so on)

the economic and social life of the United States. Because of their massive power and the absence of Presidential supervision and direction, independent agencies pose a significant threat to individual liberty and to the constitutional system of separation of powers and checks and balances. To help mitigate the risk to individual liberty, the independent agencies, although not checked by the President, have historically been headed by multiple commissioners, directors, or board members who act as checks on one another. Each independent agency has traditionally been established, in the Supreme Court's words, as a 'body of experts appointed by law and informed by experience.' Humphrey's Executor, 295 U.S. at 624 (internal quotation marks omitted) [p. 920]. The multi-member structure reduces the risk of arbitrary decisionmaking and abuse of power, and thereby helps protect individual liberty.

"In other words, to help preserve individual liberty under Article II, the heads of executive agencies are accountable to and checked by the President, and the heads of independent agencies, although not accountable to or checked by the President, are at least accountable to and checked by their fellow commissioners or board members. No head of either an executive agency or an independent agency operates unilaterally without any check on his or her authority. Therefore, no independent agency exercising substantial executive authority has ever been headed by a single person. Until now.

". . . Because the CFPB is an independent agency headed by a single Director and not by a multi-member commission, the Director of the CFPB possesses more unilateral authority—that is, authority to take action on one's own, subject to no check—than any single commissioner or board member in any other independent agency in the U.S. Government. Indeed, as we will explain, the Director enjoys more unilateral authority than any other officer in any of the three branches of the U.S. Government, other than the President. At the same time, the Director of the CFPB possesses enormous power over American business, American consumers, and the overall U.S. economy. The Director unilaterally enforces 19 federal consumer protection statutes, covering everything from home finance to student loans to credit cards to banking practices. The Director alone decides what rules to issue; how to enforce, when to enforce, and against whom to enforce the law; and what sanctions and penalties to impose on violators of the law. . . .

"The question before us is whether we may extend the Supreme Court's Humphrey's Executor precedent to cover this novel, single-Director agency structure for an independent agency. To analyze that issue, we follow the history-focused approach long applied by the Supreme Court in separation of powers cases where, as here, the constitutional text alone does not resolve the matter. . . . [In striking down the double for-cause protection enjoyed by the PCAOB in Free Enterprise] . . . the Court emphasized, among other things, the novelty of the of the Board's structure. . . . [H]istory and tradition are critical factors in separation of powers cases where the constitutional text does not otherwise resolve the matter. [citing Noel Canning] . . . In this case, the single-Director structure of the CFPB represents a gross departure from settled historical practice. Never before has an independent agency exercising substantial executive authority been headed by just one person.

"The CFPB's concentration of enormous executive power in a single, unaccountable, unchecked Director not only departs from settled historical practice, but also poses a far greater risk of arbitrary decisionmaking and abuse of power, and a far greater threat to individual liberty, than does a multi-member independent agency. The overarching constitutional concern with independent agencies is that the agencies are unchecked by the President, the official who is accountable to the people and who is responsible under Article II for the exercise of executive power. Recognizing the broad and unaccountable power wielded by independent agencies, Congresses and Presidents of both political parties have therefore long endeavored to keep independent agencies in check through other statutory means. In particular, to check independent agencies, Congress has traditionally required multi-member bodies at the helm of every independent agency. In lieu of Presidential control, the multi-member structure of independent agencies acts as a critical substitute check on the excesses of any individual independent agency head—a check that helps to prevent arbitrary decisionmaking and thereby to protect individual liberty. This new agency, the CFPB, lacks that critical check and structural constitutional protection, yet wields vast power over the U.S. economy. . . . [W]e conclude that Humphrey's Executor cannot be stretched to cover this novel agency structure."

Taking a further page from Free Enterprise, the PHH court held that the appropriate remedy to address the constitutional infirmities in the CFPB's structure was simply to excise the for-cause removal protection for the CFPB Director, making the President free to remove the Director at will. As this left the CFPB operational, the panel assessed PHH Corporation's additional challenges to the CFPB's action at issue and agreed that the CFPB had misinterpreted governing statutes and violated due process. Concurring, Judge Randolph argued that the ALJ who had presided over PHH Corporation's administrative adjudication was an inferior officer who had not been appointed in accordance with the Appointments Clause. Concurring in part, Judge Henderson argued that there was no need to reach the constitutional question, as the court agreed with PHH Corporation's non-constitutional claims and therefore vacated the CFPB's decision.

Do you agree with the PHH panel that granting removal protection to a single-headed regulatory agency goes beyond constitutional bounds? What is the constitutional basis for requiring Congress use the multi-member form if it creates an independent agency? In your view, is the President's capacity to oversee a multi-member commission with tenure protected by "for-cause" removal constraints likely greater than his capacity to oversee a single administrator similarly protected? Moreover, how far does the logic of the decision extend: many multi-member independent commissions also have bipartisan requirements, mandating that no more than a bare majority of commissioners can be from one party (eg, 3 of 5 commissioners). Are such bipartisan provisions also constitutionally required? Why not?

Note the prominent functionalist character of the panel's opinion. Doesn't the opinion's argument largely boil down to the argument that there need to be adequate checks on an agency's power and if those checks can't be provided by the President through the threat of removal, the checks must be constructed internally in the shape of a multi-member commission heading the agency? Ensuring power is adequately checked is a classic functionalist concern. This functionalist turn is notable compared to the formalist unitary executive approach in Free Enterprise—all the more so because the double for-cause prohibition adopted in Free Enterprise was initially proposed by Judge Kavanaugh's dissent in Free Enterprise at the D.C. Circuit before the case went up to the Court. What do you think explains his functionalist turn here? Note also that Judge Kavanaugh's reasoning, like that in Humphrey's Executor, places the CFPB wholly outside the President's oversight authority, "not accountable to or checked by the President." Can this reasoning be reconciled with the Supreme Court's reasoning in PCAOB about the President's relationship to the SEC?

One intervening Supreme Court decision was Noel Canning, and the PHH court relies heavily on Noel Canning's emphasis on historical practice to invalidate what it calls the CFPB's "novel" structure.[43] But Noel Canning involved an assertion of presidential power against Congress, without any underlying statute in support, and it was necessary to rely on historical practice in the absence of other express statements of congressional and presidential understandings. Is this challenge to the CFPB, an entity created by statute with congressional and presidential approval, analogous? And even if analogous, should historical practice be given so much weight in separation of powers analysis? The CFPB was part of a major financial regulatory reform in the wake of the worst national financial crisis since the Great Depression. The panel decision identified three other examples of independent agencies sharing the CFPB's structure—the Social Security Administration, the Office of Special Counsel (which enforces personnel rules against government employers and employees), and the Federal Housing Finance Agency—but gave these examples little weight on the grounds that all were relatively recent creations. Does this approach risk forcing the political branches to adhere to out-of-date institutional designs?

(5) *Is Innovative Agency Design Constitutionally Disfavored?* Professor LEAH M. LITMAN, in DEBUNKING ANTINOVELTY, 66 Duke L.J. 1407, 1423, 1427–29 (2017) criticizes this growing anti-novelty rhetoric in federalism and separation of powers challenges. She notes that it is "unclear whether the Court uses novelty as a 'factor' in its analysis or as an on-off switch that adjusts whether a statute is presumed constitutional or presumed unconstitutional." Separate from this lack of clarity, she attacks the logic underlying anti-novelty rhetoric: "The primary justification that has been offered . . . is that legislative novelty suggests that previous Congresses assumed similar legislation was unconstitutional. The presumption is 'that if Congress possessed a particular power, it would have

---

[43] Noel Canning and PHH Corp. share an additional tie. Although Noel Canning involved recess appointments to the NLRB, perhaps President Obama's most contentious recess appointee was his appointment of Richard Cordray as the CFPB Director.

exercised it. . . . But enacting federal laws is difficult, and the nature of the legislative process requires Congress to select from among many different priorities and make compromises. Moreover, . . .[j]udicial decisions may make some legislative choices more attractive than others, different areas of federal regulation may be better suited to different forms of regulation, and new factual or legal developments may change reasonable people's assessments about how to accommodate the pertinent constitutional values.' " Professor GILLIAN E. METZGER, in APPOINTMENTS, INNOVATION AND THE JUDICIAL-POLITICAL DIVIDE, 64 Duke L.J. 1607, 160–11 (2015), adds that the Supreme Court's Burkean anti-innovation turn is particularly troublesome given growing political polarization. "Not only has deepening polarization instigated many novel congressional and executive measures, . . . but efforts to mitigate polarization in Congress are also likely to entail further structural changes. . . . The Court's resistance to innovation might appear a useful prophylactic against efforts to bend the Constitution in the name of political expediency. But such a general suspicion of innovation lacks a constitutional basis [and] . . . given the political transformations occurring in response to polarization . . . sets the Court on a course of confrontation with the other two branches that is hard to justify."

Do you agree with these critiques? The judicial resistance to novelty and innovation accords with an originalist approach to constitutional interpretation. But are there also good non-originalist and functional reasons for the courts to look skeptically at structural innovations from Congress and the President? For a detailed description of recent innovations in legislation and administration, see Abbe R. Gluck, Anne J. O'Connell, & Rosa Po, Unorthodox Lawmaking, Unorthodox Rulemaking, 115 Colum. L. Rev. 1789 (2015).

(6) *Free Enterprise and Removal Protections for ALJs.* The constitutionality of removal protections for inferior officers was initially established in the context of a military appointment in Perkins, p. 918, and reaffirmed in Morrison, p. 934. Today, as Justice Breyer's Free Enterprise dissent points out, at least 48 agencies are headed by officers who can be removed only for cause. And those agencies have large numbers of other positions that also have for-cause protection: members of the Senior Executive Service (SES) who fill important managerial positions, ALJs, and members of the competitive service. Chief Justice Roberts disputes that all of these positions are analogous to the Board. He insists that "[n]othing in our opinion . . . should be read to cast doubt on the use of what is colloquially known as the civil service system within independent agencies." For discussion of whether ALJs should be seen as inferior officers or employees, see p. 886. Many of the current issues challenging ALJs' appointments as not conforming to the Appointments Clause also contend that if ALJs are independent officers, they violate Free Enterprise's prohibition on double-for-cause removal protection for officers, because of the heavy protections of independence ALJs enjoy.

Do you read Free Enterprise and Chief Justice Roberts' footnote on ALJs as leaving open the question of whether ALJs raise a similar double-for-cause problem or as suggesting that administrative adjudication might be analyzed differently? In Duka v. SEC, 103 F.Supp.3d 382, 393–96 (S.D.N.Y. 2015),[44] the District Court concluded that even if ALJs were inferior officers, Free Enterprise did not adopt a categorical rule forbidding two levels of good-cause protection. Instead, using the functional approach drawn from Morrison, the court concluded that "restrictions upon the President's ability to remove 'quasi-judicial' agency adjudicators are unlikely to interfere with the President's ability to perform his executive duties" and emphasized the distinction between ALJs' adjudicative functions and PCAOB's policymaking and enforcement functions. See also Bandimer v. SEC, 844 F.3d 1168 (10th Cir. 2016) (Judge McKay, dissenting, argued that finding ALJs to be inferior officers would create a Free Enterprise double-for-cause problem).

NOTES ON THE IMPLICATIONS OF FREE ENTERPRISE FOR INDEPENDENT AGENCIES

(1) ***Constitutionality Confirmed?*** Despite the Court's careful statement that it was not reexamining Myers and Humphrey's Executor, does Free Enterprise nonetheless signal that the long-running battle over the constitutionality of independent agencies is really over? Doesn't the remedy of curing the constitutional defect by making Board members removable at will by SEC Commissioners necessarily imply that one level of for-cause removal protection is not inconsistent with the President's Take Care duty? If such removal provisions were constitutionality invalid, wouldn't the Court be constrained to construe silence in the SEC Act in a way that *avoids* the constitutional problem? On the other hand, what should we make of the fact that Justice Scalia joined the majority opinion, without even a separate concurrence, despite his vigorous dissent in Morrison? Does this suggest that Free Enterprise should not be read too broadly—or does it signal that even vocal proponents of broad presidential power now accept independent agencies as a feature of the federal administrative state?

For the view that "if there is anything revolutionary about the PCAOB decision it may be that the independence of independent agencies appears to have achieved a quasi-constitutional status, such that Congress would have to explicitly grant the President unlimited removal power to overcome the presumption of protection," see Jack M. Beerman, Essay: An Inductive Understanding of Separation of Powers, 63 Admin. L. Rev. 467 (2011); see also Gary Lawson, Stipulating the Law, 109 Mich. L. Rev. 1191 (2011) (analyzing the legitimacy of the Court's relying on a stipulation of for-cause protection for SEC Commissioners). For a contrasting view that the case could presage decisions that further shift the balance of power over Administration to the President, see Richard H. Pildes, Free Enterprise Fund, Boundary-Enforcing Decisions, and the Unitary Executive Branch Theory of Government Administration, 6 Duke J. Const. L. & Pub. Pol'y 1 (2010); Neomi Rao, A Modest Proposal: Abolishing Agency Independence in Free Enterprise Fund v. PCAOB, 79 Fordham L. Rev. 2541 (2011).

---

[44] The District Court subsequently found that ALJs were inferior officers not appointed as required under the Appointments Clause and granted a preliminary injunction against the SEC adjudicative proceeding, 124 F.Supp.3d 287 (S.D.N.Y. 2015), which was vacated and remanded on jurisdictional grounds (2d Cir. 15–2732, June 13, 2016), see p. 1398.

(2) *Another Chapter in the Meaning of "For Cause."* In Humphrey's Executor, statutory provisions permitting removal only for cause were seen as the touchstone of "independence." Yet Morrison describes the good-cause removal provision as "ample authority to assure that the [independent] counsel is competently performing her statutory responsibilities in a manner that comports with the provisions of the Act." And, if you read Bowsher, p. 860, recall that a majority of the Court concluded there that the Comptroller General was under Congress's control because he could be removed by joint resolution for "permanent disability; inefficiency; neglect of duty; malfeasance; or a felony or conduct involving moral turpitude." Hence the more modern cases suggested that the Court might be crafting a new, more capacious understanding of what constitutes "cause" for removal.

Where does Free Enterprise come down on this question? On the one hand, the Court concludes that if the SEC Commissioners could remove Board members at will the President would be able to hold them accountable for supervising the Board—as the President can hold them accountable for "everything else" the SEC does—even though the Commissioners themselves can be removed only for cause. This suggests agreement with the Morrison/Bowsher view that for-cause protection still allows ample room for presidential oversight. On the other, the Court expressly rejects the possibility that the Commissioners' "simple disagreement with the Board's policies or priorities could constitute 'good cause' for its removal" because this would be at odds with Humphrey's Executor. Is the decision best read as indicating that the President need not be able to remove principal officers on the basis of policy disagreement with how they exercise their statutory authority in order to exercise constitutionally adequate supervision over their actions?

(3) *What Makes an Independent Agency Independent?* The traditional view equates independence with for-cause removal protection. An important strand of the literature emphasizes that "independence" is a far more complex and subtle phenomenon than the traditional view recognizes. KIRTI DATLA & RICHARD L. REVESZ, DECONSTRUCTING INDEPENDENT AGENCIES (AND EXECUTIVE AGENCIES), 98 Cornell L. Rev. 769, 772, 825–26 (2013): "The binary conception of agencies as either 'independent' or 'executive' is incorrect. . . . [A]gencies cannot be divided into two categories based on their common structural or functional features." The authors "systematically survey the enabling statutes of both independent and executive agencies [to identify] . . . a broad set of indicia of independence: removal protection, specified tenure, multimember structure, partisan balance requirements, litigation authority, budget and congressional communication authority, and adjudication authority." They find "that there is no single feature—not even a for-cause removal provision—that every agency commonly thought of as independent shares. . . . Instead of falling into two categories, agencies fall along a continuum . . . [that] ranges from most insulated to least insulated from presidential control. An agency's place along that continuum is based on both structural insulating features as well as functional realities. And that placement need not be static. It can shift depending on statutory

amendments or an increased (or decreased) presidential focus on the agency's mission."

Professor Rachel E. Barkow, in Insulating Agencies: Avoiding Capture Through Institutional Design, 89 Tex. L. Rev. 15, 18 (2010), offers a similar view in the context of consumer protection agencies. She argues that removal provisions and other traditional indicia of "independence" may be less significant than such features as funding source, qualifications for appointment and post-employment restrictions, relationship with other federal and state entities, and "various political tools, including the agency's ability to generate politically powerful information, its ability to recruit political benefactors, and the potential for public advocates to become part of the agency structure." See also David E. Lewis & Jennifer L. Selin, in Political Control and the Forms of Agency Independence, 83 Geo. Wash. L. Rev. 1487, 1490–91 (2015) (" 'for cause' protections are widely used across the executive establishment in executive departments in single-headed administrative units as well as the normal 'independent' agencies . . . and a comprehensive survey of the executive establishment reveals an amazing diversity of statutory devices designed to limit political influence and applied to a variety of different agencies"); Lisa Schultz Bressman & Robert B. Thompson, The Future of Agency Independence, 63 Vand. L. Rev. 599, 600 (2010) (critiquing the binary executive-independent agency divide and describing several mechanisms through which independent agencies have become more responsive to presidential preferences).

(4) *Real World Political Complexity.* The persistent legal battles over for-cause removal protections suggest that statutory provisions for agency "independence" make a real world difference. Justice Scalia articulates the view of many unitary executive theorists: "The independent agencies are sheltered not from politics but from the President, and it has often been observed that their freedom from presidential oversight (and protection) has simply been replaced by increased subservience to congressional direction." FCC v. Fox Televisions Stns., 556 U.S. 502, 524 (2009) (Scalia J., dissenting).

For decades, scholars of law, political science, and public administration have debated the accuracy of this picture, arguing that political reality often tempers statutory independence features. PETER L. STRAUSS, THE PLACE OF AGENCIES IN GOVERNMENT: SEPARATION OF POWERS AND THE FOURTH BRANCH, 84 Colum. L. Rev. 573, 586–95 (1984): "Even in executive agencies, the layer over which the President enjoys direct control of personnel is very thin and political factors may make it difficult for him to exercise even those controls to the fullest. An administrator with a public constituency and mandate cannot be discharged—and understands that he cannot be discharged—without substantial political cost. Also for political reasons, . . . independent [agencies often] . . . consult[ ] with the White House about appointments[,] . . . voluntarily participate in the Regulatory Council, publish regular agendas of rulemaking, are attentive to White House inquiries about their progress, and otherwise behave as if they were in fact subject to the discipline from which they have been excused. The reasons for this acceptance of presidential input are clear. . . . It can be useful to be associated with national policy, to have a big and politically powerful 'friend,' when appearing before Congress. [They] need goods the President can provide: budgetary and legislative support, assistance in dealing with other agencies, legal services, office space, and advice on national policy. They share a commitment to achieving the public interest, and are likely to respect the President's motives and appreciate his political responsibility and support. They are flattered when their own advice is sought, and respectful of office when they are advised. In the circumstances, it is not surprising that the independent commissions can be susceptible to substantial presidential oversight."

Recent empirical studies similarly reveal a more complex story than unitary executive fears of presidential insulation and congressional domination. Adam Candeub and Eric Hunnicutt, Political Control of Independent Agencies: Evidence from the FCC (July 16, 2010), available at http://ssrn.com/abstract=1640285, analyze 35 years of FCC orders and individual votes to conclude that "independent agencies constitute a place at which Presidential and Congressional power compete"—especially in periods of divided government. Similarly, Christopher R. Berry & Jacob E. Gersen, Agency Design and Political Control, 126 Yale L.J. 1002, 1036 (2017), analyzing more than 30 years of data on distribution of federal funds, conclude that "[a]gencies with more political appointees are more responsive to moves into or out of the President's party when making spending allocations. Moreover, agencies with more Senate confirmed appointees are more responsive to the membership in the majority party than the President's party, while agencies with more non-Senate-confirmed appointees are more responsive to the President's party than the majority party." Brian D. Feinstein notes that "agencies with two characteristics commonly associated with independence—fixed terms and qualification requirements for appointees—receive less oversight attention" and concludes that "these design features not only restrict presidential control over agencies, but also congressional control." Designing Executive Agencies for Congressional Control, 69 Admin. L. Rev. 259, 285 (2017). Finally, Neal Devins and David E. Lewi, examining data on appointments to twelve different independent regulatory commissions from President Harding to President George W. Bush, found that, in all but one agency, presidents on average obtained a majority on the Commissions within 9–10 months of taking office (although the length of time was increasing as part of a larger story about growing delay in filling agency positions, see Note 6, p. 913). Not-So Independent Agencies: Party Polarization and the Limits of Institutional Design, 88 B.U. L. Rev. 459 (2008).

c.   Presidential Direction of Regulatory Outcomes

> *PRESIDENTIAL MEMORANDUM—*
> *POWER SECTOR CARBON*
> *POLLUTION STANDARDS*
>
> *PRESIDENTIAL EXECUTIVE ORDER*
> *ON PROMOTING ENERGY*
> *INDEPENDENCE AND ECONOMIC*
> *GROWTH*
>
> *(1) The Emergence and Mechanisms of*
>   *Presidential Directory Authority*
>
> *(2) The Legal Basis for Presidential*
>   *Directory Authority*
>
> *(3) Presidential Directory Authority in*
>   *Context*

Unlike early statutory delegations that empowered the President personally to make decisions about tariffs and other international trade issues, modern regulatory statutes typically delegate decisional authority to some named federal official—a Cabinet Secretary, an Administrator, or members of an independent commission. Do these statutes vest the power of decision in the named official specifically, meaning that although she may be influenced by the President's wishes, the responsibility to decide is ultimately hers alone? If she persists in a decision at odds with the President's preferences, may the President nullify the decision? May the President make the decision himself or herself? The President's ability to fire recalcitrant officials and replace them with more compliant decisionmakers is explored in Section 3.b. Here, we consider the more fundamental question: what is the scope of the President's power to direct particular regulatory outcomes if the statutory delegation to a named official is silent as to the President's role? We begin with two recent exercises of presidential directory authority, one by President Obama and one by President Trump, both addressing greenhouse gas regulation and climate change. We then provide an overview of how the directory authority has emerged in recent administrations, and we consider possible legal bases for such presidential power. Finally, we examine presidential direction in specific contexts.

That Presidents regularly assert such directive authority is beyond dispute. But administrative law has not kept up with the increasing centrality of the President in executive branch decisionmaking. DANIEL A. FARBER & ANNE J. O'CONNELL, THE LOST WORLD OF ADMINISTRATIVE LAW, 92 Tex. L. Rev. 1137, 1155–56 (2014): "[T]he actual workings of the administrative state have increasingly diverged from the assumptions animating the APA and classic judicial decisions that followed. . . . Those assumptions call for statutory directives to be implemented by an agency led by Senate-confirmed presidential appointees with decisionmaking authority. The implementation is presumed to be through statutorily mandated procedures and criteria, where the final result can then be reviewed by the courts to see if the reasons given by the agency at the time of action match the delegated directions. . . .

"In practice, however, both legislative enactments and presidential directives compel agency action. . . . [T]he White House . . .tr[ies] at times to direct agency action that the current Congress does not support or has not ordered. . . . [Even w]hen presidential orders are connected to an underlying statute, the statute may not be the primary driver of agency action. . . . For instance, the [Clean Air Act] was not enacted to address climate change, [yet] . . . President [Obama] used the broad regulatory authority in the Act to compel climate change regulations under a White House timeline. The primacy that administrative law places on congressional mandates, therefore, diverges from the realities of modern agency action, where presidential directives can have equal importance with statutes to agencies. Of course, the agencies may sometimes be happy enough to take actions in these areas, but the timing and framing of the policies are not under their control."

The White House
Office of the Press Secretary
For Immediate Release

June 25, 2013

PRESIDENTIAL MEMORANDUM—POWER SECTOR CARBON POLLUTION STANDARDS

ENVIRONMENTAL PROTECTION AGENCY

SUBJECT: Power Sector Carbon Pollution Standards

With every passing day, the urgency of addressing climate change intensifies. I made clear in my State of the Union address that my Administration is committed to reducing carbon pollution that causes climate change, preparing our communities for the consequences of climate change, and speeding the transition to more sustainable sources of energy. . . .

By the authority vested in me as President by the Constitution and the laws of the United States of America, and in order to reduce power plant carbon pollution, building on actions already underway in States and the power sector, I hereby direct the following:

Section 1.   Flexible Carbon Pollution Standards for Power Plants.

(a) Carbon Pollution Standards for Future Power Plants. On April 13, 2012, the EPA published a Notice of Proposed Rulemaking entitled "Standards of Performance for Greenhouse Gas Emissions for New Stationary Sources: Electric Utility Generating Units," 77 Fed. Reg. 22392. In light of the information conveyed in more than two million comments on that proposal and ongoing developments in the industry, you have indicated EPA's intention to issue a new proposal. I therefore direct you to issue a new proposal by no later than September 20, 2013. I further direct you to issue a final rule in a timely fashion after considering all public comments, as appropriate.

(b) Carbon Pollution Regulation for Modified, Reconstructed, and Existing Power Plants. To ensure continued progress in reducing harmful carbon pollution, I direct you to use your authority under sections 111(b) and 111(d) of the Clean Air Act to issue standards, regulations, or guidelines, as appropriate, that address carbon pollution from modified, reconstructed, and existing power plants and build on State efforts to move toward a cleaner power sector. In addition, I request that you:

(i)   issue proposed carbon pollution standards, regulations, or guidelines, as appropriate, for modified, reconstructed, and existing power plants by no later than June 1, 2014;

(ii) issue final standards, regulations, or guidelines, as appropriate, . . . by no later than June 1, 2015; and

(iii) include in the guidelines addressing existing power plants a requirement that States submit to EPA the implementation plans required under section 111(d) of the Clean Air Act and its implementing regulations by no later than June 30, 2016.

(c)   Development of Standards, Regulations, or Guidelines for Power Plants. In developing standards, regulations, or guidelines pursuant to subsection (b) of this section, and consistent with Executive Orders 12866 of September 30, 1993, as amended, and 13563 of January 18, 2011, you shall ensure, to the greatest extent possible, that you:

(i)   launch this effort through direct engagement with States . . . and . . . with leaders in the power sector, labor leaders, non-governmental organizations, other experts, tribal officials, other stakeholders, and members of the public, on issues informing the design of the program;

(ii) consistent with achieving regulatory objectives and taking into account other relevant environmental regulations and policies . . ., tailor regulations and guidelines to reduce costs;

(iii) develop approaches that allow the use of market-based instruments, performance standards, and other regulatory flexibilities;

(iv) ensure that the standards enable continued reliance on a range of energy sources and technologies;

(v) ensure that the standards are developed and implemented in a manner consistent with the continued provision of reliable and affordable electric power for consumers and businesses; and

(vi) work with the Department of Energy and other Federal and State agencies to promote the reliable and affordable provision of electric power through the continued development and deployment of cleaner technologies and by increasing energy efficiency . . .

Section. 2.   General Provisions.

(a) This memorandum shall be implemented consistent with applicable law, including international trade obligations, and subject to the availability of appropriations.

(b) Nothing in this memorandum shall be construed to impair or otherwise affect:

(i)   the authority granted by law to a department, agency, or the head thereof; or

(ii) the functions of the Director of the Office of Management and Budget relating to budgetary, administrative, or legislative proposals.

(c)   This memorandum is not intended to, and does not, create any right or benefit, substantive or procedural, enforceable at law or in equity by any party against the United States, its departments, agencies, or entities, its officers, employees, or agents, or any other person.

(d) You are hereby authorized and directed to publish this memorandum in the Federal Register.

BARACK OBAMA

The White House
Office of the Press Secretary
For Immediate Release

March 28, 2017

PRESIDENTIAL EXECUTIVE ORDER ON PROMOTING ENERGY INDEPENDENCE AND ECONOMIC GROWTH

EXECUTIVE ORDER

PROMOTING ENERGY INDEPENDENCE AND ECONOMIC GROWTH

By the authority vested in me as President by the Constitution and the laws of the United States of America, it is hereby ordered as follows:

Section 1.   Policy. (a) It is in the national interest to promote clean and safe development of our Nation's vast energy resources, while at the same time avoiding regulatory burdens that unnecessarily encumber energy production, constrain economic growth, and prevent job creation.

Moreover, the prudent development of these natural resources is essential to ensuring the Nation's geopolitical security.

(b) It is further in the national interest to ensure that the Nation's electricity is affordable, reliable, safe, secure, and clean, and that it can be produced from coal, natural gas, nuclear material, flowing water, and other domestic sources, including renewable sources.

(c) Accordingly, it is the policy of the United States that executive departments and agencies (agencies) immediately review existing regulations that potentially burden the development or use of domestically produced energy resources and appropriately suspend, revise, or rescind those that unduly burden the development of domestic energy resources beyond the degree necessary to protect the public interest or otherwise comply with the law.

(d) It further is the policy of the United States that, to the extent permitted by law, all agencies should take appropriate actions to promote clean air and clean water for the American people, while also respecting the proper roles of the Congress and the States concerning these matters in our constitutional republic.

(e) It is also the policy of the United States that necessary and appropriate environmental regulations comply with the law, are of greater benefit than cost, when permissible, achieve environmental improvements for the American people, and are developed through transparent processes that employ the best available peer-reviewed science and economics.

Sec. 2. Immediate Review of All Agency Actions that Potentially Burden the Safe, Efficient Development of Domestic Energy Resources. (a) The heads of agencies shall review all existing regulations, orders, guidance documents, policies, and any other similar agency actions (collectively, agency actions) that potentially burden the development or use of domestically produced energy resources, with particular attention to oil, natural gas, coal, and nuclear energy resources. Such review shall not include agency actions that are mandated by law, necessary for the public interest, and consistent with the policy set forth in section 1 of this order. . . .

(c) Within 45 days of the date of this order, the head of each agency with agency actions described in subsection (a) of this section shall develop and submit to the Director of the Office of Management and Budget (OMB Director) a plan to carry out the review required by subsection (a) of this section. . . .

(d) Within 120 days of the date of this order, the head of each agency shall submit a draft final report detailing the agency actions described in subsection (a) of this section . . . includ[ing] specific recommendations that, to the extent permitted by law, could alleviate or eliminate aspects of agency actions that burden domestic energy production.

(e) The report shall be finalized within 180 days of the date of this order, unless the OMB Director . . . extends that deadline. . . .

(g) With respect to any agency action for which specific recommendations are made in a final report pursuant to subsection (e) of this section, the head of the relevant agency shall, as soon as practicable, suspend, revise, or rescind, or publish for notice and comment proposed rules suspending, revising, or rescinding, those actions, as appropriate and consistent with law. Agencies shall endeavor to coordinate such regulatory reforms with their activities undertaken in compliance with Executive Order 13771 of January 30, 2017 (Reducing Regulation and Controlling Regulatory Costs).

Sec. 3. Rescission of Certain Energy and Climate-Related Presidential and Regulatory Actions.

(a) The following Presidential actions are hereby revoked: . . .

(ii) The Presidential Memorandum of June 25, 2013 (Power Sector Carbon Pollution Standards) . . .

(b) The following reports shall be rescinded:

(i) The Report of the Executive Office of the President of June 2013 (The President's Climate Action Plan) . . .

Sec. 4. Review of the Environmental Protection Agency's "Clean Power Plan" and Related Rules and Agency Actions. (a) The Administrator of the EPA (Administrator) shall immediately take all steps necessary to review the . . . [following] rules . . . and any rules and guidance issued pursuant to them, for consistency with the policy set forth in section 1 of this order and, if appropriate, shall, as soon as practicable, suspend, revise, or rescind the guidance, or publish for notice and comment proposed rules suspending, revising, or rescinding those rules . . .

(b) This section applies to the following final . . . rules:

(i) The final rule entitled "Carbon Pollution Emission Guidelines for Existing Stationary Sources: Electric Utility Generating Units," 80 Fed. Reg. 64661 (October 23, 2015) (Clean Power Plan) . . .

Sec. 5. Review of Estimates of the Social Cost of Carbon, Nitrous Oxide, and Methane for Regulatory Impact Analysis. . . . (b) The Interagency Working Group on Social Cost of Greenhouse Gases (IWG), which was convened by the Council of Economic Advisers and the OMB Director, shall be disbanded, and the . . . documents issued by the IWG shall be withdrawn as no longer representative of governmental policy [, including documents specifying how to measure the social cost of carbon and other greenhouse gasses for regulatory impact analyses.] . . .

(c) Effective immediately, when monetizing the value of changes in greenhouse gas emissions resulting from regulations, including with respect to the consideration of domestic versus international impacts and the consideration of appropriate discount rates, agencies shall ensure, to the extent permitted by law, that any such estimates are consistent with the guidance contained in OMB Circular A–4 of September 17, 2003 . . .

Sec. 8. *General Provisions.* (a) Nothing in this order shall be construed to impair or otherwise affect:

> (i)   the authority granted by law to an executive department or agency, or the head thereof; or

> (ii)   the functions of the Director of the Office of Management and Budget relating to budgetary, administrative, or legislative proposals.

(b)   This order shall be implemented consistent with applicable law and subject to the availability of appropriations.

(c)   This order is not intended to, and does not, create any right or benefit, substantive or procedural, enforceable at law or in equity by any party against the United States, its departments, agencies, or entities, its officers, employees, or agents, or any other person.

DONALD J. TRUMP

NOTES

(1)   ***Law? Politics? Both?*** Most of the materials you see in law casebooks are judicial decisions; in this casebook, you will also encounter (if you haven't already) other legal materials such as statutes, legislative materials, regulations, and agency guidance. These two measures represent another variety: presidential directives. They were and are key elements of the Obama and Trump Administrations' actions on climate change. Both were issued with great fanfare: President Obama announced his directive in a speech at Georgetown University early in his second term, after campaigning on promises to use administrative power to push regulatory reforms stuck in Congress. President Obama's directive led to EPA's adoption of its Clean Power Plan, which was strongly attacked by the coal industry and others as representing a "war on coal." President Trump, in turn, went to the EPA Headquarters to sign his directive, bringing along a group of coal executives and miners and promising to bring back the coal industry.

Yet these measures aren't just political theater. Both direct agency heads, and specifically the EPA Administrator, to take certain actions. Both invoke the President's authority under "the Constitution and the laws of the United States of America" and make specific reference to the Clean Air Act or binding regulations, like the Clean Power Plan. And both clearly intend to have an effect on governing law. They thus are paradigmatic examples of the way that administrative law can combine both law and politics.

(2)   ***What's in a Name?*** Note that President Obama's directive is titled a presidential memorandum, whereas President Trump's is an executive order. The substantive legal effect of executive orders and presidential memoranda is generally thought to be the same. See Office of Legal Counsel, Department of Justice, Legal Effectiveness of a Presidential Directive, as Compared to an Executive Order (Jan. 29, 2000). The executive order in

Youngstown (p. 871) looks very similar, with President Truman directing the Secretary of Commerce to seize the steel mills. However, memoranda can be more procedurally flexible. Under the Federal Register Act, 44 U.S.C. § 1505(a) (2012), executive orders must be published in the Federal Register unless they lack "general applicability and legal effect" or if they are effective only against federal officials—although many executive orders are also published and generally available online. Obama relied on presidential memoranda to issue his directives far more than executive orders; he issued only 277 executive orders, "fewer executive orders per year in office than any U.S. president in 120 years." Kristen Bialik, Obama Issued Fewer Executive Orders On Average Than Any President Since Cleveland, Pew Research Ctr, Jan. 23, 2017 (reporting on data compiled by the American Presidency Project, http://www.presidency.ucsb.edu/data/orders.php). But President Obama supplemented those executive orders with an "unprecedented" use of presidential memoranda and other issuances. See Kenneth J. Lowande, After the Orders: Presidential Memoranda and Unilateral Action, 44 Pres. Stud. Q. 724, 731 (2014). Different Presidents' approaches to directive authority are described in detail in Sec. 3.c.1.

(3) ***Parsing the Directives.*** A lot can be gleaned just by looking closely at the language of the directives. Why do you think Presidents Obama and Trump directed their EPA Administrators to take certain actions, rather than just taking those actions themselves? In this regard, note the contrast between Sections 3–5 of Trump's EO: Section 3 revokes and rescinds certain presidential documents and reports; Section 4 directs the EPA Administrator to immediately review the Clean Power Plan for consistency with the Trump administration's policy and, "if appropriate, . . . publish for notice and comment proposed rules suspending, revising, or rescinding" the Plan; Section 5 withdraws a document on the Social Cost of Carbon issued by an interagency working group convened by the Council of Economic Advisers and the OMB Director.

What explains this different language, do you think? Is it relevant that 42 U.S.C. § 7411(d), the section of the Clean Air Act under which the Clean Power Plan was issued, states "[t]he Administrator shall prescribe regulations" to implement the section? If you were EPA Administrator Gina McCarthy under President Obama or EPA Administrator Scott Pruitt under President Trump, how would you read the phrase "as appropriate" that appears in both Pres. Memo § 1(b) and EO § 4(a)? Would you feel free to decide not to take the actions listed because you thought they weren't good policy? What do you think would be the likely result? The Obama directive in some language "directs" and in other "requests." If you were EPA Administrator McCarthy, how would you understand these differences? To what extent do they impose legal obligations?

Both also make reference to "consistent with applicable law." This language is common in executive orders and presidential memoranda. Why do you think this phrase is repeated so often? One feature of the applicable law in these cases is that the decision about whether and how to regulate greenhouse gasses is statutorily delegated to the EPA Administrator. Does this language alleviate any concerns you might have that through these directives both President Obama and President Trump were trying to directly exercise authority Congress has delegated elsewhere? The legal basis of directive authority is discussed in detail below in Sec. 3.c.2. More obviously, "applicable law" includes governing substantive legal requirements, which for the relationship of the Clean Air Act and greenhouse gasses includes the Supreme Court's decision in Massachusetts v. EPA, p. 1253.

(1) The Emergence and Mechanisms of Presidential Directory Authority

The two presidents usually identified as most intent upon placing their personal stamp on federal regulatory policy are Franklin Roosevelt and Ronald Reagan. Clearly, each of them offers a model of a President determined to direct the regulatory state. Yet, most observers identify the presidency of Bill Clinton as a watershed in presidential ambitions to control regulatory outcomes. From President Clinton to President Trump, presidential efforts to direct the administrative state have expanded and taken on new forms.

(1) *The Clinton Administration: Presidential Memoranda and Unabashed Assertion of Directory Authority.* ELENA KAGAN, PRESIDENTIAL ADMINISTRATION, 114 Harv. L. Rev. 2245, 2281–82, 2290, 2298–99 (2001): "President Clinton treated the sphere of regulation as his own, and in doing so made it his own, in a way no other modern President had done. . . . [He] developed a set of practices that enhanced his ability to influence or even dictate the content of . . . a wide variety of agency action-rulemakings, more informal means of policymaking, and even certain enforcement activities. . . .

"The claim of directive authority . . . manifested itself most concretely and importantly in the frequent issuance of formal and published memoranda to executive branch agency heads instructing them to take specified action within the scope of the discretionary power delegated to them by Congress. These directives . . . enabled Clinton and his White House staff to instigate, rather than merely check, administrative action. The memoranda became, ever increasingly over the course of eight years, Clinton's primary means, self-consciously undertaken, both of setting an administrative agenda that reflected and advanced his policy and political preferences and of ensuring the execution of this program. . . .

"Even absent any assertion of directive authority, a President has many resources at hand to influence the scope and content of administrative action. Agency officials may accede to his preferences because they feel a sense of personal loyalty and commitment to him; because they desire his assistance in budgetary, legislative, and appointments matters; or in extreme cases because they respect and fear his removal power . . . Conversely, even given the assertion of directive authority, a President may face considerable constraints in imposing his will on administrative actors. Their resistance to or mere criticism of a directive may inflict political costs on the President as heavy as any that would result from an exercise of the removal power. This fact of political life accounts in part for the consultations and compromises that prefaced many of the Clinton White House's uses of directive authority. In this context, to put the matter simply, persuasion may be more than persuasion and command may be less than command—making the line between the two sometimes hard to discover.

"All that said, a line remains, and by so often asserting legal authority to direct regulatory decisions, President Clinton crossed from one side of it to the other. . . . The unofficial became official, the subtle blatant and the veiled transparent. . . . But more, the change in form likely led to a change in substance . . . [T]he explicit and repeated assertion of directive authority probably alters over time what Peter Strauss has called the 'psychology of government'—the understanding of agency and White House officials alike of their respective roles and powers. This change, in turn, makes presidential intervention in regulatory matters ever more routine and agency acceptance of this intervention ever more ready. The Clinton White House's use of presidential directives thus created the conditions for a significant enhancement of presidential power over regulatory matters."

(2) *The George W. Bush Administration: Signing Statements and Politicized Agencies.* Debate about the scope of presidential directory authority in domestic and foreign affairs was a constant during the Bush administration. The White House espoused a strong view of unitary executive theory, and that became the proffered constitutional justification for both unilateral presidential initiatives and vigorous resistance to power sharing with Congress.

(a) *Signing Statements.* One of the most controversial practices was President Bush's use of "signing statements" when signing legislation into law. Presidents have long used signing statements as political messages, praising enactment of the legislation or criticizing its inadequacy and exhorting Congress to further measures. The Bush administration controversy involved a very different use of signing statements: to identify constitutional problems the President perceived in the legislation he had just signed into law and to signal how he would "remediate" these problems. Sometimes this entailed construing the law to avoid such issues; other times, it was a direction to executive officials on how the new law should (or should not) be implemented. After comparing President Bush's signing statements with those of his predecessors, political scientist Christopher Kelley concluded that the Bush-era statements were distinctive because of the number of separate provisions in each bill that were said to interfere with presidential constitutional prerogatives. Because of the sheer volume of challenges, Professor Kelley observes, their effectiveness varied: "[T]here are certain policy areas that are critical to the president's agenda, and in those areas he and his staff will see to it that the substance of the signing statement is implemented by bureaucratic agents. In other areas deemed important to Congress, or at least to some members of Congress, the president and his staff will not spend the energy fighting a losing battle." Christopher S. Kelley, The Law: Contextualizing the Signing Statement, 37 Presidential Stud. Q. 737, 738 (2007); see also Presidential Signing Statements Accompanying the Fiscal Year 2006 Appropriations Acts 9 (2007) (identifying six instances in which, it concluded, agencies did not execute the new statutes as written); Kevin A. Evans, Challenging Law: Presidential Signing Statements and the Maintenance of Executive Power, 38 Cong. & the Pres. 217, 220 (2011) (concluding that President Bush used signing statements "to protect issue areas of traditional presidential influence—foreign policy and defense—and to combat various forms of congressional oversight").

Debate about President Bush's enhanced use of signing statements was fierce and polarized. An ABA Task Force study was harshly critical, calling "the issuance of presidential signing statements that claim the authority to disregard or decline to enforce all or part of a law" contrary to separation of powers and the rule of law. Am. Bar. Ass'n, Task Force on Presidential Signing Statements and the Separation of Powers Doctrine 1 (2006). At the opposite end of the spectrum: "Signing statements provide public information about a president's views of a statute and thus would seem to promote dialogue and accountability. Furthermore, courts pay little attention to signing statements; as a result, it is not clear how they can increase the president's authority vis-à-vis Congress. . . . [I]t is already widely recognized that the president has considerable authority to allocate enforcement resources . . . He certainly does not need a signing statement to do this . . ." Curtis A. Bradley & Eric A. Posner, Presidential Signing Statements and Executive Power, 23 Const. Comment. 307, 310 (2006). Signing statements have continued to be a focus of legal and political science scholarship in the years since. See, e.g., Daniel Rodriquez, Edward Stiglitz & Barry Weingast, Executive Opportunism, Presidential Signing Statements, and the Separation Of Powers, 8 J. Legal Analysis 95 (2016) (arguing that signing statements interpreting a statute upset the constitutional vision of lawmaking and exacerbate legislative gridlock); Christopher S. Yoo, Presidential Signing Statements, 164 U. Pa. L. Rev. 1801 (2016) (arguing that constitutional and interpretive signing statements are both appropriate and interpretive statements reflect the President's role as an essential participant in the legislative process).

(b) *Politicization of Agency Decision Makers.* President Bush also sought to exert greater control over administrative agencies by politicizing agency decision makers. In a famous article, presidential scholar Terry Moe identified agency politicization—populating agencies with officials who are politically responsive to the President—as one of two main techniques that Presidents use to gain control over administrative government. The other technique, centralization, is evident in the growth of centralized regulatory review (see Ch. IV, Sec. 4.d). Terry M. Moe, The Politicized Presidency, in The New Direction in American Politics 235, 244–45 (John E. Chubb & Paul E. Peterson eds., 1985).

According to now-judge DAVID J. BARRON, writing in FROM TAKEOVER TO MERGER: REFORMING ADMINISTRATIVE LAW IN AN AGE OF AGENCY POLARIZATION, 76 Geo. Wash. L. Rev. 1095, 1096 (2008), "for the last three decades, Presidents have been . . . making novel and aggressive use of their powers of appointment to remake agencies in their own image. As a result, agencies increasingly want to align their own judgments with the White House view—even if top agency officials are not ordered to do so by the political aides working at 1600 Pennsylvania Avenue. Agencies are now to an unprecedented extent governed by a thick cadre of political appointees; these individuals have been chosen either for having close ties to the President or for making strong prior commitments to his regulatory vision. For all the debate over the legality of a White House hostile takeover, therefore, the real story may be that Presidents have effected a peaceful merger with the federal bureaucracy by transforming the nation's administrative agencies from within." Professors David E. Lewis and Jennifer L. Selen agree: "Presidents have used the increasing number of appointees and their enhanced White House capacity for personnel selection to 'implant their DNA throughout the government' (to borrow a phrase from a George W. Bush aide). This is the essence of the politicization strategy. Presidents strategically politicize the agencies that control budgets, regulation, communication with Congress, and personnel." Political Control and the Forms of Agency Independence, 83 Geo. Wash. L. Rev. 1487, 1499 (2015).

Public administration scholars Daniel P. Moynihan and Alastair S. Roberts, in The Triumph of Loyalty over Competence: The Bush Administration and the Exhaustion of the Politicized Presidency, 70 Pub. Admin. Rev. 572, 573–74 (2010), maintain that the Bush administration "quickly demonstrated its commitment to the strategy of politicized control" through a variety of means, including: "expanding the number of political appointees; . . . giving more weight to loyalty than to merit in hiring decisions; . . . transferring untrustworthy bureaucrats out of key positions or pressuring them to resign; by excluding career officials from decision making" as well as "by centralizing authority over key policy decisions in the White House." Some of the Bush politicization efforts generated extensive public controversy, such as politicization of hiring at the Department of Justice and the suppression as well as manipulation of agency science on a range of issues, including global warming, day-after contraception, endangered species protection, and environmental hazard regulation. "[A] group of sixty scientists, including 20 Nobel Laureates, issued a joint statement condemning the administration of

President George W. Bush for distorting scientific knowledge to achieve political ends." Michele Estrin Gilman, The President as Scientist-in-Chief, 45 Willamette L. Rev. 565, 565 (2009); Peter L. Strauss, Possible Controls Over the Bending of Regulatory Science in Gordon Anthony, et. al, eds., Values in Global Administrative Law (2011).

The strategy of regulatory direction through politicization of agency decision makers also raised concerns about poor performance. Political scientist David Lewis found that the thicker layer of political appointees was not a stable, across-the-board phenomenon, but instead varied across agencies and over time—depending on how closely the agency's policy views or priorities were perceived to be aligned with the President's. David E. Lewis, The Politics of Presidential Appointments: Political Control and Bureaucratic Performance 202–03, 205 (2008). But this strategy for increasing presidential direction had costs: More politicized programs did more poorly on two numerical measures devised by the Administration itself to grade program performance. On both the Program Assessment Rating Tool and the Federal Human Capital Survey, systematically lower scores were achieved by programs *headed* by political appointees rather than career managers and by programs with higher *percentages* of appointees on the management team. Id. at 172–95.

(3) *The Obama Administration: "We Can't Wait" and Presidential Administration in an Era of Political Polarization.* Presidential administration arguably reached an all-time high during President Obama's two terms in office. Early on, President Obama expressly rejected some moves of the Bush Administration, issuing memoranda defending scientific integrity and limiting the use of signing statements, and signaled a possible retrenchment form politicization of the regulatory review process. But over his two terms in office, Obama employed many of the tools of presidential administration used by his predecessors. Within the first year of his administration, President Obama had issued signing statements challenging, among other things, format requirements for budget requests, limits on who may be appointed to a regulatory commission, restrictions on putting troops under United Nations command, and directions to U.S. negotiators to press certain policies in negotiations with the International Monetary Fund and World Bank.

(a) *Following in Clinton and Bush's Footsteps: President Obama's Use of Centralized Regulatory Review and Directives.* Professor KATHRYN WATTS, in CONTROLLING PRESIDENTIAL CONTROL, 114 Mich. L. Rev. 683, 698–700 (2016), describes how Obama "leverag[ed] existing tools for regulatory control like OMB review and presidential directives. . . . Obama—much like Bush—has heavily depended on OMB review. Indeed, Obama has relied on OMB even more intensely—and even more controversially—than Clinton did. Two aspects of Obama's aggressive approach to OMB review are notable. First, under Obama, OIRA has seized on delay as a significant means of aggressively controlling the regulatory state. . . . Second, much like the Bush administration, the Obama administration has not followed various transparency requirements set forth in Executive Order 12,866, such as the requirement that documents exchanged between OMB and the agency during review are to be made publicly available at the end of the rulemaking." Compare also Lisa Heinzerling, A Pen, a Phone, and the U.S. Code, 103 Geo. L.J. Online 59, 60–61 (2014) (a critical view of the operations of OIRA under Obama) with Cass R. Sunstein, Commentary, The Office of Information and Regulatory Affairs: Myths and Realities, 126 Harv. L. Rev. 1838 (2013) (a favorable view, written by the former head of OIRA under Obama).

Watts further reports that "Obama—like Clinton—has relied extensively on presidential directives. Such directives generally have taken the form of written memoranda posted to WhiteHouse.gov and published in the Federal Register. . . . Obama's heavy use of directives . . . continued throughout his presidency. In the first seven months of 2014 alone, Obama did as follows: gave a public speech about retirement savings while surrounded by steel workers in Pennsylvania and signed a memorandum that directed the Secretary of Treasury to create a myRA retirement program; gave a public speech at a Safeway Distribution Center in Maryland and issued a written report directing the EPA and DOT to issue new fuel efficiency standards for heavy trucks; delivered a speech at the White House about the importance of raising minimum wages and then issued an Executive Order requiring that the minimum wage for workers on new federal contracts be raised; directed the Secretary of Labor to update overtime pay provisions; directed various federal agencies to improve the entry process for international arrivals via a presidential memorandum; gave a speech at the White House about making college more affordable and signed a memorandum directing the Department of Education to change its regulations governing the repayment of student debt; and issued an Executive Order that prohibited discrimination based on gender identity and sexual orientation in federal employment. These directives illustrate how Obama—taking a cue from Clinton—relied extensively on positive command to turn the administrative state into an extension of the White House." Watts, supra, at 700–02; see also Andrew Rudalevige, The Obama Administrative Presidency: Some Late-Term Patterns, 46 Pres. Stud. Q. 868, 871–72 (2016). Perhaps the most prominent of all of President Obama's directives was his instruction to EPA reproduced above on issuing greenhouse gas emissions for power plants, see p. 951.

(b) *Newer Mechanisms of Presidential Influence: Czars, Nonenforcement, and Creative Statutory Interpretation.* Another mechanism used by the Obama Administration to assert presidential control over policy was the creation of special White House policy advisors or "czars." This mechanism was particularly prominent early on, with roughly twenty major czars being appointed at the outset of Obama's first term. A "striking and unusual" feature was appointment of "the more experienced and higher-profile policymaker . . . as 'czar' and the junior [appointee being] in the cabinet." The use of czars generally, and particularly the "appointment of Elizabeth Warren to lead a team of 30–40 Treasury Department officials in 'standing up' the new Consumer Financial Protection Bureau," sparked controversy, with "[t]he focal point of debate . . . [being that] czars are considered part of the President's personal staff and so are outside the requirement of confirmation." Aaron Saiger, Obama's "Czars" for Domestic Policy and the Law of the White House Staff, 79 Fordham L. Rev. 2577, 2594–95 (2011) Whether czars actually enhance presidential direction of regulatory decisionmaking is a matter of some debate. Compare Paul C. Light, Opinion: Nominate and Wait N.Y. Times, Mar. 23, 2009 ("Most have more stalemates than successes, hardly ever receive the presidential attention they were promised and often quit in frustration") with Saiger, supra, at 2594–95 (czars "increase the *capacity* of the president to jawbone, lobby, and directly supervise agency activities. . . . This sort of capacity for influencing the bureaucracy is opaque to political accountability and judicial review").

By contrast, the Obama Administration's use of nonenforcement strategies became more important as his presidency progressed. Perhaps his Administration's most famous use of nonenforcement came in the context of immigration, with the administration promulgation of deferred action programs allowing up to 5 million immigrants in the country unlawfully to apply for relief from deportation for a period of three years. (See p. 357) President Obama outlined the policy in a televised address to the Nation, and it was implemented by memoranda from the Secretary of the Department of Homeland Security. "The President's decision to defer the deportation of millions of immigrants sparked sharp debate among scholars and political figures about his authority to create such a large-scale relief program. The Administration provided an unusually meaty framework for the debate by releasing an opinion, prepared by the Office of Legal Counsel (OLC) in the Department of Justice, concluding that the initiative was well within the Administration's statutory and constitutional authorities. Critics disagreed with OLC's conclusion, decrying President Obama's actions as not just unwise but unconstitutional—the latest installment in the rise of an imperial presidency." ADAM B. COX & CRISTINA M. RODRÍGUEZ, THE PRESIDENT AND IMMIGRATION LAW REDUX, 125 Yale L.J. 104, 107–08 (2015).

The Obama Administration also used nonenforcement in the form of delayed application of several requirements of the Affordable Care Act, a signature initiative of the President. The Administration delayed implementation of the ACA's employer mandate, market reforms, and out-of-pocket caps. Nicholas Bagley, Legal Limits and Implementation of the Affordable Care Act, 164 U. Pa. L. Rev. 1715, 1721–23 (2016): "Delays in rolling out large government programs are of course common. But none of these delays were the result of an agency's failure to meet a deadline or its inability to implement a congressional instruction. Instead, they resulted from conscious decisions to delay the dates on which congressional statutes directed at private actors would take effect. . . [T]hese delays represented 'bald efforts to avoid unwanted consequences associated with full implementation of the ACA.' "

In other contexts, the Obama Administration formally waived statutory requirements. Although based on express statutory grants of waiver authority, these waivers often served to fundamentally rewrite the statutes at issue in line with the administration's priorities. See David J. Barron and Todd D. Rakoff, In Defense of Big Waiver, 113 Colum. L. Rev. 265 (2013). This happened most prominently with respect to the No Child Left Behind Act, under which the Administration had granted more than forty states waivers before Congress replaced the statute with new legislation. The Administration also used waivers to encourage states to expand their Medicaid programs, thereby again helping to ensure successful implementation of the ACA. The Obama Administration's grants of waivers to states are also part of a broader phenomenon of executive federalism, under which "policymaking [occurs] through intergovernmental negotiation by executives at different levels of a federal system." Moreover, given the public salience of the policies at issue and their salience to the President's agenda, the White House is often central to these negotiations. See Jessica Bulman-Pozen, Executive Federalism Comes to America, 102 Va. L. Rev. 953 (2016).

The Obama Administration justified these measures as legitimate exercises of enforcement discretion, highlighting another feature of Obama's presidential administrativism: "the frequent use of administrative statutory interpretation to drive . . . [the Administration's executive] actions, whether by producing legal opinions, issuing guidance documents, or more formal rulemaking." Rudalevige, supra, at 869. In some instances, the administration appeared to revise its own prior interpretations to meet a policy goal. A prime example was the Obama Administration's interpretation of the ACA's method for funding critical cost-sharing subsidies. Despite initially seeking annual appropriations for these subsidies, when Congress refused to fund them despite the statutory mandate, the administration determined that the subsidies could be funded through an ACA permanent appropriations. This interpretation sparked a lawsuit by the House of Representatives and a determination by the D.C. District Court that the Obama Administration had spent billions in unappropriated funds. See House v. Burwell, 185 F.Supp.3d 165 (D.D.C. 2016), appeal held in abeyance, 2016 WL 8292200 (D.C. Cir. Dec. 5, 2016).

(c) *Presidential Administration and Polarization.* President Obama's strong assertion of administrative power came against a background of extreme partisanship and polarization in national politics.

"[A] major consequence of polarization . . . [is] an increase in presidential assertions of policymaking authority and control over agencies. . . . Moreover, Presidents assert such policy control in the knowledge that Congress is unlikely to succeed in legislating limits in response. Hence, polarization contributes to the rise of presidential unilateralism as a central governance phenomenon." Gillian E. Metzger, Agencies, Polarization, and the States, 115 Colum. L. Rev. 1739, 1752 (2015); see also Abbe R. Gluck, Anne J. O'Connell, & Rosa Po, Unorthodox Lawmaking, Unorthodox Rulemaking, 115 Colum. L. Rev. 1789 (2015) (arguing that, in addition to polarization, President Obama's assertions of administrative power reflected the need to coordinate policymaking across multiple delegations and in a world of fiscal constraints).

President Obama invoked partisan divides and gridlock in Congress as justification for his administrative turn. KENNETH S. LOWANDE & SIDNEY M. MILKIS, "WE CAN'T WAIT": BARACK OBAMA, PARTISAN POLARIZATION, AND THE ADMINISTRATIVE PRESIDENCY, 12 The Forum 3, 9 (2014): "After the summer of 2011, . . . when Obama and congressional Republicans reached an impasse on fiscal policy and the House Republicans refused to raise the debt-ceiling, threatening to bring the government into default, the White House began to plot the course that led to the We Can't Wait Campaign. In an October speech, President Obama proclaimed 'we can't wait for an increasingly dysfunctional Congress to do its job. Where they won't act, I will.' . . . From October 2011 to October 2012, the administration announced 45 distinct executive actions that were packaged under the 'We Can't Wait' brand." The turn to administration in the face of congressional inaction explains some features of Obama's approach to presidential control; in particular, the reliance on new statutory interpretations reflected the need to adapt old statutes to meet new problems because new legislation was stalled in Congress. See Jody Freeman & David B. Spence, Old Statutes, New Problems, 163 U. Pa. L. Rev. 1 (2014). But Lowande and Milkis, supra, at 4–5, argue that rather than being just "a prisoner of partisan rancor in Congress," Obama "actively . . . embraced the role of party leader, even in the management of the bureaucracy, . . . [and] occasionally resorted to unilateral action as a *first* resort in bringing about non-incremental policy change."

Not surprisingly, President Obama's assertive use of administrative power provoked significant political pushback. Republicans in Congress accused the President of "lawlessness" and seizing "unparalleled executive power." Andrew Rudavelige, Old Laws, New Meanings: Obama's Brand of Presidential "Imperialism," 66 Syracuse L. Rev. 1, 3 (2016). Some academics voiced concern about expanding presidential power as well, from both sides of the political spectrum. See David E. Bernstein, Lawless: The Obama Administration's Unprecedented Assault on the Constitution and the Rule of Law (2015); William P. Marshall, Actually We Should Wait: Evaluating the Obama

Administration's Commitment to Unilateral Executive-Branch Action, 2014 Utah L. Rev. 773 (2014).

Do you think the actions of President Obama represented an assertion of administrative power categorically different from the presidents who preceded him? Or are his actions more accurately described as representing a "difference in degree, not in kind. Past presidents provided the template; Obama used it, and pushed at its edges; presidents after Obama will be guided by its possibilities as well." Rudavelige, Old Laws, supra, at 3. Should President Obama's actions be viewed as a constitutionally defensible form of self-help, in the face of a polarized and recalcitrant Congress? See David E. Pozen, Self-Help and the Separation of Powers, 124 Yale L.J. 2, 7 (2014).

(4) ***President Trump's Early Days.*** President Trump's Administration, coming to power at a time of unified national government under Republican control, may show whether President Obama left a lasting imprint on the scope of presidential power or was a temporary expansion in response to partisan polarization and divided government. As this edition casebook goes to press, it is too soon to tell how the Trump Administration will play out. However, Trump has already asserted substantial presidential directive authority, issuing 31 executive orders targeting regulations, 28 presidential memoranda, and 30 proclamations in his first 100 days in office. Rebecca Harrington, Trump Signed 90 Executive Actions in His First 100 Days—Here's What Each One Does, Business Insider, May 3, 2017. The Trump White House has also suggested at times that the members of the federal bureaucracy are working to undermine his agenda. See, e.g., Mark Hensch, Spicer Won't Reject Idea That 'Deep State' Opposes Trump, The Hill, Mar. 10, 2017.

The most prominent of Trump's executive orders to date have been his orders imposing bans on travel to the United States from individuals in a number of majority-Muslim states and a temporary halt to refugees. The Trump White House issued an initial broad ban and a second narrower version, both of which were challenged and enjoined. . . When the Trump Administration issued a third permanent measure in September 2017, the Supreme Court vacated these decisions and remanded for the cases to be dismissed as moot. See Hawaii v. Trump, 859 F. 3d 741 (9th Cir. 2017), 2017 WL 4782860 (Sup. Ct. 2017); Int'l Refugee Assistance Project v. Trump, 857 F.3d 554 (4th Cir. 2017), vacated, 2017 WL 4518553 (Sup. Ct. 2017). As this casebook goes to press, the third measure, Pres. Proc. No. 9645, 82 Fed. Reg. 45161 (Sept. 27, 2017), has also been enjoined by a district court and appeal is pending. Int'l Refugee Assistance Project v. Trump, 2017 WL 4674314 (D. Md. Oct. 17, 2017).

Trump has also issued numerous executive orders targeting regulation, which direct cabinet secretaries to reconsider many existing regulations, implement statutes and regulations in a particular fashion, and produce reports on several policy issues. Even broader is Exec. Order 13771, titled Reducing Regulation and Controlling Regulatory Costs. See 82 Fed. Reg. 9339 (Feb. 3, 2017), which applies across agencies and areas. It provides that "[u]nless prohibited by law, . . . whenever an executive department or agency . . . publicly proposes for notice and comment or otherwise promulgates a new regulation, it shall identify at least two existing regulations to be repealed." Sec. 2. In addition, the EO imposes a regulatory budget requirement, providing that the regulatory costs associated with a new measure not exceed the costs saved by the regulations being repealed (with no mention of regulatory benefits). The EO also authorizes the Director of OMB to cap total incremental cost of all new regulations in future fiscal years and requires that any regulations adopted by agencies be included in the annual regulatory plan. In quickly promulgated guidance, OMB excluded independent agencies and limited the new requirements to apply only to regulations qualifying as significant under Exec. Order 12866. For further discussion of the executive order's impact on rulemaking, see Ch. IV, Sec. 4.d.

Offering an early assessment, Peter L. Strauss in American Administrative Law under the Presidency of Donald Trump 4, 18 (unpublished draft, 2017): "President Trump's campaign rhetoric and initial actions have suggested. . . . [a] view that the President is not just politically responsible to oversee, but constitutionally entitled to command, the work of executive government." Professor DANIEL A. FARBER, in PRESIDENTIAL ADMINISTRATION UNDER TRUMP 5 (August 8, 2017), available at https://ssrn.com/abstract=3015591, concurs in viewing the Trump Administration as asserting a strong view of presidential power and argues that "experience [under Trump] should lead . . . to reject[ing] . . . call[s] for a more expansive view of the president's power to issue legally binding dictates to agencies, as well as . . . argument[s] that presidential involvement in an agency action should lead to greater judicial deference. On the contrary, the need for a check against White House disregard for the rule of law and expert knowledge should lead to a presumption that the president does not have this type of directive power over agencies unless Congress specifically grants that power."

In a study of presidential administration across the Obama and Trump Administrations, Professor JERRY L. MASHAW and DAVID BERKE identify "continued bold attempts to accrete executive power beyond Clinton-era presidentialism . . . ; presidential administration insinuating itself more and more into areas like prosecution/adjudication and government science; and the rise of organizational techniques, like policy czars and "shadow cabinets," to codify presidential control beyond episodic directive authority." They also see "a general lack of durability for presidential policy actions across these two Administrations. Indeed, the speed with which presidential administration in the Obama era has been undone in the early Trump Administration has proven, in many

instances, impressive." PRESIDENTIAL ADMINISTRATION IN A REGIME OF
SEPARATED POWERS: AN ANALYSIS OF RECENT AMERICAN EXPERIENCE, 35
Yale J. On Reg. (forthcoming 2018), at 79-81, https://ssrn.com/
abstract=3018618.

(5) ***Speaking for the President.*** All the previous discussion has
spoken of *presidential* direction. Yet the President rarely is personally
involved in efforts to control regulatory outcomes. Around 2,500–4,500
rules are published each year by about 250–400 agencies.[45] There are
vast numbers of agency formal and informal adjudications through which
regulatory policy decisions are also made. How is presidential directory
authority operationalized in such an environment?

i.   The Polyphonic Executive. Surveys and interviews of top Bush
and Clinton EPA political appointees conducted by Professors LISA
BRESSMAN and MICHAEL VANDERBERGH provide a rare empirical window
into how agency heads experience "presidential" direction. Responses to
a number of questions designed to elicit their perceptions of presidential
control revealed that these officials experienced control as emanating
from several locations within "the White House," not only from the
President (who was relatively rarely personally an actor) and OIRA.
Often, these various offices (the authors identified 19 involved in EPA
rulemaking) competed with one another, "enlisting other offices, the vice
president, and even the president himself to mediate the disputes."
Moreover, with respect to the most formalized type of White House
oversight—regulatory review of proposed regulations (see Ch. IV, Sec.
4.d)—they perceived OIRA career staff as exercising significant
judgment independent of, and unguided by, that of the OIRA
Administrator or the President. INSIDE THE ADMINISTRATIVE STATE: A
CRITICAL LOOK AT THE PRACTICE OF PRESIDENTIAL CONTROl, 105 Mich.
L. Rev. 47, 873, 740–82 (2006).

A recent, much broader empirical study provides a surprising degree
of confirmation that the upper echelons of the Executive Branch do not
speak with a single voice. Noting the "considerable scholarly agreement"
among political scientists that "the ideological preferences of [Cabinet
Secretaries] have important consequences for public policy," Anthony M.
Bertelli & Christian R. Grose, The Lengthened Shadow of Another
Institution? Ideal Point Estimates for the Executive Branch and
Congress, 55 Am. J. Pol. Sci. 767, 767 (2011), examined the degree of
ideological congruence between the President and his Cabinet in the
George H.W. Bush and Clinton administrations. They used various
publicly available data to construct "ideal point estimates"[46] of Cabinet

---

[45] See Maeve P. Carey, Cong. Res. Serv., R43056, Counting Regulations: An Overview of
Rulemaking, Types of Federal Regulations, and Pages in the Federal Register (2016) ; David E.
Lewis & Jennifer L. Selin, Admin. Conf. of the U.S., Sourcebook: Sourcebook of United States
Executive Agencies 14–15 (1st ed. 2012) (noting "[t]here is no authoritative list of government
agencies").

[46] "Ideal point estimation" is a statistical method of locating an individual (e.g., President,
Supreme Court Justice, legislator) in a multidimensional policy space based on observed

members, the President, and members of the House and Senate between 1991 and 2004. The results? Sixty-nine percent of the George H. W. Bush administration cabinet and 85 percent of the Clinton administration cabinet had ideological ideal point estimates significantly different from the President who appointed them. Moreover, "inner cabinet secretaries" (Justice, State, Treasury, and Defense) "appear no more ideologically proximate to their presidents than outer cabinet agencies." Divided government made a difference: More ideological diversity was present within the Cabinet in periods of unified government than when the opposite party held the House, Senate, or both. Reporting on early months of the President Trump administration suggests that he has adopted a "team of rivals" approach that embeds such divergence at the highest levels of the White House. "Set up two rival teams. Watch them clash. Pick a winner and punish the losers. It was Donald Trump's approach on The Apprentice. It was how he structured his campaign leadership. And now, it appears to be the staffing strategy [he's]... take[n] ... to the White House," with clashes between "White House chief of staff Reince Priebus, the party stalwart, ...chief strategist Steve Bannon, the populist firebrand," and Trump son-in-law and senior presidential advisor Jared Kushner. Matthew Nussbaum, Trumpsition Day 35: The Apprentice: White House Edition, POLITICO, Dec. 14, 2016.

ii. The Institutional Presidency. HUGH HECLO, THE CHANGING PRESIDENTIAL OFFICE, IN THE MANAGERIAL PRESIDENCY 23, 23–24 (James P. Pfiffner ed., 2d ed. 1999): "Our most familiar image of the presidency finds a man, sitting alone, in the dimly lit Oval Office. Against this shadowy background the familiar face ponders that ultimate expression of power, a presidential decision. It is a compelling and profoundly misleading picture. Presidential decisions are obviously important. But a more accurate image would show a presidency composed of at least a thousand people—a jumble of personal loyalists, professional technocrats, and bureaucratic staff with one man struggling, often vainly, to stay abreast of it all. What that familiar face ponders in the Oval Office is likely to be a series of conversations with advisers or a few pages of paper containing several options. These represent the last distillates produced from immense rivers of information flowing from sources-and condensed in ways—about which the president probably knows little."

CYNTHIA R. FARINA, FALSE COMFORT AND IMPOSSIBLE PROMISES: UNCERTAINTY, INFORMATION OVERLOAD, AND THE UNITARY EXECUTIVE, 12 U. Pa. J. Const. L. 357, 407–09, 413–14 (2010): "[T]he trajectory of modern government has been mirrored within the presidency: constantly pressed by the expanding scope and complexity of the federal policy agenda and the entities charged with pursuing it, Presidents develop new

---

behavior (e.g., roll call votes, congressional testimony). Since the 1980s, it has been increasingly used as a measure of ideology by political scientists instead of self-reported liberal or conservative beliefs.

structures to compile and analyze information, provide advice, and assert control. Those structures ramify, growing in size and specialization as the task of supervision grows. . . . The evolution of this large, multi-layered structure to assist the President in understanding and controlling the government—which some political scientists are now calling the 'presidential branch'—has two significant consequences . . . First, the contrast drawn by unitary executive theorists between the efficient, representationally direct singularity of presidential leadership on the one hand, and the chaotic, democratically deficient collectivity of congressional action on the other, is over-simplified to the point of inaccuracy. In important ways, modern presidential leadership is constituted through, and carried out by, a large and diverse group of White House advisers and staff. . . . Second, overseeing this multi-layered support structure is itself a formidable management imperative for the President. . . . Academic and insider accounts of White House operations describe an intensely absorbed, highly energized atmosphere generated by staff units with distinct expertise and perspectives. At their best, they robustly debate the multiple substantive and political implications of policy options; at their worst, they vie for advantage and influence. Even under the most optimistic assumptions of universal, disinterested competence and good judgment, the information flowing up to the President about implications and options will be imperfect—and the message flowing down to agency officials about 'what the President wants done' will at times be ambiguous, even contradictory."

(2) The Legal Basis for Presidential Directory Authority

As noted above, see p. 881, the Court frequently invokes the tripartite framework of Justice Jackson's *Youngstown* concurrence in analyzing presidential power claims. Under that framework, whether Congress has authorized or prohibited the presidential action in question is centrally important. When a statute expressly delegates authority to the President, Congress's authorization of presidential action is clear. But far more commonly, statutes delegate authority to a Secretary of a Department or a head of an agency, and the President is not mentioned. The critical questions then become whether the President has independent constitutional authority to control the policymaking at issue and whether the relevant statutes should be read to allow such a role. The precedent and academic commentary discussed below address these questions.

(1) *Precedent on Presidential Directory Authority.* In contrast to the President's removal power (see Sec. 3.b), the President's directory authority has so far provided little occasion for judicial review. Two decisions often invoked to analyze presidential power in this area substantially predate the advent of the modern national administrative state. How much guidance do they provide for assessing contemporary assertions of presidential directory authority?

(a) MARBURY V. MADISON, 5 U.S. (1 Cranch) 137, 165–66 (1803) (MARSHALL, C.J.): "By the constitution of the United States, the president is invested with certain important political powers, in the exercise of which he is to use his own discretion, and is accountable only to his country in his political character, and to his own conscience. To aid him in the performance of these duties, he is authorized to appoint certain officers, who act by his authority and in conformity with his orders. In such cases, their acts are his acts; and whatever opinion may be entertained of the manner in which executive discretion may be used, still there exists, and can exist, no power to control that discretion. . . . But when the legislature proceeds to impose on that officer other duties; when he is directed peremptorily to perform certain acts; when the rights of individuals are dependent on the performance of those acts; he is so far the officer of the law; is amenable to the laws for his conduct. . . .

"The conclusion from this reasoning is, that where the heads of departments are the political or confidential agents of the executive, merely to execute the will of the president, or rather to act in cases in which the executive possesses a constitutional or legal discretion, nothing can be more perfectly clear than that their acts are only politically examinable. But where a specific duty is assigned by law, and individual rights depend upon the performance of that duty, it seems equally clear that the individual who considers himself injured has a right to resort to the laws of his country for a remedy."

(b) MYERS V. UNITED STATES, 272 U.S. 52, 132–35 (1926) (Taft, C.J.): "The degree of guidance in the discharge of their duties that the President may exercise over executive officers varies with the character of their service as prescribed in the law under which they act. The highest and most important duties which his subordinates perform are those in which they act for him. In such cases they are exercising not their own but his discretion. This field is a very large one. It is sometimes described as political. Each head of a department is and must be the President's alter ego in the matters of that department where the President is required by law to exercise authority. . . . In all such cases, the discretion to be exercised is that of the President in determining the national public interest and in directing the action to be taken by his executive subordinates to protect it. In this field his cabinet officers must do his will. . . .

". . . The ordinary duties of officers prescribed by statute come under the general administrative control of the President by virtue of the general grant to him of the executive power, and he may properly supervise and guide their construction of the statutes under which they act in order to secure that unitary and uniform execution of the laws which article 2 of the Constitution evidently contemplated in vesting general executive power in the President alone. . . . Of course there may be duties so peculiarly and specifically committed to the discretion of a particular officer as to raise a question whether the President may overrule or revise the officer's interpretation of his statutory duty in a particular instance."

Note that Chief Justice Marshall ascribes presidential control to situations in which the acts of executive officers like the secretary of state "are his acts; and whatever opinion may be entertained of the manner in which executive discretion may be used, still there exists, and can exist, no power to control that discretion," and Chief Justice Taft's first paragraph addresses the same setting. How does Chief Justice Taft extend the same reasoning, in his second paragraph, to officers who act under statutory authority and not as presidential surrogates whose acts are beyond judicial control?

(2) ***Directory Authority and Unitary Executive Theory.*** STEVEN G. CALABRESI & SAIKRISHNA B. PRAKASH, THE PRESIDENT'S POWER TO EXECUTE THE LAWS, 104 Yale L.J. 541 (1994): "Because the President alone has the constitutional power to execute federal law, it would seem to follow that, notwithstanding the text of any given statute, the President must be able to execute that statute, interpreting it and applying it in concrete circumstances.... Under the Constitution, executive officers can act only in the President's stead, since it is the President and the President alone who can delegate to them the constitutional power that they must have if they are to execute laws. For example, if Congress establishes by statute a Treasury Secretary with the power and responsibility to expend appropriations and also provides a degree of discretion in an appropriations act, it is a mistake to view that statute as creating any duty or authority that belongs to the Secretary, even if the statute is written that way. Rather, it is the President, under our Constitution, who must always be the ultimate empowered and responsible actor. This is because the Constitution establishes that the President *exclusively* controls the power to execute all federal laws, and therefore it must be the case that all inferior executive officers act in his stead. A statute stating that the Secretary of the Treasury and other Treasury personnel will execute appropriation and tax laws only establishes that these particular officers will assist the President in carrying those laws into execution. Congress lacks constitutional power to do anything more.

"If the President may make a decision that a statute purports to reserve for an inferior executive officer, by the same logic, the President must be able to nullify an action taken by an inferior executive officer. [For] example, suppose the Secretary of the Treasury, in the exercise of her purportedly exclusive statutory discretion, decided to fine a bank for violation of certain banking laws. Because the Treasury Secretary would be ultimately exercising the President's 'executive power,' the President must be able, in effect, to reverse or nullify the Secretary's decision by withdrawing his delegation of the executive power, which the Constitution gives to him alone."

Would the same reasoning apply to a presidential decision ordering the Treasury Secretary to fine a bank that the Secretary would not otherwise sanction? Early in the 19th Century, the ninth and longest serving Attorney General, William Wirt, counseled President Monroe that congressional assignment of duties to others was an element of the laws for whose faithful execution the President was responsible. His successor, Roger Taney, gave President Andrew Jackson the same advice that his prerogative was limited to removing an official who would not act as he preferred. The Jewels of the Princess of Orange, p. 984. Thus, when President Jackson wanted to have U.S. moneys removed from the Second Bank of the United States following his reelection in 1832, as a statute gave the Secretary of Treasury discretion to do, Jackson was forced to remove two Secretaries of the Treasury before he found an official (also Roger Taney, as Acting Secretary) who was willing to take that step. The immediate result was a Senate motion of censure, and the defeat of nominations of Taney to be Secretary of Treasury and, subsequently, Associate Justice of the Supreme Court. The by-election of 1834 produced a Senate willing to withdraw the motion of censure and to confirm Taney as Chief Justice.

(3) *A Different Constitutional Justification for Directory Authority.* LAWRENCE LESSIG & CASS R. SUNSTEIN, THE PRESIDENT AND THE ADMINISTRATION, 94 Colum. L. Rev. 1, 2 (1994): "We think that the view that the framers constitutionalized anything like this vision of the executive is just plain myth. . . . We believe [however] that there is . . . a plausible structural argument on behalf of the hierarchical conception of the unitary executive. . . . [T]he national government has changed dramatically since the founding, and so too has the national presidency. In light of these changes, mechanical application of the founding understanding—to allow independent officials to engage in tasks that the framers never foresaw—may well disserve the very commitments that underlay the founding itself. Under current circumstances, a strongly unitary executive is the best way of keeping faith with the most fundamental goals of the original scheme. . . .

"[A]n argument for the strongly unitary executive under modern conditions takes the following form. . . . Where the framers allocated a power that they thought of as political, that power was allocated to people who were themselves politically accountable. This was part of the fundamental commitments to accountability and avoidance of factionalism. At the founding period, the existence of a degree of independence in administration could not realistically have been thought to compromise these commitments. Today, by contrast, a strong presumption of unitariness is necessary in order to promote the original constitutional commitments. The legislative creation of domestic officials operating independently of the President but exercising important discretionary policymaking power now stands inconsistent with founding commitments."

Professors LESSIG and SUNSTEIN would, however, permit Congress to immunize specific regulatory policymaking from presidential directory authority. In particular, they justify independence for the Federal Reserve Board because of the risk that "the money supply would be manipulated by the President for political reasons. Even a perception of this sort would have corrosive effects on democratic processes. . . . [I]t would likely have adverse effects on the economy as well." Id. at 108. Can the Fed be so easily distinguished on *constitutional* grounds from all other agencies?

(4) *More Skeptical Views.* PETER L. STRAUSS, OVERSEER OR THE DECIDER? THE PRESIDENT IN ADMINISTRATIVE LAW, 75 Geo. Wash. L. Rev. 696, 702–05 (2007): "The Constitution itself is at best ambivalent on the question. On the one hand, the opening words of Article II locate all executive power in the President. . . . On the other hand, the Constitution twice refers to 'duties' or 'powers' assigned to other officers. Article II in terms gives the President only the right to seek from those officers a written opinion about their exercise of those duties (i.e., it does not say he may command their exercise of the duties assigned to them), and it concludes that he is responsible to see to it that the laws 'be faithfully executed'—i.e., as if by others. . . .

"[I]n ordinary administrative law contexts, where Congress has assigned a function to a named agency subject to its oversight and the discipline of judicial review, the President's role—like that of the Congress and the courts—is that of overseer and not decider . . . The difference between oversight and decision can be subtle, particularly when the important transactions occur behind closed doors and among political compatriots who value loyalty and understand that the President who selected them is their democratically chosen leader. Still, there is a difference between ordinary respect and political deference, on the one hand, and law-compelled obedience, on the other. The subordinate's understanding which of these is owed, and what is her personal responsibility, has implications for what it means to have a government under laws."

ROBERT V. PERCIVAL, PRESIDENTIAL MANAGEMENT OF THE ADMINISTRATIVE STATE: THE NOT-SO-UNITARY EXECUTIVE, 51 Duke L.J. 963, 998–99 (2001): "The president's appointment and removal powers and the Framers' decision to vest executive authority in the president presumably give him considerable ability to influence decisions by executive officers. However, this does not provide a compelling case for concluding that the president may dictate decisions entrusted by Congress to the heads of executive agencies. Article II, Section 2's requirement that presidential appointments of executive officers be subject to the advice and consent of the Senate would have little meaning if the president simply could dictate the decisions such officers are required by law to make. By requiring Senate confirmation of the president's nominees to head cabinet agencies, the Constitution presumably envisions that these officers will have some degree of independence that makes it necessary for them to be acceptable not only to the president, but also to the Senate, one of the entities largely responsible for defining the powers, duties, and functions of their agencies."

GILLIAN E. METZGER, THE CONSTITUTIONAL DUTY TO SUPERVISE 124 Yale L.J. 1836, 1875–80 (2015): "The Take Care Clause is particularly relevant . . . Two points seem evident from its text. The first, indicated by the Clause's use of the passive voice and the sheer practical impossibility of any other result, is that the actual execution of the laws will be done by others. Despite vesting the executive power in the President, the Framers did not expect that the President would be personally implementing the laws . . . The second point is that the presidential oversight role is mandatory. . . . [T]he mandatory character of the Take Care Clause is worth underscoring . . . This feature, combined with the Clause's oversight phrasing, means that the Take Care Clause represents the clearest constitutional statement of a duty to supervise. . . .

"These two features of the Take Care Clause—provision for presidential oversight and language signaling that such oversight is obligatory—combine to imply a hierarchical structure for federal administration, under which lower government officials act subject to higher-level superintendence. Article II's other provisions echo that hierarchy. A prime example is the Appointments Clause, with its differentiation between 'Officers of the United States' and 'inferior Officers,' the latter subject to appointment by (and thus implicitly subservient to) Heads of Department. . . . The Opinion Clause also conveys the importance of oversight, as the President's power to require written opinions from principal officers both signals that the President was expected to play an oversight role and ensures that such officers cannot keep the President in the dark about how their departments are operating. . . .

"Unitary executive scholars claim that Article II's hierarchy requires broad presidential authority to control all executive-branch decisionmaking or at least at-will presidential removal power over those executing federal law. But such a claim of broad presidential authority mistakenly elides the President's right and duty to supervise law execution with the scope of such supervision. The structural principle of hierarchy entails that supervision up to the President must occur; it does not require that such supervision take the form of full presidential decisionmaking control. Only if supervision could not otherwise occur— a dubious proposition, given the variety of forms supervision takes today—would such a broad claim of presidential power necessarily follow."

(5) *Directory Authority as Statutory Presumption?* ELENA KAGAN, PRESIDENTIAL ADMINISTRATION, 114 Harv. L. Rev. 2245, 2319 (2001): "I

believe . . . that the unitarians have failed to establish their claim for plenary control as a matter of constitutional mandate. . . . But [this] does not require the conclusion. . .that the President lacks all power to direct administrative officials as to the exercise of their delegated discretion. That Congress could bar the President from directing discretionary action does not mean that Congress has done so; whether it has is a matter of statutory construction. If Congress, in a particular statute, has stated its intent with respect to presidential involvement, then that is the end of the matter. But if Congress, as it usually does, simply has assigned discretionary authority to an agency official, without in any way commenting on the President's role in the delegation, then an interpretive question arises. One way to read a statute of this kind is to assume that the delegation runs to the agency official specified and to that official alone. But a second way to read such a statute is to assume that the delegation runs to the agency official specified, rather than to any other agency official, but still subject to the ultimate control of the President. . . .

"When the delegation in question runs to the members of an independent agency, the choice between these two interpretive principles seems fairly obvious. . . . When the delegation runs to an executive branch official, however, Congress's intent (to the extent it exists) may well cut in the opposite direction. Congress knows, after all, that executive officials stand in all other respects in a subordinate position to the President, given that the President nominates them without restriction, can remove them at will, and can subject them to potentially far-ranging procedural oversight. All these powers establish a general norm of deference among executive officials to presidential opinions, such that when Congress delegates to an executive official, it in some necessary and obvious sense also delegates to the President. . . ."

Compare KEVIN M. STACK, THE PRESIDENT'S STATUTORY POWERS TO ADMINISTER THE LAWS, 106 Colum. L. Rev. 263, 267, 276 (2006): "If Congress's legislative practice were to name only an agency official or the President alone as the statutory delegate, then the difference between a delegation to an independent agency and an executive agency would provide a basis to embrace the view that the President has directive authority. . . . Congress, however, has a more varied [delegating] practice . . . than Kagan acknowledges. . . . From the earliest days of the republic, [Congress] has delegated authority to an agency to act subject to the President's control. Congress also has delegated authority to the President to act though a specified agent, and to the President to act upon the recommendation of a cabinet secretary or the joint recommendation of cabinet secretaries. . . . [Therefore] delegations to executive officials alone . . . should not be read to grant directive authority to the President. . . . [A]s a matter of statutory construction the President has directive authority-that is, the power to act directly under the statute or to bind the discretion of lower level officials—only when the statute expressly grants power to the President in name." For a similar view, see Thomas O. Sargentich, The Emphasis on the Presidency in U.S. Public Law: An Essay Critiquing Presidential Administration, 59 Admin. L. Rev. 1, 24 (2007).

(6) ***Enhancing Democratic Accountability?*** Both strong unitary executive theorists and other defenders of presidential directory authority argue that it is needed to make regulation democratically accountable. But what does "accountability" mean in our constitutional history and culture?

(a) PETER M. SHANE, POLITICAL ACCOUNTABILITY IN A SYSTEM OF CHECKS AND BALANCES: THE CASE OF PRESIDENTIAL REVIEW OF RULEMAKING, 48 Ark. L. Rev. 161, 196 (1995): "[I]t is a striking feature of most of the 'unitary executive' literature that it gives little sustained attention to what 'accountability' means. The connection between presidential control of administration and accountability is offered as self-evident. Of course, if one simply defines 'accountability' as the vesting of ultimate decisional authority in a person who is elected, not appointed, it is, indeed, self-evident that the President is elected, and bureaucrats are not. Voters have one—albeit no more than one—opportunity to vote 'No' on extending a President's White House stay. Bureaucrats do not run for office. But no adequate analysis can rest entirely on that observation. The point of accountability, by definition, must surely be the actual operational capacity of any decisionmaker to be held to account. It is not at all self-evident that the President is more accountable in this sense than other public officials."

(b) JERRY L. MASHAW, CENTER AND PERIPHERY IN ANTEBELLUM FEDERAL ADMINISTRATION: THE MULTIPLE FACES OF POPULAR CONTROL, 12 U. Pa. J. Const. L. 331, 354–56 (2010): "[Part of a larger project on the history of federal administration, this article examines how the norm of democratic control of administration was 'operationalized in the organization of the early Republic.'] [I]t seems fair to conclude that popular control of bureaucratic elites has a number of meanings . . . In one, government is popular because those who have authority are under the control of political actors who are popularly elected. This is true of both presidential and congressional control of administration and also of decentralized administration through state and local officials. The second general approach is to insinuate 'the people' into administration itself. [In this early period, this happened in several ways that 'blur[red] the distinction between laymen and officials,' including the use of citizens to perform inspections, resolve valuation disputes, and undertake private enforcement actions.]

"These visions of popular control not only compete with unitary presidential control by weakening the capacity of central officials under presidential direction to manage implementation effectively, they also compete normatively as independently attractive means for limiting bureaucratic excesses, guiding bureaucratic judgment and enforcing bureaucratic loyalty. . . . Every vision of popular control . . . has both strengths and well-known defects. Strong control by the Chief Executive can promote democratic accountability; it can also degenerate into lawlessness or authoritarian excess. The participation of regulated parties or beneficiaries in the administration of federal law can provide a needed corrective to bureaucratic tunnel vision; it can also facilitate the seizure of public power by private interests. Local control of administration can harmonize national policy with local political culture; it can also obstruct the effective implementation of national goals."

(c) CYNTHIA R. FARINA, FALSE COMFORT AND IMPOSSIBLE PROMISES: UNCERTAINTY, INFORMATION OVERLOAD, AND THE UNITARY EXECUTIVE, 12 U. Pa. J. Const. L. 357, 385 (2010): "[N]o one institution of government is authorized, or able, to speak for the people and to manage singlehandedly the enterprise of contemporary regulatory government. We must expect and challenge all the institutions of government—Congress, the President, the courts, and agencies themselves—to be part of an ongoing process through which democratic legitimacy is created and effective policy discovered, a process that must seek new and more effective ways to inform and engage citizens. A fundamental danger of unitary executive theory is that we will be lulled into thinking that this unwieldy, constant, and demanding work need not be done, so long as we select the 'right' person to be President."

(7) **_Transparency._** Does the accountability argument for presidential directive authority depend at all on the specifics of presidential involvement being publicly known? NINA A. MENDELSON, DISCLOSING "POLITICAL" OVERSIGHT OF AGENCY DECISION MAKING, 108 Mich. L. Rev. 1127 (2010): "[P]ublic information about the content of executive supervision of an agency decision itself, such as through regulatory review, is surprisingly rare. . . . [D]espite the several hundred economically significant rules that were modified during the review process, the Bush Administration OMB posted only forty-two review and return letters that explain its problems with the agency rule under review. President Obama's OIRA appears to be even less committed to disclosure. . . . Between January 20, 2009 and January 20, 2010, Obama's OIRA reviewed 120 economically significant proposed or final rules. Of these, only 8 were issued without change; 46 were issued consistent with change; and 12 were withdrawn. In other words, over 90 percent of economically significant rules underwent some change or withdrawal during the OIRA review process. . . . [Yet] no review or return letters of any sort appeared to have been posted electronically by Obama's OIRA during that time." For further discussion of the effect of presidential involvement on transparency, see Ch. VI, Sec. 4.d.

Lack of transparency emerged as a theme in surveys and interviews with top EPA political appointees from both the George H.W. Bush and Clinton administrations. BRESSMAN &VANDENBERGH, supra, at 80–82: "90% [of officials surveyed] answered that the White House was more able than the EPA to shield its actions from public view" and "68% said that the EPA represented the public's views more often than the White House." That even political appointees would believe that their own agency was more open and public-regarding than White House overseers is not, in itself, surprising. But their reasons are noteworthy: these officials emphasized (i) "the notice-and-comment rule-making procedures of the Administrative Procedure Act" [see Ch. IV, Sec. 4.d]; (ii) "various [public] stakeholder and regional meetings"; (iii) "Federal Advisory Committee Act [transparency] requirements" that do not apply to meetings with White House staff; and (iv) the greater "general media and trade press" coverage of regulatory action as compared to White House intervention. Finally, "according to 63% of [respondents,] only rarely or sometimes were changes arising from White House involvement apparent in the [administrative] record available to reviewing courts." More recently, Professor Lisa Heinzerling (a senior political appointee in EPA during the Obama administration) repeated these themes, complaining that "OIRA is the stumbling block when it comes to transparency. Agencies know full well that they are not to be too transparent. OIRA reprimanded the EPA when the EPA accidentally posted interagency comments on its proposal to regulate coal ash impoundments." Inside EPA: A Former Insider's Reflections on the Relationship Between the Obama EPA and the Obama White House, 31 Pace Envtl. L. Rev. 325, 363 (2014). For the contrasting view (from a former OIRA Administrator) that "OIRA has a high degree of transparency," see Cass R. Sunstein, The Office of Information and Regulatory Affairs: Myths and Realities, 126 Harv. L. Rev. 1838, 1860–61 (2013).

(3) Presidential Directory Authority in Context

Are assertions of presidential directory authority more defensible in certain administrative contexts than others? Some settings where such authority seem obviously appropriate are those where, in Chief Justice Marshall's words, "the heads of departments are the political or confidential agents of the executive, merely to execute the will of the president, or rather to act in cases in which the executive possesses a constitutional or legal discretion, nothing can be more perfectly clear than that their acts are only politically examinable." Three more ordinary procedural contexts worth examining individually are adjudication, regulation, and enforcement. A fourth context, budget, is an often overlooked area of presidential control, but one that has become increasingly more important over time.

(1) ***Adjudication.*** The question of presidential involvement in formal adjudication was squarely presented in PORTLAND AUDUBON SOCIETY V. THE ENDANGERED SPECIES COMMITTEE, 984 F.2d 1534 (9th Cir. 1993) (also discussed on p. 523). The case was part of long and complex litigation concerning timber sales in the habitat of the northern spotted

owl, an endangered species living in the old growth forests of Oregon. The Endangered Species Act stringently regulates federal (and other) activity affecting such habitats. Under the Act, *only* a high-level committee may authorize exemptions from the Act, after a process based on a record compiled in an on-the-record hearing before an ALJ, a report by the Secretary of the Interior, and any other hearings or written submissions the committee may request. This so-called God Committee (given its control over species preservation) is made up of the Secretaries of Agriculture, the Army, and the Interior, the Administrators of EPA and the National Oceanic and Atmospheric Administration (NOAA), the Chair of the Council of Economic Advisors, and presidential appointees from the affected state(s) with one collective vote. Granting an exemption requires five (out of seven) votes. After the Committee authorized a number of timber sales affecting northern spotted owl habitat under a 5–2 vote—only the second exemption ever authorized under the ESA—environmental groups sought discovery to show the Committee's decision was the product of improper ex parte contacts with White House staff. They alleged a number of such contacts had occurred with the NOAA Administrator, who ultimately voted in favor and whose vote, if he had voted against, would have been decisive.[47]

In an opinion written by JUDGE REINHARDT, the Ninth Circuit held that ex parte contacts by the President and White House, if they had occurred, would be inappropriate but remanded to Committee for evidentiary hearing rather than discovery. The court first held that the Committee's proceedings were subject to the ex parte communications ban of 5 U.S.C. § 557(d)(1), which prohibits any ex parte communications relevant to the merits of an agency proceeding between "any member of the body comprising the agency" or any agency employee who "is or may reasonably be expected to be involved in the decisional process" and any "interested person outside the agency." According to the court, "[e]x parte contacts are antithetical to the very concept of an administrative court reaching impartial decisions through formal adjudication. . . . Basic fairness requires that ex parte communications play no part in Committee adjudications, which involve high stakes for all the competing interests and concern issues of supreme national importance. See Professional Air Traffic Controllers Org. v. Federal Labor Relations Auth., 672 F.2d 109, 113 (D.C. Cir. 1982) (PATCO), [p. 508]."

Judge Reinhardt then turned to the government's claim that communications from the President and his staff are not covered by § 557(d)(1): "Although the APA's ban on ex parte communications is absolute and includes no special exemption for White House officials, the government advances three arguments in support of its position that section 557(d)(1) does not apply to the President and his staff. . . . The government does not contest the validity of PATCO as it applies to

---

47 The environmental groups alleged that White House staff had met with and called the EPA Administrator as well, but the Administrator ultimately voted against the exemptions.

Cabinet level officials and below. However, it argues that the President's broader policy role places him [and White House staff] beyond the reach of the 'interested person' language. . . . We believe the President's position at the center of the Executive Branch renders him, ex officio, an 'interested person' . . . in every agency proceeding. No ex parte communication is more likely to influence an agency than one from the President or a member of his staff. No communication from any other person is more likely to deprive the parties and the public of their right to effective participation in a key governmental decision at a most crucial time. The essential purposes of the statutory provision compel the conclusion that the President and his staff are 'interested persons' within the meaning of 5 U.S.C. § 557(d)(1)."

The government also argued that "the President and his staff do not fall within the terms of section 557(d)(1) because the President's interest as the Chief of the Executive Branch is no different from that of his subordinates on the Committee." The court rejected this argument as well: "The government's . . . [argument that] the President is, for all intents and purposes, a 'member' of the Committee and may attempt to influence its decisions . . . amounts to a contention that the President is not 'outside the agency' for the purposes of APA § 557(d)(1). The Supreme Court soundly rejected the basic logic of this argument in United States ex rel. Accardi v. Shaughnessy, 347 U.S. 260 (1954). The Court held that where legally binding regulations delegated a particular discretionary decision to the Board of Immigration Appeals, the Attorney General could not dictate a decision of the Board, even though the Board was appointed by the Attorney General, its members served at his pleasure, and its decision was subject to his ultimate review. Here, the Endangered Species Act explicitly vests discretion to make exemption decisions in the Committee and does not contemplate that the President or the White House will become involved in Committee deliberations. The President and his aides are not a part of the Committee decision-making process. They are . . . covered by section 557's prohibition and are not free to attempt to influence the decision-making processes of the Committee through ex parte communications. . . .

"The government next contends that any construction of APA § 557(d)(1) that includes presidential communications within the ban on ex parte contacts would constitute a violation of the separation of powers doctrine. It relies on language in Myers v. United States that states that the President has the constitutional authority to 'supervise and guide' Executive Branch officials in 'their construction of the statutes under which they act.' 272 U.S. 52, 135 (1926) [p. 918]. The government argues that including the President and his staff within the APA's ex parte communication ban would represent Congressional interference with the President's constitutional duty to provide such supervision and guidance to inferior officials. We reject this argument out of hand."

"The Supreme Court established the test for evaluating whether an act of Congress improperly interferes with a presidential prerogative in Nixon v. Administrator of Gen. Services, 433 U.S. 425 (1977). First, a court must determine whether the act prevents the executive branch from accomplishing its constitutional functions. If the potential for such disruption exists, the next question is whether the impact is justified by an overriding need to promote objectives within the constitutional authority of Congress. We conclude that Congress in no way invaded any legitimate constitutional power of the President in providing that he may not attempt to influence the outcome of administrative adjudications through ex parte communications and that Congress' important objectives reflected in the enactment of the APA would, in any event, outweigh any de minimis impact on presidential power.

". . . [C]arried to its logical conclusion the government's position would effectively destroy the integrity of all federal agency adjudications. It is a fundamental precept of administrative law that when an agency performs a quasi-judicial (or a quasi-legislative) function its independence must be protected. . . . Myers itself clearly recognizes that "there may be duties of a quasi-judicial character imposed on executive officers and members of executive tribunals whose decisions after hearing affect interests of individuals, the discharge of which the President can not in a particular case properly influence or control." 272 U.S. at 135. And in Humphrey's Executor v. United States, the Court observed that "[t]he authority of Congress, in creating quasi-legislative or quasi-judicial agencies, to require them to act in discharge of their duties independently of executive control cannot well be doubted. 295 U.S. 602, 629 (1935) [p. 920]. The government's position in this case is antithetical to and destructive of these elementary legal precepts, and we unequivocally reject it. . . . [W]e hold that communications between the Committee and the President or his staff are subject to the APA's prohibition on ex parte contacts."[48]

Although particularly adamant in rejecting White House involvement in administrative adjudication, Portland Audubon has company in suggesting that presidential involvement in adjudication is particularly problematic. Even Myers, the high-water mark of presidential directory power, acknowledged that the President might not be able to direct the results in administrative adjudications (though it allowed the President to remove agency adjudicators who made decisions with which the President disagreed). At least as early as 1823, the President's chief legal adviser had opined that the President lacked the power to direct the outcome of an agency proceeding in an individual case. See The President and Accounting Officers, 1 Op. A.G. 624 (1823)

---

[48] Judge Goodwin concurred, agreeing that "all of the executive and cabinet level officials involved here are subject to the APA's ban on ex parte communications," but finding there was no need to reach the question of whether "the President is himself subject to the APA's ban on ex parte communications—a question which presents troubling separation of powers problems."

(William Wirt) (opinion of Attorney General William Wirt to President Monroe).

Yet agencies often establish public policy through adjudication; the NLRB, for example, has developed national labor policy almost entirely through formal adjudications. (See p. 258). If the President has a constitutional claim to at least oversee the development of national policy, even if not control all executive decisionmaking, should adjudication be pulled out of the President's ambit so strongly? To the extent the prohibition on presidential interference in adjudication rests on due process and fairness concerns, should such a prohibition be limited to contexts in which the adjudication involves traditional liberty or property interests or entitlements that trigger due process—rather than, as in Portland Audubon, the discretionary grant of a regulatory exemption?

Such an approach would still leave the conflict the Portland Audubon court identified between White House and presidential contacts and § 557(d)(1)'s requirements. But can § 557(d)(1) plausibly be read to allow such contacts? Should the Ninth Circuit have read the provision more leniently? Finally, it is worth considering what the impact of Portland Audubon would be on informal administrative adjudication—*i.e.*, administrative adjudication *not* subject to § 557(d)(1). Would presidential and White House ex parte contacts still be prohibited, and if so on what basis? See also Harold J. Krent, Presidential Control of Adjudication within the Executive Branch, 65 Case W. Res. L. Rev. 1083 (2015) (arguing that Congress should have more leeway to insulate adjudicative officials as opposed to those involved in regulation and enforcement).

(2) *Enforcement.* If adjudication is the hardest context in which to imagine presidential power to direct administrators to reach particular outcomes, what about the seemingly easiest context—exercises of prosecutorial discretion? In 1831, the Attorney General advised President Andrew Jackson that he could direct the U.S. Attorney in New York to discontinue prosecution of an action to condemn certain stolen jewels brought into the country in violation of the revenue laws. The context implicated the President's independent constitutional role in foreign affairs—the true owner of the jewels was the Princess of Orange, who had requested their return—but the Attorney General relied not on that ground but rather on "the general supervisory powers which belong to his office, and which are necessary to enable him to perform the duty imposed upon him, of seeing that the law is faithfully executed." The Jewels of the Princess of Orange, 2 Op. A.G. 482 (1931) (William D. Mitchell) . (Notably, in light of strong unitary executive claims, the Opinion advised Jackson that while he could direct, he could not himself effect the dismissal of the prosecution. Rather, presidential authority was limited to removing from office any U.S. Attorney who did not do his bidding.)

Still, even in the area of prosecution—where the President's claim to directory authority might seem strongest—our politico-legal culture is uncomfortable with direct presidential disruption of the "standard operating procedure" for investigating and enforcing the law. Would the President's legitimate prerogatives be invaded if Congress enacted a statute directing the Internal Revenue Service to select tax returns for audit strictly upon objective criteria and making it a felony for anyone (including any elected or appointed official) to coerce or induce the administrator to audit, or cease to audit, any particular person? In thinking about presidential authority here, it is helpful to draw a distinction between priority setting and particular actions. Priority setting, like budget recommendation control, is at the very heart of seeing to the faithful execution of the law, given the reality that appropriations cannot/will not permit full enforcement. But choosing particular targets is another thing entirely. In the spring and summer of 2017, the strong norms against presidential involvement in particular investigations— and their potential liability on obstruction of justice or other charges if they do—were sharply in the public spotlight amid testimony from the former FBI Director James Comey that President Trump sought to end the criminal investigation of his first National Security Advisor, Michael Flynn.

Professor KATE ANDRIAS, in THE PRESIDENT'S ENFORCEMENT POWER, 88 N.Y.U. L. Rev. 1031, 1033–36 (2013), notes that "[w]hile enforcement of law is at the very core of executive responsibility, the formal apparatus of presidential administration concerns itself little with it. No office or staff in the White House or the Executive Office of the President (EOP) attends systematically to the enforcement of rules after they have been promulgated—that is, to problems of regulatory compliance," as there is with OIRA for rulemaking. Still, "notwithstanding the absence of an office dedicated to enforcement, under both Republican and Democratic administrations the White House has long influenced administrative enforcement efforts within and across executive branch agencies. . . . Nonenforcement in particular, which is subject to few judicial checks, has proved to be an important tool for advancing the presidential agenda. . . .

"In the modern era, ...Presidents have legitimately exercised great influence over agency enforcement policy. Yet they have failed to ensure that their administrations' policy decisions are well-disclosed and therefore have not always been held sufficiently accountable for uses of enforcement discretion. . . . While concerns about political involvement in enforcement actions should be taken seriously, and while it is critical that law enforcement be nonpartisan, it is naïve to imagine that administrative enforcement can or should be insulated from the President. Such a view fails to account for the pervasiveness and inevitability of policy judgments in enforcement, sacrifices potential gains in regulatory compliance that could be achieved through greater coordination, and ignores the structural factors that make presidential involvement in administration so entrenched. By acknowledging the President's role in, and responsibility for, enforcement, we can create the structure and transparency that will promote appropriate presidential influence."

Although presidential involvement in enforcement was long an understudied aspect of presidential administration, it has received significant attention of late as a result of President Obama's turn to enforcement—and often nonenforcement—as a central mechanism by which to advance his administration's policies. See, e.g., Zachary S. Price, Enforcement Discretion and Enforcement Duty, 67 Vand. L. Rev. 671 (2014); Patricia L. Bellia, Faithful Execution and Enforcement Discretion, 164 U. Pa. L. Rev. 1753 (2016); Leigh Osofsky, The Case for Categorical Nonenforcement, 69 Tax L. Rev. 73 (2015).

(3) *Rulemaking.* Rulemaking presents the most challenging context for specifying the appropriate scope and nature of presidential directory authority. Some things seem clear. The Opinion Clause[49] authorizes the President to require agencies to provide information about their proposed rulemakings. Thus, even though the Court in Whitman v. American Trucking, p. 791, held that the Clean Air Act precludes EPA from considering costs in setting national air quality emission standards (NAAQS) under 42 U.S.C. § 7409(b),[50] surely the President can require an Administrator to calculate and report cost data as a part of the regulatory review of proposed new standards required by Executive Order 12866. The President's take care duty and supervisory responsibilities also support such requests for information and the coordinative aspects of the centralized regulatory review under the executive order.

But could a President direct the EPA Administrator not to set NAAQS at a certain level because of the cost such a regulation would impose? Could the President do so for an emissions provision of the CAA that does not preclude consideration of costs but grants authority to set emission standards at issue to the EPA Administrator and the EPA Administrator has decided that a proposed standards' benefits outweighed its costs? Like its predecessors, Executive Order 12866 is careful to avoid the question of whether the President may *control* agency rulemaking outcomes. At the same time, it certainly provides a means by which the President might effectively do so, as by failing to approve the agency's regulatory plan or delaying indefinitely OIRA's response to a submitted draft or final impact analysis. (See Ch. IV, Sec. 4.d.)

---

[49] "[H]e may require the Opinion, in writing, of the principal Officer in each of the executive Departments, upon any subject relating to the Duties of their respective Offices." U.S. Const., Art. II, § 1.

[50] Subsequently, in Michigan v. EPA, 135 S.Ct. 2699 (2015), p. 1094, the Court held that another section of the CAA did require the EPA to consider costs.

It also seems clear (except perhaps to the most ardent unitary executive theorist) that when Congress has authorized an agency to develop regulations on a particular topic, adoption of the regulation requires the agency's acquiescence. If the relevant Secretary or Administrator is unwilling to sign the final rulemaking document, it cannot meet the terms of the statutory authorization. But can the agency head sign and cause to be published a rule to which the President objects? For example, in 2011, EPA proposed a NAAQS for ozone of 60–70 ppm; although this standard was recommended by EPA's science advisory committee, business interests strongly opposed it as too costly. After reviewing the proposed standard under the Executive Order 12866 process, OIRA Administrator Cass Sunstein returned the rule to EPA at President Obama's direction. EPA pulled the proposed standard.[51] Could EPA Administrator Lisa Jackson nonetheless have adopted the rejected emissions standard? Can the President control publication of such a rule in the Federal Register, if adopted by the Administrator, by instructions to the Office of the Federal Register? The EO does appear to assert this prerogative, and an unpublished rule cannot take effect.

Alternatively, if the rulemaking at issue is one undertaken by an independent agency, can the President force the agency to submit the rule for centralized review? The general view that when Congress delegates rulemaking authority to an independent agency, it does not intend the President to exercise that kind of control. See Kagan, supra, at 2319. Note that EO 12866 expressly exempts independent agencies from the requirement that agencies must submit rules for OIRA review but subjects them to the requirement that they provide a regulatory agenda. See p. 417. OMB similarly issued guidance exempting independent agencies from President Trumps regulatory EO. Thus, they avoid the question of whether, and to what extent, the Constitution protects the President's ability to intervene in specific independent agency rulemakings. As for EO 12866's requirement that independent agencies submit regulatory agendas along with other agencies, can you think of a clear constitutional basis on which the President could require independent agencies to provide that information? The absence of centralized review doesn't mean that Presidents stay out of independent agency rulemaking, however—as evident with respect to the FCC's 2015 rule on net neutrality, for which President Obama issued a video and a statement urging the FCC Commissioners to "implement the strongest possible rules to protect net neutrality." See Net Neutrality, President Obama's Plan for a Free and Open Internet, https://obamawhite house.archives.gov/node/323681.

There is little precedent on the appropriate scope of the presidential role in rulemaking. A rare and influential decision is SIERRA CLUB V. COSTLE, 657 F.2d 298 (D.C. Cir. 1981), which addressed standards EPA

---

[51] For a description of this episode, see Kathryn A. Watts, Controlling Presidential Control, 114 Mich. L. Rev. 683, 714–15 (2016).

issued for emissions of sulfur dioxide and particulates by new coal-fired power stations. The economic stakes of the standards were high and the rulemaking process underlying the new standards had been long and contentious. A lower ceiling on sulfur dioxide emissions would have been possible but would have impaired the market for coal produced in the Eastern, Midwest, and Northern Appalachian coal regions. In one of many challenges to the standards, the Environmental Defense Fund (EDF) asserted that EPA initially chose a lower ceiling but had backed away under an "ex parte blitz" from the coal industry, President Carter, and Senator Robert Byrd. At the time, Byrd was Senate majority leader representing West Virginia; he was naturally and deeply interested in the economic health of the Northern Appalachian coal region. The "blitz" occurred partly through the submission of late comments and partly through high-level meetings with Executive branch officials (including one meeting with the President himself) and congressional officials (including two with Senator Byrd).[52]

In an over 100-page opinion for the court (about 90 percent of which is devoted to a detailed review of EPA's publicly stated reasoning), CHIEF JUDGE PATRICIA WALD rejected the argument that such ex parte contacts were improper: "We note initially that § 307 makes specific provision for including in the rulemaking docket the 'written comments' of other executive agencies along with accompanying documents on any proposed draft rules circulated in advance of the rulemaking proceeding. Drafts of the final rule submitted to an executive review process prior to promulgation, as well as all 'written comments,' 'documents,' and 'written responses' resulting from such interagency review process, are also to be put in the docket prior to promulgation. This specific requirement does not mention informal meetings or conversations concerning the rule which are not part of the initial or final review processes, nor does it refer to oral comments of any sort. Yet it is hard to believe Congress was unaware that intra-executive meetings and oral comments would occur throughout the rulemaking process. We assume, therefore, that unless expressly forbidden by Congress, such intra-executive contacts may take place, both during and after the public comment period; the only real issue is whether they must be noted and summarized in the docket.

"The court recognizes the basic need of the President and his White House staff to monitor the consistency of executive agency regulations with Administration policy. He and his White House advisers surely must be briefed fully and frequently about rules in the making, and their contributions to policymaking considered. The executive power under our Constitution, after all, is not shared—it rests exclusively with the President. The idea of a 'plural executive,' or a President with a council of state, was considered and rejected by the Constitutional Convention. Instead the Founders chose to risk the potential for tyranny inherent in

---

[52] That part of the decision concerning Senator Byrd's involvement is discussed in the materials on ex parte comments in rulemaking, p. 453.

placing power in one person, in order to gain the advantages of accountability fixed on a single source. . . .

"The authority of the President to control and supervise executive policymaking is derived from the Constitution; the desirability of such control is demonstrable from the practical realities of administrative rulemaking. Regulations such as those involved here demand a careful weighing of cost, environmental, and energy considerations. They also have broad implications for national economic policy. Our form of government simply could not function effectively or rationally if key executive policymakers were isolated from each other and from the Chief Executive. Single mission agencies do not always have the answers to complex regulatory problems. An overworked administrator exposed on a 24-hour basis to a dedicated but zealous staff needs to know the arguments and ideas of policymakers in other agencies as well as in the White House.

"We recognize, however, that there may be instances where the docketing of conversations between the President or his staff and other Executive Branch officers or rulemakers may be necessary to ensure due process. This may be true, for example, where such conversations directly concern the outcome of adjudications or quasi-adjudicatory proceedings; there is no inherent executive power to control the rights of individuals in such settings. [Citing Myers v. United States, p. 918.] Docketing may also be necessary in some circumstances where a statute like this one *specifically requires* that essential 'information or data' upon which a rule is based be docketed. But in the absence of any further Congressional requirements, we hold that it was not unlawful in this case for EPA not to docket a face-to-face policy session involving the President and EPA officials during the post-comment period, since EPA makes no effort to base the rule on any 'data or information' arising from that meeting. . . .

"The purposes of full-record review which underlie the need for disclosing ex parte conversations in some settings do not require that courts know the details of every White House contact, including a Presidential one, in this informal rulemaking setting. After all, any rule issued here with or without White House assistance must have the requisite *factual support* in the rulemaking record, and under this particular statute the Administrator may not base the rule in whole or in part on any '*information or data*' which is not in the record, no matter what the source. . . . Of course, it is always possible that undisclosed Presidential prodding may direct an outcome that *is* factually based on the record, but different from the outcome that would have obtained in the absence of Presidential involvement. In such a case, it would be true that the political process did affect the outcome in a way the courts could not police. But we do not believe that Congress intended that the courts convert informal rulemaking into a rarified technocratic process, unaffected by political considerations or the presence of Presidential power. In sum, we find that the existence of intra-Executive Branch meetings during the post-comment period, and the failure to docket one such meeting involving the President, violated neither the procedures mandated by the Clean Air Act nor due process."[53]

Do you agree with how the Costle court viewed ex parte presidential contacts? The Costle court holds that ex parte contacts do not need to be disclosed unless Congress (or constitutional due process) so requires. Should the presumption instead be that such contacts must be disclosed unless Congress prohibits disclosure (and due process allows such a prohibition)? Does the fact that any resulting rule will need to have sufficient factual support to survive judicial review alleviate concerns about "presidential prodding" in the absence of disclosure? Note also that the Costle court states "we assume . . . unless expressly forbidden by Congress, such intra-executive contacts may take place." Given its reasoning, do you think the Costle court believed Congress constitutionally could prohibit such contacts? How would you analyze that constitutional question?

(4) **Budget.** ELOISE PASACHOFF, THE PRESIDENT'S BUDGET AS A SOURCE OF AGENCY POLICY CONTROL, 125 Yale L.J. 2182, 2186–93 (2016): "Reviewing regulations is not the only policy lever OMB has to control executive agencies' policy choices. In fact, it may not even be the main one. The budget itself—the core reason for OMB's existence—is a key tool for controlling agencies. Yet the mechanisms of control through the executive budget process remain little discussed and insufficiently understood. . . . Much writing on the budget process focuses solely on legislative procedures and general fiscal policy, attending very little to the executive's role. . . . When the administrative law literature discusses the budget, it tends to do so through the lens of institutional battles between Congress and the President rather than by examining the budget as a method through which the White House can control agencies' policymaking. When the literature does discuss the intra-executive role of the budget, it tends to focus on blunt tools and discrete moments in time: the President's ability to propose the funding levels and associated policy choices that Congress acts on, to 'recommend budget cuts for agencies that fail to follow administration preferences (and budget increases for those that comply),' and ultimately to veto appropriations legislation not to his liking."

According to Pasachoff, this ignores how "OMB's budget work serves as a regularized and pervasive form of agency control." Understanding this dynamic requires "focus[ing] not on the appropriations process but instead on the periods leading up to the annual submission of the President's budget to Congress and following the passage of the budget." Moreover, the critical OMB players here are not OIRA but OMB's five

---

[53] The court cautioned that it was not addressing situations "in which administration or inter-agency contacts serve as mere conduits for private parties in order to get the latter's off-the-record views into the proceeding," noting that "the Department of Justice Office of Legal Counsel has taken the position that it may be improper for White House advisers to act as conduits for outsiders."

"Resource Management Offices (RMOs), . . . [which] collectively contain more than four times as many staff members as OIRA. Working directly with budget and policy officials in each agency, the RMO staff play a large role in overseeing—indeed, at times in directing—the work of agencies throughout the administrative state because they have primary responsibility for pulling the . . . levers [of agency control] associated with budget preparation, budget execution, and management initiatives. . . .

"Three key points about centralized executive control emerge from this study of the RMOs. First, the RMOs provide a direct line into agencies. Each agency has identifiable RMO staff responsible for its work and a regular mode of communication with that staff. The RMOs therefore can serve as a conduit for policy and political direction from the President, the White House policy councils and other White House political advisors, and the OMB Director. If there is a message to be conveyed to agencies, the RMOs are a good way to convey it. The RMOs therefore work to ensure conformity with the President's policy program and political interests . . . . Second, the RMOs are not simply a conduit of information from the top down. They also serve as a source of deep and valuable knowledge of agency programs and practices. . . .Third, the RMOs reach many decisions about agency action on their own, since much agency oversight does not require elevation. . . . In this sense, whether the RMOs' work is a form of presidential control is less clear. At times, the RMOs' work may instead reflect OMB control, or RMO-intuited versions of presidential control as applied to particular situations, with case-specific value judgments obscured."

Presidential budget authority has a well-established historical and statutory basis. It dates back to the Budget and Accounting Act of 1921, which created the initial Bureau of the Budget that is now OMB.[54] By statute, 31 U.S.C. § 1105, the President is responsible for developing and submitting a consolidated budget to Congress no later than the first Monday in February prior to the start of the fiscal year. As a result, Pasachoff writes, "the RMOs' work, unlike OIRA's, is undoubtedly legal. . . . There is also little doubt that the RMOs play an important role in coordinating the sprawling administrative state. In doing so, the RMOs further core administrative law values of efficiency, effectiveness, and to some extent, accountability. On the negative side, however, three aspects of the RMOs' work collectively weaken their accountability. First, the RMOs' work is far too opaque. The lack of transparency surrounding the RMOs' interactions with agencies and third parties makes it difficult for the public and for Congress to monitor their actions. Second, the structure of the RMOs' work empowers OMB's civil servants relative to politically appointed agency officials and obscures ultimate responsibility for agency decisions. Third, because the RMOs' work seems dry and

---

[54] The same statute established the GAO as the congressional agency responsible for supervising budget implementation—a potential check to the new authority given the President.

technical from the outside—the kind of work associated with the bean-counter, green-eyeshade stereotype of budget bureaucrats—its substantive nature and potential for partisan politicization are ignored."

d. Internal Separation of Powers

> **(1) Charting Internal Checks on Executive Power**
> **(2) Assessing the Internal Separation of Powers**

As you've seen throughout this chapter, separation of powers debates often focus on the relationships among the three branches of national government and the various "webs of control" they construct over administrative agencies. Peter L. Strauss, The Place of Agencies in Government: Separation of Powers and the Fourth Branch, 84 Colum. L. Rev. 573, 636 (1984). But there is also an important "internal" dimension to the separation of powers that reflects the complicated structures and relationships that exist within the executive branch. Often these represent checks on presidential and administrative power, but they can serve to enhance authority as well. The materials that follow examine the internal side of agencies, the subject of a wide array of recent administrative law scholarship, and assess the relevance of this internal dimension—most entirely absent from the Constitution's text—to contemporary separation of powers disputes.

(1) Charting Internal Checks on Executive Power

(1) **The Civil Service.** The civil service is perhaps the most ubiquitous internal force within the executive branch, present in all agencies. The federal government is the nation's largest employer, with around 1.4 million civilian employees (excluding the Postal Service) in 2014.[55] Roughly 97 percent work in the executive branch. Although the number of political appointees has been growing, only around 4,000 of these were political appointees in 2016. The executive branch civil service has three main components: (1) the "competitive service" (also called the "classified civil service"), positions filled through a competitive, merit-based examination that represent the largest component; (2) the "excepted service," a miscellaneous set of positions excluded from competitive examination, many of which involve national security or intelligence gathering but which also include patent examiners, agency attorney positions, and special assistants; and (3) the Senior Executive Service

---

[55] See Executive Branch Civilian Employment since 1940, available at: https://www.opm.gov/policy-data-oversight/data-analysis-documentation/federal-employment-reports/historical-tables/executive-branch-civilian-employment-since-1940/. There are an additional 640,000 postal service employees, both political and career. See U.S. Postal Serv., About: Size and Scope, available at: https://about.usps.com/who-we-are/postal-facts/size-scope.htm.

(SES), top-level management and professional jobs that include a mixture of career employees and political appointees, created by the Civil Service Reform Act of 1978. The civil service system dates back to the late nineteenth century, when in 1883 the Pendleton Act created the Civil Service Commission to oversee merit-based hiring via competitive examinations. The Pendleton Act did not include a general for-cause removal protection; this was added by the Lloyd-LaFollette Act of 1912. Today the vast majority of civilian federal employees enjoy some form of removal protection, although only about half are covered by the general civil service system. The remainder enjoy largely equivalent protection under statutes specific to their departments or agencies. See David E. Lewis, The Politics of Presidential Appointments: Political Control and Bureaucratic Performance 20–26 (2008); see also Comm. on Oversight and Gov't Reform, 114th Cong., 2d. Sess. United States Government Policy and Supporting Positions (Comm. Print 2016) (the "Plum Book") (providing data on leadership positions in the federal legislative and executive branches that are subject to noncompetitive appointment).

Increasingly, contemporary scholars are emphasizing the importance of the civil service as a check on executive branch abuse of power. JON D. MICHAELS, AN ENDURING, EVOLVING, SEPARATION OF POWERS, 115 Colum. L. Rev. 515, 540–43 (2015): "The first administrative counterweight is the professional civil service. Civil servants are politically insulated. They often spend their entire careers as government employees. And they are well positioned to push back on any tendency agency leaders might have to skirt laws and promote hyperpartisan interests. Three factors explain the civil service's potential effectiveness as an institutional rival. First, as suggested, its members are capable of speaking truth to power without fear of serious reprisal. . . . Second, agency heads must take civil servants seriously. Appointed leaders in all federal domestic agencies necessarily rely on civil servants to help develop and carry out the presidential administration's agenda. . . . Third, the independent and much relied-upon civil service has institutional, cultural, and legal incentives to insist that agency leaders follow the law, embrace prevailing scientific understandings, and refrain from partisan excesses. That is to say, these professional civil servants regularly do have reason to 'choose' to hold agency leaders accountable."

NEAL KUMAN KATYAL, INTERNAL SEPARATION OF POWERS: CHECKING TODAY'S MOST DANGEROUS BRANCH, 115 Yale L.J. 2314 (2006): "A critical mechanism to promote internal separation of powers is bureaucracy. Much maligned by both the political left and right, bureaucracy creates a civil service not beholden to any particular administration and a cadre of experts with a long-term institutional worldview. These benefits have been obscured by the nowdominant, caricatured view of agencies as simple antichange agents. . . . A well-functioning bureaucracy contains agencies with differing missions and objectives that intentionally overlap to create friction. Just as the standard separation-of-powers paradigms (legislature v. courts, executive v. courts, legislature v. executive) overlap to produce friction, so too do their internal variants. When the State and Defense Departments have to convince each other of why their view is right, for example, better decision-making results. . . . [T]he executive is the home of two different sorts of legitimacy: political (democratic will) and bureaucratic (expertise). [The goal should be] to allow each to function without undermining the other."

(2) *Internal Dissent Mechanisms.* Civil servants may be willing to stand up to executive branch excesses, but what if agency leaders are nonresponsive? Civil servants rely on a number of mechanisms, some legal and some not, to bring their concerns to public attention. (Many of these mechanisms also relate to government transparency and are discussed in Ch. VI.) To begin with, many career officials have connections to members of Congress and staff on the committees that oversee their agencies, including from the party opposite of the President's. They often also have relationships with civil society groups, affected businesses, state and local officials, and so on to whom they can turn. A number of statutory and bureaucratic measures protect government employees who raise concerns through certain channels. For example, a number of whistleblower laws—like the Whistleblower Protection Act of 1989, Pub. L. No. 101–12, 103 Stat. 16 (codified as amended in scattered sections of 5 U.S.C.)—protect executive branch employees who disclose information regarding alleged abuses to responsible agency officials or congressional committees under specified procedures, and the Office of Special Counsel was created in 1978 to protect civil service employees from retaliatory action for lawful disclosures under whistleblower statutes. However, these statutes offer less protection for disclosure of national security information and do not confer disclosures to the press.

Some agencies have established procedures through which lower level employees can voice concerns about decisions and actions of their superiors. The most well known of these may be the dissent channel at the State Department, which "gives any officer in any embassy the ability . . . to disagree with the position taken by the ambassador," provides that all dissents must be sent to high-level staff, including the Secretary of State, and requires a quick response. KATYAL, supra, at 2328–29. During President Obama's administration, over four dozen employees used the dissent channel to encourage military strikes in Syria, and at the outset of the Trump administration hundreds of State Department employees signed a dissent channel memorandum expressing their opposition to President Trump's ban on travel into the United States by citizens of a number of Muslim-majority countries. See Daniel A. Farber & Anne Joseph O'Connell, Agencies as Adversaries, 105 Cal L. Rev. 1375, 1381 (2017).

Government employees also commonly leak their concerns to the press. DAVID E. POZEN, THE LEAKY LEVIATHAN: WHY THE GOVERNMENT CONDEMNS AND CONDONES UNLAWFUL DISCLOSURES OF INFORMATION, 127 Harv. L. Rev. 512, 513–18 (2013): "Ours is a polity saturated with, vexed by, and dependent upon leaks. The Bay of Pigs, the Pentagon Papers, warrantless wiretapping by the National Security Agency at home, targeted killings by the Central Intelligence Agency abroad: the contours of these and countless other government activities have emerged over the years through anonymous disclosures of confidential information to the press. . . . Mass releases of classified defense documents and diplomatic cables through WikiLeaks [and leaks by Edward Snowden are more recent examples] . . . [E]ven though the Espionage Act of 1917 and other statutes broadly criminalize the gathering, receipt, and dissemination of national defense-related information and even though every modern President has decried the practice, an enormous amount of leaking to the press appears to go unpunished. The federal government has brought roughly a dozen media leak prosecutions in the ninety-six years since the Espionage Act was enacted, eight of them under the [Obama] Administration. . . ."

Pozen disagrees with the standard view that leaks are rarely prosecuted because of the difficulty identifying leakers or First Amendment prohibitions on prosecuting journalists who knowingly publish leaked information. Instead, "[t]he leak laws are so rarely enforced not only because it is difficult to punish violators, but also because key institutional players share overlapping interests in vilifying leakers while maintaining a permissive culture of classified information disclosures. . . . The executive's 'leakiness' is often taken to be a sign of institutional failure. It may be better understood as an adaptive response to key external liabilities—such as the mistrust generated by presidential secret keeping and media manipulation—and internal pathologies—such as overclassification and fragmentation across a sprawling bureaucracy—of the modern administrative state. . . . Leakiness is a product not only of external and organizational constraints but also of deliberate choices made by high-level officials within those constraints. These choices have helped an ever-growing executive to secure the necessary leeway and legitimacy for governance."

(3) *Government Lawyers and Professional Norms.* The government employs a large number of professionals with specialized expertise, including many lawyers and scientists. Lawyers in particular are located throughout the executive branch, with thousands of lawyers in general counsel offices in every agency, as well as in the Department of Justice and the White House. Legal and public administration scholars emphasize the importance of professional norms in motivating the behavior of government lawyers and other civil servants: "By and large civil servants see themselves as professional public servants. That is, they see themselves as engineers, economists, chemists, biologists,

attorneys, social workers, accountants, etc.—and. . . 'often feel bound by legal, moral, or professional norms to certain courses of action and these courses of action may be at variance with the president's agenda.'" Jon D. Michaels, Of Constitutional Custodians and Regulatory Rivals: An Account of the Old and New Separation of Powers, 91 N.Y.U. L. Rev. 227, 238 (2008) (quoting Lewis, supra, at 30).

Moreover, internal executive branch norms can serve to give special weight to the views of professionals. For example, traditionally "legal opinions [from the Office of Legal Counsel in DOJ] are treated as authoritative and binding within the executive branch unless 'overruled' by the Attorney General or the President. OLC generally will not provide legal advice if there is doubt about whether it will be followed." Trevor W. Morrison, Constitutional Alarmism, 124 Harv. L. Rev. 1688, 1711 (2011). According to OLC's MEMORANDUM ON BEST PRACTICES FOR OLC LEGAL ADVICE AND WRITTEN OPINIONS, "OLC's central function is to provide, pursuant to the Attorney General's delegation, controlling legal advice to Executive Branch officials in furtherance of the President's constitutional duties to preserve, protect, and defend the Constitution, and to 'take Care that the Laws be faithfully executed.' To fulfill this function, OLC must provide advice based on its best understanding of what the law requires—not simply an advocate's defense of the contemplated action or position proposed by an agency or the Administration. Thus, in rendering legal advice, OLC seeks to provide an accurate and honest appraisal of applicable law, even if that appraisal will constrain the Administration's or an agency's pursuit of desired practices or policy objectives. This practice is critically important to the Office's effective performance of its assigned role, particularly because it is frequently asked to opine on issues of first impression that are unlikely to be resolved by the courts—a circumstance in which OLC's advice may effectively be the final word on the controlling law." For discussion of whether OLC and government lawyers actually can play a checking role in practice, see Sec. 3.d.2.

(4) *Internal Watchdogs and Internal Administrative Law.* Congress has created a number of additional internal institutional checks on the executive branch, ranging from offices expressly given oversight roles to indirect checks that result from program and regulatory design. Some of these, like independent agencies or the procedural constraints of the APA, are likely already familiar to you, but others you may not have encountered yet. Two examples bear special notes and appear in many agencies, but there are a number of other similar institutions sprinkled throughout the executive branch:

First are offices within agencies that are tasked with ensuring that the agency attends to concerns that might not otherwise get adequate weight, what Professor MARGO SCHLANGER calls "Offices of Goodness" in OFFICES OF GOODNESS: INFLUENCE WITHOUT AUTHORITY IN FEDERAL AGENCIES, 36 Cardozo L. Rev. 53, 60–61 (2014). The Department of

Homeland Security's Office for Civil Rights and Civil Liberties, where Schlanger worked, is an example: "First, Offices of Goodness are advisory rather than operational. Offices of Goodness help other parts of the agency get work done; they are not the offices . . . that themselves carry out the agency's mission. This means that Offices of Goodness must operate by persuasion or coercion of others. . . . Second, Offices of Goodness are value-infused. The observations here apply to offices that are explicitly assigned to further a particular value that is not otherwise primary for the agency in which they sit. That value could be civil rights, consumer welfare, fiscal rectitude, etc. . . . Where the value in question is 'lawfulness,' the Office of Goodness is likely to be the agency's Office of General Counsel . . . Third, Offices of Goodness are internal and dependent on their agency. The dynamics of a fully internal office are very different from one that has structural separation and independence."

Second are Inspector Generals. Created by the Inspector General Act of 1978 with a mandate to "prevent and detect fraud and abuse" in agency programs, IGs now exist in over fifty federal agencies, including many working on national security. Professor SHIRIN SINNAR, in PROTECTING RIGHTS FROM WITHIN: INSPECTOR GENERALS AND NATIONAL SECURITY OVERSIGHT, 65 Stan. L. Rev. 1027, 1031, 1034–35 (2013), argues that "IGs stand out in two ways. First . . . IGs enjoy several statutory protections from agency interference. The Inspector General Act provides for presidential appointment and Senate confirmation of IGs [on a nonpartisan basis] . . . While the President can remove an IG without cause, the Act requires that the President communicate to Congress the reasons for any removal no later than thirty days before[hand] . . . Even more significantly, IGs have a dual-reporting role that requires them to serve their agencies as well as Congress. . . . Second, IGs enjoy broad investigative powers. The Act authorizes IGs to undertake and carry out audits and investigations without interference from agency leadership and to access documents within and beyond their agencies." Based on an analysis of five case studies of IGs in national security contexts, Sinnar "conclude[s] that in certain cases IGs played a surprisingly significant role in protecting rights. . . . At the same time, . . . IG reviews . . . also displayed important limitations. Even the strongest reviews rarely led to individual relief for most victims, repercussions for high-level executive officials, or significant rights-protective constraints on agency discretion[, and] . . . IG reviews varied significantly: while some exhibited independence and a willingness to critique executive national security conduct, others faced obstruction or lacked rigor." See also Jack Goldsmith, Power and Constraint 95–108 (2012); Paul C. Light, Monitoring Government: Inspectors General and the Search for Accountability (1993).

Internal agency structure is important more broadly, for example, in prioritizing certain perspectives in agency decision-making or ensuring agency staff adhere to legal and policy constraints. One important element is how authority delegated to an agency is then subdelegated through the agency's structure. JENNIFER NOU, SUBDELEGATING POWERS, 117 Colum. L. Rev. 473, 475–81 (2017): "As a result [of subdelegation], tenure-protected career staff and lower-level political officials often make decisions initially granted to their superiors . . . [and have] signature authority—literally, the authority to affix one's signature and sign off on an agency action without higher-level oversight." According to Nou, "[a]gency subdelegation of this nature is a more pervasive phenomenon than commonly recognized." For example, the SEC has reported more than 376 separate rules subdelegating a range of authority to a variety of actors, and the EPA at one point reported 500 subdelegations. "Subdelegations to career civil servants . . . weaken [centralized presidential control as a] mechanism of executive power. When administrations turn over, subdelegations remain in place until and unless they are repealed." On the other hand, Nou cautions that subdelegation raises questions for internal separation of powers scholarship extolling "the counterbalances offered by various agency actors. This literature often presents career staff as nonpartisan keepers of professional norms. Considering such staff members as recipients of delegated authority with their own preferences and biases, however, calls into question the extent to which they facilitate, rather than buffer, fights between their political principals."

Nou describes these agency structures as a form of internal administrative law. GILLIAN E. METZGER and KEVIN STACK in INTERNAL ADMINISTRATIVE LAW, 115 Mich. L. Rev. 1239, 1252–53 (2017), agree, arguing that "many internal measures, ranging from substantive guidelines to management structures that allow for oversight of agency operations, qualify as forms of law. These measures not only bind and are perceived as binding by agency officials; they also encourage consistency, predictability, and reasoned argument in agency decisionmaking." They argue that recognition of internal administrative law's role in controlling agency power is essential for the legitimacy of administrative governance: "A legal regime that envisions external control as the only protection against administrative abuse is fundamentally at odds with the logic of contemporary administrative governance. Such a regime will never be able to ease anxieties about the administrative state or successfully regulate the exercise of administrative power." For a detailed investigation of the role of internal administrative law over time, see Jerry L. Mashaw, Creating the Administrative Constitution (2012).

(5) *Interagency Conflict.* Professors DANIEL FARBER and ANNE JOSEPH O'CONNELL, in AGENCIES AS ADVERSARIES, supra, at 1378–79, 1383–85, 1429, analyze the different interagency relationships found in the executive branch and emphasize the internal separation of powers benefits of inter-agency conflict: "Beneath the surface of the administrative state are constant battles, between and within

agencies. . . . Wh[en] the [FBI] . . . fought in court to force Apple to hack the iPhone of a perpetrator of the 2015 mass shooting in San Bernardino, California, it . . . faced resistance from other government agencies [which] . . . expressed grave concerns about weakening encryption technologies . . . The State Department negotiates laboriously to persuade foreign countries to accept a [Guantanamo] detainee. Once it succeeds, however, a new struggle begins with the Defense Department [over release]. . . . Fights are not limited to core executive branch agencies. The [SEC] and the Commodity Futures Trading Commission (CFTC) have long tussled over jurisdiction, including . . . disputes over which agency should regulate futures contracts based on securities . . .

"[M]uch of [the academic and policy] literature has denigrated agency conflict. . . . But conflict plays an important and often productive role in the functioning of the modern administrative state. . . .[C]onflicts, whatever their motivations, can be most constructive when they bring differing expertise, information bases, constituencies, and values into policy decisions. Such conflicts have the greatest prospects for enhancing expertise and ensuring that all points of view are heard—two key goals of administrative law. . . . In theory, checks between branches may be preferable . . ., but using them as a benchmark for judging the desirability of other mechanisms seems inappropriate in the present political era. Because of intense political polarization, periods of divided government may prevent Congress from making effective use of its powers to check the president, while periods of unified party government may eliminate Congress's motivation to do so. Thus, checks and balance may either cause an impasse between branches or fail to work at all. Consequently, . . . we think the question is not whether agency conflict compares well in terms of democratic norms with interbranch checks and balances, but rather whether agency conflict has desirable effects given the possibility that interbranch checks are ineffective."

(2) Assessing the Internal Separation of Powers

A multitude of independent forces and checks thus exist within the executive branch; despite being single-headed by the President, the reality is the executive branch is very much a "they, not an it," just like Congress. See Kenneth A. Shepsle, Congress Is a "They," Not an "It": Legislative Intent as Oxymoron, 12 Int'l Rev. L. & Econ. 239 (1992). But this leaves the question of whether, and to what extent, these internal forces check or constrain the President: Is there really an internal separation of powers that has bite? And if internal checks with real bite exist, are such arrangements constitutional?

(1) *Do Internal Measures Check or Empower?* Several studies of internal institutional arrangements raise questions about the extent to which supposed checks actually constrain the President. This concern has been raised particularly forcefully in regard to executive branch lawyers, in part in response to failures of executive branch legal

institutions like OLC to stop presidential abuses of power, such as the use of torture under the Bush Administration. Some suggest that these supposed checks may actually have the opposite effect and enhance presidential power by "writ[ing] up learned opinions that vindicate the constitutionality of their most blatant power grabs [and] . . . publicly rubber-stamp presidential actions." Bruce Ackerman, The Decline and Fall of the American Republic 9–10, 88 (2010). "Torture, indefinite detention, extraordinary rendition, targeted killing, profiling of Arab and Muslim men, and warrantless surveillance all occurred with the ex ante approval of government lawyers." Norman W. Spaulding, Independence and Experimentation at the Department of Justice, 63 Stan. L. Rev. 409, 410 (2011). Others view such accounts as exaggerated and fault them for giving insufficient weight to OLC's professionalism and its culture of giving independent legal advice, contrasting OLC with presidential-controlled legal offices like the White House Counsel. See Trevor W. Morrison, Constitutional Alarmism, 124 Harv. L. Rev. 1688 (2011).

The multiplicity of legal offices throughout the national administrative state is a sign of the importance of legal constraints in presidential and agency decisionmaking. But could the very number of legal offices serve to undermine the ability of executive branch lawyers to check presidential overreach? DAPHNA RENAN, in THE LAW PRESIDENTS MAKE, 103 Va. L. Rev. 805, 809–10, 812 (2017), argues that executive branch legal institutions may be sidelined or see their decisionmaking role reduced by the White House. "While the myth of a supreme OLC dispensing formal legal opinions persists, the reality is a less insulated, more diffuse, and more informal set of institutional arrangements. OLC's opinion-writing institution is withering. And on questions of special salience to the president, there is growing reliance on a more policy- and politics-infused legal apparatus, directed by the White House but reliant on a diffusion of ambiguously overlapping legal interpreters. Rather than OLC supremacy, legal views are developed by a collection of administrative actors. OLC usually has a seat at the table. But it is no longer the decider." In her view, "executive branch legalism has never been an external, or exogenous, constraint on presidential power. It has always been a tool of presidential administration itself. The president today looks to executive branch legal review to forge pathways to policy and political compromise in highly-contested, con-sequential, and increasingly legalistic terrain."

The concern that Presidents may be able to evade internal constraints by choosing among agencies is not limited to the executive lawyering context. "The United States Code is riddled with 'duplicative delegations'—delegations in separate statutes or statutory provisions that may reasonably be construed as granting the same regulatory authority to different agencies." Jason Marisam, Duplicative Delegations, 63 Admin. L. Rev. 181 (2011). In addition, "[i]t is quite common for Congress to create situations where an agency with the exclusive authority to regulate or manage a problem cannot proceed without first consulting, or taking comment from, another agency whose mission is implicated in the action agency's decisionmaking." Jody Freeman & Jim Rossi, Agency Coordination in Shared Regulatory Space, 125 Harv. L. Rev. 1131, 1157–60 (2013). Such duplicative delegations and interagency consultation or consent requirements might seem to create internal checks, as they force agencies with different programmatic perspectives and culture to agree on a policy before going forward—if only to not have their regulatory efforts be at cross purposes. Regulatory redundancy and a lack of unified control might also yield benefits in protecting against regulatory gaps. See Anne Joseph O'Connell, The Architecture of Smart Intelligence: Structuring and Overseeing Agencies in the Post-9/11 World, 94 Calif. L. Rev. 1655 (2006); see also Jacob E. Gersen, Overlapping and Underlapping Jurisdiction in Administrative Law, 2006 Sup. Ct. Rev. 201, 211–16 (2006) (exploring why Congress might create overlapping and underlapping jurisdiction).

But such duplicative and overlapping responsibilities may operate to enhance presidential power as well. Professor JASON MARISAM, in THE PRESIDENT'S AGENCY SELECTION POWERS, 65 Admin. L. Rev. 821, 838–39, 860–63 (2013), argues that "the most important aspect of overlapping jurisdictions among agencies is how presidents manipulate the overlapping jurisdiction to select which agency in the shared space they want to perform tasks." He further contends that, when available, "presidents' agency selection powers operate as a less costly alternative to the removal power. . . . [A]gency selection powers are less broad in two key ways. . . . [W]hile the removal power enables presidents to change who is in charge of the entire portfolio of an agency office, a president can only use his agency selection powers for a more limited set of tasks . . . [and] can only choose from among the existing set of agencies and the officers who staff them." But "agency selection powers . . . are broader . . . when it comes to independent agencies . . . [and] while the President cannot use his removal power to replace civil servants en masse, he can use his agency selection powers to transfer authority from one agency to another when he is dissatisfied with the performance of the first agency's civil servants."

(2) **_The Interdependence of Internal and External Checks._** Is the problem with arguments for the internal separation of powers that real internal checks on executive power don't exist, or instead that they don't exist in isolation from more traditional external constraints?

GILLIAN E. METZGER, THE INTERDEPENDENT RELATIONSHIP BETWEEN INTERNAL AND EXTERNAL SEPARATION OF POWERS, 59 Emory L.J. 423, 425–26 (2009). "[A]ttending to internal constraints alone is too narrow a focus because it excludes the crucial relationship between internal and external checks on the Executive Branch. Internal checks can be, and often are, reinforced by a variety of external forces—including not just Congress and the courts, but also state and foreign governments, international bodies, the media, and civil society organizations. Moreover, the reinforcement can also work in reverse, with internal constraints serving to enhance the ability of external forces, in particular Congress and the courts, to exert meaningful checks on the Executive Branch. Greater acknowledgment of this reciprocal relationship holds import both for fully understanding the separation of powers role played by internal constraints and for identifying effective reform strategies."

Professor AZIZ Z. HUQ agrees on the importance of the interbranch dynamic but would go further, arguing for "moving beyond the unit of the 'branch' to more granular determinants of interbranch relations." THE PRESIDENT AND THE DETAINEES, 165 U. Pa. L. Rev. 499, 506–07, 518 (2017). Drawing on a detailed case study of President Obama's effort to close Guantanamo Bay, which he concludes was "derailed by an interbranch alliance between the military bureaucracy and a legislative faction hostile to the new President's agenda," Huq contends that "bureaucratic actors are salient not because of internal dynamics but only because of their outward-facing influence on Congress and the judiciary. They are complements to, not substitutes for, interactions among the three branches. Intrabranch checks . . . are partially caused by and mediated through bureaucratic forces. Hence, legislative resistance to presidential pressure to close Guantánamo hinged on information produced by the bureaucracy" and "[l]egislative barriers to transfers depended upon the executive for their efficacy. These statutes elaborated new opportunities for bureaucratic foot-dragging and resistance to the presidential agenda."

Moving beyond this case study, Huq argues that "[t]here is a dense, and systematically significant, ecosystem of internal and external interest groups, ideological factions, and institutional actors that Jon Michaels and I elsewhere label the 'thick political surround.' Dynamic interactions between diverse elements of the thick political surround (such as bureaucrats and legislative factions) can check presidential initiatives even when bilateral interbranch interactions (between the executive branch and Congress) cannot. The account offered here thus draws attention to the institutionally granular determinants of interbranch relations. These help explain how Presidents can be thwarted even absent divided government." (quoting Aziz Z. Huq & Jon D. Michaels, The Cycles of Separation-of-Powers Jurisprudence, 126 Yale L.J. 342 (2016)).

(3) *Internal Separation of Powers and the Unitary Executive.* From a unitary executive perspective, the very idea of executive branch institutions and officials opposing presidential policy might seem constitutionally problematic. But are all of the internal checks identified above troublesome to a unitarian? Note that many—professional expertise, reputational concerns, agency offices without removal protection, interagency consultation requirements—involve what we might call "soft" constraints, rather than the hard constraints of

statutory removal independence. Moreover, might Presidents actually find internal separation of powers to be an asset, ensuring that they receive expert advice from a variety of different perspectives and that problems in agencies may be more likely to get the attention of high-level agency officials? Consider in this regard the "Team of Rivals" approach President Trump took among his closest advisors, p. 969. Trump is not the first President to adopt such an approach; President Lincoln famously incorporated leaders of diverse factions in his party into his cabinet. See Doris Kearns Goodwin, Team of Rivals: The Political Genius of Abraham Lincoln (2005). Although sparking concerns of turmoil and paralysis in the White House, O'Connell and Farber argue that a team of rivals approach can also motivate improved performance and information acquisition and ensure that important issues are escalated for presidential attention. See Agencies as Adversaries, supra, at 1425.

Do accounts suggesting that the power of internal checks come from interaction with external entities, often entities that are themselves constitutionally created and exercising their constitutional powers, alleviate or worsen the unitary executive concern? On the one hand, these accounts suggest that internal checks have limited effect independent of the constitutional separation of powers structure, as opposed to representing a novel and nonconstitutional form of constraint. On the other, they also suggest that Congress may be able to aggrandize its powers at the President's expense by building internal checks into the executive branch that it can later exploit.

(4) *The World of the Second Best.* Should the efficacy of internal separation of powers constraints be assessed in isolation or in comparison to how well external separation of powers are working today? Put differently, however limited, do internal checks on presidential power remain an essential aspect of modern administrative government under a theory of the second best? "The first-best concept of 'legislature v. executive' checks and balances must be updated to contemplate second-best 'executive v. executive' divisions," given the reality today that "major decisions are going to be made by the President." KATYAL. supra at 2316.

DAWN E. JOHNSEN, FAITHFULLY EXECUTING THE LAWS: INTERNAL LEGAL CONSTRAINTS ON EXECUTIVE POWER, 54 UCLA L. Rev. 1559 (2006): "Our recent history, . . . has demonstrated the inherent inadequacies of the courts and Congress as external checks on the President. An approach of issue-by-issue review and oversight even by a vigilant judiciary and Congress will incompletely constrain a President who, in the name of national security, is willing to undermine the rule of law. . . . The obstacles to judicial or congressional review of particular executive branch actions on matters of war and national security—especially during times of crisis—are familiar. The courts face (and create) difficult justiciability requirements, in part out of respect for executive authority and expertise. . . . With regard to Congress, oversight obviously tends to be least effective when the President's political party dominates, but . . . Congress tends to defer strongly to the commander-in-chief on matters of war and national security even in times of divided government. Legislative efforts face the possibility of a filibuster or a presidential veto. . . . When Congress already has legislated and the President unjustifiably threatens nonenforcement, Congress is left with the options of resource-intensive oversight to attempt to police compliance, indirect retribution (such as through appropriations and appointments), and the blunt instrument of impeachment. Executive branch secrecy further hinders both judicial and congressional review. . . .

"The proposition that the President's own legal advisors can provide an effective constraint on unlawful action understandably engenders a high degree of skepticism . . . Internal checks alone, of course, are insufficient. But we debase our commitment to democracy and justice if we do not view legal advice from within the executive branch as an essential component of efforts to safeguard civil liberties, the constitutional allocation of governmental authority, and the rule of law."

SECTION 4. CONSTITUTIONAL FRAMEWORKS FOR ADMINISTRATIVE ADJUDICATION

> ***STERN v. MARSHALL***
> ***Crowell v. Benson***
> ***CFTC v. Schor***
> ***Notes on the Public/Private Rights Distinction and the Right to a Jury Trial***

The judicial Power of the United States, shall be vested in one supreme Court, and in such inferior Courts as the Congress may from time to time ordain and establish. The Judges, both of the supreme and inferior Courts, shall hold their Offices during good Behavior, and shall, at stated Times, receive for their Services, a Compensation, which shall not be diminished during their Continuance in Office.

U.S. Const., Art. III, § 1

In Suits at common law, where the value in controversy shall exceed twenty dollars, the right of trial by jury shall be preserved . . .

U.S. Const., Amend. 7

The judicial power of the United States—the Article III power to resolve specified categories of "Cases" and "Controversies" particularly important to the national government—is as clearly vested by the Constitution in the federal judiciary as the legislative power is in Congress. Hence, when Congress assigns adjudication of disputes to agencies, the problem is not that the legislative branch is giving away some of its own power. Rather, it is reallocating what seemingly ought to be judicial business—a possibly hostile interference with the work of a coordinate (perhaps especially vulnerable) branch. Similar concerns can arise when Congress appears to be giving the Article III courts too much power by assigning them what appear to be non-judicial duties.

The Constitution clearly envisions substantial congressional power to structure the institutions that do the judicial work of the national government. Indeed, the text of Article III implies that Congress need not create lower federal courts at all, and the Supreme Court has long held that it may withhold parts of the Article III power from whatever lower courts it does create. Even the Supreme Court's appellate jurisdiction is subject to "such Exceptions, and . . . such Regulations as the Congress shall make." Art. III, § 2, cl. 2. From your study of constitutional law or federal courts, you may be aware that defining the extent of Congress's authority in this area is one of the knottiest questions in constitutional jurisprudence, and one the Court steadfastly avoids. But what if Congress decides to create federal institutions to adjudicate claims within the federal judicial power—but not to give those adjudicators the Article III protections of life tenure and guarantee against reduction in compensation? These institutions may be designated "courts" (e.g., the Bankruptcy Court, the Court of Federal Claims) and the adjudicators may be called "judges" or "administrative law judges," but they are not part of the judicial branch established by the Constitution. Institutions like the Court of Federal Claims are referred to as Article I courts, but most of the non-Article III institutions created to adjudicate cases under federal law are simply called agencies.

Why would Congress take such a step? LOUIS L. JAFFE and NATHANIEL NATHANSON, ADMINISTRATIVE LAW: CASES AND MATERIALS 133–36 (1961), describe the genesis of the workers' compensation board, one of the earliest forms of an adjudicating administrative agency. These boards implemented state legislative decisions to displace the common law of torts with a substantively and procedurally simpler—and more employee-favoring—statutory scheme for compensating harms suffered from accidents in the workplace.

Nothing functionally intrinsic to the scheme, at least as at first conceived, required the creation of a new agency. Indeed, in some states, New Jersey was one, workmen's compensation was originally administered by the courts, but in most states, and finally in nearly all, specialized boards were set up. The courts were thought to be hostile to the purposes of the legislation and were incidentally too expensive and too much taken up with other business. What was needed was an agency which was sympathetic, which cost the worker little or nothing and had no other business. In what sense is such an agency administrative, as distinguished from a court? We see at once that the answer must run as much in terms of our constitutional system as in generic or functional terms. A court and a compensation board are fundamentally alike in that they determine controversies under the law upon the basis of evidence received in a hearing between the parties. . . . They are different in that a court as we know it today is a court of general jurisdiction, the board is restricted to one subject. . . . [T]hough expertness came to be an important aspect of its specialization, it came perhaps as a byproduct. It was the advocate rather than the expert who was sought. . . .

Can Congress vest regulatory adjudicatory authority in bodies that are not constitutional courts without violating separation of powers? The materials that follow explore this question, one on which the Court has varied over time. Before 1982, the answer seemed pretty clearly yes, at least so long as the federal courts retained certain relationships of oversight with agency adjudication. The ruling precedent was Crowell v. Benson, p. 1015, a 1932 decision that rejected a series of constitutional challenges to the federal longshoreman and harborworkers compensation program, modeled on state workers' compensation programs. This understanding was upset in 1982, however, when a fractured Supreme Court in Northern Pipeline Construction Co. v. Marathon, p. 1022, declared the system of bankruptcy courts unconstitutional. Within a few Terms, the Court decided two cases—Thomas v. Union Carbide, p. 1023, and Commodity Future Trading Comm. v. Schor, p. 1018—that appeared to reaffirm the constitutionality of regulatory adjudication despite Northern Pipeline. But twenty-five years later the Court decided the next principal case, Stern v. Marshall, which echoed Northern Pipeline and held unconstitutional an aspect of the bankruptcy system.

STERN v. MARSHALL

Supreme Court of the United States (2011).
564 U.S. 462.

■ CHIEF JUSTICE ROBERTS delivered the opinion of the Court.

. . . This is the second time we have had occasion to weigh in on this long-running dispute between Vickie Lynn Marshall [known to the public as Anna Nicole Smith] and E. Pierce Marshall over the fortune of J. Howard Marshall II, a man believed to have been one of the richest people in Texas. . . . Known to the public as Anna Nicole Smith, Vickie was J. Howard's third wife and married him about a year before his death. Although J. Howard bestowed on Vickie many monetary and other gifts during their courtship and marriage, he did not include her in his will. Before J. Howard passed away, Vickie filed suit in Texas state probate court, asserting that Pierce—J. Howard's younger son— fraudulently induced J. Howard to sign a living trust that did not include her, even though J. Howard meant to give her half his property. Pierce denied any fraudulent activity and defended the validity of J. Howard's trust and, eventually [after J. Howard's death,], his will. . . .

After J. Howard's death, Vickie filed a petition for bankruptcy in the Central District of California. Pierce filed a complaint in that bankruptcy proceeding, contending that Vickie had defamed him by inducing her lawyers to tell members of the press that he had engaged in fraud to gain control of his father's assets. . . . Vickie responded to Pierce's initial complaint by asserting truth as a defense to the alleged defamation and by filing a counterclaim for tortious interference with the gift she expected from J. Howard. . . .[T]he Bankruptcy Court issued an order granting Vickie summary judgment on Pierce's claim for defamation [and eventually] . . . issued a judgment on Vickie's counterclaim in her favor[, awarding her . . . over $400 million in compensatory damages and $25 million in punitive damages. [In post-trial proceedings, Pierce argued that Vicki's counterclaim was not a "core proceeding" under 28 U.S.C. § 157(b)(2)(C) and hence was outside the Bankruptcy Court's statutory jurisdiction. The Court of Appeals agreed that the bankruptcy court lacked jurisdiction over Vickie's counterclaim.]

II

[The Court first held that Vicki's counterclaim was a "core proceeding" within the Bankruptcy Court's statutory jurisdiction under 28 U.S.C. § 157(b)(2)(C).]

III

A

Although we conclude that § 157(b)(2)(C) permits the Bankruptcy Court to enter final judgment on Vickie's counterclaim, Article III of the Constitution does not. . . . Article III is "an inseparable element of the constitutional system of checks and balances" that "both defines the power and protects the independence of the Judicial Branch." Northern Pipeline, 458 U.S., at 58 (plurality opinion). . . . In establishing the system of divided power in the Constitution, the Framers considered it essential that "the judiciary remain[] truly distinct from both the legislature and the executive." The Federalist No. 78, p. 466 (C. Rossiter ed. 1961) (A. Hamilton). . . . We have recognized that the three branches are not hermetically sealed from one another, see Nixon v. Administrator of General Services, 433 U.S. 425, 443 (1977), but it remains true that Article III imposes some basic limitations that the other branches may not transgress. Those limitations serve two related purposes. "Separation-of-powers principles are intended, in part, to protect each branch of government from incursion by the others. Yet the dynamic between and among the branches is not the only object of the Constitution's concern. The structural principles secured by the separation of powers protect the individual as well." Bond v. United States, 564 U.S. [211, 222] (2011) [p. 152].

Article III protects liberty not only through its role in implementing the separation of powers, but also by specifying the defining characteristics of Article III judges. . . . Article III could neither serve its purpose in the system of checks and balances nor preserve the integrity of judicial decisionmaking if the other branches of the Federal Government could confer the Government's "judicial Power" on entities outside Article III. That is why we have long recognized that, in general, Congress may not "withdraw from judicial cognizance any matter which, from its nature, is the subject of a suit at the common law, or in equity, or admiralty." Murray's Lessee v. Hoboken Land & Improvement Co., 59 U.S. 272 (1856). When a suit is made of "the stuff of the traditional actions at common law tried by the courts at Westminster in 1789," Northern Pipeline, 458 U.S. [50,] 90 [(1982)] (Rehnquist, J., concurring in judgment)[p. 1022], and is brought within the bounds of federal jurisdiction, the responsibility for deciding that suit rests with Article III judges in Article III courts. . . .

B

This is not the first time we have faced an Article III challenge to a bankruptcy court's resolution of a debtor's suit. In Northern Pipeline, we considered whether bankruptcy judges serving under the Bankruptcy Act of 1978—appointed by the President and confirmed by the Senate, but lacking the tenure and salary guarantees of Article III—could "constitutionally be vested with jurisdiction to decide [a] state-law contract claim" against an entity that was not otherwise part of the bankruptcy proceedings. 458 U.S., at 53, 87, n. 4 (plurality opinion); see id., at 89–92 (Rehnquist, J., concurring in judgment). The Court concluded that assignment of such state law claims for resolution by those judges "violates Art. III of the Constitution." Id., at 52, 87 (plurality opinion); id., at 91 (Rehnquist, J., concurring in judgment).

The plurality in Northern Pipeline recognized that there was a category of cases involving "public rights" that Congress could constitutionally assign to "legislative" courts for resolution. That opinion concluded that this "public rights" exception extended "only to matters arising between" individuals and the Government "in connection with the performance of the constitutional functions of the executive or legislative departments . . . that historically could have been determined exclusively by those" branches. Id., at 67–68 (internal quotation marks omitted). A full majority of the Court, while not agreeing on the scope of the exception, concluded that the doctrine did not encompass adjudication of the state law claim at issue in that case. Id., at 69–72; see id., at 90–91 (Rehnquist, J., concurring in judgment) . . . A full majority of Justices in Northern Pipeline also rejected the debtor's argument that the bankruptcy court's exercise of jurisdiction was constitutional because the bankruptcy judge was acting merely as an adjunct of the district court or court of appeals. . . .

C

Vickie and the dissent argue that the Bankruptcy Court's entry of final judgment on her state common law counterclaim was constitutional, despite the similarities between the bankruptcy courts under the 1978

Act and those exercising core jurisdiction under the 1984 Act. We disagree. . . .

Vickie's counterclaim cannot be deemed a matter of "public right" that can be decided outside the Judicial Branch. . . . We first recognized the category of public rights in Murray's Lessee. That case involved the Treasury Department's sale of property belonging to a customs collector who had failed to transfer payments to the Federal Government that he had collected on its behalf. Id., at 274, 275. The plaintiff . . . objected that the Treasury Department's calculation of the deficiency and sale of the property was void, because it was a judicial act that could not be assigned to the Executive under Article III. Id., at 274–275, 282–283. . . . The Court . . . recognized that ". . . there are matters, involving public rights, which may be presented in such form that the judicial power is capable of acting on them, and which are susceptible of judicial determination, but which congress may or may not bring within the cognizance of the courts of the United States, as it may deem proper." Ibid. As an example of such matters, the Court referred to "[e]quitable claims to land by the inhabitants of ceded territories" and cited cases in which land issues were conclusively resolved by Executive Branch officials. Ibid. . . . In those cases "it depends upon the will of congress whether a remedy in the courts shall be allowed at all," so Congress could limit the extent to which a judicial forum was available. . . .

Subsequent decisions from this Court contrasted cases within the reach of the public rights exception—those arising "between the Government and persons subject to its authority in connection with the performance of the constitutional functions of the executive or legislative departments"—and those that were instead matters "of private right, that is, of the liability of one individual to another under the law as defined." Crowell v. Benson, 285 U.S. 22, 50, 51 (1932).[6] . . .

Shortly after Northern Pipeline, the Court rejected the limitation of the public rights exception to actions involving the Government as a party. The Court has continued, however, to limit the exception to cases in which the claim at issue derives from a federal regulatory scheme, or in which resolution of the claim by an expert government agency is deemed essential to a limited regulatory objective within the agency's authority. In other words, it is still the case that what makes a right

---

[6]   Although the Court in Crowell went on to decide that the facts of the private dispute before it could be determined by a non-Article III tribunal in the first instance, subject to judicial review, the Court did so only after observing that the administrative adjudicator had only limited authority to make specialized, narrowly confined factual determinations regarding a particularized area of law and to issue orders that could be enforced only by action of the District Court. In other words, the agency in Crowell functioned as a true "adjunct" of the District Court. That is not the case here.

Although the dissent suggests that we understate the import of Crowell in this regard, the dissent itself recognizes—repeatedly—that Crowell by its terms addresses the determination of facts outside Article III. Crowell may well have additional significance in the context of expert administrative agencies that oversee particular substantive federal regimes, but we have no occasion to and do not address those issues today. . . .

"public" rather than private is that the right is integrally related to particular federal government action.

Our decision in Thomas v. Union Carbide Agricultural Products Co., [473 U.S. 568 (1985) p. 1023], for example, . . . held that the [FIFRA] scheme did not violate Article III, explaining that "[a]ny right to compensation . . . results from [the statute] and does not depend on or replace a right to such compensation under state law." [473 U.S. 568,] 584 [(1985)]. . . . [In] Commodity Futures Trading Commission v. Schor[, 478 U.S. 833 (1986), the Court rejected the Article III challenge] only after observing that (1) the claim and the counterclaim concerned a "single dispute"—the same account balance; (2) the CFTC's assertion of authority involved only "a narrow class of common law claims" in a " 'particularized area of law' "; (3) the area of law in question was governed by "a specific and limited federal regulatory scheme" as to which the agency had "obvious expertise"; (4) the parties had freely elected to resolve their differences before the CFTC; and (5) CFTC orders were "enforceable only by order of the district court." Id., at 844, 852–855. Most significantly, given that the customer's reparations claim before the agency and the broker's counterclaim were competing claims to the same amount, the Court repeatedly emphasized that it was "necessary" to allow the agency to exercise jurisdiction over the broker's claim, or else "the reparations procedure would have been confounded." Id., at 856.

The most recent case in which we considered application of the public rights exception—and the only case in which we have considered that doctrine in the bankruptcy context since Northern Pipeline—is Granfinanciera, S.A. v. Nordberg, 492 U.S. 33 (1989) [p. 1027]. In Granfinanciera we rejected a bankruptcy trustee's argument that a fraudulent conveyance action filed on behalf of a bankruptcy estate against a noncreditor in a bankruptcy proceeding fell within the "public rights" exception. We explained that, "[i]f a statutory right is not closely intertwined with a federal regulatory program Congress has power to enact, and if that right neither belongs to nor exists against the Federal Government, then it must be adjudicated by an Article III court." Id., at 54–55. We reasoned that fraudulent conveyance suits were "quintessentially suits at common law that more nearly resemble state law contract claims brought by a bankrupt corporation to augment the bankruptcy estate than they do creditors' hierarchically ordered claims to a pro rata share of the bankruptcy res." Id., at 56. As a consequence, we concluded that fraudulent conveyance actions were "more accurately characterized as a private rather than a public right as we have used those terms in our Article III decisions." Id., at 55.

Vickie's counterclaim—like the fraudulent conveyance claim at issue in Granfinanciera—does not fall within any of the varied formulations of the public rights exception in this Court's cases. It is . . . one under state common law between two private parties. It does not "depend[ ] on the will of congress," Murray's Lessee, supra, at 284; Congress has nothing to do with it. In addition, Vickie's claimed right to relief does not flow from a federal statutory scheme, as in Thomas, 473 U.S., at 584–585, or Atlas Roofing, 430 U.S., at 458. It is not "completely dependent upon" adjudication of a claim created by federal law, as in Schor. And in contrast to the objecting party in Schor, Pierce did not truly consent to resolution of Vickie's claim in the bankruptcy court proceedings. He had nowhere else to go if he wished to recover from Vickie's estate. See Granfinanciera, supra, at 59, n. 14.

Furthermore, the asserted authority to decide Vickie's claim is not limited to a "particularized area of the law," as in Crowell, Thomas, and Schor. Northern Pipeline, 458 U.S., at 85 (plurality opinion). We deal here not with an agency but with a court, with substantive jurisdiction reaching any area of the corpus juris. See ibid.; id., at 91 (Rehnquist, J., concurring in judgment). This is not a situation in which Congress devised an "expert and inexpensive method for dealing with a class of questions of fact which are particularly suited to examination and determination by an administrative agency specially assigned to that task." Crowell, 285 U.S., at 46; see Schor, supra, at 855–856. The "experts" in the federal system at resolving common law counterclaims such as Vickie's are the Article III courts, and it is with those courts that her claim must stay. . . .

We recognize that there may be instances in which the distinction between public and private rights—at least as framed by some of our recent cases—fails to provide concrete guidance as to whether, for example, a particular agency can adjudicate legal issues under a substantive regulatory scheme. Given the extent to which this case is so markedly distinct from the agency cases discussing the public rights exception in the context of such a regime, however, we do not in this opinion express any view on how the doctrine might apply in that different context.

What is plain here is that this case involves the most prototypical exercise of judicial power: the entry of a final, binding judgment by a court with broad substantive jurisdiction, on a common law cause of action, when the action neither derives from nor depends upon any agency regulatory regime. If such an exercise of judicial power may nonetheless be taken from the Article III Judiciary simply by deeming it part of some amorphous "public right," then Article III would be transformed from the guardian of individual liberty and separation of powers we have long recognized into mere wishful thinking. . . .

Vickie additionally argues that the Bankruptcy Court's final judgment was constitutional because bankruptcy courts under the 1984 Act are properly deemed "adjuncts" of the district courts. Brief for Petitioner 61–64. We rejected a similar argument in Northern Pipeline, and our reasoning there holds true today. . . . The new bankruptcy courts, like the old, do not "ma[k]e only specialized, narrowly confined factual determinations regarding a particularized area of law" or engage in "statutorily channeled factfinding functions." Northern Pipeline, 458 U.S., at 85. Instead, bankruptcy courts under the 1984 Act resolve "[a]ll matters of fact and law in whatever domains of the law to which" the parties' counterclaims might lead. Id., at 91 (Rehnquist, J., concurring in judgment). In addition, . . . a bankruptcy court resolving a counterclaim . . . has the power to enter "appropriate orders and judgments"— including final judgments—subject to review only if a party chooses to appeal. . . . Given that authority, a bankruptcy court can no more be deemed a mere "adjunct" of the district court than a district court can be deemed such an "adjunct" of the court of appeals. . . .

D

Finally, Vickie and her amici predict as a practical matter that restrictions on a bankruptcy court's ability to hear and finally resolve compulsory counterclaims will create significant delays and impose additional costs on the bankruptcy process. It goes without saying that "the fact that a given law or procedure is efficient, convenient, and useful in facilitating functions of government, standing alone, will not save it if it is contrary to the Constitution." INS v. Chadha, 462 U.S. 919, 944 (1983). In addition, we are not convinced that the practical consequences of such limitations on the authority of bankruptcy courts to enter final judgments are as significant as Vickie and the dissent suggest. . . .

If our decision today does not change all that much, then why the fuss? Is there really a threat to the separation of powers where Congress has conferred the judicial power outside Article III only over certain counterclaims in bankruptcy? The short but emphatic answer is yes. A statute may no more lawfully chip away at the authority of the Judicial Branch than it may eliminate it entirely. . . . We cannot compromise the integrity of the system of separated powers and the role of the Judiciary in that system, even with respect to challenges that may seem innocuous at first blush.

■ JUSTICE SCALIA, concurring.

I agree with the Court's interpretation of our Article III precedents, and I accordingly join its opinion. I adhere to my view, however, that— our contrary precedents notwithstanding—"a matter of public rights . . . must at a minimum arise between the government and others," Granfinanciera, S.A. v. Nordberg, 492 U.S. 33, 65 (1989) (SCALIA, J., concurring in part and concurring in judgment) . . . Leaving aside certain adjudications by federal administrative agencies, which are governed (for better or worse) by our landmark decision in Crowell v. Benson, in my view an Article III judge is required in all federal adjudications, unless there is a firmly established historical practice to the contrary. . . . Vicki points to no historical practice that authorizes a non-Article III judge to adjudicate a counterclaim of the sort at issue here.

■ JUSTICE BREYER, with whom JUSTICE GINSBURG, JUSTICE SOTOMAYOR, and JUSTICE KAGAN, join dissenting.

. . . My disagreement with the majority's conclusion stems in part from my disagreement about the way in which it interprets, or at least emphasizes, certain precedents. In my view, the majority overstates the current relevance of statements this Court made in an 1856 case, Murray's Lessee v. Hoboken Land & Improvement Co., and it overstates the importance of an analysis that did not command a Court majority in Northern Pipeline . . . and that was subsequently disavowed. At the same time, I fear the Court understates the importance of a watershed opinion widely thought to demonstrate the constitutional basis for the current authority of administrative agencies to adjudicate private disputes, namely, Crowell v. Benson. And it fails to follow the analysis that this Court more recently has held applicable to the evaluation of claims of a kind before us here, namely, claims that a congressional delegation of adjudicatory authority violates separation-of-powers principles derived from Article III. See Thomas v. Union Carbide Agricultural Products Co.; Commodity Futures Trading Comm'n v. Schor. . . .

Crowell has been hailed as "the greatest of the cases validating administrative adjudication." Bator, The Constitution as Architecture: Legislative and Administrative Courts Under Article III, 65 Ind. L.J. 233, 251 (1990). Yet, in a footnote, the majority distinguishes Crowell as a case in which the Court upheld the delegation of adjudicatory authority to an administrative agency simply because the agency's power to make the "specialized, narrowly confined factual determinations" at issue arising in a "particularized area of law," made the agency a "true 'adjunct' of the District Court." Were Crowell's holding as narrow as the majority suggests, one could question the validity of Congress' delegation of authority to adjudicate disputes among private parties to other agencies such as the National Labor Relations Board, the Commodity Futures Trading Commission, the Surface Transportation Board, and the Department of Housing and Urban Development . . .

The majority, in my view, overemphasizes the precedential effect of the plurality opinion in Northern Pipeline. . . . Rather than leaning so heavily on the approach taken by the plurality in Northern Pipeline, I would look to this Court's more recent Article III cases Thomas and Schor—cases that commanded a clear majority. In both cases the Court took a more pragmatic approach to the constitutional question. It sought to determine whether, in the particular instance, the challenged delegation of adjudicatory authority posed a genuine and serious threat that one branch of Government sought to aggrandize its own constitutionally delegated authority by encroaching upon a field of authority that the Constitution assigns exclusively to another branch. . . .

This case law . . . requires us to determine pragmatically whether a congressional delegation of adjudicatory authority to a non-Article III judge violates the separation-of-powers principles inherent in Article III. That is to say, we must determine through an examination of certain relevant factors whether that delegation constitutes a significant encroachment by the Legislative or Executive Branches of Government upon the realm of authority that Article III reserves for exercise by the Judicial Branch of Government. Those factors include (1) the nature of the claim to be adjudicated; (2) the nature of the non-Article III tribunal; (3) the extent to which Article III courts exercise control over the proceeding; (4) the presence or absence of the parties' consent; and (5) the nature and importance of the legislative purpose served by the grant of adjudicatory authority to a tribunal with judges who lack Article III's tenure and compensation protections. The presence of "private rights" does not automatically determine the outcome of the question but requires a more "searching" examination of the relevant factors. Insofar as the majority would apply more formal standards, it simply disregards recent, controlling precedent.

Applying Schor's approach here, I conclude that the delegation of adjudicatory authority before us is constitutional. . . . First, I concede that the nature of the claim to be adjudicated argues against my conclusion. Vickie Marshall's counterclaim—a kind of tort suit— resembles "a suit at the common law." Murray's Lessee, 18 How., at 284. . . . At the same time the significance of this factor is mitigated here by the fact that bankruptcy courts often decide claims that similarly resemble various common-law actions. . . . Second, the nature of the non-Article III tribunal argues in favor of constitutionality. That is because the tribunal is made up of judges who enjoy considerable protection from improper political influence. Unlike the 1978 Act which provided for the appointment of bankruptcy judges by the President with the advice and consent of the Senate, current law provides that the federal courts of appeals appoint federal bankruptcy judges. . . . Third, the control exercised by Article III judges over bankruptcy proceedings argues in favor of constitutionality. Article III judges control and supervise the bankruptcy court's determinations—at least to the same degree that Article III judges supervised the agency's determinations in Crowell, if not more so. Any party may appeal those determinations to the federal district court, where the federal judge will review all determinations of fact for clear error and will review all determinations of law de novo [and] may "withdraw, in whole or in part, any case or proceeding referred [to the Bankruptcy Court] . . . on its own motion or on timely motion of any party, for cause shown." 28 U.S.C. § 157(d) . . . Fourth, the fact that the parties have consented to Bankruptcy Court jurisdiction argues in favor of constitutionality, and strongly so. Fifth, the nature and importance of the legislative purpose served by the grant of adjudicatory authority to bankruptcy tribunals argues strongly in favor of constitutionality.

SIGNIFICANT CASES

CROWELL v. BENSON
285 U.S. 22 (1932).

This case, on the threshold of the New Deal era, was the Court's first important engagement with the constitutionality of using agencies as primary adjudicators. The Longshoremen's and Harbor Workers' Act provided a federal tort-substitute for injuries arising in certain maritime employments. Crowell, deputy commissioner of the United States Employees' Compensation Commission, ordered Benson to compensate injured Knudsen. Benson denied that Knudsen was acting as his employee at the time of injury. Under the Act, Commission decisions were reviewable in the district courts, which had plenary authority to redecide any questions of law but only limited authority to review conclusions of fact. Benson claimed that this scheme violated both due process and Article III. The District Court below held that a de novo hearing on the facts and law was constitutionally required and ruled that Knudsen was not an employee of Benson.

■ CHIEF JUSTICE HUGHES wrote for the Court:

"Apart from cases involving constitutional rights to be appropriately enforced by proceedings in court, there can be no doubt that the Act contemplates that as to questions of fact, arising with respect to injuries to employees within the purview of the Act, the findings of the deputy commissioner, supported by evidence and within the scope of his authority, shall be final. To hold otherwise would be to defeat the purpose of the legislation to furnish a prompt, continuous, expert, and inexpensive method for dealing with a class of questions of fact which are peculiarly suited to examination and determination by an administrative agency assigned to that task. The object is to secure within the prescribed limits of the employer's liability an immediate investigation and a sound practical judgment, and the efficacy of the plan depends upon the finality of the determinations of fact with respect to the circumstances, nature, extent, and consequences of the employee's injuries and the amount of compensation that should be awarded. . . . The use of the administrative method for these purposes, assuming due notice, proper opportunity to be heard, and that findings are based upon evidence, falls easily within the principle of the decisions sustaining similar procedure against objections under the due process clauses of the Fifth and Fourteenth Amendments. . . .

"The contention based upon the judicial power of the United States . . . (Const. Art. III) presents a distinct question. . . . The question in the instant case, in this aspect, can be deemed to relate only to determinations of fact. . . . The Congress did not attempt to define questions of law, and the generality of the description leaves no doubt of the intention to reserve to the Federal court full authority to pass upon all matters which this Court had held to fall within that category. There is thus no attempt to interfere with, but rather provision is made to facilitate, the exercise by the court of its jurisdiction to deny effect to any administrative finding which is without evidence or 'contrary to the indisputable character of the evidence,' or where the hearing is 'inadequate,' or 'unfair,' or arbitrary in any respect. . . .

"As to determinations of fact, the distinction is at once apparent between cases of private right and those which arise between the Government and persons subject to its authority in connection with the performance of the constitutional functions of the executive or legislative departments. The Court referred to this distinction in Murray's Lessee v. Hoboken Land and Improvement Company, 18 How. 272, pointing out that 'there are matters, involving public rights, which may be presented in such form that the judicial power is capable of acting on them, and which are susceptible to judicial determination, but which Congress may or may not bring within the cognizance of the courts of the United States, as it may deem proper.' Thus the Congress, in exercising the powers confided to it, may establish 'legislative' courts (as distinguished from 'constitutional courts in which the judicial power conferred by the Constitution can be deposited') which are . . . to serve as special tribunals 'to examine and determine various matters, arising between the government and others, which from their nature do not require judicial determination and yet are susceptible of it.' But 'the mode of determining matters of this class is completely within congressional control. Congress may reserve to itself the power to decide, may delegate that power to executive officers, or may commit it to judicial tribunals.' Ex parte Bakelite Corporation, 279 U.S. 438, 451. Familiar illustrations of administrative agencies created for the determination of such matters are found in connection with the exercise of the congressional power as to interstate and foreign commerce taxation, immigration, the public lands, public health, the facilities of the post office, pensions and payments to veterans.

"The present case does not fall within the categories just described but is one of private right, that is, of the liability of one individual to another under the law as defined. But in cases of that sort, there is no requirement that, in order to maintain the essential attributes of the judicial power, all determinations of fact in constitutional courts shall be made by judges. On the common law side of the Federal courts, the aid of juries is not only deemed appropriate but is required by the Constitution itself. In cases of equity and admiralty, it is historic practice to call to the assistance of the courts, without the consent of the parties, masters and commissioners or assessors, to pass upon certain classes of questions, as, for example, to take and state an account or to find the amount of damages. While the reports of masters and commissioners in such cases are essentially of an advisory nature, it has not been the practice to disturb their findings when they are properly based upon evidence, in the absence of errors of law, and the parties have no right to demand that the court shall redetermine the facts thus found. . . .

"The statute has a limited application, being confined to the relation of master and servant, and the method of determining the questions of fact, which arise in the routine of making compensation awards to employees under the Act, is necessary to its effective enforcement. . . . For the purposes stated, we are unable to find any constitutional obstacle to the action of the Congress in availing itself of a method shown by experience to be essential in order to apply its standards to the thousands of cases involved, thus relieving the courts of a most serious burden while preserving their complete authority to insure the proper application of the law.

"What has been said thus far relates to the determination of claims of employees within the purview of the act. A different question is presented where the determinations of fact are fundamental or 'jurisdictional,' in the sense that their existence is a condition precedent to the operation of the statutory scheme. These fundamental requirements are that the injury occurs upon the navigable waters of the United States, and that the relation of master and servant exists. These conditions are indispensable to the application of the statute, not only because the Congress has so provided explicitly . . . but also because the power of the Congress to enact the legislation turns upon the existence of these conditions. . . .

"In relation to these basic facts, the question is not the ordinary one as to the propriety of provision for administrative determinations. Nor have we simply the question of due process in relation to notice and hearing. It is rather a question of the appropriate maintenance of the federal judicial power in requiring the observance of constitutional restrictions. It is the question whether the Congress may substitute for constitutional courts, in which the judicial power of the United States is vested, an administrative agency—in this instance a single deputy commissioner—for the final determination of the existence of the facts upon which the enforcement of the constitutional rights of the citizen depend. The recognition of the utility and convenience of administrative agencies for the investigation and finding of facts within their proper province, and the support of their authorized action, does not require the conclusion that there is no limitation of their use, and that the Congress could completely oust the courts of all determinations of fact by vesting the authority to make them with finality in its own instrumentalities or in the executive department. That would be to sap the judicial power as it exists under the federal Constitution, and to establish a government of a bureaucratic character alien to our system, wherever fundamental rights depend, as not infrequently they do depend, upon the facts, and finality as to facts becomes in effect finality in law. . . . In cases brought to enforce constitutional rights, the judicial power of the United States necessarily extends to the independent determination of all questions, both of fact and law, necessary to the performance of that supreme function."[56]

JUSTICE BRANDEIS, joined by Justices Stone and Roberts, dissented, arguing that Article III had no "bearing upon the question presented" and that "[i]f there be any controversy to which the judicial power extends that may not be subjected to the conclusive determination of administrative bodies or federal legislative courts, it is not because of [Article III] . . . but because, under certain circumstances, the constitutional requirement of due process is a requirement of judicial process."

COMMODITY FUTURES TRADING COMMISSION v. SCHOR
478 U.S. 833 (1986)

The Commodity Futures Trading Commission is an independent regulatory commission that regulates and oversees the commodities markets. Section 14 provides that any person injured by violations of the Commodities Exchange Act or CFTC regulations may apply to the Commission for an order directing the offender to pay reparations to the complainant and may enforce that order in federal district court. The remedy is, however, non-exclusive; no rule prevents such a plaintiff from seeking arbitration or bringing a judicial action.

Schor traded commodities futures through a broker at Conti, a firm regulated by the CFTC, and owed Conti a substantial sum as a result of trades. Schor sought reparations before the CFTC, alleging that this debt was the result of Conti's violations of the CEA, and Conti counterclaimed to recover Schor's debt. The ALJ in Schor's reparations proceeding ruled in Conti's favor on both Schor's claims and Conti's counterclaims and rejected Schor's subsequently raised challenge that it lacked jurisdiction over the counterclaims.

JUSTICE O'CONNOR delivered the opinion of the Court. She first addressed whether Schor had waived any Article III claim by initiating the action before the CFTC. Identifying Article III, as "serving both to protect the role of the independent judiciary within the constitutional scheme of tripartite government and to safeguard litigants right to have claims decided before judges who are free from potential domination by other branches of government" (internal quotations omitted), she held that the latter guarantee "of an impartial and independent federal adjudication" was a personal right subject to waiver, and Schor indisputably had waived it. But to the extent Article III § 1's structural role was implicated in a given case, "notions of consent and waiver cannot

---

[56] [Ed.] The jurisdictional facts aspect of Crowell has been especially controversial. The distinction between "jurisdictional" (or "constitutional") and other facts has been elusive at best. Although never formally overruled, the proposition that Article III courts must make a de novo determination of such facts is rarely replied upon. See generally Henry P. Monaghan, Constitutional Fact Review, 85 Colum. L. Rev. 229, 249–56 (1985).

be dispositive because the limitations serve institutional interests that the parties cannot be expected to protect."

"... Schor claims that [Article III] prohibit[s] Congress from authorizing the initial adjudication of common law counterclaims by the CFTC, an administrative agency whose adjudicatory officers do not enjoy the tenure and salary protections embodied in Article III. . . . Although our precedents in this area do not admit of easy synthesis, they do establish that the resolution of claims such as Schor's cannot turn on conclusory reference to the language of Article III. Rather, the constitutionality of a given congressional delegation of adjudicative functions to a non-Article III body must be assessed by reference to the purposes underlying the requirements of Article III. This inquiry, in turn, is guided by the principle that 'practical attention to substance rather than doctrinaire reliance on formal categories should inform application of Article III.' Thomas v. Union Carbide Agricultural Products Co., 473 U.S. 568, 587 (1985) [p. 1023]. . . .

"... In determining the extent to which a given congressional decision to authorize the adjudication of Article III business in a non-Article III tribunal impermissibly threatens the institutional integrity of the Judicial Branch, the Court has declined to adopt formalistic and unbending rules. Although such rules might lend a greater degree of coherence to this area of the law, they might also unduly constrict Congress' ability to take needed and innovative action pursuant to its Article I powers. Thus, in reviewing Article III challenges, we have weighed a number of factors, none of which has been deemed determinative, with an eye to the practical effect that the congressional action will have on the constitutionally assigned role of the federal judiciary. Among the factors upon which we have focused are the extent to which the essential attributes of judicial power' are reserved to Article III courts, and, conversely, the extent to which the non-Article III forum exercises the range of jurisdiction and powers normally vested only in Article III courts, the origins and importance of the right to be adjudicated, and the concerns that drove Congress to depart from the requirements of Article III.

"... [T]he congressional scheme [here] does not impermissibly intrude on the province of the judiciary. The CFTC's adjudicatory powers depart from the traditional agency model in just one respect: the CFTC's jurisdiction over common law counterclaims. While wholesale importation of concepts of pendent or ancillary jurisdiction into the agency context may create greater constitutional difficulties, we decline to endorse an absolute prohibition on such jurisdiction out of fear of where some hypothetical 'slippery slope' may deposit us. . . . The CFTC, like the agency in Crowell v. Benson deals only with a particularized area of law, whereas the jurisdiction of the bankruptcy courts found unconstitutional in Northern Pipeline extended to broadly 'all civil proceedings arising under title 11 or arising in or related to cases under title 11.' CFTC orders, like those of the agency in Crowell, but unlike those of the bankruptcy courts are enforceable only by order of the District Court. CFTC orders are also reviewed under the same 'weight of the evidence' standard sustained in Crowell, rather than the more deferential 'clearly erroneous' standard found lacking in Northern Pipeline. The legal rulings of the CFTC, like the legal determinations of the agency in Crowell, are subject to de novo review. Finally, the CFTC, unlike the bankruptcy courts under the 1978 Act, does not exercise 'all ordinary powers of district courts,' and thus may not, for instance, preside over jury trials or issue writs of habeas corpus.

"Of course, the nature of the claim has significance. . . . [It] is a 'private' right for which state law provides the rule of decision. It is therefore a claim of the kind assumed to be at the 'core' of matters normally reserved to Article III courts. . . . Yet this conclusion does not end our inquiry; just as this Court has rejected any attempt to make determinative for Article III purposes the distinction between public rights and private rights, there is no reason inherent in separation of powers principles to accord the state law character of a claim talismanic power in Article III inquiries. . . . Accordingly, where private, common law rights are at stake, our examination of the congressional attempt to control the manner in which those rights are adjudicated has been searching. In this case, however, . . .[i]t is clear that Congress has not attempted to 'withdraw from judicial cognizance' the determination of Conti's right to the sum represented by the debit balance in Schor's account. Congress gave the CFTC the authority to adjudicate such matters, but the decision to invoke this forum is left entirely to the parties and the power of the federal judiciary to take jurisdiction of these matters is unaffected. . . . This is not to say, of course, that if Congress created a phalanx of non-Article III tribunals equipped to handle the entire business of the Article III courts without any Article III supervision or control and without evidence of valid and specific legislative necessities, the fact that the parties had the election to proceed in their forum of choice would necessarily save the scheme from constitutional attack. But this case obviously bears no resemblance to such a scenario . . .

". . . [The] reparations scheme itself is of unquestioned constitutional validity. It was only to ensure the effectiveness of this scheme that Congress authorized the CFTC to assert jurisdiction over common law counterclaims. . . . It also bears emphasis that . . . CFTC adjudication of common law counterclaims is incidental to, and completely dependent upon, adjudication of reparations claims created by federal law, and in actual fact is limited to claims arising out of the same transaction or occurrence as the reparations claim."

JUSTICE BRENNAN dissented, joined by Justice Marshall: "Article III's prophylactic protections were intended to prevent . . . abdication to claims of legislative convenience. The Court requires that the legislative interest in convenience and efficiency be weighed against the competing interest in judicial independence. In doing so, the Court pits an interest the benefits of which are immediate, concrete, and easily understood against one, the benefits of which are almost entirely prophylactic, and thus often seem remote and not worth the cost in any single case. Thus, while this balancing creates the illusion of objectivity and ineluctability, in fact the result was foreordained, because the balance is weighted against judicial independence. The danger of the Court's balancing approach is, of course, that as individual cases accumulate in which the Court finds that the short-term benefits of efficiency outweigh the long-term benefits of judicial independence, the protections of Article III will be eviscerated. . . ."

NOTES

(1) ***Methodology: Formalist or Functionalist?*** There is a sharp methodological divide between Stern on the one hand and Crowell and Schor on the other. Stern takes on the whole a very formalist approach. The majority insists on a strict separation of public and private rights, treating the public rights and adjunct lines as distinct analyses. Although acknowledging that administrative adjudication may be necessary for a regulatory scheme like that in Schor to function, the majority dismisses efficiency concerns about splitting claims in bankruptcy and warns about allowing even seemingly innocuous deviations from Article III.

Crowell similarly treats the public rights and adjunct lines as distinct lines of inquiry but takes an openly functionalist approach in assessing the role of the Employees' Compensation Commission, justifying deference to the commission's ordinary factual determinations as necessary so as not to "defeat the purpose of the legislation." Schor meanwhile is even more functionalist: it counts the public or private nature of the right and the extent to which a non-Article III court is functioning as an adjunct as simply factors to be weighed against others in an overall balancing test and expressly rejects adopting "formalistic and unbending rules" out of fear "they might also unduly constrict Congress."

Which approach, formalism or functionalism, is the appropriate stance to take in assessing possible encroachments on Article III? Note that the balancing test of Schor bears a close resemblance to Morrison p. 934, which assesses whether restrictions on the President "are of such a nature that they impede the President's ability to perform his constitutional duty." Both are highly functionalistic analyses and polar opposites to the formalistic approach to congressional power the Court took in Chadha, p. 831, or Bowsher, p. 860—the latter decided on the same day as Schor.

Are questions of the scope of presidential and judicial power distinguishable from legislative power in a way that might explain this difference? Does the broad availability of judicial review mean that the Article III courts will be able to protect their turf if need be, making a case-by-case balancing approach more appropriate? Or, as Chief Justice Roberts suggests in Stern (and Justice Brennan argued before him in Northern

Pipeline), is there a need to prophylactically enforce Article III's ambit strictly, because in each individual case the incursion on Article III will seem innocuous but the aggregate effect may eviscerate the courts?

Significantly, just as Stern takes a more formalistic approach to judicial power than Schor, Free Enterprise takes a much more formalistic approach to presidential power than Morrison. Thus, perhaps the best explanation of these methodological changes is variation in the composition of the Court and the Roberts Court's predilection for a more formalist analysis.

(2) **Does Stern Call Crowell and Schor into Question?** These methodological differences underlie Justice Breyer's concern that Stern calls Crowell and Schor into question. Reaction to Stern among administrative law scholars has generally been to emphasize the several places Chief Justice Roberts seems careful to distinguish the bankruptcy context from regulatory adjudication—and, accordingly, to predict that the constitutionality of garden-variety administrative adjudication remains solidly established by the Crowell/Schor line of precedent.

Is this wishful thinking? What is the significance of Stern's bringing 19th century decisions back into the foreground? Is Justice Breyer's concern about the fate of Crowell overstated? What do you make of the majority's description, in a footnote, of Crowell as a situation in which "the agency . . . functioned as a true 'adjunct' of the District Court"? It remains generally true that agency adjudications result in "orders that could be enforced only by action of" an Article III court. But can contemporary regulatory adjudication be defined as "only limited authority to make specialized, narrowly confined factual determinations regarding a particularized area of law"?

(3) **Is Bankruptcy Special?** One important distinction of Stern from Schor and Crowell is that Stern did not involve administrative adjudication but instead arose in bankruptcy. And it relied heavily on NORTHERN PIPELINE CONSTRUCTION CO. v. MARATHON PIPE LINE CO., 458 U.S. 50 (1982), also a bankruptcy case, involving a bankruptcy court's assertion of jurisdiction over a state law contract claim. Writing for a plurality, JUSTICE BRENNAN began by identifying three narrow categories where non-Article III adjudication historically had been allowed: (i) the creation of "territorial courts" in "geographical areas in which no State operated as sovereign"; (ii) the establishment of "courts-martial," which "involves a constitutional grant of power that has been historically understood as giving the political Branches of Government extraordinary control over the precise subject matter at issue"; and (iii) legislative courts and administrative agencies created by Congress to adjudicate cases involving "public rights," which required that the government be a party. In invalidating the bankruptcy court's jurisdiction, his opinion emphasized the breadth of jurisdiction given to bankruptcy courts, arguing that Congress had vested "bankruptcy judges with powers over Northern's state-created right that far exceed the powers that it has vested in administrative agencies that adjudicate only rights of Congress' own creation." Chief Justice Rehnquist, concurring, emphasized the state law nature of the right at issue, stating that "[n]one of [the Courts prior] cases has gone so far as to sanction the type of adjudication to which Marathon will be subjected against its will."

One way to read Northern Pipeline and Stern is that they turn on unique features of bankruptcy: the broad range of claims that bankruptcy courts can hear, the immediate enforceability of their determinations, and the limited review of core bankruptcy claims by Article III courts. By contrast, administrative adjudicators often have a limited scope of jurisdiction, hearing only claims related to a specific area of expertise, and their decisions are often not self-enforcing, so agencies have to go into court for an order of enforcement. Should Stern be viewed primarily as a bankruptcy case?

Is bankruptcy more threatening to Article III values of independence than administrative adjudication, or vice versa? Note that bankruptcy courts work closely with district courts and are often located at federal courthouses; administrative adjudicators, by contrast, are agency employees. If you've studied the APA's provisions on adjudication (Ch. V), you know that the APA allows the head of an agency to review ALJ determinations de novo. Does that allow in too much room for agency bias? For a recent discussion of Article III's stakes in bankruptcy and a proposal for a new approach, see Anthony J. Casey & Aziz Z. Huq, The Article III Problem in Bankruptcy, 82 U. Chi. L. Rev. 1155 (2015).

(4) ***The Evolving Meaning of Public Rights.*** Although the cases all invoke the category of "public right," do they define public rights the same way? Crowell specified that a public right was one involving the government as a party, a definition that Northern Pipeline adopted too.

But the Court took a different approach in THOMAS V. UNION CARBIDE AGRICULTURAL PRODUCTS CO., 473 U.S. 568 (1985). At issue in Thomas were the binding arbitration provisions of the Federal Insecticide, Fungicide and Rodenticide Act (FIFRA). FIFRA authorizes EPA to use one manufacturer's data about health, safety, and environmental effects of its product in considering another manufacturer's later application to register a similar product, but it requires the follow-on registrant to compensate the initial manufacturer for use of this data and provides for binding arbitration when the parties cannot agree on amount.

JUSTICE O'CONNOR'S opinion for the Court rejected the claim that this arrangement violated Article III, holding that: "Congress, acting for a valid legislative purpose pursuant to its constitutional powers under Article I, may create a seemingly 'private' right that is so closely integrated into a public regulatory scheme as to be a matter appropriate for agency resolution with limited involvement by the Article III judiciary." In reaching this conclusion, she argued that "[t]he enduring lesson of Crowell is that practical attention to substance, rather than doctrinaire reliance on formal categories, should inform application of Article III. . . . If the identity of the parties alone determined the requirements of Article III, under appellees' theory, the constitutionality of many quasi-adjudicative activities carried on by administrative agencies involving claims between individuals would be thrown into doubt. . . . [T]he right created by FIFRA is not a purely 'private' right, but bears many of the characteristics of a 'public' right. Use of a registrant's data to support a follow-on registration serves a public purpose as an integral part of a program safeguarding the public health." No one dissented. Justice Brennan (the author of the Northern Pipeline plurality) concurred, noting: "In one sense the question of proper compensation . . . is . . . a dispute about 'the liability of one individual to another under the law as defined.' Crowell v. Benson. But the dispute arises in the context of a federal regulatory scheme that virtually occupies the field. . . ."

Although Schor deemed Conti's counterclaim a private right, it relied heavily on Thomas and echoed Thomas's pragmatic approach in refusing to draw a strict line between public and private rights. Granfinanciera, S.A. v. Paul C. Nordberg, 492 U.S. 33 (1989) (p. 1027), was a subsequent decision involving the Seventh Amendment that deviated from Thomas and Schor in putting heavy emphasis on a sharp distinction between public rights and private rights. But it nonetheless followed Thomas in defining a public right as a "right that is so closely integrated into a public regulatory scheme as to be a matter appropriate for agency resolution with limited involvement by the Article III judiciary."

How does Stern define public right? Note that Stern, too, rejects the limitation of public right to matters in which the government is a party. In describing the public rights exception, Chief Justice Roberts states that it is limited "to cases in which the claim at issue derives from a federal regulatory scheme, or in which resolution of the claim by an expert government agency is deemed essential to a limited regulatory objective within the agency's authority. In other words, it is still the case that what makes a right 'public' rather than private is that the right is integrally related to particular federal government action."

If the Court continues to define public right this broadly, how constraining will the decision be for administrative adjudication? Where would the counterclaim in Schor fall under Stern's categorization: Would it still be deemed a matter of private right, as the Schor Court held? Or might it now be considered public because it was "integrally related to particular federal government action" and "resolution of the claim by an expert government agency is . . . essential to a limited regulatory objective within the agency's authority"?

For a thoughtful examination of the historical meaning of public and private rights, see Caleb Nelson, Adjudication in the Political Branches, 107 Colum. L. Rev. 559 (2007).

(5) *The Importance of Judicial Review.* How important is it that a non-Article III court's determination be subject to judicial review, even if limited? The Court's decisions vary somewhat on this point, but all give the availability (or not) of judicial review substantial weight. The availability of judicial review was central to upholding the administrative adjudication at issue in Crowell under the adjunct theory and also emphasized by the Court in applying Schor's balancing test. Moreover, both the Northern Pipeline plurality and Stern majority emphasized the limited review of the bankruptcy court's determinations—as did the Stern dissent, maintaining that the substantial degree of Article III oversight counted towards allowing the bankruptcy court to adjudicate.

Thomas is a slight outlier. The Court there considered the fact that "the FIFRA arbitration scheme incorporates its own system of internal sanctions and relies only tangentially, if at all, on the Judicial Branch for enforcement" as counting towards its constitutionality. It stated that "[t]he danger of Congress or the Executive encroaching on the Article III judicial powers is at a minimum when no unwilling defendant is subjected to judicial enforcement power as a result of the agency 'adjudication.' " But the Thomas Court proceeded to underscore that "FIFRA limits but does not preclude review of the arbitration proceeding by an Article III court. We conclude that, in the circumstances, the review afforded preserves the 'appropriate exercise of the judicial function.' Crowell, 285 U.S. at 54. FIFRA at a minimum allows private parties to secure Article III review of the arbitrator's 'findings and determination' for fraud, misconduct, or misrepresentation. This provision protects against arbitrators who abuse or exceed their powers or willfully misconstrue their mandate under the governing law. Moreover, review of constitutional error is preserved, and FIFRA, therefore, does not obstruct whatever judicial review might be required by due process."

According to Professor Richard H. Fallon, Jr., in Of Legislative Courts, Administrative Agencies, and Article III, 101 Harv. L. Rev. 915 (1988), judicial review is the key to the constitutionality of non-Article III adjudication: "A better accommodation of article III with the functional imperatives of contemporary government focuses on the reviewability of the decisions of non-article III federal tribunals by article III courts. Thus the central claim of my appellate review theory: adequately searching appellate review of the judgments of legislative courts and administrative agencies is both necessary and sufficient to satisfy the requirements of article III." Do you agree?

Professor Mila Sohoni, in AGENCY ADJUDICATION AND JUDICIAL NONDELEGATION: AN ARTICLE III CANON, 107 Nw. U. L. Rev. 1569, 1573–75 (2013), argues that "courts should be guided by the Article III divide between public and private rights in determining the extent of their deference in adjudicative contexts." Currently, "[t]he extent of deference courts owe to agencies does not vary if the underlying right being adjudicated is 'public' or 'private' in the Article III sense of those terms. . . . Article III jurisprudence should prompt us to question that uniformity of approach. . . . The principle derivable from Article III jurisprudence is that in private rights cases the judicial review available to an Article III court must be meaningful. . . . Specifically, federal courts should be more stringent in policing agency reasoning, agency fact-finding procedure, and the factual basis for the agency action in private rights contexts than in public rights contexts. On fact and mixed questions, the federal court's review must be functionally much closer to de novo review if courts are to honor Article III values when reviewing initial agency adjudication of private rights."

(6) ***Stern's Aftermath.*** The Court continues to try to settle the waters roiled by Stern. In Executive Benefits Insurance Agency v. Arkinson, 134 S.Ct. 2165 (2014), the Court unanimously held that when Article III does not permit a bankruptcy court to enter final judgment on a core bankruptcy claim, that court may issue proposed findings and conclusions to be reviewed

de novo by a district court. But it left unresolved whether consent to litigate in the bankruptcy court can obviate an Article III objection.

That question was addressed the following term, in WELLNESS INTERNATIONAL NETWORK LTD. V. SHARIF, 135 S.Ct. 1932 (2015), which held that Article III permits bankruptcy judges to adjudicate Stern claims if the parties knowingly and voluntarily consent. The Seventh Circuit had held that a Stern claim could not be waived. Justice Sotomayor's opinion for a 6–3 court repeatedly invoked Schor and Thomas: Schor established that "[t]he entitlement to an Article III adjudicator is a personal right and thus ordinarily subject to waiver," and "allowing Article I adjudicators to decide claims submitted to them by consent does not offend the separation of powers so long as Article III courts retain supervisory authority over the process." (internal quotations omitted). The question for the Court thus was "whether allowing bankruptcy courts to decide Stern claims by consent would 'impermissibly threate[n] the institutional integrity of the Judicial Branch,' . . . [a] question that must be decided not by 'formalistic and unbending rules,' but 'with an eye to the practical effect that the' practice 'will have on the constitutionally assigned role of the federal judiciary.'" (quoting Schor). Stern was distinguished as a case where consent was founding to be lacking.

Emphasizing the power District Courts have to refer or withdraw matters from bankruptcy court jurisdiction, Justice Sotomayor's opinion concluded that "separation of powers concerns are diminished" when, as here, "the decision to invoke [a non-Article III] forum is left entirely to the parties and the power of the federal judiciary to take jurisdiction" remains in place. The opinion, joined by Justices Kennedy, Ginsburg, Breyer, and Kagan, also held that consent need not be express and urged reading Stern narrowly. Justice Alito agreed that express consent was possible but would have reserved the issue of implied consent.

Chief Justice Roberts dissented, joined by Justice Scalia and (in part) Justice Thomas. He would have resolved the case on the "narrow" ground that the particular kind of claim involved was in fact not "the stuff of the traditional actions at common law tried by the courts at Westminster in 1789" (quoting Stern). He strongly disagreed with the majority that consent of the parties could cure an Article III violation and criticized the majority for its "imaginative reconstruction of Stern." Justice Thomas wrote separately to argue that the consent question was more complex than either of the other opinions indicated. After a determined effort to untangle the "historical understanding" of public and private rights, Justice Thomas concluded that "the inalienable core of the judicial power vested by Article III in the federal courts is the power to adjudicate private rights disputes." But, given parties may consent to "dispose of their own private rights freely," just as they may waive their right to a jury trial, it was still necessary to determine if there are "other aspects of the adjudication that demand the exercise of the judicial power, such as the entry of a final judgment enforceable without any further action by an Article III court." Justice Thomas also raised a question about Congress's authority to establish the bankruptcy courts. The Bankruptcy Clause does not expressly authorize the establishment of courts, and Thomas expresses wariness at concluding that every grant of lawmaking authority includes the power to establish legislative courts. Closer attention to "historical understandings of the bankruptcy power" is required. Hence, Justice Thomas would reserve the consent question until the parties and Court can fully consider its complexities.

(7) ***Article III and SEC Adjudication.*** The recent constitutional attacks on increased SEC use of administrative adjudication—which have primarily focused on claims based on the Appointments Clause (p. 886) and removal power (p. 945)—have included arguments that such adjudication violates Article III. DAVID ZARING, ENFORCEMENT DISCRETION AT THE SEC, 94 Tex. L. Rev. 1155, 1202–04 (2016), notes that at first glance, bankruptcy cases like Stern and Northern Pipeline "seem to have little to do with the SEC's use of ALJs. Unlike the bankruptcy cases, the SEC administrative proceedings do not involve common law counterclaims, but instead involve purely statutory violations. A civil penalty for a violation of the securities acts is not 'a suit . . . made of 'the stuff . . . tried by the courts at Westminster in 1789.' (quoting Stern) Moreover, the securities laws are an area where the SEC has special expertise. And in practice, many other agencies use ALJs to adjudicate claims that would otherwise come within the jurisdiction of the federal courts. . . . But the SEC's use of ALJs might be . . . different in some ways. It requires analogizing the heavy fines and penalties, and the frequent follow-on nature of the penalties, to something that looks close enough to being part of a criminal case to raise constitutional questions. It is clear that the Supreme Court's jurisprudence in cases like Northern Pipeline would prevent an administrative agency from hearing criminal cases." "The lack of consent and seriously punitive, criminal-related role, might, in some follow-on cases involving disgorgement and . . . defendants [who have not registered with the SEC], combine to look like something constitutionally troubling."

Zaring describes this argument as "the best doctrinal case against the agency's authority, even if it is still not particularly strong." What do you think?

NOTES ON THE PUBLIC/PRIVATE RIGHTS DISTINCTION AND THE RIGHT TO A JURY TRIAL

(1) ***"Public Rights" and the Seventh Amendment.*** Stern was not the first post-Schor reappearance of the "public"/"private" rights distinction. In GRANFINANCIERA, S.A. v. PAUL C. NORDBERG, 492 U.S. 33 (1989), discussed in Stern, the context was again bankruptcy but the constitutional concern was a jury trial. The trustee in bankruptcy had sued in district court to recover money allegedly fraudulently transferred by the bankrupt to Granfinanciera. The district judge referred the action to the bankruptcy court, which refused Granfinanciera's request for a jury trial on grounds that the fraud claim was equitable.

After determining that the trustee's claim was legal, not equitable, in nature, JUSTICE BRENNAN (writing for five justices) framed the Seventh Amendment question as "requiring the same answer as the question whether Article III allows Congress to assign adjudication of that action to a non-

Article III tribunal." Surprisingly, given Thomas and Schor, the most recent precedents on Article III at the time, both questions were said to turn on the public right/private right distinction: "Congress may only deny trials by jury in actions at law . . . in cases where 'public rights' are litigated." However, reflecting the evolution in the meaning of public rights detailed above, these categories were redrawn in a way particularly relevant to administrative adjudication: "The crucial question, in cases not involving the Federal Government, is whether 'Congress, acting for a valid legislative purpose pursuant to its constitutional powers under Article I, [has] create[d] a seemingly 'private' right that is so closely integrated into a public regulatory scheme as to be a matter appropriate for agency resolution with limited involvement by the Article III judiciary." (quoting Justice Brennan's concurrence in Thomas). In this case, the trustee's claim was neither against the Federal Government nor "closely intertwined with a federal regulatory program Congress has the power to enact." Thus it concerned a "private right" and the Seventh Amendment guarantee applied. (The Court was careful not to decide before whom—the bankruptcy judge or the district judge—the jury trial must be held.)

JUSTICE SCALIA, concurring in part and concurring in the judgment, would have pushed the "public rights" doctrine in the opposite direction: "In my view a matter of 'public rights,' whose adjudication Congress may assign to tribunals lacking the essential characteristics of Article III courts, 'must at a minimum arise between the government and others.'. . . It is clear that what we meant by public rights [in Murray's Lessee] were not rights important to the public, or rights created by the public, but rights of the public—that is, rights pertaining to claims brought by or against the United States. For central to our reasoning was the device of waiver of sovereign immunity . . . [which] can only be implicated . . . in suits where the Government is a party." Justice White and Justice Blackmun (joined by Justice O'Connor) dissented.

(2) *The Seventh Amendment and Congress's Choice of Adjudicator.*
Early cases suggested that the Seventh Amendment jury trial right would rarely attach to "typical" regulatory programs. NLRB V. JONES & LAUGHLIN STEEL CORP., 301 U.S. 1 (1937), was a multi-pronged constitutional attack on the National Labor Relations Act and the NLRB. (You may have read the decision in constitutional law for its holding on the Congress's commerce power.) The Court rejected the Seventh Amendment challenge, reasoning tersely that the Amendment applied only to proceedings "in the nature of a suit at common law"—and NLRA proceedings were—unknown to the common law. Reinstatement of the employee and payment for time lost are requirements imposed for violation of the statue and are remedies appropriate for its enforcement.

Eventually, however, the Court cut back the breadth of this reasoning. In CURTIS V. LOETHER, 415 U.S. 189 (1974), a suit for damages for violation of the fair housing provisions of the Civil Rights Act of 1968, the Court insisted that "[t]he Seventh Amendment does apply to actions enforcing statutory rights. . . ." Its analysis seemed to turn on Congress's choice of primary enforcement forum: "[I]f the statute creates legal rights and remedies, enforceable in the ordinary courts of law," then an opportunity for jury trial must be provided. On the other hand, citing Jones and Laughlin, "the Seventh Amendment is generally inapplicable in administrative proceedings where jury trials would be incompatible with the whole concept of administrative adjudication . . ."

Three years later, this distinction was further developed in ATLAS ROOFING CO., INC. V. OCCUPATIONAL SAFETY AND HEALTH REVIEW COMMISSION, 430 U.S. 442 (1977). Two employers, Atlas Roofing and Irey, had been cited by an OSHA inspector for worksite violations that had resulted, in each case, in an employee's death. Irey was assessed a $7500 "civil penalty"; Atlas, a $600 penalty. They claimed that the statutory assessment scheme (in which the inspector proposes the penalty and the employer can contest the penalty order in a [juryless] hearing by an ALJ of the Occupational Health and Safety Review Commission) violated their Seventh Amendment rights. JUSTICE WHITE wrote for a unanimous Court (Justice Blackmun not participating): ". . . Petitioners claim that a suit in a federal court by the Government for civil penalties for violation of a statute is a suit for a money judgment which is classically a suit at common law, . . . We disagree. At least in cases in which 'public rights' are being litigated— e.g., cases in which the Government sues in its sovereign capacity to enforce public rights created by statutes within the power of Congress to enact—the Seventh Amendment does not prohibit Congress from assigning the factfinding function and initial adjudication to an administrative forum with which the jury would be incompatible.

". . . Congress is not required by the Seventh Amendment to choke the already crowded federal courts with new types of litigation or prevented from committing some new types of litigation to administrative agencies with special competence in the relevant field. This is the case even if the Seventh Amendment would have required a jury where the adjudication of those rights is assigned to a federal court of law instead of an administrative agency. . . .

"[Petitioners argue] that the right to jury trial was never intended to depend on the identity of the forum to which Congress has chosen to submit a dispute; otherwise, it is said, Congress could utterly destroy the right to a jury trial by always providing for administrative rather than judicial resolution of the vast range of cases that now arise in the courts. The argument is well put, but it overstates the holdings of our prior cases and is in any event unpersuasive. Our prior cases support administrative factfinding in only those situations involving 'public' rights . . . Wholly private tort, contract, and property cases, as well as a vast range of other cases as well are not at all implicated. . . .

". . . Congress found the common-law and other existing remedies for work injuries resulting from unsafe working conditions to be inadequate to protect the Nation's working men and women. It created a new cause of action, and remedies therefor, unknown to the common law, and placed their enforcement in a tribunal supplying speedy and expert resolutions of the issues involved. The Seventh Amendment is no bar to the creation of new rights or to their enforcement outside the regular courts of law." For criticism of the Court's approach, see, e.g., Martin H. Redish & Daniel J. La Fave, Seventh Amendment Right to Jury Trial in Non-Article III Proceedings: A Study in Dysfunctional Constitutional Theory, 4 Wm. & Mary Bill Rts. J. 407 (1995); Ellen E. Sward, Legislative Courts, Article III and the Seventh Amendment, 77 N. Car. L. Rev. 1037 (1999); Suja A. Thomas, A Limitation on Congress: "In Suits at Common Law," Ohio St. L.J. 1071 (2010).

Claims that administrative adjudication violate the Seventh Amendment were largely dormant, even after Granfinaciera, given Atlas Roofing and the Court's broad definition of public rights. Nonetheless, here too the recent attacks on SEC administrative adjudication have prompted a resurgence. See Hill v. SEC, 114 F.Supp.3d 1297, 1315–16 (N.D. Ga. 2015) (rejecting Seventh Amendment claim based on Atlas Roofing), rev'd on other grounds, 825 F.3d 1236 (11th Cir. 2016); see also Gideon Mark, SEC and CFTC Administrative Proceedings 19 U. Pa. J. Const. L. 45, 93–98 (2016).

(3) *The Sixth Amendment and Criminal Sanctions.* If, as Justice Scalia argued in Granfinanciera, "public rights" are those in which the government is a party, could Congress choose to enforce the criminal law outside the regular courts of law? WONG WING V. UNITED STATES, 163 U.S. 228 (1896): In the blatantly racist series of Chinese Exclusion Acts, Congress first (i) excluded Chinese people from entering the country; then (ii) forbade the reentry of legally resident Chinese individuals who had left the country temporarily; then (iii) required all Chinese residents to register with the Internal Revenue Service; and finally (iv) required that noncomplying Chinese persons "shall be imprisoned at hard labor for a period not exceeding one year, and thereafter removed from the United States." This sanction was imposed by immigration officials without judicial trial or review. After sustaining all the other measures as constitutional, the Court finally held that Congress exceeded its powers. "We regard it as settled by our previous decisions that the United States can, as a matter of public policy, by congressional enactment, [accomplish (i) through (iii) above.] But when Congress sees fit to further promote such a policy by subjecting the persons of such aliens to infamous punishment at hard labor, or by confiscating their property, we think such legislation, to be valid, must provide for a judicial trial to establish the guilt of the accused. . . . It is not consistent with the theory of our government that the legislature should, after having defined an offense as an infamous crime, find the fact of guilt, and adjudge the punishment by one of its own agents."

Obviously, the fines imposed on Irey and Atlas are significantly different from the hard labor imposed by an agency adjudicator upon Mr. Wong Wing. But, contemporary criminal statutes often provide for sanctions that include fines. How do the fines imposed by OSHA differ from such fines? Are they civil sanctions because Congress has chosen to label them such? United States v. Harper, 490 U.S. 435 (1989), suggested that any penalty greater than that necessary to compensate the government qualifies as a punishment rather than a civil penalty. Harper was a Double Jeopardy case, and its method of separating civil and criminal punishments for that purpose was overruled in Hudson v. United States, 522 U.S. 93 (1997). Hudson returned to a multi-factor test used prior to Harper; most relevant for our purposes, the Court stated that the fact that authority to impose the penalty "was conferred upon [an] administrative agenc[y] is prima facie evidence that Congress intended to provide for a civil sanction."

PART 5

JUDGING THE WORK OF AGENCIES

CHAPTER VIII

SCOPE OF REVIEW OF ADMINISTRATIVE ACTION

Sec. 1.	**The Baseline Norm of Legal Regularity**
Sec. 2.	**Support for Agency Decisions**
Sec. 3.	**The Framework of the Governing Statutes**

We turn now to the questions raised when courts are asked to review directly the substance of an agency's action. The fact that courts are in this business has an impact on many of the doctrines addressed elsewhere in this book—for instance, on the questions raised several times in the chapters on rulemaking and adjudication, of what procedures agencies must follow in order to build an adequate record for this review process. And if you have studied those chapters, you will already have met some of the doctrines you will also meet here— doctrines signaled by terms such as "arbitrary and capricious," "reasonable interpretation," "substantial evidence" and the like. But now we will look at the relationship of court and agency, concerning matters of substance, in a systematic way. Traditionally this is known as the question of "scope of review," but it might just as well be called an inquiry into "intensity of review."

As Louis Jaffe, a famous administrative law scholar, once wrote: "The availability of judicial review is the necessary condition, psychologically if not logically, of a system of administrative power which purports to be legitimate, or legally valid."[1] But when judicial review occurs, on what subjects and how closely is the court to inquire? To what degree are the various elements of decision—jurisdiction, facts, judgment, policy, law—left to the agency? To what extent are they to be decided by the reviewing court? One might imagine two polar positions: that the administrative determination at issue is conclusive or that the court should make the determination by itself "de novo." Neither of these is readily described as "review" at all; they represent conclusions that the matter at issue is the unique business of the agency or of the courts, rather than a shared concern to be allocated between them. But we should expect most matters to be of shared concern, if only because Congress routinely provides both for agency determination of matters in the first instance and for judicial review of those determinations. Most

---

[1] Louis L. Jaffe, Judicial Control of Administrative Action 320 (1965).

matters fall at neither pole, and thus a more nuanced determination of the proper allocation must be made.

Congress has usually, but not always, placed review of important administrative decisions in the courts of appeals. These courts are, of course, already in the business of reviewing the non-administrative-law determinations of the federal trial courts, and so one is tempted to draw an analogy between the appellate court/trial court relationship and the appellate court/administrative agency relationship. There are some similarities—for instance, both trial courts and agencies are equipped to hold evidentiary hearings, while appellate courts are not. But there are also important differences. For example, agencies, unlike district courts, have been told by Congress to initiate and carry out specific programs, and are subject to oversight by the Congress and the President. And many agencies, again unlike district courts, have been given the power, not just to decide cases, but to make regulations as well.

Considerations like these—considerations based on the systematic structural features of courts, agencies, and the other branches of government—form the groundwork on which a law of "scope of review" of administrative determinations can be built. Judges create and refine doctrine on the assumption that there is such a law, and as one of the founding editors of this casebook wrote: "We should not assume that our judges are dissemblers."[2]

Yet there is also a strong counter-tradition on this subject, to be met both among scholars and practitioners. As once pithily stated: "The rules governing judicial review have no more substance at the core than a seedless grape."[3] On that view, whatever judges say, judicial review comes down to whether the judges do, or do not, agree with the agency on the underlying merits (or politics) of the substantive decision—and nothing more. There is no "deference," but only agreement or disagreement. Even on this view, however, it behooves the student to learn the lingo used to describe judicial review, in order, as a lawyer, to play her or his assigned part in the supposed charade.

As you study this chapter, you will of course be forming your own view of the announced law of judicial review. But if you are tempted by the cynical view, you should at least consider a third possibility: that the aspiration to have a solid law of judicial review is valuable, and what needs to be done is not to abandon the goal, but rather to do a better job of reaching it. It may be right both that there are substantial structural issues that do imply that judges ought to interfere more here, and less there, and that the particular doctrines presently articulated by the courts do not properly reflect these considerations as well as they should.

---

[2]   Clark Byse, Scope of Judicial Review in Informal Rulemaking, 33 Admin. L. Rev. 183, 193 (1981).

[3]   Ernest Gellhorn & Glen O. Robinson, Perspectives in Administrative Law, 75 Colum. L. Rev. 771, 780–81 (1975).

SECTION 1.   THE BASELINE NORM OF LEGAL REGULARITY

> **SHAW'S SUPERMARKETS, INC. v. NLRB**

SHAW'S SUPERMARKETS, INC. v. NATIONAL LABOR RELATIONS BOARD

United States Court of Appeals for the First Circuit (1989).
884 F.2d 34.

■ BREYER, CIRCUIT JUDGE.

The National Labor Relations Board (the "Board") found that Shaw's Supermarkets ("Shaw") violated National Labor Relations Act ("NLRA") § 8(a)(1) during a representation election held at Shaw's Wells, Maine distribution facility in January 1987. In the election, 71 votes were cast for no union, 46 votes for a Teamsters local, and one vote for an independent union. The finding of violation rested primarily upon the fact that five days before the election, a Shaw vice president [made statements to employees that in the Board's view,] taken in context, constituted a "threat of reprisal" against collective organizing . . . The Board ordered a new election. The Board now asks us to enforce its order.

. . . Under NLRA § 7, employees have the right to "self-organization, to form, join, or assist labor organizations, to bargain collectively through representatives of their own choosing . . ." Employers may not "interfere with, restrain, or coerce employees in the exercise of" those rights. NLRA § 8(a)(1). Moreover, the NLRA expressly states that a "threat of reprisal or force or promise of benefit" does not constitute otherwise protected "express[ion]." NLRA § 8(c). Thus the NLRA prohibits employer speech during an election campaign which contains a "threat of reprisal" and thereby "interfere[s] with, restrain[s] or coerce[s]" employees in the exercise of their rights to "form, join or assist" labor unions. See NLRB v. Gissel Packing Co., Inc., 395 U.S. 575, 618 (1969). Whether any particular employer speech amounts to such a "threat of reprisal" depends upon the context in which the speech is uttered. And, as a general rule, the law gives the Board, not the courts, the authority to examine the circumstances, to find the facts, and to decide whether the remarks, in context, amounted to an unlawful threat. . . .

In January 1987, in the midst of a union representation campaign, and five days before the election, Charles Wyatt, Shaw's vice president for distribution, held three meetings with three different groups of employees. In response to questions at the first meeting, Wyatt said that if a union won "the employees would be guaranteed minimum wages and workmen's comp and that's where our collective bargaining process would begin." He made the same statement to the other two groups of employees. Wyatt also told all the employees that "typically the art of collective bargaining is a give and take process and that . . . we would start with minimum wages and workmen's comp and build from that point." Wyatt referred to a union as a "third party." He also said that "the first contract is generally the toughest or hardest to negotiate . . . and that generally it could take up to a year." Wyatt's audience contained both full-time employees, then earning up to $11.70 an hour, and part-time employees, then earning about $5.00 an hour; the federal minimum wage at that time was $3.55 an hour.

The Board found no other unfair labor practices committed by Shaw during this election campaign. We can find nothing else in the record that might sharpen the details or color the background of the "context" of the bargaining campaign, either in the Board's or the company's favor. And as Board counsel told us at oral argument, neither can the Board.

Were the Board writing on a blank slate, were there no set of Board cases on the subject, we should likely find sufficient basis in the record to sustain the Board's conclusion. Statements like those at issue here— that the company will "begin" its bargaining at "minimum wages and workmen's comp," that it will "build from that point"—might, depending on the context, innocently represent a legal truth about how the collective bargaining process works, legitimately remind employees that a union might trade certain payments or benefits that many workers now enjoy in order to obtain other payments or benefits, or improperly constitute a threat that, if the union wins, the employer will strip benefits back to the minimum, forcing the union to struggle even to keep the status quo. In deciding how to react to these statements, a court must recognize that the Board is expert, not simply about the factual context of the individual case, but also about how employees are likely to understand certain forms of words in the mine-run of cases. Thus, if the Board were to conclude that it should always assume that employees would reasonably take words of the sort at issue here as threats of regressive bargaining in the absence of added employer explanation to the contrary, we believe (though we need not, and do not decide) that a court could not easily say the Board was acting outside the authority that the law grants it.

The problem in this case for the Board, however, is that (a) it is not writing on a blank slate, but has written on the subject often in the past; (b) the Board has not said that it wishes to depart from its several prior cases on the subject; yet (c) as we shall discuss below, the prior cases dictate a result in Shaw's favor.

The law that governs an agency's significant departure from its own prior precedent is clear. . . . The agency has a

> duty to explain its departure from prior norms. The agency may flatly repudiate those norms, deciding, for example, that changed circumstances mean that they are no longer required in order to effectuate congressional policy. Or it may narrow the zone in which some rule will be applied, because it appears that

a more discriminating invocation of the rule will best serve congressional policy. Or it may find that, although the rule in general serves useful purposes, peculiarities of the case before it suggest that the rule not be applied in that case. *Whatever the ground for departure from prior norms, however, it must be clearly set forth so that the reviewing court may understand the basis of the agency's action and so may judge the consistency of that action with the agency's mandate.* . . .

[If] the agency distinguishes earlier cases[, it must] assert . . . distinctions that, when fairly and sympathetically read in the context of the entire opinion of the agency, reveal the policies it is pursuing.

Atchison, Topeka & Santa Fe Railway Co. v. Wichita Board of Trade, 412 U.S. 800, 808–09 (1973) (plurality opinion) (emphasis added).

It is, of course, true that the Board is free to adopt new rules of decision and that the new rules of law can be given retroactive application. Nevertheless the Board may not depart sub silentio from its usual rules of decision to reach a different, unexplained result in a single case. . . . "[T]here may not be a rule for Monday, another for Tuesday, a rule for general application, but denied outright in a specific case." Mary Carter Paint Co. v. FTC, 333 F.2d 654, 660 (5th Cir. 1964) (Brown, J., concurring), rev'd on other grounds, 382 U.S. 46 (1965). "[A]n inadequately explained departure solely for purposes of a particular case, or the creation of conflicting lines of precedent governing the identical situation, is not to be tolerated."

NLRB v. International Union of Operating Engineers, Local 925, 460 F.2d 589, 604 (5th Cir. 1972) (citations omitted).

The Board says that Wyatt's statements fell within a category it calls "bargaining from scratch." It has held the making of such statements unlawful when, in context, a reasonable employee would take them as a coercive threat that an employer will engage in "regressive bargaining," by removing wages and benefits if the union wins. The Board has distinguished lawful from unlawful "bargaining from scratch" statements by ascribing importance to the varying elements of the factual contexts embodied in its past precedent.

[The court reviewed eight NLRB cases, from 1968–1986, in which the Board had concluded that an employer's "bargaining from scratch" statement did *not*, in context, amount to a threat of "regressive bargaining."] In many of these cases . . . the statements in context seem to us just as threatening (if not more so) than those in the present case. We do not see how, after reading the record in this case and the opinions in the cases we have just mentioned, one could reasonably find no violation in those earlier cases yet find a violation in this case. Wyatt used language virtually identical to that used in the cases just listed. . . .

The record does not reveal any other elements suggesting regressive bargaining. Indeed, Board counsel at oral argument simply stated that he "did not know" just what it was in the context of the prior cases finding no violation that "made these same statements" benign there, yet harmful here. Counsel's statement, in our view, honestly reflects the circumstances, for we do not see how one can distinguish prior cases in which the Board found "no violation."

Of course, there are other cases in which the Board found that a "bargaining from scratch" statement violated the law. [The court reviewed four NLRB decisions from the 1977–86 period.] . . . In almost all these cases, the "bargaining from scratch" speech was accompanied by other serious unfair labor practices, such as the discriminatory treatment of labor organizers. . . . [Moreover,] the language and context suggested, far more strongly than here, a threat to eliminate benefits before bargaining. . . .

In finding the Board's decision in this case inconsistent with its precedents, we do not intend to impose upon the Board the time consuming obligation of microscopically examining prior cases; nor to encourage counsel to examine past precedent with an eye towards raising hosts of legalistic arguments and distinctions. Here, however, the past cases trace a relatively clear line. Nor do we believe that past cases are a straitjacket, inhibiting experimentation or change. . . . [T]he Board remains free to modify or change its rule; to depart from, or to keep within, prior precedent, as long as it focuses upon the issue and explains why change is reasonable. Unless an agency either follows or consciously changes the rules developed in its precedent, those subject to the agency's authority cannot use its precedent as a guide for their conduct; nor will that precedent check arbitrary agency action.

For these reasons we decline to enforce the Board's order, and we remand the case to the Board.

NOTES

(1) ***Why Does Consistency Matter?*** Judge (now Justice) Breyer gives two reasons: "Unless an agency either follows or consciously changes the rules developed in its precedent, those subject to the agency's authority cannot use its precedent as a guide for their conduct; nor will that precedent check arbitrary agency action." Taking the former of these reasons first, it suggests the possibility that Shaw's vice president was briefed by counsel about the intricacies of the Board's "bargaining from scratch" doctrine before meeting with Shaw's employees. But how does that emphasis on possible reliance mesh with Breyer's concession that, if it had properly explained what it was doing, the NLRB could have changed its doctrine by means of adjudication—a concession authoritatively grounded in the Chenery case, p. 249 above? Judge Breyer might answer that, if the Board had overtly faced up to the fact of change, then it would also realize that it had to take into account this possible private-party reliance. Agencies have, in such situations, sometimes

reduced the penalty on parties now determined to have, to their surprise, disobeyed the law. Consider, for example, what the FCC did in the Fox case, p. 1100 below. And if the agency does not do that, then, because the change is apparent, perhaps a reviewing court will do it instead. See, e.g., Epilepsy Foundation of Northeast Ohio v. NLRB, 268 F.3d 1095 (2001), in which the D.C. Circuit, considering another change in Labor Board policy, upheld the Board's change of mind as "clear and reasonable" but refused to give it retroactive application.

(2) **Beyond Reliance.** TODD D. RAKOFF, SHAW'S SUPERMARKETS, INC. V. NLRB—A FIRST CIRCUIT OPINION, 128 Harv. L. Rev. 477, 479–80 (2014): "The more important claim is that judicially requiring conscious attention to existing precedents will 'check arbitrary agency action.' Here, I think, we must distinguish two possible meanings of 'arbitrary.' One possible claim is that requiring an agency to address its existing rules and precedents will prevent it from doing mindless acts, acts in which it simply gives no thought to the fact that in other cases it has done things differently. Whatever might be the force of this idea elsewhere, it seems to me to have little force in the situation at hand. Labor Board cases are formally structured, contested affairs, much like civil trials; it would seem safe to rely on one party or another to draw to the attention of the Board its prior decisions. Assuming competent counsel, it is unlikely the precedents will remain hidden.

"What is at stake is not the 'mindless' form of arbitrary action, but rather the 'willful' form—the form that says: 'We're doing it now differently from what we did before because that's what we want to do—period!' The court's corresponding claim, as said in one of the cases that Judge Breyer quotes, is that 'there may not be a rule for Monday, another for Tuesday.'

"Now, it is not inherently arbitrary to do one thing on Monday and another on Tuesday. We do it all the time. Indeed, sometimes the reason for doing a particular thing on Tuesday is precisely that it is different from what we did on Monday. 'We had pizza for dinner yesterday' is a reason for not having pizza for dinner today, not a reason for having it again. The claim that having done something one way yesterday is a prima facie reason for doing it the same way today is not an unalterable claim of all rational thinking, but rather a claim of a specific cultural form. It is a claim of the legal order for action to be justified based on reasoning of a specific sort.

"Whether governmental administration of the economy, 'regulation,' comprises acts of will or acts of reason—or perhaps better put, the extent to which it comprises acts of will and acts of reason—is a classic question of administrative law. It is often seen through the lens of the structural Constitution, and converted into the question of whether there are administrative law 'substitutes' for the separation of powers set out in Articles I, II, and III. But Judge Breyer cites no constitutional provision, nor indeed any provision of the Administrative Procedure Act, to support his claims, and it is probably fairer to say that he is simply relying on what he sees as a fundamental demand of the legal order. (If one wanted a constitutional text, I suppose it would be 'due process' seen in its most general form, as a claim to official action having to be grounded on a legal regime.) . . .

"The legal order in question is not a legal order that plays out primarily in the courts, but rather one that fundamentally takes place within the agency. Ordering a new election on these facts may be, as Judge Breyer assumes, within the constitutional and statutory power of the agency, but the agency has to think about its task, and justify its task, in a certain way. Thus, after holding that the Board's order cannot be enforced, the rescript is to remand the case to the Board. The agency has to act as if it were part of the legal regime—and should be given another chance to do so. The court's job is to provide a context that encourages the agency so to act. . . ."

(3) ***Adherence to Agency Regulations.*** Now, what if the agency's prior position is represented by a rule rather than a set of cases? The general principle is that an agency must follow its own regulations until they are validly amended or rescinded. This principle is often called the "Accardi doctrine" from the case in which it first played a prominent role;[4] its most dramatic applications come from the Watergate scandal. When Attorney General Robert Bork, on President Nixon's order, fired Archibald Cox as Watergate Special Prosecutor, Judge Gerhardt Gesell held the action unlawful. Although the Attorney General ordinarily had the power to fire a federal prosecutor at will, he had limited his own authority by promulgating a regulation that the Watergate Special Prosecutor would be fired only "for extraordinary improprieties." As Cox had not engaged in such behavior, the Attorney General had no power to fire him. Nader v. Bork, 366 F.Supp. 104 (D.D.C. 1973). When Cox's successor, Leon Jaworski, obtained a subpoena ordering President Nixon to produce certain tape recordings, and Nixon refused to comply on grounds of executive privilege, the President argued that the judiciary could not intervene in an "intra-executive dispute." The Supreme Court unanimously held that, because the Attorney General had explicitly delegated to the Special Prosecutor the power to contest any invocation of executive privilege in connection with his investigations, "the Executive Branch is bound by" that regulation. United States v. Nixon, 418 U.S. 683 (1974).

How does one explain holding an agency to a rule that it was under no duty to adopt in the first place? A rule upon which, given the particular context, there could be no private reliance? THOMAS W. MERRILL, THE *ACCARDI* PRINCIPLE, 74 Geo. Wash. L. Rev. 569, 598–99 (2006):

> What is the status in law of the principle that agencies have a legal duty to comply with regulations that have a status analogous to statutes? Is this a proposition of constitutional law, statutory interpretation, administrative common law, or what? The most honest answer is that it is just one of those shared postulates of the legal system that cannot be traced to any provision of enacted law. In this sense, it is like the rule of stare decisis, or the understanding that majority rule prevails in multimember courts. . . . These rules are not written down in any authoritative text. They are simply foundational assumptions vital to the operations of our legal system.

---

4   Accardi v. Shaughnessy, 347 U.S. 260 (1954).

Whatever is the source of this "foundational assumption," it is reflected in the APA. As we shall see in the State Farm case (p. 1069 below), an agency rescinding a binding regulation has to adopt the rescission as if it were adopting a new rule. Of course, under the APA not all rules have what Merrill refers to as "a status analogous to statutes." Some rules are merely "interpretative rules" or "policy statements" that can be adopted informally. (See Ch IV, Sec. 3b above.) As to them, the agency may not be bound to follow the rule on the books until it formally takes the rule off the books. But to avoid being considered "arbitrary and capricious" it may still have an obligation to explain why it is departing from such an interpretation in the case at hand. For further discussion of the Accardi principle, see Elizabeth Magill, Agency Self-Regulation, 77 Geo. Wash. L. Rev. 859, 873 ff. (2009).

(4) *Legal Regularity and Enforcement Choices.* Determining that a party has violated the law is, of course, only a part of an agency's adjudicatory process; there is also the initial determination to bring an enforcement proceeding, and, if a violation is found, the ultimate determination of the appropriate sanction. Are they, too, subject to consistency-demanding rule-of-law constraints? As to the decision to initiate a proceeding, unless the particular organic statute provides differently, agencies in general enjoy a broad, presumptively unreviewable discretion. See Ch IX, Sec. 2b(3). As to the sanction to be levied, court review is available, but claims of inconsistency have not received favorable treatment in the Supreme Court.

Typical is BUTZ V. GLOVER LIVESTOCK COMMISSION CO., INC., 411 U.S. 182 (1973). Glover Livestock sold cattle under consignment on a commission basis; the Department of Agriculture found that it continually, carelessly, underweighed the cattle consigned to it (and therefore underpaid for them). The Department suspended Livestock's business license for 20 days. The Eighth Circuit upheld the finding that the Packers and Stockyards Act had been violated but set aside the suspension on the ground that the Department's practice in like cases was only to issue a cease-and-desist order when the violations had not been intentional. But, said JUSTICE BRENNAN for the Supreme Court: "The fashioning of an appropriate and reasonable remedy is for the Secretary, not the court." 411 U.S. at 186–88:

"We read the Court of Appeals' opinion to suggest that the sanction was 'unwarranted in law' because 'uniformity of sanctions for similar violations' is somehow mandated by the Act. We search in vain for that requirement in the statute. The Secretary may suspend 'for a reasonable specified period' any registrant who has violated any provision of the Act. 7 U.S.C. § 204. Nothing whatever in that provision confines its application to cases of 'intentional and flagrant conduct' or denies its application in cases of negligent or careless violations. Rather, the breadth of the grant of authority to impose the sanction strongly implies a congressional purpose to permit the Secretary to impose it to deter repeated violations of the Act, whether intentional or negligent. The employment of a sanction within the authority of an administrative agency is thus not rendered invalid in a particular case because it is more severe than sanctions imposed in other cases.

"Moreover, the Court of Appeals may have been in error in acting on the premise that the Secretary's practice was to impose suspensions only in cases of 'intentional and flagrant conduct.' The Secretary's practice, rather, apparently is to employ that sanction as in his judgment best serves to deter violations and achieve the objectives of that statute. Congress plainly intended in its broad grant to give the Secretary that breadth of discretion. Therefore, mere unevenness in the application of the sanction does not render its application in a particular case 'unwarranted in law.'"

(5) *And What About Mass Justice?* "Government is at its most arbitrary when it treats similarly situated people differently"[5]—an axiom that Judge Friendly called "the most basic principle of jurisprudence." Henry J. Friendly, Indiscretion About Discretion, 31 Emory L.J. 747, 758 (1982). Although generally (if not universally) acknowledged as an essential condition of a just legal system, the principle of "like treatment of like cases" can be surprisingly difficult to realize: recall the difficulties first-year law students have in deciding if fact patterns are, or are not, distinguishable. But Judge Breyer could at least work from formal, published NLRB opinions. What of less formal agency determinations?

In DAVIS V. COMMISSIONER, 69 T.C. 716 (1978), the Internal Revenue Service had disallowed part of a small charitable deduction claimed by Professor K.C. Davis for books received from West Publishing Co., used, and then donated to the University of Chicago Law Library. Contesting this position in the Tax Court, Davis (a famous professor of administrative law) obtained through discovery IRS "letter rulings" issued to Members of Congress who received free copies of the Congressional Record, gave them to charitable organizations, and deducted the value of the gifts.[6] After receiving four such rulings, Davis—insisting that the agency must act evenhandedly—sought additional discovery of all pertinent letter rulings (at that time, not generally available to the public) in the IRS's "reference file." Discovery was denied. As another Tax Court judge had said two years earlier in a similar effort by Professor Davis over a different deduction (Davis v. Commissioner, 65 T.C. 1014, 1022–23 (1976)):

> It has long been the position of this Court that our responsibility is to apply the law to the facts of the case before us . . .; how the Commissioner may have treated other taxpayers has generally been considered irrelevant in making that determination. Any change in that position would have widespread ramifications in the administration and application of the Federal tax laws and in the conduct of our work. . . . Over 11,000 new cases were commenced in this Court in the past year, and although many of those cases are settled, the Court still has a herculean task to keep abreast of its caseload. Were we to embrace the principles urged by Mr. Davis, the task would be magnified. Every trial would be extended, for it

---

[5]   Etelson v. OPM, 684 F.2d 918, 926 (D.C. Cir. 1982).

[6]   "Letter rulings" are issued with less structured intra-agency review than "revenue rulings," which are officially published and on which all taxpayers are encouraged to rely. The IRS considers itself bound by revenue rulings until revoked but bound by letter rulings only as to the addressee taxpayer.

would then become necessary to allow the petitioner to inquire into the Commissioner's treatment of other similarly situated taxpayers. . . . [T]he notion of equal justice has strong appeal in our society and might lead to the conclusion that his position should ultimately be adopted. Yet, a full appreciation of the ramifications of this matter makes abundantly clear that it should be approached cautiously.

We might further consider the prospects of achieving evenhandedness in a massive benefits regime like the Social Security disability program. Professor Jerry Mashaw's several writings on the administration of this program illuminate these issues. His first study, completed in 1978, produced a damning indictment from a perspective much like Professor Davis': individual cases were being decided without discernible pattern. "The inconsistency of the disability process is patent. Indeed, it is widely believed that the outcome of cases depends more on who decides the case than on what the facts are."[7] But, as Mashaw explored in his later work, Bureaucratic Justice (1983), intolerance of *any* degree of inconsistency is premised on a "model of individual justice." An alternative, a "model of bureaucratic rationality," would frame the issues as whether *gross* errors have been avoided and marginal errors *evenly distributed* (that is, about as many wrongful grants as wrongful denials) at reasonable cost. These conditions would maximize the extent to which programmatic purposes are achieved and, one might say, would represent "fairness" in a different, overall sense. If one takes this view, for the "similarly situated" people at the margin of eligibility, inconsistent treatment is a necessary cost of a workable scheme; all that can realistically be asked—that the judgment on eligibility not be "too wrong"—will have been achieved.

(6) ***Effect of Prior Court Rulings.*** And while we are on the topic of consistency—what is the obligation of an agency in deciding a later case to follow the ruling of a court in an earlier case? Partly, of course, that depends on exactly what the court said in the first case. See the discussion of National Cable & Telecommunications Ass'n v. Brand X Internet Services, p. 1162 below. It also depends on what court was saying it; no agency would say that it was not bound to follow the rulings of the Supreme Court. But agencies sometimes do say that they are not bound by the final rulings of lower courts, including the Courts of Appeals, especially when considering cases beyond the geographical jurisdiction of those courts. Is this practice of "nonacquiescence," which can well introduce regional variation into national programs, to be permitted? Insofar as the Supreme Court has addressed this issue, it has stated the law in terms of the doctrine of collateral estoppel.

In UNITED STATES V. STAUFFER CHEMICAL CO., 464 U.S. 165 (1984), the Supreme Court held that "the doctrine of mutual defensive collateral estoppel is available against the government to preclude relitigation of the same issue already litigated against the same party in another case involving virtually identical facts." 464 U.S. at 169. That, of course, still left the

---

[7]   Jerry L. Mashaw, Charles J. Goetz, Frank I. Goodman, Warren F. Schwartz, Paul R. Verkuil & Milton M. Carrow, Social Security Hearings and Appeals: A Study of the Social Security Administration Hearing System xxi (1978).

government free to litigate the same issue with other parties. Might those other parties be able to preclude litigation of an issue under the doctrine of nonmutual (and perhaps even "offensive") collateral estoppel, as is increasingly recognized in ordinary civil litigation? If so, the civil procedure doctrine of issue preclusion might well settle the administrative law question of nonacquiescence. But in Stauffer's companion case, UNITED STATES v. MENDOZA, 464 U.S. 154 (1984), the Court said that no such result was contemplated. Per Justice Rehnquist (464 U.S. at 159–61):

"We have long recognized that 'the Government is not in a position identical to that of a private litigant,' both because of the geographic breadth of Government litigation and also, most importantly, because of the nature of the issues the Government litigates. It is not open to serious dispute that the Government is a party to a far greater number of cases on a nationwide basis than even the most litigious private entity; in 1982, the United States was a party to more than 75,000 of the 206,193 filings in the United States District Courts. In the same year the United States was a party to just under 30% of the civil cases appealed from the District Courts to the Court of Appeals. Government litigation frequently involves legal questions of substantial public importance; indeed, because the proscriptions of the United States Constitution are so generally directed at governmental action, many constitutional questions can arise only in the context of litigation to which the Government is a party. Because of those facts the Government is more likely than any private party to be involved in lawsuits against different parties which nonetheless involve the same legal issues.

"A rule allowing nonmutual collateral estoppel against the Government in such cases would substantially thwart the development of important questions of law by freezing the first final decision rendered on a particular legal issue. Allowing only one final adjudication would deprive this Court of the benefit it receives from permitting several courts of appeals to explore a difficult question before this Court grants certiorari. Indeed, if nonmutual estoppel were routinely applied against the Government, this Court would have to revise its practice of waiting for a conflict to develop before granting the Government's petitions for certiorari.

". . . The Court of Appeals faulted the Government in this case for failing to appeal a decision that it now contends is erroneous. But the Government's litigation conduct in a case is apt to differ from that of a private litigant. Unlike a private litigant who generally does not forego an appeal if he believes that he can prevail, the Solicitor General considers a variety of factors, such as the limited resources of the Government and the crowded dockets of the courts, before authorizing an appeal. The application of nonmutual estoppel against the Government would force the Solicitor General to abandon those prudential concerns and to appeal every adverse decision in order to avoid foreclosing further review.

"In addition to those institutional concerns traditionally considered by the Solicitor General, the panoply of important public issues raised in governmental litigation may quite properly lead successive administrations of the Executive Branch to take differing positions with respect to the resolution of a particular issue. While the Executive Branch must of course defer to the Judicial Branch for final resolution of questions of constitutional law, the former nonetheless controls the progress of Government litigation through the federal courts. It would be idle to pretend that the conduct of Government litigation in all its myriad features, from the decision to file a complaint in the United States district court to the decision to petition for certiorari to review a judgment of the court of appeals, is a wholly mechanical procedure which involves no policy choices whatever. . . ."

For a thorough analysis of the analytical and policy issues involved in nonacquiescence, see Samuel Estreicher & Richard L. Revesz, Nonacquiescence by Federal Administrative Agencies, 98 Yale L.J. 679 (1989).

SECTION 2.   SUPPORT FOR AGENCY DECISIONS

> *a.* **Review of the Basic Facts**
> *b.* **Review of the Flow of Reasoning and Judgment**

As we have just seen, the most basic element of judicial review of agency action is the demand that the agency act with legal regularity. No one doubts that judicial review goes further than that. But how much further?

As ordinary civil procedure shows, the tradition of the law is to give a differentiated, rather than flat, answer to a question of this sort. Appellate courts review trial court decisions in ordinary civil cases using a variety of standards modulated according to particular features of the situation; scrutiny is most intense regarding trial courts' rulings on questions of law, less so on their findings of fact in trials without a jury, and least intense (or put another way, most deferential) regarding determinations of fact made by a jury.

If we were to imagine a similar scale of intensity for judicial review of agency decisions, we might then ask ourselves, what features of agency decisions should we correlate with more or less judicial scrutiny? Should we divide agency decisionmaking into its various formal components— jurisdiction, law, fact, discretion, policy, etc.—and propound different standards for each? Or should we instead develop a scale of the social and economic importance of various agency decisions and ask the judges to spend greater energy on the more important ones? Or should we try to allocate to agencies those aspects of decisionmaking that call for scientific, commercial, or industrial expertise and give to the judges those aspects accessible to legal reasoning and ordinary common sense?

Although Congress sometimes stipulates particular review standards in specific organic statutes, its general answer to this set of questions is set out in § 706 of the APA:

Scope of Review

To the extent necessary to decision and when presented, the reviewing court shall decide all relevant questions of law, interpret constitutional and statutory provisions, and determine the meaning or applicability of the terms of an agency action. The reviewing court shall—

(1) compel agency action unlawfully withheld or unreasonably delayed; and

(2) hold unlawful and set aside agency action, findings, and conclusions found to be—

  (A) arbitrary, capricious, an abuse of discretion, or otherwise not in accordance with law;

  (B) contrary to constitutional right, power, privilege, or immunity;

  (C) in excess of statutory jurisdiction, authority, or limitations, or short of statutory right;

  (D) without observance of procedure required by law;

  (E) unsupported by substantial evidence in a case subject to sections 556 and 557 of this title or otherwise reviewed on the record of an agency hearing provided by statute; or

  (F) unwarranted by the facts to the extent that the facts are subject to trial de novo by the reviewing court.

In making the foregoing determinations, the court shall review the whole record or those parts of it cited by a party, and due account shall be taken of the rule of prejudicial error.

This statute gives us some language to work with; but the language Congress used assumes as much as it answers. One ground for setting aside agency action, for example, is if it is "arbitrary" or "capricious," but these terms are given no further specification within the text of the statute. They must be explicated by the courts in the light of tradition, policy, or the needs of the case.

We begin with what is perhaps the most specific of the § 706 standards: the stipulation that the courts should set aside agency action if it is "unsupported by substantial evidence in a case subject to sections 556 and 557 of this title or otherwise reviewed on the record of an agency hearing provided by statute"—which is to say, we begin with the test for determinations of fact made in an on-the-record, trial-type hearing.

a. Review of the Basic Facts

> **UNIVERSAL CAMERA CORP. v. NLRB**
> **Notes on the Substantial Evidence Test**
> **Notes on "Arbitrary or Capricious" in**
> **Comparison to "Substantial Evidence"**

UNIVERSAL CAMERA CORP. v. NATIONAL LABOR RELATIONS BOARD

Supreme Court of the United States (1951).
340 U.S. 474.

■ JUSTICE FRANKFURTER delivered the opinion of the Court.

[The question before the National Labor Relations Board was whether an employee had been fired because he had testified in support of the union's position in an NLRB representation proceeding, or solely because subsequently he had accused the company's personnel manager of drunkenness. The trial examiner, crediting the employer's testimony and finding that antiunion animus had not entered into the discharge, recommended dismissing the complaint. A divided Board made the opposite finding and held the discharge to be an unfair labor practice. The Second Circuit also divided, granting enforcement per Judge Learned Hand but with express misgivings about the Board's assessment of the evidence; Judge Hand's opinion voiced views at odds with those of the Sixth Circuit, whose decision was reviewed in a companion case.]

The essential issue raised by this case and its companion . . . is the effect of the Administrative Procedure Act and the legislation colloquially known as the Taft-Hartley Act, 5 U.S.C. § 1001 et seq.; 29 U.S.C. § 141 et seq., on the duty of Courts of Appeals when called upon to review orders of the National Labor Relations Board. . . .

I.

Want of certainty in judicial review of Labor Board decisions partly reflects the intractability of any formula to furnish definiteness of content for all the impalpable factors involved in judicial review. But in part doubts as to the nature of the reviewing power and uncertainties in its application derive from history, and to that extent an elucidation of this history may clear them away.

The Wagner Act [the original National Labor Relations Act] provided: "The findings of the Board as to the facts, if supported by evidence, shall be conclusive." Act of July 5, 1935, § 10(e). This Court read "evidence" to mean "substantial evidence," and we said that "(s)ubstantial evidence is more than a mere scintilla. It means such relevant evidence as a reasonable mind might accept as adequate to support a conclusion." Consolidated Edison Co. v. National Labor Relations Board, 305 U.S. 197, 229. Accordingly, it "must do more than create a suspicion of the existence of the fact to be established. . . . it must be enough to justify, if the trial were to a jury, a refusal to direct a verdict when the conclusion sought to be drawn from it is one of fact for the jury." NLRB v. Columbian Enameling & Stamping Co., 306 U.S. 292, 300.

The very smoothness of the "substantial evidence" formula as the standard for reviewing the evidentiary validity of the Board's findings established its currency. But the inevitably variant applications of the standard to conflicting evidence soon brought contrariety of views and in due course bred criticism. Even though the whole record may have been canvassed in order to determine whether the evidentiary foundation of a determination by the Board was "substantial," the phrasing of this Court's process of review readily lent itself to the notion that it was enough that the evidence supporting the Board's result was "substantial" when considered by itself. It is fair to say that by imperceptible steps regard for the fact-finding function of the Board led to the assumption that the requirements of the Wagner Act were met when the reviewing court could find in the record evidence which, when viewed in isolation, substantiated the Board's findings. . . .

Criticism of so contracted a reviewing power reinforced dissatisfaction felt in various quarters with the Board's administration of the Wagner Act in the years preceding the war. The scheme of the Act was attacked as an inherently unfair fusion of the functions of prosecutor and judge. Accusations of partisan bias were not wanting. The "irresponsible admission and weighing of hearsay, opinion, and emotional speculation in place of factual evidence" was said to be a "serious menace." No doubt some, perhaps even much, of the criticism was baseless and some surely was reckless.[6] What is here relevant, however, is the climate of opinion thereby generated and its effect on Congress. Protests against "shocking injustices" and intimations of judicial "abdication" with which some courts granted enforcement of the Board's order stimulated pressures for legislative relief from alleged administrative excesses.

The strength of these pressures was reflected in the passage in 1940 of the Walter-Logan Bill. It was vetoed by President Roosevelt, partly because it imposed unduly rigid limitations on the administrative process, and partly because of the investigation into the actual operation of the administrative process then being conducted by an experienced committee appointed by the Attorney General. It is worth noting that despite its aim to tighten control over administrative determinations of fact, the Walter-Logan Bill contented itself with the conventional formula that an agency's decision could be set aside if "the findings of fact are not supported by substantial evidence."

---

[6]   Professor Gellhorn and Mr. Linfield reached the conclusion in 1939 after an extended investigation that "the denunciations find no support in fact." Gellhorn and Linfield, Politics and Labor Relations, 39 Col. L. Rev. 339, 394.

The final report of the Attorney General's Committee was submitted in January, 1941. The majority concluded that "(d)issatisfaction with the existing standards as to the scope of judicial review derives largely from dissatisfaction with the fact-finding procedures now employed by the administrative bodies." Departure from the "substantial evidence" test, it thought, would either create unnecessary uncertainty or transfer to courts the responsibility for ascertaining and assaying matters the significance of which lies outside judicial competence. Accordingly, it recommended against legislation embodying a general scheme of judicial review.[12]

Three members of the Committee registered a dissent. Their view was that the "present system or lack of system of judicial review" led to inconsistency and uncertainty. They reported that under a "prevalent" interpretation of the "substantial evidence" rule "if what is called 'substantial evidence' is found anywhere in the record to support conclusions of fact, the courts are said to be obliged to sustain the decision without reference to how heavily the countervailing evidence may preponderate—unless indeed the stage of arbitrary decision is reached. Under this interpretation, the courts need to read only one side of the case and, if they find any evidence there, the administrative action is to be sustained and the record to the contrary is to be ignored." Their view led them to recommend that Congress enact principles of review applicable to all agencies not excepted by unique characteristics. One of these principles was expressed by the formula that judicial review could extend to "findings, inferences, or conclusions of fact unsupported, upon the whole record, by substantial evidence." So far as the history of this movement for enlarged review reveals, the phrase "upon the whole record" makes its first appearance in this recommendation of the minority of the Attorney General's Committee. This evidence of the close relationship between the phrase and the criticism out of which it arose is important, for the substance of this formula for judicial review found its way into the statute books when Congress with unquestioning—we might even say uncritical—unanimity enacted the Administrative Procedure Act.

One is tempted to say "uncritical" because the legislative history of that Act hardly speaks with that clarity of purpose which Congress supposedly furnishes courts in order to enable them to enforce its true will. On the one hand, the sponsors of the legislation indicated that they were reaffirming the prevailing "substantial evidence" test. But with equal clarity they expressed disapproval of the manner in which the

---

[12] Referring to proposals to enlarge the scope of review to permit inquiry whether the findings are supported by the weight of the evidence, the majority said: ". . . [T]he wisdom of a general change to review of the 'weight of evidence' is questionable. If the change would require the courts to determine independently which way the evidence preponderates, administrative tribunals would be turned into little more than media for transmission of the evidence to the courts. It would destroy the values of adjudication of fact by experts or specialists in the field involved. It would divide the responsibility for administrative adjudications." Final Report, 91–92.

courts were applying their own standard. The committee reports of both houses refer to the practice of agencies to rely upon "suspicion, surmise, implications, or plainly incredible evidence," and indicate that courts are to exact higher standards "in the exercise of their independent judgment" and on consideration of "the whole record."[17]

Similar dissatisfaction with too restricted application of the "substantial evidence" test is reflected in the legislative history of the Taft-Hartley Act [amending the National Labor Relations Act in 1947]. . . . Early committee prints in the Senate provided for review by "weight of the evidence" or "clearly erroneous" standards. But, as the Senate Committee Report relates, "it was finally decided to conform the statute to the corresponding section of the Administrative Procedure Act where the substantial evidence test prevails. In order to clarify any ambiguity in that statute, however, the committee inserted the words 'questions of fact, if supported by substantial evidence on the record considered as a whole. . . .' "[21] This phraseology was adopted by the Senate. The House conferees agreed. . . .

It is fair to say that in all this Congress expressed a mood. And it expressed its mood not merely by oratory but by legislation. As legislation that mood must be respected, even though it can only serve as a standard for judgment and not as a body of rigid rules assuring sameness of applications. Enforcement of such broad standards implies subtlety of mind and solidity of judgment. But it is not for us to question that Congress may assume such qualities in the federal judiciary.

From the legislative story we have summarized, two concrete conclusions do emerge. One is the identity of aim of the Administrative Procedure Act and the Taft-Hartley Act regarding the proof with which the Labor Board must support a decision. The other is that now Congress

---

[17] The following quotation from the report of the Senate Judiciary Committee indicates the position of the sponsors. "The 'substantial evidence' rule set forth in section 10(e) is exceedingly important. As a matter of language, substantial evidence would seem to be an adequate expression of law. The difficulty comes about in the practice of agencies to rely upon (and of courts to tacitly approve) something less—to rely upon suspicion, surmise, implications, or plainly incredible evidence. It will be the duty of the courts to determine in the final analysis and in the exercise of their independent judgment, whether on the whole record the evidence in a given instance is sufficiently substantial to support a finding, conclusion, or other agency action as a matter of law. In the first instance, however, it will be the function of the agency to determine the sufficiency of the evidence upon which it acts—and the proper performance of its public duties will require it to undertake this inquiry in a careful and dispassionate manner. Should these objectives of the bill as worded fail, supplemental legislation will be required." S. Rep. No. 752, 79th Cong., 1st Sess. 30–31. The House Committee Report is to substantially the same effect. H.R. Rep. No. 1980, 79th Cong., 2d Sess. 45

[21] S. Rep. No. 105, 80th Cong., 1st Sess. 26–27. The Committee did not explain what the ambiguity might be. . . . Senator Taft gave this explanation to the Senate of the meaning of the section: "In the first place, the evidence must be substantial; in the second place, it must still look substantial when viewed in the light of the entire record. That does not go so far as saying that a decision can be reversed on the weight of the evidence. It does not go quite so far as the power given to a circuit court of appeals to review a district-court decision, but it goes a great deal further than the present law, and gives the court greater opportunity to reverse an obviously unjust decision on the part of the National Labor Relations Board." 93 Cong. Rec. 3839.

has left no room for doubt as to the kind of scrutiny which a court of appeals must give the record before the Board to satisfy itself that the Board's order rests on adequate proof. . . .

Whether or not it was ever permissible for courts to determine the substantiality of evidence supporting a Labor Board decision merely on the basis of evidence which in and of itself justified it, without taking into account contradictory evidence or evidence from which conflicting inferences could be drawn, the new legislation definitively precludes such a theory of review and bars its practice. The substantiality of evidence must take into account whatever in the record fairly detracts from its weight. This is clearly the significance of the requirement in both statutes that courts consider the whole record. Committee reports and the adoption in the Administrative Procedure Act of the minority views of the Attorney General's Committee demonstrate that to enjoin such a duty on the reviewing court was one of the important purposes of the movement which eventuated in that enactment.

To be sure, the requirement for canvassing "the whole record" in order to ascertain substantiality does not furnish a calculus of value by which a reviewing court can assess the evidence. Nor was it intended to negative the function of the Labor Board as one of those agencies presumably equipped or informed by experience to deal with a specialized field of knowledge, whose findings within that field carry the authority of an expertness which courts do not possess and therefore must respect. Nor does it mean that even as to matters not requiring expertise a court may displace the Board's choice between two fairly conflicting views, even though the court would justifiably have made a different choice had the matter been before it de novo. Congress has merely made it clear that a reviewing court is not barred from setting aside a Board decision when it cannot conscientiously find that the evidence supporting that decision is substantial, when viewed in the light that the record in its entirety furnishes, including the body of evidence opposed to the Board's view.

There remains, then, the question whether enactment of these two statutes has altered the scope of review other than to require that substantiality be determined in the light of all that the record relevantly presents. A formula for judicial review of administrative action may afford grounds for certitude but cannot assure certainty of application. Some scope for judicial discretion in applying the formula can be avoided only by falsifying the actual process of judging or by using the formula as an instrument of futile casuistry. It cannot be too often repeated that judges are not automata. The ultimate reliance for the fair operation of any standard is a judiciary of high competence and character and the constant play of an informed professional critique upon its work.

Since the precise way in which courts interfere with agency findings cannot be imprisoned within any form of words, new formulas attempting to rephrase the old are not likely to be more helpful than the old. There are no talismanic words that can avoid the process of judgment. The difficulty is that we cannot escape, in relation to this problem, the use of undefined defining terms.

Whatever changes were made by the Administrative Procedure and Taft-Hartley Acts are clearly within this area where precise definition is impossible. Retention of the familiar "substantial evidence" terminology indicates that no drastic reversal of attitude was intended.

But a standard leaving an unavoidable margin for individual judgment does not leave the judicial judgment at large even though the phrasing of the standard does not wholly fence it in. The legislative history of these Acts demonstrates a purpose to impose on courts a responsibility which has not always been recognized. Of course it is a statute and not a committee report which we are interpreting. But the fair interpretation of a statute is often "the art of proliferating a purpose," revealed more by the demonstrable forces that produced it than by its precise phrasing. The adoption in these statutes of the judicially-constructed "substantial evidence" test was a response to pressures for stricter and more uniform practice, not a reflection of approval of all existing practices. To find the change so elusive that it cannot be precisely defined does not mean it may be ignored. . . .

We conclude, therefore, that the Administrative Procedure Act and the Taft-Hartley Act direct that courts must now assume more responsibility for the reasonableness and fairness of Labor Board decisions than some courts have shown in the past. Reviewing courts must be influenced by a feeling that they are not to abdicate the conventional judicial function. Congress has imposed on them responsibility for assuring that the Board keeps within reasonable grounds. That responsibility is not less real because it is limited to enforcing the requirement that evidence appear substantial when viewed, on the record as a whole, by courts invested with the authority and enjoying the prestige of the Courts of Appeals. The Board's findings are entitled to respect; but they must nonetheless be set aside when the record before a Court of Appeals clearly precludes the Board's decision from being justified by a fair estimate of the worth of the testimony of witnesses or its informed judgment on matters within its special competence or both.

From this it follows that enactment of these statutes does not require every Court of Appeals to alter its practice. Some—perhaps a majority—have always applied the attitude reflected in this legislation. To explore whether a particular court should or should not alter its practice would only divert attention from the application of the standard now prescribed to a futile inquiry into the nature of the test formerly used by a particular court.

Our power to review the correctness of application of the present standard ought seldom to be called into action. Whether on the record as a whole there is substantial evidence to support agency findings is a question which Congress has placed in the keeping of the Courts of

Appeals. This Court will intervene only in what ought to be the rare instance when the standard appears to have been misapprehended or grossly misapplied.

II.

. . . The decision of the Court of Appeals is assailed on two grounds. It is said (1) that the court erred in holding that it was barred from taking into account the report of the examiner on questions of fact insofar as that report was rejected by the Board, and (2) that the Board's order was not supported by substantial evidence on the record considered as a whole, even apart from the validity of the court's refusal to consider the rejected portions of the examiner's report.

The latter contention is easily met. . . . [I]t is clear from the court's opinion in this case that it in fact did consider the "record as a whole," and did not deem itself merely the judicial echo of the Board's conclusion. The testimony of the company's witnesses was inconsistent, and there was clear evidence that the complaining employee had been discharged by an officer who was at one time influenced against him because of his appearance at the Board hearing. On such a record we could not say that it would be error to grant enforcement. The first contention, however, raises serious questions to which we now turn.

III.

The Court of Appeals deemed itself bound by the Board's rejection of the examiner's findings because the court considered these findings not "as unassailable as a master's."[24] They are not. . . . The responsibility for decision . . . placed on the Board is wholly inconsistent with the notion that it has power to reverse an examiner's findings only when they are "clearly erroneous." Such a limitation would make so drastic a departure from prior administrative practice that explicitness would be required.

The Court of Appeals concluded from this premise "that, although the Board would be wrong in totally disregarding his findings, it is practically impossible for a court, upon review of those findings which the Board itself substitutes, to consider the Board's reversal as a factor in the court's own decision. This we say, because we cannot find any middle ground between doing that and treating such a reversal as error, whenever it would be such, if done by a judge to a master in equity." Much as we respect the logical acumen of the Chief Judge of the Court of Appeals, we do not find ourselves pinioned between the horns of his dilemma.

We are aware that to give the examiner's findings less finality than a master's and yet entitle them to consideration in striking the account, is to introduce another and an unruly factor into the judgmatical process of review. But we ought not to fashion an exclusionary rule merely to

---

[24]   Rule 53(e)(2), Fed. Rules Civ. Proc., gives finality to the findings of a master unless they are clearly erroneous.

reduce the number of imponderables to be considered by reviewing courts.

The Taft-Hartley Act provides that "The findings of the Board with respect to questions of fact if supported by substantial evidence on the record considered as a whole shall be conclusive." Surely an examiner's report is as much a part of the record as the complaint or the testimony. According to the Administrative Procedure Act, "All decisions (including initial, recommended, or tentative decisions) shall become a part of the record . . ." § 557(c). We found that this Act's provision for judicial review has the same meaning as that in the Taft-Hartley Act. The similarity of the two statutes in language and purpose also requires that the definition of "record" found in the Administrative Procedure Act be construed to be applicable as well to the term "record" as used in the Taft-Hartley Act.

It is therefore difficult to escape the conclusion that the plain language of the statutes directs a reviewing court to determine the substantiality of evidence on the record including the examiner's report. The conclusion is confirmed by the indications in the legislative history that enhancement of the status and function of the trial examiner was one of the important purposes of the movement for administrative reform.

This aim was set forth by the Attorney General's Committee on Administrative Procedure: "In general, the relationship upon appeal between the hearing commissioner and the agency ought to a considerable extent to be that of trial court to appellate court. Conclusions, interpretations, law, and policy should, of course, be open to full review. On the other hand, on matters which the hearing commissioner, having heard the evidence and seen the witnesses, is best qualified to decide, the agency should be reluctant to disturb his findings unless error is clearly shown."

Apparently it was the Committee's opinion that these recommendations should not be obligatory. For the bill which accompanied the Final Report required only that hearing officers make an initial decision which would become final in the absence of further agency action, and that agencies which differed on the facts from their examiners give reasons and record citations supporting their conclusion. This proposal was further moderated by the Administrative Procedure Act. It permits agencies to use examiners to record testimony but not to evaluate it, and contains the rather obscure provision that an agency which reviews an examiner's report has "all the powers which it would have in making the initial decision."

But this refusal to make mandatory the recommendations of the Attorney General's Committee should not be construed as a repudiation of them. Nothing in the statutes suggests that the Labor Board should not be influenced by the examiner's opportunity to observe the witnesses he hears and sees and the Board does not. Nothing suggests that reviewing courts should not give to the examiner's report such probative force as it intrinsically commands. . . .

We do not require that the examiner's findings be given more weight than in reason and in the light of judicial experience they deserve. The "substantial evidence" standard is not modified in any way when the Board and its examiner disagree. We intend only to recognize that evidence supporting a conclusion may be less substantial when an impartial, experienced examiner who has observed the witnesses and lived with the case has drawn conclusions different from the Board's than when he has reached the same conclusion. The findings of the examiner are to be considered along with the consistency and inherent probability of testimony. The significance of his report, of course, depends largely on the importance of credibility in the particular case. To give it this significance does not seem to us materially more difficult than to heed the other factors which in sum determine whether evidence is "substantial." . . .

We therefore remand the cause to the Court of Appeals. On reconsideration of the record it should accord the findings of the trial examiner the relevance that they reasonably command in answering the comprehensive question whether the evidence supporting the Board's order is substantial. But the court need not limit its reexamination of the case to the effect of that report on its decision. We leave it free to grant or deny enforcement as it thinks the principles expressed in this opinion dictate.

Judgment vacated and cause remanded.

■ JUSTICE BLACK and JUSTICE DOUGLAS concur with parts I and II of this opinion but as to part III agree with the opinion of the court below, 2 Cir., 179 F.2d 749, 753.

NOTES ON THE SUBSTANTIAL EVIDENCE TEST

(1) *How Do You Create Usable Doctrine?* "Weight of the evidence," "clearly erroneous," "substantial evidence"—can you tell the labels apart? If so, *how* do you tell them apart—by comparing them with one another, by relating them to a known institutional process (such as the deference given to a jury verdict), or by reformulating them? Justice Frankfurter has a serious jurisprudential problem. He believes that Congress has indeed said *something* in enacting the APA (and the Taft-Hartley Act): "It is fair to say that in all this Congress expressed a mood. And it expressed its mood not merely by oratory but by legislation." But he also believes that "the precise way in which courts interfere with agency findings cannot be imprisoned within any form of words." If you were a Court of Appeals judge (or her clerk), would you be confident you now understand your role?

(2) *Does This Help?* In DICKINSON V. ZURKO, 527 U.S. 150 (1999), Justice Breyer distinguishes between what he labels "court/court" review of findings of fact (by which he means appellate review of findings of fact made by a trial judge, not a jury) and "court/agency" review. He then writes (527 U.S. at 162–

163): "This Court has described the APA court/agency 'substantial evidence' standard as requiring a court to ask whether a 'reasonable mind might accept' a particular evidentiary record as 'adequate to support a conclusion.' Consolidated Edison, 305 U.S., at 229. It has described the court/court 'clearly erroneous' standard in terms of whether a reviewing judge has a 'definite and firm conviction' that an error has been committed. United States v. United States Gypsum Co., 333 U.S. 364 (1948). And it has suggested that the former is somewhat less strict than the latter. Universal Camera, 340 U.S., at 477, 488 (analogizing 'substantial evidence' test to review of jury findings and stating that appellate courts must respect agency expertise). At the same time the Court has stressed the importance of not simply rubberstamping agency factfinding. Id., at 490. The APA requires meaningful review; and its enactment meant stricter judicial review of agency factfinding than Congress believed some courts had previously conducted. Ibid.

"The upshot in terms of judicial review is some practical difference in outcome depending upon which standard is used. The court/agency standard, as we have said, is somewhat less strict than the court/court standard. But the difference is a subtle one—so fine that (apart from the present case) we have failed to uncover a single instance in which a reviewing court conceded that use of one standard rather than the other would in fact have produced a different outcome. Cf. International Brotherhood of Electrical Workers v. NLRB, 448 F.2d 1127, 1142 (C.A.D.C. 1971) (Leventhal, J., dissenting) (wrongly believing—and correcting himself—that he had found the 'case dreamed of by law school professors' where the agency's findings, though 'clearly erroneous,' were 'nevertheless' supported by 'substantial evidence').

"The difficulty of finding such a case may in part reflect the basic similarity of the reviewing task, which requires judges to apply logic and experience to an evidentiary record, whether that record was made in a court or by an agency. It may in part reflect the difficulty of attempting to capture in a form of words intangible factors such as judicial confidence in the fairness of the factfinding process. Universal Camera, supra, at 489. It may in part reflect the comparatively greater importance of case-specific factors, such as a finding's dependence upon agency expertise or the presence of internal agency review, which factors will often prove more influential in respect to outcome than will the applicable standard of review."

Relying on the fact that the Federal Circuit has a much narrower, more specialized scope of jurisdiction—focused on trademark and patent decisions—than the other Circuit Courts of Appeals, Justice Breyer then continues with the following remark (527 U.S. at 163): "These features of review underline the importance of the fact that, when a Federal Circuit judge reviews PTO [Patent and Trademark Office] factfinding, he or she often will examine that finding through the lens of patent-related experience—and properly so, for the Federal Circuit is a specialized court. That comparative expertise, by enabling the Circuit better to understand the basis for the PTO's finding of fact, may play a more important role in assuring proper review than would a theoretically somewhat stricter standard."

(3) While we are on the matter, is it a good idea that judicial review of administrative action usually is done by courts with a large, general jurisdiction? Harold Bruff, Specialized Courts in Administrative Law, 443 Admin. L. Rev. 329, 331 (1991):

> A premise of our nation's usual resort to courts of general jurisdiction is that sound decisionmaking results from exposure to a wide range of problems, rather than from initiation into an arcane set of mysteries. Generalization has two related benefits. Some loosely related legal issues may produce direct cross-fertilization of insights. More often, a wider perspective aids judgment by forestalling the exaggerated importance that long immersion may lend to some social problem. A broadened perspective may be especially important in those who review the action of bureaucracies that are themselves narrowly focused.

Are you convinced? European countries typically rely on specialized courts to review regulatory decisions—and even we have our Federal Circuit and our Tax Court.

(4) ***How Far Does "Evidence" Go?*** What is the boundary of the "substantial evidence" test? In some respects this question is not unlike the question raised in the law of torts, as to the determination of "negligence": at what point is negligence a finding of fact, to be left to the jury; at what point is it a determination of law, to be made by the judge; and in this interplay of judge and jury, who does the essential job of interpreting how the facts should be understood? A recent administrative law case worth considering in this regard is NLRB v. PIER SIXTY, LLC, 855 F.3d 115 (2d Cir. 2017).

Pier Sixty is a catering company in New York; its workers were holding a hotly contested campaign to unionize. As the court stated the facts:

> Two days before that election, Hernan Perez was working as a server at a Pier Sixty venue. A supervisor, Robert McSweeney, gave Perez and two other servers various directions in what the NLRB's opinion describes as a "harsh tone." These directions included "Turn your head that way [towards the guests] and stop chitchatting," and "Spread out, move, move." McSweeney's attitude in delivering these instructions upset Perez, who viewed them as the latest instance of the management's continuing disrespect for employees. About forty-five minutes later, during an authorized break from work, Perez used his iPhone to post the following message on his Facebook page:
>
>> Bob is such a NASTY MOTHER FUCKER don't know how to talk to people! ! ! ! ! ! Fuck his mother and his entire fucking family! ! ! ! What a LOSER! ! ! ! Vote YES for the UNION! ! ! ! ! ! !
>
> "Bob" referred to McSweeney. Perez knew that his Facebook "friends," including ten coworkers, would be able to see the post; the post was also publicly accessible, although Perez may not have known so at the time.

Perez was fired for his outburst and in turn filed a charge with the NLRB alleging management retaliation for protected activities. Employees are protected in their union-related activity by the National Labor Relations Act; but they can lose that protection by "opprobrious conduct." The ALJ found in Perez's favor, and the NLRB affirmed.

As in determining negligence in torts, several questions were intertwined—what was the legal standard for determining "opprobrious conduct;" what had happened; and how should what had happened be interpreted? The employer did not challenge the Board's legal standard, so the Second Circuit focused instead on the other two questions and upheld the Board's determination. The court said that the Board could "reasonably determine" that Perez's statement was part of the debate surrounding the election. The Board could rely on the ALJ's crediting of employee testimony that McSweeney himself cursed at employees daily and could reasonably decide, as the ALJ did, that "Perez's comments 'were not a slur against McSweeney's family but, rather, an epithet directed at McSweeney himself.'" In this workplace, no employee had previously been sanctioned for profanity. And Perez's comments, while perhaps visible to the world, were not made "in the immediate presence of customers." With all this, "[w]e . . .affirm the NLRB's determination that Pier Sixty violated [the Act] by discharging Hernan Perez since Perez's conduct was not so 'opprobrious' as to lose the protection of the NLRA. Our decision rests heavily on the deference afforded to NLRB factual findings, made following a six-day bench trial informed by the specific social and cultural context in this case. We note, however, that Perez's conduct sits at the outer-bounds of protected, union-related comments."

(5) ***The Role of the ALJ's Determinations.*** In its treatment of the examiner's (now ALJ's) report, the Universal Camera Court suggests a principle of allocation of responsibility as between examiner and agency. It places significant weight on the apoliticality of the examiner's place and function in the agency, a characteristic that lends "impartiality" to her judgments—impartiality is, if you like, what her participation contributes. The agency, on the other hand, has responsibility for the development and implementation of policy in light of its experience and statutory powers. This responsibility may lead the agency to develop policy-laden principles or presumptions for interpreting fact patterns that commonly arise in the course of its work. A simple issue of witness credibility, on the one hand, evokes the examiner's objectivity as well as her presence when the testimony was given. On the other hand, the idea that sudden and drastic employment actions are associated with anti-union animus is not based only in objective fact; policy-based commitments to the protection of union organizing activity contribute to it—and if such commitments are statutorily appropriate, one may see that such an inference is grounded in the agency's responsibilities, not the examiner's. Judge Frank explained the distinction on remand in Universal Camera in the following terms (190 F.2d 429, 432 (2d Cir. 1951)):

> An examiner's finding binds the Board only to the extent that it is a "testimonial inference," or "primary inference," i.e., an inference that a fact to which a witness orally testified is an actual fact

because the witness so testified and because observation of the witness induces a belief in that testimony. The Board, however, is not bound by the examiner's "secondary inferences," or "derivative inferences," i.e., facts to which no witness orally testified but which the examiner inferred from facts orally testified by witnesses whom the examiner believed. The Board may reach its own "secondary inferences" and we must abide by them unless they are irrational; in that way, the Board differs from a trial judge (in a jury-less case) who hears and sees the witnesses, for although we are usually bound by his "testimonial inferences" we need not accept his "secondary inferences" even if rational, but where other rational "secondary inferences" are possible, we may substitute our own.

(6) *Primary v. Secondary Inferences.* PENASQUITOS VILLAGE, INC. V. NLRB, 565 F.2d 1074 (9th Cir. 1977) exemplifies both the distinction between "primary" and "secondary" inferences and the frequent difficulty of drawing such a line. Once again the question for the Board was whether a challenged discharge reflected employee misbehavior or employer anti-union animus. A supervisor testified that he had observed two discharged employees loafing on the job; one had a few months earlier been suspended for similar misconduct. After verifying that he had the authority to fire them, he did so. The employees presented evidence of their status as union organizers and of alleged coercive interrogation. At least one of the employees was shown to have testified untruthfully in important respects, and the ALJ resolved "clear-cut questions of credibility" in favor of the employer. The case was also marked, however, by circumstances (abrupt employment discipline occurring very shortly after union organizing activity had come to light) that past Board decisions had identified as signs of anti-union animus. Disagreeing with its ALJ's assessment, the Board concluded that the discharges had been improper. Were the Board's derivative inferences, based on general experience and labor policy, enough to constitute "substantial evidence" on the record as a whole, when opposed to the ALJ's testimonial inferences that the employer's witnesses had been truth tellers, and the employees not, in describing the circumstances that led up to the discharges?

Judge Wallace, for the majority, 565 F.2d at 1078 et seq.: "Even when the record contains independent, credited evidence supportive of the Board's decision, a reviewing court will review more critically the Board's findings of fact if they are contrary to the administrative law judge's factual conclusions. . . . All aspects of the witness's demeanor—including the expression of his countenance, how he sits or stands, whether he is inordinately nervous, his coloration during critical examination, the modulation or pace of his speech and other non-verbal communication—may convince the observing trial judge that the witness is testifying truthfully or falsely. These same very important factors, however, are entirely unavailable to a reader of the transcript, such as the Board or the Court of Appeals. But it should be noted that the administrative law judge's opportunity to observe the witnesses' demeanor does not, by itself, require deference with regard to his or her derivative inferences. Observation of demeanor makes weighty only the observer's testimonial inferences.

"Deference is accorded the Board's factual conclusions for a different reason—Board members are presumed to have broad experience and expertise in labor-management relations. . . . Further, it is the Board to which Congress has delegated administration of the Act. The Board, therefore, is viewed as particularly capable of drawing inferences from the facts of a labor dispute. Accordingly, it has been said that a Court of Appeals must abide by the Board's derivative inferences, if drawn from not discredited testimony, unless those inferences are 'irrational' . . .

". . . [I]n this case, credibility played a dominant role. The administrative law judge's testimonial inferences reduce significantly the substantiality of the Board's contrary derivative inferences. Particularly, removing the Board's finding of anti-union animus based upon alleged unlawful threats and interrogations, leaves poorly substantiated the Board's other conclusion that the discharges were improperly motivated. Considering the record as a whole, we conclude that the Board's conclusion that Penasquitos committed unlawful labor practices is not supported by substantial evidence and must, therefore, be set aside."

Judge Duniway's partial dissent expressed doubt, 565 F.2d at 1084–85: "The notion that special deference is owed to the determination of a trier of fact, . . . is deeply imbedded in the law. . . . As a generalization, it is unassailable. . . . [Yet] I venture to suggest that, as to every one of the factors that Judge Wallace lists, one trier of fact may take it to indicate that the witness is truthful and another may think that it shows that the witness is lying. . . . Every trial lawyer knows, and most trial judges will admit, that it is not unusual for an accomplished liar to fool a jury (or, even, heaven forbid, a trial judge) into believing him because his demeanor is so convincing. The expression of his countenance may be open and frank; he may sit squarely in the chair, with no squirming; he may show no nervousness; his answers to questions may be clear, concise and audible, and given without hesitation; his coloration may be normal—neither pale nor flushed. In short, he may appear to be the trial lawyer's ideal witness. He may also be a consummate liar."

(7) *In Support of Legal Regularity?* As Justice Frankfurter's opinion in Universal Camera suggests, the "substantial evidence" test rests in part on an underlying belief that its enforcement furthers the fairness of the agency's adjudicatory process, helping to protect it against the forces of willfulness, politics, and personal antagonism. Might it also contribute to the "rule of law"? The Court suggested as much in ALLENTOWN MACK SALES AND SERVICE, INC. V. NLRB, 522 U.S. 359 (1998):

Mack Trucks had a small branch dealership in Allentown, Pa., that it sold; it was reorganized as an independent company, Allentown Mack Sales and Service, Inc. Thirty-two of the original 45 employees were hired by the new entity. The employees at the old branch had been unionized, and normally the union would represent them in the new company, too. But the new company held a secret poll of its employees, and the union lost, 19 to 13.

The question in the case was whether the employer, before the poll was conducted, had the "good faith reasonable doubt" of support for an existing union that, in the interest of labor relations stability, was required by Board precedent to justify holding such a poll. The ALJ held that Allentown Mack had not had the requisite "good faith reasonable doubt," that the poll should not have been held, and that the company therefore had to bargain with the union. The Board adopted the ALJ's findings and conclusions. The Court of Appeals enforced the bargaining order. But the Supreme Court, 5–4, reversed.

The majority, per Justice Scalia, looked rather hard at the evidence of "doubt" that was presented to the ALJ. For example, 522 U.S. at 369:

> For one thing, the ALJ and the Board totally disregarded the effect upon Allentown of the statement of an eighth employee, Dennis Marsh, who said that "he was not being represented for the $35 he was paying." The ALJ, whose findings were adopted by the Board, said that this statement "seems more an expression of a desire for better representation than one for no representation at all." It seems to us that it is, more accurately, simply an expression of dissatisfaction with the union's performance—which could reflect the speaker's desire that the union represent him more effectively, but could also reflect the speaker's desire to save his $35 and get rid of the union. The statement would assuredly engender an uncertainty whether the speaker supported the union, and so could not be entirely ignored.

To which the dissent, per Justice Breyer, countered, 522 U.S. at 392:

> Consider Marsh's statement. Marsh said, as the majority opinion notes, that "'he was not being represented for the $35 he was paying.'" The majority says that the ALJ was wrong not to count this statement in the employer's favor. But the majority fails to mention that Marsh made this statement to an Allentown manager while the manager was interviewing Marsh to determine whether he would, or would not, be one of the 32 employees whom Allentown would re-employ. The ALJ, when evaluating all the employee statements, wrote that statements made to the Allentown managers during the job interviews were "somewhat tainted as it is likely that a job applicant will say whatever he believes the prospective employer wants to hear." In so stating, the ALJ was reiterating the Board's own normative general finding that employers should not "rely in asserting a good-faith doubt" upon "[s]tatements made by employees during the course of an interview with a prospective employer." Middleboro Fire Apparatus, Inc., 234 N.L.R.B. 888, 894 enf'd, 590 F.2d 4 (1st Cir.1978). The Board also has found that "'[e]mployee statements of dissatisfaction with a union are not deemed the equivalent of withdrawal of support for the union.'" Either of these general Board findings (presumably known to employers advised by the labor bar), applied by the ALJ in this particular case, provides more than adequate support for the ALJ's conclusion that the employer could not properly rely upon

Marsh's statement as help in creating an "objective" employer doubt.

But, as is evident in this comparison, behind these contrasting analyses of the "facts" is a dispute as to how the agency should be allowed to "read" the facts. Justice Scalia:

> [This would be] a fairly straightforward administrative-law case, except for the contention that the Board's factfinding here was not an aberration. . . . The Board . . . does defend its factfinding in this case by saying that it has regularly rejected similarly persuasive demonstrations of reasonable good-faith doubt in prior decisions. The Court of Appeals in fact accepted that defense, relying on those earlier, similar decisions to conclude that the Board's findings were supported by substantial evidence here. . . .

> It is certainly conceivable that an adjudicating agency might consistently require a particular substantive standard to be established by a quantity or character of evidence so far beyond what reason and logic would require as to make it apparent that the *announced* standard is not *really* the effective one. And it is conceivable that in certain categories of cases an adjudicating agency which purports to be applying a preponderance standard of proof might so consistently demand in fact more than a preponderance, that all should be on notice from its case law that the genuine burden of proof is more than a preponderance. The question arises, then, whether, if that should be the situation that obtains here, we ought to measure the evidentiary support for the Board's decision against the standards consistently applied rather than the standards recited. As a theoretical matter (and leaving aside the question of legal authority), the Board could certainly have raised the bar for employer polling or withdrawal of recognition by imposing a more stringent requirement than the reasonable-doubt test, or by adopting a formal requirement that employers establish their reasonable doubt by more than a preponderance of the evidence. Would it make any difference if the Board achieved precisely the same result by formally leaving in place the reasonable-doubt and preponderance standards, but consistently applying them as though they meant something other than what they say? We think it would. . . .

> Reasoned decisionmaking, in which the rule announced is the rule applied, promotes sound results, and unreasoned decisionmaking the opposite. The evil of a decision that applies a standard other than the one it enunciates spreads in both directions, preventing both consistent application of the law by subordinate agency personnel (notably administrative law judges), and effective review of the law by the courts. . . .

And Justice Breyer:

> [T]he majority has failed to focus upon the ALJ's actual conclusions, it has failed to consider all the evidence before the ALJ,

it has transformed the actual legal standard that the Board has long administered without regard to the Board's own interpretive precedents, and it has ignored the guidance that the Board's own administrative interpretations have sought to provide to the bar, to employers, to unions, and to its own administrative staff. The majority's opinion will, I fear, weaken the system for judicial review of administrative action that this Court's precedents have carefully constructed over several decades.

Which Justice do you think has a better view of what the rule of law—in the context of administrative law—requires?

(8) Finally, quite apart from evidence or "substantial evidence," Justice Frankfurter's opinion is an excellent example of what can be done to construe a statute using legislative history in both senses of the term: the documents that Congress produced, and the problems and controversies that produced the act. (See p. 167 above.) The opinion also seems to many readers to be verbose and overly stylized. It is one of the most famous decisions in this casebook. Did you like it?

NOTES ON "ARBITRARY OR CAPRICIOUS" IN COMPARISON TO "SUBSTANTIAL EVIDENCE"

(1) *How Should We Read the Various APA Provisions on Judicial Review?* To understand the reach of the substantial evidence test, it is useful to spend a few moments looking at the structure of § 706(2) of the APA, reprinted just before the Universal Camera opinion. Six distinct standards of review are there articulated. For purposes of considering review of factual propositions, we can put to one side standards (B), relating to consistency with the Constitution, (C), relating to consistency with statutes, and (D), relating to procedure. Subsection (E) states the substantial evidence standard but by its reference to §§ 556 and 557 limits that standard to review of formal proceedings decided on a closed record.

Where, then, are the standards for reviewing the factual predicates for informal agency action, and especially for notice-and-comment rulemaking? The only other specific reference to "facts" is in standard (F), and that refers to a trial de novo. Could it be that the factual propositions underlying rules are to be tried de novo in court? Whether or not that is what the drafters had in mind, it is too awful to contemplate. Apart from the consummate inefficiency involved, review of rulemaking is typically assigned by statute to the courts of appeals, which of course lack the means for de novo fact finding. And so we turn to the catch-all standard (A), and even though its terms seem to refer to action "not in accordance with law," we say that the words "arbitrary" and "capricious" also cover informal agency action not sufficiently in accordance with the facts. Having massaged the statute this far, we then have this problem: what is the relationship of that "arbitrary or capricious" review of the facts to the substantial evidence test?

(2) In a much-cited opinion for the D.C. Circuit, ASSOCIATION OF DATA PROCESSING SERVICE ORGANIZATIONS, INC. V. BOARD OF GOVERNORS OF THE

FEDERAL RESERVE SYSTEM, 745 F.2d 677, 683–84 (1984)), then-JUDGE SCALIA wrote as follows:

> "[I]n their application to the requirement of factual support the substantial evidence test and arbitrary or capricious test are one and the same. The former is only a specific application of the latter. . . . The 'scope of review' provisions of the APA, § 706(2), are cumulative. Thus, an agency action which is supported by the required substantial evidence may in another regard be 'arbitrary, capricious, an abuse of discretion, or otherwise not in accordance with law'—for example, because it is an abrupt and unexplained departure from agency precedent. Paragraph (A) of subsection 706(2)—the 'arbitrary or capricious' provision—is a catch-all, picking up administrative misconduct not covered by the other more specific paragraphs. Thus, in those situations where paragraph (E) has no application (informal rulemaking, for example, which is not governed by §§ 556 and 557 to which paragraph (E) refers), paragraph (A) takes up the slack, so to speak, enabling the courts to strike down, as arbitrary, agency action that is devoid of needed factual support. When the arbitrary or capricious standard is performing that function of assuring factual support, there is no *substantive* difference between what it requires and what would be required by the substantial evidence test, since it is impossible to conceive of a 'nonarbitrary' factual judgment supported only by evidence that is not substantial in the APA sense—i.e., not 'enough to justify, if the trial were to a jury, a refusal to direct a verdict when the conclusion sought to be drawn . . . is one of fact for the jury.' " Illinois Central R.R. v. Norfolk & Western Ry., 385 U.S. 57, 66 (1966) (quoting NLRB v. Columbian Enameling & Stamping Co., 306 U.S. 292, 300 (1939)).

> "We have noted on several occasions that the distinction between the substantial evidence test and the arbitrary or capricious test is 'largely semantic,' and have indeed described that view as 'the emerging consensus of the Court of Appeals' . . . . The distinctive function of paragraph (E)—what it achieves that paragraph (A) does not—is to require substantial evidence to be found *within the record of closed-record proceedings* to which it exclusively applies. . . ."

(3) *Equivalence?* In the case, Judge Scalia also wrote that "[t]here is surely little appeal, [to creating a] new ineffable review standard," appearing to argue that between "unsupported" and "supported by a preponderance of the evidence" there could be room for only one judicial standard of review, whatever it was called. Do you agree? Reconsider Dickinson v. Zurko, noted p. 1057 above, drawing significance from the difference between the two existing standards of review for court/court and court/agency factual findings, and reconsider as well Justice Frankfurter's conclusion that "substantial evidence" reflects a mood requiring greater intensity of attention to factual support. Some later courts would find the same "mood" when dealing with organic statutes that specifically provided that review of informal rulemaking—706(2)(A), normally—required instead "substantial evidence" review. For example, when EPA argued that for informal rulemaking under the Toxic Substances Control Act, the statutory substantial evidence standard "tend[s] to converge" with the arbitrary and

capricious standard, it lost. Corrosion Proof Fittings v. EPA, 947 F.2d 1201, 1213 n. 13 (5th Cir. 1991): "Considering that Congress specifically rejected the arbitrary and capricious standard in the TSCA context, we will not act now to read that same standard back in by holding that the two standards are in fact one and the same." The 1976 House Conference Report had included this: "The conferees recognize that in rulemaking proceedings such as those . . . in this bill . . . the traditional standard of review is that of 'arbitrary and capricious.' However, the conferees have adopted the 'substantial evidence' test because they intend that the reviewing court focus on the rulemaking record to see if the . . . action is supported by that record." (1976 U.S.C.C.A.N. (90 Stat.) 4539, 4581). Similarly, in 1992 the Eleventh Circuit reversed a major OSHA rulemaking after holding that, given the statute's "substantial evidence" language, the court "must take a 'harder look' at OSHA's action than we would if we were reviewing the action under the more deferential arbitrary and capricious standard," AFL-CIO v. OSHA, 965 F.2d 962 (11th Cir. 1992).

(4) *The Type of Record.* Judge Scalia said that the choice between "substantial evidence" and "arbitrary or capricious" is "largely semantic." (Yes, Scalia!) Perhaps the bigger factors that affect review of the basis for rules made after notice and comment are the kind of record, the kind of factual issues, and the kind of result that typify informal rulemaking and distinguish it from formal adjudication. Consider Judge McGowan in INDUSTRIAL UNION DEP'T, AFL-CIO v. HODGSON, 499 F.2d 467, 474–76 (D.C. Cir. 1974), again facing the problem of review of informal rulemaking per a statute that specified "substantial evidence" review:

"[I]n some degree the record approaches the form of one customarily conceived of as appropriate for substantial evidence review. In other respects, it does not. . . . From extensive and often conflicting evidence, the Secretary in this case made numerous factual determinations. With respect to some of those questions, the evidence was such that the task consisted primarily of evaluating the data and drawing conclusions from it. The court can review that data in the record and determine whether it reflects substantial support for the Secretary's findings. But some of the questions involved in the promulgation of these standards are on the frontiers of scientific knowledge, and consequently as to them insufficient data is presently available to make a fully informed factual determination. Decisionmaking must in that circumstance depend to a greater extent upon policy judgments and less upon purely factual analysis. Thus, in addition to currently unresolved factual issues, the formulation of standards involves choices that by their nature require basic policy determinations rather than resolution of factual controversies. . . . Regardless of the manner in which the task of judicial review is articulated, policy choices of this sort are not susceptible to the same type of verification or refutation by reference to the record as are some factual questions. Consequently, the court's approach must necessarily be different no matter how the standards of review are labeled. That does not mean that such decisions escape exacting scrutiny, for, as this court has stated in a similar context: 'This exercise need be no less searching and strict in its weighing of whether the agency has performed in accordance with the Congressional purposes, but, because it is addressed to different materials, it inevitably varies from the adjudicatory model. The paramount objective is to see whether the agency, given an essentially legislative task to perform, has carried it out in a manner calculated to negate the dangers of arbitrariness and irrationality in the formulation of rules for general application in the future.' Automotive Parts and Accessories Ass'n v. Boyd, 407 F.2d 330, 338 (D.C.Cir.1968). . . .

"What we are entitled to at all events is a careful identification by the Secretary, when his proposed standards are challenged, of the reasons why he chooses to follow one course rather than another. Where that choice purports to be based on the existence of certain determinable facts, the Secretary must, in form as well as substance, find those facts from evidence in the record. By the same token, when the Secretary is obliged to make policy judgments where no factual certainties exist or where facts alone do not provide the answer, he should so state and go on to identify the considerations he found persuasive."

(5) For rules that rest heavily on scientific or technical data, one possible strategy for determining the "facts" is to convene a panel of experts. Agencies sometimes do this because their governing statute tells them to—for example, the EPA must consult its permanent Clean Air Scientific Advisory Committee for some of its rulemaking. And agencies sometimes do this on their own, as a matter of good practice. In either case, if the agency's final rule departs from what the panel of experts recommends, or adopts a view held by only a minority of the panel, is the agency being "arbitrary or capricious"? "The short answer," says Professor ADRIAN VERMEULE, "is that the cases are somewhat schizophrenic." THE PARLIAMENT OF THE EXPERTS, 58 Duke L.J. 2231, 2241 (2009). The right answer, he suggests, id. at 2266, is to analogize this aspect of rulemaking to the problem of Universal Camera:

> The APA's background obligation of reasoned fact-finding and decisionmaking is best understood to require that the agency either defer to the expert panel as to factual matters or else give a reason to think that it, rather than the expert panel, is in the best epistemic position to determine relevant facts. This was the implicit logic of Universal Camera, in which the Court said that reviewing judges could look behind agency findings to consider whether the agency had given adequate reason for refusing to credit the contrary findings of a specialized hearing examiner. The Court's discussion, as amplified and clarified by Learned Hand and Jerome Frank in opinions on remand, suggests that examiners are usually best situated to determine witness credibility and demeanor, and that to reject their findings, the agency must give a reason that "results from the [agency's] rational use of the [agency's] specialized knowledge." . . . On this approach the key issue . . . involves comparative epistemic competence: whether the agency or expert is best positioned to determine relevant facts, where reviewing courts who lack direct knowledge themselves should place their epistemic bets, and more generally how fact-

finding authority should be allocated between agencies and their expert advisors.

b. Review of the Flow of Reasoning and Judgment

> *MOTOR VEHICLE MFRS ASS'N v.*
>   *STATE FARM MUT. AUTOMOBILE*
>   *INS. CO.*
> *Notes on the State Farm Test*
> *Notes on the Background to State Farm*
> *Notes on the Wisdom (or Not) of Serious*
>   *Arbitrary and Capricious Review*
> *Notes on Cost/Benefit Analysis as a*
>   *Possible Element of "Arbitrary and*
>   *Capricious" Review*
> *Notes on "Politics" as a Possible*
>   *Element of "Arbitrary and Capricious"*
>   *Review*
> *FCC v. FOX TELEVISION STATIONS*

MOTOR VEHICLE MANUFACTURERS ASS'N v. STATE FARM MUTUAL AUTOMOBILE INS. CO.

Supreme Court of the United States (1983).
463 U.S. 29.

■ JUSTICE WHITE delivered the opinion of the Court.

The development of the automobile gave Americans unprecedented freedom to travel, but exacted a high price for enhanced mobility. Since 1929, motor vehicles have been the leading cause of accidental deaths and injuries in the United States. In 1982, 46,300 Americans died in motor vehicle accidents and hundreds of thousands more were maimed and injured. While a consensus exists that the current loss of life on our highways is unacceptably high, improving safety does not admit to easy solution. In 1966, Congress decided that at least part of the answer lies in improving the design and safety features of the vehicle itself. But much of the technology for building safer cars was undeveloped or untested. Before changes in automobile design could be mandated, the effectiveness of these changes had to be studied, their costs examined, and public acceptance considered. This task called for considerable expertise and Congress responded by enacting the National Traffic and Motor Vehicle Safety Act of 1966, 15 U.S.C. § 1381. The Act, created for the purpose of "reduc[ing] traffic accidents and deaths and injuries to persons resulting from traffic accidents," § 1381, directs the Secretary of Transportation or his delegate to issue motor vehicle safety standards that "shall be practicable, shall meet the need for motor vehicle safety, and shall be stated in objective terms." § 1392(a). In issuing these standards, the Secretary is directed to consider "relevant available motor vehicle safety data," whether the proposed standard "is reasonable, practicable and appropriate" for the particular type of motor vehicle, and the "extent to which such standards will contribute to carrying out the purposes" of the Act. § 1392(f)(1), (3), (4).[3]

The Act also authorizes judicial review under [APA § 706] of all "orders establishing, amending, or revoking a Federal motor vehicle safety standard," § 1392(b). Under this authority, we review today whether NHTSA acted arbitrarily and capriciously in revoking the requirement in Motor Vehicle Safety Standard 208 that new motor vehicles produced after September 1982 be equipped with passive restraints to protect the safety of the occupants of the vehicle in the event of a collision. . . .

I

The regulation whose rescission is at issue bears a complex and convoluted history. Over the course of approximately 60 rulemaking notices, the requirement has been imposed, amended, rescinded, reimposed, and now rescinded again.

As originally issued by the Department of Transportation in 1967, Standard 208 simply required the installation of seatbelts in all automobiles. It soon became apparent that the level of seatbelt use was too low to reduce traffic injuries to an acceptable level. The Department therefore began consideration of "passive occupant restraint systems"— devices that do not depend for their effectiveness upon any action taken by the occupant except that necessary to operate the vehicle. Two types of automatic crash protection emerged: automatic seatbelts and airbags. The automatic seatbelt is a traditional safety belt, which when fastened to the interior of the door remains attached without impeding entry or exit from the vehicle, and deploys automatically without any action on the part of the passenger. The airbag is an inflatable device concealed in the dashboard and steering column. It automatically inflates when a sensor indicates that deceleration forces from an accident have exceeded a preset minimum, then rapidly deflates to dissipate those forces. The life-saving potential of these devices was immediately recognized, and in 1977, after substantial on-the-road experience with both devices, it was estimated by NHTSA that passive restraints could prevent approximately 12,000 deaths and over 100,000 serious injuries annually.

In 1969, the Department formally proposed a standard requiring the installation of passive restraints . . . and in 1972, the agency amended the Standard to require full passive protection for all front seat occupants of vehicles manufactured after August 15, 1975. In the interim, vehicles built between August 1973 and August 1975 were to carry either passive restraints or lap and shoulder belts coupled with an "ignition interlock"

---

[3]   The Secretary's general authority to promulgate safety standards under the Act has been delegated to the Administrator of the National Highway Traffic Safety Administration (NHTSA). 49 C.F.R. § 1.50(a). . . .

that would prevent starting the vehicle if the belts were not connected. On review, the agency's decision to require passive restraints was found to be supported by "substantial evidence" and upheld. Chrysler Corp. v. Department of Transportation, 472 F.2d 659 (C.A.6 1972).[5]

In preparing for the upcoming model year, most car makers chose the "ignition interlock" option, a decision which was highly unpopular, and led Congress to amend the Act to prohibit a motor vehicle safety standard from requiring or permitting compliance by means of an ignition interlock or a continuous buzzer designed to indicate that safety belts were not in use. Motor Vehicle and Schoolbus Safety Amendments of 1974. The 1974 Amendments also provided that any safety standard that could be satisfied by a system other than seatbelts would have to be submitted to Congress where it could be vetoed by concurrent resolution of both Houses.

The effective date for mandatory passive restraint systems was extended for a year until August 31, 1976. But in June 1976, Secretary of Transportation William Coleman, Jr., initiated a new rulemaking on the issue. After hearing testimony and reviewing written comments, Coleman extended the optional alternatives indefinitely and suspended the passive restraint requirement.[8] Although he found passive restraints technologically and economically feasible, the Secretary based his decision on the expectation that there would be widespread public resistance to the new systems. He instead proposed a demonstration project involving up to 500,000 cars installed with passive restraints, in order to smooth the way for public acceptance of mandatory passive restraints at a later date.

Coleman's successor as Secretary of Transportation disagreed. Within months of assuming office, Secretary Brock Adams decided that the demonstration project was unnecessary. He issued a new mandatory passive restraint regulation [that] mandated the phasing in of passive restraints beginning with large cars in model year 1982 and extending to all cars by model year 1984. The two principal systems that would satisfy the Standard were airbags and passive belts; the choice of which system to install was left to the manufacturers. In Pacific Legal Foundation v. Department of Transportation, 593 F.2d 1338, cert. denied, 444 U.S. 830 (1979), the Court of Appeals upheld Modified Standard 208 as a rational, nonarbitrary regulation consistent with the agency's mandate under the Act. The Standard also survived scrutiny by Congress, which did not

---

[5]   The court did hold that the testing procedures required of passive belts did not satisfy the Safety Act's requirement that standards be "objective."

[8]   [Ed.] In a step unprecedented except by his own similar actions on other matters (e.g., landing rights in the United States for supersonic airliners), Secretary Coleman personally presided over these hearings. Persons familiar with the hearings were impressed by his complete preparation and command of all material. The final decision was directly his own to a degree that is becoming rare even among leading judges. When one of your editors asked ex-Secretary Coleman how other high officials could possibly find the time to perform as he had, the response was: "Fewer cocktail parties."

exercise its authority under the legislative veto provision of the 1974 Amendments.

Over the next several years, the automobile industry geared up to comply with Modified Standard 208.... In February 1981, however, Secretary of Transportation Andrew Lewis reopened the rulemaking due to changed economic circumstances and, in particular, the difficulties of the automobile industry. Two months later, the agency ordered a one-year delay in the application of the Standard to large cars, extending the deadline to September 1982 and at the same time, proposed the possible rescission of the entire Standard. After receiving written comments and holding public hearings, NHTSA issued a final rule (Notice 25) that rescinded the passive restraint requirement contained in Modified Standard 208.

II

In a statement explaining the rescission, NHTSA maintained that it was no longer able to find, as it had in 1977, that the automatic restraint requirement would produce significant safety benefits.... In 1977, the agency had assumed that airbags would be installed in 60% of all new cars and automatic seatbelts in 40%. By 1981 it became apparent that automobile manufacturers planned to install the automatic seatbelts in approximately 99% of the new cars. For this reason, the lifesaving potential of airbags would not be realized. Moreover, it now appeared that the overwhelming majority of passive belts planned to be installed by manufacturers could be detached easily and left that way permanently. Passive belts, once detached, then required "the same type of affirmative action that is the stumbling block to obtaining high usage levels of manual belts." For this reason, the agency concluded that there was no longer a basis for reliably predicting that the Standard would lead to any significant increased usage of restraints at all.

In view of the possibly minimal safety benefits, the automatic restraint requirement no longer was reasonable or practicable in the agency's view. The requirement would require approximately $I billion to implement and the agency did not believe it would be reasonable to impose such substantial costs on manufacturers and consumers without more adequate assurance that sufficient safety benefits would accrue. In addition, NHTSA concluded that automatic restraints might have an adverse effect on the public's attitude toward safety. Given the high expense and limited benefits of detachable belts, NHTSA feared that many consumers would regard the Standard as an instance of ineffective regulation, adversely affecting the public's view of safety regulation and, in particular, "poisoning ... popular sentiment toward efforts to improve occupant restraint systems in the future." ...

[The D.C. Circuit Court of Appeals held the agency's action to be arbitrary and capricious.]

III

Unlike the Court of Appeals, we do not find the appropriate scope of judicial review to be the "most troublesome question" in [this case]. Both the [1966] Act and the 1974 Amendments concerning occupant crash protection standards indicate that motor vehicle safety standards are to be promulgated under the informal rulemaking procedures of § 553 of the Administrative Procedure Act. The agency's action in promulgating such standards therefore may be set aside if found to be "arbitrary, capricious, an abuse of discretion, or otherwise not in accordance with law." 5 U.S.C. § 706(2)(A). Citizens to Preserve Overton Park v. Volpe, 401 U.S. 402, 414 (1971). We believe that the rescission or modification of an occupant-protection standard is subject to the same test. Section 103(b) of the Act states that the procedural and judicial review provisions of the Administrative Procedure Act "shall apply to all orders establishing, amending, or revoking a Federal motor vehicle safety standard," and suggests no difference in the scope of judicial review depending upon the nature of the agency's action.

Petitioner Motor Vehicle Manufacturers Association (MVMA) disagrees, contending that the rescission of an agency rule should be judged by the same standard a court would use to judge an agency's refusal to promulgate a rule in the first place—a standard petitioner believes considerably narrower than the traditional arbitrary-and-capricious test. . . . We reject this view. The Motor Vehicle Safety Act expressly equates orders "revoking" and establishing safety standards; neither that Act nor the APA suggests that revocations are to be treated as refusals to promulgate standards. . . . Moreover, the revocation of an extant regulation is substantially different than a failure to act. Revocation constitutes a reversal of the agency's former views as to the proper course. A "settled course of behavior embodies the agency's informed judgment that, by pursuing that course, it will carry out the policies committed to it by Congress. There is, then, at least a presumption that those policies will be carried out best if the settled rule is adhered to." Atchison, T. & S.F.R. Co. v. Wichita Bd. of Trade, 412 U.S. 800, 807–808 (1973). Accordingly, an agency changing its course by rescinding a rule is obligated to supply a reasoned analysis for the change beyond that which may be required when an agency does not act in the first instance.

In so holding, we fully recognize that "[r]egulatory agencies do not establish rules of conduct to last forever," American Trucking Ass'ns., Inc. v. Atchison, T. & S.F.R. Co., 387 U.S. 397, 416 (1967), and that an agency must be given ample latitude to "adapt their rules and policies to the demands of changing circumstances." Permian Basin Area Rate Cases, 390 U.S. 747, 784 (1968). But the forces of change do not always or necessarily point in the direction of deregulation. In the abstract, there is no more reason to presume that changing circumstances require the rescission of prior action, instead of a revision in or even the extension of current regulation. If Congress established a presumption from which judicial review should start, that presumption—contrary to petitioners' views—is not *against* safety regulation, but *against* changes in current policy that are not justified by the rulemaking record. While the removal of a regulation may not entail the monetary expenditures and other costs of enacting a new standard, and, accordingly, it may be easier for an agency to justify a deregulatory action, the direction in which an agency chooses to move does not alter the standard of judicial review established by law.

The Department of Transportation . . . argues that under [the "arbitrary and capricious" standard], a reviewing court may not set aside an agency rule that is rational, based on consideration of the relevant factors, and within the scope of the authority delegated to the agency by the statute. We do not disagree with this formulation.[9] The scope of review under the "arbitrary and capricious" standard is narrow and a court is not to substitute its judgment for that of the agency. Nevertheless, the agency must examine the relevant data and articulate a satisfactory explanation for its action including a "rational connection between the facts found and the choice made." Burlington Truck Lines, Inc. v. United States, 371 U.S. 156, 168. . . . Normally, an agency rule would be arbitrary and capricious if the agency has relied on factors which Congress has not intended it to consider, entirely failed to consider an important aspect of the problem, offered an explanation for its decision that runs counter to the evidence before the agency, or is so implausible that it could not be ascribed to a difference in view or the product of agency expertise. The reviewing court should not attempt itself to make up for such deficiencies; we may not supply a reasoned basis for the agency's action that the agency itself has not given. SEC v. Chenery Corp., 332 U.S. 194, 196 (1947). . . . For purposes of this case, it is also relevant that Congress required a record of the rulemaking proceedings to be compiled and submitted to a reviewing court, § 1394, and intended that agency findings under the Act would be supported by "substantial evidence on the record considered as a whole." . . .

IV

[The course of Congressional consideration of this matter does not suggest application of any special standard of review.]

V

The ultimate question before us is whether NHTSA's rescission of the passive restraint requirement of Standard 208 was arbitrary and capricious. . . .

---

    [9]   The Department of Transportation suggests that the arbitrary-and-capricious standard requires no more than the minimum rationality a statute must bear in order to withstand analysis under the Due Process Clause. We do not view as equivalent the presumption of constitutionality afforded legislation drafted by Congress and the presumption of regularity afforded an agency in fulfilling its statutory mandate.

A

The first and most obvious reason for finding the rescission arbitrary and capricious is that NHTSA apparently gave no consideration whatever to modifying the Standard to require that airbag technology be utilized. Standard 208 sought to achieve automatic crash protection by requiring automobile manufacturers to install either of two passive restraint devices: airbags or automatic seatbelts. There was no suggestion in the long rulemaking process that led to Standard 208 that if only one of these options were feasible, no passive restraint standard should be promulgated. Indeed, the agency's original proposed standard contemplated the installation of inflatable restraints in all cars. Automatic belts were added [in 1971] as a means of complying with the Standard because they were believed to be as effective as airbags in achieving the goal of occupant crash protection. . . . At that time, the passive belt approved by the agency could not be detached. Only later, at a manufacturer's behest, did the agency approve of the detachability feature—and only after assurances that the feature would not compromise the safety benefits of the restraint. Although it was then foreseen that 60% of the new cars would contain airbags and 40% would have automatic seatbelts, the ratio between the two was not significant as long as the passive belt would also assure greater passenger safety.

The agency has now determined that the detachable automatic belts will not attain anticipated safety benefits because so many individuals will detach the mechanism. Even if this conclusion were acceptable in its entirety, . . . standing alone it would not justify any more than an amendment of Standard 208 to disallow compliance by means of the one technology which will not provide effective passenger protection. . . . Given the effectiveness ascribed to airbag technology by the agency, the mandate of the Act to achieve traffic safety would suggest that the logical response to the faults of detachable seatbelts would be to require the installation of airbags. At the very least this alternative way of achieving the objectives of the Act should have been addressed and adequate reasons given for its abandonment. But the agency not only did not require compliance through airbags, it also did not even consider the possibility in its 1981 rulemaking. Not one sentence of its rulemaking statement discusses the airbags-only option. . . . [W]hat we said in Burlington Truck Lines, Inc. v. United States, 371 U.S., at 167, is apropos here: "There are no findings and no analysis here to justify the choice made, no indication of the basis on which the [agency] exercised its expert discretion. We are not prepared to and the Administrative Procedure Act will not permit us to accept such . . . practice. . . . Expert discretion is the lifeblood of the administrative process, but 'unless we make the requirements for administrative action strict and demanding, *expertise,* the strength of modern government, can become a monster which rules with no practical limits on its discretion.' " We have frequently reiterated that an agency must cogently explain why it has exercised its discretion in a given manner, and we reaffirm this principle again today.

The automobile industry has opted for the passive belt over the airbag, but surely it is not enough that the regulated industry has eschewed a given safety device. For nearly a decade, the automobile industry waged the regulatory equivalent of war against the airbag and lost—the inflatable restraint was proven sufficiently effective. Now the automobile industry has decided to employ a seatbelt system which will not meet the safety objectives of Standard 208. This hardly constitutes cause to revoke the Standard itself. Indeed, the Act was necessary because the industry was not sufficiently responsive to safety concerns. . . .

. . . [P]etitioners recite a number of difficulties that they believe would be posed by a mandatory airbag standard. These range from questions concerning the installation of airbags in small cars to that of adverse public reaction. But these are not the agency's reasons for rejecting a mandatory airbag standard. Not having discussed the possibility, the agency submitted no reasons at all. . . .

Petitioners also invoke our decision in Vermont Yankee Nuclear Power Corp. v. NRDC, 435 U.S. 519 (1978) [p. 295] as though it were a talisman under which any agency decision is by definition unimpeachable. Specifically, it is submitted that to require an agency to consider an airbags-only alternative is, in essence, to dictate to the agency the procedures it is to follow. Petitioners both misread Vermont Yankee and misconstrue the nature of the remand that is in order. In Vermont Yankee, we held that a court may not impose additional procedural requirements upon an agency. We do not require today any specific procedures which NHTSA must follow. Nor do we broadly require an agency to consider all policy alternatives in reaching decision. It is true that a rulemaking "cannot be found wanting simply because the agency failed to include every alternative device and thought conceivable by the mind of man . . . regardless of how uncommon or unknown that alternative may have been. . . ." 435 U.S., at 551. But the airbag is more than a policy alternative to the passive restraint Standard; it is a technological alternative within the ambit of the existing Standard. We hold only that given the judgment made in 1977 that airbags are an effective and cost-beneficial life-saving technology, the mandatory passive restraint rule may not be abandoned without any consideration whatsoever of an airbags-only requirement.

B

Although the issue is closer, we also find that the agency was too quick to dismiss the safety benefits of automatic seatbelts. NHTSA's critical finding was that, in light of the industry's plans to install readily detachable passive belts, it could not reliably predict "even a 5 percentage point increase as the minimum level of expected usage increase." The Court of Appeals rejected this finding because there is "not one iota" of evidence that Modified Standard 208 will fail to increase nationwide seatbelt use by at least 13 percentage points, the level of increased usage necessary for the Standard to justify its cost. Given the lack of probative evidence, the court held that "only a well-justified refusal to seek more evidence could render rescission non-arbitrary." 680 F.2d, at 232.

Petitioners object to this conclusion. In their view, "substantial uncertainty" that a regulation will accomplish its intended purpose is sufficient reason, without more, to rescind a regulation. We agree with petitioners that just as an agency reasonably may decline to issue a safety standard if it is uncertain about its efficacy, an agency may also revoke a standard on the basis of serious uncertainties if supported by the record and reasonably explained. Rescission of the passive restraint requirement would not be arbitrary and capricious simply because there was no evidence in direct support of the agency's conclusion. It is not infrequent that the available data does not settle a regulatory issue and the agency must then exercise its judgment in moving from the facts and probabilities on the record to a policy conclusion. Recognizing that policymaking in a complex society must account for uncertainty, however, does not imply that it is sufficient for an agency to merely recite the terms "substantial uncertainty" as a justification for its actions. . . . [T]he agency must explain the evidence which is available, and must offer a "rational connection between the facts found and the choice made." Burlington Truck Lines, Inc. v. United States, supra, 371 U.S. at 168. Generally, one aspect of that explanation would be a justification for rescinding the regulation before engaging in a search for further evidence. . . .

We start with the accepted ground that if used, seatbelts unquestionably would save many thousands of lives and would prevent tens of thousands of crippling injuries. Unlike recent regulatory decisions we have reviewed, the safety benefits of wearing seatbelts are not in doubt, and it is not challenged that were those benefits to accrue, the monetary costs of implementing the standard would be easily justified. We move next to the fact that there is no direct evidence in support of the agency's finding that detachable automatic belts cannot be predicted to yield a substantial increase in usage. The empirical evidence on the record, consisting of surveys of drivers of automobiles equipped with passive belts, reveals more than a doubling of the usage rate experienced with manual belts.[16] Much of the agency's rulemaking statement—and much of the controversy in this case—centers on the conclusions that should be drawn from these studies. The agency maintained that the

---

[16] Between 1975 and 1980, Volkswagen sold approximately 350,000 Rabbits equipped with detachable passive seatbelts that were guarded by an ignition interlock. General Motors sold 8,000 1978 and 1979 Chevettes with a similar system, but eliminated the ignition interlock on the 13,000 Chevettes sold in 1980. NHTSA found that belt usage in the Rabbits averaged 34% for manual belts and 84% for passive belts. Regulatory Impact Analysis (RIA) at IV–52, App. 108. For the 1978–1979 Chevettes, NHTSA calculated 34% usages for manual belts and 72% for passive belts. On 1980 Chevettes, the agency found these figures to be 31% for manual belts and 70% for passive belts.

doubling of seatbelt usage in these studies could not be extrapolated to an across-the-board mandatory standard because the passive seatbelts were guarded by ignition interlocks and purchasers of the tested cars are somewhat atypical.[17] Respondents insist these studies demonstrate that Modified Standard 208 will substantially increase seatbelt usage. We believe that it is within the agency's discretion to pass upon the generalizability of these field studies. This is precisely the type of issue which rests within the expertise of NHTSA, and upon which a reviewing court must be most hesitant to intrude.

But accepting the agency's view of the field tests on passive restraints indicates only that there is no reliable real-world experience that usage rates will substantially increase. To be sure, NHTSA opines that "it cannot reliably predict even a 5 percentage point increase as the minimum level of expected increased usage." But this and other statements that passive belts will not yield substantial increases in seatbelt usage apparently take no account of the critical difference between detachable automatic belts and current manual belts. A detached passive belt does require an affirmative act to reconnect it, but—unlike a manual seatbelt—the passive belt, once reattached, will continue to function automatically unless again disconnected. Thus, inertia—a factor which the agency's own studies have found significant in explaining the current low usage rates for seatbelts[18]—works in *favor* of, not *against*, use of the protective device. Since 20% to 50% of motorists currently wear seatbelts on some occasions, there would seem to be grounds to believe that seatbelt use by occasional users will be substantially increased by the detachable passive belts. Whether this is in fact the case is a matter for the agency to decide, but it must bring its expertise to bear on the question. . . .

The agency also failed to articulate a basis for not requiring nondetachable belts under Standard 208. It is argued that the concern of the agency with the easy detachability of the currently favored design would be readily solved by a continuous passive belt, which allows the occupant to "spool out" the belt and create the necessary slack for easy extrication from the vehicle. The agency did not separately consider the continuous belt option, but treated it together with the ignition interlock device in a category it titled "Option of Adoption of Use-Compelling

---

[17] "NHTSA believes that the usage of automatic belts in Rabbits and Chevettes would have been substantially lower if the automatic belts in those cars were not equipped with a use-inducing device inhibiting detachment." Notice 25, 46 Fed. Reg. at 53422 (1981). [The "atypicality" was also that small car owners used seatbelts more than others did, and most owners with passive belts in these cars had voluntarily paid extra for them.]

[18] NHTSA commissioned a number of surveys of public attitudes in an effort to better understand why people were not using manual belts and to determine how they would react to passive restraints. The surveys reveal that while 20% to 40% of the public is opposed to wearing manual belts, the larger proportion of the population does not wear belts because they forgot or found manual belts inconvenient or bothersome. In another survey, 38% of the surveyed group responded that they would welcome automatic belts, and 25% would "tolerate" them. NHTSA did not comment upon these attitude surveys in its explanation accompanying the rescission of the passive restraint requirement.

Features." The agency was concerned that use-compelling devices would "complicate extrication of [an] occupant from his or her car." "[T]o require that passive belts contain use-compelling features," the agency observed, "could be counterproductive [given] . . . widespread, latent and irrational fear in many members of the public that they could be trapped by the seatbelt after a crash." In addition, based on the experience with the ignition interlock, the agency feared that use-compelling features might trigger adverse public reaction.

By failing to analyze the continuous seatbelts in its own right, the agency has failed to offer the rational connection between facts and judgment required to pass muster under the arbitrary-and-capricious standard. . . . NHTSA did not suggest that the emergency release mechanisms used in nondetachable belts are any less effective for emergency egress than the buckle release system used in detachable belts. In 1978, when General Motors obtained the agency's approval to install a continuous passive belt, it assured the agency that nondetachable belts with spool releases were as safe as detachable belts with buckle releases. NHTSA was satisfied that this belt design assured easy extricability: "[t]he agency does not believe that the use of [such] release mechanisms will cause serious occupant egress problems. . . ." While the agency is entitled to change its view on the acceptability of continuous passive belts, it is obligated to explain its reasons for doing so.

The agency also failed to offer any explanation why a continuous passive belt would engender the same adverse public reaction as the ignition interlock, and, as the Court of Appeals concluded, "every indication in the record points the other way." We see no basis for equating the two devices: the continuous belt, unlike the ignition interlock, does not interfere with the operation of the vehicle. More importantly, it is the agency's responsibility, not this Court's, to explain its decision.

VI

"An agency's view of what is in the public interest may change, either with or without a change in circumstances. But an agency changing its course must supply a reasoned analysis. . . ." Greater Boston Television Corp. v. FCC, 444 F.2d 841, 852 (1970), cert. denied, 403 U.S. 923 (1971). We do not accept all of the reasoning of the Court of Appeals but we do conclude that the agency has failed to supply the requisite "reasoned analysis" in this case. Accordingly, we vacate the judgment of the Court of Appeals and remand the case to that court with directions to remand the matter to the NHTSA for further consideration consistent with this opinion.

■ JUSTICE REHNQUIST, with whom the CHIEF JUSTICE, JUSTICE POWELL, and JUSTICE O'CONNOR join, concurring in part and dissenting in part.

I join parts, I, II, III, IV, and V-A of the Court's opinion. In particular, I agree that, since the airbag and continuous spool automatic seatbelt were explicitly approved in the Standard the agency was rescinding, the agency should explain why it declined to leave those requirements intact. In this case, the agency gave no explanation at all. . . .

I do not believe, however, that NHTSA's view of detachable automatic seatbelts was arbitrary and capricious. . . . [T]he agency's explanation, while by no means a model, is adequate. The agency acknowledged that there would probably be some increase in belt usage, but concluded that the increase would be small and not worth the cost of mandatory detachable automatic belts. . . .

The agency's changed view of the standard seems to be related to the election of a new President of a different political party. It is readily apparent that the responsible members of one administration may consider public resistance and uncertainties to be more important than do their counterparts in a previous administration. A change in administration brought about by the people casting their votes is a perfectly reasonable basis for an executive agency's reappraisal of the costs and benefits of its programs and regulations. As long as the agency remains within the bounds established by Congress,* it is entitled to assess administrative records and evaluate priorities in light of the philosophy of the administration.

NOTES ON THE STATE FARM TEST

(1) *The Direct Consequences of State Farm.* One year after State Farm, NHTSA issued a rule requiring passive restraints unless by April 1989 two-thirds of the nation's population were covered by state laws that both required use of seatbelts and met other criteria including educational efforts and enforcement. Most states enacted seat belt laws—but most of these laws did not satisfy the other criteria. Thus, a federal passive restraint requirement finally became effective in 1989. Most automakers chose to meet the requirement with airbags, and in 1991 Congress made the airbags requirement permanent, effective in 1996. Pub. L. No. 102–240, § 2508. For a fuller view of both the before and the after of the litigation, see Jerry L. Mashaw, The Story of Motor Vehicle Manufacturers Association of the U.S. v. State Farm Mutual Automobile Insurance Co.: Law, Science and Politics in the Administrative State, in ed. Peter L. Strauss, Administrative Law Stories (2006).

(2) *Applying the Standard of Review.* State Farm is the leading case on the meaning of "arbitrary and capricious" review; probably its most quoted

---

* Of course, a new administration may not refuse to enforce laws of which it does not approve, or to ignore statutory standards in carrying out its regulatory functions. But in this case, as the Court correctly concludes, . . . Congress has not required the agency to require passive restraints.

line is Justice White's restatement of that standard: "Normally, an agency rule would be arbitrary and capricious if the agency has relied on factors which Congress has not intended it to consider, entirely failed to consider an important aspect of the problem, offered an explanation for its decision that runs counter to the evidence before the agency, or is so implausible that it could not be ascribed to a difference in view or the product of agency expertise." Looking at the Court's actual use of its test, it bears noting that all nine Justices agreed that it was arbitrary and capricious not to consider the alternatives of air bags only or of continuous spooling automatic seatbelts; but only five of the nine thought the same about the agency's rejection of detachable automatic seatbelts. Analytically, there would seem to be quite a gap between the two conclusions: recognizing the first two alternatives does not require more than the ability to read the preexisting regulation, whereas Justice White's discussion of detachable belts turns heavily on recognizing the importance of inertia in human behavior in the real world as developed in studies appearing in the record. All nine Justices agreed with Justice White's statement of the basic legal standard. So in practice the question would seem to be: how hard a look at what the agency has done (and said) should a court take? Considered as a "mood," to use Justice Frankfurter's term from Universal Camera, how does this case compare with that one?

(3) *What Must an Agency Consider?* One aspect of the just-stated question lies in implementing the Court's statement that an agency has acted arbitrarily if it "has relied on factors which Congress has not intended it to consider [or has] entirely failed to consider an important aspect of the problem." Is the proper set of considerations determined by some notion of what makes for good policy, or is it determined by the framework of the legal regime? And if the latter, by the agency's organic statute or by the U.S. Code in general? Consider PENSION BENEFIT GUARANTY CORP. v. LTV CORP., 496 U.S. 633 (1990) (p. 533). PBGC is a federal agency established by the Employee Retirement Income Security Act of 1974 (ERISA) to insure certain pension benefits—somewhat like the FDIC's insuring of bank deposits. The lower court found that the agency, which often acts in situations in which bankruptcy and labor law are relevant, in this case had "focused inordinately on ERISA" and given too little consideration to those other areas of law. But Justice Blackmun for the Supreme Court said that the requirement imposed on PBGC by the lower court was irreconcilable with the statute's "plain language." He continued (496 U.S. at 646):

> Even if Congress' directive to the PBGC had not been so clear, we are not entirely sure that the Court of Appeals' holding makes good sense as a general principle of administrative law. The PBGC points up problems that would arise if federal courts routinely were to require each agency to take explicit account of public policies that derive from federal statutes other than the agency's enabling act. To begin with, there are numerous federal statutes that could be said to embody countless policies. If agency action may be disturbed whenever a reviewing court is able to point to an arguably relevant statutory policy that was not explicitly considered, then a very

large number of agency decisions might be open to judicial invalidation.

The Court of Appeals' directive . . . is questionable for another reason as well. Because the PBGC can claim no expertise in the labor and bankruptcy areas, it may be ill-equipped to undertake the difficult task of discerning and applying the 'policies and goals' of those fields.

Similarly, agencies are expected to defend their actions in terms of the policies made relevant by their governing statutes. See, e.g., Independent U.S. Tanker Committee v. Dole, 809 F.2d 847 (D.C. Cir. 1987) (p. 341) (the Secretary "is not free to substitute new goals in place of the statutory objectives without explaining how these actions are consistent with the authority under the statute.")

(4) *Identifying Alternatives.* In the same vein, what is the agency's obligation, in cases less clear than State Farm, to identify the alternatives it must consider? At stake in DEPARTMENT OF TRANSPORTATION V. PUBLIC CITIZEN, 541 U.S. 752 (2004), was a determination by the Federal Motor Carrier Safety Administration, pursuant to the National Environmental Policy Act (NEPA), that its issuance of new safety rules applicable to Mexican trucks entering the United States would have no substantial environmental impact. Thomas, J., for a unanimous Court, 541 U.S. at 764–65:

. . . We begin by explaining what this case does not involve. What is not properly before us, despite respondents' argument to the contrary, is any challenge to the EA [Environmental Assessment] due to its failure properly to consider possible alternatives to the proposed action (i.e., the issuance of the challenged rules) that would mitigate the environmental impact of the authorization of cross-border operations by Mexican motor carriers. Persons challenging an agency's compliance with NEPA must "structure their participation so that it . . . alerts the agency to the [parties'] position and contentions," in order to allow the agency to give the issue meaningful consideration. None of the respondents identified in their comments any rulemaking alternatives beyond those evaluated in the EA, and none urged FMCSA to consider alternatives. Because respondents did not raise these particular objections to the EA, FMCSA was not given the opportunity to examine any proposed alternatives to determine if they were reasonably available. Respondents have therefore forfeited any objection to the EA on the ground that it failed adequately to discuss potential alternatives to the proposed action.

Admittedly, the agency bears the primary responsibility to ensure that it complies with NEPA, and an EA's . . . flaws might be so obvious that there is no need for a commentator to point them out specifically in order to preserve its ability to challenge a proposed action. But that situation is not before us.

(5) *How Much Explanation Is Enough?* In FEDERAL ENERGY REGULATORY COMMISSION V. ELECTRIC POWER SUPPLY ASSOCIATION, 136 S.Ct. 760, 782–84 (2016), the Supreme Court reviewed a rule issued by FERC that required the operators of wholesale electricity markets to pay the same amount to "demand response providers" for conserving electricity as they paid to generators for making it. ("Demand response providers" were large companies, or aggregations of multiple users, which at times of high demand for electricity promised to lower their usage by a set amount at a set time, thus helping to balance supply and demand by reducing demand, just as electricity generators who upped their output helped to create balance by increasing supply.) Most of the opinion dealt with, and approved, FERC's claiming jurisdiction to issue the rule in the first place. JUSTICE KAGAN continued:

"These cases present a second, narrower question: Is FERC's decision to compensate demand response providers at LMP [the locational marginal price]—the same price paid to generators—arbitrary and capricious? Recall here the basic issue. Wholesale market operators pay a single price—LMP—for all successful bids to supply electricity at a given time and place. The Rule orders operators to pay the identical price for a successful bid to conserve electricity so long as that bid can satisfy a "net benefits test"—meaning that it is sure to bring down costs for wholesale purchasers. In mandating that payment, FERC rejected an alternative proposal under which demand response providers would receive LMP minus G (LMP – G), where G is the retail rate for electricity. According to EPSA and others favoring that approach, demand response providers get a windfall—a kind of "double-payment"—unless market operators subtract the savings associated with conserving electricity from the ordinary compensation level. EPSA now claims that FERC failed to adequately justify its choice of LMP rather than LMP – G.

"In reviewing that decision, we may not substitute our own judgment for that of the Commission. The 'scope of review under the "arbitrary and capricious" standard is narrow.' Motor Vehicle Mfrs. Assn. of United States, Inc. v. State Farm Mut. Automobile Ins. Co., 463 U.S. 29, 43 (1983). A court is not to ask whether a regulatory decision is the best one possible or even whether it is better than the alternatives. Rather, the court must uphold a rule if the agency has 'examine [d] the relevant [considerations] and articulate[d] a satisfactory explanation for its action[,] including a rational connection between the facts found and the choice made.' *Ibid*. And nowhere is that more true than in a technical area like electricity rate design: '[W]e afford great deference to the Commission in its rate decisions.' *Morgan Stanley,* 554 U.S., at 532.

"Here, the Commission gave a detailed explanation of its choice of LMP. Relying on an eminent regulatory economist's views, FERC chiefly reasoned that demand response bids should get the same compensation as generators' bids because both provide the same value to a wholesale market. FERC noted that a market operator needs to constantly balance supply and demand, and that either kind of bid can perform that service cost-effectively—*i.e.,* in a way that lowers costs for wholesale purchasers. A compensation system, FERC concluded, therefore should place the two kinds of bids 'on a competitive par.' With both supply and demand response available on equal terms, the operator will select whichever bids, of whichever kind, provide the needed electricity at the lowest possible cost. See Rehearing Order, 137 FERC, at 62,301–62,302, ¶ 68 ('By ensuring that both . . . receive the same compensation for the same service, we expect the Final Rule to enhance the competitiveness' of wholesale markets and 'result in just and reasonable rates').

"That rationale received added support from FERC's adoption of the net benefits test. The Commission realized during its rulemaking that in some circumstances a demand response bid—despite reducing the wholesale rate—does *not* provide the same value as generation. . . . Thus, under the Commission's approach, a demand response provider will receive the same compensation as a generator only when it is in fact providing the same service to the wholesale market.

"The Commission responded at length to EPSA's contrary view that paying LMP, even in that situation, will overcompensate demand response providers because they are also 'effectively receiv[ing] "G," the retail rate that they do not need to pay.' FERC explained that compensation ordinarily reflects only the value of the service an entity provides—not the costs it incurs, or benefits it obtains, in the process. So when a generator presents a bid, 'the Commission does not inquire into the costs or benefits of production.' Different power plants have different cost structures. And, indeed, some plants receive tax credits and similar incentive payments for their activities, while others do not. But the Commission had long since decided that such matters are irrelevant: Paying LMP to all generators—although some then walk away with more profit and some with less—'encourages more efficient supply and demand decisions.' And the Commission could see no economic reason to treat demand response providers any differently. Like generators, they too experience a range of benefits and costs—both the benefits of not paying for electricity and the costs of not using it at a certain time. But, FERC again concluded, that is immaterial: To increase competition and optimally balance supply and demand, market operators should compensate demand response providers, like generators, based on their contribution to the wholesale system.

"Moreover, FERC found, paying LMP will help demand response providers overcome certain barriers to participation in the wholesale market. Commenters had detailed significant start-up expenses associated with demand response, including the cost of installing necessary metering technology and energy management systems. The Commission agreed that such factors inhibit potential demand responders from competing with generators in the wholesale markets. It concluded that rewarding demand response at LMP (which is, in any event, the price reflecting its value to the market) will encourage that competition and, in turn, bring down wholesale prices.

"Finally, the Commission noted that determining the 'G' in the formula LMP—G is easier proposed than accomplished. Retail rates vary across and even within States, and change over time as well. Accordingly, FERC concluded, requiring market operators to incorporate G into their prices, 'even though perhaps feasible,' would 'create practical difficulties.' Better, then, not to impose that administrative burden.

"All of that together is enough. The Commission, not this or any other court, regulates electricity rates. The disputed question here involves both technical understanding and policy judgment. The Commission addressed that issue seriously and carefully, providing reasons in support of its position, and responding to the principal alternative advanced. In upholding that action, we do not discount the cogency of EPSA's arguments in favor of LMP—G. Nor do we say that in opting for LMP instead, FERC made the better call. It is not our job to render that judgment, on which reasonable minds can differ. Our important but limited role is to ensure that the Commission engaged in reasoned decisionmaking—that it weighed competing views, selected a compensation formula with adequate support in the record, and intelligibly explained the reasons for making that choice. FERC satisfied that standard."

NOTES ON THE BACKGROUND TO STATE FARM

(1) **Overton Park.** Justice White's analysis in State Farm builds on the important, and still cited, case of CITIZENS TO PRESERVE OVERTON PARK, INC. V. VOLPE, 401 U.S. 402 (1971). There, the Secretary of Transportation approved the building of an interstate highway through a public park in Memphis; the relevant statute said that park land could not be used for this purpose unless there was "no feasible and prudent alternative to the use of such land." In what was treated as, in APA terms, an informal adjudication, the Secretary approved the highway but made no contemporaneous statement as to why he considered the statute satisfied. Instead, the Department defended the decision in court based on "affidavits, prepared specifically for this litigation, which indicated that the Secretary had made the decision and that the decision was supportable." Based partly on its interpretation of the substantive meaning of the statute, the Supreme Court, deciding the case in a very short period of time, overturned the Secretary's decision. (See Peter L. Strauss, Citizens to Preserve Overton Park v. Volpe— Of Politics and Law, Young Lawyers and the Highway Goliath in ed. Peter L. Strauss, Administrative Law Stories (2006)). But the case is famous for its various statements about the course of judicial review:

(a) First, as to the meaning of APA "arbitrary or capricious" review, 401 U.S. at 415–16:

... [T]he generally applicable standards of § 706 require the reviewing court to engage in a substantial inquiry. Certainly, the Secretary's decision is entitled to a presumption of regularity. But that presumption is not to shield his action from a thorough, probing, in-depth review.

The court is first required to decide whether the Secretary acted within the scope of his authority. This determination naturally begins with a delineation of the scope of the Secretary's authority and discretion. As has been shown, Congress has specified only a small range of choices that the Secretary can make. Also involved in this initial inquiry is a determination of whether on the facts the Secretary's decision can reasonably be said to be within that range. The reviewing court must consider whether the Secretary properly construed his authority to approve the use of parkland as limited to situations where there are no feasible alternative routes or where feasible alternative routes involve uniquely difficult problems. And the reviewing court must be able to find that the Secretary could have reasonably believed that in this case there are no feasible alternatives or that alternatives do involve unique problems.

Scrutiny of the facts does not end, however, with the determination that the Secretary has acted within the scope of his statutory authority. Section 706(2)(A) requires a finding that the actual choice made was not "arbitrary, capricious, an abuse of discretion, or otherwise not in accordance with law." To make this finding the court must consider whether the decision was based on a consideration of the relevant factors and whether there has been a clear error of judgment. . . . Although this inquiry into the facts is to be searching and careful, the ultimate standard of review is a narrow one. The court is not empowered to substitute its judgment for that of the agency.

Is this the same as the test State Farm enunciated, albeit in different words? Or not?

(b) Second, as to the materials to which the standard of review should be applied, 401 U.S. at 419–20:

. . . Moreover, there is an administrative record that allows the full, prompt review of the Secretary's action that is sought without additional delay which would result from having a remand to the Secretary.

That administrative record is not, however, before us. The lower courts based their review on the litigation affidavits that were presented. These affidavits were merely "post hoc" rationalizations, Burlington Truck Lines v. United States, 371 U.S. 156, 168–169 (1962), which have traditionally been found to be an inadequate basis for review. SEC v. Chenery Corp., 318 U.S. 80, 87 (1943). And they clearly do not constitute the "whole record" compiled by the agency: the basis for review required by § 706 of the Administrative Procedure Act.

Thus it is necessary to remand this case to the District Court for plenary review of the Secretary's decision. That review is to be based on the full administrative record that was before the Secretary at the time he made his decision.

The APA does not require an "informal" proceeding to be on the record; but yet it does say that judicial review per § 706 shall be based on the "whole record." How do these provisions go together? Does Overton Park interpret the APA rightly?

(c)   Third, what should be done if the "administrative record" does not provide the information needed to determine "whether the decision was based on a consideration of the relevant factors and whether there has been a clear error of judgment"? 401 U.S. at 420:

> . . .[S]ince the bare record may not disclose the factors that were considered or the Secretary's construction of the evidence it may be necessary for the District Court to require some explanation in order to determine if the Secretary acted within the scope of his authority and if the Secretary's action was justifiable under the applicable standard.
>
> The court may require the administrative officials who participated in the decision to give testimony explaining their action. Of course, such inquiry into the mental processes of administrative decisionmakers is usually to be avoided. United States v. Morgan, 313 U.S. 409, 422 (1941). [p. 503 above] And where there are administrative findings that were made at the same time as the decision, as was the case in Morgan, there must be a strong showing of bad faith or improper behavior before such inquiry may be made. But here there are no such formal findings and it may be that the only way there can be effective judicial review is by examining the decisionmakers themselves.

The immediate result of this language was a 27-day trial held by the district court on remand, including affidavits from the Secretary and testimony of subordinates.

Shortly thereafter, this language was distinguished by the Court in CAMP V. PITTS, 411 U.S. 138 (1973), which concerned the denial by the Comptroller of the Currency of an application to organize a new national bank; the proceeding was "informal" but the applicant was send a brief letter of explanation. The Court wrote, 411 U.S. at 142–43:

> The appropriate standard for review was, accordingly, whether the Comptroller's adjudication was arbitrary, capricious, an abuse of discretion, or otherwise not in accordance with law, as specified in 5 U.S.C. § 706(2)(A). In applying that standard, the focal point for judicial review should be the administrative record already in existence, not some new record made initially in the reviewing court. . . .
>
> If, as the Court of Appeals held and as the Comptroller does not now contest, there was such failure to explain administrative action as to frustrate effective judicial review, the remedy was not to hold a de novo hearing but, as contemplated by Overton Park, to obtain from the agency, either through affidavits or testimony, such additional explanation of the reasons for the agency decision as may prove necessary. We add a caveat, however. Unlike Overton Park, in the present case there was contemporaneous explanation of the agency decision. The explanation may have been curt, but it surely indicated the determinative reason for the final action taken: the finding that a new bank was an uneconomic venture in

light of the banking needs and the banking services already available in the surrounding community. The validity of the Comptroller's action must, therefore, stand or fall on the propriety of that finding, judged, of course, by the appropriate standard of review. If that finding is not sustainable on the administrative record made, then the Comptroller's decision must be vacated and the matter remanded to him for further consideration. See SEC v. Chenery Corp., 318 U.S. 80 (1943).

Few agencies have difficulty choosing between the 27-day trial-on-remand in Overton Park itself and the alternative of making at least a basic administrative record as suggested in the preceding paragraph!

(d)   Finally, Overton Park also spoke famously about the narrowness of any exceptions to the presumption that administrative action is subject to judicial review. See p. 1399 below.

(2)   *"Hard Look" Review.* As the Court in State Farm says, the petitioners claimed that requiring NHTSA to consider the airbags only possibility would collide with Vermont Yankee's prohibition on the judicial creation of additional procedural burdens in rulemaking. (Vermont Yankee, decided five years before State Farm, is set out at p. 295.) This apparent confusion of substance and procedure can be more easily understood in light of the flow of judicial review decisions in the decade or so before the principal case.

In the oft-cited case (indeed, cited in State Farm itself) Greater Boston Television Corp. v. FCC, 444 F.2d 841 (D.C. Cir. 1970), Judge Leventhal said in 1970 that "[t]he function of the court is to assure that the agency has given reasoned consideration to all the material facts and issues." In spelling out this idea, he explained, 444 F.2d at 851:

> Its supervisory function calls on the court to intervene not merely in case of procedural inadequacies, or bypassing of the mandate in the legislative charter, but more broadly if the court becomes aware, especially from a combination of danger signals, that the agency has not really taken a "hard look" at the salient problems, and has not genuinely engaged in reasoned decision-making. If the agency has not shirked this fundamental task, however, the court exercises restraint and affirms the agency's action even though the court would on its own account have made different findings or adopted different standards.

In the succeeding years, this set of ideas was taken up by other judges, in the D.C. Circuit and elsewhere, to frame their process of review, especially of informal rulemaking. "As originally articulated," Judge Wald wrote in 1980, "the words 'hard look' described the agency's responsibility and not the court's. However, the phrase subsequently evolved to connote the rigorous standard of judicial review applied to increasingly utilized informal rulemaking proceedings or to other decisions made upon less than a full trial-type record." National Lime Assoc. v. EPA, 627 F.2d 416, 451 n. 126 (D.C. Cir. 1980).

As can be seen from Judge Leventhal's statement, the "hard look" approach did not necessarily distinguish possible procedural requirements from possible substantive ones, and indeed terms like "quasi-procedural, quasi-substantive" were sometimes used to describe various items. Different judges gave different emphases, some more to the procedural side, some to the substantive. The structure of the problem can be seen in the Nova Scotia Food Products case, decided in 1977 and already set out at p. 322. There, one of Judge Gurfein's objections was that the agency should have explained why it rejected a salient alternative urged on it in the comment process. Was this requirement to address alternatives based on APA § 553(c), requiring the agency to "incorporate in the rules adopted a concise general statement of their basis and purpose"? Was it based on APA § 706(2)(A), telling the court to "set aside agency action . . . found to be . . . arbitrary, capricious . . . or otherwise not in accordance with law"? Or was it based on neither of these and justified only if the reviewing courts had the power to create a common law of judicial review? Judge Gurfein, writing before Vermont Yankee was decided, did not have to be explicit.

What the State Farm petitioners hoped was that the Supreme Court would conclude that the "hard look" techniques were a result of courts of appeals' asserting a common-law-like power to revise agency processes. Then Vermont Yankee—which emphatically denied the existence of such a power—would be the death of "hard look." (Insofar as the Overton Park case also had "hard look" elements, petitioners also hoped the Court would narrow Overton Park in light of Vermont Yankee.) Correspondingly, the refusal of the Court to adopt petitioners' point of view has led later courts and commentators to speak of the State Farm test as embodying "hard look" review even though Justice White does not use the phrase.

(3) *Pacific States Box & Basket.* As stated in footnote 9 of the opinion, the Government also attempted to equate "arbitrary and capricious" review of agency action with the relaxed "rationality" review given to ordinary legislation. This claim can be traced back to PACIFIC STATES BOX & BASKET CO. V. WHITE, 296 U.S. 176 (1935). That case concerned a rule of the Oregon Division of Plant Industry fixing official standards for containers used to package raspberries and strawberries—standards that could not be met by the fruit baskets petitioner made. The circumstances suggested, but no finding stated, that the Oregon board might have found that use of a single container type (among the 34 available) would enhance consumer protection against short measures. Acknowledging that no such finding would be required of a legislature, petitioner urged that findings were constitutionally requisite for the actions of administrators wielding delegated powers. A unanimous court, speaking through Justice Brandeis, found that that contention was "without support in authority or reason, and rests upon misconception. Every exertion of the police power, either by the legislature or by an administrative body, is an exercise of delegated power. . . . Where the regulation is within the scope of authority legally delegated, the presumption of the existence of facts justifying its specific exercise attaches alike to statutes . . . and to orders of administrative bodies. . . . [T]he statute did not require special findings; doubtless because the regulation authorized was general legislation, not an administrative order in the nature of a judgment directed against an individual concern." 296 U.S. at 185–86. But

that was then and this was now; the State Farm court thought it sufficient to reply laconically: "We do not view as equivalent the presumption of constitutionality afforded legislation drafted by Congress and the presumption of regularity afforded an agency in fulfilling its statutory mandate."

NOTES ON THE WISDOM (OR NOT) OF SERIOUS ARBITRARY AND CAPRICIOUS REVIEW

(1) *Is It a Good Idea for Courts to Review Rather Intensively the Course of Reasoning of an Agency? Yes:* "It is a great tonic," wrote WILLIAM PEDERSEN, former Deputy General Counsel of the EPA, "to discover that even if a regulation can be slipped or wrestled through various layers of internal or external review [inside the bureaucracy] without significant change, the final and most prestigious reviewing forum of all—a circuit court of appeals—will inquire into the minute details of methodology, data sufficiency and test procedure and will send the regulations back if these are lacking. The effect of such judicial opinions within the agency reaches beyond those who were concerned with the specific regulations reviewed. They serve as a precedent for future rulewriters and give those who care about well-documented and well-reasoned decisionmaking a lever with which to move those who do not." FORMAL RECORDS AND INFORMAL RULEMAKING, 85 Yale L.J. 38, 60 (1975).

And No: JACOB GERSEN AND ADRIAN VERMEULE, THIN RATIONALITY REVIEW, 114 MICH. L. REV. 1355 (2016): "Under the Administrative Procedure Act, courts review and set aside agency action that is 'arbitrary [and] capricious.' In a common formulation of rationality review, courts must either take a 'hard look' at the rationality of agency decisionmaking, or at least ensure that agencies themselves have taken a hard look. We will propose a much less demanding and intrusive interpretation of rationality review—a thin version. Under a robust range of conditions, rational agencies have good reason to decide in a manner that is inaccurate, nonrational, or arbitrary. Although this claim is seemingly paradoxical or internally inconsistent, it simply rests on an appreciation of the limits of reason, especially in administrative policymaking. Agency decisionmaking is nonideal decisionmaking; what would be rational under ideal conditions is rarely a relevant question for agencies. Rather, agencies make decisions under constraints of scarce time, information, and resources. Those constraints imply that agencies will frequently have excellent reasons to depart from idealized first-order conceptions of administrative rationality."

(2) *The "Ossification" Issue.* SIDNEY SHAPIRO and RICHARD MURPHY, EIGHT THINGS AMERICANS CAN'T FIGURE OUT ABOUT CONTROLLING ADMINISTRATIVE POWER, 61 Admin. L. Rev. 5, 13–15 (2009): "According to critics of the current judicial review regime, undue ossification of rulemaking flows largely from the analytical demands that courts have placed on agencies in an effort to make the APA's skeletal requirements on notice-and-comment meaningful. This judicial effort has both procedural and substantive aspects . . .

"[J]udicial review of the rationality of agency policies has, by and large, intensified considerably since the time of the APA's adoption in 1946. . . . [T]he Supreme Court approved this form of review in State Farm. . . . The majority then proceeded to engage in a painstaking (one might say picky) review of the evidence. . . . In keeping with this approach, the meaning of hard look review has evolved somewhat-it is now commonly understood to require courts to take a hard look at agency rationality rather than to require courts to check whether the agency took a hard look at a problem.

"Thus, agencies must respond to any comment that they think a court might, during post hoc review, find significant, and their responses must be sufficiently detailed and persuasive to survive open-ended substantive review by a set of generalist judges who may have no particularly relevant technical expertise. This combination creates a minefield given that administrative records, at least for controversial or difficult rules, are chock-full of contestable arguments and evidence. Threading this minefield requires agencies to offer justifications for their rules that are, often enough, interminable and detailed rather than 'concise' and 'general' as the APA contemplated. As a result, it can take many years for an agency to create a significant, controversial rule via notice-and-comment."

(3) MARK SEIDENFELD, DEMYSTIFYING DEOSSIFICATION: RETHINKING RECENT PROPOSALS TO MODIFY JUDICIAL REVIEW OF NOTICE AND COMMENT RULEMAKING, 75 Tex. L. Rev. 483, 500–02 (1997): "I am skeptical . . . whether a more deferential attitude toward agency decisionmaking will relieve the problems created by hard look review without forfeiting the benefits that flow from such review. . . . [R]aising the level of deference to agency rulemaking may not reduce an agency's incentives to engage in excessive data collection and analysis. Simply making review more 'agency friendly' will not tell the agency how to perform its analyses in a manner sufficient to pass judicial review. Moreover, without delving into the details of a rulemaking record and questioning the agency's rationale in light of data and arguments submitted by challengers of the rule, most judges lack the expertise with the substantive areas of agency regulation to know whether the agency, in adopting the rule, has reached a reasonable decision. Hence, even under a more deferential standard of review, courts will have to consult the record and ensure that it is consistent with the agency's reasoning. This in turn sends a message to the agency that its chances of success on review increase if it collects additional data and performs more analysis. Thus, significant incentives remain for an agency to overtax its scarce regulatory resources.

"[Finally], easing of judicial review may have a detrimental impact on the agency deliberative process. For example, courts could dramatically reduce the uncertainty created by judicial review simply by eliminating meaningful review; they could affirm any rule that was not wholly irrational. That would still leave congressional and presidential review to ensure against unwise agency rulemaking. But both congressional and presidential review increase the propensity for agency rules to benefit groups with narrow interests. By demanding that agencies publicly justify their rules, however, judicial review can discourage the adoption and interpretation of rules preferred by special interest groups. Increasing the likelihood that a rule will be upheld by relaxing the requirements that an agency explain its decision to a court might, by the same token, increase the proportion of rules driven by pressure from special interest groups or an agency agenda that is at odds with the general public's desire for regulation."

(4)   Yet another view of the costs engendered by "hard look" review is provided in MATTHEW STEPHENSON, A COSTLY SIGNALING THEORY OF "HARD LOOK" JUDICIAL REVIEW, 58 Admin. L. Rev. 753, 772 (2006). Perhaps, argues Professor Stephenson, the costs of the process are part of the point: ". . . What does this sort of hard look review accomplish? One possibility is that it facilitates the court's efforts to learn what the agency knows about the true payoff of the regulation, or at least to verify the agency's conclusion that the regulation is substantially justified. . . . Another possibility is that judicial scrutiny of the administrative record is an elaborate charade in which courts find justifications for making the decisions they would have made anyway. . . . This Article advances another possibility: The quality of the agency's explanation and justification for its decision—a variable I will refer to as record quality—can act as a costly signal to the court of the agency's information about the true payoff. That is, when the reviewing court scrutinizes the evidence and analysis marshaled by an agency in support of a proposed rule, the court may be neither learning about the accuracy of the agency's conclusions, nor observing a substantively reliable indicator of reasoned decisionmaking. The court nonetheless may be learning something about the agency's willingness to invest resources into providing the kind of detailed record and lawyerly analysis that courts consider in hard look cases. If so, and if the benefit of a given regulation to the agency is positively correlated with the expected benefit of that regulation to the court, then a record of sufficient quality can induce a court to uphold a regulation that it would otherwise oppose."

(5)   *Some Data.* ANNE JOSEPH O'CONNELL, POLITICAL CYCLES OF RULEMAKING: AN EMPIRICAL PORTRAIT OF THE MODERN ADMINISTRATIVE STATE, 94 Va. L. Rev. 889, 964–65 (2008): "If costs to rulemaking were as high as feared, agencies presumably would engage in little notice-and-comment rulemaking and what rulemaking they did undertake would take at least several years to complete. From 1983 to 2002, federal agencies, however, commenced and completed substantial notice-and-comment rulemaking. From 1983 to 2000 and in 2002 federal agencies issued more than 690 official NPRMs each year . . . In addition, the average duration of completed rulemakings for nine of the ten agencies used in this Article's regression analyses was under two years. These empirical findings suggest that the administrative state is not greatly ossified.

"These findings, of course, are not determinative of the ossification debate. Most importantly, they do not test how costly rulemaking is to agencies. Agencies could still face considerable costs when they undertake rulemaking. We do not know how much rulemaking would occur if agencies faced less scrutiny by the courts . . . or how much rulemaking is optimal in terms of social welfare. Assuming that more rulemaking would be beneficial, rulemaking is ossified, to some extent. In addition, the generally constant level of rulemaking described here could be squared with the ossification theory if the growing complexity of the administrative state had led to increased rulemaking and canceled out the decrease we would expect from ossification. Finally, the findings do not assess the quality or significance of the rules that agencies do produce. Agencies may be promulgating low-quality rules or rules that slightly modify earlier regulations."

(6)   Finally, consider the possible impact judicial review may be having on agency structure itself. PAUL R. VERKUIL, THE WAIT IS OVER: *CHEVRON* AS THE STEALTH *VERMONT YANKEE* II, 75 Geo. Wash. L. Rev. 921, 928–29 (2007): "For me, even more troubling . . . are the consequences to the agency reasoning process that result from preparing impossibly long statements of basis and purpose. . . . The use of consultants to prepare rules for review has become a common practice. But it is not costless. Consultants undermine the quality of an agency's reasoning process when they are given increasingly expansive roles. They often summarize the comments submitted to agencies during rulemaking, write the agencies' analyses and statements of basis and purpose, and present complete rulemaking records to the agency officials. They are increasingly playing roles normally performed in-house. Agency officials, overwhelmed by a workload produced in part by perceived views of hard-look review requirements, are increasingly delegating the rationality assignment to private contractors and signing off on the results. . . .

"The use of private contractors is not just an unintended consequence of demands by reviewing courts, of course; it is caused by personnel ceilings, which limit agency staff, and by the larger trend toward the privatization of government functions. Still, by forcing more work on the agencies, hard look review may, ironically, hurt rulemaking rationality as much as it helps. The essential purpose of hard-look review is to require agency officials to be thoughtful and engaged. Reviewing judges expect the hard look to be taken by agency officials themselves. If, however, the effect is to farm out the analysis and drafting functions, then this intellectual exercise is not happening. Rationality review by the agency may be fast becoming a misnomer."

NOTES ON COST-BENEFIT ANALYSIS AS A POSSIBLE ELEMENT OF "ARBITRARY AND CAPRICIOUS" REVIEW

(1)   While "gut instincts" or "common sense" might do for many of life's decisions, State Farm says it will not do when an agency makes a rule; there we expect to find a serious analysis of the situation, overtly expressed. But there is more than one way to do a "serious analysis." In light of the increasing importance of cost-benefit analysis in the intellectual mores of the society as a whole, we might ask whether cost-benefit analysis is also part of what judicial review requires of an agency announcing a new rule.

(Cost-benefit analysis of this type can be very roughly described as entailing (1) consideration of all the consequences of adopting a rule—both the costs it will directly or indirectly impose and the benefits it will directly or indirectly generate; (2) conversion of each of those costs and benefits into a quantified, commensurable measure, almost always money; and (3) summation of those sums across the entire relevant domain, generally done without regard to how the costs or the benefits are distributed. A rule is then seen as cost-benefit justified if the benefits outweigh the costs. Of course, there are many technicalities, and some judgment calls, involved in doing such an analysis to a professional standard—for example, in deciding how many dollars saving a "statistical life" is worth.)

(2)   Cost-benefit analysis is already commonplace in the federal rulemaking process. You will have already seen it if you have studied the OIRA process for executive review of agency rulemaking, p. 434 above. But the OIRA process does not apply to all agencies, and in any case it is specifically limited not to "affect any otherwise available judicial review of agency action." E.O. 12866, § 10. So the questions for the judges remain open: should they require a cost/benefit analysis; if so, how intensely should they review its adequacy; and in any case, what is their authority for so acting?

(3)   *Cost-Benefit Analysis and the Courts.* "Normally," says State Farm, "an agency rule would be arbitrary and capricious if the agency has relied on factors which Congress has not intended it to consider [or] entirely failed to consider an important aspect of the problem." At first blush, this standard would seem to throw the matter of cost-benefit analysis back to what Congress intended when it wrote the particular substantive statute in question. And so, it would seem, the Supreme Court thought in 2001 in Whitman v. American Trucking Ass'ns, Inc. (p. 791 above). Whitman held, as a matter of statutory construction per Justice Scalia, that the specifically applicable provisions of the Clean Air Act did not permit taking costs into account in setting National Ambient Air Quality Standards.

What statutory language does trigger cost-benefit analysis? A statute passed in 1996 required the SEC in various rulemakings to consider whether the proposed rule would "promote efficiency, competition, and capital formation." A series of cases in the D.C. Circuit in subsequent years interpreted this language to require consideration of economic effects generally, went on to formulate that requirement in the terms of a technical cost/benefit analysis, and then found flaws in the SEC's various justifications for its rules. The rules at issue were then struck down as "arbitrary and capricious" per State Farm. The most well-known such case was Business Roundtable v. SEC, 647 F.3d 1144 (D.C. Cir. 2011), as to which the leading treatise on administrative law remarked: "The SEC had devoted many pages of analysis to the economic effects of the rule. It is hard to imagine how much more consideration it would take to convince the court that the agency had adequately considered the economic effects of the rule." Kristin E. Hickman and Richard Pierce, Jr., Administrative Law Treatise 5th Ed., 2017 Cumulative Supp. 158. Other critiques of this line of D.C. Circuit cases have been, if anything, harsher. See John C. Coates, IV, Cost-Benefit Analysis of Financial Regulation, 124 Yale L.J. 882, 912 ff. (2015). But these cases still relied on rather particular Congressional language.

In 2015, the Clean Air Act and costs were again before the Supreme Court in MICHIGAN V. EPA, 135 S.Ct. 2699 (2015). Again JUSTICE SCALIA wrote the majority opinion. The issue, he said, was that the "Clean Air Act directs the Environmental Protection Agency to regulate emissions . . . from power plants if the Agency finds regulation 'appropriate and necessary.' We must decide whether it was reasonable for EPA to refuse to consider cost when making this finding." Id. at 2701. Held: it was not reasonable. While in some sense this is again a matter of interpreting particular statutory language, the Court this time wrote broadly about a broad (and not uncommon) statutory term, id. at 2707–08:

> Congress instructed EPA to add power plants to the [particular regulatory] program if (but only if) the Agency finds regulation "appropriate and necessary." § 7412(n)(1)(A). One does not need to open up a dictionary in order to realize the capaciousness of this phrase. In particular, "appropriate" is "the classic broad and all-encompassing term that naturally and traditionally includes consideration of all the relevant factors." Although this term leaves agencies with flexibility, an agency may not "entirely fai[l] to consider an important aspect of the problem" when deciding whether regulation is appropriate. State Farm.

> Read naturally in the present context, the phrase "appropriate and necessary" requires at least some attention to cost. One would not say that it is even rational, never mind "appropriate," to impose billions of dollars in economic costs in return for a few dollars in health or environmental benefits. . . . No regulation is "appropriate" if it does significantly more harm than good.

> There are undoubtedly settings in which the phrase "appropriate and necessary" does not encompass cost. But this is not one of them. Section 7412(n)(1)(A) directs EPA to determine whether "*regulation* is appropriate and necessary." (Emphasis added.) Agencies have long treated cost as a centrally relevant factor when deciding whether to regulate. Consideration of cost reflects the understanding that reasonable regulation ordinarily requires paying attention to the advantages *and* the disadvantages of agency decisions. . . . Against the backdrop of this established administrative practice, it is unreasonable to read an instruction to an administrative agency to determine whether "regulation is appropriate and necessary" as an invitation to ignore cost.

At the same time. id. at 2711:

> Our reasoning so far establishes that it was unreasonable for EPA to read § 7412(n)(1)(A) to mean that cost is irrelevant to the initial decision to regulate power plants. The Agency must consider cost—including, most importantly, cost of compliance—before deciding whether regulation is appropriate and necessary. We need not and do not hold that the law unambiguously required the Agency, when making this preliminary estimate, to conduct a formal cost-benefit analysis in which each advantage and disadvantage is assigned a monetary value. It will be up to the Agency to decide (as always, within the limits of reasonable interpretation) how to account for cost.

(JUSTICE KAGAN's dissent did not disagree with the principles involved, see id. at 2717; it argued instead that the agency, considering the whole regulatory process in question and not just the initial decision to regulate power plants, had taken costs into account in substantial ways.)

(4) **Where Does This Leave Matters?** Here are three "takes" on that question:

(a) ADRIAN VERMEULE, LAW'S ABNEGATION 177–78 (2016):

Proponents of quantified cost-benefit analysis point to seemingly broad language in the opinion, as when the majority opined that "[o]ne would not say that it is even rational, never mind 'appropriate,' to impose billions of dollars in economic costs in return for a few dollars in health or environmental benefits." On the broadest possible reading, this could mean that it is arbitrary and capricious for agencies not to conduct quantified and monetized cost-benefit analysis where possible. Yet this is an interpretation the Court took pains to disavow later in the opinion. Justice Scalia went out of his way to emphasize that while rationality may require "paying attention to the advantages and the disadvantages of agency decisions," that is not the same as requiring quantification of the advantages and disadvantages . . . Michigan v. EPA is clearly alert to the distinction between the colloquial, informal sense of "costs and benefits," on the one hand, and formalized quantified and monetized cost-benefit analysis, on the other. The decision is principally an interpretive holding, about the meaning of the phrase "appropriate and necessary" in a particular section of the Clean Air Act. But insofar as it addresses issues of rationality review in passing, it stands only for the unobjectionable proposition that rationality requires consideration of both "the advantages and the disadvantages of agency decisions."

(b) CASS SUNSTEIN, COST-BENEFIT ANALYSIS AND ARBITRARINESS REVIEW 12, Harvard Public Law Working Paper No.16–12 (2016):

Surely it would not be sufficient for an agency simply to announce that it has simply "considered" costs and decided to proceed. It would have to explain that decision in some way. The Court seemed to be suggesting that such an explanation could be given even if the agency does not produce "a formal cost-benefit analysis."

Even with this qualification, Michigan v. EPA has the great virtue of identifying the fatal weakness in a tempting objection to any effort to question an agency's failure to engage with costs and benefits. The objection would be that courts lack the authority to impose procedural requirements beyond those in the APA, and cost-benefit analysis is a procedural requirement, not found in the APA, which thus cannot be imposed by courts. The problem with the objection is that under the APA, an arbitrary decision is unlawful. If an agency ignores costs, or imposes a risk that is greater than the risk that it is reducing, it would seem to be acting arbitrarily. The fact that courts cannot add procedural requirements is

At the sa acknowledged that
EPA was hardly embraced cost-
imalism. ER, COST-BENEFIT ANALYSIS
HAN S. M. lic Law Working Paper No.
AL ROLE

does it r It is not clear, but there
not to cc —or will soon think—that
to believ Court did not reach the
CBA is ndated only because the
of whet it need not consider costs
taken t aid that the agency must
n additi gulation is 'appropriate' if
r" costs od."

ignifica at the Court required only
rian V fashion) and stopped short
encies monetize those costs. But
uirin bes significantly more harm
lining cessarily requires comparing
ood," a The only way for an agency
agnit fits is to quantify them and
urt) t —in effect, to monetize them.
slate t explicitly, the Supreme Court
s, eve a rule that agencies must
for a efits.
ntify

A POSSIBLE ELEMENT
NOT PRICIUS" REVIEW

O st para ph of Justice Re nquist's
hould sugges that "[a] change in
al co ple casti their votes is perfectly
nistr ncy's rea aisal of the cos
onab s." Justice hite, for his part, co
efits behind th scillations of NHTSA's
have tement of i istory in Part I of the
andar agraph, to r e the successive views
inion an adminis ons. But his opinion
the the new ru apolitical terms. It
sists equiring an a cy to offer a formal
seems, reflect the age s actual motivation.
defens
Was h ADMINISTRATI LAW: RETHINKING
(2) 63–65 (1990): e Supreme Court
JUDI terms of the igm of expertise,
anal consideration' b of arbitrary and
app luded that NHT red by failing to
capi

agency
giving
cratic,
atively
can be
mpt in
layed a
sonally
ment of
tutory,
esident

unts as
nded to
ecutive
ces are
d. . . .

hat any
action.
y action
lthough
ences is
as those
values,
hat seek
ay to the
ple, that
llowed to
g his pro-
rescind a
ney from
ounds, to
ould not
'provider
o rescind
for their

AGENCY
d Edley
centive
may be
chosen
t may
ch as a
est or is
tive to
ease in
tatute,

a judicially enforceable procedural requirement "that a significant agency rule include at least a summary of the substance of executive supervision." Id. at 1130.)

FEDERAL COMMUNICATIONS COMMISSION v. FOX TELEVISION STATIONS, INC.

Supreme Court of the United States (2009).
556 U.S. 502.

■ JUSTICE SCALIA delivered the opinion of the Court, except as to Part III-E.

Federal law prohibits the broadcasting of "any . . . indecent . . . language," 18 U.S.C. § 1464, which includes expletives referring to sexual or excretory activity or organs, see FCC v. Pacifica Foundation, 438 U.S. 726 (1978). This case concerns the adequacy of the Federal Communications Commission's explanation of its decision that this sometimes forbids the broadcasting of indecent expletives even when the offensive words are not repeated.

I. Statutory and Regulatory Background

The Communications Act of 1934, 47 U.S.C. § 151 *et seq.*, established a system of limited-term broadcast licenses subject to various "conditions" designed "to maintain the control of the United States over all the channels of radio transmission," § 301. Twenty-seven years ago we said that "[a] licensed broadcaster is granted the free and exclusive use of a limited and valuable part of the public domain; when he accepts that franchise it is burdened by enforceable public obligations." CBS, Inc. v. FCC, 453 U.S. 367, 395 (1981).

One of the burdens that licensees shoulder is the indecency ban—the statutory proscription against "utter[ing] any obscene, indecent, or profane language by means of radio communication," 18 U.S.C. § 1464—which Congress has instructed the Commission to enforce between the hours of 6 a.m. and 10 p.m. Congress has given the Commission various means of enforcing the indecency ban, including civil fines and license revocations or the denial of license renewals.

The Commission first invoked the statutory ban on indecent broadcasts in 1975, declaring a daytime broadcast of George Carlin's "Filthy Words" monologue actionably indecent. Pacifica Foundation, 56 F.C.C.2d 94. At that time, the Commission announced the definition of indecent speech that it uses to this day, prohibiting "language that describes, in terms patently offensive as measured by contemporary community standards for the broadcast medium, sexual or excretory activities or organs, at times of the day when there is a reasonable risk that children may be in the audience." Id., at 98.

In FCC v. Pacifica Foundation, we upheld the Commission's order against statutory and constitutional challenge. . . .

In the ensuing years, the Commission took a cautious, but gradually expanding, approach to enforcing the statutory prohibition against indecent broadcasts. . . .Although the Commission had expanded its enforcement beyond the "repetitive use of specific words or phrases," it preserved a distinction between literal and nonliteral (or "expletive") uses of evocative language. In re Pacifica Foundation, Inc., 2 FCC Rcd., at 2699, ¶ 13. The Commission explained that each literal "description or depiction of sexual or excretory functions must be examined in context to determine whether it is patently offensive," but that "deliberate and repetitive use . . . is a requisite to a finding of indecency" when a complaint focuses solely on the use of nonliteral expletives. Ibid. . . .

In 2004, the Commission took one step further by declaring for the first time that a nonliteral (expletive) use of the F- and S-Words could be actionably indecent, even when the word is used only once. The first order to this effect dealt with an NBC broadcast of the Golden Globe Awards, in which the performer Bono commented, " 'This is really, really, f* * *ing brilliant.' " In re Complaints Against Various Broadcast Licensees Regarding Their Airing of the "Golden Globe Awards" Program, 19 FCC Rcd. 4975, 4976, n. 4 (2004) (Golden Globes Order). Although the Commission had received numerous complaints directed at the broadcast, its enforcement bureau had concluded that the material was not indecent because "Bono did not describe, in context, sexual or excretory organs or activities and . . . the utterance was fleeting and isolated." Id., at 4975–4976, ¶ 3. The full Commission reviewed and reversed the staff ruling.

The Commission first declared that Bono's use of the F-Word fell within its indecency definition, even though the word was used as an intensifier rather than a literal descriptor. "[G]iven the core meaning of the 'F-Word,' " it said, "any use of that word . . . inherently has a sexual connotation." Id., at 4978, ¶ 8. The Commission determined, moreover, that the broadcast was "patently offensive" because the F-Word "is one of the most vulgar, graphic and explicit descriptions of sexual activity in the English language," because "[i]ts use invariably invokes a coarse sexual image," and because Bono's use of the word was entirely "shocking and gratuitous." Id., at 4979, ¶ 9.

The Commission observed that categorically exempting such language from enforcement actions would "likely lead to more widespread use." Ibid. Commission action was necessary to "safeguard the well-being of the nation's children from the most objectionable, most offensive language." The order noted that technological advances have made it far easier to delete ("bleep out") a "single and gratuitous use of a vulgar expletive," without adulterating the content of a broadcast. Id., at 4980, ¶ 11.

The order acknowledged that "prior Commission and staff action have indicated that isolated or fleeting broadcasts of the 'F-Word' . . . are not indecent or would not be acted upon." It explicitly ruled that "any such interpretation is no longer good law." Ibid., ¶ 12. . . . Because, however, "existing precedent would have permitted this broadcast," the Commission determined that "NBC and its affiliates necessarily did not have the requisite notice to justify a penalty." Id., at 4981–4982, ¶ 15.

II.   The Present Case

This case concerns utterances in two live broadcasts aired by Fox Television Stations, Inc., and its affiliates prior to the Commission's Golden Globes Order. The first occurred during the 2002 Billboard Music Awards, when the singer Cher exclaimed, "I've also had critics for the last 40 years saying that I was on my way out every year. Right. So f* * * 'em." Brief for Petitioners 9. The second involved a segment of the 2003 Billboard Music Awards, during the presentation of an award by Nicole Richie and Paris Hilton, principals in a Fox television series called "The Simple Life." Ms. Hilton began their interchange by reminding Ms. Richie to "watch the bad language," but Ms. Richie proceeded to ask the audience, "Why do they even call it 'The Simple Life?' Have you ever tried to get cow s* * * out of a Prada purse? It's not so f* * *ing simple." Id., at 9–10. Following each of these broadcasts, the Commission received numerous complaints from parents whose children were exposed to the language.

[Proceedings followed, before the Commission and in the Second Circuit, resulting in a new Commission Order: In re Complaints Regarding Various Television Broadcasts Between February 2, 2002, and March 8, 2005, 21 FCC Rcd. 13299 (2006) (Remand Order).] The order first explained that both broadcasts fell comfortably within the subject-matter scope of the Commission's indecency test because the 2003 broadcast involved a literal description of excrement and both broadcasts invoked the "F-Word," which inherently has a sexual connotation. The order next determined that the broadcasts were patently offensive under community standards for the medium. Both broadcasts, it noted, involved entirely gratuitous uses of "one of the most vulgar, graphic, and explicit words for sexual activity in the English language." Id., at 13305, ¶ 17, 13324, ¶ 59. It found Ms. Richie's use of the "F-Word" and her "explicit description of the handling of excrement" to be "vulgar and shocking," as well as to constitute "pandering," after Ms. Hilton had playfully warned her to " 'watch the bad language.' " Id., at 13305, ¶ 17. And it found Cher's statement patently offensive in part because she metaphorically suggested a sexual act as a means of expressing hostility to her critics. The order relied upon the "critically important" context of the utterances, noting that they were aired during prime-time awards shows "designed to draw a large nationwide audience that could be expected to include many children interested in seeing their favorite music stars," id., at 13305, ¶ 18, 13324, ¶ 59. Indeed, approximately 2.5 million minors witnessed each of the broadcasts. Id., at 13306, ¶ 18, 13326, ¶ 65. . . .

The order explained that the Commission's prior "strict dichotomy between 'expletives' and 'descriptions or depictions of sexual or excretory functions' is artificial and does not make sense in light of the fact that an 'expletive's' power to offend derives from its sexual or excretory meaning." Id., at 13308, ¶ 23. In the Commission's view, "granting an automatic exemption for 'isolated or fleeting' expletives unfairly forces viewers (including children)" to take " 'the first blow' " and would allow broadcasters "to air expletives at all hours of a day so long as they did so one at a time." Id., at 13309, ¶ 25. Although the Commission determined that Fox encouraged the offensive language by using suggestive scripting in the 2003 broadcast, and unreasonably failed to take adequate precautions in both broadcasts, the order again declined to impose any forfeiture or other sanction for either of the broadcasts.

Fox returned to the Second Circuit for review of the Remand Order, and various intervenors including CBS, NBC, and ABC joined the action. The Court of Appeals reversed the agency's orders, finding the Commission's reasoning inadequate under the Administrative Procedure Act. The majority was "skeptical that the Commission [could] provide a reasoned explanation for its 'fleeting expletive' regime that would pass constitutional muster," but it declined to reach the constitutional question. 489 F.3d at 462. Judge Leval dissented. We granted certiorari.

III. Analysis

A.   Governing Principles

The Administrative Procedure Act, 5 U.S.C. § 551 et seq., . . . permits (insofar as relevant here) the setting aside of agency action that is "arbitrary" or "capricious," 5 U.S.C. § 706(2)(A). . . .

In overturning the Commission's judgment, the Court of Appeals here relied in part on Circuit precedent requiring a more substantial explanation for agency action that changes prior policy. The Second Circuit has interpreted the Administrative Procedure Act and our opinion in State Farm as requiring agencies to make clear " 'why the original reasons for adopting the [displaced] rule or policy are no longer dispositive' " as well as " 'why the new rule effectuates the statute as well as or better than the old rule.' " 489 F.3d, at 456–457. The Court of Appeals for the District of Columbia Circuit has similarly indicated that a court's standard of review is "heightened somewhat" when an agency reverses course. NAACP v. FCC, 682 F.2d 993, 998 (1982).

We find no basis in the Administrative Procedure Act or in our opinions for a requirement that all agency change be subjected to more searching review. The Act mentions no such heightened standard. And our opinion in State Farm neither held nor implied that every agency action representing a policy change must be justified by reasons more substantial than those required to adopt a policy in the first instance. . . .

To be sure, the requirement that an agency provide reasoned explanation for its action would ordinarily demand that it display awareness that it *is* changing position. An agency may not, for example, depart from a prior policy sub silentio or simply disregard rules that are still on the books. See United States v. Nixon, 418 U.S. 683, 696 (1974). And of course the agency must show that there are good reasons for the new policy. But it need not demonstrate to a court's satisfaction that the reasons for the new policy are *better* than the reasons for the old one; it suffices that the new policy is permissible under the statute, that there are good reasons for it, and that the agency *believes* it to be better, which the conscious change of course adequately indicates. This means that the agency need not always provide a more detailed justification than what would suffice for a new policy created on a blank slate. Sometimes it must—when, for example, its new policy rests upon factual findings that contradict those which underlay its prior policy; or when its prior policy has engendered serious reliance interests that must be taken into account. It would be arbitrary or capricious to ignore such matters. In such cases it is not that further justification is demanded by the mere fact of policy change; but that a reasoned explanation is needed for disregarding facts and circumstances that underlay or were engendered by the prior policy.

In this appeal from the Second Circuit's setting aside of Commission action for failure to comply with a procedural requirement of the Administrative Procedure Act, the broadcasters' arguments have repeatedly referred to the First Amendment. If they mean to invite us to apply a more stringent arbitrary-and-capricious review to agency actions that implicate constitutional liberties, we reject the invitation. The so-called canon of constitutional avoidance is an interpretive tool, counseling that ambiguous statutory language be construed to avoid serious constitutional doubts. We know of no precedent for applying it to limit the scope of authorized executive action. In the same section authorizing courts to set aside "arbitrary [or] capricious" agency action, the Administrative Procedure Act separately provides for setting aside agency action that is "unlawful," 5 U.S.C. § 706(2)(A), which of course includes unconstitutional action. We think that is the only context in which constitutionality bears upon judicial review of authorized agency action. If the Commission's action here was not arbitrary or capricious in the ordinary sense, it satisfies the Administrative Procedure Act's "arbitrary [or] capricious" standard; its lawfulness under the Constitution is a separate question to be addressed in a constitutional challenge.

B.   Application to This Case

Judged under the above described standards, the Commission's new enforcement policy and its order finding the broadcasts actionably indecent were neither arbitrary nor capricious. First, the Commission forthrightly acknowledged that its recent actions have broken new ground, taking account of inconsistent "prior Commission and staff action" and explicitly disavowing them as "no longer good law." Golden

Globes Order, 19 FCC Rcd., at 4980, ¶ 12. To be sure, the (superfluous) explanation in its Remand Order of why the Cher broadcast would even have violated its earlier policy may not be entirely convincing. But that unnecessary detour is irrelevant. There is no doubt that the Commission knew it was making a change. That is why it declined to assess penalties; and it relied on the Golden Globes Order as removing any lingering doubt. Remand Order, 21 FCC Rcd., at 13308, ¶ 23, 13325, ¶ 61.

Moreover, the agency's reasons for expanding the scope of its enforcement activity were entirely rational. It was certainly reasonable to determine that it made no sense to distinguish between literal and nonliteral uses of offensive words, requiring repetitive use to render only the latter indecent. As the Commission said with regard to expletive use of the F-Word, "the word's power to insult and offend derives from its sexual meaning." Id., at 13323, ¶ 58. And the Commission's decision to look at the patent offensiveness of even isolated uses of sexual and excretory words fits with the context-based approach we sanctioned in Pacifica. Even isolated utterances can be made in "pander[ing,] . . . vulgar and shocking" manners, Remand Order, 21 FCC Rcd., at 13305, ¶ 17, and can constitute harmful "'first blow[s]'" to children, id., at 13309, ¶ 25. It is surely rational (if not inescapable) to believe that a safe harbor for single words would "likely lead to more widespread use of the offensive language," Golden Globes Order at 4979, ¶ 9.

When confronting other requests for per se rules governing its enforcement of the indecency prohibition, the Commission has declined to create safe harbors for particular types of broadcasts. The Commission could rationally decide it needed to step away from its old regime where nonrepetitive use of an expletive was per se nonactionable because that was "at odds with the Commission's overall enforcement policy." Remand Order at 13308, ¶ 23.

The fact that technological advances have made it easier for broadcasters to bleep out offending words further supports the Commission's stepped-up enforcement policy. Golden Globes Order at 4980, ¶ 11. And the agency's decision not to impose any forfeiture or other sanction precludes any argument that it is arbitrarily punishing parties without notice of the potential consequences of their action.

C.   The Court of Appeals' Reasoning

The Court of Appeals found the Commission's action arbitrary and capricious on three grounds. First, the court criticized the Commission for failing to explain why it had not previously banned fleeting expletives as "harmful 'first blow[s].'" . . . .There are some propositions for which scant empirical evidence can be marshaled, and the harmful effect of broadcast profanity on children is one of them. One cannot demand a multiyear controlled study, in which some children are intentionally exposed to indecent broadcasts (and insulated from all other indecency), and others are shielded from all indecency. It is one thing to set aside agency action under the Administrative Procedure Act because of failure to adduce empirical data that can readily be obtained. See, e.g., State Farm, 463 U.S., at 46–56 (addressing the costs and benefits of mandatory passive restraints for automobiles). It is something else to insist upon obtaining the unobtainable. Here it suffices to know that children mimic the behavior they observe—or at least the behavior that is presented to them as normal and appropriate. Programming replete with one-word indecent expletives will tend to produce children who use (at least) one-word indecent expletives. Congress has made the determination that indecent material is harmful to children, and has left enforcement of the ban to the Commission. If enforcement had to be supported by empirical data, the ban would effectively be a nullity. . . .

The court's second objection is that fidelity to the agency's "first blow" theory of harm would require a categorical ban on *all* broadcasts of expletives; the Commission's failure to go to this extreme thus undermined the coherence of its rationale. . . . More fundamentally, however, the agency's decision to consider the patent offensiveness of isolated expletives on a case-by-case basis is not arbitrary or capricious. . . . The agency's decision to retain some discretion does not render arbitrary or capricious its regulation of the deliberate and shocking uses of offensive language at the award shows under review—shows that were expected to (and did) draw the attention of millions of children.

Finally, the Court of Appeals found unconvincing the agency's prediction (without any evidence) that a *per se* exemption for fleeting expletives would lead to increased use of expletives one at a time. But even in the absence of evidence, the agency's predictive judgment (which merits deference) makes entire sense. To predict that complete immunity for fleeting expletives, ardently desired by broadcasters, will lead to a substantial increase in fleeting expletives seems to us an exercise in logic rather than clairvoyance. The Court of Appeals was perhaps correct that the Commission's prior policy had not yet caused broadcasters to "barrag[e] the airwaves with expletives." That may have been because its prior permissive policy had been confirmed (save in dicta) only at the staff level. In any event, as the Golden Globes order demonstrated, it did produce more expletives than the Commission (which has the first call in this matter) deemed in conformity with the statute. . . .

D.   Respondents' Arguments

Respondents press some arguments that the court did not adopt. . . .

E.   The Dissents' Arguments

Justice Breyer purports to "begin with applicable law," but in fact begins by stacking the deck. He claims that the FCC's status as an "independent" agency sheltered from political oversight requires courts to be "all the more" vigilant in ensuring "that major policy decisions be based upon articulable reasons." Not so. The independent agencies are sheltered not from politics but from the President, and it has often been observed that their freedom from presidential oversight (and protection) has simply been replaced by increased subservience to congressional direction. Indeed, the precise policy change at issue here was spurred by significant political pressure from Congress.[4] . . .

Regardless, it is assuredly not "applicable law" that rulemaking by independent regulatory agencies is subject to heightened scrutiny. The Administrative Procedure Act, which provides judicial review, makes no distinction between independent and other agencies, neither in its definition of agency, 5 U.S.C. § 701(b)(1), nor in the standards for reviewing agency action, § 706. . . .

Justice Breyer and Justice Stevens rely upon two supposed omissions in the FCC's analysis that they believe preclude a finding that the agency did not act arbitrarily. Neither of these omissions could undermine the coherence of the rationale the agency gave, but the dissenters' evaluation of each is flawed in its own right.

First, both claim that the Commission failed adequately to explain its consideration of the constitutional issues inherent in its regulation. [We don't agree.]

Second, Justice Breyer looks over the vast field of particular factual scenarios unaddressed by the FCC's 35-page Remand Order and finds one that is fatal: the plight of the small local broadcaster who cannot afford the new technology that enables the screening of live broadcasts for indecent utterances. The Commission has failed to address the fate of this unfortunate, who will, he believes, be subject to sanction.

We doubt, to begin with, that small-town broadcasters run a heightened risk of liability for indecent utterances. In programming that they originate, their down-home local guests probably employ vulgarity less than big-city folks; and small-town stations generally cannot afford or cannot attract foul-mouthed glitteratae from Hollywood. Their main exposure with regard to self-originated programming is live coverage of news and public affairs. But the Remand Order went out of its way to

---

[4]   A Subcommittee of the FCC's House Oversight Committee held hearings on the FCC's broadcast indecency enforcement on January 28, 2004. "Can You Say That on TV?": An Examination of the FCC's Enforcement with respect to Broadcast Indecency, Hearing before the Subcommittee on Telecommunications and the Internet of the House Committee on Energy and Commerce, 108th Cong., 2d Sess. Members of the Subcommittee specifically "called on the full Commission to reverse [the staff ruling in the Golden Globes case]" because they perceived a "feeling amongst many Americans that some broadcasters are engaged in a race to the bottom, pushing the decency envelope to distinguish themselves in the increasingly crowded entertainment field." Id., at 2 (statement of Rep. Upton); see also, e.g., id., at 17 (statement of Rep. Terry), 19 (statement of Rep. Pitts). They repeatedly expressed disapproval of the FCC's enforcement policies, see, e.g., id., at 3 (statement of Rep. Upton) ("At some point we have to ask the FCC: How much is enough? When will it revoke a license?"); id., at 4 (statement of Rep. Markey) ("Today's hearing will allow us to explore the FCC's lackluster enforcement record with respect to these violations").

About two weeks later, on February 11, 2004, the same Subcommittee held hearings on a bill increasing the fines for indecency violations. Hearings on H. R 3717 before the Subcommittee on Telecommunications and the Internet of the House Committee on Energy and Commerce, 108th Cong., 2d Sess. All five Commissioners were present and were grilled about enforcement shortcomings. . . .

note that the case at hand did not involve "breaking news coverage," and that "it may be inequitable to hold a licensee responsible for airing offensive speech during live coverage of a public event," 21 FCC Rcd., at 13311, ¶ 33. As for the programming that small stations receive on a network "feed": This *will* be cleansed by the expensive technology small stations (by Justice Breyer's hypothesis) cannot afford.

But never mind the detail of whether small broadcasters are uniquely subject to a great risk of punishment for fleeting expletives. The fundamental fallacy of Justice Breyer's small-broadcaster gloomy scenario is its demonstrably false assumption that the Remand Order makes no provision for the avoidance of unfairness-that the single-utterance prohibition will be invoked uniformly, in all situations. The Remand Order made very clear that this is not the case. It said that in determining "what, if any, remedy is appropriate" the Commission would consider the facts of each individual case . . . .

There was, in sum, no need for the Commission to compose a special treatise on local broadcasters.[8] And Justice Breyer can safely defer his concern for those yeomen of the airwaves until we have before us a case that involves one.

IV. Constitutionality

The Second Circuit did not definitively rule on the constitutionality of the Commission's orders, but respondents nonetheless ask us to decide their validity under the First Amendment. . . . We decline to address the constitutional questions at this time.

* * *

The Second Circuit believed that children today "likely hear this language far more often from other sources than they did in the 1970's when the Commission first began sanctioning indecent speech," and that this cuts against more stringent regulation of broadcasts. Assuming the premise is true (for this point the Second Circuit did not demand empirical evidence) the conclusion does not necessarily follow. The Commission could reasonably conclude that the pervasiveness of foul language, and the coarsening of public entertainment in other media such as cable, justify more stringent regulation of broadcast programs so as to give conscientious parents a relatively safe haven for their children. In the end, the Second Circuit and the broadcasters quibble with the Commission's policy choices and not with the explanation it has given. We decline to "substitute [our] judgment for that of the agency," State

---

[8]   Justice Breyer posits that the FCC would have been required to give more explanation had it used notice-and-comment rulemaking, which "should lead us to the same conclusion" in this review of the agency's change through adjudication. Even assuming the premise, there is no basis for incorporating all of the Administrative Procedure Act's notice-and-comment procedural requirements into arbitrary-and-capricious review of adjudicatory decisions. Cf. Vermont Yankee.

Farm, 463 U.S., at 43, and we find the Commission's orders neither arbitrary nor capricious.

The judgment of the United States Court of Appeals for the Second Circuit is reversed, and the case is remanded for further proceedings consistent with this opinion.

[Six opinions were filed in this case. The opinions of Justice Thomas concurring with Justice Scalia, Justice Kennedy concurring in all but part III-E of Scalia's opinion, Justice Stevens dissenting, and Justice Ginsburg dissenting are omitted. Justices Stevens and Ginsburg also signed on to Justice Breyer's opinion, see below.]

■ JUSTICE BREYER, with whom JUSTICE STEVENS, JUSTICE SOUTER, and JUSTICE GINSBURG join, dissenting.

In my view, the Federal Communications Commission failed adequately to explain *why* it *changed* its indecency policy from a policy permitting a single "fleeting use" of an expletive, to a policy that made no such exception. Its explanation fails to discuss two critical factors, at least one of which directly underlay its original policy decision. Its explanation instead discussed several factors well known to it the first time around, which by themselves provide no significant justification for a *change* of policy. Consequently, the FCC decision is "arbitrary, capricious, an abuse of discretion." 5 U.S.C. § 706(2)(A); State Farm; Overton Park. And I would affirm the Second Circuit's similar determination.

I

I begin with applicable law. That law grants those in charge of independent administrative agencies broad authority to determine relevant policy. But it does not permit them to make policy choices for purely political reasons nor to rest them primarily upon unexplained policy preferences. Federal Communications Commissioners have fixed terms of office; they are not directly responsible to the voters; and they enjoy an independence expressly designed to insulate them, to a degree, from "'the exercise of political oversight.'" Freytag v. Commissioner, 501 U.S. 868, 916 (1991) (Scalia, J., concurring in part and concurring in judgment.) That insulation helps to secure important governmental objectives, such as the constitutionally related objective of maintaining broadcast regulation that does not bend too readily before the political winds. But that agency's comparative freedom from ballot-box control makes it all the more important that courts review its decisionmaking to assure compliance with applicable provisions of the law—including law requiring that major policy decisions be based upon articulable reasons. . . .

To explain a change requires more than setting forth reasons why the new policy is a good one. It also requires the agency to answer the question, "Why did you change?" And a rational answer to this question typically requires a more complete explanation than would prove satisfactory were change itself not at issue. An (imaginary) administrator explaining why he chose a policy that requires driving on the right side, rather than the left side, of the road might say, "Well, one side seemed as good as the other, so I flipped a coin." But even assuming the rationality of that explanation for an *initial* choice, that explanation is not at all rational if offered to explain why the administrator *changed* driving practice, from right-side to left-side, 25 years later.

In State Farm, a unanimous Court applied these commonsense requirements to an agency decision that rescinded an earlier agency policy. . . . It said that the law required an explanation for such a *change* because the earlier policy, representing a " 'settled course of behavior[,] embodies the agency's informed judgment that, by pursuing that course, it will carry out the policies . . . best if the settled rule is adhered to.' " State Farm at 41–42. Thus, the agency must explain *why* it has come to the conclusion that it should now change direction. Why does it now reject the considerations that led it to adopt that initial policy? What has changed in the world that offers justification for the change? What other good reasons are there for departing from the earlier policy?

Contrary to the majority's characterization of this dissent, it would not (and State Farm does not) require a *"heightened standard"* of review. Rather, the law requires application of the *same standard* of review to different circumstances, namely circumstances characterized by the fact that *change* is at issue. It requires the agency to focus upon the fact of change where change is relevant, just as it must focus upon any other relevant circumstance. It requires the agency here to focus upon the reasons that led the agency to adopt the initial policy, and to explain why it now comes to a new judgment.

I recognize that *sometimes* the ultimate explanation for a change may have to be, "We now weigh the relevant considerations differently." But at other times, an agency can and should say more. Where, for example, the agency rested its previous policy on particular factual findings, or where an agency rested its prior policy on its view of the governing law, or where an agency rested its previous policy on, say, a special need to coordinate with another agency, one would normally expect the agency to focus upon those earlier views of fact, of law, or of policy and explain why they are no longer controlling. Regardless, to say that the agency here must answer the question "why change" is not to require the agency to provide a justification that is *"better* than the reasons for the old [policy]." It is only to recognize the obvious fact that *change* is sometimes (not always) a relevant background feature that sometimes (not always) requires focus (upon prior justifications) and explanation lest the adoption of the new policy (in that circumstance) be "arbitrary, capricious, an abuse of discretion." . . .

II

We here must apply the general standards set forth in State Farm and Overton Park to an agency decision that changes a 25-year-old "fleeting expletive" policy from (1) the old policy that would normally permit broadcasters to transmit a single, fleeting use of an expletive to (2) a new policy that would threaten broadcasters with large fines for transmitting even a single use (including its use by a member of the public) of such an expletive, alone with nothing more. The question is whether that decision satisfies the minimal standards necessary to assure a reviewing court that such a change of policy is not "arbitrary, capricious, [or] an abuse of discretion," 5 U.S.C. § 706(2)(A), particularly as set forth in, e.g., State Farm and Overton Park. The decision, in my view, does not satisfy those standards.

Consider the requirement that an agency at least minimally "consider . . . important aspect[s] of the problem." State Farm at 43. The FCC failed to satisfy this requirement, for it failed to consider two critically important aspects of the problem that underlay its initial policy judgment (one of which directly, the other of which indirectly). First, the FCC said next to nothing about the relation between the change it made in its prior "fleeting expletive" policy and the First-Amendment-related need to avoid "censorship," a matter as closely related to broadcasting regulation as is health to that of the environment. The reason that discussion of the matter is particularly important here is that the FCC had *explicitly* rested its prior policy in large part upon the need to avoid treading too close to the constitutional line.

[The agency failed to justify sufficiently its new approach to the Supreme Court's ruling in F.C.C. v. Pacifica.]

Second, the FCC failed to consider the potential impact of its new policy upon local broadcasting coverage. This "aspect of the problem" is particularly important because the FCC explicitly took account of potential broadcasting impact. Golden Globe Order at 4980, ¶ 11 ("The ease with which broadcasters today can block even fleeting words in a live broadcast is an element in our decision"). Indeed, in setting forth "bleeping" technology changes (presumably lowering bleeping costs) as justifying the policy change, it implicitly reasoned that lower costs, making it easier for broadcasters to install bleeping equipment, made it less likely that the new policy would lead broadcasters to reduce coverage, say by canceling coverage of public events.

What then did the FCC say about the likelihood that smaller independent broadcasters, including many public service broadcasters, still would not be able to afford "bleeping" technology and, as a consequence, would reduce local coverage, indeed cancel coverage, of many public events? It said nothing at all. . . .

The plurality acknowledges that the Commission entirely failed to discuss this aspect of the regulatory problem. But it sees "no need" for discussion in light of its, *i.e.,* the plurality's, own "doubt[s]" that "small-town broadcasters run a heightened risk of liability for indecent utterances" as a result of the change of policy. The plurality's "doubt[s]" rest upon its views (1) that vulgar expression is less prevalent (at least among broadcast guests) in smaller towns; (2) that the greatest risk the new policy poses for "smalltown broadcasters" arises when they broadcast local "news and public affairs," and (3) that the *Remand Order* says "little about how the Commission would treat smaller broadcasters who cannot afford screening equipment," while also pointing out that the new policy " 'does not . . . impose undue burdens on broadcasters' " and emphasizing that the case before it did not involve " 'breaking news.' "

As to the first point, about the prevalence of vulgarity in small towns, I confess ignorance. But I do know that there are independent stations in many large and medium sized cities. See Television & Cable Factbook, Directory of Television Stations in Operation 2008. As to the second point, I too believe that coverage of local public events, if not news, lies at the heart of the problem.

I cannot agree with the plurality, however, about the critical third point, namely that the new policy obviously provides smaller independent broadcasters with adequate assurance that they will not be fined. The new policy removes the "fleeting expletive" exception, an exception that assured smaller independent stations that they would not be fined should someone swear at a public event. In its place, it puts a policy that places all broadcasters at risk when they broadcast fleeting expletives, including expletives uttered at public events. The Remand Order says that there "is *no outright news exemption from our indecency rules.*" 21 FCC Rcd., at 13327, ¶ 71 (emphasis added). The best it can provide by way of assurance is to say that "it *may* be inequitable to hold a licensee responsible for airing offensive speech during live coverage of a public event *under some circumstances.*" Id., at 13311, ¶ 33 (emphasis added). It does list those circumstances as including the "possibility of human error in using delay equipment." Id., at 13313, ¶ 35. But it says *nothing* about a station's *inability to afford* delay equipment (a matter that in individual cases could itself prove debatable). All the FCC had to do was to *consider* this matter and either grant an exemption or explain why it did not grant an exemption. But it did not. And the result is a rule that may well chill coverage—the kind of consequence that the law has considered important for decades, to which the broadcasters pointed in their arguments before the FCC, and which the FCC nowhere discusses.

Had the FCC used traditional administrative notice-and-comment procedures, 5 U.S.C. § 553, the two failures I have just discussed would clearly require a court to vacate the resulting agency decision. See ACLU v. FCC, 823 F.2d 1554, 1581 (C.A.D.C. 1987) ("Notice and comment rulemaking procedures obligate the FCC to respond to *all* significant comments, for the opportunity to comment is meaningless unless the agency responds to significant points raised by the public"). Here the agency did not make new policy through the medium of notice and comment proceedings. But the same failures here—where the policy is important, the significance of the issues clear, the failures near complete—should lead us to the same conclusion. The agency's failure to discuss these two "important aspect[s] of the problem" means that the resulting decision is "'arbitrary, capricious, an abuse of discretion'" requiring us to remand the matter to the agency. State Farm, 463 U.S., at 43; Overton Park, 401 U.S., at 416.

III

The three reasons the FCC did set forth in support of its change of policy cannot make up for the failures I have discussed. . . .

[T]he FCC found that the new policy was better in part because, in its view, the new policy better protects children against what it described as "'the first blow'" of broadcast indecency that results from the "'pervasive'" nature of broadcast media. . . . The difficulty with this argument, however, is that it does not explain the *change*. The FCC has long used the theory of the "first blow" to justify its regulation of broadcast indecency. Yet the FCC has also long followed its original "fleeting expletives" policy. Nor was the FCC ever unaware of the fact to which the majority points, namely that children's surroundings influence their behavior. So, to repeat the question: What, in respect to the "first blow," has changed?

The FCC points to no empirical (or other) evidence to demonstrate that it previously understated the importance of avoiding the "first blow." Like the majority, I do not believe that an agency must always conduct full empirical studies of such matters. But the FCC could have referred to, and explained, relevant empirical studies that suggest the contrary. One review of the empirical evidence, for example, reports that "[i]t is doubtful that children under the age of 12 understand sexual language and innuendo; therefore it is unlikely that vulgarities have any negative effect." Kaye & Sapolsky, Watch Your Mouth! An Analysis of Profanity Uttered by Children on Prime-Time Television, 2004 Mass Communication & Soc'y 429, 433 (Vol.7) (citing two studies). The Commission need not have accepted this conclusion. But its failure to discuss this or any other such evidence, while providing no empirical evidence at all that favors its position, must weaken the logical force of its conclusion.

The FCC also found the new policy better because it believed that its prior policy "would as a matter of logic permit broadcasters to air expletives at all hours of a day so long as they did so one at a time." Remand Order, 21 FCC Rcd., at 13309, ¶ 25. This statement, however, raises an obvious question: Did that happen? The FCC's initial "fleeting expletives" policy was in effect for 25 years. Had broadcasters during those 25 years aired a series of expletives "one at a time?" If so, it should not be difficult to find evidence of that fact. But the FCC refers to none. Indeed, the FCC did not even claim that a change had taken place in this respect. It spoke only of the pure "logic" of the initial policy "permitting" such a practice. That logic would have been apparent to anyone, including the FCC, in 1978 when the FCC set forth its initial policy. . . .

IV

Were the question a closer one, the doctrine of constitutional avoidance would nonetheless lead me to remand the case. . . . Unlike the majority, I can find no convincing reason for refusing to apply a similar doctrine here. The Court has often applied that doctrine where an agency's regulation relies on a plausible but constitutionally suspect interpretation of a statute. The values the doctrine serves apply whether the agency's decision does, or does not, rest upon a constitutionally suspect interpretation of a statute. And a remand here would do no more than ask the agency to reconsider its policy decision in light of the concerns raised in a judicial opinion. . . .

V

In sum, the FCC's explanation of its change leaves out two critically important matters underlying its earlier policy, namely Pacifica and local broadcasting coverage. Its explanation rests upon three considerations previously known to the agency ("coarseness," the "first blow," and running single expletives all day, one at a time). With one exception, it provides no empirical or other information explaining why those considerations, which did not justify its new policy before, justify it now. Its discussion of the one exception (technological advances in bleeping/delay systems), failing to take account of local broadcast coverage, is seriously incomplete.

I need not decide whether one or two of these features, standing alone, would require us to remand the case. Here all come together. And taken together they suggest that the FCC's answer to the question, "Why change?" is, "We like the new policy better." This kind of answer, might be perfectly satisfactory were it given by an elected official. But when given by an agency, in respect to a major change of an important policy where much more might be said, it is not sufficient. State Farm, 463 U.S., at 41–42.

NOTES

(1) *What Is the Doctrine?* Both Justice Scalia's opinion and Justice Breyer's opinion treat State Farm as the governing law. Scalia says that State Farm does not impose a "heightened standard" of judicial review when an agency changes its course, and while he says that Justice Breyer imposes such a heightened standard, Justice Breyer specifically abjures doing so. Justice Scalia goes on to concede that in appropriate cases an agency must supply "a reasoned explanation . . . for disregarding facts and circumstances that underlay or were engendered by the prior policy." What more than that does Justice Breyer want? He says that the agency has to answer the question "Why did you change?" and then goes on to give a hypothetical about the imaginary administrator choosing, at time one, driving on the right side of the road, and then at time two, twenty five years later, changing the rule to driving on the left side. More, he says, has to be said at time two. But even at time one, there probably was a prior custom or, if the rule is federal, a set

of background state laws, and we would expect the administrator to discuss that custom (as either supporting his choice or having to be overcome by it); and if the point is that by time two there has been increased reliance on the uniform federal rule, isn't that additional fact precisely the kind of reliance "engendered by the prior policy" that Justice Scalia also says would have to be addressed? Is there a difference in principle between the opinions, or simply a different response to the particular way the F.C.C. did, or didn't, address specific questions? The Justices think they have a serious quarrel—do they? If so, what is the status of the State Farm test now? Has "arbitrary and capricious" review been made less intensive?

(2) *Is Judicially Inferred Common Sense Enough?* Part of the F.C.C.'s rationale was that a complete exemption for "fleeting expletives" would lead to significantly more of them. As Justice Breyer points out, the experience of the prior 25 years would seem to be relevant on the point, but the F.C.C. produced no such evidence—relying instead on the "logic" of the policy. Justice Scalia agrees that it is "an exercise in logic rather than clairvoyance"—going on to say that the fact that the prior policy had not yet had the predicted result "may have been because its prior permissive policy had been confirmed . . . only at the staff level." Is this failure to produce evidence, and this need for a Justice to conjecture what "may have been" to fill in the gap, consistent with State Farm? Is it justified by the fact that State Farm was the product of a notice-and-comment rulemaking while this case comes up from a set of agency adjudications? Or is Justice Breyer right when he says that on a change of policy of this sort, this procedural difference should not be allowed to make a substantive difference? Consider this evaluation of F.C.C. v. Fox in Enrique Armijo, Politics, Rulemaking, and Judicial Review, 62 Admin. L. Rev. 573, 580 (2010): "The case's greatest impact may be to encourage agencies to take up 'soft' regulatory topics like indecency in adjudications rather than rulemakings, where the agency (1) can avoid the burden of 'responding to all significant comments' by regulated entities and the public, and (2) may more freely draw its own conclusions based on its reasoning and expertise, so long as it makes a rational effort to justify those conclusions."

(3) *What Explanation Is Not Enough for A Change in Policy?* In ENCINO MOTORCARS, LLC v. NAVARRO, 136 S.Ct. 2117 (2016), the Department of Labor issued in 2011 a final rule (after a notice-and-comment proceeding) that said that, under the Fair Labor Standards Act, "service advisors" in automobile dealerships were entitled to overtime compensation. This changed the previous official policy (stated in an opinion letter) that service advisors were exempt from this provision; that policy had been consistently followed since 1978. Did that longstanding practice matter? 136 S.Ct. at 2126–27:

> The retail automobile and truck dealership industry had relied since 1978 on the Department's position that service advisors are exempt from the FLSA's overtime pay requirements. See National Automobile Dealers Association, Comment Letter on Proposed Rule Updating Regulations Issued Under the Fair Labor Standards Act (Sept. 26, 2008). Dealerships and service advisors negotiated and

structured their compensation plans against this background understanding. Requiring dealerships to adapt to the Department's new position could necessitate systemic, significant changes to the dealerships' compensation arrangements. See Brief for National Automobile Dealers Association et al. as *Amici Curiae* 13–14. Dealerships whose service advisors are not compensated in accordance with the Department's new views could also face substantial FLSA liability . . . . In light of this background, the Department needed a more reasoned explanation for its decision to depart from its existing enforcement policy.

The Department said that, in reaching its decision, it had "carefully considered all of the comments, analyses, and arguments made for and against the proposed changes." 76 Fed.Reg. 18832. And it noted that, since 1978, it had treated service advisors as exempt in certain circumstances. *Id.,* at 18838. It also noted the comment from the National Automobile Dealers Association stating that the industry had relied on that interpretation. *Ibid.*

But when it came to explaining the "good reasons for the new policy," Fox Television Stations, 556 U.S. at 515, the Department said almost nothing. It stated only that it would not treat service advisors as exempt because "the statute does not include such positions and the Department recognizes that there are circumstances under which the requirements for the exemption would not be met." 76 Fed.Reg. 18838. It continued that it "believes that this interpretation is reasonable" and "sets forth the appropriate approach." *Ibid.* Although an agency may justify its policy choice by explaining why that policy "is more consistent with statutory language" than alternative policies, Long Island Care at Home, 551 U.S., at 175 (internal quotation marks omitted), the Department did not analyze or explain why the statute should be interpreted to exempt dealership employees who sell vehicles but not dealership employees who sell services (that is, service advisors). And though several public comments supported the Department's reading of the statute, the Department did not explain what (if anything) it found persuasive in those comments beyond the few statements above.

It is not the role of the courts to speculate on reasons that might have supported an agency's decision. "[W]e may not supply a reasoned basis for the agency's action that the agency itself has not given." State Farm, 463 U.S., at 43 (citing SEC v. Chenery Corp., 332 U.S. 194 (1947)). Whatever potential reasons the Department might have given, the agency in fact gave almost no reasons at all. In light of the serious reliance interests at stake, the Department's conclusory statements do not suffice to explain its decision. See Fox Television Stations, 556 U.S., at 515–516.

(4)   *What about the First Amendment in Fox?* GILLIAN E. METZGER, ORDINARY ADMINISTRATIVE LAW AS CONSTITUTIONAL COMMON LAW, 110 Colum. L. Rev. 479, 484–86 (2010): ". . . Justice Scalia's majority opinion focused on defeating the suggestion that an agency necessarily faces a higher burden to explain a change in existing policy than to adopt a new policy when none previously had existed. But the opinion also denied that agency decisions implicating constitutional liberties trigger more stringent arbitrary and capricious review. Instead, the Court said, whether an agency action is 'arbitrary and capricious' and whether it is unconstitutional are 'separate question[s].' Arguing that the canon of constitutional avoidance applied only to judicial review of statutory language, Justice Scalia stated that 'the only context in which constitutionality bears upon judicial review of authorized agency action' is when a court determines the agency action is unconstitutional. He dismissed the dissent's suggestion that the agency be required to reconsider its policy in light of constitutional concerns. . . .

"Simply stated, my argument here is that Fox is wrong in positing a strict separation between constitutional and ordinary administrative law.... [T]he benefits of addressing constitutional concerns through ordinary administrative law are especially evident with respect to the form of administrative constitutionalism condemned in Fox: judicial use of ordinary administrative law to encourage agencies to take constitutional concerns seriously in their own decisionmaking. Administrative agencies today are responsible for much of the federal government's decisionmaking. Excluding such primary decisionmakers from a judicially enforceable obligation to include significant constitutional concerns in their deliberations is at odds with the structural imperatives of our constitutional system. Agencies are not only well positioned to enforce constitutional norms effectively, but they are also better able than courts to determine how to incorporate constitutional concerns into a given regulatory scheme with the least disruption. In addition, it is far easier for agencies to respond to judicial decisions remanding administrative actions for failure to take account of constitutional concerns than for Congress to respond to judicial invalidation of measures on constitutional grounds or judicial narrowing of statutes through the application of constitutional canons."

(5) **And What Finally Happened?** On remand in Fox Television Stations, Inc. v. F.C.C., 613 F.3d 317 (2d. Cir. 2010), the Second Circuit said that the flexibility that the FCC's approach contained, especially as regards to what would qualify as exonerating "bona fide news" or "artistic necessity," was not permissible, considering that speech was at issue. "We now hold that the FCC's policy violates the First Amendment because it is unconstitutionally vague, creating a chilling effect that goes far beyond the fleeting expletives at issue here. Thus, we grant the petition for review and vacate the FCC's order and the indecency policy underlying it." 613 F.3d at 319. But the Supreme Court was not happy with this result, either. The Circuit's judgment was again accepted by the High Court for review and was vacated by the Court. In a second Fox case, F.C.C. v. Fox Television Stations, Inc., 567 U.S. 239 (2012), the Court held that, because the broadcasts at issue happened before the F.C.C. adopted its new approach to fleeting expletives, the network did not have the notice of its potential violation that the due process clause required. "This would be true with respect to a regulatory change this abrupt on any subject, but it is surely the case when applied to

the regulations in question, regulations that touch upon 'sensitive areas of basic First Amendment freedoms.'" In response to the Commission's argument that the Court should not concern itself with possible reliance because, after all, the Commission itself had decided there would be no penalties to pay, the Court said that there was a sufficient chance of ancillary sanctions, and of reputational injury, to warrant altogether setting aside the finding of a violation. "Given this disposition, it is unnecessary for the Court to address the constitutionality of the current indecency policy as expressed in the *Golden Globes* Order and subsequent adjudications. The Court adheres to its normal practice of declining to decide cases not before it."

SECTION 3.   THE FRAMEWORK OF THE GOVERNING STATUTES

> *a. Historical Building Block Cases*
> *b. The Present-Day Framework*

a.   Historical Building Block Cases

> *NLRB v. HEARST PUBS., INC.*
> *SKIDMORE v. SWIFT & CO.*

Whether an agency's action has adequate support—the subject of the preceding section—depends, of course, not just on how strong that support is but also on whether that support connects with what the agency is authorized to do. Agencies exist, and their responsibilities are delineated, by statutes. In Chapter II we considered the methods courts use as a general matter to construe statutes. We now take up a more particular question: how do the issues look different when there is an agency that has already had to, as part of what it did, construe the statute before the matter gets to court? We start our inquiry with a pair of cases that, as much as any, defined for an earlier generation an appropriate framework. Both predate—by a couple of years—passage of the APA; but here, unlike with its requirement of substantial evidence on the record as a whole, the APA was, at least initially, treated as merely restating prior practice.[9]

---

[9]   When the APA was passed in 1946, the House conferees said its provisions on review would "preclude" various decisions, specifically including the first of our cases, Hearst. Justice Frankfurter noted this in the Universal Camera opinion (see footnote 22 of the original) but seemed to think that as to this particular case the conferees were confused. In any case, the Court treated Hearst, at least for a while, as unimpaired by passage of the APA. Of course, if the case had come up after 1946, some of its phrasing would have differed.

NATIONAL LABOR RELATIONS BOARD v. HEARST PUBLICATIONS, INC.

Supreme Court of the United States (1944).
322 U.S. 111.

■ JUSTICE RUTLEDGE delivered the opinion of the Court.

These cases arise from the refusal of respondents, publishers of four Los Angeles daily newspapers, to bargain collectively with a union representing newsboys who distribute their papers on the streets of that city. Respondents' contention that they were not required to bargain because the newsboys are not their "employees" within the meaning of that term in the National Labor Relations Act, 29 U.S.C. § 152,[1] presents the important question which we granted certiorari to resolve . . . [T]he Board made findings of fact and concluded that the regular full-time newsboys selling each paper were employees within the Act and that questions affecting commerce concerning the representation of employees had arisen. It designated appropriate units and ordered elections. 28 N.L.R.B. at 1006. At these the union was selected as their representative by majorities of the eligible newsboys. [Respondents then refused to bargain with the union, and the Board found this refusal was an unfair labor practice; the court of appeals refused enforcement, deciding that "employee" was to be interpreted consistently with the tests of the common law, and under those tests the newsboys were not employees.]

The papers are distributed to the ultimate consumer through a variety of channels, including . . . newsboys who sell on the streets of the city and its suburbs. . . . The newsboys work under varying terms and conditions. They may be "bootjackers," selling to the general public at places other than established corners, or they may sell at fixed "spots." They may sell only casually or part-time, or full-time; and they may be employed regularly and continuously or only temporarily. The units which the Board determined to be appropriate are composed of those who sell full-time at established spots. Those vendors, misnamed boys, are generally mature men, dependent upon the proceeds of their sales for their sustenance, and frequently supporters of families. Working thus as news vendors on a regular basis, often for a number of years, they form a stable group with relatively little turnover, in contrast to schoolboys and others who sell as bootjackers, temporary and casual distributors.

[The Court then set forth several paragraphs of detail about the newsboys' supervision, compensation, and conditions of work.]

In this pattern of employment the Board found that the newsboys are an integral part of the publishers' distribution system and circulation organization. And the record discloses that the newsboys and checkmen

---

[1] Section 2(3) of the Act provides that "The term 'employee' shall include any employee, and shall not be limited to the employees of a particular employer, unless the Act explicitly states otherwise. . . ."

feel they are employees of the papers and respondents' supervisory employees, if not respondents themselves, regard them as such.

I

The principal question is whether the newsboys are "employees." Because Congress did not explicitly define the term, respondents say its meaning must be determined by reference to common-law standards. In their view "common-law standards" are those the courts have applied in distinguishing between "employees" and "independent contractors" when working out various problems unrelated to the Wagner Act's purposes and provisions.

The argument assumes that there is some simple, uniform and easily applicable test which the courts have used, in dealing with such problems, to determine whether persons doing work for others fall in one class or the other. Unfortunately this is not true. Only by a long and tortuous history was the simple formulation worked out which has been stated most frequently as "the test" for deciding whether one who hires another is responsible in tort for his wrongdoing. But this formula has been by no means exclusively controlling in the solution of other problems. And its simplicity has been illusory because it is more largely simplicity of formulation than of application. . . . [The various tests] have arisen principally, first, in the struggle of the courts to work out common-law liabilities where the legislature has given no guides for judgment, more recently also under statutes which have posed the same problem for solution in the light of the enactment's particular terms and purposes. . . . [W]ithin a single jurisdiction a person who, for instance, is held to be an "independent contractor" for the purpose of imposing vicarious liability in tort may be an "employee" for the purposes of particular legislation, such as unemployment compensation. . . .

Two possible consequences could follow. One would be to refer the decision of who are employees to local state law. The alternative would be to make it turn on a sort of pervading general essence distilled from state law. Congress obviously did not intend the former result. It would introduce variations into the statute's operation as wide as the differences the forty-eight states and other local jurisdictions make in applying the distinction for wholly different purposes. Persons who might be "employees" in one state would be "independent contractors" in another. . . . Persons working across state lines might fall in one class or the other, possibly both, depending on whether the Board and the courts would be required to give effect to the law of one state or of the adjoining one, or to that of each in relation to the portion of the work done within its borders.

Both the terms and the purposes of the statute, as well as the legislative history, show that Congress had in mind no such patchwork plan for securing freedom of employees' organization and of collective bargaining. The Wagner Act is federal legislation, administered by a national agency, intended to solve a national problem on a national scale. . . .

II

Whether, given the intended national uniformity, the term "employee" includes such workers as these newsboys must be answered primarily from the history, terms and purposes of the legislation. The word "is not treated by Congress as a word of art having a definite meaning . . ." Rather "it . . . must be read in the light of the mischief to be corrected and the end to be attained." South Chicago Coal & Dock Co. v. Bassett, 309 U.S. 251.

Congress, on the one hand, was not thinking solely of the immediate technical relation of employer and employee. It had in mind at least some other persons than those standing in the proximate legal relation of employee to the particular employer involved in the labor dispute. It cannot be taken, however, that the purpose was to include all other persons who may perform service for another or was to ignore entirely legal classifications made for other purposes. Congress had in mind a wider field than the narrow technical legal relation of "master and servant," as the common law had worked this out in all its variations, and at the same time a narrower one than the entire area of rendering service to others. The question comes down therefore to how much was included of the intermediate region between what is clearly and unequivocally "employment," by any appropriate test, and what is as clearly entrepreneurial enterprise and not employment. . . .

Congress . . . sought to find a broad solution, one that would bring industrial peace by substituting, so far as its power could reach, the rights of workers to self-organization and collective bargaining for the industrial strife which prevails where these rights are not effectively established. Yet only partial solutions would be provided if large segments of workers about whose technical legal position such local differences exist should be wholly excluded from coverage by reason of such differences. Yet that result could not be avoided, if choice must be made among them and controlled by them in deciding who are "employees" within the Act's meaning. Enmeshed in such distinctions, the administration of the statute soon might become encumbered by the same sort of technical legal refinement as has characterized the long evolution of the employee-independent contractor dichotomy in the courts for other purposes. The consequences would be ultimately to defeat, in part at least, the achievement of the statute's objectives. Congress no more intended to import this mass of technicality as a controlling "standard" for uniform national application than to refer decision of the question outright to the local law.

The Act, as its first section states, was designed to avert the "substantial obstructions to the free flow of commerce" which result from "strikes and other forms of industrial strife or unrest" by eliminating the causes of that unrest. It is premised on explicit findings that strikes and industrial strife themselves result in large measure from the refusal of employers to bargain collectively and the inability of individual workers to bargain successfully for improvements in their "wages, hours, or other working conditions" with employers who are "organized in the corporate or other forms of ownership association." Hence the avowed and the interrelated purposes of the Act are to encourage collective bargaining and to remedy the individual worker's inequality of bargaining power by "protecting the exercise . . . of full freedom of association, self-organization, and designation of representatives of their own choosing, for the purpose of negotiating the terms and conditions of their employment or other mutual aid or protection." 49 Stat. 449, 450.

The mischief at which the Act is aimed and the remedies it offers are not confined exclusively to "employees" within the traditional legal distinctions separating them from "independent contractors." Myriad forms of service relationship, with infinite and subtle variations in the terms of employment, blanket the nation's economy. Some are within this Act, others beyond its coverage. Large numbers will fall clearly on one side or on the other, by whatever test may be applied. But intermediate there will be many, the incidents of whose employment partake in part of the one group, in part of the other, in varying proportions of weight. And consequently the legal pendulum, for purposes of applying the statute, may swing one way or the other, depending upon the weight of this balance and its relation to the special purpose at hand.

. . . Interruption of commerce through strikes and unrest may stem as well from labor disputes between some who, for other purposes, are technically "independent contractors" and their employers as from disputes between persons who, for those purposes, are "employees" and their employers. . . . Inequality of bargaining power in controversies over wages, hours and working conditions may as well characterize the status of the one group as of the other. The former, when acting alone, may be as "helpless in dealing with an employer," as "dependent . . . on his daily wage" and as "unable to leave the employ and to resist arbitrary and unfair treatment" as the latter. For each, "union . . . [may be] essential to give . . . opportunity to deal on equality with their employer." And for each, collective bargaining may be appropriate and effective for the "friendly adjustment of industrial disputes arising out of differences as to wages, hours, or other working conditions." 49 Stat. 449. In short, when the particular situation of employment combines these characteristics, so that the economic facts of the relation make it more nearly one of employment than of independent business enterprise with respect to the ends sought to be accomplished by the legislation, those characteristics may outweigh technical legal classification for purposes unrelated to the statute's objectives and bring the relation within its protections. . . .

It is not necessary in this case to make a completely definitive limitation around the term "employee." That task has been assigned primarily to the agency created by Congress to administer the Act. Determination of "where all the conditions of the relation require protection" involves inquiries for the Board charged with this duty. Everyday experience in the administration of the statute gives it familiarity with the circumstances and backgrounds of employment relationships in various industries, with the abilities and needs of the workers for self organization and collective action, and with the adaptability of collective bargaining for the peaceful settlement of their disputes with their employers. The experience thus acquired must be brought frequently to bear on the question who is an employee under the Act. Resolving that question, like determining whether unfair labor practices have been committed, "belongs to the usual administrative routine" of the Board. Gray v. Powell, 314 U.S. 402, 411. . . .

In making that body's determinations as to the facts in these matters conclusive, if supported by evidence, Congress entrusted to it primarily the decision whether the evidence establishes the material facts. Hence in reviewing the Board's ultimate conclusions, it is not the court's function to substitute its own inferences of fact for the Board's, when the latter have support in the record. . . . Undoubtedly questions of statutory interpretation, especially when arising in the first instance in judicial proceedings, are for the courts to resolve, giving appropriate weight to the judgment of those whose special duty is to administer the questioned statute. But where the question is one of specific application of a broad statutory term in a proceeding in which the agency administering the statute must determine it initially, the reviewing court's function is limited. Like the commissioner's determination under the Longshoremen's & Harbor Workers' Act, that a man is not a "member of a crew" or that he was injured "in the course of his employment" and the Federal Communications Commission's determination that one company is under the "control" of another, the Board's determination that specified persons are "employees" under this Act is to be accepted if it has "warrant in the record" and a reasonable basis in law.

In this case the Board found that the designated newsboys work continuously and regularly, rely upon their earnings for the support of themselves and their families, and have their total wages influenced in large measure by the publishers who dictate their buying and selling prices, fix their markets and control their supply of papers. Their hours of work and their efforts on the job are supervised and to some extent prescribed by the publishers or their agents. Much of their sales equipment and advertising materials is furnished by the publishers with the intention that it be used for the publisher's benefit. Stating that "the primary consideration in the determination of the applicability of the statutory definition is whether effectuation of the declared policy and purposes of the Act comprehend securing to the individual the rights guaranteed and protection afforded by the Act," the Board concluded that the newsboys are employees. The record sustains the Board's findings and there is ample basis in the law for its conclusion. . . .

The judgments are reversed and the causes are remanded . . .

■ [JUSTICE REED concurred in the result. JUSTICE ROBERTS dissented:]

. . . I think it plain that newsboys are not "employees" of the respondents within the meaning and intent of the National Labor Relations Act. When Congress, in § 2(3) said: "The term 'employee' shall include any employee, . . ." it stated as clearly as language could do it that the provisions of the Act were to extend to those who, as a result of decades of tradition which had become part of the common understanding of our people, bear the named relationship. Clearly also Congress did not delegate to the National Labor Relations Board the function of defining the relationship of employment so as to promote what the Board understood to be the underlying purpose of the statute. The question who is an employee, so as to make the statute applicable to him, is a question of the meaning of the Act and, therefore, is a judicial and not an administrative question. . . .

NOTES

(1) **When Should a Court Defer?** Hearst is a carefully written opinion. Justice Rutledge treats some of the questions he considers as matters for the Court to decide for itself and some as matters for which "the reviewing court's function is limited." Can you pinpoint the place in the opinion where he shifts from one stance to the other? Can you say why?

(2) Compare the nearly contemporaneous PACKARD MOTOR CAR CO. V. NLRB, 330 U.S. 485 (1947). Packard's 1100 foremen wanted to organize as a unit of the Foremen's Assn. of America, representing supervisory employees exclusively. The foremen supervised Packard's 32,000 rank-and-file workers, represented by the United Auto Workers; foremen were relatively highly paid and responsible for maintaining quantity and quality of production under overall control by management; foremen could not hire or fire but could discipline and recommend promotion, demotion, etc. The NLRB decided the foremen were "employees," and then decided that they constituted an appropriate bargaining unit. Packard refused to bargain, claiming foremen were not "employees."

"The question presented by this case," said JUSTICE JACKSON for the court, "is whether foremen are entitled as a class to these rights of self-organization [and] collective bargaining . . . assured to employees generally by the National Labor Relations Act." The Act, as we have seen, provided that " 'employee' shall include any employee" but also said that " 'employer' includes any person acting in the interest of an employer, directly or indirectly . . . ." How to put these two provisions together, in relation to foremen, was, said the Court, a "naked question of law" as to which "administrative interpretation" (which had waivered over time on the question) was irrelevant. The Court affirmed the Board. None of the Justices deferred to the Board on this "tremendously important" policy affecting industry nationwide, but a majority agreed with the Board about how the Act should be read to treat foremen. Consistent with Hearst? (Hearst was cited only once, by the dissent, and only for the proposition that "the term 'employee' must be considered in the context of the Act.")[10]

(3) ROY A. SCHOTLAND, SCOPE OF REVIEW OF ADMINISTRATIVE ACTION—REMARKS BEFORE THE D.C. CIRCUIT JUDICIAL CONFERENCE, 34 Fed. B. J. 54, 58 (1975): "[T]he phrases 'questions of fact' and 'questions of law' are not only misleading, but also tend to invite focus on the wrong factors. The inquiry, when deciding what is the appropriate scope of review, of course should be not into the nature of the issue to be decided, e.g., fact or law, but rather should focus upon how much of the resolution of the issue is to be by the judge, how much by the agency. Thus, we should speak of factfinding, which obviously is mainly for the administrator; law-declaring, which has to do with general construction of a statute wholly independently of the particular controversy at bar, which will be mainly, and very often entirely, for our best experts at such matters as statutory construction, you judges; and the last function, spoken of in the familiar but muddling way as 'mixed question,' is what I call law-applying, or applying a statute or other item of law to the particular facts at bar, a function which in the normal course is mainly for the agency because in the normal course, the decisions will have little bearing on any other decision. That is, it's part of the normal particularized administration of the statute and its resolution belongs mainly to the body with the first-line responsibility for that administration."

SKIDMORE v. SWIFT & CO.

Supreme Court of the United States (1944).
323 U.S. 134.

■ JUSTICE JACKSON delivered the opinion of the Court.

Seven employees of the Swift and Company packing plant at Fort Worth, Texas, brought an action under the Fair Labor Standards Act, to recover overtime, liquidated damages, and attorneys' fees, totaling approximately $77,000. . . .

It is not denied that the daytime employment of these persons was working time within the Act. . . . Under their oral agreement of employment, however, petitioners undertook to stay in the fire hall on the Company premises, or within hailing distance, three and a half to four nights a week. This involved no task except to answer alarms, either because of fire or because the sprinkler was set off for some other reason. No fires occurred during the period in issue, the alarms were rare, and the time required for their answer rarely exceeded an hour. For each alarm answered the employees were paid in addition to their fixed compensation an agreed amount, fifty cents at first, and later sixty-four cents. The Company provided a brick fire hall equipped with steam heat and air-conditioned rooms. It provided sleeping quarters, a pool table, a

---

[10] Congress promptly amended the definition of "employee" to exclude "supervisory employees."

domino table, and a radio. The men used their time in sleep or amusement as they saw fit, except that they were required to stay in or close by the fire hall and be ready to respond to alarms. It is stipulated that "they agreed to remain in the fire hall and stay in it or within hailing distance, subject to call, in event of fire or other casualty, but were not required to perform any specific tasks during these periods of time, except in answering alarms." The trial court found the evidentiary facts as stipulated; it made no findings of fact as such as to whether under the arrangement of the parties and the circumstances of this case, which in some respects differ from those of [a companion case], the fire hall duty or any part thereof constituted working time. It said, however, as a "conclusion of law" that "the time plaintiffs spent in the fire hall subject to call to answer fire alarms does not constitute hours worked, for which overtime compensation is due them under the Fair Labor Standards Act, as interpreted by the Administrator and the Courts," and in its opinion observed, "of course we know pursuing such pleasurable occupations or performing such personal chores does not constitute work." The Circuit Court of Appeals affirmed.

For reasons set forth in [that companion case], we hold that no principle of law found either in the statute or in Court decisions precludes waiting time from also being working time. We have not attempted to, and we cannot, lay down a legal formula to resolve cases so varied in their facts as are the many situations in which employment involves waiting time. Whether in a concrete case such time falls within or without the Act is a question of fact to be resolved by appropriate findings of the trial court. . . . This involves scrutiny and construction of the agreements between the particular parties, appraisal of their practical construction of the working agreement by conduct, consideration of the nature of the service, and its relation to the waiting time, and all of the surrounding circumstances. Facts may show that the employee was engaged to wait, or they may show that he waited to be engaged. His compensation may cover both waiting and task, or only performance of the task itself. Living quarters may in some situations be furnished as a facility of the task and in another as a part of its compensation. The law does not impose an arrangement upon the parties. It imposes upon the courts the task of finding what the arrangement was. . . .

Congress did not utilize the services of an administrative agency to find facts and to determine in the first instance whether particular cases fall within or without the Act. Instead, it put this responsibility on the courts. . . . But it did create the office of Administrator [of the Wage and Hour Division of the Department of Labor], impose upon him a variety of duties, endow him with powers to inform himself of conditions in industries and employments subject to the Act, and put on him the duties of bringing injunction actions to restrain violations. Pursuit of his duties has accumulated a considerable experience in the problems of ascertaining working time in employments involving periods of inactivity and a knowledge of the customs prevailing in reference to their solution. From these he is obliged to reach conclusions as to conduct without the law, so that he should seek injunctions to stop it, and that within the law, so that he has no call to interfere. He has set forth his views of the application of the Act under different circumstances in an interpretative bulletin and in informal rulings. They provide a practical guide to employers and employees as to how the office representing the public interest in its enforcement will seek to apply it. Wage and Hour Division, Interpretative Bulletin No. 13. . . .

There is no statutory provision as to what, if any, deference courts should pay to the Administrator's conclusions. And, while we have given them notice, we have had no occasion to try to prescribe their influence. The rulings of this Administrator are not reached as a result of hearing adversary proceedings in which he finds facts from evidence and reaches conclusions of law from findings of fact. They are not, of course, conclusive, even in the cases with which they directly deal, much less in those to which they apply only by analogy. They do not constitute an interpretation of the Act or a standard for judging factual situations which binds a district court's processes, as an authoritative pronouncement of a higher court might do. But the Administrator's policies are made in pursuance of official duty, based upon more specialized experience and broader investigations and information than is likely to come to a judge in a particular case. They do determine the policy which will guide applications for enforcement by injunction on behalf of the Government. Good administration of the Act and good judicial administration alike require that the standards of public enforcement and those for determining private rights shall be at variance only where justified by very good reasons. The fact that the Administrator's policies and standards are not reached by trial in adversary form does not mean that they are not entitled to respect. This Court has long given considerable and in some cases decisive weight to Treasury Decisions and to interpretative regulations of the Treasury and of other bodies that were not of adversary origin.

We consider that the rulings, interpretations and opinions of the Administrator under this Act, while not controlling upon the courts by reason of their authority, do constitute a body of experience and informed judgment to which courts and litigants may properly resort for guidance. The weight of such a judgment in a particular case will depend upon the thoroughness evident in its consideration, the validity of its reasoning, its consistency with earlier and later pronouncements, and all those factors which give it power to persuade, if lacking power to control.

The court in the [companion] case weighed the evidence . . . in the light of the Administrator's rulings and reached a result consistent therewith. The evidence in this case in some respects, such as the understanding as to separate compensation for answering alarms, is different. Each case must stand on its own facts. But in this case,

District court did not consider all enough & thorough wasn't thorough

although the District Court referred to the Administrator's Bulletin, its evaluation and inquiry were apparently restricted by its notion that waiting time may not be work, an understanding of the law which we hold to be erroneous. Accordingly, the judgment is reversed and the cause remanded for further proceedings consistent herewith.

NOTES

(1) *What Are the Administrator's Interpretations of the Act Worth?* SAMUEL HERMAN, THE ADMINISTRATION AND ENFORCEMENT OF THE FAIR LABOR STANDARDS ACT, 6 Law & Contemp. Probs. 368, 378–80 (1939). "A rule-making power had been contained in the Act as originally introduced. The issuance of 'interpretative bulletins' by the Wage and Hour Division stemmed from the failure of Congress to include a rule-making provision in the Act. The bulletins were the creature of necessity . . . [and] self-denying as witnessed by the following typical statement:

> . . . [I]nterpretations announced by the Administrator, except in certain specific instances where the statute directs the Administrator to make various regulations and definitions, serve only to indicate the construction of the law which will guide the Administrator in the performance of his administrative duties, unless he is directed otherwise by the authoritative rulings of the courts, or unless he shall subsequently decide that a prior interpretation is incorrect.

". . . The interpretative bulletins are not binding on industry; they are merely legal advice—good, perhaps the best. While industry is advised to comply, if in doubt, the employer is not immune if, in reliance upon an interpretative bulletin, he concludes that the Act is not applicable to him. He may be subsequently prosecuted under Section 16(a), sued by an employee under Section 16(b), or enjoined under Section 17."

(2) *What Is the Doctrine of Skidmore?* Justice Jackson's penultimate paragraph is—as we shall see—much quoted, and it has a lot of prior precedent supporting it. Peter L. Strauss, In Search of Skidmore, 83 Fordham L. Rev. 789, 789–90 (2014). It is also well written. But, what exactly does it mean? The weight to be given the Administrator's interpretation by the trial court on remand, we are told, depends on "those factors which give it power to persuade." Does this mean that if the court is persuaded that the Administrator is right, it should follow his interpretation (which is now, since the court has been persuaded, also the court's interpretation)—and if not, it should not? This is not news. It is also not deference. The court will simply be doing in its own voice what it now thinks it is right to do. We would not say that a court persuaded by the excellent brief of a private litigant to decide in its favor is deferring to the litigant's lawyers.

(3) If you responded to the previous Note by saying to yourself that, whatever the words, Justice Jackson did mean for the court to give some extra weight to the agency's judgments, to defer to them to some extent, then how do you get by the point, also in the paragraph, that these interpretations are "not controlling upon the courts by reason of their authority." Is the

crucial word here "controlling"—so that a court can still *choose* to defer to the opinion of the agency much as a trial court might defer to the opinion of an expert witness once convinced the witness was really an expert?

(4) Does it bother you, in the Court's deciding to give some weight to the Administrator's interpretations, that Congress did not give the Administrator the power to make rules? Does it bother you that no law gave Swift & Co. an opportunity to be heard before the agency on the interpretive question presented? (Recall, if you have studied them, the materials on interpretative rules and policy statements, Ch IV, Sec. 3.b.)

(5) How does "Skidmore deference" fit with your interpretation of the Hearst case?

TRANSITIONAL NOTE

We now move to cases decided in the last thirty-plus years, starting with a case that is perhaps the most famous, or at least most-cited, case in modern administrative law, the Chevron case. Whether, and if so to what effect, Chevron and its progeny have changed the framework set out in the older cases is, of course, one of the topics that remains on the table.

b. The Present-Day Framework

> *CHEVRON, USA, INC. v. NRDC, INC.*
> *Notes on the Importance of Chevron*
> *Notes on the Operation of Chevron's Doctrine*
> *Notes on the Relationship Between Chevron and State Farm*
> *Notes on the Wisdom (or Not) of Chevron's Doctrine*
> *Notes on the Relationship Between Chevron and Judicial Statutory Precedent*
> *Notes on the Practical Impact of Chevron*

CHEVRON, U.S.A., INC. v. NATURAL RESOURCES DEFENSE COUNCIL, INC.

Supreme Court of the United States (1984).
467 U.S. 837.

■ JUSTICE STEVENS delivered the opinion of the Court.

In the Clean Air Act Amendments of 1977, Pub. L. 95–95, 91 Stat. 685, Congress enacted certain requirements applicable to States that had not achieved the national air quality standards established by the Environmental Protection Agency (EPA) pursuant to earlier legislation. The amended Clean Air Act required these "nonattainment" States to establish a permit program regulating "new or modified major stationary sources" of air pollution. Generally, a permit may not be issued for a new or modified major stationary source unless several stringent conditions are met. The EPA regulation promulgated to implement this permit requirement allows a State to adopt a plantwide definition of the term "stationary source." Under this definition, an existing plant that contains several pollution-emitting devices may install or modify one piece of equipment without meeting the permit conditions if the alteration will not increase the total emissions from the plant. The question presented by this case is whether EPA's decision to allow States to treat all of the pollution-emitting devices within the same industrial grouping as though they were encased within a single "bubble" is based on a reasonable construction of the statutory term "stationary source."

I

The EPA regulations containing the plantwide definition of the term stationary source were promulgated on October 14, 1981. 46 Fed. Reg. 50766. Respondents filed a timely petition for review in the United States Court of Appeals for the District of Columbia Circuit pursuant to 42 U.S.C. § 7607(b)(1). The Court of Appeals set aside the regulations. Natural Resources Defense Council, Inc. v. Gorsuch, 685 F.2d 718 (1982).

The court observed that the relevant part of the amended Clean Air Act "does not explicitly define what Congress envisioned as a 'stationary source,' to which the permit program . . . should apply," and further stated that the precise issue was not "squarely addressed in the legislative history." In light of its conclusion that the legislative history bearing on the question was "at best contradictory," it reasoned that "the purposes of the nonattainment program should guide our decision here."[5] Based on two of its precedents concerning the applicability of the bubble concept to certain Clean Air Act programs, the court stated that the bubble concept was "mandatory" in programs designed merely to maintain existing air quality, but held that it was "inappropriate" in programs enacted to improve air quality. Since the purpose of the permit program—its "raison d'etre," in the court's view—was to improve air quality, the court held that the bubble concept was inapplicable in this case under its prior precedents. It therefore set aside the regulations embodying the bubble concept as contrary to law. We . . . now reverse.

The basic legal error of the Court of Appeals was to adopt a static judicial definition of the term stationary source when it had decided that Congress itself had not commanded that definition. . . .

II

When a court reviews an agency's construction of the statute which it administers, it is confronted with two questions. First, always, is the question whether Congress has directly spoken to the precise question at

---

    5   The court remarked in this regard: "We regret, of course, that Congress did not advert specifically to the bubble concept's application to various Clean Air Act programs, and note that a further clarifying statutory directive would facilitate the work of the agency and of the court in their endeavors to serve the legislators' will."

issue. If the intent of Congress is clear, that is the end of the matter; for the court, as well as the agency, must give effect to the unambiguously expressed intent of Congress.[9] If, however, the court determines Congress has not directly addressed the precise question at issue, the court does not simply impose its own construction on the statute, as would be necessary in the absence of an administrative interpretation. Rather, if the statute is silent or ambiguous with respect to the specific issue, the question for the court is whether the agency's answer is based on a permissible construction of the statute.[11]

"The power of an administrative agency to administer a congressionally created . . . program necessarily requires the formulation of policy and the making of rules to fill any gap left, implicitly or explicitly, by Congress." Morton v. Ruiz, 415 U.S. 199, 231 (1974). If Congress has explicitly left a gap for the agency to fill, there is an express delegation of authority to the agency to elucidate a specific provision of the statute by regulation. Such legislative regulations are given controlling weight unless they are arbitrary, capricious, or manifestly contrary to the statute. Sometimes the legislative delegation to an agency on a particular question is implicit rather than explicit. In such a case, a court may not substitute its own construction of a statutory provision for a reasonable interpretation made by the administrator of an agency.

We have long recognized that considerable weight should be accorded to an executive department's construction of a statutory scheme it is entrusted to administer, and the principle of deference to administrative interpretations

has been consistently followed by this Court whenever decision as to the meaning or reach of a statute has involved reconciling conflicting policies, and a full understanding of the force of the statutory policy in the given situation has depended upon more than ordinary knowledge respecting the matters subjected to agency regulations. See e.g., Labor Board v. Hearst Publications, Inc., 322 U.S. 111; Securities & Exchange Comm'n v. Chenery Corp., 332 U.S. 194. . . . If this choice represents a reasonable accommodation of conflicting policies that were committed to the agency's care by the statute, we should not disturb it unless it appears from the statute or its legislative history that the accommodation is not one that Congress would have sanctioned.

United States v. Shimer, 367 U.S. 374, 382, 383 (1961).

---

[9] The judiciary is the final authority on issues of statutory construction and must reject administrative constructions which are contrary to clear congressional intent. If a court, employing traditional tools of statutory construction, ascertains that Congress had an intention on the precise question at issue, that intention is the law and must be given effect.

[11] The court need not conclude that the agency construction was the only one it permissibly could have adopted to uphold the construction, or even the reading the court would have reached if the question initially had arisen in a judicial proceeding.

In light of these well-settled principles it is clear that the Court of Appeals misconceived the nature of its role in reviewing the regulations at issue. Once it determined, after its own examination of the legislation, that Congress did not actually have an intent regarding the applicability of the bubble concept to the permit program, the question before it was not whether in its view the concept is "inappropriate" in the general context of a program designed to improve air quality, but whether the Administrator's view that it is appropriate in the context of this particular program is a reasonable one. Based on the examination of the legislation and its history which follows, we agree with the Court of Appeals that Congress did not have a specific intention on the applicability of the bubble concept in these cases, and conclude that the EPA's use of that concept here is a reasonable policy choice for the agency to make.

[III, IV, V]

[The Court reviewed the legislative history of the Clean Air Act and its Amendments at length. It remarked that the issue before it concerned "one phrase" from a "small portion" of "a lengthy, detailed, technical, complex, and comprehensive response to a major social issue," the Clean Air Act Amendments of 1977, that in turn was only part of a much larger statutory scheme under EPA's administration. "The legislative history of the portion of the 1977 Amendments dealing with nonattainment areas," it stated, "does not contain any specific comment on the 'bubble concept' or the question whether a plantwide definition of a stationary source is permissible under the permit program. It does, however, plainly disclose that in the permit program Congress sought to accommodate the conflict between the economic interest in permitting capital improvements to continue and the environmental interest in improving air quality."]

VI

[Turning to the administrative history of implementation of the Clean Air Act Amendments of 1977, the Court noted that EPA had at first proposed interpretations like that under challenge.]

In August 1980, however, the EPA adopted a regulation that, in essence, applied the basic reasoning of the Court of Appeals in this case. The EPA took particular note of the two then-recent Court of Appeals decisions, which had created the bright-line rule that the bubble concept should be employed in a program designed to maintain air quality but not in one designed to enhance air quality. Relying heavily on those cases, EPA adopted a dual definition of "source" for nonattainment areas that required a permit whenever a change in either the entire plant, or one of its components, would result in a significant increase in emissions even if the increase was completely offset by reductions elsewhere in the plant. . . .

In 1981 a new administration took office and initiated a "Governmentwide reexamination of regulatory burdens and complexities." 46 Fed. Reg. 16281. In the context of that review, the EPA reevaluated the various arguments that had been advanced in connection with the proper definition of the term "source" and concluded that the term should be given the same definition in both nonattainment areas and PSD [preventing significant deterioration] areas.

In explaining its conclusion, the EPA first noted that the definitional issue was not squarely addressed in either the statute or its legislative history and therefore that the issue involved an agency "judgment as how to best carry out the Act." It then set forth several reasons for concluding that the plantwide definition was more appropriate. It pointed out that the dual definition "can act as a disincentive to new investment and modernization by discouraging modifications to existing facilities" and "can actually retard progress in air pollution control by discouraging replacement of older, dirtier processes or pieces of equipment with new, cleaner ones." Moreover, the new definition "would simplify EPA's rules by using the same definition of 'source' for PSD, nonattainment new source review and the construction moratorium. This reduces confusion and inconsistency." Finally, the agency explained that additional requirements that remained in place would accomplish the fundamental purposes of achieving attainment . . . as expeditiously as possible. These conclusions were expressed in a proposed rulemaking in August 1981 that was formally promulgated in October.

VII

[The Court turned to arguments offered by the respondents to show that the statute had a clear meaning.]

Statutory Language

We are not persuaded that parsing of general terms in the text of the statute will reveal an actual intent of Congress. We know full well that this language is not dispositive; the terms are overlapping and the language is not precisely directed to the question of the applicability of a given term in the context of a larger operation. To the extent any congressional "intent" can be discerned from this language, it would appear that the listing of overlapping, illustrative terms was intended to enlarge, rather than to confine, the scope of the agency's power to regulate particular sources in order to effectuate the policies of the Act.

Legislative History

Based on our examination of the legislative history, we agree with the Court of Appeals that it is unilluminating. The general remarks pointed to by respondents "were obviously not made with this narrow issue in mind and they cannot be said to demonstrate a Congressional desire . . ." Jewell Ridge Coal Corp. v. Mine Workers, 325 U.S. 161, 168–169 (1945). . . . We find that the legislative history as a whole is silent on the precise issue before us. It is, however, consistent with the view that the EPA should have broad discretion in implementing the policies of the 1977 Amendments.

More importantly, that history plainly identifies the policy concerns that motivated the enactment; the plantwide definition is fully consistent with one of those concerns—the allowance of reasonable economic growth—and, whether or not we believe it most effectively implements the other, we must recognize that the EPA has advanced a reasonable explanation for its conclusion that the regulations serve the environmental objectives as well. Indeed, its reasoning is supported by the public record developed in the rulemaking process, as well as by certain private studies.[37]

Our review of the EPA's varying interpretations of the word "source"—both before and after the 1977 Amendments—convince us that the agency primarily responsible for administering this important legislation has consistently interpreted it flexibly—not in a sterile textual vacuum, but in the context of implementing policy decisions in a technical and complex arena. The fact that the agency has from time to time changed its interpretation of the term "source" does not, as respondents argue, lead us to conclude that no deference should be accorded the agency's interpretation of the statute. An initial agency interpretation is not instantly carved in stone. On the contrary, the agency, to engage in informed rulemaking, must consider varying interpretations and the wisdom of its policy on a continuing basis. Moreover, the fact that the agency has adopted different definitions in different contexts adds force to the argument that the definition itself is flexible, particularly since Congress has never indicated any disapproval of a flexible reading of the statute.

Significantly, it was not the agency in 1980, but rather the Court of Appeals that read the statute inflexibly to command a plantwide definition for programs designed to maintain clean air and to forbid such a definition for programs designed to improve air quality. The distinction the court drew may well be a sensible one, but our labored review of the problem has surely disclosed that it is not a distinction that Congress ever articulated itself, or one that the EPA found in the statute before the courts began to review the legislative work product. We conclude that it was the Court of Appeals, rather than Congress or any of the decisionmakers who are authorized by Congress to administer this legislation, that was primarily responsible for the 1980 position taken by the agency.

Policy

The arguments over policy that are advanced in the parties' briefs create the impression that respondents are now waging in a judicial

---

[37] "Economists have proposed that economic incentives be substituted for the cumbersome administrative-legal framework. The objective is to make the profit and cost incentives that work so well in the marketplace work for pollution control. . . . [The 'bubble' or 'netting' concept] is a first attempt in this direction. By giving a plant manager flexibility to find the places and processes within a plant that control emissions most cheaply, pollution control can be achieved more quickly and cheaply." L. Lave & G. Omenn, Cleaning the Air: Reforming the Clean Air Act 28 (1981) (footnote omitted).

forum a specific policy battle which they ultimately lost in the agency and in the 32 jurisdictions opting for the bubble concept, but one which was never waged in the Congress. Such policy arguments are more properly addressed to legislators or administrators, not to judges.

In this case, the Administrator's interpretation represents a reasonable accommodation of manifestly competing interests and is entitled to deference: the regulatory scheme is technical and complex, the agency considered the matter in a detailed and reasoned fashion, and the decision involves reconciling conflicting policies. Congress intended to accommodate both interests, but did not do so itself on the level of specificity presented by this case. Perhaps that body consciously desired the Administrator to strike the balance at this level, thinking that those with great expertise and charged with responsibility for administering the provision would be in a better position to do so; perhaps it simply did not consider the question at this level; and perhaps Congress was unable to forge a coalition on either side of the question, and those on each side decided to take their chances with the scheme devised by the agency. For judicial purposes, it matters not which of these things occurred.

Judges are not experts in the field, and are not part of either political branch of the Government. Courts must, in some cases, reconcile competing political interests, but not on the basis of the judges' personal policy preferences. (In contrast, an agency to which Congress has delegated policy-making responsibilities may, within the limits of that delegation, properly rely upon the incumbent administration's views of wise policy to inform its judgments.) While agencies are not directly accountable to the people, the Chief Executive is, and it is entirely appropriate for this political branch of the Government to make such policy choices—resolving the competing interests which Congress itself either inadvertently did not resolve, or intentionally left to be resolved by the agency charged with the administration of the statute in light of everyday realities.

When a challenge to an agency construction of a statutory provision, fairly conceptualized, really centers on the wisdom of the agency's policy, rather than whether it is a reasonable choice within a gap left open by Congress, the challenge must fail. In such a case, federal judges—who have no constituency—have a duty to respect legitimate policy choices made by those who do. The responsibilities for assessing the wisdom of such policy choices and resolving the struggle between competing views of the public interest are not judicial ones: "Our Constitution vests such responsibilities in the political branches." TVA v. Hill, 437 U.S. 153, 195 (1978).

We hold that the EPA's definition of the term "source" is a permissible construction of the statute which seeks to accommodate progress in reducing air pollution with economic growth. "The Regulations which the Administrator has adopted provide what the agency could allowably view as . . . [an] effective reconciliation of these twofold ends. . . ." United States v. Shimer, 367 U.S., at 383.

The judgment of the Court of Appeals is reversed.

■ JUSTICE MARSHALL and JUSTICE REHNQUIST did not participate in the consideration or decision of these cases.

■ JUSTICE O'CONNOR did not participate in the decision of these cases.

NOTES ON THE IMPORTANCE OF CHEVRON

(1) *How Important Is Chevron?* Sound bites on Chevron's importance:

(a) "Chevron is this generation's *Erie*. . . . *Erie* rested on a judicial recognition that the law is not 'a brooding omnipresence in the sky.' . . . Chevron is closely parallel. When statutes are ambiguous, a judgment about their meaning rests on no brooding omnipresence in the sky, but on assessments of both policy and principle. There is no reason to allow those assessments to be made by federal courts rather than executive officers. So, at least, Chevron holds." Cass R. Sunstein, Beyond *Marbury*: The Executive's Power to Say What the Law Is, 115 Yale. L. J. 2580, 2598 (2006).

(b) "Now for you agency case lawyers. Chevron is the password. In every case involving statutory interpretation, think Chevron." Judge Patricia Wald, speaking on "Advocacy from the Viewpoint of an Appellate Judge," Fourth Annual Appellate Advocacy Program, Washington D.C., Oct. 28, 1994, at 9.

(c) "Chevron is the doctrinal apotheosis of the modern legal era. It signals a resounding shift of the center of the law's gravity away from judge-made law toward statutes and their primary administrators." Abbe R. Gluck, What 30 Years of Chevron Teach Us About the Rest of Statutory Interpretation, 83 Fordham L. Rev. 607, 631 (2014).

(2) Compare ROBERT V. PERCIVAL, ENVIRONMENTAL LAW IN THE SUPREME COURT: HIGHLIGHTS FROM THE MARSHALL PAPERS, 23 Envtl. L. Rep. 10606, 10613 (1993): "One surprise is the absence of any evidence in the written record indicating that the Justices realized the full implications of their landmark administrative law decision in . . . Chevron. There is no comment in the written exchanges among the Justices that reflects any appreciation of the major change in administrative law the decision effected. . . . [T]he Marshall papers indicate that the decision was reached without any significant debate over Justice Stevens' draft opinion, which was initially circulated among the Justices on June 11, 1984. On June 12, Justices Rehnquist and Marshall circulated notes indicating without explanation that they were recusing themselves from the case. [Justice O'Connor also recused herself because a family estate owned stock in one of the parties. By June 18, all others had joined the opinion.] The only comment in the memos concerning the substance of [the] opinion is the statement by Chief Justice Burger that 'I am now persuaded you have the correct answer to this case.' "

NOTES ON THE OPERATION OF CHEVRON'S DOCTRINE

(1) *When Does the Chevron Test Even Apply?* There is a threshold issue of when the Chevron framework applies to an agency's proposed construction of a statute. That issue is sometimes referred to as Chevron step zero. See Cass R. Sunstein, Chevron Step Zero, 92 Va. L. Rev. 187 (2006); see also Thomas W. Merrill and Kristin E. Hickman, Chevron's Domain, 89 Geo. L. J. 833 (2001). For example, what does it mean to say that an agency "administers" a statute? Does the fact that an agency had reason to interpret the statute mean that it administers it? The answer to that question is surely, "No." (See, for example, the discussion of agency interpretations of the APA, p. 242.) But what is the test for determining that the agency does have the kind of administering power over a statute that might entitle it to Chevron deference in interpreting it? Relatedly, what does it mean to say that an agency has offered an interpretation of a statute that it administers? For example, does the interpretation have to be offered in a certain form to even count as an interpretation? We consider these threshold questions at various points in this chapter; as it turns out they have no simple answer. In fact, the answers to them are, if anything, becoming harder and harder to articulate, given the various carve outs and exceptions to Chevron that the Court has begun to identify. But, there is still no doubt that the Chevron test does apply much (maybe even most) of the time, and so it is important to understand how the test works.

(2) *How Does the Chevron Test Work?* The first paragraph of Part II of the Chevron opinion—the "two questions"—will be familiar to anyone who has the slightest acquaintance with modern administrative law. (It is referred to in many places throughout this book.) But Justice Stevens' opinion seems somewhat awkward for a case that is a leading case. He presents his test as if it were simply a statement of "well-settled principles," which seems unfounded. (While there were prior cases that adopted a similarly deferential approach to statutory construction, there were others that did not; and in any case the phrasing was new.) The statements in the opinion that might furnish a rationale for the test are diverse—referring variously to the regulatory scheme's being "technical and complex," to the need for "reconciling conflicting policies," to Congress's having "delegated policy-making responsibilities" to the agency, to the lack of expertise on the part of judges, to the President's being electorally responsible, and to the fact that federal judges "have no constituency." And there seems to be little effort made to connect these various considerations to the formality of the test itself. One set of issues, then, is whether the Chevron test is applicable to every case in which "a court reviews an agency's construction of the statute which it administers" (to use Justice Steven's lead-in phrase), or whether its applicability is conditioned by the presence (or absence) of some of these other factors.

A second set of issues concerns the application of the test on its own terms. Perhaps its most important feature, considered strictly as a matter of doctrinal analysis, is that the test has two steps. This provokes two important questions: First, how do we know whether we are in step one or step two? Second, what is the difference in approach between the two steps?

Let us begin with the first of these questions. To use Justice Stevens' formulations, we are in step one "if the intent of Congress is clear," while we are in step two "if the statute is silent or ambiguous." Clarity or ambiguity is the test. Of course, all language is ambiguous with regard to something, but Stevens definitely states that the test is ambiguity (or not) with regard to "the precise question at issue." And in a footnote he indicates that the way to determine whether Congress had, or did not, have a clear intent, is by using "traditional tools of statutory construction."

This formulation makes it rather plain that Chevron deference is not predicated on there being an inextricable mixture of fact and law in the problem at hand. As one commentator has said: "The distinction is not between issues of law and fact, which does not seem to have much to do with Chevron. The distinction is between issues of law and policy, which is at the core of Chevron." Michael Herz, Deference Running Riot: Separating Interpretation and Lawmaking under Chevron, 6 Admin L. J. 187, 223 (1992). Even if this claim is a bit overstated, its basic implication—that under Chevron, agencies get to make decisions that from a traditional law/fact/mixed question analysis are only about questions of law—obviously raises questions of legitimacy. (Of these questions, more later; for the moment we are looking simply at the question of how to employ the doctrine.)

Assuming that ambiguity means ambiguity as to the meaning of the statute itself (which seems to be the case), much turns on how one thinks judges should ascribe meaning to statutory language. Thus, many of the subsequent controversies regarding Chevron-in-practice have been, in effect, contests between different theories of statutory construction—between, for example, those who think that recourse to "legislative history" is useful and those who do not. (Recall, if you studied it, the discussion of that issue at in Chapter II, Section 3.e.)

Turning now to the question of the differences in operation between the two steps of the test, Stevens' formulation of the question under the second step is "whether the agency's answer is based on a permissible construction of the statute." Is this just a broader statement of the outer limits of what the statute will permit, requiring thinking similar to that done in determining Congress's intent for step one? Some have read it that way—so that the whole Chevron test, in effect, is whether the agency's interpretation of the statute is "reasonable." Or, at the other extreme, does this language signal the kind of thinking that lies behind application of the "arbitrary and capricious" standard? Some have read it that way, too—so that in effect Chevron and State Farm (p. 1069) merge at step two. Or do we have to consider Chevron step one thinking, which is different from Chevron step two thinking, which is different from State Farm thinking? There are advocates for that position, too.

It would doubtless be a mistake to think that all these issues were in Justice Stevens' mind when he wrote Chevron or that we would find definite answers to them if only we read his opinion with exquisite care. The questions have been, and remain, much alive. In the notes that follow, some possible analyses will be suggested. But all of the later principal cases in this

Chapter were written in Chevron's shadow, and so they, too, are authorities on how the Chevron test is understood at the present time.

(3) **_Are the Two Parts of the Chevron Test Different in Kind or Only Degree?_** JUDGE WILLIAMS, 30 F.3d at 193, on the denial of rehearing in SWEET HOME CHAPTER V. BABBITT, 17 F.3d 1463 (D.C. Cir. 1994), reversed, 515 U.S. 687 (1995):

> The government faults the panel for failing to specify whether the regulation's excess of statutory authority failed under the first or second "step" of the analysis set forth in Chevron and in a more general way for failing to give the agency the deference that is its due under Chevron. Because the court in determining whether Congress "unambiguously expressed" its intent on the issue is to employ all the "traditional tools of statutory construction," the factors involved in the first "step" are also pertinent to whether an agency's interpretation is "reasonable." Thus the exact point where an agency interpretation falls down may be unclear. (Indeed, the Chevron Court itself never specified which step it was applying at any point in its analysis.)

Compare JUDGE SILBERMAN in the same case (30 F.3d at 194–95):

> I quite agree with the panel that "the factors involved in the first 'step' are also pertinent to whether an agency's interpretation is 'reasonable' "; but when thinking of the statute at that second step, one must assume that the statute has more than one plausible construction as it applies to the case before you. If the agency offers one—it prevails.

> While the Supreme Court clearly says in Chevron that there are two steps, "with perhaps one exception, AT&T Corp. v. Iowa Utilities Bd., 119 S.Ct. 721, 734–36 (1999), the Supreme Court has never invalidated an agency construction of a statute at step two of Chevron. The lower court Chevron step two cases follow a similar, though not as overwhelming, pattern. Consequently, opinions rarely contain a self-conscious explanation of exactly what a court should examine at step two. Because Chevron step two invalidations are extremely rare, it is also difficult to determine the relative importance of the many factors that courts can rely on when they uphold interpretations." Elizabeth Magill, Step Two of Chevron v. Natural Resources Defense Council, in A Guide to Judicial and Political Review of Federal Agencies 85, 99 (John F. Duffy & Michael Herz eds., 2005).

For an argument that the two steps are really just one, consider: MATTHEW C. STEPHENSON & ADRIAN VERMEULE, _CHEVRON_ HAS ONLY ONE STEP, 95 Va. L. Rev. 597, 598–99 (2009): "Chevron divides the . . . inquiry—whether the agency's interpretation of the statute is valid—into two steps. At Step One, the court must ask whether, after 'employing traditional tools of statutory construction' it is evidence that 'Congress has directly spoken to the precise question at issue.' If so, the statute is 'unambiguous.' If, however, the court decides at Step One that the statute is ambiguous, the court proceeds to Step Two. At Step Two, the court must uphold the agency's interpretation so long as it is 'based on a permissible construction of the statute.' . . .

"This structure artificially divides one inquiry into two steps. The single question is whether the agency's construction is permissible as a matter of statutory interpretation; the two Chevron steps both ask this question, just in different ways. As a result, the two steps are mutually convertible.

"If an agency's construction of the statute is 'contrary to clear congressional intent . . . on the precise question at issue,' then the agency's construction is a fortiori not 'based on a permissible construction of the statute.' Step One is therefore nothing more than a special case of Step Two, which implies that all Step One opinions could be written in the language of Step Two."

For a different view, consider: KENNETH A. BAMBERGER & PETER L. STRAUSS, *CHEVRON*'S TWO STEPS, 95 Va. L. Rev. 611, 616 (2009): "In cases reviewing agency interpretations that are, in fact, permitted by the statutory text, this [step-one, step-two] distinction may bear little consequence on the resolution of the case at hand: the agency's interpretation is vindicated. Yet the systemic implications of such a difference for administration are real. . . . [A] judicial precedent holding that a particular interpretation is either required or precluded fixes statutory meaning to that extent, foreclosing future agency constructions to the contrary. By contrast, a judicial determination that an agency interpretation embodies one option within the zone of indeterminacy makes it possible for the agency to put forth a different interpretation at a later time."

If there is a difference between the two steps, how might we describe that difference? Professor Magill identifies two possibilities. See Magill, Step Two of Chevron, at 87–102. One possibility is that the first step focuses on whether the statute is clear or ambiguous in answering the precise question at issue, while the second step focuses on whether the agency's proposed answer to that precise question is a permissible one, given the range of possible answers that the statutory ambiguity permits. A difficulty with this way of understanding step two, however, is that, as she points out, step two then arguably just replicates step one. After all, if the agency's proposed answer is not a permissible one, then presumably that is because the precise question that the agency was answering was one that Congress had clearly answered at step one. Id., at 87–93. Another possibility is that step two of Chevron differs from step one by focusing on the reasoning or logic underlying the agency's proposed resolution of the ambiguity. Thus, in theory, even if the agency's interpretation is one that falls within the zone of ambiguity permitted by the statute's text and purposes, the agency must still explain why it chose that particular interpretation as opposed to some other permissible one that fell within the permissible zone. And so the agency must provide a coherent explanation for why it chose the interpretation that it selected. On this understanding, State Farm and Chevron arguably converge at step two of Chevron, as we discuss further below. See Magill, Step Two of Chevron, 93–102.

(4) *Is there a Step One-and-a-Half?* "The Supreme Court says that Chevron has two steps: Is the statute ambiguous (Step One) and if so, is the agency's interpretation of the ambiguous provision a permissible one (Step Two)? Yet over the last three decades, the D.C. Circuit has inserted an intermediate step between Steps One and Two: Did the agency recognize that the statutory provision is ambiguous? If not, then the D.C. Circuit refuses to proceed to Chevron Step Two and remands the matter to the agency. This doctrine—which we dub 'Chevron Step One-and-a-Half'—has led to dozens of agency losses in the D.C. Circuit and D.C. federal district court, but it has gone entirely unmentioned in administrative law casebooks and is rarely referenced in the academic literature. The few who have not ignored the doctrine have treated it with skepticism. Chief among those skeptics is now-Chief Justice John Roberts, who while a D.C. Circuit judge sternly criticized his colleagues for applying the doctrine." DANIEL J. HEMEL AND AARON L. NEILSON, CHEVRON STEP ONE-AND-A-HALF (forthcoming 2017).

This intermediate step raises the question whether an agency gets deference for its interpretation only if it knows that it is making an interpretive choice. How can that choice be said to be a reasoned one if it is not a choice at all and is instead just the product of the agency's mistaken judgment that the statute clearly compelled the agency's interpretation? On the other hand, if the agency's interpretation rests on a reasonable but mistaken view that the statute was clear, and that interpretation is in fact one that the statute would permit the agency to adopt, does it make sense to penalize the agency for that mistake? Isn't the agency's mistaken but reasonable judgment about the statute's clarity itself a non-arbitrary reason for choosing the interpretation that the agency adopts? And wouldn't it be a bit much to add to the Chevron inquiry an assessment of whether it was clear that the statute was ambiguous?

(5) *Step-ing Out.* NATIONAL CREDIT UNION ADMIN. V. FIRST NAT. BANK, 522 U.S. 479 (1998), is a good example of Chevron's "step one" in action. Section 109 of the Federal Credit Union Act stipulates, "Federal credit union membership shall be limited to groups having a common bond or association, or to groups within a well-defined neighborhood, community, or rural district." Beginning in 1982, the National Credit Union Administration allowed credit unions to be composed of more than one employer group, each having its own "common bond." In the instant case, NCUA approved amendments to the charter of AT&T Family Federal Credit Union, which had expanded to include not only employees of AT&T, but also employees of Duke Power, American Tobacco, Lee Apparel, and so forth; five commercial banks and the American Bankers Association brought suit. (Regarding the standing issues in the case, see p. 1360.) THOMAS, J., for the Court, 522 U.S. at 499–503:

"Turning to the merits, we must judge the permissibility of the NCUA's current interpretation of § 109 by employing the analysis set forth in Chevron. Under that analysis, we first ask whether Congress has 'directly spoken to the precise question at issue.' . . . Because we conclude that Congress has made it clear that the same common bond of occupation must unite each member of an occupationally defined federal credit union, we hold that the NCUA's contrary interpretation is impermissible under the first step of Chevron.

"As noted, § 109 requires that '[f]ederal credit union membership shall be limited to groups having a common bond of occupation or association, or to groups within a well-defined neighborhood, community, or rural district.' Respondents [i.e., the banks] contend that because § 109 uses the article 'a'—i.e., 'one'—in conjunction with the noun 'common bond,' the 'natural reading' of § 109 is that all members in an occupationally defined federal union must be united by one common bond. Petitioners [i.e., the NCUA and the credit union] reply that because § 109 uses the plural noun 'groups,' it permits multiple groups, each with its own common bond, to constitute a federal credit union.

"Like the Court of Appeals, we do not think that either of these contentions, standing alone, is conclusive. The article 'a' could be thought to convey merely that one bond must unite only the members of each group in a multiple-group credit union, and not all of the members in the credit union taken together. Similarly, the plural word 'groups' could be thought to refer not merely to multiple groups in a particular credit union, but rather to every single 'group' that forms a distinct credit union under the NCUA. Nonetheless, as the Court of Appeals correctly recognized, additional considerations compel the conclusion that the same common bond of occupation must unite all of the members of an occupationally defined federal credit union.

"First, the NCUA's current interpretation makes the phrase 'common bond' surplusage when applied to a federal credit union made up of multiple unrelated employer groups, because each 'group' in such a credit union already has its own 'common bond.' To use the facts of this case, the employees of AT & T and the employees of the American Tobacco Company each already had a 'common bond' before being joined together as members of ATTF. . . . If the phrase 'common bond' is to be given any meaning when these employees are joined together, a different 'common bond'—one extending to each and every employee considered together—must be found to unite them. Such a 'common bond' exists when employees of different subsidiaries of the same company are joined together in a federal credit union; it does not exist, however, when employees of unrelated companies are so joined. . . .

"Second, the NCUA's interpretation violates the established canon of construction that similar language contained within the same section of a statute must be accorded a consistent meaning. Section 109 consists of two parallel clauses: Federal credit union membership is limited 'to groups having a common bond of occupation or association, *or* to groups within a well defined neighborhood, community, or rural district' (emphasis added). The NCUA concedes that even though the second limitation permits geographically defined credit unions to have as members more than one 'group,' all of the groups must come from the same 'neighborhood, community, or rural district.' The reason that the NCUA has never interpreted, and does not contend that it could interpret, the geographical limitation to allow a credit union to be composed of members from an unlimited number of unrelated geographic units, is that to do so would render the geographical limitation meaningless. Under established principles of statutory interpretation, we must interpret the occupational limitation in the same way.

"... Reading the two parallel clauses in the same way, we must conclude that, just as all members of a geographically defined federal credit union must be drawn from the same 'neighborhood, community or rural district,' members of an occupationally defined federal credit union must be united by the same 'common bond of occupation.'

"Finally, by its terms, § 109 requires that membership in federal credit unions 'shall be limited.' The NCUA's interpretation—under which a common bond of occupation must unite only the members of each unrelated employer group—has the potential to read these words out of the statute entirely. The NCUA has not contested that, under its current interpretation, it would be permissible to grant a charter to a conglomerate credit union whose members would include the employees of every company in the United States. Nor can it: Each company's employees would be a 'group,' and each such 'group' would have its own 'common bond of occupation.' Section 109, however, cannot be considered a *limitation* on credit union membership if at the same time it permits such a *limitless* result.

"For the foregoing reasons, we conclude that the NCUA's current interpretation of § 109 is contrary to the unambiguously expressed intent of Congress and is thus impermissible under the first step of Chevron."

(6) Contrast ENTERGY CORP. V. RIVERKEEPER, INC., 556 U.S. 208 (2009): At issue were EPA regulations regarding installations that used very large quantities of water to cool power plants; the regulations set substantial standards for such installations but stopped short of requiring the technology most protective of aquatic wildlife because the differential costs involved in achieving the very greatest level of protection were not (in the agency's view) justified by the differential benefits. The Supreme Court granted certiorari on the question whether the Clean Water Act authorized the EPA "to compare costs with benefits" in applying the statutory requirement of "the best technology available for minimizing adverse environmental impact" to "cooling water intake structures" and, in an opinion by JUSTICE SCALIA, answered as follows, 556 U.S. at 217–19:

"In setting the Phase II national performance standards and providing for site-specific cost-benefit variances, the EPA relied on its view that § 1326(b)'s 'best technology available' standard permits consideration of the technology's costs, and of the relationship between those costs and the environmental benefits produced. That view governs if it is a reasonable interpretation of the statute—not necessarily the only possible interpretation, nor even the interpretation deemed *most* reasonable by the courts. Chevron.

"As we have described, § 1326(b) instructs the EPA to set standards for cooling water intake structures that reflect 'the best technology available for minimizing adverse environmental impact.' The Second Circuit took that language to mean the technology that achieves the greatest reduction in adverse environmental impacts at a cost that can reasonably be borne by the industry. That is certainly a plausible interpretation of the statute. The 'best' technology—that which is 'most advantageous,' Webster's New International Dictionary 258 (2d ed. 1953)—may well be the one that produces the most of some good, here a reduction in adverse environmental impact. But 'best technology' may also describe the technology that *most efficiently* produces some good. In common parlance one could certainly use the phrase 'best technology' to refer to that which produces a good at the lowest per-unit cost, even if it produces a lesser quantity of that good than other available technologies.

"Respondents contend that this latter reading is precluded by the statute's use of the phrase 'for minimizing adverse environmental impact.' Minimizing, they argue, means reducing to the smallest amount possible, and the 'best technology available for minimizing adverse environmental impacts,' must be the economically feasible technology that achieves the greatest possible reduction in environmental harm. But 'minimize' is a term that admits of degree and is not necessarily used to refer exclusively to the 'greatest possible reduction.' For example, elsewhere in the Clean Water Act, Congress declared that the procedures implementing the Act 'shall encourage the drastic minimization of paperwork and interagency decision procedures.' 33 U.S.C. § 1251(f). If respondents' definition of the term 'minimize' is correct, the statute's use of the modifier 'drastic' is superfluous.

"Other provisions in the Clean Water Act also suggest the agency's interpretation. When Congress wished to mandate the greatest feasible reduction in water pollution, it did so in plain language: The provision governing the discharge of toxic pollutants into the Nation's waters requires the EPA to set 'effluent limitations [which] shall require the *elimination* of discharges of all pollutants if the Administrator finds . . . that such elimination is technologically and economically achievable,' § 1311(b)(2)(A) (emphasis added). Section 1326(b)'s use of the less ambitious goal of 'minimizing adverse environmental impact' suggests, we think, that the agency retains some discretion to determine the extent of reduction that is warranted under the circumstances. . . . It seems to us, therefore, that the phrase 'best technology available,' even with the added specification 'for minimizing adverse environmental impact,' does not unambiguously preclude cost-benefit analysis."

After the reference to Chevron in the above quote, Justice Scalia dropped the following footnote:

"The dissent finds it 'puzzling' that we invoke this proposition (that a reasonable agency interpretation prevails) at the 'outset,' omitting the supposedly prior inquiry of 'whether Congress has directly spoken to the precise question at issue.' (Opinion of Stevens, J.) (quoting Chevron, 467 U.S., at 842). But surely if Congress has directly spoken to an issue then any agency interpretation contradicting what Congress has said would be unreasonable."

(7)   By the way, in case you had any doubt, Chevron also applies to agency construction of statutes that takes place, not in rulemaking, but in the course

of case-by-case adjudication. E.g., I.N.S. v. Aguirre-Aguirre, 526 U.S. 415 (1999).

NOTES ON THE RELATIONSHIP BETWEEN CHEVRON AND STATE FARM

(1) *Does Chevron Step Two Recapitulate State Farm?* In STATE FARM, p. 1074, the Court wrote, in what has become the standard paragraph describing "arbitrary and capricious" review:

> Normally, an agency rule would be arbitrary and capricious if the agency has relied on factors which Congress has not intended it to consider, entirely failed to consider an important aspect of the problem, offered an explanation for its decision that runs counter to the evidence before the agency, or is so implausible that it could not be ascribed to a difference in view or the product of agency expertise. The reviewing court should not attempt itself to make up for such deficiencies; we may not supply a reasoned basis for the agency's action that the agency itself has not given. SEC v. Chenery Corp., 332 U.S. 194, 196 (1947).

Does the inquiry required under Chevron Step Two, to decide whether an agency's interpretation of a statute is "permissible," merely restate this test in other words? Sometimes Justices speak as if this were so. For example, JUSTICE KAGAN, writing for the Court in JUDULANG V. HOLDER, 565 U.S. 42, 52 n. 7 (2011), invalidated a ruling of the Board of Immigration Appeals under State Farm as arbitrary and capricious and then added in a footnote: "The Government urges us instead to analyze this case under the second step of the test we announced in Chevron U.S.A. Inc. v. Natural Resources Defense Council, Inc., 467 U.S. 837 (1984), to govern judicial review of an agency's statutory interpretations. See Brief for Respondent 19. Were we to do so, our analysis would be the same, because under Chevron step two, we ask whether an agency interpretation is 'arbitrary or capricious in substance.' Mayo Foundation for Medical Ed. and Research v. United States, 562 U.S. ___ (2011) (quoting Household Credit Services, Inc. v. Pfennig, 541 U.S. 232, 242 (2004)). . . ." Nevertheless, the Court has not definitively weighed in on the issue, and scholars have spilled much ink on the topic, advocating all of the conceivable answers. Here are some of the issues:

> (a) How much overlap is there? One of the State Farm questions, whether the explanation offered by the agency "runs counter to the evidence" produced in the proceeding, seems unconnected to the Chevron question whether the agency's reading of the statute is reasonable. By contrast, whether the agency has "relied on factors which Congress has not intended it to consider" is intimately connected to interpreting the statute and might well be viewed through the lens of either case.

> (b) On the possible overlap questions, does it matter which case—Chevron or State Farm—we use to provide the reviewing lens? Are the materials used to provide the predicates for review different? Is the degree of stringency of review different? Should agency

litigators embrace Chevron Step Two as the easier test—and those challenging agency action press for State Farm's "hard look"?

(c)   Finally, should Chevron Step Two proceed from the agency's own "reasoned basis" for its choice, the way State Farm (through its citation of the Chenery case) requires for its test? KEVIN M. STACK, THE CONSTITUTIONAL FOUNDATIONS OF *CHENERY*, 116 Yale L.J. 952, 1005 (2007): "The clearest point of connection between Chevron and Chenery is that compliance with the Chenery principle operates as a condition for the agency to receive deference in Chevron Step Two. Simply put, a court should not defer to an agency's construction of a statute at Chevron Step Two unless the agency embraced that construction at the time it acted, not merely in litigation. The basic logic of this structure seems relatively clear: the deference the Court applies at Step Two is implicitly conditioned on the agency's having worked through the problem, with reason-giving as the overt expression of its exercise of discretion and expertise." Is that right?

(2)   ARENT V. SHALALA, 70 F.3d 610 (D.C. Cir. 1995): The Nutrition Labeling and Education Act of 1990, enforced by the FDA, required manufacturers of food to provide various items of nutritional information on the foods' labels. For raw produce and fish—not manufactured items—it established voluntary guidelines under which the retail stores provide nutritional information to the customer. The Act then required the FDA to convert this voluntary scheme into a mandatory set of labeling requirements if it found that food stores were not in "substantial compliance" with the guidelines. What constituted "substantial compliance" was to be defined by regulation, as follows:

> The regulation shall provide that there is not substantial compliance if a significant number of retailers have failed to comply with the guidelines. The size of the retailers and the portion of the market served by retailers in compliance with the guidelines shall be considered in determining whether the substantial-compliance standard has been met.

The regulation at issue provided that individual stores would be considered in compliance if they provided information for at least 90% of their fish and vegetables, and the industry as a whole would be in compliance if at least 60% of the surveyed stores were in compliance; the size of the stores and the markets they served were taken into account in determining the protocol for the stipulated survey.

This suit challenged both the validity of the regulation and of the subsequent determination by the FDA, based on its survey, that the industry was indeed in "substantial compliance."

EDWARDS, C.J., for the majority (70 F.3d at 614–17):

"Although the parties argue this case in terms of both Chevron analysis and arbitrary and capricious review, they interpret the case as one involving review of an agency's construction of a statute and look primarily to Chevron for the appropriate analytical framework. We, however, do not find Chevron controlling. In challenging the FDA's regulation defining 'substantial compliance,' appellants seek traditional arbitrary and capricious review governed by Motor Vehicle Manufacturers Ass'n v. State Farm Mutual Automobile Insurance Co., 463 U.S. 29 (1983). We recognize that, in some respects, Chevron review and arbitrary and capricious review overlap at the margins. But it would be a mistake to view this case as one involving typical Chevron review.

"Chevron is principally concerned with whether an agency has authority to act under a statute. Thus, a reviewing court's inquiry under Chevron is rooted in statutory analysis and is focused on discerning the boundaries of Congress' delegation of authority to the agency; and as long as the agency stays within that delegation, it is free to make policy choices in interpreting the statute, and such interpretations are entitled to deference. . . . In such a case, the question for the reviewing court is whether the agency's construction of the statute is faithful to its plain meaning, or, if the statute has no plain meaning, whether the agency's interpretation 'is based on a permissible construction of the statute.'

"In the present case, however, there is no question that the FDA had authority to define the circumstances constituting food retailers' substantial compliance with the NLEA's voluntary labeling guidelines. The only issue here is whether the FDA's discharge of that authority was reasonable. Such a question falls within the province of traditional arbitrary and capricious review under 5 U.S.C. § 706(2)(A) (1988). Thus, in the present case, State Farm is controlling regarding the standard of review.

"In State Farm, the Court held: [long quotation omitted]. Under this standard of review, it is clear that the FDA's regulations must be upheld.

"The FDA certainly took account of the relevant factors in devising its sixty-percent, industry-wide standard for food retailers' 'substantial compliance' under the NLEA. . . . The FDA also has articulated an explanation for its decision that demonstrates its reliance on a variety of relevant factors and represents a reasonable accommodation in light of the facts before the agency. . . . Given the record before the agency, the FDA's sixty-percent figure is not unreasonable and it certainly does not reveal 'a clear error of judgment.' Overton Park, 401 U.S. at 416. Moreover, the statutory intent was not to assure one-hundred-percent compliance, but rather 'substantial' compliance, and the FDA's sixty-percent standard does ensure that a major portion of the retail food market will receive nutritional information. . . ."

WALD, J., concurring (70 F.3d at 619–620):

"While I agree with the panel's conclusion that the Food and Drug Administration's ('FDA') rule is justifiable, I would resolve the case under the Chevron step two challenge which was presented by the parties and addressed by the trial court, rather than grounding our decision on a different facet of Administrative Procedure Act ('APA') review. . . .

"Chevron allocates power to interpret statutes among the branches of government by creating a presumption that agencies, rather than the courts, are the preferred institution for filling in statutory gaps. The first step of

Chevron is straightforward; if the statutory language is clear, it controls. The second step, where in my view the majority goes astray, entrusts agencies with authority to interpret statutory ambiguities, provided they do so in a manner that is reasonable and consistent with the language and purposes of the statute. By contrast, garden-variety APA review under § 706 focuses more heavily on the agency's decisionmaking process; to survive arbitrary and capricious review, 'the agency must examine the relevant data and articulate a satisfactory explanation for its action, including a rational connection between the facts found and the choice made.' State Farm.

"Given these differences in the central concerns behind the two analytic frameworks, there are certainly situations where a challenge to an agency's regulation will fall squarely within one rubric, rather than the other. For example, we might invalidate an agency's decision under Chevron as inconsistent with its statutory mandate, even though we do not believe the decision reflects an arbitrary policy choice. Such a result might occur when we believe the agency's course of action to be the most appropriate and effective means of achieving a goal, but determine that Congress has selected a different—albeit, in our eyes, less propitious—path. Conversely, we might determine that although not barred by statute, an agency's action is arbitrary and capricious because the agency has not considered certain relevant factors or articulated any rationale for its choice. . . .

"But I agree with the panel that despite these distinctions, the Chevron and State Farm frameworks often do overlap. . . . The case before us arguably falls within this area of overlap. In reviewing the FDA's regulations, our task was to determine whether the agency rationally considered the factors set forth in the NLEA when it defined 'substantial compliance.' Accordingly, I would not argue that State Farm is altogether irrelevant to our analysis, but given the scope and function of Chevron step two analysis, neither would I find State Farm applicable to the exclusion of Chevron, as the majority does. Petitioners' appeal ultimately does stand or fall on whether the FDA heeded Congress' admonitions that it may not find 'substantial compliance' if 'a significant number of retailers' have failed to comply, and that it must consider '[t]he size of the retailers and the portion of the market served by retailers in compliance with the guidelines' when making this determination. This language is sufficiently concrete to permit review of whether the agency's interpretation is reasonable and consistent with Congress' purpose in enacting the NLEA. In fact, I believe it well within the bounds of typical Chevron step two analysis, which is why the majority's opinion troubles me somewhat. If this case falls totally outside Chevron, many other cases marching under its banner must be similarly exiled. The majority's unequivocal rejection of the Chevron analytic framework utilized by the parties and the trial court in this case provides no clues as to the boundary lines for Chevron and APA review."

(3) *Are the Doctrines the Same, or Do They Just Intersect?* As we have already seen in the Notes accompanying the Fox Television case, pp. 1114–1118 above, in ENCINO V. NAVARRO MOTORCARS, LLC, 136 S.Ct. 2117 (2016), the Court ruled:

> It is not the role of the courts to speculate on reasons that might
> have supported an agency's decision. "[W]e may not supply a
> reasoned basis for the agency's action that the agency itself has not
> given." State Farm, 463 U.S., at 43 (citing SEC v. Chenery Corp.,
> 332 U.S. 194 (1947)). Whatever potential reasons the Department
> might have given, the agency in fact gave almost no reasons at all.
> In light of the serious reliance interests at stake, the Department's
> conclusory statements do not suffice to explain its decision. See Fox
> Television Stations, 556 U.S., at 515–516.

The court then went on to draw the following corollary:

> This lack of reasoned explication for a regulation that is
> inconsistent with the Department's longstanding earlier position
> results in a rule that cannot carry the force of law. See 5 U.S.C.
> § 706(2)(A); State Farm, supra, at 42–43. It follows that this
> regulation does not receive Chevron deference in the interpretation
> of the relevant statute.

How would you phrase this relationship of State Farm and Chevron?

(4)   As we saw in the "Notes on Cost-Benefit Analysis As a Possible Element
of 'Arbitrary and Capricious' Review," p. 1094, the most recent relevant
Supreme Court case on that topic is MICHIGAN V. EPA, 135 S.Ct. 2699 (2015).
There, the Clean Air Act told the EPA to require a first set of controls over
power plants, to study the effect of that first set, and then to further regulate
power plants "if the Administrator [of the agency] finds such regulation is
appropriate and necessary after considering the results of the study." 42
U.S.C. § 7412(n)(1)(A). The EPA made this determination that regulation
was "appropriate and necessary" without considering the cost to the industry
that regulation would entail; it did, however, consider cost in several ways
when determining, later on, precisely what regulations the plants had to
meet. "[T]he phrase 'appropriate and necessary,'" said the Court, "requires
at least some attention to cost" in making the initial decision to regulate.

> Here is Justice Scalia's rendition of the conceptual framework involved,
> 135 S.Ct. at 2706–07:

> Federal administrative agencies are required to engage in
> "reasoned decisionmaking." Allentown Mack Sales & Service, Inc.
> v. NLRB, 522 U.S. 359, 374 (1998). "Not only must an agency's
> decreed result be within the scope of its lawful authority, but the
> process by which it reaches that result must be logical and
> rational." *Ibid.* It follows that agency action is lawful only if it rests
> "on a consideration of the relevant factors." Motor Vehicle Mfrs.
> Assn. of United States, Inc. v. State Farm Mut. Automobile Ins. Co.,
> 463 U.S. 29, 43 (1983).

> EPA's decision to regulate power plants under § 7412 allowed the
> Agency to reduce power plants' emissions of hazardous air
> pollutants and thus to improve public health and the environment.
> But the decision also ultimately cost power plants, according to the
> Agency's own estimate, nearly $10 billion a year. EPA refused to
> consider whether the costs of its decision outweighed the benefits.

The Agency gave cost no thought *at all,* because it considered cost irrelevant to its initial decision to regulate.

EPA's disregard of cost rested on its interpretation of § 7412(n)(1)(A), which, to repeat, directs the Agency to regulate power plants if it "finds such regulation is appropriate and necessary." The Agency accepts that it *could* have interpreted this provision to mean that cost is relevant to the decision to add power plants to the program. Tr. of Oral Arg. 44. But it chose to read the statute to mean that cost makes no difference to the initial decision to regulate. See 76 Fed.Reg. 24988 (2011) ("We further interpret the term 'appropriate' to not allow for the consideration of costs"); 77 Fed.Reg. 9327 ("Cost does not have to be read into the definition of 'appropriate' ").

We review this interpretation under the standard set out in Chevron U.S.A. Inc. v. Natural Resources Defense Council, Inc., 467 U.S. 837 (1984). Chevron directs courts to accept an agency's reasonable resolution of an ambiguity in a statute that the agency administers. *Id.,* at 842–843. Even under this deferential standard, however, "agencies must operate within the bounds of reasonable interpretation." Utility Air Regulatory Group v. EPA, 573 U.S. ___, ___ (2014). EPA strayed far beyond those bounds when it read § 7412(n)(1) to mean that it could ignore cost when deciding whether to regulate power plants.

What is the relationship of State Farm and Chevron in this passage? And by the way, if a statute's text is unclear as to whether costs should be considered, why isn't the issue of whether and how to consider costs exactly the type of issue about which judges should defer to agency choices? In fact, isn't it the very type of decision that was at issue in Chevron itself?

(5) JACK M. BEERMANN, END THE FAILED *CHEVRON* EXPERIMENT NOW: HOW *CHEVRON* HAS FAILED AND WHY IT CAN AND SHOULD BE OVERRULED, 42 Conn. L. Rev. 781, 807 (2010): "If the Supreme Court were to choose to make only one clarification to the Chevron doctrine, it should clarify the interaction between Chevron and judicial review of agency policy decisions. If Chevron deference is really about deference to agency policy decisions, then it seems to be running on a parallel track to review under the arbitrary, capricious standard with no reasoning as to which is the proper track in any particular case. If it is not about deference to policy decisions, then the Court needs to explain the proper standard of review for policy decisions that are connected with questions of statutory meaning."

NOTES ON THE WISDOM (OR NOT) OF CHEVRON'S DOCTRINE

(1) *In Light of Precedent.* In a footnote, Chevron provided a long string of citations that dated back to 1827 to support its assertion that "[w]e have long recognized that considerable weight should be accorded to an executive department's construction of a statutory scheme it is entrusted to administer." The footnote reads: "Aluminum Co. of America v. Central Lincoln Peoples' Until Dist., ante, at 389; Blum v. Bacon, 457 U.S. 132, 141

(1982); Union Electric Co. v. EPA, 427 U.S. 245, 256 (1976); Investment Company Institute v. Camp, 401 U.S. 617, 626–627 (1971); Unemployment Compensation Comm'n v. Aragon, 329 U.S., at 153–154; NLRB v. Hearst Publications, Inc., 322 U.S. 111, 131 (1944); McLaren v. Fleischer, 256 U.S., at 480–481; Webster v. Luther, 163 U.S., at 342; Brown v. United States, 113 U.S. 568, 570–571 (1885); United States v. Moore, 95 U.S. 760. 763 (1878); Edwards' Lessee v. Darby, 12 Wheat. 206, 210 (1827)." But do those precedents support Chevron's particular approach to deference?

For an argument that they do not, consider ADITYA BAMZAI, THE ORIGINS OF JUDICIAL DEFERENCE TO EXECUTIVE INTERPRETATION, 126 Yale L.J. 910 (2017): "[T]he prevailing interpretive methodology of nineteenth-century American courts was not a form of judicial deference, as it has come to be understood in the post-Chevron era. Under the traditional interpretive approach, American courts 'respected' longstanding and contemporaneous executive interpretations of law as part of a practice of deferring to longstanding and contemporaneous interpretation generally. It was the pedigree and contemporaneity of the interpretation, in other words, that prompted 'respect'; the fact that the interpretation had been articulated by an actor within the executive branch was relevant, but incidental.

"Nor was nineteenth-century mandamus practice based on any interpretive methodology that required judicial deference to the executive qua executive. While the modern reader may hear echoes of Chevron in mandamus—because the mandamus standard precluded judicial intervention when an executive official engaged in an 'executive duty' (including statutory interpretation) that required the exercise of judgment and discretion—the analogy is mistaken. As the Court put it in the foundational case of Decatur v. Paulding, if an issue of statutory construction were to arise outside of the mandamus context—where the standards for obtaining the writ did not apply—'the Court certainly would not be bound to adopt the construction given by the head of a department.' Courts, in other words, applied the mandamus standard only because they were confronting a writ of mandamus (or another extraordinary writ). Where there was no writ of mandamus, there would be no comparable interpretive deference.

". . . . [W]hen the modern trend toward generalized judicial deference to executive interpretation began during the fifth decade of the twentieth century, the Court did not rely primarily on the principle that courts 'respected' contemporaneous and customary executive constructions, nor on the principle that the mandamus standard required deference to executive action. Instead, the Court invoked longstanding precedents addressing judicial deference to agency factual determinations and analogized questions of law requiring agency expertise to questions of fact. In doing so, the Court drew on preexisting scholarship suggesting that a formal distinction between 'law' and 'fact' in administrative review was illusory. By embracing this legal-realist perspective on the law-fact distinction, and thereby blurring the line between factual determinations and legal questions, the Court incrementally expanded the domain of agency discretion in a manner that ultimately led to the Chevron doctrine."

(2) *In Light of the Constitutional Design.* CYNTHIA R. FARINA, STATUTORY INTERPRETATION AND THE BALANCE OF POWER IN THE ADMINISTRATIVE STATE, 89 Colum. L. Rev. 452, 487–88 (1989): "The great success with which nondelegation analysis evolved to accommodate a regulation-favoring political consensus has, unfortunately, produced an insidious 'bottom-line' myopia—a tendency to focus only on the consequence that Congress may broadly delegate regulatory power, while ignoring the doctrinal construct that developed to make this outcome possible. A belief in legislative primacy obviously occupied an important place in that construct. Congress was accorded great deference to transfer power and thereby radically restructure American government. But the Court's long struggle to reconcile the growth of agencies with the Constitution yielded a solution far more complex than carte blanche for Congress to give agencies whatever power it wishes them to have. The administrative state became constitutionally tenable because the Court's vision of separation of powers evolved from the simple (but constraining) proposition that divided powers must not be commingled, to the more flexible (but far more complicated) proposition, that power may be transferred *so long as* it will be adequately controlled.

"A crucial aspect of the capacity for external control upon which the permissibility of delegating regulatory power hinged was judicial policing of the terms of the statute. . . . Judge Leventhal expressed the point most succinctly: 'Congress has been willing to delegate its legislative powers broadly—and the courts have upheld such delegation—because there is court review to assure that the agency exercises the delegated power within statutory limits.' Whether or not Judge Leventhal correctly interpreted the legislature's motives, he aptly characterized the course of nondelegation theory in the courts. The constitutional accommodation ultimately reached in the nondelegation cases implied that principal power to say what the statute means must rest *outside* the agency in the courts.

"Hence, a key assumption of Chevron's 'judicial usurpation' argument— that Congress may give agencies primary responsibility not only for making policy within the limits of their organic statutes, but also for defining those limits whenever the text and surrounding legislative materials are ambiguous—is fundamentally incongruous with the constitutional course by which the Court came to reconcile agencies and separation of powers. Of course, to demonstrate that one of Chevron's central premises cannot be squared with the doctrinal structure built in the nondelegation cases is not necessarily to establish that this structure was worth preserving. Was it merely a delusion that separation of powers could be honored through a theory of nondelegation that permitted the concentration of great policymaking and executing authority in administrative agencies, but which insisted that agencies could not then also hold the power to say what their organic statutes mean? An examination of the origins and content of that constitutional principle suggests not. The vision of separation of powers embodied in mature nondelegation analysis—a vision that came to ask whether power was being adequately checked, rather than whether powers were remaining divided-was in essence true to the constitutional vision."

(3) ***In Light of Democratic Accountability.*** JERRY L. MASHAW, GREED, CHAOS AND GOVERNANCE 152–53 (1997): "Strangely enough, it may make sense to imagine the delegation of political authority to administrators as a device for improving the responsiveness of government to the desires of the general electorate. This argument can be made even if we accept many of the insights of the political and economic literature that premises its predictions of congressional and voter behavior on a direct linkage between benefits transferred to constituents and the election or reelection of representatives. All we need do is not forget there are also presidential elections and that, as the Supreme Court reminds us in Chevron, presidents are heads of administrations.

"Assume then that voters view the election of representatives to Congress through the lens of the most cynical interpretation of the modern public choice literature on congressional behavior. In short, the voter chooses a representative for that representative's effectiveness in supplying governmental goods and services to the local district, including the voter. The representative is a good representative or a bad representative depending upon his or her ability to provide the district with at least its fair share of governmental largesse. In this view, the congressperson's position on various issues of national interest is of modest, if any, importance. The only question is, Does he or she 'bring home the bacon.'

"The voter's vision of presidential electoral politics is arguably quite different. The president has no particular constituency to which he or she has special responsibility to deliver benefits. Presidents are hardly cut off from pork-barrel politics. Yet issues of national scope and the candidates' positions on those issues are the essence of presidential politics. Citizens vote for a president based almost wholly on a perception of the difference that one or another candidate might make to general governmental policies.

"If this description of voting in national elections is reasonably plausible, then the utilization of vague delegations to administrative agencies takes on significance as a device for facilitating responsiveness to voter preferences expressed in presidential elections. The high transactions costs of legislating specifically suggests that legislative activity directed to the modification of administration mandates will be infrequent. Agencies will thus persist with their statutory empowering provisions relatively intact over substantial periods of time.

"Voter preferences on the direction and intensity of governmental activities, however, are not likely to be so stable. Indeed, one can reasonably expect that a president will be able to affect policy in a four-year term only because being elected president entails acquiring the power to exercise, direct, or influence policy discretion. The group of executive officers we commonly call 'the administration' matters only because of the relative malleability of the directives that administrators have in their charge. If congressional statutes were truly specific with respect to the actions that administrators were to take, presidential politics would be a mere beauty contest."

(4) ***In Light of the APA.*** Justice Stevens' opinion in Chevron does not discuss the APA. Do you think Chevron is consistent with the text of § 706?

Recall the relevant portions of its text:

To the extent necessary to decision and when presented, *the reviewing court shall decide all relevant questions of law, interpret* constitutional and *statutory provisions*, and *determine the meaning or applicability of the terms of an agency action.* The reviewing court shall—. . .

(2) hold unlawful and set aside agency action, findings, and conclusions found to be—

(A) arbitrary, capricious, an abuse of discretion, or otherwise not in accordance with law; . . .

(C) *in excess of statutory jurisdiction, authority, or limitations, or short of statutory right;*

(emphasis added). This language rather clearly ratifies—does it not?—the longstanding proposition—reiterated by the Court shortly before the passage of the APA—that "[t]he interpretation of the meaning of statutes, as applied to justiciable controversies, is exclusively a judicial function." United States v. American Trucking Ass'ns, 310 U.S. 534, 544 (1940). The language might allow consideration of agency interpretations as data used to inform a court's own judgment, as indeed American Trucking emphasized. But does it allow giving to agency interpretations the authority that Chevron specifies?

(5) Consider CASS R. SUNSTEIN, LAW AND ADMINISTRATION AFTER *CHEVRON*, 90 Colum. L. Rev. 2071, 2085–88 (1990): "When Congress has expressly said that deference is or is not appropriate, the matter is relatively simple. As stated above, the text and background of the APA suggest a firm belief in the need for judicial checks on administration, particularly with respect to the interpretation of law. The view that courts should always defer to agency interpretation is, therefore, a poor reconstruction of the instructions of the APA. It remains possible, however, that particular substantive statutes displace the APA and accord law-interpreting power to the agency. If so, the courts should defer in such cases on the ground that the relevant law *is* what the agency says that it is. The APA's provision for independent judicial interpretation of law is not inconsistent, then, with Chevron's deference to the agency's interpretation if Congress has, under particular statutes, granted the relevant authority to administrative agencies.

"Frequently, however, Congress does not speak in explicit terms on the question of deference. When this is so, the court's task is to make the best reconstruction that it can of congressional instructions. And if Congress has not made a clear decision one way or the other, the choice among the alternatives will call for an assessment of which strategy is the most sensible one to attribute to Congress under the circumstances. This assessment is not a mechanical exercise of uncovering an actual legislative decision. It calls for a frankly value-laden judgment about comparative competence, undertaken in light of the regulatory structure and applicable constitutional considerations.

"If all this is so, the Chevron approach might well be defended on the ground that the resolution of ambiguities in statutes is sometimes a question of policy as much as it is one of law, narrowly understood, and that agencies are uniquely well situated to make the relevant policy decisions. In some cases, there is simply no answer to the interpretive question if it is posed as an inquiry into some real or unitary instruction of the legislature. Sometimes congressional views cannot plausibly be aggregated in a way that reflects a clear resolution of regulatory problems, many of them barely foreseen or indeed unforeseeable. In these circumstances, legal competence, as narrowly understood, is insufficient for decision. The resolution of the ambiguity calls for an inquiry into something other than the instructions of the enacting legislature. And in examining those other considerations, the institution entrusted with the decision must make reference to considerations of both fact and policy.

"Chevron nicely illustrates the point. The decision about whether to adopt a plantwide definition of 'source' required distinctly administrative competence because it called for a complex inquiry, not foreseen by Congress, into the environmental and economic consequences of the various possibilities. If regulatory decisions in the face of ambiguities amount in large part to choices of policy, and if Congress has delegated basic implementing authority to the agency, the Chevron approach might reflect a belief, attributable to Congress in the absence of a clear contrary legislative statement, in the comparative advantages of the agency in making those choices.

"At least as a general rule, these suggestions argue powerfully in favor of administrative rather than judicial resolution of hard statutory questions. The factfinding capacity and electoral accountability of the administrators are far greater than those of courts. Chevron is best understood and defended as a frank recognition that sometimes interpretation is not simply a matter of uncovering legislative will, but also involves extratextual considerations of various kinds, including judgments about how a statute is best or most sensibly implemented. Chevron reflects a salutary understanding that these judgments of policy and principle should be made by administrators rather than judges."

(The idea that Chevron only provides a default rule is, by the way, not merely theoretical. Occasionally since the decision Congress has provided for a different standard of review. See, e.g., 15 U.S.C. § 6714(e) (regarding differences between state and federal insurance regulation).)

(6)   Or, following on our consideration of the resonances between Chevron Step Two and State Farm (p. 1145 above), can we construct a reading of § 706 that supports Chevron by focusing, not on the words that emphasize the review of statutory interpretation, but rather on the idea of overturning arbitrary and capricious action. "Normally," said State Farm, "an agency rule would be arbitrary and capricious if the agency has relied on factors which Congress has not intended it to consider, entirely failed to consider an

important aspect of the problem, offered an explanation for its decision that runs counter to the evidence before the agency, or is so implausible that it could not be ascribed to a difference in view or the product of agency expertise." Note how Justice Stevens' Chevron opinion invokes the agency's responsibility for "policy" and frames the judicial relationship to that element as one of oversight for reasonableness, not independent decision. Does the inquiry required under Chevron Step Two, to decide whether an agency's interpretation of a statute is "permissible," merely restate this test in other words—leaving in judicial hands the decision of what the statute can permissibly mean, and primarily in agency hands the responsibility for particular application within that bounded space? If so, how comforting is that way of understanding Chevron given how broad the "bounded" space may be?

(7) JONATHAN T. MOLOT, THE JUDICIAL PERSPECTIVE IN THE ADMINISTRATIVE STATE: RECONCILING MODERN DOCTRINES OF DEFERENCE WITH THE JUDICIARY'S STRUCTURAL ROLE, 53 Stan. L. Rev. 1, 76–79 (2000): "The error in Chevron's logic lies in its equating any statutory ambiguity at all with a failure on the part of Congress to legislate. Chevron posits that whenever Congress's statutory instructions do not resolve an interpretive question conclusively, this must mean Congress either failed to 'consider the question,' 'was unable to forge a coalition on either side of the question,' or else consciously decided to delegate the question to the relevant agency. Chevron thus ignores the reality that the Founders highlighted over two centuries ago: Even when a majority of legislators *do* contemplate a legislative issue broadly conceived and *do* agree to address it with substantive instructions, statutory ambiguity may nonetheless remain over the particular questions that will arise under that statute. Recall Madison's observation that '[a]ll new laws, though penned with the greatest technical skill and passed on the fullest and most mature deliberation, are considered as more or less obscure and equivocal, until their meaning be liquidated and ascertained by a series of particular . . . adjudications.'[127] . . .

"It is beyond controversy that statutes often are ambiguous and that outside the administrative context judges are responsible for resolving those ambiguities. Whether Congress may be said to have 'delegated' legislative authority to the judiciary each time it leaves an ambiguity is unimportant: Courts must make decisions using traditional tools of statutory interpretation regardless of the label attached. Thus the very same statutory instructions, yielding the very same level of ambiguity that Chevron treats as a delegation in the administrative context, will be treated outside the administrative context as ordinary legislation subject to ordinary judicial interpretation.

"There is a substantial cost to treating as a 'delegation' the sort of ordinary statutory instructions that would be subject to ordinary judicial interpretation outside the administrative context. . . . [S]ince virtually '[a]ll new laws' start out ambiguous as applied to various circumstances and do not become clear until interpreted in 'particular . . . adjudications,'

---

[127] The Federalist No. 37 (James Madison).

legislators historically have had incentives to engage in careful deliberation and drafting to guide judicial resolution of statutory ambiguities. This careful deliberation and drafting not only appropriately ensures some legislative control over law application, but also may have the corollary benefit of improving the laws that legislators enact.

"But the sort of careful deliberation and drafting that legislators might use to guide judicial interpretation will be wasted on an administrative agency. The agency will tend to choose among reasonable interpretive options based on political considerations and policy concerns rather than anything in Congress' statute. As a result, legislators wishing to guide administrative decisions under Chevron must resort to . . . tactics that differ significantly from the careful deliberation and drafting they might use to guide judges.

"[As one such tactic,] legislators may decide to engage in what scholars have dubbed 'micromanagement' of administrative regulation. If conventional drafting tools generally cannot eliminate ambiguity (and the administrative leeway that goes with it under Chevron), legislators nonetheless have tried in some instances to go beyond conventional drafting. They have drafted statutory provisions with such 'striking specificity' as to preclude deference at Chevron Step I and compel administrative outcomes in keeping with their legislative bargains. . . .

"But if highly specific drafting of detailed statutory provisions succeeds in securing legislative control over administrative outcomes, such drafting by no means ensures the fair, sensible laws that our constitutional structure was designed to promote. . . ."

(8) ***A Different Rationale.*** PETER L. STRAUSS, ONE HUNDRED FIFTY CASES PER YEAR: SOME IMPLICATIONS OF THE SUPREME COURT'S LIMITED RESOURCES FOR JUDICIAL REVIEW OF AGENCY ACTION, 87 Colum. L. Rev. 1093, 1121 (1987): ". . . [I]t is helpful to view Chevron through the lens of the Supreme Court's severely restricted capacity directly to enforce uniformity upon the courts of appeals in those courts' review of agency decisionmaking. When national uniformity in the administration of national statutes is called for, the national agencies responsible for that administration can be expected to reach single readings of the statutes for which they are responsible and to enforce those readings within their own framework. . . . If, however, one accepts not only that language is imprecise, but also that congressional language (in particular) is frequently indeterminate, it follows that that reading could never be demonstrably correct, but merely reasonable if within the range of indeterminacy, or incorrect if beyond it. Any reviewing panel of judges from one of the twelve circuits, if made responsible for precise renditions of statutory meaning, could vary in its judgment from the agency's, and from the judgments of other panels in other circuits, without being wrong. The variance might even occur in predictable ways, if simple diversity were overlaid by geographical bias. The Supreme Court's practical inability in most cases to give its own precise renditions of statutory meaning virtually assures that circuit readings will be diverse. By removing the responsibility for precision from the courts of appeals, the Chevron rule

subdues this diversity, and thus enhances the probability of uniform national administration of the laws.

"Rather than see Chevron just as a rule about agency discretion . . . it can be seen as a device for managing the courts of appeals that can reduce (although not eliminate) the Supreme Court's need to police their decisions for accuracy."

(9) *A Revolt from Below?* Then-judge NEIL GORSUCH, the newest Justice on the Supreme Court, wrote a widely noticed concurrence questioning the constitutional basis for Chevron shortly before he was nominated to the Supreme Court by President Trump. He argued in GUTIERREZ-BRIZUELA V. LYNCH, 834 F.3d 1142 (10th Cir. 2016): "Not only is Chevron's purpose seemingly at odds with the separation of legislative and executive functions, its effect appears to be as well. . . . First, we know that, consistent with the separation of powers, Congress may condition the application of a new rule of general applicability on factual findings to be made by the executive (so, for example, forfeiture of assets might be required if the executive finds a foreign country behaved in a specified manner). See Cargo of the Brig Aurora v. United-12-States, 11 U.S. (7 Cranch) 382, 388 (1813). Second, we know Congress may allow the executive to resolve 'details' (like, say, the design of an appropriate tax stamp). See In re Kollock, 165 U.S. 526, 533 (1897). Yet Chevron pretty clearly involves neither of these kinds of executive functions and, in this way and as a historical matter, appears instead to qualify as a violation of the separation of powers. See Michigan v. EPA, 135 S.Ct. 2699, 2713–14 (2015) (Thomas, J., concurring); cf. City of Arlington v. FCC, 133 S.Ct. 1863, 1877–79 (2013) (Roberts, C.J., dissenting); Nichols, 784 F.3d at 671–72 (Gorsuch, J., dissenting from the denial of rehearing en banc). Of course, in relatively recent times the Court has relaxed its approach to claims of unlawful legislative delegation. . . . But even taking the forgiving intelligible principle test as a given, it's no small question whether Chevron can clear it. For if an agency can enact a new rule of general applicability affecting huge swaths of the national economy one day and reverse itself the next (and that is exactly what Chevron permits, see 467 U.S. at 857–59), you might be forgiven for asking: where's the 'substantial guidance' in that? And if an agency can interpret the scope of its statutory jurisdiction one way one day and reverse itself the next (and that is exactly what City of Arlington's application of Chevron says it can), you might well wonder: where are the promised 'clearly delineated boundaries' of agency authority? . . . . Even under the most relaxed or functionalist view of our separated powers some concern has to arise, too, when so much power is concentrated in the hands of a single branch of government. See The Federalist No. 47 (James Madison) ('The accumulation of all powers, legislative, executive, and judiciary, in the same hands . . . may justly be pronounced the very definition of tyranny.'). After all, Chevron invests the power to decide the meaning of the law, and to do so with legislative policy goals in mind, in the very entity charged with enforcing the law. . . . I would have thought powerful and centralized authorities like today's administrative agencies would have warranted less deference from other branches, not more. None of this is to suggest that Chevron is 'the very definition of tyranny.' But on any account it certainly

seems to have added prodigious new powers to an already titanic administrative state . . . . It's an arrangement, too, that seems pretty hard to square with the Constitution of the founders' design and, as Justice Frankfurter once observed, '[t]he accretion of dangerous power does not come in a day. It does come, however slowly, from the generative force of unchecked disregard of the restrictions' imposed by the Constitution. Youngstown Sheet & Tube Co. v. Sawyer, 343 U.S. 579, 594 (1952) (Frankfurter, J., concurring). . . ."

Similar views were also expressed by Judge Kent Jordan in his concurring opinion in EGAN V. DELAWARE RIVER PORT AUTHORITY, No. 16–1471 (3d Cir. 2017): "The deference required by Chevron not only erodes the role of the judiciary, it also diminishes the role of Congress. Under Chevron, '[s]tatutory ambiguity . . . becomes an implicit delegation of rule-making authority, and that authority is used not to find the best meaning of the text, but to formulate legally binding rules to fill in gaps based on policy judgments made by the agency rather than Congress.' Michigan v. Envtl. Prot. Agency, 135 S.Ct. 2699, 2713 (2015) (Thomas, J., concurring). And we in the courts have abetted that process, largely 'abdicat[ing] our duty to enforce [the] prohibition' against Congressional delegation of legislative power to executive agencies. Department of Transp. v. Ass'n of Am. R.R., 135 S.Ct. 1225, 1246 (2015) (Thomas J., concurring). The consequent aggrandizement of federal executive power at the expense of the legislature leads to perverse incentives, as Congress is encouraged to pass vague laws and leave it to agencies to fill in the gaps, rather . . . than undertaking the difficult work of reaching consensus on divisive issues."

(10) *A Revolt in Congress?* Bills have been introduced in the House to in effect overrule Chevron. Here is the text of a bill introduced in January 2017:

SECTION 1. SHORT TITLE.

This Act may be cited as the "Separation of Powers Restoration Act of 2017".

SEC. 2. JUDICIAL REVIEW OF STATUTORY AND REGULATORY INTERPRETATIONS.

Section 706 of title 5, United States Code, is amended—

    (1)   by striking "To the extent necessary" and inserting "(a) To the extent necessary";

    (2)   by striking "decide all relevant questions of law, interpret constitutional and statutory provisions, and";

    (3)   by inserting after "of the terms of an agency action" the following "and decide de novo all relevant questions of law, including the interpretation of constitutional and statutory provisions, and rules made by agencies. Notwithstanding any other provision of law, this subsection shall apply in any action for judicial review of agency action authorized under any provision of law. No law may exempt any such civil action from the application of this section except by specific reference to this section"; and

    (4)   by striking "The reviewing court shall—" and inserting the following:

    "(b)   The reviewing court shall—".

———————

There is no doubt that the sponsors of this bill intend for it to overturn Chevron. But would this legislation actually succeed in doing so, or would it be possible to construe it to be consistent with Chevron? Might it have an effect such as Justice Frankfurter suggested in Universal Camera (p. 1052) that the new terms of the APA substantial evidence test had: by setting a new "mood."

And can Congress control the courts on this matter? The proposed bill was accompanied by the following official statement regarding Congress's constitutional authority to enact it: "Congress has the power to enact this legislation pursuant to the following: Article III, Section 1, Sentence 1, and Section 2, Clauses 1 and 4 of the Constitution, in that the legislation defines or affects judicial powers and cases that are subject to legislation by Congress; Article 1, Section 1, Clause 1 of the United States Constitution, in that the legislation concerns the exercise of legislative powers generally granted to Congress by that section, including the exercise of those powers when delegated by Congress to the Executive; and, Article 1, Section 8, Clause 18 of the United States Constitution, in that the legislation exercises legislative power granted to Congress by that clause "to make all laws which shall be necessary and proper for carrying into execution the foregoing powers, and all other powers vested by this Constitution in the Government of the United States, or in any Department or Officer thereof." Do you see any constitutional problem with Congress precluding courts from deferring to agency interpretations of ambiguous statutes?

(11) ***What Would Happen if Chevron Were Overruled?*** Here is then-JUDGE GORSUCH, again from his concurrence in GUTIERREZ-BRIZUELA V. LYNCH, 834 F.3d at 1158: "All of which raises this question: what would happen in a world without Chevron? If this goliath of modern administrative law were to fall? Surely Congress could and would continue to pass statutes for executive agencies to enforce. And just as surely agencies could and would continue to offer guidance on how they intend to enforce those statutes. The only difference would be that courts would then fulfill their duty to exercise their independent judgment about what the law is. Of course, courts could and would consult agency views and apply the agency's interpretation when it accords with the best reading of a statute. But de novo judicial review of the law's meaning would limit the ability of an agency to alter and amend existing law. It would avoid the due process and equal protection problems of the kind documented in our decisions. It would promote reliance interests by allowing citizens to organize their affairs with some assurance that the rug will not be pulled from under them tomorrow, the next day, or after the next election. And an agency's recourse for a judicial declaration of the law's meaning that it dislikes would be precisely the recourse the Constitution prescribes—an appeal to higher judicial authority or a new law enacted consistent with bicameralism and presentment. We managed to live with the

administrative state before Chevron. We could do it again. Put simply, it seems to me that in a world without Chevron very little would change—except perhaps the most important things."

For a different take on what a world without Chevron would be like, consider JEFF POJANOWSKI, WITHOUT DEFERENCE, 81 Mo. L. Rev. (2016) at 2: "To be clear, abandoning Chevron is not the same thing as abolishing deference. Deference of a different kind existed before Chevron, and if the Court were to abandon Chevron tomorrow, the Court may revert to something like that preexisting, milder form of deference. Nevertheless, imagining a regime without any deference clarifies the stakes of reforming judicial review of agencies' legal conclusions. Thus, for present purposes, and present purposes only, I equate abandoning Chevron with abandoning judicial deference on agencies' legal interpretations.

"I argue that such an alternative regime has appealing features but may not bring as much practical change as casual critiques or defenses of Chevron contemplate, at least immediately. The more immediate change would arise at the level of theory and rhetoric, which, in turn, may lead to greater practical changes in the longer run. The theoretical presuppositions underwriting a regime of non-deferential review are far more classical in cast than the moderate legal realism underwriting Chevron. Rejecting deference, therefore, would change how courts talk about the difference between law and policy in the administrative state. The resurrection of the classical distinction between interpreting and making law might therefore alter the way courts think about that relationship. If that is the case, rejecting deference could lead to a more robust judicial role on close questions of interpretation.

"Alternatively, some courts may already be quite aggressive on questions of interpretation, usually through a vigorous application of Step One. This is often the case, for example, at the Supreme Court. To the extent this is so, abandoning deference would bring the courts' skeptical rhetoric about the law/policy divide in line with their practice on the ground. This would reveal that interpreters are less skeptical about the line between law and policy than their rhetoric suggests. In short, it would show we are not, in fact, all legal realists now, at least with respect to problems amenable to the lawyers' traditional toolkit. Either way, the more traditional character of the theoretical orientation underwriting the case against deference may also shed light on the rise and (partial) fall of Chevron in administrative legal thought."

NOTES ON THE RELATIONSHIP BETWEEN CHEVRON AND JUDICIAL STATUTORY PRECEDENT

(1) *What Happens if an Agency Addresses a Statutory Issue Judges Have Already Decided?* Justice Stevens' opinion in Chevron tells us that the D.C. Circuit decided against the EPA based on two of that court's own precedents interpreting the Clean Air Act. "The basic legal error of the Court of Appeals was to adopt a static judicial definition of the term stationary source when it had decided that Congress itself had not commanded the

definition." How are we to differentiate between the forbidden "static judicial definition" and the presumably still proper rules of *stare decisis*?

(2) The Supreme Court went out of its way to answer the preceding question in NATIONAL CABLE & TELECOMMUNICATIONS ASS'N V. BRAND X INTERNET SERV., 545 U.S. 967 (2005). The underlying issue was how to classify cable companies that provided broadband internet services to consumers. The Communications Act of 1934, 47 U.S.C. § 151 et seq., distinguished between the provision of "information service" and "telecommunications service." If what the companies offered was only an "information service," they would be essentially free from regulation; if what they offered was also classified as a "telecommunications service," they would be subject to mandatory regulation by the Federal Communications Commission as a common carrier. The reality was that what the companies offered was an integrated product combining the information-processing capacity of the internet with a high speed wire. How should it be classified? The FCC said the companies did not provide "telecommunications service" and so were free from common-carrier regulation. The Ninth Circuit rejected the FCC's interpretation of the Communications Act based specifically on the precedential effect of its holding in AT & T Corp. v. Portland, 216 F.3d 871 (9th Cir. 2000), a case which had not involved the FCC. The Supreme Court reversed and upheld the agency against multiple challenges. Three Justices dissented, claiming that the FCC was attempting to impose a new regime of competition rather than regulation under the guise of statutory construction.

As regards the Ninth Circuit precedent relied on by the court below, the Supreme Court might simply have stated that it disagreed with the holding in that lower-court case; or it might have distinguished it as arising from other than a review of FCC proceedings; or it might have placed emphasis on the fact that the case at hand had nationwide importance and was only fortuitously adjudicated in the Ninth Circuit. But, acknowledging that "[t]here is genuine confusion in the lower courts over the interaction between the Chevron doctrine and *stare decisis* principles," 545 U.S. at 985, the Court, in an opinion by JUSTICE THOMAS, spoke more broadly. (545 U.S. at 982–85):

"The Court of Appeals declined to apply Chevron because it thought the Commission's interpretation of the Communications Act foreclosed by the conflicting construction of the Act it had adopted in Portland. It based that holding on the assumption that Portland's construction overrode the Commission's, regardless of whether Portland had held the statute to be unambiguous. That reasoning was incorrect.

"A court's prior judicial construction of a statute trumps an agency construction otherwise entitled to Chevron deference only if the prior court decision holds that its construction follows from the unambiguous terms of the statute and thus leaves no room for agency discretion. This principle follows from Chevron itself. Chevron established a 'presumption that Congress, when it left ambiguity in a statute meant for implementation by an agency, understood that the ambiguity would be resolved, first and foremost, by the agency, and desired the agency (rather than the courts) to possess whatever degree of discretion the ambiguity allows.' Smiley v. Citibank (South Dakota), N.A. 517 U.S. 734, 740–741 (1996). Yet allowing a judicial precedent to foreclose an agency from interpreting an ambiguous statute, as the Court of Appeals assumed it could, would allow a court's interpretation to override an agency's. Chevron's premise is that it is for agencies, not courts, to fill statutory gaps. The better rule is to hold judicial interpretations contained in precedents to the same demanding Chevron step one standard that applies if the court is reviewing the agency's construction on a blank slate: Only a judicial precedent holding that the statute unambiguously forecloses the agency's interpretation, and therefore contains no gap for the agency to fill, displaces a conflicting agency construction.

"A contrary rule would produce anomalous results. It would mean that whether an agency's interpretation of an ambiguous statute is entitled to Chevron deference would turn on the order in which the interpretations issue: If the court's construction came first, its construction would prevail, whereas if the agency's came first, the agency's construction would command Chevron deference. Yet whether Congress has delegated to an agency the authority to interpret a statute does not depend on the order in which the judicial and administrative constructions occur. . . .

"Against this background, the Court of Appeals erred in refusing to apply Chevron to the Commission's interpretation of the definition of 'telecommunications service,' 47 U.S.C. 153(46). Its prior decision in Portland held only that the *best* reading of § 153(46) was that cable modem service was a 'telecommunications service,' not that it was the *only permissible* reading of the statute. . . . Before a judicial construction of a statute, whether contained in a precedent or not, may trump an agency's, the court must hold that the statute unambiguously requires the court's construction. Portland did not do so."

To which idea, that an agency would be entitled to disregard a court's prior determination as to what is the *best* interpretation of a statute, JUSTICE SCALIA had the following to say, in dissent (545 U.S. at 1017–20):

"Article III courts do not sit to render decisions that can be reversed or ignored by Executive officers. . . .

"[T]oday's novelty . . . creates many uncertainties to bedevil the lower courts. A court's interpretation is conclusive, the Court says, only if it holds that interpretation to be 'the *only permissible* reading of the statute,' and not if it merely holds it to be 'the *best* reading.' Does this mean that in future statutory-construction cases involving agency-administered statutes courts must specify (presumably in dictum) which of the two they are holding? And what of the many cases decided in the past, before this dictum's requirement was established? . . . Does the 'unambiguous' dictum produce *stare decisis* effect even when a court is *affirming,* rather than *reversing,* agency action— so that in the future the agency *must adhere* to that affirmed interpretation? If so, does the victorious agency have the right to appeal a Court of Appeals judgment in its favor, on the ground that the text in question is in fact not (as the Court of Appeals held) unambiguous, so the agency should be able to change its view in the future?

"It is indeed a wonderful new world that the Court creates, one full of promise for administrative-law professors in need of tenure articles and, of course, for litigators. I would adhere to what has been the rule in the past: When a court interprets a statute without Chevron deference to agency views, its interpretation (whether or not asserted to rest upon an unambiguous text) is the law. I might add that it is a great mystery why any of this is relevant here. *Whatever* the *stare decisis* effect of AT & T Corp. v. Portland, 216 F.3d 871 (C.A.9 2000), in the Ninth Circuit, it surely does not govern this Court's decision. . . . [T]he Ninth Circuit would already be obliged to abandon *Portland's* holding in the face of *this Court's* decision that the Commission's construction of 'telecommunications service' is entitled to deference and is reasonable. It is a sadness that the Court should go so far out of its way to make bad law."

To which, JUSTICE THOMAS responded (545 U.S. at 983–84):

"The dissent answers that allowing an agency to override what a court believes to be the best interpretation of a statute makes 'judicial decisions subject to reversal by Executive officers.' It does not. Since Chevron teaches that a court's opinion as to the best reading of an ambiguous statute an agency is charged with administering is not authoritative, the agency's decision to construe that statute differently from a court does not say that the court's holding was legally wrong. Instead, the agency may, consistent with the court's holding, choose a different construction, since the agency remains the authoritative interpreter (within the limits of reason) of such statutes. In all other respects, the court's prior ruling remains binding law (for example, as to agency interpretations to which Chevron is inapplicable). The precedent has not been 'reversed' by the agency, any more than a federal court's interpretation of a State's law can be said to have been 'reversed' by a state court that adopts a conflicting (yet authoritative) interpretation of state law."

(3)   This last remark builds on an analogy with the Erie doctrine first made by KENNETH A. BAMBERGER in PROVISIONAL PRECEDENT: PROTECTIVE FLEXIBILITY IN ADMINISTRATIVE POLICYMAKING, 77 N.Y.U. L. Rev. 1272, 1308 (2002):

> [I]n nearly every instance in which a federal court is faced with an open state law question, it decides it. Those decisions are clearly authoritative for the parties to the case and have "binding precedential effect" on other federal courts, "absent a subsequent state court decision or [legislative] amendment" adopting a contrary construction. But once a state exercises its primary authority to make such a decision or amendment, the federal interpretation is no longer binding. Its precedential value is, literally, *provisional.*
>
> . . . Certainly, the federalism concerns structuring the relation between federal courts and state actors do not govern the administrative law context. Yet the model of federal adjudication of state law issues provides a functional framework for reconciling the doctrinal conflicts raised by judicial interpretation of

administrative statutes, and for preserving flexibility in policymaking.

(4) Then-JUDGE GORSUCH had real constitutional concerns with Brand X, as he explained in his concurrence in GUTIERREZ-BRIZUELA V. LYNCH, 834 F.3d at 1150: "Founders meet Brand X. Precisely to avoid the possibility of allowing politicized decisionmakers to decide cases and controversies about the meaning of existing laws, the framers sought to ensure that judicial judgments 'may not lawfully be revised, overturned or refused faith and credit by' the elected branches of government. Chi. & S. Air Lines v. Waterman S.S. Corp., 333 U.S. 103, 113 (1948); see also Hayburn's Case, 2 U.S. (2 Dall.) 409, 410 n* (1792) ('[B]y the Constitution, neither the Secretary . . . nor any other Executive officer, nor even the Legislature, are authorized to sit as a court of errors on the judicial acts or opinions of this court.'). Yet this deliberate design, this separation of functions aimed to ensure a neutral decisionmaker for the people's disputes, faces more than a little pressure from Brand X. Under Brand X's terms, after all, courts are required to overrule their own declarations about the meaning of existing law in favor of interpretations dictated by executive agencies. Nat'l Cable & Telecomms. Ass'n v. Brand X Internet Servs., 545 U.S. 967, 982–85 (2005). By Brand X's own telling, this means a judicial declaration of the law's meaning in a case or controversy before it is not 'authoritative,' id. at 983, but is instead subject to revision by a politically accountable branch of government. . . .

"When the political branches disagree with a judicial interpretation of existing law, the Constitution prescribes the appropriate remedial process. It's called legislation. Admittedly, the legislative process can be an arduous one. But that's no bug in the constitutional design: it is the very point of the design. The framers sought to ensure that the people may rely on judicial precedent about the meaning of existing law until and unless that precedent is overruled or the purposefully painful process of bicameralism and presentment can be cleared. Indeed, the principle of stare decisis was one 'entrenched and revered by the framers' precisely because they knew its importance 'as a weapon against . . . tyranny.' Michael B.W. Sinclair, Anastasoff Versus Hart: The Constitutionality and Wisdom of Denying Precedential Authority to Circuit Court Decisions, 64 U. Pitt. L. Rev. 695, 707 (2003). Yet even as now semi-tamed (at least in this circuit), Brand X still risks trampling the constitutional design by affording executive agencies license to overrule a judicial declaration of the law's meaning prospectively, just as legislation might—and all without the inconvenience of having to engage the legislative processes the Constitution prescribes. A form of Lawmaking Made Easy, one that permits all too easy intrusions on the liberty of the people."

Then-JUDGE GORSUCH states: "When the political branches disagree with a judicial interpretation of existing law, the Constitution prescribes the appropriate remedial process. It's called legislation." But does this argument beg the question Brand X presents? After all, if Chevron is justified by a congressional delegation of power to an agency to administer a statute by resolving ambiguities in it, then doesn't the Constitution prescribe that courts must respect that congressional grant of authority to the agency? And, if so, then on what basis could a court ignore an agency interpretation that is within the permissible range of possible interpretations that Congress itself provided for in the statute at issue? Does the Constitution really require that a court's best guess as to an ambiguous statute's meaning must forever bind the agency charged with administering that statute just because the court guessed first? Unless Chevron itself is unconstitutional, wouldn't the court have to defer to the agency if it beat the court to the punch?

NOTES ON THE PRACTICAL IMPACT OF CHEVRON

(1) *Chevron Is Famous, but Did It Change Things? Impact on Litigation.* One can start by asking whether it matters in the lower courts if the Supreme Court announces a new doctrinal formulation regarding the standard for judicial review. Professors Peter H. Schuck and E. Donald Elliott examined almost 2,000 courts of appeals decisions from 1984–85 and 1988. In To The *Chevron* Station: An Empirical Study of Federal Administrative Law, 1990 Duke L.J. 984, they reported "strong evidence" that outcomes changed from a pre-Chevron affirmance rate of 71% to a post-Chevron rate of 81%, between the six months before Chevron came down in 1984 and a six-month period in 1985. By 1988, the affirmance rate was 76% (with remands twice as frequent as reversals, whereas in 1984–85 they had been about equal).

A later study of all the courts of appeals decisions from 1995 and 1996 that cited Chevron reported that agency interpretations were upheld 73% of the time. Of those that were rejected, 59% failed step one; in 18%, the statute was declared ambiguous but the agency's interpretation was ruled unreasonable, failing step two; and in 23%, the agency's interpretation failed a general test of "reasonability," which conflated steps one and two. Orin S. Kerr, Shedding Light on *Chevron*: An Empirical Study of the *Chevron* Doctrine in the U.S. Courts of Appeals, 15 Yale J. on Reg. I (1998).

Another study, about a decade later, analyzed 253 courts of appeals decisions from 1990 through 2004 in Chevron cases involving the EPA and the NLRB. This study found that the average validation rate was about 64%—markedly lower than either of the other studies, and even lower than pre-Chevron. Thomas J. Miles & Cass R. Sunstein, Do Judges Make Regulatory Policy? An Empirical Study of Chevron, 73 U. Chi. L. Rev. 823, 849 (2006). (It is notable that the authors intentionally chose for their study agencies that tended to produce "politically contentious decisions"; this may explain, in part, the low affirmation rate.) Finally, an even more recent draft study—of 1,558 instances of agency interpretation (across many agencies) in the courts of appeals from 2003 to 2013—found that the agency prevailed about 77% of the time when the court applied Chevron, 56% when Skidmore [p. 1125] applied, and only 39% on de novo review. These findings led the authors to conclude that "the application of the *Chevron* framework seems to make a meaningful difference as to whether agencies prevail on the interpretive question." Kent H. Barnett & Christopher J. Walker, Chevron in the Circuit Courts, 116 Mich. L. Rev. 1 (2017).

Of course, rates of affirmance and reversal do not tell the whole story. They are affected not only by what the courts do but by which cases lawyers choose to bring to court. If Chevron made it easier for agencies to win, it correspondingly made it more risky to bring an action challenging an agency decision (or, in the case of an agency enforcement action, to choose to oppose). In other words, the potential value of winning would have to be discounted to a greater extent to represent the increased likelihood of losing. Accordingly, one would expect over time for counsel representing parties opposed to agency action to bring fewer marginal cases. Assuming the costs of bringing an action against an agency remain constant (litigation costs plus the more practical costs of opposing an agency one deals with), and assuming that the amounts at stake in proceedings on average also remain constant, over the long run the rates of affirmance and reversal might be expected to return to their prior state—even if the courts were using a different standard of review—since those rates would represent the discounted value of bringing actions. So if the combined story of the studies just decided is that rates of judicial affirmance went up immediately after Chevron, and then fell back to roughly the prior levels, the case may still have had a long-run effect—but on the kinds of cases brought and not brought, rather than on the overall rates of success or failure.

(2) ***Impact on Regulations.*** Another consequence of Chevron—perhaps an intentional consequence—would seem to be a reduction in the stability of administrative regulations over time. Recall the long history of policy vacillation regarding airbags in the State Farm case and Justice Rehnquist's partial dissent stressing that "[t]he agency's changed view of the standard seems to be related to the election of a new President of a different political party. . . . A change in administration brought about by the people casting their votes is a perfectly reasonable basis for an executive agency's reappraisal of the costs and benefits of its programs and regulations . . . within the bounds established by Congress."

In Chevron, a case where, once again, the agency's position had shifted over time, all six voting Justices signed on to Justice Stevens' observation endorsing agency reliance, within the limits established by delegation, "upon the incumbent administration's views of wise policy," and two of the non-participating Justices had been among the State Farm partial dissenters. This judicial proposition has substantial implications for relationships between the executive and legislative branches. For if each administration's present choice can survive judicial review, Congress will be unable to change it unless it can secure either presidential agreement or the votes necessary to override a veto. Thus a change of administration may bring in its wake new "interpretations" that, however unwelcome to Congress, cannot easily be overcome.

RUST V. SULLIVAN, 500 U.S. 173 (1991), presents a particularly dramatic example of this effect of Chevron. Title X of the Public Health Service Act, 42 U.S.C. §§ 300–300a–6, had provided, since enactment in 1970, for federal grant support of family planning clinics. While grantees were supposed to "offer a broad range of acceptable and effective family planning methods and services," the Act also stipulated that none of the grant money "shall be used in programs where abortion is a method of family planning." How far did this prohibition go? The initial regulations under the statute, issued in 1971, simply required that a Title X project "not provide abortions." Further guidelines issued in the mid-1970's expressly permitted non-directive counseling of pregnant women as to their options, including the availability of abortions elsewhere. Guidelines issued in 1981 mandated such counseling upon a patient's request. But in 1988, after a notice-and-comment proceeding, the Department of Health and Human Services promulgated new regulations that at every turn required grant recipients to avoid giving advice or making referrals concerning abortion. If a patient asked for information, the grantee was allowed to say that "the project does not consider abortion an appropriate method of family planning."

The Court sustained the regulations, 5 to 4. Much of Justice Rehnquist's opinion for the majority was devoted to answering the challengers' claim that the regulations violated constitutional guarantees of free speech and substantive due process. But, as even this brief history shows, he had to address substantial questions of statutory interpretation and administrative discretion, too. As to the statute, the reach of its reference to "programs where abortion is a method of family planning" was uncertain and not clarified by the legislative history. "The broad language of Title X" he said, "plainly allows the Secretary's construction of the statute." JUSTICE REHNQUIST continued (500 U.S. at 186–87):

"Petitioners argue, however, that the regulations are entitled to little or no deference because they 'reverse a longstanding agency policy that permitted nondirective counseling and referral for abortion,' and thus represent a sharp break from the Secretary's prior construction of the statute. . . .

"This Court has rejected the argument that an agency's interpretation 'is not entitled to deference because it represents a sharp break with prior interpretations' of the statute in question. Chevron, 467 U.S. at 862. In Chevron, we held that a revised interpretation deserves deference because '[a]n initial agency interpretation is not instantly carved in stone' and 'the agency, to engage in informed rulemaking, must consider varying interpretations and the wisdom of its policy on a continuing basis.' An agency is not required to 'establish rules of conduct to last forever,' Motor Vehicle Mfrs. Assn. of United States v. State Farm Mutual Automobile Ins. Co., but rather 'must be given ample latitude to "adapt [its] rules and policies to the demands of changing circumstances.' "

"We find that the Secretary amply justified his change of interpretation with a 'reasoned analysis.' Motor Vehicle Mfrs. The Secretary explained that the regulations are a result of his determination, in the wake of the critical reports of the General Accounting Office (GAO)[11] and the Office of the Inspector General (OIG), that prior policy failed to implement properly the statute and that it was necessary to provide 'clear and operational guidance to grantees to preserve the distinction between Title X programs and abortion as a method of family planning.' 53 Fed. Reg. 2923–2924 (1988). He

---

[11] [Ed.] Now The Government Accountability Office.

also determined that the new regulations are more in keeping with the original intent of the statute, are justified by client experience under the prior policy, and are supported by a shift in attitude against the 'elimination of unborn children by abortion.' We believe that these justifications are sufficient to support the Secretary's revised approach. Having concluded that the plain language and legislative history are ambiguous as to Congress' intent in enacting Title X, we must defer to the Secretary's permissible construction of the statute."

The dissenting Justices wrote three opinions. Much of Justice Blackmun's opinion was devoted to arguing that the regulations violated the first and fifth amendments. Justice Stevens' rested on the first step of the Chevron test: "I am convinced that the 1970 Act did not authorize the Secretary to censor the speech of grant recipients or their employees." JUSTICE O'CONNOR, making a point Justice Blackmun had also made, based her dissent on a "long-standing canon of statutory construction" (500 U.S. at 223–25):

" '[W]here an otherwise acceptable construction of a statute would raise serious constitutional problems, the Court will construe the statute to avoid such problems unless such construction is plainly contrary to the intent of Congress.' Edward J. DeBartolo Corp. v. Florida Gulf Coast Building & Construction Trades Council, 485 U.S. 568, 575 (1988). . . . In these cases, we need only tell the Secretary that his regulations are not a reasonable interpretation of the statute; we need not tell Congress that it cannot pass such legislation. If we rule solely on statutory grounds, Congress retains the power to force the constitutional question by legislating more explicitly. It may instead choose to do nothing. That decision should be left to Congress; we should not tell Congress what it cannot do before it has chosen to do it. It is enough in this case to conclude that neither the language nor the history of § 1008 compels the Secretary's interpretation, and that the interpretation raises serious First Amendment concerns. On this basis alone, I would . . . invalidate the challenged regulations."

If we view this debate in terms of its allocations of power to various institutions, Justice O'Connor's opinion would have required action on the part of both Congress and the President (or an extraordinary majority in Congress) to reinstate the prohibitions contained in the regulations. By contrast, Chief Justice Rehnquist's deference to the agency put a similar burden of action on those who would have removed the prohibitions. This, as it turned out, was not merely a theoretical point. In 1992, Congress passed a bill requiring Title X projects to provide their clients with non-directive counseling on various matters, including termination of pregnancy. But it was vetoed by President Bush on September 25, 1992, 28 Weekly Comp. Pres. Doc. 1759, with the consequence that even though both Houses of Congress opposed the regulations, they remained in force.

On February 5, 1993—very shortly after President Clinton took office— the new Secretary of HHS published an "Interim Rule," effective immediately for "good cause" pending a new notice and comment proceeding, which said in part:

". . . [T]he Secretary suspends the 1988 rules and announces that, on an interim basis, the agency's nonregulatory compliance standards that existed prior to February 2, 1988 . . . will be used to administer the Family Planning Program.

"Under these compliance standards, Title X projects would be required, in the event of an unplanned pregnancy and where the patient requests such action, to provide nondirective counseling to the patient on options relating to her pregnancy, including abortion, and to refer her for abortion, if that is the option she selects."

(3) *Impact on Agency Behavior.* Not surprisingly, Chevron may also have changed what lawyers inside agencies do. Here's the report of E. DONALD ELLIOTT, General Counsel of the EPA during the administration of the first President Bush: CHEVRON MATTERS: HOW THE CHEVRON DOCTRINE REDEFINED THE ROLES OF CONGRESS, COURTS AND AGENCIES IN ENVIRONMENTAL LAW, 16 Vill. Envtl. L.J. 1, 11–12 (2005): "The fundamental difference between the role of EPA OGC [Office of General Counsel] (and probably in any other agency as well) pre-Chevron and post-Chevron is this: pre-Chevron, OGC usually gave its legal advice as a point estimate, e.g., 'the statute means this . . . you must follow what we in OGC tell you is the correct/best interpretation of the statue or you will lose in court.' . . . This 'single-meaning' conception of statutes created a very powerful rule for lawyers and OGC within agencies. The privileged role for lawyers in defining what the statute required on every issue in turn led to a great deal of implicit policy-making by lawyers in OGC. They may have in all good faith believed that they were diving the one true and correct meaning of the statute, but intentionally or unintentionally, they may have smuggled a great deal of their policy preferences into their legal advice. . . .

"Post-Chevron, the form of OGC opinions is no longer a simple point estimate of what a statute means. Rather, OGC opinions now attempt to describe a permissible range of agency policy-making discretion that arises out of a statutory ambiguity. Post-Chevron, statutes no longer possess a single prescriptive meaning on many questions; rather, they describe what I call a 'policy space,' a range of permissible interpretive discretion, within which a variety of decisions that the agency might make would be legally defensible to varying degrees. . . .

"Chevron opened up and validated a policy-making dialogue within agencies about what interpretation the agency should adopt for policy reasons, rather than what interpretation the agency must adopt for legal reasons. I believe that this expanded policy dialogue is productive and that it takes place more inside EPA today than it did pre-Chevron, and normatively, that is a good thing. For example, it is good that Chevron has increased the weight given to the views of air pollution experts in the air program office relative to the lawyers in OGC."

In this same vein, a recent survey of 148 rule drafters, across seven executive departments and two independent agencies, found that nearly 94% of them knew about Chevron deference by name. Christopher J. Walker, Inside Agency Statutory Interpretation, 67 Stan. L. Rev. 999, 999–1000,

1061–63 (2015). And 90% of the drafters reported that the Chevron doctrine played a role in their drafting decisions. Id. The survey even found that "two in five rule drafters surveyed agreed or strongly agreed—and another two in five somewhat agreed—that a federal agency is more aggressive in its interpretive efforts if it is confident that Chevron deference (as opposed to Skidmore deference or de novo review) applies."

A FINAL NOTE ON CHEVRON

After reviewing the tasks State Farm assigned to courts and to agencies, and the tasks Chevron assigned to courts and to agencies, then-First-Circuit-Judge Stephen Breyer asked of the combination: "Is this not the exact opposite of a rational system?" Judicial Review of Questions of Law and Policy, 38 Admin. L. Rev. 363, 397 (1986).

MCI TELECOMM. CORP. v. AT&T CO.

Notes on the Relationship Between Chevron and the Theories and Tools of Statutory Interpretation

Notes on Chevron and Deference to Major Policy Changes

Notes on Chevron and the Approach Agencies Should Use When Interpreting Statutes

Notes on Chevron and Its Application to Agency Interpretations of Criminal Law

---

MCI TELECOMMUNICATIONS CORP. v. AMERICAN TELEPHONE AND TELEGRAPH CO.

Supreme Court of the United States (1994).
512 U.S. 218.

■ JUSTICE SCALIA delivered the opinion of the Court.

Section 203(a) of Title 47 of the United States Code requires communications common carriers to file tariffs with the Federal Communications Commission, and § 203(b) authorizes the Commission to "modify" any requirement of § 203. These cases present the question whether the Commission's decision to make tariff filing optional for all nondominant long distance carriers is a valid exercise of its modification authority.

I

[The Communications Act of 1934 requires long distance carriers to file their tariffs with the FCC and to charge only the filed rates. When the Act was passed, AT&T monopolized long distance service, but in the 1970s technological advances made it possible for others, like MCI, to compete. In a series of orders from 1980 on, the FCC responded to the increased competition by relaxing the filing requirements for nondominant carriers—that is, for everyone but AT&T. The policy ran into some difficulty with the D.C. Circuit Court of Appeals, but the agency persisted. In 1992, the Commission concluded a rulemaking proceeding by declaring that filing of tariffs was optional for all nondominant carriers and that the Communications Act authorized this deregulation. The D.C. Circuit reversed per curiam; MCI and the United States petitioned for certiorari, and the Court granted the petitions. The key question concerned Chevron Step One and whether the statute was clear or ambiguous in the relevant respect. Justice Scalia thought it was and thus rejected the FCC's interpretation. Justice Stevens disagreed.]

II

Section 203 of the Communications Act contains both the filed rate provisions of the Act and the Commission's disputed modification authority. It provides in relevant part:

(a) Filing; public display.

Every common carrier, except connecting carriers, shall, within such reasonable time as the Commission shall designate, file with the Commission and print and keep open for public inspection schedules showing all charges . . ., whether such charges are joint or separate, and showing the classifications, practices, and regulations affecting such charges. . . .

(b) Changes in schedule; discretion of Commission to modify requirements.

(1) No change shall be made in the charges, classifications, regulations, or practices which have been so filed and published except after one hundred and twenty days notice to the Commission and to the public, which shall be published in such form and contain such information as the Commission may by regulations prescribe.

(2) The Commission may, in its discretion and for good cause shown, modify any requirement made by or under the authority of this section either in particular instances or by general order applicable to special circumstances or conditions except that the Commission may not require the notice period specified in paragraph (1) to be more than one hundred and twenty days.

(c) Overcharges and rebates.

No carrier, unless otherwise provided by or under authority of this chapter, shall engage or participate in such communication unless schedules have been filed and published in accordance with the provisions of this chapter and with the regulations made thereunder; and no carrier shall (1) charge, demand, collect, or receive a greater or less or different compensation for such communication . . . than the charges specified in the schedule then in effect, or (2) refund or remit by any means or device any portion of the charges so specified, or (3) extend to any person any privileges or facilities in such communication, or employ or enforce any classifications, regulations, or practices affecting such charges, except as specified in such schedule.

47 U.S.C. § 203 (1988 ed. and Supp. IV).

The dispute between the parties turns on the meaning of the phrase "modify any requirement" in § 203(b)(2). Petitioners argue that it gives the Commission authority to make even basic and fundamental changes in the scheme created by that section. We disagree. The word "modify"—like a number of other English words employing the root "mod-" (deriving from the Latin word for "measure"), such as "moderate," "modulate," "modest," and "modicum"—has a connotation of increment or limitation. Virtually every dictionary we are aware of says that "to modify" means to change moderately or in minor fashion. See, e.g., Random House Dictionary of the English Language 1236 (2d ed. 1987) ("to change somewhat the form or qualities of; alter partially; amend"); Webster's Third New International Dictionary 1452 (1976) ("to make minor changes in the form or structure of; alter without transforming"); 9 Oxford English Dictionary 952 (2d ed. 1989) ("[t]o make partial changes in; to change (an object) in respect of some of its qualities; to alter or vary without radical transformation"); Black's Law Dictionary 1004 (6th ed. 1990) ("[t]o alter; to change in incidental or subordinate features; enlarge; extend; amend; limit; reduce").

In support of their position, petitioners cite dictionary definitions contained in or derived from a single source, Webster's Third New International Dictionary 1452 (1976) ("Webster's Third"), which includes among the meanings of "modify," "to make a basic or important change in." Petitioners contend that this establishes sufficient ambiguity to entitle the Commission to deference in its acceptance of the broader meaning, which in turn requires approval of its permissive detariffing policy. See Chevron U.S.A. Inc. v. Natural Resources Defense Council, Inc., 467 U.S. 837, 843 (1984). In short, they contend that the courts must defer to the agency's choice among available dictionary definitions, citing National Railroad Passenger Corp. v. Boston and Maine Corp., 503 U.S. 407 (1992).

Most cases of verbal ambiguity in statutes involve, as Boston and Maine did, a selection between accepted alternative meanings shown as such by many dictionaries. One can envision (though a court case does not immediately come to mind) having to choose between accepted alternative meanings, one of which is so newly accepted that it has only been recorded by a single lexicographer. (Some dictionary must have been the very first to record the widespread use of "projection," for example, to mean "forecast.") But what petitioners demand that we accept as creating an ambiguity here is a rarity even rarer than that: a meaning set forth in a single dictionary (and, as we say, its progeny) which not only supplements the meaning contained in all other dictionaries, but contradicts one of the meanings contained in virtually all other dictionaries. Indeed, contradicts one of the alternative meanings contained in the out-of-step dictionary itself—for as we have observed, Webster's Third itself defines "modify" to connote both (specifically) major change and (specifically) minor change. It is hard to see how that can be. When the word "modify" has come to mean both "to change in some respects" and "to change fundamentally" it will in fact mean neither of those things. It will simply mean "to change," and some adverb will have to be called into service to indicate the great or small degree of the change.

If that is what the peculiar Webster's Third definition means to suggest has happened—and what petitioners suggest by appealing to Webster's Third—we simply disagree. "Modify," in our view, connotes moderate change. It might be good English to say that the French Revolution "modified" the status of the French nobility—but only because there is a figure of speech called understatement and a literary device known as sarcasm. And it might be unsurprising to discover a 1972 White House press release saying that "the Administration is modifying its position with regard to prosecution of the war in Vietnam"—but only because press agents tend to impart what is nowadays called "spin." Such intentional distortions, or simply careless or ignorant misuse, must have formed the basis for the usage that Webster's Third, and Webster's Third alone, reported.[3] It is perhaps gilding the lily to add this: In 1934, when the Communications Act became law-the most relevant time for determining a statutory term's meaning-Webster's Third was not yet even contemplated. To our knowledge all English dictionaries provided the narrow definition of "modify," including those published by G. & C. Merriam Company. See Webster's New International Dictionary 1577 (2d ed. 1934); Webster's Collegiate Dictionary 628 (4th ed. 1934). We have not the slightest doubt that is the meaning the statute intended.

Beyond the word itself, a further indication that the § 203 authority to "modify" does not contemplate fundamental changes is the sole exception to that authority which the section provides. One of the requirements of § 203 is that changes to filed tariffs can be made only after 120 days' notice to the Commission and the public. § 203(b)(1). The only exception to the Commission's § 203(b)(2) modification authority is as follows: "except that the Commission may not require the notice period specified in paragraph (1) to be more than one hundred and twenty days." Is it conceivable that the statute is indifferent to the Commission's power to eliminate the tariff-filing requirement entirely for all except one firm in the long-distance sector, and yet strains out the gnat of extending the waiting period for tariff revision beyond 120 days? We think not. The exception is not as ridiculous as a Lilliputian in London only because it is to be found in Lilliput: in the smallscale world of "modifications," it is a big deal.

---

[3] That is not an unlikely hypothesis. Upon its long-awaited appearance in 1961, Webster's Third was widely criticized for its portrayal of common error as proper usage. . . .

Since an agency's interpretation of a statute is not entitled to deference when it goes beyond the meaning that the statute can bear, see, e.g., Pittston Coal Group v. Sebben, 488 U.S. 105, 113 (1988); Chevron, 467 U.S., at 842843, the Commission's permissive detariffing policy can be justified only if it makes a less than radical or fundamental change in the Act's tariff-filing requirement. The Commission's attempt to establish that no more than that is involved greatly understates the extent to which its policy deviates from the filing requirement, and greatly undervalues the importance of the filing requirement itself.

To consider the latter point first: For the body of a law, as for the body of a person, whether a change is minor or major depends to some extent upon the importance of the item changed to the whole. Loss of an entire toenail is insignificant; loss of an entire arm tragic. The tariff-filing requirement is, to pursue this analogy, the heart of the common-carrier section of the Communications Act. In the context of the Interstate Commerce Act, which served as its model, this Court has repeatedly stressed that rate filing was Congress's chosen means of preventing unreasonableness and discrimination in charges: "[T]here is not only a relation, but an indissoluble unity between the provision for the establishment and maintenance of rates until corrected in accordance with the statute and the prohibitions against preferences and discrimination." Texas and Pacific R. Co. v. Abilene Cotton Oil Co., 204 U.S. 426, 440 (1907).

. . . Rate filings are, in fact, the essential characteristic of a rate-regulated industry. It is highly unlikely that Congress would leave the determination of whether an industry will be entirely, or even substantially, rate-regulated to agency discretion—and even more unlikely that it would achieve that through such a subtle device as permission to "modify" rate-filing requirements.

Bearing in mind, then, the enormous importance to the statutory scheme of the tariff-filing provision, we turn to whether what has occurred here can be considered a mere "modification." The Commission stresses that its detariffing policy applies only to nondominant carriers, so that the rates charged to over half of all consumers in the long-distance market are on file with the Commission. It is not clear to us that the proportion of customers affected, rather than the proportion of carriers affected, is the proper measure of the extent of the exemption (of course all carriers in the long-distance market are exempted, except AT & T). But even assuming it is, we think an elimination of the crucial provision of the statute for 40% of a major sector of the industry is much too extensive to be considered a "modification." What we have here, in reality, is a fundamental revision of the statute, changing it from a scheme of rate regulation in long-distance common-carrier communications to a scheme of rate regulation only where effective competition does not exist. That may be a good idea, but it was not the idea Congress enacted into law in 1934.

Finally, petitioners earnestly urge that their interpretation of § 203(b) furthers the Communications Act's broad purpose of promoting efficient telephone service. They claim that although the filing requirement prevented price discrimination and unfair practices while AT & T maintained a monopoly over long-distance service, it frustrates those same goals now that there is greater competition in that market. Specifically, they contend that filing costs raise artificial barriers to entry and that the publication of rates facilitates parallel pricing and stifles price competition. We have considerable sympathy with these arguments (though we doubt it makes sense, if one is concerned about the use of filed tariffs to communicate pricing information, to require filing by the dominant carrier, the firm most likely to be a price leader). . . . But our estimations, and the Commission's estimations, of desirable policy cannot alter the meaning of the Federal Communications Act of 1934. For better or worse, the Act establishes a rate-regulation, filed-tariff system for common-carrier communications, and the Commission's desire "to 'increase competition' cannot provide [it] authority to alter the well-established statutory filed rate requirements," Maislin Industries, U.S., Inc. v. Primary Steel, Inc., 497 U.S. 116, 135 (1990). As we observed in the context of a dispute over the filed-rate doctrine more than 80 years ago, "such considerations address themselves to Congress, not to the courts," Armour Packing Co. v. United States, 209 U.S. 56, 82 (1908).

We do not mean to suggest that the tariff-filing requirement is so inviolate that the Commission's existing modification authority does not reach it at all. Certainly the Commission can modify the form, contents, and location of required filings, and can defer filing or perhaps even waive it altogether in limited circumstances. But what we have here goes well beyond that. It is effectively the introduction of a whole new regime of regulation (or of free-market competition), which may well be a better regime but is not the one that Congress established.

The judgment of the Court of Appeals is affirmed.

■ JUSTICE O'CONNOR took no part in the consideration or decision of these cases.

■ JUSTICE STEVENS, with whom JUSTICE BLACKMUN and JUSTICE SOUTER join, dissenting.

The communications industry has an unusually dynamic character. In 1934, Congress authorized the Federal Communications Commission (FCC) to regulate "a field of enterprise the dominant characteristic of which was the rapid pace of its unfolding." National Broadcasting Co. v. United States, 319 U.S. 190, 219 (1943). The Communications Act (the Act) gives the FCC unusually broad discretion to meet new and unanticipated problems in order to fulfill its sweeping mandate "to make available, as far as possible, to all the people of the United States, a rapid, efficient, Nationwide and world-wide wire and radio communication service with adequate facilities at reasonable charges." 47 U.S.C. § 151. This Court's consistent interpretation of the Act has afforded the

Commission ample leeway to interpret and apply its statutory powers and responsibilities. The Court today abandons that approach in favor of a rigid literalism that deprives the FCC of the flexibility Congress meant it to have in order to implement the core policies of the Act in rapidly changing conditions.

I

At the time the Communications Act was passed, the telephone industry was dominated by the American Telephone & Telegraph Company and its affiliates. Title II of the Act, which establishes the framework for FCC regulation of common carriers by wire, was clearly a response to that dominance. As the Senate Report explained, "[u]nder existing provisions of the Interstate Commerce Act the regulation of the telephone monopoly has been practically nil. This vast monopoly which so immediately serves the needs of the people in their daily and social life must be effectively regulated." S. Rep. No. 781, 73d Cong., 2d Sess., 2 (1934).

. . . Congress doubtless viewed the filed rate provisions as an important mechanism to guard against abusive practices by wire communications monopolies. But it is quite wrong to suggest that the mere process of filing rate schedules—rather than the substantive duty of reasonably priced and nondiscriminatory service—is "the heart of the common-carrier section of the federal Communications Act."

II

In response to new conditions in the communications industry, including stirrings of competition in the long-distance telephone market, the FCC in 1979 began reexamining its regulatory scheme. . . .

III

. . . The Commission plausibly concluded that any slight enforcement benefits a tariff-filing requirement might offer were outweighed by the burdens it would put on new entrants and consumers. Thus, the sole question for us is whether the FCC's policy, however sensible, is nonetheless inconsistent with the Act.

In my view, each of the Commission's detariffing orders was squarely within its power to "modify any requirement" of § 203. Subsection 203(b)(2) plainly confers at least some discretion to modify the general rule that carriers file tariffs, for it speaks of "any requirement." Subsection 203(c) of the Act, ignored by the Court, squarely supports the FCC's position; it prohibits carriers from providing service without a tariff "unless otherwise provided by or under authority of this Act." Subsection 203(b)(2) is plainly one provision that "otherwise provides" and thereby authorizes service without a filed schedule. The FCC's authority to modify § 203's requirements in "particular instances" or by "general order applicable to special circumstances or conditions" emphasizes the expansive character of the Commission's authority: modifications may be narrow or broad, depending upon the Commission's appraisal of current conditions. From the vantage of a Congress seeking to regulate an almost completely monopolized industry, the advent of competition is surely a "special circumstance or condition" that might legitimately call for different regulatory treatment.

The only statutory exception to the Commission's modification authority provides that it may not extend the 120-day notice period set out in § 203(b)(1). See § 203(b)(2). The Act thus imposes a specific limit on the Commission's authority to stiffen that regulatory imposition on carriers, but does not confine the Commission's authority to relax it. It was no stretch for the FCC to draw from this single, unidirectional statutory limitation on its modification authority the inference that its authority is otherwise unlimited.

According to the Court, the term "modify," as explicated in all but the most unreliable dictionaries, rules out the Commission's claimed authority to relieve nondominant carriers of the basic obligation to file tariffs. Dictionaries can be useful aids in statutory interpretation, but they are no substitute for close analysis of what words mean as used in a particular statutory context. Even if the sole possible meaning of "modify" were to make "minor" changes, further elaboration is needed to show why the detariffing policy should fail. The Commission came to its present policy through a series of rulings that gradually relaxed the filing requirements for nondominant carriers. Whether the current policy should count as a cataclysmic or merely an incremental departure from the § 203(a) baseline depends on whether one focuses on particular carriers' obligations to file (in which case the Commission's policy arguably works a major shift) or on the statutory policies behind the tariff-filing requirement (which remain satisfied because market constraints on nondominant carriers obviate the need for rate-filing). When § 203 is viewed as part of a statute whose aim is to constrain monopoly power, the Commission's decision to exempt nondominant carriers is a rational and "measured" adjustment to novel circumstances—one that remains faithful to the core purpose of the tariff-filing section. See Black's Law Dictionary 1198 (3d ed. 1933) (defining "modification" as "A change; an alteration which introduces new elements into the details, or cancels some of them, but leaves the general purpose and effect of the subject-matter intact").

The Court seizes upon a particular sense of the word "modify" at the expense of another, long-established meaning that fully supports the Commission's position. That word is first defined in Webster's Collegiate Dictionary 628 (4th ed. 1934) as meaning "to limit or reduce in extent or degree."[5] The Commission's permissive detariffing policy fits comfortably

---

[5]   See also 9 Oxford English Dictionary 952 (2d ed. 1989) ("2. To alter in the direction of moderation or lenity; to make less severe, rigorous, or decided; to qualify, tone down. . . ."); Random House Dictionary of the English Language 1236 (2d ed. 1987) ("5. to reduce or lessen in degree or extent; moderate; soften; to modify one's demands"); Webster's Third New International Dictionary 1452 (1981) ("I: to make more temperate and less extreme: lessen the severity of; . . . 'traffic rules were modified to let him pass' "); Webster's New Collegiate

within this common understanding of the term. The FCC has in effect adopted a general rule stating that "if you are dominant you must file, but if you are nondominant you need not." The Commission's partial detariffing policy—which excuses nondominant carriers from filing on condition that they remain nondominant—is simply a relaxation of a costly regulatory requirement that recent developments had rendered pointless and counterproductive in a certain class of cases.

A modification pursuant to § 203(b)(1), like any other order issued under the Act, must of course be consistent with the purposes of the statute. On this point, the Court asserts that the Act's prohibition against unreasonable and discriminatory rates "would not be susceptible of effective enforcement if rates were not publicly filed." That determination, of course, is for the Commission to make in the first instance. But the Commission has repeatedly explained that (i) a carrier that lacks market power is entirely unlikely to charge unreasonable or discriminatory rates, (ii) the statutory bans on unreasonable charges and price discrimination apply with full force regardless of whether carriers have to file tariffs, (iii) any suspected violations by nondominant carriers can be addressed on the Commission's own motion or on a damages complaint filed pursuant to § 206, and (iv) the FCC can reimpose a tariff requirement should violations occur. The Court does not adequately respond to the FCC's explanations, and gives no reason whatsoever to doubt the Commission's considered judgment that tariff-filing is altogether unnecessary in the case of competitive carriers; the majority's ineffective enforcement argument lacks any evidentiary or historical support.

The filed tariff provisions of the Communications Act are not ends in themselves, but are merely one of several procedural means for the Commission to ensure that carriers do not charge unreasonable or discriminatory rates. The Commission has reasonably concluded that this particular means of enforcing the statute's substantive mandates will prove counterproductive in the case of nondominant long distance carriers. Even if the 1934 Congress did not define the scope of the Commission's modification authority with perfect scholarly precision, this is surely a paradigm case for judicial deference to the agency's interpretation, particularly in a statutory regime so obviously meant to maximize administrative flexibility. Whatever the best reading of § 203(b)(2), the Commission's reading cannot in my view be termed unreasonable. It is informed (as ours is not) by a practical understanding of the role (or lack thereof) that filed tariffs play in the modern regulatory climate and in the telecommunications industry. Since 1979, the FCC has

---

Dictionary 739 (1973) ("I. to make less extreme; MODERATE"); Webster's Seventh New Collegiate Dictionary 544 (1963) (same); Webster's Seventh New International Dictionary 1577 (2d ed. 1934) ("2. To reduce in extent or degree; to moderate; qualify; lower; as, to modify heat, pain, punishment"); N. Webster, American Dictionary of the English Language (1828) ("To moderate; to qualify; to reduce in extent or degree. Of his grace He modifies his first severe decree. *Dryden*").

sought to adapt measures originally designed to control monopoly power to new market conditions. It has carefully and consistently explained that mandatory tariff-filing rules frustrate the core statutory interest in rate reasonableness. The Commission's use of the "discretion" expressly conferred by § 203(b)(2) reflects "a reasonable accommodation of manifestly competing interests and is entitled to deference: the regulatory scheme is technical and complex, the agency considered the matter in a detailed and reasoned fashion, and the decision involves reconciling conflicting policies." Chevron U.S.A. Inc. v. Natural Resources Defense Council, Inc., 467 U.S. 837, 865 (1984). The FCC has permissibly interpreted its § 203(b)(2) authority in service of the goals Congress set forth in the Communications Act. We should sustain its eminently sound, experience-tested, and uncommonly well explained judgment.

I respectfully dissent.

NOTES ON THE RELATIONSHIP BETWEEN CHEVRON AND THE THEORIES AND TOOLS OF STATUTORY INTERPRETATION

(1) *How Do Various Modes of Statutory Interpretation Bear on the Chevron Doctrine?* In their respective opinions in the MCI case, both Justice Scalia and Justice Stevens claim to be faithful to Chevron—Justice Scalia in his conclusion that he should not defer to the FCC's interpretation because "it goes beyond the meaning that the statute can bear" and Justice Stevens in his that "the FCC has permissibly interpreted" its statutory authority. Chevron made statutory meaning—clear or ambiguous—the doctrinal gatekeeper to judicial deference and referred to "traditional tools of statutory construction." But there is more than one traditional tool, and whether "the intent of Congress is clear" may look different when seen through different tools.

While statutory interpretation, like common-law case analysis, is a complex and to some extent artistic endeavor, the recent literature tends to separate the possible approaches into three broad categories. (You have already delved into this if you studied Chapter II.) The first, known as textualism, emphasizes the words specifically included in the statute. The second, known as purposivism, emphasizes what Congress was trying to do when it passed the statute. And the third, known as pragmatism, emphasizes the meaning that will produce the best practical result (dynamic statutory intereptation, which is in some respects a variant of pragmatic interpretation, is also sometimes identified as a fourth category in its own right, see Chapter II, Sec. 2.c). Chevron, when it is applicable, would seem to say that the third method is for the agency and not the courts, but that still leaves judges a choice between the other two.

To some extent the disagreement between these camps turns on different views of how Congress acts. Textualists tend to emphasize the bargaining nature of the legislative process, with the only definitely-agreed-to item being the final text, while purposivists emphasize more the public issues that provided the impetus for legislating in the first place. Correspondingly, the two groups have differed on the use to be made of Committee Reports, floor debates, and other sources of "legislative history." See Ch. II, Sec. 3.e. Perhaps more important, however, is what unites them: both textualists and purposivists claim to be faithful to the statute Congress has passed. As such, both groups also claim to be faithful to the judge's role as set out in Chevron. Which produces what is, for lawyers and also for students, perhaps the most important point: neither view has succeeded in triumphing over the other. While textualism has become more important in the last quarter century than it was in the half-century before that, variants of both approaches are constantly in play in the judicial review of agency action. (And there remains the suspicion among some observers that the method of selecting what will, in the judges' views, produce the best practical result still accounts for many of the cases.)

This situation persists even on the Supreme Court because, as ABBE R. GLUCK points out in THE STATES AS LABORATORIES OF STATUTORY INTERPRETATION, 119 Yale L.J. 1750, 1765–66 (2010): "[T]he Court does not give stare decisis effect to *any* statements of statutory interpretation methodology. The interpretive rule used in one case ('purpose trumps text' or 'committee statements are not reliable legislative history') is not viewed as 'law' for the next case. The Justices appear not to believe that they can bind other Justices' (and future Justices') methodological choices. Scholars across the spectrum who divide on the question of whether this way of approaching statutory interpretation is problematic nevertheless all agree both that a single controlling approach does not currently exist and that prior methodological statements do not carry into future cases with the force of precedent."

(2) *How Far Does Purpose Go at Step One?* ZUNI PUBLIC SCHOOLS DISTRICT NO. 89 V. DEPARTMENT OF EDUCATION, 550 U.S. 81 (2007): Public schools in the United States are typically funded at the local level, supplemented by aid from state governments. The federal government's Impact Aid Act also provides assistance to local school districts whose budgets are impacted by a large federal presence—because, for example, there is a large amount of federal land exempt from local taxation or because a military installation increases the number of school-age children. To make this assistance real at the local level, the federal statute prohibits the states from reducing their aid to the same districts. But if the state's aid program is intended to equalize per-pupil expenditures among districts—if, that is, it is meant to accomplish a purpose that overlaps with the purpose of the federal program—then the states can offset their aid to account for the federal aid.

To implement the Act, it thus becomes important to know whether a state aid program counts as a scheme that equalizes expenditures among local districts. A 1974 statute instructed the Secretary of Education to adopt regulations defining what would count as "equalizing expenditures" by state governments, and the Secretary promptly did so. These regulations provided for a comparison of expenditures—after state aid—between the best funded and poorest districts in the state, to see if expenditures were being equalized.

In doing so, the regulations excluded from consideration statistical outliers: the districts containing the 5% of students in the state for whom the least was spent and those containing the 5% for whom most was spent.

In 1994, at the Secretary's instance, Congress reenacted this body of legislation. Now the statute itself required the Secretary of Education, in making the needed calculations, to

> disregard local educational agencies with per-pupil expenditures or revenues above the 95th percentile or below the 5th percentile of such expenditures or revenues in the State. 20 U.S.C. § 7709(b)(2)(B)(i).

It is the meaning of this language that was at stake in this case.

In Justice Breyer's words, 550 U.S. at 91: "No one at the time—no Member of Congress, no Department of Education official, no school district or state—expressed the view that this statutory language (which, after all, was supplied by the Secretary) was intended to require, or did require, the Secretary to change the Department's system of calculation, a system that the Department and school districts across the Nation had followed for nearly 20 years, without (as far as we are told) any adverse effect." And so, after enactment, the Department did not change its regulations. It continued to construe the relevant percentiles (above the 95th or below the 5th) to cut off 5% of the number of students (in however many school districts were needed to make that total). In actual practice in New Mexico, which had 89 school districts, the Department excluded the 17 richest districts and the 6 poorest districts; compared the top per-pupil expenditure in the remaining 66 districts with the bottom per-pupil expenditure; found that those expenditures were close enough to count, under the regulations, as equalized; and according allowed New Mexico to reduce its state aid to those districts receiving federal aid.

But the challengers (Zuni Public Schools District) said that the new statutory language did not permit this method of calculation. In their view, it compelled the agency to cut off the richest or poorest 5% of the number of districts, without regard to how many students were in those districts. If this had been done, 5 districts would have been cut off at each end of the distribution; the disparities among the remaining 79 districts would have been greater than what the regulations counted as equalized, and the state would not be entitled to reduce its aid to those districts receiving federal aid.

The Court, in an opinion by Justice Breyer, sustained the Department's regulation as constituting "a reasonable, hence permissible, implementation of the statute. See Chevron." (550 U.S. at 100.) For Justice Scalia, dissenting, "The plain language of the federal Impact Aid statute clearly and unambiguously forecloses the Secretary of Education's preferred methodology. . . . Her selection of that methodology is therefore entitled to zero deference under Chevron." (550 U.S. at 108.)

A large part of the opinions in this case discuss, not surprisingly, the meaning of the words Congress used in the text quoted above—including the implications of "per" in "per-pupil" and the proper referent of "such." But the Justices also exhibited a flurry of approaches to statutory construction. As a result, the opinions offer a rich exploration into the role that a purposive—as opposed to a textualist—approach may play in determining whether Congress has spoken to the precise question at issue or whether the statute is ambiguous, such that the agency's interpretation may be eligible for Chevron deference and whether, in the event of ambiguity, the agency's interpretation is a permissible one that commands deference.

JUSTICE BREYER'S opinion, after stating the facts, began as follows, 550 U.S. at 89–91:

> Zuni's strongest argument rests upon the literal language of the statute. Zuni concedes, as it must, that if the language of the statute is open or ambiguous—that is, if Congress left a "gap" for the agency to fill—then we must uphold the Secretary's interpretation as long as it is reasonable. See Chevron. For purposes of exposition, we depart from a normal order of discussion, namely an order that first considers Zuni's statutory language argument. Instead, because of the technical nature of the language in question, we shall first examine the provision's background and basic purposes. That discussion will illuminate our subsequent analysis. It will also reveal why Zuni concentrates its argument upon language alone.

> Considerations other than language provide us with unusually strong indications that Congress intended to leave the Secretary free to use the calculation method before us and that the Secretary's chosen method is a reasonable one. For one thing, the matter at issue—*i.e.,* the calculation method for determining whether a state aid program "equalizes expenditures"—is the kind of highly technical, specialized interstitial matter that Congress often does not decide itself, but delegates to specialized agencies to decide. . . .

> For another thing, the history of the statute strongly supports the Secretary. . . .

> Finally, viewed in terms of the purpose of the statute's disregard instruction, the Secretary's calculation method is reasonable, while the reasonableness of a method based upon the number of districts alone (Zuni's proposed method) is more doubtful. . . .

Only after deciding that the Secretary's method was "reasonable" in light of "the history and purpose" of the statute did he then say:

> But what of the provision's literal language? The matter is important, for normally neither the legislative history nor the reasonableness of the Secretary's method would be determinative if the plain language of the statute unambiguously indicated that Congress sought to foreclose the Secretary's interpretation. And Zuni argues that the Secretary's formula could not possibly effectuate Congress' intent since the statute's language literally forbids the Secretary to use such a method. Under this Court's precedents, if the intent of Congress is clear and unambiguously

expressed by the statutory language at issue, that would be the end of our analysis. See Chevron. A customs statute that imposes a tariff on "clothing" does not impose a tariff on automobiles, no matter how strong the policy arguments for treating the two kinds of goods alike. But we disagree with Zuni's conclusion, for we believe that the Secretary's method falls within the scope of the statute's plain language.

JUSTICE KENNEDY, joined by Justice Alito, concurring in the opinion, had this to say about Justice Breyer's approach, 550 U.S. at 107:

> In this case, the Court is correct to find that the plain language of the statute is ambiguous. It is proper, therefore, to invoke Chevron's rule of deference. The opinion of the Court, however, inverts Chevron's logical progression. Were the inversion to become systemic, it would create the impression that agency policy concerns, rather than the traditional tools of statutory construction, are shaping the judicial interpretation of statutes. It is our obligation to set a good example; and so, in my view, it would have been preferable, and more faithful to Chevron, to arrange the opinion differently. Still, we must give deference to the author of an opinion in matters of exposition; and because the point does not affect the outcome, I join the Court's opinion.

But that didn't satisfy JUSTICE SCALIA, joined by Chief Justice Roberts, Justice Thomas, and in part by Justice Souter, dissenting, 550 U.S. at 108:

> In Church of the Holy Trinity v. United States, 143 U.S. 457 (1892), this Court conceded that a church's act of contracting with a prospective rector fell within the plain meaning of a federal labor statute, but nevertheless did not apply the statute to the church: "It is a familiar rule," the Court pronounced, "that a thing may be within the letter of the statute and yet not within the statute, because not within its spirit, nor within the intention of its makers." *Id.*, at 459. That is a judge-empowering proposition if there ever was one, and in the century since, the Court has wisely retreated from it, in words if not always in actions. But today Church of the Holy Trinity arises, Phoenix-like, from the ashes. The Court's contrary assertions aside, today's decision is nothing other than the elevation of judge-supposed legislative intent over clear statutory text.

The very structure of the Court's opinion provides an obvious clue as to what is afoot. . . .

To which JUSTICE STEVENS (who concurred with Breyer) responded, 550 U.S. at 105–07:

> . . . [Justice Scalia] correctly observes that a judicial decision that departs from statutory text may represent "policy-driven interpretation." As long as that driving policy is faithful to the intent of Congress (or, as in this case, aims only to give effect to such intent)—which it must be if it is to override a strict interpretation of the text—the decision is also a correct

performance of the judicial function. Justice Scalia's argument today rests on the incorrect premise that every policy-driven interpretation implements a judge's personal view of sound policy, rather than a faithful attempt to carry out the will of the legislature. Quite the contrary is true of the work of the judges with whom I have worked for many years. If we presume that our judges are intellectually honest—as I do—there is no reason to fear "policy-driven interpretation[s]" of Acts of Congress.

In Chevron we acknowledged that when "the intent of Congress is clear [from the statutory text], that is the end of the matter." But we also made quite clear that "administrative constructions which are contrary to clear congressional intent" must be rejected. In that unanimous opinion, we explained: "If a court, employing traditional tools of statutory construction, ascertains that Congress had an intention on the precise question at issue, that intention is the law and must be given effect."

Analysis of legislative history is, of course, a traditional tool of statutory construction. There is no reason why we must confine ourselves to, or begin our analysis with, the statutory text if other tools of statutory construction provide better evidence of congressional intent with respect to the precise point at issue.

As the Court's opinion demonstrates, this is a quintessential example of a case in which the statutory text was obviously enacted to adopt the rule that the Secretary administered both before and after the enactment of the rather confusing language found in 20 U.S.C. § 7709(b)(2)(B)(i). That text is sufficiently ambiguous to justify the Court's exegesis, but my own vote is the product of a more direct route to the Court's patently correct conclusion. This happens to be a case in which the legislative history is pellucidly clear and the statutory text is difficult to fathom. Moreover, it is a case in which I cannot imagine anyone accusing any Member of the Court of voting one way or the other because of that Justice's own policy preferences.

Given the clarity of the evidence of Congress' "intention on the precise question at issue," I would affirm the judgment of the Court of Appeals even if I thought that petitioners' literal reading of the statutory text was correct. The only "policy" by which I have been driven is that which this Court has endorsed on repeated occasions regarding the importance of remaining faithful to Congress' intent.

To which, JUSTICE SCALIA, 550 U.S. at 116–17:

Justice Stevens is quite candid on the point: He is willing to contradict the text. But Justice Steven's candor should not make his philosophy seem unassuming. He maintains that it is "a correct performance of the judicial function" to "override a strict interpretation of the text" so long as policy-driven interpretation "is faithful to the intent of Congress." But once one departs from "strict interpretation of the text" (by which Justice Stevens means the actual meaning of the text) fidelity to the intent of Congress is a chancy thing. The only thing we know for certain both Houses of Congress (and the President, if he signed the legislation) agreed upon is the text. Legislative history can never produce a "pellucidly clear" picture of what a law was "intended" to mean, for the simple reason that it is never voted upon-or ordinarily even seen or heard-by the "intending" lawgiving entity, which consists of both Houses of Congress and the President (if he did not veto the bill). See U.S. Const., Art. I, §§ 1, 7. Thus, what judges believe Congress "meant" (apart from the text) has a disturbing but entirely unsurprising tendency to be whatever judges think Congress *must* have meant, *i.e., should* have meant. . . . [T]he system of judicial amendatory veto over texts duly adopted by Congress bears no resemblance to the system of lawmaking set forth in our Constitution.

Justice Stevens takes comfort in the fact that this is a case in which he "cannot imagine anyone accusing any Member of the Court of voting one way or the other because of that Justice's own policy preferences." I can readily imagine it, given that the Court's opinion begins with a lengthy description of why the system its judgment approves is the *better* one. But even assuming that, in this rare case, the Justices' departure from the enacted law has nothing to do with their policy view that it is a bad law, nothing in Justice Stevens' separate opinion limits his approach to such rarities. Why should we suppose that in matters more likely to arouse the judicial libido-voting rights, antidiscrimination laws, or environmental protection, to name only a few-a judge in the School of Textual Subversion would not find it convenient (yea, *righteous!*) to assume that Congress *must* have meant, not what it said, but what he knows to be best?

To which (perhaps), JUSTICE BREYER, 550 U.S. at 98:

The remainder of the dissent's argument, colorful language to the side, rests upon a reading of the statutory language that ignores its basic purpose and history.

And finally, JUSTICE SOUTER (who, like Justice Scalia, was in dissent), 550 U.S. at 123:

I agree with the Court that Congress probably intended, or at least understood, that the Secretary would continue to follow the methodology devised prior to passage of the current statute in 1994. But . . . I find the statutory language unambiguous and inapt to authorize that methodology, and I therefore [dissent].

(3) ***More on Legislative History and Chevron.*** Is legislative history relevant to the step one inquiry? The opinions in *Zuni* just excerpted take differing positions on that question. JUDGE KAREN LECRAFT HENDERSON offers some reasons for so using legislative history in her concurring opinion in COUNCIL FOR UROLOGICAL INTERESTS V. BURWELL, 790 F.3d. 212, 230–31 (D.C. Cir. 2015): "Much ink has been spilled on the propriety of using legislative history to cloud a clear text under Chevron. See, e.g., Zuni Pub.

Sch. Dist. No. 89 v. Dep't of Educ., 550 U.S. 81, 90 (2007); id. at 105–06 & n. 2 (Stevens, J., concurring); id. at 108 (Scalia, J., dissenting); see also Halbig v. Burwell, 758 F.3d 390, 406 (D.C. Cir. 2014) (identifying 'a fork in our precedent' on this issue), reh'g en banc granted, judgment vacated, No. 14–5018, 2014 WL 4627181 (D.C. Cir. Sept. 4, 2014). But the converse—consulting legislative history to clarify an ambiguous text—ought to be uncontroversial. The chief objection to legislative history is that it can be undemocratic: the Congress qua Congress approves only the text of a statute and the legislative history might reflect a distinctly minority view. See Exxon Mobil Corp. v. Allapattah Servs., Inc., 545 U.S. 546, 568 (2005). In the Chevron context, however, a failure to consult legislative history would leave the text ambiguous and thereby transfer authority to an administrative agency, whose democratic accountability is nil. See Free Enter. Fund v. PCAOB, 561 U.S. 477, 499 (2010) ('The growth of the Executive Branch . . . heightens the concern that it may slip from the Executive's control, and thus from that of the people.'). And at least some types of legislative history 'shed a reliable light on' the views of a majority of the enacting Congress. Allapattah Servs., 545 U.S. at 568; see also Simpson v. United States, 435 U.S. 6, 17 (1978) (Rehnquist, J., dissenting) ('[S]ome types of legislative history are substantially more reliable than others. The report of a joint conference committee of both Houses of Congress, for example, . . . is accorded a good deal more weight than the remarks . . . on the floor of the chamber.'). Legislative history is also criticized for being 'murky, ambiguous, and contradictory,' an exercise of 'looking over a crowd and picking out your friends.' Allapattah Servs., 545 U.S. at 568. But again, this criticism loses force under Chevron. If legislative history is 'ambiguous'—i.e., if both the petitioner and the agency have 'friends' they can pick out—then, by definition, the agency prevails under Chevron Step One. See, e.g., Catawba Cnty., 571 F.3d at 38. Sometimes, however, the legislative history is clear, reliable and uncontroverted; if it is, we would be wrong to ignore it."

Even some who support the use of legislative history, however, have suggested that there are limits to how it may be used at step one. For example, Justice Kagan in Milner v. Department of Navy, 562 U.S. 562 (2011), writing for the Court, explains: "Those of us who make use of legislative history believe that clear evidence of congressional intent may illuminate ambiguous text. We will not take the opposite tack of allowing ambiguous legislative history to muddy clear statutory language." But notice the artful dodge: may clear legislative history render ambiguous what otherwise seems like clear text?

And what about step two? Is legislative history particularly relevant at that stage, if only because it may require the agency to explain how its favored interpretation is a reasonable one insofar as that interpretation deviates from strong indications of legislative intent reflected in the legislative history? Again, the opinions at *Zuni* address that issue. Does it make more sense to consider legislative history at Step Two then Step One? Or, is Step Two more about policy than law, such that legislative history is of more relevance at the first of Chevron's steps. For a general discussion of the role that legislative history plays within the Chevron framework, see

John F. Manning, Chevron and Legislative History, 82 Geo. Wash. L. Rev. 1517 (2014).

(4) ***Systemic Consequences of Various Interpretive Approaches under Chevron?*** Is one or another interpretive method more likely to produce Chevron deference? Consider THOMAS W. MERRILL, TEXTUALISM AND THE FUTURE OF THE *CHEVRON* DOCTRINE, 72 Wash. U. L.Q. 351, 354, 372–73 (1994):

". . . [T]extualism triumphant would lead to a permanent subordination of the Chevron doctrine.

"This has to do with the style of judging associated with textualism. Intentionalism mandates an 'archeological' excavation of the past, producing opinions written in the style of the dry archivist sifting through countless documents in search of the tell-tale smoking gun of congressional intent. Textualism, in contrast, seems to transform statutory interpretation into a kind of exercise in judicial ingenuity. The textualist judge treats questions of interpretation like a puzzle to which it is assumed there is one right answer. The task is to assemble the various pieces of linguistic data, dictionary definitions, and canons into the best (most coherent, most explanatory) account of the meaning of the statute. This exercise places a great premium on cleverness. In one case the outcome turns on the placement of a comma, in another on the inconsistency between a comma and rules of grammar, in a third on the conflict between quotation marks and the language of the text. One day arguments must be advanced in support of broad dictionary definitions; the next day in support of narrow dictionary definitions. New canons of construction and clear statement rules must be invented and old ones reinterpreted.

"This active, creative approach to interpretation is subtly incompatible with an attitude of deference toward other institutions—whether the other institution is Congress or an administrative agency. In effect, the textualist interpreter does not *find* the meaning of the statute so much as *construct* the meaning. Such a person will very likely experience some difficulty in deferring to the meanings that other institutions have developed.

". . . By changing the focus from what Congress intended to what the ordinary reader would understand, textualism adopts, at least implicitly, a model of the court as an autonomous interpreter, applying its own judicially prescribed conventions and canons for understanding the code that Congress has built up over the years. Once the Court grows comfortable with the autonomous interpreter model, its creativity in matters of statutory interpretation begins to expand apace, exemplified perhaps most clearly by the proliferating use of canons.

"Whatever the explanation for the active, creative style associated with textualism, it is fair to say that this attitude is out of sync with the Chevron doctrine, based as it is on a generalized model of the courts as faithful agents of the politically accountable branches of government. To the extent this change in style explains what appears to be an inverse relationship between the rise of textualism and the waning of Chevron, it suggests that the eclipse of the deference doctrine is likely to last as long as textualism remains dominant."

(5) A study of the Courts of Appeals cases that relied on Chevron in 1995 and 1996 tried to test the prediction that judges from different interpretive schools would apply Chevron differently—to test, that is, whether "textualist" judges would be less likely to find ambiguity under the first part of the Chevron test. Judges appointed by Presidents Reagan and Bush, who presumably were more likely to be textualist than those appointed by Presidents Carter and Clinton, in fact found ambiguity at very nearly the same rate as the other group; no statistically significant differences were found. ORIN S. KERR, SHEDDING LIGHT ON *CHEVRON*: AN EMPIRICAL STUDY OF THE *CHEVRON* DOCTRINE IN THE U.S. COURTS OF APPEALS, 15 Yale J. on Reg. I, 42 (1998). The author comments, 15 Yale J. on Reg. at 57–59:

"I propose that [the prediction] errs by understating the degree to which theories of statutory interpretation are normative, rather than descriptive. I submit that jurists internalize interpretative norms based on their largely intuitive understandings of the proper role of the judiciary in a constitutional democracy, not on their personal answer to the hermeneutic question of how much meaning can be extracted from text. Roughly speaking, those judges who follow text more closely tend to profess a belief in a more limited, rule-following judiciary, while those who endorse a more dynamic interpretative method tend to appreciate judicial rule-making power. Whether a judge advocates or rejects textualism does not reflect the judge's capacity to find more or less meaning in text. Instead, it means that the judge believes that the body politic is better served by judges who try more or less hard to find what meaning may be there.

"The reason that [the prediction] fails in the Chevron context, then, is that Chevron asks judges an interpretive question in a context that disrupts the usual relationship between the outcomes served and the political theories that typically inform judges' interpretive methods. Chevron upsets the usual relationship between interpretation and the judicial role in two ways. First, statutory ambiguity no longer expands judicial power; it constricts it, limiting the judicial role to deferential review for unreasonableness. Conversely, finding meaning in the text no longer limits judicial power; it expands it by granting to the courts plenary review of administrative action. Second, Chevron transforms a judge's degree of commitment to the text from a means of allocating power between the legislature and the judiciary (its usual function) into a means of allocating power between the judiciary and the executive. Finding meaning in the text no longer enhances the power of the legislature over the judiciary; instead, it emphasizes the power of the judiciary over the executive. I propose that these disruptions of the typical association between interpretative method and the judicial role explains why judges do not approach Chevron's first step with their usual interpretive associations intact. Chevron's atypical interpretive context in effect suspends judges' normative associations between their approaches to text and political theory.

"Consider the case of a judge who adopts an expansive view of the judicial function and believes that the proper judicial role is to ensure that the broad policy concerns of Congress are carried out in a fair and just way. Because textualism requires a judge to adhere to text instead of purpose and justice, the judge would likely eschew textualism and instead find that most texts were ambiguous enough to allow the judge to fashion a just remedy. In the Chevron context, however, the ambiguity that would normally allow the judge to fashion a just remedy backfires. A finding of ambiguity instead binds the judge to accept a wide range of agency action, even if the judge perceives that action as unjust. Ambiguity ceases to be an engine of judicial authority and becomes an engine of uncabined executive power.

"In the absence of the usual forces pulling and pushing judges toward different interpretive approaches, judges who typically are influenced by very different normative interpretive traditions adopt roughly equivalent understandings of how ambiguous is ambiguous enough at step one. This does not mean that all judges will agree in every case, of course (although most cases are unanimous), but it does mean that no one set of judges will be led to adopt a particularly different vision of Chevron."

NOTES ON CHEVRON AND DEFERENCE TO MAJOR POLICY CHANGES

(1) *Is the MCI Case Really Driven Only by Its Approach to Statutory Interpretation?* PETER STRAUSS, ON RESEGREGATING THE WORLDS OF STATUTE AND COMMON LAW, 1994 Sup. Ct. Rev. pp. 429, 495–97: "Perhaps the root issue for Justice Scalia [in the MCI case] is one of delegation—a factor that has been important to him in other contexts. It is not merely the largeness of the change being effected, but also that accepting it will entail accepting that an agency can be empowered to change its mandate. For Justice Stevens, author of striking passages in Chevron strongly endorsing delegation, the FCC has 'unusually broad discretion to meet new and unanticipated problems in order to fulfill its sweeping mandate'; this power to 'modify' is no different in kind from the Commission's responsibility to allocate licenses and otherwise act in accordance with 'public convenience, interest, or necessity.' Justice Scalia accepts broad delegations only because he cannot imagine a judicially manageable standard for telling the good from the bad, a handicap he does not face if he can plausibly construe an agency's authority in a narrow way. It is revealing in this respect that he never explains how he concludes that the New Deal Congress that so broadly empowered all the agencies it created, not just the FCC, intended here only a narrow grant of authority.

"The result, in any event, is essentially formal and text-bound. Whether the FCC has rightly caught the implications of new market conditions and adapted its regulatory regime to them are not issues for the Court. '[O]ur estimations, and the Commission's estimations, of desirable policy cannot alter the meaning of the Federal Communications Act of 1934. . . . [A] whole new regime of regulation (or of free-market competition) . . . may well be a better regime but is not the one that Congress established.' Of course, the validity of the 'but is not' clause depends on one's conclusions about the meaning of 'modify,' one's general estimation of the breadth of authority Congress bestowed on the Commission, and also on one's acceptance or not of agency and/or judicial authority to follow Congress's lead by using existing text to adapt law to changing circumstances. . . . Looking to the general climate of change, in regulation and in technology, it is hard to imagine that the FCC erred. The general trend of legislation, the absence of any legislative effort to correct the Commission, indeed the Commission's dogged persistence in its deregulatory course despite prior discouragement from the courts—all suggest that this was the right reading. It was one that both ancient and contemporary understandings of 'modify' would permit. The insistence that Congress unmistakably act tends, again, to deny the coherence-building judicial function."

(2) *Chevron and the Tobacco Litigation.* "In 1996, the Food and Drug Administration (FDA), after having expressly disavowed any such authority since its inception, asserted jurisdiction to regulate tobacco products." So began FDA v. BROWN & WILLIAMSON TOBACCO CORP., 529 U.S. 120 (2000). The Food, Drug and Cosmetic Act (FDCA), the opinion continued, 529 U.S. at 126–27, "grants the FDA . . . the authority to regulate, among other items, 'drugs' and 'devices.' The Act defines 'drug' to include 'articles (other than food) intended to affect the structure or any function of the body.' It defines 'device,' in part, as 'an instrument, apparatus, implement, machine, contrivance, . . . or other similar or related article, including any component, part, or accessory, which is . . . intended to affect the structure or any function of the body.' The Act also grants the FDA the authority to regulate so-called 'combination products,' which 'constitute a combination of a drug, device, or biological product.' " In the rulemaking under review, "[t]he FDA determined that nicotine is a 'drug' and that cigarettes and smokeless tobacco are 'drug delivery devices,' and therefore it had jurisdiction under the FDCA to regulate tobacco products."

The opinion by JUSTICE O'CONNOR for five members of the court held that the FDA's assertion of jurisdiction was unwarranted. First, the FDCA was premised on ensuring that drugs were either safe or taken off the market. The FDA's own approach to cigarettes—involving regulation of advertising, labeling, and promotion, but not banning sale to adults—would do neither. "The inescapable conclusion is that there is no room for tobacco products within the FDCA's regulatory scheme." Second, since 1965 Congress had enacted six statutes regarding tobacco, each time acting on the premise, supported by the FDA at the time, that the FDA lacked jurisdiction. "Under these circumstances, it is clear that Congress' tobacco-specific legislation has effectively ratified the FDA's previous position that it lacks jurisdiction to regulate tobacco." She continued (529 U.S. at 159–161):

"Finally, our inquiry into whether Congress has directly spoken to the precise question at issue is shaped, at least in some measure, by the nature of the question presented. Deference under Chevron to an agency's construction of a statute that it administers is premised on the theory that a statute's ambiguity constitutes an implicit delegation from Congress to the agency to fill in the statutory gaps. In extraordinary cases, however, there may be reason to hesitate before concluding that Congress has intended such an implicit delegation.

"This is hardly an ordinary case. Contrary to its representations to Congress since 1914, the FDA has now asserted jurisdiction to regulate an industry constituting a significant portion of the American economy.... Owing to its unique place in American history and society, tobacco has its own unique political history. Congress, for better or for worse, has created a distinct regulatory scheme for tobacco products, squarely rejected proposals to give the FDA jurisdiction over tobacco, and repeatedly acted to preclude any agency from exercising significant policymaking authority in the area. Given this history and the breadth of the authority that the FDA has asserted, we are obliged to defer not to the agency's expansive construction of the statute, but to Congress' consistent judgment to deny the FDA this power.

"Our decision in MCI Telecommunications Corp. v. American Telephone & Telegraph Co., 512 U.S. 218 (1994), is instructive. That case involved the proper construction of the term 'modify' in § 203(b) of the Communications Act of 1934. The FCC contended that, because the Act gave it the discretion to 'modify any requirement' imposed under the statute, it therefore possessed the authority to render voluntary the otherwise mandatory requirement that long distance carriers file their rates. We rejected the FCC's construction, finding 'not the slightest doubt' that Congress had directly spoken to the question. In reasoning even more apt here, we concluded that '[i]t is highly unlikely that Congress would leave the determination of whether an industry will be entirely, or even substantially, rate-regulated to agency discretion—and even more unlikely that it would achieve that through such a subtle device as permission to "modify" rate-filing requirements.'

"As in MCI, we are confident that Congress could not have intended to delegate a decision of such economic and political significance to an agency in so cryptic a fashion. To find that the FDA has the authority to regulate tobacco products, one must not only adopt an extremely strained understanding of 'safety' as it is used throughout the Act—a concept central to the FDCA's regulatory scheme—but also ignore the plain implication of Congress' subsequent tobacco-specific legislation. It is therefore clear, based on the FDCA's overall regulatory scheme and the subsequent tobacco legislation that Congress has directly spoken to the question at issue and precluded the FDA from regulating tobacco products."

Compare JUSTICE BREYER'S dissent for four (529 U.S. at 190–91):

"[O]ne might claim that courts, when interpreting statutes, should assume in close cases that a decision with 'enormous social consequences' should be made by democratically elected Members of Congress rather than by unelected agency administrators. Cf. Kent v. Dulles, 357 U.S. 116, 129 (1958) (assuming Congress did not want to delegate the power to make rules interfering with exercise of basic human liberties). If there is such a background canon of interpretation, however, I do not believe it controls the outcome here.

"Insofar as the decision to regulate tobacco reflects the policy of an administration, it is a decision for which that administration, and those politically elected officials who support it, must (and will) take responsibility.

And the very importance of the decision taken here, as well as its attendant publicity, means that the public is likely to be aware of it and to hold those officials politically accountable. Presidents, just like Members of Congress, are elected by the public. Indeed, the President and Vice President are the only public officials whom the entire Nation elects. I do not believe that an administrative agency decision of this magnitude—one that is important, conspicuous, and controversial—can escape the kind of public scrutiny that is essential in any democracy. And such a review will take place whether it is the Congress or the Executive Branch that makes the relevant decision."

Whichever view you favor, is MCI now to be understood as precedent only for a certain type of situation? If so, does it represent purposive reasoning in a textualist disguise? How would you characterize Justice Scalia's pithy aphorism in Whitman v. American Trucking Associations, Inc., 531 U.S. 457, 468 (2001), p. 791, for which he cited MCI as well as Brown and Williamson: "Congress, we have held, does not alter the fundamental details of a regulatory scheme in vague terms or ancillary provisions—it does not, one might say, hide elephants in mouseholes."

(3)   *Chevron and the Affordable Care Act (ACA):* In KING V. BURWELL, 135 S.Ct. 2480 (2015) (set out at p. 97), the Court refused to extend Chevron deference to the IRS's regulation interpreting the ACA's tax-credit provision—despite the ACA's express grant of authority to the IRS to 'prescribe such regulations as may be necessary to carry out' the ACA's tax credits. CHIEF JUSTICE ROBERTS wrote for the Court, 135 S.Ct. at 2488–89: "When analyzing an agency's interpretation of a statute, we often apply the two-step framework announced in Chevron, 467 U.S. 837. Under that framework, we ask whether the statute is ambiguous and, if so, whether the agency's interpretation is reasonable. Id., at 842–843. This approach 'is premised on the theory that a statute's ambiguity constitutes an implicit delegation from Congress to the agency to fill in the statutory gaps.' FDA v. Brown & Williamson Tobacco Corp., 529 U.S. 120, 159 (2000). 'In extraordinary cases, however, there may be reason to hesitate before concluding that Congress has intended such an implicit delegation.' Ibid.

"This is one of those cases. The tax credits are among the Act's key reforms, involving billions of dollars in spending each year and affecting the price of health insurance for millions of people. Whether those credits are available on Federal Exchanges is thus a question of deep 'economic and political significance' that is central to this statutory scheme; had Congress wished to assign that question to an agency, it surely would have done so expressly. Utility Air Regulatory Group v. EPA, 573 U.S. ___, ___ (2014) (slip op., at 19) (quoting Brown & Williamson, 529 U.S., at 160). It is especially unlikely that Congress would have delegated this decision to the IRS, which has no expertise in crafting health insurance policy of this sort. See Gonzales v. Oregon, 546 U.S. 243, 266–267 (2006). This is not a case for the IRS.

"It is instead our task to determine the correct reading of Section 36B. If the statutory language is plain, we must enforce it according to its terms. Hardt v. Reliance Standard Life Ins. Co., 560 U.S. 242, 251 (2010). But oftentimes the 'meaning—or ambiguity—of certain words or phrases may only become evident when placed in context.' Brown & Williamson, 529 U.S., at 132. So when deciding whether the language is plain, we must read the words 'in their context and with a view to their place in the overall statutory scheme.' Id., at 133. Our duty, after all, is 'to construe statutes, not isolated provisions.' Graham County Soil and Water Conservation Dist. v. United States ex rel. Wilson, 559 U.S. 280, 290 (2010)."

Is this the kind of question that is so important that it would have to have been delegated expressly to any agency in order to trigger the Chevron test? Or is Chief Justice Roberts saying that the problem is just that the question concerned health policy, and so the IRS could not be presumed to have been delegated the power to resolve this particular question? And what does Chief Justice Roberts mean by delegated "expressly"?

Chief Justice Roberts goes on to determine that the crucial piece of statutory text at issue in King v. Burwell is "ambiguous" and then says: "Given that the text is ambiguous, we must turn to the broader structure of the Act to determine the meaning of [the disputed section]." Given that structure, he then identifies what he calls the "fair reading" of the Act. Is he saying that, if deference were warranted, we would be using Chevron Step Two? Or is he suggesting that, in the end, this case really was a Step One case, even though the clear meaning of the statute required a lot of interpretive work in order to unearth it? Is "ambiguous" itself an ambiguous term?

NOTES ON CHEVRON AND THE APPROACH AGENCIES SHOULD USE WHEN INTERPRETING STATUTES

Does Chevron Have Implications for How Agencies Should Interpret Statutes? Chevron said that within the possible meanings of a statute, a reviewing court should accept any reasonable meaning given by the agency. As the MCI case emphasizes, what the universe of reasonable meanings might be is, within the Chevron framework, a question for the courts to decide. But Chevron did not discuss how the agency was to do its own interpretive work or how it was to choose among the reasonable meanings, and the issue has only slowly been recognized as an important feature of the post-Chevron landscape. Three possibilities might be suggested, none of which is without its difficulties:

(1) The agency could act as if it were a court interpreting the language in question without regard to the Chevron doctrine. In other words, the agency could ask what is the best interpretation of the statute that Congress wrote, using the same types of interpretive methods used by courts in handling statutes that are not administered by any agency. This would have the virtue of making "statutory interpretation" a unified subject, whether done by court or agency. But it is subject to several objections. First, insofar as the agency is asked to simply mimic what a court would do, the reasons for having a court defer to the agency's conclusion—that is, the Chevron principle—seem doubtful. Second, in many of the cases arising under Chevron Step Two— cases of statutory ambiguity—there may not be enough materials to make interpretation of the judicial sort more than a flip-a-coin proposition. Finally, and most importantly, this approach fails to take account of the different

institutional roles of courts and agencies. For example, as pointed out in JERRY MASHAW, NORMS, PRACTICES AND THE PARADOX OF DEFERENCE: A PRELIMINARY INQUIRY INTO AGENCY STATUTORY INTERPRETATION, 57 Admin. L. Rev. 501, 507 (2005), courts and agencies are very differently situated in their relationship to the President: "Save in those rare instances where presidents have been given clear statutory or constitutional authority to guide judicial interpretation by presidential pronouncement, the failure of the court to exercise interpretive judgment independent of presidential preferences would be to abandon what we imagine to be the constitutionally appropriate role of the federal judiciary. By contrast, for agencies of the executive branch to ignore legitimate presidential instruction would be for them to ignore their appropriate place in the constitutional order." Thus, this most straightforward answer to how agencies should interpret statutes— mimic how the courts interpret statutes—may be too simple.

(2)   A second possibility is for agencies to follow the approach courts use in applying Chevron, but once having determined that the statute is ambiguous, then choose among the possible "permissible" interpretations on a purely policy-preference basis. Here is how Professor RICHARD PIERCE describes this approach in HOW AGENCIES SHOULD GIVE MEANING TO THE STATUTES THEY ADMINISTER: A RESPONSE TO MASHAW AND STRAUSS, 59 Admin. L. Rev. 197, 202–04 (2007): "The proper roles for agencies in conforming to Chevron follow logically and inevitably from the Court's instructions to reviewing courts in Chevron. Because a reviewing court will apply step one of Chevron first, a prudent agency must apply step one itself. To maximize the chances of having its action upheld, the agency must do its best to determine whether Congress resolved the question before the agency. Although this process definitely is interpretive, it is one in which the agency has no practical choice but to attempt to anticipate and replicate the interpretive process a reviewing court will use. Additionally, the agency should use the same 'traditional tools of statutory construction' that it expects a reviewing court to use. . . . To the best of its ability, the agency should attempt to use exactly the same interpretive process a court would use—any intentional variation from that judicial interpretive process would be a self-defeating exercise in futility.

"The agency's task in minimizing its risk of reversal through application of Chevron step two is totally different from its task in attempting to minimize its risk of reversal through application of step one. An agency's efforts to minimize the risk of judicial reversal through application of Chevron step two has little to do with statutory interpretation. Rather, the agency's task is to use a comprehensive and transparent policymaking process in which it identifies and explains each step in its decisionmaking process, relates each decision to the available data relevant to the decision, and explains why it rejected alternatives to, or criticisms of, the decisions it made.

"Depending on the context in which the agency makes the decision to give the ambiguous statutory term a particular meaning, the policymaking process that maximizes the likelihood of judicial approval through application of Chevron step two will require an agency to use tools made available by fields like economics, statistics, chemistry, toxicology, epidemiology, meteorology, etc. There is only one link between this policymaking process and the process of statutory interpretation. In the course of explaining why it made the decisions it made, the agency must refer to decisional factors that the underlying statute makes permissible. For that purpose, the agency must engage in statutory interpretation to the extent necessary to explain why it believes that a decisional factor it applies is statutorily permissible. In other words, a court will—and should—reverse an agency action if the agency relies on a decisional factor that is logically relevant to its decision in the abstract but one that Congress has forbidden the agency to consider. . . . Here again, however, the agency must do its best to anticipate and to replicate the interpretive process a reviewing court will use to minimize the agency's risk of judicial reversal of its action. A court will reverse an agency if the agency relies on a decisional factor the court determines to be impermissible."

But this approach will seem too policy driven for some. Consider GARY LAWSON, DIRTY DANCING—THE FDA STUMBLES WITH THE *CHEVRON* TWO-STEP, 93 Cornell L. Rev. 927, 932–33 (2008): "[Under Chevron,] reviewing courts are not looking to see whether agencies got the *right* answer but only whether they got a *permissible* answer. Could an agency take advantage of this deference and say, 'In construing this statute, we are going to pick the interpretation that we like on policy grounds, even though we think that a different interpretation represents the best reading of the statute, because we can get away with it on judicial review?' Such reasoning would be a clear abuse of the deferential standard of review. Deferential review is premised on the initial decision maker's good-faith effort to get the right answer. . . . [I]t would be just as outrageous for an agency to use Chevron deference as a tool to protect its *initial law findings* as it would be for an agency to use the substantial evidence standard as a tool to protect its *initial fact findings*."

More broadly, this second approach may rely too strongly on separating policy determinations from legal determinations. At least that is Professor JERRY L. MASHAW'S view, in AGENCY-CENTERED OR COURT-CENTERED ADMINISTRATIVE LAW? A DIALOGUE WITH RICHARD PIERCE ON AGENCY STATUTORY INTERPRETATION, 59 Admin. L. Rev. 889, 898 (2007): "Administrative agency personnel must ask and answer at least five basic questions: (1) What are the goals of the statute that we are implementing? (2) How does the current state of the world differ from those goals? (3) What policy choices are likely to move the future state of the world closer to our statutorily specified goals? (4) What instruments have we been given with which to articulate and implement our chosen policies? (5) What constraints—procedural, analytic, temporal, etc.-have been placed on our development and implementation of our policies? Although questions two and three can be addressed without interpreting the agency's statute, the remaining questions are all saturated with interpretive issues. The notion that policy choice is not interpretive simply ignores many of the necessary mental operations involved in administrative implementation."

(3) Which leaves us with a third possibility: that the process by which agencies interpret statutes should be modeled neither on what judges do

when they interpret a statute directly nor on what judges do under Chevron. In other words, perhaps the most responsible way for agencies to proceed in their institutional context is, at least in some respects, different from the most responsible way for courts to proceed in theirs. Consider, for example, Professor PETER L. STRAUSS' discussion of the difference between the ways courts and agencies relate to legislative history in WHEN THE JUDGE IS NOT THE PRIMARY OFFICIAL WITH RESPONSIBILITY TO READ: AGENCY INTERPRETATION AND THE PROBLEM OF LEGISLATIVE HISTORY, 66 Chi.-Kent L. Rev. 321, 346–47 (1990): "Responsible in some sense for all law, a court has infrequent occasion to consider the meaning of any particular part of the law, and no responsibility for continuing, proactive attention to its development. If it comes to the legislative history at all, it comes to that history cold, without a developed institutional sense of the state of play. It does not participate in, indeed very likely is utterly unaware of, what occurs in drafting, hearings, debates, or a continuing course of oversight hearings, presidential guidance, and frustrated efforts at securing legislative change; a court is not continually studying issues of statutory meaning and adjusting outcomes—as administrators responsible for a program must. For the agency, of course, the reverse is generally true; its closeness to the legislative process, continued involvement, and responsibility are . . . precisely the reasons courts have long given its readings of statutory meaning special weight. Delegitimating reference to legislative history for the agency, then, not only reduces its defenses to contemporary political oversight; it encourages it to ignore, in acting, what in an important sense it already knows.

". . . The enduring and multifaceted character of the agency's relationship with Congress contributes to the agency's capacity to distinguish reliably those considerations that served to shape the legislation, the legislative history, from the more manipulative chaff."

On this view, the interpretive space provided by Chevron deference is based on a recognition of the differential engagement of agencies and courts in parts of a complex process of statutory interpretation.

How far does this notion of agencies using a distinct mode of interpretation go? Consider this, on the differing relations of courts and agencies to the Constitution, from JERRY MASHAW, NORMS, PRACTICES AND THE PARADOX OF DEFERENCE: A PRELIMINARY INQUIRY INTO AGENCY STATUTORY INTERPRETATION, 57 Admin. L. Rev. 501, 507 (2005): "American administrative agencies are obviously bound by the Constitution and must often implement it directly. Agency hearing processes, for example, must satisfy constitutional due process requirements. And, federal law enforcement officials make thousands of decisions every day that require an interpretation of the Fourth Amendment's search and seizure provisions. But how should the potential for constitutional difficulty influence an agency's construction of some statute that it is charged with implementing? We know that there is a judicial canon of statutory construction, based on principles of constitutional comity, which counsels courts to avoid constructions of statutes that would raise serious constitutional questions about their validity. Are agencies in a similar position?

"Arguably not. They have no general responsibility for constitutional review of congressional action whose aggressive or imprudent exercise might threaten the legitimacy of judicial review and thereby weaken the constitutional order. Indeed, were agencies intensely attentive to avoiding constitutional questions when interpreting the statutes entrusted to their care, they would often foreclose authoritative resolution of constitutional questions by the judiciary. To put the point in its strongest form, an administrative apparatus that operated in the shadow of the avoidance canon would set itself up operationally as the arbiter of the constitutionality of congressional action. . . . Obviously, administrators who fail to pursue implementation any time a constitutional issue looms on their horizon could not possibly carry out their legislative mandates effectively. Constitutionally timid administration both compromises faithful agency and potentially usurps the role of the judiciary in harmonizing congressional power and constitutional command."

On this subject—the impact of the Constitution on the best interpretation of the statute—a court is unlikely to defer to the agency's judgment. So one difficulty with the idea that responsible agency interpretation might follow a different set of norms from responsible judging is that, as Professor Mashaw has himself recognized, "responsible judging may reject an interpretation generated by responsible administration." Agency-Centered or Court-Centered Administrative Law?, supra, p. 1196 at 903.

NOTES ON CHEVRON AND ITS APPLICATION TO AGENCY INTERPRETATIONS OF CRIMINAL LAW

(1) *Courts Have Held that Chevron Deference Does Not Apply to Criminal Law.* See Abramski v. United States, 134 S.Ct. 2259, 2274 (2014) ("criminal laws are for the courts, not for the Government, to construe"); *see also* United States v. Apel, 134 S.Ct. 1144, 1151 (2014) ("we have never held that the Government's reading of a criminal statute is entitled to any deference"). Driven by the separation of powers concerns that one branch of government should not make, interpret and enforce the law, courts have outlined numerous reasons to explain why the judiciary does not employ Chevron deference in criminal law. See generally Dan M. Kahan, Is Chevron Relevant to Federal Criminal Law?, 110 Harv. L. Rev 469 (1996).

First, there may be "rule of law" concerns about ensuring the public is on notice of what the criminal law demands. "[W]hile courts recognize the inevitability and, in certain contexts, the desirability of legislation that leaves some details to be resolved as the statute is applied, there are limits. Those limits are most graphic in cases involving criminal sanctions. In the criminal context, courts have traditionally required greater clarity in draftsmanship than in civil contexts, commensurate with the bedrock principle that in a free country citizens who are potentially subject to criminal sanctions should have clear notice of the behavior that may cause sanctions to be visited upon them. That is to say, the law of crimes must be clear. There is less room in a statute's regime for flexibility, a characteristic so familiar to us on this court in the interpretation of statutes entrusted to agencies for administration. We are, in short, far outside *Chevron* territory here." UNITED STATES V. McGOFF, 831 F.2d 1071, 1077 (D.C. Cir. 1987).

Second, there may be reason to doubt that Congress intended to delegate interpretive power over criminal law to the executive branch. "[A] criminal statute, is not administered by any agency but by the courts. It is entirely reasonable and understandable that federal officials should make available to their employees legal advice regarding its interpretation; and in a general way all agencies of the Government must interpret it in order to assure that the behavior of their employees is lawful—just as they must interpret innumerable other civil and criminal provisions in order to operate lawfully; but that is not the sort of specific responsibility for administering the law that triggers Chevron." CRANDON V. UNITED STATES, 494 U.S. 152, 177 (1990) (SCALIA, J., concurring in the judgment).

Third, the rule of lenity, which counsels in favor of reading grievous ambiguities in criminal statutes narrowly, arguably conflicts with Chevron. "Any responsible lawyer advising on whether particular conduct violates a criminal statute will obviously err in the direction of inclusion rather than exclusion—assuming, to be on the safe side, that the statute may cover more than is entirely apparent. That tendency is reinforced when the advice-giver is the Justice Department, which knows that if it takes an erroneously narrow view of what it can prosecute the error will likely never be corrected, whereas an erroneously broad view will be corrected by the courts when prosecutions are brought. Thus, to give persuasive effect to the Government's expansive advice-giving interpretation would turn the normal construction of criminal statutes upside-down, replacing the doctrine of lenity with a doctrine of severity." *Id.* at 177–78.

For a contrary view, consider the arguments Professor Kahan makes. Kahan explains that federal criminal law statutes are broad and require interpretation in order to have meaning. He cites the Racketeer Influenced Corrupt Organizations Act (RICO) as an example of a statute in which Congress did not define the elements of the crime, and thus delegated authority to courts, as well as prosecutors, to bring meaning to the statute. The resulting judicial doctrines that comprise RICO law "should be understood not as bare 'interpretations' of the statute, but rather as exercises of federal common law-making power." KAHAN, IS CHEVRON RELEVANT TO FEDERAL CRIMINAL LAW?, 110 Harv. L. Rev at 473. He acknowledges the benefits of delegating power, including increased efficiency and decreased practical and political costs, as well as the losses of delegating power, such as unresolved disagreement between different courts and prosecutorial overreach. To maintain benefits while reducing these costs, he argues that the judiciary should embrace Chevron deference in criminal law: the executive branch—specifically the Department of Justice—has both greater expertise and democratic accountability than the judiciary and is therefore the more appropriate branch to interpret criminal law.

KAHAN explains: "Combining the authority to make, enforce and interpret law in the hands of a single actor, it is said, is a blueprint for tyranny. Yet it is exactly this concentration of functions that I want to defend. Federal criminal law would be better by any conceivable measure . . .

if the executive branch were treated as an authoritative law-expositor, and not merely an authoritative law-enforcer. . . . Applying the Chevron doctrine would improve the content of federal criminal law by shifting to the Justice Department the delegated lawmaking powers now exercised jointly by the courts and individual prosecutors. This transfer of authority would preserve essentially all the benefits associated with delegation, and, at the same time, effectively treat all of the pathologies that afflict it. The Justice Department has greater law-making expertise than do courts because it comes into contact with all manner of crimes at all stages of the justice system. Its readings are more likely to be uniform that those of courts because it is a single, integrated agency. Finally, the Department is less likely to overreach than are individual U.S. Attorneys because it has less incentive to pander to local interests and is more likely to internalize the costs of unduly broad statutory readings."

Responding to the specific criticisms raised in Crandon and McGoff, Kahan argues that neither the "rule of law" argument nor appropriate delegation concern is logical. With regard to the "rule of law" concern, Kahan responds that "the question isn't whether these statutes will be given shape by someone other than Congress, but only whether courts or the Justice Department will be doing the shaping." *Id.* at 491–92. Requiring Justice to interpret laws prior to prosecution would enhance, not hinder, the rule of law. *Id.* at 500–501. And as to delegation, Kahan argues that Congress never states which branch should exercise delegated power in criminal statutes. Because of this, courts should weigh whether the judicial or executive branch is "better situated to exercise delegated criminal law-making power." *Id.* at 491. Justice, with greater criminal law expertise, is better positioned than the judiciary to manage both of these worries, according to Kahan.

(2) ***What about Regulations that May Have Both Civil and Criminal Consequences?*** In Babbitt v. Sweet Home Chapter, Communities for Great Ore., the Supreme Court deferred to the Secretary of the Interior's definition of a term in the Endangered Species Act of 1973 and criminal sanctions turned on the Secretary's interpretation. 515 U.S. 687 (1995). However, the question is not settled. Justice Scalia wrote in 2014, joined by Justice Thomas in respecting the denial of certiorari in Whitman v. United States, that he would be "receptive" to granting a petition seeking review of deference to an agency's interpretation that has criminal and administrative penalties. 135 S.Ct. 352 (2014). "With deference to agency interpretations of statutory provisions to which criminal prohibitions are attached, federal administrators can in effect create (and uncreate) new crimes at will, so long as they do not roam beyond ambiguities that the laws contain. . . . Babbitt's drive-by ruling, in short, deserves little weight." *Id.* at 353–354.

In ESQUIVEL-QUINTANA V. LYNCH, the Sixth Circuit considered whether a conviction under a state criminal rape statute for consensual intercourse between Juan Esquivel-Quintana, a twenty-one-year-old noncitizen, and a seventeen-year-old was "sexual abuse of a minor" under a federal civil immigration statute; under the civil statute, an immigration judge ruled that Esquivel-Quintana would be deported. 810 F.3d 1019 (6th Cir. 2016). The majority, under *Chevron,* deferred to the Board of Immigration and Appeal's interpretation of the civil statute and denied Esquivel-Quintana's petition for review of the immigration judge's decision. JUDGE JEFFREY SUTTON dissented in part, discussing the application of Chevron to statutes that have civil and criminal implications: "Chevron permits agencies to fill gaps in *civil* statutes that Congress has delegated authority to the agency to interpret. . . . But Chevron has no role to play in construing *criminal* statutes. . . . The doctrine does not give the Department of Justice (or for that matter any other federal agency) *implied* gap-filling authority over ambiguous criminal statutes. Otherwise, that would leave this distasteful combination: The prosecutor would have the explicit (executive) power to enforce the criminal laws, an implied (legislative) power to fill policy gaps in ambiguous criminal statutes, and an implied (judicial) power to interpret ambiguous criminal laws. And it would permit this aggregation of power in the one area where its division matters most: the removal of citizens from society. . . . But what happens when the same statute has criminal *and* civil applications? May Congress sidestep these requirements by giving criminal statutes a civil application? The answer is no. The courts must give dual-application statutes just one interpretation, and the criminal application controls. Statutes are not 'chameleon[s]' that mean one thing in one setting and something else in another. Time, time, and time again, the Court has confirmed that the one-interpretation rule means that the criminal-law construction of the statute (with the rule of lenity) prevails over the civil-law construction of it (without the rule of lenity)." *Id.* 1027–1028 (emphasis in original).

The Supreme Court granted certiorari in *Esquivel-Quintana* but held that the statute, in context, unambiguously foreclosed the government's interpretation of it; "[t]herefore, neither the rule of lenity nor Chevron applies." Esquivel-Quintana v. Sessions, 137 S.Ct. 1562 (2017).

(3) Finally, for an argument that Chevron does not apply to the Department of Justice's interpretation of criminal statutes reveals that Chevron cannot be made to fit within the constitutional framework, here is then-JUDGE GORSUCH again from GUTTIEREZ-BIZUELA V. LYNCH: "What I suspect about Chevron's compatibility with the separation of powers finds confirmation in what I know. The Supreme Court has expressly instructed us not to apply Chevron deference when an agency seeks to interpret a criminal statute. Why? Because, we are seemingly told, doing so would violate the Constitution by forcing the judiciary to abdicate the job of saying what the law is and preventing courts from exercising independent judgment in the interpretation 2250 (2001); See, e.g., Abramski v. United States, 134 S.Ct. 2259, 2274 (2014) ('Whether the Government interprets a criminal statute too broadly . . . or too narrowly . . . a court has an obligation to correct its error.'). An admirable colleague has noted that the same rationale would appear to preclude affording Chevron deference to agency interpretations of statutes that bear both civil and criminal applications. See, e.g., Esquivel-Quintana v. Lynch, 810 F.3d 1019, 1027–32 (6th Cir. 2016) (Sutton, J., concurring in part and dissenting in part); Carter v. Welles-Bowen Realty, Inc., 736 F.3d 722, 729–36 (6th Cir. 2013) (Sutton, J., concurring). A category that covers a great many (most?) federal statutes today. And try as I might,

I have a hard time identifying a principled reason why the same rationale doesn't also apply to statutes with purely civil application. After all, the APA doesn't distinguish between purely civil and other kinds of statutes when describing the interpretive duties of courts. Neither did the founders reserve their concerns about political decisionmakers deciding the meaning of existing law to criminal cases; Article III doesn't say judges should say what the law is or decide whether legal rights have or haven't vested and been violated only when a crime is alleged. And certainly Marbury did not speak so meekly: it affirmed the judiciary's duty to say what the law is in a case that involved the interpretation of, yes, a civil statute affecting individual rights. Some have suggested that criminal statutes should be treated differently when it comes to Chevron because they are not 'administered' by an agency. See Gonzales v. Oregon, 546 U.S. 243, 264–65 (2006). I take this as a roundabout way of suggesting that Congress hasn't 'delegated' its legislative authority in the criminal context like it has in the civil. But as we've seen, the claim that Congress has delegated legislative authority even in the civil context is no more than a fiction. And for that matter it's hard to see why the Justice Department doesn't 'administer' criminal statutes in much the same way other agencies 'administer' various civil statutes. See, e.g., Crandon v. United States, 494 U.S. 152, 177 (1990) (Scalia, J., concurring in the judgment) (acknowledging that '[t]he Justice Department . . . has a very specific responsibility to determine for itself what this statute means, in order to decide when to prosecute'). Of course, criminal law enforcement takes place in the courts, not before administrative agencies. But often enough civil administrative actions also depend on court approval for their effectiveness, and as we've seen this may be a matter not merely of statutory but sometimes constitutional imperative. . . .

"Other arguments for rejecting Chevron deference (only) in criminal matters seem equally shaky. Some suggest that principles of due process and equal protection demand that the criminal law be clear and clearly given by judges. Others suggest that prosecutorial agencies have too many incentives to interpret criminal statutes expansively. But while concerns about due process and fair notice surely reach their apex in the criminal context, I am uncertain why we would view that as a license to neglect attending to them in the civil context. See Clinton v. City of New York, 524 U.S. 417, 450 (1998) (Kennedy, J., concurring) ('Liberty is always at stake when one or more of the branches seek to transgress the separation of powers.'). Especially given the power our modern administrative state already enjoys, even without Chevron, to penalize persons in ways that can destroy their livelihoods and intrude on their liberty even when exercising only purely civil powers. And given that the line between 'criminal' and 'civil' statutes has often proven tricky enough to administer. See, e.g., Hudson v. United States, 522 U.S. 93, 99–100 (1997) (suggesting the use of a balancing test composed of seven non-exclusive factors to tell the difference between civil and criminal statutory penalties). Neither, too, are prosecutorial agencies known to be alone in their capacity and willingness to interpret statutes aggressively."

Does then-Judge Gorsuch's argument depend on the premise that the Department of Justice does "administer" the criminal laws and thus that

Congress did delegate the power to interpret them to the Department, just like Congress delegated a similar power to an agency that administers its organic statute? How strong is that premise?

> SWANCC v. U.S. ARMY CORPS OF
>   ENGINEERS
> Notes on the Logic of the SWANCC
>   Opinions
> Notes on Canons of Construction and
>   Chevron
> Notes on Federalism and Agency Action

SOLID WASTE AGENCY OF NORTHERN COOK COUNTY v. U.S. ARMY CORPS OF ENGINEERS

Supreme Court of the United States (2001).
531 U.S. 159.

■ CHIEF JUSTICE REHNQUIST delivered the opinion of the Court.

Section 404(a) of the Clean Water Act (CWA or Act), 33 U.S.C. § 1344(a), regulates the discharge of dredged or fill material into "navigable waters." The United States Army Corps of Engineers (Corps) has interpreted § 404(a) to confer federal authority over an abandoned sand and gravel pit in northern Illinois which provides habitat for migratory birds. We are asked to decide whether the provisions of § 404(a) may be fairly extended to these waters, and, if so, whether Congress could exercise such authority consistent with the Commerce Clause, U.S. Const., Art. I, § 8, cl. 3. We answer the first question in the negative and therefore do not reach the second.

Petitioner, the Solid Waste Agency of Northern Cook County (SWANCC), is a consortium of 23 suburban Chicago cities and villages that united in an effort to locate and develop a disposal site for baled nonhazardous solid waste. The Chicago Gravel Company informed the municipalities of the availability of a 533-acre parcel, bestriding the Illinois counties Cook and Kane, which had been the site of a sand and gravel pit mining operation for three decades up until about 1960. Long since abandoned, the old mining site eventually gave way to a successional stage forest, with its remnant excavation trenches evolving into a scattering of permanent and seasonal ponds of varying size (from under one-tenth of an acre to several acres) and depth (from several inches to several feet).

The municipalities decided to purchase the site for disposal of their baled nonhazardous solid waste. By law, SWANCC was required to file for various permits from Cook County and the State of Illinois before it could begin operation of its balefill project. In addition, because the operation called for the filling of some of the permanent and seasonal ponds, SWANCC contacted federal respondents (hereinafter respondents), including the Corps, to determine if a federal landfill permit was required under § 404(a) of the CWA.

Section 404(a) grants the Corps authority to issue permits "for the discharge of dredged or fill material into the navigable waters at specified disposal sites." The term "navigable waters" is defined under the Act as "the waters of the United States, including the territorial seas." § 1362(7). The Corps has issued regulations defining the term "waters of the United States" to include

> waters such as intrastate lakes, rivers, streams (including intermittent streams), mudflats, sandflats, wetlands, sloughs, prairie potholes, wet meadows, playa lakes, or natural ponds, the use, degradation or destruction of which could affect interstate or foreign commerce. . . . 33 CFR § 328.3(a)(3).

In 1986, in an attempt to "clarify" the reach of its jurisdiction, the Corps stated that § 404(a) extends to intrastate waters:

> a.   Which are or would be used as habitat by birds protected by Migratory Bird Treaties; or
>
> b.   Which are or would be used as habitat by other migratory birds which cross state lines; or
>
> c.   Which are or would be used as habitat for endangered species; or
>
> d.   Used to irrigate crops sold in interstate commerce. 51 Fed.Reg. 41217.

This last promulgation has been dubbed the "Migratory Bird Rule."[1]

The Corps initially concluded that it had no jurisdiction over the site because it contained no "wetlands," or areas which support "vegetation typically adapted for life in saturated soil conditions," 33 CFR § 328.3(b). However, after the Illinois Nature Preserves Commission informed the Corps that a number of migratory bird species had been observed at the site, the Corps reconsidered and ultimately asserted jurisdiction over the balefill site pursuant to subpart (b) of the "Migratory Bird Rule." The Corps found that approximately 121 bird species had been observed at the site, including several known to depend upon aquatic environments for a significant portion of their life requirements. Thus, on November 16, 1987, the Corps formally "determined that the seasonally ponded, abandoned gravel mining depressions located on the project site, while not wetlands, did qualify as 'waters of the United States' . . . based upon the following criteria: (1) the proposed site had been abandoned as a gravel mining operation; (2) the water areas and spoil piles had developed a natural character; and (3) the water areas are used as habitat by migratory bird *[sic]* which cross state lines." U.S. Army Corps

---

[1]   The Corps issued the "Migratory Bird Rule" without following the notice and comment procedures outlined in the Administrative Procedure Act, 5 U.S.C. § 553.

of Engineers, Chicago District, Dept. of Army Permit Evaluation and Decision Document.

[SWANCC obtained the necessary local and state permits but was denied a federal permit for failure to meet various regulatory specifications. It brought suit under the APA. The district court held that the Corps had jurisdiction over the site; SWANCC does not challenge denial of the federal permit if indeed the Corps has jurisdiction.]

The Court of Appeals began its analysis with the constitutional question, holding that Congress has the authority to regulate such waters based upon "the cumulative impact doctrine, under which a single activity that itself has no discernible effect on interstate commerce may still be regulated if the aggregate effect of that class of activity has a substantial impact on interstate commerce." 191 F.3d 845, 850 (C.A.7 1999). The aggregate effect of the "destruction of the natural habitat of migratory birds" on interstate commerce, the court held, was substantial because each year millions of Americans cross state lines and spend over a billion dollars to hunt and observe migratory birds. Ibid. The Court of Appeals then turned to the regulatory question. The court held that the CWA reaches as many waters as the Commerce Clause allows and, given its earlier Commerce Clause ruling, it therefore followed that respondents' "Migratory Bird Rule" was a reasonable interpretation of the Act.

We granted certiorari, and now reverse.

Congress passed the CWA for the stated purpose of "restor[ing] and maintain[ing] the chemical, physical, and biological integrity of the Nation's waters." 33 U.S.C. § 1251(a). In so doing, Congress chose to "recognize, preserve, and protect the primary responsibilities and rights of States to prevent, reduce, and eliminate pollution, to plan the development and use (including restoration, preservation, and enhancement) of land and water resources, and to consult with the Administrator in the exercise of his authority under this chapter." § 1251(b). Relevant here, § 404(a) authorizes respondents to regulate the discharge of fill material into "navigable waters," 33 U.S.C. § 1344(a), which the statute defines as "the waters of the United States, including the territorial seas," § 1362(7). Respondents have interpreted these words to cover the abandoned gravel pit at issue here because it is used as habitat for migratory birds. We conclude that the "Migratory Bird Rule" is not fairly supported by the CWA.

This is not the first time we have been called upon to evaluate the meaning of § 404(a). In United States v. Riverside Bayview Homes, Inc., 474 U.S. 121 (1985), we held that the Corps had § 404(a) jurisdiction over wetlands that actually abutted on a navigable waterway. In so doing, we noted that the term "navigable" is of "limited import" and that Congress evidenced its intent to "regulate at least some waters that would not be deemed 'navigable' under the classical understanding of that term." Id., at 133. But our holding was based in large measure upon Congress' unequivocal acquiescence to, and approval of, the Corps' regulations interpreting the CWA to cover wetlands adjacent to navigable waters. We found that Congress' concern for the protection of water quality and aquatic ecosystems indicated its intent to regulate wetlands "inseparably bound up with the 'waters' of the United States." Id., at 134.

It was the significant nexus between the wetlands and "navigable waters" that informed our reading of the CWA in Riverside Bayview Homes. Indeed, we did not "express any opinion" on the "question of the authority of the Corps to regulate discharges of fill material into wetlands that are not adjacent to bodies of open water. . . ." Id., at 131–132, n. 8. In order to rule for respondents here, we would have to hold that the jurisdiction of the Corps extends to ponds that are *not* adjacent to open water. But we conclude that the text of the statute will not allow this.

Indeed, the Corps' *original* interpretation of the CWA, promulgated two years after its enactment, is inconsistent with that which it espouses here. Its 1974 regulations defined § 404(a)'s "navigable waters" to mean "those waters of the United States which are subject to the ebb and flow of the tide, and/or are presently, or have been in the past, or may be in the future susceptible for use for purposes of interstate or foreign commerce." 33 CFR § 209.120(d)(1). The Corps emphasized that "[i]t is the water body's capability of use by the public for purposes of transportation or commerce which is the determinative factor." § 209.260(e)(1). Respondents put forward no persuasive evidence that the Corps mistook Congress' intent in 1974.

. . . In July 1977, the Corps formally adopted 33 CFR § 323.2(a)(5) (1978), which defined "waters of the United States" to include "isolated wetlands and lakes, intermittent streams, prairie potholes, and other waters that are not part of a tributary system to interstate waters or to navigable waters of the United States, the degradation or destruction of which could affect interstate commerce." Respondents argue that Congress was aware of this more expansive interpretation during its 1977 amendments to the CWA. . . .

Although we have recognized congressional acquiescence to administrative interpretations of a statute in some situations, we have done so with extreme care. . . .

We conclude that respondents have failed to make the necessary showing that the failure of the 1977 House bill demonstrates Congress' acquiescence to the Corps' regulations or the "Migratory Bird Rule," which, of course, did not first appear until 1986. . . . Beyond Congress' desire to regulate wetlands adjacent to "navigable waters," respondents point us to no persuasive evidence that the House bill was proposed in response to the Corps' claim of jurisdiction over nonnavigable, isolated, intrastate waters or that its failure indicated congressional acquiescence to such jurisdiction.

We thus decline respondents' invitation to take what they see as the next ineluctable step after Riverside Bayview Homes: holding that isolated ponds, some only seasonal, wholly located within two Illinois counties, fall under § 404(a)'s definition of "navigable waters" because they serve as habitat for migratory birds. As counsel for respondents conceded at oral argument, such a ruling would assume that "the use of the word navigable in the statute . . . does not have any independent significance." Tr. of Oral Arg. 28. We cannot agree that Congress' separate definitional use of the phrase "waters of the United States" constitutes a basis for reading the term "navigable waters" out of the statute. We said in Riverside Bayview Homes that the word "navigable" in the statute was of "limited import" 474 U.S., at 133, and went on to hold that § 404(a) extended to nonnavigable wetlands adjacent to open waters. But it is one thing to give a word limited effect and quite another to give it no effect whatever. The term "navigable" has at least the import of showing us what Congress had in mind as its authority for enacting the CWA: its traditional jurisdiction over waters that were or had been navigable in fact or which could reasonably be so made.

Respondents—relying upon all of the arguments addressed above contend that, at the very least, it must be said that Congress did not address the precise question of § 404(a)'s scope with regard to nonnavigable, isolated, intrastate waters, and that, therefore, we should give deference to the "Migratory Bird Rule." We find § 404(a) to be clear, but even were we to agree with respondents, we would not extend Chevron deference here.

Where an administrative interpretation of a statute invokes the outer limits of Congress' power, we expect a clear indication that Congress intended that result. See Edward J. DeBartolo Corp. v. Florida Gulf Coast Building & Constr. Trades Council, 485 U.S. 568, 575 (1988). This requirement stems from our prudential desire not to needlessly reach constitutional issues and our assumption that Congress does not casually authorize administrative agencies to interpret a statute to push the limit of congressional authority. This concern is heightened where the administrative interpretation alters the federal-state framework by permitting federal encroachment upon a traditional state power. See United States v. Bass, 404 U.S. 336, 349 (1971) ("[U]nless Congress conveys its purpose clearly, it will not be deemed to have significantly changed the federal-state balance"). Thus, "where an otherwise acceptable construction of a statute would raise serious constitutional problems, the Court will construe the statute to avoid such problems unless such construction is plainly contrary to the intent of Congress." DeBartolo, supra, at 575.

Twice in the past six years we have reaffirmed the proposition that the grant of authority to Congress under the Commerce Clause, though broad, is not unlimited. See United States v. Morrison, 529 U.S. 598 (2000); United States v. Lopez, 514 U.S. 549 (1995). Respondents argue that the "Migratory Bird Rule" falls within Congress' power to regulate intrastate activities that "substantially affect" interstate commerce. They note that the protection of migratory birds is a "national interest of very nearly the first magnitude," Missouri v. Holland, 252 U.S. 416, 435 (1920), and that, as the Court of Appeals found, millions of people spend over a billion dollars annually on recreational pursuits relating to migratory birds. These arguments raise significant constitutional questions. For example, we would have to evaluate the precise object or activity that, in the aggregate, substantially affects interstate commerce. . . .

These are significant constitutional questions raised by respondents' application of their regulations, and yet we find nothing approaching a clear statement from Congress that it intended § 404(a) to reach an abandoned sand and gravel pit such as we have here. Permitting respondents to claim federal jurisdiction over ponds and mudflats falling within the "Migratory Bird Rule" would result in a significant impingement of the States' traditional and primary power over land and water use. Rather than expressing a desire to readjust the federal-state balance in this manner, Congress chose to "recognize, preserve, and protect the primary responsibilities and rights of States . . . to plan the development and use . . . of land and water resources. . . ." 33 U.S.C. § 1251(b). We thus read the statute as written to avoid the significant constitutional and federalism questions raised by respondents' interpretation, and therefore reject the request for administrative deference.

We hold that 33 CFR § 328.3(a)(3) (1999), as clarified and applied to petitioner's balefill site pursuant to the "Migratory Bird Rule," 51 Fed. Reg. 41217 (1986), exceeds the authority granted to respondents under § 404(a) of the CWA. The judgment of the Court of Appeals for the Seventh Circuit is therefore reversed.

■ JUSTICE STEVENS, with whom JUSTICE SOUTER, JUSTICE GINSBURG, and JUSTICE BREYER join, dissenting.

In 1969, the Cuyahoga River in Cleveland, Ohio, coated with a slick of industrial waste, caught fire. Congress responded to that dramatic event, and to others like it, by enacting the Federal Water Pollution Control Act (FWPCA) Amendments of 1972, 33 U.S.C. § 1251 *et seq.*, commonly known as the Clean Water Act (Clean Water Act, CWA, or Act). . . .

It is fair to characterize the Clean Water Act as "watershed" legislation. The statute endorsed fundamental changes in both the purpose and the scope of federal regulation of the Nation's waters. In § 13 of the Rivers and Harbors Appropriation Act of 1899 (RHA), Congress had assigned to the Army Corps of Engineers (Corps) the mission of regulating discharges into certain waters in order to protect their use as highways for the transportation of interstate and foreign commerce; the scope of the Corps' jurisdiction under the RHA accordingly extended only to waters that were "navigable." In the CWA, however, Congress broadened the Corps' mission to include the purpose of protecting the quality of our Nation's waters for esthetic, health, recreational, and environmental uses. The scope of its jurisdiction was therefore redefined to encompass all of "the waters of the United States, including the territorial seas." § 1362(7). That definition requires neither actual nor potential navigability.

The Court has previously held that the Corps' broadened jurisdiction under the CWA properly included an 80-acre parcel of low-lying marshy land that was not itself navigable, directly adjacent to navigable water, or even hydrologically connected to navigable water, but which was part of a larger area, characterized by poor drainage, that ultimately abutted a navigable creek. United States v. Riverside Bayview Homes, Inc., 474 U.S. 121 (1985). Our broad finding in Riverside Bayview that the 1977 Congress had acquiesced in the Corps' understanding of its jurisdiction applies equally to the 410-acre parcel at issue here. Moreover, once Congress crossed the legal watershed that separates navigable streams of commerce from marshes and inland lakes, there is no principled reason for limiting the statute's protection to those waters or wetlands that happen to lie near a navigable stream.

In its decision today, the Court draws a new jurisdictional line, one that invalidates the 1986 migratory bird regulation as well as the Corps' assertion of jurisdiction over all waters except for actually navigable waters, their tributaries, and wetlands adjacent to each. Its holding rests on two equally untenable premises: (1) that when Congress passed the 1972 CWA, it did not intend "to exert anything more than its commerce power over navigation"; and (2) that in 1972 Congress drew the boundary defining the Corps' jurisdiction at the odd line on which the Court today settles.

As I shall explain, the text of the 1972 amendments affords no support for the Court's holding, and amendments Congress adopted in 1977 do support the Corps' present interpretation of its mission as extending to so-called "isolated" waters. Indeed, simple common sense cuts against the particular definition of the Corps' jurisdiction favored by the majority.

I

The significance of the FWPCA Amendments of 1972 is illuminated by a reference to the history of federal water regulation. . . .

The shift in the focus of federal water regulation from protecting navigability toward environmental protection reached a dramatic climax in 1972, with the passage of the CWA. The Act, which was passed as an amendment to the existing FWPCA, was universally described by its supporters as the first truly comprehensive federal water pollution legislation. The "major purpose" of the CWA was "to establish a comprehensive long-range policy for the elimination of water pollution."

S. Rep. No. 92–414, p. 95 (1971) . . . Strikingly absent from its declaration of "goals and policy" is *any* reference to avoiding or removing obstructions to navigation. Instead, the principal objective of the Act, as stated by Congress in § 101, was "to restore and maintain the chemical, physical, and biological integrity of the Nation's waters." 33 U.S.C. § 1251. Congress therefore directed federal agencies in § 102 to "develop comprehensive programs for preventing, reducing, or eliminating the pollution of the navigable waters and ground waters and improving the sanitary condition of surface and underground waters." 33 U.S.C. § 1252. The CWA commands federal agencies to give "due regard," not to the interest of unobstructed navigation, but rather to "improvements which are necessary to conserve such waters for the protection and propagation of fish and aquatic life and wildlife [and] recreational purposes." Ibid.

Because of the statute's ambitious and comprehensive goals, it was, of course, necessary to expand its jurisdictional scope. Thus, although Congress opted to carry over the traditional jurisdictional term "navigable waters" from the RHA and prior versions of the FWPCA, it broadened the *definition* of that term to encompass all "waters of the United States." § 1362(7).[6] Indeed, the 1972 conferees arrived at the final formulation by specifically deleting the word "navigable" from the definition that had originally appeared in the House version of the Act.[7] The majority today undoes that deletion. . . .

The majority's reading drains all meaning from the conference amendment. . . . The activities regulated by the CWA have nothing to do with Congress' "commerce power over navigation." Indeed, the goals of the 1972 statute have nothing to do with *navigation* at all. . . .

The majority accuses respondents of reading the term "navigable" out of the statute. But that was accomplished by Congress when it deleted the word from the § 502(7) definition. . . .

II

As the majority correctly notes, when the Corps first promulgated regulations pursuant to § 404 of the 1972 Act, it construed its authority as being essentially the same as it had been under the 1899 RHA. The reaction to those regulations in the federal courts, in the Environmental Protection Agency (EPA), and in Congress convinced the Corps that the statute required it "to protect water quality to the full extent of the [C]ommerce [C]lause" and to extend federal regulation over discharges "to many areas that have never before been subject to Federal permits or to this form of water quality protection." 40 Fed. Reg. 31320 (1975). . . .

---

[6]   The definition of "navigable water" in earlier versions of the FWPCA had made express reference to navigability. § 211, 80 Stat. 1253.

[7]   The version adopted by the House of Representatives defined "navigable waters" as "the navigable waters of the United States, including the territorial seas." H.R. 11896, 92d Cong., 2d Sess., § 502(8) (1971). The CWA ultimately defined "navigable waters" simply as "the waters of the United States, including the territorial seas." 33 U.S.C. § 1362(7).

The Corps' broadened reading of its jurisdiction provoked opposition among some Members of Congress. As a result, in 1977, Congress considered a proposal that would have limited the Corps' jurisdiction under § 404 to waters that are used, or by reasonable improvement could be used, as a means to transport interstate or foreign commerce and their adjacent wetlands. H.R. 3199, 95th Cong., 1st Sess., § 16(f) (1977). A bill embodying that proposal passed the House but was defeated in the Senate. The debates demonstrate that Congress was fully aware of the Corps' understanding of the scope of its jurisdiction under the 1972 Act. . . .

III

Although it might have appeared problematic on a "linguistic" level for the Corps to classify "lands" as "waters" in Riverside Bayview, 474 U.S., at 131–132, we squarely held that the agency's construction of the statute that it was charged with enforcing was entitled to deference under Chevron. Today, however, the majority refuses to extend such deference to the same agency's construction of the same statute. This refusal is unfaithful to both Riverside Bayview and Chevron. For it is the majority's reading, not the agency's, that does violence to the scheme Congress chose to put into place.

Contrary to the Court's suggestion, the Corps' interpretation of the statute does not "encroac[h]" upon "traditional state power" over land use. "Land use planning in essence chooses particular uses for the land; environmental regulation, at its core, does not mandate particular uses of the land but requires only that, however the land is used, damage to the environment is kept within prescribed limits." California Coastal Comm'n v. Granite Rock Co., 480 U.S. 572, 587 (1987). The CWA is not a land-use code; it is a paradigm of environmental regulation. Such regulation is an accepted exercise of federal power.

It is particularly ironic for the Court to raise the specter of federalism while construing a statute that makes explicit efforts to foster local control over water regulation. Faced with calls to cut back on federal jurisdiction over water pollution, Congress rejected attempts to narrow the scope of that jurisdiction and, by incorporating § 404(g), opted instead for a scheme that encouraged States to supplant federal control with their own regulatory programs. . . . Because Illinois could have taken advantage of the opportunities offered to it through § 404(g), the federalism concerns to which the majority adverts are misplaced. The Corps' interpretation of the statute as extending beyond navigable waters, tributaries of navigable waters, and wetlands adjacent to each is manifestly reasonable and therefore entitled to deference.

IV

. . . Whether it is necessary or appropriate to refuse to allow petitioner to fill those ponds is a question on which we have no voice. Whether the Federal Government has the power to require such permission, however, is a question that is easily answered. If, as it does, the Commerce Clause empowers Congress to regulate particular "activities causing air or water pollution, or other environmental hazards that may have effects in more than one State," Hodel, 452 U.S., at 282, it also empowers Congress to control individual actions that, in the aggregate, would have the same effect. There is no merit in petitioner's constitutional argument.

Because I would affirm the judgment of the Court of Appeals, I respectfully dissent.

NOTE ON THE LOGIC OF THE SWANCC OPINIONS

(1)   This case deals with legal materials at five levels of authority:

>   (a)   A Constitutional provision: Art. I, § 8, cl. 3 (the Commerce Clause);

>   (b)   A statute: the Clean Water Act, notably § 404(a) (Corps authority over discharge of fill into "the navigable waters") and § 1362(7) (definition of "navigable waters" as "waters");

>   (c)   An agency "legislative" regulation: 33 CFR § 328.3(a)(3) ("waters" goes as far as "wetlands, sloughs, prairie potholes" etc.);

>   (d)   An agency "interpretative" regulation: the "Migratory Bird Rule"; and

>   (e)   An agency adjudication: the "Permit Evaluation and Decision Document" asserting the Corps' jurisdiction over the particular site.

Justice Stevens says that the agency's interpretation of its authority (developed in items c, d, and e) is a "manifestly reasonable" interpretation of the statute (item b) and "therefore entitled to deference"; this is a standard Chevron argument. Independently, Justice Stevens concludes that the statute (item b) is constitutional under the Commerce Clause (item a).

By contrast, the Court's opinion says two things. The first is that the language of the statute (b) clearly rejects the agency's assertion of authority (c, d, and e). This point, like Justice Stevens', is a standard Chevron analysis, differing only in the way the statute is read.

But the Court also says that "even were we to agree" that the statute was ambiguous, "we would not extend Chevron deference here." This is something different. The Court continues: "Where an administrative interpretation of a statute invokes the outer limits of Congress' power, we expect a clear indication that Congress intended that result." Ambiguity no longer helps the agency; it hurts its case.

Is this because of the relationship of the courts to Congress—because courts should interpret statutes in light of the canon of construction of avoiding Constitutional difficulties, such that an otherwise ambiguous statute now becomes clear? Or is this because of the relationship of the agencies to Congress—because Congress would not want agencies to test the limits of Congress' own authority? Justice Rehnquist asserts both rationales:

"This requirement stems from our prudential desire not to needlessly reach constitutional issues and our assumption that Congress does not casually authorize administrative agencies to interpret a statute to push the limit of congressional authority."

NOTES ON CANONS OF CONSTRUCTION AND CHEVRON

(1) *How Are Canons to be Handled under Chevron?* Linguistic canons—see p. 135—would seem to be fully applicable at Chevron Step One. It is in part by applying those canons that a statute may be determined to be clear or ambiguous. And both textualists and purposivists agree that canons are among the ordinary tools of statutory interpretation.

More controversial are the substantive canons, see p. 151. Probably the most well known of these is the canon Justice Rehnquist quotes in the SWANCC case: "where an otherwise acceptable construction of a statute would raise serious constitutional problems, the Court will construe the statute to avoid such problems unless such construction is plainly contrary to the intent of Congress." Edward J. DeBartolo Corp. v. Florida Gulf Coast Building & Constr. Trades Council, 485 U.S. 568, 575 (1988). As can be seen from his and Justice Stevens' opinions, this canon requires, by its own terms, a determination of whether a potential constitutional difficulty is "serious"; this element of judgment has often led Justices who all agree with the canon in principle to differ on its application in particular cases.

(2) Because substantive canons are based on assumed general policies of the law, their use in cases involving judicial review of agency action comes up against another assumed general policy of the law, the Chevron principle. The Chevron doctrine, after all, has the same structural consequence of resolving statutory ambiguity in a particular direction—to be specific, in the direction of agency authority. In SWANCC, Justice Rehnquist defends the proposition that the avoid-serious-constitutional-doubt principle should dominate the Chevron principle.

Other cases have faced the same issue with respect to other substantive canons and Chevron. For example, in EEOC v. Arabian American Oil Co., 499 U.S. 244 (1991), the Court held that the "[l]ong-standing principle of American law 'that legislation of Congress, unless a contrary intent appears, is meant to apply only within the territorial jurisdiction of the United States'" overrode any deference due under Chevron to the EEOC's interpretation of Title VII as applying extraterritorially. But sometimes the answer is not so clear. Compare Muscogee (Creek) Nation v. Hodel, 851 F.2d 1439 (D.C. Cir. 1988), cert. denied, 488 U.S. 1010 (1989) (applying the canon that ambiguous statutes should be construed in favor of American Indians, and noting that but for the canon deference to the agency's interpretation would have been appropriate) with Haynes v. United States, 891 F.2d 235 (9th Cir.1989) (declining to apply the same canon when Chevron deference was appropriate, on the grounds that the canon is a guideline, not substantive law, and that extended administrative practice deserves deference).

Immigration law is another area where the tension between Chevron and a substantive canon may be acute. Long before Chevron was decided, there was a principle of construing immigration statutes mandating deportation—now known as removal—narrowly. But if that rule of construction still applies, then how could Chevron ever operate in a case concerning whether Congress intended for an alien to be subject to removal? Whenever it was not clear whether Congress did intend for one of its statutes to require removal, the canon would seem to kick in to clarify the ambiguity in the alien's favor. In fact, however, Chevron is alive and well in the area of immigration, although there is no Supreme Court decision addressing what happened to the rule of immigration lenity post-Chevron. See Brian G. Slocum, The Immigration Rule of Lenity and Chevron Deference, 17 Geo. Imm. L. Rev. 515 (2003).

(3) *An Intermediate Answer?* KENNETH A. BAMBERGER, NORMATIVE CANONS IN THE REVIEW OF ADMINISTRATIVE POLICYMAKING, 118 Yale L.J. 64, 66–69 (2008): "Judicial application of normative canons . . . fits uncomfortably with the fundamental premise of Chevron U.S.A. Inc. v. Natural Resources Defense Council, Inc. . . . Under the preexisting canons regime, courts resolve statutory ambiguity conclusively, by resort to judge-made canonic presumptions. Yet after Chevron, when a statute is unclear, the resulting discretion belongs generally to the agency charged with its administration. . . .

"This tension has split courts and commentators. A majority, including the Supreme Court, argues that courts should continue to interpret legislation independently when normative canons would apply, even when Congress has charged a particular agency with the statute's administration. Canons, they conclude, involve the type of legal question best resolved by independent courts, rather than political agencies. More specifically, canons operate simply as clear-statement rules that constrain interpretive discretion and simply turn politically sensitive questions back to Congress. Accordingly, they leave no space for agency input, and judges should continue to fix statutory meaning independently when canonic values are implicated.

"A minority, including the Ninth Circuit, takes the opposite stance. Relying on Chevron's generalized understandings about superior agency expertise and political accountability, this account decries any continued judicial role in policing normative canons. It leaves to agencies the task of balancing both those goals reflected in statutory language and those left out.

"This Article rejects both all-or-nothing approaches. . . .

"The categorical approaches to resolving the Chevron-canons conflict ignore both the variability in canon application and the contingency of agency capacity. Specifically, a rule excluding agencies entirely from resolving statutory ambiguity when canonic norms are implicated fails to justify an all-or-nothing preference for judicial, rather than agency, discretion in three important ways. First, such a rule ignores the fact that agencies, in some circumstances, may possess greater capacity than courts for norm balancing. Second, it fails to provide any incentive for agencies to account for those values in their own decisionmaking. Such incentive would further the canons' strong policy of judicial restraint by obviating the need for judicial canon application in an important set of cases, as well as promote canons' goal of norm protection in the range of agency actions that never reach a courtroom. Third, it disregards important limits on judicial authority. . . .

"At the same time, a rule eliminating the judicial role in policing the application of normative canons after Chevron fails to recognize the unreliability of the agency contribution, especially in protecting values which are systemically underenforced. Such a rule removes incentives for agencies to account for such norms and constitutes, as a practical matter, a determination that certain important public values need not be consistently reflected in public policy.

"[This article] therefore concludes that the goals of both normative canons and Chevron require a contextual analysis—an institutionally sensitive framework that takes into account the particularity of governing doctrine and actual agency behavior in each case. . . . Incorporating a context-sensitive, case-by-case application of normative canons into Chevron's secondstep reasonableness analysis offers the best framework for enlisting the comparative strengths of both courts and agencies."

NOTES ON FEDERALISM AND AGENCY ACTION

(1) *Is There a Canon Regarding Federalism Applicable to Agency Action?* The Corps' authority over landfill under the Clean Water Act came before the Court again in RAPANOS V. UNITED STATES, 547 U.S. 715 (2006), with the Court again holding that the agency had overreached. JUSTICE SCALIA'S plurality opinion for the Court had this to say about the SWANCC principles, 547 U.S. at 737–738:

> Even if the phrase "the waters of the United States" were ambiguous as applied to intermittent flows, our own canons of construction would establish that the Corps' interpretation of the statute is impermissible. As we noted in SWANCC, the Government's expansive interpretation would "result in a significant impingement of the States' traditional and primary power over land and water use." Regulation of land use, as through the issuance of the development permits sought by petitioners . . . is a quintessential state and local power. The extensive federal jurisdiction urged by the Government would authorize the Corps to function as a de facto regulator of immense stretches of intrastate land—an authority the agency has shown its willingness to exercise with the scope of discretion that would befit a local zoning board. We ordinarily expect a "clear and manifest" statement from Congress to authorize an unprecedented intrusion into traditional state authority. The phrase "the waters of the United States" hardly qualifies.
>
> Likewise, just as we noted in SWANCC, the Corps' interpretation stretches the outer limits of Congress's commerce power and raises

difficult questions about the ultimate scope of that power. (In developing the current regulations, the Corps consciously sought to extend its authority to the farthest reaches of the commerce power. See 42 Fed. Reg. 37127 (1977).) Even if the term "the waters of the United States" were ambiguous as applied to channels that sometimes host ephemeral flows of water (which it is not), we would expect a clearer statement from Congress to authorize an agency theory of jurisdiction that presses the envelope of constitutional validity. See Edward J. DeBartolo Corp. v. Florida Gulf Coast Building & Constr. Trades Council, 485 U.S. 568, 575 (1988).

Both this passage and Justice Scalia's further reference to "these two clear-statement rules," 547 U.S. at 738, n. 9, suggest the existence of a federalism canon of construction separate in some way from the constitutional avoidance canon—a federalism canon that requires a clear statement from Congress to authorize an agency's doing something that trenches on "a quintessential state and local power" even if that interference would be unquestionably constitutional. (For a similar result when agency action is not at issue, see Bond v. United States, p. 152.)

(2)   What is the source of the extra respect for federalism implied by having a canon beyond constitutional avoidance? Shouldn't we rather have just that respect for state authority that the Constitution itself—with its carefully balanced structure of specifically named Congressional powers, equal Senatorial representation by state, a Supremacy Clause, and the like—stipulates? And, in any event, how does a federalism canon—insofar as it supports a presumption that Congress did not intend to preempt state and local regulation—interact with Chevron, insofar as the agency intends to be preemptive? In WATTERS V. WACHOVIA BANK, N.A., 550 U.S. 1 (2007), which concerned the scope of federal preemption of state laws that deal with the local mortgage lending activities of national banks, JUSTICE STEVENS, albeit in dissent, had this to say, 550 U.S. at 41:

> Even if the OCC [the relevant federal agency] did intend its regulation to preempt the state laws at issue here, it would still not merit Chevron deference. No case from this Court has ever applied such a deferential standard to an agency decision that could so easily disrupt the federal-state balance. To be sure, expert agency opinions as to which state laws conflict with a federal statute may be entitled to "some weight," especially when "the subject matter is technical" and "the relevant history and background are complex and extensive." Geier v. American Honda Motor Co., 529 U.S. 861, 883 (2000). But "[u]nlike Congress, administrative agencies are clearly not designed to represent the interests of States, yet with relative ease they can promulgate comprehensive and detailed regulations that have broad preemption ramifications for state law." Id., at 908 (Stevens, J., dissenting). For that reason, when an agency purports to decide the scope of federal preemption, a healthy respect for state sovereignty calls for something less than Chevron deference.

(3)   Even if we are persuaded that federalism does deserve an extra boost, how will we know "a quintessential state and local power" when we meet it? SWANCC and Rapanos emphasize property law—but is that more inherently local than contract law or tort law, which are the staples of state common law? Pretty much all federal agency action that is "regulatory" prohibits something that state common law allows—that is indeed the most likely reason that it is seen as "regulatory." How far does the federalism principle extend? When the question is not simply adding a federal regulatory requirement on top of state requirements but rather concluding that the federal requirement abrogates state law as contrary to a comprehensive federal scheme—the effect commonly referred to as "preemption"—the judicial "presumption against preemption" does extend beyond property law. For example, in WYETH V. LEVINE, 555 U.S. 555 (2009), the basic situation was this (555 U.S. at 558):

> Directly injecting the drug Phenergan into a patient's vein creates a significant risk of catastrophic consequences. A Vermont jury found that petitioner Wyeth, the manufacturer of the drug, had failed to provide an adequate warning of that risk and awarded damages to respondent Diana Levine to compensate her for the amputation of her arm. The warnings on Phenergan's label had been deemed sufficient by the federal Food and Drug Administration (FDA) when it approved Wyeth's new drug application in 1955 and when it later approved changes in the drug's labeling. The question we must decide is whether the FDA's approvals provide Wyeth with a complete defense to Levine's tort claims.

In the course of deciding that the approvals did not provide the defense that Wyeth claimed—which is to say, that this agency action did not preempt the state common law of torts—the Court repeated its statement from earlier cases, 555 U.S. at 565:

> [i]n all pre-emption cases, and particularly in those in which Congress has "legislated . . . in a field which the States have traditionally occupied," . . . we "start with the assumption that the historic police powers of the States were not to be superseded by the Federal Act unless that was the clear and manifest purpose of Congress."

(4)   ***Where Is the Authority to Preempt Best Placed?*** GILLIAN E. METZGER, ADMINISTRATIVE LAW AS THE NEW FEDERALISM, 57 Duke L.J. 2023, 2077–2083 (2008): "Public choice and institutional competency arguments are . . . raised against federal agencies' ability to serve as reliable representatives for state regulatory interests. One such argument asserts that agencies are primarily interested in expanding their own policymaking power and achieving their programmatic goals, which sets them in conflict with state regulatory autonomy. Another contends that agencies are overly responsive to particular industry or other constituencies and will privilege those constituencies' interests over state claims to regulatory authority. A third maintains that federal agencies' specific programmatic focus makes

them ill equipped to consider general issues of the appropriate federal-state balance. . . .

". . . It is hard to dispute the risk that federal agencies will privilege their specific programmatic goals over more general concerns relating to government structure, or may be unduly beholden to particular regulated entities. After all, administrative tunnel vision and agency capture are hardly unknown phenomena. It is similarly plausible that at least in some contexts federal agencies view state regulators as competitors and seek to use preemption to advance their institutional interests. The spate of aggressive preemption efforts by numerous different agencies during the Bush administration-the OCC, FDA, Consumer Product Safety Administration, the National Highway Safety Administration, and the Federal Railroad Administration-raises real concerns about the potential for federal bureaucratic empire building at the expense of the states.

"Yet public choice accounts of agency motivation become unduly simplistic, to the extent that they portray federal agency officials as motivated solely by desire for greater resources and power without consideration of what represents the best regulatory policy. It also is mistaken to think that agency self-interest always lies on the side of expanding federal regulatory power at state expense. Even in public choice terms that account rings hollow, as the potential for congressional retaliation or the desire to avoid new responsibilities may lead rational agency officials to a different account of where their parochial interests lie. The view that agencies will advance the interests of favored regulatory constituencies at the expense of the states is similarly oversimplified. Too many instances exist of federal agencies refusing to preempt or seeking to expand state regulatory autonomy to conclude that federal agencies are categorically insensitive or hostile to preserving a state regulatory role. This is not to deny that federal agencies are able to aggrandize themselves at the expense of the states when so inclined. But the fact that federal agencies frequently are not so inclined merits emphasis, and underscores that the explanation for federal agency behavior is more complicated.

"One crucial variable the public choice account omits is politics. An agency's political agenda is likely to affect whether the agency will seek to accord states a regulatory role or instead centralize control in Washington. Thus, recent efforts to preempt state tort actions are in line with the Bush administration's support for tort reform and restrictions. At least some of these preemption efforts were rejected under prior presidential administrations with different political agendas. Indeed, politics rather than institutional position often seems to be the driving force behind federal administrative limitations on (or deference to) the states. In that regard, agencies appear little different from Congress or even the courts.

"As that suggests, the real issue here is one of comparative institutional competency. Which institution—Congress, federal agencies, or the courts— is best situated to make the relevant political choices? Which will give greatest weight to preserving a meaningful state regulatory role? Constitutionally, Congress is the federal institution with primary policy-setting responsibility, and Congress is also the institution most structured to represent state interests. Yet it is not clear that Congress offers significantly more sensitivity to state regulatory prerogatives than federal agencies do. In any event, insisting that Congress itself resolve all federal-state questions is a nonstarter. Congress simply lacks the resources and foresight to resolve all the federalism issues that can arise in a given regulatory scheme. Requiring Congress to do so would impose a significant obstacle to federal regulation, something the Court's delegation cases indicate it is not prepared to do.

"As a result, in many ways the critical comparison is between federal agencies and federal courts; given that Congress will delegate broadly, one of the other institutions will need to resolve the federalism disputes that inevitably will arise. Moreover, it is hard to contest that of these two, agencies are more competent to make overt political choices. Yet a case nonetheless could be made that the courts have a comparative advantage over agencies in resolving federalism questions. Unlike specialized, program-focused agencies, the federal courts are generalist institutions that have special responsibilities to enforce constitutional structures and values. In practice, however, it is not at all clear that the federal courts have been more sensitive to state regulatory interests than agencies have been, and at times courts have been strong enforcers of federal uniformity over state control. Indeed, several commentators have noted the Rehnquist Court's willingness to curtail state regulatory authority in a variety of contexts.

"This leaves for consideration the claim that agencies simply lack expertise in determining the proper balance between federal and state regulation, particularly as compared to courts. Here, much turns on how the question of expertise is framed. Agencies have no special claim to expertise in assessing the proper federal-state balance in the abstract, divorced from a particular regulatory scheme or statute. But federalism disputes are unlikely to surface in such a form—whether before agencies, the federal courts, or Congress. Instead, . . . these questions arise in particular regulatory contexts. In such contexts, questions about the appropriate federal-state balance are not easily separated from substantive policy determinations on which agencies do have expertise. . . . The difficulty in separating substantive policy and federalism also undermines the institutional competency arguments in favor of courts, for courts are comparatively ill-equipped to assess the substantive impact that preserving a state role may have on a particular regulatory regime."

(5) *Is This Only a Chevron Issue?* Consider WILLIAM W. BUZBEE, PREEMPTION, HARD LOOK REVIEW, REGULATORY INTERACTION, AND THE QUEST FOR STEWARDSHIP AND INTERGENERATIONAL EQUITY, 77 Geo. Wash. L. Rev. 1521, 1556–58 (2009): "Agency claims of preemptive power and effect also virtually always contain an empirical footing with numerous factual and linked policy assumptions or findings: what about baseline conditions calls for preemptive action, and how do real world circumstances before and after an assertion of preemptive impact link to concerns made relevant by the underlying federal statute's criteria? Agency preemption claims sometimes also contain assertions about benefits and harms of allowing multiple regulatory voices or displacing all but a single, federal regulatory actor. If

the claim is that state regulation or tort law will invariably create conflict and defeat statutory ends, is there a basis for this? Might state enforcement of parallel laws further federal ends rather than frustrate or conflict with them? . . .

"Agencies largely failed to explore these questions in late Bush Administration agency assertions of preemptive power and effect. They also seldom sought public comment on whether to preempt. Yet these are all fundamentally empirical, fact-dominated questions where neither agencies nor reviewing courts have all relevant information. The content of those factual and policy questions and claims necessarily must be shaped by what a federal statute deems relevant, but they remain contestable and provable. The question is how such claimed effects should be reviewed by courts and, relatedly, what kinds of procedures agencies should utilize if they wish to claim preemptive power and effect. . . .

"Determining the standard of review for agency factual and policy determinations claimed to justify preemption relates both to doctrinal room left to articulate the standard of review and to normative goals in devising the standard. Although the Supreme Court has not explicitly spoken in terms of hard look review in the setting of agency preemption claims, preemption precedents and related administrative and constitutional law precedents support adoption of preemption hard look review. Explicitly embracing such a reviewing framework would constitute only a modest movement in existing doctrine, more clarification than change. Second, normative goals of encouraging agency transparency, accountability, and open process are furthered by hard look review. Such rigorous review, and the underlying regulatory process it would likely provoke, would also act to check preemption assertions. Ossification of regulation is often criticized, but in an area where the Supreme Court has long stated a presumption disfavoring preemption, a procedural brake on preemption finds a doctrinal footing. Finally, the regulatory interactions fostered by such review would shine scrutiny on arguments for preemptive effect that, by their nature, will often be motivated by interest group entreaties for relief from state regulatory or common law. Illuminating such entreaties and deliberation would enhance the likelihood of public-regarding behavior. . . .

"The basics of ordinary hard look review are well established and were first squarely embraced by the Supreme Court in State Farm."

(6) "THE WHITE HOUSE, May 20, 2009 / MEMORANDUM FOR THE HEADS OF EXECUTIVE DEPARTMENTS AND AGENCIES

"SUBJECT: Preemption . . .

"The purpose of this memorandum is to state the general policy of my Administration that preemption of State law by executive departments and agencies should be undertaken only with full consideration of the legitimate prerogatives of the States and with a sufficient legal basis for preemption. Executive departments and agencies should be mindful that in our Federal system, the citizens of the several States have distinctive circumstances and values, and that in many instances it is appropriate for them to apply to themselves rules and principles that reflect these circumstances and values.

As Justice Brandeis explained more than 70 years ago, '[i]t is one of the happy incidents of the federal system that a single courageous state may, if its citizens choose, serve as a laboratory; and try novel social and economic experiments without risk to the rest of the country.'

"... Heads of departments and agencies should review regulations issued within the past 10 years that contain statements in regulatory preambles or codified provisions intended by the department or agency to preempt State law, in order to decide whether such statements or provisions are justified under applicable legal principles governing preemption. Where the head of a department or agency determines that a regulatory statement of preemption or codified regulatory provision cannot be so justified, the head of that department or agency should initiate appropriate action, which may include amendment of the relevant regulation. . . .

"BARACK OBAMA"

> *U.S. v. MEAD CORP.*
> *Notes on the Logic of the Mead Opinions*
> *Notes on Putting the Mead Test for*
>   *Chevron Deference into Action*
> *Notes on the Theory of the Mead*
>   *Decision*
> *Notes on Agencies' Interpretations of*
>   *Their Own Regulations*

UNITED STATES v. MEAD CORPORATION

Supreme Court of the United States (2001).
533 U.S. 218.

■ JUSTICE SOUTER delivered the opinion of the Court.

The question is whether a tariff classification ruling by the United States Customs Service deserves judicial deference. The Federal Circuit rejected Customs's invocation of Chevron U.S.A. Inc. v. Natural Resources Defense Council, Inc., 467 U.S. 837 (1984), in support of such a ruling, to which it gave no deference. We agree that a tariff classification has no claim to judicial deference under Chevron, there being no indication that Congress intended such a ruling to carry the force of law, but we hold that under Skidmore v. Swift & Co., 323 U.S. 134 (1944), the ruling is eligible to claim respect according to its persuasiveness.

I

A

Imports are taxed under the Harmonized Tariff Schedule of the United States (HTSUS), 19 U.S.C. § 1202. Title 19 U.S.C. § 1500(b) provides that Customs "shall, under rules and regulations prescribed by the Secretary [of the Treasury] . . . fix the final classification and rate of duty applicable to . . . merchandise" under the HTSUS. Section 1502(a) provides that

> [t]he Secretary of the Treasury shall establish and promulgate such rules and regulations not inconsistent with the law (including regulations establishing procedures for the issuance of binding rulings prior to the entry of the merchandise concerned), and may disseminate such information as may be necessary to secure a just, impartial, and uniform appraisement of imported merchandise and the classification and assessment of duties thereon at the various ports of entry.[1]

The Secretary provides for tariff rulings before the entry of goods by regulations authorizing "ruling letters" setting tariff classifications for particular imports. 19 CFR § 177.8 (2000). A ruling letter

> represents the official position of the Customs Service with respect to the particular transaction or issue described therein and is binding on all Customs Service personnel in accordance with the provisions of this section until modified or revoked. In the absence of a change of practice or other modification or revocation which affects the principle of the ruling set forth in the ruling letter, that principle may be cited as authority in the disposition of transactions involving the same circumstances.

§ 177.9(a).

After the transaction that gives it birth, a ruling letter is to "be applied only with respect to transactions involving articles identical to the sample submitted with the ruling request or to articles whose description is identical to the description set forth in the ruling letter." § 177.9(b)(2). As a general matter, such a letter is "subject to modification or revocation without notice to any person, except the person to whom the letter was addressed," § 177.9(c), and the regulations consequently provide that "no other person should rely on the ruling letter or assume that the principles of that ruling will be applied in connection with any transaction other than the one described in the letter," *ibid.* Since ruling letters respond to transactions of the moment, they are not subject to notice and comment before being issued, may be published but need only be made "available for public inspection," 19 U.S.C. § 1625(a), and, at the time this action arose, could be modified without notice and comment under most circumstances, 19 CFR § 177.10(c).

Any of the 46 port-of-entry Customs offices may issue ruling letters, and so may the Customs Headquarters Office. . . . Most ruling letters contain little or no reasoning, but simply describe goods and state the appropriate category and tariff. A few letters, like the Headquarters ruling at issue here, set out a rationale in some detail.

---

[1] The statutory term "ruling" is defined by regulation as "a written statement . . . that interprets and applies the provisions of the Customs and related laws to a specific set of facts." 19 CFR § 177.1(d)(1).

B

Respondent, the Mead Corporation, imports "day planners," three-ring binders with pages having room for notes of daily schedules and phone numbers and addresses, together with a calendar and suchlike. The tariff schedule on point falls under the HTSUS heading for "[r]egisters, account books, notebooks, order books, receipt books, letter pads, memorandum pads, diaries and similar articles," HTSUS subheading 4820.10, which comprises two subcategories. Items in the first, "[d]iaries, notebooks and address books, bound; memorandum pads, letter pads and similar articles," were subject to a tariff of 4.0% at the time in controversy. Objects in the second, covering "[o]ther" items, were free of duty.

Between 1989 and 1993, Customs repeatedly treated day planners under the "other" HTSUS subheading. In January 1993, however, Customs changed its position, and issued a Headquarters ruling letter classifying Mead's day planners as "Diaries . . ., bound" subject to tariff under subheading 4820.10.20. That letter was short on explanation, but after Mead's protest, Customs Headquarters issued a new letter, carefully reasoned but never published, reaching the same conclusion. This letter considered two definitions of "diary" from the Oxford English Dictionary, the first covering a daily journal of the past day's events, the second a book including "printed dates for daily memoranda and jottings; also . . . calendars. . . ." Customs concluded that "diary" was not confined to the first, in part because the broader definition reflects commercial usage and hence the "commercial identity of these items in the marketplace." As for the definition of "bound," Customs concluded that HTSUS was not referring to "bookbinding," but to a less exact sort of fastening described in the Harmonized Commodity Description and Coding System Explanatory Notes to Heading 4820, which spoke of binding by "reinforcements or fittings of metal, plastics, etc."

Customs rejected Mead's further protest of the second Headquarters ruling letter, and Mead filed suit in the Court of International Trade (CIT). The CIT granted the Government's motion for summary judgment, adopting Customs's reasoning without saying anything about deference. 17 F.Supp.2d 1004 (1998).

Mead then went to the United States Court of Appeals for the Federal Circuit. . . .

The Federal Circuit . . . reversed the CIT and held that Customs classification rulings should not get Chevron deference. . . . Rulings are not preceded by notice and comment as under the Administrative Procedure Act (APA), 5 U.S.C. § 553, they "do not carry the force of law and are not, like regulations, intended to clarify the rights and obligations of importers beyond the specific case under review." 185 F.3d, at 1307. The appeals court thought classification rulings had a weaker Chevron claim even than Internal Revenue Service interpretive rulings, to which that court gives no deference; unlike rulings by the IRS,

Customs rulings issue from many locations and need not be published. 185 F.3d, at 1307–1308.

The Court of Appeals accordingly gave no deference at all to the ruling classifying the Mead day planners and rejected the agency's reasoning as to both "diary" and "bound." It thought that planners were not diaries because they had no space for "relatively extensive notations about events, observations, feelings, or thoughts" in the past. Id., at 1310. And it concluded that diaries "bound" in subheading 4810.10.20 presupposed "unbound" diaries, such that treating ring-fastened diaries as "bound" would leave the "unbound diary" an empty category. Id., at 1311.

We granted certiorari, in order to consider the limits of Chevron deference owed to administrative practice in applying a statute. We hold that administrative implementation of a particular statutory provision qualifies for Chevron deference when it appears that Congress delegated authority to the agency generally to make rules carrying the force of law, and that the agency interpretation claiming deference was promulgated in the exercise of that authority. Delegation of such authority may be shown in a variety of ways, as by an agency's power to engage in adjudication or notice-and-comment rulemaking, or by some other indication of a comparable congressional intent. The Customs ruling at issue here fails to qualify, although the possibility that it deserves some deference under Skidmore leads us to vacate and remand.

II

A

When Congress has "explicitly left a gap for an agency to fill, there is an express delegation of authority to the agency to elucidate a specific provision of the statute by regulation," Chevron, 467 U.S., at 843–844, and any ensuing regulation is binding in the courts unless procedurally defective, arbitrary or capricious in substance, or manifestly contrary to the statute. APA, 5 U.S.C. §§ 706(2)(A), (D). But whether or not they enjoy any express delegation of authority on a particular question, agencies charged with applying a statute necessarily make all sorts of interpretive choices, and while not all of those choices bind judges to follow them, they certainly may influence courts facing questions the agencies have already answered. "[T]he well-reasoned views of the agencies implementing a statute 'constitute a body of experience and informed judgment to which courts and litigants may properly resort for guidance,'" Bragdon v. Abbott, 524 U.S. 624, 642 (1998) (quoting Skidmore, 323 U.S., at 139–140), and "[w]e have long recognized that considerable weight should be accorded to an executive department's construction of a statutory scheme it is entrusted to administer...." Chevron, *supra*, at 844. The fair measure of deference to an agency administering its own statute has been understood to vary with circumstances, and courts have looked to the degree of the agency's care, its consistency, formality, and relative expertness, and to the persuasiveness of the agency's position. The approach has produced a spectrum of judicial responses, from great respect at one end, to near indifference at the other. Justice Jackson summed things up in Skidmore v. Swift & Co.:

> The weight [accorded to an administrative] judgment in a particular case will depend upon the thoroughness evident in its consideration, the validity of its reasoning, its consistency with earlier and later pronouncements, and all those factors which give it power to persuade, if lacking power to control. 323 U.S., at 140.

Since 1984, we have identified a category of interpretive choices distinguished by an additional reason for judicial deference. This Court in Chevron recognized that Congress not only engages in express delegation of specific interpretive authority, but that "[s]ometimes the legislative delegation to an agency on a particular question is implicit." 467 U.S., at 844. Congress, that is, may not have expressly delegated authority or responsibility to implement a particular provision or fill a particular gap. Yet it can still be apparent from the agency's generally conferred authority and other statutory circumstances that Congress would expect the agency to be able to speak with the force of law when it addresses ambiguity in the statute or fills a space in the enacted law, even one about which "Congress did not actually have an intent" as to a particular result. Id., at 845. When circumstances implying such an expectation exist, a reviewing court has no business rejecting an agency's exercise of its generally conferred authority to resolve a particular statutory ambiguity simply because the agency's chosen resolution seems unwise, but is obliged to accept the agency's position if Congress has not previously spoken to the point at issue and the agency's interpretation is reasonable; cf. 5 U.S.C. § 706(2) (a reviewing court shall set aside agency action, findings, and conclusions found to be "arbitrary, capricious, an abuse of discretion, or otherwise not in accordance with law").

We have recognized a very good indicator of delegation meriting Chevron treatment in express congressional authorizations to engage in the process of rulemaking or adjudication that produces regulations or rulings for which deference is claimed. It is fair to assume generally that Congress contemplates administrative action with the effect of law when it provides for a relatively formal administrative procedure tending to foster the fairness and deliberation that should underlie a pronouncement of such force.[11] Thus, the overwhelming number of our cases applying Chevron deference have reviewed the fruits of notice-and-

---

[11] See Merrill & Hickman, Chevron's Domain, 89 Geo. L.J. 833, 872 (2001) ("[I]f Chevron rests on a presumption about congressional intent, then Chevron should apply only where Congress would want Chevron to apply. In delineating the types of delegations of agency authority that trigger Chevron deference, it is therefore important to determine whether a plausible case can be made that Congress would want such a delegation to mean that agencies enjoy primary interpretational authority").

comment rulemaking or formal adjudication.[12] That said, and as significant as notice-and-comment is in pointing to Chevron authority, the want of that procedure here does not decide the case, for we have sometimes found reasons for Chevron deference even when no such administrative formality was required and none was afforded, see, *e.g.,* NationsBank of N.C., N.A. v. Variable Annuity Life Ins. Co., 513 U.S. 251, 256–257, 263 (1995).[13] The fact that the tariff classification here was not a product of such formal process does not alone, therefore, bar the application of Chevron.

There are, nonetheless, ample reasons to deny Chevron deference here. The authorization for classification rulings, and Customs's practice in making them, present a case far removed not only from notice-and-comment process, but from any other circumstances reasonably suggesting that Congress ever thought of classification rulings as deserving the deference claimed for them here.

B

No matter which angle we choose for viewing the Customs ruling letter in this case, it fails to qualify under Chevron. On the face of the statute, to begin with, the terms of the congressional delegation give no indication that Congress meant to delegate authority to Customs to issue classification rulings with the force of law. We are not, of course, here making any global statement about Customs's authority, for it is true that the general rulemaking power conferred on Customs, see 19 U.S.C. § 1624, authorizes some regulation with the force of law, or "legal norms." It is true as well that Congress had classification rulings in mind when it explicitly authorized, in a parenthetical, the issuance of "regulations establishing procedures for the issuance of binding rulings prior to the entry of the merchandise concerned," 19 U.S.C. § 1502(a). The reference to binding classifications does not, however, bespeak the legislative type of activity that would naturally bind more than the parties to the ruling, once the goods classified are admitted into this country. And though the statute's direction to disseminate "information" necessary to "secure" uniformity, 19 U.S.C. § 1502(a), seems to assume that a ruling may be precedent in later transactions, precedential value alone does not add up to Chevron entitlement; interpretive rules may sometimes function as precedents, see Strauss, The Rulemaking Continuum, 41 Duke L.J. 1463, 1472–1473 (1992), and they enjoy no Chevron status as a class. In any event, any precedential claim of a classification ruling is counterbalanced by the provision for independent review of Customs classifications by the CIT, see 28 U.S.C. §§ 2638–2640 . . . .

---

[12] For rulemaking cases, see, e.g., [19 cases cited]. For adjudication cases, see e.g., [8 cases cited].

[13] In NationsBank of N.C., N.A. v. Variable Annuity Life Ins. Co., 513 U.S. 251, 256–257 (1995), we quoted longstanding precedent concluding that "[t]he Comptroller of the Currency is charged with the enforcement of banking laws to an extent that warrants the invocation of [the rule of deference] with respect to his deliberative conclusions as to the meaning of these laws" (internal quotation marks omitted).

It is difficult, in fact, to see in the agency practice itself any indication that Customs ever set out with a lawmaking pretense in mind when it undertook to make classifications like these. Customs does not generally engage in notice-and-comment practice when issuing them, and their treatment by the agency makes it clear that a letter's binding character as a ruling stops short of third parties; Customs has regarded a classification as conclusive only as between itself and the importer to whom it was issued, 19 CFR § 177.9(c), and even then only until Customs has given advance notice of intended change, §§ 177.9(a), (c). Other importers are in fact warned against assuming any right of detrimental reliance. § 177.9(c).

Indeed, to claim that classifications have legal force is to ignore the reality that 46 different Customs offices issue 10,000 to 15,000 of them each year. Any suggestion that rulings intended to have the force of law are being churned out at a rate of 10,000 a year at an agency's 46 scattered offices is simply self-refuting. Although the circumstances are less startling here, with a Headquarters letter in issue, none of the relevant statutes recognizes this category of rulings as separate or different from others; there is thus no indication that a more potent delegation might have been understood as going to Headquarters even when Headquarters provides developed reasoning, as it did in this instance.

In sum, classification rulings are best treated like "interpretations contained in policy statements, agency manuals, and enforcement guidelines." Christensen v. Harris County, 529 U.S. 576, 587 (2000). They are beyond the Chevron pale.

C

To agree with the Court of Appeals that Customs ruling letters do not fall within Chevron is not, however, to place them outside the pale of any deference whatever. Chevron did nothing to eliminate Skidmore's holding that an agency's interpretation may merit some deference whatever its form, given the "specialized experience and broader investigations and information" available to the agency, 323 U.S., at 139, and given the value of uniformity in its administrative and judicial understandings of what a national law requires, id., at 140.

There is room at least to raise a Skidmore claim here, where the regulatory scheme is highly detailed, and Customs can bring the benefit of specialized experience to bear on the subtle questions in this case: whether the daily planner with room for brief daily entries falls under "diaries," when diaries are grouped with "notebooks and address books, bound; memorandum pads, letter pads and similar articles," HTSUS subheading 4820.10.20; and whether a planner with a ring binding should qualify as "bound," when a binding may be typified by a book, but also may have "reinforcements or fittings of metal, plastics, etc.," Harmonized Commodity Description and Coding System Explanatory Notes to Heading 4820, p. 687. A classification ruling in this situation may therefore at least seek a respect proportional to its "power to persuade." Such a ruling may surely claim the merit of its writer's thoroughness, logic and expertness, its fit with prior interpretations, and any other sources of weight.

D

Underlying the position we take here, like the position expressed by Justice Scalia in dissent, is a choice about the best way to deal with an inescapable feature of the body of congressional legislation authorizing administrative action. That feature is the great variety of ways in which the laws invest the Government's administrative arms with discretion, and with procedures for exercising it, in giving meaning to Acts of Congress. Implementation of a statute may occur in formal adjudication or the choice to defend against judicial challenge; it may occur in a central board or office or in dozens of enforcement agencies dotted across the country; its institutional lawmaking may be confined to the resolution of minute detail or extend to legislative rulemaking on matters intentionally left by Congress to be worked out at the agency level.

Although we all accept the position that the Judiciary should defer to at least some of this multifarious administrative action, we have to decide how to take account of the great range of its variety. If the primary objective is to simplify the judicial process of giving or withholding deference, then the diversity of statutes authorizing discretionary administrative action must be declared irrelevant or minimized. If, on the other hand, it is simply implausible that Congress intended such a broad range of statutory authority to produce only two varieties of administrative action, demanding either Chevron deference or none at all, then the breadth of the spectrum of possible agency action must be taken into account. Justice Scalia's first priority over the years has been to limit and simplify. The Court's choice has been to tailor deference to variety. This acceptance of the range of statutory variation has led the Court to recognize more than one variety of judicial deference, just as the Court has recognized a variety of indicators that Congress would expect Chevron deference.[18]

Our respective choices are repeated today. Justice Scalia would pose the question of deference as an either-or choice. On his view that Chevron rendered Skidmore anachronistic, when courts owe any deference it is Chevron deference that they owe. Whether courts do owe deference in a given case turns, for him, on whether the agency action (if reasonable) is "authoritative." The character of the authoritative derives, in turn, not from breadth of delegation or the agency's procedure in implementing it, but is defined as the "official" position of an agency, and may ultimately be a function of administrative persistence alone.

---

[18] It is, of course, true that the limit of Chevron deference is not marked by a hard-edged rule. But Chevron itself is a good example showing when Chevron deference is warranted, while this is a good case showing when it is not. Judges in other, perhaps harder, cases will make reasoned choices between the two examples, the way courts have always done.

The Court, on the other hand, said nothing in Chevron to eliminate Skidmore's recognition of various justifications for deference depending on statutory circumstances and agency action; Chevron was simply a case recognizing that even without express authority to fill a specific statutory gap, circumstances pointing to implicit congressional delegation present a particularly insistent call for deference. Indeed, in holding here that Chevron left Skidmore intact and applicable where statutory circumstances indicate no intent to delegate general authority to make rules with force of law, or where such authority was not invoked, we hold nothing more than we said last Term in response to the particular statutory circumstances in Christensen, to which Justice Scalia then took exception, just as he does again today.

We think, in sum, that Justice Scalia's efforts to simplify ultimately run afoul of Congress's indications that different statutes present different reasons for considering respect for the exercise of administrative authority or deference to it. Without being at odds with congressional intent much of the time, we believe that judicial responses to administrative action must continue to differentiate between Chevron and Skidmore, and that continued recognition of Skidmore is necessary for just the reasons Justice Jackson gave when that case was decided.[19]

. . .

Since the Skidmore assessment called for here ought to be made in the first instance by the Court of Appeals for the Federal Circuit or the Court of International Trade, we go no further than to vacate the judgment and remand the case for further proceedings consistent with this opinion.

■ JUSTICE SCALIA, dissenting.

Today's opinion makes an avulsive change in judicial review of federal administrative action. Whereas previously a reasonable agency application of an ambiguous statutory provision had to be sustained so long as it represented the agency's authoritative interpretation, henceforth such an application can be set aside unless "it appears that Congress delegated authority to the agency generally to make rules carrying the force of law," as by giving an agency "power to engage in adjudication or notice-and-comment rulemaking, or . . . some other [procedure] indicati[ng] comparable congressional intent," and "the agency interpretation claiming deference was promulgated in the exercise of that authority." What was previously a general presumption of authority in agencies to resolve ambiguity in the statutes they have been authorized to enforce has been changed to a presumption of no such authority, which must be overcome by affirmative legislative intent to

---

[19] Surely Justice Jackson's practical criteria, along with Chevron's concern with congressional understanding, provide more reliable guideposts than conclusory references to the "authoritative" or "official." Even if those terms provided a true criterion, there would have to be something wrong with a standard that accorded the status of substantive law to every one of 10,000 "official" customs classifications rulings turned out each year from over 46 offices placed around the country at the Nation's entryways.

the contrary. And whereas previously, when agency authority to resolve ambiguity did not exist the court was free to give the statute what it considered the best interpretation, henceforth the court must supposedly give the agency view some indeterminate amount of so-called Skidmore deference. We will be sorting out the consequences of the Mead doctrine, which has today replaced the Chevron doctrine, for years to come. I would adhere to our established jurisprudence, defer to the reasonable interpretation the Customs Service has given to the statute it is charged with enforcing, and reverse the judgment of the Court of Appeals.

I

Only five years ago, the Court described the Chevron doctrine as follows: "We accord deference to agencies under Chevron . . . because of a presumption that Congress, when it left ambiguity in a statute meant for implementation by an agency, understood that the ambiguity would be resolved, first and foremost, by the agency, and desired the agency (rather than the courts) to possess whatever degree of discretion the ambiguity allows," Smiley v. Citibank (South Dakota), N.A., 517 U.S. 735, 740–741 (1996). Today the Court collapses this doctrine, announcing instead a presumption that agency discretion does not exist unless the statute, expressly or impliedly, says so. While the Court disclaims any hard-and-fast rule for determining the existence of discretion-conferring intent, it asserts that "a very good indicator [is] express congressional authorizations to engage in the process of rulemaking or adjudication that produces regulations or rulings for which deference is claimed." Only when agencies act through "adjudication[,] notice-and-comment rulemaking, or . . . some other [procedure] indicati[ng] comparable congressional intent [whatever that means]" is Chevron deference applicable—because these "relatively formal administrative procedure[s] [designed] to foster . . . fairness and deliberation" bespeak (according to the Court) congressional willingness to have the agency, rather than the courts, resolve statutory ambiguities. Once it is determined that Chevron deference is not in order, the uncertainty is not at an end—and indeed is just beginning. Litigants cannot then assume that the statutory question is one for the courts to determine, according to traditional interpretive principles and by their own judicial lights. No, the Court now resurrects, in full force, the pre-Chevron doctrine of Skidmore deference. . . . The Court has largely replaced Chevron, in other words, with that test most beloved by a court unwilling to be held to rules (and most feared by litigants who want to know what to expect): th'ol' "totality of the circumstances" test.

The Court's new doctrine is neither sound in principle nor sustainable in practice.

A

As to principle: The doctrine of Chevron—that all *authoritative* agency interpretations of statutes they are charged with administering deserve deference—was rooted in a legal presumption of congressional intent, important to the division of powers between the Second and Third Branches. When, Chevron said, Congress leaves an ambiguity in a statute that is to be administered by an executive agency, it is presumed that Congress meant to give the agency discretion, within the limits of reasonable interpretation, as to how the ambiguity is to be resolved. By committing enforcement of the statute to an agency rather than the courts, Congress committed its initial and primary interpretation to that branch as well. . . .

The basis in principle for today's new doctrine can be described as follows: The background rule is that ambiguity in legislative instructions to agencies is to be resolved not by the agencies but by the judges. Specific congressional intent to depart from this rule must be found—and while there is no single touchstone for such intent it can generally be found when Congress has authorized the agency to act through (what the Court says is) relatively formal procedures such as informal rulemaking and formal (and informal?) adjudication, and when the agency in fact employs such procedures. . . . [T]he Court's principal criterion of congressional intent to supplant its background rule seems to me quite implausible. There is no necessary connection between the formality of procedure and the power of the entity administering the procedure to resolve authoritatively questions of law. The most formal of the procedures the Court refers to—formal adjudication—is modeled after the process used in trial courts, which of course are not generally accorded deference on questions of law. The purpose of such a procedure is to produce a closed record for determination and review of the facts—which implies nothing about the power of the agency subjected to the procedure to resolve authoritatively questions of law. . . .

B

As for the practical effects of the new rule:

(1)

The principal effect will be protracted confusion. As noted above, the one test for Chevron deference that the Court enunciates is wonderfully imprecise: whether "Congress delegated authority to the agency generally to make rules carrying the force of law, . . . as by . . . adjudication[,] notice-and-comment rulemaking, or . . . some other [procedure] indicati[ng] comparable congressional intent." But even this description does not do justice to the utter flabbiness of the Court's criterion, since, in order to maintain the fiction that the new test is really just the old one, applied consistently throughout our case law, the Court must make a virtually open-ended exception to its already imprecise guidance: In the present case, it tells us, the absence of notice-and-comment rulemaking . . . is not enough to decide the question of Chevron deference, "for we have sometimes found reasons for Chevron deference even when no such administrative formality was required and none was afforded." The opinion then goes on to consider a grab bag of other factors—including the factor that used to be the sole criterion for

Chevron deference: whether the interpretation represented the *authoritative* position of the agency. It is hard to know what the lower courts are to make of today's guidance.

(2)

Another practical effect of today's opinion will be an artificially induced increase in informal rulemaking. Buy stock in the GPO. Since informal rulemaking and formal adjudication are the only more-or-less safe harbors from the storm that the Court has unleashed; and since formal adjudication is [often] not an option . . . informal rulemaking . . . will now become a virtual necessity. As I have described, the Court's safe harbor requires not merely that the agency have been given rulemaking authority, but also that the agency have *employed* rulemaking as the means of resolving the statutory ambiguity. (It is hard to understand why that should be so. Surely the mere *conferral* of rulemaking authority demonstrates—if one accepts the Court's logic-a congressional intent to allow the agency to resolve ambiguities. And given that intent, what difference does it make that the agency chooses instead to use another perfectly permissible means for that purpose?) Moreover, the majority's approach will have a perverse effect on the rules that do emerge, given the principle (which the Court leaves untouched today) that judges must defer to reasonable agency interpretations of their own regulations. Agencies will now have high incentive to rush out barebones, ambiguous rules construing statutory ambiguities, which they can then in turn further clarify through informal rulings entitled to judicial respect.

(3)

Worst of all, the majority's approach will lead to the ossification of large portions of our statutory law. Where Chevron applies, statutory ambiguities remain ambiguities subject to the agency's ongoing clarification. They create a space, so to speak, for the exercise of continuing agency discretion. As Chevron itself held, the Environmental Protection Agency can interpret "stationary source" to mean a single smokestack, can later replace that interpretation with the "bubble concept" embracing an entire plant, and if that proves undesirable can return again to the original interpretation. For the indeterminately large number of statutes taken out of Chevron by today's decision, however, ambiguity (and hence flexibility) will cease with the first judicial resolution. Skidmore deference gives the agency's current position some vague and uncertain amount of respect, but it does not, like Chevron, *leave* the matter within the control of the Executive Branch for the future. Once the court has spoken, it becomes *unlawful* for the agency to take a contradictory position; the statute now *says* what the court has prescribed. . . .

One might respond that such ossification would not result if the agency were simply to readopt its interpretation, after a court reviewing it under Skidmore had rejected it, by repromulgating it through one of the Chevron-eligible procedural formats approved by the Court today.

Approving this procedure would be a landmark abdication of judicial power. It is worlds apart from Chevron proper, where the court does not *purport* to give the statute a judicial interpretation—except in identifying the scope of the statutory ambiguity, as to which the court's judgment is final and irreversible. (Under Chevron proper, when the agency's authoritative interpretation comes within the scope of that ambiguity—and the court therefore approves it—the agency will not be "overruling" the court's decision when it later decides that a different interpretation (still within the scope of the ambiguity) is preferable.) By contrast, under this view, the reviewing court will not be holding the agency's authoritative interpretation within the scope of the ambiguity; but will be holding that the agency has not used the "delegation-conferring" procedures, and that the court must therefore *interpret the statute on its own*—but subject to reversal if and when the agency uses the proper procedures. . . .

There is, in short, no way to avoid the ossification of federal law that today's opinion sets in motion. What a court says is the law after according Skidmore deference will be the law forever, beyond the power of the agency to change even through rulemaking.

(4)

And finally, the majority's approach compounds the confusion it creates by breathing new life into the anachronism of Skidmore, which sets forth a sliding scale of deference owed an agency's interpretation of a statute that is dependent "upon the thoroughness evident in [the agency's] consideration, the validity of its reasoning, its consistency with earlier and later pronouncements, and all those factors which give it power to persuade, if lacking power to control"; in this way, the appropriate measure of deference will be accorded the "body of experience and informed judgment" that such interpretations often embody, 323 U.S., at 140. Justice Jackson's eloquence notwithstanding, the rule of Skidmore deference is an empty truism and a trifling statement of the obvious: A judge should take into account the well-considered views of expert observers.

It was possible to live with the indeterminacy of Skidmore deference in earlier times. But in an era when federal statutory law administered by federal agencies is pervasive, and when the ambiguities (intended or unintended) that those statutes contain are innumerable, totality-of-the-circumstances Skidmore deference is a recipe for uncertainty, unpredictability, and endless litigation. To condemn a vast body of agency action to that regime (all except rulemaking, formal (and informal?) adjudication, and whatever else might now and then be included within today's intentionally vague formulation of affirmative congressional intent to "delegate") is irresponsible.

II

The Court's pretense that today's opinion is nothing more than application of our prior case law does not withstand analysis. . . .

III

To decide the present case, I would adhere to the original formulation of Chevron. "'The power of an administrative agency to administer a congressionally created . . . program necessarily requires the formulation of policy and the making of rules to fill any gap left, implicitly or explicitly, by Congress,'" 467 U.S., at 843 (quoting Morton v. Ruiz, 415 U.S. 199, 231 (1974)). We accordingly presume—and our precedents have made clear to Congress that we presume—that, absent some clear textual indication to the contrary, "Congress, when it left ambiguity in a statute meant for implementation by an agency, understood that the ambiguity would be resolved, first and foremost, by the agency, and desired the agency (rather than the courts) to possess whatever degree of discretion the ambiguity allows," Smiley, 517 U.S., at 740–741. Chevron sets forth an across-the-board presumption, which operates as a background rule of law against which Congress legislates: Ambiguity means Congress intended agency discretion. Any resolution of the ambiguity by the administering agency that is authoritative—that represents the official position of the agency—must be accepted by the courts if it is reasonable.

Nothing in the statute at issue here displays an intent to modify the background presumption on which Chevron deference is based. . . .

There is no doubt that the Customs Service's interpretation represents the authoritative view of the agency. Although the actual ruling letter was signed by only the Director of the Commercial Rulings Branch of Customs Headquarters' Office of Regulations and Rulings, the Solicitor General of the United States has filed a brief, cosigned by the General Counsel of the Department of the Treasury, that represents the position set forth in the ruling letter to be the official position of the Customs Service. No one contends that it is merely a "post hoc rationalizatio[n]" or an "agency litigating positio[n] wholly unsupported by regulations, rulings, or administrative practice."[6]

There is also no doubt that the Customs Service's interpretation is a reasonable one, whether or not judges would consider it the best. I will

---

[6]   The Court's parting shot, that "there would have to be something wrong with a standard that accorded the status of substantive law to every one of 10,000 'official' customs classifications rulings turned out each year from over 46 offices placed around the country at the Nation's entryways" misses the mark. I do not disagree. The "authoritativeness" of an agency interpretation does not turn upon whether it has been enunciated by someone who is actually employed by the agency. It must represent the judgment of central agency management, approved at the highest levels. I would find that condition to have been satisfied when, a ruling having been attacked in court, the general counsel of the agency has determined that it should be defended. If one thinks that that does not impart sufficient authoritativeness, then surely the line has been crossed when, as here, the General Counsel of the agency and the Solicitor General of the United States have assured this Court that the position represents the agency's authoritative view. . . .

not belabor this point, since the Court evidently agrees: An interpretation that was unreasonable would not merit the remand that the Court decrees for consideration of Skidmore deference.

IV

. . . For the reasons stated, I respectfully dissent from the Court's judgment. I would uphold the Customs Service's construction of Subheading 4820.10.20 of the Harmonized Tariff Schedule of the United States, 19 U.S.C. § 1202, and would reverse the contrary decision of the Court of Appeals. I dissent even more vigorously from the reasoning that produces the Court's judgment, and that makes today's decision one of the most significant opinions ever rendered by the Court dealing with the judicial review of administrative action. Its consequences will be enormous, and almost uniformly bad.

NOTES ON THE LOGIC OF THE MEAD OPINIONS

(1) ***Where Is Mead Coming From?*** Just one year before Mead, in CHRISTENSEN V. HARRIS COUNTY, 529 U.S. 576 (2000), the Court considered the status of an opinion letter issued by the Department of Labor's Wage and Hour Division applying the Fair Labor Standards Act to a particular set of circumstances. Holding against the agency's interpretation, the Court, in an opinion by JUSTICE THOMAS, refused to give it Chevron deference. 529 U.S. at 587:

> Here . . . we confront an interpretation contained in an opinion letter, not one arrived at after, for example, a formal adjudication or notice-and-comment rulemaking. Interpretations such as those in opinion letters—like interpretations contained in policy statements, agency manuals, and enforcement guidelines, all of which lack the force of law—do not warrant Chevron-style deference.

Instead, the interpretation was entitled to Skidmore deference, but in applying that standard Justice Thomas found the agency's interpretation "unpersuasive."

Justice Thomas spoke for five members of the Court. Justice Scalia agreed with the result reached, not because he would refuse Chevron deference but because even granting that deference he considered the agency's statutory interpretation unreasonable. In terms not unlike those used in Mead, he specifically abjured Skidmore deference. Justices Stevens, Breyer, and Ginsburg dissented in two opinions, the gist of which was that the Department got it right, whether viewed as a matter of Skidmore or Chevron.

Christensen was, thus, in some sense a dress-rehearsal for Mead. But in Mead, Justice Souter speaks with the authority of eight Justices and delivers an opinion in which Skidmore deference is clearly part of the holding, since it forms the basis for the instructions to the court below upon remand.

(2)   PETER L. STRAUSS, PUBLICATION RULES IN THE RULEMAKING SPECTRUM: ASSURING PROPER RESPECT FOR AN ESSENTIAL ELEMENT, 53 Admin. L. Rev. 803, 822–23 (2001): "The Supreme Court's recent decision in Christensen v. Harris County and its very recent decision in United States v. Mead Corp. have focused attention on how one might articulate the way in which agency judgments on matters of law or policy should influence reviewing courts. Putting aside the possibility of treating agency views as simply irrelevant, two models live in the cases. The first might be described as 'obedience'— courts encountering agency decisions they conclude the agencies were authorized to take must accept the conclusions they embody rather than displace them with their own independent judgment on the matter. The second, as 'weight'—the court is responsible for decision of a matter; but, in so deciding it will treat the agency views as constituent elements of its own decision, as persuasive if not controlling material whose force derives from the agency's office and the dignity of its action. The 'obedience' model is firmly associated in the Court's canon with its decision in Chevron U.S.A., Inc. v. Natural Resources Defense Council that, within the possibilities of meaning a statute's language could be given, a matter for the courts to decide, a reviewing court must accept any reasonable interpretation given that language by the agency Congress has empowered to implement the statute. The 'weight' model was best articulated by Justice Jackson in Skidmore v. Swift & Co. . . . .

"Christensen, which arose in precisely the same context as Skidmore, held that Skidmore weight rather than Chevron obedience remained the correct measure of the force of an agency upon judicial interpretation of text where the agency interpretation was expressed in a publication rule. Mead Corp., which concerned a Customs Service tariff classification ruling, reiterated the point, with rather more (and more satisfactory) attention to the nature of that weight and its influence on judicial judgment."

(3)   *How Do You Understand Justice Souter's Opinion?* The particulars of the two tests are worked out in the Notes following Skidmore (pp. 1128– 1129) and Chevron (pp. 1136–1171). But what do you make of Justice Souter's way of presenting the landscape of deference in Section II of his opinion? Is Skidmore's multifactored analysis of deference now the core principle, with Chevron representing merely the limiting case of "most" deference because "an additional reason for judicial deference applies"? Or is Skidmore merely a clean-up principle, kept alive so as to give judges more choices than Chevron or nothing? More broadly, are judges now to employ a "spectrum of judicial responses" or is it Chevron—or Skidmore—or nothing?

In S.D. Warren Co. v. Maine Board of Environmental Protection, 547 U.S. 370 (2006), the statutory question was whether river water that collects behind a dam and then flows through turbines back into the riverbed constituted a "discharge" into the river under the Clean Water Act; if it did, additional environmental licenses were needed. The Maine Board of Environmental Protection, a state agency charged with licensing S. D. Warren's dams, said that the additional licenses were needed. In the subsequent litigation, the Court supported the agency. Partly it looked to common usage as shown in a dictionary ("the Hudson discharges its waters into the bay"). But partly it looked to statements appearing in a federal Environmental Protection Agency handbook and in a Federal Energy Regulatory Commission adjudication. "Warren," wrote Justice Souter, "is, of course, entirely correct in cautioning us that because neither the EPA nor FERC has formally settled the definition, or even set out agency reasoning, these expressions of agency understanding do not command deference from this Court [references to Chevron and Skidmore.] But even so, the administrative usage of 'discharge' in this way confirms our understanding of the everyday sense of the term." 547 U.S. at 377–78.

Is there something that is even less than Skidmore deference and still more than nothing?

(4)   Justice Souter's paragraph presenting "an additional reason for judicial deference," just referred to, ends with the statement that a court in such circumstances "is obliged to accept the agency's position if Congress has not previously spoken to the point at issue and the agency's interpretation is reasonable," followed by a citation to, and quotation from, the portion of the APA establishing the "arbitrary and capricious" standard of review. Is the opinion very quietly trying to solve the question whether Chevron is compatible with the APA? If so, is it solving it by making Chevron Step Two congruent with the State Farm "arbitrary and capricious" test? Refer back to the discussion in the Notes to Chevron, pp. 1145–1150

(5)   *Why Have a Test Before We Get to Chevron?* The Mead case, in addition to affirming the continued viability of Skidmore, holds that there is a prerequisite to according agency action Chevron deference. At this level of abstraction, even Justice Scalia agrees that "there would have to be something wrong with a standard that accorded the status of substantive law to every one of 10,000 'official' customs classifications rulings turned out each year from over 46 offices placed around the country at the Nation's entryways." See footnote 6 (majority opinion) and footnote 7 (Scalia's dissent). Assuming that the officials issuing these rulings are doing something they are authorized to do (in the ordinary bureaucratic sense of "authorized"), why is this need for an additional prerequisite obvious to all the Justices? Assuming there ought to be an additional test, do you prefer Justice Scalia's "authoritative view of the agency" test or Justice Souter's "delegation meriting Chevron treatment" test as a way of sorting agency action that deserves Chevron deference from agency action that does not? (By the way, because of its prerequisite nature, the Court's test in Mead is sometimes referred to as establishing a "Chevron step zero." Refer back to the discussion in the Notes to Chevron, p. 1137 You should know the term— but it might be argued that what Mead really establishes is a "Chevron step one-plus"; presumably Chevron Step One—if Congress has directly spoken to the point, that is the end of the issue for agency and for court—remains true for all cases.)[12]

---

[12]   Paez, J., in Northern California River Watch v. Wilcox, 633 F.3d 766 (2011): "We begin our analysis with the 'familiar two-step procedure' laid out in Chevron. At step one, we evaluate whether Congressional intent regarding the meaning of the text in question is clear from the statute's plain language. If it is, we must give effect to that meaning. If the statute is ambiguous, and an agency purports to interpret the ambiguity, prior to moving on to step two, we must

NOTES ON PUTTING THE MEAD TEST FOR CHEVRON DEFERENCE INTO PRACTICE

(1) *How Does the Mead Prerequisite Work?* The Court states its holding as follows:

> We hold that administrative implementation of a particular statutory provision qualifies for Chevron deference when it appears that Congress delegated authority to the agency generally to make rules carrying the force of law, (and) that the agency interpretation claiming deference was promulgated in the exercise of that authority. Delegation of such authority may be shown in a variety of ways, as by an agency's power to engage in adjudication or notice-and-comment rulemaking, or by some other indication of a comparable congressional intent.

Perhaps as important as any of these words are the connectors in the sentences: the "and" following the comma in the first and the "or" following the second comma in the second. The complexity of the resulting apparatus perhaps illustrates Justice Souter's comment, in a footnote, "It is, of course, true that the limit of Chevron deference is not marked by a hard-edged rule."

The Court's opinion says that "the overwhelming number of our cases applying Chevron deference have reviewed the fruits of notice-and-comment rulemaking or formal adjudication." These are situations in which both sides of the "and"—authority to make determinations with the force of law *and* procedural exercise of that authority—will inherently go together under the APA or comparable requirements in organic statutes. (The rarely required APA "formal" rulemaking would also qualify.) In cases like Mead, by contrast, neither side of the couple will normally be satisfied. The "ruling letter," says the Court, is "best treated like interpretations contained in policy statements, agency manuals, and enforcement guidelines." This is the closest we get to an answer of how the "ruling letter" would be classified under the APA. Probably it is an interpretative rule of particular effect, but possibly it could be labeled an informal adjudication. In either case, while not irrelevant, it would normally not have a strong "force of law" and under the APA not have to be adopted with procedural formality.

But the APA does not always link the two together. For example, § 553 allows an agency to avoid the notice-and-comment process when adopting even ordinary "legislative-type" rules if it "for good cause" finds that the process is "impracticable, unnecessary, or contrary to the public interest." If the agency appropriately determines there is such "good cause," is the second part of Mead's "and" test excused? Or is there a value in public process that entitles the resulting rule to Chevron deference only if the process actually occurs?

Similarly, what of agency rules of procedure—which are exempted from § 553 processes (although an agency can, of course, consistent with Vermont

---

determine whether the agency meets the requirements set forth in Mead: (1) that Congress clearly delegated authority to the agency to make rules carrying the force of law, and (2) that the agency interpretation was promulgated in the exercise of that authority. If both of these requirements from Mead are met, then we proceed to step two."

Yankee, choose to hold a notice-and-comment proceeding if it wants to)? Procedural rules are often held to bind the agency, however adopted—and in that sense the agency's power to adopt them meets the first part of the test, before the "and." But what of the second part?

(2) ***The Barnhart Factors.*** The Court's willingness to accord Chevron deference beyond the confines of notice-and-comment rulemaking or formal adjudication appeared a year after Mead in BARNHART V. WALTON, 535 U.S. 212 (2002). In an opinion written by JUSTICE BREYER and joined by all but Justice Scalia, the Court sustained an interpretation of the Social Security Administration that had appeared in many documents—rulings and official manuals—over many years. This interpretation, said the Court in what was either an alternate holding or a very-well-considered dictum, was entitled to Chevron deference even though not the product of a notice-and-comment proceeding (535 U.S. at 222):

> In this case, the interstitial nature of the legal question, the related expertise of the Agency, the importance of the question to administration of the statute, the complexity of that administration, and the careful consideration the Agency has given the question over a long period of time all indicate that Chevron provides the appropriate legal lens through which to view the legality of the Agency interpretation here at issue. See Mead.

(3) ***Chaos?*** "When the Supreme Court decided United States v. Mead Corp.," wrote LISA SCHULTZ BRESSMAN, "Justice Scalia predicted that judicial review of agency action would devolve into chaos. This Article puts that prediction to the test by examining the court of appeals decisions applying the decision. Justice Scalia actually understated the effect of Mead." HOW *MEAD* HAS MUDDLED JUDICIAL REVIEW OF AGENCY ACTION, 58 Vand. L. Rev. 1443, 1443–44 (2005). Among her other findings, Professor Bressman reports that two divergent lines of cases have developed in the lower courts regarding how to draw the Chevron/Skidmore dividing line (id. at 1459):

> . . . [T]he courts can be sorted into two groups: those that consider Mead-inspired factors and those that consider Barnhart-inspired factors [referring to Barnhart v. Walton, discussed in the previous note]. Some courts consider whether an interpretation reflects binding effect, either alone or together with deliberation (via public participation)—the factor that Mead made determinative. Other courts consider whether an agency interpretation reflects careful consideration, either alone or together with agency expertise and statutory complexity—the factor that Barnhart made relevant. The problem . . . is that these tests are not necessarily equivalent. Nor do the courts generally acknowledge that they have chosen one over another. As a result, Chevron deference seems to turn more on which test a court prefers than on which procedure an agency uses.

The Supreme Court itself has continued to employ the distinction between Chevron and Skidmore deference, but without much further guidance as to how to do so in close cases. E.g., Alaska Dep't of Environmental Conservation v. EPA, 540 U.S. 461, 487 (2004) (EPA interpretive guides, published, consistent over long period—Skidmore but not Chevron). There may be some comfort in knowing (or at least the Supreme Court has sometimes taken comfort in knowing) that if a statutory reading is either "clearly right" or "clearly wrong," the Chevron/Skidmore issue can simply be sidestepped. See General Dynamics Land Systems, Inc. v. Cline, 540 U.S. 581, 600 (2004). Is this irresponsible? No, said Professor CASS SUNSTEIN in CHEVRON STEP ZERO, 92 Va. L. Rev. 187, 229 (2006):

> The first and simplest solution stems from a recognition that Chevron and Skidmore are not radically different in practice; in most cases, either approach will lead to the same result. If the agency's interpretation runs afoul of congressional instructions or is unreasonable, the agency will lose even under Chevron. If the agency's interpretation is not evidently in conflict with congressional instructions, and if it is reasonable, the agency's interpretation will be accepted even under Skidmore. These observations suggest the easiest path for questions on which Mead and Barnhart give inadequate guidance: Resolve the case without answering the question whether it is governed by Chevron or Skidmore. For most cases, the choice between Chevron and Skidmore is not material, and hence it is not worthwhile to worry over it.

But does the case stand for the same thing—is it a well-conceived precedent—if the court does not specify if it is deciding or deferring? See the discussion of the Brand X case, p. 1162.

(4) **_Or Stability?_** A different view of the legal landscape was provided a few years later in KRISTIN E. HICKMAN, THE THREE PHASES OF MEAD, 83 Fordham L. Rev. 527 (2014): "Consistent with the complaints of Mead critics, the Court's vacillating rhetoric about the interaction of Mead, Chevron, and Skidmore has undoubtedly sowed some amount of confusion. It is unclear, however, that the practical impact of that confusion has been especially great.

"For all of the Court's rhetorical inconsistency, much of its Mead jurisprudence is pretty unremarkable, at least as regards Mead itself. A quick survey shows that, over thirteen Terms, thirty-nine Supreme Court cases offer opinions that cite Mead. Only a few of those cases featured clearly articulated disagreements among the justices over the standard of review to be applied. Brand X and City of Arlington . . . were particularly contentious, with the phases of Mead all spectacularly displayed. . . .

"By comparison, most of the cases in which the Court cited Mead offered little or no disagreement in either extending Chevron review to obviously eligible notice-and-comment rulemaking and formal (or formal-ish) adjudications and applying Skidmore to informal guidance and similarly nonbinding interpretations. Indeed, post-Mead, the Court has never actually extended Chevron deference to interpretations lacking with notice-and-comment rulemaking or relatively formal adjudication procedures. . . .

"Far more important, given the limited size of the Court's docket, is how the justices' differing views of Mead, Chevron, and Skidmore have influenced the federal circuit courts. Are they just as divided? Have the Court's varying rhetorical flourishes yielded the muddled doctrinal mess predicted by Justice Scalia? . . . I would assert that Mead overall has had a stabilizing effect on the lower courts' Chevron jurisprudence. More often than not, the circuit courts of appeals seem to follow a relatively rote version of . . . Mead, Chevron, and Skidmore, rather than the more fluid and open-ended version advocated by Justice Breyer. While this approach is not always doctrinally precise and unanswered questions remain, it is also relatively easy to apply and yields consistent outcomes in most cases."

(5) *Or Just Plain Ad Hoc?* After reading every Supreme Court opinion between 1984 and 2006 that considered an agency's interpretation of a statute, WILLIAM N. ESKRIDGE JR. and LAUREN E. BAER concluded that, whatever instructions the Supreme Court was giving to lower courts, the Court itself was applying a broad continuum of deference regimes. THE CONTINUUM OF DEFERENCE: SUPREME COURT TREATMENT OF AGENCY STATUTORY INTERPRETATIONS FROM *CHEVRON* TO *HAMDAN*, 96 Geo. L. J. 1083, 1157 (2008): "Perhaps most of all, our study reveals that the Supreme Court itself is not settled as to what is the correct approach to agency statutory interpretations. At one extreme, Justice Scalia would unify the Court's deference jurisprudence around Chevron, whose two-step framework would be applicable to all interpretations (except litigating positions) that are ratified by an agency head. At the other extreme, Justice Breyer would unify the Court's deference jurisprudence around Skidmore, with delegated lawmaking authority (the Chevron trigger) being another deference 'plus' for the agency. In the middle, Justices such as Stevens . . ., Kennedy. . ., and Souter (Mead) recognize Chevron as a different regime than Skidmore, are comfortable with the doctrines' coexistence, but apply both regimes unpredictably and episodically. . . .

"Should the Justices be concerned? Our intuition, from reading the opinions in 1014 cases and from knowing many of the Justices who authored them, is that the Justices sense the messiness of this jurisprudence but (except for Justice Scalia) are not deeply troubled by it. From their point of view, the Court's inconsistent and confusing deference practice has not disabled the Court from carrying out its primary goals, nor has it created any kind of governance crisis. One normative judgment that can be drawn from our empirical analysis is that the substantially ad hoc approach to agency deference the Court has followed is workable for the Justices. Indeed, the abstract advantages of a more coherent and consistently applied jurisprudence of deference may not be attainable among the current collection of Justices (or perhaps among almost any nine sophisticated jurists with different professional and ideological backgrounds). To the extent the Court does follow an 'approach,' it is ad hoc: the amount of deference the Justices afford an agency interpretation in a particular case depends on several factors, including congressional delegation of lawmaking authority, agency expertise and consistency, and perhaps other background norms. Our empirical study suggests that, whatever approach the Court *says* it is following, the Justices will tend to be ad hoc in their actual practice."

NOTES ON THE THEORY OF THE MEAD DECISION

(1) *What Have the Scholars Thought of the Mead Doctrine?* Here is a sample. THOMAS W. MERRILL, THE MEAD DOCTRINE: RULES AND STANDARDS, META-RULES AND META-STANDARDS, 54 Admin. L. Rev. 807, 833–34 (2002): "On the whole, 'the Mead doctrine' is a sound development. Mead clarifies that Chevron rests on congressional intent, and correctly concludes from this that Chevron applies only when Congress has given some signal that the agency, rather than the court, is to be the primary interpreter of statutory ambiguity. The decision also correctly concludes that the relevant signal of Congress's intent in this regard is a delegation of power to act with the force of law. By linking Chevron and congressional intent, Mead helps achieve a reconciliation between Chevron and the judicial review provisions of the APA. Indeed, by insisting that the agency gets strong deference only when it acts within the scope of delegated power to act with the force of law, and not otherwise, Mead goes part way toward restoring an important aspect of the nondelegation doctrine. . . .

"To be sure, the decision comes up short in terms of articulating a meta-rule to guide lower courts in future controversies. Mead says Chevron applies only when Congress has delegated authority to an agency to act with the force of law, but it treats 'force of law' as (at most) a standard to be applied by looking to a variety of factors. The Court's decision to treat 'force of law' as a standard rather than a rule is regrettable. But nothing the Court did or said precludes future decisions that brush away the fuzziness in the majority's exposition, leaving us with a clear and defensible meta-rule."

(2) JACK M. BEERMANN, THE TURN TOWARD CONGRESS IN ADMINISTRATIVE LAW, 89 B.U. L. Rev. 727, 745–46 (2009): "The Court . . . relies on an apparently fictional account of congressional intent in establishing the domain of Chevron—that is, when the Chevron doctrine applies. Under what has been called Chevron Step Zero, before applying the Chevron doctrine, the reviewing court must determine whether the Chevron framework applies to the particular agency interpretation under review. The entire inquiry is wrapped in a cloak of congressional intent because, as the Court puts it, Chevron applies only when Congress intends to empower the agency to make interpretations that have the force of law. While the Court has expressly disavowed limitations on the factors relevant to whether Chevron applies, the main criterion that the Supreme Court applies to this is the formality of agency process, not explicitly because they tend to lead to more reliable results, but rather because when Congress prescribes a relatively formal process, this formality is purportedly indicative of Congress's intent to delegate to the agency the power to issue interpretations with the force of law.

"It is exceedingly difficult to evaluate whether the formality criterion, or any factor other than the text or legislative history of a particular statute or the APA, accurately reflects congressional intent regarding the status of agency interpretations. The Court's most important opinion on this matter [Mead] makes it clear that the doctrine is built on an assumption concerning Congress's intent, not actual evidence of that intent. No opinion of the Court cites direct evidence such as statutory language, legislative reports or legislative debates for the relevance of formality to that inquiry. Further, although there are suggestions in early decisions that procedural formality may be relevant to the deference issue, the Court does not offer a shared tradition that procedural formality signals actual congressional intent to delegate, so that Congress might be presumed to have legislated against that background. Rather, the criterion seems to fit the Court's own logic about when agency interpretations should receive Chevron deference, regardless of congressional intent."

(3) Considering Mead in light of her earlier work on whether those who actually draft legislation (as contrasted with Senators or Representatives) know the principles that judges announce, see p. 148 ABBE GLUCK had this to say (WHAT 30 YEARS OF *CHEVRON* TEACH US ABOUT THE REST OF STATUTORY INTERPRETATION, 83 Fordham L. Rev. 607, 621–22 (2014): "The [earlier] study surveyed 137 congressional counsels on their familiarity with the judicial doctrines of interpretation and delegation and on whether the doctrines (regardless of staffer familiarity with them) substantially reflected the realities of the legislative drafting process. As we detailed, congressional staffers knew few of the non-administrative law canons of statutory interpretation and rejected several that they did know (such as presumptions of consistent-term usage) as unrealistic assumptions about congressional drafting.

"The administrative law canons, however, fared better. For example, the rule announced in Mead, although the case was virtually unknown by name of as a doctrine that courts employ, was overwhelmingly validated as a good signal on which to rest assumptions about congressional delegation. Chevron was the most known of *all* the canons by name, and the majority of respondents said they understood Chevron's consequences when drafting. Even some of the lesser generally known and hotly contested administrative law doctrines, such as the major questions rule (i.e., do not presume from mere ambiguity that Congress delegates major economic, policy, or political statements to agencies) were validated by our respondents as realistic assumptions about delegation."

(4) DAVID J. BARRON & ELENA KAGAN, CHEVRON'S NONDELEGATION DOCTRINE, 2001 S.Ct. Rev. 201, 203–05: "We . . . argue in this article that an inquiry into actual congressional intent, of the kind the Mead Court advocated, cannot realistically solve this question of the proper scope of Chevron. Although Congress has broad power to decide what kind of judicial review should apply to what kind of administrative action, Congress so rarely discloses (or, perhaps, even has) a view on this subject as to make a search for legislative intent chimerical and a conclusion regarding that intent fraudulent in the mine run of cases. . . . Given the difficulty of determining actual congressional intent, some version of constructive—or perhaps more frankly said, fictional—intent must operate in judicial efforts to delineate the scope of Chevron. After considering other alternatives, we aver that this construction should arise from and reflect candid policy judgments, of the kind evident in Chevron itself, about the allocation of

interpretive authority between administrators and judges with respect to various kinds of agency action.

"Underneath the rhetoric of legislative intent, an approach of this kind in fact animates the Mead decision, but the Court's reliance on the two stock dichotomies of administrative process failed to generate the most appropriate distribution of interpretive power. The Court emphasized most heavily the divide between formal and informal procedures, suggesting that, except in unusual circumstances, only decisions taken in formal procedural contexts merit Chevron deference. But this preference for formality in administration, even in cases when not statutorily required, fails to acknowledge the costs associated with the procedures specified in the APA, which only have increased in significance since that statute's enactment. The Court similarly noted at times the divide between generality and particularity in administrative decision making, suggesting that actions exhibiting the former trait should receive greater judicial deference. But administrative law doctrine long has resisted, for good reason, the temptation to pressure the choice between general and particular decision making, in light of the many and fluctuating considerations, usually best known to an agency itself, relevant to this choice. None of this is to say that interpretive authority in areas of statutory ambiguity or silence always should rest with agency officials; it is only to say that in allocating this power in a way consistent with important administrative values, courts can do better than to rely on the two usual (indeed, hoary) 'either-ors' of agency process.

"We contend that the deference question should turn on a different feature of agency process, traditionally ignored in administrative law doctrine and scholarship—that is, the position in the agency hierarchy of the person assuming responsibility for the administrative decision. More briefly said, the Court should refocus its inquiry from the 'how' to the 'who' of administrative decision making. If the congressional delegatee of the relevant statutory grant of authority takes personal responsibility for the decision, then the agency should command obeisance, within the broad bounds of reasonableness, in resolving statutory ambiguity; if she does not, then the judiciary should render the ultimate interpretive decision. This agency nondelegation principle serves values familiar from the congressional brand of the doctrine, as well as from Chevron itself: by offering an incentive to certain actors to take responsibility for interpretive choice, the principle advances both accountability and discipline in decisionmaking. . . .

"The aspect of institutional design we emphasize here—call it the high level/low level distinction—justifies the result the Court reached in Mead, but only by fortuity. In other cases our approach would diverge significantly from the Court's—in granting deference even in the absence of formality or generality and, conversely, in refusing deference even in the face of these attributes. This approach also would diverge from Justice Scalia's, given the nearly unlimited deference he favors. But oddly enough, we see our approach as in some sense, even if in a sense unrecognized by the Justices themselves, present in all of their different views on the issue: because this is so, we see some potential for the Court to move toward, and even converge on, the . . . doctrine we advocate. . . ."

NOTES ON AGENCIES' INTERPRETATIONS OF THEIR OWN REGULATIONS

(1) ***What about Justice Scalia's Objections?*** Whether or not, after Mead, use of informal rulemaking will give agencies a "safe harbor," as Justice Scalia claims, the case surely does give agencies an incentive (if they are authorized to do so) to issue "legislative" rules through the notice-and-comment process rather than "interpretative" rules issued more informally. One might argue that this incentive serves as a useful antidote to the pressures towards "ossification" of the notice-and-comment process created by hard look review. (See p. 1090.) But Justice Scalia goes in another direction: he says that the result will have a "perverse effect," for "[a]gencies will now have high incentive to rush out barebones, ambiguous rules construing statutory ambiguities" which they will then clarify informally. To understand his argument, one must understand the rules governing agencies' interpretations of their own regulations.

(2) ***The Developing Doctrine.*** In BOWLES V. SEMINOLE ROCK & SAND CO., 325 U.S. 410, 414–15 (1945), while determining the effect of a World War II price control regulation, the Supreme Court had said: "Since this involves an interpretation of an administrative regulation a court must necessarily look to the administrative construction of the regulation if the meaning of the words used is in doubt. The intention of Congress or the principles of the Constitution in some situations may be relevant in the first instance in choosing between various constructions. But the ultimate criterion is the administrative interpretation, which becomes of controlling weight unless it is plainly erroneous or inconsistent with the regulation." And in Udall v. Tallman, 380 U.S. 1, 16 (1965), still prior to Chevron, the Court had said: "When the construction of an administrative regulation rather than a statute is in issue, deference is even more clearly in order." What effect would Chevron's deference to agency statutory construction in the initial formulation of the regulation have on this matter? Would it reduce deference to an agency's construction of its own regulations, on the theory that the agency was now already receiving deference in its construction of its organic statute; would it increase deference to an agency's construction of its own regulation, on the theory that the agency was now more clearly the legitimate author of its regulations; or would it make no difference?

In THOMAS JEFFERSON UNIV. V. SHALALA, 512 U.S. 504, 512 (1994), after Chevron, the Court, per Justice Kennedy, followed these prior cases, and, quoting several of them, wrote:

> . . . [T]he agency's interpretation must be given "controlling weight unless it is plainly erroneous or inconsistent with the regulation." In other words, we must defer to the Secretary's interpretation unless an "alternative reading is compelled by the regulation's plain language or by other indications of the Secretary's intent at the time of the regulation's promulgation." This broad deference is

all the more warranted when, as here, the regulation concerns "a complex and highly technical regulatory program," in which the identification and classification of relevant "criteria necessarily require significant expertise and entail the exercise of judgment grounded in policy concerns."

Dissenting, Justice Thomas, joined by Justices Stevens, O'Connor, and Ginsburg, found that the regulation was "hopelessly vague" and unworthy of deference (512 U.S. at 525):

> . . . [T]he Secretary has merely replaced statutory ambiguity with regulatory ambiguity. It is perfectly understandable, of course, for an agency to issue vague regulations, because to do so maximizes agency power and allows the agency greater latitude to make law through adjudication than through the more cumbersome rulemaking process.

The dissenters in Thomas Jefferson University received support in JOHN F. MANNING, CONSTITUTIONAL STRUCTURE AND JUDICIAL DEFERENCE TO AGENCY INTERPRETATIONS OF AGENCY RULES, 96 Colum. L. Rev. 612, 617 (1996):

> If an agency's rules mean whatever it says they mean (unless the reading is plainly erroneous), the agency effectively has the power of self-interpretation. This authority permits an agency to supply the meaning of regulatory gaps or ambiguities of its own making and relieves the agency of the cost of imprecision that it has produced. This state of affairs makes it that much less likely that an agency will give clear notice of its policies either to those who participate in the rulemaking process prescribed by the Administrative Procedure Act or to the regulated public. The present arrangement also contradicts a major premise of our constitutional scheme and of contemporary separation of powers case law that a fusion of lawmaking and law-exposition is especially dangerous to our liberties.

Professor Manning further explicated the difference he saw between Chevron and a case like Thomas Jefferson University in this fashion, 96 Colum. L. Rev. at 639:

> In a Chevron case, the reviewing court asks whether agency action—usually the promulgation of a rule, an agency enforcement action, or an adjudication—is consistent with an authorizing statute. If the reviewing court is effectively bound by the agency's interpretation of the statute, separation remains between the relevant lawmaker (Congress) and at least one entity (the agency) with independent authority to interpret the applicable legal text. In contrast, [in a case like Thomas Jefferson University] the reviewing court asks whether the agency action—typically an enforcement action or adjudication—is consistent with an agency regulation. In those circumstances, if the court is bound by the agency's interpretation of the meaning of its own regulation, there is no independent interpreter; the agency lawmaker has effective

control of the exposition of the legal text that it has created. In short, whereas Chevron retains *one* independent interpretive check on lawmaking by Congress, [this other line of cases] leaves in place *no* independent interpretive check on lawmaking by an administrative agency.

(3) **_The Current Controversy._** The hostile sentiments towards the Seminole Rock line of precedent were amplified in a series of concurrences in PEREZ V. MORTGAGE BANKERS ASSN., 135 S.Ct. 1199 (2015), set out on p. 385. JUSTICE SCALIA'S concurrence started things off, 135 S.Ct. 1211–13: "Heedless of the original design of the APA, we have developed an elaborate law of deference to agencies' interpretations of statutes and regulations. Never mentioning § 706's directive that the 'reviewing court . . . interpret . . . statutory provisions,' we have held that *agencies* may authoritatively resolve ambiguities in statutes. Chevron U.S.A. Inc. v. Natural Resources Defense Council, Inc., 467 U.S. 837, 842–843 (1984). And never mentioning § 706's directive that the 'reviewing court . . . determine the meaning or applicability of the terms of an agency action,' we have—relying on a case decided before the APA, Bowles v. Seminole Rock & Sand Co., 325 U.S. 410 (1945)—held that *agencies* may authoritatively resolve ambiguities in regulations. Auer v. Robbins, 519 U.S. 452, 461 (1997).

"By supplementing the APA with judge-made doctrines of deference, we have revolutionized the import of interpretive rules' exemption from notice-and-comment rulemaking. Agencies may now use these rules not just to advise the public, but also to bind them. After all, if an interpretive rule gets deference, the people are bound to obey it on pain of sanction, no less surely than they are bound to obey substantive rules, which are accorded similar deference. Interpretive rules that command deference *do* have the force of law.

"The Court's reasons for resisting this obvious point would not withstand a gentle breeze. . . . So long as the agency does not stray beyond the ambiguity in the text being interpreted, deference *compels* the reviewing court to "decide" that the text means what the agency says. . . . Of course an interpretive rule must meet certain conditions before it gets deference—the interpretation must, for instance, be reasonable—but once it does so it is every bit as binding as a substantive rule. So the point stands: By deferring to interpretive rules, we have allowed agencies to make binding rules unhampered by notice-and-comment procedures.

"The problem is bad enough, and perhaps insoluble if Chevron is not to be uprooted, with respect to interpretive rules setting forth agency interpretation of statutes. But an agency's interpretation of its own regulations is another matter. By giving that category of interpretive rules *Auer* deference, we do more than allow the agency to make binding regulations without notice and comment. Because the agency (not Congress) drafts the substantive rules that are the object of those interpretations, giving them deference allows the agency to control the extent of its notice-and-comment-free domain. To expand this domain, the agency need only write substantive rules more broadly and vaguely, leaving plenty of gaps to be filled in later, using interpretive rules unchecked by notice and comment. The APA does not remotely contemplate this regime. . . .

"I would . . . restore the balance originally struck by the APA with respect to an agency's interpretation of its own regulations, not by rewriting the Act in order to make up for Auer, but by abandoning Auer and applying the Act as written. The agency is free to interpret its own regulations with or without notice and comment; but courts will decide—with no deference to the agency—whether that interpretation is correct."

JUSTICE THOMAS joined in with a concurrence of his own, 135 S.Ct. at 1217–24: "Seminole Rock . . . represents a transfer of judicial power to the Executive Branch, and it amounts to an erosion of the judicial obligation to serve as a 'check' on the political branches.

"When a party properly brings a case or controversy to an Article III court, that court is called upon to exercise the "judicial Power of the United States." Art. III, § 1. . . .[T]he judicial power, as originally understood, requires a court to exercise its independent judgment in interpreting and expounding upon the laws.

". . . Courts act as 'an intermediate body between the people and the legislature, in order, among other things, to keep the latter within the limits assigned to their authority.' Federalist No. 78, at 467 (A. Hamilton). The Legislature and Executive may be swayed by popular sentiment to abandon the strictures of the Constitution or other rules of law. But the Judiciary, insulated from both internal and external sources of bias, is duty bound to exercise independent judgment in applying the law.

"Interpreting agency regulations calls for that exercise of independent judgment. Substantive regulations have the force and effect of law. . . . Just as it is critical for judges to exercise independent judgment in applying statutes, it is critical for judges to exercise independent judgment in determining that a regulation properly covers the conduct of regulated parties. Defining the legal meaning of the regulation is one aspect of that determination.

"Seminole Rock deference, however, precludes judges from independently determining that meaning. Rather than judges' applying recognized tools of interpretation to determine the best meaning of a regulation, this doctrine demands that courts accord 'controlling weight' to the agency interpretation of a regulation, subject only to the narrow exception for interpretations that are plainly erroneous or inconsistent with the regulation. That deference amounts to a transfer of the judge's exercise of interpretive judgment to the agency. . . .

"Seminole Rock is constitutionally questionable for an additional reason: It undermines the judicial "check" on the political branches. . . . [T]he Judiciary has one primary check on the excesses of political branches. That check is the enforcement of the rule of law through the exercise of judicial power. . . . Article III judges cannot opt out of exercising their check.

". . . But we have not consistently exercised the judicial check with respect to administrative agencies. . . . [W]e have deferred to the executive agency that both promulgated the regulations and enforced them. . . . When courts refuse even to decide what the best interpretation is under the law, they abandon the judicial check. That abandonment permits precisely the accumulation of governmental powers that the Framers warned against. See The Federalist No. 47, at 302 (J. Madison).

". . .*Seminole Rock* deference [also cannot be justified on the grounds] . . .that Congress has delegated to agencies the authority to interpret their own regulations. This justification fails because Congress lacks authority to delegate th[is] power. . . .[T]he Constitution does not empower Congress to issue a judicially binding interpretation of the Constitution or its laws. Lacking the power itself, it cannot delegate that power to an agency. To hold otherwise would be to vitiate the separation of powers and ignore the "sense of a sharp necessity to separate the legislative from the judicial power . . . [that] triumphed among the Framers of the new Federal Constitution." Plaut v. Spendthrift Farm, Inc., 514 U.S. 211, 221 (1995)."

Does the fact that Justice Thomas feels compelled to assert that Congress could not constitutionally authorize Seminole Rock suggest that the argument against that doctrine rests on premises that are necessarily fairly deeply at odds with those underlying contemporary administrative law? And, if you are not convinced that Congress *is* barred from authorizing this doctrine, does that suggest that the real question is simply whether Congress has authorized it? Finally, if that is really the question, then what are we to make of the fact that this doctrine of deference has been around for a long time without Congress having done anything to undo it?

Whatever the force of the argument against judges conferring Seminole Rock or Auer deference, the Court has not yet accepted it. The "controlling unless plainly erroneous or inconsistent with the regulation" standard for review of an agency's interpretation of its own regulation continues to be regularly used. (It is sometimes called the *Seminole Rock* standard of review, for the case (from 1945) where it originated, and sometimes called the *Auer v. Robbins* standard, for the case (from 1997) most often cited recently.)

(It is also worth mentioning that an agency's interpretation of its own regulations seems to have a favored status as regards the "no post-hoc rationalization" rule, see p. 1086. Justice Sotomayor speaking for a unanimous Court in Chase Bank USA v. McCoy, 562 U.S. 195 (2011): "Under Auer v. Robbins, we defer to an agency's interpretation of its own regulation, advanced in a legal brief, unless that interpretation is 'plainly erroneous or inconsistent with the regulation.' ").

(4) ***Decision Avoided.*** A recent dispute over transgender bathroom rights almost brought some of these questions to a head but ultimately reached an anticlimactic conclusion (at least as far as the Auer doctrine goes). In Gloucester County School Bd. v. G.G. ex rel. Grimm, 822 F.3d 709 (4th Cir. 2016), the Fourth Circuit ruled that the Department of Education's interpretation (in an opinion letter) of its own regulation (itself an interpretation of Title IX), finding that a school "generally must treat transgender students consistent with their gender identity," merited Auer deference. The School Board petitioned for certiorari to the Supreme Court in August 2016, requesting consideration of three questions: "(1) Should this

Court retain the Auer doctrine despite the objections of multiple Justices who have recently urged that it be reconsidered and overruled?; (2) If Auer is retained, should deference extend to an unpublished agency letter that, among other things, does not carry the force of law and was adopted in the context of the very dispute in which deference is sought?; (3) With or without deference to the agency, should the Department's specific interpretation of Title IX and 34 C.F.R. § 106.33 be given effect?"

In October 2016, the Court granted the School Board's petition with respect to questions 2 and 3; however, it declined to grant the petition with respect to the first question (which invited the court to abandon the Auer doctrine). Then, after a change of Administrations in Washington, the Department of Education rescinded its earlier interpretation of Title IX—potentially rendering the case moot. And in March 2017, the Court declined to proceed with the case, remanding it to the Fourth Circuit "in light of the guidance document issued by the Department of Education." Thus, after the many twists and turns in the Gloucester litigation, the Auer doctrine remains safe—for now.

(5)   But can it be that an informal agency interpretation of an ambiguity in its organic statute will, under Mead, get only Skidmore (or perhaps no) deference, while an informal agency interpretation of the same ambiguity in one of its own regulations will do much better? GONZALES V. OREGON, 546 U.S. 243 (2006), perhaps represents an attempt to respond to Justice Scalia's concern that such a situation would simply encourage issuance of "barebones, ambiguous rules." "The question before us," wrote JUSTICE KENNEDY for the Court, "is whether the Controlled Substances Act allows the United States Attorney General to prohibit doctors from prescribing regulated drugs for use in physician-assisted suicide, notwithstanding a state law permitting the procedure." 546 U.S. at 248–49. The answer, said the Court, was "no." A long-standing regulation under the CSA required that any prescription for a controlled substance "be issued for a legitimate medical purpose," 21 C.F.R. § 1306.04(a). One of the Attorney General's arguments was that his new interpretive rule, which said that "assisting suicide" was not a "legitimate medical purpose" within the regulation, deserved the deference due an agency's interpretation of its own regulations. But, said the Court, the statute itself required that prescriptions of controlled drugs have "a currently accepted medical use," 21 U.S.C. § 812(b), and the government did not contend that the interpretation of what was medically proper turned on any difference between the statutory and regulatory language. "Simply put, the existence of a parroting regulation does not change the fact that the question here is not the meaning of the regulation but the meaning of the statute. An agency does not acquire special authority to interpret its own words when, instead of using its expertise and experience to formulate a regulation, it has elected merely to paraphrase the statutory language." 546 U.S. at 257.

(What, then, about the possibility that the Attorney General's rule could be upheld as a proper interpretation of the statute itself? The Court also turned this claim down, providing a plethora of reasons that it never quite knitted into a single fabric:

(a)   The Controlled Substances Act was really meant to control "recreational drugs" and "drug abuse" in the common sense of the term, and not medical practice more broadly;

(b)   Medical practice is primarily supervised by the states, and we would expect Congress, as a matter of "commonsense," to speak clearly before giving the Attorney General power to determine its contours;

(c)   Proper practice is a matter of medical, not legal, expertise and falls within the authority the Act gives to the Secretary of Health and Human Services, not the Attorney general;

(d)   The Interpretive Rule was issued without any public process;

(e)   For the foregoing reasons, among others, the A.G. was not authorized to issue regulations governing this matter that were entitled, under Mead, to Chevron deference. "We need not decide whether Chevron deference would be warranted for an interpretation issued by the Attorney General concerning matters closer to his role under the CSA, namely, preventing doctors from engaging in illicit drug trafficking. . . .[T]he CSA does not give the Attorney General authority to issue [this] Interpretive Rule as a statement with the force of law."

(f)   And under Skidmore, deference is "tempered by the Attorney General's lack of expertise in this area and the apparent absence of any consultation with anyone outside the Department of Justice who might aid in a reasoned judgment." For these reasons, among others, "we do not find the Attorney General's opinion persuasive.")

(6)   ***The Cumulation of Deference.*** Can there be deference on top of deference? Yes. The way deference principles can cumulate shows up clearly in this passage from Coeur Alaska, Inc. v. Southeast Alaska Conservation Council, 557 U.S. 261, 277–78 (2009), discussing the question whether an EPA regulation under the Clean Water Act applied to the discharge of fill material from a mining operation into a lake and applying the Auer doctrine:

> We address in turn the statutory text of the CWA, the agencies' regulations construing it, and the EPA's subsequent interpretation of those regulations. Because Congress has not "directly spoken" to the "precise question" of whether an EPA performance standard applies to discharges of fill material, the statute alone does not resolve the case. Chevron. We look first to the agency regulations, which are entitled to deference if they resolve the ambiguity in a reasonable manner. Chevron; Mead. But the regulations, too, are ambiguous, so we next turn to the agencies' subsequent interpretation of those regulations. Mead; Auer v. Robbins. In an internal memorandum the EPA explained that its performance standards do not apply to discharges of fill material. That interpretation is not "plainly erroneous or inconsistent with the regulation[s]," and so we accept it as correct. Auer v. Robbins.

And no. Side by side with this approach is a line of lower-court cases that protect regulated parties from being penalized for agency enforcement of standards of which they had no fair notice. If a regulation is sufficiently ambiguous, it may not give adequate notice of what it requires (although of course the agency's enforcement personnel may have given actual notice of the agency's interpretation in interactions with the regulated party). Absent such actual notice, it is possible to have (a) a properly adopted regulation, to which the court will defer as a reasonable interpretation of an ambiguous statute; (b) a less formal agency interpretation of that regulation, to which the court will defer as an interpretation of an ambiguous regulation; (c) conditions which violate the agency's interpretation of the law; but (d) no liability because the combined ambiguity in (a) and (b)—even though overcome by the combined deference in (a) and (b)—prevents the regulated party from having had fair notice of what it was required to do. For an example, see Beaver Plant Operations, Inc. v. Herman, 223 F.3d 25 (1st Cir. 2000).

(7)   **Consistency and Informal Rulings.** The Mead Court points out that the Customs Service was careful to make clear in its ruling letter that the ruling could be modified without notice and that no one should rely on it except the person to whom it was issued for the transaction particularly described. Can the agency avoid its obligation to be consistent, see pp. 1040–1047, that easily?

(8)   Suppose we take a yet more extreme case: Someone in an agency advises a private party as to the law governing her situation, and the agency later determines that the advice was improvident or wrong? Suppose, for example, that a taxpayer was advised by an IRS agent over the phone that she will not have to pay taxes if she does thus-and-so, and an IRS auditor later determines that that advice was incorrect. If the private party has relied on the agency's advice in the interim, can she estop the agency? (You will notice that this, in effect, is the Mead situation in reverse: the agency wants to disavow the effect of an informal interpretation of the law made by a subordinate employee while the outside party wants to assert its binding effect.)

The short answer to the question, ninety-some-percent reliable, is that the government cannot be estopped. The longer answer is that the Supreme Court has made a practice of always stopping short of saying "never" while at the same time refusing actually to find an estoppel in any particular set of facts before it; and the lower courts have occasionally found a set of facts extreme enough to convince them. Some of the fact patterns that the Supreme Court has found insufficient seem at first glance (or maybe even later) to be rather compelling. In one leading case, an agent for a federal crop insurance plan told a farmer that a particular kind of crop was insurable; the farmer insured it with the government; after the drought hit, the government determined that a regulation not known to the agent or the farmer prevented coverage, and refused payment; held: no estoppel. Federal Crop Ins. Corp. v. Merrill, 332 U.S. 380 (1947). In another, a retired Navy employee consulted with the Navy's personnel department before taking another job that might threaten his disability annuity and was told it would not, took the job, and then lost payments under his annuity because, although not reflected in the Navy's own manuals, a few years earlier

Congress had amended the statute to tighten eligibility requirements; *held*: no estoppel. Office of Personnel Management v. Richmond, 496 U.S. 414 (1990).

The Court's attitude can be better understood if the consequences of allowing lower level employees to estop the government are considered. In effect such a ruling would allow bad advice plus private reliance to take the place of the otherwise applicable law—to override the terms of a statute or the limitations of an appropriation. Moreover, liability for bad advice might well create an incentive for agencies to give no advice—in which case the cure might be worse than the disease.

In an appropriate case, of course, the facts that might establish an estoppel might also be recharacterized in the terms of some other doctrine that seems to threaten less far-reaching consequences—perhaps in terms of the government's having "waived" a right, or in terms of the government's abusing its discretion in not taking its own course of advice into account when deciding what to do, or in terms, as discussed in a note above, of the government's having failed to give "fair notice" of what its regulations require.

MASSACHUSETTS v. EPA

Notes on the Decision in Massachusetts v. EPA

Notes on Judicial Review: Law or Politics

MASSACHUSETTS v. ENVIRONMENTAL PROTECTION AGENCY

Supreme Court of the United States (2007).
549 U.S. 497.

■ JUSTICE STEVENS delivered the opinion of the Court.

A well-documented rise in global temperatures has coincided with a significant increase in the concentration of carbon dioxide in the atmosphere. Respected scientists believe the two trends are related. For when carbon dioxide is released into the atmosphere, it acts like the ceiling of a greenhouse, trapping solar energy and retarding the escape of reflected heat. It is therefore a species—the most important species—of a "greenhouse gas."

Calling global warming "the most pressing environmental challenge of our time," a group of States, local governments, and private organizations, alleged in a petition for certiorari that the Environmental Protection Agency (EPA) has abdicated its responsibility under the Clean Air Act to regulate the emissions of four greenhouse gases, including carbon dioxide. Specifically, petitioners asked us to answer two questions concerning the meaning of § 202(a)(1) of the Act: whether EPA has the statutory authority to regulate greenhouse gas emissions from new motor vehicles; and if so, whether its stated reasons for refusing to do so are consistent with the statute.

In response, EPA, supported by 10 intervening States and six trade associations, correctly argued that we may not address those two questions unless at least one petitioner has standing to invoke our jurisdiction under Article III of the Constitution. Notwithstanding the serious character of that jurisdictional argument and the absence of any conflicting decisions construing § 202(a)(1), the unusual importance of the underlying issue persuaded us to grant the writ.

I

Section 202(a)(1) of the Clean Air Act provides:

> The [EPA] Administrator shall by regulation prescribe (and from time to time revise) in accordance with the provisions of this section, standards applicable to the emission of any air pollutant from any class or classes of new motor vehicles or new motor vehicle engines, which in his judgment cause, or contribute to, air pollution which may reasonably be anticipated to endanger public health or welfare. . . .

The Act defines "air pollutant" to include "any air pollution agent or combination of such agents, including any physical, chemical, biological, radioactive . . . substance or matter which is emitted into or otherwise enters the ambient air." § 7602(g). "Welfare" is also defined broadly: among other things, it includes "effects on . . . weather . . . and climate." § 7602(h).

When Congress enacted these provisions, the study of climate change was in its infancy. In 1959, shortly after the U.S. Weather Bureau began monitoring atmospheric carbon dioxide levels, an observatory in Mauna Loa, Hawaii, recorded a mean level of 316 parts per million. This was well above the highest carbon dioxide concentration—no more than 300 parts per million—revealed in the 420,000-year-old ice-core record. By the time Congress drafted § 202(a)(1) in 1970, carbon dioxide levels had reached 325 parts per million.

In the late 1970's, the Federal Government began devoting serious attention to the possibility that carbon dioxide emissions associated with human activity could provoke climate change. In 1978, Congress enacted the National Climate Program Act, 92 Stat. 601, which required the President to establish a program to "assist the Nation and the world to understand and respond to natural and man-induced climate processes and their implications," id., § 3. President Carter, in turn, asked the National Research Council, the working arm of the National Academy of Sciences, to investigate the subject. The Council's response was unequivocal: "If carbon dioxide continues to increase, the study group finds no reason to doubt that climate changes will result and no reason to believe that these changes will be negligible. . . . A wait-and-see policy may mean waiting until it is too late."

Congress next addressed the issue in 1987, when it enacted the Global Climate Protection Act, 101 Stat. 1407. . . . Congress directed EPA to propose to Congress a "coordinated national policy on global climate change," § 1103(b), and ordered the Secretary of State to work "through the channels of multilateral diplomacy" and coordinate diplomatic efforts to combat global warming, § 1103(c). Congress emphasized that "ongoing pollution and deforestation may be contributing now to an irreversible process" and that "[n]ecessary actions must be identified and implemented in time to protect the climate." § 1102(4).

Meanwhile, the scientific understanding of climate change progressed. In 1990, the Intergovernmental Panel on Climate Change (IPCC), a multinational scientific body organized under the auspices of the United Nations, published its first comprehensive report on the topic. Drawing on expert opinions from across the globe, the IPCC concluded that "emissions resulting from human activities are substantially increasing the atmospheric concentrations of . . . greenhouse gases [which] will enhance the greenhouse effect, resulting on average in an additional warming of the Earth's surface."

Responding to the IPCC report, the United Nations convened the "Earth Summit" in 1992 in Rio de Janeiro. The first President Bush attended and signed the United Nations Framework Convention on Climate Change (UNFCCC), a nonbinding agreement among 154 nations to reduce atmospheric concentrations of carbon dioxide and other greenhouse gases for the purpose of "prevent[ing] dangerous anthropogenic [i.e., human-induced] interference with the [Earth's] climate system." S. Treaty Doc. No. 102–38, Art. 2, p. 5 (1992). The Senate unanimously ratified the treaty.

Some five years later—after the IPCC issued a second comprehensive report in 1995 concluding that "[t]he balance of evidence suggests there is a discernible human influence on global climate"—the UNFCCC signatories met in Kyoto, Japan, and adopted a protocol that assigned mandatory targets for industrialized nations to reduce greenhouse gas emissions. Because those targets did not apply to developing and heavily polluting nations such as China and India, the Senate unanimously passed a resolution expressing its sense that the United States should not enter into the Kyoto Protocol. President Clinton did not submit the protocol to the Senate for ratification.

II

On October 20, 1999, a group of 19 private organizations filed a rulemaking petition asking EPA to regulate "greenhouse gas emissions from new motor vehicles under § 202 of the Clean Air Act." . . . As to EPA's statutory authority, the petition observed that the agency itself had already confirmed that it had the power to regulate carbon dioxide. In 1998, Jonathan Z. Cannon, then EPA's General Counsel, prepared a legal opinion concluding that "CO_2 emissions are within the scope of EPA's authority to regulate," even as he recognized that EPA had so far declined to exercise that authority. Cannon's successor, Gary S. Guzy, reiterated that opinion before a congressional committee just two weeks before the rulemaking petition was filed.

Fifteen months after the petition's submission, EPA requested public comment on "all the issues raised in [the] petition," adding a "particular" request for comments on "any scientific, technical, legal, economic or other aspect of these issues that may be relevant to EPA's consideration of this petition." 66 Fed.Reg. 7486, 7487 (2001). EPA received more than 50,000 comments over the next five months.

Before the close of the comment period, the White House sought "assistance in identifying the areas in the science of climate change where there are the greatest certainties and uncertainties" from the National Research Council, asking for a response "as soon as possible." The result was a 2001 report titled Climate Change: An Analysis of Some Key Questions (NRC Report), which, drawing heavily on the 1995 IPCC report, concluded that "[g]reenhouse gases are accumulating in Earth's atmosphere as a result of human activities, causing surface air temperatures and subsurface ocean temperatures to rise. Temperatures are, in fact, rising." NRC Report 1.

On September 8, 2003, EPA entered an order denying the rulemaking petition. 68 Fed. Reg. 52922. The agency gave two reasons for its decision: (1) that contrary to the opinions of its former general counsels, the Clean Air Act does not authorize EPA to issue mandatory regulations to address global climate change; and (2) that even if the agency had the authority to set greenhouse gas emission standards, it would be unwise to do so at this time.

In concluding that it lacked statutory authority over greenhouse gases, EPA observed that Congress "was well aware of the global climate change issue when it last comprehensively amended the [Clean Air Act] in 1990," yet it declined to adopt a proposed amendment establishing binding emissions limitations. Id., at 52926. Congress instead chose to authorize further investigation into climate change. EPA further reasoned that Congress' "specially tailored solutions to global atmospheric issues," id.—in particular, its 1990 enactment of a comprehensive scheme to regulate pollutants that depleted the ozone layer—counseled against reading the general authorization of § 202(a)(1) to confer regulatory authority over greenhouse gases.

EPA stated that it was "urged on in this view" by this Court's decision in FDA v. Brown & Williamson Tobacco Corp., 529 U.S. 120 (2000). In that case, relying on "tobacco['s] unique political history," id., at 159, we invalidated the Food and Drug Administration's reliance on its general authority to regulate drugs as a basis for asserting jurisdiction over an "industry constituting a significant portion of the American economy," ibid.

EPA reasoned that climate change had its own "political history": Congress designed the original Clean Air Act to address *local* air pollutants rather than a substance that "is fairly consistent in its concentration throughout the *world's* atmosphere," 68 Fed. Reg. 52927; declined in 1990 to enact proposed amendments to force EPA to set carbon dioxide emission standards for motor vehicles; and addressed global climate change in other legislation. Because of this political history, and because imposing emission limitations on greenhouse gases would have even greater economic and political repercussions than regulating tobacco, EPA was persuaded that it lacked the power to do so. In essence, EPA concluded that climate change was so important that unless Congress spoke with exacting specificity, it could not have meant the agency to address it.

Having reached that conclusion, EPA believed it followed that greenhouse gases cannot be "air pollutants" within the meaning of the Act. See ibid. . . . The agency bolstered this conclusion by explaining that if carbon dioxide were an air pollutant, the only feasible method of reducing tailpipe emissions would be to improve fuel economy. But because Congress has already created detailed mandatory fuel economy standards subject to Department of Transportation (DOT) administration, the agency concluded that EPA regulation would either conflict with those standards or be superfluous.

Even assuming that it had authority over greenhouse gases, EPA explained in detail why it would refuse to exercise that authority. The agency began by recognizing that the concentration of greenhouse gases has dramatically increased as a result of human activities, and acknowledged the attendant increase in global surface air temperatures. EPA nevertheless gave controlling importance to the NRC Report's statement that a causal link between the two " 'cannot be unequivocally established.' " Ibid. (quoting NRC Report 17). Given that residual uncertainty, EPA concluded that regulating greenhouse gas emissions would be unwise.

The agency furthermore characterized any EPA regulation of motor-vehicle emissions as a "piecemeal approach" to climate change, and stated that such regulation would conflict with the President's "comprehensive approach" to the problem, id., at 52932. That approach involves additional support for technological innovation, the creation of nonregulatory programs to encourage voluntary private-sector reductions in greenhouse gas emissions, and further research on climate change—not actual regulation. According to EPA, unilateral EPA regulation of motor-vehicle greenhouse gas emissions might also hamper the President's ability to persuade key developing countries to reduce greenhouse gas emissions.

III

Petitioners . . . sought review of EPA's order in the United States Court of Appeals for the District of Columbia Circuit [which upheld the Administrator].

IV

[Massachusetts has standing to pursue this litigation. This portion of the opinion appears at p. 1355.]

V

The scope of our review of the merits of the statutory issues is narrow. As we have repeated time and again, an agency has broad discretion to choose how best to marshal its limited resources and personnel to carry out its delegated responsibilities. See Chevron. That discretion is at its height when the agency decides not to bring an enforcement action. Therefore, in Heckler v. Chaney, 470 U.S. 821 (1985), [p. 1407] we held that an agency's refusal to initiate enforcement proceedings is not ordinarily subject to judicial review. Some debate remains, however, as to the rigor with which we review an agency's denial of a petition for rulemaking.

There are key differences between a denial of a petition for rulemaking and an agency's decision not to initiate an enforcement action. See American Horse Protection Assn., Inc. v. Lyng, 812 F.2d 1, 3–4 (C.A.D.C.1987). In contrast to nonenforcement decisions, agency refusals to initiate rulemaking "are less frequent, more apt to involve legal as opposed to factual analysis, and subject to special formalities, including a public explanation." Id., at 4; see also 5 U.S.C. § 555(e). They moreover arise out of denials of petitions for rulemaking which (at least in the circumstances here) the affected party had an undoubted procedural right to file in the first instance. Refusals to promulgate rules are thus susceptible to judicial review, though such review is "extremely limited" and "highly deferential." National Customs Brokers & Forwarders Assn. of America, Inc. v. United States, 883 F.2d 93, 96 1989). . . .

VI

On the merits, the first question is whether § 202(a)(1) of the Clean Air Act authorizes EPA to regulate greenhouse gas emissions from new motor vehicles in the event that it forms a "judgment" that such emissions contribute to climate change. We have little trouble concluding that it does. In relevant part, § 202(a)(1) provides that EPA "shall by regulation prescribe . . . standards applicable to the emission of any air pollutant from any class or classes of new motor vehicles or new motor vehicle engines, which in [the Administrator's] judgment cause, or contribute to, air pollution which may reasonably be anticipated to endanger public health or welfare." 42 U.S.C. § 7521(a)(1). Because EPA believes that Congress did not intend it to regulate substances that contribute to climate change, the agency maintains that carbon dioxide is not an "air pollutant" within the meaning of the provision.

The statutory text forecloses EPA's reading. The Clean Air Act's sweeping definition of "air pollutant" includes "*any* air pollution agent or combination of such agents, including *any* physical, chemical . . . substance or matter which is emitted into or otherwise enters the ambient air. . . ." § 7602(g) (emphasis added). On its face, the definition embraces all airborne compounds of whatever stripe, and underscores that intent through the repeated use of the word "any." Carbon dioxide, methane, nitrous oxide, and hydro-fluorocarbons are without a doubt "physical [and] chemical . . . substance[s] which [are] emitted into . . . the ambient air." The statute is unambiguous.

. . . That subsequent Congresses have eschewed enacting binding emissions limitations to combat global warming tells us nothing about what Congress meant when it amended § 202(a)(1) in 1970 and 1977. . . .

EPA's reliance on Brown & Williamson Tobacco Corp., 529 U.S. 120 (2000) [p. 1191] is similarly misplaced. In holding that tobacco products are not "drugs" or "devices" subject to Food and Drug Administration (FDA) regulation pursuant to the Food, Drug and Cosmetic Act (FDCA), we found critical at least two considerations that have no counterpart in this case.

First, we thought it unlikely that Congress meant to ban tobacco products, which the FDCA would have required had such products been classified as "drugs" or "devices." Here, in contrast, EPA jurisdiction would lead to no such extreme measures. EPA would only *regulate* emissions, and even then, it would have to delay any action "to permit the development and application of the requisite technology, giving appropriate consideration to the cost of compliance," § 7521(a)(2). However much a ban on tobacco products clashed with the "common sense" intuition that Congress never meant to remove those products from circulation, there is nothing counterintuitive to the notion that EPA can curtail the emission of substances that are putting the global climate out of kilter.

Second, in Brown & Williamson we pointed to an unbroken series of congressional enactments that made sense only if adopted "against the backdrop of the FDA's consistent and repeated statements that it lacked authority under the FDCA to regulate tobacco." Id., at 144. We can point to no such enactments here: EPA has not identified any congressional action that conflicts in any way with the regulation of greenhouse gases from new motor vehicles. Even if it had, Congress could not have acted against a regulatory "backdrop" of disclaimers of regulatory authority. Prior to the order that provoked this litigation, EPA had never disavowed the authority to regulate greenhouse gases, and in 1998 it in fact affirmed that it *had* such authority. There is no reason, much less a compelling reason, to accept EPA's invitation to read ambiguity into a clear statute.

EPA finally argues that it cannot regulate carbon dioxide emissions from motor vehicles because doing so would require it to tighten mileage standards, a job (according to EPA) that Congress has assigned to DOT. See 68 Fed. Reg. 52929. But that DOT sets mileage standards in no way licenses EPA to shirk its environmental responsibilities. EPA has been charged with protecting the public's "health" and "welfare," 42 U.S.C. § 7521(a)(1), a statutory obligation wholly independent of DOT's mandate to promote energy efficiency. The two obligations may overlap, but there is no reason to think the two agencies cannot both administer their obligations and yet avoid inconsistency.

While the Congresses that drafted § 202(a)(1) might not have appreciated the possibility that burning fossil fuels could lead to global warming, they did understand that without regulatory flexibility, changing circumstances and scientific developments would soon render the Clean Air Act obsolete. The broad language of § 202(a)(1) reflects an intentional effort to confer the flexibility necessary to forestall such obsolescence. Because greenhouse gases fit well within the Clean Air Act's capacious definition of "air pollutant," we hold that EPA has the statutory authority to regulate the emission of such gases from new motor vehicles.

VII

The alternative basis for EPA's decision—that even if it does have statutory authority to regulate greenhouse gases, it would be unwise to do so at this time—rests on reasoning divorced from the statutory text. While the statute does condition the exercise of EPA's authority on its formation of a "judgment," 42 U.S.C. § 7521(a)(1), that judgment must relate to whether an air pollutant "cause[s], or contribute[s] to, air pollution which may reasonably be anticipated to endanger public health or welfare," ibid. Put another way, the use of the word "judgment" is not a roving license to ignore the statutory text. It is but a direction to exercise discretion within defined statutory limits.

If EPA makes a finding of endangerment, the Clean Air Act requires the agency to regulate emissions of the deleterious pollutant from new motor vehicles. Ibid. (stating that "[EPA] shall by regulation prescribe . . . standards applicable to the emission of any air pollutant from any class of new motor vehicles"). EPA no doubt has significant latitude as to the manner, timing, content, and coordination of its regulations with those of other agencies. But once EPA has responded to a petition for rulemaking, its reasons for action or inaction must conform to the authorizing statute. Under the clear terms of the Clean Air Act, EPA can avoid taking further action only if it determines that greenhouse gases do not contribute to climate change or if it provides some reasonable explanation as to why it cannot or will not exercise its discretion to determine whether they do. To the extent that this constrains agency discretion to pursue other priorities of the Administrator or the President, this is the congressional design.

EPA has refused to comply with this clear statutory command. Instead, it has offered a laundry list of reasons not to regulate. For example, EPA said that a number of voluntary executive branch programs already provide an effective response to the threat of global warming, 68 Fed. Reg. 52932, that regulating greenhouse gases might impair the President's ability to negotiate with "key developing nations" to reduce emissions, id., at 52931, and that curtailing motor-vehicle emissions would reflect "an inefficient, piecemeal approach to address the climate change issue," ibid.

Although we have neither the expertise nor the authority to evaluate these policy judgments, it is evident they have nothing to do with whether greenhouse gas emissions contribute to climate change. Still less do they amount to a reasoned justification for declining to form a scientific judgment. In particular, while the President has broad authority in foreign affairs, that authority does not extend to the refusal to execute domestic laws. . . .

Nor can EPA avoid its statutory obligation by noting the uncertainty surrounding various features of climate change and concluding that it would therefore be better not to regulate at this time. See 68 Fed. Reg. 52930–52931. If the scientific uncertainty is so profound that it precludes EPA from making a reasoned judgment as to whether greenhouse gases contribute to global warming, EPA must say so. That EPA would prefer not to regulate greenhouse gases because of some residual uncertainty . . . is irrelevant. The statutory question is whether sufficient information exists to make an endangerment finding.

In short, EPA has offered no reasoned explanation for its refusal to decide whether greenhouse gases cause or contribute to climate change. Its action was therefore "arbitrary, capricious, . . . or otherwise not in accordance with law." 42 U.S.C. § 7607(d)(9)(A). We need not and do not reach the question whether on remand EPA must make an endangerment finding, or whether policy concerns can inform EPA's actions in the event that it makes such a finding. We hold only that EPA must ground its reasons for action or inaction in the statute.

VIII

The judgment of the Court of Appeals is reversed, and the case is remanded for further proceedings consistent with this opinion.

■ Chief Justice Roberts, with whom Justice Scalia, Justice Thomas, and Justice Alito join, dissenting.

Global warming may be a "crisis," even "the most pressing environmental problem of our time." Pet. for Cert. 26, 22. Indeed, it may ultimately affect nearly everyone on the planet in some potentially adverse way, and it may be that governments have done too little to address it. It is not a problem, however, that has escaped the attention of policymakers in the Executive and Legislative Branches of our

Government, who continue to consider regulatory, legislative, and treaty-based means of addressing global climate change.

Apparently dissatisfied with the pace of progress on this issue in the elected branches, petitioners have come to the courts claiming broad-ranging injury, and attempting to tie that injury to the Government's alleged failure to comply with a rather narrow statutory provision. I would reject these challenges as nonjusticiable. Such a conclusion involves no judgment on whether global warming exists, what causes it, or the extent of the problem. Nor does it render petitioners without recourse. This Court's standing jurisprudence simply recognizes that redress of grievances of the sort at issue here "is the function of Congress and the Chief Executive," not the federal courts. Lujan v. Defenders of Wildlife, 504 U.S. 555, 576 (1992). I would vacate the judgment below and remand for dismissal of the petitions for review. . . .

■ JUSTICE SCALIA, with whom THE CHIEF JUSTICE, JUSTICE THOMAS, and JUSTICE ALITO join, dissenting.

I join the Chief Justice's opinion in full, and would hold that this Court has no jurisdiction to decide this case because petitioners lack standing. The Court having decided otherwise, it is appropriate for me to note my dissent on the merits.

I

A

The provision of law at the heart of this case is § 202(a)(1) of the Clean Air Act (CAA), which provides that the Administrator of the Environmental Protection Agency (EPA) "shall by regulation prescribe . . . standards applicable to the emission of any air pollutant from any class or classes of new motor vehicles or new motor vehicle engines, which *in his judgment* cause, or contribute to, air pollution which may reasonably be anticipated to endanger public health or welfare." 42 U.S.C. § 7521(a)(1) (emphasis added). As the Court recognizes, the statute "condition[s] the exercise of EPA's authority on its formation of a 'judgment.' " There is no dispute that the Administrator has made no such judgment in this case.

The question thus arises: Does anything *require* the Administrator to make a "judgment" whenever a petition for rulemaking is filed? Without citation of the statute or any other authority, the Court says yes. Why is that so? When Congress wishes to make private action force an agency's hand, it knows how to do so. Where does the CAA say that the EPA Administrator is required to come to a decision on this question whenever a rulemaking petition is filed? The Court points to no such provision because none exists.

Instead, the Court invents a multiple-choice question that the EPA Administrator must answer when a petition for rulemaking is filed. The Administrator must exercise his judgment in one of three ways: (a) by concluding that the pollutant *does* cause, or contribute to, air pollution that endangers public welfare (in which case EPA is required to regulate); (b) by concluding that the pollutant *does not* cause, or contribute to, air pollution that endangers public welfare (in which case EPA is *not* required to regulate); or (c) by "provid[ing] some reasonable explanation as to why it cannot or will not exercise its discretion to determine whether" greenhouse gases endanger public welfare (in which case EPA is *not* required to regulate).

I am willing to assume, for the sake of argument, that the Administrator's discretion in this regard is not entirely unbounded-that if he has no reasonable basis for deferring judgment he must grasp the nettle at once. The Court, however, with no basis in text or precedent, rejects all of EPA's stated "policy judgments" as not "amount[ing] to a reasoned justification," effectively narrowing the universe of potential reasonable bases to a single one: Judgment can be delayed *only* if the Administrator concludes that "the scientific uncertainty is [too] profound." The Administrator is precluded from concluding *for other reasons* "that it would . . . be better not to regulate at this time." Such other reasons—perfectly valid reasons—were set forth in the agency's statement.

> We do not believe . . . that it would be either effective or appropriate for EPA to establish [greenhouse gas] standards for motor vehicles at this time. As described in detail below, the President has laid out a comprehensive approach to climate change that calls for near-term voluntary actions and incentives along with programs aimed at reducing scientific uncertainties and encouraging technological development so that the government may effectively and efficiently address the climate change issue over the long term. . . .

> [E]stablishing [greenhouse gas] emission standards for U.S. motor vehicles at this time would . . . result in an inefficient, piecemeal approach to addressing the climate change issue. The U.S. motor vehicle fleet is one of many sources of [greenhouse gas] emissions both here and abroad, and different [greenhouse gas] emission sources face different technological and financial challenges in reducing emissions. A sensible regulatory scheme would require that all significant sources and sinks of [greenhouse gas] emissions be considered in deciding how best to achieve any needed emission reductions.

> Unilateral EPA regulation of motor vehicle [greenhouse gas] emissions could also weaken U.S. efforts to persuade developing countries to reduce the [greenhouse gas] intensity of their economies. . . . Unavoidably, climate change raises important foreign policy issues, and it is the President's prerogative to address them. 68 Fed.Reg. 52929–52931 (footnote omitted).

The Court dismisses this analysis as "rest[ing] on reasoning divorced from the statutory text." "While the statute does condition the exercise of

EPA's authority on its formation of a 'judgment,' . . . that judgment must relate to whether an air pollutant 'cause[s], or contribute[s] to, air pollution which may reasonably be anticipated to endanger public health or welfare.'" True but irrelevant. When the Administrator *makes* a judgment whether to regulate greenhouse gases, that judgment must relate to whether they are air pollutants that "cause, or contribute to, air pollution which may reasonably be anticipated to endanger public health or welfare." 42 U.S.C. § 7521(a)(1). But the statute says *nothing at all* about the reasons for which the Administrator may *defer* making a judgment—the permissible reasons for deciding not to grapple with the issue at the present time. Thus, the various "policy" rationales that the Court criticizes are not "divorced from the statutory text," except in the sense that the statutory text is silent, as texts are often silent about permissible reasons for the exercise of agency discretion. The reasons the EPA gave are surely considerations executive agencies *regularly* take into account (and *ought* to take into account) when deciding whether to consider entering a new field: the impact such entry would have on other Executive Branch programs and on foreign policy. There is no basis in law for the Court's imposed limitation. . . .

B

Even on the Court's own terms, however, the same conclusion follows. As mentioned above, the Court gives EPA the option of determining that the science is too uncertain to allow it to form a "judgment" as to whether greenhouse gases endanger public welfare. Attached to this option (on what basis is unclear) is an essay requirement: "If," the Court says, "the scientific uncertainty is so profound that it precludes EPA from making a reasoned judgment as to whether greenhouse gases contribute to global warming, EPA must say so." But EPA *has* said precisely that—and at great length, based on information contained in a 2001 report by the National Research Council (NRC) entitled Climate Change Science: An Analysis of Some Key Questions:

> As the NRC noted in its report, concentrations of [greenhouse gases (GHGs)] are increasing in the atmosphere as a result of human activities (pp. 9–12). It also noted that "[a] diverse array of evidence points to a warming of global surface air temperatures" (p. 16). The report goes on to state, however, that "[b]ecause of the large and still uncertain level of natural variability inherent in the climate record and the uncertainties in the time histories of the various forcing agents (and particularly aerosols), a [causal] linkage between the buildup of greenhouse gases in the atmosphere and the observed climate changes during the 20th century cannot be unequivocally established. The fact that the magnitude of the observed warming is large in comparison to natural variability as simulated in climate models is suggestive of such a linkage, but

it does not constitute proof of one because the model simulations could be deficient in natural variability on the decadal to century time scale" (p. 17). . . .

The science of climate change is extraordinarily complex and still evolving. Although there have been substantial advances in climate change science, there continue to be important uncertainties in our understanding of the factors that may affect future climate change and how it should be addressed. As the NRC explained, predicting future climate change necessarily involves a complex web of economic and physical factors including: Our ability to predict future global anthropogenic emissions of GHGs and aerosols; the fate of these emissions once they enter the atmosphere (e.g., what percentage are absorbed by vegetation or are taken up by the oceans); the impact of those emissions that remain in the atmosphere on the radiative properties of the atmosphere; changes in critically important climate feedbacks (e.g., changes in cloud cover and ocean circulation); changes in temperature characteristics (e.g., average temperatures, shifts in daytime and evening temperatures); changes in other climatic parameters (e.g., shifts in precipitation, storms); and ultimately the impact of such changes on human health and welfare (e.g., increases or decreases in agricultural productivity, human health impacts). The NRC noted, in particular, that "[t]he understanding of the relationships between weather/climate and human health is in its infancy and therefore the health consequences of climate change are poorly understood" (p. 20). Substantial scientific uncertainties limit our ability to assess each of these factors and to separate out those changes resulting from natural variability from those that are directly the result of increases in anthropogenic GHGs.

Reducing the wide range of uncertainty inherent in current model predictions will require major advances in understanding and modeling of the factors that determine atmospheric concentrations of greenhouse gases and aerosols, and the processes that determine the sensitivity of the climate system. 68 Fed. Reg. 52930.

I simply cannot conceive of what else the Court would like EPA to say.

II

A

Even before reaching its discussion of the word "judgment," the Court makes another significant error when it concludes that "§ 202(a)(1) of the Clean Air Act *authorizes* EPA to regulate greenhouse gas emissions from new motor vehicles in the event that it forms a 'judgment' that such emissions contribute to climate change" (emphasis added). For such authorization, the Court relies on what it calls "the Clean Air Act's capacious definition of 'air pollutant.' "

"Air pollutant" is defined by the Act as "any air pollution agent or combination of such agents, including any physical, chemical, . . . substance or matter which is emitted into or otherwise enters the ambient air." 42 U.S.C. § 7602(g). The Court is correct that "[c]arbon dioxide, methane, nitrous oxide, and hydrofluorocarbons," fit within the second half of that definition: They are "physical, chemical, . . . substance[s] or matter which [are] emitted into or otherwise ente[r] the ambient air." But the Court mistakenly believes this to be the end of the analysis. In order to be an "air pollutant" under the Act's definition, the "substance or matter [being] emitted into . . . the ambient air" must also meet the *first* half of the definition—namely, it must be an "air pollution agent or combination of such agents." The Court simply pretends this half of the definition does not exist.

. . . As that argument goes, anything that *follows* the word "including" must necessarily be a subset of whatever *precedes* it. Thus, if greenhouse gases qualify under the phrase following the word "including," they must qualify under the phrase preceding it. . . .

That is certainly one possible interpretation of the statutory definition. The word "including" can indeed indicate that what follows will be an "illustrative" sampling of the general category that precedes the word. Often, however, the examples standing alone are broader than the general category, and must be viewed as limited in light of that category. The Government provides a helpful (and unanswered) example: "The phrase 'any American automobile, including any truck or minivan,' would not naturally be construed to encompass a foreign-manufactured [truck or] minivan." Brief for Federal Respondent 34. The general principle enunciated—that the speaker is talking about *American* automobiles—carries forward to the illustrative examples (trucks and minivans), and limits them accordingly, even though in isolation they are broader. Congress often uses the word "including" in this manner. . . .

In short, the word "including" does not require the Court's (or the petitioners') result. It is perfectly reasonable to view the definition of "air pollutant" in its entirety: An air pollutant *can* be "any physical, chemical, . . . substance or matter which is emitted into or otherwise enters the ambient air," but only if it retains the general characteristic of being an "air pollution agent or combination of such agents." This is precisely the conclusion EPA reached: "[A] substance does not meet the CAA definition of 'air pollutant' simply because it is a 'physical, chemical, . . . substance or matter which is emitted into or otherwise enters the ambient air.' It must also be an 'air pollution agent.' " 68 Fed. Reg. 52929, n. 3. Once again, in the face of textual ambiguity, the Court's application of Chevron deference to EPA's interpretation of the word "including" is nowhere to be found. Evidently, the Court defers only to those reasonable interpretations that it favors.

B

Using (as we ought to) EPA's interpretation of the definition of "air pollutant," we must next determine whether greenhouse gases are "agent[s]" of "air pollution." If so, the statute would authorize regulation; if not, EPA would lack authority.

Unlike "air pollutants," the term "air pollution" is not itself defined by the CAA; thus, once again we must accept EPA's interpretation of that ambiguous term, provided its interpretation is a "permissible construction of the statute." Chevron. . . . EPA began with the commonsense observation that the "[p]roblems associated with atmospheric concentrations of CO_2," id., at 52927, bear little resemblance to what would naturally be termed "air pollution": . . . In other words, regulating the buildup of CO_2 and other greenhouse gases in the upper reaches of the atmosphere, which is alleged to be causing global climate change, is not akin to regulating the concentration of some substance that is *polluting* the *air*.

We need look no further than the dictionary for confirmation that this interpretation of "air pollution" is eminently reasonable. The definition of "pollute," of course, is "[t]o make or render impure or unclean." Webster's New International Dictionary 1910 (2d ed.1949). And the first three definitions of "air" are as follows: (1) "[t]he invisible, odorless, and tasteless mixture of gases which surrounds the earth"; (2) "[t]he body of the earth's atmosphere; esp., the part of it near the earth, as distinguished from the upper rarefied part"; (3) "[a] portion of air or of the air considered with respect to physical characteristics or as affecting the senses." Id., at 54. EPA's conception of "air pollution"—focusing on impurities in the "ambient air" "at ground level or near the surface of the earth"—is perfectly consistent with the natural meaning of that term.

In the end, EPA concluded that since "CAA authorization to regulate is generally based on a finding that an air pollutant causes or contributes to air pollution," 68 Fed. Reg. 52928, the concentrations of CO_2 and other greenhouse gases allegedly affecting the global climate are beyond the scope of CAA's authorization to regulate. "[T]he term 'air pollution' as used in the regulatory provisions cannot be interpreted to encompass global climate change." Once again, the Court utterly fails to explain why this interpretation is incorrect, let alone so unreasonable as to be unworthy of Chevron deference. . . .

The Court's alarm over global warming may or may not be justified, but it ought not distort the outcome of this litigation. This is a straightforward administrative-law case, in which Congress has passed a malleable statute giving broad discretion, not to us but to an executive agency. No matter how important the underlying policy issues at stake, this Court has no business substituting its own desired outcome for the reasoned judgment of the responsible agency.

NOTES ON THE DECISION IN MASSACHUSETTS v. EPA

(1) *What Is Driving This Decision?* The statutory provision at issue in this case says that the EPA Administrator "shall" act in certain situations that "in his judgment" cause pollution. As one emphasizes "in his judgment" the Administrator's discretion inflates; as one emphasizes "shall," it deflates. Doesn't this balloon-like command create exactly the ambiguity for which Chevron deference was created? Or is it that, because one alternative reading would constitute a command to the Administrator to do something he does not want to do, his judgment cannot be trusted? Or is it that the agency's 2003 view of its very authority to regulate is too much driven by politics? Or is it that the topic is too important for the Supreme Court to dispose of on "deference" grounds?

(2) Massachusetts v. EPA implicates doctrines found throughout this book. You might want to review (or look at for the first time) the materials on public initiation of rulemaking (p. 402) and on the reviewability of an agency's refusal to act (p. 1407), especially the reviewability of an agency's refusal to initiate rulemaking (p. 1411). The treatment of standing in the principal case itself is considered at p. 1355.

(3) *How Does the Decision Relate to the Politics of Global Warming?* A Response to Massachusetts v. EPA from the Bush administration:

"Office of the Press Secretary, White House, May 14, 2007:

"Today, President Bush directed the U.S. Environmental Protection Agency (EPA) and the U.S. Departments Of Energy (DOE), Transportation (DOT), and Agriculture (USDA) to take the first steps toward regulations using the 'Twenty In Ten' Plan as a starting point. The President has directed these agencies to take the first steps toward regulations that would cut gasoline consumption and greenhouse gas emissions from motor vehicles. . . .

"In the State Of The Union address, the President announced his 'Twenty In Ten' goal to cut U.S. gasoline consumption by 20 percent over the next ten years. By increasing the supply of alternative fuels and making motor vehicles more energy efficient, the President's 'Twenty in Ten' plan provides a framework to address energy security and reduce greenhouse gas emissions from motor vehicles and off-road engines and equipment. . . .

"On April 2, 2007, the Supreme Court ruled that the EPA must take action under the Clean Air Act regarding greenhouse gas emissions from motor vehicles.

"In response to the Supreme Court's ruling, the President directed cabinet agencies to take the first steps toward regulations based on 'Twenty In Ten' that will make our economy stronger, our environment cleaner, and our nation more secure for generations to come.

"The President has directed members of his administration to complete this process by the end of 2008. The President has asked Administration officials to listen to public input; carefully consider safety, science, and available technology; and evaluate benefits and costs before they reach any decisions. This is a complicated legal and technical matter that will take time to fully resolve. Yet it is important to move forward.

"The President also signed an Executive Order requiring coordination among federal agencies tasked with the development of any regulations affecting greenhouse gas emissions from motor vehicles. The Executive Order will ensure coordinated agency efforts on regulatory actions aimed at protecting the environment with respect to greenhouse gas emissions from motor vehicles, nonroad vehicles, and nonroad engines proceed in a manner consistent with sound science, analysis of benefits and costs, public safety, and economic growth.

"The steps the President announced today are not a substitute for effective legislation. The Administration will redouble its efforts to work with Congress on a bipartisan 'Twenty in Ten' bill."

(4)   A Response to Massachusetts v. EPA from the Obama administration (74 Fed. Reg. 66496):

"Endangerment and Cause or Contribute Findings for Greenhouse Gases Under Section 202(a) of the Clean Air Act

Tuesday, December 15, 2009

"AGENCY: Environmental Protection Agency (EPA).

"ACTION: Final rule.

"SUMMARY: The Administrator finds that six greenhouse gases taken in combination endanger both the public health and the public welfare of current and future generations. The Administrator also finds that the combined emissions of these greenhouse gases from new motor vehicles and new motor vehicle engines contribute to the greenhouse gas air pollution that endangers public health and welfare under CAA section 202(a). These Findings are based on careful consideration of the full weight of scientific evidence and a thorough review of numerous public comments received on the Proposed Findings published April 24, 2009."

(5)   The Statement of Basis and Purpose accompanying these 2009 findings included this, 74 Fed. Reg. 66500–501:

"Many commenters urge EPA to delay making final findings for a variety of reasons. They note that the Supreme Court did not establish a deadline for EPA to act on remand. Commenters also argue that the Supreme Court's decision does not require that EPA make a final endangerment finding, and thus that EPA has discretionary power and may decline to issue an endangerment finding, not only if the science is too uncertain, but also if EPA can provide 'some reasonable explanation' for exercising its discretion. These commenters interpret the Supreme Court decision not as rejecting all policy reasons for declining to undertake an endangerment finding, but rather as dismissing solely the policy reasons EPA set forth in 2003. Some commenters cite language in the Supreme Court decision regarding EPA's discretion regarding 'the manner, timing, content, and coordination of its regulations,' and the Court's declining to rule on 'whether policy concerns can inform EPA's actions in the event that it makes' a CAA section 202(a) finding to support their position.

"Commenters then suggest a variety of policy reasons that EPA can and should make to support a decision not to undertake a finding of endangerment under CAA section 202(a)(1). For example, they argue that a finding of endangerment would trigger several other regulatory programs . . . that would impose an unreasonable burden on the economy and government, without providing a benefit to the environment. Some commenters contend that EPA should defer issuing a final endangerment finding while Congress considers legislation. Many commenters note the ongoing international discussions regarding climate change and state their belief that unilateral EPA action would interfere with those negotiations. Others suggest deferring the EPA portion of the joint U.S. Department of Transportation (DOT)/EPA rulemaking because they argue that the new Corporate Average Fuel Economy (CAFE) standards will effectively result in lower greenhouse gas emissions from new motor vehicles, while avoiding the inevitable problems and concerns of regulating greenhouse gases under the CAA.

"Other commenters argue that the endangerment determination has to be made on the basis of scientific considerations only. These commenters state that the Court was clear that '[t]he statutory question is whether sufficient information exists to make an endangerment finding,' and thus, only if 'the scientific uncertainty is so profound that it precludes EPA from making a reasoned judgment as to whether greenhouse gases contribute to global warming,' may EPA avoid making a positive or negative endangerment finding. Many commenters urge EPA to take action quickly. They note that it has been 10 years since the original petition requesting that EPA regulate greenhouse gas emissions from motor vehicles was submitted to EPA. They argue that climate change is a serious problem that requires immediate action.

"EPA agrees with the commenters who argue that the Supreme Court decision held that EPA is limited to consideration of science when undertaking an endangerment finding, and that we cannot delay issuing a finding due to policy concerns if the science is sufficiently certain (as it is here). The Supreme Court stated that 'EPA can avoid taking further action only if it determines that greenhouse gases do not contribute to climate change or if it provides some reasonable explanation as to why it cannot or will not exercise its discretion to determine whether they do.' 549 U.S. at 533. Some commenters point to this last provision, arguing that the policy reasons they provide are a 'reasonable explanation' for not moving forward at this time. However, this ignores other language in the decision that clearly indicates that the Court interprets the statute to allow for the consideration only of science. For example, in rejecting the policy concerns expressed by EPA in its 2003 denial of the rulemaking petition, the Court noted that 'it is evident [the policy considerations] have nothing to do with whether greenhouse gas emissions contribute to climate change. Still less do they amount to a reasoned justification for declining to form a scientific judgment' Id. at 533–34 (emphasis added).

"Moreover, the Court also held that '[t]he statutory question is whether sufficient information exists to make an endangerment finding.' Id. at 534. Taken as a whole, the Supreme Court's decision clearly indicates that policy reasons do not justify the Administrator avoiding taking further action on the question here."

If the EPA of the Obama administration had wanted not to take action, do you think the reading proposed by the first set of commenters was foreclosed? If the EPA had some latitude to act or not to act, did it help it (in an obviously contested situation) to be able to rely so heavily on the Court's decision?

(6) JODY FREEMAN & ADRIAN VERMEULE, MASSACHUSETTS V. EPA: FROM POLITICS TO EXPERTISE, 2007 Sup. Ct. Rev. 51, 96–97: "On the view we attribute to the MA v. EPA majority, courts have a role to play not only through ex post judicial review of agency decisions, but also through expertise-forcing when agencies are deciding not to decide because of political pressures. If agencies refuse to exercise their first-order expertise, in any direction, because issues are politically too controversial, or because they fear that an expert judgment would point in the direction of politically costly action—a plausible description of what occurred when EPA considered whether to regulate greenhouse gases—courts can review the reasons agencies give for postponing their first-order decisions in order to flush out these socially harmful motivations. Where agencies have no valid reason for further delay, courts will indirectly force them to make the first-order expert judgment they have been avoiding.

"MA v. EPA seems to adopt this perspective when it makes two important findings. The first is that *rulemaking denials are reviewable. . . .*

"The second crucial point is that *agency decisions not to decide are (presumptively) subject to 'hard look' review.* At least absent a clear statutory command to the contrary, the reviewing court will require the agency to offer a nonarbitrary reason for the decision not to decide. One type of arbitrariness is legal error: agencies must consider only those factors made relevant by the particular statute at hand. In other words, hard look review applies *both* to the agency's decision about whether to make a threshold determination in the first place, *and* to the agency's decision about whether the threshold has been crossed. When making both the first-order judgment under § 202 and the second-order decision about whether to decide, EPA may not consider extraneous non-statutory factors such as foreign policy, or its preference for other regulatory or nonregulatory approaches that might fit better with the President's priorities. Rather, the agency is to focus primarily on information, scientific uncertainty, and the costs and benefits of acquiring further information. Does the state of the science enable the EPA to make a rational judgment now, in either direction, about the health and welfare effects of a given pollutant? What are the costs of deciding not to decide, as against the informational advantages that would arise from postponing the first-order judgment until the science is solidified?

"Of course the case does not answer all questions. Crucial to the holding is the point that § 202(a) excludes nonscientific and nontechnical factors from the agency's initial decision-making calculus. Some statutes can plausibly be read to share that feature; others presumably cannot. All organic statutes are different; in some settings statutes will be read to give agencies more or less discretion to decide not to decide. The main contribution of the decision, however, is to clarify that there is nothing magic about such initial decisions. They are reviewable on the ordinary terms of administrative law. Properly understood, MA v. EPA is . . . State Farm for a new generation."

If, as Freeman and Vermeule say, "all organic statutes are different," what is the precedential force of the principal case? They obviously think it represents a significant general development. But could this be a one-time-only Supreme Court response to an issue too important, and in the Court's judgment, too mishandled, to pass up? If it were, would that be objectionable? Or is that what the Supreme Court ought to do when certain "really big" cases come its way? Conversely, would the doctrine as restated by Freeman and Vermeule be good or bad if used in the mine run of cases?

(7)   By the way, the official list of lawyers who participated in this case—the list of government lawyers, the private bar, and lawyers for public interest organizations—totals an astonishing 103 lawyers in all. (And that does not count all those who helped write the briefs but did not get named!)

NOTES ON JUDICIAL REVIEW: LAW OR POLITICS?

Is It All Politics? When judges review an agency's decision, are they really applying "the law," or are they simply deciding what outcome they think most accords with their views of policy and justice, and disguising their preferences under a facade of doctrine? (Justice Scalia, in the case we just read, charged: "Evidently, the Court defers only to those reasonable interpretations it favors.") The only thing that can be said for certain about this question, is that it is much debated.

Insofar as the question is addressed to the behavior of the U.S. Supreme Court, you can to some extent decide for yourself by looking at the series of judicial review opinions set forth in this chapter. But the Supreme Court is probably not a representative test case. Its role is primarily to decide cases of first impression, and the most obvious basis for granting certiorari is precisely that the courts below have given contrary answers to the question at hand; it is to be expected that such a court will often have to reach beyond existing doctrine to find its grounds for decision. What about the lower courts—or, of special importance for administrative law, what about the U.S. Courts of Appeals, where much review of administrative agencies starts and almost all of it stops?

(1)   Here, from 1991, is the view of Judge Harry Edwards, a well-known member of the Court of Appeals for the District of Columbia Circuit, a court that, because of its location and some specific statutory assignments, does a disproportionate share of administrative review work. HARRY T. EDWARDS, THE JUDICIAL FUNCTION AND THE ELUSIVE GOAL OF PRINCIPLED DECISIONMAKING, 1991 Wis. L. Rev. 837, 838–39, 849, 855–57: "Today, more than eleven years after becoming a judge, . . . I still believe in and subscribe

to principled decisionmaking, but it is no longer entirely clear to me that partisan politics and ideological maneuvering have no meaningful influence on judicial decisionmaking. . . . [I]n my view, most judges still share a belief that principled decisionmaking is the essence of the judicial function. What has changed, I think, is the nature of certain external pressures felt by judges; these pressures are both created and exacerbated by the continuing distortion of public perceptions, in which the judicial function is increasingly viewed as just one more 'political' enterprise. . . .

"The more that judges are assessed in terms of 'political' (result-oriented) decisionmaking, the more likely it is that this will become a self-fulfilling prophecy. Even if judges are able to resist the temptation to conform to the false perception, continued assessments of judicial performance in political terms will promote a 'new reality,' for most people will come to believe that the judicial function is nothing more than a political enterprise. No matter how good the intentions of its servants, the judiciary will be sharply devalued and incompetent to fulfill its role as mediator in a society with lofty but sometimes conflicting ambitions. This would be a horror to behold.

". . . I have felt damned by an increasingly common image of the judiciary, and particularly of the D.C. Circuit, as a fundamentally political body. . . .

"Fortunately, the present reality of decisionmaking on the D.C. Circuit does not match the public perception. There is no doubt that there are ideological differences among the judges and that these differences may have an impact in the disposition of certain 'very hard' (and even 'hard') cases. . . . Perhaps the most fundamental reality of D.C. Circuit decisionmaking is that, contrary to popular belief, circuit judges rarely disagree with one another over the disposition of particular cases. The vast majority of case dispositions involve unanimous decisions. In the court's 1983–84 year, for instance, dissents were filed in only 5.8% of the total cases decided; of those cases decided by full opinion, only 13% generated a dissent. A statistical analysis of 1989–90 reveals that dissents were filed in only 2.6% of the total cases decided; of those cases decided by full opinion, only roughly 10% included a dissent. Thus, the rate of dissents in 1989–90 actually dropped below the rate for 1983–84. Most notably, the dissent rate on what I call 'mixed panels'—panels with judges appointed by Presidents of different political affiliations—did not exceed the general dissent rate in either year. Clearly, the image of an ideologically divided circuit court on which judges heed some political call to action is far from the truth.

"In my view, most cases are 'easy,' in that the pertinent legal rules are readily identified and applied to the facts at hand, revealing a single 'right answer.' . . . [R]oughly one-half of the cases I hear each year are 'easy' and virtually all of these are disposed of without dissent. . . . In a second category of [the 'hard' cases] . . . each party is able to advance at least one plausible legal argument in its favor. . . . [But after] . . . research and review . . . the arguments of one party to a 'hard' case seem to me demonstrably stronger than those of the other, and the case is decided accordingly. . . . [A]pproximately 35 to 45% of the cases before the court are 'hard' in this sense. In my experience, judges hearing these cases generally feel themselves bound by their view of the law, and identify the sounder arguments without recourse to their own political opinions. Not surprisingly, therefore, there is substantial agreement among judges as to the proper disposition of 'hard' cases.

"That leaves from 5 to 15% of our cases in the 'very hard' category, making it by far the smallest of the three. In this narrow set of cases, careful research and reflection fail to yield conclusive answers. The relevant legal materials, thoroughly studied, show only that the competing arguments advanced by the parties are equally strong, and the judges who must decide are left in a state of equipoise. Disposition of this small number of cases, then, requires judges to exercise a measure of discretion, drawing to some degree on their own social and moral beliefs. That judges may find themselves in disagreement as to the outcome of these 'very hard' cases is thus to be expected, and represents something quite different from stark political decisionmaking.

"The important point, I think, is that so-called 'very hard' cases are viewed as such not because they raise situations in which judges are inclined to engage in result-oriented decisionmaking, but, rather, because these cases admit of no clear answer. And when there is no discernible 'right' answer to a case, it is more likely (although not inevitable) that decisionmaking may be influenced by political or ideological considerations."

(2)   In the last twenty years there have been a great many academic studies that have challenged Edwards' point of view. For students of administrative law, of special interest are a series of studies carried out by Thomas Miles and Cass Sunstein that looked at the degree to which politics impacted the application of Chevron and of arbitrary and capricious review. Here is their description of their method (CASS R. SUNSTEIN & THOMAS J. MILES, DEPOLITICIZING ADMINISTRATIVE LAW, 58 Duke L. J. 2193, 2199–2201 (2009)): "Within the courts of appeals, our focus has been on judicial review of decisions by the Environmental Protection Agency (EPA) and the National Labor Relations Board (NLRB). . . . [In the case of agency interpretations of law, we examined all cases citing Chevron between 1990 and 2004 (253 in total); in the case of arbitrariness review, we examined all arbitrariness and substantial evidence cases between 1996 and 2006 (653 in total).] There are of course real difficulties in deciding how to 'code' agency decisions in political terms. It is hard to undertake such coding in the abstract; it is even harder to do so when the real question is not whether the agency has proceeded in a 'liberal' fashion, but how the particular controversy, before a court, should be evaluated in political terms. Let us begin by describing our choice and then explaining it.

"In brief, we attempted to categorize agency decisions as 'liberal' or 'conservative' by asking whether the challenge was made by a company or instead by a public interest group or a labor union. If, for example, the Sierra Club objected to an EPA decision, the decision was coded as conservative; if General Motors made the objection, the decision was coded as liberal. This method has several important advantages. It greatly simplifies the coding exercise, avoids controversial judgments that might divide reviewers, and thus improves administrability and replicability. It can also be defended in principle. What matters is not whether the agency's decision is liberal or conservative in the abstract, but the political valence of the particular challenge before the court. If, for example, the EPA has issued a ruling that some people consider 'liberal,' but that is challenged by a public interest group that is attempting to increase regulation, the ruling is relevantly conservative, in the sense that judges are being asked to hold that it is unlawfully weak. . . .

"We also examined whether judicial votes were issued by Republican or Democratic appointees to the federal bench, with the hypothesis that the division should operate as a proxy for political predilections and with the further thought that the effect of the political affiliation of the appointing president is of considerable independent interest. With this method, we can investigate 'liberal voting rates' for Democratic and Republican appointees in different domains. We can also compare the validation rate of both sets of appointees for conservative agency decisions and for liberal agency decisions. In addition to studying the effects of party, we can study the effects of panels by asking whether the votes of Democratic or Republican appointees are affected by the political affiliation of the president who appointed the two other judges on the panel. Do Democratic appointees show especially liberal voting patterns when they sit only with other Democratic appointees? How do the voting patterns of Republican appointees differ depending on whether they are sitting with no, one, or two Democratic appointees?

"The baseline case, for purposes of studying neutrality and partisanship, would show no significant disparities between Republican and Democratic appointees. If no such disparities were shown, existing administrative law doctrines would be 'working' in the sense that they would be serving to filter out any effect from the most obvious and salient difference among appointees to the federal bench."

And here is their description of their principal results (58 Duke L.J. 2193, 2201–05):

"Within the courts of appeals, politicized voting is unmistakable in Chevron cases. Consider three different ways to demonstrate this point:

1. When the agency's decision is liberal, the Democratic validation rate is 74 percent; when the agency's decision is conservative, the Democratic validation rate falls to 51 percent. The pattern is the opposite for Republican appointees—very close to the mirror image. When the agency's decision is liberal, the Republican validation rate is 59.5 percent. When the agency's decision is conservative, the Republican validation rate jumps to 70 percent.

2. When the agency's decision is liberal, Democratic appointees are 14 percent more likely to vote to validate it than are Republican appointees. When the agency's decision is conservative, Democratic appointees are 19 percent less likely to validate it than are Republican appointees.

3.   The overall liberal voting rate is 67 percent for Democratic appointees; for Republican appointees, it is 50 percent.

"To be sure, differences of these magnitudes are inconsistent with the proposition that in administrative law cases judicial voting is thoroughly politicized. It remains true that Republican appointees vote to uphold liberal interpretations well over 50 percent of the time, and that Democratic appointees are more likely than not to uphold conservative interpretations. Nonetheless, the disparities are significant. What produces them?

"Intriguingly, they are driven in large part by the radically different behavior of both sets of appointees on unified panels-that is, panels consisting solely of Democratic appointees (DDD panels) or solely of Republican appointees (RRR panel). When Democratic appointees are on DDD panels, the validation rate for liberal agency decisions is 86 percent; when Democratic appointees are on DDD panels, the validation rate for conservative agency decisions is 54 percent. . . . When Republican appointees are on RRR panels, the validation rate for liberal agency decisions is 51 percent; and on such panels, the validation rate for conservative agency decisions is a remarkable 100 percent.

"Because of the relatively small sample size, the particular numbers here should be taken with a grain of salt, but they should be sufficient to show that unified panels are playing a large role in driving the results. . . . On mixed panels, politicized voting is greatly reduced; the behavior of Democratic appointees, on such panels, is very close to that of Republican appointees. . . . Group polarization is the typical pattern within deliberating groups, and it occurs in a wide range of settings. If Democratic appointees show especially liberal voting patterns on panels consisting solely of Democratic appointees, it is likely because the judges' initial inclinations are amplified, rather than moderated, by learning about the conclusions and arguments of other judges. On mixed panels, by contrast, a whistleblower effect may occur, in the form of presentation of counterarguments based (for example) on the principle of Chevron deference. . . .

"The pattern is strikingly similar in arbitrariness cases. Here the question is not whether the agency's decision conforms to the governing statute, but whether its judgments of policy or fact are arbitrary on the merits (or unsupported by substantial evidence). Return to our three key tests for politicized voting, and notice the closely analogous pattern in Chevron cases:

1.   When the agency's decision is liberal, the Democratic validation rate is 72 percent; when the agency's decision is conservative, the rate falls to 55 percent. The pattern is the opposite for Republican appointees—very close to the mirror image. When the agency's decision is liberal, the validation rate is 58 percent; when the agency's decision is conservative, the validation rate jumps to 72 percent.

2.   When the agency's decision is liberal, Democratic appointees are 14 percent more likely to vote to validate it than are Republican appointees. When the agency's decision is conservative, Democratic

appointees are 17 percent less likely to validate it than are Republican appointees.

3.   The overall liberal voting rate is 69 percent for Democratic appointees; for Republican appointees, it is 56 percent.

"One of the most striking features of these findings is their similarity to those under Chevron; different areas of administrative law have produced parallel voting patterns. And here too, unified panels explain a significant part of these disparities. . . ."

"To say the least," the authors comment, "this seems to be a disturbing and somewhat embarrassing state of affairs. Whatever one's view of the foundational questions in administrative law, no one should approve of a situation in which judicial voting patterns are highly politicized. On the contrary, it is reasonable to read existing doctrines as an explicit effort to prevent such patterns from emerging. Most prominently, Chevron U.S.A. Inc. v. Natural Resources Defense Council, Inc. establishes that courts must uphold agency interpretations of ambiguous statutory provisions so long as those interpretations are reasonable. Chevron is naturally read to say that resolution of statutory ambiguities calls for a policy judgment, with the suggestion that such judgments should be made by administrators, not judges. It is disconcerting, to say the least, to find that when judges review agency interpretations of law, judicial policy judgments continue to be playing a significant role." 58 Duke L. J. at 2195–96.

An additional study of seventy environmental law cases in the courts of appeals between 2003 and 2005 was conducted in 2008. The study found, consistent with the Miles & Sunstein study, that the political ideology of judges (as measured through the GHP scale, which is based on the ideology of the senators in that judge's state at the time of his or her appointment, or of the appointing president) appears to play a statistically significant role in their decisions. The more "liberal" a judge, the more likely they were to vote in support of the environmental agency, while the more "conservative" a judge, the *less* likely they were to cast a vote in favor of the agency. Indeed, the authors found that liberal judges had voted in favor of the agency about 53% of the time. Conservative judges voted in favor only 36% of the time. Jason J. Czarnezki, An Empirical Investigation of Judicial Decisionmaking, Statutory Interpretation, and the Chevron Doctrine in Environmental Law, 79 U. Colo. L. Rev. 767, 793–95 (2008).

(3)   Judge Edwards is not, however, convinced. In an article responding to the work of Miles and Sunstein, and to other studies (HARRY T. EDWARDS & MICHAEL A. LIVERMORE, PITFALLS OF EMPIRICAL STUDIES THAT ATTEMPT TO UNDERSTAND THE FACTORS AFFECTING APPELLATE DECISIONMAKING, 58 Duke L. J. 1895 (2009)), he stuck by his original analysis of easy, hard, and very hard cases, and quarreled in part with the methodology the empirical scholars employed. He also took issue with the underlying view of "law" and "politics" he thought was encapsulated in their studies (58 Duke L. J. at 1945–48): "The crudeness of the measures used to support the ideology thesis rest on an implausibly formalistic and positivistic conception of law. The hypothesis that judicial decisionmaking is influenced by the ideology of

judges is remarkable only if and to the extent that ideology is extrinsic to law. If we do not subscribe to this assumption, then both law and ideology can influence outcomes, and greater contributions from the later tell us nothing about the contribution of the former. The crude measure of 'ideology' fails to discriminate between forms of moral/political reasoning intrinsic to law and those extrinsic to law. It is well understood that legal reasoning partakes of moral judgment in cases in which judges routinely exercise delegated or common law-making authority. This need not, and generally does not, take the form of personal whim or preference. Rather, in cases where the law requires it, judicial decisionmaking can include a situated and disciplined elaboration of the conventional norms of the American political community. This occurs in both 'hard' and 'very hard' cases, including, for example, cases involving judicial resolutions of disputes in areas of law ranging from constitutional interpretation to the administration of the antitrust laws. This reality might be contested by some, but it is far and away the dominant understanding of how adjudication works in our judicial system.

"On this account, some play for inherently contestable political judgments is simply built into law and strikes us as a normal constituent of good judging. It is obvious—to the point of being mundane—to suggest that there is a correlation between how individual judges will carry out this aspect of judicial reasoning and their 'ideologies.' When positive law is imprecise and judges are required to exercise delegated or common law-making authority in hard or very hard cases, they often are obliged to refer to the conception of our community's political morality that strikes them as the most compelling. Good examples of this are seen in the political . . . conception of free speech that animated the Supreme Court's seminal decision New York Times v. Sullivan, in the neoclassical conception of economics that triumphed with the . . . 'public welfare' understanding of antitrust law, and in the extensive jurisprudence surrounding the enforcement of collective bargaining agreements pursuant to section 301 of the Labor Management Relations Act. The judging that gave rise to those conceptions of law can be described as either (1) not ideological in any manner opposed to law or (2) ideological in a manner intrinsic to law itself. . . .

"Judges who exercise delegated or common law-making authority to decide cases of this sort . . . are obliged to rely—and to do so self-consciously and overtly—on political and ideological values in their legal reasoning. This cannot seriously be doubted, nor can it reasonably be seen as surprising. It is merely part of the judicial function. If one accepts that such reasoning is legal reasoning, then any regression model that uses a crude measure of ideology that spills over to evaluative reasoning of this sort will produce results that merely state the obvious, i.e., that judicial disagreement over how to understand the law helps explain variations in case outcomes.

"Empirical studies of this sort, in sum, assume not only that judicial decisionmaking is sometimes influenced by the ideology of judges, but also that ideology is invariably extrinsic to law. But this turns out, surprisingly, to be a normative claim . . . in the guise of an empirical one. The fact is that most members of the legal profession—judges, lawyers, and scholars-subscribe to a conception of law that sees forms of moral or political reasoning as intrinsic to law in some circumstances. Thus, empirical scholars can convince us to accept their central claim (that extralegal judicial 'ideology' explains variation in some legal outcomes) only if they first convince us that we are wrong in our view that some political and ideological questions are intrinsic to law itself. In other words, empirical ideologists must convince us that we should adopt a formalistic or 'hard' positivistic theory that insists that legal questions never subsume moral or political questions. But, of course, if empirical scholars could do this (assuming they wanted to), they would not be showing that judges have been substituting their ideology for law but, rather, that judges have been following a conception of law that we should reject for normative reasons."

(4) As is evident from his examples, Judge Edwards does not distinguish what he considers to be the appropriate judicial method in general from a judicial method that might be especially applicable to review of administrative decisions. The passage from Sunstein and Miles, with its reliance on Chevron, suggests that we should make that distinction. Who has the better of that part of the argument?

(5) In many legal systems abroad, being a judge is a career, and selection proceeds more or less on bureaucratic criteria such as tests (which themselves perhaps incorporate the worldview of an elite stratum). Federal judges in our system are nominated by the President and confirmed by the Senate. Does that say something about how we expect our judges to behave?

(6) Finally, there is this from Seventh Circuit Judge Richard Posner (Some Realism About Judges: A Reply to Edwards and Livermore, 59 Duke L. J. 1177, 1180 (2010)): "Even Judge Edwards says that 5 to 15 percent of cases decided by his court are indeterminate from a legalist standpoint. If one cumulates those figures over many years and many courts, it is apparent that an immense number of decisions are legalistically indeterminate; and among them . . . are the decisions that have made the law what it is today."

> *CITY OF ARLINGTON v. F.C.C.*

CITY OF ARLINGTON, TEXAS v. FEDERAL COMMUNICATIONS COMMISSION

Supreme Court of the United States (2013).
569 U.S. 290.

■ JUSTICE SCALIA delivered the opinion of the Court.

We consider whether an agency's interpretation of a statutory ambiguity that concerns the scope of its regulatory authority (that is, its jurisdiction) is entitled to deference under Chevron U.S.A. Inc. v. Natural Resources Defense Council, Inc., 467 U.S. 837 (1984).

I

Wireless telecommunications networks require towers and antennas; proposed sites for those towers and antennas must be approved by local zoning authorities. In the Telecommunications Act of 1996, Congress "impose[d] specific limitations on the traditional authority of state and local governments to regulate the location, construction, and modification of such facilities," Rancho Palos Verdes v. Abrams, 544 U.S. 113, 115 (2005), and incorporated those limitations into the Communications Act of 1934. Section 201(b) of that Act empowers the Federal Communications Commission to "prescribe such rules and regulations as may be necessary in the public interest to carry out [its] provisions." 47 U.S.C. § 201(b). Of course, that rulemaking authority extends to the subsequently added portions of the Act.

The Act imposes five substantive limitations, which are codified in 47 U.S.C. § 332(c)(7)(B); only one of them, § 332(c)(7)(B)(ii), is at issue here. That provision requires state or local governments to act on wireless siting applications "within a reasonable period of time after the request is duly filed." Two other features of § 332(c)(7) are relevant. First, subparagraph (A), known as the "saving clause," provides that nothing in the Act, except those limitations provided in § 332(c)(7)(B), "shall limit or affect the authority of a State or local government" over siting decisions. Second, § 332(c)(7)(B)(v) authorizes a person who believes a state or local government's wireless-siting decision to be inconsistent with any of the limitations in § 332(c)(7)(B) to "commence an action in any court of competent jurisdiction."

In theory, § 332(c)(7)(B)(ii) requires state and local zoning authorities to take prompt action on siting applications for wireless facilities. But in practice, wireless providers often faced long delays. In July 2008, CTIA—The Wireless Association, which represents wireless service providers, petitioned the FCC to clarify the meaning of § 332(c)(7)(B)(ii)'s requirement that zoning authorities act on siting requests "within a reasonable period of time." In November 2009, the Commission, relying on its broad statutory authority to implement the provisions of the Communications Act, issued a declaratory ruling responding to CTIA's petition. In re Petition for Declaratory Ruling, 24 FCC Rcd. 13994, 14001. The Commission found that the "record evidence demonstrates that unreasonable delays in the personal wireless service facility siting process have obstructed the provision of wireless services" and that such delays "impede the promotion of advanced services and competition that Congress deemed critical in the Telecommunications Act of 1996." Id., at 14006, 14008. A "reasonable period of time" under § 332(c)(7)(B)(ii), the Commission determined, is presumptively (but rebuttably) 90 days to process a collocation application (that is, an application to place a new antenna on an existing tower) and 150 days to process all other applications. Id., at 14005.

Some state and local governments opposed adoption of the Declaratory Ruling on the ground that the Commission lacked "authority to interpret ambiguous provisions of Section 332(c)(7)." Id., at 14000. Specifically, they argued that the saving clause, § 332(c)(7)(A), and the judicial review provision, § 337(c)(7)(B)(v), together display a congressional intent to withhold from the Commission authority to interpret the limitations in § 332(c)(7)(B). Asserting that ground of objection, the cities of Arlington and San Antonio, Texas, petitioned for review of the Declaratory Ruling in the Court of Appeals for the Fifth Circuit.

Relying on Circuit precedent, the Court of Appeals held that the Chevron framework applied to the threshold question whether the FCC possessed statutory authority to adopt the 90- and 150-day timeframes. 668 F.3d 229, 248 (C.A.5 2012). Applying Chevron, the Court of Appeals found "§ 332(c)(7)(A)'s effect on the FCC's authority to administer § 332(c)(7)(B)'s limitations ambiguous," 668 F.3d, at 250, and held that "the FCC's interpretation of its statutory authority" was a permissible construction of the statute. Id., at 254. On the merits, the court upheld the presumptive 90- and 150-day deadlines as a "permissible construction of § 332(c)(7)(B)(ii) and (v) . . . entitled to Chevron deference." Id., at 256.

We granted certiorari limited to the first question presented: "Whether . . . a court should apply Chevron to . . . an agency's determination of its own jurisdiction." Pet. for Cert. in No. 11–1545, p. i.

II

A

As this case turns on the scope of the doctrine enshrined in Chevron, we begin with a description of that case's now-canonical formulation. "When a court reviews an agency's construction of the statute which it administers, it is confronted with two questions." 467 U.S., at 842. First, applying the ordinary tools of statutory construction, the court must determine "whether Congress has directly spoken to the precise question at issue. If the intent of Congress is clear, that is the end of the matter; for the court, as well as the agency, must give effect to the unambiguously expressed intent of Congress." Id., at 842–843. But "if the statute is silent or ambiguous with respect to the specific issue, the question for the court is whether the agency's answer is based on a permissible construction of the statute." Id., at 843.

Chevron is rooted in a background presumption of congressional intent: namely, "that Congress, when it left ambiguity in a statute" administered by an agency, "understood that the ambiguity would be resolved, first and foremost, by the agency, and desired the agency (rather than the courts) to possess whatever degree of discretion the ambiguity allows." Smiley v. Citibank (South Dakota), N.A., 517 U.S. 735, 740–741 (1996). Chevron thus provides a stable background rule against which Congress can legislate: Statutory ambiguities will be resolved, within the bounds of reasonable interpretation, not by the courts but by the administering agency. Congress knows to speak in plain terms when it wishes to circumscribe, and in capacious terms when it wishes to enlarge, agency discretion.

B

The question here is whether a court must defer under Chevron to an agency's interpretation of a statutory ambiguity that concerns the scope of the agency's statutory authority (that is, its jurisdiction). The argument against deference rests on the premise that there exist two distinct classes of agency interpretations: Some interpretations—the big, important ones, presumably—define the agency's "jurisdiction." Others—humdrum, run-of-the-mill stuff—are simply applications of jurisdiction the agency plainly has. That premise is false, because the distinction between "jurisdictional" and "nonjurisdictional" interpretations is a mirage. No matter how it is framed, the question a court faces when confronted with an agency's interpretation of a statute it administers is always, simply, whether the agency has stayed within the bounds of its statutory authority.

The misconception that there are, for Chevron purposes, separate "jurisdictional" questions on which no deference is due derives, perhaps, from a reflexive extension to agencies of the very real division between the jurisdictional and nonjurisdictional that is applicable to courts. In the judicial context, there is a meaningful line: Whether the court decided correctly is a question that has different consequences from the question whether it had the power to decide at all. Congress has the power (within limits) to tell the courts what classes of cases they may decide, but not to prescribe or superintend how they decide those cases. A court's power to decide a case is independent of whether its decision is correct, which is why even an erroneous judgment is entitled to res judicata effect. Put differently, a jurisdictionally proper but substantively incorrect judicial decision is not ultra vires.

That is not so for agencies charged with administering congressional statutes. Both their power to act and how they are to act is authoritatively prescribed by Congress, so that when they act improperly, no less than when they act beyond their jurisdiction, what they do is ultra vires. Because the question—whether framed as an incorrect application of agency authority or an assertion of authority not conferred—is always whether the agency has gone beyond what Congress has permitted it to do, there is no principled basis for carving out some arbitrary subset of such claims as "jurisdictional."

An example will illustrate just how illusory the proposed line between "jurisdictional" and "nonjurisdictional" agency interpretations is. Imagine the following validly-enacted statute:

COMMON CARRIER ACT

SECTION 1. The Agency shall have jurisdiction to prohibit any common carrier from imposing an unreasonable condition upon access to its facilities.

There is no question that this provision—including the terms "common carrier" and "unreasonable condition"—defines the Agency's jurisdiction. Surely, the argument goes, a court must determine de novo the scope of that jurisdiction.

Consider, however, this alternative formulation of the statute:

COMMON CARRIER ACT

SECTION 1. No common carrier shall impose an unreasonable condition upon access to its facilities.

SECTION 2. The Agency may prescribe rules and regulations necessary in the public interest to effectuate Section 1 of this Act.

Now imagine that the Agency, invoking its Section 2 authority, promulgates this Rule: "(1) The term 'common carrier' in Section 1 includes Internet Service Providers. (2) The term 'unreasonable condition' in Section 1 includes unreasonably high prices. (3) A monthly fee greater than $25 is an unreasonable condition on access to Internet service." By this Rule, the Agency has claimed for itself jurisdiction that is doubly questionable: Does its authority extend to Internet Service Providers? And does it extend to setting prices? Yet Section 2 makes clear that Congress, in petitioners' words, "conferred interpretive power on the agency" with respect to Section 1. Brief for Petitioners in No. 1545, p. 14. Even under petitioners' theory, then, a court should defer to the Agency's interpretation of the terms "common carrier" and "unreasonable condition"—that is to say, its assertion that its "jurisdiction" extends to regulating Internet Service Providers and setting prices.

In the first case, by contrast, petitioners' theory would accord the agency no deference. The trouble with this is that in both cases, the underlying question is exactly the same: Does the statute give the agency authority to regulate Internet Service Providers and cap prices, or not? The reality, laid bare, is that there is no difference, insofar as the validity of agency action is concerned, between an agency's exceeding the scope of its authority (its "jurisdiction") and its exceeding authorized application of authority that it unquestionably has. . . .

This point is nicely illustrated by our decision in National Cable & Telecommunications Assn., Inc. v. Gulf Power Co., 534 U.S. 327 (2002). That case considered whether the FCC's "jurisdiction" to regulate the rents utility-pole owners charge for "pole attachments" (defined as attachments by a cable television system or provider of telecommunications service) extended to attachments that provided both cable television and high-speed Internet access (attachments for so-called "commingled services"). We held, sensibly, that Chevron applied. Whether framed as going to the scope of the FCC's delegated authority or the FCC's application of its delegated authority, the underlying question was the same: Did the FCC exceed the bounds of its statutory authority to regulate rents for "pole attachments" when it sought to regulate rents for pole attachments providing commingled services?

The label is an empty distraction because every new application of a broad statutory term can be reframed as a questionable extension of the agency's jurisdiction. One of the briefs in support of petitioners explains, helpfully, that "[j]urisdictional questions concern the who, what, where, and when of regulatory power: which subject matters may an agency regulate and under what conditions." Brief for IMLA Respondents 18–19. But an agency's application of its authority pursuant to statutory text answers the same questions. Who is an "outside salesman"? What is a "pole attachment"? Where do the "waters of the United States" end? When must a Medicare provider challenge a reimbursement determination in order to be entitled to an administrative appeal? These can all be reframed as questions about the scope of agencies' regulatory jurisdiction—and they are all questions to which the Chevron framework applies. See Christopher v. SmithKline Beecham Corp., 567 U.S. ___ (2012); National Cable & Telecommunications Assn., supra, at 331, 333; United States v. Riverside Bayview Homes, Inc., 474 U.S. 121, 123, 131 (1985); Sebelius v. Auburn Regional Medical Center, 568 U.S. ___ (2013).

In sum, judges should not waste their time in the mental acrobatics needed to decide whether an agency's interpretation of a statutory provision is "jurisdictional" or "nonjurisdictional." Once those labels are sheared away, it becomes clear that the question in every case is, simply, whether the statutory text forecloses the agency's assertion of authority, or not. The federal judge as haruspex, sifting the entrails of vast statutory schemes to divine whether a particular agency interpretation qualifies as "jurisdictional," is not engaged in reasoned decisionmaking.

C

Fortunately, then, we have consistently held "that Chevron applies to cases in which an agency adopts a construction of a jurisdictional provision of a statute it administers." 1 R. Pierce, Administrative Law Treatise § 3.5, p. 187 (2010). One of our opinions explicitly says that no "exception exists to the normal [deferential] standard of review" for "'jurisdictional or legal question[s] concerning the coverage'" of an Act. NLRB v. City Disposal Systems, Inc., 465 U.S. 822, 830, n. 7 (1984). . . .

Similar examples abound. . . .

Our cases hold that Chevron applies equally to statutes designed to curtail the scope of agency discretion. . . .

The U.S. Reports are shot through with applications of Chevron to agencies' constructions of the scope of their own jurisdiction. And we have applied Chevron where concerns about agency self-aggrandizement are at their apogee: in cases where an agency's expansive construction of the extent of its own power would have wrought a fundamental change in the regulatory scheme. In FDA v. Brown & Williamson Tobacco Corp., 529 U.S. 120 (2000), the threshold question was the "appropriate framework for analyzing" the FDA's assertion of "jurisdiction to regulate tobacco products," id., at 126, 132—a question of vast "economic and political magnitude," id., at 133. "Because this case involves an administrative agency's construction of a statute that it administers," we held, Chevron applied. 529 U.S., at 13. Similarly, in MCI Telecommunications Corp. v. American Telephone & Telegraph Co., 512 U.S. 218 (1994), we applied the Chevron framework to the FCC's assertion that the statutory phrase "modify any requirement" gave it authority to eliminate rate-filing requirements, "the essential characteristic of a rate-regulated industry," for long-distance telephone carriers.

The false dichotomy between "jurisdictional" and "nonjurisdictional" agency interpretations may be no more than a bogeyman, but it is dangerous all the same. Like the Hound of the Baskervilles, it is conjured by those with greater quarry in sight: Make no mistake—the ultimate target here is Chevron itself. Savvy challengers of agency action would play the "jurisdictional" card in every case. Some judges would be deceived by the specious, but scary-sounding, "jurisdictional"-"nonjurisdictional" line; others tempted by the prospect of making public policy by prescribing the meaning of ambiguous statutory commands. The effect would be to transfer any number of interpretive decisions—archetypal Chevron questions, about how best to construe an ambiguous term in light of competing policy interests—from the agencies that administer the statutes to federal courts.[4] We have cautioned that "judges ought to refrain from substituting their own interstitial lawmaking" for that of an agency. Ford Motor Credit Co. v. Milhollin, 444 U.S. 555, 568 (1980). That is precisely what Chevron prevents.

III

A

One group of respondents contends that *Chevron* deference is inappropriate here because the FCC has "assert[ed] jurisdiction over matters of traditional state and local concern." Brief for IMLA Respondents 35. But this case has nothing to do with federalism. Section 332(c)(7)(B)(ii) explicitly supplants state authority by *requiring* zoning authorities to render a decision "within a reasonable period of time," and the meaning of that phrase is indisputably a question of federal law. We rejected a similar faux-federalism argument in the *Iowa Utilities Board* case, in terms that apply equally here: "This is, at bottom, a debate not about whether the States will be allowed to do their own thing, but about whether it will be the FCC or the federal courts that draw the lines to which they must hew." 525 U.S., at 379, n. 6. These lines will be drawn

---

⁴ The Chief Justice's discomfort with the growth of agency power, see *post*, is perhaps understandable. But the dissent overstates when it claims that agencies exercise "legislative power" and "judicial power." The former is vested exclusively in Congress, U.S. Const., Art. I, § 1, the latter in the "one supreme Court" and "such inferior Courts as the Congress may from time to time ordain and establish," Art. III, § 1. Agencies make rules ("Private cattle may be grazed on public lands *X, Y,* and *Z* subject to certain conditions") and conduct adjudications ("This rancher's grazing permit is revoked for violation of the conditions") and have done so since the beginning of the Republic. These activities take "legislative" and "judicial" forms, but they are exercises of—indeed, under our constitutional structure they *must be* exercises of—the "executive Power." Art. II, § 1, cl. 1.

either by unelected federal bureaucrats, or by unelected (and even less politically accountable) federal judges. "[I]t is hard to spark a passionate 'States' rights' debate over that detail." *Ibid*.

B

A few words in response to the dissent. The question on which we granted certiorari was whether "a court should apply Chevron to review an agency's determination of its own jurisdiction." Pet. for Cert. i. Perhaps sensing the incoherence of the "jurisdictional-nonjurisdictional" line, the dissent does not even attempt to defend it, but proposes a much broader scope for de novo judicial review: Jurisdictional or not, and even where a rule is at issue and the statute contains a broad grant of rulemaking authority, the dissent would have a court search provision-by-provision to determine "whether [that] delegation covers the 'specific provision' and 'particular question' before the court."

The dissent is correct that United States v. Mead Corp., 533 U.S. 218 (2001), requires that, for Chevron deference to apply, the agency must have received congressional authority to determine the particular matter at issue in the particular manner adopted. No one disputes that. But Mead denied Chevron deference to action, by an agency with rulemaking authority, that was not rulemaking. What the dissent needs, and fails to produce, is a single case in which a general conferral of rulemaking or adjudicative authority has been held insufficient to support Chevron deference for an exercise of that authority within the agency's substantive field. There is no such case, and what the dissent proposes is a massive revision of our Chevron jurisprudence.

Where we differ from the dissent is in its apparent rejection of the theorem that the whole includes all of its parts—its view that a general conferral of rulemaking authority does not validate rules for all the matters the agency is charged with administering. Rather, the dissent proposes that even when general rulemaking authority is clear, every agency rule must be subjected to a de novo judicial determination of whether the particular issue was committed to agency discretion. It offers no standards at all to guide this open-ended hunt for congressional intent (that is to say, for evidence of congressional intent more specific than the conferral of general rulemaking authority). It would simply punt that question back to the Court of Appeals, presumably for application of some sort of totality-of-the-circumstances test—which is really, of course, not a test at all but an invitation to make an ad hoc judgment regarding congressional intent. Thirteen Courts of Appeals applying a totality-of-the-circumstances test would render the binding effect of agency rules unpredictable and destroy the whole stabilizing purpose of Chevron. The excessive agency power that the dissent fears would be replaced by chaos. There is no need to wade into these murky waters. It suffices to decide this case that the preconditions to deference under Chevron are satisfied because Congress has unambiguously vested the FCC with general authority to administer the Communications Act through rulemaking and adjudication, and the agency interpretation at issue was promulgated in the exercise of that authority.

* * *

Those who assert that applying Chevron to "jurisdictional" interpretations "leaves the fox in charge of the henhouse" overlook the reality that a separate category of "jurisdictional" interpretations does not exist. The fox-in-the-henhouse syndrome is to be avoided not by establishing an arbitrary and undefinable category of agency decisionmaking that is accorded no deference, but by taking seriously, and applying rigorously, in all cases, statutory limits on agencies' authority. Where Congress has established a clear line, the agency cannot go beyond it; and where Congress has established an ambiguous line, the agency can go no further than the ambiguity will fairly allow. But in rigorously applying the latter rule, a court need not pause to puzzle over whether the interpretive question presented is "jurisdictional." If "the agency's answer is based on a permissible construction of the statute," that is the end of the matter. Chevron, 467 U.S., at 842.

The judgment of the Court of Appeals is affirmed.

■ JUSTICE BREYER, concurring in part and concurring in the judgment.

I agree with the Court that normally "the question a court faces when confronted with an agency's interpretation of a statute it administers" is, "simply, whether the agency has stayed within the bounds of its statutory authority." Ante. In this context, "the distinction between 'jurisdictional' and 'non-jurisdictional' interpretations is a mirage." Ante.

Deciding just what those statutory bounds are, however, is not always an easy matter, and the Court's case law abounds with discussion of the subject. A reviewing judge, for example, will have to decide independently whether Congress delegated authority to the agency to provide interpretations of, or to enact rules pursuant to, the statute at issue—interpretations or rules that carry with them "the force of law." United States v. Mead Corp., 533 U.S. 218, 229 (2001). If so, the reviewing court must give special leeway or "deference" to the agency's interpretation.

We have added that, if "[e]mploying traditional tools of statutory construction," INS v. Cardoza-Fonseca, 480 U.S. 421, 446 (1987), the court determines that Congress has spoken clearly on the disputed question, then "that is the end of the matter," Chevron U.S.A. Inc. v. Natural Resources Defense Council, Inc., 467 U.S. 837, 842 (1984). The agency is due no deference, for Congress has left no gap for the agency to fill. If, on the other hand, Congress has not spoken clearly, if, for example it has written ambiguously, then that ambiguity is a sign—but not always a conclusive sign—that Congress intends a reviewing court to pay particular attention to (i.e., to give a degree of deference to) the agency's interpretation. See Gonzales v. Oregon, 546 U.S. 243, 258–269 (2006); Mead, supra, at 229.

I say that the existence of statutory ambiguity is sometimes not enough to warrant the conclusion that Congress has left a deference-warranting gap for the agency to fill because our cases make clear that other, sometimes context-specific, factors will on occasion prove relevant. (And, given the vast number of government statutes, regulatory programs, and underlying circumstances, that variety is hardly surprising.) In Mead, for example, we looked to several factors other than simple ambiguity to help determine whether Congress left a statutory gap, thus delegating to the agency the authority to fill that gap with an interpretation that would carry "the force of law." 533 U.S., at 229–231. Elsewhere, we have assessed "the interstitial nature of the legal question, the related expertise of the Agency, the importance of the question to administration of the statute, the complexity of that administration, and the careful consideration the Agency has given the question over a long period of time." Barnhart v. Walton, 535 U.S. 212, 222 (2002).

The subject matter of the relevant provision—for instance, its distance from the agency's ordinary statutory duties or its falling within the scope of another agency's authority—has also proved relevant. See Gonzales, supra, at 265–266.

Moreover, the statute's text, its context, the structure of the statutory scheme, and canons of textual construction are relevant in determining whether the statute is ambiguous and can be equally helpful in determining whether such ambiguity comes accompanied with agency authority to fill a gap with an interpretation that carries the force of law. Statutory purposes, including those revealed in part by legislative and regulatory history, can be similarly relevant.

Although seemingly complex in abstract description, in practice this framework has proved a workable way to approximate how Congress would likely have meant to allocate interpretive law-determining authority between reviewing court and agency. The question whether Congress has delegated to an agency the authority to provide an interpretation that carries the force of law is for the judge to answer independently. The judge, considering "traditional tools of statutory construction," will ask whether Congress has spoken unambiguously. If so, the text controls. If not, the judge will ask whether Congress would have intended the agency to resolve the resulting ambiguity. If so, deference is warranted. See Mead, supra, at 229. Even if not, however, sometimes an agency interpretation, in light of the agency's special expertise, will still have the "power to persuade, if lacking power to control," Skidmore v. Swift & Co., 323 U.S. 134 (1944).

The case before us offers an example. The relevant statutory provision requires state or local governments to act on wireless siting applications "within a reasonable period of time after" a wireless service provider files such a request. 47 U.S.C. § 332(c)(7)(B)(ii). The Federal Communications Commission (FCC) argued that this provision granted it a degree of leeway in determining the amount of time that is reasonable. Many factors favor the agency's view: (1) the language of the Telecommunications Act grants the FCC broad authority (including rulemaking authority) to administer the Act; (2) the words are open-ended—i.e. "ambiguous"; (3) the provision concerns an interstitial administrative matter, in respect to which the agency's expertise could have an important role to play; and (4) the matter, in context, is complex, likely making the agency's expertise useful in helping to answer the "reasonableness" question that the statute poses.

On the other side of the coin, petitioners point to two statutory provisions which, they believe, require a different conclusion—namely, that the FCC lacked authority altogether to interpret § 332(c)(7)(B)(ii). First, a nearby saving clause says: "Except as provided in this paragraph, nothing in this chapter shall limit or affect the authority of a State or local government or instrumentality thereof over decisions regarding the placement, construction, and modification of personal wireless service facilities." § 332(c)(7)(A). Second, a judicial review provision, says: "Any person adversely affected by any final action or failure to act by a State or local government or any instrumentality thereof that is inconsistent with this subparagraph may, within 30 days after such action or failure to act, commence an action in any court of competent jurisdiction." § 332(c)(7)(B)(v).

In my view, however, these two provisions cannot provide good reason for reaching the conclusion advocated by petitioners. The first provision begins with an exception, stating that it does not apply to (among other things) the "reasonableness" provision here at issue. The second simply sets forth a procedure for judicial review, a review that applies to most government actions. Both are consistent with a statutory scheme that gives States, localities, the FCC, and reviewing courts each some role to play in the location of wireless service facilities. And neither "expressly describ[es] an exception" to the FCC's plenary authority to interpret the Act. American Hospital Assn. v. NLRB, 499 U.S. 606, 613 (1991).

For these reasons, I would reject petitioners' argument and conclude that § 332(c)(7)(B)(ii)—the "reasonableness" statute—leaves a gap for the FCC to fill. I would hold that the FCC's lawful efforts to do so carry "the force of law." Mead, 533 U.S., at 229. The Court of Appeals ultimately reached the same conclusion (though for somewhat different reasons), and the majority affirms the lower court. I consequently join the majority's judgment and such portions of its opinion as are consistent with what I have written here.

■ CHIEF JUSTICE ROBERTS, with whom JUSTICE KENNEDY and JUSTICE ALITO join, dissenting.

My disagreement with the Court is fundamental. It is also easily expressed: A court should not defer to an agency until the court decides, on its own, that the agency is entitled to deference. Courts defer to an agency's interpretation of law when and because Congress has conferred on the agency interpretive authority over the question at issue. An agency cannot exercise interpretive authority until it has it; the question whether an agency enjoys that authority must be decided by a court, without deference to the agency.

I

One of the principal authors of the Constitution famously wrote that the "accumulation of all powers, legislative, executive, and judiciary, in the same hands, . . . may justly be pronounced the very definition of tyranny." The Federalist No. 47, p. 324 (J. Cooke ed. 1961) (J. Madison). Although modern administrative agencies fit most comfortably within the Executive Branch, as a practical matter they exercise legislative power, by promulgating regulations with the force of law; executive power, by policing compliance with those regulations; and judicial power, by adjudicating enforcement actions and imposing sanctions on those found to have violated their rules. The accumulation of these powers in the same hands is not an occasional or isolated exception to the constitutional plan; it is a central feature of modern American government.

The administrative state "wields vast power and touches almost every aspect of daily life." Free Enterprise Fund v. Public Company Accounting Oversight Bd., 561 U.S. ___ (2010). The Framers could hardly have envisioned today's "vast and varied federal bureaucracy" and the authority administrative agencies now hold over our economic, social, and political activities. Ibid. . . . And the federal bureaucracy continues to grow; in the last 15 years, Congress has launched more than 50 new agencies. . . .

Although the Constitution empowers the President to keep federal officers accountable, administrative agencies enjoy in practice a significant degree of independence. As scholars have noted, "no President (or his executive office staff) could, and presumably none would wish to, supervise so broad a swath of regulatory activity." Kagan, Presidential Administration, 114 Harv. L. Rev. 2245, 2250 (2001) . . .

As for judicial oversight, agencies enjoy broad power to construe statutory provisions over which they have been given interpretive authority. In Chevron U.S.A. Inc. v. Natural Resources Defense Council, Inc., we established a test for reviewing "an agency's construction of the statute which it administers." 467 U.S. 837, 842 (1984). If Congress has "directly spoken to the precise question at issue," we said, "that is the end of the matter." Ibid. A contrary agency interpretation must give way. But if Congress has not expressed a specific intent, a court is bound to defer to any "permissible construction of the statute," even if that is not "the reading the court would have reached if the question initially had arisen in a judicial proceeding." Id., at 843, and n. 11.

When it applies, Chevron is a powerful weapon in an agency's regulatory arsenal. Congressional delegations to agencies are often ambiguous—expressing "a mood rather than a message." Friendly, The Federal Administrative Agencies: The Need for Better Definition of Standards, 75 Harv. L. Rev. 1263, 1311 (1962). By design or default, Congress often fails to speak to "the precise question" before an agency. In the absence of such an answer, an agency's interpretation has the full force and effect of law, unless it "exceeds the bounds of the permissible." Barnhart v. Walton, 535 U.S. 212, 218 (2002).

It would be a bit much to describe the result as "the very definition of tyranny," but the danger posed by the growing power of the administrative state cannot be dismissed. . . . What the Court says in footnote [1] of its opinion is good, and true (except of course for the "dissent overstates" part). The Framers did divide governmental power in the manner the Court describes, for the purpose of safeguarding liberty. And yet . . . the citizen confronting thousands of pages of regulations—promulgated by an agency directed by Congress to regulate, say, "in the public interest"—can perhaps be excused for thinking that it is the agency really doing the legislating. And with hundreds of federal agencies poking into every nook and cranny of daily life, that citizen might also understandably question whether Presidential oversight—a critical part of the Constitutional plan—is always an effective safeguard against agency overreaching.

It is against this background that we consider whether the authority of administrative agencies should be augmented even further, to include not only broad power to give definitive answers to questions left to them by Congress, but also the same power to decide when Congress has given them that power.

Before proceeding to answer that question, however, it is necessary to sort through some confusion over what this litigation is about. The source of the confusion is a familiar culprit: the concept of "jurisdiction," which we have repeatedly described as a word with " 'many, too many, meanings.' " Union Pacific R. Co. v. Locomotive Engineers, 558 U.S. 67, 81 (2009).

The Court states that the question "is whether a court must defer under Chevron to an agency's interpretation of a statutory ambiguity that concerns the scope of the agency's statutory authority (that is, its jurisdiction)." Ante. That is fine—until the parenthetical. The parties, amici, and court below too often use the term "jurisdiction" imprecisely, which leads the Court to misunderstand the argument it must confront. That argument is not that "there exist two distinct classes of agency interpretations," some "big, important ones" that "define the agency's 'jurisdiction,' " and other "humdrum, run-of-the-mill" ones that "are simply applications of jurisdiction the agency plainly has." Ibid. The argument is instead that a court should not defer to an agency on whether Congress has granted the agency interpretive authority over the statutory ambiguity at issue.

You can call that "jurisdiction" if you'd like, as petitioners do in the question presented. But given that the term is ambiguous, more is required to understand its use in that question than simply "having read it." It is important to keep in mind that the term, in the present context, has the more precise meaning noted above, encompassing congressionally delegated authority to issue interpretations with the force and effect of law. And that has nothing do with whether the statutory provisions at issue are "big" or "small."

II

"It is emphatically the province and duty of the judicial department to say what the law is." Marbury v. Madison, 1 Cranch 137, 177 (1803). The rise of the modern administrative state has not changed that duty. Indeed, the Administrative Procedure Act, governing judicial review of most agency action, instructs reviewing courts to decide "all relevant questions of law." 5 U.S.C. § 706.

We do not ignore that command when we afford an agency's statutory interpretation Chevron deference; we respect it. We give binding deference to permissible agency interpretations of statutory ambiguities because Congress has delegated to the agency the authority to interpret those ambiguities "with the force of law." United States v. Mead Corp., 533 U.S. 218, 229 (2001); see also Monaghan, Marbury and the Administrative State, 83 Colum. L.Rev. 1, 27–28 (1983) ("the court is not abdicating its constitutional duty to 'say what the law is' by deferring to agency interpretations of law: it is simply applying the law as 'made' by the authorized law-making entity").

But before a court may grant such deference, it must on its own decide whether Congress—the branch vested with lawmaking authority under the Constitution—has in fact delegated to the agency lawmaking power over the ambiguity at issue. Agencies are creatures of Congress; "an agency literally has no power to act . . . unless and until Congress confers power upon it." Louisiana Pub. Serv. Comm'n v. FCC, 476 U.S. 355, 374 (1986). Whether Congress has conferred such power is the "relevant question[ ] of law" that must be answered before affording Chevron deference. 5 U.S.C. § 706.

III

A

Our precedents confirm this conclusion—beginning with Chevron itself. In Chevron, the EPA promulgated a regulation interpreting the term "stationary sources" in the Clean Air Act. An environmental group petitioned for review of the rule, challenging it as an impermissible interpretation of the Act. Finding the statutory text "not dispositive" and the legislative history "silent on the precise issue," we upheld the rule. 467 U.S. at 862, 866.

In our view, the challenge to the agency's interpretation "center[ed] on the wisdom of the agency's policy, rather than whether it is a reasonable choice within a gap left open by Congress." Id., at 866. Judges, we said, "are not experts in the field, and are not part of either political branch of the Government." Id., at 865. Thus, because Congress had not answered the specific question at issue, judges had no business providing their own resolution on the basis of their "personal policy preferences." Ibid. Instead, the "agency to which Congress ha[d] delegated policymaking responsibilities" was the appropriate political actor to resolve the competing interests at stake, "within the limits of that delegation." Ibid.

Chevron's rule of deference was based on—and limited by—this congressional delegation. And the Court did not ask simply whether Congress had delegated to the EPA the authority to administer the Clean Air Act generally. We asked whether Congress had "delegat[ed] authority to the agency to elucidate a specific provision of the statute by regulation." Id., at 843–844 (emphasis added); see id., at 844 (discussing "the legislative delegation to an agency on a particular question" (emphasis added)). We deferred to the EPA's interpretation of "stationary sources" based on our conclusion that the agency had been "charged with responsibility for administering the provision." Id., at 865 (emphasis added).

B

We have never faltered in our understanding of this straightforward principle, that whether a particular agency interpretation warrants Chevron deference turns on the court's determination whether Congress has delegated to the agency the authority to interpret the statutory ambiguity at issue. . . .

In Mead, we again made clear that the "category of interpretative choices" to which Chevron deference applies is defined by congressional intent. Id., at 229. Chevron deference, we said, rests on a recognition that Congress has delegated to an agency the interpretive authority to implement "a particular provision" or answer " 'a particular question.' " Ibid. (quoting Chevron, 467 U.S., at 844). An agency's interpretation of "a particular statutory provision" thus qualifies for Chevron deference only "when it appears that Congress delegated authority to the agency generally to make rules carrying the force of law, and that the agency interpretation claiming deference was promulgated in the exercise of that authority." 533 U.S., at 226–227.

The Court did not defer to the agency's views but instead determined that Congress had not delegated interpretive authority to the Customs Service to definitively construe the tariff schedule through classification rulings. Neither the statutory authorization for the classification rulings, nor the Customs Service's practice in issuing such rulings, "reasonably suggest[ed] that Congress ever thought of [such] classification rulings as deserving the deference claimed for them." Id., at 231. And in the absence of such a delegation, we concluded the interpretations adopted in those rulings were "beyond the Chevron pale." Id., at 234. . . .

[These cases] thus confirm that Chevron deference is based on, and finds legitimacy as, a congressional delegation of interpretive authority. An agency interpretation warrants such deference only if Congress has delegated authority to definitively interpret a particular ambiguity in a particular manner. Whether Congress has done so must be determined by the court on its own before Chevron can apply. . . .

In other words, we do not defer to an agency's interpretation of an ambiguous provision unless Congress wants us to, and whether Congress wants us to is a question that courts, not agencies, must decide. Simply put, that question is "beyond the Chevron pale." Mead, supra, at 234.

IV

Despite these precedents, the FCC argues that a court need only locate an agency and a grant of general rulemaking authority over a statute. Chevron deference then applies, it contends, to the agency's interpretation of any ambiguity in the Act, including ambiguity in a provision said to carve out specific provisions from the agency's general rulemaking authority. If Congress intends to exempt part of the statute from the agency's interpretive authority, the FCC says, Congress "can ordinarily be expected to state that intent explicitly." Brief for Federal Respondents 30 (citing American Hospital Assn. v. NLRB, 499 U.S. 606 (1991)).

If a congressional delegation of interpretive authority is to support Chevron deference, however, that delegation must extend to the specific statutory ambiguity at issue. The appropriate question is whether the delegation covers the "specific provision" and "particular question" before the court. Chevron, 467 U.S., at 844. A congressional grant of authority over some portion of a statute does not necessarily mean that Congress granted the agency interpretive authority over all its provisions. See Adams Fruit, 494 U.S., at 650.

An example that might highlight the point concerns statutes that parcel out authority to multiple agencies, which "may be the norm, rather than an exception." Gersen, Overlapping and Underlapping Jurisdiction in Administrative Law, 2006 S.Ct. Rev. 201, 208. The Dodd-Frank Wall Street Reform and Consumer Protection Act, for example, authorizes rulemaking by at least eight different agencies. When presented with an agency's interpretation of such a statute, a court cannot simply ask whether the statute is one that the agency administers; the question is whether authority over the particular ambiguity at issue has been delegated to the particular agency.

By the same logic, even when Congress provides interpretive authority to a single agency, a court must decide if the ambiguity the agency has purported to interpret with the force of law is one to which the congressional delegation extends. A general delegation to the agency to administer the statute will often suffice to satisfy the court that Congress has delegated interpretive authority over the ambiguity at issue. But if Congress has exempted particular provisions from that authority, that exemption must be respected, and the determination whether Congress has done so is for the courts alone.

The FCC's argument that Congress "can ordinarily be expected to state that intent explicitly," Brief for Federal Respondents 30 (citing American Hospital, supra), goes to the merits of that determination, not to whether a court should decide the question de novo or defer to the agency. Indeed, that is how the Court in American Hospital considered it. It was in the process of "employing the traditional tools of statutory construction" that the Court said it would have expected Congress to speak more clearly if it had intended to exclude an entire subject area—employee units for collecting bargaining—from the NLRB's general rulemaking authority. Id., at 613, 614. The Court concluded, after considering the language, structure, policy, and legislative history of the Act on its own—without deferring to the agency—that the meaning of the statute was "clear and contrary to the meaning advanced by petitioner." Id., at 609–614. To be sure, the Court also noted that "[e]ven if we could find any ambiguity in [the provision] after employing the traditional tools of statutory construction, we would still defer to Board's reasonable interpretation." Id., at 614 (emphasis added). But that single sentence of dictum cannot carry the day for the FCC here.

V

As the preceding analysis makes clear, I do not understand petitioners to ask the Court—nor do I think it necessary—to draw a "specious, but scary-sounding" line between "big, important" interpretations on the one hand and "humdrum, run-of-the-mill" ones on the other. Ante. Drawing such a line may well be difficult. Distinguishing between whether an agency's interpretation of an ambiguous term is reasonable and whether that term is for the agency to interpret is not nearly so difficult. . . . More importantly, if the legitimacy of Chevron deference is based on a congressional delegation of interpretive authority, then the line is one the Court must draw.

The majority's hypothetical Common Carrier Acts do not demonstrate anything different. The majority states that in its second Common Carrier Act, Section 2 makes clear that Congress " 'conferred interpretative power on the agency' " to interpret the ambiguous terms "common carrier" and "unreasonable condition." Ante. Thus, it says, under anyone's theory a court must defer to the agency's reasonable interpretations of those terms. Correct.

The majority claims, however, that "petitioners' theory would accord the agency no deference" in its interpretation of the same ambiguous terms in the first Common Carrier Act. Ante. But as I understand petitioners' argument—and certainly in my own view—a court, in both cases, need only decide for itself whether Congress has delegated to the agency authority to interpret the ambiguous terms, before affording the agency's interpretation Chevron deference.

For the second Common Carrier Act, the answer is easy. The majority's hypothetical Congress has spoken clearly and specifically in Section 2 of the Act about its delegation of authority to interpret Section 1. As for the first Act, it is harder to analyze the question, given only one section of a presumably much larger statute. But if the first Common Carrier Act is like most agencies' organic statutes, I have no reason to doubt that the agency would likewise have interpretive authority over the same ambiguous terms, and therefore be entitled to deference in construing them, just as with the second Common Carrier Act. There is no new "test" to worry about; courts would simply apply the normal rules of statutory construction.

That the question might be harder with respect to the first Common Carrier Act should come as no surprise. The second hypothetical Congress has more carefully defined the agency's authority than the first. Whatever standard of review applies, it is more difficult to interpret an unclear statute than a clear one. My point is simply that before a court can defer to the agency's interpretation of the ambiguous terms in either Act, it must determine for itself that Congress has delegated authority to the agency to issue those interpretations with the force of law.

The majority also expresses concern that adopting petitioners' position would undermine Chevron 's stable background rule against which Congress legislates. That, of course, begs the question of what that stable background rule is. . . .

VI

The Court sees something nefarious behind the view that courts must decide on their own whether Congress has delegated interpretative authority to an agency, before deferring to that agency's interpretation of law. What is afoot, according to the Court, is a judicial power-grab, with nothing less than "Chevron itself" as "the ultimate target." Ante.

The Court touches on a legitimate concern: Chevron importantly guards against the Judiciary arrogating to itself policymaking properly left, under the separation of powers, to the Executive. But there is another concern at play, no less firmly rooted in our constitutional structure. That is the obligation of the Judiciary not only to confine itself to its proper role, but to ensure that the other branches do so as well.

An agency's interpretive authority, entitling the agency to judicial deference, acquires its legitimacy from a delegation of lawmaking power from Congress to the Executive. Our duty to police the boundary between the Legislature and the Executive is as critical as our duty to respect that between the Judiciary and the Executive. In the present context, that means ensuring that the Legislative Branch has in fact delegated lawmaking power to an agency within the Executive Branch, before the Judiciary defers to the Executive on what the law is. That concern is heightened, not diminished, by the fact that the administrative agencies, as a practical matter, draw upon a potent brew of executive, legislative, and judicial power. And it is heightened, not diminished, by the dramatic shift in power over the last 50 years from Congress to the Executive—a shift effected through the administrative agencies.

We reconcile our competing responsibilities in this area by ensuring judicial deference to agency interpretations under Chevron—but only after we have determined on our own that Congress has given interpretive authority to the agency. Our "task is to fix the boundaries of delegated authority," Monaghan, 83 Colum. L.Rev., at 27; that is not a task we can delegate to the agency. We do not leave it to the agency to decide when it is in charge.

* * *

In these cases, the FCC issued a declaratory ruling interpreting the term "reasonable period of time" in 47 U.S.C. § 332(c)(7)(B)(ii). The Fifth Circuit correctly recognized that it could not apply *Chevron* deference to the FCC's interpretation unless the agency "possessed statutory authority to administer § 332(c)(7)(B)(ii)," but it erred by granting *Chevron* deference to the FCC's view on that antecedent question. See 668 F.3d, at 248. Because the court should have determined on its own whether Congress delegated interpretive authority over § 332(c)(7)(B)(ii) to the FCC before affording *Chevron* deference, I would vacate the decision below and remand the cases to the Fifth Circuit to perform the proper inquiry in the first instance.

I respectfully dissent.

NOTES

(1)   City of Arlington is the most recent Supreme Court case that plumbs the basic questions involved in courts' deferring to agencies. There is much discussion in the opinions about Chevron, but where is Skidmore deference? See Peter L. Strauss, In Search of Skidmore, 83 Fordham L. Rev. 789, 792 (2014): "In Justice Scalia's majority opinion and Chief Justice Roberts's dissent for himself and Justices Kennedy and Alito, 184 years of what we have recently been calling Skidmore deference simply disappeared. Save once in Justice Breyer's lonely concurrence in the result, there is not a mention of the concept . . . in opinions signed by eight of the Justices." Is this a meaningful omission? Or is it just a reflection of the abstractness of the question presented, at least as seen by all the Justices other than Breyer?

(2)   Chief Justice Roberts suggests that the only way to make Chevron consistent with the APA standards for judicial review is to adopt his

approach. Is he right? Even if he is, should he also have said something about Skidmore? Even if the job of deciding whether Congress had delegated substantive authority to the agency on the matter at hand was for the independent judgment of the courts, didn't Skidmore and its many predecessors say that the courts, in exercising that independent judgment, should consider what weight the agency's expert view might have? Wouldn't the FCC have some insight into the interrelationship of local, state, and federal authorities in this industry that would help the court understand why Congress set up this statutory provision in the way it did? In fact, if Chief Justice Roberts would follow Skidmore, wouldn't that strengthen his argument by making it more sensitive to the practical difficulties judges may have in resolving ambiguities?

(3)   Are there echoes in the dispute here of the proposition that courts can sometimes identify issues that are of such importance as to require congressional determination? Justice Scalia makes fun of the idea that the courts would be asked to distinguish between "two distinct classes of agency interpretations": "the big, important ones" that would constitute jurisdictional matters and the "humdrum, run-of-the-mill stuff" that would be "simply applications of jurisdiction." The distinction, he says, is a "mirage." And Chief Justice Roberts abjures making any such distinction. But fun aside, is it so crazy to say that courts should treat differently an agency's "big, important" decisions from its "run-of-the-mill" stuff? Is it, in fact, so different from Justice Scalia's own principle of statutory interpretation, to be used in applying Chevron, that "Congress . . . does not alter the fundamental details of a regulatory scheme in vague terms of ancillary provisions—it does not, one might say, hide elephants in mouseholes"? (Whitman v. American Trucking Ass'ns, Inc., p. 791) (His treatment of "modify" in MCI v. AT&T, p. 1171 supra, is to similar effect.) To apply this principle, mustn't courts be able to tell what is, and isn't, an "elephant"?

(4)   Go back now and read (or reread, if you have already encountered it), King v. Burwell, p. 97, and consider whether the Chief Justice's refusal to use Chevron in the service of the conclusion he reaches has a similar impetus.

CHAPTER IX
ACCESS TO JUDICIAL REVIEW: JUSTICIABILITY

> **Sec. 1. Standing**
> **Sec. 2. Reviewability, Timing, and Remedies**

As Chapter VIII makes clear, judicial review gives courts substantial power to affect what agencies can do and don't do, as well as how they operate. Who can invoke this power against the agency? For what sorts of claims? When? With what kinds of remedies? Such questions are answered by the various doctrines of justiciability. For those of you who have taken the course in Federal Courts, many of these materials will be familiar. But the focus here is on approaching justiciability with an eye to how rules about access to judicial review may affect the regulatory process.

We begin in this chapter with materials on the threshold question of whether a plaintiff has standing to sue. Standing is the most common justiciability question, and as you'll see the Supreme Court has rooted the core requirements for standing in Article III of the Constitution. The materials on standing begin by going over the basic doctrinal framework for standing and then look in more detail at how the Court has applied the three core requirements of Article III—injury, causation, and redressability—in regulatory contexts. We next take up additional standing problems, in particular questions about when governments have standing to sue and about prudential standing doctrines, which are non-constitutional requirements for standing.

The second half of the chapter turns to an additional set of justiciability doctrines. One is the requirement that the agency action at issue be reviewable, which includes both that plaintiffs have a source of authority to sue, such as a right of action in a statute, and that judicial review not be precluded. Even if an agency action is potentially reviewable, the availability of review may be subject to timing limitations. Some questions we'll cover on timing are whether a plaintiff can challenge an agency regulation before it is finalized or enforced, and whether she needs to exhaust administrative remedies before turning to court. At the end of the chapter we turn from the front end to the back end of judicial review, briefly examining what types of judicial remedies are available for unlawful agency action.

As you go through these materials, try not to lose sight of the regulatory impact of the doctrines you are studying have on different actors in the regulatory process and regulatory outcomes. So, for example, think about how rules of standing affect: (1) the agency, (2) the regulated community, (3) those who are intended beneficiaries of the regulatory program, and (4) those who might benefit incidentally from the regulation. The various justiciability doctrines discussed in this chapter operate to allocate among these actors access to, or protection from, judicial review. Do you think the doctrines are making the right allocations?

SECTION 1.   STANDING

> a. **The Basic Doctrinal Framework**
> b. **Defining Injury in Regulatory Settings**
> c. **Causation and Redressability in Regulatory Settings**
> d. **Governmental Standing**
> e. **Standing Under the APA**

a.   The Basic Doctrinal Framework

> *LUJAN v. DEFENDERS OF WILDLIFE*
> *Notes on Lujan and the Basic Standing Framework*
> *Notes on Standing Doctrine's Constitutional Basis*

LUJAN v. DEFENDERS OF WILDLIFE

Supreme Court of the United States (1992).
504 U.S. 555.

■ JUSTICE SCALIA delivered the opinion of the Court with respect to Parts I, II, III-A, and IV, and an opinion with respect to Part III-B in which CHIEF JUSTICE REHNQUIST, JUSTICE WHITE, and JUSTICE THOMAS join.

[Section 7(a)(2) of the Endangered Species Act of 1973 (ESA) divides responsibility for protecting endangered species between the Secretary of the Interior and the Secretary of Commerce. Federal agencies must consult with one or the other Secretary when funding an action that might jeopardize the existence or habitat of any endangered or threatened species. The Secretaries initially promulgated a joint regulation interpreting § 7(a)(2) to apply to actions taken in foreign nations; then, they jointly revised the rule to limit the section's geographic scope to the United States and the high seas. Wildlife conservation and other environmental organizations sued, claiming that the revised rule misinterpreted the statute. The district court dismissed for lack of standing; the court of appeals reversed. On remand, the district court held for the plaintiffs on the merits and the court of appeals affirmed.]

This case involves a challenge to a rule promulgated by the Secretary of the Interior interpreting § 7 of the [ESA] . . . The preliminary issue, and the only one we reach, is whether respondents here, plaintiffs below, have standing to seek judicial review of the rule.

II

While the Constitution of the United States divides all power conferred upon the Federal Government into "legislative Powers," Art. I, § 1, "[t]he executive Power," Art. II, § 1, and "[t]he judicial Power," Art. III, § 1, it does not attempt to define those terms. . . . Obviously, then, the Constitution's central mechanism of separation of powers depends largely upon common understanding of what activities are appropriate to legislatures, to executives, and to courts. . . . One of th[e] landmarks, setting apart the "Cases" and "Controversies" that are of the justiciable sort referred to in Article III . . . is the doctrine of standing. Though some of its elements express merely prudential considerations that are part of judicial self-government, the core component of standing is an essential and unchanging part of the case-or-controversy requirement of Article III. See, e.g., Allen v. Wright, 468 U.S. 737, 751 (1984) [p. 1340].

Over the years, our cases have established that the irreducible constitutional minimum of standing contains three elements. First, the plaintiff must have suffered an "injury in fact"—an invasion of a legally protected interest which is (a) concrete and particularized; and (b) actual or imminent, not conjectural or hypothetical. Second, there must be a causal connection between the injury and the conduct complained of—the injury has to be "fairly . . . trace[able] to the challenged action of the defendant, and not . . . th[e] result [of] the independent action of some third party not before the court." Simon v. EKWRO, 426 U.S. 26, 41–42 (1976) [p. 1345]. Third, it must be "likely," as opposed to merely "speculative," that the injury will be "redressed by a favorable decision." Id. The party invoking federal jurisdiction bears the burden of establishing these elements. . . .

When the suit is one challenging the legality of government action or inaction, the nature and extent of facts that must be averred (at the summary judgment stage) or proved (at the trial stage) in order to establish standing depends considerably upon whether the plaintiff is himself an object of the action (or forgone action) at issue. If he is, there is ordinarily little question that the action or inaction has caused him injury, and that a judgment preventing or requiring the action will redress it. When, however, as in this case, a plaintiff's asserted injury arises from the government's allegedly unlawful regulation (or lack of regulation) of someone else, much more is needed. In that circumstance, causation and redressability ordinarily hinge on the response of the regulated (or regulable) third party to the government action or inaction—and perhaps on the response of others as well. The existence of one or more of the essential elements of standing "depends on the unfettered choices made by independent actors not before the courts and whose exercise of broad and legitimate discretion the courts cannot presume either to control or to predict," ASARCO Inc. v. Kadish, 490 U.S. 605, 615 (1989) (opinion of Kennedy, J.), and it becomes the burden of the plaintiff to adduce facts showing that those choices have been or will be made in such manner as to produce causation and permit redressability of injury. Thus, when the plaintiff is not himself the object of the government action or inaction he challenges, standing is not precluded, but it is ordinarily "substantially more difficult" to establish. . . .

III

. . . Respondents' claim to injury is that the lack of consultation with respect to certain funded activities abroad "increas[es] the rate of extinction of endangered and threatened species." Of course, the desire to use or observe an animal species, even for purely aesthetic purposes, is undeniably a cognizable interest for purpose of standing. See, e.g., Sierra Club v. Morton, [405 U.S. 727 (1972) p. 1338]. "But the 'injury in fact' test requires more than an injury to a cognizable interest. It requires that the party seeking review be himself among the injured." Id. . . .

. . . [T]he Court of Appeals focused on the affidavits of two Defenders' members—Joyce Kelly and Amy Skilbred. Ms. Kelly stated that she traveled to Egypt in 1986 and "observed the traditional habitat of the endangered nile crocodile there and intend[s] to do so again, and hope[s] to observe the crocodile directly," and that she "will suffer harm in fact as a result of [the] American . . . role . . . in overseeing the rehabilitation of the Aswan High Dam on the Nile . . . and [in] develop[ing] . . . Egypt's . . . Master Water Plan." Ms. Skilbred averred that she traveled to Sri Lanka in 1981 and "observed th[e] habitat" of "endangered species such as the Asian elephant and the leopard" at what is now the site of the Mahaweli Project funded by the Agency for International Development (AID), although she "was unable to see any of the endangered species;" "this development project," she continued, "will seriously reduce endangered, threatened, and endemic species habitat including areas that I visited . . . [, which] may severely shorten the future of these species;" that threat, she concluded, harmed her because she "intend[s] to return to Sri Lanka in the future and hope[s] to be more fortunate in spotting at least the endangered elephant and leopard." When Ms. Skilbred was asked at a subsequent deposition if and when she had any plans to return to Sri Lanka, she reiterated that "I intend to go back to Sri Lanka," but confessed that she had no current plans: "I don't know [when]. There is a civil war going on right now. I don't know. Not next year, I will say. In the future."

We shall assume for the sake of argument that these affidavits contain facts showing that certain agency-funded projects threaten listed species—though that is questionable. They plainly contain no facts, however, showing how damage to the species will produce "imminent" injury to Ms. Kelly and Skilbred. That the women "had visited" the areas of the projects before the projects commenced proves nothing. As we have said in a related context, "[p]ast exposure to illegal conduct does not in itself show a present case or controversy regarding injunctive relief . . . if unaccompanied by any continuing, present adverse effects." And the affiants' profession of an "inten[t]" to return to the places they had visited before—where they will presumably, this time, be deprived of the opportunity to observe animals of the endangered species—is simply not enough. Such "some day" intentions—without any description of concrete plans, or indeed even any specification of when the some day will be—do not support a finding of the "actual or imminent" injury that our cases require.

[The Court rejected "a series of novel standing theories" including "ecosystem nexus" (standing for someone who uses any part of a "contiguous ecosystem" adversely affected by a funded activity) and "animal nexus" (standing for someone with an interest in studying or seeing the endangered animals anywhere) and "vocational nexus" (standing for someone with a professional interest in the animal).]

[Part III-B of the opinion, joined by only Justices White and Thomas and Chief Justice Rehnquist, concluded that Defenders also failed to meet the redressability requirements of standing. The agencies involved in the particular projects were not named defendants, and Justice Scalia saw no reason to expect they would in fact consult simply because a court ordered the Secretaries to return to the extraterritorial interpretation. Justice Stevens protested that no agency would ignore an authoritative construction of the ESA by the Supreme Court; Justice Scalia responded that, as standing must be determined at the outset of the lawsuit, "it could certainly not be known [at that point] that the suit would reach this Court."]

IV

The Court of Appeals found that respondents had standing for an additional reason: because they had suffered a "procedural injury." The so called "citizen-suit" provision of the ESA provides, in pertinent part, that "any person may commence a civil suit on his own behalf (A) to enjoin any person, including the United States and any other governmental instrumentality or agency . . . who is alleged to be in violation of any provision of this chapter." 16 U.S.C. § 1540(g). The court held that, because § 7(a)(2) requires interagency consultation, the citizen-suit provision creates a "procedural righ[t]" to consultation in all "persons"—so that anyone can file suit in federal court to challenge the Secretary's (or presumably any other official's) failure to follow the assertedly correct consultative procedure, notwithstanding their inability to allege any discrete injury flowing from that failure. To understand the remarkable nature of this holding one must be clear about what it does *not* rest upon: This is not a case where plaintiffs are seeking to enforce a procedural requirement the disregard of which could impair a separate concrete interest of theirs (e.g., the procedural requirement for a hearing prior to denial of their license application, or the procedural requirement for an environmental impact statement before a federal facility is constructed next door to them).[7] Nor is it simply a case where concrete injury has been suffered by many persons, as in mass fraud or mass tort situations. Nor, finally, is it the unusual case in which Congress has created a concrete private interest in the outcome of a suit against a private party for the government's benefit, by providing a cash bounty for the victorious plaintiff. Rather, the court held that the injury-in-fact requirement had been satisfied by congressional conferral upon all persons of an abstract, self-contained, noninstrumental "right" to have the Executive observe the procedures required by law. We reject this view.[8]

We have consistently held that a plaintiff raising only a generally available grievance about government—claiming only harm to his and every citizen's interest in proper application of the Constitution and laws, and seeking relief that no more directly and tangibly benefits him than it does the public at large—does not state an Article III case or controversy. . . .

To be sure, our generalized-grievance cases have typically involved Government violation of procedures assertedly ordained by the Constitution rather than the Congress. But there is absolutely no basis for making the Article III inquiry turn on the source of the asserted right. Whether the courts were to act on their own, or at the invitation of Congress, in ignoring the concrete injury requirement described in our cases, they would be discarding a principle fundamental to the separate and distinct constitutional role of the Third Branch—one of the essential elements that identifies those "Cases" and "Controversies" that are the business of the courts rather than of the political branches. "The province

---

[7] There is this much truth to the assertion that "procedural rights" are special: The person who has been accorded a procedural right to protect his concrete interests can assert that right without meeting all the normal standards for redressability and immediacy. Thus, under our case-law, one living adjacent to the site for proposed construction of a federally licensed dam has standing to challenge the licensing agency's failure to prepare an Environmental Impact Statement, even though he cannot establish with any certainty that the Statement will cause the license to be withheld or altered, and even though the dam will not be completed for many years. (That is why we do not rely, in the present case, upon the Government's argument that, even if the other agencies were obliged to consult with the Secretary, they might not have followed his advice.) What respondents' "procedural rights" argument seeks, however, is quite different from this: standing for persons who have no concrete interests affected—persons who live (and propose to live) at the other end of the country from the dam.

[8] The dissent's discussion of this aspect of the case distorts our opinion. We do not hold that an individual cannot enforce procedural rights; he assuredly can, so long as the procedures in question are designed to protect some threatened concrete interest of his that is the ultimate basis of his standing. The dissent, however, asserts that there exist "classes of procedural duties . . . so enmeshed with the prevention of a substantive, concrete harm that an individual plaintiff may be able to demonstrate a sufficient likelihood of injury just through the breach of that procedural duty." If we understand this correctly, it means that the government's violation of a certain (undescribed) class of procedural duty satisfies the concrete-injury requirement by itself, without any showing that the procedural violation endangers a concrete interest of the plaintiff (apart from his interest in having the procedure observed). We cannot agree. . . .

of the court," as Chief Justice Marshall said in Marbury v. Madison, 1 Cranch 137, 170 (1803), "is, solely, to decide on the rights of individuals." Vindicating the public interest (including the public interest in government observance of the Constitution and laws) is the function of Congress and the Chief Executive. The question presented here is whether the public interest in proper administration of the laws (specifically, in agencies' observance of a particular, statutorily prescribed procedure) can be converted into an individual right by a statute that denominates it as such, and that permits all citizens (or, for that matter, a subclass of citizens who suffer no distinctive concrete harm) to sue. If the concrete injury requirement has the separation-of-powers significance we have always said, the answer must be obvious: To permit Congress to convert the undifferentiated public interest in executive officers' compliance with the law into an "individual right" vindicable in the courts is to permit Congress to transfer from the President to the courts the Chief Executive's most important constitutional duty, to "take Care that the Laws be faithfully executed," Art. II, § 3. It would enable the courts, with the permission of Congress, "to assume a position of authority over the governmental acts of another and co-equal department," and to become "virtually continuing monitors of the wisdom and soundness of Executive action." Allen, 468 U.S. at 760. We have always rejected that vision of our role:

> When Congress passes an Act empowering administrative agencies to carry on governmental activities, the power of those agencies is circumscribed by the authority granted. This permits the courts to participate in law enforcement entrusted to administrative bodies only to the extent necessary to protect justiciable individual rights against administrative action fairly beyond the granted powers. . . . This is very far from assuming that the courts are charged more than administrators or legislators with the protection of the rights of the people. Congress and the Executive supervise the acts of administrative agents. . . . But under Article III, Congress established courts to adjudicate cases and controversies as to claims of infringement of individual rights whether by unlawful action of private persons or by the exertion of unauthorized administrative power.

Stark v. Wickard, 321 U.S. 288 (1944). "Individual rights," within the meaning of this passage, do not mean public rights that have been legislatively pronounced to belong to each individual who forms part of the public.

Nothing in this contradicts the principle that "[t]he . . . injury required by Art. III may exist solely by virtue of 'statutes creating legal rights, the invasion of which creates standing.'" Warth, 422 U.S. at 500 . . . [These other cases] involved Congress's elevating to the status of legally cognizable injuries concrete, de facto injuries that were previously inadequate in law. . . As we said in Sierra Club , "[Statutory] broadening [of] the categories of injury that may be alleged in support of standing is a different matter from abandoning the requirement that the party seeking review must himself have suffered an injury." . . .

We hold that respondents lack standing to bring this action and that the Court of Appeals erred in denying the summary judgment motion filed by the United States. The opinion of the Court of Appeals is hereby reversed, and the cause remanded for proceedings consistent with this opinion.

■ JUSTICE KENNEDY, with whom JUSTICE SOUTER joins, concurring in part and concurring in the judgment.

Although I agree with the essential parts of the Court's analysis, I write separately to make several observations.

I agree with the Court's conclusion in Part III-A that, on the record before us, respondents have failed to demonstrate that they themselves are "among the injured." . . . While it may seem trivial to require that Ms. Kelly and Skilbred acquire airline tickets to the project sites or announce a date certain upon which they will return, this is not a case where it is reasonable to assume that the affiants will be using the sites on a regular basis, see Sierra Club v. Morton, nor do the affiants claim to have visited the sites since the projects commenced. . . .

In light of the conclusion that respondents have not demonstrated a concrete injury here sufficient to support standing under our precedents, I would not reach the issue of redressability that is discussed by the plurality in Part III-B.

I also join Part IV of the Court's opinion with the following observations. As government programs and policies become more complex and farreaching, we must be sensitive to the articulation of new rights of action that do not have clear analogs in our common-law tradition. Modern litigation has progressed far from the paradigm of Marbury suing Madison to get his commission. . . . In my view, Congress has the power to define injuries and articulate chains of causation that will give rise to a case or controversy where none existed before, and I do not read the Court's opinion to suggest a contrary view. In exercising this power, however, Congress must at the very least identify the injury it seeks to vindicate and relate the injury to the class of persons entitled to bring suit. The citizen-suit provision of the Endangered Species Act does not meet these minimal requirements, because while the statute purports to confer a right on "any person . . . to enjoin . . . the United States and any other governmental instrumentality or agency . . . who is alleged to be in violation of any provision of this chapter," it does not of its own force establish that there is an injury in "any person" by virtue of any "violation."

The Court's holding that there is an outer limit to the power of Congress to confer rights of action is a direct and necessary consequence of the case and controversy limitations found in Article III. I agree that it would exceed those limitations if, at the behest of Congress and in the absence of any showing of concrete injury, we were to entertain citizen-suits to vindicate the public's nonconcrete interest in the proper administration of the laws. While it does not matter how many persons have been injured by the challenged action, the party bringing suit must show that the action injures him in a concrete and personal way. This requirement is not just an empty formality. It preserves the vitality of the adversarial process by assuring both that the parties before the court have an actual, as opposed to professed, stake in the outcome, and that "the legal questions presented . . . will be resolved, not in the rarified atmosphere of a debating society, but in a concrete factual context conducive to a realistic appreciation of the consequences of judicial action." Valley Forge Christian College v. Americans United for Separation of Church and State, Inc., 454 U.S. 464, 472 (1982). In addition, the requirement of concrete injury confines the Judicial Branch to its proper, limited role in the constitutional framework of Government.

[Justice Stevens concurred in the judgment on grounds that the new rule correctly interpreted the intended geographical scope of the ESA. He concluded respondents did have standing.]

■ JUSTICE BLACKMUN, with whom JUSTICE O'CONNOR joins, dissenting.

[Justice Blackmun concluded that the allegations and depositions of Ms. Skilbred and Ms. Kelly were sufficient to survive a motion for summary judgment, then turned to the second claim.]

The Court . . . rejects the view that the "injury-in-fact requirement . . . [is] satisfied by congressional conferral upon all person of an abstract, self-contained, noninstrumental 'right' to have the Executive observe the procedures required by law." Whatever the Court might mean with that very broad language, it cannot be saying that "procedural injuries" as a class are necessarily insufficient for purposes of Article III standing.

Most governmental conduct can be classified as "procedural." Many injuries caused by governmental conduct, therefore, are categorizable at some level of generality as "procedural" injuries. Yet, these injuries are not categorically beyond the pale of redress by the federal courts. . . . The Court expresses concern that allowing judicial enforcement of "agencies' observance of a particular, statutorily prescribed procedure" would "transfer from the President to the courts the Chief Executive's most important constitutional duty, to 'take Care that the Laws be faithfully executed,' Art. II, § 3." In fact, the principal effect of foreclosing judicial enforcement of such procedures is to transfer power into the hands of the Executive at the expense—not of the courts—but of Congress, from which that power originates and emanates.

Under the Court's anachronistically formal view of the separation of powers, Congress legislates pure, substantive mandates and has no business structuring the procedural manner in which the Executive implements these mandates. . . . In complex regulatory areas, however, Congress often legislates, as it were, in procedural shades of gray. That is, it sets forth substantive policy goals and provides for their attainment by requiring Executive Branch officials to follow certain procedures, for example, in the form of reporting, consultation, and certification requirements. . . . Congress could simply impose a substantive prohibition on executive conduct; it could say that no agency action shall result in the loss of more than 5% of any listed species. Instead, Congress sets forth substantive guidelines and allows the Executive, within certain procedural constraints, to decide how best to effectuate the ultimate goal. . . . Just as Congress does not violate separation of powers by structuring the procedural manner in which the Executive shall carry out the laws, surely the federal courts do not violate separation of powers when, at the very instruction and command of Congress, they enforce these procedures.

. . . Ironically, this Court has previously justified a relaxed review of congressional delegation to the Executive on grounds that Congress, in turn, has subjected the exercise of that power to judicial review. INS v. Chadha, 426 U.S. 919, 953–54 n. 16 (1983) [p. 831]. The Court's intimation today that procedural injuries are not constitutionally cognizable threatens this understanding upon which Congress has undoubtedly relied. . . .

. . . There may be factual circumstances in which a congressionally imposed procedural requirement is so insubstantially connected to the prevention of a substantive harm that it cannot be said to work any conceivable injury to an individual litigant. But, as a general matter, the courts owe substantial deference to Congress' substantive purpose in imposing a certain procedural requirement. . . . There is no room for a per se rule or presumption excluding injuries labeled "procedural" in nature.

NOTES ON LUJAN AND THE BASIC STANDING FRAMEWORK

(1) *The Majority Position in Lujan.* What exactly do a majority of the justices hold in Lujan? Only three other justices (Chief Justice Rehnquist, Justice White, and Justice Thomas) joined Justice Scalia's opinion in full. Justices Blackmun and O'Connor (dissenting) and Justice Stevens (concurring in the judgment) concluded that Defenders of Wildlife had standing. Justice Kennedy, with Justice Souter, "joined" Part IV of the opinion but strongly reiterated the well-established views that: (i) Congress can create new injuries where none had previously existed for Article III purposes; and (ii) "it does not matter how many persons have been injured by the challenged action."

Given this head count, how accurate is it to refer to the procedural injury analysis—or, for that matter, the discussion of Article II as creating a barrier to standing here—as holdings of the Court? Professor Richard Pierce considers Justice Scalia's opinion to be a "plurality opinion." III Pierce,

Administrative Law Treatise 1433–37 (5th ed. 2010). Do you agree? Moreover, the procedure at issue here was consultation between agencies. Is that a procedure in which the plaintiffs had any personal claim to participation? If not, might that limit the import of Lujan's procedural injury analysis for cases that involve procedures where plaintiffs can make such a claim, such as notice and comment rulemaking procedures or procedures for filing a request for information under the Freedom of Information Act? In a case involving congressionally created procedures that authorize such personal participation, do you think that Justices Kennedy and Souter might find standing?

(2) *The Constitutional Core of Standing.* Standing is an essential ingredient for ability to sue. A plaintiff without standing cannot bring suit in federal court and a defendant without standing can't appeal. Lujan's description of the constitutional requirements for standing is now canonical as a matter of doctrine: Standing requires a "concrete and particularized" injury that is "actual and imminent," as opposed to speculative; a causal connection establishing that the injury is "fairly traceable" to the conduct being challenged; and a likelihood that a favorable decision would redress the injury. Often reduced to the tripartite shorthand of injury-in-fact, causation, and redressability, these requirements represent the constitutional core of standing that the Court has derived from Article III's "case" or "controversy" requirement for the exercise of judicial power.

(3) *Standing versus Merits.* As the Lujan Court stated at the outset, a plaintiff's standing to sue is a preliminary jurisdictional question that is deemed to be distinct from whether she should win on the merits. The separation of standing from merits came in Association of Data Processing Organizations v. Camp, 397 U.S. 150 (1970) (Data Processing) (p. 1366). There, the appeals court had denied a data processing providers organization's standing to challenge a rule allowing national banks to provide data processing services on the grounds that the providers had no legal interest under the governing statute. The Supreme Court reversed, stating: "The 'legal interest' test goes to the merits. The question of standing is different. It concerns, apart from the 'case' or 'controversy' test, the question whether the interest sought to be protected by the complainant is arguably within the zone of interests to be protected or regulated by the statute or constitutional guarantee in question. . . . That interest, at times, may reflect aesthetic, conservational, and recreational as well as economic values. . . . We mention these noneconomic values to emphasize that standing may stem from them as well as from . . . economic injury." Provided "[t]he plaintiff alleges that the challenged action has caused him injury in fact, economic or otherwise," satisfaction of the zone of interest test was all that was needed to challenge the rule under the APA.

(4) *The Two-Level Structure of Standing Law: Constitutional and Prudential Standing.* Lujan distinguished between the constitutional requirements for standing and "prudential" limitations. Writing for the majority in UNITED STATES V. WINDSOR, 133 S.Ct. 2675, 2685 (2013) (p. 1358), Justice Kennedy stated: "The Court has kept these two strands separate: Article III standing, which enforces the Constitution's case-or-

controversy requirement, see Lujan; and prudential standing, which embodies judicially self-imposed limits on the exercise of federal jurisdiction. Unlike Article III requirements—which must be satisfied by the parties before judicial consideration is appropriate—the relevant prudential factors that counsel against hearing [a] case are subject to countervailing considerations [that] may outweigh the concerns underlying the usual reluctance to exert judicial power." Prominent examples of prudential standing restrictions are the requirement that plaintiffs fall within the zone-of-interests protected by a statute (a requirement also imposed by the APA, see Sec. 1.e), and the general rule against third-party standing. In Windsor itself, the Court held that prudential standing concerns raised by the executive branch's refusal to defend the constitutionality of the Defense of Marriage Act were overcome by the presence of able, adverse argument from congressional leadership and the need for a definitive constitutional ruling from the Court.

Moreover, it's clear that Congress can direct courts to disregard prudential standing limitations (see Note 5, p. 1368). Is it equally clear that the core constitutional elements are beyond Congress's ability to affect? Not exactly. Although Congress cannot direct federal courts to ignore the requirements of injury, causation, and redressability, it "has the power to define injuries and articulate chains of causation that will give rise to a case or controversy." Lujan (Kennedy, J., concurring.) However, as explored in Sections 1.b and 1.c below, the precise extent of this power is sharply contested among the justices.

(5) *Standing Doctrine's Historical Background.* Scholarly examinations of constitutional history and early federal practice largely agree that standing doctrine is a recent creation, constructed over the course of the twentieth century. Professor-turned-Judge WILLIAM A. FLETCHER identifies two "overlapping developments" as fueling standing doctrine's rise. One was "the growth of the administrative state . . . As private entities increasingly came to be controlled by statutory and regulatory duties, many kinds of plaintiffs and would-be plaintiffs sought the articulation and enforcement of new and existing rights in the federal courts. . . . Among the difficult questions posed by the enormous growth of administrative agencies, . . . one of the most prominent was how to determine who could sue to enforce the legal duties of an agency." The second development was "an increase in litigation to articulate and enforce public, primarily constitutional, values. . . . [F]ederal litigation in the 1960's and 1970's increasingly involved attempts to establish and enforce public, often constitutional, values by litigants who were not individually affected by the conduct of which they complained in any way markedly different from most of the population." THE STRUCTURE OF STANDING, 98 YALE L.J. 221, 225–28 (1988). Other scholars similarly identify the emergence of the modern administrative state as central, but rather than emphasizing judicial efforts to restrict suits by regulatory beneficiaries, they maintain that standing doctrine began as an effort by liberal justices to insulate progressive and New Deal legislation from judicial review. See Cass R. Sunstein, What's Standing After Lujan? Of Citizen Suits, "Injuries," and Article III, 91 MICH. L. REV. 163, 180 (1992);

Stephen L. Winter, The Metaphor of Standing and the Problem of Self-Governance, 40 Stan. L. Rev. 1371, 1456–57 (1988). A recent empirical study of every contested standing issue decided by the Supreme Court from 1921 to 2006 concludes that "the insulation thesis does not fully explain the conception or invention of the modern standing doctrine," given progressive and conservative unanimity in standing decisions in the 1920s, but does a better job in explaining standing doctrine's development in the 1930s and 1940s, when progressive justices disproportionately voted against standing. See Daniel E. Ho & Erica L. Ross, Did Liberal Justices Invent the Standing Doctrine? An Empirical Study of the Evolution of Standing, 1921–2006, 62 Stan. L. Rev. 591, 595–96 (2010).

NOTES ON STANDING DOCTRINE'S CONSTITUTIONAL BASIS

Lujan is part of a long stream of precedent identifying standing's requirements of injury, causation, and redressability as constitutionally mandated. (By contrast, prudential standing requirements, discussed below in Section 1.e, are not considered constitutional; they stem from judge-made doctrines or statutes). Yet the constitutional basis of standing doctrine remains a matter of debate. Both judges and scholars continue to dispute which aspects of current standing doctrine—if any—have a constitutional basis and what that constitutional basis might be.

(1) **Standing and Article III's Case or Controversy Requirement.** Lujan based standing requirements in Article III. But injury-in-fact, causation, and redressability are nowhere expressly referenced in the text of Article III. Instead, Lujan argues that these requirements follow from Article III's limitation of the federal judicial power to "cases" and "controversies." In so doing it followed the earlier precedent, in particular ALLEN V. WHITE, 468 U.S. 737 (1984) (p. 1340), which involved an IRS policy, rooted in the Internal Revenue Code, of denying charitable tax-exempt status to racially discriminatory schools. In a 5–3 opinion by JUSTICE O'CONNOR, the Court emphasized standing doctrine's constitutional roots in holding that the parents of minority children lacked standing to challenge the IRS's failure to enforce the policy:

"Article III of the Constitution confines the federal courts to adjudicating actual 'cases' and 'controversies.' As the Court explained in Valley Forge Christian Coll. v. Americans United for Separation of Church and State, Inc., 454 U.S. 464, 471–476 (1982), the 'case or controversy' requirement defines with respect to the Judicial Branch the idea of separation of powers on which the Federal Government is founded. The several doctrines that have grown up to elaborate that requirement are 'founded in concern about the proper—and properly limited—role of the courts in a democratic society.' Warth v. Seldin, 422 U.S. 490, 498 (1975). . . . The case-or-controversy doctrines state fundamental limits on federal judicial power in our system of government," of which standing doctrine "is perhaps the most important. . . . Standing doctrine embraces several judicially self-imposed limits on the exercise of federal jurisdiction, such as the general prohibition on a litigant's raising another person's legal rights, the rule barring adjudication of generalized grievances more appropriately addressed in the representative branches, and the requirement that a plaintiff's complaint fall within the zone of interests protected by the law invoked. The requirement of standing, however, has a core component derived directly from the Constitution. A plaintiff must allege personal injury fairly traceable to the defendant's allegedly unlawful conduct and likely to be redressed by the requested relief."

Must an individual have suffered an actual and particular injury or satisfy causation and redressability for a judicially cognizable case or controversy to exist? Why isn't it enough that a dispute centers on the meaning of a statute as in Lujan or of the lawfulness of governmental conduct as in Allen? Put differently, even if Article III's case and controversy requirement is understood as restricting the federal courts to distinctly legal disputes, does current doctrine do a good job at identifying which disputes are really legal—weren't the plaintiffs in both Lujan and Allen raising legal questions?

In addition, does the lack of historical support for standing (see Note 5, p. 1310) undermine the Court's claim that standing requirements stem from Article III's case or controversy requirement? The answer to that question might depend on the extent to which you believe that the Constitution must be read in keeping with the original public meaning of its terms. For those who view the Constitution's meaning as evolving over time, the lack of historical support for constitutional standing doctrine may be less important. Interestingly, however, some of the Court's most rigorous enforcers of constitutional standing requirements, like Justice Scalia, have been originalists. (For Justice Thomas's effort to construct an originalist defense of standing doctrine, see his concurrence in Spokeo v. Robins, p. 1324.)

(2) *Standing Doctrine and Judicial Capacity.* Alternatively, the "case or controversy" requirement could be understood as limiting the federal courts to those legal disputes that the courts will be able to resolve accurately and effectively. In his Lujan concurrence, Justice Kennedy argued that the concrete injury requirement "preserves the vitality of the adversarial process by assuring both that the parties before the court have an actual, as opposed to professed, stake in the outcome, and that 'the legal questions presented . . . will be resolved, not in the rarified atmosphere of a debating society, but in a concrete factual context conducive to a realistic appreciation of the consequences of judicial action.' Valley Forge Christian College v. Americans United for Separation of Church and State, Inc., 454 U.S. 464, 472 (1982)."

Do you agree? Even if some degree of concreteness is needed for the Court to have an accurate sense of the issues at stake, does that justify the injury-in-fact requirement of standing doctrine? Do you think the Court in Lujan could not have accurately and effectively determined the meaning of the ESA's consultation requirement without further evidence of Joyce Kelly and Amy Skilbred's plans to return to project sites? And if Kelly and Skilbred were to add more concrete details on their plans to return—purchasing plane tickets, perhaps—would that concrete detail in any way inform the Court's consideration of whether the ESA's consultation requirement was violated? See David M. Driesen, Standing for Nothing: The Paradox of Demanding

Concrete Context for Formalist Adjudication, 89 Cornell L. Rev. 808, 839–55 (2004).

Moreover, isn't a national public interest organization like the Defenders of Wildlife, an organization which often litigates ESA claims and whose mission is to protect wildlife, more likely to present a strong argument against the government's position than a landowner who happens to own property abutting a government-funded project? Yet under current standing doctrine, isn't the landowner more likely to have standing? (This issue is discussed further in Sierra Club v. Morton, p. 1338.)

In any event, should ensuring adequate presentation of the legal issues involved be seen primarily as a matter of constitutional or prudential standing? In United States v. Windsor (p. 1358), Justice Kennedy argued for a prudentialist approach and relied on the "the participation of amici curiae prepared to defend with vigor the constitutionality of the legislative act" to assure "adversarial presentation of the issues." 133 S.Ct. at 2687. Is taking such contextual factors into account as part of a prudentialist analysis a better approach for sifting out those cases unconducive to judicial resolution without barring those cases that courts are able to address?

(3) *Standing and the Separation of Powers.* Fundamentally, both Lujan and Allen root standing doctrine in the separation of powers. Professor HEATHER ELLIOT, in THE FUNCTIONS OF STANDING, 61 Stan. L. Rev. 459, 461–63 (2008) argues that "[t]he Court seems to mean at least three different things when it uses standing to promote separation of powers . . . First, and most familiarly, the Court uses standing doctrine 'to restrict the cases heard . . . to those that are properly "cases" and "controversies" under Article III, . . . [thereby] keeping courts to their role qua courts' . . . Second, the Court has said, standing doctrine allows the courts to refuse cases better suited to the political process. . . Thus, the Court frequently 'has refrained from adjudicating abstract questions of wide public significance which amount to generalized grievances, pervasively shared and most appropriately addressed in the representative branches.' [Valley Forge, 454 U.S. at 475]. . . Third, the Court (and particularly Justice Scalia) has suggested that standing acts as a bulwark against congressional overreaching, preventing Congress from conscripting the courts in its battles with the executive branch."

The first of these functions—ensuring disputes are presented to courts in a manner they are capable of resolving—was discussed in the previous note. Insofar as the function of limiting the courts to their role qua courts means something more than that, it seems indistinguishable from the second function of courts not inappropriately intruding on the political process. Can we assess whether standing doctrine ensures the federal courts adhere to their proper constitutional role without subscribing to a particular view about what that role is—a matter of contestation and debate going back to the Constitution's adoption? For example, in Lujan Justice Scalia quotes Marbury v. Madison's famous statement that "[t]he province of the court is, solely, to decide on the rights of individuals." 5 U.S. (1 Cranch) 137, 170 (1803). Yet Marbury also famously stated that "[i]t is emphatically the province and duty of the judicial department to say what the law is," id. at

177. Such a law declaring function is not necessarily cabined to cases involving private rights of individuals.

In an article written before he joined the Supreme Court, THE DOCTRINE OF STANDING AS AN ESSENTIAL ELEMENT OF THE SEPARATION OF POWERS, 17 SUFFOLK U. L. REV. 881, 897 (1983), JUSTICE SCALIA argued that standing doctrine "functionally" served the separation of powers by "roughly restrict[ing] courts to their traditional undemocratic role of protecting individuals and minorities against impositions of the majority, and exclud[ing] them from the even more undemocratic role of prescribing how the other two branches should function in order to serve the interest of the majority itself. Thus, when an individual who is the very object of a law's requirement or prohibition seeks to challenge it, he always has standing. That is the classic case of the law bearing down upon the individual himself, and the court will not pause to inquire whether the grievance is a 'generalized' one." Justice Scalia contrasted "that classic form of court challenge with the increasingly frequent administrative law cases in which the plaintiff is complaining of an agency's unlawful failure to impose a requirement or prohibition upon someone else. [T]hat harm alone is, so to speak, a majoritarian one. The plaintiff may care more about it . . . [b]ut that does not establish that he has been harmed distinctively—only that he assesses the harm as more grave, which is a fair subject for democratic debate in which he may persuade the rest of us. Since our readiness to be persuaded is no less than his own (we are harmed just as much) there is no reason to remove the matter from the political process and place it in the courts." Judicial enforcement is additionally anti-democratic because when "the courts . . . enforce upon the executive branch adherence to legislative policies that the political process itself would not enforce, they are likely (despite the best of intentions) to be enforcing the political prejudices of their own class. . . ."

Are you convinced that the proper role of courts in regulatory settings is limited to protecting individuals against overzealous enforcement? Are the separation of powers and democratic rule advanced by limiting the extent to which individuals can challenge lax enforcement in court? Compare CASS R. SUNSTEIN, WHAT'S STANDING AFTER LUJAN? OF CITIZEN SUITS, "INJURIES," AND ARTICLE III, 91 Mich. L. Rev. 163, 165 (1992): "In a case of beneficiary or citizen standing, courts are not enforcing 'executive branch adherence to legislative policies that the political process itself would not enforce.' Instead, they are requiring the executive branch to adhere to the law, that is, to outcomes that the political process has endorsed. . . . Standing would produce 'legislative policies that the political process itself would not enforce' only if courts systematically misinterpreted statutes. But this seems to be an unsupportable assumption."

(4) *Standing and Article I.* In assessing whether such a beneficiary suit would be undemocratic or exceed the proper role of the courts, does it matter if Congress has expressly provided for broader enforcement challenges, as for example by enacting a citizen suit provision as it did in the ESA? Lujan was the first case to deny standing in the context of a statutory citizen suit provision and to constitutionalize a ban on generalized grievances. Notably,

Allen (p. 1340) had described the generalized grievances bar as a prudential limitation, meaning it could be waived by Congress.

By constitutionalizing the ban on generalized grievances, is it actually Lujan that undermines majoritarian rule and the separation of powers? Several scholars have argued that constitutionalizing standing requirements unjustifiably intrudes on congressional authority, and that instead the only question in regulatory contexts should be whether Congress has provided a cause of action: "[S]uperimposing an 'injury in fact' test upon an inquiry into the meaning of a statute is a way for the Court to enlarge its powers at the expense of Congress. . . . For the Court to limit the power of Congress to create statutory rights enforceable by certain groups of people—to limit, in other words, the power of Congress to create standing—is to limit the power of Congress to define and protect against certain kinds of injury that the Court thinks it improper to protect against." FLETCHER, supra, at 233; see also SUNSTEIN, supra, at 167–69.

Do you agree? In assessing the relationship of standing doctrine to congressional authority, think about the likely impact on policy of a regulatory regime in which regulated parties can sue agencies but regulatory beneficiaries cannot. Might agencies become more attentive to the complaints of regulated parties about excessive enforcement for fear of being hauled into court and correspondingly inattentive to complaints of insufficient enforcement from regulatory beneficiaries? These concerns led the courts to ease barriers to suit in the 1960s and 1970s (see Data Processing, p. 1366).

Recall that in his Lujan concurrence, Justice Kennedy also underscored the importance of congressional authority. Although he agreed that Article III limited Congress to only conferring rights of action where concrete injury existed, he emphasized that "Congress has the power to define injuries and articulate chains of causation that will give rise to a case or controversy where none existed before," provided Congress "identif[ies] the injury it seeks to vindicate and relate[s] the injury to the class of persons entitled to bring suit." The scope of this congressional power over standing is explored in the materials in the next subsection.

(5) *Standing, Article II, and the President's Duty to Take Care that the Laws Be Faithfully Executed.* In Lujan, Justice Scalia offered two arguments as to why Congress's inclusion of a broad citizen suit provision in the ESA, authorizing any person to sue to enforce the act, did not resolve the standing inquiry. One was to argue that Congress cannot grant jurisdiction over suits that fall outside of Article III's case or controversy requirement. The other was to contend that "[t]o permit Congress to convert the undifferentiated public interest in executive officers' compliance with the law into an 'individual right' vindicable in the courts is to permit Congress to transfer from the President to the courts the Chief Executive's most important constitutional duty, to 'take Care that the Laws be faithfully executed,' Art. II, § 3." In Federal Election Commission v. Akins (p. 1317, in which the Court upheld Congress's power to provide for suit by voters challenging the FEC's enforcement of the Federal Election Campaign Act, Justice Scalia made this argument the central claim of his dissent. As you

will see if you study Chapter VII, arguments about the meaning and impact of the Article II Vesting and Take Care Clauses are at the heart of the debate over unitary executive theory and presidential control over administration.

In what way does legislation authorizing a suit to enforce a governing statute violate the President's take care duty? That duty, after all, requires the President to ensure that the laws are faithfully executed. Insofar as a citizen suit seeks to force an agency to comply with a governing statute, isn't that furthering rather than undermining faithful execution of the laws? Justice Blackmun made this argument in his Lujan dissent: "Just as Congress does not violate separation of powers by structuring the procedural manner in which the Executive shall carry out the laws, surely the federal courts do not violate separation of powers when, at the very instruction and command of Congress, they enforce these procedures." Was he right?

Moreover, Lujan suggests that there would be standing if the individual plaintiffs had provided greater evidence of their likely return to the project sites in the near future. But if a citizen suit seeking enforcement interferes with the President's Article II powers, why is such a suit constitutionally acceptable when an individual can demonstrate injury-in-fact? According to Justice Scalia in Akins, this insistence on individual injury is critical: "A system in which the citizenry at large could sue to compel Executive compliance with the law would be a system in which the courts, rather than the President, are given the primary responsibility to 'take Care that the Laws be faithfully executed.' We do not have such a system . . ." As you read Akins and the materials on congressional power to create new injury in the next subsection, think about whether you agree.

b. Defining Injury in Regulatory Settings

> *(1) The Requirement of Particularized Injury*
>
> *(2) The Requirement of Concrete and Imminent Injury*
>
> *(3) Procedural Rights and Associational Standing*

Having laid out standing's basic framework and potential constitutional underpinnings, what remains is to look more in detail about how it works in practice, with special attention to the impact of standing doctrine in regulatory and administrative settings. A first set of questions to explore concerns the type of injury required for standing. Lujan prohibited suits based on "generalized grievances" and required that injury must be "concrete and particular," as well as "actual and imminent, as opposed to speculative." What do these terms mean in practice: are they distinguishable, what kinds of suits do they allow or prohibit, and how good a job has the Court done in applying them? This subsection addresses these issues, focusing on implications of standing requirements in modern regulatory contexts.

(1) The Requirement of Particularized Injury

***FEDERAL ELECTION COMMISSION v.
AKINS***

FEDERAL ELECTION COMMISSION v. AKINS

Supreme Court of the United States (1998).
524 U.S. 11.

■ JUSTICE BREYER delivered the opinion of the Court.

The Federal Election Commission (FEC) has determined that the American Israel Public Affairs Committee (AIPAC) is not a "political committee" as defined by the Federal Election Campaign Act of 1971 (FECA or Act), 2 U.S.C. § 431(4), and, for that reason, the FEC has refused to require AIPAC to make disclosures regarding its membership, contributions, and expenditures that FECA would otherwise require. We hold that respondents, a group of voters, have standing to challenge the Commission's determination in court, and we remand this case for further proceedings.

[FECA attempts to remedy actual or perceived corruption of the electoral process by limiting the amounts that individuals, corporations, "political committees" (including political action committees), and political parties can contribute to a candidate for federal office. A less well-known but equally important part of the Act requires public disclosure of campaign finance information. Groups within the definition of "political committee" (more familiarly, political action committees, or PACs) must register with the FEC, appoint a treasurer, keep names and addresses of contributors, track the amount and purpose of disbursements, and file detailed reports that include names of donors giving in excess of $200 per year, contributions, expenditures, and other disbursements. The FEC is required to make these reports available for public review and copying within 48 hours of receipt. In addition, data from the reports are entered in a database (now accessible online) that sorts and aggregates the information in a variety of ways.

[Akins et al. described themselves as a group of voters with views opposed to those of AIPAC. They filed a complaint with the FEC, alleging that AIPAC was a "political committee" but had failed to register and to make the required disclosures. AIPAC moved to dismiss, arguing that it was not a "political committee" within the meaning of FECA. The FEC then interpreted the statutory definition to include only organizations that have as a "major purpose" the nomination or election of candidates. AIPAC's focus, it concluded, was issue-oriented lobbying not election-related activities, and so it dismissed the complaint. Akins et al. sought judicial review. The district court and a panel of the D.C. Circuit affirmed the FEC. The Circuit then took the case en banc and reversed, concluding that the FEC misinterpreted the Act. The government sought certiorari on standing as well as the merits.]

II

. . . Congress has specifically provided in FECA that "[a]ny person who believes a violation of this Act . . . has occurred, may file a complaint with the Commission." § 437g(a)(1). It has added that "[a]ny party aggrieved by an order of the Commission dismissing a complaint filed by such party . . . may file a petition" in district court seeking review of that dismissal. § 437g(a)(8)(A). [The Court first concluded that Akins et al satisfied prudential standing requirements and fell within the zone of interest of FECA.] . . .

[We do not] agree with the FEC or the dissent that Congress lacks the constitutional power to authorize federal courts to adjudicate this lawsuit. Article III, of course, limits Congress' grant of judicial power to "cases" or "controversies." That limitation means that respondents must show, among other things, an "injury in fact" . . .

The "injury in fact" that respondents have suffered consists of their inability to obtain information—lists of AIPAC donors (who are, according to AIPAC, its members), and campaign-related contributions and expenditures—that, on respondents' view of the law, the statute requires that AIPAC make public. There is no reason to doubt their claim that the information would help them (and others to whom they would communicate it) to evaluate candidates for public office, especially candidates who received assistance from AIPAC, and to evaluate the role that AIPAC's financial assistance might play in a specific election. Respondents' injury consequently seems concrete and particular. Indeed, this Court has previously held that a plaintiff suffers an "injury in fact" when the plaintiff fails to obtain information which must be publicly disclosed pursuant to a statute. Public Citizen v. Dep't of Justice, 491 U.S. 440, 449 (1989) (failure to obtain information subject to disclosure under Federal Advisory Committee Act "constitutes a sufficiently distinct injury to provide standing to sue"). . . .

The FEC's strongest argument is its contention that this lawsuit involves only a "generalized grievance." . . . The FEC points out that respondents' asserted harm (their failure to obtain information) is one which is " 'shared in substantially equal measure by all or a large class of citizens.' " (quoting Warth v. Seldin, 422 U.S. 490, 499 (1975)). This Court, the FEC adds, has often said that "generalized grievance[s]" are not the kinds of harms that confer standing. Whether styled as a constitutional or prudential limit on standing, the Court has sometimes determined that where large numbers of Americans suffer alike, the political process, rather than the judicial process, may provide the more appropriate remedy for a widely shared grievance.

The kind of judicial language to which the FEC points, however, invariably appears in cases where the harm at issue is not only widely shared, but is also of an abstract and indefinite nature—for example, harm to the "common concern for obedience to law." L. Singer & Sons v. Union Pacific R. Co., 311 U.S. 295, 303 (1940); see also Allen [v. Wright],

468 U.S. [737,] 754 [(1984), p. 1340], Cf. Lujan [v. Defenders of Wildlife, 504 U.S. 555,] 572–78 [(1992), p. 1300] (injury to interest in seeing that certain procedures are followed not normally sufficient by itself to confer standing). The abstract nature of the harm—for example, injury to the interest in seeing that the law is obeyed—deprives the case of the concrete specificity that characterized those controversies which were "the traditional concern of the courts at Westminster," Coleman [v. Miller], 307 U.S. [433,] 460 [(1939)] (Frankfurter, J., dissenting); and which today prevents a plaintiff from obtaining what would, in effect, amount to an advisory opinion.

Often the fact that an interest is abstract and the fact that it is widely shared go hand in hand. But their association is not invariable, and where a harm is concrete, though widely shared, the Court has found "injury in fact." See Public Citizen, 491 U.S., at 449–450 ("The fact that other citizens or groups of citizens might make the same complaint after unsuccessfully demanding disclosure . . . does not lessen [their] asserted injury"). Thus the fact that a political forum may be more readily available where an injury is widely shared (while counseling against, say, interpreting a statute as conferring standing) does not, by itself, automatically disqualify an interest for Article III purposes. Such an interest, where sufficiently concrete, may count as an "injury in fact." This conclusion seems particularly obvious where (to use a hypothetical example) large numbers of individuals suffer the same common-law injury (say, a widespread mass tort), or where large numbers of voters suffer interference with voting rights conferred by law. Cf. Shaw v. Hunt, 517 U.S. 899 (1996). We conclude that, similarly, the informational injury at issue here, directly related to voting, the most basic of political rights, is sufficiently concrete and specific such that the fact that it is widely shared does not deprive Congress of constitutional power to authorize its vindication in the federal courts.

[The Court then rejected the argument that traceability and redressability were lacking because "it is possible that even had the FEC agreed with respondents' view of the law, it would still have decided in the exercise of its discretion not to require AIPAC to produce the information." Justice Breyer pointed out that "those adversely affected by a discretionary agency decision generally have standing to complain that the agency based its decision upon an improper legal ground," citing Citizens to Preserve Overton Park, Inc. v. Volpe, p. 1085, and SEC v. Chenery Corp., p. 249. Finally, in response to the argument that the FEC's decision not to undertake enforcement action was unreviewable because it was "committed to agency discretion by law," APA § 701(a)(2) (see Sec. 2.b.3) the Court concluded that the FECA "explicitly indicates the contrary." On the merits, the Court remanded the case to the FEC for reconsideration in light of intervening new rules about other sections of FECA that would, if applicable to AIPCA, moot the case.]

■ JUSTICE SCALIA, with whom JUSTICE O'CONNOR and JUSTICE THOMAS join, dissenting.

The provision of law at issue in this case is an extraordinary one, conferring upon a private person the ability to bring an Executive agency into court to compel its enforcement of the law against a third party. . . . If provisions such as the present one were commonplace, the role of the Executive Branch in our system of separated and equilibrated powers would be greatly reduced, and that of the Judiciary greatly expanded. [Justice Scalia argued that FECA did not "intend" to give every person who can file administrative complaints the right also to obtain judicial review if the complaint is rejected. He then turned to the majority's standing analysis.]

What is noticeably lacking in the Court's discussion of our generalized-grievance jurisprudence is all reference to two words that have figured in it prominently: "particularized" and "undifferentiated." "Particularized" means that "the injury must affect the plaintiff in a personal and individual way." Lujan. If the effect is undifferentiated and common to all members of the public, . . . the plaintiff has a "generalized grievance" that must be pursued by political, rather than judicial, means. These terms explain why it is a gross oversimplification to reduce the concept of a generalized grievance to nothing more than "the fact that [the grievance] is widely shared," thereby enabling the concept to be dismissed as a standing principle by such examples as "large numbers of individuals suffer[ing] the same common-law injury (say, a widespread mass tort), or . . . large numbers of voters suffer[ing] interference with voting rights conferred by law." The exemplified injuries are widely shared, to be sure, but each individual suffers a particularized and differentiated harm. One tort victim suffers a burnt leg, another a burnt arm—or even if both suffer burnt arms they are different arms. One voter suffers the deprivation of his franchise, another the deprivation of hers. With the generalized grievance, on the other hand, the injury or deprivation is not only widely shared but it is undifferentiated. The harm caused to . . . Mr. Akins by the allegedly unlawful failure to enforce FECA is precisely the same as the harm caused to everyone else: unavailability of a description of AIPAC's activities.

. . . A system in which the citizenry at large could sue to compel Executive compliance with the law would be a system in which the courts, rather than the President, are given the primary responsibility to "take Care that the Laws be faithfully executed." We do not have such a system because the common understanding of the interest necessary to sustain suit has included the requirement . . . that the complained-of injury be particularized and differentiated, rather than common to all the electorate. When the Executive can be directed by the courts, at the instance of any voter, to remedy a deprivation that affects the entire electorate in precisely the same way—and particularly when that deprivation (here, the unavailability of information) is one inseverable part of a larger enforcement scheme—there has occurred a shift of political responsibility to a branch designed not to protect the public at large but to protect individual rights. . . . If today's decision is correct, it is within the power of Congress to authorize any interested person to manage (through the courts) the Executive's enforcement of any law that includes a requirement for the filing and public availability of a piece of paper. This is not the system we have had, and is not the system we should desire.

NOTES

(1) *Is the Court Drawing Consistent Lines?* Do you think Akins can be squared with Lujan? How easy will it be for courts to distinguish between "broadly shared injuries" and "generalized grievances" going forward?

According to Justice Breyer, Akins did not involve a generalized grievance simply because every voter in the country shared the same information injury, arguing that a generalized grievance involves not just a broadly shared injury but in addition assertion of an abstract interest, such as an interest in having the government follow the law. Here, however, the Akins plaintiffs were asserting a concrete interest in having information on AIPAC's donors, contributions, and expenditures that would help them evaluate candidates. Does this argument suffice to distinguish Lujan? Weren't the plaintiffs there also alleging a concrete interest, namely the interest in having government agencies undertake ESA consultations?

Is the difference instead that Akins involved an effort to get the government to provide something—information—to individuals outside of government on which those individuals could then act, whereas Lujan involved an effort simply to get government agencies to do something—consult with one another? On the other hand, didn't Lujan also involve an effort to change actions outside of government, in that the goal was to stop projects that endangered protected species from going forward and consultation would increase the chances of that result? A separate issue is whether such an impact is too attenuated, but that concern goes more to causation and redressability than the presence of injury-in-fact. See Sec. 1.c.

Perhaps, then, what makes the difference is that the plaintiffs sought information that might change how they themselves acted, as opposed to change how others acted. In Akins, the Court emphasizes the plaintiffs' claim that the information being sought "would help them . . . evaluate candidates for public office." Moreover, the procedure in Lujan—interagency consultation—lacked this element of personal participation.

(2) *The Goals of Information Disclosure.* But is it clear that the goal of information disclosure under the FECA is simply to allow voters to be better informed? That is certainly one purpose for disclosure, but couldn't disclosure also be used to reduce the influence of interest group money in elections, either because interest groups will be discouraged from making large contributions and expenditures for fear of public outcry or because candidates will be more willing to take positions at odds with their donors' interests for fear of being seen as bought? If so, is the situation in Akins

really that different from Lujan, where consultation was similarly a regulatory strategy used to protect endangered species? Alternatively, public disclosure requirements might function as a way to use private resources to enhance enforcement, allowing private parties to notify the agency of potential violations or go to court to ensure compliance. Does the Constitution prevent Congress from "crowdsourcing" enforcement of regulatory violations in this fashion? For a discussion of information disclosure as a regulatory strategy, see Chapter VI.

(3) *Taxpayer Standing.* One area where the Court has fairly consistently rejected standing involves lawsuits by taxpayers challenging government expenditures as unlawful. A prominent denial of taxpayer standing came in UNITED STATES V. RICHARDSON, 418 U.S. 166 (1974). There, a federal taxpayer brought suit challenging the statutory exemption on reporting the CIA's expenditures as violating Art. I, § 9, cl. 7, of the Constitution: "No Money shall be drawn from the Treasury, but in Consequence of Appropriations made by Law; and a regular Statement and Account of the Receipts and Expenditures of all public Money shall be published from time to time." The Court held that he lacked standing: "Respondent's claim is that, without detailed information on CIA expenditures—and hence its activities—he cannot intelligently follow the actions of Congress or the Executive, nor can he properly fulfill his obligations as a member of the electorate in voting for candidates seeking national office. This is surely . . . a generalized grievance . . . since the impact on him is plainly undifferentiated and 'common to all members of the public.' Ex parte Levitt, 302 U.S. 633, 634 (1937)." Chief Justice Burger's opinion in Richardson goes so far as to say that the apparent absence of any other viable plaintiff is good evidence that the matter does not belong in the courts. Other constitutional standing cases have echoed this position. Note that Richardson was a suit based on the Constitution rather than a statute with a specific citizen suit provision. Does that suffice to distinguish Akins?

Should taxpayer suits be deemed inherently generalized grievances, or are there some such suits where the injury is more limited or where other factors provide special ground for taxpayer standing? In the past the Court has sanctioned municipal taxpayer standing, relying on "the peculiar relation of the corporate taxpayer to the corporation" to distinguish such a case from the general bar on taxpayer suits. Commonwealth of Massachusetts v. Mellon, 262 U.S. 447, 487 (1923). But it has recently rejected state taxpayer standing even where taxpayers are allowed to sue in state courts. See DaimerChrysler Corp. v. Cuno, 547 U.S. 332 (2006). In the past, the Court has also upheld federal taxpayer suits alleging congressional exercise of the spending power violated Establishment Clause on the ground that the "Establishment Clause . . . operates as a specific constitutional limitation upon the exercise by Congress of the taxing and spending power conferred by Art. I, § 8." Flast v. Cohen, 392 U.S. 83, 103–04 (1968). But over time it has narrowed this exemption from the usual ban on taxpayer standing almost out of existence. See Arizona Christian School Tuition Org'n v. Winn, 563 U.S. 125 (2011); Hein v. Freedom from Religion Foundation, Inc., 551 U.S. 587 (2007).

(4) ***Qui Tam and Civil Penalty Actions.*** Note that Lujan distinguishes "the unusual case in which Congress has . . . provid[ed] a cash bounty for the victorious plaintiff" as one where concerns about permitting private enforcement may be diminished. These "qui tam" statutes originated in England and have existed in the United States since the founding. See Marvin v. Trout, 199 U.S. 212, 225 (1905). Typically, they establish a penalty for official wrongdoing and provide that anyone who brings such a wrongdoing to the attention of the court will receive a share of the penalty. "These statutes provided a common mechanism to regulate, by judicial sanction, governmental officials where there was likely to be no aggrieved party with a private cause of action." Winter, supra, at 1407; Evan Caminker, The Constitutionality of Qui Tam Actions, 99 Yale L.J. 341 (1989). VERMONT AGENCY OF NATURAL RESOURCES V. U.S. EX REL. STEVENS, 529 U.S. 765 (2000), held that a qui tam suit under the False Claims Act satisfied Article III standing requirements. Writing for the Court, JUSTICE SCALIA focused on the long history of such actions in Anglo-American jurisprudence and reasoned that injury-in-fact arose from the status of the "qui tam relator [as], in effect, suing as a partial assignee of the United States." However, footnote 8 warns: "In so concluding, we express no view on the question whether qui tam suits violate Article II, in particular the Appointments Clause of § 2 and the Take Care Clause of § 3," citing Lujan.

Would the generalized grievance concern in Lujan disappear if Congress had amended the citizen-suit provision of ESA to provide that a successful plaintiff would receive a reward of $1,000? In STEEL CO. V. CITIZENS FOR A BETTER ENVIRONMENT, 523 U.S. 83 (1998), the Court held that the Emergency Planning and Community Right-to-Know Act could not constitutionally authorize private suits to complain of *past* violations of the Act's requirement that companies file annual reports about the nature and quantity of hazardous chemical use. JUSTICE SCALIA's opinion reasoned that a statutory scheme in which the only available remedies were noncompliance penalties payable to the United States, rather than to the private complainants, ran afoul of Lujan. JUSTICE STEVENS, concurring only in the judgment, responded: "[U]nder the Court's own reasoning, respondent would have had standing if Congress had authorized some payment to respondent. . . . Yet it is unclear why the separation of powers question should turn on whether the plaintiff receives monetary compensation. In either instance, a private citizen is enforcing the law."

Contrast Steel Co. with FRIENDS OF THE EARTH, INC. (FOE) V. LAIDLAW ENVIRONMENTAL SERVICES, 528 U.S. 167 (2000), (see also p. 1347) where the Court held by 7–2 decision that an environmental organization had standing to seek civil penalties under the Clean Water Act's citizen suit provision for unlawful discharges of mercury that were ongoing when the complaint was filed. Writing for the majority, JUSTICE GINSBURG found that "the affidavits and testimony [from FOE's members] assert that Laidlaw's discharges, and the affiant members' reasonable concerns about the effects of those discharges, directly affected those affiants' recreational, aesthetic, and economic interests." Justice Ginsburg rejected the contention that "the reasoning of our decision in Steel Co., directs the conclusion that citizen plaintiffs have no standing to seek civil penalties under the Act . . . Steel Co. held that private plaintiffs, unlike the Federal Government, may not sue to assess penalties for wholly past violations, but our decision in that case did not reach the issue of standing to seek penalties for violations that are ongoing at the time of the complaint and that could continue into the future if undeterred."

In dissent, JUSTICE SCALIA insisted that allowing private individuals to sue for civil penalties violated Article II: "A Clean Water Act plaintiff pursuing civil penalties acts as a self-appointed mini-EPA. Where, as is often the case, the plaintiff is a national association, it has significant discretion in choosing enforcement targets. . . . And once the target is chosen, the suit goes forward without meaningful public control. . . . Elected officials are entirely deprived of their discretion to decide that a given violation should not be the object of suit at all, or that the enforcement decision should be postponed. . . . The undesirable and unconstitutional consequence of today's decision is to place the immense power of suing to enforce the public laws in private hands." Concurring, Justice Kennedy stated that whether Article II allows private litigants to sue for public fines present "[d]ifficult and fundamental questions" but emphasized those questions had not been briefed or decided below.

Are qui tam actions or citizen suits for civil penalties really distinguishable from generalized grievances? Does the presence of individual gain—financial bounties in the case of qui tam, and cessation and deterrence of unlawful conduct in the case of civil penalties—make a constitutional difference in your view? Focusing just on the Article III concern, doesn't FOE suggest that the generalized grievance bar is more of a pleading requirement than a real constitutional prohibition? If Defenders of Wildlife and its members had averred more detail on their injury from nonenforcement of the ESA consultation requirement for international projects, would they too have been able to sue?

Note also the trend post-Lujan, evident in Akins, Vermont Agency, and FOE, to reprise the generalized grievance concern in Article II rather than Article III terms. To date, the claim that allowing private enforcement of the law violates Article II has yet to garner majority support. Should it? What weight should be given to the fact that private enforcement in the form of qui tam statutes was present going back to the Founding?

(2) The Requirement of Concrete and Imminent Injury

SPOKEO V. ROBINS, 136 S.Ct. 1540 (2016), dealt with the Fair Credit Reporting Act (FCRA), which required consumer reporting agencies to follow reasonable procedures to ensure maximum accuracy in consumers' credit reports. The Act provides that an agency that willfully fails to comply with the FCRA with respect to an individual is liable to that individual for either actual damages or statutory damages of $100–1,000 per violation, in addition to other penalties. Spokeo is a "people search engine," allowing users to enter a person's name, a phone number, or an email address and search approximately 12 billion accumulated public records for information about the subject of the search. Thomas Robins conducted a search about himself and claimed that some of the information Spokeo had gathered was incorrect; in particular, Robins alleged his report stated that he had a job, was relatively affluent, and had a graduate degree, all of which were untrue. Robins "filed a complaint on his own behalf and on behalf of a class of similarly situated individuals," alleging violations of the FCRA. The district court dismissed the complaint for a lack of standing and the Ninth Circuit reversed.

Writing for the Court, JUSTICE ALITO first discussed the "irreducible constitutional minimum" of standing, noting that the case at hand hinged on the injury-in-fact requirement. In order to show an injury-in-fact, a plaintiff must demonstrate that "he or she suffered 'an invasion of a legally protected interest' that is 'concrete and particularized' and 'actual or imminent, not conjectural or hypothetical.'" Lujan, 504 U.S., at 560. He then addressed the differences between the requirements of particularization and concreteness, finding that the Ninth Circuit had failed to distinguish between the two:

"[T]he Ninth Circuit concluded that Robins' complaint alleges 'concrete, de facto' injuries for essentially two reasons. First, the court noted that Robins 'alleges that Spokeo violated his statutory rights, not just the statutory rights of other people.' Ibid. Second, the court wrote that 'Robins's personal interests in the handling of his credit information are individualized rather than collective.' Ibid. (emphasis added). Both of these observations concern particularization, not concreteness. We have made it clear time and time again that an injury-in-fact must be both concrete and particularized. . . .

"A 'concrete' injury must be 'de facto'; that is, it must actually exist. See Black's Law Dictionary 479 (9th ed. 2009). When we have used the adjective 'concrete,' we have meant to convey the usual meaning of the term—'real,' and not 'abstract.' Webster's Third New International Dictionary 472 (1971); Random House Dictionary of the English Language 305 (1967). Concreteness, therefore, is quite different from particularization. . . . 'Concrete' is not, however, necessarily synonymous with 'tangible.' Although tangible injuries are perhaps easier to recognize, we have confirmed in many of our previous cases that intangible injuries can nevertheless be concrete. . . . In determining whether an intangible harm constitutes injury-in-fact, both history and the judgment of Congress play important roles. Because the doctrine of standing derives from the case-or-controversy requirement, and because that requirement in turn is grounded in historical practice, it is instructive to consider whether an alleged intangible harm has a close relationship to a harm that has traditionally been regarded as providing a basis for a lawsuit in English or American courts. In addition, because Congress is well positioned to identify intangible harms that meet minimum Article III requirements, its judgment is also instructive and important. Thus, we said in Lujan that Congress may 'elevat[e] to the status of legally cognizable injuries concrete, de facto injuries that were previously inadequate in law.' 504 U.S., at 578. Similarly, Justice Kennedy's concurrence in that case explained that 'Congress has the power to define injuries and articulate chains of causation that will give rise to a case or controversy where none existed before.' Id., at 580.

"Congress' role in identifying and elevating intangible harms does not mean that a plaintiff automatically satisfies the injury-in-fact requirement whenever a statute grants a person a statutory right and purports to authorize that person to sue to vindicate that right. Article III standing requires a concrete injury even in the context of a statutory violation. For that reason, Robins could not, for example, allege a bare procedural violation, divorced from any concrete harm, and satisfy the injury-in-fact requirement of Article III. . . . This does not mean, however, that the risk of real harm cannot satisfy the requirement of concreteness. For example, the law has long permitted recovery by certain tort victims even if their harms may be difficult to prove or measure. Just as the common law permitted suit in such instances, the violation of a procedural right granted by statute can be sufficient in some circumstances to constitute injury-in-fact. In other words, a plaintiff in such a case need not allege any additional harm beyond the one Congress has identified."

Justice Alito then turned to Robins' case, finding that while "Congress plainly sought to curb the dissemination of false information by adopting procedures designed to decrease that risk[,] . . . Robins cannot satisfy the demands of Article III by alleging a bare procedure violation[, which] . . . may result in no harm." Justice Alito also seemed skeptical of the idea that all incorrect information would result in harm, noting that "[i]t is difficult to imagine how the dissemination of an incorrect zip code, without more, could work any concrete harm." Because the Ninth Circuit failed to conduct a complete analysis of Robins' standing, the Court vacated the judgment of the Ninth Circuit and remanded the case for further proceedings.

JUSTICE THOMAS concurred in the Court's opinion but wrote separately to note that, while common-law courts have historically "possessed broad power to adjudicate suits involving the alleged violation of private rights, even when plaintiffs alleged only the violation of those rights and nothing more[,]" they have traditionally "required a further showing of injury for violations of 'public rights'—rights that involve duties owed 'to the whole community.' " Justice Thomas then traced the historical differences to modern standing doctrine: "These differences between legal claims brought by private plaintiffs for the violation of public and private rights underlie modern standing doctrine and explain the Court's description of the injury-in-fact requirement. This requirement applies with special force when a plaintiff files suit to require an executive agency to 'follow the law' . . . But the concrete-harm requirement does not apply as rigorously when a private plaintiff seeks to vindicate his own private rights. Our contemporary decisions have not required a plaintiff to assert an actual injury beyond the violation of his personal legal rights to satisfy the 'injury-in-fact' requirement. . . . The separation-of-powers concerns underlying our public-rights decisions are not implicated when private individuals sue to redress violations of their own private rights. . . .

". . . Congress can create new private rights and authorize private plaintiffs to sue based simply on the violation of those private rights. A plaintiff seeking to vindicate a statutorily created private right need not allege actual harm beyond the invasion of that private right. See Havens Realty Corp. v. Coleman, 455 U.S. 363, 373–374 (1982) [p. 1328] (recognizing standing for a violation of the Fair Housing Act). A plaintiff seeking to vindicate a public right embodied in a federal statute, however, must demonstrate that the violation of that public right has caused him a concrete, individual harm distinct from the general population. See Lujan, 502 U.S. at 578.

"Given these principles, I agree with the Court's decision to vacate and remand. . . . If Congress has created a private duty owed personally to Robins to protect his information, then the violation of the legal duty suffices for Article III injury-in-fact. If that provision, however, vests any and all consumers with the power to police the 'reasonable procedures' of Spokeo, without more, then Robins has no standing to sue for its violation absent an allegation that he has suffered individualized harm."

JUSTICE GINSBURG, joined by Justice Sotomayor, dissented from the Court's decision to remand but agreed with the Court's holding that Robins met "the particularity requirement for standing under Article III . . . [,] that Congress has the authority to confer rights and delineate claims for relief where none existed before[, and that] Congress' connection of procedural requirements to the prevention of substantive harm . . . is 'instructive and important.' " However, Justice Ginsburg found that Spokeo's misrepresentation of Robins' age, marital status, employment, and parental status constituted a "concrete" injury which could harm Robin's employment prospects.

NOTES

(1) *Should the Court Have Remanded?* Given the allegations in Robins' complaint, should the Court have remanded for the Ninth Circuit to determine standing? On these allegations alone, has Robins alleged adequate actual injury to have standing—and if so, why do you think a majority insisted on remanding? Could the fact that Robins brought his suit as a class action have played a role? As mentioned above, FCRA provides that any person who willfully fails to comply with the FCRA with respect to an individual is liable to that individual for either actual damages or statutory damages of $100–1,000 per violation, in addition to other penalties.

Given the estimated 12 billion public records Spokeo contained, the total could add up to several billion dollars.

(2) ***Intangible Harm and the Concrete Injury Requirement.*** In Spokeo, the Court reaffirmed that the concrete injury requirement did not require tangible harm, and "Congress may 'elevat[e] to the status of legally cognizable injuries concrete, de facto injuries that were previously inadequate in law.' (quoting Lujan). The Supreme Court has stated in the past that non-economic injury is cognizable; in particular, the Court has shown a willingness to recognize injury to aesthetic and conservational interests, a spiritual stake in First Amendment values, the inability to compete on an equal footing, and—possibly—stigma or indignity as bases of Article III injury." RACHEL BAYEFSKY, PSYCHOLOGICAL HARM AND CONSTITUTIONAL STANDING, 81 BROOK. L. REV. 1555, 1557–58 (2016).

What about pure psychological injury? Does recognizing these forms of standing entail recognizing psychological effect as a potential injury-in-fact, in that "the harmful nature of these intangible injuries seems to stem at least partially from their psychological effects on plaintiffs." Bayefsky, supra, at 1558. But would acknowledging psychological harm on its own eviscerate the prohibition on generalized grievances as a basis for standing? See Hein v. Freedom from Religion, Inc., 551 U.S. 587, 619 (2007) (Scalia, J., concurring in the judgment) (arguing that it would in the context of a taxpayer's Establishment Clause challenge to spending).

(3) ***Congressional Power to Create New Injuries.*** A key question underlying Spokeo concerns the extent to which Congress can create new injuries. The Court has long emphasized that "Congress may create a statutory right or entitlement the alleged deprivation of which can confer standing to sue even where the plaintiff would have suffered no judicially cognizable injury in the absence of statute" Warth v. Seldin 422 U.S. 490, 514 (1975). If this were not the case, wouldn't standing doctrine operate to freeze the set of injuries capable of legal redress to those recognized at common law? Recall Justice Kennedy's statement in his Lujan concurrence, p. 1306: "As government programs and policies become more complex and far-reaching, we must be sensitive to the articulation of new rights of action that do not have clear analogs in our common-law tradition." Were you surprised to see him join the majority in Spokeo?

In HAVENS REALTY CORP v. COLEMAN, 455 U.S. 363 (1982), the Court found that a black tester who was discriminated against by being denied information about available housing opportunities had standing to sue for violations of the Fair Housing Act (FHA), even though he did not actually want to rent any property. In so holding, the Court stated: "Congress has thus conferred on all 'persons' a legal right to truthful information about available housing. This congressional intention cannot be overlooked in determining whether testers have standing to sue. As we have previously recognized, '[t]he actual or threatened injury required by Art. III may exist solely by virtue of statutes creating legal rights, the invasion of which creates standing. . . .' Warth, 422 U.S. at 500." Similarly, in TRAFFICANTE V. METROPOLITAN LIFE INS. CO., 409 U.S. 212 (1972), the Court held that two tenants, one black and one white, had standing to sue the owner of their apartment complex alleging that it had engaged in racially discriminatory housing practices because the alleged practices deprived them of the "important benefits of interracial association." (The Court reaffirmed its precedent on the breadth of the FHA's cause of action recently in Bank of America v. City of Miami, 137 S.Ct. 1296 (2017), p. 1279.

Is Spokeo consistent with Havens Realty and Trafficante? In addition to reaffirming that intangible injury can satisfy Article III, Spokeo underscored that "because Congress is well positioned to identify intangible harms that meet minimum Article III requirements, its judgment is also instructive and important." On the other hand, Spokeo also emphasized that congressional grant of a statutory right and authorization to sue is not enough; concrete injury must also exist, although it allowed that in some circumstances the violation of statutory right alone is enough to create the requisite injury-in-fact. Would the actual denial of information on housing opportunities in Havens Realty suffice to provide standing under Spokeo, even though the tester had not actually wanted to rent an apartment?

Are there certain injuries that Congress cannot elevate to the level of potential injuries-in-fact sufficient for suit? The majority seems to say there are: "[N]ot all inaccuracies cause harm or present any material risk of harm. An example that comes readily to mind is an incorrect zip code. It is difficult to imagine how the dissemination of an incorrect zip code, without more, could work any concrete harm." But what if a plaintiff alleged that a reporting agency's dissemination of an incorrect zip code caused companies that had obtained information on her credit status, such as mortgage lenders or credit card companies, to send letters and solicitations to the wrong address? How much of a limit on Congress is the majority imposing in practice?

(4) **_Are Private Rights Different?_** Justice Thomas, relying on historical practice, would allow the mere violation of a statutorily granted private right to be adequate for suit. A number of scholars have emphasized that the "injury-in-fact requirement" was "historically unwarranted" in "cases alleging the violation of a private right. . . . Although the Court has claimed that its standing requirements are necessary to preserve the traditional limits on the judiciary, those requirements have precluded claims that courts historically would have permitted." ANDREW HESSICK, STANDING, INJURY IN FACT, AND PRIVATE RIGHTS, 93 CORNELL L. REV. 275, 277–78 (2008). Given that the majority also underscored the importance of historical practice to determining if standing exists, should it too have acknowledged that violation of a statutorily granted private right, absent more, satisfied the requirements of Article III?

On the other hand, many scholars dispute Justice Thomas' claim that individualized concrete injury was historically required to allow private individuals to enforce public rights. See Note 5, p. 1310; contra Woolander & Nelson, supra. Moreover, "for several decades in the middle of the [twentieth] century, Congress was allowed to authorize legal challenges to government action by parties whose only cognizable interest was just that: that the government abide by the law. . . . In its cases, the Supreme Court acknowledged that these parties had no legally cognizable injury—no legal rights—but it held nonetheless that Congress could authorize such parties to, as the Supreme Court itself said, bring the government's 'legal errors' to the attention of the federal courts 'on behalf of the public.'" ELIZABETH MAGILL, STANDING FOR THE PUBLIC: A LOST HISTORY, 95 Va. L. Rev. 1131, 1133 (2009). Should this mid-twentieth century approach count in assessing historical practice?

(5) *When Is an Alleged Injury Too Speculative to Qualify as Concrete?* As the challenged actions had occurred in Spokeo, the Court had no occasion to address when an alleged injury is sufficiently imminent and actual to satisfy Article III—although the majority noted that a "risk of real harm" can be adequate. Consider two recent decisions in which the Court has taken up this question. (A third decision on point, Summers v. Earth Island Institute, follows as the next main case.)

First, in CLAPPER V. AMNESTY INTERNATIONAL, INC., 568 U.S. 398 (2013), the Court by a 5–4 vote held that a group of attorneys, human rights organizations, and others lacked standing to challenge a provision of the Foreign Intelligence Surveillance Act (FISA), § 1881a, as violating the Fourth Amendment. The provision authorizes the Attorney General and the Director of National Intelligence to acquire foreign intelligence information by jointly authorizing the surveillance of individuals who are not "United States persons" and are reasonably believed to be located outside the United States, provided that (in most circumstances) they first obtain the Foreign Intelligence Surveillance Court's approval. The plaintiffs had alleged that their work required them to engage in communications with clients, sources, and others located abroad whom they believed were "likely to be targets of surveillance" under the provision; that the provision "compromised their ability to locate witnesses, cultivate sources, obtain information, and communicate confidential information to their clients"; and that they had stopped engaging in communications as a result. The Court held these to be "too speculative to satisfy the well-established requirement that threatened injury must be certainly impending." Quoting Lujan, the Court noted that "[a]lthough imminence is concededly a somewhat elastic concept, it cannot be stretched beyond its purpose, which is to ensure that the alleged injury is not too speculative for Article III purposes—that the injury is certainly impending." 504 U.S. at 565, n. 2. Here, "respondents' argument rests on their highly speculative fear that: (1) the Government will decide to target the communications of non-U.S. persons with whom they communicate; (2) in doing so, the Government will choose to invoke its authority under § 1881a rather than utilizing another method of surveillance; (3) the Article III judges who serve on the Foreign Intelligence Surveillance Court will conclude that the Government's proposed surveillance procedures satisfy § 1881a's many safeguards and are consistent with the Fourth Amendment; (4) the Government will succeed in intercepting the communications of respondents' contacts; and (5) respondents will be parties to the particular communications that the Government intercepts. . . . [R]espondents' theory of standing, which relies on a highly attenuated chain of possibilities, does not satisfy the requirement that threatened injury must be certainly impending."

The second decision, SUSAN B. ANTHONY LIST (SBA) V. DRIEHAUS, 134 S.Ct. 2334 (2014), was issued the next term. Congressman Driehaus filed a complaint with the Ohio Elections Commission alleging that SBA had violated an Ohio law that criminalizes certain false statements made during a political campaign. Driehaus based his complaint on SBA materials opposing his candidacy that stated his vote for the Affordable Care Act was a vote for "taxpayer funded abortion." The complaint was dismissed when Driehaus lost the election. However, SBA continued to pursue a separate suit in federal court challenging the law on First Amendment grounds. Both lower courts concluded the case was nonjusticiable, but the Supreme Court reversed, holding that SBA's pre-enforcement challenge to the Ohio law alleged sufficiently imminent injury for Article III purposes. JUSTICE THOMAS wrote for a unanimous Court: "First, petitioners have alleged 'an intention to engage in a course of conduct arguably affected with a constitutional interest' . . . [and] pleaded specific statements they intend to make in future election cycles. SBA has already stated that representatives who voted for the ACA supported 'taxpayer-funded abortion,' and it has alleged an 'inten[t] to engage in substantially similar activity in the future.' . . . Next, petitioners' intended future conduct is 'arguably. . . proscribed by [the] statute' they wish to challenge. . . . SBA's insistence that the allegations in its press release were true did not prevent the Commission panel from finding probably cause to believe that SBA had violated the law the first time around. And there is every reason to think that similar speech in the future will result in similar proceedings . . . . Finally, the threat of future enforcement of the false statement statute is substantial. . . . We have observed that past enforcement against the same conduct is good evidence that the threat of enforcement is not 'chimerical.' Here, the threat is even more substantial given that the Commission panel actually found probable cause to believe that SBA's speech violated the false statement statute." The facts that the Ohio statute allows "any person" to file a complaint with the Commission and that "[c]ommission proceedings are not a rare occurrence" bolsters the credibility of the threat.

In your view, can Clapper and SBA be reconciled? Are their different outcomes explained by the different facts involved and the greater certainty of eventual injury in SBA than in Clapper? Do you think the subject matters of the underlying lawsuits—national security surveillance and the First Amendment—played a role in some of the justices' views on whether sufficient injury-in-fact had been alleged? VICKI C. JACKSON, STANDING AND THE ROLE OF FEDERAL COURTS: TRIPLE ERROR DECISIONS IN CLAPPER V. AMNESTY INTERNATIONAL USA AND CITY OF LOS ANGELES V. LYONS, 23 Wm. & Mary Bill Rts. J. 127, 144 (2014): "It is because of the necessary secrecy of government operations to obtain foreign intelligence that the plaintiffs could not say, with absolute certainty, that they were being surveilled; only in unsuccessful covert surveillances could such a plaintiff emerge."

"Edward Snowden's disclosures of NSA metadata and mass data collection activities were first reported June 5, 2013, less than four months after Clapper came down." Do you think the Clapper Court would have reached the same result if the case were decided after Snowden's disclosures?

For that matter, could the result in Clapper have affected Snowden's decision to disclose? "The possible impact of the Clapper decision on Snowden's disclosures is suggested by the report that one of Snowden's first questions to his attorney . . . in July of 2013 was "Do you have standing now?" Id. 160 n. 132.

(3) Procedural Rights and Associational Standing

> *SUMMERS v. EARTH ISLAND*
>   *INSTITUTE*
> **Notes on Procedural Rights**
> **Notes on Associational Standing**

SUMMERS v. EARTH ISLAND INSTITUTE

Supreme Court of the United States (2009).
555 U.S. 488.

■ JUSTICE SCALIA delivered the opinion of the Court.

[The Forest Service Decisionmaking and Appeals Reform Act (Act) requires the Forest Service to establish a notice, comment, and appeal process for proposed Forest Service actions related to land and resource management plans. The Forest Service's regulations implementing the Act provided that certain activities, including "fire rehabilitation activities" and timber salvage sales prompted by "small" forest fires, would be categorically exempt from the notice, comment, and appeal process as well as from environmental impact assessment requirements. A group of environmental organizations sued to challenge the regulation exempting these sales as at odds with the Act. Standing initially rested on the affidavit of one organizational member who had hiked in a particular area of the Sequoia National Forest, the Burnt Ridge site, where a small fire had occurred and a timber sale was pending.]

[The affidavit alleged that the member] had repeatedly visited the Burnt Ridge site, that he had imminent plans to do so again, and that his interests in viewing the flora and fauna of the area would be harmed if the Burnt Ridge Project went forward without incorporation of the ideas he would have suggested if the Forest Service had provided him an opportunity to comment. The Government concedes this was sufficient to establish Article III standing with respect to Burnt Ridge. . . . After the District Court had issued a preliminary injunction, however, the parties settled their differences on that score . . . [and the member's] injury in fact with regard to that project has been remedied . . . We know of no precedent for the proposition that when a plaintiff has sued to challenge the lawfulness of certain action or threatened action but has settled that suit, he retains standing to challenge the basis for that action (here, the regulation in the abstract), apart from any concrete application that threatens imminent harm to his interests. . . .

Respondents have identified no other application of the invalidated regulations that threatens imminent and concrete harm to the interests of their members. The only other affidavit relied on was that of Jim Bensman, . . . which asserts that he has visited many National Forests and plans to visit several unnamed National Forests in the future. . . . [It fails] to allege that any particular timber sale or other project claimed to be unlawfully subject to the regulations will impede a specific and concrete plan of Bensman's to enjoy the National Forests. The National Forests occupy more than 190 million acres, an area larger than Texas. . . . [W]e are asked to assume not only that Bensman will stumble across a project tract unlawfully subject to the regulations, but also that the tract is about to be developed by the Forest Service in a way that harms his recreational interests, and that he would have commented on the project but for the regulation. Accepting an intention to visit the National Forests as adequate to confer standing to challenge any Government action affecting any portion of those forests would be tantamount to eliminating the requirement of concrete, particularized injury in fact. . . .

Respondents argue that they have standing to bring their challenge because they have suffered procedural injury, namely, that they have been denied the ability to file comments on some Forest Service actions and will continue to be so denied. But deprivation of a procedural right without some concrete interest that is affected by the deprivation—a procedural right in vacuo—is insufficient to create Article III standing. Only a "person who has been accorded a procedural right to protect his concrete interests can assert that right without meeting all the normal standards for redressability and immediacy." Lujan, 504 U.S., at 572, n. 7. . . .

It makes no difference that the procedural right has been accorded by Congress. That can loosen the strictures of the redressability prong of our standing inquiry—so that standing existed with regard to the Burnt Ridge Project, for example, despite the possibility that Earth Island's allegedly guaranteed right to comment would not be successful in persuading the Forest Service to avoid impairment of Earth Island's concrete interests. Unlike redressability, however, the requirement of injury in fact is a hard floor of Article III jurisdiction that cannot be removed by statute. . . .

The dissent proposes a hitherto unheard-of test for organizational standing: whether, accepting the organization's self-description of the activities of its members, there is a statistical probability that some of those members are threatened with concrete injury. . . . This novel approach to the law of organizational standing would make a mockery of our prior cases, which have required plaintiff-organizations to make specific allegations establishing that at least one identified member had suffered or would suffer harm. . . .

■ JUSTICE KENNEDY, concurring.

. . . This case would present different considerations if Congress had sought to provide redress for a concrete injury 'giv[ing] rise to a case or controversy where none existed before.' Lujan v. Defenders of Wildlife at 580 (Kennedy, J., concurring in part and concurring in judgment). Nothing in the statute at issue here, however, indicates Congress intended to identify or confer some interest separate and apart from a procedural right.

■ JUSTICE BREYER, with whom JUSTICES STEVENS, SOUTER, and GINSBURG join, dissenting.

. . . The majority assumes, as do I, that these unlawful Forest Service procedures will lead to substantive actions, namely the sales of salvage timber on burned lands, that might not take place if the proper procedures were followed. . . . How can the majority credibly claim that salvage-timber sales, and similar projects, are unlikely to harm the asserted interests of the members of these environmental groups? . . . The majority . . . argu[es] that the Forest Service actions are not "imminent"—a requirement more appropriately considered in the context of ripeness or the necessity of injunctive relief. I concede that the Court has sometimes used the word "imminent" in the context of constitutional standing. But it has done so primarily to emphasize that the harm in question . . . was merely "conjectural" or "hypothetical" or otherwise speculative. Where the Court has directly focused upon the matter, i.e., where, as here, a plaintiff has already been subject to the injury it wishes to challenge, the Court has asked whether there is a realistic likelihood that the challenged future conduct will, in fact, recur and harm the plaintiff. . . .

. . . [A] threat of future harm may be realistic even where the plaintiff cannot specify precise times, dates, and GPS coordinates. . . . The Forest Service admits that it intends to conduct thousands of further salvage-timber sales and other projects exempted under the challenged regulations "in the reasonably near future." How then can the Court deny that the plaintiffs have shown a "realistic" threat that the Forest Service will continue to authorize (without the procedures claimed necessary) salvage-timber sales, and other Forest Service projects, that adversely affect the recreational, esthetic, and environmental interests of the plaintiffs' members? Respondents allege, and the Government has conceded, that the Forest Service took wrongful actions (such as selling salvage timber) "thousands" of times in the two years prior to suit. . . . The Complaint alleges, and no one denies, that the organizations, the Sierra Club for example, have hundreds of thousands of members who use forests regularly across the Nation for recreational, scientific, esthetic, and environmental purposes. The Complaint further alleges, and no one denies, that these organizations (and their members), believing that actions such as salvage-timber sales harm those interests, regularly oppose salvage-timber sales (and similar actions) in proceedings before the agency. And the Complaint alleges, and no one denies, that the organizations intend to continue to express their opposition to such actions in those proceedings in the future. . . . The Bensman affidavit does not say which particular sites will be affected by future Forest Service projects, but the Service itself has conceded that it will conduct thousands of exempted projects in the future. Why is more specificity needed to show a "realistic" threat that a project will impact land Bensman uses? To know, virtually for certain, that snow will fall in New England this winter is not to know the name of each particular town where it is bound to arrive. The law of standing does not require the latter kind of specificity. . . .

[Justice Breyer criticized the Court's refusal to consider additional affidavits offered by the plaintiffs after judgment was entered below, after the Burnt Ridge challenge had settled and at the point when the government challenged their standing to continue with the case.] The affidavits in question describe a number of then-pending Forest Service projects, all excluded from notice, comment, and appeal under the Forest Service regulations and all scheduled to take place on parcels that the plaintiff organizations' members use. . . . The affidavits also describe, among other things, the frequency with which the organizations' members routinely file administrative appeals of salvage-timber sales and identify a number of proposed and pending projects that certain Sierra Club members wished to appeal. These allegations and affidavits more than adequately show a "realistic threat" of injury to plaintiffs brought about by reoccurrence of the challenged conduct—conduct that the Forest Service thinks lawful and admits will reoccur. Many years ago the Ninth Circuit warned that a court should not "be blind to what must be necessarily known to every intelligent person." In re Wo Lee, 26 F. 471, 475 (1886). Applying that standard, I would find standing here.

NOTES

(1) **What Would It Have Taken for Standing?** Suppose the Summers plaintiffs decided to file a new challenge to the Forest Service's exempting regulations. What facts would they need to allege to have standing? Do you think the affidavits they tried to submit after settling the Burnt Ridge dispute would suffice—and if so, should the Court then have accepted the new affidavits as a basis for standing?

For that matter, should the settlement of the Burnt Ridge timber sale been given the weight the majority gave it? If the Government had simply provided the procedures sought on its own initiative, thereby "mooting" the dispute, the Burnt Ridge challenge might still have been able to go forward under the exception to mootness for actions capable of repetition yet evading review. Is a settlement so different as to preclude any consideration of Burnt Ridge, even for purposes of standing analysis?

(2) **The Distinction Between Regulated Parties and Regulatory Beneficiaries.** The Court's reluctance to find standing in Summers seems

at first glance in sharp tension with its decision in SBA (p. 1331). In SBA the Court upheld standing, emphasizing—much like Justice Breyer's dissent in Summers—that the challenged governmental action had occurred in the past and that whether a plaintiff has already been subject to the injury it wishes to challenge gets substantial weight in assessing whether future injury is speculative. Can you square the two decisions?

One key difference between the two cases is that the plaintiff in SBA was a regulated party directly subject to enforcement for violations of Ohio's election laws whereas the plaintiffs in Summers were regulated beneficiaries. Recall that Lujan emphasized this factor in standing analysis (p. 1301). But does this distinction justify the different standing outcomes in these cases? After all, whether SBA would be subject to future enforcement depends on the actions of third parties who file complaints with Ohio's Election Commission, and the plaintiffs in Summers had hundreds of thousands of members who regularly use the national forests. Is the likelihood of future injury in Summers really more speculative? Moreover, what are the effects on regulatory programs if the courts draw such a distinction between regulation parties and regulatory beneficiaries?

NOTES ON PROCEDURAL RIGHTS

(1) ***Procedural Rights and Injury.*** In Summers, Congress had provided interested persons with a procedural right to comment on Forest Service actions, which according to the plaintiffs included the sales and rehabilitation activities related to small forest fires that the Forest Service had exempted. No doubt existed that the Forest Service was denying plaintiffs and others the ability to comment. According to Justice Scalia's majority opinion, the uncontroverted denial of plaintiffs' procedural right to comment was not enough to give them sufficient injury to sue: "[D]eprivation of a procedural right without some concrete interest that is affected by the deprivation—a procedural right in vacuo—is insufficient to create Article III standing."

But why not? As you now know, procedural rights abound in administrative law: rights to get notice, to be given information about what the agency considers relevant, to submit comments or present evidence, to get a statement of the agency's reasons, etc. Why create so many procedural rights, unless they are believed to be useful in affecting administrative behavior? Indeed, a field of political science scholarship, positive political theory, maintains that one of the central mechanisms by which Congress exerts control over the executive branch is by providing procedural rights. Among other things, these rights enable interest groups to try to influence agency decisionmaking and to monitor agency actions, raising "fire alarms" with members of Congress if they see anything amiss. (See Note 2, p. 823.)

In short, a good basis exists on which to conclude that even a "procedural right in vacuo" may well be valuable. Why then does Justice Scalia dismiss out of hand the possibility that violation of a procedural right alone could create sufficient injury to sue?

Equally important, how do we distinguish a statute that creates a "procedural right in vacuo" from one that also gives rise to substantive interests? Does 5 U.S.C. § 553's provision that agencies must provide notice and allow "interested persons" an opportunity to comment in rulemaking simply provide a "procedural right in vacuo," as the notice-and-comment requirement in Summers was held to do, or does it create more? Or what about 5 U.S.C. § 552(a)(3), providing that "upon . . . request," an agency shall make non-exempted records available to the person requesting?

(2) ***Real Procedural Rights vs. the General Interest in Government Obeying the Law.*** Perhaps the most prominent decision to reject standing based simply on an interest in enforcing a procedural right was Lujan (p. 1300), on which Summers relied. But are Summers and Lujan analogous in terms of the procedural rights at stake? Whatever its intended geographical scope, the ESA consultation requirement at issue in Lujan is, apparently, a completely internal executive branch process. The agencies involved were not required to allow interested persons to comment on the consultation process, as in Summers. Indeed, none of the agencies or officials involved in the ESA consultation process were required to produce an assessment, report, or other document for or about the consultation that was to be released for public review. (Compare the spending and contribution information required by the Federal Election Campaign Act in Akins, p. 1317).

This suggests that the problem in Lujan was not that "procedural" rights/injuries were involved but rather that *no* rights were involved—other than the "abstract, self-contained . . . right," Lujan, 504 U.S. at 573, long regarded as nonjusticiable, to have government obey the law? If so, does Summers go significantly beyond Lujan in holding that violation of a procedural right to comment alone is insufficient injury for standing? Or would allowing standing based simply on such a procedural right also risk opening up the courts to suits brought simply to ensure the government obeys the law?

(3) ***Procedural Rights and Redressability.*** Summers makes clear that procedural rights can ease the standing inquiry with respect to the redressability prong of standing analysis, so that if the plaintiffs had a separate concrete injury from a particular fire sale, they could claim that the ability to comment would adequately redress their injury notwithstanding that the Forest Service might have simply ignored their views. This use of procedural rights is discussed below in Section 1.c.2.

NOTES ON ASSOCIATIONAL STANDING

(1) ***Associational Standing and Probabilities.*** As you know from reading cases in this and other chapters, organizations often sue to challenge agency action or inaction. In such cases, the standing question is one of associational standing: HUNT V. WASHINGTON APPLE ADVERTISING COMM. 432 U.S. 333, 343 (1977): "[W]e have recognized that an association has standing to bring suit on behalf of its members when: (a) its members would otherwise have standing to sue in their own right; (b) the interests it seeks

to protect are germane to the organization's purpose; and (c) neither the claim asserted nor the relief requested requires the participation of individual members in the lawsuit."

What this means is that associational standing is derivative of the standing of the association's individual members. But as Summers demonstrates, that still leaves a question of how to determine the likelihood that one of an association's members has standing. Should the Court require evidence of harm to specific members, or should it be enough that the government acknowledges it is going to take a challenged action in the future and an organization has so many members that the odds are high one will be affected? Does Article III prohibit such a probabilistic approach? The issue of risk and probability of harm appears again when in assessing causation and redressability. See Sec. 1.c.

(2) *Sierra Club v. Morton and the Ideological Associational Plaintiff.* One of the earliest cases on associational standing in the regulatory context, SIERRA CLUB V. MORTON, 405 U.S. 727 (1972), involved a challenge to the Forest Service's decision to permit Walt Disney Enterprises to construct a year-round recreational facility in the theretofore pristine wilderness area of Mineral King Valley in the Sierra Nevada Mountains. Sierra Club sought to use the case to establish clear precedent for organizational standing to represent the public interest, and it deliberately avoided pleading facts—such as its founder John Muir's having a cabin in the affected area—that would have placed individual members personally in the pathway of environmental impact. Instead, the Club claimed that it had standing based on its "special interest in the conservation and the sound maintenance of the national parks, game refuges and forests of the country." In a 4–3 decision (two justices not participating), JUSTICE STEWART rejected the concept of an ideological plaintiff:

"[I]f a 'special interest' in this subject were enough to entitle the Sierra Club to commence this litigation, there would appear to be no objective basis upon which to disallow a suit by any other bona fide 'special interest' organization however small or short-lived. . . . The requirement that a party seeking review must allege facts showing that he is himself adversely affected . . . serve[s] as at least a rough attempt to put the decision as to whether review will be sought in the hands of those who have a direct stake in the outcome. That goal would be undermined were we to construe the APA to authorize judicial review at the behest of organizations or individuals who seek to do no more than vindicate their own value preferences through the judicial process. . . ." Justices Black, Brennan, and Douglas dissented.

Would a disappointed competitor of Walt Disney Enterprises, who had submitted a more modest development proposal, have standing to complain that the Forest Service decision inadequately protected the wilderness environment? How about a company that offered guided wilderness hiking tours through the area? Is the harm to Sierra Club's organizational commitments really so different from these economic injuries? For that matter, are any of these better plaintiffs than Sierra Club for reliably litigating the environmental issues raised by development of Mineral King? LOUIS L. JAFFE, THE CITIZEN AS LITIGANT IN PUBLIC ACTIONS: THE

NONHOHFELDIAN OR IDEOLOGICAL PLAINTIFF, 116 U. PA. L. REV. 1033, 1037–
38 (1968): "If it were thought that self-aggrandizement is a more dependable
motive than ideological interest, I would point out that it usually requires a
financial outlay to undertake a lawsuit. . . . But the very fact of investing
money in a lawsuit from which one is to acquire no further monetary profit
argues, to my mind, a quite exceptional kind of interest, and one peculiarly
indicative of a desire to say all that can be said in support of one's contention.
From this I would conclude that, insofar as the argument for a traditional
plaintiff runs in terms of the need for effective advocacy, the argument is not
persuasive." (Sierra Club ultimately got standing to challenge the Mineral
King project on remand, alleging the individual injuries of its members, but
as Summers demonstrates, that will not always be so easy.)

c.   Causation and Redressability in Regulatory Settings

> **(1) The Impact of Sanctions and
>   Incentives**
> **(2) Probabilities, Risk, and
>   Incrementalism**

The final constitutionally required elements of standing—causation
and redressability—are closely interlinked: if a challenged act causes a
plaintiff's injury, prohibiting the act will redress the harm. As with
injury, debates about the causation and redressability elements of
regulatory standing disproportionately affect beneficiary standing. The
causal chain between stopping the agency and stopping the injury will
usually be obvious for those whose conduct is being regulated. But is it
so clear that ordering the agency to regulate more vigorously the conduct
of, for example, polluting industries will stop the harm suffered by the
intended beneficiaries of the program? Recall Lujan's statement, p. 1301,
that when "a plaintiff's asserted injury arises from the government's
allegedly unlawful regulation (or lack of regulation) of someone else, . . .
causation and redressability ordinarily hinge on the response of the
regulated (or regulable) third party to the government action or
inaction—and perhaps on the response of others as well." Lujan suggests
that beneficiary standing should be curtailed as a result: "[W]hen the
plaintiff is not himself the object of the government action or inaction he
challenges, standing is not precluded, but it is ordinarily substantially
more difficult to establish." As you read the materials in this subsection,
consider whether this higher burden is actually justified, how difficult it
is in practice to meet, and the potential impact of such asymmetric
standing thresholds on regulatory policy.

Causation and redressability cases fall largely into two categories.
The first category concerns assessing the impact of sanctions and
incentives on the behavior of regulated parties. Suppose an agency acts
as a plaintiff wishes—enforces a statute more vigorously, for example.
Would regulated parties' behavior likely change, and how certain must a

court be that it would? The second category concerns contexts that are characterized by probabilities and incremental effects. How certain must a court be that an agency's action or inaction is contributing to the plaintiff's injury? Must the harm be entirely remediated, or is it enough that the plaintiff is somewhat better off? For that matter, must remediation be certain, or is a reasonable probability enough? Finally, a question underlying both categories is what should be the impact of congressional choices: Should courts defer to congressional assessments on the impact of certain policies or measures?

(1) The Impact of Sanctions and Incentives

> ### *ALLEN v. WRIGHT*

ALLEN v. WRIGHT

Supreme Court of the United States (1984).
468 U.S. 737.

■ JUSTICE O'CONNOR delivered the opinion of the Court.

[Allen was previously discussed in Note 1, p. 1311. As described there, the IRS had a formal policy of denying charitable tax-exempt status to racially discriminatory schools. (In Bob Jones Univ. v. United States, 461 U.S. 574 (1983), the Court held that this policy correctly interpreted the Internal Revenue Code.) Parents of African-American children attending public schools in districts undergoing court-ordered desegregation sued the IRS, seeking more vigorous enforcement of the policy. Unlike the situation in Lujan, Congress had not supplied a citizen suit provision through which to challenge the IRS's actions. While the case was pending, the IRS proposed new procedures to tighten its requirements for eligibility for tax-exempt status for private schools, but Congress blocked any strengthening of the IRS guidelines through an appropriations measure.[16]]

Respondents allege in their complaint that many racially segregated private schools were created or expanded in their communities at the time the public schools were undergoing desegregation. According to the complaint, many such private schools, including 17 schools or school systems identified by name in the complaint (perhaps some 30 schools in all), receive tax exemptions. . . . Respondents allege that . . . some of the tax-exempt racially segregated private schools created or expanded in desegregating districts in fact have racially discriminatory policies. . . .

---

[16] . . . Section 615 of the Treasury, Postal Service, and General Government Appropriations Act of 1980, 93 Stat. 562, 577, specifically forbade the use of funds to carry out the IRS's proposed procedures while Section 103 more generally forbade the use of funds to make the requirements for tax-exempt status of private schools more stringent than those in effect prior to the IRS's proposal of its new procedures. These provisions expired on October 1, 1980[, but Congress maintained similar limitations on funding for several years thereafter, though none was in force at the time of the Court's decision.]

Respondents allege that the challenged Government conduct harms them in two ways. The challenged conduct

(a) constitutes tangible federal financial aid and other support for racially segregated educational institutions, and

(b) fosters and encourages the organization, operation and expansion of institutions providing racially segregated educational opportunities for white children avoiding attendance in desegregating public school districts and thereby interferes with the efforts of federal courts, HEW and local school authorities to desegregate public school districts which have been operating racially dual school systems.

[Complaint at 38–39] Thus, respondents do not allege that their children have been the victims of discriminatory exclusion from the schools whose tax exemptions they challenge as unlawful. Indeed, they have not alleged at any stage of this litigation that their children have ever applied or would ever apply to any private school. Rather, respondents claim a direct injury from the mere fact of the challenged Government conduct and, as indicated by the restriction of the plaintiff class to parents of children in desegregating school districts, injury to their children's opportunity to receive a desegregated education. The latter injury is traceable to the IRS grant of tax exemptions to racially discriminatory schools, respondents allege, chiefly because contributions to such schools are deductible from income taxes . . . and the "deductions facilitate the raising of funds to organize new schools and expand existing schools in order to accommodate white students avoiding attendance in desegregating public school districts." . . .

. . . We conclude that neither [injury] suffices to support respondents' standing. The first fails . . . because it does not constitute judicially cognizable injury. The second fails because the alleged injury is not fairly traceable to the assertedly unlawful conduct of the IRS.[19]

1

[Justice O'Connor rejected respondents' first claim of injury essentially on generalized grievance grounds, emphasizing that only those personally denied equal treatment have standing to challenge racial discrimination. Otherwise, "standing would extend nationwide to all members of the particular racial groups against which the Government was alleged to be discriminating by its grant of a tax exemption to a racially discriminatory school, regardless of the location of that school. . . . A black person in Hawaii could challenge the grant of a tax exemption to a racially discriminatory school in Maine. Recognition

---

[19] The "fairly traceable" and "redressability" components of the constitutional standing inquiry were initially articulated by this Court as "two facets of a single causation requirement." C. Wright, Law of Federal Courts § 13, p. 68 n. 43 (4th ed. 1983). To the extent there is a difference, it is that the former examines the causal connection between the assertedly unlawful conduct and the alleged injury, whereas the latter examines the causal connection between the alleged injury and the judicial relief requested. . . .

of standing in such circumstances would transform the federal courts into 'no more than a vehicle for the vindication of the value interests of concerned bystanders.' United States v. SCRAP, 412 U.S. 669, 687 (1973)."]

2

It is in their complaint's second claim of injury that respondents allege harm to a concrete, personal interest that can support standing in some circumstances. The injury they identify—their children's diminished ability to receive an education in a racially integrated school—is, beyond any doubt, not only judicially cognizable but, as shown by cases from Brown v. Board of Educ., 347 U.S. 483 (1954), to Bob Jones Univ. v. United States, 461 U.S. 574 (1983), one of the most serious injuries recognized in our legal system. . . . [Here, however,] respondents' second claim of injury cannot support standing because the injury alleged is not fairly traceable to the Government conduct respondents challenge as unlawful.

The illegal conduct challenged by respondents is the IRS's grant of tax exemptions to some racially discriminatory schools. The line of causation between that conduct and desegregation of respondents' schools is attenuated at best. . . . The diminished ability of respondents' children to receive a desegregated education would be fairly traceable to unlawful IRS grants of tax exemptions only if there were enough racially discriminatory private schools receiving tax exemptions in respondents' communities for withdrawal of those exemptions to make an appreciable difference in public-school integration. Respondents have made no such allegation. It is, first, uncertain how many racially discriminatory private schools are in fact receiving tax exemptions. Moreover, it is entirely speculative, as respondents themselves conceded [below] . . . whether withdrawal of a tax exemption from any particular school would lead the school to change its policies. It is just as speculative whether any given parent of a child attending such a private school would decide to transfer the child to public school as a result of any changes in educational or financial policy made by the private school once it was threatened with loss of tax-exempt status. It is also pure speculation whether, in a particular community, a large enough number of the numerous relevant school officials and parents would reach decisions that collectively would have a significant impact on the racial composition of the public schools.

The links in the chain of causation between the challenged Government conduct and the asserted injury are far too weak for the chain as a whole to sustain respondents' standing. . . . The idea of separation of powers that underlies standing doctrine explains why our cases preclude the conclusion that respondents' alleged injury "fairly can be traced to the challenged action" of the IRS. Simon v. Eastern Kentucky Welfare Rights Org'n, 426 U.S. 26 (1984). That conclusion would pave the way generally for suits challenging, not specifically identifiable

Government violations of law, but the particular programs agencies establish to carry out their legal obligations. . . .

"When a plaintiff seeks to enjoin the activity of a government agency, even within a unitary court system, his case must contend with 'the well-established rule that the Government has traditionally been granted the widest latitude in the dispatch of its own internal affairs.' Cafeteria Workers v. McElroy, 367 U.S. 886, 896 (1961)." [Rizzo v. Goode, 423 U.S. 362, 378–79 (1976).]

. . . [T]hat principle, grounded as it is in the idea of separation of powers, counsels against recognizing standing in a case brought, not to enforce specific legal obligations whose violation works a direct harm, but to seek a restructuring of the apparatus established by the Executive Branch to fulfill its legal duties. The Constitution, after all, assigns to the Executive Branch, and not to the Judicial Branch, the duty to "take Care that the Laws be faithfully executed." U.S. Const., Art. II, § 3. We could not recognize respondents' standing in this case without running afoul of that structural principle.

. . . The judgment of the Court of Appeals is accordingly reversed, and the injunction issued by that court is vacated.

[Justice Marshall did not participate; Justice Brennan's dissenting opinion is omitted.]

■ JUSTICE STEVENS, with whom JUSTICE BLACKMUN joins, dissenting.

. . . An organization that qualifies for preferential treatment under § 501(c)(3) of the Internal Revenue Code, because it is "operated exclusively for . . . charitable . . . purposes," is exempt from paying federal income taxes, and [under § 170] persons who contribute to such organizations may deduct the amount of their contributions when calculating their taxable income. Only last Term [in Bob Jones, supra], we explained the effect of this preferential treatment:

> Both tax exemptions and tax-deductibility are a form of subsidy that is administered through the tax system. A tax exemption has much the same effect as a cash grant to the organization of the amount of tax it would have to pay on its income. Deductible contributions are similar to cash grants of the amount of a portion of the individual's contributions.

The purpose of this scheme, like the purpose of any subsidy, is to promote the activity subsidized . . . If the granting of preferential tax treatment would "encourage" private segregated schools to conduct their "charitable" activities, it must follow that the withdrawal of the treatment would "discourage" them. . . .

This causation analysis is nothing more than a restatement of elementary economics: when something becomes more expensive, less of it will be purchased. . . . [W]ithout tax exempt status, private schools will either not be competitive in terms of cost, or have to change their admissions policies, hence reducing their competitiveness for parents seeking "a racially segregated alternative" to public schools, which is what respondents have alleged many white parents in desegregating school districts seek. In either event the process of desegregation will be advanced . . . Thus, the laws of economics, not to mention the laws of Congress embodied in §§ 170 and 501(c)(3), compel the conclusion that the injury respondents have alleged—the increased segregation of their children's schools because of the ready availability of private schools that admit whites only—will be redressed if these schools' operations are inhibited through the denial of preferential tax treatment.

Considerations of tax policy, economics, and pure logic all confirm the conclusion that respondents' injury in fact is fairly traceable to the Government's allegedly wrongful conduct. The Court therefore is forced to introduce the concept of "separation of powers" into its analysis. . . . The Court could mean one of three things by its invocation of the separation of powers. First, it could simply be expressing the idea that if the plaintiff lacks Article III standing to bring a lawsuit, then there is no "case or controversy" within the meaning of Article III and hence the matter is not within the area of responsibility assigned to the Judiciary by the Constitution. . . . While there can be no quarrel with this proposition, in itself it provides no guidance for determining if the injury respondents have alleged is fairly traceable to the conduct they have challenged.

Second, the Court could be saying that it will require a more direct causal connection when it is troubled by the separation of powers implications of the case before it. That approach confuses the standing doctrine with the justiciability of the issues that respondents seek to raise. . . . If a plaintiff presents a nonjusticiable issue, or seeks relief that a court may not award, then its complaint should be dismissed for those reasons, and not because the plaintiff lacks a stake in obtaining that relief and hence has no standing. . . .

Third, the Court could be saying that it will not treat as legally cognizable injuries that stem from an administrative decision concerning how enforcement resources will be allocated. This surely is an important point. . . . The Executive requires latitude to decide how best to enforce the law, and in general the Court may well be correct that the exercise of that discretion, especially in the tax context, is unchallengeable.[1] However, as the Court also recognizes, this principle does not apply when suit is brought "to enforce specific legal obligations whose violation works a direct harm." . . . Here, respondents contend that the IRS is violating a specific constitutional limitation on its enforcement discretion. There is a solid basis for that contention. . . . Similarly, respondents claim that the Internal Revenue Code itself, as construed in Bob Jones, constrains enforcement discretion. . . . Surely the question whether the Constitution

---

[1] [Ed.] The following Term in Heckler v. Chaney, p. 1407, the Court held that an agency's decision not to take enforcement action is presumptively nonreviewable.

or the Code limits enforcement discretion is one within the Judiciary's competence. . . .

NOTES

(1) *Incentives and Causation.* Is there any real world doubt that the conditions legally attached to charitable tax-exempt status are designed to induce socially desirable behavior that would benefit people like the plaintiffs in Allen? Or, that as a matter of "elemental economics," as Justice Stevens put it, such financial incentives often will increase the likelihood of the desired behavior? Does it then follow that denial of these incentives through nonenforcement likely injures the purported beneficiaries? FRANK H. EASTERBROOK, FOREWORD: THE COURT AND THE ECONOMIC SYSTEM, 98 HARV. L. REV. 4, 40–41 (1984): "The [Allen] Court concludes that the plaintiffs, black parents and children in public schools who disclaimed interest in attending the bigoted private schools, were unaffected by the IRS's policies. . . . [I]t is hard to take seriously the claim that enforcement of legal rules does not affect bystanders. The rule against murder is designed to prevent other people from slaying me, as well as others, and I suffer an injury if the police announce that they will no longer enforce that rule in my neighborhood. I will keep off the streets, hire guards, pay for locks, and still face an increased chance of being killed. Only a judge who secretly believes that the law does not influence behavior would find no injury."

Similar instances of nonenforcement exist in other prominent cases where the Court has found causation lacking. SIMON V. EASTERN KENTUCKY WELFARE RIGHTS ORGANIZATION, 426 U.S. 26 (1984), cited in Allen, similarly involved tax incentives. When the IRS removed an existing requirement that hospitals wishing charitable tax-exempt status provide free care to indigents, low-income persons and organizations representing them sued, arguing that the new interpretation violated the Internal Revenue Code. Although the plaintiffs alleged "specific occasions on which each . . . sought but was denied hospital services solely due to his indigency" and that the IRS "had 'encouraged' hospitals to deny services to indigents [by removing the free care requirement.] . . . But it . . . is purely speculative whether the denials of service specified in the complaint fairly can be traced to petitioners' 'encouragement' or instead result from decisions made by the hospitals without regard to the tax implications. It is equally speculative whether the desired exercise of the court's remedial powers in this suit would result in the availability to respondents of such services. . . . [I]t is just as plausible that the hospitals to which respondents may apply for service would elect to forgo favorable tax treatment to avoid the undetermined financial drain of an increase in the level of uncompensated services."

Another precursor to Allen, LINDA R.S. V. RICHARD D., 410 U.S. 614 (1973), involved criminal penalties. Article 602 of the Texas Penal Code provided that "[a]ny parent who shall willfully desert, neglect or refuse to provide for the support and maintenance of his or her child . . . shall be guilty of a misdemeanor." Texas courts read the provision as applying only when the child's parents were married. The mother of a child born out of wedlock attempted to enjoin the local district attorney from refusing to prosecute the father of her child for support payments, arguing that the distinction between children born to married and unmarried parents violated the Equal Protection Clause. In a 5–4 decision written by JUSTICE MARSHALL, the Court held "that, in the unique context of a challenge to a criminal statute, appellant has failed to allege a sufficient nexus between her injury and the government action which she attacks to justify judicial intervention.... [She] has made no showing that her failure to secure support payments results from the nonenforcement, as to her child's father, of Art. 602. . . . On the contrary, if appellant were granted the requested relief, it would result only in the jailing of the child's father. The prospect that prosecution will, at least in the future, result in payment of support can, at best, be termed only speculative. . . . The Court's prior decisions consistently hold that a citizen lacks standing to contest the policies of the prosecuting authority when he himself is neither prosecuted nor threatened with prosecution. Although these cases arose in a somewhat different context, they demonstrate that, in American jurisprudence at least, a private citizen lacks a judicially cognizable interest in the prosecution or nonprosecution of another."

(2) ***Causation in Fact vs. Causation in Law.*** What might lead the Court to refuse to give legal effect to causal relationships that make intuitive sense empirically? In Linda R.S., Justice Marshall's opinion refers to "the special status of criminal prosecutions in our system" and the "unique context of a challenge to [the non-enforcement of] a criminal statute." (Note also, a *state* criminal statute—which added a federalism dimension; compare the presumption of unreviewability that applies to agency refusals to take enforcement action. See Heckler v. Chaney, p. 1407.) In Simon, Justice Stewart wrote separately, stating that he "could not now imagine a case, at least outside the First Amendment area, where a person whose own tax liability was not affected ever could have standing to litigate the federal tax liability of someone else." Are there not compelling policy justifications for judicial hesitation to open the proverbial floodgates to suits by victims unhappy with prosecutors' decisions not to prosecute (or to accept pleas for lesser offenses)? Or to suits complaining that someone else got better tax treatment than they deserved?

(3) ***Standing Causation and Proximate Causation.*** Does causation for standing purposes entail the same requirement of proximate causation that surfaces in common law actions alleging a loss, like a tort suit for damages? In BANK OF AMERICA V. CITY OF MIAMI, 137 S.Ct. 1296 (2017), discussed at greater length on p. 1279, the Supreme Court addressed this question in the context of a suit for damages under the Fair Housing Act (FHA). JUSTICE BREYER wrote for the Court in concluding that proximate causation is required under the FHA and "requires some direct relation between the injury asserted and the injurious conduct alleged. . . . 'Proximate-cause analysis is controlled by the nature of the statutory cause of action. The question it presents is whether the harm alleged has a sufficiently close connection to the conduct the statute prohibits.' Lexmark [Int'l v. Static Control Components, Inc., 134 S.Ct. 1377 (2014), p. 1368]."

Justice Breyer emphasized that "[w]e assume Congress is familiar with the common-law rule and does not mean to displace it sub silentio in federal causes of action. A claim for damages under the FHA—which is akin to a tort action—is no exception." However, what appeared to be driving the Court's causation holding was concern about the potential breadth of liability under the FHA if the test of causation were simply foreseeability: "In the context of the FHA, foreseeability alone does not ensure the close connection that proximate cause requires. The housing market is interconnected with economic and social life. A violation of the FHA may, therefore, be expected to cause ripples of harm to flow far beyond the defendant's misconduct. Nothing in the statute suggests that Congress intended to provide a remedy wherever those ripples travel. And entertaining suits to recover damages for any foreseeable result of an FHA violation would risk massive and complex damages litigation." Justice Thomas, joined by Justices Kennedy and Alito, concurred that foreseeability was not enough but disagreed with the Court's decision to remand for a causation determination, concluding that the City could not meet the requirement of proximate causation.

(4) **_Legislative Judgments about Causation and the Separation of Powers._** Neither Allen, Simon, or Linda R.S. involved statutes with a broad statutory standing and review provision. How much should it matter that Congress explicitly considered the issue of private enforcement and wrote a broad standing provision into a regulatory program's implementing architecture?

The Court stressed the presence of such a legislative judgment in FRIENDS OF THE EARTH (FOE) V. LAIDLAW ENVIRONMENTAL SERVICE, INC. 528 U.S. 167 (2000), also discussed above p. 1323, which involved an effort by FOE, an environmental organization, to seek civil penalties for a company's discharges of mercury in violation of the Clean Water Act. The company argued that because civil penalties are paid to the government, such penalties offer no redress to private plaintiffs and standing was lacking. Writing for the majority in a 5–4 decision, JUSTICE GINSBURG disagreed. "We have recognized on numerous occasions that all civil penalties have some deterrent effect. More specifically, Congress has found that civil penalties in Clean Water Act cases do more than promote immediate compliance by limiting the defendant's economic incentive to delay its attainment of permit limits; they also deter future violations. This congressional determination warrants judicial attention and respect. . . . It can scarcely be doubted that, for a plaintiff who is injured or faces the threat of future injury due to illegal conduct ongoing at the time of suit, a sanction that effectively abates that conduct and prevents its recurrence provides a form of redress. . . . [The dissent's argument that it is availability rather than imposition of civil penalties that deters continued pollution] overlooks the interdependence of the availability and the imposition; a threat has no deterrent value unless it is credible that it will be carried out. . . . A would-be polluter may or may not be dissuaded by the existence of a remedy on the books, but a defendant once hit in its pocketbook will surely think twice before polluting again." Acknowledging "that there may be a point at which the deterrent effect of a claim for civil penalties becomes so insubstantial or so remote that it cannot support citizen standing," the Court found that here "the civil penalties sought by FOE carried with them a deterrent effect that made it likely, as opposed to merely speculative, that the penalties would redress FOE's injuries by abating current violations and preventing future ones." The District Court had assessed a penalty of $405,800.

Was FOE's emphasis on congressional authorization of citizen suits for civil penalties appropriate? Dissenting, JUSTICE SCALIA maintained that "a plaintiff's desire to benefit from the deterrent effect of a public penalty for past conduct can never suffice to establish a case or controversy of the sort known to our law. Such deterrent effect is, so to speak, 'speculative as a matter of law.' Even if that were not so, however, the deterrent effect in the present case would surely be speculative as a matter of fact." Emphasizing that deterrence comes from fear of penalties for future pollution, Justice Scalia argued that the company's fear on this score was already "near the top of the graph," given that the Act was "regularly and notoriously enforced," the company had already been subject to public suit and state penalties for pollution. "The deterrence on which the plaintiffs must rely for standing in the present case is the marginal increase in Laidlaw's fear of future penalties that will be achieved by adding federal penalties for Laidlaw's past conduct. I cannot say for certain that this marginal increase is zero; but I can say for certain that it is entirely speculative whether it will make the difference between these plaintiffs' suffering injury in the future and these plaintiffs' going unharmed." Justice Scalia also invoked the Take Care Clause in arguing that allowing FOE to sue for civil penalties would unconstitutionally put public enforcement powers in private hands.

Should courts defer to congressional judgments on causality—at least so long as the statutory judgment is within the "outer limits" of plausibility—as the FOE majority did? Is there any reason why such judgments should not receive the same degree of deference—i.e., accepted so long as minimally rational—that the Court gives to other tactical choices Congress makes when structuring a regulatory program? After all, legislatures can redefine causation requirements in tort by, for example, removing certain defenses (e.g., assumption of the risk) or specifying how contributory negligence will be treated. Why can't they also redefine causation for standing purposes? Do the separation of powers concerns invoked by Justice O'Connor in her majority opinion in Allen, or the President's Take Care duty raised by Justice Scalia in his FOE dissent, justify not deferring to congressional judgments on causation specifically? Why? Recall Justice Kennedy's concurring opinion in Lujan: "In my view, Congress has the power to define injuries and articulate chains of causation that will give rise to a case or controversy where none existed before . . ." (emphasis added).

(5) **The Relationship Between Defining the Injury and Finding Causation.** To what extent could the difficulty in finding causation with respect to regulatory beneficiaries be solved by changing the definition of the injury at stake? GENE R. NICHOL, JR., RETHINKING STANDING, 72 Calif. L. Rev. 68, 79–81 (1984): "[Linda R.S. and Simon] demonstrate the ease with which the Court, by toying with the scope of the injury at issue, can raise or lower the redressability hurdle. . . . In Linda R.S., the Court refused jurisdiction because even a decree requiring nondiscriminatory enforcement would not ensure support. But why was obtaining the payment of child

support considered the relevant injury? The mother in Linda R.S. sought to be treated on an equal basis with married mothers. Her injury—denial of equal treatment—would undoubtedly have been redressed by an affirmative decree requiring enforcement of child support obligations against unmarried fathers. . . . The indigents in [Simon] had no objection to receiving hospital access, but the interest they asserted would more appropriately be described as having hospital decisions concerning the services offered to indigents accurately reflect an earlier incentive structure implicitly approved by the Congress. Again, that injury would have been redressed by the claim presented."

Is there any reason why the injuries in Linda R.S. and Simon can't be redefined in this way? Note that in challenges to affirmative action programs, the Court has defined the relevant injury as "the inability to compete on an equal footing" and thereby avoided the need to address whether the challengers would have gained admittance in the absence of the program. Northeastern Fla. Chap. of Assoc. Gen. Contractors v. Jacksonville, 508 U.S. 656, 666 (1993). Similarly, note that in tort contexts a decreased probability of benefit or increased probability of harm suffices for recovery.

(2) Probabilities, Risk, and Incrementalism

MASSACHUSETTS V. EPA, 549 U.S. 497 (2009), which you may already have encountered as a principal case in Chapter VIII, p. 1253, arose out of an effort by environmental organizations to get EPA to regulate greenhouse gas emissions from new motor vehicles. The groups petitioned EPA to undertake a rulemaking, arguing that greenhouse gas emissions constituted an air pollutant that EPA was required to regulate under the Clean Air Act. When EPA denied the petition, the groups sued, joined by a number of states and localities. The D.C. Circuit upheld EPA's refusal to regulate, but the Supreme Court reversed in a sharply contested 5–4 decision. Before reaching the merits, the Court rejected several challenges to the plaintiffs' standing.

In his majority opinion, JUSTICE STEVENS first rejected the claim that any injury from global warming was nonjusticiable because widely shared, emphasizing Massachusetts' status as a sovereign state (see p. 1355). He also held that petitioners' allegations of loss of Massachusetts coastline due to global warming sufficed to show the requisite injury-in-fact for standing: "According to petitioners' unchallenged affidavits, global sea levels rose somewhere between 10 and 20 centimeters over the 20th century as a result of global warming. These rising seas have already begun to swallow Massachusetts' coastal land. . . . The severity of that injury will only increase over the course of the next century," with "a significant fraction of coastal property" predicted to be permanently or temporarily lost through inundation and flooding, imposing significant remediation costs on the state. Justice Stevens then turned to the questions of causation and redressability:

"EPA does not dispute the existence of a causal connection between man-made greenhouse gas emissions and global warming. At a minimum, therefore, EPA's refusal to regulate such emissions 'contributes' to Massachusetts' injuries. EPA nevertheless maintains that its decision not to regulate greenhouse gas emissions from new motor vehicles contributes so insignificantly to petitioners' injuries that the agency cannot be haled into federal court to answer for them. For the same reason, EPA does not believe that any realistic possibility exists that the relief petitioners seek would mitigate global climate change and remedy their injuries. That is especially so because predicted increases in greenhouse gas emissions from developing nations, particularly China and India, are likely to offset any marginal domestic decrease.

"But EPA overstates its case. Its argument rests on the erroneous assumption that a small incremental step, because it is incremental, can never be attacked in a federal judicial forum. Yet accepting that premise would doom most challenges to regulatory action. Agencies, like legislatures, do not generally resolve massive problems in one fell regulatory swoop. See Williamson v. Lee Optical, 348 U.S. 483, 489 (1955) ('[A] reform may take one step at a time, addressing itself to the phase of the problem which seems most acute to the legislative mind'). They instead whittle away at them over time, refining their preferred approach as circumstances change and as they develop a more-nuanced understanding of how best to proceed.

"And reducing domestic automobile emissions is hardly a tentative step. Even leaving aside the other greenhouse gases, the United States transportation sector emits an enormous quantity of carbon dioxide into the atmosphere—according to the MacCracken affidavit, more than 1.7 billion metric tons in 1999 alone. That accounts for more than 6% of worldwide carbon dioxide emissions. To put this in perspective: Considering just emissions from the transportation sector, which represent less than one-third of this country's total carbon dioxide emissions, the United States would still rank as the third-largest emitter of carbon dioxide in the world, outpaced only by the European Union and China. Judged by any standard, U.S. motor-vehicle emissions make a meaningful contribution to greenhouse gas concentrations and hence, according to petitioners, to global warming. . . .

"While it may be true that regulating motor-vehicle emissions will not by itself reverse global warming, it by no means follows that we lack jurisdiction to decide whether EPA has a duty to take steps to slow or reduce it. . . . Because of the enormity of the potential consequences associated with man-made climate change, the fact that the effectiveness of a remedy might be delayed during the (relatively short) time it takes for a new motor-vehicle fleet to replace an older one is essentially irrelevant. Nor is it dispositive that developing countries such as China and India are poised to increase greenhouse gas emissions substantially over the next century: A reduction in domestic emissions would slow the pace of global emissions increases, no matter what happens elsewhere. . . .

"In sum—at least according to petitioners' uncontested affidavits—the rise in sea levels associated with global warming has already harmed and will continue to harm Massachusetts. The risk of catastrophic harm, though remote, is nevertheless real. That risk would be reduced to some extent if petitioners received the relief they seek. We therefore hold that petitioners have standing to challenge the EPA's denial of their rulemaking petition."

CHIEF JUSTICE ROBERTS, joined by Justices Scalia, Thomas, and Alito, strongly dissented from the majority's conclusion that standing requirements were met. In addition to arguing that global warming was almost by definition a generalized grievance, the Chief Justice argued that Massachusetts' sovereign status was irrelevant to the standing inquiry and any "inference of actual loss of Massachusetts coastal land [was] . . . pure conjecture," complaining that "accepting a century-long time horizon and a series of compounded estimates renders requirements of imminence and immediacy utterly toothless." Roberts further insisted that the requisite causality and redressability were lacking:

"Petitioners' reliance on Massachusetts's loss of coastal land as their injury in fact for standing purposes creates insurmountable problems for them with respect to causation and redressability. . . . First, it is important to recognize the extent of the emissions at issue here. Because local greenhouse gas emissions disperse throughout the atmosphere and remain there for anywhere from 50 to 200 years, it is global emissions data that are relevant. According to one of petitioners' declarations, domestic motor vehicles contribute about 6 percent of global carbon dioxide emissions and 4 percent of global greenhouse gas emissions. The amount of global emissions at issue here is smaller still; § 202(a)(1) of the Clean Air Act covers only new motor vehicles and new motor vehicle engines, so petitioners' desired emission standards might reduce only a fraction of 4 percent of global emissions.

"This gets us only to the relevant greenhouse gas emissions; linking them to global warming and ultimately to petitioners' alleged injuries next requires consideration of further complexities. As EPA explained in its denial of petitioners' request for rulemaking,

> predicting future climate change necessarily involves a complex web of economic and physical factors including: our ability to predict future global anthropogenic emissions of [greenhouse gases] and aerosols; the fate of these emissions once they enter the atmosphere (e.g., what percentage are absorbed by vegetation or are taken up by the oceans); the impact of those emissions that remain in the atmosphere on the radiative properties of the atmosphere; changes in critically important climate feedbacks (e.g., changes in cloud cover and ocean circulation); changes in temperature characteristics (e.g.,

average temperatures, shifts in daytime and evening temperatures); changes in other climatic parameters (e.g., shifts in precipitation, storms); and ultimately the impact of such changes on human health and welfare (e.g., increases or decreases in agricultural productivity, human health impacts).

"Petitioners are never able to trace their alleged injuries back through this complex web to the fractional amount of global emissions that might have been limited with EPA standards. In light of the bit-part domestic new motor vehicle greenhouse gas emissions have played in what petitioners describe as a 150-year global phenomenon, and the myriad additional factors bearing on petitioners' alleged injury—the loss of Massachusetts coastal land—the connection is far too speculative to establish causation.

"Redressability is even more problematic. To the tenuous link between petitioners' alleged injury and the indeterminate fractional domestic emissions at issue here, add the fact that petitioners cannot meaningfully predict what will come of the 80 percent of global greenhouse gas emissions that originate outside the United States. As the Court acknowledges, 'developing countries such as China and India are poised to increase greenhouse gas emissions substantially over the next century,' so the domestic emissions at issue here may become an increasingly marginal portion of global emissions, and any decreases produced by petitioners' desired standards are likely to be overwhelmed many times over by emissions increases elsewhere in the world. . . . No matter, the Court reasons, because any decrease in domestic emissions will 'slow the pace of global emissions increases, no matter what happens elsewhere.' Every little bit helps, so Massachusetts can sue over any little bit.

"The Court's sleight-of-hand is in failing to link up the different elements of the three-part standing test. What must be likely to be redressed is the particular injury in fact. The injury the Court looks to is the asserted loss of land. The Court contends that regulating domestic motor vehicle emissions will reduce carbon dioxide in the atmosphere, and therefore redress Massachusetts's injury. But even if regulation does reduce emissions—to some indeterminate degree, given events elsewhere in the world—the Court never explains why that makes it likely that the injury in fact—the loss of land—will be redressed."

NOTES

(1) *Big Problems and Incrementalism.* Who has the better of the argument on causation and redressability, the majority or the dissent? Justice Stevens' opinion adopts an approach to causation and redressability calibrated to the size and complexity of the problem of global warming: Because the problem is so large and multi-faceted, anything EPA could do would necessarily be incremental and partial—but the agency contributes to the problem's continuation by not using *whatever* power it has to abate global

warming. Chief Justice Roberts' opinion agrees with the size and complexity of the problem of global warming but draws the opposite conclusion: Global warming is a problem too big to be justiciable; nothing EPA could do would make any appreciable change that would palpably benefit any individual or entity over any reasonably imminent timeframe. This kind of problem is a political, not a judicial, question.

Either view seems plausible. Can you select between them without referring to some normative theory about the appropriateness of centralized regulatory government and the roles and relationships among Congress, the President, and the courts? What are the implications of requiring more than some incremental benefit, given the multi-causal, complex, and often global nature of many major policy issues today?

(2) **Specific or General Causal Chains.** Is the Chief Justice correct to require a tight connection between the alleged injury and the specific action challenged, namely Massachusetts' loss of coastline and EPA's failure to regulate greenhouse gas emissions from new motor vehicles? Or, given that global warming has multiple causes, is it enough to show that Massachusetts will likely lose coastline due to global warming and that greenhouse gas emissions from new motor vehicles contribute to global warming, without showing any more specific connection between the two?

(3) **The Role of Probability in Standing Analysis.** Note that probability factors into the standing analysis in Massachusetts in several ways. Two involve causation and redressability, specifically the probability that EPA's failure to regulate greenhouse gas emissions caused Massachusetts' injury and the probability that EPA's undertaking such regulation will remedy that injury. But probability also surfaces in the disagreement between the majority and dissent over whether Massachusetts has suffered a sufficiently imminent injury. According to Justice Stevens, given that "the harms associated with climate change are serious and well recognized," including rising sea levels, the plaintiffs' allegations of loss of coastline over the next century was sufficiently likely; to Chief Justice Roberts, it was "pure conjecture" and made the imminence inquiry "utterly toothless." This debate echoes other disagreements over whether allegations of injury are too speculative, such as those in Summers (p. 1332), Clapper (p. 1330), and SBA (p. 1331), all of which involve assessments of the probability and imminence of injury.

(4) **Redressability,   Probability,   and   Procedural   Rights.**   In Massachusetts, the Court cited Lujan for the proposition that the presence of a procedural right can ease the redressability prong analysis for standing: "a litigant to whom Congress has 'accorded a procedural right to protect his concrete interests'—here, the right to challenge agency action unlawfully withheld, § 7607(b)(1)—'can assert that right without meeting all the normal standards for redressability and immediacy.' When a litigant is vested with a procedural right, that litigant has standing if there is some possibility that the requested relief will prompt the injury-causing party to reconsider the decision that allegedly harmed the litigant." 549 U.S. at 517–18; see also Summers (p. 1332) to the same effect. But if these normal standards for

redressability and immediacy are core Article III standing requirements, how can they be dispensable in the case of procedural rights?

The classic redressability problem with procedural rights is the inability to predict, with any degree of confidence, whether procedural regularity would yield the regulatory outcome *on the merits* desired by the plaintiff—here, whether even a properly focused EPA decision would ultimately produce a global warming regulation. But isn't there yet another level of uncertainty in this case: namely, whether the plaintiff's harm would be remediated *even if it obtains the desired regulatory outcome on the merits*? This is the level at which Chief Justice Roberts attacks the majority's finding of standing. Note that his attack assumes that the substantive harm grounding Massachusetts' standing claim is the loss *in fact* of its shoreline land. By contrast, the majority seems to conceptualize the injury as EPA's failure to *decrease the probability* of such a loss. If the disagreement between majority and dissent is really part of the larger debate about how to frame the injury from under-regulation (see Note 5, p. 1348), then is the discussion of "procedural rights" a red herring?

According to RICHARD J. PIERCE, JR., MAKING SENSE OF PROCEDURAL INJURY, 62 Admin. L. Rev. 1, 2–3 (2010), after Lujan "circuit court opinions fall in two categories with respect to the nature of the causal relationship they require between the omitted procedure and a substantive result that is unfavorable to the petitioner. In many cases, a petitioner prevails by alleging only that it was unlawfully deprived of a procedural right that might plausibly have changed the outcome of a substantive dispute. In other cases, however, a petitioner loses because a court concludes that it did not demonstrate that 'it is substantially probable that the procedural breach will cause the essential injury to the plaintiff's own interest.' The choice of the causal test to apply is outcome determinative. When a court applies the plausibility standard, it holds that the petitioner has standing because it is almost always plausible that provision of a procedural safeguard will change the outcome of a case. Conversely, when a court applies the probability standard, it holds that the petitioner lacks standing because it is usually impossible to prove that provision of a procedural safeguard will probably change the outcome." Professor Pierce advocates for use of the plausibility test, arguing that given this impossibility, the probability approach "devalue[s] the procedures required by the Constitution and by statutes by encouraging agencies to deny procedural safeguards in all close cases."

d. Governmental Standing

Up to now, we've focused on suits brought by private individuals and organizations. But what about when governments are plaintiffs? Do the same standing rules apply? Should they? The question of governmental standing has arisen recently with a significant expansion in suits by states challenging national administrative action. This expansion reflects the dramatic political polarization that divides the country, with red states repeatedly challenging Obama Administration actions and blue states likely to do the same under the Trump Administration. See

Jessica Bulman-Pozen, *Partisan Federalism*, 127 Harv. L. Rev. 1077 (2014).

(1) *Massachusetts and State Standing.* As noted above p. 1349, in MASSACHUSETTS V. EPA, 549 U.S. 497 (2007), JUSTICE STEVENS' majority opinion emphasized Massachusetts' state status as a reason for granting standing: "We stress here . . . the special position and interest of Massachusetts. It is of considerable relevance that the party seeking review here is a sovereign State and not, as it was in Lujan, a private individual. Well before the creation of the modern administrative state, we recognized that States are not normal litigants for the purposes of invoking federal jurisdiction. . . . Georgia v. Tennessee Copper Co., 206 U.S. 230, 237 (1907), [was] a case in which Georgia sought to protect its citizens from air pollution originating outside its borders. . . . Just as Georgia's 'independent interest . . . in all the earth and air within its domain' supported federal jurisdiction a century ago, so too does Massachusetts' well-founded desire to preserve its sovereign territory today. That Massachusetts does in fact own a great deal of the 'territory alleged to be affected' only reinforces the conclusion that its stake in the outcome of this case is sufficiently concrete to warrant the exercise of federal judicial power.

"When a State enters the Union, it surrenders certain sovereign prerogatives. Massachusetts cannot invade Rhode Island to force reductions in greenhouse gas emissions, it cannot negotiate an emissions treaty with China or India, and in some circumstances the exercise of its police powers to reduce in-state motor-vehicle emissions might well be pre-empted. . . . These sovereign prerogatives are now lodged in the Federal Government, and Congress has ordered EPA to protect Massachusetts (among others) by prescribing standards applicable to the 'emission of any air pollutant from any class or classes of new motor vehicle engines, which in [the Administrator's] judgment cause, or contribute to, air pollution which may reasonably be anticipated to endanger public health or welfare.' 42 U.S.C. § 7521(a)(1). Congress has moreover recognized a concomitant procedural right to challenge the rejection of its rulemaking petition as arbitrary and capricious. § 7607(b)(1). Given that procedural right and Massachusetts' stake in protecting its quasi-sovereign interests, the Commonwealth is entitled to special solicitude in our standing analysis."

According to CHIEF JUSTICE ROBERTS in dissent, however, Massachusetts' status as a state was entirely irrelevant to the case: "Relaxing Article III standing requirements because asserted injuries are pressed by a State . . . has no basis in our jurisprudence, and support for any such 'special solicitude' is conspicuously absent from the Court's opinion. The general judicial review provision cited by the Court, 42 U.S.C. § 7607(b)(1), affords States no special rights or status. . . . Congress knows how to do that when it wants to, see, e.g., § 7426(b) (affording States the right to petition EPA to directly regulate certain sources of pollution), but it has done nothing of the sort here. Under the law on which petitioners rely, Congress treated public and private litigants exactly the same.

"Nor does the case law cited by the Court provide any support for the notion that Article III somehow implicitly treats public and private litigants differently. . . . Tennessee Copper [stands] for nothing more than a State's right, in an original jurisdiction action, to sue in a representative capacity as parens patriae. Nothing about a State's ability to sue in that capacity dilutes the bedrock requirement of showing injury, causation, and redressability to satisfy Article III. A claim of parens patriae standing is distinct from an allegation of direct injury. Far from being a substitute for Article III injury, parens patriae actions raise an additional hurdle for a state litigant: the articulation of a 'quasi-sovereign interest' apart from the interests of particular private parties. Just as an association suing on behalf of its members must show not only that it represents the members but that at least one satisfies Article III requirements, so too a State asserting quasi-sovereign interests as parens patriae must still show that its citizens satisfy Article III. Focusing on Massachusetts's interests as quasi-sovereign makes the required showing here harder, not easier."

Even supposing special solicitude for the states is justified, what does it mean? After invoking it, the majority opinion proceeded to invoke the tripartite injury-causation-redressability framework of Lujan and to find standing based on Massachusetts' loss of coastline, a loss to which the majority found EPA's failure to regulate greenhouse gas emissions from new motor vehicles contributed and targeting this failure would redress. The Court also applied the Lujan tripartite framework in a suit brought by the Arizona State Legislature. Arizona State Legislature v. Arizona Independent Redistricting Commission, 135 S.Ct. 2652, 2662–63 (2015). Special solicitude for the states thus does not appear to mean application of a different analytic framework. It might mean, however, that the standard framework is applied more leniently.

(2) *Should States Get Special Solicitude in Standing Analysis?* Is a different or more lenient standing analysis for states justified? Does it matter what claim the states might be raising? See TARA LEIGH GROVE, WHEN CAN A STATE SUE THE UNITED STATES?, 101 Cornell L. Rev. 851 (2016): "States are entitled to 'special solicitude' in the standing analysis in only one context: when they seek to enforce or defend state law. . . . States have broad standing to challenge federal statutes and regulations that preempt, or otherwise undermine the continued enforceability of, state law. But States do not have a special interest in the manner in which the federal executive enforces federal law. . . . In sum, I argue that States have broad standing to protect federalism principles, not the constitutional separation of powers." By contrast, GILLIAN E. METZGER, FEDERALISM AND FEDERAL AGENCY REFORM, 111 Colum. L. Rev. 1 (2011), argues in favor of assigning states a special role in policing federal

agencies. "[T]he delegation of extensive policymaking responsibilities to agencies eviscerates the political checks traditionally relied upon to defend state interests. On this account, ensuring states access to federal court to challenge federal administrative action is necessary to preserve constitutional federalism in the administrative era." But noting that "[a]llowing states greater access to challenge federal agency policy and functioning in federal court . . . would entail potentially significant trumping of . . . separation of powers concerns in the name of federalism," Metzger argues that the courts should focus on whether "Congress . . . [has] assign[ed] states a special role in particular federal regulatory schemes" instead of undertaking that assignment on judicial initiative alone.

(3) *Congressional Standing.* Does a different analysis apply to suits by Congress? The question of whether Congress, the House and Senate respectively, or members of Congress have standing to challenge alleged executive branch failure to follow the law has surfaced periodically, often closely tied to the question of whether such a suit represents a nonjusticiable political question.

In RAINES V. BYRD, 521 U.S 811 (1996), six members of Congress sued to challenge the Line Item Veto Act as unconstitutionally altering the effect of their votes on legislation subject to the Act and undermining the constitutional separation of powers. Although the Act expressly provided for just such a suit, the Court found that the members of Congress lacked Article III standing because they failed to establish a "personal, particularized, concrete, and otherwise judicially cognizable" injury: "[They] have not been singled out for specially unfavorable treatment as opposed to other Members of their respective bodies. Their claim is that the Act causes a type of institutional injury (the diminution of legislative power), which necessarily damages all Members of Congress and both Houses of Congress equally." In so holding, the Court distinguished two precedents: Powell v. McCormack, 395 U.S. 486 (1969), in which the Court had held that Congressman Adam Clayton Powell could sue to challenge his exclusion from the House of Representatives, and Coleman v. Miller, 307 U.S. 433 (1939), which found that twenty members of the Kansas Senate, who had voted against a proposed amendment to the U.S. Constitution banning child labor, had standing to challenge the inclusion of the Lieutenant Governor's vote. According to the Raines Court, Powell represented a case where a member was specially signaled out and denied something to which he was personally entitled, whereas Coleman stood "(at most, . . .) for the proposition that legislators whose votes would have been sufficient to defeat (or enact) a specific legislative Act have standing to sue if that legislative action goes into effect (or does not go into effect), on the ground that their votes have been completely nullified." (Although not emphasized in Raines, it is worth noting that Coleman proceeded to find that the senators' challenge was a nonjusticiable political question.)

At the same time, both the House and Senate and their committees have long asserted the power to sue in an official capacity to demand information from the executive branch in furtherance of Congress's oversight role, and courts have long held they have standing to do so. See, e.g., United States v. AT&T, 551 F.2d 384 (D.C.Cir. 1976); Comm. on Oversight and Gov. Reform v. Holder, 979 F.Supp.2d 1, 4 (D.D.C. 2013).

(4) ***Congressional Standing to Challenge Executive Branch Nondefense and Nonexecution.*** As is true with respect to state standing, congressional standing has risen to the fore of late, a result of intense political disagreement between the Democratic and Republican parties and each party controlling at least one of the major political branches.

In UNITED STATES V. WINDSOR, 133 S.Ct. 2675 (2013), also discussed in Note 4 p. 1309, the Bipartisan Legal Advisory Group (BLAG), composed of the leaders of the House and the Senate, sought to challenge the Obama Administration's refusal to defend § 3 of the Defense of Marriage Act. Concluding that the United States government had standing to appeal the lower courts' decisions holding § 3 unconstitutional, despite agreeing with that result, a majority of the Supreme Court never reached the question of BLAG's standing. Justice Alito wrote separately, dissenting from the Court's determination that § 3 was unconstitutional and holding that BLAG had standing. In so holding, Justice Alito drew on Coleman and on INS v. Chadha, 462 U.S. 919 (1983) (p. 831) where the Court had allowed the House and the Senate to intervene to defend the constitutionality of the legislative veto in the face of executive nondefense. According to Justice Alito, just as the invalidation of the one-house legislative veto impaired Congress's power, so too invalidation of § 3 "impairs Congress' legislative power by striking down an Act of Congress." Also dissenting, Justice Scalia disagreed with Justice Alito on this score, arguing that allowing "Congress . . . [to] hale the Executive before the courts not only to vindicate its own institutional powers to act, but to correct a perceived inadequacy in the execution of its laws" would unconstitutionally expand the role of the courts. Instead, Congress's "only recourse is to confront the President directly. . . . If majorities in both Houses of Congress care enough about the matter, they have available innumerable ways to compel executive action without a lawsuit."

Subsequent to Windsor, the Court by a 5–4 vote found legislative standing in a case involving a state legislature's constitutional attack on an enacted citizen's initiative that transferred redistricting authority form the legislature to an independent commission. ARIZONA STATE LEGISLATURE V. ARIZONA INDEPENDENT REDISTRICTING COMMISSION, 135 S.Ct. 2652 (2015). The majority, written by Justice

Ginsburg, found Coleman "closer to the mark than Raines, because the effect of the initiative was to "completely nullify any vote by the Legislature, now or in the future, purporting to adopt a redistricting plan." 135 S.Ct. at 2665. However, the Court emphasized that "[t]he case before us does not touch or concern the question whether Congress has standing to bring a suit against the President." Id. at 2665 n. 12. Chief Justice Roberts and Justices Scalia, Thomas, and Alito would not have found standing.

A third major dispute over congressional standing recently arose with respect to the Affordable Care Act (ACA). In 2014, the House of Representatives passed a resolution that authorized Speaker John Boehner to sue President Obama claiming unconstitutional abuse of power in connection with unilateral executive action to implement the Act. All but five Republicans and no Democrats voted for the resolution. The resulting lawsuit—U.S. HOUSE OF REPRESENTATIVES V. BURWELL, 130 F.Supp.3d 53 (D.D.C. 2015), naming the Secretaries of HHS and Treasury as defendants rather than the President—challenged both the administration's delay of the effective date of the ACA's employer mandate and the payment of cost-sharing reduction payments to insurers allegedly without congressional appropriation. The District Court held that the House had standing to assert its claim that the executive branch's actions violated the Appropriations Clause. Relying on Coleman and Arizona State Legislature to distinguish Raines, the District Court emphasized that here "the House of Representatives as an institution is the plaintiff" and "because the House occupies a unique role in the appropriations process prescribed by the Constitution, . . . perversion of that process inflicts on the House a particular injury." The District Court rejected the House's further claim of standing to challenge the executive branch's failure to implement the ACA, and thus the House could not challenge the delay of the employer mandate. Subsequently, the District Court ruled on the merits that the government's payment of cost-sharing reduction payments violated the Appropriations Clause. U.S. House of Representatives v. Burwell, 130 F.Supp.3d 53 (D.D.C. 2016). Although the Obama Administration appealed, among other points challenging the court's decision that the House had standing, the D.C. Circuit had not heard the appeal before President Trump took office. The D.C. Circuit granted the House of Representatives' motion to hold the appeal in abeyance and also allowed several states to intervene. The case was still pending when this edition went to press.

e. Standing Under the APA

> NCUA v. FIRST NAT'L BANK & TRUST

A person suffering legal wrong because of agency action, or adversely affected or aggrieved by agency action within the meaning of a relevant statute, is entitled to judicial review thereof.

5 U.S.C. § 702

NATIONAL CREDIT UNION ADMIN. (NCUA) v. FIRST NAT'L BANK & TRUST CO.

Supreme Court of the United States (1998).
522 U.S. 479.

■ JUSTICE THOMAS delivered the opinion of the Court. . . .[2]

Section 109 of the Federal Credit Union Act (FCUA), 48 Stat. 1219, 12 U.S.C. § 1759, provides that "[f]ederal credit union membership shall be limited to groups having a common bond of occupation or association, or to groups within a well-defined neighborhood, community, or rural district." Since 1982, the National Credit Union Administration (NCUA), the agency charged with administering the FCUA, has interpreted § 109 to permit federal credit unions to be composed of multiple unrelated employer groups, each having its own common bond of occupation. In this action, respondents, five banks and the American Bankers Association, have challenged this interpretation on the ground that § 109 unambiguously requires that the *same* common bond of occupation unite every member of an occupationally defined federal credit union. . . .

II

Respondents claim a right to judicial review of the NCUA's chartering decision under § 10(a) of the APA [§ 702, above] . . . We have interpreted § 10(a) of the APA to impose a prudential standing requirement in addition to the requirement, imposed by Article III of the Constitution, that a plaintiff have suffered a sufficient injury in fact. See, e.g., Association of Data Processing Service Organizations, Inc. v. Camp, 397 U.S. 150, 152 (1970) (Data Processing). For a plaintiff to have prudential standing under the APA, "the interest sought to be protected by the complainant [must be] arguably within the zone of interests to be protected or regulated by the statute . . . in question." *Id.*, at 153. . . .

Although our prior cases have not stated a clear rule for determining when a plaintiff's interest is "arguably within the zone of interests" to be protected by a statute, they nonetheless establish that we should not inquire whether there has been a congressional intent to benefit the would-be plaintiff. In Data Processing, . . . the Office of the Comptroller

---

[2]   [Ed.] Justice Thomas' opinion was the opinion of the Court except for footnote 6, which Justice Scalia did not join and which examined the legislative history of § 109.

of the Currency (Comptroller) had interpreted the National Bank Act's incidental powers clause . . . to permit national banks to perform data processing services for other banks and bank customers. . . . The plaintiffs, a data processing corporation and its trade association, alleged that this interpretation was impermissible . . . . In holding that the plaintiffs had standing [in Data Processing], we stated that § 10(a) of the APA required only that "the interest sought to be protected by the complainant [be] arguably within the zone of interests to be protected or regulated by the statute . . . in question." Id., at 153. In determining that the plaintiffs' interest met this requirement, we noted that although the relevant federal statutes . . . did not "in terms protect a specified group[,] . . . their general policy is apparent; and those whose interests are directly affected by a broad or narrow interpretation of the Acts are easily identifiable." Data Processing, 397 U.S., at 157. "[A]s competitors of national banks which are engaging in data processing services," the plaintiffs were within that class of "aggrieved persons" entitled to judicial review of the Comptroller's interpretation. Ibid.

Less than a year later, we applied the "zone of interests" test in Arnold Tours, Inc. v. Camp, 400 U.S. 45 (1970) (per curiam) (Arnold Tours). There, certain travel agencies challenged a ruling by the Comptroller, similar to the one contested in Data Processing, that permitted national banks to operate travel agencies. See 400 U.S., at 45. In holding that the plaintiffs had prudential standing under the APA, we . . . explained:

> In Data Processing . . . [w]e held that § 4 arguably brings a competitor within the zone of interests protected by it. Nothing in the opinion limited § 4 to protecting only competitors in the data-processing field. When national banks begin to provide travel services for their customers, they compete with travel agents no less than they compete with data processors when they provide data-processing services to their customers." Ibid.

A year later, we decided Investment Company Institute v. Camp, 401 U.S. 617 (1971) (ICI). In that case, an investment company trade association and several individual investment companies alleged that the Comptroller had violated, inter alia, § 21 of the Glass-Steagall Act, 1932, by permitting national banks to establish and operate what in essence were early versions of mutual funds. We held that the plaintiffs, who alleged that they would be injured by the competition resulting from the Comptroller's action, had standing under the APA and stated that the case was controlled by Data Processing. See 401 U.S., at 621. . . .

Our fourth case in this vein was Clarke v. Securities Industry Assn., 479 U.S. 388 (1987) (Clarke). There, a securities dealers trade association sued the Comptroller, this time for authorizing two national banks to offer discount brokerage services both at their branch offices and at other locations inside and outside their home States. The plaintiff contended that the Comptroller's action violated the McFadden Act, which permits national banks to carry on the business of banking only at authorized branches, and to open new branches only in their home States and only to the extent that state-chartered banks in that State can do so under state law. We again held that the plaintiff had standing under the APA. . . .

Our prior cases, therefore, have consistently held that for a plaintiff's interests to be arguably within the "zone of interests" to be protected by a statute, there does not have to be an "indication of congressional purpose to benefit the would-be plaintiff." Id., at 399–400 (citing ICI) . . . The proper inquiry is simply "whether the interest sought to be protected by the complainant is *arguably* within the zone of interests to be protected . . . by the statute." Data Processing, 397 U.S., at 153 (emphasis added). Hence in applying the "zone of interests" test, we do not ask whether, in enacting the statutory provision at issue, Congress specifically intended to benefit the plaintiff. Instead, we first discern the interests "arguably . . . to be protected" by the statutory provision at issue; we then inquire whether the plaintiff's interests affected by the agency action in question are among them.

. . . By its express terms, § 109 limits membership in every federal credit union to members of definable "groups." Because federal credit unions may, as a general matter, offer banking services only to members, . . . § 109 also restricts the markets that every federal credit union can serve. . . . Thus, even if it cannot be said that Congress had the specific purpose of benefiting commercial banks, one of the interests "arguably . . . to be protected" by § 109 is an interest in limiting the markets that federal credit unions can serve. . . . As competitors of federal credit unions, respondents certainly have an interest in limiting the markets that federal credit unions can serve, and the NCUA's interpretation has affected that interest . . .

. . . Petitioners attempt to distinguish this action [from Clarke, ICI, Arnold Tours, and Data Processing] principally on the ground that there is no evidence that Congress, when it enacted the FCUA, was at all concerned with the competitive interests of commercial banks, or indeed at all concerned with competition. Indeed, petitioners contend that the very reason Congress passed the FCUA was that "[b]anks were simply not in the picture" as far as small borrowers were concerned, and thus Congress believed it necessary to create a new source of credit for people of modest means.

The difficulty with this argument is that similar arguments were made unsuccessfully in each of Data Processing, Arnold Tours, ICI, and Clarke. . . . We therefore cannot accept petitioners' argument that respondents do not have standing because there is no evidence that the Congress that enacted § 109 was concerned with the competitive interests of commercial banks. To accept that argument, we would have to reformulate the "zone of interests" test to require that Congress have specifically intended to benefit a particular class of plaintiffs before a plaintiff from that class could have standing under the APA to sue. We have refused to do this in our prior cases, and we refuse to do so today.

Petitioners also mistakenly rely on our decision in Air Courier Conference v. Postal Workers, 498 U.S. 517 (1991). In Air Courier, we held that the interest of Postal Service employees in maximizing employment opportunities was not within the "zone of interests" to be protected by the postal monopoly statutes, and hence those employees did not have standing under the APA to challenge a Postal Service regulation suspending its monopoly over certain international operations. See id., at 519. We stated that the purposes of the statute were solely to increase the revenues of the Post Office and to ensure that postal services were provided in a manner consistent with the public interest, see id., at 526–527. Only those interests, therefore, and not the interests of Postal Service employees in their employment, were "arguably within the zone of interests to be protected" by the statute. We further noted that although the statute in question regulated competition, the interests of the plaintiff employees had nothing to do with competition. See id. at 528, n. 5 . . . . In this action, not only do respondents have "competitive and direct injury," but, as the foregoing discussion makes clear, they possess an interest that is "arguably . . . to be protected" by § 109. . . .

III

[Justice Thomas, writing for the majority, proceeded to hold on the merits that the NCUA's interpretation of the common bond requirement was impermissible under the first step of Chevron. See p. 1141.]

■ JUSTICE O'CONNOR, with whom JUSTICE STEVENS, JUSTICE SOUTER, and JUSTICE BREYER join, dissenting.

In determining that respondents have standing under the zone-of-interests test to challenge the NCUA's interpretation of the "common bond" provision of the FCUA, the Court applies the test in a manner that is contrary to our decisions and, more importantly, that all but eviscerates the zone-of-interests requirement. . . .

Respondents brought this suit under § 10(a) of the APA, 5 U.S.C. § 702. To establish their standing to sue here, . . . respondents must show that they are "adversely affected or aggrieved," *i.e.,* have suffered injury in fact. . . . In addition, respondents must establish that the injury they assert is "within the meaning of a relevant statute," *i.e.,* satisfies the zone-of-interests test. . . . Specifically, "the plaintiff must establish that the injury he complains of (*his* aggrievement, or the adverse effect *upon him*), falls within the 'zone of interests' sought to be protected by the statutory provision whose violation forms the legal basis for his complaint." [Lujan v.] National Wildlife Federation, [497 U.S. 871,] 883 [(1990)]. . . .

. . . The relevant question under the zone-of-interests test, then, is whether injury to respondents' commercial interest as a competitor "falls within the zone of interests sought to be protected by the [common bond] provision." . . . The Court adopts a quite different approach to the zone-of-interests test today, eschewing any assessment of whether the common bond provision was intended to protect respondents' commercial interest. . . .

. . . Under the Court's approach, every litigant who establishes injury in fact under Article III will automatically satisfy the zone-of-interests requirement, rendering the zone-of-interests test ineffectual. . . . The crux of the Court's zone-of-interests inquiry . . . is simply that the plaintiff must "have" an interest in enforcing the pertinent statute. . . . A party, however, will invariably have an interest in enforcing a statute when he can establish injury in fact caused by an alleged violation of that statute. . . . Our decision in Air Courier, likewise, cannot be squared with the Court's analysis in this action. . . . [T]he postal employees would have established standing under the Court's analysis in this action: The employees surely "had" an interest in enforcing the statutory monopoly, given that suspension of the monopoly caused injury to their employment opportunities. . . .

Contrary to the Court's suggestion, its application of the zone-of-interests test in this action is not in concert with the approach we followed in a series of cases in which the plaintiffs, like respondents here, alleged that agency interpretation of a statute caused competitive injury to their commercial interests. [Data Processing, Arnold Tours, ICI, and Clarke] In each of those cases, we focused . . . on whether competitive injury to the plaintiff's commercial interest fell within the zone of interests protected by the relevant statute. . . . It is true, as the Court emphasizes repeatedly, . . . that we did not require in this line of decisions that the statute at issue was designed to benefit the particular party bringing suit. . . . In each of the competitor standing cases, though, we found that Congress had enacted an "anti-competition limitation," see Bennett, 520 U.S., at 176 (discussing Data Processing), or, alternatively, that Congress had "legislated against . . . competition," see Clarke, supra, at 403; ICI, supra, at 620–621, and accordingly, that the plaintiff-competitor's "commercial interest was sought to be protected by the anti-competition limitation" at issue, Bennett, supra, at 176. . . . The Court fails to undertake that analysis here.

Applying the proper zone-of-interests inquiry to this action, I would find that competitive injury to respondents' commercial interests does not arguably fall within the zone of interests sought to be protected by the common bond provision. . . . There is no indication in the text of the provision or in the surrounding language that the membership limitation was even arguably designed to protect the commercial interests of competitors. . . . The circumstances surrounding the enactment of the FCUA also indicate that Congress did not intend to legislate against competition through the common bond provision. . . . The requirement of a common bond was . . . meant to ensure that each credit union remains a cooperative institution that is economically stable and responsive to its members' needs. As a principle of internal governance designed to secure the viability of individual credit unions in the interests of the membership, the common bond provision was in no way designed to impose a restriction on all credit unions in the interests of institutions that might one day become competitors. . . .

. . . The pertinent question under the zone-of-interests test is whether Congress *intended* to protect certain interests through a particular provision, not whether, irrespective of congressional intent, a provision may have the *effect* of protecting those interests. . . . In this light, I read our decisions as establishing that there must at least be *some* indication in the statute, beyond the mere fact that its enforcement has the effect of incidentally benefiting the plaintiff, from which one can draw an inference that the plaintiff's injury arguably falls within the zone of interests sought to be protected by that statute. The provisions we construed in Clarke, ICI, and Data Processing allowed such an inference: Where Congress legislates against competition, one can properly infer that the statute is at least arguably intended to protect competitors from injury to their commercial interest, even if that is not the statute's principal objective. . . . The same cannot be said of respondents in this action, because neither the terms of the common bond provision, nor the way in which the provision operates, nor the circumstances surrounding its enactment, evince a congressional desire to legislate against competition. This, then, is an action "the plaintiff's interests are so marginally related to or inconsistent with the purposes implicit in the statute that it cannot reasonably be assumed that Congress intended to permit the suit." Clarke, 479 U.S., at 399.

NOTES

(1) ***Data Processing and the Birth of the Zone of Interest Test.*** As noted above, p. 1310, standing doctrine is a modern creation. The traditional jurisprudential approach did not recognize standing as an inquiry separate from the case on the merits. See Alexander Sprunt & Son v. United States, 281 U.S. 249 (1930). The Supreme Court clearly rejected the view that a "legal right" is constitutionally required in an important set of cases under the Communications Act of 1934, which authorizes judicial review of FCC's decisions on license applications at the behest of either the applicant or "any other person aggrieved or whose interests are adversely affected by any decision of the Commission granting or refusing any such application." See FCC v. Sanders Bros., 309 U.S. 470 (1940); Scripps-Howard Radio Inc. v. FCC, 316 U.S. 4, 14 (1942); Elizabeth Magill, Standing for the Public: A Lost History, 95 Va. L. Rev. 1131 (2009).

Sanders Bros. and Scripps-Howard represented a major conceptual shift in thinking about who could seek judicial review of agency compliance with statutory requirements. But their immediate impact on regulatory standing was limited because they rested on the relatively atypical phrasing of § 402(b). Then in 1946 Congress enacted the APA. Underscoring the fact that "standing" had not yet gained currency as a distinct jurisprudential concept, the APA nowhere uses the term. However, a major interpretive controversy ensued about the meaning of § 702, originally enacted as § 10a of the APA, which made judicial review available to a person "adversely affected or aggrieved by agency action within the meaning of the relevant statute." Prominent judicial review scholar Louis Jaffe (and many lower courts) took the position that § 702 merely codified existing standing law—that is, a "legal interest" is required unless the particular organic statute (like the Communications Act) empowers "aggrieved" persons to sue. Louis L. Jaffe, Judicial Control of Administrative Action 528–30 (1965). On the other side, influential commentator Professor Kenneth Davis pointed to legislative history that described § 702 as "confer[ring] a right of review upon any person adversely affected in fact by agency action or aggrieved within the meaning of any statute" and argued that Congress intended to broaden regulatory standing by adopting the Sanders Bros./Scripps-Howard approach across the board in the APA. Kenneth C. Davis, Judicial Control of Administrative Action: A Review, 66 Colum. L. Rev. 635, 668–69 (1966).

Nearly a quarter-century after the APA was enacted, ASSOCIATION OF DATA PROCESSING SERVICE ORGANIZATIONS, INC. V. CAMP, 397 U.S. 150 (1970) (Data Processing) settled the question. There, in an opinion by JUSTICE DOUGLAS, the Court stated: "The first question is whether the plaintiff alleges that the challenged action has caused him injury in fact, economic or otherwise." This inquiry, Justice Douglas insisted, was not the same as determining whether the plaintiff had a legal interest at stake. "The 'legal interest' test goes to the merits. The question of standing is different. It concerns, apart from the 'case' or 'controversy' test, the question whether the interest sought to be protected by the complainant is arguably within the zone of interests to be protected or regulated by the statute or constitutional guarantee in question. Thus the Administrative Procedure Act grants standing to a person 'aggrieved by agency action within the meaning of a relevant statute.' 5 U.S.C. § 702. That interest, at times, may reflect aesthetic, conservational, and recreational as well as economic values. . . . We mention these noneconomic values to emphasize that standing may stem from them as well as from the economic injury on which petitioners rely here. Certainly he who is 'likely to be financially' " injured, FCC v. Sanders Bros. Radio Station, 309 U.S. 470 (1940), may be a reliable private attorney general to litigate the issues of the public interest in the present case. . . . Where statutes are concerned, the trend is toward enlargement of the class of people who may protest administrative action. The whole drive for enlarging the category of aggrieved 'persons' is symptomatic of that trend."

Concurring in the result, JUSTICE BRENNAN dissented from the zone-of-interests inquiry the majority adopted for not opening up standing enough: "The Court's approach to standing . . . , set out in Data Processing, has two steps: (1) . . . determine 'whether the plaintiff alleges that the challenged action has caused him injury in fact;' (2) determine 'whether the interest sought to be protected by the complainant is arguably within the zone of interests to be protected or regulated by the statute or constitutional guarantee in question.' My view is that the inquiry in the Court's first step is the only one that need be made to determine standing. . . . By requiring a second, nonconstitutional step, the Court comes very close to perpetuating the discredited requirement that conditioned standing on a showing by the plaintiff that the challenged governmental action invaded one of his legally protected interests."

Data Processing represented an effort to expand access to the courts at a time of expansion in agencies' regulatory responsibilities and growing concern about agencies being captured by the very industries and entities they regulated. Ironically, however, the first part of Data Processing's analysis, the requirement of an injury-in-fact, has become an obstacle for standing. In Lujan (p. 1301), the Court inexplicably reinserted the legal interest requirement into the definition of injury-in-fact, stating that for standing a "plaintiff must have suffered an 'injury in fact'—an invasion of a *legally protected interest* which is (a) concrete and particularized, and (b) actual and imminent. . . ." (emphasis added). But it was in Spokeo's requirement of actual injury that the potential restrictiveness of identifying "injury-in-fact" as a constitutional requirement became more apparent. See Andrew Hessick, Standing, Injury in Fact, and Private Rights, 93 Cornell L. Rev. 275, 299–306 (2008).

(2) ***Finding Surrogates to Speak for the Intended Beneficiaries of Regulation.*** In general, courts are extremely reluctant to allow a party to litigate anyone's interest but her own. Recall that Allen (p. 1311) identifies the "jus tertii" principle—no raising the rights of third parties—as one of the prudential restrictions on standing. Presumably, the intended beneficiaries of the common bond requirement are credit union members, who benefit insofar as the common bond requirement ensures credit unions' financial strength. Why shouldn't the intended beneficiaries of regulation speak for themselves? Do you think anyone in this group could establish standing to complain that the Comptroller's approach might allow credit unions to get too big and threaten their financial security? Recall that, under Lujan and Spokeo, standing requires an individualized, actual injury caused by the Comptroller's decision.

If it's unlikely that intended beneficiaries could get (or would be motivated to seek) standing—perhaps because the collective nature of the regulatory goods produced makes it difficult to establish individualized injury—does that justify allowing competitors to sue as a surrogate? On the other hand, if expanding the scope of what counts as a common bond actually enhances credit union financial strength, as the NCUA argued, why should banks be able to sue to assert their competitive interests to the potential disadvantage of credit union members, the provision's intended beneficiaries?

(3) ***Is the Zone of Interests Requirement Doing Any Work?*** Dissenting in NCUA, Justice O'Connor complains that the majority's approach to the zone of interest test makes it meaningless; any plaintiff who meets the Article III standing requirements will fall within the zone of interest. Is she right? How often will plaintiffs be outside of the zone-of-interests under the majority's approach? And if Justice O'Connor is right, is that a bad thing? After all, Justice Brennan argued in Data Processing that a plaintiff need

only satisfy the requirements of Article III to bring suit under the APA. Is that a plausible reading of the text of APA § 702?

(4) *Is the Court Drawing Consistent Lines?* One case where the zone-of-interest test operated to prevent suit was AIR COURIER CONFERENCE OF AMERICA V. AMERICAN POSTAL WORKERS UNION, AFL-CIO, 498 U.S. 517 (1991). There, as discussed in NCUA, postal employee unions tried to challenge a Postal Service rule allowing private couriers to deliver foreign address letters to foreign post offices as violating Private Express Statutes (PES), which gave the Postal Service a statutory monopoly over the carriage of mail. The Court ruled that the unions did not fall within the PES' zone of interests: "[T]he provisions [of the PES] . . . indicate that the congressional concern was not with opportunities for postal workers but with the receipt of necessary revenues for the Postal Service. . . . The PES enable the Postal Service to fulfill its responsibility to provide service to all communities at a uniform rate. . . . If competitors could serve the lower cost segment of the market, leaving the Postal Service to handle the high-cost services, the Service would lose lucrative portions of its business, thereby increasing its average unit cost and requiring higher prices to all users. The postal monopoly, therefore, exists to ensure that postal services will be provided to the citizenry at large, and not to secure employment for postal workers."

The NCUA majority insisted that Air Courier was distinguishable, but can the result in Air Courier really be squared with the result in NCUA? Are the interests of the national banks in NCUA—essentially, to advance their own economic interests at the expense of credit unions—more plausibly within the zone of interests of the FCUA than the postal employees' interests are within the zone of interests of the PES? For that matter, is Air Courier distinguishable from other precedent—specifically, Data Processing, Arnold Tours, ICI, and Clarke—in which the Court found the zone-of-interests test satisfied? For a discussion of the Court's zone-of-interests precedent and an argument that the zone is currently applied incoherently and courts should instead allow any plaintiffs with standing to sue unless Congress has adopted a more restrictive rule, see Jonathan R. Siegel, Zone of Interests, 92 Geo. L.J. 317 (2004).

(5) *Statutory Abrogation of the Zone Requirement.* Because the zone restriction is prudential, Congress can dispense with it. Bennett v. Spear, 520 U.S. 154 (1997) involved one type of statutory provision now understood as expressing congressional intent to confer standing to the full extent Article III permits: citizen suit provisions. See Lujan, p. 1300.

(6) *The Current Status of the Zone-of-Interests Test.* In LEXMARK INTERNATIONAL V. STATIC CONTROL COMPONENTS, INC., 134 S.Ct. 1377 (2014), a recent unanimous decision addressing whether a manufacturer who alleged lost sales and damage to its business reputation had prudential standing to bring a challenge under the Lanham Act, JUSTICE SCALIA cast doubt on the concept of prudential standing in general. Calling "prudential standing" a "misleading" label, the Court stated that the question of "[w]hether a plaintiff comes within 'the zone of interests' is an issue that requires us to determine, using traditional tools of statutory interpretation, whether a legislatively conferred cause of action encompasses a particular

plaintiff's claim." Justice Scalia proceeded to note that the Court "ha[d] said, in the APA context, that the test is not especially demanding. In that context we have often conspicuously included the word 'arguably' in the test to indicate that the benefit of any doubt goes to the plaintiff, and have said that the test forecloses suit only when a plaintiff's interests are so marginally related to or inconsistent with the purposes implicit in the statute that it cannot reasonably be assumed that Congress authorized that plaintiff to sue. That lenient approach is an appropriate means of preserving the flexibility of the APA's omnibus judicial-review provision, which permits suit for violations of numerous statutes of varying character that do not themselves include causes of action for judicial review."

Does Lexmark raise questions about the future status of the zone-of-interests test for standing under the APA? Does the test add much to Article III standing requirements as Lexmark describes it? Note that eight justices signed onto an opinion applying the APA's zone-of-interest test two years before Lexmark (and the lone dissenter disagreed on a different ground). In MATCH-E-BE-NASH-SHE-WISH BAND OF POTTAWATOMI INDIANS V. PATCHAK, 567 U.S. 209 (2012), the Court held that a neighboring landowner fell within the zone of interests of the Indian Reorganization Act to challenge the Secretary of the Interior's ability to take title to the property on behalf of a non-federally recognized tribe. Justice Kagan's majority opinion emphasized that the statute concerned itself not only with land acquisition but also with land use, and therefore the landowner's allegations of economic, environmental, and aesthetic injury resulting from the planned establishment of a casino fell into the zone of interests to be protected by the IRA. Does such a near-unanimous application of the APA zone-of-interests test right before Lexmark suggest that the test likely remains alive and well?

In BANK OF AMERICA V. CITY OF MIAMI, 137 S.Ct. 1296 (2017), the Court quoted Lexmark (and its prior precedent on the scope of the Fair Housing Act cause of action, p. 1328) in concluding that a suit by Miami against Bank of America and Wells Fargo for allegedly engaging in predatory lending practices against Latino and African-American communities fell within the FHA's zone of interests. Miami claimed that the banks' predatory practices had led to a concentration of foreclosures and vacancies in those communities, which in turn hindered the City's efforts to create integrated, stable neighborhoods, increased demand for city services, and diminished the City's property tax revenue by reducing property values. According to the Court, in an opinion by Justice Breyer, "the City's claims of financial injury. . .—specifically, lost tax revenue and extra municipal expenses—satisfy the 'cause-of-action' (or 'prudential standing') requirement. To use the language of Data Processing, the City's claims of injury it suffered as a result of the statutory violations are, at the least, 'arguably within the zone of interests' that the FHA protects." Justice Thomas dissented on this point, joined by Justices Kennedy and Alito, and the Court remanded for the lower court to apply the correct causation analysis, p. 1346.

SECTION 2.   REVIEWABILITY, TIMING, AND REMEDIES

> *a. Methods of Obtaining Review*
> *b. Preclusion of Judicial Review*
> *c. Timing of Review*
> *d. Remedies*

The lawyer considering a lawsuit to challenge agency action must resolve many of the same questions that occur in planning any federal litigation. In addition to standing, discussed in the preceding section, these include:

- Which courts are available? (jurisdiction and venue) If more than one is available, what are the advantages and disadvantages of each forum?

- What causes of action are possible? (reviewability) Are some claims more desirable than others, in the procedural advantages they offer and the substantive claims and defenses they permit?

- When can the action be brought? When is too early? (exhaustion, finality, ripeness) When is too late? (statute of limitations and mootness)

- What remedies are available, and do the remedies vary with different causes of action and different defendants? (remedies) Here, plaintiffs face an obstacle not present in federal-question suits between private parties: sovereign immunity. The federal government (and its agencies) is immune from suit *unless* Congress has given consent.

These questions are explored in this section. We begin with a brief overview of different bases of jurisdiction and of the background presumption of reviewability the Supreme Court found in the APA. We then turn to issues of preclusion of judicial review, timing of judicial review, and the different remedies available. You'll see that, whereas standing doctrine is heavily constitutional and judge-made, in this section the APA is often of paramount importance. Critical language from the APA is reproduced at the outset of each subsection where relevant below, but before going further you may find it helpful to read through the APA's provisions on judicial review in their entirety, 5 U.S.C. §§ 701–706, located in the Appendix.

a. Methods of Obtaining Review

> *(1)   Special Statutory Review*
> *(2)   General Statutory Review*
> *(3)   "Nonstatutory" Review*

The methods of obtaining review of agency action are conventionally grouped into three categories, which are described in order below:

1. Special Statutory Review: Review authorized by the particular organic statute(s) under which the agency is acting.

2. General Statutory Review: Review authorized by the APA.

3. "Nonstatutory Review": The somewhat confusing name for the category that originally comprised common-law and equity forms of action but now also includes actions authorized by statutes *other* than the agency's organic statute or the APA.

(1) Special Statutory Review

The form of proceeding for judicial review is the special statutory review proceeding relevant to the subject matter in a court specified by statute or, in the absence or inadequacy thereof, any applicable form of legal action . . .

5 U.S.C. § 703

Not surprisingly, regulatory statutes often contain provisions specifically authorizing judicial review of at least some of the actions in which the agency engages. A good example is 29 U.S.C. § 160(f), which provides that "[a]ny person aggrieved by a final order of the [NLRB] granting or denying in whole or in part the relief sought may obtain a review of such order in [the appropriate] United States court of appeals."

Searching the relevant organic statute(s) for such provisions—which define what § 703 terms a "special statutory review proceeding"—is the lawyer's first step. Why? Such provisions often designate the level of the court system (i.e., district or appellate) at which review is to be initiated. Moreover, they are usually interpreted as performing several other important tasks, in particular, granting subject matter jurisdiction, providing a cause of action, and waiving sovereign immunity for claims within their scope. In addition, these provisions might also specify venue, set a statute of limitations, determine whether certain intra-agency remedies must be exhausted, confer standing, and provide supplementary or alternative standards of review.

Unlike ordinary civil litigation, the typical special statutory review proceeding (evident in 29 U.S.C. § 160(f)'s text above) begins directly in the court of appeals, by filing a petition for review.[3] The reason Congress so often chooses to site review in the circuit courts is that the record on which agency action is reviewed is almost always the record created *at the agency*. Therefore, there is no need for the district court's capacity to hold evidentiary hearings.

Another important species of special statutory review proceeding is the "enforcement action." Even agencies that are broadly authorized to investigate and adjudicate alleged wrongdoing and impose sanctions are usually not empowered to use self-help to enforce those sanctions. If the regulated entity does not voluntarily accept the penalty imposed, the agency typically has to petition the court for a judicial order of enforcement. Here again, a good example involves the NLRB, which 29 U.S.C. § 160(e) provides "shall have power to petition any court of appeals of the United States . . . for the enforcement of [an unfair labor practice order]." In deciding whether to issue this order, the court reviews the agency's decision just as if an aggrieved person had filed a petition for review and indeed often confronts cross-petitions for review—one from the agency seeking to have its sanction enforced and one from the regulated entity seeking to have it vacated.

APA § 703 expressly acknowledges that a special statutory review proceeding might be "absen[t] or inadequa[te]." The first of these situations occurs when the relevant statute does not mention judicial review at all. Such silence is usually construed as not precluding general statutory (APA) or nonstatutory review. (See § 2.a.2 below) Alternatively, the statute might provide for review of agency actions *other than* the particular type about which the litigant wishes to complain. Here, too, selective silence is usually not interpreted to preclude other avenues of review. Whether alternative forms of review are available will depend on the court's assessment in light of the legislative evidence and regulatory objectives of the particular administrative scheme, and whether Congress intended the special review proceeding to be exclusive—even with its alleged shortcomings.

---

[3]   Some statutes, especially in the environmental area, consolidate review in the D.C. Circuit. Otherwise, the petition can usually be filed in any circuit in which the petitioner resides or the cause of action arose, but through a combination of statutory direction and litigant choice, the D.C. Circuit hears the lion's share of petitions for review of rules. There are also important instances of special statutory review sited in the district court, such as review of Social Security benefit denials or terminations, see 42 U.S.C. §§ 405(g), 421(d).

(2) General Statutory Review

Agency action made reviewable by statute and final agency action for which there is no other adequate remedy in a court are subject to judicial review.

5 U.S.C. § 704

If a special statutory review proceeding is absent, inadequate, or deemed non-exclusive, the cause of action most commonly used is the one created by the APA itself in § 704. But the APA is not a grant of subject matter jurisdiction. Califano v. Sanders, 430 U.S. 99 (1977). Typically, this is easily remedied by pleading 28 U.S.C. § 1331, the general federal-question statute. It means, however, that such a review proceeding under the APA typically begins in the trial court. This almost invariably means a longer course of litigation. Ambiguity about whether a special statutory proceeding applies, or is intended to be exclusive, tends to be resolved in favor of the special statutory process.

There is one significant exception to the rule that general statutory review begins in the district court. In the important and widely followed decision Telecommunications Research & Action Center v. FCC, 750 F.2d 70 (D.C. Cir.1984) (TRAC), the D.C. Circuit held that where an organic statute commits review of *final* agency action to the court of appeals, that court has exclusive jurisdiction over *all* suits seeking relief that "might affect" its future statutory review power. If you studied the materials in Chapter VIII on dealing with judicial review of agency inaction and unreasonable delay, you've already seen a context in which the TRAC principle can operate to locate APA-based review immediately in the appeals court.

(3) "Nonstatutory" Review

Nonstatutory review has produced some of our most important opinions defining the legitimate scope of government action: Marbury v. Madison, 5 U.S. (1 Cranch) 137 (1803), Osborn v. Bank of the United States, 22 U.S. (9 Wheat.) 738 (1824), and Youngstown Sheet and Tube Co. v. Sawyer, 343 U.S. 579 (1952) (p. 871). Born of the need to provide some avenue for judicial review of official conduct when sovereign immunity had not been waived, nonstatutory review proceeds against the official individually. When the 1976 amendments established unambiguously that APA-based review could proceed against agencies by name without sovereign immunity concerns, the need for nonstatutory forms of review disappeared in the typical case seeking review of rulemaking or administrative adjudication.

However, APA-based review does not serve every need. The government official or entity whose action is challenged may not be within the purview of the APA. Or, the action complained of may not be reachable under that statute. Finally, the injured party may find the APA cause of action insufficient because she principally desires compensation rather than prospective relief. In such circumstances, and lacking any usable special statutory review proceeding, the lawyer looks for an appropriate form of "nonstatutory review."[4]

Today, statutes codify, supplement, or sometimes even supplant the original nonstatutory forms. As a result, "nonstatutory review" is a term of art that includes certain obviously statutory proceedings. Equitable actions for relief against officers are an important form of nonstatutory review that remains uncodified and are often based on the Supreme Court's decision in Ex parte Young, 209 U.S. 123 (1908). Other forms of nonstatutory relief include actions for declaratory relief and the prerogative writs, of which habeas and mandamus remain the most relevant. Here a statutory basis exists for such "nonstatutory" relief, in the Declaratory Judgment Act, 28 U.S.C. § 2201, the All Writs Act, 28 U.S.C. § 1651, and 28 U.S.C. §§ 1361, 2255. Another important form of relief is damages actions against federal officers for violation of legal rights. These different forms of action are described in greater detail in Section 2.d on Remedies.

b.   Preclusion of Judicial Review

> *(1) The Presumption That Agency Action Is Reviewable*
> *(2) Statutory Preclusion of Review*
> *(3) Committed to Agency Discretion by Law*

This chapter [i.e., §§ 701–706] applies, according to the provisions thereof, except to the extent that—

> *(1) statutes preclude judicial review; or*
>
> *(2) agency action is committed to agency discretion by law.*

5 U.S.C. § 701(a)

If the organic statute does not expressly authorize judicial review of a particular agency action—either because it's completely silent on review or because its review provisions don't expressly mention the type of action complained of—the court must determine whether review is nonetheless available. The answer almost invariably begins with the framework established by first case below, Abbott Labs v. Gardner. Like the Data Processing opinion on standing three years later, p. 1366, it

---

[4]   For a lucid and illuminating examination of the history and forms of nonstatutory review, see Jonathan R. Siegel, Suing the President: Nonstatutory Review Revisited, 97 Colum. L. Rev. 1612 (1997).

substantially altered existing concepts of justiciability and laid the groundwork for the contemporary era of judicial review.

Abbott Labs is a watershed case on both *whether* review is available and *when* it can occur. The second of these, the issue of "ripeness," is taken up in Section 2.c.3. Here, we focus on reviewability per se. As Abbott explains, the APA strongly favors review but does not universally guarantee it. Section 701 establishes two sets of circumstances in which, notwithstanding the "presumption" of review, the APA will not assist a party seeking judicial scrutiny of agency behavior. These circumstances—when statutes preclude judicial review and when an agency action is committed to agency discretion by law—are explored in the materials that follow.

(1) The Presumption That Agency Action Is Reviewable

> **ABBOTT LABORATORIES v. GARDNER**
> **Note on the Constitutionality of**
> **Precluding Review**

ABBOTT LABORATORIES v. GARDNER

Supreme Court of the United States (1967).
387 U.S. 136.

■ JUSTICE HARLAN delivered the opinion of the Court.

[Consumers today are widely aware that "Advil" and "ibuprofen" are the same drug, and so they can decide whether to buy the cheaper store-brand version. We now take such information for granted, but the story of its availability begins with the 1962 amendments to the Federal Food, Drug, and Cosmetic Act. The amendments required manufacturers of prescription drugs to print the "established [i.e., generic] name" of the drug "prominently and in type at least half as large as that used thereon for any proprietary [i.e., brand] name or designation for such drug" on labels and other printed material. FDA conducted a rulemaking on how to implement the new amendments, and adopted the following requirement:

> If the label or labeling of a prescription drug bears a proprietary name or designation for the drug or any ingredient thereof, the established name, if such there be, corresponding to such proprietary name or designation, shall accompany *each appearance* of such proprietary name or designation. (emphasis added)

The so-called "every time" standard was also applied to advertisements. Shortly after the rule became final, 37 drug manufacturers and the Pharmaceutical Manufacturers Association (which included more than 90 percent of U.S. prescription drug manufacturers) sued, arguing that FDA had exceeded its statutory authority. The district court agreed and granted declaratory and injunctive relief; the court of appeals reversed on grounds that (i) pre-enforcement review was not authorized by the Act; and (ii) because none of the plaintiffs had yet been accused of violating the rule, no "actual case or controversy" existed.]

The first question we consider is whether Congress by the Federal Food, Drug, and Cosmetic Act intended to forbid pre-enforcement review of this sort of regulation promulgated by the Commissioner. The question is phrased in terms of "prohibition" rather than "authorization" because a survey of our cases shows that judicial review of a final agency action by an aggrieved person will not be cut off unless there is persuasive reason to believe that such was the purpose of Congress. Early cases in which this type of judicial review was entertained have been reinforced by the enactment of the Administrative Procedure Act, which embodies the basic presumption of judicial review to one "suffering legal wrong because of agency action, or adversely affected or aggrieved by agency action within the meaning of a relevant statute," 5 U.S.C. § 702, so long as no statute precludes such relief or the action is not one committed by law to agency discretion, 5 U.S.C. § 701(a). The Administrative Procedure Act provides specifically not only for review of "[a]gency action made reviewable by statute" but also for review of "final agency action for which there is no other adequate remedy in a court," 5 U.S.C. § 704. The legislative material elucidating that seminal act manifests a congressional intention that it cover a broad spectrum of administrative actions,[2] and this Court has echoed that theme by noting that the Administrative Procedure Act's "generous review provisions" must be given a "hospitable" interpretation. Shaughnessy v. Pedreiro, 349 U.S. 48, 51. Again in Rusk v. Cort, 369 U.S. 367, 379–380, the Court held that only upon a showing of "clear and convincing evidence" of a contrary legislative intent should the courts restrict access to judicial review.

Given this standard, we are wholly unpersuaded that the statutory scheme in the food and drug area excludes this type of action. The Government relies on no explicit statutory authority for its argument that pre-enforcement review is unavailable, but insists instead that because the statute includes a specific procedure for such review of certain enumerated kinds of regulations, not encompassing those of the kind involved here, other types were necessarily meant to be excluded from any pre-enforcement review. The issue, however, is not so readily resolved; we must go further and inquire whether in the context of the entire legislative scheme the existence of that circumscribed remedy evinces a congressional purpose to bar agency action not within its purview from judicial review. As a leading authority in this field has noted, "The mere fact that some acts are made reviewable should not suffice to support an implication of exclusion as to others. The right to

---

2   See H.R. Rep. No. 1980, 79th Cong., 2d Sess., 41 (1946):

To preclude judicial review under this bill a statute, if not specific in withholding such review, must upon its face give clear and convincing evidence of an intent to withhold it. The mere failure to provide specially by statute for judicial review is certainly no evidence of intent to withhold review.

review is too important to be excluded on such slender and indeterminate evidence of legislative intent." Louis Jaffe, Judicial Control of Administrative Action 357 (1965). . . .

II

A further inquiry must, however, be made. The injunctive and declaratory judgment remedies are discretionary, and courts traditionally have been reluctant to apply them to administrative determinations unless these arise in the context of a controversy "ripe" for judicial resolution. Without undertaking to survey the intricacies of the ripeness doctrine it is fair to say that its basic rationale is to prevent the courts, through avoidance of premature adjudication, from entangling themselves in abstract disagreements over administrative policies, and also to protect the agencies from judicial interference until an administrative decision has been formalized and its effects felt in a concrete way by the challenging parties. The problem is best seen in a twofold aspect, requiring us to evaluate both the fitness of the issues for judicial decision and the hardship to the parties of withholding court consideration.

As to the former factor, we believe the issues presented are appropriate for judicial resolution at this time. First, all parties agree that the issue tendered is a purely legal one: whether the statute was properly construed by the Commissioner to require the established name of the drug to be used *every time* the proprietary name is employed. Both sides moved for summary judgment in the District Court, and no claim is made here that further administrative proceedings are contemplated. It is suggested that the justification for this rule might vary with different circumstances, and that the expertise of the Commissioner is relevant to passing upon the validity of the regulation. This of course is true, but the suggestion overlooks the fact that both sides have approached this case as one purely of congressional intent, and that the Government made no effort to justify the regulation in factual terms.

Second, the regulations in issue we find to be "final agency action" within the meaning of [APA] § 704, as construed in judicial decisions. . . . The regulation challenged here . . . was made effective upon publication, and the Assistant General Counsel for Food and Drugs stated in the District Court that compliance was expected. . . .

This is also a case in which the impact of the regulations upon the petitioners is sufficiently direct and immediate as to render the issue appropriate for judicial review at this stage. These regulations purport to give an authoritative interpretation of a statutory provision that has a direct effect on the day-to-day business of all prescription drug companies; its promulgation puts petitioners in a dilemma that it was the very purpose of the Declaratory Judgment Act to ameliorate. As the District Court found on the basis of uncontested allegations, "Either they must comply with the every time requirement and incur the costs of changing over their promotional material and labeling or they must follow their present course and risk prosecution." . . . If petitioners wish to comply . . . they must destroy stocks of printed matter and they must invest heavily in new printing type and new supplies. The alternative to compliance—continued use of material which they believe in good faith meets the statutory requirements, but which clearly does not meet the regulation of the Commissioner—may be even more costly. That course would risk serious criminal and civil penalties for the unlawful distribution of "misbranded" drugs.

It is relevant at this juncture to recognize that petitioners deal in a sensitive industry, in which public confidence in their drug products is especially important. To require them to challenge these regulations only as a defense to an action brought by the Government might harm them severely and unnecessarily. Where the legal issue presented is fit for judicial resolution, and where a regulation requires an immediate and significant change in the plaintiffs' conduct of their affairs with serious penalties attached to noncompliance, access to the courts under the Administrative Procedure Act and the Declaratory Judgment Act must be permitted, absent a statutory bar or some other unusual circumstance. . . .

Finally, the Government urges that to permit resort to the courts in this type of case may delay or impede effective enforcement of the Act. We fully recognize the important public interest served by assuring prompt and unimpeded administration of the Pure Food, Drug, and Cosmetic Act, but we do not find the Government's argument convincing. First, in this particular case, a pre-enforcement challenge by nearly all prescription drug manufacturers is calculated to speed enforcement. If the Government prevails, a large part of the industry is bound by the decree; if the Government loses, it can more quickly revise its regulation.

. . . [I]t is important to note that the institution of this type of action does not by itself stay the effectiveness of the challenged regulation. There is nothing in the record to indicate that petitioners have sought to stay enforcement of the "every time" regulation pending judicial review. See 5 U.S.C. § 705. If the agency believes that a suit of this type will significantly impede enforcement or will harm the public interest, it need not postpone enforcement of the regulation and may oppose any motion for a judicial stay on the part of those challenging the regulation. It is scarcely to be doubted that a court would refuse to postpone the effective date of an agency action if the Government could show, as it made no effort to do here, that delay would be detrimental to the public health or safety.

[On the merits, the Court remanded the case to allow the court of appeals to decide the statutory authority question. Shortly before reargument there, the FDA and industry reached a settlement that produced the rule still in effect today: the generic name must appear every time the brand name is "featured," but the rule for "running text" is much looser. For illuminating behind-the-scenes details of the litigation, see Ronald M. Levin, The Story of the Abbott Labs Trilogy: The Seeds of the Ripeness Doctrine 430, in Administrative Law Stories (P. Strauss ed. 2006).]

[On the same day as Abbott Laboratories, the Court decided two companion cases, TOILET GOODS ASS'N, INC. V. GARDNER and GARDNER V. TOILET GOODS ASS'N, INC. The majority denied pre-enforcement review in the first and allowed it in the second; these holdings are considered further below in the materials on ripeness, Section 2.c.3.]

■ JUSTICE FORTAS, dissented in Gardner v. Toilet Goods Ass'n, in an opinion that applied to Abbott Labs as well:[5]

. . . The Court, by today's decisions[,] . . . has opened Pandora's box. Federal injunctions will now threaten programs of vast importance to the public welfare. . . . [I]t can hardly be hoped that some federal judge somewhere will not be moved as the Court is here, by the cries of anguish and distress of those regulated, to grant a disruptive injunction.

. . . [T]he Court has concluded that the damage to petitioners if they have to engage in the required redesign and reprint of their labels and printed materials without threshold review outweighs the damage to the public of deferring during the tedious months and years of litigation a cure for the possible danger and asserted deceit of peddling plain medicine under fancy trademarks and for fancy prices which, rightly or wrongly, impelled the Congress to enact this legislation. I submit that a much stronger showing is necessary than the expense and trouble of compliance and the risk of defiance. Actually, if the Court refused to permit this shotgun assault, experience and reasonably sophisticated common sense show that there would be orderly compliance without the disaster so dramatically predicted by the industry, reasonable adjustments by the agency in real hardship cases, and where extreme intransigence involving substantial violations occurred, enforcement actions in which legality of the regulation would be tested in specific, concrete situations. I respectfully submit that this would be the correct and appropriate result. Our refusal to respond to the vastly overdrawn cries of distress would reflect not only healthy skepticism, but our regard for a proper relationship between the courts on the one hand and Congress and the administrative agencies on the other. It would represent a reasonable solicitude for the purposes and programs of the Congress. And it would reflect appropriate modesty as to the competence of the courts.

NOTES

(1) **Does the APA Support a Presumption of Reviewability?** Is the APA best read as embodying a presumption of judicial review, as the Abbott Labs Court held? No, says Professor NICHOLAS BAGLEY in THE PUZZLING PRESUMPTION OF REVIEWABILITY, 127 Harv. L. Rev. 1285, 1304–06 (2014):

---

[5]   [Ed.] Justice Brennan did not participate in decisions of any of the three cases.

"Per § 701(a), the sections providing for judicial review apply 'except to the extent that . . . statutes preclude judicial review.' Preclusion is a threshold inquiry: only where Congress has not precluded judicial review do § 702 and § 704 call for review as the default. . . . The point is significant. A presumption must be overcome: to reject it, an interpreter must point to affirmative evidence (how much evidence depends on the strength of the presumption) that Congress meant something other than what it is presumed to have meant. That's not what the APA tells courts to do, however. Instead, the APA establishes a default rule favoring review where no statute precludes it. In other words, it supplies a rule of decision only after a court determines that the statute, fairly read, doesn't shut off review. . . . [T]he APA does not tell courts to discard the best interpretation of a statute in favor of a second- or third-best alternative that would allow for judicial review." For earlier criticisms of the presumption, see e.g., Kenneth C. Davis, Administrative Law of the Seventies § 28.08 at 631 (1976); Administrative Law Treatise § 28.09 at 495 (1982 Supp.).

Do you agree that the APA simply imposes a default rule favoring review if the best reading of the statute does not preclude it? Couldn't the language of § 701(a), stating that the APA's judicial review provisions apply *except* if "statutes *preclude* judicial review" or the "action is committed to agency discretion," be read as providing that judicial review should be available unless there is some affirmative basis in the governing statute (e.g., preclusion, discretion) to conclude otherwise? Does a presumption in favor of reviewability require more?

Abbott Labs does not delve much into the APA's legislative history, but in a subsequent case, BOWEN V. MICHIGAN ACADEMY OF FAMILY PHYSICIANS, 476 U.S. 667 (1986) the Court quoted the legislative reports on the APA in support of a strong endorsement of the presumption: "In undertaking the comprehensive rethinking of the place of administrative agencies in a regime of separate and divided powers that culminated in the passage of the [APA], the Senate Committee on the Judiciary remarked:

> Very rarely do statutes withhold judicial review. It has never been the policy of Congress to prevent the administration of its own statutes from being judicially confined to the scope of authority granted or to the objectives specified. Its policy could not be otherwise, for in such a case statutes would in effect be blank checks drawn to the credit of some administrative officer or board.

The Committee on the Judiciary of the House of Representatives agreed that Congress ordinarily intends that there be judicial review and emphasized the clarity with which a contrary intent must be expressed:

> The statutes of Congress are not merely advisory when they relate to administrative agencies, any more than in other cases. To preclude judicial review under this bill a statute, if not specific in withholding such review, must upon its face give clear and convincing evidence of an intent to withhold it. The mere failure to provide specially by statute for judicial review is certainly no evidence of intent to withhold review.

How clear are these legislative materials? If you have read the materials in Chapter III on the history of the APA, you know that the APA represented a hard-fought compromise between opponents and defenders of the New Deal administrative state. As a result, the legislative reports have long been thought "demonstrably unreliable guides to what Congress meant the APA to accomplish." Bagley, supra, at 1307. Expansive access to judicial review had been the mantra of the administrative state's opponents, but by the time the APA was enacted, the courts were full of judges appointed by FDR who accepted the constitutionality of administrative action. See George B. Shepherd, Fierce Compromise: The Administrative Procedure Act Emerges from New Deal Politics, 90 Nw. U. L. Rev. 1557, 1644 (1995). In addition, by 1946 the Democrats' hold on the White House looked more imperiled and conservative Democrats as well as Republicans were pushing for administrative controls. This history might support the presumption, but on the other hand it might also mean that members of Congress from both camps were content to leave the question of whether to preclude judicial review in Congress's hands. See Daniel Rodriguez, The Presumption of Reviewability: A Study in Canonical Construction and Its Consequences, 45 Vand. L. Rev. 743, 752–57 (1992). Perhaps more importantly, when Abbot Labs was decided, "[s]ome twenty years or so after the APA was passed, liberals and conservatives changed teams. Where the spectre of judicial review had seemed so threatening to New Dealers, liberals in the public interest era understood that federal administrative agencies and a Republican President presented their own set of dangers." Id. at 758.

(2) ***Are Reviewability and Timing Separate Questions?*** Justice Harlan treats the questions of reviewability and timing as separate questions in Abbott Labs. But is that accurate? Is there any doubt that the every-time standard would be reviewable in an enforcement action brought by FDA against a drug manufacturer who refused to comply? Given that review was indisputably available at enforcement, should the Court have invoked the presumption of reviewability as a basis for upholding pre-enforcement review?

In conflating timing and reviewability, Abbott Labs is hardly unusual. Many preclusion cases involve statutes that provide for judicial review, but at a later juncture. See the discussion of alternative avenues to review, Note 5, p. 1396.

(3) ***Is the Presumption of Reviewability Justified?*** Separate from questions about its basis in the APA, is the presumption of reviewability articulated in Abbott Labs nonetheless justified? Here again, Professor BAGLEY, supra, at 1287–88, answers in the negative: "As with any canon of statutory construction that serves a substantive end, it should find a source in history, positive law, the Constitution, or sound policy considerations. None of these, however, offers a plausible justification for the presumption. As for history, the sort of judicial review that the presumption favors— appellate-style arbitrariness review—was not only unheard of prior to the twentieth century, but was commonly thought to be unconstitutional. . . . [A]lthough the text and structure of the Constitution may prohibit Congress from precluding review of constitutional claims, a presumption responsive to

constitutional concerns would favor review of constitutional claims, not any and all claims of agency wrongdoing.

"As for policy considerations, judicial review might improve the fairness, quality, and legality of agency decisionmaking. But it also introduces delay, diverts agency resources, upsets agency priorities, and shifts authority within agencies toward lawyers and away from policymakers. Congress has the constitutional authority, democratic legitimacy, and institutional capacity to understand and to trade off these competing values. Courts do not. Nor is there reason to think that the presumption allows courts to better capture Congress's intent. . . . As Justice Frankfurter put it seventy years ago, 'engraft[ing] upon remedies which Congress saw fit to particularize . . . impliedly denies to Congress the constitutional right of choice in the selection of remedies.' Dishonoring Congress's choices limits its ability to tailor its administrative and regulatory schemes to their particular contexts." See also Daniel Rodriguez, The Presumption of Reviewability: A Study in Canonical Construction and Its Consequences, 45 Vand. L. Rev. 743, 766–67 (1992) (arguing that the presumption imposes costs on courts and Congress).

If you've read Chapter VIII on judicial review, you'll have seen particular concerns raised about the broad availability of judicial review in the context of rulemaking, which a number of scholars contend has "ossified" the rulemaking process and led agencies to pursue less open and effective methods of policymaking. See Notes 2–5, pp. 1090–1092. Abbott Labs, in creating a presumption in favor of pre-enforcement judicial review, was a critical jurisdictional development that helped fuel the modern expansion of judicial review of rulemaking.

Do you agree with Professor Bagley that the costs of the presumption outweigh its benefits? The difficult issue of whether, and if so when, the Constitution requires judicial review is discussed in the Note below. But separate from any constitutional requirement, does this argument give adequate weight to the importance of judicial review in legitimating administrative action? Consider Professor Louis L. Jaffe's famous statement that "[t]he availability of judicial review is the necessary condition, psychologically if not logically, of a system of administrative power which purports to be legitimate, or legally valid." Judicial Control of Administrative Action 320 (1965). If he's right, does that justify the presumption?

Whether the presumption has a historical basis is also a matter of debate. In Bowen, 476 U.S. at 670, the Supreme Court traced the presumption back to the origins of judicial review: "In Marbury v. Madison, 5 U.S. 163 (1803), a case itself involving review of executive action, Chief Justice Marshall insisted that '[t]he very essence of civil liberty certainly consists in the right of every individual to claim the protection of the laws.' " Later, in the lesser known but nonetheless important case of United States v. Nourse, 34 U.S. 8, 28–29 (1835), the Chief Justice noted the traditional observance of this right and laid the foundation for the modern presumption of judicial review:

> It would excite some surprise if, in a government of laws and of principle, furnished with a department whose appropriate duty it

is to decide questions of right, not only between individuals, but between the government and individuals, a ministerial officer might, at his discretion, issue this powerful process . . . leaving to the debtor no remedy, no appeal to the laws of his country, if he should believe the claim to be unjust. But this anomaly does not exist; this imputation cannot be cast on the legislature of the United States.

Although these sources emphasize the historical importance of judicial review of executive action, scholars have emphasized that such suits fell into narrow categories: either an action for a prerogative writ, usually mandamus, that was rarely granted, or a common law suit against an officer, which could impose damages. Officer suits also could take the form of actions for equitable relief. See Jerry L. Mashaw, Creating the Administrative Constitution 24–25 (2012); Thomas W. Merrill, Article III, Agency Adjudication, and the Origins of the Appellate Review Model of Administrative Law, 111 Colum. L. Rev. 939, 946–53 (2011). Professor Bagley argues that these actions do not support the presumption because they were quite limited and did not take the form of appellate review of agency action, the common form of judicial review after enactment of the APA and the context in which the presumption is applied today. Are you convinced?

NOTE ON THE CONSTITUTIONALITY OF PRECLUDING REVIEW

As mentioned above, concern about the constitutionality of precluding all judicial review is often invoked to justify the presumption of reviewability. Several leading reviewability decisions often note constitutional concerns as one reason to find judicial review not precluded. But whether some form of judicial review is constitutionally required is the subject of extensive scholarship and one of the most difficult questions in the course on federal courts. To date, only two Supreme Court decisions have directly rejected clear statutory preclusion as unconstitutional, United States v. Klein, 80 U.S. 128 (1871), and Boumediene v. Bush, 553 U.S. 723 (2008), with the former being notoriously opaque on its reasoning and the latter resting on restrictions the Constitution imposes on suspending the writ of habeas corpus in Article I, § 9, rather than on Article III. The Federal Courts course addresses this question in depth; what follows merely sketches the contours of the debate.

The problem begins with the language of Article III. Although contemporary lawyers take the extensive federal court system for granted, very little of that system is explicitly mandated by the Constitution. Article III, § 1 provides, "The judicial Power of the United States shall be vested in one Supreme court, and in such inferior Courts as the Congress *may from time to time ordain and establish*." (emphasis added) This language, known as the "Madisonian Compromise," was adopted as a compromise between framers who initially sought a full system of federal courts and those who resisted lower federal courts altogether and preferred federal judicial business to take place in state courts. Moreover, even with respect to the

Supreme Court, Article III confers "appellate Jurisdiction, both as to Law and Fact, *with such Exceptions, and under such Regulations as the Congress shall make.*" (emphasis added). Hence, even if the Supreme Court's narrow original jurisdiction is constitutionally protected, Article III makes access to the Supreme Court's much broader appellate jurisdiction contingent on congressional authorization.

The traditional view is that Congress has plenary power over the jurisdiction of both Supreme and lower federal courts. This view draws some support from history and precedent. Early on, the Court took the position that Article III is not self-executing—i.e., the federal courts, even the Supreme Court, require an affirmative *statutory* grant of jurisdiction. In all the years since the Constitution was adopted, the full range of federal judicial power defined in Article III has never been statutorily vested in either the Supreme Court or the lower federal courts.[6] And there is language in the few Supreme Court cases on point that supports the view that Congress has plenary power view over the jurisdiction of the lower courts[7] and the Supreme Court's appellate jurisdiction.[8] Those adhering to the plenary power interpretation of Article III typically urge that Congress *should not* use its power to withdraw jurisdiction but insist that the power does exist as part of the constitutional system of checks and balances.[9] Notably, however, the plenary power view does not entail accepting that there could be *no* judicial forum for asserting constitutional claims. Rather, as Henry Hart put it, the concern that Congress might leave constitutional rights without a remedy is answered by "[t]he state courts. In the scheme of the Constitution, they are the primary guarantors of constitutional rights, and in many cases they may be the ultimate ones."[10] By contrast, opponents of the plenary power view argue that Article III's text and Supreme Court opinions supporting the plenary power view can all be read more narrowly.[11] They also emphasize limitations on state court jurisdiction over federal officials and federal agencies.[12]

---

[6] For example, the statutory grant of diversity jurisdiction has always included an amount in controversy limitation.

[7] See Sheldon v. Sill, 49 U.S. (8 How.) 441 (1850).

[8] See Ex parte McCardle, 74 U.S. (7 Wall.) 506 (1868).

[9] See, e.g., Paul Bator, Congressional Power Over the Jurisdiction of the Federal Courts, 27 Vill. L. Rev. 1030, 1037–41 (1982); Gerald Gunther, Congressional Power to Curtail Federal Court Jurisdiction: An Opinionated Guide to the Ongoing Debate, 36 Stan. L. Rev. 895, 908–12 (1984).

[10] See Henry Hart, The Power of Congress to Limit the Jurisdiction of the Federal Courts: An Exercise in Dialectic, 66 Harv. L. Rev. 1362, 1401 (1953).

[11] See, e.g., James Pfander, One Supreme Court: Supremacy, Inferiority, and the Judicial Power of the United States (Oxford University Press, 2009) (arguing that the Supreme Court must have sufficient appellate jurisdiction to preserve its hierarchically superior role in the federal court system); Leonard Ratner, Majoritarian Constraints on Judicial Review: Congressional Control of Supreme Court Jurisdiction, 27 Vill. L. Rev. 929 (1982) (arguing that an "exception" could not destroy the "essential characteristics" of the subject to which it applies, while authority to adopt a "regulation" did not confer the power of complete prohibition.).

[12] Several early cases seem to establish that state courts cannot employ habeas corpus or mandamus to remedy the illegal acts of federal officials. On the other hand, damage awards and, apparently, orders for possession of specific property are possible. Injunctive relief is an open question. See generally Richard S. Arnold, The Power of State Courts to Enjoin Federal Officers, 73 Yale L.J. 1385 (1964).

Two principal types of theories have emerged as alternatives to the traditional, plenary power view. One type, "essential function" arguments, uses constitutional history, structure, and purpose to insist that Congress cannot withdraw jurisdiction when the result would be to vitiate the essential functions of the federal judiciary.[13] The second type, "independent unconstitutionality" arguments, finds limits on Congress's jurisdiction-withdrawing power in constitutional provisions outside Article III. On the most basic level, virtually all commentators (including traditional plenary power advocates) agree that Congress cannot limit judicial review through a restriction that itself violates some specific constitutional right—for example, closing the courthouse doors to African Americans or Jews. "Independent unconstitutionality" theorists argue for even broader limitations, for example with some contending that the equal protection clause, and perhaps substantive due process, prevent Congress from withdrawing jurisdiction over particular kinds of cases (e.g., school prayer challenges) because of hostility to the Court's holdings in the area.[14] The Supreme Court has signaled that due process may prohibit certain forms of preclusion, holding that "where a determination made in an administrative proceeding is to play a critical role in the subsequent imposition of a criminal sanction, there must be *some* meaningful review of the administrative proceeding."[15] But the scope of any such limits remain murky,[16] in no small part because the Supreme Court bends over backwards to read preclusion provisions so as to avoid constitutional concerns.

In the administrative context, judges and scholars have also suggested that separation of powers principles beyond Article III might justify a requirement of some judicial review of agency action. This argument emphasizes that under the Constitution agencies can only wield power that Congress has delegated to them, and therefore individuals subject to agency action have a constitutional right to challenged agency action as unauthorized. See, e.g., Ethyl Corp. v. EPA, 541 F.2d 1, 68 (1976) (Leventhal, J., concurring) ("Congress has been willing to delegate its legislative powers broadly and courts have upheld such delegation because there is court review to assure that the agency exercises the delegated power within statutory limits, and that it fleshes out objectives within those limits by an

---

[13] See, e.g., Theodore Eisenberg, Congressional Authority to Restrict Lower Federal Court Jurisdiction, 83 Yale L.J. 498 (1974); Ratner, supra note 11; Lawrence Sager, Constitutional Limitations on Congress' Authority to Regulate the Jurisdiction of the Federal Courts, 95 Harv. L. Rev. 17 (1981). The central debate sparked by these arguments is, of course, how to define the "essential functions" of the federal judiciary, with these scholars adopting different views on that score. See also Martin Redish, Constitutional Power to Regulate Supreme Court Appellate Jurisdiction Under the Exceptions Clause: An Internal and External Examination, 27 Vill. L. Rev. 900, 911 (1982) (critiquing the essential functions approach on this ground).

[14] See, e.g. Laurence H. Tribe, Jurisdictional Gerrymandering: Zoning Disfavored Rights Out of the Federal Courts, 14 Harv. C.R.-C.L. L. Rev. 129 (1981).

[15] United States v. Mendoza-Lopez, 481 U.S. 828 (1987). Cf. Zadvydas v. Davis, 533 U.S. 678, 692 (2001) ("This Court has suggested . . . that the Constitution may well preclude granting an administrative body the unreviewable authority to make determinations implicating fundamental rights.").

[16] See United States v. Falbo, 320 U.S. 549 (1944) (upholding criminal sanctions for failure to comply with an administrative order of a local draft board). But see Estep v. United States, 327 U.S. 114 (1946) (allowing defendant to challenge local draft board's order after exhausting all remedies).

administration that is not irrational or discriminatory.") Yet such an argument runs into a number of obstacles, ranging from the Supreme Court's insistence that the constitutionality of a delegation turns solely on whether Congress has provided sufficient guidance and not on alternative checks against agency abuse of power.[17] In addition, this delegation argument would seem to require Congress to create lower federal courts, at odds with plenary power view, and further would call into question Congress's power to ever preclude judicial review, at odds with longstanding doctrine and the APA.[18]

(2) Statutory Preclusion of Review

> **BOWEN v. MICHIGAN ACADEMY OF FAMILY PHYSICIANS**
> **Block v. Community Nutrition Institute (CNI)**

BOWEN v. MICHIGAN ACADEMY OF FAMILY PHYSICIANS

Supreme Court of the United States (1986).
476 U.S. 667.

■ JUSTICE STEVENS delivered the opinion of the Court.

[Michigan Academy, an association of family physicians, and several individual family physicians challenged a regulation of the Secretary of Health and Human Services that set higher Medicare reimbursement levels for "board certified" family physicians than for identical services performed by non-board certified family physicians. They claimed this distinction violated both the Medicare Act and the Fifth Amendment. The lower courts agreed with their statutory argument and hence did not reach the constitutional claim. In seeking certiorari, the Secretary did not challenge the decision on the merits but contended only that the Act precluded review.]

We begin with the strong presumption that Congress intends judicial review of administrative action. From the beginning "our cases [have established] that judicial review of a final agency action by an aggrieved person will not be cut off unless there is persuasive reason to believe that such was the purpose of Congress." Abbott Laboratories v. Gardner, 387 U.S. 136, 140 (1967). [Justice Stevens traced the presumption back to Marbury v. Madison, 5 U.S. 163 (1803) and United States v. Nourse, 34 U.S. 8, 9 Pet. 8, 28–29 (1835), and also emphasized that "[c]ommittees of both Houses of Congress have endorsed this view" in the APA.] Taking up the language in the House Committee Report [on the APA, Abbott Labs] reaffirmed . . . that "only upon a showing of 'clear and convincing evidence' of a contrary legislative intent should the courts

---

[17] See Whitman v. American Trucking Assns., 531 U.S. 457 (2001), p. 791.
[18] See Thomas W. Merrill, Delegation and Judicial Review, 33 Harv. J.L. & Pub. Pol'y 73 (2010).

restrict access to judicial review." This standard has been invoked time and again when considering whether the Secretary has discharged "the heavy burden of overcoming the strong presumption that Congress did not mean to prohibit all judicial review of his decision," Dunlop v. Bachowski, 421 U.S. 560, 567 (1975).[3]

Subject to constitutional constraints, Congress can, of course, make exceptions to the historic practice whereby courts review agency action. The presumption of judicial review is, after all, a presumption, and "like all presumptions used in interpreting statutes, may be overcome. . . ." Block v. Community Nutrition Institute, 467 U.S. 340, 349 (1984) [p. 1390]. In this case, the Government asserts that two statutory provisions remove the Secretary's regulation from review under the grant of general federal-question jurisdiction found in 28 U.S.C. § 1331. [The first of the Government's arguments was for implicit preclusion, the second for express preclusion.]

II

[The Government rested its implied preclusion argument on a distinction between Part A of the Medicare program, which established a federally administered insurance plan (mandatory for all Medicare participants) that covers a portion of costs such as hospitalization, and Part B, which established an optional coverage plan, provided by private insurance carriers under contract with HHS, that Medicare participants can purchase to supplement Part A benefits. The challenged regulation was promulgated under Part B. The government argued that 42 U.S.C. § 1395ff implicitly forecloses review of any Part B determination because it explicitly provides for review of comparable Part A determinations:

> (a) *Entitlement to and amount of benefits.* The determination of whether an individual is entitled to benefits under part A or part B, and the determination of the amount of benefits under part A, shall be made by the Secretary in accordance with regulations prescribed by him.
>
> (b) *Appeal by individuals.* Any individual dissatisfied with any determination under subsection (a) of this section as to
>
>> (A) whether he meets the [eligibility requirements for Part A], or
>>
>> (B) whether he is eligible to enroll and has enrolled pursuant to the provisions of part B . . ., or,
>>
>> (C) the amount of the benefits under part A (including a determination where such amount is determined to be zero)

---

[3] Of course, this Court has "never applied the 'clear and convincing evidence' standard in the strict evidentiary sense;" nevertheless, the standard serves as "a useful reminder to courts that, where substantial doubt about the congressional intent exists, the general presumption favoring judicial review of administrative action is controlling." Block v. Community Nutrition Inst., 467 U.S. 340, 350–51 (1984) [p. 1390].

shall be entitled to a hearing thereon by the Secretary . . . and to judicial review of the Secretary's final decision after such hearing. . . .]

Section 1395ff on its face is an explicit authorization of judicial review, not a bar. As a general matter, " '[t]he mere fact that some acts are made reviewable should not suffice to support an implication of exclusion as to others. The right to review is too important to be excluded on such slender and indeterminate evidence of legislative intent.' " Abbott Laboratories v. Gardner, 387 U.S. at 141 (quoting L. Jaffe, Judicial Control of Administrative Action 357 (1965)).

In the Medicare program, however, the situation is somewhat more complex . . . . Subject to an amount-in-controversy requirement, individuals aggrieved by delayed or insufficient payment with respect to benefits payable under Part B are afforded an "opportunity for a fair hearing by the *carrier*," § 1395u (emphasis added); in comparison, and subject to a like amount-in-controversy requirement, a similarly aggrieved individual under Part A is entitled "to a hearing thereon by the *Secretary* . . . and to judicial review," § 1395ff(b). "In the context of the statute's precisely drawn provisions," we held in United States v. Erika, Inc., 456 U.S. 201, 208 (1982), that the failure "to authorize further review for determinations of the amount of Part B awards . . . provides persuasive evidence that Congress deliberately intended to foreclose further review of such claims." Not limiting our consideration to the statutory text, we investigated the legislative history which "confirm[ed] this view," and disclosed a purpose to " 'avoid overloading the courts' " with " 'trivial matters,' " a consequence which would " 'unduly ta[x]' " the federal court system with " 'little real value' " to be derived by participants in the program (quoting 118 Cong. Rec. 33992 (1972) (remarks of Sen. Bennett)).

Respondents' federal-court challenge to the validity of the Secretary's regulation is not foreclosed by § 1395ff as we construed that provision in Erika. The reticulated statutory scheme, which carefully details the forum and limits of review of "any determination . . . of . . . the amount of benefits under part A," § 1395ff(b), and of the "amount of . . . payment" of benefits under Part B, § 1395u, simply does not speak to challenges mounted against the *method* by which such amounts are to be determined rather than the *determinations* themselves. As the Secretary has made clear, "the legality, constitutional or otherwise, of any provision of the Act or regulations relevant to the Medicare Program" is not considered in a "fair hearing" held by a carrier to resolve a grievance related to a determination of the amount of a Part B award. As a result, an attack on the validity of a regulation is not the kind of administrative action that we described in Erika as an "amount determination" which decides "the amount of the Medicare payment to be made on a particular claim" and with respect to which the Act impliedly denies judicial review.

That Congress did not preclude review of the method by which Part B awards are computed (as opposed to the computation) is borne out by the very legislative history we found persuasive in Erika. [Justice Stevens quotes the House and Senate Reports on the original legislation and the Conference Committee Report on pertinent 1972 amendments, all referring to complaints regarding "the amount of benefits."] Senator Bennett's introductory explanation to the amendment confirms that preclusion of judicial review of Part B awards—designed "to avoid overloading the courts with quite minor matters"—embraced only "decisions on a claim for payment for a given service." The Senator feared that "[i]f judicial review is made available where any claim is denied, as some court decisions have held, the resources of the Federal court system would be unduly taxed and little real value would be derived by the enrollees. The proposed amendment would merely clarify the original intent of the law and prevent the overloading of the courts with trivial matters because the intent is considered unclear." . . .

Careful analysis of the governing statutory provisions and their legislative history thus reveals that Congress intended to bar judicial review only of determinations of the amount of benefits to be awarded under Part B. Congress delegated this task to carriers who would finally determine such matters in conformity with the regulations and instructions of the Secretary. We conclude, therefore, that those matters which Congress did *not* leave to be determined in a "fair hearing" conducted by the carrier-including challenges to the validity of the Secretary's instructions and regulations-are not impliedly insulated from judicial review by [§ 1395ff].

III

In light of Congress' express provision for carrier review of millions of what it characterized as "trivial" claims, it is implausible to think it intended that there be *no* forum to adjudicate statutory and constitutional challenges to regulations promulgated by the Secretary. The Government nevertheless maintains that this is precisely what Congress intended to accomplish [when it incorporated by reference § 405(h) of the Social Security Act into § 1395ii of the Medicare Act. Section 405(h) provides:]

Finality of Secretary's decision

The findings and decision of the Secretary after a hearing shall be binding upon all individuals who were parties to such hearing. No findings of fact or decision of the Secretary shall be reviewed by any person, tribunal, or governmental agency except as herein provided. No action against the United States, the Secretary, or any officer or employee thereof shall be brought under section 1331 or 1346 of title 28 to recover on any claim arising under this subchapter.

The Government contends that the third sentence of § 405(h) by its terms prevents any resort to the grant of general federal-question jurisdiction contained in 28 U.S.C. § 1331. . . . Respondents counter that . . . Congress' purpose was to make clear that whatever specific procedures it provided for judicial review of final action by the Secretary were exclusive, and could not be circumvented by resort to the general jurisdiction of the federal courts.

. . . [W]e need not pass on the meaning of § 405(h) in the abstract to resolve this case. Section 405(h) does not apply on its own terms to Part B of the Medicare program, but is instead incorporated *mutatis mutandis* by § 1395ii. The legislative history of both the statute establishing the Medicare program and the 1972 amendments thereto provides specific evidence of Congress' intent to foreclose review only of "amount determinations"—i.e., those "quite minor matters," (remarks of Sen. Bennett), remitted finally and exclusively to adjudication by private insurance carriers in a "fair hearing." By the same token, matters which Congress did *not* delegate to private carriers, such as challenges to the validity of the Secretary's instructions and regulations, are cognizable in courts of law. In the face of this persuasive evidence of legislative intent, we will not indulge the Government's assumption that Congress contemplated review by carriers of "trivial" monetary claims, but intended no review at all of substantial statutory and constitutional challenges to the Secretary's administration of Part B of the Medicare program. This is an extreme position, and one we would be most reluctant to adopt without "a showing of 'clear and convincing evidence,'" Abbott Laboratories v. Gardner, 397 U.S. at 141, to overcome the "strong presumption that Congress did not mean to prohibit all judicial review" of executive action, Dunlop v. Bachowski, 421 U.S. at 567. We ordinarily presume that Congress intends the executive to obey its statutory commands and, accordingly, that it expects the courts to grant relief when an executive agency violates such a command. That presumption has not been surmounted here.[12]

The judgment of the Court of Appeals is affirmed.

■ JUSTICE REHNQUIST took no part in the consideration or decision of this case.

SIGNIFICANT CASE

BLOCK v. COMMUNITY NUTRITION INSTITUTE (CNI)
467 U.S. 340 (1984).

The Agricultural Marketing Agreement Act directs the Secretary of Agriculture to adopt "milk marketing orders" setting minimum prices

---

[12] Our disposition avoids the "serious constitutional question" that would arise if we construed § 1395ii to deny a judicial forum for constitutional claims arising under part B of the Medicare program. . . .

that milk handlers must pay to milk producers. These "orders" are formulated through a rulemaking process that includes public hearing and comment, but can become effective only on the vote of a majority of handlers and a supermajority of producers. In general, milk to be sold as fresh milk falls into higher price categories than milk to be processed into cheese or yogurt. An order formulated several years before this lawsuit had assigned reconstituted milk (milk made by adding water to milk powder) to one of the higher price classes.

The plaintiffs—who included consumers and a nonprofit organization promoting good nutrition for lower income families—petitioned the Secretary to begin a rulemaking to reclassify reconstituted milk to a lower price category. The Secretary invited comments on this proposal, but there the process stalled. Eventually, plaintiffs filed suit challenging both inaction on their rulemaking petition and the original marketing order. This prompted the Secretary to announce that he would not proceed further with the proposed rulemaking, and the inaction claim was dismissed as moot. The district court held that the consumers and nonprofit organization had no standing to challenge the marketing order, and that review was precluded. The court of appeals reversed on both issues; as to reviewability, it concluded that the structure and purposes of the Act did not reveal "the type of clear and convincing evidence of congressional intent needed to overcome the presumption in favor of judicial review."

The Supreme Court unanimously reversed (Justice Stevens did not participate). JUSTICE O'CONNOR:

"The presumption favoring judicial review of administrative action is just that—a presumption. [It] may be overcome by specific language or specific legislative history that is a reliable indicator of Congressional intent[,] contemporaneous judicial construction barring review and the congressional acquiescence in it, or the collective import of legislative and judicial history behind a particular statute. More important for purposes of this case, the presumption favoring judicial review of administrative action may be overcome by inferences of intent drawn from the statutory scheme as a whole. See, e.g., Switchmen v. National Mediation Board, 320 U.S. 297 (1943) [p. 1393]. . . .

"This Court has . . . never applied the 'clear and convincing evidence' standard in the strict evidentiary sense the Court of Appeals thought necessary in this case. Rather, the Court has found the standard met, and the presumption favoring judicial review overcome, whenever the congressional intent to preclude judicial review is 'fairly discernible in the statutory scheme.' [Data Processing], 397 U.S. at 157 [p. 1366]. In the context of preclusion analysis, the 'clear and convincing evidence' standard is not a rigid evidentiary test but a useful reminder to courts that, where substantial doubt about the congressional intent exists, the general presumption favoring judicial review of administrative action is controlling. That presumption does not control in cases such as this one, however, since the congressional intent to preclude judicial review is 'fairly discernible' in the detail of the legislative scheme . . ."

Justice O'Connor noted that the original 1933 statute contained no judicial review provision; a 1935 amendment provided that handlers could seek review of marketing orders, but only after exhausting specified administrative remedies; consumers are not mentioned in the amendment. "Nowhere in the Act . . . is there an express provision for participation by consumers in any proceeding. In a complex scheme of this type, the omission of such a provision is sufficient reason to believe that Congress intended to foreclose consumer participation in the regulatory process. . . . To be sure, the general purpose sections of the Act allude to general consumer interests. . . . But the preclusion issue does not only turn on whether the interests of a particular class like consumers are implicated. Rather, the preclusion issue turns ultimately on whether Congress intended for that class to be relied upon to challenge agency disregard of the law. . . .

"Allowing consumers to sue the Secretary would severely disrupt this complex and delicate administrative scheme. It would provide handlers with a convenient device for evading the statutory requirement that they first exhaust their administrative remedies. A handler may also be a consumer and, as such, could sue in that capacity. Alternatively, a handler would need only to find a consumer who is willing to join in or initiate an action in the district court. The consumer or consumer-handler could then raise precisely the same exceptions that the handler must raise administratively. . . . For these reasons, we think it clear that Congress intended that judicial review of market orders issued under the Act ordinarily be confined to suits brought by handlers in accordance with 7 U.S.C. § 608c(15).

". . . [P]reclusion of consumer suits will not threaten realization of the fundamental objectives of the statute. Handlers have interests similar to those of consumers. Handlers, like consumers, are interested in obtaining reliable supplies of milk at the cheapest possible prices. Handlers can therefore be expected to challenge unlawful agency action and to ensure that the statute's objectives will not be frustrated. . . ."

NOTES

(1) *Are Bowen and CNI Consistent?* Bowen was issued two years after CNI. Are the two decisions consistent in their approach to finding preclusion and the presumption of reviewability? In CNI, the Court downplayed the presumption of reviewability, whereas the Bowen Court put heavy emphasis on the presumption. What are we to make of the fact that neither opinion drew separate concurrences or dissents (although Justice Stevens, author of the latter opinion, did not participate in the former case)?

Is the statutory basis for preclusion stronger in CNI than in Bowen? Note that in CNI, no one argued that marketing orders, as a category of agency action, were unreviewable; the 1935 amendments expressly provided for their review. The focus was on *who* can get review, with CNI's reference to whether a "class" was entitled to invoke judicial review sounding more aligned with a zone-of-interests inquiry than preclusion (see Sec. 1.e). By contrast, in Bowen, the issue was whether there would be any review of regulations setting out reimbursement methodology, a clearer case of preclusion of a category of agency action.

Does this difference make the presumption of reviewability more relevant in Bowen, and the argument for preclusion more troubling? Or does the fact that review was already available in CNI make the Court's decision to deny review at consumers' behest more puzzling? Here it's worth emphasizing that the handlers could get judicial review but first had to exhaust administrative remedies. (For discussion of exhaustion, see Sec. 2.c.1.) Is the concern that direct suit by consumers might allow handlers to avoid this exhaustion requirement? If so, another way to address this concern would be to allow consumers to sue but subject them also to the exhaustion requirement. Is extending exhaustion a less plausible reading of the statute than finding preclusion?

Perhaps the difference is simply, as Justice O'Connor argues, that foreclosing consumer suits "will not threaten realization of the fundamental objectives of the statute," given the availability of some judicial review. This fits with her argument that handlers will be adequate surrogates for consumers. But do you think they will be? Or is the better justification for preclusion in CNI that the Agricultural Marketing Agreement Act and its provisions for judicial review represent a carefully wrought compromise between milk producers and handlers that excludes consumers? Does that fit with the Act's provision for public hearings and comment? Note that at the time the Act was adopted in the 1930s, consumer suits were not with legal contemplation. In any event, why isn't the same legislative compromise point available with respect to Medicare and its carefully articulated opportunities for review?

(2) ***"Implied" Preclusion: A Wrong Turn in APA Interpretation?*** Both Bowen and CNI involved claims for implied statutory preclusion. Look again at the language of § 701(a)(1). Should this provision *ever* be satisfied by anything short of an *explicit* statutory direction that review not occur? For a historical argument that the correct answer to this question is no, see Daniel Rodriguez, The Presumption of Reviewability: A Study in Canonical Construction and Its Consequences, 45 Vand. L. Rev. 743, 754–57 (1992).

Abbott Labs admits the possibility that a statute could implicitly foreclose review. However, the opinion set what seemed like such a formidable standard for preclusion that, for many years, courts and commentators looking for a Supreme Court implied preclusion case had to fall back on the pre-APA opinion in SWITCHMEN'S UNION V. NATIONAL MEDIATION BOARD., 320 U.S. 297 (1943). The Switchmen's Union lost a representation battle with a rival union and sought to challenge a decision of the National Mediation Board that had disadvantaged it in the election and that rested, it claimed, on the Board's misconstruction of the statute. Writing for four of the seven Justices who participated, JUSTICE DOUGLAS reviewed the legislative history of the disputed portion of the statute:

"Commissioner Eastman, draftsman of the 1934 amendments, . . . stated that whether one organization or another was the proper representative of a particular group of employees was 'one of the most controversial questions in connection with labor organization matters.' He stated that it was very important 'to provide a neutral tribunal which can make the decision and get the matter settled.' . . . Accordingly [the provision] was drafted so as to give to the Mediation Board the power to 'appoint a committee of three neutral persons who after hearing shall within ten days designate the employees who may participate in the election.' That was added so that the Board's 'own usefulness of settling disputes that might arise thereafter might not be impaired.' Where Congress took such great pains to protect the Mediation Board in its handling of an explosive problem, we cannot help but believe that if Congress had desired to implicate the federal judiciary and to place on the federal courts the burden of having the final say on any aspect of the problem, it would have made its desire plain. . . . [T]he intent seems plain— the dispute was to reach its last terminal point when the administrative finding was made. There was to be no dragging out of the controversy into other tribunals of law."

(3) *Narrow Reading of Express Preclusion Provisions.* Bowen also involved a statutory provision expressly precluding review, 42 U.S.C. § 405(h) of the Social Security Act (incorporated into the Medicare Act). Should the preclusion analysis be the same when there is an express preclusion provision? In particular, should the presumption of reviewability apply in this context?

As Bowen suggests, the Supreme Court has read express preclusion clauses narrowly and applied the presumption of reviewability. In JOHNSON V. ROBISON, 415 U.S. 361 (1974), a conscientious objector claimed that the First and Fifth Amendments were violated by a statutory provision denying generally available veterans' educational benefits to conscientious objectors who had completed alternative service. Invoking Abbott Labs' clear and convincing evidence standard for finding preclusion, the Court ruled that 38 U.S.C. § 211(a), providing that the Veterans Affairs Administrator's "decisions . . . on any question of law or fact under any law administered by the Veterans' Administration providing benefits for veterans . . . shall be final and conclusive and no . . . court of the United States shall have power or jurisdiction to review any such decision," did not preclude judicial review of his claims.

Writing for a unanimous Court, JUSTICE BRENNAN began by stating that construing § 211(a) as "bar[ring] federal courts from deciding the constitutionality of veterans' benefits legislation . . . would, of course, raise serious questions concerning the constitutionality of § 211(a), and in such case it is a cardinal principle that this Court will first ascertain whether a construction of the statute is fairly possible by which the [constitutional] question[s] may be avoided. Plainly, no explicit provision of § 211(a) bars judicial consideration of appellee's constitutional claims. . . . The prohibitions would appear to be aimed at review only of those decisions of law or fact that arise in the *administration* by the Veterans' Administration of a *statute* providing benefits for veterans. A decision of law or fact 'under' a statute is made by the Administrator in the interpretation or application of a particular provision of the statute to a particular set of facts. Appellee's constitutional challenge is not to any such decision of the *Administrator*, but rather to a decision of *Congress* to create a statutory class entitled to benefits that does not include . . . conscientious objectors who performed alternate civilian service." Subsequently, in Traynor v. Turnage, 485 U.S. 535 (1988), the Court held that "[t]he text and legislative history of § 211(a) . . . provide no clear and convincing evidence of any congressional intent to preclude a suit claiming that § 504 of the Rehabilitation Act, a statute applicable to all federal agencies, has invalidated an otherwise valid regulation issued by the Veterans' Administration."

Compare CUOZZO SPEED TECHNOLOGIES, LLC. v. LEE, 136 S.Ct. 2131 (2016), where the Court found that 35 U.S.C. § 314(d), stating that the "determination by the [Patent Office on] whether to institute an inter partes review under this section shall be final and nonappealable," precluded "judicial review of the kind of mine-run claim at issue here, involving the Patent Office's decision to institute inter partes review." Writing for a 7–2 majority on the issue, JUSTICE BREYER argued that the § 314(d)'s text and purpose required preclusion. "We recognize the 'strong presumption' in favor of judicial review that we apply when we interpret statutes, including statutes that may limit or preclude review. Mach Mining, LLC v. EEOC, 135 S.Ct. 1645, 1650–51 (2015) [p. 1405] This presumption, however, may be overcome by 'clear and convincing' indications, drawn from 'specific language,' 'specific legislative history,' and 'inferences of intent drawn from the statutory scheme as a whole,' that Congress intended to bar review. Block v. CNI, 467 U.S. 340, 349–350 (1984) [p. 1390]. That standard is met here. . . . Nevertheless, in light of § 314(d)'s own text and the presumption favoring review, we emphasize that our interpretation applies where the grounds for attacking the decision to institute inter partes review consist of questions that are closely tied to the application and interpretation of statutes related to the Patent Office's decision to initiate inter partes review. . . . This means that we need not, and do not, decide the precise effect of § 314(d) on appeals that implicate constitutional questions, that depend on other less closely related statutes, or that present other questions of interpretation that reach, in terms of scope and impact, well beyond 'this section.' Cf. Johnson v. Robison, 415 U.S. 361, 367 (1974)."

(4) *All Claims Are Not Equal.* RONALD M. LEVIN, UNDERSTANDING UNREVIEWABILITY IN ADMINISTRATIVE LAW, 74 Minn. L. Rev. 689, 739–40 (1990): "[T]he Court tends to allow some issues to be precluded more readily than other issues. At the top of the scale, . . . the presumption against preclusion of constitutional grievances against an agency is practically irrebuttable. The Court also has proved less willing to find preclusion in cases involving administrative rules than in cases involving agency adjudication, and less willing to foreclose legal challenges than factual ones, especially where the legal issues are not within the administering agency's expertise. At the bottom of the hierarchy are issues of fact and application of law to fact, which the Court allows to be precluded more readily than any others.

"In most of these cases, the Court also found technical grounds for reading the statutes to support these results; thus the Court's lawmaking was peripheral and somewhat covert. Yet these holdings clearly have been informed by practical judgments about the relative importance of judicial review of various kinds of issues. One would have been astonished if the Court had adopted any of the opposite distinctions—for example, if it had made factual contentions reviewable in a situation in which legal issues were unreviewable."

(5) *The Effect of Alternative Avenues for Review.* In THUNDER BASIN COAL CO. V. REICH, 510 U.S. 200 (1994), a mine owner whose workforce was not unionized refused to post information about two United Mine Workers Union employees who had been designated the miners' "representatives"— despite the fact that a Department of Labor regulation required posting. The owner then filed suit in the district court, seeking to enjoin enforcement of the regulation against him. Relying on CNI, the Court held that "[i]n cases involving delayed judicial review, we shall find that Congress has allocated initial review to an administrative body where such intent is fairly discernible in the statutory scheme" and "petitioner's claims are of the type Congress intended to be reviewed within this statutory structure." Id. at 207, 210.

Applying this test, the Court unanimously held that there was no jurisdiction over the employer's suit. Under the Federal Mine Safety and Health Amendments Act, challenges to enforcement are first reviewed by the Federal Mine Safety and Health Review Commission (an independent agency created exclusively to adjudicate Mine Act disputes) and then by the appropriate court of appeals. The statute is silent about pre-enforcement review and explicitly provides for review in the district court only in two specific (inapplicable) circumstances. JUSTICE BLACKMUN's opinion concluded that the statute's comprehensive scheme of enforcement and administrative review implicitly precluded a pre-enforcement challenge. The mine owner could obtain review by refusing to comply with the order and forcing the agency to begin enforcement proceedings: "Although the Act's civil penalties unquestionably may become onerous if petitioner chooses not to comply, the Secretary's penalty assessments become final and payable only after full review by both the Commission and the appropriate Court of Appeals."

More recent Supreme Court decisions have split on their willingness to find delayed review schemes to be exclusive. FREE ENTERPRISE FUND V. PUBLIC CO. ACCOUNTING OVERSIGHT BD., 561 U.S. 477 (2010) (PCAOB) [p. 922], held that a separation-of-powers challenge to the structure of PCAOB, an agency created by the Sarbanes-Oxley Act as part of reforms of the accounting industry, was not precluded. The Act makes PCAOB's rules and orders reviewable by the SEC, whose rules and orders are in turn reviewable by the courts of appeals; "[n]o objection . . . may be considered by the court unless it was urged before the Commission or there was reasonable ground for failure to do so." 15 U.S.C. §§ 78y(a)(1), (b)(1), (c)(1). The Government argued that this was the exclusive avenue for review. No Justice dissented from the conclusion that petitioners' action for declaratory and injunctive relief was not precluded under Thunder Basin's test. "We do not see how petitioners could meaningfully pursue their constitutional claims under the Government's theory. Section 78y provides only for judicial review of Commission action, and not every Board action is encapsulated in a final Commission order or rule." The Court rejected the Government's argument that the petitioners could have precipitated a Board decision imposing sanctions by refusing to provide requested information and then raised the constitutional challenge on appeal. "We normally do not require plaintiffs to bet the farm by taking the violative action before testing the validity of the law." The constitutional claims did not turn on "fact-bound inquiries" that were within the SEC's special competence or "require 'technical considerations of [agency] policy.' Johnson v. Robison, 415 U.S. 361, 373 (1974). They are instead standard questions of administrative law, which the courts are at no disadvantage in answering."

By contrast, in ELGIN V. DEP'T OF TREASURY, 567 U.S. 1 (2012), the Court ruled that the statute outlined the exclusive route to judicial review. Elgin concerned the Civil Service Reform Act (CSRA), which sets forth a comprehensive structure for reviewing personnel actions taken against federal employees. Under the CSRA, federal employees who suffer adverse employment actions may seek a hearing before the Merit Systems Protection Board (MSPB), whose decision is then reviewed by the Federal Circuit. Male employees who had been discharged because they failed to register for the military draft filed suit in federal district court alleging that the Military Selective Service Act and the corresponding statute barring them from federal employment were facially unconstitutional under the Equal Protection and the Bill of Attainder Clauses. In a 6–3 decision written by JUSTICE THOMAS, the Court held that "the CSRA's elaborate framework . . . indicates that extrastatutory review is not available to those employees to whom the CSRA grants administrative and judicial review." The Court further held that meaningful review was available for the plaintiffs' claims because "the CSRA provides review in the Federal Circuit, an Article III court fully competent to adjudicate petitioners' [constitutional] claims" and rejected the plaintiffs' argument that their constitutional challenges were "wholly collateral" to the CSRA scheme. It also rejected the plaintiffs' assertion "that their constitutional claims are not the sort that Congress intended to channel through the MSPB because they are outside the MSPB's expertise," arguing that the plaintiffs "overlook the many threshold questions that may accompany a constitutional claim and to which the MSPB can apply its expertise. Of particular relevance here, preliminary questions unique to the employment context may obviate the need to address the constitutional challenge." Justice Alito dissented, joined by Justices Ginsburg and Kagan.

Recently, a number of constitutional challenges to the SEC's administrative proceedings have raised the issue of whether a statutory administrative and judicial review scheme precludes immediate access to court. By statute, the SEC can seek civil enforcement of the federal securities laws either by bringing a civil action in federal district court or by initiating an administrative enforcement proceeding. The SEC expanded its use of administrative proceedings after the Dodd-Frank Wall Street Reform and Consumer Protection Act expanded the remedies available to it, sparking a raft of constitutional challenges brought in federal court by defendants seeking to prevent the administrative proceedings from going forward. In JARKESY V. SEC, 803 F.3d 9 (D.C. Cir. 2015), the D.C. Circuit held that "Congress has implicitly precluded Jarkesy's district-court suit by channeling his challenges through the securities laws' scheme of administrative adjudication and judicial review in a court of appeals." In so holding, the appeals court emphasized the comprehensiveness of the adjudication structure contained in the securities laws and the inseparability of Jarkesy's constitutional challenges from the administrative enforcement proceeding. The D.C. Circuit distinguished Free Enterprise on the ground that "[t]o have his claims heard through the agency route, Jarkesy would not have to erect a Trojan-horse challenge to an SEC rule or 'bet the farm' by subjecting himself to unnecessary sanction under the securities laws. Jarkesy is already properly before the Commission by virtue of his alleged violations of those laws. Indeed, the existence of the enforcement proceedings gave rise to Jarkesy's challenges. And, should the Commission's final order run against him, a court of appeals is available to hear those challenges." Accord, Bebo v. SEC, 799 F.3d 765 (7th Cir. 2015), cert denied, 136 S.Ct. 1500 (2016); Tilton v. SEC, 824 F.3d 276 (2nd Cir. 2016), pet'n for cert filed, No. 16–906; Hill v. SEC, 825 F.3d 1236 (11th Cir. 2016); Bennett v. SEC, 844 F.3d 174 (4th Cir. 2016).

(6) ***Preclusion by Statute, Not Regulation.*** KACANA V. HOLDER, 558 U.S. 233 (2010): An unusual twist on preclusion produced an unusual degree of agreement among the Justices. One of the review-limiting provisions of the Illegal Immigration Reform and Immigrant Responsibility Act of 1996 (IIRIRA) states that no court shall have jurisdiction to review actions of the Attorney General, "the authority for which is specified under this subchapter to be in the discretion of the Attorney General." The Board of Immigration Appeals had denied Agron Kucana's motion to reopen his removal proceeding on grounds of new evidence to support his plea for asylum. By regulation, the Attorney General had declared that decisions on such motions were "discretionary" actions. The Seventh Circuit held that it could not review. Writing for all members of the Court but Justice Alito, who concurred in the judgment, JUSTICE GINSBURG concluded that the preclusion provision applied only to determinations made discretionary by statute. "If the Seventh Circuit's construction were to prevail, the Executive would have a free hand to shelter its own decisions from abuse-of-discretion appellate court review simply by issuing a regulation declaring those decisions 'discretionary.' Such an extraordinary delegation of authority cannot be extracted from the statute Congress enacted."

(3) Committed to Agency Discretion by Law

> **WEBSTER v. DOE**
> **Notes on the Reviewability of Agency**
> ** Refusals to Act**

WEBSTER v. DOE

Supreme Court of the United States (1988).
486 U.S. 592.

■ CHIEF JUSTICE REHNQUIST delivered the opinion of the Court.

[John Doe had been employed by the CIA for nine years, during which he was consistently rated an excellent or outstanding employee and was promoted from clerk-typist to covert electronics technician. After Doe voluntarily informed the CIA that he was gay, he was placed on paid administrative leave. He was extensively questioned about possible security breaches in connection with sexual activity and a polygraph indicated that his denials were truthful. The CIA's Office of Security then told Doe that his homosexuality posed a threat to security, although it declined to explain the nature of the danger. When Doe refused to resign, the Office recommended his dismissal to the CIA Director. After reviewing Doe's records and evaluations, the Director dismissed him, invoking § 102(c) of the National Security Act of 1947. Doe sued, alleging that the dismissal (i) was arbitrary and capricious and an abuse of discretion in violation of the APA, and (ii) deprived him of his constitutional rights. He sought reinstatement or, at least, an order that the Director reevaluate the termination and provide a statement of reasons.]

Section 102(c) . . . provides that:

[T]he Director of Central Intelligence may, in his discretion, terminate the employment of any officer or employee of the Agency whenever he shall deem such termination necessary or advisable in the interests of the United States . . .

In this case we decide whether, and to what extent, the termination decisions of the Director under § 102(c) are judicially reviewable . . .

In Citizens to Preserve Overton Park, Inc. v. Volpe, 401 U.S. 402 (1971) [p. 1085] this Court explained the distinction between §§ 701(a)(1) and (a)(2). Subsection (a)(1) is concerned with whether Congress expressed an intent to prohibit judicial review; subsection (a)(2) applies "in those rare instances where 'statutes are drawn in such broad terms that in a given case there is no law to apply.'" (quoting S.Rep. No. 752, 79th Cong., 1st Sess., 26 (1945)).

We further explained what it means for an action to be "committed to agency discretion by law" in Heckler v. Chaney, 470 U.S. 821 (1985) [p. 1407]. . . . We noted that, under § 701(a)(2), even when Congress has not affirmatively precluded judicial oversight, "review is not to be had if the statute is drawn so that a court would have no meaningful standard against which to judge the agency's exercise of discretion." . . .

Both Overton Park and Heckler emphasized that § 701(a)(2) requires careful examination of the statute on which the claim of agency illegality is based. In the present case, respondent's claims against the CIA arise from the Director's asserted violation of § 102(c) of the NSA. As an initial matter, it should be noted that § 102(c) allows termination of an Agency employee whenever the Director "shall *deem* such termination necessary or advisable in the interests of the United States" (emphasis added), not simply when the dismissal *is* necessary or advisable to those interests. This standard fairly exudes deference to the Director, and appears to us to foreclose the application of any meaningful judicial standard of review . . .

So too does the overall structure of the NSA. Passed shortly after the close of the Second World War, the NSA created the CIA and gave its Director the responsibility "for protecting intelligence sources and methods from unauthorized disclosure." Section 102(c) is an integral part of that statute, because the Agency's efficacy, and the Nation's security, depend in large measure on the reliability and trustworthiness of the Agency's employees . . . Section 102(c) exhibits the Act's extraordinary deference to the Director in his decision to terminate individual employees.

We thus find that the language and structure of § 102(c) indicate that Congress meant to commit individual employee discharges to the Director's discretion, and that § 701(a)(2) accordingly precludes judicial review of these decisions under the APA . . .

In addition to his claim that the Director failed to abide by the statutory dictates of § 102(c), . . . [r]espondent charged that petitioner's termination of his employment deprived him of property and liberty interests under the Due Process Clause of the Fifth Amendment, denied him equal protection of the laws, and unjustifiably burdened his right to privacy. Respondent asserts that he is entitled, under the APA, to judicial consideration of these claimed violations.

. . . It is difficult, if not impossible, to ascertain from the amended complaint whether respondent contends that his termination, based on *his* homosexuality, is constitutionally impermissible, or whether he asserts that a more pervasive discrimination policy exists in the CIA's employment practices regarding *all* homosexuals. This ambiguity in the amended complaint is no doubt attributable in part to the inconsistent explanations respondent received from the Agency itself regarding his termination. Prior to his discharge, respondent had been told by two CIA security officers that his homosexual activities themselves violated CIA regulations. In contrast, the Deputy General Counsel of the CIA later informed respondent that homosexuality was merely a security concern that did not inevitably result in termination, but instead was evaluated on a case-by-case basis.

Petitioner maintains that, no matter what the nature of respondent's constitutional claims, judicial review is precluded by the language and intent of § 102(c). In petitioner's view, all Agency employment termination decisions, even those based on policies normally repugnant to the Constitution, are given over to the absolute discretion of the Director, and are hence unreviewable under the APA. We do not think § 102(c) may be read to exclude review of constitutional claims. We emphasized in Johnson v. Robison, 415 U.S. 361 (1974) [p. 1394], that where Congress intends to preclude judicial review of constitutional claims its intent to do so must be clear . . . We require this heightened showing in part to avoid the "serious constitutional question" that would arise if a federal statute were construed to deny any judicial forum for a colorable constitutional claim. See Bowen v. Michigan Academy of Family Physicians, 476 U.S. 667, 681, n. 12 (1986) [p. 1386].

Our review of § 102(c) convinces us that it cannot bear the preclusive weight petitioner would have it support. [T]he section . . . precludes challenges to [termination] decisions based upon the statutory language of § 102(c), [but] nothing in § 102(c) persuades us that Congress meant to preclude consideration of colorable constitutional claims arising out of the actions of the Director pursuant to that section; we believe that a constitutional claim based on an individual discharge may be reviewed by the District Court . . .

Petitioner complains that judicial review even of constitutional claims will entail extensive "rummaging around" in the Agency's affairs to the detriment of national security. But petitioner acknowledges that Title VII claims attacking the hiring and promotion policies of the Agency are routinely entertained in federal court, and the inquiry and discovery associated with those proceedings would seem to involve some of the same sort of rummaging. Furthermore, the District Court has the latitude to control any discovery process which may be instituted so as to balance respondent's need for access to proof which would support a colorable constitutional claim against the extraordinary needs of the CIA for confidentiality and the protection of its methods, sources, and mission. . . .

The judgment of the Court of Appeals is affirmed in part, reversed in part, and the case is remanded for further proceedings consistent with this opinion.

■ JUSTICE KENNEDY took no part in the consideration or decision of this case.

■ JUSTICE O'CONNOR, concurring in part and dissenting in part.

I agree that the APA does not authorize judicial review [here] . . . I do not understand the Court to say that the exception in § 701(a)(2) is necessarily or fully defined by reference to statutes "drawn in such broad terms that in a given case there is no law to apply." See Citizens to Preserve Overton Park, Inc. v. Volpe, 401 U.S. 402, 410 (1971) . . . I disagree, however, with the Court's conclusion that a constitutional claim challenging the validity of an employment decision covered by § 102(c) may nonetheless be brought in a federal district court. Whatever may be the exact scope of Congress' power to close the lower federal courts to constitutional claims in other contexts, I have no doubt about its authority to do so here . . .

■ JUSTICE SCALIA, dissenting.

I agree with the Court's apparent holding, that the Director's decision to terminate a CIA employee is "committed to agency discretion by law" . . . Though I subscribe to most of that analysis, I disagree with the Court's description of what is required to come within subsection (a)(2) of § 701 . . . Our precedents amply show that "commit[ment] to agency discretion by law" includes, but is not limited to, situations in which there is "no law to apply. . . ."

The key to understanding the "committed to agency discretion *by law*" provision of § 701(a)(2) lies in contrasting it with the "*statutes* preclude judicial review" provision of § 701(a)(1). Why "statutes" for preclusion, but the much more general term "law" for commission to agency discretion? The answer is, as we implied in [Heckler v.] Chaney, that the latter was intended to refer to "the 'common law' of judicial review of agency action" 470 U.S. at 832—a body of jurisprudence that had marked out, with more or less precision, certain issues and certain areas that were beyond the range of judicial review. That jurisprudence included principles ranging from the "political question" doctrine, to sovereign immunity (including doctrines determining when a suit against an officer would be deemed to be a suit against the sovereign), to official immunity, to prudential limitations upon the courts' equitable powers, to what can be described no more precisely than a traditional respect for the functions of the other branches reflected in the statement in Marbury v. Madison, 1 Cranch 137, 170–71 (1803), that "[w]here the head of a department acts in a case, in which executive discretion is to be exercised; in which he is the mere organ of executive will; it is again repeated, that any application to a court to control, in any respect, his conduct, would be rejected without hesitation." . . .

All this law, shaped over the course of centuries and still developing in its application to new contexts, cannot possibly be contained within the phrase "no law to apply." It is not surprising, then, that although the Court recites the test it does not really apply it. Like other opinions relying upon it, this one essentially announces the test, declares victory and moves on. It is not really true "'that a court would have no meaningful standard against which to judge the agency's exercise of discretion,'" supra, quoting Chaney. The standard set forth in § 102(c) . . . at least excludes dismissal out of personal vindictiveness, or because the Director wants to give the job to his cousin. Why, on the Court's theory, is respondent not entitled to assert the presence of such excesses, under the "abuse of discretion" standard of § 706? . . .

II.

[Justice Scalia then turned to reviewability of Doe's constitutional claim.] The first response to the Court's grave doubt about the constitutionality of denying all judicial review to a "colorable constitutional claim" is that the denial of all judicial review is not at issue here, but merely the denial of review in United States district courts. As to that, the law is, and has long been, clear. Article III, § 2, of the Constitution extends the judicial power to "all Cases . . . arising under this Constitution." But Article III, § 1, provides that the judicial power shall be vested "in one supreme Court, *and in such inferior Courts as the Congress may from time to time ordain and establish*" (emphasis added). We long ago held that the power not to create any lower federal courts at all includes the power to invest them with less than all of the judicial power . . . Sheldon v. Sill, 49 U.S. (8 How.) 441, 449 (1850). Thus, if there is any truth to the proposition that judicial cognizance of constitutional claims cannot be eliminated, it is, at most, that they cannot be eliminated from state courts, and from this Court's appellate jurisdiction over cases from state courts . . .

It can fairly be argued, however, that our interpretation of § 701(a)(2) indirectly implicates the constitutional question whether state courts can be deprived of jurisdiction, because if they cannot, then interpreting § 701(a)(2) to exclude relief here would impute to Congress the peculiar intent to let state courts review Federal Government action that it is unwilling to let federal district courts review . . . I turn, then, to the substance of the Court's warning that judicial review of all "colorable constitutional claims" arising out of the respondent's dismissal may well be constitutionally required. What could possibly be the basis for this fear? Surely not some general principle that *all* constitutional violations must be remediable in the courts. The very text of the Constitution refutes that principle, since it provides that "[e]ach House shall be the Judge of the Elections, Returns and Qualifications of its own Members," Art. I, § 5, and that "for any Speech or Debate in either House, [the Senators and Representatives] shall not be questioned in any other Place," Art. I, § 6. Claims concerning constitutional violations committed in these contexts—for example, the rather grave constitutional claim that an election has been stolen—cannot be addressed to the courts. Even apart from the strict text of the Constitution, we have found some constitutional claims to be beyond judicial review because they involve "political questions." The doctrine of sovereign immunity—not repealed by the Constitution, but to the contrary at least partly reaffirmed as to the States by the Eleventh Amendment—is a monument to the principle that some constitutional claims can go unheard. No one would suggest that, if Congress had not passed the Tucker Act, the courts would be able to order disbursements from the Treasury to pay for property taken under lawful authority (and subsequently destroyed) without just compensation . . . In sum, it is simply untenable that there must be a judicial remedy for every constitutional violation . . .

. . . It seems to me clear that courts would not entertain, for example, an action for backpay by a dismissed Secretary of State claiming that the reason he lost his Government job was that the President did not like his religious views—surely a colorable violation of the First Amendment. I am confident we would hold that the President's choice of his Secretary of State is a "political question." But what about a similar suit by the Deputy Secretary of State? Or one of the Under Secretaries? Or an Assistant Secretary? Or the head of the European Desk? Is there really a constitutional line that falls at some immutable point between one and another of these offices at which the principle of unreviewability cuts in, and which cannot be altered by congressional prescription? I think not. . . .

Perhaps, then, a constitutional right is by its nature so much more important to the claimant than a statutory right that a statute which plainly excludes the latter should not be read to exclude the former unless it says so. That principle has never been announced—and with good reason, because its premise is not true. An individual's contention that the Government has reneged upon a $100,000 debt owing under a contract is much more important to him—both financially and, I suspect, in the sense of injustice that he feels—than the same individual's claim that a particular federal licensing provision requiring a $100 license denies him equal protection of the laws, or that a particular state tax violates the Commerce Clause. . . . [A]s between executive violations of statute and executive violations of the Constitution both of which are equally unlawful, and neither of which can be said, *a priori*, to be more harmful or more unfair to the plaintiff—[there is no reason why] one or the other category should be favored by a presumption against exclusion of judicial review . . .

NOTES

(1) ***Does Webster's Half-Unreviewable Solution Make Sense?*** The Webster Court is unanimous in reading § 102(c) to preclude judicial review of the Director's exercises of discretion under the National Security Act, but it divided 6–2 in holding that § 102(c) allowed judicial review of constitutional claims. Note that § 701(a) appears to sanction such partial reviewability, stating that judicial review is precluded "to the extent that" judicial review is precluded by statute or "agency action is committed to agency discretion by law." But what about § 102(c): Is it plausible to read the provision's text as splitting preclusion this way? The majority invokes the canon of constitutional avoidance to justify its split reading, but that canon does not apply if the meaning of a provision is clear, see p. 1207.

Justice Scalia faults the majority for invoking the constitutional avoidance canon on another ground: in his view, it is clearly constitutional for Congress to preclude judicial review of some constitutional claims. Do you agree? See Note on the Constitutionality of Precluding Review, p. 1383.

(2) ***Squaring § 701(a)(2) with § 706(2)(A).*** Professor LEVIN, supra, at 695, writes that ". . .a straightforward reading of the text of section 701(a)(2) would be totally unacceptable. At face value, the clause seems to say that every enabling statute that grants some discretion to an agency creates a sphere of administrative conduct that the courts must not examine. That conclusion, however, would be absurd: everyday reality teaches that judicial review of agencies' exercises of discretionary judgment is routine. Indeed, the APA contains compelling internal evidence that the literal interpretation was not intended. Section 706(2)(A) provides that an agency action may be set aside for 'abuse of discretion.' If the existence of statutory discretion made the challenged action unreviewable, that provision would become meaningless. Accordingly, the need for a restrictive, and perhaps artificial, reading of the phrase 'committed to agency discretion' has been universally acknowledged since the earliest days of the APA."

Another way of addressing the tension between § 701(a)(2) and § 706(2)(A) would be to conclude that the term "discretion" has different meanings in the two sections; a strong and much rarer "DISCRETION" form for § 701(a)(2) and a much more common and weaker "discretion" version for § 706(2)(A), the exercise of which is subject to judicial review. See Peter L. Strauss, Presidential Rulemaking, 72 Chi.-Kent L. Rev. 965, 975–78 (1997).

(3) ***Reviewable, but Narrowly.*** Would a better approach have been to read § 102(c) as not precluding all review of any claims but as restricting reviewing courts to very narrow and deferential review given the broad discretion expressly granted the agency? The Court took such an approach in MACH MINING, LLC V. EEOC, 135 S.Ct. 1645 (2015), a non-APA case involving a suit by the EEOC against a mining company for discriminating against women in hiring in violation of Title VII of the Civil Rights Act. Under Title VII, EEOC is required to try to conciliate a claim before filing suit but can sue if it is unable to secure from the respondent a conciliation agreement "acceptable to the Commission." In a unanimous opinion by JUSTICE KAGAN, the Court rejected EEOC's argument that judicial review of its conciliation efforts was precluded but emphasized the limited scope of appropriate judicial scrutiny:

"Congress rarely intends to prevent courts from enforcing its directives to federal agencies. For that reason, this Court applies a 'strong presumption' favoring judicial review of administrative action. . . . Title VII, as the Government acknowledges, imposes a duty on the EEOC to attempt conciliation of a discrimination charge prior to filing a lawsuit. That obligation is a key component of the statutory scheme. . . . Courts routinely enforce such compulsory prerequisites to suit in Title VII litigation (and in many other contexts besides). An employee, for example, may bring a Title VII claim only if she has first filed a timely charge with the EEOC . . . Absent [judicial] review, the Commission's compliance with the law would rest in the Commission's hands alone. We need not doubt the EEOC's trustworthiness, or its fidelity to law, to shy away from that result. We need only know—and know that Congress knows—that legal lapses and violations occur, and especially so when they have no consequence. That is why this Court has so long applied a strong presumption favoring judicial review of administrative action. Nothing overcomes that presumption with respect to the EEOC's duty to attempt conciliation of employment discrimination claims.

"[But w]hat is the proper scope of judicial review of the EEOC's conciliation activities? . . . The appropriate scope of review enforces the statute's requirements as just described—in brief, that the EEOC afford the employer a chance to discuss and rectify a specified discriminatory practice—but goes no further. Such limited review respects the expansive discretion that Title VII gives to the EEOC over the conciliation process, while still ensuring that the Commission follows the law." For similar conclusions that particular types of agency actions are reviewable but subject to very deferential scrutiny, see the Notes on the Reviewability of Agency Refusals to Act, p. 1407.

(4) *Nonreviewability and Nondelegation.* What is the relationship between § 701(a)(2) and nondelegation doctrine? Recall that under nondelegation doctrine, Congress is required to provide an intelligible principle in order for a delegation of power to an agency to be constitutional. See Whitman v. Am. Trucking Assns, p. 791. If there is "no law to apply" does this mean that the delegation is unconstitutional because it is lacking an "intelligible principle"? As Webster demonstrates, courts have distinguished between nonreviewability and nondelegation, holding that actions are unreviewable under § 701(a)(2) without calling the underlying delegation of authority pursuit to which such delegations are taken into question. But why not?

One way to resolve the doctrinal tension here is to note that "no law to apply" actually means no law for *courts* to apply. That is, § 102(c) of the National Security Act instructs the Director how to exercise his power to fire: he must determine that "such termination [is] necessary or advisable in the interests of the United States." This instruction is certainly intelligible to the Director—it is simply not a principle that courts will enforce, because Congress has vested exercise of that discretion exclusively in an executive official. Although we tend to equate "legal obligation" with judicial enforcement, in fact many very important statutory and constitutional requirements that govern executive action are not enforced by courts (for example, in areas of military and foreign affairs, as well as national security), and yet we recognize them as law. More to the point, we expect executive officials to regard them as binding constraints, not merely precatory admonitions about using delegated power.

Is this explanation satisfying? It is in line with the Court's insistence in Whitman that what matters for nondelegation purposes is that *Congress* lay down an intelligible principle, not whether agencies limit their delegated authority—nor, by extension, whether courts are able to police agencies' exercises of delegated authority. (See p. 793.) But if you see judicial review as more central to the constitutionality of delegations, is § 701(a)(2) more problematic? Or are constitutional delegation concerns adequately addressed by "a system of . . . remedies adequate to keep government generally within the bounds of law," Richard H. Fallon, Jr. & Daniel J. Meltzer, New Law, Non-Retroactivity, and Constitutional Remedies, 104 Harv. L. Rev. 1731, 1778–79 (1991), even if some exercises of agency discretion are not reviewable?

Note that not every court has treated nonreviewability and nondelegation as distinct. See South Dakota v. Department of the Interior, 69 F.3d 878 (8th Cir. 1995) (p. 803) (concluding that statute underlying agency action represented an unconstitutional delegation based on agency's claims that its actions applying the statute were unreviewable under § 701(a)(2), rev'd and remanded without opinion upon the Solicitor General's retraction of its § 701(a)(2) argument, 519 U.S. 919 (1996).

(5) ***Regulations as "Law to Apply."*** What if the agency adopts a regulation that provides judicially manageable standards for how it will go about exercising its discretion? It is then likely to lose its § 701(a)(2) defense to judicial review. E.g., Smirko v. Ashcroft, 387 F.3d 279 (3d Cir. 2004); Haoud v. Ashcroft, 350 F.3d 201 (1st Cir. 2003); Center for Auto Safety v. Dole, 846 F.2d 1532 (D.C. Cir. 1988). Is this simply application of the principle that agencies must follow their own regulations? See p. 1042. Consider, however, the resulting disincentives for agencies to exercise self-discipline through discretion-constraining regulations; doing so will expose them to judicial review where none might otherwise exist. Recognizing this, might a reviewing court hesitate before interpreting an agency statement as a binding commitment to limit its own power? Alternatively, should the court be willing to look to interpretive rules and statements of policy as also possible sources of "law to apply"? See Gillian Metzger & Kevin Stack, Internal Administrative Law, 115 Mich. L. Rev. 1239, 1295 (2017).

NOTES ON THE REVIEWABILITY
OF AGENCY REFUSALS TO ACT

One area where § 701(a)(2) frequently arises involves agency inaction. The Supreme Court has found some forms of agency inaction to be unreviewable, or presumptively so, whereas it has upheld the reviewability of others. As you read through these notes, can you identify a consistent theme or set of factors that leads the Court to come down in favor of or against reviewability?

(1) ***Decisions Not to Take Enforcement Action.*** HECKLER V. CHANEY, 470 U.S. 821 (1985), was an attempt by prisoners on death row to persuade the Food and Drug Administration to regulate the use of drugs for human execution. The FDA refused on grounds that (1) its jurisdiction in the area was unclear but should not be exercised to interfere with state criminal justice practices; and (2) enforcement in the area of unapproved use of approved drugs was generally initiated "only when there is a serious danger to the public health or a blatant scheme to defraud," neither of which was present here. The D.C. Circuit found the refusal reviewable, focusing both on the Abbott presumption of reviewability and on an FDA Policy Statement that the agency was "obligated" to investigate unapproved uses of approved

drugs when such uses became "widespread" or "endanger[ed] the public health." JUSTICE REHNQUIST wrote for the eight-justice majority:

"This Court has recognized on several occasions over many years that an agency's decision not to prosecute or enforce, whether through civil or criminal process, is a decision generally committed to an agency's absolute discretion. This recognition is attributable in no small part to the general unsuitability for judicial review of agency decisions to refuse enforcement.

"The reasons for this general unsuitability are many. First, an agency decision not to enforce often involves a complicated balancing of a number of factors which are peculiarly within its expertise. Thus, the agency must not only assess whether a violation has occurred, but whether agency resources are best spent on this violation or another, whether the agency is likely to succeed if it acts, whether the particular enforcement action requested best fits the agency's overall policies, and, indeed, whether the agency has enough resources to undertake the action at all. An agency generally cannot act against each technical violation of the statute it is charged with enforcing. The agency is far better equipped than the courts to deal with the many variables involved in the proper ordering of its priorities . . .

"In addition to these administrative concerns, we note that when an agency refuses to act it generally does not exercise its *coercive* power over an individual's liberty or property rights, and thus does not infringe upon areas that courts often are called upon to protect . . . Finally, we recognize that an agency's refusal to institute proceedings shares to some extent the characteristics of the decision of a prosecutor in the Executive Branch not to indict—a decision which has long been regarded as the special province of the Executive Branch, inasmuch as it is the Executive who is charged by the Constitution to 'take Care that the Laws be faithfully executed.' U.S. Const., Art. II, § 3.

". . . [W]e emphasize that the decision is only presumptively unreviewable; the presumption may be rebutted where the substantive statute has provided guidelines for the agency to follow in exercising its enforcement powers.[4] . . . Congress may limit an agency's exercise of enforcement power if it wishes, either by setting substantive priorities, or by otherwise circumscribing an agency's power to discriminate among issues or cases it will pursue . . ." But Justice Rehnquist ruled that neither limit was present here.

JUSTICE BRENNAN concurred to point out that "the Court properly does not decide today that nonenforcement decisions are unreviewable in cases where (1) an agency flatly claims that it has no statutory jurisdiction to reach certain conduct; (2) an agency engages in a pattern of nonenforcement of clear statutory language; (3) an agency has refused to enforce a regulation

---

[4] We do not have in this case a refusal by the agency to institute proceedings based solely on the belief that it lacks jurisdiction. Nor do we have a situation where it could justifiably be found that the agency has 'consciously and expressly adopted a general policy' that is so extreme as to amount to an abdication of its statutory responsibilities. Although we express no opinion on whether such decisions would be unreviewable under § 701(a)(2), we note that in those situations the statute conferring authority on the agency might indicate that such decisions were not 'committed to agency discretion.'

lawfully promulgated and still in effect; or (4) a nonenforcement decision violates constitutional rights." What justifies this set of "exceptions" to the nonreviewability presumption—presumed congressional intent? Judicial manageability? The APA itself?

JUSTICE MARSHALL, concurring only in the judgment, objected strongly to the notion that judicial review is more important when the agency acts *against* members of the regulated community than when it refuses to act *for* regulated beneficiaries: "[A]ttempting to draw a line for purposes of judicial review between affirmative exercises of coercive agency power and negative agency refusals to act is simply untenable; one of the very purposes fueling the birth of administrative agencies was the reality that governmental refusal to act could have just as devastating an effect upon life, liberty, and the pursuit of happiness as coercive governmental action." He argued that "refusals to enforce, like other agency actions, are reviewable in the absence of a 'clear and convincing' congressional intent to the contrary, but that such refusals warrant deference when, as in this case, there is nothing to suggest that an agency with enforcement discretion has abused that discretion."

In announcing a (rebuttable) § 702(a) presumption against reviewability of agency enforcement decisions, should the Court have discussed other provisions of the APA—in particular, § 551(13), which defines "agency action" as including "failure to act," or § 706, which expressly makes "agency action unlawfully withheld or unreasonably delayed" subject to judicial review? Does the majority's reasoning reduce the view that regulatory beneficiaries have less claim to judicial review of government behavior than regulated entities? Compare Justice Scalia's similar view on standing for beneficiaries in Lujan v. Defenders of Wildlife, p. 1301. For an argument that Heckler v. Chaney represents "a Lochner-like view of the judicial role," see Cass R. Sunstein, Reviewing Agency Inaction After Heckler v. Chaney, 52 U. Chi. L. Rev. 653 (1985).

Chaney thus establishes that nonenforcement decisions are presumptively nonreviewable, but what counts as a nonenforcement decision? This issue arose in TEXAS V. UNITED STATES, 809 F.3d 134 (5th Cir. 2015) (p. 357), aff'd by an equally divided Supreme Court, United States v. Texas, 136 S.Ct. 2271 (2016), which involved a challenge to President Obama's Deferred Action for Parents of Americans and Lawful Permanent Residents program ("DAPA"). Under the program, certain categories of immigrants in the country illegally could apply for a grant of deferred action status, under which the government would not seek to deport them for three years. The total number of immigrants subject to the program was estimated at 4.3 million. Twenty-six states, led by Texas, challenged the program as violating the immigration laws and the President's Take Care duty.

Invoking Chaney, the government argued that a grant of "deferred action . . . is a presumptively unreviewable exercise of prosecutorial discretion," but the Fifth Circuit disagreed, in a 2–1 decision written by JUDGE SMITH: "Deferred action . . . is much more than nonenforcement: It would affirmatively confer 'lawful presence' and associated benefits on a class of unlawfully present aliens. Though revocable, that change in designation would trigger . . . eligibility for federal benefits—for example, under title II and XVIII of the Social Security Act—and state benefits—for example, driver's licenses and unemployment insurance—that would not otherwise be available to illegal aliens. . . . DAPA would also toll the duration of the recipients' unlawful presence under the INA's reentry bars . . . [and recipients of deferred action status were eligible to work under a governing regulation.] . . . DAPA 'provides a focus for judicial review, inasmuch as the agency must have exercised its power in some manner. The action at least can be reviewed to determine whether the agency exceeded its statutory powers.' Chaney, 470 U.S. at 832." In a footnote, the majority added that "[b]ecause the challenged portion of DAPA's deferred-action program is not an exercise of enforcement discretion, we do not reach the issue of whether the [Chaney] presumption against review of such discretion is rebutted."

In dissent, JUDGE KING argued that "[d]eferred action decisions, such as those contemplated by the DAPA Memorandum, are quintessential exercises of prosecutorial discretion. . . . To the extent the exercise of deferred action 'trigger[s]' other benefits, . . . those benefits are a function of statutes and regulations that were enacted by Congresses and administrations long past—statutes and regulations which, vitally, Plaintiffs do not challenge in this action. . . . [B]oth 'lawful presence' and 'deferred action' refer to nothing more than DHS's tentative decision, revocable at any time, not to remove an individual for the time being—i.e., the decision to exercise prosecutorial discretion." The dissent further maintained that Chaney's exception for when an agency had " 'consciously and expressly adopted a general policy' that is so extreme as to amount to an abdication of its statutory responsibilities," 470 U.S. at 833 n. 4, was not applicable, given the Obama administration's record number of deportations.

(2) *Only Where the Failure to Act Involves a Discrete and Required Action.* NORTON V. SOUTHERN UTAH WILDERNESS ALLIANCE, 542 U.S. 55 (2004), involved an effort by environmental groups to challenge the Bureau of Land Management's failure to take action to limit off-road-vehicle usage on federal lands in Utah. In a unanimous opinion, JUSTICE SCALIA set forth general criteria that agency failures must meet to be reviewable under the APA:

"Failures to act are sometimes remediable under the APA, but not always. . . . Sections 702, 704, and 706(1) all insist upon an 'agency action,' either as the action complained of (in §§ 702 and 704) or as the action to be compelled (in § 706(1)). The definition of that term begins with a list of five categories of decisions made or outcomes implemented by an agency— 'agency rule, order, license, sanction [or] relief.' § 551(13). All of those categories involve circumscribed, discrete agency actions, as their definitions make clear: 'an agency statement of . . . future effect designed to implement, interpret, or prescribe law or policy' (rule); 'a final disposition . . . in a matter other than rule making' (order); a 'permit . . . or other form of permission' (license); a 'prohibition . . . or . . . taking [of] other compulsory or restrictive action' (sanction); or a 'grant of money, assistance, license, authority,' etc., or 'recognition of a claim, right, immunity,' etc., or 'taking of other action on the application or petition of, and beneficial to, a person' (relief). §§ 551(4), (6), (8), (10), (11).

"The terms following those five categories of agency action are not defined in the APA: 'or the equivalent or denial thereof, or failure to act.' § 551(13). But an 'equivalent . . . thereof' must also be discrete (or it would not be equivalent), and a 'denial thereof' must be the denial of a discrete listed action (and perhaps denial of a discrete equivalent). . . .

"The final term in the definition, 'failure to act,' is in our view properly understood as a failure to take an agency action—that is, a failure to take one of the agency actions (including their equivalents) earlier defined in § 551(13). Moreover, even without this equation of 'act' with 'agency action' the interpretive canon of ejusdem generis would attribute to the last item ('failure to act') the same characteristic of discreteness shared by all the preceding items. . . . A 'failure to act' is not the same thing as a 'denial.' The latter is the agency's act of saying no to a request; the former is simply the omission of an action without formally rejecting a request-for example, the failure to promulgate a rule or take some decision by a statutory deadline. The important point is that a 'failure to act' is properly understood to be limited, as are the other items in § 551(13), to a discrete action. A second point central to the analysis of the present case is that the only agency action that can be compelled under the APA is action legally required. This limitation appears in § 706(1)'s authorization for courts to "compel agency action unlawfully withheld." . . .

"Thus, a claim under § 706(1) can proceed only where a plaintiff asserts that an agency failed to take a discrete agency action that it is required to take. These limitations rule out several kinds of challenges[, such as] . . . the kind of broad programmatic attack we rejected in Lujan v. National Wildlife Federation, 497 U.S. 871 (1990)."

Is SUVA's exclusion of more general agency failure to act and programmatic attacks on agency functioning appropriate? Or should courts train their attention on inaction cases precisely to this level and not interfere with specific instances of inaction? Isn't SUVA in tension with Chaney's footnoted suggestion that the APA's exception for action committed to agency discretion might not apply when "it could justifiably be found that the agency has consciously and expressly adopted a general policy that is so extreme as to amount to an abdication of its statutory responsibilities"? Chaney n. 4, p. 1408. For an argument that current doctrine gets reviewability backwards here and it would be better to review general failures over specific ones, see Gillian E. Metzger, The Constitutional Duty to Supervise, 124 Yale L.J. 1836 (2015).

(3) **Refusal to Initiate Rulemaking.** Another form of agency refusals to act are refusal to engage in rulemaking. Should such refusals be treated like specific enforcement decisions and presumptively unreviewable under Chaney? In MASSACHUSETTS V. EPA, 549 U.S. 497, 527–28 (2007), after finding that Massachusetts had standing to challenge EPA's refusal to engage in a rulemaking on greenhouse gas emissions from new motor vehicles (pp. 1349, 1355), JUSTICE STEVENS's majority opinion made clear that such rulemaking refusals are reviewable: "As we have repeated time and again, an agency has broad discretion to choose how best to marshal its limited resources and personnel to carry out its delegated responsibilities.

See Chevron U.S.A. Inc. v. Natural Resources Defense Council, Inc., 467 U.S. 837, 842–845 (1984). That discretion is at its height when the agency decides not to bring an enforcement action. Therefore, in Heckler v. Chaney, 470 U.S. 821 (1985), we held that an agency's refusal to initiate enforcement proceedings is not ordinarily subject to judicial review. Some debate remains, however, as to the rigor with which we review an agency's denial of a petition for rulemaking.

"There are key differences between a denial of a petition for rulemaking and an agency's decision not to initiate an enforcement action. See American Horse Protection Assn., Inc. v. Lyng, 812 F.2d 1, 3–4 (D.C. Cir. 1987). In contrast to nonenforcement decisions, agency refusals to initiate rulemaking 'are less frequent, more apt to involve legal as opposed to factual analysis, and subject to special formalities, including a public explanation.' Id., at 4; see also 5 U.S.C. § 555(e). They moreover arise out of denials of petitions for rulemaking which (at least in the circumstances here) the affected party had an undoubted procedural right to file in the first instance. Refusals to promulgate rules are thus susceptible to judicial review, though such review is 'extremely limited' and 'highly deferential.' National Customs Brokers & Forwarders Assn. of America, Inc. v. United States, 883 F.2d 93, 96 (D.C. Cir. 1989)."

(4) *Refusal to Spend Money.* In LINCOLN V. VIGIL, 508 U.S. 182 (1993), JUSTICE SOUTER for a unanimous Court described § 701(a)(2) jurisprudence as recognizing "certain categories of administrative decisions that courts traditionally have regarded as 'committed to agency discretion.'" He listed: (i) decisions not to take enforcement action; (ii) refusals to grant reconsideration of an action because of material error; and (iii) decisions to terminate an employee in the interests of national security—and then added another: decisions about allocating funds from a lump-sum appropriation.

The Indian Health Service decided to phase out a program that directly provided evaluative and clinical services to handicapped Native American children in the Southwest in favor of what it described as a "nationwide" program. Children who had been receiving services sued, claiming that the decision violated various organic statutes, the APA, and the Fifth Amendment. They also argued that the Service had represented the Program's continuation to Congress, and Congress had appropriated funds on that representation. The Court's opinion pointed out that Congress had made a lump-sum appropriation, not a program-specific appropriation. As in Chaney, the Court noted, "Congress may always circumscribe agency discretion to allocate resources by putting restrictions in the operative statutes . . . But as long as the agency allocates funds from a lump-sum appropriation to meet permissible statutory objectives, § 701(a)(2) gives the courts no leave to intrude. [T]o [that] extent, the decision to allocate funds 'is committed to agency discretion by law.' § 701(a)(2)." Compare the complicated issue of presidential power to make programmatic impoundments of appropriated funds, p. 855.

c. Timing of Review

> *(1) Exhaustion of Administrative Remedies*
> *(2) Finality*
> *(3) Ripeness*

Timing problems can bedevil any federal court litigant: For both Article III and prudential reasons, the case must be brought neither too early nor too late. For those seeking review of agency action, though, three timing doctrines stand out as especially important:

- *Exhaustion:* Whether the agency has internal procedures for remediating errors that should be used before coming to court; the nature of the inquiry very much depends on whether the statute under which the claim is brought expressly addresses exhaustion (e.g., § 704).

- *Finality*: Whether the action complained of is complete and authoritative, rather than part of a larger decisional process still ongoing.

- *Ripeness*: Whether the action is fit for judicial examination now as opposed to waiting for some future event, often (but not always) raised in the context of pre-enforcement challenges to rules.

Although these three timing doctrines are distinct, they serve overlapping purposes. As a result, they are not always easy to separate. A good example of the overlapping nature of timing doctrines is Ticor Title Insurance Co. v. Federal Trade Commission, 814 F.2d 731 (D.C. Cir. 1987) where the court was unanimous in holding that the suit was premature, but the three judges each offered a different basis as to why, with one concluding that the suit was barred by failure to exhaust administrative remedies, one holding that the requisite finality was lacking, and one ruling that the challenge was unripe.

(1) Exhaustion of Administrative Remedies

DARBY v. CISNEROS

. . . Except as otherwise expressly required by statute, agency action otherwise final is final for the purposes of this section whether or not there has been presented or determined an application for a declaratory order, for any form of reconsideration, or, unless the agency otherwise requires

by rule and provides that the action meanwhile is inoperative, for an
appeal to superior agency authority.

5 U.S.C. § 704

DARBY v. CISNEROS

Supreme Court of the United State (1993).
509 U.S. 137.

■ JUSTICE BLACKMUN delivered the opinion of the Court.[19]

[Darby, a real estate developer, sought review of an ALJ decision that he had engaged in improper financial practices and should be barred from participating in Housing and Urban Development programs for 18 months. Under HUD regulations, an ALJ's decision "shall be final unless . . . the Secretary or the Secretary's designee, within 30 days of receipt of a request decides as a matter of discretion to review the [ALJ's] finding. . . . Any party may request such a review in writing within 15 days of receipt of the [ALJ's] determination." The agency argued that Darby's failure to request this review foreclosed judicial review.:]

This case presents the question whether federal courts have the authority to require that a plaintiff exhaust available administrative remedies before seeking judicial review under the Administrative Procedure Act, where neither the statute nor agency rules specifically mandate exhaustion as a prerequisite to judicial review. At issue is the relationship between the judicially created doctrine of exhaustion of administrative remedies and the statutory requirements of § [704] of the APA. . . .

Petitioners argue that this provision means that a litigant seeking judicial review of a final agency action under the APA need not exhaust available administrative remedies unless such exhaustion is expressly required by statute or agency rule. . . . Respondents contend that [the section] is concerned solely with timing, that is, when agency actions become 'final,' and that Congress had no intention to interfere with the courts' ability to impose conditions on the timing of their exercise of jurisdiction to review final agency actions. . . . It perhaps is surprising that it has taken over 45 years since the passage of the APA for this Court definitively to address this question. . . .

. . . [T]he text of the APA leaves little doubt that petitioners are correct . . . While federal courts may be free to apply, where appropriate, other prudential doctrines of judicial administration to limit the scope and timing of judicial review, [§ 704], by its very terms, has limited the availability of the doctrine of exhaustion of administrative remedies to that which the statute or rule clearly mandates.

---

[19]   [Ed.] Chief Justice Rehnquist and Justices Scalia and Thomas did not join in a portion of the opinion that discussed the APA's legislative history.

. . . Congress clearly was concerned with making the exhaustion requirement unambiguous so that aggrieved parties would know precisely what administrative steps were required before judicial review would be available. If courts were able to impose additional exhaustion requirements beyond those provided by Congress or the agency, the last sentence of [§ 704] would make no sense. . . . Of course, the exhaustion doctrine continues to apply as a matter of judicial discretion in cases not governed by the APA." Because neither the governing statute nor HUD regulations *mandated* an appeal to the Secretary, the Court held that Darby's action must be permitted to go forward.

NOTES

(1) ***Statutory and Common Law Exhaustion.*** As Darby indicates, exhaustion requirements come in both a statutory and common law guise. In MCCARTHY V. MADIGAN, 503 U.S. 140 (1992), the Court laid out the common law exhaustion inquiry in an opinion by JUSTICE BLACKMUN: "Exhaustion is required because it serves the twin purposes of protecting administrative agency authority and promoting judicial efficiency. . . . Notwithstanding these substantial institutional interests, federal courts are vested with a 'virtually unflagging obligation' to exercise the jurisdiction given them. Cohens v. Virginia, 19 U.S. 264, 6 Wheat. 264, 404 (1821). Accordingly, this Court has declined to require exhaustion in some circumstances even where administrative and judicial interests would counsel otherwise.

"In determining whether exhaustion is required, federal courts must balance the interest of the individual in retaining prompt access to a federal judicial forum against countervailing institutional interests favoring exhaustion. . . . [Our] precedents have recognized at least three broad sets of circumstances in which the interests of the individual weigh heavily against requiring administrative exhaustion. First, requiring resort to the administrative remedy may occasion undue prejudice to subsequent assertion of a court action. Such prejudice may result, for example, from an unreasonable or indefinite timeframe for administrative action . . . . [or] when an individual's failure to exhaust may preclude a defense to criminal liability. McKart v. United States, 395 U.S. [185,] 197 [(1969)]. . . . Second, an administrative remedy may be inadequate 'because of some doubt as to whether the agency was empowered to grant effective relief.' Gibson v. Berryhill, 411 U.S. [564,] 575 n. 14 [(1973)]. For example, an agency [may] lack[ ] institutional competence to resolve the particular type of issue presented, such as the constitutionality of a statute. . . . Third, an administrative remedy may be inadequate where the administrative body is shown to be biased or has otherwise predetermined the issue before it. . . ."

Recently, in ROSS V. BLAKE, 136 S.Ct. 1850 (2016), the Supreme Court in an opinion by JUSTICE KAGAN reiterated that statutory exhaustion provisions displace the common-law analysis: "No doubt, judge-made exhaustion doctrines, even if flatly stated at first, remain amenable to judge-made exceptions. But a statutory exhaustion provision stands on a different footing. There, Congress sets the rules—and courts have a role in creating

[handwritten margin note: 3x indiv ints > instit ints]

exceptions only if Congress wants them to. For that reason, mandatory exhaustion statutes like the [Prison Litigation Reform Act] establish mandatory exhaustion regimes, foreclosing judicial discretion." However, judges still need to interpret the scope of any exceptions in the statute. In the PLRA, "the exhaustion requirement hinges on the 'availab[ility]' of administrative remedies[,] . . . [which means that] an inmate is required to exhaust those, but only those, grievance procedures that are 'capable of use' to obtain 'some relief for the action complained of.' Booth [v. Churner,] 532 U.S. [731,] 738 [(2001)]. . . . Building on our own and lower courts' decisions, we note as relevant here three kinds of circumstances in which an administrative remedy, although officially on the books, is not capable of use to obtain relief. . . . First, as Booth made clear, an administrative procedure is unavailable when (despite what regulations or guidance materials may promise) it operates as a simple dead end—with officers unable or consistently unwilling to provide any relief to aggrieved inmates. . . . Next, an administrative scheme might be so opaque that it becomes, practically speaking, incapable of use. . . . And finally, . . . when prison administrators thwart inmates from taking advantage of a grievance process through machination, misrepresentation, or intimidation."

For an ambitious argument that exhaustion and ripeness doctrines (among other things) are inappropriate vestiges of judicial common law making that should be recognized as completely supplanted by the APA, see John F. Duffy, Administrative Common Law in Judicial Review, 77 Tex. L. Rev. 113 (1998). On exhaustion in rulemaking contexts, see ACUS, Issue Exhaustion in Preenforcement Judicial Review of Administrative Rulemaking, Statement No. 19 (Sept. 25, 2015).

(2) *Exhaustion and Rulemaking.* Darby, McCarthy, and Ross involved adjudication. Does exhaustion have any role to play in review of rules? Unlike adjudication, there is nothing like "party" status in rulemaking. In the typical regulatory context, neither statute nor regulation *requires* that persons seeking to challenge the rule in court must have participated in the notice-and-comment process. Exhaustion in this context, therefore, focuses on whether the challenge sought be brought in litigation was raised by someone during the rulemaking proceeding and with sufficient specificity. For example, the Clean Air Act provides that "[o]nly an objection to a rule . . . raised with reasonable specificity during the period for public comment . . . may be raised during judicial review." 42 U.S.C. § 7607(d)(7)(B).

In EPA V. EME HOMER CITY GENERATION L.P., 134 S.Ct. 1584 (2014), the Supreme Court sidestepped the question of whether exhaustion applies in rulemaking by deciding that EPA had committed a procedural default of its own. EPA had argued that states and other parties challenging the Transport Rule had failed the CAA's "reasonable specificity" standard and that this failure at the administrative level deprived the court of jurisdiction to hear their challenges on review. Referring to the Court's general reluctance to consider restrictions "jurisdictional," JUSTICE GINSBURG's opinion pointed out that "[a] rule may be 'mandatory,' yet not 'jurisdictional'. . . The [CAA] 'does not speak to a court's authority, but only to a party's procedural obligations.' As such, the procedural default (if it had occurred) could be waived. EPA had done so by failing to press the reasonable specificity argument in the court of appeals. 'Before the D. C. Circuit, it indicated only that the 'reasonable specificity' prescription might bar judicial review. We therefore do not count the prescription an impassable hindrance to our adjudication of the respondents' attack on EPA's interpretation of the Transport Rule.' "

Some lower courts have refused to consider challenges to rules when those claims were not raised during the rulemaking or the court below. The D.C. Circuit has stated that "[i]t is a hard and fast rule of administrative law, rooted in simple fairness, that issues not raised before an agency are waived and will not be considered by a court on review." Nuclear Energy Inst. Inc. v. EPA, 373 F.3d 1251 1297–98 (D.C. Cir. 2004); accord Nat'l Ass'n of Clean Air Agencies v. E.P.A., 489 F.3d 1221, 1231 (D.C. Cir. 2007). By contrast, in American Forest & Paper Ass'n v. EPA, 137 F.3d 291 (5th Cir.1998), where the issue appeared to concern an agency's legal authority per se, the Fifth Circuit refused to impose any requirement that the party (or anyone else) have flagged the issue in the rulemaking. These cases conspicuously lack discussion of whether, when, why, or how exhaustion doctrine developed in the context of agency adjudication should be applied to rulemaking.

(3) ***Exhaustion, Preclusion of Pre-enforcement Review, and Primary Jurisdiction.*** Notice the close relationship between exhaustion and decisions holding that pre-enforcement review is precluded, like Thunder Basin, Elgin, and Jarkesy (Note 5, p. 1396). Practically speaking, the result of the two is the same: a plaintiff must pursue administrative remedies before seeking judicial review.

The doctrine of primary jurisdiction is also related to, though distinct from, exhaustion of administrative remedies. Under this doctrine, when an agency and a court have concurrent jurisdiction, a court may abstain to allow the agency to first address the matter. According to JUSTICE BREYER, concurring in part and concurring in judgment in PHARMACEUTICAL RESEARCH & MFRS. OF AMERICA V. WALSH, 538 U.S. 644, 673 (2003): "The legal doctrine of 'primary jurisdiction' permits a court itself to 'refer' a question to the Secretary. That doctrine seeks to produce better informed and uniform legal rulings by allowing courts to take advantage of an agency's specialized knowledge, expertise, and central position within a regulatory regime. United States v. Western Pacific R. Co., 352 U.S. 59, 63–65 (1956). 'No fixed formula exists' for the doctrine's application. Id., at 64, 77 S.Ct. 161. Rather, the question in each instance is whether a case raises 'issues of fact not within the conventional experience of judges,' but within the purview of an agency's responsibilities; whether the 'limited functions of review by the judiciary are more rationally exercised, by preliminary resort' to an agency 'better equipped than courts' to resolve an issue in the first instance; or, in a word, whether preliminary reference of issues to the agency will promote that proper working relationship between court and agency that the primary jurisdiction doctrine seeks to facilitate. Far East Conference v. United States, 342 U.S. 570, 574–75 (1952)."

Note also that all three doctrines often share the feature of implicitly upholding the adequacy of the combined administrative and judicial remedial arrangement to which the plaintiff will be subject, in the course of concluding that direct suit is not immediately available. How important do you think this feature is to assessing the acceptability of these doctrines?

(2) Finality

> SACKETT v. EPA

Agency action made reviewable by statute and final agency action for which there is no other adequate remedy in a court are subject to judicial review.

5 U.S.C. § 704

Finality is the most amorphous of the several doctrines through which courts regulate the timing of judicial review. A legal grab bag, the finality rubric is applied to an assortment of questions about the appropriateness of intervention at a particular moment in the administrative process.

SACKETT v. EPA

Supreme Court of the United States (2012).
566 U.S. 120.

■ JUSTICE SCALIA delivered the opinion of the Court.

[The Clean Water Act (CWA) prohibits "the discharge of any pollutant by any person," § 1311, without a permit, into the "navigable waters" § 1344. Upon determining that a violation has occurred, the EPA may either issue a compliance order or initiate a civil enforcement action. When the EPA prevails in a civil action, the Act provides for a civil penalty of up to $37,500 per day per violation, but that can be doubled for a person who was previously issued a compliance order but failed to comply. The Sacketts received a compliance order from the EPA, which stated that their residential lot contained navigable waters and that their construction project violated the Act. The compliance order further required the Sacketts to immediately restore the property pursuant to an EPA work plan. The EPA denied the Sacketts' request for a hearing regarding the compliance order. The Sacketts then challenged the compliance order in Federal District Court as "arbitrary [and] capricious" under the APA and as a due process violation of the Fifth Amendment. The District Court dismissed for lack of subject-matter jurisdiction. The Ninth Circuit affirmed, concluding that the CWA precluded pre-enforcement judicial review of compliance orders and that such preclusion was not a due process violation.]

II

. . . We consider first whether the compliance order is final agency action. There is no doubt it is agency action, which the APA defines as including even a "failure to act." §§ 551(13), 701(b)(2). But is it *final*? It has all of the hallmarks of APA finality that our opinions establish. Through the order, the EPA "determined" "rights or obligations." Bennett v. Spear, 520 U.S. 154, 178 (1997). By reason of the order, the Sacketts have the legal obligation to "restore" their property according to an agency-approved Restoration Work Plan, and must give the EPA access to their property and to "records and documentation related to the conditions at the Site." App. 22, ¶ 2.7. Also, " 'legal consequences . . . flow' " from issuance of the order. Bennett, supra, at 178 (quoting Marine Terminal, supra, at 71). For one, according to the Government's current litigating position, the order exposes the Sacketts to double penalties in a future enforcement proceeding. It also severely limits the Sacketts' ability to obtain a permit for their fill from the Army Corps of Engineers, see 33 U.S.C. § 1344. The Corps' regulations provide that, once the EPA has issued a compliance order with respect to certain property, the Corps will not process a permit application for that property unless doing so "is clearly appropriate." 33 CFR § 326.3(e)(1)(iv) (2011).

The issuance of the compliance order also marks the " 'consummation' " of the agency's decisionmaking process. Bennett, supra, at 178 (quoting Chicago & Southern Air Lines, Inc. v. Waterman S.S. Corp., 333 U.S. 103 (1948)). As the Sacketts learned when they unsuccessfully sought a hearing, the "Findings and Conclusions" that the compliance order contained were not subject to further agency review. The Government resists this conclusion, pointing to a portion of the order that invited the Sacketts to "engage in informal discussion of the terms and requirements" of the order with the EPA and to inform the agency of "any allegations [t]herein which [they] believe[d] to be inaccurate." App. 22–23, ¶ 2.11. But that confers no entitlement to further agency review. The mere possibility that an agency might reconsider in light of "informal discussion" and invited contentions of inaccuracy does not suffice to make an otherwise final agency action nonfinal.

The APA's judicial review provision also requires that the person seeking APA review of final agency action have "no other adequate remedy in a court," 5 U.S.C. § 704. In CWA enforcement cases, judicial review ordinarily comes by way of a civil action brought by the EPA under 33 U.S.C. § 1319. But the Sacketts cannot initiate that process, and each day they wait for the agency to drop the hammer, they accrue, by the Government's telling, an additional $75,000 in potential liability. The other possible route to judicial review—applying to the Corps of Engineers for a permit and then filing suit under the APA if a permit is denied—will not serve either. The remedy for denial of action that might be sought from one agency does not ordinarily provide an "adequate remedy" for action already taken by another agency. . . .

III

Nothing in the CWA *expressly* precludes judicial review under the APA or otherwise. But in determining "[w]hether and to what extent a particular statute precludes judicial review," we do not look "only [to] its express language." Block v. Community Nutrition Institute, 467 U.S. 340, 345 (1984). The APA, we have said, creates a "presumption favoring judicial review of administrative action," but as with most presumptions, this one "may be overcome by inferences of intent drawn from the statutory scheme as a whole." Id., at 349. The Government offers several reasons why the statutory scheme of the . . . Act precludes review.

. . . The Government argues that, because Congress gave the EPA the choice between a judicial proceeding and an administrative action, it would undermine the Act to allow judicial review of the latter. But that argument rests on the question-begging premise that the relevant difference between a compliance order and an enforcement proceeding is that only the latter is subject to judicial review. There are eminently sound reasons other than insulation from judicial review why compliance orders are useful. The Government itself suggests that they "provid[e] a means of notifying recipients of potential violations and quickly resolving the issues through voluntary compliance." Brief for Respondents 39. It is entirely consistent with this function to allow judicial review when the recipient does not choose "voluntary compliance." The Act does not guarantee the EPA that issuing a compliance order will always be the most effective choice.

The Government also notes that compliance orders are not self-executing, but must be enforced by the agency in a plenary judicial action. It suggests that Congress therefore viewed a compliance order "as a step in the deliberative process[,] . . . rather than as a coercive sanction that itself must be subject to judicial review." Id., at 38. But the APA provides for judicial review of all final agency actions, not just those that impose a self-executing sanction. And it is hard for the Government to defend its claim that the issuance of the compliance order was just "a step in the deliberative process" when the agency rejected the Sacketts' attempt to obtain a hearing and when the *next* step will either be taken by the Sacketts (if they comply with the order) or will involve judicial, not administrative, deliberation (if the EPA brings an enforcement action). As the text (and indeed the very name) of the compliance order makes clear, the EPA's "deliberation" over whether the Sacketts are in violation of the Act is at an end; the agency may still have to deliberate over whether it is confident enough about this conclusion to initiate litigation, but that is a separate subject.

The Government further urges us to consider that Congress expressly provided for prompt judicial review, on the administrative record, when the EPA assesses administrative penalties after a hearing, . . . but did not expressly provide for review of compliance orders. But if the express provision of judicial review in one section of a long and complicated statute were alone enough to overcome the APA's presumption of reviewability for all final agency action, it would not be much of a presumption at all. . . .

Finally, the Government notes that Congress passed the CWA in large part to respond to the inefficiency of then existing remedies for water pollution. . . . The Government warns that the EPA is less likely to use [compliance] orders if they are subject to judicial review. That may be true—but it will be true for all agency actions subjected to judicial review. The APA's presumption of judicial review is a repudiation of the principle that efficiency of regulation conquers all. And there is no reason to think that the CWA was uniquely designed to enable the strong-arming of regulated parties into "voluntary compliance" without the opportunity for judicial review—even judicial review of the question whether the regulated party is within the EPA's jurisdiction. Compliance orders will remain an effective means of securing prompt voluntary compliance in those many cases where there is no substantial basis to question their validity.

* * *

We conclude that the compliance order in this case is final agency action for which there is no adequate remedy other than APA review, and that the Clean Water Act does not preclude that review. We therefore reverse the judgment of the Court of Appeals and remand the case for further proceedings consistent with this opinion.

[Justice Ginsburg concurred to note that the opinion did not resolve whether the Sacketts could challenge the terms and conditions of the compliance order at the pre-enforcement stage.]

[Justice Alito concurred to argue that Congress "should provide a reasonably clear rule regarding the reach of the CWA."]

NOTES

(1) *Finality of Initial Agency Determinations.* Sackett involves the question of when an initial agency determination is final. A similar issue, in the judicial context, concerns when an interlocutory appeal is available. There is a presumption against such interlocutory appeals. Should there be a similar presumption against judicial review of agency determinations until the administrative process is completed? Why or why not?

The Court adhered to its approach in Sackett in UNITED STATES ARMY CORPS OF ENGINEERS V. HAWKES CO., 136 S.Ct. 1807 (2016). There, in an opinion by CHIEF JUSTICE ROBERTS, the Court held that a jurisdictional determination that a property comes under CWA because it contains "waters of the United States," when it represents the agency's definitive view, constitutes final agency action and is judicially reviewable under the APA. The government did not contest that such a jurisdictional determination marked the culmination of the Army Corp's decisionmaking process but argued that the jurisdictional determination alone had no legal consequences. CHIEF JUSTICE ROBERTS disagreed, emphasizing that under a Memorandum of Understanding between the Army Corps and EPA, a determination that a property does not contain waters of the United States (a negative determination), would generally bind the government for five years, preventing an enforcement action for CWA violations. "It follows that affirmative [jurisdictional determinations] have legal consequences as well: They represent the denial of the safe harbor that negative [determinations] afford. . . . This conclusion tracks the 'pragmatic' approach we have long taken to finality." Roberts also rejected the government's further argument that property owners' ability to apply for a permit and seek review if denied, or discharge pollutants and challenge the jurisdictional determination in an enforcement action, represented adequate alternatives to direct judicial review of the determination under the APA.

(2) *Multiple Regulatory Actors.* Another sort of finality problem occurs when a regulatory program requires several officials each to play a part in the regulatory decision. *Whose* actions constitute "final agency action"? The Supreme Court has encountered several statutory schemes in which the President is the ultimate official actor. It generally invokes lack of finality in refusing to review the actions of other officials prior to presidential involvement. In Franklin v. Massachusetts, 505 U.S. 788 (1992), Massachusetts attempted to regain a seat lost in the House because of the decennial reapportionment; five Justices concluded that the Secretary of Commerce's Census Report was not final action: "In this case, the action that creates an entitlement to a particular number of Representatives and has a direct effect on the reapportionment is the President's statement to Congress, not the Secretary's report to the President." However, because the President is not an "agency" within the meaning of the APA, review is not available once the action does become final by presidential decision. Similarly, Dalton v. Specter, 511 U.S. 462 (1994), held that the actions of the Secretary of Defense and the Base Closing Commission are not "final agency action" since their reports identifying military bases for closure have "no direct consequences."

Are these cases explained by judicial solicitude for preserving the President's constitutionally unique freedom to act? Cf. Japan Whaling Ass'n v. American Cetacean Soc., 478 U.S. 221 (1986) (holding final and reviewable the Secretary of Commerce's certification to the President that another country was endangering fisheries; the certification automatically triggered sanctions, regardless of any discretionary action the President might choose to take). Absent direct involvement of the President, would (should?) other officials be able to avoid review on finality grounds by pointing out that their decision was a necessary, but not sufficient, component of a complex regulatory action?

(3) *Finality and Guidance Documents.* Yet another dimension of finality appears when a party insists that the agency has definitively committed itself to a position, but this position has not been expressed in a form conventionally understood as having the force of law. In CENTER FOR AUTO SAFETY V. NHTSA, 452 F.3d 798 (D.C. Cir. 2006) (p. 368), Judge Edward's opinion for the panel appears to hold that guidance documents are

never reviewable (at least under the APA): Such documents "cannot be viewed as 'final agency action' under § 704 of the APA unless they mark the consummation of the agency's decisionmaking process" and either determine " 'rights or obligations' or result in 'legal consequences.' " Center for Auto Safety relies heavily on Bennett v. Spear, 520 U.S. 154, 178 (1997), from which the internally quoted language in the above passage comes. In fact, Bennett—which involved a Fish and Wildlife Service Biological Opinion recommending certain actions to the Bureau of Reclamation that was challenged by ranchers and others who would lose the use of water for irrigation if those actions were taken—posed a "multiple regulatory actor" type of finality problem rather than a guidance document problem. Strikingly, Judge Edwards' opinion in Center for Auto Safety does not cite National Park Hospitality Ass'n v. Dep't of the Interior, p. 1428, which described guidance as "final agency action" in the course of holding that a challenge to the guidance was unripe.

Particularly if guidance is produced through some sort of formal agency process—such as the notice-and-comment procedure used by National Park Service and increasingly used by agencies either as a matter of "best practices" or by statutory compulsion, see p. 380—does it make sense to label such a document not "final" based on a definition of finality developed to deal with a different kind of finality problem? More fundamentally, why should the availability of review of guidance be approached differently than the inquiry under the Declaratory Judgment Act, 28 U.S.C. § 2201, which reflects a general congressional willingness to allow "pre-enforcement" review of an actual and imminent controversy assessed on the basis of the *practical* consequences for the moving party of delaying review? See Peter L. Strauss, Publication Rules in the Rulemaking Spectrum: Assuring Proper Respect for an Essential Element, 53 Admin. L. Rev. 803 (2001) (addressing the desirability of finding finality for guidance in situations satisfying declaratory judgment standards as an alternative to requiring notice and comment rulemaking).

Compare Center for Auto Safety with the approach to finality and guidance offered thirty-five years earlier in NATIONAL AUTOMATIC LAUNDRY & CLEANING COUNCIL V. SHULTZ, 443 F.2d 689 (D.C. Cir. 1971). The Council had requested a letter ruling from the Administrator of the Wage and Hour Division of the Department of Labor to "confirm" that laundromat employees were not covered by recent amendments to the Fair Labor Standards Act. When the ruling took the opposite position, it sought a declaratory judgment that the Administrator had misinterpreted the statute. At the time, the Division issued about 750,000 letter rulings annually, fewer than 1.5 percent of which were signed by the Administrator himself and the bulk of which came from regional or field offices. According to JUDGE LEVENTHAL: "There are sound reasons why such advisory letters and opinions should not be subject to judicial review . . . There is surely a need for such informality in the administration of the Fair Labor Standards Act, a law deemed 'full of baffling questions of application.' . . . [I]t would be unfortunate if the prospect of judicial review were to make an agency reluctant to give them.

"There are two separate matters involved. One of these is the need for authoritative determination within the office or agency before its ruling can be termed final. . . . But there seems little room for the application of that doctrine when the interpretative ruling is signed by the head of the agency. In this situation we are not troubled by the questions that might arise as to the nature or extent of delegation to a subordinate official. . . . [Second, e]ven the head of an agency, it may be contended, operates on more than one level of deliberativeness. And it may be urged that a ruling made without that kind of assurance of deliberativeness that is presented by a hearing, or a structured controversy, may be the kind of ruling that is more truly subject to reconsideration. Certainly we know that the head of an agency may make tentative rulings and may reconsider rulings previously made. . . . We think the sound course is to accept the ruling of a board or commission, or the head of an agency, as presumptively final. If it does not indicate on its face that it is only tentative, it would be likely to be accepted as authoritative, and given [judicial] deference. . . . This presumption could be negatived, of course, if the agency adopted a rule prescribing its procedure in such a way as to identify certain actions as tentative and subject to reconsideration, prescribing the means of obtaining such reconsideration. Indeed, even in the absence of such structuring in regulations prescribing agency procedures, a court might decline to entertain a litigation if it was presented not with legal defenses interposed by counsel, but with an affidavit of the agency head advising the court that the ruling in question was tentative, and outlining the method of seeking reconsideration."

(3) Ripeness

> **ABBOTT LABORATORIES v. GARDNER**
> **GARDNER v. TOILET GOODS ASS'N, INC.**
> **TOILET GOODS ASS'N, INC. v. GARDNER**

ABBOTT LABORATORIES v. GARDNER
387 U.S. 136 (1967).
p. 1377.

GARDNER v. TOILET GOODS ASS'N, INC.
387 U.S. 167 (1967) (FORTAS, J., dissenting).
p. 1379.

TOILET GOODS ASS'N, INC. v. GARDNER
387 U.S. 158 (1967).

[Abbott Labs established the modern framework for ripeness analysis, under which a court must "evaluate both the fitness of the issues for judicial decision and the hardship to the parties of withholding court consideration." To some extent, ripeness overlaps with the standing inquiry, when suit is brought too prematurely and the plaintiff's injury is speculative. But as Abbott Labs makes clear, ripeness also has a prudential element, so that even if the plaintiff has standing, the suit may still be unripe if the issues remain unfit for judicial resolution or the hardships from delay are minimal.

In Toilet Goods v. Gardner, a companion case to Abbott Labs, the Court denied pre-enforcement review under the Abbott Labs framework. Cosmetic manufacturers sought pre-enforcement review of regulations requiring them to give FDA inspectors access to their manufacturing processes and formulas for making color additives. If access were denied, the FDA Commissioner "may immediately suspend" the manufacturer's certificate to sell additives and "may continue such suspension until adequate corrective action has been taken." The Court, with only Justice Douglas dissenting, held that this challenge was not ripe. Per JUSTICE HARLAN:]

. . . [T]here can be no question that this regulation . . . is "final agency action" . . . Also, we recognize the force of petitioners' contention that the issue as they have framed it presents a purely legal question: whether the regulation is totally beyond the agency's power under the statute. . . . These points which support the appropriateness of judicial resolution are, however, outweighed by other considerations. The regulation serves notice only that the Commissioner *may* under certain circumstances order inspection of certain facilities and data, and that further certification of additives *may* be refused to those who decline to permit a duly authorized inspection until they have complied in that regard. At this juncture we have no idea whether or when such an inspection will be ordered and what reasons the Commissioner will give to justify his order. The statutory authority asserted for the regulation is the power to promulgate regulations "for the efficient enforcement" of the Act. Whether the regulation is justified thus depends . . . on whether the statutory scheme as a whole justified promulgation of the regulation. This will depend not merely on an inquiry into statutory purpose, but concurrently on an understanding of what types of enforcement problems are encountered by the FDA, the need for various sorts of supervision in order to effectuate the goals of the Act, and the safeguards devised to protect legitimate trade secrets. We believe that judicial appraisal of these factors is likely to stand on a much surer footing in the context of a specific application of this regulation than could be the case in the framework of the generalized challenge made here.

We are also led to this result by considerations of the effect on the petitioners of the regulation . . . This is not a situation in which primary conduct is affected—when contracts must be negotiated, ingredients tested or substituted, or special records compiled. This regulation merely states that the Commissioner may authorize inspectors to examine certain processes or formulae; no advance action is required of cosmetics manufacturers . . . Moreover, no irremediable adverse consequences flow from requiring a later challenge to this regulation by a manufacturer who refuses to allow this type of inspection. Unlike the other regulations challenged in this action, in which seizure of goods, heavy fines, adverse publicity for distributing "adulterated" goods, and possible criminal liability might penalize failure to comply, a refusal to admit an inspector here would at most lead only to a suspension of certification services to the particular party, a determination that can then be promptly challenged through an administrative procedure, which in turn is reviewable by a court.

NOTES

(1) *The Benefits and Costs of Pre-enforcement Review.* Recall that Justice Fortas dissented in Abbott Labs and Gardner v. Toilet Goods, contending that by allowing pre-enforcement review the Court had "opened Pandora's box." (p. 1379). Pre-enforcement review would be frequently granted, "threaten[ing] programs of vast importance to the public welfare," and was based on "vastly overdrawn cries of distress" by the drug manufacturers. As he predicted, Abbott Labs has inaugurated an era in which pre-enforcement review is common. But is it unjustified?

According to RICHARD J. PIERCE, JR., SEVEN WAYS TO DEOSSIFY AGENCY RULEMAKING, 47 Admin. L. Rev. 59, 89–91 (1995), "many scholars believe that the Court's 1967 opinion in Abbott was one of the major causes of the ensuing significant increase in the stringency of judicial review of legislative rules. Before Abbott, . . . [c]ourts typically relied on the record of the enforcement proceeding as the primary basis for review of the rule, and most rules were upheld. . . . Proponents of reversal of Abbott believe that the unavailability of pre-enforcement review . . . will deossify rulemaking by restoring the legal environment that existed prior to Abbott. . . . [In addition, they anticipate that the] lack of availability of pre-enforcement review of rules will deter parties from seeking review. . . . Violation of a rule that is held to be valid often exposes the regulatee to the risk of large civil and criminal penalties, as well as other adverse regulatory and public relations consequences. Those risks are likely to induce regulatees to comply with a rule, even if they believe the rule to be invalid. . . . [Finally, r]eversal of Abbott also could deossify rulemaking in a third way. Beneficiaries of regulatory statutes can obtain judicial review of agency rules only in the pre-enforcement context. Thus, reversal of Abbott would have effects identical to those created by elimination of beneficiaries' standing to obtain judicial review of rules."

Should Congress therefore get rid of pre-enforcement review? Pierce argues no. Given the adverse consequences to regulated entities of losing an enforcement action, "agencies often could predict with confidence that a rule will never be subject to judicial review"; hence, "reversal of Abbott could produce a legal environment in which agencies frequently issue rules that conflict with statutes or with the Constitution." By contrast, JERRY L. MASHAW and DAVID L. HARFST in THE STRUGGLE FOR AUTO SAFETY 246–47 (1990) answer yes with respect to the auto safety program overseen by the National Highway Transportation Safety Administration. They acknowledge that pre-enforcement review brings several benefits: "Costs of compliance with invalid rules are saved, uncertainty about the legality of regulation is more quickly removed, all affected parties receive similar treatment (no one need comply while a challenge is pending, and weak or disfavored organizations cannot be singled out by the agency for enforcement action), and regulators are held strictly accountable because they cannot suppress legal contests through enforcement compromises." At the same time, Mashaw and Harfst argued that pre-enforcement review's costs to the auto safety were great: Difficulty getting rules through judicial review led NHTSA to abandon rulemaking in favor of a far less rational and effective reliance on recalls. In addition, "[b]ecause delaying review shifts incentives, it promotes the development of more credible information on both compliance costs and engineering feasibility. Judicial review will be better informed on the critical issues that are now routinely presented but seldom substantiated by more than industry and agency conjecture."

(2) ***Pre-enforcement Review and Beneficiary Challenges.*** Regulatory beneficiaries have a significant stake in the preservation of pre-enforcement review. Under Heckler v. Chaney, p. 1407, beneficiaries are presumptively precluded from challenging agencies' nonenforcement decisions. Even if an enforcement action is brought, would a beneficiary group be permitted to intervene and argue that because the rule isn't stringent enough, even greater sanctions should be imposed against the defendant than the agency proposes? See generally Nina A. Mendelson, Regulatory Beneficiaries and Informal Agency Policymaking 92 Cornell L. Rev. 408 (2007).

LUJAN V. NATIONAL WILDLIFE FED., 497 U.S. 871, 890–94 (1990), demonstrates the obstacles that ripeness can pose to beneficiary challenges. Environmentalists challenged what they described as an unlawful Bureau of Land Management "program" of opening previously protected public lands to private development. JUSTICE SCALIA's opinion for the five-member majority concluded that they did not have standing but went on to articulate a more general theory of ripeness that also foreclosed review: "The term 'land withdrawal review program' . . . does not refer to a single BLM order or regulation, or even to a completed universe of particular BLM orders and regulations. . . . It is no more an identifiable 'agency action'—much less a 'final agency action'—than a 'weapons procurement program' of the Department of Defense or a 'drug interdiction program' of the Drug Enforcement Administration. . . .

"Under the terms of the APA, respondent must direct its attack against some particular 'agency action' that causes it harm. Some statutes permit broad regulations to serve as the 'agency action,' . . . [but a]bsent such a provision . . . a regulation is not ordinarily considered the type of agency action 'ripe' for judicial review under the APA until the scope of the controversy has been reduced to more manageable proportions, and its factual components fleshed out, by some concrete action applying the regulation to the claimant's situation in a fashion that harms or threatens to harm him. (The major exception, of course, is a substantive rule which as a practical matter *requires the plaintiff to adjust his conduct immediately.* Such agency action is 'ripe' for review at once, whether or not explicit statutory review apart from the APA is provided.)"(emphasis added). See also Norton v. Southern Utah Wilderness Alliance, p. 1410.

Note that the italicized description applies principally—if not exclusively—to members of the regulated community. Where, in this description, do challenges by beneficiaries fit? In RENO V. CATHOLIC SOC. SERV., INC., 509 U.S. 43, 68–71, 78 (1993), immigrants' rights groups, in class actions on behalf of certain aliens residing in the country illegally, challenged INS regulations that narrowly interpreted two of the four statutory criteria for an amnesty program established by the Immigration Reform and Control Act of 1986. The interpretations rendered the plaintiff classes ineligible for amnesty. The majority held that most of the challenges were not constitutionally ripe until an immigrant had applied for benefits and been denied.[20] Concurring, Justice O'Connor stated that she "would not go so far as to state that a suit challenging a benefit conferring rule is necessarily unripe simply because the plaintiff has not yet applied for the benefit. . . . If it is 'inevitable' that the challenged rule will 'operat[e]' to the plaintiff's disadvantage—if the court can make a firm prediction that the plaintiff will apply for the benefit, and that the agency will deny the application by virtue of the rule—then there may well be a justiciable controversy that the court may find prudent to resolve."

(3) ***Ripeness and Statutorily Required Pre-enforcement Review?*** Sometimes Congress tries to ensure prompt determination of the validity of regulations by imposing strict statutory time limits (typically, 30–90 days from promulgation) for seeking judicial review. Unexcused failure to obtain pre-enforcement review precludes later attacks on the rule—even as a defense to civil or criminal enforcement proceedings. "Excusable" failure includes situations in which the challenge would not have been ripe within the statutory period. See Eagle-Picher Indus. v. EPA, 759 F.2d 905, 914 (D.C. Cir. 1985).

(4) ***Ripeness and Guidance.*** NATIONAL PARK HOSPITALITY ASS'N V. DEPARTMENT OF THE INTERIOR, 538 U.S. 803 (2003), was rooted in a power struggle between two Department of Interior agencies—the Board of Contract Appeals (BCA) and the National Park Service (NPS)—over whether contracts to run concessions in national parks fall under the Contract Disputes Act of 1978 (CDA). BCA, which has a role in that dispute procedure, insisted that concession contracts are covered. NPS, in the course of a notice-and-comment rulemaking to implement its authority under the National Parks Omnibus Management Act of 1998, took the opportunity at the same time to codify its contrary view in § 53.1 of the new regulations, which stated, "Concession contracts are not contracts within the meaning of [the Contract Disputes Act]." A trade association of concessioners that do business in the national parks sought judicial review of § 51.3. Both lower courts sustained

---

[20] The Court remanded for exploration of allegations that the INS engaged in a practice of "front-desking," in which employees refused even to accept applications from immigrants whom the agency considered ineligible under the challenged interpretation. "[A] class member whose application was 'front-desked' would have felt the effects of the [challenged regulations] in a particularly concrete manner, for his application for legalization would have been blocked then and there; his challenge to the regulation should not fail for lack of ripeness."

the regulation but the Supreme Court, sua sponte, asked the parties to address whether the case was ripe.

JUSTICE THOMAS began by noting that Abbott Labs two-part inquiry governed the determination if the challenge was ripe. He wrote for the Court: "We turn first to the hardship inquiry. . . . The task of applying the CDA rests with agency contracting officers and boards of contract appeals, as well as the Federal Court of Claims, the Court of Appeals for the Federal Circuit, and, ultimately, this Court. . . . Consequently, we consider § 51.3 to be nothing more than a 'general statemen[t] of policy' designed to inform the public of NPS' views on the proper application of the CDA[, and not an interpretive rule.] . . . Viewed in this light, § 51.3 does not create adverse effects of a strictly legal kind . . . . [It] does not command anyone to do anything or to refrain from doing anything; it does not grant, withhold, or modify any formal legal license, power, or authority; it does not subject anyone to any civil or criminal liability; and it create no legal rights or obligations. Moreover, § 51.3 does not affect a concessioner's primary conduct. Unlike the regulation at issue in Abbott Laboratories, . . . the regulation here leaves a concessioner free to conduct its business as it sees fit. . . . All the regulation does is announce the position NPS will take with respect to disputes arising out of concession contracts. Petitioner contends that delaying judicial resolution of this issue will result in real harm because the applicability vel non of the CDA is one of the factors a concessioner takes into account when preparing its bid for NPS concession contracts. . . . We are not persuaded. If we were to follow petitioner's logic, courts would soon be overwhelmed with requests for what essentially would be advisory opinions because most business transactions could be priced more accurately if even a small portion of existing legal uncertainties were resolved.

"We consider next whether the issue in this case is fit for review. Although the question presented here is 'a purely legal one' and § 51.3 constitutes 'final agency action' within the meaning of § 10 of the APA, 5 U.S.C. § 704, we nevertheless believe that further factual development would significantly advance our ability to deal with the legal issues presented. . . .[T]he federal respondents . . . acknowledge that certain types of concession contracts might come under the broad language of the CDA. Similarly, . . . [both] petitioner and respondent Xanterra Parks & Resorts, LLC . . . rely on specific characteristics of certain types of concession contracts to support their positions. In light of the foregoing, we conclude that judicial resolution of the question presented here should await a concrete dispute about a particular concession contract."

Justice Stevens, concurring in the judgment, concluded that petitioners had no standing but thought the dispute was ripe: "Whichever view may better reflect the intent of the Congress that enacted the CDA, it is perfectly clear that this question of statutory interpretation is as 'fit' for judicial decision today as it will ever be." Justice Breyer, dissenting in an opinion in which Justice Ginsburg joined, argued that the Association had sufficiently alleged "concrete monetary harm," either now or in the foreseeable future, "primarily in the form of increased bidding costs," sufficient to ground both standing *and* ripeness.

Note that although Justice Thomas uses the fact that § 51.3 "creates no legal rights or obligations" in assessing hardship to the parties, he discusses its operation *on the particular facts* and goes on to discuss fitness of the issues before concluding that the case was not ripe. Moreover, he compares and contrasts § 51.3 to what were uncontestably legislative rules in earlier cases—with no suggestion that this factor in itself was dispositive. Inasmuch as Justices Stevens, Breyer, and Ginsburg thought the Association's challenge *was* ripe, it appears open to other litigants to establish, on different facts, that guidance documents are ripe for review. In addition, isn't this case a good example of the partial review that can occur even when justiciability doctrines like ripeness are invoked? If you were counsel for the Association reading Justice Thomas' opinion, would you think you had lost?

(5)   ***The Coming End of Prudential Ripeness Doctrine?*** In a surprising development of uncertain impact, a unanimous opinion of the Supreme Court has cast doubt on the "continuing validity of the prudential ripeness doctrine." SUSAN B. ANTHONY LIST V. DRIEHAUS, 134 S.Ct. 2334 (2014), involved a pre-enforcement challenge to the constitutionality of an Ohio statute criminalizing certain kinds of false statements during a political campaign. After concluding that SBA satisfied the requirements for standing, p. 1331, JUSTICE THOMAS turned to the question of whether the challenge was ripe: "Respondents contend that these 'prudential ripeness' factors confirm that the claims at issue are nonjusticiable. . . . But we have already concluded that petitioners have alleged a sufficient Article III injury. To the extent respondents would have us deem petitioners' claims nonjusticiable 'on grounds that are 'prudential,' rather than constitutional,' '[t]hat request is in some tension with our recent reaffirmation of the principle that a federal court's obligation to hear and decide cases within its jurisdiction is virtually unflagging.' Lexmark Int'l, Inc. v. Static Control Components, Inc., 134 S.Ct. 1377, 1386 (2014). . . .

"In any event, we need not resolve the continuing vitality of the prudential ripeness doctrine in this case because the 'fitness' and 'hardship' factors are easily satisfied here. First, petitioners' challenge to the Ohio false statement statute presents an issue that is 'purely legal, and will not be clarified by further factual development.' Thomas v. Union Carbide Agricultural Products Co., 473 U.S. 568, 581 (1985). And denying prompt judicial review would impose a substantial hardship on petitioners, forcing them to choose between refraining from core political speech on the one hand, or engaging in that speech and risking costly Commission proceedings and criminal prosecution on the other."

d. Remedies

> *(1)   Injunctive and Declaratory Relief*
> *(2)   Suits for Damages*

Standing, reviewability, and timing are all doctrines that target the front end of a judicial action challenging administrative action. They go to the question of what claims a particular plaintiff can bring at a particular time. Remedies, by contrast, are focused on the back end question of what relief a court can and should grant upon finding that an agency acted unlawfully. Yet remedies also have an important front-end dimension. The availability of different types of relief often turns on the type of legal action that is brought, and a court's inability to grant any relief—or, put in different terms, a lack of redressability—can result in a finding of no standing. Hence, in addition to thinking about standing and reviewability, attorneys need to give thought to what remedial relief might be available in constructing a lawsuit to challenge actions by an agency or agency official.

Remedies for unlawful governmental conduct fall into two general camps: (1) injunctive and declaratory relief, and (2) damages. These are also common forms of relief in suits targeting private conduct, but suits against the government face a unique hurdle: sovereign immunity. Under the doctrine of sovereign immunity, the federal government cannot be sued without its consent. State governments also enjoy freedom from suit in federal court without their consent, protected by the Eleventh Amendment and constitutional principles of federalism but subject to abrogation by Congress in some contexts. As you'll see in the materials that follow, Congress has broadly waived sovereign immunity and courts have designed doctrines to mitigate its impact, with the result that sovereign immunity is rarely a barrier in suits for injunctive or declaratory relief. However, it can pose a barrier to suits for damages.

Courts and Congress have also devised some unique remedies for actions challenging administrative action. Prime among these is remand without vacatur, a relatively recent remedial mechanism, which you may have seen already in Chapter IV. Other uniquely governmental remedies are the prerogative writs, particularly of habeas and mandamus, which have existed since before the founding, with habeas enjoying constitutional protection. U.S. Const. Art. I, § 9.

(1) Injunctive and Declaratory Relief

Federal courts have long provided relief against unlawful governmental action. The traditional form of such relief was an officer's suit, a creation of the federal court's equitable powers that traced back to the English petition of right. In an early famous example, United States v. Lee, 106 U.S. 196 (1882), the federal government took General Robert E. Lee's Arlington property for unpaid taxes during the Civil War and turned it into Arlington Cemetery. The Supreme Court allowed Robert E. Lee's son to bring an ejectment action against the two military officers who had control of the property, concluding the suit was not barred by sovereign immunity. As noted above in Section 2.a.3's discussion of nonstatutory review, suits against government officials based on the writs of habeas corpus[21] or mandamus,[22] if successful, also result in grants of injunctive relief. Habeas corpus, used to challenge the legality of physical custody, has recently become prominent for its capacity to obtain review of the detention of aliens and persons in military custody. However, the scope of these writs is narrow: habeas is limited to actions seeking release of an individual claimed to be unlawfully in custody, and traditionally mandamus was available only for plaintiffs seeking to force a governmental official to perform a ministerial, nondiscretionary duty.[23]

In American School of Magnetic Healing v. McAnnulty, 187 U.S. 94 (1902), the Supreme Court upheld a grant of injunctive relief against a federal postmaster. The subsequent decision in Ex parte Young, 209 U.S. 123 (1908), has come to stand for the broader principle that sovereign immunity does not bar injunctive relief against governmental officials acting unlawfully. Such suits rest on the fiction that ordering an official to conform his (official) behavior to law is not a suit against the sovereign because the sovereign does not authorize its agents to violate the law. Although Ex parte Young involved a state official, its principle has long been applied to federal officials as well, as the Court recently reaffirmed in Free Enterprise Fund v. PCAOB, p. 922. Official immunity doctrines which limit government officers' personal liability in damages actions are thought not to apply in actions for prospective relief, such as injunctive or declaratory relief.

As the Supreme Court recently remarked, "[t]he ability to sue to enjoin unconstitutional actions by state and federal officers is the creation of courts of equity" and a "judge-made remedy." Armstrong v. Exceptional Child Center, Inc., 135 S.Ct. 1378 (2015). Enactment of the Declaratory Judgment Act in 1934, 28 U.S.C. §§ 2201–02, made declaratory relief available as well, and the APA in 1946 provided an express cause of action in § 702 in lieu of the implied equitable action. Further, § 703 states that in the absence or inadequacy of a special statutory review proceeding, "any applicable form of legal action, including actions for declaratory judgments or writs of prohibitory or mandatory injunction or habeas corpus, in a court of competent jurisdiction" can be brought.[24] Given that § 702 expressly authorizes specific relief against the agency itself, the nonstatutory forms retain

---

[21] 28 U.S.C. § 2241.

[22] 28 U.S.C. § 1361. In addition, 28 U.S.C. § 1651(a), the All Writs Act, authorizes the Supreme Court and the lower federal courts to "issue all writs necessary or appropriate in aid of their respective jurisdictions and agreeable to the usages and principles of law." The prerogative writs other than habeas and mandamus are quo warranto (usually limited to challenging an official's right to office), prohibition (used to prevent a judicial or quasi-judicial body from exceeding its jurisdiction when no other remedy is available), and certiorari (used to require a lower tribunal to certify the record of its proceedings to a higher tribunal for purposes of review).

[23] See, e.g., United States ex rel. Dunlap v. Black, 128 U.S. 40, 46 (1888) (quoting Kendall v. United States ex rel. Stokes, 12 Pet. 524, 613 (1838)).

[24] Section 702 requires that "any mandatory or injunctive decree shall specify the Federal officer or officers (by name or by title), and their successors in office, personally responsible for compliance."

little independent practical significance for cases that can be brought under the APA, but the traditional nonstatutory avenues for declaratory and injunctive relief, and for mandamus, continue to function where the APA is not available.[25]

As originally enacted, the APA did not contain a waiver of sovereign immunity, but one was added in 1976. This waiver, contained in § 702, provides:

> An action in a court of the United States seeking relief other than money damages and stating a claim that an agency or an officer or employee thereof acted or failed to act in an official capacity or under color of legal authority shall not be dismissed nor relief therein be denied on the ground that it is against the United States or that the United States is an indispensable party. . . .

In addition, § 703 provides, "If no special statutory proceeding is applicable, the action for judicial review may be brought against the United States, the agency by its official title, or the appropriate officer." As a result, today most garden-variety administrative review claims now proceed against the agency, by name, without any sovereign immunity concerns. Because the consent to suit excludes suits seeking "money damages," injunctive relief cannot be used to obtain a payment of money unless the challenged administrative decision itself involves such a payment.[26]

The APA also contains provisions addressing more specifically the type of relief a court can grant. To begin with, § 705 expressly authorizes interim relief:

> On such conditions as may be required and to the extent necessary to prevent irreparable injury, the reviewing court . . . may issue all necessary and appropriate process to postpone the effective date of an agency action or to preserve status or rights pending conclusion of the review proceedings.

In addition, § 706, which sets out the scope of review under the APA, also provides that "the reviewing court shall . . . hold unlawful and set aside agency action, findings, and conclusions found to be" arbitrary and capricious, outside of constitutional and statutory authority, at odds with governing procedures or unsupported by substantial evidence (where applicable, and that "due account shall be taken of the rule of prejudicial error." Finally, § 702 makes clear that general doctrines governing the grant of injunctive and declaratory relief continue to apply. Thus, notwithstanding the APA's authorization of actions for injunctive and

---

[25] See, e.g., Duncan v. Muzyn, 833 F.3d 567 (6th Cir. 2016); Chamber of Commerce of U.S. v. Reich, 74 F.3d 1322 (D.C. Cir. 1996).

[26] See Bowen v. Massachusetts, 487 U.S. 879 (1988) (construing § 702 to permit Massachusetts to contest an HHS decision denying the state $6,000,000 in Medicaid reimbursements).

declaratory relief, "[n]othing herein (1) affects . . . the power or duty of a court to . . . deny relief on any . . . appropriate legal or equitable ground; or (2) confers authority to grant relief if any other statute that grants consent to suit expressly or impliedly forbids the relief which is sought."

NOTES

(1) *Preclusion of Injunctive and Declaratory Relief.* The APA's provisions generally ensure that declaratory and injunctive relief are available in actions against agencies. However, Congress can always preclude certain types of relief by statute, and some statutory grants of a specific basis for suit expressly contain such limitations. For example, the America Invents Act at 35 U.S.C. Sec 324(e) precludes judicial review of the director's decision regarding whether to institute post-grant review of the patent.

In addition, the Court has found that injunctive relief is sometimes implicitly precluded by statute. ARMSTRONG V. EXCEPTIONAL CHILD CENTER, 135 S.Ct. 1378 (2015), provides a recent example. There, the Court in a 5–4 decision written by JUSTICE SCALIA, rejected an effort by providers of habilitation services to enjoin Idaho's Medicaid reimbursement rates as preempted by § 30A of the Medicaid Act: "The power of federal courts of equity to enjoin unlawful executive action is subject to express and implied statutory limitations. 'Courts of equity can no more disregard statutory and constitutional requirements and provisions than can courts of law.' INS v. Pangilinan, 486 U.S. 875, 883 (1988). . . . Two aspects of § 30(A) establish Congress's 'intent to foreclose' equitable relief. Verizon Md., Inc. v. Public Serv. Comm'n of Md., 535 U.S. 635, 647 (2002). First, the sole remedy Congress provided for a State's failure to comply with Medicaid's requirements . . . is the withholding of Medicaid funds by the Secretary of Health and Human Services. 42 U.S.C. § 1396c. As we have elsewhere explained, the 'express provision of one method of enforcing a substantive rule suggests that Congress intended to preclude others.' Alexander v. Sandoval, 532 U.S. 275, 290 (2001)." The second is "the judicially unadministrable nature of § 30(A)'s text. It is difficult to imagine a requirement broader and less specific than § 30(A)'s mandate that state plans provide for payments that are 'consistent with efficiency, economy, and quality of care,' all the while 'safeguard[ing] against unnecessary utilization of . . . care and services.' Explicitly conferring enforcement of this judgment-laden standard upon the Secretary alone establishes, we think, that Congress 'wanted to make the agency remedy that it provided exclusive.' Gonzaga Univ. v. Doe, 536 U.S. 273, 292 (2002) (Breyer, J., concurring in judgment). The sheer complexity associated with enforcing § 30(A), coupled with the express provision of an administrative remedy, § 1396c, shows that the Medicaid Act precludes private enforcement of § 30(A) in the courts."

(2) *Interim Relief and Stays of Rules.* Section 705 also expressly authorizes interim relief, such as a stay pending review. The relevant organic statute under which an agency operates may also authorize a stay. If all else fails, the Supreme Court has suggested that the power to issue a stay does not depend upon specific authorization but is "part of [the court's]

traditional equipment for the administration of justice." ScrippsHoward Radio, Inc. v. FCC, 316 U.S. 4, 9–10 (1942). In deciding whether or not to actually grant a stay of agency action pending appeal, courts consider factors typically at issue in requests for preliminary relief, such as whether the petitioner has made a strong showing of likely success and of irreparable harm, and whether a stay would substantially harm other interested parties and the public interest. See Virginia Petroleum Jobbers Ass'n v. FPC, 259 F.2d 921, 925 (D.C. Cir. 1958); see also eBay Inc. v. MercExchange, L.L.C., 547 U.S. 388 (2006) (setting out the traditional factors).

How willing should courts be to stay rules pending judicial challenge? This question rose to the fore with respect to the Obama Administration's Clean Power Plan: the D.C. Circuit denied a stay but was reversed by the Supreme Court on a 5–4 vote. West Virginia v. EPA, 136 S.Ct. 1000 (2016). According to Professor RONALD A. CASS, in STAYING AGENCY RULES: CONSTITUTIONAL STRUCTURE AND RULE OF LAW IN THE ADMINISTRATIVE STATE, 69 Admin. L. Rev.225, 228-29 (2017)), stays should be granted more freely in the context of rules that impose significant obligations: "Allowing these rules to apply immediately often gives the individuals and entities that are subject to them a choice between investing in costly compliance or risking serious sanctions, including potential criminal liability; to the extent that this induces compliance with rules that were not well-grounded in law, courts' ability to provide an effective check on administrative officials can be substantially eroded. Obviously, expensive, time-consuming litigation contesting the legality of an administrative decision is a far less attractive option if the only remedy at the end of the case is a Pyrrhic declaration of victory. Once a rule's targets decide that the risk of sanctions requires immediate compliance, the only "remedy" a court can offer is recognition that the litigants need not have spent the millions already invested in complying with an illegal rule, were under no lawful obligation to have undertaken economically damaging modifications of their operations, or need not have made other disruptive changes to their lives. However satisfying it is to hear someone say, 'you're right, the barn door should have stayed shut,' it's more rewarding to get confirmation while the horse is still inside."

Are you persuaded? Cass argues that regulated parties will be less likely to challenge rules in court if they will have to invest significantly in compliance regardless in the interim, and knowing they are unlikely to be sued gives agency officials incentives to exceed their authority. But isn't the opposite also true: making stays more easily available will give regulated parties incentive to bring excessive and unwarranted challenges to rules, if nothing else than to delay the time at which they have to comply. Between agencies and regulated parties, who should the courts favor with respect to interim relief? Is the current case-by-case assessment about the propriety of interim relief better than a categorical approach? If so, should lower courts receive substantial deference in making such discretionary assessments?

(3) *The Propriety and Scope of Injunctive Relief.* If a court is not precluded from granting injunctive relief by statute, must it do so upon finding that an agency has acted unlawfully? And what is the proper geographic scope of such injunctive relief?

Professor RONALD M. LEVIN, in "VACATION" AT SEA: JUDICIAL REMEDIES AND EQUITABLE DISCRETION IN ADMINISTRATIVE LAW, 53 Duke L.J. 291, 334–35, 340 (2003), argues that the equitable tradition remains strong in administrative law. He concludes that "[t]he teaching of the [Supreme Court's] cases, broadly speaking, is that equity does not always require the court to issue such an injunction, even if the court has found the defendant to be in breach of the statute. . . . Their collective message is that a court may not rely on equity to repudiate a statutory objective outright, but it has some leeway to decide whether or not to grant an injunction as a means of achieving compliance with the statutory scheme." Levin's assessment relies heavily on WEINBERGER V. ROMERO-BARCELO, 456 U.S. 305, 314 (1982), a case in which a district court found that the U.S. Navy was required to obtain a permit for its training exercises under the Federal Water Pollution Control Act but refused to grant an injunction and simply ordered the Navy to obtain a permit. The Court sustained the district court's decision, emphasizing "an injunction is an equitable remedy. It is not a remedy which issues as of course . . . The Court has repeatedly held that the basis for injunctive relief in the federal courts has always been irreparable injury and the inadequacy of legal remedies. . . . Unless a statute in so many words, or by a necessary and inescapable inference, restricts the court's jurisdiction in equity, the full scope of that jurisdiction is to be recognized and applied." The Court distinguished Tennessee Valley Authority v. Hill, 437 U.S. 153 (1978), the case in which the Court had required construction of a dam be enjoined to protect the snail darter, as an instance where an injunction was the only means available to vindicate Congress's choice. Some commentators have expressed concern about the Court's approach in Romero-Barcelo as being too tied to equitable jurisprudence and insufficiently attentive to the underlying statute. See Daniel A. Farber, Equitable Discretion, Legal Duties, and Environmental Injunctions, 45 U. Pitt. L. Rev. 513, 515 (1984).

The question of the proper geographic scope of injunctive relief arose in the context of TEXAS V. UNITED STATES, 809 F.3d 134, 188 (2015) (p. 357), aff'd by an evenly divided Supreme Court, UNITED STATES V. TEXAS, 136 S.Ct. 2271 (2016), a challenge brought by twenty-six states to DAPA, one of the Obama administration's immigration deferred action initiatives. Upon finding that the Department of Homeland Security should have adopted the initiative using notice-and-comment rulemaking, the district court had issued a nationwide injunction. The Fifth Circuit upheld the injunction as within the district court's discretion, arguing that "partial implementation" would undermine uniformity in immigration regulation, at odds with the integrated scheme of regulation Congress created, and "would be ineffective because DAPA beneficiaries would be free to move among states." The court also emphasized that a district court exercises the federal judicial power that "is not limited to the district wherein the court sits but extends across the country. It is not beyond the power of a court, in appropriate circumstances, to issue a nationwide injunction."

The practice of the nationwide injunction is strongly criticized in SAMUEL L. BRAY, MULTIPLE CHANCELLORS: REFORMING THE NATIONAL INJUNCTION, 131 Harv. L. Rev. (forthcoming, Dec. 2017), available at SSRN:

https://ssrn.com/abstract=2864175. Bray argues that the ability of any federal court to grant such relief leads to forum-shopping and defendants facing conflicting injunctions. Instead, "[a] federal court should give what might be called a 'plaintiff-protective injunction,' enjoining the defendant's conduct only with respect to the plaintiff. No matter how important the question and no matter how important the value of uniformity, a federal court should not award a national injunction. This principle, if adopted by the courts or by Congress, would solve the forum-shopping problem. It would restore the percolation of legal questions through the different courts of appeals, allowing each circuit to reach its own conclusion pending resolution by the Supreme Court. It would nearly eliminate the risk of directly conflicting injunctions." Bray argues that this principle is rooted in the judicial power given by Article III and in traditional equity.

Do you agree that courts should only give plaintiff-specific relief? Such a narrow approach could increase dramatically the number of suits that are brought on the same issue, consuming judicial and plaintiff resources and raising fairness concerns for plaintiffs who face barriers to suing. Does the option of declaratory relief adequately address these concerns, or can the government be relied upon to treat individualized relief as applying to all similarly situated without being ordered to do so? Are there other alternatives, such as district or circuit wide relief, worth considering that might accommodate the relevant concerns?

(4)   *The Ordinary Remand Rule and Remand without Vacatur.* What about the opposite extreme: If a court finds an agency erred, is it ever justified in ignoring the error as harmless or allowing the action to remain in while remanding to the agency for corrective action? The ordinary rule, often traced back to SEC v. Chenery Corp. (Chenery II), 332 U.S. 194, 196 (1947) (p. 249), is that upon finding error a court will remand back to the agency rather than addressing the issue itself. See Christopher J. Walker, The Ordinary Remand Rule and the Judicial Toolbox for Agency Dialogue, 82 Geo. Wash. L. Rev. 1553 (2014).

Although courts frequently vacate before remanding, the use of remand without vacatur is now a fairly routine practice in judicial review. "[T]he decision whether to vacate depends on the seriousness of the . . . deficiencies (and thus the extent of doubt whether the agency chose correctly) and the disruptive consequences of an interim change that may itself be changed." Allied-Signal, Inc. v. NRC, 988 F.2d 146, 150–51 (D.C. Cir. 1993). This approach is often invoked when the court identifies a defect in an agency's explanation for its decision that the court concludes the agency can readily cure on remand. Vacating a rule in such contexts can undo extensive agency effort for little substantive benefit and unduly reward marginal appeals. It also can be significantly disruptive, particularly when the new rule has already gone into effect, and create regulatory gaps given the limits the Supreme Court has put on retroactive rulemaking (see Note 3, p. 264).

But does the APA give courts authority to adopt remand without vacatur? Judicial authority for the practice was disputed in CHECKOSKY V. SEC, 23 F.3d 452 (D.C. Cir. 1994), which arose out of an agency adjudication rather than a rulemaking. Dissenting from the panel's decision to remand without vacating an SEC order that all judges agreed was arbitrary and capricious, JUDGE RANDOLPH argued that remand without vacatur violated the APA. Once the conclusion had been reached, he said, "the Administrative Procedure Act requires the court—in the absence of any contrary statute—to vacate the agency's action. . . . Section 706(2)(A) provides that a 'reviewing court' faced with an arbitrary and capricious agency decision 'shall'—not may—'hold unlawful and set aside' the agency action. Setting aside means vacating; no other meaning is apparent." 23 F.3d at 491; see also Comcast Corp. v. FCC, 579 F.3d 1, 10–11 (D.C. Cir. 2009) (Randolph, J., concurring). By contrast, JUDGE SILBERMAN insisted that the APA only requires a court to set aside an agency decision it finds to be arbitrary and capricious but does not preclude a court from remanding a decision to an agency for fuller explanation without making that determination. Checkosky, 23 F.3d at 462–63. No Supreme Court decision has directly considered whether remand without vacatur is authorized by the APA.

Professor NICHOLAS BAGLEY in REMEDIAL RESTRAINT IN ADMINISTRATIVE LAW, 117 Colum. L. Rev. 253, 309 (2017), has identified an additional basis of support in the APA for remand without vacatur: § 706's instruction that "due account shall be taken of the rule of prejudicial error." This means that "[s]o far as the APA is concerned, reviewing courts are authorized to hold agency errors harmless, much as they can hold trial errors harmless. There's nothing to the argument that the APA, by its terms, strips courts of the authority to leave procedurally defective agency rules intact." According to Bagley, what's anomalous is not a court's decision not to vacate in this context, but instead its decision to remand to the agency for correction of harmless errors. "An agency response to a remand order is often little more than a formal ritual signifying obeisance to the reviewing court's authority. Giving low priority to that kind of ritual is completely reasonable . . . Fixing minor mistakes is no trivial matter." As a result, "the problem with remand without vacatur may not be that agencies don't respond expeditiously to remand orders. The problem may be that they're ordered to respond at all. The prominence of remand without vacatur has displaced a forthright discussion of the possibility that some errors should be excused as harmless." For additional commentary, see Ronald M. Levin, "Vacation" at Sea: Judicial Remedies and Equitable Discretion in Administrative Law, 53 Duke L. J. 291 (2003); Kristina Daugirdas, Note, Evaluating Remand Without Vacatur: A New Judicial Remedy for Defective Agency Rulemakings, 80 N.Y.U. L. Rev. 278, 293–97 (2005).

Do you think the logic of Chenery requires an initial agency determination of whether the error would make a difference to its decisionmaking, even if the reviewing court concludes that the error didn't change the result the agency reached? The significance of an error sounds like the kind of question that draws on agency expertise, but is it also a question going to the court's expertise about the judicial review process? Do you agree that § 706's reference to taking "due account . . . of the rule of prejudicial error," in the context of an instruction to courts to "hold unlawful and set aside agency action, findings, and conclusions found to be . . .arbitrary, capricious, an abuse of discretion, or otherwise not in accordance with law," justifies courts in developing harmless error doctrines? Do you think this language precludes harmless error analysis? Given that Chenery is a judge-made doctrine, isn't it open to further judicial refinements that are consistent with the governing statute?

(5) *How Should Administrative Law Approach Remedial Questions: Remedial Purity, Remedial Restraint, or Somewhere in the Middle?* Recent debates about the grant of national injunctions, interim stays, and remand without vacatur showcase the importance of the remedial dimension of administrative law. Yet remedial questions are rarely engaged in depth by courts or scholars.

Professor BAGLEY, supra at 255, 263, 309, faults administrative law for this "systematic inattention to remedial questions," and more substantively for a tacit "norm of remedial purity" that he identifies in administrative law decisions: "With rare exceptions, [such as remand without vacatur], agency actions that contravene the APA are invalidated and returned to the agency. Across a range of cases, the remedy appears disproportionate to the underlying infraction. The courts' strict approach could perhaps be justified on prophylactic grounds: Better a hard rule that encourages procedural fastidiousness than a remedial standard that might tempt agencies to cut corners." But "[w]hatever the merits of that approach, its costs are large. When a court vacates an agency action, the agency must decide whether to correct whatever deficiency the court has identified. Rectifying the mistake may be no mean feat, especially if doing so requires the agency to trudge through the procedural thicket surrounding notice and comment. In the meantime, the agency action will be put on hold . . . In the end, the agency might choose to abandon the action altogether: Its priorities may have changed, its staff may have been reassigned, or the external groups supporting action may have dispersed. Judicial review can thus derail or delay significant government programs, sometimes at substantial cost to the public welfare. The harshness of the vacate-and-remand remedy may also affect the standards that courts employ to gauge the legality of agency action. . . .[T]the prospect of invalidation may push courts to narrow the scope of what counts as arbitrary."

In response, Professor CHRISTOPHER J. WALKER, in AGAINST REMEDIAL RESTRAINT IN ADMINISTRATIVE LAW, 117 Columbia Law Review Online 106, 117, 120 (2017), agrees that Professor "Bagley is no doubt correct that the current rule-based approach to remand in administrative law leads to some additional costs, including a heightened risk of false positives—cases in which relatively harmless agency errors are remanded to the agency, resulting in additional delay or even the agency's abandonment of the regulatory effort. . . . But for those of us concerned about bureaucracy and distrust, we are much more troubled about false negatives—cases in which there are harmful agency errors that nevertheless are ignored because the court erroneously finds no prejudice." Walker adds, "we are [also] much less likely to find agency errors harmless—especially errors related to the structures and procedures that attempt to compensate for the regulatory state's democratic deficits." Indeed, Walker argues that "[m]any of the agency errors Bagley highlights as meriting a more searching prejudice inquiry can be structural errors," which fall outside of harmless error in the criminal context. "On the rulemaking front, if the agency is required to utilize notice-and-comment rulemaking but fails to do so . . . that goes to the heart of the administrative process."

Who has the better argument? Does the choice between remedial restraint and remedial purity inevitably turn on the degree of trust one has in administrative government? Are both acceptable interpretations of the APA? If so, would the best course be neither extreme but instead to grant lower courts broad discretion to determine administrative law remedies?

(2) Suits for Damages

Historically, if an administrative action invaded liberty or property interests protected by the common law, the injured citizen sued the responsible official in tort or contract. When the official defended against the suit by citing his or her statutory authority, the court could examine the scope of that authority and resolve allegations of its abuse. If the action was not justified under the legal authority claimed, the official would be liable personally for the damages caused. See, e.g., North Am. Cold Storage Co. v. Chicago, p. 615. This system applied to federal officials as well as state officials, but federal officials can remove state court suits against them to federal court if they can assert a federal defense.[27]

Of course, such a regime tends to be hard on government officials whose personal assets are at risk in the event of a mistaken administrative decision. Although Congress often enacted private bills indemnifying the officers involved, that did not always occur.[28] Consequently, courts developed "official immunity" defenses that protected official judgment in varying degrees, with executive officials other than the President generally received qualified immunity. See, e.g., Harlow v. Fitzgerald, 457 U.S. 800 (1982). The Supreme Court has held that some governmental contractors may qualify for immunity as well, Boyle v. United Techs. Corp., 487 U.S. 500 (1988), an issue that has arisen recently with respect to actions by private military contractors in Iraq.[29]

Eventually, legislatures intervened to provide alternative or supplanting causes of action against the government itself. At the federal level, officials now have complete statutory immunity for torts committed "while acting within the scope of [their] office or employment." 28 U.S.C. § 2679(b)(1). The exclusive remedy is against the United States, on a respondeat superior theory, under the Federal Tort Claims Act (FTCA).

---

[27] See 28 U.S.C. § 1442(a)(1); Mesa v. California, 489 U.S. 121 (1989); Tennessee v. Davis, 100 U.S. 257 (1879).

[28] See James E. Pfander & Jonathan L. Hunt, Public Wrongs and Private Bills: Indemnification and Government Accountability in the Early Republic, 85 N.Y.U. L. REV. 1862 (2010).

[29] Saleh v. Titan Corp., 580 F.3d 1 (D.C. Cir. 2009).

However, the statutory consent to liability in the FTCA has significant procedural restrictions and substantive gaps, including not applying to performance of a discretionary function or actions taken outside of the United States.[30] For claims "not sounding in tort"—most importantly, contract and takings claims—a remedy directly against the United States can be sought under the Tucker Act in the Court of Claims.

Damages actions against government officials in their personal capacity remain important for constitutional violations committed in the course of their duties. In the case of federal officials, the cause of action (if any) comes directly from the Constitution. See Bivens v. Six Unknown Federal Narcotics Agents, 403 U.S. 388 (1971). The FTCA immunity from personal liability does *not* extend to constitutional wrongs, 28 U.S.C. § 2679(b)(2)(A), although the official will have the benefit of official immunity defenses. "Bivens actions" cannot be brought against the agency as an entity[31] or against top agency officials merely on the basis of their supervisory position.[32] Even where the official himself is being sued on a theory of individual, intentional unconstitutional behavior, the Court has become decidedly less willing to imply new Bivens actions. Recently, Ziglar v. Abbasi, 137 S.Ct. 1843, 1856–57 (2017), the Court stated that Bivens was "settled law" in the "search-and-seizure context in which it arose," but emphasized that "expanding the Bivens remedy is now a disfavored judicial activity."[33]

In the case of state and local officials, the cause of action for damages from constitutional violations is statutory: 42 U.S.C. § 1983.[34] Here, we can sketch only the basic contours of what has become a massive body of law: (i) Damages claims against state and local officials, in their individual capacity, are subject to the same official immunity defenses available to federal officials in Bivens actions; (ii) The statute can be used to seek damages against government entities below the level of the state itself; these entities (counties, municipalities, etc.) can assert no immunity defenses, but their liability for their employees' actions is

---

[30]   28 U.S.C. §§ 2680(a), (k). In such circumstances, victims are remitted to whatever relief they can obtain through administrative settlement, see 28 U.S.C. §§ 2672, 2675, or from Congress via a private bill.

[31]   Federal Deposit Ins. Corp. v. Meyer, 510 U.S. 471 (1994); Correctional Services Corp. v. Malesko, 534 U.S. 61 (2001).

[32]   Ashcroft v. Iqbal, 556 U.S. 662 (2009).

[33]   A cause of action will not be implied when either (1) Congress has provided an alternative remedy deemed equally effective; or (2) the court perceives "special factors counseling hesitation." Recently, the Court appears to have added a third situation: "difficulty in defining a workable cause of action." Wilkie v. Robbins, 551 U.S. 537 (2007). In Ziglar, 137 S.Ct. at 1858, the Court emphasized that Courts must consider the systemwide effects of implying a Bivens remedy and reiterated that "if there are sound reasons to think that Congress might doubt the efficacy or necessity of a damages remedy . . ., the courts must refrain from creating [one]."

[34]   "Every person who, under color of any statute, ordinance, regulation, custom, or usage, of any State or Territory . . . subjects, or causes to be subjected, any citizen of the United States or other person within the jurisdiction thereof to the deprivation of any rights, privileges, or immunities secured by the Constitution and laws, shall be liable to the party injured in an action at law, suit in equity, or other proper proceeding for redress."

limited in a number of ways;[35] and (iii) States (and state agencies) cannot be sued under this statute.

Finally, a number of federal statutes—for example, the Family and Medical Leave Act or the Americans with Disabilities Act—provide for a right of action against state and local (as well as private) entities that violate statutory requirements. Even where federal statutes are silent on enforcement, § 1983 has been used to obtain damages for violations, although the Supreme Court has significantly restricted the availability of § 1983 to enforce statutory obligations and has also pulled back significantly from implying rights of action from statutes directly.[36]

Sovereign immunity is often a barrier to suits against state and local governments for violations of federal statutes. The Court has held that the Eleventh Amendment bars damages suits based on federal statutes unless Congress validly abrogates state sovereign immunity and that Article I overwhelming does not give Congress authority to abrogate.[37] Subsequently, the Court extended this holding, first to suits brought by private parties in state court to enforce federal law, and subsequently to attempts by private parties to force states to appear before federal agencies to answer for federal regulatory violations.[38] Congress can abrogate state sovereign immunity when it legislates pursuant to the remedial authority of section 5 of the Fourteenth Amendment. However, the Court has set fairly stringent standards of "congruence and proportionality" for invoking this authority and many regulatory programs have not qualified.[39]

There remain a few ways by which regulatory obligations can be enforced against states and their agencies in the many regulatory programs enacted under the Commerce Clause, Spending Clause, and other Article I provisions. First, States cannot assert sovereign immunity in actions by the United States or its agencies.[40] Thus, immunity will not be a problem in the very common enforcement paradigm in which the federal agency itself, or the U.S. Attorney, brings the complaint. Second, as noted above, in cases of ongoing violations private individuals can often seek injunctive or declaratory relief, although not if such actions

---

[35] Most significantly, there is no respondeat superior liability; the wrongdoing must be pursuant to official policy or custom. Monell v. Dep't of Social Serv., 436 U.S. 658, 691 (1978). Also, punitive damages may not be recovered. City of Newport v. Fact Concerts, 453 U.S. 247 (1981).

[36] See Gonzaga Univ. v. Doe, 536 U.S. 273 (2002) (limiting use of § 1983 for statutory violations); Alexander v. Sandoval, 532 U.S. 275, 288–89 (2001) (restricting statutory implied rights of action).

[37] See Seminole Tribe of Fla. v. Florida, 517 U.S. 44 (1996). But see Central Virginia Community College v. Katz, 546 U.S. 356 (2006) (holding that Congress may abrogate state sovereign immunity under the Bankruptcy Clause of Article I).

[38] Alden v. Maine, 527 U.S. 706 (1999); Federal Maritime Com'n v. South Carolina Ports Auth., 535 U.S. 743 (2002).

[39] See, e.g., Coleman v. Court of Appeals of Maryland, 566 U.S. 30 (2012); Bd. of Trustees of Univ. of Alabama v. Garrett, 531 U.S. 356 (2001).

[40] E.g., Alden v. Maine, 527 U.S. 706, 755–56 (1999); United States v. Texas, 143 U.S. 621, 644–45 (1892).

really seek retrospective, compensatory relief that requires the payment of money from the state treasury.[41] Finally, Congress can enact an express requirement that states consent to suit in order to obtain some benefit the federal government is not otherwise required to confer upon them,[42] although the Court requires such conditions to be very clear and unambiguous to the recipient entity, germane to the purpose of the funds, and to not be coercive.[43]

---

[41] Edelman v. Jordan, 415 U.S. 651 (1974).

[42] See, e.g., NFIB v. Sebelius, 567 U.S. 519 (2012); South Dakota v. Dole, 483 U.S. 203 (1987).

[43] See, e.g., Arlington Central Sch. Dt. Bd. of Educ. v. Murphy, 548 U.S. 291 (2006); NFIB v. Sebelius, 567 U.S. 519, 576 (2012).

APPENDIX

CONSTITUTION OF THE UNITED STATES OF AMERICA

We the People of the United States in Order to form a more perfect Union, to establish Justice, insure domestic Tranquility, provide for the common defense, promote the general Welfare, and secure the Blessings of Liberty to ourselves and our Posterity, do ordain and establish this Constitution for the United States of America.

ARTICLE I

Section 1

All legislative Powers herein granted shall be vested in a Congress of the United States, which shall consist of a Senate and House of Representatives.

Section 2

[1] The House of Representatives shall be composed of Members chosen every second Year by the People of the several States, and the Electors in each State shall have the Qualifications requisite for Electors of the most numerous Branch of the State Legislature.

[2] No Person shall be a Representative who shall not have attained to the Age of twenty-five Years, and been seven Years a Citizen of the United States, and who shall not, when elected, be an Inhabitant of that State in which he shall be chosen.

[3] Representatives and direct Taxes shall be apportioned among the several States which may be included within this Union, according to their respective Numbers, which shall be determined by adding to the whole Number of free Persons, including those bound to Service for a Term of Years, and excluding Indians not taxed, three fifths of all other Persons. The actual Enumeration shall be made within three Years after the first Meeting of the Congress of the United States, and within every subsequent Term of ten Years, in such Manner as they shall by Law direct. The Number of Representatives shall not exceed one for every thirty Thousand, but each State shall have at Least One Representative; and until such enumerations shall be made, the State of New Hampshire

shall be entitled to chuse three, Massachusetts eight, Rhode Island and Providence Plantations one, Connecticut five, New York six, New Jersey four, Pennsylvania eight, Delaware one, Maryland six, Virginia ten, North Carolina five, South Carolina five, and Georgia three.

[4] When vacancies happen in the Representation from any State, the Executive Authority thereof shall issue Writs of Election to fill such Vacancies.

[5] The House of Representatives shall chuse their Speaker and other Officers, and shall have the sole Power of Impeachment.

Section 3

[1] The Senate of the United States shall be composed of two Senators from each State, chosen by the Legislature thereof, for six Years; and each Senator shall have one Vote.

[2] Immediately after they shall be assembled in Consequence of the first Election, they shall be divided as equally as may be into three Classes. The Seats of the Senators of the first Class shall be vacated at the Expiration of the second Year, of the second Class at the Expiration of the fourth Year, and of the third class at the Expiration of the sixth Year, so that one third may be chosen every second Year; and if Vacancies happen by Resignation, or otherwise, during the Recess of the Legislature of any State, the Executive thereof may make temporary Appointments until the next Meeting of the Legislature, which shall then fill such Vacancies.

[3] No Person shall be a Senator who shall not have attained to the Age of thirty Years, and been nine Years a Citizen of the United States, and who shall not, when elected, be an Inhabitant of that State for which he shall be chosen.

[4] The Vice President of the United States shall be President of the Senate, but shall have no Vote, unless they be equally divided.

[5] The Senate shall chuse their other Officers, and also a President pro tempore, in the Absence of the Vice President, or when he shall exercise the Office of President of the United States.

[6] The Senate shall have the sole Power to try all Impeachments. When sitting for that Purpose, they shall be on Oath or Affirmation. When the President of the United States is tried, the Chief Justice shall preside: And no Person shall be convicted without the Concurrence of two thirds of the Members present.

[7] Judgment in Cases of Impeachment shall not extend further than to removal from Office, and disqualification to hold and enjoy any Office of honor, Trust or Profit under the United States: but the Party convicted shall nevertheless be liable and subject to Indictment, Trial, Judgment and Punishment, according to Law.

Section 4

[1]   The Times, Places and Manner of holding Elections for Senators and Representatives, shall be prescribed in each State by the Legislature thereof; but the Congress may at any time by Law make or alter such Regulations, except as to the Places of chusing Senators.

[2]   The Congress shall assemble at least once in every Year, and such Meeting shall be on the first Monday in December, unless they shall by Law appoint a different Day.

Section 5

[1]   Each House shall be the Judge of the Elections, Returns and Qualifications for its own Members, and a Majority of each shall constitute a Quorum to do Business; but a smaller Number may adjourn from day to day, and may be authorized to compel the Attendance of absent Members, in such Manner, and under such Penalties as each House may provide.

[2]   Each House may determine the Rules of its Proceedings, punish its Members for disorderly Behaviour, and, with the Concurrence of two thirds, expel a Member.

[3]   Each House shall keep a Journal of its Proceedings, and from time to time publish the same, excepting such Parts as may in their Judgment require Secrecy; and the Yeas and Nays of the Members of either House on any questions shall, at the Desire of one fifth of those Present, be entered on the Journal.

[4]   Neither House, during the Session of Congress, shall, without the Consent of the other, adjourn for more than three days, nor to any other Place than that in which the two Houses shall be sitting.

Section 6

[1]   The Senators and Representatives shall receive a Compensation for their Services, to be ascertained by Law, and paid out of the Treasury of the United States. They shall in all Cases, except Treason, Felony and Breach of the Peace, be privileged from Arrest during their Attendance at the Session of their respective Houses, and in going to and returning from the same; and for any Speech or Debate in either House, they shall not be questioned in any other Place.

[2]   No Senator or Representative shall, during the Time for which he was elected, be appointed to any civil Office under the Authority of the United States, which shall have been created, or the Emoluments whereof shall have been encreased during such time; and no Person holding any Office under the United States, shall be a Member of either House during his Continuance in Office.

Section 7

[1] All Bills for raising Revenue shall originate in the House of Representatives; but the Senate may propose or concur with Amendments as on other Bills.

[2] Every Bill which shall have passed the House of Representatives and the Senate, shall, before it become a Law, be presented to the President of the United States; If he approve he shall sign it, but if not he shall return it with his Objections to that House in which it shall have originated, who shall enter the Objections at large on their Journal, and proceed to reconsider it. If after such Reconsideration two thirds of the House shall agree to pass the Bill, it shall be sent, together with the Objections, to the other House, by which it shall likewise be reconsidered, and if approved by two thirds of that House, it shall become a Law. But in all such Cases the Votes of both Houses shall be determined by Yeas and Nays, and the Names of the Persons voting for and against the Bill shall be entered on the Journal of each House respectively. If any Bill shall not be returned by the President within ten Days (Sundays excepted) after it shall have been presented to him, the Same shall be a Law, in like Manner as if he had signed it, unless the Congress by their Adjournment prevent its Return, in which Case it shall not be a Law.

[3] Every Order, Resolution, or Vote to Which the Concurrence of the Senate and House of Representatives may be necessary (except on a question of Adjournment) shall be presented to the President of the United States; and before the Same shall take Effect, shall be approved by him, or being disapproved by him, shall be repassed by two thirds of the Senate and House of Representatives, according to the Rules and Limitations prescribed in the Case of a Bill.

Section 8

[1] The Congress shall have Power To lay and collect Taxes, Duties, Imports and Excises, to pay the Debts and provide for the common Defence and general Welfare of the United States; but all Duties, Imports and Excises shall be uniform throughout the United States;

[2] To borrow money on the credit of the United States;

[3] To regulate Commerce with foreign Nations, and among the several States, and with the Indian Tribes;

[4] To establish a uniform Rule of Naturalization, and uniform Laws on the subject of Bankruptcies throughout the United States;

[5] To coin Money, regulate the value thereof, and of foreign Coin, and fix the Standard of Weights and Measures;

[6] To provide for the Punishment of counterfeiting the Securities and current Coin of the United States;

[7] To establish Post Offices and post Roads;

[8]   To promote the Progress of Science and useful Arts, by securing for limited Times to Authors and Inventors exclusive Right to their respective Writings and Discoveries;

[9]   To constitute Tribunals inferior to the supreme Court;

[10] To define and punish Piracies and Felonies committed on the high Seas, and Offences against the Law of Nations;

[11] To declare War, grant Letters of Marque and Reprisal, and make Rules concerning Captures on Land and Water;

[12] To raise and support Armies, but no Appropriation of Money to that Use shall be for a longer Term than two Years;

[13] To provide and maintain a Navy;

[14] To make Rules for the Government and Regulation of the land and naval Forces;

[15] To provide for calling forth the Militia to execute the Laws of the Union, suppress Insurrections and repel Invasions;

[16] To provide for organizing, arming, and disciplining, the Militia and for governing such Part of them as may be employed in the Service of the United States, reserving to the States respectively, the Appointment of the Officers, and the Authority of training the Militia according to the discipline prescribed by Congress;

[17] To exercise exclusive Legislation in all Cases whatsoever, over such District (not exceeding ten Miles square) as may, by Cession of particular States, and the Acceptance of Congress, become the Seat of the Government of the United States, and to exercise like Authority over all Places purchased by the Consent of the Legislature of the State in which the Same shall be, for the Erection of Forts, Magazines, Arsenals, dock-Yards, and other needful buildings;—And

[18] To make all Laws which shall be necessary and proper for carrying into Execution the foregoing Powers, and all other Powers vested by this Constitution in the Government of the United States, or in any Department or Officer thereof.

Section 9

[1]   The Migration or Importation of such Persons as any of the States now existing shall think proper to admit, shall not be prohibited by the Congress prior to the Year one thousand eight hundred and eight, but a Tax or duty may be imposed on such Importation, not exceeding ten dollars for each Person.

[2]   The privilege of the Writ of Habeas Corpus shall not be suspended, unless when in Cases of Rebellion or Invasion the public Safety may require it.

[3]   No Bill of Attainder or ex post facto Law shall be past.

[4]   No Capitation, or other direct, Tax shall be laid, unless in Proportion to the Census on Enumeration herein before directed to be taken.

[5]   No Tax or Duty shall be laid on Articles exported from any State.

[6]   No Preference shall be given by any Regulation of Commerce or Revenue to the Ports of one State over those of another: nor shall Vessels bound to, or from, one State, be obliged to enter, clear or pay Duties in another.

[7]   No money shall be drawn from the Treasury, but in Consequence of Appropriations made by Law, and a regular Statement and Account of the Receipts and Expenditures of all public Money shall be published from time to time.

[8]   No Title of Nobility shall be granted by the United States: And no Person holding any Office of Profit or Trust under them, shall, without the Consent of the Congress, accept of any present, Emolument, Office, or Title, of any kind whatever, from any King, Prince, or foreign State.

Section 10

[1]   No State shall enter into any Treaty, Alliance, or Confederation; grant Letters of Marque and Reprisal; coin Money; emit Bills of credit; make any Thing but gold and silver Coin a Tender in Payment of Debts; pass any Bill of Attainder, ex post facto Law, or Law impairing the Obligation of Contracts, or grant any Title of Nobility.

[2]   No State shall, without the Consent of Congress, lay any Imposts or Duties on Imports or Exports, except what may be absolutely necessary for executing its inspection Laws: and the net Produce of all Duties and Imposts, laid by any State on Imports and Exports, shall be for the Use of the Treasury of the United States; and all such Laws shall be subject to the Revision and Controul of the Congress.

[3]   No State shall, without the Consent of Congress, lay any Duty of Tonnage, keep Troops, or Ships of War in time of Peace, enter into any Agreement or Compact with another State, or with a foreign Power, or engage in War, unless actually invaded, or in such imminent Danger as will not admit of delay.

ARTICLE II

Section 1

[1]   The executive Power shall be vested in a President of the United States of America. He shall hold his Office during the Term of four Years, and, together with the Vice President, chosen for the same Term, be elected, as follows:

[2]   Each State shall appoint, in such Manner as the Legislature thereof may direct, a Number of Electors, equal to the whole Number of Senators and Representatives to which the State may be entitled in the

Congress: but no Senator or Representative, or Person holding an Office of Trust or Profit under the United States, shall be appointed an Elector.

[3] The Electors shall meet in their respective States, and vote by Ballot for two Persons, of whom one at least shall not be an Inhabitant of the same State with themselves. And they shall make a List of all the Persons voted for, and of the Number of Votes for each; which List they shall sign and certify, and transmit sealed to the Seat of the Government of the United States, directed to the President of the Senate. The President of the Senate shall, in the Presence of the Senate and House of Representatives, open all the Certificates, and the Votes shall then be counted. The Person having the greatest Number of Votes shall be the President, if such Number be a Majority of the whole Number of Electors appointed; and if there be more than one who have such Majority, and have an equal Number of Votes, then the House of Representatives shall immediately chuse by Ballot one of them for President; and if no Person have a Majority, then from the five highest on the List the said House shall in like Manner chuse the President. But in chusing the President, the Votes shall be taken by States, the Representation from each State having one Vote; a quorum for this Purpose shall consist of a Member or Members from two thirds of the States, and a Majority of all the States shall be necessary to a Choice. In every Case, after the Choice of the President, the Person having the greatest Number of Votes of the Electors shall be the Vice President. But if there should remain two or more who have equal Votes, the Senate shall chuse from them by Ballot the Vice President.

[4] The Congress may determine the Time of chusing the Electors, and the Day on which they shall give their Votes; which Day shall be the same throughout the United States.

[5] No Person except a natural born Citizen, or a Citizen of the United States, at the time of the Adoption of this Constitution, shall be eligible to the Office of President; neither shall any Person be eligible to that Office who shall not have attained to the Age of thirty five Years, and been fourteen Years a Resident within the United States.

[6] In case of the removal of the President from Office, or of his Death, Resignation or Inability to discharge the Powers and Duties of the said Office, the Same shall devolve on the Vice President, and the Congress may by Law provide for the Case of Removal, Death, Resignation or Inability, both of the President and Vice President, declaring what Officer shall then act as President, and such Officer shall act accordingly, until the Disability be removed, or a President shall be elected.

[7] The President shall, at stated Times, receive for his Services, a Compensation, which shall neither be increased nor diminished during the Period for which he shall have been elected, and he shall not receive within that Period any other Emolument from the United States, or any of them.

[8]   Before he enter on the Execution of his Office, he shall take the following Oath or Affirmation: "I do solemnly swear (or affirm) that I will faithfully execute the Office of President of the United States, and will to the best of my Ability, preserve, protect and defend the Constitution of the United States."

Section 2

[1]   The President shall be Commander in Chief of the Army and Navy of the United States, and of the Militia of the several States, when called into the actual Service of the United States; he may require the Opinion, in writing, of the principal Officer in each of the executive Departments, upon any Subject relating to the Duties of their respective Offices, and he shall have Power to grant Reprieves and Pardons for Offences against the United States, except in Cases of Impeachment.

[2]   He shall have Power, by and with the Advice and Consent of the Senate, to make Treaties, provided two thirds of the Senators present concur; and he shall nominate, and by and with the Advice and Consent of the Senate, shall appoint Ambassadors, other public Ministers and Consuls, Judges of the supreme Court, and all other Officers of the United States, whose Appointments are not herein otherwise provided for, and which shall be established by Law: but the Congress may by Law vest the Appointment of such inferior Officers, as they think proper, in the President alone, in the Courts of Law, or in the Heads of Departments.

[3]   The President shall have Power to fill up all Vacancies that may happen during the Recess of the Senate, by granting Commissions which shall expire at the End of their next Session.

Section 3

He shall from time to time give to the Congress Information of the State of the Union, and recommend to their Consideration such Measures as he shall judge necessary and expedient; he may, on extraordinary occasions, convene both Houses, or either of them, and in Case of Disagreement between them, with Respect to the time of Adjournment, he may adjourn them to such Time as he shall think proper; he shall receive Ambassadors and other public Ministers, he shall take Care that the Laws be faithfully executed, and shall Commission all the Officers of the United States.

Section 4

The President, Vice President and all civil Officers of the United States, shall be removed from Office on Impeachment for, and Conviction of Treason, Bribery, or other high Crimes and Misdemeanors.

ARTICLE III

Section 1

The judicial Power of the United States, shall be vested in one supreme Court, and in such inferior Courts as the Congress may from time to time ordain and establish. The Judges, both of the supreme and inferior Courts, shall hold their Offices during good Behaviour, and shall, at stated Times, receive for their Services, a Compensation, which shall not be diminished during their Continuance in Office.

Section 2

[1]   The judicial Power shall extend to all Cases, in Law and Equity, arising under the Constitution, the Laws of the United States, and Treaties made, or which shall be made, under their Authority;—to all Cases affecting Ambassadors, other public Ministers and Consuls;—to all Cases of admiralty and maritime Jurisdiction;—to Controversies to which the United States shall be a Party;—to Controversies between two or more States;—between a State and Citizens of Another State;—between Citizens of different States;—between Citizens of the same State claiming Lands under Grants of different States, and between a State, or the Citizens thereof, and foreign States, Citizens or Subjects.

[2]   In all Cases affecting Ambassadors, other public Ministers and Consuls, and those in which a State shall be Party, the supreme Court shall have original Jurisdiction. In all the other Cases before mentioned, the supreme Court shall have appellate Jurisdiction, both as to Law and Fact, with such Exceptions, and under such Regulations as the Congress shall make.

[3]   The trial of all Crimes, except in Cases of Impeachment, shall be by Jury; and such Trial shall be held in the State where the said Crimes shall have been committed; but when not committed within any State, the Trial shall be at such Place or Places as the Congress may by Law have directed.

Section 3

[1]   Treason against the United States, shall consist only in levying War against them, or in adhering to their Enemies, giving them Aid and Comfort. No Person shall be convicted of Treason unless on the Testimony of two Witnesses to the same overt Act, or on Confession in open Court.

[2]   The Congress shall have Power to declare the Punishment of Treason, but no Attainder of Treason shall work Corruption of Blood, or Forfeiture except during the Life of the Person attained.

ARTICLE IV

Section 1

Full Faith and Credit shall be given in each State to the public Acts, Records, and judicial Proceedings of every other State. And the Congress may by general Laws prescribe the Manner in which such Acts, Records and Proceedings shall be proved, and the Effect thereof.

Section 2

[1]   The Citizens of each State shall be entitled to all Privileges and Immunities of Citizens in the several States.

[2]   A Person charged in any State with Treason, Felony, or other Crime, who shall flee from Justice, and be found in another State, shall on demand of the executive Authority of the State from which he fled, be delivered up, to be removed to the State having Jurisdiction of the Crime.

[3]   No Person held to Service or Labour in one State, under the Laws thereof, escaping into another, shall, in Consequence of any Law or Regulation therein, be discharged from such Service or Labour, but shall be delivered up on Claim of the Party to whom such Service or Labour may be due.

Section 3

[1]   New States may be admitted by the Congress into this Union, but no new State shall be formed or erected within the Jurisdiction of any other State; nor any State be formed by the Junction of two or more States, or Parts of States, without the Consent of the Legislatures of the States concerned as well as of the Congress.

[2]   The Congress shall have Power to dispose of and make all needful Rules and Regulations respecting the Territory or other Property belonging to the United States; and nothing in this Constitution shall be so constructed as to Prejudice any claims of the United States, or of any particular State.

Section 4

The United States shall guarantee to every State in this Union a Republican Form of Government, and shall protect each of them against Invasion; and on Application of the Legislature, or of the Executive (when the Legislature cannot be convened) against domestic Violence.

ARTICLE V

The Congress, whenever two thirds of both Houses shall deem it necessary, shall propose Amendments to this Constitution, or, on the Application of the Legislature of two thirds of the several States, shall call a Convention for proposing Amendments, which, in either Case, shall be valid to all Intents and Purposes, as part of this Constitution, when ratified by the Legislatures of three fourths of the several States, or by Conventions in three fourths thereof, as the one or the other Mode of Ratification may be proposed by the Congress; Provided that no Amendment which may be made prior to the Year One thousand eight hundred and eight shall in any Manner affect the first and fourth Clauses in the Ninth Section of the first Article; and that no State, without its Consent, shall be deprived of its equal Suffrage in the Senate.

ARTICLE VI

[1] All Debts contracted and Engagements entered into, before the Adoption of this Constitution, shall be as valid against the United States under this Constitution, as under the Confederation.

[2] This Constitution, and the Laws of the United States which shall be made in Pursuance thereof; and all Treaties made, or which shall be made, under the Authority of the United States, shall be the supreme Law of the Land; and the Judges in every State shall be bound thereby, any Thing in the Constitution or Laws of any State to the Contrary notwithstanding.

[3] The Senators and Representatives before mentioned, and the Members of the several State Legislatures, and all executive and judicial Officers, both of the United States and of the several States, shall be bound by Oath or Affirmation, to support this Constitution; but no religious Test shall ever be required as a Qualification to any Office or public Trust under the United States.

ARTICLE VII

The Ratification of the Conventions of nine States, shall be sufficient for the Establishment of this Constitution between the States so ratifying the Same.

AMENDMENT 1 [1791]

Congress shall make no law respecting an establishment of religion, or prohibiting the free exercise thereof; or abridging the freedom of speech, or of the press; or the right of the people peaceably to assemble, and to petition the Government for a redress of grievances.

AMENDMENT 2 [1791]

A well regulated Militia, being necessary to the security of a free State, the right of the people to keep and bear Arms, shall not be infringed.

AMENDMENT 3 [1791]

No Soldier shall, in time of peace be quartered in any house, without the consent of the Owner, nor in time of war, but in a manner to be prescribed by law.

AMENDMENT 4 [1791]

The right of the people to be secure in their persons, houses, papers, and effects, against unreasonable searches and seizures, shall not be violated, and no Warrants shall issue, but upon probable cause, supported by Oath or affirmation, and particularly describing the place to be searched, and the persons or things to be seized.

AMENDMENT 5 [1791]

No person shall be held to answer for a capital, or otherwise infamous crime, unless on a presentment or indictment of a Grand Jury, except in cases arising in the land or naval forces, or in the Militia, when in actual service in time of War or public danger; nor shall any person be subject for the same offence to be twice put in jeopardy of life or limb; nor shall be compelled in any criminal case to be a witness against himself, nor be deprived of life, liberty, or property, without due process of law; nor shall private property be taken for public use, without just compensation.

AMENDMENT 6 [1791]

In all criminal prosecutions, the accused shall enjoy the right to a speedy and public trial, by an impartial jury of the State and district wherein the crime shall have been committed, which district shall have been previously ascertained by law, and to be informed of the nature and cause of the accusation; to be confronted with the witnesses against him; to have compulsory process for obtaining witnesses in his favor, and to have the Assistance of Counsel for his defence.

AMENDMENT 7 [1791]

In Suits at common law, where the value in controversy shall exceed twenty dollars, the right of trial by jury shall be preserved, and no fact tried by a jury, shall be otherwise re-examined in any Court of the United States, than according to the rules of the common law.

AMENDMENT 8 [1791]

Excessive bail shall not be required, nor excessive fines imposed, nor cruel and unusual punishments inflicted.

AMENDMENT 9 [1791]

The enumeration in the Constitution, of certain rights, shall not be construed to deny or disparage others retained by the people.

AMENDMENT 10 [1791]

The powers not delegated to the United States by the Constitution, nor prohibited by it to the States, are reserved to the States respectively, or to the people.

AMENDMENT 11 [1798]

The Judicial power of the United States shall not be construed to extend to any suit in law or equity, commenced or prosecuted against one of the United States by Citizens of another State, or by Citizens or Subjects of any Foreign State.

AMENDMENT 12 [1804]

The Electors shall meet in their respective states and vote by ballot for President and Vice-President, one of whom, at least, shall not be an inhabitant of the same state with themselves; they shall name in their ballots the person voted for as President, and in distinct ballots the person voted for as Vice-President, and they shall make distinct lists of all persons voted for as President, and of all persons voted for as Vice-President, and of the number of votes for each, which lists they shall sign and certify, and transmit sealed to the seat of the government of the

United States, directed to the President of the Senate;—The President of the Senate shall, in the presence of the Senate and House of Representatives, open all the certificates and the votes shall then be counted;—The person having the greatest number of votes for President, shall be the President, if such number be a majority of the whole number of Electors appointed; and if no person have such majority, then from the persons having the highest numbers not exceeding three on the list of those voted for as President, the House of Representatives shall choose immediately, by ballot, the President. But in choosing the President, the votes shall be taken by states, the representation from each state having one vote; a quorum for this purpose shall consist of a member or members from two-thirds of the states, and a majority of all the states shall be necessary to a choice. And if the House of Representatives shall not choose a President whenever the right of choice shall devolve upon them, before the fourth day of March next following, then the Vice-President shall act as President, as in the case of the death or other constitutional disability of the President.—The person having the greatest number of votes as Vice-President, shall be the Vice-President, if such number be a majority of the whole number of Electors appointed, and if no person have a majority, then from the two highest numbers on the list, the Senate shall choose the Vice-President; a quorum for the purpose shall consist of two-thirds of the whole number of Senators, and a majority of the whole number shall be necessary to a choice. But no person constitutionally ineligible to the office of President shall be eligible to that of Vice-President of the United States.

AMENDMENT 13 [1865]

Section 1

Neither slavery nor involuntary servitude, except as a punishment for crime whereof the party shall have been duly convicted, shall exist within the United States, or any place subject to their jurisdiction.

Section 2

Congress shall have power to enforce this article by appropriate legislation.

AMENDMENT 14 [1868]

Section 1

All persons born or naturalized in the United States, and subject to the jurisdiction thereof, are citizens of the United States and of the State wherein they reside. No State shall make or enforce any law which shall abridge the privileges or immunities of citizens of the United States; nor shall any State deprive any person of life, liberty, or property, without due process of law; nor deny to any person within its jurisdiction the equal protection of the laws.

Section 2

Representatives shall be apportioned among the several States according to their respective numbers, counting the whole number of persons in each State, excluding Indians not taxed. But when the right to vote at any election for the choice of electors for President and Vice President of the United States, Representatives in Congress, the Executive and Judicial officers of a State, or the members of the Legislature thereof, is denied to any of the male inhabitants of such State, being twenty-one years of age, and citizens of the United States, or in any way abridged, except for participation in rebellion, or other crime, the basis of representation therein shall be reduced in the proportion which the number of such male citizens shall bear to the whole number of male citizens twenty-one years of age in such State.

Section 3

No person shall be a Senator or Representative in Congress, or elector of President and Vice President, or hold any office, civil or military, under the United States, or under any State, who, having previously taken an oath, as a member of Congress, or as an officer of the United States, or as a member of any State legislature, or as an executive or judicial officer of any State, to support the Constitution of the United States, shall have engaged in insurrection or rebellion against the same, or given aid or comfort to the enemies thereof. But Congress may by a vote of two-thirds of each House, remove such disability.

Section 4

The validity of the public debt of the United States, authorized by law, including debts incurred for payment of pensions and bounties for services in suppressing insurrection or rebellion, shall not be questioned. But neither the United States nor any State shall assume or pay any debt or obligation incurred in aid of insurrection or rebellion against the United States, or any claim for the loss of emancipation of any slave; but all such debts, obligations and claims shall be held illegal and void.

Section 5

The Congress shall have the power to enforce, by appropriate legislation, the provisions of this article.

AMENDMENT 15 [1870]

Section 1

The right of citizens of the United States to vote shall not be denied or abridged by the United States or by any State on account of race, color, or previous condition of servitude.

Section 2

The Congress shall have power to enforce this article by appropriate legislation.

AMENDMENT 16 [1913]

The Congress shall have power to lay and collect taxes on incomes, from whatever source derived, without apportionment among the several States, and without regard to any census or enumeration.

AMENDMENT 17 [1913]

[1] The Senate of the United States shall be composed of two Senators from each State, elected by the people thereof for six years, and each Senator shall have one vote. The electors in each State shall have the qualifications requisite for electors of the most numerous branch of the State legislatures.

[2] When vacancies happen in the representation of any State in the Senate, the executive authority of such State shall issue writs of election to fill such vacancies: Provided, That the legislature of any State may empower the executive thereof to make temporary appointments until the people fill the vacancies by election as the legislature may direct.

[3] This amendment shall not be so construed as to affect the election or term of any Senator chosen before it becomes valid as part of the Constitution.

AMENDMENT 18 [1919]

Section 1

After one year from the ratification of this article the manufacture, sale, or transportation of intoxicating liquors within, the importation thereof into, or the exportation thereof from the United States and all territory subject to the jurisdiction thereof for beverage purposes is hereby prohibited.

Section 2

The Congress and the several States shall have concurrent power to enforce this article by appropriate legislation.

Section 3

This article shall be inoperative unless it shall have been ratified as an amendment to the Constitution by the legislatures of the several States as provided in the Constitution, within seven years from the date of the submission hereof to the States by the Congress.

AMENDMENT 19 [1920]

[1] The right of citizens of the United States to vote shall not be denied or abridged by the United States or by any State on account of sex.

[2] Congress shall have power to enforce this article by appropriate legislation.

AMENDMENT 20 [1933]

Section 1

The terms of the President and Vice President shall end at noon on the 20th day of January, and the terms of Senators and Representatives at noon on the 3d day of January, of the years in which such terms would have ended if this article had not been ratified; and the terms of their successors shall then begin.

Section 2

The Congress shall assemble at least once in every year, and such meeting shall begin at noon on the 3d day of January, unless they shall by law appoint a different day.

Section 3

If, at the time fixed for the beginning of the term of the President, the President elect shall have died, the Vice President elect shall become President. If a President shall not have been chosen before the time fixed for the beginning of his term, or if the President elect shall have failed to qualify, then the Vice President elect shall act as President until a President shall have qualified; and the Congress may by law provide for the case wherein neither a President elect nor a Vice President elect shall have qualified, declaring who shall then act as President, or the manner in which one who is to act shall be selected, and such person shall act accordingly until a President or Vice President shall have qualified.

Section 4

The Congress may by law provide for the case of the death of any of the persons from whom the House of Representatives may choose a President whenever the right of choice shall have devolved upon them, and for the case of the death of any of the persons from whom the Senate may choose a Vice President whenever the right of choice shall have devolved upon them.

Section 5

Sections 1 and 2 shall take effect on the 15th day of October following the ratification of this article.

Section 6

This article shall be inoperative unless it shall have been ratified as an amendment to the Constitution by the legislatures of three-fourths of the several States within seven years from the date of its submission.

AMENDMENT 21 [1933]

Section 1

The eighteenth article of amendment to the Constitution of the United States is hereby repealed.

Section 2

The transportation or importation into any State, Territory, or possession of the United States for delivery or use therein of intoxicating liquors, in violation of the laws thereof, is hereby prohibited.

Section 3

This article shall be inoperative unless it shall have been ratified as an amendment to the Constitution by conventions in the several States, as provided in the Constitution, within seven years from the date of the submission hereof to the States by the Congress.

AMENDMENT 22 [1951]

Section 1

No person shall be elected to the office of the President more than twice, and no person who has held the office of President, or acted as President, for more than two years of a term to which some other person was elected President shall be elected to the office of President more than once. But this Article shall not apply to any person holding the office of President when this Article was proposed by the Congress, and shall not prevent any person who may be holding the office of President, or acting as President, during the term within which this Article becomes operative from holding the office of President or acting as President during the remainder of such term.

Section 2

This article shall be inoperative unless it shall have been ratified as an amendment to the Constitution by the legislatures of three-fourths of the several States within seven years from the date of its submission to the States by the Congress.

AMENDMENT 23 [1961]

Section 1

The District constituting the seat of Government of the United States shall appoint in such manner as the Congress may direct:

A number of electors of President and Vice President equal to the whole number of Senators and Representatives in Congress to which the District would be entitled if it were a State, but in no event more than the least populous State; they shall be in addition to those appointed by the States, but they shall be considered, for the purposes of the election of President and Vice President, to be electors appointed by a State; and they shall meet in the District and perform such duties as provided by the twelfth article of amendment.

Section 2

The Congress shall have power to enforce this article by appropriate legislation.

AMENDMENT 24 [1964]

Section 1

The right of citizens of the United States to vote in any primary or other election for President or Vice President, for electors for President or Vice President, or for Senator or Representative in Congress, shall not be denied or abridged by the United States or any State by reason of failure to pay any poll tax or other tax.

Section 2

The Congress shall have power to enforce this article by appropriate legislation.

AMENDMENT 25 [1967]

Section 1

In case of the removal of the President from office or of his death or resignation, the Vice President shall become President.

Section 2

Whenever there is a vacancy in the office of the Vice President, the President shall nominate a Vice President who shall take office upon confirmation by a majority vote of both Houses of Congress.

Section 3

Whenever the President transmits to the President pro tempore of the Senate and the Speaker of the House of Representatives his written declaration that he is unable to discharge the powers and duties of his office, and until he transmits to them a written declaration to the contrary, such powers and duties shall be discharged by the Vice President as Acting President.

Section 4

Whenever the Vice President and a Majority of either the principal officers of the executive departments or of such other body as Congress may by law provide, transmit to the President pro tempore of the Senate and the Speaker of the House of Representatives their written declaration that the President is unable to discharge the powers and duties of his office, the Vice President shall immediately assume the powers and duties of the office as Acting President.

Thereafter, when the President transmits to the President pro tempore of the Senate and the Speaker of the House of Representatives his written declaration that no inability exists, he shall resume the powers and duties of his office unless the Vice President and a majority of either the principal officers of the executive department or of such other body as Congress may by law provide, transmit within four days to the President pro tempore of the Senate and the Speaker of the House of Representatives their written declaration that the President is unable to discharge the powers and duties of his office. Thereupon Congress shall decide the issue, assembling within forty-eight hours for that purpose if not in session. If the Congress, within twenty-one days after receipt of the latter written declaration, or, if Congress is not in session, within twenty-one days after Congress is required to assemble, determines by two-thirds vote of both Houses that the President is unable to discharge the powers and duties of his office, the Vice President shall continue to discharge the same as Acting President; otherwise, the President shall resume the powers and duties of his office.

AMENDMENT 26 [1971]

Section 1

The right of citizens of the United States, who are eighteen years of age or older, to vote shall not be denied or abridged by the United States or by any State on account of age.

Section 2

The Congress shall have the power to enforce this article by appropriate legislation.

AMENDMENT 27 [1992]

No law, varying the compensation for the services of the Senators and Representatives, shall take effect, until an election of Representatives shall have intervened.

ADMINISTRATIVE PROCEDURE ACT[1]

§ 551.   Definitions

For the purpose of this subchapter—

(1)   "agency" means each authority of the Government of the United States, whether or not it is within or subject to review by another agency, but does not include—

(A)   the Congress;

(B)   the courts of the United States;

(C)   the governments of the territories or possessions of the United States;

(D)   the government of the District of Columbia;

or except as to the requirements of section 552 of this title—

(E)   agencies composed of representatives of the parties or of representatives of organizations of the parties to the disputes determined by them;

(F)   courts martial and military commissions;

(G)   military authority exercised in the field in time of war or in occupied territory; or

(H)   functions conferred by sections 1738, 1739, 1743, and 1744 of title 12; chapter 2 of title 41; subchapter II of chapter 471 of title 49; or sections 1884, 1891–1902, and former section 1641(b)(2), of title 50, appendix;

(2)   "person" includes an individual, partnership, corporation, association, or public or private organization other than an agency;

(3)   "party" includes a person or agency named or admitted as a party, or properly seeking and entitled as of right to be admitted as a party, in an agency proceeding, and a person or agency admitted by an agency as a party for limited purposes;

(4)   "rule" means the whole or a part of an agency statement of general or particular applicability and future effect designed to implement, interpret, or prescribe law or policy or describing the organization, procedure, or practice requirements of an agency and includes the approval or prescription for the future of rates, wages, corporate or financial structures or reorganization thereof, prices, facilities, appliances, services or allowances therefor or of valuations, costs, or accounting, or practices bearing on any of the foregoing;

---

[1]   Public Law 404—79th Congress, approved June 11, 1946, 60 Stat. 237; as codified by An Act to enact title 5, United States Code, September 6, 1966, Public Law 89–554, 80 Stat. 378; and as amended through P.L. 107–245 (2002).

(5) "rule making" means agency process for formulating, amending, or repealing a rule;

(6) "order" means the whole or a part of a final disposition, whether affirmative, negative, injunctive, or declaratory in form, of an agency in a matter other than rule making but including licensing;

(7) "adjudication" means agency process for the formulation of an order;

(8) "license" includes the whole or a part of an agency permit, certificate, approval, registration, charter, membership, statutory exemption or other form of permission;

(9) "licensing" includes agency process respecting the grant, renewal, denial, revocation, suspension, annulment, withdrawal, limitation, amendment, modification, or conditioning of a license;

(10) "sanction" includes the whole or a part of an agency—

(A) prohibition, requirement, limitation, or other condition affecting the freedom of a person;

(B) withholding of relief;

(C) imposition of penalty or fine;

(D) destruction, taking, seizure, or withholding of property;

(E) assessment of damages, reimbursement, restitution, compensation, costs, charges, or fees;

(F) requirement, revocation, or suspension of a license; or

(G) taking other compulsory or restrictive action;

(11) "relief" includes the whole or a part of an agency—

(A) grant of money, assistance, license, authority, exemption, exception, privilege, or remedy;

(B) recognition of a claim, right, immunity, privilege, exemption, or exception; or

(C) taking of other action on the application or petition of, and beneficial to, a person;

(12) "agency proceeding" means an agency process as defined by paragraphs (5), (7), and (9) of this section; and

(13) "agency action" includes the whole or a part of an agency rule, order, license, sanction, relief, or the equivalent or denial thereof, or failure to act.

(14)[2]"Ex parte communication" means an oral or written communication not on the public record with respect to which reasonable prior notice to all parties is not given, but it shall not

---

[2]   Added by P.L. 94–409, 90 Stat. 1241 (1976) and subsequently amended.

include requests for status reports on any matter or proceeding covered by this subchapter.

§ 552.   Public information; agency rules, opinions, orders, records, and proceedings[3]

(a) Each agency shall make available to the public information as follows:

(1) Each agency shall separately state and currently publish in the Federal Register for the guidance of the public—

(A) descriptions of its central and field organization and the established places at which, the employees (and in the case of a uniformed service, the members) from whom, and the methods whereby, the public may obtain information, make submittals or requests, or obtain decisions;

(B) statements of the general course and method by which its functions are channeled and determined, including the nature and requirements of all formal and informal procedures available;

(C) rules of procedure, descriptions of forms available or the places at which forms may be obtained, and instructions as to the scope and contents of all papers, reports, or examinations;

(D) substantive rules of general applicability adopted as authorized by law, and statements of general policy or interpretations of general applicability formulated and adopted by the agency; and

(E) each amendment, revision, or repeal of the foregoing.

Except to the extent that a person has actual and timely notice of the terms thereof, a person may not in any manner be required to resort to, or be adversely affected by, a matter required to be published in the Federal Register and not so published. For the purpose of this paragraph, matter reasonably available to the class of persons affected thereby is deemed published in the Federal Register when incorporated by reference therein with the approval of the Director of the Federal Register.

(2) Each agency, in accordance with published rules, shall make available for public inspection and copying—

(A) final opinions, including concurring and dissenting opinions, as well as orders, made in the adjudication of cases;

---

[3]   The more limited provisions respecting publication and public records contained in § 3 of the original APA, which became § 552, have been replaced by the following language and by the Freedom of Information Act, which begins at § 552(a)(3) and is by far the longest element of the APA. It is set out in full at p. 1479.

(B) those statements of policy and interpretations which have been adopted by the agency and are not published in the Federal Register; and

(C) administrative staff manuals and instructions to staff that affect a member of the public;

(D) copies of all records, regardless of form or format, which have been released to any person under paragraph (3) and which, because of the nature of their subject matter, the agency determines have become or are likely to become the subject of subsequent requests for substantially the same records; and

(E) a general index of the records referred to under subparagraph (D);

unless the materials are promptly published and copies offered for sale. For records created on or after November 1, 1996, within one year after such date, each agency shall make such records available, including by computer telecommunications or, if computer telecommunications means have not been established by the agency, by other electronic means. . . . Each agency shall also maintain and make available for public inspection and copying current indexes providing identifying information for the public as to any matter issued, adopted, or promulgated after July 4, 1967, and required by this paragraph to be made available or published. . . . A final order, opinion, statement of policy, interpretation, or staff manual or instruction that affects a member of the public may be relied on, used, or cited as precedent by an agency against a party other than an agency only if—

(i) it has been indexed and either made available or published as provided by this paragraph; or

(ii) the party has actual and timely notice of the terms thereof.

[The remainder of this section is set out under the FREEDOM OF INFORMATION ACT, p. 1479.]

§ 552a. Records maintained on individuals

[This section, also known as the Privacy Act, is omitted.]

§ 552b. Open meetings

[This section, also known as the GOVERNMENT IN THE SUNSHINE ACT, is set out at p. 1494.]

§ 553.   Rule making

(a) This section applies, according to the provisions thereof, except to the extent that there is involved—

(1) a military or foreign affairs function of the United States; or

(2) a matter relating to agency management or personnel or to public property, loans, grants, benefits, or contracts.

(b) General notice of proposed rule making shall be published in the Federal Register, unless persons subject thereto are named and either personally served or otherwise have actual notice thereof in accordance with law. The notice shall include—

(1) a statement of the time, place, and nature of public rule making proceedings;

(2) reference to the legal authority under which the rule is proposed; and

(3) either the terms or substance of the proposed rule or a description of the subjects and issues involved.

Except when notice or hearing is required by statute, this subsection does not apply—

(A) to interpretative rules, general statements of policy, or rules of agency organization, procedure, or practice; or

(B) when the agency for good cause finds (and incorporates the finding and a brief statement of reasons therefor in the rules issued) that notice and public procedure thereon are impracticable, unnecessary, or contrary to the public interest.

(c) After notice required by this section, the agency shall give interested persons an opportunity to participate in the rule making through submission of written data, views, or arguments with or without opportunity for oral presentation. After consideration of the relevant matter presented, the agency shall incorporate in the rules adopted a concise general statement of their basis and purpose. When rules are required by statute to be made on the record after opportunity for an agency hearing, sections 556 and 557 of this title apply instead of this subsection.

(d) The required publication or service of a substantive rule shall be made not less than 30 days before its effective date, except—

(1) a substantive rule which grants or recognizes an exemption or relieves a restriction;

(2) interpretative rules and statements of policy; or

(3) as otherwise provided by the agency for good cause found and published with the rule.

(e) Each agency shall give an interested person the right to petition for the issuance, amendment, or repeal of a rule.

§ 554. Adjudications

(a) This section applies, according to the provisions thereof, in every case of adjudication required by statute to be determined on the record after opportunity for an agency hearing, except to the extent that there is involved—

(1) a matter subject to a subsequent trial of the law and the facts de novo in a court;

(2) the selection or tenure of an employee, except an administrative law judge appointed under section 3105 of this title;

(3) proceedings in which decisions rest solely on inspections, tests, or elections;

(4) the conduct of military or foreign affairs functions;

(5) cases in which an agency is acting as an agent for a court; or

(6) the certification of worker representatives.

(b) Persons entitled to notice of an agency hearing shall be timely informed of—   *- Notice*

(1) the time, place, and nature of the hearing;

(2) the legal authority and jurisdiction under which the hearing is to be held; and

(3) the matters of fact and law asserted.

When private persons are the moving parties, other parties to the proceeding shall give prompt notice of issues controverted in fact or law; and in other instances agencies may by rule require responsive pleading. In fixing the time and place for hearings, due regard shall be had for the convenience and necessity of the parties or their representatives.

(c) The agency shall give all interested parties opportunity for—   *- Procedure*

(1) the submission and consideration of facts, arguments, offers of settlement, or proposals of adjustment when time, the nature of the proceeding, and the public interest permit; and

(2) to the extent that the parties are unable so to determine a controversy by consent, hearing and decision on notice and in accordance with sections 556 and 557 of this title.

(d) The employee who presides at the reception of evidence pursuant to section 556 of this title shall make the recommended decision or initial decision required by section 557 of this title, unless he becomes unavailable to the agency. Except to the extent required for the disposition of ex parte matters as authorized by law, such an employee may not—   *- Decision*

(1) consult a person or party on a fact in issue, unless on notice and opportunity for all parties to participate; or

(2) be responsible to or subject to the supervision or direction of an employee or agent engaged in the performance of investigative or prosecuting functions for an agency.

An employee or agent engaged in the performance of investigative or prosecuting functions for an agency in a case may not, in that or a factually related case, participate or advise in the decision, recommended decision or agency review pursuant to section 557 of this title, except as witness or counsel in public proceedings. This subsection does not apply—

(A) in determining applications for initial licenses;

(B) to proceedings involving the validity or application of rates, facilities, or practices of public utilities or carriers; or

(C) to the agency or a member or members of the body comprising the agency.

(e) The agency, with like effect as in the case of other orders, and in its sound discretion, may issue a declaratory order to terminate a controversy or remove uncertainty.

§ 555. Ancillary matters

(a) This section applies, according to the provisions thereof, except as otherwise provided by this subchapter.

(b) A person compelled to appear in person before an agency or representative thereof is entitled to be accompanied, represented, and advised by counsel or, if permitted by the agency, by other qualified representative. A party is entitled to appear in person or by or with counsel or other duly qualified representative in an agency proceeding. So far as the orderly conduct of public business permits, an interested person may appear before an agency or its responsible employees for the presentation, adjustment, or determination of an issue, request, or controversy in a proceeding, whether interlocutory, summary, or otherwise, or in connection with an agency function. With due regard for the convenience and necessity of the parties or their representatives and within a reasonable time, each agency shall proceed to conclude a matter presented to it. This subsection does not grant or deny a person who is not a lawyer the right to appear for or represent others before an agency or in an agency proceeding.

(c) Process, requirement of a report, inspection, or other investigative act or demand may not be issued, made, or enforced except as authorized by law. A person compelled to submit data or evidence is entitled to retain or, on payment of lawfully prescribed costs, procure a copy or transcript thereof, except that in a nonpublic investigatory proceeding the witness may for good cause be limited to inspection of the official transcript of his testimony.

(d) Agency subpenas authorized by law shall be issued to a party on request and, when required by rules of procedure, on a statement or showing of general relevance and reasonable scope of the evidence sought. On contest, the court shall sustain the subpena or similar process or demand to the extent that it is found to be in accordance with law. In a proceeding for enforcement, the court shall issue an order requiring the appearance of the witness or the production of the evidence or data within a reasonable time under penalty of punishment for contempt in case of contumacious failure to comply.

(e) Prompt notice shall be given of the denial in whole or in part of a written application, petition, or other request of an interested person made in connection with any agency proceeding. Except in affirming a prior denial or when the denial is self-explanatory, the notice shall be accompanied by a brief statement of the grounds for denial.

§ 556.   Hearings; presiding employees; powers and duties; burden of proof; evidence; record as basis of decision   *- Procedural Rights*

(a)   This section applies, according to the provisions thereof, to hearings required by section 553 or 554 of this title to be conducted in accordance with this section.

(b)   There shall preside at the taking of evidence

    (1)   the agency;

    (2)   one or more members of the body which comprises the agency; or

    (3)   one or more administrative law judges appointed under section 3105 of this title.

This subchapter does not supersede the conduct of specified classes of proceedings, in whole or in part, by or before boards or other employees specially provided for by or designated under statute. The functions of presiding employees and of employees participating in decisions in accordance with section 557 of this title shall be conducted in an impartial manner. A presiding or participating employee may at any time disqualify himself. On the filing in good faith of a timely and sufficient affidavit of personal bias or other disqualification of a presiding or participating employee, the agency shall determine the matter as a part of the record and decision in the case.

(c)   Subject to published rules of the agency and within its powers, employees presiding at hearings may—

    (1)   administer oaths and affirmations;

    (2)   issue subpenas authorized by law;

    (3)   rule on offers of proof and receive relevant evidence;

    (4)   take depositions or have depositions taken when the ends of justice would be served;

    (5)   regulate the course of the hearing;

    (6)   hold conferences for the settlement or simplification of the issues by consent of the parties or by the use of alternative means of dispute resolution as provided in subchapter IV of this chapter [5 U.S.C. §§ 571 et seq.];

    (7)   inform the parties as to the availability of one or more alternative means of dispute resolution, and encourage use of such methods;

    (8)   require the attendance at any conference held pursuant to paragraph (6) of at least one representative of each party who has authority to negotiate concerning resolution of issues in controversy;

(9)   dispose of procedural requests or similar matters;

(10) make or recommend decisions in accordance with section 557 of this title; and

(11) take other action authorized by agency rule consistent with this subchapter.

(d)   Except as otherwise provided by statute, the proponent of a rule or order has the burden of proof. Any oral or documentary evidence may be received, but the agency as a matter of policy shall provide for the exclusion of irrelevant, immaterial, or unduly repetitious evidence. A sanction may not be imposed or rule or order issued except on consideration of the whole record or those parts thereof cited by a party and supported by and in accordance with the reliable, probative, and substantial evidence. The agency may, to the extent consistent with the interests of justice and the policy of the underlying statutes administered by the agency, consider a violation of section 557(d) of this title sufficient grounds for a decision adverse to a party who has knowingly committed such violation or knowingly caused such violation to occur.[4] A party is entitled to present his case or defense by oral or documentary evidence, to submit rebuttal evidence, and to conduct such cross-examination as may be required for a full and true disclosure of the facts. In rule making or determining claims for money or benefits or applications for initial licenses an agency may, when a party will not be prejudiced thereby, adopt procedures for the submission of all or part of the evidence in written form.

(e)   The transcript of testimony and exhibits, together with all papers and requests filed in the proceeding, constitutes the exclusive record for decision in accordance with section 557 of this title and, on payment of lawfully prescribed costs, shall be made available to the parties. When an agency decision rests on official notice of a material fact not appearing in the evidence in the record, a party is entitled, on timely request, to an opportunity to show the contrary.

§ 557.   Initial decisions; conclusiveness; review by agency; submissions by parties; contents of decisions; record

(a)   This section applies, according to the provisions thereof, when a hearing is required to be conducted in accordance with section 556 of this title.

(b)   When the agency did not preside at the reception of the evidence, the presiding employee or, in cases not subject to section 554(d) of this title, an employee qualified to preside at hearings pursuant to section 556 of this title, shall initially decide the case unless the agency requires, either in specific cases or by general rule, the entire record to be certified to it for decision. When the presiding employee makes an initial decision, that decision then becomes the decision of the agency without further

---

[4]   This sentence added by P.L. 94–409, 90 Stat. 1247 (1976).

proceedings unless there is an appeal to, or review on motion of, the agency within time provided by rule. On appeal from or review of the initial decision, the agency has all the powers which it would have in making the initial decision except as it may limit the issues on notice or by rule. When the agency makes the decision without having presided at the reception of the evidence, the presiding employee or an employee qualified to preside at hearings pursuant to section 556 of this title shall first recommend a decision, except that in rule making or determining application for initial licenses—

(1)   instead thereof the agency may issue a tentative decision or one of its responsible employees may recommend a decision; or

(2)   this procedure may be omitted in a case in which the agency finds on the record that due and timely execution of its functions imperatively and unavoidably so requires.

(c)   Before a recommended, initial, or tentative decision, or a decision on agency review of the decision of subordinate employees, the parties are entitled to a reasonable opportunity to submit for the consideration of the employees participating in the decisions—

(1)   proposed findings and conclusions; or

(2)   exceptions to the decisions or recommended decisions of subordinate employees or to tentative agency decisions; and

(3)   supporting reasons for the exceptions or proposed findings or conclusions.

The record shall show the ruling on each finding, conclusion, or exception presented. All decisions, including initial, recommended, and tentative decisions, are a part of the record and shall include a statement of—

(A)   findings and conclusions, and the reasons or basis therefor, on all the material issues of fact, law, or discretion presented on the record; and

(B)   the appropriate rule, order, sanction, relief, or denial thereof.

(d)(1)[5]   In any agency proceeding which is subject to subsection (a) of this section, except to the extent required for the disposition of ex parte matters as authorized by law—

(A)   no interested person outside the agency shall make or knowingly cause to be made to any member of the body comprising the agency, administrative law judge, or other employee who is or may reasonably be expected to be involved in the decisional process of the proceeding, an ex parte communication relevant to the merits of the proceeding;

(B)   no member of the body comprising the agency, administrative law judge, or other employee who is or may reasonably be expected to be involved in the decisional process of the proceeding, shall make

---

[5]   Subsection (d) was added by P.L. 94–409, 90 Stat. 1247 (1976).

or knowingly cause to be made to any interested person outside the agency an ex parte communication relevant to the merits of the proceeding;

(C) a member of the body comprising the agency, administrative law judge, or other employee who is or may reasonably be expected to be involved in the decisional process of such proceeding who receives, or who makes or knowingly causes to be made, a communication prohibited by this subsection shall place on the public record of the proceeding:

> (i) all such written communications;

> (ii) memoranda stating the substance of all such oral communications; and

> (iii) all written responses, and memoranda stating the substance of all oral responses, to the materials described in clauses (i) and (ii) of this subparagraph;

(D) upon receipt of a communication knowingly made or knowingly caused to be made by a party in violation of this subsection, the agency, administrative law judge, or other employee presiding at the hearing may, to the extent consistent with the interests of justice and the policy of the underlying statutes, require the party to show cause why his claim or interest in the proceeding should not be dismissed, denied, disregarded, or otherwise adversely affected on account of such violation; and

(E) the prohibitions of this subsection shall apply beginning at such time as the agency may designate, but in no case shall they begin to apply later than the time at which a proceeding is noticed for hearing unless the person responsible for the communication has knowledge that it will be noticed, in which case the prohibitions shall apply beginning at the time of his acquisition of such knowledge.

(2) This subsection does not constitute authority to withhold information from Congress.

§ 558. Imposition of sanctions; determination of applications for licenses; suspension, revocation, and expiration of licenses

(a) This section applies, according to the provisions thereof, to the exercise of a power or authority.

(b) A sanction may not be imposed or a substantive rule or order issued except within jurisdiction delegated to the agency and as authorized by law.

(c) When application is made for a license required by law, the agency, with due regard for the rights and privileges of all the interested parties or adversely affected persons and within a reasonable time, shall set and complete proceedings required to be conducted in accordance with sections 556 and 557 of this title or other proceedings required by law and shall make its decision. Except in cases of willfulness or those in which public health, interest, or safety requires otherwise, the withdrawal, suspension, revocation, or annulment of a license is lawful only if, before the institution of agency proceedings therefor, the licensee has been given—

(1)   notice by the agency in writing of the facts or conduct which may warrant the action; and

(2)   opportunity to demonstrate or achieve compliance with all lawful requirements.

When the licensee has made timely and sufficient application for a renewal or a new license in accordance with agency rules, a license with reference to an activity of a continuing nature does not expire until the application has been finally determined by the agency.

§ 559.   Effect on other laws; effect of subsequent statute

This subchapter, chapter 7, and sections 1305, 3105, 3344, 4301(2)(E), 5372, and 7521, and the provisions of section 5335(a)(B) of this title that relate to administrative law judges, do not limit or repeal additional requirements imposed by statute or otherwise recognized by law. Except as otherwise required by law, requirements or privileges relating to evidence or procedure apply equally to agencies and persons. Each agency is granted the authority necessary to comply with the requirements of this subchapter through the issuance of rules or otherwise. Subsequent statute may not be held to supersede or modify this subchapter, chapter 7, sections 1305, 3105, 3344, 4301(2)(E), 5372, or 7521, or the provisions of section 5335(a)(B) of this title that relate to administrative law judges, except to the extent that it does so expressly. . . .

§ 701.   Application; definitions

(a)   This chapter applies, according to the provisions thereof, except to the extent that—

(1)   statutes preclude judicial review; or

(2)   agency action is committed to agency discretion by law.

(b)(1)   ["agency" is defined precisely as in § 551(1)(A) through (H), above];

(2)   "person", "rule", "order", "license", "sanction", "relief", and "agency action" have the meanings given them by section 551 of this title.

§ 702.   Right of review

A person suffering legal wrong because of agency action, or adversely affected or aggrieved by agency action within the meaning of a relevant statute, is entitled to judicial review thereof.[6] An action in a court of the United States seeking relief other than money damages and stating a

---

[6]   Material after first sentence added by P.L. 94–574, 90 Stat. 2721 (1976).

claim that an agency or an officer or employee thereof acted or failed to act in an official capacity or under color of legal authority shall not be dismissed nor relief therein be denied on the ground that it is against the United States or that the United States is an indispensable party. The United States may be named as a defendant in any such action, and a judgment or decree may be entered against the United States: Provided, That any mandatory or injunctive decree shall specify the Federal officer or officers (by name or by title), and their successors in office, personally responsible for compliance. Nothing herein (1) affects other limitations on judicial review or the power or duty of the court to dismiss any action or deny relief on any other appropriate legal or equitable ground; or (2) confers authority to grant relief if any other statute that grants consent to suit expressly or impliedly forbids the relief which is sought.

§ 703.   Form and venue of proceeding

The form of proceeding for judicial review is the special statutory review proceeding relevant to the subject matter in a court specified by statute or, in the absence or inadequacy thereof, any applicable form of legal action, including actions for declaratory judgments or writs of prohibitory or mandatory injunction or habeas corpus, in a court of competent jurisdiction. If no special statutory review proceeding is applicable, the action for judicial review may be brought against the United States, the agency by its official title, or the appropriate officer.[7] Except to the extent that prior, adequate, and exclusive opportunity for judicial review is provided by law, agency action is subject to judicial review in civil or criminal proceedings for judicial enforcement.

§ 704.   Actions reviewable

Agency action made reviewable by statute and final agency action for which there is no other adequate remedy in a court are subject to judicial review. A preliminary, procedural, or intermediate agency action or ruling not directly reviewable is subject to review on the review of the final agency action. Except as otherwise expressly required by statute, agency action otherwise final is final for the purposes of this section whether or not there has been presented or determined an application for a declaratory order, for any form of reconsideration, or, unless the agency otherwise requires by rule and provides that the action meanwhile is inoperative, for an appeal to superior agency authority.

§ 705.   Relief pending review

When an agency finds that justice so requires, it may postpone the effective date of action taken by it, pending judicial review. On such conditions as may be required and to the extent necessary to prevent irreparable injury, the reviewing court, including the court to which a case may be taken on appeal from or on application for certiorari or other writ to a reviewing court, may issue all necessary and appropriate

---

[7]   Preceding sentence added by P.L. 94–574, 90 Stat. 2721 (1976).

process to postpone the effective date of an agency action or to preserve status or rights pending conclusion of the review proceedings.

§ 706. Scope of review

To the extent necessary to decision and when presented, the reviewing court shall decide all relevant questions of law, interpret constitutional and statutory provisions, and determine the meaning or applicability of the terms of an agency action. The reviewing court shall—

(1) compel agency action unlawfully withheld or unreasonably delayed; and

(2) hold unlawful and set aside agency action, findings, and conclusions found to be—

(A) arbitrary, capricious, an abuse of discretion, or otherwise not in accordance with law;

(B) contrary to constitutional right, power, privilege, or immunity;

(C) in excess of statutory jurisdiction, authority, or limitations, or short of statutory right;

(D) without observance of procedure required by law;

(E) unsupported by substantial evidence in a case subject to sections 556 and 557 of this title or otherwise reviewed on the record of an agency hearing provided by statute; or

(F) unwarranted by the facts to the extent that the facts are subject to trial de novo by the reviewing court.

In making the foregoing determinations, the court shall review the whole record or those parts of it cited by a party, and due account shall be taken of the rule of prejudicial error.

§ 1305. Administrative law judges[8]

For the purpose of sections 3105, 3344, 4301(2)(D), and 5372 of this title and the provisions of section 5335(a)(B) of this title that relate to administrative law judges, the Office of Personnel Management may, and for the purpose of section 7521 of this title, the Merit Systems Protection Board may investigate, prescribe regulations, appoint advisory committees as necessary, recommend legislation, subpena witnesses and records, and pay witness fees as established for the courts of the United States.

§ 3344. Details; administrative law judges

An agency as defined by section 551 of this title which occasionally or temporarily is insufficiently staffed with administrative law judges appointed under section 3105 of this title may use administrative law

---

[8]   Substitution of "administrative law judge" for "hearing examiner," here and elsewhere in the APA, was effected by P.L. 95-251, 92 Stat. 183 (1978).

judges selected by the Office of Personnel Management from and with the consent of other agencies.

§ 5372.   Administrative law judges[9]

(a)   For the purposes of this section, the term "administrative law judge" means an administrative law judge appointed under section 3105.

(b)(1)(A) There shall be 3 levels of basic pay for administrative law judges (designated as AL–1, 2, and 3, respectively), and each such judge shall be paid at 1 of those levels, in accordance with the provisions of this section. . . .

(c)   The Office of Personnel Management shall prescribe regulations necessary to administer this section.

§ 7521.   Actions against administrative law judges[10]

(a)   An action may be taken against an administrative law judge appointed under section 3105 of this title by the agency in which the administrative law judge is employed only for good cause established and determined by the Merit Systems Protection Board on the record after opportunity for hearing before the Board. . . .

(b)   [This section covers removals, suspensions, reductions in grade or pay, and furloughs of 30 days or less, with some exceptions.]

---

[9]   Added by P.L. 101–509, Title V, § 529, 104 Stat. 1445 (1990) with succeeding amendments through P.L. 106–97, § 1 (1999); the section it replaced authorized OPM to set pay levels "independently of agency recommendations or ratings" and in accordance with general civil service practice.

[10]   As amended by the Civil Service Reform Act of 1978, P.L. 95–454, 92 Stat. 1137.

FREEDOM OF INFORMATION ACT[11]

5 U.S.C. § 552. Public information; agency rules, opinions, orders, records, and proceedings

(a) . . .

[§§ 552(a)(1), (2) are set out at p. 1466]

(3)(A)　Except with respect to the records made available under paragraphs (1) and (2) of this subsection, and except as provided in subparagraph (E), each agency, upon any request for records which (i) reasonably describes such records and (ii) is made in accordance with published rules stating the time, place, fees (if any), and procedures to be followed, shall make the records promptly available to any person.

(B)　In making any record available to a person under this paragraph, an agency shall provide the record in any form or format requested by the person if the record is readily reproducible by the agency in that form or format. Each agency shall make reasonable efforts to maintain its records in forms or formats that are reproducible for purposes of this section.

(C)　In responding under this paragraph to a request for records, an agency shall make reasonable efforts to search for the records in electronic form or format, except when such efforts would significantly interfere with the operation of the agency's automated information system.

(D)　For purposes of this paragraph, the term "search" means to review, manually or by automated means, agency records for the purpose of locating those records which are responsive to a request.

(E)　An agency, or part of an agency, that is an element of the intelligence community (as that term is defined in section 3(4) of the National Security Act of 1947 (50 U.S.C. 401a(4))) shall not make any record available under this paragraph to—

(i)　any government entity, other than a State, territory, commonwealth, or district of the United States, or any subdivision thereof; or

(ii)　a representative of a government entity described in clause (i).

(4)(A)(i) In order to carry out the provisions of this section, each agency shall promulgate regulations, pursuant to notice and receipt of public comment, specifying the schedule of fees applicable to the processing of requests under this section and establishing procedures and guidelines for determining when such fees should be

---

[11]　As amended by the FOIA Improvement Act of 2016.

waived or reduced. Such schedule shall conform to the guidelines which shall be promulgated, pursuant to notice and receipt of public comment, by the Director of the Office of Management and Budget and which shall provide for a uniform schedule of fees for all agencies.

(ii) Such agency regulations shall provide that—

(I) fees shall be limited to reasonable standard charges for document search, duplication, and review, when records are requested for commercial use;

(II) fees shall be limited to reasonable standard charges for document duplication when records are not sought for commercial use and the request is made by an educational or noncommercial scientific institution, whose purpose is scholarly or scientific research; or a representative of the news media; and

(III) for any request not described in (I) or (II), fees shall be limited to reasonable standard charges for document search and duplication.

In this clause, the term "a representative of the news media" means any person or entity that gathers information of potential interest to a segment of the public, uses its editorial skills to turn the raw materials into a distinct work, and distributes that work to an audience. In this clause, the term "news" means information that is about current events or that would be of current interest to the public. Examples of news-media entities are television or radio stations broadcasting to the public at large and publishers of periodicals (but only if such entities qualify as disseminators of "news") who make their products available for purchase by or subscription by or free distribution to the general public. These examples are not all-inclusive. Moreover, as methods of news delivery evolve (for example, the adoption of the electronic dissemination of newspapers through telecommunications services), such alternative media shall be considered to be news-media entities. A freelance journalist shall be regarded as working for a news-media entity if the journalist can demonstrate a solid basis for expecting publication through that entity, whether or not the journalist is actually employed by the entity. A publication contract would present a solid basis for such an expectation; the Government may also consider the past publication record of the requester in making such a determination.

(iii) Documents shall be furnished without any charge or at a charge reduced below the fees established under clause

(ii) if disclosure of the information is in the public interest because it is likely to contribute significantly to public understanding of the operations or activities of the government and is not primarily in the commercial interest of the requester.

(iv) Fee schedules shall provide for the recovery of only the direct costs of search, duplication, or review. . . . Review costs may not include any costs incurred in resolving issues of law or policy that may be raised in the course of processing a request under this section. No fee may be charged by any agency under this section—

> (I)   if the costs of routine collection and processing of the fee are likely to equal or exceed the amount of the fee; or

> (II) for any request described in clause (ii)(II) or (III) of this subparagraph for the first two hours of search time or for the first one hundred pages of duplication.

(vii) In any action by a requester regarding the waiver of fees under this section, the court shall determine the matter de novo: Provided, That the court's review of the matter shall be limited to the record before the agency.

(B) On complaint, the district court of the United States in the district in which the complainant resides, or has his principal place of business, or in which the agency records are situated, or in the District of Columbia, has jurisdiction to enjoin the agency from withholding agency records and to order the production of any agency records improperly withheld from the complainant. In such a case the court shall determine the matter de novo, and may examine the contents of such agency records in camera to determine whether such records or any part thereof shall be withheld under any of the exemptions set forth in subsection (b) of this section, and the burden is on the agency to sustain its action. In addition to any other matters to which a court accords substantial weight, a court shall accord substantial weight to an affidavit of an agency concerning the agency's determination as to technical feasibility under paragraph (2)(C) and subsection (b) and reproducibility under paragraph (3)(B).

(C) Notwithstanding any other provision of law, the defendant shall serve an answer or otherwise plead to any complaint made under this subsection within thirty days after service upon the defendant of the pleading in which such complaint is made, unless the court otherwise directs for good cause shown. . . .

(E)(i)   The court may assess against the United States reasonable attorney fees and other litigation costs reasonably incurred in any case under this section in which the complainant has substantially prevailed.

(ii) For purposes of this subparagraph, a complainant has substantially prevailed if the complainant has obtained relief through either—

(I) a judicial order, or an enforceable written agreement or consent decree; or

(II) a voluntary or unilateral change in position by the agency, if the complainant's claim is not insubstantial.

(F)(i) Whenever the court orders the production of any agency records improperly withheld from the complainant and assesses against the United States reasonable attorney fees and other litigation costs, and the court additionally issues a written finding that the circumstances surrounding the withholding raise questions whether agency personnel acted arbitrarily or capriciously with respect to the withholding, the Special Counsel shall promptly initiate a proceeding to determine whether disciplinary action is warranted. . . . The administrative authority shall take the corrective action that the Special Counsel recommends.

(ii) The Attorney General shall—

(I) notify the Special Counsel of each civil action described under the first sentence of clause (i); and

(II) annually submit a report to Congress on the number of such civil actions in the preceding year.

(iii) The Special Counsel shall annually submit a report to Congress on the actions taken by the Special Counsel under clause (i).

(5) Each agency having more than one member shall maintain and make available for public inspection a record of the final votes of each member in every agency proceeding.

(6)(A) Each agency, upon any request for records made under paragraph (1), (2), or (3) of this subsection, shall—

(i) determine within 20 days (excepting Saturdays, Sundays, and legal public holidays) after the receipt of any such request whether to comply with such request and shall immediately notify the person making such request of

(I) such determination and the reasons therefor;

(II) the right of such person to seek assistance from the FOIA Public Liaison of the agency; and

(III) in the case of an adverse determination—

(aa) the right of such person to appeal to the head of the agency, within a period determined by the head of the agency that is not less than 90 days after the date of such adverse determination; and

(bb) the right of such person to seek dispute resolution services from the FOIA Public Liaison of the agency or the Office of Government Information Services; and

(ii) make a determination with respect to any appeal within twenty days (excepting Saturdays, Sundays, and legal public holidays) after the receipt of such appeal. If on appeal the denial of the request for records is in whole or in part upheld, the agency shall notify the person making such request of the provisions for judicial review of that determination under paragraph (4) of this subsection.

The 20-day period under clause (i) shall commence on the date on which the request is first received by the appropriate component of the agency, but in any event not later than ten days after the request is first received by any component of the agency that is designated in the agency's regulations under this section to receive requests under this section. The 20-day period shall not be tolled by the agency except—

(I) that the agency may make one request to the requester for information and toll the 20-day period while it is awaiting such information that it has reasonably requested from the requester under this section; or

(II) if necessary to clarify with the requester issues regarding fee assessment. In either case, the agency's receipt of the requester's response to the agency's request for information or clarification ends the tolling period.

(B)(i) In unusual circumstances as specified in this subparagraph, the time limits prescribed in either clause (i) or clause (ii) of subparagraph (A) may be extended by written notice to the person making such request setting forth the unusual circumstances for such extension and the date on which a determination is expected to be dispatched. No such notice shall specify a date that would result in an extension for more than ten working days, except as provided in clause (ii) of this subparagraph.

(ii) With respect to a request for which a written notice under clause (i) extends the time limits prescribed under clause (i) of subparagraph (A), the agency shall notify the person making the request if the request cannot be processed within the time limit specified in that clause and shall provide the person an opportunity to limit the scope of the request so that it may be processed within that time limit or an opportunity to arrange with the agency an alternative time frame for processing the request or a modified request. . . . Refusal by the person to reasonably modify the request or arrange such an alternative time frame shall be considered as a factor in determining whether exceptional circumstances exist for purposes of subparagraph (C).

(iii) As used in this subparagraph, "unusual circumstances" means, but only to the extent reasonably necessary to the proper processing of the particular requests—

(I) the need to search for and collect the requested records from field facilities or other establishments that are separate from the office processing the request;

(II) the need to search for, collect, and appropriately examine a voluminous amount of separate and distinct records which are demanded in a single request; or

(III) the need for consultation, which shall be conducted with all practicable speed, with another agency having a substantial interest in the determination of the request or among two or more components of the agency having substantial subject-matter interest therein.

(iv) Each agency may promulgate regulations, pursuant to notice and receipt of public comment, providing for the aggregation of certain requests by the same requestor, or by a group of requestors acting in concert, if the agency reasonably believes that such requests actually constitute a single request, which would otherwise satisfy the unusual circumstances specified in this subparagraph, and the requests involve clearly related matters. Multiple requests involving unrelated matters shall not be aggregated.

(C)(i)   Any person making a request to any agency for records under paragraph (1), (2), or (3) of this subsection shall be deemed to have exhausted his administrative remedies with respect to such request if the agency fails to comply with the applicable time limit provisions of this paragraph. If the Government can show exceptional circumstances exist and that the agency is exercising due diligence in responding to the request, the court may retain jurisdiction and allow the agency additional time to complete its review of the records. Upon any determination by an agency to comply with a request for records, the records shall be made promptly available to such person making such request. Any notification of denial of any request for records under this subsection shall set forth the names and titles or positions of each person responsible for the denial of such request.

(ii) For purposes of this subparagraph, the term "exceptional circumstances" does not include a delay that results from a predictable agency workload of requests under this section, unless the agency demonstrates reasonable progress in reducing its backlog of pending requests.

(iii) Refusal by a person to reasonably modify the scope of a request or arrange an alternative time frame for processing a request (or a modified request) under clause (ii) after being given an opportunity to do so by the agency to whom the person made the request shall be considered as a factor in determining whether exceptional circumstances exist for purposes of this subparagraph.

(D)(i)   Each agency may promulgate regulations, pursuant to notice and receipt of public comment, providing for multitrack processing of requests for records based on the amount of work or time (or both) involved in processing requests. . . .

(E)(i)   Each agency shall promulgate regulations, pursuant to notice and receipt of public comment, providing for expedited processing of requests for records—

(I)   in cases in which the person requesting the records demonstrates a compelling need; and

(II) in other cases determined by the agency.

(ii) Notwithstanding clause (i), regulations under this subparagraph must ensure—

(I)   that a determination of whether to provide expedited processing shall be made, and notice of the determination shall be provided to the person making the request, within 10 days after the date of the request; and

(II) expeditious consideration of administrative appeals of such determinations of whether to provide expedited processing.

(iii) An agency shall process as soon as practicable any request for records to which the agency has granted expedited processing under this subparagraph. Agency action to deny or affirm denial of a request for expedited processing pursuant to this subparagraph, and failure by an agency to respond in a timely manner to such a request shall be subject to judicial review under paragraph (4), except that the judicial review shall be based on the record before the agency at the time of the determination.

(iv) A district court of the United States shall not have jurisdiction to review an agency denial of expedited processing of a request for records after the agency has provided a complete response to the request.

(v) For purposes of this subparagraph, the term "compelling need" means—

(I) that a failure to obtain requested records on an expedited basis under this paragraph could reasonably be expected to pose an imminent threat to the life or physical safety of an individual; or

(II) with respect to a request made by a person primarily engaged in disseminating information, urgency to inform the public concerning actual or alleged Federal Government activity.

(vi) A demonstration of a compelling need by a person making a request for expedited processing shall be made by a statement certified by such person to be true and correct to the best of such person's knowledge and belief.

(F) In denying a request for records, in whole or in part, an agency shall make a reasonable effort to estimate the volume of any requested matter the provision of which is denied, and shall provide any such estimate to the person making the request, unless providing such estimate would harm an interest protected by the exemption in subsection (b) pursuant to which the denial is made.

(7) Each agency shall—

(A) establish a system to assign an individualized tracking number for each request received that will take longer than ten days to process and provide to each person making a request the tracking number assigned to the request; and

(B) establish a telephone line or Internet service that provides information about the status of a request to the person making the request using the assigned tracking number, including—

(i) the date on which the agency originally received the request; and

(ii) an estimated date on which the agency will complete action on the request.

(8)(A) An agency shall—

(i) withhold information under this section only if—

(I) the agency reasonably foresees that disclosure would harm an interest protected by an exemption described in subsection (b); or

(II) disclosure is prohibited by law; and

(ii)(I)   consider whether partial disclosure of information is possible whenever the agency determines that a full disclosure of a requested record is not possible; and

(II) take reasonable steps necessary to segregate and release nonexempt information; and

(B) Nothing in this paragraph requires disclosure of information that is otherwise prohibited from disclosure by law, or otherwise exempted from disclosure under subsection (b)(3).

(b) This section does not apply to matters that are—

(1) (A) specifically authorized under criteria established by an Executive order to be kept secret in the interest of national defense or foreign policy and (B) are in fact properly classified pursuant to such Executive order;

(2) related solely to the internal personnel rules and practices of an agency;

(3) specifically exempted from disclosure by statute (other than section 552b of this title), if that statute—

(A)(i)   requires that the matters be withheld from the public in such a manner as to leave no discretion on the issue; or

(ii) establishes particular criteria for withholding or refers to particular types of matters to be withheld; and

(B) if enacted after the date of enactment of the OPEN FOIA Act of 2009, specifically cites to this paragraph.

(4) trade secrets and commercial or financial information obtained from a person and privileged or confidential;

(5) inter-agency or intra-agency memorandums or letters which that would not be available by law to a party other than an agency in litigation with the agency, provided that the deliberative process privilege shall not apply to records created 25 years or more before the date on which the records were requested;

(6) personnel and medical files and similar files the disclosure of which would constitute a clearly unwarranted invasion of personal privacy;

(7) records or information compiled for law enforcement purposes, but only to the extent that the production of such law enforcement records or information (A) could reasonably be expected to interfere with enforcement proceedings, (B) would deprive a person of a right to a fair trial or an impartial adjudication, (C) could reasonably be

expected to constitute an unwarranted invasion of personal privacy, (D) could reasonably be expected to disclose the identity of a confidential source, including a State, local, or foreign agency or authority or any private institution which furnished information on a confidential basis, and, in the case of a record or information compiled by criminal law enforcement authority in the course of a criminal investigation or by an agency conducting a lawful national security intelligence investigation, information furnished by a confidential source, (E) would disclose techniques and procedures for law enforcement investigations or prosecutions, or would disclose guidelines for law enforcement investigations or prosecutions if such disclosure could reasonably be expected to risk circumvention of the law, or (F) could reasonably be expected to endanger the life or physical safety of any individual;

(8) contained in or related to examination, operating, or condition reports prepared by, on behalf of, or for the use of an agency responsible for the regulation or supervision of financial institutions; or

(9) geological and geophysical information and data, including maps, concerning wells.

Any reasonably segregable portion of a record shall be provided to any person requesting such record after deletion of the portions which are exempt under this subsection. The amount of information deleted, and the exemption under which the deletion is made, shall be indicated on the released portion of the record, unless including that indication would harm an interest protected by the exemption in this subsection under which the deletion is made. If technically feasible, the amount of the information deleted, and the exemption under which the deletion is made, shall be indicated at the place in the record where such deletion is made.

(c)(1)   Whenever a request is made which involves access to records described in subsection (b)(7)(A) and—

(A) the investigation or proceeding involves a possible violation of criminal law; and

(B) there is reason to believe that (i) the subject of the investigation or proceeding is not aware of its pendency, and (ii) disclosure of the existence of the records could reasonably be expected to interfere with enforcement proceedings,

the agency may, during only such time as that circumstance continues, treat the records as not subject to the requirements of this section.

(2) Whenever informant records maintained by a criminal law enforcement agency under an informant's name or personal identifier are requested by a third party according to the informant's name or personal identifier, the agency may treat the records as not

subject to the requirements of this section unless the informant's status as an informant has been officially confirmed.

(3) Whenever a request is made which involves access to records maintained by the Federal Bureau of Investigation pertaining to foreign intelligence or counterintelligence, or international terrorism, and the existence of the records is classified information as provided in subsection (b)(1), the Bureau may, as long as the existence of the records remains classified information, treat the records as not subject to the requirements of this section.

(d) This section does not authorize withholding of information or limit the availability of records to the public, except as specifically stated in this section. This section is not authority to withhold information from Congress.

(e)(1) On or before February 1 of each year, each agency shall submit to the Attorney General of the United States and to the Director of the Office of Government Information Services a report which shall cover the preceding fiscal year and which shall include [comprehensive information on the agency's performance under the statute, including median and average times for processing requests, pending requests, refusals to comply with requests, appeals, and other matters. These reports are available at: https://www.justice.gov/oip/reports-1]. . .

(6)(A) The Attorney General of the United States shall submit to the Committee on Oversight and Government Reform of the House of Representatives, the Committee on the Judiciary of the Senate, and the President a report on or before March 1 of each calendar year, which shall include for the prior calendar year—

(i) a listing of the number of cases arising under this section;

(ii) a listing of—

(I) each subsection, and any exemption, if applicable, involved in each case arising under this section;

(II) the disposition of each case arising under this section; and

(III) the cost, fees, and penalties assessed under subparagraphs (E), (F), and (G) of subsection (a)(4); and

(iii) a description of the efforts undertaken by the Department of Justice to encourage agency compliance with this section. . . .

(f) For purposes of this section, the term—

(1) "agency" as defined in section 551(1) of this title includes any executive department, military department, Government

corporation, Government controlled corporation, or other establishment in the executive branch of the Government (including the Executive Office of the President), or any independent regulatory agency; and

(2) "record" and any other term used in this section in reference to information includes—

   (A) any information that would be an agency record subject to the requirements of this section when maintained by an agency in any format, including an electronic format; and

   (B) any information described under subparagraph (A) that is maintained for an agency by an entity under Government contract, for the purposes of records management.

(h)(1)   There is established the Office of Government Information Services within the National Archives and Records Administration. The head of the Office shall be the Director of the Office of Government Information Services.

   (2)   The Office of Government Information Services shall—

   (A) review policies and procedures of administrative agencies under this section;

   (B) review compliance with this section by administrative agencies; and

   (C) identify procedures and methods for improving compliance under this section.

(3) The Office of Government Information Services shall offer mediation services to resolve disputes between persons making requests under this section and administrative agencies as a nonexclusive alternative to litigation and may issue advisory opinions at the discretion of the Office or upon request of any party to a dispute.

(4)(A)   Not less frequently than annually, the Director of the Office of Government Information Services shall submit to the Committee on Oversight and Government Reform of the House of Representatives, the Committee on the Judiciary of the Senate, and the President [a comprehensive report on its activities]. . . .

(i)   The Government Accountability Office shall conduct audits of administrative agencies on the implementation of this section and issue reports detailing the results of such audits.

(j)(1)   Each agency shall designate a Chief FOIA Officer who shall be a senior official of such agency (at the Assistant Secretary or equivalent level).

   (2)   The Chief FOIA Officer of each agency shall, subject to the authority of the head of the agency—

(A) have agency-wide responsibility for efficient and appropriate compliance with this section;

(B) monitor implementation of this section throughout the agency and keep the head of the agency, the chief legal officer of the agency, and the Attorney General appropriately informed of the agency's performance in implementing this section;

(C) recommend to the head of the agency such adjustments to agency practices, policies, personnel, and funding as may be necessary to improve its implementation of this section;

(D) review and report to the Attorney General, through the head of the agency, at such times and in such formats as the Attorney General may direct, on the agency's performance in implementing this section;

(E) facilitate public understanding of the purposes of the statutory exemptions of this section by including concise descriptions of the exemptions in both the agency's handbook issued under subsection (g), and the agency's annual report on this section, and by providing an overview, where appropriate, of certain general categories of agency records to which those exemptions apply;

(F) offer training to agency staff regarding their responsibilities under this section;

(G) serve as the primary agency liaison with the Office of Government Information Services and the Office of Information Policy; and

(H) designate 1 or more FOIA Public Liaisons.

(3) The Chief FOIA Officer of each agency shall review, not less frequently than annually, all aspects of the administration of this section by the agency to ensure compliance with the requirements of this section, including—

(A) agency regulations;

(B) disclosure of records required under paragraphs (2) and (8) of subsection (a);

(C) assessment of fees and determination of eligibility for fee waivers;

(D) the timely processing of requests for information under this section;

(E) the use of exemptions under subsection (b); and

(F) dispute resolution services with the assistance of the Office of Government Information Services or the FOIA Public Liaison.

(k)(1)   There is established in the executive branch the Chief FOIA Officers Council (referred to in this subsection as the 'Council').

(2) The Council shall be comprised of the following members:

(A) The Deputy Director for Management of the Office of Management and Budget.

(B) The Director of the Office of Information Policy at the Department of Justice.

(C) The Director of the Office of Government Information Services.

(D) The Chief FOIA Officer of each agency.

(E) Any other officer or employee of the United States as designated by the Co-Chairs.

(3) The Director of the Office of Information Policy at the Department of Justice and the Director of the Office of Government Information Services shall be the Co-Chairs of the Council.

(4) The Administrator of General Services shall provide administrative and other support for the Council.

(5)(A)   The duties of the Council shall include the following:

(i) Develop recommendations for increasing compliance and efficiency under this section.

(ii) Disseminate information about agency experiences, ideas, best practices, and innovative approaches related to this section.

(iii) Identify, develop, and coordinate initiatives to increase transparency and compliance with this section.

(iv) Promote the development and use of common performance measures for agency compliance with this section.

(B) In performing the duties described in subparagraph (A), the Council shall consult on a regular basis with members of the public who make requests under this section.

(6)(A)   The Council shall meet regularly and such meetings shall be open to the public unless the Council determines to close the meeting for reasons of national security or to discuss information exempt under subsection (b).

(B) Not less frequently than annually, the Council shall hold a meeting that shall be open to the public and permit interested persons to appear and present oral and written statements to the Council.

(C) Not later than 10 business days before a meeting of the Council, notice of such meeting shall be published in the Federal Register.

(D) Except as provided in subsection (b), the records, reports, transcripts, minutes, appendices, working papers, drafts, studies, agenda, or other documents that were made available to or prepared for or by the Council shall be made publicly available.

(E) Detailed minutes of each meeting of the Council shall be kept and . . . shall be redacted as necessary and made publicly available.

(*l*) FOIA Public Liaisons shall report to the agency Chief FOIA Officer and shall serve as supervisory officials to whom a requester under this section can raise concerns about the service the requester has received from the FOIA Requester Center, following an initial response from the FOIA Requester Center Staff. FOIA Public Liaisons shall be responsible for assisting in reducing delays, increasing transparency and understanding of the status of requests, and assisting in the resolution of disputes.

(m)(1) The Director of the Office of Management and Budget, in consultation with the Attorney General shall ensure the operation of a consolidated online request portal that allows a member of the public to submit a request for records under subsection (a) to any agency from a single website. The portal may include any additional tools the Director of the Office of Management and Budget finds will improve the implementation of this section.

(2) This subsection shall not be construed to alter the power of any other agency to create or maintain an independent online portal for the submission of a request for records under this section. The Director of the Office of Management and Budget shall establish standards for interoperability between the portal required under paragraph (1) and other request processing software used by agencies subject to this section.

GOVERNMENT IN THE SUNSHINE ACT[12]

5 U.S.C. § 552b. Open meetings

(a) For purposes of this section—

(1) the term "agency" means any agency, as defined in section 552(e) of this title, headed by a collegial body composed of two or more individual members, a majority of whom are appointed to such position by the President with the advice and consent of the Senate, and any subdivision thereof authorized to act on behalf of the agency;

(2) the term "meeting" means the deliberations of at least the number of individual agency members required to take action on behalf of the agency where such deliberations determine or result in the joint conduct or disposition of official agency business, but does not include deliberations required or permitted by subsection (d) or (e); and

(3) the term "member" means an individual who belongs to a collegial body heading an agency.

(b) Members shall not jointly conduct or dispose of agency business other than in accordance with this section. Except as provided in subsection (c), every portion of every meeting of an agency shall be open to public observation.

(c) Except in a case where the agency finds that the public interest requires otherwise, the second sentence of subsection (b) shall not apply to any portion of an agency meeting, and the requirements of subsections (d) and (e) shall not apply to any information pertaining to such meeting otherwise required by this section to be disclosed to the public, where the agency properly determines that such portion or portions of its meeting or the disclosure of such information is likely to—

(1) disclose matters that are (A) specifically authorized under criteria established by an Executive order to be kept secret in the interests of national defense or foreign policy and (B) in fact properly classified pursuant to such Executive order;

(2) relate solely to the internal personnel rules and practices of an agency;

(3) disclose matters specifically exempted from disclosure by statute . . .

(4) disclose trade secrets and commercial or financial information obtained from a person and privileged or confidential;

---

[12] P.L. 94–409, 90 Stat. 1247 (1976).

(5) involve accusing any person of a crime, or formally censuring any person;

(6) disclose information of a personal nature where disclosure would constitute a clearly unwarranted invasion of personal privacy;

(7) disclose investigatory records compiled for law enforcement purposes, or information which if written would be contained in such records, . . .

(8) disclose information contained in or related to examination, operating, or condition reports prepared by, on behalf of, or for the use of an agency responsible for the regulation or supervision of financial institutions;

(9) disclose information the premature disclosure of which would—

(A) in the case of an agency which regulates currencies, securities, commodities, or financial institutions, be likely to (i) lead to significant financial speculation in currencies, securities, or commodities, or (ii) significantly endanger the stability of any financial institution; or

(B) in the case of any agency, be likely to significantly frustrate implementation of a proposed agency action, . . .

or

(10) specifically concern the agency's issuance of a subpena, or the agency's participation in a civil action or proceeding, an action in a foreign court or international tribunal, or an arbitration, or the initiation, conduct, or disposition by the agency of a particular case of formal agency adjudication pursuant to the procedures in section 554 of this title or otherwise involving a determination on the record after opportunity for a hearing.

(d)(1) Action under subsection (c) shall be taken only when a majority of the entire membership of the agency (as defined in subsection (a)(1)) votes to take such action. . . .

(e)(1) In the case of each meeting, the agency shall make public announcement, at least one week before the meeting, of the time, place, and subject matter of the meeting, whether it is to be open or closed to the public, and the name and phone number of the official designated by the agency to respond to requests for information about the meeting. . . .

(f)(1) For every meeting closed pursuant to paragraphs (1) through (10) of subsection (c), the General Counsel or chief legal officer of the agency shall publicly certify that, in his or her opinion, the meeting may be closed to the public and shall state each relevant exemptive provision. . . .

(h)(1) The district courts of the United States shall have jurisdiction to enforce the requirements of subsections (b) through (f) of this section.

EXECUTIVE ORDER 12866 REGULATORY PLANNING AND REVIEW

58 Fed. Reg. 51735

The American people deserve a regulatory system that works for them, not against them: a regulatory system that protects and improves their health, safety, environment, and well-being and improves the performance of the economy without imposing unacceptable or unreasonable costs on society; regulatory policies that recognize that the private sector and private markets are the best engine for economic growth; regulatory approaches that respect the role of State, local, and tribal governments; and regulations that are effective, consistent, sensible, and understandable. We do not have such a regulatory system today.

With this Executive order, the Federal Government begins a program to reform and make more efficient the regulatory process. The objectives of this Executive order are to enhance planning and coordination with respect to both new and existing regulations; to reaffirm the primacy of Federal agencies in the regulatory decision-making process; to restore the integrity and legitimacy of regulatory review and oversight; and to make the process more accessible and open to the public. In pursuing these objectives, the regulatory process shall be conducted so as to meet applicable statutory requirements and with due regard to the discretion that has been entrusted to the Federal agencies.

Accordingly, by the authority vested in me as President by the Constitution and the laws of the United States of America, it is hereby ordered as follows:

Sec. 1. Statement of Regulatory Philosophy and Principles.

(a) The Regulatory Philosophy. Federal agencies should promulgate only such regulations as are required by law, are necessary to interpret the law, or are made necessary by compelling public need, such as material failures of private markets to protect or improve the health and safety of the public, the environment, or the well-being of the American people. In deciding whether and how to regulate, agencies should assess all costs and benefits of available regulatory alternatives, including the alternative of not regulating. Costs and benefits shall be understood to include both quantifiable measures (to the fullest extent that these can be usefully estimated) and qualitative measures of costs and benefits that are difficult to quantify, but nevertheless essential to consider. Further, in choosing among alternative regulatory approaches, agencies should select those approaches that maximize net benefits (including potential economic, environmental, public health and safety, and other advantages; distributive impacts; and equity), unless a statute requires another regulatory approach.

(b) The Principles of Regulation. To ensure that the agencies' regulatory programs are consistent with the philosophy set forth above, agencies should adhere to the following principles, to the extent permitted by law and where applicable:

(1) Each agency shall identify the problem that it intends to address (including, where applicable, the failures of private markets or public institutions that warrant new agency action) as well as assess the significance of that problem.

(2) Each agency shall examine whether existing regulations (or other law) have created, or contributed to, the problem that a new regulation is intended to correct and whether those regulations (or other law) should be modified to achieve the intended goal of regulation more effectively.

(3) Each agency shall identify and assess available alternatives to direct regulation, including providing economic incentives to encourage the desired behavior, such as user fees or marketable permits, or providing information upon which choices can be made by the public.

(4) In setting regulatory priorities, each agency shall consider, to the extent reasonable, the degree and nature of the risks posed by various substances or activities within its jurisdiction.

(5) When an agency determines that a regulation is the best available method of achieving the regulatory objective, it shall design its regulations in the most cost-effective manner to achieve the regulatory objective. In doing so, each agency shall consider incentives for innovation, consistency, predictability, the costs of enforcement and compliance (to the government, regulated entities, and the public), flexibility, distributive impacts, and equity.

(6) Each agency shall assess both the costs and the benefits of the intended regulation and, recognizing that some costs and benefits are difficult to quantify, propose or adopt a regulation only upon a reasoned determination that the benefits of the intended regulation justify its costs.

(7) Each agency shall base its decisions on the best reasonably obtainable scientific, technical, economic, and other information concerning the need for, and consequences of, the intended regulation.

(8) Each agency shall identify and assess alternative forms of regulation and shall, to the extent feasible, specify performance objectives, rather than specifying the behavior or manner of compliance that regulated entities must adopt.

(9) Wherever feasible, agencies shall seek views of appropriate State, local, and tribal officials before imposing regulatory requirements that might significantly or uniquely affect those governmental entities. Each agency shall assess the effects of Federal regulations on State, local, and tribal governments, including specifically the availability of resources to carry out those mandates, and seek to minimize those burdens that uniquely or significantly affect such governmental entities, consistent with achieving regulatory objectives. In addition, as appropriate, agencies shall seek to harmonize Federal regulatory actions with related State, local, and tribal regulatory and other governmental functions.

(10) Each agency shall avoid regulations that are inconsistent, incompatible, or duplicative with its other regulations or those of other Federal agencies.

(11) Each agency shall tailor its regulations to impose the least burden on society, including individuals, businesses of differing sizes, and other entities (including small communities and governmental entities), consistent with obtaining the regulatory objectives, taking into account, among other things, and to the extent practicable, the costs of cumulative regulations.

(12) Each agency shall draft its regulations to be simple and easy to understand, with the goal of minimizing the potential for uncertainty and litigation arising from such uncertainty.

Sec. 2. Organization. An efficient regulatory planning and review process is vital to ensure that the Federal Government's regulatory system best serves the American people.

(a) The Agencies. Because Federal agencies are the repositories of significant substantive expertise and experience, they are responsible for developing regulations and assuring that the regulations are consistent with applicable law, the President's priorities, and the principles set forth in this Executive order.

(b) The Office of Management and Budget. Coordinated review of agency rulemaking is necessary to ensure that regulations are consistent with applicable law, the President's priorities, and the principles set forth in this Executive order, and that decisions made by one agency do not conflict with the policies or actions taken or planned by another agency. The Office of Management and Budget (OMB) shall carry out that review function. Within OMB, the Office of Information and Regulatory Affairs (OIRA) is the repository of expertise concerning regulatory issues, including methodologies and procedures that affect more than one agency, this Executive order, and the President's regulatory policies. To the extent permitted by law, OMB shall provide guidance to agencies and assist the President, the Vice President, and other regulatory policy advisors to the President in regulatory planning and shall be the entity that reviews individual regulations, as provided by this Executive order.

(c) The Vice President. The Vice President is the principal advisor to the President on, and shall coordinate the development and presentation of recommendations concerning, regulatory policy, planning, and review, as set forth in this Executive order. In fulfilling their responsibilities under this Executive order, the President and the Vice President shall be assisted by the regulatory policy advisors within the Executive Office of the President and by such agency officials and personnel as the President and the Vice President may, from time to time, consult.

Sec. 3. Definitions. For purposes of this Executive order:

(a) "Advisors" refers to such regulatory policy advisors to the President as the President and Vice President may from time to time consult, including, among others: (1) the Director of OMB; (2) the Chair (or another member) of the Council of Economic Advisers; (3) the Assistant to the President for Economic Policy; (4) the Assistant to the President for Domestic Policy; (5) the Assistant to the President for National Security Affairs; (6) the Assistant to the President for Science and Technology; (7) the Assistant to the President for Intergovernmental Affairs; (8) the Assistant to the President and Staff Secretary; (9) the Assistant to the President and Chief of Staff to the Vice President; (10) the Assistant to the President and Counsel to the President; (11) the Deputy Assistant to the President and Director of the White House Office on Environmental Policy; and (12) the Administrator of OIRA, who also shall coordinate communications relating to this Executive order among the agencies, OMB, the other Advisors, and the Office of the Vice President.

(b) "Agency," unless otherwise indicated, means any authority of the United States that is an "agency" under 44 U.S.C. 3502(1), other than those considered to be independent regulatory agencies, as defined in 44 U.S.C. 3502(10).

(c) "Director" means the Director of OMB.

(d) "Regulation" or "rule" means an agency statement of general applicability and future effect, which the agency intends to have the force and effect of law, that is designed to implement, interpret, or prescribe law or policy or to describe the procedure or practice requirements of an agency. It does not, however, include:

> (1) Regulations or rules issued in accordance with the formal rulemaking provisions of 5 U.S.C. 556, 557;
>
> (2) Regulations or rules that pertain to a military or foreign affairs function of the United States, other than procurement regulations and regulations involving the import or export of non-defense articles and services;

(3) Regulations or rules that are limited to agency organization, management, or personnel matters; or

(4) Any other category of regulations exempted by the Administrator of OIRA.

(e) "Regulatory action" means any substantive action by an agency (normally published in the Federal Register) that promulgates or is expected to lead to the promulgation of a final rule or regulation, including notices of inquiry, advance notices of proposed rulemaking, and notices of proposed rulemaking.

(f) "Significant regulatory action" means any regulatory action that is likely to result in a rule that may:

(1) Have an annual effect on the economy of $100 million or more or adversely affect in a material way the economy, a sector of the economy, productivity, competition, jobs, the environment, public health or safety, or State, local, or tribal governments or communities;

(2) Create a serious inconsistency or otherwise interfere with an action taken or planned by another agency;

(3) Materially alter the budgetary impact of entitlements, grants, user fees, or loan programs or the rights and obligations of recipients thereof; or

(4) Raise novel legal or policy issues arising out of legal mandates, the President's priorities, or the principles set forth in this Executive order.

Sec. 4. Planning Mechanism. In order to have an effective regulatory program, to provide for coordination of regulations, to maximize consultation and the resolution of potential conflicts at an early stage, to involve the public and its State, local, and tribal officials in regulatory planning, and to ensure that new or revised regulations promote the President's priorities and the principles set forth in this Executive order, these procedures shall be followed, to the extent permitted by law:

(a) Agencies' Policy Meeting. Early in each year's planning cycle, the Vice President shall convene a meeting of the Advisors and the heads of agencies to seek a common understanding of priorities and to coordinate regulatory efforts to be accomplished in the upcoming year.

(b) Unified Regulatory Agenda. For purposes of this subsection, the term "agency" or "agencies" shall also include those considered to be independent regulatory agencies, as defined in 44 U.S.C. 3502(10). Each agency shall prepare an agenda of all regulations under development or review, at a time and in a manner specified by the Administrator of OIRA. The description of each regulatory action shall contain, at a minimum, a regulation identifier number, a brief summary of the action, the legal authority for the action, any legal deadline for the action, and the name and telephone number of a knowledgeable agency official.

Agencies may incorporate the information required under 5 U.S.C. 602 and 41 U.S.C. 402 into these agendas.

(c) The Regulatory Plan. For purposes of this subsection, the term "agency" or "agencies" shall also include those considered to be independent regulatory agencies, as defined in 44 U.S.C. 3502(10).

(1) As part of the Unified Regulatory Agenda, beginning in 1994, each agency shall prepare a Regulatory Plan (Plan) of the most important significant regulatory actions that the agency reasonably expects to issue in proposed or final form in that fiscal year or thereafter. The Plan shall be approved personally by the agency head and shall contain at a minimum:

(A) A statement of the agency's regulatory objectives and priorities and how they relate to the President's priorities;

(B) A summary of each planned significant regulatory action including, to the extent possible, alternatives to be considered and preliminary estimates of the anticipated costs and benefits;

(C) A summary of the legal basis for each such action, including whether any aspect of the action is required by statute or court order;

(D) A statement of the need for each such action and, if applicable, how the action will reduce risks to public health, safety, or the environment, as well as how the magnitude of the risk addressed by the action relates to other risks within the jurisdiction of the agency;

(E) The agency's schedule for action, including a statement of any applicable statutory or judicial deadlines; and

(F) The name, address, and telephone number of a person the public may contact for additional information about the planned regulatory action.

(2) Each agency shall forward its Plan to OIRA by June 1st of each year.

(3) Within 10 calendar days after OIRA has received an agency's Plan, OIRA shall circulate it to other affected agencies, the Advisors, and the Vice President.

(4) An agency head who believes that a planned regulatory action of another agency may conflict with its own policy or action taken or planned shall promptly notify, in writing, the Administrator of OIRA, who shall forward that communication to the issuing agency, the Advisors, and the Vice President.

(5) If the Administrator of OIRA believes that a planned regulatory action of an agency may be inconsistent with the President's priorities or the principles set forth in this Executive order or may be in conflict with any policy or action taken or planned by another

agency, the Administrator of OIRA shall promptly notify, in writing, the affected agencies, the Advisors, and the Vice President.

(6) The Vice President, with the Advisors' assistance, may consult with the heads of agencies with respect to their Plans and, in appropriate instances, request further consideration or inter-agency coordination.

(7) The Plans developed by the issuing agency shall be published annually in the October publication of the Unified Regulatory Agenda. This publication shall be made available to the Congress; State, local, and tribal governments; and the public. Any views on any aspect of any agency Plan, including whether any planned regulatory action might conflict with any other planned or existing regulation, impose any unintended consequences on the public, or confer any unclaimed benefits on the public, should be directed to the issuing agency, with a copy to OIRA.

(d) Regulatory Working Group. Within 30 days of the date of this Executive order, the Administrator of OIRA shall convene a Regulatory Working Group ("Working Group"), which shall consist of representatives of the heads of each agency that the Administrator determines to have significant domestic regulatory responsibility, the Advisors, and the Vice President. The Administrator of OIRA shall chair the Working Group and shall periodically advise the Vice President on the activities of the Working Group. The Working Group shall serve as a forum to assist agencies in identifying and analyzing important regulatory issues (including, among others (1) the development of innovative regulatory techniques, (2) the methods, efficacy, and utility of comparative risk assessment in regulatory decision-making, and (3) the development of short forms and other streamlined regulatory approaches for small businesses and other entities). The Working Group shall meet at least quarterly and may meet as a whole or in subgroups of agencies with an interest in particular issues or subject areas. To inform its discussions, the Working Group may commission analytical studies and reports by OIRA, the Administrative Conference of the United States, or any other agency.

(e) Conferences. The Administrator of OIRA shall meet quarterly with representatives of State, local, and tribal governments to identify both existing and proposed regulations that may uniquely or significantly affect those governmental entities. The Administrator of OIRA shall also convene, from time to time, conferences with representatives of businesses, nongovernmental organizations, and the public to discuss regulatory issues of common concern.

Sec. 5. Existing Regulations. In order to reduce the regulatory burden on the American people, their families, their communities, their State, local, and tribal governments, and their industries; to determine whether regulations promulgated by the executive branch of the Federal Government have become unjustified or unnecessary as a result of changed circumstances; to confirm that regulations are both compatible with each other and not duplicative or inappropriately burdensome in the aggregate; to ensure that all regulations are consistent with the President's priorities and the principles set forth in this Executive order, within applicable law; and to otherwise improve the effectiveness of existing regulations:

(a)   Within 90 days of the date of this Executive order, each agency shall submit to OIRA a program, consistent with its resources and regulatory priorities, under which the agency will periodically review its existing significant regulations to determine whether any such regulations should be modified or eliminated so as to make the agency's regulatory program more effective in achieving the regulatory objectives, less burdensome, or in greater alignment with the President's priorities and the principles set forth in this Executive order. Any significant regulations selected for review shall be included in the agency's annual Plan. The agency shall also identify any legislative mandates that require the agency to promulgate or continue to impose regulations that the agency believes are unnecessary or outdated by reason of changed circumstances.

(b)   The Administrator of OIRA shall work with the Regulatory Working Group and other interested entities to pursue the objectives of this section. State, local, and tribal governments are specifically encouraged to assist in the identification of regulations that impose significant or unique burdens on those governmental entities and that appear to have outlived their justification or be otherwise inconsistent with the public interest.

(c)   The Vice President, in consultation with the Advisors, may identify for review by the appropriate agency or agencies other existing regulations of an agency or groups of regulations of more than one agency that affect a particular group, industry, or sector of the economy, or may identify legislative mandates that may be appropriate for reconsideration by the Congress.

Sec. 6.   Centralized Review of Regulations. The guidelines set forth below shall apply to all regulatory actions, for both new and existing regulations, by agencies other than those agencies specifically exempted by the Administrator of OIRA:

(a)   Agency Responsibilities.

(1)   Each agency shall (consistent with its own rules, regulations, or procedures) provide the public with meaningful participation in the regulatory process. In particular, before issuing a notice of proposed rulemaking, each agency should, where appropriate, seek the involvement of those who are intended to benefit from and those expected to be burdened by any regulation (including, specifically, State, local, and tribal officials). In addition, each agency should afford the public a meaningful opportunity to comment on any proposed regulation, which in most cases should include a comment

period of not less than 60 days. Each agency also is directed to explore and, where appropriate, use consensual mechanisms for developing regulations, including negotiated rulemaking.

(2) Within 60 days of the date of this Executive order, each agency head shall designate a Regulatory Policy Officer who shall report to the agency head. The Regulatory Policy Officer shall be involved at each stage of the regulatory process to foster the development of effective, innovative, and least burdensome regulations and to further the principles set forth in this Executive order.

(3) In addition to adhering to its own rules and procedures and to the requirements of the Administrative Procedure Act, the Regulatory Flexibility Act, the Paperwork Reduction Act, and other applicable law, each agency shall develop its regulatory actions in a timely fashion and adhere to the following procedures with respect to a regulatory action:

(A) Each agency shall provide OIRA, at such times and in the manner specified by the Administrator of OIRA, with a list of its planned regulatory actions, indicating those which the agency believes are significant regulatory actions within the meaning of this Executive order. Absent a material change in the development of the planned regulatory action, those not designated as significant will not be subject to review under this section unless, within 10 working days of receipt of the list, the Administrator of OIRA notifies the agency that OIRA has determined that a planned regulation is a significant regulatory action within the meaning of this Executive order. The Administrator of OIRA may waive review of any planned regulatory action designated by the agency as significant, in which case the agency need not further comply with subsection (a)(3)(B) or subsection (a)(3)(C) of this section.

(B) For each matter identified as, or determined by the Administrator of OIRA to be, a significant regulatory action, the issuing agency shall provide to OIRA:

(i) The text of the draft regulatory action, together with a reasonably detailed description of the need for the regulatory action and an explanation of how the regulatory action will meet that need; and

(ii) An assessment of the potential costs and benefits of the regulatory action, including an explanation of the manner in which the regulatory action is consistent with a statutory mandate and, to the extent permitted by law, promotes the President's priorities and avoids undue interference with State, local, and tribal governments in the exercise of their governmental functions.

(C) For those matters identified as, or determined by the Administrator of OIRA to be, a significant regulatory action within the scope of section 3(f)(1), the agency shall also provide to OIRA the following additional information developed as part of the agency's decision-making process (unless prohibited by law):

(i) An assessment, including the underlying analysis, of benefits anticipated from the regulatory action (such as, but not limited to, the promotion of the efficient functioning of the economy and private markets, the enhancement of health and safety, the protection of the natural environment, and the elimination or reduction of discrimination or bias) together with, to the extent feasible, a quantification of those benefits;

(ii) An assessment, including the underlying analysis, of costs anticipated from the regulatory action (such as, but not limited to, the direct cost both to the government in administering the regulation and to businesses and others in complying with the regulation, and any adverse effects on the efficient functioning of the economy, private markets (including productivity, employment, and competitiveness), health, safety, and the natural environment), together with, to the extent feasible, a quantification of those costs; and

(iii) An assessment, including the underlying analysis, of costs and benefits of potentially effective and reasonably feasible alternatives to the planned regulation, identified by the agencies or the public (including improving the current regulation and reasonably viable nonregulatory actions), and an explanation why the planned regulatory action is preferable to the identified potential alternatives.

(D) In emergency situations or when an agency is obligated by law to act more quickly than normal review procedures allow, the agency shall notify OIRA as soon as possible and, to the extent practicable, comply with subsections (a)(3)(B) and (C) of this section. For those regulatory actions that are governed by a statutory or court-imposed deadline, the agency shall, to the extent practicable, schedule rulemaking proceedings so as to permit sufficient time for OIRA to conduct its review, as set forth below in subsection (b)(2) through (4) of this section.

(E) After the regulatory action has been published in the Federal Register or otherwise issued to the public, the agency shall:

(i) Make available to the public the information set forth in subsections (a)(3)(B) and (C);

(ii) Identify for the public, in a complete, clear, and simple manner, the substantive changes between the draft submitted to OIRA for review and the action subsequently announced; and

(iii) Identify for the public those changes in the regulatory action that were made at the suggestion or recommendation of OIRA.

(F) All information provided to the public by the agency shall be in plain, understandable language.

(b) OIRA Responsibilities. The Administrator of OIRA shall provide meaningful guidance and oversight so that each agency's regulatory actions are consistent with applicable law, the President's priorities, and the principles set forth in this Executive order and do not conflict with the policies or actions of another agency. OIRA shall, to the extent permitted by law, adhere to the following guidelines:

(1) OIRA may review only actions identified by the agency or by OIRA as significant regulatory actions under subsection (a)(3)(A) of this section.

(2) OIRA shall waive review or notify the agency in writing of the results of its review within the following time periods:

(A) For any notices of inquiry, advance notices of proposed rulemaking, or other preliminary regulatory actions prior to a Notice of Proposed Rulemaking, within 10 working days after the date of submission of the draft action to OIRA;

(B) For all other regulatory actions, within 90 calendar days after the date of submission of the information set forth in subsections (a)(3)(B) and (C) of this section, unless OIRA has previously reviewed this information and, since that review, there has been no material change in the facts and circumstances upon which the regulatory action is based, in which case, OIRA shall complete its review within 45 days; and

(C) The review process may be extended (1) once by no more than 30 calendar days upon the written approval of the Director and (2) at the request of the agency head.

(3) For each regulatory action that the Administrator of OIRA returns to an agency for further consideration of some or all of its provisions, the Administrator of OIRA shall provide the issuing agency a written explanation for such return, setting forth the pertinent provision of this Executive order on which OIRA is relying. If the agency head disagrees with some or all of the bases for the return, the agency head shall so inform the Administrator of OIRA in writing.

(4) Except as otherwise provided by law or required by a Court, in order to ensure greater openness, accessibility, and accountability in

the regulatory review process, OIRA shall be governed by the following disclosure requirements:

(A) Only the Administrator of OIRA (or a particular designee) shall receive oral communications initiated by persons not employed by the executive branch of the Federal Government regarding the substance of a regulatory action under OIRA review;

(B) All substantive communications between OIRA personnel and persons not employed by the executive branch of the Federal Government regarding a regulatory action under review shall be governed by the following guidelines:

(i) A representative from the issuing agency shall be invited to any meeting between OIRA personnel and such person(s);

(ii) OIRA shall forward to the issuing agency, within 10 working days of receipt of the communication(s), all written communications, regardless of format, between OIRA personnel and any person who is not employed by the executive branch of the Federal Government, and the dates and names of individuals involved in all substantive oral communications (including meetings to which an agency representative was invited, but did not attend, and telephone conversations between OIRA personnel and any such persons); and

(iii) OIRA shall publicly disclose relevant information about such communication(s), as set forth below in subsection (b) (4)(C) of this section.

(C) OIRA shall maintain a publicly available log that shall contain, at a minimum, the following information pertinent to regulatory actions under review:

(i) The status of all regulatory actions, including if (and if so, when and by whom) Vice Presidential and Presidential consideration was requested;

(ii) A notation of all written communications forwarded to an issuing agency under subsection (b)(4)(B)(ii) of this section; and

(iii) The dates and names of individuals involved in all substantive oral communications, including meetings and telephone conversations, between OIRA personnel and any person not employed by the executive branch of the Federal Government, and the subject matter discussed during such communications.

(D) After the regulatory action has been published in the Federal Register or otherwise issued to the public, or after the agency has announced its decision not to publish or issue the regulatory action, OIRA shall make available to the public all documents exchanged between OIRA and the agency during the review by OIRA under this section.

(5) All information provided to the public by OIRA shall be in plain, understandable language.

Sec. 7. Resolution of Conflicts. To the extent permitted by law, disagreements or conflicts between or among agency heads or between OMB and any agency that cannot be resolved by the Administrator of OIRA shall be resolved by the President, or by the Vice President acting at the request of the President, with the relevant agency head (and, as appropriate, other interested government officials). Vice Presidential and Presidential consideration of such disagreements may be initiated only by the Director, by the head of the issuing agency, or by the head of an agency that has a significant interest in the regulatory action at issue. Such review will not be undertaken at the request of other persons, entities, or their agents.

Resolution of such conflicts shall be informed by recommendations developed by the Vice President, after consultation with the Advisors (and other executive branch officials or personnel whose responsibilities to the President include the subject matter at issue). The development of these recommendations shall be concluded within 60 days after review has been requested.

During the Vice Presidential and Presidential review period, communications with any person not employed by the Federal Government relating to the substance of the regulatory action under review and directed to the Advisors or their staffs or to the staff of the Vice President shall be in writing and shall be forwarded by the recipient to the affected agency(ies) for inclusion in the public docket(s). When the communication is not in writing, such Advisors or staff members shall inform the outside party that the matter is under review and that any comments should be submitted in writing.

At the end of this review process, the President, or the Vice President acting at the request of the President, shall notify the affected agency and the Administrator of OIRA of the President's decision with respect to the matter.

Sec. 8. Publication. Except to the extent required by law, an agency shall not publish in the Federal Register or otherwise issue to the public any regulatory action that is subject to review under section 6 of this Executive order until (1) the Administrator of OIRA notifies the agency that OIRA has waived its review of the action or has completed its review without any requests for further consideration, or (2) the applicable time period in section 6(b)(2) expires without OIRA having notified the agency that it is returning the regulatory action for further consideration under section 6(b) (3), whichever occurs first. If the terms of the preceding sentence have not been satisfied and an agency wants to publish or otherwise issue a regulatory action, the head of that agency may request Presidential consideration through the Vice President, as provided under section 7 of this order. Upon receipt of this request, the Vice President shall notify OIRA and the Advisors. The guidelines and time period set forth in section 7 shall apply to the publication of regulatory actions for which Presidential consideration has been sought.

Sec. 9. Agency Authority. Nothing in this order shall be construed as displacing the agencies' authority or responsibilities, as authorized by law.

Sec. 10. Judicial Review. Nothing in this Executive order shall affect any otherwise available judicial review of agency action. This Executive order is intended only to improve the internal management of the Federal Government and does not create any right or benefit, substantive or procedural, enforceable at law or equity by a party against the United States, its agencies or instrumentalities, its officers or employees, or any other person.

Sec. 11. Revocations. Executive Orders Nos. 12291 and 12498; all amendments to those Executive orders; all guidelines issued under those orders; and any exemptions from those orders heretofore granted for any category of rule are revoked.

WILLIAM J. CLINTON

THE WHITE HOUSE
September 30, 1993.

EXECUTIVE ORDER 13771 REDUCING REGULATION AND CONTROLLING REGULATORY COST

82 Fed. Reg. 9339

By the authority vested in me as President by the Constitution and the laws of the United States of America, including the Budget and Accounting Act of 1921, as amended (31 U.S.C. 1101 et seq.), section 1105 of title 31, United States Code, and section 301 of title 3, United States Code, it is hereby ordered as follows:

Section 1.   Purpose. It is the policy of the executive branch to be prudent and financially responsible in the expenditure of funds, from both public and private sources. In addition to the management of the direct expenditure of taxpayer dollars through the budgeting process, it is essential to manage the costs associated with the governmental imposition of private expenditures required to comply with Federal regulations. Toward that end, it is important that for every one new regulation issued, at least two prior regulations be identified for elimination, and that the cost of planned regulations be prudently managed and controlled through a budgeting process.

Sec. 2.   Regulatory Cap for Fiscal Year 2017.

(a) Unless prohibited by law, whenever an executive department or agency (agency) publicly proposes for notice and comment or otherwise promulgates a new regulation, it shall identify at least two existing regulations to be repealed.

(b) For fiscal year 2017, which is in progress, the heads of all agencies are directed that the total incremental cost of all new regulations, including repealed regulations, to be finalized this year shall be no greater than zero, unless otherwise required by law or consistent with advice provided in writing by the Director of the Office of Management and Budget (Director).

(c) In furtherance of the requirement of subsection (a) of this section, any new incremental costs associated with new regulations shall, to the extent permitted by law, be offset by the elimination of existing costs associated with at least two prior regulations. Any agency eliminating existing costs associated with prior regulations under this subsection shall do so in accordance with the Administrative Procedure Act and other applicable law.

(d) The Director shall provide the heads of agencies with guidance on the implementation of this section. Such guidance shall address, among other things, processes for standardizing the measurement and estimation of regulatory costs; standards for determining what qualifies as new and offsetting regulations; standards for determining the costs of existing regulations that are considered for elimination; processes for accounting for costs in different fiscal years; methods to oversee the issuance of rules with costs offset by savings at different times or different agencies; and emergencies and other circumstances that might justify individual waivers of the requirements of this section. The Director shall consider phasing in and updating these requirements.

Sec. 3. Annual Regulatory Cost Submissions to the Office of Management and Budget.

(a) Beginning with the Regulatory Plans (required under Executive Order 12866 of September 30, 1993, as amended, or any successor order) for fiscal year 2018, and for each fiscal year thereafter, the head of each agency shall identify, for each regulation that increases incremental cost, the offsetting regulations described in section 2(c) of this order, and provide the agency's best approximation of the total costs or savings associated with each new regulation or repealed regulation.

(b) Each regulation approved by the Director during the Presidential budget process shall be included in the Unified Regulatory Agenda required under Executive Order 12866, as amended, or any successor order.

(c) Unless otherwise required by law, no regulation shall be issued by an agency if it was not included on the most recent version or update of the published Unified Regulatory Agenda as required under Executive Order 12866, as amended, or any successor order, unless the issuance of such regulation was approved in advance in writing by the Director.

(d) During the Presidential budget process, the Director shall identify to agencies a total amount of incremental costs that will be allowed for each agency in issuing new regulations and repealing regulations for the next fiscal year. No regulations exceeding the agency's total incremental cost allowance will be permitted in that fiscal year, unless required by law or approved in writing by the Director. The total incremental cost allowance may allow an increase or require a reduction in total regulatory cost.

(e) The Director shall provide the heads of agencies with guidance on the implementation of the requirements in this section.

Sec. 4. Definition. For purposes of this order the term "regulation" or "rule" means an agency statement of general or particular applicability and future effect designed to implement, interpret, or prescribe law or policy or to describe the procedure or practice requirements of an agency, but does not include:

(a) regulations issued with respect to a military, national security, or foreign affairs function of the United States;

(b) regulations related to agency organization, management, or personnel; or

(c) any other category of regulations exempted by the Director.

Sec. 5.   General Provisions.

(a) Nothing in this order shall be construed to impair or otherwise affect:

    (i)   the authority granted by law to an executive department or agency, or the head thereof; or

    (ii) the functions of the Director relating to budgetary, administrative, or legislative proposals.

(b) This order shall be implemented consistent with applicable law and subject to the availability of appropriations.

(c) This order is not intended to, and does not, create any right or benefit, substantive or procedural, enforceable at law or in equity by any party against the United States, its departments, agencies, or entities, its officers, employees, or agents, or any other person.

DONALD J. TRUMP

THE WHITE HOUSE

January 30, 2017.

INDEX

References are to Pages

ADMINISTRATIVE LAW JUDGES (ALJ'S)

ADMINISTRATIVE PROCEDURE ACT (APA)

ADMINISTRATIVE STATE